Sweden and National Liberation in Southern Africa

Sweden and National Liberation in Southern Africa

Volume II:
Solidarity and Assistance 1970–1994

Tor Sellström

Nordiska Afrikainstitutet, Uppsala 2002

Indexing terms

Churches
Foreign relations
National liberation movements
Solidarity organizations
Trade unions
Youth organizations

ANC
FRELIMO
Inkatha
MPLA
PAC
PAIGC
SWAPO
UDF
ZANU
ZAPU

Angola
Guinea-Bissau
Mozambique
Namibia
South Africa
Sweden
Zimbabwe

Language checking: Elaine Almén
Cover: Adriaan Honcoop

© The author and Nordiska Afrikainstitutet 2002
ISBN 91-7106-448-6
Printed in Sweden by Elanders Gotab, Stockholm, 2002

Contents

Tables and Graphs

Bibliography

Appendices

Name Index

Acronyms

AALC	African-American Labor Center (United States)
AAPSO	Afro-Asian Peoples Solidarity Organization
ABF	Workers Educational Association/Arbetarnas Bildningsförbund (Sweden)
ADRA	Action for Rural Development and the Environment/Acção para o Desenvolvimento Rural e Ambiente (Angola)
AET	Africa Educational Trust (Great Britain)
AGIS	Africa Groups in Sweden/Afrikagrupperna i Sverige
AI	Amnesty International
AIC	International Centre of the Swedish Labour Movement/Arbetarrörelsens Internationella Centrum
AIS	International Support Committee of the Labour Movement/Arbeiderbevegelsens Internasjonale Støttekomité (Norway)
AME	African Methodist Episcopal Church
AMS	Swedish Labour Market Board/Arbetsmarknadsstyrelsen
ANC	African National Congress (South Africa)
ANC-Z	African National Council-Zimbabwe
APLA	Azanian People's Liberation Army (South Africa)
ARO	Recruitment Organization of the Africa Groups/Afrikagruppernas Rekryteringsorganisation (Sweden)
AWEPAA	Association of West European Parliamentarians for Action against Apartheid
AZACTU	Azanian Confederation of Trade Unions (South Africa)
AZAPO	Azanian People's Organization (South Africa)
BAWU	Black Allied Workers Union (South Africa)
BCMA	Black Consciousness Movement of Azania (South Africa)
BCP	Black Community Programmes (South Africa)
BF	Bread and Fishes/Brödet och Fiskarna (Sweden)
BOSS	Bureau of State Security (South Africa)
BPC	Black People's Convention (South Africa)
CANU	Caprivi African National Union (Namibia)
CAYCO	Cape Youth Congress (South Africa)
CCHA	Consultative Committee on Humanitarian Assistance/Beredningen för humanitärt bistånd (Sweden)
CCM	Christian Council of Mozambique
CCM	Chama Cha Mapinduzi (Tanzania)
CCN	Council of Churches in Namibia
CDS	Centre for Development Studies (South Africa)
CFTC	Commonwealth Fund for Technical Cooperation
CI	Christian Institute (South Africa)
CIA	Central Intelligence Agency (United States)
CIIR	Catholic Institute for International Relations (Great Britain)
CIO	Central Intelligence Organization (Rhodesia)
COD	Congress of Democrats (South Africa)
CODESA	Convention for a Democratic South Africa
CONCP	Conference of Nationalist Organizations in the Portuguese Colonies/Conferência das Organizações Nacionalistas das Colónias Portuguêsas
COREMO	Revolutionary Committee of Mozambique/Comité Revolucionário de Moçambique
COSAS	Congress of South African Students
COSATU	Congress of South African Trade Unions
COSAW	Congress of South African Writers
COTRALESA	Congress of Traditional Leaders of South Africa
CPC	Coloured People's Congress (South Africa)
CPSA	Communist Party of South Africa
CSA	Church of Sweden Aid/Lutherhjälpen

CSLA	Supreme Council for the Liberation of Angola/Conselho Supremo da Libertação de Angola
CSM	Church of Sweden Mission
CUF	Centre Party Youth League/Centerpartiets Ungdomsförbund (Sweden)
CUSA	Council of Unions of South Africa
DAC	Department of Arts and Culture of ANC
DHAC	Durban Housing Areas Action Committee (South Africa)
DHF	Dag Hammarskjöld Foundation (Sweden)
DIP	Department of Information and Publicity of ANC
DONS	Department of National Security (South Africa)
DRC	Dutch Reformed Church (South Africa)
DTA	Democratic Turnhalle Alliance (Namibia)
EAWU	Engineering and Allied Workers Union (South Africa)
ECC	End Conscription Campaign (South Africa)
ELC	Evangelical Lutheran Church (South Africa)
ELCIN	Evangelical Lutheran Church in Namibia
ELCZ	Evangelical Lutheran Church of Zimbabwe
ELOK	Evangelical Lutheran Ovambo-Kavango Church (Namibia)
ERIP	Education Resource and Information Project (South Africa)
FCWU	Food and Canning Workers Union (South Africa)
FLING	Front for the Liberation and Independence of Guinea/Frente para a Libertação e Independência da Guiné (Guinea-Bissau)
FNLA	National Front for the Liberation of Angola/Frente Nacional de Libertação de Angola
FOSATU	Federation of South African Trade Unions
FPJ	Foundation for Peace and Justice (South Africa)
FPU	Liberal Party Youth League/Folkpartiets Ungdomsförbund (Sweden)
FRELIMO	Mozambique Liberation Front/Frente de Libertação de Moçambique
FRG	Federal Republic of Germany
FROLIZI	Front for the Liberation of Zimbabwe
FUF	Swedish Development Forum/Föreningen för Utvecklingsfrågor
GATT	General Agreement on Tariffs and Trade
GAWU	General and Allied Workers Union (South Africa)
GDR	German Democratic Republic
GWU	General Workers Union (South Africa)
HUF	Moderate Party Youth League/Högerns Ungdomsförbund (Sweden)
IAS	Industrial Aid Society (South Africa)
ICAAS	International Campaign Against Apartheid Sport
ICEIDA	Icelandic International Development Agency
ICFTU	International Confederation of Free Trade Unions
ICJ	International Court of Justice
ICRC	International Committee of the Red Cross
ICSA	International Committee against Apartheid, Racism and Colonialism in Southern Africa
IDAF	International Defence and Aid Fund for Southern Africa
IDASA	Institute for a Democratic Alternative in South Africa
IFP	Inkatha Freedom Party (South Africa)
ILO	International Labour Organization
IDEA	International Institute for Democracy and Electoral Assistance (Sweden)
ISAK	Isolate South Africa Committee/Isolera Sydafrika-Kommittén (Sweden)
ISC	International Student Conference
IUEF	International University Exchange Fund
IUSY	International Union of Socialist Youth
JMC	Joint Military Command (Zimbabwe)
JODAC	Johannesburg Democratic Action Committee (South Africa)
KF	Co-operative Union and Wholesale Society/Kooperativa Förbundet (Sweden)
KRISS	Christian Student Movement in Sweden/Kristna Studentrörelsen i Sverige

LLA	Lesotho Liberation Army
LO	Swedish Trade Union Confederation/Landsorganisationen i Sverige
LPC	Left Party Communists (Sweden)
LWF	Lutheran World Federation
MANWU	Metal and Allied Namibian Workers Union
MAWU	Metal and Allied Workers Union (South Africa)
MFA	Movement of the Armed Forces/Movimento das Forças Armadas (Portugal)
MIF	Miners International Federation
MK	Umkhonto we Sizwe/The Spear of the Nation (South Africa)
MMD	Movement for Multiparty Democracy (Zambia)
MONAP	Mozambique-Nordic Agricultural Programme
MPLA	Popular Movement for the Liberation of Angola/Movimento Popular de Libertação de Angola
MUF	Moderate Party Youth Leage/Moderata Ungdomsförbundet (Sweden)
MUN	Mineworkers Union of Namibia
MWASA	Media Workers Union of South Africa
NAAWU	National Automobile and Allied Workers Union (South Africa)
NACTU	National Council of Trade Unions (South Africa)
NADEL	National Association of Democratic Lawyers (South Africa)
NAFAU	Namibian Food and Allied Union
NANSO	Namibian National Students Organization
NAPSA	Namibia Private School Association
NAPWU	Namibia Public Workers Union
NATO	North Atlantic Treaty Organization
NAWU	Namibian Workers Union
NAYCO	Natal Youth Congress (South Africa)
NDP	National Democratic Party (Zimbabwe)
NEC	National Executive Committee of ANC
NEU	Namibian Extension Unit
NEUM	Non-European Unity Movement (South Africa)
NIC	Natal Indian Congress (South Africa)
NIEO	New International Economic Order
NIP	Namibia Independence Party
NIR	International Council of Swedish Industry/Näringslivets Internationella Råd
NIS	National Intelligence Service (South Africa)
NNF	Namibia National Front
NOK	Norwegian Kroner
NORAD	Norwegian Agency for International Development
NP	National Party (South Africa)
NPF	National Patriotic Front of Namibia
NRC	National Reception Committee (South Africa)
NTUC	Nordic Trade Union Council
NUM	National Union of Mineworkers (South Africa)
NUMSA	National Union of Metalworkers of South Africa
NUNW	National Union of Namibian Workers
NUSAS	National Union of South African Students
NWC	National Working Committee of ANC
OAU	Organization of African Unity
OMA	Angolan Women's Organization/Organização das Mulheres de Angola
OPIC	Olof Palme International Center (Sweden)
PAC	Pan Africanist Congress of Azania (South Africa)
PAI	African Independence Party/Partido Africano de Independência (Guinea-Bissau)
PAICV	African Independence Party of Cape Verde/Partido Africano para a Independência do Cabo Verde
PAIGC	African Independence Party of Guinea and Cape Verde/Partido Africano para a Independência da Guiné e Cabo Verde
PASA	Post-Apartheid South Africa

PCR	Programme to Combat Racism
PDA	Democratic Party of Angola/Partido Democrático Angolano
PEYCO	Port Elizabeth Youth Congress (South Africa)
PF	Patriotic Front (Zimbabwe)
PFP	Progressive Federal Party (South Africa)
PIDE	International and State Defence Police/Policía Internacional e de Defesa do Estado (Portugal)
PLAN	People's Liberation Army of Namibia
PSP	Socialist Party of Portugal/Partido Socialista de Portugal
RB	Save the Children/Rädda Barnen (Sweden)
RENAMO	Mozambique National Resistance/Resistência Nacional Moçambicana
RF	Swedish Sports Confederation/Sveriges Riksidrottsförbund
RMC	Release Mandela Campaign (South Africa)
RRV	Swedish National Audit Bureau/Riksrevisionsverket
SAAU	South African Artists United
SAAWU	South African Allied Workers Union
SABA	South African Black Alliance
SABC	South African Broadcasting Corporation
SACC	South African Council of Churches
SACHED	South African Council of Higher Education
SACL	South African Confederation of Labour
SACP	South African Communist Party
SACPO	South African Coloured People's Organization
SACTU	South African Congress of Trade Unions
SADC	Southern African Development Community
SADCC	Southern Africa Development Coordination Conference
SADF	South African Defence Force
SAF	Swedish Employers Confederation/Svenska Arbetsgivareföreningen
SAIC	South African Indian Congress
SAIRR	South African Institute of Race Relations
SAK	Central Organization of Finnish Trade Unions/Suomen Ammattiliittojen Keskus- järjestö
SAR	South African Rands
SARDC	Southern African Research and Documentation Centre
SAREC	Swedish Agency for Research Cooperation with Developing Countries
SASCO	South African Students Congress
SASM	South African Students Movement
SASO	South African Students Organization
SASPRO	South African Studies Project
SAUF	South Africa United Front
SAYCO	South African Youth Congress
SCC	South African State Security Council
SCC	Swedish Co-operative Centre/Kooperation Utan Gränser
SDF	Students Development Fund (Sweden)
SDP	Social Democratic Party (Sweden)
SECO	Swedish Union of Secondary School Students/Sveriges Elevers Centralorganisation
SEK	Swedish Kronor
SEN	Swedish Ecumenical Council/Svenska Ekumeniska Nämnden
SFN	United Nations Association of Sweden/Svenska FN-förbundet
SFS	Swedish National Union of Students/Sveriges Förenade Studentkårer
SI	Socialist International
SIDA	Swedish International Development Authority
SIF	Federation of Swedish Industries/Sveriges Industriförbund
SIF	Union of Industrial Employees/Svenska Industritjänstemannaförbundet (Sweden)
SILC	Swedish International Liberal Center/Liberalt Utvecklingscentrum
SIPU	Swedish National Institute for Civil Service Training and Development/Statens Institut för Personalutveckling

SIV	Swedish Immigration Board/Statens Invandrarverk
SKP	Communist Party of Sweden/Sveriges Kommunistiska Parti
SKTF	Union of Municipal Employees/Sveriges Kommunaltjänstemannaförbund (Sweden)
SL	Swedish Teachers Association/Sveriges Lärarförbund
SLU	Swedish University of Agricultural Sciences/Sveriges Lantbruksuniversitet
SOMAFCO	Solomon Mahlangu Freedom College (ANC/Tanzania)
SOYCO	Soweto Youth Congress (South Africa)
SRB	Shipping Research Bureau (Holland)
SSAK	Swedish South Africa Committee/Svenska Sydafrikakommittén
SSF	Support Group for the People of South Africa/Stödgruppen för Sydafrikas Folk (Sweden)
SSRC	Soweto Students Representative Council (South Africa)
SSU	Social Democratic Youth League/Sveriges Socialdemokratiska Ungdomsförbund (Sweden)
SUL	National Council of Swedish Youth/Sveriges Ungdomsorganisationers Landsråd
SWANLIF	South West African National Liberation Front
SWANU	South West Africa National Union
SWANUF	South West Africa National United Front
SWAPO	South West Africa People's Organization
SWAPO-D	SWAPO-Democrats
SWATUL	South West Africa Trade Union League
SWEDTEL	Swedish Telecommunication Consulting AB
SYL	SWAPO Youth League
TCO	Central Organization of Salaried Employees/Tjänstemännens Centralorganisation (Sweden)
TEC	Transitional Executive Council (South Africa)
TGNU	Transitional Government of National Unity (Namibia)
TRC	Truth and Reconciliation Commission (South Africa)
TUACC	Trade Union Advisory and Coordinating Council (South Africa)
TUC	Trades Union Congress (Great Britain)
TUCSA	Trade Union Council of South Africa
UANC	United African National Council (Zimbabwe)
UAW	United Automobile Workers (South Africa)
UDF	United Democratic Front (South Africa)
UDI	Unilateral Declaration of Independence (Rhodesia)
UFF	Development Aid from People to People in Sweden/U-landshjälp från Folk till Folk i Sverige
UMSA	Unity Movement of South Africa
UNCN	United Nations Council for Namibia
UNETPSA	United Nations Educational and Training Programme for Southern Africa
UNHCR	United Nations High Commissioner for Refugees
UNICEF	United Nations Children's Fund
UNIN	United Nations Institute for Namibia
UNITA	National Union for the Total Independence of Angola/União Nacional para a Independência Total de Angola
UNOMSA	United Nations Observer Mission in South Africa
UNTA	National Union of Angolan Workers/União Nacional dos Trabalhadores de Angola
UNTAG	United Nations Transitional Assistance Group (Namibia)
UNZA	University of Zambia
UPA	Union of the Peoples of Angola/União das Populações de Angola
USD	United States Dollar
UWC	University of the Western Cape (South Africa)
UWUSA	United Workers Union of South Africa
VAT	Victims Against Terrorism (South Africa)
VEETU	Voter Education and Elections Training Unit (South Africa)
VUF	Left Party Youth League/Vänsterpartiets Ungdomsförbund (Sweden)
WACL	World Anti-Communist League

WAY	World Assembly of Youth
WCC	World Council of Churches
WCG	Western Contact Group
WCL	World Confederation of Labour
WFTU	World Federation of Trade Unions
WHO	World Health Organization
WPC	World Peace Council
WUS	World University Service
ZANLA	Zimbabwe African National Liberation Army
ZANU	Zimbabwe African National Union
ZAPU	Zimbabwe African People's Union
ZCRS	Zambian Christian Refugee Service
ZIPA	Zimbabwe People's Army
ZIPRA	Zimbabwe People's Revolutionary Army
ZIRIC	Zimbabwe Research and Information Centre
ZLC	Zimbabwe Liberation Council
ZUM	Zimbabwe Unity Movement
ZWT	Zimbabwe Welfare Trust

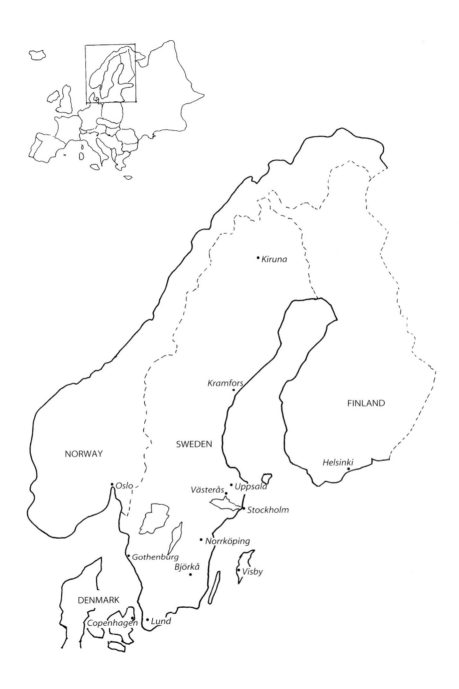

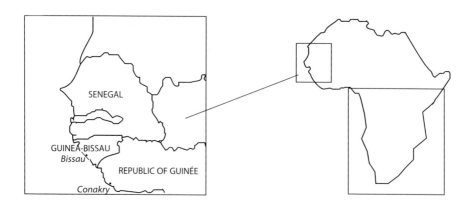

Chronological overview 1950–1994

1954	Publication of Herbert Tingsten's book *Problemet Sydafrika* (the following year published in Great Britain as *The Problem of South Africa*).
1959 (September)	Launch of the Swedish Fund for the Victims of Racial Oppression in South Africa.
1959 (December)	Windhoek 'Old Location' shootings, Namibia.
1960 (March)	Sharpeville massacre, South Africa.
1960 (April)	ANC and PAC banned.
1960 (April)	First consumer boycott of South African goods declared by the Swedish Trade Union Confederation and the Cooperative Union and Wholesale Society.
1961 (Feb–March)	Armed uprisings by MPLA and UPA (FNLA) in Angola mark the beginnings of the Thirty Years' War in Southern Africa.
1961 (March)	Swedish South Africa Committee established.
1961 (December)	Nobel Peace Prize to Albert Luthuli. Launch of Umkhonto we Sizwe in South Africa.
1962	Swedish Agency for International Assistance (NIB).
1962 (May)	Address by Oliver Tambo to the Labour Day demonstrations in Gothenburg, Sweden.
1962 (August)	Afro-Scandinavian Youth Congress in Oslo, Norway.
1963 (March)	Consumer boycott campaign against South Africa launched by the National Council of Swedish Youth.
1964 (May)	'Refugee million' adopted by the Swedish parliament.
1964 (August)	Consultative Committee on Education Support to African Refugee Youth—later Consultative Committee on Humanitarian Assistance—appointed.
1964 (September)	Eduardo and Janet Mondlane's first visit to Sweden.
1964 (September)	FRELIMO launches armed struggle in Mozambique.
1965 (January)	First parliamentary motions on economic sanctions against South Africa.
1965 (May)	First Swedish grant to the Mozambique Institute, Tanzania.
1965 (July)	Swedish International Development Authority (SIDA).
1965 (November)	Ian Smith's Unilateral Declaration of Independence, Rhodesia.
1966 (March)	First international conference on Namibia in Oxford, England.
1966 (April)	ZANU begins military operations in Zimbabwe.
1966 (August)	SWAPO launches armed struggle for the liberation of Namibia.
1967	First FRELIMO representative based in Sweden.
1968 (May)	Demonstrations in Båstad against a Davis Cup match between Sweden and Rhodesia.
1969	World Council of Churches launches its Programme to Combat Racism.
1969 (May)	Endorsement by the Swedish parliament of official humanitarian support to African liberation movements.
1969 (July)	Swedish legislation against economic transactions with Rhodesia.
1969/70	First Swedish allocation to PAIGC of Guinea-Bissau.
1969/70	First Swedish allocation to ZANU/Zimbabwe Welfare Trust.
1970/71	First Swedish allocation to SWAPO of Namibia.

1970 (September)	First MPLA representative to the Nordic countries (Stockholm).
1971	First SWAPO representative to the Scandinavian countries, West Germany and Austria (Stockholm).
1971 (June)	International Court of Justice rules that South Africa's occupation of Namibia is illegal.
1971/72	First Swedish allocation to MPLA of Angola.
1971/72	Direct cooperation programme with FRELIMO of Mozambique.
1972/73 (Feb. 1973)	First Swedish allocation to ANC of South Africa.
1972/73 (Feb. 1973)	First Swedish allocation to ZAPU of Zimbabwe.
1973 (April)	UN/OAU Conference on Southern Africa in Oslo, Norway.
1973 (June)	ILO International Conference of Trade Unions against Apartheid in Geneva, Switzerland.
1974	First ANC Chief Representative to the Scandinavian countries (Stockholm).
1974 (April)	Military coup in Portugal.
1974 (September)	Independence of the Republic of Guinea-Bissau.
1975 (June)	Independence of the People's Republic of Mozambique.
1975 (November)	Independence of the People's Republic of Angola.
1976 (June)	Soweto uprising, South Africa.
1976 (October)	Patriotic Front between ZAPU and ZANU.
1977 (September)	Steve Biko killed in detention in South Africa.
1978 (March)	Nordic Programme of Action against Apartheid/Oslo Plan.
1978 (May)	South African massacre of SWAPO refugees at Kassinga, Angola.
1978 (September)	UN Security Council adopts Resolution 435 on Namibia.
1978 (September)	'Total strategy' adopted as official South African state policy.
1979 (July)	Sweden bans new investments in South Africa and Namibia.
1979 (Sept–Dec)	Lancaster House Conference on Zimbabwe, London.
1980 (January)	South African infiltration of IUEF revealed.
1980 (April)	Independence of the Republic of Zimbabwe.
1983 (August)	UDF of South Africa launched.
1984 (March)	Nkomati Accord between South Africa and Mozambique.
1984 (December)	Nobel Peace Prize to Desmond Tutu.
1986 (February)	Swedish People's Parliament against Apartheid in Stockholm.
1986 (February)	Olof Palme assassinated.
1987 (July)	Swedish trade embargo on South Africa and Namibia.
1988 (December)	New York accords between Angola, Cuba and South Africa lead to independence process in Namibia.
1990 (February)	ANC, PAC, SACP, UDF and other organizations unbanned. Nelson Mandela released.
1990 (March)	Independence of the Republic of Namibia.
1993 (December)	Nobel Peace Prize to Nelson Mandela and Frederik Willem de Klerk.
1994 (April–May)	Elections in South Africa. ANC-led Government of National Unity. Nelson Mandela President.

Acknowledgements

During the course of this study, I have incurred debts to so many individuals, institutions and organizations—both in Sweden and Southern Africa—that it is impossible to mention them all. Those to whom I am most indebted for assistance, contributions and comments during the first phase have been acknowledged in the introductions to the volumes *Formation of a Popular Opinion (1950–1970)* and the accompanying *Regional and Swedish Voices*. Many of them have also been extremely helpful during the second phase, making possible the following text on *Solidarity and Assistance (1970–1994)*.

Extending over seven years, a project like the one which is now being brought to a close could not have been sustained without generous financial and moral support. The Swedish International Development Cooperation Agency not only provided the initial funds, but the responsible officials—Sten Rylander and, later, Lars Ekengren—on several occasions showed patience and confidence by granting additional resources. At the Ministry for Foreign Affairs, Jan Cedergren's support will always be remembered. In 1992, the entire project on *National Liberation in Southern Africa: The Role of the Nordic Countries*—of which the Swedish study forms part—originated in conversations with him and Ibbo Mandaza of the Southern Africa Regional Institute for Policy Studies in Harare. Once the project was launched, Cedergren spurred me on, extending the necessary advice and encouragement to make me persevere.

As coordinator of the Nordic project, I was based at the Nordic Africa Institute from August 1994 to June 2001. Here, the support, understanding and friendship accorded by its Director, Lennart Wohlgemuth, was remarkable. I am also grateful to many former colleagues, among them Karl Eric Ericson and the staff at the publications department; Jan Pettersson at the library; Karin Andersson-Schiebe, who compiled the name index; and—associated with the institute in a freelance capacity—Elaine Almén, who kept a watchful eye on my English.

If there is one person without whose efforts and inputs this study would not have seen the light of day, it is Charlotta Dohlvik, who worked as my research assistant from mid-1996. Willingly assuming a number of tedious administrative tasks—often working outside normal schedules—her dedication to detail, incisive comments, good spirits and, in general, ability to communicate with all those involved and consulted have in a crucial way pulled the project out of the dark tunnel where it at times seemed to be stuck.

At the institute, Charlotta Dohlvik and I worked closely with research teams in the other Nordic countries. In this context, the study on Sweden benefited greatly from the contacts and exchange with Christopher Munthe Morgenstierne in Denmark; Pekka Peltola and Iina Soiri in Finland; and Tore Linné Eriksen and Eva Helene Østbye in Norway. Special thanks go to Eva Østbye for her constructive comments.

The text that follows is far from comprehensive and will be criticized both for what is included and for what is omitted. It is not an 'official' account of Sweden's relations with the Southern African liberation movements, nor an 'authorized' interpretation of the role of the state or the non-state actors. The author is solely responsible for the views and conclusions expressed. This said, I have—in addition to the recorded interviews—tried to accommodate viewpoints from a number of centrally placed actors in Sweden, as well as in Southern Africa.

In February 1999, the first volume and drafts of the present text covering the former Portuguese colonies and Zimbabwe were presented at a conference on Robben Island, South Africa, where a great number of the participants had either played prominent parts in the regional liberation struggles or as Swedish government officials or NGO activists had supported them.[1] Throughout the ensuing drafting process—covering the sections on SWAPO and ANC—the following, in particular, made valuable comments, contributions or corrections to one or more chapters: Roland Axelsson, Gunilla von Bahr, Birgitta Berggren, Axel-Ivar Berglund, Tore Bergman, Bodil Dreifaldt, Mark Gevisser, Sven Hamrell, Bertil Högberg, Anders Johansson, Lena Johansson, Anton Johnston, Ola Jämtin, Folke Löfgren, Birgitta Karlström Dorph, Uazuvara Katjivena, Tomas Ledin, Henning Melber, Anders Möllander, Sten Rylander, Anders Stendalen, Raymond Suttner, Bengt Säve-Söderbergh, Roy Unge, Mikael Wiehe and Ann Wilkens. Their inputs and views are greatly appreciated and acknowledged.

In addition, private photos were kindly provided by Gittan Arwén, Tore Bergman, Paul Carlsson, Ingalill Colbro, Georg Dreifaldt, Eva Ehlin, Christer Johansson, Josef Jonsson, Folke Löfgren, Stig Lövgren, Carin Norberg, Bengt Nordenbrand, Bertil Odén, Mai Palmberg, Kaj Persson, Pierre Schori and Bertil Sörberg.

Research and writing are hard on family and friends. Whenever possible, I took my files and withdrew to the soothing environment of Väddö, where the sky meets the sea. During four summer periods, my sister Ebba, Olle, Tomas and Anna did everything possible to make me feel at ease. In memory of those summers and the times spent together in Southern Africa, I dedicate this book to them.

Uppsala, August 2001

Tor Sellström

---

1. *Nordic Solidarity with the Liberation Struggles in Southern Africa and Challenges for Democratic Partnerships into the 21st Century.* The texts submitted on Angola, Mozambique, Namibia, South Africa and Zimbabwe were respectively discussed by Maria da Conceição Neto and Alberto Ribeiro-Kabulo; Sérgio Vieira; Ben Amathila; Lindiwe Mabuza and Raymond Suttner; and Addmore Kambudzi. The members of the Swedish delegation were: Anna Brodin, Jan Cedergren, Anders Johansson, Mats Karlsson, Sören Lindh, Annika Lysén, Anders Möllander, Carin Norberg, Thomas Ohlson, Margareta Ringström and Per Wästberg. Among others, Roland Axelsson and Bo Heinebäck were also present. Together with South Africa's Deputy President Thabo Mbeki, Foreign Minister Anna Lindh addressed the opening of the conference.

Prologue

Background

This book is the second in a two-volume study on Sweden and the struggles for human dignity, majority rule and national independence in Southern Africa. Volume I[1] was mainly concerned with the formation of the broad and active political opinion which in May 1969 was behind the Swedish parliament's decision to endorse a policy of direct, official humanitarian assistance to the Southern African liberation movements.[2] The present text will discuss *how* the support was expressed from around 1970 until the democratic elections in South Africa in 1994. Chiefly based on unresearched primary sources, it attempts an intelligible presentation of empirical data, events and plots to the general reader interested in Sweden's relations with the liberation movements in the region.

Although official Swedish humanitarian support had been granted to Southern Africa since the mid-1960s, the year 1969 was a turning point.[3] That it came about at the close of the decade was in an international context not specific to Sweden. On the contrary, the intransigence of the white minority regimes and the mounting pressure for change by the nationalist movements were towards the end of the 1960s increasingly seen as threats to world peace, forcing the main regional and global actors to define their positions vis-à-vis the situation in Southern Africa. To place the Swedish position in the contemporary international context, a brief presentation of some of these standpoints at the time of the parliamentary decision should thus be made.

1960 was proclaimed 'Africa Year' by the United Nations. The same year, the UN General Assembly adopted the Decolonization Declaration, affirming that "the subjection of peoples to alien subjugation, domination and exploitation constitutes a denial of fundamental human rights, [which] is contrary to the Charter of the United Nations and an impediment to the promotion of world peace and cooperation".[4] Many former European colonies in Africa were in quick succession granted national independence at the beginning of the 1960s. In 1960 alone, seventeen African states were admitted to the United Nations. In Southern Africa, however, the quest for democracy and independence was firmly opposed by Portugal, the white settlers in Rhodesia and the South African apartheid regime.

---

1. Tor Sellström: *Sweden and National Liberation in Southern Africa: Formation of a Popular Opinion (1950-1970)*, Nordiska Afrikainstitutet, Uppsala, 1999. The first part of the study is referenced below as 'Sellström Volume I'.
2. And to PAIGC of Guinea-Bissau and Cape Verde.
3. In October 1969, Olof Palme was elected to lead the ruling Social Democratic Party, becoming Prime Minister of Sweden. For many years deeply concerned with the issues of national liberation and the right of small nations to self-determination, Palme—at the time the youngest Premier in Europe, representing a new political generation—would be closely identified with Sweden's policy towards Southern Africa. His appointment did not go unnoticed in the region. In an article headlined "Sweden's new premier is protest leader [and] anti-SA", the liberal South African newspaper *Rand Daily Mail* presented Palme as the "bane of [Sweden's] cosy middle classes", adding that he "on racial matters [...] spearheads the general Scandinavian condemnation of discrimination in South Africa and Rhodesia" (*Rand Daily Mail*, 14 October 1969).
4. 'Declaration on the Granting of Independence to Colonial Countries and Peoples' in *Yearbook of the United Nations: 1960*, Office of Public Information, United Nations, New York, 1961, p. 49.

Determined to keep Southern Africa under white rule, the minority regimes not only rejected popular democratic demands, but intensified the oppression of the black populations. At the beginning of 1959, emergency legislation was introduced throughout the Federation of Rhodesia and Nyasaland, followed by massive arrests and the banning of the leading nationalist organizations in Malawi (Nyasaland), Zambia (Northern Rhodesia) and Zimbabwe (Southern Rhodesia). In December 1959, thirteen people opposing forced eviction were killed by the South African police in Windhoek, Namibia (South West Africa). The Windhoek shootings were followed four months later—in March 1960—by the Sharpeville massacre in South Africa, where close to seventy people peacefully demonstrating against the apartheid pass laws were shot dead and two hundred wounded. After the shootings, the Pretoria regime proclaimed a state of emergency and banned ANC and PAC.[1] Similarly, in Angola a series of arrests and clampdowns on the nationalist movement from March 1959 culminated in June 1960 in the Catete massacre, where over thirty demonstrators were killed and another two hundred maimed by Portuguese soldiers. Finally, in June 1960 a staggering five hundred unarmed demonstrators were mown down by the Portuguese at Mueda in northern Mozambique.

Excluded from universally recognized democratic rights, oppressed in their own lands and having exhausted the limited peaceful avenues at their disposal, the peoples of Southern Africa eventually found no other solution than to embark on violent struggles for liberation. What has aptly been called the 'Thirty Years' War' in the region[2] started in Angola in February-March 1961, when MPLA attacked the prisons in Luanda in an attempt to free its jailed leaders and FNLA inspired popular insurrections in the northern parts of the country. Towards the end of the year, ANC of South Africa also abandoned the principle of non-violence, formed Umkhonto we Sizwe with its main allies and launched a campaign of armed sabotage and propaganda. FRELIMO initiated the armed struggle in Mozambique in September 1964, and in 1965-66—after Ian Smith's Unilateral Declaration of Independence in Rhodesia (Zimbabwe)—ZANU and ZAPU similarly decided to take up arms.[3] In Namibia, SWAPO's first military encounter with the South African occupation forces took place in August 1966.

From the mid-1960s, Southern Africa[4] became the scene of armed struggles between intransigent white minority regimes and national liberation movements pushed to use organized violence to achieve legitimate demands for democracy and national self-determination. The struggles were not confined to Southern Africa proper, but extended into Africa and, eventually, to the world at large. Forced by

---

1. For the full names behind the acronyms, see the list above. In the text, the liberation movements are mentioned by their acronyms only, i.e. without the definite article.
2. John S. Saul: *Recolonization and Resistance: Southern Africa in the 1990s*, Africa World Press, Trenton, 1993, p. ix.
3. 'The Battle of Sinoia' (now Chinhoyi) on 28 April 1966—when freedom fighters from ZANU clashed with Ian Smith's security forces—is in Zimbabwe officially considered as the beginning of the liberation war. However, ZAPU's former head of military intelligence, Dumiso Dabengwa, has stressed that "[c]ontrary to claims that ZANU started the armed struggle in 1966 in Chinhoyi, the fact is that ZAPU's armed struggle started in 1965 when [...] small units were sent into the country" (Dumiso Dabengwa: 'ZIPRA in the Zimbabwe War of National Liberation' in Ngwabi Bhebe and Terence Ranger (eds): *Soldiers in Zimbabwe's Liberation War*, Volume I, University of Zimbabwe Publications, Harare, 1995, p. 27).
4. Although Bechuanaland (Botswana), Basutoland (Lesotho) and Swaziland stayed outside the direct conflict between the Southern African white minority regimes and the nationalist forces, they were from the beginning drawn into the regional struggles. Under British sovereignty and economically dependent on South Africa, they offered only limited room for political manoeuvre to the liberation movements. Nevertheless, the so called BLS territories—Bechuanaland in particular—were both important as escape routes for persecuted nationalists from South Africa, Namibia and Zimbabwe and as host countries for refugee students from these countries.

bannings and political repression in their home countries, the liberation movements had from the early 1960s set up exile bases in independent Africa. Throughout the decade, increasing flows of refugees joined them there, with growing humanitarian concerns as a result. Tanzania, Zambia and—in the case of Angola—the two Congos became important political rearguard areas and host nations, both for the Southern African nationalist organizations and the refugee populations. The fact that the minority regimes enjoyed support from the major Western powers and that the liberation movements in their search for military training and arms supplies received assistance from the Soviet Union, China and other East bloc countries also introduced a divisive ideological Cold War dimension into the nationalist struggles.

Despite progress on the ground—particularly in Angola and Mozambique—the nationalist organizations were at the end of the 1960s confronted with major political and military challenges. In South Africa, the apartheid regime had effectively crushed the internal opposition[1], and ANC's efforts to penetrate the country via Zimbabwe through military cooperation with ZAPU in the 1967 Wankie campaign had ended in defeat. With regard to Namibia, the South African parliament passed the South West Africa Affairs Bill in March 1969 with the objective to reduce the country to the status of a South African province.[2] In Zimbabwe, repeated talks between the British Prime Minister Harold Wilson and Ian Smith appeared to be just talks, without any acceptable solution to the white settler rebellion in sight.

Finally, in the Portuguese colonies of Angola and Mozambique—as well as in Guinea-Bissau in West Africa—the Lisbon regime steadily increased its military presence. At the end of the decade, the Portuguese troops in the three colonies exceeded 120,000.[3] That Portugal's resolve to keep the 'overseas provinces' went beyond the self-proclaimed 'national borders' was illustrated in February 1969, when the FRELIMO President Eduardo Mondlane was assassinated in the Tanzanian capital Dar es Salaam, provoking a serious crisis in the Mozambican liberation movement and dramatically indicating to all Southern African nationalists that exile was far from a safe haven.[4]

Encouraged by the military offensives, in April 1969 the Portuguese Prime Minister Marcelo Caetano embarked on a tour of Angola, Guinea-Bissau and Mozambique. The African tour—the first ever by a Portuguese Premier—was warmly welcomed by his South African counterpart John Vorster, who declared that Caetano's assurances that Portugal would continue its established policy in Africa "helped to strengthen morale" in other countries too, that is, mainly in South

---

1. In 1999, ANC's Raymond Suttner commented: "We may sometimes forget how difficult the periods were before we had rebuilt our structures [...]. I was a student in the 1960s, and by 1969 there appeared to be no presence whatsoever of the ANC within the country" (Raymond Suttner: 'Response, South Africa' in Robben Island Museum, Mayibuye Centre and Nordic Africa Institute: *Conference Report: Nordic Solidarity with the Liberation Struggles in Southern Africa, and Challenges for Democratic Partnerships into the 21st Century,* Robben Island, 11-14 February 1999, p. 87.

2. The move was immediately countered by the United Nations. Also in March 1969, the UN Security Council terminated South Africa's mandate over Namibia, declaring its continued presence in the country illegal (UN Security Council Resolution No. 264 of 20 March 1969).

3. Letter from Gunnar Dryselius, Swedish ambassador to Portugal, to the Ministry for Foreign Affairs, Lisbon, 6 March 1969 (MFA). Portugal mobilized no less than 1 per cent of its total population to the three military theatres in Africa, but "simply could not sustain this domestic manpower drain" (John P. Cann: *Counterinsurgency in Africa: The Portuguese Way of War, 1961-1974,* Greenwood Press, Westport, Connecticut and London, 1997, p. 106). By 1974, a total of 150,000 Portuguese soldiers were waging a losing war against an estimated number of 6,000 guerrillas for PAIGC, 10,000 for FRELIMO and 4,500 for MPLA. At the same time, FNLA and UNITA combined had a military force of about 1,500 (ibid., pp. 91 and 107).

4. See, for example, the interview with Ben Amathila, p. 64. Unless otherwise stated, the interviews referred to appear in Tor Sellström (ed.): *Liberation in Southern Africa-Regional and Swedish Voices: Interviews from Angola, Mozambique, Namibia, South Africa, Zimbabwe, the Frontline and Sweden,* Nordiska Afrikainstitutet, Uppsala, 1999.

Africa and Ian Smith's Rhodesia.[1] Shortly thereafter, the secret services in the three countries started to coordinate their counter-insurgency policies.[2]

Such was, in broad outline, the situation when the main international actors in the ensuing Southern African drama at the close of the 1960s defined their positions vis-à-vis the regional liberation struggles.

International Standpoints

After the March 1960 Sharpeville massacre in South Africa, the UN Security Council had in April for the first time discussed apartheid as an international issue, and in December the General Assembly adopted the Decolonization Declaration. Under increasing influence from the Afro-Asian group of member states, the United Nations would from the mid-1960s also address the issue of humanitarian support to the peoples under apartheid, foreign occupation and colonialism. Resolutions passed by the General Assembly regularly urged the member states to render moral and material assistance to the peoples of Southern Africa in their struggles for freedom and independence.[3] The decision taken by the Swedish parliament in May 1969 referred directly to the assembly resolutions, stating that

> with regard to liberation movements in Africa, humanitarian assistance [...] should not be in conflict with [international law] in cases where the United Nations unequivocally has taken a stand against oppression of peoples striving for national freedom. This [is] deemed to be the case [with regard to] South West Africa, Rhodesia and the African territories under Portuguese suzerainty. Concerning assistance to the victims of the policy of apartheid, such support can *inter alia* be motivated by the explicit condemnation by the United Nations of South Africa's policy.[4]

In the 1960s, several influential international organizations went through a process similar to that of the UN General Assembly. The World Council of Churches (WCC), for example, became increasingly concerned with the issue of racism in general and the situation in Southern Africa in particular. After convening the historic Cottesloe meeting in South Africa in December 1960—which rejected all forms of racial discrimination and provoked a break with the Dutch Reformed Church of South Africa—the WCC assembly in New Dehli, India, declared in 1961 that "racism [...] often causes oppressed people to resort to violence when they have no other option" and that "[t]he churches should identify themselves with the oppressed race".[5]

Establishing close relations with several of the Southern African liberation movements—in particular ANC of South Africa and FRELIMO of Mozambique[6]—

1. Cited in Colin Legum and John Drysdale: *Africa Contemporary Record: Annual Survey and Documents 1969-1970*, Africa Research Limited, Exeter, 1970, p. C 26.
2. In July 1969, senior representatives from Portugal's PIDE, Rhodesia's Security Police and South Africa's BOSS met in the Portuguese capital Lisbon. Such tripartite meetings were regularly held until the fall of the Caetano regime in April 1974.
3. Towards the end of the 1960s, the appeals for support by the UN General Assembly were often issued in favour of the national liberation movements in the respective countries. Usually, the member states were asked to coordinate the requested assistance with the Organization of African Unity.
4. Swedish Parliament 1969: Statement No. 82/1969 by the Appropriations Committee, pp. 23-24.
5. Cited in Baldwin Sjollema: 'The Initial Challenge' in Pauline Webb (ed.): *A Long Struggle: The Involvement of the World Council of Churches in South Africa*, WCC Publications, Geneva, 1994, p. 5.
6. Several prominent Southern African nationalist leaders were closely involved with the World Council of Churches. This was, notably, the case with Z.K. Matthews, former member of the ANC National Executive Committee, who in 1962 joined the WCC staff as secretary of its Division of Inter-Church Aid, Refugee and World Service. Also the FRELIMO President Eduardo Mondlane had early links to WCC. As early as in 1954, Mondlane was a youth representative to the WCC assembly and would until his death in 1969 often participate in various WCC meetings.

Dancing outside the cathedral: Archbishops Desmond Tutu and Bertil Werkström from the Church of Sweden in Uppsala, June 1989 (Photo: Jim Elfström/IKON, Svenska kyrkans bildbyrå)

the ecumenical world body went further. At its fourth assembly in Uppsala, Sweden, it was in 1968 decided that WCC should "undertake a crash programme to guide the council and member churches in the urgent matter of racism".[1] The decision led the following year to the establishment of WCC's Ecumenical Programme to Combat Racism—commonly referred to as the Programme to Combat Racism (PCR)—through which the member churches from 1970 would channel direct humanitarian support to the Southern African liberation movements.[2]

The stand provoked vehement reactions from advocates of apartheid and colonialism in Southern Africa, ironically portraying themselves as defenders of a

1. Sjollema in Webb (ed.) op. cit., p. 10.
2. The first grants—in total amounting to 120,000 USD—were given in favour of education and health projects and channelled to the following nine African liberation movements: FNLA, MPLA and UNITA of Angola, PAIGC of Guinea-Bissau, FRELIMO of Mozambique, SWAPO of Namibia, ANC of South Africa and ZANU and ZAPU of Zimbabwe (Marianne Rappe: '10 Frågor till Ärkebiskopen'/'10 Questions to the Archbishop' in *Rapport från SIDA*, No. 3, 1971, p. 10). At first, the Nordic churches experienced quite widespread internal opposition to PCR and the support to the liberation movements. In the case of Sweden, Tore Bergman, former Africa secretary of the official Church of Sweden Mission (CSM), stated in 1997 that CSM "received very heavy criticism from certain quarters in Sweden" because of its contributions to PCR. The criticism "resulted in a loss of contributions towards the general work of the Church of Sweden, and the Church of Sweden Mission was branded by some people as pro-Communist and as a movement propagating armed violence" (Interview with Tore Bergman, p. 264). The South African church leader and activist Beyers Naudé described in 1995 the initial attitude of the Nordic churches as "over-cautious", which he attributed to "the fact that in the Nordic churches the pietistic, evangelistic movement has always played [...] a very strong role. The danger of pietism is always to be non-political, non-controversial and to withdraw from any political debate and discussion" (Interview with Beyers Naudé, p. 183). Eventually, however, the Norwegian and Swedish churches extended considerable support to PCR (Interview with Barney Pityana, p. 189). In the case of Sweden, the bulk of the funds was from 1970/71 allocated by SIDA through the Swedish Ecumenical Council.

'Christian civilization'. The South African Prime Minister John Vorster accused WCC of being infiltrated by Communists and providing "terrorist organizations with funds for buying arms".[1] Similar views were expressed during the following years by many leading Western politicians and military strategists.[2] They were strongly rejected by prominent representatives of the South African churches. While stating his position that "there is no way in which a Christian can be a member of the Communist Party", the 1984 Nobel Peace Prize laureate Desmond Tutu, Anglican Archbishop and General Secretary of the South African Council of Churches, emphasized that

> [i]t was not Communists who oppressed us, it was not Communists who thought up apartheid [and] it was not Communists who killed our people in Sharpeville [...]. It was Christians who killed us [and] it was Christians who [created] apartheid.[3]

Closer to the conflict areas in Southern Africa, thirteen independent states in East and Central Africa[4] defined their position during a summit meeting held in the Zambian capital Lusaka in April 1969. Chaired by the Zambian President Kenneth Kaunda and attended by his Tanzanian colleague Julius Nyerere, the summit adopted the so called Lusaka Manifesto on Southern Africa. In this important document—drafted by the Zambian and Tanzanian leaders[5]—the assembled African heads of state and government stated that

> we do not accept that any one group within a society has the right to rule any society without the continuing consent of all the citizens. [...] [T]he principle of human equality, and all that flows from it, is either universal or it does not exist. [...] Our objectives in Southern Africa stem from our commitment to [the] principle of human equality. [...] [W]e can neither surrender, nor compromise. We have always preferred, and we still prefer, to achieve [liberation in the region] without physical violence. We would prefer to negotiate rather than destroy, to talk rather than kill. We do not advocate violence. We advocate an end to the violence against human dignity which is now being perpetrated by the oppressors of Africa. [...]

> If peaceful progress to emancipation were possible, or if changed circumstances were to make it possible in the future, we would urge our brothers in the resistance movements to use peaceful methods of struggle even at the cost of some compromise on the timing of change. But while peaceful progress is being blocked by actions of those at present in power in the states of Southern Africa, we have no choice but to give to the peoples of those territories all the support of which we are capable in their struggle against their oppressors.[6]

1. Baldwin Sjollema: 'Eloquent Action' in Webb (ed.) op. cit., p. 15.
2. For example, by the British General Walter Walker, former NATO Commander-in-Chief, Allied Forces, Northern Europe, in his *The Bear at the Back Door: The Soviet Threat to the West's Lifeline in Africa*, Foreign Affairs Publishing Co., Surrey, 1978.
3. Desmond Tutu: *The Essential Desmond Tutu*, compiled by John Allen, David Philip Publishers and Mayibuye Books, Cape Town, 1997, pp. 55-56.
4. Malawi participated in the summit, but did not sign the manifesto. As the only independent state in Southern Africa, Malawi had in 1967 established diplomatic relations with South Africa.
5. Thomas G. Karis and Gail M. Gerhart: *From Protest to Challenge: A Documentary History of African Politics in South Africa, 1882-1990; Volume 5: Nadir and Resurgence, 1964-1979*, Indiana University Press, Bloomington & Indianapolis, 1997, p. 34.
6. 'The Lusaka Manifesto on Southern Africa' in J. Ayo Langley: *Ideologies of Liberation in Black Africa, 1856-1970: Documents on Modern African Political Thought from Colonial Times to the Present*, Rex Collings, London, 1979, pp. 782-84.

Although the manifesto was far from satisfactory to the Southern African liberation movements[1], the fact that it was promoted by Presidents Kaunda and Nyerere—their two most important hosts in exile—made it particularly significant. Later in the year, the Lusaka Manifesto was endorsed by both the Organization of African Unity and the UN General Assembly. In the case of Sweden—which maintained particularly close relations with Zambia and Tanzania—the Social Democratic government welcomed the willingness to search for peaceful solutions to the problems of Southern Africa. In a statement in March 1970, Foreign Minister Torsten Nilsson expressed admiration for "the African leaders for being so far-sighted in their attitude, even though they are exposed to great provocation from the white oppressor regimes. The high-minded principles they profess in this manifesto make it a Magna Carta for all who live in Southern Africa".[2]

Also in 1969, both the Soviet Union (indirectly) and the United States (covertly) defined their views on Southern Africa. The position of the Soviet Union was not new. It was on an initiative taken by the Soviet leader Nikita Khrushchev that the UN General Assembly in December 1960 adopted the historic Decolonization Declaration, and the Soviet Union had together with its allies from the early 1960s extended assistance to the liberation movements in Southern Africa, not least in the military field. Nevertheless, what became clearer at the close of the 1960s was the preference accorded to certain nationalist organizations.

In January 1969—three months before the African summit meeting which adopted the Lusaka Manifesto—a first International Conference of Solidarity with the Peoples of Southern Africa and the Portuguese Colonies[3] was sponsored by the Soviet Union and jointly organized by the Afro-Asian Peoples Solidarity Organization[4] and the World Peace Council[5] in the Sudanese capital Khartoum. In addition to leading nationalists from Southern Africa, it assembled more than two hundred delegates from over fifty countries. Although most of the delegates represented Communist organizations, there were also representatives from the Labour Party in

---

1. The liberation movements were not consulted during the drafting of the Lusaka Manifesto, which, in addition, did not recognize them as important actors. In general, the movements objected to the emphasis on peaceful change. In the case of South Africa, the manifesto further appeared to undermine the view held by both ANC and PAC that the apartheid regime was illegal, acknowledging that "the Republic of South Africa is [...] an independent sovereign state and a member of the United Nations". However, given their dependence on—in particular—Zambia and Tanzania, none of the Southern African liberation movements publicly criticized the manifesto. Nevertheless, at its consultative conference in Morogoro, Tanzania, ANC ten days later addressed a number of the uncertainties introduced by the declaration. (On the Lusaka Manifesto and ANC, see Karis and Gerhart op. cit., pp. 34-35 and Scott Thomas: *The Diplomacy of Liberation: The Foreign Relations of the ANC since 1960*, Tauris Academic Studies, I.B. Tauris Publishers, London and New York, 1996, pp. 128-30.)
2. 'Extract from a statement by the Foreign Minister', 20 March 1970, in The Royal Ministry for Foreign Affairs: *Documents on Swedish Foreign Policy: 1970*, Stockholm, 1971, p. 105.
3. The conference also covered Guinea-Bissau. PAIGC was represented by its Secretary General, Amílcar Cabral.
4. The Afro-Asian Peoples Solidarity Organization (AAPSO) traced its origins to the Conference of Afro-Asian Nations held in Bandung, Indonesia, in April 1955. The Bandung conference was the first major political expression of cooperation between recently independent Third World nations, giving definition to some of the basic principles of Afro-Asian solidarity, such as anti-colonialism, anti-imperialism and non-alignment. The 'Bandung spirit' later guided the Afro-Asian group at the United Nations and inspired the Non-Aligned Movement, formed in Belgrade, Yugoslavia, in September 1961. With headquarters in Cairo, Egypt, AAPSO was founded in December 1957. Working through national committees in a great number of African, Asian and—mainly—Eastern European countries, its aims were *inter alia* to eliminate colonialism and consolidate genuine independence.
5. The World Peace Council (WPC) was closely linked to the Soviet Union and the Communist movement. With headquarters in Prague, Czechoslovakia, WPC was founded in Warsaw, Poland, in November 1950, having as its main objectives to eliminate weapons of mass destruction, prohibit foreign military bases and promote the right to sovereignty and national independence. Members were national committees, as a rule based within Communist or Communist-aligned political parties in various countries. In Western Europe, WPC maintained an important office in Helsinki, Finland.

Britain, the British Anti-Apartheid Movement and the London-based International Defence and Aid Fund.[1] Presenting a report on behalf of the invited liberation movements[2], the FRELIMO President Eduardo Mondlane—who only two weeks later would be killed by a parcel bomb in Dar es Salaam—stressed the hope that the conference would "stimulate a new interest [in the liberation struggles], primarily among [the] African independent states. As a matter of fact", Mondlane said,

> following the Addis Ababa heads of state conference in 1963, much enthusiasm and zeal were stimulated in Africa on the question of liberation.[3] During the last few years, however, that enthusiasm has been allowed to cool down as African countries have come to give priority to their own internal problems and contradictions. [...]
>
> It is hoped [that] a conference like this will prove highly beneficial in warming up [the] energies for the liberation struggle. [...] [W]e need a great deal more material assistance from Africa and our friends abroad. In order to have a decisive victory over our enemy, we will have to move out of the guerrilla phase of our struggle to a regular army phase. This will need more and better weapons [and it] implies heavier commitments on the part of our friends. [...] We must not fall into the usual mistake of previous conferences, satisfying ourselves with [...] strong resolutions against the enemy and thinking that in this way we will frighten him into retreating from our lands. The liberation movements believe that the shortest and only path to freedom is to be cleared by fire.[4]

The critical and militant statement by the liberation movements influenced the discussions and was reflected in the conference resolutions. They called on "democratic forces everywhere to support the political demands of the liberation movements for independence, democracy and unqualified and immediate implementation of majority rule", as well as "urging maximum material and moral support for the armed struggle in Southern Africa and the Portuguese colonies".[5] While emphasis on armed struggle in the era of the Vietnam war was far from exceptional, the decision to extend exclusive recognition only to the invited liberation movements would have significant consequences. Thus, the conference made an appeal

> to recognize as the sole official and legitimate authority of the respective countries the following fighting movements: MPLA (Angola), PAIGC (Guinea-Bissau), FRELIMO (Mozambique), ANC (South Africa), SWAPO (Namibia) and ZAPU (Zimbabwe), and to recognize them as the accredited representatives of the people's organizations in these countries.[6]

---

1. Thomas op. cit., p. 19. IDAF's founder and director, Canon John Collins, submitted a paper on 'Material Aid' to the conference.
2. The Southern African movements were represented by Robert Resha (ANC), Eduardo Mondlane (FRELIMO), Agostinho Neto (MPLA), Sam Nujoma (SWAPO) and Stephen Nkomo (ZAPU).
3. At the inaugural OAU meeting in Addis Ababa, Ethiopia, in May 1963, it was decided to establish a Coordinating Committee for the Liberation of Africa. In recognition of Tanzania's role, the OAU Liberation Committee was based in Dar es Salaam. During the first ten years, the efficiency of the committee was seriously affected by divergent political views between the OAU member states, as well as by organizational constraints and—above all—a lack of financial resources. For a study on the OAU Liberation Committee during the initial years, see Franz Ansprenger: *Die Befreiungspolitik der Organisation für Afrikanische Einheit (OAU), 1963 bis 1975* ('The Liberation Policy of the Organization of African Unity (OAU), 1963 to 1975'), Studien zum Konflikt im Südlichen Afrika, Chr. Kaiser Verlag, Munich, 1975.
4. 'Joint Statement of the Liberation Movement[s] of [the] Portuguese Colonies and Southern Africa', International Conference in Support of the Peoples of [the] Portuguese Colonies and Southern Africa (sic), Khartoum, 18-20 January, 1969, pp. 1 and 4 (NAI).
5. Cited in 'The Khartoum Conference: First International Conference of Solidarity' in Legum and Drysdale op. cit., p. C 155. The conference also called upon "the progressive and anti-imperialist forces of the entire world to back the armed struggles which have been forced upon [the freedom fighters of the Portuguese colonies and Southern Africa] as the only alternative to slavery" (ibid.).
6. Ibid.

What was called the Khartoum alliance of 'sole official and legitimate'—or 'authentic'—liberation movements was at the same time a confirmation of long-standing political and ideological affinities between the six movements and existing relations with the Soviet Union in the military field.[1] For the Soviet Union, the formal constitution of an allied group of the leading Southern African liberation movements was highly significant, not least in the ongoing ideological struggle with the People's Republic of China for influence in Africa.[2] For the movements themselves—from then on often appearing as a group—it strengthened their international standing, in particular vis-à-vis the Communist countries and the Non-Aligned Movement, but also within many solidarity organizations in the West.[3] At the same time, however, the alliance added propaganda arguments to those Western interests that were opposed to democracy and national independence in Southern Africa and Guinea-Bissau. They would regularly label the nationalist organizations as 'Soviet-backed', 'Communist' or 'terrorist'.[4] The exclusive recognition of one liberation movement in each country was also contrary to the official OAU position.[5]

The constitution of the Khartoum alliance increased the cleavage between its members and competing nationalist organizations, notably in the cases of ANC and PAC of South Africa and ZAPU and ZANU of Zimbabwe.[6] This was to prove particularly costly in Zimbabwe, where ZANU—a 'non-authentic' movement—emerged as the dominant political force. After Zimbabwe's independence in 1980, the Soviet Union and its Eastern allies, as well as MPLA-ruled Angola and ANC of South Africa, were initially kept at arm's length by the ZANU-led government,

---

1. In this context, SWAPO appeared as a more uncertain partner. It had close relations with UNITA of Angola and was neutral in the Sino-Soviet conflict. Much closer to the alliance partners, FRELIMO maintained good relations with both the Soviet Union and the People's Republic of China.

2. A short-lived group—known as the Congo alliance—had in the early 1960s been formed around FNLA of Angola, UDENAMO of Mozambique, SWAPO of Namibia, PAC of South Africa and—from 1963—ZANU of Zimbabwe. In response to the Khartoum initiative, China attempted at the end of the decade to support the formation of a rival group composed of UNITA, COREMO of Mozambique, SWANU of Namibia, PAC and ZANU, but it never achieved the cohesion of the Khartoum alliance. Within the group supported by China, PAC and ZANU maintained particularly close relations.

3. Often in a sectarian manner, the 'authentic' movements of the Khartoum alliance blocked the non-alliance members from participation in solidarity meetings. In the case of ZANU in Sweden, see the interview with Sydney Sekeramayi, p. 228.

4. The successful 'non-authentic' movements, similarly, did not escape the epithets. In an article in the US journal *Foreign Affairs*, the ZANU leader Robert Mugabe—then Prime Minister of Zimbabwe—wrote, for example, in late 1987 that "[d]uring our war of liberation I was accused of leading surrogate Russian forces, when in fact the Russian government adamantly refused to give us a single gun or [R]uble. [I]n 1978, they even refused me permission to pass through the Moscow airport in transit" (Robert Mugabe: 'Struggle for Southern Africa' in *Foreign Affairs*, Vol. 66, No. 2, Winter 1987, p. 320).

5. Although OAU recognized more than one liberation movement in a given country, the policy of the Liberation Committee was to unite them into one common front. For a critique of this policy, see the interviews with Ottilie Abrahams (pp. 59-62) and Mishake Muyongo (pp. 88-89). On the Khartoum resolution and the OAU policy, cf. also Ibbo Mandaza: 'The State and Democracy in Southern Africa: Towards a Conceptual Framework' in *Southern Africa Political and Economic Monthly*, No. 6, 1991, where the Zimbabwean scholar comments that "at the end of the day, it was a question of which of the two [i.e. the Soviet Union or China] would provide material support for a struggle that was essentially nationalist in character". Looking beyond political independence, he adds: "[T]o the extent that the main thrust and nature of the liberation struggle in Southern Africa purported to be based upon Marxism-Leninism and the idea of a 'sole' and 'authentic' vanguard party, so too did this provide both the justification and the impetus towards a *One-Party State* in the post-colonial period" (p. 48).

6. In the political report by the ANC National Executive Committee to the Morogoro consultative conference, UNITA and FNLA of Angola, COREMO of Mozambique, PAC of South Africa and ZANU of Zimbabwe were three months later characterized as "spurious stooge organizations", created and maintained by "the imperialists" (Oliver Tambo: *Preparing for Power: Oliver Tambo Speaks*, Compiled by Adelaide Tambo, Heinemann, London, 1987, p. 74).

while PAC and SWAPO were welcomed into the country.[1] Later criticizing the decision adopted by the Khartoum conference, Ilona and Hans-Georg Schleicher—the latter *inter alia* representing the German Democratic Republic (GDR) in Zambia, Zimbabwe and Namibia—have commented that

> the policy of exclusion blocked all possibility of cooperation with liberation movements that maintained links with China. It was an admission of failure as regards political foresight by the Soviet Union and its allies, among them GDR. [...] For a long time, it hopelessly blocked a mutual rapprochement [between] GDR and ZANU.[2]

Sweden did not extend formal recognition to the Southern African liberation movements in the spirit of the Khartoum conference.[3] It is, nevertheless, relevant for the following discussion that both the Social Democratic (1969-1976 and 1982-91) and the non-socialist (1976-1982 and 1991-1994) governments granted official assistance to the Khartoum alliance members, that is, to the very same movements that were given preferential treatment by the Soviet Union. There was, however, one important exception. In the case of Zimbabwe, ZANU was from the very beginning an important recipient of Swedish support. The Southern African liberation movements that were directly assisted by Sweden and *de facto* increasingly were regarded as 'governments-in-waiting' by different Swedish governments[4]— irrespective of the political parliamentary majorities—were thus MPLA of Angola, FRELIMO of Mozambique, SWAPO of Namibia, ANC of South Africa and both ZANU and ZAPU of Zimbabwe. These movements—all of them waging armed struggle—would eventually lead their peoples to majority rule and national independence. Direct official Swedish support was never channelled to competing organizations, such as FNLA and UNITA of Angola, PAC of South Africa or UANC of Zimbabwe.[5]

Following the Khartoum conference and the African summit in Lusaka, the new Republican US administration under President Richard Nixon, finally, clarified its position on Southern Africa. Due to the pre-eminence of the United States in the Western world, it was to have a deep and lasting impact on the developments in the region.

At the time of Nixon's investiture in January 1969, US concerns about South and Southern Africa were virtually at their nadir. It was the war in Vietnam and its repercussions at home that preoccupied the new administration. Nevertheless, in

---

1. ZANU's views did not affect SWAPO or FRELIMO. After its formation in 1963, ZANU maintained close relations with SWAPO, and from 1970 ZANU and FRELIMO coordinated their military activities. In fact, in the early 1970s FRELIMO tried to establish cooperation with its Khartoum partner ZAPU, but "could not find them. [...] No one was forthcoming". Instead, a close and decisive alliance was established with ZANU (Interview with Sérgio Vieira, p. 56). As stated by the FRELIMO leader Marcelino dos Santos, both practical realities and history proved that ZANU was an 'authentic' liberation movement (Interview with Marcelino dos Santos, p. 49).
2. Ilona and Hans-Georg Schleicher: *Die DDR im südlichen Afrika: Solidarität und Kalter Krieg* ('GDR in Southern Africa: Solidarity and Cold War'), Institut für Afrika-Kunde, Hamburg, 1997, p. 101. This important study covers GDR's relations with ANC and SACP of South Africa, ZAPU and ZANU of Zimbabwe and SWAPO of Namibia. Hans-Georg Schleicher served as GDR's ambassador to Zimbabwe in the 1980s and led the GDR observer mission to Namibia in 1989-90. Under the title *Special Flights: The GDR and Liberation Movements in Southern Africa*, the study was in 1998 published in English by SAPES Books, Harare. The quotes are translations from the original German text.
3. In November 1972, the UN General Assembly recognized PAIGC as 'the sole and authentic representative of the people of the territory' of Guinea-Bissau and in December 1973 SWAPO was similarly recognized as the 'authentic representative of the Namibian people'.
4. Cf. the interview with Thabo Mbeki, pp. 153-56.
5. To the extent that they were assisted by the United Nations and international NGOs, such as IDAF, IUEF, WUS and others, these movements did, however, indirectly receive official Swedish support.

April 1969 Nixon initiated a comprehensive review of the United States policies towards Southern Africa, to be implemented by the staff of the national security adviser Henry Kissinger. Contemporary observers eagerly awaited the outcome of the review, noting that it was "far from clear in which direction Kissinger would steer President Nixon [...], [whether] towards strengthening the Lusaka Manifesto's approach or towards killing the whole of its spirit".[1] Both positions had influential American advocates. Senator Edward Kennedy strongly supported the Lusaka Manifesto, which he saw as "a convincing plea for the basic principles of human dignity and equality [...] long associated with the liberal traditions of the West and the noblest aspirations of man".[2] The former Secretary of State Dean Acheson understood the Western values differently, emphasizing that the United States, "as the principal responsible power in the free world", had a

> duty and responsibility to encourage good will, cooperation and stability in Southern Africa. It [would be] the height of folly to sacrifice these desirable ends to an aggressive reformist intervention in the internal affairs of these states, [...] designed to force upon them electoral practices that none of the black African or Communist states and few of the Asians accept.[3]

It was eventually the Acheson view that the Nixon administration endorsed, killing the spirit of the Lusaka Manifesto. Of the different options outlined in Kissinger's secret National Security Study Memorandum 39 ('NSSM 39'), it was the following scenario that was adopted as US policy in January 1970:

> The whites are here to stay and the only way that constructive change can come about is through them. There is no hope for the blacks to gain the political rights they seek through violence, which will only lead to chaos and increased opportunities for the Communists. We can, by selective relaxation of our stance toward the white regimes, encourage some modification of their current racial and colonial policies and through more substantial economic assistance to the black states [...] help to draw the two groups together and exert some influence on both for peaceful change. Our tangible interests form a basis for our contacts in the region and these can be maintained at an acceptable political cost.[4]

Based on this assessment, the Nixon administration would quietly improve US relations with apartheid South Africa, eschew pressuring Portugal regarding independence for its colonies, modulate American statements on Southern Africa at the United Nations and—to balance these moves—increase aid to the independent African states. Leading the Western alliance—but in contrast to the stand taken by the United Nations, the Organization of African Unity and major international organizations such as the World Council of Churches—the United States effectively came to the rescue of the increasingly isolated Southern African minority regimes at a crucial time. As in the case of the policy of 'constructive engagement' under President Ronald Reagan in the 1980s, the stated objective was to increase communication with the white regimes in order to convince them to alter their positions. This

---

1. Colin Legum: 'America's Year in Africa' in Legum and Drysdale op. cit., p. A 45.
2. Cited in ibid., p. A 43.
3. Cited in ibid., p. A 42.
4. *The Kissinger Study on Southern Africa*, Spokesman Books, Nottingham, 1975, p. 66. NSSM 39 was not made public by the US government. The main points of the study were leaked to the press and the full text—including revealing views on the Southern African liberation movements—was brought to light in the autumn of 1974.

policy was to prove both "a gross miscalculation"[1] and "extremely myopic".[2] To the peoples of Southern Africa, its consequences were utterly painful, leading to untold suffering over the following two and a half decades.

Scope and Layout

Taking an opposite stand to the United States, Sweden became the first—and for several years the only—industrialized Western country to extend direct official assistance to the Southern African liberation movements.[3] Until the 1994 democratic elections in South Africa, a total of around 4 billion Swedish Kronor (SEK)—in current figures[4]—was channelled by the Swedish government as official humanitarian assistance to the region.[5] Of this amount, 1.7 billion—more than 40 per cent—was under bilateral agreements granted directly to ANC, FRELIMO, MPLA, SWAPO, ZANU and ZAPU.[6]

Attempting to identify the actors and factors behind the decision taken by the Swedish parliament in May 1969, Volume I addressed the question *why* Sweden became concerned with the liberation struggles in Southern Africa. The text that follows will discuss *how* the concern was expressed, focusing on the direct official assistance to the nationalist movements during the increasingly pro-active period that began around 1970. It mainly draws on hitherto restricted official primary

---

1. Thomas Karis: 'United States Policy toward South Africa' in Gwendolen M. Carter and Patrick O'Meara (eds): *Southern Africa: The Continuing Crisis*, The Macmillan Press, London and Basingstoke, 1979, p. 334.
2. Kema Irogbe: *The Roots of United States Foreign Policy toward Apartheid South Africa, 1969-1985*, The Edwin Mellen Press, Lewiston, Queenston and Lampeter, 1997, p. 71. On the US 'policy of communication', see also the doctoral dissertation by Hans Abrahamsson: *Seizing the Opportunity: Power and Powerlessness in a Changing World Order—The Case of Mozambique*, Department of Peace and Development Research, University of Gothenburg, 1997, pp. 165-70.
3. Among the Nordic countries, Finland and Norway decided in 1973 to grant direct official humanitarian support to the liberation movements. In the case of Finland, assistance to FRELIMO and SWAPO started in 1974 and to ANC in 1978. A smaller contribution was given to PAC in 1983. The Norwegian support was more comprehensive and substantial. Regular official assistance to FRELIMO, SWAPO, ZANU and ZAPU started in 1974 and to ANC and PAC in 1977. In 1977, Norway also granted UANC of Zimbabwe a financial contribution. As was later the case with other Western governments, Denmark did not extend direct official assistance to the liberation movements, but channelled considerable official resources via Danish and international non-governmental organizations. It could be noted that the Organization of African Unity during the first half of the 1970s regularly urged the Swedish government to channel its support via the OAU Liberation Committee. As the movements themselves were opposed to the idea (cf. the interview with ZANU's former Deputy Secretary of Finance Didymus Mutasa, pp. 218-19), this was, however, never implemented. Against the background of well established bilateral relations, in March 1974 the Ministry for Foreign Affairs concluded that support via OAU should only be given "under particular circumstances, for example, [...] in favour of a recipient that otherwise cannot be reached, or to satisfy a need which in any other way could not possibly be met" (Letter ('Bistånd till befrielserörelser via OAU?'/'Assistance to liberation movements via OAU?') from Anders Möllander to the Swedish embassy in Dar es Salaam, Ministry for Foreign Affairs, Stockholm, 20 March 1974) (SDA).
4. Figures given in the text refer to current amounts. For easy reference, a conversion table between the Swedish Krona (SEK) and the United States Dollar (USD) is appended.
5. Based on disbursement figures according to SIDA's audited annual accounts and established by Ulla Beckman for this study. Considerable amounts were, in addition, granted for emergencies, cultural activities, information, research etc. outside the bilateral regular assistance programmes.
6. The direct, official humanitarian assistance to the liberation movements was administered by SIDA. The disbursements to the Southern African movements and PAIGC within the regular assistance programmes are given in the accompanying tables. In 1995, the Swedish International Development Authority, with the acronym in capital letters, became the Swedish International Development Cooperation Agency, with the same acronym in small letters. As this study discusses events before 1995, the upper case version—i.e. SIDA—is used.

Anti-imperialist march
in central Stockholm,
December 1982: Veteran
activist and academic
Björn Beckman with the
placard 'Support ANC
and the Liberation
Struggle in South Africa'
(Courtesy of ISAK)

sources.[1] The important role played by the organized Swedish solidarity movement and other non-governmental organizations also forms part of the narration. Partly to avoid too many repetitions, the main NGO actors are in this respect given closer attention where their contributions have been particularly significant or conspicuous.[2]

Related issues, such as Sweden at the United Nations and official development assistance to the independent Southern African states—which may be studied in various open sources—feature only to the extent that they are relevant to the core subject.[3] Instead, the presentation includes discussions on humanitarian assistance

1. Documents regarding Swedish humanitarian assistance to Southern Africa were as a rule classified as confidential by the Ministry for Foreign Affairs or SIDA. The author is most grateful for having been granted access to these sources, without which the study could not have been undertaken. Notes, letters, memoranda etc. written under confidentiality are by historians often considered to be less influenced by secondary considerations than corresponding open documents and to represent a more direct or genuine view of the subject discussed. When reading the text below, in the case of quotations from internal Swedish records from meetings with representatives of the Southern African liberation movements at least three important considerations should, however, be borne in mind, namely a) that the document quoted reflects interpretations made by one party to the discussion; b) that the responsible official acts within a given political context; and—above all—c) that he or she represents a friendly or potential donor. Views expressed by a representative of a liberation movement may in the Swedish document appear as distorted, particularly as the Southern African interlocutor seeking financial or diplomatic support is likely to adjust his or her arguments to the donor's known position or perceived wish.
2. The youth and student movements are presented in the context of Mozambique, while the Africa Groups (AGIS) are introduced in the case of Angola. The contributions by the initially Christian-inspired Emmaus communities and Bread and Fishes, as well as by the Church of Sweden (CSM and CSA), feature prominently in the chapters on Zimbabwe and Namibia. In the cases of Namibia and South Africa, the role of the trade union movement (LO/TCO) is, similarly, emphasized. Throughout the text, the role of Swedish journalists and film-makers is conspicuous. While all the constituent parts of the wider solidarity movement joined forces in the anti-apartheid struggle, the text on South Africa, finally, underlines the significance of culture and the roles played by the International Centre of the Swedish Labour Movement (AIC)—later renamed the Olof Palme International Center (OPIC)—and the Isolate South Africa Committee (ISAK).
3. The issue of sanctions against Portugal, Rhodesia and—particularly—South Africa is highly relevant. As noted in the introduction to Volume I, while the Swedish sanctions debate—which mainly was conducted in open fora—forms a necessary part of the narration, it has, however, been documented elsewhere and will not be given prime attention. See, for example, Ove Nordenmark: *Aktiv Utrikespolitik: Sverige-Södra Afrika, 1969-1987* ('Active Foreign Policy: Sweden-Southern Africa, 1969-1987'), Acta Universitatis Upsalienses No. 111, Almqvist & Wiksell International, Stockholm, 1991. This doctoral dissertation in political science studies the Swedish political parties and the three main sanctions laws adopted in 1969 (against Rhodesia), 1979 (South Africa and Namibia) and 1987 (South Africa and Namibia).

and human rights;[1] opposition against the official policy;[2] and attempts to thwart the Swedish assistance to the liberation forces.[3]

The objectives, contexts and limitations of the study were outlined in the introductory chapter to Volume I. The reader of this volume should be reminded that it in no way purports to be a study of the liberation struggles in Southern Africa, nor an official version of Sweden's support to those struggles. The history of the Thirty Years' War in Southern Africa should primarily be written by scholars from the region.[4] Although the author for many years was involved with Swedish humanitarian assistance and the study has been financially supported by the government, there is, in addition, no 'official history' of the events discussed below. The representation of the past always carries the fingerprints of the individual interpreter.

The presentation roughly follows the sequence in which Swedish official assistance to the liberation movements was granted and—coincidentally—the order in which they became victorious in their respective countries, ending the protracted struggles for majority rule and national independence by assuming state power. It thus starts in the Portuguese colonies. Although Guinea-Bissau does not form part of Southern Africa, the assistance to PAIGC will on account of its wider significance—not least regarding the content and structure of Sweden's cooperation with the liberation movements—be presented in an introductory chapter. Sweden's involvement with Mozambique (FRELIMO), Angola (MPLA)[5], Zimbabwe (ZANU and ZAPU), Namibia (SWAPO) and South Africa (ANC) will thereafter be discussed.

Postscript

As new contradictions appeared after independence, the young Southern African states faced huge challenges. While Mozambique and South Africa on the threshold of the 21th century seemed to be constructively grappling with their violent pasts, in Angola MPLA and UNITA were still engaged in the open warfare that had rav-

---

1. See the chapters on Zimbabwe and—especially—Namibia.
2. Particularly in the context of the Swedish right wing and UNITA in the chapter on Angola.
3. In this respect, notably South Africa's infiltration of the International University Exchange Fund (IUEF), an international NGO supported by Sweden.
4. In his study on the Soviet Union and ANC of South Africa, Vladimir Shubin shares this view. Less convincing is his addendum that "of non-South African historians, it is perhaps Soviet/Russian scholars who are best placed to undertake [...] a comprehensive history of the ANC [...] because of the multi-faceted relationship that developed between Moscow and the South African liberation movement" (Vladimir Shubin: *ANC: A View from Moscow*, Mayibuye History and Literature Series No. 88, Mayibuye Books, University of the Western Cape, Bellville, 1999, p. 7). As Shubin himself eloquently describes, the Soviet support was, however, dominated by the armed struggle and the relations with the South African Communist Party. While the Soviet Union's assistance to ANC and the other 'authentic' liberation movements in Southern Africa was of fundamental importance to sustain military pressure, the non-military Swedish and Nordic support was arguably more diverse and significant. Thabo Mbeki, the President of South Africa, has stated that it was not merely complementary, but decisive also with regard to the armed struggle. Interviewed in 1995, he argued that "the position of Sweden created more space than the African or non-aligned position. It created space for ANC to be able to deal with the rest of the Western world. And not just the Western world, but even with regard to the Eastern world and the relationship [...] with those countries. [...] They called you a liberation movement, but they had a conception of that [...] movement as an opposition party. The notion that you could defeat a government that represented a system and have it replaced by the liberation movement might have been there theoretically. But, in practice, it was different, whereas Oliver Tambo could go to Sweden and be met by the Prime Minister, who understood that he represented a system that must replace the one in power" (Interview with Thabo Mbeki, pp. 154-55). This understanding was a result of ANC's close and extensive dialogue with the Swedish government, different political parties and the NGO community over a number of years.
5. In the case of Angola, the narration goes beyond the date of formal independence, covering aspects of Sweden's relations with UNITA in the 1970s and 1980s.

aged the country since Portugal's departure. In Namibia, the SWAPO government was increasingly criticized by both victims of abuse during the liberation struggle and upholders of the 1990 independence dispensation, opposing Sam Nujoma's third term as head of state. In Zimbabwe, ZANU's authoritarian rule under Robert Mugabe provoked widespread opposition. Clampdowns by the state against the press, trade unions and—in general—dissident citizens were recurrent. Angola, Namibia and Zimbabwe had at the same time dispatched military forces to the war in the Democratic Republic of Congo (ex-Zaire), straining weak economic resources and under the guise of national security restricting domestic criticism.

Post-independence developments raise questions regarding Sweden's assistance to the victorious liberation movements. Some Southern African scholars have suggested that seeds of authoritarian policies were sown by the external support during the liberation struggles, arguing that "the Nordic solidarity movement did not, as a matter of practice [...], promote a democratic culture as a critical component of [the] assistance".[1] Did the substantial involvement by the Swedish state and civil society thus mask shortcomings within the nationalist organizations, encouraging an uncritical, romantic representation of their political practices and evading serious dialogues concerning human rights, transparency and post-independence democratic visions? Did the assistance strengthen authoritarian orientations within and by the liberation movements? Did the nationalist leaders exploit Sweden's *de facto* recognition, using it to cement their positions and hold internal oppositions and competing forces at bay?

Concerned with Sweden's policies vis-à-vis the overriding historical contradiction in Southern Africa between, on the one hand, colonialism and minority rule and, on the other, national self-determination and majority rights, the study only indirectly addresses these important questions.[2] During the liberation wars, both the nationalist movements and their African host countries often sacrificed democratic debate and individual liberties for the sake of unity and purpose in working

---

1. Jonathan Moyo: 'Future Challenges' in Robben Island Museum, Mayibuye Centre and Nordic Africa Institute op. cit., p. 17. Mainly referring to Zimbabwe—his native country—Moyo added that "ruling personalities have hijacked the movement and are doing totally unacceptable things in the name of national liberation" (ibid.). It could, ironically, be noted that one year later Moyo appeared as ZANU-PF's strategist during the election campaign in Zimbabwe. Seriously marred by violence and intimidation from Mugabe's ruling party, the campaign was internationally denounced for its lack of fair play and transparency. Furthermore, after the June 2000 elections Moyo accepted President Mugabe's offer to become Minister of Information and Publicity. In another paper to the same conference, Addmore Kambudzi—also from Zimbabwe—suggested that "selective recognition and support reinforced the ego in [the] dominant nationalist movements to take all power for themselves once the colonial regime ceased" (A. M. Kambudzi: 'Zimbabwe: Nordic Solidarity, National Liberation and Post-Independence Problems and Prospects in Southern Africa' in ibid., p. 67). While not specifically discussing Sweden or the Nordic countries, in her critical study on SWAPO the Canadian scholar Lauren Dobell has similarly argued that "few, if any, serious inquiries were made by the providers of 'solidarity aid' into the 'inner life' of the movement" (Lauren Dobell: *SWAPO's Struggle for Namibia, 1960-1991: War by Other Means*, Basel Namibia Studies Series No. 3, P. Schlettwein Publishing, Basel, 1998, p. 64).

2. They were, however, raised in several of the interviews carried out for the study. Billy Modise, ANC's former Chief Representative to Sweden, emphasized, for example, that Swedes "at all levels spent time discussing the struggle with our leaders, the Tambos of this world. Sweden was [thus] in its own way able to influence them how they should handle things. In the minds of our leaders, Sweden helped to confirm that the basis of the struggle was to create democracy. The interaction between Sweden and ANC strengthened the democratic urge of the ANC leadership" (Interview with Billy Modise, p. 160). It could further be noted that both 'Pik' Botha, South Africa's former Foreign Minister, and Dirk Mudge, leader of the Democratic Turnhalle Alliance of Namibia, expressed the opinion that the Nordic support to ANC and SWAPO influenced the liberation movements in a democratic direction (Interviews with Roelof 'Pik' Botha, pp. 114-18, and Dirk Mudge, p. 83).

towards the principal goal of national independence.[1] Sweden—under Social Democratic or non-socialist governments and whether at the official or at the NGO level—more or less uncritically accepted this situation.[2] In addition to purely humanitarian concerns, from a political point of view it was the ultimate objective—national liberation and majority rule—that determined the stand of a broad opinion.[3] As stated by Olof Palme to the UN Security Council in March 1977:

> Neutrality towards the existing and coming struggles in Southern Africa is impossible. [...] Action must be taken [...] to end a system which is both evil in itself and a threat to peace. [...] The right kind of foreign intervention is that which will support the liberation struggle and reduce the resistance of the forces which still cling to the idea of maintaining white supremacy. [...] The liberation of the Africans will be their own work, and that liberation will inevitably come some day. But the international community can contribute to shortening that struggle and making it more peaceful, with less human suffering.[4]

The text focuses on that aspect of Sweden's contribution to the nationalist struggles in Southern Africa which is least documented, that is, the direct, official assistance to the liberation movements. As such, it is far from comprehensive. After the largely re-active beginnings in the 1970s—mainly covering the commodity aid to PAIGC, FRELIMO, MPLA and ZANU and ZAPU—the close and pro-active involvement with SWAPO and ANC from the 1980s included substantial components in favour of transparency and democracy which merit further discussion. Within the bilateral cooperation programmes with SWAPO and ANC, emphasis was increasingly given to financial management, administration and, in general, to broad, participatory capacity-building. Together with the other Nordic countries—notably Norway—Sweden, SWAPO and ANC embarked on extensive consultations on a number of strategic issues, including their countries' future constitutional dispensations.

With official support, considerable efforts and resources were, finally, channelled via Swedish and international NGOs to independent organizations inside Namibia and, above all, in South Africa. Working within oppressive and hostile environments, church organizations, community newspapers, cultural associations, human rights centres, trade unions, women's groups and many other suppressed voices were assisted. In the case of South Africa alone, around 1.6 billion SEK—almost twice the amount disbursed to ANC—was over the years through various channels granted by the Swedish government to hundreds of popularly based,

---

1. For a preliminary discussion on "the wedge which was always liable to be forced between 'liberation' and 'democracy' in the course of the region's war", see John Saul: 'Liberation without Democracy?: Rethinking the Experiences of the [S]outhern African Liberation Movements' in Jonathan Hyslop (ed.): *African Democracy in the Era of Globalisation*, Witwatersrand University Press, Johannesburg, 1999, pp. 167-78.
2. This was notably the case with regard to the so called 'Shipanga affair' in SWAPO between 1976 and 1978.
3. Several examples could be quoted. In November 1978, the Swedish historian Per Lundvall published a highly critical article on SWAPO in the conservative newspaper *Svenska Dagbladet*, entitled 'Millions to murderers' (Per Lundvall: 'Miljoner åt mördare' in *Svenska Dagbladet*, 27 November 1978). David Wirmark—a Liberal MP and government spokesperson on aid questions—replied to the article. He brushed aside the criticism concerning internal conflicts within SWAPO and the issue of armed struggle, stressing that "it is the *objective* of the struggle that should determine our judgement" (David Wirmark: 'Kamp och bistånd med samma mål'/ 'Struggle and assistance with the same objectives' in *Svenska Dagbladet*, 5 December 1978).
4. 'No neutrality towards the struggle in Southern Africa', Statement made by Mr. Olof Palme, leader of the Social Democratic Party in Sweden, at the meeting of the Security Council on 25 March 1977 during the consideration of the question of South Africa, UN Centre Against Apartheid, Notes and Documents, United Nations, New York, April 1977, pp. 1-6.

democratic organizations and other anti-apartheid structures, from the Alexandra Art Centre and the Grahamstown Rural Committee via the Congress of Traditional Leaders to the Afrikaans-language *Vrye Weekblad* and the Muslim association Call of Islam.[1]

According to ANC's Raymond Suttner, this support was not only "vital" for the anti-apartheid struggle, but also a significant contribution towards a democratic post-apartheid society.[2] Commenting on the assistance to the popular movements in South Africa, Suttner—a leading member of the internal opposition[3]—stated in 1999 that the support from Sweden and the other Nordic countries

> was directed towards organizations based in communities. By providing funding, they contributed towards long-term democratic governance in South Africa. [...] [T]hey helped root democratic practices [...] that will be essential if we are to have long-term accountable government, popular participation and continued respect for human rights.[4]

A closer examination of this involvement falls outside the scope of the present study.[5] It is hoped, however, that future inquiries will look into the broader relations between Sweden and Southern Africa. In a tribute to the assassinated Swedish Social Democratic Prime Minister Olof Palme, they were in 1988 characterized by the ANC leader Oliver Tambo as "a natural system [...] from people to people" and as "a system of international relations which is not based on the policies of any

---

1. Examples of South African organizations directly or indirectly supported by the Swedish government are given in an accompanying appendix. See also Ingrid Puck Åberg: *Att Skapa Något Slags Hopp: Om Svenskt Humanitärt Bistånd i Södra Afrika* ('To Create Some Kind of Hope: On Swedish Humanitarian Assistance to Southern Africa'), SIDA, Stockholm, 1992.
2. Suttner in Robben Island Museum, Mayibuye Centre and Nordic Africa Institute op. cit., p. 88.
3. Intermittently imprisoned or under house arrest for ANC activities (1975-83 and 1986-88), Suttner—a lawyer by formation—headed ANC's Department of Political Education during the crucial years 1990-94. He became in 1991 both a member of ANC's National Executive Committee and of the Central Committee of the South African Communist Party. An ANC member of the National Assembly after the democratic elections in 1994, he chaired the parliamentary Committee on Foreign Affairs. In 1997, he was appointed ambassador to Sweden.
4. Suttner in Robben Island Museum, Mayibuye Centre and Nordic Africa Institute op. cit., p. 88.
5. Seven years after the democratic elections in South Africa, the roles played by the organized Swedish solidarity movement, the churches, trade unions and other major non-governmental actors during the regional Thirty Years War remained largely undocumented. Among the Nordic countries, Norway was here leading the way, both with regard to academic inquiries and to popular accounts. Where only brief Swedish presentations existed in the form of summary booklets—commonly sponsored by Sida—more comprehensive Norwegian studies had been undertaken, often by centrally placed participants. In 1995, for example, Trond Bakkevig published a study on the Norwegian church and South Africa (*Den Norske Kirke og Kampen mot Apartheid*/'The Church of Norway and the Struggle against Apartheid', Mellomkirkelig Råd, Oslo; also issued in English in 1996), which in the same year was followed by a general overview edited by Inger A. Heldal (*Sammen for Demokrati: Norsk Støtte til Kampen mot Apartheid*/'Together for Democracy: Norwegian Support for the Struggle against Apartheid; in English published as *From Cape to Cape Against Apartheid: Norwegian Support for Democracy in South Africa*, Mayibuye Books, Cape Town, 1996). Vesla Vetlesen's account of the trade union assistance appeared in 1998 (*Frihet for Sør-Afrika: LO og Kampen mot Apartheid*/'Freedom for South Africa: LO and the Struggle against Apartheid', Tiden Norsk Forlag, Oslo), and in a richly illustrated book Nina Drolsum documented in 1999 the history of the Norwegian solidarity movement's umbrella organization, the Council for Southern Africa (*For et Fritt Afrika: Solidaritet mot Kolonialisme og Apartheid for Menneskeverd og Rettferdighet-Fellesrådet 1967-2000*/'For a Free Africa: Solidarity against Colonialism and Apartheid for Human Dignity and Justice', Fellesrådet for Afrika, Solidaritet Forlag, Oslo). In connection with its 20th anniversary, in 2000, finally, Trond Andresen and Steinar Sætervadet published a study of the Namibia Association of Norway (*Fra Dugnad till Bistand: Namibiaforeningen gjennom 20 År*/'From Community Work to Assistance: The Namibia Association through 20 Years', Namibiaforeningen, Elverum). The studies by Vetlesen and Drolsum are summarized in Tore Linné Eriksen (ed.): *Norway and National Liberation in Southern Africa*, Nordiska Afrikainstitutet, Uppsala, 2000, which also contains a contribution by Eva Helene Østbye on the Namibia Association. Similar studies on the Swedish churches, the Emmaus movement, Bread and Fishes, LO/TCO, AIC/OPIC, AGIS and ISAK would cover important aspects and events only indirectly addressed below.

party that might be in power in Sweden at any particular time".[1] Such studies should try to assess the impact of the relations built during the liberation struggles on the post-independence societies in Southern Africa, as well as on Sweden itself.[2]

1. Oliver Tambo: 'Olof Palme and the Liberation of Southern Africa' in Kofi Buenor Hadjor (ed.): *New Perspectives in North-South Dialogue: Essays in Honour of Olof Palme*, I. B. Tauris Publishers, London, 1988, p. 258.

2. How and to what extent did three decades of popular solidarity with the liberation struggles in Southern Africa affect Sweden? What lasting imprints—if any—did the involvement have? On what basis could new North-South relations be established? The difference vis-à-vis the Eastern European countries is here conspicuous. Describing how the "Soviet government['s] relations with the ANC deteriorated slowly, but steadily" from the late 1980s, Shubin, for example, attributes this to "the fact that Soviet citizens [had been] involved in South African affairs only as members of the [Communist Party] or party-controlled trade unions and other NGOs". This, in turn, led to an "absence of a broad-based anti-apartheid movement" (Shubin op. cit., pp. 382 and 408-09). ANC's Garth Strachan, a member of the South African Communist Party who in 1984/85 studied at the Institute of Social Sciences (better known as the International Lenin School) in Moscow, similarly stated in 1995 that "when you came across ordinary people in the [...] Soviet Union, they were not necessarily in agreement with the support for the liberation movements. And—sometimes quite alarmingly—there were massive problems with racism directed to ANC and black people" (Interview with Garth Strachan, p. 194). In the case of Sweden, the official support channelled via various NGOs significantly broadened and strengthened the important popular anti-apartheid movement.

PAIGC of Guinea-Bissau:
Breaking the Ground

Focus on the Portuguese Colonies

The situation in apartheid South Africa dominated the Swedish Southern Africa debate during the first half of the 1960s. On his second visit to Sweden, in September 1965 Eduardo Mondlane, the President of FRELIMO of Mozambique, openly criticized the emergent solidarity movement for what he saw as an almost exclusive concentration on South Africa, arguing that

> it is an illusion to believe that the problem of South Africa is independent of the Portuguese territories of Angola and Mozambique, or of Southern Rhodesia, and that it can be solved without their freedom. It is [...] to be desired that the [Swedish] South Africa movement also will include these territories in its activities.[1]

Largely as a result of Mondlane's criticism, the situation was reversed towards the end of the 1960s. In early 1966, the Lund South Africa Committee decided "after mature consideration" that the information bulletin *Syd- och Sydvästafrika* from then on should also cover "the other countries in Southern Africa", explaining that "it has appeared that their problems are closely connected to the situation in South Africa".[2] This marked the beginning of an increasingly intense coverage of the liberation struggles in the Portuguese colonies, while the situation in South Africa and Namibia was relegated to the background. Following the successful campaign against the participation of the Swedish company ASEA in the Cabora Bassa project in Mozambique in 1968-69[3], in the era of the Vietnam war this led the reorganized solidarity movement to be almost entirely concerned with the armed struggle in the Portuguese colonies.[4]

At a conference between the first Africa Groups of Arvika, Gothenburg, Lund, Stockholm and Uppsala, it was in June 1971 decided "to concentrate [the] propaganda on the Portuguese colonies".[5] The following year, *Södra Afrika Informationsbulletin*—the successor to *Syd- och Sydvästafrika*; jointly edited and published by the Africa Groups—stated that its main objective was to disseminate "current information on the struggle in Angola, Guinea-Bissau and Mozambique; develop-

---

1. Mondlane in *Dagens Nyheter*, 17 September 1965.
2. Lund South Africa Committee: 'Klubbmeddelande' ('Information to the members'), No. 2/66, Lund, 22 April 1966 (AJC).
3. See Sellström Volume I, pp. 483-502.
4. Sören Lindh, a leading representative of the Africa Groups, later stated that "we gave priority to the armed struggle in the Portuguese colonies. [...] That also meant that we staved off demands to recognize this and that organization in other areas, although we were, of course, in solidarity with their struggle" (Interview with Sören Lindh, p. 305).
5. The Africa Groups in Sweden: 'Circular Letter No. 4', [no place], 23 September 1971 (AGA). In October 1970, the Africa Groups started to issue circular letters in English about their activities, distributing them to the offices of the liberation movements and to like-minded solidarity organizations, mainly in Europe. The informative letters—including comments on Sweden's official assistance to the liberation movements—were produced on an *ad hoc* basis until 1977. Beginning in mid-1984, a more formal and ambitious quarterly *Scandinavian Newsletter on Southern Africa* was, similarly, produced. It provided general information on the relations between Denmark, Norway, Sweden and Southern Africa, but concentrated on the issue of sanctions against South Africa.

ments in Portugal; Swedish interests in Portugal and Africa; [and] on the role of US imperialism in Africa".[1] Several of Sweden's major publishing houses dedicated at the same time a number of books to the Portuguese colonies. In a study on the liberation struggles in Southern Africa, Gun-Britt Andersson noted in 1973 that "it has in Sweden often been easier to get information about the Portuguese colonies than about South Africa".[2]

Behind the shift were the changing realities in Southern Africa. While the apartheid regime had effectively crushed the democratic opposition inside South Africa and the nationalist struggles in Namibia and Zimbabwe were in their infancy, the liberation movements in Angola and Mozambique had by the mid-1960s managed to establish a precarious, but real presence. Rising against the fascist dictatorship of Salazar's Portugal and drawing unequivocal support from the 1960 UN Decolonization Declaration, their cause received increasing international attention during the second half of the 1960s. The United Nations regularly appealed to the member states to extend assistance to the peoples in the Portuguese colonies, and in its liberation strategy the Organization of African Unity accorded priority to the territories, considered as the weakest links in the chain of colonial and white minority rule.[3]

In Sweden, the first parliamentary motions proposing official support to the African liberation organizations were introduced from 1967 in favour of the movements in the Portuguese colonies.[4] Once the policy of official assistance had been endorsed by the Swedish parliament in 1969, it was these movements that until the

1. *Södra Afrika Informationsbulletin*, No. 15-16, May 1972, p. 2. A book on the liberation struggles in Africa published by the Africa Groups in January 1972 was almost exclusively dedicated to the Portuguese colonies. While it contained a short chapter on South Africa (critical to ANC), it did not, for example, discuss the situation in Zimbabwe (AGIS: *Afrika: Imperialism och Befrielsekamp*/'Africa: Imperialism and Liberation Struggle', Lund). Reflecting the developments in Africa and the changing focus of the Africa Groups after the attainment of independence in Angola, Cape Verde, Guinea-Bissau, Mozambique and São Tomé and Príncipe, in August 1977 AGIS issued a new book, entitled *Befrielsekampen i Afrika* ('The Liberation Struggle in Africa', Stockholm). Collectively written by various members guided by Mai Palmberg, it included chapters on Namibia and Zimbabwe. A revised and updated edition was published in English in 1983 (Mai Palmberg (ed.): *The Struggle for Africa*, Zed Press, London).
2. Gun-Britt Andersson: *Befrielse i Södra Afrika* ('Liberation in Southern Africa'), Världspolitikens Dagsfrågor, No. 3, 1973, Utrikespolitiska Institutet, Stockholm, 1973, p. 33. As first secretary at the Ministry for Foreign Affairs, Andersson led the Swedish delegation to the UN/OAU Oslo conference on Southern Africa in April 1973. Holding various positions at SIDA and SAREC—the Swedish Agency for Research Cooperation with Developing Countries—she served as SIDA's representative to Tanzania in 1983-84. In 1994, she was appointed Under-Secretary of State in the Ministry of Social Affairs. In 1999, she became Under-Secretary of State for International Development Cooperation in the Ministry for Foreign Affairs.
3. The so called 'domino strategy' was outlined at a meeting of the OAU Liberation Committee in Dar es Salaam in June 1964. In this view—based on an analysis of the strength of the colonial and white regimes—OAU (and, consequently, international) support should first be given to the struggles in the Portuguese colonies, then to Zimbabwe, Namibia and, finally, South Africa. In a domino chain of events, the liberation of one nation was supposed to encourage the independence process in the subsequent countries. Not surprisingly, accorded lowest priority ANC of South Africa strongly criticized the OAU strategy, stating that "we are opposed to the strategic theory that the intensification of the struggle in South Africa must await the liberation of Southern Rhodesia and Mozambique and Angola. Indeed, to starve the South African liberation movement of assistance pending the liberation of other territories is, in our view, to play into the hands of the unholy alliance [between South Africa, Rhodesia and Portugal]" (cited in Thomas op. cit., pp. 92-93). Nevertheless, the actual liberation of Southern Africa would follow OAU's domino scenario.
4. It was the Left Party Communists that introduced the first parliamentary motions in favour of Swedish official assistance to the liberation movements in the Portuguese colonies. In January 1967, the future party leader Lars Werner and other members of what was still called the Communist Party of Sweden submitted a motion in favour of FRELIMO of Mozambique, which was rejected by the Standing Committee on Foreign Affairs. Together with C.H. Hermansson, the chairman of the renamed Left Party Communists, Werner again introduced a motion in January 1968, this time in support of "the liberation movement in the Portuguese colonies via CONCP", that is, the alliance of FRELIMO, MPLA and PAIGC (Swedish Parliament 1968: Motion No. 507 in the First Chamber (Werner) and Motion No. 633 in the Second Chamber (Hermansson and others), Riksdagens Protokoll, 1968, pp. 12 and 1-3). This initiative was also turned down by the parliamentary majority. The following year, similar motions by the ruling Social Democratic Party and the opposition Left Party Communists, the Centre Party and the Liberal Party were, however, supported, paving the way for the historic decision by the parliamentary Standing Committee on Appropriations in May 1969.

mid-1970s were granted practically all the resources. Of the 67.5 million SEK (MSEK) disbursed as direct official humanitarian support to the liberation movements in Southern Africa and PAIGC from the financial year 1969/70[1] until 1974/75, no less than 64.5 million—an overwhelming 96 per cent—was channelled to MPLA of Angola, FRELIMO of Mozambique and PAIGC of Guinea-Bissau and Cape Verde.[2] During the same period, ANC of South Africa, SWAPO of Namibia and ZANU and ZAPU of Zimbabwe together received a mere 3 million.[3] In fact, the assistance to the latter was initially seen as a political counterbalance to the concentration on the Portuguese colonies, motivated by a concern to increase the international credibility of Sweden's general policy towards the liberation movements. Assessing the first two years of the new policy, the Department for International Development Cooperation in the Ministry for Foreign Affairs concluded in September 1971 that "the emphasis [...] given to the Portuguese territories [...] should be maintained". At the same time, it stated that

> the token support to the smaller movements from the southern parts of the continent should [also] continue, on humanitarian and moral grounds, but also [for] political [reasons], as [it] shows that Sweden does not follow an anti-Portuguese line, but one that supports liberation.[4]

From the late 1960s until the collapse of the Lisbon regime in April 1974 and the subsequent independence of Angola, Guinea-Bissau and Mozambique, both the Swedish government and the solidarity movement focused their attention on the liberation movements in the Portuguese colonies.[5] The struggle by PAIGC—the African Independence Party of Guinea and Cape Verde[6]—and the political skills and stature of its Secretary General, Amílcar Cabral, had a major impact in this regard. The considerable future involvement with the liberation movements in Southern Africa—with which close relations already existed—was to a significant extent guided by the encounter with the struggle in a small West African country which before 1969 was practically unknown.

---

1. During the period covered in this study, the Swedish financial year started on 1 July and ended on 30 June.
2. See the accompanying tables on disbursements from SIDA to the Southern African liberation movements and PAIGC.
3. In Sweden, it was liberal intellectuals and newspapers that first raised their voices against apartheid South Africa. Significantly, it was also the opposition Centre and Liberal parties that first advocated direct official support to ANC, SWAPO, ZANU and ZAPU in the Swedish parliament. In January 1969—i.e. before the policy was endorsed—the Centre leader Gunnar Hedlund and the Liberal leader Sven Wedén submitted a joint parliamentary motion in favour of the movements in Southern Africa that "strive for social and economic justice. Particularly relevant in this context are the movements that operate in Rhodesia, [...] Mozambique, Angola, Portuguese Guinea, Namibia and South Africa" (Swedish Parliament 1969: Motion No. 511 in the Second Chamber, Riksdagens Protokoll 1969, p. 16). Similar motions were introduced in 1970 and 1971 by the non-socialist 'middle parties', and in January 1972 the new leaders of the Centre and Liberal parties, Thorbjörn Fälldin and Gunnar Helén, again advocated support to the liberation movements in South Africa, Namibia and Zimbabwe. In their joint submission, Fälldin and Helén stated that they "largely" supported that Swedish assistance had until then mainly been channelled to the liberation movements in the Portuguese colonies, but found it "urgent" that the South African, Namibian and Zimbabwean movements "are given Swedish assistance, although their successes so far have been modest" (Swedish Parliament 1972: Motion No. 934, Riksdagens Protokoll 1972, p. 16). In broad terms, it could be concluded that in the early 1970s the Swedish left gave priority to the liberation movements in the Portuguese colonies, while the non-socialist political centre was in favour of increased support to the nationalists in South Africa, Namibia and Zimbabwe. As stated in Volume I, it should be noted that the ruling Social Democratic Party did not take the parliamentary initiative vis-à-vis any of the African liberation movements officially supported by Sweden (Sellström Volume I, p. 424).
4. [Ethel] Ringborg: Memorandum ('Stöd till befrielserörelser'/'Support to liberation movements'), Ministry for Foreign Affairs, Stockholm, 7 September 1971 (MFA). From a handwritten note, it appears that it was written as "background information" for the Foreign Minister, attending the Consultative Committee on Humanitarian Assistance (CCHA) two weeks later.
5. Official assistance—albeit small—to ANC (starting in 1973), SWAPO (1970), ZANU (1969) and ZAPU (1973) preceded the recognition accorded these movements by AGIS by three to six years.
6. In Portuguese, *Partido Africano para a Independência da Guiné e Cabo Verde*.

The Liberation Struggle in Guinea-Bissau

Like the other Portuguese-held territories in Africa, what was then 'Portuguese Guinea' and the islands of Cape Verde[1] were in 1951 constitutionally incorporated as 'overseas provinces' with metropolitan Portugal. The move—mainly a device by the Portuguese regime to perpetuate colonial rule—did not lead to any improvements for the inhabitants. On the contrary, commenting on "the absurdity of our situation", Cabral stated in 1961 that

> the Portuguese colonialists try [...] to convince the world that they have no colonies and that our African countries are 'provinces of Portugal'. [...] [W]hen the colonizing country has a fascist government; when the people of that country are largely illiterate and neither know nor enjoy [...] fundamental human rights [...]; [and] when furthermore the economy of the metropolis is under-developed, as is the case in Portugal, then violence and lies reach an unparalleled height and [the] lack of respect for the African people knows no limits.[2]

As in Angola and Mozambique, Portugal ruled with an iron fist over Guinea-Bissau and any protests were severely crushed. Towards the end of the 1950s, the regime's secret police—the infamous PIDE[3]—was established in Bissau and started to build up a network of informers matching that already operating in Portugal itself. As a result, 'Portuguese Guinea' was not spared the violent police repression and massacres that the African populations in the southern parts of the continent had to experience in 1959-60. In August 1959, some 50 dock workers on strike at Pijiguiti were killed by the Portuguese police. As with similar events in Southern Africa, the massacre had far-reaching consequences. One month after the killings, PAIGC militants held a meeting in Bissau where they decided to liberate Guinea and Cape Verde "by all possible means, including war".[4]

PAIGC was the oldest of the leading liberation movements in the Portuguese colonies in Africa. Originally named the African Independence Party (PAI)[5], it was formed by a small group of predominantly Cape Verdean activists around Amílcar Cabral in Bissau in September 1956, three months before MPLA of Angola was founded. Although other nationalist organizations existed and emerged—notably FLING, the Front for the Liberation and Independence of Guinea[6]—they were mainly based in neighbouring Senegal and inactive inside Guinea-Bissau.[7] As in the case of FRELIMO of Mozambique—but in contrast to MPLA of Angola—PAIGC was the all dominant liberation movement. Combined with the fact that it pursued

---

1. Situated in the Atlantic, some 600 kilometres north-west of Guinea, the islands of Cape Verde had at the beginning of the 1960s a total population of just over a quarter of a million, mostly of mixed Portuguese and African descent. From the late 15th century, Portuguese colonialism linked the islands closely to Guinea on the African mainland. Many Cape Verdeans were active within PAIGC, not least at the leadership level. Although born in Guinea, Amílcar Cabral himself was of Cape Verdean descent. As the name indicates, PAIGC emphasized the unity of the two territories, but apart from political propaganda and some labour activities the liberation movement never attempted to extend the open liberation struggle to the islands. Cape Verde remained under effective Portuguese rule until the Lisbon coup in April 1974. This contributed to the widening gap between Cape Verde and Guinea-Bissau after independence, eventually leading to a formal break in early 1981.
2. Amílcar Cabral: *Revolution in Guinea: An African People's Struggle,* Stage 1, London, 1969, p. 10.
3. In Portuguese, *Polícia Internacional e de Defesa do Estado* (International and State Defence Police).
4. Basil Davidson: *The Liberation of Guiné: Aspects of an African Revolution,* Penguin African Library, Harmondsworth, 1969, p. 32
5. In Portuguese, *Partido Africano de Independência.*
6. In Portuguese, *Frente para a Libertação e Independência da Guiné.*
7. FLING concentrated much of its limited energies on criticism of PAIGC's 'non-African' leadership, i.e. the fact that Cabral and other leaders were *mestiço* Cape Verdeans. Based in the Senegalese capital Dakar, FLING received considerable support from President Léopold Senghor, who throughout the liberation war in Guinea-Bissau kept his political options open by spreading his favours between FLING and PAIGC.

Birgitta Dahl, Social Democratic MP, and PAIGC Secretary General Amílcar Cabral in Conakry, Guinée, November 1970. Behind Cabral is Lars Rudebeck of the Uppsala Africa Group (Photo: Knut Andreassen)

a strategy based on clear politico-military precepts[1], Cabral's organization gave the liberation struggle a remarkably high degree of cohesion. Important in this context was that the anti-colonial cause in Guinea-Bissau was uncomplicated by any significant settler dimension. The number of Portuguese residents was extremely low. There were never more than about 2,000 European civilians in the territory, the majority being colonial administrators rather than colonists.[2]

Under the leadership of Amílcar Cabral[3], PAIGC assumed a high profile at the time of the Pijiguiti strike, in which the organization was deeply involved. However, the ensuing repression forced the leadership out of the country. In 1960, Cabral established PAIGC's exile headquarters in Conakry, the capital of Guinea-Bissau's southern neighbour, the francophone Republic of Guinée.[4] There followed a period of intense political mobilization of the peasantry in southern Guinea-Bissau, combined with acts of sabotage and civil disobedience, and in January 1963 the armed phase of PAIGC's struggle for national liberation began with an attack on the Portuguese barracks at Tite.

1. See Lars Rudebeck: *Guinea-Bissau: A Study of Political Mobilization*, Scandinavian Institute of African Studies, Uppsala, 1974.
2. Norrie MacQueen: *The Decolonization of Portuguese Africa: Metropolitan Revolution and the Dissolution of Empire*, Longman, London and New York, 1997, p. 37.
3. Born in Guinea-Bissau in 1924, Cabral went to Lisbon in 1945 to study at the Higher Institute of Agronomy (*Instituto Superior de Agronomía*), graduating with outstanding marks in 1952. In Portugal, Cabral actively participated in clandestine African political and cultural groups and formed—together with Mário de Andrade and Agostinho Neto of Angola and Marcelino dos Santos of Mozambique—the Centre for African Studies (*Centro dos Estudos Africanos*) in Lisbon in 1951. Described as the 'cradle of African leadership', the Centre for African Studies brought the future leaders of PAIGC, MPLA and FRELIMO together and paved the way for future organizations, such as the Anti-Colonial Movement (*Movimento Anti-Colonialista*), formed by de Andrade, dos Santos and Cabral in 1957, and—eventually—the Conference of Nationalist Organizations in the Portuguese Colonies (*Conferência das Organizações Nacionalistas das Colónias Portuguêsas*; CONCP) in 1961. After graduation, Cabral went to Guinea to take charge of a research station near Bissau, conducting an agricultural survey of the colony in 1953-54. The mission, as well as repeated visits to Angola as an agricultural consultant for various companies between 1955 and 1959, brought him into direct contact with the realities of the African peasantry, a crucial experience for the development of his political ideas. Together with Aristides Pereira, his brother Luís and a few others, Cabral founded PAI/PAIGC in Bissau in September 1956, eventually becoming its Secretary General. Later in the year, he also participated in the process leading to the formation of MPLA in Luanda, Angola. After the Pijiguiti massacre in August 1959, the PAIGC leadership was forced into exile and Cabral settled in Conakry, the capital of the neighbouring Republic of Guinée, in May 1960, from where he led the liberation struggle. On 20 January 1973, Cabral was assassinated in Conakry. On the life of Amílcar Cabral, see Patrick Chabal: *Amílcar Cabral: Revolutionary Leadership and People's War*, African Studies Series, Cambridge University Press, Cambridge, 1983.
4. To distinguish the independent Republic of Guinea from 'Portuguese' Guinea, the former is referred to by its French name, that is, Guinée. MPLA of Angola also established its exile headquarters in Conakry in 1960, moving to Léopoldville (Congo) the following year.

PAIGC's military victories came in quick succession. Within six months of the beginning of the war, the Portuguese Minister of Defence, General Gomes de Araújo, startled his government by publicly admitting that the nationalists had gained control over a significant portion of the colony.[1] In early 1964, Lisbon's morale was further damaged when PAIGC repulsed a major counter-attack against the island of Como—which the nationalists had occupied early in the military offensive—involving at least 3,000 Portuguese soldiers.[2] The battle for Como marked a turning point. From then on, the liberated areas of southern Guinea-Bissau remained firmly in the hands of PAIGC, while the Portuguese—eventually building up a military presence of some 30,000 men[3] in a country with just over half a million inhabitants—concentrated their attention on the defence of the capital, a number of fortified positions and the use of air power.

By the mid-1960s—when the military situation began to stabilize—PAIGC controlled about half of the national territory, where it was running its own administration and social services, including education and health care. It was primarily for these activities that the movement sought outside assistance.[4] And it was in response to that call that the Swedish government in mid-1969 decided to extend humanitarian support to PAIGC.

Early Contacts

While Sweden had various historical, economic and ecclesiastical links to the five Southern African countries discussed in this study, relations with Guinea-Bissau were until the establishment of a humanitarian assistance programme with PAIGC non-existent. Although both Sweden and Portugal had joined EFTA in 1960 and the trade exchange between the two rapidly increased during the 1960s[5], this did not translate into major economic transactions with the Portuguese colonies in Africa. In the case of Guinea-Bissau, there were no Swedish investments and the trade exchange was infinitesimal.

Before the 1970s, Guinea-Bissau did not appear as a specific entry in the Swedish trade statistics. Data for the country were until then registered with those for Angola, São Tomé and Príncipe and Cape Verde under the heading 'Portuguese West Africa'. Within this group, it can safely be assumed that the bulk of the Swedish trade exchange took place with the more important economy of Angola. Nevertheless, the figures were extremely low. In 1950, the value of Swedish exports to 'Portuguese West Africa' amounted to 1.8 MSEK, representing 0.03 per cent of total Swedish foreign sales. The import value was at the same time 2.3 million, corresponding to 0.04 per cent of Sweden's imports. Ten years later, the exchange was still marginal. In 1960, Swedish imports from 'Portuguese West Africa' reached 3.8 MSEK—a stable share of the total of 0.03 per cent—while the value of Sweden's exports had increased to 10.7 million, corresponding to 0.08 per cent of the total.[6]

1. MacQueen op. cit., p. 38.
2. Chabal op. cit., p. 59.
3. MacQueen op. cit., p. 39.
4. In addition, PAIGC was responsible for the maintenance of growing numbers of refugees in both the Republic of Guinée and Senegal.
5. See Sellström Volume I, pp. 370-71.
6. For 1950: Kommerskollegium: *Handel: Berättelse för år 1950*, Volume I, Sveriges Officiella Statistik, Norstedt & Söner, Stockholm, 1952. For 1960: Statistiska Centralbyrån: *Handel: Berättelse för år 1960*, Volume II, Stockholm, 1963.

The trade between Sweden and Guinea-Bissau must against this background have been virtually nil. This is confirmed by the statistics established after independence. Between 1975 and 1980, annual exports from Guinea-Bissau to Sweden fluctuated between 2,000 and 270,000 SEK, amounts too low to be meaningfully expressed as shares of total Swedish imports. Registered annual exports from Sweden, on the other hand, grew during the period from 3.2 to 20.0 MSEK.[1] They did not, however, reflect normal commercial transactions, but deliveries under Swedish aid grants.[2]

Without historical, commercial or other links, it is not surprising that the encounter between PAIGC and Sweden only took place towards the end of the 1960s, at a time when popular support for the nationalist struggles in Africa had won broad recognition and the Guinean liberation movement was already established as a decisive force. The pace with which both the Swedish Social Democratic government and the organized solidarity movement—across cultural and linguistic divides—embraced the cause of PAIGC is, however, remarkable. So is the fact that although the two interpreted PAIGC's struggle differently—even antagonistically[3]—they managed to mobilize their respective constituencies for the same cause. The diplomatic skills of Amílcar Cabral were in this regard highly significant.

PAIGC's first known contact with Sweden was made before the launch of the armed struggle in January 1963. The background was that the Conference of Nationalist Organizations in the Portuguese Colonies (CONCP)[4] in June 1961 appealed to the Swedish newspaper *Expressen* for assistance to the Angolan refugees who in abject condition crossed the border into Congo (Zaire).[5] In response, *Expressen* carried out an important campaign called 'Angola Help'[6] between July and September 1961.[7] Through the campaign, the liberal newspaper managed to

---

1. Quoted from Lars Rudebeck: 'Some facts and observations on relations between the Nordic countries and the officially Portuguese-speaking countries of Africa', Paper presented to a conference on the Portuguese-speaking countries in Africa organized by the *Stiftung Wissenschaft und Politik*, Ebenhausen, West Germany, February 1986.
2. The aid-financed exports from Sweden represented during the period between 5 and 10 per cent of Guinea-Bissau's total imports (Rudebeck op. cit.).
3. To the Africa Groups and the wider socialist left in Sweden, PAIGC's armed struggle formed part of the global battle against imperialism and capitalism. The struggle against colonialism in Guinea-Bissau and the struggle against capitalism in Sweden—including the Social Democratic government—were seen as parts of the same cause. In a report to an international solidarity conference in Oxford, England, AGIS presented their outlook as follows in April 1974: "In the Swedish Africa Groups, we base our work on the fact that Sweden is an imperialist state where the workers are oppressed by the same system as that which oppresses the peoples of Africa. Therefore, we do not primarily appeal to the feeling of pity for the suppressed peoples, but we emphasize the fairness of the armed struggle, the [...] construction of a new, non-exploitative society in the liberated areas and the common interest to fight the imperialist system" (AGIS: 'Report from the Swedish Africa Groups', Africa Solidarity Conference, Oxford, Easter 1974) (AGA).
4. *A Conferência das Organizações Nacionalistas das Colónias Portuguêsas* (CONCP) was an umbrella organization representing nationalist movements in the Portuguese colonies, mainly in Africa, but also, for example, in Goa, India. The prime movers behind CONCP were MPLA and PAIGC. Tracing its origins to MAC (and, before that, to the Centre for African Studies in Lisbon), CONCP was formed at a conference in Casablanca, Morocco, in April 1961, i.e. shortly after the start of the liberation war in Angola. Mário de Andrade of MPLA served as President of the Consultative Council. CONCP's Secretariat was set up in Rabat, Morocco, with Marcelino dos Santos of Mozambique as Secretary General and Amílcar Cabral—based in Conakry, Republic of Guinée—as Deputy Secretary General. Seven years after *Expressen*'s Angola campaign, one of the first Swedish parliamentary motions for official support to the liberation movements in Southern Africa was submitted in 1968 by the Left Party Communists in favour of CONCP.
5. The former Belgian Congo was renamed Zaire in 1965. In 1997, it became the Democratic Republic of Congo.
6. In Swedish, *Angola-Hjälpen*.
7. See Sellström Volume I, pp. 389-92.

procure some 4.5 tons of medical drugs, mainly penicillin, for the refugees in the Lower Congo region. The assistance was channelled via MPLA. In his capacity as Deputy Secretary General of CONCP, Amílcar Cabral was well aware of the campaign and approached *Expressen* with a similar request in favour of PAIGC. Preparing the launch of the armed struggle, he sent a telegram to the Swedish journalist and author Anders Ehnmark requesting assistance in the form of medicines[1], adding that "we are also liberating ourselves".[2] At the time, PAIGC and the situation in Guinea-Bissau were, however, little known. Ehnmark later commented that "I knew who Amílcar was, but nothing more happened. It was, after all, a bit early".[3]

The "wall of silence"[4] built by the Portuguese around their colonies in Africa was during the first half of the 1960s particularly effective with regard to Guinea-Bissau. It was only in 1964 that the British journalist and historian Basil Davidson[5] and his French counterpart Gérard Chaliand[6] published a profile of Amílcar Cabral and an account of PAIGC's liberation struggle. In Sweden, it was the Lund South Africa Committee and the editorial board of the bulletin *Syd- och Sydvästafrika*—heeding the advice of Eduardo Mondlane—that two years later broke through the wall of silence, reproducing a summary of PAIGC's programme and a report by Cabral in an issue entirely dedicated to Portugal and its wars in Africa.[7] The Lund committee and the bulletin of the Swedish solidarity movement would thus initiate a long and sustained information effort regarding the struggles in the Portuguese colonies, later continued by the second generation Africa Group in Lund and the *Södra Afrika Informationsbulletin*.[8]

Shortly thereafter, the ruling Social Democratic Party had a decisive encounter with PAIGC and the liberation struggle in Guinea-Bissau. After establishing direct links with the FRELIMO President Eduardo Mondlane[9]—and having visited Portugal on an "undercover" fact-finding mission for the Socialist International[10]—Pierre Schori concluded in the official party journal *Tiden* in mid-1967 that "our support to the liberation movements in the Portuguese colonies can be increased. Above all", the Social Democratic international secretary wrote, "we should intensify the contacts with the nationalists within PAIGC".[11]

At about the same time, a number of Swedes—representing both the wider NGO solidarity movement and the Social Democratic Party—contacted PAIGC in

---

1. Anders Ehnmark: *Resan till Kilimanjaro: En Essä om Afrika efter Befrielsen* ('The Trip to Kilimanjaro: An Essay about Africa after Liberation'), Norstedts, Stockholm, 1993, p. 8 and Anders Ehnmark, letter to the author, [Taxinge, January 1997].
2. Letter from Anders Ehnmark to the author, [Taxinge, January 1997].
3. Ibid.
4. Foreword by Amílcar Cabral to Davidson op. cit., p. 9.
5. Basil Davidson: 'Profile of Amílcar Cabral' in *West Africa*, 28 April 1964.
6. Gérard Chaliand: *Guinée 'portugaise' et Cap Vert en Lutte pour leur Indépendence* ("'Portuguese' Guinea and Cape Verde Struggling for their Independence'), Maspero, Paris, 1964.
7. *Syd- och Sydvästafrika*, No. 4, 1966, pp. 11-14.
8. Reflecting the broadening of the Swedish solidarity movement's attention, the information bulletin *Syd- och Sydvästafrika*—published in Lund from January 1964—was in 1967 changed into *Södra Afrika Informationsbulletin* (and in 1975 to *Afrikabulletinen*, the official organ of the Africa Groups in Sweden).
9. See Sellström Volume I, pp. 475-77.
10. Ibid, p. 481.
11. Pierre Schori: 'Portugal' in *Tiden*, No. 8, 1967, p. 495.

Birgitta Dahl accompanying
PAIGC into the liberated areas
of Guinea-Bissau, November 1970
(Photo: Knut Andreassen)

order to visit the liberated areas of Guinea-Bissau.[1] Widely publishing their experiences, early visits were notably undertaken by Rolf Gustavsson of the Lund South Africa Committee in 1968[2]; the writer Göran Palm and Bertil Malmström of the Uppsala South Africa Committee in 1969[3]; the academic Lars Rudebeck in1970[4]; and the Social Democratic MP Birgitta Dahl together with the journalist Knut

1. In contrast to other liberation movements, PAIGC was "particularly open and accessible to outside visitors", such as journalists, writers, film crews, lawyers and academics, and "made every effort to allow these visitors to travel inside the country during the war" (Chabal op. cit., p. 6). Access from Guinea-Conakry—and Senegal—was easy and the small size of the country made it possible for the visitors to travel on foot through large sections of the territory in a relatively short period of time. As the first international journalist ever, Anders Johansson from the liberal Swedish newspaper *Dagens Nyheter* had in February 1968 visited the liberated areas in northern Mozambique together with FRELIMO's President Eduardo Mondlane (see Sellström Volume I, pp. 484-87). And in July-August 1969, the journalist and vice chairman of the Liberal Party Youth League, Olle Wästberg, accompanied FNLA on a mission into northern Angola (ibid. pp. 414-16). The frequent visits by Swedish journalists and activists to the liberated areas of the Portuguese colonies in 1968-70 largely contributed to focusing public attention on these territories.
2. Rolf Gustavsson: 'Besök hos Gerillan 1968' ('Visit to the Guerrillas in 1968') in *Södra Afrika Informationsbulletin*, No. 7, 1970, pp. 9-13. In addition to a number of radio programmes and newspaper articles on Guinea-Bissau, Gustavsson—a well-known Africanist and reporter with the Swedish television—later published an important anthology entitled *Kapitalismens Utveckling i Afrika: Studier i Afrikas Moderna Ekonomiska Historia* ('The Development of Capitalism in Africa: Studies on the Modern Economic History of Africa'), Cavefors, Lund, 1971.
3. Göran Palm: 'Besök hos Gerillan 1969: Kampen Enar Folket' ('Visit to the Guerrillas in 1969: The Struggle Unites the People') in *Södra Afrika Informationsbulletin*, No. 7, 1970, pp. 37-41. Palm subsequently edited a book in Swedish with texts by Amílcar Cabral: *Vår Kamp Er Kamp* ('Our Struggle Your Struggle'), Bokförlaget PAN/Norstedts, Stockholm, 1971. The PAIGC leader had first been introduced to the general Swedish public through Anders Ehnmark's anthology *Guerilla* (Bokförlaget PAN/Norstedts, Stockholm, 1968), which included Cabral's 'Kampen i Guinea' ('The Struggle in Guinea').
4. Rudebeck was active in the Uppsala South Africa Committee/Africa Group. He returned to Guinea-Bissau in 1972. Later associate professor of political science at the University of Uppsala, in 1974 Rudebeck published the widely acknowledged book *Guinea-Bissau: A Study of Political Mobilization* (op. cit.).

Andreassen, also in 1970.[1] With later accounts[2], their vivid reports guided the Swedish government and sustained public support to PAIGC's struggle.[3] The nationalist cause in the little known Portuguese colony was soon compared to that of Vietnam. In the absence of international media coverage, the direct, personal Swedish testimonies were highly significant. By 1972, the number of visitors from Sweden to the liberated areas of Guinea-Bissau exceeded that from any other country.[4]

Towards Official Support to PAIGC

The visitors described how PAIGC was building a democratic society in the liberated areas while the armed struggle against the Portuguese was in progress. The construction of the new society—in which provision of education and health care played prominent parts—was, however, not only threatened by constant aerial bombardments, but also by a severe lack of supplies for the rural schools and clinics that were being set up. Against this background, PAIGC turned to Sweden for assistance. A first request on behalf of the liberation movement was forwarded in October 1968 by the British historian Basil Davidson[5] to Per Wästberg[6], a leading member of the government-appointed Swedish Consultative Committee on Humanitarian Assistance.[7] In turn, Wästberg submitted the request to the Ministry

---

1. Knut Andreassen and Birgitta Dahl: *Guinea-Bissau: Rapport om ett Land och en Befrielserörelse* ('Guinea-Bissau: Report about a Country and a Liberation Movement'), Prisma, Stockholm, 1971. Dahl—at the time an official with SIDA—later served as Minister of Energy (1982-90) and of the Environment (1986-91). She became Speaker of the Swedish parliament in 1994.
2. Such as Bengt Ahlsén: *Portugisiska Afrika: Beskrivning av ett Kolonialimperium och dess Sönderfall* ('Portuguese Africa: Presentation of a Colonial Empire and Its Demise'), Svenska Utbildningsförlaget Liber AB, Stockholm, 1972. After a visit to the liberated areas in late 1971, Anders Ehnmark and the photographer Jean Hermanson published *Exemplet Guinea-Bissau: Ett Reportage om en Befrielserörelse* ('The Example of Guinea-Bissau: A Report about a Liberation Movement'), Bokförlaget PAN/Norstedts, Stockholm, 1973. The Norwegian journalist Johan Thorud accompanied them, publishing his own accounts in Norway (*Geriljasamfunnet: Guinea-Bissaus Kamp mot Portugal*/'The Guerrilla Society: Guinea-Bissau's Struggle against Portugal', Tiden, Oslo, 1972).
3. As SIDA's knowledge about PAIGC and the situation in the liberated areas was limited, Palm and Dahl were asked to supply the aid agency with reports from their visits. Their reports also played an important role for the decision to extend direct official assistance to MPLA of Angola (Sellström Volume I, pp. 429-32).
4. Marianne Rappe: Memorandum ('Samtal med Folke Löfgren på SIDA den 21.4.1972: PAIGC'/'Conversation with Folke Löfgren at SIDA 21.4.1972: PAIGC'), SIDA, Stockholm, 24 April 1972 (MFA).
5. Closely involved with the nationalist cause in the Portuguese colonies since the 1950s, Davidson visited the liberated areas in Guinea-Bissau in 1967. His account—*The Liberation of Guiné*—was published in 1969 in Swedish as *Frihetskampen i Guinea-Bissau* (Natur och Kultur, Stockholm).
6. Wästberg's important role for the development of the early Swedish solidarity movement with Southern Africa is discussed in Volume I, passim.
7. On the consultative committee, see Sellström Volume I, pp. 71-72. Originally set up in 1964 to advise the government on Swedish education support to African refugee youth, the officially appointed CCHA members represented the Ministry for Foreign Affairs, SIDA, larger NGOs and individual expertise on Southern Africa. Per Wästberg, for example, belonged to the latter category. The committee played a crucial role with regard to beneficiaries of Swedish humanitarian assistance. Beginning with the parliamentary decision to extend direct official assistance to the African liberation movements, its mandate and membership were over the years regularly expanded. In addition to Southern Africa, CCHA later advised the government on humanitarian assistance to Latin America. Swedish support to Vietnam and the nationalist movements in Indochina was, however, never part of CCHA's mandate. SIDA's Director General chaired the committee, which relied on a small secretariat—composed of SIDA and Foreign Ministry officials—to prepare the meetings and the items to be discussed, as a rule recommending decisions in memoranda based on submissions received and comments requested from relevant actors. Working under strict confidentiality, CCHA only registered decisions reached, not discussions held. With few exceptions, the recommendations by the secretariat were followed by the committee and endorsed by the government for implementation by SIDA. Over a period of 18 months in 1981/82-1982/83, for example, CCHA discussed 100 requests—in total representing some 270 MSEK—at 13 meetings. In 91 cases, the committee followed the secretariat's advice, while it proposed higher allocations in 2 cases and decreased support or outright rejection in 7 cases (SIDA/Kjellmer: Memorandum ('Beredningen för humanitärt bistånd: Ärenden 1981/82 och 1982/83'/'The Consultative Committee on Humanitarian Assistance: Items 1981/82 and 1982/83'), SIDA, Stockholm, 17 February 1983) (SDA).

for Foreign Affairs.[1] In his letter, Davidson—emphasizing that he only acted as "an intermediary", but that he could arrange "a direct discussion with PAIGC whenever [so] wished"[2]—stressed that "there is urgent need for certain forms of non-military aid [...] in the liberated zones", adding that:

> My feeling is that it would be really helpful if our friends in Sweden could rapidly produce money for the purchase of goods relating to 1) medical supplies, and 2) dried milk and canned meat. [...] My second thought is that the emphasis at the moment should be on speed rather than large quantity. I think especially of the many napalm cases they have, of their almost total deficiency in essential stores, of the fact that they are getting only minimal military aid (as I understand) and almost none at all of a non-military sort.[3]

Invited by the Social Democratic Party, PAIGC's Secretary General paid his first of many visits to Sweden less than two months later.[4] Marking the beginning of close links between Cabral's organization and the Swedish ruling party—as well as with the organized solidarity movement[5]—it took place at a particularly crucial time. The campaign against the Cabora Bassa project in Mozambique had gained broad support, and in late November 1968 activists in Gothenburg initiated 'direct actions' against ASEA. They were soon followed by demonstrations against both the company and the Social Democratic government all over Sweden.[6] In the midst of the domestic Cabora Bassa debate, the government voted on 29 November 1968 in favour of the UN General Assembly Resolution 2395 on the Portuguese colonies. By so doing, it officially expressed concern over "the continued and intensified activities of foreign economic, financial and other interests which impede the realization of the legitimate aspirations of the African peoples in those territories". It also supported the appeal "to grant the peoples of the territories under Portuguese domination the moral and material assistance necessary for the restoration of their inalienable rights".[7]

1. Letter from Per Anger, Ministry for Foreign Affairs, to Olof Ripa, Swedish ambassador to Liberia, Stockholm, 19 December 1968 (MFA).
2. Letter from Basil Davidson to Per Wästberg, London, 17 October 1968 (MFA).
3. Ibid.
4. *Arbetet*, 13 December 1968. During his visit to Sweden in late November 1968, Amílcar Cabral also met C.H. Hermansson, the chairman of the Left Party Communists (Uppsala South Africa Committee: 'Protokoll' /'Minutes', Uppsala, 8 November 1968) (UPA). According to Onésimo Silveira, PAIGC's resident representative to Sweden, "the contacts with the Western Communist parties were [,however,] weak" and PAIGC did "not wish to get involved in their struggle" (ibid).
5. The Social Democratic Party and PAIGC had established contacts before Cabral's visit to Sweden in late 1968. Earlier in the year, the ruling party had, for example, donated 10,000 SEK to the liberation movement from its International Solidarity Fund, set up in October 1967 (Pierre Schori in *Arbetet*, 13 December 1968). Through Onésimo Silveira, who lived and studied in Uppsala, close contacts had also been established with the active South Africa Committee in the university town, which would lead the Swedish solidarity movement's support to PAIGC. In mid-1968, for example, an X-ray unit was sent through the committee to PAIGC in Conakry (Uppsala South Africa Committee: 'Protokoll'/'Minutes', Uppsala, 30 June 1968) (UPA). Cabral also visited Uppsala during his stay in Sweden, *inter alia* appearing at a public meeting co-arranged by the South Africa Committee, the Social Democratic Laboremus association, the Verdandi student association and the Left Party Youth League (VUF) at the university on 27 November ('Amílcar Cabral: Demonstrationer inte nog - Vi behöver konkret hjälp'/'Amílcar Cabral: Demonstrations are not enough - We need concrete aid' in *Upsala Nya Tidning*, 28 November 1968). In 1969, the Uppsala South Africa Committee started a nationwide fund-raising campaign for PAIGC (*Södra Afrika Informationsbulletin*, No. 12, 1971, p. 49) and, as noted above, several members of the committee—notably Bertil Malmström, Lars Rudebeck and Birgitta Dahl—visited the liberated areas of Guinea-Bissau in 1969-70. Protesting against the state visit to Sweden by the Senegalese President Léopold Senghor—seen as treacherous towards PAIGC—in May 1970 the Uppsala South Africa Committee and a number of political organizations staged spectacular demonstrations in connection with his appearance at the university ('En Diktare och Diktator Besöker Norden'/'A Poet and Dictator Visits the Nordic Countries' in *Södra Afrika Informationsbulletin*, No. 9, 1970, pp. 5-8 and 'Senghor-rättegången'/ 'The Senghor Trial' in *Södra Afrika Informationsbulletin*, No. 14, 1972, pp. 23-25).
6. See Sellström Volume I, pp. 493-96.
7. United Nations General Assembly Resolution 2395 (XXIII) of 29 November 1968, cited in *Yearbook of the United Nations: 1968*, Office of Public Information, United Nations, New York, 1971, p. 804.

While Prime Minister Tage Erlander's government did not act according to its internationally declared position with regard to the first issue—refusing to intervene against ASEA—it immediately did so in the case of assistance to the liberation movements. Ten days later—on 9 December 1968—Foreign Minister Torsten Nilsson made what was to become a pivotal statement of intent, declaring that

> Sweden is among the states that have urged [for] greater efforts to terminate South Africa's policy of racial discrimination and Portugal's out-of-date and crudely provocative colonial policy. But, as everyone knows, we cannot [...] count on any steps being taken in the near future to remedy these abuses. What, then, can we do as visible proof of the solidarity we feel with those oppressed peoples? [...] Sweden has for a long time made financial contributions for the education of refugees from Southern Africa. Moreover, for a number of years we have helped to pay for legal aid for those charged with offences under the so called 'apartheid laws' in South Africa. We have [also] maintained dependants of people who have been imprisoned or detained under those laws. [...]
>
> These contributions have been made in support of the oppressed peoples of Africa who have [...] not obtained their freedom. The struggle is still continuing and we are in touch with a number of the leaders of the African liberation movements. Some of them have asked us for assistance. We are prepared to help [...], in the same way as we help the liberation front in South Vietnam with drugs and medical supplies. Educational assistance to the members of the liberation movements via their organizations would also be conceivable. It is humanitarian aid that is in question. [A]id that puts the members of those movements in a better position to continue their struggle for the liberty of their people.[1]

Referring to contacts with the leaders of the African liberation movements, it is more than likely that Nilsson had the recent discussions with Amílcar Cabral uppermost in his mind. Pierre Schori—who participated in the discussions with the PAIGC leader—later described Cabral as "a master of diplomacy [...], a formidable person and a great international figure, [who] carried an extremely good message".[2] That it was Cabral who after years of close Swedish contacts with the nationalist leaders of Southern Africa ultimately broke the ice regarding direct official assistance is indicated by the speed with which the government after his visit proceeded to give Nilsson's announcement form and content. Less than two weeks later, Sweden's ambassador to Liberia, Olof Ripa, was instructed to contact the government in Conakry to find out whether direct Swedish assistance to PAIGC would be acceptable to the host government.[3] Ripa replied in February 1969 that Sékou Touré's government supported PAIGC and "without the slightest doubt willingly [would] participate in forwarding consignments of humanitarian aid from Sweden to [the liberation movement]".[4]

During his stay in Stockholm, Cabral also visited SIDA, where he confirmed the general content of the request submitted through Basil Davidson and further specified PAIGC's needs in the areas of health, education and basic necessities, such as food and textiles.[5] Following these discussions and on the basis of the government's declaration of intent, SIDA's Director General Ernst Michanek decided in April 1969—before the Swedish parliament had made its pronouncement on this very

1. 'Speech by the Foreign Minister', 9 December 1968, in The Royal Ministry for Foreign Affairs: *Documents on Swedish Foreign Policy: 1968*, Stockholm, 1969, p. 116.
2. Interview with Pierre Schori, p. 333.
3. Letter from Per Anger, Ministry for Foreign Affairs, to Olof Ripa, Swedish ambassador to Liberia, Stockholm, 19 December 1968 (MFA).
4. Letter from Olof Ripa, Swedish ambassador to Liberia, to Per Anger, Ministry for Foreign Affairs, Monrovia, 19 February 1969 (MFA).
5. Kerstin Oldfelt: Memorandum ('Humanitärt bistånd till Partido Africano da Independência da Guiné e Cabo Verde (PAIGC)'/'Humanitarian assistance to PAIGC'), SIDA, Stockholm, 22 July 1969 (SDA).

principle—to send a fact-finding mission to Senegal and the Republic of Guinée.[1] The purpose was to "study the conditions for [...] aid deliveries to PAIGC".[2]

The official mission—led by Curt Ström, head of SIDA's education division—went to West Africa in mid-May 1969, at the same time as the parliamentary Standing Committee on Appropriations[3] was discussing the general issue of Swedish support to African liberation movements. The conclusion was that such assistance was in accordance with international law "in cases where the United Nations unequivocally has taken a stand against oppression of peoples striving for national freedom".[4] Sweden would thus become the first industrialized Western country to endorse a policy of direct official humanitarian assistance to the liberation movements in the Portuguese colonies, Zimbabwe, Namibia and South Africa.[5] In the case of 'Portuguese Guinea', the pronouncement explicitly referred to PAIGC and to the preparatory steps initiated regarding Swedish assistance, stating that

> according to the information received by the committee, practical possibilities are being explored how to extend [Swedish] humanitarian and educational assistance to the victims of the struggle conducted under the leadership of the Partido Africano da Independência da Guiné e Cabo Verde (PAIGC) to liberate Portuguese Guinea from Portugal's suzerainty. The committee is—*inter alia* with reference to the support which already is being extended to the Mozambique Institute[6]—positive to such assistance if the practical problems can be overcome, assuming that [the government] will utilize the possibilities that may appear.[7]

Guinea-Bissau does not form part of Southern Africa. In a narrow sense, Sweden's relations with PAIGC should therefore not be part of this study. PAIGC was, however, closely linked to MPLA of Angola and FRELIMO of Mozambique. Together with its CONCP allies and SWAPO of Namibia, ANC of South Africa and ZAPU of Zimbabwe, it formed, in addition, part of the so called Khartoum group of 'authentic' liberation movements. In an international context, the liberation struggle in the small Portuguese colony on the West African coast was against this background often juxtaposed with the struggles in Southern Africa, which it to a large extent both encouraged and drew inspiration from.

The importance of the cooperation with PAIGC for Sweden's involvement in Southern Africa cannot be overstated. The very first Swedish comprehensive programme of direct, official humanitarian assistance to an African liberation movement was developed with PAIGC, which in turn was deeply engaged in armed warfare against a European nation that maintained formal commercial links with Sweden. This determined the character and limits of the assistance. Despite strong appeals by the non-governmental solidarity movement and the wider socialist left in favour of 'unconditional support'—that is, cash resources to be used by PAIGC as it saw fit—a basic humanitarian orientation was upheld. Nevertheless, the authorities would soon equate 'humanitarian' assistance with 'non-military', or 'civilian', assistance and considerably widen the scope of the cooperation.

---

1. Curt Ström: 'Reserapport' ('Travel report'), SIDA, Stockholm, 13 June 1969 (SDA).
2. Ibid.
3. In Swedish, *Statsutskottet*.
4. Swedish Parliament 1969: Statement No. 82/1969 by the Appropriations' Committee, p. 24.
5. Ironically, the MP who signed the historic statement by the Standing Committee on Appropriations was Gösta Bohman. The following year, he became chairman of the conservative Moderate Party, the only traditional Swedish party to remain outside the broader partnership with the liberation movements in Southern Africa.
6. Official Swedish support to FRELIMO's Mozambique Institute in Dar es Salaam, Tanzania, had been extended since 1965. On Sweden and the Mozambique Institute, see Sellström Volume I, pp. 453-59 and the following chapter.
7. Swedish Parliament 1969: Statement No. 82/1969 by the Appropriations' Committee, p. 24.

Particularly significant is that the interpretation made by the Swedish government and SIDA of the humanitarian assistance to PAIGC was subsequently applied to the liberation movements in Southern Africa. The cooperation with PAIGC not only defined the general content and structure of Sweden's official assistance to the liberation movements, but created an institutional culture within SIDA and between SIDA and the Ministry for Foreign Affairs. It is therefore relevant to outline the cooperation between the Swedish government and PAIGC.[1]

A Decisive Breakthrough

Curt Ström's fact-finding mission in May 1969 largely shaped Sweden's future assistance to PAIGC. On his way to the Republic of Guinée, Ström first visited Senegal, where more than 50,000 refugees from Guinea-Bissau were living at the time.[2] He found that the refugees were well received by the Senegalese authorities. In addition, the United Nations High Commissioner for Refugees had financed the building of thirty schools for the refugee children.[3] Against this background, Ström concluded that "there is no reason for SIDA to support the aid activities in favour of the refugees in Senegal".[4]

Sweden had no official representation in the Republic of Guinée[5] and no development assistance had been extended to the former French colony. Ström's initial discussions with the authorities in Conakry were in this context "not without frictions".[6] While confirming that assistance to PAIGC would be welcome, they made it clear that Guinée expected some support in return. In his report, SIDA's representative concluded that "contributions in favour of PAIGC without satisfying some of the many needs pointed out by [the government of Guinée] do not appear as very advisable".[7] The Swedish government eventually conceded to this view, granting limited support to the education sector in the Republic of Guinée. According to Stig Lövgren—later responsible for SIDA's procurement programme to PAIGC—"we had to enter into a special arrangement with Guinea-Conakry in order to get things moving. [...] The price Sweden had to pay was the provision of a complete printing press for the education sector".[8]

---

1. Chiefly included as an introduction to the subject of Swedish assistance to the Southern African liberation movements, the 'detour' via PAIGC and Guinea-Bissau is far from comprehensive. While examples are given to illustrate the scope and character of the Swedish government's assistance, the important role played by the Social Democratic Party, the Africa Groups and other solidarity organizations is not properly represented. In addition to what was noted above, it should *inter alia* be mentioned that the Social Democratic Party and the Social Democratic Youth League at the end of the 1960s through the campaign 'ABC for PAIGC' raised funds for the production of PAIGC's first schoolbooks in Portuguese. The first book—PAIGC: *O Nosso Livro: 1a Classe* ('Our Book: Form One')—was printed in 1970 by Wretmans Boktryckeri, Uppsala, in 20,000 copies. The same year, *O Nosso Livro: 2a Classe* ('Our Book: Form Two') was printed by Wretmans in 25,000 copies. Next to the Swedish printer's name, the title page of the second book stated that it was issued by PAIGC in "the liberated areas of Guinea".
2. Curt Ström: 'Reserapport' ('Travel report'), SIDA, Stockholm, 13 June 1969 (SDA).
3. Ibid. Fifteen of the schools were built through contributions from Norway.
4. Ibid. During his visit to Senegal, Ström also met Benjamin Pinto-Bull, the leader of the Dakar-based rival Guinean liberation organization FLING. Pinto-Bull asserted that his organization had "stronger support among the people [in Guinea-Bissau] than PAIGC", but Ström was neither convinced, nor impressed by the FLING leader.
5. During his meetings in Conakry, Ström discovered that both the government of Guinée and PAIGC were "deeply suspicious" of the local Swedish consul. Amílcar Cabral stated that he did not want the consul to have anything to do with possible future Swedish assistance (ibid).
6. Ibid.
7. Ibid.
8. Interview with Stig Lövgren, p. 314. The Swedish government did not encounter similar demands in Southern Africa, where it had diplomatic representations and the countries hosting the liberation movements were important recipients of Swedish development assistance.

Ström's meetings with PAIGC were straightforward. In his report, he described the PAIGC Secretary General Amílcar Cabral as "a cheerful, young agronomist; elegant, intellectual [and] with a quick and lively way of talking. No pathetic appeals or solemn declarations. His statements seem objective, clear and to the point".[1] Ström was also impressed by the atmosphere at PAIGC's headquarters in Conakry: "The work was, as far as we could judge, marked by determination and efficiency".[2] SIDA's representative did not cross into the liberated areas of Guinea-Bissau and a planned visit to PAIGC's hospital in Boké in northern Guinée had to be cancelled on instructions from the host government. He did, however, assess the situation at two PAIGC schools in Conakry, where he found the material conditions wanting, but the spirit and general environment "commendable".[3]

The discussions on possible future assistance from Sweden to PAIGC were held directly with Cabral. According to Ström's report, Cabral emphasized that the need for assistance was almost unlimited and that it was "easier to state what he did not wish from Sweden".[4] That was, notably, arms, military supplies and scholarships[5], which PAIGC could obtain from other sources.[6] Referring to the request discussed with SIDA during Cabral's visit to Sweden in November 1968, the parties eventually agreed on a proposal covering the areas of health, education and basic necessities "within and outside the combat areas".[7] The envisaged support was in the form of deliveries of goods and equipment, to be shipped to PAIGC in Conakry.[8] PAIGC had, according to Cabral, the necessary storage capacity in the capital of Guinée and the material assistance would be transported into Guinea-Bissau by PAIGC's department of logistics, composed of some 150 people and having at its disposal a number of trucks donated by OAU and the Soviet Union.[9]

Before Ström's return to Sweden, PAIGC supplied him with detailed lists of the items requested. With regard to basic necessities, they included both food—such as dried milk and canned fish and meat—and consumer goods in the form of textiles, blankets, household utensils and agricultural tools. The goods were intended for the 'people's stores'[10] that PAIGC had set up in the liberated areas. It was from the outset evident that the bulk of the proposed Swedish humanitarian assistance was destined for the liberation movement's civilian activities inside Guinea-Bissau.

Despite the problems encountered vis-à-vis the authorities in Conakry, Ström's report to SIDA's Director General recommended in June 1969—after the clarifying statement by the Swedish parliament—that an amount of 1 million SEK should be

---

1. Curt Ström: 'Reserapport' ('Travel report'), SIDA, Stockholm, 13 June 1969 (SDA).
2. Ibid.
3. Ibid.
4. Ibid.
5. PAIGC later made exceptions to this general stand on scholarships. With funds from SIDA, Amílcar Cabral's younger brother Fernando Cabral began medical studies in thoracic surgery in Stockholm at the end of 1972 (Letter from Onésimo Silveira to Marianne Rappe, Uppsala, 21 October 1972) (SDA).
6. In his report, Ström stated that PAIGC's most important donors were the Organization of African Unity, the Soviet Union, the German Democratic Republic and Czechoslovakia. The assistance from the People's Republic of China had come to an end five years earlier, a fact which Cabral commented as follows: "It is true that we need assistance, but no masters" (Curt Ström: 'Reserapport'/'Travel report', SIDA, Stockholm, 13 June 1969) (SDA).
7. Ibid.
8. There were very few transport connections between Sweden and the Republic of Guinée. In the beginning, SIDA had difficulties in finding a shipping line with regular sailings to the country, but eventually used a Danish company with a regular service to some West African ports, among them Conakry (Interview with Stig Lövgren, p. 314).
9. Curt Ström: 'Reserapport' ('Travel report'), SIDA, Stockholm, 13 June 1969 (SDA).
10. In Portuguese, *armazéns do povo*.

allocated to PAIGC for the procurement of various items within the indicated areas during the financial year 1969/70.[1] Supported by the Consultative Committee on Humanitarian Assistance[2], the recommendation was in July 1969 forwarded by Michanek to Foreign Minister Nilsson, who also gave it his seal of approval. The first shipment within a comprehensive official Swedish support programme to an African liberation movement left Rotterdam, Holland, for PAIGC on 29 September 1969.[3] Amílcar Cabral was at the time again visiting Sweden, now to attend the congress of the Social Democratic Party.[4] Ten months after his first visit to Sweden, he could thus register on the spot the results of his diplomatic efforts.[5]

Civilian Needs and Swedish Responses

From the beginning, PAIGC gave proof of high efficiency with regard to adminis-tration, distribution and reporting of the goods received from Sweden. After a visit by a SIDA delegation to Conakry in late 1971, a memorandum to the Consultative Committee on Humanitarian Assistance concluded, for example, that the "previ-ous Swedish commodity support has been utilized in an optimal way. A rapid deci-sion system, detailed commodity orders, good storage and bookkeeping characterize PAIGC".[6] PAIGC's written reports to SIDA were, similarly, of the highest standard. Every year, Amílcar Cabral himself—and after his death in 1973, Aristides Pereira—made general comments on the assistance and submitted detailed lists of the goods received, including breakdowns of the distribution between the var-ious schools, clinics and people's stores in the liberated areas.[7] According to SIDA's Stig Lövgren, PAIGC was "some sort of ideal organization for us".[8]

At the same time, PAIGC faced enormous challenges. In 1971, it was estimated that 400,000 people lived in the liberated areas of Guinea-Bissau.[9] The majority

1. Curt Ström: 'Reserapport' ('Travel report'), SIDA, Stockholm, 13 June 1969 (SDA).
2. CCHA: 'Protokoll' ('Minutes'), Stockholm, 5 June 1969 (SDA). On this occasion, Curt Ström made a verbal presentation of his findings during the visits to Senegal and the Republic of Guinée.
3. SIDA: 'Fortsatt svenskt stöd till Partido Africano da Independência da Guiné e Cabo Verde' ('Continued Swedish support to PAIGC'), Stockholm, 19 November 1970 (SDA). As will be seen from the accompanying tables, SIDA's accounts do not reflect any disbursements to PAIGC during the financial year 1969/70. The deliveries made in 1969/70 were first debited in 1970/71. In a comprehensive report dated 19 May 1970, Cabral, however, acknowledged receipt and recorded the distribution of the Swedish assistance during the financial year 1969/70 (PAIGC: 'Sur l'aide humanitaire de la Suède à notre parti: Rapport bref et proposition d'aide' ('On the humanitarian aid from Sweden to our party: Brief report and aid proposal'), Conakry, 19 May 1970) (SDA).
4. The congress elected Olof Palme as party leader and Prime Minister. Less than a month earlier, ASEA had withdrawn from the controversial Cabora Bassa project in Mozambique. The ruling Social Democratic Party could thus point at real Swedish commitments to the cause of Africa's liberation to both the invited FRE-LIMO leader Marcelino dos Santos and the Secretary General of PAIGC, Amílcar Cabral. For Palme, this was highly significant. He started his term as Prime Minister of Sweden without major economic complications in Southern Africa, with a parliamentary pronouncement in favour of direct official support to the African liber-ation movements and a first concrete example of such support. It is, against this background, not surprising that he as a person became identified to a large extent with Sweden's assistance to the liberation movements in Africa.
5. Cabral returned to Stockholm in June 1970 to discuss PAIGC's request for continued Swedish assistance in 1970/71 (SIDA: 'Fortsatt svenskt stöd till Partido Africano da Independência da Guiné e Cabo Verde'/'Con-tinued Swedish support to PAIGC', Stockholm, 19 November 1970) (SDA).
6. SIDA: 'Fortsatt stöd till Partido [Africano] da Independência da Guiné e Cabo Verde (PAIGC)'/'Continued support to PAIGC', Stockholm, 5 September 1972 (SDA).
7. The reports were written in French. Swedish support also went to PAIGC in the Republic of Guinée, notably to the PAIGC schools and—above all—to the Solidarity Hospital in Boké, in the north of the country. In addi-tion, vehicles, office equipment and stationery for PAIGC's headquarters in Conakry formed part of the sup-port.
8. Interview with Stig Lövgren, p. 312.
9. SIDA: 'Fortsatt svenskt stöd till Partido Africano da Independência da Guiné e Cabo Verde' ('Continued Swedish support to PAIGC'), Stockholm, 28 October 1971 (SDA).

were peasants and artisans. The illiteracy rate was around 80 per cent and the general health situation difficult. Large sections of the population—children in particular—suffered from malnutrition.[1] Trying to build a new society in the liberated areas by providing social services and developing the economy, PAIGC—which, above all, was engaged in a generalized war against NATO-backed Portugal—assumed the functions of a government and administration in an independent state.[2] In marked contrast to an independent state, the liberation movement was, however, not in control of the national resources or in a position to carry out international trade.[3] On the contrary, in a country with a huge fishery potential, the people in the liberated areas suffered from protein deficiency, which, paradoxically, led PAIGC to include important deliveries of canned fish under the Swedish aid programme. In addition, PAIGC could not impose taxes on the population in the liberated areas. There was, in the first place, no overall taxable surplus produced. More importantly, the monetary economy had been abolished and replaced by a barter system in which the people's stores played an economically crucial and politically sensitive role.

The *armazéns do povo* were designed to serve as trade centres, or depots, where the villagers could exchange their agricultural products for other essential commodities and consumer goods, such as textiles, cooking oil, soap, matches, household utensils, agricultural tools or cigarettes.[4] As pointed out by Rudebeck, this was "a highly political function. [I]f it [was] not performed to the people's satisfaction, the entire credibility of the PAIGC in the people's eyes [would] suffer".[5] The barter system could only operate properly if the PAIGC stores had an adequate supply of goods.[6]

Enjoying broad political support, facing next to unlimited needs and giving proof of good administrative capacity, PAIGC would during the first half of the 1970s become dominant among the African liberation movements receiving official Swedish assistance. The initial grant of 1 million SEK was increased to 1.75 million in 1970/71, 4.5 in 1971/72, 10 in 1972/73, 15 in 1973/74 and to 22 MSEK in 1974/75.[7] As noted above, of the 67.5 MSEK actually disbursed by Sweden as direct official humanitarian assistance to the liberation movements in Southern Africa and PAIGC between 1969/70 and 1974/75, 64.5 million—corresponding to 96 per cent—was paid out in favour of MPLA of Angola, FRELIMO of Mozambique and PAIGC of Guinea-Bissau and Cape Verde, indicating a clear concentration on the Portuguese colonies. Out of the total, no less than 45.2 MSEK benefited PAIGC. During the first six years of official assistance to the liberation movements, PAIGC received two thirds of the funds disbursed. It is thus not surprising that the Southern African liberation movements with which Sweden had had closer relations during a longer period of time felt disadvantaged. Interviewed in 1996, the

1. Ibid.
2. PAIGC: 'Sur l'aide humanitaire de la Suède à notre parti: Rapport bref et proposition d'aide' ('On the humanitarian aid from Sweden to our party: Brief report and aid proposal'), Conakry, May 1972 (SDA).
3. Within the economy of the people's stores, PAIGC did, nevertheless, organize limited exports to the neighbouring countries, mainly of kola nuts and rice, but also of peanuts, palm oil and other agricultural products.
4. The system was also intended to achieve economic justice by keeping the barter prices lower than the cash prices in the Portuguese stores in the non-liberated areas. The first *armazém do povo* was set up in 1964. By 1968, there were fifteen such stores in the liberated areas. The number had in 1973 more than doubled.
5. Rudebeck op. cit., p. 179.
6. On the people's stores, see Rudebeck op. cit., pp. 178-86 and Chabal op. cit., pp. 112-14.
7. SIDA: 'Stöd till PAIGC' ('Assistance to PAIGC'), Stockholm, 25 June 1974 (SDA).

MPLA leader Lúcio Lara stated that the support to PAIGC "even made us a little jealous", adding that "we compared the figures [...] and saw the difference".[1]

With regard to non-military assistance, the Swedish government arguably became PAIGC's most important donor.[2] That was over the years often acknowledged by the Guinean leadership, in particular when compared to the stand by other Western countries.[3] Noting that the United States had extended aid to Portugal of almost 500 million USD, Cabral wrote, for example, in 1972 that the "rich example of the Swedish people and its government influences, and will increasingly influence, the attitude of other peoples and governments in favour of the struggle against foreign domination, colonialism and racism in our continent".[4] In the case of PAIGC, it was, however, comparatively uncontroversial for the Swedish government to take a firm stand. The liberation struggle did not constitute a threat to Sweden's national security and the affinity with PAIGC's objectives was strong. There were, in addition, no conflicting considerations concerning economic opportunity.[5] Finally, from the point of view of public legitimacy, the official policy enjoyed broad support.[6] Nevertheless, viewed against the Cold War situation prevailing in the early 1970s, the Swedish assistance to PAIGC was more political than a strict interpretation of the term 'humanitarian support' would suggest.[7] This also had a bearing on the cooperation with the liberation movements in Southern Africa.

Besides the military struggle, PAIGC had through the barter system based on the people's stores engaged in an economic battle against Portugal. Cabral was also keen to point out that "with hospitals and schools we can win the war".[8] Far from a defensive reaction to Portuguese colonialism and oppression, the economic, health and education sectors were integral and pro-active parts of the liberation effort. It was to these sectors that the bulk of the Swedish assistance was channelled. Initially restricted to purely humanitarian goods, the commodities included in the procurement programmes would in step with the growing allocations

---

1. Interview with Lúcio Lara, p. 19. The Swedish support to MPLA during the same period amounted to a mere 2.3 MSEK, i.e. 5 per cent of the support extended to PAIGC. Lara attributed the difference to the qualities of the PAIGC Secretary General: "The reason was the presence of Amílcar Cabral. He was very dynamic and always on top of the events" (ibid.).

2. In the absence of comprehensive PAIGC accounts, this remains to be documented. The conclusion is based on statements by PAIGC, SIDA and the United Nations.

3. Lövgren later commented that the Swedish commodity support according to Cabral was "the best form of aid that Sweden could give. [...] They had no use for money at the time. [...] Everything that they needed for the war they received from the socialist bloc, but they did not have any resources when it came to food, medicines, school equipment etc. for the civilian part of the struggle. They were totally dependent on countries like Sweden for these items, because they could not procure them on the international market" (Interview with Stig Lövgren, p. 310).

4. PAIGC: 'Sur l'aide humanitaire de la Suède à notre parti: Rapport bref et proposition d'aide' ('On the humanitarian aid from Sweden to our party: Brief report and aid proposal'), Conakry, May 1972 (SDA).

5. See the interview with Bengt Säve-Söderbergh, in which the former Social Democratic Under-Secretary of State for Foreign Affairs (1985-91) states that "Angola was of interest to those who were looking for money. We knew that nobody really cared about Guinea-Bissau and [that] some only marginally cared about Mozambique. Angola was the interesting case and therefore the hottest country in terms of the East-West divide" (p. 338).

6. On Sweden, the African liberation movements and the determining factors of national security, ideological affinity, economic opportunity and public legitimacy, see the concluding chapter in Sellström Volume I, pp. 512-519.

7. To Cabral, all assistance to PAIGC was humanitarian, "irrespective of form and content, because it is extended in favour of political, economic, social and cultural progress of mankind and of peace" (Letter from Amílcar Cabral to SIDA, Conakry, 28 July 1971) (SDA).

8. Cabral cited in Chabal op. cit., p. 114.

increasingly meet more political needs.[1] The programmes were drawn up between PAIGC and SIDA. The Consultative Committee on Humanitarian Assistance and the Swedish government would as a rule follow SIDA's recommendations.

Defining Humanitarian Assistance

At PAIGC's request, official Swedish assistance was over the years almost exclusively extended in the form of commodity support. It did not involve major components of technical assistance, project activities or cash support.[2] As there was no SIDA representation in Conakry, annual negotiations regarding the support normally took place in Stockholm. Amílcar Cabral himself took a keen interest in the discussions and would in the beginning lead PAIGC's delegations. Later, Stig Lövgren recalled how Cabral

> would come to Stockholm. He stayed in a hotel under an assumed name for security reasons and was working with us at SIDA to establish a list of articles, goods, equipment etc. that they needed. It was a very simple procedure and not very controversial, because at that time the list just covered food, medicines, hospital and school equipment and so on. [...] Amílcar Cabral [...] was extremely engaged in this kind of detail. [H]e felt that it was something that he had to attend to. [...] We did not question their needs very much. After all, the funds allocated in those days were not that big and Curt Ström, who was the official in charge at SIDA, was of the opinion that we should not question too much.[3]

Once the commodity lists had been established, SIDA acted as a tender board for PAIGC, inviting bids from different suppliers in Sweden and internationally. PAIGC's representative in Sweden generally took part in this work. When the supplier had been identified, SIDA paid for the goods and organized the shipments to Conakry.[4]

It was important that the assistance was not seen as support to the military struggle. In the case of PAIGC, this was far from obvious. The bulk of the assistance went to the liberated areas inside Guinea-Bissau, where the population was

---

1. The Swedish solidarity movement was in the early 1970s highly critical of how the official support to the liberation movements was designed. A book published by the Africa Groups argued in January 1972 that "SIDA's contribution is not given unconditionally to the liberation movements. It is only given for 'humanitarian purposes', i.e. to health, education and the like. This means that the liberation movements are not recognized as representatives of their respective peoples and that the military side of the liberation movements' activity is not supported" (AGIS op. cit., p. 194). At about the same time, a document written by the Africa Groups in English for an international solidarity conference with FRELIMO, MPLA and PAIGC, held in Lund in early 1972, stated that "by refusing to see the military aspect as an integral part of the struggle, the Swedish government is giving a false picture of the situation. Another restriction is that material through [SIDA] is given in kind, selected from a list and purchased (in Sweden) by SIDA officials. This is a severe form of *paternalism*, which can be explained only by the desire to keep the flourishing economic links with Portugal as long as possible and by the desire to achieve a neo-colonialist solution in the [Portuguese] colonies" (Draft: 'Swedish imperialism in Portugal and Africa', The Easter Conference, Lund, 1972) (AGA). It should be noted that the official assistance was *not* tied to procurement in Sweden. Nor did SIDA procure goods in Portugal for the liberation movements in the Portuguese colonies (Interview with Stig Lövgren, p. 314).
2. The issue of cash support would be raised particularly by FRELIMO of Mozambique. In November 1972, SIDA decided that 5 per cent of the annual allocations to the liberation movements could be transferred as cash support for local procurement and running costs. In the case of PAIGC, it corresponded in 1972/73 to 0.5 MSEK.
3. Interview with Stig Lövgren, pp. 309-12.
4. With its wide network and considerable experience, SIDA's procurement division was able to identify the best suppliers and press prices in favour of PAIGC and the Southern African liberation movements. It later arranged training courses for the movements in international procurement. Acknowledging the importance of well-functioning procurement routines in general and the significant contribution to PAIGC by Stig Lövgren in particular, shortly after independence Luís Cabral, the first President of Guinea-Bissau, invited Lövgren to become responsible for national imports and public procurement in the new country (Anders Möllander: *Sverige i Södra Afrika: Minnesanteckningar 1970-80* ('Sweden in Southern Africa: Memories 1970-80'), SIDA, Stockholm, 1982, p. 19 and interview with Stig Lövgren, 313).

Food and propaganda: Sardines
from Sweden with PAIGC label
(Courtesy of Stig Lövgren)

engaged in a war. Freedom fighters and villagers alike benefited from the schools, health clinics and people's stores that PAIGC was running and which to an important extent were supplied through Swedish assistance. In addition, SIDA was in no position to regularly visit the liberated areas and could not verify whether the end-users were soldiers or civilians.[1] The line between 'humanitarian' and 'military' support was therefore drawn as the commodity lists were established. The main criterion was the character of the commodity. Initially, this often led to quite absurd considerations, such as whether torches that clicked[2] or a certain type of boots[3] could be considered military. Stig Lövgren has given a good illustration of the dilemma:

> [The issue of military and non-military supplies] was very much discussed during the early years. Curt Ström, especially, was always very nervous that we might send things that could be used for military purposes. I remember very well one meeting with Amílcar Cabral at SIDA. We were discussing the lists that we had prepared earlier and which Ström should approve. When we came to machetes, he was very concerned and said that they could be used to kill people. Amílcar Cabral then took up a pen and said: 'This is a weapon too...'.[4]

That even such an obviously non-military commodity as sardines could play an important role in the wider liberation struggle would, in addition, become evident. In an interview in 1996, Lövgren recalled:

> We supplied a lot of food, especially tinned food, to PAIGC. At one stage, we bought something like a hundred tons of tinned fish—quite a considerable quantity—from a Swedish factory. The supplier—Strömstad Canning—asked me if we wanted a special label for the consignment. I thought that it was a good idea, so I contacted Onésimo Silveira, who was then the PAIGC representative in Sweden. He became so enthusiastic! It was not until later that I realized why he became ecstatic. He decided on a label with the PAIGC flag and with the text 'From the liberated areas of Guinea-Bissau'. Years afterwards, I was told that [PAIGC] had arranged for these tins to appear in different places in the areas where the Portuguese still held

---

1. Interview with Stig Lövgren, p. 311: "[W]e did not and could not visit the liberated areas. We tried to, but in most cases [PAIGC] politely found some excuse for not letting us go there. Basically for security reasons, of course".
2. Möllander op. cit., p. 17.
3. Interview with Mishake Muyongo (ex-SWAPO), p. 87.
4. Interview with Stig Lövgren, p. 310.

power. They even distributed some of the tins in Bissau, the capital. You can imagine what an effective psychological weapon this was.[1]

The Swedish authorities would, however, soon "roughly equate humanitarian with civilian assistance"[2] and, according to Lövgren, "in the end we did not pay any attention to [the problem]. After all, we did not supply weapons or ammunition".[3] In fact, the definition of 'civilian'—or 'non-military'—assistance was given a wide interpretation. When Amílcar Cabral in July 1971 asked SIDA to supply a mobile radio station in support of PAIGC's education efforts[4] the request was approved without misgivings. Eventually mounted on two Mercedes Benz trucks—also supplied by Sweden—two transmitters and the accompanying studio equipment were purchased in March 1972. After installation and training of PAIGC personnel by the official consultancy firm SWEDTEL[5], the liberation movement could on 19 September 1972 start regular broadcasting services to Guinea-Bissau and Cape Verde from different locations in northern Guinée.[6]

Nevertheless, in the early days of the support to the liberation movements a more serious discussion took place concerning the supply of vehicles, particularly trucks. Anders Möllander—who as secretary to the Consultative Committee on Humanitarian Assistance closely followed the debate—later wrote that "some argued that means of transport, such as trucks, could always be used for military purposes and therefore should not be provided as part of the Swedish support".[7] The counter-argument by PAIGC and the liberation movements in Southern Africa was that they could not move and distribute the goods received without adequate transport facilities. It was the latter view that prevailed. Lövgren later commented that

[t]he basic reason why trucks were finally supplied was [...] that the goods [...] provided by SIDA had to be transported in one way or the other from the ports to the stores at the PAIGC bases. After all, we found that it would be reasonable to provide a limited number of trucks at

1. Ibid. One of many ironies of the war in Guinea-Bissau was that canned sardines—a typically Portuguese product—had to be procured in Sweden and shipped to the fish-rich country. The tins weighed 225 grams each. The 'propaganda consignment' with the PAIGC flag thus consisted of some 400,000 tins. No wonder, then, that PAIGC re-routed part of it from the people's stores to the Portuguese-held areas. In addition to misspelling 'liberated areas' (*zonas libertas* instead of *zonas libertadas*), the label, however, clearly identified both the Swedish supplier and Sweden as the country of origin. Cigarettes were also delivered to the people's stores. Produced in Sweden under the propaganda label *Nô Pintcha*, PAIGC, similarly, designed the packet. The provision of this non-essential commodity under the humanitarian support was strongly criticized. The Swedish National Association for Information on the Harmful Effects of Tobacco (*Nationalföreningen för Upplysning om Tobakens Skadeverkningar* - NTS) wrote to the Minister for International Development Cooperation, Gertrud Sigurdsen, demanding that she "immediately instruct SIDA that the planned exportation of cigarettes to Guinea-Bissau is replaced by assistance in the form of more essential goods" (Letter from Eric Carlens and Lars Ramström, NTS, to Gertrud Sigurdsen, Stockholm, 25 June 1974) (SDA). Noting that the cigarettes only represented 185,000 SEK out of a total allocation to PAIGC of 15 million and that they played an important role in the barter economy of the *armazéns do povo*, the minister, however, replied that goods to the people's stores formed part of "Sweden's explicit support to the work of the liberation movement" and that it "must, in cases like this, be SIDA's responsibility to assess what is suitable" (Letter from Gertrud Sigurdsen to NTS, Stockholm, 2 July 1974) (SDA). Cf. Möllander op. cit., pp. 16-17 and the interview with Stig Lövgren, pp. 310-11).
2. Möllander op. cit., p. 17.
3. Interview with Stig Lövgren, p. 310. In Portugal—where there were vehement reactions against Sweden's decision to extend assistance to the liberation movements—the humanitarian character of the support was never accepted. The newspaper *Diário de Notícias* noted, for example, in early 1971 that Swedish exports of pocket-knives to the 'terrorists' in Africa had increased considerably (*Diário de Notícias*, 16 January 1971). This was taken as proof of Sweden's bellicose intentions (see the editorial 'O apoio do Sr. Olof Palme ao terrorismo em África'/'Mr. Olof Palme's support to terrorism in Africa' in *Diário de Notícias*, 19 January 1971).
4. Letter from Amílcar Cabral to SIDA, Conakry, 28 July 1971 (SDA).
5. Swedish Telecommunication Consulting AB, a subsidiary of the Swedish Telecommunications Administration.
6. SWEDTEL: 'Broadcasting station in Guinea: Final report', Stockholm, December 1972 (SDA). Hundreds of transistor radios were subsequently supplied by SIDA for the liberated areas in Guinea-Bissau.
7. Möllander op. cit., p. 18.

the same time as we were supplying large quantities of goods. [...] [W]e [thus] supplied Land Rovers and other four-wheel drive vehicles. After a few years, there was no discussion about that. We even provided both Volvo and Scania vehicles specifically designed for the Swedish army, but made available in a civilian version too.[1]

In fact, the provision of vehicles occupied a prominent—and highly appreciated—part of the Swedish government's support to the liberation movements.[2] In the case of PAIGC, the transport component represented as early as in 1970/71 11 per cent of the total value of the assistance.[3] Three years later—in 1973/74—the share had increased to 18 per cent.[4] From the point of view of costs, transport was then the second biggest component of the assistance programme, after food, but before medical drugs and school supplies.[5] That year alone it included the provision of 12 larger (Volvo) and 6 smaller (GAZ 66) trucks, 15 jeeps (Unimog) with trailers, 2 ambulances (Peugeot) and 2 estate cars (Peugeot), as well as spare parts, tyres, oils and lubricants etc.[6] In addition, 10 outboard motors for river transport by pirogue and 500 bicycles were supplied.[7]

Amílcar Cabral and the Swedish Assistance

The cooperation with PAIGC of Guinea-Bissau dominated official Swedish assistance to the African liberation movements during the first half of the 1970s. Starting at a comparatively high level[8], the commodity support steadily increased over the years. In spite of cultural differences and generally difficult circumstances, it was based on mutual trust between the parties and implemented to the satisfaction of both donor and recipient. The experience from the cooperation with PAIGC served as a positive example with regard to humanitarian assistance to the liberation movements in Southern Africa.[9]

That the PAIGC Secretary General himself was deeply involved in the design, implementation and follow-up of the official assistance naturally facilitated the

---

1. Interview with Stig Lövgren, p. 310.
2. See, for example, the interviews with SWAPO's Aaron Mushimba (p. 84) and ZANU's Kumbirai Kangai (p. 213-14). Although not tied to procurement in Sweden, the transport support would over the years with regard to heavy trucks substantially benefit the Swedish companies Scania and Volvo, which were often given preference by the liberation movements. For example, when the MPLA President Agostinho Neto and Prime Minister Olof Palme met in Lusaka, Zambia, in September 1971, Neto reacted to the news that SIDA would supply German or French trucks to his movement, stating that he "could not understand why [it] would not rather deliver Swedish vehicles" (Pierre Schori: Memorandum, Stockholm, 1 October 1971) (MFA). In addition to Scania and Volvo trucks, SIDA supplied many German (Mercedes Benz) and French (Berliet) heavy vehicles. British (Land Rover) and Japanese (Toyota) manufacturers dominated in the case of lighter four-wheel drive cars. Looking back, the former head of SIDA's procurement division, Stig Lövgren, commented in 1996: "One thing that I regret very much is that instead of supplying the liberation movements with Swedish trucks, we should have supplied them with Russian trucks. At the time, you could get almost three Russian trucks for one Swedish [...]. That was really a waste of money. They should not have received so many of these very technical and sophisticated Swedish machines, but [as] simple trucks as possible" (Interview with Stig Lövgren, p. 315).
3. SIDA: 'Fortsatt svenskt stöd till Partido Africano da Independência da Guiné e Cabo Verde' ('Continued Swedish support to PAIGC'), Stockholm, 28 October 1971 (SDA).
4. SIDA: 'Stöd till PAIGC' ('Support to PAIGC'), Stockholm, 22 August 1973 (SDA).
5. Out of a total allocation of 15 million SEK, the following were the eight major components of the Swedish assistance to PAIGC in 1973/74: food (20%), transport (18%), textiles and sewing equipment (15%), items for the people's stores (13%), clothes and shoes (11%), medical drugs (5%), hygienic articles (3%) and school supplies (2.5%) (ibid.).
6. SIDA: 'Stöd till PAIGC' ('Support to PAIGC'), Stockholm, 25 June 1974 (SDA).
7. Ibid.
8. The first allocation to PAIGC in 1969/70 was 1 million SEK. The initial grant to SWAPO of Namibia in 1970/71 amounted to 30,000 SEK and the regular assistance to ANC of South Africa started with 150,000 SEK in 1972/73.
9. Cabral's influence on the decision to extend Swedish support to MPLA of Angola is discussed in Sellström Volume I, pp. 429-35.

cooperation.[1] So did the fact that PAIGC before the relationship started had a resident representative in Sweden, who actively participated in the debate and with whom SIDA often consulted. Onésimo Silveira was, however, dismissed in November 1972[2] and only two months later—on 20 January 1973—Amílcar Cabral was assassinated.[3]

By that time, the cooperation with PAIGC was solidly established. The assassination of Cabral did not provoke an open crisis within the liberation movement, motivating the Swedish government to withhold the assistance as had been the case after the murder of the FRELIMO President Eduardo Mondlane in February 1969. Both Cabral's successor as Secretary General, Aristides Pereira, and his brother, Luís Cabral, the future President of independent Guinea-Bissau, had from the beginning worked closely with SIDA and would after the murder take over his contacts with the aid agency.[4] SIDA resumed the aid shipments to Conakry as early as in mid-February 1973.[5]

Cabral's death made a deep impact in Sweden.[6] Described as "the most theoretically profound of the nationalist leaders in Portuguese Africa"[7], he had with extraordinary skills managed to raise support for PAIGC over a broad political spectrum, ranging from the extra-parliamentary left to the Liberal Party. He

---

1. Cabral firmly opposed the idea of receiving official Swedish assistance via the OAU Liberation Committee (Marianne Rappe: Memorandum ('Samtal med Folke Löfgren på SIDA den 21.4.1972: PAIGC'/'Conversation with Folke Löfgren at SIDA 21.4.1972: PAIGC'), SIDA, Stockholm, 24 April 1972) (MFA). Direct, bilateral relations did not only enhance the liberation movement's influence over the support programme, but also strengthened its international standing. To this should be added OAU's administrative shortcomings. All the Southern African liberation movements supported by Sweden shared Cabral's view in this regard. In the case of Zimbabwe, ZANU's former Deputy Secretary of Finance Didymus Mutasa later explained: "We had to a great extent [...] experienced the bureaucracy within OAU. They would say that we must wait for the summit meeting of the Heads of State, which then would take quite a long time to decide whether it was necessary for us to pursue the liberation struggle. In the meanwhile, we would be sitting under the sun, waiting and hoping that the assistance would arrive. [...] So, we felt, well, why do we not get the money directly" (Interview with Didymus Mutasa, p. 218). Cf. Ansprenger op. cit.

2. According to Aristides Pereira—who visited Stockholm in early January 1973—the dismissal of Silveira was a "disciplinary action", motivated by the fact that he had refused to travel to Guinée for discussions with PAIGC. The movement was, however, "very satisfied with Silveira's work in Sweden" (Anders Möllander: Memorandum ('Minnesanteckningar från besök 1973 01 02 av Aristides Pereira, PAIGC'/'Notes from visit 1973 01 02 by Aristides Pereira, PAIGC'), Stockholm, 4 January 1973) (SDA). The new PAIGC representative, Gil Fernandes, was introduced in a letter from Pereira shortly thereafter (Letter from Aristides Pereira to SIDA, Conakry, 11 January 1973) (SDA). He paid his first visit to SIDA together with Fernando Cabral, the brother of the recently murdered PAIGC leader, in mid-February 1973 (Letter ('Svenskt varubistånd till PAIGC'/'Swedish commodity support to PAIGC') from Marianne Rappe, SIDA, to Gun-Britt Andersson, Ministry for Foreign Affairs, Stockholm, 26 February 1973) (SDA). When it came to the PAIGC representation in Sweden, there was, thus, no major break in the relations. Silveira later worked with the United Nations in various African countries. In November 1998, he formed a new political party—*Partido do Trabalho e da Solidariedade* (Labour and Solidarity Party; PTS)—in his native Cape Verde.

3. The Portuguese government knew that PAIGC planned to declare Guinea-Bissau independent in 1973, fearing that it would lead to greater pressure for decolonization in Angola and Mozambique and challenge its authority in Portugal. The assassination of Cabral was the outcome of an operation initiated by PIDE, working through a group of PAIGC dissidents. Cabral was shot in broad daylight in front of the PAIGC office in Conakry by a former PAIGC naval commander (see Chabal op. cit., pp. 132-43).

4. At the PAIGC congress at Boé in eastern Guinea-Bissau, Aristides Pereira was in July 1973 confirmed as the new Secretary General and Luís Cabral as Deputy Secretary General.

5. Letter ('Svenskt varubistånd till PAIGC'/'Swedish commodity support to PAIGC') from Marianne Rappe, SIDA, to Gun-Britt Andersson, Ministry for Foreign Affairs, Stockholm, 26 February 1973 (SDA).

6. Cabral's memory was *inter alia* honoured by Prime Minister Palme in parliament ('Extract from the opening speech by the Prime Minister, Mr. Palme, in the general political debate in the Riksdag', 31 January 1973, in Ministry for Foreign Affairs: *Documents on Swedish Foreign Policy: 1973*, Stockholm, 1976, pp. 19-20). Palme had earlier sent his condolences to PAIGC and to the widow of the murdered Secretary General, characterizing him as "one of the foremost leaders of the Third World" (Cable from the Ministry for Foreign Affairs to the Swedish UN delegation in New York, Stockholm, 22 January 1973) (MFA). Indicative of the strained relations between the solidarity movement and the government at the time, Palme's sympathy was described by the Africa Groups as "an unpleasant attempt to take advantage of PAIGC's worldwide good name and reputation in a moment of grief" (*Södra Afrika Informationsbulletin*, No. 19, 1973, p. 9).

7. MacQueen op. cit., p. 21.

became particularly close to the Social Democratic leadership around Prime Minister Palme, but also maintained warm relations with SIDA and the solidarity movement. Arguing that "ideology was above all knowing what one wanted in one's own particular circumstances"[1], his rich ideas would, however, often be quoted—and misquoted—in favour of particular political positions.

The Africa Groups considered Cabral as being "one of the foremost revolutionary leaders of our times" and PAIGC's struggle as "one of the nails in the coffin of imperialism".[2] While the solidarity movement and the Swedish left in general were highly critical of the Social Democratic government's humanitarian assistance—in the spirit of the 1969 Khartoum conference demanding unconditional cash support and a clear stand in favour of PAIGC's armed struggle[3]—it was, however, Cabral himself who was the chief architect behind the commodity programme. Supplied with arms from the Soviet Union and its allies, he had from the outset ruled out the idea of military support from Sweden, designing instead a programme of civilian cooperation that at the close of the 1960s was met by no other country. As predicted by him, the Swedish humanitarian assistance eventually broadened PAIGC's international support and paved the way for similar aid from other Western countries. This was notably the case with the NATO member Norway, which in 1972 defied the Western alliance's common cause with Portugal and introduced a highly significant dissent in the form of direct official assistance to PAIGC.[4]

Sweden and the Soviet Union were the largest donors to PAIGC.[5] While the former was predominant on the civilian side, the latter was the leading supplier to the military struggle.[6] There was an uncoordinated—but, nevertheless, real—*de facto* division of functions between the two, which to a large extent later was reproduced with regard to the Southern African liberation movements.[7] That Sweden in the eyes of the United States and other leading Western countries was seen to

---

1. Carlos Lopes: *Guinea Bissau: From Liberation Struggle to Independent Statehood*, Westview Press, Boulder, Colorado and Zed Books, London and New Jersey, 1987, pp. 57-58.
2. *Södra Afrika Informationsbulletin*, No. 19, 1973, pp. 2 and 9.
3. In January 1972, the chairman of the Left Party Communists, C.H. Hermansson, submitted a parliamentary motion demanding the "termination of the guardianship principle for the humanitarian assistance [to the liberation movements in the Portuguese colonies] in favour of a principle of unconditional support" (Swedish Parliament 1972: Motion No. 57, Riksdagens Protokoll, 1972, p. 5). Interviewed in 1996, Hermansson explained that "[i]n our opinion, [the liberation movements] should, for example, have the possibility of buying arms—all that they needed in their struggle—with the Swedish assistance" (Interview with C.H. Hermansson, p. 291).
4. The government of Norway decided in March 1972 to allocate 1 million Norwegian Kroner to PAIGC. The grant was in 1973 increased to 1.5 million NOK. On Norway and PAIGC, see Tore Linné Eriksen: 'The Origins of a Special Relationship: Norway and Southern Africa 1960-1975' in Eriksen (ed.) op. cit., pp. 72-77. Before the Finnish government in 1973 took a principled decision in favour of direct support to the African liberation movements, Cabral paid a visit to Helsinki. Invited by a broadly based *ad hoc* NGO committee chaired by the future Social Democratic Prime Minister Kalevi Sorsa, he was in October 1971 officially received by President Urho Kekkonen. According to Soiri and Peltola, Cabral "was the first leader of the [African] liberation movement[s] who was treated as a statesman [in Finland]". The visit "was a success [and] united for the first time the [Finnish] political parties around the question of ending colonialism in Africa" (Iina Soiri and Pekka Peltola: *Finland and National Liberation in Southern Africa*, Nordiska Afrikainstitutet, Uppsala, 1999, pp. 51-52).
5. Marianne Rappe: Memorandum ('Samtal med Folke Löfgren på SIDA den 21.4.1972: PAIGC'/'Conversation with Folke Löfgren at SIDA 21.4.1972: PAIGC'), SIDA, Stockholm, 24 April 1972 (SDA). SIDA requested information on other donors from PAIGC and the Southern African liberation movements. The information was regularly included in the documents submitted to the Consultative Committee on Humanitarian Assistance.
6. In the later stage of the liberation war, the Soviet Union supplied PAIGC with ground-to-air missiles, decisively giving the liberation movement the upper hand. The missiles were first used in March 1973, when PAIGC shot down two fighter bombers supplied by the Federal Republic of Germany. Over the following year, thirty-six planes were lost by the Portuguese (Rudebeck op. cit., pp. 52-53).
7. In the case of ZANU of Zimbabwe, the main supplier of arms was the People's Republic of China.

'Portugal out of Africa':
The author Göran Palm (left) picketing
in Stockholm, February 1973
(Photo: Ragnhild Haarstad/
Scanpix Sverige AB)

make common cause with the Communist bloc did not discourage the Swedish parliament and government from extending non-military assistance.[1]

In the early 1970s, the strongest criticism levelled against the Social Democratic
government—both by the non-socialist opposition Liberal Party[2] and the solidarity
movement—concerned Sweden's commercial relations with its EFTA partner Portugal. It was seen as both highly immoral and contradictory to extend official humanitarian assistance to PAIGC and its CONCP allies at the same time as trade with the
Portuguese colonial power was allowed to expand.[3] To the Africa Groups, it
showed that the government "protected [the interests of] Swedish imperialists".[4]
The writer and activist Göran Palm—who after a visit to the liberated areas of
Guinea-Bissau in late 1969 had written enthusiastically that he had been received
"as a prince" due to the Swedish assistance[5]—concluded in 1971 that "Sweden
gives with the left social democratic hand, but takes back with the right capitalist
hand".[6]

Palm's conclusion was presented in the introduction to a book with texts in
Swedish by Amílcar Cabral, published as *Our Struggle Your Struggle*. The title was
taken from a speech given in 1964, in which Cabral stated that imperialism was the
common enemy of the international working class and the national liberation
movements. It should, therefore, be fought in "a common struggle".[7] Cabral's
speech—included in Anders Ehnmark's anthology *Guerrilla*[8]—was widely quoted

1. See, for example, the interviews with SIDA's former Director General (1965-79) Ernst Michanek (p. 323) and
    the former Minister for International Development Cooperation (1985-91) and for Foreign Affairs (1994-98)
    Lena Hjelm-Wallén (p. 293). In 1998, Hjelm-Wallén became Deputy Prime Minister.
2. On the Liberal Party, Portugal and EFTA, see Sellström Volume I, pp. 479-83.
3. This view was also held by important groups within the ruling Social Democratic Party. Birgitta Dahl, for
    example, raised the question of legislation against investments in Portugal and its colonies in the Swedish par-
    liament ('Reply by the Foreign Minister to an interpellation by Mrs. Dahl', 10 December 1973, in Ministry
    for Foreign Affairs: *Documents on Swedish Foreign Policy: 1973*, Stockholm, 1976, pp. 155-59).
4. AGIS op. cit., p. 194.
5. Göran Palm: 'Rapport från Guinea-Bissau'/'Report from Guinea-Bissau' [no place or date] (SDA). On Palm's
    visit and his report to SIDA, see Sellström Volume I, pp. 429-30.
6. Introduction by Göran Palm to Cabral (1971) op. cit., p. 25.
7. Cabral (1971) op. cit., p. 37.
8. Ehnmark (1968) op. cit., pp. 139-58.

by the Swedish anti-imperialist movement. At a conference in Stockholm between the Africa Groups of Arvika, Gothenburg, Stockholm and Uppsala—describing themselves as "anti-imperialist working groups"[1] and defining as one of their main objectives "to study and combat imperialism, especially Swedish, in Africa"[2]—it was in January 1971 adopted as a "guideline [for the groups'] activities".[3] After the conference, the groups wrote to the headquarters of FRELIMO, MPLA and PAIGC, informing them that the work of the Swedish solidarity movement was based on "the principle formulated by comrade Amílcar Cabral", namely that

> the best way of proving your solidarity is to fight against imperialism in your countries in Europe. It is good to send us medicines, but that is only a secondary issue.[4]

Irrespective of their views on imperialism, in the case of Sweden it is doubtful whether the leaders of PAIGC, FRELIMO and MPLA in early 1971 were encouraged by the application of a general statement made in 1964 to the concrete situation then prevailing.[5] It is, in addition, improbable that they considered humanitarian support of secondary importance, or that they at all viewed Sweden as an imperialist country.[6] The quoted PAIGC leader had been deeply involved with the Swedish assistance. Cabral also appeared as remarkably broad-minded regarding Sweden's relations with Portugal. During his first visit in late 1968, he had—according to Pierre Schori—stated that Portugal should not be excluded from EFTA as "it would only mean that [it] could act even more freely".[7] As recorded in the Swedish notes from a meeting with the UN representative Sverker Åström[8], Cabral should in February 1970 further have expressed the opinion that he

> greatly understood that Portugal's membership of EFTA imposed certain limitations on [Sweden], [but] was keen to emphasize that he in no way wanted to recommend a break of [the] commercial relations with Portugal, which he knew that radical youth circles in Sweden demanded.[9]

Leading a successful liberation struggle and intent on maintaining and developing international relations after the independence of Guinea-Bissau, Cabral's diplomacy was characterized by pragmatic realism. According to the Guinean scholar Carlos Lopes, his basic guiding dictum was that "our ideology is nationalism, to get our independence, absolutely, and to do all we can with our own forces, but to cooperate with all other peoples in order to realize the development of our country".[10] This position not only contrasted with the ideological interpretation made

---

1. 'Protokoll'/'Minutes' ('Konferens mellan Afrikagrupperna i Sverige, 2-3 januari 1971'/'Conference between the Africa Groups in Sweden, 2-3 January 1971') [no place or date] (AGA).
2. The Africa Groups in Sweden: 'Circular letter No. 3', [no place], 8 April 1971 (AGA).
3. Ibid. See also *Södra Afrika Informationsbulletin*, No. 11, 1971, p. 2.
4. Letter (in French) on behalf of the Africa Groups in Arvika, Lund, Stockholm and Uppsala from Dick Urban Vestbro to FRELIMO, MPLA and PAIGC, Stockholm, 3 January 1971 (AGA).
5. On the contrary, appearing with Göran Palm at Uppsala university in November 1968, Cabral said: "Do not just demonstrate. Also do something concrete. [...] Send us medicines and other necessities" (*Upsala Nya Tidning*, 28 November 1968). The very first appeal for Swedish assistance to the liberation struggle in the Portuguese colonies in Africa was made by Marcelino dos Santos on behalf of MPLA in 1961. It concerned medicines for the Angolan refugees in the Lower Congo region. Noting *Expressen*'s positive response, Cabral also turned to the Swedish liberal newspaper for medical supplies.
6. Cf. the interviews with MPLA's Lúcio Lara (pp. 18-21) and FRELIMO's Marcelino dos Santos (pp. 47-52).
7. Cited in 'Portugal's argumentnöd bevisar: Kolonialkrigen går dåligt!' ('Portugal's lack of arguments proves that the colonial wars are not going well!') in *Arbetet*, 13 December 1968.
8. On the possible shortcomings of internal Swedish records, see the Prologue.
9. Letter ('Samtal med Amílcar Cabral om läget i Portugisiska Guinea'/'Conversation with Amílcar Cabral on the situation in Portuguese Guinea') from Sverker Åström to the Swedish Ministry for Foreign Affairs, New York, 26 February 1970 (SDA).
10. Cabral cited in Lopes op. cit., p. 57.

of the nationalist struggle by the Swedish solidarity movement, but on occasion led Cabral to downplay important international initiatives in PAIGC's favour. This was notably demonstrated prior to the UN General Assembly meeting in November 1972, when he out of strategic deference to Sweden and the other Nordic countries turned down the possibility to address the full assembly as the first representative of a liberation movement.

The background was that the United Nations Decolonization Committee[1]— also known as the Committee of 24—in April 1972 organized a unique fact-finding visit to Guinea-Bissau "[i]n order to defy [the Portuguese] myth [that there was nothing like liberated areas] and give legitimacy to the [African] liberation movements".[2] The delegation consisted of three young UN diplomats, of whom one— Folke Löfgren, first secretary at the permanent mission in New York—represented Sweden.[3] Sweden was at the time the only Western European member of the Decolonization Committee.[4] As the Swedish government bilaterally extended considerable humanitarian support to PAIGC, the initiative was followed with great interest at the Ministry for Foreign Affairs in Stockholm. Organized in "a subterranean manner"[5], the UN mission provoked an outcry in Portugal.[6] During the visit, the Portuguese intensified the aerial bombings and general military activities against the liberated areas. Löfgren later stated that "we were naive enough not to believe that it was possible that Portugal could treat the United Nations in such a way".[7]

The UN mission was "impressed by the enthusiastic and wholehearted cooperation which PAIGC receives from the people in the liberated areas and the extent to which the latter are participating in the administrative machinery set up by the [liberation movement]"[8], concluding that PAIGC not only militarily controlled, but effectively governed the liberated territory. Löfgren could on the spot also register that the Swedish humanitarian assistance—not least in the form of educational supplies, such as the text books *O Nosso Livro*—reached the population inside the country.[9] In general, the mission confirmed the popular support enjoyed by PAIGC

---

1. That is, the United Nations Special Committee on the Situation with Regard to the Implementation of the Declaration on the Granting of Independence to Colonial Countries and Peoples, or the UN committee set up to monitor developments referring to the 1960 Decolonization Declaration.

2. Interview with Salim Ahmed Salim, p. 244. At the time, Salim was the chairman of the UN Decolonization Committee. Close to the African liberation movements, he later became Foreign Minister (1980-84) and Prime Minister (1984-85) of Tanzania. In 1989, Salim was elected Secretary General of OAU.

3. The UN mission was led by Horacio Sevilla-Borja from Ecuador. The third member was Kamel Belkhiria from Tunisia. Accompanied by a large PAIGC military escort, the three diplomats were joined by a secretary and a photographer. The visit took place from 2 to 8 April 1972.

4. Letter from Brita Åhman to the Ministry for Foreign Affairs, New York, 7 March 1972 (MFA). Sweden's membership of the UN Decolonization Committee was of great importance for its contacts with and policies towards the African liberation movements. For example, in April 1972 the Swedish representative—Brita Åhman—participated in the committee's discussions with a total of fifteen movements in Conakry (Guinée), Lusaka (Zambia) and Addis Ababa (Ethiopia). In an extensive report from the 'hearings' to the Swedish Ministry for Foreign Affairs, she assessed the policies and strength of the various liberation movements, giving valuable guidance to the Swedish government (Brita Åhman: Memorandum ('Kolonialkommitténs session i Afrika 1972'/'The Decolonization Committee's session in Africa 1972'), New York, 19 June 1972) (MFA).

5. Interview with Salim Ahmed Salim, p. 244.

6. Notably, the Swedish ambassador to Portugal, Karl Fredrik Almqvist, also repudiated the initiative. While the UN Secretary General Kurt Waldheim congratulated the mission members on their difficult and successful visit, Almqvist described it as an "infringement of another country's sovereignty", arguing that the mission had "violated international law" and that the Swedish participation could undermine Sweden's "international goodwill" (Letter from Karl Fredrik Almqvist to the Ministry for Foreign Affairs, Lisbon, 14 April 1972) (MFA).

7. Cited in Marianne Rappe: Memorandum ('Samtal med Folke Löfgren på SIDA den 21.4.1972: PAIGC'/'Conversation with Folke Löfgren at SIDA 21.4.1972: PAIGC'), SIDA, Stockholm, 24 April 1972 (SDA).

8. United Nations: 'Report of the United Nations Special Mission to Guinea (Bissau)', Reprint from *Objective: Justice*, Vol. 4, No. 3, New York, September 1972, p. 12.

9. Johnny Flodman: 'Svensk FN-diplomat jagades av portugiser i Guinea' ('Swedish UN diplomat was chased by [the] Portuguese in Guinea') in *Svenska Dagbladet*, 17 April 1972.

Representing UN in the PAIGC-
held areas: Folke Löfgren with
pupils at the Areolino Lopes
Cruz bush school consulting
the text book *O Nosso Livro*
from Uppsala, April 1972
(Courtesy of Folke Löfgren)

in the areas visited, recommending recognition of the planned declaration of independence of Guinea-Bissau.[1] Based on its findings, at a meeting in Conakry attended by Amílcar Cabral the UN Decolonization Committee on 10 April 1972 adopted a resolution recognizing PAIGC as

> the only and authentic representative of the territory [of Guinea-Bissau], [...] requesting all states and specialized agencies and other organizations within the UN system to take this into consideration when dealing with matters pertaining to Guinea (Bissau) and Cape Verde.[2]

This was a major political and diplomatic success for PAIGC and, more generally, "a dramatic breakthrough in the international understanding [...] of greater legitimacy to the [African] liberation movements vis-à-vis the United Nations".[3] Based on the mission report, the UN Decolonization Committee could now call for recognition of the liberation movements as observers and not merely as petitioners.[4] More importantly, for the first time in the history of the United Nations it made it possible for a representative of a liberation movement to directly address the UN General Assembly. The honour would have fallen upon Amílcar Cabral, but due to Swedish and Nordic reservations that was not to be the case. In an interview in 1995, the chairman of the UN Decolonization Committee, Salim Ahmed Salim of Tanzania, recalled:

> Amílcar Cabral [...] came to New York and we were trying to get him to address the UN General Assembly. In those days it was inconceivable for a representative of a liberation movement to address the General Assembly, but we had the necessary support. However, the Nordic countries had reservations. I remember the ambassador of Sweden and the other Nordic ambassadors telling me: 'Look, we are not happy with this. Legally, it gives us problems if representatives of the liberation movements address the General Assembly. It has not been done

1. The mission visited Guinea-Bissau at a time when preparations for the first national elections in the country were being carried out by PAIGC in the liberated areas. Elections to regional councils were held from August 1972. The councillors subsequently elected the members of a National Assembly.
2. United Nations: *Secretariat News*, Vol. XXVII, No. 10, New York, 31 May 1972, p. 9.
3. Interview with Salim Ahmed Salim, p. 244.
4. Ibid.

before and it causes a lot of problems.'[1] So I went to Amílcar Cabral and said: 'Mr. Secretary General, if you want to address the General Assembly we have the votes. We have the necessary support of the African countries, of the Asian countries and of a number of the Latin American countries. But I want you to know that the Nordic countries are very unhappy about it. What do we do?' Cabral then said: 'Look, the Nordic countries are our friends. They have supported us through thick and thin and we do not want to embarrass them. I will not address the General Assembly'. [...]

There was so much respect for the position of the Nordic countries. There was no question of doubting their integrity or their sincerity towards the liberation movements. If any other country or combination of countries had said no, we would have pushed the matter to the General Assembly and received the necessary votes. [...] [W]e knew that the Nordic countries' position was to support the liberation movements in a practical manner. [...] That was also the only way in which I could understand Cabral's position. Amílcar Cabral was one of those luminaries—a giant among people—and he did not hesitate [...]. It shows the respect which he had for the Nordic countries, and, of course, those of us who were supporting him and the struggle shared that respect.[2]

Independence and beyond

PAIGC's diplomacy was largely guided by the objective to gain the broadest possible international support for the forthcoming declaration of independence, scheduled for early 1973. Confident of victory in a not too distant future, Cabral's pragmatism should be seen in this light.[3] In the case of Sweden and the other Nordic countries, his willingness to compromise was, however, not reciprocated by an early recognition of Guinea-Bissau's independence.

Amílcar Cabral did not live to witness his country's independence and the end of Portuguese colonialism in Africa. *De facto* controlling the major part of Guinea-Bissau, PAIGC had from the early 1970s discussed how the situation could be translated into a *de jure* international recognition of national independence. The question had, for example, been raised by Cabral during a meeting at the Ministry for Foreign Affairs in Stockholm as early as in July 1971.[4] Recognition of an independent state of Guinea-Bissau had also been recommended by the UN fact-finding mission in April 1972.

PAIGC organized popular elections in the liberated areas in August-October 1972. One year later—on 24 September 1973—the first National Assembly of the People of Guinea convened in the eastern region of Boé, proclaiming the state of Guinea-Bissau a "sovereign, republican, democratic, anti-colonialist and anti-imperialist state" within the same borders as continental 'Portuguese' Guinea.[5] Luís

---

1. According to the Swedish UN delegation, it conveyed to Cabral that "Sweden naturally would vote positively [on the question of his proposed address to the General Assembly], but [...] called his attention to the fact that it seemed obvious that Cabral's own cause would not benefit if such a proposal became the subject of divided opinions and a vote" (Cable from the Swedish UN representation to the Ministry for Foreign Affairs, New York, 24 October 1972) (MFA).
2. Interview with Salim Ahmed Salim, pp. 244-45.
3. Representing the African liberation movements, in 1972 Cabral participated in the preparations for the UN/OAU International Conference of Experts for the Support of Victims of Colonialism and Apartheid in Southern Africa, held in Oslo, Norway, in April 1973. Discussing the agenda and "aiming at achieving 'realism' instead of wasting time on fierce polemics", he argued that the conference in addition to humanitarian assistance should concentrate on political and diplomatic issues, while it should be left to individual governments to consider the issue of military support (Eriksen in Eriksen (ed.) op. cit., p. 59).
4. [Ethel] Ringborg: Memorandum, Stockholm, 6 July 1971 (MFA). At the time, the responsible Foreign Ministry officials concluded that "there is reason to already now examine how such a proclamation [of independence] should be considered from the point of view of international law. This should not least be of interest due to Sweden's membership of the UN Decolonization Committee" (ibid.).
5. The independence proclamation did not encompass the islands of Cape Verde.

Cabral was elected President. As the only Western journalists present[1], the solemn ceremony was documented by the Swedish film-makers Lennart Malmer and Ingela Romare.[2] Their unique one-hour film—'The Birth of a Nation'[3]—was televised by the official Swedish TV company.[4] Despite the fact that the Portuguese remained in control of the capital Bissau and the major centres, the new state was immediately recognized by a great number of nations. By early October 1973, diplomatic recognition had been extended by more than sixty governments and on 19 November 1973 the independent Republic of Guinea-Bissau was formally accepted as the forty-second member state of the Organization of African Unity.[5]

Inter alia applying the principle of full territorial control[6], the Swedish government was, however, reluctant to recognize the new state. This provoked strong reactions by the Africa Groups and the Left Party Communists[7], but also within the ruling party itself. In December 1973, the Social Democratic MP Birgitta Dahl—who in late 1970 had visited the liberated areas of Guinea-Bissau—confronted Foreign Minister Sven Andersson[8] in parliament, demanding information on the government's position.[9] Less than six months later, the issue was, however, solved by the 'revolution of the carnations' in Portugal. Largely influenced by the African wars—particularly in Guinea-Bissau[10]—the Movement of the Armed Forces[11] overthrew the fascist Caetano regime on 25 April 1974, paving the way for democracy at home and the granting of national independence to the colonies in Africa. An official statement of intent to the latter effect was issued at the end of July. Ten days later—on 9 August 1974—the Swedish government recognized the Republic of Guinea-Bissau.[12] Formal independence from Portugal was granted on 10 Septem-

---

1. Telephone conversation with Lennart Malmer, 7 October 1999.
2. Malmer and Romare had in 1971-72 introduced the Mozambican liberation struggle to the Swedish TV viewers (see the following chapter).
3. Lennart Malmer and Ingela Romare: 'En Nations Födelse', Sveriges Television (SVT).
4. At the time, there were no commercial television networks in Sweden. In 1973, Malmer and Romare also produced a documentary on the children and the liberation struggle in Guinea-Bissau for the public TV company, called 'Guinea-Bissau Är Vårt Land' ('Guinea-Bissau Is Our Country'), Sveriges Television (SVT). After independence, they *inter alia* produced the television documentaries 'Guinea-Bissau: Ett Exempel' ('Guinea-Bissau: An Example') and 'Guinea-Bissau efter Självständigheten' ('Guinea-Bissau after Independence'), Sveriges Television (SVT), 1976.
5. Rudebeck op. cit., p. 55.
6. Other considerations of the Swedish government concerned the relations with Portugal and the situation in Cape Verde.
7. Cf. 'Reply by the Foreign Minister to a question in the Riksdag by Mr. Måbrink', 25 October 1973, in Ministry for Foreign Affairs: *Documents on Swedish Foreign Policy: 1973*, Stockholm, 1976, p. 155.
8. Succeeding Krister Wickman (1971-73), Sven Andersson served as Minister for Foreign Affairs in the crucial period between 1973 and 1976.
9. 'Reply by the Foreign Minister to an interpellation by Mrs. Dahl', 10 December 1973, in Ministry for Foreign Affairs: *Documents on Swedish Foreign Policy: 1973*, Stockholm, 1976, pp. 155-59.
10. Several of the leading officers behind the Lisbon coup—such as General António de Spínola and Captain Otelo Saraiva de Carvalho—had spent longer periods in 'Portuguese' Guinea. Spínola—who in February 1974 as an important prelude to the coup published his famous book *Portugal and the Future*—became President of Portugal in May 1974, but left the scene four months later. He had served as Governor and Commander-in-Chief in Bissau between 1968 and 1973. Otelo de Carvalho worked in the information and propaganda section of Spínola's headquarters in Guinea, where he became convinced of the moral and political injustice of the colonial wars. Other influential MFA officers had been posted to Angola or Mozambique. Admiral Rosa Coutinho had, for example, served in Angola, where he also led the military government after the April 1974 coup.
11. In Portuguese, *Movimento das Forças Armadas* (MFA).
12. 'Press release', 9 August 1974, in Ministry for Foreign Affairs: *Documents on Swedish Foreign Policy: 1974*, Stockholm, 1976, p. 180. Chabal—and other observers after him—is thus mistaken when he states that "not a single Western government [...] recognized Guinea-Bissau until the new Portuguese government did so" (Chabal op. cit., p. 131).

ber 1974[1] and the following week the new state joined the United Nations.[2] Centuries of colonial oppression had come to an end. Guinea-Bissau could finally take its legitimate place among the independent nations of the world, embarking on the difficult road to turn swords into ploughshares.

PAIGC was the first African liberation movement with which the Swedish government established a comprehensive cooperation programme. Although the first contacts between the two were only made in the late 1960s and the humanitarian support just covered a period of half a decade, the relations with PAIGC would in a significant way break new ground and prepare the terrain for Sweden's ensuing involvement with the liberation movements in Southern Africa. Possible assistance to PAIGC was explicitly mentioned in the historic pronouncement by the Swedish parliament in May 1969. Assessing the new policy two years later, the Ministry for Foreign Affairs stated that "the experiences of the Swedish direct support [...] have to date been mainly positive", adding that "the solidarity with the developing countries—of which the assistance to the liberation movements is an example—results in goodwill [which] in the longer term will probably be of growing importance to Sweden".[3] Largely seen as a political investment rather than humanitarian charity, the assessment concluded that "there is every reason to continue as before, but with increasing amounts".[4]

At the close of the 1960s, the decision to extend direct official assistance to PAIGC and the Southern African liberation movements was not politically controversial in Sweden. The conservative Moderate Party would, however, soon turn against the very arguments that in 1969 had informed the unanimous parliamentary Standing Committee on Appropriations, chaired by its future leader Gösta Bohman. In marked contrast to the other parliamentary parties, the Moderate Party drew negative conclusions from the first years of cooperation with the liberation movements. In 1972, for example, the party asserted in the parliamentary Standing Committee on Foreign Affairs that

> to actively support revolutionary movements [...] is not in agreement with the international legal principle of non-intervention, nor with the Swedish policy of neutrality. [...] Considerable international doubts [...] exist with regard to the idea of [extending] assistance to the African population in the form of support to a certain liberation movement. Particularly a state which wishes to conduct a credible policy of neutrality should desist from designing its assistance in this way.[5]

The Moderate Party—at the time representing around 15 per cent of the electorate—was the only parliamentary party opposed to the policy of direct official humanitarian assistance to the liberation movements.

---

1. The Swedish Minister for Foreign Affairs, Sven Andersson, made a statement on Portuguese television on the day of Guinea-Bissau's independence from Portugal ('Statement by the Foreign Minister, Mr. Sven Andersson, for the Portuguese television on the occasion of the declaration of Guinea-Bissau's independence from Portugal', 10 September 1974, in Ministry for Foreign Affairs: *Documents on Swedish Foreign Policy: 1974*, Stockholm, 1976, pp. 180-81).
2. The process towards independence in Cape Verde was more complicated. After elections to a national assembly, the islands became the independent Republic of Cape Verde on 5 July 1975. PAIGC was the ruling party in Guinea-Bissau and Cape Verde until the break in January 1981, when PAIGC was replaced on the islands by PAICV (*Partido Africano para a Independência do Cabo Verde*, the African Independence Party of Cape Verde).
3. [Ethel] Ringborg: Memorandum ('Stöd till befrielserörelser'/'Support to liberation movements'), Ministry for Foreign Affairs, Stockholm, 7 September 1971 (MFA).
4. Ibid.
5. Cited in Olav Stokke: *Sveriges Utvecklingsbistånd och Biståndspolitik* ('Sweden's Development Assistance and Development Policy'), Scandinavian Institute of African Studies, Uppsala, 1978, p. 17.

From the modest beginnings in 1969, the Swedish government would over the years—in current figures—channel a total of 53.5 MSEK to PAIGC.[1] Designed by PAIGC as a commodity support programme, the assistance grew quickly, eventually covering most branches of the liberation movement's civilian activities, with a concentration on food, transport, education and health, in addition to a wide range of supplies to the people's stores. From an administrative point of view, planning methods similar to those applied for the development cooperation programmes with independent countries were introduced. This made it easy to transform the humanitarian assistance into a programme of development assistance upon Guinea-Bissau's independence. As would later be the case with the Southern African liberation movements, the humanitarian support to the struggle for majority rule and national independence paved the way for longer term cooperation.

As a result of the support to PAIGC during the liberation struggle, Guinea-Bissau was—as the only country in West Africa—from the financial year 1974/75 included among the so called 'programme countries' for Swedish development assistance.[2] With mixed results[3], total Swedish assistance to independent Guinea-Bissau during the period 1974/75-1994/95 amounted—in fixed prices (1995)—to 2.5 billion SEK[4], placing Sweden among the top three largest donors to the country.[5]

1. See the accompanying table on disbursements from SIDA to PAIGC.
2. The Republic of Cape Verde would from 1974/75 receive increasing grants from Sweden. Expressed in fixed prices (1994), the assistance amounted in July 1994 to a total of 1.4 billion SEK (SIDA: *Bistånd i Siffror och Diagram* ('Development Assistance in Figures and Graphs'), Stockholm, January 1995, p. 60). It should be noted that Portugal for a shorter period received Swedish development assistance from 1975/76.
3. Swedish development assistance to independent Guinea-Bissau has not been particularly successful. For a factual assessment, see Peter Svedberg, Anders Olofsgård and Björn Ekman: *Evaluation of Swedish Development Co-operation with Guinea-Bissau*, Secretariat for Analysis of Swedish Development Assistance (SASDA), Report No. 3, Ds 1994:77, Ministry for Foreign Affairs, Stockholm, 1994. As early as in 1980, Patrik Engellau—who served as SIDA's representative to Guinea-Bissau in the late 1970s—published a thoughtful novel about the trials and tribulations of a Swedish aid worker in the fictitious republic of Candjambari. Unmistakably placed in Guinea-Bissau, it depicts the problems and pitfalls encountered by the liberation movement after assuming state power, as well as those met by the well-intentioned donor country (Patrik Engellau: *Genom Ekluten* ('Through the Mill'), Atlantis, Stockholm). Returning to Guinea-Bissau twenty years after his visit to PAIGC's liberated areas, in 1993 Anders Ehnmark, similarly, reflected upon liberation and liberty, independence and development, dreams and realities, in his essay 'The Trip to Kilimanjaro', concluding that "something which was not predicted has taken place" (Ehnmark (1993) op. cit., p. 113). In 1998, economic failures and unresolved ethnic and social divisions resulted in civil war in Guinea-Bissau. Tragically, the unifying example set by Amílcar Cabral and PAIGC during the struggle for liberation came to a violent end.
4. Sida: *Development in Partnership: Sida and Swedish Bilateral Development Cooperation in Africa*, Sida, Stockholm, 1997, p. 23. The corresponding amounts for Tanzania and the Swedish priority countries in Southern Africa were: Tanzania 20.3 billion SEK, Mozambique 11.5, Zambia 6.9, Angola 3.9, Zimbabwe 3.8 and Botswana 3.2.
5. Svedberg, Olofsgård and Ekman op. cit., p. 20.

FRELIMO of Mozambique:
Clearing a Way

The Mondlanes, Sweden and the Struggle in Mozambique

While broader contacts between Sweden and the liberation movement in Guinea-Bissau were only established towards the end of the 1960s, the relations with PAIGC's Mozambican CONCP partner FRELIMO[1] were of longer standing. Also initiated at the highest political level, they went as far back as September 1964, when the FRELIMO President Eduardo Mondlane paid his first visit to Sweden.[2] In fact, Mondlane was the first incumbent leader of a Southern African liberation movement to directly present his case to the Swedish public, soon building a support base in the country.

Initially addressing the youth and student movements, the FRELIMO President and his wife Janet—the Director of the Mozambique Institute in Dar es Salaam, Tanzania—skillfully managed to widen the Swedish debate to encompass the situation in the Portuguese colonies. As a result, the Mozambique Institute was during the financial year 1964/65 included among the institutions benefiting from the very first official Swedish budgetary allocation for humanitarian assistance to Southern Africa, the so called 'refugee million'.[3] Extended as cash support, the first contribution to the education activities at the Mozambique Institute was granted in May 1965. The support was suspended after the closure of the institute's secondary school in March 1968.[4] By that time, 1.7 MSEK had been disbursed, roughly corresponding to 15 per cent of total Swedish humanitarian assistance to Southern Africa during the five years 1964/65-1968/69. Hence, FRELIMO was via the institute a major recipient of official Swedish support years before the parliamentary decision on direct support to the Southern African liberation movements and PAIGC had been taken. Indeed, the positive experience from the support to the FRELIMO school influenced the decision in 1969. The statement by the parliamen-

---

1. In Portuguese, *Frente de Libertação de Moçambique* (Mozambique Liberation Front).
2. On the early political and aid relations between Sweden and FRELIMO, see Sellström Volume I, pp. 439-72.
3. On the 1964 'refugee million', see ibid., pp. 70-79. In 1999, Thord Palmlund—who served as the first secretary to the Consultative Committee on Humanitarian Assistance—published his reminiscences of the beginnings of the official Swedish humanitarian support to Southern Africa, including 'the refugee million' (Thord Palmlund: 'Ullas Miljon och Så Vidare'/'Ulla's Million and So On' in Sida-seniorerna: ... *Och Världen Växte: Biståndet Som Vi Minns Det!'*... And the World Grew: Aid As We Remember It', Sida-seniorerna, Uppsala, 1999, pp. 268-80).
4. The Mozambique Institute was originally set up as a secondary school. During the second half of the 1960s, it developed into a technical and fund-raising institution, coordinating FRELIMO's civilian activities in the fields of education, health, social welfare and economic development among the Mozambican refugees in Tanzania as well as in the liberated areas of northern Mozambique. The Swedish support to the institute referred to both the secondary school in Dar es Salaam—also known as the Mozambique Institute—and to the education activities inside Mozambique. While the other activities continued, it was the secondary school in Dar es Salaam that was closed in March 1968.

Director Janet Rae
Mondlane in her office
at the Mozambique
Institute in Dar es Salaam
in the early 1970s
(Photo: Aftonbladet Bild)

tary Standing Committee on Appropriations made explicit reference to "the support [...] already [...] extended to the Mozambique Institute".[1]

The relations established in Sweden by Eduardo and Janet Mondlane in the mid-1960s went far beyond humanitarian support. Close political contacts were established with both the ruling Social Democratic Party and the opposition Liberal Party. Mondlane's contacts with the Social Democratic Party were particularly significant. After attending a congress of the Socialist International in Stockholm in May 1966—where the British Labour Party clashed with the invited representatives of ZANU and ZAPU over Ian Smith's Unilateral Declaration of Independence in Rhodesia[2]—the FRELIMO leader wrote a letter to the party secretary Sten Andersson, stating that

> I gathered the impression [at the congress] that the socialists of Western Europe as a whole are too over-concentrated on the problems of their own continent to be interested in the problems of the rest of the world. The only exception [...] was the attitude of the leaders of your own party. [...] [W]e had a strong impression that the Swedish socialists are not only not afraid of hearing the Africans speak, but are actually actively interested in stimulating a constant intercourse of ideas between the two continents. [...] If you could allow me to make a suggestion in this connection, I would say the following: That the present good relations existing between the Swedish Social Democratic Party and many African socialist parties, especially, in East and Southern Africa, must be encouraged. [...]
>
> In so far as they affect Mozambique, FRELIMO is deeply interested in cultivating a special relationship with your party. [...] I should [therefore] like to propose that a high officer of FRELIMO be invited, either officially or unofficially, to Sweden to set up an information centre to provide the Swedish people and other Scandinavians with fresh information from Mozambique [and] to learn as much as he can from the Social Democratic Party of Sweden about the organization, administration, information and other activities of the party [...] so that he may help to apply these things in the structure of FRELIMO.[3]

---

1. Swedish Parliament 1969: Statement No. 82/1969 by the Appropriations' Committee, p. 24.
2. See Sellström Volume I, pp. 338-43.
3. Letter from Eduardo Mondlane to Sten Andersson, [Dar es Salaam], 2 June 1966 (MHA). Cf. the interview with Marcelino dos Santos, in which the former FRELIMO Vice-President stated that "the relations with Sweden were initiated at [the] meeting [...] of the Socialist International [...] in 1966" (pp. 47-48).

Mondlane's interest in a special relationship with the ruling party opened a new chapter in Sweden's interaction with the Southern African liberation movements. His proposal was the first politically motivated initiative to have a representative of a liberation movement formally accredited to the Social Democratic Party and to the country at large. Lourenço Mutaca, FRELIMO's Secretary for Financial and Economic Affairs—thus responsible for the economic activities in the liberated areas in northern Mozambique—was chosen for the task. He took up the position towards the end of 1967, effectively contributing to the consolidation of FRELIMO's popular support in Sweden and in the other Nordic countries.[1]

Founded as a broad political front in 1962, FRELIMO was initially fraught with internal contradictions. Nevertheless, after the launch of the armed struggle in the province[2] of Cabo Delgado in September 1964, the unresolved divisions were relegated to the background. In spite of breakaways and the appearance of rival organizations[3], FRELIMO managed in 1965 to advance where it really mattered, that is, inside Mozambique, establishing what it at the time called 'semi-liberated zones'[4] in Cabo Delgado and Niassa, the two provinces south of the Tanzanian border. It consolidated its position as the genuine liberation movement of Mozambique and was confirmed as such by the Organization of African Unity.[5] In Sweden, the first parliamentary motion for direct official support to an African liberation movement was introduced in favour of FRELIMO by the then Communist Party in January 1967.[6]

Successfully confronting the counterattacks by the Portuguese military forces, FRELIMO would over the following years extend its presence in the northern provinces, setting up its own administration, schools, clinics and a trading system with people's stores similar to that introduced by PAIGC in Guinea-Bissau.[7] In March 1968, Mondlane announced the opening of a new military front in the Tete province—the site of the Cabora Bassa project—and four months later FRELIMO held

---

1. Active and popular in Sweden, Mutaca surprisingly resigned from FRELIMO during the post-Mondlane leadership struggle. As FRELIMO did not appoint a successor to Mutaca, the official relations with Sweden (and the other Nordic countries) were from then on handled at the embassy level in Dar es Salaam and through frequent diplomatic visits, in particular by Janet Mondlane. Publicly siding with Uria Simango, Mutaca was in mid-February 1970 suspended from FRELIMO. Informing the Swedish embassy in Dar es Salaam about the decision, Marcelino dos Santos explained that the underlying reason for Mutaca's break with FRELIMO was that he had refused to visit the liberated areas in northern Mozambique. He, however, added that Mutaca had "done a good job, both as Financial Secretary in FRELIMO and as our representative in Sweden" (Telex from the Swedish embassy to the Ministry for Foreign Affairs, Dar es Salaam, 18 February 1970) (MFA). Shortly before the Lisbon coup in April 1974, Mutaca was welcomed back to FRELIMO.
2. As Mozambique officially was a 'province' of Portugal, the term 'district' formed part of the colonial parlance. In early documents, FRELIMO intermittently used 'province' and 'district' for the same administrative area. The same applied to MPLA in Angola.
3. Notably, the Revolutionary Committee of Mozambique (*Comité Revolucionário de Moçambique*; COREMO), founded in June 1965. Supported by the People's Republic of China, COREMO set up headquarters in Lusaka, Zambia, and conducted an independent, but low-level, guerrilla campaign in central Mozambique in the late 1960s and early 1970s. As early as in June 1966, COREMO addressed a first unsuccessful request for financial support to the Swedish government (Letter from Mazunzo M. Bobo, COREMO National Secretary for Foreign Affairs, to Ernst Michanek, Director General of SIDA, Lusaka, 15 June 1966) (SDA). Initially given some attention by the Swedish solidarity movement, COREMO again approached Sweden for official support in January 1969 (Letter from Olof Kaijser, Swedish ambassador to Zambia, to the Ministry for Foreign Affairs, Lusaka, 10 January 1969) (MFA). The brief response by the Foreign Ministry in Stockholm was, however, that "COREMO is not to be considered for Swedish assistance" (Letter from Per Anger to the Swedish embassy in Lusaka, 22 January 1969) (MFA).
4. Iain Christie: *Machel of Mozambique*, Zimbabwe Publishing House, Harare, 1988, p. 37.
5. FRELIMO was recognized by OAU in 1963.
6. Swedish Parliament 1967: Motion No. 466 in the First Chamber (Werner) and Motion No. 590 in the Second Chamber (Hector and others), Riksdagens Protokoll, 1967, pp. 1-2.
7. In Mozambique, the stores were called *lojas do povo*.

its second congress at Machedje in Niassa.[1] During the Khartoum conference in January 1969 the movement was recognized by the Afro-Asian Peoples Solidarity Organization and the Soviet-sponsored World Peace Council as "the sole and legitimate authority" of Mozambique.[2] At the same time, FRELIMO was together with ANC of South Africa, MPLA of Angola, PAIGC of Guinea-Bissau, SWAPO of Namibia and ZAPU of Zimbabwe grouped among the so called 'authentic' liberation movements.[3]

With solid political and aid relations established by the Mondlanes, FRELIMO was towards the end of the 1960s in a better position than any other Southern African liberation movement to receive direct, official Swedish assistance. When the Swedish parliament in May 1969 endorsed such a policy, the Mozambican movement was, however, in the midst of a deep crisis. An open conflict—leading to the suspension of the Swedish assistance—had broken out at the Mozambique Institute's secondary school in Dar es Salaam in early 1968. It was in many respects a prelude to the internal struggle that culminated in the assassination of Eduardo Mondlane by a parcel bomb in Dar es Salaam on 3 February 1969 and which ultimately was not solved until Samora Machel assumed the presidency in May 1970.

FRELIMO Crisis and Portuguese Counter-Offensive

The contradictions inherent in FRELIMO's front structure burst forth in 1968. A group of "traditionalists who wanted [...] a less political campaign"[4] and maintained "a narrow nationalist posture with racialist and tribalist overtones"[5] openly turned against the FRELIMO majority around President Mondlane.[6] The dissident group was led by Lázaro Nkavandame, FRELIMO's provincial secretary for Cabo Delgado, who at the leadership level had links to the Vice-President, Reverend Uria

---

1. Very few outsiders had at the time visited the liberated areas in northern Mozambique. Accompanying Eduardo Mondlane on his first entry into the country as President of FRELIMO, Anders Johansson of the Swedish liberal newspaper *Dagens Nyheter* became in February 1968 the first international journalist to report on the situation in the province of Cabo Delgado. His articles had a major impact, not only in Sweden, but around the world (Sellström Volume I, pp. 484-87). The British journalist and historian Basil Davidson attended the FRELIMO congress in Niassa in July 1968. In September-October 1968, a team of six students from the University of Dar es Salaam—led by the future President of Uganda, Yoweri Museveni—travelled extensively in both Cabo Delgado and Niassa. Museveni was highly impressed with what he encountered and wrote an important essay for the university journal, subsequently published in a book edited by the Zimbabwean academic and politician Nathan Shamuyarira (Yoweri T. Museveni: 'Fanon's Theory on Violence: Its Verification in Liberated Mozambique' in N. M. Shamuyarira (ed.): *Essays on the Liberation of Southern Africa*, University of Dar es Salaam, Studies in Political Science, No. 3, Tanzania Publishing House, Dar es Salaam, 1972, pp. 1-24). Through the international attention given to the Cabora Bassa project, FRELIMO's struggle and the situation in northern Mozambique were increasingly covered from 1968.
2. Cited in 'The Khartoum Conference: First International Conference of Solidarity' in Legum and Drysdale op. cit., p. C 155.
3. FRELIMO managed to stay in favour with both Moscow and Beijing. Cf. the interviews with Janet Mondlane (p. 43) and Joaquim Chissano (p. 40).
4. Malyn Newitt: *A History of Mozambique*, Hurst & Company, London, 1995, pp. 524-25.
5. Allan Isaacman and Barbara Isaacman: *Mozambique: From Colonialism to Revolution, 1900-1982*, Westview Press, Boulder, Colorado, 1983, p. 97.
6. On the FRELIMO crisis in 1968-70, see Christie op. cit., pp. 48-60. For the contradictions at the level of production, see Bertil Egerö: *Mozambique: A Dream Undone: The Political Economy of Democracy, 1975-84*, Nordiska Afrikainstitutet, Uppsala, 1987, pp. 17-27. Nkavandame and most of his followers were Makonde from northern Mozambique, opposing the radical positions defended by leaders from the southern parts of the country, notably Eduardo Mondlane, Marcelino dos Santos, Samora Machel and Joaquim Chissano. Supported by certain members of the Tanzanian government, the Nkavandame group strongly turned against FRELIMO's white members, managing to have some of them expelled from the country in May 1968. On the difficult situation for the white female members at the time, see the interview with Janet Mondlane, p. 44. Cf. also the interview with Pamela dos Santos in Hilda Bernstein: *The Rift: The Exile Experience of South Africans*, Jonathan Cape, London, 1994, pp. 387-391. Married to Marcelino dos Santos in 1968, Pamela dos Santos of ANC of South Africa worked at the SIDA office in Dar es Salaam in the mid-1960s. She later joined FRELIMO's Department of Information and Propaganda.

Funeral of FRELIMO President Eduardo Mondlane in Dar es Salaam, February 1969: President Nyerere with Janet Mondlane and the Mondlanes' three children (Photo: Uhuru Publications, Dar es Salaam)

Simango, and at the Mozambique Institute was supported by the Catholic priest and teacher Mateus Gwenjere. It was Gwenjere who in January 1968 incited the students at the institute's secondary school to go on strike, accusing Janet Mondlane of CIA connections and turning against both the white Mozambican and expatriate teachers. In the meantime, Nkavandame started to enlist support for a separatist movement in Cabo Delgado. Refusing to attend FRELIMO's second congress in July 1968, he further demonstrated his opposition by trying to prevent any freedom fighters from crossing into 'his' province from the movement's camps in southern Tanzania.[1]

Faced with an open rebellion, FRELIMO's Executive Committee stripped Nkavandame of his functions in early January 1969. With the help of the Portuguese secret police, PIDE[2], Nkavandame immediately made his way to Mozambique, where he joined the colonial regime and throughout the rest of the war served as one of Lisbon's leading propagandists. Less than a month later, Eduardo Mondlane was assassinated by a parcel bomb known to have passed through the hands of Nkavandame's associates. Although the assassins have never been caught, circumstantial evidence indicates that PIDE was behind the murder.[3]

In terms of seniority, Uria Simango should have succeeded Mondlane. With links to Nkavandame and Gwenjere, he was, however, deeply mistrusted, and when the FRELIMO Central Committee convened in April 1969 Simango was unable to muster the necessary support. Instead, a triumvirate Council of the Presidency was formed, composed of Simango, the Secretary for External Affairs Marcelino dos Santos and the Commander-in-Chief Samora Machel. The uneasy troika did not last long. In November 1969, Simango published a widely spread polemic with fierce attacks on dos Santos, Machel, Joaquim Chissano, Janet Mondlane and oth-

---

1. In December 1968, Nkavandame's followers murdered Paulo Kankhomba, Samora Machel's deputy chief of staff, as he was about to cross the Rovuma river.
2. Isaacman and Isaacman op. cit., p. 98.
3. A former PIDE officer, Rosa Casaco, confirmed in February 1998 PIDE's direct involvement (*Expresso*, 21 February 1998).

ers, accusing them of plotting to kill him.[1] The Executive Committee responded by suspending Simango from the Council of the Presidency.[2] Finally, in May 1970 the Central Committee elected Samora Machel[3] as President and Marcelino dos Santos[4] as Vice-President of FRELIMO.

The Portuguese—heavily involved in the events leading up to the assassination of Mondlane—tried to take advantage of the FRELIMO crisis. In the areas exposed to nationalist activities, a policy of grouping the population into fortified villages— so called *aldeamentos*—was intensified. It had been introduced in Cabo Delgado shortly after the outbreak of the war. As early as in 1966, some 250,000 people had been resettled in 150 *aldeamentos*.[5] The programme to force the African population into 'strategic hamlets' was now extended to Niassa and Tete, with the result that about half the population in the three provinces were confined behind barbed wire at the close of the 1960s.[6] This policy—which was no more successful in Mozambique than in Vietnam—was combined with a strategy of establishing a network of European, paramilitary settler communities (*colonatos*) in areas of guerrilla activity. To stem the nationalist tide, the Lisbon government envisioned resettling one million Portuguese in northern Mozambique by the year 2000, primarily along the banks of the Zambezi river.[7] This plan too—in which the Cabora Bassa scheme played a strategic role[8]—failed. By 1973, only a few hundred poor Portuguese immigrants—primarily from the island of Madeira—had been lured to the *colonatos*.[9]

Above all, the Portuguese military presence and activities were reinforced. In 1961, there were 4,000 Portuguese soldiers in Mozambique, mainly stationed in the provincial capitals.[10] At the beginning of 1969, the size of the military had increased to 41,000[11] and by the early 1970s it exceeded 70,000.[12] Backed by such

---

1. Uria Simango: 'Gloomy Situation in FRELIMO', [no place], 3 November 1969 (NAI). Janet Mondlane, white and American-born, was particularly singled out by Simango. In the document, he accused her of direct participation in assassinations, of "being the source of massive corruption" and of "being [an] agent and financial channel of imperialist activities to paralyse in a more subtle way the struggle of the people of Mozambique against colonialism and imperialism" (ibid.).
2. Simango subsequently joined COREMO, occupying the position of Secretary for Foreign Relations.
3. Machel's background was different from that of most of the nationalist leaders of the Portuguese colonies. Born in the southern Mozambican Gaza province in 1933, he attended a Catholic rural school and began a nursing course in Lourenço Marques (Maputo) in 1952. After graduating in 1954, Machel started to work as a full-time nurse in the capital. In 1961, he met Eduardo Mondlane—visiting Lourenço Marques as a UN official—and was highly impressed by him. At about the same time, PIDE began operating in Mozambique. High on PIDE's list, Machel left Mozambique in March 1963. Travelling via Swaziland, South Africa and Botswana, he joined FRELIMO in Tanzania, from where he proceeded to Algeria for military training. Returning to Tanzania, he was in April 1964 placed in charge of FRELIMO's military training camp at Kongwa, directing the preparations for the launch of the armed struggle in Cabo Delgado in September of the same year. Machel entered the war zones in November 1965, when he opened a front in the eastern part of the Niassa province. Quickly rising through the ranks, he was appointed Secretary of Defence in November 1966, joining the FRELIMO leadership and working from the movement's new camp in Nachingwea in southern Tanzania (on the life of Samora Machel, see Christie op. cit.).
4. On Marcelino dos Santos, see Sellström Volume I, pp. 442-44.
5. Newitt op. cit., p. 525.
6. Isaacman and Isaacman op. cit., p. 101.
7. Ibid.
8. On the Cabora Bassa scheme and the involvement by the Swedish company ASEA, see Sellström Volume I, pp. 483-502.
9. Isaacman and Isaacman op. cit., p. 101. In southern Mozambique—that is, outside the combat areas—the number of Portuguese immigrants increased right up to the 1974 Lisbon coup. Between 1950 and 1974, it quadrupled, growing from 50,000 to almost 200,000 (James Ciment: *Angola and Mozambique: Postcolonial Wars in Southern Africa*, Facts on File, New York, 1997, p. 34).
10. Isaacman and Isaacman op. cit., p. 102.
11. Letter from Gunnar Dryselius, Swedish ambassador to Portugal, to the Ministry for Foreign Affairs, Lisbon, 6 March 1969 (MFA).
12. Isaacman and Isaacman op. cit., p. 102.

strength, the Lisbon regime decided to deliver a final blow to FRELIMO, launching the operation code-named Gordian Knot[1] from May to October 1970.[2] The man chosen to deliver the blow was General Kaúlza de Arriaga, who from the outbreak of the war in Angola in 1961 had vociferously argued for a massive military effort in the Portuguese 'overseas provinces' in Africa.

In March 1970, de Arriaga was appointed military commander in Mozambique, immediately starting the preparations for *Nó Górdio*, which was to be the largest single military campaign carried out by the Portuguese in Africa during the wars of national liberation from 1961 to 1974.[3] Encompassing paratroop attacks on FRELIMO bases in Cabo Delgado and Niassa followed by ground operations by some 30,000 soldiers[4], the operation did, however, not achieve its main objective. "Melting before the onslaught, the bulk of [FRELIMO's] guerrilla forces escaped either north across the Rovuma to Tanzania or south through Malawi [...] into Tete".[5] Outmanoeuvring de Arriaga's stationary conventional forces, Machel's mobile freedom fighters hit behind the back of the Portuguese. In October 1970, FRELIMO crossed the Zambezi, for the first time threatening the European settler areas. The 'final blow' against FRELIMO was instead turned into a decisive breakthrough for the Mozambican liberation movement. As FRELIMO at about the same time started to coordinate its military activities with ZANU, the thrust into central Mozambique would also radically impact on the liberation struggle in Zimbabwe.[6]

Youth and Student Solidarity

It was, paradoxically, during the crisis between 1968 and 1970 that FRELIMO came to enjoy widespread popular support in Sweden. As a combined effect of Eduardo and Janet Mondlane's information activities from the mid-1960s and the intense public debate regarding ASEA's proposed participation in the Cabora Bassa project in 1968-69, a number of youth, student and solidarity organizations launched important campaigns for FRELIMO. They were carried out at a time when the Swedish government's assistance to the Mozambique Institute was suspended. In the case of FRELIMO, the non-governmental organizations' solidarity initiatives would—during a difficult period for the liberation movement—play a particularly important role. Talking about the Swedish secondary students' 1969 Operation Day's Work, Janet Mondlane recalled almost thirty years later

---

1. In Portuguese, *Nó Górdio*.
2. At the height of the Gordian Knot operation, the Lisbon regime suffered a major diplomatic setback when the FRELIMO Vice-President Marcelino dos Santos together with the MPLA President Agostinho Neto and the PAIGC Secretary General Amílcar Cabral on 1 July 1970 were received by the Pope at the Vatican in Rome.
3. Cann op. cit., p. 80.
4. MacQueen op. cit., p. 47.
5. Ibid.
6. ZANU was not a member of the Khartoum alliance of 'authentic' liberation movements. Although "dealing with ZANU was like consorting with the devil" (Christie op. cit., p. 78), it became obvious to FRELIMO that ZANU was a determined and serious liberation movement which enjoyed broad popular support. Initially, FRELIMO offered ZAPU the possibility of using its trails to the Zimbabwe border, but ZAPU was at the time in a deep crisis and did not respond to the offer. FRELIMO then turned to ZANU, and in July 1970 the first ZANU guerrillas entered northern Tete to operate alongside FRELIMO. It was from its bases in Tete that ZANU in December 1972 launched the protracted—and eventually successful—liberation war in Zimbabwe (see the interviews with Joaquim Chissano (p. 41), Marcelino dos Santos (p. 49) and Sérgio Vieira (p. 56)).

how a kind of mass consciousness about what was happening in Mozambique really began. [...] It was not just the money that was important, but the sensitization of the whole population. [...] It was a big event. [...] After that, things began to snowball.[1]

Inspired by Eduardo Mondlane, a first FRELIMO support group had been formed in Uppsala as early as at the end of 1966.[2] Having as its main objective to raise unconditional support for FRELIMO, it was, however, not particularly successful and dissolved at the beginning of 1970. By that time, more consistent solidarity initiatives had been launched. The Social Democratic Youth League, for example, had started to distribute a Swedish version of FRELIMO's English-language journal *Mozambique Revolution* and Emmaus-Björkå had begun its deliveries of clothes to the Mozambican refugees under FRELIMO's care in Tanzania.[3]

In November 1968, Sören Lindh—later one of the leading members of the Africa Groups in Sweden—formed a support group for FRELIMO among the public servants at his workplace, the Swedish Agency for Administrative Development.[4] Still active thirty years later, it was this group that more than any other consistently promoted FRELIMO's cause in Sweden. Lindh did not have previous contacts with the Mozambican liberation movement. Concerned with the wider issue of international solidarity and influenced by the articles published on Mozambique by Anders Johansson in *Dagens Nyheter*, he decided to set up a FRELIMO group, as "[s]upport for Vietnam was not politically realistic at [the] government

---

1. Interview with Janet Mondlane, p. 42.
2. On the Uppsala based *Svenska FRELIMO-gruppen* and the NGO activities in favour of FRELIMO at the end of the 1960s, see Sellström Volume I, pp. 461-67.
3. The Swedish Emmaus groups would from the late 1960s make highly significant contributions to the liberation movements in Southern Africa. Closely cooperating with the Africa Groups, Emmaus-Björkå in southern Sweden was particularly active, sending huge amounts of clothes to the movements. For the importance of the support, see, for example, the interviews with ZANU's Kumbirai Kangai (pp. 215-16) and ANC's Rica Hodgson (p. 133). Interviewed in 1996, the Mozambican President Joaquim Chissano remembered how—during his visit to Sweden as far back as in November 1970—he had "worked particularly with Emmaus-Björkå" (Interview with Joaquim Chissano, p. 40). According to a study by SIDA, the value of the clothes sent by Emmaus-Björkå to FRELIMO in 1972 alone amounted to almost 1.7 MSEK, i.e. as much as the total Swedish official humanitarian assistance to the Mozambique Institute from 1965 to 1968. The same year, Emmaus-Björkå delivered clothes to a value of 1.1 MSEK to MPLA of Angola, 0.9 million to PAIGC of Guinea-Bissau, 0.5 million to SWAPO of Namibia and 75,000 to ZANU of Zimbabwe, or a combined value of well over 4 MSEK to the five liberation movements. This, in turn, corresponded to approximately 8 per cent of the total amount donated by Swedish NGOs to the entire continent of Africa in 1972 (Jörgen Knudtzon and Miriam Magnusson: 'Svenska icke-statliga organisationers u-hjälp 1972'/'Development aid by Swedish non-governmental organizations 1972', SIDA [no place or date] (SDA). Several other Swedish solidarity organizations—notably Bread and Fishes (*Brödet och Fiskarna*) and the Africa Groups—would later follow the example set by Emmaus-Björkå. In the case of Bread and Fishes, which like the Emmaus groups had a religious base and was inspired by the ideas of abbé Pierre, the total value of the material support in the form of clothes, shoes, health equipment etc. to the liberation movements in Namibia, South Africa and Zimbabwe from 1974 to 1993 has been estimated at between 300 and 400 MSEK (Bertil Högberg: 'Det materiella stödet till befrielserörelserna från Brödet och Fiskarna'/'The material support to the liberation movements from Bread and Fishes', [Uppsala], 7 March 1997) (BHC). In January 1989, the Emmaus groups in Björkå, Stockholm and Sundsvall joined forces with the Västerås based Bread and Fishes, forming the national organization Practical Solidarity (*Praktisk Solidaritet*). By that time, the collection of clothes and other items had grown into a veritable 'solidarity industry'. During its first year, Practical Solidarity collected 4,000 tons of clothes, mainly for ANC, SWAPO and the independent countries in Southern Africa. It corresponded in monetary terms to a value of some 120 MSEK (Lasse Ström: 'Fler Idealister Behövs!'/'More Idealists Are Needed!' in *Afrikabulletinen*, No. 4, June 1991, p. 34). Beginning in 1973/74, through SIDA the Swedish government contributed to the transportation costs of the clothes and other items collected by various NGOs in favour of the liberation movements. During the eighteen years until 1990/91, a total amount of 85.3 MSEK was paid out for this purpose (Disbursement figures according to SIDA's audited annual accounts, established by Ulla Beckman for this study).
4. In Swedish, *Statskontoret*.

agency".[1] The main purpose was fund-raising. The members agreed to set aside part of their salaries for FRELIMO, and by August 1971 an amount of 23,000 SEK had been raised.[2] The funds were in the beginning mainly used to cover freight costs to Tanzania of clothes collected by Emmaus-Björkå for the Mozambican liberation movement[3], but were later transferred directly to FRELIMO. Lindh and other members subsequently formed a sub-group of the Stockholm Africa Group, which organized a subscription service for *Mozambique Revolution* and "set a standard for the Africa Groups' external work, with fund-raising and information activities".[4]

During the crisis of 1968-1970, it was the university and secondary school students who decisively turned FRELIMO into a household name in Sweden. In April 1968, the student organizations at the University of Stockholm decided to grant no less than 100,000 SEK to FRELIMO's education projects in the liberated areas of Mozambique, and the following month about half of that amount was donated for the same purpose by teachers and staff members at the University of Gothenburg. In the wake of the May 1968 student revolt, the Båstad demonstrations[5] and the announcement of ASEA's participation in the tendering for the Cabora Bassa project, the university students' support grew further in 1968-69. It largely centred on the question of how to use the ten Swedish Kronor all students were paying as part of their membership fee to the student unions for humanitarian causes. After intense debates, it was agreed to give 'a tenner to FRELIMO', and in February 1969 the Students Development Fund (SDF)[6] allocated 80,000 SEK to the Mozambique Institute's education activities in Tanzania and the liberated areas.[7]

At about the same time—immediately after the death of Eduardo Mondlane—the Swedish Union of Secondary School Students (SECO)[8] decided to dedicate the 1969 Operation Day's Work[9] to the health and education projects carried out by the Mozambique Institute. Influential behind the decision was Janet Mondlane,

---

1. Interview with Sören Lindh, p. 304. In spite of diverging views between the solidarity movement and the Swedish government, the two were firmly in support of FRELIMO. Marcelino dos Santos later declared that he never felt inhibited by either party (Interview with Marcelino dos Santos, p. 50). Elsewhere in Europe, FRELIMO often encountered a different situation. After attending a solidarity conference in Oxford, England, in April 1974, Janet Mondlane wrote to FRELIMO, saying that the conference "went quite well, except for the constant quarrelling among the West German groups. [B]ut since it happens every year, it was a surprise for no one" (Letter from Janet Rae Mondlane to [FRELIMO], London, 29 April 1974) (MHA). Interviewed in 1996, she remembered "going to European solidarity conferences where you had the far left and the middle-of-the-road, edging over to the right. The liberation movements would just sit back and watch the things that were going on between the various solidarity groups. It really was not our problem. It was theirs" (Interview with Janet Mondlane, p. 44).
2. *Södra Afrika Informationsbulletin*, No. 12, 1971, p. 29.
3. Ibid.
4. Interview with Sören Lindh, p. 304.
5. On the Båstad demonstrations against the Davis Cup match in tennis between Sweden and Rhodesia in May 1968, see Sellström Volume I, pp. 348-53.
6. The Students Development Fund (with no designation in Swedish) was the branch for international assistance of the Swedish university student unions.
7. After a visit to FRELIMO in Tanzania, in late 1969 the SDF president Åke Magnusson published a series of articles on the Mozambican liberation movement in the liberal Swedish daily *Sydsvenska Dagbladet*. Also in 1969, he summarized his views in the booklet *Moçambique*, issued by the Nordic Africa Institute, Uppsala. Magnusson would later play a prominent role with regard to Sweden's relations with South Africa.
8. In Swedish, *Sveriges Elevers Centralorganisation*. Reorganized in 1982, it changed its name to *Elevorganisationen i Sverige* (The Swedish [Secondary] School Students Union).
9. In Swedish, *Operation Dagsverke*. Operation Day's Work was an important institution, regularly taking place in September or October. All secondary school students in Sweden were once a year given a day off to carry out various jobs for interested private or public companies or institutions against a remuneration below normal rates. The proceeds of the work were subsequently channelled to one or more international projects. In 1998, Operation Day's Work was dedicated to Angola.

Operation Day's Work
for FRELIMO's
Mozambique
Institute: Street
theatre and fund-
raising at a Stockholm
underground station,
October 1969
(Photo: Leif Engberg/
Pressens Bild)

who during a visit to Sweden in December 1968 had met representatives of SECO[1]
and raised the idea of a campaign for Mozambique. In early 1969, SECO issued a
comprehensive brief to all the secondary schools, stating that

> this year the subject of our campaign is the Mozambique Institute. It is an organization which
> is mainly concerned with health and education in an area [...] in northern Mozambique which
> has been liberated from the colonial power of Portugal [and which] is in dire need of financial
> support. Through our action we do not only want to contribute funds. We also wish to [...]
> spread knowledge about [...] people who under very difficult conditions are fighting for the
> right to their country, an existence worthy of humans and the possibility to decide their own
> future.[2]

The actual Operation Day's Work was held at the beginning of October 1969,
preceded by information campaigns and wide coverage in the press, radio and
television. Janet Mondlane took part in the activities, addressing meetings in different schools.[3] The SECO action coincided with a visit to Sweden by the FRE-
LIMO leader Marcelino dos Santos, who together with PAIGC's Secretary
General Amílcar Cabral had been invited to attend the Social Democratic Party
congress. Dos Santos—who unlike Cabral did not discuss official Swedish assistance during his stay[4]—could witness the school children's fund-raising efforts and
was "markedly moved by the solidarity action".[5] The results were, indeed, impressive.
The secondary school students managed through one major effort to raise no less than
2 MSEK for the FRELIMO institute[6], or more than the total government support

1. Janet Mondlane also met representatives of the Finnish secondary school students, who joined their counterparts in Sweden and organized an important *taksvärkki* in October 1969 (Soiri and Peltola, op. cit., pp. 34-
   43).
2. SECO: 'SECO's insamling 1969: FRELIMO-Moçambique Institute' ('SECO's fund-raising campaign 1969:
   FRELIMO-Mozambique Institute') [no place or date, but 1969] (AJC).
3. Interview with Janet Mondlane, p. 42.
4. The Swedish government had in mid-1969 decided to allocate 1 million SEK to PAIGC during the financial
   year 1969/70.
5. Sture Lidén: 'Om FRELIMO och PAIGC' ('About FRELIMO and PAIGC') in *Östersunds-Posten*, 13 October
   1969.
6. Elevorganisationen i Sverige: Reply to a questionnaire from the Nordic Africa Institute, 29 July 1996.

between 1965 and 1968.[1] As stated by Janet Mondlane, it was not just the money that was important, but the fact that the 1969 *Operation Dagsverke* brought FRELIMO and the liberation struggle in Mozambique into homes and workplaces all over Sweden.

FRELIMO's cause was further enhanced by SECO's decision to let the Swedish Save the Children[2] administer the funds collected. It was a well established and influential NGO, which could hardly be accused of subversive activities or Communist leanings. This marked the beginning of a close relationship between the Mozambique Institute and *Rädda Barnen*. When SECO in 1972 decided to carry out yet another Operation Day's Work for Mozambique—now raising 450,000 SEK[3]—Save the Children not only agreed to continue as the operating partner, but also allocated funds of its own via the Mozambique Institute to the Mozambican refugee children at FRELIMO's Tunduru camp in southern Tanzania.[4] The cooperation was based on trust. In April 1973, Staffan Bodemar, head of *Rädda Barnen*'s finance section, wrote to Janet Mondlane that "we do not find it necessary for you to send us long detailed reports, but are satisfied to receive a summary covering all your activities, from which can be seen how the SECO-RB money [has] been used".[5] That was in marked contrast to SIDA's reporting requirements.

Enjoying broad popular support and with solid political connections established by the Mondlanes to both the ruling Social Democratic Party and the opposition Liberal Party, FRELIMO's position in Sweden was not negatively affected by the 1968-70 crisis. Nevertheless, in a letter to the future member of FRELIMO's Political Bureau, Jacinto Veloso, Anders Johansson wrote in November 1969 that "people in Sweden are somewhat confused about FRELIMO [at] the moment [...], following Simango's statement and accusations against Samora [Machel] and Marcelino [dos Santos]".[6] But the questions never turned into doubts. Even the surprise resignation and expulsion from the movement of FRELIMO's highly popular representative to Sweden, Lourenço Mutaca, in February 1970 did not provoke major reactions. The Swedish conservative press did, however, highlight Mutaca's case. An article in the national paper *Svenska Dagbladet* presented FRELIMO as "a severely divided movement, where assassinations, escapes and desertions are the order of the day". It quoted Mutaca as saying that "the present

1. In 1968-69, the Swedish university and secondary school students together raised around 2.3 MSEK in favour of FRELIMO. Fund-raising activities were also carried out by FRELIMO-Sweden from November 1968. Significant contributions in the form of used clothes to the Mozambican refugees in Tanzania were, in addition, made by Emmaus-Björkå. It has not been possible to reliably establish the total value of the Swedish NGO support to FRELIMO and the other Southern African liberation movements. It was, however, in the early 1970s higher than the official humanitarian assistance through SIDA. Total transfers from Sweden to the Southern African liberation movements thus exceeded by a wide margin the official figures given in the text.
2. In Swedish, *Rädda Barnen* (RB).
3. Elevorganisationen i Sverige: Reply to a questionnaire from the Nordic Africa Institute, 29 July 1996 and letter from Staffan Bodemar and Margareta Tullberg, *Rädda Barnen*, to Janet Mondlane, Mozambique Institute, [no place], 18 April 1973 (MHA).
4. Letter from Staffan Bodemar and Margareta Tullberg, *Rädda Barnen*, to Janet Mondlane, Mozambique Institute, [no place], 18 April 1973 and letter from Janet Rae Mondlane, Mozambique Institute, to Save the Children Federation, [no place], 4 April 1974 (MHA).
5. Letter from Staffan Bodemar and Margareta Tullberg, *Rädda Barnen*, to Janet Mondlane, Mozambique Institute, [no place], 18 April 1973 (MHA).
6. Letter from Anders Johansson to Jacinto Veloso, London, 15 November 1969 (AJC). Together with independent Mozambique's first Minister of Health, Dr. Helder Martins, Fernando Ganhão and Birgitta Karlström—a young Swedish volunteer at the Mozambique Institute—Veloso had been expelled from Tanzania in May 1968 (see Sellström Volume I, pp. 457-58). All of them were white and targets of Mateus Gwenjere's attacks. Living in Algiers, Algeria, Veloso replied to Johansson that he had talked to Samora Machel over the phone and that "everything is OK. [...] The struggle continues as before. Inside [Mozambique], nobody supports Simango. His force is outside, in Tanzania, among Mozambicans and Tanzanians (the same that expelled Birgitta and the others)" (Letter from Jacinto Veloso to Anders Johansson, Algiers, 5 December 1969) (AJC).

leadership [...] is working to eliminate all opposition [...]. Those who have not yielded to the given course are [either] killed or run away from Tanzania", according to him "increasingly to the Portuguese side".[1]

Desertions certainly did take place, but in the opposite direction and all the way to Sweden. The first deserter from the war in Mozambique to publicly appear in Sweden was the Portuguese Captain Jaime Morais, who stated his case to the press in early February 1971. A commanding officer during Operation Gordian Knot, Morais denounced the Portuguese "war of aggression against innocent people" and declared that "FRELIMO has the support of the [Mozambican] population".[2] He arrived in Sweden at the beginning of 1971. The previous year, around thirty—according to some sources about a hundred[3]—Portuguese war-resisters had made their way to the country, attracted by "Sweden's criticism of Portugal's colonialism".[4] Morais' case—and the Swedish stand towards the war—provoked an uproar in Portugal and was highlighted in *Mozambique Revolution*.[5] More importantly, the liberation movement's Portuguese-language publication *A Voz da Revolução* ('Voice of the Revolution')—distributed inside Mozambique—gave publicity to the deserters.[6] In Sweden, Portuguese Deserters' Committes[7] were formed in Lund, Stockholm and Uppsala. In addition to the demand for political asylum, the committees joined forces with the local Africa Groups in actively advocating support for PAIGC, MPLA and FRELIMO, strengthening the political arguments in favour of the nationalist movements.[8]

Resumption of the Swedish Support

Following the disturbances at the Mozambique Institute, FRELIMO decided to move the secondary school to Bagamoyo—some 70 kilometres north of Dar es Salaam—where it eventually re-opened in late October 1970.[9] The official Swedish

---

1. Ingmar Lindmarker: 'FRELIMO är splittrad—Allt fler deserterar' ('FRELIMO is divided—More and more desert') in *Svenska Dagbladet*, 26 February 1970. Lindmarker went on a three week tour to Southern Africa, where he visited South Africa, Mozambique, Namibia and Zimbabwe. His impressions were first published in a series of articles under the heading 'White Africa' in *Svenska Dagbladet* and later in 1971 in a book with the same title (Ingmar Lindmarker: *Det Vita Afrika: Sydafrika och Dess Grannar /*'White Africa: South Africa and Its Neighbours', Gebers/Almqvist & Wiksell, Stockholm, 1971). Lindmarker's article on Mozambique was particularly indicative of a Swedish conservative opinion. Headlined 'Miscegenation is here honourable', it was an enthusiastic praising of a dynamic country without racism, but exposed to "a war difficult to explain". Quoting Portuguese military sources, Lindmarker conveyed to the readers of *Svenska Dagbladet* that "out of 83 major tribes in the colony, only 3 or 4 [are] affected by the war". The Swedish assistance to FRELIMO was particularly criticized. Lindmarker wrote that "there is only a slight difference between the Swedish support and the Russian and Chinese deliveries of war equipment". According to his sources, the assistance did not go to humanitarian purposes, but "to the [FRELIMO] leaders themselves, to their propaganda and their travels". The Mozambique Institute in Dar es Salaam—which Lindmarker did not visit—was, finally, presented as "only a cover. [The] Swedish funds go somewhere else" (Ingmar Lindmarker: 'Här är rasblandning hedervärt' in *Svenska Dagbladet*, 20 March 1971 and Lindmarker op. cit., pp. 124-126).
2. Erik Eriksson: 'Portugisisk kapten söker asyl här: Jag vägrar bränna byar i Afrika' ('Portuguese captain asks for asylum here: I refuse to burn villages in Africa') in *Aftonbladet*, 1 February 1971.
3. *Södra Afrika Informationsbulletin*, No. 12, 1971, p. 7.
4. Eriksson in *Aftonbladet*, 1 February 1971. A certain number of Portuguese who had left Portugal to avoid conscription and had stayed in France and other countries on their way to Sweden—i.e. not deserters from the war fronts—were denied asylum and returned to their first country of refuge. As these countries—including Denmark—were NATO members and the war- resisters were likely to be sent back to Portugal, there emerged a strong opinion in their favour. Between 1967 and 1975, Sweden also received around 800 US Vietnam deserters and war-resisters.
5. 'Portuguese Soldier in Africa, Listen!' in *Mozambique Revolution*, No. 46, January-April 1971, pp. 16-17.
6. 'Um Capitão Nosso Aliado' ('A Captain Our Ally') in *A Voz da Revolução*, June 1971, p. 3.
7. In Portuguese, *Comités de Desertores Portugueses.*
8. *Södra Afrika Informationsbulletin*, No. 12, 1971, pp. 7-10 and No. 13, 1971, pp. 6-8.
9. Meanwhile, the institute as such remained at Kurasini in the capital.

The Stockholm Portuguese
Deserters' Committee
demonstrating against
Portugal, October 1973
(Photo: Aftonbladet Bild)

cash support to the Mozambique Institute had been discontinued after the closure of the school in March 1968. However, Janet Mondlane stayed in close contact with the Swedish government and SIDA during her many visits to Sweden, and it was understood that the support would resume once the situation so allowed.

Shortly after the re-opening of the school, Joaquim Chissano and Anselmo Anaiva visited Sweden. Chissano, the future President of Mozambique[1], was at the time FRELIMO's representative in Tanzania and a member of the movement's Politico-Military Committee, while Anaiva was responsible for supplies in the liberated areas.[2] The main purpose of their visit in mid-November 1970 was to explain the political and military situation after the assassination of Eduardo Mondlane and the Portuguese Gordian Knot offensive[3], both to the government and the solidarity movement.[4]

In addition to discussions at the Ministry for Foreign Affairs[5], Chissano and Anaiva had meetings with the Social Democratic Party[6], the Africa Groups[7], Emmaus-Björkå[8] and with the independent socialist monthly *Kommentar*.[9] They also visited SIDA, where Chissano—who besides his political tasks had been teaching mathematics at the FRELIMO school[10]—presented the budget of the Mozam-

1. Prime Minister in the transitional government that led Mozambique to independence from September 1974 to June 1975, Chissano served as Minister for Foreign Affairs from 1975 to 1986. After the death of Samora Machel in October 1986, Chissano was appointed President of FRELIMO and of the People's Republic of Mozambique.
2. Inga Lagerman: 'Minnesanteckningar från besök av representanter för FRELIMO den 13.11 1970 på SIDA' ('Notes from visit by representatives of FRELIMO on 13.11 1970 at SIDA'), SIDA, 17 November 1970 (SDA).
3. See the interview with Joaquim Chissano, p. 40.
4. Organized by the Social Democratic Party, the visit by Chissano and Anaiva also included the other Nordic countries. In June 1971, President Samora Machel went on a similar information tour to the Soviet Union, GDR, Bulgaria, Romania and Italy (Christie op. cit., p. 70).
5. Göran Hasselmark: Memorandum ('Besök av representanter för FRELIMO'/'Visit by representatives of FRELIMO'), Ministry for Foreign Affairs, 20 November 1970 (MFA).
6. Social Democratic Party: 'Verksamheten 1970' ('Activities 1970'), p. 81 (LMA).
7. The Africa Groups in Sweden: 'Circular Letter No. 2', [no place], 17 December 1970 (AGA).
8. Interview with Joaquim Chissano, p. 40.
9. See 'Folkets Krig i Moçambique: Misslyckad Portugisisk Offensiv mot FRELIMO' ('The People's War in Mozambique: Abortive Portuguese Offensive against FRELIMO') in *Kommentar*, No. 1, 1971, pp. 16-17.
10. Mozambique Institute: 'Mozambique Institute: 1965', [no place or date], p. 2.

bique Institute for 1971, particularly emphasizing the need for support to the health and education sectors.[1] The establishment of people's shops in the liberated areas was also mentioned.[2] On behalf of SIDA, Stig Abelin responded positively, asking FRELIMO to submit a formal request and stating that possible assistance would be extended in the form of commodity aid.[3]

Janet Mondlane submitted a request in early January 1971.[4] Official Swedish assistance to FRELIMO was discussed the following month by SIDA's Deputy Director General Anders Forsse with the Director of the Mozambique Institute and FRELIMO's Vice-President Marcelino dos Santos in Dar es Salaam. Forsse was, however, far from impressed. In his report to the Consultative Committee on Humanitarian Assistance, he characterized the post-Mondlane crisis as internal "squabbling"[5], in the same breath stating that the organization was "evolving from Danton to Robespierre".[6] Janet Mondlane was described as a "decoration"[7], while his opinion of Marcelino dos Santos was coloured by the hearsay that he had "recently received a high Soviet order of distinction".[8] Concluding his findings, Forsse stated that FRELIMO's "interest in receiving material assistance from us is markedly weaker than our manifest interest in extending such support".[9]

As vice-chairman of the Consultative Committee on Humanitarian Assistance, Forsse's opinions carried great weight. Nevertheless, when the question of resumed assistance to FRELIMO was discussed by the committee in early March 1971, the views expressed in his report did not prevail.[10] Instead, CCHA recommended that direct official Swedish support to an amount of 750,000 SEK should be allocated to the movement through the Mozambique Institute. Based on SIDA's positive experiences from the cooperation with PAIGC, it was further recommended to extend the support "in kind", primarily to the education and health sectors, as well as to contribute towards the daily necessities of the Mozambican refugees in Tanzania.[11] Thus, the committee followed the priorities indicated by Chissano four months earlier.

CCHA's recommendation was endorsed by the government, and on 17 March 1971 SIDA set aside 750,000 SEK for the financial year 1971/72.[12] The Swedish government's assistance to FRELIMO—which via the Mozambique Institute in 1965 had been the first Southern African liberation movement to receive official

---

1. Inga Lagerman: Memorandum ('Minnesanteckningar från besök av representanter för FRELIMO den 13.11 1970 på SIDA'/'Notes from visit by representatives of FRELIMO on 13.11 1970 at SIDA'), SIDA, Stockholm, 17 November 1970 (SDA).
2. Ibid.
3. Ibid.
4. Marianne Rappe: Memorandum ('Beslut om fortsatt stöd till Mozambique Institute, (FRELIMO), Dar es Salaam'/'Decision on continued support to the Mozambique Institute, (FRELIMO), Dar es Salaam'), SIDA, Stockholm,16 May 1971 (SDA).
5. In Swedish, "*kivet inom FRELIMO*".
6. Anders Forsse: Memorandum ('Om samtal med FRELIMO-representanter'/'On conversations with FRELIMO representatives'), SIDA, Stockholm, 1 March 1971 (SDA).
7. In Swedish, *kuttersmycke*. Quoting diplomatic sources, Forsse added—in English—that "[s]he will be admitted as long as she is a good fund-raiser" (ibid.).
8. Ibid.
9. Ibid.
10. Per Wästberg, the influential member of the Consultative Committee on Humanitarian Assistance, held a radically different view. Visiting Tanzania in early 1971, he published a highly informative article on FRELIMO, the Mozambique Institute and the liberation struggle in Mozambique in *Dagens Nyheter* (Per Wästberg: 'Det är en befrielse att gå över gränsen'/'It is a relief to cross the border' in *Dagens Nyheter*, 10 April 1971).
11. CCHA: 'Protokoll' ('Minutes'), SIDA, Stockholm, 10 March 1971 (SDA).
12. Marianne Rappe: Memorandum ('Beslut om fortsatt stöd till Mozambique Institute, (FRELIMO), Dar es Salaam'/'Decision on continued support to the Mozambique Institute, (FRELIMO), Dar es Salaam'), SIDA, Stockholm, 16 May 1971 (SDA).

Swedish support—was thus resumed. In contrast to the cooperation programme with PAIGC, the Swedish assistance to FRELIMO would, however, during the first years not be without "discords".[1] This largely explains why the official support to the Mozambican movement—despite its broad and strong sympathy in Sweden— never reached the levels of the assistance to PAIGC. In the case of Mozambique, both the form of the assistance and Sweden's general stand towards the liberation struggle was initially debated by the cooperating partners.

Commodity or Cash Support?

From 750,000 SEK, the official humanitarian support to FRELIMO was increased to 2 million in 1972/73, 5 million in 1973/74 and—when a broad political under-standing and well functioning routines had been established—to 15 MSEK in 1974/75.[2] In the latter year, the allocation was almost four times as big as the 4 million granted to MPLA, approaching the 22 million extended to PAIGC. Of the 67.5 MSEK actually disbursed by Sweden to PAIGC and the Southern African lib-eration movements between 1969/70 and 1974/75, 17.1 million—corresponding to 25 per cent—was paid out in favour of FRELIMO.[3] Although the annual alloca-tions were modest[4], FRELIMO was the second largest recipient, well behind PAIGC, but far ahead of all the other movements in Southern Africa.

There were, nevertheless, frictions.[5] The main disagreement concerned the form of the assistance. Until the suspension of the support in 1968, the Swedish contri-butions had been extended in cash. Influenced by PAIGC and the efficient routines established with Amílcar Cabral, the Swedish authorities decided that continued assistance from 1971/72 should be extended in the form of commodities. Accord-ing to SIDA, several arguments spoke in favour of a commodity programme. After a visit to Dar es Salaam in December 1971, a SIDA delegation led by Curt Ström— the official who together with Cabral had designed the support to PAIGC—con-cluded that FRELIMO's experience of international procurement was inadequate and that the administrative capacity to efficiently handle large quantities of goods was low.[6] In addition, if SIDA managed procurements and freight, the main admin-istrative costs would not be charged against the FRELIMO allocation, but be borne by Sweden. Other Southern African liberation movements who faced similar administrative constraints—notably MPLA and SWAPO—had, finally, welcomed the idea of commodity support.[7]

While not opposing support in kind as such, FRELIMO argued that a substan-tial part of the assistance should be given in the form of cash to cover local pro-curement in Tanzania; costs related to the reception and distribution of the commodities; and running costs at the Mozambique Institute. Such local costs

---

1. Letter from Göran Hasselmark to the Ministry for Foreign Affairs, Dar es Salaam, 18 June 1973 (MFA).
2. CCHA: Memorandum ('Biståndet till Guinea-Bissau och Moçambique'/'The assistance to Guinea-Bissau and Mozambique'), SIDA, Stockholm, 13 November 1974 (SDA).
3. See the accompanying tables on disbursements from SIDA to the Southern African liberation movements and PAIGC. Including the early support to the Mozambique Institute and payments registered after Mozambique's independence, the total official Swedish assistance to FRELIMO amounted to 24.7 MSEK.
4. Cf. the interview with Jacinto Veloso, p. 52: "[T]he support was limited and today we can say that it was very limited. [...] The Nordic countries could have done much more."
5. The administration of the Swedish support was handled by SIDA. The Mozambique Institute acted on behalf of FRELIMO.
6. Anders Möllander: Memorandum ('Ansökan från Frente de Libertação de Moçambique, FRELIMO, om fort-satt svenskt stöd'/'Request from FRELIMO regarding continued Swedish support'), SIDA-CCHA, Stockholm, 5 September 1972 (SDA).
7. Ibid.

included, for example, fresh food, medicines, wharfage and storage fees, petrol and vehicle repairs and telephone and electricity bills.[1] During the first year of cooperation, SIDA would, however, not change its position.

In September 1971, the responsible official at SIDA, Marianne Rappe, concluded that the experience from the 1971/72 programme was "not particularly positive".[2] Against this background, the Swedish authorities reviewed their position. In November 1972, it was decided that a small component of the support—amounting to 5 per cent of the annual allocation—could be disbursed in cash and used for local procurement and running costs.[3] Although SIDA's detailed reporting requirements subsequently became another bone of contention[4], this was a victory for Janet Mondlane and the Mozambique Institute. As the decision applied to all liberation movements receiving official Swedish humanitarian support, it was also a battle won on their behalf. Once cash support had been included in the assistance to the movements, its share of the cooperation programmes increased continuously. It should be noted that the future SIDA routine of quarterly payments in advance was first raised in discussions between the Swedish embassy in Dar es Salaam and FRELIMO in mid-1973.[5]

The question of cash support—or, rather, of a cash component within the support—initially played a prominent part in the dialogue between SIDA and FRE-LIMO, at times diverting the attention from more pressing issues, as well as threatening to undermine the trust between the parties. In retrospect, the debate could be seen as a significant Swedish learning process. After repeatedly explaining his movement's position, Vice-President Marcelino dos Santos expressed the opinion during a visit to the Ministry for Foreign Affairs in Stockholm in April 1973 that "Sweden has by now started to know FRELIMO and its situation. The assistance, therefore, should be adapted to the needs of the movement".[6] That would increasingly also be the case. Looking back in 1996, Janet Mondlane—who *de facto* served as FRELIMO's Cooperation Minister—recalled:

> [Y]ou cannot hit people over the head in the beginning. You have to ease them into the situation. [...] Contributions in kind were very good, because we needed the goods, but they were [...] difficult to administer. [...] It is much easier to report on money spent than on things

1. Janet Mondlane: Memorandum ('Grants-in-Aid, Cash and Kind') to SIDA, Dar es Salaam, 22 March 1972 (SDA). The Director of the Mozambique Institute described the introduction of commodity aid as "a shock to [its] financial system [...]. The [...] switch from cash to kind resulted in the Institute finding itself in serious financial difficulties, which continue until today" (ibid.).
2. Message from Marianne Rappe to Curt Ström, SIDA, Stockholm, 1 September 1972 (SDA). Only two thirds of the 1971/72 allocation was actually used.
3. SIDA: 'Beslut' ('Decision'), UND-E, No. 97/72, SIDA, Stockholm, 20 November 1972 (SDA).
4. Olof Milton: Memorandum ('FRELIMO: Redovisning av 1972/73 års kontantbidrag samt aktuellt om utformningen av 1973/74 års SIDA-bidrag'/'FRELIMO: Report on the 1972/73 cash contribution and the present situation regarding the design of SIDA's contribution for 1973/74'), SIDA, Stockholm, 3 September 1973 (SDA).
5. Letter from Göran Hasselmark to the Ministry for Foreign Affairs, Dar es Salaam, 18 June 1973 (MFA). Funds allocated to the Southern African liberation movements for local expenditures were as a rule disbursed each quarter by the SIDA office in the country concerned. According to the established procedure, disbursements for the third quarter of the financial year were made upon satisfactory reporting on funds used during the first quarter; for the fourth quarter after reports from the second, etc. The quarterly payments were thus made in advance, on a rolling basis allowing the local offices of the liberation movements three months to prepare and submit financial statements with supporting vouchers. In the case of local project activities supported by Sweden, the financial statement was to be accompanied by a quarterly progress report. The quarterly statements and progress reports were, finally, forwarded by the organizations and SIDA offices to their respective headquarters, forming the basis for financial control and budgeting at the official annual negotiations between the parties. Over the years, the flexible system proved both educational and efficient.
6. Anders Möllander: Memorandum ('Minnesanteckningar från samtal 1973 04 17 med representanter för FRE-LIMO'/'Notes from conversations 1973 04 17 with representatives of FRELIMO'), CCHA, Stockholm, 26 April 1973 (MFA).

received. We were supposed to show how every little thing was distributed. That is hard when you are running a big operation. The Mozambique Institute included the Tunduru refugee centre, Dr. Américo Boavida Hospital and activities in the liberated areas inside Mozambique. How can you put your word on the line and say: 'Yes, I know that those books went off to such and such a place?' But it worked out. We had to go slowly. In the end, a lot of confidence inspired our working relationship and reached such an extent that we received cash funds. But it had to go slowly, because there was no previous Swedish experience.[1]

That also the shipment of goods from Sweden was part of a political reality was illustrated in late 1973, when the Portuguese authorities impounded two Scania trucks in the Mozambican port of Beira.[2] The trucks were part of the 1973/74 procurement programme. Openly marked 'FRELIMO, c/o Mozambique Institute, Dar es Salaam', they were transported on the Norwegian ship *Drammensfjord*. Unbeknown to SIDA, en route to Dar es Salaam the ship called on Beira, where the cargo caused an outrage and the Portuguese security police ordered the captain to surrender the trucks.[3]

Although SIDA immediately replaced the vehicles—increasing FRELIMO's 1973/74 allocation from 5 to 5.1 MSEK[4]—the experience underlined the importance of reliable transport routes. Commenting upon the incident, the owner of *Drammensfjord*—the Scandinavian East Africa Line—wrote to the Norwegian Shipowners' Association[5], conveying the captain's view that "if we continue to take cargo for the liberation movement, we must be ready to face great difficulties down here".[6] In the letter, the shipping company stated that the incident "only was to be expected", adding that "it is difficult for us to understand that trucks can form part of the concept of humanitarian assistance [...], but SIDA goes possibly further than NORAD[7] in its support to the 'liberation movement'".[8] Subsequently, SIDA mostly used the Besta Line from the Soviet Union for shipments of goods to FRELIMO and the other liberation movements in Dar es Salaam.[9]

Armed Struggle and Humanitarian Assistance

While Amílcar Cabral and the PAIGC leadership generally adopted a pragmatic attitude to potentially divisive issues such as Sweden's economic relations with Portugal and its opposition to violence as a means to solve conflicts, the FRELIMO leaders were more critical. Ever since his first visits to Sweden in the mid-1960s, Eduardo Mondlane regularly and forcefully raised the questions of military assistance to the Mozambican struggle and of Portugal's expulsion from EFTA.[10] After

1. Interview with Janet Mondlane, pp. 43-44.
2. See the interview with Stig Lövgren, pp. 312-13.
3. Letter from the captain of *Drammensfjord* to the Scandinavian East Africa Line, Beira, 30 October 1973 (Ministry of Foreign Affairs of Norway).
4. Letter ('Ang. beslagtagna bilar till FRELIMO'/'Re. impounded vehicles for FRELIMO') from Astrid Bergquist, SIDA, to Olof Milton, Swedish embassy in Dar es Salaam, SIDA, Stockholm, 26 November 1973 (SDA).
5. In Norwegian, *Norges Rederforbund*.
6. Letter from the captain of *Drammensfjord* to the Scandinavian East Africa Line, Beira, 30 October 1973 (Ministry of Foreign Affairs of Norway).
7. The Norwegian Agency for International Development.
8. Letter from Arne M. Hansson, Scandinavian East Africa Line, to the Norwegian Shipowners' Association, [no place], 5 November 1973 (Ministry of Foreign Affairs of Norway).
9. Interview with Stig Lövgren, p. 314.
10. See Sellström Volume I, pp. 473-75.

his death in February 1969, the same position was taken by Marcelino dos Santos, Joaquim Chissano and other Mozambican representatives.[1]

More than any other Southern African liberation movement supported by Sweden, FRELIMO consistently maintained a critical stance towards the separation between humanitarian and military support and vis-à-vis Sweden's international economic relations.[2] On both accounts, it was strongly backed by the Swedish solidarity movement. Talking about Sweden and the armed struggle—"the principal form of struggle that history imposed on Mozambique"[3]—Marcelino dos Santos later explained that FRELIMO never felt that there were any ideological conditions attached to the Swedish assistance. However,

> we always said that we did not agree with the Swedish position of being in support of peace, and therefore not being able to help us to wage war. We said: 'The war which we are waging, is it not for peace?' [...] [However,] [w]e never questioned Sweden's right to state that 'since we are in favour of peace, we cannot give you arms'.[4]

Also of the opinion that "there was [no Swedish] ideological pressure on us"[5], President Chissano similarly stated in May 1996:

> We were in favour of the approach by the Swedish solidarity groups that the help should be unconditional. The only condition was to assist the struggle against Portuguese colonialism. [...] [W]e tried to use the influence of the public opinion to change the [Swedish] position. In our view, the humanitarian position of Sweden should be expanded to include an understanding of the nature of our struggle, which was in defence against aggression and violations of human rights by Portuguese colonialism. [...] [B]ut we also understood that Sweden and the other Scandinavian countries could not just change the opinion without going through a democratic process. They faced a public opinion which should be convinced. They had parliaments and many political parties. They were not obliged to have the same understanding of the situation in Mozambique as we had.[6]

In the case of the assistance to PAIGC, there was no permanent Swedish presence in Guinée-Conakry and SIDA was in no position to monitor the utilization of the support in the liberated areas of Guinea-Bissau. In this respect, the situation regarding the cooperation with FRELIMO was quite different. Sweden had a significant presence in Tanzania. Although the SIDA officials at the embassy in Dar es Salaam

---

1. For example, by Joaquim Ribeiro de Carvalho in September 1973. Visiting Sweden in connection with the 'Southern Africa Week' organized by AGIS, de Carvalho—who would become independent Mozambique's first Minister for Agriculture and at the time was responsible for commerce and production in the liberated areas—demanded a Swedish investment ban against Mozambique and economic isolation of Portugal (Peo Österholm: 'FRELIMO-ledare anklagar: Sverige är inkonsekvent'/'FRELIMO leader accuses: Sweden is inconsistent' in *Dagens Nyheter*, 26 September 1973, and Bengt Säve-Söderbergh: Memorandum: 'Samtal med en besökande FRELIMO-ledare'/'Conversation with a visiting FRELIMO leader', Ministry for Foreign Affairs, Stockholm, 28 September 1973) (MFA). There were no Swedish investments in Mozambique. At the time of de Carvalho's visit, press reports, however, indicated that the Portuguese Lisnave construction and repair yard—in which the Swedish companies Kockums and Eriksbergs together controlled about one fifth of the capital—was planning to build a shipyard in Nacala ('Svenskvarv utreder Moçambique-satsning'/'Swedish yards study venture in Mozambique' in *Dagens Nyheter*, 21 September 1973). Stating the view that Swedish investments in both Portugal and in the Portuguese colonies were "not desirable", three months later Foreign Minister Sven Andersson informed the Swedish parliament that the government was "studying the feasibility of preventing Swedish investment in the Portuguese colonies" ('Reply by the Foreign Minister to an interpellation by Mrs. Dahl', 10 December 1973, in Ministry for Foreign Affairs: *Documents on Swedish Foreign Policy: 1973*, Stockholm, 1976, p. 158).
2. Cf. the interview with Jorge Rebelo, p. 46.
3. Interview with Marcelino dos Santos, p. 49.
4. Ibid., p. 48.
5. Interview with Joaquim Chissano, p. 40. Chissano further stated: "Actually, even ideologically we were close to Sweden. The support constituted a balance to the tendencies of copying what one could see in countries where there had been revolutions, like in the Soviet Union or China. We found a middle point in Sweden which we could refer to" (ibid.).
6. Ibid., pp. 39-40.

could not cross into the liberated areas of northern Mozambique, they did, how-ever, regularly visit FRELIMO's refugee camp at Tunduru[1] and the Dr. Américo Boavida Hospital in Mtwara.[2] Just north of the Mozambican border and with FRELIMO's main military base at Nachingwea between the two, the Tunduru set-tlement and the Mtwara hospital were directly exposed to the liberation struggle. Opened in June 1970, the hospital became a medical centre for the population in the combat areas.

While SIDA in the case of PAIGC could not verify whether the end-users of the humanitarian assistance were civilians or soldiers, this was with regard to FRELIMO in Tanzania not only possible, but also done. Interviewed in 1996, Chis-sano noted that

> [Sweden] gave us medicines to treat civilians, but we said that humanitarianism means that a man with a gun also has a right to life and to be treated when he is wounded. A wounded civil-ian could come to the hospital for treatment, but a soldier could not be treated with the same medicine. This was shocking to us and on that point we had to be sharp. [...]

> [W]e used to receive the medicines and we tried to do our best until we could convince the Swedes that this was impossible, particularly in the clinics in Dar es Salaam and at our hospital in Mtwara. The Swedes would visit and say that 'these are medicines from Sweden. They can-not go to that patient, because he is a military'. That was very powerful! It was impossible! We have a soldier [...] who is fighting. His child is in the Tunduru camp, receiving medicines and clothing from Sweden. When his father comes, he cannot be clothed or fed with [the same] assistance [...]. It was so strange! [...] We tried to say [...] that they were supporting a struggle for liberation, but they chose to support just one aspect of it. We [, however,] could not sepa-rate the diplomatic, social or military areas. It was impossible.[3]

The Swedish authorities eventually assumed a more flexible attitude. Also in this regard, the dialogue with FRELIMO contributed to adjusting the humanitarian assistance to the realities of the Southern African liberation movements. With the definitions reached within the support to PAIGC, a broader interpretation would guide the non-military assistance to ANC of South Africa, SWAPO of Namibia and ZANU and ZAPU of Zimbabwe from the mid-1970s. In the case of FRELIMO itself, the official assistance was from 1973 not only significantly increased, but chiefly channelled to the liberated areas inside Mozambique.

In the meantime, severe criticism of Sweden's humanitarian assistance was pub-licly expressed in mid-1972 by Tanzanian voices. It came as a surprise. The ruling Social Democratic Party maintained particularly close bonds with President Nyerere's TANU party[4] and Prime Minister Olof Palme had in September 1971 paid an official visit to Tanzania to an enthusiastic welcome. During the visit, he *inter alia* addressed the TANU congress in Dar es Salaam, stating that "in countries still subject to colonial oppression, no tactically calculated advances for the mainte-

---

1. For example, 'Reserapport'/'Travel report': 'Besök i FRELIMO's läger i Tunduru, 1-2 mars 1973'/'Visit to FRELIMO's camp at Tunduru, 1-2 March 1973', SIDA/Swedish embassy, Dar es Salaam, 26 March 1973 (SDA).
2. Olof Milton: Memorandum ('Besök vid FRELIMOs sjukhus i Mtwara (Dr. Américo Boavida Hospital) 1972 10 10'/'Visit to FRELIMO's hospital in Mtwara (Dr. Américo Boavida Hospital) 1972 10 10'), SIDA/Swedish embassy, Dar es Salaam, 13 October 1972 (SDA).
3. Interview with Joaquim Chissano, p. 40. FRELIMO's Secretary for Information Jorge Rebelo in June 1972 expressed the same opinion in an interview with the independent socialist monthly *Kommentar* ('Verklig Hjälp Måste Stödja Vårt Befrielsekrig'/'Real Assistance Must Support Our Liberation War' in *Kommentar*, No. 11-12, 1972, pp. 18-23).
4. See Sellström Volume I, pp. 80-82.

nance of a balanced international development can be substituted for the demand
for national liberation"[1], adding that

> [a]s far as Sweden is concerned, we support the liberation movements in the Portuguese-occu-
> pied territories, i.e. PAIGC, FRELIMO and MPLA. We have supplied humanitarian aid in the
> form of medical equipment, educational materials, food, textiles and other consumer goods, as
> well as means of transportation. We have been criticized for this. But we shall continue to fol-
> low the demands of solidarity and the recommendations of the United Nations. [...] In our
> opinion, the European nations must take [...] a much more active and [...] decisive line of
> action in these questions. [...] The Swedish government is prepared to further increase its
> assistance.[2]

Nine months later, the official newspaper *Sunday News* published a major article
by a certain TANU Study Group under the heading 'The secret behind humanitarian aid' in which Sweden was singled out. Among other things, it asserted that

> [c]ognisant of the fact that the African peoples in [the Portuguese] colonies are winning greater
> and greater victories each passing day, imperialism has lately been extending its ugly hand of
> 'friendship' to the liberation movements, offering them what it shamelessly calls 'humanitarian
> aid'. The truth of the matter is that this 'aid' is nothing but a carrot intended to blind the fight-
> ing peoples [to] the inhuman activities imperialism perpetrates against them, albeit under a
> guise of Portuguese fascism. [...] Sweden, for example, is one of the countries whose economic
> interests in Portugal have recently been growing at a tremendous rate. [...] Imperialism may
> change its colour and tactics, but it cannot change its essence. It will always be inhuman, what-
> ever 'humanitarian' facades it may show at times.[3]

The article prompted the Swedish ambassador, Sven Fredrik Hedin, to seek an
explanation from the Tanzanian government. According to Foreign Minister John
Malecela, the TANU Study Group was a group of scholars who made political
analyses for the ruling party, but "the publication of the report was an accident".[4]
Nevertheless, shortly thereafter the organ of the TANU Youth League at the University of Dar es Salaam—*Maji Maji*—published an article by 'a correspondent'
entitled 'Swedish imperialism'.[5] It stated that

> [t]he official [Swedish] support to FRELIMO, PAIGC and MPLA has clear limitations [...].
> First of all, it is restricted to 'humanitarian assistance', which means that only one part of the
> liberation struggle is recognized. By refusing to see the military aspect as an integral part of the
> struggle, the Swedish government is giving a false picture of the situation. Another restriction
> is that material [aid] through [...] SIDA is given in kind, selected from a list and purchased (in
> Sweden) by SIDA officials. This is a severe form of paternalism, which can be explained only
> by the desire to keep the flourishing economic links with Portugal as long as possible and by
> the desire to achieve a neo-colonialist solution in the colonies.[6]

---

1. Cited in Pierre Schori: *The Impossible Neutrality-Southern Africa: Sweden's Role under Olof Palme*, David
   Philip Publishers, Cape Town, 1994, p. 5.
2. 'Speech by the Prime Minister at the TANU Congress in Dar-es-Salaam', 26 September 1971, in The Royal
   Ministry for Foreign Affairs: *Documents on Swedish Foreign Policy: 1971*, Stockholm, 1972, p. 65.
3. *Sunday News*, 11 June 1972.
4. Letter from Sven Fr. Hedin to the Ministry for Foreign Affairs, Dar es Salaam, 30 June 1972 (MFA).
5. *Maji Maji*, No. 6, June 1972, pp. 19-21.
6. Ibid., p. 21.

Swedish film-maker Lennart Malmer with FRELIMO's Joaquim Chissano (right) in the liberated areas of Cabo Delgado, Mozambique, November 1971 (Courtesy of Lennart Malmer)

This was unmistakably the wording of the Swedish Africa Groups.[1] As the article did not reflect the views of the Tanzanian ruling party or the liberation movements, it was decided by the Swedish Foreign Ministry to let the matter rest.[2]

De Facto Recognition and Expanded Support

The initial discords notwithstanding, SIDA and FRELIMO established close and well functioning aid relations.[3] At the political level, the interaction between the Social Democratic government and the liberation movement had since the mid-1960s been extensive and the relations developed further in the early 1970s. Looking back, President Chissano stated in 1996 that "Olof Palme was one of our staunch supporters" and that "[t]he Swedes often had a better understanding of our situation [than many African countries]".[4] A close dialogue between the parties contributed to this situation, but also that a number of Swedish journalists visited the liberated areas in the company of leading FRELIMO representatives. Their impressions were widely disseminated via the established media in Sweden.

In November 1971, for example, Lennart Malmer and Ingela Romare[5]—who

1. Cf. Draft: 'Swedish imperialism in Portugal and Africa', The Easter Conference, Lund, 1972 (AGA). At the time, members of AGIS contributed to *Maji Maji* (Letter from Mai Palmberg, Malung, 24 June 1974; addressee unknown) (AGA).
2. Handwritten notes on a letter ('Svensk imperialism'/'Swedish imperialism') from Nils G. Rosenberg, Swedish embassy, to the Ministry for Foreign Affairs, Dar es Salaam, 21 August 1972 (MFA). The humanitarian support was at the same time strongly criticized by the business community. For example, in a letter to the Ministry for Foreign Affairs the South African agent of the Swedish company Boliden—AE & CI—wrote in December 1972 that "our office in Lourenço Marques informs us that our customer, Beira Waterworks Company, will no longer be purchasing your aluminium sulphate. They have taken this attitude in view of your government's support for [the] terrorist movements in [the] Portuguese territories" (Letter from AE & CI to the Ministry for Foreign Affairs, [no place], 13 December 1972) (MFA).
3. See the interview with Stig Lövgren (SIDA): "We had an excellent cooperation" (p. 312). Also the interview with Janet Mondlane: "In the end, a lot of confidence inspired our working relationship" (p. 44).
4. Interview with Joaquim Chissano, p. 39.
5. As early as in 1969, Malmer and Romare visited Beira to make a television programme about the Portuguese colonial system, but were expelled after four days (Lennart Malmer and Ingela Romare: 'Filming the New Society' in *Mozambique Revolution*, No. 49, October-December 1971, p. 18, and Malmer and Romare: 'Das Mais Belas Experiencias das Nossas Vidas'/'Among the Best Experiences of Our Lives' in *A Voz da Revolução*, No. 6, November-December 1971).

for three weeks were accompanied by Joaquim Chissano[1]—shot a documentary
film for the official Swedish television company in the province of Cabo Delgado.
With their earlier productions on the liberation struggles in Southern Africa[2], the
one hour long documentary—televised in early 1972 with the title 'In Our Country
the Bullets Start to Blossom'[3]—"played an extraordinarily important role for the
formation of the [Swedish] opinion".[4] In June 1974, Anders Johansson of *Dagens
Nyheter* also returned to the areas he had first visited with Eduardo Mondlane in
February 1968, documenting FRELIMO's advances to a wide readership.[5]

The year 1973 would to a large extent represent an official breakthrough for
FRELIMO in Sweden and the other Nordic countries. In April 1973, the UN/OAU
Conference on Colonialism and Apartheid in Southern Africa[6] was hosted by the
government of Norway.[7] Described by FRELIMO as "a remarkable gathering of
the forces of worldwide public opinion in support of the liberation struggle in
Africa"[8], the Mozambican movement was particularly pleased. Visiting the Foreign
Ministry in Stockholm after the conference, Vice-President dos Santos described it
as "a victory", notably with regard to the liberation movements' right to represent
the peoples of their countries.[9] FRELIMO's official organ *Mozambique Revolution*
underlined the fact that the liberation movements had "attended the conference on
a basis of full equality with the representatives of independent states".[10] And in
June 1973, FRELIMO's Secretary for Information Jorge Rebelo stated to the
United Nations Decolonization Committee in New York that

> the fact that [the conference] was strongly supported by the [Nordic][11] countries and, indeed,
> took place in a country that happens to be a member of NATO, marks a new phase in our
> international relations. [...] We wish to express our appreciation for the role which was played
> by the [Nordic] countries. [...] There is nothing strange in this, as Sweden, Norway, Denmark
> and Finland have been consistently supporting our struggle. But we consider that the new

1. Telephone conversation with Lennart Malmer, 7 October 1999, and FRELIMO: *Boletim de Informacão*, No. 71, 30 December 1971, p. 9 (MHA). In May 1996, President Chissano vividly recalled the visit by the Swedish television team (Interview with Joaquim Chissano, p. 39).
2. In 1969, Malmer and Romare produced two documentaries on Southern Africa for the Swedish public television company, entitled 'Södra Afrika: Ett Nytt Vietnam?' ('Southern Africa: Another Vietnam?') and 'Vi Älskar Frihet Mer än Fred' ('We Love Freedom More than Peace'). The latter introduced ANC of South Africa, SWAPO of Namibia and FRELIMO to the TV viewers. In 1971, their 'Moçambique Är Vårt Land' ('Mozambique Is Our Country')—a production in five parts about FRELIMO and the Mozambican liberation struggle—further familiarized the public with the nationalist cause in Mozambique.
3. Lennart Malmer och Ingela Romare: 'I Vårt Land Börjar Kulorna Blomma', Sveriges Television (SVT), 1972.
4. Ulf von Strauss: 'Till Olydnadens Lov: Lennart Malmers Filmskap' ('Praising Disobedience: Lennart Malmer's Film-Making Craft') in *Film & TV*, No. 2, 1991, p. 8.
5. See Anders Johansson: 'På marsch med gerillan' ('Marching with the guerrillas') in *Dagens Nyheter*, 19 July 1974. Like the impressions of Malmer and Romare, Johansson's reports were highlighted by FRELIMO. See Anders Johansson: 'The People Are Still Being Bombed' in *Mozambique Revolution*, No. 59, April-June 1974, p. 6, and Johansson: 'O Progresso É Evidente'/'Progress Is Obvious' in *A Voz da Revolução*, No. 22, May-July 1971, p. 12.
6. The actual title of the UN/OAU conference was the International Conference of Experts for the Support of Victims of Colonialism and Apartheid in Southern Africa.
7. On the Oslo conference, see Eriksen in Eriksen (ed.) op. cit., pp. 56-72. The conference documents were published in two volumes by the Scandinavian Institute of African Studies (Olav Stokke and Carl Widstrand (eds): *The UN-OAU Conference on Southern Africa, Oslo, 9-14 April 1973*, Scandinavian Institute of African Studies, Uppsala, 1973).
8. 'The Oslo Conference: A Major Victory' in *Mozambique Revolution*, No. 55, April-June 1973, p. 19.
9. Anders Möllander: Memorandum ('Minnesanteckningar från samtal 1973 04 17 med representanter för FRELIMO'/'Notes from conversations 1973 04 17 with representatives of FRELIMO'), CCHA, Stockholm, 26 April 1973 (MFA).
10. *Mozambique Revolution*, No. 55, April-June 1973, p. 19. France, Great Britain and the United States declined invitations to attend the UN/OAU conference.
11. 'Scandinavian' in the original text.

approach they are taking—now supporting us politically and not only on a humanitarian basis—is an important development.[1]

In Sweden, the wider recognition was immediately manifest. Proceeding from Oslo, representatives of eight liberation movements recognized by OAU[2] travelled to Stockholm, where a number of meetings and activities were arranged by the government and NGOs.[3] The visit was given prominent attention by the newspapers[4], radio and television, and Foreign Minister Krister Wickman hosted a reception for the representatives at the Ministry for Foreign Affairs.[5] As a reflection of the significance accorded to the liberation movements in the Portuguese colonies[6], Wickman, in addition, invited the MPLA President Agostinho Neto, the FRELIMO Vice-President Marcelino dos Santos and Lucette Andrade Cabral from PAIGC[7] to a separate working luncheon.[8]

Shortly thereafter, the situation in Mozambique dramatically occupied the headlines all over the world when on 10 July 1973 in *The Times* in London the British priest Adrian Hastings published information gathered from Spanish Catholic missionaries about a massacre at the village of Wiriyamu, south of the provincial capital Tete. According to Hastings' sources, a staggering 400 villagers had been slaughtered there by Portuguese paratroopers in mid-1972.[9] The information—published in connection with the Portuguese Premier Caetano's state visit to Britain in July 1973—was far from the only account of massacres in Mozambique[10], but caused an international uproar. In Sweden, the news set in motion a chain of reactions which further isolated Portugal and enhanced the cause of FRELIMO.

Interviewed by the social democratic evening paper *Aftonbladet*, Foreign Minister Wickman announced four days after the publication of Hastings' report that Sweden would "initiate a broad political action against Portugal's colonial wars in Africa".[11] He also criticized the Swedish private companies' investments in Portugal, which he characterized as "offensive" and the result of "dubious and short-sighted speculation".[12] The same day, Wickman stated on Swedish radio that as a first step he had requested an extraordinary meeting of the UN Decolonization Committee and that official exchanges with Portugal at ministerial level were "out

1. United Nations: 'Statement by Mr. Jorge Rebelo, Frente de Libertação de Moçambique (FRELIMO), at the 915th meeting of the Special Committee of 24, on 13 June 1973' (MFA).
2. FNLA and MPLA of Angola, PAIGC of Guinea-Bissau and Cape Verde, FRELIMO of Mozambique, SWAPO of Namibia, ANC of South Africa and ZANU and ZAPU of Zimbabwe.
3. Anders Möllander: Memorandum ('Besök 1973 04 17-18 av representanter för afrikanska befrielserörelser'/ 'Visit 1973 04 17-18 by representatives of African liberation movements'), CCHA, Stockholm, 16 April 1973 (SDA).
4. See, for example, Per Wästberg: 'Oslokonferensen om Sydafrikas rastyranni: Apartheid hot mot världsfreden' ('The Oslo conference on South Africa's racial tyranny: Apartheid threat against world peace') in *Dagens Nyheter*, 19 April 1973.
5. Cf. the interview with Ben Amathila (SWAPO): "After the [Oslo] conference [...], Krister Wickman held a reception for all the liberation movements' representatives at the Foreign Ministry in Stockholm. After that, Sweden almost recognized the liberation movements as official representatives of their peoples. That was a very significant development towards recognition and support" (p. 65).
6. The focus on the Portuguese colonies by the solidarity movement was similarly illustrated when AGIS arranged a public meeting where only Agostinho Neto (MPLA), Marcelino dos Santos (FRELIMO) and Gil Fernandes (PAIGC) addressed the audience.
7. PAIGC's Secretary General Amílcar Cabral was assassinated on 20 January 1973.
8. Gun-Britt Andersson: Memorandum ('Besök i Sverige av befrielserörelserepresentanter'/'Visit to Sweden by representatives of liberation movements'), Ministry for Foreign Affairs, Stockholm, 25 May 1973 (MFA).
9. Hastings' research was published in 1974 in Great Britain by Search Press under the title *Wiriyamu*. It was published the same year in Swedish (Adrian Hastings: *Wiriyamu*, Gummessons Bokförlag, Falköping, 1974).
10. Cf. 'Wiriyamu: Not an Isolated Crime' in *Mozambique Revolution*, No. 55, April-June 1973, pp. 23-24.
11. Gunnar Fredriksson: 'Sverige till attack mot Portugals kolonialkrig' ('Sweden launches attack against Portugal's colonial wars') in *Aftonbladet*, 14 July 1973.
12. Ibid.

of the question".[1] The news of the Wiriyamu massacre was, similarly, received with disgust and anger by the Swedish liberal opposition. The future chairman of the Liberal Party and Deputy Prime Minister Per Ahlmark[2]—who as early as in 1961 had condemned Portugal's colonial wars and EFTA membership[3]—was particularly outspoken. Reacting to the news, he wrote an open letter in the liberal newspaper *Expressen* to the managing directors of the Swedish companies with significant economic interests in Portugal[4], stating that

> you contribute to prolonging the bloodbaths in three areas of Africa. In practice, you economically assist the Caetano regime to commit genocide. [...] Will you continue to [...] pump money into the Portuguese economy or do you draw any new conclusions from the debate and reports of the last week?[5]

The news of the massacre galvanized the Swedish political opinion against Portugal, which at the United Nations was characterized by the government as "a tottering and ramshackle colonial empire".[6] Wickman's initiative to launch a broad action enjoyed wide support. His proposal to convene a special meeting of the UN Decolonization Committee was, similarly, supported by the member countries. The Committee of 24 met in New York on 20 July 1973. In his statement to the UN body, ambassador Kaj Björk declared that

> the Swedish government had suggested that a meeting [...] would be useful in order to stress the duty of the Portuguese government to allow [an] impartial international investigation into all aspects of its warfare in the African territories still under its domination. [...] [A]ll states must take part in the campaign to abolish every remnant of colonial exploitation [, of which] Portugal's African dependencies are the most striking example. [...] International pressure must be increased in order to bring an end to this shameful state of affairs [and] [a]id to the liberation movements [...] must be granted by the industrialized states. [...] The future of Angola, Mozambique and Guinea-Bissau must be decided by their respective peoples.[7]

The Decolonization Committee supported the proposal for an international commission of inquiry. In turn, the proposal was adopted by the Nordic Foreign Ministers at a meeting in Stockholm on 30 August 1973[8], and a draft resolution to this effect was in early November 1973 submitted by Sweden to the UN General Assembly.[9] Endorsed by the assembly, the UN investigators were, however, barred

---

1. Ministry for Foreign Affairs: 'Intervju med utrikesminister Krister Wickman i Dagens Eko, 14.7 1973' ('Interview with Foreign Minister Krister Wickman in [the news programme] Dagens Eko, 14.7 1973'), Press department, Stockholm, 24 July 1973 (MFA).
2. At the time a Liberal MP, Ahlmark served as chairman of the Liberal Party from 1975 to 1978. He was Deputy Prime Minister and Minister of Labour between 1976 and 1978.
3. 'Portugal ur EFTA!' ('Portugal out of EFTA!') in *Dagens Nyheter*, 1 July 1961. As a young parliamentarian for the opposition Liberal Party, Ahlmark was in the mid-1960s the most active Swedish politician against Portugal's EFTA membership and a strong supporter of assistance to the Southern African liberation movements (see Sellström Volume I, pp. 479-83). In a book published in 1994—*Vänstern och Tyranniet* ('The Left and the Tyranny'), Timbro, Stockholm—he vehemently criticized Swedish "fellow travellers" with Communism and totalitarianism during what he called the "crazy quarter century" from the end of the 1960s until the beginning of the 1990s. In the process, he seems to have forgotten his own political past.
4. The companies were: Algots, Billeruds, Eriksbergs, Gefa, Kockums, Mölnlycke, STAB, Wicanders and Öberg & Co.
5. Per Ahlmark: 'Ni stöder portugisernas massmord' ('You support the genocide by the Portuguese') in *Expressen*, 18 July 1973.
6. Ministry for Foreign Affairs: 'Speech by ambassador Kaj Björk at the UN Special Committee of 24 meeting concerning Mozambique in New York, 20 July 1973', Press department, Stockholm, 23 July 1973 (MFA).
7. Ibid.
8. 'Press release', 4 October 1973, in Ministry for Foreign Affairs: *Documents on Swedish Foreign Policy: 1973*, Stockholm, 1976, p. 150. It should be noted that Denmark, Iceland and Norway together with Portugal formed part of the NATO alliance.
9. 'Press release', 7 November 1973, in Ministry for Foreign Affairs: *Documents on Swedish Foreign Policy: 1973*, Stockholm, 1976, p. 152.

by the Caetano regime from entry into any of the Portuguese colonies. In the case of the Wiriyamu massacre, they, however, conducted investigations in Europe and Tanzania and found Hastings' revelations to be true.[1]

Sweden's initiative against Portugal was combined with expanded political and material support for the liberation movements in Angola, Guinea-Bissau and Mozambique. In his speech to the UN Decolonization Committee, ambassador Björk had on 20 July 1973 urged the Western countries to extend assistance to the nationalist organizations. To set an example, the Swedish government decided the same day to more than double the allocation to FRELIMO, which was increased from 2 MSEK in 1972/73 to 5 million in 1973/74.[2] More significant than the amount—which was still quite modest—was that the focus of the support from then on shifted from FRELIMO's refugee programmes in Tanzania to the movement's non-military activities in the liberated areas in Mozambique. This approach—recommended by the Oslo conference[3]—had been requested by Marcelino dos Santos during his visit to Stockholm in April 1973.[4]

The changed focus was underlined by Foreign Minister Wickman in an interview with the French journal *Afrique-Asie* in September 1973, where he stated that "the goal of [Sweden's assistance] is to support the civilian activities of the liberation movements in the liberated areas". In the interview—where Wickman also spoke about Vietnam and stressed the community of interests between non-aligned Sweden and the liberation movements in the Cold War context—he explained that

> it is essential for [Sweden]—from the point of view of our own policy of neutrality—to uphold the rights of small states to independence against any power or group of powers that may threaten their autonomy. Moreover, the Swedish government is convinced that the demands of the oppressed peoples [...] will not be silenced. [...] A long-term peace policy must be based on the will to meet the demands of the oppressed peoples for change. This means that within the framework of what is politically possible and practical, Sweden supports the political liberation of peoples from colonialism and other outside pressures. For this reason, the material and moral support we extend to the national liberation movements becomes a natural element in Sweden's foreign policy. [...]
>
> [The] UN recommendations constitute a political and formal basis for Sweden's assistance [to] the liberation movements in Africa. The goal of our assistance, which has a humanitarian form and content, is to support the civilian activities of the liberation movements in the liberated areas. [...] Over and above our own disbursement of aid, Sweden makes use of the diplomatic and political means which we consider appropriate.[5]

The nationalist organizations were at the same time granted broader recognition in other respects. The increased allocations to the movements in the Portuguese colonies—and the extension of official assistance also to ANC of South Africa and ZAPU of Zimbabwe[6]—were combined in 1973 with new politico-administrative

1. Thomas H. Henriksen: *Mozambique: A History*, Rex Collings, London, with David Philip, Cape Town, 1978, p. 216.
2. Ministry for Foreign Affairs: 'Beslut' ('Decision'): 'Bistånd till FRELIMO' ('Assistance to FRELIMO'), Stockholm, 20 July 1973 (MFA).
3. The 'Programme of Action' adopted at the April 1973 Oslo conference stated that "[s]pecial reference should be made to the large-scale needs in the liberated areas for the provision of essential supplies for the populations and for national reconstruction" (cited in Stokke and Widstrand (eds) op. cit. (Vol. I), p. 32).
4. Ernst Michanek: 'Brev till Konungen' ('Letter to the King'): 'Stöd till Frelimo' ('Support to FRELIMO'), SIDA, Stockholm, 19 July 1973 (SDA).
5. 'Interview (September) with the Foreign Minister, Mr. Wickman, in the special [issue on Sweden] of the journal *Afrique-Asie*' in Ministry for Foreign Affairs: *Documents on Swedish Foreign Policy: 1973*, Stockholm, 1976, pp. 62-64.
6. In February 1973, the Swedish government decided to extend official assistance to ANC of South Africa and ZAPU of Zimbabwe.

procedures. Based on the regulatory framework for Sweden's official aid relations with independent states, a routine of official annual negotiations with the liberation movements was introduced. Doing away with *ad hoc* requests and decisions throughout the financial year, the annual negotiations became important events between donor and recipients, encompassing political discussions, follow-up of previous grants and plans for continued assistance.

The annual negotiations were initially held in Dar es Salaam, Tanzania, or Lusaka, Zambia.[1] While the Swedish delegations normally included officials from the Ministry for Foreign Affairs and SIDA[2], the liberation movements were as a rule represented at the highest political level.[3] The deliberations were formalized through a signed protocol—agreed minutes—which together with a detailed budget served as the steering document for the cooperation during the following year.[4] The routine did not only introduce a significant—and highly appreciated[5]—element of stability in the aid relationship[6], but amounted to an informal, official recognition of the liberation movements.[7] On a par with the independent countries receiving Swedish development assistance, they were from 1973 from the point of view of protocol and official administration for all practical purposes approached as bilateral partners. In brief, the liberation movements were not only seen as resistance organizations against oppressive regimes, but as legitimate 'governments-in-waiting'.

Concentration on the Liberated Areas

By 1973, FRELIMO had assumed the position of a *de facto* government in large areas of northern Mozambique. In addition to the projects set up by the Mozam-

---

1. The annual negotiations with ZANU of Mozambique and SWAPO of Namibia were later held in Maputo, Mozambique, and Luanda, Angola, respectively.
2. Remarkably, Ernst Michanek, SIDA's Director General until 1979—at the same time chairing the Consultative Committee on Humanitarian Assistance—never led a Swedish delegation to official negotiations with a Southern African liberation movement.
3. In the case of FRELIMO, Janet Mondlane led the first official negotiations with Sweden in September 1973. She was *inter alia* seconded by Daniel Mbanze, who in July 1975 became Vice-Minister for Home Affairs in independent Mozambique. In May 1974, the FRELIMO delegation was led by Marcelino dos Santos and Joaquim Chissano. On the often unequal balance between the official delegations from Sweden and the liberation movements, see the interview with Lindiwe Mabuza (ANC), p. 137.
4. The cycle of annual negotiations was initiated through negotiations with FRELIMO, MPLA, SWAPO and ZANU in September 1973 (Letter from Anders Möllander ('Bistånd till FRELIMO'/'Assistance to FRELIMO') to the Swedish embassy in Dar es Salaam, Stockholm, 23 August 1973) (SDA). Adjusted to the Swedish financial year, negotiations were held in May 1974 with PAIGC (in Conakry), ANC, FRELIMO and MPLA (in Dar es Salaam) and with SWAPO, ZANU and ZAPU (in Lusaka) (Letter from Astrid Bergqvist ('Överläggningar med FRELIMO ang. biståndsprogram för 1974/75'/'Negotiations with FRELIMO re. cooperation programme for 1974/75') to the Swedish embassy in Dar es Salaam, Stockholm, 20 March 1974) (SDA).
5. See, for example, the interviews with ZANU's Kumbirai Kangai (p. 213) and SWAPO's Aaron Mushimba (pp. 84-85).
6. During the negotiations with FRELIMO in Dar es Salaam in September 1973, the Swedish delegation raised the question of longer term commitments to the liberation movement (CCHA: Memorandum ('Stöd till FRELIMO'/'Support to FRELIMO'), SIDA, Stockholm, 5 November 1973) (SDA). The idea was that the annual allocation for a given year should serve as a firm planning figure for the following year. In January 1975, Per Ahlmark and Billy Olsson of the Liberal Party submitted a parliamentary motion to that effect, "requesting long-term agreements" [with the Southern African liberation movements] which will secure rapidly growing Swedish assistance" (Swedish Parliament 1975: Motion No. 1165, Riksdagens Protokoll 1975, p. 16). The principle was implemented in the case of ANC of South Africa and SWAPO of Namibia from the early 1980s.
7. In 1973, the Danish, Norwegian and Swedish diplomatic and aid representations in Dar es Salaam started to coordinate their positions towards FRELIMO, discussing shared financial support to the running costs of the Mozambican liberation movement's civilian institutions in Tanzania (Letter from Göran Hasselmark ('Bistånd till Frelimo'/'Assistance to FRELIMO') to the Ministry for Foreign Affairs, Dar es Salaam, 6 August 1973) (SDA). The discussions—held with FRELIMO's Vice-President Marcelino dos Santos—paved the way for joint Nordic development assistance projects in independent Mozambique, such as the Mozambique-Nordic Agricultural Programme (MONAP).

bique Institute in favour of the refugees in Tanzania—notably the secondary school in Bagamoyo, the refugee centre and primary school at Tunduru and the Dr. Américo Boavida Hospital at Mtwara[1]—the movement administrated the liberated areas "as a proto-independent state, with external trade, diplomatic relations and services to the inhabitants".[2] While engaged in a war, FRELIMO—like PAIGC—laid the foundations for a new society by providing social services and developing the rural economy. A publication by the Mozambique Institute noted in 1971 that "our life has two major aspects: the armed struggle against Portuguese colonialism and the gigantic undertaking of constructing a new nation, socially, economically and politically".[3]

The challenges were enormous. In 1971, it was estimated that about one million people lived in the liberated areas of Mozambique.[4] Denied access to education and health care under the Portuguese, many had their situation dramatically changed through FRELIMO's efforts. As early as in 1966, more than 100,000 villagers in the Cabo Delgado province were, for example, inoculated against smallpox[5], and by 1971 FRELIMO had established 40 health clinics with more than 400 medical workers in the liberated areas.[6] Three years later, the number of open-air clinics had grown to 150, with a combined staff of around 750.[7] The achievements in the field of primary education and adult literacy were, similarly, impressive. By 1966, more than 10,000 students were attending FRELIMO classes, and by 1970 the number had trebled.[8] Many more participated in the literacy programmes. In 1974, there were some 200 'bush schools' in the FRELIMO-controlled areas,[9] often kept mobile to escape bombings by the Portuguese.

To turn the liberated zones into viable economic entities—able to feed the local population as well as support the freedom fighters[10]—FRELIMO paid serious attention to agricultural production. Various co-operative systems were introduced and—largely inspired by PAIGC—a barter economy with people's stores was established.[11] The first *lojas do povo* were set up in 1966.[12] They were created to serve the peasants with imported goods, such as textiles, agricultural tools and household utensils, which were bartered for agricultural products. Until the early 1970s, the system was, however, affected by a lack of supplies.[13] Nevertheless, a functioning exchange network was established, eventually resulting in exports of cashew nuts, sesame seeds and Makonde wood carvings to Tanzania. In 1973, FRELIMO organized exports of more than 200 tons of cashew nuts and 500 tons of sesame seeds.[14]

1. Situated just north of the Mozambican border, the Dr. Américo Boavida Hospital largely served the population in the liberated areas of Cabo Delgado. It was named after a prominent black Angolan doctor, killed in a Portuguese helicopter attack on MPLA in eastern Angola in 1968.
2. Henriksen op. cit., p. 204.
3. The Mozambique Institute: *Mozambique and the Mozambique Institute 1972*, Dar es Salaam, [no date], p. 1.
4. Ibid, p. 57.
5. Isaacman and Isaacman op. cit., p. 95.
6. The Mozambique Institute op. cit., p. 6.
7. Letter from Janet Rae Mondlane, Mozambique Institute, to Save the Children Federation, [no place], 4 April 1974 (MHA).
8. Isaacman and Isaacman op. cit., p. 93.
9. Henriksen op. cit., p. 203.
10. In 1971, FRELIMO was reported to have 15,000 guerrilla fighters and 20,000 villagers in para-military militia (The Mozambique Institute op. cit., p. 1).
11. Both Portuguese and Tanzanian currencies were used, but the most common medium of exchange was salt (Mozambique Institute op. cit., p. 53). From 1973, Sweden supplied large quantities of salt to FRELIMO under the humanitarian assistance programme.
12. Isaacman and Isaacman op. cit., p. 96.
13. The Mozambique Institute op. cit., p. 53.
14. Henriksen op. cit., p. 203.

Official negotiations between the Swedish government and FRELIMO were held in Dar es Salaam in mid-September 1973, shortly after Foreign Minister Wickman's statement that assistance primarily should be channelled to the liberated areas. The expanded cooperation programme for 1973/74 reflected this approach. Of the 5 MSEK granted, not less than 3.1 million—two thirds of the allocation—was set aside for the areas held by FRELIMO.[1] Under the heading 'social welfare', an amount of 1.8 MSEK was allocated for the supply of clothes to an estimated number of 10,000 children under the age of twelve, as well as for condensed milk, tinned food and dried fruit.[2] A wide range of goods to a total value of 1.3 MSEK—including tools for agriculture, salt production, bee-keeping and wood carving in addition to salt, blankets, torches, transistor radios and watches—was, similarly, allocated to the people's stores as 'equipment for production and commerce'.[3] Of the remaining 1.9 MSEK, a total of 1.3 million was set aside as cash support for the running of the Mozambique Institute and of FRELIMO's Tunduru refugee centre in southern Tanzania[4], while 0.3 million was earmarked for goods to FRELIMO's medical and health programmes in Tanzania and Mozambique.[5] The same amount was, finally, set aside for the movement's agricultural farm in Zambia, covering the supply of trucks, tractors, seeds and agricultural equipment.[6]

Sweden's relations with FRELIMO from 1973 cleared the way for a more proactive assistance to the liberation movements in Southern Africa. With positive experiences from 1973/74[7], the wider approach was maintained in 1974/75, when the grant to FRELIMO was trebled from 5 to 15 MSEK. Of this amount, 6.4 million was set aside for children in the liberated areas and 2.4 million for goods to the *lojas do povo*.[8] The remaining balance was allocated as cash[9], commodities to FRELIMO's health and information sectors in Tanzania[10] and in the form of transport support, that is, mainly vehicles.[11]

In addition, outside the 1974/75 allocation the Swedish government decided in February 1975 to grant FRELIMO emergency assistance in the form of no less than

1. CCHA: Memorandum ('Stöd till Frelimo'/'Support to FRELIMO'), SIDA, Stockholm, 5 November 1973 (SDA).
2. Ibid. and Attachment No. 1 (SDA).
3. Ibid.
4. Ibid. The balance from the 1972/73 allocation should be used to provide the Tunduru camp with drinking water ('Agreed minutes of discussions on cooperation between delegations from Sweden and FRELIMO', Dar es Salaam, [no date, but September 1973]) (SDA).
5. CCHA: Memorandum ('Stöd till FRELIMO'/'Support to FRELIMO'), SIDA, Stockholm, 5 November 1973 and Attachment No. 1 (SDA).
6. Ibid. Also Lars M. Hultkvist: Memorandum ('Follow up [of] purchase programme - FRELIMO'), SIDA, Lusaka, 15 January 1975 (SDA). ZANU of Zimbabwe used the facilities offered by FRELIMO at its farm in Zambia (Interview with Joaquim Chissano, p. 41). As will be noted, the Swedish government later purchased a farm for ZANU not far from Lusaka.
7. Torgil Ringmar, Acting Director General of SIDA: 'Brev till Konungen' ('Letter to the King'): 'Stöd till FRELIMO' ('Support to FRELIMO'), SIDA, Stockholm, 10 July 1974 (SDA).
8. Ibid.
9. Ibid. The cash support to FRELIMO, the Mozambique Institute and the Tunduru settlement amounted to 2.6 MSEK in 1974/75. After the April 1974 coup in Portugal, it was agreed to re-allocate the funds for the procurement of up to fifteen trucks, to be used for the repatriation of people and equipment to Mozambique (Letter from Marcelino dos Santos to Knut Granstedt, Swedish ambassador to Tanzania, Dar es Salaam, 4 April 1975 and reply ('Exchange of letters') from Knut Granstedt to Marcelino dos Santos, Dar es Salaam, 4 April 1975) (SDA).
10. Ringmar: 'Brev till Konungen' ('Letter to the King') op. cit. The amount for the health sector was 1.1 MSEK and for FRELIMO's printing press 0.4 MSEK.
11. Ibid. The allocation for vehicles amounted to 0.7 MSEK.

20,000 tons of wheat.[1] The decision was in response to an urgent appeal by the liberation movement, underlining the difficult food situation in northern and southern Mozambique. While the impending return of some 110,000 refugees from Tanzania, Malawi and Zambia added to the challenge of resettling tens of thousands of *aldeamento* villagers in the north, floods in the Limpopo valley had caused near famine among a further 250,000 people in the south.[2]

From the resumption of the assistance to FRELIMO in 1971 until Mozambique's independence in June 1975, a total of 23 MSEK—including outstanding commitments—was disbursed in favour of the liberation movement.[3] In the absence of comprehensive FRELIMO accounts[4], it is difficult to assess the significance of the official Swedish assistance for the movement's civilian programmes in Tanzania and in the liberated areas of Mozambique. In the latter case, a FRELIMO commission concluded in the early 1970s that the plan to "raise the standard of living and to widen the internal market by producing those items which will help the people [to] become more self-reliant" as a minimum would need inputs estimated at around 60 million Tanzanian Shillings, at the time corresponding to 37.5 MSEK.[5] As the Swedish support to the liberated areas from mid-1973 to mid-1975 amounted to around 12 MSEK, it could be deduced that it did play a major role. Later statements by leading FRELIMO representatives confirm that this was the case. Interviewed in April 1996, the former Mozambican cabinet member Sérgio Vieira[6] said, for instance, that there was "a tremendous need" of assistance in the form of medicines, clothes and food:

> I would say as much as weapons. Weapons alone do not change life, but the clothes supplied [...] helped us to present something to the peasant in the liberated areas. He could get something in return for his production. It was fundamental to create a base of economic development and self-reliance.[7]

Jorge Rebelo, Mozambique's former Minister for Information, has similarly emphasized the wider context of the Swedish—and Nordic—support:

> We [...] knew that the West was not a monolithic entity and in our mobilization work we told the people that not all the capitalist countries were enemies. There were countries belonging to the Western bloc that supported the liberation struggle. That is why it was important that the Scandinavian countries supported us. Instead of talking in abstract terms, we could show that not all the Western countries were bad. But we had to prove it. When the people through the Mozambique Institute saw the medicines and books, we could say that they came from Sweden or Norway. It then became concrete. It helped us in our effort to break the dichotomy bad-good, West-East. [...] [The support] helped us to educate our people and change their image that the West was bad and that all the Eastern countries were our friends. We knew that it was

---

1. Beslut' ('Decision'): 'Svensk vetegåva till FRELIMO' ('Swedish donation of wheat to FRELIMO'), Ministry for Foreign Affairs, Stockholm, 6 February 1975 (SDA). Similar emergency donations in the form of food or clothes were often granted by the Swedish government to the liberation movements in Southern Africa, particularly after military attacks on the refugee settlements. The value of such relief assistance is not included in the disbursement figures given in the study.
2. Henriksen op. cit., p. 226.
3. See the accompanying table on disbursements from SIDA to FRELIMO.
4. Contained in a steel cabinet, the documents from the Mozambique Institute were lost in the port of Dar es Salaam. Loaded on a ship that was transporting the institute's possessions to Lourenço Marques (Maputo) after Mozambique's independence, the cabinet fell overboard (Conversation with Janet Mondlane, Maputo, 30 April 1996).
5. The Mozambique Institute op. cit., p. 55.
6. After independence, Vieira was *inter alia* responsible for security matters and served as Minister for Agriculture.
7. Interview with Sérgio Vieira, p. 55.

not so, but we needed something to substantiate that with. I think that it was at that moment that the seeds of the future relations were sown. [...]

The Nordic support enabled us to carry out programmes in education, health and information. Through cash contributions [...] we could develop economic activities in the liberated zones. It was important, because it is a fact that you cannot win a war by just firing against the enemy. We wanted to create a new life. For this we needed support. We could mobilize the people to cultivate, to produce maize and products which they could eat, but it was difficult for us to supply soap, medicines and other basics. The support from the Nordic countries filled this gap. [...] After independence, the Nordic support was thus seen as a continuity.[1]

In this context, it could be noted that the official Nordic support was perceived as being extended without any political or ideological conditions attached[2], while the crucial military assistance from the Soviet Union and China was seen in a different light. In the interview quoted above, Rebelo made it clear that

we knew that it was not because the Soviet Union liked Mondlane or the Mozambicans that they were giving us support. Nor China. They had their geo-strategic interests. There were certain moments —in fact many moments—when their support was given under very strict conditions. The basic condition was to support their policies and condemn [...] imperialism. Mobilizing our people, we wanted them to be aware of [this] situation. We received support from the socialist countries, but they had their reasons for that. They wanted something in return, either at that moment or later. On the other hand, they were our friends [...]. We depended absolutely on their support for the war effort. If we had questioned the reasons why they were giving the support, it could have been a disaster. But we knew.[3]

Independent Mozambique: The Relations Continue

On 25 April 1974, the Movement of the Armed Forces overthrew the Caetano regime in Portugal.[4] While FRELIMO's forces continued their forward advance—pushing into the Zambézia province in July 1974—soon after the coup MFA officers initiated political discussions with the Mozambican liberation movement. They culminated on 7 September 1974 in the signing of the Lusaka Accord, allowing for unequivocal transfer of power to FRELIMO without prior elections after nine months of transitional government.[5] The transitional government, led by Prime Minister Joaquim Chissano and composed of six FRELIMO and four Portuguese members, was installed on 20 September 1974. It served as a caretaker government until the formal independence of the People's Republic of Mozambique on 25 June 1975, when Samora Machel assumed the presidency.[6] FRELIMO's Vice-President, Marcelino dos Santos, was five days later appointed Minister for Development and Economic Planning, while Joaquim Chissano became independent Mozambique's first Minister for Foreign Affairs.

1. Interview with Jorge Rebelo, pp. 45-47.
2. See, for example, the interviews with Joaquim Chissano (p. 40), Janet Mondlane (p. 44) and Marcelino dos Santos (p. 48).
3. Interview with Jorge Rebelo, p. 45.
4. Janet Mondlane was at the time visiting Sweden for discussions with SIDA (Torgil Ringmar: 'Brev till Konungen'/'Letter to the King': 'Stöd till FRELIMO'/'Support to FRELIMO', SIDA, Stockholm, 10 July 1974) (SDA).
5. Two days after the Lusaka Accord, a white settler movement attempted a coup in Lourenço Marques (Maputo). Supported by some military commandos, the self-proclaimed 'Dragons of Death' captured the radio station and blew up an arsenal outside the capital. The rebellion was crushed by a joint force of Portuguese and FRELIMO troops. Further disturbances took place in October 1974.
6. Sweden officially recognized the People's Republic of Mozambique on 25 June 1975 (Ministry for Foreign Affairs: *Documents on Swedish Foreign Policy: 1975*, Stockholm, 1977, p. 267).

Thanking the Africa Groups:
FRELIMO Vice-President
Marcelino dos Santos with
Sören Lindh in Stockholm,
April 1975 (Photo: Anders
Gunnartz)

Consultations between the Swedish government and FRELIMO on future bilateral relations—including development cooperation—were initiated in early 1975. Leading a large delegation, Marcelino dos Santos visited Stockholm in mid-April 1975.[1] In addition to meetings with the Ministry for Foreign Affairs[2], SIDA and AGIS—which were all invited to the independence celebrations in June—he was received by Prime Minister Palme.

Underlining the close links with FRELIMO, Palme stated that people "in Sweden had identified with FRELIMO's struggle not only as a struggle against colonialism, but also due to the social and ideological objectives expressed in FRELIMO's programme".[3] In his response, dos Santos described Sweden as "a model" for other Western countries, stating that it had a particularly important role to play within the Non-Aligned Movement.[4] The FRELIMO Vice-President also explained that the government of independent Mozambique would follow the United Nations decision on sanctions against Rhodesia[5], as well as extend political support to ANC of South Africa. However, Mozambique's position made it difficult to make "too many statements" regarding South Africa.[6] On the latter point, Palme mentioned that he had recently met Oliver Tambo and that the ANC leader had ex-

1. The delegation visited all the Nordic countries. In an interview in May 1996, Marcelino dos Santos said that "[w]e went to thank everybody for the support they had given us during the struggle for national liberation" (Interview with Marcelino dos Santos, p. 51).

2. Ann Wilkens and Arne Ström: Memorandum ('FRELIMO-besök i Sverige'/'FRELIMO visit to Sweden'), Ministry for Foreign Affairs, Stockholm, 6 May 1975 (SDA).

3. Ann Wilkens and Mikael Dahl: Memorandum ('Besök av FRELIMO-delegation hos statsministern'/'Visit by FRELIMO delegation to the Prime Minister'), Ministry for Foreign Affairs, Stockholm, 14 May 1975 (SDA). The meeting between dos Santos and Palme took place on 18 April 1975.

4. Ibid.

5. After repeated military incursions by Rhodesian forces into Mozambique, the Maputo government closed the border with Rhodesia in March 1976. This notably meant that the Smith regime no longer could use the ports of Beira and Maputo for exports and imports.

6. Ibid. Dos Santos referred *inter alia* to the fact that some 150,000 Mozambicans worked as migrant labourers in South Africa.

pressed fears that South Africa "would be forgotten in the process which is now taking place in Southern Africa".[1] Against this background, Palme concluded, it was "important to show solidarity, even if the liberation of the South African people to all appearances would take a long time".[2]

Before Mozambique's formal independence, Palme thus initiated discussions with its leaders on support for the continued liberation struggles in Southern Africa. The close, personal exchange of ideas—sometimes candidly sincere and critical, such as after the Nkomati Accord between Mozambique and South Africa in March 1984[3]—remained a permanent feature until 1986, when the Swedish Prime Minister was assassinated and the Mozambican President Machel died in a mysterious plane crash. Considerable Swedish resources were in the meantime channelled via SIDA as official humanitarian assistance to ZANU and ANC in Mozambique. Direct and indirect assistance would notably be extended in favour of Zimbabwean refugees in the country. In 1977 alone, no less than 22.5 MSEK was allocated to ZANU, the Mozambican government and UNHCR.[4]

In his independence address to the Mozambican nation, President Machel stated on 25 June 1975 that "we [...] consider it important to develop our relations with the Scandinavian countries, Finland and Holland, which were able to understand the justness of the anti-colonial cause". [5] In the case of Sweden, the humanitarian support to FRELIMO was transformed into development assistance to independent Mozambique, which was included among the priority countries for Sweden's development cooperation. The transition was, according to Marcelino dos Santos, "completely natural".[6]

Ten years after receiving the first Swedish grant to the Mozambique Institute in Dar es Salaam, Janet Mondlane could in her new capacity as National Director of International Cooperation in the Ministry for Development and Economic Planning maintain her contacts with Sweden and from a different platform discuss a

1. This was at the time of the so called 'détente exercise' in response to the developments in Angola and Mozambique. During his first visit to Sweden in November-December 1974, ANC's Thabo Mbeki had criticized Joaquim Chissano for having allegedly stated that "apartheid was an internal South African question in which the government of [independent] Mozambique had no intention of getting involved" (Arne Ström: Memorandum ('Minnesanteckningar från möte med Thabo Mbeki, informationssekreterare till ANC's exekutiv'/'Notes from meeting with Thabo Mbeki, information secretary on ANC's executive'), SIDA, Stockholm, 2 December 1974) (SDA). In November 1974, Portuguese newspapers referred to a secret non-aggression treaty between FRELIMO and South Africa. Some observers—quoting FRELIMO sources—have claimed that such an agreement did exist. South Africa is said to have agreed not to intervene in Mozambique, in return for which independent Mozambique would not allow ANC to operate from its territory (Hans Abrahamsson and Anders Nilsson: *Mozambique: The Troubled Transition*, Zed Books, London and New Jersey, 1995, pp. 40-41 and 241. See also David Martin and Phyllis Johnson: *The Struggle for Zimbabwe*, Faber and Faber, London and Boston, 1981, pp. 138-40). After Mozambique's independence, the presence of ANC in the country was fraught with difficulties.
2. Wilkens and Dahl: Memorandum (op. cit.), 14 May 1975.
3. On the Nkomati accord, Sweden, Mozambique and ANC, see the chapter 'Attacks and Assistance in the Forward Areas: Swaziland and Mozambique'.
4. CCHA: 'Biståndsframställning från UANC/Zimbabwe' ('Request for assistance from UANC/Zimbabwe'), Ministry for Foreign Affairs, Stockholm, 27 January 1978 (SDA).
5. Cited in *Mozambique Revolution*, No. 61, June 1975, p. 23. See also the interviews with Jorge Rebelo (p. 47) and Marcelino dos Santos. In the latter interview, dos Santos explained that the only Western governments that were formally invited to the independence celebrations were those of the Nordic countries and Holland. However, using "trickery" (*artimanha*) the British Minister of International Cooperation—who was visiting Mozambique at the time—also "managed to infiltrate" the festivities (pp. 50-51).
6. Interview with Marcelino dos Santos, p. 50.

longer term relationship. Initially focused on agriculture[1] and education[2], but with important components of technical assistance and budget support, the assistance to independent Mozambique grew quickly. During the period from 1974/75 to 1994/95, it amounted—in fixed prices (1995)—to a total of 11.5 billion SEK.[3] From the point of view of total resource transfers, Mozambique in the late 1980s became the most important recipient of official Swedish assistance. From the very beginning, the country also attracted a number of non-governmental organizations. A particularly appreciated role was to be played by the Africa Groups, which from 1976 with official financial support followed up their campaigns during the liberation struggle by recruiting qualified 'solidarity workers'[4] for placement in Mozambique.[5]

One year after Mozambique's independence, the Social Democratic Party lost the parliamentary elections in Sweden and a non-socialist coalition government led by the leader of the Centre Party, Thorbjörn Fälldin, was installed. The change in government did not, however, result in a change in Sweden's policies towards Southern Africa. In addition to Fälldin himself[6], his cabinet included several members who had been actively involved in the early solidarity movement with Southern Africa in general and with FRELIMO in particular. This was notably the case with Ola Ullsten from the Liberal Party, who became Minister for International Development Cooperation.[7] When President Samora Machel paid his first official

---

1. One of the first, major development initiatives was the joint Mozambique-Nordic Agricultural Programme, coordinated by SIDA. It should be noted that the government of Iceland also contributed to the programme.
2. As later would be the case in Angola, Zimbabwe, Namibia and South Africa, many cabinet members in Mozambique had through official Swedish humanitarian support directly or indirectly entered into contacts with Sweden. The Minister for Education and Culture, Graça Simbine—the future wife of President Machel (and, in 1998, of President Mandela of South Africa)—had, for example, left Mozambique on a Methodist scholarship to study in Portugal, from where she joined FRELIMO and the Mozambique Institute in Tanzania in late 1972. The Methodist scholarship programme was largely financed by the Swedish government (Sellström Volume I, pp. 459-61).
3. Sida op. cit., p. 27.
4. According to AGIS, "to be a 'solidarity worker' means something more than to have a suitable profession. It means, for example, [...] to see the solidarity work in Africa as [...] part of the anti-imperialist work that is done both in Africa and within the solidarity work in Sweden" (AGIS: 'Recruitment activities by the Africa Groups of Sweden', Stockholm, December 1976; English original) (AGA).
5. An agreement between the government of Mozambique and the Africa Groups (AGIS) was entered into on 1 March 1977 ('Agreement between the Government of the People's Republic of Mozambique and the Africa Groups of Sweden concerning recruitment in Sweden of trained personnel [...] for work, on a solidarity basis, in Mozambique') (AGA). Three months later, the annual congress of the solidarity organization decided to organize the recruitment as an independent activity, eventually forming the Recruitment Organization of the Africa Groups, or—in Swedish—*Afrikagruppernas Rekryteringsorganisation* (ARO). Beginning with 10 solidarity workers in 1977, ARO from the early 1980s would annually have around 70 professionals—including medical doctors, engineers etc.—working in Mozambique, Angola, Guinea-Bissau, Cape Verde and Zimbabwe ('ARO: En Historia om Bistånd'/'ARO: A Story of Assistance' in *Afrikabulletinen*, No. 2, May 1989, pp. 4-5). Many of them made important contributions in the ANC and SWAPO settlements in Tanzania and Angola. Involved with practical solidarity and financed by SIDA, from the latter part of the 1970s ARO played an important role for the bridging of the initial gap between the NGO solidarity movement, SIDA and the Swedish government.
6. On Fälldin and his early contacts with Southern Africa, see Sellström Volume I, pp. 90-91. From the early 1970s, Fälldin had together with the chairman of the Liberal Party, Gunnar Helén, submitted parliamentary motions in favour of increased official Swedish support to the Southern African liberation movements.
7. On Ullsten and Southern Africa, see Sellström Volume I, pp. 103, 196 and 224-25. After a visit to Tanzania in 1964, Ullsten—at the time chairman of the Liberal Party Youth League—wrote in *Dagens Nyheter* that "it is difficult to find a better planned project than [the Mozambique Institute]" (Ola Ullsten: 'Strid flyktingström från Moçambique' ('Strong refugee stream from Mozambique') in *Dagens Nyheter*, 13 December 1964).

Enjoying a sauna at the Prime Minister's Harpsund residence in April 1977 (from left): Chief of protocol Sven Fredrik Hedin, Prime Minister Thorbjörn Fälldin, Mozambican President Samora Machel, Cooperation Minister Ola Ullsten and chargé d'affaires (Maputo) Göran Hasselmark (Photo: Sören Lindell/Folket)

visit to Sweden in April 1977, he was thus received as a national friend.[1] Invited to a sauna at the Prime Minister's summer residence at Harpsund, the Marxist-Leninist[2] Mozambican guerrilla leader and the non-socialist Swedish sheep-farmer found a lot of common ground.[3] The picture of President Machel, Prime Minister Fälldin and Cooperation Minister Ullsten having cold drinks after the sauna illustrates the close and non-partisan relationship established between the Southern African nationalist leaders and the Swedish government.

1. Interviewed in April 1996, Sérgio Vieira recalled: "[I]n 1977, there was a conservative government in Sweden. The Prime Minister was Mr. Fälldin. I was charged by our government to prepare an official visit and I went to Sweden before Samora Machel arrived. I discussed with our Swedish friends and was received by the Prime Minister. At a certain point I said: 'Mr. Prime Minister, there is something very sensitive that I really would like to ask you. During a long time, Olof Palme was a very close friend of ours and today he is the leader of the opposition. Would it be improper for President Machel to meet Olof Palme?' I received an answer that symbolized what Sweden was for us. He said: 'We would be surprised otherwise. Olof Palme is the one who contributed to the consensus in Sweden around our relationship with FRELIMO. Please, do see him'" (Interview with Sérgio Vieira, pp. 55-56). It could be noted that the situation was reversed when Vice-President Marcelino dos Santos in January 1983 paid an official visit to Sweden. Hosted by the Social Democratic government under Prime Minister Olof Palme—which had won the 1982 elections—at dos Santos' request he met Thorbjörn Fälldin. Fälldin had paid an official visit to Mozambique as Prime Minister in August 1981.
2. At the third FRELIMO congress in February 1977, the liberation front was transformed into a Marxist-Leninist party.
3. Machel's reception in April 1977 made a deep impression. Visiting Cuba in October 1977, he raised the question of Sweden with Fidel Castro. Late one evening, Castro and Machel called the Swedish chargé d'affaires, Lars-Hjalmar Wide, "praising the strong commitment by [...] Ola Ullsten and [...] Olof Palme for the countries in Southern Africa". At the same time, Machel recalled that he had been invited to a sauna by Prime Minister Fälldin, "which apparently had been an appreciated part of his visit to Sweden" (Letter by Lars-Hjalmar Wide to the Ministry for Foreign Affairs, Havanna, 12 October 1977) (MFA).

MPLA of Angola:
A Rockier Road

Limited Assistance

The Southern African Thirty Years' War for majority rule and national liberation started in February-March 1961 in Angola—'the jewel in the Portuguese imperial crown'[1]—when the Popular Movement for the Liberation of Angola (MPLA)[2] attacked the prisons in Luanda and FNLA[3] inspired rural insurrections in the northern parts of the country. The events led the same year to the first broader popular Swedish solidarity manifestation with the nationalist cause in the region[4], the so called 'Angola Help' launched by the liberal newspaper *Expressen* in favour of MPLA.[5] For a brief period, the campaign received an extraordinary response. However, the Angolan struggle was soon overshadowed by the question of apartheid South Africa and until the mid-1960s largely forgotten. Re-introduced by the Lund South Africa Committee and the *Syd- och Sydvästafrika* information bulletin in 1966, the solidarity movement would from then on support Agostinho Neto's MPLA, while the ruling Social Democratic Party at about the same time had brief, but close, contacts with Jonas Savimbi's UNITA[6] and the opposition Liberal Party towards the end of the 1960s established more lasting relations with Holden Roberto's FNLA.[7]

Nevertheless, without direct links to the leaders of the Angolan organizations[8] and in the absence of a major domestic mobilizing issue—such as the Mozambican Cabora Bassa project[9]—the situation in Angola was at the close of the 1960s less

---

1. Pedro Pezerat Correia: *Descolonização de Angola: A Jóia da Corona do Império Português* ('Decolonization of Angola: The Jewel in the Portuguese Imperial Crown'), Inquérito, Lisbon, 1991.
2. In Portuguese, *Movimento Popular de Libertação de Angola*. On the formation of MPLA, see Lúcio Lara: *Um Amplo Movimiento...: Itinerário do MPLA através de Documentos e Anotações* ('A Broad Movement...: MPLA's Itinerary through Documents and Notes'), Volume I - Until February 1961, LitoTipo, Luanda, 1998. This compilation by one of the foremost Angolan intellectuals and political leaders is a unique source on the origins of the Angolan nationalist movement.
3. In Portuguese, *Frente Nacional de Libertação de Angola*. UPA (*União das Populações de Angola*; Union of the Peoples of Angola) was behind the insurrections in northern Angola in March 1961. Together with the small Democratic Party of Angola (PDA), it formed the National Front for the Liberation of Angola (FNLA) the following year.
4. The Fund for the Victims of Racial Oppression in South Africa had been set up in September 1959 and the Swedish South Africa Committee was formed in March 1961 (see Sellström Volume I, pp. 137-46).
5. Ibid., pp. 384-94.
6. In Portuguese, *União Nacional para a Independência Total de Angola* (National Union for the Total Independence of Angola).
7. See Sellström Volume I, pp. 412-19.
8. Jonas Savimbi paid a short visit to Sweden in June 1967. Agostinho Neto's first visit took place in July 1970, after the International Conference of Support to the Peoples of the Portuguese Colonies, held in Rome, Italy. Olof Palme and the MPLA President also met in Lusaka during the Prime Minister's official visit to Zambia in September 1971. Neto would over the following years pay several visits to Sweden. Holden Roberto, finally, visited Sweden for the first time in November 1971.
9. There were no Swedish investments in Angola and the trade exchange between the two countries was marginal. When the international solidarity movement in response to an appeal from MPLA in the early 1970s launched a boycott against Angolan coffee, the Africa Groups responded that "there is no basis for [such] a campaign [in Sweden] yet" (Swedish Africa Groups: 'Circular letter No. 7', [no place], 20 December 1972) (AGA). Cf. the interview with Hillevi Nilsson, p. 328.

known in Sweden than the struggles in Guinea-Bissau or Mozambique. Thus, while the situation in Angola was not explicitly mentioned, both PAIGC and FRELIMO's Mozambique Institute were referred to when the Swedish parliament in May 1969 endorsed a policy of official humanitarian assistance to the liberation movements.[1] While support to PAIGC was extended from mid-1969, it was only in March 1971—at the same time as the assistance to FRELIMO was resumed—that MPLA was included among the liberation movements receiving humanitarian aid. The decision was largely influenced by the leaders of the Guinean and Mozambican organizations, notably PAIGC's Amílcar Cabral.[2] Of the three CONCP partners, MPLA was, however, the least favoured, with grants well below those given to PAIGC and FRELIMO. In addition, with combined allocations of 10 MSEK for the period 1971/72-1974/75[3], total disbursements to MPLA during the four years only amounted to 2.3 million, representing less than a quarter of the available funds.[4]

Several factors contributed to the limited allocations and to the low utilization of the Swedish assistance to MPLA. Contrary to the situation in both Guinea-Bissau and Mozambique—where PAIGC and FRELIMO were unchallenged—the wider Angolan nationalist movement was, in the first place, deeply divided. To the initial rivalry between MPLA and FNLA was added from 1966 the appearance of UNITA. Even before the collapse of the Lisbon regime in April 1974, the conflicts between the three reached an intensity that often suggested civil war rather than a joint nationalist effort. This had an impact in Sweden. The basic understanding between the ruling Social Democratic Party and the opposition Liberal Party regarding support to the liberation movements in the Portuguese colonies was in the case of Angola questioned by influential liberal voices[5], who also advocated assistance to FNLA.[6]

---

1. The first parliamentary motion explicitly mentioning MPLA was submitted by the Left Party Communists in January 1969 (Swedish Parliament 1969: Motion No. 404 in the First Chamber (Werner) and Motion No. 465 in the Second Chamber (Hermansson and others), Riksdagens Protokoll, 1969, pp. 10 and 4-6).
2. On the background to the decision, see Sellström Volume I, pp. 424-29. Cf. the interview with Paulo Jorge, p. 15.
3. For 1971/72: 0.5; 1972/73: 2.0; 1973/74: 3.5; and 1974/75: 4.0 MSEK.
4. Excluding the multi-bilateral aid to the MPLA school at Dolisie in Congo-Brazzaville through UNESCO. During the same period, 43.5 and 17.1 MSEK were disbursed in favour of PAIGC and FRELIMO, respectively.
5. Notably by David Wirmark and Olle Wästberg. As secretary general of the World Assembly of Youth (1958-64), Wirmark—a Liberal MP between 1971 and 1973—established close relations with Holden Roberto in the early 1960s. Wästberg—who as vice chairman of the Liberal Party Youth League accompanied FNLA on a mission into northern Angola in July-August 1969—was particularly active in favour of Roberto's movement during the first half of the 1970s. He became a Liberal MP in 1976. Carl Tham—SIDA's former Director General (1985-94)—served as the Liberal Party secretary from 1969 to 1976. Commenting upon the support to FNLA, he said in 1997 that "it was a reflection of a more anti-Communist position within the party, specifically by Olle Wästberg. [...] I guess that [he] was the one who demanded assistance to FNLA and that the party supported him. But the broader liberal opinion was very divided on this point" (Interview with Carl Tham, p. 342).
6. This argument was strengthened in December 1972, when MPLA and FNLA under the auspices of the Organization of African Unity formed a Supreme Council for the Liberation of Angola in Kinshasa, Zaire (*Conselho Supremo da Libertação de Angola*; CSLA). According to the agreement, Roberto of FNLA would preside over the CSLA, with Neto of MPLA as Vice-President. The agreement further stipulated that the two movements should immediately end all hostile acts towards each other and that membership of all bodies of the CSLA was to be based on parity. While the agreement initially drew pan-African applause, it proved, however, costly for MPLA. In the eyes of the Soviet Union, it "immediately lowered the prestige of MPLA [and the Soviet] assistance was suspended" (Conversation with Vladimir Shubin, p. 250). One of the main reasons why MPLA signed the agreement was that it would make it possible to use Zaire as a rear base. However, it soon transpired that the Mobutu government was not willing to open its territory to MPLA. MPLA guerrillas were not permitted to transit and its members were still subject to arrest in Zaire. Against this background, the agreement became hollow and eventually broke down.

Secondly, although MPLA via Zambia in May 1966 had opened an eastern front in the Angolan province of Moxico[1]—from there carrying the liberation effort to the central parts of the country—the concept of liberated zones was in these sparsely populated areas[2] less tangible than in Guinea-Bissau or in northern Mozambique. It was, in addition, only in mid-1972—four years after similar visits to PAIGC- and FRELIMO-held zones—that the first Swedish observers visited the MPLA-controlled areas in eastern Angola. Thirdly, MPLA itself became torn by internal divisions from 1973, eventually resulting in the breakaway of the so called Eastern Revolt[3] and Active Revolt[4] factions. Reminiscent of the divisions within FRELIMO in 1968-70, the MPLA crisis came openly to the fore after the Lisbon coup of 25 April 1974. This made the situation more ominous, provoking the intervention of the African states hosting the Angolan liberation movements, notably Congo-Brazzaville, Tanzania, Zaire and Zambia. The position taken by Zambia would in this context have a negative impact on the Swedish assistance to MPLA.

Last but not least, while PAIGC from the beginning appeared as an 'ideal organization' and the initial discords with FRELIMO regarding the form of the Swedish assistance were soon ironed out, MPLA approached the issue of humanitarian assistance in a less focused manner. As acknowledged by the MPLA leader Lúcio Lara, PAIGC's successful aid diplomacy was largely due to the direct, personal involvement by its Secretary General, Amílcar Cabral.[5] In the case of FRELIMO, Janet Mondlane and the Mozambique Institute were similarly vested with the authority to negotiate on behalf of the liberation movement. Despite close—and in the Western world unique—political contacts between President Agostinho Neto and other MPLA leaders with the Social Democratic Party and government, the aid

---

1. Barred from using Zairean territory to supply its forces inside Angola, Zambia's independence in October 1964 offered new possibilities to MPLA. An office was opened in Lusaka in 1965, preparing the activities on the eastern front (*frente leste*). On 18 May 1966—two months after the UNITA founding conference at Muangai in the same province—MPLA began military operations in the Cazombo area of Moxico. After UNITA attacks on the Benguela railway, Zambia broke the relations with Savimbi's organization in July 1967, instead supporting MPLA. MPLA established rearguard structures in western Zambia, and in January 1968 Neto announced that MPLA was moving its headquarters inside Angola. In August 1968—at about the same time as Mondlane presided over FRELIMO's second congress in the liberated areas in northern Mozambique—Neto led an MPLA conference in eastern Angola. As a result, MPLA moved its main military and civilian structures from Congo-Brazzaville and Tanzania to the border areas of eastern Angola/western Zambia, where it organized local village militias, cadre training, 'bush schools', health clinics, food production and 'people's stores'. As in Guinea-Bissau and Mozambique, the Portuguese responded by launching 'search and destroy campaigns'. With 56,000 soldiers, the Lisbon regime had at the beginning of 1969 concentrated almost half of its military forces in Africa to Angola (Letter from Gunnar Dryselius, Swedish ambassador to Portugal, to the Ministry for Foreign Affairs, Lisbon, 6 March 1969) (MFA). Entering into a truce with UNITA in the early 1970s—whereby the colonial army would leave Jonas Savimbi's movement alone as long as it attacked MPLA—the *tropa tuga* mounted increasing military campaigns against MPLA's positions, culminating in the so called Operation Attila in February 1972. "Raining napalm and defoliants in a 'scorched earth' assault on nationalist villages [in eastern Angola], they inflicted serious defeats on MPLA forces" (John Marcum: *The Angolan Revolution: Exile Politics and Guerrilla Warfare (1962-1976)*, Volume II, The MIT Press, Cambridge, Massachusetts, and London, England, 1978, p. 201). MPLA survived the assault, but the ensuing 're-adjustment movement' revealed internal contradictions, manifested in the appearance of Daniel Chipenda's Eastern Revolt faction. It should, however, be noted that MPLA had a strong urban base, particularly in the capital Luanda.
2. It was only in the 1930s that the Portuguese extended effective control over the eastern parts of Angola, described as 'the lands at the end of the world' (*as terras do fim do mundo*).
3. In Portuguese, *Revolta do Leste*.
4. In Portuguese, *Revolta Activa*.
5. Interview with Lúcio Lara: "We compared the figures [...] and saw the difference. The reason was the presence of Amílcar Cabral. He was very dynamic and always on top of [the] events" (p. 19).

relationship between the two, however, suffered from the lack of a focal point within the Angolan organization.[1]

More than any other liberation movement supported by Sweden, MPLA would over the years via visiting representatives or its offices in Stockholm, Dar es Salaam and Lusaka submit additional requests or amendments to already made agreements, introducing a high degree of indecision into the assistance.[2] Looking back in 1996, the former head of SIDA's procurement division, Stig Lövgren, described the cooperation with MPLA as his "greatest disappointment", explaining that

> I felt that we did not come anywhere [...]. Time just went on and on and nothing really happened. The specifications and the lists we received were so unrealistic. We tried to establish a close cooperation with the MPLA representatives in Stockholm and they were supposed to be in contact with their leaders. However, it did not work very well. It was very frustrating. [...] I often got the impression that the political decision [...] that Sweden should provide assistance to MPLA in itself was the most important. They did not seem to care very much about the content of the assistance. I am afraid that during these first years the technical side of the support to MPLA was not very effective.[3]

The first official Swedish grant to MPLA amounted to 500,000 SEK and covered the period from 1 July 1971 until 30 June 1972. Of the amount, 460,000 SEK—over 90 per cent—was utilized before the end of the financial year.[4] Based on this experience, the government increased the allocation to 2 MSEK in 1972/3.[5] However, from the beginning of 1973 the disbursements almost came to a standstill, reaching the extremely low total of 100,000 SEK—a mere 5 per cent of the funds available—by 30 June 1973.[6] Carried over to the following years, large unutilized balances would from then on complicate the administration of the assistance.[7]

Active NGO Solidarity

While the flow of official aid was reduced to a trickle, the opposition Centre and Liberal parties requested humanitarian assistance also to FNLA. Their main argument was that both MPLA and FNLA were recognized by OAU.[8] Joint parliamentary motions to that effect were submitted by the respective party chairmen in

---

1. The problem was compounded by the fact that it was Daniel Chipenda, the future leader of the *Revolta do Leste* faction, who was responsible for MPLA's contacts with foreign donors (see the interview with Paulo Jorge, p. 17).
2. In relation to the actual assistance, the documentation held at Sida and the Ministry for Foreign Affairs—with requests, counter-requests, comments and correspondence between various Swedish embassies and MPLA offices—is very substantial.
3. Interview with Stig Lövgren, pp. 312-15.
4. See the accompanying disbursement table for MPLA.
5. CCHA: Memorandum ('Svenskt bistånd till afrikanska flyktingar och nationella befrielserörelser'/'Swedish assistance to African refugees and national liberation movements'), SIDA, Stockholm, 26 June 1975 (SDA).
6. See the accompanying disbursement table.
7. 10 MSEK was allocated during the period 1971/72-1974/75, but only 2.3 million was actually disbursed. Of the accumulated balance of 7.7 MSEK, 1.5 million was via UNESCO in 1975/76 paid out in favour of the MPLA school at Dolisie. A final decision on the utilization of the remaining 6.2 million was not reached until October 1975.
8. UNITA was only recognized by OAU in late 1974, after the Lisbon coup.

1971, 1972 and 1973.[1] Decreasing aid and increasing attention to Holden Roberto's movement suggested that MPLA was being politically marginalized in Sweden in the early 1970s. This was, however, not the case. The motions in favour of FNLA were rejected by the parliamentary majority, which, on the contrary, voted for increased allocations to MPLA. At the party level, the ruling Social Democratic Party had at the beginning of the decade established privileged relations with MPLA, similar to those with PAIGC and FRELIMO. Agostinho Neto's movement received financial support from both the Social Democratic Party's International Solidarity Fund[2] and the youth league.[3] In October 1972, Lúcio Lara—MPLA's influential Secretary for Organization and Cadres—was, in addition, invited to the Social Democratic Party congress in Stockholm together with PAIGC's Secretary General Amílcar Cabral.[4]

At the level of the wider non-governmental solidarity movement, MPLA enjoyed increasing support. In 1971-72, the Emmaus-Björkå community in southern Sweden collected and dispatched more than 60 tons of clothes to MPLA[5], and in 1972 the student unions at the universities of Lund and Umeå decided to raise funds for Agostinho Neto's organization.[6] The efforts were to a large extent the result of the information and lobbying work carried out by a small, dedicated core of activists within the Lund and Stockholm Africa Groups[7] and by the independent socialist monthly *Kommentar*. Ten years later, Sören Lindh concluded in a personal

---

1. The Centre and Liberal parties advocated support to *both* MPLA and FNLA. In the case of the Liberal Party Youth League, token financial contributions were given to MPLA and FNLA in 1970 and in 1972, that is, before and after the official decision to support MPLA (For 1970: Letter ('Svensk hjälp till Angola'/'Swedish aid to Angola') from Dag Malm, Ministry for Foreign Affairs, to the Swedish ambassador to Zaire, Olof Bjurström, Stockholm, 9 April 1970 (MFA). For 1972: Knudtzon and Magnusson op. cit.). Joint parliamentary motions in favour of Swedish official support to MPLA and FNLA were introduced by the Centre and Liberal party leaders Gunnar Hedlund and Gunnar Helén in January 1971 (Swedish Parliament 1971: Motion No. 472, Riksdagens Protokoll, 1971, p. 16); by the new Centre Party chairman Thorbjörn Fälldin and Helén in January 1972 (Swedish Parliament 1972: Motion No. 934, Riksdagens Protokoll, 1972, pp. 15-16); and by Fälldin and Helén in January 1973 (Swedish Parliament 1973: Motion No. 1101, Riksdagens Protokoll, 1973, p. 10). Helén and other leading Liberal MPs—among them the future Foreign and Prime Minister Ola Ullsten—submitted a similar motion in January 1974 (Swedish Parliament 1974: Motion No. 657, Riksdagens Protokoll, 1974, p. 5). It should be noted that the motions by the opposition 'middle parties' also requested official support/increased assistance to SWAPO of Namibia, ANC of South Africa and ZANU and ZAPU of Zimbabwe.
2. For example, Socialdemokraterna: 'Verksamheten 1972' ('Activities 1972'), p. 90 (LMA). Agostinho Neto informed the MPLA members of the financial support received through the Social Democratic Party's International Solidarity Fund (Interview with Paulo Jorge, p. 16).
3. For example, SSU: 'Verksamheten 1970' ('Activities 1970'), p. 27 and SSU: 'Verksamheten 1972-74' ('Activities 1972-74'), p. I:47 (LMA).
4. See the interview with Lúcio Lara, where he recalls how he in connection with the congress participated in a solidarity march for the liberation movements together with Madame Nguyen Thi Binh from the National Liberation Front (FNL) of South Vietnam (p. 18). In October 1972, the veteran MPLA leader—who first visited Stockholm in November 1971 for talks on the Dolisie school project in Congo-Brazzaville—discussed the political situation in Angola with first secretary Pierre Schori at the Ministry for Foreign Affairs (Pierre Schori: Memorandum ('Samtal med Lúcio Lara, MPLA'/'Conversation with Lúcio Lara, MPLA'), Ministry for Foreign Affairs, Stockholm, 4 October 1972) (MFA).
5. Africa Groups: 'Circular letters Nos. 4, 5 and 6', [no place], 23 September 1971; Lund, 6 February 1972; and [no place], 25 July 1972 (AGA). According to the SIDA study earlier quoted, the value of the clothes sent by Emmaus-Björkå to MPLA in 1972 corresponded to 1.1 MSEK, i.e. twice as much as the total official humanitarian support disbursed to the Angolan movement during the two financial years 1971/72 and 1972/73. In 1972, six NGOs together contributed 1.5 MSEK to MPLA. Emmaus-Björkå's share was almost 75 per cent. Only one organization—the Liberal Party Youth League—supported FNLA, granting the sum of 2,500 SEK. The value of the NGO support to FRELIMO was for 1972 estimated at around 1.7 MSEK, while the corresponding amount in favour of PAIGC was 1.1 MSEK (Knudtzon and Magnusson op. cit.).
6. In 1972, the university students in Lund raised 16,000 SEK for MPLA. The corresponding figure at the university of Umeå was 1,700 SEK (Knudtzon and Magnusson op. cit.).
7. In 1970, the Africa Groups had less than a hundred members (Sören Lindh: 'AGIS' organisatoriska historia: En subjektiv beskrivning'/'The history of the AGIS organization: A subjective description', Diskussionsunderlag/Material for discussion, AGIS, Winter conference 1982 [no place or date]) (AGA). Ten years later—when the local groups had increased from four to seventeen— the number had almost reached a thousand (ibid).

reflection on the history of the Swedish Africa Groups that "the most important contribution during the initial stages [from 1970 until 1974] was probably the political analysis of the situation in Angola and the support for MPLA".[1] Looking back in 1997, he added that the "Africa Groups did thorough homework on the Angolan [situation]. [...] It influenced not only the left, but a number of organizations".[2] Hillevi Nilsson similarly said that "we perhaps did the most important things at the beginning of the 1970s. Information was an important part of this. The fact that we tried to analyze the different organizations in Angola. [...] [W]e [...] made a study on the different movements [...] and I think that some people in the Social Democratic Party read it".[3]

This is also how developments in Sweden were understood by MPLA. In 1996, Alberto Ribeiro-Kabulu, for example, said that the solidarity organizations

> knew us very well. They had been with us in the liberated area and they had played an important role for the official aid [...]. Even if we sometimes faced constraints and limitations—for instance, regarding four-wheel drive vehicles, which could be used for military purposes—the insistence of the solidarity movement always helped us to get things right. [...]
>
> When I recall my personal ties with the Nordic countries—first of all with Sweden, Denmark and Norway—the support always began through the people, students, workers and trade-unionists. It was the civil society in those countries that channelled the message to their governments. In other cases, for instance, in the socialist countries, the support came straight from the governments and from parties in one-party states. In the case of the Nordic countries, it first came through contacts from people to people. It was the civil society that was in touch with us. It made a big difference in relation to the support.[4]

Focusing the attention on the liberation struggles in the Portuguese colonies, the Lund South Africa Committee had from 1966 followed the situation in Angola.[5] Towards the end of the 1960s, the socialist monthly *Kommentar*—launched in 1968—also formed a study group on Africa. After initial attention to Ethiopia, Kenya and Zimbabwe[6], it came into contact with Angola and MPLA through the visits to Stockholm by Daniel Chipenda and Agostinho Neto in 1970.[7] In addition, in early 1970 the Stockholm-based Angola-MPLA Group[8] published a document on 'The so called problem of the unification of the nationalists in Angola', which underlined the role played by MPLA.[9] The initiatives coalesced in late 1970—at a time when the Consultative Committee on Humanitarian Assistance was discussing requests from both FNLA and MPLA—in a longer analysis in the *Södra Afrika*

1. Ibid.
2. Interview with Sören Lindh, p. 306.
3. Interview with Hillevi Nilsson, pp. 327-29.
4. Interview with Alberto Ribeiro-Kabulu, pp. 29-30. See also the interview with Paulo Jorge, p. 15.
5. In 1966, the Lund South Africa Committee—from 1970 Africa Group—was visited by Pedro Gomes Higino from MPLA and later in the year the *Syd- och Sydvästafrika* information bulletin published an update on MPLA and a profile of Agostinho Neto (*Syd- och Sydvästafrika*, Nos. 7-8 and 10, 1966). Several articles on Angola and MPLA were subsequently published by the bulletin, which in 1967 changed its name to *Södra Afrika Informationsbulletin*.
6. Interview with Hillevi Nilsson, p. 326.
7. Ibid. In 1969, Dick Urban Vestbro—a leading representative of the Swedish South Africa Committees/Africa Groups and a member of the editorial board of the *Södra Afrika Informationsbulletin*—wrote a number of full-page articles on MPLA in the socialist weekly *Tidsignal* (see Sellström Volume I, p.408). Together with Hillevi Nilsson, Vestbro was the most active MPLA advocate in Sweden at the close of the 1960s/beginning of the 1970s.
8. With largely overlapping membership, the *Kommentar* study group on Africa and the Angola-MPLA Group would in 1970-71—at the same time as the FRELIMO Group—join forces with the Stockholm Africa Group. While the solidarity work for Guinea-Bissau had its centre in Uppsala, the Stockholm group would coordinate the work for Angola and Mozambique.
9. Angola-MPLA Gruppen: 'Det s.k. problemet med nationalisternas enande i Angola', Document No. 3, [Stockholm], 1970 (AJC).

Studying Angola: British historian Basil Davidson visiting the Africa Groups in Stockholm, October 1977. Taking notes in the centre is Dick Urban Vestbro (Photo: Anders Gunnartz)

Informationsbulletin under the heading 'Who Leads the Struggle in Angola?'.[1] Addressing the question, the four Africa Groups then existing concluded that "MPLA is the only movement in Angola that [...] deserves our support", adding that they felt "a duty to reject the propaganda which the representatives of FNLA and UNITA, as well as their Swedish supporters, disseminate in different newspapers in Sweden".[2]

Backing the parliamentary initiatives by younger Social Democratic MPs, such as Birgitta Dahl and Lena Hjelm-Wallén[3], the active advocacy of MPLA's cause by the Africa Groups and *Kommentar* contributed to the official decision taken in March 1971. The mobilizing effort was maintained over the following years. Although the Africa Groups gave primacy to political support and information activities over monetary assistance[4], a conference held in June 1971 decided to launch a fund-raising campaign in favour of unconditional support to MPLA.[5] Coordinated by the Stockholm Africa Group, the campaign raised over the following two years the modest amount of 46,000 SEK.[6] However, in connection with the fund-raising activities, information on MPLA and the struggle in Angola was widely disseminated. The Africa Groups were also active during the UN Conference on the Human Environment, held in Stockholm in June 1972, where the alter-

1. 'Vem Leder Kampen i Angola?' in *Södra Afrika Informationsbulletin*, No. 10, 1970, pp. 19-32 (see Sellström Volume I, p. 423).
2. Ibid., p. 32. Five years later, the analysis was updated, expanded and reproduced. See *För ett Fritt Angola: En Analys av MPLA, FNLA och UNITA* ('For a Free Angola: An Analysis of MPLA, FNLA and UNITA'), Afrikagruppernas Skriftserie, No. 4, Stockholm, August 1975.
3. In January 1971, Birgitta Dahl submitted the decisive parliamentary motion in favour of direct official assistance to MPLA. It was co-signed, among others, by the future Foreign Minister Lena Hjelm-Wallén (Swedish Parliament 1971: Motion No. 667, Riksdagens Protokoll, 1971, pp. 15-17).
4. The Stockholm Africa Group argued in the early 1970s that "the easiest way to collect large amounts of money is to appeal strictly to the emotions of people. But this creates no understanding of the reasons why money is needed. [...] The most important [aspect] is not the coin, but the political acknowledgement of a people's right to an armed fight for their defence and liberation" (Stockholm Africa Group: 'Support to the liberation movements in the Portuguese colonies from Swedish non-governmental organizations, 1971', Stockholm [no date, but probably February 1973]; original in English) (AGA).
5. Africa Groups: 'Protokoll: Konferens mellan Afrikagrupperna i Sverige i Arvika den 5-6 juni 1971' ('Minutes: Conference between the Africa Groups in Sweden in Arvika 5-6 June 1971'), [no place or date], p. 14 (AGA).
6. Ulf Carlqvist: 'MPLA-insamlingen: Redovisning för tiden 23/8 1971-7/6 1973' ('The MPLA collection: Accounts for the period 23 August 1971-7 June 1973'), Spånga, 7 June 1973 (AGA).

native People's Forum paid attention to the situation in the Portuguese colonies, not least with regard to Portugal's use of napalm, defoliants and other chemical products in the wars against the liberation movements.[1] Together with Armando Panguene from FRELIMO[2], MPLA's Pedro Van-Dunem[3] and José Eduardo dos Santos—the future President of Angola[4]—participated in the well covered events. They also attended solidarity meetings "in several parts of Sweden".[5]

The solidarity movement did not limit the activities to information. Within the Stockholm Africa Group, a small number of engineers active in a so called 'materials group'[6] assisted MPLA with procurement of technical equipment and advice.[7] Little known is that the group made important contributions to MPLA's military squadron for radio and telecommunications services.[8] When MPLA captured radio units from the Portuguese on the eastern front and needed equipment to change the frequencies, it was, for example, supplied by the group.[9] More significant was that the Stockholm Africa Group actively contributed to the codification and protection of MPLA's communications between the front in eastern Angola and its offices in Africa. Interviewed in 1996, the former Director of MPLA's Service for Radio and Telecommunications, Alberto Ribeiro-Kabulu, explained the wider context and significance of the assistance:

> I was asked by President Neto to protect our communications network as much as I could, because we were talking all across Africa, from Dar es Salaam to Brazzaville. Neto was very clear on one aspect. He asked me to invent something new and not follow the roads given to our trainees in the socialist countries. Our people who went for training in the Soviet Union, Cuba and so on brought us some knowledge of codes and cryptography. But Neto told me: 'Look, I don't want to use this. Try to invent something new'. When I finished my masters degree in [West] Germany[10], I had been working with computers and I had gained some knowledge related to that. However, I needed books on cryptography and mathematics, which I got through the solidarity groups. It was a very useful and little known support, including from Lars and Hillevi [Nilsson of the Stockholm Africa Group]. With [these] books [...] we created our own code.
>
> Some of our friends were not at all happy with that. In particular, of course, the liaison officials from the socialist countries. They also wanted to know what was going on. But it was Neto's clear position that 'we have to keep our own secrets and we will use this system'. Until the end of the war we used our own codes. We also used the equipment we had captured in action

---

1. Africa Groups: 'Circular letter No. 6', [no place], 25 July 1972 (AGA).
2. On 1 July 1975, Panguene was appointed Vice-Minister for Foreign Affairs in the first government of independent Mozambique.
3. Van-Dunem ('Loy') was later closely involved with the official Swedish assistance to MPLA. In the 1980s, he became Minister of Oil and, from 1986, Minister of Production. He was appointed Foreign Minister in 1989.
4. As Foreign Minister, dos Santos returned to Sweden in January 1976. After the death of Agostinho Neto, he became President of MPLA and of the People's Republic of Angola in September 1979.
5. Africa Groups: 'Circular letter No. 6', [no place], 25 July 1972 (AGA).
6. In Swedish, *materialgrupp*.
7. Interview with Hillevi Nilsson, p. 329.
8. In Portuguese, *Serviço de Rádio e Telecomunicações*. Alberto Ribeiro-Kabulu directed the SRT from 1968 to 1974. He was after independence appointed Secretary of State for Communications and Transport and in 1978 Minister of Industry and Energy. José Eduardo dos Santos formed part of the SRT from 1970 to 1974.
9. Interview with Alberto Ribeiro-Kabulu, p. 28.
10. It is worthy of note that President Neto appointed Ribeiro-Kabulu as head of the sensitive communications sector. Contrary to many MPLA cadres, Ribeiro-Kabulu was not educated in Eastern Europe, but in the Federal Republic of Germany, where he received a masters degree from the Aachen Technical University and also worked as a computer engineer between 1965 and 1968. He later said that "[i]t was Neto who insisted that I should have this responsibility, but in the days of the Cold War it had its limitations. I had no access to the Communist countries. I was not chosen for further training in the Soviet Union and I was only able to visit the socialist countries after our independence" (Interview with Alberto Ribeiro-Kabulu, p. 27). President Neto's sister Ruth—a leading representative of the Angolan Women's Organization (OMA)—also studied and worked in West Germany until 1968, when she joined her brother in Tanzania and, subsequently, at the eastern front in Angola (see the interview with Ruth Neto, p. 21).

against the Portuguese to control things.[1] [...] The Portuguese were very surprised when we met for the cease-fire in Mozico [in October 1974], seeing that we had such a well organized service, not only with regard to communications, but also to intelligence. [...] [I]t was not only through our own achievement, but very much that of the solidarity committees, in this case specifically in Sweden.[2]

The first Swedes to report from the MPLA-held areas in eastern Angola were members of the Africa Groups. Active within *Kommentar*'s study group on Africa, Elisabeth Hedborg[3] and Hillevi Nilsson[4] were in early 1971 asked by the Verdandi association to participate in the writing of a book about Zambia.[5] In Lusaka, they together with the medical doctor Bertil Sörberg were invited by Daniel Chipenda to visit MPLA's base areas close to the Angolan border.[6] Travelling to western Zambia in July 1971, they were profoundly impressed by the logistical problems faced by MPLA.[7] Practically all the supplies for the eastern front were moved from the port in Dar es Salaam, Tanzania, in three stages, first by truck 2,000 kilometres to Lusaka[8] and then by four-wheel drive vehicles via northern Zambia on gravel roads and sandy tracks another 1,300 kilometres to the Angolan border.[9] The goods and equipment had, finally, to be carried across savanna and rivers—always subject to possible Portuguese attacks—into the MPLA-controlled areas inside Angola. This could take up to a month and a half. To get proper treatment, wounded freedom fighters and civilian medical patients from Angola had in the same way to be transported by teams of carriers to MPLA's clinics in western Zambia.[10] Re-visiting the area in 1972, Hedborg and Nilsson wrote:

---

1. The Africa Groups recruited a telecommunications engineer to work with MPLA. Ribeiro-Kabulu later recalled: "To my surprise I met a very quiet person, but a brilliant engineer. He came to see us in Lusaka and immediately started to work with us. We assembled the radios which we captured from the enemy [...] [t]o understand what was going on and to get intelligence from listening to their radio emissions" (Interview with Alberto Ribeiro-Kabulu, p. 28).
2. Interview with Alberto Ribeiro-Kabulu, p. 28. Some of the Swedish engineers who assisted MPLA during the liberation struggle joined the Ministries of Defence and Industry at Angola's independence in November 1975. Among them was Lars Nilsson.
3. Hedborg later became a prominent journalist with the Swedish public television company.
4. No Swede has had longer and closer relations with MPLA than Hillevi ('Vivi') Nilsson. Active in *Kommentar*'s study group on Africa from the late 1960s, she came into contact with the organization when Daniel Chipenda and the future MPLA representative to Sweden, António Alberto Neto, visited Stockholm in May 1970. She joined the Stockholm Africa Group and would after her visits to western Zambia and eastern Angola in 1971-72 become closely involved with the Angolan struggle. In addition to her work with the Africa Groups, she served as secretary at the MPLA office in Stockholm and assisted the resident MPLA representatives to Sweden (António Alberto Neto 1970-73, Saydi Mingas 1973-75 and Maria Jesus de Haller 1975). When Mingas returned to Angola in early 1975, he *de facto* appointed Nilsson as acting MPLA representative until the arrival of de Haller in the early autumn (Saydi Mingas: 'Kreditivbrev/Fullmakt' - 'Credentials/Letter of attorney', Stockholm, 22 January 1975) (AGA). Together with her husband, Lars Nilsson, she moved to Luanda in November 1975 and worked in Angola for nine years, *inter alia* at MPLA's printing press and with the Angolan Writers' Union (*União dos Escritores Angolanos*) (see the interview with Hillevi Nilsson, pp. 326-30).
5. Föreningen Verdandis Zambiagrupp: *Zambia: Ett Gränsfall* ('Zambia: A Border Case'), Folkuniversitetets förlag/Föreningen Verdandi, Stockholm, 1972.
6. Interview with Hillevi Nilsson, p. 326. The first decision on official Swedish assistance to MPLA had been taken a couple of months earlier. Nilsson later said that "the very invitation made to us by Chipenda perhaps was because of the Swedish support. As I see it afterwards, it could have been" (ibid., p. 327).
7. Hillevi Nilsson: 'En Vecka med MPLA' ('One Week with MPLA') in *Kommentar*, No. 8, 1971, pp. 14-15. Also Hillevi Nilsson: '15 År med MPLA' ('15 Years with MPLA') in *Kommentar*, No. 5-6, 1983, pp. 22-35.
8. Upgrading and tarring of the Great North Road from Lusaka to Dar es Salaam had for the most part been completed by the end of 1970. The Tanzania-Zambia Railway only started to operate in 1975.
9. The distance from Dar es Salaam to the Angolan border equalled that between Stockholm and northern Morocco. The distance from the port of entry to the end-users in central Angola corresponded to almost one tenth of the circumference of the globe.
10. MPLA faced incomparably more difficult logistical problems than PAIGC or FRELIMO. Responsible for logistics in MPLA's Steering Committee, Daniel Chipenda thereby wielded considerable power over the developments on the eastern front.

Collecting information on the Angolan struggle: Hillevi Nilsson of the Stockholm
Africa Group in the MPLA-held areas of eastern Angola, July 1972 (Courtesy of Bertil
Sörberg)

We saw people of all ages—men, women and children—who were marching, loaded with supplies of different kinds. There is in Europe sometimes a tendency—it might concern Vietnam or
Angola—to consider the liberation struggle in a romantic way. It is easy to primarily think [of
it] in terms of weapons, combat etc. But it was in many ways confirmed to us that what is
needed above all in the Angolan liberation struggle is very hard work.[1]

Hedborg, Nilsson and Sörberg returned to Africa in July 1972, this time to accompany MPLA on the long supply route from Dar es Salaam into Angola.[2] The situation in mid-1972 was, however, radically different from the one encountered a
year earlier. After securing a truce with UNITA[3], the Portuguese had in February
1972 launched the Operation Attila offensive against MPLA and—as in Guinea-
Bissau and Mozambique—intensified the programme to force the African population
into 'strategic hamlets'.[4] Nevertheless, after a meeting with President Neto in Lusaka
the visitors could in late July 1972—shortly after Knut Andreassen from the Lund
Africa Group—cross the border into Angola.[5] More or less visiting the same areas,
the members of the Lund and Stockholm Africa Groups could in the midst of the

1. Hillevi Nilsson and Elisabeth Hedborg: 'Segern Är Säker!: Om Folkets Kamp i Angola' ('Victory Is Certain!:
   On the People's Struggle in Angola') in *Kommentar*, No. 9, 1972, p. 6. In late 1971, representatives from the
   SIDA office in Lusaka also visited MPLA's rearguard areas in western Zambia. Like Hedborg and Nilsson,
   they were awed by the transport and logistical problems, but positively impressed by MPLA's administration.
   They concluded that the needs for assistance to the MPLA schools and clinics in the border areas were considerable (CCHA: Memorandum ('Ansökan från Movimento [Popular] de Libertação de Angola, MPLA, om
   fortsatt svenskt varubistånd'/'Request from MPLA for continued Swedish commodity support'), SIDA, Stockholm, 5 September 1972) (SDA).
2. Nilsson op. cit. in *Kommentar*, No. 5-6, 1983, p. 28. See also the interview with Hillevi Nilsson, p. 327.
3. Cann op. cit., p. 135. On UNITA's collaboration with the Portuguese colonial army, see William Minter:
   Operation Timber: Pages from the Savimbi Dossier, Africa World Press, Trenton, New Jersey, 1988. Vestbro
   had as early as in mid-1969 written that there was "evidence that [UNITA] collaborates with the Portuguese"
   (Dick Urban Vestbro: 'Sydafrikas akilleshäl' ('South Africa's Achilles' heel') in *Tidsignal*, No. 28, 1969, p. 7).
4. By February 1973, almost a million Angolans had been relocated by force into 2,000 *aldeamentos* in the eastern parts of the country (Cann op. cit., p. 156).
5. The visit by Hedborg, Nilsson and Sörberg was organized by MPLA's Information Director Paulo Jorge.
   Succeeding José Eduardo dos Santos, Jorge served as Angola's Minister for Foreign Affairs from 1976 until
   1984.

Portuguese offensive give positive accounts of MPLA's efforts to build a new society, particularly in the fields of education and health.[1]

Emphasis on Transport

Like PAIGC, MPLA did not question the commodity form of the Swedish support or raise objections against the fact that it was restricted to non-military purposes. The wider issue of transport would, however, soon feature prominently in the aid dialogue. As stated by Anders Möllander, "with the [Swedish] assistance to MPLA, the question of transport support was brought to a head".[2]

MPLA's first request for Swedish assistance envisaged support to the educational and medical activities in the MPLA-controlled areas inside Angola. It was presented by Daniel Chipenda during a visit to Sweden in May 1970 and further discussed with President Neto in Stockholm two months later. Based on the request and the subsequent clarifications by the MPLA leaders, the first decision on official assistance to MPLA was eventually taken in March 1971. An amount of 500,000 SEK was granted for educational and medical supplies during the financial year 1971/72.[3]

Agostinho Neto was from the very beginning in favour of a clearer emphasis on transport support. He had raised this concern with SIDA during his visit to Stockholm in July 1970, underlining MPLA's logistical problems and assuring that there was "no risk that transport means possibly donated by Sweden would be used for military [purposes]".[4] Thanking SIDA's Director General for the decision taken in March 1971, he reiterated his position in a letter in late July. He then requested increased commodity assistance from Sweden, with priority given to four-wheel drive vehicles, inflatable rubber boats and outboard motors, ambulances, food and medical supplies.[5] At about the same time, the Swedish aid agency decided to make an allowance for heavy-duty trucks within the support to MPLA, which was

---

1. Nilsson and Hedborg op. cit. in *Kommentar*, No. 9, 1972. The Norwegian photographer Knut Andreassen was active in the Swedish solidarity movement with Southern Africa. He had in late 1970 visited the liberated areas of Guinea-Bissau with the Social Democratic MP Birgitta Dahl. Travelling to the MPLA-held areas in eastern Angola in June-July 1972, his photos and impressions were published in 1973 in the book *Kamrater i Angola* ('Comrades in Angola'), Hermod, Malmö. Finally, in July-August 1973, Leif Biureborgh—a Swedish journalist representing the trade union press—spent a month with MPLA in western Zambia and eastern Angola. He shared his impressions with the Swedish labour movement in the article 'Över 500 Års Portugisiskt Förtryck i Västra Afrika' ('More than 500 Years of Portuguese Oppression in Western Africa') in *Fackföreningsrörelsen*, the official organ of the Swedish Trade Union Confederation (LO), No. 22 A, 1973, pp. 12-15. Commenting upon the Swedish assistance to MPLA, Biureborgh concluded that the 1972/73 allocation of 2 MSEK constituted "modest, but well utilized funds. In the future we can do more. This also applies to the Swedish trade union movement" (ibid., p. 15). Biureborgh's visit took place after the Chipenda crisis had openly broken out. Strongly supporting the leadership around Agostinho Neto, he reported his findings to the Swedish Ministry for Foreign Affairs in September 1973 (Elisabet Borsiin: Memorandum ('Samtal med Leif Biureborgh angående befrielserörelsen MPLA den 11 september 1973'/'Conversation with Leif Biureborgh regarding the liberation movement MPLA, 11 September 1973'), Ministry for Foreign Affairs, Stockholm, 21 September 1973) (MFA).
2. Möllander op. cit., p. 29.
3. See Sellström Volume I, pp. 426-29.
4. Birgitta Dahl: Memorandum ('Sammanträffande mellan representanter för MPLA och SIDA på SIDA den 3.7 1970'/'Meeting between representatives of MPLA and SIDA at SIDA, 3 July 1970'), SIDA, Stockholm, 9 July 1970 (SDA).
5. Letter from Agostinho Neto to SIDA's Director General, [no place], 22 July 1971; original in French (SDA). In the letter—in which he addressed SIDA's Director General as "dear comrade"—Neto also requested no less than 5 tons of cigarettes, corresponding to over 20,000 cartons.

Problems of transportation and logistics: Casualties along the 'hell run' between Dar es Salaam, Tanzania, and Lusaka, Zambia, during the 1969 rainy season (Photo: IKON, Svenska kyrkans bild-byrå)

acknowledged with appreciation by Neto when he met Prime Minister Palme in Lusaka in September 1971.[1]

Finally, in November-December 1971, a SIDA delegation including Curt Ström, Marianne Rappe and Stig Lövgren discussed the technical aspects of the changed preferences in meetings with MPLA in Lusaka and Dar es Salaam.[2] At the end of 1971—with a delay of almost a year—a commodity support programme for 1971/72 was thus established. With more than half of the available funds earmarked for the transport sector, the renegotiated agreement reflected the priorities set by Neto. Of the 500,000 SEK granted, 250,000 was allocated for the procurement of trucks, motorbikes and bicycles; 140,000 for four-wheel drive ambulances and medical supplies; 50,000 for food and agricultural tools; and only 20,000 for equipment to the education sector.[3] Whenever possible, the items were to be procured locally, that is, mainly in Tanzania and Zambia.

1. Pierre Schori: Memorandum: 'Samtal med Agustino Neto, generalsekreterare för MPLA (*sic*), Angola, i State House, Lusaka, 24 september 1971' ('Conversation with Agustino Neto, General Secretary of MPLA, Angola, State House, Lusaka, 24 September 1971'), Ministry for Foreign Affairs, Stockholm, 1 October 1971 (MFA). During the meeting—which on the Swedish side was also attended by Pierre Schori and Per Wästberg—Palme said that the support to the liberation movements would be substantially increased: "MPLA [could] count on a positive attitude from the Swedish government [and] the assistance to MPLA [would] at least be doubled" (ibid.).
2. The first meeting with MPLA in Lusaka did not lead anywhere. Stig Lövgren later recalled: "There was a meeting scheduled with the MPLA leaders, but nobody seemed to be there when we arrived. We were later told that we had to wait for one of the commanders from the province in Angola bordering with Zambia [...], Daniel Chipenda. [...] The MPLA people in Lusaka did not dare to discuss with us, because everything had to be decided by Chipenda himself. [He] had to take a domestic flight to Lusaka, but [...] did not have any money. We had to provide him with a ticket. After a few days, he turned up and we had a meeting with him. But he was not prepared for the discussions [...]. Frankly speaking, he did not seem to know very much about us and what the purpose of our meeting was" (Interview with Stig Lövgren, pp. 311-12).
3. CCHA: Memorandum: 'Ansökan från Movimento [Popular] de Libertação de Angola, MPLA, om fortsatt svenskt varubistånd' ('Request from MPLA for continued Swedish commodity support'), SIDA, Stockholm, 5 September 1972 (SDA). The balance of 40,000 SEK was set aside for freight costs, *inter alia* of a considerable amount of shoes donated by the Swedish Labour Market Board (*Arbetsmarknadsstyrelsen*; AMS) over and above SIDA's contribution. On the inadequacy of the footwear donated by AMS, see the interview with Hillevi Nilsson, p. 327.

Local procurement and deliveries from Sweden under the agreed commodity support programme were carried out without complications during the first half of 1972. As a result, the Swedish government decided to increase the allocation to MPLA from 0.5 to 2 MSEK in 1972/73. The actual content of the support was largely based on President Neto's letter to SIDA of July 1971 and finally established by the local SIDA office and MPLA's Pedro Van-Dunem ('Loy') in Lusaka in December 1972.[1] For the financial year 1972/73, MPLA, however, again changed the emphasis to the social sectors.[2] Of the 1.8 MSEK available after deduction for freight and related costs, 0.7 million—around 40 per cent—was set aside for education, including the procurement of a printing press and stationery for MPLA in Congo-Brazzaville. With 0.3 million, the health sector was second on the priority list. The remaining 0.8 million was more or less equally divided between clothes, footwear and textiles[3]; food[4]; and means of transport, in addition to the cash component of 5 per cent which on FRELIMO's insistence in November 1972 had been included in the Swedish support to the liberation movements. Although given less emphasis, the transport support was still considerable. It included 2 heavy-duty trucks with trailers (Scania), 4 four-wheel drive vehicles (Land Rovers), 1 large barge[5], 10 smaller boats and 5 inflatable rubber boats with outboard motors.[6]

After completing a year of successful cooperation and having reached an agreement on expanded support for 1972/73, the direct assistance ground, however, almost to a halt at the beginning of 1973.[7] Several factors contributed to this situation. The formal agreement between FNLA and MPLA in Kinshasa on 13 December 1972—signed shortly after the Lusaka offices of SIDA and Agostinho Neto's movement had established the second commodity support programme—would, in the first place, introduce a considerable element of uncertainty with regard to the future bilateral relationship. The implications of the Kinshasa agreement—which led to the suspension of the Soviet Union's support to MPLA—would over the following months figure prominently in the Swedish government's dialogue with

---

1. MPLA's needs had been discussed with Lúcio Lara during his visit to Stockholm in October 1972 (Göran Hasselmark: Memorandum ('Samtal med Lúcio Lara'/'Conversation with Lúcio Lara'), Ministry for Foreign Affairs, Stockholm, 4 October 1972) (MFA). Lara confirmed that the supplies to MPLA's eastern front despite Portugal's counter-offensive were regularly and well received along what was described as "the Agostinho Neto trail" with reference to the so called Ho Chi Minh trail in Vietnam (ibid.).

2. Interviewed by Elisabeth Hedborg and Hillevi Nilsson in Lusaka in July 1972, Neto stated that MPLA's transport problems had eased: "We have in a satisfactory way been able to expand our transport system. We now have a much greater number of vehicles, which we have received from several different countries. [...] But the roads are the same. They are very bad, especially during the rainy season" ('Vårt Folk Är Alltid Berett att Fortsätta Kampen' ('Our People Are Always Ready to Continue the Struggle'), Interview with Agostinho Neto in *Kommentar*, No. 9, 1972, p. 8).

3. *Inter alia*, 20,000 blankets, 30,000 metres of cotton material, 2,000 pairs of socks, 1,000 pairs of rubber boots and 500 pairs of plastic sandals.

4. 100 tons of maize flour, 100 tons of tinned fish and 50 tons of beans, cooking oil, salt and sugar.

5. According to the agreed specification, the barge was designed to carry 8 to 12 tons of supplies on the rivers and canals from western Zambia into Angola. MPLA's rearguard areas in western Zambia were flooded annually during the rainy season by the Zambezi river.

6. Letter from Kurt Kristiansson ('MPLA purchase programme for 1972/73') to SIDA Stockholm, Lusaka, 5 December 1972; original in English (SDA).

7. The multi-bilateral assistance extended via UNESCO to the MPLA school in Dolisie, Congo-Brazzaville, continued without complications.

MPLA.[1] As it became clear that the agreement was without consequence due to Zaire's reluctance to open its territory to MPLA, other—more ominous—doubts appeared, however, as a result of the internal MPLA struggles which followed upon the 1972 Portuguese counter-offensive and the agreement with FNLA. In the case of Sweden, a first indication of MPLA's internal strains came in mid-May 1973, when Pascal Luvualu, head of MPLA's Department of External Relations, through a circular letter from Dar es Salaam communicated that MPLA's resident representative in Stockholm, António Alberto Neto,

> is no more [a] militant of our movement. [He] is therefore no more [the] MPLA representative in [the] Scandinavian countries, namely Sweden, Norway, Finland, Denmark, Netherlands, England and others.[2]

Shortly thereafter, Agostinho Neto informed the Swedish embassy in Lusaka that "comrade Daniel Chipenda is suspended from all [MPLA] functions and prerogatives until [a final] decision is taken".[3] Finally, in early July the SIDA representative to Zambia, Kurt Kristiansson[4], submitted a report on the MPLA crisis to the Ministry for Foreign Affairs.[5] This started a series of meetings and an intense correspondence between the Lusaka embassy, the Foreign Ministry and MPLA regarding the internal situation in the Angolan movement. The discussions—also involving the Zambian government—continued for almost a year. As later stated by Paulo Jorge, the crisis led to "a kind of paralysis".[6] During that period, formal aid negotiations with MPLA were in a state of suspension. At the very moment when Swe-

---

1. Notably with Alfonso Van-Dunem ('Mbinda') and with Agostinho Neto himself. Van-Dunem—who had participated in the Kinshasa talks—visited Stockholm in February 1973 (CCHA: 'Minnesanteckningar från samtal 1973 02 02 med António Alberto Neto och Alfonso Van-Dunem, MPLA'/'Memorandum on conversation with António Alberto Neto and Alfonso Van-Dunem, 2 February 1973', SIDA, Stockholm, 19 February 1973) (SDA). The question of the FNLA-MPLA agreement was widely covered when the MPLA President after the Oslo conference in April 1973 visited Stockholm. Although acknowledging "many difficulties", Neto strongly defended the agreement. In a meeting at the Ministry for Foreign Affairs, the MPLA President stated—according to the Swedish notes—that "a process towards cooperation [between MPLA and FNLA] now had been initiated [and that it] was irrevocable". The situation in Angola was such that "the liberation movement could not afford to be divided". Neto further explained that "the northern front [in Angola] had the highest priority" and that "if MPLA does not agree to the conditions set by Zaire, it would also in the future be locked out from access to the most important parts of [the country]" (Gun-Britt Andersson: Memorandum ('Samtal med MPLA's president Agostinho Neto'/'Conversation with MPLA's President Agostinho Neto'), Ministry for Foreign Affairs, Stockholm, 25 May 1973) (MFA).
2. Circular letter from Pascal Luvualu, responsible for the MPLA Department of External Relations, Dar es Salaam, 20 May 1973; original in English (MFA). In the same circular, Luvualu introduced Neto's successor as MPLA representative to Sweden and the Nordic countries, Saydi Mingas. António Alberto Neto served as MPLA's representative from September 1970 to May 1973. He resurfaced on the Angolan political scene as the leader of the Angolan Democratic Party (*Partido Democrático Angolano*) before the presidential and parliamentary elections in September 1992. In the presidential elections, Neto received 2.2% of the votes, far behind José Eduardo dos Santos of MPLA (49.6%) and Jonas Savimbi of UNITA (40.1%), but before Holden Roberto of FNLA (2.1%) and Daniel Chipenda of the Liberal Democratic Party of Angola (*Partido Liberal Democrático de Angola*) (0.5%) (Inge Tvedten: *Angola: Struggle for Peace and Reconstruction*, Westview Press, Boulder, Colorado and Oxford, 1997, p. 59). Mingas, independent Angola's first Finance Minister (Secretary of State for Finance), was assassinated during the abortive coup led by Nito Alves on 27 May 1977.
3. Agostinho Neto: 'Communiqué' ('*Ordem de serviço*'), Lusaka, 4 June 1973 (SDA).
4. As chairman of the National Council of Swedish Youth (*Sveriges Ungdomsorganisationers Landsråd*; SUL), Kristiansson had in March 1963 launched the Swedish consumer boycott campaign against South Africa (see Sellström Volume I, pp. 190-98).
5. Letter from Kurt Kristiansson ('Splittring inom MPLA'/'Split within MPLA') to the Ministry for Foreign Affairs, Lusaka, 5 July 1973 (MFA). In the letter, Kristiansson reported from a meeting with Agostinho Neto and 'Iko' Carreira in Lusaka on 23 June. They had conveyed that a conspiracy against the MPLA leadership was discovered in April 1973; that it was led by Chipenda; and that Chipenda had been suspended (ibid.). Before the crisis became known, the Swedish government allocated an amount of 3.5 MSEK for the financial year 1973/74. The same day as the meeting between Neto, Carreira and Kristiansson was held, the MPLA President submitted a detailed proposal regarding the utilization of the allocation (Letter with attachments from Agostinho Neto to the SIDA Director, Lusaka, 23 June 1973) (SDA).
6. Interview with Paulo Jorge, p. 17.

den accorded higher political priority to the Southern African liberation movements, the cooperation with MPLA came under serious strain.

Crisis and Standstill

What was later to be known as the Eastern Revolt faction emerged towards the end of 1972. It was denounced by the leadership around Agostinho Neto six months later. On 3 June 1973, Neto informed the Zambian government that

> as in the cases of FRELIMO and PAIGC[1], the Portuguese secret police (PIDE) infiltrated [a] large number of agents into our movement, with the aim of collecting information, demoralizing the militants and organizing plots. [...] [D]uring the past year, the tribalists of [Ovimbundu] origin organized a plot to destroy MPLA and obstruct unity with FNLA. [They were] tribally motivated and [acted] to avoid alleged domination of [the] 'South' by the 'North'.[2] [...]

> This plot has long-standing antecedents. For some years now, Daniel Chipenda, [MPLA] head of logistics, provided arms for UNITA for tribal reasons, [...] closely aligning himself with the counter-revolution. [...] Two attempts were made to kill the leaders of the movement, one in October 1972 and another in January 1973. [...] In April this year, [the] plot was discovered and subversive elements began to be detained. At present, [they] are prisoners in [our] Kalombo camp [in western Zambia]. They have all confessed that [...] Chipenda was [the] head [of the plot], that the objective was to physically eliminate the President of MPLA and that Chipenda should be [the new] President. [...]

> MPLA [now] requests the following of the Zambian government: [...] That the Zambian authorities should not interfere in the question of the prisoners in [the] Kalombo camp[3], [and] that Daniel Chipenda should not be authorized to leave Zambia before MPLA has taken a decision on [the] question. We also inform the Zambian government that he has already been suspended from his activities in the leadership of the movement.[4]

Kenneth Kaunda's government did not comply with the requests. Chipenda denied involvement in any assassination plans, opposed what he termed Neto's "authoritarian presidentialism" and was given protection by the Zambian authorities. Not without significant support among MPLA's military cadres[5], he managed to secure a political stalemate between the main body of MPLA around President Neto and his own Eastern Revolt faction. From mid-1973, there were two 'MPLA representations' in Zambia. This, in turn, led to a deadlock with regard to the Swedish assistance.

Until the outbreak of the MPLA crisis, the Zambian government encouraged assistance to Agostinho Neto's movement. As late as in March 1973, Foreign Minister Elijah Mudenda made, for example, a personal "appeal" to the SIDA representative in Lusaka to "come to MPLA's aid".[6] When the crisis began, the Zam-

---

1. PAIGC's Secretary General Amílcar Cabral was assassinated on 20 January 1973 in an operation instigated by PIDE.
2. Eventually, Chipenda—although of Ovimbundu origin—did not join UNITA, but FNLA.
3. It was later reported that the five imprisoned dissident leaders had been executed by MPLA. Among them was Commander Paganini, who accompanied the British historian Basil Davidson on his visit to eastern Angola in 1970 (see Basil Davidson: *In the Eye of the Storm: Angola's People*, Longman, London, 1972). The executions contributed to the deterioration of the relations between the Zambian government and MPLA. On the question of liberation movements taking the law into their own hands in Zambia, see the interview with Kenneth Kaunda, p. 240.
4. Cited in Marcum op. cit. (Vol. II), pp. 202-03.
5. Marcum estimates that Chipenda counted on the loyalty of some 2,000-3,000 guerrillas (ibid., p. 251), while MacQueen sets the number at 1,500-2,000 (MacQueen op. cit., p. 171).
6. Letter from E.H.K. Mudenda, Minister of Foreign Affairs, to Kurt Kristiansson, SIDA, Lusaka, 26 March 1973 (SDA). Cf. the interview with Kenneth Kaunda, where the former Zambian President commented upon his relations with Agostinho Neto as follows: "I loved that man. He was a Marxist-Leninist and I am a Christian, but we were very good friends" (p. 241).

bian position dramatically changed. At a meeting with the Swedish ambassador Iwo Dölling in August 1973, Mudenda strongly criticized Agostinho Neto's leadership, surprisingly adding that "UNITA could not be overlooked". In fact, according to Mudenda Zambia "would hold nothing against the formation of a common front between UNITA and the other two movements", that is, FNLA and MPLA.[1] In mid-1973, Kaunda's government thus unexpectedly introduced Jonas Savimbi's UNITA movement into the Angolan equation. As Nyerere at about the same time extended a special invitation to Holden Roberto[2] and the Soviet Union withdrew its support to MPLA[3], Agostinho Neto's position was increasingly precarious.

Of particular significance to the Swedish government was that Kaunda and Nyerere—the two African leaders that were closest to Sweden and who Prime Minister Palme had visited in mid-1971—appeared to change their political allegiances. Zambia and Tanzania were, in addition, important recipients of Swedish development assistance. When the Swedish embassy in Lusaka at the beginning of September 1973 proposed that aid negotiations with MPLA-Neto should be held on a tripartite basis together with the Zambian government, it therefore seemed a constructive way to break the stalemate. The Ministry for Foreign Affairs was, however, of a different opinion and issued a counter-directive. It thereby established a fundamental political principle for Sweden's relations with the Southern African liberation movements and their host governments. The instruction stated:

> We understand the need [for] close contacts with the Zambian government, but negotiations should be held directly with MPLA's official representatives. It does [...] not appear as appropriate to formally act via the Zambian government. A departure [from this principle] may in our opinion run the risk of interference [in the form of] conflicting interests by [the] third party. [In] a similar [...] case [regarding] FRELIMO after Mondlane's death [...], we received a parallel proposal [from] the Tanzanian government, which was declined. This was acknowledged by the Tanzanians.[4]

In spite of the uncertain and fluid situation, the Swedish government only recognized the official MPLA representation—that is, the leadership around Agostinho Neto—as a legitimate counterpart. At the level of the embassy in Lusaka, this was only reluctantly accepted. Through the second half of 1973 and early 1974, ambassador Dölling and SIDA's representative Kristiansson maintained that no support should be extended to MPLA. Giving voice to official Zambian positions, they argued that "Neto and his collaborators could not forward the assistance to those that it mainly concerned, [...] the militants of the liberation movement and their families, [as well as to] the camps, schools and hospitals". Chipenda, on the other hand, "had the means to do so, but any assistance to him could possibly increase

1. Letter ('Utrikesminister Mudenda om MPLA'/'Foreign Minister Mudenda on MPLA') from Iwo Dölling, Swedish ambassador to Zambia, to the Ministry for Foreign Affairs, Lusaka, 20 August 1973 (MFA).
2. The FNLA President made a high-profile four-day visit to Dar es Salaam in July 1973 (Marcum op. cit. (Vol. II), p. 227) and FNLA opened offices in both Tanzania and Zambia in 1974.
3. Agostinho Neto later told Anders Bjurner, second secretary at the Swedish embassy in Lusaka, that the Soviet Union via its embassy in the Zambian capital had extended support to Chipenda (Letter ('Minnesanteckning angående samtal med MPLA's ordförande'/'Memorandum on conversation with the MPLA President') from Anders Bjurner to the Ministry for Foreign Affairs, Lusaka, 24 April 1975) (MFA).
4. Cable from Bengt Säve-Söderbergh, Ministry for Foreign Affairs, to the Swedish embassy in Lusaka, 13 September 1973 (MFA). Säve-Söderbergh was at the time first secretary in the Department for International Development Cooperation. Official Swedish assistance to the liberation movements had in principle to be accepted by the host countries. On the tripartite relations between Sweden, the liberation movements and their host countries, cf. below and the interview with Thabo Mbeki (ANC), pp. 155-56.

the difficulties for an agreement [with Neto]".[1] With little support from the embassy and no aid from Sweden in Zambia, MPLA feared that the assistance had been unilaterally cancelled. Hillevi Nilsson later recalled:

> I was in Lusaka at the beginning of January 1974. [...] I [had] met Neto [in Dar es Salaam] and he asked me if I would go with him to Lusaka for a meeting. [...] Kurt Kristiansson was the SIDA representative in the Swedish embassy in Lusaka. [...] MPLA told me that Chipenda through Kristiansson had managed to cut off the Swedish government's support from October or November 1973. MPLA wondered if this was done on instructions from the Swedish government, asking me to meet either Kristiansson or the Swedish ambassador, Iwo Dölling. But [...] [i]t was Christmas time and they were on holiday. [...] I then proposed that I would take the matter to Sweden and that [the MPLA representative], Saydi Mingas, and I would go to the Ministry for Foreign Affairs and talk to Bengt Säve-Söderbergh. Returning to Sweden, we did so. At the Ministry for Foreign Affairs, they said that the aid had not been cut off from Sweden. It had been done in Lusaka.[2]

The assistance to MPLA had, however, not been cancelled. In addition to the support via UNESCO to the Dolisie school in Congo-Brazzaville[3] and to some minor bilateral projects in Sweden[4], aid deliveries[5] and local procurement to MPLA in Tanzania continued throughout 1973/74. In fact, disbursements made by SIDA in favour of MPLA during the financial year amounted to 0.9 MSEK, reaching a higher total than previous years.[6]

Nevertheless, due to the Zambian government's opposition and to the strained relations between MPLA and the Swedish embassy in Lusaka, no local procurement was carried out in Zambia. More importantly, the Swedish authorities did not process MPLA's request for continued assistance—submitted by President Neto in June 1973—or invite the organization to formal aid negotiations. The cooperation was *de facto* in a state of suspension. Increasingly marginalized, the situation was of great concern to MPLA. It was also seen as most unsatisfactory by both SIDA in Dar es Salaam and at SIDA's headquarters in Stockholm. After a meeting with Pedro Petroff, MPLA's deputy representative to Tanzania, Olof Milton, SIDA's acting representative, wrote a sharp letter to SIDA Stockholm in late January 1974, requesting information with regard to the status of MPLA's submission of June 1973. In the letter, he pointedly added:

> As far as [the SIDA office in Dar es Salaam] is aware, it has from different quarters been recommended to freeze the assistance to MPLA due to the internal problems in the movement. Any confirmation that this actually has been done can, however, not be found in the available documents [...]. [We] would therefore appreciate such information on the matter that will

---

1. Letter ('Utrikesministern om MPLA'/'The Foreign Minister on MPLA') from Iwo Dölling, Swedish ambassador to Zambia, to the Ministry for Foreign Affairs, Lusaka, 9 January 1974 (MFA). The letter was written after a meeting with Zambia's newly appointed Foreign Minister, Vernon Mwaanga. He recommended the Swedish government to "desist from aid discussions with or aid deliveries to MPLA" (ibid.).
2. Interview with Hillevi Nilsson, p. 328. Nilsson's meeting with Säve-Söderbergh took place on 21 January 1974 (Anders Möllander: Memorandum: 'Agostinho Neto om splittringen inom MPLA'/'Agostinho Neto on the split within MPLA', Ministry for Foreign Affairs, Stockholm, 22 January 1974) (MFA).
3. On the assistance to MPLA's school at Dolisie, Congo-Brazzaville, see Sellström Volume I, pp. 398-400.
4. Such as the translation from Swedish into Portuguese of a textbook in physics, to be used at the Dolisie school.
5. For example, in early 1974 SIDA delivered two trucks to MPLA (Astrid Bergquist: Memorandum ('Minnesanteckningar förda vid diskussion den 29.1.1974 angående det svenska stödet till befrielserörelserna'/'Notes from discussion regarding the Swedish support to the liberation movements, 29 January 1974'), SIDA, Stockholm, 12 February 1974) (SDA).
6. See the accompanying disbursement table.

make it possible for us to respond to the questions [raised] by the MPLA office in a correct way.[1]

SIDA shared this concern. In a policy memorandum on the assistance to MPLA, the aid agency underlined in early April 1974 that "the wait and see attitude which presently dominates the Swedish position towards MPLA must come to an end. It only plays into the hands of MPLA's opponents".[2]

Agreement and Postponements

The stalemate was broken when Agostinho Neto in late April 1974—on the eve of the Lisbon coup[3]—unexpectedly paid a surprise visit to Stockholm. At the time, MPLA's international fortunes had reached their nadir.[4] The MPLA President was, however, received at both the Ministry for Foreign Affairs and SIDA, where he forcefully raised the question of Swedish aid. It was established that a total amount of no less than 3.7 MSEK under previous bilateral agreements remained at MPLA's disposal. For the 1974/75 financial year, another 2.5 million out of an indicative planning frame of 4 MSEK was to be added.[5] Total financial resources available to MPLA thus amounted to 6.2 MSEK. Indicating preference for an agricultural project in Congo-Brazzaville, vehicles and vehicle repair facilities, supplies to MPLA's education and health programmes, as well as for food, Neto proposed that no future aid should be delivered to MPLA in Zambia[6], but only in Tanzania and Congo-Brazzaville. It was, finally, decided that formal negotiations between Sweden and MPLA should take place in Dar es Salaam the following month.[7] The drawn-out *de facto* suspension of the bilateral aid relationship appeared to be coming to an end.

As agreed, official discussions were held in the Tanzanian capital on 24-25 May 1974.[8] The Lisbon coup had taken place exactly one month earlier, but the MPLA

1. Letter from Olof Milton ('MPLA's framställning: Vad har hänt?'/'MPLA's request: What has happened?') to SIDA Stockholm, Dar es Salaam, 24 January 1974 (SDA).
2. Astrid Bergquist: Memorandum ('Angående bistånd till MPLA'/'Regarding assistance to MPLA'), SIDA, Stockholm, 11 April 1974 (SDA).
3. Cf. the interview with Bengt Säve-Söderbergh: "Neto was sitting in my kitchen in Stockholm the famous evening of 24 April 1974. He had no idea of what was going to happen in Portugal. He was not informed about the revolt. The following morning he left for Canada" (p. 338).
4. Cf. the interview with Hillevi Nilsson: "Neto came to Sweden in April 1974. He was really worried at that time. We had a meeting with the Africa Groups at our place in Vällingby. Rolf Gustavsson was present, as well as people from the different Africa Groups in Sweden and from *Kommentar*. Neto then asked us straight out: 'What are we going to do? You are the only ones that we can trust in this situation. We cannot trust the Soviet Union, the Swedish government or anyone. What are we going to do? Can you as a solidarity movement tell us?' But, of course, we could not answer. [...] [T]hose who eventually resolved the problem were not the solidarity organizations. It was the people in Luanda" (pp. 329-30).
5. On 13 March 1974, CCHA recommended an allocation of 4 MSEK to MPLA for the financial year 1974/75. Of that amount, 1.5 million was set aside for the Dolisie school (CCHA: 'Protokoll'/'Minutes' ('Sammanträde med beredningen för studiestöd och humanitärt bistånd till afrikanska flyktingar och nationella befri-elserörelser'/'Meeting of the committee on education support and humanitarian assistance to African refugees and national liberation movements'), SIDA, Stockholm, 18 April 1974) (SDA).
6. Apart from local procurement of food for the Angolan refugees in MPLA's Zambian camps.
7. Letters from Agostinho Neto to Lennart Klackenberg, Ministry for Foreign Affairs, Stockholm, 21 and 22 April 1974 (SDA); Astrid Bergquist: Memorandum ('Minnesanteckningar förda vid diskussioner angående bistånd till MPLA den 22.4 [1974]'/'Notes from discussions regarding assistance to MPLA, 22 April [1974]'), SIDA, Stockholm, 26 April 1974 (SDA); Anders Möllander: Memorandum ('Besök av MPLA:s president'/'Visit by the MPLA President'), Ministry for Foreign Affairs, Stockholm, 26 April 1974 (SDA) and 'Agreed minutes of discussions on cooperation between Movimento Popular de Libertação de Angola (MPLA) and Sweden'; Dar es Salaam, [no date, but drafted 25 May 1974]; original in English (SDA).
8. The MPLA delegation was led by Pedro Van-Dunem ('Loy'), representing the movement's Commission for International Cooperation, while Göran Hasselmark, first secretary at the Swedish embassy in Dar es Salaam, headed the Swedish delegation.

delegation confirmed that the priorities given by Neto during his visit to Stockholm "in principle were still valid".[1] Emphasis was given to food, transport and agriculture, with estimated budget shares of around 25, 20 and 15 per cent, respectively. Specifications were made with regard to the requested assistance in most areas, although details concerning the proposed agricultural project in Congo-Brazzaville would be submitted later.[2] Worthy of note considering the earlier, limited, Swedish commodity support to MPLA was that the Angolan movement requested technical assistance in the form of agricultural and transport experts from Sweden.[3]

Finally, the parties agreed that "all assistance would [...] be given subject to approval by any African host country concerned". MPLA "undertook to present [such] evidence".[4] In the critical case of Zambia, it was, however, noted that the authorities did not issue documents to that effect. Against this background, it was proposed from the Swedish side that the OAU Liberation Committee could "act as an intermediary"[5], although it was also underlined that Sweden would need "an assurance that they did not get on the wrong side of the Zambian authorities".[6] A written statement was subsequently obtained from the head office of the OAU Liberation Committee in Dar es Salaam. According to the statement, "all humanitarian assistance considered [by] SIDA [...] to MPLA will be [delivered] without any hindrance. This is in accordance with the clear and unequivocal position by the host authorities and their total commitment towards all the liberation movements recognized by OAU".[7]

Before the comprehensive agreement had been formally endorsed by the Swedish government, the assistance was, however, once again deferred. Due to the rapidly changing situation after the fall of the Caetano regime[8], MPLA turned to Sweden with a request for renewed consultations.[9] In late September 1974, President Neto wrote to Prime Minister Palme, explaining that

> the present situation in our country [calls for] a new strategy concerning the assistance received from certain friendly countries, the intention being to channel [it] to the zones liberated by MPLA. [...] We will as soon as possible [send] you a complete outline of the redefinition of the plans which we have already submitted.[10]

Towards Independence and Understanding

The process towards independence in Angola was considerably more complex and disruptive than in Guinea-Bissau or Mozambique. Deeply divided, the nationalist

1. 'Agreed minutes', op. cit., Dar es Salaam, [25 May 1974] (SDA).
2. Three weeks later, Van-Dunem submitted what he himself called a "more or less detailed application" regarding the agricultural project. However, it was now designed as a project on MPLA's northern front inside Angola (Letter ('Swedish assistance to MPLA for the year 1974/75') from Pedro Van-Dunem ('Loy') to SIDA, Dar es Salaam [no date, but received by the Swedish embassy in Dar es Salaam on 21 June 1974]) (SDA).
3. 'Agreed minutes', op. cit., Dar es Salaam, [25 May 1974] (SDA).
4. Ibid.
5. Ann Wilkens: Memorandum ('Minnesanteckningar från förhandlingar med MPLA den 24-25 maj 1974'/ 'Notes from negotiations with MPLA, 24-25 May 1974'), attached to letter ('Bistånd till MPLA'/'Assistance to MPLA') from Knut Granstedt, Swedish ambassador to Tanzania, to the Ministry for Foreign Affairs, Dar es Salaam, 31 May 1974 (SDA).
6. Ibid.
7. Statement by the OAU Coordinating Committee for the Liberation of Africa to the Swedish embassy, Dar es Salaam, 27 May 1974; original in French (SDA).
8. On 7 September 1974, Portugal and FRELIMO signed the Lusaka Accord, allowing for transfer of power to the Mozambican liberation movement after nine months of transitional government.
9. Letter ('Bistånd till MPLA för budgetåret 1974/75'/'Assistance to MPLA during the financial year 1974/75') from Ernst Michanek, Director General of SIDA, to the Ministry for Foreign Affairs, SIDA, Stockholm, 27 January 1975 (SDA).
10. Letter from Agostinho Neto to Olof Palme, Lusaka, 25 September 1974; original in French (MFA).

movement, in the first place, did not constitute a military threat with enough power to force Portugal into immediate negotiations. While PAIGC in 1973 intensified the liberation effort in Guinea-Bissau and the FRELIMO forces in 1974 accelerated their southward thrust into the settler areas of Mozambique, the un-coordinated campaigns by FNLA, MPLA and UNITA in Angola were largely contained. Secondly, incomparably richer and with a larger Portuguese settler community[1], the Lisbon Junta of National Salvation[2] led by General António de Spínola did not initially contemplate Angola's departure from 'the Portuguese space'. For Spínola and his supporters, "the loss of Guinea was regrettable, the loss of Mozambique a tragedy [...], but the abandonment of Angola was unthinkable".[3] As late as in September 1974—just before he resigned as President of Portugal—Spínola warned the Angolan nationalists that they must learn to distinguish "the line separating liberation from usurpation", foreseeing that

> there will soon be born in the South Atlantic a new Portuguese-speaking state which will constitute, with Brazil and Portugal, the enclosing triangle of a sea which carved out our histories and which will perpetuate the links which in the future once more will unite our three brother countries.[4]

Finally, through the activities of transnational corporations, such as the Gulf Oil company of the United States, Angola's wealth had brought the country into much closer contacts with the global economy than the other Portuguese colonies. In addition to Portuguese and Southern African geo-strategic dimensions, there was, thus, an important involvement by international economic forces which could be expected to resist dramatic change.

In a complex and seemingly never-ending struggle, MPLA would from late 1975 with direct Cuban assistance and resumed Soviet support confront FNLA and UNITA, South Africa and the West. At the time of the April 1974 Lisbon coup, the future ruling Angolan movement was, however, in a deep crisis. Agostinho Neto's leadership was not only challenged by Chipenda's *Revolta do Leste*, but had also been abandoned by the Soviet Union and increasingly questioned by Tanzania and Zambia. In May 1974—two weeks after the coup in Portugal—a group of Brazzaville-based MPLA members around the brothers Mário and Joaquim de Andrade—prominent intellectuals of MPLA's founding generation—also broke with Neto's executive, forming the so called *Revolta Activa* faction.

One month later—at the same time as Savimbi's UNITA, by far the weakest of the Angolan nationalist movements[5], formally concluded a cease-fire with Portugal—MPLA met with the two factions in Lusaka to restore unity, but the effort failed. The question was brought to OAU, which mandated the governments of Congo-Brazzaville, Tanzania, Zaire and Zambia to oversee a process of reconciliation. Hosting both the MPLA executive and Chipenda's faction, Zambia was detailed to bring the parties together. In mid-August 1974, amid rumours that

---

1. Angola was a major producer of oil, coffee, diamonds and iron ore. In 1974, there were some 335,000 white settlers in Angola. The corresponding figure for Mozambique was 200,000 and for Guinea-Bissau 2,000 (Ciment op. cit., p. 34).
2. In Portuguese, *Junta de Salvação Nacional*.
3. Richard A.H. Robinson: *Contemporary Portugal: A History*, George Allen and Unwin, London, 1979, p. 212.
4. Cited in MacQueen op. cit., p. 169.
5. MacQueen op. cit., p. 159. Founded in 1966, UNITA did not appear as a major actor in Angola until after the coup in Portugal in April 1974.

Agostinho Neto had resigned[1], 400 representatives—of whom 165 for Neto, 165 for Chipenda and 70 for de Andrade—gathered under Zambian supervision at a military camp outside Lusaka.

After eleven days of bitter disputes, the conference aborted.[2] In this situation, the MPLA executive convened an Inter-Regional Conference of Militants at Lundoje in the Angolan province of Moxico from 12 to 21 September 1974. Here, delegates from the MPLA-controlled areas inside Angola, the country's urban centres and exile proceeded without outside pressure to elect a new Central Committee and a Political Bureau.[3] They also adopted a political strategy for the transitional phase ahead, emphasizing self-reliance and a non-aligned international course. It was, finally, agreed to establish closer links with social democratic movements and parties, including the Swedish government.[4]

Neto's letter to Palme anticipating a new strategy for the Swedish assistance was written in this context. As Chipenda after his political defeat found new friends in Zaire[5] and the *Revolta Activa* faction sought accommodation with MPLA, Neto's ascendancy removed the last obstacles to Zambian recognition. In early October 1974, representatives of the Norwegian[6] and Swedish embassies in Lusaka were informed during a meeting at the Zambian Ministry of Defence that "the Zambian government [no longer] had any objections to direct assistance to MPLA". However, the spokesperson—Major Mulopa—underlined that "it should be in the donors' interest to take advice from the Zambian authorities". According to Mulopa—who, as an example, said that petrol could not be given directly to a liberation movement—no particular movement would in that way "be unfairly favoured".[7] Neto also took part in the meeting. His view was that MPLA—"notwithstanding the Zambian attitude towards assistance to MPLA"—maintained good relations with the official Norwegian and Swedish aid agencies. "[T]hrough a

---

1. Letter from Kurt Kristiansson to the Ministry for Foreign Affairs, Lusaka, 7 August 1974 (MFA). Kristiansson got his information from the Zambian Foreign Minister Vernon Mwaanga.
2. After the conference, President Kaunda invited Agostinho Neto to the State House in Lusaka. According to Kaunda, "[w]e met for sixteen hours [...]. No breaks for lunch, only tea and scones. I tried to persuade my brother and said: 'Look, you are an organizer. Please, bring all the parties together. It must be possible to do that, because for the time being you need a coalition government'. But I believe that he was under pressure from the Soviet Union. We could not accept that at all" (Interview with Kenneth Kaunda, p. 241).
3. The elected members of the Political Bureau were: Agostinho Neto, Carlos Rocha ('Dilolwa'), Henrique Carreira ('Iko'), Jacob Caetano João ('Monstro Imortal'), João Luís Neto ('Xietu'), Joaquim Kapango, José Eduardo dos Santos, Lopo do Nascimento, Lúcio Lara, Pedro Maria Tonha ('Pédalé') and Rodrigues João Lopes ('Ludy').
4. Letter from Anders Bjurner to the Ministry for Foreign Affairs, Lusaka, 10 October 1974 (MFA). Travelling on a SIDA grant, having close links with IUEF in Geneva, Switzerland, and claiming to represent the Swedish Social Democratic Party, the journalist Leif Biureborgh attended MPLA's Inter-Regional Conference in Moxico. His role would subsequently become controversial. While Neto in a letter to Palme appreciated Biureborgh's presence in Moxico (Letter from Agostinho Neto to Olof Palme, Lusaka, 25 September 1974) (MFA) and the Soviet Union according to Vladimir Shubin—at the time secretary for African affairs of the Soviet Afro-Asian Solidarity Committee—partly based its decision to resume assistance to MPLA on information supplied by IUEF (Conversation with Vladimir Shubin, p. 250), he was not representing the Swedish ruling party (Letter from Sverker Åström, Under-Secretary of State for Foreign Affairs, to Iwo Dölling, Swedish ambassador to Zambia, Stockholm, 27 November 1974) (MFA). During his visit to Zambia and Angola in September 1974, Biureborgh had before the Inter-Regional Conference spoken against the Swedish embassy and also antagonized the Finnish diplomatic representation in Lusaka (Letter from Iwo Dölling to the Ministry for Foreign Affairs, Lusaka, 6 September 1974) (MFA). Biureborgh settled in Luanda after Angola's independence, but was declared *persona non grata* in 1977. He was later welcomed back to the country.
5. Chipenda was formally expelled from MPLA at the end of November 1974.
6. In August 1972, the government of Norway granted 50,000 USD for the construction of a boarding school for Angolan refugee children under MPLA's care at Sikongo in western Zambia. A similar grant was made in early 1973 for MPLA's Augusto Ngangula centre at Chavuma on the Angolan border in the northwestern part of the country. On Norway's assistance to MPLA, see Eriksen in Eriksen (ed.) op. cit., pp. 77-87.
7. Anders Bjurner: Memorandum ('Besök på försvarsministeriet ang. fortsatt bistånd till MPLA'/'Visit to the Ministry of Defence re continued assistance to MPLA'), Lusaka, 10 October 1974 (SDA).

MPLA President
Agostinho Neto with
SIDA's Carin Norberg
in Lusaka, October 1974
(Courtesy of Carin
Norberg)

perhaps too legalistic interpretation", they had, nevertheless, "been made difficult".[1]

It was soon thereafter agreed to hold renewed official negotiations between Sweden and MPLA in Lusaka in mid-December 1974. "In the absence of [the] revised request" anticipated by Neto in his letter to Palme, the Ministry for Foreign Affairs and SIDA decided, however, "not to send a delegation to Lusaka".[2] The consultations were therefore held between the local embassy and MPLA, the former represented by ambassador Iwo Dölling and the SIDA representative Carin Norberg and the latter by Carlos Rocha ('Dilolwa')[3], Garcia Neto[4] and Olga Lima[5]. Before the meeting, MPLA submitted a brief statement, explaining that "the recent cease-fire agreement between MPLA and [the] Portuguese authorities"— signed in mid-October 1974—"has created a new situation which impose[s] a very deep change in our way to see and concept[ualize] the future of our country".[6]

No revolutionary proposals were, however, presented by MPLA. On the contrary, proceeding "very simply and quickly"[7] the negotiations largely confirmed the May agreement. The only major changes introduced by MPLA were that the movement wished to cancel or decrease the proposed assistance for vehicle repairs, school equipment and warehouse facilities in Tanzania and Zambia in favour of expanded transport support in the form of additional vehicles. This was accepted by the Swedish delegation.[8] Of the available amount of 6.2 MSEK, the transport component was increased from 1.4 to 1.8 million, representing a share of almost 30 per cent and encompassing the delivery of 14 lighter four-wheel drive vehicles and 8

1. Cited in ibid.
2. Instruction ('Bistånd till MPLA'/'Assistance to MPLA') from the Ministry for Foreign Affairs to Iwo Dölling, Swedish ambassador to Zambia, Stockholm, 19 November 1974 (SDA).
3. A veteran MPLA instructor, Rocha was elected at the Inter-Regional Conference in September 1974 to the movement's Political Bureau. He became Minister of Economic Planning and Coordination in the first independent Angolan government in November 1975. Dropped from his state and party positions in December 1978, he had just published the important study *Contribuição à História Económica de Angola* ('Contribution to the Economic History of Angola'), INA, Luanda, 1978.
4. Neto was at the time heading MPLA's Commission for International Cooperation.
5. In January 1975, Lima succeeded Manuel Alexandre Rodrigues ('Kito') as MPLA's representative to Zambia.
6. Letter from Garcia Neto to SIDA, Lusaka, 9 December 1974; original in English (SDA).
7. Letter ('MPLA-bistånd 1974/75'/'MPLA Assistance 1974/75') from Anders Bjurner to the Ministry for Foreign Affairs, Lusaka, 17 December 1974 (MFA).
8. 'Agreed minutes of discussions on cooperation between Movimento Popular de Libertação de Angola (MPLA) and Sweden', Lusaka, 10 December 1974 (SDA).

heavy-duty trucks.[1] In addition, an amount of 300,000 SEK—corresponding to 5 per cent of the available funds—was set aside as a cash component, to be disbursed to MPLA in favour of "welfare activities and maintenance of families in need".[2]

After years of trials and tribulations, the Swedish government decided on 13 February 1975 to endorse the understanding reached in Lusaka in December 1974.[3] While it caught up with "the agreements earlier entered into with MPLA"[4], the decision had by then largely been overtaken by the political events regarding the Portuguese colony. The Alvor Agreement had been signed between Portugal, FNLA, MPLA and UNITA on 15 January 1975. Following the agreement, a transitional government formed by the four parties—vested with the powers to prepare for Angola's full independence by 11 November 1975—was installed two weeks later. The decision by the Social Democratic government was against this background strongly contested by the opposition parties, arguing that it constituted undue interference in favour of one political actor in a sensitive process.[5]

When the decision was eventually reached, MPLA had already moved its structures to Luanda.[6] Outstanding technical details and other questions regarding the assistance package could no longer be settled in Lusaka or Dar es Salaam.[7] As the agreement envisaged local procurement of a number of items and there was no official Swedish representation in Angola, urgent humanitarian needs in the areas of food and health could not be met. To solve the problem, SIDA's procurement division in Stockholm entered into "extensive contacts" with various companies in Angola[8], but in May 1975 had to conclude that "the result [...] has been extremely

---

1. Astrid Bergquist: Memorandum ('Bistånd till MPLA under budgetåret 1974/75'/'Assistance to MPLA during the financial year 1974/75'), SIDA, Stockholm, 16 January 1975 (SDA).
2. Letter from S-G Henricsson ('Bistånd till MPLA budgetåret 1974/75'/'Assistance to MPLA in the financial year 1974/75') to SIDA Lusaka, SIDA, Stockholm, 3 March 1975 (SDA).
3. Cable ('Re bistånd till MPLA'/'Re assistance to MPLA') from the Ministry for Foreign Affairs to the Swedish embassy in Lusaka, Stockholm, 12 February 1975 (SDA).
4. Ibid.
5. The debate for or against official assistance to MPLA was given prime space in the major Swedish newspapers. In February-March 1975, the liberal daily *Dagens Nyheter* published, for example, an exchange of opinions between the writer Per Wästberg, a member of the Consultative Committee on Humanitarian Assistance, and David Wirmark of the Liberal Party. Wästberg had visited Angola in early 1975. He was "impressed by MPLA's organization and discipline and frightened by FNLA's superficial militarism and propagandistic and lavish spending". Wästberg described MPLA as a movement which was "independent in its African socialism", with members "who are not primarily soldiers, but ideologically educated workers, peasants and intellectuals who know why they are fighting and have a vision of the society they want. [...] My heart and reason are [therefore] with MPLA" (Per Wästberg: 'Stödet till Angola'/'The support to Angola' in *Dagens Nyheter*, 21 February 1975). Wirmark—who from 1974 had criticized the Swedish government for "flagrantly sabotaging OAU's unity efforts by only extending support to MPLA" (David Wirmark: 'Sverige saboterar OAU?'/'Sweden sabotages OAU?' in *Göteborgs-Posten*, 11 April 1974)—held, however, the opinion that "it is not for [Sweden] to choose between the movements". With close relations to Holden Roberto, he saw FNLA as a genuine liberation movement worthy of Swedish support, adding that assistance "possibly" should also be extended to UNITA (David Wirmark: 'Inte vår sak att välja mellan rörelserna!'/'It is not for us to choose between the movements!' in *Dagens Nyheter*, 5 March 1975). In a lengthy rejoinder, Wästberg, finally, commented that "Sweden has supported MPLA for ten years. I do not think that we—in the words of the [Liberal Party]—would help 'the whole population and the nation in its entirety' if we were to transfer part of our assistance to putschists and terrorists" (Per Wästberg: 'Sverige har rätt att välja sida!'/'Sweden has a right to take a stand!' in *Dagens Nyheter*, 11 March 1975).
6. Lúcio Lara returned to Luanda in December 1974 and on 4 February 1975—twenty-four years after the 1961 uprisings—Agostinho Neto was received by hundreds of thousands of people in the Angolan capital.
7. At the same time, uncoordinated MPLA initiatives in Tanzania and Zambia complicated the situation. For example, in March 1975 Pedro Petroff, MPLA's representative in Dar es Salaam, visited the Swedish embassy and stated that Neto's 1974 agricultural proposal for Congo-Brazzaville—which had later been moved to northern Angola—was now to be implemented in the Cabinda enclave and should be supported (Letter from Anders Möllander ('Samtal med MPLA's Dar es Salaam-representant'/'Conversation with MPLA's Dar es Salaam representative') to SIDA, Dar es Salaam, 13 March 1975) (SDA).
8. Garcia Neto visited SIDA from Angola in April 1975 (Marianne Sundh: Memorandum ('Minnesanteckningar angående biståndet till MPLA under budgetåret 1974/75'/'Notes regarding the assistance to MPLA for the financial year 1974/75'), SIDA, Stockholm, 16 September 1975) (SDA).

disappointing. Either no replies have been received or no goods have been offered".[1] By mid-1975, vehicles and food to a total value of just over one million SEK had been procured.[2]

With the agreed independence date of 11 November 1975 quickly approaching and in the midst of the turbulence reigning in Luanda in mid-1975, Anders Bjurner, second secretary at the Swedish embassy in Lusaka[3], was asked at the end of June to go to the Angolan capital to prepare the terrain for final implementation of the December 1974 agreement. Since his arrival in Lusaka in mid-1974, Bjurner had established close relations with MPLA and the other liberation movements repre-sented in Zambia. In Luanda, he was, however, confronted with a difficult task. The clashes between FNLA and MPLA leading to the 'battle of Luanda' from 9 July 1975—eventually ending with the expulsion of Holden Roberto's movement from the capital—had begun. The 300,000 Portuguese were preparing to leave, abandoning administrative functions, closing businesses and bringing the port to near chaos.[4] Together with Garcia Neto of MPLA's Commission for International Cooperation, Bjurner, however, managed to carry out an initial survey of possible procurement alternatives on the dwindling and unreliable Angolan market.

After submitting a first report to SIDA in mid-July 1975[5], Bjurner returned to Luanda. He held formal consultations with MPLA in the Angolan capital in Octo-ber 1975.[6] Less than two weeks before Angola's independence date—at a time when the Swedish government, on the one hand, was under heavy criticism from the Africa Groups for not disbursing the outstanding assistance to MPLA[7] and, on the other, from the parliamentary opposition for doing just that[8]—SIDA was on 30 October 1975, at long last, in a position to take a final decision.[9] At the same time, the Minister for International Development Co-operation, Gertrud Sigurdsen, declared that "the [Swedish] government will fulfil its undertakings to the MPLA

---

1. Stig Lövgren: Memorandum ('Angående stöd till MPLA 1974/75'/'Regarding support to MPLA 1974/75'), SIDA, Stockholm, 13 May 1975 (SDA).
2. Astrid Bergquist: Memorandum ('Biståndssituationen' /'Status of the assistance'), SIDA, Stockholm, 26 August 1975 (SDA).
3. A leading Swedish diplomatic expert on Southern Africa, Bjurner was in 1994 appointed Deputy Under-Secre-tary of State for Foreign Affairs. As will be evident throughout the text, he played a particularly decisive role regarding Sweden's relations with the region's liberation movements in the mid-1970s.
4. For a masterly description of Luanda in mid-1975, see Ryszard Kapuscinski: *Another Day of Life*, Picador/ Pan Books, London, 1988, pp. 13-19.
5. Letter ('MPLA's biståndsprogram 1974/75'/'MPLA's assistance programme 1974/75') from Anders Bjurner to SIDA, Lusaka, 10 July 1975 (SDA).
6. SIDA: 'Beslut' ('Decision'), No. 658/75, SIDA, Stockholm, 30 October 1975 (SDA).
7. The Africa Groups held their first national congress in Stockholm in May 1975. As a first priority, the con-gress decided to launch a solidarity campaign for MPLA (AGIS: 'Protokoll från Afrikagruppernas i Sverige kongress i Stockholm 17-19.5 1975'/'Minutes from the congress of the Africa Groups in Sweden, 17-19 May 1975', [no place], 22 July 1975) (AGA). Coinciding with the arrival of Maria Jesus de Haller, MPLA's new representative to Sweden, the campaign was carried out in Gothenburg, Lund, Malmö, Stockholm, Umeå, Uppsala and Växjö in October 1975. At the same time, AGIS wrote an open letter to the Swedish government and SIDA, demanding that "the outstanding [funds to MPLA for 1974/75] are accorded without further delay" (AGIS: 'Öppet Brev till Regeringen och SIDA: Stödet till MPLA Måste Fortsätta!'/'Open Letter to the Government and SIDA: The Support to MPLA Must Continue!' in *Afrikabulletinen*, No. 29-30, October 1975, p. 3).
8. In May 1975, a unanimous parliamentary Standing Committee on Foreign Affairs—i.e., including the Social Democratic members—stated that "it would be extremely inappropriate if Sweden extended support to one of the parties in Angola, which could be interpreted as a Swedish stand on an internal Angolan matter" (cited in Stokke op. cit., p. 18). Arguing that a decision on support to MPLA would disqualify Sweden from being impartial—and thus from participation in a possible UN intervention in Angola—the representatives of the Centre and Liberal parties reiterated the position at a meeting with the select Advisory Council on Foreign Affairs on 27 October 1975 (*Dagens Nyheter*, 28 October 1975). The question of partiality versus UN partic-ipation would later be discussed in connection with the independence process in Namibia.
9. SIDA: 'Beslut' ('Decision'), No. 658/75, SIDA, Stockholm, 30 October 1975 (SDA).

liberation movement in Angola".[1] The bulk of the 6.2 MSEK allocation to MPLA discussed with Agostinho Neto in Stockholm on the eve of the Lisbon coup was thus committed at the eleventh hour. The actual disbursements—*inter alia* covering local procurement of food, ambulances and medical equipment, as well as newsprint supplied from Sweden[2]—were made after Angola's independence. They amounted in total to 5.4 MSEK during the financial year 1975/6.[3] The balance was paid out in 1976/77, mainly as part of emergency and development assistance to independent Angola.

Independence, Neto and Palme

The Swedish humanitarian support to MPLA was never significant in quantitative terms. In addition, by mid-1975, only 2.3 MSEK had been disbursed, corresponding to a mere 5 per cent of the assistance paid out in favour of PAIGC of Guinea-Bissau or 13 per cent of the funds channelled to FRELIMO of Mozambique. By far the least favoured of the seven African liberation movements supported by Sweden, the official aid relationship did, nevertheless, amount to a *de facto* recognition of MPLA as Angola's legitimate 'government-in-waiting'. This is also how it was understood by the leadership of MPLA[4], as well as by the competing FNLA[5] and UNITA[6] movements. Despite mutual frustrations regarding the implementation of the humanitarian support and against the position taken by other actors close to Sweden—notably the Zambian government—the Social Democratic government never broke with MPLA or established official links with Daniel Chipenda's *Revolta do Leste*, FNLA or UNITA. The relations established through the Swedish assistance made it possible for the two parties to find common ground and establish a lasting political relationship.

When in 1973 the Soviet Union suspended its support to MPLA, Sweden was together with Cuba and Yugoslavia among the few countries that maintained close political relations with Agostinho Neto's movement.[7] After the intervention of the superpowers in the drama which escalated as Angola's independence was approaching[8], MPLA would in the West commonly be regarded as a Moscow-backed Communist organization. This was, however, the outcome of preconceived Cold War ideas rather than a stand based on familiarity with the aims and objectives of the nationalist organization. Describing "the bonds between the MPLA leadership and [the] Swedish Social Democracy" as "unique in the [W]estern

---

1. 'Statement by the Minister for International Development Cooperation, Mrs. Sigurdsen, concerning assistance to the MPLA in Angola', 30 October 1975, in Ministry for Foreign Affairs: *Documents on Swedish Foreign Policy: 1975*, Stockholm, 1977, p. 227.
2. Ibid.
3. See the accompanying disbursement table.
4. Interview with Lúcio Lara, p. 21.
5. Interview with Holden Roberto, p. 33.
6. Interview with Jorge Valentim, p. 35.
7. Interview with Paulo Jorge, p. 17.
8. In October 1975, a force of some 3,000 South African/UNITA/FNLA-Chipenda troops invaded Angola and advanced up the coast towards Luanda, while joint Zairean/FNLA forces attacked from Zaire. The objective—planned by the US intelligence agency CIA (John Stockwell: *In Search of Enemies: A CIA Story*, W.W. Norton, New York, 1978)—was to forestall an MPLA victory and take Luanda by 11 November 1975. When the South African invasion was a fact, MPLA requested military assistance from Cuba. Under *Operación Carlota*, the first Cuban contingent arrived in Luanda on 10 November 1975. To support the MPLA/Cuban troops, military hardware was at the same time supplied by the Soviet Union (on the Cuban intervention, see Gabriel García Márquez: 'The Cuban Mission to Angola' in *New Left Review*, No.101-2, pp. 123-37, February-April 1977).

world", Pierre Schori[1]—who from the mid-1960s was closely involved with the liberation struggles in Southern Africa—has written that

> Neto often turned to us for advice on various issues, both international and domestic. To us he seemed anything but an implacable Marxist revolutionary. I came to know [him] as a shy, responsive person, firm in matters of principle, but always ready to compromise.[2]

Of all the tragic elements in the Angolan drama, one of the most salient is that MPLA's non-aligned ambition was not recognized by the Western powers. As stated by MPLA's Alberto Ribeiro-Kabulu,

> the dynamics of the Cold War and the fact that [...] Portugal was secluded by a fascist regime which did not allow any kind of contact with the rest of the world [...] placed our liberation struggle and its political motivations one-sidedly [...] in the socialist camp, when, indeed, it was genuinely non-aligned.[3]

Socialist perspectives[4] and non-alignment brought MPLA and the ruling Swedish Social Democratic Party closer together. According to Ribeiro-Kabulu,

> [t]he neutrality of Sweden was very important for [our] relationship. We were looking for support outside the Cold War polarization and it could only come from the Nordic countries. [...] In addition, Neto was somehow seduced by Olof Palme, Sweden and the Nordic countries regarding the way that they understood the nationalist interest of their own countries, based on moral principles and independence in the divided bipolar world.[5]

In his letter to Palme quoted above, the victorious—and confident—MPLA President stated to the Swedish Premier and party leader after the Inter-Regional Conference in late September 1974 that

> we have [during the conference] reflected on the need to render the relations between our two organizations closer, since our [...] countries in a near future, definitely, are destined to establish important links of cooperation in areas of common interest. The relations which now exist forecast a good development of this cooperation. We [...] do not think that certain misunderstandings with MPLA at the level of the [Swedish] diplomatic mission in Lusaka have [...] affected the good relations developed [in] Stockholm [and elsewhere].[6]

In connection with the tenth anniversary of Zambia's independence, Neto met the Swedish Minister for Transport and Communications, Hans Gustafsson, a month later, and in early December 1974 Palme formally replied to the MPLA President. Friendly[7] and correct, his letter did not, however, discuss the relations between

---

1. Attached to the national board of the Social Democratic Party in 1965, Schori served as its international secretary from 1967 to 1971 and between 1977 and 1982. He was Under-Secretary of State for Foreign Affairs from 1982 to 1991 and became Minister for International Development Co-operation in 1994.
2. Schori op. cit., p. 12.
3. Letter from Alberto Ribeiro-Kabulu to the author, [Harare], 26 May 1998.
4. In an interview with the British journalist Victoria Brittain in *The African Communist*, Lúcio Lara—considered as MPLA's leading ideologue—explained in 1996: "[O]ur 'socialist' choice [...] had its roots in our history. We had very simple aims, which struck a chord with peasants and workers alike: to end exploitation and to give the people [...] power to have control over their own lives. Socialism [...] appeared [...] the most obvious way to achieve these objectives. [...] MPLA had come from the bush with socialist ideas, but we lacked the organization to achieve socialism. [...] [We have been regarded] as Communists, which is false. [...] We had terrible problems with the Soviets. [...] We had problems every time the Russians tried to use their approach [...] to force our country to do something. We always reacted with outrage. The Soviets withdrew their support from the MPLA when we returned to Angola. [...] It wasn't until later, when we got the support of Cuba—which we asked for—that [the] relations with Russia improved. [W]e've always been very independent, even with regard to our allies. The Soviets had misgivings and wanted to impose their party line on us, [but] we never accepted" ('Eighteen Years Later... Speaking to Lúcio Lara' in *The African Communist*, No. 143, First Quarter 1996, pp. 55-61).
5. Interview with Alberto Ribeiro-Kabulu, pp. 29-30.
6. Letter from Agostinho Neto to Olof Palme, Lusaka, 25 September 1974; original in French (MFA).
7. Palme addressed Neto as "dear friend".

MPLA and the Social Democratic Party, nor the future bilateral relations with Angola. Instead, it focused on the question of Swedish aid to MPLA—an issue also raised by Neto—underlining that "it will be necessary to have renewed, practical discussions on the subject".[1] As earlier noted, official aid consultations were held in Lusaka the following week.

Closely connected to Mário Soares'[2] Socialist Party and at the same time following the developments in Angola, Guinea-Bissau and Mozambique, Palme and the ruling party would in 1974-75 pay particular attention to the situation in Portugal. In May 1974—only two weeks after the MFA coup—a delegation from the Nordic labour movements visited Lisbon. At the beginning of October 1974—shortly after the departure of General Spínola—the Social Democratic Party launched a solidarity campaign with the democratic forces in Portugal, and at the end of the month Palme paid a visit to the country.[3] The visit included discussions with MFA's Rosa Coutinho and Foreign Minister Mário Soares. The political situation in Portugal at the time was volatile, not least due to the decolonization process and to the arrival of thousands of Portuguese *retornados* from Africa. Respecting Portugal's role in the negotiations with the liberation movements, Schori later commented that

> [i]t was inevitable that Portugal [...] had to take responsibility for tens of thousands of Portuguese [...] The political situation in Portugal was difficult and could have turned against the government, bringing the conservatives back into power. It was [...] a national, domestic question for Portugal and we fully understood that. What we tried to do was to get the different parties [in Portugal and the colonies] together. For that purpose, I acted several times as a go-between, sending messages back and forth between Soares and some African leaders. I think that it was important. [...] I trusted both sides and Mário Soares really tried to work things out.[4]

After the agreement on Angola's independence signed at Alvor in Portugal on 15 January 1975, the Swedish government kept a low profile with regard to the developments in the country. It, however, remained in regular contact with MPLA via the Swedish embassy in Lusaka and through visits to Luanda, not least concerning the finalization of the outstanding humanitarian support. Nevertheless, the fragility of the Angolan process was such that when MPLA in May 1975 proposed an official visit to Sweden by Agostinho Neto, it was considered inopportune.[5] However, other important MPLA delegations went there for discussions with the ruling party. In October 1975, for example, Roberto de Almeida and Paulo Jorge attended the Social Democratic Party congress together with the movement's resident representative, Maria Jesus de Haller.[6] When on 11 November 1975 Agostinho Neto pro-

1. Letter from Olof Palme to Agostinho Neto, Stockholm, 3 December 1974; original in French (MFA).
2. Responsible for the decolonization negotiations, Soares served as Foreign Minister in the post-Caetano government from 1974 to 1975. For FRELIMO's, MPLA's and UNITA's relations with Mário Soares and the Socialist Party of Portugal, see the interviews with Marcelino dos Santos (pp. 51-52), Lúcio Lara (pp. 19-20) and Jorge Valentim (p. 35).
3. On the Swedish Social Democratic Party and Portugal, see Pierre Schori: *Dokument Inifrån: Sverige och Storpolitiken i Omvälvningarnas Tid* ('Documents from Within: Sweden and Big Politics in the Era of Upheavals'), Tidens Förlag, Stockholm, 1992, pp. 221-50.
4. Interview with Pierre Schori, p. 334.
5. Letter from Ann Wilkens, Ministry for Foreign Affairs, to the Swedish embassy in Lusaka, Stockholm, 27 May 1975 (SDA). The situation in Mozambique was very different. In mid-April 1975, FRELIMO's Vice-President Marcelino dos Santos led a large delegation to Sweden and the other Nordic countries.
6. Socialdemokraterna: 'Verksamheten 1975' ('Activities 1975'), p. 79 (LMA).

Agostinho Neto
proclaiming the
People's Republic of
Angola, Luanda,
11 November 1975
(Photo: Georg Dreifaldt)

claimed Angola's independence in the besieged capital[1], he had thus well-founded hopes that the Social Democratic government would recognize the new People's Republic of Angola.[2]

Although Sven Andersson, the Minister for Foreign Affairs, on the day of independence "with great satisfaction [...] welcome[d] Angola as an independent nation"—noting that "today the last vestiges of the centuries-old Portuguese colonial regime in Africa have disappeared"[3]—Sweden would, however, along with most Western and African countries[4] withhold official recognition. In his statement, the Foreign Minister declared that "the question as to how we are to arrange our relations with the independent state of Angola must be left open, pending a stabilization of [the] political conditions there".[5] Two weeks later, he declared in parliament that

> according to the principle followed by Sweden and many other countries, the government which is recognized must exercise effective control over the territory and have a certain measure of stability. The situation on 11 November was such that neither MPLA, UNITA or FNLA could be regarded as exercising [...] effective control. [...] Sweden's views [...] are the same today as they were on 11 November. [...] I wish [, however,] to stress that the question of establishing diplomatic relations has nothing to do with our sympathies for the one or the

1. At the time, the combined South African/UNITA/FNLA-Chipenda forces stood only some 200 kilometres south of Luanda, while the Zairean/FNLA troops were less than 50 kilometres north of the capital. The Portuguese government was largely responsible for the crisis. Not responding to the South African and Zairean military interventions, the Lisbon government simply abandoned the scene. On 10 November 1975, the Portuguese High Commissioner eventually folded the flag and "in a pathetic end to centuries of colonial rule stole out of besieged Luanda [...], leaving the Angolans to fight it out" (Marcum op. cit. (Vol. II), p. 271). There was no Portuguese presence at the following day's independence ceremony in Luanda. Notably, Rosa Coutinho—the former Portuguese commander in Angola, close to MPLA and at that point leading the Portuguese government—regretted that his position in Lisbon prevented an acceptance of Agostinho Neto's personal invitation (MacQueen op. cit., p. 197). Portugal only recognized the MPLA government on 22 February 1976, i.e. after Sweden. The relations broke down in April and were not re-established until 30 September 1976.

2. In recognition of the solidarity work carried out by the Africa Groups, MPLA invited the organization to the independence celebrations. While Hillevi Nilsson and other members by that time were living in Luanda, AGIS was represented by Georg Dreifaldt. Dreifaldt—whose long involvement with Southern Africa as an activist and a SIDA official will be obvious throughout this study—captured the historic moment when Neto proclaimed the People's Republic of Angola on widely published photos.

3. 'Statement by the Foreign Minister, Mr. Andersson', 11 November 1975, in Ministry for Foreign Affairs: *Documents on Swedish Foreign Policy: 1975*, Stockholm, 1977, p. 201.

4. It was not until 11 February 1976 that OAU decided to welcome Angola as a member.

5. Ibid. On 11 November 1975, FNLA and UNITA proclaimed their own Democratic People's Republic of Angola in Nova Lisboa (now Huambo). Patched together to counter MPLA's initiative, it was not recognized by any nation and soon fell apart.

other movement. The government's view is that MPLA is the political movement [which has] roots among the people [and] has combined the struggle for independence with efforts to establish social and economic justice in Angola.[1]

The position caused great disappointment in Luanda. After a meeting with Agostinho Neto on 12 November 1975, a friend working for the Swedish television wrote to Pierre Schori that "the President and the comrades are disappointed and unhappy about Sweden's silence". Neto asked him to convey to Schori that "in the absence of a Swedish recognition within a reasonable period of time, Angola would be forced to recall MPLA's representative [from Sweden]".[2] At about the same time, the Angolan leadership was, however, encouraged by Prime Minister Palme's stand.

Visiting the United States as the Angolan independence crisis was unfolding, Palme strongly opposed the opinion that MPLA was a Communist organization. According to the *Saint Louis Post*, the Swedish Premier—"as usual talking to the Americans like a Dutch uncle"—said during a press conference in New York that "it was a gross distortion to call [MPLA] Marxist", adding that "American emphasis on Soviet support for the movement overlooked the fact that Sweden and other nations had supported [it] before the Soviet Union did". Palme also warned that "dire predictions about Angola being on the road to becoming a Soviet satellite could easily turn [the country] into another Congo, with white mercenaries fighting black guerrillas in a new arena of East-West combat".[3]

The MPLA government acknowledged Palme's stand. Before an official Swedish recognition of the People's Republic of Angola had been extended, Foreign Minister José Eduardo dos Santos thus led an important delegation to Sweden in late January 1976.[4] In Stockholm, dos Santos was received by both his counterpart and the Minister for Development Cooperation.[5] He also raised the issue of humanitarian assistance to independent Angola with SIDA's Director General Ernst Michanek.[6] Noting that the direct support to MPLA was about to be "smoothly" finalized[7], he particularly emphasized the need for support in the areas of medicines and food.[8] The request was received in a positive spirit. The Swedish government was via

---

1. 'Reply by Mr. Andersson, Minister for Foreign Affairs, to questions put by Mr. Granstedt and Mr. Takman', 2 December 1975, in Ministry for Foreign Affairs: *Documents on Swedish Foreign Policy: 1975*, Stockholm, 1977, p. 202.
2. Letter from [Gaetano] Pagano to Pierre Schori, Luanda, 18 November 1975; original in Spanish (LMA).
3. *Saint Louis Post*, 13 November 1975. Palme's worries were not unfounded. A significant number of mainly American and British mercenaries participated in the war against the MPLA government. Thirteen of them were brought to trial in Luanda in June 1976 and four were later sentenced to death. One of them was a US citizen. On 30 June 1976, the US Secretary of State Henry Kissinger delivered an urgent message to Olof Palme via the United States embassy in Sweden, asking him "to persuade President Neto to rescind the death sentence" (Cable from the Ministry for Foreign Affairs to the Swedish embassy in Washington, Stockholm, 30 June 1976) (LMA). Forming part of the Swedish government's intermediary mission between Angola, Cuba and the United States, the question was raised by Pierre Schori in discussions with President Neto in Luanda (Schori (1994) op. cit., pp. 15-16). The proceedings of the Angolan tribunal against the captured mercenaries were followed by an international commission. Lars Rudebeck, associate professor in political science at the University of Uppsala, participated in the commission (Lars Rudebeck: 'På de anklagades bänk i Angola'/'On the bench of the accused in Angola' in *Dagens Nyheter*, 1 July 1976).
4. The delegation included the future Foreign Minister (1984-89) Alfonso Van-Dunem ('Mbinda'), Ambrósio Lukoki—then secretary to President Neto—and Pascal Luvualu, member of MPLA's Central Committee and leader of the MPLA-aligned National Union of Angolan Workers (*União Nacional dos Trabalhadores de Angola*; UNTA).
5. Ministry for Foreign Affairs: Memorandum ('Sverige-Angola'/'Sweden-Angola'), Political department, Stockholm, 17 April 1978 (MFA).
6. Marianne Sundh: Memorandum ('Besök av MPLA's utrikesminister José Eduardo dos Santos'/'Visit by MPLA's Foreign Minister José Eduardo dos Santos'), SIDA, Stockholm, 27 January 1976 (SDA).
7. The last delivery from Sweden under the October 1975 understanding with MPLA—covering newsprint—was made on 8 January 1976 (ibid.).
8. Ibid.

SIDA subsequently to grant 25 MSEK to Angola in the form of emergency aid.[1] The amount was raised to 40 million during the financial year 1976/77.[2] A large part of the funds was used for the procurement of trucks, raft-bridges and ferries to rebuild the war-ravaged transport network.[3]

Diplomatic Relations and Mediation

On 18 February 1976—shortly after dos Santos' visit—Sweden officially recognized the People's Republic of Angola.[4] Although South African armoured columns were still in the country[5] and the UNITA, FNLA and Chipenda forces were fighting MPLA, Foreign Minister Andersson declared that "today it can be said that the government in Luanda exercises effective control [...]. [T]hus, according to Swedish practice, the basic requirement for our diplomatic recognition [...] is now fulfilled".[6] Expanding on his statements made in the United States in November 1975, Palme had by that time reduced recognition to a formality. In an article in the Swedish liberal newspaper *Dagens Nyheter*, on 4 February 1976 he gave an overview of the Social Democratic Party's historical relations with the cause of national liberation in Africa, particularly discussing the Angolan struggle. It was, in his own words, "an attempt at an ideological analysis".[7]

In the prominent article—published on the anniversary of the Angolan insurrection of 1961—the Prime Minister stated that

> MPLA is almost consistently described as 'Marxist', pro-Soviet or—in the [Swedish conservative] press—even as Communist. This is a propagandistic simplification. Marxism has historically been of little significance to African socialism [and] MPLA does not markedly differ from other liberation movements. [...] At any rate, Communists have until this year constituted a very small minority in MPLA. [...]

> MPLA visited most countries in the Western world trying to get weapons for the struggle against the Portuguese. The answer was no. They then turned to the Soviet Union and the answer was yes. Lately, MPLA has received massive military support from the Soviet Union and Cuba. [...] We are critical of this, just as we are critical of all other foreign intervention. [...]

> The Swedish position has been completely clear. We are against all foreign interference in the internal affairs of Angola. It must stop. Angola should be given the possibility to [achieve] national independence, a non-aligned position and the opportunity to form its internal development by itself. I am convinced that this is in accordance with MPLA's own objectives. [...]

> It is important to remember that the war waged in Angola is not between 'the Free World' and 'Communism' [and] that it must not in a prejudiced way be viewed on the basis of the clichés of the Cold War or from the perspective of the conflicts between the super powers. It is funda-

---

1. Stokke op. cit., p. 175.
2. Ibid.
3. Ministry for Foreign Affairs: Memorandum ('Sverige-Angola'/'Sweden-Angola'), Political department, Stockholm, 17 April 1978 (MFA).
4. 'Sweden recognizes the People's Republic of Angola' in Ministry for Foreign Affairs: *Documents on Swedish Foreign Policy: 1976*, Stockholm, 1978, p. 242. Immediately thereafter, Anders Thunborg of the Foreign Ministry visited Luanda for talks on the future relations between Sweden and Angola (cf. Carin Norberg: 'Reserapport från besök i Angola 7-14 juni 1976'/'Travel report from visit to Angola, 7-14 June 1976'), Swedish embassy, Lusaka, 12 July 1976) (SDA).
5. Pushed back by the combined MPLA-Cuban forces, the South Africans retreated to Namibia on 27 March 1976.
6. 'Sweden recognizes the People's Republic of Angola' in Ministry for Foreign Affairs: *Documents on Swedish Foreign Policy: 1976*, Stockholm, 1978, p. 242.
7. Pierre Schori: Memorandum ('Samtal statsministern - Kubas ambassadör den 30 april 1976'/'Conversation [between] the Prime Minister [and the] Cuban ambassador, 30 April 1976'), Ministry for Foreign Affairs, Stockholm, [no date] (MFA).

mentally a continuation of the long liberation struggle that was embarked upon one and a half decades ago and which in its final phase has had a tragic course due to internal divisions and foreign intervention.[1]

Palme also raised the question of violence in the African liberation struggles. Noting that "there is hardly any doubt that the great majority of [the liberation movements] have tried to achieve independence by way of peaceful negotiation", he added that

> [t]here has been very little revolutionary romanticism in their way of thinking. [...] If violence has had to be used as a last resort, it has, in my opinion, essentially been due to the colonial power. The liberation movements have been put in a position where all other avenues seemed closed. Armed violence [thus] appeared as inevitable to achieve national independence. [...] As President Nyerere has pointed out, they could hardly fight the colonial armies—well equipped by certain Western states—with bows and arrows. The Western countries simply gave them no option.[2]

Finally, Palme discussed the role of Cuba in the Angolan conflict. Sweden had since 1971 extended official development assistance to Cuba and the Prime Minister had as recently as in June 1975 paid a highly successful visit to the country. When the Cuban presence in Angola became known, the Swedish non-socialist opposition parties demanded that the assistance should be cancelled.[3] Palme took issue with such views, arguing that it was "dangerous to use development assistance as an instrument of sudden punishment or award with regard to foreign policy elements of [the] recipient countries. This is", Palme stated, "quite incompatible with a long-term development cooperation policy".[4] Furthermore,

> [t]he substantial Cuban intervention took place after it was clear that the South African regime had strongly intervened with military forces on the side of UNITA and FNLA. [...] It has ideologically been motivated as support to the Third World in the struggle against colonialism and racism. A Swedish act of reprisal could in such a situation be regarded as [a] rich, white country's need to reprimand the Third World.[5]

Palme's article made a great impact.[6] It was brought to the attention of the Cuban Premier Fidel Castro, who took it as a point of departure to explain the motives

---

1. Olof Palme: 'Kriget i Angola: Befrielsekampens fortsättning' ('The war in Angola: Continuation of the liberation struggle') in *Dagens Nyheter*, 4 February 1976. In the article, Palme only mentioned FNLA and UNITA in connection with the support they were receiving from the United States and South Africa. It is interesting to note that Demba Paku Zola, responsible for FNLA's foreign relations, on 10 February 1976—at a time when the embassy had not yet received the article—visited the Swedish embassy in Kinshasa to formally protest against "Palme's statement" (Letter ('FNLA-protest mot statsminister Palmes uttalande om Angola'/'Protest by FNLA against Prime Minister Palme's statement on Angola') from Sture Theolin, second secretary at the Swedish embassy in Kinshasa, to the Ministry for Foreign Affairs, Kinshasa, 11 February 1976) (MFA). After FNLA's defeat in the 1975-76 power struggle, the influence of the movement quickly declined.
2. Palme in *Dagens Nyheter*, 4 February 1976. On Palme and his early commitment to the cause of national liberation in Africa and Asia, see Sellström Volume I, pp. 91-96.
3. In particular, the Moderate and the Liberal parties. See, for example, 'Reply by the Minister for Foreign Affairs to Mr. Björck's interpellation on the presence of Cuban troops in Angola and to Mr. Ullsten's question on Swedish repudiation of foreign interference in the fighting in Angola', Ministry for Foreign Affairs, Press department, Stockholm, 10 February 1976 (MFA). Anders Björck represented the Moderate Party and Ola Ullsten the Liberal Party. In 1977—ironically at the same time as regular development cooperation with Angola started—the non-socialist government under Prime Minister Thorbjörn Fälldin excluded Cuba from the group of so called 'programme countries', substituting grant assistance for other forms of cooperation.
4. Palme in *Dagens Nyheter*, 4 February 1976.
5. Ibid.
6. President Nyerere—with whom Palme maintained regular correspondence—was of the opinion that the Swedish Premier "really looked upon the matter in the right way [...], *inter alia* rejecting all this talk about Communism". Nyerere also made sure that Palme's article was published in Tanzania (Letter ('Samtal med president Nyerere om Angola och Rhodesia - Vädjan om svenskt bistånd'/'Conversation with President Nyerere about Angola and Rhodesia - Appeal for Swedish assistance') from Knut Granstedt, Swedish ambassador to Tanzania, to the Ministry for Foreign Affairs, Dar es Salaam, 16 February 1976) (MFA).

President Neto hosting an informal dinner for Swedish Social Democratic visitors in Luanda, 1978: On Neto's right is Gertrud Sigurdsen and on his left Pierre Schori (Courtesy of Pierre Schori)

behind the intervention in Angola. Through the Cuban ambassador to Sweden, Castro delivered a long message to Palme on 30 April 1976.[1] It marked the beginning of an intensive diplomatic exchange between Cuba, Sweden, Angola, Portugal[2] and the United States, continuing until the end of September. Pierre Schori—who served as a link between Palme, Neto and the Socialist Party of Portugal[3] and also participated in the meetings with the Cubans and the Americans—has described the sequence of the events.[4] In addition to Castro and Palme, the Angolan President Agostinho Neto and the US Secretary of State Henry Kissinger played prominent roles in the diplomatic exercise, in which the MPLA government at the same time sought to establish normal relations with the United States[5] and mend fences with Portugal.[6] In the case of the Angolan-US relations, the initiative eventually failed. On 16 September 1976—a week before the Social Democratic Party lost the parliamentary elections in Sweden—Kissinger, nevertheless, wrote a letter to Palme, acknowledging his "assistance in developing the groundwork for a [...] dia-

1. Pierre Schori: Memorandum ('Samtal statsministern - Kubas ambassadör den 30 april 1976'/'Conversation [between] the Prime Minister [and the] Cuban ambassador 30 April 1976'), Ministry for Foreign Affairs, Stockholm, [no date] (MFA). Of general interest is that Castro in his message emphasized that Neto had requested Cuban military assistance; that the number of Cuban soldiers was appreciably higher than the figure of 15,000 mentioned by international media; and that it was a purely bilateral action. According to Castro, "you could indeed say that it was Cuba which through its support to Angola involved the Soviet Union" (ibid.).
2. Angola and Portugal did not maintain diplomatic relations from mid-May until the end of September 1976. The Social Democratic Party's contact in Portugal was Rui Mateus, the international secretary of the Socialist Party, who had "lived as a refugee in Lund and spoke fluent Swedish" (Schori (1994) op. cit.). Foreign Minister Mário Soares—the leader of the Socialist Party—was largely regarded by the Angolans as responsible for the strained relationship (Pierre Schori: Memorandum ('Samtal i Luanda den 15-17 juni 1976'/'Conversations in Luanda, 15-17 June 1976'), Cabinet Office, Stockholm, 23 June 1976 (LMA) and Anders Bjurner: Memorandum ('Samtal med Paulo Jorge, president Netos utrikespolitiske rådgivare'/'Conversation with Paulo Jorge, President Neto's foreign policy adviser'), Swedish embassy, Luanda, 12 May 1976) (MFA).
3. Invited by the Angolan President, Schori visited Luanda for talks with Agostinho Neto and Paulo Jorge, then foreign policy adviser in the President's Office, in mid-June 1976.
4. Schori (1994) op. cit., pp. 6-19. Schori's booklet on Southern Africa originally appeared in Swedish as a chapter in his *Dokument Inifrån: Sverige och Storpolitiken i Omvälvningarnas Tid*, published in 1992.
5. Pierre Schori: Memorandum [on conversation with Mrs. de Haller, Angola's ambassador to Sweden, no date, but 30 August 1976] (MFA). There was, in Neto's view, "a great future for bilateral relations between Angola and USA".
6. Schori (1994) op. cit., p. 14.

logue with the government of Angola. [...] Given the respect accorded Sweden throughout the Third World, your cooperation [has been] both helpful and very much appreciated".[1]

At the same time as these multilateral efforts took place, an official Swedish representation was established in Luanda[2] and a number of official delegations visited Angola to discuss the future bilateral relationship between the two countries, including the question of development assistance.[3] As in the case of Mozambique, the issue of support to the Southern African liberation movements hosted by the newly independent country—notably SWAPO of Namibia, ANC of South Africa and ZAPU of Zimbabwe—was raised in this context. In June 1976, Paulo Jorge explained to representatives from the Ministry for Foreign Affairs and SIDA that "nothing prevented any of the movements [supported by Sweden] from receiving goods in Angola".[4] Deliveries under the Swedish humanitarian assistance to SWAPO and ANC in Angola started soon thereafter.

Non-Socialist Continuity and UNITA

In September 1976, the Social Democratic Party lost the parliamentary elections to a non-socialist coalition led by the Centre Party chairman Thorbjörn Fälldin. Karin Söder of the Centre Party was appointed Minister for Foreign Affairs and Ola Ullsten of the Liberal Party Minister for International Development Cooperation. As the non-socialist parties—notably through Fälldin and Ullsten—had for many years advocated Swedish support to FNLA, there were in Angola well-founded reasons to be concerned about the relationship with its main Western supporter.[5] There was, however, to be no change in Sweden's official policy.[6] Fälldin's government proceeded to accord Angola the status of core 'programme country'. As early

---

1. Letter from Henry Kissinger to Olof Palme, [no place], 16 September 1976 (MFA). Discussing the actors and events leading up to the Angolan crisis of 1975-76, twenty years later Kissinger wrote that Jonas Savimbi "had accepted support from wherever it was available, which, in his case, for a long time was China and, to a lesser extent, admirers from Scandinavia, mostly from Sweden" (Henry Kissinger: *Years of Renewal*, Simon & Schuster, New York, 1999, p. 794). With regard to Sweden, the statement by the former US Secretary of State is inaccurate. It was only in the mid-1980s that a group of right wing Swedes expressed political support for UNITA. There is no evidence that Savimbi's organization during the first half of the 1970s received material or financial assistance from Swedish sources.
2. A Swedish embassy was opened in October 1976.
3. Anders Bjurner: Memorandum ('Samtal med Paulo Jorge, president Neto's utrikespolitiske rådgivare'/'Conversation with Paulo Jorge, President Neto's foreign policy adviser'), Swedish embassy, Luanda, 12 May 1976 (MFA).
4. Ann Wilkens: Memorandum ('Samtal med Paulo Jorge om stöd till befrielserörelser verksamma i Angola'/'Conversation with Paulo Jorge on support to liberation movements active in Angola'), Ministry for Foreign Affairs, Stockholm, 23 June 1976 (MFA). The meeting with Jorge took place in Luanda on 10 June 1976. Meetings were also held with ANC's representatives in Luanda, Cassius Make and Max Moabi (ibid.). In parallel talks with Schori, Neto confirmed in mid-June 1976 that "Angola had given [SWAPO] bases, where they [...] have a great deal of armed forces" (Pierre Schori: Memorandum ('Samtal i Luanda den 15-17 juni 1976'/'Conversations in Luanda, 15-17 June 1976'), Cabinet Office, Stockholm, 23 June 1976) (LMA). Schori also met representatives of ANC, SWAPO and ZAPU during his visit.
5. In discussions with Rui Mateus of the Socialist Party of Portugal, Neto at the beginning of September 1976 expressed concern about a possible Social Democratic defeat in the Swedish elections (Cable from the Swedish embassy in Portugal to the Ministry for Foreign Affairs, Lisbon, 6 September 1976) (MFA).
6. Although the Liberal Party advocated support to both FNLA and MPLA, there were strong voices in favour of the latter within the wider Swedish liberal movement. After the proclamation of Angola's independence, the liberal theoretical journal *Liberal Debatt* noted in an editorial that "FNLA and UNITA consider their objectives well compatible with [...] assistance from Portuguese mercenaries [and] regular South African military forces". In this situation, the journal stated, "the MPLA government in Luanda appears as the only legitimate representative of free Angola", concluding with the following appeal: "The Swedish support to the Angolan people's liberation struggle must not cease at this decisive moment. No diplomatic subtleties can excuse the termination of Swedish expressions of solidarity. Recognize the new government in Luanda! Support MPLA!" ('Stöd MPLA!'/'Support MPLA!' in *Liberal Debatt*, No. 8, 1975, p. 3).

as in May 1977, Ullsten visited Angola on an exploratory mission together with SIDA's Director General Michanek.[1] The first regular, bilateral agreement covered grant assistance of no less than 50 MSEK during the financial year 1977/78. It was signed by Paulo Jorge[2] and—considering the Liberal Party's earlier stand—somewhat ironically by Ullsten.[3] In the non-military field, Sweden would from then on become Angola's most important donor, contributing more than 40 per cent of total bilateral aid to the country at the end of the 1980s.[4] Including initial emergency assistance, the support to Angola during the period from 1975/76 to 1994/95 amounted—in fixed prices (1995)—to a total of 3.9 billion SEK.[5]

As in the cases of Guinea-Bissau and Mozambique, the early relations established with the nationalist movement during the liberation struggle made it possible for the non-socialist government to see beyond the Cold War East-West divide also with regard to the more complex Angolan situation. Among the Western countries, Sweden played a unique role in Angola. Fälldin's government—which as a junior partner included the conservative Moderate Party—would during the late 1970s both continue and expand the official support initiated by its Social Democratic predecessor in 1971. This, in turn, brought Sweden closer to Southern Africa. In a speech to the Center for Strategic and International Studies at the Georgetown University in Washington, USA, Foreign Minister Karin Söder—by the American audience possibly seen as a 'Dutch aunt'—declared in September 1978 that

> it is perhaps true to say that Africa [...] plays a comparatively greater role in our foreign policy than in yours. It most certainly does in our public opinion. Sweden was the first country to reach the goal of one per cent of the gross national product for development aid [...]. We are still topping the list of per capita donors, although we are anxious to meet more competition in this field. [...]
>
> When Angola, Cape Verde, Guinea-Bissau and Mozambique became independent, they [...] became recipients of Swedish aid. This followed as a matter of course from our earlier humanitarian aid to the liberation movements in these countries. Here, aid was a pressing need as so many vital functions of society had been disrupted as a result of the lengthy armed struggle and the massive flight of European know-how and capital. We are not surprised by the radical stand of some of these countries. Fifteen years of guerrilla warfare has shaped their political outlook. During this time, they got their support from various socialist states and precious little from the West. To them, the West was basically an ally of their colonizer, Portugal. Sweden was one of the very few Western countries that gave these liberation movements direct political

---

1. Ministry for Foreign Affairs: Memorandum ('Sverige-Angola'/'Sweden-Angola'), Political department, Stockholm, 17 April 1978 (MFA).
2. Jorge was appointed Minister of Foreign Affairs in November 1976, holding that position until 1984.
3. Jorge later stated that he was "pleased" by the fact that "the first agreement between Angola and Sweden was signed by me and the minister from the Liberal Party" (Interview with Paulo Jorge, p. 17).
4. Inge Tvedten: *Country Analysis: Angola*, SIDA, Stockholm, 1992, p. 81. Until the end of the 1980s, most of the Swedish assistance went to the fishery and health sectors, as well as to commodity aid. Of the total net official development assistance to Angola—i.e. from bilateral and multilateral sources—the Swedish contribution was in 1989 roughly 25 per cent (ibid.).
5. Sida op. cit., p. 24. It could be noted that the situation in Angola in 1998 brought AGIS and the historical MPLA leadership together anew. In May 1998, the Swedish [Secondary] School Students Union carried out an Operation Day's Work for Angolan children and schools. The actual support was implemented by AGIS in cooperation with the Angolan NGO ADRA (*Acção para o Desenvolvimento Rural e Ambiente*/Action for Rural Development and the Environment). Preparing for the secondary school students' campaign, the Africa Groups invited Lúcio Lara to Sweden. In October 1997, the veteran MPLA leader toured the country with the equally seasoned solidarity activist Hillevi Nilsson. Coincidentally, their tour took place twenty-six years after Lara's first visit to Sweden and Nilsson's first direct contacts with MPLA in western Zambia. It was the question of Swedish support to the MPLA school at Dolisie (Congo-Brazzaville) which in November 1971 brought Lara to Sweden and MPLA's education activities on the eastern front that had largely impressed Nilsson in July 1971.

and humanitarian support. This was not without importance, since it gave them and their leaders a Western outlet and an alternative.[1]

Discussing the situation in Zimbabwe, Namibia and South Africa, she continued:

> Leading Western countries should [...] worry less about the contact[s] that the liberation movements have with various socialist countries.[2] [...] Our [relations] with the nationalist leaders give us the definite impression that their foremost interest is [...] freedom and independence [...] and that they are anxious to keep their contacts open with all countries. It should be natural for us who believe in democracy to support those who struggle for [...] freedom and independence. [...] [T]he West must treat Africa as a continent in its own right [and] not as an object of big power politics.[3]

South African, US and general Western support to Jonas Savimbi's UNITA movement would, however, plunge Angola further into the Cold War abyss. Never enjoying full freedom and national independence, Angola's first war of liberation (1961-75) was followed by a second (1975-90) and—when UNITA in October 1992 rejected the outcome of the parliamentary and presidential elections—a third (1992 onwards). More than anywhere else in Southern Africa, the Swedish stand was in the process isolated and in conflict with that of the West.[4] This was illustrated as early as in October 1977, when Savimbi accused Fälldin's government of ferrying Cuban troops for military operations against UNITA.

In May 1977, the Angolan Prime Minister Lopo do Nascimento asked Minister Ullsten if Sweden could participate in relief operations in favour of thousands of destitute Zairean refugees in eastern Angola[5], preferably by putting a transport plane at the disposal of the operation.[6] The proposal was well received. From the end of September until the first week of November 1977, a C 130 Hercules aircraft from the Swedish air force operated an air bridge between Luanda and Dundo (Chitato) in northeastern Angola, transporting food and basic supplies under the auspices of the UN High Commissioner for Refugees (UNHCR) and the League of

---

1. 'Speech by Mrs. Karin Söder, Minister for Foreign Affairs, at the Center for Strategic and International Studies, Georgetown University, Washington', 27 September 1978, in Ministry for Foreign Affairs: *Documents on Swedish Foreign Policy: 1978*, Stockholm, 1982, pp. 93-95. On the question of Sweden's role for the broadening of MPLA's and the Angolan government's international contacts, see the interview with Lúcio Lara, p. 21.
2. The US government only recognized Angola in May 1993, eighteen years after independence.
3. 'Speech by Mrs. Karin Söder', op. cit., p. 99. It should be noted that the Centre Party Foreign Minister in her address further stated that "the Swedish government believes in the peaceful solution of international conflicts. Considering the uncompromising attitude of the [Southern African] white minority governments and their increased repression it is, however, understandable that the African nationalists see no other choice than to continue the quest for independence by armed struggle" (ibid., p. 96).
4. The Swedish position differed from that of its Nordic neighbours. Non-aligned Finland did not extend humanitarian support to MPLA. Soiri and Peltola state that it "never made any serious commitment to the Angolan cause" (Soiri and Peltola op. cit., p. 107). Finland recognized the People's Republic of Angola in February 1977, but did not establish a bilateral development assistance programme with the independent country (ibid.). Although Norway—a member of NATO—in the early 1970s granted support to MPLA schools in Zambia, it only established diplomatic relations with Angola in October 1977. It would, however, take another five years before the first Norwegian ambassador visited Luanda to submit his credentials (Eriksen in Eriksen (ed.) op. cit., pp. 86-87). Nevertheless, Finland and—in particular—Norway granted considerable resources to SWAPO in Angola. Limited by the absence of their own diplomatic missions, both governments largely used the Swedish embassy as a broker and intermediary channel. From the early 1980s, the Danish government also channelled substantial assistance via SIDA to SWAPO's refugee settlement in the Angolan province of Kwanza Sul.
5. Due to unrest in the Zairean province of Shaba (ex-Katanga), some 220,000 people fled across the border into the Angolan provinces of Lunda and Moxico from March 1977.
6. Ministry for Foreign Affairs: Memorandum ('Sverige-Angola'/'Sweden-Angola'), Political department, Stockholm, 17 April 1978 (MFA).

Facing Savimbi's threats:
Sven Lampell of the
Red Cross coordinating
relief operations for
Zairean refugees,
Luanda, October 1977
(Photo: Anders Johansson)

Red Cross Societies.[1] UNICEF and the United Nations World Food Programme participated in the operation, respectively contributing 20 tons of medicines and 1,245 tons of food.[2]

Despite its eminently humanitarian objectives, Savimbi denounced the relief operation. On 12 October 1977—in his first television interview for two years—the UNITA leader stated to the British Independent Television News that "Sweden is militarily involved on the side of MPLA [...], lifting troops from Luanda [and] aiding the Cubans in the war against [us]".[3] In further statements, Savimbi—who at the time was visiting Togo—threatened to "liquidate" the Swedish aircraft.[4]

Pursuing his threats, Savimbi wrote a long letter to the Senegalese President Léopold Senghor, alleging that the aircraft was used by the Angolan army for flights to Huambo in central Angola. According to the UNITA leader, "Sweden was embarrassed because it did not know what the Luanda government was doing with the plane", adding that the Swedish government showed "contempt for the fate of the 3 million Angolans who are with UNITA, only being interested in the [MPLA] minority in Luanda and in 55,000 refugees from Katanga".[5] With close links to the Socialist International, Senghor forwarded the letter to Olof Palme, emphasizing that Savimbi was "a sincere man" and that Palme ought to "carry out an investiga-

1. The operation was led by the retired Swedish colonel Sven Lampell, representing the League of Red Cross Societies. Employed by UNHCR, the author participated in the operation (Tor Sellström: 'Ponte aérea para os refugiados'/'Air bridge for the refugees' in *Jornal de Angola*, 17 November 1977).

2. Elisabeth Wiechel: 'UNITA attack: Sverige deltar i Angola-kriget' ('UNITA attack: Sweden participates in the Angolan war') in *Göteborgs-Posten*, 13 October 1977. The costs of the air bridge—amounting to 1.2 MSEK—were covered by the Swedish government (Anders Johansson: 'Sabotagevakt på hjälpplanet'/'Guard against sabotage on the aid plane' in *Dagens Nyheter*, 14 October 1977).

3. Transcript of interview by Michael Nicholson with Jonas Savimbi for Independent Television News, attached to letter ('UNITA-ledaren Savimbis uttalande om det svenska Hercules-planet i Angola'/'The statement by the UNITA leader Savimbi on the Swedish Hercules plane in Angola') from the Swedish embassy in London to the Ministry for Foreign Affairs, London, 20 October 1977 (MFA).

4. Anders Johansson: 'Sabotagevakt på hjälpplanet' ('Guard against sabotage on the aid plane') in *Dagens Nyheter*, 14 October 1977.

5. Letter from Jonas Savimbi to Léopold Senghor, Kinshasa, 27 October 1977; original in French (copied to the UNHCR Branch Office in Luanda. Author's private collection).

tion into the question".[1] As Savimbi's statements were without foundation, it was decided by both the Social Democratic Party and the non-socialist government to let the matter rest.

The Swedish Right Wing Enters the Scene

Savimbi did not bury his aversion towards Sweden. Ten years later—when the Social Democratic Party had returned to power[2] and a group of Moderate Party MPs actively backed UNITA—he went from words to action. In September 1987, UNITA took three Swedish aid workers as hostages. One of them was killed. During the negotiations to release the remaining two, Savimbi's wrath was in particular targeted at Pierre Schori, the Social Democratic Under-Secretary of State for Foreign Affairs who twenty years earlier had welcomed the UNITA leader to Sweden. At the height of the Cold War, UNITA's action introduced new domestic and international dimensions into Sweden's involvement in Southern Africa. More than any other single event—arguably barring South Africa's infiltration into IUEF in the late 1970s[3]—the kidnapping and subsequent developments underlined that Swedish aid workers and projects were far from immune from attacks.[4] They also revealed that UNITA and South Africa had committed right wing supporters in Sweden.

By 1979, UNITA had been effectively defeated by the MPLA government.[5] Its political presence in Sweden was extremely marginal. Resurrected and supplied by the South African regime—as well as encouraged by the Reagan administration in the United States—from the early 1980s Savimbi's organization could, however, register increasing military achievements. After establishing its headquarters at Jamba across the Namibian border in southeastern Angola, in 1980 UNITA was able to cross the Benguela railway. Two years later, it was "disrupting life in large areas of Angola".[6] At the same time, the movement intensified its international diplomacy. In the case of Sweden, the efforts were coordinated by Jorge Sangumba[7], UNITA's representative in London, who via IUEF had established contacts with the Swedish student movement in the mid-1960s and accompanied Savimbi on his visit to Stockholm in May 1967.[8]

While the UNITA leader had been invited by the ruling Social Democratic Party in 1967 and his movement during the first half of the 1970s enjoyed some sympa-

---

1. Letter from Léopold Senghor to Olof Palme, Dakar, 17 November 1977; original in French (copied to the UNHCR Branch Office in Luanda. Author's private collection).
2. Ending six years of non-socialist rule, the Social Democratic Party won the parliamentary elections in September 1982 and, again, in September 1985. Olof Palme was assassinated in February 1986. He was replaced as party leader and Premier by Ingvar Carlsson. A non-socialist coalition government was formed by the Moderate Party leader Carl Bildt after the elections in September 1991.
3. The IUEF affair is discussed in the chapter 'Black Consciousness, IUEF and 'Operation Daisy".
4. In December 1984, Per Martinsson, a Swedish aid worker employed by ARO, was killed in southern Mozambique by the anti-government MNR (Mozambique National Resistance), better known as RENAMO (*Resistência Nacional Moçambicana*). See 'Mordet på Per Martinsson' ('The Assassination of Per Martinsson') in *Afrikabulletinen*, No. 1, 1985, p. 23.
5. Joseph Hanlon: *Apartheid's Second Front: South Africa's War against Its Neighbours*, Penguin Books, Harmondsworth, 1986, p. 68.
6. Ibid., p. 69.
7. Interview with Miguel N'Zau Puna, p. 26.
8. See Sellström Volume I, pp. 396 and 402-08.

thy among Maoist organizations[1], the situation in the early 1980s was radically different. Shunned by the parliamentary parties and the wider solidarity movement, UNITA's initial diplomatic endeavours only found an echo in extreme right wing circles. Prominent among these was a group around *Contra*, a journal established in 1975.[2] Some of the most active and outspoken Swedish UNITA advocates—such as Tommy Hansson and Birger Hagård—belonged to this group, which also included Anders Larsson and Bertil Wedin.[3] Common to all of them was that they had been—or still were—active within the World Anti-Communist League (WACL)[4], an international right wing umbrella organization set up in the late 1960s.[5] Birger Hagård and Bertil Wedin also had old links to Southern Africa.

While chairing the Moderate Party Youth League[6] between 1963 and 1965, Hagård had been a leading member of the Swedish Katanga Committee.[7] Wedin— who at about the same time was a member of the Swedish UN contingent during the Congo conflict—was recruited in 1980 by the South African intelligence officer Craig Williamson, serving as a paid undercover agent for the apartheid regime in

---

1. Notably the Communist League Marxist-Leninists (*Kommunistiska Förbundet Marxist-Leninisterna*; KFML) and the Clarté Association. See the interview with Hillevi Nilsson, p. 328.
2. *Contra* was established by people with a past in the Moderate Party Youth League and Democratic Alliance (*Demokratisk Allians*), the latter set up in the late 1960s in support of the US war in Vietnam. From the second half of the 1970s, the journal devoted increasing attention to Southern Africa, defending the white minority regimes and denouncing the liberation movements as terrorist, Communist and/or controlled by the Soviet Union or China. Above all, *Contra* conducted a veritable crusade against Olof Palme. In his study of contemporary Swedish Nazism and right wing extremism, Karl Alvar Nilsson concludes that *Contra* went further than other publications in expressing outright hatred of the Social Democratic leader (Karl N. Alvar Nilsson: *Överklass, Nazism och Högerextremism: 1945-1995* /'Upper Class, Nazism and Right Extremism: 1945-1995', Carlsson Bokförlag, Stockholm, 1998, p. 240). As noted in the main text, the journal *inter alia* supported the South African backed RENAMO of Mozambique and, primarily, UNITA. As early as in March 1980, Géza Mólnár—one of the founders of *Contra*— published an enthusiastic presentation of RENAMO under the title 'The Freedom Struggle Has Started in Mozambique' ('Frihetskampen Har Börjat i Mozambique' in *Contra*, No. 2, 1980, pp. 6-7). The first major article on UNITA appeared in mid-1984, in an issue which on the cover carried a portrait of Olof Palme designed as a shooting target (Peter Hornung: 'Moskvas Vänner Inträngda i Hörnet'/'Moscow's Friends Pushed into the Corner' in *Contra*, No. 4, 1984, pp. 8-9). Exalting presentations of RENAMO, UNITA and other right wing movements were also included in a number of books published by *Contra*. See, for example, Bertil Häggman: *Frihetskämpar: Motstånd på Kommunistiskt Territorium* ('Freedom Fighters: Resistance on Communist Territory'), Contra Förlag, Stockholm, 1987, and Tommy Hansson: *Slaveri i Vår Tid: En Handbok i Totalitär Socialism* ('Slavery in Our Time: A Manual in Totalitarian Socialism'), Contra Förlag, Stockholm, 1989. In the latter book—written by the chairman of the Swedish Angola Groups after a visit to UNITA's headquarters in August 1988—Jonas Savimbi was described as "probably the most intelligent and dynamic leader on the African continent" (p. 177).
3. Larsson and Wedin were both later mentioned in connection with the investigations into the assassination of Prime Minister Palme. See, for example, Nilsson op. cit., pp. 256-65 and various Swedish press reports in September-October 1996.
4. Nilsson op. cit., p. 258.
5. Hagård was present when WACL was founded in Taiwan in 1967 (ibid., p. 143). Interviewed by the regional newspaper *Östgöta-Correspondenten* in October 1986, Hagård—at the time a Moderate Party MP—confirmed that he served as WACL's contact person in Sweden. According to Hagård, "we encourage the struggle against Communism, for example, by supporting the Contras in Nicaragua, [RENAMO] in Mozambique and UNITA in Angola" (Jan Hederén: 'Birger Hagård medlem i antikommunistiskt förbund'/'Birger Hagård member of an anti-Communist league' in *Östgöta-Correspondenten*, 7 October 1986). WACL was led in the mid-1980s by the US General John Singlaub from CIA's Covert Action Staff, that is, the structure which channelled military assistance to UNITA. Clive Derby-Lewis represented South Africa in WACL. He was later found guilty of the assassination of the ANC leader Chris Hani, Secretary General of the South African Communist Party, who was murdered in April 1993. In 1990, WACL changed name to the World League for Freedom and Democracy (WLFD).
6. At the time, *Högerns Ungdomsförbund* (HUF).
7. Sellström Volume I, pp. 52-53. See also the interview with Birger Hagård, p. 273.

London at the beginning of the decade.[1]

Possibly through WACL and/or South Africa, towards the mid-1980s UNITA established close relations with the group around *Contra*.[2] By that time, the London representative Jorge Sangumba had "sent Luís Antunes to Sweden"[3], from where he was subsequently to act on behalf of the movement in Scandinavia. Hagård was for the first time approached by Antunes in 1984.[4] The UNITA representative gave him "a lot of material [and] it all developed from there".[5] Hagård—a Moderate MP—"found that something had to be done and wrote [a parliamentary] motion in January 1985".[6]

Over the following seven years, Hagård annually submitted motions against Swedish development assistance to Angola, advocating humanitarian support to UNITA.[7] In the beginning, he acted individually, but by January 1988 no fewer

1. See, for example, Leif Kasvi: 'Craig Williamson avslöjar sitt hemliga agentnät' ('Craig Williamson reveals his secret network of agents') and Lennart Håård: 'Svenske agenten berättar om mötena med Williamson' ('Swedish agent talks about the meetings with Williamson') in *Aftonbladet*, 29 September 1996. According to Swedish police sources, Wedin had established contacts with South Africa's intelligence services in the 1970s (Viveka Hansson and Annika Folcker: 'Han var en känd Palme-hatare'/'He was a known Palme hater' in *Expressen*, 2 October 1996). It was, however, during a visit to South Africa in 1980—shortly after Williamson's exposure at IUEF—that he was recruited to the services' foreign operations. Williamson confirmed in October 1996 that "I recruited him and sent him to London as part of the European operation I was setting up" (Peta Thornycroft: 'Palme's murder still a mystery' in *Mail & Guardian*, 4-10 October 1996). Williamson's main agent in London was Peter Casselton—also mentioned in connection with Palme's assassination—who *inter alia* had provided the intelligence for the Rhodesian attack on ZANU's Chimoio camp in Mozambique in November 1977 (Jacques Pauw: *Into the Heart of Darkness: Confessions of Apartheid's Assassins*, Jonathan Ball Publishers, Johannesburg, 1997, p. 213-14). As 'John Wilson', Wedin worked in London under Casselton. In July-August 1982, the two organized burglaries of the London offices of ANC of South Africa and SWAPO of Namibia. Casselton was subsequently jailed, while Wedin was acquitted by a British court. He later settled in Cyprus, but continued to write for *Contra*. He also remained active within the South Africa-linked organization Victims Against Terrorism (VAT). Presented as 'Morgan', the story of Wedin was first published by the Swedish journalist Anders Hasselbohm in 1995 (Anders Hasselbohm: 'Svensken Som Spionerade för Sydafrika'/'The Swede Who Spied for South Africa' in *Vi*, No. 11, 1995, pp. 5-11. See also Nos. 12 and 13, 1995).
2. At about the same time, some prominent members of the Swedish non-socialist parties entered into contact with UNITA via other international anti-Communist organizations. This was notably the case with Andres Küng, who served as a member of the national board of the Liberal Party between 1982 and 1993. Küng was chairman of the Swedish section of Resistance International (RI), which started its activities in March 1985 (Nilsson op. cit., p. 262). RI had been set up in Paris in 1982 with the objective to "promote political, humanitarian and material support to democratic resistance movements" (cited in Anne-Marie Gustafsson: 'Liberalt Stöd till Terror'/'Liberal Support for Terror' in *Afrikabulletinen*, No. 6, 1985, p. 4). Both UNITA and RENAMO of Mozambique were founder members of Resistance International, which like WACL *inter alia* actively advocated support to the Contras in Nicaragua. Interviewed by AGIS in mid-1985, Küng stated that he supported UNITA's political demands, while refusing to dissociate himself from RENAMO ('Vad Menar Du Andres Küng?'/'What Do You Mean Andres Küng?' in *Afrikabulletinen*, No. 6, 1985, p. 5). Küng received *Contra*'s 'freedom prize' in 1986 (Nilsson op. cit., p. 252).
3. Interview with Miguel N'Zau Puna, p. 26.
4. Interview with Birger Hagård, p. 274.
5. Ibid., pp. 274-75.
6. Ibid., p. 275.
7. The motions introduced by Hagård were: No. 844 in 1984/85, No. U 213 in 1985/86, No. U 235 in 1986/87, No. U 220 in 1987/88, No. U 233 in 1988/89, No. U 658 in 1989/90, No. U 237 in 1990/91 and No. U 224 in 1991/92. Towards the end of the 1970s—when the Moderate Party formed part of the ruling non-socialist coalition—a number of Moderate MPs actively turned against the official Swedish policy of humanitarian support to the Southern African liberation movements. In November 1996, Hagård requested the Parliamentary Committee on the Constitution—of which he was a member—to retroactively examine whether the official assistance to the anti-apartheid struggle over the years had been compatible with constitutional principles (Birger Hagård: 'Anmälan till Konstitutionsutskottet'/'Submission to the Parliamentary Committee on the Constitution', Stockholm, 5 November 1996, published in Swedish Parliament/Konstitutionsutskottets betänkande ('Report by the Parliamentary Committee on the Constitution'), No. 1997/98: KU 25, Part II, Stockholm, 1998, p. 343). According to Hagård, there had been no parliamentary control over the Consultative Committee on Humanitarian Assistance (Interview with Birger Hagård, p. 274). His claims were, however, rejected (Swedish Parliament/Konstitutionsutskottets betänkande op. cit., Part I, pp. 159-168).

than 17 fellow conservative backbenchers co-signed his motion.[1] While this only corresponded to 5 per cent of the 349 Swedish parliamentarians, it represented almost a fourth of the 76 Moderate MPs. Hagård—who was honorary president of the pro-UNITA Swedish Angola Groups and in July 1987 with his Moderate colleague Göran Allmér launched a campaign called 'Angola Help'[2]—thus managed to rally a significant conservative constituency behind his demands. This, in turn, was not whole-heartedly welcomed by the Moderate leadership around Carl Bildt. Interviewed in 1996, Hagård stated that

> you may say that I was 'the first mover'. I never asked the party leadership for any support at all. [...] It was very interesting, because there was some kind of a conflict between me and Carl Bildt. He said that the motion was okey, but that I could not have so many co-signatories, because it [then] almost became a party motion. But I think that there was a majority for my position in the [Moderate] parliamentary group. Many colleagues came to me and asked if they could have their names on the motion. [...] [This] was very unique.[3]

In his first motion Hagård described the MPLA government as "a totalitarian dictatorship [...] which in no way meets the requirements concerning democratic development and respect for human rights". UNITA, on the other hand, was said to have a political programme in accordance with "Western democratic principles". Savimbi was characterized as "one of the foremost personalities in Africa". According to Hagård, his movement was "not dependent on South African support". In fact, Hagård stated, "no close contacts exist between UNITA and South Africa, [and Pretoria] has no part in the confrontation between MPLA and UNITA". Against this background, he argued that "there is no ground for Sweden as almost the only Western country to support MPLA's attempts to maintain the power it has usurped through deceit and violence". Warning that "the safety of Swedish aid workers no longer can be guaranteed"[4], he proposed that humanitarian assistance should instead be channelled to the areas held by UNITA.[5]

Hagård further criticized the Swedish companies Saab-Scania and Volvo for selling trucks to the MPLA government, arguing that the vehicles "in certain cases

---

1. Among the co-signatories were Göran Allmér, Elisabeth Fleetwood and Gullan Lindblad. The motion requested that the agreement on development assistance between Sweden and Angola be "brought to an end as soon as possible" and that humanitarian support be channelled to "the whole of Angola, including the areas liberated by UNITA" (Swedish Parliament 1987/88: Motion No. U 220, Riksdagens Protokoll 1987/88, p. 4).

2. In Swedish, *Angola-Hjälpen*. It is striking how the right wing pro-UNITA supporters in the 1980s used designations close to those established by the solidarity movement. While the organized NGO movement for Southern Africa was represented by AGIS, the structure advocating support for UNITA was called the Swedish Angola Groups. In the case of the 'Angola Help' launched by Hagård and Allmér, the name was the same as that of the campaign by the liberal newspaper *Expressen* in favour of MPLA in the early 1960s (Sellström Volume I, pp. 386-92).

3. Interview with Birger Hagård, p. 275. In 1996, Jorge Valentim, UNITA's former Secretary for Information, underlined the significance of the Moderate support: "[T]here was a tendency in Sweden towards a different approach. I think that there was some weakness of the Social Democratic Party in power which made it possible for the other side to come out strongly. The [Moderate] members of the Swedish parliament who [subsequently] visited Angola helped us a lot. They helped to change the perception in the world at large, because people were getting the impression that every single Swedish person was against UNITA. Later, they realized that this was due to party politics" (Interview with Jorge Valentim, pp. 35-36).

4. It should be emphasized that it was UNITA policy to take foreign hostages. In the early 1980s, Savimbi's movement had in separate actions *inter alia* kidnapped great numbers of Czech and British aid workers and their families—including women and children—marching them to Jamba under severe hardship. This was hardly unknown to Hagård and the Swedish pro-UNITA advocates. Interviewed in 1996, UNITA's former Secretary General Miguel N'Zau Puna explained: "No one spoke about the struggle we were fighting. [...] [W]e thought that if we kidnapped some foreigners, the international community would perhaps become more aware of our struggle. [...] We kidnapped Swedes, Englishmen and many others. [...] After some time, we stopped [...]. [W]e reached a point where it was not worth it" (Interview with Miguel N'Zau Puna, p. 26).

5. Swedish Parliament 1984/85: Motion No. 844, Riksdagens Protokoll 1984/85, pp. 3-7.

have come to direct military use".[1] This point was often raised by the pro-UNITA lobby. Quoting an Angolan military deserter, in October 1985 Tommy Hansson conveyed to the readers of the conservative regional newspaper *Nya Wermlands-Tidningen* that "all the Russian and Cuban officers [in Angola] are using Swedish cars".[2]

Within the wider conservative movement a climate was created whereby UNITA was depicted as a democratic alternative. "Mainly led by Moderate politicians", pro-UNITA Angola Groups were formed, "spreading propaganda in favour of both UNITA and South Africa".[3] According to a contemporary comment by the political observer Olle Svenning in the social democratic newspaper *Arbetet*,

> the Angola Groups are quite candid. They frankly say that they accept UNITA's right to kidnap aid workers and foreign businessmen. The responsibility is laid on the aid agencies and the companies, not on the terrorists.[4]

Threats, Hostages and Murder

Although backed by apartheid South Africa and extending its influence through far from democratic methods, UNITA could at about the same time register major international successes. In July 1985, the US Congress repealed the Clark Amendment—which had prohibited overt assistance to the movement—and in early 1986 Savimbi was given a hero's welcome in Washington by President Reagan. Together with the US support to the Contras in Nicaragua, these developments prompted Pierre Schori to criticize the Reagan administration's foreign policy, describing the Contras and UNITA as "American clients" and "terrorists".[5] Encouraged by Washington's recognition and the support extended by Swedish right wing and Moderate circles, the UNITA representative Luís Antunes reacted vehemently to the statement by the Under-Secretary of State for Foreign Affairs. Threatening to recommend action against the Swedes working and living in Angola[6], in April 1986 he issued a press release, declaring that

> Schori has attacked and defamed the Angolan people. Sweden's attitude [...] will have negative consequences for those Swedes who work for the non-elected, illegal regime in Luanda.[7]

---

1. Ibid., p. 6.
2. Tommy Hansson: 'Kuba utnyttjar barn för slavarbete' ('Cuba uses children for slave labour') in *Nya Wermlands-Tidningen*, 10 October 1985. Complementing Hagård's parliamentary activities, Hansson wrote prolifically about Angola, MPLA and UNITA in various Swedish newspapers in the second half of the 1980s. In March 1987, for example, he denounced the MPLA government's "cruelties against religious believers" in the Christian daily paper *Dagen*, close to the Christian Democrats (Tommy Hansson: 'MPLA förföljer troende i Angola'/'MPLA persecutes believers in Angola' in *Dagen*, 31 March 1987). With a past in the Democratic Alliance and links to the World Anti-Communist League, Tommy Hansson was elected in 1991 to the city council of Södertälje as a member of the 'protest party' New Democracy (Nilsson op. cit., p. 203). He soon thereafter became chief editor of *Contra* (ibid., p. 255).
3. Olle Svenning: 'Moderater stöder terrorister' ('Moderates support terrorists') in *Arbetet*, 3 May 1985.
4. Ibid. Svenning concluded: "One is [...] left to wonder who finances the Moderate dominated Angola Groups, whose analyses almost completely coincide with South Africa's and whose concern more often than not is how the 'South African Republic' shall survive" (ibid.). Membership of the Angola Groups largely coincided with that of the pro-Pretoria *Sverige-Sydafrikasällskapet* ('Sweden-South Africa Society'). Representing its Stockholm and Södertälje branches, Tommy Hansson was, for example, very active within the society towards the end of the 1980s, regularly contributing to its publication *Sydafrika-Nytt* ('News from South Africa'). Cf. Tommy Hansson: 'Sydafrikas Krigsmakt Effektivast i Afrika' ('South Africa's Military Most Efficient in Africa') in *Sydafrika-Nytt*, No. 2, April 1989.
5. Bosse Schön: 'Schori gjorde UNITA till Sveriges fiende' ('Schori turned UNITA into Sweden's enemy') in *Aftonbladet*, 9 September 1987.
6. There were at the time some 285 Swedes in the country (ibid.).
7. Cited in Ola Liljedahl: 'UD varnades för 17 månader sedan' ('The Foreign Ministry was warned 17 months ago') in *Expressen*, 9 September 1987.

Schori's statement was relayed to Savimbi. As the Africa Groups at the same time demanded that Antunes should be expelled from Sweden[1], the UNITA leader repeated the threats. Interviewed in Jamba by the social democratic evening paper *Aftonbladet*, Savimbi announced in May 1987:

> I am warning Pierre Schori. If he expels UNITA's representative [...], I will take Swedes in Angola as hostages. There is nothing Sweden can do to get them back. The Swedes will remain [with us] until the war is over. [...]

> We have had contacts with many Swedes. I met Pierre Schori in Sweden [in 1967].[2] He was then our friend. We are not against [the fact] that Sweden blindly supports MPLA. That is [a] choice which must be respected. But Sweden must know that [it] takes a risk.[3]

Although the Swedish government did not institute legal proceedings against Antunes, less than four months later Savimbi went from words to action. The target was a 200 MSEK rural electrification project in the Dembos region northeast of the capital Luanda.[4] Partly financed by SIDA, the project had been implemented by the Swedish companies Transelectric and Bygg-Paul. Extending electricity to some 30,000 villagers, it was completed in mid-1987 and officially inaugurated in the presence of the Swedish Minister for International Development Cooperation, Lena Hjelm-Wallén, in Quibaxe on 5 September 1987.[5] Two days later—on 7 September, while Hjelm-Wallén was still in Angola—UNITA attacked a convoy of eight vehicles returning from Quibaxe to Luanda, some 110 kilometres north of the capital. Swedish construction workers from Bygg-Paul were travelling with the convoy. Three of them—Kent Andersson, Göran Larsson and Gunnar Sjöberg—were taken hostage by the attackers, while others managed to escape.[6]

What subsequently became known as 'the Angolan hostage drama' triggered off hectic activities. While the Swedish embassy in Luanda[7] together with the Angolan

---

1. Editorial in *Afrikabulletinen*, No. 3, 1986, p. 1. After the UNITA attack, the Ministry for Foreign Affairs examined whether Antunes could be prosecuted for the threats issued in April 1986 (Ove Bring: Memorandum ('Kan UNITAs representant i Sverige åtalas?'/'Can UNITA's representative in Sweden be prosecuted?'), Ministry for Foreign Affairs, Stockholm, 17 September 1987) (MFA). Due to the sensitive negotiations to release the hostages, no legal action was taken against Antunes.

2. In the interview, Savimbi stated that he met Schori in Sweden in 1968 and 1969. The only known meeting between the two took place, however, in Stockholm at the end of May 1967.

3. Ritva Rönnberg: 'Jag kan gripa svensk gisslan' ('I can take Swedes hostage') in *Aftonbladet*, 17 May 1987. Savimbi acknowledged that UNITA was receiving "certain assistance" from South Africa.

4. According to Ritva Rönnberg from *Aftonbladet*, the electrification project had been specifically mentioned by Savimbi during her interview with him in May 1987. The UNITA leader was said to have stated: "If you electrify close to the capital Luanda, it is not for the people, but [for] a city where there is no peace. Sweden takes a risk" (Ritva Rönnberg: 'Gerillaledarens hot blev verklighet'/'Guerrilla leader's threats became real' in *Aftonbladet*, 9 September 1987).

5. Ulf Hagman: 'Svenskt projekt i Angola hotas av UNITA-gerillan' ('Swedish project in Angola is threatened by the UNITA guerrilla') in *Svenska Dagbladet*, 5 September 1987.

6. Cable ('Saknade svenskar i Angola'/'Missing Swedes in Angola') from Sten Rylander, Swedish ambassador to Angola, to the Ministry for Foreign Affairs, Luanda, [no date, but 8 September 1987] (MFA). After their release, the surviving hostages stated that UNITA "knew that the [Swedish] Cooperation Minister had been to Quibaxe [...]. They say that it was a routine attack, but [we] are convinced that it was planned [...] to [kidnap] Swedes and possibly other foreigners" (Peter Carlberg, Torgny Hinnemo and Roger Magnergård: 'UNITA-fångarna hemma idag'/'The UNITA prisoners home today' in *Svenska Dagbladet*, 3 December 1987).

7. At the Swedish embassy, Svend Thomsen served as the responsible liaison officer. It was Thomsen who five weeks later located Larsson's body.

UNITA hostages Gunnar Sjöberg (left) and Kent Andersson paraded before the press, Jamba, Angola, November 1987 (Photo: Pressens Bild/Reuter)

authorities tried to establish the condition and whereabouts of the missing Swedes[1], UNITA—in particular through Luís Antunes—launched a sustained disinformation campaign. In his first comment on the events, Antunes stated to the Swedish press that "we took the Swedes as hostages to protect them. If we had not taken them, MPLA would probably have [...] killed [them] and put the blame on UNITA".[2] Three days later, he declared that the Swedes "are our guests. We give them food and shelter until we reach the liberated areas".[3] When five weeks after the attack the body of Göran Larsson was found in a shallow grave some 15 kilometres away[4]—also causing serious concern with regard to the other missing Swedes— Antunes claimed that the news amounted to "false information spread by the [MPLA] government [and] a rumour [designed] to denigrate [...] UNITA even more".[5]

The Swedish pro-UNITA lobby supported the action taken against the aid workers. While admitting that "kidnappings, of course, are not good", the Moderate MP Göran Allmér—with Birger Hagård one of the initiators of the 'Angola

1. In their search for the Swedes, the Angolan authorities assumed that UNITA was taking them north to Zaire, while they in reality were taken east towards Malanje and then south to Jamba. Serving as election observers in Angola in September 1992, Sten Rylander—the Swedish ambassador to Luanda at the time of the hostage drama—and the author coincidentally travelled with the UNITA commander who was responsible for the attack and the transfer of the Swedes to Jamba. The exact itinerary could then be established. When Rylander observed to Commander Chimuko that he had caused Sweden a lot of pain and problems, the UNITA military stiffly replied: "That was the whole idea" (Author's recollection).

2. Cited in Rönnberg op. cit. in *Aftonbladet*, 9 September 1987. Tommy Hansson repeated the astonishing statement in an article published by the conservative national newspaper *Svenska Dagbladet* in mid-November 1987 (Tommy Hansson: 'Carl Tham leker med fångarnas liv'/'Carl Tham is playing with the prisoners' lives' in *Svenska Dagbladet*, 11 November 1987).

3. Annika Creutzer: 'Vi kan inte säga när gisslan släpps' ('We can't say when the hostages will be released') in *Aftonbladet*, 12 September 1987.

4. Bittan Svensson: 'Göran Larsson död' ('Göran Larsson dead') in *Östgöta-Correspondenten*, 14 October 1987. Larsson was shot in a leg and the stomach during the UNITA attack. He died the following day. According to later statements by Andersson and Sjöberg, he could have survived, but UNITA refused to give him proper medical care (Carlberg, Hinnemo and Magnergård op. cit. in *Svenska Dagbladet*, 3 December 1987).

5. Bittan Svensson: 'UNITA's representant: Det är bara ett rykte' ('UNITA's representative: It is only a rumour') in *Östgöta-Correspondenten*, 14 October 1987. The UNITA leadership in Jamba had immediately been informed about Larsson's death (Carlberg, Hinnemo and Magnergård op. cit. in *Svenska Dagbladet*, 3 December 1987). Antunes claimed to be in constant contact with Jamba.

Help' campaign—maintained that UNITA was fighting "a just cause".[1] Hagård repeated Antunes' statements. After the news of Larsson's death, he "doubt[ed] the information from [the Swedish embassy] in Angola", adding that "there is a civil war [going on]. [...]. Every Swede who goes [to Angola] must understand that".[2] Antunes and Hagård also tried to force the Swedish government into direct negotiations with UNITA, linking the release of the hostages to a suspension of the official development assistance to Angola.[3]

The Social Democratic government did not negotiate with Savimbi's movement. In addition to contacts through the International Committee of the Red Cross, indirect channels were instead opened via the US and Portuguese governments. At the time of the UNITA attack, Prime Minister Ingvar Carlsson was paying an official visit to the United States. In spite of their diverging views on Angola, he appealed to President Reagan to intervene in favour of the kidnapped Swedes.[4] Under political pressure due to the parallel situation of US citizens being held hostage in Lebanon, the Reagan administration took the appeal seriously. After the denouement of the hostage drama, the Swedish Minister for Foreign Affairs, Sten Andersson, thus singled out the decisive role played by Vice President George Bush, who "had personally committed himself to the fate of the Swedes [...], issuing a direct demand to [...] Jonas Savimbi".[5] An appeal was also made to the Portuguese President Mário Soares, whose son João maintained close relations with UNITA.[6] João Soares would eventually accompany the Swedish government representatives to Jamba in early December 1987.[7]

The two surviving hostages reached UNITA's headquarters in mid-November 1987, after travelling 63 days on foot and 4 on trucks over more than 1,400 kilometres through the Angolan bush.[8] They were released by UNITA 20 days later. Ambassador Annie Marie Sundbom and Assistant Under-Secretary Anders Bjurner represented Sweden at the handover in Jamba.[9] They both had a long involvement with Swedish support to the liberation struggles in Southern Africa. While Sundbom as secretary general of the National Council of Swedish Youth had been active in the anti-apartheid boycott movement in the early 1960s, Bjurner had as second

---

1. Cited in Christer Bergström and Michael Berwick: 'Han stöder kidnappargerillan' ('He supports the kidnapping guerrilla') in *Folket*, 9 September 1987.
2. Cited in Torbjörn Westerlund: 'UNITA's trovärdighet är körd i botten' ('UNITA's credibility is at rock bottom') in *Östgöta-Correspondenten*, 14 October 1987. While acknowledging that UNITA's attack was "a mistake", ten years later Hagård insisted: "You could say that this was some kind of terrorist attack, but on the other hand it was the same kind of methods that the MPLA was using all the time. There was a civil war situation in Angola and the three Swedes must have been quite aware of the dangers. It happened, but that did not change our views" (Interview with Birger Hagård, p. 275).
3. 'Statement by the Minister for Foreign Affairs, Mr. Sten Andersson, in response to a communiqué from UNITA', 19 October 1987, in Ministry for Foreign Affairs: *Documents on Swedish Foreign Policy: 1987*, Stockholm, 1990, pp. 212-13 and cable ('Samtal med president dos Santos'/'Conversation with President dos Santos') from Sten Rylander, Swedish ambassador to Angola, to the Ministry for Foreign Affairs, Luanda, 26 October 1987 (MFA). Cf. Mikael Svensson: 'Hagård låg bakom moderaternas UNITA-plan' ('Hagård was behind the Moderate UNITA plan') in *Blekinge Läns Tidning*, 2 December 1987.
4. Bert Willborg: 'Besked i morse: Vi skall hjälpa er' ('Confirmation this morning: We shall help you') in *Aftonbladet*, 10 September 1987.
5. Peter Carlberg: 'Gerillan har ljugit upprepade gånger' ('The guerrilla has lied on repeated occasions') in *Svenska Dagbladet*, 3 December 1987.
6. Several influential members of the Socialist Party of Portugal (PSP) supported UNITA. When Luís Antunes on 15 October 1987—that is, after the news of Göran Larsson's death—organized a press conference in Stockholm, PSP was represented by José Brandão. He had six months earlier visited UNITA's headquarters in Jamba together with João Soares (Cable ('UNITA') from Lennart Rydfors, Swedish ambassador to Portugal, to the Ministry for Foreign Affairs, Lisbon, [no date, but probably 17 October 1987]) (MFA).
7. Carlberg, Hinnemo and Magnergård op. cit. in *Svenska Dagbladet*, 3 December 1987.
8. Michael Sullivan and Bo Westmar: 'Vi behandlades väl av gerillan' ('We were well treated by the guerrilla') in *Dagens Nyheter*, 13 November 1987.
9. Åke Ekdahl: 'Sundbom till Angola' in *Dagens Nyheter*, 29 November 1987.

secretary at the Swedish embassy in Lusaka in the mid-1970s established close contacts with MPLA. Despite disapproval by the Moderate Party[1], the Swedish government was represented by highly informed officials with well established relations to the genuine liberation forces in the region.

Exit UNITA

The Angolan hostage drama represented at the same time both the apex and nadir for UNITA and the Swedish right wing on the centre stage of the domestic Southern Africa debate. With the final act of the drama, Antunes disappeared from the political scene, while the pro-UNITA lobby withdrew to the rear chambers from where it had made its appearance a couple of years earlier. Close contacts were certainly maintained with Savimbi's movement. As chairman of the Swedish Angola Groups,
Hansson, for example, visited UNITA's headquarters in Jamba in August 1988[2] and Hagård went there in April 1989, impressed by UNITA's "high morale and motivation".[3]

UNITA's credibility within the wider Swedish conservative opinion was, however, irreparably damaged. While 17 Moderate MPs co-signed Hagård's Angola motion in January 1988, only 6 did so the following year.[4] And when the Moderate Party after the parliamentary elections in September 1991 became the leading partner in a new non-socialist coalition government—holding both the premiership and the Ministry for Foreign Affairs[5]—it did not phase out the Swedish bilateral development assistance to the MPLA government. In fact, with an amount of 200 MSEK Prime Minister Carl Bildt's first budget for 1991/92 maintained the country allocation to Angola at the level established by the Social Democratic government. The following year, it was even increased to 210 MSEK.[6]

The ultimate blow to UNITA's democratic pretensions was, finally, administered by Savimbi himself, when in October 1992 he rejected the outcome of the multiparty parliamentary and presidential elections held at the end of September. Declared free and fair by the United Nations and various international observer teams, MPLA won the parliamentary elections with 53.7 per cent of the votes, while UNITA received 34.1. In the elections to the presidency, MPLA's incumbent José Eduardo dos Santos got 49.6 and Savimbi 40.1 per cent of the votes. However, the UNITA leader accused the MPLA government of widespread fraud, mobilized

1. The Moderate Party leader Carl Bildt proposed that Anders Wijkman, the head of the Swedish Red Cross and a member of his party, should travel to Jamba (ibid.). Cf. Hans O. Alfredsson: 'Frigivningen utlöste ordkrig mellan Andersson och Bildt' ('The release provoked a war of words between Andersson and Bildt') in *Svenska Dagbladet*, 3 December 1987.
2. Tommy Hansson: *Åter till det Kalla Kriget* ('Return to the Cold War'), Contra Förlag, Stockholm, 1993, pp. 10 and 48-51.
3. Tommy Hansson: 'Man Måste Beundra UNITA's Höga Moral och Motivation' ('One Has to Admire UNITA's High Morale and Motivation') in *Angola-Rapport*, No. 1, 1990, p. 1. Cf. the author's interview with Hagård, in which the Moderate MP stated that he found the meeting with the head of UNITA's interrogation services—"a very intelligent man"—particularly "interesting" (Interview with Birger Hagård, p. 276).
4. Swedish Parliament 1988/89: Motion No. U 233, Riksdagens Protokoll 1988/89, pp. 6-8.
5. Margaretha af Ugglas from the Moderate Party became Minister for Foreign Affairs, while Alf Svensson—the leader of the Christian Democrats—was appointed Minister of International Development Cooperation.
6. Sida: 'Sida's International Development Cooperation: Statistical Summary of Operations 1997', Sida, Stockholm, 1997, p. 34 (referenced below as Sida 1997 b). Following the outbreak of war in late 1992—leading to the evacuation from Angola of the Swedish aid personnel—the regular allocation was cut down to 160 MSEK in 1993/94 and to 60 MSEK in 1994/95. It was again raised to 210 MSEK in 1995/96.

his military forces and launched a devastating offensive throughout the country. Angola's first ever democratic elections came to a tragic end.

One year later—in September 1993—a unanimous UN Security Council imposed sanctions on UNITA. Welcoming the decision, the Moderate Foreign Minister Margaretha af Ugglas concluded that "UNITA and its leader Jonas Savimbi bear a heavy responsibility for the large-scale human suffering and material destruction [...] in Angola", adding that "[i]t [is] my sincere hope that the firmness of the Security Council [...] to introduce further sanctions against UNITA will bring the war to an end and ensure that the peace process is resumed".[1] While this was not to be, af Ugglas' party colleague Birger Hagård and the other Moderate backbenchers would, however, eventually—and reluctantly[2]—cease their open pro-UNITA advocacy in Sweden.

---

1. 'We hope that sanctions will lead to peace in Angola' - 'Statement by the Minister for Foreign Affairs, Mrs. Margaretha af Ugglas', 16 September 1993, in Ministry for Foreign Affairs: *Documents on Swedish Foreign Policy: 1993*, Stockholm, 1994, p. 343.
2. Interviewed in 1996, Hagård stated that "I doubt if the elections really could be called free and fair". He also put the blame for the resumption of the war on the MPLA government: "After the elections, UNITA was attacked in Luanda. Many of the leaders were killed by MPLA. One of them was a General Mango, who had visited Sweden some years before. I found him a very interesting man" (Interview with Birger Hagård, p. 276).

ZANU and ZAPU of Zimbabwe:
On Separate Trails

Early Attention

Zimbabwe occupies a prominent—and largely exceptional—place in the history of Sweden's involvement with the struggles for majority rule and self-determination in Southern Africa. Official support to Zimbabwean refugee students started before Ian Smith's Unilateral Declaration of Independence (UDI) in November 1965.[1] Special allocations for legal aid to political prisoners and their families were granted immediately thereafter.[2] Until the achievement of national sovereignty in April 1980, considerable resources were extended to the country's two dominant liberation movements, Robert Mugabe's Zimbabwe African National Union (ZANU) and Joshua Nkomo's Zimbabwe African People's Union (ZAPU). According to the ZANU leader Nathan Shamuyarira, the Swedish support represented in the late 1970s around 40 per cent of his movement's civilian budget.[3] In his memoirs, Nkomo concludes that "Sweden, especially through its official agency SIDA, was the most generous of all donors of food and clothing for our refugees".[4]

Although Swedish assistance in the early 1970s was primarily channelled to the liberation movements in the Portuguese colonies, the Zimbabwean cause was not relegated to the background. On the contrary, the close and frequent contacts established with the nationalist movement in Zimbabwe during the mid-1960s[5] were maintained when in May 1969 the parliament endorsed a general policy of official support to the African liberation organizations. In fact, support to ZANU was recommended by the Consultative Committee on Humanitarian Assistance as early as in June 1969, at the same time as assistance to PAIGC of Guinea-Bissau.[6] ZANU would thereby become the first liberation movement in Southern Africa proper to receive humanitarian assistance from the Swedish government.[7] Support

---

1. See Sellström Volume I, pp. 320-23.
2. Ibid, pp. 324-26.
3. Author's conversation with Nathan Shamuyarira, Harare, 29 July 1995. ZANU's former Deputy Secretary of Finance, Didymus Mutasa, has stated that the Swedish government's support "at one time [...] was greater than [that of] all the other Western governments put together" (Interview with Didymus Mutasa, p. 217).
4. Joshua Nkomo: *The Story of My Life*, Methuen, London, 1984, p. 181. Occupying the position as Vice-President of Zimbabwe, Nkomo died on 1 July 1999.
5. Sellström Volume I, pp. 336-48.
6. CCHA: 'Protokoll' ('Minutes'), Stockholm, 5 June 1969 (SDA).
7. In April 1970, ZANU requested SIDA to support the establishment of a representation in Stockholm which would cover the Scandinavian countries (Letter from Richard Hove to SIDA, Lusaka, 21 August 1972) (SDA). Eventually, ZANU was to be represented by Sydney Sekeramayi, who had come to Sweden in June 1964 and was a medical student at Lund university. Sekeramayi also served as Secretary General of the Zimbabwe Students' Union in Europe. Claude Chokwenda—another ZANU student in Sweden—became ZANU's resident representative from June 1974 (Letter from Mukudzei Mudzi, Lusaka, 23 September 1974) (MFA).

to ZAPU was "in principle" recommended four months later.[1] Due to the 1970-71 ZAPU leadership crisis[2], the recommendation was, however, not implemented. Direct support to ZAPU was only granted from February 1973.[3]

As in Angola, the wider Zimbabwean liberation movement was plagued from the early 1960s by internal divisions. Deepened by the fact that the principal ZANU and ZAPU leaders were held in detention camps and prisons between 1964 and 1974[4]—as well as by regional, ethnically based, ambitions—the cleavages were capitalized upon by Ian Smith's intelligence services.[5] The divisions prompted at the same time an exceptionally active intervention by concerned African governments, principally Tanzania and Zambia. At the beginning of the 1970s, the Zimbabwean liberation movement appeared as particularly fragmented. In his thesis on Zimbabwe's liberation struggle until the early 1970s, Shamuyarira—who himself left ZAPU for ZANU in 1963; joined FROLIZI[6] in 1971; and returned to ZANU in the mid-1970s[7]—noted that

> in African capitals and at international or regional conferences, the leaders of ZANU and ZAPU [have] devoted more time to their inter-party rivalry than to the fight against the common enemy.[8]

Presidents Kaunda of Zambia and Nyerere of Tanzania often expressed similar opinions. As late as in May 1977, Nyerere told the Swedish ambassador to Tanzania, Lennart Eckerberg, that the Zimbabweans "only talked about the liberation struggle. They preferred conferences [and] wanted to travel around, meeting politicians".[9] It is against this background not surprising that potentially sympathetic donors—governments and solidarity organizations alike—were hesitant for a long time regarding support to the Zimbabwean liberation movements. In the case of Finland, Soiri and Peltola have noted that "the complexities of the liberation struggle [...] were not well understood. [...] [A]ll those alliances and factions did not really become clear in the eyes of the ordinary people or [...] the foreign policy deci-

---

1. CCHA: 'Protokoll från sammanträde 14 oktober 1969' ('Minutes from meeting on 14 October 1969'), Stockholm, 16 October 1969 (SDA).

2. On the ZAPU crisis, see Sellström Volume I, pp. 361-63.

3. SIDA: Decision ('Stöd till African National Congress (ANC), Sydafrika, samt Zimbabwe African People's Union (ZAPU), Rhodesia'/'Support to ANC and ZAPU'), Stockholm, 2 February 1973 (SDA).

4. Among them Ndabaningi Sithole and Robert Mugabe from ZANU and Joshua Nkomo from ZAPU.

5. See Ken Flower: *Serving Secretly: An Intelligence Chief on Record—Rhodesia into Zimbabwe 1964 to 1981*, Juhn Murray, London, 1987. Remarkably, Flower served continuously as Director General of the country's Central Intelligence Organization (CIO) from 1964 to 1981, i.e. under the British, Ian Smith, Bishop Muzorewa and Robert Mugabe.

6. The Front for the Liberation of Zimbabwe (FROLIZI) was formed by dissident members of ZANU and ZAPU in Zambia in October 1971. Although part of the December 1974 Lusaka Unity Accord, it was ignored by the OAU Liberation Committee and soon disintegrated.

7. A prominent journalist, academic and politician, Shamuyarira became Administrative Secretary of ZANU in 1978. He was appointed Minister of Information and Tourism in Zimbabwe's first independent government in 1980.

8. Nathan Shamuyarira: *National Liberation through Self-Reliance in Rhodesia, 1956-1972*, Ph.D. thesis, Princeton University, 1972, cited in Douglas G. Anglin and Timothy M. Shaw: *Zambia's Foreign Policy: Studies in Diplomacy and Dependence*, Westview Press, Boulder, Colorado, 1979, p. 250.

9. Letter ('Samtal med president Nyerere'/'Conversation with President Nyerere') from Lennart Eckerberg, Swedish ambassador to Tanzania, to Karin Söder, Minister for Foreign Affairs, Dar es Salaam, 14 May 1977 (MFA).

sion makers".[1] As a result, the Finnish government never extended official assistance to the Zimbabwean nationalist organizations.[2]

From the early 1970s, the Swedish government maintained frequent contacts with the Zimbabwean nationalists. In addition to regular consultations at the United Nations in New York and at the level of the embassies in Dar es Salaam, Lusaka and Gaborone—as well as later in Luanda and Maputo—high-ranking delegations often visited Stockholm, where they were received at the Ministry for Foreign Affairs and SIDA.[3] In late 1972, for example, representatives of ZANU, ZAPU, FROLIZI and the African National Council (ANC)[4]—the four organizations that in December 1974 signed the Lusaka Unity Accord—travelled separately to Sweden to "inform about their respective activities and [give] their views on the situation in Rhodesia".[5] These early, direct contacts and—above all—the cooperation with ZANU and ZAPU would over the years place Sweden in a unique position[6], not only compared with Britain and other Western powers, but also with the Soviet Union and its allies, which restricted their relations to ZAPU. After the 1980 independence elections, Anders Möllander—who as CCHA secretary, SIDA programme officer in Dar es Salaam and first secretary at the Swedish embassy in Lusaka had closely followed the events in Zimbabwe—asserted that

---

1. Soiri and Peltola op. cit., p. 134.

2. The Nordic governments adopted different policies vis-à-vis UDI and the Zimbabwean liberation movements. While both Finland and Sweden responded to UDI by imposing sanctions and breaking off diplomatic ties with Rhodesia, it was only Sweden that subsequently embarked on a policy of direct support to the liberation movements. The NATO members Denmark and Norway were much slower in severing their economic and diplomatic links. There were a number of Danish settler farmers in Rhodesia, but Norway too—which did not have any direct interests in the country—only closed its consulate when Ian Smith declared Rhodesia an independent republic in March 1970 (Wolf Lorenz: 'Norway and "Rhodesia": 1965-1980' in Eriksen (ed.) op. cit., p. 180). Following Sweden, Norway would, however, from 1974 extend official assistance to ZANU and ZAPU. Bishop Muzorewa—who had a Norwegian Methodist missionary as personal assistant—also enjoyed considerable support in Norway, particularly in the Christian People's Party (*Kristelig Folkeparti*). In 1977, Muzorewa's UANC was granted a one-off contribution by the Norwegian government. He visited the country on several occasions in the late 1970s, *inter alia* in October 1978—i.e. as a member of Ian Smith's Executive Council—when he was received privately by the Social Democratic Foreign Minister Frydenlund (Eva Kettis: Memorandum ('Besök i Norge av Muzorewa'/'Visit to Norway by Muzorewa'), Ministry for Foreign Affairs, Stockholm, 1 November 1978) (MFA).

3. Among the ZANU leaders who were in close contact with Sweden or visited the country in the 1960s and 1970s—in some cases already as students—were Herbert Chitepo, Henry Hamadziripi, Richard Hove, Ernest Kadungure, Kumbirai Kangai, Moton Malianga, Sally Mugabe, Didymus Mutasa, Simon Muzenda and Sydney Sekeramayi. In the case of ZAPU, some of the leading representatives were Ruth Chinamano, Dumiso Dabengwa, Phineas Makhurane, Daniel Matzimbamuto, J.Z. Moyo, Joseph Msika, Edward Ndlovu, John Nkomo, Isaac Nyathi and George Silundika.

4. The African National Council was formed in December 1971, originally as a pressure group opposing the Anglo-Rhodesian settlement proposals signed three weeks earlier. Two Methodist ministers—Abel Muzorewa and Canaan Banana—led the umbrella movement. In March 1972, ANC reconstituted itself as a permanent political organization under Bishop Muzorewa. It was renamed United African National Council (UANC) on the eve of the 1976 Geneva conference. During the conference, Canaan Banana—independent Zimbabwe's first President—left UANC and joined the ZANU delegation. In September 1975, ZAPU broke with ANC (Muzorewa) and formed the rival African National Council - Zimbabwe (ANC-Z) inside the country. In exile, ANC-Z normally translated as ANC-ZAPU.

5. CCHA: 'Framställning om bistånd från Zimbabwe-rörelserna ZANU, ZAPU och FROLIZI' ('Request for assistance from the Zimbabwean movements ZANU, ZAPU and FROLIZI'), Ministry for Foreign Affairs, Stockholm, 10 January 1973 (SDA).

6. Kumbirai Kangai, ZANU's former Secretary of Transport and Social Welfare, later said that "[e]ach time I visited Sweden, or I had a Swedish delegation in my office, you would feel like you were speaking to another comrade in the organization" (Interview with Kumbirai Kangai, p. 213).

Sweden through its cooperation [...] with the liberation movements had had better possibilities than even the former colonial power to form an idea of who the principal actors on the [Zimbabwean] political scene would be after the first free elections.[1]

Sweden, Britain and Zimbabwe

The relations established between the Swedish government and the wider Zimbabwean liberation movement were based on the common position that the 'Rhodesia question' was not an internal British concern, but part of the independence process in Africa as established by the UN General Assembly in the Decolonization Declaration of December 1960. As a young student leader, Olof Palme had raised the issue of Zimbabwe's independence as early as in 1953[2] and representatives of the Liberal Party would from the late 1950s share this view.[3] On this crucial point, the ruling Social Democratic Party stood out from the mid-1960s not only among the Nordic governments, but also embarked on a collision course with the British.[4]

In its relations with the three main actors on the Zimbabwean scene—the Smith regime, the British government and the nationalist movement—Sweden became progressively critical of the British stand and supportive of the latter's position.[5] The Anglo-Rhodesian Settlement Proposals entered into between Sir Alec Douglas Home and Ian Smith in November 1971 were, for example, rejected by Foreign Minister Krister Wickman, who described them as "a heavy blow to the force working for equality between the races".[6] This position was in turn strengthened by the affinity established between the Social Democratic Party and the ruling par-

---

1. Möllander op. cit., p. 45. The following anecdote could illustrate Möllander's statement: Olof Palme—then in opposition—visited London for a meeting with the Socialist International shortly before the 1980 independence elections. Very few British observers expected that ZANU would gain an outright majority, counting instead on a coalition between ZAPU and UANC. Palme's colleagues in the British Labour Party asked him about his views. Closely following the Zimbabwean events—*inter alia* through regular correspondence with Presidents Nyerere and Kaunda—and basing his prediction on Swedish diplomatic reports (Anders Möllander: Memorandum ('Samtal med Robert Mugabe'/'Conversation with Robert Mugabe'), Lusaka, 14 February 1980) (MFA), Palme said to his incredulous interlocutors that ZANU would win between 55 and 60 of the 80 contested seats. Two or three days later, it was announced that ZANU had won 57 seats, ZAPU 20 and UANC 3. Together with the Swedish representative Jan Eliasson and Anders Möllander, the author participated in the meeting with Mugabe in the ZANU leader's residence in Salisbury (now Harare) on 12 February 1980, i.e. two weeks before the elections. Mugabe predicted that ZANU would win 58 seats, ZAPU 20 and UANC 2 (Tor Sellström: Memorandum ('Samtal med Robert Mugabe i Salisbury 1980 02 12'/'Conversation with Robert Mugabe in Salisbury, 12 February 1980'), Lusaka, 14 February 1980) (SDA). During the pre-election period, Eliasson served as head of the Swedish liaison office in Salisbury, while Möllander and Sellström visited from Zambia. In Lusaka, their impressions on the Zimbabwean election campaign and the prospects of a ZANU victory were keenly sought by other interested parties, not least by ANC of South Africa and the Cuban embassy.
2. See Sellström Volume I, pp. 95-96.
3. As secretary general of the World Assembly of Youth, David Wirmark of the Liberal Party had befriended Joshua Nkomo as early as in 1958 (ibid., pp. 101-02).
4. Finland "regarded the Rhodesia/Zimbabwe question as an internal [British] issue" (Soiri and Peltola op. cit., p. 134). Despite its support to ZANU and ZAPU, "if a choice *had to be made*" the Norwegian government would in case of a breakdown at the 1979 Lancaster House independence negotiations, similarly, let the relations with Britain "prevail" (Lorenz in Eriksen (ed.) op. cit., p. 190). While the Zimbabwean liberation movements regularly urged Sweden to put pressure on the British, Britain conversely "worked to persuade [its] Norwegian colleagues to seek to moderate [their] demands" (ibid.).
5. Cf. the interview with Didymus Mutasa: "Most of our time was taken up by explaining the activities of the British government [...] and we believe that [the Swedes] in turn quietly approached the British and said: 'Why are things happening that way?'" (p. 219). Invited to Sweden by Amnesty International, Mutasa—who at the time was studying in England—visited the Ministry for Foreign Affairs in June 1973, requesting the Swedish government to take legal proceedings against Britain for breaching the European Convention on Human Rights (Ann Wilkens: Memorandum ('Samtal med sydrhodesier som önskar svenskt stöd för aktion i Europarådet'/'Conversation with Southern Rhodesian who wishes Swedish support for action in the European Council'), Ministry for Foreign Affairs, Stockholm, 18 June 1973) (MFA).
6. 'Statement by the Foreign Minister', 25 November 1971, in The Royal Ministry for Foreign Affairs: *Documents on Swedish Foreign Policy: 1971*, Stockholm, 1972, p. 162.

ties in Tanzania and Zambia.[1] Shortly after Wickman's criticism of the joint British and Rhodesian proposals, Nyerere wrote to Palme, describing them as "window-dressing for the establishment of a second South Africa", adding that "Tanzania will continue to support the nationalist movements of Rhodesia".[2] Concluding his long and detailed letter, he stated that

> we regard the almost inevitable legalising of Ian Smith's regime by Britain as a setback to African freedom and as an indication of where Britain stands in the almost inevitable confrontation between free Africa and Southern Africa. I can say no more.[3]

Palme responded in late January 1972, stating that "much of what you say coincides with our own thinking". In his opinion, the implication of the Anglo-Rhodesian proposals appeared to "support [...] the Rhodesian policy [of] continu[ing] to deprive the African majority of its fundamental democratic rights". Against this background, Palme explained, "we are, of course, continuing our support in the form of humanitarian assistance [to] the Rhodesian liberation movements".[4]

After UDI, Sweden and Britain also differed over the issue of sanctions against the Smith regime. At the beginning of the 1960s, there were only marginal Swedish economic interests in Rhodesia and the trade exchange between the two countries was almost insignificant.[5] Reacting to UDI, it was comparatively uncomplicated for the Swedish government to immediately follow the UN Security Council's recommendation of 20 November 1965 and impose a total ban on all trade with the rebel colony.[6] Largely seen as a test case for international sanctions against apartheid South Africa, Sweden sought, however, to go further. In December 1965, the Swedish representative to the United Nations, Sverker Åström, circulated a letter to the members of the Security Council, stating that "the present situation in Southern Rhodesia constitutes a threat to peace and that [...] the Security Council should [...] take mandatory decisions relating [...] to economic sanctions against Rhodesia".[7] Warning Stockholm that such a decision could lead to an "appeal in favour of mandatory sanctions also against [South Africa]"[8], Harold Wilson's British Labour government strongly opposed the initiative, conveying that the proposed Swedish "drastic measures" had "caused concern in London".[9]

---

1. Palme had in September 1971 paid official visits to Zambia and Tanzania. The situation in Zimbabwe featured prominently in his talks with Kaunda and Nyerere. During his stay in Zambia, Palme visited the Victoria Falls, where he described the Zambezi as "the border of human decency", separating independent Africa from the white-ruled South.
2. Letter from Julius Nyerere to Olof Palme, Dar es Salaam, 4 December 1971 (MFA).
3. Ibid.
4. Letter from Olof Palme to Julius Nyerere, Stockholm, 24 January 1972 (MFA). On the latter point, Palme's statement was not entirely correct. Official Swedish assistance was at the time only extended to ZANU.
5. See Sellström Volume I, pp. 55-57.
6. Ibid., p. 335. In the absence of a specific instrument on economic sanctions, a government committee was appointed to prepare such legislation. In December 1966, the UN Security Council made selective sanctions against Rhodesia compulsory. While Sweden maintained a total trade ban against the country, the committee submitted its final proposal in March 1968. After extensive parliamentary discussions, the main points were adopted in May 1969. The Rhodesia Law of 29 May 1969 thus became Sweden's first piece of legislation on economic sanctions against another country. It should, however, be noted that several South Africa-based Swedish subsidiary companies continued to trade with Rhodesia (Sven-Ivan Sundqvist: *Sydafrikas Guldålder/* 'South Africa's Golden Age', Askild & Kärnekull, Borås, 1974, pp. 190-92). This strengthened the demands in Sweden for unilateral sanctions against the apartheid regime.
7. 'Press release', 14 December 1965, in The Royal Ministry for Foreign Affairs: *Documents on Swedish Foreign Policy: 1965*, Stockholm, 1966, p. 130.
8. Leif Belfrage: Promemoria' ('Memorandum'), Ministry for Foreign Affairs, Stockholm, 22 December 1965 (MFA).
9. Ibid.

A widening gap would from then on appear between Britain and Sweden regarding Zimbabwe and, more broadly, Southern Africa.[1] While Britain stalled on the question of broader sanctions, Sweden repeatedly demanded a decision to that effect by the Security Council. In October 1974—at a time when the 'détente exercise' was under way—the Swedish UN representative Brita Åhman underlined, for example, that it "was clear that the United Kingdom had assumed the task of continuing to be a stumbling block", but that it was "the duty of the international community to support the liberation movements in their struggle for freedom by respecting the policy of sanctions".[2] As a member of the Security Council, Sweden insisted on this demand.[3] In March 1976, Palme's Social Democratic government stated in its annual foreign policy declaration that

> it is imperative that majority rule [is] established in Rhodesia at the earliest possible moment. The demands for independence put forward by the liberation movements must be met. In the meantime, Sweden advocates that the sanctions against Rhodesia should be made more severe.[4]

Commending the newly independent Mozambican government for closing its frontier with Ian Smith's Rhodesia, in April 1976 Sweden asserted in the Security Council that it was "now for the [...] Council and the Sanctions Committee to make sure that all loopholes [against Rhodesia] were closed".[5] This view was not only held by the Social Democratic Party. After winning the parliamentary elections later in the year, it was upheld by Thorbjörn Fälldin's non-socialist coalition government. In its first major declaration on Swedish foreign policy, in March 1977 it made it clear that "we give wholehearted support to economic sanctions against Rhodesia and will work for them to be strengthened".[6]

Shortly thereafter, the non-socialist government substantially increased the direct official allocations to ZANU and ZAPU, granting them 2.5 MSEK each in 1976/77.[7] To ease the plight of the Zimbabwean refugees in Botswana and, above all, in Mozambique, considerable contributions were in addition made to these countries' refugee programmes. In 1977 alone, a total of 35 MSEK was directly and

---

1. As noted in Volume I, the opposing views held by the British Labour Party and the Swedish Social Democratic Party became manifest at the congress of the Socialist International in Stockholm in May 1966 (Sellström Volume I, pp. 339-41).
2. 'Summary of a speech by Mrs. Brita Åhman in the Fourth Committee of the UN General Assembly', 23 October 1974, in Ministry for Foreign Affairs: *Documents on Swedish Foreign Policy: 1974*, Stockholm, 1976, p. 176.
3. A particularly heated exchange regarding sanctions on South Africa took place in June 1975 between Sweden on the one hand and France, United Kingdom and United States on the other during the Namibia debate in the Security Council. On this occasion, the three permanent Western council members utilized for the second time in the history of the United Nations a joint veto, opposing a mandatory arms embargo on the apartheid regime.
4. 'Government Declaration in the *Riksdag* debate on foreign affairs', 31 March 1976, in Ministry for Foreign Affairs: *Documents on Swedish Foreign Policy: 1976*, Stockholm, 1978, p. 24.
5. 'Summary of speech by ambassador Sundberg in the Security Council concerning sanctions against Rhodesia', 6 April 1976, in Ministry for Foreign Affairs: *Documents on Swedish Foreign Policy: 1976*, Stockholm, 1978, p. 191.
6. 'Government Statement [in] the *Riksdag* debate on foreign policy', 30 March 1977, in Ministry for Foreign Affairs: *Documents on Swedish Foreign Policy: 1977*, Stockholm, 1978, p. 25.
7. Ministry for Foreign Affairs: Decision ('Stöd till Zimbabwe African National Union (ZANU) och Zimbabwe African People's Union (ZAPU)'/'Assistance to ZANU and ZAPU'), Stockholm, 16 June 1977 (SDA). Taken late in the financial year, the decision retroactively applied to 1976/77. Due to the 'détente exercise', the Lusaka Unity Accord and to the crisis following the assassination of Herbert Chitepo, no Swedish assistance was allocated to ZANU and ZAPU during the financial year 1975/76. Under the Social Democratic government, the last allocation to ZANU in 1974/75 amounted in total to 860,000 SEK (SIDA: Decision ('Biståndsprogram för ZANU för budgetåret 1974/75'/'Assistance programme to ZANU during the financial year 1974/75'), Stockholm, 25 June 1974) (SDA). The corresponding grant to ZAPU only amounted to 50,000 SEK (SIDA: Decision ('Bistånd till ZAPU'/'Assistance to ZAPU'), Stockholm, 27 June 1974) (SDA).

indirectly allocated as official Swedish humanitarian assistance to the Zimbabwean liberation movements and refugees.[1] The changeover from Olof Palme's Social Democratic government to the Centre Party leader Thorbjörn Fälldin's non-socialist coalition in September 1976 did not negatively affect the official support to the Zimbabwean cause. On the contrary, maintaining the basic policy towards Zimbabwe, the Fälldin government would at the end of the 1970s regularly increase the assistance to ZANU and ZAPU, granting the two Patriotic Front partners equal resources.[2]

Exceptional Relations

The continuity of Sweden's position might have surprised outside observers. It was, however, quite a natural outcome of the early encounter with the Zimbabwean liberation struggle, which from the late 1960s was actively supported by the broader liberal camp.[3] While the Social Democratic Party and the organized solidarity movement focused on the independence struggles in the Portuguese colonies, in the case of Zimbabwe it was the Centre and Liberal parties that advocated official support. As early as at the beginning of 1968, the Liberal Party Youth League (FPU)[4] organized a campaign in favour of Joshua Nkomo's ZAPU.[5] Announcing the campaign, the party review *Liberal Debatt* stated that

> Swedish liberalism must practically support the liberation of Zimbabwe. [...] While waiting for official contributions [by the government], FPU has decided to start its own fund-raising campaign. Its central point is the direct assistance to ZAPU. It should be supported by all liberals. Every success for ZAPU is a defeat for white racial fascism in Southern Africa.[6]

Several younger Liberal politicians—among them Per Ahlmark and Ola Ullsten; the latter Minister for International Development Cooperation in Fälldin's coalition government and later Prime Minister (1978-79) and Foreign Minister (1979-82)—took active part in the ZAPU campaign. Towards the end of 1968, FPU followed up the initiative by demanding direct, official humanitarian assistance to the Zimbabwean "resistance movements".[7]

It was, however, not only the Liberal youth that advocated support. In January 1969—before the very principle was endorsed—the chairmen of the Centre and Liberal parties, Gunnar Hedlund and Sven Wedén, submitted a joint parliamentary motion in favour of official assistance to the movements in Southern Africa that

---

1. CCHA: 'Biståndsframställning från UANC/Zimbabwe' ('Request for assistance from UANC/Zimbabwe'), Ministry for Foreign Affairs, Stockholm, 27 January 1978 (SDA).
2. Fälldin's 1976 coalition government between the Centre Party, the Liberal Party and—in a junior position— the Moderate Party was formed just prior to the decision by ZANU and ZAPU to jointly appear as the Patriotic Front. In the corridors of the Geneva conference in late 1976, it was thus representatives of Fälldin's non-socialist government that conferred with representatives of the Patriotic Front, a novel situation in the relations between Sweden and the Zimbabwean nationalist movements. However, the opposition leader Olof Palme also visited the Geneva conference.
3. On the change of government in 1976 and the continuity of the Swedish support to the liberation movements, see the interviews with Lena Hjelm-Wallén (Social Democratic Party) (p. 294), Pär Granstedt (Centre Party) (p. 271), Carl Tham (ex-Liberal Party) (pp. 342-43) and Birger Hagård (Moderate Party) (p. 274). See also the interviews with Anders Johansson (p. 299) and Åke Magnusson (pp. 317-18).
4. In Swedish, *Folkpartiets Ungdomsförbund*.
5. The initiative was launched a couple of months after ZAPU and ANC of South Africa carried out the joint military Wankie campaign in Zimbabwe.
6. Editorial: 'Liberalt Stöd åt Zimbabwes Frigörelse' ('Liberal Support for the Liberation of Zimbabwe') in *Liberal Debatt*, No. 2, 1968, p. 2.
7. Letter from FPU to the Swedish government, signed by Olle Wästberg and Lennart Rydberg, Stockholm, 7 November 1968 (MFA). At the time, the Centre and Liberal parties preferred to talk of 'resistance'—not liberation—movements.

"strive for social and economic justice. Particularly relevant in this context are the movements that operate in Rhodesia [...], Mozambique, Angola [...], Namibia and South Africa".[1] Similar motions were introduced in 1970[2] and 1971[3] by the non-socialist 'middle parties', and in January 1972 the new Centre and Liberal party leaders, Thorbjörn Fälldin and Gunnar Helén, repeated the demand, stating that

> the Swedish support to the liberation movements has so far mainly been extended to movements in the Portuguese colonies in Africa. Considering the successes achieved by the resistance movements in Mozambique, Angola and, above all, in Guinea-Bissau, on the whole we endorse this priority. [...] Taking into account that the United Nations in its resolutions has requested the member states to [...] support resistance movements in Namibia, Rhodesia and South Africa, we [, however,] find it important that the movements in these [countries also] receive Swedish assistance, even if their successes so far have been modest. Even smaller contributions may here have a greatly stimulating effect.[4]

When Fälldin's coalition government came to power in 1976, the two main partners—the Centre and Liberal parties—had for many years advocated increased support to the liberation movements in Zimbabwe (and in Namibia and South Africa). The Prime Minister himself had actively raised the issue in parliament.[5] This was not only exceptional from an international point of view, but also had an impact on the Swedish debate.

Concentrating their attention on the Portuguese colonies and largely viewing the struggle in Zimbabwe as a wider liberal concern, both the Left Party Communists and the organized solidarity movement downplayed its significance until the second half of the 1970s. The first parliamentary motion submitted by the Left Party concerning Zimbabwe was only introduced by its chairman, C.H. Hermansson, in January 1976. In general terms, it stated that official Swedish assistance "ought to be possible" in the case of Bishop Muzorewa's by then controversial African National Council.[6] No parliamentary initiative had previously been taken by the party in favour of either ZANU or ZAPU.

---

1. Swedish Parliament 1969: Motion No. 511 in the Second Chamber, Riksdagens Protokoll 1969, p. 16. It should be noted that the Liberal Party at its congress in 1968 had approved a proposal by Per Ahlmark, Gustaf Lindencrona and David Wirmark to draw up guidelines for support to "resistance movements of various kinds". A working group chaired by Wirmark was appointed in November 1968. It submitted its report—*Support to Resistance Movements*—in May 1969, that is, at the time when the Swedish parliament approved the policy of official assistance to PAIGC and the liberation movements in Southern Africa. Endorsed by the board of the Liberal Party, the Wirmark report explicitly advocated Swedish support to the liberation movements in Mozambique, Zimbabwe, Angola and South Africa (Sellström Volume I, pp. 234-36).
2. In 1970, Per Ahlmark and Ola Ullsten of the Liberal Party submitted a motion in which they saw it as "self-evident that the Swedish support to the resistance movements shall be substantially increased", adding that they in particular had ZANU and ZAPU of Zimbabwe, FNLA and MPLA of Angola and ANC of South Africa in mind (Swedish Parliament 1970: Motion No. 624 in the Second Chamber, Riksdagens Protokoll 1970, p. 7).
3. In 1971, Thorbjörn Fälldin (Centre Party) and Gunnar Helén (Liberal Party) introduced a joint motion in favour of increased support to the liberation movements, explicitly mentioning FNLA and MPLA of Angola and ANC of South Africa (Swedish Parliament 1971: Motion No. 472, Riksdagens Protokoll 1971, p. 16). At the same time, the Liberal Party submitted a motion signed by Per Ahlmark and David Wirmark, which advocated support to ZAPU and ZANU of Zimbabwe, FNLA and MPLA of Angola, the "resistance movement" of Namibia and ANC of South Africa (Swedish Parliament 1971: Motion No. 683, Riksdagens Protokoll 1971, p. 3).
4. Swedish Parliament 1972: Motion No. 934, Riksdagens Protokoll 1972, p. 16.
5. Fälldin had come into contact with the struggle in Zimbabwe through his friendship with Alexander Chikwanda of Zambia's UNIP party at the end of 1964 (Sellström Volume I, pp. 90-91).
6. Swedish Parliament 1975/76: Motion No. 350, Riksdagens Protokoll 1976, p. 5. ANC had *de facto* collapsed after the abortive Victoria Falls conference in August 1975. While the exiled leadership of ZANU was detained in Zambia, ZAPU decided to remove Muzorewa, forming the African National Council-Zimbabwe in September 1975.

In spite of the spectacular Båstad demonstrations against the tennis match between Sweden and Rhodesia in May 1968[1], the post-Vietnam Africa Groups, similarly, paid very little attention to Zimbabwe.[2] When the leaders of PAIGC and the Southern African liberation movements in April 1973 made a highly publicized visit to Stockholm after the Oslo Conference on Colonialism and Apartheid, the solidarity movement did not, for example, invite Herbert Chitepo from ZANU or Jane Ngwenya from ZAPU to address its public meeting.[3] It was only at its second congress in June 1976 that the reorganized solidarity movement decided to launch a Zimbabwe campaign, without taking sides for any nationalist organization.[4] Instead, the support was, generally, to be channelled to "the guerrilla struggle".[5]

In the case of Sweden and Zimbabwe, it was primarily at the level of the state that the issue of humanitarian support to ZANU and ZAPU was discussed and defined. Instrumental behind the decisions taken to extend direct government support to ZANU and ZAPU in 1969 and 1971/73 were the opposition non-socialist Centre and Liberal parties. While ZANU towards the end of the 1960s had established a platform in Sweden[6], the active role played by the Liberal Party in favour of ZAPU was in this context particularly significant. Within the so called Khartoum alliance of 'authentic' liberation movements, ZAPU was given exclusive recognition by the Soviet Union from 1969. It had established close links with Moscow and, notably, East Germany at the beginning of the 1960s[7] and in the Nordic region it was initially represented through the Soviet-aligned World Peace Council in Helsinki.[8] As later stated by ZAPU's former Administrative Secretary, John Nkomo, "we tended to develop a much firmer leaning to the East than to the West".[9] The pro-Western Liberal Party would, nevertheless, more than any other Swedish political organization defend ZAPU's cause from the late 1960s. Parliamentary motions to that effect were even submitted at the height of ZAPU's internal crisis in 1970-71.

Although the Liberal Party was closer to ZAPU than to ZANU, it did not shut the door on ZANU[10], advocating instead official support to the two Zimbabwean

---

1. See Sellström Volume I, pp. 348-53.
2. As earlier noted, the book—*Afrika: Imperialism och Befrielsekamp* ('Africa: Imperialism and Liberation Struggle')—published by the Africa Groups in early 1972 did not discuss Zimbabwe.
3. Nor were Oliver Tambo from ANC of South Africa or Moses Garoeb and Andreas Shipanga from SWAPO of Namibia invited. The speakers at the Africa Groups' meeting represented MPLA of Angola (Agostinho Neto), FRELIMO of Mozambique (Marcelino dos Santos) and PAIGC of Guinea-Bissau (Lucette Andrade Cabral). The representatives from Namibia, South Africa and Zimbabwe did, however, address a public meeting arranged by the UN Association and the Social Democratic Party branches in Stockholm (Gun-Britt Andersson: Memorandum ('Besök i Sverige av befrielserörelserepresentanter'/'Visit to Sweden by representatives of liberation movements'), Ministry for Foreign Affairs, Stockholm, 25 May 1973 (MFA).
4. AGIS: 'Protokoll från AGIS' kongress, 5-7 juni 1976, i Björkå' ('Minutes from the AGIS' congress, 5-7 June 1976, at Björkå') [no date] (AGA).
5. Letter from Dick Urban Vestbro to *Fellesrådet for det sørliga Afrika* (The Norwegian Council for Southern Africa), 3 October 1976 [no place] (AGA).
6. See Sellström Volume I, pp. 336-38.
7. Nkomo op. cit., pp. 173-176 and Schleicher op. cit., pp. 75-150. In his memoirs, Joshua Nkomo states that his first visit to Moscow—after initial contacts in London and at the United Nations in New York—was made in 1961. The Schleichers also date the first direct contact between ZAPU and GDR to 1961.
8. Cf. the interview with Dumiso Dabengwa: "We were [...] part of the Helsinki World Peace Council. That is, to a very large extent, how we got in touch with the Nordic countries. After that it spread to Sweden, where we had a representative" (p. 210).
9. Interview with John Nkomo, p. 223.
10. *Liberal Debatt*, the Liberal Party review, opened its pages to ZANU. In early 1970, for example, it published an article by Sydney Sekeramayi which was highly critical of ZAPU, characterizing the rival organization as a "reactionary, conservative group" (S.T. Sekeramayi: 'Zimbabwe African National Union' in *Liberal Debatt*, No. 3, 1970, pp. 34-36).

liberation movements that were recognized by OAU.[1] There was thus a strong resemblance to the Liberal Party's views on humanitarian support to Angola, where it called for official assistance to both FNLA and MPLA. The Zimbabwean situation could, however, hardly be compared to that of Angola. Although the relations between ZANU and ZAPU were strained, they did not assume the antagonistic character that separated the two Angolan organizations. Differing on tactics[2], ZANU and ZAPU were ideologically close and they both enjoyed support from Tanzania and Zambia, the two independent African countries with which Sweden maintained particularly friendly bonds.[3] Above all, in the case of Zimbabwe the Liberal Party advocated support to a movement which was close to MPLA, PAIGC and FRELIMO and therefore almost by definition enjoyed sympathy in Sweden, while the advocacy of Holden Roberto's FNLA met widespread and strong opposition.

Closely aligned with ANC of South Africa, ZAPU had, in addition, from the mid-1960s been invited to Sweden by the ruling Social Democratic Party and the organization had been promoted by the Swedish solidarity movement's first generation South Africa Committees. As early as in 1966, Joshua Nkomo's European representatives Nelson Samkange and Nicholas Chitsiga had addressed the traditional Labour Day celebrations.[4] Later in the year, the NGO solidarity movement's *Syd- och Sydvästafrika* bulletin published a special issue on Zimbabwe in connection with a visit by ZANU's Tarisai Ziyambi and ZAPU's Lawrence Vambe.[5]

Above all, it was in reaction to an appeal by ZAPU's National Secretary George Nyandoro that the local South Africa Committees in Lund and Uppsala with support from a wide range of political youth and student organizations demonstrated in May 1968 against the tennis match between Sweden and Rhodesia. Immediately after the 'battle at Båstad', the Social Democratic Youth League granted ZAPU an amount of 5,000 SEK.[6] There was, as a consequence, at the end of the 1960s far from a principled uncertainty regarding ZAPU. Both ZANU and ZAPU were seen

---

1. Both ZANU and ZAPU were recognized by the OAU Liberation Committee in December 1963. According to David Wirmark, the Social Democratic Party "did not want to support more than one [liberation] movement in each country", while the Liberal Party was open to assistance to several organizations (Interview with David Wirmark, p. 348). In Wirmark's view, it was on this point—rather than on the ideological orientation of the liberation movements—that the Social Democratic Party and the Liberal Party differed.
2. Broadly speaking, ZAPU was amenable to political solutions, while ZANU developed a strong conviction that independence could only be achieved through armed struggle. Joshua Nkomo would on a number of occasions enter into negotiations with Ian Smith. As stated by John Nkomo, "[t]he military effort was simply a tool to pressurize the others to come to the table and talk" (Interview with John Nkomo, p. 225). Different ethnic constituencies and conflicts at the leadership level—combined with the fact that ZAPU was supported by the Soviet Union while ZANU relied on China—further separated the two.
3. Also in very general terms, Tanzania was closer to ZANU and Zambia to ZAPU. While Zambia during the second half of the 1960s clearly showed a preference for Joshua Nkomo's organization, the situation changed after the 1970-71 ZAPU crisis and the opening of ZANU's eastern front. Discussing the situation in Zimbabwe, in March 1973, for example, the Zambian Minister of State for Foreign Affairs, Timothy Kankasa—representing Zambia at the OAU Liberation Committee—told the Swedish ambassador in Lusaka that "ZANU's activities were completely dominant" and that ZAPU "did not play any active role". At the same time, Kankasa gave Sweden the advice to "forget about FROLIZI" (Letter ('Frihetsrörelserna i Sydrhodesia'/'The freedom movements in Southern Rhodesia') from the Swedish ambassador to Zambia, Iwo Dölling, to the Ministry for Foreign Affairs, Lusaka, 9 March 1973) (MFA). In connection with the 'détente exercise', Zambia would once again give political priority to ZAPU. The ZANU leadership and more than a thousand ZANU followers were detained in Zambia after the assassination of Herbert Chitepo in March 1975. With regard to FROLIZI, CCHA shortly after the meeting between Kankasa and Dölling recommended that a renewed request for Swedish assistance should "be left without attention" (Stig Abelin: Letter ('Angående FROLIZI'/'Regarding FROLIZI') to SIDA Lusaka, SIDA, Stockholm, 26 June 1973) (SDA).
4. Socialdemokratiska Partistyrelsen (The National Board of the Social Democratic Party): 'Berättelse för år 1966' ('Report for the year 1966'), p. 7 (LMA).
5. Sellström Volume I, pp. 344-45.
6. *Dagens Nyheter*, 15 May 1968.

Robert Mugabe—then representing ZAPU of Zimbabwe—at a meeting of the Pan-African Freedom Movement for East, Central and Southern Africa, Mbeya, Tanzania, May 1962 (Photo: Maelezo, Dar es Salaam)

as genuine liberation movements. As stated by the Social Democratic Party's former international secretary Pierre Schori:

> [W]e refused to give unilateral recognition to one movement. We thought that both ZANU and ZAPU were authentic movements and that there was no reason for us to follow the demand of one or the other. When one of them asked for unilateral support, we said that 'we do not give you unilateral recognition, because that is not up to us to do. We see two movements and we hope that you can work together'.[1]

Broad political relations and contacts with the Zimbabwean nationalist movement exceptionally prepared the terrain for official assistance to both ZANU and ZAPU. Of the five countries covered in this study, it was only in Zimbabwe that Sweden extended direct support to more than one movement. Of all the Southern African liberation movements receiving Swedish humanitarian assistance, it was, in addition, only ZANU that did not form part of the so called 'authentic alliance' recognized by the Soviet Union. That ZANU[2] played a particular role was further

---

1. Interview with Pierre Schori, p. 332. The stand was strengthened by FRELIMO's position. FRELIMO and ZANU worked together from 1970 and it was this cooperation that made it possible for ZANU to open its eastern front in late 1972. Criticizing the decision taken at the 1969 Khartoum conference, Marcelino dos Santos stated in 1996: "In the case of Zimbabwe, we were [...] wrong. Reality and history showed that ZANU, in fact, was an authentic movement" (Interview with Marcelino dos Santos, p. 49).
2. ZANU was formed in August 1963 by dissident members of ZAPU. At the inaugural congress in May 1964, Ndabaningi Sithole was elected President, Leopold Takawira Vice-President and Robert Mugabe Secretary General. Between 1964 and 1974, Sithole and Mugabe spent a decade in detention camps and prisons in Zimbabwe. Takawira died in detention in June 1970. Until the release of Sithole and Mugabe, Herbert Chitepo—who in 1964 had been appointed National Chairman *in absentia*—represented ZANU abroad, setting up headquarters in Lusaka in early 1966. After the assassination of Chitepo in March 1975, the detained ZANU leaders deposed Sithole and declared their loyalty to Mugabe, appointing him leader of the organization. While Sithole attempted to regain control through his chairmanship of the Zimbabwe Liberation Council (ZLC)—formed as the external wing of ANC in Dar es Salaam in July 1975—Mugabe was confirmed in early 1977 as Secretary General and "leader of ZANU". In September 1977, an enlarged Central Committee meeting, finally, elected Mugabe President of ZANU, with Simon Muzenda as Vice-President and Edgar Tekere as Secretary General. It should be noted that ZANU at the annual negotiations with Sweden over the years was either represented by Chitepo in Zambia or—from 1977—by Mugabe in Mozambique. Sithole never took part in the consultations. Similarly, Joshua Nkomo never led a ZAPU delegation to official aid negotiations with the Swedish government. Among the Southern African 'historical leaders', he was in this respect an exception.

underlined by the fact that it was the first Zimbabwean movement to formally request Swedish official assistance and that it became the first of the Southern African liberation movements with which the government signed a formal protocol on humanitarian cooperation.[1]

The aid relations with ZANU and ZAPU will be discussed below. It should, nevertheless, be noted that Sweden's particular links to Zimbabwe's leading nationalist movements by the mid-1970s prompted intense diplomatic efforts to bring the two closer together. Also in this regard Zimbabwe occupies an exceptional place in the history of Sweden's involvement with the Southern African liberation movements.[2] In 1996, SIDA's former Director General Ernst Michanek stated that

> I was myself active, talking to Joshua Nkomo and Robert Mugabe on several occasions. [...] [A]fter some trial and error [we] told each of them that 'unless you find a way of working together, we cannot support either of you'. That was more or less the beginning of the Patriotic Front between ZAPU and ZANU. I think that we almost demanded that the front should be created. [...]

> [T]he situation was very [...] delicate, so we had to take a position. Outside the military field, Sweden was by far the largest and most important financial supporter of both ZAPU and ZANU [and] Stockholm was a very important meeting point between the Zimbabwean liberation movements and international actors. I think that we played a prominent role in this connection and [that] whatever decisions we took had been considered very thoroughly. [...] [W]e [eventually] came to the conclusion that we had to steer in a way that we otherwise did not like to do. It was sometimes rather unpleasant, but necessary.[3]

Prisoners and War

The official Swedish support to ZANU and ZAPU can be divided into three phases. The first phase covers the period from the parliamentary pronouncement in May 1969 until March 1975, when Sweden—mainly at Zambia's insistence—due to the 'détente exercise' decided to suspend the assistance. The second phase corresponds to the troubled détente period and to the aftermath of the assassination of Herbert Chitepo in March 1975, when direct assistance was suspended. The third phase, finally, begins after the formation of the Patriotic Front in October 1976, when the support was substantially increased and extended in equal amounts to both ZANU and ZAPU.

Sweden's relations with the Zimbabwean liberation movements were during the first half of the 1970s chiefly maintained at the level of the embassy in Lusaka, where both ZANU and ZAPU had set up external headquarters while Reverend Sithole, Robert Mugabe and Joshua Nkomo were in detention. Consultations with ZANU were held with its National Chairman, Herbert Chitepo.[4] The principal ZAPU contact—before and after the 1970-71 leadership struggle—was Edward Ndlovu,

---

1. Möllander op. cit., p. 37.
2. Representatives of the Church of Sweden Mission would in an unusual way also add their voices to a proactive Swedish involvement with both ZANU and ZAPU.
3. Interview with Ernst Michanek, p. 323. Cf. the interview with Pierre Schori, p. 332.
4. Born in 1923, Chitepo was one of Southern Africa's most outstanding nationalist leaders. After studies at Adam's College and Fort Hare University College in South Africa, he qualified in 1954 as a barrister at King's College, London, while at the same time working as a research assistant at the School of Oriental and African Studies. As the country's first black barrister, he returned to Zimbabwe the same year, often defending African nationalists in court. In December 1960, he served as Joshua Nkomo's legal adviser at the Federal Constitutional Review Conference in London. Going into voluntary exile in Tanganyika (Tanzania) in May 1962, he established close relations with Julius Nyerere and became the country's first black Director of Public Prosecutions. Appointed ZANU National Chairman *in absentia* in 1964, he resigned from his position in Tanzania and moved to Lusaka, Zambia, in January 1966, subsequently leading ZANU's external organization.

the organization's National Secretary.[1] Mainly due to the ZAPU crisis and to Chitepo's active diplomacy[2], the period was dominated by the relations with ZANU, which received the bulk of the initially modest official Swedish resources.

Until the suspension of the assistance in March 1975, disbursements to ZANU amounted in total to slightly more than 1.1 MSEK, while corresponding payments to ZAPU only reached 100,000 SEK.[3] In spite of the formation of the African National Council inside Zimbabwe in December 1971—and that ZANU and ZAPU under pressure from the OAU Liberation Committee had set up a Joint Military Command (JMC) in March 1972; in early 1973 followed by a decision in principle to unite the two movements[4]—there was a clear preference in favour of ZANU. This, in turn, resulted from frequent contacts and an extraordinary openness from the organization regarding its military plans and humanitarian concerns.

The first appeals by ZANU and ZAPU were made before the launch of the armed struggle and concerned the political prisoners in Zimbabwe. Even before Ian Smith's proclamation of 'independence', there were an estimated 1,700 African nationalists held in jails and prison camps throughout the country and more arrests were carried out after UDI in November 1965. Against this background, the newly established SIDA was approached in late 1965 by the two organizations to extend relief assistance to the families of the prisoners.[5] SIDA responded positively. In December 1965, an initial amount of 150,000 SEK was granted "in favour of the families of political prisoners [in Zimbabwe]", to be channelled through the Church of Sweden Aid and the World Council of Churches.[6] At the same time as a high-profile Stockholm group of Amnesty International—joined by Per Wästberg, member of the officially appointed CCHA and active within the International Defence and Aid Fund[7]—adopted Robert Mugabe as a prisoner of conscience[8], the

---

1. Both Chitepo and Ndlovu had links to Sweden. The ZANU Chairman paid his first visit to the country in April 1966—attending a seminar in Uppsala when the 'battle of Sinoia' took place—while Ndlovu had received his education through the Church of Sweden Mission. During Joshua Nkomo's detention, J.Z. Moyo led ZAPU from Lusaka.

2. Between October 1972 and November 1974, Chitepo made three visits to Sweden. He also led ZANU's delegations to official negotiations with Sweden in 1973 and 1974. In Sweden itself, ZANU's cause was successfully promoted by Sydney Sekeramayi. Sally Mugabe, the wife of the detained ZANU leader, made the first of her six nationwide tours of Sweden in February 1973. Her important information activities—which continued until May 1979—were organized by SIDA (Sellström Volume I, pp. 327-28).

3. See the accompanying tables on disbursements from SIDA to ZANU and ZAPU. During the first seven years of assistance from 1969/70—that is, under Social Democratic governments—a total of 1.2 MSEK was disbursed to ZANU and ZAPU. The allocations were substantially increased by the Fälldin government. During the five years from 1976/77 until 1980/81, no less than 87.2 MSEK—excluding extraordinary allocations—was disbursed to the two Patriotic Front partners.

4. The 1972-73 agreements were imposed on the Zimbabwean liberation movements by the OAU Liberation Committee. As in the case of the December 1972 Kinshasa agreement between FNLA and MPLA—on which they were largely modelled—the JMC and the March 1973 Lusaka agreement between ZANU and ZAPU never became operational. In addition, they did not envisage joint management of humanitarian assistance. In a letter to SIDA in November 1972—i.e., shortly after Herbert Chitepo's crucial visit to Sweden—J.Z. Moyo underlined that "welfare and other problems remain the responsibility of ZAPU and ZANU separately, as individual parties" (Letter from J.Z. Moyo, ZAPU National Treasurer, to SIDA, Lusaka, 8 November 1972) (SDA).

5. SIDA: 'Protokoll från styrelsemöte' ('Minutes from board meeting'), Stockholm, 21 December 1965 (SDA).

6. Ibid.

7. Co-founder of the Swedish branch of Amnesty International in 1963, Wästberg served as its vice-president between 1964 and 1972.

8. The Swedish Amnesty group No. 34—led by the journalist Eva Moberg—took up the case of Mugabe in 1965 (Sellström Volume I, pp. 326-27). In 1970, Didymus Mutasa was another leading ZANU member to be adopted by a Swedish Amnesty group. He later said that the "experience gave us an understanding of the Swedish people, which was very different from others. We could see that they were absolutely concerned about us and would like our situation to change" (Interview with Didymus Mutasa, p. 218).

Swedish government would grant considerable amounts to both the Zimbabwean prisoners and their dependants, primarily via Christian Care[1] and IDAF.

It was, similarly, in favour of dependants of ZANU members who had been killed or imprisoned in Zimbabwe that the first allocation to ZANU was made in June 1969. Strictly speaking, the allocation—amounting to 50,000 SEK—was not made directly to ZANU, but to the Zimbabwe Welfare Trust (ZWT), formally an independent, private organization. As in the case of FRELIMO's Mozambique Institute in Dar es Salaam, ZWT was, however, for all practical purposes a ZANU institution. Together with the prominent Zambian lawyer Edward Shamwana, Herbert Chitepo was a ZWT trustee and the deed established that the trustees "shall be elected at annual meetings of the Zimbabwe African National Union".[2]

The humanitarian support to the detained ZANU leaders led to closer political contacts and to a frank and open exchange. Immediately after the signing of the Anglo-Rhodesian Settlement Proposals in late November 1971, ZANU President Ndabaningi Sithole managed, for example, to smuggle a letter out of prison to Prime Minister Palme. It was forwarded by Chitepo at the end of January 1972. In his long address, Sithole listed eleven arguments against the agreement reached between Sir Alec Douglas Home and Ian Smith, ending by stating that

> we would, therefore, Mr. Prime Minister, earnestly urge you to exert the necessary diplomatic pressures on Britain to desist from undermining the very fabric of international values by granting legal independence to the Rhodesian white minority at the expense of the black majority of Zimbabwe.[3]

In his covering letter, Chitepo was considerably more personal and to the point, emphasizing that

> the current situation in Zimbabwe is grave. Many of our people have been shot in cold blood for demonstrating against the Home-Smith conspiracy to enslave them. [...] We believe that the current political atmosphere is ripe for a sustained effort to liberate ourselves. Your direct assistance to make this possible is urgently sought. [...] This is not the time to wait for explanations. We need money, weapons and other war requirements. Do not fail us at this hour![4]

While Palme some days earlier had confirmed to President Nyerere that the Swedish government would continue its support to the Zimbabwean liberation movements[5], military assistance was out of the question.[6] Later in the year, Chitepo—who as chairman of ZANU's Revolutionary Council (*Dare re Chimurenga*) was responsible for the coordination of the armed struggle—would, nevertheless, in a

---

1. Christian Care was formed in 1967 as a welfare organization of the Rhodesian Christian Council, providing relief and legal aid to political prisoners and their families. During its first year, about half of the council's external resources were provided by the Swedish government (Christian Care, Rhodesia: '1968', Report attached to a letter from the Swedish section of the Lutheran World Federation to the Ministry for Foreign Affairs, Lidingö, 13 December 1968) (MFA).
2. Zimbabwe Welfare Fund: 'Trust Deed' [no date], attached to letter from Simpson Mtambanengwe, ZANU, to Torsten Nilsson, Minister for Foreign Affairs, Stockholm, 4 February 1969 (MFA). ZANU's Zimbabwe Welfare Trust was set up in 1967. ZAPU had in 1966 already formed a similar trust, called the Zimbabwe African People's Trust. It was to this institution that the first Swedish allocation to ZAPU was disbursed at the beginning of 1973 (Letter from Edward Ndlovu, ZAPU National Secretary, to Anders Möllander, SIDA, Lusaka, 12 February 1973) (SDA).
3. Handwritten letter from Ndabaningi Sithole to Olof Palme [no date or place], forwarded with letter from Herbert Chitepo, Lusaka, 27 January 1972 (MFA).
4. Letter from Herbert Chitepo to Olof Palme, Lusaka, 27 January 1972 (MFA).
5. Letter from Olof Palme to Julius Nyerere, Stockholm, 24 January 1972 (MFA). At the time, official Swedish assistance was, however, only extended to ZANU. As late as in June 1972, CCHA turned down ZAPU's requests, while at the same time recommending an allocation of 70,000 SEK to ZANU/ZWT (CCHA: 'Protokoll' ('Minutes'), SIDA, Stockholm, 22 June 1972) (SDA). Direct support to ZAPU was only granted from February 1973.
6. There is no evidence that Palme replied to Chitepo's letter.

remarkable display of trust inform the Swedish government of his movement's military plans.

Allied within the Khartoum group of 'authentic movements', FRELIMO had at the beginning of the 1970s invited ZAPU to join forces with the Mozambican freedom fighters to penetrate Zimbabwe via the liberated areas in northern Mozambique. Primarily due to the internal crisis which broke out in February 1970, ZAPU was, however, in no position to respond to the invitation.[1] As FRELIMO "started to look for ZAPU, but could not find them"[2], the invitation was passed on to ZANU.[3] From the FRELIMO-held areas in the Mozambican province of Tete, ZANU began preparations for the launch of a protracted struggle in north-eastern Zimbabwe. The military campaign started in December 1972, when guerrillas from ZANU's military wing—the Zimbabwe African National Liberation Army (ZANLA)—attacked the Altena farm in the Centenary area, some 200 kilometres north of Salisbury (Harare). It was to be a decisive turning point. As later pointed out by Ken Flower, the head of Ian Smith's intelligence services,

> the guerrilla war had moved into its second stage. [...] The point we missed was that ZANU [...] would have a much better chance of mobilising support in the north-eastern area bordering Mozambique [...]. From a winning position between 1964 and 1972, [the] Rhodesian Forces were [now] entering the stage of the 'no-win' war, which lasted from December 1972 to 1976. After that, they were fighting a losing war.[4]

A Significant Visit

While ZANU secretly prepared for the armed struggle on the eastern front, Herbert Chitepo came to Sweden in early October 1972. It was a remarkable visit, with far-reaching consequences. Chitepo was not only ZANU's highest representative in exile and chairman of its Revolutionary Council, but also the head of the Joint Military Command which had been formed with ZAPU in February 1972.[5] At the Ministry for Foreign Affairs, he was received by first secretary Pierre Schori, "in the strictest confidence" informing him about the cooperation established between ZANU and FRELIMO and of the decision to shift the armed struggle to the eastern front.[6] Subsequently meeting Anders Möllander, then assistant secretary to the Consultative Committee on Humanitarian Assistance, the ZANU

---

1. Dumiso Dabengwa, ZAPU's head of military intelligence, has stated that "it was during this crisis that ZAPU lost its important and strategic contact with FRELIMO" (Dabengwa in Bhebe and Ranger (eds) op. cit. (Vol. I), p. 31).
2. Interview with Sérgio Vieira, p. 56.
3. See the interview with Marcelino dos Santos, p. 49. Cf. also Martin and Johnson op. cit., pp. 14-20.
4. Flower op. cit., pp. 111 and 119.
5. The JMC remained a paper construction. According to Dumiso Dabengwa, "the main commanders of ZAPU deliberately chose not to be involved in the implementation of the agreement. [...] Our view at that stage was that ZANU must disband and rejoin ZAPU. [...] [W]e thought [that] ZANU needed to confess its failure as a splinter party" (Dabengwa in Bhebe and Ranger (eds) op. cit. (Vol. I), p. 29-30).
6. Pierre Schori: Memorandum ('Besök av ZANU's ordförande'/'Visit by ZANU's Chairman'), Ministry for Foreign Affairs, Stockholm, 31 October 1972 (MFA). Chitepo's visit at the Ministry for Foreign Affairs took place on 9 October 1972. According to Chitepo, it was the Tanzanian President Julius Nyerere who was behind the cooperation between ZANU and FRELIMO and who had taken the initiative of a Zimbabwean eastern front as he considered that "the pressure upon Zambia was very difficult for Kaunda" (ibid.). From the meeting between Chitepo and Schori, it should also be noted that the ZANU Chairman was particularly grateful for the deliveries of used clothes made by Emmaus-Björkå to ZANU. "To be able to offer clothes to the soldiers and the civilian population", Chitepo said, "strengthens both the morale to fight and the basis for recruitment and support" (ibid.). The non-governmental Emmaus-Björkå association started to send clothes to ZANU in 1971, at the same time as deliveries were made to FRELIMO, MPLA, PAIGC, SWAPO and FNL of Vietnam ('Framgångar för Emmaus-Björkå'/'Successes for Emmaus-Björkå' in *Kommentar*, No. 5-6, 1983, p. 43). See also the chapter 'Patriotic Front: ZANU and ZAPU towards Independence'.

Chairman amazed the junior SIDA official by telling him that ZANU had "decided to launch a new offensive" and that "the liberation struggle would begin at the turn of the year".[1] Anticipating harsh counter-measures against the civilian population by the Smith regime and increasing flows of refugees into independent Zambia, Chitepo wanted to inform about possible future humanitarian needs, including medical care. Against this background, he "appealed for increased Swedish assistance to ZANU".[2]

Ten years later—after Zimbabwe's independence—Möllander wrote that

> I found what Chitepo told me almost unbelievable. I could not understand that he came to us to tell us about a guerrilla struggle which would [only] begin in a couple of months. He must have had the security risks in mind, calculating them against [ZANU's] need to be able to care for the refugees.[3]

Sydney Sekeramayi was at the time a leading ZANU spokesperson in Sweden, facilitating Chitepo's visit. Asked about the extraordinary trust showed by Chitepo towards a Western government with regard to ZANU's closely held military plans, the Zimbabwean Minister of State for National Security said in 1995 that the ZANU leader

> was very clear that [...] we could not discuss military support, but [that] we should be honest: 'Let us tell them that we are going to wage an armed struggle. Where we will get the arms from is none of their business, but from the moral and political point of view we want them to support us.' When he talked about launching the armed struggle in Rhodesia, it was really part of a policy that there were certain people whom you could tell the truth, because it would not help if you hid [it] from them. They would later find out and think that you were not quite honest in the presentation of your case. So we agreed: 'Tell them that the struggle is on the way and that we expect non-military support.'[4]

From blunt to honest, Chitepo's diplomacy was successful. His presentation of ZANU's case and of the consequences of the December 1972 offensive proved true. In January 1973, ZANU's Secretary for External Affairs, Richard Hove[5], wrote to SIDA that "the Smith regime has [...] over-reacted to the events [...], bombing [...] areas suspected to harbour freedom fighters. The net result", Hove stated, "is that

> we have hundreds of people fleeing the country. [...] [W]e are overwhelmed [by] the problems of feeding and clothing them. We have among these people women and children. The problem of medicines and medical care has become terribly acute, and I am writing to request whether you could [supply us with] medicines, a mobile clinic, tinned food [and] second-hand clothing.[6]

After a meeting with Kurt Kristiansson, SIDA's representative in Lusaka, Hove renewed ZANU's request in early March 1973, giving a breakdown of the 1,300

---

1. Möllander op. cit., p. 35.
2. Ibid.
3. Ibid. Cf. the interview with Kenneth Kaunda, p. 241.
4. Interview with Sydney Sekeramayi, pp. 227-28. Robert Mugabe continued this policy. For example, in a meeting with the principal ZANLA commanders in Maputo in July 1979, Rex Nhongo—ZANU's Deputy Chief of Defence—told the Swedish ambassador to Mozambique, Lennart Dafgård, that "he had received orders from Mugabe to be open towards us and tell us as much as possible [about the military situation]" (Letter ('Samtal med ZANU's militära befälhavare'/'Conversation with ZANU's military commanders') from Lennart Dafgård to the Ministry for Foreign Affairs, Maputo, 16 July 1979) (MFA).
5. A former student at CSM schools in his native Mberengwa region, Hove too had early links to Sweden. Based in London as ZANU's representative to the United Kingdom and Western and Eastern Europe, he was in close contact with the Swedish government from the late 1960s and visited Stockholm in 1970. Hove became Minister of the Public Service in 1980.
6. Letter from Richard Hove to SIDA, Lusaka, 24 January 1973 (SDA). A detailed list of medical needs was attached to the letter.

Zimbabwean refugees who by then had fled into Zambia. In the same letter, he explained that "Zambia, naturally, wants to protect its citizens and they will neither allow us to make public knowledge of [the] refugees, nor allow us to invite international organizations to assist with such cases".[1] He, however, added that "we can [...] make an undertaking to SIDA that as soon as the situation [so] permits, we will invite [you] to see some of the cases".[2] As Hove together with Chitepo would represent ZANU at the upcoming UN/OAU Oslo Conference on Colonialism and Apartheid in Southern Africa, he, finally, suggested that they in that connection should meet CCHA.

Chitepo and Hove came to Stockholm from Oslo in April 1973.[3] In addition to the request presented in January, they informed SIDA and the Ministry for Foreign Affairs that ZANU planned to purchase a piece of land in Zambia to take care of the newly arrived refugees, adding that they would probably seek assistance from the Swedish government to start agricultural activities and build schools.[4] As ZANU at the same time requested continued support to the Zimbabwe Welfare Trust[5], CCHA recommended in June a total Swedish contribution to ZANU of 300,000 SEK for the financial year 1973/74, of which 100,000 to ZWT and 200,000 as commodity support.[6]

Support to Zimbabwean refugees was a new component in Sweden's cooperation with ZANU. To define its content, official negotiations were held between the two parties in Lusaka in mid-September 1973. ZANU had during the previous week held its regular biennial review conference. In addition to Herbert Chitepo—who had been confirmed as Chairman—its delegation included three officials from the newly elected eight-member Revolutionary Council, namely Henry Hamadziripi, Mukudzei Mudzi and Noel Mukono. Also Richard Hove formed part of the ZANU delegation.[7] The movement thus attached great importance to the consultations. The Swedish delegation was led by Kristiansson and included Stig Lövgren from SIDA's procurement section in Stockholm and Anders Möllander from the Ministry for Foreign Affairs.[8]

Apart from political discussions on the situation in Zimbabwe—during which the ZANU leaders were confident that the armed struggle would prove successful

---

1. Letter from Richard Hove to SIDA Lusaka, Lusaka, 9 March 1973 (SDA). Zimbabweans fleeing to Zambia were formally considered British subjects and not eligible for refugee status, including assistance through UNHCR.

2. Ibid.

3. Like FRELIMO, ZANU was pleased with the Oslo conference. Speaking on behalf of all the liberation movements represented, Chitepo stated during the concluding session that they had "feared that a meeting sponsored by the United Nations [...] might underplay or endeavour to shift us from our commitment to armed struggle". However, according to Chitepo, "one of the cardinal successes of [the] conference has been its acceptance of the inevitability of armed struggle and its support for that struggle" (cited in Stokke and Widstrand (eds) op. cit. (Vol. I), p. 69). Chitepo and Hove represented ZANU, while George Silundika, Secretary for Publicity and Information, headed ZAPU's delegation (ibid., p. 272).

4. Ministry for Foreign Affairs: Memorandum ('Samtal med representanter för ZANU'/'Conversation with representatives of ZANU'), Stockholm, 3 May 1973 (MFA). The meeting at the Foreign Ministry took place on 17 or 18 April 1973.

5. Gun-Britt Andersson: Memorandum ('Stöd till ZANU'/'Support to ZANU'), Ministry for Foreign Affairs, Stockholm, 7 June 1973 (SDA).

6. CCHA: 'Protokoll' ('Minutes'), SIDA, Stockholm, 5 July 1973 (SDA).

7. 'Agreed minutes of discussions between delegations from ZANU and Sweden', Lusaka, 20 September 1973 (SDA). Hamadziripi—who also had early links to Sweden—was Secretary of Finance and Mudzi Administrative Secretary. Mukono replaced Hove as Secretary of External Affairs. ZANU's 1973 conference was *inter alia* important in that it elected for the first time a military cadre to the *Dare re Chimurenga*. Josiah Tongogara became Chief of Defence. The remaining positions on the Revolutionary Council were held by Rugare Gumbo (Information and Publicity), Kumbirai Kangai (Labour, Social Services and Welfare) and John Mataure (Chief Political Commissar).

8. Ibid.

and declared that Bishop Muzorewa's attempts to reach a negotiated settlement with Ian Smith were "doomed to fail"[1]—the Swedish delegation was, as promised by Richard Hove in March, given the opportunity to meet Zimbabwean refugees and discuss their needs. Möllander could thus verify that the predictions made by Chitepo in Stockholm in October 1972 had come true. Returning to Stockholm, he wrote that

> the needs for assistance were in glaring contrast to the ZANU leadership's political self-confidence [...]. We visited about a hundred refugees—mostly women and children—who had fled [...] the military excesses by the minority regime. Several of the women and the children had been taken to Zambia to be treated for gunshot injuries. [...] For these refugees—in total estimated to exceed a thousand—[...] ZANU needed clothing, food and medicines.[2]

ZANU looked upon the refugee problem in a longer term perspective. During the negotiations, the ZANU leaders declared that "the highest priority was given to the purchase of a farm in Zambia where [the movement] would house dependants of ZANU members and others who [...] fled from Rhodesia and sought refuge with ZANU".[3] Against this background, it was—subject to the Swedish government's approval—agreed to set aside two thirds of the available allocation of 200,000 SEK for the procurement of a farm, with the balance for food. If the farm project could not be supported, the entire allocation should be used for food, with minor allocations for clothes, medicines and "publicity material", such as cameras, dark-room equipment and paper.[4]

As a result of the close relations established with ZANU—and at a time when it expressed a firmer commitment to "support the civilian activities of the [African] liberation movements in the liberated areas"[5]—the Swedish government was in mid-1973 faced with a major, novel problem: How to deal with the procurement of land in favour of a liberation movement in a friendly, sovereign country? The question would feature prominently in the dialogue with Zambia over the following years.[6] Approached as an uncomplicated humanitarian concern[7]—and coupled with the experiences from the 1973-74 MPLA crisis—it would brusquely awaken the Swedish aid officials to the vulnerable security situation of the independent Southern African states.

---

1. Anders Möllander: Memorandum ('Samtal med ZANU-ledare'/'Conversations with ZANU leaders'), Ministry for Foreign Affairs, Stockholm, 1 October 1973 (SDA).
2. Ibid. See also Möllander op. cit., p. 36.
3. 'Agreed minutes', Lusaka, 20 September 1973 (SDA).
4. Ibid. Remarkably, ZANU did not include transport support in the form of vehicles.
5. 'Interview (September) with the Foreign Minister, Mr. Wickman, in the special [issue on Sweden] of the journal *Afrique-Asie* in Ministry for Foreign Affairs: *Documents on Swedish Foreign Policy: 1973*, Stockholm, 1976, p. 64. Cf. the chapter on Mozambique.
6. During the official negotiations with ZAPU in May 1974, Nkomo's movement also made an appeal for funds to purchase a farm in Zambia ('Agreed minutes of discussions on cooperation between Sweden and Zimbabwe African People's Union', Lusaka, 11 June 1974) (SDA). As will be seen below, both SWAPO of Namibia and ANC of South Africa were, in addition, in 1974-75 discussing farm projects in Zambia with the Swedish government.
7. According to the available documentation, the Swedish authorities did not discuss the fact that the farm could be used for military training or as a ZANLA transit point. However—as later confirmed by President Chissano of Mozambique—to launch the military offensive on the eastern front in late 1972 ZANU had used FRELIMO's farm in Zambia and subsequently needed its own base to sustain the war effort. Interviewed in May 1996, Chissano explained: "ZANU started in 1972. They were then utilizing our farm in Zambia, but they were looking for another farm as a transit camp. We knew about that. I was then in charge of the military contacts between ZANU and FRELIMO together with Samora Machel" (Interview with Joaquim Chissano, p. 41).

Following the negotiations in Lusaka, SIDA decided in late October 1973 to approve the farm project, setting aside 135,000 SEK for the purpose.[1] The farm identified by ZANU was situated some 25 kilometres west of the capital and had an area of about 2,000 acres. The private Zambian owner had agreed to sell the property and ZANU had through a proxy paid a firm deposit. After due assessments of the farm and the price, it was agreed that SIDA should pay the outstanding purchase sum to ZANU's Zambian lawyer Edward Shamwana, who through ZWT would finalize the transaction. At the same time, SIDA was to "ensure that the Zambian state [did] not oppose the land acquisition".[2]

As the Zambian authorities did not [3], ZANU bought the farm with Swedish funds in early 1974.[4] SIDA had at that time also agreed to channel support to a farm purchased by SWAPO of Namibia.[5] However, the acquisition of land by ZANU and SWAPO[6] soon became a much more complicated issue than originally envisaged. While the Zambian government initially did not raise any objections— and final commitments on that basis were made by Sweden to the two liberation movements[7]—essential national security aspects were introduced into the equation.[8]

During a meeting at the Zambian Ministry of Defence in mid-April 1974, President Kaunda's newly appointed Minister of State, the army chief General Kingsley Chinkuli[9], asked SIDA to "wait and see", explaining that the Zambian government had "not yet defined a final policy on where in the country [...] the liberation movements could be established".[10] Two weeks later, Foreign Minister Vernon Mwaanga told the Swedish ambassador Iwo Dölling that the farm projects were

1. SIDA: Decision ('Biståndsprogram för ZANU 1973/74'/'Assistance programme for ZANU 1973/74'), SIDA, Stockholm, 23 October 1973 (SDA).
2. Bo Wilén: Memorandum ('Biståndsprogram för ZANU 1973/74'/'Assistance programme for ZANU 1973/74'), Swedish embassy, Lusaka, 23 October 1973 (SDA).
3. Letter ('Det svenska biståndet till SWAPO/ZANU-farmerna'/'The Swedish assistance to the SWAPO/ZANU farms') from the Swedish ambassador to Zambia, Iwo Dölling, to the Ministry for Foreign Affairs, Lusaka, 6 May 1974 (SDA).
4. Visiting Stockholm in March 1974, ZANU's Information and Publicity Secretary Rugare Gumbo particularly thanked SIDA for making it possible to purchase the farm (Astrid Bergquist: Memorandum ('Minnesanteckningar från samtal med Mr. Gumbo och Mr. Chokwenda'/'Notes from conversation with Mr. Gumbo and Mr. Chokwenda'), SIDA, Stockholm, 6 March 1974) (SDA). Cf. the interview with Kumbirai Kangai: "ZANU [...] acquired a farm not far from Lusaka, which the Swedes paid for. That is when we really started to rehabilitate our refugees, carrying out quite a number of activities" (p. 213).
5. The same day as the decision on ZANU's farm project was taken, SIDA decided on the recommendation of CCHA to assist SWAPO with the construction of a school, a clinic and houses at what came to be known as the organization's 'old farm', some 40 kilometres southwest of Lusaka (SIDA: Decision ('Biståndsprogram för SWAPO 1973/74'/'Assistance programme for SWAPO 1973/74'), Stockholm, 23 October 1973) (SDA). Due to the Zambian government's opposition, the construction plans could not be carried out. In December 1975, SWAPO eventually had to abandon the farm, but was instead allocated land at Nyango in Zambia's Western Province (see the chapter 'Transport, Home Front, Churches and Trade Unions').
6. As well as by ANC of South Africa.
7. Letter ('Det svenska biståndet till SWAPO/ZANU-farmerna'/'The Swedish assistance to the SWAPO/ZANU farms') from the Swedish ambassador to Zambia, Iwo Dölling, to the Ministry for Foreign Affairs, Lusaka, 6 May 1974 (SDA).
8. After the opening of ZANU's eastern front in December 1972, the tensions between Zambia and Rhodesia rapidly increased. The border between the countries was closed in February 1973.
9. Due to the rapidly deteriorating security situation, President Kaunda himself had at the time assumed the position of Minister of Defence.
10. Letter from Iwo Dölling to the Ministry for Foreign Affairs, Lusaka, 6 May 1974 (SDA). The Southern African liberation movements had offices in the so called Liberation Centre in Lusaka, established in 1965. While a certain amount of clandestine military training was tolerated in the country, in contrast with Tanzania, Zambia did not grant the movements specially defined military camps, or areas. As noted by Anglin and Shaw, "the Zambian government was determined to ensure that it exercised adequate control over freedom fighter interactions with each other, with the Zambian population and even with the Southern African regimes" (Anglin and Shaw op. cit., p. 245). In 1971, President Kaunda—a devout Ghandian pacifist by nature and conviction—stated that "Zambia cannot, and does not, tolerate the use of its soil as a base for military or paramilitary operations" (ibid., p. 244).

not acceptable, explaining that "the new [Zambian] stand expressed an ambition to establish a security policy towards the presence and activities of the liberation movements in the country". Reflecting on the problem, Mwaanga explained, the Zambian government had concluded that "the establishment of liberation movements in the vicinity of Lusaka implied non-acceptable security risks". In addition, the Zambian government was "not totally convinced by [the movements'] arguments regarding self-sufficiency" and, in general, "not particularly keen that the liberation movements acquired farms on Zambian territory".[1]

In his comments to the Swedish Ministry for Foreign Affairs, ambassador Dölling wrote that

> what we possibly [can] learn is that while the Zambian side earlier did not have a policy [...] regarding [...] the presence of liberation movements in the country—giving them rather free space to manoeuvre—the conditions have now changed. In the future, there is [every] reason to ensure that the cooperation with the liberation movements on Zambian soil takes place with the full understanding of the Zambian authorities.[2]

By that time, ZANU had already procured the farm with Swedish funds. Nowhere, however, did SIDA or the Swedish government appear as the buyer. When the Zambian government after the assassination of Chitepo in March 1975 impounded the property, there was, consequently, nothing that Sweden could legally do. Through Shamwana, the imprisoned ZANU leaders tried to retain the property, but lost their case.[3] In the meantime, Sweden would be keenly aware of Zambia's policies, both with regard to ZANU in 1975-76 and to SWAPO in mid-1976. As the two movements respectively transferred their headquarters to Mozambique and Angola, the Swedish government shifted the bulk of the humanitarian assistance from Zambia to the two former Portuguese colonies. From the late 1970s, only ZAPU and ANC of South Africa maintained external headquarters in Lusaka.

ZAPU: Sluggish Beginnings and Persistent Doubts

The Swedish government had in the meantime also decided to extend humanitarian assistance to ZAPU. A first recommendation to that effect was made as early as in October 1969. Due to the organization's leadership struggle, it was never implemented and the bilateral contacts were for a long time suspended. In October 1971, however, ZAPU's National Secretary Edward Ndlovu addressed a letter to the Swedish ambassador in Lusaka, expressing the wish to re-establish the relations:

> You have been following, be it remotely, the internal crisis in ZAPU, which for almost two years threw the credibility of our organization into doubt internationally. We are pleased to inform you that the generators of the crisis have since quit and also [been] expelled from the party, [i.e.] James Chikerema and George Nyandoro.[4] [...] [W]e look forward to resuming normal relations with your mission, that is, without the cloud of a crisis hanging over [us].[5]

Two months later, ZAPU submitted a substantial, non-budgeted request to SIDA, covering vehicles, office equipment and cash support.[6] As it did not have a clear humanitarian content—principally designed to assist ZAPU as an organization—

---

1. Letter from Iwo Dölling to the Ministry for Foreign Affairs, Lusaka, 6 May 1974 (SDA). In January 1974, Mwaanga requested Sweden to stop the assistance to MPLA of Angola.
2. Ibid.
3. Conversation with Kumbirai Kangai, Harare, 19 July 1995.
4. Chikerema and Nyandoro subsequently joined FROLIZI.
5. Letter from Edward Ndlovu to the Swedish ambassador to Zambia, Lusaka, 9 October 1971 (MFA).
6. Letter from K.D. Nyamupingidza to SIDA Lusaka, Lusaka, 18 January 1972 (SDA).

the request was not supported.[1] After frequent contacts at the level of the embassy in Lusaka, ZAPU then decided to present its case directly to the government in Stockholm.

Edward Ndlovu visited Sweden in September-October 1972. Pointing out that he had attended schools run by the Church of Sweden Mission at Manama and Masase, he made a special appeal for unspecified cash support to ZAPU.[2] Better informed about the principles governing Sweden's assistance to the liberation movements, during his stay Ndlovu submitted a detailed humanitarian request, covering food requirements, household items, clothes, office equipment, vehicles, medicines and educational supplies.[3] Above all, before returning to Lusaka ZAPU's National Secretary addressed a long letter to the Swedish Minister for Foreign Affairs. Considering that the Social Democratic government had not yet granted any assistance to ZAPU, the letter to Krister Wickman must have come as a surprise. Thus, Ndlovu stated:

> We are well aware of the sympathies of your government towards the aspirations of the people of Southern Africa for freedom from racist minority rule. We have no doubt that these arise from a deep understanding of the oppression experienced by non-white people living in that part of Africa. We are gratified that your government has already taken steps to translate its feelings into positive action [...] [and] have with great interest watched the evolution of your party—the Social Democratic Party—and your government's sympathetic policy for the oppressed masses of our country. [...]
>
> We are convinced that there are sufficient grounds for the establishment of bilateral relations between your country and our liberation movement, ZAPU. We therefore propose to appoint a representative in Sweden. [W]ith your permission, we would [like to] submit the name of Dr. Phineas Makhurane, who is currently a research fellow at the University of Uppsala, as our acting representative.[4]

Ndlovu wrote his letter on the very same day that Chitepo visited the Ministry for Foreign Affairs. ZAPU's National Secretary and ZANU's National Chairman were visiting Stockholm at the same time and with the same purpose, to obtain support for the Zimbabwean liberation struggle.[5] In spite of the Joint Military Command between the two organizations, there is, however, no evidence of a common approach towards the Swedish government. While Chitepo through his open diplo-

---

1. Letter from Curt Ström, SIDA, to ZAPU, Stockholm, 4 August 1972 (SDA).
2. Anders Möllander: Memorandum ('Samtal 1972 09 27 med Edward Ndlovu, Zimbabwe African People's Union, ZAPU, samt Gun-Britt Andersson, UD, och Anders Möllander, SIDA'/'Conversation 27 September 1972 between Edward Ndlovu, ZAPU, Gun-Britt Andersson, Ministry for Foreign Affairs, and Anders Möllander, SIDA'), CCHA/SIDA, Stockholm, [no date] (MFA).
3. ZAPU: 'Humanitarian request submitted to the government of Sweden', attached to letter from Edward Ndlovu to Foreign Minister Krister Wickman, Stockholm, 9 October 1972 (SDA).
4. Letter from Edward Ndlovu to Krister Wickman, 9 October 1972 (SDA). Makhurane was subsequently appointed ZAPU representative to Sweden and the Scandinavian countries. Based in Uppsala, he stayed in Sweden until mid-1973 when he was succeeded by Aggrippa Madhlela. Like Ndlovu, Makhurane was a product of the CSM school system in south-western Zimbabwe. As representative of IUEF in Zambia and Botswana, he would during the 1970s maintain close links with Sweden. After independence, Makhurane served as Pro Vice-Chancellor of the University of Zimbabwe and was at the beginning of the 1990s appointed Vice-Chancellor of the National University of Science and Technology in Bulawayo.
5. Jacob Moyo of ANC had in late August 1972 visited the Ministry for Foreign Affairs (Gun-Britt Andersson: Memorandum ('Besök av Jacob Moyo, ANC, Rhodesia, den 22 och 23 augusti 1972'/'Visit by Jacob Moyo, ANC Rhodesia, 22 and 23 August 1972'), Ministry for Foreign Affairs, Stockholm, 4 September 1972) (MFA). Immediately after Ndlovu's and Chitepo's visits, George Nyandoro would, in addition, request assistance to FROLIZI (Gun-Britt Andersson: Memorandum ('Besök av George Nyandoro från rhodesiska befrielserörelsen FROLIZI den 24 oktober 1972'/'Visit by George Nyandoro from the Rhodesian liberation movement FROLIZI on 24 October 1972'), Ministry for Foreign Affairs, Stockholm, 25 October 1972) (MFA). Similarly uncoordinated visits to Stockholm would over the following years frequently be made by high-ranking representatives of the various Zimbabwean nationalist organizations.

macy made a lasting impression on his Swedish hosts, there is no indication that Ndlovu's initiative prepared the terrain for closer relations between ZAPU and the Social Democratic party or government. In spite of its relations with the Soviet Union and its insistence on armed struggle[1], ZAPU was mainly supported by the opposition Liberal Party, while the ruling party had already established links to ZANU. The Social Democratic Youth League (SSU) had, for example, started to grant ZANU financial support from its international solidarity fund in the early 1970s.[2] Through SSU, ZANU had, in addition, begun to take an active part in the social democratic International Union of Socialist Youth (IUSY), with headquarters in Vienna, Austria.[3]

Nevertheless, as the Liberal and Centre parties continued to submit parliamentary motions in favour of Joshua Nkomo's organization, in January 1973 official support to ZAPU was recommended by CCHA.[4] The recommendation was endorsed on 2 February 1973.[5] A modest amount of 50,000 SEK was allocated to "ZAPU members and their dependants in Zambia" during the financial year 1973/74, or from 1 July 1973. Reflecting doubts about ZAPU, SIDA's decision, however, explicitly stated that the contribution was made "on condition that control over the use of the funds can be guaranteed".[6]

The grant was disbursed to ZAPU's Zimbabwe African People's Welfare Trust. When ZAPU in January 1974 accounted for the contribution, it appeared that the funds contrary to SIDA's decision had been channelled to activities inside Zimbabwe.[7] This did not strengthen ZAPU's case. The doubts expressed by SIDA were confirmed. When ZAPU requested a substantially increased allocation for 1974/75—including funds for medical clinics, a research centre and a farm in Zambia[8]—it was not supported. While ZANU was granted a total of 860,000 SEK, *inter alia* covering vehicles, food, medicines, clothes and supplies for information activities[9],

---

1. In his letter to Wickman in October 1972, Ndlovu stated, for example, that "it has become clear to us [...] that the only effective method to dislodge the minority racist regime from power is the armed revolutionary struggle".
2. See SSU: 'Verksamheten 1972-74' ('Activities 1972-74'), p. I:47 (LMA). While not granting any financial contributions to ZAPU, SSU continued its exclusive support to ZANU over the period 1975-77 (SSU: 'Verksamheten 1975-77'/'Activities 1975-77'), p. I:49 (LMA).
3. Through Johan Ahnberg, international secretary of SSU and general secretary of IUSY, Claude Chokwenda made the ZANU youth movement a member of the social democratic international organization (Carl F. Hallencreutz: 'Religion and War in Zimbabwe - and Swedish Relationships' in C. F. Hallencreutz and S. Axelson (eds): *Annual Report 1992 of Uppsala Studies of Mission*, Faculty of Theology, University of Uppsala, Uppsala, 1993, p. 21). In 1975—after the Lusaka Unity Accord—Chokwenda represented IUSY at the Social Democratic Party congress (Socialdemokraterna: 'Verksamheten 1975' ('Activities 1975'), p. 78) (LMA). In mid-1977, finally, Henry Hamadziripi—at the time ZANU's Secretary for Manpower Planning—sought assistance from the Swedish Social Democrats to "rebuild ZANU as a party". Approaching Lars-Gunnar Eriksson, IUEF's Director in Geneva, he suggested that a person from the then Swedish opposition party "should spend a period of time in Mozambique, advising and training, or that one or two people from ZANU should spend some time in Sweden, or, possibly, a combination of the two approaches" (Letter from Lars-Gunnar Eriksson to Pierre Schori, Geneva, 20 July 1977) (LMA). The proposal, however, never materialized, one of the main possible reasons being that the Social Democratic Party recognized ZANU and ZAPU on equal terms within the Patriotic Front. On ZANU and the Swedish Social Democratic Party, see also the interview with Sydney Sekeramayi, p. 228.
4. Official Swedish assistance to ANC of South Africa was at the same time recommended by CCHA. The first allocation to ANC—amounting to 150,000 SEK—was granted in February 1973.
5. SIDA: Decision ('Stöd till African National Congress (ANC), Sydafrika, samt Zimbabwe African People's Union (ZAPU), Rhodesia'/'Support to ANC and ZAPU'), Stockholm, 2 February 1973 (SDA).
6. Ibid.
7. CCHA: Memorandum ('Stöd till ZAPU'/'Support to ZAPU'), SIDA, Stockholm, 11 February 1974 (SDA).
8. 'Agreed minutes of discussions on cooperation between Sweden and Zimbabwe African People's Union', Lusaka, 11 June 1974 (SDA).
9. SIDA: Decision ('Biståndsprogram för ZANU under budgetåret 1974/75'/'Assistance programme for ZANU during the financial year 1974/75'), Stockholm, 25 June 1974 (SDA).

the ZAPU contribution was maintained at a mere 50,000 SEK.[1] As in 1973/74, it was, furthermore, disbursed to ZAPU's welfare trust, not directly to the organization.

As a result of the December 1974 Lusaka Unity Accord between ANC (Muzorewa), FROLIZI (Chikerema), ZANU (Sithole) and ZAPU (Nkomo), the Swedish assistance to ZANU and ZAPU was suspended in March 1975. It was only resumed by Fälldin's government in June 1977. During the first half of the 1970s, ZAPU received a total of a mere 100,000 SEK as official Swedish assistance, or less than 10 per cent of the 1.1 million disbursed to ZANU. Of all the Southern African liberation movements supported by Sweden, ZAPU was until 1975 by far the least privileged.[2] Although this situation radically changed from June 1977[3], a lack of trust characterized the relations.[4] In 1976-77—when the assistance to both ZANU and ZAPU was suspended—leading ZAPU representatives criticized the Swedish government for allegedly giving preference to ZANU.[5] And in April 1978, Joshua Nkomo publicly censured the government for being "afraid"[6], according to him showing "a humiliating and wanting trust" in his organization.[7] In contrast to the other Southern African liberation movements that received official Swedish support, the relations with ZAPU were, thus, over the years often strained.[8]

With ZANU towards Détente

Meanwhile, the Social Democratic government's relations with Herbert Chitepo and ZANU were further consolidated during the months preceding the 'détente exercise'. Negotiations regarding humanitarian assistance—which was trebled from 300,000 SEK in 1973/74 to 860,000 in 1974/75[9]—were held in Lusaka in May

---

1. SIDA: Decision ('Bistånd till ZAPU'/'Assistance to ZAPU'), Stockholm, 27 June 1974 (SDA).
2. Official assistance to ANC of South Africa started at the same time as the assistance to ZAPU. By 30 June 1975, 570,000 SEK had been disbursed to ZAPU's South African ally (see the accompanying disbursement tables).
3. With equal allocations, disbursements to ZAPU exceeded those to ZANU in 1977/78 and 1978/79 (see the accompanying disbursement tables).
4. Cf. the interview with Garth Strachan (ANC/SACP), p. 193. The presentation of Strachan in the first edition of the accompanying interview volume is not correct. Between 1978 and 1990, Strachan served as administrator and secretary to ANC's Revolutionary Council/Politico-Military Council in Lusaka and Harare.
5. Several examples could be given. At the 1976 Geneva conference, both Joshua Nkomo and Edward Ndlovu strongly criticized Sweden for having granted more assistance to ZANU than to ZAPU (Bo Heinebäck: Memorandum ('Det svenska biståndet till de zimbabwiska nationalistgrupperna'/'The Swedish assistance to the Zimbabwean nationalist groups'), Ministry for Foreign Affairs, Stockholm, 9 November 1976) (SDA). Just before Nkomo's visit to Sweden in May 1977, his political assistant Daniel Madzimbamuto similarly asked the Swedish embassy in Maputo whether "Sweden still only supported ZANU" (Bo Westman: Memorandum ('Samtal med Daniel Madzimbamuto, ZAPU, 1 april 1977'/'Conversation with Daniel Madzimbamuto, ZAPU, 1 April 1977'), Swedish embassy, Maputo, 4 April 1977) (SDA). George Silundika, member of ZAPU's National Executive, stated at the same time to the Swedish embassy in Luanda that "Sweden discriminated against ZAPU by continuing to [only] support ZANU" (Cable from the Swedish embassy in Luanda to the Ministry for Foreign Affairs, Luanda, 18 April 1977) (SDA). It should, however, be noted that no official Swedish assistance was granted to either ZANU or ZAPU between March 1975 and June 1977.
6. Interview with Joshua Nkomo by Bengt Persson ('Ni i Sverige är rädda'/'You in Sweden are afraid') in *Aftonbladet*, 3 April 1978. Cf. the interview with Dumiso Dabengwa: "[Sweden was] not brave enough to come out and say: 'Yes, your armed effort is also justified'" (p. 211).
7. Cable from the Swedish embassy in Lusaka to the Ministry for Foreign Affairs, Lusaka, 11 April 1978 (SDA). Cf. the interview with Tore Bergman, p. 264.
8. Also the Swedish NGOs that supported the so called 'authentic' liberation movements were closer to ZANU than to ZAPU. Various reasons for ZAPU's weak performance in Sweden are advanced in the interviews with Tore Bergman of the Church of Sweden Mission (p. 264), Anders Johansson of *Dagens Nyheter* (p. 300), Sören Lindh of AGIS (p. 306) and Pierre Schori of the Social Democratic Party (p. 333).
9. At ZANU's request, 315,000 SEK was channelled as cash support to the Zimbabwe Welfare Trust, while 545,000 SEK was set aside as commodity support.

On television: ZANU
Chairman Herbert
Chitepo with
Cooperation Minister
Gertrud Sigurdsen at
the Ministry for
Foreign Affairs, Stock-
holm, November 1974

1974[1], and in mid-November the ZANU Chairman again went to Sweden, where in addition to meetings at SIDA he held top level discussions with Foreign Minister Sven Andersson and Prime Minister Olof Palme.

Before going to Stockholm, Chitepo met the Swedish Minister of Transport and Communications, Hans Gustafsson, in Lusaka at the end of October 1974.[2] The Lusaka Accord on Mozambique's independence had been signed in the Zambian capital the previous month. On 23 October—just before the meeting between Chitepo and Gustafsson—the South African Prime Minister John Vorster also made his first public speech on détente in Southern Africa. Together, the two events heralded major changes in the Southern African region, particularly focusing on Zimbabwe.

While the agreed independence of Mozambique under FRELIMO was naturally positive for the Zimbabwean liberation cause, Vorster's speech indicated to Chitepo political realignments that could prove "more problematic".[3] Behind the new developments—in the ZANU Chairman's view—was Britain, attempting to implement what he called a "soft solution". ANC under Bishop Muzorewa could become a vehicle for the British strategy.[4] In this situation, Chitepo said, Britain was "in a certain sense more dangerous to ZANU than [Ian] Smith", and it was necessary to intensify the armed liberation struggle. He therefore asked the Swedish government to "reject any possible British initiatives [that] did not consider complete majority rule [...], continue to support ZANU as the most important force in Zimbabwe[5] [and] considerably increase its [humanitarian] assistance".[6]

1. 'Agreed minutes of discussions on cooperation between Sweden and Zimbabwe African National Union, ZANU', Lusaka, 29 May 1974 (SDA). The Swedish delegation was led by ambassador Iwo Dölling, with Herbert Chitepo as his counterpart. Gumbo, Hamadziripi and Kangai formed part of the ZANU delegation. The final decision on the allocation of 860,000 SEK to ZANU in 1974/75 was taken by SIDA in late June 1974.
2. Gustafson represented the Swedish government at the celebrations of the tenth anniversary of Zambia's independence.
3. Swedish embassy in Lusaka: Memorandum ('Samtal med ZANU's ordförande'/'Conversation with ZANU's chairman'), Lusaka, 31 October 1974 (MFA).
4. Ibid.
5. Chitepo described ZAPU as "powerless and with a very limited military capacity" (ibid.).
6. Ibid.

On behalf of the Social Democratic Party, its international secretary Bernt Carlsson had at the same time invited Chitepo to Sweden.[1] At a particularly critical juncture in Southern Africa, ZANU's National Chairman responded positively to the invitation. His meetings in Stockholm between 16 and 20 November 1974 were not limited to the ruling party. Chitepo was *de facto* received as a head of government, with official, scheduled meetings with Prime Minister Palme, Foreign Minister Andersson, Cooperation Minister Sigurdsen and SIDA's Director General Michanek.[2] His reception at the Ministry for Foreign Affairs was covered on national television and a longer interview with him was screened by the TV 2 channel.[3] In mid-November 1974—less than a month before the signing of the Lusaka Unity Accord and only four months before Chitepo's violent death in the Zambian capital; provoking a drastic clampdown on his organization—ZANU was seen as a genuine nationalist alternative.

However, before Chitepo's visit, something inconceivable had happened. Under pressure from South Africa, Ian Smith had agreed to temporarily release the detained ZANU and ZAPU leaders[4] for consultations with Kenneth Kaunda, Seretse Khama of Botswana, Julius Nyerere and Samora Machel.[5] For the first time in more than ten years, Chitepo met the ZANU President Ndabaningi Sithole[6] in Lusaka and Dar es Salaam immediately prior to his departure for Stockholm.[7]

Although the moves between South Africa and Zambia were conducted in great secrecy[8], they, naturally, affected the ZANU Chairman. As was his custom vis-à-vis the Swedish government, on 19 November 1974 Chitepo informed Foreign Minister Andersson "in the strictest confidence" about the latest "remarkable" developments, which had been "arranged in advance" by Vorster and Kaunda.[9] Kaunda had told the temporarily released Zimbabwean nationalist leaders that Smith in Vorster's opinion was ready to accept majority rule and that they had been brought

---

1. Letter from Bernt Carlsson to Herbert Chitepo, Stockholm, 25 October 1974 (MFA). Sam Nujoma, the President of SWAPO of Namibia—similarly hosted by Zambia and affected by the 'détente policy'—was at about the same time invited to Sweden for political consultations by the ruling Social Democratic Party. Preceding that of Chitepo, Nujoma's visit took place between 29 October and 2 November 1974 ('Press release', Ministry for Foreign Affairs, Stockholm, 28 October 1974) (MFA). Like Chitepo, Nujoma held discussions with the Prime Minister, the Foreign Minister and the Cooperation Minister. Although given less attention by the Social Democratic Party and the government, in November 1974 both the KwaZulu leader Gatsha Buthelezi and ANC's Thabo Mbeki also visited Sweden.

2. Ministry for Foreign Affairs: 'Preliminärt program för ZANU's ordförande Herbert Chitepo under besöket i Stockholm, 16-20 november 1974'/'Preliminary programme for the ZANU Chairman Herbert Chitepo during his visit to Stockholm, 16-20 November 1974', Stockholm, 12 November 1974 (MFA).

3. On 18 November 1974, Chitepo was interviewed on TV 2's news programme *Rapport*. Asked how ZANU could increase the international attention to the Zimbabwean cause, he firmly rejected the use of what he called "terror tactics", such as hijackings, kidnappings and indiscriminate violence against whites. Four months later to the day, the so called 'terrorist' was himself assassinated by the Smith regime.

4. The nationalist leaders were released on the understanding that they would return to detention after the consultations in Lusaka.

5. This was the original group of Frontline State Presidents. Agostinho Neto joined the group after independence and OAU's recognition of Angola.

6. Unbeknown to the outside world, a majority of the detained members of the ZANU Central Committee had on 1 November 1974 suspended Sithole as President, appointing Secretary General Robert Mugabe as acting leader. Mugabe was thus released and flown to Lusaka. The Frontline State Presidents did not, however, recognize Mugabe, accusing him of a coup within ZANU. Without being able to see his colleagues in Zambia, Mugabe was immediately flown back to detention at Que Que (now Kwekwe). Instead, Sithole was released. Reinstated pending a congress decision, he subsequently represented ZANU during the consultations and signed the Lusaka Unity Accord (Martin and Johnson op. cit., pp. 147-52).

7. On 14 November 1974, Chitepo and Tongogara accompanied Sithole to Dar es Salaam, where they met President Nyerere (ibid., p. 151).

8. It was only on 3 December 1974 that the London *Financial Times* broke the news that the Zimbabwean nationalist leaders had been released from detention to meet the Frontline State Presidents.

9. Knut Thyberg: Memorandum ('Samtal med ZANU's ordförande'/'Conversation with ZANU's Chairman'), Ministry for Foreign Affairs, Stockholm, 19 November 1974 (MFA).

to Lusaka to discuss how a peaceful process towards that objective could be implemented. Chitepo was, however, far from convinced. Stating that ZANU's military offensive had been more successful than expected, he feared that the Vorster-Kaunda initiative would set in motion a process towards the establishment of a "puppet regime"[1] and that ZANU could quickly be "overtaken by events".[2] Once again, he asked for increased assistance, principally in the form of cash support.[3]

Indicative of the close relationship established with ZANU, Prime Minister Palme, the Ministry for Foreign Affairs and SIDA were all positive to Chitepo's appeal.[4] An extraordinary allocation of 50 per cent of the 860,000 SEK already granted for 1974/75 was suggested[5], with the proviso that a formal request be submitted through the Swedish embassy in Lusaka.[6] On his return, Chitepo presented the request on 12 December 1974. To meet ZANU's "ever-increasing commitments arising [from] the intensification and expansion of our struggle" and to "take advantage of the new political opportunities [...] looming on the horizon", he requested 350,000 SEK in cash and 150,000 for food and four Land Rovers.[7]

Between Chitepo's visit to Stockholm and his formal request, the Unity Accord was, however, signed at State House in Lusaka on 7 December 1974. Under the Zambian-sponsored agreement, ANC, FROLIZI, ZANU and ZAPU decided to "unite in ANC", recognizing the organization led by Bishop Muzorewa "as the unifying force of the people of Zimbabwe" and agreeing to "take steps to merge their respective [...] structures into ANC before [a] congress [is held] within four months".[8] Despite the commitments made by Prime Minister Palme and the authorities in Stockholm, in the light of the accord the Swedish embassy in Lusaka strongly advised against any additional support to ZANU. Commenting upon Chitepo's request, second secretary Anders Bjurner wrote that "great importance must be attached to the [unity] agreement [...], the spirit of which [...] is that other organizations [than ANC] no longer exist as independent entities".[9] In addition, Bjurner wrote,

> ZANU has earlier received considerably more resources from Sweden than ZAPU. The reasons [...] appear mainly to be a larger documented civilian activity and a more prominent (and successful) liberation [effort] within Zimbabwe. Against the background of the latest developments, these motives for additional assistance seem in the present situation less valid. An 'unbalanced' allocation [...] could possibly be seen as a particular support to one party of the agreement.[10]

1. Ibid.
2. Cable from the Ministry for Foreign Affairs to the Swedish UN delegation in New York, Stockholm, 19 November 1974 (MFA).
3. During a subsequent meeting at SIDA, Claude Chokwenda, the resident ZANU representative, underlined on 10 January 1975—i.e. after the Lusaka Accord—that ZANU only could count on substantial assistance from Sweden (Astrid Bergquist: Memorandum ('Promemoria med anledning av skrivelse från ambassaden i Lusaka angående extra bistånd till ZANU under innevarande budgetår'/'Memorandum in view of communication from the embassy in Lusaka regarding additional assistance to ZANU during the current financial year'), SIDA, Stockholm, 14 January 1975) (SDA).
4. Ibid.
5. Ibid.
6. Letter from Herbert Chitepo to the SIDA office in the Swedish embassy in Lusaka, Lusaka, 12 December 1974 (SDA).
7. Ibid.
8. 'Zimbabwe's Seven-Point Unity Pact', [Lusaka, 7 December 1974] (MFA). Sithole signed the Lusaka Unity Accord on behalf of ZANU. Both Chitepo and Mugabe formed part of the ZANU delegation. The unity accord stated that "the leaders recognize the inevitability of continued armed struggle and [of] all other forms of struggle until [the] total liberation of Zimbabwe".
9. Letter ('Framställning från ZANU'/'Request from ZANU') from Anders Bjurner, Swedish embassy in Lusaka, to the Ministry for Foreign Affairs, Lusaka, 19 December 1974 (MFA).
10. Ibid.

This position eventually prevailed. Referring to the endorsement of the Lusaka Unity Accord by the OAU Liberation Committee, the Ministry for Foreign Affairs communicated on 16 January 1975 that the ZANU request could not be approved.[1] The following day, the Zambian Foreign Minister Vernon Mwaanga— "annoyed by Chitepo's continuous acting in the name of ZANU"[2]—told the Swedish ambassador that ANC was the only Zimbabwean nationalist organization recognized by OAU and that both ZANU and ZAPU had "ceased to exist".[3] In no uncertain terms, Mwaanga requested that "Swedish assistance to ZANU as soon as possible should be suspended and that current deliveries [to the organization] should be deposited with OAU or the Zambian authorities".[4] Due to the friendly and close relations to both the Zambian host government and ZANU, Mwaanga's stern directive put the embassy in a difficult situation. In the process of placing local orders for a large consignment of maize to ZANU, it cabled its predicament to the Ministry for Foreign Affairs in Stockholm, requesting instructions on how to proceed. In the meantime, it stated, "we have deliberately avoided contacts with ZANU".[5]

After diplomatic consultations with Zambia and Tanzania, Sweden eventually agreed to the first part of Mwaanga's request. In the midst of considerable confusion regarding the interpretation of the Unity Accord and the stand taken by Zambia, Tanzania, Mozambique and OAU, CCHA concluded on 11 March 1975—one week before the assassination of Herbert Chitepo—that "conditions for support to liberation movements in Southern Rhodesia do not exist".[6] Without recognizing ANC as the legitimate nationalist movement in Zimbabwe, the humanitarian assistance to both ZANU and ZAPU was suspended.[7]

Détente and the Chitepo Assassination

The so called 'détente exercise' around Zimbabwe was a reaction to ZANU's offensive in Zimbabwe from December 1972; FRELIMO's steady military advances in Mozambique; and the fall of the Portuguese regime—one of the three pillars of the Southern African white citadel—in April 1974. Presaging a radical change in the regional correlation of forces, the developments set in motion a political process in which the long-term objectives of the South African regime—to build a dependable line of defence around apartheid[8]—and the short-term interests of Zambia—to avoid being drawn into an escalating conflict in Zimbabwe—coincided. Through secret diplomacy, Vorster and Kaunda reached an understanding that the only alternative to Zimbabwe being slowly bled to death was a constitutional settlement. This, in turn, supposed that South Africa accepted that white minority rule in Zim-

---

1. Cable from the Ministry for Foreign Affairs to the Swedish embassy in Lusaka, Stockholm, 16 January 1975 (MFA).
2. Ann Wilkens: Memorandum ('Bistånd ZANU/ZAPU'/'Assistance ZANU/ZAPU'), Ministry for Foreign Affairs, Stockholm, 4 February 1975 (MFA).
3. Ibid.
4. Ibid.
5. Cable from Anders Bjurner, Swedish embassy in Lusaka, to the Ministry for Foreign Affairs, Lusaka, 27 January 1975 (MFA).
6. CCHA: 'Protokoll' ('Minutes'), SIDA, Stockholm, 13 March 1975 (SDA). It has been implied by both Hallencreutz (in Hallencreutz and Axelson op. cit., p. 22) and Möllander (op. cit., p. 37) that it was the assassination of Chitepo that led the Swedish government to suspend the assistance to ZANU and ZAPU. It was, however, the Lusaka Unity Accord.
7. As the funds for 1974/75 had been disbursed to ZAPU, the decision only affected ZANU.
8. Inside South Africa, there was at the same time a resurgence of opposition. As the Black Consciousness Movement increasingly confronted the state, more than 60,000 workers went on strike in Durban in early 1973.

babwe must end and that Zambia agreed to the establishment of a moderate black government in the neighbouring country.

It was South Africa's role to convince Ian Smith, and Zambia's to do likewise vis-à-vis independent Africa, bringing ZANU's military campaign to an end and uniting the Zimbabwean nationalist organizations under a formula acceptable to both Smith and Vorster. Publicly confirming the understanding, Prime Minister Vorster stated to the South African Senate on 23 October 1974 that "Southern Africa is at the crossroads and should now choose between peace and escalating violence". "Rhodesia", Vorster said, was "the key to peace", adding that "now is the time for all who have influence to bring it to bear on all parties concerned to find a durable, just and honourable situation".[1] Three days later, Kaunda responded by describing the statement as "the voice of reason for which Africa and the rest of the world have waited for many years".[2] The stage had been set. It remained, however, to persuade the principal political Zimbabwean actors to take part.

South Africa kept its part of the understanding by forcing Ian Smith to release Sithole, Mugabe, Nkomo and other detained nationalist leaders. Zambia reciprocated by acting on behalf of the Frontline States, prevailing upon the Zimbabwean nationalist movements to enter into the Lusaka Unity Accord under the chairmanship of Muzorewa.[3] Eventually, however, this had little impact.[4] The Smith regime was neither a convinced nor a formal party to the initiative and all the deeply divided Zimbabwean movements soon pursued their own, separate policies.

Although joint ANC representations were initially formed in Lusaka[5] and elsewhere, the four organizations did not merge their respective structures and no constituent unity congress was ever held.[6] Rather than laying the foundation for sustained unity, the Lusaka Accord contributed to further division, deepening the rifts between the signatories, as well as between the political organizations and the guerrilla forces. As the ZANU[7] and ZANLA leaders were detained in Zambia after the assassination of Herbert Chitepo, the liberation struggle was practically brought to a standstill.[8] Despite repeated approaches by Bishop Muzorewa and

---

1. Cited in James Barber and John Barratt: *South Africa's Foreign Policy: The Search for Status and Security 1945-1988*, Cambridge University Press, Cambridge, 1990, p. 183.

2. Ibid.

3. Muzorewa and Smith had initiated bilateral consultations as early as in July 1973. They continued until March 1974.

4. The détente policy culminated in the extraordinary—and aborted—Victoria Falls Conference in late August 1975, where Smith, Chikerema, Muzorewa, Nkomo and Sithole in the presence of Vorster and Kaunda tried to negotiate a settlement in a South African railway carriage perched on the bridge between Zambia and Zimbabwe. The exercise died two months later, when South African military forces invaded Angola.

5. In Lusaka, ZANU's Simon Muzenda and ZAPU's John Nkomo represented ANC under the Unity Accord. They had frequent contacts with the Swedish embassy.

6. On the contrary, inside Zimbabwe ZAPU proceeded in September 1975 to hold its own congress, ousting Muzorewa and reconstituting the African National Council as ANC Zimbabwe (ANC-Z) under Joshua Nkomo's leadership. Shortly thereafter, Nkomo—the only nationalist leader to return to Zimbabwe—embarked on bilateral talks with Ian Smith. This, in turn, sealed the end of the Unity Accord.

7. With the notable exception of Ndabaningi Sithole, who by endorsing the clampdown on ZANU irrevocably broke with his own organization, subsequently acting as Chairman of the Zimbabwe Liberation Council, formed as the military wing of ANC (Muzorewa) in July 1975.

8. In a famous BBC interview, Mugabe stated in London in January 1976 that "President Kaunda has been the principal factor in slowing down our revolution", adding that "he has arrested our men, locked them up, and within his prisons and restriction areas there have been cases of poisoning [and] murders" (cited in Martin and Johnson op. cit., p. 210).

Reverend Sithole[1], no direct official Swedish humanitarian assistance was extended during this period to the wider Zimbabwean nationalist movement.[2]

Leading a successful guerrilla war, the externally based ZANU leaders had reluctantly agreed to the Lusaka Unity Accord. Chitepo, in particular, did not hide his criticism. In addition to the leadership dispute between Sithole and Mugabe, there were obvious contradictions between the ZANU President and the National Chairman. "To sow further dissension"[3] and put an end to ZANU's military struggle, Ian Smith's Central Intelligence Organization (CIO) capitalized on the situation. Immediately after the Unity Accord, it used "willing conspirators"[4] to launch the so called Nhari rebellion at ZANLA's Chifombo base on the Zambian border with Mozambique. Above all, however, "for CIO and many other interested parties, Chitepo [...] became the prime target".[5] As later acknowledged by Ian Smith's intelligence chief Ken Flower,

> CIO considered him the biggest obstacle to ending the war and, in the circumstance then prevailing in Zambia, it became clear to us that if Chitepo were to be eliminated the blame could be laid at any number of doors. Accordingly, CIO gave the 'green light' to a carefully prepared physical and psychological operation.[6]

On 18 March 1975—four months after his high-profile visit to Sweden—Chitepo was killed in Lusaka by a bomb fitted to his car by CIO operatives.[7] Having prepared the operation by "feed[ing] disinformation to the Zambian Special Branch [...], the extent of the reaction in Zambia astounded even CIO".[8] Drawing the conclusion that the assassination formed part of ethnically motivated internal ZANU struggles, the Zambian government vigorously and violently turned against the entire organization.[9] While ZANU was banned, over the following weeks its leaders and members were rounded up by the Zambian army and police. At the Swedish embassy, Anders Bjurner followed the events. In early May 1975, he reported to

---

1. In July 1975, Sithole made a first appeal for Swedish assistance to 'his ZANU' outside ANC (Letter ('Bistånd till ZANU'/'Assistance to ZANU') from Anders Bjurner, Swedish embassy in Lusaka, to the Ministry for Foreign Affairs, Lusaka, 30 July 1975) (SDA). And in January 1976, Muzorewa submitted a request for no less than 7 MSEK in favour of ANC (Letter ('ANC (Zimbabwe): Request for assistance programme from SIDA for the year 1975/76') from Bishop Abel T. Muzorewa to SIDA Stockholm, Lusaka, 30 January 1976) (SDA).
2. In mid-1975, SIDA decided, however, to support dependants of ZANU detainees in Zambia.
3. Flower op. cit., p. 146.
4. Ibid.
5. Ibid., p. 147.
6. Ibid.
7. See David Martin and Phyllis Johnson: *The Chitepo Assassination*, Zimbabwe Publishing House, Harare, 1985, and Peter Stiff: *See You in November*, Galago Paperback, Alberton, 1987, pp. 124-43. Stiff's account—based on primary sources—was originally published by Galago in 1985. Reacting "with abhorrence and sorrow" to the news of Chitepo's death, the Swedish Foreign Minister Sven Andersson stated: "Chitepo visited Sweden many times and I had the opportunity of talking to him a couple of months ago. [...] On several occasions, we have earlier witnessed how leaders of liberation movements in Africa have been murdered during their efforts [to achieve] independence. Amílcar Cabral from Guinea-Bissau was murdered two years ago. Eduardo Mondlane of FRELIMO of Mozambique was eliminated in the same violent way. Guinea-Bissau is today a free country [and] Mozambique will become so in a couple of months. Violent deeds cannot stop the necessary development towards sovereignty and independence [in Zimbabwe]" (Ministry for Foreign Affairs: Press communiqué ('Uttalande av utrikesminister Sven Andersson med anledning av mordet på den sydrhodesiska befrielserörelsen ZANU's ledare Herbert Chitepo'/'Statement by Foreign Minister Sven Andersson in view of the assassination of the [...] ZANU leader Herbert Chitepo'), Stockholm, 19 March 1975) (MFA).
8. Flower op. cit., p. 147.
9. Interviewed in 1995, Kaunda claimed that at the time he did not know "that one of my own ministers actually had been persecuting ZANU, because he was a supporter of ZAPU. [...] Well, my minister was not supporting ZAPU as such. He was an agent of Ian Smith's, informing on ZANU. He was given instructions to disorganize ZANU within Zambia" (Interview with Kenneth Kaunda, p. 242). The minister in question was Aaron Milner, who served as Kaunda's Minister of Home Affairs between 1973 and 1977. In 1980, the Zambian government discovered arms caches on a farm owned by Milner south of Lusaka. The discovery led to charges of treason. Born in Southern Rhodesia, Milner subsequently left Zambia for Zimbabwe. Cf. also the interview with Sydney Sekeramayi, p. 230.

the Ministry for Foreign Affairs that a staggering number of 1,660 ZANU members had been arrested.[1] Around 930 had been taken to the Zambian army camp at Mboroma outside Kabwe[2], while another 600 were held in detention camps in eastern Zambia. ZANU's political and military leaders were at the same time detained at the Mukobeko maximum security prison and at the Mpima prison camp in Kabwe, some 140 kilometres north of Lusaka.[3] Bjurner further reported that "outright torture [seems] to take place".[4]

Closely involved with the events in Angola, Bjurner would at the same be concerned with the issue of the ZANU detainees in Zambia. Twenty years later, Kumbirai Kangai—a leading member of the *Dare re Chimurenga* detained at Mpima—recalled that

> Anders Bjurner had arrived [in] Lusaka and I had just started to work with him when [the clampdown] happened. All of a sudden [...] I was detained. I managed to send a note to Bjurner, introducing one of our comrades. I said to this comrade: 'Please, take this to the Swedish embassy. Give it to Bjurner and simply say that we have some women and children who are at place so-and-so. They need medical attention and welfare assistance.' They [subsequently] received [...] assistance right through the time when we were in detention.[5]

Sweden and the ZANU Detainees

Bjurner had access to the detained ZANU leaders[6] and was well informed on their situation.[7] When Simon Muzenda—who as ZANU's ANC representative in Lusaka was still at liberty[8]—made a plea in June 1975 for extraordinary Swedish humanitarian assistance to the destitute family members of the detainees in Zambia,

1. Letter ('ZANU-militanter i fängsligt förvar'/'ZANU militants in detention') from Anders Bjurner, Swedish embassy in Lusaka, to the Ministry for Foreign Affairs, Lusaka, 8 May 1975 (MFA).
2. After the outbreak of the 1975-76 SWAPO crisis, up to two thousand PLAN fighters and SYL members were a year later detained by the Zambian army at the Mboroma camp. Cf. the chapter 'The Shipanga Affair and Beyond: Humanitarian Assistance and Human Rights'.
3. Letter from Bjurner (op. cit.), 8 May 1975.
4. Ibid.
5. Interview with Kumbirai Kangai, p. 215. Kangai, ZANU's Secretary of Labour, Social Services and Welfare, visited Sweden less than three weeks before the assassination of Herbert Chitepo. During a meeting at the Ministry for Foreign Affairs, he *inter alia* said on 27 February 1975 that the Lusaka Unity Accord only implied that the four Zimbabwean organizations had agreed that ANC as an umbrella body should coordinate the negotiations with Ian Smith, but that they as separate movements should continue their own military and welfare activities (Ann Wilkens: Memorandum ('Besök av ZANU-representant'/'Visit by ZANU representative'), Ministry for Foreign Affairs, Stockholm, 7 March 1975) (MFA).
6. Interview with Kumbirai Kangai: "[The Swedes] came to visit us [in prison]" (p. 215).
7. Several of the imprisoned ZANU leaders—such as Hamadziripi and Gumbo—had long-standing relations with Sweden. Through Bjurner's contacts, the Swedish government received firsthand information of their endorsement of Robert Mugabe as head of ZANU. In late January 1976, the Swedish embassy in Lusaka could, for example, provide the ministry with a copy of a letter from Rugare Gumbo, Kumbirai Kangai and Josiah Tongogara, written at the Mpima prison on 24 January 1976. In this important letter, the three *Dare re Chimurenga* detainees—who in turn were coordinated with two of the remaining four members of the Revolutionary Council, namely Henry Hamadziripi and Mukudzei Mudzi, thus representing a majority—explained how they had come "to the conclusion that Ndabaningi Sithole had betrayed the revolution and as such was not fit to lead [the] party". Instead, the letter stated, "we are in a position to make a formal declaration, calling upon you to immediately take over the party leadership" (Letter from Rugare Gumbo, Kumbirai Kangai and Josiah Tongogara to Robert Mugabe, Mpima prison, Kabwe, 24 January 1976, attached to memorandum ('Samtal med Simon Muzenda, representant för ANC/ZANU i Lusaka'/'Conversation with Simon Muzenda, ANC/ZANU representative in Lusaka'), Swedish embassy in Lusaka [no author or date]) (MFA). Kangai confirmed the authenticity of the letter to the author in Harare on 19 July 1995.
8. Muzenda was at the time ZANU's Deputy Organizing Secretary. Leaving Zambia for Mozambique in 1976, in September 1977 he was elected Vice-President of ZANU and represented ZANU/Patriotic Front at the Social Democratic Party congress in Stockholm in September 1978. In that connection, he had meetings at the Ministry for Foreign Affairs (Marika Fahlén: Memorandum ('Besök av ZANU's vicepresident Muzenda'/ 'Visit by ZANU's Vice-President Muzenda'), Ministry for Foreign Affairs, Stockholm, 20 September 1978) (SDA). At Zimbabwe's independence in April 1980, Muzenda became Deputy Prime Minister and Minister of Foreign Affairs.

Bjurner backed the request.[1] It was also supported by the authorities in Stockholm. After the March 1975 decision to suspend the assistance to the Zimbabwean liberation movements, there remained an unspent balance of 260,000 SEK in favour of ZANU. In spite of the general ruling, a total of 35,000 was exceptionally disbursed from the balance to the detained ZANU members' dependants.[2]

Through Bjurner and his contacts, the Swedish government became increasingly aware and concerned about the conditions of the detained ZANU leaders. From mid-1975—when Reverend Sithole's endorsement of the detentions and the fact that ZANU did not enjoy support from the Soviet-aligned countries or organizations combined to give marginal attention to their situation—the young diplomat actively pleaded their case in his reports to Stockholm. In late August 1975, he strongly questioned Zambia's stand vis-à-vis the Zimbabwean liberation movements, pointing out that although both ZANU and ZAPU had been banned in the country, ZAPU was *de facto* allowed to function.[3] In addition, Bjurner stated, "I would personally be extremely surprised if the majority of the [ZANU] detainees have been involved [in the Chitepo assassination]".[4] There were, in his view, "several reasons to assume" that the detainees had been subjected to what "probably can be characterized as 'torture'".[5] Against this background, he concluded that "the detentions have paralyzed the military mobilization for the continuation of the struggle for [Zimbabwe's] independence".[6]

Two months later, Bjurner was—"under secrecy, to say the least"[7]—contacted by Beatrice Ngonomo, a ZANU defence counsel. She gave him further details regarding the detainees' conditions, appealing for Swedish assistance.[8] There were 57 ZANU leaders in detention. Josiah Tongogara, ZANU's Chief of Defence, was according to the Zambian government the prime instigator behind the assassination of Chitepo.[9] The case against him and two ZANU members[10] was to open in late 1975. Convinced about the urgency of legal and humanitarian assistance—and at the same time fully aware of its sensitivity vis-à-vis the Zambian government—Bjurner asked the Swedish government to raise the matter with international human rights' organizations.[11] The Ministry for Foreign Affairs followed his recommendation, approaching the International Defence and Aid Fund, the International Commission of Jurists and Amnesty International. Canon John Collins, the

---

1. Cable from Anders Bjurner, Swedish embassy in Lusaka, to the Ministry for Foreign Affairs, Lusaka, 17 June 1975 (MFA).
2. SIDA: Decision ('Bistånd till ANC (Zimbabwe)'/'Assistance to ANC (Zimbabwe)'), Stockholm, 17 September 1975 (SDA). Although presented by Muzenda in his capacity as ANC representative, the request was in favour of ZANU family members in Zambia. Considerable infighting would take place over the following months between Muzorewa and Sithole with regard to the remaining balance of 225,000 SEK. In November 1975, SIDA decided to allocate the amount for the Zimbabwean refugees in Mozambique via OAU (SIDA: Decision ('Bistånd till African National Council - ANC (Zimbabwe)'/'Assistance to ANC (Zimbabwe)'), Stockholm, 27 November 1975) (SDA).
3. Although formally banned, ZAPU was, for example, given ZANU's regular slot on the Zambian radio.
4. Letter ('Ex-ZANU i fängsligt förvar'/'Ex-ZANU in detention') from Anders Bjurner, Swedish embassy in Lusaka, to the Ministry for Foreign Affairs, Lusaka, 28 August 1975 (MFA).
5. Ibid.
6. Ibid.
7. Letter ('Samtal med försvarsadvokaten för de ZANU-fängslade'/'Conversation with the defence lawyer for the ZANU detainees') from Anders Bjurner, Swedish embassy in Lusaka, to the Ministry for Foreign Affairs, Lusaka, 10 October 1975 (MFA).
8. Ibid.
9. It could, as a curiosity, be noted that Tongogara—who left Zimbabwe for Zambia in 1961—started his political career in Kenneth Kaunda's ruling UNIP party.
10. Joseph Chimurenga, a ZANLA commander, and 'Sadat' Kufa Mazuva, Chitepo's only surviving bodyguard.
11. Indirect reference: Letter from Anders Bjurner to Bo Heinebäck, Lusaka, 10 October 1975 (MFA).

IDAF Director, however, told the Swedish embassy in London that it "was doubtful whether the case fell under [the fund's] sphere of activities"[1], while Amnesty stated that they were already in contact with the Zambian authorities.[2]

Not satisfied, Bjurner insisted on legal assistance and the presence of international observers at the proceedings. In mid-January 1976, he emphasized to the Ministry for Foreign Affairs in Stockholm that this "request [is] increasingly urgent".[3] His efforts were eventually crowned with success. Via the Swedish section of Amnesty International[4], the government contributed behind the scenes to covering the costs of a British counsel, who participated in the defence of Tongogara, Chimurenga and Kufa Masuva ('Sadat').[5] Ten years after the first Swedish contributions for legal assistance to imprisoned Zimbabwean nationalists, official funds were again set aside for the purpose.[6] While the assistance in the mid-1960s was motivated by Ian Smith's repression, the support in the mid-1970s was, however, in a bewildering turn of events secretly channelled in defence of Zimbabweans detained and tortured in an independent African host country with which Sweden maintained close and friendly relations.[7]

On 20 October 1976, the case in the High Court of Zambia charging Josiah Tongogara and his two ZANU colleagues with the murder of Chitepo was dismissed due to "unfair and improper conduct on the part of the [Zambian] police authorities".[8] The other ZANU detainees—including the ZANLA soldiers—had by then been released and transferred to independent Mozambique. After nineteen

---

1. Cable from the Swedish embassy in London to the Ministry for Foreign Affairs, London, 20 November 1975 (MFA). It should be noted that President Kaunda was one of IDAF's more prominent patrons.
2. Ibid.
3. Cable from Anders Bjurner to the Ministry for Foreign Affairs, Lusaka, 15 January 1976 (MFA).
4. The Swedish section of Amnesty International (AI) had been deeply involved with ZANU detainees since the mid-1960s. As earlier noted, Robert Mugabe was in 1965 adopted as a prisoner of conscience by an Amnesty group in Stockholm. Didymus Mutasa was also supported by a Swedish Amnesty group. It should in this context be noted that a major controversy appeared between the ZANU government and Amnesty International in the mid-1980s. As Amnesty reacted strongly against the Harare government's military campaigns in Matabeleland, Mugabe, Mutasa and other former beneficiaries of the human rights organization vehemently condemned what they saw as undue interference into independent Zimbabwe's own affairs. Thomas Hammarberg, AI's Swedish Secretary General, was particularly censured (Letter from Thomas Hammarberg to Senator Sam Whaley, Amnesty International, London, 9 June 1986) (SDA). In order to uphold its mandate and stay independent vis-à-vis possible official influence, AI would over the years oppose assistance from any government source whatsover. In the case of Southern Africa, however, from the early 1970s financial support was sought from the governments of Norway and Sweden. A first initial grant—amounting to 100,000 SEK— was extended by the Swedish government in 1971 (Thomas Hammarberg and Marianne Eyre: Memorandum ('Framställning om förnyat bidrag för de politiska fångarna och deras familjer i södra Afrika'/'Request for continued contribution in favour of the political prisoners and their families in Southern Africa'), Swedish Amnesty Fund, Stockholm, 4 July 1974) (SDA). Two years later, the grant was raised to 300,000 SEK. By that time, the official contribution from Sweden corresponded to more than half of AI's central operating budget (Anders Möllander: Memorandum ('Samtal med ordföranden i svenska Amnesty, Thomas Hammarberg'/ 'Conversation with the head of Swedish Amnesty, Thomas Hammarberg'), Ministry for Foreign Affairs, Stockholm, 14 January 1974) (SDA).
5. Letter from Karl-Axel Elmqvist, Amnesty International Sweden, to the Ministry for Foreign Affairs, Stockholm, 26 May 1976 (MFA) and letter ('Rättegång mot f.d. ZANU-medlemmar'/'Trial against ex-ZANU members') from Anders Bjurner, Swedish embassy in Lusaka, to the Ministry for Foreign Affairs, Lusaka, 14 September 1976 (MFA). See also the interview with Kumbirai Kangai, p. 215.
6. It was only in June 1976—well over a year after the clampdown on ZANU—that AGIS formally voiced its concern. The second national congress of the Swedish solidarity movement with Southern Africa then sent a protest letter to President Kaunda, demanding "the immediate release of the detained former ZANU militants" (Letter ('Detention of members of [the] ZANU leadership') from the Africa Groups in Sweden to [President Kaunda], [no date or place, but June 1976]) (AGA).
7. The issue was complicated by the fact that Kaunda appointed a 'Special International Commission on the Assassination of Herbert Wiltshire Chitepo'. Stage-managed by Zambia, the commission presented its report in March 1976. It was on the basis of the commission's work—described by Ken Flower as "a farce from start to finish" (Flower op. cit., p. 148)—that Tongogara was charged with the murder of Chitepo.
8. Cited in Martin and Johnson (1981) op. cit., p. 181.

months in detention, ZANU's Chief of Defence joined them there, subsequently coordinating the military struggle against the Smith and Muzorewa regimes.[1]

By that time, the Patriotic Front had been formed. After two years of uncertainties regarding ZANU's leadership, Robert Mugabe had, in addition, definitely taken over the reins of the movement. One week after the assassination of Chitepo, ZANU's Central Committee members at liberty in Salisbury (Harare) decided that he and Edgar Tekere should quietly cross the border into Mozambique[2], where they arrived in early April 1975.

As a political prisoner, Mugabe had for a decade corresponded with a high-profile Swedish Amnesty group, and his wife had through the official aid agency made important information tours in Sweden. Mugabe himself had, however, not had any direct contacts with the Swedish government or the humanitarian assistance to ZANU. Nevertheless, after a first meeting with the embassy in Maputo in late February 1976[3] he attached particular attention to the bilateral relations. During the Geneva conference at the end of 1976, he met both the Social Democratic opposition leader Olof Palme and representatives of the Swedish government. Above all—like Amílcar Cabral of PAIGC, but in marked contrast to his Patriotic Front partner Joshua Nkomo—from 1977 Mugabe personally led ZANU's delegations to all the aid negotiations with Sweden. This was in the tradition of Herbert Chitepo. Addressing the visiting SIDA board members in Maputo in February 1979, the ZANU leader stated that

> our close and friendly relations [...] date back several years, when the late comrade Chitepo and other members of our Dare [...] worked to cultivate them. Although these relations suffered a severe setback in 1975-76 as a result of the near destruction of our party and the disruption of the armed struggle [...] by Zambia, we were, nevertheless, able to resuscitate them firmly in 1977.[4]

---

1. In the light of the accusations against Tongogara, it is ironic that during the decisive Lancaster House negotiations in late 1979 he was hailed by Zambia and OAU for his constructive efforts. Less than a week after the Lancaster House agreement on Zimbabwe's independence, he died in a road accident in Mozambique in late December 1979.
2. Martin and Johnson (1985) op. cit., p. 79.
3. Anders Möllander: Memorandum ('Samtal med en syd-rhodesisk nationalistledare'/'Conversation with a Southern Rhodesian nationalist leader'), Swedish embassy, Maputo, 27 February 1976 (SDA).
4. Robert Mugabe: 'Brief statement to the members of the board of SIDA', ZANU, Maputo, 7 February 1979 (MFA).

Patriotic Front:
ZANU and ZAPU towards Independence

End of Détente

The regional developments around Zimbabwe during the détente period not only brought the liberation struggle to a standstill, but also the Swedish humanitarian assistance to ZANU and ZAPU. With close links to Zambia and Tanzania, the Social Democratic government followed their advice and suspended the ongoing support. However, towards the end of 1975 and during the first half of 1976, the understanding between South Africa, Zambia and the Frontline States would rapidly break down, leading to the formation of the Patriotic Front between the two movements in October 1976 and to renewed contacts with Sweden at the Geneva conference later in the month.

Détente in Southern Africa died with the South African invasion of Angola in October 1975. Returning to Zimbabwe, Joshua Nkomo had by then initiated bilateral contacts with Ian Smith. On 1 December 1975, the two signed a declaration of intent to negotiate a settlement.[1] Their talks led, however, nowhere, and in March 1976—as the invading South African army was pushed back by combined Angolan and Cuban forces and newly independent Mozambique in accordance with UN resolutions closed its borders with Zimbabwe—the contacts broke down conclusively. ZAPU would from then on join ZANU in mainly pursuing a military solution to the national question, re-launching its armed campaign from Zambia in June 1976.[2] The majority of the detained ZANLA cadres in Zambia had by that time been released and transferred to Mozambique, where they under the auspices of the host government and Tanzania together with ZIPRA formed the Zimbabwe People's Army (ZIPA) in November 1975.[3] From bases in Mozambique, ZIPA started

---

1. Martin and Johnson (1981) op. cit., p. 227.
2. On 5 June 1976, soldiers from the Zimbabwe People's Revolutionary Army (ZIPRA) attacked the Bumi Hills' airstrip on the southern shore of Lake Kariba. See J.K. Cilliers: *Counter-Insurgency in Rhodesia*, Croom Helm, London, Sydney and Dover, New Hampshire, 1985, p. 30. The real breakthrough for ZAPU on the western front came in 1977. During 1977-78, almost 2,000 ZIPRA guerrillas were infiltrated across the Zambezi, rapidly extending their operational areas inside Zimbabwe (Jeremy Brickhill: 'Daring to Storm the Heavens: The Military Strategy of ZAPU 1976 to 1979' in Bhebe and Ranger (eds) op. cit. (Vol. I), p. 51).
3. ZIPA—also called the 'Third Force'—was set up in Mozambique. It was led by an eighteen-member military committee, composed of nine representatives each from ZANLA and ZIPRA. Rex Nhongo, the most senior ZANLA leader at liberty, served as ZIPA's Commander and Alfred 'Nikita' Mangena from ZIPRA held the position of Political Commissar. There were, however, from the beginning deep divisions between the ZANLA and ZIPRA members, leading to armed clashes in the training camps in Mozambique and Tanzania. As a number of ZIPRA cadres were killed, a majority of their colleagues withdrew from ZIPA and returned to Zambia. By mid-1976, ZIPA was for all practical purposes a ZANU/ZANLA structure. With the release of the 'old guard' ZANU leadership from Zambian prisons in late October 1976, ZIPA *de facto* ceased to exist. It was formally dissolved in January 1977. On ZIPA, see, for example, Martin and Johnson (1981) op. cit., pp. 215-63; Dabengwa in Bhebe and Ranger (eds) op. cit. (Vol. I), pp. 33-35; and David Moore: 'The Zimbabwe People's Army: Strategic Innovation or More of the Same?' in ibid, pp. 73-86. See also David Moore: 'The Zimbabwean People's Army and ZANU's Interregnum: Innovative Military, Ideological and Political Strategies' in Hallencreutz and Axelson op. cit., pp. 33-57. The latter draws substantially from SIDA documents. When the Africa Groups in June 1976 decided to launch a Zimbabwe campaign, it was ZIPA—not ZANU or ZAPU—that attracted their attention (Sellström Volume I, pp. 364-66).

military operations against the Smith regime in January 1976.[1]

By mid-1976, the Zimbabwean liberation war resumed on two fronts, through ZIPRA from Zambia and Botswana[2] and through ZIPA/ZANLA from Mozambique. As before, the eastern front constituted the major threat to the rebel settler regime. In addition to the freedom fighters transferred from Zambia, hundreds of ZANLA cadres from the training grounds in Tanzania could after Mozambique's independence transit to the combat areas in eastern Zimbabwe.[3] Increasing numbers of Zimbabwean refugees were at the same time received by the FRELIMO government and hosted in settlements, where many joined the rapidly growing liberation army. The focus of the liberation struggle shifted from Zambia to Mozambique.

Trying to stem the nationalist tide, in early 1976—even before the bilateral talks with Nkomo broke down—the Smith regime initiated military cross-border raids into Mozambique.[4] On 9 August 1976—less than two months after the Soweto massacre in South Africa—they culminated in an attack by the infamous Selous Scouts[5] on the Zimbabwean settlement at Nyadzonia in the Mozambican province of Manica, where more than 1,000 refugees were brutally mown down.[6] If the South African military invasion of Angola the previous year had left any doubts about the intentions of the white minority regimes, Soweto and Nyadzonia confirmed that they would stop at nothing to defend their interests. The Nyadzonia massacre was the first in a series of similar cross-border attacks against Zimbabwean and Namibian refugee camps in Mozambique, Zambia and Angola in the late 1970s. War—not détente—dominated the Zimbabwean and the wider Southern African scene.

After their débâcle in Angola, the United States and South Africa insisted on an 'internal solution' to the Zimbabwean question by putting pressure on Ian Smith and trying to "trick the genuine liberation movements into accepting a ceasefire without transferring power to them".[7] From April 1976, the US Secretary of State Henry Kissinger embarked on 'shuttle diplomacy' between Pretoria, Salisbury,

---

1. Between January and April 1976, three major ZIPA groups crossed into Zimbabwe (Cilliers op. cit., p. 27).

2. The front through Botswana was opened by ZIPRA without the permission of Seretse Khama's government. Dumiso Dabengwa later noted that "at times the Botswana army intercepted ZIPRA forces who were using the front, but at others they were ignored and permitted to proceed" (Dabengwa in Bhebe and Ranger (eds) op. cit. (Vol. I), p. 34).

3. According to the Tanzanian President, 1,200 freedom fighters from Tanzania and 800 from Zambia were transferred to Mozambique at the end of 1975 (Letter ('Samtal med president Nyerere om Angola och Rhodesia - Vädjan om svenskt bistånd'/'Conversation with President Nyerere - Appeal for Swedish assistance') from Knut Granstedt, Swedish ambassador to Tanzania, to the Ministry for Foreign Affairs, Dar es Salaam, 16 February 1976) (MFA).

4. Inside Zimbabwe, the Rhodesian government had in 1974 started to force the rural population into so called 'protected villages', particularly in the north-eastern parts of the country. By mid-1977, an estimated 300,000 people lived within chain-link fencing enclosures under constant watch by Rhodesian soldiers.

5. Led by Ron Reid Daly, the Selous Scouts Regiment of Rhodesia was set up as a semi-autonomous counterinsurgency unit in 1973. It would be responsible for many of the worst atrocities committed during the Zimbabwean war.

6. Martin and Johnson (1981) op. cit., p. 241. Reid Daly has given a glorified account of the massacre in his *Selous Scouts: Top Secret War* (Galago Publishing, Alberton, 1982).

7. Nathan Shamuyarira: 'Tanzania' in Douglas G. Anglin, Timothy M. Shaw and Carl G. Widstrand (eds): *Conflict and Change in Southern Africa: Papers from a Scandinavian-Canadian Conference*, University Press of America, Washington, 1978, p. 23.

Lusaka and Dar es Salaam[1], eventually leading to the Zimbabwe conference in Geneva from late October to mid-December 1976. Convened by the British government, a reluctant Ian Smith—the key to the initiative—left the conference after less than a week. Instead, Geneva's lasting significance became—quite unintentionally—closer cooperation between Robert Mugabe's ZANU and Joshua Nkomo's ZAPU, a marriage of convenience contracted in Maputo two weeks earlier as the Patriotic Front. Originally formed with the limited objective to coordinate the movements' positions at the conference[2], the Patriotic Front effectively marginalized Abel Muzorewa's UANC and Ndabaningi Sithole's rump ZANU organization. Without liberation armies, Muzorewa and Sithole subsequently approached Ian Smith, ending up as junior partners in a non-recognized internal dispensation in March 1978.

Pro-Active Initiatives with Limitations

Discussing the Western involvement at a conference on the relations between Canada, Scandinavia and Southern Africa, in 1978 Nathan Shamuyarira described Sweden as a "relay station of imperialism".[3] While this characterization contrasted with statements made by Mugabe and other ZANU leaders[4], there is no evidence that the Swedish government—whether under Palme or Fälldin—found Kissinger's initiative or the subsequent Anglo-American proposals by David Owen and Andrew Young satisfactory.[5] On the contrary, closely guided by the Southern Afri-

---

1. In late May 1976, Kissinger paid an official visit to Sweden. Meeting Prime Minister Palme on 24 May, they *inter alia* discussed the recent developments in Angola and Zimbabwe. With regard to Zimbabwe, Kissinger conveyed the message that "we will try to say to the South Africans that they can establish their African credentials by certain [positive] actions". At the same time, the US Secretary of State declared that his government had to take domestic American opinion into consideration. Apparently more concerned about the white opinion in the United States than about the democratic rights of the black majority in Zimbabwe, Kissinger told Palme that "many in the [...] [US] southern states identify their own problems with those of the white Rhodesians. I am being very frank with you on this [and] I would appreciate if you did not tell [...] the press". In his comments, Palme emphasized that colonialism and racism must be abolished as "an unavoidable historical process". On Kissinger's contacts with South Africa, Palme further said that "it is your country that can bring pressure to bear. We Swedes only maintain good contacts with the black Africans. We have no leverage vis-à-vis Pretoria" (Pierre Schori: Memorandum ('Överläggningar mellan utrikesminister Kissinger och statsminister Palme den 24 maj 1976'/'Deliberations between Secretary of State Kissinger and Prime Minister Palme on 24 May 1976'), Ministry for Foreign Affairs, Stockholm, 4 June 1976) (LMA).
2. The joint communiqué issued by ZANU and ZAPU on 9 October 1976 stated: "Cognisant of the need of presenting a common and solid approach to national matters and [...] determined that our different political identities shall not be a barrier to cooperation in promoting the revolutionary process in Zimbabwe [...], our two organizations [...] have resolved that they shall, with a singularity of purpose, adopt a common approach to all issues arising from the [...] current constitutional talks. [...] We shall proceed to such talks as a joint delegation under a joint leadership" (Cable from the Swedish embassy in Lusaka to the Ministry for Foreign Affairs, Lusaka, 11 October 1976) (MFA). The Patriotic Front's position was that "the colonial power, which is the United Kingdom, [should] transfer power to the people of Zimbabwe. Such transfer must be total and immediate" (ibid.).
3. Shamuyarira in Anglin, Shaw and Widstrand (eds) op. cit., p. 27. At the same time, the ZANU leader acknowledged that "the Scandinavian countries have given open and public support to the liberation movements" (ibid., p. 26).
4. Visiting Angola in October 1978, Mugabe, characterized Sweden as "ZANU's most reliable source of assistance" (Letter ('Samtal med ZANU's president om Zimbabwe, ZANU och Angola'/'Conversations with ZANU's President on Zimbabwe, ZANU and Angola') from Anders Bjurner, Swedish embassy in Luanda, to the Ministry for Foreign Affairs, Luanda, 1 November 1978) (SDA).
5. The British government was keen to have Sweden's support for its different initiatives with regard to Zimbabwe. In a letter to the Foreign Minister Karin Söder, Foreign Secretary David Owen stated in late September 1977 that "it is important to me to have Sweden's backing for our proposal. Your principled stand on the issues of Southern Africa has given you a powerful voice both in Africa itself and at the United Nations. I hope I can count on your active support" (Letter from David Owen to Karin Söder, attached to letter from the British ambassador to Sweden, Jeffrey Petersen, to the Ministry for Foreign Affairs, Stockholm, 26 September 1977) (MFA). Sweden and Britain held, however, not only different views on ZANU and ZAPU, but also on the issue of effective sanctions against the Smith regime.

can Frontline States—Mozambique and Tanzania in particular—Sweden would diplomatically support the Patriotic Front partners and disregard frequent appeals by UANC and ZANU-Sithole.[1] In marked contrast to the situation prevailing at the end of the 1960s, the missions in Angola, Mozambique, Tanzania and Zambia would in this context take a pro-active stand, conveying the opinion that official support to ZANU and ZAPU should be resumed.[2] The outstanding question remained, however, how the humanitarian assistance practically could be channelled to the liberation movements. In this regard, both the Swedish government and the Zimbabwean organizations depended on the approval and cooperation of the Southern African host governments. In a conclusive way, such a clearance would only be forthcoming in mid-1977. In the meantime, a number of official initiatives were taken to break the statement.

As early as in May 1975—only two months after the decision to suspend the support to ZANU and ZAPU—Anders Bjurner at the Swedish embassy in Lusaka started to explore the possibilities of resuming the humanitarian assistance in discussions with ANC's Lusaka representatives Simon Muzenda from ZANU and John Nkomo from ZAPU. In Bjurner's opinion, an amount of "at least two million [SEK] should soonest be [allocated]".[3] Due to the negative stand by Tanzania and Zambia, as well as to the divisions between the parties to the December 1974 Lusaka Accord, his proposal was, however, not supported.

It was not until the changing circumstances brought about by Mozambique's independence and the end of the détente exercise that official Swedish support was again proposed. While the Zambian government prepared the trial of Josiah Ton-

1. In 1976-78, a number of delegations visited Sweden on behalf of Muzorewa and Sithole. Far from diplomatic and constructive, they would almost without exception not only turn against ZANU and ZAPU, but also criticize Tanzania and Zambia in the harshest of terms. Requesting Swedish assistance, in August 1976—just before the Geneva conference—ANC's George Nyandoro, chairman of its Finance and Property Committee, and Simpson Mtambanengwe, chairman of the Diplomatic Committee, "dedicated the major part [of a meeting at the Ministry for Foreign Affairs] to intense slander of the governments of Tanzania and, above all, Mozambique" (Ann Wilkens: Memorandum ('Besök av representanter för ANC/ZLC'/'Visit by representatives of ANC/ZLC'), Ministry for Foreign Affairs, Stockholm, 27 August 1976) (SDA). It is against this background not surprising that they had to leave empty-handed. Undeterred, UANC continued to denounce the Patriotic Front and the Frontline States, while at the same time seeking financial support from the Swedish government. After the March 1978 Salisbury agreement between Smith, Chirau, Muzorewa and Sithole, Muzorewa addressed a request from Salisbury to Foreign Minister Söder. In the letter, the UANC leader stated that his party was "supported by 80 per cent of the population and preparing to become the future government of Zimbabwe". He added that "you may hear a lot [...] about guerrilla activities, [but] we can assure you—and would invite you to come and see for yourselves—that the majority of the fighters are supporting us [and the Salisbury] agreement. A lot of negative, but largely uninformed criticism has been made of [the] agreement, spearheaded [particularly by the leaders of] the externally based Patriotic Front, who see no virtue in any development unless they gain personally in their blind ambition to become [...] leaders of independent Zimbabwe. Also [the] so called Frontline States—[who are] playing their own big brother politics—will not accept what the overwhelming masses of Zimbabwe accept unless their own candidates stand to gain". Muzorewa requested Swedish humanitarian assistance to the tune of 800,000 US Dollars, mainly in favour of destitute people in the militarily administered 'protected villages' and for UANC offices "throughout the country for the purposes of electioneering" (Letter from Abel Muzorewa to Karin Söder, Salisbury, 6 June 1978) (SDA). As noted, Sweden never extended support to Muzorewa's organization. In 1977, Norway channelled some 380,000 NOK via ANC as official humanitarian assistance to the 'protected villages'. At the same time, Norway contributed 70,000 NOK to Muzorewa's representation in Stockholm (Jon Bech: 'Norsk Bistand til Frigjøringsbevegelsene i det Sørlige Afrika' ('Norwegian Assistance to the Liberation Movements in Southern Africa') in *Forum for Utviklingsstudier*, No. 10, 1978, Norsk Utenrikspolitisk Institutt, Oslo, p. 17).
2. The Swedish ambassador to Botswana, Bo Kälfors, was less convinced. In April 1977, he quoted South African press reports and local UANC sources concerning an alleged "power struggle within ZANU" during which Rex Nhongo was said to have been killed by Henry Hamadziripi. His view was that Sweden "should wait and see before assistance is given directly to any nationalist organization in [Zimbabwe]" (Letter ('Maktstrid inom ZANU'/'Power struggle within ZANU') from Bo Kälfors to the Ministry for Foreign Affairs, Gaborone, 29 April 1977) (SDA).
3. Cable from Anders Bjurner, Swedish embassy in Lusaka, to the Ministry for Foreign Affairs, Lusaka, 4 June 1975 (MFA).

gogara, the Tanzanian President Nyerere thus pleaded for general Swedish assistance to the Zimbabwean nationalists in mid-February 1976.[1] After a first meeting with Robert Mugabe in Maputo the same month, the newly established Swedish embassy in the Mozambican capital similarly appealed to Stockholm for humanitarian assistance. In early May 1976, chargé d'affaires Göran Hasselmark[2] wrote to the Ministry for Foreign Affairs that

> it is urgent that disbursement of the remaining Swedish assistance [...] soonest be carried out, preferably that a decision also can be reached on replenishment [of the grant]. [...] The final end-user is a movement whose leaders at least formally are anonymous and whose structures are unknown. The possibilities of establishing contact with its representatives in Maputo are extremely limited. This road should, nevertheless, be explored. The Swedish assistance is humanitarian, and the need for the commodities in question is according to unanimous sources very great. [T]he risk of [improper] utilization appears to be limited.[3]

Following the independence of Guinea-Bissau, Mozambique and Angola, the Swedish government had by that time initiated a comprehensive review of the humanitarian assistance to Southern Africa. As ruling parties, PAIGC, FRELIMO and MPLA were no longer eligible for such support. The initial focus on the Portuguese colonies had shifted to Zimbabwe, Namibia and South Africa. Although official support had already been extended to SWAPO and ANC, as well as to ZANU and ZAPU, the changing geo-political situation in Southern Africa and increasing Swedish budgetary allocations for humanitarian assistance[4] motivated the review.[5]

As part of the exercise, three officials from SIDA and the Ministry for Foreign Affairs attached to the Consultative Committee on Humanitarian Assistance—Olof Milton, Marianne Sundh and Ann Wilkens—undertook a fact-finding mission to Southern Africa from early March until the beginning of April 1976.[6] The question of official Swedish humanitarian support to the Zimbabwean movements featured prominently during their talks in the Frontline States. After a series of meetings with government and OAU officials, various humanitarian organizations and repre-

---

1. Letter ('Samtal med president Nyerere om Angola och Rhodesia - Vädjan om svenskt bistånd'/'Conversation with President Nyerere - Appeal for Swedish assistance') from Knut Granstedt, Swedish ambassador to Tanzania, to the Ministry for Foreign Affairs, Dar es Salaam, 16 February 1976 (MFA).
2. As Sweden's ambassador to Zambia, Hasselmark would from 1979 closely follow the unravelling of the Zimbabwean drama.
3. Letter ('Bistånd till Zimbabwe'/'Assistance to Zimbabwe') from Göran Hasselmark, Swedish embassy in Maputo, to the Ministry for Foreign Affairs, Maputo, 10 May 1976 (MFA).
4. As will be seen in the accompanying disbursement tables, actual payments decreased in 1975/76-1976/77. This was largely due to the suspension of the assistance to ZANU and ZAPU.
5. As leader of the opposition, Olof Palme forcefully engaged the Social Democratic Party and the Socialist International (SI) for the cause of national liberation and majority rule in Southern Africa. His "crusade against racism" (Schori (1994) op. cit., p. 22) will be discussed in the context of South Africa below. It should, however, be noted that the question of Zimbabwe played a prominent part in what Schori has described as "an unparalleled offensive" (ibid., p. 21). After visiting the Geneva conference in late 1976, Palme met most of the Zimbabwean nationalist leaders who came to Sweden during 1977. In March 1977, he took part in the UN Security Council's apartheid debate in New York; in May, he attended the international conference on Namibia and Zimbabwe in Maputo; and in August the UN conference against apartheid in Lagos, Nigeria. In September 1977, Palme also led an SI mission to Southern Africa. Observing the damage caused by the Rhodesian attacks against Zambia across the Zambezi river, he described them as "small scale terror" in his diary from the journey. "In the midst of the Western mumblings", Palme wrote, "one [has] to be crystal clear on a number of points [...]. The armed struggle is justified if all other possibilities have been exhausted and if it is combined with a willingness to negotiate a settlement when the opportunity arises. There can be no 'purchasing' guarantees of the continuance of the apartheid system in South Africa by means of settlements in Namibia and Zimbabwe (as was attempted by Kissinger). [W]hat is at stake in Zimbabwe and Namibia also concerns the future of South Africa" (Olof Palme: 'Här går gränsen för mänsklig värdighet: Palme's afrikanska dagbok'/'Here goes the border of human decency: Palme's African diary' in *Aftonbladet-Magasinet*, 9 October 1977. Also Schori (1994) op. cit., p. 21).
6. Wilkens also visited South Africa, where she held a series of important meetings with a range of anti-apartheid organizations. She returned to South Africa in mid-1976.

sentatives of the liberation movements[1], they concluded in mid-April 1976 that "the practical details regarding [...] assistance [to the Zimbabwean nationalist movement] do not as yet appear as entirely clear". Nevertheless, in their view Swedish support "ought primarily to be channelled via the government of Mozambique, perhaps [...] in cooperation with the OAU Liberation Committee". To balance the recommended assistance via the Mozambican government, they also considered it "appropriate" to grant support to "those groups—mainly belonging to former ZAPU—which are active in Zambia".[2]

The government supported the mission's conclusions and the plea made by Hasselmark the following month. In a letter in late August 1976—shortly after the Nyadzonia massacre—Thord Palmlund, Assistant Under-Secretary in the Foreign Ministry, summarized the situation and instructed the embassy in Maputo as follows:

> The situation in the Zimbabwean liberation movement has for a long time been unclear. Reports about new factions [and] divisions continue to pour in. Here in Stockholm, different [Zimbabweans] turn up, demanding [...] assistance as representatives of the authentic liberation struggle. The grand total of the information [...] appears, however, to be the same as earlier this year, [that is,] that possible Swedish assistance should be channelled to the camps in Mozambique in consultation with the Mozambican government and given an OAU label. This means an arrangement whereby the OAU Liberation Committee is kept informed and in agreement, but does not in practice administer the [actual] channelling of the assistance. Commodity support directly to Maputo or Beira appears from a practical point of view as the most adequate option. Against this background, the embassy is [herewith] requested to once again raise the issue of [Swedish] assistance to the Zimbabwean camps in Mozambique with the Mozambican authorities.[3]

By that time, Rex Nhongo[4], the Commander of ZIPA, had made an appeal for Swedish assistance.[5] In late July 1976, initial discussions were also held between Göran Hasselmark and Robert Mugabe at the Swedish embassy in Maputo. During the meeting, Mugabe gave an account of the recent clashes between ZIPRA and ZANLA soldiers in the training camps in Tanzania, explaining that ZIPA—or as he preferred to call it, the 'Third Force'—due to ZAPU's withdrawal had *de facto* become part of ZANU. While acknowledging Mozambique's support for the liberation of Zimbabwe, Mugabe "cautiously" criticized President Machel's "theories on the protracted struggle" and the view that outside assistance should be channelled via OAU. ZANU/the 'Third Force', Mugabe declared, was "keen to establish direct contacts with the donors".[6]

---

1. After their mission, Milton, Sundh and Wilkens submitted over 30 memoranda totalling 150 pages to CCHA. The documentation constitutes a remarkable source of information on the refugee situation and the liberation movements in Southern Africa in early 1976.
2. Ann Wilkens: Memorandum ('Bistånd till ANC/Zimbabwe: Sammanfattning'/'Assistance to ANC/Zimbabwe: Summary'), CCHA/MFA, Stockholm, 17 April 1976 (SDA). While the report in accordance with the December 1974 Lusaka Accord formally treated ANC as the overall Zimbabwean umbrella organization, it made it clear that Swedish assistance to a request presented by Bishop Muzorewa in January 1976 should not be supported.
3. Letter ('Bistånd till Zimbabwe'/'Assistance to Zimbabwe') from Thord Palmlund to the Swedish embassy in Maputo, Ministry for Foreign Affairs, Stockholm, 31 August 1976 (SDA).
4. Known as Rex Nhongo during the liberation struggle, in the mid-1980s the former ZIPA Commander and—following the death of Josiah Tongogara—ZANLA Commander-in-Chief changed his name to Solomon Mujuru. After independence, Mujuru became Commander of the Zimbabwean army.
5. Letters from Rex Nhongo ("To whom it may concern"), Dar es Salaam, 14 and 15 July 1976 (SDA).
6. Letter ('Samtal med Robert Mugabe, ANC-Zimbabwe'/'Conversation with Robert Mugabe, ANC-Zimbabwe') from Göran Hasselmark, Swedish chargé d'affaires in Maputo, to the Ministry for Foreign Affairs, Maputo, 23 July 1976 (SDA).

Due to conflicting signals from the OAU Liberation Committee and the Front-line States, another four months would lapse before the Swedish embassy and the Mozambican government towards the end of 1976 could start in earnest discussing humanitarian assistance to the Zimbabweans. The political situation had in the meantime drastically changed in Sweden and in the wider Zimbabwean nationalist movement, as well as internationally. In late September 1976, Olof Palme's Social Democratic Party lost the parliamentary elections to Thorbjörn Fälldin's non-socialist coalition. Two weeks later, ZANU and ZAPU formed the Patriotic Front, and at the end of October the Geneva conference opened. After the establishment of direct contacts between the Fälldin government and ZANU and ZAPU in Geneva, support to the two Patriotic Front partners resumed in mid-1977.

The Fälldin Government and the Patriotic Front

The new Swedish government's first official contacts with the Zimbabwean nation-alist movement took place immediately after the formation of the Patriotic Front, when both ZANU and ZAPU appealed for financial assistance to cover outlays dur-ing the forthcoming Geneva conference.[1] More detailed information regarding the funding of the conference was gathered during the opening session in Geneva in meetings with the British government, the nationalist delegations and the Frontline States by the Swedish observer from the Ministry for Foreign Affairs, Bo Heine-bäck. Confirming the need for general financial assistance, all of them welcomed Swedish support. The representatives of the Frontline States emphasized, however, that possible contributions must be equally divided between the four participant nationalist delegations, that is, ZANU, ZAPU, UANC and Reverend Sithole's ZANU group.[2] A decision to that effect was announced by Foreign Minister Karin Söder on 1 November 1976.[3] An amount of 140,000 SEK was to be shared between the four delegations.[4]

Taking place only a month after the formation of Fälldin's non-socialist coali-tion government, the Geneva conference presented an opportunity to clarify the new government's position on Zimbabwe. On behalf of the Ministry for Foreign Affairs this was initially done by Heinebäck[5], who in late October 1976 explained to the Zimbabwean nationalist delegations that

> the new Swedish government continued the principled policy of the former regarding support to the developing world in general. With regard to Southern Africa, the government had in its [political] declaration stated that it intended to increase the assistance for the liberation of the region. This policy did not represent a particular [political] party, but was firmly anchored in the general Swedish popular opinion.[6]

---

1. Cable from the Swedish embassy in Lusaka to the Ministry for Foreign Affairs, Lusaka, 11 October 1976 (MFA). Also memorandum ('Svenskt bidrag till Rhodesia-konferensen'/'Swedish contribution to the Rhodesia conference') by Bo Heinebäck, Ministry for Foreign Affairs, Stockholm, 2 November 1976 (MFA). The Brit-ish government covered the costs for nine participants from each of the four nationalist delegations.
2. Memorandum by Heinebäck, Stockholm, 2 November 1976. The other participating delegations represented the British and the Rhodesian governments.
3. Memorandum by Heinebäck, Stockholm, 2 November 1976.
4. Minutes from cabinet meeting ('Bidrag till Rhodesia-konferensen i Genève'/'Contribution to the Rhodesia conference in Geneva'), Ministry for Foreign Affairs, Stockholm, 2 December 1976 (MFA). Additional contri-butions to the conference were channelled by Denmark, Norway and Sweden via IUEF.
5. In the mid-1970s, Heinebäck served as a substitute member of CCHA. He became the first Swedish ambassa-dor to independent Zimbabwe in 1980.
6. Bo Heinebäck: Memorandum ('Det svenska biståndet till de zimbabwiska nationalistgrupperna'/'The Swedish assistance to the Zimbabwean nationalist groups'), Ministry for Foreign Affairs, Stockholm, 9 November 1976 (SDA).

Heinebäck also discussed how to practically channel official humanitarian assistance to the Zimbabwean refugees in Southern Africa with the representatives of Mozambique, Tanzania and Zambia.[1] They all made it clear that they supported the four Zimbabwean nationalist organizations and that any Swedish support should be extended through OAU.[2] The Mozambican delegation, however, indicated that "it should be possible to channel purely humanitarian assistance directly to the [Zimbabwean] camps [in the country]".[3] This was a longed-for opening with regard to the outstanding question of how to assist the rapidly increasing numbers of refugees from Zimbabwe, who at the time amounted to around 30,000 in Mozambique alone.[4]

Two weeks later—while the Geneva conference was still in progress[5]—Göran Hasselmark and SIDA's representative to Mozambique, Jan Cedergren, were in a new position to discuss humanitarian efforts with the Maputo government. Meeting the Mozambican Chief of Cabinet, Sérgio Vieira, on 20 November 1976, they were told that Mozambique did not wish to give preference to any particular Zimbabwean organization, as it had "difficulties in seeing the political differences between the various factions". There were, however, "positive and regular contacts with ZIPA". Against that background, Vieira promised to look into ZIPA's needs with regard to a possible commodity support programme.[6]

The following month—immediately after the adjournment of the Geneva conference—Vieira came back to the Swedish embassy with an official request for assistance to the Zimbabwean refugees in Mozambique, signed by the Ministry for Development and Economic Planning. He also submitted a comprehensive list of items needed, established by David Todhlana, ZIPA's Deputy Director of Logistics, Supplies and Social Aid.[7] It covered a wide range of items, from clothes, blankets, food and medicines to vehicles and office equipment.[8] The request, however, never materialized. Following the breakdown of the Geneva talks, in early January 1977 the Frontline States agreed to support the Patriotic Front, dissociating themselves from Muzorewa's UANC and Sithole's ZANU group. ZIPA was at the same time formally dissolved. The Mozambican submission to the Swedish government was accordingly withdrawn.[9]

The Frontline States' decision to pledge political support to the Patriotic Front coalition put a definitive end to the uncertainties introduced by the December 1974 Lusaka Accord. On equal terms, Mugabe's ZANU and Nkomo's ZAPU were from then onwards recognized as the genuine Zimbabwean liberation movements. Thus clarified, the developments around Zimbabwe rapidly opened up. During an official visit to Tanzania and Zambia in February-March 1977, the Liberal Minister for

---

1. The Mozambican delegation was led by Oscar Monteiro, the Tanzanian by Salim Ahmed Salim and the Zambian by Mark Chona.
2. Memorandum by Heinebäck, Stockholm, 9 November 1976.
3. Ibid.
4. Martin and Johnson (1981) op. cit., p. 276.
5. The Geneva talks ended inconclusively in mid-December 1976.
6. Jan Cedergren: Memorandum ('Stöd till Zimbabwes befrielserörelser - Sammanträffande med Sérgio Vieira, presidentens kabinettschef'/'Assistance to the Zimbabwean liberation movements - Meeting with Sérgio Vieira, Chief of the President's Office'), Maputo, 22 November 1976 (MFA).
7. Letter ('Ansökan om stöd till Zimbabwe-flyktingar i Moçambique samt ansökan om humanitärt stöd till ZIPA'/'Request for support to Zimbabwe refugees in Mozambique and request för humanitarian support to ZIPA') from the Swedish ambassador to Mozambique, Knut Granstedt, to the Ministry for Foreign Affairs, Maputo, 20 December 1976 (SDA).
8. Letter ('Urgent appeal for aid') from David Todhlana, ZIPA, to the Swedish government, Chimoio, 25 November 1976 (SDA).
9. Telex from Jan Cedergren to SIDA Stockholm, Maputo, 18 March 1977 (SDA).

International Development Cooperation, Ola Ullsten, was assured that there was no longer any objection to direct humanitarian assistance to the Patriotic Front partners.[1] The same position was expressed by President Machel during his state visit to Sweden in April 1977.[2] When Bishop Muzorewa in February and Reverend Sithole in April 1977, respectively, turned up in Stockholm, the government thus only paid protocollary attention to their appeals for support.[3] Visiting the Swedish capital in mid-May, Joshua Nkomo's requests on behalf of ZAPU were, however, immediately acknowledged. Earlier submissions by ZANU had been received in the same spirit.[4]

The clarifying stand by the Frontline States made it possible for the Fälldin government to officially state its intention to *de facto* recognize the Patriotic Front and increase the humanitarian assistance to ZANU and ZAPU. In fact, the two Zim-

1. Ove Heyman: Memorandum ('Biståndsministerns samtal med president Kaunda 1977 03 02'/' The Cooperation Minister's conversation with President Kaunda on 2 March 1977'), Swedish embassy, Lusaka, 7 March 1977 (MFA). During his trip, Ullsten had several meetings with representatives of the Patriotic Front. In Dar es Salaam he met ZANU's Rugare Gumbo and Edgar Tekere, the latter serving as the movement's Chief Representative to Mozambique, on 22 February 1977 (Helena Ödmark: Memorandum ('Biståndsminister Ullsten sammanträffar med representanter för Patriotiska Fronten'/'Cooperation Minister Ullsten meets representatives of the Patriotic Front'), Swedish embassy, Dar es Salaam, 25 February 1977) (MFA). The following week, he had a joint meeting with ZANU and ZAPU in Lusaka. ZANU was *inter alia* represented by Simon Muzenda and Richard Hove, while ZAPU's delegation included Joseph Msika (Secretary General) and John Nkomo (Administrative Secretary) (Elisabeth Michanek: Memorandum ('Möte med representanter för Patriotiska Fronten den 28 februari 1977'/'Meeting with representatives of the Patriotic Front on 28 February 1977'), Swedish embassy, Lusaka, 7 March 1977) (MFA). During the meetings, Ullsten explained the Swedish government's views on Zimbabwe, indicating a resumption and increase of the humanitarian assistance to the Patriotic Front partners.

2. During his visit to Sweden, Machel was rather of the opinion that assistance should be extended to the Patriotic Front as a joint structure, and not to ZANU and ZAPU separately (Bo Heinebäck: Memorandum ('Besök av representanter för ZANU'/'Visit by ZANU representatives'), Ministry for Foreign Affairs, Stockholm, 6 May 1977) (MFA). Subsequent efforts to set up joint Patriotic Front offices in the Frontline States did not succeed.

3. Bishop Muzorewa was invited to Sweden by the Methodist youth movement. On 4 February 1977, he was also received by Foreign Minister Karin Söder for a courtesy visit (Jan af Sillén: Memorandum ('Biskop Muzorewa hos utrikesministern'/'Bishop Muzorewa with the Foreign Minister'), Ministry for Foreign Affairs, Stockholm, 4 February 1977) (MFA). Coming from Norway and Finland, Muzorewa's visit to Sweden was not well timed. After the decision by the Frontline States to recognize the Patriotic Front, the OAU Liberation Committee took the same position during his stay in Stockholm. Claiming support from 90 to 95 per cent of Zimbabwe's black population, OAU's stand was vehemently denounced by the UANC leader. In a statement to the Swedish press, he declared that "the formation of the so called Patriotic Front [...] was the brainchild of President Kaunda, designed to force the leadership of Mr. Nkomo on the people of Zimbabwe. [...] It is a well known fact [...] that [Nkomo and Mugabe] have no support worth talking about in Zimbabwe. [...] We appeal to all democratic people of the world to condemn the Frontline States' decision as [an] undemocratic, arbitrary [and] unwarranted interference in the internal affairs of Zimbabwe and [as] usurpation of the inalienable right of the people of Zimbabwe to choose who their leader shall be" ('Press statement by Bishop Abel T. Muzorewa', Stockholm, February 1977) (SDA). See also Anders Johansson: 'Fortsatt väpnad kamp vårt enda alternativ' ('Continued armed struggle our only alternative') in *Dagens Nyheter*, 5 February 1977, and Ulf Hagman: 'Jag har stödet i Rhodesia' ('I have the support in Rhodesia') in *Svenska Dagbladet*, 5 February 1977. Ndabaningi Sithole's visit in April 1977 was mainly of a private character. His daughter lived in Stockholm and he went to visit her (Interview with Ndabaningi Sithole, p. 232). Sithole too paid a courtesy call on Foreign Minister Söder (Cable from the Ministry for Foreign Affairs to the Swedish embassies in London and Washington, Stockholm, 22 April 1977) (MFA). Like Muzorewa, Sithole denounced the Patriotic Front as an "external creation". Inside Zimbabwe, he stated, it was he and Muzorewa who enjoyed popular support (Marika Fahlén: Memorandum ('ZANU-ledaren Ndabaningi Sithole på Sverige-besök'/'The ZANU leader Ndabaningi Sithole visiting Sweden'), Ministry for Foreign Affairs, Stockholm, 25 April 1977) (MFA).

4. In mid-April 1977, Simon Muzenda submitted a request to SIDA for no less than 15 MSEK. It was instantly processed, and on 5 May 1977—that is, before Nkomo's visit—SIDA suggested that CCHA should recommend an allocation of 2 MSEK to ZANU (Marianne Sundh: Memorandum ('Ansökan från Zimbabwe African National Union avseende budgetåret 1976/77'/'Request from ZANU for the financial year 1976/77'), SIDA, Stockholm, 5 May 1977) (SDA). While the government's decision on support to ZANU and ZAPU was made in mid-June, already on 12 April SIDA allocated 25,000 SEK to ZANU's office in Stockholm and on 18 May 1977 another 8,000 SEK to its office in Maputo (SIDA: Decisions Nos. 232/77 and 324/77 by the Country Division) (SDA). Of the two Patriotic Front partners, initially ZANU thus enjoyed more sympathy than ZAPU within the Swedish aid agency.

Against the Patriotic
Front: Bishop Abel
Muzorewa invited by
the Swedish Methodist
youth, Stockholm,
February 1977 (Photo:
Anders Gunnartz)

babwean movements were accorded special attention by the incoming government.[1] In its first comprehensive parliamentary foreign policy declaration, it stressed on 30 March 1977 that

> we give wholehearted support to the economic sanctions against Rhodesia and will work for them to be strengthened. [...] We are [also] prepared to give increased humanitarian assistance to the liberation movements in Southern Africa, which are [...] involved in the struggle for their peoples' political and economic rights and the independence of their countries. We have, primarily, in mind ZANU and ZAPU within the Patriotic Front.[2]

The pledge was swiftly honoured. On 12 May 1977, CCHA recommended support of 2.5 MSEK each to ZANU and ZAPU as retroactive humanitarian assistance during the financial year 1976/77, that is, until 30 June 1977.[3] The recommendation was endorsed by Minister Ullsten on 16 June.[4] Official negotiations regarding the content of the assistance were held with ZAPU in Lusaka in July and with ZANU in Maputo in August 1977. Three months later, CCHA proposed an increase of the grants to each of the two movements to 5 MSEK in 1977/78, a recommendation that was also approved.[5] To ease Mozambique's extraordinary burden as host to tens of thousands of Zimbabwean refugees, it was at the same time decided—in

---

1. Forming part of Fälldin's non-socialist coalition, the Moderate Party did not share the Centre-Liberal views regarding official Swedish support to the Southern African liberation movements. In a remarkable editorial comment, the conservative theoretical journal *Svensk Tidskrift* argued in early 1977 that Ullsten in the case of Zimbabwe "out of the quarrelling groups" had "opted for [the one] qualified to kill most whites in Rhodesia [...]. He has travelled the same simple road as his predecessor. The most Communist-supported [group], the so called Patriotic Front, is to receive Swedish financial assistance. [...]. It is unbelievable how much the concept of neutrality can cover. [...] Palme's government introduced support to revolutionary movements from the aid budget. The idea could have been raised in Moscow. Those who took up arms for socialism [...] were supported. [...] Mr. Ullsten innocently continues along Mr. Palme's road" ('Ola Ullstens biståndspolitik'/'Ola Ullsten's aid policy' in *Svensk Tidskrift*, No. 3, 1977, pp. 101-102). Margaretha af Ugglas was at the time a member of the moderate journal's editorial board. She became Minister for Foreign Affairs in 1991, holding that position until 1994.
2. 'Government statement [in] the *Riksdag* debate on foreign policy', 30 March 1977, in Ministry for Foreign Affairs: *Documents on Swedish Foreign Policy: 1977*, Stockholm, 1978, pp. 25-26.
3. CCHA: 'Protokoll från sammanträde' ('Minutes from meeting'), SIDA, Stockholm, 1 June 1977 (SDA).
4. Ministry for Foreign Affairs: Decision ('Stöd till Zimbabwe African National Union (ZANU) och Zimbabwe African People's Union (ZAPU)'/'Support to ZANU and ZAPU'), Stockholm, 16 June 1977 (MFA).
5. CCHA: 'Protokoll från sammanträde' ('Minutes from meeting'), SIDA, Stockholm, 16 November 1977 (SDA).

addition to substantial grants via UNHCR, WFP, WCC and LWF—to give the Maputo government a direct contribution of 8 MSEK for its humanitarian work.[1]

Once the political conditions in Southern Africa so allowed, the Swedish government would in a significant way materially express its support to what it saw as the genuine forces for Zimbabwe's national liberation. Formally extended to the Patriotic Front, the assistance to ZANU and ZAPU was granted in equal amounts. In current figures, from 1 July 1977 until independence in April 1980 a total of 87 MSEK was disbursed under bilateral agreements to the two Patriotic Front partners as direct official humanitarian support through SIDA.[2]

The Africa Groups and Zimbabwe

Zimbabwe occupies a particular place in the history of Sweden's involvement with the liberation struggles in Southern Africa. The fact that two national movements were supported and that one of them did not belong to the group of 'authentics' has been mentioned. Official assistance to ZANU and ZAPU in the mid-1970s was, in addition, exceptional in that it was not actively promoted by the leading Swedish solidarity organization. Until 1978, the Africa Groups in Sweden paid limited attention to the Zimbabwean cause, expressing serious doubts about ZANU, ZAPU and the Patriotic Front. Important constituent parts of the wider solidarity opinion—particularly the Emmaus groups and Bread and Fishes—had, however, established close relations with ZANU in the early 1970s. Largely through their influence, the national solidarity organization eventually embarked on support campaigns for the Patriotic Front. Nevertheless, Sweden's pro-active policy in favour of ZANU and ZAPU originated chiefly at the level of the state. This was, in turn, to a large extent the result of an unusual involvement by the Church of Sweden Mission and interaction between the state and the church.[3] As has been concluded by Hallencreutz, "the missionary factor was an important element in the new moves [by the government]".[4]

During the first half of the 1970s, the Africa Groups focused their solidarity on the armed liberation struggles in the Portuguese African colonies. After the victories in Guinea-Bissau, Mozambique and Angola, they shifted their attention to Namibia, South Africa and Zimbabwe. The transition was neither easy nor smooth.[5] While the South Africa Committees of the 1960s—particularly in Lund,

---

1. Ibid. In January 1977, a first grant of 5 MSEK was for the same purpose extended to the Mozambican government (Marianne Sundh: Memorandum ('Ansökan från Zimbabwe African National Union avseende budgetåret 1976/77'/'Request from ZANU for the financial year 1976/77'), SIDA, Stockholm, 5 May 1977) (SDA). The same amount was granted to the government of Botswana (Marika Fahlén: Memorandum ('Biståndsframställning från UANC/Zimbabwe'/'Request for assistance by UANC/Zimbabwe'), Ministry for Foreign Affairs, Stockholm, 27 January 1978) (SDA). After the Rhodesian attacks against ZAPU in Zambia from October 1978, the Zambian government was also given additional financial resources to cater for the Zimbabwean refugees in the country.
2. See the disbursement tables for ZANU and ZAPU. In the same period, a total of 90 MSEK was disbursed to SWAPO of Namibia and 58 to ANC of South Africa.
3. Over the years, several CSM representatives served on CCHA or on the SIDA board, acting as intermediaries between the state and the church. This was, notably, the case with Gunnar Helander (see Sellström Volume I, pp. 71 and 112-13), but also, for example, with Carl Fredrik Hallencreutz and Tore Bergman.
4. Hallencreutz in Hallencreutz and Axelson op. cit., p. 26. Carl Fredrik Hallencreutz acted in the early 1970s as Southern Africa secretary of the Church of Sweden Mission. In the mid-1970s, he was a member of the SIDA board. He served as professor of religious studies at the University of Zimbabwe in the latter half of the 1980s, returning there in 1995 to take up an assignment as visiting professor at the Institute of Development Studies. In 1998, Hallencreutz published the study *Religion and Politics in Harare 1890-1980* (Studia Missionalia Upsaliensia No. LXXIII, Swedish Institute of Missionary Research, Uppsala). He died in March 2001.
5. On the internal AGIS debate in the mid-1970s, see the interview with Sören Lindh, p 305-06.

Stockholm and Uppsala[1]—maintained good contacts with ZANU and ZAPU, the second generation, post-Vietnam solidarity movement was markedly critical towards the established Zimbabwean organizations. On behalf of AGIS national executive committee, Dick Urban Vestbro later explained that the Africa Groups until their congress in May 1977 "rejected all solutions which were not based upon armed struggle".[2]

Against this background, ZANU's resident representative in Sweden, Claude Chokwenda, took the initiative in forming a Swedish ZANU Committee.[3] With the stated objectives to "disseminate information [...] about Zimbabwe; support ZANU in its struggle for the liberation of Zimbabwe from colonial oppression; support the building of an independent, democratic, African state; and work for cultural exchange and [...] friendship between the peoples of Zimbabwe and Sweden", the solidarity committee was formed in Stockholm in February 1975.[4] It was quite active during the first half of 1975, arranging a number of public meetings and—above all—distributing ZANU's information bulletin *Zimbabwe Chimurenga*.[5]

At their second national congress in June 1976, AGIS decided to launch a solidarity campaign for Zimbabwe.[6] Still reluctant to support either ZANU or ZAPU, the board decided to raise money for "the guerrilla struggle" and that the assistance should be channelled to Mozambique, "where we have FRELIMO's word that [it] will reach those who are fighting".[7] Coordinated by the Africa Group in Gothenburg, a first Zimbabwe campaign took place in December 1976. The solidarity organization had in the meantime received an "appeal for Zimbabwean refugees and cadres in Mozambique and Tanzania" from Crispen Mandizvidza, a member of ZANU's Central Committee based in Mozambique. Mandizvidza explained that ZANLA operated in the name of ZIPA and that ZIPA was "run by the party's Central Committee, headed by comrade Robert Mugabe, in conjunction with the ZIPA High Command and party administrators".[8] In spite of the letter—and that ZANU and ZAPU in early October had formed the Patriotic Front—AGIS stated in November 1976 that they did "not take sides with any exile organization", preferring to "cooperate directly with ZIPA".[9] Inviting ZIPA to send a representative to

1. Sellström Volume I, pp. 338 and 344-48.
2. Letter from Dick Urban Vestbro to ZAPU, Stockholm, 2 August 1977 (AGA).
3. In Swedish, *ZANU-kommittén*.
4. ZANU-kommittén: 'Stadgar antagna vid konstituerande möte söndagen den 23 februari 1975' ('Statutes adopted at constituent meeting, Sunday 23 February 1975') (MFA). In the mid-1970s, the resident representatives of ANC of South Africa and SWAPO of Namibia would, similarly, react to the Africa Groups' initial passivity by promoting alternative solidarity committees or working with other organizations. In the case of ANC, the Support Group for the People of South Africa (*Stödgruppen för Sydafrikas Folk*) was formed in January 1975 (*Phambili*, No. 1, March-May 1975, p. 29). Finding the Africa Groups "very lukewarm on Namibia", the SWAPO representative Ben Amathila opted to work through the Swedish UN Association. Thus, he initially "tapped not the mainstream, but the off-stream of the support groups" (Interview with Ben Amathila, pp. 65-66).
5. Letter ('Svenska Zanukommittén'/'The Swedish ZANU Committee') from Birgitta Johansson to the Swedish embassy in Lusaka, Ministry for Foreign Affairs, Stockholm, 9 June 1975 (MFA). Some issues of *Zimbabwe Chimurenga* were published in Swedish as "the official organ of ZANU's office in Scandinavia".
6. AGIS: 'Protokoll från AGIS' kongress, 5-7 juni 1976, i Björkå' ('Minutes from the AGIS' congress, 5-7 June 1976, at Björkå') [no date] (AGA).
7. Letter from Dick Urban Vestbro to *Fellesrådet for det sørlige Afrika* (The Norwegian Council for Southern Africa), 3 October 1976 [no place] (AGA).
8. Letter ('An appeal for Zimbabwe refugees and cadres in Mozambique and Tanzania') from C.P. Mandizvidza to the Africa Groups, Quelimane, 8 October 1976 (AGA).
9. Letter from Dick Urban Vestbro to KEG [Kommunistiska Enhetsgruppen], 1 November 1976 [no place] (AGA).

the forthcoming Zimbabwe campaign, a letter was at the same time addressed to "ZANU-ZIPA" in Mozambique.[1]

As ZIPA by then had been neutralized, it is not surprising that the Africa Groups in spite of "several letters and cables [...] did not receive a reply".[2] The Zimbabwe campaign itself, did, in addition, "meet with a weak response among most local [Africa] groups".[3] The issue of Zimbabwe was, however, largely downplayed also at the national level. When ZAPU's Edward Ndlovu in December 1976 made an appeal for material support[4], his letter was, for example, not acknowledged until August 1977.[5] In the reply from AGIS' national executive committee, it explained that a "contributing reason" for the delay was that "the situation [regarding] the liberation movement of Zimbabwe was not very clear to us at [the] time".[6] At the third national AGIS congress, held in Uppsala in May 1977, the organization had in the meantime decided to express its "support for ZANU's and ZAPU's efforts towards unification within the Patriotic Front".[7]

There were, however, still strong doubts regarding the Zimbabwean movements. In the letter to ZAPU, Vestbro stated that "we do not yet regard the Patriotic Front as a stable political organization".[8] In fact, while the congress resolved to divide any material assistance equally between ZANU and ZAPU, it added that

> if the Patriotic Front is dissolved, the support shall not automatically continue [to be extended] to [the two movements]. In such a case, the board shall in consultation with local [Africa] groups [...] determine how the future support shall be designed.[9]

ZAPU reacted to the letter, criticizing the solidarity movement for "meddling in the way they conducted the struggle" and for "judging the situation one-sidedly".[10] The relations with the Patriotic Front (PF) improved in 1977-78, but the two resident PF representatives, ZANU's John Shoniwa and ZAPU's Frank Mbengo, remained—according to the annual report by the AGIS board—"dissatisfied" and of the opinion that "we have done too little for Zimbabwe".[11] The board agreed with the criticism. Assessing the Zimbabwe campaign carried out in late 1977, it concluded that "there was no [real] campaign at all".[12] At a more general level, it, furthermore, self-critically acknowledged that

> we have been lacking updated and penetrating knowledge. The most serious miss concerns the assessment of the situation in Namibia and Zimbabwe. We have not in a sufficiently attentive

1. Letter from Ola Jämtin to Zimbabwe [African] National Union (ZANU-ZIPA), Stockholm, 5 November 1976 (AGA). Jämtin was from 1979 directly involved with the liberation movements as SIDA programme officer at the Swedish embassy in Lusaka. In mid-1980, he was transferred to Salisbury (Harare), where he prepared the opening of SIDA's Zimbabwe office.
2. AGIS: 'Verksamhetsberättelse för AGIS' styrelse 1976-77' ('Activity report by the AGIS' board'), p. 20 [no place or date] (AGA).
3. Ibid.
4. Letter from Edward Ndlovu to Dick Urban Vestbro, Stockholm Africa Group, Lusaka, 8 December 1976 (AGA). Ndlovu's letter was addressed under ANC's old letterhead.
5. Letter from Dick Urban Vestbro to ZAPU, Stockholm, 2 August 1977 (AGA).
6. Ibid. The situation was not much clearer in mid-1977. In his letter to ZAPU, Vestbro explained that the money collected for ZIPA during the Zimbabwe campaign at the end of 1976 "should be sent to the ZIPA address in Quelimane" (ibid.). ZIPA had, however, been dissolved in January 1977.
7. AGIS: 'Beslutsprotokoll från Afrikagruppernas kongress 1977' ('Minuted decisions from the congress of the Africa Groups 1977') [no place or date] (AGA).
8. Letter from Dick Urban Vestbro to ZAPU, Stockholm, 2 August 1977 (AGA).
9. AGIS: 'Beslutsprotokoll från Afrikagruppernas kongress 1977' ('Minuted decisions from the congress of the Africa Groups 1977') [no place or date] (AGA).
10. AGIS: 'Styrelsens verksamhetsberättelse 1977-78' ('Activity report by the board'), p. 4 [no place or date, but presented to AGIS' fourth congress, held in Gothenburg in May 1978] (AGA).
11. Ibid.
12. Ibid., p. 6.

way followed the escalation of the liberation struggle, and not in a sufficiently quick and force-ful manner observed the neo-colonial manoeuvres in these states.[1]

Emphasizing that "SWAPO and PF [now] appear as clearly revolutionary move-ments [and as] the only legitimate representatives of their respective peoples", the AGIS board, however, stated in its annual report that "the uncertainty at the 1977 congress regarding the stability of [the Patriotic Front] does [no longer] need to pre-vail, although ZANU and ZAPU still must take many steps to achieve full unity".[2] On this basis, it recommended the delegates from the fifteen Africa groups in Swe-den[3] to intensify the solidarity work for Zimbabwe. The slogans adopted in May 1978—that is, after the Salisbury agreement between Smith, Chirau, Muzorewa and Sithole—were: "We demand that the Swedish government denounce the so called internal solution in Zimbabwe! No neo-colonial solutions [...]! Support the Patriotic Front!".[4]

These were in the official Swedish context far from revolutionary demands. From being largely isolated with regard to Zimbabwe, the Africa Groups arrived at a position which essentially had been adopted by Fälldin's non-socialist coalition government two years before. Launching a series of important efforts in support of the Zimbabwean liberation struggle, AGIS subsequently concentrated its work on traditional NGO activities, such as information, fund-raising[5] and collection of clothes and medical equipment. In addition to regular articles on Zimbabwe in *Afrikabulletinen*, the solidarity organization initiated close cooperation with other Swedish NGOs, supplying them with information. When the Swedish Union of Sec-ondary School Students (SECO) decided to dedicate the 1979 Operation Day's Work to education in the Zimbabwean refugee camps in Southern Africa, AGIS contributed background information to the campaign. As in 1969—when Janet Mondlane addressed the schools in connection with SECO's *Operation Dagsverke* for the Mozambique Institute[6]—the wife of a nationalist leader would again play a prominent part in the youth effort. Invited by the Swedish government and with financial support from SIDA, Sally Mugabe made one of her six tours through Swe-den in April-May 1979, appearing in secondary schools throughout the country.[7] Lena Johansson of the Africa Groups accompanied her as interpreter, in addition representing SECO's cooperating organization.[8]

With the Swedish government, the Africa Groups came to share the opinion that any support to Zimbabwe should be equally divided between the two Patriotic

1. Ibid., p. 1.
2. Ibid.
3. Ibid., p. 9.
4. AGIS: 'Protokoll fört vid Afrikagruppernas i Sverige fjärde ordinarie kongress i Göteborg, 13-15 maj 1978' ('Minutes from the fourth ordinary congress of the Africa Groups in Sweden, Gothenburg, 13-15 May 1978') [no place or date] (AGA).
5. As in the cases of AGIS' fund-raising campaigns for the other liberation movements in Southern Africa, the monetary results were modest. Between May 1978 and April 1979, a total of 44,500 SEK was raised for the Patriotic Front (AGIS: 'Verksamhetsberättelser [till] AGIS' femte ordinarie kongress, Karlstad, 2-4 juni 1979'/ 'Activity reports [to] AGIS' fifth ordinary congress, Karlstad, 2-4 June 1979' [no place or date]) (AGA). Another 40,000 SEK was raised from May 1979 until the independence elections in February 1980 (AGIS: 'Verksamhetsberättelser [till] AGIS' sjätte ordinarie kongress, Lund, 24-26 maj 1980'/'Activity reports [to] AGIS' sixth ordinary congress, Lund, 24-26 May 1980', [no place or date], p. 15) (AGA).
6. See Sellström Volume I, pp. 467-72 and the chapter on Mozambique.
7. On 1 May 1979, Sally Mugabe joined Olof Palme as one of the main speakers at the Labour Day celebrations in Stockholm (Hallencreutz in Hallencreutz and Axelson op. cit., p. 21).
8. AGIS: 'Verksamhetsberättelser [till] AGIS' femte ordinarie kongress, Karlstad, 2-4 juni 1979'/'Activity reports [to] AGIS' fifth ordinary congress, Karlstad, 2-4 June 1979' [no place or date] (AGA). Employed by the Africa Groups, Johansson later joined SIDA. In 1991, she took up the position as SIDA's coordinator of humanitar-ian assistance in Southern Africa, initially based in Lusaka and later in Pretoria.

Front partners. From May 1978 until April 1979, AGIS collected clothes and medical equipment for the Zimbabwean movements of a total value of about 3 MSEK.[1] Lacking its own channels to forward the material assistance, the organization relied heavily on the Emmaus communities in Björkå, Fnysinge and Stockholm, and, above all, on Bread and Fishes in Västerås.[2] In the case of Zimbabwe, these groups traditionally supported ZANU. In its unitary stand vis-à-vis the two established Zimbabwean liberation movements, this became somewhat ironically a problem for AGIS. In November 1978, the national board found it "unfortunate" that Bread and Fishes had taken a decision to only continue supporting ZANU, as "they [present] their collection as support to [the Patriotic Front] and have received contributions for freight from SIDA under that designation. What do we [then] do to pursue our fairness, not being disadvantageous to ZAPU?", the board asked.[3]

Practical Solidarity: Emmaus and Bread and Fishes

While the Africa Groups in the early 1970s focused on the Portuguese colonies, Emmaus-Björkå constituted an exception within the wider Swedish anti-imperialist movement in that it was, in addition, also involved with practical solidarity for Zimbabwe, Namibia *and* Vietnam.

Forming part of the international Emmaus movement founded by abbé Pierre in France after the Second World War, the Emmaus-Björkå community was set up close to Åseda in southern Sweden in 1965.[4] From the start, the solidarity work focused on the collection of used clothes, which via the Church of Sweden Aid[5]— the relief organization of the official Church of Sweden—were initially sent to different areas in the world where the Lutheran church was involved.[6] Towards the end of the 1960s, the community came to the conclusion that "solidarity with the Third World [was] best expressed by supporting the liberation movements"[7], and in 1971 Emmaus-Björkå started its own shipments of clothes to FRELIMO, MPLA, PAIGC, ZANU, SWAPO and FNL of Vietnam.[8] Via the Church of Sweden Aid, contacts had been made with Zimbabwe, but it was mainly through Sydney Sekeramayi—at the time a student in Lund—that direct relations with ZANU were established.

Together with other Emmaus communities in the country, Emmaus-Björkå not only played a significant role for Sweden's relations with ZANU, but also with the wider Southern African nationalist movement. In 1972, for example, the value of

---

1. Ibid.
2. AGIS: 'Protokoll från styrelsemöte' ('Minutes from board meeting'), Uppsala, 25-26 November 1978 (AGA).
3. Ibid. AGIS' fund-raising and information activities were divided equally between ZANU and ZAPU. During the second half of 1979, the solidarity movement organized important information tours in Sweden by ZAPU teachers and representatives from the ZAPU women's league to balance ZANU's dominance. Immediately after the agreement on Zimbabwe's independence at Lancaster House in December 1979, the organization took the initiative in forming a broad, representative Swedish *ad hoc* committee called 'Friends of the Patriotic Front' (*Patriotiska Frontens Vänner*). Together with Bread and Fishes and Emmaus-Björkå, the Africa Groups delivered a considerable amount of election material to ZANU and ZAPU, and six AGIS representatives were present in Zimbabwe during the election campaign in early 1980. The efforts were greatly appreciated by the PF partners, who both invited AGIS to the independence celebrations in April. Stefan Olsson and Magnus Walan represented the Africa Groups at the celebrations (AGIS: 'Verksamhetsberättelser [till] AGIS' sjätte ordinarie kongress, Lund, 24-26 maj 1980'/'Activity reports [to] AGIS' sixth ordinary congress, Lund, 24-26 May 1980', [no place or date]) (AGA).
4. Emma Leijnse makes a general presentation of Emmaus-Björkå in *Solidaritetens Ansikte: Historien om Emmaus Björkå* ('The Face of Solidarity: The History of Emmaus Björkå'), Leijnse Förlag, Stockholm, 2000.
5. In Swedish, *Lutherhjälpen*.
6. 'Framgångar för Emmaus-Björkå' ('Successes for Emmaus-Björkå') in *Kommentar*, No. 5-6, 1983, p. 43.
7. Ibid.
8. Ibid.

From second-hand clothes to political victory: Christer Johansson of Emmaus-Björkå with ZANU's Kumbirai Kangai, Minister of Labour and Social Services, at Zimbabwe's independence, Harare, April 1980 (Courtesy of Christer Johansson)

the clothes sent to the liberation movements from Mozambique, Angola, Guinea-Bissau, Zimbabwe and Namibia amounted to well over 4 MSEK, representing almost one tenth of the total amount donated by Swedish NGOs to the entire continent of Africa.[1] By 1983—when ANC of South Africa had been included among the recipients—Emmaus-Björkå had delivered around 4,000 tons of clothes, shoes and other material assistance to an estimated value of 100 MSEK.[2] As the solidarity work was combined with information on the liberation struggles, the community's sustained efforts at the local grass roots level in southern Sweden can hardly be exaggerated. Years later, Sekeramayi emphasized that Emmaus-Björkå "was the organization which really got into the homes of the Swedish people, especially appealing for clothes, which we would sort out and send over [to ZANU]".[3]

ZANU and Emmaus-Björkå established particularly close bonds. Visiting the Ministry for Foreign Affairs in Stockholm, the ZANU Chairman Herbert Chitepo had as early as in 1972 on behalf of the liberation movement stressed the importance of Emmaus' work.[4] Many ZANU leaders—among them Simon Muzenda and

1. Jörgen Knudtzon and Miriam Magnusson: 'Svenska icke-statliga organisationers u-hjälp 1972' ('Development aid by Swedish non-governmental organizations in 1972'), SIDA [no place or date] (SDA).
2. Op. cit. in *Kommentar*, No. 5-6, 1983, p. 43.
3. Interview with Sydney Sekeramayi, p. 228. In the interview, the Zimbabwean Minister of State for National Security added: "[A]fter I got to Mozambique [...], I really became very scared [...] because in 1978 the Rhodesians were beginning to poison clothes. Imagine if they had poisoned the clothes that we were sending at that time! We were sending them to people who were in prison, [...] to our leaders. It would have been a really terrible situation. I thought about it and said: 'Oh, help me God if anything happens!' The Rhodesians would just have been very happy. They would have poisoned the clothes and accused the Scandinavians of sending poisoned clothes" (ibid.). The technique of impregnating clothes, blankets and other textiles with chemicals affecting the human respiratory system, provoking suffocation and death, was invented by the Rhodesians at the Chikurubi prison in Salisbury (Harare). It was widely used against freedom fighters in Zimbabwe and later by the Pretoria regime against anti-apartheid activists in South Africa. In the case of Zimbabwe, Ken Flower has related how one of CIO's paid agents, Reverend Arthur Kadonereka of the Methodist Church—who in 1976 accompanied Bishop Muzorewa to the Geneva conference—used to recruit young men for the liberation struggle and supply them with poisoned clothes: "The men would be sent on their way to the guerrilla training camps, but before reaching their destination would die a slow death in the African bush. Many hundreds of recruits became victims of this operation. It became so diabolically successful that exposure seemed inevitable and so the principal perpetrators had to be eliminated. [...] [S]o it was that the bullet-riddled body of [Kadonereka] was found in a motor vehicle in the Salisbury area in 1978" (Flower op. cit., p. 137). Sekeramayi's fears appear well founded. Through the international network of the Moral Re-Armament movement (MRA), Kadonereka visited Sweden in March 1977, staying in Uppsala and Stockholm and addressing local MRA groups. He also met James Dickson of the Moderate Party and some of his fellow MPs (Hallencreutz in Hallencreutz and Axelson op. cit., p. 24).
4. Pierre Schori: Memorandum ('Besök av ZANU's ordförande'/'Visit by ZANU's Chairman'), Ministry for Foreign Affairs, Stockholm, 31 October 1972 (MFA).

Didymus Mutasa[1]—were over the years received by the community members at the former glassworks in the province of Småland, where they shared their frugal way of living and participated in practical activities.

Based outside Västerås in central Sweden, Bread and Fishes[2] (BF) had a similar background. It was formed in 1972 as "a Christian group which wanted to run social activities".[3] Soon branching out into international solidarity work, BF—like Emmaus-Björkå—decided to collect clothes, shoes, medical equipment and other basic items for movements struggling for national liberation, eventually giving priority to SWAPO of Namibia, ZANU of Zimbabwe and ANC of South Africa. Over the years, important amounts in the form of cash support were also extended to these movements.[4] In addition, the organization embarked on project work, notably a health project for SWAPO in Angola together with the Africa Groups from 1980. A first shipment of 5 tons of clothes was made to SWAPO in Zambia in August 1974.[5] Similar shipments to ZANU—initially to Zambia and later to Mozambique—started in early 1975[6], and at the time of Zimbabwe's independence in April 1980 around 300 tons of clothes alone had been delivered to the movement.[7] From the modest beginnings in 1974 until 1993, BF's material assistance to the three Southern African liberation movements represented a combined estimated value of between 300 and 400 MSEK.[8]

Like Emmaus-Björkå, Bread and Fishes continued to assist ZANU during the Southern African 'détente exercise'.[9] In contrast to the Swedish government—which suspended the official support to ZANU and ZAPU between March 1975 and June 1977—and to the Africa Groups—which did not give serious attention to Zimbabwe until early 1978—the two, initially Christian-inspired[10], local NGOs carried the wider Swedish solidarity during a particularly crucial period in the Zimbabwean liberation struggle.[11] Their contribution was emphasized by Kumbirai Kangai, ZANU's former Secretary of Transport and Social Welfare, in July 1995:

> What the solidarity groups perhaps do not realize is the relief caused by the bales of clothes which they shipped. In 1977, the Chimoio refugee camp was attacked. [...] I immediately rushed back to the camp. The little hut where I was staying was burnt. Everything was burnt, my medical books and equipment, stethoscopes and blood pressure cuffs. Everything was destroyed. I remained with the pair of trousers that I had. It was raining very heavily. [...] I [...] went to Beira. I looked around and saw some bales of clothes which had arrived from Sweden. I quickly took them, rushed back to the camp and distributed the clothes to the people [...].

1. Interview with Didymus Mutasa, pp. 216-17.
2. In Swedish, *Brödet och Fiskarna*.
3. 'Bread and Fishes', speech by Eva Strimling [no place or date, but 1982]. Documents on Bread and Fishes have kindly been made available by Bertil Högberg, former chairman of the organization. The source of the material supplied by this leading member of BF, AGIS and ISAK is referenced as BHC.
4. Until Namibia's independence, Bread and Fishes raised 700,000 SEK as cash support to SWAPO. The corresponding amount to ZANU until 1980 was 440,000 and to ANC until 1993 130,000 SEK (Bertil Högberg: 'Det materiella stödet till befrielserörelserna från Brödet och Fiskarna'/'The material support from Bread and Fishes', [Uppsala], 7 March 1997) (BHC).
5. Bread and Fishes: 'Verksamhetsberättelse 1974' ('Annual report 1974') [no place or date] (BHC).
6. Bread and Fishes: 'Verksamhetsberättelse 1975' ('Annual report 1975'), Västerås, January 1976 (BHC).
7. Bertil Högberg: 'Det materiella stödet till befrielserörelserna från Brödet och Fiskarna' ('The material support to the liberation movements from Bread and Fishes'), [Uppsala], 7 March 1997 (BHC).
8. Ibid.
9. In early 1976, however, BF decided to temporarily suspend the deliveries to the Zimbabwean refugees. After consultations with Tore Bergman and Emmaus-Björkå, they were resumed during the second half of the year. The bales of clothes sent to Mozambique were on ZANU's advice addressed to 'MURE', or to MUgabe and TekeRE (Letter from Bertil Högberg to the author, Uppsala, 17 March 1999).
10. Emmaus-Björkå and Bread and Fishes soon followed a socialist orientation.
11. The two organizations received substantial contributions from SIDA to finance their shipments to Southern Africa. It is possible that the combination of their exclusive assistance to ZANU and SIDA's financial support in 1976-77 led ZAPU to believe that Sweden officially supported ZANU.

Mutton stew in a rebuilt pigsty: Robert Mugabe at Bread and Fishes in Västerås, September 1977 (Photo: Pressens Bild)

> I tell you, it was a big relief! I am mentioning this to illustrate what actually happens to a person in the bush who has no alternative. He has no money to buy anything. And all of a sudden somebody comes and says: 'Hey! Here is another pair![1]

BF's role was notably acknowledged by the newly appointed ZANU President Robert Mugabe[2] when he came to Sweden for the first time in mid-September 1977. Invited by the government[3], he insisted after a long journey on first going to Västerås, some 120 kilometres west of Stockholm.[4] In marked contrast to his later high-profile official visits as Prime Minister of independent Zimbabwe[5], immediately upon arrival "Mugabe and his colleagues squeezed into a Volkswagen minibus to go to Västerås to call on [...] Bread and Fishes, [where they] had mutton stew [...] in a rebuilt pigsty".[6]

During his stay in September 1977, the internationally largely unknown—and as a 'terrorist' often vilified—ZANU leader also visited the headquarters of the Church of Sweden Mission in Uppsala. Mugabe's appearance at the official ecclesiastical centre was a result of remarkable contacts initiated in early 1976. A year later—in January 1977—influential representatives of CSM had, in addition, entered into direct contact with Joshua Nkomo following the exodus of students from the Manama secondary school in south-western Zimbabwe. At the beginning of 1977—as the Swedish government prepared a resumption of the assistance to the

---

1. Interview with Kumbirai Kangai, pp. 215-16.
2. Mugabe was appointed President at ZANU's enlarged Central Committee meeting in Chimoio, Mozambique, on 4 September 1977.
3. 'Vi accepterar bara en kolonial motpart' ('We only accept one colonial counterpart') in *Upsala Nya Tidning*, 20 September 1977.
4. Conversation with Bo Heinebäck, Sweden's ambassador to South Africa, Cape Town, 6 February 1999.
5. As Prime Minister, Mugabe paid his first official visit to Sweden in September 1981.
6. Anders Mellbourn: 'Mugabe mötte regeringen, hustrun Afrikagrupperna' ('Mugabe met the government, his wife the Africa Groups') in *Dagens Nyheter*, 25 September 1981.

PF partners—important links concerning humanitarian concerns had thus already been established between CSM and ZANU and ZAPU.[1]

A Novel Dimension: Church of Sweden Mission and ZANU

Mugabe left Zimbabwe together with Edgar Tekere—who in September 1977 became Secretary General of ZANU[2]—shortly after the Chitepo murder. Crossing the border into Mozambique through the assistance of the Catholic church[3], they were in early April 1975 received by local FRELIMO cadres and taken to a camp in Manica province. This was at the time of the clampdown on ZANU in Zambia and during the latter stage of the transition preceding Mozambique's independence. Although Mugabe and Tekere managed to carry out political work among the Zimbabwean refugees in the area, their presence was kept secret. Due to the leadership struggle within ZANU and to the developments in Zambia, Mugabe was "viewed with great suspicion by FRELIMO's leadership".[4] Immediately after Mozambique's independence in late June 1975, the two ZANU leaders were transferred to Quelimane in the province of Zambézia—far from the Zimbabwe border—where they had no contacts with the outside world. The situation only changed in January 1976, when Mugabe was allowed to visit Britain.[5]

Mugabe's situation and whereabouts caused concern in Sweden. Sally Mugabe —who again visited the country in May-June 1975—reported that she did not know where her husband was.[6] The Foreign Ministry therefore asked the embassies in Tanzania and Zambia for possible information.[7] As no conclusive evidence was forthcoming[8], Per Wästberg decided to publicly raise the issue in the liberal newspaper *Dagens Nyheter*. Wästberg was particularly well placed to do so. He had not only maintained close contacts with the nationalist movement in Zimbabwe since the late 1950s[9], but as a member of the official CCHA, Amnesty International and IDAF he was well informed about the developments after Chitepo's death. Above all, the well-known author and leading journalist belonged to the Swedish Amnesty group which as early as in 1965 had adopted Mugabe as a prisoner of conscience and for a period of ten years regularly corresponded with him.

---

1. Ngwabi Bhebe's study *The ZAPU and ZANU Guerrilla Warfare and the Evangelical Lutheran Church in Zimbabwe* (Mambo Press, Gweru, in association with Studia Missionalia Upsaliensia, Uppsala, 1999) was not available at the time of writing the following text on the Church of Sweden Mission and the Zimbabwean liberation movements. Bhebe largely draws on SDA and CSA primary sources. Confirming the general conclusions reached with regard to CSM and the role of official Swedish assistance to ZANU and ZAPU, minor discrepancies and different emphases in Bhebe's study are mainly due to the fact that he did not have access to the documentation held at the Swedish Ministry for Foreign Affairs.
2. In April 1980, Tekere was appointed Minister of Manpower Planning and Development in independent Zimbabwe's first government. Involved in the murder of a white farm manager, he was detained in August 1980 and brought to trial. Although acquitted, he left the government in January and lost his position as Secretary General of ZANU in August 1981. In May 1987, Tekere was removed from ZANU's Central Committee, subsequently forming the opposition Zimbabwe Unity Movement (ZUM).
3. Janice McLaughlin: *On the Frontline: Catholic Missions in Zimbabwe's Liberation War*, Baobab Books, Harare, 1996, pp. 26-27.
4. Martin and Johnson (1981) op. cit., p. 208.
5. Ibid., p. 209.
6. Cable from Bengt Säve-Söderbergh, Ministry for Foreign Affairs, to the Swedish embassies in Dar es Salaam and Lusaka, 14 May 1975 (MFA).
7. Ibid.
8. According to the information obtained in Zambia, Mugabe had been arrested by the transitional government in Mozambique (Cable from Anders Bjurner, Swedish embassy in Lusaka, to the Ministry for Foreign Affairs, Lusaka, 16 May 1975) (MFA).
9. See Sellström Volume I, pp. 307-10.

Touring Swedish schools: Sally Mugabe with Kerstin Rimmerfors at Lundskolan in Järfälla outside Stockholm, September 1977 (Photo: Paul Rimmerfors)

Under the heading 'Where is Robert Mugabe?', Wästberg's call was published on 1 June 1975. It was at the same time a portrait of the ZANU leader and a critical comment on the détente policy in Southern Africa. Introducing Mugabe to the Swedish public, Wästberg wrote that "many observers have seen him as the best possible leader of a united African front and as the first President of Zimbabwe".[1] Now he had disappeared, rumoured to be under arrest in Mozambique: "No official communiqués mention his fate. [...] I have tried to inquire of [the Mozambican] Prime Minister Chissano [...], but I do not get an answer. [...] Is [Mugabe] a victim of the détente policy in Southern Africa?", Wästberg asked.[2]

Accused of uncritically taking sides with ZANU and Mugabe, Wästberg repeated his questions one week later, stating that

> the secret diplomacy which in Southern Africa now has assumed Kissingerian proportions must have its limits, despite the exceptionally complicated game which is going on. [...] A man disappears. Some months pass. His family is not notified. No lawyer is called. Officially it is not known in which country he is. [...] Perhaps Southern Africa in its history has never been confronted with such decisive decisions for the future as now. [...] It would be a pity if this dramatic course of events is not fully observed by the press and the [public] opinion.[3]

At the same time, Sally Mugabe raised the question of her husband's whereabouts. Addressing the congress of the Centre Party women's league in Sundsvall in northern Sweden together with the future Prime Minister Thorbjörn Fälldin, she confirmed in mid-June 1975 that she did not know where Robert Mugabe was.[4]

Mugabe's first meeting with representatives of the Swedish government took place in Maputo in late February 1976, when he with Göran Hasselmark and Anders Möllander from the local embassy discussed the events leading up to the

1. Per Wästberg: 'Var finns Robert Mugabe?' ('Where is Robert Mugabe?') in *Dagens Nyheter*, 1 June 1975.
2. Ibid.
3. Per Wästberg: 'Mugabe och den hemliga diplomatin' ('Mugabe and the secret diplomacy') in *Dagens Nyheter*, 6 June 1975.
4. Ingrid Marklund: 'Afrikas kvinnor jämlika i kampen' ('Africa's women equal in the struggle') in *Sundsvalls Tidning*, 15 June 1975. A visit by Sally Mugabe to Sweden in November 1975 was cancelled on short notice when she was called to Mozambique to meet her husband after more than eleven years of separation (Hallencreutz in Hallencreutz and Axelson op. cit., p. 20).

Chitepo assassination and a possible resumption of the direct assistance to ZANU.[1] Through Didymus Mutasa and Guy Clutton-Brock[2]—who he had visited in Britain the previous month—Mugabe had by that time made a request for humanitarian assistance to the Church of Sweden Mission.[3] The circular call—'Appeal for aid for young Zimbabwe'—was addressed to CSM's Africa secretary and former missionary educationalist in Zimbabwe, Tore Bergman. According to the appeal,

> Mr. Robert Mugabe is seeking aid to help maintain the thousands of young Africans who have now crossed the border from Rhodesia into Mozambique. They are young patriots, mostly boys and girls in their teens, who are driven to desperation by the conditions prevailing in their country [...]. In the grip of the 'police state' maintained by the rebel colonialist regime, they see no way of gaining freedom for their country other than by training themselves across its borders to liberate it from without.[4]

In his personal capacity[5], Bergman replied to Clutton-Brock in mid-March 1976. Having visited the CSM missionary area in Mberengwa-Gwanda-Mtetengwe in southern Zimbabwe in November 1975, Bergman noted that "some of the youngsters in Mozambique are members of the Lutheran church or come from that area. [...] I met some of their parents in November and shared [...] their anxiety over their children, of whom, of course, they had heard nothing after their departure".[6] He further stated that he would like to "attempt to secure some help in response to your appeal, either from my own organization or others with which I [am in] contact".[7] In order to proceed, he asked for more information regarding the assistance needed.

In response, Clutton-Brock wrote that after consultations with Mutasa he concluded that "it might be best if you were to be in touch direct with Robert Mugabe [in Quelimane]", adding that "a close colleague of Robert's is Edgar Tekere, who might also be one to correspond [with]. Both are wholly reliable and would certainly ensure that any aid sent would be used for the purpose for which it is given".[8] The following week, Bergman wrote to Mugabe, stating that he had "no great illusions about the help I can give or obtain, but a few lines from you or one of your colleagues would be very encouraging and helpful".[9] Apprehensive about the reactions his contact with the ZANU leader could cause both within the Church of Sweden Mission and within the Evangelical Lutheran Church of Zimbabwe

---

1. Anders Möllander: Memorandum ('Samtal med en syd-rhodesisk nationalistledare'/'Conversation with a Southern Rhodesian nationalist leader'), Swedish embassy, Maputo, 27 February 1976 (SDA). See also Möllander op. cit., p. 38.
2. Together with Mutasa, the Anglican missionary Guy Clutton-Brock set up the non-racial, Christian-inspired Cold Comfort Farm Society in eastern Zimbabwe. Deemed subversive, the society was declared an unlawful organization and totally dispossessed in early 1971. Mutasa, the chairman of the society, was at the same time imprisoned and Clutton-Brock deported to Britain (see Guy and Molly Clutton-Brock: *Cold Comfort Confronted*, Mowbrays, London and Oxford, 1972, and Didymus Mutasa: *Rhodesian Black behind Bars*, Mowbrays, London and Oxford, 1974). After independence, Mutasa founded a new Cold Comfort Farm Society outside Harare. Actively engaged against apartheid, it was *inter alia* supported by Sweden (see the interview with Didymus Mutasa, p. 220).
3. On the Church of Sweden Mission in Zimbabwe, see Sellström Volume I, pp. 311-19.
4. Guy Clutton-Brock: 'Appeal for aid for young Zimbabwe', Clwyd, January 1976 (CSA).
5. Bergman explained in 1997 that he, "due to the criticism [the church] received for providing funds to [the World Council of Churches'] Programme to Combat Racism and CSM's contacts with armed movements" decided to write in a personal capacity (Interview with Tore Bergman, p. 265).
6. Letter from Tore Bergman to Guy Clutton-Brock, [no place, but Uppsala], 12 March 1976 (CSA).
7. The letter was copied to Helge Alm of the Swedish Methodist church. Bergman was also in close contact with Bread and Fishes (Letter from Bertil Högberg to the author, Uppsala, 17 March 1999).
8. Letter from Guy Clutton-Brock to Tore Bergman, Clwyd, 26 March 1976 (CSA).
9. Letter from Tore Bergman to Robert Mugabe, Uppsala, 1 April 1976 (CSA).

(ELCZ), shortly thereafter the CSM Africa secretary also had a letter delivered to the ELCZ Bishop Jonas Shiri in Bulawayo.[1] In the letter, Bergman wrote:

> [T]here is bound to be a question asked here in Sweden, [namely] whether the assistance [proposed] is not de facto, indirectly, assistance for arms and soldiers. Can a church and a mission organization involve itself in this? The reply [...] is not so easy. Are we not already as whites involved against the blacks? Who started the fighting—the strong man show—in Rhodesia? If we remain passive, are we not already taking sides, even militarily? But church people here cannot be convinced. [...] I would [...] be glad to have your reactions and, if possible, recommendations.[2]

Mugabe replied from Quelimane on 12 April 1976. While appreciating the concern for the Zimbabwean refugees, he openly discussed the armed struggle and thus did not make Bergman's personal commitment to assist less difficult. "It is", Mugabe stated, "because the settler community has adamantly denied us the right to acquire full political rights in our own country that we have resorted to an armed confrontation as the only feasible method of attaining our objectives".[3] By clarifying that the younger refugees were not being trained for the guerrilla war, Mugabe, however, left an opening for strictly humanitarian assistance:

> [S]everal thousands [of] young men and women have crossed the Rhodesian border into Mozambique to offer themselves for military training. The present number of people we are handling exceeds 20,000, distributed among several camps in Mozambique and Tanzania. [...] Certainly, those below seventeen are still too tender for the rigours of military life [...] so we must continue to cater for their educational needs. Each camp in Mozambique has [...] an educational project, plus [...] a serious agricultural project based on co-operative self-help [and] a medical side. Our humanitarian needs are thus many and varied. [They] cover educational supplies, agricultural implements [and] medical supplies, over and above welfare needs, such as food, clothing, blankets [and] shoes. My fellow worker Edgar Tekere is writing to give you more detail[s]. Please help us.[4]

Tekere—who at the time served as secretary and treasurer of ZANU's Camps' Relief Committee—followed up Mugabe's letter by sending Bergman a long and detailed account ten days later. Giving a breakdown of the Zimbabwean refugees in Mozambique, he indicated that 7 per cent—or 1,400—were between seven and fifteen years of age and therefore not eligible for military training. To cater for their educational needs, ZANU was in the process of setting up a specialist education committee, to be based in Britain.[5] Ending his comprehensive presentation of ZANU's needs in Zimbabwe, Tekere stated:

> I did take note of your modest remark about not being able to do very much for us in relation to the size of our needs. I however thought it best to give you as complete a view as possible. Perhaps it will give you an interesting talking [point] while you make friends on our behalf.[6]

Tekere's letter "rather overwhelmed" Bergman, who "had not quite thought in those terms".[7] Directly informed about the situation in Mozambique, he tried

---

1. In 1975, Shiri succeeded CSM's Sigfrid Strandvik as the first African Bishop of ELCZ.
2. Letter from Tore Bergman to Reverend Jonas Shiri, [no place or date, but according to a handwritten note delivered at the beginning of April 1976] (CSA). The letter was forwarded by a visitor from Sweden. Conscious of the fact that it could have serious consequences, Bergman asked Shiri to "destroy it" after reading (ibid.). Bishop Shiri visited Uppsala later in 1976 (Letter from Tore Bergman to Reverend Jonas Shiri, Uppsala, 16 September 1976) (CSA).
3. Letter from Robert Mugabe to Tore Bergman, Quelimane, 12 April 1976 (CSA).
4. Ibid.
5. Letter from Edgar Tekere to Tore Bergman, Quelimane, 23 April 1976 (CSA).
6. Ibid.
7. Interview with Tore Bergman, p. 265.

through various channels to mobilize support. He forwarded Tekere's account to SIDA[1] and initiated a discussion within the Church of Sweden regarding the Zimbabwean refugee youth in Mozambique. Interviewed in 1997, the former CSM Africa secretary explained:

> During my visits to Zimbabwe [...] and through correspondence I was in contact with the parents of some of these children, who expressed concern over what had happened to them and how they were being cared for. Addressing meetings in Sweden, I tried to question the attitude among some church people that those who had left Zimbabwe for political reasons and taken refuge in other countries were being called terrorists, as was then the term. Why should the act of crossing the border change our attitude to them?[2]

At a time when the official Swedish humanitarian assistance to the Zimbabwean liberation movements was suspended and the Africa Groups still talked about the defunct ZIPA, together with Emmaus-Björkå and Bread and Fishes Bergman placed ZANU at the centre of the Swedish Zimbabwe debate, particularly within the church. Although "not much came of it at that time" and he was "unable to find sources of support"[3], his active concern had important consequences. Advocating support for those who had gone into exile, his views were, notably, accepted by the Church of Sweden Mission Board[4], which marked the beginning of CSM's indirect, but substantial, involvement with the liberation movements in Southern Africa. As early as in April 1976, Bergman approached the General Secretary of the recently established Christian Council of Mozambique (CCM), Reverend Isaac Mahlalela, to explore the possibilities of channelling support to the Zimbabwean refugee children in the country.[5] Soon thereafter, CSM started to support CCM to enable the organization to administer assistance to the Zimbabwean camps.[6] At about the same time, the Lutheran World Federation established an office in Maputo through which assistance was also channelled.[7]

Bergman's correspondence with Mugabe and Tekere led ZANU to send a delegation to Sweden in September 1976, immediately prior to the formation of the Patriotic Front. It included Didymus Mutasa, Rex Chiwara, ZANU's representative to Western Europe, and Ruvimbika Tekere, Edgar Tekere's wife and at the time in charge of the ZANU women's affairs in London.[8] They held meetings with CSM in Uppsala[9] and SIDA in Stockholm.[10] The delegation also visited Emmaus-Björkå in southern Sweden.[11] The meeting in Uppsala was the first in a series of contacts which one year later—in September 1977—culminated in the ZANU President's appearance at the CSM headquarters with a high-profile ZANU delegation.[12]

---

1. Hallencreutz in Hallencreutz and Axelson op. cit., p. 23.
2. Interview with Tore Bergman, p. 265.
3. Ibid.
4. Ibid.
5. Letter from Tore Bergman to the Christian Council of Mozambique, [no place, but Uppsala], 29 April 1976 (CSA).
6. Interview with Tore Bergman, p. 265.
7. Ibid.
8. Ibid.
9. Ibid.
10. Hallencreutz in Hallencreutz and Axelson op. cit., p. 24.
11. Interview with Didymus Mutasa, p. 216.
12. Among those who visited Uppsala with Mugabe in September 1977 were Sally Mugabe, Mukudzei Mudzi (ZANU Secretary for External Affairs) and Rugare Gumbo (Secretary for Information and Publicity). Before the consultations with CSM, Mugabe addressed a public meeting in Uppsala arranged by the Nordic Africa Institute (Tord Harlin: 'Minnesanteckningar förda vid samtalen mellan representanter för den Patriotiska Frontens ZANU-grupp, Lutherska Världsförbundets svenska sektion och Svenska Kyrkans Mission'/'Notes from the discussions between representatives of the ZANU group of the Patriotic Front, the Swedish section of the Lutheran World Federation and the Church of Sweden Mission', Uppsala, 19 September 1977) (CSA).

Visiting Sweden for the first time: ZANU President Robert Mugabe welcomed by Bo Heinebäck (left) and David Wirmark of the Foreign Ministry at Arlanda airport, Stockholm, September 1977 (Photo: Paul Rimmerfors)

Mainly as a result of the contacts established with Bergman, Mugabe—himself a Catholic—included a visit to the Lutheran centre in Uppsala during his first stay in Sweden. The meeting with the Church of Sweden Mission was chaired by Carl Fredrik Hallencreutz and *inter alia* attended by Tore Bergman, Tord Harlin—who had been involved with ZAPU concerning Zimbabwean refugees in Zambia—and Hugo Söderström. In his address on the role of the church, Mugabe gave a historical account of the churches and liberation, also discussing the issue of religion in an independent Zimbabwe. With regard to the armed struggle, he stated that "we do not say that you necessarily have to support [it], but the churches are duty bound to support the cause of justice. They must, at the very least, loudly denounce the regime". Mugabe commended the Catholic Bishops' Conference, the Christian Council and Christian Care[1], but criticized his hosts. "The Swedish mission", he said, "has not distinguished itself by denouncing the regime"[2], adding that

> it is true that we receive support from the government and SIDA, but we appreciate the assistance even more when it comes from people like yourselves. A government is a government. We would like to have our cause as deeply rooted in the hearts of the [Swedish] people as possible. [...] You who have been [to Zimbabwe] can better than others explain [...] how the people there are dehumanized. [...] We would like to get much more support and wish to continue to stay in contact.[3]

Manama: CSM and ZAPU 'Going to Geneva'

That a delegation from ZANU—a liberation movement waging armed struggle against the secular rulers of a country in which the official Church of Sweden Mission had a significant presence[4]—was received in Uppsala as early as in September

---

1. As much as half of Christian Care's external resources were provided by the Swedish government.
2. Hugo Söderström, a CSM missionary who had lived many years in Zimbabwe, shared Mugabe's critical view, stating that "we have to admit that we have not done as much as the Roman Catholic church when it comes to protests against the regime" (Tord Harlin: 'Minnesanteckningar...'/'Notes...', Uppsala, 19 September 1977) (CSA).
3. Ibid.
4. In August 1976, however, there remained only twelve Swedish missionaries in Zimbabwe (Letter from Bo Kälfors ('Missionärer varnas i Rhodesia'/'Missionaries are warned in Rhodesia'), Swedish ambassador to Botswana, to the Ministry for Foreign Affairs, Gaborone, 24 August 1976) (MFA).

1976 was significant. The Smith regime had by then begun its general clampdown on the missionary societies in Zimbabwe. In August 1976—one month before the visit—Hilary Squires, Smith's Minister of Law and Order, warned in the Salisbury House of Assembly that "the government is ready to act against missions which become involved in the aiding and abetting of terrorists". "There is", he said, "a limit to what can be tolerated in the name of freedom of religion and expression of opinion".[1]

The repressive measures against the churches in the mid-1970s forced the CSM missionaries to become more closely involved with the nationalist cause.[2] In the case of ELCZ, a number of Zimbabwean pastors and other church members had been imprisoned as a result of political activities.[3] Their Swedish colleagues stayed in close contact with them. Regularly reporting on his attendance at court cases and prison visits, Hugo Söderström, in particular, kept the Church of Sweden Mission abreast of the developments regarding the detainees.[4] Others informed them about the security forces' cruelties in the missionary area.[5]

Three ELCZ pastors and one youth secretary[6] were notably held as political prisoners at the Wha Wha detention camp outside Gwelo (now Gweru) from mid-1975. One of them was an outspoken ZAPU supporter.[7] Söderström raised their case, and one year later he was in a position to report that one of the detainees—Reverend Arote Vellah—had "a distinct chance to get permission to go overseas for studies if the Church of Sweden Mission would take the responsibility for all the expenses which will arise".[8] CSM guaranteed the necessary funds. Not only Vellah, but also the remaining ELCZ members were subsequently released and brought to Sweden, where they stayed with different congregations.[9] In Uppsala, Vellah added his voice to the Africa Groups' denunciation of the Smith regime.[10]

What eventually brought about CSM's direct humanitarian cooperation with the Patriotic Front—in this case ZAPU—was the so called 'Manama exodus' in late January 1977.[11] This event—and the subsequent involvement by the Swedish church—has been interpreted by the ZAPU leadership as a breakthrough not only in the relations with the official missionary society, but with Sweden in general.

---

1. *The Herald*, 19 August 1976.
2. Other events brought CSM on a collision course with the Rhodesian regime. On behalf of the Swedish Ecumenical Council, CSM was in the mid-1970s collecting information on Swedish companies in South Africa, preparing a policy statement on sanctions. Extending the study to include Swedish subsidiaries in Rhodesia, the missionary society was censured by the Smith regime. In February 1975, for example, CSM's Lester Wikström was denied entry into the country and as a 'prohibited immigrant' expelled from the airport in Bulawayo (Letter to the author from Lester Wikström, Uppsala, 26 May 1999).
3. Interview with Tore Bergman, p. 264.
4. For example, letter from Hugo Söderström to Tore Bergman, [no place], 23 February 1976 (CSA). Söderström noted that "many Africans seem to be afraid to visit the prisoners, for fear of getting into trouble themselves". He also stated that "this government will hardly stay long in power".
5. In August 1976, Ernst Timm informed CSM "about a couple of cases where civilians have been hideously tortured [and that] a man died at the Mnene hospital after being beaten" (Letter from Ernst Timm to Tore Furberg, Bulawayo, 19 August 1976) (CSA).
6. Reverends E. Masiyane, N. Ramakgapola, A. Vellah and A. Malala.
7. Interview with Tore Bergman, p. 264. In his capacity as CSM's Africa secretary, Bergman also visited the prisoners at Wha Wha (ibid.).
8. Letter from Hugo Söderström to the Church of Sweden Mission Board, Salisbury, 11 September 1976 (CSA).
9. Interview with Tore Bergman, p. 264.
10. 'Från Wha Wha Fängelset till Uppsala' ('From the Wha Wha Prison to Uppsala') in *Afrikabulletinen*, No. 1, 1979, pp. 14-15. Vellah returned to Zimbabwe after independence and became the headmaster of the Manama secondary school, which together with his own case had played such a central role for the involvement of CSM in the liberation struggle (Tord Harlin: *Trons Öga* ('The Eye of Faith'), Verbum, Stockholm, 1991, p. 49).
11. Tore Bergman stated in 1997 that "[i]n the case of ZAPU, it was the Manama exodus that initiated our contacts" (Interview with Tore Bergman, p. 266).

Although he acknowledged that Sweden probably "had a much wider focus", ZAPU's former Secretary of Administration John Nkomo said in 1995:

> I think that what encouraged Sweden to really come out in full force was the exodus of the population in Mberengwa and Gwanda, which is predominantly Lutheran. What they did later on was to try [to] provide as much comfort as possible to the people that they regarded as part of their community.[1]

The background to the church's active involvement was that the liberation war reached the CSM missionary area in southern Matabeleland in 1976. More and more young people left the area to either join ZANU in Mozambique or ZAPU in Zambia. Towards the end of January 1977, the Manama secondary school became one of the first schools to move, involving more than three hundred pupils, seven teachers, three nurses and an ELCZ pastor. Paulos Matjaka was one of the teachers. He later wrote:

> We left in the evening of the first Sunday of the first term of the academic year. Some children in Form I were less than 13 years old. After travelling through the bush in pitch darkness throughout the night, sunrise found us crossing the Shashi river into Botswana en route to Zambia.[2] We called it 'going to Geneva'. [...] We had two armed guerrillas in our company.[3] [...] With the assistance of the international world, we finally forced our way through from Botswana to Zambia. We all cherished the idea that we would [...] train in guerrilla warfare and return to liberate our country.[4]

The Manama students were far from being the only ones to 'go to Geneva' at that time. In 1977, thousands of recruits and refugees poured out across Zimbabwe's western border, as they had done earlier—and were still doing—in the east. Crowding the refugee camps in Botswana, most of them were transported to Zambia. At its peak in mid-1977, an airlift to Zambia carried almost a thousand Zimbabwean refugees a week.[5] Assisted by the Zambian authorities, ZAPU set up two school camps outside Lusaka for the children, the 'Victory Camp' for girls and the 'J.Z. Moyo Camp' for boys, the latter named in honour of ZAPU's Vice-President, killed by a Rhodesian parcel bomb in Lusaka on 22 January 1977.[6]

The Manama exodus affected the Church of Sweden Mission deeply. The CSM station at Manama had been founded as early as in 1938 and many missionaries had been active there. Tore Bergman had set up the Manama secondary school in the early 1960s and soon thereafter Tord Harlin became its headmaster and vicar.[7]

---

1. Interview with John Nkomo, p. 224.
2. Manama is situated some 40 kilometres from the Botswana border.
3. The Manama exodus has often been presented as 'abduction'. The term is, for example, used by Hallencreutz (in Hallencreutz and Axelson op. cit., p. 22) and was certainly in the minds of those involved at the Church of Sweden Mission. It has, however, never been conclusively established whether the action was voluntarily organized by the students or forcibly imposed by ZIPRA/ZAPU.
4. Paulos Matjaka Nare: 'Education and the War' in Ngwabi Bhebe and Terence Ranger (eds): *Society in Zimbabwe's Liberation War*, Volume II, University of Zimbabwe Publications, Harare, 1995, p. 130.
5. Via the Lutheran World Federation (LWF) and the Zambian Christian Refugee Service (ZCRS), the Church of Sweden Mission and the Church of Sweden Aid contributed substantial amounts and efforts to the airlift from Botswana to Zambia. At the time, the LWF representative in Zambia was the Swede Nils-Göran Gussing, while the Norwegian Øystein Tveter served as the local director of ZCRS (see Björn Ryman: 'Utökad Lutherhjälp till Flyktingarna'/'Increased Lutheran Assistance to the Refugees' in *Lutherhjälpen*, No. 3, 1978, p. 7).
6. Jason Moyo was an outspoken advocate of the armed struggle and of unity between ZANU and ZAPU. He played a key role in creating the Patriotic Front and in keeping it together at the 1976 Geneva conference. Commenting upon his death, Smith's CIO Director Ken Flower wrote that it "spelt the end of attempts at unity between the fighting forces of the nationalist movement. [T]hereafter ZIPRA went its own way" (Flower op. cit., p. 179).
7. After serving as a CSM missionary in Zimbabwe, Harlin worked for the Church of Sweden Aid (CSA) between 1975 and 1985. He was consecrated Bishop of Uppsala in 1990 and chaired CSA from 1992 until 1995.

ZANLA guerrillas posing for Tord Harlin of the Church of Sweden Aid close to the Masase mission, Matabeleland, prior to the 1980 independence elections (Photo: Tord Harlin/IKON, Svenska kyrkans bildbyrå)

The youngsters who 'went to Geneva' were known to CSM, which subsequently received "disconsolate letters" from parents asking for information and help.[1] Over the years, many future Zimbabwean nationalist leaders had, in addition, attended CSM schools at Manama. This was, notably, the case with Edward Ndlovu, former ZAPU Secretary General and at the time Acting Secretary for Foreign Affairs.[2] The motivation and necessary political contacts for a direct humanitarian effort were thus at hand.

The Church of Sweden Mission Board decided on 1 March 1977 that Harlin should travel to Zimbabwe, Botswana and Zambia to "try to get as much information as possible regarding the fate of the Manama youth".[3] At the end of March, he met Joshua Nkomo together with John Nkomo and Edward Ndlovu in Lusaka. Explaining that he was about to go to Sweden—and that he wished to meet both the Church of Sweden Mission and the Swedish section of the Lutheran World Federation—the ZAPU President explained that his organization was preparing an educational project called 'New Manama' in favour of the Zimbabwean refugee youth in Zambia. A request to CSM for financial support would be submitted.[4]

Before returning to Sweden, Harlin received ZAPU's comprehensive 'New Manama' project proposal, which included the construction of school buildings, educational equipment, text books etc. for an estimated amount of around 10 MSEK. ZAPU wanted Sweden to take care of the project via CSM "so that the contact with 'their' people from Manama could be maintained". Concluding his impressions from the journey, the future Uppsala Bishop wrote in his report that

1. Harlin op. cit., p. 48.
2. Ndlovu had since 1969 been closely involved with the Swedish government and SIDA (see Sellström Volume I, pp. 358-64). In the absence of Joshua Nkomo, between July 1977 and January 1980 he led the ZAPU delegations to four out of six official aid negotiations with Sweden. On the remaining two occasions, ZAPU was represented by Dumiso Dabengwa (December 1977) and John Nkomo (May 1979).
3. Tord Harlin: 'Rapport från Tord Harlins resa till södra Afrika den 21 mars-6 april 1977' ('Report on Tord Harlin's journey to Southern Africa, 21 March-6 April 1977'), Uppsala, 19 April 1977 (CSA).
4. Ibid.

the question of principle whether CSM could or should assist the Manama youth through the political organization ZAPU—which [...] conducts a guerrilla war against the Smith regime—must be weighed against the factual situation, which is that there is no alternative [way] to help [...]. CSM is probably the first organization to receive a request of this kind. CSM has, in addition, had the possibility of influencing the [proposed] curricula, with the result that religious instruction has been included.[1]

Recommending direct CSM support to ZAPU's 'New Manama' project, Harlin added that—"in order to underline the political neutrality of the [Swedish] church and mission"—he found it "important that assistance of this magnitude is balanced by support [also] through ZANU and, to a certain extent, UANC".[2]

Acting swiftly, CSM resolved on 19 April 1977 to consider the project in a positive spirit, although it found the cost estimates "unreasonably high" and that the proposal ought to be reformulated.[3] It was at the same time agreed to approach the Lutheran World Federation, the Ministry for Foreign Affairs and SIDA regarding possible funding.[4] A letter to that effect was sent a week later to ZAPU in Lusaka.[5] When Joshua Nkomo visited Sweden in early May 1977, the 'New Manama' project was thus high on the agenda. At a meeting between the ZAPU President, CSM and the Swedish section of LWF in Stockholm,[6] Nkomo stated on 10 May that "the Church of Sweden after many years of missionary work constituted a link between the peoples of Zimbabwe and Sweden".[7] ZAPU and CSM had a particular responsibility for the children and he hoped that support for the 'New Manama' project would be forthcoming. After Harlin's visit to Zambia, ZAPU had, however, considerably reduced the original project proposal. It now focused on basic needs, as well as on educational facilities. A modified request—'Urgent requirements for children from 5 to 15 years'—was therefore submitted by Nkomo. It included clothes, blankets, toiletries, food, text books, bibles etc. for 2,000 girls and 4,000 boys.[8]

Two weeks later—on 25 May 1977—the CSM board decided to grant the equivalent of 80,000 SEK for the procurement of text books, educational equipment and bibles for the refugee youth in Zambia.[9] It was at the same time agreed that the funds should be channelled via the Lutheran World Federation in Geneva.[10] With SIDA support, more substantial amounts were later extended via LWF, the Zambian Christian Refugee Service and the Church of Sweden Aid.[11] Initially, however, the contacts established between CSM and ZAPU after the Man-

---

1. Ibid.
2. Ibid. The information gathered by Harlin indicated that there were even more ELCZ members among the refugees in Mozambique (ibid.). CSM never channelled any support to UANC. According to Tore Bergman, Muzorewa "was regarded by both ZANU and ZAPU as something of an upstart [who] could not be relied upon. [...] UANC [...] was not seen by the liberation movements as the answer to the problems in [Zimbabwe]" (Interview with Tore Bergman, p. 265).
3. Tore Bergman: Memorandum ('Project New Manama'), [no place, but Uppsala], 26 April 1977 (CSA).
4. Ibid.
5. Letter from Tore Bergman [signed by Birgitta Lebel] to Edward Ndlovu, Uppsala, 27 April 1977 (CSA).
6. The CSM representatives to the meeting were Tore Furberg, Biörn Fjärstedt, Carl Fredrik Hallencreutz and Hugo Söderström. Ebbe Arvidsson, Tord Harlin, Thorsten Månson and Björn Ryman represented CSA/LWF. Marika Fahlén from the Ministry for Foreign Affairs and Marianne Sundh from SIDA also attended the meeting.
7. Tord Harlin: 'Minnesanteckningar från överläggningar i Klara församlings kyrkorådsrum den 10 maj 1977' ('Notes from deliberations at the church council's room, Klara congregation, 10 May 1977'), Stockholm, 10 May 1977 (CSA). A cousin of Joshua Nkomo had served as school headmaster at CSM's Mnene mission in the late 1950s.
8. Ibid.
9. Letter from Tore Bergman to Brian Neldner, Lutheran World Federation, Uppsala, 1 June 1977 (CSA).
10. Ibid.
11. Letter from Tore Bergman to Edward Ndlovu, Uppsala, 2 January 1979 (CSA).

ZAPU President Joshua Nkomo addressing the press, Stockholm, May 1977. Seated on his left is Madi Gray of the Africa Groups (Photo: Anders Gunnartz)

ama exodus only resulted in a modest and indirect contribution. Nevertheless, the decision by the Church of Sweden was reached one month before the Swedish government resolved to resume its direct official assistance to the Patriotic Front. It thus contributed to a massive effort, rooted in a broad opinion.

Official Aid to ZANU and ZAPU

Direct, official Swedish humanitarian assistance to the Patriotic Front partners[1] was extended on equal terms from mid-1977.[2] After initial allocations of 2.5 MSEK—granted in June 1977 and made retroactive for the financial year 1976/ 77—the contributions were raised to 5 million each at the end of 1977. Due to increasing numbers of refugees and repeated Rhodesian attacks against the Zimbabwean settlements in Mozambique and Zambia, the assistance was doubled the following two years. The total amounts set aside for each of the two movements in 1978/79 and 1979/80 were, respectively, 10 and 21 MSEK. From 1 July 1977 until Zimbabwe's independence in April 1980, a total of 87 MSEK in current figures was disbursed to ZANU and ZAPU under official cooperation agreements.[3]

Visiting Stockholm in May 1977, Joshua Nkomo was the first of the two Patriotic Front leaders to submit a request for resumed Swedish assistance. Although the visit was made on his own initiative[4], the ZAPU President was *de facto* received as

---

1. Although ZANU and ZAPU had formed the Patriotic Front and in 1979 jointly attended the Lancaster House conference under that banner, they remained two separate entities. Contesting the 1980 elections, ZANU was registered as ZANU-PF, while ZAPU appeared as PF-ZAPU. The names were kept as official designations after Zimbabwe's independence. The relations between the two went from uneasy to hostile during the first half of the 1980s. A series of bilateral talks culminated, however, in the signing of a unity pact in December 1987. Subsequently, the parties amalgamated under the name ZANU-PF.
2. Non-socialist governments—headed by Thorbjörn Fälldin from the Centre Party and Ola Ullsten from the Liberal Party—were in power during the entire period of official Swedish assistance to the Patriotic Front.
3. To this should be added direct assistance outside the agreements, which covered, for example, support to ZAPU's research unit (Zimbabwe Research and Information Centre; ZIRIC) via SAREC; the delivery of a field hospital to ZAPU in late 1978; and significant donations of clothes and shoes to ZANU and ZAPU from the government's stores in 1978 and 1979.
4. Marika Fahlén: Memorandum ('Inför ZAPU-ledaren Nkomos besök i Sverige'/'In view of the visit to Sweden by the ZAPU leader Nkomo'), Ministry for Foreign Affairs, Stockholm, 5 May 1977 (SDA).

a government representative.[1] During a period of two days, Nkomo held in quick succession official meetings with SIDA, the Ministry for Foreign Affairs, Cooperation Minister Ola Ullsten and Foreign Minister Karin Söder.[2] He also met the opposition leader Olof Palme.[3] In addition to discussions with the Church of Sweden Mission regarding the 'New Manama' project, Nkomo emphasized the need for urgent humanitarian support in the form of food, clothes, medicines and vehicles.[4] During the meeting with Foreign Minister Söder, he also expressed the wish to enter into longer term cooperation with Sweden, *inter alia* in the agricultural field.[5] Although the Swedish authorities advised against the suggestion, Nkomo, finally, declared that ZAPU wanted to send cadres to Sweden for higher education.[6] This seemingly minor question would lead the following year to major misunderstandings between the ZAPU leader and the Swedish government.

Official aid negotiations with ZAPU were held in Lusaka in July 1977 and with ZANU in Maputo the following month.[7] At the time, the estimated numbers of Zimbabwean refugees in Zambia and Mozambique were, respectively, 10,000 and 35,000.[8] Apart from the United Nations, international observers had until then not been allowed by the host governments to visit the refugee settlements.[9] The actual needs were therefore left to be specified until a closer assessment of the refugee situation could be made. Nevertheless, at the negotiations Sweden set aside 2.5 MSEK each to the Patriotic Front partners.

Official visits to the refugee camps took place in September-October 1977. After clearance from the Zambian government[10], Anders Möllander and Elisabeth Michanek from the embassy in Lusaka could report from a visit to a well organ-

---

1. Invited by the Swedish government, in September 1977 Robert Mugabe was accorded the same protocollary recognition. During his stay, the ZANU leader discussed humanitarian assistance with SIDA and political issues with Foreign Minister Söder (Bo Heinebäck: Memorandum ('Robert Mugabe besöker utrikesministern'/'Robert Mugabe visits the Foreign Minister'), Ministry for Foreign Affairs, Stockholm, 23 September 1977) (MFA). In their conversations with Söder, both Nkomo and Mugabe strongly criticized the Anglo-American—so called 'Owen-Young'—initiative on Zimbabwe.
2. Marika Fahlén: Memorandum ('Sverige-besök av Joshua Nkomo 9-10 maj 1977'/'Visit to Sweden by Joshua Nkomo, 9-10 May 1977'), Ministry for Foreign Affairs, Stockholm, 13 May 1977 (SDA).
3. Cable from Bo Heinebäck to the Swedish embassy in Lusaka, Ministry for Foreign Affairs, Stockholm, 6 May 1977 (MFA).
4. Marianne Sundh: Memorandum ('Besök av Joshua Nkomo den 9 maj 1977'/'Visit by Joshua Nkomo, 9 May 1977'), SIDA, Stockholm, 9 May 1977 (SDA).
5. Bo Heinebäck: Memorandum ('Utrikesministern samtalar med Joshua Nkomo'/'The Foreign Minister talks to Joshua Nkomo'), Ministry for Foreign Affairs, Stockholm, 16 May 1977 (MFA).
6. Marika Fahlén: Memorandum, 13 May 1977.
7. On the negotiations with ZAPU, see 'Agreed minutes of discussions on cooperation between Sweden and the Zimbabwe African People's Union, ZAPU (The Patriotic Front)', Lusaka, 11 July 1977 (SDA). At the negotiations, the Swedish government was represented by Elisabeth Michanek and Anders Möllander, while ZAPU took part through Edward Ndlovu and Dumiso Dabengwa. The negotiations with ZANU are summarized in 'Agreed minutes of discussions regarding cooperation between the Zimbabwe African National Union, ZANU (Patriotic Front) and Sweden', Maputo, 17 August 1977 (SDA). Jan Cedergren and Bo Westman from the Swedish embassy represented Sweden. Robert Mugabe led the ZANU delegation, which in addition included Simon Muzenda, Kumbirai Kangai and the Health Secretary Herbert Ushewokunze. With the notable absence of Joshua Nkomo, both ZANU and ZAPU were from the very beginning represented at the highest political level at the discussions on Swedish assistance.
8. In Mozambique, there were in addition around 18,000 people in ZANU's military camps, bringing the total Zimbabwean population in the country to more than 50,000 (Jan Cedergren: Memorandum ('Rapport från besök i flyktingläger i Moçambique'/'Report from visit to refugee camps in Mozambique'), Swedish embassy, Maputo [no date, but forwarded to SIDA Stockholm with covering letter dated 27 October 1977]) (SDA).
9. Marika Fahlén: Memorandum, 13 May 1977.
10. The government of Zambia formally stated in late July 1977 that it had "no objection to humanitarian assistance being extended to the Patriotic Front, ZAPU wing, by [Sweden]" (Letter ('Assistance to the Patriotic Front (ZAPU wing)') from F.P. Muyawala, Permanent Secretary, Office of the President, Defence Division, to the Swedish ambassador to Zambia, Lusaka, 26 July 1977) (SDA).

Jan Cedergren, SIDA's representative to Mozambique, and ZANU cadres distributing Swedish relief assistance to Zimbabwean refugees, Tronga refugee camp, Manica province, March 1979 (Photo: Paul Rimmerfors)

ized, but destitute women's camp outside the Zambian capital.[1] The following week, Jan Cedergren, SIDA's representative in Maputo[2], participated in a fact-finding mission organized by the FRELIMO government to the refugee settlements at Tronga and Doroi, respectively situated in the Mozambican provinces of Sofala and Manica.[3] In his comprehensive report, Cedergren noted that the refugees in the two camps—who exceeded 30,000—lacked most basic necessities, such as food, medicines and clothing. There was, in addition, a general lack of heavy-duty vehicles to transport possible assistance to the camps on a regular basis.[4]

As the general conditions for the Zimbabwean refugees in Mozambique and Zambia were similar, the Swedish assistance programmes to ZANU and ZAPU

1. Elisabeth Michanek: Memorandum ('Rapport från besök vid ett av ZAPU's läger strax utanför Lusaka'/ 'Report from visit to one of the ZAPU camps just outside Lusaka'), Swedish embassy, Lusaka, 29 September 1977 (SDA).
2. Cedergren established a close working relationship with ZANU in Mozambique. Didymus Mutasa, ZANU's Deputy Secretary of Finance, later reminisced: "[Cedergren] would sit down with us and very generously give us the things we asked for. [...] He said: '[...] [A]s long as you can account for it and as long as you can give me a list of the things that you need, I will buy some of the things and give you the money to buy the other things. But you must definitely account for it'. [...] The man was absolutely sympathetic to our cause. [...] Here was a Swedish man, who—because he trusted us and we trusted him—actually was walking with us more than just one mile. You asked him to go one mile and he came two miles with us" (Interview with Didymus Mutasa, p. 217). As a leading SIDA official, Cedergren would over the following decade and a half—in Sweden and in Southern Africa—play a prominent role with regard to Sweden's relations with and assistance to SWAPO of Namibia and ANC of South Africa. From 1980 to 1982, he served as SIDA's first representative to Zimbabwe. He later became head of SIDA's industry division in Stockholm, Deputy Director General of the aid agency and—in 1995—Director General (*utrikesråd*) for International Development Cooperation at the Ministry for Foreign Affairs.
3. In June 1977, the Mozambican government took direct charge of the administration of the three civilian refugee camps in the country (Doroi, Mavudzi and Tronga), setting up a specialized unit in the President's Office (*Núcleo de apoio aos refugiados e movimentos de libertação*, or Unit in support of the refugees and liberation movements). It also coordinated the assistance to the military camps administered by ZANU.
4. Jan Cedergren: Memorandum attached to letter to SIDA Stockholm dated 27 October 1977. The visit to the refugee camps took place from 5 to 8 October 1977.

would have a close resemblance. From mid-1977 until the Lancaster House Agreement in December 1979, food—particularly in the form of maize meal—and vehicles were by far the two most important items for both ZANU and ZAPU. Of the 67 MSEK allocated to the two movements before the start of the repatriation exercise in early 1980, no less than 40 million—corresponding to 60 per cent of the funds—was set aside for the procurement of food, mainly in the host countries.[1] As in the case of the assistance to PAIGC, transport was with regard to costs the second biggest component. More than 10 MSEK—around 15 per cent—was used by the two organizations for the procurement of trucks, jeeps and lighter vehicles.[2] Over the two and a half years, the combined assistance in the form of clothes (2.5 MSEK), medicines (2 MSEK) and educational supplies (1 MSEK) was considerably smaller.[3]

Towards the end of the 1970s, Sweden had become the most important supplier of non-military assistance to both ZANU and ZAPU, particularly with regard to food and vehicles. The wider impact of the support is difficult to measure. In the case of food supplies, ZANU's former Deputy Secretary of Finance Didymus Mutasa concluded in an interview in 1995 that without the Swedish contribution the liberation movement "would have been inundated with people that we could not have fed" and that "the Mozambican government [...] would have [...] found it difficult to carry on".[4] In late 1977, it was estimated that the annual costs just to provide maize meal to the civilian refugees in Mozambique amounted to 10 MSEK.[5] Through its direct assistance to the Mozambican government and ZANU, as well as via significant contributions to UNHCR and the World Food Programme, Sweden covered an important part of these costs. In addition to the strictly humanitarian aspect, there was, however, also a military dimension to the support. Commenting upon the assistance received from Sweden and the other Nordic countries[6], ZANLA's former Political Commissar Josiah Tungamirai has later stated that ZANU in Mozambique

> faced three major problems, namely, food, clothing and medicine[s]. And here the Nordic countries helped us tremendously. [...] [A]t that stage we were no longer recruiting [military cadres] from home, but from the refugee camps and if the refugees had not been fed, if they had not been clothed and if they had had no medical care, then our source of recruitment would have dried up. [...]

> Before 1977—when the leadership had not yet taken a grip of the refugee situation—[...] [w]e [...] had some camps [in Mozambique] which recorded an average of over twenty people dying

---

1. Based on the budgets established with ZANU and ZAPU at the annual and extraordinary negotiations on Swedish humanitarian assistance. In the case of ZANU, 18.5 MSEK in total was allocated for the procurement of food, while the corresponding figure for ZAPU was 21.5 million. As towards the end of the liberation war there were three times as many Zimbabwean refugees in Mozambique than in Zambia, it follows that the Swedish assistance in this respect had a greater impact among the refugees administered by ZAPU. In addition to food, significant quantities of cooking oil were supplied by Sweden to the two movements.
2. Before the repatriation exercise, ZANU used 4.8 and ZAPU 5.3 MSEK for the procurement of vehicles.
3. With regard to clothing, SIDA allocated important amounts in favour of shipments organized by various Swedish NGOs, notably Emmaus-Björkå and Bread and Fishes. Considerable donations of clothes and shoes were, in addition, made to ZANU and ZAPU by the Swedish government outside the bilateral cooperation programmes. In 1978, for example, 5,000 pairs of trousers were donated to ZAPU and 15,000 to ZANU (Letter ('Beredskapslager av byxor till befrielserörelserna'/'Trousers from the government's stores to the liberation movements') from SIDA Stockholm to the SIDA offices in Dar es Salaam, Luanda, Lusaka and Maputo, Stockholm, 21 December 1978) (SDA). Regarding medical supplies, a complete field hospital was—as will be seen below—airlifted to ZAPU in Zambia in late 1978.
4. Interview with Didymus Mutasa, p. 219.
5. Jan Cedergren: Memorandum attached to letter to SIDA Stockholm dated 27 October 1977.
6. Like Sweden, Norway extended direct support to ZANU (and ZAPU), while the Danish government channelled its assistance via NGOs. Finland did not support the Zimbabwean liberation movements.

each day due to lack of food.[1] That is when the Nordic countries came in full force, giving us food, medicines and clothing. And that is also why the ZANU leadership never went to Sweden, Denmark or Norway saying: 'Could you give us some guns?' [...] I also think that that is why they managed to support us, because I do not think that they would have been able to continue if they had said that they were going to support the liberation [struggle] straight out. [...]

The importance of this assistance went even further. For example, in what we called the North-East—which is now Mashonaland Centre and part of Mashonaland East—there were areas where we had fought the war and everybody had gone into the bush. The cultivation of the land had come to a standstill, so we had to take food from Mozambique into Zimbabwe to feed the ordinary people, the poor, the masses. We fed them and clothed them with the supplies that we had got from external sources like Sweden, Norway and Denmark.[2]

With regard to vehicles and the wider issue of transport[3], the Swedish support was even more conspicous. According to Kumbirai Kangai, ZANU's Secretary of Transport and Social Welfare, "each [year] we would get three or four new trucks. It really made a tremendous impact on our people as far as the Swedish and the Nordic peoples are concerned".[4] Interviewed in 1995, Kangai also underlined how the untied transport support gave ZANU an "international posture". When an allocation for vehicles to ZANU was made in 1978, he was thus

sent to Europe to look for transport, Land Rovers, lorries and things like that. The British had actually outlawed any sale of Land Rovers to Mozambique. I got to the UK and posed as somebody from West Africa. I went to Southampton, where they assemble Land Rovers. I talked to the management [and] they said: 'How are you going to pay?' I said: 'I have a bank in Sweden. I will just tell it to transfer the money to your account.' I tell you, I was given VIP treatment by those people! [...]

I [then] got on the train, went back to London, called Mozambique to inform comrade Mugabe what I had got and then called SIDA to simply say: 'Can you transfer X amount of money to account so-and-so in London?' Everything just went smoothly. When I got back to Southampton, these British people checked their account and saw that the money had been transferred. [...] I packed my vehicles and shipped them to Mozambique. [...] It was, I think, four Land Rovers, one ambulance and one fast vehicle, a Range Rover. [...] You can see the type of relationship we had. To simply call from London and say: 'My name is Kumbirai Kangai from the sector for transport and welfare of ZANU. [...] Can you transfer the money from SIDA to account so-and-so in the UK?' And it was done![5]

Although heavy-duty trucks to transport the assistance to the refugee camps in Mozambique and Zambia featured prominently, Sweden also supplied both ZANU

---

1. After leaving Sweden in September 1975, Sydney Sekeramayi took up a position at the University Teaching Hospital in Lusaka. He joined Herbert Ushewokunze as one of ZANU's only two medical doctors in Mozambique in 1977. Respectively appointed Secretary and Deputy Secretary of Health in September 1977, at Zimbabwe's independence in April 1980 Ushewokunze became Minister of Health and Sekeramayi Minister of Lands, Resettlement and Rural Development. Sekeramayi later succeeded Ushewokunze as Health Minister.
2. Interview with Josiah Tungamirai, pp. 234-35. In the case of Sweden and ZANU, the extraordinary allocation of 2 MSEK in late 1978 was granted "especially to cater for the population in the liberated areas within Zimbabwe" ('Agreed minutes of discussions on utilization of an additional Swedish grant to the Zimbabwe African National Union, ZANU (Patriotic Front)', Maputo, 19 December 1978) (SDA). The year of the agreement is wrongly given as 1979, but should read 1978 (see covering letter ('Agreed minutes - Bistånd ZANU'/'Agreed minutes - Assistance ZANU') from Lennart Dafgård, Swedish ambassador to Mozambique, to the Ministry for Foreign Affairs, Maputo, 20 December 1978) (SDA).
3. Considerable amounts were allocated by the Swedish government to ZAPU for the onward transportation—normally by air—of Zimbabwean refugees from Botswana to Zambia. For the financial year 1978/79, for example, in June 1978 an amount of 2.8 MSEK was set aside for this purpose ('Agreed minutes of discussions on cooperation between Sweden and the Zimbabwe African People's Union, Patriotic Front, 1978/79', Lusaka, 15 June 1978) (SDA).
4. Interview with Kumbirai Kangai, p. 213.
5. Ibid., pp. 213-14.

and ZAPU with a great number of jeeps and lighter vehicles. Only for the financial year 1979/80, it was, for example, agreed with ZAPU in May 1979 that SIDA would provide 7 larger Volvo trucks, 14 Volvo jeeps and 7 Volvo station wagons.[1] The effort would in turn attract the attention of the Rhodesian intelligence and counter-insurgency forces. While CIO's principal operative against the Zimbabwean liberation movements in Zambia—*inter alia* directly responsible for the assassination of Herbert Chitepo—posed as a Scania representative[2], attacks on ZANU and ZAPU often targeted their vehicle fleets. In mid-April 1979, one of the Rhodesian units carrying out military raids against ZAPU in Lusaka[3] was almost left behind when it refused to obey orders to withdraw, stating that "there's still some Scanias left to deal with [...], gifts from those shithouses in Sweden".[4]

Differences, Disputes and Extraordinary Support to ZAPU

Extended on equal terms and with a remarkably similar content with regard to the humanitarian core of the cooperation programmes, Sweden's assistance to ZANU and ZAPU also showed clear differences and was against that background differently interpreted by the Patriotic Front partners. The major contrast was that the assistance to ZANU—much along the lines of the assistance to SWAPO of Namibia and ANC of South Africa—developed into a broader support programme to the movement as such, with important components for administration, information and publicity.

Under the bilateral programmes to the two organizations, the government gave administrative support to the ZAPU offices in Luanda and Gaborone[5], and as early as in 1977 the official Swedish Agency for Research Cooperation with Developing Countries assisted ZAPU's Zimbabwe Research and Information Centre in Lusaka outside the core programme.[6] Nevertheless, the contributions were small compared to the support extended to ZANU. Until the Lancaster House Agreement, only 1 MSEK was allocated to ZAPU for administration. The corresponding amount

---

1. 'Agreed minutes from discussions on the cooperation between the Zimbabwe African People's Union (ZAPU) and the Swedish International Development Authority (SIDA)', Lusaka, 18 May 1979 (SDA). The support to the liberation movements was not tied to procurement in Sweden. Nevertheless, ZAPU gave almost exclusive preference to Volvo vehicles. While choosing Japanese lighter vehicles—normally procured in Swaziland—and British four-wheel drive vehicles (Land Rover), ZANU, on the other hand, requested SIDA as a rule to supply Scania trucks. This, in turn, reflected the fact that Volvo was better represented on the Zambian market, while Scania enjoyed a similar advantage in Mozambique.
2. Stiff op. cit., p. 96.
3. In mid-April 1979, the Rhodesians carried out combined attacks against Joshua Nkomo's residence and ZAPU's offices at the Liberation Centre in Lusaka. Several of the Rhodesians and South Africans whose names later appeared in connection with the investigations into the Palme assassination were present in Lusaka or took active part in the attacks. This was, notably, the case with the South African Craig Williamson, at the time Deputy Director of IUEF, but also with Anthony ('Ant') White, the Rhodesian Selous Scout who was chosen by CIO to kill the ZAPU President. Interviewed in 1996, Williamson admitted that he and the South Africans "had given information to [the Rhodesians] of where to strike" (Interview with Craig Williamson, p. 202). Present in Lusaka at the time of the attacks, the following morning Williamson visited the Liberation Centre together with Laban Oyaka, Assistant Executive Secretary of the OAU Liberation Committee. A somewhat blurred photo of the two looking at the debris was taken by an employee at the Swedish embassy. It should here be noted that Peter Casselton—Williamson's main contact and Bertil Wedin's superior in London in the early 1980s (see the chapter on Angola)—in 1977 had provided the intelligence for the massacre at ZANU's Chimoio camp in Mozambique.
4. Cited in Stiff op. cit., p. 296.
5. Sweden also covered the costs for the ZANU and ZAPU offices in Stockholm.
6. SAREC's initial contribution to ZIRIC for the financial year 1977/78 was 200,000 SEK (Letter ('Begäran om svenskt bidrag till ett planerat Zimbabwe-institut'/'Request for Swedish assistance to a planned Zimbabwe Institute') from Ove Heyman, Swedish ambassador to Zambia, to the Ministry for Foreign Affairs, Lusaka, 19 April 1978) (SDA). In 1977, ZIRIC's Director, Isaac Nyathi, served for a short time as ZAPU's representative in Sweden. Cf. the interview with John Nkomo, p. 224.

Shaky picture of a shady figure: IUEF's Deputy Director Craig Williamson (right) inspecting the Liberation Centre in Lusaka after giving the Rhodesians information on where to strike, April 1979. With Williamson is Laban Oyaka of the OAU Liberation Committee (Author's collection)

granted to ZANU was 4.7 million, representing 14 per cent of the total assistance to the organization, only marginally less than the allocation for transport. Over the years, the support mainly consisted of supplies of paper and stationery to the ZANU office in Maputo, but in June 1979 the Swedish government also agreed to allocate 1.4 MSEK for the production of ZANU's official organ *Zimbabwe News* and 0.3 million for the procurement of two mobile film units, photographic equipment and other supplies to the movement's Department of Information and Publicity.[1] Above all, by 1979 the assistance to ZANU had taken the form of support to its different civilian departments, assuming a more political character than the basically humanitarian assistance to ZAPU.[2]

It is against this background not surprising that the assistance to ZANU and ZAPU was viewed differently by the two movements. In ZANU's case, the main observation did not concern the content of the cooperation programme, nor did the movement consider that there were any political conditions attached to the support.[3] Instead, it concerned the financial parity accorded the two Patriotic Front organizations. Although the question has later been downplayed by leading ZANU representatives[4], in the late 1970s—as there were considerably more Zimbabwean refugees in Mozambique than in Zambia—it regularly prompted the ZANU leadership to request more resources to ZANU than to ZAPU. The issue was, for example, forcefully raised by Mugabe's political adviser Nathan Shamuyarira in discussions with Swedish diplomats in mid-1977[5] and at the Foreign Ministry in late 1978.[6] It was also raised by the ZANU President himself, stating to the visiting SIDA board members in Maputo in February 1979 that

1. 'Agreed minutes of discussions on cooperation between the Zimbabwe African National Union (ZANU) and the Swedish International Development Authority (SIDA)', Maputo, 4 June 1979 (SDA).
2. Ibid.
3. In interviews carried out in 1995, leading representatives of both ZANU and ZAPU emphasized that the assistance granted by the Swedish government was given without any political conditions. See the interviews with Dumiso Dabengwa (ZAPU) (p. 210), Kumbirai Kangai (ZANU) (p. 214) and Didymus Mutasa (ZANU) (p. 218).
4. Cf. the interviews with Kumbirai Kangai (p. 215) and Didymus Mutasa (p. 219).
5. Örjan Landelius: Memorandum ('Uppteckning av samtal med Nathan Shamuyarira, medlem av patriotiska fronten i Zimbabwe'/'Notes from conversation with Nathan Shamuyarira, member of the Patriotic Front of Zimbabwe'), Swedish embassy, Brussels, 21 June 1977 (MFA).
6. Hans Alldén: Memorandum ('Besök av ZANU-representanter'/'Visit by ZANU representatives'), Ministry for Foreign Affairs, Stockholm, 13 November 1978 (MFA).

Strains, but also smiles: Director
General Ernst Michanek with ZAPU
President Joshua Nkomo in SIDA's
corridors, Stockholm, May 1977
(Photo: Paul Rimmerfors)

while you are entitled to use the criterion of equality and equal treatment [...] between ZANU and ZAPU, our view is that [it] operates unfairly in respect of the two sets of refugees and the two parties in charge of them. Therefore, it does not yield the desired effect of equal treatment, but rather that of [inequality]. A more equitable basis of apportionment would, in our opinion, be one which takes the size of the population to be catered for as the criterion, viewed against the background of the existing general needs. [...] [T]he [Swedish] allocation could be on a per capitum basis, thus ensuring a much fairer distribution, first among the victims of the oppressive racial system themselves and, secondly, [...] between our two political parties.[1]

Despite the close relations with Mugabe's movement, from 1977 the Swedish government did not, however, abandon the policy of equal financial allocations to ZANU and ZAPU. The Africa Groups maintained a similar position.

In ZAPU's case, more serious criticism had as early as in June 1977—even before the resumption of the official assistance—been made by President Nkomo. Although his initial observations concerned the marginal question of scholarships, it would in 1978 escalate into open, uneasy relations between the ZAPU leader and Sweden. Publicly raised via the press and finding its way into the Swedish parliament, Nkomo's criticism stands out as exceptional. No other leader of a Southern African liberation movement supported by Sweden challenged the Swedish government in a similar way.

The source of the disagreement was that the Swedish authorities during Nkomo's visit to Stockholm in May 1977 had been reluctant to allocate funds for scholarships in Sweden under the planned cooperation programme with ZAPU. The main argument was that Sweden was already the main supplier of funds to various international educational programmes, such as the United Nations Educational and Training Programme for Southern Africa (UNETPSA), the Africa Educational Trust (AET), the International University Exchange Fund (IUEF) and

---

1. Robert Mugabe: 'Brief statement to the members of the board of SIDA', ZANU, Maputo, 7 February 1979 (MFA).

the World University Service (WUS).[1] Returning to Lusaka, Nkomo, however,
approached the Swedish ambassador and "vehemently" criticized his government
for unilaterally trying to "steer" the proposed assistance to ZAPU.[2] Although he
did not participate in the negotiations with Sweden in July and December 1977, in
early April 1978 the ZAPU President suddenly and publicly turned against SIDA
and the Fälldin government.[3] In an interview with the social democratic evening
paper *Aftonbladet*, he stated that

> in Sweden, [they] are afraid. [...] [T]he Swedish government has for a long time been sympa-
> thetic towards our struggle, but like the Norwegians and the Danes, [the Swedes] never dare to
> concretely show that they support us. [...] [They] do not want to sell arms to us, [and when] we
> some time back asked [...] to place some of our youth [members] at [their] universities [...] we
> did not get a reply. [...] That is the way it is the whole time. [The] assistance comes through
> SIDA, but it seems that you have to extract the funds with pincers [...] Why can [they] not talk
> and act in a straightforward manner? As things now stand, [the Swedes] are very difficult to
> deal with.[4]

Nkomo made his statement less than two months before the scheduled aid negotiations between Sweden and ZAPU for 1978/79. It immediately set in motion intense
contacts with the ZAPU leadership. Although questions were raised by the Social
Democratic opposition in the Swedish parliament[5] and Dumiso Dabengwa—who,
in contrast to Nkomo, had taken part in the two rounds of negotiations with Sweden in 1977—expressed the opinion that "the Swedish assistance worked well"[6],
the ZAPU President did not budge. During a meeting with Sweden's ambassador to
Zambia a week after the *Aftonbladet* interview, he intensified his criticism, characterizing the Swedish support as "humiliating" and as a sign of "wanting trust".[7] At
the end of the month, he repeated his views in a telephone conversation with the
Liberal MP David Wirmark, a personal friend since the late 1950s.[8]

Against this background, it was decided to make a particular effort to clarify
the principles governing Swedish humanitarian assistance to the ZAPU President. A
long and detailed letter to that effect was delivered by the Swedish ambassador in
Lusaka, Ove Heyman, in mid-May 1978. With regard to the core issue of the reluctance to grant scholarships to ZAPU, the letter stated:

> For several years, Sweden operated a programme of individual scholarships for studies in Swe-
> den [...]. After evaluation, this programme was, however, discontinued. [...] The decision [...]
> coincided with a recommendation passed by an OAU conference in Addis Ababa in 1967,
> [advocating] placement in Africa for African refugee students. The Swedish government has

---

1. Official Swedish contributions to UNETPSA, AET, IUEF and WUS regularly exceeded 50 per cent of their
   respective Southern Africa programmes.
2. Cable from Ove Heyman, Swedish ambassador to Zambia, to the Ministry for Foreign Affairs, Lusaka, 9
   June 1977 (SDA).
3. At a meeting with CSM's Africa secretary Tore Bergman in Lusaka in March 1978, Nkomo had criticized the
   Swedish government for being "too particular about its funding" (Interview with Tore Bergman, p. 266).
4. Interview with Joshua Nkomo by Bengt Persson ('Ni i Sverige är rädda'/'You in Sweden are afraid') in *Aftonbladet*, 3 April 1978.
5. On 12 April 1978, the Social Democratic MP Mats Hellström repeated Nkomo's criticism of SIDA during the
   parliamentary debate on Swedish foreign aid. According to Craig Williamson, much of the background material for Hellström's address had been drafted by Williamson himself and submitted to Hellström through the
   IUEF Director Lars-Gunnar Eriksson (see the interview with Craig Williamson by Knut-Göran Källberg: 'Jag
   lurade skjortan av dem'/'I took them for a ride' in *Expressen*, 5 October 1996). Hellström was actively
   involved in the Swedish Southern Africa debate. In 1983, he was appointed Minister of Foreign Trade and
   served as Minister of Agriculture between 1986 and 1991.
6. Cable from Ove Heyman, Swedish ambassador to Zambia, to the Ministry for Foreign Affairs, Lusaka, 11
   April 1978 (SDA).
7. Ibid.
8. Thord Palmlund: Memorandum ('Samtal med Nkomo'/'Conversation with Nkomo'), Ministry for Foreign
   Affairs, Stockholm, 27 April 1978 (SDA).

since supported several educational programmes in Africa. A request by ZAPU to use some of the Swedish funds to finance studies in African countries would, no doubt, be received favourably by my government.[1]

Although leading ZAPU representatives during the following months raised the scholarship issue[2], it was not given priority at the formal aid negotiations. Bilateral scholarships were not included in the cooperation programme. What essentially was a storm in a teacup soon subsided.[3] When SIDA's Deputy Director General Anders Forsse at the beginning of October 1978 visited Lusaka, Nkomo was full of praise regarding the Swedish assistance, asking: "What would we have done without you?"[4]

As the Rhodesian regime later that month began massive military attacks on ZAPU's refugee settlements and bases in Zambia[5], the Swedish government responded to the movement's appeals for extraordinary assistance. Unlike the raids on ZANU in Mozambique—which took place far away from the capital—in Zambia the bombings were directly experienced by the local embassy staff. First secretary Anders Möllander later wrote:

> With horrid precision, the minority regime in Rhodesia started in 1978 to attack the refugee camps in Zambia. Some of them were so close to the capital that we through the embassy win-

1. Letter ('Principles governing Swedish cooperation with liberation movements') from Ove Heyman, Swedish ambassador to Zambia, to Joshua Nkomo, Lusaka, 10 May 1978 (SDA). Informing Nkomo about the approaching aid negotiations in May 1979, a similar letter was submitted by SIDA's Director General Ernst Michanek in March 1979 (Letter from Ernst Michanek to Joshua Nkomo, Stockholm, 16 March 1979) (SDA).
2. It was, for example, discussed by ZAPU's General Secretary Joseph Msika with the Ministry for Foreign Affairs (Ingrid Hjelt af Trolle: Memorandum ('Besök av ZAPU's generalsekreterare Joseph Msika'/'Visit by the ZAPU General Secretary Joseph Msika'), Ministry for Foreign Affairs, Stockholm, 31 May 1978) (SDA) and at a meeting with Cooperation Minister Ullsten in Stockholm in mid-May 1978 (Ingrid Hjelt af Trolle: Memorandum ('ZAPU's generalsekreterare besöker biståndsministern'/'ZAPU's General Secretary visits the Cooperation Minister'), Ministry for Foreign Affairs, Stockholm, 1 June 1978) (SDA).
3. The background to ZAPU's emphasis on scholarships for higher education was that in 1977 the organization reviewed its strategy. The new course involved the training of regular military units, who would establish themselves in the semi-liberated areas in Zimbabwe. The new strategy also involved "the training of non-military personnel to provide legal, medical, educational and administrative services" to the population in these areas (Dabengwa in Bhebe and Ranger (eds) op. cit. (Vol. I), p. 35). In 1995, ZAPU's former Head of Military Intelligence, Dumiso Dabengwa, confirmed that Nkomo's critical statements should be seen in that context: "One of his main thrusts was to get that kind of support, because that was the time when we were looking at the creation of liberated zones. Obviously, we were going to require an infrastructure when we created such zones. We would have to take over the schools. We would have to take over all the social functions of the Rhodesian government in those areas. It was for this kind of support that [Nkomo] to a very large extent was appealing" (Interview with Dumiso Dabengwa, p. 212).
4. Cable from Ove Heyman, Swedish ambassador to Zambia, to the Ministry for Foreign Affairs, Lusaka, 5 October 1978 (SDA).
5. Rhodesian military units had been operating with the Portuguese in Mozambique since 1969 (Cilliers op. cit., p. 175). The first major attack on ZANU in independent Mozambique was the Nyadzonia massacre in August 1976. Similar raids were later *inter alia* carried out on Zimbabwean settlements at Mapai in June and at Chimoio in November 1977. Although the real figure will never be established, it has been estimated that around 3,500 Zimbabwean refugees in Mozambique were killed during the raids in 1977-78 alone (ibid., p. 182). In the case of ZAPU and Zambia, the large scale Rhodesian military strikes started in October 1978, when the settlement at Mkushi and the movement's Freedom Camp outside Lusaka were bombed. According to the Rhodesian CIO Director Ken Flower, 1,600 nationalists lost their lives during the combined operation (Flower op. cit., p. 214). Air strikes were also carried out on ZAPU/ZIPRA at Mulungushi in Zambia in December 1978 and at Luena in Angola in February 1979. In April 1979, overland attacks on Zimbabwe House and the Liberation Centre took place in central Lusaka. The Rhodesian operations against Mozambique, Zambia and Angola—which included major attacks on roads, bridges, railways and other so called "economic targets"—were coordinated with South Africa's military intelligence (ibid., p. 138 and interview with Craig Williamson, p. 202). The Pretoria regime also embarked on direct air strikes to stem the nationalist tide in Southern Africa. The SWAPO settlement at Kassinga in southern Angola was bombed in May 1978, with more than 600 Namibian refugees—mostly young women and children— killed (Mvula ya Nangolo and Tor Sellström: *Kassinga: A Story Untold*, Namibia Book Development Council, Windhoek, 1995). In the case of Zambia, it should be noted that the Rhodesian raids began after the Salisbury agreement between Smith, Chirau, Muzorewa and Sithole.

dows could see the smoke clouds from the bombs. Ambulances shuttled back and forth. Hundreds of refugees died and many more were left wounded. The Zambian hospitals became overloaded [...].[1]

In late October 1978—after the first Rhodesian raids—ZAPU made an appeal for extraordinary assistance in the form of mobile field hospitals to ease Zambia's burdens and be in a position on its own to give medical treatment to the hundreds of wounded Zimbabweans. According to ZAPU, the movement had its own doctors and the necessary medical personnel for such hospitals.[2] While SIDA contacted the Swedish UN emergency unit and the air force, the government supported the idea to send a mobile hospital, ambulances, medicines and food by air to Zambia. The formal decision to allocate 2 MSEK as emergency assistance to ZAPU was taken on 10 November 1978.[3]

On 8 November, President Kaunda had in a discussion with ambassador Heyman endorsed the proposed emergency operation.[4] In view of the difficult security situation, he, however, underlined "that no publicity [should be] given [to it]".[5] After necessary clearances, two C 130 Hercules carriers from the Swedish air force took off for Zambia on 29 November and 8 December, respectively.[6] They carried a complete mobile hospital, consisting of eighteen tents with a capacity to care for a hundred in-patients and two hundred out-patients; a power plant; refrigerators; two cross-country ambulances; medicines and food.[7] Led by Wing Commander S.E. Nauclér, the subsequent operation—carried out in great secrecy "to avoid detection or even destruction [by the Rhodesians]"[8]—was a unique event in Sweden's humanitarian cooperation with the Southern African liberation movements. Involving the transport and placement of the mobile hospital 40 kilometres outside Lusaka, it brought military personnel from the Swedish air force, the Zambian army and ZAPU/ZIPRA together at a particularly tense and crucial moment in the Zimbabwean liberation struggle.[9] In 1995, ZAPU's former Administrative Secretary John Nkomo—who received the first Swedish air force carrier and the mobile hospital—commented that "[t]hese are some of the things that a lot of people do not know".[10]

Possibly encouraged by this intervention, the ZAPU President would one year later again show little understanding of the Swedish policy on humanitarian assist-

1. Möllander op. cit., p. 39.
2. Cable from the Swedish embassy in Lusaka to SIDA, Lusaka, 30 October 1978 (SDA).
3. Ministry for Foreign Affairs: Decision ('Katastrofbistånd till Patriotiska fronten'/'Emergency assistance to the Patriotic Front'), Stockholm, 10 November 1978 (SDA). The same amount was allocated to ZANU in Mozambique. Two weeks later, it was in addition decided to grant the government of Zambia an amount of 1 MSEK for the procurement of medical supplies and hospital equipment (Kurt Kristiansson: Memorandum ('Reserapport'/'Travel report'), SIDA, Stockholm, 28 February 1979) (SDA).
4. Kurt Kristiansson: Memorandum ('Reserapport'/'Travel report'), SIDA, Stockholm, 28 February 1979 (SDA).
5. Ibid.
6. From the end of September until the first week of November 1977, a Hercules from the Swedish air force had operated an air bridge in Angola under the auspices of UNHCR and the League of Red Cross Societies.
7. S.E. Nauclér: 'Brief description of the mobile hospital', Lusaka, 2 December 1978 (SDA).
8. Interview with John Nkomo, p. 226.
9. Kurt Kristiansson: Memorandum ('Reserapport'/'Travel report'), SIDA, Stockholm, 28 February 1979 (SDA). Dabengwa later stated that the mobile hospital "was very useful" (Interview with Dumiso Dabengwa, p. 211). Mainly due to the fact that ZAPU—contrary to what was stated in the original appeal—did not have the qualified medical personnel to run the hospital, the Swedish assessment was less positive (cf. Kristiansson: 'Travel report'). Anders Möllander—who participated in the operation—later concluded: "I [...] doubt that the most advanced part of the equipment [...] came to use" (Möllander op. cit., p. 41). Möllander also mentions that ZAPU received another field hospital "from West Germany", giving the impression that it was donated by the FRG government. It was, however, supplied by a German NGO. In early 1979, the Swedish mobile hospital was moved to a ZAPU camp outside Solwezi in north-western Zambia.
10. Interview with John Nkomo, p. 226.

ance. On 24 December 1979—immediately after the signing of the Lancaster House Agreement—he made a political "appeal for assistance from [Sweden] in order to ensure victory [in the forthcoming elections]". It amounted to no less than 50 MSEK and included the supply of 20 trucks, 40 Land Rovers, 30 Land Cruisers, 10 buses, 40 passenger cars, 5,000 motor cycles and 8,000 bicycles.[1] In mid-February 1980, he followed up the appeal by sending an urgent cable to the Minister for Foreign Affairs, stating that

> there is great need for the use of some helicopters for my election campaign. I have acquired the use of three machines through [a] contract with a Swedish company. I would be very grateful for assistance to finance the hiring and, in particular, [the] transport of the machines by air freight from Stockholm to Salisbury immediately.[2]

At the time involved in a sensitive exchange with the British government regarding Sweden's support to the Patriotic Front, the Liberal Foreign Minister Ullsten replied:

> I am obliged to tell you that, as a matter of principle, the Swedish government never engages itself in material support [to] any party or organization in its election preparations. What is open to my government to do, and what we have done, is to give humanitarian assistance in the form of food, clothes, medicin[es], agricultural tools, vehicles etc. We hope that this kind of assistance has been, and still is, of importance to your people in this very difficult period.[3]

Elections: Sweden, Britain and the Patriotic Front

Against the weight of ZANU's and ZAPU's combined military operations, after one and a half decades—and some 30,000 lives lost—Ian Smith's white rebel Rhodesian settler regime crumbled at the end of the 1970s. At the Commonwealth conference in Lusaka in August 1979, the recently elected British Conservative Prime Minister Margaret Thatcher was forced to withdraw recognition of the puppet Muzorewa government and organize genuine independence negotiations with the Patriotic Front. Convened on 10 September 1979, the Lancaster House talks in London—chaired by the British Foreign Secretary Lord Carrington—eventually, and surprisingly, ended three months later with the signing of an agreement on a cease-fire and the holding of democratic elections.[4] The final Lancaster House Agreement was signed on 21 December 1979. Through the agreement, Britain resumed direct responsibility over its former colony under Lord Soames, who was to ensure that free and fair elections supervised by the Commonwealth were organized.[5] Despite misgivings by ZAPU, the two Patriotic Front partners resolved to present themselves to the Zimbabwean electorate as separate entities, or as ZANU-PF and PF-ZAPU.

1. Letter from Joshua Nkomo to the Swedish embassy in Zambia, Lusaka, 24 December 1979 (SDA).
2. Cable from Joshua Nkomo to Ola Ullsten, Salisbury, 15 February 1980 (MFA).
3. Cable from Ola Ullsten to Joshua Nkomo, Stockholm, 15 February 1980 (MFA). The previous day, the Swedish Ministry for Foreign Affairs had been notified by the private company Osterman Aero in Stockholm that three helicopters had been rented on commercial terms by Bishop Muzorewa and flown to Salisbury. Two Swedish pilots had at the same time been employed by UANC (Cable from Anders Bjurner to the Swedish embassy in Lusaka, Ministry for Foreign Affairs, Stockholm, 15 February 1980) (MFA).
4. However, the small minority of white, coloured and Zimbabweans of Asian origin was to elect 20 members to the new parliament, while the overwhelmingly black majority—registered on a separate roll—was to select the remaining 80.
5. On the Lancaster House Agreement, see Thomas Ohlson's Ph. D. dissertation *Power Politics and Peace Politics: Intra-State Conflict Resolution in Southern Africa*, Department of Peace and Conflict Research, Uppsala University, Uppsala, 1998, pp. 82-88 and 155-60.

After a particularly conflictual and acrimonious election campaign—during which political intimidation, arrests, sabotage, assassination attempts and threats were daily occurrences[1]—the independence elections were held at the end of February 1980. They resulted in a resounding victory for Robert Mugabe's ZANU-PF, which took 57 out of the 80 parliamentary seats reserved for blacks, or an absolute majority in the 100-member assembly. Joshua Nkomo's PF-ZAPU gained 20 and Bishop Abel Muzorewa's UANC 3 seats.[2] The Commonwealth observer group endorsed the results. On 18 April 1980, the independent nation of Zimbabwe was born under Robert Mugabe's premiership. British rule in Africa came to an end.

After a decade and a half of indirect and direct relations with the Patriotic Front movements, Fälldin's government, the Social Democratic opposition and the wider Swedish solidarity movement were far from disinterested or impartial during the events culminating in the elections in late February 1980. Visiting the Ministry for Foreign Affairs in Stockholm in mid-August 1979, Bishop Muzorewa's representative to the Nordic countries, Chenzira ('Joyce') Mutasa, complained that "Sweden's policy towards Rhodesia was different from that of Denmark, Finland and Norway", who had responded positively to UANC requests for humanitarian assistance, while Sweden had not even replied to the submissions.[3]

Although the Swedish government together with the other Nordic countries had expressed political reservations to both ZAPU and ZANU[4], it was at the time of the Lancaster House conference clearly seen by the British to unreservedly support the Patriotic Front. Thatcher's Tory government did not seriously attempt to seek official backing for its 'Rhodesia policy' from Fälldin's non-socialist ruling coalition.[5] After the signing of the Lancaster House agreement, the British and the Swedish positions would, on the contrary, clash in a spectacular way, confirming the separate views held with regard to Zimbabwe and the wider Southern African question. While the differences at the time of Ian Smith's UDI were between ruling

1. The irregularities were overwhelmingly directed against ZANU-PF. In addition to a number of administrative restrictions against the party by Governor Soames, two assassination attempts on Robert Mugabe's life were made in February 1980. In his account of Zimbabwe's transition process, David Caute concludes: "The whole objective was to defeat Mugabe. The entire capacity of white Rhodesia was mobilized to achieve this one aim" (David Caute: *Under the Skin: The Death of White Rhodesia*, Allen Lane, London, 1983, p. 416).
2. Ian Smith's Rhodesian Front took all the 20 seats reserved for the 'white' roll. ZANU's founder, Reverend Sithole, failed to make any impact at all.
3. Jan Romare: Memorandum ('Besök av biskop Muzorewa's representant'/'Visit by the representative of Bishop Muzorewa'), Ministry for Foreign Affairs, Stockholm, 17 August 1979 (MFA).
4. In September 1978, ZAPU shot down a civilian Air Rhodesia plane at Kariba. Eighteen of the fifty-three passengers survived the crash, but ten of them were killed by ZIPRA guerrilllas. One of the survivors was a Danish citizen. The internationally much publicized event was discussed in the Danish parliament and also brought to the attention of the Swedish government (Letter ('Rhodesiska flygmassakern i danska folketinget'/'The Rhodesian air massacre in the Danish parliament'), from Ove Svensson, Swedish embassy in Denmark, to the Ministry for Foreign Affairs, Copenhagen, 8 September 1978) (MFA). While the event did not cause a Nordic protest, the publication of death threats against a number of perceived "black traitors"—among them Abel Muzorewa and Ndabaningi Sithole—by ZANU in November 1978, however, did. After consultations with the Norwegian government, the Ministry for Foreign Affairs instructed the Swedish embassy in Maputo to convey the disapproval of both Oslo and Stockholm directly to Mugabe (Cable from the Ministry for Foreign Affairs to the Swedish embassy in Maputo, Stockholm, 1 December 1978) (MFA). The criticism was raised with Robert Mugabe, Simon Muzenda and Richard Hove one week later. Although the ZANU President did not retract the statement, he admitted that it was "perhaps formulated a bit drastically" (Cable from Lennart Dafgård, Swedish ambassador to Mozambique, to the Ministry for Foreign Affairs, Maputo, 6 December 1978) (MFA).
5. Before the Commonwealth conference in Lusaka and Queen Elizabeth's state visit to Zambia, the Thatcher government demanded that Joshua Nkomo should leave the country. Discussing the issue, ZAPU's Central Committee recommended that—if necessary—Nkomo should go to Sweden (Cable from the Swedish embassy in Lusaka to the Ministry for Foreign Affairs, Lusaka, 27 July 1979) (MFA). Both the ZAPU President and the conference host, President Kaunda, refused, however, to give in to the British demands (cf. the interview with Kenneth Kaunda, p. 243).

labour parties, in early 1980 the opposing positions were taken by non-socialist governments.

Not a member of the Commonwealth, Sweden had no formal role during the denouement of the Zimbabwean drama. It did, however, play a prominent part. In addition to substantial contributions to UNHCR for the repatriation of refugees from Botswana, Mozambique and Zambia in the form of cash[1] and personnel[2], the Swedish government[3], the Social Democratic Party[4] and the Africa Groups maintained high profiles during the pre-election period. Sweden's role was further enhanced by the fact that additional allocations of 5 MSEK each to ZANU and ZAPU were made by the government on the recommendation of CCHA on 3 January 1980.[5] Granted for humanitarian purposes during the repatriation exercise, the allocations were viewed by the British government as undue interference, causing a major diplomatic controversy between London and Stockholm.[6]

On 25 January 1980—three weeks after the press release announcing the allocations to ZANU and ZAPU—the Foreign Office in London instructed its Stockholm ambassador, Jeffrey Petersen, to formally make a complaint. In his letter to Leif Leifland, Under-Secretary of State for Foreign Affairs, Petersen stated the British view that "money given direct to the Patriotic Front at the present stage is likely to be used for military or electioneering purposes, or both".[7] Against this background, Petersen continued,

> I am under instructions to say that it is unwelcome and unhelpful to our efforts to hold elections which will be seen to be free and fair [...] if countries like Sweden commit themselves in advance to one or another political party by means of large donations.[8]

The Swedish assistance to ZANU was particularly singled out by Petersen, who stated that

---

1. An extraordinary allocation of 5 MSEK was extended directly to UNHCR for the repatriation exercise (Cable from the Ministry for Foreign Affairs to the Swedish embassy in Lusaka, Stockholm, 24 January 1980) (SDA).
2. Gillis Herlitz, one of the UNHCR observers seconded by SIDA, later published a vivid, personal account from his experiences in *Dagbok från Zimbabwe: Rapport från en Stats Födelse* ('Diary from Zimbabwe: Report from the Birth of a Nation'), Nordiska Afrikainstitutet, Uppsala, 1981.
3. Sweden established a 'liaison office' in Salisbury (Harare) in mid-February 1980. It was led by Jan Eliasson, who in 1992 became Deputy Secretary General of the United Nations in New York and in 1994 was appointed Under-Secretary of State for Foreign Affairs in Stockholm.
4. A chain of prominent members represented the Social Democratic Party during the pre-election period in Zimbabwe. One of them was Bengt Säve-Söderbergh, who delivered messages of encouragement and financial support to both ZANU and ZAPU (Interview with Bengt Säve-Söderbergh, p. 336). Donating 200,000 SEK each to the two movements, in similarly worded letters on behalf of the Social Democratic Party to Mugabe and Nkomo, Palme wrote on 7 February 1980: "Dear comrade and friend: [...] We certainly realize the many obstacles that exist. [I]n my speech at the Socialist International meeting in Vienna a few days ago, I criticized the British administration for [its] shortcomings in the implementation of the Lancaster House Agreement. [...] [W]e have decided to give [...] 200,000 SEK from our labour movement to each of the two parties in the Patriotic Front. As you know, we [would] do much better than this modest sum if we had been in government at this time" (Letters from Olof Palme to Robert Mugabe and Joshua Nkomo, Stockholm, 7 February 1980) (OPA).
5. Ministry for Foreign Affairs: Decision ('Katastrofbistånd till Patriotiska fronten i Zimbabwe'/'Emergency assistance to the Patriotic Front in Zimbabwe'), Stockholm, 3 January 1980 (SDA).
6. SWAPO's Peter Katjavivi—who had close links to the British Labour Party—recalled in 1995 how the British "[i]n the particular case of Zimbabwe at the time of independence [...] were objecting to the Swedish humanitarian support to the liberation movements. I remember a distinguished personality in the UK saying: 'It is holding things up'. I was a bit amazed by that comment" (Interview with Peter Katjavivi, pp. 74-75).
7. Letter from Jeffrey Petersen, British ambassador to Sweden, to Leif Leifland, Stockholm, 25 January 1980 (MFA).
8. Ibid.

we are already having problems with Mr. Mugabe and ZANU. [...] Mr. Mugabe is in clear breach of the undertakings which he signed at Lancaster House and there is every reason to fear that any undertakings which you have been given regarding the use of Swedish aid funds will be similarly disregarded.[1]

On behalf of the government, Leifland replied four days later, expressing his regret at the fact that "more states have not given aid of this kind as the situation of the refugees has been very difficult, indeed".[2] In addition, he made it clear that

through detailed reporting and supervision, and furthermore after many years of trustful [...] cooperation, [we know] that none of the branches of the Patriotic Front is using the Swedish contribution in any other way than that intended, i.e. for strictly humanitarian purposes. [...] The contribution [made on 3 January] is being extended to the Patriotic Front in its capacity as the predominant channel to the refugees. The Swedish government has [...] no reason whatsoever to suspect that the funds might be used for military or electioneering purposes.[3]

Finally, commenting upon the British government's statement on Robert Mugabe and ZANU, Leifland strongly noted:

Regarding your doubts about Mr. Mugabe's will and capability to keep agreements, we would only say that our experience is different from yours. [C]ooperation between Sweden and ZANU has always been founded on mutual respect and conscientious observance of concluded agreements.[4]

SIDA and ZANU had formally agreed on the utilization of the additional allocation of 5 MSEK at a meeting in Maputo on 9 January 1980.[5] According to the agreement, the grant was to be used for food and transport in favour of Zimbabwean returnees, as well as to assist them at the reception centres in Zimbabwe. It was further decided that the entire amount "should be paid out in cash to ZANU's [bank] account in Maputo".[6] As the ZANU leadership and the refugees soon thereafter started to return to Zimbabwe, it was, however, for practical reasons and at ZANU's request subsequently agreed to transfer the funds to the movement's newly established account in Salisbury (Harare). The transfer was made by SIDA from Stockholm on 30 January 1980.[7]

At that time, there was no official Swedish representation in Zimbabwe. Due to the strong British reaction against Sweden's assistance—in particular to ZANU—it was in early February decided to send SIDA's planning officer at the embassy in Lusaka, Tor Sellström, to verify that the funds were used in accordance with the agreement.[8] Sellström visited Salisbury on two occasions in mid-February 1980. After an introductory meeting with Robert Mugabe together with Jan Eliasson and

---

1. Ibid.
2. Letter from Leif Leifland to Jeffrey Petersen, Ministry for Foreign Affairs, Stockholm, 29 January 1980 (MFA)
3. Ibid.
4. Ibid.
5. 'Agreed minutes of discussions on utilization of an additional Swedish grant to the Zimbabwe African National Union, ZANU', Maputo, 9 January 1980 (SDA). The agreement was signed by Robert Mugabe and Johan Brisman, SIDA's representative to Mozambique.
6. Ibid.
7. Letter ('Uppföljning av katastrofbistånd om 5 mkr till Zimbabwe African National Union, ZANU: Slutrapport'/'Follow-up of emergency assistance of 5 MSEK to ZANU: Final report') from Lars-Olof Edström, SIDA's representative to Zambia, to SIDA Stockholm, Swedish embassy, Lusaka, 25 February 1980 (SDA).
8. Per Fröberg and Lennart Wohlgemuth: Instruction ('Katastrofbistånd till Zimbabwe African National Union, ZANU'/'Emergency assistance to ZANU'), SIDA, Stockholm, 8 February 1980 (SDA).

'Condemn British Colonial
Policy in Zimbabwe':
Georg Dreifaldt of the
Africa Groups addressing
a march by the Friends of the
Patriotic Front to the British
embassy in Stockholm,
February 1980 (Photo:
Anders Gunnartz)

Anders Möllander, he was referred to ZANU's Finance Secretary Ernest Kadungure.[1] The meetings with Kadungure were characterized by "complete openness [and] a high degree of trust vis-à-vis Sweden".[2] Sellström could without any restrictions examine ZANU's financial accounts and make sure that the emergency funds had indeed been used for the humanitarian purposes intended.[3]

Meanwhile, in Stockholm the relations with the British embassy did not improve. Against the background of increasing tensions and reported irregularities in Zimbabwe, some AGIS members had in early February 1980 taken the initiative in forming a broad *ad hoc* committee called Friends of the Patriotic Front.[4] On 9 February, the committee called for support to the PF movements through an appeal published in the liberal newspaper *Dagens Nyheter* and four days later it organized a march to the British embassy, where a number of solidarity organizations and the youth leagues of all the Swedish parliamentary parties except the Moderate Party demanded that "the British government assume full responsibility for the implementation of the [Lancaster House] Agreement".[5]

In particular, the appeal published in *Dagens Nyheter* incensed ambassador Petersen. It was signed by over fifty Swedes—including MPs from both the socialist opposition and the non-socialist ruling coalition[6], again with the exception of the Moderate Party—leading cultural personalities, journalists and solidarity activists, who *inter alia* noted that South African troops were still based in Zimbabwe; thousands of people remained imprisoned; Muzorewa's private army terrorized the rural population; and the Rhodesian police and army intimidated the Patriotic Front. The signatories therefore concluded that the British Governor, Lord Soames, "is allowing various violations of [the Lancaster House Agreement]".[7] Ambassador

1. Tor Sellström: Memorandum ('Samtal med Robert Mugabe i Salisbury 1980 02 12'/'Conversation with Robert Mugabe in Salisbury, 12 February 1980'), Swedish embassy, Lusaka, 14 February 1980 (SDA).
2. Tor Sellström: Memorandum ('Uppföljning av katastrofbistånd om 5 mkr till Zimbabwe African National Union, ZANU: Slutrapport'/'Follow-up of emergency assistance of 5 MSEK to ZANU: Final report'), Swedish embassy, Lusaka, 25 February 1980 (SDA).
3. Ibid. Cf. Möllander op. cit., p. 43.
4. In Swedish, *Patriotiska Frontens Vänner*.
5. 'Resolution adopted at demonstration against the British embassy, Stockholm', 13 February 1980 (SDA).
6. Among the MPs were C.H. Hermansson (Left Party Communists), Birgitta Dahl (Social Democratic Party), Pär Granstedt (Centre Party) and Olle Wästberg (Liberal Party). Advertisement: 'Stöd Patriotiska Fronten'/ 'Support the Patriotic Front' in *Dagens Nyheter*, 9 February 1980.
7. Ibid.

Petersen reacted strongly. Once again he complained to the Ministry for Foreign Affairs.[1] In addition, on 13 February 1980 Petersen addressed a long, harsh letter to all the individual signatories, rejecting their views and stating that he considered "that signatures of persons of standing like yourself should mean something real when appended to published documents".[2]

While Bishop Muzorewa accused "Sweden and Holland of sending war material and Communist propaganda to the Patriotic Front disguised as emergency aid"[3], by mid-February 1980 there was widespread concern in Sweden that the free and fair elections scheduled for 27-29 February would not be held. In fact, after contacts with the British Foreign Office, Per Lind, the Swedish ambassador in London, had on 6 February conveyed to the Foreign Ministry that "development[s] point towards [a scenario] of 'everybody against Mugabe'".[4] Reports from Zimbabwe gave increasing cause for concern as the election dates were approaching. In a statement on 21 February, the opposition leader Olof Palme noted that "the election campaign is now daily disrupted by terror and outrage", requesting the Swedish government "to convey its apprehension to the British government".[5] Five days later—on the eve of the elections—the Liberal Foreign Minister Ola Ullsten[6] repeated Palme's concern almost to the letter. Speaking on behalf of the government, Ullsten said:

> It is important [that] the elections opening tomorrow bring liberty and independence to Zimbabwe. What is at stake is not only the future of Zimbabwe, but also the prospects of [...] a positive course throughout Southern Africa. With this in mind, the Swedish government is disturbed by reports of terror and outrage disrupting the election campaign. The Lancaster House Agreement laid down the rules for the transition to a free Zimbabwe, stating among other things that all sections of opinion in the country should suffer no impediment in presenting their case to the electorate. The British government was made ultimately responsible for the maintenance of order and for ensuring fair and genuinely free elections. The parties must now live up to their responsibilities and help to ensure that the elections are conducted in such a manner that the outcome can be respected by all.[7]

The British had, however, not given up their defence of righteousness or their hope of a grand coalition in Salisbury. In a remarkable letter to the Ministry for Foreign Affairs, the British embassy in Stockholm wrote on 29 February that

> in view of [the] Swedish policy on Southern Africa, [you are] particularly well placed to support the British government in its attempts to ensure that the future government of Rhodesia (*sic*) is stable and reflects as fully as possible the aspiration of the people of Rhodesia. This will safeguard against the renewal of the war [and] can best be achieved through the formation of the most suitable coalition possible. [...]

---

1. Kaa Eneberg: 'Svenska politiker skrev under Zimbabweupprop' ('Swedish politicians signed Zimbabwe appeal') in *Dagens Nyheter*, 22 February 1980.
2. Circular letter from Jeffrey Petersen, Stockholm, 13 February 1980 (MFA).
3. 'Muzorewa: Vapen svensk hjälp' ('Muzorewa: Arms Swedish aid') in *Dagens Nyheter*, 12 February 1980. Muzorewa referred to election material and relief goods sent to the Patriotic Front movements by the Dutch NGO Holland Committee on Southern Africa and the Swedish NGOs Emmaus-Björkå and Bread and Fishes. The cargo arrived at Salisbury airport on 31 January, but was not cleared until mid-February 1980.
4. Cable from Per Lind, Swedish ambassador to Great Britain, to the Ministry for Foreign Affairs, London, 6 February 1980 (MFA).
5. 'Palmeprotest: Valkampen störs av terror' ('Palme protest: The election campaign is disrupted by terror') in *Dagens Nyheter*, 22 February 1980.
6. After serving as Prime Minister between October 1978 and October 1979, Ullsten became Minister for Foreign Affairs in Thorbjörn Fälldin's new non-socialist coalition government. He held that position from October 1979 until October 1982, when the Social Democratic Party returned to power.
7. 'Statement by the Foreign Minister, Mr. Ullsten, concerning the forthcoming elections in Zimbabwe-Rhodesia', 26 February 1980, in Ministry for Foreign Affairs: *Documents on Swedish Foreign Policy: 1980*, Stockholm, 1982, p. 189.

[T]here is no obligation on the [British] Governor to invite the leader of the largest party to form the government, unless that party has an absolute majority of the seats in the House of Assembly. We hope that the Swedish government will take every opportunity to explain to African governments that even if Mr. Mugabe's party wins the most seats, it will not necessarily enter the government, perhaps referring to the fact that the largest single party in Sweden is in opposition.[1]

This communication marked the end of British diplomacy towards Sweden with regard to 'the Rhodesia question'.[2] Against all the odds and Western predictions[3], ZANU achieved an absolute majority. Mugabe was thus invited to form independent Zimbabwe's first government. While the Union Jack was lowered, the longstanding relations between Sweden and the Zimbabwean nationalist movement continued.

Independence and New Relations

Discussions on development cooperation were initiated between representatives of the incoming government of independent Zimbabwe and Sweden before independence on 18 April 1980. The parties agreed to use a Swedish allocation of 17 million SEK until 30 June 1980 for government-to-government cooperation "to alleviate the short-term difficulties in Zimbabwe" (10 million), for NGO support (5 million) and for UNHCR's programme in favour of internally displaced persons (2 million).[4] It was an early and comparatively modest beginning of a development cooperation programme under which Sweden until 1994/95—in fixed prices (1995)—would disburse a total of 3.8 billion SEK, mainly to the education, health, transport and public administration sectors.[5]

Zimbabwe's independence radically altered the regional correlation of forces in favour of majority rule in Namibia and South Africa. Strategically situated in the heart of Southern Africa—touching the former and bordering the latter—the newly independent state would over the following decade and a half play a prominent role with regard to the liberation struggles in the two remaining bastions of white supremacy. In the case of South Africa, ZANU's background as a 'non-authentic' movement outside the Khartoum alliance—as well as increasingly tense relations with the 'authentic' ZAPU—initially favoured PAC.

When SIDA in late June 1980 opened an office in the Zimbabwean capital, it assisted ANC in establishing a presence in the country. The future South African President Thabo Mbeki was closely involved in the drawn out process, which eventually was crowned with success. During the second half of the 1980s, Zimbabwe

---

1. Letter from the British embassy in Stockholm to the Ministry for Foreign Affairs, Stockholm, 29 February 1980 (MFA).
2. The British Foreign Secretary, Lord Carrington, visited Sweden in August 1980. In his internal preparatory notes, Jan Eliasson wrote that "international attention must now be focused on Namibia. South Africa's stalling tactics must be exposed and rejected. From the Swedish side, we are not supporting the idea that South Africa would be given time to 'absorb' the events in Zimbabwe. On the contrary, pressure on South Africa must increase to [force it] to accept the UN plan for free Namibian elections" (Jan Eliasson: Memorandum ('Bakgrundspapper om södra Afrika inför brittiske utrikesministerns besök, 18-20 augusti 1980'/'Background paper to the visit by the British Foreign Secretary, 18-20 August 1980'), Ministry for Foreign Affairs, Stockholm, 15 August 1980) (MFA).
3. Cf. Möllander op. cit., p. 45 and Anders Möllander: Memorandum: 'Är Robert Mugabe känd i Rhodesia?: Några intryck' ('Is Robert Mugabe known in Rhodesia?: Some impressions'), Swedish liaison office, Salisbury, 12 February 1980 (MFA).
4. 'Agreed minutes from discussions on development cooperation 1980 between the government of Zimbabwe and the government of Sweden', Salisbury, 21 April 1980 (SDA).
5. Sida op. cit., p. 26.

would become of crucial importance to ANC, both from a military and a political point of view.

Although SWAPO belonged to the Khartoum alliance of 'authentic' liberation movements, there was in the case of Namibia no competing force to the movement led by Sam Nujoma. The relations between ZANU and SWAPO had, in addition, traditionally been close and friendly.[1] As early as in June 1981, the Zimbabwean government challenged the Pretoria regime by arranging a nationwide solidarity week for Namibia, attended by the SWAPO President. The Namibian movement was soon thereafter officially invited to open an office in the country, as well as to use the Zimbabwe Broadcasting Corporation's facilities for radio programmes to Namibia.[2]

SWAPO's Chief Representative to Zambia, Aaron Mushimba, was in February 1982 accredited as 'ambassador' to Zimbabwe. Within the regular, official humanitarian assistance to SWAPO, Swedish support was extended for the running of the office, information activities[3] and to assist the increasing number of Namibian refugees who were sent by SWAPO to the country for schooling and vocational training. Before turning to Sweden's relations with the Namibian liberation struggle, it could be noted that Sam Nujoma in his frequent exchange of views with Swedish government representatives often held up Zimbabwe as an example for independent Namibia.[4]

---

1. In addition to the fact that SWAPO and ZANU maintained close relations, there were many similarities between the political developments in Namibia and Zimbabwe. While Namibia was occupied by South Africa and the white minority in Zimbabwe *de facto* declared the country independent, both countries were ultimately controlled by the Pretoria regime, which in a parallel process tried to engineer 'internal solutions' by co-opting black political representatives into a dependent dispensation.
2. Jan Cedergren: Memorandum ('SWAPO i Zimbabwe'), Salisbury, 26 February 1982, attached to letter ('SWAPO's representation i Zimbabwe') from Bo Heinebäck, Swedish ambassador to Zimbabwe, to the Ministry for Foreign Affairs, Salisbury, 26 February 1982 (MFA).
3. Sweden financed *inter alia* the production of the bimonthly publication *SWAPO News and Views*, issued in Harare.
4. For example, in conversations with the Swedish ambassador to Angola, Leif Sjöström, in 1983-84. According to Sjöström, the SWAPO President was extremely critical of the decolonization process in Angola and Mozambique, as well as of the administrative system inherited from the Portuguese (Letter ('Samtal med Sam Nujoma'/'Conversation with Sam Nujoma') from Leif Sjöström to the Ministry for Foreign Affairs, Luanda, 6 June 1983 (MFA) and letter ('Samtal med Sam Nujoma') from Leif Sjöström to the Ministry for Foreign Affairs, Luanda, 23 January 1984) (MFA).

SWAPO of Namibia:
Tentative Steps towards Firm Relations

A Land in Anger

Namibia has been described as "the land God made in anger".[1] Predominantly Christian[2], it has been far from blessed with divine political fortunes. Colonized with brutal zeal by imperial Germany between 1884 and 1915, the administration of the territory was in 1921—after the German defeat in the First World War—entrusted by Great Britain to South Africa under a League of Nations mandate. Betraying the trust, Pretoria would over the following decades *de facto* incorporate Namibia as a fifth South African province, strengthen racial segregation and suppress mounting demands for national independence. These developments notwithstanding, South Africa's mandate was extended under the umbrella of the United Nations.[3]

After years of fruitless nationalist representations[4], the South West Africa People's Organization (SWAPO) initiated armed resistance against South Africa's occupation in August 1966. Two months later, the UN General Assembly resolved to terminate the international mandate, declaring that South Africa "has no [...] right to administer the territory and that henceforth [Namibia] comes under the direct responsibility of the United Nations".[5] The resolution was confirmed in March 1969 by the Security Council, which determined that "the continued presence of South Africa in Namibia is illegal", requesting the Pretoria government to "immediately withdraw its administration".[6] The UN resolutions were in turn upheld by the International Court of Justice (ICJ), which in June 1971 not only declared South Africa's administration illegal under international law, but expressed the opinion that "the members of the United Nations are under obligation to recognize the illegality of South Africa's presence in Namibia".[7]

Thus began two decades of glaring paradox. While the main Western powers opposed effective action to enforce the UN and ICJ rulings—notably economic

---

1. Jon Manchip White: *The Land God Made in Anger: Reflections on a Journey through South West Africa*, George Allen and Unwin, London, 1969.
2. Like the Nordic countries and Germany, Namibia is mainly an Evangelical-Lutheran country. This partly explains the close Nordic relations with the country. The Finnish Missionary Society established a significant presence in Ovamboland after 1870. See Carl-Johan Hellberg: *Mission, Colonialism and Liberation: The Lutheran Church in Namibia 1840-1966*, New Namibia Books, Windhoek, 1997. On the Namibian churches and the independence cause, cf. also Peter Katjavivi, Per Frostin and Kaire Mbuende (eds): *Church and Liberation in Namibia*, Pluto Press, London (UK) and Winchester (USA), 1989.
3. South Africa's proposal to formally incorporate Namibia was rejected by the UN General Assembly in December 1946. In July 1950, the International Court of Justice ruled that the mandate was still in force.
4. In 1960 alone, the United Nations received 120 messages and petitions demanding that Namibia be granted independence or placed under direct international control (IDAF: *Namibia: The Facts*, IDAF Publications, London, 1989, p. 16).
5. UN General Assembly Resolution 2145 (XXI) of 27 October 1966, cited in UNIN: *Namibia: A Direct United Nations Responsibility*, United Nations Institute for Namibia, Lusaka, 1987, p. 317.
6. UN Security Council Resolution 264 of 20 March 1969, cited in ibid., p. 332.
7. Advisory opinion of the International Court of Justice, 21 June 1971, cited in IDAF op. cit., p. 17.

measures[1]—apartheid South Africa could with impunity strengthen its illegal hold on Namibia. Using the territory as a strategic buffer against a perceived 'Communist onslaught' from Angola, the Pretoria regime embarked on a three-pronged strategy to a) "combat SWAPO with military means so as to weaken its domestic and international credibility and legitimacy", b) "seek to build support inside Namibia for [an] internal solution" and c) "continue a diplomatic dialogue with external parties in order to buy time and stall [...] negotiations".[2] In the process, the United Nations direct responsibility became for all practical purposes a dead letter[3] and the question of Namibia part of regional and global Cold War politics that the nationalist movement in crucial ways could do little to influence.[4] It was only after South Africa's military setbacks at Cuito Cuanavale in Angola in early 1988—which decisively changed the regional balance of power—that the Pretoria government recognized the urgency of a diplomatic settlement. The events led to the December 1988 New York accords with Cuba and Angola, and to independence elections in accordance with UN Security Council Resolution 435, adopted already in September 1978. At the elections in November 1989, SWAPO won an absolute majority of 57.3 per cent, while its main contender DTA got 28.6 per cent of the votes. Under SWAPO's President Sam Nujoma, Namibia achieved its independence on 21 March 1990.

Although a straightforward question of decolonization, national independence in Namibia would over the years—more than elsewhere in Southern Africa—turn into a complicated and multi-layered conflict. Formally, the United Nations played a specific role. Prominent in the equation from the mid-1970s was, however, the Cold War dimension of the wars in Angola, on the one hand involving the MPLA government, Cuba, the Soviet Union and SWAPO, and on the other South Africa,

---

1. On this point, Thomas Ohlson quotes William Zartman, who in his study *Ripe for Resolution: Conflict and Intervention in Africa* (Oxford University Press, New York, 1989) states that "when sanctions of any kind are feared more by those who would apply them than by the target, it is clear that deadlines are in the hands of the latter" (cited in Ohlson op. cit., p. 93). Cf. the author's interview with 'Pik' Botha, where the former South African Foreign Minister emphasized that "I managed the Rhodesian [...] and the Namibian situation without incurring sanctions. We never got sanctions on Namibia and/or Rhodesia. We got them on apartheid in South Africa, which was not my function" (Interview with Roelof 'Pik' Botha, p. 116).

2. Ohlson op. cit., p. 92.

3. In May 1967, the UN Council for Namibia (UNCN)—then South West Africa—was established to administer Namibia until independence. It was not recognized by South Africa and never allowed to establish a presence in the country it was supposed to govern. Sweden had from the beginning doubts about the council, considering its mandate "unrealistic" (Eva Nauckhoff: Memorandum ('Sveriges röstning i södra Afrika-frågorna 1967-70'/'Sweden's votes on Southern African questions 1967-70'), Ministry for Foreign Affairs, Stockholm, 20 November 1970) (MFA).

4. SWAPO was in December 1973 recognized by the UN General Assembly as "the authentic" and in December 1976 as "the sole and authentic representative of the Namibian people" (UNIN op. cit., pp. 381-382). A prime party to the Namibian conflict, SWAPO was, however, not invited to sign the December 1988 New York accords. Although SWAPO was the only Namibian political organization to receive official Swedish support—and thus *de facto* recognition—pending a democratic verdict by the Namibian people Sweden did not accord the movement the status of 'sole and authentic representative'. Instead, it was, for example, characterized by the Social Democratic government as "the leading movement in Namibia [...], which ha[s] articulated the people's demand for freedom" ('Summary of speech by Ambassador Rydbeck during the UN Security Council debate on Namibia', 29 January 1976, in Ministry for Foreign Affairs: *Documents on Swedish Foreign Policy: 1976*, Stockholm, 1978, p. 190). Similarly, Thorbjörn Fälldin's non-socialist coalition treated SWAPO as "the only really national political force in Namibia" ('Government statement at the Riksdag debate on foreign policy', 30 March 1977, in Ministry for Foreign Affairs: *Documents on Swedish Foreign Policy: 1977*, Stockholm, 1978, p. 24).

the United States and UNITA. A strong believer in the United Nations, granting development assistance to Angola and to the Southern African Frontline States, as well as extending humanitarian support to SWAPO, Sweden supported the former constellation.

The following narration does not attempt to disentangle all the knots of Sweden's involvement in the Namibian drama. It focuses on the direct, official assistance to SWAPO. Related questions—notably the issue of sanctions against the Pretoria regime; for which SWAPO campaigned together with ANC—will be addressed in the subsequent text on South Africa. It should be noted, however, that the economic relations with Namibia were extremely marginal. During the 1970s and 1980s, the registered commodity exchange between the two countries never exceeded 0.003 per cent of Sweden's total external trade.[1] As SWAPO—following the 1969 resolution by the UN Security Council—vowed not to accept official assistance from countries with significant interests in Namibia, this was not without importance. For example, when in January 1974 the Tanzanian and Zambian press reported[2] that SWAPO had asked the government of the Federal Republic of Germany to support its refugee settlement in Zambia, the organization reacted strongly, declaring that

SWAPO [has] never approached the Bonn government or any private [German] organization for any aid or assistance toward any of its projects. It is [...] not our policy to seek any aid, be it financial or otherwise, from imperialists or their supporters. It [would] amount to a betrayal of the national armed struggle if we seek or accept money or any kind of assistance from the

1. Of the five Southern African countries covered in this study, Namibia was from an economic point of view the least important to Sweden. There were no direct investments and although some Swedish-owned companies in South Africa (*inter alia* Atlas Copco, Skega and SKF) established outlets there, the *registered* trade was almost non-existent. Most probably, however, products of Swedish manufacture did find their way to Namibia through South Africa. Data for Namibia were until 1971 included in the statistics for South Africa. In that year, Sweden exported goods—mainly wood products—for a trifling value of 1 million, while imports—almost exclusively in the form of pelts (*SWAKARA* fur coats)—amounted to 0.6 MSEK (Ministry of Trade: 'Memorandum', Stockholm, 16 March 1972) (MFA). In absolute terms, the exchange increased in the 1970s. With Swedish exports remaining at a stable 1 million, by 1980 the value of imported Namibian goods had grown almost seven times, reaching 3.9 MSEK (Statistiska Centralbyrån: *Utrikeshandel 1980* ('Foreign Trade 1980'), Liber/Allmänna Förlaget, Stockholm, 1982, Table 9, p. 182). While this corresponded to a mere 0.003 per cent of Sweden's total imports, the increase provoked strong protests by the solidarity movement and members of parliament. In January 1982, for example, Pär Granstedt of the Centre Party introduced a motion demanding a ban on Swedish trade with Namibia (Swedish Parliament 1981/82: Motion No. 1715, Riksdagens Protokoll, 1982, pp. 10-11). As the Swedish imports towards the end of the 1970s included some base metals, in January 1983 Hans Göran Franck, Anna Lindh, Monica Andersson and other MPs of the ruling Social Democratic Party invoked the UN Council for Namibia's Decree No. 1 (1974) on 'Protection of the Natural Resources of Namibia', demanding a total trade ban (Swedish Parliament 1982/83: Motion No. 721, Riksdagens Protokoll, 1983, pp. 9-11). However, by 1982 the exchange had dwindled. The value of exports to Namibia was then 0.7 million, while the imports—now exclusively in the form of pelts—had fallen drastically to a mere 0.3 MSEK (Erich Erichsen, Bertil Högberg and Arne Tostensen: 'Scandinavia and Namibia: Contradictions of Policies and Actions' in Allan D. Cooper (ed.): *Allies in Apartheid: Western Capitalism in Occupied Namibia*, Macmillan Press, London, 1988, table 6.1, p. 140). Nevertheless, it should be noted that the Swedish shipping company Transatlantic in contravention of the UN Council of Namibia's decree regularly transported Namibian minerals—notably lead ore—from the port of Walvis Bay (Örjan Berner: Memorandum ('Handel med Namibia'/'Trade with Namibia'), Ministry for Foreign Affairs, Stockholm, 14 February 1975) (MFA).

2. 'SWAPO asks for 1.3 m aid' in *Daily News*, Dar es Salaam, 18 January 1974 and 'SWAPO may have Lusaka centre' in *Zambia Daily Mail*, Lusaka, 18 January 1974.

very regime which sells guns and other sophisticated instruments of war to racist South Africa to kill and massacre our people.[1]

Namibia in Sweden

Sweden's contacts with the Namibian nationalist movement go back to the early 1960s[2], when the South West Africa National Union (SWANU) formed part of the South Africa United Front and the SWANU President Jariretundu Kozonguizi visited the country with Oliver Tambo of ANC and Nana Mahomo of PAC of South Africa. Leading SWANU members—among them Uatja Kaukuetu, Charles Kauraisa and Zedekia Ngavirue—were at about the same time granted scholarships in Sweden. With close links to the emerging solidarity movement, the SWANU students-cum-diplomats played major roles in the development of the Swedish anti-apartheid opinion, placing Namibia at the centre of the debate. The solidarity movement's first regular information bulletin was thus entitled *Syd- och Syd-västafrika* ('South and South West Africa'). Often invited to address the traditional First of May demonstrations, the SWANU leaders[3] established privileged relations with the ruling Social Democratic Party, in particular through the future international secretaries Pierre Schori and Bernt Carlsson.[4] According to Schori, "the first close contact that the Swedish Social Democratic Party had with any liberation movement in Southern Africa was really with SWANU", adding that "you could say that [the SWANU students] opened the eyes of both the party and of the public opinion to the situation in that part of the world".[5]

Under the 'refugee million', in 1964 the Swedish government embarked upon a humanitarian assistance programme which to a large extent targeted Namibian students. Via the Lutheran World Federation, the Church of Sweden Aid (CSA) had by then established direct contacts with its Namibian sister churches, notably the

---

1. SWANU: 'Press release', Lusaka, 18 January 1974 (MFA). Due to the German colonization and the significant number of German citizens and German-speakers in Namibia, there was a special relationship between the two. Nevertheless, SWAPO's representative to the Federal Republic of Germany (FRG) was placed in Sweden from 1971, covering the Nordic countries, FRG and Austria. SWAPO's President Sam Nujoma visited FRG prior to the country's admission to the United Nations in September 1973. During the non-official stay, he requested the Bonn government to close its consulate in Namibia and to "discontinue all its economic, cultural and military connections and interventions in Namibia" (ibid.). The Swedish honorary consulate in Windhoek was closed in 1966, following UN General Assembly Resolution 2145 (Cable from the Ministry for Foreign Affairs to the Swedish UN delegation, Stockholm, 22 June 1970) (MFA). Exploiting Cold War divisions between West (FRG) and East (GDR) Germany, SWAPO moved closer to the latter in the mid-1970s (Ilona and Hans-Georg Schleicher op. cit., pp. 151-57). The organization would at the same time increasingly denounce West Germany. The June 1976 report by the 'John Ya-Otto Commission of Inquiry into Circumstances Which Led to the Revolt of SWAPO Cadres between June 1974 and April 1976' concluded that "evidence [...] clearly demonstrates that the Bonn government devised schemes aimed at subverting SWAPO both internally and externally". According to the report, the "recruitment" of the SWAPO leader Andreas Shipanga was central to the "West German imperialistic intrigues" (SWAPO: 'Report of the Findings and Recommendations of the John Ya-Otto Commission of Inquiry', Lusaka, 4 June 1976, p. 6) (MFA). On SWAPO's relations with the Federal Republic of Germany, see also the interviews with its representatives Ben Amathila (1971-77) (p. 67) and Hadino Hishongwa (1977-82) (p. 69).
2. See Sellström Volume I, pp. 146-52, 157-58 and 261-71.
3. Kaukuetu and Kauraisa arrived in Sweden in late 1960 and Ngavirue at the beginning of 1962. At the time, Kaukuetu was Vice-President of SWANU. In 1965, Ngavirue became Chairman of SWANU's External Council while Kauraisa was elected Foreign Secretary. In 1968, Kauraisa succeeded Ngavirue as head of the External Council. At Namibia's independence in March 1990, President Nujoma appointed Ngavirue Director General of the National Planning Commission, *inter alia* in charge of foreign aid coordination.
4. After serving as international secretary of the Swedish Social Democratic Party (1971-76) and Secretary General of the Socialist International (1976-83), Carlsson was in 1987 appointed UN Commissioner for Namibia. On his way to witness the signing of the New York accords between Angola, Cuba and South Africa, he was killed in the Lockerbie air disaster in December 1988.
5. Interview with Pierre Schori, p. 330.

'The Swedish Labour Movement Pays Tribute to the UN': Foreign Minister Torsten Nilsson (in light overcoat) and SWANU President Jariretundu Kozonguizi in Gothenburg on First of May 1965 (Photo: Kamera-reportage)

Evangelical Lutheran Church in Namibia (ELCIN).[1] The first CSA project in the country—the construction of the Oshigambo High School—was launched in 1964. With the information activities carried out by the resident SWANU leaders, this led to a growing political concern for Namibia. The Swedish stand was recognized by the organizers of the first ever International Conference on South West Africa, held in Oxford, England, in March 1966. Olof Palme—then Minister of Transport and Communications—was invited to chair the deliberations. Representatives from all the Swedish parliamentary parties except the Moderate Party took part in the conference, where for the first time broad and close contacts were established with SWAPO.[2]

It was also in 1966 that the social democratic newspapers *Aftonbladet* and *Arbetet* launched a fund-raising campaign for SWANU and SWAPO.[3] Shortly before the first armed encounter between SWAPO and the South African security forces at Omgulumbashe in Ovamboland on 26 August 1966, the two Namibian

---

1. ELCIN—which as ELOK (Evangelical Lutheran Ovambo-Kavango Church) became independent in 1957—grew out of the Finnish mission. It joined the Lutheran World Federation in 1961. Two years later, the head of ELOK/ELCIN, Bishop Leonard Auala, became a member of the federation's executive committee. Auala maintained contacts with the Church of Sweden and was during his visits to the country received at the Ministry for Foreign Affairs, where he expressed sympathy for SWAPO. For example, in November 1974—ten days after a high-profile visit by the SWAPO President—he supported Nujoma's request for continued Swedish support to the Namibian refugees under SWAPO's care in Zambia (Ann Wilkens: Memorandum ('Samtal med namibisk biskop'/'Conversation with Namibian bishop'), Ministry for Foreign Affairs, Stockholm, 19 November 1974) (MFA).

2. On the Oxford conference, see Sellström Volume I, pp. 273-77. It was formally organized by the exiled South African Ronald Segal with assistance from the British Anti-Apartheid Movement and the Africa Bureau in London. According to the Namibian historian Peter Katjavivi, it was through Palme's active involvement that the conference took place (Interview with Peter Katjavivi, p. 72).

3. The decision to organize the campaign was taken in reaction to a negative stand by the International Court of Justice, which on 18 July 1966 refused to pass a verdict regarding South Africa's mandate over Namibia.

nationalist organizations, finally, met in Uppsala, Sweden, to form a National Union of South West African Students. The SWAPO delegation was led by President Sam Nujoma, who in connection with the meeting held bilateral talks with the acting Swedish Minister for Foreign Affairs, Olof Palme.

Through armed resistance, active diplomacy and support from OAU, SWAPO would from 1966 establish itself as the main Namibian liberation movement in the eyes of the Swedish solidarity opinion.[1] In the case of the ruling Social Democratic Party, Schori later explained that "there was an initial transition period, but we came to believe that SWAPO had more roots and that it was more anchored in the people. [...] There was no particular incident behind this development. It was simply based on reality".[2]

South Africa's massive clampdown on SWAPO decisively contributed to that realization. In a series of 'terrorism trials', from 1968 the apartheid regime sentenced scores of the movement's leaders and freedom fighters—among them the legendary Andimba Toivo ya Toivo—to life imprisonment or decades of detention on Robben Island outside Cape Town, where they joined Nelson Mandela, Walter Sisulu, Robert Sobukwe and other South African political prisoners. Considering the trials and sentences "a travesty of justice"[3], the Swedish Foreign Ministry regularly instructed its legation in Pretoria to be present at the court proceedings. Behind the scenes, Foreign Minister Torsten Nilsson granted official funds to the International Defence and Aid Fund and Church of Sweden Aid to cover legal defence costs and assist the families of the prisoners. The contacts broadened the understanding of the Namibian liberation struggle in Sweden, bringing the government and the church closer to SWAPO.

From Uneasy Beginnings to Privileged Attention

SWAPO was among the first African liberation movements to approach Sweden for direct, official assistance.[4] On the basis of repeated declarations by the UN General Assembly, in May 1969 the Swedish parliament endorsed such a policy, which in the West was both unique and controversial. In the case of Namibia, the parliamentary decision was validated only three months later by the highest organ of the world organization. Recalling its March 1969 resolution on the illegality of South Africa's presence in Namibia, the UN Security Council defined in August 1969 South Africa's "continued occupation" as "an aggressive encroachment on the authority of the United Nations, a violation of the territorial integrity and a denial

---

1. The OAU Liberation Committee withdrew its recognition of SWANU in 1965. Kauraisa later said that the committee "wanted us to make a clear statement that SWANU was embarking on armed struggle. This we could not do" (Interview with Charles Kauraisa, p. 78).
2. Interview with Pierre Schori, p. 331. Ngavirue in 1995 gave the following comment to the shift in the Swedish opinion: "I am not so sure that it was a question of recognition and non-recognition. I do know that SWAPO really was being seen as having the guerrilla fighters, doing the actual fighting. OAU had at that point indicated support for SWAPO and I think that organizations that were sympathetic to the Namibian cause felt that they should follow the guidelines set by the Organization of African Unity" (Interview with Zedekia Ngavirue, p. 94).
3. 'Press release', 13 February 1968, in The Royal Ministry for Foreign Affairs: *Documents on Swedish Foreign Policy: 1968*, Stockholm, 1969, p. 104.
4. During a visit to Sweden, SWAPO's Secretary General Jacob Kuhangua had as early as in September 1965 asked SIDA for support to assist a group of Namibian refugees in Tanzania. In May 1966, SIDA decided to allocate an amount of 200,000 SEK to the Tanganyika Christian Refugee Service in favour of the refugees. Although not extended directly to SWAPO, the support was initiated by the liberation movement and could be seen as a first expression of humanitarian cooperation between the Swedish government and SWAPO (Sellström Volume I, pp. 272-73).

of the political sovereignty of the people of Namibia". More importantly, the Security Council recognized

> the legitimacy of the struggle of the people of Namibia against the illegal presence of the South African authorities, [requesting] all states to increase their moral and material assistance to the people of Namibia in their struggle against foreign occupation.[1]

While SWANU at the time had practically disappeared from the official Swedish political scene[2], SWAPO responded to the parliamentary statement and to the Security Council's call by submitting a request for financial support in September 1969.[3] It covered such different items as travel and accommodation in connection with the movement's pending consultative congress at Tanga in Tanzania; procurement of land for the settlement of Namibian refugees in Zambia; scholarships; and equipment for SWAPO's offices.[4] At its meeting in October 1969, CCHA decided to recommend support for the delivery of office equipment.[5] Although not of a human-itarian character, the recommendation was approved, and in early 1970 consignments to the value of 15,000 SEK each were delivered to the SWAPO offices in Dar es Salaam and Lusaka.[6] This was the first, modest step on a long journey jointly embarked upon by the Swedish government and SWAPO.[7]

In the early 1970s, the Swedish government gave almost exclusive attention to the liberation movements in the Portuguese colonies. In September 1971, the Minis-

---

1. UN Security Council Resolution 269 of 12 August 1969, cited in United Nations: *Yearbook of the United Nations: 1969*, Office of Public Information, United Nations, New York, 1972, p. 697. The resolution was adopted with 11 votes in favour and 4 abstentions. Against the background of Finland's policy towards Namibia, it could be noted that it abstained from voting together with France, UK and USA. Cf. Soiri and Pel-tola (op. cit., pp. 86-87), who note that the policy of Finland at the time was that "no support should be given [to] violent movements" and that it did not recognize SWAPO or any other liberation organization. Official Finnish humanitarian assistance to SWAPO was, however, granted from 1974.

2. According to an unsigned note by a Foreign Ministry official, written after the meetings held by UNCN in Stockholm in June 1971, "SWANU has not made its presence known for the last three years" ('SWANU-kon-takter'/'SWANU contacts', Stockholm, [no date, but June 1971]) (MFA).

3. Despite the early relations established with the Social Democratic Party, it was only in 1976 and then in Botswana that SWANU approached the Swedish government for support. At the beginning of the year, John Rikondja Tjirare, SWANU Secretary General, and Joseph Kambamunu Havanga, Chairman of the SWANU Youth League, presented an unspecified appeal to the Swedish embassy in Gaborone, which was rather directed against SWAPO than in favour of SWANU. The appeal emphasized that "the choice is yours [to] either support the united liberation movement of Namibia or to support a single liberation movement, which is tribally orientated and thus [i]mpose[s] domination of one tribe upon the entire nation" (SWANU: 'The political developments in Namibia', submitted to the Swedish embassy in Gaborone and attached to a letter from Tore Zetterberg ('Cirkulärskrivelse från SWANU-Namibiska flyktingar i Botswana'/'Circular letter from SWANU-Namibian refugees in Botswana') to the Ministry for Foreign Affairs, Gaborone, 15 April 1976) (SDA). Two years later, Charles Kauraisa—then also representing the Namibia National Front (NNF)—contacted the Ministry for Foreign Affairs to "enquire about the possibilities of receiving a [financial] contribution towards a visit to Namibia" (Marika Fahlén: Memorandum ('Besök av Charles Kauraisa, Namibia National Front (NNF)'/'Visit by Charles Kauraisa, NNF)', Ministry for Foreign Affairs, Stockholm, 4 April 1978) (SDA). Neither request was granted. Together with a number of SWANU members, Kauraisa went to Namibia later in 1978, finally settling there in 1981 (Interview with Charles Kauraisa, p. 79).

4. CCHA: Memorandum ('Framställning från SWAPO'/'Request by SWAPO') by Kerstin Oldfeldt, Stockholm, 9 October 1969 (SDA).

5. CCHA: 'Protokoll' ('Minutes'), Stockholm, 16 October 1969 (SDA).

6. Letter of acknowledgement from SWAPO's Acting Treasurer-General, Joseph Ithana, to SIDA's Director [General], Dar es Salaam, 29 September 1970 (MFA). The first allocation to SWAPO of 30,000 SEK was granted for the financial year 1970/71. In 1972, SWAPO moved its exile headquarters from Dar es Salaam to Lusaka.

7. In their study *Namibia's Liberation Struggle: The Two-Edged Sword* (James Currey, London, and Ohio University Press, Athens, 1995), Colin Leys and John Saul acknowledge that "little is said [...] about SWAPO's diplomatic accomplishments, although this is an intriguing theme that deserves more research" (p. 3). Studies on SWAPO and the liberation struggle in Namibia are on this point both weak and wanting. Quoting a South African newspaper report, Dobell, for example, merely states in a footnote that "in 1975 (*sic*) the Swedish government set a precedent of giving direct aid to SWAPO" (Dobell op. cit., p. 64). In the book—based on her masters thesis and presented as "the first in-depth study on the history of [SWAPO]" (p. 10)—Dobell argues that "the extent and sources of [the] material support are critical to understanding SWAPO's thinking" (p. 64). The inquisitive student of Namibian affairs is, however, left wondering about the possible impact of the substantial Swedish—and later Nordic—support.

try for Foreign Affairs confirmed this orientation, in a policy document adding, however, that a "token support" to "the smaller movements from the southern parts of the continent" should be maintained, "as [it] shows that Sweden does not follow an anti-Portuguese line, but one that supports liberation".[1] Together with ZANU of Zimbabwe, SWAPO was the first Southern African liberation movement outside the Portuguese colonial sphere to benefit from the official policy. In December 1971, CCHA recommended a second regular, annual allocation to SWAPO for the financial year 1971/72.[2] Subsequently approved, it amounted to 100,000 SEK and covered the delivery of medicines, medical equipment, clothes and food supplies in favour of an estimated 3,000 Namibian refugees in Zambia.[3]

For the following year, in June 1972 SWAPO requested continued commodity support to the tune of 200,000 SEK.[4] The majority of the Namibian refugees had by then been moved by the Zambian authorities to a camp administered by UNHCR near Solwezi in the north-western part of the country. In addition, CCHA was not convinced that SWAPO was adequately organized to handle increased commodity aid, expressing the opinion that "it is still too early to assess SWAPO's capacity to make use of [the] assistance and [to] determine the effects of the support granted so far."[5] Against this background, in September 1972 it was decided to leave the request without further action.[6] Although deliveries under the 1971/72 programme continued[7], no official support was granted for 1972/73.

As the history of Sweden's cooperation with the Southern African liberation movements would later show, this expression of non-confidence was exceptional.[8] In all the cases where official support was postponed, suspended or interrupted— that is, to FRELIMO in 1968-71, ZAPU in 1969-73, MPLA in 1973-74[9] and to ZANU and ZAPU in 1975-77—the decision was due to internal struggles or external demands, not to doubts concerning the recipient's administrative competence. From 1973/74—when the Swedish government allocated 500,000 SEK to

---

1. [Ethel] Ringborg: Memorandum ('Stöd till befrielserörelser'/'Support to liberation movements'), Ministry for Foreign Affairs, Stockholm, 7 September 1971 (MFA).
2. CCHA: 'Protokoll' ('Minutes'), Stockholm, 27 December 1971 (SDA).
3. CCHA: Memorandum ('Stöd till SWAPO'/'Support to SWAPO') by Anders Möllander, Stockholm, 6 June 1973 (SDA).
4. CCHA: Memorandum ('Ansökan från South West Africa People's Organization, SWAPO, om fortsatt svenskt varubistånd'/'Request by SWAPO for continued Swedish commodity aid') by Gun-Britt Andersson, [Stockholm], 1 September 1972 (MFA).
5. Ibid.
6. CCHA: 'Protokoll' ('Minutes'), Stockholm, 19 September 1972 (SDA).
7. The principle applied by Sweden was that funds allocated for a given financial year were carried over to the next year.
8. The decision is noteworthy in the light of the developments inside Namibia in 1971-72, characterized by Katjavivi as "a turning point" (Peter Katjavivi: *A History of Resistance in Namibia*, James Currey, London, OAU, Addis Ababa and Unesco Press, Paris, 1988, pp. 65-71). In response to the June 1971 advisory opinion by the ICJ on the illegality of South Africa's presence, there was an upsurge of nationalist resistance. It culminated in a historic, general strike against the contract labour system from mid-December 1971 to late January 1972, involving between 13,000 and 20,000 workers. Organized by "ordinary workers" (Katjavivi op. cit., p. 70), the strike was largely inspired by students from the SWAPO Youth League. On the 1971-72 strike, see Gretchen Bauer: *Labor and Democracy in Namibia, 1971-1996*, Ohio University Press, Athens, and James Currey, London, 1998, pp. 18-50; Gillian and Suzanne Cronje: *The Workers of Namibia*, International Defence and Aid Fund for Southern Africa, London, 1979, pp. 77-89; and Pekka Peltola: *The Lost May Day: Namibian Workers Struggle for Independence*, The Finnish Anthropological Society in association with the Nordic Africa Institute, Jyväskylä, 1995, pp. 108-23. Triggered by dismissals and forced repatriation of striking Ovambo contract workers, a rural revolt followed in Ovamboland in February 1972. It was savagely repressed by the authorities, including the South African army. The strike and the rural revolt led in 1973 to an increasing exodus from Namibia, which after the fall of the Portuguese regime grew to a flood from mid-1974.
9. The assistance to MPLA was never formally interrupted. Due to the Chipenda revolt and to the Zambian government's position, the cooperation was, however, in a state of suspension from late 1973 until mid-1974.

SWAPO[1]—the confidence was restored. Despite a number of outstanding doubts, official assistance to SWAPO was not suspended, but, surprisingly, more than doubled after the outbreak of the internal crisis and the 'Shipanga affair' in 1976.

SWAPO and the ruling Social Democratic Party had established close political relations towards the end of the 1960s.[2] Invited to Sweden by Palme and Schori after the 1966 Oxford conference, the founder member and leader Andreas Shipanga stayed with the future UN Commissioner for Namibia, Bernt Carlsson.[3] As early as in October 1967, SWAPO also appointed a resident representative to Sweden. However, Paul Helmuth—who was formally introduced in late 1968—fell out with the movement at its consultative Tanga congress at the turn of 1969-1970.[4] It was only at the beginning of 1971 that Ben Amathila—who at Tanga had been elected Assistant Secretary for Education and Culture—arrived in Stockholm to open SWAPO's mission to the Scandinavian countries, West Germany and Austria.[5] The Namibia question was at the time high on the agenda. Shortly after Amathila's arrival, Sweden hosted an important meeting of the UN Council for Namibia.[6] It was attended by Sam Nujoma, who over the following years regularly paid visits to the country for political consultations. Assisted by his wife Libertine[7], Amathila would at the same time through patient and skillful diplomacy constructively contribute to rapidly increasing aid allocations to SWAPO.

SWAPO had initially to overcome considerable resistance in Sweden. Nevertheless, after the April 1973 UN/OAU conference on Southern Africa in Oslo it soon became a major recipient of direct official humanitarian assistance. While no Swedish assistance was granted in 1972/73, an amount of 500,000 SEK was, as noted,

---

1. 'Agreed minutes of discussions between delegations from SWAPO and Sweden', Lusaka, 20 September 1973 (SDA) and SIDA: Decision ('Biståndsprogram för SWAPO 1973/74'/'Assistance programme to SWAPO 1973/74'), Stockholm, 23 October 1973 (SDA).
2. Via its International Solidarity Fund—set up in 1967—the Social Democratic Party regularly granted financial assistance to SWAPO. Contrary to the stand taken by the official CCHA, the support was not suspended in 1972 (Socialdemokraterna: 'Verksamheten 1972'/'Activities 1972', p. 90) (LMA). Starting at a modest level, the party's contribution to SWAPO steadily increased and was on average more important than that to ANC of South Africa. In 1977, for example, the grants to SWAPO and ANC amounted, respectively, to 78,500 and 30,000 SEK (Socialdemokraterna: 'Verksamheten 1977', p. 77) (LMA). In 1978, the financial support to SWAPO was 120,000 SEK, representing more than 20 per cent of the payments from the fund (Socialdemokraterna: 'Verksamheten 1978'/'Activities 1978', p. 103) (LMA). The support was utilized for "political organization, educational work, assistance to political prisoners and their families, as well as for medicines" (ibid.).
3. Interview with Andreas Shipanga, p. 97. A founder member of SWAPO's forerunner, the Ovamboland People's Congress (set up in Cape Town in 1958), Shipanga was at the time the movement's representative to the United Arab Republic, based in Cairo. He was also the editor of the SWAPO publication *Solidarity*.
4. See Sellström Volume I, pp. 288-89.
5. On the background to the decision and Amathila's initial trials and tribulations, see the interview with Ben Amathila, p. 63. Appointed SWAPO Secretary for Economic Affairs, Amathila returned to Zambia in 1977. In 1990, he became Minister of Trade and Industry in the first government of independent Namibia.
6. As noted, the Swedish government expressed doubts about the mandate and functions of UNCN. Both Zambia—holding the chairmanship—and SWAPO, however, wanted Sweden to join the council. Immediately after the ICJ ruling in mid-June 1971, UNCN held a series of consultations with SWANU, SWAPO, so called 'independent Namibians' and the Swedish government in Stockholm. The SWAPO delegation was led by Sam Nujoma and included Ben Amathila, Peter Katjavivi (Secretary for Economic and Legal Affairs and Chief Representative to the United Kingdom and Western Europe), Evald Katjivena (member of SWAPO's Executive Committee and Chief Representative to Algeria) and Alpo Mbamba (member of the Central Committee and Deputy Representative to Scandinavia, West Germany and Austria) (United Nations: 'Report of the United Nations Council for Namibia', General Assembly, Official Records from the Twenty-Sixth Session, Supplement No. 24, United Nations, New York, 1971, pp. 69 and 81-84) (MFA). As a curiosity, it could be noted that SWANU strongly opposed the change of name from South West Africa to Namibia—adopted by the United Nations in 1968—demanding "a plebiscite in the territory" (ibid., p. 82).
7. Née Appolus, Libertine Amathila—a medical doctor by profession—held the position of Assistant Secretary for Health and Social Welfare. She was also the Director of SWAPO's Women's Council. At Namibia's independence in 1990, she was appointed Minister of Local Government and Housing.

SWAPO representative Ben Amathila and Olof Palme leading a march organized by the Social
Democratic Youth League in Stockholm, October 1976 (Photo: Lars Groth/Pressens Bild)

allocated for the financial year 1973/74. It was increased to 750,000 in 1974/75[1], 3
million in 1975/76[2] and to a total of 5.9 MSEK in 1976/77.[3] As early as in August
1975, Nujoma underlined the significance of the support, stating in a letter to the
Swedish ambassador to Zambia that "I feel that Sweden will go down in the history
of the Namibian people as one of the most reliable friends, who stood by us during
the most trying period of our national liberation struggle".[4] By 1976, Sweden had
according to SWAPO's Finance Secretary and representative to Tanzania, Hifikepunye Pohamba[5], become "SWAPO's largest donor outside the socialist bloc".[6] One

1. To an original allocation of 600,000 during 1974/75 (SIDA: Decision ('Bistånd till SWAPO'/'Assistance to
   SWAPO'), Stockholm, 28 June 1974) (SDA) was added in April 1975 150,000 SEK (SIDA: Decision ('Ytterligare stöd till SWAPO för budgetåret 1974/75'/'Additional support to SWAPO for the financial year 1974/
   75'), Stockholm, 7 April 1975) (SDA).
2. The first grant of 2 MSEK for 1975/76 (SIDA: Decision ('Bistånd till SWAPO under budgetåret 1975/76'/
   'Assistance to SWAPO during the financial year 1975/76'), Stockholm, 14 October 1976) (SDA) was
   increased in April 1976 to 3 million (SIDA: Decision ('Framställning från SWAPO om ytterligare stöd under
   1975/76'/'Request from SWAPO re additional support in 1975/76'), Stockholm, 29 April 1976) (SDA).
3. An amount of 5 MSEK was in September 1976 allocated to SWAPO for 1976/77 (SIDA: Decision ('Bistånd
   till SWAPO under budgetåret 1976/77'/'Assistance to SWAPO during the financial year 1976/77'), Stockholm, 24 September 1976) (SDA). An additional grant of 900,000 was decided by the government in June
   1977 (Ministry for Foreign Affairs: Decision ('Stöd till SWAPO'/'Support to SWAPO'), Stockholm, 16 June
   1977) (SDA).
4. Letter from Sam Nujoma to the Swedish ambassador to Zambia, Lusaka, 14 August 1975 (MFA).
5. Secretary for Finance and Administration on SWAPO's Political Bureau, Hifikepunye ('Lukas') Pohamba in
   mid-1977 took up the position as National Treasurer at the organization's provisional headquarters in
   Lusaka. Keeping that position until Namibia's independence, he moved to Luanda in mid-1981. As head of
   SWAPO's Treasury Department, from the late 1970s Pohamba was more closely involved with Swedish assistance than anybody else in the movement, regularly leading SWAPO's delegations to the annual aid negotiations and often visiting Sweden. At Namibia's independence in 1990, he was appointed Minister of Home
   Affairs. Cf. the interviews with Hifikepunye Pohamba (pp. 94-96) and Roland Axelsson, SIDA's regional
   coordinator of humanitarian assistance between 1984 and 1991 (pp. 252-56).
6. Letter ('Samtal med chefen för SWAPO's kontor i Dar es Salaam'/'Conversation with the head of the SWAPO
   office in Dar es Salaam') from Per Lindström, Swedish embassy, to the Ministry for Foreign Affairs, Dar es
   Salaam, 16 March 1976 (MFA). The Soviet Union was according to Pohamba the largest donor among the
   socialist countries.

year later—in February 1977—Pohamba informed Foreign Minister Karin Söder's political adviser Pär Granstedt that the Swedish government had grown into "the largest, or second largest, donor" overall.[1]

In September 1976, the Social Democratic Party lost the Swedish parliamentary elections. Succeeded by Thorbjörn Fälldin's non-socialist coalition between the Centre, Liberal and Moderate parties, it was widely expected that the new government would depart from the pro-active policy towards national liberation in Southern Africa and scale down the direct support to the nationalist movements. Sensing a changing wind after the election results, the head of the South African legation in Stockholm, ambassador Endemann, requested a meeting with the Ministry for Foreign Affairs. Raising the issue of the detention of Andreas Shipanga, Solomon Mifima and other SWAPO leaders, he expressed the hope that the new government would follow "a more balanced policy" vis-à-vis South Africa and Namibia. He was, however, told by the head of the political department, ambassador Leif Leifland, that "such prospects were as good as non-existent. Sweden's policies towards South Africa", Leifland explained, "were based on a very unequivocal [...] opinion and no changes were to be expected".[2]

Endemann was "markedly disappointed" by the answer, commenting that "I had at least hoped that the new government would not go out of its way to seek confrontation".[3] Requesting a second meeting, one month later he himself took a confrontational course, criticizing a statement on Namibia made by the former Social Democratic Foreign Minister Sven Andersson in August 1976. According to Endemann, it could only "diminish Sweden's reputation in South Africa". Commenting that it was "a price [Sweden] was ready to pay", Leifland reminded the South African diplomat that the statement in question was made by a representative of the previous government, but that he, nevertheless, "should rest assured that the new government in no respect was less critical to South Africa's apartheid policy than the former".[4]

In fact—as in the case of the Zimbabwean Patriotic Front—the Fälldin government sharply increased the assistance to SWAPO (and to ANC of South Africa). Supported by the opposition Social Democratic Party and the Africa Groups—who in June 1976 decided to embrace SWAPO—in 1977/78 the annual allocation to SWAPO was raised from 5.9 to a total of 14.5 million[5], in 1978/79 to 22 million[6]

1. Anders Möllander: Memorandum ('Samtal med SWAPO-representant' /'Conversation with SWAPO representative'), Swedish embassy, Dar es Salaam, 11 February 1977 (MFA). Interviewed in 1995, Pohamba stated: "Being responsible for the aid programmes to SWAPO from various countries, I rated [them]. When I did that, the SIDA assistance was the largest" (Interview with Hifikepunye Pohamba, p. 95).

2. Bo Heinebäck: Memorandum ('Sydafrikanske ambassadören besöker polchefen'/'The South African ambassador visits the head of the political department'), Ministry for Foreign Affairs, Stockholm, 30 September 1976 (MFA).

3. Ibid.

4. Bo Heinebäck: Memorandum ('Sydafrikanske ambassadören besöker polchefen'/'The South African ambassador visits the head of the political department'), Ministry for Foreign Affairs, Stockholm, 29 October 1976 (MFA).

5. SIDA: Decision ('Bistånd till SWAPO under budgetåret 1977/78'/'Assistance to SWAPO during the financial year 1977/78'), Stockholm, 4 October 1977 (SDA); Ministry for Foreign Affairs: Decision ('Katastrofbistånd till SWAPO'/'Emergency assistance to SWAPO'), Stockholm, 23 February 1978 (SDA); and 'Agreed minutes of discussions on the cooperation between the South West Africa People's Organization (SWAPO) and Sweden, 1978/79', Lusaka, 31 May 1978 (SDA).

6. SIDA: Decision ('Bistånd till SWAPO under budgetåret 1978/79'/'Assistance to SWAPO during the financial year 1978/79'), Stockholm, 27 July 1978 (SDA) and Ministry for Foreign Affairs: Decision ('Tilläggsanslag till SWAPO'/'Additional allocation to SWAPO'), Stockholm, 23 May 1979 (SDA).

Clothes from Emmaus
and Bread and Fishes
stored at the SWAPO
settlement in Kwanza
Sul, Angola, 1983
(Photo: Charlotte
Thege)

and in 1979/80 to 27 MSEK.[1] Welcoming the Swedish delegation to the annual aid consultations in Luanda, Nujoma noticed in May 1980 that

> you only need to meet a group of four Namibian civilian refugees [to be] immediately struck by the fact that two of the four are either dressed in Swedish [clothes], eating Swedish food [...] or travelling in a Swedish-made vehicle.[2]

After the independence of Guinea-Bissau, Mozambique and Angola, SWAPO became in the mid-1970s the most important recipient of official Swedish humanitarian assistance among the Southern African liberation movements.[3] Although the organization for many years faced difficulties in absorbing the support—until the mid-1980s accumulating huge unspent balances—from 1976/77 actual disbursements regularly exceeded those registered for ZANU and ZAPU of Zimbabwe and ANC of South Africa.[4] At the time of Namibia's independence in March 1990, the cumulative direct bilateral assistance to SWAPO amounted—in current figures—to a total of 669 million, while bilateral payments to ANC of South Africa by then had reached 506 MSEK.[5] From the point of view of official financial transfers, SWAPO was for a decade and a half given privileged attention by Social Democratic and non-socialist Swedish governments alike.

This becomes more manifest if contributions via the United Nations and various international organizations—including the Commonwealth[6]—are taken into account. Considerable public resources channelled to SWAPO and to SWAPO-aligned organi-

1. SIDA: Decision ('Bidrag till SWAPO under budgetåret 1979/80'/'Contribution to SWAPO during the financial year 1979/80'), Stockholm, 11 July 1979 (SDA).
2. Sam Nujoma: 'Welcoming address to the delegation of SIDA', Luanda, 13 May 1980 (SDA).
3. In SIDA's corridors, it was jokingly said in the early 1980s that the acronym SWAPO translated as 'Sweden's Africa Policy' (Author's recollection).
4. See the accompanying disbursement tables.
5. Ditto.
6. Although not a member of the Commonwealth—the association of Great Britain and the former British colonies—Sweden was from the early 1980s a major contributor to its Fund for Technical Cooperation (CFTC), supporting various educational programmes for Namibians. By 1984, more than 12 MSEK had been paid out by Sweden to CFTC in favour of scholarships for Namibian (and Zimbabwean) students, telecommunication courses in India and vocational training courses in Malta (Elisabeth Lewin: 'The Commonwealth Fund for Technical Cooperation: An evaluation with special reference to the Namibia programme', SIDA, Stockholm, 17 December 1984) (SDA). In addition to the support via UN, Sweden was also a leading donor to the educational programmes in favour of Namibian students administered by AET, WCC and WUS.

zations in Namibia via Swedish solidarity organizations, churches and trade unions should also be added. For 1981/82—when the direct support to the movement was 41 MSEK (as compared to 23 million to ANC of South Africa)—it has been estimated that the total Swedish assistance extended to SWAPO amounted to 63 MSEK.[1] Measured against the Namibian domestic and exile population, the direct official Swedish support to SWAPO exceeded by far that to the other Southern African liberation movements.[2]

Questions and Doubts

The particular attention accorded to SWAPO was, ultimately, a combined result of UN decisions and Swedish concerns regarding the world organization's credibility[3]; the view that Namibia was the key to unlocking the apartheid question in South Africa[4]; the abject oppression and the steady exodus from the country; as well as the fact that the movement assumed responsibility for the welfare of the Namibian refugees in exile. It remains, however, that SWAPO initially had to overcome significant obstacles. Paradoxically, the Southern African liberation movement with the smallest popular, active Swedish support base would over the years become the largest recipient of official assistance.[5] Leys and Saul have on a more general level commented that

> it stands as a remarkable achievement that a small group of Namibians [...] could set in motion a movement that would [...] so challenge South Africa's illegal presence in South West Africa and so establish its own political coherence, military presence and international credibility as to emerge, by 1990, as the governing party of an independent Namibia.[6]

Against the background of initial doubts and persistent questions, the SWAPO leadership's ability to continuously convince the Swedish authorities to raise the annual aid allocations must, similarly, be regarded as extraordinary. While SIDA over the years regularly found reason to criticize SWAPO's financial reports, only on one

1. Elisabeth Michanek: Memorandum ('Swedish assistance to SWAPO/Namibia'), SIDA, Stockholm, 20 September 1982; original in English (SDA).
2. SWAPO was granted privileged attention also by other major donors. In value terms, the non-military assistance extended by the German Democratic Republic to SWAPO between 1975 and 1989 was, for example, almost twice as important as that to ANC of South Africa. Compared with ANC, the resources spent by GDR on education and training in favour of SWAPO in the 1980s were, in addition, five times as high (Ilona and Hans-Georg Schleicher op. cit., pp. 177-78).
3. As a member of the UN Security Council, in January 1976, the Swedish representative stated: "There are certain principles [...] on which it is impossible to compromise. The illegality of South Africa's presence in Namibia, UN sovereignty over the area, the duty of South Africa to withdraw, the inalienable right of the Namibian people to self-determination [...] and the independence of Namibia as a unitary state. [...] The credibility of the UN itself is at stake, owing to its special responsibility" ('Summary of speech by ambassador Rydbeck during the UN Security Council debate on Namibia', 29 January 1976, in Ministry for Foreign Affairs: *Documents on Swedish Foreign Policy: 1976*, Stockholm, 1978, p. 190).
4. From the mid-1960s, Sweden defended the view that the Security Council as a matter of course should impose mandatory sanctions against South Africa if it failed to respect the verdicts by ICJ or the council's resolutions. Already in April 1965, the former Swedish Foreign Minister Östen Undén had argued that "South Africa's position with regard to the apartheid policies in South West Africa is essentially much weaker than in the case of [its] racial policies in South Africa" (Östen Undén: 'Då har FN rätt att ingripa'/'In that case the UN has the right to intervene' in *Stockholms-Tidningen*, 28 April 1965). Subsequent Swedish initiatives in this regard were, however, regularly opposed by the major Western powers. Following a proposal to impose a binding arms embargo on South Africa during the Security Council's Namibia debate in June 1975, the British representative—"almost desperately attempting to eschew [the issue]"—expressed "in vehement terms great indignation" over the Swedish position (Cable from the Swedish UN representative Olof Rydbeck to the Ministry for Foreign Affairs, New York, 2 June 1975 (MFA).
5. That is, until Namibia's independence in 1990.
6. Leys and Saul op. cit., p. 3.

occasion was it decided not to increase the support, and then for other reasons.[1] Obvious contradictions between SWAPO's internal wing[2] and the leadership in exile; the 1975-76 crisis and the Shipanga affair; the expulsion of Vice-President Muyongo[3]; and allegations of human rights' abuses in the 1980s, similarly, did not affect SWAPO's solid standing or change the decision makers' positive disposition towards the movement.[4]

Contradictions relating to the expanding assistance will be addressed below. Meanwhile, it should be noted that in addition to the general, aid-related issue of administrative capacity, politico-military concerns—notably SWAPO's relations with the Angolan UNITA movement and the question of liberated areas—were regularly discussed between the two cooperating partners during the first half of the 1970s.

The question of SWAPO's administration and its capacity to handle external aid goes beyond the initial cooperation stages. As noted, through a unique decision in September 1972 it was decided by the Swedish authorities to discontinue the support initiated in 1970 due to doubts in this regard.[5] Although the decision was reversed one year later, many questions remained. After concluding in January 1975 that SWAPO's "administrative capacity to coordinate [assistance] is, as testified, very weak"[6], in a comprehensive analysis Anders Bjurner at the Swedish embassy in Lusaka reported after the outbreak of the internal crisis in August 1976 that

[e]very sympathizer with SWAPO's struggle for a free Namibia appears to be faced with a dilemma. [...] On the one hand, it is said that SWAPO represents the only possibility of achieving freedom in Namibia. [...] On the other, it is regretted that the [...] problems—which were given concrete expression with the breakaway of the dissidents and [by] their complaints—have not been cleared. The tactics of the leadership have largely been to sweep [the problems] under the carpet'. Allegations of corruption have not been investigated, in spite of the fact that

---

1. Due to huge accumulated balances within the SWAPO programme, it was decided to maintain the 1985/86 allocation at the 1984/85 level, i.e. 50 MSEK. As will be seen from the accompanying tables, no less than 112 million was disbursed in 1985/86, leaving room for a new increase in 1986/87.

2. SWAPO was formally never banned in Namibia. For all practical purposes, the organization was, however, treated as such by the South African regime.

3. At SWAPO's consultative Tanga congress in 1969-70, the Caprivian leaders Bredan Simbwaye and Mishake Muyongo were elected Vice-President and Acting Vice-President. As Simbwaye had been detained in 1964, Muyongo *de facto* became Vice-President, signing his official letters as such.

4. It should be noted that neither the affiliation to the Communist-dominated World Federation of Trade Unions (WFTU) by the SWAPO-aligned National Union of Namibian Workers (NUNW) nor NUNW's exiled condition in Angola in the early 1980s precluded bilateral support—including technical assistance—from the Swedish LO/TCO Council of International Trade Union Cooperation. However, LO/TCO would at the very same time not extend support to the South African Congress of Trade Unions (SACTU), using the arguments that SACTU was a member of WFTU and an organization in exile. The Swedish trade union support to Namibia and South Africa will be discussed below.

5. Interviewed in 1995, Muyongo recalled the beginnings of the cooperation with Sweden: "Accountability in exile was not very easy. We ran into a lot of problems with the SIDA people. [...] If there was one Dollar or one Kwacha missing, they would say: 'What happened? Did you buy sweets?' [...] But when I think of it now, I think that they were right. They were telling us that 'one day you are going to run a country, and if you do not look after the resources of your country you are going to run into problems'" (Interview with Mishake Muyongo, p. 87).

6. Anders Bjurner: Memorandum ('Biståndsframställning från SWAPO'/'Request for assistance from SWAPO'), Swedish embassy, Lusaka, 29 January 1975 (SDA).

irregularities without doubt have occurred [...].[1] A lack of political guidelines and strategy remains. One of the really burning issues—the cooperation with UNITA—has been completely avoided. [...]

[Certain] SWAPO leaders have stated [to us] that the absence of self-criticism by the leadership has been almost complete and that several of the fundamental problems [...] remain unresolved. [...] SWAPO today is not 'united and strong'.[2]

Nevertheless, despite the critical assessment Bjurner proposed continued humanitarian assistance. To suspend the support would in his view be "most unfortunate".[3] Such a decision would not only "not affect the leadership", but be regarded by both SWAPO and "other African countries" as undue interference in internal affairs.[4] He, however, emphasized that "controls against misuse [...] must be strict".[5]

Seven years later—when SWAPO had moved its exile headquarters to Luanda; the allocation amounted to 47 MSEK; and the cooperation included longer term projects—SIDA's education division noted that

SWAPO is a weak counterpart for discussions regarding concrete projects. The organization is hierarchical, with sparing [internal] dissemination of information, few [people] with whom responsibilities can be shared and an almost complete lack of coordination. [...] Cooperation of a traditional kind requires that fairly clear lines may be perceived in [an] education system. That is not the case with SWAPO.[6]

In order to carry out a growing number of proposed education projects, it was found that SIDA—both in Stockholm and at the level of the Swedish embassy in Luanda—must take a more interventionist part than usually was the case in Swedish development assistance.[7] The same applied to other projects with SWAPO. The movement's politico-administrative weaknesses did thus not lead to decreasing Swedish assistance. Instead, the growing support from the mid-1980s was coupled with measures designed to strengthen SWAPO's management capacity.

UNITA and Liberated Areas

Both the Social Democratic and the non-socialist governments acknowledged that SWAPO had been forced to take up arms against the South African regime. In

---

1. Bjurner did not expand on this important question, indicating whether the irregularities involved SIDA funds. However, while the UN Commissioner for Namibia, Séan MacBride, in April 1976 confirmed to the Swedish UN representation in New York that "the SWAPO leadership was guilty of financial irregularities", he also stated that it *inter alia* concerned official Swedish cash support intended for aid in Namibia (Letter from Kaj Sundberg, Swedish UN representation, to the Ministry for Foreign Affairs, New York, 13 April 1976) (MFA). In his autobiography, Shipanga implies that Nujoma and other SWAPO leaders were "working rackets" in Zambia, also misappropriating Swedish aid (Andreas Shipanga: *In Search of Freedom*, The Andreas Shipanga Story as told to Sue Armstrong, Ashanti Publishing, Gibraltar, 1989, pp. 100-101). According to the author's interview with Shipanga, he had raised this issue with the Swedish ambassador to Zambia around 1975 (Interview with Andreas Shipanga, p. 98). There is, however, no explicit reference to misuse of Swedish assistance in the documents consulted.
2. Anders Bjurner: Memorandum ('Läget inom SWAPO'/'The situation within SWAPO'), Swedish embassy, Lusaka, 25 August 1976 (MFA). *Inter alia*, Bjurner based his report on discussions with Ben Amathila, described as "one of the most articulate critics".
3. Bjurner referred to comments made by Pierre Schori, who had proposed a suspension of the Swedish assistance (ibid.).
4. Ibid.
5. Ibid.
6. SIDA's Education Division: 'Instruktion för programdiskussioner med SWAPO angående undervisningssamarbete' ('Instruction for programme discussions with SWAPO regarding education cooperation'), SIDA, Stockholm, 3 November 1983 (SDA).
7. Ibid.

November 1977, for example, the representative of the Fälldin government stated
at the United Nations that

> we recognize that the Namibian people have seen no other way out than to resort to armed
> struggle to free itself from foreign occupation. We know that this struggle is pursued with the
> goal [of creating] an independent and united Namibia. [It] has the full support of the Swedish
> government.[1]

As was the case with the other Southern African liberation movements, the official
Swedish humanitarian assistance was, however, strictly civilian. The activities of
SWAPO's military wing—the People's Liberation Army of Namibia (PLAN)—fell
outside the support.[2] This said, during the first half of the 1970s there were two
aspects of SWAPO's military campaigns that due to the precedent of Sweden's
involvement with the liberation movements in the Portuguese colonies caused concerns and questions, namely its relations with UNITA of Angola and the absence of
liberated or semi-liberated areas inside Namibia.

SWAPO formed part of the 1969 Khartoum alliance of the so called 'authentic'
liberation movements together with MPLA. Historically, it was, however, closer to
Jonas Savimbi's UNITA movement than to the organization led by Agostinho
Neto.[3] This was partly due to cultural affinities between SWAPO's main Ovambo
constituency in northern Namibia[4] and UNITA's Ovimbundu following in central
Angola[5], but primarily to mutual interests and exigencies during their respective
armed campaigns. In order to penetrate Ovamboland from its base areas in western
Zambia, PLAN had to pass through regions in Angola where UNITA was operating. UNITA, on the other hand, was isolated inside Angola and barred from Zambia.[6] In exchange for logistic support to reach the home front, SWAPO could
supply UNITA with necessary external supplies. On this basis, the two movements
established a largely hushed up, but well-known association. Interviewed in 1996,
UNITA's former Secretary General Miguel N'Zau Puna described it as "a strategic
and tactical alliance", adding that

> we did not have any weapons or external support. [...] From time to time, our friends in
> SWAPO—which was recognized by OAU and received weapons, but did not have the men in
> Namibia to fight with those weapons—helped us. That is how UNITA was growing stronger.

1. Cable from the Ministry for Foreign Affairs to the Swedish UN delegation, Stockholm, 4 November 1977
   (MFA). Sweden would not vote in favour of UN General Assembly resolutions which called for support of
   armed force. Under the UN Charter, only the Security Council was—and remains—mandated to endorse
   armed action. In the General Assembly, this often led Sweden to abstain or vote against resolutions on Southern Africa where it otherwise supported the core issue. The reasons were normally understood by the OAU
   and the Southern African liberation movements. Cf. the interviews with Salim Ahmed Salim, p. 244, and Ben
   Amathila, p. 67.
2. As noted by Muyongo, SIDA was extremely watchful for any possible signs of assistance being used by the
   military. However, "when food was bought or given, they did not mind whether you shared it with the people
   at the front" (Interview with Mishake Muyongo, p. 87). SWAPO's former Treasurer Hifikepunye Pohamba
   has similarly said that "when [the Nordic countries] gave us food, it went to the camps and the camps were
   also the reserves of the PLAN cadres. It would therefore not be wrong to say that the people of the Nordic
   world also assisted PLAN. But they never gave us guns" (Interview with Hifikepunye Pohamba, p. 96). For
   ZANU of Zimbabwe and ANC of South Africa on this point, cf. the interviews with Josiah Tungamirai
   (ZANU), pp. 234-235, and Lindiwe Mabuza (ANC), p.136.
3. It was through SWAPO's assistance that Savimbi returned to Angola in July 1968, armed with "one Soviet-
   made Tokarev pistol given to [him] in Dar es Salaam by Sam Nujoma" (Fred Bridgland: *Jonas Savimbi: A Key
   to Africa*, Mainstream Publishing Company, Edinburgh, 1986, p. 35). On Swedish contacts with UNITA and
   support for Savimbi's return, see Sellström Volume I, pp. 402-10.
4. The largest Ovambo sub-group, the Kwanyama, straddle the border between Namibia and Angola.
5. In 1996, the former UNITA leader N'Zau Puna explained: "SWAPO had fraternal bonds with us. A common
   culture and a common past. In those days, we did not go in for ideology. We looked at ethnic affinity and,
   above all, regional affinity" (Interview with Miguel N'Zau Puna, pp. 25-26).
6. After repeated attacks against the Benguela railway, in mid-1967 UNITA was barred from entering Zambia.

[...] Many soldiers from UNITA fought with SWAPO. We also made some incursions into Namibian territory under UNITA's General Commander Samuel Chiwale [...].[1]

It was a controversial arrangement. UNITA was not only barred from SWAPO's main host country, Zambia, but had in the early 1970s entered into a truce with the Portuguese according to which the colonial army would leave Savimbi's organization alone as long as it fought against MPLA. Although indirectly, SWAPO became connected with UNITA in the Angolan drama.[2] Not surprisingly, SWAPO's Khartoum partner MPLA reacted in the strongest of terms. In a letter to the Zambian government, President Agostinho Neto requested in June 1973

> that the Zambian authorities intensify their struggle against UNITA, and [in this regard] [...] take into account that it is SWAPO which is the large-scale supplier of arms to UNITA and provides [it with] Zambian travel documents [...] under the completely false pretext that UNITA [controls] [s]outh [e]ast Angola.[3]

As the Swedish government extended humanitarian assistance to both SWAPO and MPLA, it regularly raised the issue of UNITA in political discussions with the two movements. As late as in April 1975, Neto told Bjurner that "MPLA did not have any regular relations with SWAPO", adding that he personally found the SWAPO leadership "ideologically unclear".[4] While MPLA expressed outspoken distrust of SWAPO[5], the Namibians would for a long time downplay the relations with UNITA or give contradictory information. After going into exile via Angola, SWAPO's Acting Secretary General John Ya-Otto, for example, stated in September 1974 to the Foreign Ministry in Stockholm that "the earlier cooperation with UNITA"—which in his view "mainly [was] based on personal relations"—had been "abandoned".[6] In January 1975, however, SWAPO informed the embassy in Lusaka that it had sought and received assurances from UNITA that the movement could open an office in southern Angola "after independence".[7] Shortly thereafter, Andreas Shipanga confirmed that "the contacts with UNITA were good".[8] That was also the embassy's understanding. In August 1975—that is, at the time of the open conflicts between FNLA, MPLA and UNITA—ambassador Dölling reported

---

1. Interview with Miguel N'Zau Puna, pp. 26 and 25-26. As UNITA later took an active part in South Africa's military campaigns against the Namibian liberation movement, official or semi-official SWAPO historiography tends as a rule not to mention, or minimize, the relations. Affirming that "there was [...] no alliance between SWAPO and UNITA", Katjavivi, for example, cautiously stated in 1988 that "the likelihood of SWAPO and UNITA units interacting [had] caused some problems between SWAPO and MPLA" (Katjavivi op. cit., p. 86).
2. And, by extension, on the side of Portugal and South Africa. In a complex turn of events, the involvement would become more direct after South Africa's invasion of Angola in October 1975. This, in turn, was one of the major factors behind the SWAPO crisis of 1976.
3. Cited in Marcum op. cit. (Vol. II), p. 203.
4. Letter ('Minnesanteckning angående samtal med MPLA's ordförande'/'Memorandum on conversation with the MPLA President') from Anders Bjurner to the Ministry for Foreign Affairs, Lusaka, 24 April 1975 (MFA).
5. After Angola's independence, Bjurner reported from discussions in Luanda in March 1976 that "MPLA [still] regards SWAPO as an organization which only in a limited way has tried to mobilize the population, raising the political consciousness of its members. In addition, MPLA considers that principles which can be called socialist [are] absent in SWAPO's programme. [...] The ideological misgivings [...] and the criticism against [SWAPO's] cooperation with UNITA still remain and several MPLA leaders are not slow to express them" (Anders Bjurner: Memorandum ('Namibia') to the Ministry for Foreign Affairs, Swedish embassy, Lusaka, 8 March 1976) (MFA).
6. Anders Möllander: Memorandum ('Diskussion med SWAPO-representanter om Namibia'/'Discussion with SWAPO representatives about Namibia'), Ministry for Foreign Affairs, Stockholm, 25 September 1974 (MFA).
7. Anders Bjurner : Memorandum ('Biståndsframställning från SWAPO'/'Request for assistance from SWAPO'), Swedish embassy, Lusaka, 29 January 1975 (MFA).
8. Ann Wilkens: Memorandum ('Samtal med SWAPO-talesman i Lusaka'/'Conversation with SWAPO spokesman in Lusaka'), Ministry for Foreign Affairs, Stockholm, 16 April 1975 (MFA).

to the Foreign Ministry that "now as before, SWAPO's contacts are significantly better with UNITA than with MPLA", noting that "Savimbi during his regular visits to Lusaka normally meets Nujoma".[1]

After South Africa's UNITA-backed invasion of Angola in October 1975, SWAPO adapted to the changing geopolitical realities.[2] Although not without considerable internal strains, it eventually approached the new MPLA government. In March 1976, Hifikepunye Pohamba told the Swedish ambassador to Tanzania that SWAPO "at the time of Angola's independence had begun to understand that South Africa and UNITA were collaborating, [...] seeing the danger of working with [the latter]".[3] Invaded by South Africa, the besieged MPLA government welcomed SWAPO's realignment. During a visit by Pierre Schori to Luanda in June 1976, President Neto informed Prime Minister Palme's envoy that "Angola had given [SWAPO] bases where they [...] have a great number of armed forces".[4] And in November 1976, Nujoma confirmed that SWAPO's "cooperation with the Angolan army was excellent", adding that PLAN "assisted in identifying UNITA elements, in particular those who operated from Namibian territory".[5]

Closely followed by the Swedish government during the complex Southern African détente period between 1974 and 1976, SWAPO's association with UNITA did not affect the assistance to the Namibian movement.[6] From the point of view of official aid policy, more contentious was instead that SWAPO did not administer liberated areas, such as those established by PAIGC in Guinea-Bissau, FRELIMO in Mozambique and, to a lesser extent, MPLA in Angola. Namibia's political geography and South Africa's military power did not allow for the establishment of such areas. Nor could SWAPO create semi-liberated zones as ZANU and ZAPU did in

---

1. Cable from Iwo Dölling, Swedish ambassador to Zambia, to the Ministry for Foreign Affairs, Lusaka, 20 August 1975 (MFA).

2. On the 'shifting alliances' between SWAPO, MPLA and UNITA in 1974-76, see Ronald Dreyer: *Namibia and Southern Africa: Regional Dynamics of Decolonization 1945-1990*, Kegan Paul International, London and New York, 1994, pp. 78-104.

3. Letter ('Samtal med chefen för SWAPO's kontor i Dar es Salaam'/'Conversation with the head of the SWAPO office in Dar es Salaam') from Per Lindström to the Ministry for Foreign Affairs, Swedish embassy, Dar es Salaam, 16 March 1976 (MFA).

4. Pierre Schori: Memorandum ('Samtal i Luanda den 15-17 juni 1976'/'Conversations in Luanda, 15-17 June 1976'), Cabinet Office, Stockholm, 23 June 1976 (MFA). SWAPO opened an office in Luanda in June 1976. The MPLA government welcomed at the same time Swedish humanitarian assistance to SWAPO in Angola (Carin Norberg: Memorandum ('Reserapport från besök i Angola 7-14 juni 1976'/'Travel report from visit to Angola, 7-14 June 1976'), Swedish embassy, Lusaka, 12 July 1976) (SDA). SWAPO's exile headquarters were moved from Lusaka to Luanda in late 1979.

5. Letter ('Samtal med SWAPO's president'/'Conversation with SWAPO's President') from Kaj Falkman, Swedish ambassador to Angola, to the Ministry for Foreign Affairs, Luanda, 30 November 1976 (MFA). The following year, SWAPO's Secretary of Defence, Peter Nanyemba, confirmed that "SWAPO had captured many UNITA soldiers [and] handed them over to [the Angolan army]" (Anders Bjurner: Memorandum ('Synpunkter från SWAPO'/'Points of view from SWAPO'), Swedish embassy, Luanda, 13 July 1977) (SDA). Nevertheless, distrust remained. As late as in June 1978, SWAPO's Chief Representative to Angola, Aaron Mushimba, told the Swedish ambassador in Luanda that "there, unfortunately, were suspicions [by] MPLA that SWAPO maintained contacts with UNITA" (Cable ('Samtal 1978 06 07 med Mushimba, SWAPO'/'Conversation 7 June 1978 with Mushimba, SWAPO') from Kaj Falkman, Swedish ambassador to Angola, to the Ministry for Foreign Affairs, Luanda, 8 June 1978) (MFA).

6. It did, however, strongly influence the Africa Groups. Backing MPLA, the solidarity organization would not recognize SWAPO until the movement had been acknowledged by the independent Angolan government.

parts of Zimbabwe, which sufficiently excluded security forces to ensure a consolidated presence of freedom fighters.[1]

Recognizing that "the needs of the [Southern African] liberation movements vary from territory to territory, depending on the stage and the nature of the struggle", the Programme of Action adopted by the UN/OAU Oslo conference on Southern Africa concluded in April 1973 that "special reference should be made to the large-scale needs in the liberated areas".[2] The recommendation was largely influenced by the position of the OAU Liberation Committee and by the nationalist struggles in the Portuguese colonies. With considerable aid programmes to PAIGC, FRELIMO and MPLA, it would also guide the Swedish Social Democratic government's policy towards the liberation movements. In an interview with the French journal *Afrique-Asie*, Foreign Minister Krister Wickman stated in September 1973 that "the [objective] of [Sweden's assistance] is to support the civilian activities of the liberation movements in the liberated areas".[3]

The orientation was, naturally, of concern to SWAPO—and to ANC of South Africa—which did not control any self-administered areas. According to Ben Amathila, "it became an issue". Looking back, he commented in 1995 that

> OAU was very forceful that liberation movements with a liberated territory should be given priority. The case of Vietnam was well established in Sweden. Now, where do I come in with SWAPO? It would have been easy for me to tell a story and state that we had liberated areas, but I thought that it was not correct and I refrained from it.[4]

Although it was mainly at the level of the non-governmental solidarity movement that the question of liberated areas became 'an issue'[5], it was also raised by the Swedish authorities. For example, asked to comment shortly after Foreign Minister Wickman's statement Nujoma informed SIDA that "SWAPO [had] set up clinics and schools in areas where military activities were going on", but that the movement "was not in complete command of those areas".[6] Again visiting Stockholm in

---

1. In Namibia, PLAN was during the first phase of the liberation war (1966-75) mainly forced to concentrate its activities to the Caprivi and, to a lesser extent, the Okavango regions in the north-eastern parts of the country. From bases in western Zambia, PLAN soldiers carried out 'hit-and-run' operations against the South African Defence Force (SADF) or acts of sabotage on government installations. The situation changed after Angola's independence in late 1975, when it became possible for PLAN to penetrate deep into the populous Ovambo region and beyond, establishing a more continuous presence (1976-80). SADF's strength and South Africa's rapid militarization of Ovamboland prevented, however, the establishment of permanent guerrilla positions inside Namibia. After carrying out their missions, the PLAN forces would as a rule withdraw to bases in southern Angola. Starting in the late 1970s—and continuously from 1980—SADF, finally, took the war to Namibia's northern neighbour, striking both against the Angolan army and SWAPO, as well as providing backing for UNITA. Namibia's war of national liberation would from then on chiefly be fought on Angolan soil.
2. Stokke and Widstrand (eds) op. cit. (Vol. I), p. 32. The recommendations made at the Oslo conference were endorsed in May 1973 by the OAU Council of Ministers (ibid., p. 37).
3. 'Interview (September) with the Foreign Minister, Mr. Wickman, in the special [issue on Sweden] of the journal *Afrique-Asie*', in Ministry for Foreign Affairs: *Documents on Swedish Foreign Policy: 1973*, Stockholm, 1976, p. 64.
4. Interview with Ben Amathila, p. 65.
5. According to Amathila, "especially the Africa Groups, were very lukewarm on Namibia. [...] because we did not have liberated territories" (ibid.). Once the solidarity movement had embraced SWAPO, it, however, fell into the other extreme, exaggerating SWAPO's military achievements. In June 1978, for example, *Afrikabulletinen* published an article by Per Sandén entitled 'På Väg in i Befriade Områden' ('Entering Liberated Areas') (No. 42, 1978, pp. 4-5). AGIS' report to the annual congress in June 1979 stated, similarly, that "SWAPO's struggle has developed strongly during the year. [The movement] now operates over the entire country and has also proclaimed liberated areas, with reasonably well functioning administration, schools and medical services" (AGIS: 'Verksamhetsberättelser [till] AGIS' femte ordinarie kongress, Karlstad, 2-4 juni 1979'/ 'Activity reports [to] AGIS' fifth ordinary congress, Karlstad, 2-4 June 1979' [no place or date]) (AGA).
6. Astrid Bergquist: Memorandum ('Minnesanteckningar förda vid samtal med SWAPO-representanterna Sam Nujoma och Ben Amathila'/'Notes from talks with the SWAPO representatives Sam Nujoma and Ben Amathila'), SIDA, Stockholm, 13 November 1973 (SDA).

November 1974, Nujoma explained that SWAPO did not administer any liberated areas, but that there were "operational zones" in which the local population was assisted.[1]

By that time, Sweden had already embarked on a growing humanitarian assistance programme to SWAPO in exile. A formal request had in April 1973 been submitted by the Namibian delegation that visited Stockholm after the Oslo conference. In spite of the quoted conference recommendation and Sweden's declared policy, it was subsequently approved. In a memorandum introducing the request to CCHA, in June 1973 Anders Möllander convincingly argued that

> it is in Sweden's interest to try to comply with the [United Nations] call in support of the liberation efforts in Namibia. The absence of liberated areas makes it for the time being impossible to extend assistance of the kind given to the liberation movements in the Portuguese colonies. [...] At the same time, it is urgent to support those political movements that [...] are forced to operate in exile. SWAPO's important role, both for the discussion of the Namibia question internationally and for actions inside the country, is undisputed. The assistance requested by SWAPO for activities in Zambia [is thus] well justified.[2]

In the case of Namibia, the decisive factor for official Swedish support was the principled question of national self-determination established by the United Nations, rather than the strategic considerations raised by the OAU Liberation Committee. As SWAPO's Chief Representative to Sweden, from 1971 Amathila consciously pursued the UN policy. In the era of Vietnam and the liberation wars in the Portuguese African colonies, SWAPO experienced "a problem of penetration" in Sweden. "My strategy", Amathila later said, was therefore

> to use the Namibian legal position at the UN and take the resolutions of the United Nations as a way of presenting the legitimacy of the SWAPO struggle to the Swedish public. In order to do that, I had to rely on the Swedish UN Association.[3] [...] I think that SWAPO's position gradually became clear to quite a number of people who had an option between supporting what they saw as 'direct blood-letting activities' and the UN endorsement of the right of the Namibian people to self-determination. [...] We actually tapped not the mainstream, but the off-stream of the support groups. Those who looked at the UN as an authority, just as OAU was seen as an authority. [...]
>
> I [also] came to realize that the Swedish government [...] did not really need the public to push it into a certain direction. Most of the people I dealt with were internationalists, who understood what was taking place, and they formulated a policy in line with SWAPO's expectations.[4]

The chapters which follow focus on Sweden's official policy towards Namibia and the bilateral cooperation with SWAPO until independence in 1990. To place the

---

1. Astrid Bergquist: Memorandum ('Minnesanteckningar från överläggningar med en SWAPO-delegation den 1 november 1974'/'Notes from deliberations with a SWAPO delegation, 1 November 1974'), SIDA, Stockholm, 25 November 1974 (SDA).
2. CCHA: Memorandum by Anders Möllander ('Stöd till SWAPO'/'Support to SWAPO'), [Stockholm], 6 June 1973 (SDA).
3. In 1972, the Swedish UN Association issued a stencilled publication on Namibia, drafted with assistance from the SWAPO office in Stockholm (Svenska FN-förbundets aktivitetskommitté: 'Namibia', [no place], 1972 (MFA); cf. the interview with Ben Amathila, p. 66). The early role played by the UN Association is underlined by the fact that when the SWAPO President in October-November 1974 was invited to Sweden by the Social Democratic Party, a meeting with the association was included in the programme. In addition to the ruling party and the UN Association, Nujoma held talks with Prime Minister Palme, Foreign Minister Andersson, Cooperation Minister Sigurdsen and SIDA. In marked contrast to later visits, he did not meet the Africa Groups (Cable ('SWAPO-delegation besöker Sverige'/'SWAPO delegation visits Sweden') from the Ministry for Foreign Affairs to the Swedish embassies in Dar es Salaam, Lusaka, New York and Pretoria, Stockholm, 28 October 1974) (MFA).
4. Interview with Ben Amathila, pp. 66 and 63.

narrative within its wider national context, a brief presentation of some of the major Swedish actors in the Namibian liberation struggle in the 1970s should first be made.

Parliament and 'Off-Stream'

Amathila's recollection of a non-accommodating 'mainstream' within the wider Swedish solidarity movement chiefly referred to the Africa Groups, the most active and influential pressure organization. At the level of the established political parties and among the support groups focusing on practical solidarity, SWAPO did, however, enjoy considerable support. With the exception of the Left Party Communists[1] and the Moderate Party[2], all parties represented in parliament had by the early 1970s recommended official assistance to the Namibian liberation movement. As in the case of Zimbabwe (and South Africa), it was the opposition Centre and Liberal parties that first raised the demand, regularly submitting joint motions to this effect from 1969.[3] Their position was underlined in January 1975 when the chairman of the Liberal Party, Gunnar Helén, in a parliamentary motion requested that "in the case of Namibia, a major effort should be made in favour of SWAPO". At the same time, he proposed that "longer term agreements" on official support should be concluded between the government and the liberation movements in Namibia (SWAPO), South Africa (ANC) and Zimbabwe (ZANU and ZAPU).[4]

In addition, among the 'off-stream support groups'—just as in the case of Zimbabwe—both the Christian-inspired Emmaus communities and the Bread and Fishes foundation had committed themselves to practical solidarity in favour of SWAPO during the first half of the 1970s. Initially, Emmaus-Björkå played a particularly significant role. It had as early as in 1971 started to organize shipments of used clothes to FRELIMO, MPLA, PAIGC, ZANU, SWAPO and FNL of Vietnam. Combining door-to-door collection of clothes in the Swedish 'bible belt' of the southern province of Småland with information on the liberation struggles, Emmaus-Björkå's pioneering efforts on SWAPO's behalf were considerable. For example, in 1972 alone—at a time when the initially very modest official Swedish

---

1. It was only in January 1976 that the Left Party Communists explicitly advocated official Swedish assistance to SWAPO in a parliamentary motion, submitted by the party chairman C.H. Hermansson (Swedish Parliament 1975/76: Motion No. 350, Riksdagens Protokoll 1975/76, p. 5).
2. The conservative Moderate Party never supported the nationalist struggles in Southern Africa. Towards the end of the 1970s—when it formed part of the ruling non-socialist coalition—the party actively turned against the official policy of humanitarian assistance to the liberation movements. In January 1978, for example, the Moderate MP Allan Åkerlind demanded in a parliamentary motion that "no development aid shall be accorded to so called liberation movement[s]", arguing that "it cannot be in the interest of Sweden to financially maintain fighting guerrilla units in other countries" (Swedish Parliament 1977/78: Motion No. 532, Riksdagens Protokoll 1977/78, p. 1). Two years later, Åkerlind disparagingly described SWAPO and ANC of South Africa as mere "guerrilla groups", stating that "Sweden cannot afford to play [the role of a] super power and conduct wars through [such] proxies". In a remarkable motion, he demanded that "the allocation to liberation movements and refugees [...] in Southern Africa be completely discontinued" (Swedish Parliament 1979/80: Motion No. 1626, Riksdagens Protokoll 1979/80, p. 1). In 1982, Tore Nilsson of the Moderate Party introduced a motion which characterized SWAPO as "a terrorist organization with highly remunerated agents in a great number of cities, including Europe", requesting an end to further Swedish assistance (Swedish Parliament 1981/82: Motion No. 1249, Riksdagens Protokoll 1981/82, p. 7).
3. Cf. the joint parliamentary motion introduced by the chairmen of the Centre and Liberal parties, Gunnar Hedlund and Sven Wedén, in January 1969, that is, before the endorsement of the policy of official Swedish support to the Southern African liberation movements (Swedish Parliament 1969: Motion No. 511 in the Second Chamber, Riksdagens Protokoll 1969, p. 16). Joint or coordinated motions were also presented in 1971, 1972, 1973 and 1974. Cf., for example, the submission by the new Centre and Liberal party leaders, Thorbjörn Fälldin and Gunnar Helén, in January 1973 (Swedish Parliament 1973: Motion No. 1101, Riksdagens Protokoll 1973, p. 10). To the attentive observer of Swedish politics, the stand taken by the non-socialist government from 1976 should thus not have come as a surprise.
4. Swedish Parliament 1975: Motion No. 730, Riksdagens Protokoll 1975, p. 30.

Practical solidarity throughout the years and seasons: Bread and Fishes collecting clothes and other items for SWAPO around Västerås during a winter in the early 1980s (Photo: Bread and Fishes)

assistance was temporarily suspended—together with the Emmaus community in Stockholm it delivered clothes to the SWAPO refugees in Zambia to a value of no less than 650,000 SEK[1], or five times the total amount granted by the Swedish government during the two financial years 1970/71 and 1971/72. When the first official Swedish delegation in September 1973 visited SWAPO's 'old farm' outside Lusaka, the immediate impression was how the Namibian refugees

> gathered around a truck [...] from which clothes were handed out. [I]t turned out that they came from Sweden. They were collected by Emmaus, who send them to the liberation movements with [financial support] from SIDA. A shirt received by a proud teenager [displayed the text] 'Elfsborg Swimming Team'.[2]

Quantitatively and qualitatively more important in the longer term perspective was the practical solidarity in favour of SWAPO initiated in 1974 by Emmaus' sister organization Bread and Fishes (BF), based in Västerås. While Emmaus-Björkå had established privileged contacts with ZANU of Zimbabwe, BF and SWAPO developed particularly close relations. Also active within the Africa Groups, Bertil Högberg—a prominent representative of the organization—was, for example, employed by SWAPO at the movement's Stockholm office between 1977 and 1979.[3] BF also supported ZANU and—to a lesser extent—ZAPU of Zimbabwe, as well as ANC of South Africa (from 1980), but throughout the 1970s and the 1980s SWAPO was by far the most important recipient. It accounted on average for as much, or more, material and financial assistance than that extended to the other Southern African liberation movements taken together.

A first shipment of 5 tons of clothes to SWAPO was made by BF in August 1974.[4] By 1980, 210 tons of clothes and shoes had been sent to the movement, and

---

1. Jörgen Knudtzon and Miriam Magnusson: 'Svenska icke-statliga organisationers u-hjälp 1972' ('Development aid by Swedish non-governmental organizations in 1972'), SIDA [no place or date] (SDA). Emmaus-Björkå's share was 450,000 SEK, while the clothes collected by Emmaus-Stockholm represented a value of 200,000 SEK.
2. Anders Möllander: Memorandum ('Besök på SWAPO's farm utanför Lusaka i Zambia'/'Visit to SWAPO's farm outside Lusaka in Zambia'), Ministry for Foreign Affairs, Stockholm, 29 October 1973 (SDA).
3. Telephone conversation with Bertil Högberg, Uppsala, 10 May 1999.
4. Bread and Fishes: 'Verksamhetsberättelse 1974' ('Annual report 1974') [no place or date] (BHC).

at Namibia's independence in 1990 the total amount was slightly below 1,000 tons.[1] Working closely with the Africa Groups, BF did not only collect clothes and footwear, but a whole range of items, including stationery, educational supplies and hospital equipment. By 1990, the value of the material assistance corresponded to 6 MSEK.[2] From 1975, Bread and Fishes also carried out fund-raising activities. Over the years, some 700,000 SEK was raised as cash support in favour of SWAPO.[3]

One of BF's principal activities from the mid-1970s was the collection and shipment of medical supplies and hospital equipment to SWAPO's refugee centres in Zambia and Angola. In 1978, for example, it participated together with the local Africa Group and five secondary schools in Västerås in an Operation Day's Work which resulted in the procurement of two Land Rover ambulances for SWAPO.[4] The focus on practical solidarity in the health sector brought Bread and Fishes into closer cooperation with the Africa Groups in Sweden[5] concerning a major project in SWAPO's Kwanza Sul settlement in Angola. An agreement on a multi-million project—called 'Health Care to SWAPO'[6]—was signed between BF, AGIS and SWAPO in Angola in December 1979.[7] With Bread and Fishes as the responsible Swedish coordinator, the implementation of the project depended on financial contributions from SIDA.[8]

The required support—during the initial project phase amounting to 1.4 MSEK—was granted by SIDA in July 1980.[9] It was a significant decision, underlining the increasing cooperation between the state and the non-governmental Southern Africa solidarity movement that gradually developed during the second half of the 1970s.[10] In fact, for the Africa Groups 'Health Care to SWAPO' was the very first project activity carried out with financial support from SIDA.[11] An important component of the project was technical assistance in the form of medical personnel supplied by the Africa Groups' Recruitment Organization (ARO). Also in this

1. Bertil Högberg: 'Det materiella stödet till befrielserörelserna från Brödet och Fiskarna' ('The material support to the liberation movements from Bread and Fishes'), [Uppsala], 7 March 1997 (BHC). Assuming that an average of 25,000 Namibian refugees over the years benefited from the assistance, this means that BF supplied each refugee with some 40 kilograms of clothes and shoes. Other Swedish NGOs also collected clothes and shoes for SWAPO. This was notably the case with *U-landshjälp från Folk till Folk i Sverige* (Development Aid from People to People in Sweden; UFF). UFF started to support SWAPO in 1982 and by 1996 it had delivered no less than 1,089 tons (UFF: Reply to a questionnaire from the Nordic Africa Institute, 4 November 1996). The quantity of clothes supplied before Namibia's independence is, however, not known.
2. Högberg op. cit., 7 March 1997.
3. Ibid.
4. Bread and Fishes: 'Verksamhetsberättelse 1978' ('Annual report 1978') [no place or date] (BHC).
5. AGIS had established a medical committee, based in Uppsala. Similar committees were formed in other cities too.
6. In Swedish, *Sjukvård till SWAPO*.
7. Agreement between Bread and Fishes (Bertil Högberg), Africa Groups in Sweden (Georg Dreifaldt) and SWAPO's Department of Health and Social Welfare (Dr. Iyambo Indongo), Kwanza Sul, 21 December 1979 (SDA).
8. Ibid.
9. [AGIS, Bread and Fishes and ISAK]: *Sjukvård till SWAPO*, Stockholm, 1980, p. 12. During the initial phase, the Swedish non-governmental organizations contributed some 400,000 SEK (ibid.).
10. In mid-1978, AGIS' national board noted that "SIDA's [financial] contributions have become a cornerstone of AGIS' economy" (AGIS: 'Styrelsens verksamhetsberättelse 1977-78'/'Activity report by the board, 1977-78' [no place or date], p. 14) (AGA). From the end of the 1970s, it became increasingly common that leading SIDA officials were active within the Africa Groups and that prominent AGIS activists joined SIDA. At the AGIS congress in Lund in May 1980, Jan Cedergren—later Deputy Director General of SIDA and in 1995 Director General for International Development Cooperation at the Ministry for Foreign Affairs—became, for example, a substitute member of the solidarity organization's national board, forming part of its working committee (AGIS: 'Kongress 81'/'Congress 81', Eskilstuna, 6-8 June 1981) (AGA). Conversely, in late 1988 Georg Dreifaldt of the Africa Groups joined SIDA to coordinate official assistance to SWAPO at the Swedish embassy in Luanda, and in 1991 AGIS' Lena Johansson took up the position as SIDA's regional coordinator of humanitarian assistance to ANC, initially based in Lusaka and later in Pretoria.
11. AGIS: 'Kongress 80' ('Congress 80'), Lund, 24-26 May 1980, p. 15 (AGA).

respect, the project marked a new beginning. ARO's two medical doctors, a nurse and a laboratory assistant recruited with funds from SIDA[1], commenced their work in Kwanza Sul in February 1980. They were the first ARO solidarity workers to directly assist a liberation movement.[2] Soon thereafter, SIDA granted financial resources for ARO personnel working with ANC in Tanzania. As later observed by Sören Lindh—one of the main initiators behind ARO—"we [...] were quickly regarded as professional by [...] SIDA and the Ministry for Foreign Affairs. They came to respect us".[3]

Supporting the same liberation movements—SWAPO and ANC—and engaged in joint projects, the "rather antagonistic"[4] relationship which during the first half of the 1970s prevailed between the Swedish post-Vietnam solidarity movement for Southern Africa and the state came to an end. Instead, the role of AGIS and aligned NGO organizations became that of "expert, lobbying" groups[5], primarily pressurizing the government to legislate a complete ban on any Swedish links to South Africa and Namibia.

From the early 1970s, SWAPO's cause also enjoyed considerable sympathy among Swedish media representatives. The role played by Per Sandén[6] should be underlined.[7] Following in the footsteps of a number of pioneering journalists, photographers and fellow film-makers—such as Anders Ehnmark, Elisabeth Hedborg and Hillevi Nilsson with regard to Angola; Anders Johansson, Lennart Malmer and Ingela Romare in Mozambique; and Rolf Gustavsson, Göran Palm and Knut Andreassen in Guinea-Bissau[8]—Sandén travelled with SWAPO in the operational areas. His television documentaries not only reached a broad Swedish and international public, but provoked major reactions by the South African regime. He placed Namibia at the centre of the debate at a time when the liberation struggle in the country was overshadowed by events in and around Angola, Mozambique and Zimbabwe. This was notably the case in late July 1974, when the official Swedish Broadcasting Corporation/TV 2 on its television news programme *Rapport* screened extracts from a film shot by Sandén and his colleague Rudi Spee in the Caprivi region, documenting a massacre carried out by the South African army.

SWAPO had in 1972 invited the Swedish television company to send a team to north-eastern Namibia "in order that the Swedes and the world at large should have first-hand knowledge of the [...] situation in [the] country".[9] Accompanied by

1. SIDA: Decision ('Bidrag till Afrikagruppernas [R]ekryteringsorganisation för korttidsanställning av voluntärer till SWAPO's läger i Angola'/'Grant to the Recruitment Organization of the Africa Groups for short-term employment of volunteers to SWAPO's settlement in Angola'), Stockholm, 1 November 1979 (SDA).
2. [AGIS, Bread and Fishes and ISAK] op. cit., p. 15.
3. Interview with Sören Lindh, p. 309. On 'Health Care to SWAPO', see the chapter 'Cold War, Total Strategy and Expanded Assistance'.
4. Interview with Birgitta Berggren, p. 259: "Returning from Tanzania in 1978 to work with the Consultative Committee on Humanitarian Assistance, I found that there was no cooperation at all [with the solidarity movement], or at least very little. The atmosphere was rather antagonistic, which I thought was unnecessary. We definitely needed to cooperate, because the work was growing very fast. All the good forces had to cooperate to do a good job".
5. Interviews with Sören Lindh, p. 308, and Hillevi Nilsson, p. 330.
6. Sandén's active involvement with Southern Africa started in the mid-1960s, when he as a young student in Skinnskatteberg chaired the local South Africa Committee. In the late 1980s, he served as an instructor at SWAPO's film and video training unit in Lusaka, *inter alia* producing material for the movement's election campaign.
7. See the interviews with Ben Amathila, p. 66, and Hadino Hishongwa, p. 70. Cf. also the interview with Ottilie Abrahams, p. 61.
8. Ehnmark, Malmer and Romare also covered the liberation struggle in Guinea-Bissau.
9. SWAPO: Press communiqué ('Massacres in Namibia'), Lusaka, 9 August 1974 (SDA).

Documenting apartheid massacres: Swedish film-maker Per Sandén (left) and Rudi Spee exhibiting photos of South African attacks on Namibian villagers, Stockholm, July 1974 (Photo: Birgitta Rydbeck/ Pressens Bild)

PLAN soldiers, Sandén and Spee visited Caprivi in January 1974. Shooting a longer documentary film[1], they came across the remains of a village where more than a hundred men, women and children had been killed in September 1973 for assisting SWAPO freedom fighters.[2] When shown on Swedish television, Sandén's footage was rejected as "mere nonsense" by South Africa's Defence Minister P.W. Botha[3], and in early August 1974 Foreign Minister Hilgard Muller extended an invitation to the Swedish Broadcasting Corporation to participate in an "investigation" into the situation in Caprivi.[4]

Despite the fact that Sweden did not recognize South Africa's administration over Namibia, on SWAPO's advice[5] the official television company accepted the invitation, demanding that Sandén and Spee be accompanied by representatives of the United Nations Commissioner for Namibia.[6] This was not acceptable to the apartheid regime, which proceeded to organize a stage-managed tour to Caprivi for South African and selected international journalists. Not surprisingly, the "investigation" found no evidence of a massacre.[7]

Four years later—after the Kassinga massacre in southern Angola—Sandén could once again record the atrocities perpetrated by the South African military and the successes won by the People's Liberation Army of Namibia.[8] Contrary to the situation in 1974, his unique documentation was widely disseminated by and

1. Per Sandén and Rudi Spee: 'Frihetskampen i Namibia' ('The Freedom Struggle in Namibia'), Documentary film, 1974 (Distributed by Filmcentrum).
2. SWAPO: Press communiqué ('Massacres in Namibia'), Lusaka, 9 August 1974 (SDA).
3. Ministry for Foreign Affairs: Cable ('Massakern i Namibia'/'The massacre in Namibia') to the Swedish UN delegation, Stockholm, 26 July 1974 (MFA).
4. Letter from Olle Berglund, Deputy Controller, Swedish Broadcasting Corporation/TV 2, to R.H. Coaton, Minister at the South African legation in Sweden, Stockholm, 7 August 1974 (MFA).
5. SWAPO: 'The Atrocities Committed by Racist South African Troops against the Innocent Civilian Namibian People', [no place or date, but Lusaka, August 1974] (SDA).
6. Letter from Olle Berglund (op. cit.) (MFA). In August 1974, Sandén and Spee reported their findings to the UN Commission for Human Rights in Geneva, Switzerland (*Aftonbladet*, 25 July 1974 and telephone conversation with Sandén, 24 November 1999).
7. 'Swedish TV was duped says author at Caprivi' in *Rand Daily Mail*, 21 August 1974. In his memoirs, Andreas Shipanga—who as SWAPO's Secretary for Information was responsible for the visit by the Swedish television crew—presents the Caprivi massacre as a successful disinformation ploy. According to him, Sandén and Spee were taken by SWAPO to a village inside Angola which had been wiped out by the Portuguese (Shipanga op. cit., pp. 96-97).
8. Per Sandén: 'Här Är Namibia' ('Here Is Namibia'), Documentary film, 1978 (Distributed by AV-Centralerna).

within the organized Swedish solidarity movement. Sandén's film was also shown by SWAPO at a meeting of the Organization of African Unity in Dar es Salaam in June 1978.[1]

'Mainstream'

Until the second half of the 1970s, the Africa Groups did not form part of the active Swedish solidarity movement in favour of SWAPO. Due to their concentration on the liberation struggles in Angola, Guinea-Bissau and Mozambique; SWAPO's association with UNITA; and what was perceived as a lack of a clear politico-military strategy, AGIS did not advocate support to Nujoma's organization until June 1976. Albeit with a very small margin, at its second national congress the organization then agreed to "support SWAPO in its struggle for independence".[2] As in the cases of the Zimbabwean Patriotic Front partners ZANU and ZAPU and ANC of South Africa, the reorganized post-Vietnam solidarity organization only recognized SWAPO years after the Swedish government had initiated official support to the movement. During Amathila's term as resident SWAPO representative between 1971 and 1977, the relations between the nationalist movement and the solidarity organization were strained. Looking back, Amathila later recalled that

> especially the Africa Groups were very lukewarm on Namibia [...]. Some people believed that we did not have the seriousness of movements like Guinea-Bissau's PAIGC, Angola's MPLA and Mozambique's FRELIMO, because we did not have liberated territories. They were seen not only as 'ideologically clear' between Moscow and Beijing, but they also met the OAU criteria. [To the Africa Groups], I was a 'newcomer' to the politics of the outside world, who 'understood very little about the ideological differences of the Soviet Union and the Chinese and the imperialistic policies of the West. Marxism-Leninism was new to me'. So, it was very difficult. I always found it very difficult to pretend [to be] what I was not. The active solidarity groups had a network, and in order to work through that network you had to prove [that] you were a Marxist-Leninist.[3] [...]
>
> Gradually, [however, the Africa Groups] began to ignore some of the things that were not acceptable to them, and started to embrace SWAPO. Well, I should not say that they had rejected SWAPO. They did not. It was only that I, as a person, did not say the things that they expected to hear and then, of course, [there was] the UNITA question.[4]

Inviting its members to a first formal meeting with Amathila in July 1974, the Stockholm Africa Group noted that "Namibia, unfortunately, seems to be a relatively bare patch to many of us".[5] This was in striking contrast to the situation in

---

1. Cable ('Re film till SWAPO'/'Re film to SWAPO') from the Ministry for Foreign Affairs to the Swedish embassy in Dar es Salaam, Stockholm, 14 June 1978 (MFA).
2. AGIS: 'Protokoll från AGIS' kongress, 5-7 juni [1976], i Björkå' ('Minutes from the AGIS congress, 5-7 June [1976], at Björkå'), [no date] (AGA). The decision to support SWAPO was passed with 20 votes in favour and 13 against. It should be noted that it was taken at the height of SWAPO's 1975-76 crisis. There is, however, no evidence of the turmoil and detentions in AGIS' contemporary documents. Thus, in a letter to Zambia's President Kenneth Kaunda the congress requested "the immediate release" of the ZANU members who were arrested after the assassination of Herbert Chitepo (AGIS: Letter to President Kaunda ('Detention of members of [the] ZANU leadership'), [no place or date]) (AGA). No similar action was taken in the case of the SWAPO detainees.
3. In this respect, Amathila's characterization is exaggerated. Although generally forming part of the New Left current, barring Emmaus-Björkå (cf. Leijnse op. cit., pp. 34-38) no Swedish solidarity organization involved with Southern Africa embraced Marxism-Leninism as a guiding principle, nor was any of them institutionally linked to—or dominated by—a Marxist political party. The members of the Africa Groups and aligned organizations were overwhelmingly independent socialists and anti-imperialists. In the case of the various Emmaus communities and Bread and Fishes, the activists often had a Christian background.
4. Interview with Ben Amathila, pp. 65-66.
5. Stockholm Africa Group: 'Kallelse till medlemmar' ('Summons to members'), Stockholm, [no date] (AGA).

'For a free Namibia – Support
SWAPO': Members of the Africa Groups
handing out pamphlets in connection
with the Stockholm Open tennis
tournament, 1977
(Photo: Anders Gunnartz)

the early 1960s, when the resident SWANU students in Sweden actively participated in the local, as well as in the national South Africa Committees[1] and the situation in what was then known as South West Africa was widely discussed. During
the first half of the 1970s, few articles on Namibia were, however, published by the
Africa Groups in *Södra Afrika Informationsbulletin* and its successor *Afrikabulletinen*.[2] As late as in mid-1977, the AGIS' board acknowledged that "the cooperation
with SWAPO's representative[3] is [...] weak".[4]

Although the Stockholm Africa Group together with SWAPO shortly thereafter
embarked on internal studies on Namibia and organized public activities for the
liberation movement on 'Namibia Day' in August 1977[5], the relations remained

1. Zedekia Ngavirue was from 1962 a member of the national board of the Swedish South Africa Committee
   (SSAK: 'Verksamhetsberättelse för perioden [augusti] 1962 till mars 1964'/'Activity report for the period
   [August] 1962 to March 1964', Uppsala, 23 March 1964) (AJC).
2. In fact, only twice was Namibia covered, namely in No. 14, 1972 on the general strike ('Strejken i Namibia:
   Hårt Slag mot Sydafrika'/'The Strike in Namibia: Hard Blow against South Africa') and in No. 31, 1975 on
   the Turnhalle process ('Skenval och Vackra Löften: Sydafrika Spelar Falskt i Namibia'/'Mock Elections and
   Beautiful Promises: South Africa's Foul Play in Namibia'). No articles on SWAPO were published until the
   late 1970s.
3. Amathila was succeeded in April 1977 by Hadino Hishongwa. Based in Stockholm, he represented SWAPO in
   the Nordic countries, Austria and the Federal Republic of Germany until late 1982. Hishongwa became Deputy Minister of Labour and Manpower Development at Namibia's independence in 1990. After his term in
   Sweden, SWAPO established a separate office in Bonn for FRG and Austria. Hishongwa's successor, Joseph
   Jimmy, only represented SWAPO in the Nordic countries.
4. AGIS: 'Verksamhetsberättelse för AGIS' styrelse 1976-77' ('Activity report by the AGIS board 1976-77') [no
   place or date], p. 24 (AGA). In an overview of the history of the Swedish solidarity movement with Southern
   Africa, Dick Urban Vestbro—a founder member and leading representative of AGIS—wrote in 1978: "The
   strong concentration on Portugal's colonies led the Africa Groups to neglect the work for South Africa,
   Namibia and Zimbabwe. Ignorance [...] of ANC and SWAPO prevailed in the early 1970s, and disparaging
   comparisons in favour of MPLA and FRELIMO were made in the name of the Africa Groups. This strongly
   obstructed the cooperation with ANC and SWAPO, further delaying the solidarity work in favour of the rising struggle in South Africa and Namibia" (Dick Urban Vestbro: 'Svenska Solidaritetsrörelsen och Södra
   Afrika: Från Anti-Apartheid till Anti-Imperialism'/'The Swedish Solidarity Movement and Southern Africa:
   From Anti-Apartheid to Anti-Imperialism' in *Kommentar*, No. 2, 1978, p. 7).
5. AGIS: 'Protokoll från AU-möte 25.7 1977' ('Minutes from meeting of the working committee, 25 July 1977')
   [no place or date] (AGA). In commemoration of the freedom fighters who fell during SWAPO's first military
   encounter with the South Africans in 1966, 26 August was annually celebrated as 'Namibia Day'.

uneasy. Towards the end of the year, SWAPO's new representative, Hadino Hishongwa, criticized the Africa Groups for not giving Namibia sufficient attention, in his view treating his country as "an appendage" to South Africa.[1] He also threatened to "publicly dissociate himself from AGIS".[2] In its annual report to the congress in Gothenburg in May 1978, the AGIS board acknowledged that "the criticism in general terms was justified", but noted that the relations had improved.[3] Despite the fact that the Africa Groups together with Bread and Fishes at the time had initiated a wide range of campaigns for SWAPO—including the recruitment of doctors and other medical personnel to SWAPO's Kwanza Sul settlement in Angola—they would, however, soon deteriorate anew.

In connection with a visit to Sweden by President Nujoma, in August 1980 Sören Lindh on behalf of the Africa Groups and Bertil Högberg for Bread and Fishes and the Isolate South Africa Committee[4] took the unusual step of writing him a letter in which "the attitude of comrade Hishongwa" was described as having "reached the point of outright hostility". Listing a number of problem areas, the solidarity organizations criticized Hishongwa for "accusing the Africa Groups of 'not doing much for SWAPO' [and] member organizations of ISAK [...] of only dealing with South Africa". According to the letter, the resident SWAPO representative had tried to "create a separate [...] support group" in Sweden.[5] His "lack of understanding" and often "unfriendly, irritated and 'touchy' attitudes, sometimes arrogant and at times rude and insulting towards fellow activists", the letter noted, "is threatening [the] continued mobilization for SWAPO [in Sweden] and the performance of [our] ongoing projects". Against this background, the three solidarity organizations concluded that "a new, positive solution must be found, and we hope that our discussions with you might indicate how the problems can be solved".[6]

The criticism was largely inspired by the three solidarity organizations' contacts with other SWAPO leaders.[7] It was, however, far from well received by Nujoma. He handed the letter to his representative, who in turn distributed it widely in Sweden and accused Högberg of CIA connections.[8] Coordinating the important project 'Health Care to SWAPO'—and having worked at the movement's Stockholm office between 1977 and 1979—Högberg was not allowed to visit the Kwanza Sul settlement.[9] The solidarity movement's substantial assistance was, however, acknowledged by both SWAPO and the Swedish government and the conflict soon subsided.

1. AGIS: 'Protokoll från AGIS styrelsemöte 77 12 17' ('Minutes from AGIS' board meeting, 17 December 1977), Stockholm, [no date] (AGA).
2. Ibid.
3. AGIS: 'Styrelsens verksamhetsberättelse 1977-78' ('Activity report by the board, 1977-78') [no place or date], p. 4 (AGA).
4. In Swedish, *Isolera Sydafrika-Kommittén*. Set up by the Africa Groups in January 1979, ISAK was formally constituted as an independent organization with the objective to achieve a comprehensive isolation of apartheid South Africa in Sweden. In contrast to AGIS, ISAK was not based on individual membership, but made up of NGOs and branches of political parties. By 1991, 63 organizations had joined. One of ISAK's main slogans was "South Africa out of Namibia! Support SWAPO!".
5. With Nujoma in attendance, on 'Namibia Day' 1980—that is, three days later—a separate Swedish Namibia Committee was actually launched by SWAPO in Stockholm to "coordinate contacts with organizations and [political] parties in order to mobilize material and [popular] support for SWAPO" (AGIS: 'Verksamhetsberättelse för Namibia-utskottet 1980/81'/'Activity report [by] the Namibia committee 1980/81' in 'Kongress 81'/'Congress 81', Eskilstuna, 6-8 June 1981) (AGA). While the initiative illustrated the rift between the SWAPO office and the Africa Groups, the committee—largely formed around the Swedish UN Association—never got off the ground.
6. Letter to Sam Nujoma signed by Sören Lindh for the Africa Groups in Sweden and Bertil Högberg for Bread and Fishes and the Isolate South Africa Committee, [no place], 23 August 1980 (AGA).
7. Telephone conversation with Bertil Högberg, Uppsala, 10 May 1999.
8. Ibid.
9. Ibid.

In the case of Namibia, the fact remains, nevertheless, that the relations with the liberation movement were uneasy for a decade. No similar strains were experienced in the cooperation with the other Southern African nationalist movements supported by the Africa Groups.[1]

---

1. Although less acrimonious, the relations between AGIS and the local ANC office in Stockholm were not without complications in the mid-1970s.

Transport, Home Front,
Churches and Trade Unions

Beginnings of Regular Support: The 'Old Farm'

Regular official Swedish humanitarian assistance to SWAPO was, somewhat paradoxically, consolidated during the turbulent détente period 1974-76, when—as a
result of the collapse of the Portuguese colonial empire—the correlation of regional
forces radically changed; the Zambian host government restricted the activities of
the liberation movements; and the Namibian organization experienced mounting
internal strains. As in the case of ZANU of Zimbabwe, a steady flow of refugees
into Zambia and SWAPO's resolve to give the population a meaningful, self-sufficient existence in exile was in this context of decisive importance.

As noted above, no bilateral support was granted for the financial year 1972/73.
In mid-1973, however, SWAPO successfully submitted a request which marked the
beginning of a sustained, extensive bilateral cooperation programme between Sweden and the Namibian liberation movement. In addition to legal aid in favour of
detainees in Namibia and to basic commodities such as food, medicines and shelter
for the SWAPO refugees in Zambia and—later—Angola, it covered supplies and
activities within the fields of agriculture, education, health, information and transport. Transport was from the beginning a particularly important component.
Within the bilateral programme, official Swedish support was from the mid-1970s
also granted to strengthen SWAPO's political and social work inside Namibia.
Towards the end of the decade, the effort was broadened through indirect SIDA
support via church organizations and trade unions to SWAPO-aligned structures in
the country.

Meeting in Stockholm after the UN/OAU Oslo conference, in April 1973 a
SWAPO delegation led by the Administrative Secretary Moses Garoeb[1] resumed
discussions on Swedish assistance with the Ministry for Foreign Affairs and SIDA.[2]
There were at the time some 600 Namibians in Zambia under SWAPO's care.[3] To
properly cater for the refugees, the movement's National Executive Committee had
adopted a plan which "would effectively meet [their] social, economic, health and
educational needs".[4] After procuring farmland of about 2,000 acres some 40 kilo-

1. In addition to Garoeb and SWAPO's resident representative Ben Amathila, the delegation included Theo-Ben
   Gurirab (Chief Representative to the United Nations and the Americas), Peter Katjavivi (Secretary for Economic and Legal Affairs and Chief Representative to the United Kingdom and Western Europe), Solomon
   Mifima (Secretary for Labour and Chief Representative to Egypt) and Andreas Shipanga (Secretary for Information and Publicity).
2. [Gunnar] Lund: Memorandum ('Samtal med representanter för SWAPO'/'Conversation with SWAPO representatives'), Ministry for Foreign Affairs, Stockholm, 3 May 1973 (MFA).
3. Another two thousand refugees were either living in a camp administered by UNHCR at Meheba in north-
   western Zambia or among the local population in the country's Western Province. About a thousand
   Namibians had at the time also crossed into Botswana.
4. SWAPO: 'Development of the Namibia Educational and Health Centre', document attached to letter
   ('SWAPO's request for assistance from SIDA') from Ben Amathila to the Director General of SIDA, Spånga, 5
   June 1973 (SDA).

metres south-west of Lusaka—where 120 refugees had been settled[1]—SWAPO intended to establish "a model nuclear community, which would form a foundation for the future Namibian society".[2] The planned 'Namibian Education and Health Centre'[3] was "not only [...] concerned with the material well-being of the [refugees], but, more importantly, [...] with inculcating ideas of nationhood and social reconstruction".[4] As later explained by Katjavivi,

> we [...] immediately understood that it was important not to simply leave our people in the care of UNHCR. We were not ordinary refugees. We were [...] out to prepare ourselves to make a contribution towards the liberation of our country. The idea of being in a refugee camp was not to settle there indefinitely. It was an opportunity to regroup and acquire the necessary skills and competence while we were in exile.[5]

It was for the SWAPO settlement in Zambia—later known as the 'old farm'—that the visiting delegation sought Swedish assistance. The reaction was in principle positive, and at the beginning of June 1973 Ben Amathila summarized the discussions in a formal request to SIDA.[6] It envisaged financial support amounting to 500,000 SEK during 1973/74, out of which 250,000 was for the construction of a school and a health clinic and 50,000 for agricultural equipment. As the farming activities had not yet yielded any results, in addition to transport the submission included a request for food supplies.[7]

A week later, CCHA recommended support in accordance with SWAPO's request.[8] The first formal aid negotiations between the parties were held in Lusaka in mid-September 1973.[9] The Swedish delegation could then visit the farm, where it not only found SWAPO's plans and request appropriate, but due to the prevailing difficult conditions concluded that "it [is] clear that more aid resources will come to [productive] use".[10] With slight modifications[11], it was agreed to primarily utilize the 1973/74 allocation of 500,000 SEK for construction activities and agriculture.[12]

1. In *A History of Resistance in Namibia*, Katjavivi—who participated in the Stockholm talks—states that the 'old farm' was "established by SWAPO in the 1960s" and that it "by the end of 1974 [catered for] several thousand [Namibians]" (Katjavivi op. cit., p. 109). Contemporary SWAPO and SIDA documents show that the land was procured in 1973 and that the number of refugees living there increased to about 500 (Carin Norberg: Memorandum ('Rapport från besök på SWAPO-farmen 1975 01 22'/'Report from visit to the SWAPO farm 22 January 1975'), Swedish embassy, Lusaka, 30 January 1975) (SDA).
2. SWAPO: 'Development of the Namibia Educational and Health Centre', op. cit.
3. SWAPO's refugee settlements in Zambia and Angola were later known as 'health and education centres'.
4. SWAPO: 'Development of the Namibia Educational and Health Centre', op. cit.
5. Interview with Peter Katjavivi, p. 71.
6. Letter ('SWAPO's request for assistance from SIDA') from Ben Amathila to the Director General of SIDA, Spånga, 5 June 1973 (SDA).
7. Ibid.
8. CCHA: 'Protokoll [från sammanträde 12 juni 1973]' ('Minutes [from meeting 12 June 1973]'), SIDA, [Stockholm], 5 July 1973 (SDA).
9. The SWAPO delegation to the first negotiations with Sweden was led by Peter Nanyemba, Secretary for Defence and Transport. It also included Putuse Appolus from the Women's Council, Moses Garoeb and Andreas Shipanga. The Swedish team was headed by Kurt Kristiansson, SIDA's representative to Zambia. The other members were Stig Lövgren (SIDA Stockholm), Anders Möllander (Ministry for Foreign Affairs), Stig Regnell (SIDA Dar es Salaam) and Bo Wilén (SIDA Lusaka). Parallel aid negotiations between Sweden and ZANU of Zimbabwe were conducted by the team in Lusaka.
10. Anders Möllander: Memorandum ('Besök på SWAPO's farm utanför Lusaka i Zambia'/'Visit to SWAPO's farm outside Lusaka in Zambia'), Ministry for Foreign Affairs, Stockholm, 29 October 1973 (SDA). The visit took place on 18 September 1973.
11. In addition to the school and the health clinic, it was agreed that Sweden should finance the construction of dormitories for 50 children.
12. 'Agreed minutes of discussions between delegations from SWAPO and Sweden', Lusaka, 20 September 1973 (SDA). The actual discussions were held on 18 September 1973.

The agreement was confirmed by SIDA in October 1973.[1]

During parallel negotiations with ZANU, Sweden had in September 1973 agreed to finance the procurement of a farm for the Zimbabwean liberation movement.[2] With almost the same area as the 'old farm'[3], it was situated some 25 kilometres west of Lusaka. While the Zambian authorities initially did not oppose the land acquisitions by SWAPO and ZANU, essential national security aspects were, however, soon raised, and in mid-April 1974 SIDA was asked to "wait and see" concerning the assistance to the two farms.[4] Two weeks later, the Zambian Foreign Minister Vernon Mwaanga concluded that "the establishment of liberation movements in the vicinity of Lusaka implied non-acceptable security risks"[5], asking Sweden to withhold its support. The same message was conveyed to SWAPO. Immediately contacting the Swedish embassy in Lusaka, Nujoma explained that during the negotiations with Sweden SWAPO had "acted in good faith" and that the Zambian authorities at the time "were fully informed of the content of the agreement, but did not express [...] any objections".[6] He, nevertheless, hoped that a solution could be found.

Zambia's decision affected the establishment of permanent structures at the SWAPO settlement. Meeting in Lusaka for a new round of negotiations at the end of May 1974, delegations from Sweden and the Namibian liberation movement[7] noted that it "due to unforeseen circumstances had not been possible to start the building programme at the farm"[8], while food, medicines, vehicles and agricultural equipment had been delivered according to the agreement reached in September 1973. When Carin Norberg, the responsible SIDA official at the Swedish embassy in Lusaka, together with Andreas Shipanga visited the 'old farm' in January 1975[9] she found the 500 Namibians staying there—of whom 200 were school children—healthy and engaged in meaningful activities. However, the primary school con-

---

1. SIDA: Decision ('Biståndsprogram för SWAPO 1973/74'/'Assistance programme for SWAPO 1973/74'), SIDA, Stockholm, 23 October 1973 (SDA). At the time, Swedish humanitarian support to the Southern African liberation movements mainly consisted of commodity aid, which was handled by the procurement section within SIDA's country division. As the 1973/74 SWAPO programme envisaged building activities, it was decided to engage SIDA's industry division, where Johan Brisman became responsible for the Swedish assistance. Together with the education and health divisions, the industry division was thus among the first so called 'sector divisions' to be concerned with Sweden's cooperation with the liberation movements. In the case of SWAPO's 'old farm', the construction component was, however, never implemented. As SIDA's representative to Mozambique in 1980-82, Brisman was closely involved with the liberation movements, particularly with ANC of South Africa. In 1994, he became responsible for Swedish development assistance to democratic South Africa at the Swedish embassy in Pretoria.
2. See the chapter 'ZANU and ZAPU of Zimbabwe: On Separate Trails'.
3. The purchase price was in both cases approximately 20,000 Zambian Kwacha, at the time corresponding to some 130,000 SEK.
4. Letter ('Det svenska biståndet till SWAPO/ZANU-farmerna'/'The Swedish assistance to the SWAPO/ZAPU farms') from Iwo Dölling, Swedish ambassador to Zambia, to the Ministry for Foreign Affairs, Lusaka, 6 May 1974 (SDA).
5. Ibid. It should be remembered that landlocked Zambia—at least until the 'détente exercise' and the independence of Angola and Mozambique—was the most exposed host country engaged in the liberation struggle in Southern Africa. Four of the major theatres of the regional liberation wars bordered Zambian territory, namely Tete (Mozambique), the Zambezi valley (Zimbabwe), Caprivi (Namibia) and Moxico (Angola).
6. Letter ('Samtal med SWAPO-presidenten'/'Conversation with the SWAPO President') from Iwo Dölling, Swedish ambassador to Zambia, to the Ministry for Foreign Affairs, Lusaka, 6 May 1974 (SDA).
7. SWAPO's Vice-President Mishake Muyongo led the Namibian delegation, which included Ben Amathila, Peter Nanyemba and Andreas Shipanga. Ambassador Iwo Dölling headed the Swedish team, which consisted in addition of Astrid Bergquist (SIDA Stockholm), Lars Hultkvist (SIDA Lusaka), Stig Lövgren (SIDA Stockholm), Anders Möllander (Ministry for Foreign Affairs) and Bo Wilén (SIDA Lusaka).
8. 'Agreed minutes of discussions on cooperation between South West Africa People's Organization and Sweden', Lusaka, 6 June 1974 (SDA). The actual discussions were held on 20-22 May 1974.
9. Lars Hultkvist (SIDA Lusaka), Christina Jämtin (SIDA Dar es Salaam) and Maria Nordenfelt (SIDA Dar es Salaam) accompanied Norberg.

sisted of barracks, the clinic was housed in a grass structure and the majority of the refugees were living in makeshift huts or tents.[1]

SWAPO negotiated for a long time with the Zambian authorities for permission to remain at the 'old farm'. As thousands of Namibian refugees reached Zambia via Angola after the April 1974 Lisbon coup, President Kaunda's government, however, eventually decided to allocate a new site to the liberation movement. It was situated at Nyango in the Western Province, close to Kaoma and some 450 kilometres from Lusaka.[2] Here, the Zambian authorities put no less than 10,000 acres at SWAPO's disposal, also allowing the construction of permanent buildings.[3] The final decision to close the 'old farm' and move the SWAPO refugees to Nyango was taken in October 1975, at the height of the détente exercise launched by the South African Prime Minister Vorster and President Kaunda one year earlier[4]; at about the same time as the South African military invasion of Angola started; and in the midst of a mounting internal SWAPO crisis. Carried out at a particularly critical juncture, the move from the 'old farm' to Nyango was successfully implemented towards the end of 1975. In March 1976, SWAPO's Vice-President Muyongo informed a visiting Swedish delegation to Lusaka that around a thousand Namibian refugees had been settled there.[5]

1. Carin Norberg: Memorandum ('Rapport från besök på SWAPO-farmen 1975 01 22'/'Report from visit to the SWAPO farm 22 January 1975'), Swedish embassy, Lusaka, 30 January 1975 (SDA). At the time of the visit, 5 Namibian teachers were active at the primary school, while 17 nurses and midwives managed the clinic. In addition to Sweden, the Soviet Union had supplied vehicles and farm equipment. UNICEF and—remarkably—USAID had delivered books and equipment to the school, while the clinic had received medicines from Norway and Sweden (ibid.). SWAPO's medical doctors Iyambo Indongo and Libertine Amathila, respectively Secretary and Deputy Secretary for Health and Welfare, took charge of the clinic later in 1975 (Carin Norberg: Memorandum ('Minnesanteckningar från samtal [med] Hidipo Hamutenya 1975 10 15'/'Notes from conversation [with] Hidipo Hamutenya 15 October 1975'), Swedish embassy, Lusaka, 22 October 1975) (SDA).
2. SWAPO's military activities were coordinated from PLAN's 'central base' near the town of Senanga on the Zambezi river, some 300 kilometres west of Nyango.
3. Carin Norberg: Memorandum ('Minnesanteckningar från samtal [med] Hidipo Hamutenya 1975 10 15'/ 'Notes from conversation [with] Hidipo Hamutenya 15 October 1975'), Swedish embassy, Lusaka, 22 October 1975 (SDA).
4. While the détente exercise primarily concerned Zimbabwe, it affected the liberation struggle in Namibia and left the SWAPO leadership deeply concerned. As in the case of ZANU and the other Southern African liberation movements, throughout the period Sweden maintained a close dialogue with SWAPO on its possible regional consequences. The contacts between Vorster and Kaunda became publicly known in late October 1974. Sam Nujoma was immediately thereafter invited to Sweden by the ruling Social Democratic Party ('Press release', Ministry for Foreign Affairs, Stockholm, 28 October 1974) (MFA). Like ZANU's Chairman Herbert Chitepo—who visited Stockholm two weeks later—Nujoma held discussions with Prime Minister Palme, Foreign Minister Andersson and Cooperation Minister Sigurdsen on the latest developments in Southern Africa (Olof Dahlberg: 'Vorster ökar terrorväldet i Namibia'/'Vorster increases the rule of terror in Namibia' in *Dagens Nyheter*, 1 November 1974). Chitepo was assassinated in Lusaka on 18 March 1975. In subsequent discussions at the Ministry for Foreign Affairs, Ben Amathila—who ruled out the Zambian argument that the murder was due to internal ZANU conflicts, concluding that it must have been committed by the Smith regime—expressed concern about Kaunda's policy (Bengt Säve-Söderbergh: Memorandum ('Besök av SWAPO's Sverige-representant Ben Amathila'/'Visit by SWAPO's representative to Sweden, Ben Amathila'), Ministry for Foreign Affairs, Stockholm, 25 March 1975) (MFA). Later in the year—as it was reported that the Zambian government had impounded SWAPO vehicles carrying arms from Tanzania—Nujoma openly criticized Zambia in discussions with Swedish diplomats in Lusaka (Cable ('SWAPO och Namibia') from Anders Bjurner to the Ministry for Foreign Affairs, Swedish embassy, Lusaka, 19 September 1975) (MFA). And in March 1976—just before the internal SWAPO crisis broke out—Vice-President Muyongo stated that the movement "never had put up with the détente policy". Expressing deep distrust towards the host government, he told representatives of the Swedish government that SWAPO "was anxious that the information given to the Zambian authorities about the Swedish assistance should be as sparing as possible" (Marianne Sundh and Ann Wilkens: Memorandum ('Minnesanteckningar från möte med SWAPO i Lusaka den 16 mars 1976'/'Notes from meeting with SWAPO in Lusaka on 16 March 1976'), CCHA/Ministry for Foreign Affairs, Stockholm, 29 April 1976) (SDA).
5. Sundh and Wilkens op. cit.

The bulk of the Swedish assistance to SWAPO in Zambia was from then on channelled to the new health and education centre at Nyango. Aaron Mushimba— SWAPO's representative to Zambia in the early 1980s—later recalled:

> SIDA got very much involved in the Nyango settlement. We set it up and built the kindergartens, the hospital and other installations through SIDA. SIDA also paid for the clearing of the fields behind Nyango, where we were to plant millet. Our people later became self-sufficient.[1]

Mainly due to the deteriorating situation in the region—resulting both from South African activities and from hostilities between UNITA and the MPLA government in neighbouring Angola—Nyango was initially declared a "security area".[2] When the embassy in Lusaka asked for permission to visit Nyango in mid-1977, it was not granted by the Zambian Ministry for Defence.[3] Despite considerable Swedish deliveries of humanitarian assistance, no authorization to visit the camp was issued until 1978.[4] By then, SWAPO had moved great numbers of refugees to Angola, where the Kassinga and—above all—the Kwanza Sul settlements became major recipients of Swedish support.

Transport: Dominance, Doubts and New Directions

The first visible evidence of Swedish assistance encountered by Namibians released from detention and joining the movement in exile in the late 1970s and the 1980s was SWAPO's vehicle fleet. Reaching Zambia in 1977, Mushimba, for example, was struck by the transport capacity:

> You could see it from the day we were picked up at the Botswana border. [...] We could not comprehend. 'How come that SWAPO has all these vehicles?' They had new cars and four-by-fours.[5]

When Andimba Toivo ya Toivo arrived in Angola in mid-1984 after sixteen years on Robben Island, he similarly "found a lot of Volvos flooding SWAPO and our camps. All from Sweden. Volvos and Scanias". [...] As far as the question of transport is concerned, we never suffered".[6]

---

1. Interview with Aaron Mushimba, p. 85.
2. Zambia Christian Refugee Service: 'Report on Reverend K.C. Mwenda's visit to Nyango Namibian refugee camp, 4-6 June 1977', Lusaka, [no date] (SDA). At the time, a great number of the former Mboroma detainees were in addition moved to Nyango.
3. Letter ('Besök vid SWAPO's farm i Zambia'/'Visit to SWAPO's farm in Zambia') from Anders Möllander to the Ministry for Foreign Affairs, Swedish embassy, Lusaka, 22 July 1977 (SDA).
4. Letter ('SWAPO's läger i Nyango, Zambia'/'SWAPO's camp at Nyango, Zambia') from Anders Möllander to the Ministry for Foreign Affairs, Swedish embassy, Lusaka, 28 December 1977 (SDA).
5. Interview with Aaron Mushimba, p. 84.
6. Interview with Andimba Toivo ya Toivo, p. 99. In the 1995 interview, Toivo ya Toivo added: "I fell in love with the Volvos. I am still driving a Volvo now" (ibid.). Although the Swedish humanitarian support was not tied to procurement in Sweden, in the case of heavy-duty trucks the Swedish companies Scania and Volvo were often preferred by the liberation movements. Competing on the Southern African market, preferences by and links with individual movements would largely influence their post-independence presence in the various countries. While Scania via FRELIMO contacts gained a dominant position in independent Mozambique, Volvo was to enjoy a similar position in MPLA's Angola. In addition, in Mozambique ZANU often talked about the Swedish aid in terms of a 'triple S', meaning 'Sweden, SIDA and Scania', while Volvo in Angola was seen by SWAPO as a 'progressive ally' in the Namibian liberation war. Interviewed in 1995, Festus Naholo, SWAPO's former Secretary of Logistics, recalled that "the South Africans [in 1981-82] with support from the USA and Thatcher in Britain turned against the Nordic countries, Sweden in particular. They wanted to stop Volvo. It was difficult for us. We were afraid of not getting trucks from Sweden. By then, we were also receiving some Volvos which were a kind of military vehicle. They were very important to get loads into the bush and people into hospitals and clinics" (Interview with Festus Naholo, p. 90). The author remembers when in May 1978 after the Kassinga massacre he travelled with SWAPO's Defence Secretary in southern Angola. Nanyemba's driver had three badges proudly attached to his beret, respectively representing SWAPO, Lenin and Volvo.

After initial doubts, the Swedish authorities had at an early stage resolved that the supply of vehicles to the liberation movements was a necessary complement to strict humanitarian commodity aid.[1] With the exception of FRELIMO of Mozambique and ANC of South Africa, transport featured prominently within the assistance programmes to the liberation movements supported by Sweden. In the cases of PAIGC of Guinea-Bissau and ZANU and ZAPU of Zimbabwe, it occupied in monetary terms as a rule second place, representing 15 to 20 per cent of the value of the support. In the case of MPLA of Angola—which faced particularly difficult logistical problems—the transport support was dominant, over the years accounting for between 30 and 50 per cent of the assistance.

From being essentially re-active and mechanical—driven by quantitative considerations—the transport support to the Namibian movement would in the early 1980s become pro-active and forward-looking, contributing to policy re-orientation and capacity-building. With the assistance extended in the fields of education and financial administration, it illustrates how the Swedish humanitarian assistance to SWAPO in exile prepared the terrain for close cooperation with independent Namibia.

From a logistical point of view, SWAPO's challenges were similar to those faced by MPLA. In order to supply the Namibian refugees in Zambia with essential commodities, the movement had, until Angola's independence in late 1975, to establish secure lines of communication from the harbour in Dar es Salaam to Lusaka—a distance of some 2,000 kilometres—and from there to the various localities in western Zambia where the majority of the refugees initially settled. The Nyango centre was set up in late 1975. It was situated some 450 kilometres from Lusaka. Hundreds of Namibian refugees were, in addition, living in Botswana. They could only be reached from Zambia, implying additional—and extremely difficult—transports over 1,000 (Francistown) and 1,500 (Maun and Gaborone) kilometres.

Towards the end of the 1970s, SWAPO transferred the bulk of its activities to Angola. Although the organization had direct access to the harbour in Luanda, the refugee centres were far away. To reach the Kassinga settlement from the capital, SWAPO had to travel along roads damaged by war and threatened by UNITA attacks for more than 1,600 kilometres. Finally, the distance from Luanda to the Kwanza Sul settlement was about 300 kilometres.[2] Not including its military campaigns, SWAPO's area of operation was extremely extensive. In fact, with incomparably inferior roads and largely exposed to enemy attacks it approximately corresponded to the area of western Europe.

It was these circumstances which determined that over the years the supply of vehicles played such a significant role in Sweden's cooperation with the Namibian liberation movement. In 1995, SWAPO's former Treasurer Hifikepunye Pohamba summarized the aid relationship as follows:

> [I]t grew into millions of Swedish Kronor every year. It started with food and was then extended to vehicles. If the food was bought in Lusaka, it had to be transported into the camps. We did not have any vehicles, so we said: 'OK, here is the food, but we have no means to take it to the people.' SIDA then made provision for vehicles. [...] It even went to the building of [workshops] for our vehicles, which eventually became many.[3]

---

1. See the chapter on Guinea-Bissau.
2. Although the distance was only some 300 kilometres, Peltola notes that the drive from Luanda to Kwanza Sul normally took eleven hours, "but it could [also] take double that time" (Peltola op. cit., p. 143).
3. Interview with Hifikepunye Pohamba, p. 95.

Heavy-duty Scania
trucks from Sweden
for SWAPO: Transport
Secretary Maxton
Mutongolume
standing next to a
container from Bread
and Fishes, Luanda,
January 1983 (Photo:
Paul Rimmerfors)

Transport was included for the first time in the Swedish assistance to SWAPO during the financial year 1973/74. Two Mercedes Benz trucks were then supplied to the 'old farm'.[1] In that year, the support represented 25 per cent of the funds allocated.[2] The share remained approximately the same in 1974/75[3], but rose sharply to 50 per cent in 1975/76 when three heavy-duty trucks and three lighter four-wheel drive cars in addition to trailers, spare parts, lubricants etc. were included in the cooperation programme.[4] Transport had thus become by far the most important single component of the Swedish humanitarian support to SWAPO, representing more than double the combined value of food and medicines.[5] This, in turn, prompted the Ministry for Foreign Affairs to ask the Swedish embassy in Lusaka for a report on SWAPO's logistical situation and needs.[6] The embassy gave a detailed account of the problems faced by the liberation movement, stating that

> the embassy has, naturally, no possibility to control in detail for what purpose the [vehicles] are being used. Although it as a rule is not explicitly stated in the [agreed minutes], the liberation movements in question[7] are, however, fully aware that all Swedish assistance must be used for civilian, humanitarian purposes. The question of control [thus] partly becomes a question of trust between the two parties. The liberation movements are—at least in the case of Zam-

---

1. 'Agreed minutes of discussions between delegations from SWAPO and Sweden', Lusaka, 20 September 1973 (SDA).
2. Ibid.
3. 'Agreed minutes of discussions on cooperation between South West Africa People's Organization and Sweden', Lusaka, 6 June 1974 (SDA).
4. 'Agreed Minutes of discussion[s] on cooperation between Sweden and South West Africa People's Organization (SWAPO)', Lusaka, 26 August 1975 (SDA) and CCHA: Memorandum ('Biståndssamarbetet med South West Africa People's Organization, Namibia, under budgetåret 1975/76 och förslag till medelsram 1976/77'/ 'Cooperation with SWAPO during the financial year 1975/76 and proposed allocation 1976/77') by Marianne Sundh, SIDA, Stockholm, 10 May 1976 (SDA). Sam Nujoma was largely behind the emphasis given to the transport sector in 1975/76. He led—for the first time—the SWAPO delegation to the aid negotiations in Lusaka in August 1975. The other SWAPO members were Hidipo Hamutenya, Iyambo Indongo, Peter Nanyemba and Nahambo Shamena. Anders Bjurner, at the time chargé d'affaires in Lusaka, headed the Swedish team, which also included Carin Norberg and Stefan Jörgne from the local SIDA office. With regard to the early attention given to the transport sector, it should be noted that SWAPO's Secretary for Defence and Transport, Peter Nanyemba, took part in all the negotiations with Sweden between 1973 and 1976.
5. Ibid. In 1975/76, food and medicines only represented shares of 15 and 10 per cent, respectively (ibid.).
6. Letter ('Humanitärt bistånd till ANC (Sydafrika) och SWAPO'/'Humanitarian assistance to ANC (South Africa) and SWAPO') from Ove Heyman, Swedish ambassador to Zambia, to the Ministry for Foreign Affairs, Lusaka, 19 December 1975 (SDA).
7. The report also covered ANC of South Africa.

bia—also aware that the [...] 'host countries' are informed about this Swedish principle. In Zambia, it is in addition an explicit condition that information on all assistance to the liberation movements must be given to the Ministry of Defence. The Zambian government does not permit bilateral assistance of a strategic, military nature.[1]

Concluding that "even the theoretical possibility to use [the vehicles] for other than civilian purposes is [...] very limited", the embassy advised against any "restrictions on [...] the access to transport means" as it "undoubtedly would affect the [liberation movements'] civilian activities".[2]

The Swedish authorities were satisfied with the embassy report. From a political point of view, no objections were raised from then on against the substantial part transport played in Sweden's overall cooperation with SWAPO. With a budget of 4.2 million out of a total allocation of 10 MSEK, in 1977/78, for example, it still represented a share of more than 40 per cent, while food stood for 30 and medicines for less than 1 per cent.[3] As SWAPO ordered new vehicles each year under the cooperation programme[4], it was, however, eventually decided by SIDA to carry out a more technical study with regard to the status of the units already supplied. The inventory was carried out jointly with SWAPO in 1982 and covered the vehicles procured between 1975/76 and 1980/81.[5]

During the six years in question, SWAPO had received no less than 181 vehicles from Sweden, that is, an average of 30 per year. With 72 units, cross-country jeeps accounted for the largest number[6], followed by heavy-duty trucks (53)[7], Landcruisers (21)[8], station wagons (15)[9] and ambulances (15).[10] The inventory, however, revealed that only 58 of the 181 vehicles—less than a third—could be identified and that the number in working order was a mere 31, or less than 20 per cent.[11] Although SWAPO had lost many vehicles during attacks by South Africa and UNITA—as at Kassinga in May 1978—the findings sounded an alarm.[12] Commenting on the figures, Stig Lövgren, the head of SIDA's procurement division, described SWAPO's consumption of vehicles as "completely astounding". Adding that the movement's accounts regarding the Swedish transport support were "not acceptable", he concluded that "it can't be right to year after year supply SWAPO with factory-new vehicles which obviously either disappear or within too short a time are run down and remain standing".[13] As SIDA at the time had delivered another 25 vehicles to SWAPO under the 1981/82 programme and the movement

---

1. Letter from Ove Heyman to the Ministry for Foreign Affairs, op. cit.
2. Ibid.
3. CCHA: Memorandum ('Tilläggsframställning från South West Africa People's Organization, SWAPO'/'Additional request from SWAPO') by Marianne Sundh, SIDA, Stockholm, 31 January 1978 (SDA).
4. Under the Swedish assistance programme, many vehicles—especially Landcruisers and station wagons—were procured locally by SWAPO, in the beginning in Zambia and later mainly in Botswana.
5. Stig Lövgren: Memorandum ('Fordonsleveranser till SWAPO'/'Deliveries of vehicles to SWAPO'), SIDA, Stockholm, 8 July 1982 (SDA).
6. Of the lighter cross-country vehicles and jeeps, 39 were of Swedish manufacture (Volvo C 202 and C 303) and 33 Japanese (Toyota).
7. With 39 units, Volvo dominated among the heavy-duty trucks. Scania accounted for 11 trucks and Mercedes Benz for 3.
8. Toyota.
9. Volvo 6 and Toyota 9.
10. Volvo 7, Toyota 5 and Mercedes Benz/Unimog 3. One Volvo bus and four trailers were also supplied during the period. Excluding the trailers, 103 of the 177 vehicles (58%) were of Swedish manufacture (Volvo 92 and Scania 11), 68 (39%) Japanese (all Toyota) and 6 (3%) West German (Mercedes Benz).
11. Stig Lövgren: Memorandum, op. cit.
12. For security reasons, SWAPO also often had vehicles re-painted, which, eventually, made the origin difficult to establish even for the movement itself.
13. Ibid.

PLAN freedom fighters gathering around SWAPO Defence Secretary Peter Nanyemba's cross-country Volvo vehicle, Huíla province, Angola, May 1978 (Photo: The author)

had requested 43 more for 1982/83[1], Lövgren proposed a new policy to tackle the movement's transport requirements.[2]

Instead of regularly supplying new units, in Lövgren's view SIDA should rather deliver reconditioned second-hand vehicles and take a more active part in the repair and maintenance of SWAPO's transport fleet, notably by setting up vehicle workshops and by training SWAPO cadres in automechanics.[3] The proposal was in principle accepted by the liberation movement. Together with SIDA's adviser Torgny Quick, SWAPO's Secretary for Transport Maxton Mutongolume established the general framework for a re-orientation of both the Swedish support and SWAPO's transport policy by putting emphasis on maintenance and training.[4] The Quick report—which primarily envisaged the establishment of a fully equipped, modern vehicle workshop close to SWAPO's transit camp in Viana on the outskirts of

1. Ibid.
2. Lövgren was also concerned about the great number of cross-country vehicles and jeeps. The purpose of these should, in his view, "be clarified before new, substantial deliveries are made. In any case, SIDA should receive some sort of guarantee from SWAPO that these vehicles—as in the case of others financed by SIDA—are not directly used in the war operations" (ibid.). PLAN did, in fact, use a lot of Volvo cross-country vehicles in the operational areas in southern Angola. In May 1978, for example, the author travelled with SWAPO's Secretary for Defence Peter Nanyemba in his Volvo jeep in the Kassinga area. Although most likely (cf. the number of vehicles not accounted for by SWAPO), it is, however, not possible to establish beyond doubt that SWAPO used Volvo jeeps supplied by the Swedish government in the war effort. In addition to purely commercial procurements, SWAPO received many Volvo C 202's and C 303's from other donors, such as the United Nations, international organizations, government agencies and NGOs. In the case of heavy-duty trucks, Soiri and Peltola quote an example where the Finnish government—intending to tie its assistance to deliveries from Finland—offered SWAPO Sisu trucks. SWAPO, however, preferred Volvos (Soiri and Peltola op. cit., p. 121-22). Trying to standardize its transport fleet, the same applied to cross-country vehicles. According to the report given to Quick, by early 1983 SWAPO had acquired no less than 124 Volvo jeeps, or almost three times as many as the 45 supplied under the Swedish assistance programme (Torgny Quick: 'SWAPO's verkstäder och fordon i Angola: Inventering och förslag till åtgärder'/'SWAPO's workshops and vehicles in Angola: Inventory and proposed action', SIDA, Stockholm, 5 March 1983) (SDA).
3. Letter ('Fordonsleveranser till SWAPO'/'Deliveries of vehicles to SWAPO') from Stig Lövgren to the Swedish embassy in Luanda, SIDA, Stockholm, 15 July 1982 (SDA).
4. Torgny Quick op. cit. SWAPO had by 1983 acquired no fewer than 1,500 vehicles of various makes and models. Around 450 (30%) were Volvos and Scanias. According to SWAPO's inventory, the liberation movement had in addition obtained 500 (33%) West German Mercedes Benz trucks and Unimog jeeps, while the number of Japanese vehicles was 340, corresponding to 23%. The total number of vehicles supplied by the Soviet Union, East Germany, Romania and other socialist countries was surprisingly low, or around 100 (7%).

Luanda—was positively reviewed by the partners during the aid negotiations in the Angolan capital in mid-March 1983.[1]

While SWAPO—characterizing transport as "the lifeline of all activities"[2]—continued to request and receive vehicles from Sweden and other donors, from 1984 it gave increasing attention to training in automechanics and vehicle maintenance. Members were sent to Tanzania and Zambia, where they—in addition to on-the-job training at Volvo's workshop in Angola—attended specialized courses.[3] Soon thereafter[4], SIDA started to supply second-hand trucks at considerably lower costs than factory-new units. Above all, the Viana workshop became operational in September 1986. Supplied with tools and spare parts for different makes and models, it was run with assistance from the Swedish consultancy firm SWEDEC, which for training purposes seconded a workshop manager, a chief mechanic and a stores director. In May 1988, 61 SWAPO members were attached to the workshop.[5]

The Viana project was evaluated by independent consultants in May 1988. The assessment was clearly positive, concluding that the workshop "arguably is the best in the entire country" and that "SWAPO's transports would hardly function without it".[6] Although the training component according to the evaluators could improve, they found that the workshop had "become one of SWAPO's most important institutions for vocational training".[7] More importantly, since its opening the workshop had rehabilitated around 140 SWAPO vehicles. From an economic point of view, this motivated the project costs of 17 MSEK.[8]

In addition to the main workshop in Viana, Sweden financed at the same time a similar facility for SWAPO in Lusaka and less sophisticated garages at the refugee settlements in Kwanza Sul, Angola, and Nyango, Zambia. Highly appreciated by SWAPO[9], the transport policy jointly drawn up between SIDA and the Namibian liberation movement in the early 1980s prepared the terrain for forward planning and bilateral Swedish development assistance to independent Namibia. In late September 1988—before the decisive New York accords between Angola, Cuba and

---

1. 'Agreed minutes from discussions on the cooperation between SWAPO of Namibia and the Swedish International Development Authority (SIDA)', Luanda, 21 March 1983 (SDA). Hifikepunye Pohamba led the SWAPO delegation for the first time to the 1983 negotiations. He would from then on play a particularly important role in the design of the cooperation programme with Sweden.

2. 'Minutes from consultative talks held in Luanda, November 1984, between SWAPO and SIDA concerning humanitarian assistance', Luanda, [15 November] 1984 (SDA).

3. 'Minutes from programme discussions between SWAPO of Namibia and the Swedish International Development Authority (SIDA)', Luanda, [9 November] 1983 (SDA).

4. 'Minutes of understanding between SWAPO and SIDA', Luanda, 20 November 1986 (SDA).

5. SIDA: *Verkstad i Exil: SWAPOs Fordonverkstad i Angola* ('Workshop in Exile: SWAPO's Vehicle Workshop in Angola'), SIDA, Bistånd Utvärderat No. 1/89, Stockholm, 1989, p. 9. The report by Willy Damm and Lars Rylander was originally presented in English as 'The Swedish Support to the SWAPO Workshop in Viana', Scandinavian Project Managers, Stockholm, May 1988.

6. Ibid., pp. 17 and 15.

7. Ibid., p. 6.

8. Ibid., p. 14 and Ola Hällgren: Memorandum ('Fortsatt stöd till SWAPO's fordonsverkstäder under perioden 1989/04/01-1992/03/31'/'Continued support to SWAPO's vehicle workshops during the period 1 April 1989-31 March 1992'), SIDA, Stockholm, 9 April 1989 (SDA).

9. Cf. the interview with Pohamba, p. 96: "As time went by, we had a lot of vehicles bought with money not only from the Nordic countries, but also from other[s]. The problem was that we needed garages where these vehicles could be served. SIDA then agreed to establish [workshops] for us in Lusaka, Luanda and Kwanza Sul. So the fleet of vehicles was serviced by SWAPO with the assistance of SIDA experts".

South Africa—Nujoma addressed a letter to Prime Minister Carlsson. In the letter, he explained "on behalf of the Central Committee of SWAPO and the struggling people of Namibia" that it

> in anticipation of the imminent independence of Namibia [...] is extremely important that our two respective countries cooperate in some of the vital fields in which Sweden is more competent, experienced and technologically advanced.[1]

Two fields were identified by Nujoma, namely transport and communications and the establishment of a Namibian central bank.[2] Carlsson responded positively to Nujoma's letter on 1 December 1988, adding that education could become a priority sector for Swedish assistance.[3] In the case of transport and communications, SIDA subsequently procured the services of the Swedish consultancy firm SWECO, which prepared a comprehensive study. Known as the 'blue book'[4], it was released at Namibia's independence on 21 March 1990. Approved by the incoming SWAPO government, the study formed the basis for a bilateral agreement on long-term cooperation with regard to transport and communications, signed in April 1991.[5]

Repression and Diplomatic Intervention

After the 1973 UN/OAU Oslo conference, Sweden would give explicit priority to areas liberated by the Southern African nationalist movements. In the case of Namibia, the situation was, however, different from that in Angola, Mozambique and—although less obvious—Zimbabwe. Recognized as such by the Swedish authorities, they, nevertheless, emphasized the importance of assisting the internal political opposition. Recommending continued support to SWAPO, the CCHA secretariat explained in February 1974 that

> where such possibilities do exist, it is [...] essential to assist institutions and organizations in [Namibia] which—as in South Africa—try to work against the apartheid system, for racial equality and independence.[6]

Despite the fact that no objections were raised against the use of official Swedish resources for civilian purposes inside the country, SWAPO did not include such pro-

---

1. Letter from Sam Nujoma to Ingvar Carlsson, Luanda, 30 September 1988 (MFA).
2. Ibid.
3. Letter from Ingvar Carlsson to Sam Nujoma, Stockholm, 1 December 1988 (MFA).
4. [SIDA/SWECO]: 'Transport and Communications in Namibia', [A study] prepared for the Ministry of Works, Transport and Communications [of the] Republic of Namibia, Stockholm, 21 March 1990. The coordinator and principal author of the study was Nils Bruzelius. He was later closely involved with the restructuring of the transport sector in Namibia, also serving as an adviser concerning the re-incorporation of Walvis Bay.
5. Bertil Odén, Henning Melber, Tor Sellström and Chris Tapscott: *Namibia and External Resources: The Case of Swedish Development Assistance*, Research Report No. 96, Nordiska Afrikainstitutet, Uppsala, 1994, p. 81.
6. CCHA: Memorandum ('Stöd till SWAPO'/'Support to SWAPO') by Astrid Bergquist, [SIDA, Stockholm], 12 February 1974 (SDA).

posals in its requests until mid-1975.[1] Having discussed the issue with the SWAPO leadership in Lusaka, Anders Bjurner was "somewhat surprised" when in January 1975 the movement presented an emergency request which yet again made no mention of the needs inside Namibia.[2] In the absence of material assistance to SWAPO's internal wing—and apart from indirect legal aid—the support to the home front was in the mid-1970s primarily expressed at the diplomatic level. This was, for example, the case during the repression after the Ovamboland elections in 1973; as uncertainties prevailed in Angola following the April 1974 Lisbon coup; and when the UN Security Council in June 1975 debated the Namibia question.

Following the recommendations by the 1962 Odendaal Commission and in open defiance of the United Nations, South Africa proceeded towards the end of the 1960s to legislate 'territorial apartheid' in Namibia, physically separating the black inhabitants from each other along ethnic lines and, collectively, from the whites.[3] Under Pretoria's bantustan policy, eleven so called 'homelands' were to achieve self-governing status. There was widespread opposition to this divisive scheme. When elections to a legislative assembly were prepared in Ovamboland, both SWAPO and the dominant Evangelical Lutheran Church in Namibia (ELCIN)

---

1. On many occasions, the SWAPO leadership asked the Swedish government to channel financial resources to SWAPO-aligned structures inside Namibia via church organizations (cf., for example, Astrid Bergquist: Memorandum ('Minnesanteckningar förda vid samtal med SWAPO-representanterna Sam Nujoma och Ben Amathila'/'Notes from talks with the SWAPO representatives Sam Nujoma and Ben Amathila'), SIDA, Stockholm, 13 November 1973) (SDA). Outside the bilateral SWAPO programme, LWF and WCC were, in consultation with SWAPO, from the late 1960s important intermediaries of both Swedish legal aid and humanitarian support. The Swede Carl-Johan Hellberg, LWF Secretary for Africa in the Department of World Mission, played a particularly important role in this context. Hellberg had visited Ovamboland in early 1966, where he met Andimba Toivo ya Toivo. He later established close contacts with Sam Nujoma. Reflecting upon the early links with Sweden, Peter Katjavivi—who served as SWAPO's representative to the United Kingdom and Western Europe from 1968—recalled in 1995: "We were not [...] on the spot, but through the assistance we received—initially through the churches and later from the trade unions and from the youth and solidarity organizations—we were able to develop a mechanism to reinforce and strengthen our lines of communication with the colleagues inside the country. I was in the middle of that, using London as a base. [...] [It] was done through whatever opportunities we had at the time, including a number of old friends from Sweden, who were linked to the churches and able to spend time [in Namibia]" (Interview with Peter Katjavivi, pp. 71-72). The question of the exiled SWAPO leadership's relations with the internal wing and the wider struggle inside Namibia will be discussed below from a Swedish perspective. It should in this context be borne in mind that 'revisionist' studies on Namibia—notably by Leys and Saul op. cit. and Dobell op. cit.—argue that external SWAPO for reasons of self-interest was opposed to the development of a strong Namibian opposition movement. In his introduction to Dobell's study, Leys states that "the SWAPO leadership in exile was not only cut off from the people they represented inside Namibia, but actively worked to ensure that no significant SWAPO leadership emerged inside the country with an agenda that might in any way conflict with the twists and turns of their diplomatic manoeuvres at the UN and in capitals on both sides of the Iron Curtain" (Dobell op. cit., p. 11). As will be seen in the following text, although not always united the SWAPO leaders abroad were during long periods of time moderately interested in using bilateral Swedish resources for activities inside Namibia and some of the officially assisted NGO activities were only accorded token support. The lines of communication between external and internal SWAPO were, in addition, often weak. There were, however, more often than not very real reasons for this. South Africa's ironclad grip made it virtually impossible to channel financial means through other sources than the churches. Any externally supported activities outside the ecclesiastical umbrella were greatly exposed to South African security interests and repression. This said, within the official Swedish sphere of support to SWAPO there were in the 1970s and 1980s sufficiently many initiatives within and outside the bilateral cooperation programme—concerning legal aid, trade union development, independent schools, human rights centres, information and political organization—to contradict Leys' sweeping statement.

2. Letter ('Biståndsframställning från SWAPO'/'Request for assistance from SWAPO') from Anders Bjurner, Swedish embassy in Lusaka, to the Ministry for Foreign Affairs, Lusaka, 29 January 1975 (SDA).

3. The Development of Self-Government for Native Nations in South West Africa Act was passed in 1968 and the South West Africa Affairs Act in 1969.

called for a boycott.[1] The SWAPO Youth League (SYL) was particularly active in the anti-elections campaign.

The Ovamboland elections were held in early August 1973. From a political point of view, they resulted in a resounding victory for the nationalist opposition. Only 2.5 per cent of those eligible to vote did so, "and many of these were [...] bantustan policemen and officials".[2] The boycott, however, unleashed a severe repressive wave throughout Namibia, including public floggings. It targeted, in particular, the youth and SWAPO's internal leaders.[3] Even though SWAPO at no time was declared illegal or banned, hundreds of men and women were rounded up by the police, accused of being members of the organization. By the end of August 1973, the SYL leaders Jerry Ekandjo (Chairman), Jacob Ngidinua (Vice-Chairman), David Shikomba and Martin Kapewasha had been detained under the South African Sabotage Act. They were later sentenced to between six and eight years' imprisonment on Robben Island. In February 1974, SWAPO's Chairman David Meroro, the Organizing Secretary Axel Johannes, the Acting SYL Chairman Thomas Kamati and other nationalist leaders were detained under the Terrorism Act.[4] Meroro and Johannes were held in solitary confinement and physically assaulted by the security police.[5]

People accused under the Terrorism Act could be sentenced to death. Referring to the Swedish government's stand during the 1967-68 trial against Andimba Toivo ya Toivo and his colleagues[6]—which in his view "probably had [...] prevented capital punishments"—in early April 1974 SWAPO's resident representative Ben Amathila appealed to the Ministry for Foreign Affairs to intervene on behalf of Meroro and the others.[7] The response was positive, and when the SWAPO Chairman in July 1974 was set free on bail Amathila *inter alia* ascribed the release to Sweden's active diplomacy.[8]

As in the late 1960s, the Swedish government manifested its concern by instructing its diplomatic representatives in Pretoria to be present at the court proceedings. This was, for example, the case in June 1974[9] and, again, in September

1. ELCIN put out a newsletter called *Omukwetu* ('Friend' or 'Comrade') to voice its opposition to the elections. In May 1973, a bomb destroyed ELCIN's printing press at Oniipa, where the newsletter was produced. The press was again blown up in November 1980. On both occasions, it was rebuilt with assistance from CSA and LWF (Björn Ryman: *Lutherhjälpens Första 50 År* ('The First 50 Years of the Church of Sweden Aid'), Verbum Förlag, Stockholm, 1997, p. 202). Bishop Auala, the head of ELCIN, visited the Church of Sweden in Uppsala in November 1974. During the visit, he was also received at the Ministry for Foreign Affairs in Stockholm (Ann Wilkens: Memorandum ('Samtal med namibisk biskop'/ 'Conversation with Namibian bishop'), Ministry for Foreign Affairs, Stockholm, 19 November 1974) (MFA).
2. Katjavivi op. cit., p. 75.
3. For a detailed account of Pretoria's repressive rule in Namibia from the early 1970s until the mid-1980s, see David Soggot: *Namibia: The Violent Heritage*, Rex Collings, London, 1986. The study was produced with support from SIDA.
4. Circular letter from Ben Amathila, SWAPO, Stockholm, 26 March 1974 (MFA).
5. Katjavivi op. cit., pp. 80-81. Over the years, Johannes was particularly persecuted and savagely brutalized by the South African regime. Bearing visible marks of repeated torture, he left Namibia at the end of 1980. By that time—aged 35—he had spent nearly one third of his life in prison or detention without charge, often held in solitary confinement (IDAF op. cit., p. 63). At independence, he became an adviser in the Office of the President.
6. See Sellström Volume I, pp. 285-87.
7. Anders Möllander: Memorandum ('Vädjan om stöd för arresterade SWAPO-ledare'/'Appeal for support to detained SWAPO leaders'), Ministry for Foreign Affairs, Stockholm, 10 April 1974 (MFA).
8. Anders Möllander: Memorandum ('Politiska rättegångar i Namibia m.m.'/'Political trials in Namibia etc.'), Ministry for Foreign Affairs, Stockholm, 26 July 1974 (MFA).
9. Cable from [Per] Jödahl to the Ministry for Foreign Affairs, Swedish embassy, London, 12 July 1974 (MFA). Lars Schönander, first secretary at the Swedish legation in Pretoria, attended the court proceedings in Windhoek in June 1974.

1974, when the trial against Meroro opened.[1] It was also the situation during subsequent political trials, notably against SWAPO's National Organizer Aaron Mushimba, Hendrik Shikongo and others in Swakopmund in 1976.[2] Via church organizations and through SWAPO channels, financial assistance was, finally, extended to the families of several detained SWAPO members.[3]

The involvement in the political trials deepened the government's familiarity with SWAPO and the struggle inside Namibia. When Meroro in 1975 and Mushimba in 1977 left the country to join SWAPO abroad, they were known to the Swedish embassies in Southern Africa. This, in turn, contributed to a trustful relationship and made the cooperation between the parties less bureaucratic and more personal.[4] Since these developments took place at the time of the Shipanga affair, the involvement also helps to explain why the Swedish government—whether Social Democratic or non-socialist—in 1976-77 *de facto* acquiesced in SWAPO's official position on the movement's conflicts in exile.

After the fall of the Portuguese regime, Sweden intervened to facilitate the passage through Angola of Namibians who fled the repression in their country. After the Lisbon coup, hundreds of people crossed the Angolan border to join SWAPO. Initially, many were detained by the Portuguese authorities. SWAPO feared that they would be handed over to the South Africans, and in July 1974 the London representative, Peter Katjavivi, asked the Swedish government to approach the MFA government in Lisbon to secure their release.[5] With close ties to the Socialist Party of Portugal, the ruling Social Democratic Party contacted the party leader, Foreign

---

1. Cable from [Frank] Belfrage to [Axel] Edelstam, Ministry for Foreign Affairs, Stockholm, 29 August 1974 (MFA).
2. Chief Minister Elifas of Ovamboland was assassinated in August 1975. Mushimba, Shikongo and others were accused of the murder and detained under the Terrorism Act. In May 1976, Mushimba—Sam Nujoma's brother-in-law—and Shikongo were sentenced to death in Swakopmund. It was the first time that death sentences were pronounced under the Terrorism Act in Namibia. (In a book about Namibia given to the author by Mushimba in February 1982, he wrote on the flyleaf: "This was the word of the fascist judge Strydom in my case in Namibia in 1976: 'Accused No. 1: The sentence of this court is that you will be taken to the place of custody and that you will be hanged by the neck until you are dead'. Cries of consternation and wailing filled the courtroom. Mushimba and Shikongo faced the public and saluted SWAPO-style with clenched fists, a gesture answered with unanimity in the public gallery".) Due to gross irregularities during the proceedings, an appeal was, however, launched, and in an unprecedented ruling South Africa's Supreme Court set the convictions aside in March 1977. SIDA's Marianne Sundh—secretary to CCHA—was in Windhoek at the time, witnessing the jubilation and how Mushimba and Shikongo were driven around the township of Katutura followed by a procession of 3-4,000 people. "It was", Sundh wrote, "a united and strong SWAPO which assembled around Aaron and Hendrik" ([Marianne Sundh]: 'Aaron, Hendrik, Rauna och Anna friades och firades!'/'Aaron, Hendrik, Rauna and Anna were acquitted and celebrated!', SIDA, Stockholm, 28 April 1977 (SDA). (To hide Sundh's identity, her name was not attached to the report.)
3. See, for example, SWAPO: 'SIDA assistance to SWAPO: Report of expenditure for publicity, political education and information inside Namibia 1975-76', attached to letter from Mishake Muyongo to the Swedish ambassador to Zambia, Lusaka, 29 November 1976 (SDA). SWAPO reported that assistance in particular had been given to the Mushimba and Shikongo families.
4. At Namibia's independence, Mushimba—who served as SWAPO's representative to Angola in the late 1970s and to Zambia in the early 1980s—left politics to become a successful businessman. In 1995, he reflected upon his personal relations with Sweden as follows: "[W]e could feel the involvement by the SIDA officials. It was exciting. On a personal level, I developed such a good relationship with Carin [Norberg in Angola]. We became like a brother and sister. [...] It was very helpful that this relationship developed. It also developed in the camps. It helped our people to understand who the SIDA people were. You could not step on the toes of somebody from Sweden! Our people felt that they were the beloved ones. [...] Coming home to Namibia, we miss that. Namibia is now a free country and we no longer find that sort of relationship. SIDA is with the government and the diplomats are confined to their activities. Some of us who worked with them feel that it is unusual. Of course, we are invited to receptions and the ambassador will receive us, but the warmth of [the] time [in exile] has changed into something different" (Interview with Aaron Mushimba, p. 85). Similarly, SWAPO's Secretary of Logistics, Festus Naholo, later reminisced: "[The] SIDA officials] fit in with the Namibians. When we were negotiating different points, we were just exchanging views, teaching each other. That characterized our negotiations. [...] It was wonderful. People who were never involved [in that] do not realize that they missed something in their lives" (Interview with Festus Naholo, pp. 90-91).
5. Cable from [Per] Jödahl to the Ministry for Foreign Affairs, Swedish embassy, London, 12 July 1974 (MFA).

Minister Mário Soares. The issue was also raised in a meeting between Bernt Carlsson and Soares in London.[1] Soares, in turn, intervened on behalf of the Namibians, and in early August Ben Amathila confirmed to the Ministry for Foreign Affairs in Stockholm that all of them had been set free.[2]

On the Angolan side[3], the route to Zambia was thus open, which in combination with the repression in Namibia led from mid-1974 to a veritable exodus. It has been estimated that between 4,000 and 6,000 people had left Namibia by August 1975.[4] One of the first internal leaders who joined the movement in Zambia was SWAPO's Acting Secretary General John Ya-Otto. Imprisoned in South Africa under the Terrorism Act, Ya-Otto had in the late 1960s been 'adopted' by a Swedish Amnesty group.[5] In September 1974—shortly after leaving Namibia—he visited Sweden, where he was received at the Ministry for Foreign Affairs and briefed the officials about SWAPO's situation in Namibia, Angola and Zambia.[6] Appointed SWAPO Secretary for Labour in 1976, Ya-Otto later worked closely with the Swedish trade union movement.

Sweden would, finally, in the mid-1970s forcefully raise the question of Namibia at the United Nations, thereby entering into conflict with the major Western powers. With direct relations to SWAPO through the bilateral humanitarian assistance programme and insights into the situation in Namibia via its diplomatic involvement on the legal front, the Social Democratic government had by 1974 become a regular contributor to the UN Fund for Namibia[7] and an active promoter of the proposal to set up a UN Institute for Namibia.[8] This, in turn, brought the government into closer consultations with the African states. As a member of the UN Security Council and coordinating its position with the OAU countries, during the council's Namibia debate in early June 1975 the Swedish representative, Olof Rydbeck, condemned South Africa's occupation in the strongest of terms. Reminding the council that the UN General Assembly, the Security Council itself and the International Court of Justice had assumed direct responsibility for Namibia, Ryd-

1. Letter ('Namibier arresterade i Angola'/'Namibians detained in Angola') from Bengt Säve-Söderbergh to Bernt Carlsson, Ministry for Foreign Affairs, Stockholm, 14 August 1974 (MFA).
2. Ibid.
3. Fearing the impact of the fall of the facist Portuguese regime and democratization in Angola, in June 1974 the South African authorities replaced police units with army troops along Namibia's 2,250 kilometre long border with Angola and Zambia. Border fences were later erected.
4. Dobell op. cit., p. 47, quoting various sources.
5. Anders Möllander: Memorandum ('Politiska rättegångar i Namibia m.m.'/'Political trials in Namibia etc.'), Ministry for Foreign Affairs, Stockholm, 26 July 1974 (MFA).
6. Anders Möllander: Memorandum ('Diskussion med SWAPO-representanter om Namibia'/'Discussion with SWAPO representatives about Namibia'), Ministry for Foreign Affairs, Stockholm, 25 September 1974 (MFA).
7. The UN Fund for Namibia was set up by the General Assembly in 1970 to provide day-to-day assistance to Namibians in exile. It was later divided into a General Account, a Nationhood Programme Account and an Institute for Namibia Account.
8. The proposal to create a UN Institute for Namibia (UNIN) was in particular pursued by Ireland's Séan Mac-Bride, who on 1 January 1974 assumed office as UN Commissioner for Namibia. MacBride *inter alia* discussed the proposal with the Swedish government during a visit to Stockholm in May 1974 (Örjan Berner: Memorandum ('Namibiakommissariens Sean MacBride besök'/'Visit by the UN Commissioner for Namibia, Sean MacBride'), Ministry for Foreign Affairs, Stockholm, 22 May 1974) (MFA). UNIN was established by the General Assembly in September 1974 and became operational in Lusaka in August 1976. Independent Namibia's first Prime Minister, Hage Geingob, was appointed Director of UNIN. The principal objective of the institute was to provide education and training for Namibia's future public service. It also conducted research on Namibian matters. Sweden supported UNIN from the start, granting a first contribution of 500,000 SEK in November 1976 (Cable from the Ministry for Foreign Affairs to the Swedish embassy in Lusaka, Stockholm, 18 November 1976) (SDA). During the second half of the 1980s, the Nordic countries covered approximately half of the institute's budget (Per Sjögren: Memorandum ('Bidrag till FN's fonder för södra Afrika'/'Contributions to the UN funds for Southern Africa'), CCHA/Ministry for Foreign Affairs, Stockholm, 20 February 1989) (SDA).

beck concluded that "there can be no alternative to moving forward". Supporting a draft resolution which requested a mandatory arms embargo on South Africa, he continued:

> My government has carefully considered the question of how to increase the pressure against South Africa and whether the ultimate step should now be contemplated, that is, action according to Chapter VII of the United Nations Charter. We have found that several circumstances would warrant the conclusion that Article 39 is applicable [as] the situation in Namibia constitutes a threat to international peace and security. I refer here to the continued illegal occupation [by] South Africa [of] this international territory and the application of apartheid and the homelands policy.
>
> These [...] policies create a situation of dangerous tension in Africa, [...] which—if allowed to continue—will gradually become aggravated. We are therefore prepared to support the imposition of a mandatory embargo on the delivery of armaments to South Africa. [...] In regard to no other issue does the United Nations have a greater responsibility than the one which this council is [considering] today.[1]

Although in March 1969 the Security Council had resolved to "determine [...] necessary steps or measures in accordance with [...] the Charter of the United Nations" in case South Africa did not immediately withdraw its administration from Namibia[2], the permanent Western members—France, United Kingdom and United States—vetoed the proposal. It was only the second time in the history of the United Nations that a draft resolution was rejected by a triple veto.[3] The British government was particularly incensed by the Swedish stand. "In their almost desperate attempts to avoid [sanctions on South Africa]", Rydbeck later wrote, the British UN ambassador Ivor Richard "expressed [...] in vehement terms great indignation at [the fact] that Sweden after contacts with the African [states] [...] had tabled a draft resolution without consulting [them]".[4] This was not the first time that the Swedish and British governments clashed over sanctions on South Africa or the wider situation in Southern Africa.[5] On this occasion, however, the conflicting views were openly expressed at the level of the UN Security Council, which caused ambassador Rydbeck to conclude a longer letter to the Foreign Minister in Stockholm as follows:

> Sweden has assumed an even more pronounced profile vis-à-vis the great conflict in Southern Africa. We will be exposed to expectations and hopes.[6] Within the next couple of years, we will at the United Nations thus also shoulder increased responsibility for a consistent continuation of our policy.[7]

---

1. Ministry for Foreign Affairs: 'Statement by the permanent representative of Sweden to the United Nations, ambassador Olof Rydbeck, in the Security Council on 5 June 1975 on the question of Namibia', Press department, Stockholm, 5 June 1975 (MFA).
2. UN Security Council Resolution 264 (1969) of 20 March 1969, cited in UNIN op. cit., p. 332.
3. In October 1976, France, United Kingdom and United States again vetoed a draft resolution which would have imposed mandatory sanctions on South Africa.
4. Cable ('Namibia i säkerhetsrådet'/'Namibia at the Security Council') from Olof Rydbeck to the Ministry for Foreign Affairs, New York, 2 June 1975 (MFA).
5. Cf., for example, the conflicting views concerning Zimbabwe.
6. On behalf of Tanzania, Salim Ahmed Salim stated during the Security Council debate: "I want, in the name of my government and our people, to single out the delegation of Sweden, and to pay tribute to the role it played in the negotiations and to the positive vote it cast. I do so in the clear knowledge that—even when it became difficult for us to entertain some of the demands it made—it went along, convinced as it is, of the justness of our cause. I am sure that Sweden, by its vote, has lived up to the expectations of the African people and to the long and traditional friendship that it has with all the African countries, including my own" (cited in cable ('Namibia i säkerhetsrådet'/'Namibia in the Security Council') from Olof Rydbeck to the Ministry for Foreign Affairs, New York, 9 June 1975) (MFA). On the relations between Sweden and the independent African states at the United Nations, see the interview with Salim Ahmed Salim, pp. 243-48. For Sweden and SWAPO at the UN, see also the interview with Mishake Muyongo, p. 88.
7. Letter from Olof Rydbeck to the Minister for Foreign Affairs, New York, 22 July 1975 (MFA).

The Social Democratic Party lost the parliamentary elections in September 1976. The Swedish position on Namibia did not, however, change under Thorbjörn Fäll- din's non-socialist coalition. Addressing the UN General Assembly for the first time soon after the Soweto uprisings in South Africa, the new Minister for Foreign Affairs—Karin Söder of the Centre Party—declared in October 1976 that

> Sweden and many other states have characterized the situation in Southern Africa as a threat to peace. If acceptable results cannot be attained through negotiations, the Security Council should therefore impose sanctions to eliminate the threat. In the first place, we have proposed that [...] the cessation of all shipments of weapons to South Africa should be made manda- tory.[1] [...] In Namibia, South Africa upholds its illegal rule and increases the oppression of the black majority. South Africa must now be forced to accept the solutions prescribed by the United Nations, so that Namibia can at last achieve national independence as a unitary state. SWAPO must be a principal party in the negotiations towards such solutions.[2]

When South Africa within the framework of the Turnhalle scheme in early Decem- ber 1978 arranged elections to a so called 'constituent assembly' in Namibia, Söder's successor as Foreign Minister—Hans Blix of the Liberal Party[3]—empha- sized Sweden's critical position even more. Characterizing the elections as "a sham" and "an outrageous attempt to retain control over a country which the United Nations has deprived South Africa of the right to administer"[4], in an address to the Swedish Institute of International Affairs[5] he stated that the government with regard to the situation in Namibia was contemplating an exception to its tradi- tional stand on violence. Noting that Sweden—"although we sympathize with those who in desperation resort to arms against an oppressive power"—due to the UN Charter had been unable to support the General Assembly's calls in favour of armed struggle, the minister declared that

> right now we are [...] discussing whether the situation in Namibia [...] is so clearly distinguish- able from other [cases] that it is possible for us to vote in favour of a resolution which gives explicit support to the armed liberation struggle.[6]

Turnhalle and the Home Front

SWAPO's London and Stockholm representatives, Peter Katjavivi and Ben Amathila, were from the beginning of 1974 particularly active in trying to direct official Swedish assistance to the movement inside Namibia. While Anders Bjurner at the Swedish embassy in Lusaka in May 1975 wrote that SWAPO "not seldom [shows] a lack of competence to diplomatically and journalistically work towards its objectives" and concluded that "the coordination [between the external and

---

1. A mandatory arms embargo against South Africa was eventually declared by the UN Security Council in November 1977.
2. 'Speech by Mrs. Karin Söder, the Minister for Foreign Affairs, at the General Assembly of the United Nations', 13 October 1976, in Ministry for Foreign Affairs: *Documents on Swedish Foreign Policy: 1976*, Stockholm, 1978, p. 69.
3. Blix was Foreign Minister in Ola Ullsten's minority Liberal government from October 1978 until October 1979. He had been involved in the wider anti-apartheid movement since the late 1950s, when he served as president of the World Federation of Liberal and Radical Youth (see Sellström Volume I, pp. 163-64).
4. 'Statement on Namibia by the Foreign Minister, Mr. Blix', 4 December 1978, in Ministry for Foreign Affairs: *Documents on Swedish Foreign Policy: 1978*, Stockholm, 1982, pp. 321-22.
5. In Swedish, *Utrikespolitiska Institutet*.
6. 'Speech by Mr. Hans Blix, Minister for Foreign Affairs, at the Swedish Institute of International Affairs', 11 December 1978, in Ministry for Foreign Affairs: *Documents on Swedish Foreign Policy: 1978*, Stockholm, 1982, pp. 150-51.

internal SWAPO wings] often is unsatisfactory"[1], SIDA's Astrid Bergquist could after discussions with Amathila in Stockholm report that

> there were certain differences of opinion within SWAPO. The leadership based in Europe realized much more clearly than the leadership in Zambia the need to intensify the political mobilization [inside Namibia]. The SWAPO representatives in Sweden and London, among others, appear to advocate such a [policy].[2]

The initiatives by Katjavivi and Amathila intensified in early 1975. Within the wider détente policy, South Africa[3] had by that time launched preparations for and propaganda about the so called Turnhalle conference, an ethnic exercise designed to work out a 'national' Namibian constitutional arrangement. Thus, it was planned by the apartheid regime, the demands by the United Nations and the popular support enjoyed by SWAPO would be neutralized.[4] Following the repression against SWAPO in 1973-74, the initiative came at a particularly difficult time for the liberation movement. SWAPO had not made its views on a constitution for independent Namibia publicly known and the internal wing was—as stated by Amathila—"politically weak".[5] It was therefore "extremely important [...] to counter [...] South Africa's political offensive [and] as soon as possible re-activate the [...] work inside Namibia".[6]

---

1. Anders Bjurner: Memorandum ('SWAPO och Namibia'), Swedish embassy, Lusaka, 15 May 1975 (MFA).
2. Astrid Bergquist: Memorandum ('Samtal med Ben Amathila, SWAPOs representant, angående 1975/76 års bistånd till SWAPO'/'Conversation with Ben Amathila, the SWAPO representative, regarding the assistance to SWAPO in 1975/76'), SIDA, Stockholm, 12 August 1975 (SDA). From his base in Sweden, Amathila used various contacts in the Nordic countries to support the struggle inside Namibia. Interviewed in 1995, SWAPO's former Secretary for Logistics, Festus Naholo—who as the Chairman of the Inter-Church Student Conference in 1974 was actively involved in the establishment of the Namibia Students Organization and the Namibia Workers Organization, that is, the forerunners of NANSO and NUNW—recalled: "Our contacts with the Nordic countries inside Namibia started, I think, around 1974-75. We began to communicate with Ben Amathila [...]. He started to send solidarity workers to us—in particular directly to me—so that was when we started to get involved with people from Scandinavia. We carried out certain underground work to collect information, which was needed for the exposure of the apartheid crimes in Namibia. Taking photos and filming. It was dangerous work, and I wondered why these people were taking such risks to get involved with us" (Interview with Festus Naholo, p. 90).
3. Convening the conference, Dirk Mudge would later reject the conventional view that it was sponsored by South Africa. At a symposium in Freiburg, Germany, on the Namibian peace process, he stated in July 1992: "South Africa did not take the initiative on the Turnhalle conference. I did, although it is possible that they tried to hijack it" (cited in International Peace Academy/Arnold Bergstraesser Institut: *The Namibian Peace Process: Implications and Lessons for the Future*, Report on the Freiburg Symposium, 1-4 July 1992, Freiburg, 1994, p. 27). In an interview in 1995, he reiterated that "it is not true [that Turnhalle was sponsored by South Africa]. I had to fight a long and hard battle to get it started. Firstly, with my party colleagues in Namibia and, secondly, with the South African government, who had their own ideas, like: 'Let us first get Ovambo independent, then we can talk. Let us first get Kavango off, then we can talk. Let us get rid of the majority of the black people and then we can talk'. I opposed all of it and said that if we want to talk we have to involve everybody" (Interview with Dirk Mudge, p. 81). Mudge did not, however, include SWAPO in his plans.
4. Named after a German-built gymnastics hall in Windhoek, the Turnhalle constitutional conference convened there on 1 September 1975. Invited members were chosen by ethnic affiliation and sworn to secrecy. SWAPO characterized the talks as "a farce" (Katjavivi op. cit., p. 95) and the United Nations rejected them. Dirk Mudge of the all-white National Party of South West Africa—the Namibian branch of the ruling South African party—was a leading promoter of the conference. Mudge became close to the Herero chief Clemens Kapuuo, progressively advocating a change away from apartheid. On this question, he broke with the National Party and founded a new—although still all-white—Republican Party in September 1977. Two months later, Mudge formed the multi-racial Democratic Turnhalle Alliance (DTA), with himself as Chairman and Kapuuo as President (cf. the interview with Dirk Mudge, pp. 81-82). In August 1976, the Turnhalle conference proposed that a multi-racial interim government be formed by early 1977, with a provisional independence day set for 31 December 1978. Elections for a constituent assembly—boycotted by SWAPO—were held on 4 December 1978. DTA appeared as the dominant party and Mudge was subsequently appointed Chairman of the so called Namibian Council of Ministers.
5. Astrid Bergquist: Memorandum, op. cit., 12 August 1975.
6. Amathila cited in ibid.

To regain the political initiative, SWAPO intensified the discussions initiated at the 1969-70 consultative congress at Tanga, Tanzania[1], on a constitutional dispensation for independent Namibia. In early 1975, Anders Bjurner was informed by SWAPO in Lusaka that "work is progressing on a draft constitution, which is now being discussed within the two SWAPO wings".[2] Behind the scenes, the Swedish government was supporting the initiative. Peter Katjavivi—who was closely involved in the preparatory work[3]—later stated:

> I want to underline the role which the Nordic countries played in this regard. The funding sources can be traced to Nordic bodies which were actively involved in helping us [...]. I remember a number of colleagues of mine at the Swedish embassy in Lusaka and at the Swedish embassy in London. It is tremendous when you think about it. These people basically positioned themselves behind you. They were not always visible. Nobody knew about that, but the underlying interest and commitment was just tremendous. That kind of international solidarity and understanding is what helped us to do as much as we did. [...] They were prepared to reinforce the struggle by working in partnership.[4]

While the discussions on the draft constitution were going on, in Stockholm Amathila approached the government with a proposal to allocate funds under the annual SWAPO programme for political work inside Namibia. In early August 1975—that is, shortly before the opening of the Turnhalle conference—he contacted SIDA's Astrid Bergquist[5], stressing the importance of urgent support to the movement's internal wing. SWAPO in Namibia, he explained, had at the time only four members who were actively engaged with organized political work on a full-

1. Cf. Amathila: "[O]ne of the most important things that we had to tackle [at Tanga] was, obviously, to answer the question: 'After liberation: What?' There was nothing before Tanga that indicated that we were preparing ourselves to take the reins of power [...]. These were the things which were addressed [at the congress]" (Interview with Ben Amathila, p. 63).
2. Anders Bjurner: Memorandum ('SWAPO och Namibia'), Swedish embassy, Lusaka, 15 May 1975 (MFA). Little is known about the actual beginnings of the constitutional work, which subsequently appeared in various revised versions. According to Dobell, the final document—which she quotes under the title 'Discussion paper on the constitution of independent Namibia'—was drafted by the British lawyer Cedric Thornberry in consultation with Daniel Tjongarero, one of SWAPO's most prominent leaders in Namibia (Dobell op. cit., p. 45). Living in Lusaka, Thornberry was a member of the International Commission of Jurists, of which the UN Commissioner for Namibia at the time, Séan MacBride, had been the Secretary General between 1963 and 1971. Anders Bjurner at the Swedish embassy in Lusaka—who throughout the process was kept informed by SWAPO—noted in August 1975 that the version obtained by the embassy (SWAPO of Namibia: 'What kind of future?': A first discussion paper on a constitution for independent Namibia, Windhoek, July 1975) (MFA) "primarily [was] drafted by SWAPO in London [together with] one of SWAPO's executive members" (Anders Bjurner: Memorandum ('Förslag till konstitution för Namibia'/'Proposed constitution for Namibia'), Swedish embassy, Lusaka, 27 August 1975) (MFA). Finally, Peter Katjavivi, SWAPO's London representative, gave the following background in an interview in 1995: "An initiative developed within the leadership of SWAPO in Namibia and they consulted with us in exile. [...] The colleagues in Namibia wanted a discussion paper which could be used as a talking point within the country. There were meetings in Windhoek and Rehoboth, in Otjiwarongo, Okahandja, Walvis Bay and so on. We were able to organize this through Amnesty International [and] the International Defence and Aid Fund. We received funds from them and lined up a colleague to go to Namibia. I happened to be in Oslo [...] when our colleague was ready to fly to Namibia with this important document. He came to see me in Oslo. It was just a hand-written piece of paper. I called Hans Beukes [and] involved him in checking some of the wording of this paper. The original idea was to discuss it in Lusaka with some colleagues, including Moses Garoeb. Eventually [, however,] the person flew directly to Namibia. This is how the discussion paper on Namibia's future constitution started" (Interview with Peter Katjavivi, p. 72).
3. SWAPO's discussion paper proposed a parliamentary, Westminster democracy, based on a republican model, with an executive president and a one-chamber legislature. A comprehensive Bill of Rights would be entrenched. English would become the official language and—pursuing a non-aligned course—independent Namibia was to apply for membership of the Commonwealth. In the main, these proposals were repeated in 1989 in SWAPO's election manifesto. They were subsequently included in independent Namibia's constitution, adopted in February 1990.
4. Interview with Peter Katjavivi, p. 72. Returning to Namibia in 1989, Katjavivi—who in 1986 had earned a doctorate in history at Oxford university in England (Ph. D. thesis on *The Rise of Nationalism in Namibia and Its International Dimensions*)—was elected to independent Namibia's first National Assembly. In 1991, he was appointed Vice-Chancellor of the new University of Namibia.
5. Bergquist was responsible for SIDA's cooperation with SWAPO.

time basis. The organization wanted to increase the number to twelve. They would each receive a monthly salary of 120 South African Rands. Amathila wished to know if the Swedish government through SIDA could cover their salaries for a period of twelve months, in total corresponding to 120,000 SEK.[1] To raise SWAPO's profile in the country, he also proposed that Swedish funds should be set aside for the production of T-shirts with political slogans. He had been in contact with a Swedish company and estimated that another 100,000 SEK would be needed for this purpose.[2]

Amathila's initiative raised a number of questions with regard to the general principles governing official Swedish humanitarian assistance to the Southern African liberation movements. It was, in the first place, eminently political, aiming at strengthening SWAPO's organization and propaganda in Namibia. Secondly, for the first time since the official support to the liberation movements started it implied that the Swedish government—although indirectly—would pay the salaries of foreign political office-holders.[3] In fact, SWAPO's entire cadre of organizers working full-time for the movement in Namibia was according to the proposal to be financed by the Swedish government. Finally, the approach brought about questions concerning the channelling of the proposed assistance and how it should be accounted for.

Sweden had until then roughly equated humanitarian assistance with non-military, civilian support. The definition of 'civilian' had been given a wide interpretation.[4] Large numbers of vehicles had been supplied to the liberation movements, and as early as in 1971 SIDA had delivered a mobile radio station to PAIGC of Guinea-Bissau.[5] Such support, however, had either been given to the liberation movements in the African host countries or in the liberated areas, not directly for political work 'behind the enemy lines'. Nevertheless, Amathila's request was positively received. While noting the principled questions involved, the CCHA secretary Astrid Bergquist argued in a SIDA memorandum shared with the Ministry for Foreign Affairs[6] that

> the objective of the support to the liberation movements is, as we know, to contribute towards the attainment of a political goal, namely, the liberation of the country [in question]. It would thus be justified to further stretch the concept of humanitarian assistance and grant SWAPO [financial] means for straightforward political work.[7]

This view was accepted. A 'stretched' interpretation of the concept of humanitarian assistance would from then on guide the increasingly pro-active official Swedish support. This was the case with regard to the cooperation with SWAPO, but, above all, with the assistance to ANC of South Africa, where—as will be seen below—considerable amounts were allocated for political work inside the country.

1. Astrid Bergquist: Memorandum ('Samtal med Ben Amathila, SWAPOs representant, angående 1975/76 års bistånd till SWAPO'/'Conversation with Ben Amathila, the SWAPO representative, regarding the assistance to SWAPO in 1975/76'), SIDA, Stockholm, 12 August 1975 (SDA).
2. Ibid.
3. As part of the bilateral support to the liberation movements, their representatives in Sweden—normally covering the Nordic countries—were paid for by the Swedish government.
4. Demanding increased allocations to the Southern African liberation movements, in a parliamentary motion submitted in January 1973 Thorbjörn Fälldin and Gunnar Helén, the leaders of the Centre and Liberal parties, argued that "direct [official] support should not [...] be limited to refugee [assistance] alone" (Swedish Parliament 1973: Motion No. 1101, Riksdagens Protokoll 1973, p. 10).
5. See the chapter on Guinea-Bissau.
6. Bergquist consulted with Ann Wilkens at the Foreign Ministry.
7. Astrid Bergquist: Memorandum ('Samtal med Ben Amathila, SWAPOs representant, angående 1975/76 års bistånd till SWAPO'/'Conversation with Ben Amathila, the SWAPO representative, regarding the assistance to SWAPO in 1975/76'), SIDA, Stockholm, 12 August 1975 (SDA).

Amathila approached SIDA immediately before the negotiations between Sweden and SWAPO concerning the cooperation in 1975/76 were to be held in Lusaka. Bergquist conveyed the request to the Swedish embassy[1] and it was put on the agenda. Supported by the SWAPO delegation led by President Nujoma, it was agreed to set aside 240,000 of the available allocation of 2 MSEK for 1975/76 in favour of "information and educational activities inside Namibia".[2] The Swedish delegation also noted that "the item was a new and welcome field for Swedish support"[3], and the parties decided "to hold further discussions [...] to agree on specified purposes and procedures for the use of the [...] resources".[4]

Only in mid-February 1976—six months later—did the SWAPO leadership submit a specified proposal on how to use the 'home front' allocation. Dividing the grant between political education; publicity and information; and social welfare, it largely followed Amathila's original suggestion.[5] The proposal was promptly accepted by SIDA.[6] While the policy issue concerning official Swedish assistance to SWAPO's political work inside Namibia did not become problematic, the technical question of how to channel the funds, however, did.

After the negotiations in Lusaka in August 1975, Anders Bjurner—the head of the Swedish delegation—noted that "SWAPO [in this regard] is experiencing great difficulties [as] primarily the transfer [to Namibia] of financial means, but also of written messages, entails big risks".[7] The problems were compounded by SWAPO's internal struggles. Eventually, Nujoma proposed that the funds "be released to the SWAPO headquarters here in Lusaka. [They] will then be channelled through our own sources to appropriate SWAPO members inside Namibia. We feel [that] this would be the best course, given the very serious situation inside [the country]".[8] This was accepted, and in early March 1976—after agreement had been reached on the utilization of the funds—ambassador Ove Heyman handed Nujoma a cheque for the amount of 37,000 Zambian Kwacha, corresponding to 240,000 SEK.[9] In the accompanying letter, he stipulated that

> the receipt of the money in Namibia shall be confirmed by a statement [and] items purchased and other disbursements [made] out of this contribution [shall] be documented by receipts to the extent practically possible. [...] All information in this regard shall, as agreed, be treated as confidential.[10]

Vice-President Muyongo submitted a report on the allocation in November 1976. Regretting that "the risks and logistics of collecting and transporting receipts and

---

1. Letter ('Bistånd till SWAPO'/'Assistance to SWAPO') from Astrid Bergquist to Carin Norberg, SIDA, Stockholm, 12 August 1975 (SDA).
2. 'Agreed minutes of discussion[s] on cooperation between Sweden and South West Africa People's Organization (SWAPO)', Lusaka, 26 August 1975 (SDA).
3. Ibid. In his internal report on the negotiations, Bjurner observed that the reason why SWAPO included assistance to activities inside Namibia was probably "the growing demand for support made by internal SWAPO on external SWAPO. The inability to meet this demand has undoubtedly resulted in frictions between the two SWAPO wings" (Letter ('Förhandlingsprotokoll för bistånd till SWAPO 1975/76'/'Agreed minutes regarding assistance to SWAPO in 1975/76') from Anders Bjurner, Swedish embassy in Lusaka, to SIDA, Lusaka, 4 September 1975) (SDA).
4. 'Agreed minutes', op. cit., 26 August 1975.
5. Letter from Mishake Muyongo to the Swedish ambassador to Zambia, Lusaka, 11 February 1976 (SDA).
6. Cable ('Bistånd SWAPO 1975/76'/'Assistance to SWAPO') from SIDA to the Swedish embassy in Lusaka, SIDA, Stockholm, 25 February 1976 (SDA).
7. Letter from Anders Bjurner, op. cit., 4 September 1975.
8. Letter from Sam Nujoma to the Swedish ambassador to Zambia, Lusaka, 2 January 1976 (SDA).
9. According to the UN Commissioner for Namibia, Séan MacBride, it was out of this contribution that money was misappropriated by the SWAPO leadership (Letter from Kaj Sundberg, Swedish UN representation, to the Ministry for Foreign Affairs, New York, 13 April 1976) (MFA).
10. Letter from Ove Heyman, Swedish ambassador to Zambia, to Sam Nujoma, Lusaka, 4 March 1976 (SDA).

proofs of expenditure [from Namibia] to Zambia has [made reporting] impossible", without any financial or qualitative breakdowns the purely narrative report noted that the funds had been used for bus and train fares, the purchase of bicycles and the hiring of cars by SWAPO organizers (political education); the printing of posters, leaflets, booklets and stickers, as well as for the hiring of loudspeaker equipment (publicity and information); and for assistance to dependants of detained SWAPO members (social welfare).[1] In his covering letter, Muyongo stated that

> the assistance [...] has been of inestimable value in allowing us to coordinate a nationwide, consistent [...] strategy. It has been particularly important at this [point in] time, when the South African propaganda machine is desperately striving to legitimize [...] the so called [Turnhalle] constitutional talks.[2]

Thus began—with a modest amount and after considerable delays—the direct official Swedish support to SWAPO's efforts inside Namibia. Often insisted upon by Sweden rather than by SWAPO[3], the allocation for internal activities would subsequently play a prominent part within the regular cooperation programme. At the time of Namibia's independence, 89 million[4] out of the 669 MSEK extended by the Swedish government to SWAPO under bilateral agreements—that is, 13 per cent— had been allocated to what was called the 'home front component'. To this should be added direct allocations in the form of emergency assistance and—above all— substantial official Swedish resources indirectly channelled to SWAPO inside Namibia via non-governmental organizations.

Social Projects and Financial Problems

In Muyongo's report, SWAPO expressed the hope that "this type of allocation can be continued and increased in the future".[5] Nevertheless, due to internal problems and to the rapidly escalating humanitarian needs among the Namibian refugees in Zambia and Angola, financial support for political work inside Namibia was not included in SWAPO's submission for Swedish assistance in 1976/77.[6] In 1977/78, no less than 1.5 million out of a total of 14.5 MSEK was, however, disbursed by SIDA for essentially the same purposes as in 1975/76.[7]

1. SWAPO: 'SIDA assistance to SWAPO: Report of expenditure for publicity, political education and information inside Namibia 1975-76', attached to letter from Mishake Muyongo to the Swedish ambassador to Zambia, Lusaka, 29 November 1976 (SDA). According to the report, Swedish funds were not used to cover salary costs for SWAPO cadres in Namibia.
2. Letter from Mishake Muyongo to the Swedish ambassador to Zambia, Lusaka, 29 November 1976 (SDA).
3. During the second half of the 1980s, Sweden strongly advocated increased allocations to the home front.
4. Based on budgets and disbursement figures attached to the agreed minutes between Sweden and SWAPO during the period 1975/76-1989/90 (SDA).
5. SWAPO, op. cit., attached to letter from Muyongo, 29 November 1976.
6. Letter from Mishake Muyongo to the Swedish ambassador to Zambia, Lusaka, 12 August 1976 (SDA).
7. 'Agreed minutes of discussions on the cooperation between the South West Africa People's Organization (SWAPO) and Sweden, 1978/79', Lusaka, 31 May 1978 (SDA). As an amount of 440,000 SEK out of an emergency allocation of 0.9 MSEK referring to the financial year 1976/77 was disbursed for political work inside Namibia after 1 July 1977, a total of 1.9 MSEK was used for the purpose in 1977/78 (for the emergency allocation, see 'Agreed minutes of discussions on cooperation between Sweden and the South West Africa People's Organization (SWAPO)', Lusaka, 7 July 1977) (SDA).

Soon thereafter, it was on SWAPO's request agreed to change the orientation of the support. Due to yet another massive repressive wave in the country[1], in mid-1978 it was shifted from general political activities to specific social self-help projects in the fields of agriculture, health and, above all, education. At the negotiations between Sweden and SWAPO in Lusaka in May 1978, the Namibian delegation noted that

> [t]he possibilities for SWAPO to politically work smoothly inside Namibia [are] severely hampered [...] due to the arrest of [many] internal leaders [...]. Funds are [, however,] needed for SWAPO's internal work [...], especially for [...] schools, health care and agricultural projects.[2]

From the late 1970s, substantial amounts under the home front allocation were, in addition, disbursed in favour of legal aid; support to families of detained or exiled SWAPO members; released political prisoners; as well as to victims of South Africa's repression in the combat areas in northern Namibia. Information and publicity remained an important area of the Swedish assistance.

Despite the fact that there was no permanent official Swedish presence in Namibia, the authorities in Stockholm could through various channels follow the events in the country and assess SWAPO's needs and requests. Observers from both the Swedish legation in Pretoria and Sweden attended the major political trials, and representatives of Swedish church organizations and—later—trade unions worked for longer periods closely with the SWAPO-aligned opposition inside Namibia. Several prominent internal SWAPO leaders visited Sweden in the late 1970s. This was, for example, the case with Reverend Zephania Kameeta[3], who in early December 1977 was received by Cooperation Minister Ola Ullsten and in discussions at the Ministry for Foreign Affairs underlined the importance of assistance to the internal opposition, characterizing SWAPO's political and social work in Namibia as "the backbone of the movement".[4] During his stay in Stockholm, Kameeta also met representatives of the Swedish labour movement, welcoming its plans to assist SWAPO and the exiled National Union of Namibian Workers in forming a trade union organization in the country.[5]

---

1. The DTA leader Clemens Kapuuo was assassinated under unclear circumstances in March 1978. Accusing SWAPO, the South African authorities immediately brought troop reinforcements to Windhoek and started a 'mopping up' operation during which some 50 people were killed. From the beginning of April 1978, the repression was not only directed against individual SWAPO sympathizers, but also against institutions considered supportive of the liberation movement, including churches, hospitals etc. On 8 April, the Lutheran Paulineum Theological Seminary at Otjimbingwe was forced to close; on 10 April, nurses were beaten up at Okakarara hospital; and on 16 April, worshippers were evicted from St John's Apostolic Church in Windhoek. Finally, on 18 April—during the UN General Assembly special debate on Namibia—the repression was officially sanctioned by the apartheid regime through Proclamation AG 26/78, or the 'Detention for Prevention of Political Violence [Act]'. This draconian decree extended the powers of the South African security forces to detain people without charge and allowed for unlimited solitary confinement. During the following days and weeks, hundreds of SWAPO leaders and followers were rounded up, including Axel Johannes, Festus Naholo and Hendrik Witbooi. Others, such as Daniel Tjongarero, received death threats (ya Nangolo and Sellström op. cit., pp. 17-18).
2. 'Agreed minutes of discussions on the cooperation between the South West Africa People's Organization (SWAPO) and Sweden, 1978/79', Lusaka, 31 May 1978 (SDA).
3. SWAPO Secretary for Health and Social Welfare inside Namibia, Reverend Kameeta of the Evangelical Lutheran Church (ELC) was considered the leading Namibian exponent of black liberation theology. He was ordained Deputy Bishop of ELC (Rhenish Mission) in 1985. At independence, Kameeta was elected Deputy Speaker of the National Assembly.
4. Marika Fahlén: Memorandum ('Besök av Zefania Kameeta, SWAPO'/'Visit by Zefania Kameeta, SWAPO'), Ministry for Foreign Affairs, Stockholm, 7 December 1977 (MFA).
5. Letter from Kristina Persson, LO, to John Ya-Otto, National Union of Namibian Workers, Stockholm, 13 January 1978 (LMA).

This was also the case with SWAPO's Deputy Chairman Daniel Tjongarero[1] and Hendrik Witbooi[2], Secretary for Education and Culture inside Namibia, who in mid-February 1978 accompanied Sam Nujoma to Stockholm. During the visit, they primarily discussed the international aspects of the Namibia question with Foreign Minister Söder[3], but they also raised the challenges SWAPO was facing domestically. Decidedly less interested than Kameeta in the trade union plans[4], it was during this visit by the movement's external and internal leaders that the official Swedish assistance to the home front was re-designed. To present an alternative to South Africa's policy of 'bantu education', a Namibia Private School Association (NAPSA) had on SWAPO's initiative recently been set up.[5] In addition to education, NAPSA would be concerned with agriculture and health at various private, church-run and SWAPO-aligned schools in Namibia. Based at Gibeon in southern Namibia, Reverend Witbooi was a leading promoter of the initiative, for which Swedish assistance was sought. An agreement to that effect was reached during the bilateral negotiations in Lusaka three months later.

The support to the alternative NAPSA schools in Gibeon, Hoachanas and Vaalgras will be presented below. Before turning to the activities of the Swedish churches and trade unions inside Namibia, it should be noted that SWAPO at the end of the 1970s had still not established expedient, regular routines for the transfer of funds into the country. Over the following years, a number of *ad hoc* channels and methods were used[6]—including deliveries of cash via couriers[7]—until SWAPO in mid-1983 eventually "succeeded in opening the proposed bank account in London".[8] Via the account, SWAPO primarily channelled the assistance to the leaders of the main churches in Namibia, who—as was later disclosed by SWAPO's

---

1. A leading representative of SWAPO's internal wing, Tjongarero was in 1977 appointed Deputy National Chairman. At independence, he became Deputy Minister of Information and Broadcasting.

2. Reverend Witbooi of the African Methodist Episcopal Church (AME)—a great-grandson of the famous Nama chief after whom he was named—joined SWAPO in 1976, becoming Secretary for Education and Culture inside Namibia. In 1983, he was elected Acting SWAPO Vice-President. At independence, he was appointed Minister of Labour, Public Service and Manpower Development.

3. Göran Hasselmark: Memorandum ('Samtal med SWAPO-delegation'/'Conversation with SWAPO delegation'), Ministry for Foreign Affairs, Stockholm, 22 February 1978 (MFA).

4. During their stay in Stockholm, Nujoma, Tjongarero and Witbooi also met Paul Carlsson from the LO/TCO Council of International Trade Union Cooperation. At that time, the SWAPO Secretary of Labour John Ya-Otto had already agreed with LO/TCO on Swedish trade union support to Namibia and Carlsson was preparing to leave for Windhoek. Nevertheless, in a later report Carlsson noted that the three SWAPO leaders "were clearly uninterested in the project", which according to Ya-Otto had been approved by SWAPO's Central Committee (Paul Carlsson: 'Verksamhetsrapport - Namibiaprojektet'/'Activity report - The Namibia project', Stockholm, 14 August 1978) (LMA).

5. Marika Fahlén: Memorandum ('Bistånd till SWAPO'/'Assistance to SWAPO'), Ministry for Foreign Affairs, Stockholm, 22 February 1978 (SDA).

6. Huge amounts were on several occasions disbursed by SIDA to a bank account in Geneva held by Hadino Hishongwa, the SWAPO representative to the Nordic countries. In early December 1981, for example, a sum of 1.6 MSEK was transferred to his account for activities inside Namibia (Letter ('Överföring av interna medel'/'Transfer of internal funds') from Carin Norberg to the Swedish embassy in Luanda, SIDA, Stockholm, 4 December 1981) (SDA).

7. See, for example, cable ('Överföring av biståndsmedel till Namibia'/'Transfer of assistance funds to Namibia') from the Swedish embassy in Luanda to the Ministry for Foreign Affairs, Luanda, 26 October 1979 (SDA). Funds received inside Namibia attracted the attention of the South African authorities. To cover the source when assistance from Sweden was expected, at Gibeon Reverend Witbooi used to organize sham church bazaars or similar activities (Author's recollection).

8. Letter ('Transfer of funds for home front operations') from Hifikepunye Pohamba to SIDA Stockholm, Luanda, 7 June 1983 (SDA).

National Treasurer Pohamba—were the only ones who knew the origin of the funds.[1]

Reporting on the funds transferred would, however, throughout the 1980s cause concern. For reasons of security, Sweden did not require receipts or vouchers for the home front component, but a descriptive, narrative annual report. After lengthy discussions on the subject, in mid-1986 it was agreed that SWAPO should annually submit a 'home front report', which

> should be considered [...] a progress report and describe the various activities [...] supported by SIDA. A financial statement should be attached, on which a breakdown of the total amount should be given. The financial statement should be copied to [SWAPO's] Auditor General[2], who after examination will include it in his [comprehensive] report. No vouchers need to be attached to the financial statement.[3]

More often than not, the agreement was not honoured to SIDA's satisfaction. While the Swedish authorities at the annual aid negotiations—as in 1987, for example—stated their "strong interest in increasing the support to [the] home front activities"[4], they repeatedly "stressed the need for improved reporting [on the component]".[5] In the absence of adequate SWAPO reports, the necessary follow-up of the assistance was instead mainly carried out through visits to Namibia by officials from the Swedish legation in Pretoria. They were normally undertaken via established church contacts. In addition, in December 1987, Reverend Martin Amadhila—assistant to Bishop Kleopas Dumeni of ELCIN and an executive member of the Council of Churches in Namibia—took part in the consultative talks between SWAPO and SIDA in Luanda, where he reported on the developments inside the country.[6] In connection with a church conference in Sweden, six months later Amadhila also visited SIDA's headquarters in Stockholm. The issue of unsatisfactory reports on the projects supported by Sweden inside Namibia was then raised. Amadhila was aware of the problem and "promised improvements" in this regard.[7]

Church Support

Outside the direct official support to SWAPO, from the mid-1970s the Church of Sweden Aid (CSA), the Swedish Trade Union Confederation (LO) and the Central Organization of Salaried Employees (TCO) embarked upon programmes and projects to strengthen the democratic forces inside Namibia. Although the activities were kept confidential to the wider public, the involvement of these actors—all of

---

1. Georg Dreifaldt: Memorandum ('Rapport från programsamtal mellan SWAPO och SIDA i Luanda, 22 februari 1989'/'Report from consultative talks between SWAPO and SIDA in Luanda, 22 February 1989'), Swedish embassy, Luanda, 28 February 1989 (SDA). The five church leaders mentioned by Pohamba were the Bishops Kleopas Dumeni of ELCIN, Henderik Frederick of ELC, Bonifacius Hausiku of the Roman Catholic Church and James Kauluma of the Church of the Province of Southern Africa (Anglican Diocese), in addition to Reverend Witbooi of AME.
2. For auditing purposes, Sweden accepted internal examination by SWAPO's Auditor General.
3. Roland Axelsson: Memorandum ('Reporting guidelines'), Swedish embassy, Lusaka, 28 May 1986 (SDA).
4. 'Minutes of understanding between SWAPO and SIDA, December 1-3, 1987', Luanda, 5 December 1987 (SDA).
5. Ibid. As a curiosity, it could be noted that Ben Amathila—on whose initiative official Swedish support to activities inside Namibia had started twelve years earlier—signed the 1987 minutes on SWAPO's behalf. Hifikepunye Pohamba led the SWAPO delegation.
6. 'Minutes of understanding between SWAPO and SIDA, December 1-3, 1987', Luanda, 5 December 1987 (SDA).
7. Inger Jernberg: Memorandum ('Anteckningar från möte med Reverend Amadhila, lutherska kyrkan i Namibia, 1988 06 15'/'Notes from meeting with Reverend Amadhila, Lutheran church in Namibia, [on] 15 June 1988'), SIDA, Stockholm, 20 June 1988 (SDA).

them with a huge parliamentary influence[1]—would decisively consolidate Sweden's relations with SWAPO and the broader Namibian nationalist movement.

CSA had been involved in practical project work inside Namibia since 1964, when construction of the Lutheran secondary school Oshigambo High School started in Ovamboland. Two years later, it assisted in the building of a school at Nkongo in the same region.[2] Via the Lutheran World Federation, from the late 1960s CSA channelled increasing support to the Evangelical Lutheran Church in Namibia led by Bishop Auala. For example, the aid branch of the official Church of Sweden contributed towards the reconstruction of ELCIN's printing press at Oniipa in Ovamboland when it was blown up in May 1973. It also granted financial resources to cover the operational costs of various Lutheran-run schools and clinics. Between 1969 and 1982, a total of 12 MSEK was channelled by CSA to projects and programmes in Namibia.[3] As stated by Björn Ryman in his history of the Church of Sweden Aid, "the support to Namibia was unique [in Sweden] in so far as neither SIDA nor the Africa Groups could carry out any [activities there] as long as South Africa ruled".[4]

CSA's programme grew rapidly after the foundation of the Council of Churches in Namibia (CCN)—an umbrella organization of the major Namibian churches[5]—in October 1978.[6] This growth was made possible through considerable grants from SIDA. After a visit to Namibia in September 1982[7], *Lutherhjälpen* applied for financial assistance from the official aid agency in favour of four activities, namely CCN's central administration in Windhoek, its Diaconic Fund[8], the Oshigambo High School and the Martin Luther High School.[9] CCHA was positive to the request, recommending a grant of 1.5 MSEK.[10] From a financial point of view, a quantitatively more substantial involvement by CSA thus began. As the funds were channelled via LWF, there was, however, in the early 1980s at the same time a markedly diminishing direct Swedish church presence in Namibia. This was noted

1. See Sellström Volume I, p. 36.
2. Åke Kastlund: *Resa genom Svart och Vitt* ('Journey through Black and White'), Svenska Kyrkans Diakonistyrelses Bokförlag, Stockholm, 1967, p. 15.
3. Björn Ryman: 'Rapport från Lutherhjälpens studieresa till Namibia och Swaziland den 17 september-3 oktober 1982' ('Report from CSA's study trip to Namibia and Swaziland, 17 September-3 October 1982') [no place or date] (CSA).
4. Ryman op. cit., p. 202.
5. The member churches were: the African Methodist Episcopal Church, the Anglican Church-Diocese of Damaraland, the Evangelical Lutheran Church in Namibia, the Evangelical Lutheran Church-Rhenish Mission, the Methodist Church of Southern Africa, the United Congregational Church of Southern Africa-Gordonia Region and—from 1982—the Roman Catholic Church.
6. CCN was formally constituted in October 1978 and began functioning officially from 1 April 1979. The council was close to SWAPO. According to Leys and Saul, "in the 1980s the CCN became almost a leading arm of SWAPO inside Namibia, employing various SWAPO office-bearers and activists and channelling external funds to SWAPO-approved development projects" (Leys and Saul op. cit., p. 11).
7. In his report from the visit to Namibia, Björn Ryman—representing CSA's secretariat in Uppsala—wrote: "The whole of Ovamboland [...] is a war zone—an operational area—where there are South African soldiers with sophisticated weapons practically everywhere. As we approached Ovamboland, our Volkswagen bus was attacked by an Impala plane, simulating machine gun fire five metres above the ground. [...] [W]e saw thousands of soldiers along the roads. [...] The scouts followed every movement from the water towers. [...] The South Africans are totally guided by fear. All who are against them and [the] apartheid system are classified as Communists. It also applies to the missionaries" (Björn Ryman: 'Rapport från Lutherhjälpens studieresa till Namibia och Swaziland den 17 september-3 oktober 1982'/'Report from CSA's study trip to Namibia and Swaziland, 17 September-3 October 1982' [no place or date]) (CSA).
8. CCN's Diaconic Fund was set up to assist war victims, political prisoners and their families.
9. Letter ('Begäran om anslag för fyra program i Namibia'/'Request for grant for four programmes in Namibia') from Thorsten Månson, CSA, to Elisabeth Michanek, SIDA, Uppsala, 17 December 1982 (SDA). The Martin Luther High School was situated in Okombahe, Damaraland, some 70 kilometres west of Omaruru.
10. Elisabeth Michanek: Memorandum ('Ansökan från Lutherhjälpen om bidrag till det namibiska kyrkorådet'/ 'Request from Church of Sweden Aid for contributions to the Council of Churches in Namibia'), CCHA/ SIDA, Stockholm, 18 February 1983 (SDA).

with concern by Birgitta Karlström Dorph, counsellor at the Swedish legation in Pretoria[1], who after a visit to Namibia in March 1985 reported that

> a number of churches in Namibia have observed that support from churches in Sweden [...] has hardly been forthcoming during the last couple of years. A very prominent church leader [said] that he [...] had drawn the conclusion that people in Sweden were not interested in supporting programmes in Namibia. [...] Churches in Namibia have also noted that visits from [...] Swedish churches have been almost non-existent during [these] years. Visits from [their] Swedish brothers should [, however,] facilitate a closer cooperation.[2]

The concerns expressed by Karlström Dorph were noted by SIDA and conveyed to the Church of Sweden and Diakonia, the international branch of the Swedish Free Church Council, made up of seven non-Lutheran denominations.[3] While it is impossible to conclusively state that SIDA's active intervention played a decisive role in this regard[4], it can be noted that both CSA and Diakonia at about the same time approached SIDA with more substantial funding requests for activities in Namibia. Generally approved, they *inter alia* covered support to CCN's running costs (CSA); its Legal Aid and Social Services Units[5] (Diakonia); a programme to rehabilitate released political prisoners (CSA); the establishment of a Human Rights Centre at Ongwediva (CSA); and assistance to families of the mineworkers participating in the Tsumeb strike in 1987 (Diakonia).

In a report commissioned by SIDA on NGO support inside Namibia, Bertil Högberg of the Africa Groups concluded in November 1988 that "[i]t is striking how the churches and [their] missionary and aid agencies dominate the picture".[6] As both CSA and Diakonia raised considerable resources of their own, it is difficult to estimate the total monetary value of the assistance extended by the churches. In the case of CSA, the official SIDA contributions amounted to 17.5 MSEK between

---

1. Karlström Dorph played a crucial role with regard to the Swedish assistance to SWAPO, ANC and aligned organizations inside Namibia and South Africa. Based in Pretoria during the difficult years from 1982 to 1988, she was subsequently appointed ambassador to Ethiopia.
2. Birgitta Karlström Dorph: Memorandum ('SWAPO's program inne i Namibia'/'SWAPO's programmes inside Namibia'), Swedish legation, Pretoria, 4 March 1985 (SDA).
3. Author's recollection. Loosely formed in 1966, the aid council of the Swedish non-state churches was for many years known as the Swedish Free Church Aid (*Frikyrkan Hjälper*). In 1984, it adopted the name Diakonia. On the Swedish free churches and Southern Africa, see Sellström Volume I, pp. 41-42.
4. Constantly receiving requests for support from a range of NGOs in Namibia and South Africa, SIDA pursued an active policy of identifying suitable Swedish counterparts, or 'channels'. This unusual situation—whereby the state invited the civil society to engage in international solidarity work, putting the necessary financial means at its disposal—largely explains why a great number of Swedish NGOs covering a broad spectrum of activities and interests became involved in the liberation struggles in Namibia and, above all, in South Africa. In the case of Sweden, the pro-active policy in this respect undoubtedly broadened the involvement of the society at large. On this point, cf. the interview with Birgitta Berggren, former CCHA secretary and head of SIDA's Southern Africa section: "[R]egarding the question of apartheid and the situation in Southern Africa there was not much debate whether Sweden should support the struggle or not. People were generally supportive. When various requests were channelled to us—in very different ways, to say the least—we tried to look for the group, party, organization or institution that could take an interest in that very activity and identify itself with the project. For instance, if it concerned training of girls or women, we would look for a women's group in Sweden which could be especially interested, either in a political party context or as an ordinary NGO. We tried to use our imagination. We worked very hard to find people who could take such an interest that they really would work with great solidarity. I would say that the absolute majority—maybe 98-99 per cent—of those who agreed to work with the various projects did so in a fantastic way. There were hardly any leaks to the media. Neither would you hear from someone that they knew about the activities. It was kept very confidential by such a great number of people that I am still surprised that it worked so well. It was like a collective secret" (Interview with Birgitta Berggren, p. 258).
5. According to accounts submitted by Vezera Kandetu, Associate General Secretary of CCN, Diakonia's contribution to the central Social Services Unit corresponded in 1989 to 40 per cent of the total funds received (CCN report attached to letter ('Stöd till CCN'/'Support to CCN') from Margaret Bäckman, Diakonia, to SIDA, Älvsjö, 2 November 1989 (SDA).
6. Bertil Högberg: 'NGO's stöd till Namibia och planer vid ev[entuellt] oberoende för Namibia'/'NGO support to Namibia and plans in the eventuality of independence for Namibia', Uppsala, 7 November 1988 (SDA).

1985/86 and 1989/90.[1] As the involvement by CSA and Diakonia grew during the pre-independence period—when CCN under the UNTAG[2] umbrella was given responsibility for repatriation, resettlement and rehabilitation of the Namibians in exile—over the years the amount channelled by the Swedish church organizations to Namibia reached somewhere between 75 and 100 MSEK.[3]

LO/TCO and the National Union of Namibian Workers

While the involvement by the churches took place in a comparatively sheltered environment, the Swedish labour movement would towards the end of the 1970s become engaged in a much more exposed milieu. From 1977, LO, TCO and—indirectly, as a funding agency—SIDA were closely associated with the underground efforts to build a national trade union organization in Namibia. Coordinated by the LO/TCO Council of International Trade Union Cooperation[4], Swedish assistance to this endeavour was extended over the following decade. It can be divided into three phases. In the late 1970s, the support was channelled to activities inside the country. Due to the authorities' clampdown, it had, however, during the first half of the 1980s to be carried out among the Namibian refugees in Angola. After a dramatic upsurge in the labour mobilization inside Namibia in the mid-1980s, it could, finally, once again be directed to the home front.

Namibian workers had always been at the forefront of nationalist resistance to South Africa's occupation. To a large extent, SWAPO had its origins in the workers' struggles.[5] The forerunners of the political movement—the Ovamboland People's Congress and the Ovamboland People's Organization—were initially more concerned with the problems facing contract labour than the question of outright national independence.[6] Nevertheless, it was only in the late 1980s that a modern national trade union organization was formed. Although a number of attempts to organize trade unions were made from the 1920s onwards, they either failed due to the combined effects of the dispersed labour force—scattered between far-flung mines and coastal fisheries—and the disruptive contract system[7] or, above all, to the repression under the apartheid laws. While the 1952 Wage and Industrial Con-

---

1. Letter ('Slutrapportering av bidrag till Lutherhjälpen'/'Final accounts regarding contributions to the Church of Sweden Aid') from Ingalill Colbro, SIDA, to Marlene Campbell Holmberg, CSA, SIDA, Stockholm, 20 March 1992 (SDA).
2. United Nations Transitional Assistance Group.
3. Author's estimate.
4. In Swedish, *LO/TCO's Biståndsnämnd*. LO—the national Trade Union Confederation—represents the Swedish blue-collar workers, while TCO—the Central Organization of Salaried Employees—does the same with regard to civil servants and private professional employees. As noted in Volume I (pp. 35-36), the two confederations dominate the trade union scene in Sweden. Belonging to the pro-Western International Confederation of Free Trade Unions (ICFTU), in 1974 LO and TCO set up a joint international committee to coordinate assistance to trade union education in developing countries. The cooperation was institutionalized in 1977 when a secretariat—later called the LO/TCO Council of International Trade Union Cooperation—was formed. Although sharing common outlooks and working closely together, the council should not be confused with the International Centre of the Swedish Labour Movement (*Arbetarrörelsens Internationella Centrum* - AIC), later renamed the Olof Palme International Center (OPIC). Formed in 1978 by the Social Democratic Party, LO, the Swedish Co-operative Union and Wholesale Society (KF) and the Swedish Workers Educational Association (ABF), AIC's objective was to coordinate wider international matters of common interest to constituent parts of the Swedish social democratic movement.
5. As emphasized by Bauer (op. cit., pp. 29-31) and Peltola (op. cit., pp. 98-106), the leading founders of OPC/OPO/SWAPO were, however, nationalist intellectuals and although the question of contract labour played a prominent role, the organizations had a wider outlook. The following presentation of the Namibian trade union movement borrows heavily from Bauer's and Peltola's pioneering works.
6. In the late 1950s and early 1960s, OPC/OPO/SWAPO petitioned the United Nations to force South Africa to entrust Namibia to the UN Trusteeship Council. The demand for national independence came later.
7. See Ndeutala Hishongwa: *The Contract Labour System and Its Effects on Family and Social Life in Namibia: A Historical Perspective*, Gamsberg Macmillan, Windhoek, 1992.

ciliation Ordinance did provide for the organization of trade unions, it, however, excluded black workers from the definition 'employee', effectively precluding the formation of black unions.

In exile, where—as pointedly noted by Bauer—"there were no workers"[1], SWAPO made provisions for a national trade union. At the consultative Tanga congress at the turn of 1969-70, a Labour Department was created with Solomon Mifima as its first Secretary.[2] Soon thereafter, Mifima launched a National Union of Namibian Workers, which he was to officially represent at the ILO-sponsored International Trade Union Conference against Apartheid in Geneva, Switzerland, in June 1973.[3]

Together with Andreas Shipanga, Mifima was, however, held responsible for the 1975-76 SWAPO crisis and detained in April 1976.[4] The subsequent internal commission of inquiry—led by SWAPO's Acting Secretary General John Ya-Otto—concluded in June 1976 that "there is a dire need for the restructuring and reorganization of the party administration to ensure [...] the revitalization of dormant and inactive departments, [such as that of] Labour".[5] At the following Central Committee meeting at Nampundwe outside Lusaka, Ya-Otto was appointed Secretary for Labour in August 1976, replacing his detained predecessor. In marked difference to Mifima—but largely without active backing from the inner SWAPO leadership around Sam Nujoma—he immediately took an active interest in the building of a national trade union inside Namibia.

Although various union ideas had been floated in the country[6], at that time there was no concrete initiative to build on. At a SWAPO congress in Walvis Bay in late May 1976—essentially called in support of the exiled leadership after the 1975-76 crisis—labour matters were, however, discussed and the young SWAPO activist Jason Angula was elected Secretary for Economics, Labour and Natural Resources. Like Ya-Otto, Angula took his task seriously. He soon came into contact with Gerson Max, a black Lutheran pastor who worked with migrant workers all over Namibia and who—inspired by Andimba Toivo ya Toivo and the general strike of 1971-72—had come up with "the very original idea of building a general trade union based on [...] the churches".[7] Despite limited possibilities of communicating, Angula and Max established contacts with Ya-Otto in Zambia.

As a result of growing mobilization in South Africa, at about the same time the Pretoria government prepared amendments to the 1952 labour laws. The definition 'employee' was to be extended to black workers, who—at least in theory—from then on could form trade unions.[8] After years of nominal existence, the time had come to give NUNW real meaning and content. Visiting Namibia in 1977, the

---

1. Bauer op. cit., p. 45.
2. As early as in 1962, a South West Africa Trade Union League (SWATUL) had—at least in name—been formed in exile. Paul Helmuth was appointed Secretary General of SWATUL (John Marcum: *The Angolan Revolution: The Anatomy of an Explosion (1950-1962)*, Volume I, The MIT Press, Cambridge, Massachusetts, and London, England, 1969, p. 305, note 62).
3. As 'the sole and authentic representative of the Namibian people', SWAPO would—remarkably—from 1977 represent both the employers (SWAPO) and the workers (NUNW) at ILO's annual labour conferences in Geneva.
4. See the chapter 'The Shipanga Affair and Beyond: Humanitarian Assistance and Human Rights'.
5. SWAPO: 'Report of the Findings and Recommendations of the John Ya-Otto Commission of Inquiry into Circumstances Which Led to the Revolt of SWAPO Cadres between June 1974 and April 1976', [SWAPO, Lusaka], 4 June 1976, p. 17 (MFA).
6. SWAPO activists in the 1970s had tried to set up a Namibian Workers Union (NAWU). For all practical purposes, it remained, however, only a name.
7. Peltola op. cit., p. 169.
8. Trade unions were, however, prohibited from affiliating to a political party. When NUNW later applied for registration, it was turned down on account of its association with SWAPO (Peltola op. cit., p. 169).

Swedish journalist Eric Sjöquist from the liberal evening paper *Expressen* wrote in a report to the Lutheran World Federation:

> One evening I participated in a trade union meeting in a church in Windhoek, where I had been invited by pastor Max, who works among [migrant] labourers from Ovamboland. There were 25 people in the church. They discussed proposals for a constitution [of] a trade union. [...] That evening [...] was a historical event, since there have not been any trade unions in Namibia up until now. [...] The meeting started at 7 p.m. and ended at 10.30 p.m. Then the chairman said: 'We must finish now, otherwise we may risk an encounter with the police'.[1]

Such was the situation when John Ya-Otto—formally both SWAPO Labour Secretary and NUNW General Secretary—during a visit to LO in April 1977 approached the Swedish labour movement for support.[2] Soon thereafter he started to send SWAPO members for training at the International Trade Union Institute in Moscow.[3] SWAPO had, however, not yet decided to affiliate the fledgling Namibian trade union organization to the Eastern-dominated World Federation of Trade Unions, based in Prague, Czechoslovakia.[4] Although the issue of international affiliation would later provoke both confusion[5] and criticism[6], it did not prevent the ICFTU-aligned Swedish LO/TCO from entering into bilateral negotiations with

---

1. Cited in Cronje op. cit., p. 106. The report appeared as LWF Information 41/77 of 16 November 1977.
2. Ingvar Ygeman: 'Vittnesbörd på LO och Brunnsvik om Facklig Kamp i Södra Afrika' ('Testimonies at LO and Brunnsvik of Trade Union Struggles in Southern Africa') in *Statsanställd*, No. 17, 1977.
3. Peltola op. cit., p. 163, note 10.
4. Like so many other aspects concerning NUNW, the date of affiliation to WFTU is unclear. As late as in December 1978, LO/TCO was under the impression that NUNW did not belong to any international (Letter from Kristina Persson to John Ya-Otto, Stockholm, 12 December 1978) (SDA). While Bauer claims that "it is not clear exactly who made [the] decision [to affiliate to WFTU] or when" (Bauer op. cit., p. 58), Peltola affirms that it was taken by SWAPO's Central Committee in 1978 (Peltola op. cit., p. 133). According to ICFTU, NUNW only became a full member of WFTU in 1982. In a report from ICFTU's Coordinating Committee on South Africa, it was noted in April 1982 that "the ICFTU has for some years been working in cooperation with [the] National Union of Namibian Workers. However, when it was discovered that the union was to affiliate to the WFTU—the affiliation has been endorsed at the WFTU congress in Cuba early this year—it became impossible to maintain any relationship" (ICFTU: '18th meeting of the Coordinating Committee on South Africa', Brussels, 22-23 April 1982, p. 2) (LMA). Nevertheless, LO/TCO continued the relationship, concluding a bilateral agreement with NUNW in 1984 and seconding a representative to work directly with Ya-Otto in Angola. This was in marked contrast to the position held vis-à-vis the WFTU-affiliated South African Congress of Trade Unions, which—as will be seen below—did not receive any support from LO/TCO. On the question of LO/TCO and NUNW's affiliation to WFTU, cf. also the interview with the founder of Namibia's modern trade union movement, Ben Ulenga, where he states that "it was handled very nicely and diplomatically [by LO/TCO]. [...] It was essentially not a problem. There was no conditionality" (Interview with Ben Ulenga, p. 101).
5. In her study on the Norwegian trade union movement and the anti-apartheid struggle, Vesla Vetlesen—actively engaged in the international work by the Norwegian Confederation of Trade Unions (*Landsorganisasjonen i Norge* - LO) between 1980 and 1994 and Norway's Minister of Development Cooperation from 1986 to 1988—writes that "NUNW applied for support from the Nordic trade union organizations[. A]t a meeting in Zambia in 1978, where [the] Danish, Swedish and Norwegian LO [confederations], as well as ICFTU, were present, NUNW, however, declined offers of support if it was to be channelled via ICFTU" (Vetlesen op. cit., p. 106). According to the documents consulted by the author, throughout 1977 and 1978 NUNW applied *both* for bilateral support from the Nordic confederations *and* multilateral support from ICFTU (cf. Paul Carlsson: 'Verksamhetsrapport – Namibiaprojektet'/'Activity report – The Namibia project', Stockholm, 14 August 1978) (LMA). The bilateral support from LO/TCO to NUNW inside Namibia started in 1978. In 1979, the Central Organization of Finnish Trade Unions (*Suomen Ammattiliittojen Keskusjärjestö* - SAK)—also affiliated to ICFTU—began its cooperation with NUNW in Angola.
6. Although NUNW was not a full member of WFTU, SWAPO's decision to seek affiliation was, as Bauer notes, taken without consulting those who were involved in the formation of the trade union organization inside Namibia (Bauer op. cit., p. 58). Some of them—such as Arthur Pickering and Paul Carlsson—were far from happy with the decision (Peltola op. cit., pp. 190 and 194). According to Peltola, "during the early 1980s, the SWAPO officials in Luanda commented very negatively on the efforts of [the] LO/TCO representative [...] Kristina Persson to get NUNW to break [the affiliation with WFTU] and join ICFTU instead. She was said to have used material aid as a means of extortion" (ibid., p. 149). Peltola himself was actively involved in the Finnish support to NUNW. Representing the ICFTU-affiliated SAK, during his first visit to Angola in mid-1979 he and his colleague Ilkka Tahvanainen were described as 'CIA agents' by SWAPO's Administrative Secretary Moses Garoeb (ibid., p. 136).

SWAPO/NUNW. In a letter to Ya-Otto, Kristina Persson of the LO/TCO secretariat later explained that

> although it is a principle for [...] LO/TCO to cooperate on a multilateral basis, we are, as you already know, in certain cases prepared to deviate from that principle, i.e. when an organization does not belong to any international, which is the case with NUNW.[1]

The Swedish trade union support was not limited to Namibia. On the contrary, it formed part of a broader effort which concentrated on South Africa and in addition included Lesotho and Zimbabwe.[2] The campaign followed upon a study tour to South Africa by LO and TCO in January-February 1975, which recommended assistance to a number of union initiatives. Primarily implemented via ICFTU and closely coordinated with the trade union confederations in the other Nordic countries, it started on a modest scale in 1976.[3] To prepare the campaign, Kristina Persson was employed in December 1976 by the LO/TCO Committee—later Council—of International Trade Union Cooperation.[4] She went on a fact-finding mission to South Africa in January-February 1977.[5] Shortly thereafter, LO/TCO submitted a first request for financial support to CCHA. It covered support to various structures and activities in South Africa, as well as funds to prepare programmes in the field of trade union education in Lesotho, Namibia and Zimbabwe. The consultative committee endorsed the request in mid-June 1977. SIDA subsequently disbursed an initial amount of 1 MSEK to LO/TCO.[6]

Although LO/TCO's campaign was not primarily directed towards Namibia, the assistance to NUNW was unique in many ways and merits more than a passing comment. NUNW's relations with WFTU have been mentioned. To this should be added that the assistance was not channelled to an independent trade union organization, but to a branch of SWAPO. It was also implemented by the Swedish confederations in direct consultation with the Namibian liberation movement. Contrary to the support in South Africa, the involvement in Namibia was, in addition, a bilateral venture, furthermore including Swedish personnel.[7]

Last but by no means least, while LO/TCO during the preparatory stages was given the impression that a national trade union organization had already been

---

1. Letter from Kristina Persson to John Ya-Otto, Stockholm, 12 December 1978 (SDA).
2. The trade union support to South Africa will be discussed below. The modest assistance to Zimbabwe was extended in favour of trade union education at the Catholic, Jesuit-run Silveira House, while the efforts in Lesotho were primarily directed towards migrant workers in the South African mines. In monetary terms, it has within the present study not been possible to establish the overall support by the Swedish trade union movement. The contributions by the Swedish government to the trade union efforts between 1976/77 and 1994/95 amounted in total to 144.6 MSEK (Disbursement figures according to SIDA's audited annual accounts). To this should be added considerable amounts extended as 'own resources' by LO, TCO and various members, such as the Swedish Mineworkers Union. In her booklet on Swedish trade union support to South Africa, LO/TCO's Solveig Wickman estimates that by 1996 almost 200 MSEK had been channelled to that country alone (Solveig Wickman: *Sydafrika: Fackligt Bistånd*/'South Africa: Trade Union Assistance', Förlaget Trädet/LO/TCO's Biståndsnämnd, Stockholm, 1996, p. 5).
3. The very first contribution—amounting to 55,000 SEK—was disbursed in late 1976 to the Engineering and Allied Workers Union (EAWU) to strengthen the unions at the Swedish-owned companies in South Africa (Kristina Persson: 'LO/TCO's aktiviteter i Sydafrikafrågan'/'The activities of LO/TCO in regard to the South Africa question', LO/TCO International Committee, Stockholm, 14 November 1977) (LMA).
4. Ibid. After many years at LO/TCO, between 1993 and 1995 Persson represented the Social Democratic Party in the Swedish parliament and in 1995 in the European parliament. She was in August 1995 appointed governor of the county of Jämtland in northern Sweden.
5. Ibid.
6. Kristina Persson: Memorandum ('Projekt för facklig utbildning m.m. i södra Afrika budgetåret 1978/79'/ 'Projects on trade union education etc. in Southern Africa [during the] financial year 1978/79'), Stockholm, 7 April 1978 (SDA).
7. Under ICFTU's umbrella, LO/TCO recruited a Swedish project leader—Ove Johansson—for the work in Lesotho. He arrived there in 1979, staying in the country for many years.

formed in Namibia, when Paul Carlsson arrived in the country in August 1978 he dramatically found that this was far from being the case. Rather than assisting an existing organization with education programmes, he—and LO/TCO—instead became intimately involved in the actual formation of the National Union of Namibian Workers. Alone in an unfamiliar, racially divided and hostile environment, 'Palle' Carlsson—a young Swedish teacher from LO's Runö school outside Stockholm with no real previous working experience in Africa[1]—would thus play a leading role[2] during the initial phase of the historic, but difficult and dangerous, undertaking to build a union for the black Namibian workers.[3] In the history of the Swedish trade union support to the region, this was also unique. Although the efforts were eventually crushed by the South African authorities, Carlsson stands out as one of the unsung pioneers[4] in Sweden's long involvement in the struggles for human dignity, democracy and majority rule in Southern Africa.[5]

'Palle' Carlsson in Namibia

In August 1977, Kristina Persson returned to Southern Africa, where she together with John Ya-Otto drew up the general plans for LO/TCO's Namibia project. Focusing on education, the plans were further defined by SWAPO's Labour Secretary in a request for assistance submitted in early December 1977.[6] According to Ya-Otto, NUNW was the "industrial wing of [...] SWAPO, which [had] been operating in exile". It was, however, felt that

> the time is now opportune to lay the foundation for [the] building [of] sound and viable trade unions in Namibia through a two-pronged approach, [namely] education and organiz[ation]. [...] From what we have learnt about [...] trade union education, the following should be a convenient way of operating:

> [During a] first stage, a small group of Namibians (preferably not more than 3-4) are selected carefully in Namibia and sent to Nairobi and Lusaka to a) plan the project together with a Swedish expert[7] [...] and b) receive [...] training for their future tasks. [...] At the same time, study materials etc. for [the work] inside Namibia should be prepared. It should also be inves-

---

1. Letter from Bengt Säve-Söderbergh, AIC, to Martti Ahtisaari, UN Commissioner for Namibia, Stockholm, 15 August 1978 (OPA). In the letter, Säve-Söderbergh introduced Carlsson and the LO/TCO project to Ahtisaari, who in July 1978 had been appointed as the UN Secretary General's Special Representative for Namibia and was preparing a visit to the country. The visit took place in January 1979, at a time when Carlsson had temporarily returned to Sweden. Bauer—who mentions Carlsson—writes that "he had never been out of Sweden" (Bauer op. cit., p. 161, note 16). While he had not worked for a longer period in Africa, he had, however, visited Kenya, where he assisted the trade unions with the production of study materials (Letter from Kristina Persson to John Ya-Otto, Stockholm, 13 January 1978) (LMA).
2. According to Peltola, the five leaders behind the NUNW project inside Namibia between 1977 and 1980 were Jason Angula, Gerson Max, Arthur Pickering, Paul Carlsson and Henry Boonzaaier (Peltola op. cit., pp. 169-70). Carlsson was the only white person in the group.
3. Peltola writes that in September 1979 he was asked by John Ya-Otto to join Carlsson in Namibia, but declined "because I felt [that] I [would] be jailed and/or kicked out in no time. That would embarrass [the] Finnish trade unions and give a weapon to the apartheid regime" (ibid., p. 198, note 22).
4. To the author's knowledge, it is only Peltola who—partly due to his own personal involvement—in his study on the Namibian trade union movement has recognized the role played by Carlsson (ibid., pp. 167-97). No Swedish or SWAPO publication mentions his contribution, although it is well known by many trade union leaders, particularly in Namibia. See, for example, the interview with Ben Ulenga, p. 100.
5. Based in Harare and working with prominent South African trade union leaders such as Cyril Ramaphosa and James Motlatsi—and through them with Ben Ulenga in Namibia—LO/TCO's Stig Blomqvist is another 'unsung hero'. As will be seen later in the text, in the 1980s he was instrumental in the development of both the South African National Union of Mineworkers (NUM) and the Mineworkers Union of Namibia (MUN).
6. Letter from Kristina Persson to John Ya-Otto, Stockholm, 13 January 1978 (LMA).
7. Gunvor Fredriksson was mentioned in the proposal. She was at the time leading a LO/TCO project in Kenya. Under her married name Gunvor Ngarambe, in the early 1980s she worked at the SIDA office at the Swedish embassy in Luanda, being responsible for Sweden's assistance to SWAPO and ANC.

tigated if NUNW could get some help [...] from experienced trade unionists in South Africa. [...] This initial [stage] should extend over a period of 1-2 months. [...]

At stage two of the project, the Namibians return home. The Swedish expert [who will be specially recruited to assist NUNW] also leaves for Namibia [...]. Formally, the expert should be invited by the Christian Centre[1] or the Lutheran church to work at the centre as a lecturer for one year. In Windhoek, the [...] group produce[s] the study material needed and start[s] a series of seminars for trade union organizers/educators. The seminars should be on a full-time basis and cover a period of 2-3 weeks. During a period of 6 months, the instructors and the [Swedish] expert should together be able to carry out at least 15 seminars [with] 15 participants [each], [representing various sectors and] all [the] regions in Namibia. [...]

[During] the third stage [...], the 225 organizers/educators[2] [go] back to the regions [and to the] work places where they came from. Their function [...] is to build [...] local organizations. In order to do so, study circles are formed [...], [meeting] after work or at weekends. The number of participants [in each circle] could be 7-10 and the amount of time spent by each [circle] 20-30 hours, altogether. [...] In the meantime, seminars continue and additional organizers/educators are [...] trained, who in turn go back to their work places to organize and educate new members.[3]

The project should extend "over a period of at least two years". Once properly established, it should "within a few months" give basic trade union education to between 2,000 and 4,000 "members",[4] and thus to several thousand more over the project span. It would, however, soon become obvious that the ambitious plans were at odds with the political realities inside Namibia. There were, simply, no trade union structures or relevant traditions to build upon.

Nevertheless, in the meantime the project was approved by LO/TCO. In January 1978, Persson informed Ya-Otto that "your requests were met by the LO/TCO committee at a meeting on 19 December" and that "the preparations [...] continue according to previous plans".[5] Finally, in April 1978 LO/TCO submitted a request for 1.1 MSEK during the financial year 1978/79 to CCHA.[6] With a fair understanding of the situation inside Namibia and drawing upon comments by the Swedish embassy in Lusaka—which after discussions with Ya-Otto concluded that "a great lack of clarity surrounds the [...] project"[7]—the committee was, however, reluctant to recommend the entire amount, instead proposing a grant of 250,000

---

1. Set up in Windhoek in 1974 as a forum for informal cooperation among the Namibian churches, the Christian Centre was a forerunner of the Council of Churches in Namibia. CSA supported the centre from 1976, when more than half a million SEK was granted (Ryman op. cit., p. 202). There is no evidence of coordination between LO/TCO and CSA concerning the trade union project.
2. The proposal mentioned 205 organizers/educators. With 15 seminars and 15 participants in each seminar, the figure should be 225.
3. NUNW proposal cited in Kristina Persson: Memorandum ('Project for trade union education in Namibia'), Stockholm, 1 December 1977 (LMA).
4. Ibid.
5. Letter from Kristina Persson to John Ya-Otto, Stockholm, 13 January 1978 (LMA).
6. Kristina Persson: Memorandum ('PM angående projekt för facklig utbildning i Namibia budgetåret 1978/79 och 1979/80'/'Memorandum regarding [a] project on trade union education in Namibia [during] the financial year 1978/79 and [in] 1979/80'), Stockholm, 20 March 1978 (LMA) and Kristina Persson: Memorandum ('Projekt för facklig utbildning m.m. i södra Afrika budgetåret 1978/9'/'Projects on trade union education etc. in Southern Africa [during the] financial year 1978/79'), Stockholm, 7 April 1978 (SDA).
7. Letter ('Remiss angående LO's ansökan om stöd till facklig utbildning i södra Afrika'/'Observations concerning LO's request for support to trade union education in Southern Africa') from Bengt Oberger, Swedish embassy, to SIDA, Lusaka, 14 September 1978 (SDA).

SEK for continued project preparations. In October 1978, SIDA decided in accordance with this recommendation.[1]

At that time, Paul Carlsson—who had been appointed project leader by LO/TCO in consultation with SWAPO/NUNW—was already in Namibia. In spite of President Nujoma's lack of interest in the project during his visit to Stockholm in February; the fact that SWAPO's entire internal leadership—including Jason Angula—had been detained in April; serious warnings by Vice-President Muyongo in May[2]; and in the absence of suitable counterparts in the country, in June 1978 Labour Secretary Ya-Otto had given Carlsson the green light to travel to Namibia.[3] He was to liaise with Gerson Max, identify the instructors, prepare basic study materials and draw up a budget for the planned project.[4]

Thus thrown in at the deep end, Carlsson entered Namibia on a tourist visa in mid-August 1978. He immediately established contact with 'Pastor Max'—at the time chairing a NUNW 'executive committee' in Windhoek—and noted in his first report to LO/TCO, dated 5 September 1978, that

> I started my activities by speaking in the church, during the service that Max has for the migrant workers. We invited [people] to a first meeting in the evening of [...] 28 August. [...] There were around 30 people, of whom 5 women. We use the church as we don't have any other place. Closely crammed in a few rows. [...] The meetings start and end with a prayer. All conversations are held in Ovambo. [T]here is a girl who helps me with the translations. She is the only person apart from Max who speaks English. I act as leader of the meetings and as a teacher. It can be compared to an evening class.[5]

---

1. As the LO/TCO council had informed Ya-Otto that the project was approved and Paul Carlsson was already in Namibia, it was far from happy with the decision. In a letter to Elisabeth Michanek at the Swedish embassy in Lusaka, Kristina Persson stated that "people at LO and TCO [are] quite upset". Describing the decision as "extremely unsatisfactory", she added that "it cannot be reasonable that SIDA requests far-reaching assurances with regard to assessments, detailed planning and detailed knowledge about every single recipient organization" (Letter from Kristina Persson to Elisabeth Michanek, Stockholm, 20 October 1978) (SDA). Of the Swedish NGOs requesting funds from CCHA, LO/TCO was for many years among the most imperious. Often reluctant to submit the necessary background information for decisions, the trade union council jealously guarded its autonomy vis-à-vis the state. With regard to the Namibia project, for example, in April 1981 LO/TCO's Jan-Erik Norling wrote a sharp letter to the Ministry for Foreign Affairs, *inter alia* stating that "it cannot be for SIDA to 'carefully assess the conditions for trade union work [...] before a decision on possible support [...] to projects inside Namibia is taken'. That responsibility rests *exclusively* with LO/TCO [and] is a basic condition if LO and TCO shall at all be in a position to utilize public funds for [...] trade union assistance. It can, similarly, not be the task of Swedish [embassies] to supervise and control Swedish trade union assistance projects. The projects must be—and be seen to be—independent undertakings between trade union organizations, both with regard to the donor and to the recipient. It should not be unfamiliar that in many quarters it would be extremely discrediting if 'state involvement' was to be experienced in trade union cooperation" (Letter ('Stöd till fackföreningsrörelsen i Namibia'/'Support to the trade union movement in Namibia') from Jan-Erik Norling, LO/TCO, to Tom Tscherning, Ministry for Foreign Affairs, Stockholm, 10 April 1981) (SDA).
2. According to Carlsson, Muyongo—who at the time was visiting Sweden—had in a meeting with LO/TCO on 10 May 1978 "immediately advised us against going to Namibia, as the situation was so difficult. In his opinion, the people who were of interest to us [...] had already been detained. Contacts with SWAPO members would probably lead to immediate expulsion from the country [and] cause problems for [them]" (Paul Carlsson: 'Verksamhetsrapport - Namibiaprojektet'/'Activity report - The Namibia project'), Stockholm, 14 August 1978 (LMA). The report was written two days before Carlsson's arrival in Windhoek.
3. Ibid.
4. Ibid. In a country with widespread illiteracy and extremely low familiarity with the English language—the mother tongue of less than one per cent of the population—it was, remarkably, "SWAPO's wish that the [study] materials are prepared in English" (ibid.). In his report, Carlsson laconically noted that "this will be a great obstacle" (ibid.). He, however, later decided to use only local languages, disregarding English (Letter from Paul Carlsson to LO/TCO [no place or date, but Windhoek, probably in September 1979]) (LMA).
5. Letter from Paul Carlson to LO/TCO [no place or date, but Windhoek, 5 September 1978] (LMA). Pastor Max's church for migrant workers was situated in the black township of Katutura, north of Windhoek. Katutura was a no-go area for whites after sunset. In his letter, Carlsson does not mention where he stayed or how he eluded the police to attend the evening meetings in the church. According to Ben Ulenga—who at the time was imprisoned on Robben Island, but "used to hear what was happening"—Carlsson "sometimes [...] had to disguise himself as a cleric, feigning pastoral work. The title of reverend was attached to his name" (Interview with Ben Ulenga, p. 100).

Trade union organizer 'Palle' Carlsson of LO/TCO facing problems in the Namibian desert during one of his nationwide tours in 1978 (Courtesy of Paul Carlsson)

If the environment of the small Katutura church was strange to the young Swede, he must have been worried when during the initial meetings he came to realize the extent of NUNW's weakness and the lack of trade union experience and awareness among its members. The first evening, for example, "people asked whether the employers should be members of the union. [W]hen I explained [the situation to them], the next question was: 'How can we then talk to each other?'".[1] During the second meeting—held on 1 September—Carlsson wanted to discuss NUNW's constitution, but found that "nobody had seen [it] before". He also introduced the method of study circles, which "they [...] find interesting", but difficult to implement. On this point, he quoted a participant who said: "We are 8-9 people living in the same room and we have problems with [electricity]".[2]

Carlsson was, however, not discouraged. On the contrary, in his first letter to LO/TCO he wrote that while "you have to light a candle during the darkest of times, here you must ignite sparks to start a bush fire".[3] Assisted by the British secretary Justin Ellis at the Christian Centre[4], he continued the work, studying salary scales and visiting workers' compounds. He also decided to assess the situation with regard to trade unions and workers' conditions in the whole of Namibia. After less than three weeks in the country, in September 1978 he and Pastor Max embarked on a long journey to southern Namibia, where they visited factories and mines at twelve different places, from Mariental to Noordoewer on the South African border.[5] The journey took place from 7 to 25 September 1978. Before leaving Windhoek, Carlsson wrote to LO/TCO that "I am going to buy a sleeping bag as we will have to [stay overnight] wherever we can. Apartheid also works efficiently in these places according to Max".[6] He also informed them that he and Max had

---

1. Letter from Paul Carlson to LO/TCO [no place or date, but Windhoek, 5 September 1978] (LMA).
2. Ibid.
3. Ibid.
4. Ellis was deported from Namibia in December 1978. He was thereafter invited by AIC to Sweden (Letter ('Stöd till SWAPO inför ett av FN övervakat val i Namibia'/'Support to SWAPO at the prospect of UN-supervised elections in Namibia') from Bengt Säve-Söderbergh to CCHA, Stockholm, 18 January 1979) (OPA).
5. The places visited were: Mariental, Keetmanshoop, Karasburg, Warmbaad, Goodhouse, Ai-Ais, Noordoewer, Bethanie, Rosh Pinah, Aus, Lüderitz and Gibeon (Peltola op. cit., p. 193), many of which were extremely isolated and without easy access.
6. Letter from Paul Carlsson to LO/TCO [no place or date, but Windhoek, 5 September 1978] (LMA).

decided to convene a national trade union seminar in Windhoek at the end of the month.

At the end of September 1978, Kristina Persson attended the national conference of the Angolan trade union movement UNTA[1] in Luanda, where she met John Ya-Otto. Believing that he via Gerson Max was familiar with Carlsson's work in Namibia, she surprisingly found that he "altogether was very little informed about the trade union situation in the country".[2] When she gave him a summary in English of Carlsson's first report, the SWAPO Labour Secretary and NUNW General Secretary, however, became "enthusiastic, nay overjoyed. [...] [He] had apparently not believed that this was possible".[3]

In the meantime, the journey to southern Namibia was a success. Carlsson later reported that

> at every place we came to, in the compounds, locations and churches I informed [people] about trade unions. Normally it started with Max giving a short service and after that I spoke. To my surprise, it was easy to get [in] good contact with the people. I think [that] the reason was that most [of them] knew Max. He [...] served as my 'passport'.[4]

Judging from Carlsson's reports, he was not overly worried about the security police. In his first letter to LO/TCO, he wrote that "the situation is critical and unsettled"[5] and that Max "says that we have to be careful"[6], but nothing more. As early as in September 1978, the South African authorities had, however, given Pastor Max a warning, telling him that "they knew everything [that he] and the Swede were doing".[7] Undeterred, the two nevertheless organized the planned NUNW seminar at the end of September. Soon thereafter, on his own Carlsson made two more organizing trips, first to the mines in the western desert areas and then to northern Ovamboland. The Finnish missionary Anneli Hirvonen joined him in the north, where they established a first NUNW branch at Oniipa, mainly formed by construction workers at the local mission station.[8]

It was soon obvious that the warning received by Pastor Max was serious, and in early December 1978—after less than four months in Namibia—Carlsson was advised by him, Angula and Tjongarero to return to Sweden. By that time, NUNW had grown from a marginal and loose concept with 100-200 followers to the embryo of a national trade union movement with 800-1,000 members.[9] In his doctoral thesis on the Namibian trade union movement, Peltola notes:

> Branches and cells of NUNW had been established in many places. [Carlsson] had travelled the whole country and was very optimistic about the future of the project. No study circles had been established, however, and [the] production of study material[s] had not yet started.[10]

---

1. In Portuguese, *União Nacional dos Trabalhadores de Angola*, the MPLA-aligned trade union organization.
2. Letter from Kristina Persson to Elisabeth Michanek, Stockholm, 20 October 1978 (SDA).
3. Ibid.
4. Carlsson cited in Peltola op. cit., p. 193.
5. In September 1978—after Carlsson's arrival in Namibia—the UN Security Council adopted Resolution 435 under which the independence of Namibia was to be achieved through free elections under the supervision of the United Nations. In defiance of the resolution, South Africa proceeded to prepare for unilateral, internal elections to a so called Namibian 'constituent assembly'. The elections were held shortly after Carlsson's departure in December 1978.
6. Letter from Paul Carlsson to LO/TCO [no place or date, but Windhoek, 5 September 1978] (LMA).
7. Peltola op. cit., p. 194.
8. Ibid.
9. According to Peltola, NUNW had 134 members when Carlsson arrived in Namibia and more than 800 when he left in December 1978 (Peltola op. cit., pp. 192 and 194). In a report from August 1979, LO/TCO gave the figures of 200 and 1,000, respectively (Kristina Persson: 'Rapport: LO/TCO's projekt i södra Afrika'/'Report: The LO/TCO projects in Southern Africa', [Stockholm], 13 August 1979) (SDA).
10. Peltola op. cit., p. 194.

After Carlsson's departure, a number of meetings were held between LO/TCO and NUNW/SWAPO in exile. Concluding that the cooperation should continue[1], Carlsson remained as project leader in Sweden. During the first half of 1979, he was primarily busy with the production of basic, appropriate study materials based on the experiences gained in Namibia and intended for the planned study circle activities. They were regularly sent to Gerson Max for translation into local languages. After obtaining a new tourist visa, Carlsson finally returned to Namibia in August 1979. His main tasks were to recruit three to four organizers and hold seminars for study circle instructors.[2]

Back in Windhoek, Carlsson found that not much had been done during his absence. The texts sent from Sweden had not been translated[3], and although "Jason [Angula], [Gerson] Max and others [had] promised Palle when he left [in December 1978] that they would do their best to find the right people to employ for NUNW"[4], no progress had been made. Shortly after his departure in early December 1978, a major, largely spontaneous strike over salaries had, however, taken place at the Rössing uranium mine at Arandis. Two labour leaders in particular—the lawyer Arthur Pickering[5] and Henry Boonzaaier—had come to the forefront during the conflict. Detained for six months, both of them were out of prison and unemployed when Carlsson returned. He approached them and they agreed "to work full-time for the union to get it really started".[6] Their salaries were paid by LO/TCO. Noting that "if I had followed Max, we would still be on the same old spot"[7], Carlsson—who in a letter to LO/TCO acknowledged that he "worked rather undemocratically, but effectively"[8]—also proceeded to employ Philip Nembembe, a former migrant worker, and Angelina Haukongo, who had worked for SWAPO as a secretary.

Through the Catholic church, Carlsson acquired a house in Klein Windhoek—one of the white suburbs in the capital—where the LO/TCO-NUNW office was established. Thus formed, the project team resumed the work on education materials for the study circles. Strongly arguing that the group—as had been proposed in Ya-Otto's original proposal[9]—needed the services of an experienced Afrikaans-speaking South African trade unionist, Carlsson, finally, contacted FOSATU.[10] He later went to Durban together with Pickering to confer with the recently formed—and LO/TCO supported—South African trade union organization.

In the process, a rift emerged between the NUNW structure chaired by Gerson Max and the project group around Carlsson, Pickering and Boonzaaier. While Pastor Max advocated the formation of a general trade union and continued to emphasize the work among the migrant workers, the latter set out with the intention of estab-

1. LO/TCO did not request additional funds from CCHA. With its own contributions, the original allocation of 250,000 SEK was sufficient (Kristina Persson: 'Rapport: LO/TCO's projekt i södra Afrika'/'Report: The LO/TCO projects in Southern Africa', [Stockholm], 13 August 1979) (SDA).
2. Kristina Persson: Memorandum ('LO/TCO projekt i södra Afrika'/'LO/TCO projects in Southern Africa'), Stockholm, 27 March 1979 (SDA).
3. Letter from Paul Carlsson to LO/TCO [no place or date, but Windhoek, probably in September 1979] (LMA).
4. Letter from Kristina Persson to John Ya-Otto, Stockholm, 12 December 1978 (SDA).
5. Carlsson and Pickering had met during one of the seminars organized in late 1978 (see the interview with Pickering in Peltola op. cit., p. 187).
6. Ibid., p. 188.
7. Letter from Paul Carlsson to LO/TCO [no place or date, but Windhoek, probably in September 1979] (LMA).
8. Ibid.
9. The SWAPO/NUNW leadership in exile was sensitive about close relations with the South African trade union movement. FOSATU's emphasis on factory-level organization and independence vis-à-vis the political liberation movement was at odds with the views held by SWAPO/NUNW.
10. Federation of South African Trade Unions.

lishing industrial unions, with the workers on the Namibian mines as a first priority.[1] The rift was compounded by other issues. To Pickering, for example, the question of NUNW's independence vis-à-vis SWAPO was important, while Carlsson tried to exploit the fact that black trade unions were not forbidden by law. In what amounted to a declaration of intent by the team, he wrote to LO/TCO in Stockholm that

> we will not become a mass organization, but [...] a trade union with possibilities to be legally registered [and thus be able] to negotiate with [the employers]. In Lüderitz, there are two fishing unions, one for whites and one for coloureds. We believe that later it will be possible to affiliate them to NUNW.[2]

To discuss the diverging views with the SWAPO/NUNW leadership in exile, Carlsson—who maintained that "constant connection with SWAPO [...] was absolutely necessary"[3]—proposed a meeting with John Ya-Otto in Botswana. LO/TCO agreed to finance the encounter.[4] Before it was held, the security police, however, decided to move against the Swede. He was expelled from Namibia on 16 November 1979[5], exactly fifteen months after his first arrival in the country.[6] Arthur Pickering took over as project leader.[7]

In Carlsson's absence, the proposed meeting was held in Francistown, Botswana, in December 1979. It was attended by Pickering and Boonzaaier on behalf of NUNW inside Namibia, while Ya-Otto represented the SWAPO/NUNW leadership abroad. Jason Angula and Gerson Max did not participate. Nevertheless, "the Francistown meeting of trade union leaders inside and outside Namibia was actually the only one for almost a decade".[8] Little is known about the encounter, where the issues discussed ranged from SWAPO's decision to affiliate NUNW to WFTU; the relations between the liberation movement and the trade union organization; and whether NUNW should be a general union or built around industrial branches from the shop floor level. On several questions, Ya-Otto's views differed from those held by the internal trade unionists, according to Peltola bringing "into the open the almost total lack of experience of grass roots trade union work in Ya-Otto's office".[9]

---

1. NUNW's final breakthrough in Namibia in the mid-1980s occurred along the lines advocated by Carlsson, Pickering and the other members of the project group.
2. Letter from Paul Carlsson to LO/TCO [no place or date, but Windhoek, probably in September 1979] (LMA).
3. Cited in Peltola op. cit., p. 173.
4. Ibid., p. 142.
5. Kristina Persson: Memorandum ('Rapport: LO/TCO's projekt i södra Afrika verksamhetsåret 1979/80'/ 'Report: The LO/TCO projects in Southern Africa [during] the year 1979/80'), Stockholm, 20 August 1980 (SDA).
6. After his return to Sweden, Carlsson talked to "hundreds" of local trade unions and solidarity groups about Namibia and his experiences in the country (Telephone conversation with Paul Carlsson, Stockholm, 28 August 1999).
7. Pickering was far from unknown to the SWAPO leadership abroad. He had been the chairman of the SWAPO branch in Windhoek in the mid-1970s.
8. Peltola op. cit., p. 191.
9. Ibid. SWAPO's views on the role of the Namibian trade union movement should not have come as a surprise to LO/TCO. In the project proposal submitted by Ya-Otto in December 1977, he had written: "As long as the country is not yet liberated, the unions can serve as one of several means to achieve independence, at the same time as [the] workers' interests are protected. Once the Namibian people have gained freedom and democracy, [the] trade unions should [...] participate in the building [...] of a country which serves the interests of the people" (NUNW proposal cited in Kristina Persson: Memorandum ('Project for trade union education in Namibia'), Stockholm, 1 December 1977) (LMA).

The conclusions reached in Francistown were never implemented.[1] On their return to Namibia, Pickering and Boonzaaier were picked up by the security police. Gerson Max was also detained. At the same time, the police raided the house in Klein Windhoek. Documents, equipment and vehicles were confiscated and the office closed. Thus ended not only LO/TCO's first involvement with the trade union movement inside Namibia, but also the first serious attempt to build a Namibian national trade union organization.[2] How should LO/TCO's—and in particular 'Palle' Carlsson's—efforts be assessed? In his study on the Namibian trade union movement, Peltola concludes:

> The brave attempt [by] Paul Carlsson ended in failure. Everything was too open [and] the ringleaders too easy to catch. Things started to move too fast for [the] workers to follow. The Swedish project started as an educational effort, went on as an organizational effort and ended up in politics. [...] The tide of trade unionism was stemmed [...], but [...] only for six years. [...] The upsurge of trade unions beginning in 1986 was built on the previous struggles, each adding to the knowledge and to the skills, and building up the consciousness. Big and small actions had kept up the hope. Also the Swedish effort must have added to the morale, expectations and hopes of the workers who were involved. Nothing had been in vain.[3]

From Namibia to the Refugee Camps...

In spite of the detentions—and although SWAPO according to Gerson Max "was very angry with Paul [Carlsson] because we were in jail"[4]—neither Labour Secretary Ya-Otto nor LO/TCO abandoned the plans concerning an education project inside Namibia. In early June 1980, Ya-Otto contacted LO/TCO in Stockholm to inform them that he had identified a person who could replace Pickering as project leader. The LO/TCO Council of International Trade Union Cooperation reacted positively, inviting Ya-Otto and the candidate—John Akwenye—to Stockholm for further discussions. Nelago Kasuto, NUNW's auditor in Namibia, was also invited.

The Namibian delegation visited Stockholm from 13 to 18 June 1980. At the opening session, Ya-Otto stated that the LO/TCO-NUNW project in spite of the recent setbacks had been "very useful" and "of great importance both for the trade

---

1. It should be noted that John Ya-Otto in discussions with LO/TCO in Stockholm in June 1980 not only commented favourably on the Francistown meeting in general terms, but also said that it had been agreed to abandon the concept of a general organization in favour of the formation of industrial unions ([Name illegible]: 'Sammanfattning över diskussioner förda med John Ya-Otto, John Akwenye samt Nelago Kasuto från NUNW i Namibia vid deras besök i Stockholm den 13-18 juni 1980'/'Summary of discussions held with John Ya-Otto, John Akwenye and Nelago Kasuto from NUNW of Namibia during their visit to Stockholm 13-18 June 1980', LO/TCO, Stockholm, 19 June 1980) (LMA).
2. Angula, Boonzaaier, Max and Pickering would face very different fortunes. From 1978 until Namibia's independence in 1990, Jason Angula spent most of the time under house arrest or in prison, often in solitary confinement. After independence, he became SWAPO's regional representative in Swakopmund, taking up the position as first secretary at the Namibian embassy in Stockholm in June 1997. Henry Boonzaaier also spent most of the time in detention, but tragically as a victim of the SWAPO spy drama in Angola. Released by the South Africans in mid-1980, he left Namibia to join SWAPO in exile. Initially working at the SWAPO office in Luanda, he was subsequently taken to Lubango, where he spent no less than eight years as a SWAPO prisoner. He returned to Namibia after independence, joined DTA and opened a small business in the south. In 1987, the Lutheran pastor Gerson Max left Namibia for the United States, where he studied theology at Drew University. He successfully defended his doctoral thesis on the subject of the workers of Namibia in 1992. With assistance from LO/TCO, Arthur Pickering, finally, was given a WUS scholarship in 1980 to study at the university of Warwick, England. Returning to Namibia after independence, he was appointed Under-Secretary for Legal Affairs in the Ministry of Foreign Affairs.
3. Peltola op. cit., pp. 196-97. Bauer similarly notes: "[The] first efforts to organize a general trade union in Namibia did not survive long beyond the Botswana trip. [T]hey fell victim to the repression of the wider political struggle. But the idea of a NUNW and of a SWAPO-based trade union had been introduced and the groundwork for later efforts was laid" (Bauer op. cit., p. 56).
4. Max cited in Peltola op. cit., p. 179.

union and the political developments in the country".[1] Acknowledging the role played by Carlsson, the NUNW General Secretary noted that as a result of his efforts there were around 2,000 paid-up members in Namibia; that a NUNW structure had been formalized; and that organized trade union activities had begun. "Everybody", he concluded, "agrees that it would be wrong to give up now. The awareness among the workers [has] increased significantly over the past years and there [is] a great deal of enthusiasm for trade union studies".[2] The LO/TCO council shared Ya-Otto's opinion, and it was decided to employ Akwenye as project leader and Kasuto as instructor.[3] During their stay in Stockholm, Akwenye and Kasuto were also briefed by 'Palle' Carlsson.[4] On his way back to Namibia, Akwenye visited Kenya, where he was introduced by LO/TCO's Gunvor Fredriksson-Ngarambe to a trade union project using the study circle methodology.[5]

Akwenye returned to Namibia in July 1980. It soon became apparent, however, that the project was not being managed as it should. Activity and financial reports were not submitted as agreed.[6] Against this background, it was decided that Fredriksson-Ngarambe on LO/TCO's behalf should visit Namibia to assess the situation. The visit took place at the end of January 1981. During her stay in Windhoek, she found that Akwenye had been employed by a private company on a full-time basis and that he was in no position to function as project leader.[7] The activities had come to a standstill. After discussions with Nelago Kasuto and the young, white lawyer Anton Lubowski[8], Fredriksson-Ngarambe proposed that Kasuto should be appointed project leader and that Lubowski should act as an intermediary with regard to the transfer and distribution of funds from LO/TCO to NUNW.[9] It was also suggested that he should be responsible for financial follow-ups to the Swedish trade union council. While Ya-Otto was positive to the proposal, LO/TCO, however, decided to turn it down, arguing that "our experience tells us that [this] kind of [indirect] contact rarely renders any results".[10] Through this decision, the LO/TCO-NUNW project inside Namibia came to a final end in early 1981.

---

1. [Name illegible]: 'Sammanfattning över diskussioner förda med John Ya-Otto, John Akwenye samt Nelago Kasuto från NUNW i Namibia vid deras besök i Stockholm den 13-18 juni 1980' ('Summary of discussions held with John Ya-Otto, John Akwenye and Nelago Kasuto from NUNW of Namibia during their visit to Stockholm 13-18 June 1980'), LO/TCO, Stockholm, 19 June 1980 (LMA).
2. Ibid.
3. Ibid.
4. Ibid.
5. Kristina Persson: Memorandum ('Rapport: LO/TCO's projekt i södra Afrika verksamhetsåret 1979/80'/ 'Report: The LO/TCO projects in Southern Africa [during] the year 1979/80'), Stockholm, 20 August 1980 (SDA).
6. Letter ('Stöd till fackföreningsrörelsen i Namibia'/'Support to the trade union movement in Namibia') from Jan-Erik Norling, LO/TCO, to Tom Tscherning, Ministry for Foreign Affairs, Stockholm, 10 April 1981 (SDA).
7. Gunvor Ngarambe: 'Report from the Namibian trip 22 January 1981-5 February 1981', Nairobi, 10 February 1981 (LMA).
8. As far as can be ascertained, this was the first Swedish contact with Lubowski, then a young, recently graduated lawyer who had defended a number of SWAPO members in court. In 1979, Lubowski visited SWAPO in Zambia and Angola. He was thus not unknown to the SWAPO leadership—including Ya-Otto—in exile (Molly Lubowski and Marita van der Vyver: *Anton Lubowski: Paradox of a Man*, Queillerie Publishers, Strand, [no year], pp. 48-50). Lubowski joined SWAPO in 1984. In the late 1980s, he was closely involved with SWAPO projects supported by Sweden, including trade union activities. Lubowski was brutally murdered in Windhoek in September 1989.
9. As NUNW's bank account had been closed by the authorities, Lubowski proposed that his private account with the Bank of Lisbon in Cape Town, South Africa, be used as a channel. From there, transfers could be made to his account in Windhoek (Gunvor Ngarambe: 'Rapport från Namibia-resan'/'Report from the Namibia journey', [no place or date, but Nairobi in February 1981] (LMA).
10. Letter ('Stöd till fackföreningsrörelsen i Namibia'/'Support to the trade union movement in Namibia') from Jan-Erik Norling, LO/TCO, to Tom Tscherning, Ministry for Foreign Affairs, Stockholm, 10 April 1981 (SDA).

Nevertheless, the bilateral cooperation continued, albeit with new objectives and in a radically different environment. After a series of contacts, in June 1981 Ya-Otto wrote to LO/TCO, expressing the wish that "we will be able to discuss matters pertaining to the extension of assistance to NUNW activities abroad and in the refugee centres".[1] SAK from Finland—the Central Organization of Finnish Trade Unions—had since 1979 been actively involved in education projects among the Namibian refugees in SWAPO's Kwanza Sul settlement in Angola[2], but for LO/TCO this was a new and unfamiliar area. The idea was, however, accepted. Together with the SWAPO/NUNW leadership abroad, the Swedish trade union council thus went back to the drawing board to design a suitable project. The work was initiated in discussions with Ya-Otto and SWAPO's Deputy Secretary of Labour, Pejavi Muniaro, during the second half of 1981. With funds from SIDA[3], a first planning seminar with participants from the SWAPO centres in Angola and Zambia was led by Gunvor Ngarambe in Lusaka in December 1981.[4]

By that time, the interest in the Namibian trade union movement had grown considerably in Sweden. In December 1980, for example, the Brunnsvik folk high school in the province of Dalecarlia offered SWAPO two scholarships for the academic year 1981/82. One was for trade union education, while the other emphasized co-operative issues.[5] Fritz Spiegel—later Director of the Nduuvu Nangolo Trade Union Centre (NNTUC) in Kwanza Sul—studied there, and several leading SWAPO/NUNW representatives visited the school.[6] In addition, in early 1982 the Africa Groups invited a NUNW representative to an information tour around the country.[7] The highly successful visit took place in August-September 1982, when SWAPO's Deputy Labour Secretary Muniaro travelled for two weeks from Gothenburg on the west coast to Örnsköldsvik in the north. He held an impressive number of meetings with major national popular movements and with the local trade unions at several Swedish companies represented in South Africa, informing them about the situation in Namibia and demanding total sanctions against the apartheid regime.[8]

LO/TCO's support to NUNW in the Namibian refugee camps had, however, a sluggish start. After drawn out discussions, it was agreed in mid-1983 that Henry Blid—a teacher at the Brunnsvik folk high school with solid experience from vari-

---

1. Letter from John Ya-Otto to Gunvor Fredriksson-Ngarambe, Luanda, 10 June 1981 (LMA).
2. On SAK's cooperation with SWAPO/NUNW in Angola, see Peltola op. cit., pp. 133-66 and Soiri and Peltola op. cit., pp. 120-22.
3. In October 1981, CCHA recommended SIDA to allocate 200,000 SEK to LO/TCO for preparations of a trade union project among the Namibian refugees in Angola and Zambia (Elisabeth Michanek: Memorandum ('Tilläggsframställning från LO/TCO om bidrag för fackligt bistånd till södra Afrika'/'Additional request from LO/TCO regarding contributions for trade union assistance to Southern Africa'), CCHA/SIDA, Stockholm, [no date, but mid-1982]) (SDA).
4. [Gunvor Ngarambe]: 'NUNW-seminariet i Zambia 7-18 december 1981' ('The NUNW seminar in Zambia 7-18 December 1981'), [no place or date] (LMA). In 1982, Ngarambe led a second planning seminar in Dar es Salaam.
5. Letter from Henry Blid to Hadino Hishongwa, Ludvika, 23 December 1980 (SDA).
6. Henry Blid: 'Rapport för projekt 178, stöd till National Union of Namibian Workers, för tiden 24 oktober 1983-23 januari 1984' ('Report concerning project 178, support to the National Union of Namibian Workers, for the period 24 October 1983-23 January 1984'), Ludvika/Stockholm, 3 February 1984 (LMA).
7. Letter from Pejavi Muniaro to Gunvor Ngarambe, Luanda, 25 January 1982 (LMA).
8. Christer Peterson: 'National Union of Namibian Workers: Turné 30/8-12/9 1982 med Acting Secretary Pejavi Muniaro: Referat och utvärdering' ('National Union of Namibian Workers: Tour 30 August-12 September 1982 with Acting Secretary Pejavi Muniaro: Report and evaluation'), Stockholm, 6 October 1982 (AGA). During the tour, Muniaro held formal meetings with the Social Democratic Party, SSU, ABF, the LO/TCO Council of International Trade Union Cooperation, AGIS, ISAK and the national unions of the civil servants, the municipal employees, the metal workers, the transport workers and the dockworkers. In addition, Muniaro addressed the local trade unions at the Swedish companies Alfa Laval, Atlas Copco, Saab-Scania, Skega, SKF and Volvo. He also met members of parliament and the Swedish UN Association (ibid.).

ous assignments in Africa—should visit SWAPO in Angola to translate the findings of the earlier planning work into a concrete plan of action.[1] He stayed in Angola from late October 1983 until the end of January 1984, roughly dividing his time between the SWAPO headquarters in Luanda and the NNTUC school in Kwanza Sul. "In practice serving as [a] personal adviser" to Ya-Otto, Blid found their cooperation "extremely good".[2] Seeing Ya-Otto's "commitment to the cause of the workers and to the conditions of the 'grass roots' [as] evident", he, however, also concluded that "many leading [SWAPO representatives] do not know what trade union activities entail or what a trade union organization can achieve".[3] Considering the pros and cons of possible support to NUNW, he, nevertheless, recommended a bilateral effort by LO/TCO, not least to "counterbalance the one-sided education [given] by the Eastern countries".[4]

LO/TCO followed Blid's recommendation. A cooperation agreement between the Swedish confederations and NUNW was drafted with Ya-Otto in Stockholm in February 1984. Subsequently approved for the period 1 July 1984 to 30 June 1985, it envisaged

> assistance [by] a trade union education expert from LO/TCO [...]; support for trade union education and information for members and would-be members in the SWAPO centres and inside Namibia [...]; and support for the development of the organization of the Nduuvu Nangolo Trade Union Centre.[5]

On the basis of the agreement, the LO/TCO council successfully applied for a contribution from SIDA of 950,000 SEK.[6] Henry Blid was at the same time recruited as the LO/TCO expert to assist NUNW.

As during his first stay in Angola, Blid established close and trustful relations with Ya-Otto and his deputy Muniaro, later replaced by Reinhold Muremi.[7] For about half of the time, he was placed at SWAPO's headquarters in Luanda, where he worked from the same office as the NUNW General Secretary.[8] The LO/TCO-NUNW project in Angola was, however, far from a success. Working under difficult material conditions and constantly commuting between Luanda and the Kwanza Sul settlement[9], Blid achieved little during his twelve months in the country. Nevertheless, he did produce a guide for trade union education and also set up a course for union instructors. Towards the end of the course, four of the eight instructors were, however, in June 1985 suddenly ordered by the SWAPO com-

---

1. Gunvor Ngarambe had in the meantime started to work at the Swedish embassy in Luanda.
2. Henry Blid: 'Rapport för projekt 178, stöd till National Union of Namibian Workers, för tiden 24 oktober 1983-23 januari 1984' ('Report concerning project 178, support to the National Union of Namibian Workers, for the period 24 October 1983-23 January 1984'), Ludvika/Stockholm, 3 February 1984 (LMA).
3. Ibid.
4. Ibid.
5. 'Cooperation agreement' in Jan-Erik Norling: Memorandum to CCHA [no title], Stockholm, 27 April 1984 (SDA).
6. Jan-Erik Norling: Memorandum to CCHA [no title], Stockholm, 27 April 1984 (SDA) and SIDA: 'Decision', No. 265/84, SIDA, Stockholm, 26 June 1984 (SDA).
7. During Blid's assignment, Muniaro was replaced as SWAPO Deputy Secretary for Labour by Reinhold Muremi. While Muniaro's fate was unknown at the time, it later turned out that he was detained by SWAPO's security services and probably killed by them (Peltola op. cit., p. 154).
8. Henry Blid: Memorandum ('Samarbete med National Union of Namibian Workers i Angola m.m. 1984/85'/ 'Cooperation with NUNW in Angola etc. 1984/85'), Ludvika, 9 September 1985 (LMA).
9. Blid's wife and children stayed with him in Kwanza Sul. This was an exceptional arrangement as aid workers' families were not as a rule allowed to accompany them there.

mand in Kwanza Sul to "go to another camp, for some kind of education".[1] Blid had no previous information about their departure and registered in vain his protest with the SWAPO leadership in Luanda. To LO/TCO, the decision was "a serious breach of the agreement"[2] and contributed to the subsequent decision not to extend the cooperation.

The agreement between LO/TCO and NUNW also envisaged Swedish trade union assistance to "members and would-be members [...] inside Namibia". Not surprisingly, this part remained a dead letter. In his final report, Blid concluded that any activity directed towards Namibia must be based outside Angola, proposing Lusaka, Zambia, as a possible vantage point. The agreed assistance to the Nduuvu Nangolo Trade Union Centre was, finally, never carried out. Commenting upon the meagre results of LO/TCO's project with NUNW in Angola, Peltola later stated that Blid "did a lot of good work [by] helping people in their everyday problems. He also produced a booklet on study circles [...], [but] I do not know of any circles that were functioning after he left".[3] By that time, however, the revival in Namibia of the trade union movement had already begun. Via the South African National Union of Mineworkers and Stig Blomqvist, after almost a decade of support LO/TCO would be closely involved with the subsequent, final breakthrough of the National Union of Namibian Workers.

... and back to Namibia

As described by Bauer[4], the impetus to the upsurge of trade unionism inside Namibia in the mid-1980s was given by the churches and other community-based organizations, particularly in and around Windhoek, and the organizing work carried out by NUM of South Africa among the workers on the diamond fields in southern Namibia.[5] These two developments were brought together by a third—which from 1986 led to the formation of industrial unions—namely, the release of the Namibian political prisoners from Robben Island.[6] Among them were John

1. Henry Blid: Memorandum ('Samarbete med National Union of Namibian Workers i Angola m.m. 1984/85'/ 'Cooperation with NUNW in Angola etc. 1984/85'), Ludvika, 9 September 1985 (LMA). As the SWAPO spy drama (see below) "especially concerned NUNW" (Peltola op. cit., p. 155), it is possible that the four instructors were taken to Lubango and detained. In his report, Blid does not give the names of the instructors.
2. Henry Blid: Memorandum ('Samarbete med National Union of Namibian Workers i Angola m.m. 1984/85'/ 'Cooperation with NUNW in Angola etc. 1984/85'), Ludvika, 9 September 1985 (LMA).
3. Peltola op. cit., p. 149.
4. Bauer op. cit., pp. 72-95.
5. NUM later "signed over the membership" of the Namibian workers to the Mineworkers Union of Namibia (Interview with Stig Blomqvist, p. 269).
6. The release of the Namibian prisoners was largely an attempt by the South African government to relieve it of some of the international pressure and lend credibility to the internal 'transitional government' in whose name the action was taken. Andimba Toivo ya Toivo was the first to be allowed to go, after serving sixteen years of a twenty-year sentence. He was released on 1 March 1984 and taken to Windhoek. He soon joined SWAPO in Angola and in August 1984 was formally appointed Secretary General of the movement. Shortly after his arrival in Luanda, on 30 March 1984 ya Toivo accompanied Sam Nujoma to brief the Swedish ambassador on the situation in Namibia (Letter ('Samtal med Sam Nujoma och Herman Toivo ja Toivo'/ 'Conversation with Sam Nujoma and Herman Toivo ja Toivo') from Leif Sjöström, Swedish ambassador to Angola, to the Ministry for Foreign Affairs, Luanda, 4 April 1984) (MFA). Remarkably, ya Toivo and Nujoma had never met until they were united in Angola. According to Nujoma, the meeting with ambassador Sjöström at the end of March 1984 was their first formal appearance together as SWAPO leaders (ibid.). Invited to attend the Social Democratic Party congress, in September 1984 ya Toivo visited Sweden for the first time (Thus not in 1985, as later stated by him. Cf. the interview with Andimba Toivo ya Toivo, p. 99). He led the SWAPO delegation to the annual aid negotiations with Sweden in Luanda in May 1988 and in Windhoek in February 1990.

Finally meeting face to face: Prime
Minister Olof Palme and SWAPO
Secretary General Andimba Toivo ya
Toivo during the Social Democratic
Party congress, Stockholm,
September 1984
(Photo: Aftonbladet Bild)

Pandeni and Ben Ulenga[1], the latter released in November 1985. Ulenga, a former
PLAN combatant who—wounded and captured in action in the Tsumeb area—in
July 1977 had been sentenced to fifteen years imprisonment, was particularly
instrumental in the trade union work. Interviewed in 1995, he recalled:

> At the end of 1985, we were released. Especially among some of us who came from prison, it
> was of great concern that there should be greater organization among the working people.
> That is why we proceeded to persuade some colleagues on the political side to embark on a
> project to start workers' committees [...]. Initially, we did not contact anybody. We did not ask
> for assistance. Very soon [, however,] it came out that the work was being done and, of course,
> we linked up with the so-called leadership outside and also with the international trade union
> movement as far as we could. It did not take long before we were in contact with the trade
> union movement in Sweden, Norway and Finland.[2]

Peltola has noted that "the upsurge of trade unionism [in Namibia] took place
without the initiative or leading hand of SWAPO in exile, although it was fully
inspired by the liberation struggle and exclusively led by SWAPO activists".[3] In
spite of the close bilateral relations between Sweden and SWAPO, the renewed contacts with the Swedish trade union movement were established via South Africa. In
early December 1986—barely two weeks after the formation of the mineworkers
union—Anton Lubowski, National Treasurer of NUNW in Namibia[4], wrote to
LO/TCO, stating that "we have been advised by our colleagues in COSATU[5] and
NUM—with whom we [have] a very close relationship—to appeal to you for finan-

---

1. In September 1986, Pandeni became the General Secretary of the first formally constituted Namibian industrial union, the Namibian Food and Allied Union (NAFAU). The Mineworkers Union of Namibia (MUN)
   was formed two months later—in November 1986—with Ulenga as General Secretary. Two more unions
   were launched in 1987, namely, the Metal and Allied Namibian Workers Union (MANWU) in May and the
   Namibia Public Workers Union (NAPWU) in December.
2. Interview with Ben Ulenga, p. 100.
3. Peltola, op. cit., p. 207.
4. Although NUNW had not yet been formally (re)constituted, this is how Lubowski signed the letter to LO/
   TCO. At the time, the Namibian trade unions were coordinated within a Steering Committee, elected in April
   1986.
5. Congress of South African Trade Unions.

cial assistance".[1] Characterizing the emerging Namibian trade union movement's material situation as "desperate", Lubowski explained that

> we have a very high profile [...] and there [are] a lot of expectations from the workers. At this stage—[...] because we have practically only started and also [due to] the terrible situation the workers in this country find themselves in—we lack financial assistance of any sort. At the moment, we have no funds whatsoever and are for all intents and purposes standing still.[2]

Via Bengt Herrström, first secretary at the Swedish legation in Pretoria, LO/TCO had by then already extended an invitation to the emerging Namibian trade union movement.[3] In his double capacity as General Secretary of MUN and Organizing Secretary of NUNW, Ben Ulenga went to the Nordic countries in February 1987:

> Only about three or four months after the setting up of the first two unions of [...] NUNW, I went for a visit to [Sweden, Norway and Finland]. In Sweden, I was invited by LO/TCO. It was the first time that we established a direct relationship between the trade unions in Namibia—not from Luanda—and the trade unions in Sweden. That was in February 1987. We had very good meetings with the LO/TCO joint council that dealt with international cooperation. [...] What we agreed was, basically, that they were going to give us assistance for the organization of part of the unions and also for mobilization. Later, we got support from them for the setting up of our offices, projects like the Newsletter, organizing May Day celebrations, acquiring vehicles and so on.[4]

At about the same time, the fifth national congress of the South African National Union of Mineworkers—held in Johannesburg in February-March 1987—decided to assist their Namibian colleagues.[5] LO/TCO's Harare-based regional education officer Stig Blomqvist—who at an early stage had established particularly close relations with NUM's James Motlatsi and Cyril Ramaphosa—attended the congress. Through NUM, it was agreed that he should proceed from Johannesburg to Windhoek to discuss Swedish support to Namibia too.[6] Recalling the events in 1997, Blomqvist said that "there were two representatives of the Mineworkers Union of Namibia [at the congress]. We talked a lot and agreed that I should come over to discuss education activities. I went there, and when I arrived I was met by one of my oldest friends, Ben Ulenga".[7] For his part, Ulenga recalled in 1995 that

> I was [...] lucky to link up with a guy called Stig Blomqvist [...]. He was [...] very much down to earth. He understood what was happening. He was the best, as far as I am concerned. The

1. Letter from Anton Lubowski to LO/TCO, Windhoek, 5 December 1986 (LMA).
2. Ibid.
3. Ibid.
4. Interview with Ben Ulenga, p. 100. Towards the end of the 1980s, NUNW appeared as a major political force in Namibia, with concerns far beyond the strict trade union field. In a meeting between Lubowski—representing NUNW/Joint Union Committee—and LO/TCO's Urs Hauser in Stockholm in March 1988, Lubowski, for example, asked the Swedish trade union council for assistance to the private weekly opposition newspaper *The Namibian*, launched by the editor Gwen Lister in August 1985 (Urs Hauser: Memorandum ('Record of meeting on 22 March 1988 with Anton Lubowski, Joint Union Committee, Namibia'), [no place or date]) (LMA). While such a request was outside LO/TCO's mandate, at that time the Swedish government had already granted official funds to the newspaper. In May 1987, the Africa Groups requested 380,000 SEK in favour of *The Namibian*. The request was supported by CCHA and paid out by SIDA in September 1987 (CCHA: 'Ansökan från Afrikagrupperna om stöd till tidningen *The Namibian*' ('Application from the Africa Groups for support to the newspaper *The Namibian*'), SIDA, Stockholm, 3 September 1987). In the context of the historical relations between Sweden and Namibia, it could be noted that Mbatjiua Ngavirue was among *The Namibian*'s founding staff. In 1967, the then eleven-year old son of the SWANU leader Zedekia Ngavirue had in his father's absence addressed the traditional First of May rally in Stockholm (Sellström Volume I, p. 268).
5. [Stig Blomqvist]: 'Report of the MIF education officer's visit to South Africa and Namibia, 25 February-27 March 1987', [no place], June 1987 (LMA).
6. Cf. Motlatsi: "[W]e facilitated the meeting between Ben Ulenga and Stig Blomqvist" (Interview with James Motlatsi, p. 168).
7. Interview with Stig Blomqvist, p. 269.

President of the National Union of Mineworkers of South Africa, James Motlatsi, and the [future] General Secretary of ANC, Cyril Ramaphosa, worked with him. Actually, they worked out the whole support plan with Blomqvist. He did his own thing with the Swedes and pulled some strings here and there. [...] Blomqvist coordinated with the Swedish Mineworkers Union, LO/TCO and, of course, with the people in Brussels, that is, with [the Miners International Federation] and—although maybe not directly—with [ICFTU]. This cooperation continued until independence.[1]

After years of trials and tribulations, direct links were established between the Swedish and the Namibian workers. As in the case of South Africa, the relations between the mineworkers' unions were in this context particularly significant. In both South Africa and Namibia, the miners' militant actions contributed decisively to the final demise of the apartheid regime. And in both cases the Swedish Mineworkers Union[2] gave them considerable material and moral support, not least during the massive strikes that took place towards the end of the 1980s. When the workers at the important Namibian copper mine in Tsumeb went on strike in July 1987, their Swedish colleagues immediately launched a number of support and solidarity actions, ranging from interventions at the level of the British and American owners to collections for the workers' strike fund.[3] As noted by Ulenga,

> those were very interesting years. In the end, the chairman of the Swedish Mineworkers Union[4]—who at the time was also the President of the Miners International Federation—was thoroughly on the side of the Namibian Mineworkers Union. [...] [D]uring the strike we had in Tsumeb in [1987][5], [the Swedish miners] gave us some money to relieve the situation of the workers and we paid out quite a few thousand Rands to assist them. [...] The support was understood at the branch level of the union. Everybody knew. [...] If you got into the street, people were aware of the friendly relations, especially between Namibia and Sweden".[6]

---

1. Interview with Ben Ulenga, p. 100.
2. In Swedish, *Svenska Gruvindustriarbetareförbundet*.
3. Appeal ('Gruvarbetare i Namibia avskedas och vräks'/'Mineworkers in Namibia [are] dismissed and evicted') by Anders Stendalen, Swedish Mineworkers Union, Grängesberg, 19 August 1987 (OPA).
4. Anders Stendalen.
5. In the published interview it is said that the strike took place in 1978. It should be 1987.
6. Interview with Ben Ulenga, pp. 100-01. In 1989, Ulenga was elected to the Constituent Assembly and in early 1991 he was appointed Deputy Minister of Wildlife, Conservation and Tourism. A member of SWAPO's Central Committee, he later served as Namibia's high commissioner to the United Kingdom. In an unprecedented move, he resigned from his ambassadorial post in August 1998, largely in protest against President Nujoma's intention of standing for a third five-year term as head of state and against Namibia's military intervention in the conflict in the Democratic Republic of Congo. Leaving SWAPO, in March 1999 Ulenga launched a new Namibian political party, the Congress of Democrats (COD). In the third national elections in December 1999, he got 11 per cent of the votes for the presidency, far behind the 77 per cent accorded to Nujoma. At the same time, SWAPO won three quarters of the votes in the parliamentary elections, while one tenth of the Namibian electorate preferred Ulenga's COD.

The Shipanga Affair and Beyond:
Humanitarian Assistance and
Human Rights

Crisis and Detentions

In mid-September 1975, the Swedish embassy in Lusaka reported that "a tense climate" prevailed among the Namibians in Zambia.[1] The tensions were a prelude to a deep internal crisis, which in March-April 1976 culminated in an open revolt by PLAN fighters at bases in Zambia's Western Province. To quell the rebellion, the SWAPO leadership invoked the assistance of the Zambian army.[2] Up to two thousand dissident PLAN fighters[3] and eleven prominent SWAPO and SYL leaders—among them Andreas Shipanga, Solomon Mifima and Immanuel Engombe, all three members of SWAPO's National Executive Committee—were in late April 1976 rounded up and taken to the Zambian Mboroma[4] and Nam-

---

1. Cable ('SWAPO och Namibia') from Anders Bjurner to the Ministry for Foreign Affairs, Lusaka, 19 September 1975 (MFA).
2. As Sam Nujoma was not in Zambia, it was left to Vice-President Muyongo to suppress the rebellion. Interviewed in 1995, Muyongo stated: "I know the Shipanga issue very well, because I was then in charge of the SWAPO office in Lusaka. [...] [A] lot of my colleagues in SWAPO came to me and said: 'Just hand him over so that we can take him to the front', [meaning] that [he was] going to disappear. [...] I did not believe in that [and said]: '[W]hy do we not ask the Zambian authorities to keep him'. [...] I [later] personally asked the Zambian authorities to intervene with Nyerere, so that he could take [Shipanga] to Tanzania". In the same interview, the former SWAPO Vice-President added: "[W]hen we had that crisis, Sweden—or the Nordic countries—should have said: 'If this is the way you do your things, then you can forget about our assistance'. [...] I believe very strongly that [they] should have said: 'Listen, we are giving you aid for humanitarian purposes. If you start detaining each other, you can be sure that we cannot continue'. By so doing they would have driven some sense into some in the leadership of SWAPO" (Interview with Mishake Muyongo, p. 89). Closely involved in the detention of the SWAPO dissidents, Muyongo himself was, however, at the time both downplaying the issue and advocating increased Swedish assistance to SWAPO. In late August 1976, for example, he led the SWAPO delegation to the official aid negotiations with Sweden in Lusaka ('Agreed minutes of discussion[s] on cooperation between Sweden and South West Africa People's Organization (SWAPO)', Lusaka, 2 September 1976) (SDA). The Swedish delegation was headed by Anders Bjurner. There is no evidence in the agreed minutes that the SWAPO crisis or the detention of Shipanga—who two years previously had formed part of the SWAPO team to the negotiations—were discussed. On the contrary, the Swedish delegation "expressed [...] the solidarity of Sweden with SWAPO [in] its struggle, and [...] referred to statements by the Swedish Prime Minister and most recently by the Foreign Minister on [...] Namibia Day", i.e. 26 August 1976 (ibid.).
3. Quoting contemporary newspaper reports, Katjavivi states that "1,000 SWAPO fighters" were detained, "although SWAPO denied that there were this many" (Katjavivi op. cit., p. 107). Leys and Saul mention "some 1,600-1,800 combatants" (Leys and Saul op. cit., p. 49) and Dobell gives a figure of "between 1,600 and 2,000 dissident fighters" (Dobell op. cit., p. 49).
4. After the assassination of the ZANU Chairman Herbert Chitepo in March 1975, about a thousand ZANLA fighters and ZANU members had, similarly, been rounded up by the Zambian army and taken to the Mboroma camp outside Kabwe. They had just been released and transferred to Mozambique when the Namibians were brought there. When Shipanga, Mifima and the other SWAPO leaders were detained in April 1976, Josiah Tongogara and the two ZANU members charged with the murder of Chitepo were still imprisoned in Zambia. Tongogara was set free in October 1976. By that time, Shipanga had been transferred to Tanzania.

pundwe army camps.[1]

Detained at Nampundwe outside Lusaka, SWAPO's Secretary for Information Andreas Shipanga was later held responsible for the revolt.[2] While for several months the outside world was ignorant of the fate of the detainees at Mboroma[3], the case of Shipanga and his ten colleagues immediately attracted international attention. Together with Finland and Norway[4], Sweden was from the beginning closely involved in the ensuing Shipanga affair, which only ended with his release from prison in Tanzania in May 1978, more than two years later.

All the Southern African liberation movements supported by Sweden did at some moment or other experience internal strains, crises or—as in the case of SWAPO in 1975-76—open 'struggles within the struggle'.[5] Engaged in wars of national liberation and exposed to infiltration by enemy agents, human rights and democratic freedoms were often sacrificed for the sake of unity and purpose towards the principal goal of national independence. Official Swedish assistance was, however, extended on humanitarian, democratic grounds. To the extent that violation of human rights or undemocratic excesses became known to the Swedish government, they raised fundamental, principled questions with regard to the assistance.

As stated in the introduction to this study, in this connection the roles played by the Swedish government and the major non-governmental actors should be discussed.[6] How did they react to the internal struggles within the nationalist movements? By whom was the Swedish government informed? To what extent and how were such issues raised with the Southern African host countries? Were political

---

1. Several SWAPO followers were also expelled, declared *persona non grata* or forced to leave Zambia. This was in early June 1976 notably the case with the Namibian pastor Salatiel Ailonga and his Finnish missionary wife, and with the former SWAPO leader Hans Beukes and his Norwegian wife, who at the time was working for the official Norwegian aid agency NORAD. The Swedish embassy in Lusaka became involved in their situation (Letter ('Splittringen inom SWAPO: Andreas Shipanga'/'The split within SWAPO: Andreas Shipanga') from Ove Heyman, Swedish ambassador to Zambia, to the Ministry for Foreign Affairs, Lusaka, 14 June 1976) (MFA). Ailonga and Beukes would later forcefully take up the cause of the SWAPO detainees in Finland, Norway and internationally. In June 1977, Beukes was, for example, received by David Wirmark at the Ministry for Foreign Affairs in Stockholm, where he—unsuccessfully—appealed for a Swedish intervention in favour of the Mboroma detainees and the Shipanga group (Marika Fahlén: Memorandum ('Vädjan om frigivning av SWAPO-medlemmar i fängelse i Zambia och Tanzania'/'Appeal for release of SWAPO members imprisoned in Zambia and Tanzania'), Ministry for Foreign Affairs, Stockholm, 11 June 1977) (SDA). Interviewed in 1996 about Sweden and the Shipanga affair, Wirmark, however, stated that "I was not involved", adding that he did not know if Sweden had put any pressure on SWAPO or its host governments to have Shipanga tried in a court of law (Interview with David Wirmark, p. 350).
2. Due to the attention later given to Andreas Shipanga, the 1975-76 SWAPO crisis and the 1976 revolt are often termed the 'Shipanga crisis' and the 'Shipanga rebellion'. As noted by Leys and Saul, Shipanga, however, "remained a relatively minor player in the [...] drama", while three dissident groups were far more important, namely "soldiers who were in PLAN before the [1974-75] exodus [...], soldiers who came out in the exodus [...] and a group of SYL leaders who were also part of the exodus" (Leys and Saul op. cit., p. 47). As the 1976-78 case in the Zambian Supreme Court focused on Shipanga, it is, however, relevant to talk about a post-crisis 'Shipanga affair'.
3. In the substantial documentation on the SWAPO crisis and the Shipanga affair from the Swedish embassy in Lusaka, the detention of the PLAN fighters and SYL members at Mboroma is only referred to in passing. The first major article on the Mboroma detainees in Sweden appeared in the liberal newspaper *Dagens Nyheter* on 17 October 1976. Based on a letter smuggled out from the detention camp, it was written by a Namibian resident under the pseudonym of Pekka Owambo ('Gerilla fängslad i Zambia: Revolt mot SWAPO-ledare'/'Guerillas detained in Zambia: Revolt against SWAPO leaders').
4. On Finland and the Shipanga affair, see Soiri and Peltola op. cit., pp. 125-28. Norway's reactions are discussed by Eva Helene Østbye in 'The Namibian Liberation Struggle: Direct Norwegian Support to SWAPO' in Eriksen (ed.) op. cit., pp. 96-102.
5. The expression is by the Zimbabwean political scientist Masipula Sithole, who in 1979 published *Zimbabwe: Struggles-within-the-Struggle (1957-1980)*. Discussing the contradictions and conflicts within and among the Zimbabwean nationalist organizations until independence in 1980, a second edition of the study was published by Rujeko Publishers, Harare, in 1999.
6. Sellström Volume I, p. 23.

pressures or other conditions applied and, if so, in favour of which political forces and projects? Was the bilateral assistance suspended, continued or channelled to a particular faction? Were there any noticeable differences between the Social Democratic and non-socialist governments in this regard?

These questions have in a more general way been addressed with reference to FRELIMO of Mozambique, MPLA of Angola and ZANU and ZAPU of Zimbabwe. The Swedish reactions to the SWAPO crisis in 1975-76 and the Shipanga affair in 1976-78 are, however, better documented. In addition, with regard to the issue of liberation and democracy "Namibia, perhaps, provides the worst-case scenario".[1] Discussed by both Social Democratic and non-socialist governments and involving Zambia and Tanzania—two countries particularly close to Sweden—the Shipanga case may illustrate how Sweden positioned itself vis-à-vis divisions and human rights violations within the liberation movements that received official assistance. As such, it merits a more detailed presentation.

The text below does not discuss the origins and developments of the SWAPO crisis.[2] Suffice it to say that it arose in the wake of the massive 1974-75 exodus to Zambia and was mainly provoked by unsuccessful demands for a democratic congress—which according to SWAPO resolutions was due to be held before the end of 1975—and that Shipanga and his co-detainees supported the PLAN and SYL cadres who forcefully raised the issue. The congress debate came to the fore at a particularly turbulent and unsettled juncture, when Zambia embarked upon the 'détente exercise' with South Africa; the Turnhalle initiative was launched in Namibia; Zimbabwean nationalists were forced into an unpopular alliance; Kaunda's government turned against ZANU; and—above all—SWAPO's former and future allies UNITA and MPLA engaged in open warfare against each other.

The subsequent political accusation against Shipanga was that he in collusion with South Africa and West Germany[3] had "manipulated discontented SYL members [and] receptive PLAN cadres [...] to wreck the entire leadership", bring the armed struggle to an end and force SWAPO to join the Turnhalle exercise in Windhoek.[4] According to SWAPO's internal commission of inquiry, Shipanga—

---

1. Saul in Hyslop (ed.) op. cit., p. 168.
2. On the crisis, see Dobell op. cit., pp. 47-55; Siegfried Groth: *Namibia: The Wall of Silence*, Peter Hammer Verlag, Wuppertal, 1995, pp. 55-67; Colin Leys and John S. Saul: 'Liberation without Democracy?: The SWAPO Crisis of 1976' in *Journal of Southern African Studies*, No. 1, 1994, pp. 123-47; Leys and Saul op. cit., pp. 46-53; and Paul Trewhela: 'The Kissinger/Vorster/Kaunda Détente Genesis of the SWAPO 'Spy-Drama' in *Searchlight South Africa*, Parts I, No. 5, 1990, pp. 69-86 and Part II, No. 6, 1990, pp. 42-58. SWAPO's official version is contained in 'Report of the findings and recommendations of the John Ya-Otto Commission of Inquiry into circumstances which led to the revolt of SWAPO cadres between June 1974 and April 1976', [SWAPO, Lusaka], 4 June 1976, here referred to as the 'Ya-Otto Report'. Shipanga's account appears in his autobiography (Shipanga op. cit., pp. 109-47).
3. In the light of future developments, it could be noted that Shipanga *inter alia* was accused of meeting the West German Foreign Minister Hans Dieter Genscher during his official visit to Zambia in July 1975. A few years later, the SWAPO leadership established good relations with Genscher. Interviewed in 1995, Hadino Hishongwa, SWAPO's former Chief Representative to Scandinavia, West Germany and Austria (1977-83) stated: "Let me give credit to Herr Genscher [...]. He was really a good man. He was able to meet and discuss with me. First privately and later [...] we finally discussed officially. [...] He realized that the support to DTA and other elements was not to bear fruit. [...] We met in Bonn. It was then that [he] decided to give [SWAPO] some support, especially for students to study in Germany. I think that Genscher was really generous" (Interview with Hadino Hishongwa, p. 69). Sam Nujoma paid his first official visit to the Federal Republic of Germany in late October 1980, fourteen years after being received by the Swedish government (Letter ('Den namibiska befrielserörelsen SWAPO's ledare besöker Bonn'/'The leader of the Namibian liberation movement SWAPO visits Bonn') from John Wingstrand, Swedish minister to FRG, to the Ministry for Foreign Affairs, Bonn, 4 November 1980) (MFA).
4. SWAPO: 'Ya-Otto Report', pp. 4-11. Several SWAPO leaders who had—or soon would establish—close contacts with Sweden participated in the internal Ya-Otto commission of inquiry. In addition to John Ya-Otto himself, Libertine Amathila, Nahas Angula, Theo-Ben Gurirab and Kapuka Nauyala were on the commission.

Olof Palme with Andreas Shipanga (centre) and Sam Nujoma in Uppsala, August 1966 (Photo: The Uppland County Museum)

described as "a character of dubious personality and an opportunist"—was a "witting agent [...] of [an] international imperialist-South African conspiracy".[1]

To place the Swedish reactions to the Shipanga affair in their proper context, a brief summary of the main events in the ensuing drama should be made. It is in this context relevant to recall that Andreas Shipanga was far from unknown in Sweden. On the contrary, as SWAPO's representative in Léopoldville (now Kinshasa) he had as early as in 1963 established friendly relations with the Swedish ambassador, who the following year helped him and fellow Namibians to leave Congo when Moise Tshombe returned to power.[2] Later based in Cairo, Shipanga was in the mid-1960s instrumental in swaying the Swedish opinion from SWANU to SWAPO.[3] In Sam Nujoma's absence, he represented SWAPO at the first international conference on Namibia in Oxford, England, in March 1966, where he established contacts with Olof Palme, Pierre Schori[4] and other leading Social Democrats, as well as with Ola Ullsten and Per Ahlmark of the Liberal Party.[5] Together with Nujoma and Mifima, Shipanga also attended the Namibian student congress in Uppsala in August 1966, renewing his contacts with Palme.[6] Visiting Sweden on several occasions towards the end of the 1960s, he became close to a number of Swedish decision and opinion makers engaged in Southern African affairs, such as the future international secretary of the Social Democratic Party and UN Commissioner for Namibia, Bernt Carlsson, and the journalist Anders Johansson at the liberal daily *Dagens Nyheter*.

Last but not least, once official Swedish assistance to SWAPO began, Shipanga was actively involved in the design of the support. Elected Secretary for Information and Publicity at SWAPO's consultative Tanga congress in 1969-70[7], he attended the UN/OAU Oslo conference and participated—together with Solomon

1. Ibid., pp. 6 and 9.
2. See Sellström Volume I, p. 271 and the interview with Andreas Shipanga, p. 97.
3. In his memoirs, Shipanga notes that he enjoyed addressing student audiences, "especially in [the] Scandinavian countries, where they like their politics hot. It made me laugh when they challenged me: 'Hey, man, how can you call yourself a revolutionary when you wear a tie? Why don't you dress like an African revolutionary?'" (Shipanga op. cit., p. 95).
4. Shipanga later described Schori as an "old friend" (ibid., p. 145).
5. After the conference, Ahlmark wrote a profile of Shipanga for the liberal newspaper *Expressen* (Per Ahlmark: 'Om Afrika ingenting.../'On Africa nothing...' in *Expressen*, 29 March 1966).
6. See Sellström Volume I, pp. 280-81.
7. Formally, Shipanga was elected Acting Secretary.

Mifima, SWAPO's Labour Secretary—in the decisive talks on Swedish assistance in Stockholm in April 1973. More importantly, Shipanga was part of the core SWAPO delegations to the first two official aid negotiations with Sweden in Lusaka in 1973 and 1974.

Shipanga was detained in his Lusaka residence and taken to the Nampundwe camp on 21 April 1976. Held *incommunicado* and without any charges against him, his wife applied for a writ of *habeas corpus* on his behalf. This was the beginning of a long legal process with many bizarre twists and turns. The application was heard by the Lusaka High Court in mid-June. Appearing for the Zambian state, the Attorney General—at the same time Minister of Justice—Mainza Chona rejected it, arguing that Shipanga had not been detained, but placed under 'protective custody'. In Chona's opinion, there was, simply, no case of 'unlawful detention'. In addition, according to the presiding judge Shipanga was as a foreign freedom fighter not a resident under the Immigration and Deportation Act. He did therefore not enjoy normal constitutional rights and freedoms in Zambia.[1]

Shipanga's lawyer filed an appeal, set to be heard by the Zambian Supreme Court at the end of July. However, on 18 July 1976—just before the scheduled hearing—Shipanga and his ten co-detainees were taken from Nampundwe and flown to the Tanzanian capital Dar es Salaam in a Zambian air force transport carrier. In Tanzania—where the legal instrument of *habeas corpus* did not apply—they were first taken to the Ukonga prison in the capital and two weeks later sent to different places of detention in the country.[2] Shipanga and Mifima were transferred in early August to the Isanga prison in Dodoma, where they were to remain under harsh conditions for almost two years. Shipanga spent most of this time in solitary confinement.

By moving the Shipanga group to Tanzania, the Zambian government—and SWAPO[3]—hoped that the matter would be placed beyond the reach of the law. The former Zambian President Kenneth Kaunda later stated:

> It was a very difficult [decision] for us. Very difficult, indeed. We really tried as humanely as possible to maintain law and order and to do things as established by law. On the other hand, our commitment to the cause of independence and freedom of the peoples of Southern Africa was such that there were certain things that we had to do. For example, accepting to launch the armed struggle from [Zambia] was not easy at all. By the same token, it was not easy for me to defy a matter that was before the [courts] and give instructions to fly somebody who was going to appear in the [Supreme] Court of Zambia out of the country in our own plane. It was not easy at all. But when we weighed the two, it was quite clear where our duty lay. So I had to order that Shipanga and the others be taken to Tanzania.[4]

---

1. Cable ('Splittringen inom SWAPO'/'The split within SWAPO') from the Swedish embassy to the Ministry for Foreign Affairs, Lusaka, 21 June 1976 (MFA). See also Shipanga op. cit., pp. 123-25.
2. There was one woman—Ndeshi Uuyumba—in the group. She was taken to the Keko female prison in Dar es Salaam.
3. Other prominent SWAPO prisoners were at the time held in Tanzanian jails. This was notably the case with Leonard ('Castro') Phillemon, SWAPO's chief military commander from May 1967. Briefly detained by the South Africans in 1966, he had been 'played back' to SWAPO as an agent. In 1968, 'Castro' was accused of working for the Pretoria regime and handed over by SWAPO to the Tanzanian authorities. According to Tanzanian records, he was—without trial—imprisoned there in 1969 (Letter ('Freedom fighters who are detained') from the Tanzanian Ministry of Home Affairs to the UNHCR Branch Office in Dar es Salaam, Dar es Salaam, 25 January 1978, attached to letter ('Tanzania önskar frige fängslade nationalister, bl.a. Shipanga-gruppen'/'Tanzania wishes to release detained nationalists, *inter alia* the Shipanga group') from Per Lindström, Swedish embassy, to the Ministry for Foreign Affairs, Dar es Salaam, 31 January 1978) (MFA). After sixteen years, Phillemon was released in 1985. He subsequently settled in Norway (Katjavivi op. cit., pp. 61 and 136).
4. Interview with Kenneth Kaunda, p. 242. He added that "as far as I remember, we had no pressure at all from the Nordic countries" on Shipanga's behalf.

The Zambian Supreme Court, however, proceeded with the case. Arguing that "there is no principle of law [...] that enables a person to be taken into protective custody against his will"[1], in late September 1976 it ruled in Shipanga's favour, according him the right to have his case tried in a court of law. With the appellant imprisoned in another country, a new act in the drama began. While the Supreme Court ordered Shipanga's release and return to Zambia, both SWAPO and the Zambian government strongly opposed the verdict. The Supreme Court would over the following sixteen months on several occasions demand that Shipanga be brought back to the country. Contending that the request was "unjustifiable, unsound and [that it] would cause great misunderstandings between Zambia and Tanzania"[2], it was, however, left unattended by President Kaunda and his government. Convening on 6 January 1978, the court, finally, separated itself from the case, concluding that "there was nothing that could be done since all means had been exhausted".[3]

Although unbeknown to both SWAPO and the Shipanga group, at that time President Nyerere of Tanzania had indicated that he was ready to release the political prisoners and let them resettle in a third country. To SWAPO's great indignation, they were eventually released on 25 May 1978. While Shipanga himself was given political asylum in the United Kingdom and Mifima in Greece, five of the Namibians—among them the SYL President Pelao Nathanael Keshii—were received in Sweden.[4] The others settled in Finland, Norway and the United States.[5]

After grim experiences and—eventually—international exposure[6], the Mboromo detainees had by then also been set free. Given a choice of coming under the protection of UNHCR or returning to SWAPO for 'political rehabilitation', around 200 chose to leave the liberation movement. They were taken to the UNHCR refugee camp at Meheba in north-western Zambia, where they remained until 1989. The majority—between 1,200 and 1,300—opted for rehabilitation, which initially was carried out at Mboroma.[7] Most of the 'rehabilitees' were eventually moved to the SWAPO settlement at Nyango.[8] Others were transferred to Angola, "some [...]

---

1. Cited in Shipanga op. cit., p. 129.
2. Cited in *Times of Zambia*, 7 January 1978.
3. Ibid. and letter ('Shipanga-affären'/'The Shipanga affair') from Ove Heyman, Swedish ambassador to Zambia, to the Ministry for Foreign Affairs, Lusaka, 11 January 1978 (MFA).
4. The government of Tanzania availed itself of the opportunity to release other Southern African political prisoners. In addition to the five Namibians and their families, Sweden granted asylum to Eliphas Matsweru, a former member of ZANU of Zimbabwe held in Tanzania since 1972, and to Cecil Sondlo of PAC of South Africa, detained in 1976. Sondlo would subsequently appear as an assistant representative of the Pan Africanist Congress in Sweden, vociferously criticizing the assistance to ANC during the 1980s and in the early 1990s.
5. Some of the more prominent dissident leaders of the SWAPO Youth League were later quietly given political asylum in Norway and Sweden. Those who settled in Sweden were—unlike PAC's Sondlo—not particularly active and their presence did not assume political dimensions.
6. When several appeals for help to the Zambian government and the OAU Liberation Committee had failed, on 5 August 1976 the detainees at Mboroma organized what was called a 'march out of the concentration camp'. It ended in disaster. The Zambian army opened fire and three Namibians were killed. Twelve—including a pregnant woman and a baby—were severely wounded. Four of the injured later died in hospital. The shootings were four weeks later reported by the BBC (Groth op. cit., pp. 59-60).
7. Initially suppressing any news about the Mboroma detainees, in May 1977 the Zambian authorities surprisingly asked the Swedish embassy in Lusaka whether humanitarian assistance could be extended to the camp. According to Permanent Secretary Muyawala in the Zambian Ministry of Defence, to put pressure on the 'rehabilitees' SWAPO had deliberately not supplied them with sufficient food and other basic needs. They had therefore started to carry out raids in the areas surrounding the camp, becoming "a threat to the neighbouring population" (Letter ('SWAPO-dissidenter, flyktingar m.m.'/'SWAPO dissidents, refugees etc.') from Ove Heyman, Swedish ambassador to Zambia, to the Ministry for Foreign Affairs, Lusaka, 2 June 1977) (MFA).
8. Leys and Saul state that some 45 to 50 PLAN commanders "are widely believed to have been taken out of the camp [...] and killed" (Leys and Saul op. cit., pp. 49-50).

arriving in [K]assinga just before the May 1978 attack by the South Africans, in which many [...] are believed to have died".[1]

Sweden and the Shipanga Affair

Via the embassy in Lusaka and other contacts, the Swedish government could closely follow the build-up and outbreak of the crisis in the Namibian liberation movement. Anders Bjurner—who at the time was actively involved in the fate of the ZANU detainees accused of the Chitepo assassination[2]—had as early as in mid-September 1975 reported from Lusaka that tensions were mounting within SWAPO. In March 1976— after receiving copies of strongly worded SYL documents demanding a congress[3]—he expressed concerns regarding the unity of the movement.[4] His views were confirmed by the UN Commissioner for Namibia, Séan MacBride, who in mid-April 1976 approached the Swedish mission in New York.[5] According to MacBride—who "did not hide his critical attitude towards many in the SWAPO leadership, including Nujoma himself"—"a [...] gap was building up between the 'SWAPO establishment' and, in particular, the younger military cadres".[6] Stating that the US Central Intelligence Agency had "infiltrated" SWAPO and was fomenting the divisions, MacBride explained that the purpose of his communication was that the Swedish authorities "should be aware of the situation [...] to take preventive measures concerning future aid disbursements to SWAPO".[7]

While the details of the PLAN fighters' revolt in Zambia's Western Province in March-April 1976 remained unknown to the Lusaka embassy, the detention of the SWAPO and SYL leaders was immediately noted. Shipanga, in particular, had maintained close and regular contacts with the embassy. He was detained on 21 April 1976. The following week, the SWAPO Vice-President Muyongo informed the embassy that he "regrettably" had been forced to ask the Zambian authorities to take Shipanga, Mifima and the other nine leaders into protective custody, but that they were "at a farm in complete freedom".[8] Contacting the Swedish embassy in Dar es Salaam, two weeks later Hifikepunye Pohamba, SWAPO's representative to Tanzania, was more explicit. Largely expressing the views of the subsequent Ya-Otto commission, he explained that Shipanga had been in contact with both South Africa and West Germany and that he was behind the unrest provoked by the

---

1. Ibid., p. 50.
2. See the chapter 'ZANU and ZAPU of Zimbabwe: On Separate Trails'. Bjurner questioned Zambia's stand towards the Zimbabwean liberation movements in general and the crackdown on ZANU in particular.
3. At a consultative meeting held at the 'old farm' outside Lusaka, SYL had on 14 September 1975 "condemned the SWAPO [National] Executive [Committee's] failure to execute the will of the Namibian people". As the SWAPO leadership contrary to earlier decisions did not summon a congress before the end of 1975, the Youth League's opposition intensified. In January 1976, the SYL President Pelao Nathanael Keshii issued a declaration stating that "the Namibian people [...] demand [that] the present executive step down, so that they either re-mandate them or elect other people to the office" (Declaration signed on behalf of SYL by Pelao Nathanael Keshii, [Lusaka], 14 January 1976) (MFA).
4. Anders Bjurner: Memorandum ('Namibia'), Swedish embassy, Lusaka, 8 March 1976 (MFA).
5. According to MacBride, he only shared his concerns with the Finnish and Swedish UN representations.
6. Letter from Kaj Sundberg, Swedish UN representation, to the Ministry for Foreign Affairs, New York, 13 April 1976 (MFA).
7. Cited in ibid. During a visit to Lusaka the previous month, MacBride had in a meeting with Bjurner stated the opinion that the demands for a SWAPO congress were justified, but that a democratic assembly could result in a split of the movement. Against this background, he argued that a congress should not be held at that particular point in time (Anders Bjurner: Memorandum ('Namibia'), Swedish embassy, Lusaka, 8 March 1976) (MFA). Shipanga was not mentioned by MacBride in his meetings with the Swedish diplomats in Lusaka and New York in March-April 1976.
8. Letter ('Arrestering av SWAPO-ledare'/'Detention of SWAPO leaders') from Ove Heyman, Swedish ambassador to Zambia, to the Ministry for Foreign Affairs, Lusaka, 3 May 1976 (MFA).

PLAN and SYL dissidents. As if he knew MacBride's counsel to the Swedish UN mission in New York, Pohamba gave the assurance that "Shipanga's activities would not result in Swedish assistance falling into the wrong hands".[1]

The Swedish embassy in Lusaka reacted with incredulity to SWAPO's explanations of the crisis and the detention of the Shipanga group. In his comments to Muyongo's first contact, ambassador Heyman conveyed to the Ministry for Foreign Affairs in Stockholm that "our assessment is that there basically are good reasons for the critics' accusations".[2] One month later, he wrote that "the legal grounds [for] the detention may strongly be called into question".[3] And when in early June 1976 SWAPO President Sam Nujoma during a visit to the embassy stated that he had "irrefutable evidence that Shipanga was paid by South Africa to disrupt SWAPO's external wing", Heyman concluded that the situation within the liberation movement was "extremely unclear", adding that "one statement contradicts the other and it is impossible for us to establish which party is right".[4]

As Anders Bjurner in August 1976—when the Shipanga group had already been moved to Tanzania—commented that "[e]very sympathizer with SWAPO's struggle for a free Namibia appears to be faced with a dilemma"[5], the following month ambassador Heyman finally stated that

> from our perspective we are of the opinion that very strong arguments indicate that Shipanga is a 'political victim', [a] point of view which is shared by several well-informed commentators, including certain [people] within SWAPO (*inter alia* the representative to Sweden). We [therefore] also believe that Swedish attention [to his case] could further strengthen the demand for a fair trial.[6]

On 1 June 1976, Shipanga's defence counsel contacted the Swedish embassy in Lusaka to inquire whether Sweden could grant political asylum to Shipanga and his co-detainees.[7] While the bilateral assistance to SWAPO continued, the contact marked the beginning of two years of close attention to the Shipanga affair. The initial reaction by the Lusaka embassy was to wait and see. Confronted with contradictory explanations by, on the one hand, the SWAPO leadership and the Zambian government and, on the other, the dissident representatives, the embassy stressed "the SWAPO leadership's extreme sensitivity to external interference and to any expression of sympathy towards the Shipanga group", recommending the authorities in Stockholm not to take a premature decision.[8] Nevertheless, as the embassy received information that Shipanga might be brought before a SWAPO

---

1. Letter ('Arrestering av SWAPO-medlemmar'/'Detention of SWAPO members') from Knut Granstedt, Swedish ambassador to Tanzania, to the Ministry for Foreign Affairs, Dar es Salaam, 17 May 1976 (MFA).
2. Letter ('Arrestering av SWAPO-ledare'/'Detention of SWAPO leaders') from Ove Heyman to the Ministry for Foreign Affairs, Lusaka, 3 May 1976 (MFA).
3. Cable ('Om politisk asyl för SWAPO-arresterade'/'Re political asylum for SWAPO detainees') from Ove Heyman to the Ministry for Foreign Affairs, Lusaka, 2 June 1976 (MFA).
4. Letter ('Splittringen inom SWAPO'/'The split within SWAPO') from Ove Heyman to the Ministry for Foreign Affairs, Lusaka, 14 June 1976 (MFA).
5. Anders Bjurner: Memorandum ('Läget inom SWAPO'/'The situation within SWAPO'), Swedish embassy, Lusaka, 25 August 1976 (MFA).
6. Letter ('Rättegången mot SWAPO's f.d. 'informationsminister''/'The trial against SWAPO's former 'Minister of Information'') from Ove Heyman to the Ministry for Foreign Affairs, Lusaka, 24 September 1976 (MFA).
7. Cable ('Om politisk asyl för SWAPO-arresterade'/'Re political asylum for SWAPO detainees') from Ove Heyman to the Ministry for Foreign Affairs, Lusaka, 2 June 1976 (MFA). In October 1975, the Swedish embassy in Lusaka had been contacted by ZANU's defence counsel concerning assistance to Josiah Tongogara and his co-accused of the murder of Herbert Chitepo. Although the political circumstances were very different in the Tongogara and Shipanga cases, there were a number of parallels between the two. When it comes to the Swedish reactions, in both cases, for example, the government quietly approached Amnesty International and other human rights organizations.
8. Ibid.

military tribunal, it obtained authorization to grant him an entry visa to Sweden "in case his life should be in direct danger".[1]

Indeed, during a visit to Dar es Salaam President Nujoma later publicly announced that Shipanga and the members of his group would be facing the liberation movement's military tribunal and that they could be sentenced to death.[2] This, however, never happened. As noted, they were instead moved to Tanzania. Two days after their arrival, they managed to smuggle a letter to the Swedish embassy, dated 20 July and received by the embassy on 2 August 1976. Writing on behalf of his fellow prisoners, in the letter Jimmy Amupala appealed to the governments of Sweden and the other Nordic countries for political asylum. Noting that "we are [...] in jail with criminals and other outlaws [and that] the treatment we receive here is harder than in Zambia", Amupala stressed that

> since we are political offenders of neither Zambia nor Tanzania—not even of SWAPO—we are convinced that we are [the] victims of [a] gross injustice. And since the two governments seem to have taken [...] sides in our case, we expect no fair hearing while [being] here.[3]

The embassy in Dar es Salaam copied the letter to the other Nordic embassies and to the UNHCR representative in Tanzania, Dessalegn Chefeke.[4] However, the discussions with the latter did not lead very far. According to Per Lindström, first secretary at the Swedish embassy, Chefeke saw it as "unlikely that requests by him or any individual country would influence the decision taken by Tanzania". "The Frontline States", Chefeke explained,

> had taken a stand in favour of the SWAPO leadership in the present conflict. [...] The requirements of the [liberation] struggle often took precedence over other considerations. [...] It was [therefore] not improbable that the leaders of the [SWAPO] 'rebellion' would be executed, as SWAPO's President had announced.[5]

Nevertheless, the UNHCR representative promised to "cautiously" approach the Tanzanian authorities with a request to grant the Namibian detainees the necessary protection under the UN mandate. In the meantime, Per Lindström concluded that there was not much the embassy could do.[6]

The Shipanga affair was at about the same time overshadowed by important political developments and initiatives, which together strengthened the incumbent SWAPO leadership's position, not least in the Nordic countries. Despite the SWAPO crisis, Nujoma's organization could, in the first place, during the second half of 1976 register a significant increase in its following inside Namibia. Opposing the ethnic Turnhalle scheme, in August 1976 the Rehoboth Volksparty dis-

---

1. Letter ('Splittringen inom SWAPO: Andreas Shipanga'/'The split within SWAPO: Andreas Shipanga') from Ove Heyman to the Ministry for Foreign Affairs, Lusaka, 14 June 1976) (MFA).
2. Cable ('Om SWAPO'/'Re SWAPO') from Per Lindström, Swedish embassy, to the Ministry for Foreign Affairs, Dar es Salaam, 6 August 1976 (SDA).
3. Letter from Jimmy Amupala to the Swedish ambassador, Ukonga prison, Dar es Salaam, 20 July 1976, attached to letter ('Fängslade SWAPO-medlemmar i Tanzania vädjar om hjälp från Sverige'/'Detained SWAPO members in Tanzania appeal for assistance from Sweden') from Per Lindström, Swedish embassy, to the Ministry for Foreign Affairs, Dar es Salaam, 9 August 1976 (MFA).
4. Cable ('Re SWAPO-fångar'/'Re SWAPO prisoners') from Per Lindström, Swedish embassy, to the Ministry for Foreign Affairs, Dar es Salaam, 4 August 1976 (MFA).
5. Letter ('Fängslade SWAPO-medlemmar i Tanzania vädjar om hjälp från Sverige'/'Detained SWAPO members in Tanzania appeal for assistance from Sweden') from Per Lindström, Swedish embassy, to the Ministry for Foreign Affairs, Dar es Salaam, 9 August 1976 (MFA).
6. Ibid.

banded to join SWAPO.[1] Even more important was that four communities—inspired by Hendrik Witbooi and representing some 80 per cent of the Nama population in southern Namibia[2]—in October 1976 also decided to support SWAPO. Until then often accused of being a regional, Ovambo-based organization, SWAPO could thus convincingly claim to be a truly national liberation movement.[3]

Secondly—and largely in response to the recent crisis and to the demands for a congress—in July-August 1976 SWAPO organized an enlarged Central Committee meeting at Nampundwe outside Lusaka, that is, the farm where Andreas Shipanga and his co-detainees had initially been held. While the meeting closed the open SWAPO crisis, the shadow of those recently taken into detention would linger on. The meeting did not allow much room for criticism of the leadership[4]—which had been confirmed at a preceding congress of the internal SWAPO wing in Walvis Bay in late May 1976—but managed to redefine SWAPO's organization and adopt a new constitution and a political programme. Reflecting a marked turn towards socialist positions—and internationally towards the MPLA government in Angola[5] and the Soviet Union—in the political programme SWAPO "made for the first time a firm commitment to the establishment of a future classless society in Namibia"[6], pledging itself to

> unite all [the] Namibian people, particularly the working class, the peasantry and progressive intellectuals, into a vanguard party capable of safeguarding national independence and of building a classless, non-exploitative society based on the ideals and principles of scientific socialism.[7]

Thirdly, in mid-1976 the UN Commissioner for Namibia, Séan MacBride, announced his intention to resign. The ensuing search for a suitable successor deeply involved the Nordic countries, bringing the SWAPO leadership into direct diplomatic negotiations with, in particular, the Finnish and Swedish governments. While MacBride in July 1976 approached Martti Ahtisaari—then Finland's ambassador to Tanzania—as his personal choice[8], on behalf of SWAPO's National Executive Committee Vice-President Muyongo conveyed the following month the move-

---

1. The significance of the move by the Rehoboth Volksparty was reported to the Ministry for Foreign Affairs by the Swedish legation in Pretoria (Letter ('Ökad uppslutning kring SWAPO'/'Increased support for SWAPO') from Sven-Otto Allard, Swedish legation, to the Ministry for Foreign Affairs, Pretoria, 18 August 1976) (MFA).
2. Katjavivi op. cit., p. 99.
3. The claim was further strengthened in April 1977, when the Association for the Preservation of the Tjamuaha/Maharero Royal House also disbanded to join SWAPO. This brought a broad section of the Herero population into the nationalist movement.
4. In his extensive report on the Nampundwe meeting, Bjurner—who based himself on long and privileged discussions with many of the participants, among them Ben Amathila—drew the conclusion that "the absence of self-criticism by the leadership [was] almost complete and [that] several of the fundamental problems [...] remain unresolved. [...] SWAPO today is *not* 'united and strong'" (Anders Bjurner: Memorandum ('Läget inom SWAPO'/'The situation within SWAPO'), Swedish embassy, Lusaka, 25 August 1976) (MFA).
5. One of the questions discussed at Nampundwe was whether SWAPO's headquarters in exile should be moved from Lusaka to Luanda or not. According to Bjurner, a majority was in favour of such a move, but the leadership was against it. The compromise was to quietly transfer parts of SWAPO's central functions and structures to Angola, while the headquarters were officially to remain in Zambia (ibid.).
6. Katjavivi op. cit., p. 108.
7. SWAPO: *Political Programme*, cited in ibid., pp. 108-109. In spite of the strong ideological wording of the political programme, Sam Nujoma—who skillfully 'worked' both sides of the Cold War—was in the West often quick to convey a more moderate outlook. Visiting Sweden in February 1978, at a press conference in Stockholm the SWAPO President said: "Have I said that I am a socialist? It must be the press which puts words in my mouth. [In independent Namibia,] we will pursue an autonomous, progressive policy in the interest of the people. In that sense, we are socialists" ('SWAPO-chef förkastar Namibiaval'/'SWAPO chief rejects Namibian elections' in *Dagens Nyheter*, 21 February 1978).
8. Soiri and Peltola op. cit., p. 123.

ment's wish to propose a Swede for the post.[1] No suitable Swedish candidate was, however, identified.[2]

Although Norway later entered the race by proposing Tom Vraalsen—at the time chairman of the Fourth Committee of the UN General Assembly[3]—by September 1976 the issue had *de facto* been settled in Ahtisaari's favour. At the Nordic level, his candidacy gained support. After subsequent missions to Helsinki by Muyongo and MacBride, the Finnish government also "started to warm to the idea".[4] Ahtisaari was formally introduced by SWAPO to the African countries at the United Nations in mid-October 1976.[5] With strong backing from OAU and the Nordic countries, in December 1976 he was unanimously appointed UN Commissioner for Namibia by the General Assembly, taking over from Séan MacBride on 1 January 1977.

SWAPO's increased support inside Namibia, the unity maintained at the Nampundwe Central Committee meeting and the contacts with the Nordic governments concerning the Namibia Commissioner's post combined from mid-1976 to push the Shipanga issue into the background. When the Swedish Foreign Ministry in early September 1976 contacted the Nordic governments to establish how they had reacted to the SWAPO crisis and the detention of the Shipanga group, there was no indication that the official assistance to SWAPO was seriously affected. In the case of Finland—whose entire support was tied to a Namibian scholarship programme—the Foreign Ministry informed that it "in no way had intended to suspend the SWAPO assistance".[6] The Norwegian government—which had a more comprehensive assistance programme—reported that due to the SWAPO crisis it had initially withheld payments, but that it was of the opinion that the SWAPO leadership now was "in full control".[7] It therefore intended to honour the agreements made. Denmark, finally, did not extend any official, bilateral assistance to SWAPO. Furthermore, at the Danish Foreign Ministry "they did not seem to be aware that a split had taken place within the movement".[8]

In Sweden, the non-socialist coalition led by Thorbjörn Fälldin did not change the policy towards the Southern African liberation movements. The passive stance adopted by the Social Democratic government regarding the Shipanga case was also maintained. After renewed consultations between its political and legal departments, in mid-October 1976 the Foreign Ministry concluded that

> Sweden for the time being should not take any action in the Shipanga case. A Swedish intervention in this complicated issue—which also concerns the relations between Zambia and Tanzania—would be rather conspicuous. We must generally be very restrained in expressing our

1. Letter ('Svensk kandidat till Namibiakommissarie'/'Swedish candidate as Namibia Commissioner') from Anders Bjurner, Swedish embassy, to the Ministry for Foreign Affairs, Lusaka, 17 August 1976 (MFA). Among others, Per Lind—at the time Sweden's ambassador to Australia—was asked by the Foreign Ministry if he would agree to be a candidate. He, however, declined the offer.
2. The final discussions took place as the Social Democratic Party handed over the reins of government to Fälldin's non-socialist coalition.
3. Cable ('Namibia-kommissarien'/'The Namibia Commissioner') from Olof Rydbeck, Swedish UN representation, to the Ministry for Foreign Affairs, New York, 27 October 1976 (MFA).
4. Soiri and Peltola op. cit., p. 124.
5. Cable ('Namibia-kommissarien - Efterträdarfråga'/'The Namibia Commissioner - Question of successor') from Olof Rydbeck, Swedish UN representation, to the Ministry for Foreign Affairs, New York, 22 October 1976 (MFA).
6. [Olof] Poluha and [Ann] Wilkens: Memorandum ('De nordiska ländernas bistånd till SWAPO efter Shipanga-affären'/'The Nordic countries' assistance to SWAPO after the Shipanga affair'), Ministry for Foreign Affairs, Stockholm, 8 September 1976 (MFA).
7. Ibid.
8. Ibid.

opinion with regard to legal proceedings in other countries, particularly when there is no Swedish interest involved.[1]

Nevertheless, behind the scenes—and largely due to the insistence by Ove Heyman, the Swedish ambassador to Zambia—in early November 1976 the Foreign Ministry quietly contacted Amnesty International in London, in particular drawing its attention to the fact that Shipanga was held *incommunicado* and that his wife was not allowed to correspond with him.[2] Similar contacts were also taken with the Lutheran World Federation in Geneva.[3] While the Swedish solidarity movement remained silent on the Shipanga affair, various individual initiatives were at about the same time launched by people who were generally supportive of SWAPO, but reacted to the fact that the Namibians were detained without trial.[4] This was notably the case with Bishop Colin Winter, the former head of the Anglican church in Namibia[5], who via Tore Bergman at the Church of Sweden Mission in January 1977 submitted a request for Swedish intervention.[6] In Tanzania, Winter had discussed the case of the Namibian detainees with President Nyerere, who "was anxious to get them out of his hands", rhetorically asking whether they perhaps could be given asylum in Scandinavia.[7]

Nyerere, Wästberg and the Release of the Shipanga Group

Shortly thereafter, the Tanzanian President raised the matter directly with the Swedish government. During a visit to Tanzania by Ola Ullsten[8], the Liberal Minister for International Development Cooperation, in late February 1977 Nyerere spontaneously mentioned that he "on President Kaunda's personal request kept a number of SWAPO members in detention in Tanzania".[9] Although he noted that "if this is my contribution to the struggle, I will have to put up with it"[10], Nyerere was not happy with the situation, particularly as "fellows keep coming here asking about them".[11] Declaring that he was ready to raise the matter with the SWAPO

1. Letter ('SWAPO's f.d. 'informationsminister' Andreas Shipanga'/'SWAPO's former 'Information Minister' Andreas Shipanga') from Hans Danelius to Ove Heyman, Ministry for Foreign Affairs, Stockholm, 15 October 1976 (MFA).
2. Letter ('Shipanga') from Hans Danelius to Ove Heyman, Ministry for Foreign Affairs, Stockholm, 1 November 1976 (MFA). Martin Ennals, the Secretary General of Amnesty International, later personally went to Tanzania to intervene on behalf of the Shipanga group (Cable ('Re Shipanga-ärendet'/'Re the Shipanga case') from the Swedish embassy in Dar es Salaam to the Ministry for Foreign Affairs, Dar es Salaam, 23 February 1977) (MFA). Earlier in 1976, the Foreign Ministry had on the Lusaka embassy's insistence contacted Amnesty International concerning the trial of the ZANU leader Josiah Tongogara.
3. Jan Palmstierna: Memorandum ('Möte rörande SWAPO's f.d. 'informationsminister' Andreas Shipanga samt övriga tio i Tanzania fängslade SWAPO-medlemmar'/'Meeting concerning SWAPO's former 'Information Minister' Andreas Shipanga and the other ten SWAPO members detained in Tanzania'), Ministry for Foreign Affairs, Stockholm, 26 January 1977 (MFA). The Foreign Ministry contacted LWF on 6 December 1976.
4. At SIDA, Maria Nordenfelt was actively engaged in the Shipanga case.
5. Openly supporting the 1971-72 general strike in Namibia, Bishop Winter had in March 1972 been deported from the country.
6. Palmstierna op. cit., 26 January 1977.
7. Letter ('Samtal med biskop Winter 1977-01-24'/'Conversation with Bishop Winter on 24 January 1977') from Andreas Ekman, Swedish embassy, to the Ministry for Foreign Affairs, London, 24 January 1977 (MFA). While acknowledging the role played by Bishop Winter, in his memoirs Shipanga states: "Regrettably, Winter never risked his close relationship with SWAPO by speaking out publicly about our plight" (Shipanga op. cit., p. 140).
8. As deputy chairman of the March 1966 Oxford conference, Ullsten had established early relations with Shipanga and SWAPO.
9. Cable ('Re Shipanga-ärendet'/'Re the Shipanga case') from the Swedish embassy in Dar es Salaam to the Ministry for Foreign Affairs, Dar es Salaam, 23 February 1977 (MFA).
10. Ibid. In the cable, the sentence is in English.
11. Ibid. Sentence in English.

leadership, Nyerere added: "If you want them in Sweden, I'll be glad to send them".[1] Ullsten, however, made no commitments in that regard.[2] Proceeding to Zambia, a couple of days later he met Sam Nujoma. The Shipanga case was not mentioned during the discussions.[3]

In spite of President Nyerere's overtures, the Swedish government preferred to keep a low profile. With close relations also to Zambia and SWAPO, the official position was that Sweden would not "consider [...] receiving Shipanga unless all parties involved [are] in agreement".[4] This policy was endorsed by Foreign Minister Karin Söder in May 1977.[5] It would only be reluctantly abandoned in March 1978, when Tanzania unilaterally had decided to release the Namibian detainees.

The passive stance was confirmed on 21 March 1977, when two young SWAPO members—Sakarias Elago and Hizipo Shikondombolo (alias 'Moses Joseph')—appeared at the Swedish embassy in Dar es Salaam asking for political asylum in Sweden, "a country in which they had confidence".[6] During the open SWAPO crisis, Elago and Shikondombolo had been detained at the Mboroma camp in Zambia. On 11 March 1977, they managed to escape. Without any money or assistance, they walked and hitch-hiked the 2,000 kilometres to Dar es Salaam, where their first stop was at the Swedish embassy.[7] The embassy recommended them to contact the local UNHCR office, where they were informed that they had to report to the Tanzanian authorities. Aware of the fate of Shipanga and his co-detainees, they, however, did not dare to show themselves.[8] After a second unsuccessful visit to the Swedish embassy, they therefore decided to continue on foot, eventually reaching Nairobi, Kenya, where their information on the Mboroma camp in late April 1977—a year after the massive detentions—became world news.[9]

Until the end of 1977—a year dominated by the diplomatic initiative on Namibia launched in April by the Western Contact Group[10]—few developments took place regarding Sweden and the Shipanga case. In October, Solomon Mifima managed to smuggle out yet another distressed call for assistance[11], but no action was taken by the Swedish authorities. However, at about the same time Per

1. Ibid. Sentence in English.
2. Ibid.
3. Elisabeth Michanek: Memorandum ('Möte med SWAPO's president Sam Nujoma den 2 mars 1977'/'Meeting with the SWAPO President Sam Nujoma on 2 March 1977'), Swedish embassy, Lusaka, 7 March 1977 (MFA).
4. Cable ('Re Shipanga') from the Ministry for Foreign Affairs to the Swedish embassies in Dar es Salaam, London and Lusaka, Stockholm, 25 March 1977 (MFA).
5. Jan Palmstierna: Memorandum ('Föredragning inför utrikesministern rörande SWAPO's f.d. 'informations-minister' Andreas Shipanga samt övriga tio i Tanzania fängslade SWAPO-medlemmar'/'Presentation to the Foreign Minister of the case involving SWAPO's former 'Information Minister' Andreas Shipanga and the other ten SWAPO members detained in Tanzania'), Ministry for Foreign Affairs, Stockholm, 5 May 1977 (MFA).
6. Letter ('SWAPO-'avfällingar' söker asyl'/'SWAPO 'defectors' seek asylum') from Per Lindström, Swedish embassy, to the Ministry for Foreign Affairs, Dar es Salaam, 21 March 1977 (MFA).
7. Ibid.
8. Ibid.
9. 'Appeal for the release of over 1,000 Namibians in detention in Zambia and Tanzania', [Nairobi], 27 April 1977 (MFA).
10. The Contact Group was set up in early 1977 by the five Western members of the UN Security Council, that is, Canada, France, the Federal Republic of Germany, the United Kingdom and the United States. In April 1977, the group started discussions with South Africa, SWAPO and the Frontline States on the implementation of UN Security Council Resolution 385, adopted in January 1976.
11. In Mifima's letter—dated 29 August 1977—he emphasized that he and Shipanga were "living in a complete blackout, [with] no information, nothing. [...] We really feel [that] this is too much. Even prisoners of war have the right to receive presents and mail from their families and friends" (Letter from Solomon Mifima, [Isanga prison, Dodoma], 29 August 1977, obtained by Maria Nordenfelt, SIDA, and attached to an internal note ('SWAPO') by Jan af Sillén, Ministry for Foreign Affairs, Stockholm, 25 October 1977) (MFA).

Wästberg—co-founder of the Swedish section of Amnesty International and chief editor of the liberal newspaper *Dagens Nyheter*[1]—introduced the issue to the general public.[2] When Foreign Minister Karin Söder was on an official visit to Southern Africa, he published a highly critical editorial under the heading 'Blacks against blacks' in *Dagens Nyheter* on 20 October 1977. Censuring the Swedish government's passivity and the solidarity movement's silence, the veteran anti-apartheid activist forcefully stated:

> SWAPO is undeniably the dominant liberation movement in Namibia. It is recognized by the United Nations as the sole representative of the Namibian people. [...] Our crusade against apartheid's cruelties should [, however,] not cause us to keep silent when freedom fighters place themselves above human rights. The fear of altering delicate [political] balances and of playing into the hands of the enemy make many people refrain from criticism. But one should be ready to put up with criticism from a friend, without losing faith in him. [...]

> Sweden has for many years been SWAPO's friend, financially and morally supporting its struggle. Quiet diplomacy has been employed to release Shipanga and his sympathizers. It is said that the possibility of granting some of them political asylum in Sweden has been discussed, but [that it] has failed due to the SWAPO leadership's unwillingness to have competitors for power moving freely about. This fear of democratic discussion is ominous. Since discreet diplomacy has proved futile, there remains [no other option than] to give publicity to the case. [...]

> [Foreign Minister] Karin Söder will today in Zambia meet those who are responsible for this tragic and hidden drama. She should point out both the political risks and the injustices of keeping freedom fighters in detention camps out of fear for democratic elections. A movement which—with strong support from Sweden—fights the South African racist regime should not favour [the apartheid] propaganda by holding its own political prisoners. [...] Karin Söder may emphatically assert that if we—who have shown solidarity with the liberation movements and with the new black states—refrain from pointing out injustices, the enemies of black independence will greedily seize the opportunity.[3]

There is no indication that Wästberg's editorial had an effect on Söder's discussions in Southern Africa. It might, however, have influenced the Social Democratic opposition leader Olof Palme. Reporting on a recent mission to the region by the Socialist International—during which he had met both Sam Nujoma and Julius Nyerere—at a meeting organized by the Swedish Development Forum[4] and the Swedish parliament's foreign policy club, on 30 November 1977 he publicly expressed his "doubts regarding the imprisoned SWAPO members in Tanzania".[5] According to the Swedish ambassador in Dar es Salaam, Lennart Eckerberg, a second leading

---

1. During his period as chief editor of *Dagens Nyheter* from 1976 to 1982, Wästberg was not a member of the Consultative Committee on Humanitarian Assistance.

2. In a critical comment on the détente policy in Southern Africa, Wästberg had in June 1975 raised the question of Robert Mugabe's whereabouts and conditions in *Dagens Nyheter*.

3. Per Wästberg: 'Svarta mot svarta' ('Blacks against blacks') in *Dagens Nyheter*, 20 October 1977. The editorial was translated into English and published in *The Namibian Review* (No. 7, November 1977, pp. 5-6), a "journal of contemporary South West African affairs" edited by Kenneth Abrahams and issued in Stockholm.

4. In Swedish, *Föreningen för Utvecklingsfrågor* (FUF).

5. Marianne Sundh: Memorandum ('Olof Palme om södra Afrika'/'Olof Palme on Southern Africa'), SIDA, Stockholm, 12 December 1977 (SDA). At the same meeting—held at the Swedish parliament—Palme defended the Cuban presence in Angola. According to him, "it was a brilliant idea to [deploy] Cubans in Angola [as] they in a way return to their roots" (ibid.).

article by Wästberg could also have contributed to the subsequent decision by the Tanzanian government.[1] At any rate, it caused "great irritation".[2]

Published by *Dagens Nyheter*—the largest morning paper in the Nordic countries—on 9 January 1978 under the heading 'Tanzania's prisoners', Wästberg's second editorial primarily discussed the domestic situation in Tanzania, but also raised the issue of the Namibian detainees. Even more critical than the call of October 1977, it stated that

> Tanzania is a leading example in the Third World, the principal recipient of Swedish assistance and [a country which] continuously is given attention by our media. Its President, Julius Nyerere, is one of the most impressive statesmen of our time. [...] Against that background, we should be allowed to criticize Tanzania where the situation is not what it ought to be. About a thousand people are according to Amnesty imprisoned without trial. A majority [of them] are criminals who have not been sentenced. Several are Namibians [...], locked up at the request of the present leadership of the liberation movement SWAPO. [...]
>
> Human rights are ignored in a more brutal way in most developing countries. Considering the unique position that Tanzania occupies in the minds of the Swedish people, as well as the close contacts between our countries, it is, however, even more urgent not to forget those who have been kept imprisoned for years, under painful conditions and without being convicted of any crime. The political prisoners should no longer have to wait to have their cases tried.[3]

At the end of January 1978, the local UNHCR representative informed the Swedish embassy in Dar es Salaam that the Tanzanian government—if SWAPO so agreed— was prepared to release the Shipanga group, inquiring whether Sweden was willing to receive some of them.[4] A list of the detainees from Southern Africa that could be resettled in third countries had already been forwarded to the UNHCR headquarters in Geneva.[5] The Swedish government, however, steadfastly maintained its position. At a time when the international negotiations on Namibia's independence were at a crucial stage[6] and aware of the fact that SWAPO opposed the release of Shipanga and the other Namibians[7], the Foreign Ministry reacted by sending the following message to ambassador Eckerberg in Dar es Salaam:

> We are at present not prepared to state how we would react to a possible request from UNHCR concerning [acceptance] of Shipanga and/or some in his group. At this juncture, we do not [...] want to risk our possibilities to act vis-à-vis SWAPO [in order to] contribute to a peaceful solution of the Namibia question. We therefore wish rather that [you] play for time[8] with regard to a possible [acceptance]. If the Tanzanians or UNHCR raise the issue, you may perhaps answer something vague about forwarding it to Stockholm.[9]

---

1. Cable ('Frisläppande [av] SWAPO-medlemmar'/'Release of SWAPO members') from Lennart Eckerberg, Swedish ambassador to Tanzania, to the Ministry for Foreign Affairs, Dar es Salaam, 3 February 1978 (MFA). In the cable, Eckerberg wrote that "Wästberg's editorial [...] of 9 January may possibly have speeded up Nyerere's decision" (ibid.).
2. Ibid.
3. Per Wästberg: 'Tanzanias fångar' ('Tanzania's prisoners') in *Dagens Nyheter*, 9 January 1978.
4. Letter ('Tanzania önskar frige fängslade nationalister, bl.a. Shipanga-gruppen'/'Tanzania wishes to release detained nationalists, *inter alia* the Shipanga group') from Per Lindström, Swedish embassy, to the Ministry for Foreign Affairs, Dar es Salaam, 31 January 1978 (MFA).
5. Ibid.
6. In early February 1978, the Western Contact Group submitted its proposal for a settlement in accordance with UN Security Council Resolution 385. It was to be discussed by the Nordic countries and the Frontline States on 9 February 1978 (Cable ('Namibia') from the Swedish UN representation to the Ministry for Foreign Affairs, New York, 9 February 1978) (MFA).
7. These circumstances were, of course, equally—if not more—relevant to Tanzania.
8. In Swedish, *dra i långbänk*, an expression often used by Prime Minister Thorbjörn Fälldin.
9. Cable ('Polchefen om Shipanga-gruppen'/'The head of the political department re the Shipanga group') from the Ministry for Foreign Affairs to the Swedish embassy in Dar es Salaam, Stockholm, 7 February 1978 (MFA).

President Nyerere was, however, determined to release Shipanga and his co-detainees. In a meeting with Eckerberg immediately thereafter, he stated that in order to save SWAPO from possible "future embarrassment" he had decided to set some of the detainees free. He had communicated the decision to Sam Nujoma, who—according to Nyerere—initially had "become furious".[1] Eventually, however, the two leaders had agreed that

> if SWAPO convincingly could prove that certain detainees not merely were political dissidents, but really had collaborated with the enemy, Tanzania would then keep them and one day deliver them to the government of a free Namibia.[2]

Accepting the principle that enemy agents would not be released, Nyerere was thus waiting for the agreed evidence from Nujoma.[3]

Together with the internal SWAPO leaders Daniel Tjongarero and Hendrik Witbooi, Nujoma paid a visit to Stockholm from 19 to 21 February 1978. As noted above, during their stay they primarily discussed the international aspects of the Namibia question with Foreign Minister Karin Söder. The issue of the SWAPO detainees in Tanzania was not even included among the many questions prepared by the Foreign Ministry staff to be covered during the talks.[4] It was, similarly, not raised by the SWAPO delegation.[5] Less than two weeks later, the Foreign Ministry was, however, informed by the embassy in Dar es Salaam that five Namibians, one South African and one Zimbabwean had been granted asylum in Sweden and that they were imminently to be released.[6]

The news about the asylum in Sweden came as a total surprise. It subsequently turned out that the Swedish Immigration Board[7] without consulting the Ministry for Foreign Affairs on a direct appeal from UNHCR in Geneva had agreed to receive the seven detainees.[8] Tired of waiting for SWAPO's evidence of enemy collaboration, President Nyerere had in the meantime agreed to release the Shipanga group. The situation was extremely awkward for the Foreign Ministry, which reproached the Immigration Board[9] and issued instructions to the embassies in Dar es Salaam and Lusaka to contact Sam Nujoma. They should in particular emphasize that Andreas Shipanga was not part of the group accepted by the Swedish authorities.[10]

---

1. Cable ('SWAPO-fångarna i Tanzania'/'The SWAPO prisoners in Tanzania') from Lennart Eckerberg, Swedish ambassador to Tanzania, to the Ministry for Foreign Affairs, Dar es Salaam, 14 February 1978 (MFA).
2. Ibid.
3. Ibid.
4. Göran Hasselmark: Memorandum ('Samtalsunderlag vid besök av delegation från SWAPO under ledning av Sam Nujoma'/'Preparatory notes for discussions during [the] visit by [a] delegation from SWAPO led by Sam Nujoma'), Ministry for Foreign Affairs, Stockholm, 17 February 1978 (MFA).
5. Göran Hasselmark: Memorandum ('Samtal med SWAPO-delegation'/'Conversation with [a] SWAPO delegation'), Ministry for Foreign Affairs, Stockholm, 22 February 1978 (MFA).
6. Cable ('SWAPO-fångarna'/'The SWAPO prisoners') from Lennart Eckerberg, Swedish ambassador to Tanzania, to the Ministry for Foreign Affairs, Dar es Salaam, 3 March 1978 (MFA).
7. In Swedish, *Statens Invandrarverk* (SIV).
8. Jan af Sillén: Memorandum ('Shipanga-gruppen'/'The Shipanga group'), Ministry for Foreign Affairs, Stockholm, 3 March 1978 (MFA).
9. Ibid. Drawing a lesson from the experience, the head of the political department at the Ministry for Foreign Affairs concluded that "it is extremely urgent that the Director General [of SIV] [...] is kept informed of political aspects that may be of importance for the decisions by the board. That has evidently not been the situation in this case" (ibid.).
10. For example, cable from the Ministry for Foreign Affairs to the Swedish embassy in Lusaka, Stockholm, 3 March 1978 (MFA).

It was ambassador Heyman in Lusaka—himself from the beginning personally engaged in the Shipanga affair—who two weeks later eventually broke the news to the SWAPO President. According to Heyman, Nujoma's reaction was "generally negative", declaring that "friendly nations such as Sweden should not give shelter to spies [and] traitors for whom SWAPO was accountable to the Namibian people".[1] Without criticizing President Nyerere[2], he also turned against UNHCR, adding that "imperialist forces that wanted to split SWAPO and arrest the liberation struggle were [...] active within the United Nations system".[3]

Incomparably more dramatic developments would, however, soon take the edge off the Shipanga issue. On 4 May 1978, South Africa carried out combined air and ground attacks on SWAPO's settlement at Kassinga in southern Angola. SWAPO reacted by immediately withdrawing from the ongoing negotiations regarding Namibia's independence. Vice-President Muyongo was visiting Sweden at the time of the Kassinga massacre. SWAPO's humanitarian needs and the new diplomatic situation—not the impending release of the Namibian detainees—dominated his discussions with Foreign Minister Söder on 9 May.[4]

Largely as a result of the discussions, two days later the Swedish government decided to grant SWAPO an extraordinary allocation of 3 MSEK, of which half was intended for the victims of the South African attacks and half for the movement's work inside Namibia.[5] The following week, President Nujoma personally thanked the Swedish government for its prompt humanitarian assistance, which in his view was also of political significance as it demonstrated that Sweden "does not abandon SWAPO in this [difficult] situation".[6] In his report from the meeting with Nujoma, Anders Bjurner explicitly noted that "nothing was said about the Shipanga affair".[7] The issue was, similarly, not raised during the aid negotiations between Sweden and SWAPO in Lusaka on 24 May 1978, that is, the day before the release of the Shipanga group. On the contrary, the parties "expressed their satisfaction with the running and implementation of the [cooperation] programme". The Swedish delegation also announced that the Fälldin government had decided to increase the allocation to SWAPO from a total of 14.5 MSEK in 1977/78 to 20 million in 1978/79.[8]

---

1. Cable ('Om sammanträffande [med] Nujoma'/'Re meeting [with] Nujoma') from Ove Heyman, Swedish ambassador to Zambia, to the Ministry for Foreign Affairs, Lusaka, 21 March 1978 (MFA).

2. After the release of the Shipanga group, SWAPO, was, however, critical of President Nyerere. In a meeting with ambassador Kaj Falkman in Luanda, SWAPO's representative Aaron Mushimba said in early June 1978 that Tanzania had set the detainees free "without consulting SWAPO, as promised" (Cable ('Samtal 1978-06-07 med Mushimba, SWAPO'/'Conversation with Mushimba, SWAPO, on 7 June 1978') from Kaj Falkman, Swedish ambassador to Angola, to the Ministry for Foreign Affairs, Luanda, 8 June 1978) (MFA).

3. Cable ('Om sammanträffande [med] Nujoma'/'Re meeting [with] Nujoma') from Ove Heyman, Swedish ambassador to Zambia, to the Ministry for Foreign Affairs, Lusaka, 21 March 1978 (MFA).

4. Göran Hasselmark: Memorandum ('SWAPO-delegation besöker utrikesministern'/'SWAPO delegation pays a visit to the Foreign Minister'), Ministry for Foreign Affairs, Stockholm, 16 May 1978 (MFA).

5. Cable ('Extra stöd till SWAPO'/'Additional support to SWAPO') from the Ministry for Foreign Affairs to the Swedish embassy in Luanda, Stockholm, 11 May 1978 (MFA).

6. Cable ('Samtal om Namibia'/'Conversation about Namibia') from Anders Bjurner, Swedish embassy, to the Ministry for Foreign Affairs, Luanda, 18 May 1978 (MFA).

7. Ibid. Bjurner had in late 1976 been transferred from Lusaka to Luanda, where he held the position of first secretary.

8. 'Agreed minutes of discussions on the cooperation between the South West Africa People's Organization (SWAPO) and Sweden 1978/79', signed in Lusaka on 31 May 1978 (SDA). The SWAPO delegation was led by Mishake Muyongo and the Swedish team by Ove Heyman.

Founding of SWAPO-Democrats

Andreas Shipanga, Solomon Mifima and the other detainees were released by Tanzania on 25 May 1978, ironically the anniversary of the founding of the Organization of African Unity and the date designated as Africa Liberation Day. Boarding a regular SAS plane, they left Dar es Salaam the same day, travelling via Athens, Greece—where Mifima disembarked—to Copenhagen, Denmark. While Shipanga continued to London, those who had been granted asylum in Sweden proceeded to Stockholm.

If SWAPO had feared that the presence in Sweden of some of the dissidents would undermine its dominant position in the country, the following developments convincingly demonstrated that this was not to be the case. Certainly, in his first comments Shipanga stated that it was "thanks to Sweden" that he and his colleagues had been released[1], but this was hardly a correct interpretation of the events. It is true, however, that a group of Namibians resident in Sweden had carried out a campaign around the publication *The Namibian Review*[2] for the release of Shipanga and the other detainees[3], and—above all—that it was with this group

---

1. Peter Bratt: 'SWAPOs grundare fri - Sveriges förtjänst' ('SWAPO's founder free - Thanks to Sweden') in *Dagens Nyheter*, 26 May 1978. Interviewed by Bratt while in transit in Copenhagen, Shipanga stated that he owed his freedom to "the Swedish and other Nordic governments". He also emphasized the role played by Swedish non-governmental organizations and the press, in particular *Dagens Nyheter*, where the articles by Anders Johansson in his view had been of great importance (ibid.). Shipanga and Johansson had established a close working relationship in the late 1960s. In fact, in an interview in 1996 Johansson stated that his early writings on Namibia led Shipanga to propose that he "could be 'SWAPO's man in Sweden'" (Interview with Anders Johansson, p. 298).
2. The first issue of *The Namibian Review* appeared in November 1976, setting out with the intention of establishing "the broadest possible united front against foreign domination" in Namibia (*The Namibian Review*, No. 1, November 1976, p. 3). The editorial board consisted of both former SWAPO members, such as the editor Kenneth Abrahams and the treasurer Paul Helmuth, and active SWANU politicians, among them the assistant editor Godfrey Gaoseb and the secretary Moses Katjiuongua, who all resided in Sweden. Kenneth Abrahams and his wife Ottilie (assistant secretary) were the prime movers of the Namibian Review Group—also calling itself the Swedish-Namibian Association—which soon pursued a vehemently anti-SWAPO line. Abrahams and Shipanga had been very close since the late 1950s. As members of SWAPO, they were in 1961, for example, among the founders of the secret Yu Chi Chan Club in Cape Town, South Africa (see Sellström Volume I, p. 172). In 1963, they fled together from Namibia to Bechuanaland (now Botswana), where they were kidnapped by the South African police. Released after intervention by the British, Abrahams subsequently travelled to Dar es Salaam, where he and his wife were appointed members of SWAPO's Central Committee. Shipanga became at about the same time the movement's representative in Congo. Actively working for a united South West African National Liberation Front (SWANLIF), the Abrahams were, however, soon suspended from SWAPO (see the interview with Ottile Abrahams, p. 59). Later granted asylum in Sweden, the couple settled in Stockholm, where Kenneth finished his medical studies and Ottilie took a masters degree in literature. They returned to Namibia as leaders of SWAPO-D in August 1978, continuing to publish *The Namibian Review* from Windhoek. However, in early 1980 they broke with Shipanga, joining the Namibia Independence Party (NIP). Paul Helmuth formed part of the group of Namibian nationalists which was active in Cape Town at the end of the 1950s. He had in 1967 been appointed SWAPO representative in Sweden, but fell out with the movement at the Tanga consultative congress in 1969-70. Joining the marginal South West Africa National United Front (SWANUF), Helmuth was also granted asylum in Sweden, where he worked as a civil servant. Returning permanently to Namibia in 1979, he was active within the National Democratic Party (NDP). Moses Katjiuongua settled in Sweden in the mid-1960s, completing his education while at the same time being involved in political work for SWANU, where he served on the External Council. Returning to Namibia in 1982, he became President of SWANU. Chairman of the electoral alliance the National Patriotic Front of Namibia (NPF), Katjiuongua was in 1989 elected to the Constituent Assembly. Godfrey Gaoseb, finally, later left SWANU for SWAPO. At Namibia's independence in 1990, he was appointed Permanent Secretary in the Ministry of Finance.
3. See, for example, Ottilie Abrahams: 'In Defence of Andreas Shipanga' in *The Namibian Review*, No. 7, November 1977, pp. 6-7.

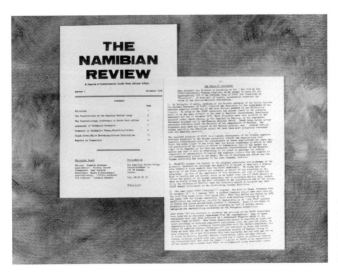

The first issue of
The Namibian Review
issued in Spånga outside
Stockholm in November
1976 and 'The SWAPO (D)
Manifesto' of May 1978

that he on 10 June 1978 founded the opposition SWAPO-Democrats (SWAPO-D) in Spånga outside Stockholm.[1]

SWAPO-D was launched without encouragement or support from the Swedish government or any other Swedish organization.[2] After the release of the detainees, Anders Mellbourn[3] at the liberal newspaper *Dagens Nyheter*, which had defended their cause during the imprisonment without trial, wrote in an editorial comment that "it is regrettable that the SWAPO leadership—as is unfortunately the case with so many other movements in a similar situation—has not managed to solve its internal problems in an acceptable way. However, at the critical juncture where [the] Namibia [question] is today, it is necessary that SWAPO is given continued

1. SWAPO-Democrats was founded in Spånga outside Stockholm—where the Abrahams lived—on 10 June 1978 (and not on 23 June as stated by Katjavivi; cf. Katjavivi op. cit., p. 108). Contrary to commonly held beliefs, the new party was not the brainchild of Andreas Shipanga. On 1 May 1978—that is, when Shipanga was still in prison in Tanzania—*The Namibian Review* released a 'SWAPO (D) Manifesto', calling for the formation of "a distinct faction so that efforts directed at rescuing SWAPO from the incompetent and megalomaniac Nujoma leadership may be better coordinated" ('The SWAPO (D) Manifesto' in *The Namibian Review*, No. 11, May 1978, p. 2). Drafted by a SWAPO (Democratic) Working Committee—which claimed to speak for "the approximately 20 per cent of the external wing of SWAPO now classified as 'dissident'" (ibid., p. 1)—the manifesto formed the basis for the discussions with Shipanga in Stockholm in June 1978. In a special edition of *The Namibian Review*, Kenneth Abrahams wrote in June 1978 that the release of the Namibian detainees "has not only given this SWAPO (D) movement a shot in the arm, but has also enabled the SWAPO (D) Working Committee to transform itself into the SWAPO (Democrats), a group with its own constitution, programme and policy" (Kenneth Abrahams: 'The Formation of the SWAPO (Democrats)' in *The Namibian Review*, No. 12, June 1978, p. 1).

2. As earlier noted, when Shipanga was asked in 1995 whether he had any support in Sweden, he emphatically responded: "No, none at all" (Interview with Andreas Shipanga, p. 98). Ottilie Abrahams similarly asserted that SWAPO-D did not enjoy any support from political organizations, the church or the youth movement in Sweden (Interview with Ottilie Abrahams, p. 61). In fact, the Swedish authorities tried to thwart Shipanga's visit to Stockholm. Having granted the Namibian Review Group/the Swedish-Namibian Association permission to use SIDA's premises for a public meeting with Shipanga on 7 June 1978, the authorization was—allegedly after representations by the resident SWAPO representative Hadino Hishongwa and after consultations with the Ministry for Foreign Affairs—withdrawn the very same day as the meeting was to take place. Concluding that "it seems obvious that SIDA is not interested in promoting friendship between Namibians and Swedes" and that the aid agency "takes instructions from SWAPO", the Namibian Review Group/the Swedish-Namibian Association—unsuccessfully—referred the matter to the Swedish Ombudsman ('Why Does SIDA Want to Stifle Shipanga?' in *The Namibian Review*, No. 12, June 1978, p. 8).

3. Mellbourn became chief editor of *Dagens Nyheter* in 1995.

strong support".[1] After the launch of SWAPO-D, Mellbourn further commented: "It is sad to see how [...] Shipanga [...] is unable to contain his bitterness, [...] embarking upon a competing political activity. That can only be a source of joy to the racist regime in South Africa".[2] Finally, in his memoirs Shipanga himself later noted:

> Soon after I arrived in London, I began to make plans to go to Sweden for the purpose of founding the SWAPO-Democrats. [...] [Mifima] and I had been founder members of the original party and we considered ourselves to be the true guardians of its principles and ideals. [...] I had formed strong links with the Swedes during my days in the SWAPO leadership, but now they seemed to find me an embarrassment. They were determined to stay loyal to SWAPO at all costs. I [even] found it hard to get a visa to visit the country [...]. However, we were not deterred [and] our new party was founded in June 1978 in Sweden.[3]

Above all, after rejecting the armed struggle the newly elected President of SWAPO-D returned to Namibia as early as in August 1978, only three months after his release.[4] To prepare the terrain, Kenneth and Ottilie Abrahams—respectively Secretary for Information and Finance and General Secretary of the new party—had gone there a couple of weeks earlier, immediately holding a meeting with Justice Marthinus Steyn, the South African Administrator General. Not surprisingly, their claim to represent SWAPO's true ideals and their talks with the representative of the apartheid regime provoked a vehement reaction. In a press release issued on 4 August 1978, SWAPO's internal Secretary for Information and Publicity, Mokganedi Thlabanello, noted that "hardly 72 hours after 15 years in exile [...] this Swedish couple [...] has the audacity to claim that their dissident group has tremendous potential in Namibia as many SWAPO supporters are SWAPO[-D]emocrats at heart and particularly the youth is going to follow them".[5]

---

1. Anders Mellbourn: 'SWAPO-medlemmarna' ('The SWAPO members') in *Dagens Nyheter*, 27 May 1978.
2. Anders Mellbourn: 'Namibia förhandlar' ('Namibia negotiates') in *Dagens Nyheter*, 19 June 1978.
3. Shipanga op. cit., p. 145.
4. In his memoirs, Shipanga notes that Canon John Collins, the Director of the International Defence and Aid Fund in London, gave him 3,000 Pounds Sterling to help him settle in Namibia (Shipanga op. cit., p. 146).
5. SWAPO: 'Stockholm-based masquerades exposed', Department of Information and Publicity, Lusaka [no date] (NAI). The leadership of SWAPO-D had highly unrealistic expectations. In a remarkable editorial comment to the formation of SWAPO-D, Kenneth Abrahams, for example, wrote in June 1978 that it was "bound to radically alter the [...] alignment of forces in Namibia. SWAPO has been effectively split into SWAPO (D) and SWAPO (Nujoma). [...] SWAPO (Nujoma) is really totally irrelevant to a reasonable and acceptable solution to the Namibian independence problem. [...] [T]his is not so much a matter of international support for SWAPO (Nujoma) as an instance where international diplomacy has tied itself in a knot over the Namibian issue, a knot which cannot be untied by diplomatic means while they have to deal with a nut like Sam Nujoma, who doesn't understand the rules of the game and whose lust for total power is greater than his feeling for 'real-politik'. [...] Rather a bilateral arrangement between the people of Namibia and South Africa than the present ridiculous set-up in which no one can move while Nujoma ponders!" (Kenneth Abrahams: 'The Formation of the SWAPO (Democrats)' in *The Namibian Review*, No. 12, June 1978, p. 7). Looking back, SWAPO-D's first Secretary General Ottilie Abrahams, however, noted in 1995 that "the formation of SWAPO-D was a mistake. [...] The problem was that [...] we were totally out of touch with the sentiments of the people of Namibia. [...] [W]hen we arrived in Namibia, we discovered that people were totally opposed to the formation of anything new [and that they] regarded SWAPO, for good reasons, as the liberating organization. There was no fertile ground for anything else. [...] As my husband said one day: 'We should actually have shut up and got onto the band-wagon'. But there are certain things you just cannot do. [...] The feeling behind [the formation of SWAPO-D] was not a mistake" (Interview with Ottilie Abrahams, pp. 61-62).

This was, however, not to be the case. SWAPO-D was from the outset marginalized in Namibia.[1] After parting company with the Abrahams[2], Mifima and other founder members, in 1983 Shipanga thus took his party into the South African supported Multi-Party Conference and in 1985 into the so called Transitional Government of National Unity (TGNU), a form of local rule under South African tutelage without any powers over the fundamental areas of constitutional affairs, foreign policy or national defence. Shipanga became TGNU Minister of Nature Conservation, Mining, Commerce and Tourism. SWANU's President Moses Katjiuongua—a former member of the *The Namibian Review* team in Sweden—occupied the position of Minister of Manpower, National Health and Welfare. Shipanga himself later acknowledged that "anyone who joined such a government could be called a puppet"[3], which is also how he was seen by the Namibian people. While SWAPO in the November 1989 independence elections obtained 386,567 votes—corresponding to 57.3 per cent of the national total—SWAPO-D received a mere 3,161. With a share of 0.5 per cent it placed the party in eighth position among the ten contenders, not even according Shipanga a seat in the Constituent—later National—Assembly.[4]

'Struggle and Assistance with the Same Objectives'

It has not been established beyond doubt that Andreas Shipanga at the time of the SWAPO crisis in 1975-76 collaborated with the South African regime.[5] It remains, however, that he and his colleagues on SWAPO's request were detained without trial under harsh conditions in Zambia and Tanzania for twenty-five months. Sub-

1. On several occasions, SWAPO-D unsuccessfully approached the Swedish government for assistance. In January 1980, for example, both Immanuel Ingombe, Secretary for Education, and Andreas Shipanga submitted requests to cover the travel costs for 37 members granted scholarships in the United States (Letters from Immanuel Ingombe and Andreas Shipanga to the Swedish legation in Pretoria, Windhoek, 2 and 14 January 1980) (MFA). Similar requests were made in March 1983 (Letter ('Namibian educational question') from André Booys, SWAPO-D Administrative Secretary, to the Swedish legation in Pretoria, Windhoek, 24 March 1983) (MFA). The representation in Pretoria did not support the requests, which was also the position adopted by CCHA (Letter ('Namibia: Framställan från SWAPO-D om stöd till utbildning'/'Namibia: Request from SWAPO-D for support to education') from Birgitta Karlström Dorph, Swedish legation in Pretoria, to the Ministry for Foreign Affairs, Pretoria, 3 May 1983) (MFA).
2. Arguing that the Abrahams had "betrayed their positions of trust by indulging in acts prejudicial to the best interests of the party", Shipanga expelled the couple from SWAPO-D in late February 1980 (Letter ('Ledarkris inom SWAPO-D'/'Leadership crisis within SWAPO-D') from Per Lindström, Swedish legation in Pretoria, to the Ministry for Foreign Affairs, Pretoria, 5 March 1980) (MFA).
3. Shipanga op. cit., p. 153. If appointed to official positions, the SWAPO-D and SWANU members who returned to Namibia had to sign an oath of allegiance to the Pretoria regime, declaring that "I will be faithful to the Republic of South Africa, observe its laws, promote all that which will advance it and oppose all that may harm it".
4. Lionel Cliffe (ed.): *The Transition to Independence in Namibia*, Lynne Rienner Publishers, Boulder and London, 1994, pp. 254-55.
5. In conversations with Swedish diplomats, Southern African political leaders often shared President Nyerere's doubts in this regard. Despite the fact that ZANU traditionally maintained close and friendly relations with SWAPO, in a meeting with the Swedish ambassador Bo Heinebäck and Tom Vraalsen from the Norwegian Ministry of Foreign Affairs Simon Muzenda—independent Zimbabwe's Foreign Minister—characterized as late as in September 1980 the charges against Shipanga as "nonsense" and "an invention by Nujoma". According to Muzenda, Shipanga was "a victim of politics". The veteran ZANU leader also remarkably told the Nordic government representatives that Shipanga "as a leader was of a significantly higher intellectual stature than Sam Nujoma". Through his return to Namibia, he had, however, politically become "a dead man" (Bo Heinebäck: Memorandum ('Samtal med utrikesminister Muzenda om södra Afrika'/'Conversation with Foreign Minister Muzenda about Southern Africa'), Swedish embassy, Salisbury, 4 September 1980) (MFA). It could be noted that Shipanga together with the former SWANU President Jariretundu Kozonguizi in March 1982 testified against SWAPO during the US Senate's attempts to depict the movement—and ANC of South Africa—as 'Communist' and 'terrorist' (*The Role of the Soviet Union, Cuba and East Germany in Fomenting Terrorism in Southern Africa*, Hearings before the Subcommittee on Security and Terrorism, Committee on the Judiciary, United States Senate, US Government Printing Office, Washington, 1982, Volume I, pp. 690-99).

sequent Swedish governments closely followed the case, but did not actively intervene.

Closest to the 'struggles within the struggle', the Swedish embassy in Lusaka doubted from the beginning SWAPO's official explanations of the crisis and the detention of the Shipanga group, drawing the conclusion that he most probably was 'a political victim'. Although in favour of a fair trial, the embassy did not recommend political action or suspension of the humanitarian assistance.[1] Swedish administrations—initially under Palme's Social Democratic Party and from October 1976 under Fälldin's non-socialist coalition—would not only follow this recommendation, but implement it in a most compliant way. The Shipanga case was never formally raised by Sweden in its close and frequent contacts with SWAPO, Zambia or Tanzania. In addition, the support to the Namibian liberation movement was not suspended or frozen, but regularly increased between 1975 and 1978.

With regard to the stricter human rights issues, the Swedish passivity was equally conspicuous. Important contacts were quietly made with both Amnesty International and the Lutheran World Federation, but mainly in response to requests by Shipanga's wife or other concerned personalities and only informally, behind the scenes. Although the Swedish embassy in Dar es Salaam via letters from the detainees or through other channels was aware of their plight, no attempt to visit or contact the detention centres was ever made. Similarly, when the escapees from the Mboroma camp asked for aid and protection, the embassy kept its doors closed twice. Eventually, it was President Nyerere who raised the matter of Shipanga and his co-detainees with the Swedish government, not the other way around. And when he decided to release the prisoners, the Ministry for Foreign Affairs was far from ready to receive them, instructing the embassy in Tanzania to 'play for time'. In fact, had the Swedish Immigration Board without the ministry's knowledge not taken a unilateral decision to grant some of the detainees asylum in Sweden, it remains an open question whether they would have been accepted there.

Several factors explain the Swedish stand. Until Wästberg in late October 1977 on grounds of principle publicly raised the issue in *Dagens Nyheter*, there were, in the first place, no active voices defending Shipanga's cause in Sweden. The Africa Groups and the wider solidarity movement upheld the SWAPO view that he was a traitor who had been taken into protective custody. So did *de facto* the Swedish political parties, trade unions and churches concerned with Namibia. Secondly, the frequent official contacts with Namibian church leaders and representatives of

---

1. Prime Minister Palme had in February 1976 on grounds of principle rejected the use of Swedish assistance as a political instrument. When the non-socialist opposition demanded that the bilateral support to Cuba should be cancelled due to its role in the Angolan conflict, Palme wrote in *Dagens Nyheter* that it was "dangerous to use [...] assistance as an instrument of sudden punishment or award", arguing that it was "quite incompatible with a long-term [...] cooperation policy" (Olof Palme: 'Kriget i Angola: Befrielsekampens fortsättning'/'The war in Angola: Continuation of the liberation struggle' in *Dagens Nyheter*, 4 February 1976). It should, nevertheless, be noted that Pierre Schori—at the time attached to the Prime Minister's Office—in mid-1976 did raise the possibility of a suspension of the Swedish aid to SWAPO (Anders Bjurner: Memorandum ('Läget inom SWAPO'/'The situation within SWAPO'), Swedish embassy, Lusaka, 25 August 1976) (MFA). Interviewed in 1996 about the Social Democratic Party's reaction to human rights violations within the liberation movements in general and the Shipanga case in particular, Schori stated: "When such excesses became clear, we raised our voices. For example, when the Social Democratic Party [in 1979] started to support SWAPO for the election campaign in Namibia, we raised it very strongly". At the same time, he added that "we did not know about human rights abuses and we had no ways of certifying what was going on. The liberation struggle was a situation of war, and we did not get very much information about it. It was like the French resistance during the Second World War. In that situation, it was natural for us to support the movement as such. [However], the Shipanga affair was a different story. It was a personal case. Shipanga had his own ambitions and his story was not entirely credible" (Interview with Pierre Schori, p. 335).

SWAPO's internal wing did not indicate a wish for an intervention on Shipanga's behalf. Finally—although Sweden was hardly risking more than Tanzania in this regard—due to the international negotiations on Namibia in 1977-78 the government did not dare to jeopardize its relations with SWAPO.

Even if the leadership around Sam Nujoma could be criticized on many accounts, it was—as stated by the UN Commissioner for Namibia, Séan Mac-Bride—of crucial importance to defend the unity of the movement[1], which in December 1976 was declared the 'sole and authentic representative of the Namibian people' by the UN General Assembly.

This also explains the common negative attitude by the Swedish authorities, non-governmental organizations and the press to the formation of SWAPO-D in Sweden in June 1978. In the opinion of the liberal newspaper *Dagens Nyheter*, it only served the interests of South Africa. Representing a party which championed individual freedoms and multi-party democracy, in an article in the conservative daily *Svenska Dagbladet* in December 1978 David Wirmark—at the time serving Ola Ullsten's Liberal minority government as an adviser on aid questions—stressed that "it is the *objective* of the struggle that should determine our judgement".[2] Brushing aside criticism levelled against SWAPO with regard to internal conflicts and the armed struggle, in his article—pregnantly entitled 'Struggle and assistance with the same objectives'—the Liberal MP and veteran anti-apartheid activist also argued that official Swedish humanitarian assistance contributed to "increased autonomy" of the movement.[3]

SWAPO's and Sweden's strategic objective—the independence of a non-aligned Namibia—was thus seen to be the same. What SWAPO set out to achieve through armed resistance and Sweden through diplomatic support and humanitarian assistance coincided. Elements seen to 'rock the common boat' were in this context of secondary importance and, thus, basically disregarded. While SWAPO dedicated its efforts to the political and military struggle, Sweden was to ease the burden by covering large portions of the movement's non-military and humanitarian needs. In general terms, this position—largely supported by Social Democratic and non-socialist Swedish governments alike, as well as by the wider solidarity movement—

---

1. Martti Ahtisaari, MacBride's successor as UN Commissioner for Namibia, later commented: "We were aware of what was going on, but I don't think [that] it had any major impact on our policy. It was simply an indication that [SWAPO had] difficulties in [...] catering for different views in the organization. The liberation struggle [...] is not the most democratic phase in the life of an organization, because you are bound to have very authoritarian ways of running [it]. [...] The justification [for supporting SWAPO] was to concentrate the efforts vis-à-vis the occupying power. That was the fact which we had to deal with" (Interview with Martti Ahtisaari, 29 January 1996, in Soiri and Peltola op. cit., pp. 184-85).

2. David Wirmark: 'Kamp och bistånd med samma mål' ('Struggle and assistance with the same objectives') in *Svenska Dagbladet*, 5 December 1978.

3. Ibid. Wirmark's article was in reply to a highly critical piece on SWAPO by the Swedish historian Per Lundvall, published under the title 'Millions to murderers'. According to Lundvall, SWAPO was a "tribally based organization [...] with little respect for democratic values [and] no Christian ideals whatsoever". *Inter alia* quoting the Shipanga case, he criticized the support extended to SWAPO by both the Swedish government and the Church of Sweden (Per Lundvall: 'Miljoner åt mördare'/'Millions to murderers' in *Svenska Dagbladet*, 27 November 1978). Towards the end of 1978—at a time when the Moderate Party was no longer represented in government—a number of national and regional conservative newspapers started to turn against SWAPO and Sweden's assistance to the movement. Often full of factual errors, some of the articles reached a low water mark in Swedish journalism on Southern Africa. For example, under the heading 'The comedy of freedom' the writer Ebbe Linde ridiculed the United Nations plans for Namibia, describing the world organization as "a farce [...] which already is swarming with Negro states". SWAPO was presented as "a Marxist, revolutionary movement founded by exile students from London, Paris and the Eastern states—mostly Hereros—who have no major connections with their home country. They have prepared the seizure of power through assassinations of [traditional] chiefs" (Linde: 'Frihetens komedi'/'The comedy of freedom' in *Norrköpings Tidningar*, 26 October 1978). Some of these remarkable statements were later repeated in parliamentary motions introduced by members of the Moderate Party.

was upheld during the SWAPO crisis in 1975-76 and through the Shipanga affair in 1976-78. Despite continuous internal SWAPO strains—*inter alia* illustrated in 1980 by the expulsion of Vice-President Mishake Muyongo[1] and, above all, in the 1980s by the hidden campaign to purge the movement of alleged spies—it was to be maintained until Namibia's independence in March 1990.

Sweden and the Spy Drama

In the context of humanitarian assistance and human rights, Sweden's reactions to the SWAPO 'spy drama'[2] in the 1980s—affecting up to two thousand members, of

---

1. In mid-July 1980, SWAPO's Central Committee resolved to expel Muyongo and eight other members, all of them Caprivians, due to "counter-revolutionary and secessionist activities aimed at dismembering Namibia's national territory [...], advocating and organizing for the breaking away of [...] Caprivi" (cited in cable ('Uteslutningar i SWAPO'/'Expulsions in SWAPO') from Ulla Boija, Swedish embassy, to the Ministry for Foreign Affairs, Luanda, 23 July 1980) (MFA). Informing the Swedish embassy in Luanda about the expulsions, SWAPO's Angola representative Aaron Mushimba said that Muyongo had been involved in the activities for about a year; that he and his fellow Caprivians were in contact with the South African regime; and that SWAPO had asked Zambia to detain him (Cable ('Uteslutningar SWAPO'/'Expulsions SWAPO') from Ulla Boija, Swedish embassy, to the Ministry for Foreign Affairs, Luanda, 24 July 1980) (MFA). This time, however, the Zambian government did not act upon SWAPO's request, allowing Muyongo to stay in the country on condition that he abstained from political activities (Letter ('Utrensningar i SWAPO'/'Purges in SWAPO') from Göran Hasselmark, Swedish ambassador to Zambia, to the Ministry for Foreign Affairs, Lusaka, 31 July 1980) (MFA). Another 'Shipanga affair' was thus avoided. Like Shipanga, Muyongo was well known to the Swedish government. As Vice-President of SWAPO, he had led the movement's delegations to the official aid negotiations with Sweden in 1974, 1976, 1977, 1978 and 1979. He had also visited Sweden on several occasions. In September 1979—less than a year before the expulsion and at a time when he was later said to have been involved in secessionist activities—Muyongo was invited by the International Centre of the Swedish Labour Movement to observe the elections in the country. Initially, therefore, the news of his expulsion caused considerable concern. Göran Hasselmark, the Swedish ambassador to Zambia, wrote that "it is unfortunate that SWAPO—which already is weak—shall suffer this depletion", adding that "it is difficult not to be sceptical of the statements made by the victorious faction within the SWAPO leadership" and that "Muyongo's standing among the Frontline States is considerably better than Nujoma's" (ibid.). However, as Muyongo—a former leader of the Caprivi African National Union (CANU), who had merged his organization with SWAPO in 1964—continued to champion the case of Caprivi (by him and his followers called Itenge) and he readily acknowledged that he had resurrected CANU, his credibility vanished (Letter ('SWAPO: Samtal med Misheck Muyongo'/'Conversation with Misheck Muyongo') from Göran Hasselmark to the Ministry for Foreign Affairs, Lusaka, 4 January 1981) (MFA). Repeated requests for Swedish assistance submitted by Muyongo on behalf of CANU were rejected (Letter ('Begäran om bistånd från Caprivi African National Union (CANU)'/'Request for assistance from CANU') from Göran Hasselmark to the Ministry for Foreign Affairs, Lusaka, 2 June 1983) (SDA). Muyongo returned to Namibia in 1985 and became Vice-President of the Democratic Turnhalle Alliance in 1987. Elected President of the DTA Party in 1991, he served as leader of the parliamentary opposition in independent Namibia. In the 1994 presidential elections, Muyongo received 24 per cent of the votes. However, in a remarkable turn of events, in June 1998 he was again accused of advocating secession for Caprivi and once more dismissed by the Central Committee of his own party. Allegedly leading an armed Caprivi Liberation Movement, in October 1998 Muyongo crossed into Botswana, where over the following months he was joined by some 2,000 followers. The events led to a diplomatic conflict between Namibia and Botswana. Muyongo's extraordinary exit from the Namibian scene appeared to be sealed in May 1999, when he was granted political asylum in distant Denmark.

2. This term has appropriately been used to describe the events in the 1980s. In Namibia itself, they are often referred to as 'the detainees issue'. On the spy drama, see Groth op. cit.; Leys and Saul op. cit., pp. 53-58; Peltola op. cit., pp. 153-61; and Trewhela op. cit. in *Searchlight South Africa*, Nos. 5 and 6, 1990. Leys and Saul characterize the events as "organized terror". SWAPO members were systematically "arrested, taken to Lubango [in southern Angola] and forced to 'confess' to being South African agents, if necessary by being beaten or otherwise tortured to the point of death, and then detained, with poor food and little or no medical care, in covered pits in the ground" (Leys and Saul op. cit., p. 55). The pits—and, in general, the detention camps—in the Lubanga area are in Namibia widely known as 'the dungeons'.

whom many were tortured and killed[1]—should, finally, be mentioned. Although the origins of the events in the 1980s largely lie in unresolved contradictions carried over from the 1970s[2], there are fundamental differences between the two crises. While the 1975-76 upheavals and the ensuing Shipanga affair led to a SWAPO commission of inquiry and was raised in the Zambian courts, the extent of the hidden drama in Angola in the 1980s remained unknown to the outside world—including prominent members of the SWAPO leadership—until the end of the decade. It was only with the return to Namibia in 1989 of a number of former SWAPO prisoners that the details of this dark chapter in SWAPO's history started to come out into the open.[3]

The 'struggles within the struggle' in the 1970s were followed and commented upon by the Swedish authorities as they unfolded. Although SIDA, a number of Swedish companies and several NGOs in the 1980s were closely involved with SWAPO in Angola[4]—often working in direct partnership with officials who would

---

1. Accurate figures are not available. While Leys and Saul estimate that "almost a thousand SWAPO members in exile were arrested" (Leys and Saul op. cit., p. 55), Soiri and Peltola state that "up to two thousand [...] are said to have gone through the horrors of the prison camps" (Soiri and Peltola op. cit., p. 131). In 1994, the former detainee Eric Biwa requested the release of a promised, official list of some 2,100 people still unaccounted for (Lauren Dobell: 'Namibia's Wall of Silence' in *Southern Africa Report*, July 1996, p. 31).

2. Working as a programme officer with UNHCR in Luanda, the author recalls how three young members of the SWAPO Youth League—two boys and one girl—in 1978 were referred to the office by the Angolan security organization DISA for resettlement in a third country. Markedly defiant and critical of the SWAPO leadership, the three SYL members had contacted DISA for protection. During the long process of finding a suitable country of asylum, they eventually decided to return to SWAPO. It was a fatal decision. A couple of days later, DISA contacted the UNHCR office with the information that they had been executed while being transported from Luanda to Lubango. Other outspoken critics were luckier. Inspired by the MPLA and FRELIMO women, Martha Ford, Secretary of SWAPO's Women's Council, launched a campaign to strengthen the position of the women in SWAPO, criticizing the male-dominated leadership's "veteranism", "scandalizing" and "double standards" (cited from documents attached to a letter from Martha Ford to the Swedish embassy in Luanda, 2 October 1978) (SDA). Establishing a close dialogue with Ulla Boija at the Swedish embassy, SIDA's Marianne Sundh and Kristina Persson from the LO/TCO Council of International Trade Union Cooperation, her ideas were, however, seen as offensive and she was soon forced to leave SWAPO. With a protective network in Angola, Ford managed to steer clear of SWAPO's security services, but did not return to Namibia at independence. On the question of the continuity between the 1975-76 crisis in Zambia and the spy drama in Angola in the 1980s, it could be noted that Mishake Muyongo—himself greatly responsible for the internal repression in 1976—in a press statement after his expulsion in August 1980 declared that the SWAPO leadership was "openly advocating [...] physical elimination of Caprivians by killing, imprisoning cadres without trial in the SWAPO underground prisons and [by] forcing our people to go to Angola at gunpoint" ('Press statement issued by Mishake Albert Muyongo', attached to letter ('Utrensningarna ur SWAPO'/'The SWAPO purges') from Göran Hasselmark, Swedish ambassador to Zambia, to the Ministry for Foreign Affairs, Lusaka, 8 October 1980) (MFA).

3. After independence, the SWAPO government consistently refused to have the detainees issue openly investigated or to establish a truth and reconciliation commission, as was done in South Africa after the democratic elections in 1994. Arguing that resurrecting the past would serve no useful purpose, the SWAPO leadership not only stifled a democratic discussion, but rejected the testimonies which appeared. When pastor Groth's book was published, President Nujoma "commandeered fifteen minutes of air time on national television to condemn [it]", while SWAPO's Secretary General Moses Garoeb rejected the account as a "false history" and its author as an "enemy of Namibia" (Dobell op. cit. in *Southern Africa Report*, July 1996, pp. 33 and 31).

4. In addition, a number of Swedish delegations visited the Kwanza Sul settlement outside the humanitarian cooperation programme. In March 1982, for example, a delegation of ten members from the Centre Party Youth League spent a couple of days in the camp (Letter ('Veckobrev SWAPO, vecka 9'/'Weekly letter SWAPO, week 9') from Jörgen Christensen, Swedish embassy, to SIDA, Luanda, 4 March 1982) (SDA).

'disappear'[1]—the purges by SWAPO's military security services[2] were, in contrast, surrounded by a "wall of silence".[3] Until the end of the decade, even indirect references to the events in the archives consulted for this study are extremely few. In his dissertation on the Namibian trade union movement, the Finnish scholar Pekka Peltola—who between 1979 and 1986 regularly visited SWAPO in Angola—states that "from 1983 onwards a paranoic atmosphere prevailed in Kwanza Sul, and probably also elsewhere in the SWAPO settlements. Practically everybody was suspected of treason".[4] Such a situation is, however, not reflected in the regular reports written by the Swedish aid workers and company representatives who lived and worked in the settlement, nor is it implied in the correspondence from the Swedish embassy in Luanda. On the contrary, taking the difficult security situation into account they were often pleasantly surprised by the SWAPO leadership's openness and the relaxed environment in Kwanza Sul.[5] Nevertheless, as allegations of deten-

---

1. Many examples could be mentioned, among them the cases of Pejavi Muniaro, Victor Nkandi and Lukas Stephanus, who were all detained in the mid-1980s and probably were killed or died in the prison camps. Muniaro had close contacts with the Swedish trade unions and the solidarity movement. As early as in September 1978, he attended an LO seminar in Stockholm. Holding the position of SWAPO Deputy Labour Secretary, in September 1982 he made a nationwide information tour of Sweden as the guest of the Africa Groups. Between October 1983 and June 1985, Henry Blid of LO/TCO worked with Muniaro at the Kwanza Sul settlement and at the SWAPO headquarters in Luanda, where they shared the same office. In his capacity as Director of SWAPO's settlements, Victor Nkandi was in constant contact with the Swedish companies and NGOs that were represented in Kwanza Sul and Viana. Lukas Stephanus, finally, was SWAPO Deputy Secretary for Education and Culture. He was directly involved with the Swedish support to the education sector, *inter alia* participating at a workshop on financial management and administrative training in Uppsala, Sweden, in January-February 1984. The case of Fritz Spiegel could be added. In the early 1980s, he studied at the Brunnsvik folk high school in Sweden, where he met Henry Blid. As Director of SWAPO's trade union school, they later worked closely together. In 1984, he was taken to Lubango, where he spent five years 'in the dungeons'. It should also be noted that Aaron Mushimba, SWAPO Chief Representative to Angola, Zambia and Senegal, Deputy Treasurer and President Nujoma's brother-in-law, in 1989 was detained and taken to Lubango, from where he, however, managed to escape. When questions were asked about counterparts and other SWAPO officials who were no longer to be found, standard replies were that they had been transferred to other duties; that they had received scholarships abroad; that they had been called up for military duties; or—in not so few cases—that they had been found to be South African agents (Author's recollection).

2. SWAPO's military intelligence and security were reorganized around 1980, following a visit in April 1979 to Czechoslovakia, the German Democratic Republic and the Soviet Union by Defence Secretary Peter Nanyemba. The East German support was highly important to SWAPO. In their informative study on GDR and Southern Africa, Ilona and Hans-Georg Schleicher—the latter a former GDR diplomat and a specialist on Southern African affairs—note that "[s]ince 1979 PLAN fighters were trained in the GDR, in particular in the field of military intelligence. [This was] a field in which the GDR had specialized with regard to its support to the liberation movements in Southern Africa" (Schleicher op. cit., pp. 206-07). Regrettably, the Schleichers do not discuss the SWAPO spy drama or GDR's possible role in the ensuing events. SWAPO's reorganized military and security services fell under the control of the Deputy Army Commander Solomon Hawala. Although strongly identified with the horrors in the 1980s, he was in 1990 appointed Commander of independent Namibia's new army, a decision which stirred up a public controversy.

3. The title of Siegfried Groth's book is *Namibia: The Wall of Silence*. The publication in Germany in 1995 led to an intensification of the debate regarding the 'detainees issue'. To prepare the launch of the book in Namibia, a Breaking the Wall of Silence (BWOS) movement was formed, comprising former detainees and their supporters. The book was eventually launched in Windhoek in late March 1996 ('Detainee book sparks strong public interest' in *The Namibian*, 1 April 1996).

4. Peltola op. cit., p. 155. Peltola worked with the Finnish support to the Namibian trade union movement in exile. In his study, he emphasizes that the purges carried out by SWAPO's military intelligence in particular targeted NUNW.

5. Bengt Svensson, who served as SIDA's representative in Angola from 1979 to 1984, wrote, for example, in August 1983: "SWAPO is [...] characterized by an openness that borders on carelessness. It is never difficult to visit the big camp in Kwanza Sul, although it requires military escort in the present security situation" (Letter ('Tankar om vårt bistånd till SWAPO och ANC: Nkosi Sikelel' iAfrika'/'Reflections on our assistance to SWAPO and ANC: Nkosi Sikelel' iAfrika') from Bengt Svensson to SIDA's Director General, Anders Forsse, Swedish embassy, Luanda, 11 August 1983) (SDA).

tions and torture were raised from the mid-1980s, the Swedish authorities' reaction merits a comment.

In mid-April 1985, the West German right wing journalist Willy Lützen-kirchen published an article in *Mannheimer Morgen*, claiming to have uncovered horrific human rights violations in SWAPO's refugee camps in Angola and Zambia.[1] Although Lützenkirchen was far from a reliable source, a couple of weeks later the Namibia Information Service in London reproduced the main points of the article.[2] This prompted the British MP Nicholas Winterton, chairman of the British All-Party Namibia Group, to turn to SIDA for comments.[3] The allegations came as a surprise to the Swedish aid agency.[4] Nevertheless, Birgitta Berggren, the head of SIDA's Southern Africa section, immediately asked the Lusaka-based coordinator of Sweden's humanitarian assistance, Roland Axelsson, to visit the Nyango settlement in western Zambia. Due to security restrictions, a similar visit to the Kwanza Sul settlement in Angola could not be arranged at short notice.[5] At the same time, SIDA asked SWAPO's Kaire Mbuende at Lund university for his opinion.[6]

Unannounced, Axelsson visited Nyango for three days in early June 1985. The refugee settlement had at the time an estimated population of 5,000. Apart from a number of familiar shortages and problems in the humanitarian field, Axelsson could not detect any signs of "maltreatment, torture [or] violence", which Lützen-kirchen had alleged to be "the order of the day" in the SWAPO camps.[7] Neither did he find any evidence of prisons or detention centres. On the contrary, "everybody seemed to be happy and to get on well, in spite of the circumstances".[8] At the same time, however, the leadership of the settlement confirmed South Africa's attempts to infiltrate SWAPO, "mentioning [the case] of Lukas Stephanus and his accomplices as one of the worst examples".[9]

With years of experience from close cooperation with SWAPO and Axelsson's recent report in hand, the official aid agency replied to Winterton on 1 July 1985. The letter stressed that "SIDA has never received reports about atrocities of the kind described in Mr. Lützenkirchens's article, nor have we ever had information

---

1. *Mannheimer Morgen*, 17 April 1985.
2. Namibia Information Service: 'Human rights violated by SWAPO claims West German journalist', Press release, London, 9 May 1985 (SDA).
3. Letter from Nicholas Winterton to Birgitta Berggren, London, 14 May 1985 (SDA).
4. In late 1984, family members in Namibia of some of the detainees had formed a Committee of Parents to demand an inquiry. It had, however, not yet written to the Namibian church leaders about human rights violations by SWAPO in exile. This happened in June 1985. After receiving no response from either SWAPO or the churches, it went public at the end of 1985.
5. In addition, as a result of escalating UNITA attacks in the area Swedes working in the Kwanza Sul settlement under SIDA contracts were withdrawn from February 1985 until March 1986.
6. Studying and lecturing in Sweden for many years, in 1986 Mbuende published his doctoral thesis *Namibia, the Broken Shield: Anatomy of Imperialism and Revolution*, Liber Förlag, Malmö. He was appointed Deputy Minister of Agriculture, Water and Rural Development at Namibia's independence in 1990. From 1994 to 1999, Mbuende served as Executive Secretary of the Southern African Development Community (SADC), based in Gaborone, Botswana.
7. Namibia Information Service: 'Human rights violated by SWAPO claims West German journalist', Press release, London, 9 May 1985 (SDA).
8. Roland Axelsson: Memorandum ('Anteckningar från besök i Nyango, 7-9 juni 1985'/'Notes from visit to Nyango, 7-9 June 1985') to SIDA, Swedish embassy, Lusaka, 17 June 1985 (SDA).
9. Ibid.

about torture or brutal oppression". However, as SIDA was aware of tensions within SWAPO[1] it left a small opening for doubts, concluding that

> the picture given by Mr. Lützenkirchen [...] does not correspond to ours after several years of humanitarian assistance and development cooperation with SWAPO. Evidently, this does not exclude that divergence of opinion exists within SWAPO, especially taking into consideration the extremely harsh conditions under which the movement has to cater for its refugee population.[2]

Mbuende gave his opinion in a letter to SIDA shortly thereafter. Stating that "the description of the situation in the settlements [made by *Mannheimer Morgen* and reproduced by the Namibia Information Service] is completely wrong", he concluded:

> There are, of course, a number of people who resign from SWAPO for a number of reasons. These individuals—who end up in the 'underground of Lusaka'—are capable of fabricating stories as a way of getting back at SWAPO.[3]

At a time of escalating South African military attacks and disinformation campaigns against SWAPO, SIDA thus made an effort to verify the allegations of human rights violations. Birgitta Berggren later commented that it was

> difficult to judge from outside what actually happened. In most cases you could not do that, because it might as well be a case of [actual] infiltration. [...] [But] we did discuss it. We raised some questions, but I do not remember that it influenced our attitude very much. It was a problem, and we understood that such problems would appear. It was, however, very difficult even to ask pertinent questions to get better knowledge of the problems. We would at the same time more or less regularly get information from groups in Germany, accusing the liberation movements of being Marxists, Leninists, oppressors etc. You could not really say that it was all that true. It was difficult to know the true picture.[4]

SWAPO reacted in early 1986. At a press briefing in London on 16 February, Theo-Ben Gurirab and Hidipo Hamutenya, respectively Secretary for Foreign Affairs and Secretary for Information and Publicity, revealed that the movement had uncovered a South African spy network, which had penetrated both its political and military wings. Around one hundred members—of whom four were represented on the Central Committee—were held by SWAPO for questioning. Videotaped confes-

---

1. The atmosphere within SWAPO in early 1985 was tense. When Berit Rylander in April 1985 took up her position as SIDA's programme officer with responsibility for humanitarian assistance to the liberation movements, she initially found Hifikepunye Pohamba and other leaders on their guard. Soon establishing a close friendship with Pohamba, he later told her that they had received information from SWAPO's security services that she was American and a spy (Conversation with Berit Rylander, Uppsala, 28 August 1999). Berit and her husband Sten, Sweden's ambassador to Angola, stayed in Luanda from 1985 until 1988. They were highly instrumental in dissipating SWAPO's doubts, as well as in consolidating the cooperation and the political relations between Sweden and SWAPO. With a strong personal commitment to SWAPO's cause, Berit Rylander even brought her retired father—Erik Andersson, a baker by profession—to Luanda to set up a bakery for the liberation movement. Pohamba, SWAPO's Finance Secretary, later recalled: "One person who I worked with and [who] really assisted me is Berit Rylander. [...] I will not forget how she assisted us. [...] She would go to the camps and assess the situation herself. Then she would come and say: 'This is what you should do'" (Interview with Hifikepunye Pohamba, p. 96). Similarly, Festus Naholo, the Secretary of Logistics, noted in 1995 that "some of the [SIDA] projects were not going well, but it later changed when Berit Rylander and Georg Dreifaldt came in. They were really wonderful people" (Interview with Festus Naholo, p. 90). Before her return to Sweden in September 1988, President Nujoma awarded Berit Rylander SWAPO's Certificate of Appreciation for her "selfless services rendered in solidarity with the legitimate struggle of the Namibian people for independence", an unusual gesture towards a diplomat. After Namibia's independence in 1990, Sten Rylander became the first Swedish ambassador to the country, while Berit Rylander was employed by UNDP as an adviser on foreign aid, based at the National Planning Commission.
2. Letter ('Re article on SWAPO's civilian settlements in Angola and Zambia'), signed by Tor Sellström for Birgitta Berggren, to Nicholas Winterton, SIDA, Stockholm, 1 July 1985 (SDA).
3. Letter from Kaire Mbuende to Ingalill Colbro, Lund, 14 July 1985 (SDA).
4. Interview with Birgitta Berggren, p. 261.

sions by some of them were shown. Thus confirming that detentions had taken place, Gurirab and Hamutenya stated that the agents would not be brought to trial. The liberation movement was fighting a war, and "we are not able to open up SWAPO for scrutiny".[1] Acknowledging that "there are concerns about the human rights of these people", they, however, strongly rejected the allegations that SWAPO was involved in injusticies against the Namibians in Angola and Zambia. Explicitly referring to the presence of Swedish, Norwegian and German teachers and nurses in the camps, Hamutenya declared:

> There is a well-calculated campaign organized by South Africa, saying that [the] SWAPO camps are concentration camps. [...] We have apprehended some of [the] agents, but we have not [...] become fascists against our own people. We have been, and will remain, committed to basic human rights.[2]

SWAPO's position was accepted by the Swedish authorities. After consideration by CCHA, in mid-April 1986 SIDA submitted its proposal for cooperation with SWAPO during the financial year 1986/87 to the Ministry for Foreign Affairs. In the covering letter, SIDA's Director General Carl Tham noted that "a spy tangle" had been uncovered within SWAPO and that "South Africa had infiltrated the movement at different levels".[3] Adding that SWAPO "has been forced to dedicate a lot of time to solve the problems", no particular Swedish course of action was in this context recommended.[4] Official aid negotiations between Sweden and SWAPO were held in Luanda the following month. Leading the delegation from Sweden, SIDA's Deputy Director General Lars-Olof Edström announced in his opening remarks that the Social Democratic government had decided to increase the allocation to SWAPO from 50 to 59 MSEK, adding that "Sweden was prepared to be flexible and extend more support whenever new needs arose".[5] While the parties thoroughly discussed the general security situation in the Kwanza Sul settlement, they did not, however, mention the human rights issues or SWAPO's recent statements on the spy network.[6]

Rumours about spies, detentions and secret prison camps—in particular in distant Lubango, where Sweden did not support any SWAPO activities—intensified over the following years. They were finally confirmed at the beginning of July 1989, when a first group of 153 detainees were released by SWAPO and repatriated to Namibia under the auspices of UNHCR. Throughout this period, SIDA and the Swedish Ministry for Foreign Affairs kept a low profile. Asked about SIDA's reactions to the rumours and whether the aid agency had discussed them with SWAPO or its host governments in Southern Africa, principally Angola[7], Tham affirmed in 1997:

---

1. Cited in *The Namibian*, 21 February 1986.
2. Ibid.
3. Letter ('Humanitärt bistånd till South West Africa People's Organization, SWAPO (Namibia), budgetåret 1986/87'/'Humanitarian assistance to SWAPO [during the] financial year 1986/87') from Carl Tham to the Ministry for Foreign Affairs, SIDA, Stockholm, 16 April 1986 (SDA).
4. Ibid.
5. 'Agreed minutes [from] consultations in Luanda in May 1986 between SWAPO of Namibia and Sweden concerning humanitarian assistance 1986/87', Luanda, 29 May 1986 (SDA). SWAPO's Administrative Secretary Moses Garoeb led the Namibian delegation.
6. Ibid.
7. The Angolan government was well aware of the situation in SWAPO's camps in the Lubango area, but did not intervene. Nor did it raise the issue with Sweden. In a conversation with the author, MPLA's Secretary General Lopo do Nascimento acknowledged in April 1996 that during his period as Governor of the Huíla province (1986-91) he had received many calls for help in the form of letters and messages from SWAPO detainees.

We did not know much about that. We knew, of course, that there were divisions, but we did not know about abuse of power in the camps. [...] SIDA was mainly a financing institution. We tried to follow events, but the implementing agents were the people involved in the churches and other NGOs. We were very much dependent on them. If they had raised the issue with SIDA, we would certainly have acted. But as far as I remember, that was never the case.[1]

However, Lena Hjelm-Wallén, the Social Democratic Minister for International Development Cooperation (1985-91), confirmed that human rights issues had been discussed with SWAPO at the highest political level. Also in 1997, she explained that she

in the late 1980s [...] raised [the detainee issue] directly with SWAPO. I remember a discussion I had with Sam Nujoma. But we never discussed it with the Angolan government.[2]

---

1. Interview with Carl Tham, p. 344.
2. Interview with Lena Hjelm-Wallén, p. 295. Cf. Pär Granstedt of the Centre Party, a former member of the SIDA board, the parliamentary Foreign Affairs Committee *(Utrikesutskottet)* and the Advisory Council on Foreign Affairs *(Utrikesnämnden)*: "Yes, [these issues] were definitely discussed. Not as a reason to stop the support, but rather as an embarrassment [...]. I suppose that it was taken up in the official contacts between Sweden and the liberation movements. I was not involved in that, but on the [Centre Party] youth side I remember, for instance, participating in discussions with representatives of SWAPO on these questions. It definitely played a role. We were eager to point out how much it hurt the case of the liberation movements and how counter-productive it was for the struggle" (Interview with Pär Granstedt, pp. 271-72). In addition to the Centre youth's cooperation with the Namibian liberation movement, in the late 1980s the Centre Party Women's League started to support the SWAPO Women's Council.

Cold War, Total Strategy and Expanded Assistance

Talks, Frustrations and Hopes

The end of the 1970s was a period of hopes and frustrations with regard to a settlement of the Namibia question. In January 1976, the UN Security Council reacted to South Africa's unilateral Turnhalle constitutional scheme by adopting Resolution 385. It condemned Pretoria's continued occupation and "all attempts [...] calculated to evade the clear demand of the United Nations for the holding of free elections under [UN] supervision and control".[1] With huge economic and strategic interests in Namibia, the permanent Western members of the Security Council— France, Great Britain and the United States—were, however, not disposed to apply pressure to enforce the decision. On the contrary, in October 1976 they vetoed a draft resolution which would have imposed mandatory sanctions against the apartheid regime.

Keen "to avoid [...] a long-drawn-out armed liberation struggle" and anxious "to maintain some international credibility"[2], together with Canada and the Federal Republic of Germany—at the time temporary council members—the three permanent members instead formed a so called Western Contact Group (WCG). Acting as a go-between, in April 1977 the group began discussions with South Africa, SWAPO and the Southern African Frontline States to find a settlement in accordance with Resolution 385 and earlier rulings by the International Court of Justice.

The talks continued over the following years. While South Africa initially agreed to set aside the Turnhalle scheme, it soon became clear that it followed "a two-track strategy, preparing the option of an internal settlement [and] continuing to explore the possibilities for a wider solution".[3] Combining intensified repression against the nationalist movement with increased militarization of the country[4], South Africa went ahead with the Turnhalle initiative and extended its grip over Namibia—appointing an Administrator General in July and annexing the port of Walvis Bay on 1 September 1977[5]—while at the same time taking part in the WCG talks.[6]

---

1. UN Security Council Resolution 385 of 30 January 1976, cited in UNIN op. cit., p. 348.
2. Katjavivi op. cit., p. 114.
3. Ibid., p. 116.
4. In early 1978, it was estimated that there were some 75,000 South African soldiers in Namibia (Kimmo and Marja-Liisa Kiljunen: 'Report on a visit to Namibia', Brighton, July 1978, p. 35) (NAI). This corresponded to more than one South African soldier to twenty Namibian inhabitants. As most of the soldiers were based in northern Namibia, the relative size of the occupation forces there was even bigger.
5. Walvis Bay has Namibia's only deep-water port and is of crucial importance to the country's economy, both as a centre of the fishing industry and for foreign trade. South Africa's claim rested on a proclamation from 1878, when the British annexed the bay and the surrounding area to prevent the port from falling into the hands of the Germans. Six years later—in 1884—the enclave was attached to the Cape Province. When South West Africa became a mandate under the League of Nations, the Union of South Africa, however, chose to make Walvis Bay an integral part of that territory. After the re-annexation in 1977, Walvis Bay assumed increasing military importance to South Africa. The question of its status featured prominently in the negotiations on Namibia's future. It was only resolved in February 1994, when South Africa formally transferred sovereignty over the area to independent Namibia.
6. During so called 'proximity talks' between WCG, South Africa and SWAPO in New York in February 1978, the South African Foreign Minister 'Pik' Botha abruptly walked out and returned to Cape Town.

The contact group submitted its final proposal to the UN Security Council in early April 1978. Although South Africa made some reservations—of which the most important related to Walvis Bay—it accepted the proposal on 25 April. However, less than two weeks later—on 4 May 1978—it showed its true colours by attacking the SWAPO settlement at Kassinga in southern Angola, killing more than 600 refugees[1] and dramatically bringing the diplomatic talks to a halt. The Security Council—which in November 1977 had imposed a mandatory arms embargo against South Africa[2]—reacted strongly by condemning Pretoria's violation of the sovereignty and territorial integrity of Angola, as well as its utilization of the international territory of Namibia as a springboard for armed invasions.[3]

Despite the Kassinga massacre and on condition that Walvis Bay was confirmed as an integral part of Namibia, SWAPO agreed to WCG's settlement proposal on 12 July 1978. Following SWAPO's acceptance, the Security Council adopted two more resolutions on Namibia. Through Resolution 431, the council requested the Secretary General to submit a report with recommendations on the implementation of the proposal, as well as to appoint a Special Representative for Namibia "in order to ensure the early independence of [the country] through free elections under the supervision and control of the United Nations".[4] Martti Ahtisaari, the Finnish diplomat who held the position as UN Commissioner for Namibia, was appointed Special Representative and instructed to visit Namibia. Resolution 432, finally, declared that "the territorial integrity and unity of Namibia must be assured through the reintegration of Walvis Bay within its territory" and that "South Africa must not use [the port] in any manner prejudicial to the independence of Namibia or the viability of its economy".[5]

Ahtisaari went on a two week survey mission to Namibia in August 1978. On the basis of his findings, the UN Secretary General submitted a report to the Security Council which was accepted by SWAPO and endorsed through Resolution 435 of 29 September 1978, subsequently known as the 'UN plan' for Namibia's independence.[6] Under the resolution, a United Nations Transitional Assistance Group (UNTAG) was established to assist the Special Representative "to carry out the mandate conferred upon him [...], namely, to ensure the early independence of

---

1. The precise number of those killed at Kassinga may never be known. While some of the wounded refugees disappeared during the attack, others who later died in foreign hospitals were not recorded as Kassinga victims. The number of dead established by SWAPO and the Angolan authorities amounted to 612, of which 298—that is, almost half—were children, 167 women and 147 men. Another 611 refugees were physically wounded, while many more were affected by gas and/or mentally traumatized. Finally, in addition to the dead and wounded the South Africans took some 200 prisoners at Kassinga and at the PLAN base at Tchetequera. They were taken to the Keikanachab military detention camp at Hardap in central Namibia, where most of them remained imprisoned for more than six years until released in October 1984 (ya Nangolo and Sellström op. cit., p. 36). On the Kassinga massacre, see also Annemarie Heywood: *The Cassinga Event*, Archeia No. 18, National Archives of Namibia, Windhoek, 1994, and below.
2. UN Security Council Resolution 418 of 4 November 1977. The mandatory arms embargo—the first action ever taken against a member state under the UN Charter's Chapter VII—was primarily introduced in reaction to the deteriorating situation in South Africa. After Steve Biko's death in detention in September, in a major crackdown the following month the Pretoria regime banned practically all the black consciousness' formations, as well as other democratic organizations, such as the Christian Institute.
3. UN Security Council Resolution 428 of 6 May 1978.
4. UN Security Council Resolution 431 of 27 July 1978, cited in UNIN op. cit., p. 361. The resolution was adopted by 13 votes to 0, with Czechoslovakia and the Soviet Union abstaining.
5. UN Security Council Resolution 432 of 27 July 1978, cited in ibid.
6. In reality, the UN plan was set out in about twenty resolutions, documents, letters, statements and informal understandings adopted between 1976 and 1989, all of which came together under the label of UN Security Council Resolution 435.

Namibia through free elections under the supervision and control of the United Nations".[1]

In the meantime, South Africa applied the brakes. Announcing his resignation on 20 September 1978, Prime Minister John Vorster at the same time rejected the Secretary General's report and declared that South Africa would go ahead with internal elections in Namibia in December 1978 "in order to establish unequivocally who had the right to speak for the people of South West Africa".[2] His successor, the former Defence Minister P.W. Botha, maintained this position. In an effort to rescue the UN plan, in mid-October the WCG Foreign Ministers travelled to South Africa to persuade him to cancel the elections. They did not succeed. Instead, they entered into a "compromise deal", according to which the proposed elections were to be regarded as a first round, to be followed by UN supervised elections.[3] This was in direct conflict with the original WCG proposal which had been endorsed by the Security Council, and the 'deal' was rejected by SWAPO and the vast majority of the UN member states. On 13 November 1978, the council adopted Resolution 439, which condemned "the decision [...] to proceed unilaterally with the holding of elections [in Namibia]" and declared "[the] elections and their results null and void".[4] All the five members of the Western Contact Group abstained from voting on the resolution.

Amidst widespread fraud and intimidation of voters, elections were held in Namibia in early December 1978. Although South Africa soon introduced new issues and problems, on 22 December it formally communicated to the Secretary General its decision to cooperate in the implementation of the UN plan. As all parties, finally, seemed to be in general agreement, in January 1979 the Special Representative went to Namibia and South Africa together with the Indian Commander of UNTAG's military component, Lieutenant-General Prem Chand, to begin consultations on the requirements for the deployment of UNTAG.

Swedish Preparations and South African Reactions

This brief account illustrates how fragile the basis was for a negotiated settlement of the Namibia question at the end of the 1970s, even before a number of crucial issues—such as the question of United Nations impartiality; that of ultimate authority during the proposed transition period; cessation of hostilities and confinement to base of the armed forces; as well as election procedures—had been resolved. In the event, the negotiations broke down in January 1981, when the South African delegation to a 'pre-implementation meeting' in Geneva, Switzerland, claimed that the United Nations was disqualified from supervising free and fair elections due to its recognition of SWAPO.[5] Soon thereafter, the new US administration under President Ronald Reagan introduced its concept of 'constructive engagement', which in the case of Namibia linked the independence process to the withdrawal of the Cuban troops from Angola. With the 'linkage policy', the

---

1. UN Security Council Resolution 435 of 29 September 1978, cited in UNIN op. cit., p. 370. Adopted by 13 votes to 0, with Czechoslovakia and the Soviet Union abstaining. The Cold War dimension of the Namibia question is illustrated by the fact that the Soviet Union and its Eastern bloc allies changed position on Resolution 435 as soon as it was pushed into the background by the United States (Ilona and Hans-Georg Schleicher op. cit., p. 164).
2. Cited in Katjavivi op. cit., p. 122.
3. UNIN op. cit., p. 214.
4. UN Security Council Resolution 439 of 13 November 1978, cited in UNIN op. cit., pp. 371-72.
5. UNIN op. cit., p. 219.

straightforward question of Namibia's national independence became part of regional Cold War politics and yet again deferred to an unknown future.

Nevertheless, in 1978-79 there were signs of a possible settlement. In Sweden's case, this led to intensified consultations with SWAPO and increased coordination with the Nordic neighbours. The fact that Martti Ahtisaari from Finland served as the UN Secretary General's Special Representative for Namibia was in this context not without significance. A number of important NGO initiatives to assist SWAPO during an election campaign were also launched, notably by AIC. These developments were not positively noted in South Africa.

As the regular humanitarian assistance was growing rapidly[1], the end of the 1970s witnessed a closer political dialogue between Sweden and SWAPO. President Nujoma and other leading SWAPO representatives continuously kept the Swedish government abreast of the twists and turns in the diplomatic talks with the Western Contact Group. When openings for a negotiated settlement of the Namibia question appeared, the parties initiated discussions on both short and longer term measures to strengthen SWAPO's administrative and planning capacity.

As early as in May 1977, Nujoma asked Sweden to use its influence vis-à-vis the recently constituted Western Contact Group[2], and in November he shared WCG's draft settlement proposal and SWAPO's informal position papers with the Swedish embassy in Luanda.[3] Cautiously optimistic, Nujoma welcomed Sweden's participation in "the substantial UN operation in Namibia".[4] While referring to the WCG as the 'gang of five', other SWAPO leaders were at the same time equally hopeful that a negotiated settlement could be reached. Also in November 1977, the Secretary for Foreign Affairs, Peter Mueshihange, conveyed to ambassador Kaj Falkman that the Soviet Union was exercising "pressure" on the liberation movement to reject the presence of UN troops during a transition period in Namibia. "Without hiding his irritation", Mueshihange said that the Soviet Union "only was interested in the continuation of the armed struggle", while SWAPO "did not wish [to wage] war for the sake of war".[5]

In addition to bilateral meetings at the level of the Swedish embassies in Luanda and Lusaka, high-level discussions were conducted in late 1977 and—above all—in 1978 during visits to Southern Africa and Sweden. The Namibia question featured prominently on Karin Söder's agenda when in October 1977 the Swedish Foreign Minister travelled to Tanzania, Zambia and Botswana. And—as earlier noted—in February 1978, she received President Nujoma and SWAPO's internal leaders Daniel Tjongarero and Hendrik Witbooi in Stockholm, immediately after the breakdown of so called 'proximity talks' between WCG, SWAPO and South Africa in

---

1. Not counting additional emergency allocations, the annual allocation to SWAPO, for example, was increased from 10 MSEK in 1977/78 to 20 million in 1978/79.
2. The SWAPO President was surprised that Canada formed part of the group. Seeing the policies of Canada and Sweden towards Southern Africa as "quite close", Nujoma asked the Swedish ambassador in Luanda whether his government could "influence" the Canadian government (Cable from Kaj Falkman, Swedish ambassador to Angola, to the Ministry for Foreign Affairs, Luanda, 13 May 1977) (MFA).
3. Letter ('Samtal med Sam Nujoma'/'Conversation with Sam Nujoma') from Kaj Falkman to the Ministry for Foreign Affairs, Luanda, 15 November 1977 (MFA).
4. Ibid.
5. Mueshihange cited in cable from Kaj Falkman to the Ministry for Foreign Affairs, Luanda, 3 November 1977 (MFA). It could be noted that the Soviet Union together with its ally Czechoslovakia abstained from voting on both the UN Security Council Resolution 431 in July 1978 and Resolution 435 in September 1978. In a meeting at the Swedish embassy in Luanda in June 1978, Aaron Mushimba, SWAPO's Chief Representative to Angola, was, similarly, concerned about the Soviet Union's position (Cable ('Samtal 1978 06 07 med Mushimba, SWAPO'/'Conversation 7 June 1978 with Mushimba, SWAPO') from Kaj Falkman to the Ministry for Foreign Affairs, Luanda, 8 June 1978) (MFA).

New York. Nujoma was soon followed by Vice-President Mishake Muyongo, who together with the former SWAPO representative in Stockholm, Ben Amathila, now Secretary for Economic Affairs, and Linekela Kalenga, Secretary for Education and Culture, visited Sweden in early May 1978 to discuss possible Swedish assistance to an independent Namibia, particularly in the field of technical assistance.[1]

This was the first time that regular development assistance to Namibia was considered by the Swedish government[2], twelve years before independence eventually was achieved. The discussions continued in Lusaka later in May, when the SWAPO delegation—led by Muyongo—during the aid negotiations emphasized the need for "further assistance and funds for planning purposes".[3] The diplomatic talks and assistance to Namibia were also raised in a meeting between SWAPO's Administrative Secretary Garoeb and Cooperation Minister Ullsten in Stockholm in August 1978[4], as well as by Foreign Secretary Mueshihange when he visited Sweden the following month.[5]

Sweden and its Nordic neighbours had also started to discuss their respective plans for future development assistance to an independent Namibia. At the level of foreign policy, the Nordic countries had for many years coordinated their positions on Southern Africa, notably at the United Nations.[6] At a meeting between the five Nordic Foreign Ministers in Helsinki, Finland, in September 1977, they went a step further, agreeing in principle on joint measures against apartheid. The agreement was formalized in Oslo, Norway, in March 1978, when a Nordic Programme of Action against Apartheid—the so called 'Oslo plan'—was adopted. At the same time, the Foreign Ministers from Denmark, Finland, Iceland, Norway and Sweden

> reiterated the willingness of the Nordic countries—within the framework of the United Nations—to make their services available for the promotion of a peaceful transition to independence and majority rule [in Namibia]. The participation of SWAPO will be decisive for the implementation of a peaceful transition [...].[7]

In November 1977, officials from the Nordic aid agencies met in Stockholm to discuss their humanitarian assistance programmes in Southern Africa, including the cooperation with the liberation movements in Zimbabwe, Namibia and South Africa.[8] One year later—in January 1979—a Nordic working group was set up to

1. Maj-Britt Amer: Memorandum ('SWAPO-delegation besöker SIDA'/'SWAPO delegation visits SIDA'), SIDA, Stockholm, 26 April 1978 (SDA). During the visit—which took place from 7 to 10 May 1978, that is, immediately after the Kassinga massacre—the SWAPO delegation conferred with Foreign Minister Söder, officials at the Ministry for Foreign Affairs and with SIDA. Discussions were also held with the ruling Centre and Liberal parties, as well as with the opposition Social Democratic Party and with the Africa Groups.
2. SIDA Country Division: Memorandum ('Svenskt stöd till SWAPO-Namibia'/'Swedish support to SWAPO-Namibia'), SIDA, Stockholm, 27 April 1978 (SDA).
3. 'Agreed minutes of discussions on the cooperation between the South West Africa People's Organization (SWAPO) and Sweden 1978/79', Lusaka, 31 May 1978 (SDA).
4. Göran Hasselmark: Memorandum ('M. Garoeb, SWAPO, besöker statsrådet Ullsten'/'M. Garoeb, SWAPO, visits Minister Ullsten'), Ministry for Foreign Affairs, Stockholm, 1 September 1978 (MFA).
5. Göran Hasselmark: Memorandum ('Samtal med SWAPO-representant'/'Conversation with SWAPO representative'), Ministry for Foreign Affairs, Stockholm, 28 September 1978 (MFA).
6. See Sellström Volume I, pp. 53-55.
7. 'Communiqué on the Nordic Foreign Ministers' meeting in Oslo', 9-10 March 1978, in Ministry for Foreign Affairs: *Documents on Swedish Foreign Policy: 1978*, Stockholm, 1982, p. 168.
8. Marika Fahlén: Memorandum ('Nordiska överläggningar om humanitärt bistånd till södra Afrika'/'Nordic deliberations on humanitarian assistance to Southern Africa'), CCHA/Ministry for Foreign Affairs, Stockholm, 30 January 1978 (SDA).

"study the conditions and forms for joint Nordic assistance to an independent Namibia".[1]

Towards the end of 1977, there was a widespread, positive feeling that the drawn out Namibian drama eventually would come to an end. SWAPO, Sweden and the Nordic countries embarked on short-term planning for a sudden break-through in the diplomatic negotiations. In Sweden, a number of initiatives were taken. In February 1978, for example, SIDA's future Director General Anders Forsse—at the time finishing an aid assignment in Tanzania—volunteered to form part of "the leadership of the Nordic military contingent" which was widely believed to be formed under a UN umbrella.[2] In mid-July 1978—immediately after SWAPO's acceptance of the WCG settlement proposal—the United Nations also approached the Swedish government with an informal request for military personnel, police and election observers.[3] In 1978-79—as in 1989—no Swedish military participation in UNTAG would, however, take place. More lasting initiatives were instead launched directly with SWAPO. This was, in particular, the case with the election support programme carried out by the International Centre of the Swedish Labour Movement.[4]

In the event of elections, SWAPO—harassed in Namibia and without any electoral experience—would be clearly disadvantaged compared with DTA and other internal political parties. In late 1978, the organization therefore approached the Social Democratic Party and LO for assistance[5], primarily with regard to the planning and organization of an election campaign, but also for the production and dissemination of information materials.[6] With close links between the Swedish social democratic movement and SWAPO—in the case of LO at the time illustrated by the support to NUNW—the request was well received and referred to the recently formed AIC for implementation.[7]

In January 1979, AIC submitted an application for financial support to CCHA.[8] It was, however, surprisingly shelved.[9] AIC's Bengt Säve-Söderbergh—who partici-

---

1. Jarl Tranaeus and Marianne Sundh: Memorandum ('Minnesanteckningar från möte om nordiskt bistånd till Namibia'/'Notes from meeting on Nordic assistance to Namibia'), Ministry for Foreign Affairs, Stockholm, 24 September 1981 (SDA). At the time, the proposal was that the Nordic countries should agree on a joint administrative model with the government of independent Namibia; that they should pool their resources; and that a joint Nordic aid office in Windhoek should be headed by Finland (ibid.).
2. Letter ('Ett eventuellt uppdrag för undertecknad i Namibia'/'A possible assignment for the undersigned in Namibia') from Anders Forsse to Leif Leifland, Under-Secretary of State for Foreign Affairs, Dar es Salaam, 12 February 1978 (MFA).
3. Klas Stenström: Memorandum ('Samråd om FN's underhandsframställning om svensk insats i Namibia'/'Consultations regarding the informal UN request for a Swedish contribution in Namibia'), Ministry for Foreign Affairs, Stockholm, 19 July 1978 (MFA).
4. Interviewed in 1997, Bengt Säve-Söderbergh, the former secretary general of AIC, stated: "The Swedish government was very much involved with the liberation movements and we had no reason to duplicate what it was doing. However, there were a number of specific projects that we carried out. For example, [...] we organized a seminar with SWAPO on elections in 1979. At the time, there was hope that something would move on the issue of Namibia" (Interview with Bengt Säve-Söderbergh, p. 336).
5. Letter ('Stöd till SWAPO inför eventuella val i Namibia'/'Support to SWAPO in the eventuality of elections in Namibia') from Bengt Säve-Söderbergh, AIC, to LO, Stockholm, 30 May 1979 (OPA).
6. Letter ('Stöd till SWAPO inför ett av FN övervakat val i Namibia'/'Support to SWAPO at the prospect of UN-supervised elections in Namibia') from Bengt Säve-Söderbergh to CCHA, Stockholm, 18 January 1979 (OPA).
7. As earlier noted, AIC was formed in 1978 by the Social Democratic Party, LO, KF and ABF. Bengt Säve-Söderbergh was its first secretary general (1978-85).
8. Letter ('Stöd till SWAPO inför ett av FN övervakat val i Namibia'/'Support to SWAPO at the prospect of UN-supervised elections in Namibia') from Bengt Säve-Söderbergh to CCHA, Stockholm, 18 January 1979 (OPA).
9. CCHA: 'Protokoll från sammanträde med beredningen för humanitärt bistånd' ('Minutes from meeting of the Consultative Committee on Humanitarian Assistance'), SIDA, Stockholm, 26 January 1979 (SDA).

Election materials for SWAPO: Tor Lindmark (standing) and Bengt Säve-Söderbergh of AIC with
SWAPO President Sam Nujoma and resident representative Hadino Hishongwa, Stockholm,
September 1980 (Photo: Paul Rimmerfors)

pated in the meeting[1]—later argued that "the request was blocked by the Minister
for Foreign Affairs with reference to impartiality in the political work".[2] While no
explicit reason for the decision can be found in the CCHA documentation[3], AIC,
instead, sought the financial means for the proposed activities from LO's ongoing
Southern Africa campaign, launched in September 1978.[4] In early June 1979, the
trade union confederation allocated 265,000 SEK to AIC and SWAPO for "election
planning, production of materials, advice etc.".[5]

The major part of the grant was used for the production of election materials.
Developed and printed by LO according to SWAPO's designs, they were eventually
shipped to Angola towards the end of 1980.[6] Before this, in June-July 1979 AIC
organized a major seminar with SWAPO at the UN Institute for Namibia in
Lusaka. Säve-Söderbergh chaired the proceedings together with Muyongo. For one

1. Holding various positions in the Swedish labour movement and government, Säve-Söderbergh was closely
   involved with the support to the Southern African liberation movements. Starting his career with SIDA, in
   1970 he joined the Ministry for Foreign Affairs, where he two years later became the head of the Africa section in the Department for International Development Cooperation. From 1976, he worked with international questions at LO, before being asked to set up AIC in 1978. After serving as AIC's secretary general
   until 1985, Säve-Söderbergh returned to the Ministry for Foreign Affairs. Between 1985 and 1991, he was
   Under-Secretary of State for International Development Cooperation. In 1995, he was appointed Secretary
   General of the International Institute for Democracy and Electoral Assistance (International IDEA) in Stockholm. Both as an official in the Ministry for Foreign Affairs and as head of AIC, Säve-Söderbergh formed part
   of CCHA.
2. Letter ('Stöd till SWAPO inför eventuella val i Namibia'/'Support to SWAPO in the eventuality of elections in
   Namibia') from Bengt Säve-Söderbergh to LO, Stockholm, 30 May 1979 (OPA). Sweden had at the time a
   Liberal minority government led by Ola Ullsten. Hans Blix served as Foreign Minister.
3. Over the years, the CCHA minutes only recorded the decisions reached, not the discussions held. A possible
   reason for the decision to postpone AIC's application could be that it was found wanting with regard to
   implementation schedules, budgets etc. As stated in 1997 by Carl Tham, the former Director General of SIDA
   and chairman of CCHA, "for each activity [supported], the decisions were so well prepared that it appears
   almost unbelievable today" (Interview with Carl Tham, p. 343).
4. See the chapter 'SACTU, Unions and Sanctions'.
5. Letter from Eva Hummelgren, LO, to AIC, Stockholm, 18 June 1979 (OPA).
6. Letter from Hadino Hishongwa to Rune Molin, LO, Stockholm, 27 November 1980 (OPA). According to
   SWAPO, the materials were "extremely well done" (ibid.).

week, three experts from the Social Democratic Party[1] shared their experiences of election procedures, campaigning and information with about 40 representatives from SWAPO.[2] The seminar was followed up with a visit to Sweden, where a SWAPO delegation led by Muyongo during a period of ten days in mid-September 1979 studied the Swedish local, regional and parliamentary elections.[3]

In the history of Swedish support to the liberation movements in Southern Africa, it is ironic that CCHA did not support the election training offered to SWAPO by AIC. The assistance was a pioneering effort, paving the way for similar projects with SWAPO at the end of the 1980s[4] and—above all—with ANC of South Africa in the early 1990s.

With financial backing from LO and the Social Democratic Party's international solidarity fund—and in spite of the fact that Vice-President Muyongo, its main SWAPO counterpart, was expelled in July 1980—AIC proceeded with its support. In January 1981, the Swedish labour movement assisted the organization during the 'pre-implementation talks' with South Africa in Geneva.[5] And in September 1982, AIC and the Social Democratic Party again invited SWAPO to follow the Swedish elections.[6] For two weeks, six SWAPO representatives toured the country, in particular familiarizing themselves with the election campaign and administrative issues at the local level, as well as studying technical aspects—such as voter registration—at the Swedish National Tax Board.[7] Organized by the labour movement, the study programme was far from partisan. In addition to discussions with the Social Democratic Party, it included deliberations with the ruling Centre and Liberal parties.[8]

The readiness displayed by Sweden and the other Nordic countries to contribute to a democratic settlement of the Namibia question was far from popular in South Africa. For example, in October 1978—when the UN request for comprehensive Swedish participation in UNTAG became official—the head of the South African legation in Stockholm, ambassador Jacobus Liebenberg, made an unconventional, direct contact with the Supreme Commander of the Swedish Armed Forces, General Lennart Ljung. Explaining that he had not discussed the question of Swedish military UNTAG participation with the Ministry for Foreign Affairs, Liebenberg made it clear that the composition of the UN forces was subject to South Africa's

---

1. In addition to Säve-Söderbergh, the Swedish seminar leaders were Sören Thunell, former head of the Social Democratic Party's information department; Rolf Theorin, for many years responsible for the planning of the party's election campaigns; and Tor Lindmark, responsible for the production of election materials (Letter from Bengt Säve-Söderbergh to Mishake Muyongo, Stockholm, 8 June 1979) (OPA).
2. Ibid.
3. Press release from AIC, signed by Bengt Säve-Söderbergh, Stockholm, 5 September 1979 (OPA). The SWAPO delegation followed the elections in Stockholm, Gothenburg and Söderhamn. In opposition since 1976, the Social Democratic Party lost the 1979 elections, which led to the Centre Party leader Thorbjörn Fälldin's second non-socialist coalition government of the Centre, Liberal and Moderate parties.
4. In September 1988, for example, eight SWAPO representatives were invited by AIC to follow the election campaign in Stockholm, the province of Södermanland and in Gothenburg (Letter ('Stöd till SWAPO inför eventuella val i Namibia'/'Support to SWAPO in the eventuality of elections in Namibia') from Elisabeth Michanek, AIC, to the Ministry for Foreign Affairs, Stockholm, 21 October 1988) (OPA).
5. Letter ('Stöd till befrielserörelsen SWAPO i Namibia ur LO's Södra Afrika-insamling'/'Support to the Namibian liberation movement SWAPO from LO's Southern Africa Campaign') from Bengt Säve-Söderbergh to LO, Stockholm, 9 January 1981 (OPA).
6. AIC: 'Protokoll från sammanträde med verkställande utskottet i I-fondens styrelse den 24 augusti 1982' ('Minutes from meeting of the executive committee of the board of the international [solidarity] fund on 24 August 1982'), [no place or date] (OPA).
7. In Swedish, *Riksskatteverket.*
8. Letter ('Ang. besök från SWAPO under den svenska valrörelsen'/'Re visit from SWAPO during the Swedish election campaign') from Conny Fredriksson, AIC, to Stellan Bäcklund, Stockholm, 6 September 1982 (OPA). The Social Democratic Party won the parliamentary elections in September 1982. Olof Palme—Prime Minister between 1969 and 1976—returned as head of government.

approval. Personnel suspected of pro-SWAPO sympathies were not welcome. Without mentioning Sweden, he stated that troops from some African countries—among them Nigeria—would not be accepted. According to Liebenberg, it was, similarly, not obvious that Pretoria would accept Finnish troops. "In any event", he added, they would "carefully scrutinize the people participating [in UNTAG]".[1]

Some months later, a number of fabricated stories on Sweden, SWAPO and UNTAG appeared in the Namibian and South African press. In mid-January 1979—shortly after Pretoria's agreement to cooperate in the implementation of UN Security Council Resolution 435—the Namibian newspaper *Die Republikein*, the DTA mouthpiece, published several reports which were reproduced in South Africa. Claiming that it was in possession of "secret SWAPO documents", *Die Republikein* alleged that Sweden "was involved in a plot" to ensure a SWAPO victory in the envisaged elections. According to the version published by *The Cape Times*, "Sweden was even prepared to risk its credibility as a member of UNTAG to aid and abet SWAPO". The Swedish government was said to have undertaken that military troops "[which] can be trusted by SWAPO would be included in the military UNTAG contingent". It was also said to have "offered to make officials available on Mr. Martti Ahtisaari's staff who would favour SWAPO". "Unlimited financial support" would, finally, "be given to SWAPO [by SIDA] and the Swedish Social Democratic Party".[2]

Due to South Africa's recalcitrance, there was no peaceful settlement of the Namibia question in 1979. When the final breakthrough eventually came ten years later, the apartheid regime opposed any Swedish military presence in Namibia. Traditionally a major contributor of troops to the United Nations peace-keeping operations, Sweden was excluded from UNTAG's military contingent in 1989-90.

Total Strategy and Constructive Engagement

Although the diplomatic efforts in favour of a peaceful solution were never completely abandoned, until the end of the 1980s the Namibia question was *de facto* relegated to the battlefields in Angola. In defence of the apartheid state, the new Prime Minister, P.W. Botha, launched the so called 'total strategy' against what was perceived as a regional 'Communist onslaught'.[3] Under this policy, Namibia was seen as a crucial buffer. Combined with containment of the nationalist movement in

---

1. Letter ('Samtal med Sydafrikas ambassadör'/'Conversation with South Africa's ambassador') from Lennart Ljung, Supreme Commander of the Armed Forces, to Leif Leifland, Under-Secretary of State for Foreign Affairs, Stockholm, 23 October 1978 (MFA).
2. *Die Republikein* and *The Cape Times* cited in cables from the Swedish legation in Pretoria to the Ministry for Foreign Affairs, Pretoria, 15 and 16 January 1979 (MFA).
3. 'Total strategy' was outlined in the South African Defence White Paper in 1977 and adopted as official state policy after the accession to the premiership of P.W. Botha in September 1978. As Minister of Defence, Botha had since 1973 repeatedly argued in favour of this security doctrine. Calling for the mobilization of all available resources against a perceived 'Communist onslaught', it was more of an ideological statement than a coherent military strategy. A publication issued by the South African authorities in Namibia in 1980 stated: "Insurgency is the military term for the infiltration of terrorists from neighbouring countries to the country which is their target. [...] A 'total insurgency onslaught' is the term used for this threat [when it] is aimed against everything and everybody, regardless of race or colour. [...] This total assault requires total resistance (by each and every one) on a basis organised by those in authority [...]. It requires a continuous and controlled reciprocal relationship between the economic, political, military, diplomatic and cultural facets of the state. [...] [A] solid front of opposition must be presented to the enemy, and this requires from everybody, also from the ordinary citizen, a larger measure of involvement and contribution than merely following the progress of the war in a newspaper" (*Counterinsurgency: A Way of Life* by SWA/Namibia Information Service, Windhoek, 1980, cited in The Catholic Institute for International Relations and the British Council of Churches: *Namibia in the 1980s*, CIIR/BCC, London, 1986, p. 77).

the country, a *cordon sanitaire* was to be established along Namibia's northern border and SWAPO militarily defeated inside Angola.[1]

Beginning with the strike against the Kassinga settlement in May 1978, South African cross-border raids and large-scale military operations into Angola were to be legion in the 1980s. With substantial support to Jonas Savimbi's proxy UNITA movement and systematic attacks on non-military 'targets', the costs of Pretoria's destabilization were enormous. In purely monetary terms, the United Nations Economic Commission for Africa estimated Angola's losses over the 1980-88 period at between 27 and 30 billion USD, corresponding to 600 per cent of the country's Gross Domestic Product in 1988.[2] During the same period, some 500,000 Angolans—a shocking 5.5 per cent of the national population in 1988—lost their lives as a direct or indirect consequence of South Africa's warfare. Two thirds of the dead were children under five years of age.[3] Towards the end of the decade, one out of two Angolans had, in addition, been displaced from their homes, while the number of wounded, mutilated and malnourished was more difficult to quantify.[4]

South Africa's aggression was largely encouraged by the British and US governments. Less than a year after his appointment, P.W. Botha found an ally in Margaret Thatcher, who as leader of the British Conservative Party became Prime Minister in 1979. Above all, in late 1980 the Republican Ronald Reagan won the US presidential elections. The two most influential members of the Western Contact Group were thereby led by governments who not only opposed economic sanctions against the apartheid regime, but were more interested in the Cold War dimension of the Angola question than in Namibia's right to self-determination.[5] Linking a withdrawal of the Cuban troops from Angola to a Namibian settlement, the latter issue was, in fact, of secondary importance. In early 1981—before the Reagan administration's policy of 'constructive engagement' had been launched—its princi-

---

1. On South Africa's 'total strategy' and regional policies, see Stephen Chan: *Exporting Apartheid: Foreign Policies in Southern Africa 1978-1988*, Macmillan Publishers, London and Basingstoke, 1990. The book contains valuable contributions by the South African scholars Peter Vale, Robert Davies and Dan O'Meara.
2. UN Economic Commission for Africa: *South African Destabilization: The Economic Cost of Frontline Resistance to Apartheid*, United Nations, New York, October 1989, pp. 4 and 6.
3. Ibid., pp. 5-6.
4. Ibid., p. 4. Angola and Mozambique were hardest hit by South Africa's military attacks and general destabilization policies. For the region as a whole, the economic losses over the 1980-88 period were estimated at more than 60 billion USD and the number of war-related deaths at 1.5 million, out of which almost 1 million were children (ibid., p. 6). Addressing the question whether South Africa's defence of Namibia had been "worthwhile", the former President F.W. de Klerk states in his autobiography: "My view [is] that it [was]. For more than two decades, we had successfully held the expansion of Soviet influence in our region at bay. We had secured the withdrawal of Cuban forces from neighbouring Angola and had ensured that the rights of all of the parties in [Namibia] had been properly protected in the independence constitution" (F.W. de Klerk: *The Last Trek: A New Beginning*, Macmillan, London and Basingstoke, 1998, p. 172). The 1993 Nobel Peace Prize laureate—a distinction shared with Nelson Mandela—does not mention the enormous human and capital losses inflicted by South Africa on Angola and Southern Africa.
5. Säve-Söderbergh later commented: "The right to self-determination was a strong and easily understandable issue, also in relation to our own country. But it was not seen like that by the Cold War representatives. For example, in [a] conversation with Chester Crocker [...] I said: 'To you, Swedish foreign policy must appear to be in a mess. In South Africa, we support the Soviets; in Zimbabwe, we support the Chinese; and in Afghanistan, we support the Americans'. He became very confused" (Interview with Bengt Säve-Söderbergh, p. 338).

pal author, the incoming US Assistant Secretary of State for African Affairs, Chester Crocker[1], asserted that

> Angola is the logical focal point for policy. It is in Angola [...] that anti-Communist forces are effectively engaged in trying to liberate their country from the new imperialism of Moscow and its allies. Not only is Jonas Savimbi's UNITA movement a genuine nationalist grouping [...]. [I]t is also succeeding in bloodying the Cubans, raising the price of adventurism to Moscow, and raising doubts in many Angolan minds about the benefits of the socialist alliance. This process should be encouraged with the aim of getting the Cubans out, so that a genuine political reconciliation can take place.

> As for Namibia, while a settlement is important there, it will not by itself end the Angolan strife, because Savimbi is by no means the tool of South Africa. He could continue to operate with the active support of other African states and governments elsewhere. [...] [T]he West should back UNITA until such time that the MPLA is prepared to negotiate and expel the Communist forces from Angola. Namibia [...] is a separate and less important issue.[2]

While many Namibians remained in Zambia, the bulk of the Swedish support was implemented in Angola, which hosted the overwhelming majority of the refugees and where SWAPO established its exile headquarters in 1979. The conditions in Angola in the 1980s were extremely difficult. SWAPO and the Namibian refugees—as well as foreigners working in the SWAPO settlements—were living under constant threat of attack by South Africa and UNITA.[3] Due to Pretoria's military operations and general destabilization policies, there was, in addition, a pronounced lack of basic commodities, including food. Practically without exception, all Swedish humanitarian assistance had to be shipped to the country.

As Sweden had established a broad development cooperation programme with the Luanda government and also extended humanitarian support to SWAPO and ANC in Angola, it was arguably in a better position than any other Western country to assess the devastating effects of South Africa's 'total strategy' and the United

---

1. Particularly in the United States, Crocker has been credited with preparing the terrain for the Namibian elections in 1989 and the Angolan elections in 1992. Although he did play an important role, such an assessment is myopic. In 1992, Crocker published his very personal accounts of the policy of 'constructive engagement' under the title *High Noon in Southern Africa: Making Peace in a Rough Neighborhood* (W. W. Norton & Company, New York). Commenting upon Crocker's role and his accounts of the events, in 1995 South Africa's former Foreign Minister 'Pik' Botha said that "Chester Crocker really tried to steal the show. A very American approach. [...] His facts are [...] not at all accurate, which surprised me. You would expect a man like that to have archives and notes that he could consult. I hope that God will give me the time and strength to write my own book, because then I would certainly reveal what really happened in the negotiations" (Interview with Roelof 'Pik' Botha, p. 116). Similarly, the main protagonists from Angola and the Southern African Frontline States would most probably describe the events in a radically different light. On Crocker's memoirs, cf. John Seiler: 'Crocker's Southern African Policy: A Critical Review' in *Journal of Contemporary African Studies*, No. 2, July 1995, pp. 193-205.
2. Chester Crocker with Mario Greznes and Robert Henderson: 'A US Policy for the '80s' in *Africa Report*, No. 1, 1981, pp. 9-10.
3. In early September 1983, for example, UNITA attacked the town of Calulo, 25 kilometres from the Kwanza Sul settlement. At the time, 15 Swedes were working there. The attacks increased towards the end of 1984. As a result, aid workers on SIDA contracts were withdrawn from the SWAPO camp between February 1985 and March 1986. As described in the context of Angola above, in September 1987 UNITA killed one and kidnapped two Swedish aid workers in the Quibaxe area.

States 'constructive engagement'.[1] Firmly opposed to the apartheid regime, the experience underlined the different views between Sweden and the major Western powers of what was 'important' and 'constructive' in Southern Africa. Denouncing the US position, in September 1984 Prime Minister Palme stated in a meeting of the Socialist International in Arusha, Tanzania, that

> we should reject the so called Cuban link, which has no part in the process for Namibian independence, and all other links or new conditions for the implementation of Resolution 435. It is an international scandal that the independence of Namibia has not yet been achieved. [...] We should [also] be more active in the work for United Nations sanctions against South Africa. [...] [S]o far, binding international sanctions through decisions by the [UN] Security Council have not been achieved, except in the limited military sphere. [Nevertheless,] big powers use sanctions against each other, and others. Evidently, they believe in the method. [...]

> In the light of history, it will be no excuse to just sit back and say that some big powers blocked a decision that the rest of us wanted, and let it rest at that.[2] We have to go the other way. Party by party, government by government, we could introduce various means of direct selective action. Such sanctions will not be [one hundred] per cent efficient, but that is not the major point. We want to put pressure on South Africa to change their system. We know that the South African government is vulnerable to international pressure. And we know that when Ian Smith finally sat down at Lancaster House, this was because of both the liberation struggle and the international sanctions.[3]

These arguments were repeated at the United Nations. Addressing the General Assembly on behalf of the Swedish government, in November 1984 the Social Democratic MP Jan Bergqvist emphasized that Resolution 435 had been adopted more than six years earlier. The fact that the Namibia question was still unresolved was characterized as "a human tragedy and an international disgrace".[4] Bergqvist also noted that the "extraneous issue [of] the 'Cuban link'" had not been invoked until several years after the adoption of the UN plan for Namibia, stating that "the Swedish government rejected these delaying tactics and considered the introduction of issues alien to the UN plan [...] unacceptable".[5] Calling for increased international assistance to SWAPO, he did the same with regard to Angola:

---

1. On various occasions in the mid-1980s, Sam Nujoma appealed to the Swedish government to use its diplomatic contacts with the United States in favour of direct talks between SWAPO and South Africa (cf. letter ('Samtal med Sam Nujoma och Herman Toivo ja Toivo'/'Conversation with Sam Nujoma and Herman Toivo ja Toivo') from Leif Sjöström, Swedish ambassador to Angola, to the Ministry for Foreign Affairs, Luanda, 4 April 1984 (MFA) and Kaj Persson: Memorandum ('Rapport från biståndsöverläggningar med SWAPO'/ 'Report from aid discussions with SWAPO'), Ministry for Foreign Affairs, Stockholm, 25 April 1984) (SDA). In the Reagan administration's Cold War perspective, Sweden was, however, not a trusted interlocutor. In 1997, Bengt Säve-Söderbergh recalled how Chester Crocker "was worried about our support to Communism", adding that he had replied that "[i]f anybody is supporting Communism in Southern Africa, it is you, Mr. Crocker. Communism is often born out of frustration and you are frustrating people by giving the wrong signals" (Interview with Bengt Säve-Söderbergh, p. 337).
2. Chairing the first ever international conference on Namibia in Oxford, England, in March 1966, Palme had warned almost twenty years earlier that "[i]t has [...] all too often happened in the history of individual countries, of the world powers [and] of the international community that they for years have seen a situation arise and inevitable developments take their course. In this respect, they have unwittingly acted as bystanders. And when the issue has burst wide open, it has seemingly come as a shock and [a] surprise. Action has then become blunt, haphazard, sometimes panicky, and with disastrous consequences" (cited in Sellström Volume I, p. 274).
3. The Socialist International: *The Arusha Conference*, Conference on Southern Africa of the Socialist International and the Socialist Group of the European Parliament with the Front Line States, ANC and SWAPO, Arusha, Tanzania, 4-5 September 1984, The Socialist International, London, 1985, pp. 40-41.
4. 'Swedish statement on Namibia to the UN General Assembly', 30 November 1984, in Ministry for Foreign Affairs: *Documents on Swedish Foreign Policy: 1984*, Stockholm, 1988, p. 196.
5. Ibid.

The question of Namibia is not a bilateral conflict, but a special responsibility for the whole of the United Nations. Angola should therefore be given increased economic assistance by the international community in order to alleviate [the] burden [of South Africa's aggression].[1]

From Kassinga to Kwanza Sul

Setting old differences aside, in early 1976 the MPLA government allocated various sites—including the abandoned mining centre at Kassinga—to SWAPO in the southern Huíla and Cunene provinces, where the organization could set up reception centres for the refugees pouring out of Namibia, as well as military bases. Critical of Zambia's role in the détente exercise with South Africa and with direct cross-border access to Namibia, SWAPO would from then on *de facto* establish the centre of its activities in Angola. Although it was not until the end of 1979 that the exile headquarters were formally moved from Lusaka to Luanda[2], in June 1976 a SWAPO office had already been opened in the Angolan capital.[3] At the enlarged Nampundwe Central Committee meeting in July-August 1976 it was, finally, agreed to transfer parts of the movement's central functions and structures to Angola.

The Swedish government established at the same time a diplomatic presence in Angola. In addition to discussions on future bilateral development cooperation, the issue of official Swedish support to SWAPO and ANC of South Africa in Angola was raised at an early stage. In June 1976, President Agostinho Neto's foreign policy adviser Paulo Jorge welcomed such support, explaining to visiting representatives from the Swedish Ministry for Foreign Affairs and SIDA that "nothing prevented any of the movements [supported by Sweden] from receiving goods in Angola".[4] Immediately thereafter, it was decided to grant SWAPO emergency assistance in the form of food supplies for the Namibian refugees in Angola, as well as a small cash contribution of 20,000 SEK for its Luanda office.[5] The Swedish government was thus among the very first to assist SWAPO in the country[6], before the specialized UN agencies[7] and even before an embassy had been properly established. The embassy—including a SIDA representative[8]—was formally opened in Luanda in October 1976.

Support to the Namibian refugees in Angola would from then on play a major part in the regular cooperation programme between Sweden and SWAPO. Submit-

---

1. Ibid.
2. Although SWAPO eventually would have established its headquarters in Luanda, the decision was forced by the fact that its offices at the Liberation Centre in Lusaka were destroyed during the Rhodesian raids against ZAPU in October 1978.
3. Herman Nangolo served as SWAPO's first Chief Representative to Angola.
4. Ann Wilkens: Memorandum ('Samtal med Paulo Jorge om stöd till befrielserörelser verksamma i Angola'/ 'Conversation with Paulo Jorge on support to liberation movements active in Angola'), Ministry for Foreign Affairs, Stockholm, 23 June 1976 (MFA).
5. 'Agreed minutes of discussion[s] on cooperation between Sweden and South West Africa People's Organization (SWAPO)', Lusaka, 2 September 1976 (SDA).
6. On a regular basis, the substantial non-military assistance from the German Democratic Republic to SWAPO in Angola only started in 1978 (Ilona and Hans-Georg Schleicher op. cit., p. 178).
7. UNICEF initiated its support to the Namibian refugees in Angola at the beginning of 1977, while UNHCR concluded an agreement with SWAPO in April 1977 (ya Nangolo and Sellström op. cit., pp. 23-24). WFP soon joined the UN effort.
8. Carin Norberg, who had been responsible for Swedish humanitarian assistance at the embassy in Lusaka between 1974 and 1976, was the first SIDA representative in Angola. Together with Anders Bjurner, she was particularly instrumental in establishing close and trustful relations between Sweden and the Southern African liberation movements in the turbulent mid-1970s. Directly involved with the support to SWAPO and ANC at SIDA's headquarters in the late 1970s and early 1980s, between 1984 and 1987 Norberg worked at the Office of the UN Commissioner for Namibia in New York.

ting the movement's request for the financial year 1976/77, in August 1976 Vice-President Muyongo noted that

> the increasing solidarity of our brothers and sisters in Angola is facilitating our efforts, but [the situation is] at the same time requiring resources which we had not anticipated. [...] Namibians have crossed [...] into Angola in large numbers. While the Angolan government is doing its best, SWAPO is primarily responsible for meeting the basic needs of [these] people. This entails food supply, medical facilities, assistance to war victims [...] and transport for the collection [...] and distribution of [the] supplies.[1]

At the annual negotiations in Lusaka later in the month, it was against this background agreed to set aside half of the original 1976/77 allocation of 5 MSEK for assistance in Angola.[2] The breakdown of the Angola budget was subsequently established in Luanda.[3] Food—mainly in the form of maize meal—was the biggest component. With an estimated Namibian refugee population in Angola of 5,000 people[4], 1.1 MSEK was used for this purpose. Transport support was—as earlier noted—also a major item. One million SEK—40 per cent of the Angola budget—was used for the procurement of trucks. The remaining 400,000 SEK was in approximately equal parts divided between educational supplies, office equipment and a cash contribution.[5] With the exception of maize meal, practically all the commodities supplied had to be purchased outside Angola.[6]

While considerable resources were still channelled to the health and education centre in Nyango, Zambia, with a rapidly increasing refugee population—and a generally deteriorating supply situation—Angola would from 1977/78 become the main target of the official Swedish assistance to SWAPO. For that year, the regular allocation to the movement was initially increased from 5 to 10 MSEK, of which it was agreed to use 6.1 million in Angola. Food and transport were again the biggest components, respectively representing shares of 49 and 46 per cent of the budget.[7]

In a letter to SIDA's Director General, Sam Nujoma wrote in September 1977 that "we now have over 10,000 Namibians of all age groups [...] under our care in Angola".[8] Most of them were settled at Kassinga, where SWAPO had established

---

1. Letter with proposed expenditures in 1976/77 from Mishake Muyongo to the Swedish ambassador to Zambia, Lusaka, 12 August 1976 (SDA).
2. 'Agreed minutes of discussion[s] on cooperation between Sweden and South West Africa People's Organization (SWAPO)', Lusaka, 2 September 1976 (SDA). It was at the same time agreed to allocate 45,000 SEK to the SWAPO office in Botswana and the more substantial amount of 170,000 SEK to SWAPO's Department of Information and Publicity in Lusaka. The latter contribution was the following year increased to 280,000 SEK, *inter alia* to be used for the production of SWAPO's official organ *Namibia Today* ('Agreed minutes of discussions on the cooperation between the South West Africa People's Organization (SWAPO) and Sweden 1977/78', Lusaka, 2 September 1977) (SDA). Support to the SWAPO office in Addis Ababa, Ethiopia, was included from 1981 and to the offices in Harare, Zimbabwe, and Brazzaville, People's Republic of the Congo, in 1982.
3. Letter ('Biståndsprogram för SWAPO 1976/77: Angola'/'Assistance programme for SWAPO 1976/77: Angola') from Carin Norberg, Swedish embassy, to SIDA, Luanda, 18 March 1977 (SDA).
4. The total number of refugees in Zambia was at the same time estimated at 3,700, most of them at the Nyango settlement.
5. 'SWAPO: Cooperation program[me] with Sweden 1976/77', financial overview attached to memorandum ('Biståndssamarbetet med South West Africa People's Organization, SWAPO, under budgetåret 1976/77 och framställning om stöd under 1977/78'/'Aid cooperation with SWAPO during the financial year 1976/77 and request for support in 1977/78') by Marianne Sundh, CCHA/SIDA, Stockholm, 3 May 1977 (SDA).
6. This included such basic commodities as soap and washing powder. In 1976/77, SIDA shipped no less than 7.5 tons of washing powder to SWAPO in Angola (Letter ('Biståndsprogram för SWAPO 1976/77: Angola'/ 'Assistance programme for SWAPO 1976/77: Angola') from Carin Norberg, Swedish embassy, to SIDA, Luanda, 18 March 1977) (SDA).
7. Marianne Sundh: Memorandum ('Information om biståndssamarbetet med South West Africa People's Organization (SWAPO) budgetåren 1976/77 och 1977/78'/'Information on the aid cooperation with SWAPO [during] the financial years 1976/77 and 1977/78'), CCHA/SIDA, Stockholm, 28 October 1977 (SDA).
8. Letter from Sam Nujoma to the Director General of SIDA, Lusaka, 7 September 1977 (SDA).

its health and education centre in the country. It was to this centre that the Swedish assistance was mainly channelled.

Situated some 250 kilometres north of the Namibian border and about 300 kilometres east of Lubango—the capital of the Huíla province—Kassinga was an old iron mining site which had been abandoned in 1975. With the arrival of thousands of refugees from Namibia, it rapidly changed. The old Portuguese colonial houses were converted into offices, schools, a clinic, warehouses, workshops etc., while new permanent structures—erected with locally made clay-bricks—thatched wooden huts and tents started to cover the ground. Fields were opened up and planted with maize, millet and vegetables.[1]

In mid-April 1978—just three weeks prior to the South African attack—a delegation from the United Nations Children's Fund (UNICEF) visited Kassinga. Observing a "flood of refugees coming directly from Namibia under pressure and repression from the South African army, which is currently attempting to establish a no-man's-land on the Angolan-Namibian frontier", the delegation estimated the number of Namibians at between 11,000 and 12,000.[2] With regard to the composition of the refugee population, the mission found that "the young population, that is to say, adolescents, children and infants, constitutes the majority. The percentage of women also seems to be considerable". Thus, the mission concluded, "the vulnerable groups apparently represent approximately 70 per cent of the total population [...]. The remainder [...] is composed of adults, with very few elderly persons". The school-going population was estimated at close to 2,500.[3]

As would be expected in any rapidly growing refugee settlement, the UNICEF mission identified a number of problem areas, particularly in the fields of nutrition, health, education and shelter. In general, however, it was positively impressed by SWAPO's organization and administration, as well as by the determination shown by the refugees:

> The term 'refugees'—by which they rightly do not like to be known—does not correspond to those of Namibia. This term makes one expect passive, destitute, lifeless people, without physical and moral resource or viable organization [...]. Although they have all the needs of [ordinary] refugees, those [from] Namibia form a category apart. They are a community, which—despite the adversity of the conditions in which they live—displays very high social organization [...] in several fields. Both men and women, as well as the young people, participate in dynamic fashion in various activities. One is struck by their physical, moral, political and military determination [...]. Their speeches, their songs, their processions, the defence of their camps and the organization of their health services, their education and sanitation [programmes] bore witness to, or were a presage of what an independent Namibia would be. [...]

> What was striking in discussions with the refugees was the constant concern to consider their present activities in all fields as the augury of their development programmes in a free Namibia. This determination galvanized them, lent strength to their activities and explained the constant priority [given by SWAPO] both to training their future cadres and to carrying out daily tasks in the social sectors [...]. Therefore, in the case of the refugees from Namibia, one should speak of cooperation rather than of assistance.[4]

Such was the situation encountered by UNICEF in the SWAPO settlement that the generals in distant Pretoria had decided to level to the ground. In official comments after the massacre, the South African government claimed that Kassinga was

1. ya Nangolo and Sellström op. cit., pp. 24-26.
2. UNICEF Area Office: 'Report on a mission to SWAPO centres for Namibian refugees in Angola from 10 to 14 April 1978', Brazzaville, 2 May 1978, cited in ya Nangolo and Sellström op. cit., p. 26.
3. Ibid., p. 27.
4. Ibid., pp. 28-29.

"SWAPO's main operational centre", from which "the intensity of acts of violence and the frequency of border violations [...] had increased dangerously".[1] "This escalation", Pretoria argued, "took place in spite of South Africa's efforts to secure a peaceful solution, and the South African government was confronted [with] urgent appeals from the leaders of South West Africa for protection".[2] Against this background, P.W. Botha stated, "a limited military operation [...] had been carried out".[3]

What the future Prime Minister called 'a limited operation' was, however, "the first true parachute attack ever carried out by the SADF".[4] The assault on Kassinga took place in the morning of 4 May 1978[5], when most of the refugees were assembled at the central, open parade ground for information and organization concerning the tasks to be performed during the day. After intense aerial bombardments—including anti-personnel fragmentation bombs and gas canisters—500 South African paratroopers descended on what remained of the settlement, carrying out 'mopping-up' operations, shooting and bayonetting refugees still surviving.[6] Almost half of the Namibians killed were children and more than a quarter women. In a statement to the South African press, a SADF spokesman subsequently declared that "many of our troops said [...] that it was hell to have to shoot at women".[7] This notwithstanding, Pretoria decorated many of its soldiers with the South African Cross of Honour for "gallantry in battle".[8]

The SWAPO health and education centre at Kassinga was no more. The thriving refugee community visited by UNICEF three weeks earlier had been blown to pieces by South Africa's military might. Visiting Kassinga after the massacre, representatives of UNHCR and WHO described it as "criminal in international law, barbaric from a moral point of view [and reminiscent of] the darkest episodes in modern history".[9] More than 600 Namibian refugees, who during the preceding months, weeks and days had fled the South African occupation of their country,

---

1. Message from the South African government to the Western Contact Group, 5 May 1978, cited in ya Nangolo and Sellström op. cit., p. 30. According to the South African Truth and Reconciliation Commission (TRC), Kassinga "housed a considerable number of combatants, including senior [PLAN] officers" (*Truth and Reconciliation Commission of South Africa Report*, Volume Two, Juta & Co. Ltd, Kenwyn, Cape Town, 1998, p. 50).
2. ya Nangolo and Sellström, op. cit., p. 30.
3. Statement by the South African Minister of Defence, P.W. Botha, on 4 May 1978, cited in ibid.
4. William Steenkamp: *Borderstrike: South Africa into Angola*, Butterworths Publishers, Durban, 1983, p. 15. In 1998, TRC characterized the attack on Kassinga as "possibly the single most controversial external operation of the Commission's mandate period", holding the following representatives of the apartheid regime accountable for "gross human rights violations against the civilian occupants of the Kassinga camp": Prime Minister Vorster, Defence Minister Botha, SADF Chief Malan, Army Chief Viljoen and Air Force Chief Rogers (TRC op. cit. (Vol. II), pp. 46 and 55).
5. After independence, Kassinga Day was declared a national holiday in Namibia.
6. For personal accounts by survivors from the massacre, see ya Nangolo and Sellström op. cit., pp. 2-5 and 38-69.
7. Cited in ibid., p. 34.
8. Steenkamp op. cit., pp. 264-66. In his account of the assault, the South African Commander Lewis Brand has given a vivid and ghastly picture of the so called 'battle'. Landing with his parachute "where the ground was thickly sown with corpses, many of them so badly mutilated by the anti-personnel bombs that even hardened veterans [...] were shocked", Brand continues: "A small toddler of about 18 months kept wandering around [...]. It kept going from body to body, obviously looking for its mother [...]. The troops began to get a bit upset, [so] I got Malcolm Blom to pick up the child and bring it to me. With the baby under my arm, I belted into the hospital and luckily found three little girls [...] hiding under a bed. I coaxed them out and gave them the baby to look after [...] Then it was back to the war" (cited in ibid., p. 68). And in a testimony to the Truth and Reconciliation Commission, Lieutenant Johan Verster stated almost twenty years later: "It was probably the most bloody exercise that we ever launched [...]. It was a terrible thing [...]. I saw many things that happened there, but I don't want to talk about it now, because I always start crying [...]. It [has] damaged my life" (cited in TRC op. cit. (Vol. II), p. 44).
9. Nicolas Bwakira, Juan Ortiz-Blasco and Tor Sellström: 'Joint report by UNHCR and WHO representatives on their visit to Cassinga and to the Namibian refugees', Luanda, 30 May 1978.

From SWAPO's health and education centre at Kassinga after the South African raid: A survivor searching in vain for her belongings, May 1978 (Photo: Sven Åsberg/Pressens Bild)

were killed by the apartheid regime in a third country. Another 600 were maimed for life, with many more affected by gas or mentally traumatized.[1] The South African paratroop commander Lewis Brand later stated:

Everything was burnt to the ground [...]. [T]he shattered trees stood out starkly against the smoke-laden sky [and] the trenches were filled with dead [...]. The smell of death lay thickly about [...], a sweet, cloying aroma that sticks in your nasal passages.[2]

The surviving Namibians were moved after the attack by SWAPO to different transit facilities allocated by the Angolan government in the vicinity of Lubango. As the movement's supplies had been destroyed[3], there was, however, an acute and massive need of food, medicines, tents and other basic commodities. In the case of Sweden, the government decided on 11 May 1978 to grant SWAPO an emergency allocation of 1.5 MSEK for urgent procurement and air transport of food from Zambia, while additional financial resources were extended to UNHCR to cover

---

1. After the retreat of the South Africans, Angolan and Cuban forces took control of the situation. The dead were laid to rest in two mass graves, one for some 120 infants and one for around 460 older children, adolescents and adults. After emergency treatment, the seriously wounded were taken to hospitals in Lubango and Luanda. Due to rapid overcrowding of the Angolan hospitals, lack of proper facilities and the complexities of the injuries—often caused by pulmonary stab wounds from bayonets—many wounded were later flown to Cuba, the German Democratic Republic and other friendly countries for specialized treatment (ya Nangolo and Sellström op. cit., pp. 35-36).
2. Cited in Steenkamp op. cit., p. 90.
3. The South Africans destroyed SWAPO's clinic and its medical stores. Above all, 4 of the 10 trained Namibian nurses and 28 of the 40 assistant nurses were killed during the massacre (ya Nangolo and Sellström op. cit., p. 36). Ironically, the nylon parachutes left behind by the South African paratroopers were later used to a great extent by the surviving medical staff to construct makeshift 'clinics' and outdoor 'wards' (Author's recollection).

other areas.[1] The Zambian operation was more complicated than expected. SIDA's Roland Axelsson later recalled how

> we chartered a British airplane in Lusaka to fly foodstuffs to Luanda as emergency assistance. We procured mealie-meal to fill five airplanes, but when we were about to load the lorries [that] we had rented from [the] Zambia National Milling [Corporation], the Zambian Minister of Agriculture gave contra-orders, saying that we could not export maize flour: 'You have to find something else to send to Angola'. Elisabeth Michanek of SIDA, the Vice-President of SWAPO [...], Mishake Muyongo, and I then had to run around in the market places in Lusaka to buy other foodstuffs. We found beans, rice, wheat etc. We needed quite a lot to fill five DC 8 aircraft, but we managed.
>
> I personally accompanied one of the flights to Luanda. [...] When we arrived at Luanda airport, Angolan military planes were already parked there. Everything was re-loaded into these military aircraft, which then flew the food to [Lubango] and the surviving Namibian refugees.[2]

As the South African attacks in southern Angola continued, thousands of SWAPO refugees were moved later in 1978 in massive operations—largely by truck—to safety in the Kwanza Sul province, more than 800 kilometres from the Namibian border. Here, in a coffee-growing area between the Kwanza river and the small town of Calulo, SWAPO was for the third time in three years faced with the challenge of building a health and education centre from scratch[3], trying to give the refugees a meaningful existence in exile.[4] Sweden would be closely involved in this venture. In fact, throughout the 1980s the Kwanza Sul settlement was the focal point of Sweden's expanding cooperation with SWAPO. Excluding commodity aid, technical assistance and various other project activities, at the end of the 1980s it was estimated that the Swedish share of the settlement's infrastructural investments was about 20 per cent of an estimated 100 MSEK.[5]

Situated about 300 kilometres south-east of Luanda, SWAPO's new health and education centre was very different from the Kassinga settlement. Initially, scores of refugees fell victim to malaria in the hot and humid environment. Largely for security reasons, the settlement was divided into a number of smaller camps, interspersed with Angolan villages and spread over a large area of approximately 200 square kilometres. About twenty camps—or 'units'—were eventually established. There were camps for administration, health, education, logistics, workers' brigades, 'labour'[6], nurseries, kindergartens etc. Agricultural activities were carried out on the banks of the Kwanza river, some 30 kilometres north of the main settlement. The production was, however, far from sufficient. With other basic commodities, huge quantities of food had to be transported by SWAPO from Luanda in convoys protected by armed PLAN units.

The Kwanza Sul settlement was established from mid-1978, and towards the end of 1979 SWAPO formally opened its exile headquarters in Luanda. There was,

---

1. As earlier noted, SWAPO's Vice-President Muyongo was visiting Sweden at the time of the Kassinga massacre. He immediately returned to Zambia. The decision taken by the Swedish government on 11 May 1978 was for 3 MSEK, of which half was intended for the victims of the South African attack and half for SWAPO's work inside Namibia (Cable ('Extra stöd till SWAPO'/'Additional support to SWAPO') from the Ministry for Foreign Affairs to the Swedish embassy in Luanda, Stockholm, 11 May 1978) (MFA).
2. Interview with Roland Axelsson, p. 256.
3. The Nyango settlement in western Zambia was started from scratch in late 1975 and the Kassinga settlement in southern Angola from mid-1976.
4. Other civilian SWAPO camps were established at Ndalatando (Kwanza Norte), Sumbe (Kwanza Sul) and Viana (Luanda). PLAN's military headquarters were in Lubango (Huíla).
5. Berit Rylander: Memorandum ('Utvecklingssamarbetet med SWAPO: D 2'/'Development cooperation with SWAPO: D 2'), Swedish embassy, Luanda, 4 February 1988 (SDA).
6. The Nduuvu Nangolo Trade Union Centre was popularly known as 'labour'.

however, to be no respite for longer term planning. In mid-January 1980, it was reported that South African troops had crossed into western Zambia[1] and shortly thereafter the South African air force started to overfly the Namibian settlement at Nyango.[2] With the Kassinga massacre fresh in mind, SWAPO decided to urgently move between 1,000 and 1,200 refugees—mainly children, women and physically handicapped—from Nyango to Kwanza Sul.[3] The refugees were to be transported by road to Lusaka and from there to Luanda by air. Outside the regular assistance programme, SIDA had earlier granted SWAPO an extraordinary allocation of 2 MSEK for the transportation of Namibians from Zambia to Angola. An unspent balance of 1.2 million was used for the emergency operation.[4]

As a result of the repression in Namibia, there was at the same time a continuous flow of refugees into southern Angola. Confronted with increasing problems to cater for the basic needs of the exiled population, in early June 1980—less than a month after the regular aid negotiations[5]—SWAPO therefore submitted an emergency appeal to Sweden for additional food supplies and blankets.[6] The request was immediately granted, and later in the month SIDA delivered 20,000 blankets, 1,600 tents for six persons each and 50 tons of food.[7] In August 1980, another 200 tons of food were shipped as emergency assistance to SWAPO in Angola.[8]

As it became increasingly evident that there was no imminent solution to the Namibia question, SWAPO and Sweden had by then initiated discussions on a comprehensive, longer term support programme for the Kwanza Sul settlement. At a time when several Swedish NGOs—ranging from the Recruitment Organization of the Africa Groups[9] and Bread and Fishes[10] via the Swedish Save the Children Asso-

---

1. Letter ('Samtal med SWAPO-ledare'/'Conversation with SWAPO leader') from Anders Möllander, Swedish embassy, to the Ministry for Foreign Affairs, Lusaka, 22 January 1980 (MFA).
2. Letter ('Flyttning ZAM-ANG'/'Move from Zambia to Angola') from Ola Jämtin, Swedish embassy, to SIDA, Lusaka, 6 February 1980 (SDA). In April 1980, Hifikepunye Pohamba showed Ola Jämtin and Anders Möllander from the Swedish embassy in Lusaka parts of a South African plane allegedly shot down by SWAPO in the Western Province (Letter ('SWAPO uppger sig ha skjutit ned sydafrikanska flygplan i Zambia'/'SWAPO states that it has shot down South African airplanes in Zambia') from Göran Hasselmark, Swedish ambassador to Zambia, to the Ministry for Foreign Affairs, Lusaka, 15 April 1980) (MFA).
3. Letter ('Flyttning ZAM-ANG'/'Move from Zambia to Angola') from Ola Jämtin, Swedish embassy, to SIDA, Lusaka, 6 February 1980 (SDA).
4. Letter ('Special fund for transportation and other related matters for Namibians from Zambia to Angola') from Hifikepunye Pohamba to Ola Jämtin, Lusaka, 6 February 1980 (SDA).
5. In mid-May 1980, the annual aid negotiations between Sweden and SWAPO were for the first time held in the Angolan capital. The Swedish delegation was led by ambassador Göte Magnusson, while President Nujoma headed the SWAPO team. Magnusson announced that the Swedish government had set aside 33 MSEK to SWAPO for the financial year 1980/81. Of this amount, it was agreed by the parties to allocate 23.6 million for Angola, 5 million for Zambia and 3 million for activities inside Namibia ('home front') ('Agreed minutes from discussions on the cooperation between the South West Africa People's Organization (SWAPO of Namibia) and the Swedish International Development Authority (SIDA)', Luanda, 15 May 1980) (SDA).
6. Letter ('Urgent request for foodstuff and blankets to SIDA from SWAPO of Namibia for emergency assistance to Namibian exiles in the People's Republic of Angola') from Aaron Mushimba to the Swedish embassy in Luanda, Luanda, 7 June 1980 (SDA).
7. Jörgen Christensen: Memorandum ('Namibia: Bk's kvartalsrapport för perioden 1980 07 01-1980 09 30'/'Namibia: Quarterly report from SIDA's development cooperation office for the period 1 July-30 September 1980'), Swedish embassy, Luanda, 14 October 1980 (SDA).
8. Ibid. In February and March 1981, additional shipments of a total of 115 tons of supplementary enriched food were made by SIDA outside the regular assistance programme (Jörgen Christensen: Memorandum ('Namibia: Kvartalsrapport för perioden 1981 01 01-1981 03 31'/'Namibia: Quarterly report for the period 1 January-31 March 1981'), Swedish embassy, Luanda, 27 April 1981) (SDA).
9. As earlier noted, recruited by ARO with financial support from SIDA two Swedish medical doctors, one nurse and one laboratory assistant started to work in February 1980 with SWAPO in Kwanza Sul.
10. In December 1979, Bread and Fishes and the Africa Groups concluded an agreement with SWAPO on health support.

ciation[1] to the National Association of Deaf People[2]—had embarked upon concrete activities with SWAPO in Angola, there was also a marked change in the official Swedish assistance in 1980. In addition to the commodity aid hitherto extended, project aid, including technical assistance and with a substantial participation of Swedish private consultancy firms and contractors, would from then on play an increasingly important role.

The starting point was a request from SWAPO in February 1980, asking SIDA for assistance to build clinics, class-rooms, staff houses and dormitories, as well as to ensure an adequate supply of electricity and water in the settlement.[3] This was the first time that SWAPO approached the Swedish government for project assistance.[4] The request paved the way for a major construction programme, which soon also received substantial financial contributions from Denmark, Norway and UNHCR. Coordinated and implemented by SIDA, it opened a new chapter in Sweden's relations with the Namibian liberation movement. Taking place in a particularly difficult environment, initially the new form of cooperation made great demands on the different partners, leading to misunderstandings, delays and frustrations. Nevertheless, the positive experiences outweighed the disadvantages, and by the mid-1980s a number of new projects had been launched by SWAPO and Sweden in both Angola and Zambia.

Constructions in Kwanza Sul

In response to SWAPO's request, SIDA contracted the Swedish architectural and planning firm White & Partners to establish preliminary plans for the proposed construction project. The consultant visited Kwanza Sul in June 1980 and submitted a draft architect's brief in September. Although the Swedish authorities were positive to the project, the feasibility study indicated that the total costs would amount to 15–20 MSEK, which at the time was beyond the available resources

---

1. In Swedish, *Rädda Barnens Riksförbund*. After the Kassinga massacre, Save the Children approached CCHA for financial support in favour of the Namibian refugee children in Angola. The request was granted in October 1978 (CCHA: 'Protokoll från sammanträde med beredningen för humanitärt bistånd'/'Minutes from meeting of the Consultative Committee on Humanitarian Assistance', SIDA, Stockholm, 17 October 1978) (SDA).
2. In Swedish, *Sveriges Dövas Riksförbund*. In 1979, SWAPO asked the Swedish National Association of Deaf People for scholarships for three deaf members at the Västanvik folk high school in Leksand. Financial resources were granted by CCHA/SIDA in February 1980 (CCHA: 'Protokoll från sammanträde med beredningen för humanitärt bistånd'/'Minutes from meeting of the Consultative Committee on Humanitarian Assistance', SIDA, Stockholm, 25 February 1980) (SDA).
3. Letter ('The Nordic clinic and school project in SWAPO's civilian settlement, Kwanza Sul, Angola') from Bengt Svensson to the UNHCR Branch Office in Luanda, Swedish embassy, Luanda, 28 August 1981 (SDA). Also Sam Nujoma: 'Welcoming address to the delegation of SIDA', Luanda, 13 May 1980 (SDA).
4. Arguing that it did not have sufficient—or sufficiently trained—personnel, until 1979 SWAPO preferred that SIDA handled the commodity aid on its behalf (cf. Marianne Sundh: Memorandum ('Information om biståndssamarbetet med South West Africa People's Organization (SWAPO) budgetåren 1976/77 och 1977/78'/'Information on the aid cooperation with SWAPO [during] the financial years 1976/77 and 1977/78'), CCHA/SIDA, Stockholm, 28 October 1977) (SDA). In a spirit of concerned partnership, at the official aid negotiations in Lusaka in May 1979 it was, however, agreed "to implement a system of advance payment [from SIDA to SWAPO] on a quarterly basis. It was further agreed that the use of [the] funds should be accounted for in the form of quarterly financial reports" ('Agreed minutes of discussions on the cooperation between the South West Africa People's Organization (SWAPO) and Sweden 1979/80', Lusaka, 18 May 1979) (SDA). SWAPO thus assumed greater responsibility for procurement of commodities under the Swedish assistance programme. The system was introduced in 1979 in all the countries in Southern Africa where SIDA assisted SWAPO (Letter ('Uppföljning av biståndsprogram med SWAPO 1979/80'/'Follow-up of the assistance programme with SWAPO 1979/80') from Carin Norberg to SIDA Luanda, SIDA, Stockholm, 12 December 1979) (SDA).

within the assistance programme to SWAPO.[1] It was therefore agreed that SIDA
and SWAPO should approach the other Nordic countries for possible co-financing.
With considerable unspent balances under its SWAPO programme, the Norwegian
government responded favourably in December 1980.[2] Whereas Finland later
designed its own programme[3], in April 1981 the Danish government—which otherwise did not extend direct official assistance to the Southern African liberation
movements—also decided to support the project.[4] At the end of 1981, finally,
UNHCR joined the Scandinavian effort.[5] With considerable delays and cost
increases, total payments under the construction project would between 1 July
1980 and 30 June 1983 eventually amount to 32.3 MSEK[6], of which Sweden contributed 19.5, Norway 8.8 and Denmark and UNHCR 2 million each.[7] Additional
allocations of some 20 MSEK were later made by SIDA for maintenance of the
buildings and for the water supply system.[8]

Based on the consultant's first assessment, in December 1980 SWAPO's Executive Committee ranged the different sub-projects in order of priority. Prime importance was given to a water supply and distribution system throughout the
settlement. Thereafter followed in decreasing order a) a central hospital, b) a
second hospital/clinic, c) school dormitories, d) a primary and secondary school,
and e) other buildings, such as a dining hall for the school and staff houses for
doctors and teachers. The construction of an electricity supply system was
accorded the lowest priority.[9] With this guidance, White & Partners returned to
Kwanza Sul to establish a detailed plan for the project. Estimating the refugee pop-

---

1. Letter ('The Nordic clinic and school project in SWAPO's civilian settlement, Kwanza Sul, Angola') from
   Bengt Svensson to the UNHCR Branch Office in Luanda, Swedish embassy, Luanda, 28 August 1981
   (SDA).
2. Østbye in Eriksen (ed.) op. cit., p. 110. Agreement on a Norwegian contribution of 9.4 million NOK for
   the period 1980-82 was signed in September 1981 (Bengt Svensson: Memorandum ('Halvårsrapport:
   Biståndet till SWAPO 1981 07 01-1981 12 31'/'Biannual report: The assistance to SWAPO 1 July-31
   December 1981'), Swedish embassy, Luanda, 2 March 1982) (SDA). As an expression of the close cooperation between Sweden, Norway and SWAPO, it could be noted that when substantial unspent balances
   occurred in the mid-1980s under the Swedish assistance programme it was agreed to channel resources to
   the Norwegian government in favour of the construction of SWAPO's secondary technical school in Loudima, People's Republic of the Congo. Swedish support to the proposed school had been raised by SWAPO
   in early 1982 (Letter ('Education programmes: SWAPO') from Jörgen Christensen to SIDA, Swedish
   embassy, Luanda, 1 March 1982) (SDA). At the annual aid negotiations in May 1982, it was, however,
   agreed that "Swedish funds would not be used for [...] the school" ('Agreed minutes from discussions on
   the cooperation between the South West Africa People's Organization (SWAPO) of Namibia and the Swedish International Development Authority (SIDA)', Lusaka, 21 May 1982) (SDA). Nevertheless, with huge
   available resources the parties agreed to allocate 5 MSEK to the school project coordinated by Norway in
   1985/86 (Letter ('Besök vid Namibia Secondary Technical School i Loudima i Folkrepubliken Kongo'/'Visit
   to the Namibia Secondary Technical School in Loudima, People's Republic of the Congo') from Berit
   Rylander to SIDA, Swedish embassy, Luanda, 19 March 1987) (SDA). On Norway and the Loudima
   school, see Østbye op. cit. pp. 112-21 and 'Pioneering Local Activism: The Namibia Association of Norway' by the same author in Eriksen (ed.) op. cit., pp. 368-70.
3. In 1983, the Finnish government started a 'Namibia Education, Health, Nutrition and Research Programme',
   which *inter alia* included a health training programme for nurses in Kwanza Sul and the production of education materials for SWAPO's primary schools (Soiri and Peltola op. cit., p. 119).
4. Letter from Bent Haakonsen, Danish Ministry of Foreign Affairs, to SIDA, Copenhagen, 9 April 1981 (SDA).
   The Danish contribution would be available in 1982.
5. Bengt Svensson: Memorandum ('Halvårsrapport: Biståndet till SWAPO 1981 07 01-1981 12 31'/'Biannual
   report: The assistance to SWAPO 1 July-31 December 1981'), Swedish embassy, Luanda, 2 March 1982
   (SDA).
6. The contributions via and by BF, AGIS and ARO are not included in this figure.
7. Ingalill Colbro: Memorandum ('Humanitärt bistånd till South West Africa People's Organization, SWAPO
   (Namibia) budgetåret 1984/85'/'Humanitarian assistance to SWAPO [during the] financial year 1984/85'),
   SIDA, Stockholm, 13 March 1984 (SDA).
8. Agreed minutes between Sweden and SWAPO for the period 1983/84-1989/90.
9. Letter ('Veckobrev Namibia/SWAPO, vecka 51'/'Weekly letter Namibia/SWAPO, week 51') from Jörgen
   Christensen to SIDA, Swedish embassy, Luanda, 16 December 1980 (SDA).

ulation at between 20,000 and 25,000—out of which slightly more than 4,000 were students[1]—the consultancy firm presented its final brief and building programme to SIDA and SWAPO in early March 1981.[2] After SWAPO's approval, later in the month SIDA invited interested construction companies to tender for the project.

The proposed undertaking was discussed during the bilateral aid negotiations between Sweden and SWAPO in Luanda in May 1981. Committed to the proposal—for which an amount of 5 MSEK was tentatively allocated during the financial year 1981/82—SIDA's representatives, however, stressed three basic preconditions before an agreement could be signed, namely that "it was necessary to obtain guarantees from the Angolan authorities regarding the continued localization of the refugee camp [in] Kwanza Sul"; that "the availability of water should be ascertained"; and that "improvement of [the access road from Calulo] is necessary [...] for deliveries of goods and [...] implementation of the water programme".[3] Although SWAPO did not foresee any problems in these regards, it would later turn out that the three points raised decisively affected the implementation of the project, with responsibility shared between the main partners. While the Angolan government requested SWAPO to move from the site originally allocated and the Swedish contractor was unable to solve the water question for years, SWAPO did not give sufficient attention to the access road. In the meantime, however, it was agreed to formally embark on the project. After SIDA with assistance from UNICEF had drilled six boreholes in the settlement, the Swedish construction firm Container Express AB was contracted in August 1981.[4]

---

1. No registration or census of the Namibian refugees was ever carried out. At the annual negotiations between Sweden and SWAPO in May 1981, the movement estimated the total number in Angola—that is, in Kwanza Sul and in various smaller transit centres—at 57,000, with an expected increase to 65,000 at the end of the year ('Agreed minutes from discussions on the cooperation between the South West Africa People's Organization (SWAPO) of Namibia and the Swedish International Development Authority (SIDA)', Luanda, 26 May 1981) (SDA). Later in the 1980s, the numbers regularly advanced by SWAPO were around 70,000 in Angola and 5,000 in Zambia. While it was clear that these estimates were exaggerated, they were, however, upheld by both the Angolan host government and UNHCR. In the case of UNHCR, as late as in August 1988 its local representative in Luanda told the Swedish embassy that the Namibian refugee population approached 90,000 (Georg Dreifaldt: Memorandum ('Repatriering av namibiska flyktingar och avveckling av SWAPO's verksamhet i Angola'/'Repatriation of Namibian refugees and phasing out of SWAPO's activities in Angola'), Swedish embassy, Luanda, 13 June 1990) (SDA). At the end of the UN-sponsored repatriation exercise in mid-1989, the total number of returnees was, however, only 42,000. During an international symposium in 1992, Martti Ahtisaari discussed the discrepancy, stating that "such a margin of error does not create confidence in the donor community". Responsible for repatriation and resettlement under UNTAG, UNHCR's Nicolas Bwakira—who in the late 1970s had served as the UN agency's representative in Angola—commented that the "great error" was due to the fact "that very often in Africa there is never a census of refugees simply because most African countries tend to receive them as brothers and sisters, never registering them" (Ahtisaari and Bwakira cited in International Peace Academy/ Arnold Bergstraesser Institut op. cit., p. 140). In the case of a liberation movement, any registration was particularly sensitive. For general political and fund-raising reasons, both Angola and SWAPO were, in addition, naturally interested in high estimates. As noted by Ahtisaari, inflated figures were, however, not conducive to proper planning. In Sweden's case, a 'pragmatic' position was adopted. Whereas SIDA *de facto* accepted the high estimates by SWAPO, Angola and UNHCR with regard to basic needs such as food, medicines and shelter—on humanitarian grounds giving the liberation movement the benefit of the doubt—more precise calculations were necessary for the planning of specific projects. This, in turn, was tacitly accepted by SWAPO. Taking future developments into account, the construction project in Kwanza Sul was, for example, designed for a refugee population of 20-25,000.
2. White Arkitekter AB: 'Civilian settlement Kwanza Sul, Angola/Clinics, primary/secondary school, electrical supply and water supply: Architect's brief and building programme', Stockholm, 1 March 1981 (SDA).
3. 'Agreed minutes from discussions on the cooperation between the South West Africa People's Organization (SWAPO) of Namibia and the Swedish International Development Authority (SIDA)', Luanda, 26 May 1981 (SDA). The Swedish delegation was led by Curt Ström, Assistant Director General of SIDA, while SWAPO's Administrative Secretary Moses Garoeb headed the Namibian team.
4. Letter ('The Nordic clinic and school project in SWAPO's civilian settlement, Kwanza Sul, Angola') from Bengt Svensson to the UNHCR Branch Office in Luanda, Swedish embassy, Luanda, 28 August 1981 (SDA).

Swedish aid to infra-
structure: New school
buildings at the SWAPO
health and education centre
in Kwanza Sul, October 1983
(Photo: Gittan Arwén)

White & Partners had designed a project where "site works and some foundations should be carried out by [the] Namibian refugees under the responsibility of
SWAPO, while buildings—[in the form of] prefabricated, light structures—and
technical equipment should be delivered and erected [...] by [the] contractor".[1] The
original contract with Container Express envisaged that the entire project would be
completed within a year.[2] A number of factors and events would, however, from
the very start obstruct the multi-million project. While prefabricated building components and construction equipment were held up in the port of Luanda[3], in
November 1981 the Angolan government—keen to develop the coffee production
in the area—decided to move the Namibian settlement a couple of kilometres from
the site originally allocated. The planned water supply system had thus to be rede-
signed. Due to Angolan priorities in favour of national reconstruction, SWAPO
was, in addition, not able to secure the agreed quantities of sand, cement and reinforced concrete to prepare the building sites. Unaccustomed to major projects, the
movement did not, finally, allocate the necessary workforce to clear the access road
from Calulo, which prevented the passage of heavy-duty construction machines
and building components.

In this situation, the relations between SWAPO and the Swedish contractor
deteriorated sharply. After an initial crisis meeting in early February 1982[4], matters
were brought to a head one month later, when the SWAPO leaders Moses Garoeb
and Peter Mueshingange felt compelled to intervene at the level of the Swedish
embassy. Raising the issue of "human relations" between Container Express and
SWAPO, they stated that they had reached a "point of breakdown". Emphasizing
their view, Garoeb and Mueshihange declared that [the refugees]

> are terrified by [the] aggressive manner of [the CE site manager], which reminds them too
> much of the attitude and behaviour of the Boers in Namibia. [...] [H]is manners are not accept-
> able. He seems not to understand the background of the Namibians and, likewise, does not

1. White Arkitekter AB: 'Civilian settlement Kwanza Sul, Angola: Clinics, primary/secondary school, electrical
   supply and water supply: Architect's brief and building programme', Stockholm, 1 March 1981 (SDA).
2. Letter ('Platschef i Civilian Settlement Project No. 1, Angola 12.1'/'Site manager of Civilian Settlement Project
   No. 1, Angola 12.1') from Rolf Folkesson to Per-Olof Libonius, SIDA, Stockholm, 6 October 1982 (SDA).
3. To implement the project, the port of entry was later changed from Luanda to Lobito, which, however,
   implied longer and less secure transports to Kwanza Sul.
4. Letter ('SWAPO: Civilian settlement, health and education project') from Jörgen Christensen to SIDA, Swedish embassy, Luanda, 3 February 1982 (SDA).

understand the difficulties under which SWAPO is working in Angola. His aggressive manners [have], among other things, had the implication that SWAPO people have refused to participate in the construction work because of fear.[1]

The criticism did not come as a surprise to SIDA's officials, who in late February had already notified the headquarters in Stockholm that the Swedish company in its relations with SWAPO acted in an "authoritarian, contemptuous and bullying way, which hardly corresponds to the behaviour we [would have] expect[ed]".[2] Following the March meeting and discussions with Container Express in Sweden, it was agreed to change the site manager with immediate effect.[3] Although a number of problems concerning the attitude of the Swedish companies towards both SWAPO and SIDA occurred over the following years[4], the action taken "immediately improved the working conditions and the atmosphere at the building site".[5]

With considerable delays, the project work entered a new phase in mid-1982. Assisted by the Swedish consultancy firm VIAK, in June UNICEF drilled for water at the new refugee site identified by the Angolan government. While clearance of the access road remained a bottleneck[6], at the same time SWAPO allocated sufficient manpower to the building programme. Six water towers delivered by the Swedish company PL-Teknik were, finally, shipped to Luanda. Originally scheduled for completion by August 1982, the building programme continued through 1983.[7] At the end of that year, the major components were finalized. In November 1983, President Nujoma and SWAPO's Deputy Secretary for Health and Welfare, Libertine Amathila, could officially inaugurate the two hospitals[8], while the school, the

---

1. [SIDA/SWAPO]: 'Minutes from the meeting 1982 03 12', [no place or date, but the Swedish embassy, Luanda, mid-March 1982] (SDA).

2. Cable ('Re civilian settlement') from Bengt Svensson to SIDA, Swedish embassy, Luanda, 24 February 1982 (SDA).

3. Letter ('SWAPO, Civilian Settlement: Byggnads- och vattenprogrammet'/'SWAPO, Civilian Settlement: The construction and water programme') from Jörgen Christensen to SIDA, Swedish embassy, Luanda, 30 March 1982 (SDA).

4. In addition to problems relating to women and alcohol, representatives of Container Express and PL-Teknik often displayed racist attitudes. In a letter to SIDA's Director General, Bengt Svensson—the head of the SIDA office in Angola—declared in August 1983 that the aid agency should take a more active part in the Swedish companies' recruitment process as he "refuse[d] to accept racist statements" (Letter ('Tankar om vårt bistånd till SWAPO och ANC: Nkosi Sikelel' iAfrika'/'Reflections on our assistance to SWAPO and ANC: Nkosi Sikelel' iAfrika') from Bengt Svensson to SIDA's Director General, Anders Forsse, Swedish embassy, Luanda, 11 August 1983) (SDA). When such incidents occurred over a certain period of time, the culprit was normally dismissed (cf., for example, cable from the Swedish embassy in Luanda to the Ministry for Foreign Affairs, Luanda, 22 June 1983) (SDA).

5. Letter ('SWAPO, Civilian Settlement: Byggnads- och vattenprogrammet'/'SWAPO, Civilian Settlement: The construction and water programme') from Jörgen Christensen to SIDA, Swedish embassy, Luanda, 30 March 1982 (SDA).

6. It was only at the aid negotiations between Sweden and SWAPO in Luanda in March 1983 that the movement decisively "undertook to supply sufficient manpower and building material in order to prevent further delays in the construction programme" ('Agreed minutes on the cooperation between SWAPO of Namibia and the Swedish International Development Authority (SIDA)', Luanda, 21 March 1983) (SDA).

7. As previously noted, in early September 1983 UNITA launched an attack on Calulo, with further hold-ups as a result.

8. Letter ('Veckobrev 48/83'/'Weekly letter 48/83') from Gunvor Ngarambe to SIDA, Swedish embassy, Luanda, 1 December 1983 (SDA). The main hospital had 40 beds, operation facilities, X-ray, laboratory etc., while the second hospital had a capacity of 30 beds, with maternity and pediatric wards. The hospital equipment was supplied by Bread and Fishes and the Africa Groups within the project 'Health Care to SWAPO'. At the end of 1983, six doctors worked at the SWAPO hospitals, which also serviced the local Angolan population. In addition to SWAPO's Iyambo Indongo (Secretary for Health and Welfare) and Libertine Amathila (Deputy Secretary for Health and Welfare), two doctors were from the German Democratic Republic and two were recruited by ARO (Hans Rosling: 'A Review of SWAPO's Health Care Service and Health Policy', A consultant study for SIDA, Uppsala, December 1983) (SDA).

dormitories, administration buildings and a library were completed soon thereafter.[1]

The water supply programme—which had been accorded highest priority by SWAPO—was, however, far from being finished. As stated in a letter from the SIDA office in Luanda to the headquarters in Stockholm, "the entire [...] programme is just a big mess, to use a mild expression".[2] While the boreholes sunk by UNICEF at the new refugee site did not yield sufficient water, when the towers supplied by PL-Teknik were eventually transported to Kwanza Sul it turned out that due to constructional faults they were leaking.[3] In early 1984, a water distribution network had been established throughout the refugee settlement, but the capacity of the wells was insufficient and the towers faulty. To supply the hospitals, school kitchens and, in general, the refugee population with water, on a daily basis SWAPO had to organize truck transports from the Kwanza river some 20 kilometres away, as well as from the wells drilled by UNICEF on the original settlement site.[4]

As late as in mid-1984, only two of the six water towers had been erected.[5] In spite of major efforts over the following months, the situation did not improve. When in February 1985—due to the unstable security situation in the area—SIDA decided to withdraw Swedish personnel from the SWAPO settlement[6], the water programme was still at square one. The restrictions were lifted in March 1986.[7] SIDA and SWAPO then agreed to redesign the entire programme. Contracting the services of VIAK, a technologically less sophisticated approach was adopted, and in July 1986 new drillings were carried out.[8] Only seven months later—in February 1987—a well functioning water supply and distribution system had been established, putting the work carried out between 1981 and 1985 to shame. The system was inaugurated by President Nujoma in May 1987[9], and in early 1988 the SIDA office in Luanda, finally, reported that "all units within the refugee camp now have regular access to water".[10]

---

1. Bo Westman: Memorandum ('Halvårsrapport: Biståndet till SWAPO-1/84'/'Biannual report: The assistance to SWAPO-1/84'), Swedish embassy, Luanda, 23 May 1984 (SDA).
2. Letter ('Vattenprogrammet, Kwanza Sul'/'The water programme, Kwanza Sul') from Gunvor Ngarambe to SIDA, Swedish embassy, Luanda, 7 September 1984 (SDA).
3. Letter ('Veckobrev 48/83'/'Weekly letter 48/83') from Gunvor Ngarambe to SIDA, Swedish embassy, Luanda, 1 December 1983 (SDA). In his consultancy study on SWAPO's health care, in December 1983 Rosling drily noted that "the reservoirs constructed have experienced a technical failure, turning them into fountains". He also noted that "insufficient water supply and water quality [have] been the main health problem [...] in the Kwanza Sul centre" (Rosling op. cit.) (SDA).
4. Bo Westman: Memorandum ('Halvårsrapport: Biståndet till SWAPO-1/84'/'Biannual report: The assistance to SWAPO-1/84'), Swedish embassy, Luanda, 23 May 1984 (SDA). The tank trucks were supplied by SIDA.
5. Ibid.
6. Letter ('Säkerhetsläget i Angola'/'The security situation in Angola') from Ingalill Colbro to DANIDA, SIDA, Stockholm, 6 March 1985 (SDA).
7. 'Agreed minutes: Consultations in Luanda in May 1986 between SWAPO of Namibia and Sweden concerning humanitarian assistance 1986/87', Luanda, 29 May 1986 (SDA).
8. Berit Rylander: Memorandum ('Utvecklingssamarbete med SWAPO: Förberedande direktionsbehandling-D 1'/'Development cooperation with SWAPO: Preparatory discussion by [SIDA's] management committee'), Swedish embassy, Luanda, 22 September 1987 (SDA).
9. 'Agreed minutes: Consultations in Stockholm in May 1987 between SWAPO of Namibia and Sweden concerning humanitarian assistance 1987/88', Stockholm, 21 May 1987 (SDA). In 1987, the official, annual aid negotiations were exceptionally held in the Swedish capital. The Swedish delegation was led by Carl Olof Cederblad, Deputy Assistant Under-Secretary in the Ministry for Foreign Affairs, while the SWAPO team was headed by Hifikepunye Pohamba, Secretary for Finance.
10. Berit Rylander: Memorandum ('Utvecklingssamarbetet med SWAPO-D 2'/'Development cooperation with SWAPO-D 2'), Swedish embassy, Luanda, 4 February 1988 (SDA). The total costs for the second phase of the water supply programme were approximately 7.5 MSEK (Agreed minutes between Sweden and SWAPO during the period 1985/86-1987/88) (SDA).

Health Care to SWAPO

The introduction of major projects within the bilateral cooperation programme called for new forms of planning, programming and management, with greater demands on both SIDA and SWAPO. This was not without initial complications. Assessing the experiences gained from the construction activities in Kwanza Sul, in September 1985 the SIDA office in Luanda bluntly described them as "bad".[1] The problems with the water supply system notwithstanding, the construction of hospitals and schools was, however, an essential contribution towards the consolidation of SWAPO's health and education centre. The parallel, but coordinated efforts by the Swedish solidarity movement within the campaign 'Health Care to SWAPO' were in this regard highly significant.

Bread and Fishes, the Africa Groups in Sweden and SWAPO had as early as in December 1979 signed a project agreement "on assistance to the SWAPO program[me] for health in the [s]ettlement in Kwanza Sul".[2] Largely dependent on financial contributions from SIDA, the project—which originally was planned for a one-year period from March 1980 to March 1981—envisaged *inter alia* the supply of prefabricated components for a small hospital and clinics, hospital equipment, medicines and an ambulance.[3] As noted above, technical assistance in the form of medical personnel through the Recruitment Organization of the Africa Groups was also part of the effort[4], which subsequently became known as 'Health Care to SWAPO'.[5] BF was responsible for administration[6], while AGIS handled information aspects, fund-raising and collection of equipment.[7]

In July 1980, SIDA allocated 1.4 MSEK to the project[8], which in its first phase was mainly dedicated to the procurement and shipment of basic hospital equipment, medicines, tents etc. for the start of SWAPO's medical services in Kwanza Sul.[9] SIDA later granted a second contribution—amounting to 1.3 MSEK—for the planned prefabricated hospital.[10] By that time, however, SWAPO had already requested the Swedish government to implement the extensive construction programme discussed above. The other Nordic governments had also been approached for possible co-financing.

1. Berit Rylander and Bo Westman: Memorandum ('Utecklingssamarbetet med SWAPO: Förberedande direktionsbehandling-D1'/'Development cooperation with SWAPO: Preparatory discussion by [SIDA's] management committee-D1'), Swedish embassy, Luanda [no date, but September 1985] (SDA).
2. Agreement between Bread and Fishes (Bertil Högberg), Africa Groups in Sweden (Georg Dreifaldt) and SWAPO's Department of Health and Social Welfare (Dr. Iyambo Indongo), Kwanza Sul, 21 December 1979 (SDA).
3. Ibid.
4. In November 1979, SIDA allocated an initial grant to ARO of 130,000 SEK for the recruitment of medical personnel (SIDA: Decision ('Bidrag till Afrikagruppernas [R]ekryteringsorganisation för korttidsanställning av voluntärer till SWAPO's läger i Angola'/'Grant to the Recruitment Organization of the Africa Groups for short-term employment of volunteers to SWAPO's settlement in Angola'), Stockholm, 1 November 1979) (SDA). The two Swedish doctors, the nurse and the laboratory assistant who started to work in Kwanza Sul in February 1980 were the first ARO solidarity workers to directly assist a liberation movement.
5. In Swedish, *Sjukvård till SWAPO*. ISAK also supported the campaign.
6. In August 1982, a mysterious fire ravaged BF's premises at Malma outside Västerås. It was the second fire within a year. Around 50 tons of clothes and medical equipment were destroyed (BF: 'Verksamhetsberättelse 1982'/'Activity report 1982', Västerås [no date]) (BHC). After the fire, ARO assumed administrative responsibility for 'Health Care to SWAPO'.
7. Eva Strimling: 'Redovisning av projektet Sjukvård till SWAPO, steg 1 och 2'/'Account of the project Health Care to SWAPO, phase 1 and 2', Bread and Fishes, Västerås, 3 November 1983 (BHC).
8. [AGIS, Bread and Fishes and ISAK] op. cit., p. 12.
9. BF: 'Verksamhetsberättelse 1980' ('Activity report 1980'), Västerås, 21 February 1981 (BHC).
10. Eva Strimling: 'Redovisning av projektet Sjukvård till SWAPO, steg 1 och 2' ('Account of the project Health Care to SWAPO, phase 1 and 2'), Bread and Fishes, Västerås, 3 November 1983 (BHC).

Against this background, SIDA proposed that the agency should coordinate the building activities, while BF and AGIS would be responsible for supplying the hospitals and schools with equipment, beds, desks, consumer articles, medicines etc. The large-scale and technologically more advanced programme designed by White & Partners was, however, "completely different from the project [BF and AGIS] had envisaged".[1] Keen to maintain their own profile, the Swedish NGOs were, in addition, reluctant to be part of an official government undertaking.[2] When they decided to withdraw from the discussions, SWAPO, however, asked BF and AGIS to take part in the programme, and in May 1981 an agreement was reached with SIDA whereby 'Health Care to SWAPO' was recognized as a parallel, but coordinated project.[3]

In close contact with the ARO medical team in Kwanza Sul[4], BF and AGIS were responsible for the furnishing and equipment of the hospitals and schools built under the SIDA programme. During the first two phases of the project—extending over the four-year period 1980-83—the total budget amounted to more than 4 MSEK, of which 2.7 million was granted by SIDA, 300,000 was contributed by the solidarity organizations themselves and the value of the collected equipment, furniture etc. was around 700,000.[5] The SIDA grants and the organizations' own financial contributions were mainly used for the procurement of medicines, medical equipment and vehicles, while the collection of second-hand items included hospital beds and school desks. As important as the commodities themselves were the wooden containers in which they were shipped. They were from the beginning of the project designed in such a way that two containers could be put together and easily converted into health clinics, maternity wards or laboratories, with the additional advantage of being mobile. In the 1980s, such 'container clinics' were set up by SWAPO's workers' brigades in various camps within the wider Kwanza Sul settlement.[6] They played a particularly important role before the completion of the two hospitals built by Container Express in late 1983.

With financial grants from SIDA and substantial contributions of their own, 'Health Care to SWAPO' continued throughout the 1980s. In monetary terms, the

---

1. Ibid.
2. There was towards the end of the 1970s increasing cooperation between the state and the NGO Southern African solidarity movements. In addition to the examples earlier quoted, it could be noted that SIDA often turned to AGIS for the organization of information tours in Sweden. In October-November 1981, for example, SWAPO's Libolius Haufiku and Pendukeni Kaulinge were invited by SIDA to visit a number of schools in the country. Reporting back to SWAPO on the successful tour, SIDA's information division noted that "[s]ince SIDA does not have the capacity to administrate such tours, [...] full responsibility [has] been given to the Africa Groups [in] Sweden (AGIS). They have administrated several of our tours in Swedish schools before and are very experienced in arrangements like this" (Letter ('SWAPO tour in Sweden 1981') from Bo Kärre to SWAPO, SIDA, Stockholm, 26 January 1982) (SDA).
3. Eva Strimling: 'Redovisning av projektet Sjukvård till SWAPO, steg 1 och 2'/'Account of the project Health Care to SWAPO, phase 1 and 2', Bread and Fishes, Västerås, 3 November 1983 (BHC).
4. The Swedish doctor Susa Beckman initially served as the project coordinator in Angola. Bertil Högberg was responsible for the coordination in Sweden. ARO also cooperated with the Finnish Africa Committee, which recruited doctors in Finland to work within the project.
5. Eva Strimling: 'Redovisning av projektet Sjukvård till SWAPO, steg 1 och 2'/'Account of the project Health Care to SWAPO, phase 1 and 2', Bread and Fishes, Västerås, 3 November 1983 (BHC).
6. Bertil Högberg has estimated that BF in addition delivered between 30 and 40 'container houses' outside the health project (Letter from Bertil Högberg to the author, Uppsala, 17 February 2000).

'Health Care to SWAPO': The ARO nurse Kina Hemlin managing an open-air under-five clinic in Kwanza Sul, January 1983. In the background a container clinic from Bread and Fishes (Photo: Charlotte Thege)

total project budget exceeded 11 MSEK.[1] More important were, however, the professional contacts and the applied technology developed by BF, AGIS and ARO. In a consultancy study for SIDA on SWAPO's health care service and policy, Hans Rosling of the International Health Care Unit at Uppsala university noted after a visit to Kwanza Sul in November 1983:

> As the Africa [G]roups since 1980 [have] two nurses and two doctors working in SWAPO's health service in [...] Kwanza Sul [...], a very close cooperation with them has been a characteristic of the project. This has made it possible [...] to ship the material in containers that can be converted into houses. [...] Some 10-20 container houses serving as clinics and wards [...] have been built [...]. [W]hen needed, they have the advantage that they are movable. Due to the rapid communications between the personnel in Angola and the project organization in Sweden, the project has [in addition] been able to solve most urgent needs regarding medicines, spare parts etc. and continuously adapts the material provided according to the rapidly changing realities. [The] project has [thereby] filled many of the gaps that have been left between the less coordinated assistance from other agencies.[2]

Undoubtedly, the 'Health Care to SWAPO' campaign effectively contributed to SWAPO's successful health care programme in the Kwanza Sul settlement.[3] It also underlined the Swedish solidarity movement's commitment to practical solidarity,

1. The budget for the third phase was 2.1 MSEK (BF: 'Verksamhetsberättelse 84 07 31-85 06 30'/'Activity report 31 July 1984-30 June 1985', Västerås, 15 September 1985) (BHC); for the fourth phase 2.2 million (BF: 'Verksamhetsberättelse 86 07 01-87 06 30'/'Activity report 1 July 1986-30 June 1987', Västerås, 25 September 1987) (BHC); and for the fifth phase 2.7 million (BF: 'Verksamhetsberättelse 88 07 01-89 06 30'/ 'Activity report 1 July 1988-30 June 1989', Västerås, 9 September 1989) (BHC). These figures do not include the value of volunteer work etc. in Sweden. Taking the costs for the drawn out water supply system into account, in monetary terms the total combined value of the construction programme and 'Health Care to SWAPO' was in the region of 50 MSEK.
2. Rosling op. cit. (SDA).
3. As early as in 1984, statistics from the Kwanza Sul (Angola) and Nyango (Zambia) settlements showed that the health situation among the Namibian refugees generally was better than that in many independent African countries. Figures for infant mortality, births and deaths were, for example, much lower than in Zambia and incomparably better than those registered in Angola (Letter ('Hälsorapport från SWAPO'/'Health report from SWAPO') from Gunvor Ngarambe to SIDA, Swedish embassy, Luanda, 4 December 1984) (SDA).

paving the way for official grants to the Africa Groups in favour of a number of Namibia projects before[1] and after independence.[2]

1. In addition to the support to SWAPO in exile, before independence the Africa Groups were in particular involved with information and the wider civil society in Namibia. As already noted, in 1987 AGIS requested and was granted SIDA funds in favour of the opposition paper *The Namibian*. The following year, it embarked on support to the Namibian National Students Organization (NANSO) (SIDA: Decision ('Ansökan från Afrikagrupperna, AGIS, om stöd till Namibia[n] National Students Organization, NANSO, samt om stöd till informationsinsats 'Namibia i Fokus"/'Request from AGIS for support to NANSO and for [the] information project 'Namibia in Focus"), Stockholm, 14 June 1988) (SDA).
2. BF and AGIS continued the support after Namibia's independence in 1990. By 1993, there were 18 Swedish solidarity workers in the country, mainly active in Ovamboland and focusing on education/teacher training, health care and forestry. After a visit to Ovamboland in February 1993, in a report to the Ministry for Foreign Affairs, Sten Rylander, the Swedish ambassador to Namibia, praised their work, concluding that "organizations such as the Africa Groups are not just needed [in Namibia], but just as much [in Sweden], where the solidarity with the poor and oppressed in the developing countries is being undermined from different quarters" (Sten Rylander: Memorandum ('Afrikagrupperna i den namibiska verkligheten'/'The Africa Groups in the Namibian reality'), Swedish embassy, Windhoek, 11 February 1993) (MFA).

With SWAPO to Victory

Partnership and Capacity-Building

By 1983, no solution to the Namibia question was in sight. The United States had in June 1982 launched the so called 'linkage policy', making the departure of the Cuban troops from Angola a precondition of South Africa's withdrawal from Namibia. Abandoned by the major Western powers[1], SWAPO saw no other option than to intensify the armed struggle and prepare for a longer exile than envisaged at the end of the 1970s. This position was widely understood in Sweden. In fact, when President Nujoma paid a visit to the country in May 1983, his programme was similar to that of a foreign head of government. In addition to discussions with Prime Minister Olof Palme and Foreign Minister Lennart Bodström[2], it covered separate meetings with the leaders of all the Swedish parliamentary parties[3]—exceptionally including the Moderate Party—and with the parliamentary Standing Committee on Foreign Affairs.[4]

SWAPO's status was also reflected at the level of Swedish aid. As earlier noted, significant institutions and popular movements—such as the churches, the trade unions and the solidarity organizations—had with their own resources and official support embarked on various projects to assist the Namibian liberation movement. A number of Swedish companies had, in addition, become involved with the regular, official cooperation programme administered by SIDA.[5] There was a marked shift from the strict commodity aid of the 1970s. Against this background, at the annual aid negotiations with SWAPO in May 1982 the Swedish delegation concluded that

> the substantial support [...] was becoming increasingly similar to long-term cooperation between [independent] so called programme countries and Sweden. It seemed appropriate, therefore, to apply procedures similar to those followed in relation to [the] programme countries. This would especially affect [the] planning [...] and presentation of formal requests. [It was] explained that such requests normally include[d] detailed reviews of previous assistance programmes, project descriptions and plans for the coming financial year.[6]

---

1. In April 1981, four draft UN Security Council resolutions calling for sanctions against South Africa were vetoed by France, the United Kingdom and the United States. In August 1981, the United States also vetoed a draft resolution condemning South Africa for its most recent military invasion of Angola.
2. The former TCO chairman (1970-82) Lennart Bodström served as Foreign Minister in the Social Democratic government between 1982 and 1985.
3. Lars Werner of the Left Party Communists, Thorbjörn Fälldin of the Centre Party, Ola Ullsten of the Liberal Party and Ulf Adelsohn of the Moderate Party.
4. Ministry for Foreign Affairs: 'Prel[iminärt] besöksprogram för Sam Nujoma, SWAPO's ordförande' ('Preliminary visiting programme for Sam Nujoma, the President of SWAPO'), Stockholm, 29 April 1983 (MFA). The visit took place between 9 and 11 May 1983. Nujoma also met SIDA's board members, CCHA and AIC.
5. Cf. SWAPO's Finance Secretary Pohamba: "There were also private companies. [A]lthough they were contracted and paid, [...] to us it was still assistance. Container Express, for example, put up building structures in our camps" (Interview with Hifikepunye Pohamba, p. 95).
6. 'Agreed minutes from discussions on the cooperation between the South West Africa People's Organization (SWAPO) of Namibia and the Swedish International Development Authority (SIDA)', Lusaka, 21 May 1982 (SDA). The Swedish delegation was led by SIDA's Director General Anders Forsse, while the future Prime Minister of independent Namibia, Hage Geingob—then Director of the UN Institute for Namibia—headed the SWAPO team.

Discussing cooperation at SIDA, Stockholm, June 1984: SWAPO President Sam Nujoma addressing a delegation led by SIDA's Director General Anders Forsse (second from left). On Forsse's right is Ingalill Colbro and on
his left Birgitta Berggren. Facing the camera at the end of the table is Elisabeth Michanek (Photo: Paul
Rimmerfors)

After consultations during 1982/83 on the implications of the proposed cooperation format, in November 1983 SIDA and SWAPO agreed that

> the size and complexity of the cooperation [...] made it necessary to start applying the same
> system as in the cooperation with independent nations. It was understood, however, that the
> new planning technique needed to be gradually introduced.[1]

Together with ANC of South Africa, from the point of view of official aid relations,
SWAPO was thus from 1982-83 *de facto* recognized on a par with the independent
core countries receiving Swedish development assistance, including its host countries in Southern Africa.[2] During the second half of the 1980s, the growing annual
appropriations to the organization also approached those extended to some of the
independent programme countries.[3] There were, however, fundamental differences.
SWAPO was a movement involved in a war of national liberation. Although
responsible for the welfare of tens of thousands of refugees, as a guest in Angola,
Zambia and other Southern African countries it had to respect the policies and priorities of the host governments and was in no position to take unilateral decisions.
In addition, it did not have access to its own economic resources and its administrative structures were weak.

In this situation, it was not surprising that the transition in the early 1980s from
commodity to project aid in combination with the introduction of more demanding
planning and reporting routines would reveal considerable shortcomings in
SWAPO's financial management system. With steadily growing Swedish appropria-

---

1. 'Minutes from programme discussions between SWAPO of Namibia and the Swedish International Development Authority (SIDA)', Luanda, [no date, but the talks were held on 8-9 November 1983] (SDA).
2. Interviewed in 1995, SWAPO's former Secretary of Logistics, Festus Naholo, commented as follows on the
   relations between Sweden, SWAPO and the host countries in Southern Africa: "SIDA [was] a government
   agency and governments have diplomatic relations. Definitely, SIDA had to act according to the wishes of the
   host government. But I suppose that they also worked to influence the host countries' attitudes towards the
   liberation movements. That was quite obvious and we really appreciated it" (Interview with Festus Naholo,
   p. 92). Cf. the interview with ANC's Thabo Mbeki, pp. 156-57.
3. For example, in 1987/88 the appropriations to SWAPO, Guinea-Bissau and Botswana were 64, 75 and 95
   MSEK, respectively.

tions, by the mid-1980s this resulted in saturation, decreasing aid utilization and increasing unspent balances. With an allocation of 47 MSEK in 1983/84, the outgoing unspent balance at the end of that financial year was no less than 22.4 million.[1] As later noted by SWAPO's Secretary of Logistics Festus Naholo[2], "the work was massive and it needed much involvement, because [at that time] we did not have the experience".[3] From 1984, financial management training was, however, included in the regular Swedish support, translating into better use of the available resources.

The role played by Hifikepunye Pohamba, SWAPO's Finance Secretary and National Treasurer, was in this context particularly important. During the transition years in the early 1980s, he had often reacted against Swedish demands for transparency and detailed financial reports.[4] Like his ANC colleague Thomas Nkobi, Pohamba, however, soon established close and trusting relations with SIDA's regional coordinator of humanitarian assistance, Roland Axelsson[5], as well as with Berit Rylander and—later—Georg Dreifaldt, both of them programme officers at the SIDA office in Luanda.[6] According to Pohamba, "these people made enormous contributions. You would sit with them and they would tell you what to do. I owe them a lot".[7] In Rylander's opinion, her working relations with Pohamba developed into a "true partnership".[8] Although the Swedish government regularly called attention to shortcomings concerning SWAPO's financial accounts—in particular with regard to funds spent inside Namibia—during the second half of the 1980s these personal relations effectively contributed to the establishment of an open and well functioning bilateral cooperation.

---

1. Ingalill Colbro: Memorandum ('Humanitärt bistånd till South West Africa People's Organization, SWAPO (Namibia), budgetåret 1985/86'/'Humanitarian assistance to SWAPO [during] the financial year 1985/86'), Draft, SIDA, Stockholm, 27 March 1985 (SDA).
2. Together with Hifikepunye Pohamba, Naholo was closely involved with the Swedish assistance to SWAPO. Leaving Namibia in 1978, three years later he was appointed assistant to the National Treasurer, with responsibility for project planning and administration. In 1986, he became Secretary of Logistics. After Namibia's independence in March 1990, Naholo—like Moses Garoeb—remained within the party structure, serving as Deputy Coordinator/Deputy Secretary General. At the congress in 1992, he became SWAPO Secretary for Economic Affairs.
3. Interview with Festus Naholo, p. 90.
4. In the early 1980s, the SIDA officials in Luanda did not dedicate much time and effort to explaining what the Swedish authorities required from SWAPO regarding financial accounts and audits. Often substituting information for criticism, this led to temporary, but serious, strains in the cooperation. When Roland Axelsson and Christina Regnell from the SIDA headquarters in Stockholm visited Luanda in March 1983 to discuss SWAPO's financial reports with Pohamba and Naholo, Pohamba was "very negative". According to Regnell's notes from the meeting, SWAPO's Finance Secretary "started by [stating] that SWAPO could not be treated as a movement as it represented a country. And [SIDA] did surely not request to look into the national accounts of recipient countries? In addition, [SWAPO's] book-keeping was designed in such a way that civilian and military expenses were mixed. [I]t was thus impossible to let SIDA look into the books without revealing military secrets. [Pohamba] stressed that everything [SWAPO] does and everything that it receives is entered into the books as a financial transaction, whether it is a gift of tins or material to blow up a bridge" (Christina Regnell: 'Minnesanteckningar från samtal med SWAPO om ekonomifrågor, 1983 03 10'/'Notes from conversation with SWAPO on financial matters, 10 March 1983', [Swedish embassy, Luanda], 11 March 1983) (SDA).
5. Axelsson served in this position from 1984 until 1991. He later stated: "I was very much trusted and allowed to study the respective systems of financial management. Neither ANC nor SWAPO accepted [...] that any other SIDA official should look through their books, so I was privileged. [...] ANC and SWAPO supported me. Thomas Nkobi, Hifikepunye Pohamba and all their co-workers supported me one hundred per cent. They trusted me, but it was, of course, in their interest that their people were fed and that the money was correctly spent" (Interview with Roland Axelsson, p. 253-54).
6. Responsible for assistance to ANC and SWAPO, Rylander represented SIDA at the Swedish embassy in Luanda between 1985 and 1988. She was replaced by Dreifaldt, who after Namibia's independence in 1990 was transferred to the Swedish embassy in Windhoek.
7. Interview with Hifikepunye Pohamba, p. 96. Cf. also the interview with Festus Naholo, p. 90.
8. Author's conversation with Berit Rylander, Uppsala, 7 September 1999.

Close friends after years
of joint financial planning
and administration:
SIDA's Roland Axelsson
with former SWAPO
National Treasurer
Hifikepunye Pohamba,
Windhoek, March 1993
(Courtesy of Roland
Axelsson)

As the extensive building programme in Kwanza Sul was coming to an end in late 1983, Sweden and SWAPO agreed that the official assistance in addition to basic needs in favour of the Namibian refugees should focus on health and education, as well as on maintenance of the infrastructure in the SWAPO settlement.[1] A programme to strengthen SWAPO's financial management capability was in this context particularly relevant.

SWAPO had already in 1982 asked SIDA for assistance regarding training of book-keepers and accountants.[2] Initially seen as a short-term measure to strengthen the movement's treasury department, in 1983 the proposal was followed up by SWAPO's Secretary for Education and Culture, Nahas Angula[3], but now as part of a more comprehensive, longer-term support to the education sector.[4] As such, it would eventually pave the way for Swedish assistance to public administration in independent Namibia, including the establishment of a central bank.

To define the basis for further consultations on a management training programme, a Swedish consultant[5] visited SWAPO in Angola and Zambia in October 1983. After discussions with Pohamba, Angula and the UN Institute for Namibia, his recommendation was that the programme should focus on three major areas, namely a) planning and implementation of development projects; b) budgeting and accounting procedures; and c) general administration and management skills.[6] The findings were discussed in December 1983 by Angula and SIDA's education division in Stockholm[7], where it was agreed to arrange a special course in financial manage-

1. 'Minutes from programme discussions between SWAPO of Namibia and the Swedish International Development Authority (SIDA)', Luanda, [no date, but November 1983] (SDA). Eventually, the parties did not enter into a specific health sector support programme. The Swedish support to the sector continued in the form of commodity aid.
2. Christina Regnell: 'Minnesanteckningar från samtal med SWAPO om ekonomifrågor, 1983 03 10'/'Notes from conversation with SWAPO on financial matters, 10 March 1983', [Swedish embassy, Luanda], 11 March 1983 (SDA).
3. Replacing Linekela Kalenga—who died in a car accident while travelling from Lusaka to the Nyango settlement—Angula was appointed SWAPO Secretary for Education and Culture in July 1981. At Namibia's independence, he became Minister of Education, Culture, Youth and Sport.
4. Letter from Nahas Angula to Lennart Wohlgemuth, head of SIDA's education division, Luanda, 29 July 1983 (SDA).
5. Anders Karlsson, representing ASK AB.
6. Anders Karlsson: Memorandum ('Management training for SWAPO officials'), [no place], 24 October 1983 (SDA).
7. Astrid Dufborg: Memorandum ('Notes from meeting with SWAPO Secretary for Education, Mr. N. Angula, and SIDA education division, December 12, 1983'), SIDA, Stockholm, 11 January 1984 (SDA).

ment for SWAPO cadres in Sweden during the academic year 1984/85. In preparation for the course, it was further agreed to hold a workshop in early 1984.[1]

The workshop was held in Uppsala, Sweden, in January-February 1984. Led by Festus Naholo, then Assistant Secretary for Finance, the SWAPO delegation included representatives from both the finance and education departments[2], who together with a Swedish team of SIDA officials and resource persons prepared a course programme. It was agreed that the course should

> improve the financial administration, as well as the administration of projects and [the] management within SWAPO, [and cover] the whole organization, including the department of finance as the coordinating unit, other departments, wings, settlements etc. involved in [the] handling of SWAPO funds and projects. [...] The target group [was] defined as both SWAPO cadres already in service, but also cadres who will take up new posts within the administrative structures [...].[3]

It was also agreed that the training should take place over a period of nine months at the Sandö U-Centre in northern Sweden. A specific agreement on education sector support—covering teacher training and the financial management course—was concluded by SIDA and SWAPO in July 1984[4], and in September a group of 11 SWAPO members started their management studies. Within the framework of the course, they produced *inter alia* a draft SWAPO 'Manual on Financial Procedures' which later was discussed at a seminar in Luanda.[5] While SIDA also financed short-term courses for SWAPO at the Eastern and Southern African Management Institute in Tanzania and at the Royal Institute for Public Administration in England, based on a positive evaluation of the first course a second tailor-made course was launched at Sandö in January 1987.[6] More ambitious than the first, it ran over a period of twelve months and was attended by 15 SWAPO cadres.[7]

The attention to capacity-building in the field of financial management had mixed results. Returning to Angola and Zambia, the SWAPO trainees strengthened and broadened the movement's administrative structures, particularly with regard to project implementation. In an internal policy memorandum, SIDA concluded in March 1987 that "the cooperation with SWAPO is going well. The movement's reception capacity has improved, which *inter alia* is reflected through decreasing [unspent] balances".[8] Similarly, at the official aid negotiations between Sweden and SWAPO in May 1987 the decreasing balances were explained "as a result of the

1. Astrid Dufborg: Project document ('Financial management course for SWAPO cadres in Sweden'), SIDA, Stockholm, 14 February 1984 (SDA).
2. Among the representatives were SWAPO's Auditor Shalongo Shimbode, the Chief Accounting Officer Letus Hausiko and the Deputy Secretary for Education and Culture Lukas Stephanus ('Conclusions [from] a workshop/preparatory discussions on financial administrative training of SWAPO staff, held in Uppsala, January 30-February 2, 1984', signed by Lennart Wohlgemuth for SIDA and Festus Naholo for SWAPO, Stockholm, 6 February 1984) (SDA).
3. Astrid Dufborg: Project document ('Financial management course for SWAPO cadres in Sweden'), SIDA, Stockholm, 14 February 1984 (SDA).
4. 'Agreement', Luanda, 16 July 1984, signed by Kerstin Fransson on behalf of SIDA and by Hifikepunye Pohamba for SWAPO (SDA).
5. 'Minutes of understanding between SWAPO and SIDA, November 18-20, 1986', Luanda, 20 November 1986 (SDA).
6. SIDA: Decision ('Anordnande av en andra kurs i 'financial management' för namibier'/'Holding of a second course in financial management for Namibians'), Stockholm, 17 June 1986 (SDA).
7. SIDA: Memorandum ('Humanitärt bistånd till South West Africa People's Organization, SWAPO (Namibia), budgetåret 1988/89'/'Humanitarian assistance to SWAPO [during] the financial year 1988/89'), Stockholm, 18 March 1988 (SDA).
8. Inger Jernberg: Memorandum ('Humanitärt bistånd till South West Africa People's Organization, SWAPO (Namibia), budgetåret 1987/88'/'Humanitarian assistance to SWAPO [during] the financial year 1987/88'), SIDA, Stockholm, 19 March 1987 (SDA).

continuous progress in the implementation of the project activities".[1] During the financial year 1985/86, the disbursements to SWAPO reached a record high of no less than 111.9 MSEK.[2] After a hiatus in 1984/85-1985/86—when the annual allocation was kept at the level of 50 million—in 1986/87 it was increased to 59 million and in 1987/88 to 64 MSEK.

At the same time, however, the Swedish authorities were still far from satisfied with SWAPO's financial accounts. In September 1987, for example, the SIDA office in Luanda remarked that "one area where SWAPO still has great shortcomings [is] financial reporting".[3] A number of initiatives had been taken to improve the situation. In early 1986, Roland Axelsson—who before joining the Swedish aid agency had worked at the Swedish National Audit Bureau[4]—dedicated a lot of attention to the problem, eventually agreeing with SWAPO on a flexible, but satisfactory reporting system.[5] The agreement was, however, not fully honoured by SWAPO, in particular with regard to auditing. Against this background, in November 1987 a Swedish financial comptroller visited SWAPO's headquarters in Luanda to study the movement's financial systems and "provide [...] relevant guidelines for financial reporting [as] required by SIDA".[6] As his efforts were largely unsuccessful too, four months later SIDA wrote to the Ministry for Foreign Affairs that "continued involvement in this area is necessary".[7]

Although Sweden at the annual negotiations with SWAPO during the second half of the 1980s repeatedly raised the need for improved financial reports, the problem remained until Namibia's independence. This was particularly the case with assistance inside Namibia. In May 1986, for example, the Swedish government delegation "stressed the need for [...] financial and activity [...] reports to be presented to SIDA in line with earlier agreements between the delegations".[8] It should be noted that the problem primarily was of a technical, administrative nature. Nowhere does the documentation give grounds for suspicions of corruption or misappropriation of funds. On the contrary, interviewed in 1996 SIDA's former

---

1. 'Agreed minutes [from] consultations in Stockholm in May 1987 between SWAPO of Namibia and Sweden concerning humanitarian assistance 1987/88', Stockholm, 21 May 1987 (SDA).
2. See the accompanying disbursement table. In the case of payments in favour of SWAPO in 1985/86, at the time the estimated overall preliminary figure established by the two parties was substantially lower, or only 62.1 MSEK ('Agreed minutes [from] consultations in Luanda in May 1986 between SWAPO of Namibia and Sweden concerning humanitarian assistance 1986/87', Luanda, 29 May 1986) (SDA).
3. Berit Rylander: Memorandum ('Utvecklingssamarbete med SWAPO: Förberedande direktionsbehandling-D1'/ 'Development cooperation with SWAPO: Preparatory discussion by [SIDA's] management committee-D1'), Swedish embassy, Luanda, 22 September 1987 (SDA).
4. In Swedish, *Riksrevisionsverket* (RRV). Cf. the interview with Roland Axelson, p. 252.
5. Roland Axelsson: 'Reporting guidelines', Swedish embassy, Lusaka, 28 May 1986 (SDA). According to the agreement, as an exception Sweden accepted SWAPO's internal audit.
6. 'Minutes of understanding between SWAPO and SIDA, December 1-3, 1987', Luanda, 5 December 1987 (SDA).
7. SIDA: Memorandum ('Humanitärt bistånd till South West Africa People's Organization, SWAPO (Namibia), budgetåret 1988/89'/'Humanitarian assistance to SWAPO [during] the financial year 1988/89'), Stockholm, 18 March 1988 (SDA).
8. 'Agreed minutes [from] consultations in Luanda in May 1986 between SWAPO of Namibia and Sweden concerning humanitarian assistance 1986/87', Luanda, 29 May 1986 (SDA). After repeated criticism, in February 1989 SWAPO did submit a brief report on the utilization of the home front allocation in 1987/88. The costs incurred were given in US Dollars. According to the report, 350,000 (13.5%) had been used to support former political prisoners and internally displaced persons, as well as for legal aid; 450,000 (17.5%) had been set aside for SWAPO's internal administration, including "house rent and daily necessities for functionaries"; and 700,000 USD (27%) had been disbursed for health and education projects via church organizations. The largest amount—1,070,000 USD (42%)—had been used for information activities, including the acquisition of a radio station. The total costs for the radio station were approximately 3 million USD. According to SWAPO's verbal report at the consultative talks, "the radio station has been very successful in mobilizing the people in Namibia. South Africa normally [tries] to jam radio stations, but [it] has not succeeded with this one" ('Minutes of understanding between SWAPO and SIDA, February 22, 1989', Luanda, 2 March 1989) (SDA).

regional coordinator of humanitarian assistance, Roland Axelsson, stated that "[e]xcept for the home front allocation, the financial control was in my opinion better and stricter than the control exercised concerning aid to independent countries [...] like Zambia or Tanzania".[1]

Nevertheless, the contradiction between the wish to improve SWAPO's reporting routines and the will to increase Sweden's financial commitment to the movement was often glaringly obvious. Discussing the support channelled to activities inside Namibia, in the minutes from the consultative talks with SWAPO in Luanda in November 1986 the Swedish delegation

> stressed the need for reporting about the home front activities, to be included in the SWAPO annual report. Emphasis should be given to description [of] the different activities. [...] The SIDA delegation furthermore confirmed the strong interest to increase the support to [the] home front activities.[2]

Financial Overview and Education Support

During the second half of the 1980s, the Swedish government regularly increased the allocation to SWAPO. The size and scope of the bilateral programme was becoming increasingly similar to Sweden's development cooperation with independent states. Covering a number of areas, in addition to SIDA's specialized divisions it involved various consultancy firms, private companies and NGOs. As the assistance was carried out in more than one country, from an administrative point of view it was, however, more complex. To this should be added the important fact that all activities and transactions were treated as confidential, often making the implementation of even matters of routine less straightforward than was the case within SIDA's regular development assistance to the programme countries.[3]

---

1. Interview with Roland Axelsson, p. 253.
2. 'Minutes of understanding between SWAPO and SIDA, November 18-20, 1986', Luanda, 20 November 1986 (SDA). The SIDA and SWAPO delegations were led by Bosse Hammarström and Hifikepunye Pohamba.
3. Security considerations were, of course, particularly relevant with regard to project activities within the SWAPO settlements. One example could be quoted. When the United Nations proclaimed 1987 as the International Year of Shelter for the Homeless (IYSH), the Swedish Ministry of Housing decided to support a self-help building scheme in the Nyango settlement in Zambia. The objective—which was welcomed by SWAPO—was to draw international attention to the plight of the Namibian refugees. Due to South African threats and fears of attacks, the intended publicity campaign had, however, to be toned down. While the project subsequently was implemented in cooperation with SIDA, SWAPO issued strict security regulations to the officials from the Ministry of Housing visiting Nyango. It was in general emphasized that "great care shall be taken at parties and during ordinary social life [as] South Africa has many agents and informants of many nationalities [in Zambia]. [...] Discretion is essential as a precaution against assassination and attack". With regard to the project and the Nyango settlement, it was stated in addition that the following information *inter alia* could not be made public: a) "any information which SWAPO has expressly stated"; b) "maps of such detail that they could be used for carrying out sabotage or an attack"; c) "information about SWAPO members, their homes, whereabouts, journey plans [etc]"; d) "details of the transportation of goods to SWAPO"; and e) "photographs—of people, for example—which have not been approved for publication by SWAPO" (Göran Tannerfeldt: Memorandum ('Security questions: The housing project for SWAPO in Nyango'), SIDA, Stockholm, 15 September 1986) (SDA). Similar instructions were issued to foreigners working in Kwanza Sul and in other Namibian refugee camps. The first houses under the IYSH self-help building project in Nyango were officially inaugurated by the Swedish Minister of Housing Hans Gustafsson and SWAPO's Hifikepunye Pohamba in April 1987 (Letter ('Bostadsminister Gustafsson besöker Zambia'/'Housing Minister Gustafsson visits Zambia') from Jan Ölander, Swedish ambassador to Zambia, to the Ministry for Foreign Affairs, Lusaka, 7 April 1987) (SDA).

In mid-1988, SWAPO and Sweden initiated a number of strategic projects for an independent Namibia, opening a new chapter in the cooperation. In the meantime, the scope of the direct, official support in the second half of the 1980s could be illustrated by the budget established by the parties for the financial year 1987/ 88. With an outgoing balance of 13.6 million from 1986/87 and an appropriation of 64 million for 1987/88, the available resources for the period 1 July 1987-30 June 1988 amounted to 77.6 MSEK. They were allocated as follows:[1]

SWAPO: SIDA budget 1987/88
(in thousands of SEK)

Country / Sector / Activity	Budgeted amount	Percentage
A) ANGOLA	(44,400)	(57.2)
Agriculture	1,000	1.3
Daily necessities	6,700	8.6
Education	7,000	9.0
Electrification at Viana	800	1.0
Food supplies	10,600	13.7
Health	2,000	2.6
Maintenance in Kwanza Sul	3,800	4.9
Transport	3,500	4.5
Vehicle workshop	9,000	11.6
B) ZAMBIA	(14,100)	(18.2)
Agriculture	1,500	1.9
Bakery	20	–
Daily necessities	8,800	11.4
Education for disabled	900	1.2
Self-help construction project	1,780	2.3
Vehicle workshop	1,100	1.4
C) NAMIBIA	(13,000)	(16.7)
Home front activities	13,000	16.7
D) OFFICES/DAILY NECESSITIES	(2,100)	(2.7)
Botswana	400	0.5
Congo	500	0.6
Sweden	600	0.8
Tanzania	200	0.3
Zimbabwe	400	0.5
E) OTHER	(4,000)	(5.2)
CFTC *	4,000	5.2
TOTAL	77,600	100.0

*) In contrast to the educational support through international organizations such as AET, WCC and WUS, the Swedish contribution to the Namibia programme of the Commonwealth Fund for Technical Cooperation (CFTC) was debited against the bilateral allocation to SWAPO.

---

1. 'Agreed minutes [from] negotiations in Luanda in May 1988 between SWAPO of Namibia and Sweden concerning humanitarian assistance 1988/89', Annex II: Financial statement, Luanda, 27 May 1988 (SDA).

Combining the budgetary figures for the different countries, in 1987/88 the official bilateral Swedish assistance to SWAPO had the following general profile:[1]

Component	MSEK	Percentage
Humanitarian commodity aid	28.1	36.3
Transport	13.6	17.5
Home front	13.0	16.7
Education	11.9	15.4
Construction/Infrastructure	6.4	8.2
Agriculture	2.5	3.2
Administration	2.1	2.7
TOTAL	77.6	100.0

Most of these components have been discussed above.[2] As education at the end of the 1980s was included among the proposed concentration areas for Swedish assistance to independent Namibia, in addition to the financial management training already mentioned a brief presentation of the support to this sector should be made.

Education played from the very beginning a prominent part in Sweden's humanitarian assistance to Southern Africa. In fact, the programme launched in 1964 targeted to a large extent Namibian students.[3] On a multilateral basis, substantial resources were also allocated over the following decades to a number of international organizations for scholarships to Namibians.[4] As already noted, the Swedish government was in addition among the leading contributors to the UN Institute for Namibia, as well as to the autonomous Namibian Extension Unit, established at

1. The table is somewhat arbitrary. The different components largely overlap and some activities could be moved from one component to another. Together with daily necessities and food supplies, health has thus been grouped under the heading humanitarian commodity aid. The reason is that there was no Swedish health sector support. The health item in the budget for Angola consisted in fact of deliveries of medicines and medical supplies. The vehicle workshops have further been included under the transport component, but they could just as well be classified as construction/infrastructure. The home front activities inside Namibia included both education and agriculture. In the absence of detailed figures, it has, however, not been possible to register the support under these two components. Finally, the education sector benefited from the maintenance programme in Kwanza Sul.
2. This is, however, not the case with agriculture, which over the years received fairly substantial amounts within the cooperation programme. As earlier noted, Swedish support to SWAPO's efforts to become self-sufficient with regard to food started at the 'old farm' in Zambia in 1973/74. While the main support to the SWAPO farms for many years was given by the Lutheran World Federation, the Swedish assistance increased rapidly from the mid-1980s. At the time of Namibia's independence, almost 20 MSEK had been disbursed in favour of agricultural activities. Although this corresponded to less than 3 per cent of the total official Swedish support, it effectively contributed to the welfare of the Namibian refugees. The support was channelled to SWAPO's farms at Makeni, Nyango and—from 1985—Namayani in Zambia and to Kwanza Sul in Angola. It was mainly extended in the form of commodity aid—including tractors, trucks, motorcycles, farm implements, water pumps, seeds, vaccines etc.—but also consisted of technical assistance in the form of consultancy services by the Swedish Agricultural University in Uppsala, as well as training courses in farm management ('Agreed minutes between Sweden and SWAPO', passim).
3. See Sellström Volume I, pp. 70-75.
4. This was notably the case with UNETPSA, AET, LWF, WCC and WUS. In 1987/88—the year chosen to illustrate Sweden's official, bilateral assistance to SWAPO—the Swedish contributions to the scholarship programmes of these organizations amounted to 23.5 MSEK ('Agreed minutes [from] consultations in Stockholm in May 1987 between SWAPO of Namibia and Sweden concerning humanitarian assistance 1987/88', Stockholm, 21 May 1987) (SDA). In the same year, a total of 9.5 MSEK was granted to the UN Fund for Namibia, the UN Institute for Namibia and the Namibia Extension Unit, while 2.5 MSEK was channelled to the Council of Churches in Namibia, largely for education support (ibid.).

UNIN in 1981.[1] Although not a member of the Commonwealth—the association of Great Britain and the former British colonies—Sweden was, finally, from the beginning of the 1980s a major donor to the vocational training programmes for Namibians administered by its fund for technical cooperation.

While a substantial bilateral support to SWAPO's education programmes in the health and education centres had regularly been extended in the form of equipment, teaching materials etc., by the early 1980s—at the time when the extensive construction project started in Kwanza Sul, which prominently included school buildings—there was, however, no direct cooperation between Sweden and SWAPO in the education field. Largely due to SWAPO's Education Secretary Nahas Angula[2], this would soon change. Preliminary discussions on direct Swedish assistance were initiated by Angula towards the end of 1981.[3] Less than a year later—in September 1982—contacts with the Dag Hammarskjöld Foundation in Uppsala resulted in a joint seminar in Lusaka on 'Education and Culture for Liberation in Namibia'.[4] Finally, in October 1982 the SIDA representative to Angola, Bengt Svensson, made a strong appeal in favour of a bilateral education support programme.[5]

The authorities in Stockholm supported the idea. For the financial year 1983/84, SIDA and SWAPO established an indicative planning frame of 2 MSEK for education support within the regular cooperation programme.[6] The funds were used to prepare the financial management training programme mentioned above, but also a pilot project on teacher training at the Namibian Education Centre in Kwanza Sul. A specific agreement on the two projects was signed in July 1984.

---

1. The chief objective of the Namibian Extension Unit (NEU) was to provide education and training opportunities to the refugees in Angola and Zambia by producing and distributing distance teaching materials to the SWAPO settlements. The teaching materials were based on correspondence courses, supplemented by tape cassettes and simple equipment. The first courses—in English and basic mathematics—were organized in early 1981. Hage Geingob, Director of UNIN and future Prime Minister of Namibia, chaired the NEU board (NEU: *Namibian Extension Unit: A Brief Account of the Distance Education Programme for Namibians*, NEU, Lusaka, January 1983, pp. 1-5) (SDA).
2. Angula was appointed Secretary for Education and Culture in mid-1981. When he later in the year initiated discussions with the SIDA office in Luanda on closer cooperation with Sweden, his interlocutor, Jörgen Christensen, described him as "a quick-witted, inventive person, who with a great amount of energy has thrown himself into the task of reviewing and planning SWAPO's education system" (Letter ('Education programme: SWAPO') from Jörgen Christensen to SIDA, Swedish embassy, Luanda, 3 November 1981) (SDA).
3. Ibid.
4. Letter ('Seminar on education and culture for liberation') from Lukas Stephanus, SWAPO Deputy Secretary for Education and Culture, to SIDA, Lusaka, 17 August 1982 (SDA) and Dag Hammarskjöld Foundation: 'Provisional report on the 1982 SWAPO/Dag Hammarskjöld Foundation seminar on education and culture for liberation in Namibia', [no place or date] (NAI). The independent Dag Hammarskjöld Foundation had since 1978 co-sponsored a seminar series on education and culture for liberation in Southern Africa. The seminar organized with SWAPO was held at the University of Zambia in Lusaka 20-25 September 1982. With over 70 participants, it provided a major occasion for SWAPO to bring together its leading educationalists from various countries to discuss and formulate educational policy relating to both the liberation struggle and the post-independence period. In addition, representatives from ANC of South Africa, Cuba, the German Democratic Republic, Mozambique, Sweden, Zambia and Zimbabwe took part in the seminar (ibid.).
5. Letter ('Förslag om fortsatta diskussioner i Sverige mellan undervisningsbyrån och SWAPO's Department of Education and Culture'/'Proposed continued discussions in Sweden between [SIDA's] education division and SWAPO's Department of Education and Culture') from Bengt Svensson to SIDA, Swedish embassy, Luanda, 20 October 1982 (SDA). Quite unusually in the context of Swedish humanitarian assistance, the Luanda embassy explicitly advanced ideological arguments in favour of closer cooperation. With a number of East German teachers in the Namibian settlements and huge training programmes in the German Democratic Republic, GDR was at the time SWAPO's most important partner in the field of education (cf. Ilona and Hans-Georg Schleicher op. cit., pp. 189-202). Against this background, the embassy argued, there was "an additional dimension of political significance [in the fact] that Swedish efforts constitute almost the only alternative to an entirely Eastern [educational] system, primarily driven by GDR" (Letter from the Swedish embassy in Luanda cited in Marianne Sundh: Memorandum ('Bistånd till SWAPO under budgetåret 1983/84'/ 'Assistance to SWAPO during the financial year 1983/84'), CCHA/Ministry for Foreign Affairs, Stockholm, 18 February 1983) (MFA).
6. 'Agreed minutes from discussions on the cooperation between SWAPO of Namibia and the Swedish International Development Authority (SIDA)', Luanda, 21 March 1983 (SDA).

As in the case of the management project, the teacher training component was prepared by a Swedish consultant.[1] He visited Kwanza Sul in August-October 1983. Finding that most of the 110 Namibian teachers in the settlement had no or insufficient training experience[2]; that a lack of integration between content and methods characterized the education system; and that there was a general shortage of equipment and teaching aids, the consultant recommended a pilot project covering in-service training of primary school teachers and local production of appropriate teaching materials.[3] The recommendations were accepted by SWAPO. After further consultations, it was agreed to implement the project in cooperation with the University of Umeå over four stages in 1984-85.[4] As SWAPO had decided to introduce English as the national language in independent Namibia and it was the medium of instruction in the refugee schools, the English teachers at the pre-school and lower primary level were chosen as the target group.[5]

With positive experiences from the pilot project, in early 1986 SIDA and SWAPO decided to launch a comprehensive Integrated Teacher Training Programme (ITTP), still with the University of Umeå as the implementing agency. Running over a period of three years (1986/87-1988/89), it started with 15 Namibian trainees in September 1986.[6] Also this undertaking was positively assessed. In a letter to Lennart Wohlgemuth, the head of SIDA's education division—proposing him as patron of a SWAPO teacher education conference to be held in Lusaka at the end of September 1989, as he had been "personally supportive of all [the] efforts"—Nahas Angula stated that the ITTP project was "an innovative success".[7] It later continued in independent Namibia, where it paved the way for a Teacher Education Reform Programme. Although limited in terms of quantity, the impact of the project was considerable. In fact, a study on Swedish development assistance to independent Namibia concluded in 1994 that it "to a large extent shaped the curricula for teacher training currently implemented in the Basic Education Teacher Diploma, [...] underlin[ing] the crucial role of Swedish assistance [to the education sector]".[8]

Official Swedish support to basic education was, finally, extended under the home front component. It concerned three private, church-run and SWAPO-aligned schools at Gibeon, Hoachanas and Vaalgras in the isolated southern parts of the country.[9] The origin of the schools was eminently political. As earlier noted, under the leadership of Reverend Hendrik Witbooi four communities representing some 80 per cent of the Nama population had in October 1976 decided to oppose the Turnhalle scheme and join SWAPO. Organized within a Nama Teachers' Association, at about the same time local teachers at the public schools in the area went

1. Lars Dahlström from the University of Umeå. Dahlström and Umeå university in northern Sweden were subsequently closely involved with teacher training and education reform in both the refugee camps and in independent Namibia.
2. According to the consultant's report, there were 2,850 students in Kwanza Sul in mid-1983. It could be noted that he estimated the total refugee population in the settlement at 30,000, while the 'official' SWAPO figure was twice as high (Lars Dahlström: 'Basic education at Kwanza Sul', [no place], October 1983) (SDA).
3. Ibid. See also Dufborg and Johansson: Project document ('In-service training of teachers and production of teaching materials at the Namibian Education Centre, Kwanza Sul'), SIDA, Stockholm, 15 February 1984 (SDA).
4. Dufborg and Johansson: Project document ('In-service training of teachers and production of teaching materials at the Namibian Education Centre, Kwanza Sul'), SIDA, Stockholm, 15 February 1984 (SDA).
5. Ibid.
6. 'Minutes of understanding, SWAPO-SIDA', Luanda, 20 November 1986 (SDA).
7. Letter ('Teacher education conference') from Nahas Angula to Lennart Wohlgemuth, SWAPO, Luanda, 13 June 1989 (SDA).
8. Odén, Melber, Sellström and Tapscott op. cit., p. 87.
9. The largest of the three, Gibeon, had in the early 1980s an estimated population of only 2,500.

on strike against the official 'bantu education' system. The two developments led to open conflicts with the apartheid authorities. Many of the teachers were either dismissed or transferred to other regions.

One of the teachers was Hendrik Witbooi. A great-grandson of the famous Nama leader with the same name[1] and a leading representative of the African Methodist Episcopal Church (AME), he had in 1976 been elected chief of the Witboois. Based at Gibeon—where SWAPO had its regional head office—Witbooi joined the nationalist organization the same year, becoming Secretary for Education and Culture inside Namibia. To present an alternative to South Africa's education system, in 1977 he established a Namibia Private School Association (NAPSA) with other AME ministers and former teacher colleagues in the area, such as Petrus Kooper at Hoachanas and Willem Konjore at Vaalgras. Under the NAPSA umbrella and with very limited means, they proceeded to set up alternative primary schools, using English as the medium of instruction, following the syllabi of Botswana and Lesotho and combining basic education with agriculture, weaving and other practical subjects.

The schools became known all over Namibia. In spite of constant harassment by the authorities, for a nominal fee parents started to send their children to Gibeon, where they could stay as boarders.[2] Following the militarization of the schools in the so called 'operational areas', this even became increasingly common in distant Ovamboland, some 800 kilometres away.[3] The NAPSA schools thus effectively contributed to bringing different Namibian communities closer together.

In mid-February 1978, Witbooi accompanied Daniel Tjongarero and Sam Nujoma to Stockholm. It was during this visit by SWAPO's external and internal leaders that the Swedish assistance to the home front was re-designed. The private school association had recently been established and SWAPO was seeking financial support for the school plans. An agreement to that effect was reached at the subsequent aid negotiations in Lusaka in May 1978, where an amount of 1.5 MSEK was set aside for internal work in Namibia during the financial year 1978/79.[4] The NAPSA schools would from then on regularly receive assistance from Sweden, *inter alia* covering building activities, maintenance, running costs, staff salaries and educational supplies.

With Swedish support through SWAPO[5], Witbooi's school at Gibeon opened in 1979. At the time, there were 12 teachers and 150 pupils, but no class-rooms.

1. Chief Hendrik Witbooi (c. 1838-1905) defiantly refused German 'protection' at the end of the 19th century. He was fatally wounded in a battle with German forces at Vaalgras near Keetmanshoop in October 1905.
2. Birgitta Karlström Dorph: Memorandum ('SWAPO's program inne i Namibia'/'SWAPO's programmes inside Namibia'), Swedish legation, Pretoria, 4 March 1985 (SDA).
3. Letter with SWAPO's request for assistance in 1984/85 from Moses Garoeb to SIDA's Director [General], [no place], 5 January 1984 (SDA).
4. 'Agreed minutes of discussions on the cooperation between the South West Africa People's Organization (SWAPO) and Sweden 1978/79', Lusaka, 31 May 1978 (SDA). The contribution formed part of an emergency allocation of 3 MSEK granted after the Kassinga massacre.
5. As SWAPO initially had difficulties in channelling funds to the schools, it was in late 1979 agreed between SWAPO, SIDA and the Immanuel Church in Stockholm that the latter should regularly transfer amounts of 100,000 SEK to the church in Gibeon (Letter from Carin Norberg to Jan-Erik Wikström, Immanuel Church, SIDA, Stockholm, 10 January 1980) (SDA). The Immanuel Church (in Swedish, *Immanuelkyrkans församling*) formed part of the independent Swedish Mission Covenant Church (*Svenska Missionsförbundet*). Its chairman, Jan-Erik Wikström, had been involved in the work against apartheid since the late 1950s. A leading member of the Liberal Party, at the time of the agreement with SIDA and SWAPO Wikström served as Minister of Education (1976-82). Unbeknown to most, there was thus an indirect, personal link between the Swedish Education Minister and SWAPO's Secretary for Education and Culture inside Namibia.

Classes were held in the AME church or "under the trees".[1] With additional funds from Danchurchaid[2] of Denmark and the West German NGO Bread for the World[3], substantial constructions were, however, erected on a community basis at both Gibeon and Hoachanas in 1981/82.[4] At Gibeon—where the number of teachers[5] and pupils in the meantime had increased to 21 and 435, respectively—eight class-rooms, three dormitories, offices and toilets were completed, while four class-rooms were built at Hoachanas.[6]

With three class-rooms, the smaller school at Vaalgras was set up in 1983. Two years later—in early 1985—Birgitta Karlström Dorph from the Swedish legation in Pretoria visited the three schools.[7] By then, additional buildings had been erected and the number of pupils had grown to a total of about 850, of which 500 were at Gibeon—where education had also started at the secondary level—250 at Hoachanas and 100 at Vaalgras. The teaching staff numbered 41.[8] Noting that the Vaalgras school through voluntary work had almost "grown out of the sand" and that "the only thing which is not lacking [at Hoachanas] is people who are willing to work for the school", the Swedish diplomat was clearly impressed by the progress made in a harsh environment and under difficult political circumstances. Recommending continued assistance, she summarized her impressions as follows:

> The schools at Gibeon, Vaalgras and Hoachanas [...] have been created through great sacrifices by the local population. They do not only offer alternative education, but they [also] systematically try to make the pupils aware, [preparing] them for a free Namibia. The management and the teachers convey the impression of being very capable. Not least the leaders at the [three] places have through the establishment of the schools shown that they possess qualities to create a common spirit among oppressed people and unite them around concrete projects.[9]

Planning for Independence

Summing up the experiences of the project-dominated assistance to SWAPO from the early 1980s, SIDA stated in a submission to the Ministry for Foreign Affairs in April 1986:

> As a growing number of project activities have been launched, the demands on both the donor and the recipient have grown. Discussions on increased Swedish participation in the planning

1. Letter with SWAPO's request for assistance in 1983/84 from Moses Garoeb to SIDA's Director [General], Luanda, 5 January 1983 (SDA). As a reflection of the expanding cooperation between Sweden and SWAPO, the detailed request—including reports on the assistance received in 1981/82—covered no less than 62 type-written pages.
2. In Danish, *Folkekirkens Nødhjælp*.
3. In German, *Brot für die Welt*.
4. Letter with SWAPO's request for assistance in 1983/84 from Moses Garoeb to SIDA's Director [General], Luanda, 5 January 1983 (SDA).
5. Two teachers were former political prisoners from Robben Island (ibid.).
6. Ibid.
7. Hendrik Witbooi visited Stockholm in mid-1983, reporting directly to SIDA on the utilization of the Swedish funds (Letter with SWAPO's request for assistance in 1984/85 from Moses Garoeb to SIDA's Director [General], [no date], 5 January 1984) (SDA).
8. There were 25 teachers at Gibeon, 10 at Hoachanas and 6 at Vaalgras (Birgitta Karlström Dorph: Memorandum ('SWAPO's program inne i Namibia'/'SWAPO's programmes inside Namibia'), Swedish legation, Pretoria, 4 March 1985) (SDA).
9. Ibid. Berit Rylander visited the Gibeon school in February 1990. The number of teachers and pupils had then grown to 28 and 750, respectively (Berit Rylander: Memorandum ('Minnesanteckningar från möten med bilaterala givare, internationella biståndsorganisationer, representanter i den namibiska skuggregeringen och från besök i landet: 30/1-8/2 1990'/'Notes from meetings with bilateral donors, international aid organizations, representatives of the Namibian shadow government and from visits in the country: 30 January-8 February 1990'), SIDA, Stockholm, 19 March 1990) (SDA). It could be noted that in 1991-94 the schools continued to receive SIDA support. It was implemented by the Africa Groups.

and implementation of projects were initially interpreted by SWAPO as [an expression] of decreased confidence [...] and reduced flexibility [...].

Important lessons have been drawn from these discussions. On the Swedish side, a more realistic view has developed concerning SWAPO's limitations with regard to [...] project preparation and implementation. Growing emphasis has in all projects been put on [capacity-building] [...]. The dialogue around these issues is often difficult and sensitive. SWAPO's high ambitions are not always [backed] by [...] trained personnel. It is not easy [for the movement] to openly recognize its shortcomings and together with a donor find solutions which can contribute to its strengthening. Progress in the dialogue has, however, been registered over the last couple of years.[1]

The relations between Sweden and SWAPO were consolidated during the second half of the 1980s. At the official aid negotiations in Luanda in May 1988, the leaders of the two delegations—Sten Rylander, Assistant Under-Secretary for Foreign Affairs, and Andimba Toivo ya Toivo, Secretary General—noted that "a strong base of solidarity and mutual trust had been built up between the parties, which was perhaps the most valuable asset when the cooperation and the policy dialogue were to be carried further".[2] What they had in mind was the transition from humanitarian assistance to policy-oriented cooperation towards independence in Namibia.

In 1987, the international negotiating process regarding Angola and Namibia had tentatively resumed, eventually leading to face-to-face talks between Angola, Cuba, South Africa and the United States in London in May 1988. Although it was far from a foregone conclusion that the talks would be successful, there were, however, in early 1988 a number of positive indications in that direction. Against this background, at the bilateral consultations in Luanda at the end of May SWAPO introduced a "strategy paper" regarding possible Swedish assistance to an independent Namibia.[3] This marked the beginning of an intense period, during which the two parties on the one hand embarked upon a number of forward-looking initiatives and on the other—once the independence process was firmly on track—started to wind up the humanitarian assistance. While Sweden at SWAPO's request as early as in June 1988 hosted a historic meeting in Stockholm between the SWAPO leadership around President Nujoma and some twenty white Namibians from different walks of life[4], in addition to a number of seminars, workshops and meetings, during the fifteen months between December 1988 and February 1990 official Swedish and SWAPO delegations met on no less than six different occasions.[5]

---

1. Letter ('Humanitärt bistånd till South West Africa People's Organization, SWAPO (Namibia), budgetåret 1986/87'/'Humanitarian assistance to SWAPO [during] the financial year 1986/87') and attachments from Carl Tham to the Ministry for Foreign Affairs, SIDA, Stockholm, 16 April 1986 (SDA).
2. 'Agreed minutes [from] negotiations in Luanda in May 1988 between SWAPO of Namibia and Sweden concerning humanitarian assistance 1988/89', Luanda, 27 May 1988 (SDA).
3. Ibid. Sweden and ANC had in 1986 started to plan for a post-apartheid South Africa (see the chapter 'Banning of Trade and Planning for Post-Apartheid').
4. See, for example, SIDA: Memorandum ('Humanitärt bistånd till South West Africa People's Organization, SWAPO (Namibia), budgetåret 1989/90'/'Humanitarian assistance to SWAPO [during] the financial year 1989/90'), SIDA, Stockholm, 30 March 1989 (SDA). The Stockholm meeting on 19-21 June 1988 was the first in a series of confidence-building initiatives taken by SWAPO vis-à-vis the white community in Namibia. It was in October 1989 followed by a similar encounter in Kabwe, Zambia. Organized by Anton Lubowski on the Namibian side, the Stockholm meeting was financed by Sweden. It brought for the first time white Namibian businessmen, academics, lawyers, journalists etc. face to face with the SWAPO leadership. It should be noted that the meeting took place six months before the decisive New York accords between Angola, Cuba and South Africa.
5. Official talks were held in Stockholm in December 1988, in Luanda on two occasions in February 1989 and again in May 1989. They continued in Windhoek in November 1989 and February 1990.

The Swedish reaction to SWAPO's introduction of a strategy paper was positive. At the May 1988 negotiations it was therefore decided to hold a joint "brainstorming seminar" with the objective to "identify some vital areas where the Swedish resource base could be used in preparing for Namibia's independence". In the meantime, the Swedish delegation "undertook to prepare a desk study [...] in the field of transport and communications", as well as "a brief paper on possible support regarding banking and monetary institutions", while SWAPO "undertook to present ideas as regards future cooperation in the fields of education [...], human resources development [and] health".[1]

The seminar was held in Sollentuna outside Stockholm in early December 1988, just before the tripartite agreement between Angola, Cuba and South Africa finally paved the way for the implementation of UN Security Council Resolution 435 on Namibia's independence. At that time, Sam Nujoma had already submitted formal requests to the five Nordic countries for assistance in the areas where SWAPO deemed that they had a particular competence. In his letter to the Swedish Prime Minister Ingvar Carlsson—dated 30 September 1988—the SWAPO President asked for support in the field of transport and communications, as well as with regard to the establishment of a central bank.[2] While Carlsson in his reply of 1 December 1988 stated that Swedish assistance was "also foreseen in some of the areas which are now part of the humanitarian assistance, such as education"[3], the seminar focused on the two issues raised by Nujoma.[4]

As already noted, in accordance with the agreement reached at the negotiations in May 1988 and President Nujoma's request, SIDA procured the services of the Swedish consultancy firm SWECO to prepare a comprehensive study on the Namibian transport and communications sector. Before turning to the Nordic countries' coordination with regard to independent Namibia—as well as to Sweden and UNTAG—it remains to comment upon the preparations for the establishment of a central bank. In addition, the joint Swedish and Norwegian support to the project 'Laws for Independent Namibia' should be mentioned. At the consultative talks between SIDA and SWAPO in Stockholm in mid-December 1988, the costs for these activities were estimated at around 5 MSEK.[5]

Occupied Namibia had been ruled from Pretoria as a *de facto* South African province. The economy was not only integrated with South Africa's, but the provincial status had left the country without such basic and vital tools for economic planning and administration as a proper system of national accounts, reliable statistics or even accurate population data. It did not have a statistics office, a customs department, an auditor general or a national bank. At the prospect of independence, among the awesome challenges faced by SWAPO was the need to urgently prepare for such institutions, drafting the necessary legal instruments and recruiting the appropriate personnel. This process had started in the mid-1970s under the umbrella of the United Nations.[6] Nevertheless, in the case of a central bank SWAPO turned to Sweden.

---

1. 'Agreed minutes [from] negotiations in Luanda in May 1988 between SWAPO of Namibia and Sweden concerning humanitarian assistance 1988/89', Luanda, 27 May 1988 (SDA).
2. Letter from Sam Nujoma to Ingvar Carlsson, Luanda, 30 September 1988 (MFA). In the letter Nujoma actually referred to the establishment of a "commercial" bank.
3. Letter from Ingvar Carlsson to Sam Nujoma, Stockholm, 1 December 1988 (MFA).
4. Letter from Per Lindström, Swedish ambassador to Angola, to SWAPO, Luanda, 20 October 1988 (SDA).
5. 'Minutes of discussion[s] between SWAPO and SIDA, December 9, 1988', Stockholm, 9 December 1988 (SDA).
6. Notably at the UN Institute for Namibia.

Reflecting on financial
strategy: Erik Karlsson,
future Governor of the
Bank of Namibia, in
Windhoek, October 1990
(Photo: Anders Gunnartz)

The Swedish authorities had started to prepare the bank project before President Nujoma's letter to Prime Minister Carlsson. In mid-September 1988, Astrid Dufborg at SIDA's education division wrote to Erik Karlsson—a former Deputy Governor of the Swedish central bank who was finishing a long-term assignment as Governor of the Bank of Lesotho—asking whether he could participate in the forthcoming 'brainstorming seminar'.[1] With experiences from Lesotho, the Common Monetary Area[2] and the Southern African Customs Union, Karlsson was particularly well placed to advise SWAPO. He responded positively, and was on his return from Lesotho in October 1988 contracted by SIDA. He subsequently drafted an outline on central bank organization and management, which was discussed at the December seminar. Immediately thereafter, Karlsson and SWAPO's Finance Secretary Pohamba met Nujoma, who concurred with Karlsson's views and asked him to continue the preparatory work.[3] This was done through a series of closed lectures, seminars and meetings with SWAPO representatives[4], for example in Luanda and Lusaka in February 1989.[5]

Karlsson continued to be in charge of the project after Namibia's independence.[6] In April 1990, he was appointed economic adviser to President Nujoma. With Karlsson as Deputy Governor, the Bank of Namibia started its operations on 1 August 1990. The veteran Swedish banker was one year later appointed Acting Governor and in November 1992 Governor. With his signature on the bank notes, the new

---

1. Letter from Astrid Dufborg to Erik Karlsson, SIDA, Stockholm, 20 September 1988 (SDA).
2. The Common Monetary Area (CMA) consisted of South Africa, Lesotho and Swaziland. The national currencies of Lesotho and Swaziland were pegged to the South African Rand. After independence, Namibia became a member of CMA. Neighbouring Botswana had moved out of CMA, pegging its Pula to a basket of currencies.
3. The meeting took place in Rome, Italy, in December 1988. Astrid Dufborg and Berit Rylander from SIDA's headquarters in Stockholm accompanied Karlsson and Pohamba to the meeting.
4. The preparatory work on the establishment of a Namibian central bank was, obviously, extremely sensitive and kept strictly confidential.
5. 'Minnesanteckningar från möte i Luanda 890212' ('Notes from meeting in Luanda on 12 February 1989') and 'Minnesanteckningar från möte på UNIN i Lusaka 890221' ('Notes from meeting at UNIN in Lusaka on 21 February 1989') (SDA). There are no names, places or dates on these notes, but they were probably drafted by Erik Karlsson. They mainly deal with planning and organization of the work.
6. Support for the establishment of the Bank of Namibia became one of the main components of Sweden's development assistance to independent Namibia. A specific agreement on the project was concluded in October 1990.

national currency—the Namibia Dollar—was, finally, introduced on 15 September 1993.[1]

In cooperation with the University of Bremen in the Federal Republic of Germany and the UN Institute for Namibia, SWAPO's Department for Legal Affairs had in 1988 worked concurrently on a so called 'Namlaw project', financed by the European Community.[2] The objective was to review the existing legislation in Namibia and prepare draft legal instruments "in the areas presently governed by laws which [after independence] may be too badly flawed to continue to apply with amendments only".[3] As the financial support from the European Community came to an end in late 1988[4], in December SWAPO's Secretary for Legal Affairs, Ernest Tjiriange, approached Sweden and Norway for continued support. They both decided to support the project, allocating 1 million SEK and 100,000 USD, respectively. SIDA administered the funds and the actual costs were shared equally between the two donors.[5]

The legal project was implemented through high-level seminars and workshops, led by Tjiriange[6] and with important inputs by the governments of Mozambique, Zambia and Zimbabwe. The first seminar was held in Lusaka in April 1989, where different tasks were assigned to a number of legal draftsmen. The work was followed up at a second seminar in Lusaka in September-October 1989, where in particular draft legal instruments regarding the Constituent Assembly, citizenship, labour relations, local government and resettlement were discussed.[7] The third and last seminar was organized in Swakopmund, Namibia, in November 1989. It was convened for a slightly different purpose, namely to review SWAPO's constitutional proposals in readiness for the forthcoming sessions of the Constituent Assembly.[8]

Finally, in January 1990 SWAPO asked for SIDA's approval to use part of the remaining funds to cover costs incurred for legal counsel during the work on the Constitution of Namibia.[9] This was accepted at the official negotiations between Sweden and SWAPO in Windhoek on 9 February 1990, that is, on the very same

1. Odén, Melber, Sellström and Tapscott op. cit., p. 75. Karlsson left Namibia in 1994. In recognition of his services, President Nujoma declared him an honorary citizen of Namibia.
2. The Namlaw project was originally organized and administered by the Centre for African Studies/Namibia Project at the University of Bremen in close cooperation with UNIN, University of Zimbabwe, the US Lawyers' Committee for Civil Rights Under Law and relevant institutions in Namibia, among them the Council of Churches and the Legal Assistance Centre.
3. Letter/request ('New laws in independent Namibia') from Ernest Tjiriange, SWAPO Secretary for Legal Affairs [no place or date]. The request was handed over to Sten Rylander from the Swedish Ministry for Foreign Affairs during a visit to Luanda in December 1988 (Per Sjögren: Memorandum ('SWAPO-ansökan om bistånd inom rättsområdet'/'SWAPO request for assistance in the legal field'), Ministry for Foreign Affairs, Stockholm, 5 January 1989) (SDA).
4. Berit Rylander: Memorandum ('Lagstiftningsarbete inför ett självständigt Namibia'/'Legal work at the prospect of an independent Namibia'), SIDA, Stockholm, 17 April 1989 (SDA).
5. Georg Dreifaldt: Memorandum ('SIDA's and Norway's support to seminars and workshops for drafting new laws for independent Namibia/Legal studies'), Swedish embassy, Windhoek, 28 December 1990 (SDA). Initially, the support was to be channelled via UNIN. As the independence process in Namibia gained momentum, it was, however, found more expedient that SIDA administered the funds through its offices in Luanda, Lusaka and Windhoek.
6. At independence, Tjiriange was appointed Minister of Justice.
7. Theo Angula: 'Brief report on SIDA-sponsored legal seminars held during the course of 1989', Ministry of Justice, Windhoek, 1 June 1990 (SDA). On behalf of SWAPO's Department for Legal Affairs, Angula had served as the project secretary.
8. Ibid.
9. To assist SWAPO with the constitutional work, three lawyers from South Africa had been engaged.

day that independent Namibia's basic charter was adopted.[1] Sweden's indirect association with the drafting of Namibia's constitution—which, as noted above, had begun as early as in 1975—was thereby brought to successful fruition. The joint Swedish-Norwegian support to SWAPO's preparatory work in the legal field had in this context played a significant role, increasing the organization's command of complex juridical matters and strengthening its negotiating capacity during the drafting process.

Nordic Coordination, UNTAG and Impartiality

The support jointly extended by the Swedish and Norwegian governments to SWAPO's legal work was one of many expressions of Nordic cooperation with regard to Namibia.[2] In addition to coordination at the political level, as early as in January 1979 a first Nordic working group had been set up to study the conditions and forms for joint assistance to an independent Namibia. As the United Nations plan was pushed into the background in the early 1980s, the group was, however, eventually dissolved. By mid-1988, there were new signs that the Namibia question was approaching a solution. In July, Angola, Cuba and South Africa released a joint statement[3], and at a meeting in Kiruna, Sweden, the Nordic Ministers of Development Cooperation decided in late August to once again establish a working group on Namibia, now under Finnish chairmanship.[4] The fact that Martti Ahtisaari from Finland in his capacity as the UN Secretary General's special representative was closely involved in the international negotiating process[5], and that Bernt Carlsson from Sweden served as UN Commissioner for Namibia, was not without importance for the decision.

---

1. 'Agreed minutes', Windhoek, 10 February 1990 (SDA). It was an historical day in other respects too. The objective of the negotiations in Windhoek in February 1990 was thus to phase out the Swedish humanitarian support to SWAPO and prepare for development assistance to independent Namibia. To mark the occasion, the Swedish delegation was led by SIDA's Director General Carl Tham, accompanied by his deputy Jan Cedergren and the Swedish counsellor in Namibia, Lena Sundh. SWAPO's Secretary General Andimba Toivo ya Toivo headed the SWAPO team, which in addition included Hifikepunye Pohamba, Nahas Angula, Hidipo Hamutenya, Maxton Mutongolume and Festus Naholo.
2. Through financial support, Sweden and Norway facilitated an important meeting between SWAPO's external and internal leaders in Harare, Zimbabwe, 25-26 February 1989 (cf. Østbye in Eriksen (ed.) op. cit., p. 125). It was held subsequent to the UN Security Council's adoption of Resolution 632—through which UNTAG was deployed in Namibia—only one month ahead of the official beginning of the transition process on 1 April 1989. Attended by Nujoma, ya Toivo, Witbooi, Bessinger, Tjongarero and many other SWAPO leaders, the meeting had two major objectives, namely to a) establish a common platform for the political work ahead and b) share experiences with the ZANU leadership on lessons learnt during the independence campaign and elections in Zimbabwe in 1980. It has been implied that the tragic events of 1 April 1989—when more than 300 PLAN fighters were killed by the South African army—resulted from advice by ZANU to send freedom fighters into Namibia given during the seminar (Cliffe op. cit., p. 88). This seems unlikely. The author of this study attended parts of the joint sessions between SWAPO and ZANU. They were eminently political, focusing on voter mobilization, election campaigning etc. Through a financial contribution to the independent Southern African Research and Documentation Centre (SARDC), SIDA also facilitated a seminar between SWAPO and key people from Zimbabwe, Britain and the Commonwealth with experience from the 1980 elections in Zimbabwe. It was held in Harare on 26-27 May 1989 in response to mounting concerns as to whether the Namibian election process would be free and fair. Based on the discussions, SARDC subsequently produced a 'Handbook for Election Observers [in Namibia]' (Letter ('SARDC: Rapport från seminariet 'The transition from Rhodesia to Zimbabwe: The lessons for Namibia', Harare, 26-27 May 1989'/'Report from the seminar 'The transition from Rhodesia to Zimbabwe...') from Tor Sellström, Swedish embassy, to SIDA, Harare, 5 October 1989) (SDA).
3. 'Principles for a Peaceful Settlement in Southwestern Africa', New York, 13 July 1988.
4. EKB (Ämbetsmannakommittén för Biståndsfrågor/The [Nordic] Committee of High Officials for Development Cooperation): 'Utvecklingssamarbetet mellan Namibia och de nordiska länderna: Förslag till samarbete och samordning' ('Development cooperation between Namibia and the Nordic countries: Proposals for cooperation and coordination'), [no place], 14 December 1988 (SDA). The Finnish diplomat David Johansson chaired the working group. Sten Rylander from the Ministry for Foreign Affairs represented Sweden.
5. Cf. Crocker op. cit., pp. 336-37 and 344.

Mandated to "plan and coordinate the Nordic countries' assistance to a future independent Namibia", the working group held regular sessions during the second half of 1988 and in early 1989. While the first Nordic working group in 1980 had suggested a joint Nordic aid programme to Namibia—"administered by one of the Nordic countries on behalf of them all"[1]—in December 1989 the re-established group concluded that "each Nordic country would have its own cooperation programme [...]. The aim is no longer Nordic cooperation for its own sake, but instead to find the ways and means to make use of the Nordic resource base as comprehensively and effectively as possible for the benefit of the recipient [government]".[2] Since 1980, all the Nordic countries except Iceland had directly or indirectly embarked upon extensive support programmes to SWAPO.[3] In the view of the working group, emphasis should now be put on active coordination to avoid duplication of work and overlaps.

In late September 1988, Sam Nujoma had on behalf of SWAPO's Central Committee approached the five Nordic countries with requests for assistance to independent Namibia. In the case of Denmark, support was envisaged in the field of agriculture. Finland was asked to concentrate on forestry and water supply, Iceland on fisheries[4] and Norway on the petroleum and fishery sectors.[5] In addition to the establishment of a central bank, the request to Sweden concerned transport and communications. While the countries individually started to prepare assistance in these respective fields, they also joined efforts as a Nordic group. When UNHCR in early 1989 presented its plans for the repatriation of the Namibian refugees, the Nordic governments, for example, decided to make a joint contribution of 10 million USD to the operation, corresponding to 25 per cent of the estimated costs.[6]

In order to facilitate planning and coordination at the non-governmental level, the working group also requested the Nordic Africa Institute in Uppsala to arrange a conference on 'Nordic NGOs in Independent Namibia'. With financial support from SIDA, it was held in Sigtuna, Sweden, on 9-10 March 1989. "Selected among those who had established contacts with SWAPO or were working in Namibia"[7], about 40 Nordic NGOs were represented at the conference, in addition to resource persons from SWAPO, the Nordic working group and representatives from the Nordic aid agencies.[8] Although a proposal to set up a joint Nordic NGO office in Namibia did not materialize, with their own funds and government support many Nordic NGOs later supported the transition process, in particular with regard to repatriation and resettlement of the Namibian refugees.

1. Cited from the English translation of EKB op. cit., Ministry for Foreign Affairs, Stockholm, 20 January 1989 (SDA).
2. Ibid.
3. The assistance from Iceland was marginal. It was only extended through the United Nations. Finland, Norway and Sweden had entered into direct, official cooperation with SWAPO, while Denmark channelled its support via NGOs. According to the working group, the total Nordic assistance to SWAPO/Namibia amounted in 1988 to 31.8 million USD. The contribution from Sweden was 15 million (47%), from Finland 6.7 million (21%), from Norway 6.5 million (20%) and from Denmark 3.6 million USD (12%) (EKB op. cit.).
4. Independent Namibia became a priority country for Iceland's bilateral development assistance. Administered by ICEIDA (Icelandic International Development Agency) in close coordination with NORAD of Norway, the support covered marine research, as well as education and training in the fishery sector.
5. EKB op. cit.
6. Per Sjögren: Memorandum ('Nordiska arbetsgruppen för bistånd till Namibia: Lägesrapport'/'The Nordic working group on assistance to Namibia: Progress report'), Ministry for Foreign Affairs, Stockholm, 14 March 1989 (SDA).
7. Bertil Högberg, Bertil Odén and Vita Sigurdson: *Nordic Organisations in Independent Namibia: Report from a Conference in Sigtuna, 9-10 March, 1989*, The Scandinavian Institute of African Studies in cooperation with Nordic Non-Governmental Organisations, Uppsala, September 1989, p. 3.
8. Ibid.

Following the signing of the New York accords between Angola, Cuba and South Africa on 22 December 1988, the independence process rapidly gained momentum.[1] When the UN Security Council on 16 February 1989 unanimously adopted the enabling Resolution 632—deciding to "implement [...] Resolution 435 (1978) in its original and definitive form"[2]—the consultations between the Nordic countries were already focusing on their respective military and civilian contributions to UNTAG, as well as on the related question of impartiality during the transition process. While all the Nordic countries sent election observers to Namibia—and Norway and Sweden contributed civilian police monitors—it was, however, only Denmark and Finland that eventually participated in UNTAG's military component, the former with a logistical unit and the latter with a full infantry battalion.[3]

Sweden had traditionally contributed troops to the United Nations peace-making and peace-keeping operations and had at an early stage declared its readiness to do so in the case of Namibia too. However, South Africa—which in 1978 had already questioned a possible Swedish participation—opposed any military forces from the country, arguing that Sweden through its support to SWAPO was partial. Informed about Pretoria's position during an official visit to Zimbabwe, Prime Minister Carlsson reacted in the strongest of terms. Addressing a conference on Southern Africa organized by the Socialist International in Harare, he stated on 15 February 1989:

> It has been reported that South Africa does not wish to see any Swedes in [the] UN operation. We have been accused of not being impartial enough. [...] Negotiations are still going on at the United Nations, but I want to make two things very clear. First: [N]o person and no nation can be neutral in the struggle against apartheid and for independence. Not even the United Nations itself is neutral, that is what [R]esolution 435 is all about.

> Second: Sweden may or may not participate in the United Nations forces in Namibia. We are still preparing to do so. But whatever the outcome of the negotiations in New York, I can assure you that South Africa will never be able to prevent the [g]overnment of Sweden, or the people of Sweden, from giving political support to the process of independence in Namibia. And our commitment to initiate development cooperation with a future independent and democratic Namibia is as firm as ever.[4]

Five days later, the UN Secretary General Javier Pérez de Cuéllar informed the Social Democratic government that due to South Africa's opposition the United Nations would not request any military contribution to UNTAG from Sweden. Back in Stockholm, Ingvar Carlsson regretted the decision, commenting that

> it goes without saying that Swedes in the service of the United Nations must act impartially. They represent the United Nations, not Sweden. It is equally natural that [the Swedish] government has condemned South Africa's illegal occupation of Namibia and [...]—in accordance with appeals from the United Nations General Assembly [...]—[has] given humanitarian assistance to the liberation movement, SWAPO. There is no contradiction between these two viewpoints. [...]

---

1. On the transition to independence in Namibia, see Cliffe op. cit.
2. UN Security Council Resolution 632 of 16 February 1989, cited in United Nations: *Yearbook of the United Nations: 1989*, Department of Public Information, United Nations, New York, 1997, p. 792.
3. The decision on the military composition of UNTAG was taken by the UN Security Council on 23 February 1989 (ibid., p. 793).
4. 'Statement by the Prime Minister, Mr. Ingvar Carlsson, at the Socialist International Conference on Southern Africa in Harare, Zimbabwe', 15 February 1989, in Ministry for Foreign Affairs: *Documents on Swedish Foreign Policy: 1989*, Stockholm, 1990, p. 49.

No Swedish UNTAG soldiers, but policewomen: Karin Edvardsson in Ondangwa during the Namibian independence elections, November 1989 (Photo: Pressens Bild)

Sweden's offer to participate in UNTAG [...] was for us a natural link between earlier and future support for Namibia's people. The amount that [the] United Nations operation was estimated to cost us —about 200 million [SEK]—will [now] be set aside for [...] development cooperation efforts for a free and independent Namibia.[1]

The issue of impartiality during the UN supervised transition period was raised at an early stage in the Nordic working group. Invited by the group to a session in Stockholm, the Swedish UN Commissioner for Namibia, Bernt Carlsson, had, for example, in late October 1988 emphasized its importance, stating that "participation in UNTAG could hardly be combined with [...] bilateral assistance to SWAPO".[2] As Denmark and Iceland did not extend any direct official support to the Namibian liberation movement, the issue only concerned Finland, Norway and Sweden. In the case of Sweden, there were—as later noted by Sten Rylander, its representative in the working group—

strong forces who pursued the line that the humanitarian assistance to SWAPO must be discontinued and that we should be neutral vis-à-vis [...] the elections under preparation. Such demands were raised internally by the [Foreign] Ministry's political department, but also indirectly by Martti Ahtisaari.[3]

They were also raised by Bernt Carlsson, an influential member of the ruling Social Democratic Party.[4] On his way to New York to attend the signing of the crucial tri-

---

1. 'Statement by the Prime Minister, Mr. Ingvar Carlsson, following the announcement on [the] implementation of the UN Plan for Namibia', 20 February 1989, in ibid., p. 327.
2. Cited in Per Sjögren: Memorandum ('Nordiskt samarbete om bistånd till Namibia'/'Nordic cooperation regarding assistance to Namibia'), Ministry for Foreign Affairs, Stockholm, 3 November 1988 (SDA).
3. Letter ('Om samarbetet med ANC och de framtida relationerna med Sydafrika: En kommentar utifrån namibiska perspektiv'/'On the cooperation with ANC and the future relations with South Africa: A comment from a Namibian perspective') from Sten Rylander, Swedish ambassador to Namibia, to the Ministry for Foreign Affairs, Windhoek, 10 May 1993 (MFA).
4. As earlier noted, Carlsson had *inter alia* served as international secretary of the Social Democratic Party, holding that position between 1971 and 1976. After a long period as Secretary General of the Socialist International (1976-83), he first worked at the Ministry for Foreign Affairs (1983-85) and then as Under-Secretary of State in the Ministry of Agriculture, also being responsible for Nordic questions (1985-87).

partite agreement between Angola, Cuba and South Africa, Carlsson was, however, tragically killed in the Lockerbie air disaster over Scotland on 21 December 1988. With his death, there was no longer any direct Swedish diplomatic connection to the ensuing UN operation.

Above all, by disqualifying Sweden from participating in UNTAG's military component South Africa silenced the internal Swedish opposition to continued assistance to SWAPO. On 22 February 1989—only two days after the UN Secretary General's communication of the decision—SIDA and SWAPO held consultative talks in Luanda on the cooperation during the financial year 1989/90.[1] Formal, official aid negotiations between the parties took place in the Angolan capital on 9-12 May 1989, respectively led by Jan Cedergren, Deputy Director General of SIDA, and the SWAPO President Sam Nujoma.[2] In fact, while most countries reduced their contacts with SWAPO, in the case of Sweden they were considerably intensified just before and during the UNTAG period, which began on 1 April 1989. As noted, official Swedish and SWAPO delegations met on no less than six occasions between December 1988 and February 1990. The direct Swedish allocation to SWAPO was, finally, increased by almost 10 per cent, or from 73 MSEK in 1988/89 to 80 million in 1989/90.[3] The budget for SWAPO's activities inside Namibia was raised from 14 to 17.5 MSEK, or by 25 per cent.[4]

At the same time, Finland and Norway reacted in different ways to the calls for impartiality and suspension of the cooperation with SWAPO. While Norway "was very careful not to give support that SWAPO could use for its election campaign"[5], it, nevertheless, extended significant official assistance to the movement's preparatory work in the legal field, as well as to important political workshops and conferences. Above all, "the official Norwegian support for ongoing SWAPO projects outside Namibia continued".[6] This was in contrast to Finland. With Ahtisaari in charge of the UNTAG operation in Windhoek and a Finnish infantry battalion deployed in northern Namibia, in 1989 the Helsinki government decided to terminate the direct, official assistance to SWAPO.[7] Although Finland at the Nordic level often claimed a "special relationship" with Namibia[8], even the contribution to SWAPO's information office in Helsinki was withdrawn.[9] The recently established

---

1. 'Minutes of understanding between SWAPO and SIDA, February 22, 1989', Luanda, 2 March 1989 (SDA).
2. 'Agreed minutes from negotiations in Luanda, May 1989, between SWAPO of Namibia and Sweden concerning humanitarian assistance 1989/90', Luanda, 12 May 1989 (SDA).
3. The official Swedish assistance to Namibia/SWAPO outside the bilateral cooperation programme amounted in 1989/90 to approximately 70 MSEK ('Agreed minutes from negotiations in Luanda, May 1989, between SWAPO of Namibia and Sweden concerning humanitarian assistance 1989/90', Luanda, 12 May 1989) (SDA).
4. Ibid.
5. Østbye in Eriksen (ed.) op. cit., p. 124.
6. Ibid. The bilateral Norwegian cooperation programme with SWAPO did not include a 'home front component' for activities inside Namibia. For all practical purposes, the substantial Norwegian assistance thus remained as before during the UNTAG period.
7. Soiri and Peltola op. cit., p. 132.
8. Ibid., p. 122.
9. At a Nordic officials' meeting on humanitarian assistance to Southern Africa, the Finnish representatives Kimmo Pulkkinen and Eija Silvola reported in early May 1989 that Finland had "ceased contributing to the SWAPO office" (Lena Johansson: Memorandum ('Nordiskt möte 10-11 maj 1989: Humanitärt bistånd i södra Afrika'/'Nordic meeting 10-11 May 1989: Humanitarian assistance in Southern Africa'), SIDA, Stockholm, 18 May 1989) (SDA).

office eventually "had to be shut down".[1] There was thus far from a coordinated Nordic position vis-à-vis SWAPO during the crucial transition period.[2]

Independence at Last

The last and final stage on Namibia's long journey towards national independence and majority rule began under United Nations supervision on 1 April 1989. It was not without serious obstacles. Those who had feared an April Fools' Day initially seemed to have their doubts confirmed. On the night before the starting date for the transition process—as Ahtisaari was arriving and UNTAG had not yet established a viable military presence in Namibia—some 2,000 PLAN fighters crossed the border from Angola. SADF immediately broke its confinement to base and "went on a hunt-and-destroy mission"[3] sanctioned by Ahtisaari and the UN Secretary General.[4] There followed in the next few days some of the bloodiest fighting in Namibia during the long war of liberation, with over 300 SWAPO and some 35-40 SADF soldiers killed.[5]

---

1. Soiri and Peltola op. cit., p. 132. After the decision, official support to the office was, however, initially channelled through the Finnish Missionary Society. Soiri and Peltola add that "SWAPO agreed with the decision" (ibid.). There is, however, abundant evidence that the suspension of the official Finnish assistance was a great disappointment. With limited resources and huge responsibilities—at the same time facing an uncertain transition process and powerful, Pretoria-backed, political opponents—SWAPO in 1989/90 was more than ever in need of friends and funds. Sten Rylander, the first Swedish ambassador to independent Namibia, later commented: "I have on several occasions during the last three years at the highest political level in Namibia been spontaneously reminded of how much they appreciated the Swedish position [...]. It could in this context be noted that Finland due to [its] opposite [stand] [...] still has to pay a political price [...]. Under pressure from Ahtisaari, Finland chose to cancel the support to SWAPO while the UNTAG process was going on. This decision provoked great embitterment and disappointment among leading SWAPO representatives" (Letter ('Om samarbetet med ANC och de framtida relationerna med Sydafrika: En kommentar utifrån namibiska perspektiv'/'On the cooperation with ANC and the future relations with South Africa: A comment from a Namibian perspective') from Sten Rylander, Swedish ambassador to Namibia, to the Ministry for Foreign Affairs, Windhoek, 10 May 1993) (MFA).
2. Although there was no particular Finnish connection to the transition process in South Africa, after the unbanning of ANC and the release of Nelson Mandela the Helsinki government would in the early 1990s act in a very similar way vis-à-vis ANC. While Norway and Sweden maintained direct cooperation and contacts, in the case of Finland "the aid was terminated and the ANC office in Helsinki was soon closed" (Soiri and Peltola op. cit., p. 154).
3. Ohlson op. cit., p. 95.
4. In an interview with Ahtisaari—then President of Finland—the UN Secretary General's former Special Representative to Namibia stated in January 1996: "[T]he only explanation [for the SWAPO soldiers crossing the border into Namibia] that I can think of was that it was an attempt to get troops inside in order to justify the claim that there was a bigger number [of PLAN fighters there]. [...] I think [that] both [the] Cubans and [the] Angolans were furious about it. [...] I was very worried [about South Africa's reaction], because they had all the reasons to stop [the independence process]. If they wanted to have an excuse, they had it. But when they didn't use it, then I was in a much stronger position [...]. [...] [T]hey could have taken the high road, actually, [...] and say 'look, this is it, out we go, end of the process, UN out'. But they didn't do it. And that then made me draw the conclusion that they [were there] to stay to the bitter end and see the whole process through. So one could say that [the] tragic death of these people served [the] purpose that it reinforced the process, finally. That was my conclusion and that of my senior colleagues as well. And that reinforced our hand in dealings with the South Africans. [...] The sad thing is that when you are in a position like I was to implement an agreement, you [have] to be as tough with your friends as [with] your foes. [A]t that time, you could hardly say that the South Africans were my friends. But you had to deal with it and, basically, you had to give them credit that they behaved correctly. [T]hey were on [1 April] all in their bases, as the agreement demanded" (Interview with Martti Ahtisaari in Soiri and Peltola op. cit., pp. 185-86). On the relations between Ahtisaari and the South African Foreign Minister Botha, see the interview with Roelof 'Pik' Botha, p. 115.
5. On the April 1989 events, see Cliffe op. cit., pp. 84-91. Unfortunately, Nujoma's memoirs (*Where Others Wavered: The Autobiography of Sam Nujoma*, Panaf Books, London, 2001) were not available when the present text on SWAPO was written. With regard to 1 April 1989, it could be noted that his judgement of Martti Ahtisaari is particularly damning. Describing the Finnish UN Special Representative as "very much a collaborator with the US and [the] British [and] more concerned with his career at the United Nations than with his responsibilities towards the oppressed people of Namibia", in his generally controversial accounts the Namibian President concludes that "[a]t this crucial and critical hour for Namibia's freedom, Ahtisaari's action betrayed our cause and resulted in the deaths of many innocent civilians" (pp. 396-97). This notwithstanding, after the country's independence Nujoma made Ahtisaari the first honorary citizen of Namibia.

The aborted cease-fire put the entire independence plan at risk. South Africa threatened to suspend its participation. On behalf of the Swedish government, Foreign Minister Sten Andersson on 6 April expressed his "profound concern about the turn of events".[1] Although a climate of mistrust and friction had been created for the following pre-election period, the crisis was, however, resolved when representatives of the Angolan, Cuban and South African governments managed to salvage the plan and get the process back on track by May 1989.[2] The election campaign proper also saw intimidation and violence.[3] Nevertheless, for the first time in Namibia's history democratic elections were held in a relatively peaceful climate on 7-11 November 1989. They were one week later declared free and fair by Ahtisaari.

As expected, SWAPO won a comfortable victory. The nationalist movement got 57.3 per cent of the votes and 41 of the 72 seats in the Constituent Assembly, while its main contender DTA got 28.6 per cent, corresponding to 21 seats. The remaining ten seats were divided between five minor parties.[4] As SWAPO did not get the two-thirds majority required to write the Namibian constitution on its own, there followed an uncertain negotiating and drafting period. Those who opposed—or did not know—SWAPO feared that the tensions during the election campaign would block the constitutional process. However, the opposite occurred. SWAPO adopted a conciliatory position, *inter alia* proposing provisions for multi-party democracy, an independent judiciary, a declaration of fundamental human rights and recognition of property rights. The differences with DTA "were quickly settled in an atmosphere characterized by a mutual will to get on with the business of running the country".[5] By late January 1990, the Constituent Assembly had finished its work and a constitution which at the time was often referred to as the "world's most democratic"[6] was unanimously adopted on 9 February 1990. Sam Nujoma was appointed to lead the new nation and on 21 March 1990 formal independence was, finally, achieved.[7]

With active Swedish official and NGO involvement, some 42,000 Namibian refugees—the chief concern of two decades of humanitarian assistance—were repatriated between June and August 1989. In addition to the physical transportation of the exiles from Angola, Botswana, Zambia and other countries, the operation coor-

---

1. 'Statement by the Minister for Foreign Affairs, Mr. Sten Andersson, on Namibia', 6 April 1989, in Ministry for Foreign Affairs: *Documents on Swedish Foreign Policy: 1989*, Stockholm, 1990, p. 331. During the aid negotiations with SWAPO in Luanda in early May, Jan Cedergren, the head of the Swedish delegation, "deplored the killings", adding that "South Africa seemed to have got away much too easily from the responsibility for [the] tragic events" ('Agreed minutes from negotiations in Luanda, May 1989, between SWAPO of Namibia and Sweden concerning humanitarian assistance 1989/90', Luanda, 12 May 1989) (SDA).
2. Angola, Cuba and South Africa had formed a joint commission to oversee the implementation of the December 1988 New York accords.
3. Cf. Cliffe op. cit., pp. 115-33. Notably, on 12 September 1989 the white SWAPO leader Anton Lubowski was shot dead outside his Windhoek home by a South African death squad. On South Africa and the assassination of Lubowski, see Pauw op. cit., pp. 12, 160 and 231-36. According to the plans, the future cabinet members Hidipo Hamutenya and Daniel Tjongarero were also to be killed (ibid., p. 229).
4. With 0.5 per cent of the votes, Shipanga's SWAPO-Democrats failed to secure a seat in the Constituent Assembly.
5. Ohlson op. cit., p. 95. Cf. the interview with Dirk Mudge, p. 83: "I think that everybody will appreciate that I played a role in the Constituent Assembly. Mr. Geingob and others have on many occasions said that they do not think that it would have been possible to write a constitution in four months if it were not for me. I always assisted in finding solutions to the problems" (p. 83).
6. Ohlson op. cit., p. 95.
7. At a meeting in Turku, Finland, the Nordic Foreign Ministers agreed in early March 1990 to lift the economic sanctions against Namibia ('Statement on South Africa and Namibia, issued at the meeting of [the] Nordic foreign ministers in Turku', 7 March 1990, in Ministry for Foreign Affairs: *Documents on Swedish Foreign Policy: 1990*, Stockholm, 1991, pp. 102-03). Sweden recognized Namibia on 21 March 1990.

dinated by UNHCR involved SWAPO's 'communal property', that is, movable assets, primarily from the Kwanza Sul and Nyango settlements. This question would soon create frictions between SWAPO and UNHCR, which only allowed for transportation to Namibia of the refugees' personal belongings.[1] When the repatriation exercise began, SWAPO had filled some 400 cargo containers with vehicles, spare parts, education supplies, medicines, food, office equipment, documents etc.[2] As UNHCR argued that the repatriation of the containers fell outside its UNTAG mandate, SWAPO turned to SIDA for assistance.[3] Most of the containers were subsequently brought back to Namibia by road. By August 1989—when the bulk of the refugees had been repatriated—there remained, however, around 80 containers in Kwanza Sul.[4]

SWAPO had in the meantime officially transferred the former health and education centre to the Angolan provincial authorities in Kwanza Sul. Its protective military forces were, however, not replaced by similarly effective Angolan troops. On the contrary, the Angolan soldiers "probably joined the local population in the wave of theft" that took place after SWAPO's withdrawal. Military raids by UNITA were also reported. In a sad comment to ten years of close cooperation between Sweden and SWAPO to turn Kwanza Sul into a well equipped and viable settlement, Georg Dreifaldt at the Swedish embassy in Luanda noted in June 1990:

> [The Angolan army's] capacity, or interest, to protect the camp has been low. The result has been a veritable cannibalization [...]. The local population—together with the [army], or at least with its consent—has cleansed it from all personal property left behind. [...] The roof sheets have disappeared and are now probably covering the houses in the neighbouring villages. In addition, [...] many containers have been broken open and emptied of everything of value. [...] The material packed by the Swedish primary school teacher project has possibly disappeared to the black market. [...] SIDA's hopes that the Kwanza Sul settlement would not fall into disrepair, but be put to continued use, were thus dashed at an early stage.[5]

The winding up of SWAPO's Nyango health and education centre in Zambia was a much longer, but also a more positive experience. Due to the centre's large population of school children under voting age and to the lack of school facilities in Namibia, it was decided by SWAPO to continue the education at the settlement beyond the transition period. At the aid negotiations in Windhoek in February 1990, it was thus agreed to set aside 3 MSEK for food and other daily necessities for some 2,400 school children, teachers and support staff during 1990/91.[6] With funds from SIDA, the refugees at Nyango and their personal belongings, as well as communal property in the form of vehicles; school, hospital and office equipment; agricultural tools etc., were between December 1990 and January 1991, finally, repatriated to independent Namibia.[7] As SWAPO handed the Nyango settlement over to the Zambian authorities, most of the former refugee children were accom-

---

1. Georg Dreifaldt: Memorandum ('Repatriering av namibiska flyktingar och avveckling av SWAPO's verksamhet i Angola'/'Repatriation of Namibian refugees and winding up of SWAPO's activities in Angola'), Swedish embassy, Luanda, 13 June 1990 (SDA).
2. Ibid.
3. Ibid.
4. Ibid. A Swedish company was contracted by SIDA to transport the containers from Kwanza Sul to Luanda, but due to the rapidly deteriorating security situation in the area it was not given the necessary permission by the Angolan authorities to carry out the task (ibid.). Once the repatriation exercise was completed, SWAPO was, similarly, not allowed to visit the Kwanza Sul settlement (ibid.).
5. Ibid.
6. 'Agreed minutes', Windhoek, 10 February 1990 (SDA).
7. Letter ('Avslutningen av Nyango-projektet'/'The termination of the Nyango project') from Georg Dreifaldt, Swedish embassy, to SIDA, Windhoek, 27 May 1991 (SDA).

On their way to the Namibian independence celebrations (from left): Swedish counsellor Lena Sundh, future ambassador Sten Rylander and Cooperation Minister Lena Hjelm-Wallén, Windhoek, 21 March 1990 (Photo: The author)

modated at a newly established school at Ruacana in northern Namibia. The Nyango project was officially closed at a small ceremony in the Namibian capital in May 1991.[1] It marked the end of twenty years of direct, official Swedish humanitarian assistance to SWAPO.

At that time, the independent Republic of Namibia had existed for more than a year. At a ceremony in a packed Windhoek stadium attended by scores of heads of state and government, foreign ministers and other international dignitaries, on 21 March 1990 the South African flag had been lowered and executive power handed over by President de Klerk to President Nujoma. Sweden was well represented at the celebrations. While the official delegation was led by Foreign Minister Sten Andersson[2] and Cooperation Minister Lena Hjelm-Wallén, a number of government officials and NGO representatives who over the years had worked closely with SWAPO also witnessed the historic moment. Among them were SIDA's former Director General Ernst Michanek; Anders Bjurner, Sten Rylander and Lena Sundh from the Ministry for Foreign Affairs; Ingalill Colbro and Berit Rylander from SIDA; Bertil Högberg from Bread and Fishes and the Africa Groups; as well as the film-maker Per Sandén.[3]

Independent Namibia was born on Sharpeville Day, exactly thirty years after the shootings outside Johannesburg which to a large extent gave rise to the anti-apartheid movement in Sweden and around the world. Sweden's relations with ANC will be discussed below. It could, however, here be noted that the ANC leader Nelson Mandela—who on 11 February 1990, only forty days earlier, had been released from imprisonment—to everybody's excitement unexpectedly appeared at

---

1. Kate Burling: 'Nyango comes home' in *The Namibian*, 27 May 1991.
2. During the independence celebrations, Foreign Minister Andersson met President de Klerk and his South African counterpart 'Pik' Botha for the first time. According to Botha, "pushing from our side [...], [w]e had a very open, fruitful and useful discussion. [...]. [Andersson] explained to us that what [Sweden] would do [vis-à-vis South Africa] would depend on how irrevocable or irreversible the change was" (Interview with Roelof 'Pik' Botha, p. 116).
3. At the time based in Harare, Zimbabwe, the author was invited by SWAPO to attend the celebrations.

the Windhoek stadium just before midnight, as the new Namibian flag was about to be hoisted.[1] Mandela had to struggle another four years before achieving his life-long dedication to majority rule in South Africa. In the meantime, he, Walter Sisulu and many other ANC leaders frequently visited Namibia for political consultations. Shortly after Namibia's independence, the SWAPO government also welcomed the establishment of an ANC office in Windhoek. It was from the beginning financially supported by Sweden.[2]

From 1970/71, the Swedish government disbursed in current figures a total amount of 671 MSEK as direct, official humanitarian assistance to SWAPO, occupying the position as the nationalist movement's main donor.[3] While it is difficult to assess the qualitative impact of the support on SWAPO's eventual victory, it could be concluded that it effectively contributed to the survival and relative welfare of the Namibian refugees in Southern Africa. The projects launched to strengthen the movement's administrative capacity were in the longer term perspective also of lasting significance. Briefing Prime Minister Ingvar Carlsson before his official visit to Namibia in early 1995, the Swedish ambassador Sten Rylander—who established close relations with the SWAPO leadership in the mid-1980s—stated:

> The long Namibian struggle for independence and national autonomy was conducted at a time and in a world which were bipolar and strongly influenced by the rivalry between two powerful and dominating super powers. [...] It may possibly sound presumptuous, but we are convinced that the close contacts with Sweden during this difficult bipolar era have been a contributing reason for [the fact that] SWAPO [after] independence has managed the transition so well. From a struggling, sometimes dogmatic, liberation movement with many faults and shortcomings, [it] has—to the best of its ability and conscious of its responsibilities—become a leading, ruling party in a constitutional democracy.[4]

As announced before independence, Namibia became a so called 'programme'—or core—country for Swedish development assistance. An initial allocation of 100 MSEK was granted for the financial year 1 July 1990-30 June 1991. The grant was raised to 110 MSEK in 1991/92, and by 30 June 1995 cumulative disbursements under the cooperation programme had—in fixed prices (1995)—reached a total of 589 MSEK.[5] Focusing on education (35 per cent), transport and communications (22 per cent), as well as on capacity-building in the public sector (16 per cent), it placed Sweden among Namibia's main donors together with the European Community and Germany.[6]

---

1. On his first trip outside Africa after his release, Mandela had visited Sweden in mid-March.
2. Established by Abbey Chikane—the brother of Frank Chikane, Secretary General of the South African Council of Churches—the ANC representation in Windhoek was subsequently accorded diplomatic status by the Namibian government. Swedish support towards furniture, office equipment, rent, running costs and daily necessities was extended from mid-1990 (Letter ('Budget för ANC Namibia för 1:a halvåret 1991'/'Budget for ANC Namibia during the first half of 1991') from Georg Dreifaldt to the Swedish embassy in Lusaka, Swedish embassy, Windhoek, 17 January 1991) (SDA).
3. See the accompanying disbursement table for SWAPO. The figure of 671 MSEK includes payments of 2.7 million registered after Namibia's independence.
4. Sten Rylander: Memorandum ('Om de svensk-namibiska relationerna'/'On the Swedish-Namibian relations'), Swedish embassy, Windhoek, 24 January 1995 (MFA).
5. Sida op. cit., p. 28.
6. Odén, Melber, Sellström and Tapscott op. cit., p. 64. The data on Namibia's donors refer to 1993.

ANC of South Africa: No Easy Walk

Early Solidarity...

Opening a conference outside Stockholm in June 1997 on a new partnership with Africa, Cooperation Minister Pierre Schori—who thirty years earlier as international secretary of the Social Democratic Party was among the first promoters of direct, official Swedish assistance to the African liberation movements[1]—affirmed that the particular involvement with South Africa represented

> the biggest, longest and most successful solidarity engagement Sweden ha[d] ever undertaken.[2]

It was the policy of apartheid that from 1948 prompted influential Swedish opinion makers to denounce racist oppression and minority rule, initially in South Africa and later in the Southern African region as a whole. As apartheid was introduced at the level of higher education, the Swedish National Union of Students (SFS)[3] started campaigns in support of their victimized black South African colleagues.[4] In the beginning, funds were partly collected through donating blood. As a student leader, Olof Palme participated in the campaigns, later describing the involvement as his "first political act".[5] Through active lobbying, SFS also managed to influence the Social Democratic government. In 1959, Foreign Minister Östen Undén took up "the worsening situation of the coloured[6] students in the Union of South Africa" in his annual address to the United Nations General Assembly.[7] It was the first time that Sweden brought the matter of apartheid to the attention of the world organization.[8]

A first organized Swedish expression of anti-apartheid solidarity outside the student movement was initiated at about the same time by Gunnar Helander, a former CSM missionary in South Africa, together with the young writer and journalist Per Wästberg. In September 1959—ten days before Undén's UN address—they launched a Fund for the Victims of Racial Oppression in South Africa.[9] Inspired by the British Defence and Aid Fund, it subsequently served as the Swedish

---

1. See Sellström Volume I, pp. 233-34.
2. Pierre Schori: 'Opening statement', Partnership Africa Conference, Saltsjöbaden, 25 June 1997 (NAI). Together with Gun-Britt Andersson (secretary), Anders Forsse (chairman), Sven Hamrell, Gunnar Helander, Anders Möllander (secretary) and Per Wästberg, on 15 January 1973 Schori participated in the CCHA meeting which for the first time recommended direct official support to ANC.
3. In Swedish, *Sveriges Förenade Studentkårer*.
4. Sellström Volume I, pp. 85-117 and 124-60.
5. Ibid., p. 86.
6. In Swedish, the term 'coloured' (*färgad*) was at the time synonymous with black or, more generally, non-white.
7. Sellström Volume I, p. 89.
8. On 15 December 1965, Sweden voted in favour of UN General Assembly Resolution 2054 A (XX), which drew "the attention of the Security Council to the fact that the situation in South Africa constitutes a threat to international peace and security; that action under Chapter VII of the Charter is essential in order to solve the problem of apartheid; and that universally applied economic sanctions are the only means of achieving a peaceful solution". While Finland, Iceland and Norway abstained, Denmark also supported the resolution. On 16 December 1966, all the Nordic countries voted in favour of UNGA Resolution 2202 A (XXI), which for the first time condemned apartheid as "a crime against humanity" (Carl Fredrik Liungman: Memorandum ('Svenska ställningstaganden till frågor berörande södra Afrika inom FN'/'Swedish standpoints on questions regarding Southern Africa at the UN'), Ministry for Foreign Affairs, Stockholm, 2 August 1968) (MFA).
9. In Swedish, *Fonden för Rasförtryckets Offer i Sydafrika*.

chapter of the International Defence and Aid Fund for Southern Africa. In a study for the United Nations, Kader and Louise Asmal noted that the Swedish fund was among the earliest anti-apartheid NGO committees in Western Europe.[1]

As in other parts of the world, the Sharpeville massacre of 21 March 1960 galvanized Swedish public opinion into greater action. Following a recommendation by the International Confederation of Free Trade Unions—at the time headed by LO's chairman Arne Geijer[2]—in April 1960 the Trade Union Confederation and the Co-operative Union and Wholesale Society declared a first consumer boycott of South African goods.[3] Finally, in March 1961 Helander, Wästberg and a group of mainly younger Social Democrats and Liberals set up a national South Africa Committee (SSAK).[4] Supporting a sustained boycott campaign launched in March 1963 by the National Council of Swedish Youth (SUL)[5], increasingly active local South Africa Committees were formed all over the country. By the mid-1960s, they had managed to place the issue of South Africa at the centre of the national political debate.[6] The first parliamentary motions demanding economic legislation against the apartheid regime were introduced by the Communist, Centre and Liberal parties in January 1965.[7] In the meantime, 20 out of Sweden's 24 regional councils had by mid-1965 decided not to procure South African products.

Through active diplomacy, resident and visiting representatives of the banned African National Congress (ANC) effectively contributed to the development of an anti-apartheid opinion. After his arrival in Sweden in January 1961, the South African student Billy Modise played a prominent role in the establishment of the influential Lund South Africa Committee, as well as in the wider solidarity movement.[8] Oliver Tambo, ANC's leader in exile, paid his first of many visits to Sweden in April 1961. On 1 May 1962, he addressed the traditional Labour Day demonstrations in Gothenburg, and in August 1962 he was received by the Social Democratic Prime Minister Tage Erlander. Shortly after going into exile, the ANC Secretary General Duma Nokwe also came to Sweden. He represented the liberation movement at the launch of SUL's boycott campaign on 1 March 1963. Often invited by

---

1. Kader and Louise Asmal: 'Anti-apartheid Movements in Western Europe', United Nations Unit on Apartheid, Notes and Documents, No. 4/74, United Nations, New York, March 1974, p. 1. A veteran ANC member, Kader Asmal—who in exile in Ireland like Helander and Wästberg in Sweden played a prominent role in IDAF—was appointed Minister of Water Affairs and Forestry after the April 1994 democratic elections in South Africa.

2. Leading LO, Geijer served as ICFTU President between 1957 and 1965. A Social Democratic MP from 1955, he also formed part of the ruling party's executive committee.

3. Sellström Volume I, pp. 141-45. In the light of the Cold War division between the Western ICFTU and the Eastern World Federation of Trade Unions (WFTU), it could be noted that the latter at the time did not support ANC's calls for a boycott of South African goods. ANC, SACTU and SACP were highly critical of the stand. According to Ilona and Hans-Georg Schleicher, "the Soviet Union's cooperation with South Africa in the [...] commercially important gold and diamond trade raises the suspicion that the leading Eastern power's economic interests constituted an important ground for [the] misgivings with regard to the boycott issue" (Schleicher op. cit., pp. 8-9).

4. In Swedish, *Svenska Sydafrikakommittén*. On SSAK, see Sellström Volume I, pp. 152-60, where it is *inter alia* noted that the Swedish police in the early 1960s had difficulties in adapting to the emerging solidarity movement, even acting against the ruling party's Labour Day marches in 1961 and 1962. In his memoirs, professor Joachim Israel—who became chairman of SSAK in August 1962—describes how he was registered by the security police due to his anti-apartheid activities (Joachim Israel: *Ett Upproriskt Liv* ('A Rebellious Life'), Norstedts Förlag, Stockholm, 1998, pp. 212-15).

5. In Swedish, *Sveriges Ungdomsorganisationers Landsråd*.

6. Sellström Volume I, pp. 215-32.

7. Ibid., p. 226. The Liberal Party motion was coordinated with that of the Centre Party. It was signed among others by Ola Ullsten, who was Prime Minister when Sweden fourteen years later—from 1 July 1979—prohibited new investments in South Africa.

8. Interviews with Billy Modise (p. 157) and Anders Johansson (p. 296).

local South Africa committees, several other leading ANC representatives visited the country during the first half of the 1960s.

By the mid-1960s, ANC had established direct contacts with the Swedish government[1], as well as with the wider solidarity movement. Although SSAK and the local South Africa committees did not formally recognize the organization, their relations were "mainly with ANC".[2] The same applied to SUL. ANC contacts were also initiated with the opposition Centre and Liberal parties[3], and in 1964 the Social Democratic Youth League (SSU) donated the modest, but significant amount of 3,000 SEK to the organization. It was "to be used in an appropriate way in the struggle against the Verwoerd regime".[4] As far as can be ascertained, the grant represented the first direct financial donation to ANC by any Swedish political organization.[5]

The struggle by ANC—Africa's oldest national liberation movement, founded in 1912—was only crowned with success in 1994, when it convincingly won the first South African non-racial, democratic elections. During the last three of the organization's eight decades of campaigns for human dignity and equality, ANC enjoyed wide support in Sweden.[6] Commenting upon his first contacts with Sweden and the other Nordic countries in the mid-1980s, Alex Boraine, founder of the Institute for a Democratic Alternative in South Africa, later noted that people "were extremely suspicious of white liberals. [...] [M]y impression was that [they] only saw the possibility of ANC overthrowing the regime".[7]

As stated by Schori, the solidarity engagement with South Africa occupies a unique place in the history of contemporary Swedish international relations. Reflecting on the role played by Sweden as Nelson Mandela in May 1994 took the presidential oath in Pretoria, SIDA's former Director General Carl Tham went further, asserting that

---

1. On 1 May 1965, Prime Minister Erlander and Oliver Tambo addressed the Labour Day demonstrations in Örebro. They, however, disagreed on the question of sanctions against South Africa (Sellström Volume I, pp. 227-29).

2. Interview with Anders Johansson, p. 296.

3. As Secretary General of the World Assembly of Youth (WAY), David Wirmark of the Liberal Party had established close relations with Oliver Tambo as early as in April 1960, only a few days after the ANC leader went into exile. On Wirmark, WAY and ANC, see Sellström Volume I, pp. 101-04.

4. See Sellström Volume I, pp. 229-30. In 1965, Thage G. Peterson—at the time SSU's vice-chairman—advocated military assistance to ANC. In his autobiography, the former minister recounts how his views were strongly criticized by Prime Minister Erlander, Foreign Minister Torsten Nilsson and the Social Democratic Party secretary Sten Andersson, as well as by some SSU members, such as Lars Engqvist. While Olof Palme "never doubted that non-violence was the principal course", Peterson, however, notes that Palme "on several occasions during our conversations expressed understanding for the [position] taken by me and SSU" (Thage G. Peterson: *Resan mot Mars: Anteckningar och Minnen* ('The Journey towards Mars: Notes and Memories'), Albert Bonniers Förlag, Stockholm, 1999, pp. 80-81).

5. As noted in the chapter 'SWAPO of Namibia: Tentative Steps towards Firm Relations', subsequent financial contributions to ANC from the Social Democratic Party's International Solidarity Fund were regularly less important than those granted to SWAPO.

6. The Swedish contacts with ANC and the liberation movements in Southern Africa incensed the apartheid regime. Several illustrations from the early 1960s are given in Sellström Volume I. In a particularly forceful broadside, the official South African Broadcasting Corporation (SABC) characterized Sweden in October 1969 as "the most strident enemy in Europe of white-ruled Southern Africa" (SABC: 'Sweden's bad dream', Current Affairs, Johannesburg, 22 October 1969, attached to letter ('Angrepp mot Sverige i sydafrikanska radion'/'Attack on Sweden on South African radio') from Eric Virgin, Swedish envoy to South Africa, to the Ministry for Foreign Affairs, Pretoria, 27 October 1969) (MFA). In March 1974, the Afrikaans-language newspaper *Die Vaderland* described the country as "the terrorists' biggest source of income" (cited in cable from the Swedish legation to the Ministry for Foreign Affairs, Pretoria, 27 March 1974) (SDA).

7. Interview with Alex Boraine, p. 107.

[n]o [other] democratic country has so consistently supported ANC and the forces of liberation. It has been of great practical and political significance. It [constitutes] one of the most
important foreign policy and cooperation efforts carried out by Sweden.[1]

In quantitative terms and current figures, at the time of the April 1994 elections
Social Democratic and non-socialist Swedish governments had over the years disbursed some 2.5 billion SEK in favour of a democratic denouement of the South
African drama. Of this amount, 896 MSEK was directly channelled to ANC under
bilateral agreements.[2] From modest beginnings, ANC became the most important
recipient of public funds among the Southern African liberation movements
assisted by Sweden. By the same token, the Swedish government became ANC's
principal donor in the non-military field. In a meeting with Prime Minister Fälldin,
Oliver Tambo noted in March 1981 that Sweden's assistance to his movement
"exceeded that from any other country, including the Soviet Union and [the German Democratic Republic]".[3] In discussions with Foreign Minister Ullsten, he
stated during the same visit to Stockholm that "ANC's strong position today would
not have been possible without the Swedish support".[4] Commenting that it "perhaps [implied] a dangerous [dependency] situation", two years later the ANC
leader concluded that the official assistance from Sweden was "absolutely decisive
for the organization's existence".[5]

As has been pointed out by Mandela's successor Thabo Mbeki—who with
Oliver Tambo maintained particularly close contacts with Sweden—from the ANC
perspective there was an important qualitative dimension to the cooperation. Interviewed in 1995, Mbeki stated that he did not think that the Swedish anti-apartheid
stand "was predicated on protest". Instead, his assessment of ANC's relationship
with Sweden—"maybe from the mid-1970s onwards"—was that it

originated in a particular theoretical and philosophical political position. [...] It changed with
the rising to the surface of the notion of the right of peoples to self-determination and, therefore, their right and duty to fight and to assert that right. As well as the duty of Sweden to support the struggle without seeking to define what the [South African] people should be. [...] The
position of Sweden created more space than the African or non-aligned position. It created
space for ANC to be able to deal with the rest of the Western world. And not just the Western
world, but even with regard to the Eastern world.[6]

... but Complex Beginnings

For many years, however, ANC was far from privileged with regard to official
Swedish assistance or NGO support. Both at the level of the state and of the reorganized, post-Vietnam solidarity movement, de facto recognition was only
extended in the mid-1970s. While the principle of direct, official humanitarian sup-

1. Carl Tham: *När Tiden Vänder* ('When the Time Turns'), Norstedts Förlag, Stockholm, 1994, p. 290.
2. See the accompanying disbursement table.
3. Anders Bjurner: Memorandum ('Samtal mellan statsminister Fälldin och ANC's ordförande Oliver Tambo'/
   'Conversation between Prime Minister Fälldin and ANC's President Oliver Tambo'), Ministry for Foreign
   Affairs, Stockholm, 27 March 1981 (MFA). The meeting took place on 5 March 1981.
4. Anders Bjurner: Memorandum ('Samtal mellan utrikesministern och ANC's ordförande Oliver Tambo'/'Conversation between the Foreign Minister and ANC's President Oliver Tambo'), Ministry for Foreign Affairs,
   Stockholm, 4 March 1981 (MFA). Ullsten and Tambo met on the same day.
5. Dag Ahlander: Memorandum ('Samtal med ANC-ledaren Oliver Tambo'/'Conversation with the ANC leader
   Oliver Tambo'), Ministry for Foreign Affairs, Stockholm, 4 May 1983 (MFA). The meeting was held on the
   same day.
6. Interview with Thabo Mbeki, pp. 153-55. Extending the horizon, ANC's Garth Strachan—a member of the
   South African Communist Party—at about the same time characterized the Nordic support to the liberation
   movements as "a model of disinterested international solidarity" (Interview with Garth Strachan, p. 194).

port to the African liberation movements in 1969 translated into cooperation with
PAIGC of Guinea-Bissau and ZANU of Zimbabwe—followed by SWAPO of
Namibia, FRELIMO of Mozambique and MPLA of Angola—it was not until February 1973 that a first, modest allocation was granted to ANC.[1] Two years later,
the 320,000 SEK disbursed to the South African liberation movement represented a
mere 2 per cent of the 16.1 million channelled to PAIGC and less than 3 per cent of
the 12.2 MSEK extended to FRELIMO.[2] In spite of Oliver Tambo's frequent visits
in the 1960s, ANC was also the last of the Southern African liberation movements
assisted by Sweden to formally appoint a representative and open an office in
Stockholm. Sobizana Mngqikana, the first Chief Representative to Sweden and the
other Scandinavian countries, arrived in early 1974.[3]

Concentrating their attention on the struggles in the Portuguese colonies, it was,
similarly, only in November 1974 that the Africa Groups for the first time recognized ANC as "the leading liberation movement in South Africa"[4], an initially controversial decision which was confirmed by the first national AGIS congress in May
1975.[5] With regard to ANC's calls for sanctions against the apartheid regime—
forcefully raised during visits to Sweden from the early 1960s—they were, in addition, only partially taken into account in mid-1979, when Prime Minister Ullsten's
minority Liberal government prohibited new investments in South Africa. A comprehensive Swedish sanctions law did not enter into effect until 1 July 1987.

The text that follows focuses on the direct cooperation between Sweden and
ANC, the only South African nationalist organization which under official, bilateral agreements was recognized *de facto* by Social Democratic and non-socialist
governments alike. While the assistance from 1973 onwards brought about a close
dialogue and rapidly expanding mutual contacts, Sweden's historical relations with
South Africa; its early encounters with legal anti-apartheid forces; and ANC's difficult survival in exile from the mid-1960s until the mid-1970s made the initial cooperation considerably more complex than that with the other Southern African
liberation movements discussed in the study. As later stated by Schori, in the case of
South Africa the Social Democratic government "thought that it was good to have
a pluralistic approach. We did not want to focus entirely on ANC".[6] Sweden's relations with allied and competing organizations should therefore also be addressed.

---

1. As well as to ANC's close ally, ZAPU of Zimbabwe.
2. The figures refer to the financial year 1974/75. See the accompanying disbursement tables.
3. As early as in December 1971—over a year before the decision to grant ANC direct assistance—CCHA
   agreed to a scholarship for an ANC representative in Sweden. The question of a formal representation was
   raised during a visit to London in May 1972 with ANC's Robert Resha by Göran Hasselmark from the Ministry for Foreign Affairs (Göran Hasselmark: Memorandum ('Samtal med ANC-representant'/'Conversation
   with ANC representative'), Ministry for Foreign Affairs, Stockholm, 18 May 1972) (SDA). ANC appointed
   Sobizana Mngqikana as Chief Representative about a year later, and final arrangements for his arrival were
   made in September 1973 (Letter ('ANC representation in Sweden') from Hallgerd Dyrssen to Lyttelton Mngqikana, SIDA, Stockholm, 20 September 1973) (SDA). He had his first meeting at the Ministry for Foreign
   Affairs in Stockholm in March 1974 (Anders Möllander: Memorandum ('Samtal med representant för African National Congress, ANC (Sydafrika)'/'Conversation with representative from ANC'), Ministry for Foreign Affairs, Stockholm, 1 April 1974) (SDA). Permanently settling in Sweden, Mngqikana was in April 1979
   replaced by Lindiwe Mabuza. When the Stockholm office was opened in 1974, there were only six formally
   established ANC missions around the world, namely in Lusaka (Zambia), Dar es Salaam (Tanzania), Algiers
   (Algeria), Cairo (Egypt/United Arab Republic), New Delhi (India) and London (UK). Offices in Washington
   and Moscow were set up in the late 1980s.
4. AGIS: 'Protokoll från Afrikagruppernas konferens i Uppsala den 16-17/11 1974' ('Minutes from the Africa
   Groups' conference in Uppsala, 16-17 November 1974') [no place or date] (AGA).
5. AGIS: 'Protokoll från Afrikagruppernas i Sverige kongress i Stockholm 17-19/5 1975' ('Minutes from the
   congress of the Africa Groups in Sweden in Stockholm, 17-19 May 1975'), [no place], 22 July 1975 (AGA).
6. Interview with Pierre Schori, p. 335. Cf. the interview with Bengt Säve-Söderbergh (p. 339): "We were never
   restricted to one movement. That was not our task. It was to find different ways".

In South Africa, the Swedish involvement was influenced by incomparably more factors and actors than elsewhere. The impact of economic interests in the apartheid republic on the business community, powerful labour voices and the government—not only with regard to the issue of sanctions, but also concerning trade union support—was, for example, conspicuous. So was ANC's marginalization at the time when the assistance began.

The interaction with the national liberation struggles earlier discussed was relatively uncomplicated. In addition to multilateral legal aid and educational support, bilateral official assistance was extended at the level of one movement—or, as in Zimbabwe, a front—fighting colonialism and occupation for the internationally recognized right of national self-determination. With the possible exception of the trade union effort in Namibia—where, however, the contacts with NUNW were coordinated with SWAPO—no direct or indirect official support was channelled in favour of political structures outside the bilateral cooperation with the *de facto* recognized 'governments-in-waiting'. Finally, in Guinea-Bissau, Mozambique, Angola, Zimbabwe and Namibia, Sweden had no particular economic interests. The trade exchange was marginal and investments infinitesimal or non-existent.

With regard to South Africa, the situation was radically different. From a *de jure* point of view, South Africa was a sovereign, independent country with which Sweden over the centuries had built extensive cultural and economic links. The Church of Sweden Mission had sent its first missionary to Zululand in the 1870s and several major South African enterprises were founded by immigrant Swedes during the second half of the 19th century. More importantly, between the First and the Second World Wars a number of Swedish manufacturing companies started production there, laying the basis for a steadily growing bilateral trade.

By 1948—when Daniel Malan's Nationalist Party came to power in Pretoria—South Africa's share of Swedish exports peaked at 2.3 per cent. Although imports from the country represented less than 1 per cent of the total, Sweden was the world's second largest buyer of South African fruit.[1] At the time of apartheid consolidation, South Africa occupied a prominent third position among Sweden's non-European trading partners, only surpassed by USA and Argentina. The importance of bilateral trade subsequently decreased[2], but investments in the country remained significant. In 1970, they represented 1.6 per cent of total Swedish assets abroad.[3]

The economic links do not only explain the opposition to ANC's calls for unilateral sanctions by leading export companies and the Moderate Party, but also by influential trade unions.[4] Against the isolation policy advocated by ANC and its WFTU-affiliated ally SACTU (South African Congress of Trade Unions), from the mid-1970s LO and TCO instead initiated direct contacts with the fledgling, non-racial South African labour movement via locally based Swedish-owned companies

---

1. Sellström Volume I, pp. 123-24. In 1948, Sweden was the world's largest consumer of South African apples, the second largest of pears and grapes and the fourth largest of oranges.
2. From the peak in 1948, South Africa's relative share of Swedish exports decreased continuously throughout the 1950s and 1960s, representing 1 per cent and 0.9 per cent in 1960 and 1970, respectively. Swedish imports from South Africa were considerably lower.
3. Sellström Volume I, p. 57.
4. Discussing the early Swedish anti-apartheid scene in the mid-1960s, Anders Johansson—a leading activist in the South Africa Committees—later said that "there was a kind of unholy alliance between the trade unions and the export companies" (Interview with Anders Johansson, p. 297). While emphasizing that it was a decision by the UN Security Council that until 1987 delayed a comprehensive Swedish sanctions law against South Africa, in 1997 the Social Democratic Foreign Minister Lena Hjelm-Wallén similarly stated that "a lot of business people and also trade unionists were not positive to [unilateral] action" (Interview with Lena Hjelm-Wallén, p. 294).

and ICFTU. Diverging opinions regarding SACTU and its significance—rather than ANC's relations with the South African Communist Party (SACP)—would, in turn, introduce a discordant Cold War dimension into the national South Africa debate.

In South Africa, the Swedish encounter with the anti-apartheid struggle preceded the 1964 'refugee million' under which official humanitarian support to Southern Africa began. In marked contrast to the situation in the other regional theatres of liberation, important NGO actors—such as the university students' movement and the churches—had as early as in the 1950s through various anti-apartheid initiatives established direct links with different South African counterparts. In fact, it was largely via these contacts that official Swedish humanitarian assistance was channelled to South Africa.

Old contacts with the National Union of South African Students (NUSAS) and the South African Council of Higher Education (SACHED) were particularly significant.[1] While Swedish missionaries in Zululand directly and through South African church organizations were in contact with Chief Gatsha Buthelezi, via the World University Service (WUS) and the International University Exchange Fund (IUEF) both the Swedish student movement and SIDA from around 1970 would channel support to the recently founded South African Students Organization (SASO) and to Steve Biko's broader black consciousness movement (BCM).[2]

By 1973—at the time of the decision to extend direct assistance to ANC in exile—ten years of officially backed relations with legal organizations inside South Africa via Swedish and international NGOs had left their mark. The contacts with Buthelezi and BCM—who between themselves developed very uneasy relations—

---

1. Supported by SFS, in 1964 SACHED became from the very beginning a major recipient of Swedish humanitarian assistance. In 1968-69, the increasingly radicalized university students' movement—particularly in Gothenburg—characterized SACHED as an 'apartheid institution', demanding instead support for FRELIMO's armed struggle in Mozambique. Many future ANC leaders were assisted by SACHED. This was, for example, the case with Thabo Mbeki, who in 1962 through SACHED was granted a scholarship to pursue studies in economics at the University of Sussex, UK (Thabo Mbeki: *Africa: The Time Has Come*, Selected speeches, Tafelberg Publishers, Cape Town/Mafube Publishing, Johannesburg, 1998, pp. viii-ix). As late as in June 1975, the Africa Groups referred to SACHED as "a project backed by the CIA" (AGIS: 'Circular letter No. 11', Stockholm, 17 June 1975) (AGA).
2. SASO—BCM's first organized expression—was formed in July 1969 by black students previously affiliated to NUSAS. Several of its leaders were medical students, among them the first SASO President Steve Biko, Mamphela Ramphele and the later Vice-President Nkosazana Dlamini-Zuma, democratic South Africa's first Minister of Health and from 1999 Minister of Foreign Affairs. Initially via NUSAS, the SASO leadership established early contacts in Sweden and Denmark, notably with Lund university with which the University of Natal Medical School had an exchange programme (Interview with Barney Pityana, p. 187). Aubrey Mokoape, SASO's Assistant Director of Publications and one of the South African exchange students, visited SIDA in Stockholm in February 1971. Introducing SASO and the emerging black consciousness movement to the Swedish authorities, he announced that SASO would submit a request for Swedish assistance to a community health services' project in the rural areas. For security reasons, any such support should, however, be channelled via WUS (Hallgerd Dyrssen: Memorandum ('Minnesanteckningar från besök av Mr. Aubrey Mokoape, SASO, den 10 februari 1971'/'Notes from visit by Mr. Aubrey Mokoape, SASO, 10 February 1971'), SIDA, Stockholm, 18 February 1971) (SDA). The project—subsequently established outside King William's Town and led by Steve Biko—was supported by the Swedish government via WUS from 1971/72, when a first, modest grant of 25,000 SEK was allocated (Letter from Stig Abelin to S. Chidambaranathan, WUS General Secretary, SIDA, Stockholm, 13 October 1971) (SDA). Increasing contributions were later extended through WUS and IUEF to SASO and BCM's Black Community Programmes (BCP). It could be noted that SASO's Vice-President Nkosazana Dlamini during a visit to Swaziland in 1975 joined ANC through Thabo Mbeki. Going into exile in September 1976, three months later she was invited by the local ANC mission to visit Stockholm, where she briefed the Swedish press about SASO, the Soweto events and the repression against black students (Ulf Hagman: 'Sydafrika: 500 studenter i landsflykt'/'South Africa: 500 students into exile' in *Svenska Dagbladet*, 16 December 1976). Addressing a solidarity meeting at SIDA on 16 December—'Heroes' Day'—she appealed for more scholarships to black students in and from South Africa (Cable from the Ministry for Foreign Affairs to the Swedish legation in Pretoria, 16 December 1976) (MFA). Supported by the Africa Educational Trust's South African programme, Dlamini-Zuma subsequently completed her medical degree at the University of Bristol, UK. Sweden was by far the largest donor to the AET programme.

Representing decades
of cooperation: Billy
Modise, South Africa's
High Commissioner to
Canada, and Anders
Möllander of the Swedish
Foreign Ministry
at Robben Island,
February 1999
(Photo: The author)

were particularly well established. As an example, it could be noted that the first direct Swedish allocation to ANC—granted for the financial year 1972/73—was 150,000 SEK, while the indirect contributions just to SASO then amounted to 175,000.[1] In 1973/74, the direct assistance to ANC was maintained at the previous level. At the same time, a total of 295,000 SEK—almost twice as much—was allocated via WUS and IUEF to SASO inside South Africa.[2]

The most important reason for the comparatively late assistance to ANC and the 'pluralistic approach', was the liberation movement's precarious situation in the early 1970s. After its banning in April 1960; the subsequent imprisonment of Nelson Mandela and most of its leaders on Robben Island; and consecutive repressive waves against SACP[3], Umkhonto we Sizwe (MK)[4], SACTU and other organizations within the ANC-led Congress Alliance[5], "by mid-1965, not only MK, but also the ANC, had effectively been destroyed within South Africa".[6] Affirming that "even the courage of our masses appeared to have [been] cowed before the tyrant's might"[7], the movement later noted that

> it was to be another eight years before there was [a] significant reconstruction of an ANC underground, and eleven years before the resumption of armed activity inside South Africa.[8]

1. Stig Abelin: Memoranda: a) 'World University Service (WUS)', CCHA/SIDA, Stockholm, 31 May 1972 (SDA); and b) 'International University Exchange Fund (IUEF)', CCHA/SIDA, Stockholm, 25 May 1972 (SDA).
2. Stig Abelin: Memorandum ('World University Service (WUS)'), CCHA/SIDA, Stockholm, 6 April 1973 (SDA) and Stig Abelin and Marianne Sundh: 'Agreed minutes of discussion on continued cooperation between SIDA and IUEF', CCHA/SIDA, [no place], 9 May 1974 (SDA).
3. Under the threat of the Suppression of Communism Act, the original Communist Party of South Africa (CPSA)—founded in 1921—dissolved itself in 1950. While it regrouped in 1953 as the underground South African Communist Party (SACP), many of its white members were active within the legal Congress of Democrats (COD). COD formed an important part of the multi-racial Congress Alliance. It was banned in 1962.
4. *Umkhonto we Sizwe*—The Spear of the Nation, or MK for short—initiated actions of armed propaganda on 16 December 1961.
5. Established in 1953, the Congress Alliance was a broad, multi-racial anti-apartheid front. Led by ANC, it included COD, the Coloured People's Congress (CPC), SACTU and the South African Indian Congress (SAIC). In June 1955, the Congress Alliance organized the Congress of the People at Kliptown, Soweto, at which the Freedom Charter was adopted.
6. ANC: 'Statement to the Truth and Reconciliation Commission', ANC Department of Information and Publicity, Johannesburg, August 1996, p. 47.
7. ANC National Executive Committee: 'Victory or Death: Statement on the Occasion of the 25th Anniversary of MK', December 1986, cited in Howard Barrell: *MK: The ANC's Armed Struggle*, Penguin Forum Series, Penguin Books, Harmondsworth, 1990, p. 16.
8. ANC (August 1996) op. cit., p. 47.

Forced into exile, ANC dates its re-emergence in South Africa to the period 1973-76, which began with unprecedented workers' strikes in and around Durban and culminated in the Soweto students' revolt outside Johannesburg. This period also saw the beginnings of Swedish assistance to ANC in Tanzania and Zambia. Although from the start the support covered basic necessities for MK cadres based at the Kongwa camp in Tanzania, it was limited, strictly humanitarian and far removed from ANC's views on how to re-establish a sustained political and military presence inside South Africa. As noted by the South African scholar and journalist Howard Barrell, in exile "ANC saw armed activity rather than the use of non-violent political methods as the main means to rebuild an internal political base and make overall progress".[1] As it did not carry burdensome responsibilities for a large refugee population[2], military training and armed support—primarily granted by the Soviet Union and its allies—were accorded first priority with regard to international assistance.[3]

Nevertheless, in response to the changes taking place in South Africa from 1973-74 Acting President Oliver Tambo[4] and leading ANC representatives of a younger generation—notably Chris Hani and Thabo Mbeki, who from different positions would be closely associated with the Swedish support—established direct contacts with the legal, internal organizations. Sweden would later assist in this process. In addition to facilitating meetings and exchanges, in mid-1976—before the Soweto uprising—the concern for a stronger internal ANC platform also led the Social Democratic government to allocate part of the annual grant for "the maintenance of [ANC's] political officials and their families inside South Africa".[5] This marked the beginning of a specific 'home front component' within the cooperation, introduced under Thorbjörn Fälldin's non-socialist coalition from the financial year 1977/78. As early as in 1978/79, it represented one third of the regular allocation.[6]

Towards the end of the 1970s, the assistance to ANC assumed a much more distinct political character than the support extended to any other Southern African liberation movement. Apart from strictly humanitarian aid, it focused on institution and capacity-building, information activities and on the extension of ANC's infrastructure inside the apartheid republic.

---

1. Barrell op. cit., p. 19. On ANC's military strategy, Barrell's unpublished Ph.D. dissertation is an invaluable source (Howard Barrell: 'Conscripts to Their Age: African National Congress Operational Strategy, 1976-1986', St Antony's College, University of Oxford, 1993). It is referenced below as 'Barrell Ph.D.'. See also the interview with Garth Strachan, pp. 192-95.

2. At the time of the first Swedish grant, ANC only catered for some 220 members in Tanzania and Zambia. Almost all of them were either politically active within the organization or undergoing military training. Also in this respect, there was a marked difference to the other Southern African liberation movements supported by Sweden, which had to assist large groups of refugees, generally with a rural background and often collectively fleeing from theatres of war. The absolute majority of the South Africans were from urban areas, who on an individual basis had left due to political persecution. When talking about its members abroad, ANC for many years opposed the term 'refugee', preferring the designation 'exile' (Author's recollection). The first massive exodus from South Africa took place after the June 1976 Soweto events, which eventually led to the establishment of ANC's settlements at Mazimbu and Dakawa in Tanzania.

3. On ANC and the Soviet Union, see Shubin op. cit. The relations with the German Democratic Republic in the 1960s have been documented by Ilona and Hans-Georg Schleicher op. cit., pp. 1-74.

4. Tambo became Acting President after the death of Chief Albert Luthuli in 1967. Ten years later, the ANC leaders imprisoned on Robben Island endorsed that he assume the full title of President-General.

5. Marianne Sundh: Memorandum ('Framställning från ANC (SA) om ytterligare stöd 1975/76'/'Request from ANC (SA) for additional support in 1975/76'), CCHA/SIDA, Stockholm, 6 May 1976 (SDA). Cf. 'Agreed minutes of discussions on cooperation between Sweden and the African National Congress of South Africa', Lusaka, 1 September 1976 (SDA). In the case of SWAPO, official Swedish support for "straightforward political work" inside Namibia had been accepted in mid-1975.

6. On the 'home front component', see the chapter 'From Beds in Exile to Organizers at Home'.

The Role of the Liberal Party and Encounters with Chris Hani

The origins of Sweden's humanitarian assistance to the Southern African liberation struggles have been discussed in Volume I of this study. It should be recalled that the official policy was supported by all the parliamentary parties except the Moderate Party. As noted in 1997 by the Social Democratic Foreign Minister Lena Hjelm-Wallén, "the support for the liberation movements [...] was much broader than the Social Democratic Party".[1] The role played by the Liberal Party in this context deserves to be underlined. Coordinating general policies with the ex-agrarian Centre Party, its long and active advocacy of the Southern African 'resistance movements'—as the party preferred to call them—explains what in an international context stands out as an extraordinary continuity between Palme's Social Democratic government and Fälldin's non-socialist coalitions, both in 1976 and in 1982.[2]

Despite its close relations with the Social Democratic Party, ANC acknowledged this otherwise often disputed or disregarded fact.[3] When the 'bourgeois' coalition in September 1982 lost the parliamentary elections to the 'socialist bloc'[4], Tambo immediately cabled sincere words of thanks to the defeated Premier Fälldin at the Centre Party headquarters in Stockholm, stating that

> following the Swedish general elections this last Sunday, the African National Congress and I personally would like to express our appreciation for the consistent political and material support accorded to us by the Swedish government and you personally. We look forward to continued cooperation between our two organizations for the liberation of Southern Africa and the restoration of a just peace in Southern Africa, Africa and the world.[5]

The particular role of the Liberal Party was highly significant vis-à-vis South Africa and ANC.[6] Although traditionally upholding the principle of free trade, as early as

---

1. Interview with Lena Hjelm-Wallén, p. 293.
2. The outcome of Sweden's parliamentary elections and the governments formed during the period under discussion are given in accompanying tables.
3. In his address on apartheid South Africa to the congress of the Christian Brotherhood Movement (in Swedish, *Broderskapsrörelsen*) in August 1976—less than two months before the Social Democratic electoral defeat—Prime Minister Palme stated: "One is moved to ask what Sweden's policy of international solidarity would have been like if we had had a bourgeois government in this country. [...] This much is clear: With a bourgeois government in power, the world would have had a very different picture of Sweden' (Olof Palme: 'Address given at the congress of the Swedish Association of Christian Social Democrats', Skövde, 6 August 1976) (LMA).
4. For a brief presentation of the Swedish party system, see Sellström Volume I, pp. 30-32.
5. Cable from Oliver Tambo to Thorbjörn Fälldin, [no place], 21 September 1982 (MFA). Tambo and Palme maintained particularly close relations. In 1996, for example, Lindiwe Mabuza, for many years ANC's Chief Representative to Sweden, concluded that "I have never known two leaders from two parts of the world being so much like brothers in the struggle" (Interview with Lindiwe Mabuza, p. 141). Cf. the interview with Bengt Säve-Söderbergh (p. 338): "[Palme's] friendship with Tambo had started in the early 1960s. There were some people that he became closer to than others and Tambo occupied a very special place". See also Mbeki op. cit., p. xix. Nevertheless, in a tribute to the assassinated Social Democratic leader, Tambo characterized in 1988, as earlier noted, the links between Sweden, Southern Africa and ANC as "a system of international relations which is not based on the policies of any party that might be in power in Sweden at any particular time" (Tambo in Hadjor (ed.) op. cit., p. 258). After nine years of Social Democratic rule (1982-91), a new bourgeois coalition was formed in October 1991. Contrary to the Fälldin-Ullsten period between 1976 and 1982, it was dominated by the Moderate Party, which had an entirely different history of relations with ANC and South Africa than the Centre and Liberal parties.
6. On the controversial and divisive issue of the Liberal Party and FNLA of Angola, see Sellström Volume I, pp. 412-19. It should also be noted that there were prominent Liberal members who openly opposed the policy of the heterogeneous party, as well as the Swedish opinion in general. In 1977—when Ola Ullsten was Cooperation Minister in the Fälldin government—Hans Hansson, a former chairman of the Gothenburg city council, accepted, for example, an invitation to the apartheid republic by the South African Foundation. The Liberal politician subsequently criticized Sweden and defended South Africa in various articles published in the two countries. This, in turn, was strongly rejected by the Swedish liberal press. See Per Wästberg: 'Folkpartist försvarar rasismen i Sydafrika' ('Liberal member defends racism in South Africa') in *Dagens Nyheter*, 17 August 1977.

in 1965 the party was among the first to demand economic sanctions against the apartheid regime. At a time when the ruling Social Democratic Party, the Left Party Communists and the organized Swedish solidarity movement concentrated their attention on the liberation struggles in the Portuguese colonies, together with the Centre Party it advocated assistance—or increased support—to the nationalist movements in Zimbabwe[1], Namibia and South Africa. In January 1970, it was the Liberal Party which submitted the very first Swedish parliamentary motion explicitly requesting official support to ANC.[2]

This demand was repeated every year during the first half of the 1970s. For example, in a joint motion in January 1973—immediately before the final decision to include ANC among the recipients of official assistance—the chairmen of the Centre and Liberal parties, the future Prime Minister Thorbjörn Fälldin and Gunnar Helén, criticized the Social Democratic government, finding it "astonishing that up to now no direct support has been extended to ANC".[3] And in January 1975—at a time when there were still doubts in the socialist camp and as the Left Party Communists for the first time submitted a motion in favour of ANC[4]—the Liberal MPs Per Ahlmark and Billy Olsson characterized ANC as "the only [South African] liberation organization of significance". In the same motion, they requested official "long-term agreements with the liberation movements in South Africa, Namibia and [Zimbabwe] [in order] to ensure rapidly increasing Swedish assistance".[5]

While ANC due to its emphasis on armed struggle and its close links to the South African Communist Party—with a largely overlapping membership between the two—was commonly shunned in the West as 'terrorist' or 'directed from Moscow', the Liberal Party did not shy away from direct, bilateral relations with the

---

1. In 1968—as ANC and ZAPU of Zimbabwe carried out joint military operations—the Liberal Party Youth League launched a Rhodesia Campaign in favour of Joshua Nkomo's movement (cf. Sellström Volume I, p. 352).
2. The motion was introduced by Ola Ullsten and Per Ahlmark (Swedish Parliament 1970: Motion No. 624 in the Second Chamber, Riksdagens Protokoll 1970, pp. 6-9). An identical motion was submitted in the First Chamber by the Liberal MPs Jan-Erik Wikström and Hans Lindblad (Swedish Parliament 1970: Motion No. 535 in the First Chamber, Riksdagens Protokoll 1970, p. 13).
3. Swedish Parliament 1973: Motion No. 1101, Riksdagens Protokoll 1973, p. 10.
4. Swedish Parliament 1975: Motion No. 1152, Riksdagens Protokoll 1975, pp. 1-3.
5. Swedish Parliament 1975: Motion No. 1165, Riksdagens Protokoll 1975, pp. 14-16. The demand for long-term agreements with the Southern African liberation movements was at the same time raised in a parallel motion by the Liberal Party chairman Gunnar Helén and other Liberal MPs (Swedish Parliament 1975: Motion No. 730, Riksdagens Protokoll 1975, pp. 30 and 37). The Liberal Party Women's League was among the first Swedish organizations to become directly involved inside South Africa. After contacts between Oliver Tambo and David Wirmark, from 1981 assistance was channelled to the Masisizane secretarial college in Soweto, for which an initial SIDA contribution of 170,000 SEK had been granted in December 1980 (Letter ('Ansökan om bidrag till Masisizane-projektet'/'Request for contribution to the Masisizane project') from Charlotte Branting, Liberal Party Women's League, to SIDA, Stockholm, 9 January 1984) (SDA). Subsequently expanded to include various women's projects initiated by the ANC-aligned United Democratic Front and the Federation of Transvaal Women, by 1990 the Liberal Women's League was one of the most important channels for Swedish internal humanitarian assistance. In addition to its own contributions, for the financial year 1990/91 alone it received no less than 2 MSEK from SIDA towards six different activities (Lena Johansson: Memorandum ('Årsansökan från Folkpartiets Kvinnoförbund om stöd till projekt i Sydafrika'/'Annual request from the Liberal Party Women's League for support to projects in South Africa'), SIDA/CCHA, [Stockholm], 24 September 1990) (SDA). It should be added that from the late 1970s the Social Democratic Women's League with support from SIDA embarked on bilateral cooperation with ANC's Women's Secretariat outside the official assistance to the liberation movement. As early as in August 1979, 500,000 SEK was granted to cover specific needs of the ANC women in the host countries in Southern Africa (CCHA: 'Protokoll [från sammanträde 22 oktober 1979]' ('Minutes [from meeting 22 October 1979]'), SIDA, [Stockholm], 29 October 1979) (SDA). Together with similar allocations for cultural activities etc., this additional support is not reflected in Appendix XIV. Over and above the regular ANC grant, through SIDA the Swedish government was thus, for example, the main contributor to the ANC women's conference in Luanda in September 1981 (Letter from Gertrude Shope to the Swedish embassy, ANC, Lusaka, 18 February 1982) (SDA).

Limpho Hani
at her desk in
the Swedish
liaison office in
Maseru, 1985
(Courtesy of
Eva Ehlin)

movement.[1] In spite of its difficulties and marginalization, years before the Africa Groups' formal recognition ANC was, for example, invited to attend the Liberal Party congress in Gothenburg in November 1972, where in Oliver Tambo's absence it was represented by a little known spokesperson introduced as Zenzile Msethu. In August 1977—when the party formed part of Fälldin's non-socialist coalition—it was Tambo himself who led ANC's delegation to the Liberal congress.[2]

Although at the time unbeknown to his Liberal hosts, it is not without historical interest to establish[3] that Msethu, the person Tambo appointed to represent him in

1. On the question of the armed struggle, David Wirmark of the Liberal Party explained in 1996: "ANC [...] changed [its] policy and entered into a period of armed struggle. The majority line within the Liberal Party was that it was up to them to decide which method they wanted to use". And on the relations with the Communist Party: "Of course, we knew that there were links between members of the liberation movements and the Communist parties or the Communist camp. But we were also convinced that they were not true Communists. They did not act like Communist party organizations. They were true national liberation movements. We never had any hesitation about ANC, for instance. [...] We were not guided by the question of whether they cooperated with the Communists. The important thing was that we were convinced that they wanted a free society and respect for human rights. They did not want a racial society. [...] ANC had taken a very clear stand. [...] They did not want to reverse the system, but a society where all citizens were equal" (Interview with David Wirmark, pp. 348-49). During his visits to Sweden, Oliver Tambo often discussed ANC's relations with the Soviet Union, both with the Social Democratic and the non-socialist governments. In a meeting with the Liberal Foreign Minister Ola Ullsten, he emphasized, for example, in March 1981 that it was both "incorrect and insulting to ANC to be regarded as a Soviet tool", adding that "it was not in ANC's interest to be classified as [belonging to] the Eastern camp" (Anders Bjurner: Memorandum ('Samtal mellan utrikesministern och ANC's ordförande Oliver Tambo'/'Conversation between the Foreign Minister and ANC's President Oliver Tambo'), Ministry for Foreign Affairs, Stockholm, 4 March 1981) (MFA). Turning against the "indecision" among the Western democracies vis-à-vis ANC and apartheid South Africa, in the government's declaration on foreign policy to the Swedish parliament Ullsten declared later in the month: "If it is the influence of the Soviet Union that they fear in the region, then there are even stronger reasons to take a stand for black Africa as soon as possible" (Swedish Parliament 1981: Debate on foreign and trade policy, 18 March 1981, Riksdagens Protokoll 1981, p. 44). With regard to the issue of armed struggle, Alex Boraine, a former leader of the South African Progressive Federal Party, recalled in 1995: "[W]e had visitors [...] from the Liberal Party of Sweden. A number of them came and a number of them were very forthright. [...] [T]hey said that the best thing that Sweden could do was to provide arms to ANC, which shocked a lot of my colleagues. It was said by a member of parliament, who later became a minister in Sweden" (Interview with Alex Boraine, p. 107).
2. Marika Fahlén: Memorandum ('Inför Oliver Tambo's besök i Sverige 26-30 augusti 1977'/'In view of Oliver Tambo's visit to Sweden, 26-30 August 1977'), Ministry for Foreign Affairs, Stockholm, 23 August 1977 (MFA). Tambo was *inter alia* accompanied by Pallo Jordan.
3. Vladimir Shubin's assistance in establishing the true identity behind Zenzile Msethu is gratefully acknowledged (Communication with Vladimir Shubin, Moscow, 5 February 2000).

1972[1], was none other than Chris Hani, the future Chief of Staff of Umkhonto we
Sizwe and General Secretary of the South African Communist Party.[2] In fact, "at
the end of 1972"—around the time he attended the Liberal congress in Gothenburg—Hani was elected SACP Assistant General Secretary at the party's extended
Central Committee meeting in Moscow.[3]

   Under the alias of Msethu, Hani—later to become a veritable bogeyman to the
apartheid regime and its Western allies—was during his first known visit to Sweden
also received at the Ministry for Foreign Affairs in Stockholm, where he gave Gun-
Britt Andersson and Bengt Säve-Söderbergh a general overview of the situation in
South Africa.[4] Keeping his alias, in early April 1973 he formed part of the ANC

---

1. Holden Roberto, the controversial leader of FNLA of Angola, also attended the 1972 Liberal Party congress
    (cf. the interview with Holden Roberto, p. 31). At the time of writing the first volume of this study, the true
    identity behind Zenzile Msethu had not yet been established. As the name was impossible to trace and Msethu
    was simply introduced as "normally based in Dar es Salaam", the author ventured the assumption that "the
    fact that Holden Roberto of FNLA attended the congress may explain Tambo's absence and ANC's junior
    representation" (Sellström Volume I, p. 251, note 5). While Hani at the time was not a senior ANC represent-
    ative, it is still possible that Tambo—who maintained close contacts with the Swedish Liberal Party—asked
    him to represent ANC under a false name in order to avoid the political embarrassment of being associated
    with FNLA.
2. Born in the Transkei in 1942, Hani graduated from the University of Fort Hare twenty years later. He
    joined the ANC Youth League in 1957, SACP in 1961 and MK in 1962. Leaving South Africa in mid-1963,
    he underwent military training in the Soviet Union and was in 1967 appointed Commissar of the Luthuli
    Detachment, which in July 1967 together with ZAPU launched military operations in Zimbabwe. Forced to
    cross into Botswana, he was detained and imprisoned there until December 1968. At the time of his first
    visits to Scandinavia in 1972-73, Hani was actively involved with MK and SACP in Tanzania and Zambia.
    Assistant SACP General Secretary from December 1972, in mid-1974 he clandestinely returned to South
    Africa to establish a political base in the eastern Cape. Later that year he settled in Lesotho, where he
    remained until mid-1982 when for security reasons he was asked to leave. In 1975—together with Thabo
    Mbeki, whose early career largely parallelled Hani's—he was elected to the ANC National Executive Com-
    mittee. While Mbeki concentrated on political work, Hani dedicated his life to the military side of the
    struggle. He became Deputy MK Commander in 1982 and MK Chief of Staff in 1987. Forming part of
    ANC's Interim Leadership Group after the unbanning of the movement in 1990, he was in 1991 elected
    SACP General Secretary. Immensely popular in South Africa, in April 1993—just a year away from the
    democratic elections—Chris Hani was assassinated by white right wing extremists outside his home in
    Dawn Park, Johannesburg. His death was *inter alia* commented by Sten Rylander, the Swedish ambassador
    to Namibia, who as SIDA's representative to Botswana and Lesotho had worked closely with him between
    1979 and 1982. Stating that he felt privileged to be "counted among Chris Hani's friends" and describing
    him as "simply a hero in a class of his own", with regard to the South African Communist Party Rylander
    wrote as follows to the non-socialist government in Stockholm: "An analysis of the historical conditions in
    South Africa [...] and of SACP's role in the political process [since] the introduction of apartheid [...] shows
    that [the party] has been able to unite many of the political forces working for a democratic change and
    that [its] profile on many central issues rather is social democratic or liberal than repressively anti-demo-
    cratic of the old Soviet Communist brand" (Letter ('Om Chris Hani'/'On Chris Hani') from Sten Rylander,
    Swedish ambassador to Namibia, to the Ministry for Foreign Affairs, Windhoek, 20 April 1993) (MFA).
    Similar views had in the 1950s been expressed by some of Sweden's most influential early anti-apartheid
    opinion makers, such as Herbert Tingsten, Gunnar Helander and Per Wästberg (see Sellström Volume I, pp.
    129, 134 and 138).
3. Shubin op. cit., pp. 121-22.
4. Gun-Britt Andersson: Memorandum ('Samtal med Zenzile Msethu från African National Congress (ANC)' i
    Sydafrika'/'Conversation with Zenzile Msethu from ANC'), Ministry for Foreign Affairs, Stockholm, 29
    November 1972 (SDA). There is no information indicating that ANC, Tambo or Msethu revealed his true
    identity to the Swedish authorities. During the meeting with Andersson and Säve-Söderbergh—which took
    place less than three months before the Swedish government's decision to extend direct assistance to ANC—
    Msethu/Hani *inter alia* said a) that it was only now that ANC was recovering from the arrests and repression
    suffered in 1963; b) that the growth of the black student movement in South Africa was important, as was the
    anti-apartheid opposition by certain churches; c) that the bantustan leaders—primarily Gatsha Buthelezi—
    with regard to single issues, such as land, could advance radical demands; d) that the objective of ANC—con-
    sidering violence as a necessary means—in the shorter term perspective was to create conditions for political
    and/or military struggles; e) that military actions had to be preceded by political mobilization; and f) that
    ANC's relations with PAC were strained due to the fact that there "within PAC were people who on good
    grounds could be suspected of being agents for the South African regime". Acknowledging the assistance
    received from the Soviet Union, Msethu/Hani, finally, stated that ANC was trying to normalize its relations
    with the People's Republic of China, passing on the information that Oliver Tambo had received an invitation
    to visit the country.

delegation to the UN/OAU Southern Africa conference in Oslo[1], and the following week he once again paid a visit to the Swedish Foreign Ministry. Based in Lesotho from 1974, Hani stayed in close contact with the Swedish government.[2] Most probably due to the alias already adopted for the Liberal Party congress in November 1972, at the time of his second visit to the Swedish Foreign Ministry he still did not reveal his true identity.[3]

Marginalization and Limited Assistance

Before the "historic watershed"[4] of the Soweto uprising[5], the prospects of closer and practical cooperation between Sweden and ANC were limited. The Social Democratic government's humanitarian assistance mainly focused on the Portuguese colonies.[6] Following the recommendations by the UN/OAU Oslo conference on Southern Africa, in September 1973—six months after the decision to assist ANC—Foreign Minister Wickman further declared that the main objective was to support the nationalist movements' civilian efforts within the areas under their control.[7] ANC held no liberated areas. To a greater extent than in the case of SWAPO, its domestic political base had been crushed by the apartheid regime.

1. Stokke and Widstrand (eds) op. cit. (Vol. I), pp. 270-71. In his study on the Soviet Union and ANC, Shubin writes: "Oslo was the first time that an ANC delegation to an international conference included Chris Hani, though he was not registered under his real name or under his *nom de guerre*. It was in Oslo that I first met him" (Shubin op. cit., p. 124). His real name was Martin Hani and his MK name Chris Nkosana. They were eventually combined into Chris Hani.
2. During his eight years in Lesotho, Hani established close working relations with the Swedish aid authorities. As the local ANC Chief Representative, from mid-1976 he coordinated the growing Swedish humanitarian assistance to the movement, regularly and openly sharing his views on the political situation in the country and in South Africa. While Hani had left at the time of South Africa's attack on Maseru in early December 1982, his Lesotho-born wife Limpho—working for the Lesotho Tourist Corporation—and their three daughters barely escaped the massacre. Joining her husband in Zambia after the attack, she returned to Lesotho towards the end of 1984. Not allowed to resume her previous employment, she was—after Swedish consultations with Chris Hani—initially employed by the local SIDA office and from 1985 by the embassy in Maseru, where she "soon became an invaluable colleague" (Tore Zetterberg: Memorandum ('Lokalanställda Limpho Hani vid ambassaden i Maseru: Samtal med [Ingalill] Colbro, SIDA'/'The locally employed Limpho Hani at the embassy in Maseru: Conversation with [Ingalill] Colbro, SIDA'), Ministry for Foreign Affairs, Stockholm, 18 February 1987) (SDA). In a rapidly deteriorating security situation and with repeated South African threats against Mrs. Hani and the Swedish embassy, her employment was—again on Chris Hani's advice and after contacts with King Moshoeshoe II—later terminated (Letter ('Ang. L. Hani'/'Re L. Hani') from Karin Roxman, chargée d' affaires, to SIDA, Swedish embassy, Maseru, 26 April 1989) (SDA). Joining her husband in South Africa after the unbanning of ANC and SACP, in the 1994 elections Limpho Hani was elected a member of parliament for ANC.
3. Gun-Britt Andersson: Memorandum ('Samtal med ANC'/'Conversation with ANC'), Ministry for Foreign Affairs, Stockholm, 25 May 1973 (MFA). The meeting with, among others, Gun-Britt Andersson, Anders Möllander and Bengt Säve-Söderbergh took place on 18 April 1973. At that time, the Swedish government had decided to grant direct assistance to ANC. The practicalities of the support occupied the major part of the conversation. In addition, Msethu/Hani strongly criticized OAU's domino theory on Southern Africa.
4. 'Political Report of the National Executive Committee to the National Consultative Conference, June 1985' in ANC: *Documents of the Second National Consultative Conference of the African National Congress: Zambia, 16-23 June 1985*, ANC, London, [no year], p. 17.
5. On 16 June 1976, police opened fire on a march of some 15,000 schoolchildren in Soweto outside Johannesburg protesting against the introduction of Afrikaans as a medium of instruction in black schools. Several marchers were killed. As a result, youths attacked police stations, administration buildings, beer-halls and other institutions associated with the apartheid state. The conflict soon escalated, spreading to Cape Town and the eastern Cape. According to official (underestimated) South African figures, 575 people—the overwhelming majority being young black students—were killed and 2,400 wounded during the uprising. As the unrest continued, the Minister of Police and Justice, James Kruger, coldly argued that "[the] police should act a bit more drastically and heavy-handedly, which will entail more deaths" (Kruger cited in ANC (August 1996) op. cit., p. 7). The following detentions and bannings forced thousands into exile, where most—perhaps as many as 5,000—joined ANC, vitally swelling the ranks of Umkhonto we Sizwe (Karis and Gerhart op. cit., p. 281).
6. Cf. the chapter on Guinea-Bissau.
7. On the issue of liberated areas, see the chapter 'SWAPO of Namibia: Tentative Steps towards Firm Relations'.

Furthermore, in exile ANC was both weak and politically isolated. While the April 1974 Lisbon coup augured independence for Angola and Mozambique under its MPLA and FRELIMO allies, OAU's 'domino strategy' accorded priority to the struggles in Zimbabwe and Namibia. This policy was strongly opposed by ANC, but *de facto* followed by Sweden.[1] Finally, the Vorster-Kaunda 'détente exercise' posed serious limitations to the establishment of meaningful projects in ANC's two main African host countries, Zambia and Tanzania, where inactivity, idleness and frustration among the members became a major concern.[2]

In Zambia—where ANC had established its 'provisional headquarters'[3]— efforts to procure a farm and plan for self-sufficiency with regard to food supplies were, as in the case of ZANU, blocked by the government.[4] In Tanzania—where the movement in the 1960s had been given the use of a plot at Morogoro—the authorities were, similarly, reluctant about land acquisitions. When the Swedish embassy in Dar es Salaam on behalf of ANC raised the issue in mid-1974 with the Prime Minister's Office, the responsible Tanzanian official "seemed to be of the opinion that [landholding] would give the movement too much security and [lead] its members to lose their motivation to continue the liberation struggle".[5] Apart from support in the form of basic, daily necessities to its members, there were few openings for a broader, non-military bilateral cooperation between Sweden and ANC.

---

1. The OAU strategy permeated the UN/OAU Oslo conference in April 1973. While the liberation movements from the Portuguese colonies—as well as ZANU—generally were pleased with the proceedings, the Swedish delegate Gun-Britt Andersson noted in her report that the nationalists from South Africa, Namibia and Zimbabwe "feel that they are being discriminated against, arguing that OAU's judgement is miscalculated" (Gun-Britt Andersson: Memorandum ('OAU/FN-konferens i Oslo till stöd för offren för kolonialism och rasåtskillnad i södra Afrika'/'OAU/UN conference in Oslo in support of the victims of colonialism and racial segregation in Southern Africa'), Ministry for Foreign Affairs, Stockholm, 3 May 1973) (MFA). The ANC delegation was led by Oliver Tambo. It included Chris Hani, who—as noted—registered under the name Zenzile Msethu. Together with several Southern African nationalist leaders, Msethu/Hani visited Stockholm after the conference. During a meeting at the Ministry for Foreign Affairs, he was extremely critical of the Organization of African Unity, stating that the 'domino strategy' was due to the fact that "many African states do not dare or wish to challenge South Africa", preferring instead "to benefit from economic cooperation [with the regime]" (Gun-Britt Andersson: Memorandum ('Samtal med ANC'/'Conversation with ANC'), Ministry for Foreign Affairs, Stockholm, 25 May 1973) (MFA). After the April 1974 Lisbon coup, the OAU Liberation Committee adjusted its strategy, but still placed the South African struggle last. Meeting in Dar es Salaam in January 1975, it recommended that "free Africa gives maximum priority to the liberation of Zimbabwe and Namibia" (OAU Coordinating Committee for the Liberation of Africa: 'The Dar es Salaam declaration on the new strategy for the liberation of Africa, the consolidation of the struggle and the reconstruction of the liberated territories', Dar es Salaam, 14 January 1975) (MFA).
2. The importance of social projects in favour of ANC's members in exile was, for example, discussed during the official aid negotiations between Sweden and ANC in Lusaka in August 1976. Chargé d'affaires Anders Bjurner led the Swedish team and Thomas Nkobi, Acting Treasurer General, the ANC delegation. According to Bjurner's covering letter to the agreed minutes, in his introductory statement Nkobi emphasized that Sweden—also taking military assistance into account—had become one of ANC's main actual supporters and that without the Swedish assistance "ANC would perhaps have disintegrated due to discontent among [its] cadres" (Letter ('Förhandlingsprotokoll för bistånd till ANC (Sydafrika) 1976/77'/'Agreed minutes on assistance to ANC (South Africa) in 1976/77') from Anders Bjurner to SIDA, Swedish embassy, Lusaka, 3 September 1976) (SDA). For a leading ANC woman's perspective on the same issue, see the interview with Sankie Mthembi-Mahanyele, pp. 169-71.
3. ANC transferred its 'provisional' headquarters from Morogoro, Tanzania, to Lusaka in the early 1970s. Much of the diplomatic activity was, however, directed from its London office. Always on the move, Oliver Tambo commuted between Lusaka, London and the world at large.
4. Mainly for security reasons, it was only in 1978-79—contradictorily at a time when the Pretoria regime adopted the policy of 'total strategy' and embarked on cross-border military operations—that Tanzania and Zambia allowed ANC to procure land and establish large-scale settlements. In the case of Tanzania, the authorities granted the movement land at Mazimbu outside Morogoro, where construction activities leading to the establishment of the Solomon Mahlangu Freedom College (SOMAFCO) started in January 1979. With Swedish funds, ANC's 1,300 hectare Chongela farm north of Lusaka was purchased in October 1978.
5. Astrid Bergquist: Memorandum ('Bistånd till ANC (Sydafrika) budgetåret 1974/75'/'Assistance to ANC (South Africa) during the financial year 1974/75'), SIDA, Stockholm, 30 September 1974 (SDA).

Invited to Sweden to attend the Social Democratic Party congress in September/
October 1975—immediately prior to the South African military invasion of
Angola, which marked the end of regional détente—Oliver Tambo acknowledged
the difficulties. In a meeting with Bengt Säve-Söderbergh, first secretary at the Ministry for Foreign Affairs, Tambo deplored that the bilateral cooperation had developed slowly, adding that this was "due to the fact that ANC under the prevailing
circumstances had not been in a position to submit any real project [proposals]".[1]
The ANC leader also criticized OAU, but above all President Kaunda and his dialogue with South Africa, underlining that the Zambians—"behaving very un-Zam-
bian"—had "gone out of their way to accommodate Vorster". Suggesting a
deteriorating scenario for ANC, Tambo even concluded that "they may ask us to
leave, but until then we intend to stay".[2]

Although he enjoyed much goodwill within the Social Democratic Party, the
message conveyed by the ANC leader was far from encouraging. Reports from the
Swedish embassies in the Frontline States and impressions from South Africa by
visitors close to the Swedish ruling party likewise did not give cause for optimism.
Asked to comment on ANC and the rival Pan Africanist Congress of Azania, in
November 1975, for example, first secretary Göran Hasselmark at the embassy in
Dar es Salaam reported to the Foreign Ministry that "weakness is their most distinguishing trait".[3] Stressing the two movements' "lack of ideas" and their respective
local leaderships' "atrophy", he concluded that "as far as can be ascertained, no
conditions for future renewal are at hand". In Hasselmark's opinion, "it seems that
to an entirely different extent the organizations which are actively working inside
South Africa—SASO, for example—have the ear of the youth".[4]

Similar viewpoints were raised from within the Swedish labour movement.
After a visit to South Africa by LO and TCO in January-February 1975[5], Jan Olsson, international secretary of the Swedish Metalworkers Union, strongly ques-

---

1. Bengt Säve-Söderbergh: Memorandum ('Samtal med Oliver Tambo, ANC, Sydafrika'/ 'Conversation with
   Oliver Tambo, ANC, South Africa'), Ministry for Foreign Affairs, Stockholm, 3 October 1975 (MFA). During
   the same meeting, Tambo said that ANC had approached the new FRELIMO government in Mozambique
   with a request to set up a vehicle workshop in Lourenço Marques (now Maputo). As later developments
   would show, the request was not granted. After independence, Samora Machel's government was far from
   accommodating to ANC. Concerns in this regard had already been raised by Tambo in conversations with
   Prime Minister Palme before Mozambique's independence in June 1975. In turn, Palme discussed the question
   with FRELIMO's Vice-President Marcelino dos Santos in Stockholm in mid-April 1975. Over the years,
   Palme would often be critical of the Machel government's policy towards ANC. This became, above all, manifest in connection with the non-aggression Nkomati Accord signed by Mozambique and South Africa in
   March 1984. See, for example, the interview with ANC's Lindiwe Mabuza (p. 142) and—for Mozambican
   viewpoints—the interviews with Jacinto Veloso (p. 54) and Sérgio Vieira (p. 57).
2. Bengt Säve-Söderbergh: Memorandum ('Samtal med Oliver Tambo, ANC, Sydafrika'/'Conversation with
   Oliver Tambo, ANC, South Africa'), Ministry for Foreign Affairs, Stockholm, 3 October 1975 (MFA).
3. Letter ('Sydafrika inför en förändrad politisk miljö'/'South Africa facing a changed political environment')
   from Göran Hasselmark to the Ministry for Foreign Affairs, Dar es Salaam, 3 November 1975 (MFA).
4. Ibid. Hasselmark—who in 1979 was appointed Swedish ambassador to Zambia, working closely with the
   ANC leadership until 1983—did not, however, suggest a change with regard to direct assistance to ANC.
   Other Swedish diplomatic representatives were less convinced, even after ANC's advances in 1976. As late as
   in April 1977, for example, Bo Kälfors, the ambassador to Botswana, asserted that "it appears [...] that ANC
   more or less [...] has had its day". Instead, he recommended that "priority [...] is given to the organizations
   within the black consciousness movement" (Letter from Bo Kälfors to SIDA, Gaborone, 13 April 1977, cited
   in letter ('African National Congress' ställning i Sydafrika'/'ANC's position in South Africa') from Anders
   Möllander to the Ministry for Foreign Affairs, Swedish embassy, Lusaka, 19 May 1977) (SDA). From his
   horizon in Botswana—sandwiched between South Africa/Namibia and Zimbabwe—Kälfors often viewed
   regional developments in a different light from that of other Swedish diplomats, SIDA and the Foreign Ministry. Also in April 1977, he cautioned against direct Swedish assistance to "any nationalist organization" in
   Zimbabwe (Letter ('Maktstrid inom ZANU'/'Power struggle within ZANU') from Bo Kälfors to the Ministry
   for Foreign Affairs, Gaborone, 29 April 1977) (SDA).
5. The visit is discussed in the chapter 'Isolation versus Involvement: Companies, Churches and Labour in the
   1970s'.

tioned ANC and its allies in the ruling party's theoretical journal *Tiden*. Turning against the calls for unilateral sanctions, he not only claimed that SACTU in South Africa was "neither seen, nor heard", but also that ANC was "not an organization to be reckoned with".[1] Instead, he too underlined the significance of SASO, the Black Allied Workers Union (BAWU) and the Black People's Convention (BPC), that is, constituent parts of the wider black consciousness movement.[2]

A Strategic Review

After the independence of Mozambique and Angola—which radically changed the regional correlation of forces—in early 1976 the Swedish authorities embarked on a comprehensive review of the humanitarian assistance to Southern Africa.[3] As ruling parties, FRELIMO and MPLA were no longer eligible for such support. Instead, the concentration on the Portuguese colonies shifted to Zimbabwe, Namibia and South Africa. In addition to rapidly evolving geo-political realities, growing parliamentary budget allocations for humanitarian assistance also motivated the exercise.

Although it largely focused on the complex situation prevailing with regard to Zimbabwe, South Africa featured prominently in the review. In addition to general humanitarian needs, attention was centred on the political relevance and prospects of BCM and Inkatha, as well as on their views of ANC, SACTU and PAC. To supplement the information provided by the Swedish diplomatic missions in Southern Africa, three officials from SIDA and the Ministry for Foreign Affairs attached to the Consultative Committee on Humanitarian Assistance[4] were appointed to gather the necessary background information. From early March until the beginning of April 1976, they undertook a regional fact-finding mission, holding an impressive number of meetings with government officials, humanitarian organizations and liberation movements in Southern Africa.[5]

On behalf of the review team, Ann Wilkens—at the time second secretary at the Ministry for Foreign Affairs—visited South Africa, where, under difficult circumstances during a short period of time she managed to meet a host of centrally placed spokespersons from various organizations and political currents, many of whom were banned. To complement her impressions, in mid-July 1976—immedi-

---

1. Jan Olsson: 'Sydafrika: Hur Förbereds Frigörelsen?' ('South Africa: How Is Liberation Being Prepared?') in *Tiden*, No. 67, 1975, pp. 443-44.
2. Ibid., p. 444. Within the wider Swedish anti-apartheid opinion, the Metalworkers Union constituted a powerful dissonant voice over the years. In addition to opposing unilateral sanctions and rejecting SACTU—positions which it shared with others in the labour movement—leading representatives of the union often publicly questioned the significance of ANC. As late as in November 1978—more than two years after the launch of Palme's 'crusade' against apartheid and at a time when LO's Southern Africa campaign had started—Göran Johansson, trade union leader at the headquarters of SKF in Gothenburg, expressed in a debate with Pierre Schori and the British historian Basil Davidson "doubts that ANC is really representing the blacks [in South Africa]" (Britt-Marie Mattsson: 'SKF's fackordförande: De svarta i Sydafrika vill att vi skall stanna'/'SKF's union chairman: The blacks in South Africa want us to remain' in *Göteborgs-Posten*, 18 November 1978). Johansson—nicknamed 'Mr. Gothenburg'—later rose to become a prominent Social Democratic politician. Chairing the local council in Sweden's second biggest city between 1989 and 1991 and again from 1994, he was mentioned in 1995 as a possible successor to the party leader and Prime Minister Ingvar Carlsson. The role of the powerful Metalworkers Union—in the debate *de facto* often siding with Swedish export interests and the Moderate Party—will be presented in the chapter 'SACTU, Unions and Sanctions'.
3. CCHA: 'Terms of reference for a study concerning Swedish aid to African refugees', [SIDA, Stockholm], 30 January 1976 (SDA).
4. Olof Milton and Marianne Sundh from SIDA and Ann Wilkens from the Ministry for Foreign Affairs.
5. As earlier noted, the mission submitted its findings in over 30 memoranda totalling some 150 pages.

ately after the Soweto uprising—Wilkens returned.[1] During her two visits, she held around twenty meetings all over the country[2], notably with Steve Biko (BCM)[3], Gatsha Buthelezi (Inkatha)[4], Drake Koka (BAWU)[5], Beyers Naudé (Christian Insti-

---

1. Wilkens' visit to South Africa in July 1976 was undertaken in a private capacity. After the official visit in March, Beyers Naudé invited her back to South Africa "to meet important people in the internal opposition" (Letter from Ann Wilkens to the author, Stockholm, 28 February 2000). Although formally private, Wilkens recorded the discussions held during the second visit too, later submitting the memoranda to CCHA and the Ministry for Foreign Affairs.

2. In addition to the meetings noted below, during her first visit Wilkens discussed the situation in South Africa with representatives of the South African Institute of Race Relations (SAIRR), the Industrial Aid Society (IAS), the Metal and Allied Workers Union (MAWU) and the Trade Union Advisory and Coordinating Council (TUACC). In July 1976, she also met BCM's Steven Carolus and Johnny Issel in Cape Town, as well as Ben Khoapa, Director of the Black Community Programmes, in Umlazi outside Durban. Her memoranda give a unique picture of the state of the South African opposition before and immediately after the June 1976 Soweto watershed. In the light of Winnie (Madikizela-) Mandela's controversial role in the late 1980s, her separation from Nelson Mandela and complex relations with the ruling party in the 1990s, it is, for example, not without interest to note the following comment by Wilkens: "During the contacts I had with ANC in Lusaka at the end of June, it appeared that Mrs. Mandela no longer is considered a reliable spokesperson for [the movement]. She is believed to play her own game and mainly work with the 'black consciousness' [organizations] in South Africa" (Ann Wilkens: Memorandum ('Samtal med Chief Buthelezi'/'Conversation with Chief Buthelezi'), Ministry for Foreign Affairs, Stockholm, 24 August 1976) (MFA).

3. Wilkens' meeting with Biko took place at the Zanempilo clinic outside King William's Town on 17 July 1976, i.e. during her second visit and after the Soweto revolt. From the discussions it could be noted that the BCM leader stressed that the time had come for the wider black consciousness movement to take a clearer ideological stand in favour of socialism and that it had to increase its international profile. Both ANC and PAC were present in South Africa, the former being the stronger of the two. Biko felt closer to ANC than to PAC, but was critical of SACP's influence over the movement. The problem with PAC, on the other hand, was that it was anti-Communist and that its leader in exile, Potlako Leballo, "was notorious [...] for having collaborated with the security police". While Biko was of the opinion that BCM—"the only important organization among the youth in South Africa" —ANC, PAC and UMSA (Unity Movement of South Africa) should join forces on an equal basis, no cooperation could, however, include Gatsha Buthelezi or Inkatha. With regard to Buthelezi and the apartheid system, Biko adamantly stated that "you cannot work with the devil in order to oppose him" (Ann Wilkens: Memorandum ('Samtal med Steve Biko, en av de ledande inom 'black consciousness'-rörelsen'/'Conversation with Steve Biko, one of the leaders of the black consciousness movement'), Ministry for Foreign Affairs, Stockholm, 8 September 1976) (MFA).

4. The meeting with Buthelezi took place at St. Francis Mission in Mahlabatini, Zululand, on 14 July 1976, also during Wilkens' second visit to South Africa. During the discussions—which lasted "several hours"— the Inkatha leader talked about his contacts with Sweden, but above all about his relations with ANC. According to Buthelezi, he was "nurtured in the ANC cradle [and] considered himself an ANC member". ANC was "still the only real liberation movement in South Africa", but the younger generation in exile "had refused to understand his difficult position". He further said that he had "always rejected" PAC proposals for cooperation and that he had had a good rapport with Steve Biko, which, however, had come to an end. Finally, Buthelezi expressed support for the emerging black trade unions. He was, however, annoyed when Wilkens confronted him with Circular No. 5/1976 by his own government, according to which "it must be stressed that trade unions are not recognized [and] therefore [...] have absolutely no official standing as far as the workers of KwaZulu are concerned" (Ann Wilkens: Memorandum ('Samtal med Chief Buthelezi'/'Conversation with Chief Buthelezi'), Ministry for Foreign Affairs, Stockholm, 24 August 1976) (MFA).

5. Wilkens met Koka in Johannesburg on 30 March and 8 July 1976. The banned BCM trade unionist was of the opinion that PAC "lacked influence inside South Africa", but that ANC had a base there. SACTU, however, was according to Koka "entirely an external organization" (Ann Wilkens: Memorandum ('Samtal med Drake Koka, grundare av Black People's Convention (BPC) och Black Allied Workers Union (BAWU), i Johannesburg 1976-03-30'/'Conversation with Drake Koka, founder of BPC and BAWU, in Johannesburg on 30 March 1976'), CCHA/Ministry for Foreign Affairs, Stockholm, 6 April 1976) (SDA). In April 1976, Koka had discussed possible Swedish trade union assistance with LO's Kristina Persson. The questions raised were followed up by Wilkens in July. BAWU, he said, had received some support from IUEF, but wished to establish direct relations with the Swedish trade union movement. Maintaining that SACTU "as an organization [did] not exist in South Africa", he also wanted to work with the SACTU leadership in exile (Ann Wilkens: Memorandum ('Samtal med Drake Koka, grundare av Black Allied Workers Union (BAWU)'/'Conversation with Drake Koka, founder of BAWU'), Ministry for Foreign Affairs, Stockholm, 7 October 1976) (MFA).

tute)[1], John Rees (SACC)[2] and Karel Tip (NUSAS).[3] She also met ANC in Lusaka[4] and various BCM representatives in Gaborone[5], but failed—as will be seen—to exchange views with Thabo Mbeki in Swaziland.

At the time of the review, the Social Democratic government had for the financial year 1975/76 increased the annual ANC allocation from 250,000 to one million SEK. Nevertheless, against the background of the organization's difficult exile conditions and, above all, the vibrant emergence of the black consciousness movement in South Africa, Wilkens' instructions were to contact "the internal opposition in order to investigate the possibilities of supporting it with Swedish assistance".[6] Thus, notwithstanding the established cooperation with ANC in exile her exploratory mission had a 'two-track' objective.

---

1. Wilkens and Naudé met in Johannesburg on 25 March and, again, on 10 and 21 July 1976. In addition to project proposals submitted to Sweden on behalf of Inkatha, the main currents of the wider anti-apartheid opinion were discussed. According to Naudé, "a peaceful solution to the racial problems in South Africa was no longer possible". Against this background, all opposition forces—black and white—had to join forces. The "external" liberation movement—ANC—and its "internal counterpart"—BCM—should be supported. While Naudé did not speak highly of PAC, his opinion of Gatsha Buthelezi was positive. In his view, "there was no doubt that [Buthelezi] should be seen as a genuine advocate of radical political change" (Ann Wilkens: Memorandum ('Samtal med Beyers Naudé, chef för Christian Institute, i Johannesburg den 25 mars 1976'/'Conversation with Beyers Naudé, head of the Christian Institute, in Johannesburg on 25 March 1976'), CCHA/ Ministry for Foreign Affairs, Stockholm, 12 April 1976) (SDA). On Wilkens' return in July 1976—after the Soweto uprising—Naudé's assessment of both ANC and Inkatha was more critical. Stressing that "[t]he ANC input is not coming across to leading black South Africans", his view was that they had concluded that they must "carry out their own revolution, regardless of the movements in exile". At the same time, Buthelezi "did not have much time at his disposal if he wished to maintain credibility among the opposition" (Ann Wilkens: Memorandum ('Samtal med Beyers Naudé, chef för Christian Institute'/'Conversation with Beyers Naudé, head of the Christian Institute'), Ministry for Foreign Affairs, Stockholm, 9 September 1976) (MFA).
2. Discussions with SACC's General Secretary John Rees and Axel-Ivar Berglund, a Swedish CSM missionary responsible for the council's education programmes, were held in Johannesburg on 24 March 1976. They focused on Swedish support to SACC's different humanitarian projects (Ann Wilkens: Memorandum ('South African Council of Churches, SACC'), CCHA/Ministry for Foreign Affairs, Stockholm, 12 April 1976) (SDA).
3. In meetings in Johannesburg on 24 and 26 March 1976, the former NUSAS President Karel Tip—who at the time together with, among others, Eddie Webster was charged under the Suppression of Communism Act— generally confirmed the impressions gathered by Wilkens. While BCM undoubtedly was a strong force, "there were still groups who identified with ANC". PAC, on the other hand, was characterized by Tip as "a movement of exiles caught up in nostalgia". While he cautioned against "a definitive conclusion with regard to [...] Buthelezi", Tip, finally, saw SACTU as an externally based trade union organization (Ann Wilkens: Memorandum ('Samtal om politiska rättegångar och politiska förhållanden med Karel Tip i Johannesburg den 24 och 26 mars 1976'/'Conversations on political trials and political conditions with Karel Tip in Johannesburg, 24 and 26 March 1976'), CCHA/Ministry for Foreign Affairs, Stockholm, 12 April 1976) (SDA).
4. The ANC delegation to meetings in Lusaka on 15 and 17 March 1976 was led by Mendy Msimang, democratic South Africa's future high commissioner to the United Kingdom. He was at the time Secretary for Administration and member of the organization's National Executive Committee. Of importance to the review was that Msimang—while stressing that "most resistance activities [in South Africa] had some kind of ANC link"—underlined that "ANC was not opposed to [the BCM] movements, [as] they [all] were working towards the same objective". At the same time, the ANC delegation rejected any relevance for Gatsha Buthelezi's Inkatha or PAC, said to be guided by "black chauvinism". The emergence of black trade unions was "of utmost importance" and ANC hoped that the Swedish labour movement would be in close contact with SACTU, which inside South Africa "for tactical reasons appear[ed] under other names" (Ann Wilkens: Memorandum ('Samtal med representanter för ANC (SA)'/'Conversation with representatives of ANC'), CCHA/Ministry for Foreign Affairs, Stockholm, 22 April 1976) (SDA). Before going to Zambia, the review mission met PAC in Dar es Salaam. According to the notes from the Swedish embassy, the PAC representatives stated that their organization did not work with BCM or the black trade unions in South Africa. In exile, they wished to form a united front with ANC (Per Lindström: Memorandum ('Samtal med representanter för Pan Africanist Congress'/'Conversation with representatives of PAC'), Swedish embassy, Dar es Salaam, 19 March 1976) (SDA).
5. The meeting with representatives of five BCM-aligned organizations in Gaborone on 21 March 1976 rather underlined political diversity than unity of purpose. All the BCM representatives were, however, strongly opposed to Gatsha Buthelezi and Inkatha (Marianne Sundh: Memorandum ('Minnesanteckningar från ett samtal i Botswana med representanter för Black Consciousness Movement (BCM)'/'Notes from a conversation in Botswana with representatives of BCM'), CCHA/SIDA, Stockholm, 8 June 1976) (SDA).
6. Ann Wilkens: Memorandum ('Intryck från Sydafrika: Sammanfattning'/'Impressions from South Africa: A summary'), CCHA/Ministry for Foreign Affairs, Stockholm, 21 April 1976 (SDA).

Wilkens did not, however, recommend a radical re-orientation of the Swedish anti-apartheid support. Sharing impressions from her visit with other officials, in April 1976 she noted in general that

> the divisions within the opposition and the lack of coordination between its internal and external parts appeared as major problems. [...] It was also evident that people with a known association to the internal [...] opposition have extremely limited possibilities of informing themselves about [...] the resistance movements in exile. [...] [It was widely believed that] nothing can be achieved without external assistance, and it was in this context felt that the Western powers would not be particularly supportive. [...] The role of Buthelezi was much discussed [...]. Where he stands politically and ideologically is still somewhat unclear, but his influence is indisputable.[1]

Three proposals for assistance were discussed during Wilkens' visit, namely an Inkatha-initiated project concerning the establishment of a 'black' newspaper, as well as requests presented by BAWU and TUACC. While she recommended assistance to the unions via the Swedish labour movement, Wilkens did not advocate direct official cooperation with BCM or Inkatha. In her view, ANC should remain Sweden's priority partner. Indeed, concluding her general overview she proposed that any official Swedish assistance to activities inside South Africa should be subject to approval by the organization led in exile by Oliver Tambo, stating that

> it seems appropriate to complement the [official Swedish] support to external ANC with assistance to different projects inside South Africa on condition that ANC does not oppose [such a policy].[2]

Shortly thereafter, Anders Bjurner at the Swedish embassy in Lusaka raised the issue directly with Tambo. Recognizing the Swedish government's sovereign rights, in the case of support to internal South African political organizations the ANC leader strongly underlined the importance of close and regular consultations, particularly at the existing juncture of "intense and rapid developments".[3] Support channelled by IUEF and other international NGOs to SASO had, for example, opened up an unfortunate gap between BCM and ANC. Against this background—and "with very great intensity"—Tambo "appealed" for official Swedish assistance to the struggle against the Vorster regime to be coordinated with ANC.[4]

After the visit to Southern Africa by the CCHA team, in mid-1976 the future assistance to the anti-apartheid opposition in general and the relations with ANC in particular were carefully assessed by the Swedish foreign policy and aid authorities. The discussions were summarized in early June by Wilkens. Noting that the wider South African anti-apartheid movement was divided, in a memorandum which essentially reflected the Social Democratic government's pluralistic approach, she wrote:

> The key question [...] is whether we at all want to [...] support groups inside South Africa which oppose the apartheid structure. If we are ready to grant such support [...], it must be

---

1. Ibid.
2. Ann Wilkens: Memorandum ('Intryck från Sydafrika: Sammanfattning'/'Impressions from South Africa: A summary'), CCHA/Ministry for Foreign Affairs, Stockholm, 21 April 1976 (SDA).
3. Letter ('Samtal med O. Tambo, ANC's t.f. ordförande'/'Conversation with O. Tambo, ANC Acting President') from Anders Bjurner, Swedish embassy, to the Ministry for Foreign Affairs, Lusaka, 21 May 1976 (MFA). The meeting took place on 2 May 1976.
4. Ibid. During the meeting, Tambo informed Bjurner that ANC's National Executive Committee had recently discussed the question of official Swedish support to ANC activities inside South Africa. Such assistance was extended from mid-1976.

seen as complementary to the assistance extended to ANC. On the other hand, as ANC operates today [Swedish support] cannot under all circumstances be subject to [its] official approval. [...]

Earlier official support to activities in South Africa has been channelled via CSM [...], WUS [...], IUEF [...] and Amnesty International.[1] It was not coordinated with ANC, and it is hard to believe that any official [ANC] approval would have been granted. [The support] has, on the other hand, not damaged our relations with [the movement]. [...]

[ANC] has to fight against enormous difficulties. It is precisely for that reason that we should [continue to] assist, and it is for the same reason that we should also support other groups which are working towards the same objective. [...] [I]t is a question of not putting all the eggs in the ANC basket, or—to be more precise—no more [...] than the basket can hold. [...]

The conclusion would thus be that the assistance to ANC should be seen as support to one of several organizations fighting against apartheid. The movement cannot [...] be considered as some kind of government-in-exile. [Nevertheless], since we are cooperating with ANC we should not support organizations which are antagonistic towards [the movement]. That would probably be the situation if Swedish support was granted to [...] PAC.[2]

Soweto erupted exactly one week later. The uprising and the ensuing massive repression prompted Prime Minister Palme in August 1976 to embark on an international 'crusade against apartheid'. In September, however, the Social Democratic Party lost the Swedish parliamentary elections and a non-socialist coalition government led by the Centre Party leader Thorbjörn Fälldin was formed. It would maintain without any drastic changes the previous government's policy towards Southern Africa. In the case of South Africa, the Fälldin government adopted the pluralistic approach outlined by Wilkens and recommended by CCHA.

As ANC's relevance and influence grew, the non-socialist coalition—backed by a broad parliamentary majority—substantially increased the direct assistance. Although not considered a government-in-exile, for all practical purposes towards the end of the 1970s ANC was seen as a potential 'government-in-waiting'. Less influenced by critical trade union voices than its Social Democratic predecessor[3], quite paradoxically the non-socialist coalition—which included the conservative Moderate Party—would from 1977/78 also extend direct assistance to SACTU, formally affiliated to the Prague-based WFTU and with a profile closer to SACP than to the broader ANC. It was, finally, under the Fälldin government that preparations for a ban against Swedish investments in South Africa were initiated.

Thabo Mbeki and Jacob Zuma in Swaziland

Swedish contacts with and assistance to the South African non-racial trade unions, PAC, Inkatha and BCM during the 1970s will be discussed below. In the meantime—as pointed out by Thabo Mbeki in the interview earlier quoted—it should be noted that despite ANC's precarious situation in exile; OAU's domino strategy; and Sweden's pluralistic approach, by the mid-1970s a special relationship was devel-

---

1. Among the examples quoted, Wilkens did not mention the substantial Swedish support to IDAF, which, however, maintained particularly close relations with ANC.
2. Ann Wilkens: Memorandum ('Svenskt stöd till ett tidningsprojekt i Sydafrika'/'Swedish support to a newspaper project in South Africa'), Ministry for Foreign Affairs, Stockholm, 9 June 1976 (SDA).
3. LO's members were collectively affiliated to the Social Democratic Party.

oping between Sweden and ANC. In Tanzania and Zambia—influential OAU member states; ANC's principal hosts in exile; and countries with which Sweden maintained particularly close relations—the Swedish embassies had, for example, acted in favour of land concessions to the organization. That Sweden already was seen to be closely associated with ANC, and that vis-à-vis independent Southern African governments it was ready to intervene on the movement's behalf in more sensitive political situations, was also illustrated during and after Ann Wilkens' first visit by a revealing episode in Swaziland. Little known and involving South Africa's future President and Deputy President, it deserves to be recounted in some detail.

The general background was that ANC from 1973-74 had started to re-build underground structures inside the country, as well as to establish a political presence in what it called the 'forward areas' of Botswana, Lesotho and Swaziland. While the internal work was carried out by a number of former political prisoners who had been released in the early 1970s—among them Harry Gwala and Jacob Zuma[1]—the initial diplomatic work in the small and exposed independent countries bordering South Africa was by the ANC leadership primarily entrusted to Chris Hani and Thabo Mbeki.

Mbeki spent the greater part of 1973 and 1974 in Botswana, where in addition to establishing links with BCM exiles he managed to obtain President Seretse Khama's permission to set up an ANC office. Isaac Makopo later took up the position as ANC Chief Representative, and in November 1975 the President's Office notified the Swedish ambassador, Bo Kälfors, that the Botswana government did not oppose humanitarian assistance to ANC in the country.[2] By that time, Chris Hani—who in mid-1974 entered South Africa to establish underground structures in the eastern Cape—had already spent about a year in Lesotho, from where he too established contacts with the black consciousness movement and the wider South African opposition. Successfully consolidating ANC's presence in Lesotho and recruiting many prominent BCM activists, as Chief Representative Hani would from mid-1976 until early 1982 administer the official Swedish support to that exposed and difficult 'forward area'.

Close to the Johannesburg-Pretoria region and strategically situated between Mozambique and Zululand/Natal, the small Kingdom of Swaziland would, finally, with the formation of a FRELIMO government and independence in the former Portuguese colony assume particular importance. Several ANC exiles were by the early 1970s living in Swaziland, among them Albert Dhlomo, Bafana Duma and Stanley Mabizela.[3] They, in turn, entered into contact with the ANC activists who started to re-build the underground structures in South Africa, notably with Jacob Zuma, who after his release from Robben Island in 1973 clandestinely entered

---

1. Gwala—released in 1972—was based in Natal, where in 1973 he was joined by Zuma. After his release in 1975, Joe Gqabi became actively involved in rebuilding ANC's underground structures in the Transvaal (Barrell Ph.D. op. cit., chapter two, p. 15).

2. Letter ('Bistånd till ANC Sydafrika i Botswana'/'Assistance to ANC South Africa in Botswana') from Bo Kälfors, Swedish ambassador to Botswana, to the Ministry for Foreign Affairs, Swedish embassy, Gaborone, 14 November 1975 (SDA).

3. Deputy headmaster of the Salesian High School in Swaziland, Mabizela had in the late 1950s/early 1960s studied at Lovedale together with Thabo Mbeki and Chris Hani and at the University of Fort Hare with Hani. Later ANC Chief Representative to Tanzania and Zimbabwe, he served on the National Executive Committee from 1988 to 1991. After the formation of the Government of National Unity in 1994, he was appointed South African high commissioner to Namibia.

Swaziland from Natal on a regular basis and eventually took refuge in the country.[1]

Already before Mozambique's independence, there was thus a significant ANC presence in Swaziland. Appointed Acting Chief Representative to the country, the young Thabo Mbeki—since 1971 Assistant Secretary to the ANC Revolutionary Council[2]—arrived there in early 1975 to coordinate the politico-military operations. In addition to contacts with FRELIMO in Mozambique, on the political side this involved discussions with BCM activists in South Africa. A number of them—such as Nkosazana Dlamini, Keith Mokoape and Tokyo Sexwale[3]—would in this way join ANC, later assuming prominent political or military positions within the movement.

On the military side, the work focused on the recruitment of new cadres to Umkhonto we Sizwe, who were sent via Swaziland and Mozambique for training in Africa, the Soviet Union or in other Eastern European countries. In this respect too, the operations were successful. According to Jacob Zuma, the ANC/MK Natal unit sent "more than a hundred" recruits through Swaziland.[4] Barrell notes that "this clandestine traffic opened up a trail between the Natal and Eastern Transvaal regions of South Africa via Swaziland to Mozambique which would become the

---

1. Like Hani and Mbeki, Zuma was born in 1942. In marked contrast to them, he did not receive any formal schooling. Growing up in rural Zululand, one of his cousins taught him to read and write, and it was—paradoxically—only as a political prisoner on Robben Island that he later managed to study formally. After joining ANC in 1959 and MK in 1962, in 1963 Zuma was arrested and sentenced to ten years on Robben Island. Working underground in Natal after his release, in 1975 he went into exile in Swaziland. Arriving in Mozambique in 1976, he later became ANC's Chief Representative to the country. Zuma rose rapidly through the ANC ranks. In 1978, he became a member of the National Executive Committee and ten years later Head of Intelligence (1988-93). Working closely with Thabo Mbeki, in the late 1980s Zuma took part in the secret talks with the South African government which in February 1990 led to the unbanning of ANC and the release of Nelson Mandela. He subsequently played a key role in the peace negotiations with the Inkatha Freedom Party. At the ANC congress in July 1991, Zuma was elected Deputy Secretary General and at the congress in December 1994 Chairperson of the movement. After the general elections in April 1994, he was appointed Minister of Economic Affairs and Tourism in the provincial government of KwaZulu/Natal. In June 1999, Jacob Zuma became Deputy President of South Africa.
2. The son of the senior ANC leader Govan Mbeki, Thabo Mbeki was born in the Transkei in 1942. During the second half of the 1950s, he attended Lovedale High School, where in 1956 he joined the ANC Youth League. Expelled in 1959, he continued his studies, first from home and later through SACHED in Johannesburg. In December 1961, he was elected secretary of the African Students Association at its founding conference in Durban, and in 1962 he joined the South African Communist Party. Later in 1962, Mbeki left South Africa, during the following four years studying at the University of Sussex, UK, where in 1966 he was awarded an MA in economics. As President of the ANC Youth and Students Section, he was subsequently attached to the ANC office in London. In 1969/70, he attended the Institute of Social Sciences (the 'International Lenin School') in Moscow and the following year he underwent military training in the Soviet Union. While studying in Moscow, in 1970 he became together with Chris Hani a member of SACP's Central Committee. Returning to Africa in 1971, he started to work as Assistant Secretary to the ANC Revolutionary Council in Lusaka. As noted in the text, between 1973 and 1976 Mbeki was actively involved in establishing links with the opposition inside South Africa, as well as in setting up ANC structures in Botswana and Swaziland. It was during this period that he came into contact with Sweden, paying his first of many visits to the country in November/December 1974. Working very closely with Acting President Oliver Tambo, in 1975 he was appointed to ANC's National Executive Committee. After serving as ANC Chief Representative to Nigeria between December 1976 and February 1978, he was recalled to Lusaka, where he took up the important position of Tambo's political secretary. A member of SACP's Political Bureau since 1977, he quickly rose as a prominent leader within the wider Congress Alliance, occupying a number of central positions. Within ANC, he served for many years as Secretary for Information and Publicity before he in 1989—following the death of Johnny Makatini—became Secretary for International Affairs. By that time, Mbeki had already made his mark as ANC's chief diplomat, leading the international talks and the secret negotiations with the Pretoria government which in 1990 led to a democratic opening in South Africa. Among the first ANC leaders to return to South Africa, in early 1990—having chaired the SACP congress in Cuba in April 1989—he let his party membership lapse. In May 1994, he was appointed First Executive Deputy President of South Africa and in June 1999 he succeeded Nelson Mandela as President. Apart from Oliver Tambo, no other ANC leader has worked as closely with Sweden as Thabo Mbeki. According to his biographer Mark Gevisser, in Mbeki's own opinion "Sweden and Swedish social democracy have had a profound effect upon his thinking" (Letter from Mark Gevisser to the Swedish embassy in Pretoria, Kensington, 4 August 1999) (MFA).
3. In 1994, Sexwale became Premier of the Gauteng province.
4. Cited in Barrell Ph.D. op. cit., chapter two, p. 31.

main conduit for [...] ANC's resumption of [the] armed struggle".[1] Later primarily associated with ANC's diplomatic work, Mbeki was closely involved in the military preparations. He had in 1970 attended an officer's military training course in the Soviet Union[2] and acted in Swaziland "as a military commander".[3]

Immediately before CCHA's fact-finding mission to Southern Africa, the ANC headquarters had submitted a request for additional Swedish assistance, stressing the need for humanitarian support in Swaziland. Assistance was sought for the maintenance of two official ANC representatives and an additional ten members, who were assisting refugees in transit from South Africa to Mozambique and Tanzania, as well as coordinating political work towards both South Africa and Mozambique. Apart from that, the ANC noted, "due to Swaziland's vulnerable position and [its] attitude towards South Africa, [our] activities [in the country] are very limited".[4]

Against this background, it was decided that Ann Wilkens in connection with her visit to South Africa should also go to Swaziland "in order to get more information concerning ANC's possibilities of working in and from [the country]".[5] As there was no official Swedish representation in Swaziland, arrangements were made directly with Mbeki.[6] On 10 March 1976, he phoned Wilkens as she was visiting the Mozambican capital Maputo. They agreed that on 25 March she should fly from Johannesburg to Manzini, Swaziland, and that Mbeki would meet her at the airport. Before 24 March, she was to cable confirmation of her arrival.[7]

Upon her arrival, Mbeki was nowhere to be seen. Wilkens was met instead by a white, plain-clothes person, introducing himself as "for one thing an immigration officer".[8] She was taken to a room in the airport building, where she was confronted with two more men and a woman, "whom I understood to be police [officers]". As later noted by Wilkens, they "were evidently informed beforehand about my contacts in Swaziland and about the objective of [my] visit". While declaring that she "at this stage" was not under arrest—but also that she could not enjoy diplomatic immunity in Swaziland since she was not accredited to the country—the 'immigration officer' proceeded to interrogate her. He not only wanted to know the reason for her visit to Swaziland, but also "the character of my activity at the Min-

1. Barrell Ph.D. op. cit., chapter two, p. 17.
2. In the Soviet Union, Mbeki underwent military training together with Max Sisulu (Adrian Hadland and Jovial Rantao: *The Life and Times of Thabo Mbeki*, Zebra Press, Rivonia, 1999, pp. 37-38).
3. Mark Gevisser: 'The bag-carrier', Part four of a six-part 'Thabo Mbeki story' in *Sunday Times*, 6 June 1999. In the same article, Gevisser quotes Zuma, recalling how "Thabo taught me how to use a gun". Hadland and Rantao, however, quote Max Sisulu saying that "Thabo was more comfortable with a book than with a gun in his hands" (Hadland and Rantao op. cit., p. 37).
4. Cited in Ann Wilkens: Memorandum ('ANC (SA)-delegation arresterad i Swaziland'/'ANC (SA) delegation arrested in Swaziland'), CCHA/Ministry for Foreign Affairs, Stockholm, 9 April 1976 (SDA).
5. Ibid. The Swedish aid authorities were fairly knowledgeable about the general refugee situation in Swaziland. Official assistance had since 1964 been extended to South African refugee youth studying in the country. The support was channelled from the financial year 1965/66 through five secondary schools, namely St. Christopher's, St. Francis', St. Michael's, the Salesian High School—where Stanley Mabizela later worked—and Waterford (Thord Palmlund: Memorandum ('Stöd till skolor i Swaziland'/'Support to schools in Swaziland'), SIDA, Stockholm, 6 December 1966) (SDA). Coordinated with Denmark and Norway, the programme was administered by a Swaziland-Scandinavian Committee. It led to assistance to the Ephesus House Bursary Committee, originally established as the Swaziland branch of IUEF.
6. Mbeki and Wilkens had met during her first visit to Sweden in late 1974 (Ann Wilkens: Memorandum ('Svenskt stöd till ett tidningsprojekt i Sydafrika'/'Swedish support to a newspaper project in South Africa'), Ministry for Foreign Affairs, Stockholm, 9 June 1976) (SDA).
7. Ann Wilkens: Memorandum ('ANC (SA)-delegation arresterad i Swaziland'/'ANC (SA) delegation arrested in Swaziland'), CCHA/Ministry for Foreign Affairs, Stockholm, 9 April 1976 (SDA).
8. Ibid. English in the original.

istry for Foreign Affairs in Stockholm". Wilkens then requested to make a telephone call to the Swedish legation in Pretoria, but "it turned out that [the lines]
were not working that day".

Eventually, Wilkens acknowledged that on behalf of the Swedish government
she worked with assistance to the liberation movements in Southern Africa and
that she had been considering contacting the official ANC delegation in Swaziland.
She was told that there was no such delegation, but that she perhaps was thinking
of "a couple of persons who had been detained [...] just recently [...] for possession
of heavy weapons, abduction from South Africa and holding of people under
duress". At this point, the Swedish diplomat declared that she wished to return to
Johannesburg. The request was granted. Accompanied by "another white man",
she was put on board the same plane with which she had arrived.[1]

Back in Johannesburg, Wilkens tried to confirm the arrests, both via the
Swedish legation and through the Swedish missionary Axel-Ivar Berglund, Director of Theological Education at the South African Council of Churches. Initially,
however, it turned out that neither ANC nor "several persons in Swaziland who
normally should have known" were aware of any detentions.[2] After repeated
attempts[3], Berglund managed to phone Swaziland's Minister of Justice. He "conceded that Thabo Mbeki and two other South Africans[4] were being kept at the
maximum security prison in Mbabane, but did not otherwise want to enter into
any details".[5]

Thus informed, on 30 March 1976 Wilkens sent a priority cable from the Swedish legation in Pretoria to the Ministry for Foreign Affairs in Stockholm, stating her
findings and asking the ministry to notify, among others, ANC's Chief Representative to Sweden, Mbeki's old friend Sobizana Mngqikana, and Zanele Mbeki, his
wife in Lusaka.[6] In a letter to Foreign Minister Sven Andersson, shortly thereafter
Mngqikana asked the Swedish government to investigate the matter further.[7] In
early May 1976, the embassy in Lusaka, however, informed the Foreign Ministry in
Stockholm that the detainees had been set free.[8]

Eventually, Mbeki, Zuma and Dhlomo "were escorted out of the country by the
Swaziland police and delivered across the border into the hands of the government
of Mozambique".[9] Until then, the prospects of being handed over instead to the
apartheid regime were both real and gruesome. In 1998, a semi-official biographical sketch of Thabo Mbeki noted that "[t]he apartheid security forces [...] were so
convinced that their scheme had succeeded that they told other activists of the
ANC, then in detention in South Africa, that at last they were going to have Mbeki

---

1. Ibid.
2. Ibid.
3. Conversation with Axel-Ivar Berglund, Uppsala, 2 February 2000. Wilkens stayed with Berglund and his wife.
   According to Berglund, he was tailed by the South African security police when he met Wilkens at the airport
   in Johannesburg. Wilkens was also watched during her stay in the city (Letter from Ann Wilkens to the
   author, Stockholm, 28 February 2000).
4. At the time, it was believed that Mbeki's detained colleagues were Albert Dhlomo and Mark Shope. In addition to Mbeki and Dhlomo—a former trade union activist from Natal—the third person was, however, Jacob
   Zuma (cf., for example, Mbeki op. cit., p. xiv and Hadland and Rantao op. cit, p. 40).
5. Ann Wilkens: Memorandum ('ANC (SA)-delegation arresterad i Swaziland'/'ANC (SA) delegation arrested in
   Swaziland'), CCHA/Ministry for Foreign Affairs, Stockholm, 9 April 1976 (SDA).
6. Cable fthe Swedish legation to the Ministry for Foreign Affairs, Pretoria, 30 March 1976 (MFA).
7. Cable from the Ministry for Foreign Affairs to the Swedish representation in Cape Town, Stockholm, 6 May
   1976 (MFA).
8. Information in cable ('Aktion för fängde ANC-medlemmar i Swaziland'/'Action in favour of detained ANC
   members in Swaziland') from Bo Heinebäck, Ministry for Foreign Affairs, to the Swedish representation in
   Cape Town, Stockholm, 13 May 1976 (MFA).
9. Mbeki op. cit., p. xiv.

in their hands".[1] What—in the tense build-up to the Soweto uprising—then would have happened to South Africa's future President and Deputy President is open to speculation. It is in this context not without relevance that ANC's Natal-based Joseph Mdluli, accused of sending MK recruits to Swaziland, died from police beatings within 24 hours of his arrest in mid-March 1976.[2] In the same month, two ANC and three PAC members were abducted from Swaziland and taken to South Africa, where they eventually were sentenced to long prison terms.[3]

It is, similarly, not possible to establish whether Wilkens' appearance in Swaziland and Sweden's knowledge of the detentions had a restraining effect on the events. Most probably, however, the government's subsequent diplomatic initiative vis-à-vis the Swazi authorities underlined that ANC enjoyed strong political support from Sweden, an old partner with regard to refugee programmes in the country and one of the most important aid donors to Southern Africa. This, in turn, may have assisted ANC in negotiating a continued, albeit precarious, presence in the country.

Towards a Special Relationship

In response to the events in Swaziland and to Mngqikana's appeal, in early May 1976 the Ministry for Foreign Affairs instructed the legation in South Africa—which at the time represented Sweden in Swaziland[4]—to contact the Swazi authorities to "inquire about the background to the detentions [...], thereby drawing [their] attention to our interest in the matter".[5] Such an approach was still considered appropriate after the news that the ANC detainees had been released. In early June, Åke Fridell visited Swaziland from Pretoria, where he handed over a diplomatic note to the Foreign Ministry in Mbabane and held discussions with Under-Secretary Mamba. The note stated:

> According to information received by the Swedish Government from various sources, members of [ANC] were arrested in Swaziland some time during the latter part of March this year. In view of the Swedish Government's keen interest in matters relating to human rights and fundamental freedoms all over the world, it would be highly appreciated if the Government of the Kingdom of Swaziland could see its way to give whatever information may be available on the background [to] the alleged arrests and the surrounding circumstances.[6]

During the following discussions, Mamba declared that he was not aware of any arrests of ANC members in Swaziland. At the same time, he emphasized that the country could not become "a springboard for guerrilla activities".[7]

Having marked its concern, the Swedish government let the matter rest. This was done on Oliver Tambo's explicit advice. In fact, while expressing his gratitude

1. Ibid. Hadland and Rantao write that there was "a growing crescendo of threats from the South African government that it was on the verge of capturing the three ANC officials" (Hadland and Rantao op. cit., p. 40).
2. Karis and Gerhart op. cit., p. 54. Four security policemen were charged with culpable homicide. Stating that Mdluli had tried to escape and "fallen over a chair", all four were, however, acquitted (TRC op. cit. (Vol. III), p. 179).
3. Ibid. (Vol. II), p. 125.
4. The relations with Swaziland were later conducted from the Swedish embassy in Maputo.
5. Cable from the Ministry for Foreign Affairs to the Swedish representation in Cape Town, Stockholm, 6 May 1976 (MFA).
6. *Aide-mémoire*, attached to letter ('ANC i Swaziland'/'ANC in Swaziland') from Åke Fridell, Swedish legation, to the Ministry for Foreign Affairs, Pretoria, 7 June 1976 (MFA).
7. Letter ('ANC i Swaziland') from Åke Fridell to the Ministry for Foreign Affairs, Pretoria, 7 June 1976 (MFA). English in the original.

Anders Bjurner of the
Swedish embassy with
Thabo Mbeki in Lusaka,
September 1976
(Courtesy of
Carin Norberg)

for Sweden's diplomatic assistance, in a meeting with Anders Bjurner in Lusaka he had in early May 1976 stressed "the very great sensitivity of the matter", being of the opinion that it should be "hushed up".[1] The ANC detainees had by that time been released, and although Tambo noted that there had been collaboration between the Swazi authorities and South Africa's security services—and that there were "certain elements within the Swazi leadership who at all costs wanted to get rid of ANC"—he was confident that the organization would be allowed to remain in the country. As this was of "significant importance", it should not be put at risk.[2]

Despite the arrests, ANC also maintained that the request for humanitarian support in Swaziland which had originally motivated Wilkens' visit to the country was still relevant.[3] And in spite of the prevailing uncertainties and of the fact that no further exploratory mission was attempted, in mid-May 1976 the consultative committee recommended that support should be granted.[4] The Social Democratic government concurred with the ANC position and CCHA's recommendation. At the official aid negotiations between Sweden and ANC in Lusaka at the end of August 1976, it was agreed to expand the scope of the assistance and include both Swaziland and Lesotho—two 'forward areas' where there were no official Swedish representations—in the cooperation programme for 1976/77.[5] This paved the way for official assistance to ANC activities inside South Africa too.

The events in Swaziland in 1976 may illustrate the special relationship that was developing between ANC and the Swedish government. In the context of the Cold War East-West divide, the relationship was exceptional. This was further underlined by the fact that it not only continued after the Social Democratic Party's elec-

1. Letter ('Samtal med O. Tambo, ANC's t.f. ordförande'/'Conversation with O. Tambo, ANC Acting President') from Anders Bjurner, Swedish embassy, to the Ministry for Foreign Affairs, Lusaka, 21 May 1976 (MFA).
2. Ibid. In subsequent ANC historiography, the detention of Dhlomo, Mbeki and Zuma has been described as "protective custody" by the Swazi authorities (cf. Mbeki, op. cit., p. xiv).
3. Marianne Sundh: Memorandum ('Framställning från ANC (SA) om ytterligare stöd 1975/76'/'Request from ANC (SA) for additional support in 1975/76'), CCHA/SIDA, Stockholm, 6 May 1976 (SDA).
4. Ibid. and CCHA: 'Protokoll [från sammanträde 18 maj 1976]' ('Minutes [from meeting 18 May 1976]'), SIDA, [Stockholm], 18 May 1976 (SDA).
5. 'Agreed minutes of discussions on cooperation between Sweden and the African National Congress of South Africa', Lusaka, 1 September 1976 (SDA).

toral defeat in September 1976, but was consolidated and expanded under Prime Minister Fälldin's non-socialist government.

The relationship was also extraordinary from a North-South perspective. As noted above, from the mid-1970s the Swedish government would *de facto* view ANC as a 'government-in-waiting', not only annually holding formal, official aid negotiations with the movement, but from a political and practical point of view relating to it in that capacity. Within Sweden's wider—and very substantial—involvement in Southern Africa, the significance of the humanitarian support to ANC was increasingly seen as equivalent to the development assistance to some of the organization's host countries in the region. In fact, with regard to Swaziland and Lesotho, the cooperation with ANC would from 1982 and 1986, respectively, take precedence over the bilateral relations with these two independent countries. This will be further illustrated below.

From the Swedish horizon, developments in Southern Africa—including issues related to bilateral development aid—were to a considerable extent assessed within the context of the wider, regional anti-apartheid struggle. With well-known and cordial relations between Sweden and ANC, there emerged an unconventional triangular interaction between the Nordic donor, the South African liberation movement and the independent countries. As noted by Thabo Mbeki, for ANC this created political space within which it was able to act. Mbeki would on ANC's behalf over the years play a prominent role in this context, as, for example, in Zimbabwe after the ZANU victory in 1980. Talking about Sweden and the other Nordic countries, in the interview quoted above he said:

> [T]he starting point was the emancipation of the people. [...] You could not sacrifice the objective of the emancipation of the people of South Africa simply to maintain good relations with the country hosting ANC, so we had to find a formula around this. [...] If [the] starting point had been different and Sweden, for instance, had wanted to create a sphere of influence and become important to [the Southern African] countries with regard to Social Democracy and the struggle against Communism or something, then, of course, if complications had appeared between ANC and Zimbabwe, [Sweden] would have said: 'Look, we cannot afford to lose our influence on Zimbabwe, so cool down ANC!' [...] But that is a different starting point. [...]

> [P]art of ANC's capacity to do things and part of the weight that was attached to ANC derived from the weight that it was given by other countries. The Nordic countries were important with regard to more than development assistance in the region of Southern Africa. Also by the nature of their relations, where a Zambia, a Zimbabwe or a Tanzania would not feel threatened or as junior partners, as they would [...] vis-à-vis the United States. You had a particular set of relations between the Nordic countries and the countries of Southern Africa. The manner in which ANC was treated [...]—[...] where [it] enjoyed a sort of official status—impacted upon the way that the countries of the region would approach [us]. They would not want to handle ANC in a manner that could upset the allies of ANC, which also happened to be their own allies.[1]

Based on early and close contacts, the political relationship with ANC developed at the level of the Swedish government. Turning to the national debate in the 1970s, it will be seen, however, that there were not only strong Swedish interests which opposed the liberation movement's calls for isolation of the apartheid regime, but also influential voices which until the end of the decade advocated support for 'alternative' South African organizations.

---

1. Interview with Thabo Mbeki, pp. 155-56.

Isolation versus Involvement:
Companies, Churches and Labour in the 1970s

A New Sanctions Debate

The quelling of the opposition not only forced the banned ANC and PAC into a precarious survival in exile, but led in the late 1960s to a marked marginalization of the wider South Africa question. In the era of Vietnam and the nationalist struggles in the Portuguese African colonies, other events overshadowed the silence of the grave in the apartheid republic. At the United Nations, for example, the committee set up by the Security Council to study possible measures against South Africa had submitted its recommendations as early as in March 1965. However, as later stated by Alva Myrdal, the former chairperson of the UN Expert Group, "thereafter the [council] fell asleep".[1] The sanctions report was never discussed. In spite of repeated resolutions by the General Assembly, it was only in November 1977 that the Security Council took action under the UN Charter's Chapter VII by imposing a mandatory arms embargo against South Africa.[2] Calls for economic sanctions were at the same time persistently rejected by the permanent Western council members.[3]

In Sweden, the marginalization of the South Africa question was reflected in dwindling attention by the established press. While the thirteen largest newspapers in 1963 published no less than 225 editorials on South Africa, the corresponding figure for 1966 was 119 and for 1969 a mere 21.[4] Albeit with some delay, the downward trend was also reflected in the publications of the solidarity organizations with Southern Africa and, above all, in those of the wider anti-imperialist movement. From the start in 1964, the information bulletin *Syd- och Sydväst-afrika*—from 1967 entitled *Södra Afrika Informationsbulletin*—had regularly contained articles on South Africa, the anti-apartheid struggle and ANC. Shifting its attention to the Portuguese colonies, between 1969 and 1974, it fell largely silent in

---

1. See Sellström Volume I, pp. 200-01.
2. UN Security Council Resolution 418 of 4 November 1977. This was the first time in the history of the United Nations that mandatory sanctions under Chapter VII were imposed against a member state. In August 1963, the Security Council had recommended the member states to cease the sale and shipment of arms, ammunition and military vehicles to South Africa. Sweden followed the recommendation, banning the export of any military commodity. At about the same time, the Swedish ball bearing manufacturer SKF was invited by the apartheid government to set up a production plant in the country, mainly for defence purposes.
3. The legal basis for the imposition of international economic sanctions is provided by Chapter VII (Articles 39-51) of the UN Charter. According to this chapter, the Security Council—consisting of five permanent members (France, the People's Republic of China, the then Soviet Union, USA and the United Kingdom; each with veto powers) and, on a rotating basis, ten elected members—could make decisions binding upon members and even non-members. Mandatory sanctions could, however, only be introduced if the Security Council had first determined that there existed "a threat to peace, breach of the peace or act of aggression".
4. Åke Magnusson: *Sverige-Sydafrika: En Studie av en Ekonomisk Relation* ('Sweden-South Africa: A Study of an Economic Relationship'), The Scandinavian Institute of African Studies, Uppsala, 1974, Diagram 3, p. 22. The main parts of this pioneering study were also published in English (Åke Magnusson: *Swedish Investments in South Africa*, Research Report No. 23, The Scandinavian Institute of African Studies, Uppsala, 1974).

this regard.[1] The independent socialist monthly *Kommentar* published no articles at all on South Africa between mid-1970 and mid-1975.[2] As was later pointed out by Dick Urban Vestbro, a leading AGIS member active on the editorial board of the Southern Africa bulletin, "the shifting focus by the public opinion from South Africa to the Portuguese colonies and the development of the solidarity movement from anti-apartheid to anti-imperialism [...] influenced [our] policy".[3]

Nowhere was the change more conspicuous than with regard to the popular boycott actions initiated against the apartheid regime in the early 1960s. In April 1963, the influential Co-operative Union and Wholesale Society had agreed to join the consumer boycott campaign launched by SUL the previous month.[4] It was a highly significant decision. With close links to the Social Democratic Party, well over a million members, more than six hundred affiliated local co-operative societies and a considerable indirect parliamentary leverage[5], KF played a crucial role in the development of Swedish anti-apartheid opinion in the 1960s. However, in September 1969—at a time when the active campaign by SUL and the South Africa Committees had long since ground to a halt—KF decided to call off the boycott. In a situation, it argued, where the government had failed to introduce official economic sanctions and the general public was showing a growing loss of interest in South Africa, it was no longer reasonable to uphold the "private sanctions" initiated more than six years earlier.[6]

Coming only four months after the parliamentary decision to grant direct official support to PAIGC and the Southern African liberation movements, KF's stand marked the end of the first, mainly re-active, boycott campaign against apartheid. Five years later, the debate resurfaced. This time, it pro-actively focused on Sweden's direct economic links with South Africa. Initially carried by the churches, it later engaged the principal actors in the labour market, the political parties and the second generation solidarity movement. By 1974-75, the issue of economic sanctions against apartheid was once more in the centre of the national political arena. Contrary to the situation ten years earlier, it was to remain there until the South African democratic elections in 1994. While the official assistance to ANC regularly increased, in the late 1970s the Africa Groups and the Isolate South Africa Committee launched a continuous consumer boycott campaign, also closely monitoring any Swedish link with the apartheid country. This, in turn, effectively contributed to the introduction of comprehensive sanctions in 1987.

At the beginning of the 1970s, the South Africa question, however, was by no means absent from the Swedish debate. Beyond the headlines, apartheid remained a

---

1. In November 1972, however, an issue dedicated entirely to South Africa was published (*Södra Afrika Informationsbulletin*, No. 17, 1972).
2. As noted in the chapter on Angola, *Kommentar* played a particularly important role with regard to MPLA. In the case of South Africa, it was, however, only towards the end of 1977—almost five years after the Swedish government and three years later than the Africa Groups—that the influential anti-imperialist journal acknowledged ANC ('Sydafrika: ANC Leder den Väpnade Kampen'/'South Africa: ANC Leads the Armed Struggle' in *Kommentar*, No. 11, 1977, pp. 35-37).
3. Dick Urban Vestbro: 'Förslag om AGIS förhållande till ANC' ('Proposal regarding AGIS' relations to ANC'), Stockholm, 21 December 1974 (AGA).
4. Sellström Volume I, p. 195.
5. In 1963, more than 30 per cent of the members of the Swedish parliament were also members of KF (Sellström Volume I, p. 36).
6. Ibid., p. 248.

matter of considerable public concern, particularly among the youth.[1] As before, official assistance in the form of legal aid, study grants etc. was channelled via the United Nations and international NGOs to various anti-apartheid organizations. In parliament, the Centre and Liberal parties advocated support to ANC.

The early humanitarian concerns primarily targeted the victims of racist repression. But in the absence of concerted international action—and as apartheid was being further consolidated—during the 1960s the South African economy recorded exceptional growth.[2] This, in turn, influenced the anti-apartheid debate. When black South African students and workers around 1970 again started to express an active internal opposition[3], the economic foundations of the apartheid state were increasingly brought into focus, as well as the directly related questions of international investments, South Africa's trade union legislation and the foreign companies' labour policies. These issues were raised in 1972-73 notably by the World Council of Churches (WCC) and the International Labour Organization (ILO).

Although Sweden by comparison with the major Western powers played a minor role in the South African economy—from the points of view of assets, company representation and trade roughly representing 1 per cent of foreign inter-

---

1. KF's decision to call off the boycott was, for example, far from uncontroversial. The board of the Social Democratic Party branch in Stockholm appealed to KF to maintain the boycott. According to an opinion poll taken at the time, one third of the general public was in favour of a continued boycott, while one third was against and the remaining one third undecided (Magnusson (1974) op. cit., pp. 44-45). Public concern was in particular expressed by the youth. At the beginning of the 1970s, letters on the situation in South Africa were often addressed to the Ministry for Foreign Affairs. In September 1971, for example, pupils at the Vattmyra secondary school in Jakobsberg outside Stockholm requested information from the ministry on international boycott actions against the country (Letter from Mona Malm, Vattmyraskolan, to the Ministry for Foreign Affairs, Jakobsberg [no date, but received on 27 September 1971] and reply ('Förfrågan ang. bojkott av Sydafrika'/'Enquiry about boycott against South Africa'), Ministry for Foreign Affairs, 5 October 1971) (MFA). Young Swedes also raised their concerns in letters to international anti-apartheid organizations and directly to ANC. In February 1971, the ANC journal *Sechaba* published a letter from the recently formed Africa Group in Arvika, a small town in central Sweden close to the Norwegian border. The letter *inter alia* stated: "We are some young boys who have formed an Africa Group. Our aim is to fight imperialism, colonialism, neo-colonialism, racialism and apartheid in Africa. Among other actions, we have sold *Sechaba* copies during a fair in Arvika. [...] Now we ask South African young refugees to write to us. Then we will give the addresses to Swedish boys and girls so that [they] can make pen-friends in Sweden. The reasons for this pen-friend action are mainly two: 1) We want Swedish youngsters to learn about [the] fight for freedom in your country, which is being oppressed by an inhuman, cruel apartheid regime; [and] 2) We want South African, Namibian and Zimbabwean refugees to know that the young people of Sweden have not forgotten them" (*Sechaba*, No. 2, February 1971, p. 23).

2. In real terms, from 1962 to 1969 South Africa's GDP grew at an annual rate of between 4.4 (1966) and 7.1 per cent (1964). The growth was, however, not translated into higher wages for the black workers. In fact, in the strategic gold mining industry real wages were lower in 1971 than in 1911 (Mats Lundahl and Lena Moritz: *Det Nya Sydafrika: Ekonomi och Politik efter Apartheid* ('The New South Africa: Economy and Politics after Apartheid'), SNS Förlag, Stockholm, 1996, pp. 34 and 37).

3. The economic growth in the 1960s had a number of important consequences. To meet the demands for sustained industrialization, the education system had to enroll more and more black students. Between 1965 and 1975, the number of blacks in secondary schools increased nearly fivefold. At the same time, there was a dramatic increase in the number of blacks employed in the manufacturing sector. Eventually, these developments led to the appearance of the black consciousness movement around 1970, the mass strikes in 1973, the Soweto revolt in 1976 and to the mass urban protests in the 1980s. As stated by the South African scholar Michael Neocosmos, "in structural terms, it was [the] period of extreme repression [in the 1960s] which was to provide, through exceptional economic growth, the seeds of the destruction of the apartheid state" (Michael Neocosmos: 'From Peoples' Politics to State Politics: Aspects of National Liberation in South Africa' in Adebayo O. Olukoshi: *The Politics of Opposition in Contemporary Africa*, Nordiska Afrikainstitutet, Uppsala, 1998, p. 200).

ests[1]—there were, nevertheless, significant Swedish investments in the apartheid republic. The issues raised by WCC and ILO in the early 1970s were thus highly relevant and had a direct impact. After intense national debates regarding 'involvement' versus 'isolation', they would towards the end of the decade lead to a substantial multilateral trade union involvement via ICFTU and to a unilateral ban on new investments.

Concerned with Sweden's official, bilateral political and aid relations with ANC and the wider South African nationalist movement, the issues of multilateral trade union assistance[2] and economic sanctions fall outside the primary scope of the present study. Nevertheless, the two interrelated issues were particularly relevant to ANC, which on the labour front was allied to SACTU and together with its partner unflaggingly called for total isolation of the Pretoria regime. To complement the narration of Sweden's direct relations with ANC, it is justified to present the positions taken in the 1970s by Sweden's most influential labour and popular movements with regard to 'isolation and involvement'.[3] The relations with SACTU and the emerging South African trade unions, as well as the first steps towards unilateral official sanctions, are discussed in the next chapter.

Sweden's 'Two Faces'

At the height of the Cold War, Sweden's stands on South Africa were often questioned by SACP and SACTU from ideological and strategic points of view. Describing "a kind of pro-Soviet hysteria" among the members of the wider Congress Alliance—as well as criticizing their "very unsophisticated, undialectic and unidimensional understanding" of the Swedish and Nordic assistance—SACP's Garth Strachan has later stated that it was commonly "characterized as imperialist and sometimes even as American support, channelled through those [Western] countries which were most amenable to [...] ANC".[4] Although this was rarely, if ever, reflected in ANC's bilateral dialogue with the Swedish authorities—in which, on the contrary, the nationalist movement regularly stressed its non-alignment and independence vis-à-vis the Soviet Union—SACP would publicly warn against the policies pursued by Olof Palme and the Social Democratic Party.[5] Even more con-

---

1. The South African authorities published statistics on foreign assets in the country until 1966. In that year, the United Kingdom accounted for 57.3% of the assets, the United States 13.1, France 5.2, Switzerland 4.4, West Germany 3.0 and Belgium/Luxemburg for 1.1%. The Swedish share was below 1% (Magnusson (1974) op. cit., Table 16, p. 71). In 1970, a total of 852 multinational corporations—i.e. concerns with production in five countries or more—operated in South Africa. Of these, 512 (60.1%) were British, 174 (20.4%) American, 58 (6.8%) West German, 33 (3.9%) Dutch, 21 (2.5%) French and 19 (2.2%) Swiss. The 13 companies registered as Swedish represented a share of 1.5% (SOU: *Förbud mot Investeringar i Sydafrika*/'Prohibition against Investments in South Africa', Stockholm, 1978, p. 66). Finally, in South Africa's foreign trade exchange imports from Sweden represented in 1973 1.7%, while exports stood for 0.5%. Sweden thus occupied 12th place among South Africa's trading partners, well below the United Kingdom, West Germany, USA, Japan, Italy, France and Holland, but also, for example, Australia (Åke Magnusson: *Sydafrika i Världen*/'South Africa in the World', Nordiska Afrikainstitutet, Uppsala, 1979, Table: 9:3, p. 251).
2. In the case of Namibia, the Swedish trade union assistance was extended on a bilateral basis.
3. These issues will be revisited in the context of the mass struggles in the 1980s.
4. Interview with Garth Strachan, p. 192.
5. For SACP's criticism of the initiative towards Southern Africa launched by Olof Palme in 1976-77, see the chapter 'SACTU, Unions and Sanctions'.

spicuous was SACTU's criticism of LO and TCO.[1] This, in turn, flowed from deep mistrust of and differences with ICFTU.[2]

Until the mid-1980s, the Swedish positions on economic sanctions and trade union assistance were not in line with ANC's and SACTU's declared policies. They were also strongly criticized by the Africa Groups, which from a recognition of ANC in late 1974 and of SACTU in mid-1977 forcefully campaigned in favour of total isolation of South Africa and support for ANC's labour ally.[3] While unilateral sanctions by the anti-apartheid movement in the Western countries which did not channel official assistance to the liberation movement were seen as an overriding objective[4], in the case of Sweden the government's hesitancy in this regard did not preclude the development of a close relationship with ANC.

Against a background of increasing direct official support—including the important 'home front' component and assistance to SACTU—ANC would in its bilateral relations with the Swedish government *de facto* downplay its insistence on comprehensive unilateral action. Although the contradiction between, on the one hand, direct support to ANC and, on the other, Swedish trade and private business links with South Africa was certainly both noted and criticized by the liberation movement[5],

1. In the interview with Strachan quoted above, he continued: "For me, it says a lot about the Nordic countries—and [...] about the Social Democratic parties in those countries [...]—that despite [the] unnuanced, unsophisticated characterization of their support [...] they a) continued to support [the liberation movements] and b) that the support was genuinely disinterested. To the best of my knowledge, there was never any effort, either in the form of literature or in the form of personal contacts or interventions, which aimed at turning around the misconception in the ranks of the liberation movements" (Interview with Garth Strachan, p. 192).
2. On account of their trade union links to ICFTU, as late as in October 1986—almost a year after the formation of COSATU—members of ANC's National Working Committee questioned the commitment and credentials of some of the internally based future leading ANC government representatives. Alec Erwin, who in 1994 became Deputy Minister of Finance, and Sydney Mufamadi, appointed at the same time Minister of Safety and Security, were among these. Stating that the members of FOSATU—of which Erwin between 1979 and 1981 had served as General Secretary—"were and still are opposed to ANC", Josiah Jele, for example, noted that Erwin "used to be [among] the most consistent attenders of ICFTU meetings". In the case of Mufamadi—former General Secretary of the General and Allied Workers Union (GAWU), who in South Africa in the early 1980s had joined SACP—it was, similarly, said that he "used to have his salary paid from ICFTU contributions" (ANC: 'Minutes of emergency NWC meeting', [Lusaka, 22 October 1986]) (MCA).
3. Although the Africa Groups—originally constituted as "anti-imperialist study groups"—during the first half of the 1970s remained hesitant vis-à-vis ANC, they soon advocated total isolation of South Africa. AGIS' 1976 programme stated: "Via Swedish investments in South Africa and [the fact] that Swedish capital to a high degree is interwoven with international capital, the workers in Sweden and in South Africa are exploited by the same capitalists. They therefore also have common interests. The only thing that in the longer term can stop the exploitation by the capitalists is that the workers and the oppressed in all countries together fight the common enemy". Against this background, the programme established as an overall objective "to expose and fight against the support to South Africa [extended] by the [Swedish] government and capital" ('Program för Afrikagrupperna i Sverige, antaget vid kongressen i Åseda den 5-7 juni 1976'/'Programme for the Africa Groups in Sweden, adopted by the congress in Åseda, 5-7 June 1976'), [no date or place] (AGA).
4. In the case of the Nordic countries, this was largely the situation in Denmark. It could be noted that comprehensive sanctions against South Africa were imposed by Denmark in 1986, while direct official assistance to ANC was granted only from 1991, after the unbanning of the movement. In Sweden, the sequence was the opposite. Official ANC assistance was extended from 1973, while an investment ban was introduced in 1979 and comprehensive sanctions in 1987.
5. Thabo Mbeki—who together with Oliver Tambo was the main architect behind the evolving political relationship between ANC and Sweden—would from the mid-1970s in no uncertain terms often emphasize the contradiction. Interviewed by the Africa Groups, in March 1978, for example, he stated that "we demand that Sweden [...] on its own takes every step [...] towards isolation of South Africa. Only then can Sweden assume the moral right to request that other countries do the same. By [focusing on] international sanctions", he said, "the Swedish government shuns its responsibility". According to Mbeki, in the meantime "the Swedish government and the company directors assume a hypocritical position" ('Sverige Flyr från Sitt Ansvar'/ 'Sweden Shuns Its Responsibility' in *Afrikabulletinen*, No. 41, 1978, p. 9). And when the Swedish government granted the first exemptions to the 1979 ban on new investments, the ANC representation in Stockholm—headed by Lindiwe Mabuza—declared that the decisions amounted to "such a disappointment that it hurts" (see below).

there is no evidence that it led to major discord or bilateral strains.[1] In the case of ANC, there was no parallel to FRELIMO's harsh denouncement in 1968-69 of ASEA's involvement in the Cabora Bassa project in Mozambique.[2]

Towards the mid-1970s, leading anti-apartheid advocates such as Per Wästberg, a government appointed CCHA member, publicly asked the question "How long can Sweden support armed liberation movements and sharply condemn apartheid without cutting off economic relations with South Africa?"[3] The contradiction was also forcefully underlined by the solidarity movement. In its diplomacy vis-à-vis the Swedish government, ANC, however, avoided placing sanctions before assistance. Although the movement maintained its principled stand and criticized the private companies which had economic interests in the apartheid republic, a pragmatic *modus vivendi* was established. In an interview with the CCHA members Gunnar Helander and Evert Svensson, Oliver Tambo, with reference to sanctions and the so called 'new strategy', declared in October 1975—at the height of the second Swedish sanctions debate—that

> it is unrealistic to believe that all investments will [be withdrawn], although it in principle appears correct to us to demand so. [...] [Y]ou can [also] understand those who pursue an apparently more pragmatic [policy], striving for more immediate results. I take a certain position, but I don't judge those who try other ways. The main thing is that we promote the cause of the oppressed.[4]

And in September 1980—after the introduction of the limited Swedish investment ban—Tambo explained to SIDA's acting representative in Zambia, Lennart Wohlgemuth, that "while foreign investments back up the apartheid regime [...], SIDA's assistance is the lifeblood [of] ANC and [the] liberation struggle".[5]

From the late 1970s spearheading the Swedish campaign for total sanctions, the Africa Groups eventually reached a similar conclusion. In a study on Sweden and South Africa written in English for an international public by Mai Palmberg—activist and student of the economic relations between the two countries[6]—the solidarity organization noted in 1985 that

---

1. When Sweden in mid-1986 fell behind Denmark and Norway with regard to comprehensive unilateral action, leading representatives of the United Democratic Front (UDF) would publicly criticize Prime Minister Ingvar Carlsson's Social Democratic government. After the discussions in the mid-1960s and the mid-1970s, the political breakthrough in the mid-1980s followed upon the third and final Swedish national debate on sanctions against apartheid.
2. See Sellström Volume I, pp. 483-502.
3. Per Wästberg: 'Svenska företag i Sydafrika ej humanare än andra' ('Swedish companies in South Africa are no more humane than others') in *Dagens Nyheter*, 23 July 1974.
4. Gunnar Helander: 'Intervju av Gunnar Helander och Evert Svensson med Sydafrikas African National Congress' ordförande Oliver Tambo, i Stockholm, 1975 10 02' ('Interview by Gunnar Helander and Evert Svensson with ANC's President Oliver Tambo, Stockholm, 2 October 1975') [no place or date] (SDA). In the frank interview, Tambo also stated that "from the point of view of [ideological] doctrine, it is irrelevant to [label] those who [...] participate in the liberation struggle. Let us not be divided between left and right, Zulu and Sotho. Let us unite against the common enemy. [...] I do not think that there is the slightest risk that South Africa [after our victory]—which is far, far away—will be dominated by Communists. When freedom comes, all kinds of groups will appear and participate in the new government".
5. Letter ('Stöd till ANC/SA'/'Support to ANC') from Lennart Wohlgemuth, Swedish embassy, to SIDA, Lusaka, 25 September 1980 (SDA). English in the original.
6. Palmberg—a citizen of Finland—joined the Africa Groups at the beginning of the 1970s. As a scholar, journalist and activist, she would over the following two decades play a prominent role in the Swedish debate on the liberation struggles in South and Southern Africa. In addition to articles in *Afrikabulletinen* and *Kommentar*, among her works could be mentioned *Befrielsekampen i Afrika* ('The Liberation Struggle in Africa', AGIS, Stockholm, 1977), edited for the Africa Groups and in 1983 published in English by Zed Press, London, as *The Struggle for Africa*. On the subject of Swedish economic interests in South Africa, her study 'Svenska Företag ut ur Sydafrika?' ('Swedish Companies out of South Africa?') was published in 1980 in Claes Brundenius, Kenneth Hermele and Mai Palmberg: *Gränslösa Affärer: Om Svenska Företag i Tredje Världen* / 'Unbounded Business: On Swedish Companies in the Third World', Liber Förlag, Stockholm.

'Involvement vs. isolation': Åke Magnusson (centre) defending his dissertation on 'South Africa in the World', Gothenburg, June 1979. Seated is Carl Lidbom of the Social Democratic Party and standing David Wirmark of the Liberal Party (Photo: Christian Tyre/Kamerareportage)

the contradictions are not to be interpreted as hypocrisy, but as a struggle between different interests. On one side is the Swedish business community, for whom South Africa is a market. On the other, a broad anti-apartheid movement for whom South Africa [...] is [an affront to] human dignity and a threat to peace. Caught in the middle is the government [...], for whom the big companies represent major power centres. In the highly export-oriented economy of Sweden, the big companies are [...] seen as important factors [in] shaping the economic basis of [the] society. It is not easy for the government to go against their interests.

Some trade unions, and notably the Metalworkers Union [...], also find [themselves] caught in the middle. [They] feel that sanctions would hurt employment in Sweden and therefore take a careful stand.[1]

Thus presenting Sweden's "two faces" vis-à-vis apartheid[2] and arguing that "it is the task of the solidarity movement to push [forward] the frontier of what is politically possible and acceptable", Palmberg concluded that

the isolation of South Africa is only a supplement to the direct support to [ANC] and [SWAPO].[3]

---

1. AGIS: *Sweden and South Africa*, Afrikagrupperna, Stockholm, September 1985, pp. 4-5. The study was financed by SIDA under a grant given to the Africa Groups in 1984 in order to "internationally inform about Sweden's South Africa policy" (Letter ('Redovisning av bidrag för internationell information om den svenska Sydafrika-politiken'/'Report on contribution for international information on the Swedish South Africa policy') from Ingvar Flink, AGIS, to SIDA, Stockholm, 11 June 1986) (SDA). Exceptional in a Western context, this official support to a critical non-governmental organization is but one example of the cooperation from the late 1970s between the Swedish state and the NGO movement around the objective of broadening the international anti-apartheid opinion. Direct official Swedish support was also granted to a number of international NGOs giving information on the anti-apartheid struggle or exposing collaboration with South Africa in various fields, such as the London-based Africa Bureau for its publication *X-Ray* (from 1975/76), the Holland Committee on Southern Africa for the news bulletin *Facts and Reports* (from 1976/77), the Norwegian-based World Campaign against Military and Nuclear Collaboration with South Africa (from the start in 1979) and the Dutch Shipping Research Bureau (also from the start in 1980).
2. Cf. Kenneth Hermele: 'Sweden and the Third World: Development Aid and Capital Involvement' in *Review of African Political Economy*, No. 23, 1982, pp. 85-100.
3. AGIS: *Sweden and South Africa* op. cit., p. 17.

Ecumenical Action and Swedish Companies

Coming to the fore in the mid-1970s—at a time when the official assistance to ANC was a fraction of that extended to the liberation movements in the Portuguese colonies and as the Africa Groups were still debating the character and significance of the movement[1]—the national debate on Sweden's economic links with the apartheid government became particularly intense and divisive, often leading to contradictions within both the ruling Social Democratic Party and the opposition Liberal Party.

More than anything, two international events provoked the Swedish debate, namely the programmes of action respectively adopted by the Central Committee of the World Council of Churches in Utrecht, Holland, in August 1972 and the International Conference of Trade Unions against Apartheid, convened by the International Labour Organization in Geneva, Switzerland, in June 1973. Involving two of the constituent parts of the wider 1960s anti-apartheid opinion—the churches[2] and the labour movement—the resolutions highlighted the presence of Swedish companies in South Africa, setting in motion a national policy debate concerning the struggle against apartheid.

While both the WCC meeting and the ILO conference upheld the UN General Assembly's calls for isolation of the apartheid regime, in the absence of mandatory sanctions the action programmes also left openings for direct involvement with the foreign companies in South Africa to force them to adopt democratic labour practices, notably by recognizing black or non-racial trade unions. The scene was thus set for an intense international debate on isolation versus involvement. Through the

---

1. Over the years, the Africa Groups would more than any other NGO be associated with unconditional popular Swedish support for ANC. In the early 1970s, the solidarity organization was, however, manifestly critical of the South African liberation movement. Dedicating its efforts to the struggles in the Portuguese African colonies—and in marked difference to the 1960s South Africa Committees—in a book published in 1972 the second generation, post-Vietnam Africa Groups criticized ANC of at the same time being influenced by Ghandi-inspired pacifism and Soviet Communism, as well as of emphasizing diplomacy rather than armed struggle (AGIS (1972) op. cit., pp. 84-86). When the leaders of the Southern African liberation movements after the UN/OAU Oslo conference on Southern Africa in April 1973 visited Stockholm, the Africa Groups arranged a public meeting to which ZANU and ZAPU of Zimbabwe, SWAPO of Namibia and ANC of South Africa were not invited. By that time, official support had already been extended to the four movements. Also with regard to ANC, *de facto* recognition by the state was thus extended long before a similar decision was taken by the principal NGO solidarity organization. While AGIS in November 1974 eventually acknowledged ANC as the leading South African liberation movement, few activities were carried out in favour of the organization. In a process similar to that experienced by the Zimbabwean and Namibian liberation movements, this in turn prompted the recently established Swedish ANC office to inspire a parallel support group, called the Support Group for the People of South Africa (*Stödgruppen för Sydafrikas Folk* - SSF), formed in January 1975 (*Phambili*, No. 1, March-May 1975, p. 29). Editing ANC's local information bulletin *Phambili*, in cooperation with individual Africa Group members—notably Mai Palmberg and Dick Urban Vestbro—it was SSF rather than AGIS that initially promoted the popular cause of ANC in Sweden. As late as in November 1976, SFF complained about its relations with AGIS, noting that "a number of unfortunate misunderstandings have appeared" (Letter from Mats Palmquist, chairman of SSF, to AGIS, Stockholm, 18 November 1976) (AGA). Critically reflecting on AGIS and ANC, Vestbro later commented that the initial assessment and "our reluctance to embark on activities in favour of ANC obstructed for at least six years the cooperation with [the movement]", adding that "[c]learly expressed self-criticism and concrete work for ANC were required by us in order to eventually gain the position as one of ANC's closest friends" (Dick Urban Vestbro: 'Afrikagrupperna och befrielserörelserna: Självkritiskt om 'kritisk solidaritet'/'The Africa Groups and the liberation movements: Self-criticism on 'critical solidarity' [no place or date]) (AGA). On AGIS and ANC in the mid-1970s, see also the interview with Sören Lindh, pp. 305-06.

2. The important role played by the official Church of Sweden and many of the independent, free churches has been discussed in Volume I of this study. With regard to the marginalization of the South Africa question, it should be noted that in the early 1970s it was mainly church-affiliated NGOs that maintained project activities in South Africa. According to the earlier quoted SIDA study by Jörgen Knudtzon and Miriam Magnusson, out of the nine Swedish NGOs active in South Africa in 1972 seven fell within this category (Knudtzon and Magnusson op. cit., p. 8). Joining forces with the anti-imperialist solidarity movement, church organizations would—as in the case of Namibia—continue to play a very prominent role. Their participation in ISAK was, for example, conspicuous.

political scientist Åke Magnusson[1], the latter option became known in Sweden as "the new strategy".[2] Although opposed by ANC and SACTU, it was eventually followed by both the Swedish churches and the trade union movement.

In Utrecht, the WCC Central Committee adopted a policy of disinvestment, not only with regard to South Africa but also vis-à-vis Namibia, Zimbabwe, Angola, Mozambique and Guinea-Bissau. By an overwhelming majority, it decided "to sell forthwith existing holdings and to make no further investments in corporations involved in or trading with [these countries]".[3] It also agreed not to deposit any of WCC's funds in banks which maintained operations there. Member churches, Christian agencies and individual Christians were, finally, urged to use their influence—including shareholders' action and disinvestment—to press international companies to withdraw from South Africa and the other countries ruled by white, racist regimes.[4] At the same time, however, some Evangelical Lutheran churches—among them the Church of Sweden—opposed a policy of complete withdrawal and advanced the alternative to work for improved conditions for black workers in the foreign owned companies, a minority position which was mentioned in the final resolution.[5]

The Church of Sweden was not only a founding member of the World Council of Churches' Programme to Combat Racism[6], but also a shareholder in several of

---

1. Based at the University of Gothenburg, Magnusson became a leading advocate of the policy of 'constructive involvement'/'the new strategy' vis-à-vis the foreign companies in South Africa. Pursuing studies in political science and specializing in the economic relations between Sweden and South Africa, in the early 1970s he joined the international 'Study Project on External Investment in South Africa and Namibia', which also covered the United States, Great Britain and the Federal Republic of Germany. In Sweden, the research was supported by the Scandinavian Institute of African Studies (later Nordic Africa Institute), which in 1974 published Magnusson's first study on Sweden and South Africa (op. cit.). The project was heavily criticized by ANC and the anti-apartheid movement (cf. Mai Palmberg: 'Det Är ANC's Kamp det Handlar Om'/'It's All about ANC's Struggle' in *Phambili*, No. 1, March-May 1975, pp. 7-9, and 'LO och TCO: För eller Emot Svenska Investeringar?'/'LO and TCO: For or Against Swedish Investments?' in *Södra Afrika Informationsbulletin*, No. 27, February 1975, pp. 4-6). Concerned with Southern Africa since the early 1960s, Magnusson's involvement with Sweden's relations towards the region has been remarkable. As chairman of the Students Development Fund, in 1968 he led the Swedish university students' fund-raising campaigns for FRELIMO. In 1973-77, he assisted the Swedish Ecumenical Council with its survey of Swedish owned companies in South Africa; in January-February 1975, he served as secretary on the LO-TCO mission to South Africa; and in 1977-78, he occupied the same position on the government appointed committee which prepared the 1979 legislation against new Swedish investments. When in June 1979 Magnusson defended his doctoral dissertation on 'South Africa in the World' (*Sydafrika i Världen* op. cit.), Carl Lidbom of the Social Democratic Party and David Wirmark of the Liberal Party—both political appointees on the committee which prepared the investment ban—served as informal discussants (Britt-Marie Mattsson: 'Lidbom om Sydafrika: Regimen dödsdömd på sikt'/'Lidbom on South Africa: The regime is in the long run condemned to death' in *Göteborgs-Posten*, 2 June 1979). Starting his career in the anti-imperialist student movement and having worked for the churches, the trade unions and the state, Magnusson had at that time already brought his knowledge and experience to big business, subsequently becoming executive director at the International Council of Swedish Industry (*Näringslivets Internationella Råd*). Cf. the interviews with Åke Magnusson (pp. 315-20) and Sören Lindh (pp. 306-07).
2. Magnusson (1974) op. cit., pp. 143-52.
3. Baldwin Sjollema: 'Eloquent Action' in Webb (ed.) op. cit., p. 20.
4. Ibid. See also Baldwin Sjollema: 'The World Council of Churches: Policies and Programmes in Support of the Liberation Struggle in Southern Africa' in Stokke and Widstrand (eds) op. cit. (Vol. II), pp. 25-32. Between 1970 and 1981, Sjollema was the first Director of WCC's Programme to Combat Racism.
5. Sjollema in Webb (ed.) op. cit., p. 20. As noted in the Prologue, the pietism of the evangelical churches initially held them back from WCC's more political positions. With regard to the Church of Sweden and the issue of investments in South Africa, it should in addition be noted that Chief Buthelezi through his long-standing relations with the Swedish mission in Zululand exercised considerable influence. Visiting the Church of Sweden Mission headquarters in Uppsala in mid-December 1972, he criticized the stand taken by WCC four months earlier, calling instead for more foreign investments (CSM: 'Minnesanteckningar från besök av Chief Gatsha Buthelezi och Rev. E. Sikakane i Uppsala den 19 december 1972'/'Notes from visit by Chief Gatsha Buthelezi and Reverend E. Sikakane, Uppsala, 19 December 1972') (CSA).
6. The initial decision to establish an ecumenical programme against racism was taken at WCC's fourth assembly meeting in Uppsala, Sweden, in 1968. Through PCR—formally set up in 1969—WCC channelled assistance to the Southern African liberation movements.

Volvo cars assembled
at the Volkswagen factory
in Uitenhage, South Africa,
1974 (Photo: Sven Ivan
Sundqvist/Pressens Bild)

the Swedish companies established on the South African market, such as ASEA, Electrolux and Volvo.[1] Thus, both the majority and the minority positions expressed at the Utrecht meeting called for action, whether in the form of disinvestment (isolation) or in favour of social and labour reforms (involvement). In order to establish a definite policy, following the WCC meeting it was therefore decided that the Swedish Ecumenical Council (SEN)[2]—the umbrella organization of the national Christian denominations through which both official and church assistance to PCR was mainly channelled[3]—should carry out a survey of the member churches' indirect economic links with the apartheid republic, as well as assess the labour conditions at the Swedish-owned companies in the country.

At the beginning of the 1970s, some twenty Swedish private companies were active in South Africa.[4] In addition to marketing firms and companies represented through local agents—in the latter category notably the car manufacturer Volvo[5]—there were eight production companies. Six of these were majority-owned, while two were controlled from Sweden through minority interests. Most of the manufacturing firms were in the strategic metal industry, cooperating with or servicing the South African mining corporations.[6] All of them formed part of Sweden's leading international business concerns. From the point of view of company employment outside Sweden, the six concerns with majority-owned South African subsidiaries[7]

---

1. Letters from the Church of Sweden Mission to the companies mentioned, Uppsala, 8 March, 11 May and 21 May 1976 (CSA).
2. In Swedish, *Svenska Ekumeniska Nämnden*. Set up in 1932, SEN was in 1992 replaced by the Christian Council of Sweden (*Sveriges Kristna Råd*).
3. Official Swedish contributions to PCR were granted from the financial year 1970/71 (CCHA: 'Ansökan från Svenska Ekumeniska Nämnden om stöd till Kyrkornas Världsråd's Program för Kampen mot Rasism'/ 'Request from SEN to WCC's PCR', SIDA, Stockholm, 8 January 1979) (SDA).
4. There were no publicly owned companies. However, the Scandinavian Airlines System (SAS)—jointly owned by the governments of Denmark, Norway and Sweden—operated a weekly air service between Copenhagen and Johannesburg. It was only in 1985 that the three Scandinavian governments put an end to the controversial traffic.
5. Volvo was represented through Lawson Motors, a local general sales agent. In 1962, Lawson Motors started to assemble Volvo passenger cars and heavy-duty trucks in South Africa. The car assembly took place at the Volkswagen factory in Uitenhage outside Port Elizabeth, while trucks were produced in Durban.
6. Sellström Volume I, pp. 122-23.
7. Alfa-Laval, Atlas Copco, Electrolux, Fagersta, Sandvik and SKF.

held overall positions between 1 and 17.[1] Four of them belonged to Sweden's six most internationalized companies, namely SKF (No. 1), Electrolux (4), Alfa-Laval (5) and Atlas Copco (6). Together with ASEA (10), these companies were, in addition, important flagships in the 'Wallenberg empire', which through its uniquely powerful position in the Swedish economy exercised considerable political leverage.[2]

While the motives behind the original establishment of the Swedish manufacturing companies had been commercial, over the years two of them—both belonging to the Wallenberg group—entered into a particularly close relationship with the apartheid state. ASEA—which with two plants and 1,150 employees was by 1972 the largest Swedish concern in South Africa[3] —produced electrical cables, transformers and isolators for the parastatal Iron and Steel Corporation (ISCOR), the country's largest steelworks.

In the case of the ball bearing manufacturer SKF, the links were closely related to South Africa's defence industry. SKF had as early as in 1914 established a marketing company in the country. In the early 1960s—when the South African government was threatened with international sanctions[4] and the economic policy of import substitution required unrestricted access to ball bearings, not least for military equipment—it requested the Swedish company to localize the manufacture of the strategic product.[5] Provided with special protection by the apartheid state[6], SKF accepted the privileged offer in 1963 and set up a plant in Uitenhage the following year. As noted by Magnusson, "even though SKF claim[ed] to be non-political" it took advantage of South Africa's "strategic security interests [...] to become involved in and partly exploit a politically sensitive situation".[7] The involvement with the apartheid state was later demonstrated by the fact that the chairman of the board of SKF South Africa was a leading member of the secretive *Afrikaner Broederbond*, with direct links to the South African government.[8]

ASEA[9] and SKF would in the 1970s and 1980s feature prominently in the Swedish sanctions debate. In ASEA's case this was far from a novel situation. The management of the Västerås-based company had in 1963 strongly condemned the consumer boycott campaign by SUL, KF and the South Africa Committees. Director Åke Vrethem had at the time characterized South Africa as "the most distinguished outpost and supporting pillar of civilization in Africa".[10] This provoked strong reactions from the Swedish solidarity movement, and in conjunction with the 1968 Båstad demonstrations and the 1968-69 Cabora Bassa debate[11] the opposition against ASEA and the wider 'Wallenberg empire' became particularly out-

---

1. Magnusson (1974) op. cit., Table 19, p. 76.
2. On the 'Wallenberg empire', see Sellström Volume I, pp. 33-34.
3. Magnusson (1974) op. cit., Table 20, p. 77.
4. In August 1963, the UN Security Council recommended all member states "to cease forthwith the sale and shipment of arms, ammunition of all types and military vehicles to South Africa" (UN Security Council Resolution 181 of 7 August 1963).
5. Self-adjusting ball bearings were a Swedish invention and the globally dominant SKF (*Svenska Kullagerfabriken*) was set up in Gothenburg in 1907. In turn, it *inter alia* paved the way for the car manufacturer Volvo ('I roll') in the 1920s.
6. An import duty of 30 per cent was imposed on American and Japanese ball bearings (Magnusson (1974) op. cit., p. 84).
7. Ibid. p. 85.
8. 'SKF's Styrelse med i Broederbond' ('SKF's Board with the Broederbond') in *Afrikabulletinen*, No. 72-73, 1983, p. 32.
9. In 1988, ASEA merged with the Swiss company Brown Boveri, subsequently operating as ABB (Asea Brown Boveri).
10. See Sellström Volume I, pp. 203 and 489.
11. Ibid., pp. 348-53 and 483-502.

spoken. When South Africa in the late 1970s within its 'total strategy' embarked on military operations against SWAPO, ANC and the Southern African Frontline States, SKF replaced ASEA as the prime target of popular criticism.[1]

SEN began its survey in June 1973. In addition to sending questionnaires to the relevant Swedish companies and holding discussions with local trade unions and the Federation of Swedish Industries[2], the responsible coordinator, Lester Wikström from the Church of Sweden Mission, enlisted the cooperation of Åke Magnusson at the University of Gothenburg. The mapping exercise proved more difficult than envisaged. At the end of the year, Wikström informed Anders Möllander from the Ministry for Foreign Affairs that "several of the Swedish companies which had been listed by WCC as active in Southern Africa had either failed to reply or had [stated] that they had no activity there".[3] Finally, only seven of the nearly twenty companies bothered to respond.[4]

Nevertheless, with regard to salary structures, union rights and general working conditions, Magnusson was through his parallel research able to conclude that nothing distinguished the Swedish companies from other companies in South Africa, adding that "it would be wrong to maintain that [they] are unaware of how most of the African labour force live. They know very well that the majority of the African employees live in social misery".[5] Sven-Ivan Sundqvist, a business editor of the liberal newspaper *Dagens Nyheter* who in 1974 during two visits to South Africa had studied the Swedish companies in the country, arrived at similar conclusions. In a book that attracted much attention, he noted in the same year that "Swedish companies have not led the way with regard to black workers' unionization". In addition, Sundqvist ventured the opinion that "the majority of the Swedish companies pay starvation wages or [only] slightly above".[6]

In spite of the 1972 WCC resolution and the Swedish parent companies' reluctance to constructively contribute to the ecumenical study, in March 1974—after the ILO conference in Geneva—SEN adopted a programme of action which rejected the isolation policy and embraced the so called 'new strategy'. Chairing the council, Archbishop Olof Sundby of the Church of Sweden explained that the official church "did not intend to sell its shares [in the Swedish companies concerned], as withdrawal [would mean] that we are completely out of the picture and, thus, unable to continue our efforts to improve the conditions in South Africa".[7] Shareholdings would instead be used to monitor the performance of the companies, which according to the programme of action

---

1. The labour links between the parent company in Gothenburg and the factory in Uitenhage were at the same time close. Cf. the interview with John Gomomo, p. 129.
2. In Swedish, *Sveriges Industriförbund* (SIF).
3. Anders Möllander: Memorandum ('Svenska Ekumeniska Nämndens undersökning av svenska börsnoterade bolags, politiska partiers, kyrkors och missionsorganisationers engagemang i södra Afrika'/'SEN's survey of the involvement in Southern Africa by Swedish companies quoted on the stock exchange, political parties, churches and missionary organizations'), Ministry for Foreign Affairs, Stockholm, 18 December 1973 (SDA). Although CSM owned almost 10,000 Volvo shares, by December 1973 the company had not reacted to the questionnaire submitted six months earlier (ibid.).
4. Johan Schück: 'Förbud i Sydafrika' ('Prohibition in South Africa') in *Dagens Nyheter*, 15 June 1974.
5. Magnusson (1974) op. cit., p. 111.
6. Sundqvist op. cit., p. 189. Recalling the situation in the mid-1970s—when he worked at the Volkswagen factory in Uitenhage where Volvo cars were assembled—in 1996 the COSATU President John Gomomo stated: "In those days, the behaviour of the management at the Swedish owned companies was no better than that at any of the South African companies. [It] was clearly the attitude of the [apartheid] government" (Interview with John Gomomo, p. 129).
7. Hans Gréen: 'Kyrkan manar företag ge lika lön i Sydafrika' ('The church calls on companies to give equal wages in South Africa') in *Dagens Nyheter*, 19 March 1974. Only in mid-1986—at the time of the third national sanctions debate—did the Church of Sweden start to sell off its shares in the Swedish South Africa companies ('Kyrkan visar vägen'/'The church shows the way' in *Arbetet*, 2 June 1986).

a) during the period 1974-1976, [...] should undertake to considerably reduce the wage differences between white and black workers; b) take rapid measures to strengthen the[ir] social
responsibility towards the black workers; and c) draw up an ethical code for corporate action. [1]

Criticized by several organizations who demanded immediate action—among them
the Christian Student Movement in Sweden[2] and the Liberal Party Youth
League[3]—the churches gave the Swedish parent companies with subsidiaries in
South Africa a respite of two years to improve the conditions for their black
employees. If the measures demanded by the companies had not been implemented
by the end of 1976, SEN would "demand [...] Swedish legislation [...] to regulate
business activities in South Africa".[4]

The Social Democratic government had in 1973 issued "special instructions" to
the Swedish legation in Pretoria "not to act in such a way as to convey the impression that investments in South Africa are supported by the Swedish authorities".[5]
While the churches monitored their subsidiaries, the parent companies, however,
hardly reacted to the public concerns. Responding to the ecumenical council's
request for a voluntary code of ethical conduct, on behalf of the manufacturing
firms represented in South Africa the powerful Federation of Swedish Industries
declared in 1974 that

> considerable efforts to improve the conditions of its African employees are already being car-
> ried out by South African industry. [...] Swedish industry is convinced that the possibility exists
> for significant economic progress for Africans in South Africa and that concrete results can and
> must be achieved within the existing legal and political framework.[6]

Thus acknowledging the apartheid 'order'[7], during the great debate on Sweden's
economic links with South Africa in the mid-1970s the dominant private business
concerns drew a line between themselves and an overwhelming public and political
opinion. As before in the mid-1960s, and later in the mid-1980s, Sweden's leading
international capital and export interests—at the political level primarily represented by the Moderate Party—not only firmly opposed economic sanctions, but
also official assistance to ANC.

1. Cited in Magnusson (1974) op. cit., p. 148.
2. In Swedish, *Kristna Studentrörelsen i Sverige* (KRISS). Cf. 'Studentprotest: En aktie räcker för insyn' ('Student protest: One share is enough for insights') in *Dagens Nyheter*, 19 March 1974.
3. Johan Schück: 'Förbud i Sydafrika' ('Prohibition in South Africa') in *Dagens Nyheter*, 15 June 1974. Chairing the Liberal Party Youth League, Schück criticized the SEN survey and action programme, demanding an investment ban.
4. Cited in Magnusson (1974) op. cit., p. 148.
5. Cited in 'Press release', 23 July 1974, in Ministry for Foreign Affairs: *Documents on Swedish Foreign Policy: 1974*, Stockholm, 1976, p. 171. In the absence of a binding resolution by the UN Security Council, the gov-ernment's position was officially to distance itself from Swedish private investments in the apartheid republic, leaving the core issues to be voluntarily decided by the companies themselves. The ambiguity was illustrated in the mid-1970s on many occasions. In February 1974, for example, a government working group submitted a memorandum on 'Guidelines for assessing permits concerning direct Swedish investments abroad'. Although they emphasized that Swedish investments in the Portuguese colonies were undesirable, in the case of South Africa the question was not discussed at all (Magnusson (1974) op. cit., p. 160).
6. Cited in Johan Schück: 'Sydafrika: Företagens Paradis och Rasförtryckets Helvete' ('South Africa: Heaven for Business and Hell for Racial Oppresssion') in *Liberal Debatt*, No. 2, 1975, p. 12.
7. Despite the Wallenberg family's motto 'To be, but not to be seen', over the years the NIR chairman Peter Wal-lenberg—who between 1959 and 1962 led Atlas Copco's operations in Rhodesia and Congo and repeatedly referred to that experience—often made extraordinary public statements with racist connotations (cf. Sell-ström Volume I, p. 43). Commenting upon apartheid and South Africa's future prospects, in a television inter-view in September 1994—that is, after ANC's electoral victory in South Africa—he not only stated that "the apartheid system [...] had some aspects that were necessary under the prevailing circumstances", but that South Africa's blacks would "absolutely not [manage without the whites]". Adding that "blacks [...] simply do not have the required competence", the leading industrialist concluded that "they are at about the level of development where we were 100 or 150 years ago" (Interview by Stina Dabrowski in 'Stina möter Peter Wal-lenberg' ('Stina meets Peter Wallenberg'), TV 4, Stockholm, 12 September 1994).

Seemingly unaware of the apartheid racist constitution, a significant, 75 page policy statement from the International Council of Swedish Industry (NIR)—partly drafted by the ubiquitous Åke Magnusson, by then attached to the business council chaired by Peter Wallenberg[1]—maintained as late as in 1983 that "South Africa is not unique" and that Swedish companies "have to follow the laws of the host country, in all essentials adapting to prevailing local business and labour customs". Turning against the 1979 Swedish investment ban, the council advanced both economic arguments and explicit political opinions. It declared that the Swedish government through its assistance to ANC not only backed "a confrontational line" which "further [...] isolates us from the Western world", but contributed to "undermining the authority and credibility of the [United Nations]".[2] At a time when hostile relations between the non-racial ANC and the Zulu-based Inkatha movement were manifest, NIR also stated that

> no consideration has been taken of [the fact that] in South Africa there are big groups of black citizens who do not at all advocate or believe in the road of violence and confrontation. The millions of blacks represented by the Inkatha movement are among these. [...] Through its decision on sanctions, Sweden has chosen to support one—but only one—of the opinions among the blacks in South Africa. By so doing, [it] has excluded the many blacks who prefer non-violent methods, economic development and political mobilization to sabotage, guerrilla warfare and, perhaps, ultimately civil war.[3]

Mbeki and Isolation

In accordance with its programme of action, SEN continued to monitor the Swedish South Africa firms. New initiatives were carried out vis-à-vis the parent companies, and in early 1975 Lester Wikström went on a fact-finding tour to South and Southern Africa.[4] Above all, using their rights as shareholders the member churches regularly attended the companies' annual meetings in Sweden. In an extraordinary exchange on ethics and profits, in March 1975 Olof Sundby, the Archbishop of the official Church of Sweden, confronted the leadership of ASEA—including Marcus

1. In addition to Magnusson, representatives from Alfa-Laval, Atlas Copco, Fagersta, Sandvik, SKF and Transatlantic formed part of the editorial board.
2. Näringslivets Internationella Råd: *Sydafrika och Svenskt Näringsliv* ('South Africa and Swedish Industry'), NIR, Lund, 1983, pp. 9 and 24-26.
3. Ibid., p. 24. With its remarkable political comments, in the Swedish context the NIR publication was exceptional. With regard to Inkatha, for example, there were in 1983 no parliamentary parties or established NGOs that advocated assistance to the movement led by Chief Buthelezi. Apart from the fact that the Zulu organization was hardly non-confrontational or non-violent, its trade union support at the Swedish owned companies in South Africa was extremely marginal. Against this background, it is far from clear what information the prestigious business council used when it in a widely disseminated policy statement on Sweden's economic links with South Africa presented Inkatha as a political alternative. In fact, the only other Swedish voice which was raised at the time in favour of the organization was that of the marginal, extreme right wing journal *Contra*. Together with its advocacy of UNITA of Angola, from 1983 the journal gave increasing attention to Buthelezi and Inkatha (cf. the interview with Buthelezi in *Contra*, No. 6, 1983).
4. Sven-Ivan Sundqvist from *Dagens Nyheter* had noted during his visits to South Africa in May and September 1974 that "all the Swedish companies in South Africa are probably aware of the fact that their products are sold to Rhodesia" (Sundqvist op. cit., p. 191). As this would have been in violation of the Swedish Rhodesia Law of June 1969, Wikström included a visit to the then Rhodesia in his tour. Although representing the Church of Sweden Mission and its close, historical connections with the country, he was as *persona non grata* denied entry by the Smith regime (Letter to the author from Lester Wikström, Uppsala, 26 May 1999).

Wallenberg—on the conditions at the biggest Swedish subsidiary in South Africa.[1] Eventually, however, the ecumenical council had to conclude that its policy of 'constructive involvement' did not lead to the desired results. In December 1976—at the end of the period of grace accorded for voluntary corporate action—Wikström reported that "no decisive improvements have taken place for the employees at [the] Swedish companies in South Africa".[2] Although still not advocating outright disinvestment, in May 1977 SEN adopted a new programme of action. Stating that the "companies which have chosen to establish [business activities] in South Africa are benefiting from legislated injustice", it concluded that

> the Swedish authorities must as soon as possible establish how the financial legislation can be changed in order to stop export of capital to South Africa. They should also establish how Sweden in other ways can minimize its economic relations with South Africa, thereby contributing to economic and political isolation [of the apartheid regime].[3]

By also proposing a severance of bilateral trade relations, the resolution was an important call for unilateral Swedish action. Combined with demands for "a considerable increase" of the official anti-apartheid support[4], the churches significantly influenced the parliamentary parties and the government. Supported by the opposition Social Democratic Party[5], in June 1977 the Fälldin government appointed a committee which essentially was mandated to study the issues raised in SEN's programme of action. Although cautious with regard to WCC's isolation policy, the 'new strategy' followed by the ecumenical council and the dominant Church of

---

1. Verbatim report attached to memorandum by Olle Dahlén ('Svenska företagsinvesteringar i Sydafrika: Diskussion vid bolagsstämman med ASEA och Volvo'/'Swedish corporate investments in South Africa: Discussion[s] at the shareholders' meeting[s] with ASEA and Volvo'), Ministry for Foreign Affairs, Stockholm, 20 May 1975 (MFA). The meeting with ASEA in Västerås took place on 14 March 1975. The Church of Sweden's involvement upset conservative opinion. When in late 1985 Bertil Werkström, Sundby's successor as Archbishop, attended a WCC meeting in Harare where sanctions against South Africa were discussed, *Svensk Tidskrift* censured the head of the official church. At the time, Margaretha af Ugglas—a Moderate member of the SIDA board (1976-89) and future Foreign Minister (1991-94)—served as chief editor of the journal. Reacting to the Archbishop's participation at the WCC meeting, in an editorial *Svensk Tidskrift* declared that "on issues of foreign policy he does [...] not speak for Sweden, nor for the Church of Sweden or even for his own diocese. He only speaks for himself" ('Ärkebiskopens Utrikespolitik'/'The Archbishop's Foreign Policy' in *Svensk Tidskrift*, No. 1, 1986, p. 6). In the same issue, the journal published an article entitled 'Don't Support ANC's Terror Policies' ('Stöd Ej ANC's Terrorpolitik') by the Swedish right wing extremist Tommy Hansson, lumping together ANC, the Soviet Union, the World Council of Churches and the Church of Sweden (pp. 67-68). It was, however, rather af Ugglas who spoke for herself. With her strong links to some of the Swedish concerns in South Africa—both through family ownership (notably in Fagersta and Sandvik) and as a member of several company boards (*inter alia* of Swedish Match AB)—she was a far from independent observer. It could be noted that Archbishop Werkström was denied a visa to South Africa in late 1986 (Carl Johan Persson: Memorandum ('Referat från möte med nordiska arbetsgruppen för åtgärder mot Sydafrika'/ 'Report from [a] meeting with the Nordic working group on measures against South Africa'), Ministry for Foreign Affairs, Stockholm, 11 December 1986) (SDA).
2. Lester Wikström: 'Rapport till SEN 8.12.1976 från IUs sekr. Lester Wikström ang. svenskt ekonomiskt engagemang i södra Afrika' ('Report to SEN, 8 December 1976, from the international committee's secretary Lester Wikström regarding Swedish economic involvement in Southern Africa'), Uppsala, 7 December 1976 (CSA).
3. 'Svenska Ekumeniska Nämndens Handlingsprogram för Svenskt Engagemang i Sydafrika' ('SEN's Programme of Action on Sweden's Involvement in South Africa') in *Svensk Missionstidskrift*, No. 3, 1977, p. 191.
4. Ibid., p. 192.
5. It should be noted that Prime Minister Palme—who the following month lost the parliamentary elections to Fälldin's coalition—in August 1976 chose the congress of the Brotherhood Movement to launch his offensive against apartheid, *inter alia* stating that "we must seriously consider the question of [Swedish] company representation and new investments in South Africa" (Olof Palme: 'Address given at the congress of the Swedish Association of Christian Social Democrats', Skövde, 6 August 1976) (LMA). Interviewed in 1996, C.H. Hermansson, the former chairman of the Swedish Communist Party/Left Party Communists, underlined the progressive role played by the churches. In his opinion, this could explain why Palme often introduced radical and largely controversial policy initiatives via the Christian Social Democrats rather than through LO. According to Hermansson, "there he had support at once. It would have been much more difficult [...] to get support at the party or trade union congresses" (Interview with C.H. Hermansson, p. 292).

Sweden thus paved the way for the 1979 ban on new investments in South Africa. In the case of the labour movement, the same policy was considerably more controversial. By focusing on the creation of black trade unions, along different paths it too, however, would effectively contribute to the eventual demise of the apartheid regime.

The Swedish trade union debate on apartheid came in particular to the fore in connection with a visit by LO and TCO to South Africa in January-February 1975. This debate will be summarized below. In the meantime, it should be underlined that the resurgence of an active Swedish anti-apartheid opinion in 1974 largely resulted from the commitment by the churches. By concentrating their attention on Sweden's economic relations with South Africa, they forced the major national political actors to take a stand. While the political parties were defining their positions and the media again dedicated significant attention to apartheid, in 1974-75 a number of conferences, meetings and visits concerning South Africa were arranged. Little known in this context is the role played by South Africa's future President Thabo Mbeki during his first visit to Sweden in November-December 1974.

As in the case two years earlier of Chris Hani (alias Zenzile Msethu), Mbeki's first visit to Sweden was made on behalf of Oliver Tambo for a meeting arranged by the Liberal Party. It took place at a time when the apartheid regime appeared to be breaking down the barriers of isolation, threatening ANC's recent diplomatic advances in Southern Africa.[1] Shortly before the visit, Prime Minister Vorster of South Africa and President Kaunda of Zambia had launched their regional 'détente exercise'.[2] In addition, Gatsha Buthelezi had just been to Sweden. In defiance of ANC's calls for economic sanctions, he had together with other homeland leaders publicly invited foreign investors to South Africa, notably through full-page advertisements in *The Economist* of London.[3] While Buthelezi's visit in early November 1974 was primarily dedicated to discussions with the Church of Sweden Mission in Uppsala[4], during his stay he repeated the appeals for investments. Finally, when Mbeki arrived in Stockholm LO and TCO—the blue- and white-collar workers' trade union confederations—had decided to carry out their fact-finding mission to South Africa.

During his stay, the rising ANC leader "engaged in some of the earliest discussions which led to the Swedish government and people evolving into some of the strongest supporters of the South African liberation struggle".[5] Standing in for

1. Mbeki had spent the greater part of 1973 and 1974 in the 'forward area' of Botswana, where he obtained permission to open an ANC office.

2. In subsequent meetings with the Swedish authorities Mbeki strongly criticized Zambia's contacts with the apartheid regime (cf. Arne Ström: Memorandum ('Minnesanteckningar från möte med Thabo Mbeki, informationssekreterare till ANC's exekutiv'/'Notes from meeting with Thabo Mbeki, information secretary on ANC's executive'), SIDA, Stockholm, 2 December 1974) (SDA). The ruling Social Democratic Party had in November 1974 invited SWAPO President Sam Nujoma and ZANU Chairman Herbert Chitepo for discussions on the political developments in Southern Africa. Nujoma's visit to Stockholm took place between 29 October and 2 November, while Chitepo stayed from 16 to 20 November. Also invited by the Social Democratic Party, Oliver Tambo came to Stockholm in early February 1975. Like Nujoma and Chitepo, he met Prime Minister Olof Palme and Foreign Minister Sven Andersson (Ulf Hagman: 'LO-TCO's Sydafrikabesök: Svart ledare kritisk'/'LO-TCO's South Africa visit: Black leader critical' in *Svenska Dagbladet*, 7 February 1975).

3. *The Economist*, 29 June 1974. In the remarkable advertisement, Buthelezi and three of his colleagues—among them Kaiser Matanzima, Chief Minister of the Transkei—stated that "South Africa has the most stable government on the African continent" and that "we do not suffer from militant trade unions". Inviting foreign investors to the homelands, they promised cash grants, low-interest loans, tax concessions and "problem-free labour resources".

4. 'Zululedare på Uppsalabesök: Underutvecklingen vårt största problem' ('Zulu leader visiting Uppsala: Underdevelopment our biggest problem') in *Upsala Nya Tidning*, 5 November 1974.

5. 'Biographical Sketch of Thabo Mbeki' in Mbeki op. cit., p. xix.

Oliver Tambo, Mbeki primarily attended an international conference on global development, co-hosted by the Swedish Liberal Party and the West German Friedrich Naumann Foundation in Stockholm between 24 and 29 November 1974. In addition, he appeared on Swedish television, participated in public debates and was received at SIDA and the Ministry for Foreign Affairs. As later stated by some of the Swedish interlocutors, his principled arguments left a lasting impression.

The international conference on 'Rich and Poor – New Approaches towards a Global Development Strategy' was attended by some 70 prominent participants from nearly 30 countries. David Wirmark of the Swedish Liberal Party chaired the proceedings. Although mainly concerned with issues of economic development, the conference also discussed political events in South and Southern Africa. Here, Mbeki was the main speaker. Warning against the illusion that apartheid had "changed [its] stripes" and emphasizing that the conflict in South and Southern Africa remained the same, he forcefully criticized any 'constructive involvement' with South Africa.[1] Stating that "it is absolutely necessary [...] to intensify [the] campaign for the isolation of South Africa", he explained:

> We would have liked to [...] come here [...] and talk about the problems of the rich and the poor. As South Africans, I think [that] we would [have spoken] from the side of the rich. Our country is very rich. [...] But, unfortunately, we cannot at this stage talk about our own contribution to the solution of the problem of the rich and the poor. There is another problem which has to be solved first. [...]
>
> I am very mindful [...] of what is happening in the rest of the world, the absence of human rights and so on. [However,] I do not think that there is any other country [...] which says: 'You, because your face is black and your hair is [not] like mine, you cannot sit in the parliament [or] vote'. I do not think that there is such a country in the world. I do not think that there is [...] a country [...] which says that 'because you are an African you cannot become a Bishop of the Dutch Reformed Church'. Such a country does not exist anywhere in the world, except South Africa. [...]
>
> The [United Nations] has [...] declared apartheid a crime against humanity, and a crime against humanity has to be punished by humanity. But what is being done? What are the people that have [...] the power to do something doing in terms of punishing this crime? There are, naturally, all sorts of pressures that can be brought to bear. [...] [T]ake up the matter of [...] withdrawal of investments from the countries which are the culprits, [t]hat is England, America, Japan and also Sweden! This is where the greatest possible attention has to be given [...].[2]

Representing the Liberal Party, David Wirmark was in July 1977 appointed by the government to the committee which the following year recommended a ban on new Swedish investments in South Africa. With close relations to ANC since the early 1960s, he later stated that it was Mbeki's intervention at the Stockholm conference in November 1974 that finally convinced him of the need for unilateral, official sanctions.[3]

During the first of his frequent visits to Sweden, Mbeki also appeared in public debates and on television. On 28 November 1974, he represented ANC at a well attended meeting on 'isolation versus the new strategy' arranged by the Swedish Development Forum. Chaired by the Social Democratic MP Birgitta Dahl, Åke Magnusson and Sven-Ivan Sundqvist, Douglas van Reis from ASEA and Anders

---

1. On this point, Mbeki *inter alia* rejected arguments advanced by Olle Engström, a member of both the Swedish Liberal Party and the Central Committee of the World Council of Churches.
2. Mbeki cited in David Wirmark (ed.): *The Rich and the Poor: New Approaches towards a Global Development Strategy*, Bokförlaget Folk och Samhälle, Stockholm, 1975, pp. 61-82.
3. Conversation with David Wirmark, Stockholm, 20 February 1996.

'Apartheid is good
for business': ANC's
Thabo Mbeki on
Swedish television,
November 1974

Pers from the Federation of Swedish Industries were also on the panel, as well as
Mai Palmberg and Dick Urban Vestbro from the Africa Groups. Here again, the
young ANC leader firmly underlined his movement's position. Noting that "it may
be that ASEA hates apartheid, but [essentially] likes profits"[1], he demanded that
the Swedish companies of their own volition should withdraw from the apartheid
economy. That would not lead to the downfall of the system, but weaken the
regime.[2] Commenting upon Buthelezi's recent statements, in an interview on Swedish television Mbeki, finally, declared that

> [n]o good can come out of [foreign] investments. We've got to understand the fact that what
> [has] attracted foreign investment to South Africa is the presence of [...] cheap, black labour.
> [...] [A]partheid is good for business. Apartheid means cheap labour. [...] The whole system is
> designed to keep the African worker in such a position that he provides cheap labour. There-
> fore, the inflow of foreign investment into South Africa [...] cannot in any sense be said to help
> the position of the black people in the country.[3]

A Controversial Mission

The ILO International Conference of Trade Unions against Apartheid was held in
Geneva in June 1973. Attended by 380 delegates from more than 200 trade union
organizations, it brought together for the first time since 1948 the three dominant
labour internationals, that is, the Western-aligned International Confederation of
Free Trade Unions (ICFTU), the Communist-dominated World Federation of Trade
Unions (WFTU) and the much smaller, Christian-inspired World Confederation of
Labour (WCL). The ICFTU-affiliated LO and TCO represented the Swedish blue-
and white-collar workers.[4] Coming from South Africa, the collaborationist Trade
Union Council of South Africa (TUCSA)—which did not accept black member
unions, opposed sanctions and welcomed foreign investments—tried hard to be

---

1. In January 1976, the Left Party Communists quoted this sentence in a parliamentary motion demanding a ban
   on Swedish investments in South Africa (Swedish Parliament 1975/76: Motion No. 1134, Riksdagens Protokoll 1975/76, p. 14).
2. 'Sydafrikadebatt: Svenska företag stärker regimen' ('South Africa debate: Swedish companies strengthen the
   regime') in *Dagens Nyheter*, 29 November 1974. On behalf of the Federation of Swedish Industries, Pers
   maintained that "if we withdraw there is no possibility of improving the situation of the black workers". This
   argument was constantly advanced by Swedish business interests against isolation. Although under public
   pressure, the Swedish companies in South Africa would, however, between 1974 and 1976 not introduce any
   decisive improvements with regard to social and labour conditions.
3. Thabo Mbeki on the news programme *Rapport*, TV 2, 5 December 1974.
4. Magnusson (1974) op. cit., p. 149.

accepted, but was effectively isolated. Instead, ANC's ally SACTU was widely seen
to represent the South African workers. Firmly advocating a policy of isolation, the
WFTU-affiliated organization managed to gain recognition beyond the Cold War
confines.[1] For the SACTU leadership in exile, the Geneva meeting represented a significant, albeit short-lived, international breakthrough.[2]

Like the WCC meeting in August 1972, the Geneva conference upheld the UN
General Assembly's calls for total isolation of the apartheid regime. As in the case
of WCC, however, the final declaration—subsequently endorsed by the General
Assembly[3]—also left openings for direct involvement by the international trade
union movement. "Strongly urg[ing] all workers and their trade union organizations—irrespective of international, continental, political or religious affiliations—
to give full support to the oppressed workers in South Africa", the resolution
emphasized the importance of

> financial, moral and material support to the workers and people of South Africa through their
> authentic trade union and political organizations.[4]

SACTU—later launching the slogan 'Direct links stink!'[5]—interpreted on good
grounds the Geneva resolution as imposing "a strong moral obligation on the
[international] trade union movement to [...] generally sever [...] communications
and, indeed, any social ties with the land of [a]partheid".[6] Under pressure from the
churches and the mounting debate on Sweden's economic links with South Africa[7],
LO and TCO, however, focused on the appeal for direct support. At a time when

---

1. The non-racial South African Congress of Trade Unions (SACTU) was formed in March 1955, in reaction to
   a decision by the South African Trades and Labour Council to exclude unions with African members and to
   reconstitute itself as the racially exclusive Trade Union Council of South Africa. With a membership of some
   20,000 workers in 19 unions in 1956, the central organization grew rapidly. By 1961, more than 53,000
   workers—including 39,000 Africans—from 51 unions were represented by SACTU. From the outset, SACTU
   argued that the struggle against economic exploitation was inextricably linked to the wider, political issue of
   the emancipation of the oppressed people as a whole. From this followed SACTU's participation in the Congress Alliance. Many of its representatives were also leading members of ANC and/or SACP. Although never
   formally proscribed, SACTU was severely attacked by the apartheid regime after the 1960 Sharpeville massacre and during the ensuing wave of repression, resulting in the arrest of around 160 activists. Many SACTU
   members had already joined MK in South Africa. When forced into exile, others opted for military training
   rather than trade union work. Shortly after its foundation in 1955, SACTU voted to affiliate to WFTU. As
   noted by Southall, however, SACTU's links with WFTU were initially loose. "It never paid any affiliation fees
   and 'for reasons of security' WFTU never regarded its association with SACTU as official. Nor is there available record of SACTU being the recipient of WFTU funding" (Roger Southall: *Imperialism or Solidarity?:
   International Labour and South African Trade Unions*, UCT Press, Rondebosch, 1995, p. 102). In fact,
   SACTU attempted to have cordial relations with both ICFTU and WFTU, but due to the former's opposition
   this balancing act was not successful. On SACTU's early history, see Ken Luckhardt and Brenda Wall: *Organize or Starve!: The History of the South African Congress of Trade Unions*, Lawrence and Wishart, London,
   1980.
2. Cf. R.E. Matajo: 'A New Weapon to Smash Trade Union Apartheid' in *The African Communist*, No. 55,
   Fourth Quarter 1973, pp. 57-68. General Secretary Mark Shope and Vice-President Moses Mabhida led the
   SACTU delegation to the conference.
3. UN General Assembly Resolution 3151 A of 14 December 1973.
4. 'Resolution for Action against Apartheid', cited in LO-TCO: *South Africa: Black Labour-Swedish Capital*, A
   Report by the LO/TCO Study Delegation to South Africa 1975, LO-TCO, Uppsala, 1975, Appendix 3, pp.
   177-78. This is the English version of the original report in Swedish, entitled *Sydafrika: Svart Arbetskraft-
   Svenskt Kapital*, LO-TCO, Uddevalla, 1975. The references below are to the English translation.
5. SACTU's publication *Workers Unity*, Nos. 30, 1982 and 40, 1984, cited in Vesla Vetlesen: 'Trade Union Support to the Struggle Against Apartheid: The Role of the Norwegian Confederation of Trade Unions' in Eriksen (ed.) op. cit., p. 334.
6. Matajo op. cit. in *The African Communist*, No. 55, 1973, p. 60.
7. Writing about the conditions at SKF's Uitenhage plant, Sundqvist concluded in 1974 that "it is hard to understand why the trade union representatives [at the parent company] in Gothenburg throughout all these years
   have avoided visiting South Africa" (Sundqvist op. cit., p. 170). In the report from the 1975 study tour to
   South Africa, LO and TCO wrote that SEN and the books by Magnusson and Sundqvist "to a great extent
   [...] [had] been conducive to the growth of the [Swedish] debate", motivating the controversial visit (LO-TCO
   op. cit., p. 8).

the Social Democratic government embarked on direct cooperation with ANC, together with its Nordic sister organizations and under the ICFTU umbrella the Swedish trade unions embraced the 'new strategy'. This would not only lead to irreconcilable differences between LO and TCO on the one side and SACTU on the other, but during the second half of the 1970s and in the early 1980s also to contradictory policies vis-à-vis ANC's labour ally between the Swedish trade union movement and the government.

While the former eschewed SACTU and—with substantial government resources—became increasingly engaged via ICFTU inside South Africa, the latter entered into direct cooperation with the exiled organization. This, in turn, stands out as a unique feature in Sweden's humanitarian support to the nationalist forces in Southern Africa. Apart from the liberation movements discussed in this study, it is only SACTU that under formal bilateral agreements received direct official Swedish assistance.[1]

The policy to explore ways and means to promote democratic labour rights and black trade unions in South Africa[2]—initially at the Swedish companies—did not exclude calls for isolation of the apartheid regime. Following the Geneva conference, in a joint statement in December 1973, for example, the LO and TCO chairmen Gunnar Nilsson and Lennart Bodström emphasized that "all measures taken by the Swedish government [...] to implement the UN Declaration on Human Rights must be supported". Stating that "Swedish investment in South Africa, Rhodesia and the Portuguese colonies [...] [contributes] to strengthening the oppressive regimes and to prolonging colonialism in Africa", the union leaders, however, put the onus for decisive action on the government. Noting that the voluntary consumer boycotts of the 1960s had proved "ineffective"[3], Nilsson and Bodström concluded that

> the governments concerned must therefore be requested to implement those UN resolutions which they themselves have jointly adopted. Only a [cessation] of economic and cultural relations with South Africa and Rhodesia, as well as efforts in every way to avoid strengthening the Portuguese colonial regimes [...], can effectively contribute to a positive turn of [events] in these countries.[4]

---

1. It will be seen below that official support was also channelled to Gatsha Buthelezi's Inkatha movement. Extended on a project basis, it was never formalized in a regular agreement. In the case of SACTU, formal aid negotiations were, however, held with the Swedish authorities. In November 1982, for example, "discussions [...] regarding [...] the programme of cooperation between the [p]arties" were summarized in agreed minutes between SACTU and SIDA ('Agreed minutes', Lusaka, 5 November 1982) (SDA). Zola Zembe, National Treasurer, signed the agreement on behalf of SACTU, while Brita Östberg, SIDA's representative to Zambia, did the same for Sweden.
2. While there were official trade unions for whites—mainly belonging to the South African Confederation of Labour (SACL); supporting apartheid—and for so called coloureds and Indians, in the early 1970s black workers did not have access to recognized bargaining machinery or to trade unions protected by law. The struggle was therefore for equal rights and non-racial, rather than black unions. However, the expression 'black trade unions' was at the time often used to distinguish the emerging, predominantly African unions from those controlled by whites. It is in this sense that the term is used. In 1977, the *South African Labour Bulletin* introduced the term 'independent trade unions', over time also indicating autonomy from both the state and the employers. In the mid-1980s, finally, 'independent' acquired a new connotation, namely vis-à-vis the liberation movement. In view thereof, from 'black' to 'independent' the non-racial, anti-apartheid unions were increasingly referred to as 'democratic' (cf. Johann Maree: 'Introduction' in Johann Maree (ed.): *The Independent Trade Unions, 1974-1984: Ten Years of the South African Labour Bulletin*, Ravan Press, Johannesburg, 1987, pp. viii-x).
3. Cf. the interview with Sören Lindh from the Africa Groups: "[In the mid-1970s], we talked to a number of people who had been active in the sanctions campaign in the 1960s. [...] An interesting thing was that the initial opposition to the idea of a boycott against South Africa came from the trade unions and other Social Democrats. They said: 'We tried it. It did not work. Do not try to do what we did, because we know that it will not work'" (Interview with Sören Lindh, p. 307).
4. 'Statement by Gunnar Nilsson, president of the LO, and Lennart Bodström, president of the TCO, on December 10, 1973' in LO-TCO op. cit., Appendix 4, p. 180.

Nevertheless, after consultations at the Nordic level and with ICFTU[1], in the meantime LO and TCO decided in late 1974 to send a joint fact-finding mission to South Africa in order to "gather information and evaluate [the] working conditions at [the] Swedish plants".[2] The question of possible trade union assistance was also on the agenda.[3] This, in turn, implied an assessment of the various anti-apartheid labour formations in South Africa, including the role and relevance of SACTU.

The mission visited South Africa between 25 January and 8 February 1975. It was from the outset highly controversial, not only provoking strong negative reactions from ANC and the solidarity movement, but also from within the LO and TCO ranks, as well as from trade unions in Southern Africa. When the decision became publicly known, in late December 1974 the resident ANC representative Sobizana Mngqikana denounced the planned study tour as "a propaganda stunt" which would be exploited by the apartheid regime.[4] Invited to Sweden by the ruling Social Democratic Party, in early February 1975—while the LO-TCO delegation was still in South Africa—Oliver Tambo similarly criticized the initiative.[5] Just before the delegation's departure, the Africa Groups characterized it as "supporting Swedish investments in South Africa"[6], and on 20 January 1975 the LO-owned, social democratic newspaper *Aftonbladet* published a longer article by Mai Palmberg under the heading 'Who has asked LO to go to South Africa?' In the article, she emphasized that the visit not only went against the resolution adopted at the 1973 Geneva conference, but also that it was contrary to the explicit appeals made by ANC and SACTU.[7]

The same arguments were raised by many LO and TCO members in the respective organs of the two trade union organizations.[8] They were also reflected in the national press.[9] Further afield, African trade unions denounced the initiative. Newstead Zimba, General Secretary of the Zambian Congress of Trade Unions, for example, commented that "it was most disheartening to see countries like Sweden break what the [Geneva] conference [...] had resolved", adding that "stern measures should be taken against European trade union movements which continue to defy the [Geneva] resolution".[10]

---

1. At a meeting in Oslo, the Nordic Trade Union Council (NTUC) decided in March 1974 to set up a working group to monitor the labour situation in South Africa and liaise with ICFTU. Also in 1974, ICFTU established a Coordinating Committee on South Africa. In May 1974, the ICFTU executive board appealed to "affiliated organizations, trade union centres, International Trade Secretariats and national unions to give material assistance to the [black] workers [in South Africa] in their efforts to establish trade unions" ('ICFTU Resolution on South Africa, Brussels, 30-31 May 1974' in LO-TCO op. cit., Appendix 1, p. 172).
2. 'LO/TCO Study Delegation to the Republic of South Africa, January 24-February 8, 1975' in LO-TCO op. cit., Appendix 6, p. 184.
3. Ibid., p. 8.
4. Anita Hansson: 'Kritik mot LO och TCO: Sydafrikaresan blir ett propagandajippo' ('Criticism of LO and TCO: The South Africa trip becomes a propaganda stunt') in *Dagens Nyheter*, 23 December 1974.
5. Ulf Hagman: 'LO-TCO's Sydafrikabesök: Svart ledare kritisk' ('LO-TCO's South Africa visit: Black leader critical') in *Svenska Dagbladet*, 7 February 1975. At the same time, the ANC leader did not reject Swedish links with Buthelezi and the homeland-based Inkatha movement.
6. AGIS: 'Uttalande om LO-TCO's resa till Sydafrika' ('Statement on LO-TCO's trip to South Africa'), [no place], 20 January 1975 (AGA).
7. Mai Palmberg: 'Vem har bett LO resa till Sydafrika?' ('Who has asked LO to go to South Africa?') in *Aftonbladet*, 20 January 1975. Palmberg was at the time in close contact with the South African journalist and scholar Ruth First, who on behalf of ANC and the Congress Alliance firmly opposed any trade union links with the apartheid republic (Letter from Mai Palmberg to the author, Uppsala, 11 August 2000).
8. Among many protest letters, cf., for example, Ann Schlyter: 'Kritik mot LO-TCO-resan till Sydafrika' ('Criticism against the LO-TCO Trip to South Africa') in *TCO-Tidningen*, No. 2, 1975, p. 18.
9. Cf. Tore Hallén: 'Fackdelegation till Sydafrika trots hård kritik' ('Trade union delegation to South Africa despite harsh criticism') in *Dagens Nyheter*, 24 January 1975.
10. Cited in 'Defiant Swedes rapped' in *Times of Zambia*, 11 February 1975, forwarded by cable from the Swedish embassy in Lusaka to the Ministry for Foreign Affairs, Lusaka, 11 February 1975 (MFA). The visit by LO-TCO had *inter alia* been preceded by visits by the British Trades Union Congress (TUC).

LO and TCO: Multilateral Involvement

In addition to the initiatives taken by the Swedish Ecumenical Council, the LO-TCO decision irreversibly brought the issue of Sweden's economic relations with apartheid South Africa to the fore. For the first time in many years, in January 1975—immediately before the study visit—both the Left Party Communists and the Liberal Party submitted parliamentary motions against the presence of Swedish companies in the country.

Together with the Centre Party, the two parties had in the mid-1960s advocated comprehensive sanctions. Ten years later their demands were less radical. Representing the Liberal Party, Per Ahlmark and Billy Olsson cautiously requested the Swedish parliament "to urge the [...] companies to phase out their interests in and relations with South Africa"[1], while the Left Party in a motion introduced by the party leader C.H. Hermansson no longer demanded a total boycott, but "prohibition against Swedish investments".[2] However, contrary to the situation during the first Swedish sanctions debate, with support from the ruling Social Democratic Party there was in 1975 a majority in favour of restrictions. Pronouncing itself on the motions submitted, at a time when Sweden formed part of the UN Security Council[3] the parliamentary Standing Committee on Foreign Affairs made it clear that it "shares the negative view of Swedish investments in South Africa, which can be interpreted as support for that country's policy of racial segregation".[4]

The companies operating in the apartheid republic were thus under severe pressure.[5] In fact, while the Moderate Party—with close links to the Federation of Swedish Industries—was the only parliamentary party which did not turn against their presence, the prevailing political climate at the time was such that even the Moderate Party Youth League (MUF)[6] did so. In an exceptional statement, MUF declared in May 1975 that

> it is morally unjust to contribute towards the strengthening of the economic position of the South African government. It is also unacceptable to operate under the race laws existing in South Africa. It is therefore up to the Swedish opinion to demand that the Swedish companies operating [there] allow their employees working conditions which will increase their economic and social status. [...] Black trade unions must be able to [negotiate]. Black [workers] must be granted the right to strike, and union activities must be permitted under decent conditions. [...]

---

1. Swedish Parliament 1975: Motion No. 331, Riksdagens Protokoll 1975, p. 16.
2. Swedish Parliament 1975: Motion No. 1152, Riksdagens Protokoll 1975, p. 3.
3. Sweden was a member of the Security Council in 1975-76.
4. Cited in 'Reply by the Minister of Commerce, Mr. Burenstam Linder, to a question in the Riksdag by Mr. Wästberg on the government's attitude to Swedish trade links with South Africa', 12 October 1976, in Ministry for Foreign Affairs: *Documents on Swedish Foreign Policy: 1976*, Stockholm, 1978, p. 195. The statement by the Standing Committee on Foreign Affairs was included in its report No. 1975:9.
5. While the main production companies at the time remained largely aloof from the public criticism, other private concerns with economic interests in South Africa felt threatened. This was, in particular, the case with the Gothenburg-based Transatlantic Shipping Company, which since 1904 had operated a regular service between the Nordic countries and Southern Africa. Its close involvement with the South African state had already in the early 1960s been singled out by the Nordic solidarity and trade union movements (Sellström Volume I, pp. 202 note 1 and 209-14). Having just entered into a new contract with the South African government to maintain its service until 1991 and planning new investments in the order of 300 MSEK, in September 1975 Transatlantic sought assurances from Trade Minister Kjell-Olof Feldt that it would be able to continue its operations. They also covered Namibia, where the Swedish company in contravention of the UN Council of Namibia's Decree No. 1 (1974) regularly carried lead ore and other minerals from Walvis Bay. Noting that the operations did not contravene the existing Swedish legislation, Feldt responded that on behalf of the Social Democratic government he advised Transatlantic not to carry out any new investments (C. Gyllenstierna: Memorandum ('Transatlantic's trafik på södra Afrika'/'Transatlantic's traffic on Southern Africa'), Ministries for Trade and Foreign Affairs, Stockholm, 23 September 1975) (MFA).
6. In Swedish, *Moderata Ungdomsförbundet*.

> While awaiting real progress [in these regards], new Swedish investments in South Africa should not be carried out.[1]

Although several of the representatives on the LO-TCO fact-finding mission found the conditions at the Swedish companies "degrading" and on their return to Sweden called for an investment ban[2], the criticism against the visit continued. Regarding the initiative as a severe breach of the calls for international isolation, ANC was particularly offended. As late as 29 September 1975—on the very same day that the LO and TCO executive boards were to decide on the delegation's findings and recommendations—TCO's chairman Lennart Bodström received a cable from the ANC headquarters in Lusaka

> strongly urg[ing] non-adoption of [the] South Africa report and [its] recommendations, because they run counter to [the] 1973 ILO resolution, [United Nations] policy, [the] objectives of [the] liberation movement and your own declared policy.[3]

Despite external opposition and internal dissent[4], the extensive report[5] was, nevertheless, adopted. Opting for a policy of indirect involvement, the joint decision by LO and TCO opened the way for the Swedish trade union movement's substantial assistance to the democratic labour forces in South Africa from the late 1970s. Although the assistance—coordinated at the Nordic level, implemented via ICFTU and mainly funded by SIDA—eventually had a considerable impact which was later acknowledged by ANC, this was at the time far from a foregone conclusion. Heading the Central Organization of Salaried Employees, Lennart Bodström—who in 1982 became Minister for Foreign Affairs in Palme's second Social Democratic government—commented just prior to the final decision that

> the TCO board is facing a dilemma. On the one hand, there is a strong wish from the union representatives at the Swedish [parent] companies to be able to do something for their black colleagues at the subsidiaries in South Africa. On the other, we have received a number of protests and sharp criticism, [saying] that we through our recommendations would be accepting the apartheid regime.
>
> [Our] opinion is that [we] must immediately stop [the] sufferings at the Swedish companies [...]. I don't think that [efforts] aiming at improving the conditions for the blacks would delay

1. Statement adopted by the board of the Moderate Party Youth League, 24-25 May 1975, reproduced in the pamphlet *Södra Afrika* ('Southern Africa') issued by MUF in June 1975, pp. 18-19. In the statement, the conservative youth also declared that the Southern African liberation movements—among them ANC—"must be recognized and supported [...] in the struggle against apartheid"; that "the liberation movements which have been recognized by OAU should receive increased Swedish support"; and that "Sweden [should] strive for international sanctions of a total nature against South Africa" (pp. 21-22). Censured by its parent party, however, MUF never actively campaigned for these demands, which it soon abandoned altogether. They do, however, reflect the widely held political views on South Africa in Sweden in the mid-1970s. Ten years later—when ANC's role was unquestionable and South Africa was in a state of popular insurrection—the conservative youth took an entirely different stand. Together with the Moderate Party, MUF then turned against both assistance to ANC and boycott actions against South Africa. In May 1986, the MUF chairperson Beatrice Ask denounced the Swedish government's South Africa policy as guided by "double standards" (Rolf Asmundsson: 'MUF-ordförande: Fel att bara stödja ANC'/'The MUF chairperson: Wrong to only support ANC' in *Barometern*, 23 May 1986).
2. Thorvald Hansson: 'Stoppa svenska pengar till Sydafrika'/'Stop Swedish money to South Africa' in *Aftonbladet*, 10 February 1975.
3. Cable from ANC to Lennart Bodström, Lusaka, 29 September 1975 (LMA).
4. The opposition against the visit and 'the new strategy' was particularly strong within TCO. When the joint draft report was discussed by the TCO board, two members—Ulla-Britta Platin from the Municipal Employees Union and John Östlund from the Public Servants Union—made reservations against its recommendations. According to Östlund, it was both "contradictory" and "strategically wrong" to try to change the black workers' situation through international trade union assistance, as it "had to be carried out on terms set by the apartheid regime" (cited in 'TCO om Sydafrika: Stöd de Svartas Fackföreningar'/'TCO on South Africa: Support the Unions of the Blacks' in *TCO-Tidningen*, No. 17, 1975, p. 4).
5. Published in book form, the English version of the report covered almost 200 pages.

a comprehensive revolution in South Africa. [...] But [we] must be careful with regard to the black organizations that [we] are to cooperate with. We [...] must see to it that we don't support quisling organizations. We must therefore call for caution. [...] I personally feel that TCO should focus on trade union support to underground organizations [like] SACTU, although we, of course, should also assist those black unions that work openly. [...] [We] must avoid internal fights with the Swedish and South African organizations that [...] oppose apartheid. TCO's policy must not be viewed with suspicion.[1]

Decisive for the stand by LO and TCO was the unacceptable labour situation at the subsidiary companies of some of Sweden's leading manufacturing firms. In this regard, the study delegation confirmed the findings made by SEN, Sven-Ivan Sundqvist and other observers. Emphasizing that in general "conditions [at] these companies are unsatisfactory", the LO-TCO mission concluded that "[s]o far [they] have not deviated from the basic rules of the apartheid policy on any crucial point" and that they "in compliance with the existing social order [...] are taking part in the current exploitation of mainly black labour".[2] On the fundamental issue of labour rights, the mission further noted that "[the Swedish] management in general refuse[s] to deal with [black] unions".[3]

In early 1975, there were no black unions at the six Swedish companies visited. On the contrary, the delegation encountered "a negative or at best a half-hearted attitude towards [b]lack trade union work. Up to now", it continued, "the Swedish managers have [...] in no way made it clear to their labour force that [b]lack trade unions are not prohibited by law", adding that "[m]oreover, several company managements seem to be ill informed as to [the] existing laws concerning trade union activities in South Africa".[4] At Atlas Copco, the management was "basically [against] dealing with this question at all".[5]

Against this background, the delegation proposed a number of steps to be taken by the Swedish trade union movement. In addition to discussions with the government to bring about "a tightening [...] of the [...] regulations concerning currency transfers in connection with investments in South Africa", as well as to increase official assistance to "the opponents and the victims of the apartheid policy"[6], they primarily involved action vis-à-vis the Swedish parent companies. LO and TCO should thus

> prevail[...] upon them in different respects to facilitate the creation of representative black trade unions at their subsidiaries in South Africa [...]; make them improve promptly and in essential respects the wages and other conditions of employment [for] the non-[w]hite labour

1. 'TCO-styrelsen i ett Dilemma' ('The TCO Board in a Dilemma') in *TCO-Tidningen*, No. 17, 1975, p. 5. Although taking a clear stand in favour of 'direct involvement', the future Foreign Minister and TCO in general were not dismissive of SACTU. Failing to mobilize sympathy among metalworkers', miners' and other industrial workers' unions, it is noteworthy that SACTU in exile primarily managed to raise support in the Western countries among white-collar unions, notably those which organized public servants. This was, for example, the case with the British National Association of Local Government Officers (NALGO). In the case of Sweden, TCO was decidedly more open to SACTU than LO. The Public Employees Union (*Statsanställdas Förbund*) was the only LO union to join ISAK. Concluding fifteen years of work to isolate South Africa, ISAK wrote in early 1995 that the trade union efforts had been "easiest on the TCO side" (*Amandla*, No. 2-3, 1995, p. 19). With direct links to the South African labour movement, the industrial unions were decidedly more pragmatic. Asked whether the issue of SACTU and WFTU had obstructed his involvement with the South African National Union of Mineworkers, Stig Blomqvist, for example, said in 1997 that he used to say: "Don't worry about that. Worry about what you yourself do or do not do" (Interview with Stig Blomqvist, p. 269). The pragmatism at the industrial union level would, however, also lead to ambiguous positions, notably by the Metalworkers Union.
2. LO-TCO op. cit., pp. 160 and 154.
3. Ibid., p. 187.
4. Ibid., pp. 145-46.
5. Ibid., p. 147.
6. Ibid., pp. 162-63.

force [...]; [and] make sure that [they] will continuously provide detailed information to the Swedish trade union organizations about their activities [...]. Among other things, this information should include data on wages and other conditions of employment.[1]

Finally, LO and TCO should

lend material assistance in appropriate forms to the [b]lack trade union movement [...] in [the] struggle for more decent working conditions. This assistance should be given chiefly in the form of contributions to [...] educational activities [...], aiming at the creation of strong, independent and well-functioning trade unions for the non-[w]hite section of the employees.[2]

Adopting the report and its recommendations, in late September 1975 LO and TCO issued a joint statement which subsequently guided the Swedish trade union movements' policy towards apartheid. Declaring "their support [for] the UN resolutions concerning the international isolation of the Republic of South Africa and call[ing] upon the Swedish government [...] to raise the question [...] in the Security Council [...] of a resolution which is binding on the member states"[3], the blue- and white-collar confederations "realize[d] that the most basic human and trade union rights are still being denied [...] the vast majority of South Africa's workers, who are excluded from the system of collective bargaining and who have no possibilities of influencing their working conditions".[4] Interpreting the 1973 ILO conference in a radically different way from ANC, SACTU and other advocates of unconditional isolation, LO and TCO made it clear that—in addition to pressures on the Swedish companies with interests in South Africa—they

[i]n agreement with the resolution taken by the International Trade Union Conference against Apartheid in Geneva [...] and a number of resolutions by ICFTU [...] will direct [...] actions towards supporting the [b]lack workers in their efforts to organize. [...] Through cooperation with [ICFTU], the International Trade Secretariats[5] and the Organization of African Trade Union Unity, [we] will continue [our] efforts to bring about international actions in support of the human rights and the trade union rights of the oppressed majority of South Africa.[6]

---

1. Ibid., p. 162.
2. Ibid., p. 163.
3. In a joint letter to Prime Minister Palme, LO's Gunnar Nilsson and TCO's Lennart Bodström demanded in February 1976 a ban on new Swedish investments in South Africa (Letter ('Hemställan'/'Request') from Gunnar Nilsson and Lennart Bodström to Prime Minister Olof Palme, Stockholm, 10 February 1976) (MFA).
4. 'Statement by the Swedish Trade Union Confederation (LO) and the Central Organization of Salaried Employees in Sweden (TCO) on South Africa, 29 September 1975' in LO-TCO op. cit., pp. i-ii.
5. The International Trade Secretariats (in Swedish, *yrkesinternationaler*) are associations which link unions of the same craft, trade or industry, such as the Miners International Federation.
6. 'Statement by [LO and TCO]' in LO-TCO op. cit., pp. ii-iii.

SACTU, Unions and Sanctions

Criticism and Contradictions

Internally based South African trade union activists—among them the future COSATU President John Gomomo, also a prominent ANC and SACP leader—would later draw positive conclusions from the initial, direct contacts with the Swedish trade unions. In 1996, he stated that

> the first visit by LO [and] TCO helped a lot. [...] After the visit [...], we managed to have an exchange between the Swedish trade unions and the workers in South Africa, which was helpful. [...] [The Swedes] went back to talk to their respective managements, saying that they must change things and that they must allow the constitution of free trade unions [...].[1]

At a time when ANC was under severe pressure and the political relations with Sweden were yet to be firmly cemented, the nationalist movement in exile was, nevertheless, decidedly critical. Striving for exclusive recognition as the sole representative of the South African majority, ANC insisted on comprehensive isolation of the apartheid regime. With weak links to the emerging internal unions, both ANC and SACTU were, in addition, suspicious of new initiatives on the labour front.

Little understanding was shown for LO's and TCO's arguments in favour of the workers at the Swedish companies in South Africa. Although Oliver Tambo maintained a flexible attitude—stressing that "the main thing is that we promote the cause of the oppressed"[2]—other ANC representatives were less accommodating. As late as in mid-1976, Thabo Mbeki, among others, turned against the LO-TCO decision taken the previous year. Interviewed in Lusaka by the Swedish Workers Educational Association[3], he and Gertrude Shope[4] expressed the opinion that

---

1. Interview with John Gomomo, p. 129. Gomomo was based in Uitenhage, where the main SKF plant was situated. His recollection of the LO-TCO visit is probably influenced by the fact that SKF Uitenhage later became a stronghold of the National Automobile and Allied Workers Union (NAAWU), where Gomomo served as Vice-President. While the contacts between the Swedish and South African workers led to positive results with regard to unionization at SKF Uitenhage, it remains that the majority of the Swedish owned companies in spite of union pressure in both South Africa and Sweden opposed to the very last the formation of democratic, non-racial trade unions. In fact, in 1980 it was only at SKF Uitenhage that the black workers' union rights were recognized. Five years later, the situation was only marginally better. In addition to SKF Uitenhage, there was in 1985 a recognized union at one of the two Sandvik plants, while the black workers at Alfa-Laval, Atlas Copco, Fagersta, SKF Johannesburg and other Swedish subsidiaries still had to channel their concerns through powerless 'liaison committees'. At the same time, it was reported that there were separate canteens and toilets for white and black employees at Atlas Copco (Anders Andersson: 'Dilemmas with Sanctions: The Policy of the Black South African Trade Unions and *Svenska Metall* towards Sanctions and Disinvestment against South Africa 1979-1993', Department of History, Gothenburg University, September 1999, pp. 22 and 35). Although the Swedish trade unions' participation in the overall, multilateral efforts to assist the South African labour movement was of significant importance, at the level of the Swedish owned companies it may be concluded that the policy adopted by LO and TCO in September 1975 largely failed. As late as in 1985, "the apartheid system [was] formally and informally still existing at the Swedish plants" (ibid.).
2. Gunnar Helander: 'Intervju av Gunnar Helander och Evert Svensson med Sydafrikas African National Congress ordförande Oliver Tambo, i Stockholm, 1975 10 02' ('Interview by Gunnar Helander and Evert Svensson with ANC's President Oliver Tambo, Stockholm, 2 October 1975') [no place or date] (SDA).
3. In Swedish, *Arbetarnas Bildningsförbund* (ABF).
4. At the time, the future head of ANC's women's section—married to SACTU's General Secretary Mark Shope—served as ANC Chief Representative to Zambia.

the Swedes wanted to give precedence to trade union work over political work, which we cannot accept. [...] Most of all we need political support. Everything else is of secondary importance. The LO-TCO delegation turned [things upside down], wanting to start from the wrong end. They should have contacted us beforehand so that we [together] could have worked out a common plan. [...] We are a bit sensitive when it comes to trade union organizations. They may have the best intentions, but their understanding is perhaps not in line with the liberation struggle in South Africa.[1]

Behind the criticism was not only that the Swedish trade union movement's 'workerist' concerns went against the calls for isolation, but, more importantly, that LO and TCO contrary to the Social Democratic government's non-aligned policy towards the Southern African nationalist movements ignored SACTU, preferring to coordinate their efforts with the Western-dominated ICFTU. As later noted by Pierre Schori, "there you had all kinds of views represented [and] it was difficult for the Swedish labour [movement] to get its views through. However, [it chose] to work through the international confederation as a point of principle. We talked a lot about this, but it was not until later that the policy was modified".[2] In the meantime, the international Cold War division between ICFTU and WFTU was reproduced in the Swedish debate, affecting the relations with SACTU.

In obvious contradiction to the isolation policy, however, the ANC leadership around Oliver Tambo soon requested official Swedish support to the independent trade union movement in South Africa. Without mentioning SACTU, in a meeting with the Liberal Cooperation Minister Ullsten in Lusaka in February 1977, Tambo, for example, stressed the need for assistance to the legal unions, which in his opinion constituted "a very important factor".[3] The Congress Alliance's conflicting views in this regard were reflected in its relations with Sweden, as well as within the wider Swedish anti-apartheid opinion. Although all the actors involved supported ANC—and the issue was cushioned by the fact that the government from 1977/78 extended direct assistance to SACTU in exile[4]—through the trade unions' opposition and the solidarity movement's advocacy the subordinate question of ANC's labour ally would until the late 1980s—when its role had long since been overtaken by internal events—form part of the national South Africa debate.

In parallel with the establishment of a special relationship with ANC at the official, political level, over the years acrimonious exchanges would characterize the relations between LO and TCO on the one hand and SACTU on the other. They culminated in the mid-1980s. Thus, in April 1984—at a time when the Swedish trade union movement was *inter alia* closely engaged with the strategically important South African National Union of Mineworkers, mainly in the field of educa-

---

1. Cited in Ann Marie Bergström: 'Politisk Kamp Är Viktigast för Facket i Sydafrika' ('Political Struggle Is Most Important for the Unions in South Africa') in *Fönstret*, No. 10, 1976.
2. Interview with Pierre Schori, p. 334.
3. Elisabeth Michanek: Draft memorandum ('Möte med ANC's (SA) president Oliver Tambo den 28 februari 1977'/'Meeting with ANC President Oliver Tambo on 28 February 1977'), Swedish embassy, Lusaka, 7 March 1977 (MFA).
4. See below. From a formal point of view, the direct support started during the financial year 1976/77. The decision to support the SACTU office in Dar es Salaam was taken in early June 1977 and the costs—amounting to 40,000 SEK—were debited against the budget allocation for 1976/77 (SIDA: 'Beslut'/'Decision', Director General's Office, No. 376/77, SIDA, Stockholm, 6 June 1977) (SDA). It was, however, from 1977/78 that the Swedish government's direct administrative assistance to SACTU became a regular feature.

tion[1]—SACTU General Secretary John Nkadimeng issued a particularly harsh statement "on interference by international trade union centres in the democratic labour movement of South Africa". Among other things, SACTU warned that

> [t]here are determined efforts by the ICFTU-affiliated unions, like the Swedish LO/TCO, Dutch FNV, Canadian Labour Congress and others, to undermine and divert the revolutionary path of struggle followed by the militant working class, [which is] locked in battle with the bosses, transnational corporations and the apartheid regime. The stake of foreign investors in our country is high and the capitalist countries live in mortal fear of any revolutionary change in South Africa. [...] What 'progress' does ICFTU want to see in our country? The birth of toothless trade unions fighting for industrial peace in the midst of apartheid exploitation? [...]

> The funding of trade unions in South Africa is aimed at corrupting and buying over the trade union leadership in order to alienate them from the workers. Such 'aid' is obviously politically motivated and has the desire to imbue our trade union movement with reformist tendencies. The exorbitant funding of workers' education is aimed at 'educating' our trade union leadership to become obedient and dedicated servants of management and bosses. [...] We shall continue to intensify our organisational capacities inside the factories, compounds, mines and on the farms. SACTU is rooted there [...] and no amount of treachery or intrigue from foreign trade union centres will change this.[2]

Bitter exchanges confirmed the rift between LO-TCO and SACTU.[3] While both advocated the cause of ANC, it was, above all, the determination to honour respective, but mutually exclusive international commitments that kept them apart. This was conclusively illustrated during enforced consultations between the two in Stockholm in March 1984.

Across the Cold War divide and as an exception, for many years SACTU received financial assistance from the Swedish government. During the aid consultations with ANC in March 1983—in which SACTU's Treasurer General Zola Zembe[4] participated—the Swedish delegation, however, declared that "direct contributions in support of trade union activities in South Africa should normally be channelled through the Swedish trade union movement [...] and that SACTU would

---

1. NUM was formed in August 1982 and held its inaugural congress four months later. Its relations with the Swedish trade union movement started as early as in August 1983. NUM's General Secretary Cyril Ramaphosa—future Secretary General of ANC—had particularly close contacts with the Mineworkers Union and LO/TCO's Council of International Trade Union Cooperation. Invited by the LO/TCO council, he paid his first of many visits to Sweden in October 1983 (Thorwald Olsson: 'Svart gruvfack i Sydafrika: De vita arbetarna vår värsta fiende'/'Black miners' union in South Africa: The white workers [are] our worst enemies' in *Dagens Nyheter*, 12 October 1983). The Swedish assistance to NUM was not channelled through ICFTU, but mainly via the Miners International Federation (MIF). During his visits to Sweden, Ramaphosa often criticized ICFTU and its dismissal of SACTU.
2. 'South African Congress of Trade Unions' statement on interference by international trade union centres in the democratic labour movement of South Africa', issued by John Nkadimeng, SACTU General Secretary, Lusaka, 27 April 1984 (LMA).
3. Contacting the Swedish embassy in Dar es Salaam, for example, Aron Pemba, Chairman of SACTU's Secretariat, complained in February 1979 that Kristina Persson of the LO/TCO Council of International Trade Union Cooperation during a visit to South Africa in late 1978 "had slandered SACTU", allegedly advising trade union activists to avoid his organization (Anna Runeborg: Memorandum ('Samtal med Mr. Aron Pemba, ordförande i SACTU, den 12 februari 1979'/'Conversation with Mr. Aron Pemba, SACTU Chairman, on 12 February 1979'), Swedish embassy, Dar es Salaam, 14 February 1979) (SDA). This prompted Rune Molin, the chairman of the LO/TCO council, to address a letter to SACTU in which he found it "astonishing that you have chosen to [...] contact the [Swedish] government and not [...] us". Stating that "it has also come to our knowledge from various sources that representatives [of] SACTU criticize LO and TCO and [their] representatives on grounds which we find rather strange, to say the least", Molin, however, expressed the hope that "the misunderstandings" could be sorted out (Letter from Rune Molin to SACTU, Stockholm, 22 May 1979) (LMA). Responding to the letter, SACTU's Administrative Secretary Eli Weinberg hastened to declare that "we hope [...] that any misunderstanding caused by ill-informed people will be ignored by you", adding that SACTU was looking forward to a "continuous friendly dialogue" (Letter from Eli Weinberg to the LO/TCO Council of International Trade Union Cooperation, Dar es Salaam, 31 May 1979) (LMA). Over the years, this kind of exchange characterized the bilateral relationship.
4. Also known as Archie Sibeko.

be welcome to discuss directly with LO/TCO the potential for continued Swedish support".[1] In the meantime, it was agreed to set aside an amount of 300,000 SEK for SACTU under the ANC allocation for 1983/84.[2]

Following the agreement, in late March 1984 the LO/TCO Council of International Trade Union Cooperation and SACTU met for discussions in Stockholm. As both parties firmly maintained that their international affiliations and policies were non-negotiable, after three days they merely agreed to disagree. While the LO/TCO council declared that it "could only enter into multilateral agreement[s]"—that is, under the ICFTU umbrella—the SACTU representatives correspondingly stated that they were "unable to enter into any multilateral agreement".[3]

The unsuccessful talks marked the end of the efforts of the Swedish authorities and ANC to bridge the gap between LO-TCO and SACTU. Although essentially contrary to the wishes of their respective labour allies, at the annual negotiations in Lusaka in April 1984 the Social Democratic government and the nationalist organization against this background felt once again obliged to accommodate SACTU within the overall ANC allocation. An amount of 350,000 SEK was set aside for SACTU activities—"primarily within South Africa"—during the financial year 1984/85.[4]

Initially seen as "a temporary exception [to] the general rule"[5], over the following six years—that is, until the unbanning of ANC and the dissolution of the labour organization[6]—support to SACTU within the ANC allocation became a permanent feature. In spite of the Swedish trade union movement's position, between 1977/78 and 1990/91 non-socialist and Social Democratic governments would directly and indirectly grant SACTU financial assistance of slightly more than 4 MSEK.[7]

Describing LO/TCO's attitude towards the organization as "lukewarm", in his autobiography Zola Zembe notes that the Swedish government was "the major source of finance for the SACTU office in London right up until the time it

---

1. 'Agreed minutes [from] consultations in Lusaka, March 1983, between the African National Congress of South Africa, ANC, and Sweden concerning humanitarian assistance', Lusaka, 25 March 1983 (SDA). The ANC delegation was led by Secretary General Alfred Nzo and SIDA's Deputy Director General Lars-Olof Edström headed the Swedish team. While Zola Zembe spoke on behalf of SACTU, there were no representatives from LO or TCO.
2. Ibid. SACTU was far from happy with the decision. In a letter to LO's chairman Gunnar Nilsson, Zembe wrote on 25 April 1983 that "SACTU is reluctant to be receiving aid from SIDA in the form of an unspecified amount which will be contained in the overall allocation [...] to the ANC. We feel that this arrangement could lead to the undermining of SACTU as an independent organisation [and] that it places an unnecessary stress on the alliance between SACTU and the ANC" (Letter from Zola Zembe, Treasurer General of SACTU, to Gunnar [Nilsson], LO, Lusaka, 25 April 1983) (LMA).
3. 'Agreed minutes [from] consultations in Stockholm on 28, 29 and 30 March, 1984 between the South African Congress of Trade Unions (SACTU) and the LO/TCO concerning financial assistance', Stockholm, 30 March 1984 (LMA). During the discussions, the LO/TCO council was represented by Jan-Erik Norling and Urs Hauser, while the SACTU delegation was composed of John Nkadimeng (General Secretary), Kay Moonsamy (National Treasurer), Zola Zembe (Coordinator for Europe) and Thozamile Botha (Administrative Secretary). Representing SIDA, the author participated at the opening and closure of the talks. The SACTU delegation was clearly bitter about the outcome. This, in turn, may explain the harsh statement quoted above, issued by Nkadimeng less than a month later. It should be noted that both ANC and SACP at the time questioned SACTU's capacity to coordinate the trade union movement inside South Africa.
4. 'Agreed minutes [from] consultations in Lusaka, April 1984, between the African National Congress of South Africa and Sweden concerning humanitarian assistance', Lusaka, 6 April 1984 (SDA). The ANC and Swedish delegations were, once again, respectively led by Alfred Nzo and Lars-Olof Edström. Kay Moonsamy represented SACTU.
5. Ibid.
6. At a meeting between SACTU and COSATU in Zambia in March 1990, it was agreed to "phase out" the former. COSATU would subsequently take its place within the Congress Alliance. On SACTU's far from glorious demise, see Zola Zembe's autobiography where he bitterly concludes that "SACTU deserved a more dignified end" (Archie Sibeko (Zola Zembe) with Joyce Leeson: *Freedom in Our Lifetime*, Indicator Press, Durban, 1996, p. 147).
7. Based on disbursement figures according to SIDA's audited annual accounts.

closed".[1] Perhaps more importantly, from the late 1970s the direct official support extended by Sweden made it possible for SACTU to establish offices in Tanzania and other Southern African countries. In fact, by the end of the 1970s the contribution via SIDA roughly covered 10 per cent of the organization's administrative budget, including salaries and travel costs.[2] Judging from the available documentation and statements by leading SACTU representatives, no other government—in the West or in the East—gave the organization equivalent support.[3]

Probably influenced by these facts, SACP's Treasurer General Kay Moonsamy—who was directly involved with the Swedish assistance to ANC from 1973 until 1994 and in the mid-1980s served as Treasurer General of SACTU; in that capacity participating in the abortive talks with LO/TCO in March 1984—later summarized the relations with the Swedish trade union movement in a surprisingly positive way. Interviewed in Johannesburg in 1995, with regard to LO and TCO he said:

> Let us be very clear: They were very supportive of ANC, SACTU and the struggle against apartheid, but their problem was that SACTU was an affiliate of WFTU [...]. They were members of ICFTU and therefore felt that they were not in a position to assist. That did not in any way sour our relationship, because through their own channels they gave support to ANC in the struggle. I think that it was important. But, unfortunately, we could not cement this in a more tangible way.[4]

SACTU in Exile

In reality, however, the bilateral relations were far from cordial.[5] From the beginning, the Swedish trade union movement eschewed ANC's labour ally. When SACTU's General Secretary John Gaetsewe visited Stockholm in December 1973—six months after the important ILO Geneva conference—he could not meet LO, which, he said, made it clear that "they didn't have the time to receive him".[6] He was, however, welcomed at the Ministry for Foreign Affairs, where he notably raised the issue of the Swedish companies in South Africa.[7] Later SACTU visitors were similarly avoided or accorded low priority at the trade union headquarters, but often received at high levels by the government authorities.[8]

---

1. Sibeko op. cit., p. 125. Although Zembe on many occasions visited Sweden and negotiated with the government, in his memoirs the official aid agency SIDA is wrongly presented as "a government funded NGO" (ibid.).
2. Letter from George Monare, SACTU General Treasurer, to the Swedish embassy in Dar es Salaam, Dar es Salaam, 26 August 1978 (SDA) and Birgitta Berggren: Memorandum ('Ansökan från South African Congress of Trade Unions, SACTU, om stöd till administrativa kostnader under 1980/81'/'Request from SACTU for support towards administrative costs in 1980/81'), CCHA/SIDA, Stockholm, 28 April 1980 (SDA).
3. Cf. the interview with Kay Moonsamy, p. 164. Norway, for example, did not grant SACTU any official support. Contrary to the situation in Sweden, in this regard the aid authorities strictly followed the recommendations of the Norwegian LO (Vetlesen (1998) op. cit., p. 85).
4. Ibid.
5. Working at the LO headquarters in Stockholm from 1976, Bengt Säve-Söderbergh, AIC's future Secretary General, later stated: "I was never a friend of SACTU. I do not know how many times we refused their requests" (Interview with Bengt Säve-Söderbergh, p. 339).
6. Cited in Astrid Bergquist: Memorandum ('Minnesanteckningar från sammanträffande på UD med SACTU-representanten John Gaetsewe'/'Notes from meeting at the Ministry for Foreign Affairs with the SACTU representative John Gaetsewe'), SIDA, Stockholm, 18 December 1973 (SDA).
7. Ibid.
8. Invited to Sweden by the Africa Groups, in March 1977, for example, SACTU's James Stuart (also known as Hermanus Loots) held discussions with Hans Blix, the Liberal Under-Secretary of State for International Development Cooperation, at the Ministry for Foreign Affairs (Marika Fahlén: Memorandum ('Besök av James Stuart, SACTU'/'Visit by James Stuart, SACTU'), Ministry for Foreign Affairs, Stockholm, 4 April 1977) (SDA). Like Nkadimeng, Moonsamy and many other SACTU officials, Stuart held high positions in ANC. At ANC's Second National Consultative Conference in Kabwe, Zambia, he was elected in June 1985 to the National Executive Committee.

In addition to the vexed ideological issue of international affiliation, two questions were often advanced in this context by LO and—less explicitly—TCO, namely that SACTU stood for political rather than strictly union objectives and that it was an exiled organization, with little or no relevance in South Africa. While the LO-TCO study delegation to South Africa concluded in early 1975 that ANC "has a great unspoken support among the oppressed in the country", it presented SACTU as a "previous[ly] existing national union".[1] On their return to Sweden, the mission members stated that SACTU did not exist in South Africa. As earlier noted, Jan Olsson, the international secretary of the Swedish Metalworkers Union, wrote in the social democratic theoretical journal *Tiden* that SACTU was "neither seen, nor heard".[2]

Most studies on the modern trade union movement in South Africa confirm this impression. While SACTU members who had managed to escape the repression in the 1960s—or were released from prison in the early 1970s—were active within the emerging unions on an individual basis, SACTU was essentially a marginalized organization in exile. In his comprehensive study *Imperialism or Solidarity?*, Roger Southall, for example, concludes that

> any claim made by SACTU to have been organisationally involved in the relaunching of open trade unions amongst African workers in the early 1970s should be regarded as hyperbole. Both the debate within the movement, as well as SACTU's contemporary advocacy of the primacy of armed struggle, clearly indicate that it was only with the explosion of labour activity in the early 1980s that SACTU really came off the fence and offered its wholehearted backing to the internal democratic unions.[3]

Southall further notes that "it is difficult to gain any sense of a distinct SACTU presence in South Africa even in the early 1980s".[4] In his dissertation on ANC's operational strategy, Howard Barrell—a former member of the movement—has noted that "trade union policy became the main blind spot in the political strategy of ANC, [...] SACP and [SACTU]", adding that "[SACTU's] external representation had almost no sources of information inside the emergent trade union movement in the late 1970s".[5] Close to SACP and SACTU, Vladimir Shubin has similarly stressed its marginalization. Characterizing SACTU as "practically leaderless", he states that by 1983

> [i]t was perfectly clear to the leaders of the SACP (and the ANC) that SACTU could not be a coordinator of the trade union movement inside the country. While it had no industrial trade unions as members, it did have a certain influence in the workers' movement and it was therefore considered a mistake to dissolve it at that stage.[6]

---

1. LO-TCO op. cit., pp. 25 and 93.
2. Jan Olsson: 'Sydafrika: Hur Förbereds Frigörelsen?' ('South Africa: How Is Liberation Being Prepared?') in *Tiden*, No. 67, 1975, p. 443. Interviewed in 1997, the delegation's secretary Åke Magnusson said: "My very firm impression is that SACTU did not exist in South Africa. Of course, sections did, but SACTU was not anchored in the minds of the working population" (Interview with Åke Magnusson, p. 319).
3. Southall op. cit., p. 227.
4. Ibid.
5. Barrell Ph. D. op. cit., chapter five, pp. 16-17. Barrell even ventures the opinion that SACTU at the end of the 1970s "was playing a spoiling role abroad to ensure that the emergent unions [in South Africa] did not receive the kind of resources that might enable them to develop into a working class political project independent of the ANC-led alliance" (ibid., chapter four, p. 3).
6. Shubin op. cit., p. 237. After visiting SACTU's office in London for discussions with General Secretary Gaetsewe, SIDA's Birgitta Berggren and Carin Norberg noted in April 1980 that "it seems that before long it will be time to let a younger generation take over" (Letter from Birgitta Berggren to Anna Runeborg, SIDA, Stockholm, 10 April 1980) (SDA). From early 1982, the Swedish authorities started to question SACTU's political relevance and administrative capacity. Nkadimeng succeeded Gaetsewe in August 1983. In his memoirs, Zembe (aka Sibeko) criticizes Nkadimeng for paying too little attention to SACTU, in practice giving priority to his ANC functions (Sibeko op. cit., p. 143).

As arguments against direct cooperation with SACTU, LO and TCO advanced its affiliation to WFTU; its political profile; and its weak position in South Africa. The very same conditions, however, did not prevent them from entering into a direct relationship with SWAPO of Namibia concerning assistance to the National Union of Namibian Workers (NUNW). From 1978, the LO/TCO Council of International Trade Union Cooperation became significantly involved in the underground efforts to establish NUNW inside Namibia. The initiative—formally coordinated with the Namibian liberation movement—was not only politically inspired, but under diffi- cult circumstances carried out in a situation where NUNW for all practical pur- poses did not exist, and certainly not as a viable national trade union organization. Finally, when NUNW's affiliation to WFTU disqualified it from multilateral ICFTU assistance, the Swedish trade unions did not suspend their bilateral assistance.[1]

Why, then, did LO and TCO—who both supported ANC—relate differently to SACTU in their joint effort? The answer mainly lies in the fact that significant Swedish production companies were established in South Africa, while the eco- nomic links with Namibia were negligible. As stated by TCO's chairman Lennart Bodström, the suffering at the Swedish companies was to be arrested, and this, it was argued, could best be achieved through coordinated action with the trade union movements in the countries with major economic interests in South Africa, that is, through ICFTU.[2] To this end, safe and reliable conduits were necessary. In this context too, SACTU appeared as far from an ideal partner.[3]

In spite of ICFTU's position, before her exploratory mission to South Africa in early 1977 LO/TCO's Kristina Persson consulted Gaetsewe and other SACTU rep- resentatives in London concerning the visit and possible assistance to the unions in South Africa. According to Persson, on both issues she "received the green light".[4] For reasons of security, however, "almost without exception" her trade union con- tacts in South Africa turned down SACTU as a possible channel, stressing that any direct relations with the organization would be "tantamount to suicide".[5] As the Swedish trade union movement together with its Nordic counterparts soon thereaf- ter started to design an aid package to South Africa via ICFTU[6], it would, in addi-

---

1. LO/TCO maintained bilateral relations with the Angolan trade union movement UNTA, the WFTU-affiliated labour wing of the ruling MPLA party. The links were unique in a Western context. In September 1978, Kris- tina Persson attended UNTA's national conference in Luanda (Letter from Kristina Persson to Elisabeth Michanek, Stockholm, 20 October 1978) (SDA). By that time, MPLA had been constituted as a Marxist-Len- inist party.
2. The ICFTU members from countries with large or substantial investments in South Africa initially formed a sub-group within the Coordinating Committee on South Africa.
3. Kristina Persson: 'LO/TCO's aktiviteter i Sydafrikafrågan' ('The activities of LO/TCO in regard to the South Africa question'), LO/TCO International Committee, Stockholm, 14 November 1977 (LMA).
4. Letter from Kristina Persson to Anna Runeborg, LO/TCO Council of International Trade Union Cooperation, Stockholm, 5 March 1979 (SDA). The visit to London took place in December 1976. Persson's letter to Runeborg in March 1979 was motivated by a series of differences between LO/TCO and SACTU.
5. Ibid.
6. In March 1977, the members of the Nordic Trade Union Council submitted a far-reaching, comprehensive 14- point anti-apartheid programme to the Nordic governments, *inter alia* calling upon them to "work towards a decision in the UN Security Council to isolate South Africa economically, socially and culturally" and to increase "humanitarian aid [...] to the movements for liberation in South Africa". On the labour front, the programme demanded that "the governments via [their] agencies for technical assistance work together with the national trade union organizations to provide the opportunity for black and coloured workers in South Africa to receive trade union education and to provide the victims of the struggle against apartheid with legal and economic support" (Programme in English, attached to letter from Thorbjörn Carlsson, head of LO's international department, to Lesley Harriman, United Nations, Stockholm, 18 April 1977) (MFA). From around 1977, the trade union movements from Denmark, Norway and Sweden constituted a leading, pro- gressive group within ICFTU, later joined by their counterparts in Finland, the Netherlands and Canada. While various initiatives developed at the level of ICFTU, these 'like-minded' movements would from 1979 channel the bulk of the foreign assistance to FOSATU and from 1985 to COSATU.

tion, acquire a negative impression of SACTU's political and practical capacity in exile. This was largely due to the organization's failure to organize a planned high-profile international solidarity conference, but also to its weak presence in Southern Africa.

Through the Swedish embassy in Lusaka, in early June 1976 SACTU had submitted a request to Sweden to finance a conference in support of the South African workers' struggle. It was to be hosted by SACTU in Lusaka during 1977. In addition to ICFTU, WCL and WFTU, representatives from the Organization of African Trade Union Unity and various national African labour movements were to be invited to a meeting which essentially was seen as a follow-up to the 1973 ILO conference.[1] The Consultative Committee on Humanitarian Assistance was positive to the request, and in January 1977 SIDA decided to allocate 140,000 SEK towards the initiative.[2] The Swedish authorities had in the meantime consulted the LO/TCO coordinating council, which—somewhat surprisingly—agreed to liaise with and channel the funds to SACTU.[3]

Nevertheless, it soon became apparent that the request expressed a political wish rather than a practical reality. As early as in December 1976, SACTU's John Gaetsewe and James Stuart explained to the Swedish embassy in Lusaka that the planned conference would no longer be held in Zambia, but probably in the Mozambican capital Maputo.[4] While asking LO/TCO to take an active part in the preparatory work, over the following years different conference venues were proposed, but nothing concrete was achieved. Visiting LO/TCO in August 1979, Zembe conceded that SACTU "in spite of repeated efforts had not managed to [get a commitment] from a [potential] host country or [a trade union] organization in Southern Africa".[5]

On a considerably smaller scale than originally envisaged, the "urgently needed solidarity conference"—proposed just before the historic Soweto uprising—was eventually held in the Ethiopian capital Addis Ababa in April 1980, almost four years after SACTU's request to Sweden and far away from the frontline in Southern Africa.[6] By that time, SACTU's marginalization in exile had become obvious not only to LO/TCO, but also to the Swedish government.[7] Due to its close involvement with ANC, the response by the official authorities was, however, not to steer away from the nationalist movement's labour ally, but—in addition to the support extended via LO/TCO to the internal unions—to assist it to establish a presence in Southern Africa. Embracing SACTU as a fully established and decisive actor, the

---

1. Arne Ström: Memorandum: 'SACTU: Ansökan om 140,000 [kronor] för genomförande av en solidaritetskonferens till stöd för de sydafrikanska arbetarnas kamp' ('SACTU: Request for 140,000 SEK for the holding of a solidarity conference in support of the South African workers' struggle'), CCHA/SIDA, Stockholm, 15 October 1976 (SDA).
2. SIDA: 'Beslut' ('Decision'), Director General's Office, No. 17/77, SIDA, Stockholm, 13 January 1977 (SDA).
3. Kristina Persson: 'LO/TCO's aktiviteter i Sydafrikafrågan' ('The activities of LO/TCO in regard to the South Africa question'), LO/TCO International Committee, Stockholm, 14 November 1977 (LMA).
4. Elisabeth Michanek: Memorandum (' Minnesanteckningar från möte med SACTU's generalsekreterare John Gaetsewe den 22 december 1976'/'Notes from meeting with SACTU's General Secretary John Gaetsewe on 22 December 1976'), Swedish embassy, Lusaka, 23 December 1976 (SDA). On a brief visit to Lusaka, Gaetsewe also informed the embassy about the meetings held with LO/TCO's Kristina Persson in London earlier in the month. She was then preparing her exploratory mission to South Africa.
5. 'Anteckningar från samtal med Zola Zembe från SACTU, 29/8 1979' ('Notes from conversations with Zola Zembe from SACTU on 29 August 1979'), attached to a letter from Kristina Persson to Birgitta Berggren, LO/TCO Council of International Trade Union Cooperation, Stockholm, 13 September 1979 (SDA).
6. Carin Norberg: Memorandum ('Ansökan från South African Congress of Trade Unions, SACTU, om finansiellt stöd 1981/82'/'Request from SACTU for financial support in 1981/82'), CCHA/SIDA, Stockholm, 27 April 1981 (SDA).
7. Cf. Ann Wilkens' memoranda from visits to South Africa in 1976.

organized solidarity movement, on the other hand, did its best to promote the organization in Sweden.

Official Support to SACTU

Following the decision to grant SACTU financial assistance for the proposed international solidarity conference, in February 1977 ANC's labour ally submitted a request for bilateral Swedish support. Signed by Eli Weinberg, the submission noted that "the recent arrests, bans, detentions [and] killings of so many of our members in South Africa have dealt a severe blow to our work".[1] Against this background, SACTU's National Executive Committee had in early January 1977 decided to set up a secretariat in Dar es Salaam "to provide contact with and direction for our activists operating in South Africa".[2] Four members had been assigned to the task, namely Aron Pemba (Chairman), Eli Weinberg (Director), George Monare (National Treasurer) and Eric Mtshali (member). However, lacking the necessary financial resources the organization asked the Swedish government "to furnish and equip an office and a residence for four people", as well as to cover their "monthly food bill".[3]

Although Kristina Persson on behalf of LO/TCO had by then made her exploratory visit to South Africa, the Consultative Committee on Humanitarian Assistance did not wait for her report, but decided in early May 1977 to support SACTU's request. An official contribution of 40,000 SEK was recommended.[4] The recommendation was endorsed by the non-socialist government, and one month later SIDA granted the amount.[5] This marked the beginning of Sweden's direct support to SACTU, which, as noted above, from 1983/84 was eventually to be included within the regular allocation to ANC.

The initial administrative support to the SACTU office in Dar es Salaam was approved at the same time as a substantial aid package via LO/TCO and ICFTU to the internal trade unions was being processed. Nevertheless, the SACTU support would over the following years develop into a unique, annual budgetary contribution. No other trade union organization in Southern Africa received similar assistance directly from Sweden, whether under Social Democratic or non-socialist rule. As the partners in the non-socialist coalition—which between October 1976 and October 1978 included the conservative Moderate Party—contrary to the Social Democratic Party had no direct links to LO or TCO, they were less susceptible to the Swedish trade unions' opposition to SACTU. In the prevailing international Cold War context, it is, however, worthy of note that they agreed to channel direct official financial support to a WFTU-affiliated labour organization in exile.[6]

To the Swedish foreign and aid authorities, it was SACTU's alliance with ANC—not its affiliation to WFTU—which was of decisive importance. In fact, over the years the reports from the Swedish embassies in Southern Africa and the memoranda on SACTU submitted for discussion by CCHA did not mention the affiliation

---

1. Letter from Eli Weinberg to Bo Göransson, Swedish embassy in Dar es Salaam, Dar es Salaam, 13 February 1977 (SDA).
2. Ibid.
3. Ibid.
4. Marianne Sundh: Memorandum ('Ansökan från South African Congress of Trade Unions, SACTU'/'Request from SACTU'), CCHA/SIDA, Stockholm, 5 May 1977 (SDA).
5. SIDA: 'Beslut' ('Decision'), Director General's Office, No. 376/77, SIDA, Stockholm, 6 June 1977 (SDA).
6. It is, of course, similarly of interest to note that SACTU—close to SACP and a staunch opponent of Western, capitalist links with South Africa—turned to Fälldin's 'bourgeois' government for bilateral assistance.

to the Communist-dominated trade union international.[1] Underlining instead its
links with ANC, direct support to SACTU was seen as a complement to the multilateral assistance extended via LO/TCO. In support of SACTU's request for 1979/
80—in which the organization asked for continued budgetary support for its work
in Tanzania, Zambia and the 'forward areas' in Southern Africa[2]—in April 1979
SIDA's Elisabeth Michanek at the Swedish embassy in Lusaka expressed, for example, the widely held opinion that official assistance to SACTU's underground activities "should [also] benefit the trade unions in South Africa which work openly and
are supported by LO/TCO".[3]

While not questioning SACTU as such, there were at the same time Foreign
Ministry officials who argued that support to the organization should either be
channelled via LO/TCO or coordinated by ANC, which was seen as the government's political counterpart.[4] Neither LO/TCO nor SACTU were, however, interested in such a proposal. On behalf of the South African organization, in
November 1978 Weinberg wrote to the Swedish embassy in Dar es Salaam that
"whilst we are very closely allied with the ANC [...], we are as a trade union organisation bound to conduct our work [...] completely independent[ly]. [...] We would
therefore much prefer it if our application would be treated on its own merit".[5]
Until the return of the Social Democratic Party in late 1982, this position was
shared by the Swedish government.

It should be noted that the embassies in Dar es Salaam and Lusaka established
cordial and constructive relations with the local SACTU representatives. Veterans
from the South African struggle—notably Eli Weinberg[6] in Dar es Salaam and Ray
Simons[7] in Lusaka—were in regular contact with Swedish officials, informing them

---

1. For example, letter from Elisabeth Michanek, Swedish embassy in Lusaka, to SIDA, Lusaka, 20 April 1979
   (SDA) and Carin Norberg: Memorandum ('Ansökan från South African Congress of Trade Unions, SACTU,
   om finansiellt stöd 1981/82'/'Request from SACTU for financial support in 1981/82'), CCHA/SIDA, Stockholm, 27 April 1981 (SDA).
2. In addition to the offices in Dar es Salaam and London, in August 1978 SACTU for the first time submitted a
   request covering residences, allowances, transport and other costs for its representatives in Zambia, Botswana
   and Swaziland (Letter from George Monare to the Swedish embassy in Dar es Salaam, Dar es Salaam, 26
   August 1978) (SDA). An amount of 125,000 SEK was subsequently granted for 1978/79 (SIDA: 'Beslut'/
   'Decision', Director General's Office, No. 72/79, SIDA, Stockholm, 31 January 1979) (SDA). The allocation
   was increased to 250,000 SEK in 1979/80 (SIDA: 'Beslut'/'Decision', Director General's Office, No. 339/79,
   SIDA, Stockholm, 1 June 1979) (SDA). It remained at the same level in 1980/81. Following SACTU's decision
   in August 1981 to move its headquarters to Lusaka, the Swedish grant was raised to 700,000 SEK in 1981/82
   (Carin Norberg: Memorandum ('Anslagsposten flyktingar och befrielserörelser i södra Afrika'/'The budgetary
   allocation for refugees and liberation movements in Southern Africa'), SIDA/CCHA, Stockholm, 11 June
   1981) (SDA).
3. Letter from Elisabeth Michanek, Swedish embassy, to SIDA, Lusaka, 20 April 1979 (SDA). In the early 1980s,
   Michanek joined AIC, where LO played a prominent role.
4. Marika Fahlén: Memorandum ('Stöd till det sydafrikanska fackförbundet SACTU'/'Support to the South
   African trade union federation SACTU'), Ministry for Foreign Affairs, Stockholm, 3 November 1978 (SDA).
5. Letter from Eli Weinberg, Administrative Secretary, to the Swedish embassy in Dar es Salaam, Dar es Salaam,
   29 November 1978 (SDA).
6. Born in Latvia, Weinberg came to South Africa in the late 1920s. From 1943 until his banning ten years later,
   he served as General Secretary of the National Union of Commercial Travellers. Following his removal from
   trade union office, Weinberg became a prominent photographer. Going into exile in 1977, he settled in Dar es
   Salaam, where he was appointed Administrative Director of SACTU. He died in 1981.
7. Also born in Latvia, Simons (née Alexander) occupies a prominent position in the history of the non-racial
   South African trade union movement. Based in Cape Town, in the early 1930s she began organizing workers
   into trade unions throughout the Cape and later also in Namibia. Her name is in particular associated with
   the strong Food and Canning Workers Union, of which she was the General Secretary until the apartheid
   regime banned her from trade union work in 1953. At its inaugural congress in 1954, Alexander-Simons was
   appointed National Secretary of the Federation of South African Women, and in the same year she was
   elected to the Cape parliament on the African roll. She was, however, prevented from taking her seat by an act
   specifically passed for this purpose. Forced into exile in the mid-1960s, she eventually settled in Lusaka,
   where she was employed by ILO from 1968. Together with her husband Jack Simons, in 1969 Ray Simons
   published the classic study *Class and Colour in South Africa 1850-1950*.

about past and present struggles on the South African labour front. Birgitta Berg-gren—later serving as secretary to the Consultative Committee on Humanitarian Assistance and heading SIDA's Southern Africa section—had, for example, her first personal encounters with the South African nationalist movement largely through SACTU in Dar es Salaam in the late 1970s. Interviewed in 1996, she recalled how

> Thomas Nkobi [from ANC] and a fellow from SACTU, George Monare, would come to the Swedish embassy. [...] They would be dressed up in suits, ties and be wearing South African hats, and the girl in the reception would call me and say: 'The uncles have arrived'. I would go out to see the 'uncles' and we would sit down and talk. So, it was in Dar es Salaam that I had my first contacts with the liberation movements. Also with people like Eli Weinberg, for instance. He had just arrived with his wife Violet. We listened to them, because they were of the older generation. They could tell the whole story of the struggle.[1]

Similarly, in Lusaka Ray Simons would regularly update the Swedish embassy with regard to SACTU's activities, labour conflicts and strike actions in South Africa.[2]

In addition to SACTU's positive diplomatic approach, initially the Swedish authorities were pleased with the organization's handling of the funds received. In April 1979, the CCHA secretariat noted that "the cooperation [...] from an admin-istrative point of view has been satisfactory, [including] detailed [financial] reports".[3] This, of course, worked in SACTU's favour. Over and above the regular budgetary support, in the early 1980s small, but significant additional requests would therefore be granted. On SACTU's behalf, in October 1980, for example, SIDA decided to purchase 500 copies of its semi-official history *Organize or Starve!*—written by Ken Luckhardt and Brenda Wall[4]—for distribution in Southern Africa. Albeit in a small way—and in spite of the well-known opinions of LO/TCO and ICFTU—SIDA would thus promote the organization.[5]

SACTU was grateful for the support. In a letter to Birgitta Berggren at SIDA, Zola Zembe concluded in January 1981 that

> what is important about the contributions from SIDA is that [they] release other monies, which we can now send into South Africa. [O]therwise, [they would] have been used [for] administration outside [the country].[6]

As the independent trade union movement in South Africa was going from strength to strength, the SACTU leadership, however, started to show signs of exile fatigue. Although extended as budget support, the utilization rate of the Swedish grant decreased.[7] SACTU would in the process become increasingly secretive. Discussing the recent developments before the annual consultations with the organization, in June 1982 the responsible official at the Ministry for Foreign Affairs, Dag

1. Interview with Birgitta Berggren, pp. 256-57.
2. Author's recollection. Closely monitoring the South African labour scene, Simons would in the late 1970s and early 1980s regularly submit handwritten notes on the latest developments to the Swedish embassy. Advising SWAPO, she was also involved in LO/TCO's assistance to NUNW of Namibia. It could be noted that she at the time led the Lusaka sub-committee of SACP's Politbureau (Shubin op. cit., p. 189).
3. Birgitta Berggren: Memorandum ('Ansökan från South African Congress of Trade Unions, SACTU, om stöd till administrativa kostnader'/'Request from SACTU for support towards administrative costs'), CCHA/SIDA, Stockholm, 24 April 1979 (SDA).
4. Luckhardt and Wall op. cit.
5. Letter from Ulf Rundin to John Gaetsewe, SIDA, Stockholm, 22 October 1980 (SDA). The financial support also covered costs for the production of SACTU's official organ *Workers Unity*. In addition, from 1978 SIDA contributed towards the information tours in Sweden that SACTU carried out under the auspices of the Africa Groups.
6. Letter from Zola Zembe to Birgitta Berggren, SIDA, London, 20 January 1981 (SDA).
7. Birgitta Berggren: Memorandum ('Ansökan från South African Congress of Trade Unions, SACTU, om stöd till administrativa kostnader under 1980/81'/'Request from SACTU for support towards administrative costs during 1980/81'), CCHA/SIDA, Stockholm, 28 April 1980 (SDA).

Ahlander, concluded that "the assistance to SACTU has not worked well. We know very little about their activities [and] [w]e have not yet received any reports on the utilization of the [latest] Swedish [contribution]".[1] Brita Östberg, SIDA's representative to Zambia, expressed at about the same time the opinion that SACTU's "unwillingness to communicate anything at all about its activities is greater than that [shown by] ANC".[2]

While the bilateral relations with ANC steadily grew, towards the end of Prime Minister Fälldin's third period of government (May 1981-October 1982) the aid authorities in Stockholm and in the field were becoming increasingly disillusioned with SACTU. In late 1982, this was carried over to Palme's incoming Social Democratic government. Although SIDA and SACTU during bilateral aid negotiations in Lusaka in November 1982 agreed on a cooperation programme of 300,000 SEK for the financial year 1982/83[3], against this background the question as to whether in principle direct, official assistance should be extended to a labour organization was raised anew.

The issue was discussed between the Foreign Ministry and SIDA in mid-February 1983. Concluding that "the government in the future should not [assist] a trade union organization which the Swedish trade union [movement] [...] was not willing to support"[4], the Ministry asked the Swedish embassies in Southern Africa for their opinion. From being positive around 1980, their responses were now decidedly critical. The embassy in Lusaka was "doubtful about continued Swedish support" and both the representations in Gaborone and Pretoria considered SACTU's role as "marginal".[5] While the Social Democratic government did not wish to end the support to SACTU altogether, at the official aid negotiations with ANC in Lusaka in March 1983 it was, as noted above, agreed to accommodate the assistance within the regular allocation to ANC. After the definitive confirmation of the rift between LO/TCO and SACTU in March 1984, this formula became a permanent feature until 1990/91.

AGIS, SACTU and LO-TCO

The Africa Groups, which only in November 1974—almost two years after the Social Democratic government's decision on direct assistance—recognized ANC as "the leading liberation movement in South Africa"[6], were from the beginning strongly opposed to the 'new strategy'. Leading representatives of the reorganized, post-Vietnam solidarity organization actively criticized the joint LO-TCO delegation's visit to South Africa. Calling for "an anti-imperialist isolation strategy"[7], in its official organ the organization denounced the delegation's report and the recom-

1. Dag Ahlander: Memorandum ('Överläggningar med SACTU'/'Consultations with SACTU'), Ministry for Foreign Affairs, Stockholm, 2 June 1982 (SDA).
2. Letter ('Bidrag till SACTU'/'Contribution to SACTU') from Brita Östberg, Swedish embassy in Lusaka, to SIDA, Lusaka, 12 August 1982 (SDA).
3. 'Agreed minutes [between SIDA and SACTU]', Lusaka, 5 November 1982 (SDA).
4. Dag Ahlander: Memorandum ('Samråd UD/SIDA om humanitärt bistånd till södra Afrika'/'Consultations between the Foreign Ministry and SIDA on humanitarian assistance to Southern Africa'), Ministry for Foreign Affairs, Stockholm, 16 February 1983 (SDA).
5. Dag Ahlander: Memorandum ('Remissvar avseende ANC's framställning för budgetåret 1983/84 samt frågan om bidrag till SACTU'/'[Comments] on ANC's request for the financial year 1983/84 and [on] the question of contributions to SACTU'), Ministry for Foreign Affairs, Stockholm, 10 March 1983 (MFA).
6. AGIS: 'Protokoll från Afrikagruppernas konferens i Uppsala den 16-17/11 1974' ('Minutes from the Africa Groups' conference in Uppsala, 16-17 November 1974') [no place or date] (AGA).
7. 'Sverige och Sydafrika: För en Anti-imperialistisk Isoleringsstrategi' ('Sweden and South Africa: For an Anti-imperialist Isolation Strategy') in *Södra Afrika Informationsbulletin*, No. 27, February 1975, pp. 3-4.

mendations adopted by the boards of the two confederations. Characterizing the policy defined by LO and TCO as an "empty threat against the Vorster regime"[1], in December 1975 AGIS urged the Swedish trade union movement to "reject [...] the recommendations and instead demand support for the resistance struggle as a whole, in cooperation with ANC and SACTU".[2]

In the mid-1970s, the solidarity organization's ideological opposition to the Swedish trade unions' reformist approach was strong. With as yet uneasy relations to ANC and marginal links to the Swedish labour movement, this initially led AGIS on an isolated course. When Prime Minister Palme shortly before the Social Democratic Party's election defeat in August 1976 outlined his vision of comprehensive social democratic action against apartheid—among other things advocating continued support to the liberation movement and for the first time officially stating that "we must seriously consider the question of [Swedish] company representation and new investments in South Africa"[3]—the ANC response was positive. Four days later, its resident Chief Representative, Sobizana Mngqikana, wrote to Palme "to commend [him] on the initiative [...] you and your government have taken on the explosive situation that is fast developing in Southern Africa".[4] AGIS, however, rejected the initiative, maintaining that

> Palme's plans will not in any way affect the developments in South Africa. As long as the government does not stop the investments in [the country], his proposals [will] just be empty talk. The only thing that can stop the [apartheid] regime is the struggle by the South African workers and peasants.[5]

The Africa Groups were at the time largely guided by SACTU's views on ICFTU and its advocacy of political and armed struggle. Direct contacts with SACTU had been established in 1975. Together with the ANC-inspired Support Group for the People of South Africa, in December 1975 AGIS' working group on South Africa hosted a visit to Sweden by Edward Ramsdale from the SACTU office in London.[6] Although it was only at its third congress in mid-1977 that the NGO movement formally recognized ANC's labour ally—describing it as "the only trade union in South Africa which has a national, underground organization and is open to all races"[7]—the June 1976 congress resolved that

> [t]rade union solidarity should [...] be expressed through support to [...] SACTU, which stands entirely free from the apartheid regime and organizes resistance [...] chiefly through underground work.[8]

1. 'LO/TCOs 'Nya Strategi': Tomt Hot mot Vorsters Regim' ('LO/TCO's 'New Strategy': Empty Threat against the Vorster Regime') in *Afrikabulletinen*, No. 31, December 1975, pp. 14-18. In May 1975, the organ of the Africa Groups changed name from *Södra Afrika Informationsbulletin* to *Afrikabulletinen*.
2. Ibid., p. 18.
3. Olof Palme: 'Address given at the congress of the Swedish Association of Christian Social Democrats', Skövde, 6 August 1976 (LMA).
4. Letter from Sobizana Mngqikana to Olof Palme, Stockholm, 10 August 1976 (LMA).
5. 'Socialdemokratisk Solidaritet' ('Social Democratic Solidarity') in *Afrikabulletinen*, No. 34, September 1976, p. 16.
6. 'SACTU-ledare i Sverige: Isolera Sydafrika' ('SACTU Leader in Sweden: Isolate South Africa') in *Afrikabulletinen*, No. 32, March 1976, p. 23. Ramsdale—a veteran trade unionist from Cape Town—was responsible for financial matters at the SACTU office in London.
7. AGIS: 'Beslutsprotokoll från Afrikagruppernas kongress 1977' ('Minutes of decisions from the 1977 congress of the Africa Groups') [no place or date] (AGA).
8. AGIS: 'Declaration adopted at the Africa Groups congress, 5-7 June 1976' [no place or date]. Original in English (AGA).

Warning against "the risks that support to openly working organizations entails"[1], in mid-1977 AGIS decided to promote SACTU politically and economically.[2] This was *inter alia* carried out through information tours by SACTU representatives, who were invited to Sweden to travel the country, meet the various Africa Groups and through them present their case to local trade unions. After the visit by Edward Ramsdale in late 1975, beginning with James Stuart in March-April 1977[3] such tours were organized on an annual basis over the following years.[4] AGIS also launched fund-raising campaigns in favour of SACTU.

At the time, the Africa Groups had, however, no support base in the Swedish trade unions.[5] While their advocacy of ANC enjoyed popular support, the promotion of SACTU combined with harsh criticism of LO and TCO tended to alienate the solidarity organization from the wider labour movement, including the Social Democratic Party. As later stated by Sören Lindh,

> [w]e [...] had to do our homework on the trade union situation. [...] [We] realized from the beginning that it was a dangerous terrain, unless it was very clear what [we] were doing.[6]

Initially, this was far from being the case. Having declared its firm support for SACTU—and after organizing James Stuart's information tour in Sweden—AGIS became uncertain about the role played by ANC's labour ally. In November 1977, Lindh wrote to Stuart in Lusaka for guidance. Noting that LO/TCO's Kristina Persson maintained that SACTU was "an exile organization only", the AGIS representative underlined that

> we *must* be able to counter [her] views. [...] [W]e need [...] 'proof' of SACTU's presence and activities inside, and advice [on] how to argue with [her] and others on this question. [Or] else, we can [be] labelled as unreliable and [as] misinformers, trying to mislead the LO and TCO members. If, on the other hand, we have been 'overselling' SACTU [...], it [would be] very tactical in the long run to present the real size and state of SACTU's work, and start from a new basis. As we are now starting to get good contacts within the LO and TCO organizations, there are reasonable prospects that we can 'survive' a 'retreat' on the issue of the clandestine trade union activities. [...]
>
> [The] irritating issue [...] whether SACTU exists inside or not must be removed from the agenda as soon as possible. If you, please, could give us documentation, contacts or other things to clarify the issue, we [could then] work with more important things[7] [...] and in closer cooperation with LO/TCO.[8]

The letter was written immediately after a seminar on trade union solidarity with South Africa had been organized by AGIS in Uppsala in mid-November 1977. In

---

1. AGIS: 'Beslutsprotokoll från Afrikagruppernas kongress 1977' ('Minutes of decisions from the 1977 congress of the Africa Groups') [no place or date] (AGA).
2. Ibid.
3. AGIS: 'Verksamhetsberättelse för AGIS' Sydafrikautskott [1977-78]' ('Activity report regarding AGIS' South Africa committee') [no place or date] (AGA).
4. Edward Ramsdale returned to Sweden in September-October 1978. William Khanyile—who was killed a year later during the South African attack on Matola outside Maputo—travelled the country on behalf of SACTU in January-February 1980. Thozamile Botha carried out a similar information tour in March 1981.
5. In 1980, the Africa Groups formed a trade union committee to "stimulate [...] solidarity with the workers' struggles in South Africa and Namibia". With only a marginal influence at the central level of the established trade unions, the committee did, however, organize some 150 individual AGIS members active within local unions all over Sweden (Dick Urban Vestbro: 'Om det fackliga utskottet'/'On the trade union committee' [no place or date]) (AGA).
6. Interview with Sören Lindh, p. 307.
7. Notably, economic sanctions.
8. Letter from Sören Lindh to James Stuart, Stockholm, 20 November 1977 (AGA). No evidence of a reply by Stuart has been found.

addition to more than 20 representatives from different local unions[1], Hans Eng-man from the TCO headquarters and Kristina Persson from the LO/TCO Council of International Trade Union Cooperation had accepted invitations to the seminar.[2] This marked the beginning of slowly improving relations between AGIS and the trade unions. Turning away from an essentially sectarian stand, as the solidarity organization started to question its exclusive advocacy of SACTU it began to self-critically re-examine its policy towards the wider Swedish labour movement. To a large extent, this was provoked by LO's decision in May 1978 to carry out a national campaign in favour of the struggling peoples in Zimbabwe, Namibia and South Africa, forcing AGIS to redefine its positions.

LO's initiative and the Africa Groups' relations to the Swedish trade union movement were discussed during AGIS' fourth congress in Gothenburg in mid-May 1978.[3] In its report to the congress, the outgoing board noted that the solidarity movement's impact in 1977-78 had been limited, concluding that

> one reason that AGIS has not succeeded better in influencing the [general] opinion is most probably that [it] is viewed as an organization which is hostile to the established labour movement. We have not recognized the progressive initiatives taken by the Social Democratic Party, LO and TCO, [nor have we] dissociated ourselves from earlier, unnuanced statements about these organizations.[4]

Keen to establish constructive relations with the labour movement—not least in order to broaden the base for sanctions against South Africa—after intensive debates the AGIS congress decided to support the LO campaign due to start in September 1978.[5] While the internal discussions were hidden to the general public, in August 1978—one month before the official launch of the campaign, which also enjoyed support from TCO and the opposition Social Democratic Party—the Africa Groups publicly dissociated themselves from positions taken in the early and mid-1970s.

Marking a clear shift in the history of the solidarity organization—as well as the foundation in Sweden of an essentially unitary anti-apartheid opinion—the self-criticism and appeals for cooperation with the social democratic movement published by *Afrikabulletinen* merit being extensively quoted. Welcoming the upcoming LO campaign, AGIS stated that

1. Ibid.
2. AGIS: 'Program för veckoslutsseminarium i Uppsala den 19-20 november 1977' ('Programme for weekend seminar in Uppsala, 19-20 November 1977') [no place or date] (AGA).
3. AGIS: 'Protokoll fört vid Afrikagruppernas i Sverige fjärde ordinarie kongress i Göteborg, 13-15 maj 1978' ('Minutes taken at AGIS' fourth regular congress in Gothenburg, 13-15 May 1978') [no place or date] (AGA).
4. AGIS: 'Styrelsens verksamhetsberättelse 1977-78' ('Activity report by the board, 1977-78') [no place or date] (AGA).
5. 'Kongress '78' ('Congress '78') in *Afrikabulletinen*, No. 42, June 1978, pp. 12-13. The discussions within the solidarity movement took place at a time when preparations for the Isolate South Africa Committee were being made. To establish a broad platform for ISAK—initially conceived as an AGIS-sponsored national campaign rather than a separate organization—constructive relations with the Social Democratic Party and LO were seen as particularly important (Letter from Bertil Högberg to the author, [Uppsala], 12 June 2000). Among those who influenced AGIS' policy shift were the board members Lennart Bengtsson (later Renöfeldt) and Bertil Högberg, who both had a base in the churches.

[our] relations [...] with LO [and the Social Democratic Party] have [...] earlier been strained, and during certain periods clearly chilly. There may be many reasons for that. The Africa Groups have criticized certain parts of the Social Democratic Party's Africa policy, in particular when it was in government. That has been the case at times when we were of the opinion that the government acted too slowly, insufficiently or wrongly. In that respect, we have among other things expressed the impatience felt by the liberation movements towards the policies of Sweden, and the Western world, in Africa. This is a natural task for a solidarity movement which is independent of any political party and acts as a pressure group in favour of the interests of the liberation movements. [...]

Stöd din kamrat i Sydafrika

1978 internationellt kampår mot apartheid.

'Support Your Comrade in South Africa': LO-TCO poster issued for the 1978 International Anti-Apartheid Year

However, in our criticism we have in some cases been guilty of indiscretions which have neither served the liberation movements, nor the common struggle against the Swedish monopoly companies' exploitation of [...] the African workers. One example is an early article [...] in which LO was equated with ICFTU and where we characterized LO as an organization for class collaboration. That is a statement alien to the Africa Groups, which is a solidarity organization and whose task is not to take a stand on socialism or the role of the labour movement in Sweden. Another example is a section [in our book on Africa] which was phrased in such a way that it could give the impression that we questioned the social democratic movement's honesty [regarding] its support to the liberation movements. [...] Our opinion work has been limited by [the fact] that we have been seen as hostile to the established labour movement. [...] [W]e therefore wish to emphasize that no such hostility exists. [...]

[T]he Africa Groups have not only ignored efforts [made] by LO and the Social Democratic Party, but also, for example, good campaigns by Christian and youth organizations. [...]

We hope [...] that these sources of irritation may be put into the historical archive [and] that we instead [...] can pay [due] attention to the good efforts that are being mutually made within the solidarity work. [...] The international campaign by LO and the Social Democratic Party in favour of the liberation struggle in Southern Africa is a good initiative. It should give extensive breadth to the solidarity actions and to the studies of what is going on in the struggle for the wealth of [the region]. [...] It is also our hope that [it] will initiate a new phase in the contacts between LO, the Social Democratic Party and the Africa Groups. [...]

With the broad popular opinion that now exists [in Sweden] for support to the liberation movements on their own conditions, we should leave our remaining differences aside. Local boycott [initiatives] [...] have shown the possibilities of cooperation. Let us continue along those lines and carry out an effective boycott campaign to isolate the Vorster regime and together mobilize support for the liberation struggle in South Africa, Namibia and Zimbabwe.[1]

Having two years earlier dismissed Palme's Southern Africa initiative as 'empty talk', this was an entirely new discourse. In spite of LO's opposition and its own doubts, AGIS, however, did not abandon its support for SACTU. During the long and successful LO campaign—which lasted from September 1978 until May 1979—the solidarity organization actively promoted ANC's labour ally. While

---

1. 'Afrikagrupperna om LO/SAP: Samarbete för Lyckad Kampanj'/'The Africa Groups on LO [and the Social Democratic Party]: Cooperation for a Successful Campaign' in *Afrikabulletinen*, No. 43, August 1978, p. 3.

SACTU in the mid-1970s had been held out as the only genuine South African trade union organization worthy of assistance, for reasons largely coinciding with those advanced by SIDA and accepted by the Fälldin government, AGIS would, nevertheless, "adjust" its views.[1] No longer denouncing the Swedish labour movement's assistance to the internal legal organizations, SACTU was now described as "the guarantor of the survival of the active South African trade unions".[2] The message became: "Give money to SACTU as well".[3]

Although this policy only produced meagre results among the LO-affiliated unions[4], it did strike an echo within TCO. Interviewed in 1997, Sören Lindh noted that

> [t]he interesting thing about [our] SACTU campaign [was] that we got allies within the Swedish trade unions. I had, for instance, contacts with the chairman of TCO, Lennart Bodström. He was concerned.[5] [...] [W]e went to the shop stewards and to the local branches and said: 'Some people in South Africa are working openly, but in disguise. Others are working underground. If you would like to have a balanced situation, how do you channel the support? To both sides'. That made sense to a lot of people. We had unions supporting our view. Then we had to face the fact that SACTU was a member of [WFTU], but most of the people who were active and interested in international affairs did not care about that.[6]

Outside the coordinated action by the joint LO/TCO council, the ICFTU-affiliated white-collar confederation would on a bilateral basis channel important financial contributions to the Eastern-aligned South African labour organization.[7] Joining the solidarity campaign for Southern Africa launched by LO and the Social Democratic Party, towards the end of 1978 TCO had raised a total of 1.8 MSEK. Largely due to the efforts of AGIS, 113,000 SEK of the amount was—in competition with support to the liberation movements in Zimbabwe, Namibia and South Africa—earmarked for SACTU by various donor unions, notably the Industrial Employees Union (SIF), TCO's largest member.[8] When AGIS started its own fund-raising campaign for SACTU, the most important contributions were, similarly, made by TCO affiliates. In 1983/84, for example, no less than 40,000 out of the 44,000 SEK received was donated by the Municipal Employees Union (SKTF).[9]

---

1. Interview with Sören Lindh, p. 307.
2. Dick Urban Vestbro: 'Om det fackliga utskottet' ('On the trade union committee') [no place or date] (AGA).
3. Interview with Sören Lindh, p. 307.
4. The powerful Metalworkers Union—to which an overwhelming majority of the workers at the Swedish parent companies with subsidiaries in South Africa belonged—was particularly dismissive of SACTU. Closely cooperating with the International Metalworkers Federation, the leadership of the union was for a long time also opposed to ANC. According to a study on the Swedish Metalworkers Union and South Africa, as late as in 1977 the executive committee rejected SACTU since it "regarded the exiled trade union as too radical and too closely connected to ANC" (Andersson op. cit., p. 21).
5. As earlier noted, shortly before the LO-TCO decision in September 1975 the future Social Democratic Foreign Minister declared that he personally felt that TCO should focus on support to "underground organizations [like] SACTU".
6. Interview with Sören Lindh, p. 307.
7. At the time, the Left Party Communists advocated a considerable increase in the official support to SACTU. In a parliamentary motion submitted in January 1979, for example, the party requested a Swedish grant to the organization of no less than 10 MSEK (Swedish Parliament 1978/79: Motion No. 590, Riksdagens Protokoll 1978/79, p. 9). The official allocation to ANC in 1978/79 amounted to 12 MSEK.
8. In Swedish, *Svenska Industritjänstemannaförbundet.* Figures quoted from *SIF-Tidningen*, No. 12, 1978, p. 54. The TCO contribution could be compared with the official grant to SACTU for the financial year 1978/79. It was 125,000 SEK, i.e. only slightly more.
9. In Swedish, *Sveriges Kommunaltjänstemannaförbund.* Figures quoted from the document ('Insamlingarna 1.5 1983-30.4 1984'/'The collections 1 May 1983-30 April 1984') attached to AGIS: 'Afrikagruppernas verksamhetsberättelse 1983/84' ('AGIS' activity report 1983/84') [no place or date] (AGA). AGIS' fund-raising efforts in favour of SACTU were not particularly successful. Between 1981/82 and 1985/86, a total of 83,000 SEK was received. Out of this amount, well over half was donated by TCO-affiliated unions (AGIS activity reports for the period) (AGA).

Thus, towards the end of the 1970s the quite extraordinary situation in Sweden with regard to the 'Communist' SACTU was that it was receiving direct official support from the non-socialist coalition government, important member unions of the ICFTU-affiliated TCO and the Africa Groups, while the blue-collar LO confederation ignored, or dismissed, the organization. All of them supported ANC. After AGIS' profound self-criticism and re-orientation in mid-1978, the views shared by SIDA and AGIS were conspicuous in this constellation between the state, prominent TCO unions and the anti-imperialist solidarity movement. With similar developments regarding the liberation struggles in Zimbabwe and Namibia, this was at the end of the 1970s but one of many expressions of the growing understanding and cooperation between the aid authorities and the solidarity movement.[1]

The Swedish trade unions' assistance to South Africa will be briefly presented below. In the meantime, it could be noted that the Africa Groups continued to promote SACTU after the government's decision to suspend the direct support to the organization. Long after the formation of the Congress of South African Trade Unions (COSATU) in December 1985, AGIS and ISAK would organize SACTU information tours in Sweden.[2] Furthermore, in February 1986 the historic People's Parliament against Apartheid[3] called on the popular movements to "intensify [their] efforts on behalf of the underground trade union organization SACTU".[4] Without mentioning COSATU, in April 1986 the new programme adopted by the Africa Groups stated that the solidarity movement "support[s] those trade union organizations which maintain close cooperation with the liberation movements, [namely] [...] SACTU in South Africa and [...] NUNW in Namibia".[5]

Although it was still an outspoken voice in the pro-sanctions campaign, by the mid-1980s the South African organization had outlived its trade union role. When LO, TCO and the wider labour movement established close and direct relations with the powerful internal union congress—and ANC in its January 1986 message[6] hailed the COSATU launch as a "victory" which the democratic movement must

---

1. Interviewed in 1997, the veteran AGIS member Hillevi Nilsson underlined that "the mainstream in the Africa Groups always wanted to be a kind of lobby group towards SIDA and the Ministry for Foreign Affairs" (Interview with Hillevi Nilsson, p. 330). And in mid-1986—before the introduction of comprehensive Swedish sanctions against South Africa—AGIS' national board noted that "the majority of the Africa Groups' demands and our global view on Southern Africa are presently shared with most of the established [political] parties and popular movements" (AGIS: 'Afrikagruppernas verksamhetsberättelse 1985/86'/'The Africa Groups' activity report for 1985/86', [no place or date], p. 4) (AGA). That in Sweden there was only one recognized NGO solidarity organization with the struggles in Southern Africa and that it maintained close working relations with the official authorities—supporting the very same liberation movements—goes a long way towards explaining the absence of ideological disputes or divisions. The situation was similar in Norway, but different in Denmark. After a visit to Scandinavia together with Oliver Tambo in March 1981, Thabo Mbeki described the state of affairs among the different Danish support groups as "confused", adding that they "apparently devoted more time to fighting the Social Democratic government than to solidarity work for Southern Africa" (Cable ('ANC om Sverigebesök'/'ANC on visit to Sweden') from Göran Hasselmark, Swedish ambassador to Zambia, to the Ministry for Foreign Affairs, Lusaka, 25 March 1981) (MFA).
2. As late as in October 1987, the Africa Groups hosted a visit to Sweden by Aron Pemba (International Secretary), Bonisile Norushe (Treasurer) and Patrick Msizi (SACTU representative to the Nordic countries) (AGIS: 'Möte med ledningen för SACTU'/'Meeting with the SACTU leadership', Stockholm [no date]) (AGA).
3. On the People's Parliament against Apartheid, see the chapter 'Culture and Popular Initiatives: From Frontline Rock to the People's Parliament'.
4. 'The Swedish People's Parliament against Apartheid in Stockholm, 21-23 February 1986', Final document, English translation [no place or date], p. 8.
5. 'Afrikagruppernas program' ('The Africa Groups' programme'), adopted at AGIS' extraordinary congress, 12-13 April 1986 [no place or date], p. 5 (AGA).
6. ANC—the oldest national liberation movement in Africa—was founded as the South African Native National Congress in Bloemfontein on 8 January 1912. On the initiative of Oliver Tambo, from 1979 ANC in exile would commemorate the anniversary by issuing 'January 8 statements'. Containing the ANC leadership's guidance to its members, followers and—in general—the people of South Africa, as a rule Thabo Mbeki drafted the political messages.

"defend at all costs"[1]—for all practical purposes the Swedish solidarity movement's lingering advocacy of SACTU in the late 1980s became mainly symbolic.

Never really debated—nor becoming divisive[2]—the calls were rather an expression of indirect support for ANC than a stand in favour of a particular tendency within the Congress Alliance. The same applied to the Social Democratic government, which *de facto* extended assistance to SACTU until its dissolution in March 1990. For its part, however, SACTU would to the very end aggressively defend its *raison d'être* vis-à-vis the Swedish and Nordic trade unions, in the process conclusively losing the sympathy it had managed to mobilize in the late 1970s and early 1980s.[3]

LO/TCO Assistance via ICFTU and to COSATU

Mainly relying on government funds[4], under the ICFTU umbrella LO and TCO would from 1977 together with their sister organizations in Denmark and Norway—later joined by the Dutch and Finnish trade unions[5]—become actively involved in the efforts to build a modern, viable South African workers' movement. Culminating in the formation of COSATU in late 1985, the history of the international support to this process has from a South African perspective been comprehensively documented by Southall[6] and—with regard to COSATU—by Baskin.[7] Largely expressing a shared Nordic experience, Vetlesen has documented the involvement by the Norwegian LO[8], while Wickman in the case of Sweden has

1. Cited in Jeremy Baskin: *Striking Back: A History of COSATU*, Verso, London and New York, 1991, p. 74. Without even mentioning SACTU, in its January 1987 message—issued on the occasion of the 75th anniversary of the nationalist movement—ANC urged the South African workers to "unite under the umbrella of COSATU" (ANC: 'Statement of the National Executive Committee of the African National Congress', Lusaka [no date], p. 7).
2. Misreading the developments on the South African labour front, in the late 1980s solidarity organizations in 'like-minded countries' advocated support to SACTU to the detriment of COSATU. In the case of Canada, for example, Linda Freeman concludes that this "meant that union loyalties and a significant part of Canadian union funds were devoted to a spent force", which, in turn, "undermined the contribution which might have gone to the trade union mainstream in South Africa during a crucial period in the struggle against apartheid" (Linda Freeman: *The Ambiguous Champion: Canada and South Africa in the Trudeau and Mulroney Years*, University of Toronto Press, Toronto, Buffalo and London, 1997, p. 142).
3. Assisted by Danish support groups, in early 1988—when the organization had long since outlived its role— SACTU opened an office in Copenhagen. Covering the Nordic countries, it was led by Patrick Msizi. In his contacts with the Nordic trade unions, Msizi denounced ICFTU, demanding recognition of and support for SACTU. At a time when COSATU had established a special relationship with the Nordic unions, not surprisingly the relations with the SACTU office turned sour from the very beginning (cf. Vetlesen (1998) op. cit., pp. 84-86).
4. Operating with official funds, like the churches, the Africa Groups and other NGOs the trade unions were for all practical purposes politically independent of government directives. Looking at the developments on the labour scene from a South African angle, Southall concludes that "despite the official sources of [the] funds, the impact of government[...] influence upon the ICFTU's programme of assistance and through that upon the South African unions themselves was, at most, indirect" (Southall op. cit., p. 181).
5. From 1979, the ICFTU-affiliated trade union confederations in Scandinavia (LO Denmark, LO Norway and LO-TCO Sweden) and Holland (FNV) shared equally the costs for the initial assistance to FOSATU. CLC of Canada and AFL-CIO of the United States joined the support programme in 1982. AFL-CIO left ICFTU in 1969, but rejoined in 1982. During the crucial years in the late 1970s, the traditionally anti-Communist American trade union confederation did not participate in the multilateral effort. After the formation of COSATU in late 1985, the so called "progressive" constellation of like-minded trade union organizations in Scandinavia and Holland coordinated the international support to the congress. SAK of Finland joined the Scandinavian and Dutch donors in 1987.
6. Southall op. cit.
7. Baskin op. cit.
8. Vetlesen (1998) op. cit. and Vetlesen in Eriksen (ed.) op. cit.

published a summary of the assistance extended via the LO/TCO Council of International Trade Union Cooperation.[1]

Not a primary focus of the present study—albeit an essential part of both Swedish official and NGO assistance to the oppressed South African majority—the purpose of the following pages is to place the Swedish trade union movement's international and national participation within the wider anti-apartheid struggle. In addition to a general overview, it is in this context—not least due to the strained relations with SACTU in exile—relevant to mention some of the union activities carried out in favour of ANC. Before summarizing the first steps towards unilateral Swedish sanctions, in anticipation of the boycott debate in the mid-1980s some conspicuous contradictions resulting from the union involvement should, finally, be mentioned.[2]

In the meantime, it could be noted that the Swedish and Nordic labour efforts via ICFTU did make a difference. Although the joint LO-TCO visit to South Africa in early 1975 was strongly censured at the time by ANC, SACTU and the Africa Groups, comparing different international actors Southall concludes that

> most assertive of all were the Swedish LO and TCO [...]. [T]hey deployed a much greater sensitivity to the historic role of SACTU and [b]lack workers' struggles, and a much more sceptical approach to TUCSA than anything the [British] TUC had been able to muster. In consequence, not only did their proposals for external assistance to emergent unions go well beyond those of the TUC by associating them openly with the struggle for democracy in South Africa, but also they were explicitly condemnatory of Swedish firms as operating 'within and in compliance with the social order'. Their [...] demand for recognition of representative [b]lack unions was [...] strident and backed up a recommendation that the Swedish [g]overnment inhibit further investment [...] and increase its support for the opponents and victims of apartheid.[3]

Between 1975 and 1978, the joint Scandinavian and Dutch contributions represented almost half of ICFTU's International Solidarity Fund.[4] In the case of South Africa and the constituent parts of COSATU, their share was even higher. As later underlined by several prominent South African trade unionists, LO-TCO and the Scandinavian confederations played a leading role.[5] Vetlesen has described the ICFTU assistance to South Africa as "no doubt [...] the single largest one in the history of trade unionism".[6] Its impact on the modern labour movement in South Africa was in 1995 summarized as follows by Southall:

1. Wickman op. cit. In her brief study—published in Swedish in 1996—Wickman notes that "the [Swedish] trade union assistance, like all other assistance to South Africa, had to be extended via secret and strictly confidential [channels]. It was [at the time] completely impossible to mention that support was given and even less, for example, to state the names of recipient organizations or contact persons in South Africa" (ibid., p. 4). While the general involvement by LO/TCO was certainly widely known—not least through frequent and public visits by prominent South African trade union representatives, such as John Gomomo, James Motlatsi and Cyril Ramaphosa, later joined by Sydney Mufamadi, Jay Naidoo and many others—the first, factual overview written by Wickman on behalf of LO/TCO raises, however, more questions than it answers. To really open the files on Sweden's substantial trade union assistance to South Africa, the initiative taken by LO and Vetlesen in Norway needs to be emulated. As stated by Wickman, in modern times South Africa has, in fact, been the single largest recipient of Swedish trade union assistance, thus deserving a more comprehensive study. This said, towards the end of the 1990s some academic studies were initiated to document certain aspects of the labour relations between Sweden and South Africa, such as Anders Andersson's discussion of the Swedish Metalworkers Union and the sanctions debate (Andersson op. cit.).
2. The Swedish labour movement's assistance to UDF and the National Union of Mineworkers will be discussed in the context of the direct involvement with the internal anti-apartheid forces towards the mid-1980s.
3. Southall op. cit., pp. 131-32.
4. Ibid., p. 181.
5. See, for example, the interviews with John Gomomo (p. 128) and James Motlatsi (pp. 166-67). Also the interview with COSATU's former General Secretary Jay Naidoo in Wickman op. cit., pp. 27-31.
6. Vetlesen in Eriksen (ed.) op. cit., p. 339.

[W]hat remains the most distinctive and vital aspect of ICFTU's programme was its early recognition of the democratic unions from the moment that they began to emerge and develop in the 1970s. In contrast to those to its left who called for the total isolation of South Africa and who queried the legitimacy and viability of the new wave of [b]lack trade unionism, the ICFTU stepped in and lent the fledgling movement critical moral and material support during its perhaps most difficult days. Indeed, it can be unambiguously stated that such was the extent of their initial dependence upon this funding that the emergent unions could scarcely have achieved the extent of their organisational reach without it.

Furthermore, whilst the machinery it established for coordinating the flow of financial aid by no means worked to the full satisfaction of the recipients, it none the less did operate in a manner which curbed competition and encouraged cooperation amongst the national centre donors, which largely eschewed imperialistic designs and which provided for the allocation of assistance to unions according to their need, their motivations and their capability. The overall result was a relatively consistent even-handedness, which avoided the favouring of any one tendency and which sought to foster unity.[1]

The beginnings of Sweden's trade union assistance to Southern Africa have been discussed in the context of Namibia above. Following the recommendations by the 1975 LO-TCO mission, in the case of South Africa the initial support targeted the Swedish owned companies. The very first contribution from the two confederations—a modest amount of 55,000 SEK—was channelled in late 1976 to the Engineering and Allied Workers Union to strengthen its work at the Swedish subsidiaries.[2] With increasing official funds at its disposal and in close coordination with its Nordic sister organizations, the LO/TCO Committee—later Council—of International Trade Union Cooperation soon extended the area of operations to the wider, national South African labour scene.

As earlier noted, on behalf of the LO/TCO council Kristina Persson went on a fact-finding mission to South Africa in January-February 1977. Shortly thereafter, the joint trade union council submitted a first request for official financial support to the Consultative Committee on Humanitarian Assistance. Focusing on trade union education, legal aid and advisory services, it covered assistance to various structures and activities in South Africa, as well as funds for project preparation in Lesotho[3], Namibia and Zimbabwe. CCHA supported the request in mid-June 1977, and SIDA subsequently disbursed an amount of 1 million SEK to LO/TCO.[4] This marked the beginning of the substantial Swedish trade union assistance to South Africa, channelled via ICFTU in Brussels, Belgium, and through different International Trade Secretariats.

During the initial years—until the formation of the Federation of South African Trade Unions—the assistance was mainly given to a number of advice bureaux, such as the General Factory Workers Benefit Fund[5], the Industrial Aid Centre, the

---

1. Southall op. cit., p. 355.
2. Kristina Persson: 'LO/TCO's aktiviteter i Sydafrikafrågan' ('The activities of LO/TCO in regard to the South Africa question'), LO/TCO International Committee, Stockholm, 14 November 1977 (LMA).
3. In the case of Lesotho, the subsequent LO/TCO assistance primarily targeted the migrant labourers working on contract for the South African mining corporations. Formally under ICFTU's umbrella, the Swede Ove Johansson was from 1979 based in the independent mountain kingdom to coordinate the project. At the time, the migrant workers from Lesotho were particularly conspicuous in the strategically important gold mining industry. Several leading representatives of the South African mineworkers were from Lesotho. This was notably the case of James Motlatsi, founder and later President of NUM.
4. Kristina Persson: Memorandum ('Projekt för facklig utbildning m.m. i södra Afrika budgetåret 1978/79'/ 'Projects on trade union education etc. in Southern Africa [during the] financial year 1978/79'), Stockholm, 7 April 1978 (SDA).
5. Also known as the Harriet Bolton Project.

Industrial Aid Society, the Institute for Industrial Education, the Trade Union Advisory and Coordinating Council[1] and the Western Province Workers Advice Bureau.[2] Already established unions—among them the Food and Canning Workers Union[3], the Metal and Allied Workers Union and the United Auto and Allied Workers Union—were also included in the first aid programme.[4] The ICFTU assistance to these structures was financed from 1977 via the labour movements in Denmark, Norway and Sweden, which each contributed one third of the costs.[5]

Less than two years later, two major events on the South African labour scene radically influenced the Swedish and Scandinavian assistance, namely the formation in April 1979 of the non-racial, national Federation of South African Trade Unions (FOSATU) and the release in May of the Wiehahn Commission's first report to the South African government, recommending the recognition of registered black unions.[6] LO/TCO supported the preparatory work for the launch of FOSATU.[7] Soon thereafter, it was decided that the new central trade union organization should become "our main South African recipient".[8] In the wake of the Wiehahn report, it was in consultations with ICFTU and FOSATU at the same time agreed to phase out the support to the advice bureaux, which essentially were incorporated into the new trade union structures.[9] Focusing on organization at the factory floor level, FOSATU emphasized the training of shop stewards. From the very beginning, the ICFTU contribution to the education effort was shared equally between the member organizations in Denmark, Norway, Sweden and the Netherlands.[10]

1. Set up in the aftermath of the 1973 Durban strikes, the Trade Union Advisory and Coordinating Council (TUACC) was more of an umbrella organization for emerging unions in Natal—and later Transvaal—than an advice bureau. TUACC was largely behind the formation of FOSATU. Alec Erwin, who in 1979 became General Secretary of FOSATU and in 1994 Deputy Minister of Finance, joined TUACC in the late 1970s. Involved in trade union education at TUACC, FOSATU, COSATU and later the National Union of Metalworkers of South Africa (NUMSA), he established close contacts with the Swedish and Nordic trade union movements.

2. Various such centres were set up in the early 1970s. Advising workers of the limited labour rights they legally possessed, but routinely were denied, they played a crucial role in and for the development of the South African trade union movement. Largely inspired by white intellectuals, veteran black trade unionists with SACTU experience were often active within these structures (Southall op. cit., pp. 57-58 and Baskin op. cit., pp. 18-21).

3. Formed by Ray Alexander-Simons in the Cape in 1941, the Food and Canning Workers Union (FCWU) would for a long time serve as a model of militant trade unionism throughout South Africa, as well as providing leadership within SACTU. FCWU was one of the few unions that managed to survive the repression in the 1960s. Although LO and TCO dismissed SACTU in exile, it should be noted that in 1977 FCWU was included among the first recipients of Swedish trade union assistance to South Africa. This, in turn, may partly explain the contacts established with the Swedish embassy in Lusaka by FCWU's founder and former General Secretary Ray Simons.

4. Kristina Persson: Memorandum ('Projekt för facklig utbildning m.m. i södra Afrika budgetåret 1978/79'/ 'Projects on trade union education etc. in Southern Africa [during the] financial year 1978/79'), Stockholm, 7 April 1978 (SDA).

5. Ibid.

6. In response to the workers' struggles from 1973 and to the pressures for change from abroad, in 1977 the Pretoria government appointed a commission led by Nic Wiehahn to look into the country's labour legislation. Its first report recommended that registration of black trade unions should be permitted as a way of controlling the emerging, militant labour movement. By an amendment to the Industrial Conciliation Act, the recommendation was subsequently enacted into law. Although the black mineworkers were initially excluded and among the existing democratic unions there followed an often bitter debate on whether to officially register or not, the result was major trade union growth in the early 1980s.

7. Kristina Persson: 'Rapport över LO/TCO's projekt i södra Afrika' ('Report on the LO/TCO projects in Southern Africa'), Stockholm, 13 August 1979 (SDA).

8. Ibid.

9. Ibid.

10. Letter from Jan-Erik Norling, LO/TCO, to CCHA, Stockholm, 8 September 1981 (SDA).

In reaction to FOSATU's non-racialism, in September 1980 a group of unions with a black exclusivist perspective formed a competing national trade union federation, the Council of Unions of South Africa (CUSA). While FOSATU did not formally join ICFTU, CUSA did. In addition to a number of independent unions[1], as well as individual FOSATU and CUSA affiliates—among the latter notably the National Union of Mineworkers[2]—CUSA would also benefit from Swedish assistance through LO/TCO and ICFTU. In the period from 1 January 1983 to 30 June 1984, for example, the budgeted LO/TCO contribution to FOSATU was 960,000 and to CUSA 400,000 SEK.[3]

This is not the place to discuss the developments on the South African labour scene in the early 1980s. Suffice it to recall that they were truly revolutionary. Together with the community-based struggles inspired by the United Democratic Front (UDF), they contributed to a state of protracted popular insurrection. As total trade union membership between 1980 and 1985 rose from around 950,000 to 1.9 million[4], increasing strike action indicated the developing strength of labour. From around 200 in 1980, the number of work stoppages grew constantly until 1987, when no less than 1,148 strikes involving a total of 600,000 workers were recorded.[5] At the same time, unity talks were held between the various democratic trade union structures, traditions and tendencies. Starting in 1981, they eventually culminated in December 1985 in the historic launch of COSATU in Durban, mainly formed around FOSATU, NUM and independent UDF-aligned unions. This, in turn, immediately led Buthelezi's Inkatha movement to set up a Zulu-based United Workers Union of South Africa (UWUSA)[6], while CUSA and the equally black exclusivist AZACTU[7] later formed a National Council of Trade Unions (NACTU).[8] Against the ethnically and racially oriented organizations, the non-racial COSATU—which in 1987 adopted the Congress Alliance's Freedom Charter—

---

1. Such as the General Workers Union (GWU), the Media Workers Union of South Africa (MWASA)—led by Zwelakhe Sisulu, son of the jailed ANC leader Walter Sisulu—and the South African Allied Workers Union (SAAWU).

2. Led by Cyril Ramaphosa and James Motlatsi, NUM later left CUSA. When COSATU was formed in December 1985, NUM was with around 100,000 members by far the largest individual member union (Baskin op. cit., p. 55).

3. Letter from Jan-Erik Norling to CCHA, Stockholm, 7 February 1983 (SDA).

4. Southall op. cit., p. 64.

5. Najwah Allie: *Directory of South African Trade Unions: A Complete Guide to All South Africa's Trade Unions*, SALDRU, Cape Town, 1991, p. 22.

6. UWUSA was set up in January 1986. Rejecting sanctions, the organization also opposed strikes and boycotts. Acting outside the ICFTU structures, representatives of the American AFL-CIO were present when the Inkatha front was formed (Vetlesen (1998) op. cit., p. 61). This led to a major row with the Nordic and Dutch members (Urs Hauser: Memorandum ('Rapport från sammanträde med FFI's koordineringskommitté för Sydafrika den 5 juni 1986'/'Report from meeting of ICFTU's Coordinating Committee on South Africa, 5 June 1986'), LO/TCO, Stockholm, 18 June 1986) (LMA). UWUSA never received any assistance from LO/TCO.

7. Azanian Confederation of Trade Unions.

8. Although with smaller amounts, via ICFTU NACTU was also supported by LO/TCO. The assistance came to an end in 1988 (Rune Molin and Hans Fogelström: Memorandum ('Sammanfattande översikt av verksamheten 1987/88'/'Summary overview of the activities in 1987/88'), LO/TCO, Stockholm, 15 November 1988) (SDA). In 1987/88, LO/TCO's budgeted core assistance to COSATU amounted to 4.8 MSEK while the overall contribution to CUSA/NACTU was 660,000 SEK (Lena Johansson: Memorandum ('Framställan från LO/TCO's biståndsnämnd angående fackligt bistånd i Sydafrika och Namibia för 1987/88'/'Request from the LO/TCO Council of International Trade Union Cooperation regarding trade union assistance in South Africa and Namibia'), SIDA/CCHA, Stockholm, 21 May 1987) (SDA).

assumed a dominant position from the beginning.[1]

Like FOSATU, COSATU did not affiliate to ICFTU, opting instead for a strict non-aligned policy.[2] Contrary to its main predecessor, the new federation also decided against any direct financial assistance from the Western trade union international. Suspicious of the intentions of some of ICFTU's member organizations—in particular the American AFL-CIO—COSATU made it clear that in its view there were both "good" and "bad" members, and that it could only negotiate with the former, not with ICFTU as such.[3] At its meeting in mid-March 1986, the COSATU stand provoked frustration and deep differences of opinion within ICFTU's Coordinating Committee on South Africa. While AFL-CIO maintained that COSATU would eventually have to reconsider its decision, the Scandinavian and Dutch members—having for years channelled the bulk of the international assistance to COSATU's main constituent parts—declared that it had to be respected. COSATU, they said, was in great need of support. To suspend the assistance would be tantamount to giving "the black workers a stab [in the back] and to reaching out hands to the apartheid regime".[4]

According to COSATU, assistance from the Scandinavian and Dutch ICFTU members was welcome.[5] In fact, at the beginning of March 1986—only two days after the first formal meeting between COSATU, ANC and SACTU in Lusaka and ten days before the turbulent ICFTU session in Brussels—a high-profile COSATU delegation arrived in Stockholm for discussions with the 'progressives' concerning the possibilities of receiving direct support from them as a group, rather than through ICFTU.[6] This was far from an uncomplicated proposition. Although closer to the ANC-aligned South African trade union movement than other Western labour organizations, as a principle the Scandinavians and the Dutch had traditionally committed themselves to working through ICFTU. Nevertheless, the COSATU delegation "convinced the Dutch and Scandinavian unionists [...], and before the trip was over [it] felt that [the] strongest links were likely to be with [the] unions in

---

1. Immediately after the COSATU launch, General Secretary Jay Naidoo attended a conference of the World Council of Churches in Harare, Zimbabwe, where he met ANC and SACTU representatives. In March 1986, a COSATU delegation held discussions with ANC and SACTU in Lusaka. It could be noted that the Swedish labour movement's early involvement with UDF often brought leading ANC and future COSATU representatives together in Sweden. For example, in May 1983—three months prior to the official UDF launch—AIC organized a seminar on sanctions at Lidingö, Stockholm. It was *inter alia* attended by Thabo Mbeki and Sydney Mufamadi. Mufamadi was at the time General Secretary of GAWU. Later a leading UDF representative, he was elected Assistant General Secretary at the COSATU launch in December 1985 (Letter ('Redovisning över kostnader i samband med internationellt seminarium om sanktionspolitiken mot Sydafrika och Namibia'/'Report on costs in connection with international seminar on sanctions policy against South Africa and Namibia') from Bengt Säve-Söderbergh to SIDA, AIC, Stockholm, 26 August 1983) (SDA). On Sweden as a meeting point, cf. the interview with Bengt Säve-Söderbergh: "At that time, AIC shared offices with the LO/TCO [c]ouncil. It was very convenient, because Cyril Ramaphosa and many others who were involved in both the trade unions and UDF were often there" (p. 339).
2. In 1997, COSATU eventually joined ICFTU. Two years later—in November 1999—ANC became a full member of the social democratic Socialist International. MPLA of Angola joined as an observer party in 1992, PAICV of Cape Verde became a full member in 1996 and FRELIMO of Mozambique—a consultative member since 1996—obtained like ANC full membership status in 1999 (Letter from Latifa Perry to the Nordic Africa Institute, Socialist International, London, 29 November 1999) (NAI).
3. Cited in Vetlesen (1998) op. cit., p. 60. See also Baskin op. cit., pp. 106-08, and Southall op. cit., pp. 310-21.
4. Vetlesen (1998) op. cit., p. 61.
5. COSATU also accepted the Canadian Labour Congress (CLC). Eventually, however, CLC was not included in the donor group.
6. Jan-Erik Norling: Memorandum ('Ang. sammanträffande med COSATU-delegation, lördagen den 8 mars 1986'/'Re. meeting with COSATU delegation, Saturday 8 March 1986'), LO/TCO, Stockholm, 7 March 1986 (LMA). The COSATU representatives were Jay Naidoo (General Secretary), Sydney Mufamadi (Assistant General Secretary), Makhulu Ledwaba (Second Vice-President) and Cyril Ramaphosa (member of the COSATU board and General Secretary of NUM).

those countries".[1] Leading the COSATU delegation, General Secretary Jay Naidoo later recalled:

> They were prepared to work with us on a bilateral basis. [...] They were forthright and open in their criticism and also in hearing us out. This laid the basis for a good relationship.[2]

After bilateral consultations between the like-minded Scandinavian and Dutch organizations, it was decided to support the South African proposal. In the case of LO and TCO, a positive decision was reached in early April 1986.[3] Coordinating their arguments, in mid-May the trade union representatives from Denmark, Norway, Sweden and the Netherlands managed to persuade the ICFTU board to abandon its strict principle of coordinated action, accepting that "disbursements could be made directly from a donor to a recipient".[4] And in June 1986, ICFTU's Coordinating Committee on South Africa endorsed the fact that the Scandinavian and Dutch members on an equal basis would from then on extend direct, budgetary support to COSATU, adding the proviso that the extent and purpose of the assistance be reported to the committee.[5] Immediately thereafter, the joint donor group and COSATU established a routine with annual consultations, rotating the secretarial function between the donors. As noted by COSATU's National Coordinator Jeremy Baskin, "[i]n one sense, the argument was [thus] academic. COSATU's financial donors coordinated their support, and they did so under the auspices of ICFTU". However,

> COSATU's relations were with the national centres concerned and not the ICFTU. Politically, this was the important point. It signified COSATU's attitude towards manipulation by 'Cold War' imperatives and declared COSATU's intention to operate a policy of 'active non-alignment'.[6]

Having embarked in the mid-1970s on a strongly questioned initiative in breach of ANC's calls for international isolation of the apartheid regime, LO and TCO had ten years later together with their Scandinavian and Dutch sister organizations established special relations with the internal, ANC-aligned trade union movement.

---

1. Baskin op. cit., p. 107.
2. Cited in ibid. The COSATU delegation visited Sweden at the time of the funeral of Olof Palme, assassinated a week earlier. In connection with the memorial services, they had further discussions with the ANC leadership and the Swedish government.
3. Letter ('Ansökan om medel för budgetåret 1986/87 för sådant stöd till verksamhet i Sydafrika som har anknytning till FFI'/'Request for funds during the financial year 1986/87 for support to such activities in South Africa that are connected to ICFTU') from Jan-Erik Norling to SIDA, LO/TCO, Stockholm, 16 April 1986 (SDA).
4. Urs Hauser: Memorandum ('Rapport från sammanträde med FFI's koordineringskommitté för Sydafrika den 5 juni 1986'/'Report from meeting of ICFTU's Coordinating Committee on South Africa, 5 June 1986'), LO/TCO, Stockholm, 18 June 1986 (SDA). In the case of South Africa, the far-reaching policy change by the ICFTU board was made easier by the fact that shortly before it was revealed that the American AFL-CIO over the preceding two years outside ICFTU's established routines had given unilateral support to no less than 29 different trade union projects in the country (ibid.). AFL-CIO—which in 1982 had awarded Gatsha Buthelezi the George Meany Prize for human rights—was present when Inkatha set up UWUSA. It could also be noted that the West German DGB (*Deutscher Gewerkschaftsbund*) was a member of ICFTU's Coordinating Committee on South Africa, but preferred to channel its assistance via the Friedrich Ebert Foundation.
5. Ibid. Thus excluded, other like-minded ICFTU members—such as the Canadian CLC—were not happy with the formula (Vetlesen (1998) op. cit., p. 61).
6. Baskin op. cit., p. 107.

To many Swedish union representatives concerned, the direct involvement with the militant labour forces inside the apartheid republic was of major importance for "the decisive role they played for [future] developments".[1]

In the absence of consolidated data regarding the international support to South Africa's trade unions from the early 1970s, it has not been possible to assess the quantitative significance of the Swedish effort reliably. In the case of Norway, Vetlesen has estimated that the contributions from the Norwegian LO from 1975 to 1985 represented between 12 and 15 per cent of ICFTU's total South African programme.[2] As the joint LO-TCO assistance was considerably higher[3], the Swedish share during the pre-COSATU period could have reached 20 to 25 per cent.[4]

It was, however, with the formation of COSATU that the Swedish trade union assistance to South Africa really took off. While the annual contributions before 1985/86 did not exceed 5 MSEK and the number of individual projects remained below 15, after the COSATU launch and the ICFTU decision both the grants and the activities supported grew. From 1985/86 to 1993/94, the annual LO/TCO contributions increased from around 10 to almost 25 MSEK, with a corresponding growth in the number of projects to approximately 40.[5] Discussing the support extended until 30 June 1996—that is, two years after the democratic elections in South Africa—Wickman notes that LO/TCO by that time had channelled almost 200 MSEK to the trade unions in the country, of which more than 60 million had been granted as legal aid or humanitarian assistance in favour of detained unionists and their dependants.[6] With more than 54 MSEK, COSATU itself was by far the most important recipient. NUM and the National Union of Metalworkers of South Africa (NUMSA) dominated among the industrial unions, receiving 37.8 and 19.6 MSEK respectively.[7]

The overwhelming part of the LO/TCO funds was granted by the government. By 1994—when the assistance had reached some 175 million—around 90 per cent of the 145 MSEK allocated as official contributions to trade union development in Southern Africa[8] had been extended to South Africa. While this indicates that less than 10 per cent of the official Swedish anti-apartheid assistance outside the bilateral support to ANC—in total amounting to approximately 1.6 billion SEK—was channelled to the South African trade unions, it also shows that the Swedish labour movement contributed substantial amounts through its own efforts. In fact, over the years LO and TCO not only carried out important campaigns in favour of the South African labour movement, but also in direct support of ANC and the nationalist struggle against apartheid. However, in the interface between wider political objectives and stricter labour concerns, doubts and contradictions would emerge, both within the Swedish and the South African trade union movements.

---

1. Anders Stendalen cited in 'Landet som Skakat Oss' ('The Country Which Shook Us'), *SIDA Rapport*, No. 3, 1994, p. 21. Cf. the opinion of the Swedish miner and MIF representative Stig Blomqvist: "Without the trade union movement, ANC would be nothing" (Interview with Stig Blomqvist, p. 268).
2. Vetlesen in Eriksen (ed.) op. cit., p. 338.
3. Compare Vetlesen (1998) op. cit., p. 68 and Wickman op. cit., p. 10. Between 1975 and 1994, the Norwegian support to the South African trade unions amounted in total to around 80 MNOK. The Swedish contribution during the same period was close to 175 MSEK.
4. Taking the Danish and Dutch contributions into account, even before 1985 the Scandinavian-Dutch share of the total ICFTU assistance exceeded 50 per cent.
5. Based on tables in Wickman op. cit., pp. 8 and 10, and CCHA documentation (passim).
6. Wickman op. cit., p. 5.
7. Ibid.
8. Disbursement figures according to SIDA's audited annual accounts.

Wider LO Solidarity

Looking back, Anders Stendalen, former chairman of the Swedish Mineworkers Union—and of the Miners International Federation—said at the time of the 1994 democratic elections in South Africa that in Sweden there had been

> a great commitment towards the South African [workers]. I don't think that we ever had such a strong response among our members to any campaign as the one we carried out for the unions in South Africa.[1]

As noted above, in May 1978 LO decided to carry out a major information and fund-raising effort in favour of the oppressed peoples in Zimbabwe, Namibia and South Africa.[2] Launched in early September 1978 and coordinated by the recently established International Centre of the Swedish Labour Movement, the campaign continued until May 1979.[3] In addition to the Africa Groups' indirect support, TCO joined the effort. In the case of South Africa, during the second half of 1978 and the beginning of 1979—a period which had been proclaimed 'International Anti-Apartheid Year' by the UN General Assembly[4]—the two dominant trade union confederations called upon their members to "support your comrade in South Africa".

Although largely focusing on the labour movement in the apartheid republic, the Swedish trade union effort was wider in scope, covering the liberation struggles in the whole of Southern Africa. Solidarity with the Zimbabwean Patriotic Front, SWAPO of Namibia and ANC featured prominently in the campaign.[5] A broad, political approach was not new to LO or TCO. In fact, through nationwide campaigns the two labour organizations had in 1959-60 played decisive roles for the development of international awareness in Sweden, preparing the terrain for official development aid.[6] With regard to apartheid, LO together with KF had in 1960 declared a boycott against South African goods.[7] What was important with the campaigns launched in 1978 was, however, that they explicitly included support for the very same liberation movements that received official Swedish assistance and were backed by the organized NGO solidarity movement. In the case of

---

1. Anders Stendalen in 'Landet som Skakat Oss' ('The Country Which Shook Us'), *SIDA Rapport*, No. 3, 1994, p. 21. From the early 1980s, Stendalen established close relations with Cyril Ramaphosa, James Motlatsi and other leaders of the South African National Union of Mineworkers. In the context of Swedish trade union doubts regarding sanctions against South Africa, it could be noted that in this 'victory interview' he stated that decisions on official sanctions and isolation of the apartheid regime should "probably have been taken earlier" (ibid.).
2. The decision was taken to commemorate the 80th anniversary of LO's founding.
3. The Norwegian labour movement had already embarked in 1976 on a similar campaign (Vetlesen (1998) op. cit., pp. 14-23). The Swedish AIC was largely modelled on the Norwegian AIS (*Arbeiderbevegelsens Internasjonale Støttekomité*/The International Support Committee of the Labour Movement), originally set up in 1969 and reorganized in 1975-76.
4. The UN International Anti-Apartheid Year covered the period from 21 March 1978 to 20 March 1979.
5. LO's campaign started with a strategy seminar organized by AIC at which these Southern African liberation movements participated ('LO Startar Nio Månaders Kampanj om Södra Afrika'/'LO Starts Nine Month Campaign on Southern Africa' in *Afrikabulletinen*, No. 43, 1978, p. 3). PAC was not invited. Although it was in general supportive of the campaign, this was criticized by the Maoist Communist Party of Sweden (SKP) ('LO-kampanj för södra Afrika'/'LO campaign for Southern Africa' in *Gnistan*, No. 38, 1978, p. 7).
6. Sellström Volume I, pp. 64-66.
7. Ibid., pp. 141-46.

South Africa, this meant ANC. Towards the end of the 1970s, there emerged a solid popular Swedish opinion behind the nationalist movement led by Oliver Tambo.[1]

While TCO at the end of 1978 had already raised among its members an amount of 1.8 million SEK towards the International Anti-Apartheid Year[2], in September 1979—at the conclusion of LO's Southern Africa campaign—the AIC-coordinated effort by the blue-collar workers' organization had not only resulted in the production of audio-visual aids, gramophone records and printed information material for further use by its more than two million members, but also in the collection of 3.3 MSEK.[3] In contrast to the official grants allocated via CCHA, these funds were not channelled to ICFTU, but deposited with the International Solidarity Fund administered by AIC.[4] In so far as they were drawn upon by LO, with regard to the South African trade unions they were set aside for direct, bilateral

---

1. Prime Minister Palme launched his initiative on South and Southern Africa in August 1976. Winning the parliamentary elections less than two months later, Fälldin's non-socialist coalition not only continued the social democratic policy, but also actively encouraged the development of a common outlook and closer links between the government and the NGO movement. In mid-March 1978—two months before LO's decision to launch a Southern Africa campaign and AGIS' self-criticism—Foreign Minister Söder took an unusual, but significant initiative. Inviting over a hundred representatives of Swedish popular movements and trade unions to a meeting at the Ministry for Foreign Affairs for an exchange of information concerning the UN Anti-Apartheid Year, she explained:

> [W]e have asked you [to come] here because we want to hear your opinions, and because we want to express our appreciation of the vital part you play in mobilizing opinion against the policy of apartheid. [...] South Africa is not an isolated problem [...]. [...] If we allow one of the states of the world to apply racism as a national ideology, how are we to combat the racial thinking which crops up now and again in other countries and which sometimes makes itself felt within our own borders? [...] [This] is an issue of conscience which concerns all of us. We have no right to be passive. We must take sides. [...] Do we want to preserve the privileges of the minority or do we want to work for global equalization? [...] [I]n order to take sides and create the solidarity which is so necessary, we need information, knowledge and debate. [T]he debate must be [...] free [and] not controlled by any official institution. This is why you as the representatives of the Swedish popular movements are so indispensable. You have the intricate network of contacts involving practically every single person in Sweden. You are governed not from the top, but by your members. [...] To us [...], it is self-evident that politics should have widespread popular support. Foreign policy is no exception. [...] The close international involvement of the popular movements has an important bearing on our ability to shape a foreign policy [which rests] on genuinely democratic foundations.

('Speech by the Foreign Minister, Mrs. Söder, at a meeting of Swedish popular movements at the Ministry for Foreign Affairs', 17 March 1978, in Ministry for Foreign Affairs: *Documents on Swedish Foreign Policy: 1978*, Stockholm, 1982, pp. 304-07).

2. *SIF-Tidningen*, No. 12, 1978, p. 54.

3. LO-skolan i Brunnsvik: 'Solidaritet med förtryckta' ('Solidarity with [the] oppressed'), Report No. 11, Ludvika, 1981, pp. 2-3 (LMA).

4. The Labour Movement's International Solidarity Fund ('I-fonden') was set up in November 1979 (AIC: Press release ('Arbetarrörelsen bildar gemensam solidaritetsfond'/'The labour movement forms a common solidarity fund'), Stockholm, 7 November 1979) (OPA). Incorporating the Social Democratic Party's solidarity fund, set up in 1967, it was governed by a board with representatives from the party—among them Sten Andersson and Pierre Schori—the co-operative movement and the trade unions. Bert Lundin, head of the Metalworkers Union, served as its first chairman. In addition to projects concerning Namibia and South Africa, during the initial years activities financed by the fund largely focused on Nicaragua, El Salvador and Poland. In 1983, the motives behind the fund and AIC's international solidarity work were described in an internal discussion document as follows: "It is [...] important that the labour movement in Sweden with all its different branches can show that it constitutes an autonomous popular movement irrespective of [the party] which holds government power. [...] In different corners of the world, there is a strong interest in Swedish democracy. There is a curiosity about the way in which the Swedish model evolved. [...] [P]erhaps it is an important task for us to share our ideology? And perhaps we would get something in return through such an exchange? [...] [Our activities] have been part of a determined ideological context. They have in a concrete way tried to express the Swedish labour movement's solidarity with those who under difficult circumstances strive for national liberation and the realization of democratic socialism in their [respective] countries" (AIC: 'Förslag till riktlinjer för AIC/I-fondens solidaritetsarbete'/'Proposed guidelines for the solidarity work by AIC/the International Solidarity Fund' [no place or date, but Stockholm, 1983]) (OPA).

assistance concerning organizational development, transport and strike funds.[1] They were, however, also used for pressing ANC needs not accommodated within the official Swedish assistance. Regularly meeting LO and the LO/TCO council during his visits to Sweden[2], from 1979 Oliver Tambo raised financial support for a number of significant ANC activities from the Swedish unions.[3] From the beginning of their active involvement in the anti-apartheid struggle, they would concurrently pursue a multilateral labour policy through ICFTU and a bilateral political course with ANC.

A number of examples could be quoted. Starting with the 1978-79 campaign, under the AIC umbrella LO soon established direct relations with ANC and the liberation movements in Namibia and Zimbabwe.[4] In the case of ANC, financial assistance over the following years was extended towards information activities, humanitarian needs and as budget support. In October 1979, for example, the LO board decided to grant the ANC Women's Secretariat 60,000 SEK for its quarterly journal *Voice of Women*, securing the production of the publication for a period of two years.[5] After the South African commando raid on Maseru, Lesotho, in December 1982—when 42 ANC activists and Lesotho nationals were killed—LO donated 75,000 SEK via ANC as emergency relief to the surviving family members.[6] Similarly, when in June 1983 the apartheid regime executed the three ANC members Simon Mogoerane, Jerry Mosololi and Thabo Motaung, a grant of 100,000 SEK was extended.[7]

Much less known—but in this context more significant—is the fact that from 1980 on several occasions LO financed and produced information material for use by ANC inside South Africa. At Tambo's request, in March 1980 LO set aside 40,000 SEK for the production of 4,000 cassette tapes with ANC's 'January 8 statement', which were subsequently smuggled into the country.[8] In June 1980, ANC's resident representative Lindiwe Mabuza repeated the request, and another 4,000 cassettes with political messages from the liberation movement were produced by the confederation's information department.[9] ANC stickers, badges and other propaganda material for underground distribution in South Africa were also sup-

1. Kristina Persson: 'Rapport över LO/TCO's projekt i södra Afrika' ('Report on the LO/TCO projects in Southern Africa'), Stockholm, 13 August 1979 (SDA). The first LO contribution from the campaign funds was disbursed at the end of 1978 in favour of striking women in Port Elizabeth, when an amount of 50,000 SEK was transferred to the National Union of Motor Assembly and Rubber Workers (*Afrikabulletinen*, No. 46, 1979, p. 7).
2. Leading high-powered ANC delegations, Tambo held, for example, bilateral talks with LO/TCO in August 1977, March 1981 and May 1983. It could be noted that in 1977 and 1981 he was invited by the non-socialist government. However, the visits included separate meetings with the opposition Social Democratic Party and the trade unions in the official programmes. Separately and jointly, over the years LO and TCO often met ANC in Lusaka.
3. The role played in this context by ANC's resident representative Lindiwe Mabuza must be underlined. Her important contribution towards a principled, unitary solidarity opinion in favour of ANC appears throughout the text.
4. AIC's support to SWAPO of Namibia financed by funds raised by LO has been discussed above. It was particularly conspicuous in 1979-80, when it focused on election training, production of information materials etc.
5. Letter from Bengt Säve-Söderbergh to Florence Mophosho, Head of the ANC Women's Secretariat, AIC, Stockholm, 31 October 1979 (OPA).
6. AIC: 'Protokoll fört vid sammanträde med I-fondens styrelse den 10 januari 1983' ('Minutes from board meeting of the International Solidarity Fund, 10 January 1983'), Stockholm [no date] (OPA).
7. AIC: Press release ('I-fonden ger stöd till ANC i Sydafrika'/'The International Solidarity Fund gives support to ANC South Africa'), Stockholm [no date] (OPA) and letter from Lindiwe Mabuza to Bengt Säve-Söderbergh, ANC, Stockholm, 28 June 1983 (OPA).
8. Letter from Bengt Säve-Söderbergh to [LO's] Gunnar Nilsson, Rune Molin, Thorbjörn Carlsson and Lars-Göran Pettersson, AIC, Stockholm, 17 April 1980 (OPA).
9. Letter ('Stöd till ANC Sydafrika'/'Support to ANC South Africa') from Bengt Säve-Söderbergh to LO, AIC, Stockholm, 23 June 1980 (OPA).

Sigvard Marjasin of the
Municipal Workers Union
handing ANC Treasurer
General Thomas Nkobi
a cheque for 1.5 million
SEK, Visby, May 1986
(Photo: Bengt Zettergren)

plied. On the occasion of ANC's 70th anniversary, in March 1982 LO allocated some 150,000 SEK for the production of such material.[1] Acknowledging receipt of the products and noting that "th[e]se seemingly unimportant details are bearing rich fruit within the country", in November 1982 Mabuza wrote to LO's secretary Rune Molin that "[t]hey will become organizing agents, as have been all the other things you have generously financed for us".[2]

The Swedish trade unions and the wider labour movement would be closely involved with ANC during the period leading up to the South African democratic elections in 1994. This will be further illustrated below. In the meantime, it could be noted that during the 1980s several individual unions launched their own anti-apartheid campaigns. Such information and fund-raising efforts were normally carried out in favour of their counterparts in South Africa. In 1987, the Mineworkers Union raised no less than 3.4 MSEK in favour of NUM.[3]

Other unions had a wider scope. Under the slogan 'One Hour for Freedom in South Africa', during the last quarter of 1985 the Municipal Workers Union[4]— LO's largest affiliate—asked its members to donate the equivalent of one hour's wages to the anti-apartheid struggle.[5] Supported by other trade unions, the campaign was a huge success. Some 60,000 members attended study circles on the situation in South Africa[6], and within three months 1.8 MSEK had been raised.[7] In this case, the union eventually decided to donate the bulk of the funds directly to ANC. During a small ceremony in Visby on the island of Gotland, in mid-May 1986 Sigvard Marjasin, the union chairman, handed ANC's Treasurer General Thomas Nkobi a cheque for 1.5 MSEK. The support from the comparatively low-paid

1. Letter ('Angående anslag ur LO's södra Afrika-insamling'/'Concerning allocations from LO's Southern Africa campaign') from Conny Fredriksson to LO, AIC, Stockholm, 11 March 1982 (OPA).
2. Letter from Lindiwe Mabuza to Rune Molin, ANC, Stockholm, 29 November 1982 (OPA).
3. *AIC-Bulletinen*, No. 6/1987-1/1988, p. 24.
4. In Swedish, *Kommunalarbetareförbundet*. In the early 1980s, *Kommunal* had some 460,000 members.
5. Leif Göbel: Circular letter ('Kampanj: En timma för frihet i Sydafrika'/'Campaign: One hour for freedom in South Africa'), Svenska Kommunalarbetareförbundet [no place], 9 September 1985 (LMA).
6. Kerstin Ostwald: 'Den största fackliga gåva vi fått' ('The biggest trade union donation we have received') in *Gotlands Tidningar*, 22 May 1986.
7. Campaign accounts on handwritten note ('En timme för fred och frihet'/'One hour for peace and freedom') [no author, place or date] (LMA).

Swedish municipal workers was, Nkobi noted, "the biggest donation [ANC had] ever received from an individual trade union organization".[1]

While both the national LO confederation and a number of its affiliates supported ANC, in the case of the Metalworkers Union direct, bilateral contacts with the South African trade unions led to contradictions and doubts.[2] Although the powerful union never managed to impose its views, to complete the picture of the Swedish labour movement and the anti-apartheid struggle this should also be taken into account.[3]

Metall's Dissonant Voice

Most of the Swedish owned manufacturing firms in South Africa were in the metal industry, and the overwhelming majority of the workers at the parent companies in Sweden belonged to the Metalworkers Union.[4] Decisions on trade union links between the Swedish companies and their subsidiaries—such as the one reached by LO and TCO in September 1975—or with regard to disinvestment and sanctions affected the union directly or indirectly. With some 450,000 members around 1980, *Metall* was not only LO's second largest affiliate, but due to its strategic position in the Swedish economy also the country's most powerful trade union organization. Its policy vis-à-vis South Africa carried significant weight.

The union's international secretary had in January-February 1975 formed part of the LO-TCO delegation to South Africa. Via the International Metalworkers Federation, the union had in 1977 also granted MAWU the—extraordinarily modest—amount of 15,000 SEK for organizational work at the Swedish owned companies.[5] Although better placed than any other affiliate, *Metall* did not play a major role during LO's Southern Africa campaign in 1978-79. It was not until the July 1979 ban on new Swedish investments that it became actively involved in the South Africa debate.[6] And when it finally did, it essentially raised a dissonant labour voice, *de facto* siding with the Swedish export companies against disinvestment and unilateral sanctions.

Leading representatives of the Swedish metalworkers' union had on several occasions during the second half of the 1970s expressed doubts concerning ANC. While the reservations were eventually toned down, the organization would until the very end oppose the calls for unilateral external measures to weaken the apart-

---

1. Per Leino: 'Direkt från Lusaka för att hämta pengarna på Gotland' ('Straight from Lusaka to fetch the money on Gotland') in *Gotlands Allehanda*, 22 May 1986. As earlier noted, it has not been possible to reliably estimate the total financial transfers from Sweden to the Southern African liberation movements, and much less to the wider national theatres of the struggle. Suffice it to say that they exceeded by far the official assistance recorded in the text and in the accompanying disbursement tables. In the case of ANC, the official assistance during the calendar year 1986 was, for example, approximately 57 MSEK. In the same year, the ANC office in Stockholm deposited Swedish voluntary contributions into the movement's account of more than 16 MSEK (Letter from Lindiwe Mabuza to Thomas Nkobi, ANC, Stockholm, 18 February 1987) (MCA). This figure, however, does not include the donation from the Municipal Workers Union or other trade union grants. In 1986, total Swedish NGO contributions to ANC thus represented one third or more of the official assistance.
2. The notes on the Metalworkers Union are to a large extent based on Andersson op. cit.
3. Addressing the question why the Swedish labour movement was late in demanding comprehensive sanctions against South Africa, C.H. Hermansson, the former chairman of the Left Party Communists, commented in November 1996: "I think that the reason why it took so long was the influence of Swedish capital in South Africa. Many of the big Swedish companies had subsidiaries [there] and they carried out an intense propaganda against sanctions, pointing out possible loss of work opportunities in Sweden. It probably made the Social Democratic Party—especially the trade union congress—cautious in these matters" (Interview with C.H. Hermansson, pp. 291-92).
4. In Swedish, *Metallindustriarbetareförbundet*, often shortened to *Metall*.
5. Andersson op. cit., p. 20.
6. Ibid., p. 23.

heid regime, arguing instead in favour of strengthening the internal trade unions. Although *Metall* "had a more cautious attitude towards sanctions and disinvestment than its South African counterparts"[1], the leadership's workerist policy was, however, largely influenced by its direct, bilateral contacts with the South African metalworkers' unions and FOSATU.[2] This, in turn, reflected real and pervasive contradictions within the wider South African anti-apartheid movement.[3]

Regular visits between the Swedish and South African metalworkers started in earnest in 1979-80.[4] From different perspectives, during these exchanges the parties came to share a number of politically controversial positions. While both of them welcomed mandatory international sanctions to end the apartheid regime, they maintained that a unilateral withdrawal of the Swedish companies would be both ineffective and counterproductive. In their view, the assets of any foreign company which in the absence of binding, universal UN resolutions withdrew from South Africa would in all likelihood be taken over by South African, or other foreign, interests, with negative consequences for the ongoing efforts to organize democratic unions.

Arguing that the assets of the foreign companies essentially belonged to the South African workers, in May 1985 FOSATU's Alec Erwin—democratic South Africa's Deputy Minister of Finance—stated that "[w]e can see absolutely no sense in handing over part of [the] social wealth of this country in order to place pressure on [the] regime".[5] Instead, he argued, the most important task was to build strong trade unions through national cooperation and links with labour organizations abroad. The question of job security played a crucial role in this context.

This was in marked contrast to ANC's declared policy. In a submission to the official Swedish commission on investments in South Africa, the liberation movement had, for example, in 1978 emphasized that

> those who wish to solve the problem of unemployment among the blacks by encouraging foreign investment oppose the liberation struggle under the guise of defending the people's interests. But the people of South Africa no longer want the scraps from the white man's table. What we want is liberation.[6]

After the formation of COSATU in late 1985, the South African trade unions' positions on disinvestment and sanctions would increasingly coincide with those held by ANC. Nevertheless, according to the Swedish Metalworkers Union it never received a clear message from its South African counterparts—MAWU, NAAWU and, later, NUMSA—to work for a withdrawal of the Swedish owned companies. Opposing the political views of both Prime Minister Palme and ANC President

1. Ibid., p. i.
2. Local branches of the Metalworkers Union were opposed to the official views, calling for disinvestment and sanctions. As a rule, however, they represented workers at companies or plants with no direct connections to the Swedish subsidiaries in South Africa (ibid.).
3. NIR's Åke Magnusson stated in 1997 that "[t]he demands for sanctions and isolation were certainly not coming from organized labour [in South Africa]. They wanted an active, dynamic presence rather than withdrawal. I know for sure that in most of the cases they did not want us to withdraw, and that is the main reason why the five or six Swedish metal companies actually did not close. The metalworkers' unions really wanted them to stay" (Interview with Åke Magnusson, p. 319).
4. In June 1979—immediately before the coming into force of the Swedish investment ban—two South African delegations visited *Metall* in Sweden, respectively led by Bernie Fanaroff from MAWU and John Gomomo from the United Automobile Workers (UAW). Torsten Wetterblad and Sven Wehlin visited South Africa in December 1980 (Andersson op. cit., pp. 21-22). In 1994, Fanaroff was appointed Deputy Director General in the Office of the President, with responsibility for the implementation of ANC's Reconstruction and Development Programme.
5. Cited in Andersson op. cit., p. 36.
6. SOU (1978) op. cit., p. 274.

Tambo, in connection with the Swedish People's Parliament against Apartheid *Metall*'s international secretary Håkan Arnelid stated in early 1986 that "[w]e must in the first place listen to our brother organizations in South Africa, and they have not asked us to pull out the Swedish companies".[1] And in an article published by the *South African Labour Bulletin*, the union chairman Leif Blomberg[2] declared later that year that "I fail to see the merits, or even morality, of a policy which gives us a clean conscience, but does not make any practical contribution to the struggle of the oppressed".[3]

Behind *Metall*'s diverging stand within the Swedish labour movement was its concern for the members' work opportunities at the targeted Swedish parent companies, but also—on behalf of its South African counterparts—at their subsidiaries. No other Swedish trade union organization was in a similar position. While LO in 1984 at the coordinated, national level in its comments to a proposed tightening up of the 1979 investment ban supported the official commission's political recommendation—"even if other countries won't follow [our example]"[4]—the union held a different view. In a separate submission it expressed "great reluctance towards unilateral Swedish measures", adding that the commission had taken the situation concerning "the jobs, particularly in South Africa, too lightly".[5] According to

Metall, the number of workers in Sweden directly involved in production for the South African market was at the time around 1,000, while some 3,000 were employed by the Swedish owned subsidiaries in South Africa.[6]

As a corollary of the employment argument, *Metall* often stated that a withdrawal of the Swedish companies would seriously affect the development of the South African trade union movement in the strategic metal industry. According to Andersson, "a common assumption [...]—foremost [among] its leadership [...]—was that Swedish companies were a better option for the black workers than South African [or] other foreign companies".[7] Although the assumption was rejected by the South African trade unions[8] and contradicted by the Swedish companies' unwillingness to adopt pioneering labour policies, from the early 1980s direct and constructive links were established between the metalworkers in the two countries. Interviewed in 1996, the UAW, NAAWU and NUMSA leader John Gomomo—in 1991 elected President of COSATU—recalled how

> we sent some shop stewards from SKF South Africa to Sweden to meet the Swedish metalworkers and learn about the company. That broadened their minds and strengthened them to come back to South Africa and speak to the management, challenging them on issues that they believed were unjust. [...] The Swedes pushed the players in the country to agree that there should be paid time for the training of shop stewards and workers. [...] That set a precedent and allowed us to push other companies to follow suit, which was great. [...] We went as far as

---

1. Cited in Andersson op. cit., p. 45.
2. Blomberg led the Mineworkers Union between 1982 and 1993. After the Social Democratic Party's electoral victory in September 1994, he was appointed Minister of Labour.
3. Cited in Andersson op. cit., p. 49.
4. Stig Malm and Hans Fogelström: Letter ('Yttrande över betänkandet Svensk Sydafrikapolitik'/'Comments on the report Swedish South Africa Policy') to the Ministry for Foreign Affairs, LO, Stockholm, [no specific date] September 1984 (MFA).
5. Leif Blomberg: Letter ('Yttrande över SOU 1984:52 Svensk Sydafrikapolitik'/'Comments on SOU 1984:52 Swedish South Africa Policy') to the Ministry for Foreign Affairs, Swedish Metalworkers Union [no place or date, but received in September 1984] (MFA).
6. Ibid. The Metalworkers Union was represented on the official commission, initially by its international secretary Torsten Wetterblad and later by his successor Bengt Jakobsson.
7. Andersson op. cit., p. 61.
8. Ibid.

to establish what we called 'multinational shop stewards' solidarity' with [the] German and Swedish companies. They met every second year.[1]

Initially conspicuously silent with regard to labour disputes and human rights' issues at the Swedish owned companies, from the mid-1980s the Metalworkers Union became more involved in the anti-apartheid struggle. In comparison with the extensive support extended by the Mineworkers Union, however, the effort was modest.[2] Nevertheless, when the workers at ASEA South Africa went on strike at the end of 1985, in a "surprisingly radical"[3] move *Metall* decided to grant MAWU 100,000 SEK.[4] And when MAWU's General Secretary Moses Mayekiso in June 1986 after a visit to Sweden was detained and charged with high treason due to his leadership of the community-based Alexandra Action Committee, the union took an active part in the international solidarity campaign for his release.[5]

From a political point of view *de facto* forming an 'unholy alliance' with Swedish business interests and expressing a minority opinion opposed to unilateral sanctions, the Metalworkers Union was in spite of its powerful position within the labour movement fighting a losing battle.[6] In October 1986—when COSATU had pronounced itself in favour of economic isolation and the third national Swedish sanctions debate was taking place—a trade union delegation from Sweden visited ANC in Lusaka to discuss the issue of the Swedish companies in South Africa. *Metall's* chairman Leif Blomberg led the delegation, which in addition to the international secretary Håkan Arnelid included Hans Fogelström from LO and Anders Stendalen from the Mineworkers Union. However, after three days of extensive talks with Oliver Tambo, Thabo Mbeki, Pallo Jordan, Ray Simons and other nationalist leaders on the pros and cons of disinvestment they had to conclude that "ANC's position on the foreign owned companies [...] does not give [any] guidance as to concrete Swedish decisions".[7]

---

1. Interview with John Gomomo, pp. 129-30.
2. On the Swedish Mineworkers Union and NUM, see the chapter 'Closer and Broader Cooperation: Projects in Exile, Mineworkers, UDF and Civics in South Africa'.
3. Andersson op. cit., p. 42.
4. Ibid.
5. Mayekiso—who during his time in detention was elected General Secretary of NUMSA—was eventually acquitted in April 1989.
6. As may be seen in the accompanying appendix, the 1979 investment legislation was strengthened in March 1985 and in May 1986.
7. Håkan Arnelid and Hans Fogelström: Memorandum ('Rapport från överläggningar m.m. med ANC i Lusaka, Zambia, 14-17 oktober 1986'/'Report on discussions etc. with ANC in Lusaka, 14-17 October 1986'), LO, Stockholm, 27 October 1986 (LMA). Bengt Säve-Söderbergh and Ulla Ström from the Ministry for Foreign Affairs attended parts of the talks. According to the notes by Arnelid (*Metall*) and Fogelström (LO), Tambo was of the opinion that "Sweden had been leading the [international] work for sanctions". Noting that unilateral Swedish measures by themselves did not have a major impact on the South African economy, the ANC delegation emphasized that they served as "good examples vis-à-vis other—in the context more important—countries". While this was far from convincing to the Swedish trade union representatives, it was, however, ANC's views on disinvestment that they above all found wanting. As ANC—without presenting concrete alternatives—at the same time called for a withdrawal of the foreign companies and opposed their possible takeover by South African interests, its stand was characterized as "ambiguous" (ibid.). It should be noted that the Swedish parent companies and *Metall* at about the same time had asked the internal unions and ANC to agree to a 'code of conduct' to guide the companies' continued operations in South Africa. While this was acceptable to the local trade unions, it was, however, rejected by the ANC leadership in Lusaka. In 1996, the COSATU President Gomomo recalled: "They asked for a code of conduct from ANC and the trade unions in South Africa. It was a hell of a struggle. We had to travel from South Africa to Lusaka to meet ANC and SACTU. Some agreed and some did not agree, but in the end they would not establish such a code. At the time of the unbanning of ANC and SACP in 1990, we were still battling. If you looked at the machines at the SKF factory they were all old, because the company could not replace them. The Swedes suffered from that. But they stuck to their guns. I praise the Swedes for all [t]hat they have done. Others tried to manoeuvre, but the Swedes did not. [...] I must say that of all the countries that supported South Africa by imposing sanctions, Sweden was number one" (Interview with John Gomomo, pp. 129-30).

Seven months later—in May 1987—the Swedish parliament not only confirmed the investment ban, but adopted comprehensive trade sanctions against South Africa. This notwithstanding, the Metalworkers Union would over the following years continue to oppose the course eventually taken by the Social Democratic government. After the unbanning of ANC, the release of Nelson Mandela and the lifting of economic sanctions by most countries—in the Nordic area notably by Finland, soon followed by Denmark[1]—from 1992 *Metall* "literally initiated a campaign for a de-escalation of the Swedish [legislation]".[2] Initially also opposed by Carl Bildt's non-socialist government—formed in October 1991 and accepting ANC's argument that sanctions should only be relaxed when the process towards democracy had been irreversibly secured—the efforts were not supported by the wider labour movement. Against the Social Democratic Party's pro-sanctions stand, in a letter to the party leader Ingvar Carlsson the *Metall* chairman Leif Blomberg complained in early February 1993 that while

> Nelson Mandela may quote employment reasons in South Africa to remove sanctions [...], we [...] cannot refer to this [argument] in favour of a policy similar to the one pursued by our main trading competitors.[3]

Towards Unilateral Sanctions

Demands for economic measures had been part of the national anti-apartheid debate since the early 1960s.[4] Although Sweden had established early relations with ANC and apartheid from 1966 was officially characterized as 'a crime against humanity', consecutive Social Democratic governments would not heed the liberation movement's calls for unilateral action. This was in accordance with a broadly anchored national security doctrine, in which defence of Sweden's non-alignment and support for the United Nations Charter were essential cornerstones.

Standing outside political and military alliances in times of peace with a view to remaining neutral in the eventuality of war[5], Sweden consistently refused to participate in, or embark upon, sanctions outside the UN framework.[6] As laid down in Chapter VII of the UN Charter, it was only the Security Council that could decide on collective punitive measures. In fact, in the Cold War era the council's mandate was of crucial importance to Sweden's policy of non-alignment. As the two opposing super powers had to be in agreement to impose sanctions, there was no risk of being forced to side with either of them against a third party. In the absence of other

---

1. Finland lifted the sanctions against South Africa in June 1991 (Soiri and Peltola op. cit., p. 154). Denmark revoked its investment ban in January 1992 and the trade sanctions in March 1992 (Cable from the Swedish embassy in Copenhagen to the Ministry for Foreign Affairs, Copenhagen, 19 March 1992) (SDA). The joint Nordic anti-apartheid policy had thereby *de facto* come to an end, an argument used by *Metall* in its campaign against the Swedish sanctions legislation.
2. Andersson op. cit., p. 77.
3. Letter from Leif Blomberg to Ingvar Carlsson, 3 February 1993. Translated from the Swedish original as cited in Andersson op. cit., p. 78, note 337. The Swedish trade ban was eventually revoked in September 1993 and the investment ban and other sanctions in late November 1993. With regard to the Metalworkers Union, it could be noted that in 1993 together with the International Council of Swedish Industry it embarked on a training programme for the employees at the Swedish-owned companies in South Africa (Andersson op. cit., p. 80).
4. See Sellström Volume I, pp. 181-205 and 215-32.
5. On Sweden's non-alignment, see ibid., pp. 45-46. In 1948, Finland signed a Treaty of Friendship, Cooperation and Mutual Assistance with the Soviet Union, and in 1949 Denmark and Norway joined the North Atlantic Treaty Organization (NATO). Iceland also became a member of NATO. As a result, Sweden was the only alliance-free state in the Nordic area.
6. In the late 1960s, for example, Sweden opposed US demands to cease trading with Cuba (Gunnar Adler-Karlsson: *Västerns Ekonomiska Krigföring 1947-1967/*'Western Economic Warfare 1947-1967', Rabén och Sjögren, Stockholm, 1970, p. 13).

international security arrangements, the UN Security Council had the function of a protective shield and its mandate was to be strictly respected and upheld. As noted by the senior diplomat Sverker Åström[1] in 1976:

> [T]hat we—without departing from our policy of neutrality—can participate in sanctions decided by the Security Council is one thing. Another question is if we can, unilaterally and without a decision of the Security Council, impose sanctions on a state which acts in contravention of international law and of whose policies we strongly disapprove. The answer to that question is, in principle, in the negative.[2]

In the case of South Africa, by 1976 a chain of events had led to rapidly escalating demands for unilateral action. Following the debate on the Swedish companies in the apartheid republic initiated by the churches, across ideologically dividing lines the Left Party Communists and the Liberal Party submitted in January 1975 parliamentary motions in this regard, respectively requesting an investment ban and official intervention in favour of voluntary withdrawal. And from within the labour movement, in February 1976 the LO and TCO chairmen Gunnar Nilsson and Lennart Bodström demanded in a strongly worded letter to Prime Minister Palme that

> the government introduces such changes in the Swedish legislation that new investments in the Republic of South Africa by Swedish concerns will be made impossible as long as the [companies] contribute to discriminating labour conditions by continuing to profit from the black and coloured labour force.[3]

These voices grew considerably stronger after the June 1976 Soweto shootings. Prime Minister Palme himself reacted in August 1976 to the events by *inter alia* declaring that the question of continued Swedish investments in South Africa must be seriously reconsidered. As the 1974-76 period of grace for labour reforms which had been accorded the Swedish South Africa companies by the ecumenical council was passing without decisive improvements, the churches too would soon demand unilateral official measures.

When the non-socialist coalition won the parliamentary elections in September 1976, it was therefore faced with considerable political pressure to tackle the issue of sanctions. While the Moderate Party—a junior partner with limited influence over foreign policy[4]—was firmly opposed to such a course[5], both Prime Minister Fälldin's Centre Party and, above all, Cooperation Minister Ullsten's Liberal Party had for many years demanded official action against apartheid. Indeed, in the case of the Liberal Party it could be argued that it "had the sanctions issue as *the* international question. They did not say very much about Vietnam, Russia or Latin America. It was South Africa".[6] As later noted by Carl Tham—then a leading member of the Liberal Party—"at that time, we looked upon the Social Democrats

1. Åström served as Sweden's ambassador to the United Nations between 1964 and 1970.
2. Sverker Åström: *Sweden's Policy of Neutrality*, The Swedish Institute, Stockholm, 1987, p. 14.
3. Letter ('Hemställan'/'Request') from Gunnar Nilsson, LO, and Lennart Bodström, TCO, to Prime Minister Olof Palme, Stockholm, 10 February 1976 (MFA).
4. Cf. the interview with Carl Tham, at the time secretary of the Liberal Party and Under-Secretary of State in the Ministry of Labour: "The Moderate Party was mainly obsessed with two foreign policy and aid questions. One was Vietnam and the other was Cuba. Southern Africa was not really on their agenda until later" (p. 343). Birger Hagård of the Moderate Party similarly noted in 1996 that the issue of Southern Africa "was a minor question [...] which had no priority within [the conservative party]" (Interview with Birger Hagård, p. 274). Staffan Burenstam Linder of the Moderate Party served as Minister of Trade in Fälldin's coalition government between October 1976 and October 1978.
5. Failing labour reforms by the Swedish companies in South Africa, in May 1975 the Moderate Party Youth League had raised the option of an investment ban.
6. Interview with Åke Magnusson, p. 318.

as not being active enough. That was our main position. Ola Ullsten of the Liberal Party and Thorbjörn Fälldin of the Centre Party were both very much engaged in these matters, so there was never a problem".[1]

Sweden was a member of the UN Security Council when the Fälldin government was formed. At the same time as the official, bilateral assistance to the Southern African liberation movements was increased, in accordance with the established foreign and security policy doctrine the non-socialist coalition initially raised the issue of sanctions at the United Nations. In addition to supporting a mandatory arms embargo[2], in her first speech to the General Assembly in mid-October 1976 Karin Söder, the new Minister for Foreign Affairs, declared that "Sweden would be prepared to support realistic proposals for further measures, including a ban on new foreign investments in South Africa and Namibia".[3] Coordinating its views with the other Nordic countries, soon thereafter—in early November 1976—Sweden together with Denmark, Finland, Iceland, Norway and a number of African and non-aligned states put forward a draft resolution in the General Assembly, demanding a stop to new investments in the apartheid republic.[4] Although adopted by a large majority, it was opposed by the Western powers in the Security Council.[5]

At the end of 1976, the Fälldin government was not yet prepared to deviate from Sweden's traditional policy and introduce unilateral measures. This was in contrast to Odvar Nordli's Social Democratic government in Norway.[6] Having co-sponsored the aborted Security Council resolution, in late November 1976 it decided to stop granting export credit guarantees and currency licences for trade with and investments in South Africa.[7] In comparison with the Swedish involvement, there were, however, only marginal direct Norwegian interests in the republic.[8] While the limited measures therefore "had little effect"[9] and could hardly be described as an 'investment ban'[10], it remains that Norway through official, unilateral anti-apartheid initiatives took the lead among the Nordic countries, also paving the way for the Swedish 1979 ban against new investments.

Influenced by the UN Security Council's opposition and the Norwegian government's stand, in January 1977 not only the Left Party Communists[11] and the ruling

---

1. Interview with Carl Tham, p. 343.
2. One year later—on 4 November 1977—the Security Council imposed a mandatory arms embargo against South Africa.
3. 'Speech by Mrs. Söder, the Minister for Foreign Affairs, at the General Assembly of the United Nations', 13 October 1976, in Ministry for Foreign Affairs: *Documents on Swedish Foreign Policy: 1976*, Stockholm, 1978, p. 69.
4. 'Summary of speech by ambassador Rydbeck in the UN General Assembly concerning new investments in South Africa', 5 November 1976, in ibid., p. 196.
5. Belgium, Canada, France, the Federal Republic of Germany, Italy, Japan, the United Kingdom and the United States already abstained from voting on the resolution in the General Assembly (United Nations: *Yearbook of the United Nations: 1976*, Office of Public Information, United Nations, New York, 1979, pp. 143-44).
6. As a member of NATO Norway pursued a different security policy to Sweden.
7. Ragnhild Narum: 'Norge og Rasekonflikten i Sør-Afrika' ('Norway and the Racial Conflict in South Africa'), University of Oslo, Oslo, 1998, p. 124. See also Olav Stokke: 'Norsk Politikk overfor det Sørlige Afrika' ('Norwegian policies towards Southern Africa') in *Internasjonal Politikk*, No. 3, 1978, p. 407.
8. While there were only marginal Norwegian investments in South Africa, Norwegian shipowners occupied a prominent position as transporters of crude oil and petroleum products to the apartheid republic. See Tore Linné Eriksen and Anita Kristensen Krokan: '"Fuelling the Apartheid War Machine": A Case Study of Shipowners, Sanctions and Solidarity Movements' in Eriksen (ed.)(ed.) op. cit., pp. 193-210.
9. Narum op. cit., p. 124.
10. Cf. Vetlesen (1998) op. cit., p. 141.
11. In its motion, the Left Party Communists demanded "a ban on Swedish investments in South Africa as long as the racial oppression continues" (Swedish Parliament 1976/77: Motion No. 56, Riksdagens Protokoll 1976/77, p. 8).

Liberal Party[1], but also the opposition Social Democratic Party[2]—making a clear break with past policies[3]—submitted parliamentary motions demanding restrictions on Sweden's economic relations with South Africa. A broad political majority in favour of unilateral action was thus at hand. As noted by the Swedish political scientist Ove Nordenmark, "the three motions indicated that a radical change [...] concerning the effects of unilateral sanctions [...] was strongly developing".[4]

The turnabout was made evident over the following months in a number of policy statements by both the government and the opposition. Strongly opposing the Swedish export companies' view that apartheid South Africa was not unique, in an address to the Federation of Swedish Industries[5] Foreign Minister Söder emphasized in May 1977 that

> we would like to see Swedish firms voluntarily abstaining from potential profits based on an inhuman system. Doing business in South Africa means, after all, that one is forced to comply with the apartheid laws and in this way be a party to racial oppression. [...] If official dissuasion is effective, there is little reason to go [as] far as to a prohibition [against new investments]. If, on the other hand, dissuasion [does] not have the desired effect, then a prohibition or other measures could be considered.[6]

Characterizing apartheid as "a unique form of evil [and] the only form of tyranny which brands a person from birth on account of the colour of his skin"[7], on behalf of the opposition Social Democratic Party Olof Palme similarly criticized the presence of Swedish companies in South Africa. During a parliamentary debate on foreign affairs, he argued in March 1977 that "free human beings are more important than free movements of capital"[8] and that Sweden instead of waiting for a UN decision should unilaterally impose an investment ban.[9] This was an entirely new Social Democratic discourse.

The Social Democratic Party's policy reorientation regarding unilateral measures started with Palme's address to the congress of the Brotherhood Movement in Skövde in August 1976.[10] It marked the beginning of what Pierre Schori has described as "an unparalleled offensive" and a "crusade against racism never before undertaken by a party leader in the industrialized world".[11] Concentrating

---

1. The motion submitted by the Liberal Party—*inter alia* signed by Olle Wästberg and Per Gahrton—urgently requested "a study on how Swedish economic sanctions against South Africa could be implemented" (Swedish Parliament 1976/77: Motion No. 676, Riksdagens Protokoll 1976/77, p. 2).
2. The Social Democratic motion was supported by the party's representatives on the parliamentary Standing Committee on Foreign Affairs. Quoting the steps taken by Norway, the motion emphasized that "in our opinion the situation in South Africa has developed in such a way that Sweden now must also consider unilateral measures of prohibition outside international decisions. As a first step, exports of [Swedish] capital to South Africa and Namibia should be prohibited" (Swedish Parliament 1976/77: Motion No. 1054, Riksdagens Protokoll 1976/77, p. 16).
3. On the Social Democratic government and the demands for sanctions against South Africa and Portugal in the mid-1960s, see Sellström Volume I, pp. 227-32 and 479-83.
4. Nordenmark op. cit., p. 79.
5. In Swedish, *Sveriges Industriförbund*.
6. 'Extract from speech by the Foreign Minister, Mrs. Söder, on 'Sweden and the World' at the annual meeting of the Federation of Swedish Industries', 4 May 1977, in Ministry for Foreign Affairs: *Documents on Swedish Foreign Policy: 1977*, Stockholm, 1978, pp. 199-200.
7. Cited in Schori (1994) op. cit., p. 25.
8. Cited in ibid., p. 27.
9. Kaa Eneberg: 'Sverige behöver inte vänta på FN' ('Sweden doesn't need to wait for the UN') in *Dagens Nyheter*, 31 March 1977.
10. Reporting on his September 1977 Southern Africa mission on behalf of the Socialist International, Palme wrote: "This trip really started one year ago, at the congress of the Brotherhood Movement in Skövde on 6 August 1976" (Olof Palme: 'Här går gränsen för mänsklig värdighet: Palme's afrikanska dagbok'/'Here goes the border of human decency: Palme's African diary' in *Aftonbladet-Magasinet*, 9 October 1977).
11. Schori (1994) op. cit., pp. 21-22.

his attention on South and Southern Africa, the Swedish opposition leader would over the following year in both his private capacity and on behalf of the Socialist International in various national and international fora forcefully advocate support to the region's liberation movements and economic sanctions against the apartheid regime.

In March 1977, Palme was invited to take part in the UN Security Council's apartheid debate in New York; in May he attended the UN-sponsored International Conference in Support of the Peoples of Zimbabwe and Namibia in Maputo, Mozambique; and in August the UN/OAU World Conference for Action against Apartheid in Lagos, Nigeria. On each of these occasions, he was asked to give a keynote address. Finally, in early September 1977 Palme led a Socialist International (SI) mission to Angola, Zambia, Mozambique and Tanzania. During the trip, representatives of ten affiliated SI parties discussed the conditions for the liberation struggles, "the crucial question of which side white Europe was *really* taking"[1] and the importance of sanctions against apartheid with the leaders of the Southern African liberation movements and the independent states.[2] In his diary, Palme noted that the delegation "everywhere had been received with overwhelming amiability and attention", but "above all with expectations that we will be able to contribute to the liberation of Africa".[3]

Palme's political initiative was, as earlier noted, welcomed by ANC, but characterized by the Africa Groups as 'empty talk'. It was also severely censured by the South African Communist Party. In order to "put the record straight", an article in the party's organ *The African Communist*—published "in the interests of African solidarity"—argued after the SI mission that

> [t]he history of the Socialist International is a history of betrayal of the interests of the working class and people of the 'developed' countries and [of] the colonial peoples. [...] The report of [the] mission to Southern Africa does show a shift of position on some points [...], [b]ut a closer look [...] raises some doubts as to the real intentions of these 'socialists'. [...] Why do they not identify the enemy of the African people clearly as imperialism, colonialism, racism and capitalism? Have the socialist countries[4] ever colonised Africa or attempted to involve themselves in a 'modern scramble for Africa'? [...] It is this 'new approach'—cynical and subtle' as it is—that has dangers for Africa. We warn the African people against these 'new friends' and their allies in Africa.[5]

---

1. Ibid., p. 23.
2. As will be seen below, a potentially historic meeting between the black consciousness leader Steve Biko, ANC's Oliver Tambo and Palme was planned to take place in Botswana during the SI mission.
3. Olof Palme: 'Här går gränsen för mänsklig värdighet: Palme's afrikanska dagbok' ('Here goes the border of human decency: Palme's African diary') in *Aftonbladet-Magasinet*, 9 October 1977.
4. That is, the Soviet Union and its allies.
5. *The African Communist*, No. 73, 1978, pp. 96-98. In his diary from the SI mission to Southern Africa, Palme wrote: "There is presently a lot of talk in Africa about Marxism-Leninism. It frightens above all the wits out of the Westerners, [but] I am pretty convinced that [the Africans] will develop their socialism according to the demands of their own countries and peoples, without being shackled by foreign lands harping on about [various] theses" (Olof Palme: 'Här går gränsen för mänsklig värdighet: Palme's afrikanska dagbok'/'Here goes the border of human decency: Palme's African diary' in *Aftonbladet-Magasinet*, 9 October 1977). During the trip, Palme notably raised ideological issues with President Agostinho Neto of Angola (cf. the chapter on Angola and the interview with Alberto Ribeiro-Kabulu, p. 29). An unusual exchange regarding ANC and its relations with the Soviet Union took place in September 1977 in the liberal *Dagens Nyheter* between the newspaper's Per Wästberg and the resident ANC representative Sobizana Mngqikana (see Per Wästberg: 'Utlandets påtryckningar kan bli avgörande'/'Pressures from abroad may be decisive' in *Dagens Nyheter*, 7 September 1977; Sobizana Mngqikana: 'Sovjet formulerar inte politiken för ANC!'/'The Soviet Union does not formulate ANC's policy!' in *Dagens Nyheter*, 17 September 1977; and Per Wästberg: 'Min skiss är kanske mer realistisk, tyvärr'/'Unfortunately, my scenario is perhaps more realistic' in ibid.).

More important than divisive Cold War echoes was, however, the fact that a broad consensus on Sweden's policy vis-à-vis apartheid was established in 1977 between the Social Democratic opposition and the ruling Centre and Liberal parties. In itself, this was far from surprising. Although deeply divided with regard to domestic issues, Olof Palme, Thorbjörn Fälldin, Ola Ullsten and many other leading representatives of the three parties belonged to a political generation that in the 1950s or in the early 1960s had already become concerned with South and Southern Africa.[1] While not yet leading their respective parties, they had on several occasions together represented Sweden at various international conferences.

For example, as early as in 1966 Palme and Ullsten had co-chaired the Oxford conference on Namibia.[2] Albeit with reversed mandates, ten years later they once again appeared together at the Maputo conference on Zimbabwe and Namibia in May and at the Lagos deliberations on apartheid in August 1977, where they essentially shared a common stand on assistance to the liberation movements and sanctions against South Africa.[3] In addition, only one month after Palme's discussions on behalf of the Socialist International with President Julius Nyerere in Dar es Salaam, on an official visit to Tanzania in October 1977 Foreign Minister Söder and Nyerere shared similar views on South and Southern Africa.[4]

A Limited Breakthrough

In early June 1977, the Swedish parliament decided to appoint two commissions to look into the question of legislated restrictions with regard to Sweden's economic relations with South Africa and Namibia. The task of the main commission—chaired by Eskil Hellner, justice at the Supreme Administrative Court[5]—was to study the issues of capital transfers and investments. The former county governor Valter Åman was at the same time appointed to discuss directly with the Swedish companies concerned a voluntary limitation of their operations in South Africa. While Åman soon reported that the companies were not interested in any self-imposed restrictions[6], against the views of the chairman and of the Moderate Party representative[7]

---

1. See Sellström Volume I, passim.
2. Ibid., pp. 273-74.
3. Cf. 'Statement by Mr. Ola Ullsten, Minister of International Development Cooperation of Sweden, at the Maputo Conference on May 19, 1977' and 'Speech by Mr. Olof Palme, Sweden, at the United Nations Conference in Maputo on May 20, 1977' in [no author or editor] *Nordic Statements on Apartheid*, Scandinavian Institute of African Studies, Uppsala, and the United Nations Centre against Apartheid, New York, 1977, pp. 37-42 and 43-53. Cf. also 'Statement by Mr. Ola Ullsten, Minister of International Development Cooperation of Sweden' in the United Nations Centre against Apartheid, Notes and Documents, World Conference for Action against Apartheid, Lagos, Nigeria, 22-26 August 1977, Conference document No. 11, United Nations, New York, November 1977, pp. 8-13 and 'Statement by Mr. Olof Palme, Vice-President of [the] Socialist International' in ibid., Conference document No. 10, pp. 1-6.
4. Asked what policy the Swedish government should pursue vis-à-vis South Africa, President Nyerere emphasized two issues in his talks with Foreign Minister Söder, namely a) "to build an international boycott" and b) "to assist the Frontline States to strengthen their economies" (Cable from Lennart Eckerberg, Swedish ambassador to Tanzania, to the Ministry for Foreign Affairs, Dar es Salaam, 13 October 1977) (MFA).
5. In Swedish, *regeringsråd*. The other members of the commission were the county governor Astrid Kristensson (Moderate Party), Carl Lidbom (MP, Social Democratic Party), David Wirmark (MP, Liberal Party) and Rolf Örjes (MP, Centre Party). Åke Magnusson from the University of Gothenburg served as secretary.
6. Nordenmark op. cit., pp. 81-82.
7. For a summary of the Moderate Party's considerations during the 1977-79 sanctions debate, see Staffan Burenstam Linder: 'Sydafrika och vi' ('South Africa and us') in *Svenska Dagbladet*, 16 January 1979.

the main commission presented its report in August 1978, recommending a ban on new investments.[1]

Soon thereafter, the Fälldin coalition fell apart and a Liberal minority government headed by the former Cooperation Minister Ola Ullsten was formed.[2] With parliamentary support from the Left Party Communists, the Social Democratic Party and the Centre Party, responsibility for the implementation of the commission's recommendations was thereby taken over by the Swedish political party which over the years had arguably been the most outspoken with regard to economic sanctions.[3] Also pushed by LO's and TCO's ongoing Southern Africa campaigns, as well as by AGIS' demands, towards the end of 1978 it was just a question of time as to when Sweden as the first industrialized Western country would unilaterally legislate against investments in the apartheid republic, in the process making an exception to a long-standing, national security policy doctrine.

Nevertheless, before taking any concrete action, in early December 1978 the new Minister of Trade, Hadar Cars, invited the Swedish companies concerned, as well as the Federation of Industries and the Employers Confederation[4], to a final round of talks on voluntary corporate action. Despite popular and political pressures, in January 1979 the companies once again "chose to refrain" from such a course.[5] Prime Minister Ullsten was at the time attending a special session of the UN Anti-Apartheid Committee in Atlanta, USA, commemorating the memory of the assassinated black American civil rights leader Martin Luther King. Expressing "great disappointment" with the Swedish companies and characterizing their stand as "short-sighted"[6], after repeated official attempts at dissuasion he announced that "a bill will be presented [...] by which Sweden unilaterally [is going to] enact legislation to prevent further investments in and financial loans to South Africa".[7] The bill was submitted to parliament in April 1979. It was passed in early June, entering

1. SOU (1978) op. cit. As the only South African organization, ANC was invited by the Hellner commission to state its views. Its strong and principled submission—demanding "an immediate ban on all further foreign investment [, as well as] a withdrawal of all existing investments" (ibid., p. 275)—was attached to the commission's official report. Looking back on ANC's relations with Sweden, Frene Ginwala—then Speaker of the democratically elected National Assembly—noted in early 1995: "I remember when we were asked by the Swedish government to write a document on our views concerning a Swedish investment ban. It was an enormous event for us. We were recognized as a partner by the Swedish government. This had not happened before in any country. We became the official South African voice" (cited in Magnus Walan: 'ISAK Hade en Viktig Betydelse för Vår Befrielse'/'ISAK Played an Important Role for Our Liberation' in *Amandla*, No. 2-3, 1995, p. 23).
2. Prime Minister Ullsten's Liberal government was in power between October 1978 and October 1979, when it was succeeded by Fälldin's second coalition between the Centre, Liberal and Moderate parties (October 1979-May 1981).
3. Against both Portugal and South Africa.
4. In Swedish, *Svenska Arbetsgivareföreningen* (SAF).
5. Nordenmark op. cit., p. 88.
6. 'Ullsten i USA om Sydafrikalagen: Jag är besviken på svensk industri' ('Ullsten in USA about the South Africa law: I am disappointed with Swedish industry') in *Kvällsposten*, 17 January 1979.
7. 'Speech by Mr. Ola Ullsten, Prime Minister of Sweden, at the Special Session of the UN [A]nti-[A]partheid [C]ommittee in Atlanta', 16 January 1979, in Ministry for Foreign Affairs: *Documents on Swedish Foreign Policy: 1979*, Stockholm, 1982, p. 11. Ullsten's statement was significant and forward-looking in other respects too. Preceding the mid-1980s discussions between Sweden and ANC on preparatory planning for a post-apartheid South Africa, he underlined that "the creation of [a non-racial] society calls for preparations in many fields, particularly in education and vocational training. We should [...] make available resources for research and studies on South African society and on the role of South Africa in the regional and global context. Such studies could also include methods and means for preparing and engaging the South African population in the process of transition to majority rule. We should not lose any time in taking up this task" (ibid., p. 12).

into force on 1 July 1979.[1] "A new element had [thereby] been added to the arsenal of Swedish foreign policy measures."[2]

Having introduced his first parliamentary motion on economic sanctions against apartheid as early as in January 1965[3], it was fitting that it was Ola Ullsten who became politically responsible for the Swedish initiative. Marking a break with past policies, it was, in addition, symbolic that he made the announcement at a UN meeting dedicated to the memory of Martin Luther King. Together with the ANC President Albert Luthuli, in September 1962 King had addressed a letter to the Social Democratic Foreign Minister Östen Undén, inviting him to co-sponsor an international anti-apartheid campaign. As the appeal contained a call for economic sanctions, Undén—firmly maintaining that only the UN Security Council was mandated to take such action—had chosen to leave the letter unanswered.[4]

The 1979 South Africa law was far from revolutionary. Seen as "an exceptional measure justified by the unique situation in South Africa"[5], its main objective was "to prevent the establishment of new [Swedish] enterprises, as well as to prevent [the companies] conducting manufacturing and other business in South Africa from expanding".[6] It was a ban on *new* investments. Commodity trade with the apartheid republic was not affected, nor did the law envisage a withdrawal of the existing Swedish companies. The companies already established on the South African market were allowed to 'hibernate'.[7] As long as they did not increase their operations, they could also apply for exemptions in order to replace worn-out equipment. The government could, in addition, allow investments to improve the working conditions at the Swedish owned plants.

Widely seen as a "weak instrument"[8] by the Swedish anti-apartheid movement, from an international point of view the legislation represented a significant step forward. No other Western country with appreciable economic interests in South Africa had at the time adopted similar measures. While this rather reflected Western acquiescence vis-à-vis the apartheid regime than a Swedish readiness to radically sever its bilateral economic relations[9], the act was warmly welcomed by ANC. On

---

1. The South Africa law also covered occupied Namibia.
2. Nordenmark op. cit., p. 91.
3. Swedish Parliament 1965: Motion No. 418 in the Second Chamber, Riksdagens Protokoll, p. 10.
4. Sellström Volume I, p. 185.
5. 'Speech by Hadar Cars, Minister of Trade, at the Symposium on Strategies in the Struggle against Apartheid', Stockholm, 13 March 1979 (LMA).
6. Ibid.
7. Although the legislation was tightened up in 1985-86 and the government in 1987 imposed a comprehensive trade boycott, the bulk of the Swedish companies which were operating in South Africa in 1979 were still in the country at the time of the democratic elections in 1994. While some—notably Volvo—had voluntarily withdrawn, through international mergers and transactions new Swedish business interests had in the meantime been indirectly established on the South African market.
8. Bertil Högberg: 'Speech delivered at the opening of the ICSA conference', Södertälje, 11 April 1980 (ISA). The London-based International Committee against Apartheid, Racism and Colonialism in Southern Africa (ICSA) held its third session in Södertälje and Stockholm in mid-April 1980. It was attended by Oliver Tambo.
9. Interviewed in 1997, Tham noted that "Swedish industry made a lot of resistance [...], which was the main reason why the Swedish sanctions laws were adopted so late. One should therefore not exaggerate our benevolence. I am quite sure that if the policy had been more dangerous to Sweden, it would have been much more controversial" (Interview with Carl Tham, p. 345).

behalf of the National Executive Committee, in late September 1979 Secretary General Alfred Nzo[1] sent a cable to the Liberal Foreign Minister Hans Blix, "congratulat[ing him] and [the Swedish] government on [their] firm stand taken in favour of economic sanctions and [an] arms embargo against Vorster's racist regime", adding that the "Swedish stand constitutes [a] timely implementation of [the] programme of action for [the] eradication of apartheid".[2] In addition to the direct assistance to the liberation movement, the limited investment ban consolidated the special relations between ANC and the Swedish government at the end of the 1970s.

ANC had without success for twenty years demanded comprehensive sanctions against South Africa. Although Sweden's increasing trade exchange with the country went against the spirit of economic isolation, the liberation movement welcomed the 1979 legislation as "a step in the right direction".[3] At a meeting in Stockholm with Prime Minister Fälldin—who had succeeded Ullsten in October 1979—Tambo noted in March 1981 that

> Sweden with regard to sanctions had gone further than any other industrialized country. [...] Sweden also played an important role as an example. ANC would [therefore] in every way try to [convince] other countries to emulate [its stand].[4]

---

1. As will be noted in the text that follows, from the late 1970s Nzo would together with Treasurer General Thomas Nkobi be closely involved in the cooperation with Sweden, on several occasions leading the ANC delegation to the annual aid negotiations. Born in 1925 in Benoni outside Johannesburg, Nzo matriculated at the Healdtown Missionary Institute, Fort Beaufort, before registering at the Fort Hare University College in 1945. Although soon leaving the university, while at Fort Hare he joined the ANC Youth League. Subsequently completing a health inspector's course, he worked in that capacity in the Johannesburg township of Alexandra from the early 1950s. At the same time, he played an increasingly prominent political role, taking active part in ANC's defiance campaigns and in the preparations for the Kliptown Congress of the People, which in June 1955 adopted the Freedom Charter. In 1958, Nzo was elected to ANC's National Executive Committee. From 1959 onwards, he was served with a series of banning orders. Imprisoned for five months in 1961 and for seven months in 1963, in March 1964 he finally joined ANC in exile. Serving as the movement's Deputy Chief Representative in Cairo, Egypt, from mid-1964, in August 1967 he was appointed Chief Representative to India, based in New Delhi. Also a member of the South African Communist Party, at the April 1969 ANC conference in Morogoro, Tanzania, Nzo replaced Duma Nokwe as Secretary General. Thus occupying the most important ANC position after that of (Acting) President Tambo, he would remain in this post for more than two decades. Following ANC's unbanning in February 1990, Nzo returned to South Africa, where he formed part of the movement's core negotiating team. At the July 1991 ANC conference in Durban, he lost his position as Secretary General to Cyril Ramaphosa, but was confirmed as a member of the National Executive Committee. After the democratic elections, he was in May 1994 appointed Minister of Foreign Affairs in President Mandela's government of national unity. In President Mbeki's first cabinet, he was replaced in June 1999 by Nkosazana Zuma. After suffering a stroke, Alfred Nzo died in Johannesburg in January 2000.

2. Cable from Alfred Nzo to the Foreign Minister of Sweden, Luanda, 30 September 1979 (MFA).

3. Anders Bjurner: Memorandum ('Samtal mellan statsminister Fälldin och ANC's ordförande Oliver Tambo'/ 'Conversation between Prime Minister Fälldin and ANC's President Oliver Tambo'), Ministry for Foreign Affairs, Stockholm, 27 March 1981 (MFA).

4. Ibid. A major consideration behind the 1979 investment ban was that it would induce other countries to follow suit. While he acknowledged that "the ban—as ANC wished—probably ought to be made more comprehensive", in his meeting with Tambo Fälldin stated that "most important was to get other countries on board" (ibid.). This only happened in the mid-1980s. It should be recalled that the Swedish investments were comparatively marginal. Estimated at roughly 490 MSEK in 1981, they represented merely 0.2 per cent of total gross foreign investments in South Africa. Swedish-owned companies stood at the same time for less than 1 per cent of the foreign firms' production in the country (Ministry for Foreign Affairs: *Prohibition of Investments in South Africa and Namibia and Other Measures against Apartheid*, Stockholm, February 1985, p. 28). Nevertheless, they played a strategic role for South Africa's economy in the mining, manufacturing and energy sectors.

In Sweden, the legislation was controversial from the outset. Firmly opposed by the export-oriented business community and the Moderate Party[1], it was at the same time not only found wanting by the organized solidarity movement, but also by the political forces which had introduced it. In fact, even when he in Atlanta announced the Liberal government's intention to submit the investment bill, Ullsten declared that "it amounts to a political gesture [which] has no major economic significance".[2] Leading liberal newspapers were also highly critical. For example, in a comment on Ullsten's announcement, under the heading 'A cheap South Africa stunt' the regional *Vestmanlands Läns Tidning*—published in Västerås, the headquarters of ASEA—wrote in an editorial that

> [t]he Swedish companies [...] should be pressurized to do more for their black employees instead of being kept on political low heat by a fussy Stockholm politician. The government's South Africa policy is as hollow as a Swiss cheese and the loopholes are there for the whole world to see.[3]

As early as in January 1980—only six months after the act had entered into force—both the opposition Social Democratic Party[4] and the Liberal Party[5] submitted parliamentary motions demanding an extension of the investment ban. Also backed by the Left Party Communists and Prime Minister Fälldin's Centre Party, in October 1980 the government decided to review the South Africa law. One year later—in December 1981—a parliamentary commission chaired by ambassador Sverker Åström was appointed. It presented its recommendations in June 1984.[6] Tighter and extended legislation—covering *inter alia* leasing arrangements, technology transfers and licensing of trade—was passed by parliament in March 1985 and in May 1986.

A closer look at the 1979 ban falls outside the scope of this study. Nevertheless, it could be noted that the main criticism was initially raised against the clause allowing Swedish parent companies to apply for exemption to replace worn-out equipment and maintain their South African operations. Campaigning for a total isolation of the apartheid regime, the clause was in particular censured by AGIS and ISAK, as well as by the ANC representation in Sweden. In early 1981—when the Fälldin government had allowed Alfa-Laval and Fagersta to transfer a total of 0.8 MSEK to their South African subsidiaries—*Phambili*, the local ANC publication issued in Swedish, declared that

---

1. Describing the Liberal government's South Africa bill as "supporting the forces which aim for a confrontation in South Africa", in May 1979 the Moderate Party leader Gösta Bohman submitted a parliamentary motion calling for a rejection of the bill (Swedish Parliament 1978/79: Motion No. 2678, Riksdagens Protokoll 1978/79, pp. 4-9). The party would over the following years tirelessly strive for a revocation of the legislation. The isolation of South Africa also encountered considerable opposition by the 'old guard' in the Ministry for Foreign Affairs. For example, in his memoirs the Swedish diplomat Bengt Rösiö wrote in 1988 that he "believed and still believe[s] that it was wrong to boycott South Africa", adding that "money doesn't smell" (Bengt Rösiö: *Yrke: Diplomat*/'Profession: Diplomat', Norstedts Förlag, Stockholm, 1988, p. 225). The most spectacular incident of diplomatic dissidence occurred in 1985, when Arne Helleryd—Sweden's representative to South Africa from 1982—decided in the midst of the state of emergency to settle in the country.
2. 'Ullsten i USA om Sydafrikalagen: Jag är besviken på svensk industri' ('Ullsten in USA about the South Africa law: I am disappointed with Swedish industry') in *Kvällsposten*, 17 January 1979.
3. 'Billigt Sydafrika-trick' ('A cheap South Africa stunt') in *Vestmanlands Läns Tidning*, 17 January 1979.
4. The Social Democratic motion was *inter alia* signed by Olof Palme, Ingvar Carlsson and Lena Hjelm-Wallén. In addition to an end to SAS flights to South Africa, it requested that prohibition of technology transfers should be investigated (Swedish Parliament 1979/80: Motion No. 1128, Riksdagens Protokoll 1979/80, p. 5).
5. The motion by the Liberal Party was introduced by Olle Wästberg. It demanded a study to "investigate the possibilities of extending the economic sanctions against South Africa" (Swedish Parliament 1979/80: Motion No. 360, Riksdagens Protokoll 1979/80, p. 11).
6. SOU (1984:52): *Svensk Sydafrikapolitik*/'Swedish South Africa Policy', Liber-Allmänna Förlaget, Stockholm, 1984.

[w]e are very disappointed, because [the exemptions] are an insult to the act [...] passed by the Swedish parliament in 1979. [...] [They] take the sting out of the Swedish solidarity, [contradicting] the good which is being done. [...] [The exemptions] constitute such a disappointment that it hurts![1]

During the five years between mid-1979 and mid-1984—when the clause had been tightened up—non-socialist and Social Democratic governments allowed five companies to invest a total of 30 MSEK in South Africa, or on average 6 million per year.[2] Although significant, these amounts were considerably lower than the company investments made in 1970-78, that is, before the South Africa law. During that period, the parent companies transferred some 220 MSEK to their South African subsidiaries, in current figures corresponding approximately to a yearly amount of 25 million.[3]

The ban on new investments did curtail the Swedish companies' direct involvement in the apartheid economy. However, a completely opposite development would at the same time take place with regard to bilateral commodity trade. Between 1977 and 1984, Swedish exports to South Africa showed a spectacular growth, in current figures increasing from 358 to no less than 1,575 MSEK, or by some 340 per cent.[4] While partly a result of transactions between the Swedish parent companies and their South African subsidiaries in circumvention of the investment ban, the expansion was much broader, involving a number of new products and actors. This was reflected in growing South African imports. Although at a lower pace, during the same period their value increased from 123 to 388 MSEK, or by around 215 per cent.[5] From 1977 to 1984, Sweden's trade surplus vis-à-vis South Africa recorded a growth of more than 400 per cent, standing at 1,187 MSEK in the latter year. From a purely economic point of view, this would be used as an argument against the demands for a comprehensive trade boycott during the third national sanctions debate in the mid-1980s.[6]

Sweden's trade relations with South Africa will be further discussed below. In the meantime, it should be noted that from the late 1970s they became the primary target of the anti-apartheid movement's attention. Closely monitoring the contacts between Sweden and South Africa, AGIS would in this regard assume a leading role. While its publication—Afrikabulletinen—had a wider scope and regularly published articles on the anti-apartheid struggle, it would over the years tirelessly campaign against the loopholes in the investment legislation and, above all, denounce the growing commercial relations between the two countries, mobilizing public opinion all over Sweden and informing the political decision makers.[7]

It was also AGIS that took the initiative to set up the Isolate South Africa Committee (ISAK) as a separate, broadly based pressure group. Formed in Stockholm in January 1979 by 25 national youth, political and Christian organizations[8] "to reveal all types of Swedish collaboration with South Africa and make these an issue

---

1. 'Vi Är Besvikna!' ('We Are Disappointed!') in *Phambili*, No. 1, 1981, p. 1. Lindiwe Mabuza was the ANC Chief Representative to Sweden at the time.
2. SOU (1984) op. cit., p. 93. SKF stood for more than half of the total amount.
3. Ibid., pp. 92-93.
4. See the table below on Swedish commodity trade with South Africa 1950-1990.
5. Ibid.
6. As will be seen in Appendix VI, South Africa played a marginal role in Sweden's total commodity trade. While in 1984 the Swedish sales to the country represented a share of 0.6 per cent, the imports from South Africa stood for merely 0.2 per cent.
7. Cf. the interview with Sören Lindh, p. 308.
8. AGIS: 'Kongress -79/Verksamhetsberättelser' ('Congress 1979/Activity reports'), Documents from AGIS' fifth ordinary congress, Karlstad, 2-4 June 1979 [no specific place or date] (AGA).

Drawing up a joint Nordic programme of action against apartheid (from left):
Foreign ministers K.B. Andersen (Denmark), Einar Augustson (Iceland), Paavo Väyrynen
(Finland), Karin Söder (Sweden) and Knut Frydenlund (Norway), Helsinki, September
1977 (Photo: Pressens Bild)

of public discussion"[1], as well as to mobilize support for ANC and SWAPO, ISAK's
growth over the following decade was as spectacular as the relations it opposed. By
June 1991, no less than 63 organizations had joined ISAK, ranging from the Communist Party Marxist-Leninists (Revolutionaries)[2] via the Methodist Church
Youth[3], Athletes Against Apartheid[4] and the Social Democratic Youth League to
the LO-affiliated Public Employees Union and the Liberal Party Women's League.[5]
Representing more than one million members[6], across ideological divides the
organization constituted a powerful solidarity front. Together with AGIS, it effectively paved the way for the trade boycott against South Africa which was eventually imposed from July 1987.

Before turning to the official political and aid relations with the wider South
African nationalist movement in the 1970s, it should be recalled that Sweden's
stand on apartheid was by tradition coordinated with its Nordic neighbours, notably at the level of the United Nations.[7] With regard to sanctions, the Nordic countries had, for example, in November 1976 co-sponsored the UN draft resolution
demanding a ban on new investments. Although at the time only Norway followed
up the initiative—and as the trade exchange between the Nordic countries and
South Africa was generally on the increase[8]—at a meeting in the Finnish capital
Helsinki in September 1977 the five Nordic Foreign Ministers "resolved to appoint

1. ISAK: 'A short presentation', Stockholm, 2 April 1980 [original in English] (ISA).
2. In Swedish, *Kommunistiska Partiet Marxist-Leninisterna (Revolutionärer)*.
3. *Metodistkyrkans Ungdom.*
4. *Idrottare Mot Apartheid.*
5. ISAK: 'Styrelsens verksamhetsberättelse 1990/91' ('Activity report by the board 1990/91') [no place or date]
   (ISA).
6. Ibid.
7. On the Nordic so called Hækkerup initiative at the United Nations in 1963—named after the Danish Foreign
   Minister Per Hækkerup—see Sellström Volume I, pp. 198-201.
8. SOU (1984) op. cit., p. 83.

a study group to investigate the feasibility of a joint action programme of wider economic measures against South Africa".[1]

Meeting six months later in Oslo, Norway, the Nordic Foreign Ministers agreed on a 'Nordic Programme of Action against Apartheid'[2], subsequently called the 'Oslo plan'. It covered seven points, namely

- prohibition or discouragement of new investments in South Africa;
- negotiations with Nordic enterprises with a view to restricting their production [...];
- recommendations that contacts with the apartheid regime [...] in the field[s] of sport[s] and culture be discontinued;
- increased Nordic support to refugees, liberation movements [and] victims of apartheid;
- work [at the United Nations] for the adoption of Security Council resolutions against new investments in South Africa;
- work for proposals in the Security Council which could result in binding resolutions against trade with South Africa; and
- work to ensure the strict observance of the Security Council's resolution on the arms embargo [...].[3]

Implemented differently by the five Nordic countries, the plan was reviewed in 1985 and—following the introduction of Nordic boycotts against South Africa— updated in 1988.[4]

1. 'Communiqué from the meeting of [the] Nordic Foreign Ministers in Helsinki', 1-2 September 1977, in Ministry for Foreign Affairs: *Documents on Swedish Foreign Policy: 1977*, Stockholm, 1978, p. 112. See also Tor Högnäs: 'Dags för nordisk aktion mot rasismen i Sydafrika' ('Time for Nordic action against racism in South Africa') in *Dagens Nyheter*, 3 September 1977.
2. Originally phrased as a programme "against South Africa", it was later changed to a plan "against apartheid".
3. 'Communiqué on the Nordic Foreign Ministers' meeting in Oslo', 9-10 March 1978, in Ministry for Foreign Affairs: *Documents on Swedish Foreign Policy: 1978*, Stockholm, 1982, pp. 167-68. See also 'Norden mot apartheid' ('The Nordic countries against apartheid') in *Dagens Nyheter*, 11 March 1978.
4. A first joint political meeting between the Foreign Ministers of the Nordic countries and the Frontline States was held in Stockholm in mid-1984. It was followed by a second encounter in Arusha, Tanzania, at the beginning of 1988.

'Looking for Alternatives':
Pan Africanist Congress

Pending Clarifications

Although Sweden established a 'special relationship' with ANC, until the end of the 1970s there were foreign affairs' officials, church voices, trade union leaders and national representatives at international organizations who advocated direct assistance to other South African political organizations. Looking back on ten years of close involvement with the nationalist struggles in Southern Africa, in mid-1980 Anders Möllander, first secretary at the embassy in Lusaka[1], observed in a "bureaucrat's testament" that

> with regard to ANC, for a long time many considered it necessary to look for alternatives. PAC, Buthelezi's Inkatha [and the] Black Consciousness Movement may be quoted as examples. The wish to look for alternatives seems to have had two main underlying motives, [namely] that ANC was seen as too insignificant inside South Africa and/or too linked to [...] the Soviet Union.[2]

Möllander wrote his retrospective in May 1980, at a time when the situation regarding the wider South African opposition had been clarified or was in the process of being confirmed. Thus, while PAC had neither enjoyed direct official nor significant NGO assistance from Sweden, at the end of the 1970s it was paralyzed by internecine struggles in exile. A deep rift had at the same time opened between ANC and the internally based Inkatha. After the death in 1977 of Steve Biko and the banning of its main constituent organizations, the black consciousness movement was also in disarray. In addition, in early 1980 the Pretoria government's penetration of the International University Exchange Fund dramatically underlined the importance of close coordination with ANC. Finally, from within the apartheid

---

1. Möllander's professional involvement with Southern Africa started in 1971, when he—at the time a young SIDA official—was appointed assistant secretary to the Consultative Committee on Humanitarian Assistance. As noted throughout the text, on behalf of CCHA, SIDA and the Ministry for Foreign Affairs he established early relations with PAIGC and the Southern African liberation movements. After working between 1975 and 1977 as a SIDA programme officer at the embassy in Dar es Salaam—also engaged in the establishment of Sweden's representation in Maputo—he was until mid-1980 first secretary at the embassy in Lusaka. Regularly forming part of official delegations to annual aid negotiations, he was particularly well placed to summarize Sweden's first ten years of assistance to the nationalist movements. His internal mid-1980 'testament' was later expanded, and in 1982 published by SIDA as *Sverige i Södra Afrika: Minnesanteckningar 1970-80* ('Sweden in Southern Africa: Memories 1970-80'). (As the struggles in Namibia and South Africa were still ongoing, the booklet did not cover the cooperation with SWAPO and ANC.) In February 1986, Möllander co-drafted Palme's historic address to the People's Parliament against Apartheid. Appointed first secretary at the legation in Pretoria, from 1987 he closely followed the denouement of the South African drama. In 1992-93, he served as ambassador to Angola. Perhaps more than any other foreign affairs' official, Möllander embodies two and a half decades of direct official Swedish cooperation with the Southern African forces of national liberation.
2. Anders Möllander: Memorandum ('Tio år med södra Afrika: En byråkrats 'testamente"/'Ten years with Southern Africa: A bureaucrat's 'testament"), Swedish embassy, Lusaka, 28 May 1980 (MFA).

Women in the forefront: Lindiwe Mabuza with Lena Johansson (left) and Mai Palmberg celebrating ANC's 70th anniversary, Stockholm, January 1982 (Courtesy of Mai Palmberg)

republic the Swedish legation reported in 1979 that ANC "undoubtedly" had become the "dominant" opposition force[1], while in Sweden its new Chief Representative, Lindiwe Mabuza, through untiring diplomatic work rapidly and successfully broadened the movement's already strong support base.[2]

One year after the introduction of the Swedish investment ban and immediately after Zimbabwe's independence, in his 'testament' Möllander advised that

> it is important that Sweden in its contacts with ANC is keenly aware of the movement's viewpoints and advice. Naturally, all assistance [to South Africa] does not necessarily have to be granted to ANC. This is also not [its] opinion. It seems, however, that it is only ANC that is in a position to determine the activities that deserve to be supported.[3]

Essentially adopting this view, from around 1980 the Swedish government— again including the Moderate Party in a junior position[4]—departed from a pluralistic approach, embarking instead on a policy which for all practical purposes accorded ANC the privileged status of a South African 'government-in-waiting'. The bilateral cooperation with ANC occupies the concluding chapters of this study. In the mean-

---

1. Gustaf Hamilton: Memorandum ('De svarta organisationernas aktivitet i dagens Sydafrika'/'The black organizations' activities in South Africa today'), Swedish legation, Pretoria, 2 March 1979 (MFA).

2. Mabuza served as ANC's Chief Representative to Sweden and the Nordic countries between 1979 and 1987. Towards the end of her assignment, ANC set up separate representations in Denmark (1985) and Norway (1986). An information office was opened in Finland in 1988. While Mabuza subsequently represented ANC in the United States, Billy Modise succeeded her in Sweden.

3. Anders Möllander: Memorandum ('Tio år med södra Afrika: En byråkrats 'testamente''/'Ten years with Southern Africa: A bureaucrat's 'testament''), Swedish embassy, Lusaka, 28 May 1980 (MFA).

4. Prime Minister Fälldin's second government of the Centre, Liberal and Moderate parties was in power from October 1979 until May 1981, when the latter left the coalition. Still under Fälldin, the 'middle' Centre and Liberal parties continued to rule until October 1982.

time, it remains to address the relations with the 'alternative' PAC, Inkatha and BCM movements.[1]

The Pan Africanist Congress and Sweden in the 1960s

From the early 1960s until the South African elections in 1994, the Pan Africanist Congress of Azania (PAC)[2] played an extremely peripheral role in Sweden. Contrary to the situation in Norway, it never received any direct official support. Whether under Social Democratic or non-socialist governments, throughout the years the Foreign Ministry, CCHA and SIDA regularly turned down its requests for assistance. No political party ever backed a parliamentary motion in favour of ANC's main rival in exile.[3] Furthermore, at the NGO level the organization did not make a significant impact. While certain Maoist-inspired organizations in the 1970s half-heartedly promoted PAC—and Emmaus-Björkå until 1980 sent clothes

1. With ANC and PAC, the loosely federated Unity Movement of South Africa (UMSA)—formerly known as the Non-European Unity Movement (NEUM) and widely regarded as South Africa's leading Trotskyist organization—could be counted among the main historical currents in the South African national liberation struggle. By the late 1960s, it had, however, lost the influence it exercised after its formation in 1943. Confined to a small following in the Western Cape, without a significant external mission and not recognized by OAU, UMSA's relations with Sweden will not form part of the narration. It could, however, be noted that the Swedish government at an early stage entered into contact with the organization. When the UMSA President Isaac Tabata in 1970 decided to revive the organization, he approached the Ministry for Foreign Affairs in Stockholm for assistance (Letter from I.B. Tabata to the Swedish Minister for Foreign Affairs, Pretoria, 26 March 1970) (MFA). Following a visit by Tabata's envoy Carl Brecker in April 1970, the request was, however, turned down (MFA annotations to ibid.). Maintaining regular contacts with the Swedish embassy in Dar es Salaam, in December 1972—immediately before the decision to grant official assistance to ANC—UMSA's Treasurer A.I. Limbada visited Bengt Säve-Söderbergh and Gun-Britt Andersson at the Foreign Ministry. Critical towards ANC and PAC—which in his view both followed a policy of "Africa for the Africans"—he asked for financial assistance to UMSA's representation in Zambia (Magnus Wernstedt: Memorandum ('Samtal med Dr. A.I. Limbada från Unity Movement of South Africa (UMSA)'/ 'Conversation with Dr. A.I. Limbada from UMSA'), Ministry for Foreign Affairs, Stockholm, 20 December 1972) (MFA). Also this request was rejected. Based in Sweden, the UMSA leader Leonard Nikani—who like ANC's Billy Modise was employed by the official aid agency SIDA; later serving at its training centre in Uppsala—subsequently raised the cause of the Unity Movement (Letter from L. Nikani on behalf of I.B. Tabata to the Director General of SIDA, Lusaka/Stockholm, 16 September 1976) (SDA). Although many CCHA members looked upon UMSA's representatives as "honest and bright" (Letter from Gunnar Helander to CCHA, Västerås, 13 December 1976) (SDA), no Swedish representation in Southern Africa backed its submissions (Marianne Sundh: Memorandum ('Framställning från All African Convention and the Unity Movement of South Africa'/'Request by AAC-UMSA'), CCHA-SIDA, Stockholm, 3 May 1977) (SDA). With even less support—but arguably more sympathy—than PAC, UMSA never became a factor in the Swedish anti-apartheid equation.

2. To mark its difference from the multi-racial ANC, the 'Africanist' PAC used the designation 'Azania' for South Africa. This was later taken over by organizations within the wider black consciousness movement. The term *Azania* is derived from old Persian, meaning 'the land of the blacks', and historically denoted the East African coast.

3. In fact, over the years only one parliamentary motion suggested official support to PAC. It was submitted in January 1984 by the former Minister of Education Jan-Erik Wikström (1976-82) and four fellow Liberal MPs. However, the general motion did not advocate exclusive assistance to PAC, but mainly increased grants to ANC and SACTU (Swedish Parliament 1983/84: Motion No. 534, Riksdagens Protokoll 1983/84, p. 14). It could as a curiosity be noted that Wikström as a member of the Swedish Mission Covenant Church Youth had met PAC President Robert Sobukwe during a visit to South Africa in November 1959. Based on an interview with him, Wikström gave a sympathetic presentation of PAC—formed only in April 1959—in the liberal newspaper *Expressen*. In the article, Sobukwe criticized ANC's policy of non-violence and its links with SACP, describing the rival movement as "not sufficiently anti-Communist" (Jan-Erik Wikström: 'Sydafrika mot katastrof'/'South Africa towards catastrophe' in *Expressen*, 19 November 1959).

to its cadres in Tanzania[1]—AGIS and ISAK preferred to pass the movement over in silence.[2] Commenting on the relations with Sweden, in 1995 PAC's Foreign Affairs Secretary Gora Ebrahim noted that "[t]here were some small organizations that we were able to contact, but we never received any substantial assistance from them. [...] To the very end, we received no assistance whatsoever from Sweden".[3]

Möllander's observation that 'many' looked towards PAC as an 'alternative' is thus exaggerated. In fact, from the point of view of political and material support, the movement's isolation from the mid-1960s was such that it could rather be left out in a study on Sweden's official, bilateral relations with the nationalist movements in Southern Africa. Karis and Gerhart's general remarks are in this context pertinent. Discussing PAC's record in exile, in their documentary history of the South African liberation struggle they conclude that it

> was not illustrious. Its scattered and quarrelsome leaders failed to create stable structures or a continuity of respected leadership. Its years in exile are primarily of interest as a case study of the perils faced by a movement unprepared for revolutionary work, dependent on foreign goodwill, only indirectly in touch with developments at home and lacking in leadership, organization, strategy and ideological clarity.[4]

As it was recognized by OAU, the United Nations and the People's Republic of China[5]; backed by Sweden's partners Tanzania and Zimbabwe; assisted by neigh-

---

1. In the 1970s, Emmaus-Björkå collected clothes and other items for both ANC and PAC. In 1977, for example, the organization shipped 11 tons to ANC and 10.5 tons to PAC ('Att Samla Lump och Kläder för Södra Afrika'/'Collecting Rags and Clothes for Southern Africa' in *Kommentar*, No. 2, 1978, p. 13). After a fact-finding mission to Tanzania and Zambia, the shipments to PAC were suspended in 1980 due to the movement's lack of organization and discipline (Telephone conversation with Christer Johansson, Emmaus-Björkå, 26 November 1999).

2. Initially, the organized solidarity movement did not explicitly reject PAC. In a letter to the Norwegian Council for Southern Africa, Dick Urban Vestbro, for example, stated on behalf of the Africa Groups in October 1976 that "we [...] have not yet officially dissociated ourselves from PAC" (Letter from Dick Urban Vestbro to *Fellesrådet for det sørlige Afrika*, [no place], 3 October 1976) (AGA). Nevertheless, in their anti-apartheid work both AGIS and ISAK would *de facto* exclude PAC. This prompted Cecil Sondlo, PAC's assistant representative to Sweden, to warn the Isolate South Africa Committee in January 1984 that it must not become an 'Isolate PAC Committee' (Letter from Cecil Sondlo to ISAK, Stockholm, 18 January 1984) (AGA). In spite of Sondlo's efforts, his organization, however, remained on the periphery. Both at the official and at the NGO level, ANC enjoyed undivided support. Neither PAC nor the BCM-inspired AZAPO (Azanian People's Organization) were invited by ISAK and the Swedish UN Association to the People's Parliament against Apartheid in Stockholm in February 1986, a fact which was criticized in both national and regional liberal newspapers (see, for example, Claes-Adam Wachtmeister: 'Ensidigt stöd till ANC förstärker splittringen'/'One-sided support to ANC deepens the division' in *Dagens Nyheter*, 18 March 1986, and Anders Davidson: 'Förmynderi i apartheidmotståndet'/'Protectionism in the resistance against apartheid' in *Vestmanlands Läns Tidning*, 22 May 1986). This, in turn, led the Africa Groups to publicly state their reasons for not supporting PAC. In a leading article in *Afrikabulletinen*, Vestbro emphasized the organization's "languishing life" in South Africa, its divisive "black power ideology" and its political "opportunism", concluding that PAC's "combination of anti-white and anti-Communist [policies] [...] prepares the terrain for [...] 'black capitalism'" (Dick Urban Vestbro: 'Därför Kan PAC Inte Få Vårt Stöd'/'For These Reasons PAC Cannot Have Our Support' in *Afrikabulletinen*, No. 3, 1986, p. 9).

3. Interview with Gora Ebrahim, pp. 120-21. According to him, Sweden was said to have taken "a decision against PAC based on [...] recommendations [by the South African security officer] Craig Williamson" (ibid., p. 120).

4. Karis and Gerhart, op. cit., p. 47.

5. On China, PAC and ANC, see Ian Taylor: 'The Ambiguous Commitment: The People's Republic of China and the Anti-Apartheid Struggle in South Africa' in *Journal of Contemporary African Studies*, No. 1, January 2000, pp. 91-106.

bouring Norway[1]; and enjoyed a certain amount of sympathy within the Western anti-apartheid movement—notably in the United States[2]—it is, nevertheless, relevant to discuss how Sweden became an almost closed area for PAC and PAC-aligned organizations in South Africa.

In the light of subsequent developments, as a point of departure it should, however, ironically be noted that PAC was the first South African liberation movement to pay a visit to Sweden, the first to submit a request for humanitarian assistance and the first to receive a significant NGO donation. As was seen in Volume I[3], this was due to the fact that in the early 1960s the organization together with ANC in exile formed part of the South Africa United Front, where it maintained a high profile and initially managed to raise political support, particularly in Africa. Discussing his 1962 Africa tour, Nelson Mandela has in his memoirs observed that "most African leaders could understand the views of the PAC better than those of the ANC". Referring to meetings with Kenneth Kaunda and other Zambian leaders, he notes that "while they knew that the ANC was stronger and more popular than the PAC, they understood the PAC's pure nationalism, but were bewildered by the ANC's non-racialism and [C]ommunist ties".[4]

PAC was founded in April 1959 by an 'Africanist' breakaway faction of ANC, led by Robert Mangaliso Sobukwe. It mainly objected to the non-racial provision in the Freedom Charter that "South Africa belongs to all who live in it, black and white", but also to the economic clauses calling for nationalization of the mines, banks and monopoly industries. Defining its vision in strongly pan-Africanist terms and aiming at the achievement of an 'Africanist socialist democracy', PAC President Sobukwe spelled out the organization's differences with ANC as follows: "To us the struggle is a national struggle, [while] those of the ANC who are its active policy makers maintain [...] that [it] is a class struggle. We are according to them

---

1. After restricting Norway's economic exchange with South Africa, from mid-1977 Odvar Nordli's Social Democratic government extended direct humanitarian assistance to both ANC and PAC in exile. Commenting that "it is not [so] easy to understand why Norway also decided to support the PAC", Østbye concludes that the decision "seems to have been the result of a combination of limited knowledge, positive recommendations [...] from the [Norwegian] embassy in Tanzania and [a resolve] to be on the safe side by supporting both organisations that were recognised by the OAU and the UN" (Eva Helene Østbye: 'The South African Liberation Struggle: Direct Norwegian Support' in Eriksen (ed.) op. cit., pp. 155 and 163). Soon, however, the Norwegian government "lost most of its faith in the PAC, [and] [a]t the beginning of the 1980s uncertainty marked the relationship" (ibid., p. 165). Nevertheless, the official support continued. It was only brought to an end in 1992, after PAC's boycott of the CODESA negotiations and when its armed wing, the Azanian People's Liberation Army (APLA), had launched indiscriminate attacks on white civilians (ibid., pp. 167-68). In comparison with that to ANC, the direct Norwegian support to PAC was small. Between 1977 and 1992, ANC received no less than 400 MNOK. The total contribution to PAC during the same period was 24 million, corresponding to 6 per cent (Eriksen (ed.) op. cit, Table VII, p. 408). While Norway's continuous cooperation with PAC was unique in the Nordic context, in 1983 the Finnish government under the Social Democratic Prime Minister Kalevi Sorsa, as an exception, granted the organization 200,000 FIM as refugee support in Tanzania (Soiri and Peltola op. cit., p. 143 and Appendix 2, p. 178).
2. Until the mid-1980s, it was PAC rather than ANC that attracted the US anti-apartheid movement's attention. As noted by Thomas, "ANC's non-racialism was contrary to the Black Power movement, which had an ideology much closer to the PAC and [BCM]". In addition, "ANC's alliance with the SACP [...] did not cause as much concern [in Europe] as it did [in the United States]" (Thomas op. cit., pp. 195 and 192).
3. Sellström Volume I, pp. 149, 157-58 and 169-75.
4. Nelson Mandela: *Long Walk to Freedom: The Autobiography of Nelson Mandela*, Macdonald Purnell, Randburg, 1994, pp. 292 and 299. Tanzania's former Foreign and Prime Minister Salim Ahmed Salim, at the time Secretary General of OAU, stated in 1995: "Over a period of years—especially from the 1970s—Tanzania's support for PAC became more *pro forma* by virtue of its obligation as headquarters of the OAU Liberation Committee. This was contrary to the early days, when there was a belief that maybe PAC was more dynamic. It was for the armed struggle when ANC was not and all that. But when Umkhonto we Sizwe started to operate, things became clear. Another thing that really turned the Tanzanian government's position regarding South Africa was that the ANC trainees in Tanzania did not remain there. They were moving into South Africa. Most of the PAC trainees remained as armchair revolutionaries" (Interview with Salim Ahmed Salim, p. 246).

oppressed as *workers*, both white and black. [...] We claim Africa for the Africans. The ANC claims South Africa for all".[1]

PAC's existence as a legal organization in South Africa was short-lived. After encouraging the demonstrations against the racial pass laws which in March 1960 ended in the Sharpeville shootings, Sobukwe was arrested and PAC together with ANC in April 1960 declared an unlawful organization. Despite their differences, in order to mobilize international support for the anti-apartheid struggle two months later—in June 1960—the exiled leaders of the banned movements formed the South Africa United Front (SAUF) together with the South African Indian Congress and SWANU of Namibia in the Ethiopian capital Addis Ababa.[2] SAUF was also short-lived. Mainly due to the rivalry between ANC and PAC, during the second half of 1961 the front began to disintegrate. After a public attack in February 1962 by PAC on ANC[3] at a conference in Addis Ababa—attended by Nelson Mandela—SAUF collapsed. It was formally disbanded by the member organizations at a meeting in London the following month. From then on, ANC and PAC embarked on separate and essentially antagonistic courses.

Although ANC was far better known in Sweden than PAC, it was through the latter's SAUF representative, Nana Mahomo, that the first direct contacts with the exiled leadership of the banned organizations were established. Responsible within the united front for relations with the student and trade union movements, in October 1960—only four months after the formation of SAUF—Mahomo paid a visit to the country, *inter alia* addressing the Social Democratic Laboremus association in Uppsala.[4] Together with ANC's Oliver Tambo and SWANU's Jariretundu Kozonguizi, he returned in April 1961. On this occasion, the three main SAUF leaders were received by the recently formed South Africa Committee (SSAK).

During subsequent visits, Mahomo established close relations with SSAK's Joachim Israel—in August 1962 appointed chairman of the committee—and through him with the Social Democratic Party. The relations continued after the break-up of the united front. Now acting on behalf of PAC, in April 1962 Mahomo approached the ruling party with a request for financial assistance to a group of South African refugees in Bechuanaland (Botswana). In a letter to the LO chairman Arne Geijer, he described the application as "the first comprehensive approach ever presented by any organization dealing with South Africa to meet the problem of refugees with a view towards its permanent solution".[5] At a time when the Swedish parliament and government had not yet decided to allocate financial resources for humanitarian assistance to Southern Africa, the submission was partly met by KF and the Metalworkers Union. In January 1963, the co-operative movement granted PAC the token amount of 100 Pounds Sterling "to help you to meet the immediate

1. Cited in Rob Davies, Dan O'Meara and Sipho Dlamini: *The Struggle for South Africa: A Reference Guide to Movements, Organizations and Institutions*, Volume II, Zed Books, London, 1984, p. 299.
2. On SAUF, see Sellström Volume I, p. 149, note 3. SWAPO was admitted in January 1961 as a member of the coordinating body. However, it never participated actively and withdrew some months later.
3. PAC's criticism was based on the same arguments that originally led to the breakaway, i.e. that ANC was dominated by white Communists and that it saw the struggle in class terms, not as a national struggle with the objective 'Africa for the Africans'.
4. Sellström Volume I, p. 157, note 5.
5. Letter from Nana Mahomo to Arne Geijer, Stockholm, 12 November 1962 (JIC).

needs of the refugees"[1], while *Metall* the same month agreed to purchase a Land Rover and ship it to the movement in Dar es Salaam.[2]

As far as can be ascertained, the trade union's donation to PAC represents the very first direct material support from a Swedish organization to a South African liberation movement.[3] It was, however, a one-off affair. Nana Mahomo—suspended from PAC in August 1964 and later expelled—did not reappear on the Swedish scene.[4] From then on, the organization would be completely overshadowed by ANC. In addition to serious doubts regarding PAC's commitment to a future non-racial South African society—and compared with ANC's successful diplomacy in this regard[5]—from late 1962 PAC's indiscriminate armed campaigns[6]; its lack of organization and accountability[7]; and, above all, its "byzantine leadership intrigues and rank-and-file rebellions" in exile, where "most of the organization's energies were devoted to internecine conflict", contributed to this.[8] From the very beginning of official Swedish assistance to the liberation movements in Southern Africa, PAC was kept at arm's length. As later stated by the leading CCHA member Per Wästberg,

> there was no question of ever supporting an organization that was more or less fraudulent and that could not take care of money. [...] PAC as an organization was never reliable. There was infighting and they were killing each other. They were absolutely impossible.[9]

---

1. Letter from J.W. Ames to Nana Mahomo, Stockholm, 2 January 1963 (JIC).
2. Sellström Volume I, p. 171. According to Bernard Leeman, a former PAC member, there was at about the same time a much more spectacular indirect link to Sweden. He has thus asserted that President Kwame Nkrumah of Ghana in late 1962 "bought a Swedish freighter for PAC [...] and had it loaded with arms in Egypt. The ship sailed south in early 1963 to land the weapons on the Transkei coast to assist the Poqo rising. [However, i]t never arrived. Later it emerged that it had been sold [...]. One high-ranking PAC official came under suspicion, but the matter was never resolved" (Letter ('Nkrumah armed the PAC') from professor Bernard Leeman, Harare, in *Mail and Guardian*, 3-9 November 2000). Eight years later, a similar initiative by ANC to land freedom fighters on the Transkeian coast was aborted.
3. Indicative of the shift from PAC to ANC, in 1964 the Social Democratic Youth League donated the modest amount of 3,000 SEK to the organization led by Oliver Tambo in exile. This, in turn, represents the first direct financial contribution to ANC by a Swedish political organization.
4. Mahomo was charged with "misappropriation of funds, attempts to create personal loyalties and sources of personal operation" (Tom Lodge: *Black Politics in South Africa since 1945*, Longman, London and New York, 1983, p. 309). PAC later accused him of CIA connections (ibid., p. 319, note 50), an allegation supported by the former South African intelligence officer Gordon Winter (Gordon Winter: *Inside BOSS, South Africa's Secret Police*, Penguin Books, Harmondsworth, 1981, p. 431). In the 1980s, Mahomo resurfaced as coordinator of the United States AFL-CIO's African-American Labor Center (AALC), working closely with Chief Gatsha Buthelezi and the Inkatha-backed United Workers Union of South Africa (UWUSA) (Anne Newman: 'Is American Support Dividing South African Labor?' in *Africa News*, June 1986, pp. 7-10).
5. Cf. the interview with Salim Ahmed Salim, where he emphasizes ANC's "tremendous work in the Nordic countries" (Interview with Salim Ahmed Salim, p. 246).
6. Sellström Volume I, p. 173.
7. Cf. Birgitta Berggren's impressions from Tanzania in the late 1970s: "Having worked in Dar es Salaam, I [...] knew that PAC was very torn by internal struggles and even killings. Already in Tanzania I knew that they could not make use of the funds which were available to them through the UN system. They were not organized enough. It was rather a tragic picture [...]" (Interview with Birgitta Berggren, pp. 257-58). See also the interview with Ernst Michanek, SIDA's former Director General and chairman of CCHA (1965-79/80): "PAC [...] developed into something rather bad, with people murdering each other even in the circles that we were dealing with. If an organization was disrupting the struggle against apartheid in the way that PAC did, then I had to be very firm. [...] Of course, the PAC leaders hated us enormously, because in the past they had had their opportunities at the expense of IDAF and therefore also of the Swedish government. [...] I should not use any derogatory words about them, because I pitied them a great deal. But what they could do with the money that they received had nothing at all to do with the struggle against apartheid in South Africa. It was far too much to be accepted" (Interview with Ernst Michanek, p. 324).
8. Lodge op. cit., pp. 343 and 310.
9. Interview with Per Wästberg, pp. 355-56.

Nevertheless, PAC would untiringly approach Sweden for financial and material assistance. As will be seen below, the contacts—more often than not amounting to "a matter of trying to incriminate ANC"[1]—were, however, never successful.

In the meantime, at the end of the 1960s a little known diplomatic event occurred which potentially could have given PAC a different platform in Sweden. In February 1969, the UN Anti-Apartheid Committee informally approached the Swedish government concerning possible political asylum for PAC's jailed President Robert Sobukwe.[2] Arrested in connection with the Sharpeville events in March 1960, Sobukwe had originally been sentenced to three years imprisonment in the Orange Free State. He was subsequently transferred to Robben Island, where under special legislation he was held in solitary confinement in a bungalow outside the main prison. After extending his detention year after year, in April 1969 the apartheid regime announced that Sobukwe would be released. It was in that connection that the approach to Sweden was made. While the Swedish UN representative Sverker Åström "found the idea worth trying"[3], Foreign Minister Torsten Nilsson was, however, "somewhat sceptical"[4] and the proposal never materialized.[5] PAC was not given a political base in Sweden.[6]

Pre-Soweto Contacts, Requests and Rejections

The relations between Sweden and PAC from the early 1970s could, roughly, be divided into four phases. Indirectly supported via the UN system, IDAF, IUEF, WCC, WUS and other international organizations[7], during a first phase—extending until the June 1976 Soweto uprising and corresponding to the Social Democratic government's initial 'pluralistic approach'—regular contacts were formally maintained. After Soweto—and coinciding with the non-socialist electoral victory in Sweden—followed a short second phase during which PAC actively approached the Swedish government and *inter alia* attempted to establish a recognized repre-

---

1. Interview with Pierre Schori, pp. 332-33.
2. Letter from Sverker Åström to Wilhelm Wachtmeister, United Nations, New York, 4 February 1969 (MFA).
3. Ibid.
4. Letter from Wilhelm Wachtmeister to Sverker Åström, Ministry for Foreign Affairs, Stockholm, 13 February 1969 (MFA).
5. "Subject to such restrictions [as] are deemed necessary for the safety of the state", Sobukwe was released from Robben Island in May 1969. Immediately banished for five years to the town of Kimberley, he was placed under rigorous house arrest. The banishment was in 1974 extended for another five years. In February 1978, Sobukwe died of cancer. On the South African government's extraordinary measures against the PAC President—who in the 1960s and 1970s together with Nelson Mandela and the jailed ANC leadership largely inspired the anti-apartheid resistance inside South Africa—see Benjamin Pogrund: *How Can Man Die Better...: Sobukwe and Apartheid*, Peter Halban Publishers, London, 1990. With regard to the indiscriminate armed campaign by the PAC-inspired Poqo movement—explicitly involving the killing of people and targeting white civilians—and PAC's exile reverses under Acting President Potlako Leballo, it could be noted that Sobukwe's biographer underlines that "by the time Poqo developed, there is no indication that [he] was still in control of the PAC. The system of communication from inside prison was proving insufficient for him to be closely in touch and to take key decisions. [...] [T]his provided the opportunity for angry young men to make the running, and for Leballo to move in and to steer them as his own" (ibid., pp. 183-84).
6. The proposal concerning Sobukwe's asylum was made at a time when the Swedish—largely Maoist-inspired—Vietnam movement was at its height and the organized solidarity movement for Southern Africa at its nadir.
7. Throughout the period discussed in this study, via multilateral channels PAC received substantial, indirect assistance from Sweden and the other Nordic countries. Cf. Gora Ebrahim: "We benefited greatly from the Nordic countries, who were the principal donors of [IDAF]. [...] IUEF recognized PAC and gave us scholarships. [...] [W]e had very good relations with IUEF. [...] The United Nations also set up a scholarship fund in which the Nordic countries played a very important role". In addition, in the 1995 interview PAC's Secretary of Foreign Affairs stated that "[w]e viewed the Nordic countries as important allies in the question of putting pressure on the apartheid regime [...]. In the international campaign to politically isolate [South Africa] and to apply sanctions against it, the Nordic countries were in the forefront. We could always count on them in international fora. [...] [They] played a very important role" (Interview with Gora Ebrahim, pp. 118-20).

sentation in the country. It ended with the outbreak of the organization's prolonged internal crisis in 1978. The 1980s constitute a third phase, when Sweden's relations with ANC were consolidated and only intermittent contacts with PAC took place at the United Nations or in connection with international conferences. A fourth phase, finally, opened with the unbanning of the two movements in February 1990.

Supported by the People's Republic of China, PAC—like the breakaway ZANU of Zimbabwe[1]—did not form part of the Khartoum alliance of 'authentic' liberation movements. Like ZANU, the organization, however, maintained cordial relations with SWAPO of Namibia. When Sweden in 1969 decided to extend direct, official humanitarian assistance to both ZANU and SWAPO, PAC too contacted the Social Democratic government for support.[2] The first serious approach to this effect was made in January 1971, when the Acting President Potlako Leballo[3] in a letter to Prime Minister Palme requested an amount of 40,000 USD "in order to propagate our just cause, cater for the victims of apartheid and provide daily needs to those deprived because of the system prevailing in our country".[4] There is, however, no evidence that Palme—who later in the year held bilateral discussions with ANC's Oliver Tambo in Lusaka[5]—or any other Swedish official ever replied to the letter. Nevertheless, after repeated, informal contacts at the level of the embassy in Dar es Salaam, in February 1973—immediately after the decision to grant direct assistance to ANC[6]—PAC's Chief Representative to Tanzania, M.K. Nkula, travelled to Sweden, where he was received at the Foreign Ministry by first secretary Bengt Säve-Söderbergh.

1. ZANU was formed in August 1963 by dissident members of ZAPU, led by Ndabaningi Sithole (President), Leopold Takawira (Vice-President) and Robert Mugabe (Secretary General). While the relations between the mother organizations ANC and ZAPU remained close over the years—in the late 1960s *inter alia* expressed through joint military operations—the bonds between the two 'non-authentic' breakaway movements PAC and ZANU became, correspondingly, particularly cordial. Both PAC and ZANU advocated pan-Africanist and—later—Maoist-inspired policies. In the late 1940s, the future PAC and ZANU leaders Robert Sobukwe and Robert Mugabe studied together at the University of Fort Hare, South Africa.
2. Contrary to most Southern African nationalist movements, PAC had no resident spokesperson in Sweden. It was only in the late 1970s that an informal representation was established. During the second half of the 1960s, the contacts were mainly pursued via the Swedish embassy in Dar es Salaam or through visits to Stockholm. PAC's National Treasurer Abednego Ngcobo—a founder member who after 1964 was based in the Tanzanian capital—had as early as in February 1967 approached the Swedish authorities with a request for financial assistance (Letter ('Resebidrag åt Pan Africanist Congress'/'Travel allowance for PAC') from Knut Granstedt, counsellor at the Swedish embassy, to the Ministry for Foreign Affairs, Dar es Salaam, 7 March 1967) (SDA). Shortly thereafter, one of PAC's recurrent internal crises broke out. "Accused of heading a clique of counter-revolutionaries and [of] promoting factionalism, tale-bearing, parochialism and tribalism", at a PAC 're-organization' meeting in Moshi, Tanzania, Ngcobo was suspended in September 1967 (Karis and Gerhart op. cit., p. 48). Due to the crisis, the request was not followed up. The contacts were far from constructively re-established in April 1968, when PAC's George Peake—former National Chairman of the South African Coloured People's Organization (SACPO)—paid a visit to the Foreign Ministry in Stockholm. He did not request material assistance, but to his interlocutor's surprise political support *against* a UN intervention in South Africa. In Peake's view, a possible UN action "would not help Africa's cause". He also condemned alleged Swedish arms deliveries to the apartheid regime. It, however, turned out that the weaponry indicated by Peake was of Swiss—not Swedish—origin (Dag Malm: Memorandum [no title], Ministry for Foreign Affairs, Stockholm, 11 April 1968) (MFA).
3. Released from detention in 1962, Leballo took over the leadership of the organization. He initially based himself in Basutoland (Lesotho), from where in March 1963 he called on Poqo to "end white South Africa". Thus providing the apartheid regime with a pretext to keep Sobukwe imprisoned and to transfer him to Robben Island (Pogrund op. cit., pp. 181-84), Leballo subsequently headed PAC's external headquarters in Dar es Salaam. His controversial leadership alienated many members, but gained the support of Julius Nyerere's government (see Sellström Volume I, p. 250). Constantly in the midst of endemic crises, in October 1979 the PAC Central Committee expelled Leballo for "reactionary and counter-revolutionary activities" (Karis and Gerhart op. cit., p. 294). He died in 1986.
4. Letter from Potlako Leballo to Olof Palme, PAC, Dar es Salaam, 28 January 1971 (SDA).
5. See Sellström Volume I, pp. 250-51.
6. The decision to support ANC was taken on 2 February 1973 (Sellström Volume I, p. 253). Nkula visited the Ministry for Foreign Affairs on 16 February 1973 (Letter from M.K. Nkula, PAC Chief Representative, to Bengt Säve-Söderbergh, PAC, Dar es Salaam, 27 February 1973) (SDA).

Back in Dar es Salaam, Nkula followed up his visit by submitting a formal request for some 200,000 SEK, covering daily necessities for an unspecified number of PAC members in Botswana, Lesotho, Tanzania and Zambia, as well as transport support and financial resources to procure a piece of land in the host country.[1] Although similar to the successful submission made earlier by ANC, the CCHA secretariat initially recommended that the request be left without further action.[2] In November 1973, the consultative committee decided, however, to first obtain additional information from Tanzania and OAU via the Swedish embassy in Dar es Salaam.[3] According to the Tanzanian Prime Minister's Office, PAC was "inefficient" and no discussions on land procurement had been held with the organization. At the same time, the OAU Liberation Committee argued that PAC was "less active" than ANC.[4] Against this background, in mid-March 1974 CCHA turned down the request.[5]

Thus informed, Nkula did not let himself be disheartened. Two months later—in May 1974—he returned to Stockholm, this time approaching SIDA. Repeating the request originally submitted in February 1973, he explained that humanitarian assistance was urgently needed in favour of some 50 members based in Tanzania, around 40 in Lesotho, a similar number in Botswana and fewer in Zambia.[6] Despite the fact that PAC's application had been rejected as recently as in March, in connection with Nkula's visit it was agreed to again raise the matter of direct, official assistance to the organization. It was discussed by CCHA in mid-June 1974. Once again the committee decided to approach the Tanzanian authorities for an advisory opinion.[7] And yet again the Prime Minister's Office in Dar es Salaam declared that PAC "did not work as efficiently as one would have wished".[8]

Tanzania's lack of enthusiasm influenced the Swedish authorities. In the mid-1970s, the embassy in Dar es Salaam was far from impressed by either ANC or PAC. In November 1975, first secretary Göran Hasselmark described the two movements' "lack of ideas" and the resident leaders' "atrophy", stating that "weakness is their most distinguishing trait".[9] Nevertheless, by that time a well functioning aid cooperation had been established with ANC, which at the political level enjoyed particular goodwill in Sweden. In September/October 1975, for example, Oliver Tambo attended the congress of the ruling Social Democratic Party.

Although Palme's government adopted a pluralistic approach towards South Africa, it never placed PAC on a par with ANC. In spite of the fact that PAC was recognized by OAU, the policy did not envisage direct support to both ANC and PAC in exile, but to ANC and, indirectly, to active, legal anti-apartheid forces inside South Africa. And—as noted above—during CCHA's fact-finding missions to

1. Ibid.
2. Stig Abelin and Marianne Sundh: Memorandum ('Stöd till Pan Africanist Congress of Azania, PAC, Sydafrika'/'Support to PAC, South Africa'), CCHA-SIDA, [Stockholm], 12 November 1973 (SDA).
3. CCHA: 'Protokoll [från sammanträde 16 november 1973]' ('Minutes [from meeting 16 November 1973]'), SIDA, [Stockholm], 19 November 1973 (SDA).
4. Astrid Bergquist: Memorandum ('Stöd till Pan Africanist Congress of Azania, PAC, Sydafrika'/'Support to PAC, South Africa'), CCHA-SIDA, [Stockholm], 5 March 1974 (SDA).
5. CCHA: 'Protokoll [från sammanträde 13 mars 1974]' ('Minutes [from meeting 13 March 1974]'), SIDA, [Stockholm], 18 April 1974 (SDA).
6. Marianne Sundh: Memorandum ('Stöd till Pan Africanist Congress of Azania, PAC, Sydafrika'/'Support to PAC, South Africa'), CCHA-SIDA, [Stockholm], 11 June 1974 (SDA).
7. CCHA: 'Protokoll [från sammanträde 17 juni 1974]' ('Minutes [from meeting 17 June 1974]'), SIDA, [Stockholm], 20 September 1974 (SDA).
8. Astrid Bergquist: Memorandum ('PAC'), CCHA-SIDA, [Stockholm], 27 September 1974 (SDA). It should be noted that the Tanzanian authorities held the same opinion with regard to ANC (ibid.).
9. Letter ('Sydafrika inför en förändrad politisk miljö'/'South Africa facing a changed political environment') from Göran Hasselmark to the Ministry for Foreign Affairs, Dar es Salaam, 3 November 1975 (MFA).

South and Southern Africa in 1976, representatives of both the black consciousness movement and Inkatha—notably Steve Biko and Gatsha Buthelezi—as well as other leading apartheid opponents[1] were highly critical of PAC. Contrary to the situation in Zimbabwe—where both ZANU and ZAPU were supported—in the case of South Africa only one liberation movement was accorded *de facto* recognition.

While the different arguments behind Sweden's stand will be summarized below, it could be noted that PAC's subsequent vexation targeted in particular the Social Democratic Party. Visiting the Foreign Ministry in Stockholm, in April 1986 the movement's Secretary of Foreign Affairs, Gora Ebrahim, characterized the policy of excluding PAC from direct assistance as "neo-colonial", emphasizing that only the South African people could choose its representatives. Without mentioning Olof Palme—assassinated less than two months earlier—Ebrahim stated that he was particularly "perturbed"[2] by the Social Democratic Party, which in his view was also responsible for PAC's "exclusion" from the Socialist International.[3] Interviewed a decade later, Ebrahim was still bitter: "[T]he [Swedish] Social Democratic Party demanded [...] multi-party democracy. Why did they then support only one [South African] political party?", he wondered.[4]

PAC's Scandinavian Offensive

A second phase in the relations between Sweden and PAC opened after the June 1976 Soweto events. As noted by Karis and Gerhart, the events

> intensified the pressures on the PAC to rebuild itself. Although it had been unable to involve itself significantly in the uprising, the movement into exile of thousands of young militants offered unprecedented opportunities for revitalization. Competition with the ANC grew as both organizations faced the prospect of winning the allegiance of members of the younger generation who had gone through the fire. Meanwhile, the qualitative change in the struggle within South Africa made other pressures on the PAC more urgent. Could it establish stability and demonstrate competence and initiative? The PAC's standing—even its existence as an exiled liberation movement—was at risk in many forums: in cooperative African states, the OAU, the Non-Aligned Movement, the United Nations, and among foreign donors.[5]

The PAC leadership responded by *inter alia* launching a diplomatic offensive vis-à-vis the Scandinavian countries, particularly Norway and Sweden. The moment was both opportune and open to opportunism. In Norway—where since 1973 the Social Democratic government had not extended direct support to any South African nationalist organization[6]—the labour movement decided in 1976 to embark on a national campaign which in addition to sanctions against apartheid aimed at "rais[ing] funds in support of the liberation movements and the trade unions in

1. Such as Beyers Naudé of the Christian Institute.
2. English in the original.
3. Anders Möllander: Memorandum ('Besök av företrädare för Pan Africanist Congress, PAC'/'Visit by representatives of PAC'), Ministry for Foreign Affairs, [Stockholm], 15 April 1986 (MFA). Ebrahim was accompanied by Count Pietersen, PAC's resident representative. They also denounced the fact that PAC had not been invited to the recently held People's Parliament against Apartheid (ibid.). With regard to the criticism of the Swedish Social Democratic Party and to PAC's 'exclusion' from the Socialist International, it should be noted that it was under a Social Democratic government that Norway in 1977 gave PAC a political platform in the Nordic countries.
4. Interview with Gora Ebrahim, p. 120.
5. Karis and Gerhart op. cit., p. 289.
6. When the Norwegian parliament in 1973 pronounced itself in favour of official support to the liberation movements in Southern Africa, it defined the recipients as "the peoples in dependent areas struggling to achieve national liberation" (Østbye in Eriksen (ed.) op. cit., p. 131). The South African liberation movements were thus not eligible for support. The restriction was revoked in June 1977 (ibid.).

Southern Africa, as well as for humanitarian aid to the victims of apartheid".[1] In Sweden—where since 1973 the Social Democratic government had granted direct assistance exclusively to ANC—the parliamentary elections in September 1976 were won by Fälldin's coalition.

In October 1976—four months after the Soweto watershed—PAC's Acting Treasurer General from the headquarters in Dar es Salaam, Mfanasekaya Gqobose[2], and its London-based representative to Europe, Vuyani Mngasa, paid a visit to Norway and Sweden, where they were received at the respective Foreign Ministries. The mission was far from successful. In Oslo, they were informed of Norway's restrictions towards South Africa[3], while in Stockholm the reaction was that the recently formed government "most likely [...] would continue with the support [to ANC]".[4] PAC, however, maintained its diplomatic initiative towards the two countries. In early May 1977, it submitted a formal request to the Norwegian government in favour of a planned transit and rehabilitation centre in Tanzania.[5] It was later in the month followed by a letter to the Swedish government from David Sibeko, the Director of Foreign Affairs, introducing the PAC member Count Pietersen—at the time living in Lund—as "the accredited Chief Representative of the Pan Africanist Congress of Azania (South Africa) [to] the Scandinavian countries [...], authorised to act as an official spokesman [...] and to negotiate [...] all forms of material assistance for [the movement]".[6]

Pietersen immediately approached the Liberal Cooperation Minister Ola Ullsten and SIDA. In the letter to Ullsten, he briefly informed the Swedish government that PAC "has decided to establish an information mission in Stockholm".[7] His letter to SIDA was more pompous. Stating that "[f]rom 1960 to date, the PAC dominates the ideological direction of the struggle for liberation and the activity of the people [in South Africa]", Pietersen claimed that

> the PAC cadres have effectively coordinated their underground work and politicised the broad masses [...] under the cloak of religion, educational projects and Black Community [activities]. [...] The PAC 'Oath of Allegiance' has taken the place of religious vows. Throughout the country, the church and other 'innocent' organisations have become the banner of the PAC underground [...].[8]

Stressing that "the objective conditions in Azania demand that we extend our international diplomatic and information work", the newly appointed PAC representative applied for assistance "to open an office in Stockholm as soon as possible". The costs during the initial year were estimated at slightly more than 200,000 SEK.

---

1. Vetlesen in ibid., p. 327.
2. Gqobose was expelled from PAC at the organization's second consultative conference, held in Arusha, Tanzania, at the end of June 1978 (Karis and Gerhart op. cit., p. 307, note 41).
3. Østbye in Eriksen (ed.) op. cit., p. 156.
4. Bo Heinebäck: Memorandum ('Besök av PAC-representanter'/'Visit by PAC representatives'), Ministry for Foreign Affairs, Stockholm, 26 October 1976 (MFA).
5. Østbye in Eriksen (ed.) op. cit., p. 156.
6. Letter ('To whom it may concern') from David Sibeko, PAC's mission to the United Nations, New York, [no date, but attached to a letter from Count Pietersen to Cooperation Minister Ola Ullsten, Lund, 26 May 1977] (MFA). To add to the confusion, in November 1978 the administrative and financial officers at the PAC headquarters in Dar es Salaam informed the Norwegian embassy that Pietersen was not authorized to raise funds for the organization's Oslo office (Østbye in Eriksen (ed.) op. cit., p. 161).
7. Letter from Count Pietersen to Ola Ullsten, Lund, 26 May 1977 (MFA).
8. Letter from Count Pietersen to SIDA, Lund, 25 May 1977 (SDA).

In addition, Pietersen announced forthcoming requests in favour of 215 PAC students who had fled from Soweto; daily necessities for "some of the Soweto victims"; the establishment of a 'Southern Africa Research, Documentation and Press Cuttings' Centre'; "assistance to help the more than 12,000 families in Azania who are depend[ent] on the PAC"; as well as air tickets to attend a number of international conferences.[1]

However, the Fälldin government was as critical of PAC as its Social Democratic predecessor. As indicated in October 1976 to the visiting PAC delegation, it would continue the policy of bilateral cooperation with ANC, subsequently increasing the annual allocations to the movement led by Oliver Tambo. As no direct, official assistance to PAC was contemplated, the negative recommendations by CCHA were regularly endorsed. PAC's request for the proposed Stockholm office was turned down in June 1977. More substantial submissions were rejected in November.[2]

The decisions were largely based on comments from the Swedish embassies in Southern Africa, as well as on discussions with visiting PAC representatives. The general assessment conveyed in mid-1977 by the Swedish diplomatic missions was that PAC was "a weak and divided organization". Most of them advised against official assistance due to "the prejudicial effect [...] it could have on Sweden's excellent and trustful relations with ANC".[3] The latter consideration was further underlined when David Sibeko during a visit to the Foreign Ministry in October 1977 stated that "no cooperation [with] ANC was even foreseeable".[4]

By 1977, the only PAC representation in Europe was the one headed by Mngasa in London. As part of its diplomatic offensive vis-à-vis the Scandinavian countries, the organization decided to open a second office in Stockholm. As late as in mid-June 1977, Count Pietersen argued that the choice of Stockholm in view of Sweden's comprehensive support to the Southern African liberation movements was "natural".[5] As the Swedish authorities at about the same time turned down PAC's request for support to the office and the Norwegian parliament revoked earlier restrictions against direct, official assistance to ANC and PAC, it was, however, decided instead to place the representation in Oslo. Headed by Pietersen, it was opened in August 1977.[6] In that connection, the Norwegian Foreign Ministry formally acknowledged PAC "as a true representative of the South African people".[7]

---

1. Ibid.
2. Cf. Marika Fahlén and Olov Poluha: Memorandum ('Bistånd till PAC'/'Assistance to PAC'), CCHA-Ministry for Foreign Affairs, [Stockholm], 4 November 1977 (SDA).
3. Marika Fahlén: Memorandum ('Bistånd till PAC'/'Assistance to PAC'), CCHA-Ministry for Foreign Affairs, [Stockholm], 8 June 1977 (SDA). The Swedish embassies in Dar es Salaam and Maputo were less negative towards PAC than the others in the region.
4. Cecilia Höglund: Memorandum ('Besök av delegation från Pan Africanist Congress of Azania (PAC), 6-7 oktober 1977'/'Visit by delegation from PAC, 6-7 October 1977'), Ministry for Foreign Affairs, Stockholm, 13 October 1977 (SDA). Before coming to Stockholm, the PAC delegation had visited Copenhagen and Oslo. Led by Sibeko, it included the Central Committee member Theo Bidi and Count Pietersen. Although confident and ready to stress the unity of their organization, both Sibeko and Bidi would over the following years fall victim to PAC's internal struggles. Together with Gqobose—who also maintained close relations with the Scandinavian countries—Bidi was expelled in June 1978 (Karis and Gerhart op. cit., p. 307, note 41). Sibeko was killed in June 1979.
5. Marika Fahlén: Memorandum ('Besök av PAC-representant'/'Visit by PAC representative'), Ministry for Foreign Affairs, Stockholm, 20 June 1977 (SDA).
6. Østbye in Eriksen (ed.) op. cit., p. 160.
7. Ibid.

While Sweden appeared as an almost closed area, towards the end of the 1970s Norway became one of the very few countries outside Africa which initiated cordial, official relations with the movement.[1]

Allocating an amount of 650,000 NOK to PAC in 1977—increased to one million in 1978[2]—and according it *de facto* recognition at a time when the organization was entering its deepest crisis, the Norwegian Social Democratic government's position differed radically from that of its Swedish non-socialist counterpart. Although continuing the official humanitarian assistance, it soon, however, "lost most of its faith".[3] The support was as a consequence reduced by half in 1979.[4] PAC's requests for financial support to the resident representation were also turned down, and in 1979 the organization eventually closed the Oslo office.[5] Without an established representation and proper administrative facilities, PAC's uphill diplomatic work in the Nordic area would thereafter be conducted from Sweden on an informal basis by Pietersen and his highly controversial assistant Cecil Sondlo[6], based respectively in Lund and Stockholm.

At Arm's Length

In marked contrast to ANC, PAC did not live up to the challenges posed by the Soweto events. Far from establishing stability and demonstrating competence, from late 1977 the leadership in exile became deeply immersed in internal power struggles. Culminating in the assassination of David Sibeko, the prolonged crisis did not subside until January 1981, when John Pokela—recently released from Robben Island—was elected Chairman.[7] With close links to Robert Mugabe's ZANU, after Zimbabwe's independence the organization was also in a better position to counter its isolation in Southern Africa by establishing a political base there. Although PAC under Pokela's chairmanship started to rebuild itself from the early 1980s, its reputation in Sweden was, however, irreparably damaged. From the outbreak of the internal struggles in 1978 until the unbanning of the organization in February 1990—constituting a third phase in the bilateral relations—the direct Swedish contacts with PAC were extremely limited.

In addition to ANC's rapidly growing strength, among the general political factors influencing the Swedish position towards PAC at the end of the 1970s were its demise in South Africa and its performance in exile. The crackdown that followed on the Soweto revolt hit the organization severely. In August 1977, founder member and former prisoner Zephania Mothopeng was detained. Other underground

1. When Norway decided in mid-1977 to extend direct assistance to PAC, the organization had according to David Sibeko only received similar bilateral support from Liberia, Libya and the United States (Cecilia Höglund: Memorandum ('Besök av delegation från Pan Africanist Congress of Azania (PAC), 6-7 oktober 1977'/'Visit by delegation from PAC, 6-7 October 1977'), Ministry for Foreign Affairs, Stockholm, 13 October 1977) (SDA). In addition to the representation in Oslo, in 1977 PAC opened offices in Canada and Liberia (Østbye in Eriksen (ed.) op. cit., p. 160).
2. Eriksen (ed.) op. cit., Table VII, p. 408.
3. Østbye in Eriksen (ed.) op. cit., p. 165.
4. Ibid., p. 159.
5. Ibid., p. 161.
6. A low-ranking PAC member, Sondlo was detained in Tanzania in 1976. Released in May 1978 together with Andreas Shipanga and other SWAPO dissidents, he was granted political asylum in Sweden. Subsequently appearing as Pietersen's assistant, he would during the 1980s and in the early 1990s actively and vociferously criticize the Swedish government and the solidarity movement. After the unbanning of PAC in 1990, Sondlo was often censured by the organization's internal leaders, but kept as representative. Like Pietersen, he did not return to South Africa after the democratic elections in 1994.
7. Pokela died in June 1985. He was succeeded by Johnson Mlambo. At PAC's congress in South Africa in December 1990, Clarence Makwetu was elected President and Mlambo First Deputy President.

cadres were subsequently picked up in widespread police raids. Mothopeng and seventeen co-detainees were put on trial in December 1977 for terrorism in Bethal, a small town in eastern Transvaal. Eventually sentenced to between five and fifteen years imprisonment, "the Bethal convictions marked the end of the PAC in the 1970s as a visible challenge to the regime".[1] Furthermore, with the death of Robert Sobukwe in February 1978 the organization lost a unifying symbol.

The detentions in South Africa and Sobukwe's death immediately led to intensified PAC power struggles in exile. Reaching new levels of vituperation and violence, they, in turn, provoked strong reactions from the governments in the Southern African host countries. Expelled from Zambia due to violent internal conflicts as early as in 1968[2], ten years later the same fate befell the organization in Swaziland, where in early April 1978 all known PAC members were rounded up and deported to Tanzania.[3] In Tanzania itself—at the time the only frontline state in which the organization was allowed an official presence—the PAC crisis had been brewing since late 1977, when the Acting President, Potlako Leballo, was challenged by his deputy, Templeton Ntantala. After it broke into the open in early 1978, the Nyerere government and the OAU Liberation Committee soon pressed for "unity and reconciliation".[4] This was also the theme of PAC's second consultative conference, held in Arusha during the last week of June 1978. However, the stormy conference[5] did not result in the restoration of unity, but in the expulsion of Ntantala and six other Central Committee officials, as well as more than sixty members.[6] What followed in Tanzania was an open struggle between two PAC factions, during which in May 1979 Leballo was initially ousted by a group led by Sibeko. In turn, Sibeko was assassinated the following month by Leballo supporters. In October 1979,

1. Karis and Gerhart op. cit., p. 289.
2. Cf. the interview with Kenneth Kaunda, p. 240. The fact that the Zambian government did not accept PAC was of importance for Sweden's position. In March 1976, the head of the Zambian army, General Kingsley Chinkuli, confirmed to the fact-finding CCHA delegation that PAC members were not welcome in the country, adding that PAC—as well as UMSA—had been infiltrated by the South African intelligence services (Marianne Sundh and Ann Wilkens: Memorandum ('Minnesanteckningar från samtal med Zambias arméchef G.K. Chinkuli angående stöd till befrielserörelser i södra Afrika'/'Notes from conversation with the Zambian army commander G.K. Chinkuli concerning support to liberation movements in Southern Africa'), CCHA, [Stockholm], 21 April 1976) (SDA).
3. According to Lennart Dafgård, the Swedish ambassador to Mozambique, the action by the Swazi authorities was due to pressure from the South African government (Göran Hasselmark: Memorandum ('Flyktingsituationen i Swaziland'/'The refugee situation in Swaziland'), Ministry for Foreign Affairs, Stockholm, 17 April 1978) (SDA).
4. Karis and Gerhart op. cit., p. 291.
5. At the time visiting Arusha on holiday and staying at the hotel where the PAC conference was being held, the author could witness at close quarters the animosity among the delegates.
6. Karis and Gerhart op. cit., p. 293. In connection with LO's Southern Africa campaign, in mid-1978 Mats Hellström, a Social Democratic MP and future Minister of Trade and Agriculture (1983-91), visited Southern Africa. In Tanzania at the time of the Arusha conference, he discussed PAC's situation with the Foreign Minister—and future President (1995-)—Benjamin Mkapa, who described the organization as "completely irrelevant". Immediately after his expulsion, Hellström also met Ntantala, who *inter alia* accused Leballo of "black racism". Summing up his recommendations to the Swedish labour movement, Hellström concluded that "the reasons for not supporting PAC in the past have become even stronger after the split at the Arusha [conference]" (Mats Hellström: 'Rapport från en resa i södra Afrika sommaren 1978' ('Report from a journey to Southern Africa in the summer of 1978'), [no place], 9 August 1978, p. 17) (OPA). With regard to ANC and the wider anti-apartheid opposition, he further advised: "Sweden and the Social Democratic movement should, as before, support the liberation movement ANC. [...] At the same time as we continue to support ANC, we should [, however,] in my opinion considerably extend [our] contacts with the organizations that are active inside South Africa". In the latter context, Hellström particularly underlined the trade unions and "the different branches of [BCM]" (ibid.). Also in August 1978, SIDA's Anna Runeborg at the Swedish embassy in Dar es Salaam discussed the situation within PAC with representatives of the Leballo faction, ANC and SACTU. The subsequent assessment by the embassy was that "PAC's prospects of surviving as a future, active liberation movement are dark" (Letter from Alf Karlsson, Swedish embassy, to the Ministry for Foreign Affairs, Dar es Salaam, 30 August 1978) (SDA).

the Central Committee eventually expelled Leballo for "reactionary and counter-revolutionary activities"[1], but the crisis continued.

As ANC responded constructively to the post-Soweto exodus by setting up the Solomon Mahlangu Freedom College (SOMAFCO), PAC took an opposite direction. Henry Isaacs—a former SASO[2] President who joined PAC in Tanzania after the student revolt—later noted how "the new recruits were drawn into the struggle and found themselves on opposing sides in a dispute of whose origins and dimensions they were largely ignorant".[3] In view of these developments, the Nyerere government started to lose its patience with the PAC leaders. After the Sibeko assassination, a high-ranking Tanzanian Foreign Affairs' official told the Norwegian ambassador that "[t]hey are all a bunch of crooks, who think of nothing else than how to enrich themselves"[4], suggesting that Norway should perhaps reconsider its support to the organization.[5]

Finally, although ZANU was close to PAC the Zimbabwean 'non-authentic' ally was, similarly, critical. In a meeting in Salisbury (Harare) with the Swedish ambassador Bo Heinebäck and Tom Vraalsen from the Norwegian Ministry of Foreign Affairs, independent Zimbabwe's Foreign Minister Simon Muzenda deplored as late as in September 1980 that PAC was "hopelessly divided".[6]

PAC's downward spiral and increasing isolation in Southern Africa were arrested when in January 1981 John Pokela took over the chairmanship. A certain stability was restored[7], and the organization could to a larger extent than before devote attention to the welfare of its members in Tanzania, as well as establish a political presence in Zimbabwe. After several years of silence[8], PAC also resumed its contacts with the Swedish aid authorities. In a rather outlandish submission to SIDA, in December 1983, for example, Count Pietersen wrote that the PAC representation in Sweden "because of the world recession [had] encountered [...] serious financial difficulties", requesting emergency assistance towards its maintenance, as well as for publicity and dissemination of information.[9] Five months later, Mfanasekaya Gqobose—who after Leballo's expulsion had been reinstated as Director of Economic Affairs and Social Welfare—submitted a more serious application for

1. Cited in Karis and Gerhart op. cit., p. 294.
2. The BCM-aligned South African Students Organization.
3. Cited in Karis and Gerhart op. cit., p. 291. Serving as PAC's representative to the United Nations, Isaacs resigned in March 1982.
4. Cited in Østbye in Eriksen (ed.) op. cit., p. 165.
5. Ibid.
6. Bo Heinebäck: Memorandum ('Samtal med utrikesminister Muzenda om södra Afrika'/'Conversation with Foreign Minister Muzenda about Southern Africa'), Swedish embassy, Salisbury, 4 September 1980 (MFA).
7. New internal struggles did, however, flare up. In May 1982, for example, David Wirmark, the Swedish ambassador to Tanzania, reported on new divisions (Letter ('Interna stridigheter inom PAC'/'Internal struggles within PAC') from David Wirmark to the Ministry for Foreign Affairs, Swedish embassy, Dar es Salaam, 31 May 1982) (SDA). At the same time, Jon Bech, chargé d'affaires at the Norwegian embassy, noted in a report to Oslo that the Tanzanian authorities questioned "whether PAC any longer could be considered a 'viable force' for the liberation of South Africa" (Jon Bech: Memorandum ('Stridigheter innen PAC'/'Struggles within PAC'), Norwegian embassy, Dar es Salaam, 26 May 1982; attached to ibid.).
8. It was not only outside South Africa that the Swedish authorities did not hear from PAC in the early 1980s. Reporting on the situation inside the apartheid republic, in December 1983, for example, the Swedish legation in Pretoria noted that "ANC's presence is both seen and heard, while silence surrounds PAC" (Cited in Tor Sellström: 'African National Congress (ANC)', SIDA, Stockholm, 1 March 1984, p. 7) (SDA).
9. Letter from Count Pietersen, Chief Representative of the PAC in the Nordic countries, to SIDA, Stockholm, 17 December 1983 (SDA). The letter was copied to the Central Committee of ZANU-PF. According to Pietersen, he had been "instructed" by the ruling party in Zimbabwe to "tell [SIDA] to give the PAC the assistance that [the aid agency] used to give to ZANU" (ibid.).

90,000 USD towards the construction of an access road to PAC's refugee settlement at Kitonga outside Bagamoyo, Tanzania.[1]

As with earlier PAC submissions, the request was turned down. After considerable delay, in October 1984 Gösta Edgren, Under-Secretary of State for International Development Cooperation, replied on behalf of the Social Democratic government that

> Swedish humanitarian assistance to Southern Africa is being channelled through various Swedish and international organizations.[2] [...] [This assistance] is to a considerable extent also benefiting individual members and supporters of the PAC, as well as projects undertaken by PAC. The Swedish authorities are for the time being not considering any change in the pattern of distribution of humanitarian aid for Southern Africa. [...] Under the circumstances, [we] are not in a position to embark on [...] direct cooperation with the PAC on project financing.[3]

Formal Arguments and Underlying Considerations

Together with ANC, PAC belonged to the wider, historical South African liberation movement. As such, it was recognized by the Organization of African Unity and the United Nations. In exile, the organization initially claimed responsibility for almost as many—or few—South African refugees as ANC. It was, in addition, supported by Tanzania—a country with which Sweden maintained particularly close relations—and allied with ZANU of Zimbabwe, one of the first Southern African liberation movements to receive direct Swedish assistance. At a crucial moment in the South African anti-apartheid struggle, it actively approached the Scandinavian countries, reaching an understanding with Norway, with which Sweden largely coordinated its aid policies in Southern Africa. Last but not least, PAC opposed the South African Communist Party and ANC's links with the Soviet Union, in a Cold War context claiming to be non-aligned, albeit close to the People's Republic of China.

In theory, there were thus several grounds for direct, official Swedish support to PAC. This was, however, not to be. Some of the reasons behind the lukewarm stand towards the organization have been mentioned. Before turning to the fourth phase of the uneasy relationship, the arguments advanced against bilateral cooperation with PAC until 1990 should be summarized.

It could, in the first place, be noted that the 'PAC issue' was constantly on the agenda. The Swedish embassies in Southern Africa regularly reported on the organization to the Ministry for Foreign Affairs and SIDA. Over the years, the reports were summarized and commented upon in a great number of memoranda submitted to CCHA. In addition, until the end of the 1970s leading PAC representatives visited Stockholm. The Pan Africanist Congress was far from an unknown entity to the officials involved with humanitarian assistance to Southern Africa.

---

1. Letter ('Urgent appeal for the construction of [an] access road to [the] PAC multi-purpose centre at Kitonga, Bagamoyo district') from Mfanasekaya Gqobose, PAC, to the Swedish embassy in Tanzania, Dar es Salaam, 10 May 1984 (SDA).
2. The organizations quoted by Edgren were: UNETPSA, UNHCR, UNTF, AET, IDAF and WUS. As earlier noted, the Swedish contributions to the Southern Africa programmes of these organizations often represented around 50 per cent of their budgets.
3. Letter ('Project for the construction of an access road to the PAC multi-purpose centre at Kitonga, Bagamoyo district') from Gösta Edgren to PAC, Ministry for Foreign Affairs, Stockholm, 15 October 1984 (SDA). The project was largely financed by Norway, which contracted the Norwegian consultancy firm NORPLAN to plan and supervise the road construction (Østbye in Eriksen (ed.) op. cit., pp. 166-67).

Secondly, despite widespread belief to the contrary in PAC circles[1] the Swedish government never took a formal decision to exclude the organization from humanitarian support. Sweden was a significant contributor to UNHCR, the various UN institutions for Southern Africa and the main international NGOs which specialized in legal aid and education support. All of them gave considerable assistance to PAC.[2] In addition, although direct requests from the organization were regularly rejected, until the open PAC crisis the policy of avoiding bilateral support did not constitute—as pointed out in January 1978 by Thord Palmlund, Under-Secretary of State for International Development Cooperation—"a definitive conclusion".[3]

Finally, the Swedish government did not extend *de jure* recognition to any liberation movement. Contrary to the Organization of African Unity, for example, Sweden did not formally 'recognize' ANC or 'not recognize' PAC. Nevertheless, while PAC was kept at arm's length official assistance was under bilateral agreements channelled from 1973 directly to ANC, which during the second half of the 1970s was *de facto* increasingly seen as a South African 'government-in-waiting'. What were then the underlying reasons against direct humanitarian support to PAC as well?

In the substantial official Swedish documentation concerning the movement, the specific reasons for dismissal are often brief and indirect. During the first phase of contacts, CCHA usually concluded that the organization's requests were insufficiently substantiated, deciding to leave them "without further action".[4] After Soweto—when PAC launched its 'Scandinavian offensive' and the quality of the submissions improved—the committee would as a rule refer instead to Sweden's contributions to the UN organizations and international NGOs.[5] As early as in 1977—before the open PAC crisis—the consideration was, however, added that direct support to PAC could negatively affect the 'special relationship' that was being established with ANC.[6]

At the very same time as direct Swedish assistance on equal terms was resumed to ZANU and ZAPU of Zimbabwe[7]—and as the government of Norway decided to officially support both ANC and PAC—the authorities drew the conclusion that aid to the latter was incompatible with assistance to the former. In addition to the argument that PAC was a weak and divided organization, this consideration would be increasingly emphasized during the 1980s. In an internal comment to PAC's request for financial assistance towards the construction of a road to its Kitonga settlement, Kaj Persson at the Ministry for Foreign Affairs—also serving as CCHA secretary—wrote in September 1984:

> For PAC, a Swedish contribution would represent a propaganda triumph. [It] could be interpreted as [...] recognition of the movement. It could also be used politically by PAC in its pro-

---

1. Cf. the interview with Gora Ebrahim, p. 120.
2. When the lives of South African refugees were in danger—as in Lesotho in 1985-86, for example—evacuation operations arranged by Sweden included PAC members.
3. Marianne Sundh: Memorandum ('Minnesanteckningar från ett särskilt möte under bkc-konferensen om södra Afrika'/'Notes from a special meeting on Southern Africa during the conference with SIDA's heads of mission'), SIDA, Stockholm, 25 January 1978 (SDA).
4. For example, Astrid Bergquist: Memorandum ('Stöd till Pan Africanist Congress of Azania, PAC, Sydafrika'/ 'Support to PAC'), CCHA-SIDA, [Stockholm], 5 March 1974 (SDA).
5. Marika Fahlén and Olov Poluha: Memorandum ('Bistånd till PAC'/'Assistance to PAC'), CCHA-Ministry for Foreign Affairs, [Stockholm], 4 November 1977 (SDA).
6. Marika Fahlén: Memorandum ('Bistånd till PAC'/'Assistance to PAC'), CCHA-Ministry for Foreign Affairs, [Stockholm], 8 June 1977 (SDA).
7. However, ZANU and ZAPU had together formed the Patriotic Front.

paganda war against ANC. Swedish [support] to PAC could [thus] at the present moment have negative effects on the relations between Sweden and ANC.[1]

While this argument was often repeated[2], there were more fundamental reasons behind the negative attitude towards PAC. In reply to a question from the Swedish ambassador to Botswana, Irene Larsson—who had asked for guidance concerning Sweden's "one-sided concentration on ANC"[3]—in May 1981 the head of the Foreign Ministry's Political Department, Jan Eliasson, reflected on the relations with the two South African liberation movements. Acknowledging that it was "not that easy to answer" Larsson's question, he summarized the underlying reasons as follows:

> [The] first reason is historical. ANC is almost the only [South African liberation movement] which since many years back has been in contact with Sweden and Swedish politicians. [Oliver] Tambo is personally [...] known to many Swedes. [Secondly], PAC's partly blurred and 'anti-white' ideology has in all probability not been of help in its few contacts with Sweden. [...] PAC's exile organization has, in addition, been very divided, which has made meaningful contacts difficult, and at times even impossible. [...] We [...] are also very doubtful regarding PAC's administrative capacity. [...] It could [, finally,] be added that no member of [the Consultative Committee on Humanitarian Assistance] has advocated support to PAC.[4]

In Sweden, PAC never appeared as an alternative or a complement to ANC. Although presenting itself as non-Communist and non-aligned, its 'blurred and anti-white' ideology—contradicting the vision of a non-racial post-apartheid society—did not prompt any response. On the contrary, interviewed in 1996 the veteran Swedish anti-apartheid activist and CCHA member Gunnar Helander noted that PAC on the fundamental issue of race

> was not neutral. [...] I found [the organization to be] black racist. [...] If we strove for a South Africa as Luthuli and Mandela wanted it— where all people would work together irrespective of colour—I did not think that PAC was the thing to support.[5]

From Unbanning towards Elections

The unbanning of PAC in February 1990 opened a new, final chapter in the history of Sweden's relations with the organization. Reacting to the new developments and with a view to "positively portraying [its] outlook and policy to both friends and foes", in early May 1990 PAC submitted a detailed request to Sweden for 0.7 MUSD towards the organization of a national congress in South Africa at the end of the year.[6] Forwarded to the Swedish legation in Pretoria for comments, in his positive reply the Swedish representative, Jan Lundvik, stated the opinion that

> it is desirable that Sweden broadens its contacts with the [...] main currents of black politics. We should not put all [our] eggs in one basket and let ourselves be identified with one party to the extent that we become isolated in the case of political changes. If we wish to contribute to

1. Kaj Persson: Memorandum ('Bistånd till PAC'/'Assistance to PAC'), Ministry for Foreign Affairs, Stockholm, 17 September 1984 (MFA).
2. For example, Karin Roxman: Memorandum ('Bistånd till PAC'/'Assistance to PAC'), Ministry for Foreign Affairs, Stockholm, 17 May 1988 (MFA).
3. Letter ('Sydafrikanska befrielserörelser'/'South African liberation movements') from Irene Larsson, Swedish ambassador to Botswana, to the Ministry for Foreign Affairs, Swedish embassy, Gaborone, 29 April 1981 (MFA).
4. Letter ('Sydafrikanska befrielserörelser'/'South African liberation movements') from Jan Eliasson to Irene Larsson, Ministry for Foreign Affairs, Stockholm, 19 May 1981 (MFA).
5. Interview with Gunnar Helander, p. 287.
6. Letter from J.R. Moabi, PAC Secretary for Finance, to the Swedish embassy, Dar es Salaam, 3 May 1990 (MFA).

Cecil Sondlo of PAC
in Stockholm, 1994
(Photo: Linnéa Öberg
Sellersjö/Pressens Bild)

> South Africa['s democratic] development, with a multi-party system and free elections [...], we should also show that we are ready to cooperate with different parties. PAC's lack of efficiency as a liberation movement is in this context irrelevant.
>
> In practice, this means that Swedish aid resources [...] also could be extended to PAC projects in South Africa. [...] If a decision is taken in favour of direct support to ANC as a political party, it is obvious that [...] contributions also ought to be made to the PAC congress.[1]

At a new and critical juncture, this was a novel line of reasoning. In Stockholm, however, the authorities remained as critical as before. At a meeting between the Foreign Ministry and SIDA, Anders Bjurner, deputy at the ministry's Political Department, argued strongly in mid-September 1990 that no direct Swedish assistance should be extended to PAC "for the same reasons as up to now, [namely,] that [the organization] [...] stands for an ideology which [CCHA] does not accept; [its] aid projects are bad; and [it is torn by] internal struggles".[2] At a time when the Swedish government was by far the biggest donor to ANC inside South Africa—decisively contributing towards its institutional set-up and administration—the Consultative Committee on Humanitarian Assistance rejected PAC's submission, motivating its decision by stating that the request envisaged "purely organizational support".[3]

In March 1991, PAC circulated a harsh attack on Sweden at the United Nations in New York, *inter alia* holding the Social Democratic government's "one-sided" ANC policy responsible for "the death of thousands of people in South Africa".[4] Despite the strained diplomatic relations that followed, inside South Africa steps towards a rapprochement between the parties were, however, taken. In late May, PAC's Second Deputy President, Dikgang Moseneke, submitted a request for "institutional support" to the Swedish legation in Pretoria.[5] After consultations with the

1. Letter ('Ansökan om stöd till PAC'/'Request for support to PAC') from Jan Lundvik, Swedish envoy to South Africa, to the Ministry for Foreign Affairs, Swedish legation, Pretoria, 16 July 1990 (MFA).
2. Christina Regnell: Memorandum ('Möte på UD 18 september 1990'/'Meeting at the Ministry for Foreign Affairs, 18 September 1990'), SIDA, Stockholm, 18 September 1990 (SDA).
3. Lena Sundh: Memorandum ('Ansökan från [PAC] om bidrag till genomförandet av organisationens kongress'/'Request from PAC for contributions towards the holding of the organization's congress'), CCHA-Ministry for Foreign Affairs, [Stockholm], 21 September 1990 (SDA).
4. Cited in letter ('Förfrågan från PAC om bistånd'/'PAC enquiry regarding assistance') from Anders Möllander to the Ministry for Foreign Affairs, Swedish legation, Pretoria, 6 June 1991 (MFA).
5. Letter ('Request for financial assistance') from Dikgang Moseneke, PAC, to the Swedish legation, Ferreirastown, 29 May 1991 (MFA).

Foreign Ministry in Stockholm, Anders Möllander at the legation met Moseneke and the head of PAC's Legal Department, Willie Seriti, for an exchange of opinions.

Contrary to ANC, PAC refused to suspend its armed operations and the members were guided by the slogan 'One settler – One bullet'. Noting that it was "impossible [...]—regardless of the historical background—to support a policy which seemed to aim at encouraging murder of a population group", Möllander suggested that the internally based PAC leadership should explain its views directly to the authorities in Sweden, informally extending an invitation to Moseneke in connection with the Swedish parliamentary elections in September 1991.[1]

Möllander's meeting with the PAC representatives took place when ANC in order to counter the ruling National Party's attempts to impose its own version of 'democratic transition' had embarked on mass campaigns and taken the initiative of forming a broad Patriotic Front. Rejecting negotiations with the apartheid regime, PAC initially supported the alliance proposed by its traditional rival.[2] During the meeting, Seriti informed Möllander about the contacts with ANC, stating that the two organizations would soon approach the Swedish government for financial assistance towards a Patriotic Front conference.[3] A joint ANC-PAC request to that effect was submitted the following month.[4]

---

1. Letter ('Förfrågan från PAC om bistånd'/'PAC enquiry regarding assistance') from Anders Möllander to the Ministry for Foreign Affairs, Swedish legation, Pretoria, 6 June 1991 (MFA). When Moseneke and other PAC officials were subsequently invited to observe the Swedish elections, in a letter to *Dagens Nyheter* the organization's resident representative, Cecil Sondlo, stated that PAC had declined the invitation. In a strong attack on the Swedish government and Sweden in general, Sondlo *inter alia* declared: "We don't want to be utilized for a propaganda stunt. We are of the opinion that the Social Democrats have used their close ANC ally [...] to fish for votes from the Swedish apartheid opponents. Since Sweden has extended sectarian support to the struggle against apartheid, it cannot expect goodwill from other black South African organizations. [...] PAC cannot respect Sweden's 'big brother' attitude [and regards its policy as] blackmail and colonial guardianship!" (Cecil Sondlo: 'Regeringen får nej av PAC'/'PAC says no to the government' in *Dagens Nyheter*, 14 August 1991). Published at a time when the Swedish government and PAC after years of uneasy relations were eventually on speaking terms, Sondlo's initiative was denounced by the PAC leadership in South Africa. While Moseneke himself due to pressure of work was not able to go to Sweden (Letter from Dikgang Moseneke to the Swedish legation, PAC, Ferreirastown, 7 August 1991) (MFA), he disavowed Sondlo as a "low-ranking official", emphasizing that he had acted "without any mandate" and that the contents of his letter were "completely without foundation" (Letter ('Mr. Sondlo och inbjudan till PAC'/'Mr. Sondlo and invitation to PAC') from the Swedish legation to the Ministry for Foreign Affairs, Pretoria, 16 August 1991) (MFA). Patricia de Lille, PAC's Secretary for Foreign Affairs, was at the same time "dismayed", adding that PAC's "bad international contacts" were of the organization's own making (Cable ('Inbjudan till PAC'/'Invitation to PAC') from the Swedish legation to the Ministry for Foreign Affairs, Pretoria, 22 August 1991) (MFA). Nevertheless, Sondlo's antics in Sweden continued. Two months after his letter to *Dagens Nyheter*, immediately after the formation of Carl Bildt's non-socialist coalition government and at a time when PAC in South Africa was appealing urgently for assistance, the unabashed PAC representative submitted a request to SIDA "for support to PAC's activities in Sweden in general and to an information office in Stockholm in particular, including [the] salary for one employee", i.e. for himself (Letter ('Ansökan'/'Request') from Cecil Sondlo, PAC, to SIDA, Stockholm, 17 October 1991) (SDA). CCHA did not need to discuss the request. Again disavowed by the PAC leadership, Deputy President Moseneke told the legation in Pretoria to leave Sondlo's submission "without action" (Cable 'Eventuell ansökan från PAC om bistånd'/'Possible PAC request for assistance') from the Swedish legation to the Ministry for Foreign Affairs, Pretoria, 14 November 1991) (MFA). The conflicting signals from PAC in South Africa and its representative in Sweden were far from conducive to a constructive relationship.

2. Convened by ANC and PAC, the Patriotic Front was launched at a conference held in Durban in late October 1991. While the 'fundamentalist' AZAPO—which eventually did not participate in the April 1994 elections—never supported the initiative, tensions soon developed between ANC and PAC. "The PAC accused the ANC of entering into secret undertakings with the government and arranging constitutional negotiations without consulting or informing its [Patriotic Front] allies" (Johannes Rantete: *The African National Congress and the Negotiated Settlement in South Africa*, J. L. van Schaik Publishers, Pretoria, 1998, p. 257). The ensuing accusations and counter-accusations resulted in PAC walking out of the preparatory CODESA meeting on 29 November 1991, followed by its withdrawal from the negotiations.

3. Letter ('Förfrågan från PAC om bistånd'/'PAC enquiry regarding assistance') from Anders Möllander to the Ministry for Foreign Affairs, Swedish legation, Pretoria, 6 June 1991 (MFA).

4. Letter ('Application for financial assistance') from ANC (Stanley Mabizela) and PAC (Willie Seriti) to the Swedish legation, PAC headquarters, Ferreirastown, 24 July 1991 (MFA).

Backed by the Swedish legation—which proposed a cash contribution of 250,000 SEK[1]—the submission occupies a unique place in the history of Sweden's relations with PAC. Albeit drawing on ANC's goodwill, it resulted for the first and only time in a decision on official assistance to the organization. Ironically, however, no funds were ever released. When the organization after two decades of trials and tribulations was formally given a positive response, it eventually led nowhere. Thus, over the years PAC never received any direct Swedish government support.

Arguing that "from a Swedish perspective it is important to broaden the support to [include] other recipients than ANC"[2], in late August 1991 SIDA decided to allocate the proposed amount of 250,000 SEK to the Patriotic Front conference.[3] Soon thereafter, PAC's Willie Seriti informed the legation in Pretoria that the organizers had already received a substantial contribution from OAU.[4] Together with a grant from Libya it more than covered the conference budget. Against this background, it was concluded that the Swedish contribution should not be disbursed.[5]

In late September 1991, the Social Democratic Party lost the parliamentary elections in Sweden, giving way to a non-socialist coalition led by the Moderate Party leader Carl Bildt. His colleague Margaretha af Ugglas became Minister for Foreign Affairs. At the very moment when the South African apartheid drama was drawing to an uncertain close, the reins of the Swedish government were in the hands of the political party which over the years had continuously opposed assistance to the Southern African liberation movements. This was viewed with considerable concern by ANC. With regard to PAC, no shift in the official policy would, however, take place, although the tentative contacts initiated in mid-1991 were maintained. They would eventually founder due to the organization's refusal to suspend the armed struggle and its ambiguous position towards a negotiated settlement.

In connection with official talks with ANC, in November 1991 Kaj Persson of the Ministry for Foreign Affairs was contacted by Moseneke. In a memorandum to the newly appointed Cooperation Minister Alf Svensson, Persson subsequently reported that he—in the light of the formation of the Patriotic Front and as "a more moderate faction seems to have taken over the PAC leadership"—had encouraged the PAC Deputy President to submit an application for financial assistance towards the negotiation process.[6] However, when the multi-party CODESA[7] talks started in late December 1991, PAC preferred to stay away. Launching an 'Operation Great Storm', one year later its armed wing—APLA—instead started to carry

---

1. Robert Rydberg: Memorandum ('Patriotic Front Conference'), Swedish legation, Pretoria, 30 July 1991 (MFA).
2. Ingalill Colbro: Memorandum ('Ansökan från Patriotic Front Conference'/'Request from the Patriotic Front Conference'), SIDA, Stockholm, 7 August 1991 (SDA).
3. SIDA: 'Decision', Office of the Director General, Stockholm, 26 August 1991 (SDA). The modest contribution could be compared to the bilateral allocation to ANC for 1991/92, amounting to 120 MSEK.
4. Letter from Willie Seriti to the Swedish legation, National Preparatory Committee for the Patriotic/United Front Conference, Johannesburg, [no date, but received on 17 September 1991] (MFA).
5. Letter ('Patriotic Front Conference') from Robert Rydberg to SIDA, Swedish legation, Pretoria, 19 September 1991 (MFA).
6. Kaj Persson: Memorandum ('Samtal om humanitärt bistånd i samband med besök i Sydafrika'/'Talks on humanitarian assistance in connection with [a] visit to South Africa'), Ministry for Foreign Affairs, Stockholm, 2 December 1991 (MFA).
7. Convention for a Democratic South Africa.

out a number of indiscriminate attacks on white civilians.[1] In this situation, Sweden suspended the contacts. They were only resumed in November 1993, when PAC's First Deputy President Johnson Mlambo and its Foreign Affairs' Secretary Gora Ebrahim requested a meeting with the Nordic diplomatic missions to South Africa.

Held at the Norwegian embassy in Pretoria, during the meeting the PAC officials appealed for financial assistance for the electoral process. With the South African elections set for April 1994, the Nordic representatives declared that a "fundamental pre-condition" for any consideration of assistance to PAC was that it unequivocally suspended the armed struggle. To this, Mlambo vaguely replied that "the issue would probably soon be resolved".[2] This reconfirmed that no direct support could be extended.[3]

In late March 1994—one month before the elections—PAC President Clarence Makwetu publicly criticized the Scandinavian countries for their "one-sided" support to ANC.[4] For him and his confident organization, the subsequent verdict was disastrous. While ANC received 62.7 per cent of the votes, PAC was supported by merely 1.3 per cent of the electorate.[5] With regard to Sweden, ANC and PAC, Gora Ebrahim—one of only five PAC MPs in the new 400-member National Assembly[6]—stated in 1995:

> We are disappointed. We had all negotiated and we were going for an election. At that crucial moment, the Swedish government made a very substantial donation to ANC for election purposes. Naturally, that influenced the election results, and we regard that as gross interference.[7]

---

1. After a series of attacks on white farmers, in late November 1992 APLA launched an assault against defenceless civilians at the local golf club in King William's Town, killing four people. Several similar operations followed thereafter. In July 1993, for example, APLA descended upon St. James Church in Cape Town, firing machine guns and throwing hand grenades at a congregation of about one thousand people. Eleven people—among them four Russian sailors—were killed and fifty-eight wounded. Appearing before the Truth and Reconciliation Commission, one of the responsible APLA operatives later justified the attack on the grounds that "whites took our country using churches and bibles" (cited in TRC op. cit. (Vol. II), p. 688).
2. Ingemar Stjernberg: Memorandum ('Pan Africanist Congress begär stöd från de nordiska länderna'/'PAC requests support from the Nordic countries'), Swedish legation, Pretoria, 12 November 1993 (MFA). PAC only announced a suspension of the armed struggle on 16 January 1994, three months before the general elections.
3. Ibid. and letter ('Pan Africanist Congress begär stöd från de nordiska länderna'/'PAC requests support from the Nordic countries') from Kaj Persson to ambassador Ingemar Stjernberg, Ministry for Foreign Affairs, Stockholm, 22 December 1993 (MFA). Indirectly, PAC benefited from the substantial Swedish and Nordic support to various organizations involved with training and preparations for the elections.
4. For example, 'PAC condemns lack of overseas poll funds' in The Citizen, 18 March 1994.
5. For an analysis of the election results—including a contribution by Saths Cooper on 'The PAC and AZAPO'—see Andrew Reynolds (ed.): Election '94 South Africa: The Campaigns, Results and Future Prospects, James Currey, London; David Philip, Cape Town and Johannesburg; and St. Martin's Press, New York, 1994.
6. The other PAC MPs were Patricia de Lille, Malcolm Dyani, Stanley Mogoba and Michael Muendane.
7. Interview with Gora Ebrahim, p. 121.

Gatsha Buthelezi and Inkatha

A Long History

In the mid-1980s, a bitter conflict broke out in Natal between Inkatha and the ANC-aligned United Democratic Front. Developing into a virtual civil war between the Zulu movement led by Chief Gatsha Buthelezi and ANC, the hostilities—in the early 1990s spreading to the black townships around Johannesburg—eventually claimed as many as 10,000 lives.[1] Financially and militarily assisted by the apartheid regime[2], Inkatha stood out as a major force against a negotiated settlement of the South African drama. In Sweden, all the major actors distanced themselves from the organization.[3]

Possibly due to massive repudiation, the history of the relations between Sweden, Buthelezi and Inkatha has not been documented.[4] What is more, in the rare cases where it has been mentioned, the relations have not only been smoothed over, but it has also incorrectly been asserted that they did not result in official support.

For example, while noting that Sweden "in the late 1970s closely followed the development of Inkatha"—simply described as "a strong cultural organization"—a report commissioned by SIDA affirmed in May 1995 that "[s]upport was, however, never considered".[5] In his personal account *In South Africa: The Journey towards Freedom*, also published in 1995, the leading South Africa expert and veteran CCHA member Per Wästberg similarly wrote that "I met Chief Gatsha Buthelezi a couple of times in Sweden in the 1970s, when he was seeking support for Inkatha

---

1. Christopher Saunders and Nicholas Southey: *Historical Dictionary of South Africa*, Second edition, The Scarecrow Press, Lanham, Maryland, and London, 2000, p. 52. In the case of KwaZulu-Natal, the Truth and Reconciliation Commission (TRC) established in 1998 that "at least three times as many victims [...] belonged to the ANC/UDF as to the [Inkatha Freedom Party] and other political groups" (TRC op. cit. (Vol. III), p. 159).
2. In July 1991, it was revealed that the National Party government for many years had secretly funded Inkatha. It had also arranged military training for members of the organization in northern Zululand and in the Caprivi area of Namibia. In addition, Inkatha received considerable financial support from right wing sources in the West, particularly in Germany. With regard to the covert training in Caprivi—which took place in 1986—TRC concluded: "Secret military intelligence documents make it clear that the project was undertaken as much to further the strategic aims of the South African government and Defence Force, as it was in response to a request from Chief Buthelezi". And in a statement to the commission, the Inkatha coordinator Daluxolo Luthuli declared that the training "aimed at equipping Inkatha supporters to kill members of the UDF/ANC" (TRC op. cit. (Vol. II), pp. 464-65).
3. As earlier noted, in 1983 the International Council of Swedish Industry opposed the official assistance to ANC, presenting instead the supposedly 'non-violent' Inkatha as an alternative. It was, however, the extreme right journal *Contra* which above all defended Buthelezi's cause in Sweden.
4. In his history of the Church of Sweden Aid (CSA), Björn Ryman does not mention the early relations established with Buthelezi and Inkatha through the Christian Institute and other organizations. The KwaZulu leader and his organization are only referred to in connection with later attacks on Sibusiso Bengu, whose family members were granted financial support by CSA (Ryman op. cit., p. 217). Receiving his primary education at a CSM mission school in Zululand, Bengu had close links with the Lutheran Church of Sweden. After doctoral studies in Switzerland, he returned to South Africa at the end of 1974. A former member of ANC, he was appointed Secretary General of Inkatha at its foundation in March 1975. Alleged to advocate mass action and BCM support, Bengu was in 1978 expelled from the movement's Central Committee. Subsequently leaving South Africa, he joined the Lutheran World Federation in Geneva, as well as ANC. In July 1991, Bengu took up the position as Vice-Chancellor of the University of Fort Hare. Three years later, he was appointed Minister of Education, Arts and Culture in South Africa's first post-apartheid cabinet.
5. Annika Lysén: 'Assisting a Democratic Process: A Report on the Swedish Humanitarian Assistance to South Africa 1962-1994', Stockholm, May 1995 , p. 19 (SDA).

from [SIDA] and the government. [...] [But h]e never received any assistance".[1]
Finally, the former CSM missionary Gunnar Helander—like Wästberg a veteran
CCHA member, *inter alia* hosting the Inkatha leader in Västerås in the late 1970s—
emphasized in 1996 with regard to Buthelezi that "it was impossible to trust that
fellow. He is hungry for power. You cannot trust his word. He is as sly as a fox".[2]

However, the Swedish government did extend official support to Inkatha, albeit
only with small amounts and not under bilateral agreements. Although never
regarded as an alternative to ANC, during the second half of the 1970s it was seen
by centrally placed officials as an important complementary anti-apartheid actor.
After initial church contacts and a complicated dialogue with the ANC leadership,
various Inkatha projects in South Africa were assisted. On a number of occasions,
Sweden also hosted secret meetings between Oliver Tambo and Gatsha Buthelezi.[3]
SIDA's Director General Ernst Michanek played a pivotal role in this context. Interviewed in 1996, he noted that

> [t]here is a long history between Sweden, Inkatha and ANC. [...] I know Gatsha Buthelezi very
> well. He was often in Sweden. He came to my office and to my home, and I had secret meet-
> ings with him in several places. [...] Inkatha and ANC also held bilateral meetings between
> themselves [...] in Sweden that were never given any publicity.[4]

In much the same way as the contacts between Tambo and Buthelezi were controversial within ANC, the assistance to Inkatha was far from enthusiastically implemented by the Swedish aid officials concerned. Looking back, SIDA's Birgitta
Berggren—at the time serving as CCHA secretary—commented in 1996 that "I was
very critical of the fact that a decision was taken to support Inkatha. [I]t was obvious that Buthelezi and the Inkatha movement were receiving support from CIA. I
could not understand why we should be involved".[5]

Sweden's official relations with Buthelezi in the 1970s may be divided into
two stages. During the first half of the 1970s, they were only indirect and mainly
sustained by the Church of Sweden Mission. After the formation of Inkatha and
the Soweto uprising, the government agreed, however, to grant it limited assistance via different international and Swedish NGOs. This policy was maintained
until the definitive split between ANC and Inkatha in mid-1980. No official,
bilateral contacts were pursued thereafter, and no parliamentary party requested
Swedish assistance to Buthelezi and his movement. At about the same time as the
contacts with PAC were suspended, the support to Inkatha was also brought to
an end.

---

1. Per Wästberg: *I Sydafrika: Resan mot Friheten*, Wahlström & Widstrand, Stockholm, 1995, p. 233. As chief
   editor of *Dagens Nyheter* between 1976 and 1982, Wästberg did not form part of the Consultative Committee on Humanitarian Assistance. Nevertheless, as an active CCHA member he had in June 1974 recommended indirect Swedish assistance to KwaZulu. When *Dagens Nyheter* in 1976 assisted SIDA/CCHA with a
   financial analysis of Inkatha's proposed newspaper, Wästberg, similarly, advocated official support to the
   project (Ernst Michanek: Memorandum ('Ang. ytterligare stöd till tidningen *The Nation* i Sydafrika'/'Re.
   additional support to *The Nation*, South Africa'), Ministry for Foreign Affairs, Stockholm, 28 December
   1979) (SDA).
2. Interview with Gunnar Helander, p. 288. In September 1979, Helander was among the CCHA members who
   supported Inkatha's citizenship project (see below).
3. See the interviews with Gunnar Helander (p. 288) and Per Wästberg (p. 356).
4. Interview with Ernst Michanek, p. 324.
5. Interview with Birgitta Berggren, p. 258.

Church of Sweden Mission, Tambo and Buthelezi

Chief of the Buthelezi Zulu clan, the enigmatic and controversial Mangosuthu Gatsha Buthelezi[1] rose to political prominence in the early 1970s. In the void created by the crushing of the nationalist movement and as the Pretoria regime proceeded to implement grand apartheid[2], his claim to represent the 'historical, non-violent ANC'[3] and his rejection of independence for KwaZulu—one of the ten black 'homelands', or bantustans, designed by the architects of separate development—initially earned him both a certain respect among black students[4] and wide acclaim from white liberals.[5] Elected in June 1970 by his fellow chiefs as Chief Executive Officer of the Zulu Territorial Authority—and confirmed as such by Pretoria—he, however, *de facto* accepted the bantustan policy. Nevertheless, Buthelezi tried to capitalize on his anti-apartheid reputation, not least internationally. Between 1971 and 1973, he made five longer trips to Africa, Europe and the United States, seeking acceptance in all quarters of the political spectrum. As noted by Massie:

> Depending on the context, Buthelezi could present himself as a reforming pragmatist, a black nationalist, a democratic politician, an ANC loyalist, a hereditary autocrat, a non-violent Christian, a descendant of Shaka the warrior, a pro-capitalist industrialist, an urbane intellectual or a Zulu traditionalist. [...] [M]any believed that even when Buthelezi said something contradictory in public, he was really, in his heart of hearts, on their side.[6]

1. On Buthelezi, Inkatha and Zulu ethnicity, see Mzala [Jabulani Nxumalo]: *Gatsha Buthelezi: Chief with a Double Agenda*, Zed Books, London and New Jersey, 1988, and Gerhard Maré: *Brothers Born of Warrior Blood: Politics and Ethnicity in South Africa*, Ravan Press, Johannesburg, 1992. Robert Kinloch Massie discusses 'the enigma of Buthelezi' between 1972 and 1975 in his *Loosing the Bonds: The United States and South Africa in the Apartheid Years*, Nan A. Talese/Doubleday, New York, 1997, pp. 333-72.
2. The policy of grand—or territorial—apartheid was implemented in various stages. Based on the 1913 Land Act, from the early 1950s territorial authorities were set up on ethnic grounds. Eight—later ten—'homelands' were subsequently created. Designed to deny black South Africans citizenship and rights of residence in the rest of the country, the 1959 Promotion of Bantu Self-Government Act provided the machinery for the territories to achieve self-government and independence, although under Pretoria's control. Transkei was the first to be accorded limited self-government in 1963. Nominal independence was later given to Transkei (1976), Bophuthatswana (1977), Venda (1979) and Ciskei (1981). In the process, around four million people were as 'aliens' through forced removals uprooted from their homes in 'white' South Africa and relocated to their respective 'homelands'. By 1980, the bantustans accounted for over half of South Africa's black population. Consisting of scattered tracts of land, five years later they together only occupied some 14 per cent of the country's total land area (Bertil Egerö: *South Africa's Bantustans: From Dumping Grounds to Battlefronts*, Discussion Paper No. 4, Nordiska Afrikainstitutet, Uppsala, 1991, pp. 8-9). On the bantustan policy, cf. also the interview with South Africa's former Foreign Minister 'Pik' Botha, regretting in 1995 that it was implemented "too late": "It was too late, because the immoral aspects of apartheid overwhelmed any merit that there might have been in the concept of complete independence for the various communities. That killed it. [...] Our plan lacked credibility and legitimacy because of apartheid. That wrecked it" (Interview with Roelof ('Pik') Botha, p. 112).
3. Buthelezi claimed to wear the mantle of ANC's founding fathers, one of whom—the future ANC President Pixley ka Isaka Seme—was his uncle. Although Mzala states that Buthelezi was never a member of ANC (Mzala op. cit., p. 66), it is generally acknowledged that he joined the ANC Youth League as a student at Fort Hare in the late 1940s. In 1985, for example, the ANC National Executive Committee described Buthelezi as "this former member of the ANC Youth League who had taken up his position in the KwaZulu bantustan after consultations with our leadership" ('Political Report of the National Executive Committee to the National Consultative Conference, June 1985' in ANC: *Documents of the Second National Consultative Conference of the African National Congress* [no year], p. 20). When Inkatha was launched in 1975, it adopted the African national anthem *Nkosi Sikelel' iAfrika* and the green, gold and black colours of ANC as its own.
4. In August 1971, Buthelezi was among the speakers at a conference held to discuss the formation of the Black People's Convention. Soon, however, a deep rift opened between him and the wider black consciousness movement. Strongly condemning the bantustans, in 1972 Steve Biko wrote with regard to Buthelezi: "For me as a black person, it is extremely painful to see a man who could easily have been my leader being so misused by the cruel and exploitative white world" (Steve Biko: *I Write What I Like*, Heinemann Educational Books, London, Ibadan and Nairobi, 1979, p. 86).
5. See Karis and Gerhart op. cit., pp. 223-26.
6. Massie op. cit., p. 343.

Still opposing nominal independence for KwaZulu[1], Buthelezi primarily appeared as a Zulu nationalist. It was in that capacity that he in December 1972 under the auspices of the Church of Sweden Mission (CSM) visited Stockholm and Uppsala, appealing for assistance.

There were many grounds for cordial relations between CSM and Buthelezi. As early as in 1882, it was the Zulu King Dinizulu—Buthelezi's maternal grandfather—who had granted the official Church of Sweden permission to carry out missionary work in Zululand.[2] In addition to its religious efforts, CSM focused on agriculture, education and health, together with other missionary endeavours—notably by the Norwegian Missionary Society—taking an active part in the socio-economic development of Zululand. Born in 1928 at the CSM hospital at Ceza and spending his early years in the rural areas, the Church of Sweden Mission was far from unknown to the future Inkatha leader. After becoming chief of the Buthelezi in 1953, he established close relations with the CSM missionary Helge Fosséus. When the Evangelical Lutheran Church in Southern Africa-Southeast Region was set up in 1961, Fosséus became its first Bishop. Soon thereafter—in 1963—Buthelezi paid his first of many visits to Sweden.[3]

ANC opposed grand apartheid and South Africa's fragmentation into divisive, tribal territories. The bantustan scheme was also firmly denounced by the Organization of African Unity and the United Nations. In December 1970, the UN General Assembly

> condemn[ed] the establishment by the racist minority government of South Africa of 'bantustans' in so called African reserves as fraudulent, a violation of the principle of self-determination and prejudicial to the territorial integrity of the state and the unity of its people.[4]

Nevertheless, after its 1969 Morogoro conference ANC tried to promote legal, democratic organizations in the 'homelands'. Through a dialogue with the bantustan leaders, it was hoped that the limited self-rule accorded by the Pretoria regime could be used to revive and shield the nationalist movement. Buthelezi and KwaZulu assumed in this context particular importance. In the political report of the National Executive Committee to the ANC conference held in Kabwe, Zambia, in June 1985, Oliver Tambo later stated that "we were of the view that [...] it was of vital importance that we should encourage the formation in the bantustans of mass democratic organizations where none existed, and urge that those which existed should be strengthened and activ[ated]".[5]

---

1. With Buthelezi as its Chief Executive Councillor, the Zulu Legislative Assembly came into being in April 1972. Five years later—in February 1977—KwaZulu moved from the status of a territorial authority to self-governance. Buthelezi served as KwaZulu's Chief Minister until the democratic elections in April 1994.
2. See Sellström Volume I, p. 121.
3. Gatsha Buthelezi: 'My role within separate development politics', Address held at a CSM seminar, Uppsala, 19 December 1972 (CSA). Gatsha Buthelezi's cousin Manas Buthelezi also had close links to CSM and Sweden. The two would, however, convey radically different messages to the Swedish church and government. After theology studies at Lund university, Manas Buthelezi returned to South Africa in the mid-1970s, where he was ordained Evangelical-Lutheran Bishop of Soweto. Closely involved in the June 1976 Soweto uprising—*inter alia* leading the subsequently banned Black Parents' Association—he briefly returned to Sweden in April 1978. Received by Foreign Minister Karin Söder, he emphasized that the possibilities of a peaceful solution to the South African situation were bleak; that Gatsha Buthelezi and Inkatha were far from close to ANC; and that economic sanctions against the apartheid regime would be effective (Ingrid Hjelt: Memoranda: a) 'Besök av biskop Manas Buthelezi'/'Visit by Bishop Manas Buthelezi', Ministry for Foreign Affairs, Stockholm, 30 April 1978 (MFA) and b) 'Biskop Buthelezi besöker utrikesministern'/'Bishop Buthelezi visits the Foreign Minister', Ministry for Foreign Affairs, Stockholm, 8 May 1978) (MFA).
4. UN General Assembly Resolution 2671 (XXV) of 8 December 1970, cited in United Nations (1994) op. cit., p. 61.
5. 'Political Report of the National Executive Committee to the National Consultative Conference, June 1985' in ANC op. cit. [no year], p. 20.

Exhibiting works at the Stockholm University College of Art, April 1965: Thobile Xakaza and Sarafina Ndlovu from the Rorke's Drift Art and Craft Centre with Per Wästberg of the Swedish South Africa Committee (Photo: Owe Sjöblom/Scanpix Sverige AB)

This concern was repeatedly conveyed in the early 1970s by ANC to the Swedish government. Meeting Prime Minister Palme in Lusaka in September 1971, Tambo particularly raised the issue of the bantustans. The British Prime Minister Edward Heath had just invited Buthelezi to London together with Lucas Mangope of Bophuthatswana and Kaiser Matanzima of the Transkei. Against this background, the ANC leader explained, he too was going to London as he "would like ANC to somehow hook onto the bantustan leaders' new attitudes".[1]

Visiting Sweden two months later, Tambo again primarily discussed the issue of the bantustans. During a meeting at the Ministry for Foreign Affairs, he noted that the discussions in London with Buthelezi, Mangope and Matanzima had been characterized by "agreement that [they and the liberation movement] were all working towards the same goal". Although the bantustan leaders had been appointed by the Pretoria regime, they "exercised a certain pressure against the government [and] could therefore no longer simply be dismissed". In addition, Buthelezi in particular enjoyed, according to Tambo, "a significant influence among the black population in general".[2]

When Bishop Fosséus and Carl Fredrik Hallencreutz of CSM at about the same time informally introduced the question of possible official assistance to KwaZulu with SIDA and CCHA, Buthulezi was thus far from regarded as hostile to the libe-

---

1. Pierre Schori: Memorandum ('Samtal med Oliver Tambo, ANC generalsekreterare i exil, i State House, Lusaka, 24.9.1971'/'Conversation with Oliver Tambo, ANC Secretary General (*sic*) in exile, State House, Lusaka, 24 September 1971'), Ministry for Foreign Affairs, Stockholm, 1 October 1971 (MFA). Pierre Schori and Per Wästberg participated in the meeting. On the conversation between Palme and Tambo, see also Sellström Volume I, pp. 250-51.

2. Ethel Ringborg: Memorandum ('Samtal med Oliver Tambo, ANC'/'Conversation with Oliver Tambo, ANC'), Ministry for Foreign Affairs, Stockholm, 18 November 1971 (MFA). The meeting with Tambo took place on 11 November 1971.

ration movement. Through official support to the Lutuli[1] Memorial Foundation, the Swedish authorities were also aware of the contacts between the KwaZulu leader and ANC.[2] Familiar with the Rorke's Drift Art and Craft Centre[3], Buthelezi was similarly conscious of official Swedish assistance to project activities in Zululand.[4]

1. For a long time, the surname of the former ANC President-General was often spelt without the letter 'h'. Thus, the foundation set up in 1970 was the Lutuli Memorial Foundation, while its 1982 successor became the Luthuli Memorial Trust/the Luthuli Cultural and Welfare Services.

2. Chief Albert Luthuli, President-General of ANC and Nobel peace laureate, died in 1967. The following year, Oliver Tambo announced that ANC was planning to honour his memory by forming a foundation to support the education of black South Africans, as well as research and information. A decision to that effect was taken by ANC's National Executive Committee later in 1968. When the Lutuli Memorial Foundation (LMF) was formally launched in November 1970, Alva Myrdal, Swedish Minister without Portfolio and former chairperson of the UN Expert Group on South Africa, became one of its international sponsors. At the same time, the Swedish government allocated an amount of 200,000 SEK to the foundation (see Sellström Volume I, p. 241). As executor of Luthuli's will, Gatsha Buthelezi was closely involved in the activities, taking a prominent part in the unveiling ceremony of Luthuli's tombstone in July 1972 and in the general administration of the foundation's South Africa branch ('Press statement', Lutuli Memorial Foundation, London, 16 November 1972) (SDA). In November 1972—just before visiting Sweden—he launched the Lutuli Memorial Trust Fund in South Africa, which was financially assisted by LMF (Gatsha Buthelezi: 'My Role within Separate Development Politics' in *Sechaba*, No. 3, March 1973, p. 21). Although on the margin of the foundation's mandate, one of the most important LMF-sponsored projects in the early 1970s was the Kurasini House for the Sick, a clinic "for South African freedom fighters" set up by ANC in Dar es Salaam, Tanzania, in 1972 ('Lutuli Memorial Foundation Fund Appeal', London, [no date]) (SDA). In March 1974, the Swedish government granted the clinic 50,000 SEK (Letter ('Bidrag till Lutuli Memorial Foundation'/'Contribution to Lutuli Memorial Foundation') from Bengt Säve-Söderbergh to the Swedish embassy in London, Ministry for Foreign Affairs, Stockholm, 13 March 1974) (SDA). From 1975, LMF's scholarship programme was partly financed through the Nobel Peace Prize awarded to Albert Luthuli in 1961. The prize money was invested in farmland in Swaziland and Luthuli's will stipulated that the land should be sold and that the interest accrued be set aside for scholarships (Lutuli Memorial Foundation: 'Memorandum on the occasion of thanking [for] the Nobel Peace Prize to the late Chief A.J. Lutuli by Mrs. N. Lutuli to representatives from the embassies of Denmark, Sweden, Norway [and] Finland', London, 13 June 1977) (SDA). Riddled with problems—notably with regard to its South Africa branch—after the split between ANC and Inkatha the largely ineffective Lutuli Memorial Foundation was reorganized in 1982 as the Luthuli Memorial Trust/the Luthuli Cultural and Welfare Services, based in London, closely connected to ANC and focusing on scholarships. Receiving official Swedish assistance both within and outside the bilateral allocation to ANC, it was, however, similarly far from successful and the support was eventually terminated in mid-1991 (Letter ('SIDA-sponsored scholarships administered by Luthuli Memorial Trust') from Jan Cedergren, Deputy Director General, to Luthuli Memorial Trust, SIDA, Stockholm, 2 July 1991) (SDA).

3. Oscarsberg, the first Church of Sweden Mission station in South Africa, was founded at Rorke's Drift in 1878. It became the centre of CSM's activities in Zululand, for a long time housing the Lutheran Theological College. The brainchild of Bishop Fosséus and the Swedish painter and textile artist Berta Hansson, an art and craft centre was opened there in 1962. Financially supported by a Swedish Committee for African Art and Craft (*Svenska Kommittén för Afrikanskt Konsthantverk*)—led by Signe Höjer, chairperson of a working group on Swedish humanitarian assistance for Government Bill No. 100: 1962 (see Sellström Volume I, pp. 67-69) and a member of the Swedish South Africa Committee—the Rorke's Drift Art and Craft Centre would arguably become "the most famous indigenous art centre in South Africa" (Lesley Paton: 'Making his mark on African art' in *The Namibian*, 18 August 1995). Highly instrumental in the development of the centre were Peder and Ulla Gowenius, Swedish art teachers who arrived there in 1963. Particularly known for its tapestries, by 1971 there were 70 black artists working at the centre's workshops, 150 people working from their homes and 30 students following courses in fine arts, handicraft or domestic science (Pat Schwartz: 'Rorke's Drift weavers strike a blow for the preservation of an age-old tradition' in *Rand Daily Mail*, 27 December 1971). Among the students was John Muafangejo, Namibia's best known printmaker. Financially supported by SIDA from 1965, the Rorke's Drift Art and Craft Centre was the first specific project in South Africa to receive official Swedish assistance (SIDA: Memorandum ('Statliga bidrag till frivilliga svenska organisationer'/'Public contributions to Swedish NGOs'), SIDA, Stockholm, 20 July 1966) (SDA). From the very beginning, the broad field of arts and culture thus played a prominent role in Sweden's humanitarian anti-apartheid assistance.

4. Just before his visit to Sweden, in November 1972, for example, Buthelezi opened an exhibition by the Rorke's Drift centre in Cape Town, emphasizing its importance as "a home industry [...] in the [h]omelands" ('Utdrag ur Chief Gatsha Buthelezi's öppningsanförande vid Rorke's Drift Art and Craft Centre's utställning i Kapstaden den 9 november 1972'/'Extracts from Buthelezi's opening statement [...] in Cape Town, 9 November 1972') (SDA).

Assisting a Bantustan?

CSM's approach to the Swedish aid authorities regarding support to KwaZulu was followed up in January 1972 during a Nordic ecumenical conference on apartheid, held in the Norwegian capital Oslo. Originally proposed by the South African journalist Colin Legum, the possibility of establishing a special trust fund to channel assistance to the territory was raised by Fosséus, Hallencreutz and CSM's Africa secretary Tore Bergman.[1] The proposal did not materialize. Instead, the Church of Sweden Mission took the initiative in inviting Buthelezi to Sweden for direct consultations.[2]

Together with Reverend Enos Sikakana, Director of the Edendale Ecumenical Centre in Pietermaritzburg, Natal, and a future Inkatha Central Committee member, Buthelezi visited Sweden in mid-December 1972.[3] Hosted by Bishop Fosséus[4] and assisted by Bergman and Hallencreutz, the purpose of the visit—which took place less than two months before the decision to extend direct, official Swedish assistance to ANC—was to "establish financial, cultural and political contacts in order to create conditions for concrete assistance to the development of KwaZulu's infrastructure and educational system".[5]

During his stay[6], the recently appointed KwaZulu Chief Executive Councillor held an impressive number of meetings. In addition to a television interview, a well attended press conference[7], a public lecture organized by the Scandinavian Institute of African Studies and discussions with the Church of Sweden Mission, Buthelezi exchanged opinions with SIDA's Director General Ernst Michanek and the Vice-Chancellor of Uppsala university, Torgny Segerstedt. As 'Prime Minister' of a non-recognized South African 'homeland', he was, however, not received at government level or at the Ministry for Foreign Affairs.

The title of Buthelezi's lecture in Uppsala was 'My Role within Separate Development Politics'.[8] Declaring that he had "great reservations about the philosophy of [a]partheid, which is behind the policies in whose implementation I am participating", the main message conveyed by Buthelezi was that

---

1. Marianne Rappe: Memorandum ('Framställning av Chief Gatsha Buthelezi om direkt svenskt stöd till Kwa-Zulu, Sydafrika'/'Request from Chief Gatsha Buthelezi for direct Swedish support to KwaZulu, South Africa'), SIDA, Stockholm, 2 May 1973 (SDA).
2. Ibid.
3. The visit formed part of a European tour during which Buthelezi also went to the Federal Republic of Germany, Great Britain, Holland and Switzerland.
4. Gatsha Buthelezi: 'My impressions of our European tour with the Revd. E.Z. Sikakane and the Hon. Mr. B.I. Dladla, November 27th to December 20th 1972' [no place or date], attached to letter from Tore Bergman to SIDA's Director General Ernst Michanek, CSM, Uppsala, 31 October 1973 (SDA). Dladla did not accompany Buthelezi to Sweden.
5. Marianne Rappe: Memorandum ('Framställning av Chief Gatsha Buthelezi om direkt svenskt stöd till Kwa-Zulu, Sydafrika'/'Request from Chief Gatsha Buthelezi for direct Swedish support to KwaZulu, South Africa'), SIDA, Stockholm, 2 May 1973 (SDA).
6. The visit took place from 17 to 20 December 1972.
7. In his invitation to the members of the media, CSM's press secretary Lester Wikström introduced Buthelezi as "[the person] who until now most forcefully has challenged the South African government's apartheid policy" (Lester Wikström: ['Invitation to a press conference'], CSM, Uppsala, 12 December 1972) (SDA).
8. ANC's ambivalence was evident when the movement in March 1973 published Buthelezi's address in its official journal *Sechaba*. After describing the bantustan policy as "a gigantic fraud", the journal explained that the text was reprinted "so that readers may see the dilemma in which some of those who are forced to serve on these institutions because of their position as chief of their people are placed" (*Sechaba*, No. 3, March 1973, p. 19). Mzala states that the address was held in Stockholm in 1973 (Mzala op. cit., p. 82). Buthelezi, however, gave his lecture at the *Södermanland-Nerike's* student fraternity in Uppsala on 19 December 1972 ('Minnesanteckningar från besök av Chief Gatsha Buthelezi och Rev. E. Sikakane i Uppsala den 19 december 1972'/'Notes from visit by Chief Gatsha Buthelezi and Reverend E. Sikakane to Uppsala, 19 December 1972', attached to letter from Tore Bergman to SIDA's Director General Ernst Michanek, CSM, Uppsala, 31 October 1973) (SDA).

[t]hose of us who have qualms of conscience about [a]partheid and yet are working within the framework of the policy do so only because it gives us the [...] opportunity of awakening our people to help themselves. We can only judge as to who are our friends not by any torrents of crocodile tears that are shed, but by concrete contributions towards our campaign as [b]lacks to try and stand on our own feet despite the situation in which we find ourselves. [...]

It is of no use to be over-righteous about [a]partheid if we get no concrete assistance while [a]partheid lasts. In other words, we feel [that] it is not enough to condemn [a]partheid as it will not crumble like the walls of Jericho merely by people shouting [...] without doing something concrete to alleviate our plight. While the problems of South Africa remain unresolved, we feel [that] we should be helped as [b]lacks to help ourselves.[1]

This view was shared by the Church of Sweden Mission. Notwithstanding slightly divergent opinions with regard to economic isolation of the apartheid regime[2] and in spite of the UN General Assembly's condemnation of the bantustan policy, during his stay in Uppsala Buthelezi and CSM—which regarded Zululand as a "colonized territory" comparable to Mozambique[3]—discussed a number of development projects and support to the KwaZulu administration. The rough proposals were followed up with Buthelezi during a visit by CSM's Africa secretary Tore Bergman to South Africa in late March 1973.[4] "On different grounds finding it justified [...] to allocate development assistance to [his] administration"[5], two months later—on 24 May—the CSM board decided to set aside some 70,000 SEK for the establishment of a newspaper in Zulu[6], and in early June 1973 the missionary society submitted a request to SIDA for support to KwaZulu.[7] Aware of the sensitivity of the submission—and in order to "avoid the political complications a direct channelling [of funds] to Chief Buthelezi's administration probably would [cause]"[8]—CSM had

---

1. Gatsha Buthelezi: 'My Role within Separate Development Politics' in *Sechaba*, No. 3, March 1973, p. 21.
2. The Central Committee of the World Council of Churches (WCC) had in August 1972 adopted a policy of disinvestment towards South Africa. The Church of Sweden and other Evangelical Lutheran churches had, however, put forward the alternative of working for improved conditions for black workers in foreign owned companies, a minority position which was acknowledged by the WCC meeting. In his discussions with CSM in Uppsala four months later, Buthelezi essentially supported the minority view. Criticizing the WCC resolution, he advocated instead a policy of involvement ('Minnesanteckningar från besök av Chief Gatsha Buthelezi och Rev. E. Sikakane i Uppsala den 19 december 1972'/'Notes from visit by Chief Gatsha Buthelezi and Reverend E. Sikakane to Uppsala, 19 December 1972', attached to letter from Tore Bergman to SIDA's Director General Ernst Michanek, CSM, Uppsala, 31 October 1973) (SDA). Nevertheless, on the overall issue of isolation versus involvement there were differences of opinion between CSM and the KwaZulu leader. They would rapidly increase when he and other bantustan leaders in 1974 publicly invited foreign investors to South Africa.
3. Tore Bergman and Carl Fredrik Hallencreutz: 'PM angående ev. ansökan om bidrag från SIDA för en Planning and Development Agency i KwaZulu'/'Memorandum regarding a possible request to SIDA for contributions towards a Planning and Development Agency in KwaZulu', CSM, Uppsala, 25 May 1973, attached to letter from Tore Bergman to SIDA's Director General Ernst Michanek, CSM, Uppsala, 31 October 1973 (SDA).
4. Ibid.
5. Ibid.
6. Ibid. At the time, CSM channelled some 2 MSEK to South Africa on an annual basis (Marianne Sundh: Memorandum ('Framställning från Svenska Kyrkans Mission om bidrag till humanitära insatser bland apartheidpolitikens offer i Sydafrika'/'Request from the Church of Sweden Mission for contributions towards humanitarian efforts in favour of the victims of the apartheid policy in South Africa'), SIDA, Stockholm, 31 May 1974) (SDA). Buthulezi's plans regarding a 'black' newspaper would subsequently feature prominently in the dialogue with the Swedish authorities. In 1973, the proposed name of the newspaper discussed with CSM was *The Black Voice*.
7. Marianne Sundh: Memorandum ('Framställning från Svenska Kyrkans Mission om bidrag till humanitära insatser bland apartheidpolitikens offer i Sydafrika'/'Request from the Church of Sweden Mission for contributions towards humanitarian efforts in favour of the victims of the apartheid policy in South Africa'), SIDA, Stockholm, 31 May 1974 (SDA).
8. Bergman and Hallencreutz op. cit., attached to letter from Tore Bergman to SIDA's Director General Ernst Michanek, CSM, Uppsala, 31 October 1973 (SDA).

Chief Buthelezi (second from left) visiting the Church of Sweden Mission in Uppsala, November 1974. Standing is CSM's Tore Bergman (Courtesy of Tore Bergman)

beforehand proposed that the assistance should be administered by the Edendale Ecumenical Centre.[1]

Giving priority to the establishment of a KwaZulu Planning and Development Agency, the CSM request coordinated with Buthelezi covered a number of areas, including English language training in the rural areas; the proposed KwaZulu newspaper; secondary schools with a technical orientation; planning for food production; and "the salary for a bodyguard to Chief Buthelezi".[2] Barring the last item, the comprehensive submission thus envisaged official assistance similar to the bilateral development cooperation with several independent countries. Buthulezi's 'Zulustan' was, however, far from an internationally recognized political entity. Despite CSM's efforts[3], it was decided to refer the unusual request to the Consultative Committee on Humanitarian Assistance.

After considerable delays, in March 1974 CCHA resolved to set up an internal working group to study the application and present an informed opinion.[4] In turn,

1. Marianne Rappe: Memorandum ('Framställning av Chief Gatsha Buthelezi om direkt svenskt stöd till KwaZulu, Sydafrika'/'Request from Chief Gatsha Buthelezi for direct Swedish support to KwaZulu, South Africa'), SIDA, Stockholm, 2 May 1973 (SDA).

2. Ibid. and Marianne Sundh: Memorandum ('Framställning från Svenska Kyrkans Mission om bidrag till humanitära insatser bland apartheidpolitikens offer i Sydafrika'/'Request from the Church of Sweden Mission for contributions towards humanitarian efforts in favour of the victims of the apartheid policy in South Africa'), SIDA, Stockholm, 31 May 1974 (SDA).

3. On behalf of CSM, in October 1973 its Africa secretary Tore Bergman argued in a letter to SIDA's Director General Ernst Michanek that it could have "detrimental consequences" if support to KwaZulu were to be discussed by CCHA "within the framework of other assistance to the struggle against racism", proposing instead that it should be regarded as an NGO matter (Letter from Tore Bergman to SIDA's Director General Ernst Michanek, CSM, Uppsala, 31 October 1973) (SDA).

4. Marianne Sundh: Memorandum ('Framställning från Svenska Kyrkans Mission om bidrag till humanitära insatser bland apartheidpolitikens offer i Sydafrika'/'Request from the Church of Sweden Mission for contributions towards humanitarian efforts in favour of the victims of the apartheid policy in South Africa'), SIDA, Stockholm, 31 May 1974 (SDA). SIDA's Astrid Bergquist, Marianne Rappe, Curt Ström, Marianne Sundh and the independent CCHA member Per Wästberg constituted the working group.

the group invited comments from a number of people. Against a positive decision were ANC's recently arrived Chief Representative Sobizana Mngqikana and BCM-SASO's Randwedzi Nengwekhulu, who paid a visit to SIDA from Botswana in March 1974. The positive voices, however, were incomparably stronger. They, notably, included Oliver Tambo, but also Canon John Collins of the London-based International Defence and Aid Fund, Colin Legum and the former CSM missionary and veteran anti-apartheid activist Gunnar Helander.[1] While concluding that "it for foreign policy reasons [was] out of the question to [officially] support the development policies of a 'bantustan government'", the working group, however, preferred to avoid the real issue, recommending an open-ended allocation of 500,000 SEK to CSM "for humanitarian efforts in favour of the victims of the apartheid policy in South Africa", to be used as CSM saw fit.[2]

In the final event, foreign policy considerations prevailed. In June 1974, CCHA decided to put CSM's request aside.[3] Nevertheless, committed to the development of KwaZulu the Church of Sweden Mission pursued its cooperation with Chief Buthelezi, who in early November 1974 returned to the missionary society's headquarters in Uppsala. Declaring that his administration was "in desperate need of continued assistance from the Church of Sweden"[4], he did not receive the same response as in 1972. In addition to increasingly critical voices regarding developments in KwaZulu, Buthelezi had in the meantime firmly turned against the disinvestment policy towards the apartheid regime. After the formation of Inkatha, CSM would with less vigour advocate aid to KwaZulu. As later stated by Tore Bergman:

> We held the view that Buthelezi to begin with stood for a positive movement in South Africa in that he refused to declare KwaZulu independent. After the formation of Inkatha, his intentions were, however, not as clear as in the beginning.[5]

Nevertheless, CSM continued to support Chief Buthelezi's plans for a 'black' newspaper. This project would during the second half of the 1970s be at the centre of a drawn-out and often confusing debate, which in addition to Buthelezi involved ANC's Oliver Tambo and Thabo Mbeki, with SIDA's Director General Ernst Michanek as an active promoter and go-between.

ANC, Inkatha and *The Nation*

Grand apartheid provided Buthelezi with a territorial base and an institutional framework. Economic development of the impoverished KwaZulu 'homeland' was, however, subject to Pretoria's budgetary allocations and financial controls, hence his calls for private investment and foreign assistance. To realize his ambitions for national political leadership, Buthelezi needed, in addition, an organization and a

---

1. Ibid.
2. Ibid.
3. CCHA: 'Protokoll [från sammanträde 17 juni 1974]' ('Minutes [from meeting 17 June 1974]'), SIDA, [Stockholm], 20 September 1974 (SDA).
4. 'Zululedare på Uppsalabesök: Underutvecklingen vårt största problem' ('Zulu leader visiting Uppsala: Underdevelopment our biggest problem') in *Upsala Nya Tidning*, 5 November 1974.
5. Interview with Tore Bergman, p. 266.

platform. Encouraged by ANC[1], in 1973 he revived the defunct cultural association *Inkatha ya ka Zulu*, originally formed by the Zulu King Solomon in the 1920s. It was formally set up in March 1975 as *Inkatha ye Nkululeko ye Sizwe*[2], with the English designation 'National Cultural Liberation Movement'. Plans were at the same time drawn up for the establishment of a newspaper, controlled by Buthelezi and targeting the black population in South Africa. As early as in May 1973, CSM decided to financially support the project[3], which the following month was included in the unsuccessful request for comprehensive Swedish development assistance to KwaZulu.

While the initial plans under the working title *The Black Voice* did not get off the ground, after the formation of Inkatha the information project assumed a new, strategic importance.[4] Embraced by Beyers Naudé and the inter-denominational Christian Institute (CI)[5], it was first raised with the Swedish aid authorities during CCHA's fact-finding mission to Southern Africa in early 1976. At meetings in Johannesburg with Naudé, Cedric Mayson, who edited CI's publication *Pro Veritate*, and Walter Felgate, Managing Director of Inkatha's Isiswe-Sechaba Publishers[6] and charged by Buthelezi with the task of launching a newspaper called *The Nation*, Ann Wilkens from the Foreign Ministry was informed of the plans in

---

1. There is very little documentation on ANC's involvement in the formation of Inkatha. In the political report to ANC's National Consultative Conference in June 1985, President Tambo briefly explained that "in the course of our discussions with [Chief Gatsha Buthelezi] we agreed that [the mobilisation of our people] would also necessitate the formation of a mass democratic organisation in the bantustan that he headed. Inkatha originated from this agreement" ('Political Report of the National Executive Committee to the National Consultative Conference, June 1985' in ANC op. cit. [no year], p. 20). Ten years later, Thabo Mbeki stated that "[t]he IFP was set up at the urging of the ANC, which spent some time at the beginning of the 1970s saying [that] it is necessary to set up a political party [...]. We said that in KwaZulu there needs to be a party. It took a bit of time for us to convince Buthelezi about this [...]. [H]e proposed that we should use the name Inkatha [...] so [that] you could present the matter to Pretoria as something traditional to the Zulu people" (Mbeki cited in 'The man who may succeed Madiba' in *The Star International Weekly*, 27 April-4 May 1995). Mbeki was closely involved in this process. In 1998, a semi-official biographical sketch of the future South African President noted that he "during the early 1970s [...] participated in discussions with Dr. M.G. Buthelezi which led to the establishment of the Inkatha Freedom Party" (Mbeki op. cit., p. xiv).

2. In English, 'Coil of the freedom of the nation'. Literally a grass coil used by women for carrying loads on their heads, in Zulu culture the *inkatha* is "a solemn symbol of unity" (Mzala op. cit., p. 116). Although non-Zulus could become members of Inkatha, leadership positions were limited to KwaZulu citizens and the movement remained for all practical purposes an exclusively Zulu organization, formally interlocked with the bantustan government. Its growth was accompanied by credible claims that membership was required for civil service positions. In fact, "unlike any black political organization in South Africa before or since, Inkatha took on the attributes of a classic political machine, building support by dispensing patronage to friends and withdrawing it from foes" (Karis and Gerhart op. cit., p. 263). In 1990, Buthelezi converted Inkatha into a political party—the Inkatha Freedom Party (IFP)—open to all races.

3. Before they were stopped by Pretoria, the Church of Sweden Aid (*Lutherhjälpen*) had, in addition, decided to support Buthelezi's plans for the establishment of a radio station (Marianne Sundh: Memorandum ('Insatser för stöd till tidningen *The Nation* och utbildningsaktiviteter i Sydafrika'/'Contributions in support of the newspaper *The Nation* and education activities in South Africa'), SIDA/CCHA, [Stockholm], 24 November 1977) (SDA).

4. Journalists were among the staunchest supporters of the black consciousness movement, and SASO—firmly opposed to Inkatha—had in the early 1970s tried to establish a black-owned newspaper. Due to lack of capital, the plans never materialized. Influenced by BCM, in 1972 black reporters, however, formed the Union of Black Journalists (UBJ). When UBJ's Percy Qoboza in 1974 became editor of the white-owned newspaper *The World*, it soon assumed increasingly challenging positions vis-à-vis the government. Together with a number of BCM organizations, UBJ was banned in October 1977. The following year, black journalists formed the Writers Association of South Africa (WASA), which was to continue where UBJ had left off. In the context of the subsequent direct assistance to Inkatha's newspaper, it should be noted that official Swedish support via LO/TCO and ICFTU was channelled to WASA from the financial year 1978/79 (Kristina Persson: 'Rapport över LO/TCO's projekt i södra Afrika'/'Report on the LO/TCO projects in Southern Africa', Stockholm, 13 August 1979) (SDA).

5. Naudé and Buthelezi had formed a close association in the early 1970s. In July 1972, the Christian Institute's magazine *Pro Veritate* admiringly described Buthelezi as "the pace-setter for the bantustans [and] the embodiment of what the Pretoria government has always feared" (cited in Karis and Gerhart op. cit., p. 261).

6. ANC's official journal in exile was called *Sechaba*.

March 1976. According to Felgate[1], the project had already been discussed with
ANC's Chief Representative to Algeria, Johnny Makatini, and a final meeting was
to be held with ANC in London the following month. Thereafter, Felgate
explained, a funding request would be submitted to Sweden.[2]

After discussions with ANC in London, Felgate, Mayson and Enos Sikakana
proceeded to Stockholm, where in late April they presented the project to the Ministry for Foreign Affairs. Affirming that through Makatini they had received ANC's
go-ahead and that the International Defence and Aid Fund in London had agreed
to serve as a channel, on 3 May 1976 they submitted an application for 1.9
MSEK.[3] It envisaged the procurement of printing equipment, as well as support
towards production and administration costs—including the training of black journalists and typographers—during an initial period of six months, after which the
newspaper was expected to be financially self-sustaining.[4]

On behalf of the Swedish aid authorities, Wilkens contacted Oliver Tambo's
close friend Canon Collins, who not only confirmed that IDAF could handle the
funds, but "gave the project the highest priority".[5] Noting that Chief Buthelezi "at
present represents a political force of such a proportion that it is difficult for the
regime to act against him", the CCHA secretariat proposed that the requested
amount should be granted.[6]

At a time when close and trusted relations with ANC were yet to be firmly
cemented, CCHA itself was ambivalent towards the initiative. The UN General
Assembly had on several occasions condemned Pretoria's bantustan policy. However, Oliver Tambo had at the same time repeatedly underlined ANC's efforts to
establish a base in the 'homelands', particularly in KwaZulu. It was, as earlier
stressed by Tambo, "ANC's most important task [...] to try to lead and coordinate
the heterogeneous expressions of opposition" in South Africa.[7] Although strongly
turning against Gatsha Buthelezi's appeals for foreign investment, during his first
visit to Sweden Thabo Mbeki had in late 1974 similarly declared that it was
"ANC's line to activate the population also within the framework of the bantustan

---

1. A former member of the Liberal Party, Felgate established through Beyers Naudé early relations with the
   KwaZulu leader and acted in the 1970s—when Naudé's passport had been withdrawn—as a messenger
   between Buthelezi and Tambo. After the break between ANC and Inkatha, he parted with Naudé and his colleagues from the Christian Institute, which had been banned in October 1977. Closely involved with Inkatha
   activities, in 1990—when the non-racial Inkatha Freedom Party (IFP) was formed—Felgate was appointed to
   its Central Committee and served on its Executive Committee, actively participating in the subsequent
   national negotiations. In April 1994, he was elected MP for IFP, but left Buthelezi and joined ANC in August
   1997.
2. Ann Wilkens: Memorandum ('Planer på att starta en tidning för svarta i Sydafrika'/'Plans for the launching of
   a newspaper for blacks in South Africa'), CCHA/Ministry for Foreign Affairs, Stockholm, 15 April 1976
   (SDA).
3. Ann Wilkens: Memorandum ('Ansökan om medel för att starta tidningar för svarta i Sydafrika'/'Request for
   funds to launch newspapers for blacks in South Africa'), CCHA/Ministry for Foreign Affairs, Stockholm, 5
   May 1976 (SDA).
4. Marianne Sundh: Memorandum ('Insatser för stöd till tidningen *The Nation* och utbildningsaktiviteter i Sydafrika'/'Contributions in support of the newspaper *The Nation* and education activities in South Africa'),
   SIDA/CCHA, [Stockholm], 24 November 1977 (SDA).
5. Ann Wilkens: Memorandum ('Ansökan om medel för att starta tidningar för svarta i Sydafrika'/'Request for
   funds to launch newspapers for blacks in South Africa'), CCHA/Ministry for Foreign Affairs, Stockholm, 5
   May 1976 (SDA).
6. Ibid.
7. Magnus Wernstedt and Gun-Britt Andersson: Memorandum ('Samtal med O. Tambo, president i ANC, M.
   Kunene och M. Legassick den 10 januari 1973'/'Conversation with O. Tambo, President of ANC, M. Kunene
   and M. Legassick, 10 January 1973'), Ministry for Foreign Affairs, Stockholm, 29 January 1973 (SDA).

policy, even if [the movement] could never accept the ['homeland'] institution".[1]

Tambo, in particular, also spoke highly of Buthelezi as a person and as a political leader. Interviewed by CCHA's Gunnar Helander and Evert Svensson, in October 1975, for example, the ANC Acting President talked about "my personal good friend Gatsha, who I like a lot"[2], and in a meeting with Anders Bjurner in Lusaka in early May 1976—at the time of the Inkatha delegation's visit to Stockholm—he described Buthelezi as "a great political leader [, who] undoubtedly enjoy[ed] big popular support". Stating that they were in regular contact, Tambo saw Buthelezi as "an important force against the Pretoria regime [whose] closeness to ANC should not be called into question". The fact that Buthelezi "largely followed ANC's principles" was, in Tambo's view, "yet another reason to support him".[3]

Similar opinions were expressed by old Swedish contacts in South Africa. In a meeting with Beyers Naudé in Johannesburg in late March 1976, the head of the Christian Institute emphasized to Wilkens that "there was no doubt that [Buthelezi] should be seen as a genuine advocate of radical political change", adding that "it is important that [his] role as a political force is anchored within ANC".[4]

In the build-up to the Soweto uprising, there were, finally, several indications that Buthelezi was publicly approaching ANC positions. While the liberation movement acknowledged that his position made any calls for armed action impossible[5], it had firmly opposed his appeals for foreign investment. However, in early March 1976 Buthelezi joined Beyers Naudé in issuing a statement which—in addition to demands for "a radical redistribution of wealth, land and political power"—asserted that "foreign investment in the central economy is devoid of all morality".[6]

1. Arne Ström: Memorandum ('Minnesanteckningar från möte med Thabo Mbeki, informationssekreterare till ANC's exekutiv'/'Notes from meeting with Thabo Mbeki, information secretary on ANC's executive'), SIDA, Stockholm, 2 December 1974 (SDA).

2. Gunnar Helander: 'Intervju av Gunnar Helander och Evert Svensson med Sydafrikas African National Congress' ordförande Oliver Tambo i Stockholm, 1975 10 02' ('Interview by Gunnar Helander and Evert Svensson with ANC's President Oliver Tambo, Stockholm, 2 October 1975') [no place or date] (SDA).

3. Letter ('Samtal med O. Tambo, ANC's t.f. ordförande'/'Conversation with O. Tambo, ANC Acting President') from Anders Bjurner, Swedish embassy, to the Ministry for Foreign Affairs, Lusaka, 21 May 1976 (MFA). During the conversation—which took place on 2 May 1976—Tambo acknowledged that there were "members [...] who wondered how the ANC leadership could accept Buthulezi's standpoints" (ibid.). In addition to opposing ANC's links with SACP, the so called 'Gang of Eight'—a group around the brothers Ambrose and Tennyson Makiwane expelled from ANC in 1975—had accused Tambo of supporting Buthelezi (Karis and Gerhart op. cit., p. 257).

4. Ann Wilkens: Memorandum ('Samtal med Beyers Naudé, chef för Christian Institute, i Johannesburg den 25 mars 1976'/'Conversation with Beyers Naudé, head of the Christian Institute, in Johannesburg on 25 March 1976'), CCHA/Ministry for Foreign Affairs, Stockholm, 12 April 1976 (SDA). The wider black consciousness movement rejected Buthelezi and his role within the bantustan system. During Wilkens' second visit to South Africa, Steve Biko adamantly told her that "you cannot work with the devil in order to oppose him", adding that the ANC leadership "due to old bonds of friendship were unable to take a stand either for or against [Buthelezi]" (Ann Wilkens: Memorandum ('Samtal med Steve Biko, en av de ledande inom 'black consciousness'-rörelsen'/'Conversation with Steve Biko, one of the leaders of the black consciousness movement'), Ministry for Foreign Affairs, Stockholm, 8 September 1976) (MFA).

5. A different matter—and a significant bone of contention—was that Buthelezi refused to facilitate the transit through KwaZulu of MK cadres and arms. The question was touched upon during the meeting between the Inkatha leader and Wilkens in July 1976, when he explained that for security reasons he had turned down ANC's requests in that regard (Ann Wilkens: Memorandum ('Samtal med Chief Buthelezi'/'Conversation with Chief Buthelezi'), Ministry for Foreign Affairs, Stockholm, 24 August 1976) (MFA).

6. 'Foreign investment in South Africa', Statement by C.F. Beyers Naudé and Gatsha Buthelezi [no place or date, but received on 12 March 1976] (CSA). The crucial words were 'the central economy'. Buthelezi rejected foreign investment in South Africa, but not in KwaZulu or the other bantustans. Nevertheless, the joint statement was heavily criticized by Kaiser Matanzima, the Chief Minister of Transkei, and Buthelezi soon returned to the pro-investment fold.

More importantly, on 14 March 1976 Buthelezi delivered what was "probably the most impassioned and radical speech of his political life"[1] before a large crowd at the Jabulani amphitheatre in Soweto. Dressed in the green, gold and black colours of ANC (and Inkatha), in the famous address—subsequently published by the Christian Institute under the title 'In This Approaching Hour of Crisis'—he declared that blacks "despised" separate development and that those who talked of dividing South Africa on the basis of ethnicity were "naive and dangerous". Dismissing the "federal formula" which later would be at the very heart of Inkatha's policy, he concluded that the time had come when "the country must move toward majority rule".[2] As stated by Buthelezi to Wilkens during their meeting at St. Francis Mission in Mahlabatini four months later: "There is no problem as to where we fit in with the ANC and the movement of liberation".[3]

It was against this background that CCHA met in mid-May 1976 to discuss Inkatha's newspaper project. Treated in a positive spirit—and in spite of the secretariat's endorsement—no decision was, however, taken as it was found that the proposal warranted further technical and financial clarifications. In addition, comments from the Swedish embassies in Southern Africa and elsewhere were invited.[4]

The comments from the Swedish embassy in Lusaka were negative. After contacts with members of ANC's National Executive Committee (NEC) and a meeting with Thabo Mbeki—under Oliver Tambo responsible for information matters on the NEC and at the time busy with the formulation of ANC's own information policy[5]—Anders Bjurner reported in late May 1976 that Mbeki had already advised against the project, "wondering how it could have emerged anew". Mbeki was "unequivocally critical of [the suggestion] that Inkatha should lead such an important project". According to Bjurner, "Mbeki's attitude towards Buthelezi was clearly critical, and much more critical than that of his President". There were in Mbeki's view "far too many questions that Inkatha had not answered or given unsatisfactory replies to". He also questioned the role played by Johnny Makatini, although acknowledging that "certain, separate contacts" had taken place between

---

1. Karis and Gerhart op. cit., p. 265.
2. Cited in ibid.
3. Ann Wilkens: Memorandum ('Samtal med Chief Buthelezi'/'Conversation with Chief Buthelezi'), Ministry for Foreign Affairs, Stockholm, 24 August 1976 (MFA; English in the original). During the meeting with the Swedish Foreign Affairs' official Buthelezi wanted in particular to "explain his position vis-à-vis ANC, since it had been misunderstood in so many quarters", not least by "the younger generation in the ANC leadership" and by "the Communists within ANC". Of interest in a historical perspective is that Buthelezi on more than one occasion mentioned the then junior ANC leader Thabo Mbeki, who according to him had been particularly critical from the early 1970s. Where Oliver Tambo had been understanding and protective, Mbeki—according to Buthelezi acting without Tambo's authorization—had been demanding, *inter alia* requesting him to support the armed struggle. Johnny Makatini, on the other hand, had been supportive, recently endorsing the newspaper project (ibid.).
4. Marianne Sundh: Memorandum ('Insatser för stöd till tidningen *The Nation* och utbildningsaktiviteter i Sydafrika'/'Contributions in support of the newspaper *The Nation* and education activities in South Africa'), SIDA/CCHA, [Stockholm], 24 November 1977 (SDA).
5. In May 1976, ANC included for the first time information support in its annual request to the Swedish government. Subsequently approved, it covered *inter alia* equipment to the movement's radio stations in Lusaka and elsewhere. ANC's wider request and Inkatha's submission in favour of a newspaper were thus presented at about the same time.

him and Buthelezi.[1]

Less categorical, the comments received from London also called for restraint. Canon Collins recommended Swedish assistance to the project in principle. At the same time, however, the head of IDAF warned against "the risk that a Swedish contribution could be depicted as support for South Africa's bantustan policy". Due to differences within the ANC leadership, it would in his view, finally, "be hard to obtain [the movement's formal] approval of the [...] project. Oliver Tambo could get into difficulties if pressurized to [make such a statement]".[2]

CCHA again discussed the newspaper project on 24 June 1976. Once more, a decision was deferred. In the light of ANC's obvious ambivalence and despite Canon Collins' comments, before a final recommendation could be made the committee felt that it was important to receive an unequivocal statement from ANC.[3] A formal endorsement of the project would, however, not be forthcoming until October 1977—almost one and a half years later—when Oliver Tambo in a letter to Ernst Michanek eventually notified him of the liberation movement's consent.[4] In the meantime, in Sweden Palme was succeeded in October 1976 by Fälldin and in South Africa *The Nation* had been launched in December 1976 as a monthly publication with contributions in English, Zulu and Sotho.

A Complementary Force

Neither ANC's silence nor the change of government in Stockholm[5] or the fact that *The Nation* began publication without Swedish assistance put an end to the saga of the Inkatha project. On the contrary, after another visit by Felgate to Sweden in

1. Letter ('Ansökan om medel för att starta tidningar för svarta i Sydafrika'/'Request for funds to launch newspapers for blacks in South Africa') from Anders Bjurner, Swedish embassy, to the Ministry for Foreign Affairs, Lusaka, 21 May 1976 (MFA). Discussing the Swedish support to ANC's own information activities, in October 1976 Mbeki told SIDA's Carin Norberg in Lusaka that ANC preferred a number of small publications to the nationwide newspaper planned by Inkatha (Carin Norberg: Memorandum ('Minnesanteckningar från samtal med Thabo Mbeki, ANC (SA), 14 oktober 1976'/' Notes from conversation with Thabo Mbeki, ANC of South Africa, 14 October 1976'), Swedish embassy, Lusaka, [no date]) (SDA).
2. Cable from the Swedish embassy to the Ministry for Foreign Affairs, London, 26 May 1976 (SDA).
3. Marianne Sundh: Memorandum ('Insatser för stöd till tidningen *The Nation* och utbildningsaktiviteter i Sydafrika'/'Contributions in support of the newspaper *The Nation* and education activities in South Africa'), SIDA/CCHA, [Stockholm], 24 November 1977 (SDA). Although not made explicit, foreign policy considerations played a major role for the deferment. It could in this context be noted that the Swedish embassy in Lusaka after official aid negotiations with ANC in late August 1976—during which support to the movement's own information activities was agreed—in a press release called for "a clear refusal of any form of recognition of the so called independent [b]antustans" (Embassy of Sweden: 'Swedish support to ANC (South Africa)', Press release, Lusaka, 1 September 1976) (SDA).
4. Ibid. and Ernst Michanek: Memorandum ('Ang. ytterligare stöd till tidningen *The Nation* i Sydafrika'/'Re. additional support to *The Nation*, South Africa'), Ministry for Foreign Affairs, Stockholm, 28 December 1979 (SDA).
5. Although not discussing Inkatha's newspaper project, in his very first meeting with the Liberal Cooperation Minister Ola Ullsten in Lusaka in February 1977 Oliver Tambo stressed that Gatsha Buthelezi must be accepted as an important actor. "He is no real puppet", the ANC leader stated (Elisabeth Michanek: Draft memorandum ('Möte med ANC's (SA) president Oliver Tambo den 28 februari 1977'/'Meeting with ANC President Oliver Tambo on 28 February 1977'), Swedish embassy, Lusaka, 7 March 1977; English in the original) (MFA). Visiting the Ministry for Foreign Affairs in Stockholm in August 1977, Tambo similarly conveyed to the non-socialist government that "the role played by Inkatha remained positive as long as it did not obstruct ANC's own work" (Marika Fahlén: Memorandum ('Besök av ordföranden i den sydafrikanska befrielserörelsen ANC, Oliver Tambo'/'Visit by the President of the South African liberation movement ANC, Oliver Tambo'), Ministry for Foreign Affairs, Stockholm, 31 August 1977) (MFA).

March[1] and—above all—ANC's belated go-ahead in October 1977, the Fälldin and Ullsten governments would not only allocate funds to the newspaper, but subsequently to other Inkatha-initiated information activities as well.

The two-year period from late 1977 until late 1979 witnessed an increasing Inkatha activity vis-à-vis Sweden.[2] Starting with a visit by Gatsha Buthelezi in November 1977—during which he held bilateral talks with Oliver Tambo[3] and was also received by Foreign Minister Karin Söder[4]—it ended abruptly after the unbridgeable split between ANC and Inkatha in London in October 1979. As in the mid-1970s, Tambo's positive attitude towards Buthelezi and the Christian Institute's backing of Inkatha were in this context of particular importance. It was, however, SIDA's Director General Ernst Michanek—*ex officio* chairing the Consultative Committee on Humanitarian Assistance—who acted as the prime mover.

According to his CCHA and IDAF colleague Gunnar Helander, "Michanek believed in Buthelezi. He thought that it was possible to talk to Buthelezi and Buthelezi put pressure on him".[5] Having established at an early stage close relations with Oliver Tambo and ANC, towards the end of the 1970s Michanek became increasingly anxious to promote Inkatha as a strong, internally based complementary force to the banned liberation movement. Addressing a meeting with SIDA's heads of mission to Southern Africa, in January 1978 he referred to Buthelezi's recent statement that it "was presumptuous of Sweden to act as a judge with regard to those who shall liberate South Africa"[6], adding his personal opinion that

> Buthelezi through the Inkatha movement perhaps represents the strongest organization. [...] [Inkatha] is from my point of view the most promising instrument and it should be strengthened. [...] It is important to back up a leadership inside South Africa.[7]

Michanek—who more than any other official had been responsible for Sweden's assistance to the Southern African liberation movements—left the official aid agency in mid-1979 to join the Ministry for Foreign Affairs.[8] Succeeded by Anders Forsse, he initially stayed on as chairman of the Consultative Committee on Humanitarian Assistance. From that position, he managed on the fringe of established procedures to secure official support to Inkatha, subsequently apportioned in far from conventional ways. Although endorsed by the Church of Sweden, the brief and limited assistance to Buthelezi's Zulu movement was rather the result of

1. Marika Fahlén: Memorandum ('Ansökan om medel från Inkatha för utgivning av en av svarta sydafrikaner kontrollerad tidning'/'Request for funds from Inkatha for the publication of a newspaper controlled by black South Africans'), Ministry for Foreign Affairs, Stockholm, 9 March 1977 (MFA). Felgate was accompanied by Gibson Thula, responsible for information matters in Inkatha.
2. There was no Inkatha representative based in Sweden.
3. No information on the matters discussed between Tambo and Buthelezi has been found in the Swedish archives consulted.
4. Marika Fahlén: Memorandum ('Biståndsansökan från KwaZulu-ledaren Gatsha Buthelezi'/'Request for assistance from the KwaZulu leader Gatsha Buthelezi'), Ministry for Foreign Affairs, Stockholm, 22 November 1977 (MFA). In the meeting with Foreign Minister Söder on 18 November 1977, Buthelezi expressed his well-known opposition to sanctions and disinvestment (ibid.).
5. Interview with Gunnar Helander, p. 288.
6. Cf. below.
7. Marianne Sundh: Memorandum ('Minnesanteckningar från ett särskilt möte under bkc-konferensen om södra Afrika'/'Notes from a special meeting on Southern Africa during the conference with SIDA's heads of mission'), SIDA, Stockholm, 25 January 1978 (SDA). Michanek's views were not unopposed. Influenced by BCM, Bo Kälfors, the Swedish ambassador to Botswana, would in particular criticize the opinion that Buthelezi was an important apartheid opponent, describing him as "a bantustan leader" and "a traitor" (ibid.).
8. After leaving SIDA, Michanek also took up the position as Vice Chairman of IDAF.

Michanek's personal efforts than the expression of an active Swedish political opinion.

Tambo wrote his go-ahead letter after a meeting in London in early October 1977 with Gibson Thula, Chairman of Inkatha's Publicity and Strategy Committee.[1] Also present was Walter Felgate, who immediately proceeded to Stockholm, where he handed over the letter to Michanek and re-introduced the issue of Swedish assistance to *The Nation*.[2]

The press project was thus high on the agenda when Buthelezi himself, Thula and other leading Inkatha officials paid a visit to Sweden in mid-November 1977.[3] During their stay, it was discussed notably with Hans Blix, Under-Secretary of State for International Development Cooperation, and Ernst Michanek at the Ministry for Foreign Affairs on 18 November.[4] In addition to appeals for scholarships in Sweden, Buthelezi submitted a new request in favour of the newspaper. Noting that "Inkatha can no longer manage to finance *The Nation* [...] without outside assistance", an amount of 1.5 to 2.5 MSEK was requested. The Swedish authorities were asked to "treat the subject as urgent, so that Inkatha's members [will] know exactly where they stand".[5]

Although the KwaZulu leader in his meeting at the Foreign Ministry described Inkatha as "an internal branch of ANC"[6]—adding that "I am an ANC man"[7]—in his public appearances he was considerably less subtle, in harsh terms criticizing Sweden's 'selective support' for ANC and calling for direct cooperation with Inkatha. Invited by the Church of Sweden Mission, on 17 November 1977 he gave a public address in Uppsala entitled 'Partnership in Development' in which he stated that

> [w]e are aware of the fact that [the Swedish] government has a praiseworthy record when it comes to supporting some of those who struggle to liberate South Africa. [...] We hope that it will also involve itself in the struggle within the borders of [the country]. [...] Selective support for one South African [b]lack group—deliberately designed to disadvantage another [b]lack group playing an active role in liberation—is no more than a partnership with Pretoria in a white divide and rule strategy. Another way of looking at selective support is to think of it as a conscience money exercise, which is done not caring two hoots about whether the struggle is carried on to success, but in order to be able to say that one does give something after all.[8]

Speaking on the same subject to the Oscar's church congregation in Stockholm the following day, Buthelezi similarly declared that

> Sweden [...] must avoid falling into the pit of [...] white political arrogance, where whites think that by divine right they alone know what is good for [b]lacks. [...] There is a false gospel

1. Letter ('*The Nation* newspaper: Application for financial assistance') from Inkatha National Cultural Liberation Movement to SIDA [no place or date, but received on 18 November 1977] (SDA).
2. Marianne Sundh: Memorandum ('Insatser för stöd till tidningen *The Nation* och utbildningsaktiviteter i Sydafrika'/'Contributions in support of the newspaper *The Nation* and education activities in South Africa'), SIDA/CCHA, [Stockholm], 24 November 1977 (SDA).
3. It is not clear from the available documentation if Buthelezi was invited to Sweden or if he and his delegation went there for the bilateral talks with Oliver Tambo.
4. Marika Fahlén: Memorandum ('Biståndsansökan från KwaZulu-ledaren Gatsha Buthelezi'/'Request for assistance from the KwaZulu leader Gatsha Buthelezi'), Ministry for Foreign Affairs, Stockholm, 22 November 1977 (MFA).
5. Letter ('*The Nation* newspaper: Application for financial assistance') from Inkatha National Cultural Liberation Movement to SIDA [no place or date, but received on 18 November 1977] (SDA).
6. Marika Fahlén: Memorandum ('Biståndsansökan från KwaZulu-ledaren Gatsha Buthelezi'/'Request for assistance from the KwaZulu leader Gatsha Buthelezi'), Ministry for Foreign Affairs, Stockholm, 22 November 1977 (MFA).
7. Ibid. English in the original.
8. Mangosuthu G. Buthelezi: 'Partnership in Development', Address held at A-huset, Drabanten, Uppsala, 17 November 1977 (CSA).

which is spread internationally and which I have encountered more than once on my visits to your country. This is the fallacy that if you give us development aid you are by so doing strengthening the apartheid system. This [...] is a severe indictment on the thinking and integrity of black people. [...] It is much better not to offer any assistance to any of the forces for liberation if offering assistance on a selective basis means playing up one or a number of forces [...] against each other. In some ways, this is worse than what Vorster is doing to us. [...]

Do not be absolutists and, for God's sake, do not play God to us. I would even plead with you that you should be prepared to make mistakes with us rather than to do things for us because you think in your wisdom from so many kilometres from South Africa that [they] are good [...].[1]

In marked contrast to PAC's criticism of Sweden's 'sectarianism' in favour of ANC, the Inkatha leader's views on 'selective support' did have an impact. Quoting extensively from Buthelezi's Stockholm address, Marianne Sundh of the CCHA secretariat argued that his words "carried great weight" and that they "[spoke] for a positive Swedish decision in favour of [the newspaper project]".[2] In the meantime, the secretariat raised the project with Tore Bergman from CSM and Thorsten Månson from CSA. The church representatives were supportive, and it was agreed that the Church of Sweden Aid could serve as a channel for assistance to *The Nation*.[3] This possible intermediary—rather than IDAF—was confirmed in follow-up discussions with Walter Felgate at SIDA in mid-December 1977.[4]

President Kaunda of Zambia—hosting ANC's external headquarters—advocated at the same time support to Buthelezi and Inkatha. In a meeting in Lusaka in early December 1977 with Ernst Michanek, David Wirmark from the Foreign Ministry and the Swedish ambassador Ove Heyman, he was of the opinion that Buthelezi "at present [is] the most important leader at liberty in South Africa" and that he "deserve[s] outside support". Explicitly asked about Inkatha's newspaper project, the Zambian President was "positive to the idea".[5] On CCHA's recommendation—and after contacts between the Liberal Cooperation Minister Ola Ullsten and the Social Democratic opposition leader Olof Palme[6]—soon thereafter the government decided to allocate 800,000 SEK to the project.[7] The ice was finally broken. After years of discussions, official Swedish assistance to Inkatha was eventually granted, albeit indirectly and not sealed by a bilateral agreement.

Controversial Requests

The heaviest crackdown on the South African anti-apartheid movement since the early 1960s occurred in mid-October 1977, when the Pretoria regime summarily banned eighteen opposition organizations. Taking place one month after the assas-

1. Buthelezi cited in Marianne Sundh: Memorandum ('Insatser för stöd till tidningen *The Nation* och utbildningsaktiviteter i Sydafrika'/'Contributions in favour of the newspaper *The Nation* and education activities in South Africa'), SIDA/CCHA, [Stockholm], 24 November 1977 (SDA).
2. Ibid.
3. Ibid.
4. Marianne Sundh: Memorandum ('Minnesanteckningar från sammanträde med Mr. Walter Felgate på SIDA den 15 december 1977 angående stöd till tidningsprojektet *The Nation* i Sydafrika'/'Notes from meeting with Walter Felgate at SIDA on 15 December 1977 re. *The Nation*'), SIDA/CCHA, [Stockholm], 16 December 1977 (SDA).
5. David Wirmark: Memorandum ('Samtal med president Kaunda om Zimbabwe och Sydafrika i Lusaka den 7 december 1977'/'Conversation with President Kaunda about Zimbabwe and South Africa in Lusaka on 7 December 1977'), Ministry for Foreign Affairs, Stockholm, 22 December 1977 (MFA).
6. Ernst Michanek: Memorandum ('Ang. ytterligare stöd till tidningen *The Nation* i Sydafrika'/'Re. additional support to *The Nation*, South Africa'), Ministry for Foreign Affairs, Stockholm, 28 December 1979 (SDA).
7. Ibid. and notes by SIDA's Birgitta Berggren [no place or date, but probably 1981] (SDA). The decision was taken in December 1977.

sination of Steve Biko, the repression primarily targeted the black consciousness movement. Among the organizations declared unlawful on 19 October 1977 were the Black People's Convention (BPC), the Black Community Programmes (BCP), the South African Students Movement (SASM), the South African Students Organization (SASO) and the Soweto Students Representative Council (SSRC). With close links to the BCM organizations, the Christian Institute was also banned. Individual banning orders were in addition issued to its Director, Beyers Naudé, and to several of his colleagues.

Inkatha was not directly affected by the crackdown, which—on the contrary—"cleared the black political arena of most of [its] open competition".[1] Leaving a vacuum to fill, what subsequently appeared as a deathblow to organized black consciousness[2] paved the way for Inkatha at the national level. With a strong and privileged base in KwaZulu, Buthelezi was not slow to take advantage of the situation. In January 1978, he drew together the South African Black Alliance (SABA) between Inkatha, the Coloured Labour Party and the Reform Party, a minority group within the South African Indian Council. Claiming that Inkatha and SABA together were the preeminent opposition force in the country, in 1978-79 the KwaZulu leader assumed increasingly radical positions, launching a number of national political campaigns. In addition to the assistance received for *The Nation*, Inkatha would also seek Swedish support for some of these activities. Beyers Naudé[3] played a crucial role in this context.

Evading his banning orders, Naudé continued to be politically active and to maintain his contacts with the Swedish legation in Pretoria. In late February 1979, he submitted a personally signed memorandum to the legation. Entitled 'A View of the Struggle for Liberation in South Africa', it had the character of a political manifesto in which he on behalf of the Christian Institute not only affirmed that "ANC

---

1. Karis and Gerhart op. cit., p. 267. In their history of black politics in South Africa, they add: "That Inkatha could emerge strengthened after the crackdown raised the question of just what Pretoria hoped to gain by permitting Buthelezi to experiment with strategies for popular mobilization and control. One answer is that Buthelezi's tough talk in South Africa and on trips abroad lent credibility to the image of South Africa as an open society where critics had nothing to fear" (ibid.).
2. To fill the gap after the banning of the BCM organizations, in May 1978 AZAPO was formed. From the outset, it was subject to both state repression and divisive internal debates.
3. Born in 1915—three years before Nelson Mandela—Naudé stands out as one of the foremost anti-apartheid and civil rights activists in South Africa. Belonging to a privileged Afrikaner family, reaching the very highest offices in the Dutch Reformed Church (DRC) and joining the secretive *Broederbond*, for the first 45 years of his life he was fiercely loyal to his *volk* and to its cause. Following the Sharpeville massacre, the bannings of ANC and PAC and the WCC Cottesloe consultation in December 1960—which condemned all forms of racial discrimination and led to a break with the pro-apartheid DRC—Naudé, however, came to reject his past. In 1963, he formed the inter-racial, inter-denominational Christian Institute of Southern Africa. Launching Spro-cas—a 'Study Project on Christianity in Apartheid Society'—with the South African Council of Churches (SACC) in 1969, he soon became involved in the promotion of black theology and the black consciousness movement. He also established early and close relations with Gatsha Buthelezi. A thorn in the government's flesh, in 1975 the Christian Institute was declared an 'affected organization', which *inter alia* meant that it could not receive financial aid from abroad. In October 1977, it was banned altogether. Naudé—who had already had his passport withdrawn in 1972—was at the same time declared 'a banned person', a condition he had to endure for the following seven years. After his unbanning in September 1984, he succeeded Desmond Tutu as General Secretary of SACC the following year. In turn, he was in 1987 succeeded by Frank Chikane. (On the life of Beyers Naudé, see Colleen Ryan: *Beyers Naudé: Pilgrimage of Faith*, David Philip, Cape Town; Wm. B. Eerdmans, Grand Rapids; and Africa World Press, Trenton, 1990). Naudé established early relations with the Church of Sweden and the Church of Sweden Mission, visiting Sweden and the other Nordic countries on several occasions in the 1950s and the 1960s (Interview with Beyers Naudé, pp. 181-82). Although banned and restricted, in South Africa he worked closely with the Swedish legation in Pretoria. As early as in March 1981 the legation described him as "our principal contact" (Letter ('Internbistånd till Sydafrika'/'Internal assistance to South Africa') from Per Lindström, Swedish legation, to the Ministry for Foreign Affairs, Pretoria, 16 March 1981) (SDA). Naudé's role was particularly significant with regard to Swedish support to the United Democratic Front, of which he had been appointed one of the patrons at its formation in 1983. (On his clandestine work and his cooperation with Cecilia Höglund, Birgitta Karlström Dorph and others from the Swedish legation, see below and the interview with Beyers Naudé, pp. 183-84.)

will one day form a government of this country", but also underlined his "personal awareness and recognition of the vital role Inkatha can and wants to play within ANC alliance politics".[1] Little known, the important document by one of South Africa's most prominent anti-apartheid activists—later General Secretary of the South African Council of Churches—deserves to be quoted at some length. Written at a crucial time in the history of the liberation struggle—shortly after the crushing of the black consciousness movement; the appointment of the former Defence Minister Pieter Willem (P.W.) Botha as Prime Minister[2]; and the introduction of his 'total strategy' doctrine—it had a major impact in Sweden, both in confirming the primacy of ANC and giving continued attention to Inkatha.

Naudé's point of departure was that "the African National Congress has already become a centre of gravity which is increasingly attracting small power advantage clusters. This process will continue, and the sooner we realise that unity necessitates harmony with the ANC, the better for all concerned". He then stated:

> The responsibility with which the ANC will wield present and future power in part rests on the extent to which there is local participation in its development at all levels. [...] We believe that not only will an ultimate armed struggle be enhanced by widespread and wide-ranging support at many levels for the ANC, but that the degree of that support at every level will directly limit the scale of violence which may one day have to be employed. [S]upport for the armed struggle would be considerably enhanced when it is recognised that it is the last resort.
>
> [W]e believe that ANC's power advantage would be served [...] if it encouraged participation in non-violent levels of activity. [A] partnership at this juncture of our history between the ANC and the ordinary men and women in South Africa is a phenomen[on] which is emerging. We believe it entirely false [...] to conceive of programmes of activity and projects on the non-violent level as an alternative to the armed struggle [...]. We do not argue this in any sense idealising the armed struggle. We recognise only that such projects which have no visible utility to the ANC necessarily fall within a liberalism which deters progress in the struggle for liberation. [...]
>
> In any field, a person could be deliberately working against the ANC. We believe it is possible to work for the ANC at all levels. [...] The Christian Institute sees itself as having moved—and is continuing to move—into ANC alliance politics. In practical terms, this has meant moving into a closer alliance with Inkatha on the one hand and black consciousness organisations [...] on the other. Every black organisation with [which] we deal has a strong ANC sentiment, either in part or a substantial part [...]. Allied objectives are therefore being pursued, whether or not these organisations have formally adopted an ANC position at the executive level.[3]

Naudé requested at the same time Swedish support in favour of four projects. Two of them were to be implemented under the auspices of the Christian Institute[4],

1. Beyers Naudé: 'A View of the Struggle for Liberation in South Africa', [no place], 28 February 1979 (attached to letter ('Rapportering från Sydafrika'/'Reporting from South Africa') from Gustaf Hamilton, to the Ministry for Foreign Affairs, Pretoria, 28 February 1979) (SDA).
2. Following the resignation of Balthazar John Vorster, P.W. Botha became Prime Minister in September 1978. With greatly increased powers, he was appointed South Africa's first executive President in 1984.
3. Naudé op. cit. PAC was not mentioned at all in the document.
4. The CI requests were in favour of a) an Institute for the Study of Parliamentary Debate, to be established under the auspices of Ravan Press, and b) support to Naudé's communication network, including salaries for three assistants (Letter ('Biståndsansökningar'/'Requests for assistance') from Gustaf Hamilton, Swedish legation, to the Ministry for Foreign Affairs, Pretoria, 2 March 1979) (SDA). Ravan Press was set up as a publishing company in November 1972. Its initial function was to act as a printer for CI's publications. The name of the company—regularly confused with the raven—was made up of elements of the names of its three founders, namely *Ra* from Peter Randall, *va* from Danie van Zyl and *n* from Beyers Naudé. Walter Felgate later joined the company board. According to Michanek, "[SIDA] supported Inkatha [...] through assistance via Ravan Press [...], which on behalf of Buthelezi had particular pages published in South African newspapers as instruction and training material for the illiterate part of the population, particularly in Soweto. That started very early and I was later closely connected to this activity" (Interview with Ernst Michanek, p. 324).

while the other two were submitted on behalf of Inkatha. All four applications were signed by him on 28 February 1979.[1]

The first Inkatha request was in favour of a feasibility study on the introduction of visual aids in KwaZulu schools.[2] The second application was more substantial. It envisaged financial assistance to a citizenship project which Buthelezi originally had launched in connection with the 'independence' of Transkei in 1976.

A central objective of grand apartheid was to deny black South Africans citizenship and residence rights. These rights were only to be exercised in their respective 'homelands'. When Transkei (1976), Bophuthatswana (1977) and Venda (1979)—later also Ciskei (1981)—opted for full, nominal independence, millions of blacks became 'aliens' in 'white' South Africa, with subsequent massive forced removals as a result. Buthelezi, however, refused independence for KwaZulu, which consequently remained under Pretoria's jurisdiction. To the annoyance of the apartheid regime, he offered KwaZulu certificates to anyone in danger of becoming stateless. By joining KwaZulu, they would remain South African citizens.

Inkatha intensified the citizenship campaign in early 1979, notably via *The Nation*. This, in turn, provoked strong reactions from Pretoria and several issues of the newspaper were banned.[3] It was in this situation that Inkatha via Naudé turned to Sweden, requesting financial assistance for the establishment of legal advice bureaux, salaries for regional organizers and distribution of information material. The requested amount for the period from June 1979 to June 1980 was 123,000 Rands, corresponding to 620,000 SEK.[4]

The Naudé-Inkatha applications soon raised questions. In the document quoted above, Naudé had stated that "we [...] seek no funding for projects which have not been fully disclosed to the ANC".[5] This was further underlined when the applications were submitted to the Swedish envoy in Pretoria, Gustaf Hamilton. In his covering letter to the Foreign Ministry in Stockholm, Hamilton noted that "the wishes expressed have been discussed and approved in contacts between ANC, the Christian Institute and Inkatha".[6] This meant through Walter Felgate, who on Naudé's behalf had close relations with Buthelezi and could travel abroad for meetings with ANC. He was also indicated as the person who could give additional information concerning the projects.[7]

In early May 1979, however, Hamilton reported on "growing distrust and suspicion of Felgate and his activities".[8] More importantly, in connection with the annual aid negotiations in Lusaka between Sweden and ANC Tambo explained two weeks later that ANC and Inkatha had recently met, but had not discussed the

1. Letter ('Biståndsansökningar'/'Requests for assistance') from Gustaf Hamilton, Swedish legation, to the Ministry for Foreign Affairs, Pretoria, 2 March 1979 (SDA).
2. Inkatha: 'Proposals for the establishment of a visual aid programme', request signed by Beyers Naudé on 28 February 1979 and attached to ibid.
3. Struggling against bannings and increasing financial constraints, *The Nation* subsequently moved from Johannesburg to Durban, where it was published in Zulu. It suspended publication in 1980.
4. [Inkatha]: 'The South African citizenship project', request signed by Beyers Naudé on 28 February 1979 and attached to letter ('Biståndsansökningar'/'Requests for assistance') from Gustaf Hamilton, Swedish legation, to the Ministry for Foreign Affairs, Pretoria, 2 March 1979 (SDA).
5. Naudé op. cit.
6. Letter ('Biståndsansökningar'/'Requests for assistance') from Gustaf Hamilton, Swedish legation, to the Ministry for Foreign Affairs, Pretoria, 2 March 1979 (SDA).
7. Ibid.
8. Cable from Gustaf Hamilton to the Ministry for Foreign Affairs, Swedish legation, Cape Town, 2 May 1979 (MFA). Hamilton added that "it is difficult to find an explanation for Beyers Naudé's close collaboration with [Felgate]" (ibid.).

projects submitted by Naudé.[1] "[I]t was not true", Tambo said, that ANC had endorsed the requests. Finding the situation "troublesome", he asked the Swedish authorities not to take a decision until Felgate's role had been clarified and ANC had discussed the issue with Inkatha.[2] With this appeal opened a confusing final chapter in the saga of Sweden's relations with Gatsha Buthelezi.

Consent and Break-up

According to Ernst Michanek, in mid-1979—at the time he left SIDA—he received Tambo's endorsement of the Inkatha projects.[3] Still chairing CCHA, in late August he was also informed by Naudé's emissary Roelf Meyer that the doubts concerning Felgate's role as intermediary between the Christian Institute, Inkatha and ANC had been confirmed. Felgate would therefore no longer be involved in project activities.[4] Against this background—and despite strong voices to the contrary; notably that of Bishop Tutu, at the time General Secretary of the South African Council of Churches[5]—Michanek insisted on Swedish assistance to Inkatha, in the first instance for the citizenship project. After contacts with ANC and the Christian Institute, together with SIDA's Birgitta Berggren—secretary to the consultative committee—in September 1979 he met Buthelezi in London for discussions regarding administration of the requested support. The Inkatha leader declared that Gibson Thula—also present during the meeting—was now responsible for the citizenship project. Walter Felgate would in the meantime continue as Managing Director of *The Nation*.[6]

After consultations with five CCHA members—among them Thomas Hammarberg, Gunnar Helander and Pierre Schori[7]—two weeks later through a SIDA

---

1. Anders Möllander: Memorandum ('Samtal med Oliver Tambo, exilpresident för African National Congress, ANC'/'Conversation with Oliver Tambo, ANC President in exile'), Swedish embassy, Lusaka, 30 May 1979 (MFA).

2. Birgitta Berggren: Memorandum ('Minnesanteckningar från samtal med Oliver Tambo, President ANC/SA, den 17 maj 1979'/'Notes from conversation with Oliver Tambo, ANC President, 17 May 1979'), SIDA, Stockholm, 18 May 1979 (SDA). Tambo was accompanied by ANC's Secretary General Alfred Nzo and Thabo Mbeki. In addition to Birgitta Berggren, SIDA's Curt Ström and Anders Möllander from the Swedish embassy took part in the meeting.

3. Ernst Michanek: Memorandum ('Ang. ytterligare stöd till tidningen *The Nation* i Sydafrika'/'Re. additional support to the newspaper *The Nation* in South Africa'), Ministry for Foreign Affairs, Stockholm, 28 December 1979 (SDA). It is not clear whether the endorsement was communicated verbally or in writing. No evidence of a written statement by ANC has been found.

4. Birgitta Berggren: Memorandum ('Minnesanteckningar från samtal med Roelf Meyer, Christian Institute, 27-28 augusti 1979'/'Notes from conversation with Roelf Meyer, Christian Institute, 27-28 August 1979'), SIDA, Stockholm, 3 September 1979 (SDA).

5. Bishop Tutu visited Sweden in August 1979. During a meeting at SIDA, he criticized Buthelezi and his bantustan role, stating that by participating in Pretoria's scheme "you become a creature of the system" (Birgitta Berggren: Memorandum ('Minnesanteckningar från samtal med biskop Desmond Tutu, South African Council of Churches, den 30 augusti 1979'/'Notes from conversation with Bishop Desmond Tutu, South African Council of Churches, 30 August 1979'), SIDA, Stockholm, 31 August 1979; English in the original) (SDA).

6. Birgitta Berggren: Memorandum ('Möte med Chief Gatsha Buthelezi i London den 10 september 1979'/'Meeting with Chief Gatsha Buthelezi in London on 10 September 1979'), SIDA, Stockholm, [no date] (SDA).

7. The other CCHA members consulted were Göran Färm and Billy Olsson. Hammarberg was at the time chairing Amnesty International's executive committee, while Schori was international secretary of the Social Democratic Party.

decision Sweden granted Inkatha in full the requested amount of 620,000 SEK for the citizenship campaign.[1] The following month, 75,000 SEK was also allocated to the visual aids project.[2] Although the amounts were small compared with the direct ANC assistance[3], at a time when the liberation movement was involved in crucial talks with Inkatha the support could be interpreted as an official recognition.[4] This assumption seemed validated when Michanek in response to a personal call by Buthelezi[5] on 2 November 1979—immediately after the aborted ANC-Inkatha consultations—again visited London, where Inkatha handed him a request for renewed assistance to *The Nation*.

The ANC-Inkatha meeting in London on 30-31 October 1979[6] was the climax of ANC's efforts to reach a broad agreement with Chief Buthelezi. Constituting the first formally planned consultation between the two movements[7], it brought together an ANC team which included President Tambo, Secretary General Alfred Nzo, Treasurer General Thomas Nkobi, Thabo Mbeki and Johnny Makatini, and a large Inkatha delegation headed by Buthelezi which comprised most of KwaZulu's cabinet members. Although disagreement was manifest on the issues of armed struggle and sanctions, according to later statements by both parties the talks were cordial and constructive. In 1995, Mbeki observed that "the one outstanding question that remained at the end [...] was how [...] Buthelezi would handle the issue of sanctions. [...] We had agreed to have a second meeting to discuss that".[8]

---

1. SIDA: 'Decision', Office of the Director General, No. 480/79, SIDA, Stockholm, 24 September 1979 (SDA). Submitted by Lennart Wohlgemuth, the decision was signed by SIDA's Acting Director General Bo Göransson.

2. Letter ('Bidrag till Inkatha för förstudie om audio-visuella hjälpmedel'/'Contribution to Inkatha for a feasibility study on audio-visual aids') from Birgitta Berggren to the Swedish legation in Pretoria, SIDA, Stockholm, 29 October 1979 (SDA) and notes by Berggren [no place or date] (SDA).

3. The ANC allocation for the financial year 1979/80 was 16 MSEK.

4. This is also how it was seen by Inkatha. In January 1980—after the split with ANC—Gibson Thula visited the Federal Republic of Germany. Quoting Sweden as an example, in his discussions with the West German authorities he argued in favour of official recognition and assistance (Birgitta Berggren: Note ('Samtal med Eva Heckscher, ambassaden i Bonn, januari 1980'/'Conversation with Eva Heckscher, the [Swedish] embassy in Bonn, January 1980'), [no place or date]) (SDA).

5. Letter from Ernst Michanek to the Foreign Minister, Ministry for Foreign Affairs, Stockholm, 5 November 1979 (SDA).

6. The meeting took place at the time of the London Lancaster House negotiations on Zimbabwe.

7. ANC and Inkatha subsequently presented different versions regarding the initiatives leading to the meeting. On behalf of ANC's National Executive Committee, Tambo briefly said in June 1985 that the meeting was held at the request of Buthelezi ('Political Report of the National Executive Committee to the National Consultative Conference, June 1985' in ANC op. cit. [no year], p. 21). Three months later, the Inkatha leader stated that "by 1978 negotiations had reached the point where I sent a formal delegation to meet with the ANC mission in exile in Stockholm [...]. [W]hen my delegation [conveyed] the request from Oliver Tambo and his executive that we meet formally, I readily agreed" (Buthelezi cited in Karis and Gerhart op. cit., p. 278, note 78). As noted in the text, a number of informal meetings were held towards the end of the 1970s between ANC and Inkatha. Interviewed in 1996, Ernst Michanek explained: "For long years, and on many occasions, Inkatha [...] tried to become clean through different missions to Stockholm and many meetings all over the place. [...] Inkatha and ANC [...] held bilateral meetings [...] in Sweden that were never given any publicity. [...] I had a very important role to play in the setting up of [the] meeting in London. On the basis of earlier discussions—including meetings in Stockholm—Oliver Tambo and Gatsha Buthelezi reached an agreement and also laid down how to treat the different parts of the agreement. However, for reasons that I could discuss for a long time without coming to a conclusion, the tragedy was that Buthelezi [...] openly and clearly broke the fundamentals of the agreement by talking to journalists about what had taken place" (Interview with Ernst Michanek, pp. 324-25).

8. Mbeki cited in 'The man who may succeed Madiba' in *The Star International Weekly*, 27 April-4 May 1995.

No follow-up meeting was, however, held.[1] In what Mbeki later described as "an act of bad faith"[2], immediately after the initial two-day session Buthelezi broke the agreed condition of confidentiality and, as noted by Mbeki, "our people reacted very strongly".[3] In his report to ANC's National Consultative Conference in Kabwe, Tambo later stated:

> Gatsha announced that we had met and explained the purpose, the contents and the results of the meeting to suit his own objectives, much to the delight of the commercial press of South Africa and other forces in the world that had, in fact, concluded that Buthelezi was possibly 'the Muzorewa' of the people of South Africa.[4]

The London consultation failed and a parting of the ways between ANC and Inkatha had eventually come. The split was confirmed in June 1980, when ANC for the first time publicly denounced Buthelezi. More significantly, at the end of July ANC President Oliver Tambo—who throughout the 1970s had consistently spoken in his favour—concluded at a press conference in Lusaka that Buthelezi had "emerged on the side of the enemy against the people".[5]

ANC had long before informed the Swedish embassy in Lusaka of the outcome of the London talks and the break with Buthelezi. In a meeting with ambassador Göran Hasselmark and first secretary Anders Möllander, on 13 December 1979 Nzo and Mbeki "appealed to Sweden not to take any action regarding support to different activities associated with Inkatha".[6] According to the two ANC leaders, "it could not be excluded that Buthelezi let himself be used by the South African government in his contacts with both ANC and Sweden". If that was the case, Pretoria "had probably endorsed the projects for which [Swedish] assistance was solicited".[7]

This, in turn, prompted Möllander to examine the decisions taken concerning Swedish assistance to Inkatha's citizenship campaign and the visual aids project. Noting that contrary to established routines they had not been documented through "customary" memoranda and that recommendations for support had not been reached at regular CCHA meetings—but only through contacts with individual committee members—he wrote a highly critical letter to the Ministry for Foreign Affairs.[8]

---

1. In fact, it was only on 19 September 1990—eleven years later—that high-ranking officials from ANC and Inkatha again held a formal meeting, this time to discuss the violence in Natal (ANC-IFP: 'Joint statement: Meeting between ANC and Inkatha Freedom Party delegations', Johannesburg, 19 September 1990). These contacts paved the way for a meeting between Nelson Mandela and Gatsha Buthelezi in Durban on 29 January 1991, where the IFP leader stated that the origins of what he called "the Inkatha/ANC conflict" lay in the "fateful meeting" in London in 1979 (cited in Karis and Gerhart op. cit., p. 271).

2. Mbeki cited in 'The man who may succeed Madiba' in *The Star International Weekly*, 27 April-4 May 1995.

3. Ibid.

4. 'Political Report of the National Executive Committee to the National Consultative Conference, June 1985' in ANC op. cit. [no year], p. 21.

5. Tambo cited in Karis and Gerhart op. cit., p. 274. In the interview quoted above, Michanek noted: "Oliver Tambo knew Gatsha Buthelezi very well from his younger days, but he could never understand why Buthelezi did what he did. [...] [He] told me several times: 'I cannot understand Gatsha. How can he do a thing like that?' But he did not say: 'I cannot see the man' or 'I hate the man'. Not at all. Instead, he said: 'How can we get together again?' That was important. However, the racial position that PAC had taken had a parallel within Inkatha and that was, of course, impossible for ANC to accept" (Interview with Ernst Michanek, p. 325).

6. Letter ('Samtal med ANC-ledare om Inkatha (Sydafrika)'/'Conversation with ANC leaders about Inkatha (South Africa)') from Göran Hasselmark, Swedish ambassador to Zambia, to the Ministry for Foreign Affairs, Swedish embassy, Lusaka, 18 December 1979 (SDA).

7. Anders Möllander: Memorandum ('ANC-Sydafrika om Inkatha'/'ANC South Africa on Inkatha'), Swedish embassy, Lusaka, 18 December 1979 (SDA).

8. Letter ('Sverige och den sydafrikanska bantustan-politiken'/'Sweden and South Africa's bantustan policy') from Anders Möllander to the Ministry for Foreign Affairs, Swedish embassy, Lusaka, 19 December 1979 (SDA). Möllander also warned against Swedish support to the International University Exchange Fund.

Despite ANC's appeal and Möllander's criticism, ambassador Michanek—the CCHA chairman—remained, however, committed to supporting Inkatha. After receiving the movement's application for renewed assistance to *The Nation*, he informed Oliver Tambo that it was "unacceptable that ANC by delaying [a decision] [...] would exercise a kind of veto [...] vis-à-vis the Swedish authorities".[1] Outside the agenda, he then verbally presented the request at a CCHA meeting in mid-December 1979.[2] Noting that no committee member was actively against the proposal, he subsequently recommended the government to allocate "without any delay" 350,000 SEK to the Inkatha newspaper, adding that "the decision should not be made public".[3]

The Liberal Foreign Minister Ola Ullsten accepted Michanek's views. Yet again without the usual background documentation and comments from the Swedish embassies in Southern Africa, on 17 January 1980 Ullsten signed the formal decision granting Inkatha the proposed amount in favour of *The Nation*.[4] The decision closed the Swedish Inkatha saga. No more official assistance would from then on be extended to Gatsha Buthelezi, Inkatha or the Inkatha Freedom Party. Michanek later acknowledged that

> [i]t was very painful to me personally, as well as to the Church of Sweden and others who had been involved, to come to the conclusion after some time that we could not continue our cooperation with Buthelezi.[5]

An Exceptional Parenthesis

The official Swedish financial assistance allocated to Inkatha between December 1977 and January 1980 amounted in total to 1.8 MSEK. In comparison with the ANC support, the assistance was modest, corresponding to 5 per cent of the grants to the liberation movement.[6]

Nevertheless, the Inkatha assistance stands out as an exceptional parenthesis in the history of Sweden's involvement with the liberation struggles in Southern Africa. It is, in the first place, only in the case of South Africa that a legal, internally based political organization was granted direct official support. Secondly, it was not motivated by humanitarian needs, such as legal aid or refugee assistance. Although Inkatha was closely linked to the KwaZulu bantustan and not recognized by OAU or the United Nations, the support was granted for its political work.[7] Thirdly, the assistance was not the result of popular or parliamentary demands, nor the effect of a particular political party effort. Albeit granted under Fälldin's first and second coalition governments, it was without objections tacitly accepted by the Social

1. Ernst Michanek: Memorandum ('Ang. ytterligare stöd till tidningen *The Nation* i Sydafrika'/'Re. additional support to the newspaper *The Nation* in South Africa'), Ministry for Foreign Affairs, Stockholm, 28 December 1979 (SDA).
2. Ibid.
3. Ibid.
4. Ministry for Foreign Affairs: 'Decision' ('Stöd till tidningen *The Nation* i Sydafrika'/'Support to the newspaper *The Nation* in South Africa'), Ministry for Foreign Affairs, Stockholm, 17 January 1980 (SDA). Taken by Foreign Minister Ullsten, the decision was countersigned by ambassador Michanek.
5. Interview with Ernst Michanek, p. 325.
6. The allocations to ANC under bilateral agreements amounted in total during the three-year period 1977/78-1979/80 to 36 MSEK.
7. Birgitta Berggren later commented: "I had a very strong feeling that [the support] was [given] to strengthen the position of Gatsha Buthelezi" (Interview with Birgitta Berggren, p. 258).

Democratic opposition.[1] Neither the government nor the opposition actively promoted Inkatha. Instead, the support was primarily due to one senior official's lobbying. Finally, the assistance was surrounded by political ambiguity and lack of
administrative transparency. In the latter respect, it was not only exceptional, but
quite unique.

Conflicting messages from Oliver Tambo, Gatsha Buthelezi, Beyers Naudé and
other central actors were for many years behind the ambiguities surrounding ANC,
KwaZulu and Inkatha. ANC's obvious ambivalence was in this context particularly
problematic. Soon after the break with Buthelezi, this was acknowledged by the
ANC President. Visiting Sweden together with Thomas Nkobi and Thabo Mbeki,
in a meeting with Foreign Ministry and SIDA officials in mid-April 1980 Tambo
discussed his organization's reluctance to unequivocally endorse Swedish assistance
to *The Nation*. Noting that "it had been difficult to comment on the matter", he
explained that "ANC could not be instrumental in creating a weapon against
itself".[2]

The non-transparent process concerning Sweden's support to the Inkatha
projects in 1979-80 has been noted. Decisions were taken without proper administrative preparations, charging SIDA with the task of apportioning the allocated
funds according to Inkatha's secretive instructions and via a number of unfamiliar
intermediaries, notably church organizations in the Netherlands. The result was far
from edifying. Disbursements from SIDA were made between September 1979 and
July 1980. As late as in March 1981, however, SIDA had not "received any information regarding implementation of the projects".[3] What is more, in some instances
the Dutch intermediaries lost track of the transfers from Sweden.[4] Responsible for
the transactions, SIDA's Birgitta Berggren stated in a retrospective memorandum on
the support to Inkatha in March 1981 that

> SIDA should not be instructed to carry out such secret transfers. [...] [I]t does not have the
> [means] to monitor with sufficient efficiency how the funds are channelled. [...] A Swedish
> government agency is not suited for this kind of activity.[5]

By that time, however, there were no longer any openings for Swedish official assistance to Inkatha or other 'alternative' or 'complementary' forces. After ANC's
break with Buthelezi and the parallel disclosure of Pretoria's penetration of the
International University Exchange Fund, the already privileged bilateral cooperation with ANC became unchallenged. Developments in South Africa further confirmed this stand. In mid-1980, Inkatha did not join the 'Free Mandela-campaign'
launched by the newspaper *The Post*, and at its Central Committee meeting in July
Buthelezi turned against ANC, stating that its "problems [were] caused [...] by a

---

1. In December 1977, Olof Palme was consulted before the decision was taken to support *The Nation*. Similarly,
   in September 1979 the party's international secretary Pierre Schori endorsed official assistance to Inkatha's citizenship project.
2. Birgitta Berggren: Memorandum ('Minnesanteckningar från samtal på SIDA den 14 april 1980 med president
   Oliver Tambo, African National Congress/South Africa'/'Notes from conversation at SIDA on 14 April 1980
   with President Oliver Tambo, ANC'), SIDA, Stockholm, 21 April 1980 (SDA). SIDA's Director General
   Anders Forsse hosted the meeting. The Ministry for Foreign Affairs was represented by Jan Eliasson and
   Anders Bjurner. While two CCHA members were present, the committee chairman Ernst Michanek did not
   participate.
3. Birgitta Berggren: Memorandum ('Utbetalning av bidrag till Inkatha, Sydafrika'/'Disbursement of contributions to Inkatha, South Africa'), SIDA, Stockholm, 4 March 1981 (SDA). It could be noted that *The Nation*
   suspended publication in October 1980.
4. Ibid.
5. Ibid.

Welcomed as a Head of State: Prime Minister Thorbjörn Fälldin with ANC President Oliver Tambo, Stockholm, March 1981 (Photo: Jan Collsiöö/ Pressens Bild)

dependence on a motley set of funding organisations and also the fact of being away from South Africa for nearly twenty years [...], operating in a vacuum forced by [...] exile".[1] In the process, Buthelezi and Inkatha lost the credibility gained through earlier identification with ANC. In a study of the movement, Sweden's envoy to South Africa, Gustaf Hamilton, noted in September 1980 that "Buthelezi's role has [....] been written off by politically conscious blacks. Many go as far as asserting that [his career] as a politician is over".[2]

Closely associated with the apartheid regime and white right wing organizations, Buthelezi's IFP would only reluctantly be drawn into South Africa's transition towards democracy. Like PAC—but from the opposite side of the political spectrum—it denounced Sweden's assistance to ANC. In January 1993, for example, the IFP National Chairman Frank Mdlalose stated that "it was a pity [that] Sweden had not taken a leaf out of the United States book by supporting democracy rather than those it would like to see in power".[3]

Joining the election process at the very last minute, IFP eventually received 10.5 per cent of the votes at the April 1994 polls, placing the party in third position after ANC (62.7 per cent) and the National Party (20.4 per cent). Ninety per cent of the votes for IFP were cast in KwaZulu-Natal, where it subsequently formed the provincial government. The national results at the same time assured Inkatha of participation in South Africa's government of national unity. In May 1994, President Mandela appointed Chief Mangosuthu Gatsha Buthelezi Minister of Home Affairs.

1. Buthelezi cited in Cecilia Höglund: Memorandum ('Kritiska röster mot Inkatha och zululedaren Buthelezi'/ 'Critical voices against Inkatha and the Zulu leader Buthelezi'), Swedish legation, Pretoria, 17 September 1980 (SDA).
2. Gustaf Hamilton: Memorandum ('Inkatha'), Swedish legation, Pretoria, 17 September 1980 (SDA).
3. Mdlalose cited in 'IFP hits Sweden's aid to ANC' in *The Citizen*, 13 January 1993.

Black Consciousness, IUEF and 'Operation Daisy'

Sweden and the Black Consciousness Movement

While PAC never received official Swedish support and Inkatha as a complementary force was eventually accorded limited and transient assistance, in the mid-1970s it was the black consciousness movement (BCM)[1] which to many appeared as an alternative to ANC. At a time when ANC in exile was still struggling to regain the political initiative, foreign affairs officials and trade unionists alike often highlighted the significance of the vibrant, internal and legal BCM opposition.[2]

No BCM organization would, however, receive direct official support. Mandated to "investigate the possibilities of supporting [the internal opposition] with Swedish assistance"[3], the 1976 CCHA fact-finding mission did not recommend bilateral aid in favour of BCM. Contrary to widespread assertions, neither did Olof Palme's Social Democratic government boost the movement as an alternative to ANC. As no political party submitted parliamentary motions in favour of BCM, this policy was maintained by the Fälldin and Ullsten governments. Although voices were raised in support of black consciousness, the Africa Groups, similarly, did not promote the movement.[4] As later stated by Sören Lindh: "We could per-

---

1. In this study, BCM refers to the broader political movement and to its various constituent parts—notably BCP, BPC, SASM and SASO—guided by the philosophy of black consciousness. In South Africa, there was no organization as such called the Black Consciousness Movement. In 1979, however, a group of exiles in London established the Black Consciousness Movement of Azania (BCMA). Chairing its Central Committee, the former Robben Island prisoner Mosibudi Mangena later represented BCMA in Botswana and Zimbabwe. In a surprise move, Mangena—since 1994 President of AZAPO—was appointed Deputy Minister of Education by President Mbeki in January 2001.
2. Bo Kälfors, Sweden's ambassador to Botswana, maintained a markedly pro-BCM stand. In April 1977, for example, he questioned the official assistance to ANC. Asserting that "it appears [...] that ANC more or less [...] has had its day", he recommended instead that "priority [...] is given to the organizations within the black consciousness movement" (Letter from Bo Kälfors to SIDA, Gaborone, 13 April 1977, cited in letter ('African National Congress' ställning i Sydafrika'/'ANC's position in South Africa') from Anders Möllander to the Ministry for Foreign Affairs, Swedish embassy, Lusaka, 19 May 1977) (SDA).
3. Ann Wilkens: Memorandum ('Intryck från Sydafrika: Sammanfattning'/'Impressions from South Africa: A summary'), CCHA/Ministry for Foreign Affairs, Stockholm, 21 April 1976 (SDA).
4. It was only in November 1974 that the Africa Groups recognized ANC as "the leading liberation movement in South Africa". The decision was confirmed by the first national AGIS congress in May 1975. After the Soweto uprising, BCM was given increasing attention. In November 1976, for example, *Afrikabulletinen* published an interview with Tsietsi Mashinini, as head of the Soweto Students Representative Council one of the most prominent leaders of the revolt. Representing the BCM-aligned South African Students Movement (SASM), in the interview Mashinini—who went into exile in August 1976—was extremely critical of ANC and PAC, *inter alia* stating that they were "completely obliterated among the students in South Africa" and that they had "nothing to do with the struggle". He also criticized ANC for refusing to recognize BCM as a liberation movement ('Studentledare: Så Startade Revolten i Soweto'/'Student Leader: Thus Began the Soweto Uprising' in *Afrikabulletinen*, No. 35, November 1976, p. 10). At a time when AGIS' relations with ANC were still uneasy, the publication of the interview in the solidarity organization's official organ was censured by the ANC representative Sobizana Mngqikana (AGIS: 'Verksamhetsberättelse för AGIS' styrelse 1976-77'/ 'Activity report by the AGIS board 1976-77' [no place or date], p. 24) (AGA). Stressing the role played by BPC and SASO, at the national congress in Uppsala in May 1977 delegates from the Umeå Africa Group criticized AGIS' "exclusive support for ANC", demanding that it should be "broadened to cover the entire liberation struggle" (AGIS: 'Kongresshäfte 77'/'Congress compendium 77' [no place or date], p. 39) (AGA). The motion was, however, defeated. The death of Steve Biko in September and the crackdown on the BCM organizations in October 1977 subsequently left the black consciousness movement in disarray. ANC's leading role would from then on not be called into question.

haps see [BCM] as John the Baptist, coming before Jesus. [B]ut they were not Jesus".[1]

Nevertheless, with links to Swedish students and youth[2] the movement inspired by Steve Biko was seen as a positive force. From the early 1970s, official funds were indirectly channelled to various BCM organizations via international NGOs, notably the International University Exchange Fund (IUEF) and the World University Service (WUS).[3] Sweden was the main contributor to both of them. Together with Denmark and Norway, it stood for almost the entire budget of the two organizations' South Africa programmes. They, in turn, largely focused on the black consciousness movement. As late as in March 1979—one and a half years after the banning of the Black People's Convention (BPC) and the other constituent BCM organizations—Ranwedzi ('Harry') Nengwekhulu[4], BPC's representative in Botswana, estimated that the three Scandinavian countries via IUEF and WUS contri-

---

1. Interview with Sören Lindh, pp. 307-08.
2. Immediately after the formation in 1948 of the apartheid Nationalist government, the Swedish National Union of Students (SFS) started to channel support to the non-racial National Union of South African Students (NUSAS) (see Sellström Volume I, pp. 85-91). The South African Students Organization (SASO)—BCM's first organized expression—was formed in July 1969 by black students previously affiliated to NUSAS. Several of the founding members—notably Steve Biko himself—studied at the University of Natal Medical School, which via SFS and NUSAS had established an exchange programme with Lund university. In 1970-71, Aubrey Mokoape, SASO's Assistant Director of Publications, studied in Lund under this programme (cf. the interview with Barney Pityana, p. 187). From the financial year 1969/70, SIDA supported WUS' scholarship programme for South African black medical students (Kerstin Oldfeldt: Memorandum ('Bilateral flyktingstipendiering och bidragsgivning till institutioner för flyktingutbildning'/'Bilateral scholarships to refugees and institutional contributions for refugee education'), CCHA/SIDA [no place], 22 May 1970) (SDA). The Swedish youth movement had fewer direct links with BCM. In the mid-1970s, the National Council of Swedish Youth (SUL) became, however, a member of the IUEF Assembly.
3. Swedish contributions to SASO via IUEF were extended from 1972/73, when an amount of 75,000 SEK was allocated (Stig Abelin: Memorandum ('International University Exchange Fund (IUEF)'), CCHA/SIDA, Stockholm, 25 May 1972) (SDA). The support to SASO via WUS started one year earlier. In addition to 50,000 for scholarships, in 1971/72 25,000 SEK was earmarked for SASO's community health programmes (Stig Abelin: Memorandum ('World University Service (WUS)'), CCHA/SIDA, Stockholm, 31 May 1972) (SDA). It should be recalled that it was not until February 1973 that the Swedish authorities decided to grant ANC direct assistance and that the first contribution only amounted to 150,000 SEK.
4. Within the BCM leadership, Nengwekhulu established particularly close contacts with Sweden. A founding member of SASO, he later served as its National Organizer. Together with Steve Biko, Barney Pityana and five other BCM leaders, he was in March 1973 declared a banned person. The bans restricted the eight for five years to their respective home districts, forbidding them to meet with more than one person at a time. Nothing they said or wrote could be published or publicly quoted. In September 1973, Nengwekhulu crossed the border into Botswana, where he subsequently represented SASO and the wider black consciousness movement. Experiencing "the need to get resources in order to provide scholarships and cater for a growing number of BC[M] people outside South Africa", he soon established close relations with IUEF (Interview with Barney Pityana, p. 187). He was also in regular contact with the Swedish embassy in Gaborone. As the most senior BCM leader in exile, Nengwekhulu visited Sweden for the first time in March 1974, strongly advising SIDA against any support to Gatsha Buthelezi (Marianne Sundh: Memorandum ('Framställning från Svenska Kyrkans Mission om bidrag till humanitära insatser bland apartheidpolitikens offer i Sydafrika'/'Request from the Church of Sweden Mission for contributions towards humanitarian efforts in favour of the victims of the apartheid policy in South Africa'), SIDA, Stockholm, 31 May 1974) (SDA). Returning in late 1976, on 1 December he was received at the Ministry for Foreign Affairs, predicting that SASO and BPC would be banned within the near future. It was therefore necessary to prepare for an underground existence. It was equally necessary to plan for armed struggle against the apartheid regime. However, BPC could not offer its members military training. Against this background, it was seeking assistance from ANC or PAC. Although ANC according to Nengwekhulu was dominated by the Communist Party, the ideological affinities with the movement led by Oliver Tambo were greater than those with PAC. BCM could thus not subscribe to PAC's exclusion of Indians and coloureds from the oppressed black majority. PAC's relations with Jonas Savimbi's UNITA movement in Angola were another divisive factor (Ann Wilkens: Memorandum ('Samtal med företrädare för 'black consciousness'-rörelsen i Sydafrika'/'Conversation with a representative from the black consciousness movement in South Africa'), Ministry for Foreign Affairs, Stockholm, 27 January 1977) (MFA). In 1977, Nengwekhulu was authorized by the internal BPC leadership to establish a formal office in Botswana. With IUEF assistance, he was at the same time closely involved in preparing meetings between Steve Biko and the ANC leadership.

buted 95 per cent of the funds towards his organization's underground activities in South Africa.[1]

In marked contrast to ANC, PAC, Inkatha and the other Southern African nationalist organizations discussed in this study[2], BCM did not develop an active policy towards Sweden. There was no authorized representative in the country, and the visits made over the years were extremely few.[3] When visits did take place, they either had the character of courtesy calls or were undertaken for purposes of general information.[4] Furthermore, at no time did any BCM organization—directly from South Africa, via representatives in exile or through contacts with the aid authorities in Stockholm—submit a formal application for bilateral support. As far as can be ascertained, the same approach was applied vis-à-vis the Africa Groups and the wider anti-apartheid movement. Neither CCHA nor AGIS, the churches[5] or other concerned NGOs were prevailed upon to take a stand on a direct call for assistance. Although enjoying a fair amount of goodwill, overshadowed by ANC and other diplomatically more active actors the black consciousness movement never established a platform in Sweden.

Even so, on account of increasing contributions via IUEF and WUS and the active, high-profile role played by IUEF's Swedish Director Lars-Gunnar Eriksson, in the mid-1970s Sweden became indirectly associated with policies aimed at establishing BCM as a 'third force'. Albeit not presented in such terms, in May 1976—before the Soweto uprising—at a meeting in Lusaka with Anders Bjurner from the Swedish embassy Oliver Tambo, for example, regretted that IUEF "uncritically" assisted the BCM organizations. SASO, in particular, had thereby "come to believe that it in the eyes of the international opinion was a very important force and therefore—contrary to the situation in the past—did not have to consult with ANC".[6] "With very great intensity", Tambo "appealed" to the Social Democratic govern-

1. Elisabeth Michanek: Memorandum ('Möte med Harry Nengwekhulu, Black People's Convention (BPC), i Gaborone den 7 mars 1979'/'Meeting with Harry Nengwekhulu, BPC, Gaborone, 7 March 1979'), Swedish embassy, Gaborone, 13 March 1979 (SDA). Explaining that the banned BPC through some 50 legal organizations was involved *inter alia* in health programmes, adult education, literacy campaigns and leadership training, Nengwekhulu particularly stressed the role of IUEF, with which he maintained "excellent relations". He also stated that it was easier to work with ANC inside the country than in exile. At the time of his visit to the Swedish Foreign Ministry in December 1976, he, finally, characterized Gatsha Buthelezi as "the most dangerous man in South Africa" (ibid.).
2. In the case of South Africa, even the marginal Unity Movement (UMSA) was in this context considerably more active.
3. In Sweden on a university exchange programme, in February 1971 SASO's Aubrey Mokoape paid a visit to SIDA. Keen to receive Swedish support for SASO's activities, he, however, stressed that for security reasons any assistance should be channelled via WUS (Hallgerd Dyrssen: Memorandum ('Minnesanteckningar från besök av Mr. Aubrey Mokoape, SASO, den 10 februari 1971'/'Notes from visit by Mr. Aubrey Mokoape, SASO, 10 February 1971'), SIDA, Stockholm, 18 February 1971) (SDA). Based in Botswana, Ranwedzi Nengwekhulu visited SIDA in March 1974 and the Ministry for Foreign Affairs in December 1976. On both occasions, he raised general political issues without requesting direct assistance.
4. Apart from Nengwekhulu, the BCM representatives who visited Sweden after the Soweto uprising did, in fact, also represent ANC. This was in December 1976 the case with SASO's Vice-President Nkosazana Dlamini and in October 1977 with Tebello Motapanyane, former Secretary General of SASM (Marika Fahlén: Memorandum ('Samtal med Tebello Motapanyane, tidigare generalsekreterare för SASM, Sydafrika'/'Conversation with Tebello Motapanyane, ex-Secretary General of SASM, South Africa'), Ministry for Foreign Affairs, Stockholm, 21 October 1977) (MFA). Motapanyane was invited to Sweden by the Africa Groups.
5. There were, however, several possible openings for Swedish church support. With close, initial links to the University Christian Movement, BCM developed a number of activities in cooperation with the Christian Institute (CI) and the South African Council of Churches. Although Beyers Naudé and CI channelled requests to Sweden on behalf of Inkatha, no similar initiatives were taken in favour of BCM.
6. Letter ('Samtal med O. Tambo, ANC's t.f. ordförande'/'Conversation with O. Tambo, ANC Acting President') from Anders Bjurner, Swedish embassy, to the Ministry for Foreign Affairs, Lusaka, 21 May 1976 (MFA).

ment to coordinate its anti-apartheid support with ANC.[1] During a visit to Sweden a year later, the ANC President made the same request to the non-socialist government.[2]

With Lars-Gunnar Eriksson in a crucial intermediary position, towards the end of the 1970s over and above the bilateral relationship Sweden and ANC would positively and negatively relate to IUEF, BCM and the wider struggle against the apartheid regime. Never documented in this context is the effort to bring Steve Biko, Oliver Tambo and Olof Palme together in Botswana in early September 1977. Much better known is the penetration of IUEF by South Africa's security services, which in early 1980 put an end to Swedish contributions to international NGOs not coordinated with ANC. At a time when the black consciousness movement was thrown into a deep crisis, contrary to the designs of the apartheid regime the end result of the IUEF débâcle was consolidated relations between Sweden and ANC.

Black Consciousness before Soweto

Largely inspired by the 1960s black power movement in the United States—but also by the writings of Frantz Fanon and the policies of Julius Nyerere in Tanzania—the philosophy of black consciousness was developed towards the end of the decade by Steve Biko[3], Barney Pityana[4] and other young black university students

---

1. Ibid.
2. Marika Fahlén: Memorandum ('Besök av ordföranden i den sydafrikanska befrielserörelsen ANC, Oliver Tambo'/'Visit by the President of the South African liberation movement ANC, Oliver Tambo'), Ministry for Foreign Affairs, Stockholm, 31 August 1977 (MFA).
3. Stephen Bantu Biko—one of South Africa's most gifted leaders—was born in King William's Town in the eastern Cape in 1946. After secondary studies at the liberal Catholic St. Francis College at Mariannhill in Natal, in 1966 he entered the University of Natal non-European medical school in Durban. Initially active in NUSAS, he was soon convinced that black students needed their own organization and together with Pityana, Nengwekhulu and other student leaders formed SASO in July 1969. Biko became its first President. Leaving his medical studies in mid-1972, he started to work for the recently established BCP in Durban. Together with seven other BCM leaders, in March 1973 he was served with banning orders. Restricted to his home district of King William's Town, he was, nevertheless, actively involved in a number of political initiatives, such as the Zanempilo clinic outside King William's Town. After the Soweto uprising, he was detained between August and December 1976. Finally, in August 1977 he was arrested once again, subsequently becoming the forty-sixth person to be killed in security police detention in South Africa. On Steve Biko, see Hilda Bernstein: *No. 46-Steve Biko*, International Defence & Aid Fund, London, 1978; Biko op. cit.; Karis and Gerhart op. cit.; Lindy Wilson: 'Bantu Stephen Biko: A Life' in Barney Pityana, Mamphela Ramphele, Malusi Mpumlwana and Lindy Wilson (eds): *Bounds of Possibility: The Legacy of Steve Biko & Black Consciousness*, David Philip Publishers, Cape Town, and Zed Books, London and New Jersey, 1991, pp. 15-77; and Donald Woods: *Biko*, Paddington Press, New York and London, 1978.
4. Pityana was born in Port Elizabeth in 1945. While studying law at the University College of Fort Hare, he became Regional Director of the University Christian Movement. Working in tandem with Steve Biko—a former secondary school classmate—Pityana was expelled from Fort Hare in 1968. The following year, he was one of the founders of SASO, becoming its Secretary General in July 1970. Like Biko, he was served with banning orders in March 1973, for the next five years restricting him to his home district in Port Elizabeth. Constantly harassed by the security police, Pityana left South Africa for the United Kingdom in 1978. Subsequently joining ANC, in the UK he resumed his academic studies. Shifting from law to religious studies and theology, he attended the universities of London and Oxford. Ordained as a priest in the Church of England in 1983, three years later he started to work for the World Council of Churches' Programme to Combat Racism (PCR) in Geneva. In 1988, Pityana was appointed Director of PCR. From the late 1980s actively involved with ANC's Department of Religious Affairs and Inter-Faith Chaplaincy, after the democratic opening in 1990 he returned to South Africa. In 1995, he defended his doctoral dissertation in theology at the University of Cape Town, and the following year he was inducted as Chairman of South Africa's Human Rights Commission (see also the interview with Barney Pityana, pp. 186-90 and 'A Steve Biko for the '90s' in Mark Gevisser: *Portraits of Power: Profiles in a Changing South Africa*, David Philip Publishers, Cape Town, in association with *Mail & Guardian*, Johannesburg, 1996, pp. 16-20).

of the post-Sharpeville generation.[1] As stated by the former BCM activists Moko-ape, Mtintso and Nhlapo,

> [t]he cornerstone of Biko's thinking was that black people must look inwardly at themselves, reflect on their history, examine the reasons for past failures and ask themselves [...]: 'What makes the black man fail to tick?'[2]

Emphasizing assertiveness and self-esteem, under the slogan 'Black man, you are on your own!' black consciousness maintained that the oppression of blacks was both psychological and physical, respectively described as 'Phase One' and 'Phase Two'.[3] During an initial period, the efforts focused on the psychological aspects. Extending until early 1973—when the apartheid regime eventually intervened against the movement by banishing Biko and other BCM leaders[4]—this period saw the formation of the student organization SASO in July 1969 and of the broader political vehicle BPC three years later.[5] Perhaps more importantly, through funds raised mainly by the Christian Institute, in January 1972 the Black Community Programmes (BCP) branch was launched, paving the way for a number of self-help projects and activities, ranging from community health programmes to leadership training schemes.[6] It was above all to these initiatives that the Scandinavian IUEF and WUS contributions were channelled.[7]

As the self-help programmes, despite increasing government harassment, were consolidated and expanded—and ANC through Chris Hani, Thabo Mbeki and others established contacts with BCM from Lesotho, Botswana and Swaziland—

---

1. It was not until 1970 that the term 'black consciousness' entered SASO's discourse, and it was only in July 1971 that SASO in its Policy Manifesto for the first time set out an explicit definition of the term: "Black consciousness is an attitude of mind, a way of life. [...] The basic tenet of [b]lack [c]onsciousness is that the [b]lack man must reject all value systems that seek to make him a foreigner in the country of his birth and reduce his basic human dignity. [...] The [b]lack man must build up his own value systems, see himself as self-defined and not as defined by others" (cited in Karis and Gerhart op. cit., p. 100). Most importantly, at the same time the manifesto declared that "South Africa is a country in which both [b]lack and [w]hite live and shall continue to live together" (ibid.). On this crucial point—the main reason for PAC's breakaway from ANC—the founding fathers of BCM shared the views expressed in the Freedom Charter. Stressing the fundamental importance of black 'psychological liberation' and self-reliance, like PAC they were, however, opposed to institutionalized cooperation with whites. Emphasis was on race, not class. Nevertheless, as their understanding of 'black' included South Africa's coloured and Indian population groups the philosophy was essentially different from PAC's 'African chauvinism'. Many South African coloured and Indian politicians who eventually joined ANC started their careers in the black consciousness movement. This is, for example, the case with the future Western Cape UDF leader Cheryl Carolus and the COSATU General Secretary Jay Naidoo.
2. Keith Mokoape, Thenjiwe Mtintso and Welile Nhlapo: 'Towards the Armed Struggle' in Pityana, Ramphele, Mpumlwana and Wilson (eds) op. cit., p. 138.
3. Ibid.
4. The philosophy of black consciousness was initially tolerated by the government as it seemed to fit in with its ideology of 'separate development'. On BCM, see, for example, Karis and Gerhart op. cit., pp. 89-188 and 311-43 and—for insiders' views—Pityana, Ramphele, Mpumlwana and Wilson (eds) op. cit.
5. The BCM-aligned Black Allied Workers Union (BAWU) was formed after the historic Durban strikes in early 1973. Led by Drake Koka, BAWU was considerably less successful than BCM's student organizations and BCP. On the question of Sweden and the promotion of a 'third force' in South Africa, it should be noted that no assistance was extended to BAWU while the SACP-inspired Food and Canning Workers Union was indirectly supported through LO/TCO and the exiled SACTU directly by the Swedish government.
6. BCM's leadership training programme was particularly successful and of lasting importance. According to Karis and Gerhart, "[n]ot since the Communist Party had developed worker night schools as a way to teach, recruit and motivate party cadres had such an effective method of organized politicization been applied among black South Africans" (Karis and Gerhart op. cit., p. 112). Among those who attended the 'formation schools' were, for example, the future UDF National Publicity Secretary, Patrick 'Terror' Lekota, and the General Secretary of the National Union of Mineworkers, Cyril Ramaphosa.
7. Cf. Pityana: "[O]ur first breakthrough came when Ben Khoapa and Steve Biko managed to [...] establish [...] BCP. Major funding was now coming to a body that was black. So, when Steve Biko was banished to King William's Town, he was able—as part of [BCP]—to establish all the projects that were based there, including the clinic and the study programmes. The funding for this came from the Nordic countries through IUEF and WUS" (Interview with Barney Pityana, p. 187).

the June 1976 Soweto uprising and the ensuing crackdown would dramatically bring the more fundamental political issue of physical oppression to the fore. While it was relatively uncomplicated to address 'Phase One', it was considerably more difficult—and in the longer term divisive—to approach 'Phase Two'. This required a clear strategic objective and definite tactics with regard to alliances and methods of struggle. Mokoape, Mtintso and Nhlapo have recalled how

> the questions relating to 'Phase [Two]' went largely unanswered [...] in BC[M] circles. [I]t was often stated that when the time came, 'the people will decide'. However, within informal sessions there was a strong recognition of the need for armed struggle. Yet, even those who agreed that this was an absolute necessity were still baffled by the 'how'.[1]

From as early as 1973—when groups of BCM members left South Africa to settle in Botswana—the answers to these questions were increasingly sought through informal contacts with ANC and PAC in exile, which both had armed structures and access to military training facilities. Acknowledging the political authority of the older movements, but convinced that "[b]lack [c]onsciousness provided a common programme [...] with which the entire liberation [process] could identify"[2], by the mid-1970s Biko and Pityana came to the conclusion that BCM on the basis of psychological understanding should work in favour of physical unity.[3] BCM should not act as a separate force, but endeavour to create a national consciousness involving all the existing political organizations against the common enemy.[4] Although they themselves were banned, BCM was not. The formal legality could, it was argued, be used to facilitate a unity process.

From his banishment in King William's Town, in May 1975 Steve Biko managed to arrange a clandestine meeting with the similarly banished PAC President Robert Sobukwe in Kimberley, obtaining his support for the proposed policy.[5] Working through various BCM emissaries, Biko also entered into contact with Griffiths Mxenge[6] and Harry Gwala, high-ranking ANC underground leaders in Natal. Plans to hold a unity meeting in South Africa after Christmas 1975 had, however, to be shelved. At about the same time, a group of BCM members in Botswana reached an agreement with PAC regarding military training in Libya.[7] This move—which had not been cleared with the leadership in South Africa—threatened

---

1. Mokoape, Mtintso and Nhlapo in Pityana, Ramphele, Mpumlwana and Wilson (eds) op. cit., p. 138.
2. Pityana cited in Wilson in ibid., p. 53.
3. Cf. the interview with Pityana: "I was never convinced that it was necessary to have both a BCM and the traditional liberation movements. When I came out [in 1978], I told everybody very clearly that that never was the intention [...]. BC[M] had a role inside South Africa at the time, but I was never convinced that I was going to come out of South Africa and become BCM" (Interview with Barney Pityana, p. 188).
4. Including UMSA, but excluding Inkatha. Firmly opposed to any cooperation with apartheid structures, BCM denounced Gatsha Buthelezi and the bantustans in the strongest of terms.
5. Karis and Gerhart op. cit., p. 149.
6. A former Robben Island prisoner, the prominent human rights lawyer and ANC member Griffiths Mxenge was in November 1981 savagely assassinated by a death squad led by Captain Dirk Coetzee. His widow, Victoria Mxenge, also a lawyer and at the time a leading UDF representative in Natal, was shot and stabbed to death in August 1985.
7. The BCM group initially contacted ANC for military training. As it was ANC's position that training could only be provided to individuals who joined the movement, the group turned to PAC. An agreement on training in Libya was reached with the PAC faction led by Templeton Ntantala. Upon arrival in Libya, the group found itself caught up in the internal power struggle between Potlako Leballo and Ntantala. Defending their independence, tensions soon developed between the BCM members and PAC. Eventually, PAC forced the Libyan government to expel the group. Before the expulsion, some of the BCM activists went for training in Syria under the auspices of the Popular Front for the Liberation of Palestine (PFLP). Returning to Botswana, further problems arose when PAC informed the government of the purpose for which the BCM members had left the country. Against this sobering background, most of them again approached ANC (Mokoape, Mtintso and Nhlapo in Pityana, Ramphele, Mpumlwana and Wilson (eds) op. cit., pp. 139-40. See also Barrell Ph.D. op. cit., chapter two, pp. 26-27).

to undermine the sensitive initiative. Against this background, after the Soweto events Biko and his closest colleagues resolved to meet ANC and PAC for discussions outside South Africa. These plans were financially supported by the IUEF Director Lars-Gunnar Eriksson.

Ann Wilkens from the Ministry for Foreign Affairs met Biko at the Zanempilo clinic outside King William's Town on 17 July 1976, just one month after the outbreak of the Soweto uprising.[1] Her notes from the meeting give a rare insight into the banished BCM leader's thoughts at that critical juncture.

According to Biko, the time had come for the black consciousness movement "to take a clear stand in favour of a socialist alternative [in South Africa]". Socialism, he said, had always formed "the basis of the movement's ideology", but had for reasons of security not been particularly highlighted. Until then, the most important task had been to "counter the apathy among the blacks" with messages similar to the ones used by the black power movement in the United States. Contrary to what appeared to be the case with the latter, slogans like 'Black is beautiful!' could, however, "in no way constitute a final position".[2]

In combination with a clearer political stand, BCM also had to increase its international profile. In the absence of representations abroad, Biko argued, BCM "had not had the international impact it deserved". A presence outside South Africa was in addition necessary as the objective was "to create a united front with ANC, PAC and UMSA". To explore this possibility, the movement had recently sent two emissaries for discussions with the organizations in exile. On their return, a final decision on external representation and cooperation would be taken.[3]

Once established outside South Africa, the black consciousness movement would be faced with the division between ANC and PAC. In this context, Biko was of the opinion that from an ideological point of view ANC was the best alliance partner. Nevertheless, "there was a risk that [BCM] would only be accepted at the cost of a total abandonment of its particular identity", which it was not prepared to sacrifice. Another problem was SACP's "dominant position".[4] BCM wanted "independent socialism". A liberation movement could not take orders from outside, and Soviet influence was not acceptable.[5]

The problem with PAC, on the other hand, was that it was anti-Communist and that its leader in exile, Potlako Leballo, "was notorious [...] for having collaborated with the security police".[6] In this context, Biko commented on the agreement reached in Botswana between BCM members and PAC regarding military training in Libya. Stating that they "wanted to learn how to play rugby, but discovered that only soccer was taught", he stressed that the group had acted on its own, without any mandate from the leadership in South Africa. Characterizing the initiative as "extremely unfortunate", he was worried that it would jeopardize the plans for a

---

1. Biko's close colleague Thenjiwe Mtintso—at the time working for the *Daily Dispatch* newspaper—was also present. Detained soon thereafter, physically tortured and continuously harassed by the security police, in December 1978 she left South Africa for Lesotho. Joining ANC and SACP, Mtintso would during the 1980s play a prominent role in Umkhonto we Sizwe.
2. Ann Wilkens: Memorandum ('Samtal med Steve Biko, en av de ledande inom 'black consciousness'-rörelsen'/ 'Conversation with Steve Biko, one of the leaders of the black consciousness movement'), Ministry for Foreign Affairs, Stockholm, 8 September 1976 (MFA).
3. Ibid.
4. According to Wilkens, Biko "had the impression that all of the ANC leaders [were] members of the Communist Party" (ibid.).
5. Ibid.
6. Ibid. As Biko at the time was in contact with Robert Sobukwe in Kimberley, it could be assumed that his views on Leballo were shared with the PAC President.

united front. At the same time, the group's negative experiences made it "even more improbable that the black consciousness movement [...] would opt for an alliance with PAC".[1]

Looking for ANC Contacts

Together with a number of BCM activists, Biko was arrested one month later. As he was held in detention between late August and December 1976, the proposed consultations with ANC and PAC had to be postponed. They were, however, not abandoned. Back in King William's Town, in January 1977 Biko was *in absentia* appointed Honorary President of the Black People's Convention to provide him with the formal authority to negotiate with the nationalist movements in exile. Ranwedzi Nengwekhulu was at the same time authorized to establish a formal BPC representation in Botswana, where divisions between various BCM groups also called for Biko's intervention.[2]

By that time, there was a clear preference for cooperation with ANC. In mid-1976, the BCM emissaries mentioned by Biko in his conversation with Wilkens made arrangements for a first meeting between the BCM leader and the Acting ANC President Oliver Tambo. According to a later statement by ANC, "[g]iven the difficulties [...] experienced at [the] time, this was like a godsend".[3] The meeting was to take place in Gaborone in connection with Botswana's independence celebrations in late September 1976.[4] As Biko was in detention, "what would have been a historic meeting"[5] did not, however, materialize. Through Nengwekhulu and Thabo Mbeki, a second encounter—this time with Barney Pityana representing BCM—was scheduled for Maseru, Lesotho, in May 1977.[6] Also this initiative came to nothing.

Finally, a third—for the apartheid regime potentially much more ominous—meeting was in utmost secrecy planned to take place in Gaborone, Botswana, in early September 1977. It was not only to involve Biko and Tambo, but also Olof Palme, the leader of the Swedish Social Democratic Party. It would have brought together South Africa's foremost internal black politician, representing the post-Sharpeville generation; the head of the strongest liberation movement, commanding a sizeable military force; and the representative of a leading donor country, also acting on behalf of a powerful international political community. As later stated by the South African security officer Craig Williamson: "That was bad news".[7]

---

1. Ibid.
2. Pityana later noted: "Steve Biko would have come out of South Africa to try to bring some order into the situation and encourage people to have a creative relationship with ANC. [...] [E]specially the situation among BC[M] people in Botswana was very bad. There were lots of factions and it was necessary that those who really did want to get involved in armed combat could be trusted. Steve would have explored the possibility of BCM engaging in open political struggle internally in South Africa and of letting those who wanted to be involved in armed struggle do so through ANC. Essentially, that is what he was going to explore. It was to bring some sort of discipline into what had been happening in exile" (Interview with Barney Pityana, pp. 188-89).
3. ANC (August 1996) op. cit., p. 49.
4. Together with Tambo, Thabo Mbeki would also have participated in the meeting (Mbeki op. cit., p. xv). In the NEC report to the 1985 Kabwe conference, Tambo stated: "This is the appropriate occasion to disclose that [...] we had, by 1976, arrived at the point where the time had come for us to meet that leading representative of the BCM, the late Steve Biko. [...] Unfortunately, it proved impossible to bring Steve out of the country for this meeting. Another attempt was made in 1977, but this also did not succeed" ('Political Report of the National Executive Committee to the National Consultative Conference, June 1985' in ANC op. cit. [no year], p. 17).
5. Mbeki op. cit., p. xv.
6. Letter from Ranwedzi Nengwekhulu to the author, [Pretoria], 7 May 1997.
7. Interview with Craig Williamson, p. 203.

Once again, however, the meeting was aborted. Less than three weeks before, Steve Biko was arrested and savagely beaten to death. And in mid-October 1977—in the heaviest crackdown since the early 1960s—BCP, BPC, SASM, SASO and a number of other BCM organizations were banned. At the time seen by the apartheid regime as the most immediate threat[1], the black consciousness movement was effectively neutralized. Launching its 'total strategy', Pretoria's attention shifted to ANC, which, in turn, was greatly strengthened by the exodus of thousands of young blacks in search of military training and political leadership.[2]

The planned meeting between Biko, Tambo and Palme in September 1977 has never been recorded. Financially facilitated by Sweden[3] and coordinated by IUEF's Lars-Gunnar Eriksson and BPC's Ranwedzi Nengwekhulu, the general outline of an initiative which could have significantly influenced the course of the anti-apartheid struggle can be presented here.[4]

Biko, Tambo and Palme: An Aborted Encounter

After losing the general election in Sweden in September 1976—and therefore less bogged down in domestic issues—as leader of the Social Democratic opposition Palme dedicated considerable time and energy to Southern Africa. Recognized by the liberation movements, OAU and the United Nations as a committed champion of national self-determination and majority rights, in 1977 he embarked—as earlier noted—on a veritable 'crusade' against white-ruled Rhodesia, Namibia and South Africa. After addressing the UN Security Council in New York in March, the UN-sponsored deliberations on Zimbabwe and Namibia in Maputo in May[5] and the UN/OAU anti-apartheid conference in Lagos in August[6], as Vice President of the Socialist International (SI) in early September 1977 he led a mission to Southern

---

1. Discussing the views held by South Africa's security establishment at the time when he joined IUEF in early 1977, Williamson explained in 1996: "We were much more worried in the mid-1970s about the [b]lack [c]onsciousness [m]ovement than about ANC. That is why we started to sabotage IUEF's support for BCM. [...] We wanted to cut the funding support to [BCM]. For two reasons. Number one, they were a problem internally. Politically, that was where the problem was, not with ANC. Number two, it was part of [a] whole process of trying to have a very clear [white] and red situation [...], paint[ing] [the liberation movements] as part of the international Soviet view of things" (ibid., pp. 199-200 and 198).
2. Mokoape, Mtintso and Nhlapo—all of them former BCM activists joining ANC and Umkhonto we Sizwe (MK)—have estimated that more than 60 per cent of the BCM organizations' active members were to be found by the 1980s in the ranks of ANC/MK (Mokoape, Mtintso and Nhlapo in Pityana, Ramphele, Mpumlwana and Wilson (eds) op. cit., pp. 141-42).
3. According to Nengwekhulu, "[t]he meeting would have been financed by Sweden through [the] Socialist International" (Letter from Ranwedzi Nengwekhulu to the author, [Pretoria], 7 May 1997). Presumably, the funds would have come from the Social Democratic Party.
4. Ranwedzi Nengwekhulu's confirmation of the evidence found in scattered Swedish archival sources is greatly acknowledged. The author is in addition indebted to Barney Pityana and Craig Williamson for their willingness—from totally opposite positions—to discuss the circumstances of Biko's intention to leave South Africa to meet with the ANC leadership and the roles played by IUEF and Sweden in this regard (cf. the interviews with Barney Pityana, pp. 187-89, and Craig Williamson, pp. 199-200 and 203). It should also be noted that IUEF and BCM earlier in 1977 were involved in an aborted attempt to bring Biko to Europe for discussions with Tambo and Palme. In 1997, Nengwekhulu revealed that "it was [...] decided to involve a right wing Dutch group [...] to invite Biko to Holland, where Biko, Tambo, Palme and myself could meet. The Dutch group had agreed to invite him, although they did not know that Biko was to meet Tambo and Palme" (Letter from Ranwedzi Nengwekhulu to the author, [Pretoria], 7 May 1997). Cf. Wilson in Pityana, Ramphele, Mpumlwana and Wilson (eds) op. cit., p. 63, where she states that Biko himself tried to procure an invitation from a Dutch visitor to King William's Town.
5. International Conference in Support of the Peoples of Zimbabwe and Namibia.
6. World Conference for Action against Apartheid.

Africa. It was during this trip that the meeting between Biko, Tambo and Palme was to have been held.[1]

The SI mission took place between 2 and 10 September 1977, with a scheduled visit to Botswana's capital Gaborone on 6-7 September, arriving from Lusaka and proceeding to Maputo.[2] While representatives from ten affiliated SI parties participated[3], according to the available documentation only Palme, SI's Secretary General Bernt Carlsson—former international secretary of the Swedish Social Democratic Party—and Pierre Schori, Carlsson's successor, were privy to the plans to meet Steve Biko.[4]

Ignoring his banning orders, on 17 August 1977 Biko drove to Cape Town for unity talks together with Peter Jones, a young coloured BPC accountant. On their way back to King William's Town, on 18 August they were stopped at a security police roadblock outside Grahamstown in the eastern Cape. Although he was taken to Port Elizabeth for interrogation, Biko's closest colleagues and friends were, however, not "unduly alarmed".[5] As later noted by Donald Woods, "Steve had been detained before, and no harm had come to him".[6] Almost one month later—on 13 September 1977—they learned that he had died.[7]

It is against this background less puzzling that the SI mission as late as on 31 August still planned to go to Botswana.[8] After discussions with Oliver Tambo and Alfred Nzo in Lusaka on 4 September[9], it was, however, decided to cancel the Botswana leg of the trip.[10] That this was a sudden decision is evident from Palme's

1. Immediately before the SI mission, Palme and Tambo had several opportunities for coordinating their views. In addition to discussions during the Lagos conference—held 22-26 August—they met in Stockholm at the end of August 1977. Officially invited to Sweden by the Liberal Cooperation Minister Ola Ullsten, during an intense and high-profile visit from 26 to 30 August the ANC President not only conferred with the non-socialist government, but also with the opposition Social Democratic Party and a number of organizations, including LO/TCO, CSM and AGIS (Marika Fahlén: Memorandum ('Inför Oliver Tambo's besök i Sverige 26-30 augusti 1977'/'In view of Oliver Tambo's visit to Sweden, 26-30 August 1977'), Ministry for Foreign Affairs, Stockholm, 23 August 1977) (MFA).
2. Socialdemokraterna: 'Pressmeddelande' ('Press communiqué'), [Stockholm], 31 August 1977 (LMA).
3. In addition to Olof Palme and Bernt Carlsson—the Secretary General of the Socialist International—the mission members were: Walter Hackler (SPÖ Austria), Wim Geldolf (PSB Belgium), Kjeld Olesen (Social Democratic Party of Denmark), José Francisco Peña Gómez (PRD Dominican Republic), Uwe Holtz (SPD Federal Republic of Germany), Jean-Pierre Raison (PSF France), Aldo Ajello (PSI Italy), Jorge Campinos (PSP Portugal), Emilio Menéndez del Valle (PSOE Spain) and Pierre Schori (Social Democratic Party of Sweden) (ibid. and Olof Palme: 'Här går gränsen för mänsklig värdighet: Palme's afrikanska dagbok'/'Here goes the border of human decency: Palme's African diary' in *Aftonbladet-Magasinet*, 9 October 1977).
4. In a "personal and confidential" letter to Bernt Carlsson—copied to Pierre Schori—Lars-Gunnar Eriksson referred to "the special visitor who will come to see you and Olof [and who] will be contactable through the [BCM] representative in Botswana, Mr. Ranwedzi (Harry) Nengwekhulu" (Letter from Lars-Gunnar Eriksson to Bernt Carlsson, [IUEF, Geneva], 24 August 1977) (LMA).
5. Woods op. cit., p. 159.
6. Ibid.
7. Ibid., p. 160. During interrogation, on 7 September 1977—after nearly three weeks of solitary confinement—Biko sustained severe head injuries. Left naked, lying on a mat and manacled to a metal grille, four days later he lapsed into semi-consciousness. The security police ordered his transfer to Pretoria. Placed on the floor of a Land Rover, in the middle of winter he was transported 1,200 kilometres from Port Elizabeth to Pretoria. No medical personnel accompanied him. Shortly after arrival, he died—naked and alone—on the floor of a cell in Pretoria Central Prison.
8. Social Democratic Party: 'Pressmeddelande' ('Press communiqué'), [Stockholm], 31 August 1977 (LMA).
9. Olof Palme: 'Här går gränsen för mänsklig värdighet: Palme's afrikanska dagbok' (Here goes the border of human decency: Palme's African diary') in *Aftonbladet-Magasinet*, 9 October 1977.
10. Nengwekhulu has briefly stated that the scheduled meeting in Gaborone "did not take place because of security concerns" (Letter from Ranwedzi Nengwekhulu to the author, [Pretoria], 7 May 1997). Interviewed in 1997, Pityana—who himself was detained three days before Biko's arrest—noted: "On his initiative, Steve Biko planned to clandestinely meet ANC abroad. And to come back. He had no intention of permanently leaving the country. I am aware that IUEF was to make it possible. Harry Nengwekhulu was part of it and he would have found some means of support from them. I do not know how advanced the plans were at the time of Steve's arrest. It had [, however,] nothing to do with that. It was due to the fact that he had breached his banning orders" (Interview with Barney Pityana, p. 188).

diary, where in the entry for 7 September he notes that "we leave Lusaka in a Mozambican military plane going to Maputo [...], arriving [there] at a totally unexpected hour".[1]

Taking place a year after the Soweto shootings, the assassination of Steve Biko and the subsequent banning of the black consciousness movement sent shock waves throughout the world. Imposing an arms embargo against South Africa, on 4 November 1977 the Security Council for the first time in the history of the United Nations applied mandatory sanctions against a member state.[2] Inside South Africa itself, the assassination provoked an outraged reaction. In spite of tight security controls, some 20,000 angry mourners attended Biko's funeral in King William's Town on 25 September 1977. Together with diplomats from ten other countries, Sven-Otto Allard represented the Swedish government.[3] The apartheid regime, however, did not budge. James Kruger, the Minister of Police and Justice, tersely commented that Biko's death "leaves me cold".[4] And at the following inquest, the presiding magistrate failed to find anyone responsible for the murder.[5]

Years later—when Craig Williamson had revealed his true identity as an officer with South Africa's security branch—ANC concluded that the planned meetings "had been betrayed [...] by [...] Williamson, who knew of the arrangements being made to take Biko to Botswana".[6] In its submission to the South African Truth and Reconciliation Commission, ANC stated in August 1996 that "information was leaked by agents of the regime such as Craig Williamson, leading to Biko's arrest and ultimate murder".[7] Although distancing himself from the actual assassination, this had by then been acknowledged by Williamson himself.[8] Interviewed in April 1996, he stated:

---

1. Olof Palme: 'Här går gränsen för mänsklig värdighet: Palme's afrikanska dagbok' ('Here goes the border of human decency: Palme's African diary') in *Aftonbladet-Magasinet*, 9 October 1977. Vividly describing the flight with the troop carrier, Palme commented: "We enter into contact with the armed struggle for the liberation of Africa" (ibid.). Flying over the Cabora Bassa dam in Mozambique, he noted that "memories flow from the Swedish debate in the 1960s on solidarity with the Third World" (ibid. Cf. Sellström Volume I, pp. 483-504). Basing themselves on information regarding the SI mission's intended itinerary, some commentators have wrongly included Botswana among the countries visited by Palme. This is, for example, the case with the Russian scholar Vladimir Shubin in his study—published under the name Vladimir Bushin—*Social Democracy and Southern Africa (1960s-1980s)*, Progress Publishers, Moscow, 1989, p. 97. The error is repeated in his study on the Soviet Union and ANC, where Palme—at the time leader of the opposition—is also incorrectly presented as Prime Minister of Sweden (Shubin (1999) op. cit., p. 180).

2. UN Security Council Resolution 418.

3. Cable ('Om Steve Biko'/'Re Steve Biko') from Sven-Otto Allard to the Ministry for Foreign Affairs, Swedish legation, Pretoria, 26 September 1977 (MFA). Among the Nordic countries, Finland was also represented at the funeral.

4. Cited in Eileen Riley: *Major Political Events in South Africa 1948-1990*, Facts on File, Oxford and New York, 1991, p. 153.

5. In his pioneering study on apartheid's death squads, Jacques Pauw concludes: "There can be little doubt that words like those of [James] Kruger, the failure of magistrates to speak out and the harsh security laws introduced by [Prime Minister] Vorster created the conditions, the climate and the state of mind that led to [the] death squads" (Jacques Pauw: *In the Heart of the Whore: The Story of Apartheid's Death Squads*, Southern Book Publishers, Halfway House, 1991, p. 105).

6. Mbeki op. cit., p. xv.

7. ANC (August 1996) op. cit., p. 9.

8. In an interview with the Swedish journalist and documentary film-maker Boris Ersson, Williamson mentioned in mid-1994 that he had reported on the planned meeting between Biko and Tambo. Extracts from the interview were shown by the Swedish Broadcasting Corporation/TV 1 on its television news programme *Aktuellt* on 30 March 1995.

[T]he reality is that Biko's detention and then death was at the time when he was secretly going to leave the country to meet Tambo. It was all funded by Swedish money through IUEF. That was bad news. [...] It was set up by the Swedes and by Lars-Gunnar [Eriksson]. I reported that it was going to happen, but I don't know if the fact that they then beat him up and killed him was based on that.[1]

Neither ANC nor Williamson mentioned Olof Palme in this context. Palme, Sweden and the other Nordic countries were, however, seen by the apartheid regime as hostile stumbling blocks. Asked to comment on South Africa's views in this regard, Williamson said:

[O]ne of the key elements of the South African security forces' war against ANC and the other liberation movements [...] was to paint them as part of the international Soviet view [...] and to discourage anti-Soviet countries and organizations [from] support[ing] them. One of the biggest problems, or hindrances, to that policy was, in fact, the Swedes and the Nordic countries. [...] What South Africa would have liked was that everybody should take a [...] white and red colour view [...], which Sweden never did. [...] [T]hat is where Olof Palme came in [...]. Palme and the people around him were a third force in this [...] political situation.[2]

To cut the support for BCM, infiltrate ANC and monitor international assistance to the wider anti-apartheid struggle[3], in the mid-1970s the South African security branch identified IUEF as a suitable target for penetration, prepared a 'legend' for its undercover agent Craig Williamson and launched 'Operation Daisy'.[4]

---

1. Interview with Craig Williamson, p. 203. Williamson's ignorance regarding the actual assassination is hardly credible. In the interview, he confirmed that he had passed on the information regarding Biko and Tambo to the very same structure that carried out the murder (ibid.). The officer in charge of Biko's arrest and 'interrogation' was Piet Goosen, who shortly thereafter was promoted to the rank of Brigadier. Transferred to Pretoria, Goosen—subsequently nicknamed 'Biko'—was appointed head of the foreign section of the South African security police. When Williamson returned to South Africa in early 1980, he became Goosen's deputy. Goosen had procured the Daisy police farm outside Pretoria with funds that Williamson diverted from IUEF (Pauw (1991) op. cit., p. 60 and below). In March 1982, Goosen, Williamson and Eugene de Kock led a team of seven operatives who bombed the ANC office in London and who were later awarded the 'Police Star for Outstanding Service' by the apartheid government (Phillip Van Niekerk: 'How we bombed London' in *The Observer*, 19 February 1995). The Swede Bertil Wedin—together with Williamson mentioned in connection with the assassination of Olof Palme—was at the time working for Williamson in London (see the chapter on Angola above).
2. Interview with Craig Williamson, pp. 197-98.
3. Williamson said in 1996 that his general objective was "to understand the whole dynamic behind the anti-apartheid support internationally. We had to sabotage it" (ibid., p. 199).
4. IUEF's assistance to BCM attracted at an early stage the attention of South Africa's security services. In February 1974, SASO's Abraham Onkgopotse Tiro—President of SASM—was killed in Botswana by an explosive device inserted into a parcel from the IUEF head office in Geneva. According to the former BOSS agent Martin Dolinchek, the parcel was intercepted and 'doctored' by the security police at the Southern African mail sorting office close to the Jan Smuts airport outside Johannesburg (TRC op. cit. (Vol. II), p. 100). Also in February 1974, John Dube, ANC's Deputy Chief Representative to Zambia and a founder member of Umkhonto we Sizwe, was killed by a letter bomb. The killings of Tiro and Dube marked the beginning of a series of cross-border assassinations carried out by the apartheid regime. Parcel bombs were often used. In August 1982, the prominent journalist, researcher and ANC-SACP member Ruth First, at the time Director of the Centre for African Studies in Maputo, was killed by such a bomb in the Mozambican capital. ANC's Jeanette Schoon and her eight-year old daughter Katryn were killed in a similar way in Lubango, Angola, in June 1984. Craig Williamson later admitted that he arranged for the preparation of the parcel bombs sent to First and Schoon (Phillip Van Niekerk: 'How we bombed London' in *The Observer*, 19 February 1995. Cf. also the interview with Craig Williamson, p. 202). In a submission to the Truth and Reconciliation Commission, he stated that he acted on instructions from Piet 'Biko' Goosen (TRC op. cit. (Vol. II), p. 107).

Sweden and the International University Exchange Fund

The story of 'Operation Daisy'[1] and its ramifications—notably the possibility of a link to the assassination of Prime Minister Olof Palme in 1986[2]—is still to be written. Unfolding in a twilight zone between concealed multilateral assistance and covert South African intelligence, it calls for a serious, comprehensive study.[3]

IUEF was an international non-governmental organization based in Geneva, Switzerland. Nevertheless, through its Director, Lars-Gunnar Eriksson, and the fact that SIDA was its largest donor, the association with Sweden was seen as particularly close. Apart from Norway—which in financial terms was a less important supporter—Sweden was, in addition, the only country among IUEF's donors which

---

1. Cf. the expression 'pushing up the daisies', meaning to be dead and buried.
2. Walking home with his wife Lisbet after having been to the movies, Palme was shot in the back and killed instantly in the centre of Stockholm at midnight on 28 February 1986. The assassination took place less than a week after the People's Parliament against Apartheid, where in the presence of ANC President Tambo he had given a particularly militant speech. During the following weeks, the Swedish police received several tip-offs about a possible South African involvement. Although similar suggestions were made over the next ten years, what became known as 'the South Africa trail' was never seriously investigated. The situation dramatically changed in September 1996, when the death squad commander Eugene de Kock stated in the Pretoria Supreme Court that the apartheid regime was behind the killing. According to de Kock, his former colleague Craig Williamson was responsible for the operation. This provoked intense activity by the Swedish media and, eventually, more serious official investigations into 'the South Africa trail'. No concrete South African connection to the unsolved assassination was, however, established. In June 1997, an internal report by the Palme Inquest (*Palmeutredningen*-PI) concluded that "[t]here is really nothing to confirm the suggestions that the murder was carried out by South African intelligence [or] security services, with Craig W[illiamson] as the organizer". Acknowledging that five sources—four of them with direct links to apartheid's death squads—maintained that it was an operation led by Williamson, PI's criminal investigators, nevertheless, added that "it is our understanding that the information [...] cannot be dismissed straight off" (cited in *Granskningskommissionens Betänkande i Anledning av Brottsutredningen efter Mordet på Statsminister Olof Palme*/'Report by the Study Commission [of] the Criminal Inquest into the Assassination of Prime Minister Olof Palme', SOU 1999:88, Ministry of Justice, Stockholm, 1999, p. 479). In the semi-official biographical sketch of Thabo Mbeki—published in 1998—it is, similarly, stated that "to this day suspicions persist that Olof Palme was assassinated because of his support for the ANC" (Mbeki op. cit., p. xix). In 1994, the Swedish government appointed a commission to examine the investigations carried out thus far by the Palme Inquest. Reorganized in 1996, it presented its report in June 1999. 'The South Africa trail' featured prominently in the report (ibid., pp. 445-81). Highly critical, the commission found it "remarkable" (p. 687) that for ten years PI had not only ignored submissions made by Foreign Affairs' officials and South Africa experts—such as Per Wästberg, who contacted PI after the murder, but was only heard in 1996—but that it had also failed to carry out a basic foreign policy analysis of possible South African motives (ibid., pp. 263, 687 and 697), adding that "[t]he shortcoming cannot be entirely rectified *a posteriori*" (ibid., p. 687).
3. South Africa's penetration of IUEF and Williamson's possible involvement in the Palme assassination were discussed in July-August 1994 by the Swedish journalist Anders Hasselbohm in five major feature articles in *Aftonbladet*. Focusing on Williamson's intelligence network and its contacts with Swedish right wing circles, they were followed up in early 1995 through a series of articles in the magazine *Vi*. With access to IUEF documents held at SIDA, Hasselbohm's investigative work highlighted a number of aspects corroborated by subsequent events and later studies. As in the case of the official Palme Inquest, it, however, lacked a comprehensive framework. Notably ignoring the much more significant direct assistance to ANC and basing himself on one-way letters from Lars-Gunnar Eriksson to leading Swedish Social Democrats such as Bernt Carlsson, Mats Hellström and Pierre Schori, Hasselbohm presented IUEF as "Olof Palme's and the Social Democratic Party's extended arm in Sweden's secret war against South Africa" (Anders Hasselbohm: 'Sydafrika hotade svenska s-politiker'/'South Africa threatened Swedish Social Democrats' in *Aftonbladet*, 31 July 1994). Carlsson, Hellström and Schori were certainly both close to and protective towards Eriksson and IUEF. There is, however, no evidence that they—and, more importantly, Palme—shared his views or actively intervened in the day-to-day activities of IUEF. While many cloak-and-dagger letters from Eriksson can be found, only rarely is there a reply from his Swedish friends. Apart from general matters concerning IUEF and financial assistance to the international NGO, the communication went almost exclusively in one direction, from Geneva to Stockholm. Although Hasselbohm's writings about Sweden and the anti-apartheid struggle represent a rare effort, they end up as a spy novel. His main contention has been that "Sweden for years conducted a secret war against the apartheid regime in South Africa. From the Social Democratic Party headquarters in Stockholm, strings were pulled for agent activities in which racial segregation was fought with rods of iron. [...] [IUEF], [a]n [...] organization directed by Sweden, [...] both smuggled money to apartheid opponents in South Africa and took part in the planning of information gathering concerning possible targets for sabotage by ANC" (Anders Hasselbohm: 'Sveriges hemliga krig mot apartheid'/'Sweden's secret war against apartheid' in *Aftonbladet*, 28 July 1994).

maintained an official cooperation programme with ANC.[1] The issue of IUEF and its activities in South Africa was regularly raised in discussions between the Swedish authorities and the liberation movement. In spite of IUEF's international status, some of the more salient aspects of what subsequently became known as the 'IUEF affair' should thus be addressed.

Far from exhaustive, the following summary focuses on the roles played by Eriksson and his deputy Williamson, their political agendas and the way in which different actors within both Sweden and ANC related to IUEF during the crucial years of infiltration and mismanagement from around 1975 until January 1980. The question of BCM as an alternative to ANC is particularly relevant. So is the often ignored fact that 'Operation Daisy' took place at a time when Sweden was ruled by non-socialist governments.[2] While Lars-Gunnar Eriksson and IUEF maintained privileged relations with some members of the opposition Social Democratic Party, there were no particular historical, institutional or personal bonds with the 'bourgeois' political parties. In fact, Eriksson often acted against both SIDA and the Fälldin and Ullsten governments.[3]

The 'IUEF affair' was not connected with the political change in Sweden in 1976.[4] Eriksson's support within the Social Democratic Party was, in addition, far from comprehensive.[5] As later stated by SIDA's Birgitta Berggren, "[i]t was

---

1. Danish and Norwegian NGOs played a much more prominent part in IUEF than Swedish organizations. When IUEF at a meeting in Copenhagen, Denmark, in May 1969 was re-organized as an association under Swiss law, the constituent organizations were the Danish National Union of Students, the Danish Refugee Council, the Norwegian National Union of Students, the Norwegian Refugee Council and the Norwegian Special Committee for Aid to Refugees from Southern Africa (IUEF: 'Statutes', IUEF, Geneva, June 1978 [p. 1]). No Swedish organization was present. With regard to government support, Sweden would, however, soon assume a leading role. In 1979/80—IUEF's last year of operation; when both the British (for the Zimbabwe programme) and the Finnish governments had decided to extend official funds to the organization—the Swedish share of the overall budget amounted to 34%. The contribution by the government of Denmark represented 25%. In descending order, the relative size of the other official allocations was: Holland 11%, United Kingdom 9%, Norway 3.5%, Canada 3% and Finland 0.2%. The remaining 14% was covered through contributions from a number of NGOs in mainly Canada, Denmark, Holland, Norway, Sweden and the United Kingdom (Telex from Piers Campbell, IUEF, to Lennart Wohlgemuth, SIDA, Geneva, 17 March 1980) (SDA). Among the Swedish NGOs which supported IUEF in 1978/79 were the Church of Sweden Mission, the Stockholm University Students' Union, the Swedish Free Church Aid and the Social Democratic Party (IUEF: 'Annual Report 1978-79', IUEF, Geneva, October 1979, p. 35).
2. In the articles quoted above, Hasselbohm, for example, discussed the IUEF affair as if the Social Democratic Party was in power in Sweden at the time.
3. As noted in the chapter on the Patriotic Front of Zimbabwe above, in April 1978, for example, Eriksson—and Williamson—encouraged the Social Democratic MP Mats Hellström to censure both the non-socialist government and SIDA during a parliamentary debate on Swedish foreign aid. In September 1979, Eriksson—who himself aspired to the directorship of IDAF—criticized in a letter to Pierre Schori the involvement of SIDA's former Director General Ernst Michanek with the London-based human rights organization, stating that "I find it somewhat remarkable that the [c]hairman of [CCHA] accepts to become part of one of the organisations that is a recipient of [official Swedish] funds" (Letter from Lars-Gunnar Eriksson to Pierre Schori, Geneva, 11 September 1979) (SDA). And in October 1979—after a meeting in Stockholm with SIDA's Lennart Wohlgemuth and Birgitta Berggren, who had raised a number of questions with regard to IUEF's administration and the role of Craig Williamson—in an internal IUEF memorandum *inter alia* copied to Williamson himself Eriksson concluded that "the main lesson one can learn from this is that there are few Swedes that one should trust too much, and some not at all" (Lars-Gunnar Eriksson: Memorandum ('Discussion with Birgitta Berggren, SIDA, October 1st 1979'), IUEF, Geneva, 26 October 1979) (SDA).
4. In fact, before 1976, Eriksson—who had left Sweden ten years earlier—often criticized the Social Democratic government for not granting IUEF sufficient support. In a letter to Bernt Carlsson—then international secretary of the ruling party—in November 1975, for example, he complained about "our dear government which seems at times to have an abundance of funds for all sorts of crazy and stillborn projects" (Letter ('Additional memorandum concerning IDAF as well as ANC and other related matters') from Lars-Gunnar Eriksson to Bernt Carlsson, Geneva, 1-2 November 1975) (SDA). As a rule, Eriksson wrote his letters in English, even when addressed to friends in Sweden.
5. From 1978 heading the International Centre of the Swedish Labour Movement (AIC), Bengt Säve-Söderbergh emphasized in 1997 that "IUEF was just one of many organizations. [...] I was not very much part of that. I was rather looking at it with some suspicion. It was led by someone who was trying to find an angle of his own" (Interview with Bengt Säve-Söderbergh, p. 339). Lars-Gunnar Eriksson only rarely corresponded with Säve-Söderbergh and the Social Democratic coordinating aid organization AIC.

mainly a question of an 'old-boys-network'"[1], involving a small group of influen-
tial party members and centrally placed officials in the Ministry for Foreign Affairs.
The absence of any political seal of approval explains the reaction in Sweden when
Williamson's true identity and Eriksson's maladministration became known.
According to Carl Tham, the Liberal Foreign Minister Ola Ullsten and his Under-
Secretary of State Hans Blix

> were furious. It must also be asked how Mats Hellström and others could be so deceived. It is
> impossible to imagine. A lot of people were after all suspicious and warned them, but they did
> not listen to the professionals.[2]

A Vehicle for Refugee Education

It was IUEF's direct involvement with BCM and the wider South African political
opposition which attracted the attention of the Pretoria regime. To put the final crisis in perspective—as well as the ensuing efforts to counter its consequences—it
should, however, be emphasized that the international NGO was primarily concerned with education support to refugees in Africa and, later, Latin America.[3]
Originally set up in 1961[4], IUEF's principal objective was "to cater to the needs—
particularly in the field of education—of refugees, with special reference to [...]
Southern Africa".[5] In addition to its scholarship programmes, the organization was
from the beginning actively involved in various refugee support activities, such as
counselling services, local integration and employment projects etc. When the Swedish government started to support IUEF under the 1964 'refugee million', it was to
these educational programmes that the funds were channelled, notably in favour of

---

1. Interview with Birgitta Berggren, p. 260.
2. Interview with Carl Tham, p. 343.
3. With an initial grant from Sweden, the Latin American programme was introduced in the mid-1970s. One of
   its main promoters was Pierre Schori, who at the time was a member of IUEF's International Board. The programme expanded quickly. In the case of Sweden, for the financial year 1979/80 the allocation towards activities in Africa amounted to 9 MSEK, while no less than 6 million was set aside for the Latin American
   programme (Birgitta Berggren: Memorandum ('IUEF'), SIDA, Stockholm, 7 February 1980) (SDA). It could
   be noted that while Bernt Carlsson and Mats Hellström were mainly following events in Southern Africa,
   Schori was chiefly concerned with Latin American affairs.
4. The International University Exchange Fund was established in Leiden, Holland, in November 1961 by
   the Western-aligned International Student Conference (ISC). NUSAS was a member of ISC. (On ISC, see
   Sellström Volume I, pp. 91-93.) Thord Palmlund from Sweden was at the same time appointed Director
   of IUEF. He served until early 1963, when he was succeeded by the Norwegian Øystein Opdahl. Lars-
   Gunnar Eriksson took over the directorship in 1966. After revelations in 1967 that ISC had received
   funds from the US Central Intelligence Agency (CIA), it was dissolved in 1969. It was, however, decided
   that IUEF should continue its operations. At a meeting in Copenhagen, Denmark, IUEF was re-organized
   in May 1969 as an independent association under Swiss law, moving its headquarters to Geneva.
   Regional sub-offices were subsequently established in London (UK, for Europe), Lusaka (Zambia, for
   Africa) and San José (Costa Rica, for Latin America). At the end of the 1970s, the organization had
   around 40 permanent staff members. According to its statutes, IUEF was governed by an Assembly and
   an International Board. Members of the Assembly were international NGOs contributing to its work,
   while the International Board was made up of individuals elected in their own right. Only one NGO
   from Sweden—the National Council of Swedish Youth (SUL)—formed part of the Assembly, while in
   1979 there were two Danish and four Norwegian member organizations. At the same time, two of the
   eleven board members—Bernt Carlsson and Astrid Bergquist—were Swedish. The Chairman of the International Board when the IUEF crisis broke out into the open was Carl Nissen, Inspector at the Danish
   Ministry of Education. To the extent that Sweden wielded a particular influence, it was thus through the
   Director and by virtue of being IUEF's major donor.
5. IUEF: 'Statutes', IUEF, Geneva, June 1978 [p. 2].

individual scholarships to students from South Africa, Namibia, Zimbabwe and Angola.[1]

Lars-Gunnar Eriksson[2] became Director of IUEF in 1966 and remained in that position until June 1980, when he resigned.[3] With financial support from the Scandinavian countries[4], Canada and the Netherlands, under his leadership the scholarship programme rapidly expanded. By 1972, the organization supported more than 1,000 students. In 1978-79, no less than 2,128 African refugees were studying on IUEF scholarships, while the number of Latin Americans was 455.[5]

The substantial scholarship programmes and IUEF's education support activities in general were highly appreciated by donors and beneficiaries alike.[6] After the exposure of Pretoria's infiltration and when the extent of Eriksson's financial mismanagement and high-handed administrative methods during the late 1970s became known, there was, however, a strong reaction against everything associated with IUEF, including its positive achievements. As noted by Enuga Reddy, Director of the UN Centre Against Apartheid, feelings of "responsibility" and "embarrassment" became widespread among IUEF's staff members, the donors and individual aid officials in the countries primarily concerned.[7]

As a general point of departure it should be recalled that IUEF in the early 1970s enjoyed a solid reputation. In 1980, the report by the Commission of Inquiry into the Espionage Activities of the South African Government in the International University Exchange Fund[8] stated that

> [t]his report necessarily focuses on what went wrong in the IUEF. What needs to be remembered is that the IUEF [...] has assisted many thousands of refugees to gain an education [with] which they have been able to contribute to the liberation and development of their countries.

---

1. See Sellström Volume I, pp. 72-75. When in 1964 Sweden started to extend official humanitarian assistance to Southern Africa, there were many links between CCHA and IUEF. In August 1964, Thord Palmlund—who from late 1961 to early 1963 served as IUEF's first Director—was appointed secretary to the consultative committee. At the same time, Lars-Gunnar Eriksson—IUEF's future Director—was a substitute CCHA member. Sven Hamrell, a full committee member, later formed part of the IUEF board and was subsequently replaced by Pierre Schori.
2. Eriksson's involvement with South and Southern Africa started in the early 1960s. A member of the national Swedish South Africa Committee (SSAK), in 1963 he became the first chairman of the Stockholm South Africa Committee. Bernt Carlsson was a member of the same committee. Serving as a substitute member of the official CCHA, Eriksson was in 1965 appointed international secretary of the Swedish National Union of Students (SFS). Via CCHA, he had already established contacts with IUEF—and through SFS with NUSAS—when in 1966 he succeeded Øystein Opdahl as IUEF Director.
3. Eriksson was on sick leave from late January 1980.
4. The government of Finland did not support IUEF until the end of the 1970s.
5. IUEF: 'Annual Report 1978-79', IUEF, Geneva, October 1979, pp. 5 and 9. The overwhelming majority of the African scholarship holders were from South Africa, Namibia and Zimbabwe. In 1978-79, no less than 1,586 of the 2,128 African students—corresponding to 75 per cent—came from these countries (ibid., p. 5).
6. Zedekia Ngavirue, former Chairman of the External Council of SWANU of Namibia, could here represent IUEF's many thousands of scholarship recipients. After exile and university attendance in Sweden from 1962, with assistance from IUEF he embarked in 1967 on doctoral studies in political science at the University of Oxford, England, where in May 1973 he obtained his degree (Letter of acknowledgement from Zedekia Ngavirue to Lars-Gunnar Eriksson, Boroko, Papua New Guinea, 5 November 1973) (SDA). In 1997—almost a quarter of a century later—his important Ph.D. thesis was published by P. Schlettwein Publishing, Basel, Switzerland with the title *Political Parties and Interest Groups in South West Africa (Namibia): A Study of a Plural Society*.
7. Enuga S. Reddy: Memorandum ('International University Exchange Fund') [no place or date], attached to memorandum ('Ang. IUEF'/'Re IUEF') by Jan Romare, Ministry for Foreign Affairs, Stockholm, 8 April 1980 (SDA).
8. The commission of inquiry was set up by the IUEF Assembly and International Board in February 1980, shortly after Williamson's exposure. Its members were David MacDonald (chairman) from Canada, former Secretary of State, Minister of Communications and MP; Sundie Kazunga from Zambia, Special Assistant to President Kaunda and member of the IUEF board; and Bertil Zachrisson from Sweden, former Minister of Education (1973-76) and at the time a Social Democratic MP.

This is something of which the IUEF can be proud, regardless of the answers given to any other questions asked about its activities.[1]

Also in 1980, Enuga Reddy emphasized that "IUEF has performed an important service for two decades", adding that "association with [the organization] should not be shameful".[2] While noting that "the perceptions of [...] Eriksson [...] as regards the nature and role of [BCM] [...] were different from mine", the prominent UN official commented:

> Starting with educational assistance in South Africa, IUEF has in [the 1970s] rapidly expanded its assistance to the [b]lack [c]onsciousness [m]ovement [...]. That involved secrecy, and IUEF became an important target for South African intelligence. [...] I believe [that] the matter should be viewed in perspective. With the resurgence of [the] student and workers' movement in South Africa ten years ago, there was a need for assistance inside. There was also a willingness, among [the] Nordic countries particularly, to provide appropriate assistance. [...] The IUEF saw the opportunities, provided the service and became the channel.[3]

In a Cold War perspective, IUEF was decidedly pro-Western and Lars-Gunnar Eriksson as anti-Communist as he was anti-apartheid. The opinion of the Russian scholar and activist Vladimir Shubin is worth noting in this context. Looking back fifteen years later, in 1995 the former head of the Africa section of the International Department of the Communist Party of the Soviet Union—described as "our best Soviet friend"[4] by SACP's Ronnie Kasrils—was of the opinion that

> one must highlight the role of IUEF. I used to know Lars-Gunnar Eriksson. I was rather friendly with him in the 1970s. [...] Of course, IUEF was very much discredited by the Craig Williamson affair, but [one] should not close the whole issue of IUEF because of that. IUEF played a very important role, although controversial. [...] A lot was done by IUEF in the early 1970s. [...] IUEF played a particular role, because they could send people inside South Africa to have a look. For example, they were a major channel of support to [SASO] and [BCM]. [...] Eriksson told me about it, and I said to him that it was about time that we also contacted them.[5]

The Swedish government's financial support to IUEF was initially limited to the scholarship programme and related activities in favour of African refugee students. Noting that the NGO "in recent years has considerably extended its field of activities and presently carries out [operations] which in principle fall within [...] the competence [...] of other [international] organizations"[6], in March 1971 CCHA reconfirmed this policy, stating that

> support to IUEF's programmes should focus on refugee scholarships, an activity for which [the organization] seem[s] to be well suited [...]. [...] Support to field projects or infrastructural

1. 'Report of the Commission of Inquiry into the Espionage Activities of the South African Government in the International University Exchange Fund' [no place or date, but 1980], p. 9 (SDA). It is referenced below as 'IUEF Commission of Inquiry'. For unknown reasons, the comprehensive report was never discussed by the Swedish Consultative Committee on Humanitarian Assistance. Sven Hamrell later remarked that "the IUEF affair was never properly reported to the committee. I think that it was a mistake. The report on the IUEF should have been made available to every member of the committee, but it was not done. That was not correct" (Interview with Sven Hamrell, p. 281).
2. Enuga S. Reddy: Memorandum ('International University Exchange Fund') [no place or date], attached to memorandum ('Ang. IUEF'/'Re IUEF') by Jan Romare, Ministry for Foreign Affairs, Stockholm, 8 April 1980 (SDA).
3. Ibid.
4. Ronnie Kasrils: 'Armed and Dangerous': My Undercover Struggle against Apartheid, Heinemann, Oxford, 1993, p. 272.
5. Conversation with Vladimir Shubin, pp. 249-50.
6. CCHA: 'Protokoll [från sammanträde 8 mars 1971]' ('Minutes [from meeting 8 March 1971]'), SIDA, [Stockholm], 10 March 1971 (SDA).

activities [is], however, not recommended, as IUEF at present appears to lack the necessary capacity for this kind of [undertaking].[1]

As late as in April 1972, the Ministry for Foreign Affairs emphasized that "an understanding [...] ha[s] been reached between Sweden and IUEF concerning a concentration of the Swedish support on refugee scholarships, [including] counselling services and [other] social measures".[2]

In addition to a number of Southern African projects of a more political nature[3]—notably in Zimbabwe[4]—soon, however, the government would support IUEF's cooperation with SASO and the wider black consciousness movement. Contributions to SASO via IUEF were extended from 1972/73, when an amount of 75,000 SEK was allocated.[5] In the process, the strict concentration on refugee education was abandoned. This was expressed as follows in April 1974 after formal discussions between SIDA and IUEF concerning assistance in 1974/75:

> With [regard] to conditions prevailing in Southern Africa, SIDA is aware that special flexibility in the administration and development of projects [...] may be called for [, and] leaves it at the d[i]scretion of IUEF to adapt [the] support to changing circumstances.[6]

Although it was added that "suggestions for major changes should [...] be referred to SIDA in writing before a decision is taken"[7], to the IUEF Director the understanding must have amounted to a *carte blanche* which he subsequently was not slow to exploit. To SIDA, it was a concession to be regretted.[8]

Handled by Eriksson himself, IUEF's support to BCM rapidly increased towards the mid-1970s. While—as noted by Enuga Reddy—there was a need to assist the anti-apartheid movement inside South Africa, by that time the Swedish government had established direct, bilateral relations with ANC in exile. In April 1976, CCHA's fact-finding mission further advised against official support to BCM, a recommen-

---

1. Ibid. Also letter ('Samarbetsområde SIDA-IUEF'/'Field of cooperation between SIDA and IUEF') from Stig Abelin to Lars-Gunnar Eriksson, SIDA, Stockholm, 27 September 1971 (SDA).

2. Gun-Britt Andersson: Memorandum ('Svenskt bistånd till IUEF'/'Swedish assistance to IUEF'), Ministry for Foreign Affairs, Stockholm, 6 April 1972 (SDA).

3. As noted in the first volume of this study, the Swedish Social Democratic Party and IUEF maintained brief, but important relations with Jonas Savimbi and his UNITA movement in the second half of the 1960s. They came to an end after Savimbi's return to Angola in mid-1968 (Sellström Volume I, pp. 402-08). In the case of Angola, IUEF subsequently established close relations with MPLA, in 1974—according to Shubin—even "help[ing] our people in Moscow to better understand the situation" (Conversation with Vladimir Shubin, p. 250). On IUEF, MPLA and the Soviet Union, see also the chapter on Angola above. It should be noted that IUEF from an early stage supported SWAPO of Namibia, PAC of South Africa (cf. the interview with Gora Ebrahim, pp. 118-20) and ZANU and ZAPU of Zimbabwe.

4. Via IUEF, Swedish support was, for example, channelled to education activities among political prisoners in Zimbabwe, as well as to trade union courses.

5. Stig Abelin: Memorandum ('International University Exchange Fund (IUEF)'), CCHA/SIDA, Stockholm, 25 May 1972 (SDA).

6. 'Agreed minutes of discussion[s] on continued cooperation between SIDA and IUEF', CCHA/SIDA, Stockholm, 9 May 1974 (SDA). SIDA was represented by Stig Abelin and Marianne Sundh, while Lars-Gunnar Eriksson negotiated on behalf of IUEF. For the financial year 1974/75, the Swedish contribution to IUEF amounted in total to 2.3 MSEK, out of which 180,000 SEK—around 8 per cent—was earmarked for BPC, SASM and SASO (ibid.).

7. Ibid.

8. As early as in November 1974—six months after negotiating with Lars-Gunnar Eriksson—Stig Abelin himself wrote a critical memorandum on Eriksson's leadership methods and IUEF's general administration.

dation followed by the ruling Social Democratic Party.[1] With funds from various sources, the IUEF Director, however, pursued his own course. This, in turn, attracted the apartheid regime's attention and paved the way for Craig Williamson's penetration.

Described by *Dagens Nyheter*'s Anders Johansson as a combination of James Bond, Robin Hood and Don Quixote[2], Eriksson "looked upon himself as a Social Democratic, anti-Communist crusader in Africa".[3] Managing IUEF high-handedly[4]—and long since removed from the broad Swedish social-liberal consensus with regard to the Southern African nationalist movements and the pragmatic view of their relations with the Soviet Union and other Communist forces—in the Cold War context he appeared as a determined anti-Communist.[5] Williamson later commented that Eriksson

> was a fanatical Social Democrat. [...] [He] liked to play. He loved intrigue and he created intrigue, but he really disliked Communists. That is why we found him useful.[6]

---

1. It has often been said that Eriksson acted as an extended arm of the Social Democratic Party. It should be noted in this context that when Mats Hellström, at the time a Social Democratic MP, after a mid-1978 visit to Southern Africa in preparation for LO's approaching Southern Africa campaign recommended that "the different branches of [BCM]" should be supported, the advice was not followed by the Social Democratic labour movement (Mats Hellström: 'Rapport från en resa i södra Afrika sommaren 1978'/'Report from a journey to Southern Africa in the summer of 1978', [no place], 9 August 1978, p. 17) (OPA).

2. Anders Johansson: 'IUEF's egen undersökning kritiserar Eriksson' ('IUEF's own investigation criticizes Eriksson') in *Dagens Nyheter*, 2 November 1980.

3. Ibid.

4. The IUEF commission of inquiry noted that "the organisation was already autocratically and arbitrarily run, with major decision-making and all responsibility centred in Geneva and in the person of the Director, before Williamson entered it. [...] Eriksson [kept] the IUEF [as] an organisation in which there was no real delegation of power or responsibility, no confidence shown in other staff members, secrecy and a reluctance to impart information" (IUEF Commission of Inquiry, p. 57).

5. In the case of ANC and the international anti-apartheid movement, Eriksson had an obsession with Communist influence. In 1975, in a letter to Bernt Carlsson—at the time international secretary of the ruling Social Democratic Party—he discussed, for example, the International Defence and Aid Fund (IDAF). The Swedish government had been since 1964 by far the largest contributor to the London-based, leading international NGO in the field of legal aid (Sellström Volume I, p. 140). Prominent Swedes—notably Dean Gunnar Helander and Per Wästberg—were actively involved in its work. This notwithstanding, in his letter Eriksson—who had the ambition to take over IDAF and merge it with IUEF—wrote that "as I have been trying to point out for now close to ten years, the [organization] is, apart from [the Director] Canon Collins [...] and his [p]ersonal [a]ssistant [...], fundamentally controlled by the South African Communist Party in cooperation with the British Communist Party [...]". Describing IDAF's South African staff members as either Communists or 'fellow travellers', in the same letter he characterized the officially appointed CCHA members Helander and Wästberg as follows: "Helander [...] has never marked himself for his intelligence and [is] at the best completely naive and at the worst a 'fellow traveller'", while Wästberg was "not a declared enemy, [but] politically unreliable" (Letter ('International Defence and Aid Fund') from Lars-Gunnar Eriksson to Bernt Carlsson [no place or date, but 1975]; original in English) (SDA). In another letter to Carlsson later in 1975, Eriksson again discussed IDAF, but above all ANC and SWAPO. The role of ANC's Acting President Oliver Tambo was said to be "ambiguous". Tambo, Eriksson argued, "is very weak as a person and, whilst not a member of SACP, certainly not in control of the organisation. He is basically being manoeuvred by the [Communist Party] hard-liners". Abdul Minty—with close links to both IDAF and Scandinavia—was characterized as SACP's "most dangerous guy", while the comment with regard to the SWAPO President Sam Nujoma was that "he is fairly sick" (Letter ('Additional memorandum concerning IDAF as well as ANC and other related matters') from Lars-Gunnar Eriksson to Bernt Carlsson, Geneva, 1-2 November 1975; original in English) (SDA). It is not clear on whose initiative and for what purpose these remarkable letters were written. Contrary to what was stated above, in this case it would, however, appear that Eriksson acted in response to questions raised by Carlsson. In the second letter, Eriksson wrote: "If you have specific further queries, let me know and I'll try to find answers. I have also asked one of my agents to collect some more data (and dirt) that might come in handy" (ibid.).

6. Interview with Craig Williamson, p. 200.

Although Steve Biko, Barney Pityana and other BCM leaders did not see black consciousness as a separate political force—and Pityana later dismissed the idea[1]—Eriksson's involvement with BCM and his distance vis-à-vis ANC and the Congress Alliance suggest that until the late 1970s he promoted the movement as an alternative, or a 'third force'.[2] In fact, it was only through Williamson's actions that IUEF in 1978—at a time when BCM was in disarray—eventually embraced ANC, the main target of 'Operation Daisy'. In a puzzling turn of events, Eriksson appeared opposed to ANC, while his deputy and confidant—soon to emerge as a South African intelligence officer—supported the movement led by Tambo.[3] Equally confusing was that ANC's political leadership was critical of IUEF's South Africa operations, while other structures appeared to give him the benefit of the doubt.

Craig Williamson and 'Operation Daisy'

Already working for the South African security police[4], in his capacity as Vice-President of NUSAS Craig Williamson first met Lars-Gunnar Eriksson and IUEF during a visit to Europe in October 1975.[5] Having established anti-apartheid credentials by running an escape route into Botswana for South African refugees, Williamson made a favourable impression on the IUEF Director. As part of the build-up of his 'legend' for 'Operation Daisy', during the same visit he also established contacts with ANC in London, volunteering to set up an 'ANC cell' on his return to South

---

1. In 1997, Pityana stated: "I think that Lars-Gunnar Eriksson recognized that there was a very new and very significant movement represented by SASO and [b]lack [c]onsciousness inside South Africa. His main interest was to recognize that movement and then to support and nurture it. [...] I do not think that [he] was thinking in terms of a 'third force', but there was on his part a recognition of BCM as a new political movement in South Africa. From talking to him I know that he felt that too many refused to acknowledge that. His insight was that BCM was a political force that had to be taken into account" (Interview with Barney Pityana, pp. 187-88).

2. In Williamson's opinion, "[t]he way Lars-Gunnar Eriksson and his friends in the Swedish Social Democratic Party saw it—putting it very simplistically—was that there is a liberation struggle in South Africa which is a just struggle. [B]ut the black political groupings have a problem, because they are dominated by ANC, which in turn is dominated by the Communist Party, which is controlled by the Soviets. [...] [Eriksson and his friends] were seeking a way to assist [the] new, younger generation of thinkers in the South African liberation struggle, and they tried to avoid being dictated to by ANC and others in determining who should be assisted" (Interview with Craig Williamson, pp. 198-99).

3. In 1996, Williamson noted: "I had to narrow [the IUEF support] down to ANC, but without being illogical. If I suddenly would have said to Lars-Gunnar that we must support this or that ANC initiative, he would immediately have thought that I was a Communist. He would have thought that this is a SACP guy. Which is what people like [Gatsha] Buthelezi and people from ZANU told him. They were not so worried about me being a spy for South Africa. They were worried that I was a white South African Communist. So, on the one hand [Eriksson] had to tell people: 'He is not a Communist'. And on the other: 'He is not working for the South Africans either'. It was a bit tricky. If I had just said: 'Look, ANC is *the* liberation movement', he would not have gone for it" (ibid., p. 200).

4. Born in Johannesburg in 1949, through family connections with Johan Coetzee—the future head of South Africa's security police—Williamson was at an early stage introduced to undercover work for the apartheid state. It could in this context be noted that his sister Lisa-Jane Williamson—between 1977 and 1979 working as secretary for the Prisoners Support Trust Fund, *inter alia* organizing visits by family members to Robben Island—was also employed by the security police (*Sunday Times*, 16 March 1980). So was his wife Ingrid, a Danish citizen who during Williamson's time at IUEF on behalf of Pretoria monitored ANC activities while working as a secretary for the World Health Organization in Geneva (*Rand Daily Mail*, 6 March 1980). After matriculation at St. John's College in Johannesburg, from May 1968 until February 1971 Williamson did his national service in the South African Police Force. It was during that time that he was recruited to the security branch. In 1972, he started studies in law and political science at the University of Witwatersrand, where he joined the local NUSAS committee and was a member of the Students Representative Council. In 1974, Williamson became a staff member at NUSAS' headquarters in Cape Town, taking up the post as finance officer. The following year, he was elected Vice-President of NUSAS (IUEF Commission of Inquiry, p. 10 and letter from Hassim Soumaré, IUEF, to the Swedish ambassador to Zambia, Lusaka, 28 January 1980) (SDA).

5. IUEF Commission of Inquiry, p. 11.

Africa. This marked the beginning of Williamson's relations with those ANC structures that coordinated the underground struggle.[1]

After his visit to Europe, Williamson made an outline of 'Operation Daisy'. In a report to his superior security officers, he presented "a strategy of appearing to get in disfavour of South Africa, fleeing the country, getting into the IUEF and from there penetrating the African National Congress".[2] Shortly thereafter, an opportunity presented itself to set the operation in motion when in late July 1976—after the Soweto uprising—he again met the IUEF Director in Botswana. As noted in an internal memorandum by Eriksson, on this occasion it was agreed "in principle that [Williamson] will be employed by the IUEF to handle our publications [...], as well as being involved with our Southern African programme in general".[3] According to Eriksson's notes, Williamson's "intention [was] to leave [South Africa] illegally at the end of the year via Botswana, where arrangements have been made with Ranwedzi [Nengwekhulu] to get him cleared".[4]

Facilitated by his superior, Johan Coetzee, Williamson's 'flight' took place in early January 1977, when he crossed the border into Botswana in the company of an anti-apartheid activist whose credibility enhanced his own.[5] Proceeding to Geneva, he—as agreed with Eriksson—initially worked for IUEF's publications department. In spite of IUEF's practice not to recruit refugees as staff members[6], Williamson soon rose to more prominent positions. The IUEF Commission of Inquiry later noted that "[w]ith Williamson's arrival [...] Eriksson appear[ed] quickly to [...] rely heavily on him for information and advice about South Africa".[7] A post of information officer was established, and Williamson was appointed to the position with retroactive effect from 1 January 1977, that is, even before the date of his arrival in Geneva.[8] As information officer, he was, however, given much more strategic tasks than the designation would indicate. In fact, together with the Director, Williamson

---

1. In a hearing with the Truth and Reconciliation Commission, Williamson later stated that he set up an 'ANC cell' consisting entirely of security police which was responsible for detonating pamphlet bombs: "Basically, if the ANC told me to put up a pamphlet bomb, I'd say 'OK, I will do it', and three weeks later it happened, and the ANC was very happy [...]. [But,] that cell was the [s]ecurity [b]ranch. [...] The people who went to London to get detonators [...] [and] pick up suitcases full of [...] propaganda material [...] were police officers [...]. People who were arrested by the flying squad after setting off a pamphlet bomb were police officers. [...] They had to recruit [...] the flying squad guys into the [s]ecurity [b]ranch to keep them quiet" (TRC op. cit. (Vol. II), pp. 696-97). Cf. Shubin, who notes that "[s]ome members of the ANC were taken in by Williamson [...]. Confidential police documents made public in 1994 [...] show that agents of the South African security forces served as couriers for a section of the ANC underground and semi-legal structures in Southern Africa" (Shubin op. cit., p. 217). In a comment on the methods developed by General Johan Coetzee and Williamson, TRC concluded that they were implemented "with deadly effect during the 1980s, [leading] to entrapment operations—in which security force personnel recruited, trained and, in some instances, armed activists before killing them—as well as [to] arson and sabotage operations conducted by the [s]ecurity [b]ranch in order to boost the credibility of agents" (TRC op. cit. (Vol. II), p. 697).
2. IUEF Commission of Inquiry, p. 12. On this point, the commission based itself on information given by the former BOSS intelligence officer Arthur McGiven. Both McGiven and Williamson were members of Witwatersrand university's Student Representative Council in 1973-74 (*Rand Daily Mail*, 23 January 1980).
3. Lars-Gunnar Eriksson: Memorandum ('File note on discussions with Craig Williamson in Botswana on 30 [July] [19]76'), IUEF, Geneva, 19 August 1976 (SDA).
4. Ibid. It should be underlined that BCM's Nengwekhulu was responsible for Williamson's clearance. Interviewed in 1997, Pityana stated that "Eriksson hired Craig Williamson with the support of ANC and against opposition from us and from the South African Council of Churches. We told him that Williamson was not a person to be trusted" (Interview with Barney Pityana, p. 187). While Williamson certainly had previous contacts with ANC and both BCM and SACC gave warnings, it is of interest to note that the IUEF contact and senior BCM representative Nengwekhulu made arrangements for his reception in Botswana and onward journey to Switzerland.
5. The journalist Eric Abraham, who had been banned by the Pretoria government and was harassed by its security police.
6. IUEF Commission of Inquiry, p. 12.
7. Ibid.
8. Ibid. The decision was taken by the Director and subsequently endorsed by IUEF's Assembly and International Board.

Craig Williamson repre-
senting IUEF at the 1978
UNHCR Executive Com-
mittee annual meeting
in Geneva (Photo from
IUEF Annual Report
1977/78)

assumed "special responsibilities [...] for [IUEF's] internal South African programmes".[1]

From the very beginning, Williamson occupied a privileged position from which
he could regularly supply the South African security forces with information on the
anti-apartheid opposition and the liberation movements in Namibia and Zimbabwe.[2] In order to consolidate his relations with ANC, behind Eriksson's back at the
same time he informed the movement about IUEF and its projects in favour of
BCM, PAC and other organizations. His role within IUEF was far from that of an
éminence grise. On the contrary, together with Eriksson—or standing in for him—
from 1977 Williamson represented IUEF at a number of international anti-apartheid conferences[3], meetings with Geneva-based UN organizations—such as
UNHCR—and in discussions with donor governments and international organizations. He paid his first of several visits to Sweden shortly after his arrival in Geneva.

With regard to South Africa, from early 1977 Williamson *de facto* acted as
Eriksson's deputy. This situation was soon formalized. At the annual meeting of the
IUEF Assembly and International Board, it was decided at the end of 1977 to insti-
tute a post of Deputy Director, to be "in full charge of all aspects of work when the
Director is absent".[4] One and a half years after leaving South Africa and with
extremely limited experience from international refugee work—in particular con-

---

1. Ibid. IUEF's activities in South Africa were coordinated at their headquarters in Geneva. There was very little
   delegation to the Lusaka office, which was primarily concerned with scholarships and counselling. Zanele
   Mbeki, the wife of Thabo Mbeki, was working from the mid-1970s at IUEF's Lusaka office. She joined IUEF
   as an administrator-cum-counsellor in September 1974 ('Contract of employment [for] staff employed outside
   Switzerland', signed by Lars-Gunnar Eriksson on 19 September and by Zanele Dlamini on 30 September
   1974, IUEF, Geneva) (SDA).
2. As noted in the chapter on the Zimbabwean Patriotic Front, Rhodesia's attacks on ZANU and ZAPU in
   Angola, Mozambique and Zambia in the late 1970s were coordinated with South Africa. Interviewed in
   1996, Williamson acknowledged that "when the Rhodesians bombed Lusaka [...] we had given information
   to them of where to strike" (Interview with Craig Williamson, p. 202). Several former Rhodesian anti-guerrilla operatives were later recruited by Williamson into South Africa's death squads. Some of them have been
   mentioned in connection with the assassination of Olof Palme.
3. As an example, Eriksson and Williamson both attended the UN/OAU World Conference for Action against
   Apartheid in Lagos, Nigeria, in August 1977.
4. 'Work description of the Deputy Director of [IUEF]', attached to letter from Per Tegmo to the members of the
   IUEF Assembly and International Board, IUEF, Geneva, 19 April 1978 (SDA).

cerning Latin America[1]—Williamson was appointed in June 1978 to the new position.[2]

By that time, Steve Biko had been killed[3] and the black consciousness movement neutralized. Although maintaining his BCM sympathies, in this situation Lars-Gunnar Eriksson became more positive towards ANC.[4] Through Williamson's lobbying[5], in June 1978 IUEF recognized ANC as the leading liberation movement in South Africa.[6] Still critical of its independent activities in the country[7], ANC reciprocated. Attending IUEF's annual meeting in Geneva in December 1978, ANC's Treasurer General Thomas Nkobi not only stated that "IUEF has become a friend [...] [which is] assisting us in many fields [that] are important for human development", but invited the organization to actively participate in the establishment of the SOMAFCO settlement in Tanzania.[8] Coming at a particularly crucial time, the shift of both IUEF's and ANC's positions momentarily arrested the mounting criticism of the international NGO and the role played by its South African Deputy Director.

In addition to political and security aspects, towards the end of the 1970s some of IUEF's major donors started to raise questions concerning the organization's finances.[9] They could, however, hardly have imagined the extent of the irregulari-

1. Within IUEF, "Williamson showed little interest in the scholarship programmes", which, however, constituted the backbone of its mandate (IUEF Commission of Inquiry, p. 27).
2. Ibid., p. 13. According to the commission report, "the only questions asked about the appointment concerned Williamson's financial and administrative competence" (ibid.).
3. The inquiry commission noted that "IUEF does not appear to have made any effort after Biko's death to ascertain if there was any connection between his funding by and association with the [organization] and his detention and murder" (ibid., p. 21).
4. After hearing Eriksson, the IUEF Commission of Inquiry noted in 1980 that his statements "indicated [...] that [...] he [...] was coming to the feeling that it would be politically wise for the IUEF to 'recognise' the ANC. The [1977] PAC arrests were a turning point, as was the moving of the external BCM towards new structures which Eriksson thought could cause trouble" (IUEF Commission of Inquiry. p. 23).
5. Williamson commented in 1996: "It took a bit of time [to push Eriksson and IUEF towards ANC]. [...] [T]he only reason it worked was that [BCM] started to have some problems of its own from 1976-78. [...] [D]uring that same period, ANC got its act together. [...] They started to look better, and at the IUEF conference in 1978 I was able to [...] move the political decision to recognize ANC" (Interview with Craig Williamson, p. 200).
6. 'IUEF Är Ingen CIA-organisation'/'IUEF Is No CIA Organization' in *Afrikabulletinen*, No. 1, 1979, p. 1. Over the years, the Africa Groups had distanced themselves from IUEF, characterizing the organization as dominated by the US Central Intelligence Agency. When IUEF recognized ANC, AGIS would, however, through the quoted editorial—published twelve months before Williamson's exposure—endorse the organization.
7. In his address to IUEF's Assembly and International Board, Thomas Nkobi stated in December 1978: "We should [...] like to emphasise that [...] the ANC thinks that the closest cooperation between ourselves and the IUEF in actually setting up [...] assistance programmes inside South Africa would add considerably to the success of such programmes" (T. T. Nkobi: 'A statement by the African National Congress of South Africa at the Board and Assembly meeting of the IUEF, held in Geneva 1st-5th December 1978' in IUEF: 'Assembly: Resolutions, Working Group Reports and Keynote Speeches', December 1978, p. 14) (SDA).
8. Ibid., pp. 13 and 15. For a short period, IUEF was closely associated with the ANC settlement in Tanzania. Although this—in the IUEF Director's characteristic way—was exaggerated, in May 1979 Eriksson told the Swedish embassy in Dar es Salaam that ANC had given IUEF the task of coordinating fund-raising for the project (Per Lindström: Memorandum ('IUEF's verksamhet i Tanzania'/'IUEF's activities in Tanzania'), Swedish embassy, Dar es Salaam, 21 May 1979) (MFA). Visiting SOMAFCO just before Williamson's exposure in January 1980, Magnus Bergmar of the Africa Groups reported that IUEF had undertaken to copy ANC's drawings of the settlement (Magnus Bergmar: 'Frihetsskolan'/'The Freedom College' in *Afrikabulletinen*, No. 3, 1980, p. 7).
9. This was, for example, the case with Denmark. When in early 1979 it was announced that the Danish state auditors were to verify the utilization of DANIDA's IUEF contributions, Lars-Gunnar Eriksson panicked. Describing the official Danish auditors as "both the dumbest and most difficult in the [W]estern world", in an internal memorandum entitled 'The storm clouds are gathering' he instructed his executive staff to take "immediate steps [...] in order to ensure that all DANIDA accounts are as clean as possible" (Lars-Gunnar Eriksson: Memorandum ('The storm clouds are gathering'), IUEF, Geneva, 16 March 1979) (SDA). In the case of Sweden, unsuccessful initiatives to examine IUEF's accounts had been taken since the early 1970s.

ties, lack of control and misappropriation of funds that came to light after the exposure of Williamson and the departure of Eriksson in early 1980.

It falls outside the scope of this study to discuss IUEF's financial administration.[1] Nevertheless, it should be noted that regular overspending on administration and projects at the level of the directorate seriously undermined the sustainability of the core scholarship programmes.[2] Above all, by becoming aware of what the IUEF Commission of Inquiry later characterized as "deliberate deception of the donors"[3] Williamson not only got a significant hold on Eriksson, but could also use the lack of financial transparency and deceptive routines to his own and Pretoria's advantage.[4] This was, in particular, the case with regard to the Southern Futures Anstalt (SFA), a slush fund set up in Vaduz, Liechtenstein, by the IUEF Director as early as in October 1976, that is, before Williamson joined the organization.[5]

Behind the donors' backs, SFA was used "as a vehicle to 'launder' transfers between IUEF project and programme accounts, [giving them] the official impression that their grants had been properly spent, whereas they had, in fact, been switched for other purposes".[6] Considerable sums were diverted from agreed humanitarian activities to all kinds of political groups, almost exclusively with a South African connection. Despite IUEF's recognition of ANC, funds were, for example, channelled by Eriksson to dissidents of the movement.[7] Much more damning was that via the slush fund he uncritically paid his deputy significant amounts in cash for various projects in South Africa, which Williamson in turn forwarded to the apartheid security police. As Williamson took the SFA files when he left Geneva in January 1980[8], the full extent of these transactions might never be known. In the case of Denmark alone, the official state auditors established in 1980 that Williamson had received more than 500,000 Swiss Francs via the Southern Futures Anstalt.[9]

As subsequently revealed by Williamson, the IUEF funds were not only used to purchase the Daisy police farm outside Pretoria—initially used by the security forces as a training and planning centre for foreign operations and later by the South African death squads—but also for bogus IUEF projects on the farm. Com-

---

1. Remarkable details of IUEF's financial mismanagement were revealed by the IUEF Commission of Inquiry (pp. 51-65) and in the parallel so called 'Moate Report' of February-March 1980 by the British accountant David Moate (SDA).
2. In mid-March 1980, IUEF's accumulated deficit was estimated at 4.4 million Swiss Francs (Roland Axelsson, Kalevi Tikkanen and Rigmor Tiranchie: Memorandum ('Report on donors' investigation into the IUEF'), SIDA, Stockholm, 14 March 1980, p. 10) (SDA).
3. IUEF Commission of Inquiry, p. 60.
4. Ibid., p. 57. See also the interview with Craig Williamson, p. 201.
5. Southern Futures Anstalt was incorporated in Liechtenstein on 13 October 1976, with full powers of attorney given to Lars-Gunnar Eriksson, Carl Nissen, the Danish Chairman of IUEF's International Board, and Leslie Rubin, a South African resident in the United States. Signing powers were, in addition, held by Neville Rubin, the son of Leslie Rubin and a former NUSAS official. Any two of them could sign bank instructions. In practice, the second signatory was always Lars-Gunnar Eriksson. Neville Rubin would sign bank instructions in blank and leave them to be used by Eriksson as and when required ('Moate Report', p. 8) (SDA). When Axelsson, Tikkanen and Tiranchie in early 1980 on behalf of the donors investigated IUEF's accounts, they found around 50 forms for bank transfers pre-signed in blank by Rubin (Roland Axelsson, Kalevi Tikkanen and Rigmor Tiranchie: Memorandum ('Report on donors' investigation into the IUEF'), SIDA, Stockholm, 14 March 1980, p. 7) (SDA). From November 1978, Craig Williamson "had control of the (SFA) books" ('Moate Report', p. 9).
6. 'Moate Report', p. 9.
7. IUEF Commission of Inquiry, p. 61.
8. Ibid., p. 58.
9. De af Folketinget Valgte Statsrevisorer: *Beretning om Anvendelsen af Bevillningen til Undertrykte Folk eller Folkegrupper ('Apartheidbevillningen')* ('Report on the Allocation for Oppressed Peoples or Population Groups ('The Apartheid Allocation')'), No. 13, 1979, Copenhagen, 1980, p. 9. See also Henrik Thomsen: 'Dansk bistand til tortur: Operation Tusindfryd' ('Danish assistance to torture: Operation Daisy') in *Morgenavisen/Jyllands-Posten*, 30 March 1997.

menting that the "complete mess" with regard to IUEF's finances was "handy" for his purposes, in 1996 he said:

> [Eriksson] created this [slush fund] in Vaduz, Liechtenstein, called Southern Futures. He then used to report to the donors: 'Look, on certain confidential projects all I can tell you is that when the money leaves IUEF's account, you have to accept that for auditing purposes it has been spent'. He would take the money out of IUEF and put it into Southern Futures [...] and, of course, he could then do what he liked with [it]. [...]
>
> Lars-Gunnar was playing a political game. So, what we did was just the same. IUEF was supposed to have a leadership training programme for white students in South Africa [...], but [...] it was a leadership training programme for the security forces, not for the anti-apartheid forces. At one stage, we ran an internal structure [...] which was financed by IUEF. People even came from Denmark and other countries and were shown the programme. They went to the farm and were very happy. [...] Paul Brandrup from [the Danish Youth Council] lived on [Daisy] farm for a while. He was told that this was the secret place we had for training of anti-apartheid activists. They all said: 'Oh, wonderful! This is in the heart of apartheid, just twenty kilometres from Pretoria. They have got a farm where they are training the opposition'. They believed in the romance of the thing.[1]

'Operation Daisy' came to a sudden end in January 1980. It was brought about by the defection from BOSS[2] of Williamson's former university colleague Arthur McGiven, who was familiar with the operation and who through a series of articles in the London *Observer* from 30 December 1979 started to give a breakdown of apartheid's security services and their foreign operations.[3] Fearing exposure by McGiven[4], the South Africans lost their nerve. During a meeting with Eriksson in Zürich on 18 January 1980, Williamson confessed to being a member of the South African security police. Also present was Brigadier Johan Coetzee, the head of the Special Branch with whom Williamson had originally planned the infiltration of IUEF. Taking considerable risks by appearing in Switzerland[5], Coetzee proposed to Eriksson that his agent should remain with IUEF for up to six months "in order to complete his mission of penetrating the ANC and the SACP", after which he would return to South Africa "with as few complications as possible for Eriksson and the IUEF".[6]

Asking for time, a couple of days later Eriksson took refuge in Sweden, where at a press conference in Stockholm on 22 January he announced Williamson's true identity. He also said that in Zürich Coetzee had threatened to take action against leading Swedish Social Democratic politicians unless his proposal was agreed to.[7] With his cover blown, together with Coetzee Williamson in the meantime returned

---

1. Interview with Craig Williamson, p. 201. Among the South African agents trained at Daisy Farm was Peter Casselton, former Rhodesian anti-guerrilla operative, future handler of the Swede Bertil Wedin in London, close friend of Eugene de Kock and mentioned in connection with the Palme assassination (Pauw (1997) op. cit., pp. 214-15).
2. Bureau of State Security. At about the same time, the name of the organization was changed to the Department of National Security (DONS). In 1980, it became the National Intelligence Service (NIS).
3. Andrew Wilson: 'BOSS agent quits to reveal spy secrets' in *The Observer*, 30 December 1979. IUEF was mentioned in general terms in the second article (Andrew Wilson: 'The British 'targets' of BOSS' in *The Observer*, 6 January 1980).
4. One year later, Williamson stated: "We now had an uncontrollable factor [...]. Here was a man who knew about the operation, knew a lot of details about it. The most fundamental rule in intelligence work is that once a man starts talking, you must assume that everything he knows is compromised" (Williamson cited by Andrew Stephen in 'Scenes in the life of a super-spy' in *The Sunday Times Magazine*, 8 February 1981).
5. As noted by the inquiry commission, unless the stakes were very high Coetzee's presence could not be easily explained (IUEF Commission of Inquiry, pp. 45-46).
6. Cited in ibid., p. 37.
7. Per Sjögren: 'Svenska politiker hotade av Sydafrikas polis' ('Swedish politicians threatened by South Africa's police') in *Dagens Nyheter*, 23 January 1980. See also Anders Hasselbohm: 'Sydafrika hotade svenska s-politiker' ('South Africa threatened Swedish Social Democratic politicians') in *Aftonbladet*, 31 July 1994.

IUEF Director
Lars-Gunnar Eriksson
revealing his deputy
Craig Williamson's true
identity at a press
conference in Stock-
holm, January 1980
(Photo: Rolf Petterson/
Aftonbladet Bild)

to South Africa[1], where as Captain Williamson he was given a hero's welcome. While Eriksson subsequently resigned from IUEF, joined the Swedish Immigration Board and kept a low profile[2], Williamson would as South Africa's 'super-spy' take a leading part in the apartheid regime's 'total strategy' against ANC. In an article published in October 1981 by the South African police magazine *Servamus*, IUEF's former 'pro-ANC' Deputy Director wrote:

> Law enforcement officers [...] understand that the [Republic of South Africa] is faced with a revolutionary onslaught which, if it is ever allowed to succeed, will plunge the southern tip of Africa into chaos. Therefore, the only real answer is secret operations against the enemy [...].[3]

---

1. Both the IUEF Commission of Inquiry and Williamson himself were surprised that Eriksson did not take any immediate action after the Zürich meeting. Thus, the commission "came to the conclusion that Eriksson and [IUEF's senior staff member Piers] Campbell made errors of judgement [...], the cumulative effects of which were to allow Williamson to leave Switzerland without being arrested and to render more difficult the handling of the affair by the rest of the IUEF staff and others associated with the organisation" (IUEF Commission of Inquiry, pp. 40-41). Interviewed in South Africa upon his return, Williamson said: "I was in my flat in Geneva all the time [after the meeting]. [I]f he had wanted to stop me [from] leaving the country [...], he could have immediately contacted the police, who could have detained me. But he did not" (Neil Hooper: 'How the spy blew his own cover' in *Sunday Times*, 27 January 1980).
2. In his letter of resignation, Eriksson referred to "a combination of personal and health reasons", defiantly stating that "I am not resigning out of a feeling of guilt in regard to the Williamson affair, nor in regard to some of the more unorthodox financial and administrative procedures and transactions for which I have been responsible" (Letter from Lars-Gunnar Eriksson to the members of IUEF's International Board and Assembly, IUEF, Geneva, 2 June 1980) (SDA). Due to the financial misappropriations, both the Danish and Swedish aid authorities examined in 1980 the possibilities of suing Eriksson for breach of contract and trust (for Sweden, see letter ('IUEF-ärendet'/'The IUEF issue') from Jarl Tranaeus to Anders Forsse, [no place], 15 August 1980) (SDA). As IUEF was an association under Swiss law and legal proceedings would be both drawn out and complicated, no action was ever taken. Eriksson died in 1990.
3. Cited in Pauw op. cit. (1991), pp. 62-63. Promoted to the rank of Major, as deputy head of the foreign section of the South African security police—led by Piet 'Biko' Goosen—Williamson would on his return immediately go into action. As admitted by Williamson himself, in March 1982 he formed part of a team which bombed the ANC office in London; in August 1982 he was behind the assassination of Ruth First in Maputo; and in June 1984 of the murder of Jeanette Schoon and her daughter in Lubango, Angola. At the same time running "an extensive African and international spy network", the South African Truth and Reconciliation Commission (TRC) noted *inter alia* that "[n]ot only was the head of the Spanish anti-apartheid movement in the 1980s an apartheid agent, but the organisation was set up at Williamson's suggestion and funded by his section" (TRC op. cit. (Vol. II), p. 99). Later appointed to the influential President's Council, Williamson left the security police in December 1985. Joining apartheid's military intelligence service, he set up the company Longreach (Pty) Ltd as a front for its foreign operations (see, for example, Peta Thornycroft: 'Little intelligence at Longreach' in *Mail & Guardian*, 4-10 October 1996). Together with the death squad commander Eugene de Kock, Williamson was in May 2000 granted amnesty by TRC for crimes committed and admitted during the apartheid era.

Early Cautions

The exposure of Williamson and the revelations of financial irregularities came as a shock to IUEF's donors.[1] To secure the scholarship programmes, a coordinated rescue operation was immediately launched. In the meantime, a number of fundamental questions were raised with regard to the underlying reasons behind the crisis.[2]

In the case of Sweden, doubts concerning IUEF's administration had been expressed by aid officials involved with the organization long before 'Operation Daisy'. Reacting to Eriksson's generous outlays on hospitality, Sven Hamrell—Director of the Dag Hammarskjöld Foundation in Uppsala, officially appointed to the Consultative Committee on Humanitarian Assistance and a member of IUEF's International Board—had, for example, in the early 1970s unsuccessfully requested the CCHA secretariat to examine the NGO's accounts.[3] More comprehensive and serious criticism was in November 1974 raised by SIDA's Stig Abelin. At the time serving as secretary to the consultative committee, in a memorandum entitled 'Points of view on IUEF's administration' he wrote that

1. To make matters worse, in late January 1980 McGiven revealed that the World University Service (WUS) had also been infiltrated by the South African security forces. The agent in question was Karl 'Zak' Edwards, a close friend of Craig Williamson who had done his national service together with him in the South African police in the early 1970s and who—like Williamson— was elected to the NUSAS executive in 1974 (Peter Bruce and David Niddrie: 'Another ex-NUSAS man named as government spy' in *Sunday Express*, 27 January 1980). Based in South Africa and working on a WUS-sponsored environmental project, Edwards served as IUEF's local contact person. Eriksson and Williamson were in close contact with him, *inter alia* supplying information on Swedish diplomatic staff. For example, even before it was formally announced that Per Lindström—first secretary at the Swedish embassy in Dar es Salaam—was moving to the legation in Pretoria, Eriksson asked Williamson to notify Edwards. Describing Lindström as "more politically mature than the [Swedish] lady [in Pretoria] at present", in an internal memorandum to his deputy Eriksson wrote: "I think that it might be an idea to warn Zak about this already now and I will let you know [more] as soon as I have [Lindström's] departure date etc." (Memorandum from Lars-Gunnar Eriksson to Craig Williamson, IUEF, Geneva, 31 May 1979) (SDA). In connection with a trial in early 1981, it appeared that Williamson on behalf of WUS in 1979 had channelled some 100,000 South African Rands to Edwards, who, however, pocketed half of the amount for himself (Letter ('IUEF-affären'/'The IUEF affair') from Gustaf Hamilton to the Ministry for Foreign Affairs, Swedish legation, Pretoria, 25 March 1981) (SDA). Edwards visited SIDA in early 1978 (Birgitta Berggren: Memorandum ('IUEF-affären och dess följder'/'The IUEF affair and its consequences'), SIDA, Stockholm, 13 March 1980) (SDA). WUS started to support the black consciousness movement before IUEF did. The Scandinavian governments were by far its largest donors. In 1996, Williamson made the following comment in this regard: "Sweden and the Nordic countries were also supporting [WUS]. [...] WUS started to support—in fact, more and more—[BCM]. [...] This became a political problem, because one had not only to try and stop the support from IUEF, but also to make sure that funding did not go into WUS, because that could defeat our goal" (Interview with Craig Williamson, p. 200).
2. The most basic question, of course, was that of Lars-Gunnar Eriksson's relationship with the apartheid regime. To the author's knowledge, it has never been seriously addressed. While the IUEF Commission of Inquiry gave damning evidence in this regard, it stopped short of implying that the IUEF Director maintained links with Pretoria. One and a half decades later, Bertil Zachrisson, the Swedish Social Democratic member of the commission, stated that "it was not just because of credulity that [...] Eriksson backed up [...] Williamson. There was another reason. It could have been [anything] from a close friendship [...] to [the fact] that he participated in activities organized by South Africa. [...] During our investigation, we read letters and documents, as well as had scores of testimonies, which indicated that Lars-Gunnar Eriksson might have worked for the South Africans. [...] We always kept that suspicion open, [b]ut as we never had any proof we did not write it straight out in the report" (cited in Anders Hasselbohm: 'Sydafrika infiltrerade FN'/'South Africa infiltrated UN' in *Aftonbladet*, 1 August 1994). Per Wästberg—who first met Eriksson in 1962—has argued that the former IUEF Director's close relations with Williamson were due to his "alcoholism, sectarianism [and] lack of judgement" (Wästberg op. cit., p. 28), while Gunnar Helander—closely involved with Wästberg at IDAF— characterized Eriksson as "an enemy" and "a traitor" who "worked for the South African racist government, in their interest and for Craig Williamson" (Interview with Gunnar Helander, p. 285). When in 1996 the author put the question directly to Williamson, he answered that Eriksson was "a fanatical Social Democrat" (Interview with Craig Williamson, p. 200).
3. Interviewed in 1996, Hamrell stated: "I was personally suspicious of the way that [IUEF] used some of the money. I had been a member of the board of IUEF and I felt that things could be kept in better order. I requested that the [s]ecretariat of [CCHA] should go through the accounts of IUEF to make sure that every Krona was used for the right purpose. However, this did not take place" (Interview with Sven Hamrell, p. 281). Instead, Hamrell was told by Øystein Opdahl, the Norwegian chairman of IUEF's International Board, that his services "were no longer needed" (Conversation with the author, Uppsala, 10 August 2000).

[t]he possibilities for the Assembly and International Board to follow or direct IUEF's activities seem limited. The decisive influence is exercised by the Director. The vague objectives stated in [the organization's] statutes have not prevented an extension of the activities to new and varied areas. A streak of empire building has [...] come to characterize IUEF, which under the present Director has turned into a 'one-man business'.[1]

Looking back on his long involvement with official humanitarian support to Southern Africa, SIDA's former Director General and CCHA chairman Ernst Michanek later stated that if there was one thing he regretted, it was that he had not given sufficient attention to Abelin's early cautions with regard to IUEF.[2] At the time, however, SIDA and the Swedish authorities in general did not heed the warnings. On the contrary, motivated by the expanding scholarship programmes the allocations to IUEF were regularly increased throughout the 1970s.

Nonetheless, several SIDA officials remained critical of IUEF's non-transparent administration. Interviewed in 1996, Roland Axelsson stated that he "as auditor at SIDA [...] in 1976-77 tried to make an audit of IUEF", but that he "was stopped by [the] government. Stig Abelin and I wanted to do that, but we were not allowed to".[3] When Birgitta Berggren started as CCHA secretary in September 1978, she too raised concerns and requested a thorough assessment of the Geneva-based NGO.[4] Her and other officials' efforts were eventually crowned with success.[5] After agreement had been reached to carry out an evaluation[6], against the background of IUEF's financial crisis in mid-December 1979 CCHA also endorsed a proposal that SIDA should set up a working group to monitor its projects and programmes.[7] By then, however, it was too late. One month later, the Zürich meeting between Eriksson, Williamson and Coetzee signalled the end of IUEF.

Combined with the political concerns raised by ANC with regard to IUEF's activities in South Africa—and with the security warnings expressed concerning Williamson—the Swedish aid authorities' reluctance to properly assess the organization and their readiness to regularly raise the financial contributions stand out as

1. Stig Abelin: Memorandum ('Synpunkter på IUEF's administration'/'Points of view on IUEF's administration'), SIDA, Stockholm, 18 November 1974 (SDA). However, six months earlier Abelin had on SIDA's behalf formally agreed with Lars-Gunnar Eriksson that "special flexibility in [IUEF's] administration and development of projects [...] may be called for", leaving it "at the discretion of IUEF to adapt [...] to changing circumstances".
2. Conversation with Ernst Michanek, Stockholm, 19 March 1996.
3. Interview with Roland Axelsson, p. 253.
4. Sceptical about Williamson, Berggren was from the beginning singled out by Eriksson as particularly threatening to IUEF. After meeting her in Dar es Salaam in early November 1978, in a memorandum to Williamson—copied to Mats Hellström and Pierre Schori—he wrote: "Craig and I and other IUEF personnel have to go out of our way to deal straight with Birgitta as she obviously has on her mind any signs of knives being stuck into her back". Berggren was married to SIDA's Director General Anders Forsse. Against this background he added: "[A]s she is a double-force through her marital connection, we will have to be extra careful" (Memorandum from Lars-Gunnar Eriksson to Craig Williamson, IUEF, Geneva, 22 November 1978) (SDA). After discussions in Stockholm a year later—when IUEF's financial crisis had become obvious and Berggren and others had eventually managed to convince CCHA of the need to evaluate the organization—Eriksson reported to Williamson and other senior IUEF staff members that "Birgitta has been made fully aware that she cannot try to knife IUEF in the back and get away with it. Her arithmetic is probably good enough for her to work out where the political majority in the [Swedish] refugee committee lies" (Lars-Gunnar Eriksson: Memorandum ('Discussion with Birgitta Berggren, SIDA, October 1st 1979'), IUEF, Geneva, 26 October 1979) (SDA). It could be noted that Berggren was a member of the Social Democratic Party.
5. Berggren later commented: "It was impossible to get any response from those who took the decisions. It took too long, and then the damage was already done. It was terrible. I am convinced that it led to the death of a number of people" (Interview with Birgitta Berggren, p. 261).
6. Birgitta Berggren: Memorandum ('Minnesanteckningar från samtal med Lars-Gunnar Eriksson, IUEF, den 4 oktober 1979'/'Notes from conversation with Lars-Gunnar Eriksson, IUEF, on 4 October 1979'), SIDA, Stockholm, 8 November 1979 (SDA).
7. CCHA: 'Protokoll [från sammanträde 14 december 1979]' ('Minutes [from meeting 14 December 1979]'), SIDA, [Stockholm], 18 January 1980 (SDA).

extraordinary. No other international NGO of a comparable status was accorded a similar *carte blanche*. This, in turn, was made possible through the IUEF Director's long-standing and privileged relations with a group of influential Social Democratic Party members and centrally placed Foreign Ministry officials. Among the former were notably Bernt Carlsson, Mats Hellström and Pierre Schori—according to Eriksson's secretary at IUEF commonly referred to as 'the three musketeers'[1]—and at the Ministry for Foreign Affairs Thord Palmlund.

In unorthodox ways, throughout the years Eriksson directly or indirectly supplied his contacts in Sweden with information intended to enhance his own and IUEF's standing, lobbying for support and trying to stave off criticism. While Hellström—from 1969 a Social Democratic MP—was an important conduit into parliament, Carlsson and Schori—old colleagues from the anti-apartheid movement in the early 1960s—would as international secretaries of the Social Democratic Party and members of IUEF's International Board be particularly courted. Within the administration, Thord Palmlund—Eriksson's predecessor as IUEF's first Director—similarly played a key role, in particular after becoming Under-Secretary of State for International Development Cooperation in 1978.[2] At the end of the 1970s, both Schori and Palmlund were full members of CCHA.

The issue of Sweden, ANC and IUEF will be discussed below. Meanwhile, it should be noted that the pervasive, uncritical view of IUEF in the 1970s was mainly a result of Eriksson's selective, but successful lobbying. Discussing the consequences of the wider IUEF affair, in a letter to the Liberal Foreign Minister Ola Ullsten SIDA's Director General Anders Forsse commented in September 1980 that although

> it may be said that the crisis was provoked by [the fact] that a leading staff member [...] turned out to be a South African spy [...], its real reasons lay in several years of mismanagement, *inter alia* expressed through disregard for basic legal concepts and conditions set by [the] donors [...], as well as suppression of critical audits [...]. The organization was essentially run by its Director, who relied directly on political connections in the donor countries. I have of late had an insight into—and an unpleasant impression of—the way in which [his] political contacts were used to neutralize justified efforts by SIDA officials to follow up the utilization of public grants.[3]

IUEF, Sweden and ANC

While doubts concerning IUEF's administration were raised from the mid-1970s by individual aid officials, in its dialogue with the Swedish authorities ANC would at the same time advise against support to its activities in South Africa. As early as in May 1976, Oliver Tambo deplored IUEF's uncritical assistance to BCM. Often shared by Swedish diplomatic representatives, ANC's politically motivated concerns—in the case of IUEF more explicit than with regard to Inkatha—did not, however, lead to decreasing allocations.

Many examples could here be quoted. In a comment to a request from IUEF, in May 1977 the Swedish embassy in Lusaka reported after discussions with ANC

---

1. Anders Hasselbohm: 'Sveriges hemliga krig mot apartheid' ('Sweden's secret war against apartheid') in *Aftonbladet*, 28 July 1994.
2. In 1980, Palmlund left the Ministry for Foreign Affairs to take up the position of Director General of the Swedish Immigration Board (SIV). Eriksson joined SIV after his resignation from IUEF.
3. Letter ('IUEF i kris'/'IUEF in crisis') from Anders Forsse to Ola Ullsten, SIDA, Stockholm, 24 September 1980 (SDA). Interviewed in 1996, Birgitta Berggren commented: "[S]ince there was this loyalty between old friends and politicians, it was difficult to bring about a change. As a plain civil servant, they would accuse you of disloyalty to the cause or whatever, which, of course, was rubbish" (Interview with Birgitta Berggren, p. 261).

that the movement was in favour of continued Swedish contributions to the scholarship programmes, but "clearly negative" about IUEF as a channel for internal "political work". Stating that there had been instances where IUEF "had used contributions with a view to opposing [the movement]", ANC recommended the Swedish authorities to adopt a "cautious" attitude regarding support via IUEF to South African organizations.[1] Against this background, ambassador Ove Heyman advocated restraint, arguing that official support to IUEF in favour of such organizations could be "counterproductive in relation to the [direct] assistance to ANC".[2] Later in the month, Anders Möllander, first secretary at the embassy, repeated the arguments.[3]

A year later—in April 1978—the support to IUEF and the organization's activities in South Africa were discussed at length during a meeting in Lusaka between SIDA[4], ANC President Tambo and Treasurer General Nkobi. On this occasion, the senior ANC leaders considerably sharpened their criticism. According to the Swedish notes from the meeting, Nkobi stressed that

> IUEF supported [...] organizations which directly opposed ANC and were spreading spiteful rumours about [the movement]. Swedish funds were thus used [...] against ANC.[5]

Expressing doubts about the motives behind the IUEF support, Nkobi added that

> the [Swedish] allocation to ANC was small compared with what was granted in support of other organizations[6], which could be said to represent the beginnings of a 'third force'. ANC's name was used [by IUEF] to raise funds for such activities. Was this intentional?[7]

Thus explicitly associating Sweden with the build-up of an internally based 'third force' against apartheid, Nkobi's harsh criticism was taken seriously by the Lusaka embassy. After further discussions with Tambo—and with Lars-Gunnar Eriksson, who visited Zambia in late April 1978[8]—Möllander wrote to the Foreign Ministry in Stockholm that "it is unfortunate—to say the least—[that] two organizations which we are supporting use the assistance to oppose one another".[9]

Although Craig Williamson already occupied a prominent position at the IUEF headquarters in Geneva, the concerns expressed by ANC—and shared by the embassy in Zambia—did not at that stage focus on security aspects, but on the contradiction between direct assistance to the liberation movement led by Tambo and

1. Cable from Ove Heyman, Swedish ambassador to Zambia, to the Ministry for Foreign Affairs, Lusaka, 3 May 1977 (SDA).
2. Ibid.
3. Letter ('African National Congress' ställning i Sydafrika'/'ANC's position in South Africa') from Anders Möllander to the Ministry for Foreign Affairs, Swedish embassy, Lusaka, 19 May 1977 (SDA).
4. The SIDA representatives at the meeting were Curt Ström from the headquarters in Stockholm and Per Kökeritz and Elisabeth Michanek from the embassy in Lusaka. Ove Heyman, the Swedish ambassador to Zambia, also took part.
5. Elisabeth Michanek: Memorandum ('Möte med Oliver Tambo den 11 april 1978'/'Meeting with Oliver Tambo on 11 April 1978'), Swedish embassy, Lusaka, 20 April 1978 (SDA).
6. In reality, however, the direct official Swedish allocation to ANC of 8 MSEK during the financial year 1977/78 was incomparably larger than the indirect contributions via IUEF, WUS and other international NGOs to any other South African political organization. In 1978/79, the ANC allocation was raised to 12 MSEK.
7. Elisabeth Michanek: Memorandum ('Möte med Oliver Tambo den 11 april 1978'/'Meeting with Oliver Tambo on 11 April 1978'), Swedish embassy, Lusaka, 20 April 1978 (SDA).
8. Anders Möllander: Memorandum ('Samtal med Lars-Gunnar Eriksson, International University Exchange Fund, IUEF'/'Conversation with Lars-Gunnar Eriksson, IUEF'), Swedish embassy, Lusaka, 4 May 1978 (SDA).
9. Anders Möllander: Memorandum ('ANC-Sydafrika och IUEF'/'ANC-South Africa and IUEF'), Swedish embassy, Lusaka, 4 May 1978 (SDA).

indirect support via IUEF to various groups in South Africa.[1] However, largely as a result of personal relations between IUEF in Geneva and aid officials in Stockholm, the authorities did not heed the calls from Lusaka. At a time when PAC had been crushed, BCM was in disarray and ANC appeared as the dominant force, Eriksson and Williamson managed to successfully argue in favour of continued grants to a loosely defined internal 'anti-apartheid opposition'.

Remarkable in this context was that the IUEF Director largely delegated the task of convincing the authorities in Sweden to Craig Williamson.[2] Arguing in favour of increased allocations to IUEF's South Africa operations, in June 1978—at the time when he was appointed Deputy Director and IUEF formally recognized ANC as the leading South African liberation movement—in a personally phrased letter[3] to the CCHA secretaries Marika Fahlén and Marianne Sundh, Williamson, for example, brushed aside ANC's criticism. Maintaining that "[t]he internal groups with which I am working are doing an incredible amount of work", he stressed that "[w]e must never assume that [the internal projects supported by SIDA] are not valuable because they do not fall under the open control of the liberation movement. In the situation in South Africa today", he continued, "work for liberation cannot be done openly [...] so other structures are used".[4]

Officially, however, IUEF stated that its activities in South Africa were endorsed by ANC. As will be seen below, for reasons of intelligence the relations between ANC, Williamson and IUEF were far from transparent and unequivocal to outsiders. Against this background, it could be argued that the support was extended against better judgement. Nevertheless, on a number of occasions from early 1979 the Swedish authorities received clear indications of contradictions between what was claimed by Eriksson and Williamson on the one hand and by ANC on the other.

Asked to comment on IUEF's submission for support during the financial year 1979/80, in March 1979, for example, SIDA's Elisabeth Michanek at the embassy in Lusaka noted after a meeting with the ANC leadership that the claim that IUEF was in close contact with the movement regarding its internal South Africa projects was "not in accordance with the reality". She therefore concluded that "IUEF should be advised that SIDA cannot take a stand [...] until consultations [between the NGO] and ANC have taken place in a way which is satisfactory to the movement".[5] Thus informed by the SIDA headquarters in Stockholm, Lars-Gunnar

---

1. A significant portion of the official ANC allocation was earmarked under the heading 'home front' for underground work in South Africa (see the chapter 'From Beds in Exile to Organizers at Home'). In 1978/79, no less than 4 out of 12 MSEK was set aside for this purpose ('Agreed minutes of discussions on the cooperation between Sweden and the African National Congress of South Africa (ANC) 1978/79', Lusaka, 26 May 1978) (SDA).
2. At the same time, Eriksson maintained his personal communication with Hellström and Schori. As a follow-up to Williamson's letter to Fahlén and Sundh, in early September 1978, for example, he wrote to Mats Hellström, asking him to intervene in favour of an increased allocation to IUEF's internal South Africa projects. Referring to "Craig's letter", he stated that "[i]n order to meet ongoing activities and new proposals we would need an additional 650,000 [SEK]. [...] [T]his must be pushed, as otherwise we are in the 'soup'. [...] [D]o what you can..." (Letter ('SIDA request/grant to IUEF 1978/79') from Lars-Gunnar Eriksson to Mats Hellström, [no place], 9 September 1978) (SDA). In January 1979, CCHA decided to recommend an additional grant of 300,000 SEK to IUEF's activities in South Africa (CCHA: 'Protokoll [från sammanträde 22 januari 1979]'/'Minutes [from meeting 22 January 1979]', SIDA, [Stockholm], 26 January 1979) (SDA).
3. The letter was simply signed 'Craig'.
4. Letter from Craig Williamson to Marika Fahlén (Ministry for Foreign Affairs) and Marianne Sundh (SIDA), Geneva, 6 June 1978 (SDA).
5. Letter ('Ansökan om bidrag från IUEF, AET och WUS'/'Request[s] for contributions from IUEF, AET and WUS') from Elisabeth Michanek to SIDA, Swedish embassy, Lusaka, 21 March 1979 (SDA).

Eriksson reacted strongly. Arguing that there had been "misunderstandings at [the] SIDA Lusaka end", in a message to the Swedish aid agency he stated that "full consultations" regarding the South Africa projects had been held with ANC's Thomas Nkobi and Mac Maharaj.[1] Williamson was at the time visiting Southern Africa. As he could "assist with further clarifications", the IUEF Director recommended a meeting between him and the embassy in Lusaka.[2]

Discussions with Williamson were subsequently arranged. In addition, in April 1979 Lars-Olof Edström, SIDA's representative to Zambia, and Elisabeth Michanek held a number of meetings with Nkobi, Maharaj and other ANC leaders. Their conclusions were that

> [t]he major part of the activities in South Africa for which IUEF is requesting [Swedish] funds has not been discussed with ANC. [The movement] does not know which groups are supported, how funds are channelled into the country, if the funds reach the [proposed] recipients or if [they] are used in an appropriate way.[3]

Once again, the embassy therefore advised against official support to IUEF's South Africa projects.[4] This notwithstanding, on 7 May 1979 the Consultative Committee on Humanitarian Assistance recommended an overall allocation to IUEF for 1979/80 of 15 MSEK[5], out of which 1.1 million—no less than 12.5 per cent of the share for Africa—was earmarked for projects in the apartheid republic.[6] Endorsed by SIDA and Ola Ullsten's minority Liberal government, the decision was not applauded by increasingly critical Swedish representatives in Southern Africa. With close relations to the ANC leadership, Anders Möllander at the embassy in Lusaka registered his concern. In a letter to the Foreign Ministry, he emphasized in June 1979 that it was "not correct" that IUEF was coordinating its South Africa activities with ANC.[7]

Basing himself on privileged ANC information, Möllander also implied that Williamson could be working for the apartheid regime.[8] This was far from a novel

---

1. Satyandranath Ragunan 'Mac' Maharaj—democratic South Africa's first Minister of Transport—was at the time serving as Secretary of ANC's Internal Policy and Reconstruction Department. Garth Strachan, who assisted Maharaj, later noted that "[t]he key [ANC] people [...] who worked with [Williamson] [...] were Mac Maharaj and to some extent Aziz Pahad and Jacob Zuma" (Interview with Garth Strachan, p. 195).
2. Telex from Lars-Gunnar Eriksson to SIDA, IUEF, Geneva, 3 April 1979 (SDA).
3. Letter ('IUEF's verksamhet i Sydafrika'/'IUEF's activities in South Africa') from Lars-Olof Edström to SIDA, Swedish embassy, Lusaka, 26 April 1979 (SDA).
4. Ibid.
5. CCHA: 'Protokoll [från sammanträde 7 maj 1979]' ('Minutes [from meeting 7 May 1979]'), SIDA, [Stockholm], 10 May 1979 (SDA).
6. Birgitta Berggren: Memorandum ('Svenskt stöd till IUEF's verksamhet i Afrika under budgetåret 1979/80'/ 'Swedish support to IUEF's activities in Africa during the financial year 1979/80'), SIDA/CCHA, [Stockholm], 23 April 1979 (SDA). Of the 9 MSEK to IUEF's Africa programmes, 4.9 million—corresponding to 54 per cent—was set aside for scholarships. For comparisons with South Africa, the Swedish contributions to IUEF's internal projects in Zimbabwe and Namibia were 464,000 and 193,000 SEK, respectively (ibid.). It could further be noted that while the officially negotiated allocation to ANC in 1979/80 amounted to 16 MSEK, the total grant to Inkatha was in the same year 1 million and the indirect contributions via IUEF to BCM and other South African organizations 1.4 MSEK.
7. Letter ('Sydafrikanska ANC och IUEF'/'South Africa's ANC and IUEF') from Anders Möllander to the Ministry for Foreign Affairs, Swedish embassy, Lusaka, 27 June 1979 (SDA). As noted in the preceding chapter, after discussions with ANC's Alfred Nzo and Thabo Mbeki in December 1979 Möllander advised against any future official assistance to Inkatha.
8. Ibid.

suggestion.[1] However, Eriksson had from the beginning vouched for his deputy and Nkobi had—as noted above—as late as in December 1978 on behalf of ANC characterized IUEF as "a friend". Against this background, in late July 1979 the Under-Secretary of State Thord Palmlund sent a strongly worded reply to Möllander, stressing that "we regard the accusations against Williamson as very serious and [are of the opinion that they] require more foundation".[2] At the same time, Palmlund personally contacted Eriksson about the matter, and in October 1979—three months before Williamson's exposure—they together met ANC's Treasurer General in Geneva. According to the subsequent IUEF Commission of Inquiry, Nkobi declared that "ANC had no suspicions against Williamson".[3]

The knots in Williamson's relations with ANC cannot be disentangled in the present study. Suffice it to note that while Maharaj and others who worked with him did not trust him[4], ANC had its own reasons for not denouncing Williamson. After consultations with Nkobi, Maharaj and Mbeki, in 1980 they were summarized as follows by the IUEF Commission of Inquiry:

> Williamson had expressed an interest [...] in joining [ANC] from the very beginning of his 'exile'.[5] [...] [T]o prove [that] he was genuine, [he] offered to feed ANC with all information he had about the struggle inside South Africa, particularly about white opposition and [BCM] activities. [...] ANC 'went along' with Williamson in part because the information [he] supplied [...] was useful [...]. [B]y comparing information [that] Williamson gave it [...] with information it secured from its own sources, ANC could gradually build up a picture of who Williamson was working for or in contact with.

> This was a slow, difficult task. While it was proceeding, the ANC headquarters did not tell even ANC representatives in other countries about its doubts about Williamson [as] the infor-

---

1. In 1980, the IUEF Commission of Inquiry noted: "It became clear to us that Williamson was taken into the IUEF and advanced to a high position [...] against a background of suspicion about his real identity and purposes and in the face of specific warnings addressed to Eriksson that he could be an agent of the South African government" (IUEF Commission of Inquiry, p. 13). In fact, suspicions about Williamson had been raised by the South African Council of Churches (SACC) as early as in 1974. At the beginning of 1977—when SACC learnt that he was to be recruited by IUEF—it alerted Lars-Gunnar Eriksson (ibid., p. 14). In the case of Sweden, in February 1977 the CSM missionary Axel-Ivar Berglund—then SACC's Director of Theological Education—conveyed specific warnings. Coming to Uppsala, to his bewilderment, however, he found that Williamson was visiting the missionary society at the same time (Conversation with Axel-Ivar Berglund, Uppsala, 2 February 2000). Warnings were also given by *inter alia* BCM (Interview with Barney Pityana, p. 187), IDAF (Interview with Rica Hodgson, p. 132) and ZANU of Zimbabwe (IUEF Commission of Inquiry, pp. 15 and 19-20). Against this background, the IUEF Commission of Inquiry concluded that "Eriksson displayed bad judgment in failing to pick up signals to which a man of his experience should have been sensitive. The key point [...] is that Eriksson received warnings which should have prompted him [...] to investigate Williamson as a security risk more thoroughly than he did" (IUEF Commission of Inquiry, p. 22). In 1996, Schori commented that "[w]e were all fooled by Williamson [...]. After [his] exposure [...], some said that they had warned Lars-Gunnar Eriksson about him. That might be true, but apparently not clearly enough" (Interview with Pierre Schori, p. 335).
2. Letter ('ANC/SA och IUEF'/'ANC/SA and IUEF') from Thord Palmlund to Anders Möllander, Ministry for Foreign Affairs, Stockholm, 24 July 1979 (SDA).
3. IUEF Commission of Inquiry, p. 16. In addition to the reasons stated below—and apart from the fact that ANC opposed IUEF's independent South Africa operations—the liberation movement was, naturally, politically interested in IUEF's recognition and financially in its resources for scholarships and refugee assistance.
4. Interview with Garth Strachan, p. 195. See also Kasrils op. cit., pp. 120-21.
5. Although Williamson often introduced himself as an ANC member (cf. Vetlesen (1998) op. cit., p. 101), the liberation movement never formally gave any grounds for substantiating such a claim (IUEF Commission of Inquiry, p. 19). In addition, ANC was not consulted either at the time of Williamson's original appointment to IUEF or when he became Deputy Director (ibid., p. 13). In a statement issued in Stockholm immediately after Williamson's exposure, ANC's Secretary General Alfred Nzo and Lindiwe Mabuza, the Chief Representative to the Scandinavian countries, declared: "Throughout his employment by the IUEF, the ANC has dealt with Williamson as a member of the staff of the IUEF, recruited by that organisation without reference to the ANC and allocated his specific and various duties by the IUEF, again without reference to the ANC" (ANC: ['Statement'], Stockholm, 25 January 1980) (SDA).

mation he was passing on was so valuable in establishing what information networks existed in South Africa and what Williamson himself was up to.[1]

To ANC, during this intelligence exercise it was important to give Lars-Gunnar Eriksson, Craig Williamson and also the donors a sense of security. When Williamson in January 1980 finally revealed his true identity and the IUEF crisis broke out into the open, in spite of earlier differences with regard to IUEF's South Africa operations, the relations with Sweden were thus not negatively affected.[2] After all, as later stated by Garth Strachan—at the time working with Maharaj on ANC's internal underground projects—"Williamson was seen as a South African who had gone to work for IUEF with the blessing of ANC".[3]

Taking place less than three months after the break between ANC and Inkatha in London, to the Swedish government South Africa's infiltration and the wider IUEF crisis was a major watershed. Discussing the IUEF affair with ANC President Oliver Tambo in Stockholm in March 1981, the Liberal Under-Secretary of State for Foreign Affairs Hans Blix concluded that "it had taught a lesson to donors and all apartheid opponents", adding—"as had become manifest after many years of cooperation"—that "ANC was a natural and appropriate channel for Swedish assistance".[4] This marked the end of official funds to internal South African organizations or activities without close, previous consultations with ANC.[5] From mid-1980, no official Swedish assistance was extended to Inkatha, BCM or any other 'alternative' organization.[6]

Aftermath

As the academic studies and general situation of IUEF's more than 2,000 scholarship holders from Africa and Latin America were threatened by the collapse of the organization, in early 1980 Sweden and the other donors mounted a rescue operation in their favour. In the beginning, there were in this context officials in the main donor countries who advocated a continuation of IUEF, albeit after necessary administrative reforms and the introduction of tighter controls. Various proposals to this effect were drafted.

From a political point of view, both IUEF's name and reputation had, however, been irreparably damaged by 'Operation Daisy' and the extent of the financial mismanagement which came to light after the exposure of Williamson and the departure of Eriksson. On behalf of the Southern African liberation movements[7], ANC's Oliver Tambo and SWAPO's Sam Nujoma strongly rejected the idea of resurrecting

1. IUEF Commission of Inquiry, p. 17.
2. Cf. the interviews with Sven Hamrell (p. 281), Lena Hjelm-Wallén (p. 295) and Pierre Schori (p. 335).
3. Interview with Garth Strachan, p. 195.
4. Henrik Salander: Memorandum ('Biståndsdiskussioner'/'Discussions on assistance'), Ministry for Foreign Affairs, Stockholm, 24 March 1981 (MFA).
5. In late 1980, the Ministry for Foreign Affairs decided to suspend indirect so called 'silent funding' of organizations in South Africa. Outside the ANC assistance, official humanitarian support was over the following years instead mainly channelled via the churches (Per Lindström: Memorandum ('Internbistånd'/'Internal assistance'), Swedish legation, Pretoria, 16 March 1981) (MFA).
6. Cf. Pityana: "After the exposure of Craig Williamson and the collapse of IUEF, it became increasingly important for the donors to make sure that any position that they took on South Africa had the support of ANC. Informally, ANC was in that way able to indicate what could and what could not be supported" (Interview with Barney Pityana, p. 188). In the case of Sweden, it should be noted that a) ANC's break with Inkatha, b) the IUEF affair and c) the controversy with the British government over ZANU of Zimbabwe all intervened between late October 1979 and mid-January 1980, forcing Fälldin's non-socialist coalition government to take a clear stand vis-à-vis the dominant liberation movements.
7. Zimbabwe became independent in April 1980.

the NGO, whether under its old or with a new name.[1] SIDA shared this view. Arguing that the organization had "lost its international credibility", in late September 1980 Director General Anders Forsse wrote to Foreign Minister Ola Ullsten, "firmly advising against Swedish [government] support for the re-establishment of IUEF, irrespective of the positions of other donor countries and whatever [a] reconstruction proposal may contain".[2] This position was in turn adopted by the Fälldin government.

From mid-1980, the Swedish authorities proposed instead that the administration of IUEF's scholarship holders should be transferred to other existing organizations specialized in this field. As IUEF's leading financier, Sweden discussed the feasibility of the proposal with the other donor countries, the IUEF staff and potentially interested international organizations. In Lusaka, Zanele Mbeki was particularly involved in the discussions.[3]

Eventually, it was decided to dissolve IUEF and transfer the African and Latin American refugee students to other organizations as from 1 April 1981. After many meetings and extensive preparatory work, convening in Copenhagen in mid-March 1981 representatives from the governments of Canada, Denmark, the Netherlands, Norway and Sweden agreed on continued financial support to the former IUEF scholarship holders. Their transfer had in the meantime been accepted by the Africa Educational Trust, the Commonwealth Fund for Technical Cooperation, the World University Service, the World Council of Churches and the Lutheran World Federation.[4]

In South Africa, 'Operation Daisy' had in the meantime claimed its first victim since Craig Williamson's return. Accused of espionage, in June 1980 Renfrew Christie—who had been detained in October 1979—was sentenced to ten years imprisonment. Williamson appeared as a state witness during the trial, presenting copies of IUEF documents allegedly drafted by Lars-Gunnar Eriksson, Neville Rubin and ANC's Frene Ginwala according to which Christie on behalf of IUEF

---

1. Anders Bjurner: Memorandum ('SWAPO och ANC om IUEF'/'SWAPO and ANC on IUEF'), Ministry for Foreign Affairs, Stockholm, 22 September 1980 (SDA). The issue of IUEF was raised in meetings with the ANC and SWAPO Presidents by Ernst Michanek and Anders Bjurner in connection with an international conference on Namibia in Paris in mid-September 1980.

2. Letter ('IUEF i kris'/'IUEF in crisis') from Anders Forsse to Ola Ullsten, SIDA, Stockholm, 24 September 1980 (SDA).

3. Acting as SIDA's representative to Zambia, in August 1980 Lennart Wohlgemuth asked Zanele Mbeki—then acting head of the local IUEF office—to reflect on the consequences of a closing-down of IUEF for its scholarship holders. Supporting the suggestion that the students at university level could be transferred to other organizations, she was more concerned about the future of the beneficiaries at the secondary level (Letter from Lennart Wohlgemuth to Birgitta Berggren at SIDA, [no place or date, but Lusaka in September 1980]) (SDA). Discussing "life without IUEF", in a subsequent memorandum to SIDA Mbeki and her colleagues *inter alia* stated: "While there are compelling political and administrative reasons why the IUEF should phase itself out at this time, we in this office believe that if this is done without creating new machinery which will undertake the 'good' aspects of the IUEF role, we shall be stepping back ten years in refugee assistance in the educational field in Africa, especially with regard to Southern Africa. This will come as a result of the loss of the pioneer and experimental role played by IUEF in educational assistance, the disappearance of a highly flexible and responsive channel for meeting felt needs and the cessation of a coordinating service for educational programming on a regional basis among the refugee agencies" (IUEF Lusaka: 'Programme role of IUEF Lusaka', Lusaka, 9 September 1980, attached to letter ('PM om IUEFs verksamhet i framtiden'/'Memorandum on IUEF's future activities') from Lennart Wohlgemuth to SIDA, Swedish embassy, Lusaka, 11 September 1980) (SDA).

4. 'Agreed minutes' and 'Press release' from the Copenhagen meeting on 12 March 1981 (SDA). Focusing their attention on the needs of the students, the donors were considerably less accommodating with regard to IUEF's former staff members. After receiving token terminal benefits, in a letter to IUEF's outgoing acting head, democratic South Africa's future First Lady Zanele Mbeki—who resigned from the organization in November 1980—characterized the role of SIDA and the other donors in May 1981 as "depressingly patronising", adding that "I feel treated like a South African black miner at the end of his contract, when he is given what is called a 'lump sum'" (Letter ('My residential status and removal costs') from Zanele Mbeki to the IUEF Director, Lusaka, 12 May 1981) (SDA).

and ANC had gathered classified information on South Africa's nuclear and electric power plants.[1]

Soon thereafter, the security police started to hand out IUEF documents collected by Williamson to the South African press. Grossly exaggerating Williamson's role and achievements as Pretoria's 'super-spy'[2]—as well as the significance of IUEF in the international anti-apartheid struggle—the subsequent newspaper coverage largely focused on Sweden. Giving his imagination a free rein, in a series of feature articles from mid-October 1980 Ken Owen, editor at the Johannesburg *Sunday Times*, alleged that the Swedish government through IUEF had been organizing "a spy ring" against South Africa.[3] Basing himself on Williamson's information, Owen notably singled out Per Lindström, counsellor at the Pretoria legation, "as a courier for clandestine operations [...] that included an espionage network".[4] However, these and other stories were never substantiated. They did not lead to any diplomatic intervention against Sweden by the South African government.[5]

---

1. Letter ('Renfrew Christie fälld för spioneri för IUEF och ANC'/'Renfrew Christie sentenced for espionage for IUEF and ANC') from Gustaf Hamilton to the Ministry for Foreign Affairs, Swedish legation, Pretoria, 11 June 1980 (SDA).
2. On Williamson and the Soviet Union, see Shubin op. cit., pp. 217-19. Cf. also Strachan, who in 1995 commented that Williamson "came across sensitive information about money and lines of supply and he probably gave a lot of political intelligence on ANC, but my impression [is] that the damage was not altogether that serious" (Interview with Garth Strachan, p. 195).
3. Ken Owen: 'Swedes named in SA spy ring' in *Sunday Times*, 19 October 1980.
4. Ibid.
5. Lindström served at the Swedish legation in Pretoria until 1982.

From Beds in Exile to Organizers at Home

Building a Special Relationship

Beginning in 1973, direct official Swedish assistance to ANC started comparatively late. It was initially seen as temporary and only modest allocations were granted. Despite voices raised in favour of alternative South African organizations, the support, however, was made permanent and soon assumed a more pro-active political character than the assistance extended to the other Southern African liberation movements discussed in this study. Based on long-standing relations, during the second half of the 1970s the cooperation between Sweden and ANC would in addition to immediate humanitarian needs focus on capacity-building and on strengthening the movement's internal political base. By the late 1970s, it had increasingly taken the form of institutional cooperation, outside the military field paving the way for support to central functions of the future South African ruling party. Looking back years later, Lindiwe Mabuza, ANC's former representative to Sweden[1], commented that

> [t]he unity of feeling and action [...] led to a deep sense of mutual inter-dependence. Each party depended on the other to ensure the success of the cooperation and [...] absolute integrity and accountability on the part of all involved [...] underpinned the relationship.[2]

Noting that "the agenda belonged to both parties" and broadening the horizon to all the Nordic countries, Mabuza—who from 1979 was particularly instrumental in consolidating and developing ANC's support base in the Nordic area—concluded in 1996 that ANC

> started with a limited view of what we were doing and that was reflected in the amounts and in the negotiations [...]. But our perspective of what ought to be accommodated [within the assistance] grew as we had more people coming out of South Africa [...]. [...] We were forming [our] departments as we were having increased assistance. The Nordic countries were actually helping us to form the nuclei of the future ministries.[3]

---

1. Born in Newcastle, Natal, in 1938, Mabuza studied in Soweto and in Lesotho before leaving South Africa in 1964 to pursue university studies in the United States. After two MA degrees— one in literature from Stanford University (1966) and another in American studies from the University of Minnesota (1968)—between 1969 and 1976 she lectured in history, English and Zulu literature at the University of Ohio. Also working for ANC, in early 1977 she returned to Africa, where she joined the movement in Lusaka and was attached to 'Radio Freedom', edited *Voice of Women*—the journal of the Women's Secretariat—and set up ANC's first cultural committee. In 1979, Mabuza was appointed ANC Chief Representative to the Nordic countries, living in Sweden for the following nine years. In 1989, she took up the same position in the United States, where she was based in Washington. Elected to South Africa's first democratic parliament in April 1994, the following year she was appointed ambassador to Germany. During her years in Sweden, Mabuza was in addition to her diplomatic and political tasks particularly active in promoting South African culture and in involving Swedish and Nordic artists in the anti-apartheid struggle. An acknowledged poet and writer, several of her poems were translated into Swedish in 1986 and included in the anthology *Malibongwe: Dikter mot Apartheid* ('Malibongwe: Poems against Apartheid'), edited by Margareta Ekström and published by Författarförlaget, Stockholm. Her poetry collection *Voices That Lead* was published by Vivlia Publishers, Florida, South Africa, in 1998. Also in 1998, Peter Hammer Verlag, Wuppertal, Germany, issued *Africa to Me*, a bilingual edition with poems in English and German (cf. the interview with Lindiwe Mabuza, pp. 134-42).
2. Lindiwe Mabuza: 'Nordic Solidarity with ANC' in Robben Island Museum, Mayibuye Centre and Nordic Africa Institute op. cit., pp. 95-96.
3. Interview with Lindiwe Mabuza, p. 138.

Sweden's assistance to ANC will be discussed in this and the following chapters. Highlighting the salient features of the official support extended over two decades, the points of departure, ANC's difficult situation and the modest beginnings of the assistance will first be recalled in order to place the rapidly growing cooperation in a proper perspective.

Points of Departure

That in 1994 more than 12 million voters in democratic elections would support ANC and that the international community would hail the inauguration of Nelson Mandela as President of South Africa were in the early 1970s distant prospects for the movement's isolated cadres and freedom fighters in Tanzania and Zambia.[1] In the era of Vietnam and with the liberation wars in the Portuguese colonies as vivid examples, ANC at the time primarily conceptualized the problem of liberation in terms of armed struggle. Although spectacular initiatives to militarily penetrate the apartheid *laager* were taken[2], until the mid-1970s ANC remained, however, weak and marginalized.[3] Beyond its triumphalist propaganda, in the dialogue with the Swedish authorities this was acknowledged by the leadership. Visiting the Ministry for Foreign Affairs in Stockholm, in January 1973, for example, Oliver Tambo regretted that his organization "had not yet managed to become a unifying factor" in the South African struggle.[4] Decisive in this context was in his opinion ANC's difficult position in Tanzania and Zambia, where the movement was facing a number of "restrictions" and a lot of energy and resources had to be devoted to maintaining its cadres and the freedom fighters returning from military training, mainly in the Soviet Union. In order to efficiently coordinate and lead the underground activities in South Africa, ANC had to build a strong external organization. This, Tambo underlined, was the "biggest immediate problem".[5]

Less than a week later—on 15 January 1973—the Consultative Committee on Humanitarian Assistance took the decision to recommend official support to the movement. Endorsed by the Social Democratic government, the stand marked the beginning of continuous cooperation. Starting at the modest level of 150,000 SEK, during the first four years the annual allocations did not exceed 1 MSEK. Although it eventually became the largest recipient of Swedish aid among the Southern African liberation movements, several factors explain why only smaller amounts were initially extended to ANC.

1. Commenting on the situation in the 1970s, Reddy Mampane—who as Reddy Mazimba served as ANC Chief Representative to Tanzania from 1976 to 1982—stated in an interview in 1995 that "[d]uring those days it was very difficult to visualize when one would be back in South Africa. There were no signs at all. The horizon was just dark" (Interview with Reddy Mampane, p. 146).
2. The most spectacular initiative—known as 'Operation J' and reminiscent of the landing of the *Granma* and the beginnings of the Cuban revolution—was launched in 1971, when ANC plans to land MK soldiers on the Transkeian coast were set in motion. An old yacht—appropriately called the *Aventura*—was purchased and a crew of Greek Communists recruited to ship the freedom fighters from Somalia to South Africa. Eventually, however, the yacht broke down off the Kenyan coast and the operation was aborted. On 'Operation J', see Kasrils op. cit., pp. 112-14 and Shubin op. cit., pp. 103-07.
3. In his dissertation on the movement's operational strategy, Barrell notes that by 1974 it was "almost wholly exiled or jailed, organisationally weak, disunited and geographically fractured. Moreover, the ANC lacked any domestic presence worthy of the term 'underground organisation'" (Barrell Ph. D. op. cit., chapter two, p. 1).
4. Magnus Wernstedt and Gun-Britt Andersson: Memorandum ('Samtal med O. Tambo, president i ANC, M. Kunene och M. Legassick den 10 januari 1973'/'Conversation with O. Tambo, ANC President, M. Kunene and M. Legassick, 10 January 1973'), Ministry for Foreign Affairs, Stockholm, 29 January 1973 (MFA).
5. Ibid.

The general policy orientation of Sweden's assistance to PAIGC and the Southern African liberation movements was, in the first place, of major importance. In the early 1970s, the Social Democratic government accorded primacy to the liberation struggles in the Portuguese colonies. As noted in the contexts of Zimbabwe and Namibia, assistance to what was described by the Foreign Ministry as "the smaller movements from the southern parts of the continent" was as late as in September 1971 mainly seen as a "token". As such, it was primarily motivated by the consideration that it "shows that Sweden does not follow an anti-Portuguese line, but one that supports liberation".[1]

While humanitarian assistance was extended to ZANU of Zimbabwe and SWAPO of Namibia, the almost exclusive attention to PAIGC of Guinea-Bissau, FRELIMO of Mozambique and MPLA of Angola was confirmed two years later by Foreign Minister Krister Wickman. In September 1973—at a time when support to ANC and ZAPU of Zimbabwe had also been initiated—he clarified that "the [objective of the Swedish effort was] to support the civilian activities of the liberation movements in the liberated areas".[2] Effectively crushed by the apartheid regime, ANC was far from being in a position to claim control over any such territory.

Secondly, during the first half of the 1970s there was no political opinion in Sweden which actively demanded a radical change in this regard. While the non-socialist opposition Liberal Party—later joined by the Centre Party—from 1970 regularly submitted parliamentary motions in favour of ANC, it did not request a re-orientation away from the assistance to the liberation movements in the Portuguese colonies. This stand was even more manifest within the organized solidarity movement and the socialist opposition. It was only in November 1974 that the Africa Groups for the first time recognized that ANC played a leading role in the South African struggle, and not until January 1975 did the Left Party Communists advocate official support to the organization.[3]

Thirdly, the late and initially modest assistance to ANC must be seen in the light of the small number of people under its care in Africa. Although thousands of South Africans had left their country in the wake of the 1960 Sharpeville shootings and the bannings of ANC and PAC, the overwhelming majority settled in Europe, notably in Great Britain. In the case of ANC—as well as of PAC—until the Soweto events in 1976 there was no massive exodus to the countries in Southern Africa.

In comparison with the influxes from Angola, Mozambique, Zimbabwe and Namibia, the number of South Africans in the independent African countries was marginal. While hundreds of thousands of Angolans had fled to Zaire, tens of thousands of Mozambicans to Tanzania and thousands of Zimbabweans to Zambia, the South African exiles in the principal host countries constituted a tiny minority. In 1973, for example, there were an estimated 3,000 Namibian refugees in Zambia alone, out of which about 600 were under SWAPO's direct care. In the entire Southern African region, PAC claimed at the same time responsibility for between 150 and 200 people, while ANC indicated that it catered for a total of 500.[4] Of

---

1. [Ethel] Ringborg: Memorandum ('Stöd till befrielserörelser'/'Support to liberation movements'), Ministry for Foreign Affairs, Stockholm, 7 September 1971 (MFA).
2. 'Interview (September) with the Foreign Minister, Mr. Wickman, in the special [issue on Sweden] of the journal *Afrique-Asie*', in Ministry for Foreign Affairs: *Documents on Swedish Foreign Policy: 1973*, Stockholm, 1976, p. 64.
3. See the chapter 'ANC of South Africa: No Easy Walk'.
4. Letter from Thomas Nkobi, Acting Treasurer General, to SIDA, ANC, Lusaka, 5 August 1973 (SDA).

these, 200—180 men and 20 women—lived in Tanzania and 150 in Zambia.[1] As late as in April 1976—just before the Soweto uprising—the estimated number of people under ANC's care in the Frontline States was below 1,000.[2]

Finally, in both Tanzania and Zambia ANC faced a number of obstacles which during the first half of the 1970s left few openings for a broader cooperation. As the Nyerere and Kaunda governments eventually stood out as not only staunch political ANC allies, but also as generous hosts to the movement's main civilian settlements, the hardships experienced at the time in the two countries should be borne in mind.

The early 1970s—later described by the movement as a "period of regrouping and recovery"[3]—were difficult years for ANC. Although militarily assisted by the Soviet Union and its allies[4], and in December 1974 together with PAC being invited by the UN General Assembly as a 'permanent observer', in the African host countries—where it mattered most—ANC was for many years a Cinderella among the Southern African liberation movements. As pointedly observed by Shubin, "[i]n the context of the high regard in which the independent African countries later held the ANC and its leaders, it is difficult to accept that [...] even acquiring a travel document was a major problem".[5]

Guided by the so called 'domino strategy'[6], until the independence of Angola and Mozambique the African states and OAU accorded with few exceptions[7] low priority to the movement precariously, but untiringly held together by Oliver Tambo. In retrospect, it should be noted that while Tanzania and Zambia granted crucial political and military sanctuary to ANC[8], on ideological grounds[9], for regional reasons[10] or due to security concerns[11] they for many years imposed limits

---

1. Ibid.
2. ANC: 'Memorandum submitted by the African National Congress (SA) to SIDA in support of a request for assistance for the year 1976/1977', Lusaka, [no date, but delivered by Thomas Nkobi to the Swedish embassy on 1 May 1976] (SDA). According to the document, in early 1976 ANC catered for 370 people in Tanzania and 280 in Zambia. It was at the same time estimated that the number of ANC members in Angola would reach 150. The remaining 200 were in more or less equal numbers in Botswana, Lesotho, Swaziland and Mozambique.
3. 'Political Report of the National Executive Committee to the National Consultative Conference, June 1985' in ANC op. cit. [no year], p. 14.
4. On ANC and the Soviet Union in the early 1970s, see Shubin op. cit., pp. 94-139.
5. Ibid., p. 131.
6. On the 'domino strategy', see the chapter 'ANC of South Africa: No Easy Walk'.
7. Distant Algeria was among ANC's strongest supporters in Africa.
8. Tanzania, but not Zambia, accorded ANC military training facilities, primarily at the Kongwa camp some 400 kilometres west of Dar es Salaam and 200 kilometres from Morogoro. In 1973, about half of the ANC members in Tanzania were freedom fighters at Kongwa.
9. Tanzania—hosting the OAU Liberation Committee—was for many years ideologically closer to PAC than to ANC (cf. the interview with Salim Ahmed Salim, p. 246). Accused of participation in an alleged coup attempt against the Nyerere government, in 1969-70 ANC was forced to close its camps in Tanzania and evacuate its military cadres to the Soviet Union (see Shubin op. cit., pp. 98-100, Sellström Volume I, p. 250 and the interview with Reddy Mampane, p. 145). Welcomed back in 1971-72, the action taken against ANC subsequently led the movement to move its exile headquarters from Morogoro, Tanzania, to Lusaka, Zambia. As noted above, initially attracted by PAC the Kaunda government in Zambia had, due to serious differences with the organization, in the meantime taken an opposite stand. After taking the law into its own hands by executing alleged South African agents, PAC was in 1968 expelled from the country.
10. After moving its headquarters from Tanzania to Zambia, during the Kaunda government's 'détente exercise' with South Africa—initiated in October 1974—ANC was again faced with serious restrictions. No action against the apartheid republic was to be undertaken from Zambian soil and the number of ANC officials in Lusaka was to be cut down to six (Shubin op. cit., p. 158). ANC's radio broadcasts to South Africa were brought to a halt at the end of the following year (Carin Norberg: Memorandum ('Minnesanteckningar från samtal med Thabo Mbeki, ANC (SA), 14 oktober 1976'/'Notes from conversation with Thabo Mbeki of ANC, 14 October 1976'), Swedish embassy, Lusaka, [no date]) (SDA).
11. Mainly for security reasons, it was only in 1978-79—contradictorily at a time when the Pretoria regime adopted the policy of 'total strategy' and embarked on cross-border military operations—that Tanzania and Zambia allowed ANC to procure land and establish civilian settlements.

on the movement's possibilities to face the challenge of establishing a strong external organization.

Barring small plots at its Tanzanian headquarters in Morogoro and outside Livingstone in Zambia[1], in contrast to other Southern African liberation movements
ANC was until the end of the 1970s neither granted land nor allowed to procure it
or the right to administer social facilities or refugee settlements.[2] Seen as freedom
fighters and not as refugees, in both Tanzania and Zambia individual ANC members were, in addition, not given work permits[3] or allowed to register their children
in local schools.[4]

In fact, in the early 1970s the authorities—notably in Tanzania—even called
ANC's need of international assistance into question. When in July-August 1972
SIDA's Olof Milton at the embassy in Dar es Salaam discussed possible assistance to
the movement with the Prime Minister's Office, the responsible Tanzanian official
disparagingly characterized ANC as a "victim of age, [...] which ha[s] abandoned
its warrior operations". Expressing doubts about the request submitted by ANC to
the Swedish government, he was of the opinion that "luxurious" food grants, work
permits and land allocations would only lead its members to "lose their sense of
blood".[5]

In addition to hosting OAU's important Liberation Committee, Tanzania was
probably the African country with which Sweden felt most affinity. Its views therefore carried particular weight. Nevertheless, despite the close links between the
Palme and Nyerere governments—and irrespective of Tanzania's views on ANC's
military prowess—after establishing contacts with the movement's headquarters,
the Swedish representatives in Dar es Salaam became aware of its difficulties and

---

1. In order to meet the movement's own requirements, but also to generate income, ANC had as early as in
   1969 launched Star Furniture in Lusaka, a carpentry company which eventually supplied office equipment also to the Zambian government. In Tanzania, a piggery and a bakery were established at
   Morogoro in the mid-1970s. In addition, the Kurasini House for the Sick—'a clinic for South African
   freedom fighters'—had with assistance from the Lutuli Memorial Foundation been set up by ANC in Dar
   es Salaam in 1972.

2. It could, for example, be recalled that FRELIMO of Mozambique since the mid-1960s had been running the
   Mozambique Institute and later administered refugee settlements and a hospital in Tanzania. In Zambia,
   SWAPO of Namibia was allocated land at Nyango in 1975.

3. In turn, this partly explains why ANC in various project activities employed Tanzanian and Zambian workers.

4. Anna Runeborg: Memorandum ('Besök hos ANC/SA i Morogoro på grisuppfödningsprojektet den 11 oktober 1977'/'Visit to ANC Morogoro and its piggery project, 11 October 1977'), Swedish embassy, Dar es
   Salaam, 4 November 1977 (SDA).

5. Olof Milton: Memorandum ('Behovet av svenskt stöd till ANC-medlemmar i exil'/'The need for Swedish
   support to ANC members in exile'), Swedish embassy, Dar es Salaam, 28 August 1972 (SDA). In January
   1970—shortly after the decision taken by the Swedish parliament to grant official support to PAIGC and
   the Southern African liberation movements—the Tanzanian Foreign Minister Mhando criticized the stand,
   generally describing the movements' representatives as corrupt coffee-shop revolutionaries (see Sellström
   Volume I, pp. 249-50). For Norwegian diplomatic reports on ANC in Tanzania and Zambia in the early
   1970s, see Østbye in Eriksen (ed.) op. cit., pp. 133-34. On Tanzania, ANC and PAC in the mid-1970s, cf.
   also ANC's former representative Reddy Mampane (aka Mazimba): "When I became the ANC Chief Representative in 1976, our relationship with Tanzania was not yet good at all. [...] You must understand that
   ANC [...] had problems with some African states, Tanzania in particular. They were saying: 'You people say
   that you are fighting against a white regime, but you have white people in your ranks. And now you allow
   whites from other countries to come and help you'. They saw PAC people as the true freedom fighters,
   because PAC maintained that black is black and did not welcome any whites" (Interview with Reddy Mampane, p. 145).

needs. Mainly dependent on limited assistance from OAU[1], it was obvious that the ANC officials and members in Tanzania were living under spartan conditions. For example, in May 1973—after the decision to grant ANC humanitarian assistance— its Administrative Secretary, Mendi Msimang, modestly approached the Swedish embassy with a request for bedsteads and mattresses for the cadres in Morogoro and Dar es Salaam, stating that "the beddings are a priority as the lot we are presently using are on loan to us and we are now required to restore them to the rightful owners".[2] Forwarding the submission to the SIDA headquarters in Stockholm, Olof Milton supported it with the comment that "decent facilities for rest and sleep must belong to the fundamental needs [of] men".[3]

Although ANC catered for very few people, their basic needs were evident. Hoping that the organization would be allowed to start self-supporting and income-generating activities in both Tanzania and Zambia, it was against this background that the Swedish government in early 1973 decided to temporarily include ANC among the Southern African liberation movements receiving direct assistance.

Breakthrough with Conditions

ANC's first comprehensive request for Swedish assistance was submitted in March 1972.[4] It envisaged local procurement of daily necessities in the form of fresh food, bread and clothes for 140 people in Tanzania and 80 in Zambia, with an estimated annual cost of about 280,000 SEK. Included in the budget were cigarettes for a total of 55,000 SEK.[5]

The request was discussed by CCHA on 1 June 1972. Far from giving it unqualified support, the committee members decided to

> recommend SIDA to instruct [its offices] in Dar es Salaam and Lusaka to gather [additional] information on the situation and needs of the ANC members, as well as on possible support from other [donors] [...]. The views of the governments of the countries of asylum on support to the ANC camps should also be established. On this basis, the committee want[s] to discuss the request anew.[6]

During the following months, the authorities in Stockholm received positive reactions from the local SIDA offices. Stating that the OAU assistance was insufficient and confirming that the governments of Tanzania and Zambia would not oppose

---

1. As was the case with other recognized liberation movements, the OAU Liberation Committee covered the rental and running costs of the ANC offices in Dar es Salaam and Morogoro. The organization also assisted ANC with transportation. In addition, the Tanzanian government supplied the MK cadres at the Kongwa camp with uniforms and one meal per day. In the early 1970s, the annual contribution to ANC from the OAU Liberation Committee and Tanzania amounted to the meagre sum of about 6,000 Pounds Sterling (ibid. and letter ('SIDA humanitarian assistance to ANC members in Zambia and Tanzania') from Marianne Rappe to the Swedish embassy in Lusaka, SIDA, Stockholm, 30 March 1973) (SDA).
2. Letter from M[endi] Msimang to the Swedish embassy in Dar es Salaam, Morogoro, 30 May 1973 (SDA). It was addressed to Roland Axelsson, at the time SIDA administrator at the embassy.
3. Letter ('Utilization of humanitarian assistance to ANC members') from Olof Milton to SIDA, Swedish embassy, Dar es Salaam, 1 June 1973 (SDA).
4. On several occasions in the 1960s—before the Swedish parliament endorsed the policy of direct support to the liberation movements—ANC had unsuccessfully approached Sweden for material and financial assistance (see Sellström Volume I, pp. 244-51).
5. Anders Möllander: Memorandum ('Framställning från African National Congress, ANC (Sydafrika)'/ 'Request from ANC'), CCHA/SIDA, Stockholm, [no date, but January 1973] (SDA).
6. CCHA: 'Protokoll [från sammanträde 1 juni 1972]' ('Minutes [from meeting 1 June 1972]'), SIDA, [Stockholm], 22 June 1972 (SDA).

Swedish commodity aid to ANC[1], in addition to fresh food and clothes they emphasized the need for medical supplies. They also recommended support for educational activities and that the movement ought to be assisted to develop its own food production. Swedish assistance to ANC, the Swedish embassy in Lusaka noted, could thereby contribute to "releasing funds for [its] political and humanitarian work in South Africa".[2]

Based on the embassy reports and after Oliver Tambo's visit at the beginning of the month, on 15 January 1973 CCHA eventually recommended official support in the form of food supplies.[3] A decision to that effect was signed two weeks later by SIDA's Acting Director General Anders Forsse.[4] After deducting the requested amount for cigarettes and taking into account that "all male ANC members are supposed to receive one uniform per person and one meal a day [from OAU] through the governments in the respective [host] countries"[5], the amount allocated for the financial year 1972/73 was 150,000 SEK.[6] Although this corresponded to two thirds of the original ANC request for food and clothing, at the time it was not envisaged that the assistance should become permanent. On the contrary, informing ANC of the decision SIDA's Curt Ström clarified that

> the humanitarian assistance [...] should be regarded as a temporary measure, to be diminished as ANC members in Zambia and Tanzania gradually make themselves self-sufficient with foodstuff. [...] SIDA [is, accordingly,] interested in following ANC's plans and measures to start agricultural production [and] is willing to consider [...] support [for] a feasibility study of such activities.[7]

In the same letter, Ström wrote that SIDA would "instruct its offices in Dar es Salaam and Lusaka to work out [...] the priorities and plans for the purchase and delivery of the goods requested [together with ANC]".[8] Thomas Nkobi, ANC's Acting Treasurer General, acknowledged the decision in a letter dated 2 March 1973, adding that "we have also taken note of your sympathetic attitude towards helping the African National Congress in its plans and measures to start agricultural projects so that we become self-sufficient".[9]

While the question of land due to the host governments' opposition would only be solved towards the end of the 1970s, Nkobi—assisted by Kay Monsamy—subsequently established routines with the SIDA office in Lusaka for local procurement in Tanzania and Zambia of the agreed food supplies.[10] This marked the beginning

---

1. While they did not oppose Swedish assistance to ANC, until the early 1980s the Tanzanian authorities often also recommended support to PAC (cf. Anna Runeborg: Memorandum ('ANC och PAC i Tanzania'/'ANC and PAC in Tanzania'), Swedish embassy, Dar es Salaam, 10 June 1980) (SDA). As earlier noted, no direct official Swedish assistance was extended to ANC's main rival in exile.
2. Anders Möllander: Memorandum ('Framställning från African National Congress, ANC (Sydafrika)'/ 'Request from ANC'), CCHA/SIDA, Stockholm, [no date, but January 1973] (SDA).
3. CCHA: 'Protokoll [från sammanträde 15 januari 1973]' ('Minutes [from meeting 15 January 1973]'), SIDA, [Stockholm], 22 January 1973 (SDA).
4. SIDA: Decision ('Stöd till African National Congress (ANC), Sydafrika, samt Zimbabwe African People's Union (ZAPU), Rhodesia'/'Support to ANC and ZAPU'), Office of the Director General, No. 47/1973, Stockholm, 2 February 1973 (SDA). The allocation to ZAPU of Zimbabwe for 1972/73 was 50,000 SEK.
5. Letter ('SIDA humanitarian assistance to ANC members in Zambia and Tanzania') from Marianne Rappe to the Swedish embassy in Lusaka, SIDA, Stockholm, 30 March 1973 (SDA).
6. For reasons of comparison, it could be noted that the 1972/73 allocations to PAIGC of Guinea-Bissau and FRELIMO of Mozambique were 10 and 2 MSEK, respectively.
7. Letter ('SIDA assistance to ANC') from Curt Ström to ANC Lusaka, SIDA, Stockholm, 14 February 1973 (SDA).
8. Ibid.
9. Letter from T[homas] Nkobi, Acting Treasurer General, to SIDA, ANC, Lusaka, 2 March 1973 (SDA).
10. Letter ('SIDA humanitarian assistance to ANC members in Zambia and Tanzania') from Bo Wilén to SIDA Stockholm, Swedish embassy, Lusaka, 18 April 1973 (SDA).

Closing of the books after two
decades of cooperation: Thomas
Nkobi seated between
SIDA's Lena Johansson and
Georg Dreifaldt, with his old
friend Roland Axelsson standing,
Johannesburg, April 1994 (Courtesy
of Lena Johansson)

of a long and close relationship between Nkobi[1], Moonsamy[2] and Sweden over the
following two decades. Largely due to the two ANC officials efficient financial
administration, they would see the official Swedish assistance grow from a modest

1. Together with Oliver Tambo and Thabo Mbeki, Thomas Titus Nkobi maintained over the years particularly
    close links with Sweden. Representing ANC at almost all bilateral aid negotiations, he led the movement's del-
    egations to the very first deliberations in Lusaka in May 1974 and to the very last in Johannesburg in Novem-
    ber 1993. Like Chief Albert Luthuli, ANC's President-General between 1952 and 1967, 'Comrade T.G.'—as
    he was fondly known—was born in Matabeleland, Zimbabwe, or more precisely in the Plumtree area in
    1922. At the age of ten, he moved to Johannesburg, where his father worked as a migrant labourer in the gold
    mines. In 1941, he went to Adams College in Natal, where he *inter alia* studied with the future ZAPU Presi-
    dent Joshua Nkomo. After matriculation at the Bantu High School in Johannesburg, he enrolled at Pope Pius
    XII University College, Roma, Lesotho, pursuing a bachelor's degree in commerce. Involved in the 1944 Alex-
    andra bus boycott, Nkobi formally joined ANC in the early 1950s. In 1955, he participated in the prepara-
    tions for the Congress of the People, subsequently attending the historic assembly which drew up the Freedom
    Charter as a delegate from Alexandra. In 1957, he was arrested for taking part in the so called 'potato boy-
    cott', organized to highlight the plight of black prisoners forced to work on private farms. Brought to court,
    he was acquitted after being defended by Nelson Mandela. The following year—in 1958—Nkobi became
    ANC National Organizing Secretary, travelling all over South Africa to implement Mandela's 'M Plan' for
    underground operations. During the 1960 state of emergency, he was once again arrested and imprisoned
    with, among others, the future ANC Secretary General Alfred Nzo. Declared a banned person in 1961, Nkobi
    left South Africa for Tanzania in April 1963. Moving to Lusaka in January 1964, he served as ANC Chief
    Representative in Zambia until 1968, when he was appointed Deputy Treasurer General. When the incum-
    bent Treasurer General Moses Kotane fell ill in 1973, Nkobi *de facto* took over ANC's finance department. In
    1977, he was formally appointed Treasurer General, together with President Tambo and Secretary General
    Nzo holding one of the three highest positions in the organization. He was confirmed in this post at all subse-
    quent ANC conferences. In April 1994, Nkobi was elected to the first democratic parliament in South Africa.
    After suffering a stroke, he died in September 1994 (see also the interview with Roland Axelsson, pp. 252-
    56).
2. Working at ANC's Treasury Department, Kesval ('Kay') Moonsamy was together with Nkobi closely involved
    with Swedish assistance from the beginning to the end. Born in 1926, he started his political career in the
    Natal Indian Congress (NIC) in the mid-1940s. Serving as NIC's Treasurer in the early 1950s, Moonsamy was
    in 1955 elected Vice-President of the organization. Also active in SACP and SACTU, he was a defendant in
    the Treason Trial from December 1956 until the charges against him were withdrawn a year later. Leaving
    South Africa in June 1965, he stayed in Botswana until 1968, when he joined Nkobi in Zambia. Commuting
    between Zambia and Tanzania, Moonsamy eventually settled in Lusaka, where he *inter alia* served as secre-
    tary to ANC's Fund-Raising Committee. In August 1976, he took part for the first time in the aid negotiations
    with Sweden, regularly attending the annual meetings until the final deliberations in South Africa. As Treas-
    urer General of SACTU, in the mid-1980s he was also actively involved in discussions with LO/TCO. After
    the unbanning of SACP, Moonsamy was appointed Treasurer General of the party (cf. the interview with Kay
    Moonsamy, pp. 161-65).

150,000 SEK in 1972/73 to no less than 127 million in 1993/94.[1] Interviewed in 1995, Moonsamy—then Treasurer General of the South African Communist Party—recalled how SIDA

> began to give us aid, a very small amount at first. I know that comrade Treasurer General [Nkobi] quite often used to refer to this. He always used to take us back to 1973, saying that there was something like 150,000 Swedish Kronor given to ANC by SIDA. [...] It was a very small [amount], but, nevertheless, it was the beginning of the massive all around aid that was given by the Swedish government, SIDA and the people of Sweden.[2]

In early 1973, however, no one could have predicted that eventually ANC would receive close to 900 MSEK from the Swedish government in the form of direct assistance. Seen as temporary, it was at the time rather a question of when the support would be phased out. This notwithstanding, and encouraged by the Swedish decision, in August 1973 Nkobi submitted a request for the financial year 1973/74. Emphasizing that "our financial situation is still critical" and that "it shall [remain] so until we start agricultural and other projects which will make us self-sufficient and self-supporting"[3], the submission was more comprehensive than the previous year. In addition to food and clothing for 200 members in Tanzania and 150 in Zambia—a combined increase of 130 people—it covered *inter alia* support in the form of household utensils, toiletries, petrol, electricity and water charges, as well as telephone costs at the Lusaka office.[4]

Despite the conditional terms established in February 1973, it was without any further comments decided in January 1974 to renew the commodity aid, although the allocation for 1973/74 was maintained at the level of 150,000 SEK.[5] Gratefully acknowledged by Nkobi, he once again reiterated that ANC was "trying fervently to get the Zambian government to allow us to have a farm where we shall be in a position to till the land and grow vegetables and other foodstuff so as to be self-supporting and self-sufficient".[6]

By that time, however, it had become increasingly apparent to the Swedish authorities that neither the Tanzanian nor the Zambian government were likely to give ANC the green light to own land and start agricultural production. Against this background—and in spite of the fact that ANC had not requested continued assistance—in late February 1974 the CCHA secretariat proposed that the consultative committee should tentatively set aside 250,000 SEK for the financial year 1974/75, "in case [the movement] submits a new application".[7] The proposal was endorsed the following month.[8] Against many odds, ANC was thereby *de facto* included among the Southern African liberation movements receiving regular

1. 'Agreed minutes from consultations held in Johannesburg, South Africa, November 1993, between the African National Congress of South Africa (ANC) and [the] Swedish International Development Authority (SIDA) concerning humanitarian assistance', Johannesburg, 2 December 1993 (SDA).
2. Interview with Kay Moonsamy, p. 161.
3. Letter from T[homas] Nkobi, Acting Treasurer General, to SIDA, ANC, Lusaka, 5 August 1973 (SDA).
4. Ibid.
5. SIDA: Decision ('Stöd till African National Congress of South Africa, ANC'/'Support to ANC'), Office of the Director General, No. 2/1974, Stockholm, 8 January 1974 (SDA).
6. Letter from T[homas] Nkobi, Acting Treasurer General, to SIDA, ANC, Lusaka, 21 January 1974 (SDA).
7. Astrid Bergquist: Memorandum ('Stöd till African National Congress of South Africa'/'Support to ANC'), CCHA/SIDA, Stockholm, 28 February 1974 (SDA). A final decision to this effect was taken by SIDA in July 1974 (SIDA: Decision ('Bistånd till ANC (Sydafrika) budgetåret 1974/75'/'Assistance to ANC during the financial year 1974/75'), Office of the Director General, No. 442/1974, Stockholm, 30 July 1974) (SDA).
8. CCHA: 'Protokoll [från sammanträde 13 mars 1974]' ('Minutes [from meeting 13 March 1974]'), SIDA, [Stockholm], 18 April 1974 (SDA).

Swedish assistance. This became a situation *de jure* in May 1974, when direct official aid negotiations between the parties were held for the very first time.[1]

Respectively led by Iwo Dölling, the Swedish ambassador to Zambia, and Thomas Nkobi[2], the historic negotiations between Sweden and ANC in Lusaka in May 1974 were uncomplicated. After reviewing the cooperation during the financial year 1973/74, the need to streamline the procedures for procurement and delivery of assistance to the ANC members in Tanzania and Zambia was discussed. For 1974/75, an amount of 87,500 SEK was set aside for local procurement in Tanzania of food, clothes and other daily necessities, while the corresponding amount for Zambia was 122,500 SEK. The remaining balance of the allocated 250,000 SEK was earmarked for the ANC representative in Stockholm.[3] In addition, the Swedish delegation confirmed that SIDA was willing to finance a feasibility study for a vocational training programme proposed by Tambo during his visit to Sweden in January 1973.[4]

The Zambian Foreign Minister Vernon Mwaanga had just before the Lusaka meeting informed ambassador Dölling that his government for reasons of national security was "not particularly keen that the liberation movements acquired farms on Zambian territory".[5] The central issue of agricultural self-sufficiency was against this background not discussed. Instead, "it was tentatively agreed that new discussions would be held between the two parties during the month of May 1975" and that "a possible new request from ANC for 1975/76 should be presented [...] before March 1975".[6] Sealed by a formal agreement, the cooperation between Sweden and ANC was thereby institutionalized.

Land Restrictions and Aid Consolidation

Still seeing the supply of food, clothes and other daily necessities as temporary palliatives, by mid-1974 neither ANC nor the Swedish government had, however, abandoned the idea that the movement in Tanzania and/or Zambia would procure land to start its own agricultural production, not only to feed its members, but also for reasons of employment and as an income-generating activity. At a time when ANC actively tried to break out of the isolation in exile—from the 'forward areas' of Botswana, Lesotho and Swaziland seeking links with BCM and the wider opposition in South Africa—its own landholdings in Southern Africa could also serve as important rearguard bases.

1. 'Agreed minutes of discussions on cooperation between Sweden and [the] African National Congress, ANC', Lusaka, 11 June 1974 (SDA). The discussions took place on 21 and 22 May 1974.
2. In addition to ambassador Dölling, Astrid Bergquist, Lars Hultkvist, Anders Möllander and Bo Wilén formed part of the Swedish delegation. Nkobi was accompanied by the recently appointed ANC representative to Sweden, Sobizana Mngqikana (ibid.).
3. Astrid Bergquist: Memorandum ('Bistånd till ANC (Sydafrika) budgetåret 1974/75'/'Assistance to ANC during the financial year 1974/75'), CCHA/SIDA, Stockholm, 30 September 1974 (SDA).
4. ANC did not include the proposal in its subsequent requests to Sweden.
5. Letter ('Det svenska biståndet till SWAPO/ZANU-farmerna'/'The Swedish assistance to the SWAPO/ZANU farms') from Iwo Dölling to the Ministry for Foreign Affairs, Swedish embassy, Lusaka, 6 May 1974 (SDA). At the time, the land issue primarily concerned the Swedish cooperation with ZANU of Zimbabwe and SWAPO of Namibia. Cf. the chapters 'ZANU and ZAPU of Zimbabwe: On Separate Trails' and 'Transport, Home Front, Churches and Trade Unions' on Namibia.
6. 'Agreed minutes of discussions on cooperation between Sweden and [the] African National Congress, ANC', Lusaka, 11 June 1974 (SDA).

In the case of Zambia, ANC had tried since 1969 to procure a piece of land, but repeated approaches to the Kaunda government had been rejected.[1] Foreign Minister Mwaanga's message to the Swedish ambassador before the negotiations in May 1974 confirmed this stand.[2] To make matters worse, shortly thereafter ANC was informed by the Tanzanian authorities that it had to close down the activities at its small agricultural plot in Morogoro.[3] When the Swedish embassy in Dar es Salaam on ANC's behalf subsequently raised the issue with the Prime Minister's Office, the responsible official seemed—as earlier noted—"to be of the opinion that [landholding] would [only] give the movement too much security and [lead] its members to lose their motivation to continue the liberation struggle".[4]

The negative attitude held at the time by the principal host countries should be seen in the context of the Southern African 'détente exercise', which behind the scenes was secretly being prepared by South Africa and Zambia after the April 1974 Lisbon coup. Radically changing the correlation of political forces in the region, the downfall of the Portuguese regime led to a tactical rapprochement between Pretoria and Lusaka which not only had major consequences for MPLA[5] and ZANU[6], but also for ANC.[7]

Visiting Sweden a month after the first public signs of an understanding between the South African Prime Minister John Vorster and the Zambian President Kenneth Kaunda, in late November 1974 Thabo Mbeki—who described ANC's efforts to procure a farm as the movement's "biggest concern"—strongly turned against Zambia's contacts with the apartheid regime, concluding that the prospects of owning land were dimmer than ever.[8] While this was soon being confirmed[9], at the height of the 'détente exercise' a year later Oliver Tambo told the Foreign Ministry in Stockholm that the Zambians "had gone out of their way to accommodate Vorster", dejectedly adding that "they may ask us to leave, but until then we intend to stay".[10] In the meantime, ANC would concentrate on information and publicity.[11] Sweden would be closely associated with this effort.

1. Magnus Wernstedt and Gun-Britt Andersson: Memorandum ('Samtal med O. Tambo, president i ANC, M. Kunene och M. Legassick den 10 januari 1973'/'Conversation with O. Tambo, ANC President, M. Kunene and M. Legassick, 10 January 1973'), Ministry for Foreign Affairs, Stockholm, 29 January 1973 (MFA).
2. In addition to national security interests, Mwaanga told ambassador Dölling that the Zambian government was "not totally convinced by [the liberation movements'] arguments regarding self-sufficiency" (Letter ('Det svenska biståndet till SWAPO/ZANU-farmerna'/'The Swedish assistance to the SWAPO/ZANU farms') from Iwo Dölling to the Ministry for Foreign Affairs, Swedish embassy, Lusaka, 6 May 1974) (SDA).
3. Astrid Bergquist: Memorandum ('Bistånd till ANC (Sydafrika) budgetåret 1974/75'/'Assistance to ANC during the financial year 1974/75'), CCHA/SIDA, Stockholm, 30 September 1974 (SDA).
4. Ibid.
5. See the chapter 'MPLA of Angola: A Rockier Road'.
6. See the chapter 'ZANU and ZAPU of Zimbabwe: On Separate Trails'.
7. As well as for SWAPO of Namibia and, in general, the struggle for national liberation in Southern Africa.
8. Arne Ström: Memorandum ('Minnesanteckningar från möte med Thabo Mbeki, informationssekreterare till ANC's exekutiv'/'Notes from meeting with Thabo Mbeki, information secretary on ANC's executive'), SIDA, Stockholm, 2 December 1974 (SDA).
9. Submitting its request for continued Swedish assistance during 1975/76, in February 1975 ANC noted that the Zambian Ministry of Defence had not given the movement the green light to procure land (Letter ('Biståndsframställning från ANC (Sydafrika)'/'Request for assistance from ANC') from Iwo Dölling, Swedish ambassador to Zambia, to the Ministry for Foreign Affairs, Swedish embassy, Lusaka, 24 April 1975) (SDA). In fact, the Zambian government was as late as in May 1978 ambivalent in this regard, neither approving nor rejecting ANC's requests. "This attitude", the Swedish embassy in Lusaka noted, "was in contrast to [the policy] towards ZAPU [of Zimbabwe]", which had been offered different farms with [already] cleared land (Anders Möllander: Memorandum ('Protokoll från biståndsöverläggningar med African National Congress of South Africa, ANC'/'Minutes from aid deliberations with ANC'), Swedish embassy, Lusaka, 31 May 1978) (SDA).
10. Bengt Säve-Söderbergh: Memorandum ('Samtal med Oliver Tambo, ANC, Sydafrika'/'Conversation with Oliver Tambo, ANC, South Africa'), Ministry for Foreign Affairs, Stockholm, 3 October 1975 (MFA).
11. Ibid.

In 1978-79, ANC was eventually granted land rights in both Zambia and Tanzania. With funds from Sweden, the 1,300 hectare Chongela farm 40 kilometres north of Lusaka was purchased in October 1978, while at about the same time the Tanzanian government put an abandoned sisal estate at the movement's disposal at Mazimbu outside Morogoro.[1] Here, bush clearing and construction activities for the Solomon Mahlangu Freedom College (SOMAFCO) started in January 1979. Both the Chongela and the Mazimbu farms would from the outset feature prominently in the Swedish assistance.

ANC's hopes of running commercially viable farms in the two countries were until then reduced to a piggery at Morogoro and a small plot outside Livingstone in southern Zambia.[2] In accordance with the Swedish authorities' undertaking to support self-sufficiency activities, these projects were in May and September 1976 temporarily included in the assistance for 1976/77, which in the meantime had grown to 3 MSEK.[3] At that time, major political developments had taken place in the Southern African region and in the apartheid republic. Respectively led by ANC's allies FRELIMO and MPLA, in 1975 Mozambique and Angola had achieved national independence from Portugal. South Africa's military invasion of Angola signalled at the same time the end of détente. In South Africa itself, the Soweto uprising of June 1976 marked the beginning of a new phase in the anti-apartheid struggle. Presenting both unprecedented responsibilities and challenges for ANC, the events prompted a re-orientation and an expansion of the Swedish assistance.

As a result of the post-Soweto exodus to Southern Africa, the budget for 'daily necessities' was raised and extended to cover several countries. Assistance to ANC in Angola was notably included in the cooperation programme. Considerable amounts were in addition set aside for transportation by air of refugees from one area to another. Information and publicity—mainly in the form of support to ANC's radio services—became a budget post of its own. Discussions on capacity-building were initiated. Last but not least, within a rapidly growing overall alloca-

---

1. The decision to grant ANC land at Mazimbu was taken in 1977.
2. Representatives of the UN system showed little understanding of ANC's efforts to become self-sufficient. In a remarkable comment on the United Nations marginal cooperation with ANC and PAC in Southern Africa, in March 1976 Winston Prattley, UNDP Resident Representative to Zambia, told the visiting CCHA fact-finding mission that the South African movements "were not particularly [important]" and that "[t]hey were mainly engaged in rearing pigs and chickens" (Ann Wilkens: Memorandum ('FN-organen och befrielserörelserna i Zambia'/'The UN agencies and the liberation movements in Zambia'), CCHA/Ministry for Foreign Affairs, Stockholm, 23 April 1976) (SDA).
3. 'Agreed minutes of discussions on cooperation between Sweden and the African National Congress of South Africa', Lusaka, 1 September 1976 (SDA). Anders Möllander from the Swedish embassy in Dar es Salaam visited ANC's recently started pig-rearing project in Morogoro in July 1975. At the time, the piggery—built from packing-cases and administered by a Tanzanian—had a stock of about 50 animals. Although ANC expected that the project would become commercially viable, Möllander was far from impressed, concluding that "the visit gave a good illustration of the relatively straitened circumstances under which the members of the liberation movement live in Tanzania, [n]ot being allowed to establish any activity which would make [them] self-sufficient" (Anders Möllander: Memorandum ('Minnesanteckningar från besök hos den sydafrikanska befrielserörelsen ANC i Morogoro'/'Notes from a visit to the South African liberation movement ANC in Morogoro'), Swedish embassy, Dar es Salaam, 28 July 1975) (SDA). After visiting the same project two years later, SIDA's Anna Runeborg was left with a much more positive impression. Partly financed through Swedish assistance, water had then been connected, permanent structures were being erected and a slaughtering facility had been installed. There were at the time more than 400 pigs, and 14 had been slaughtered and sold in Dar es Salaam the preceding week (Anna Runeborg: Memorandum ('Besök hos ANC/SA i Morogoro på gris-uppfödningsprojektet den 11 oktober 1977'/'Visit to ANC Morogoro and its piggery project, 11 October 1977'), Swedish embassy, Dar es Salaam, 4 November 1977) (SDA). This and other examples played a major role in convincing the Swedish authorities that the ANC cadres in exile—mainly coming from urban backgrounds in South Africa—despite adverse conditions were capable of managing agricultural and stock farming projects.

tion[1] the 'home front component'—covering support to the movement's underground work inside South Africa—assumed increasing weight and significance
from mid-1977.

Coinciding in time with the changeover in Sweden from Olof Palme's Social
Democratic government to Thorbjörn Fälldin's first non-socialist coalition (October 1976-October 1978), the basis was thus being laid for a special relationship
with ANC. Supported by a broad parliamentary majority[2], this policy was confirmed by Ola Ullsten's Liberal minority government (October 1978-October 1979)
and consolidated during Fälldin's second 'bourgeois' cabinet (October 1979-May
1981).

Assisting ANC in Angola

Between 1975 and 1977, the number of people under ANC's care in Southern
Africa rapidly grew from less than 600[3] to more than 4,500.[4] Behind the increase
was the exodus following upon the Soweto uprising and the ensuing repression in
South Africa.

A majority of the young refugees who crossed the borders with Botswana and
Swaziland—there seeking contact with ANC—would be transferred to Tanzania
and, above all, to Angola, where the recently independent MPLA government
assured the movement of political sanctuary and bases for military training. While
the number of people catered for by ANC increased and spread over seven countries in Southern Africa[5], as in the case of SWAPO[6] Angola would soon feature
prominently in the Swedish assistance, particularly with regard to food, clothes,
medicines and other daily necessities. In fact, as early as in September 1977 2.6 million out of a total ANC allocation for 1977/78 of 8 MSEK—corresponding to one
third—was set aside for daily necessities there.[7] This was by far the largest single
budget post overall, representing twice the amount allocated to ANC in Tanzania.[8]

In a Western context, Sweden had established unique relations with MPLA.
Against this background, it was not surprising that the ANC leadership—as later
would be the case in Zimbabwe—shortly after Angola's independence in November
1975 approached Sweden concerning possible financial assistance to set up an
office there. Anders Bjurner at the embassy in Lusaka had been closely involved

---

1. In the five-year period from 1975/76 to 1979/80, the annual allocations to ANC were as follows: 1975/76: 1
   MSEK; 1976/77: 3+2.5=5.5 MSEK; 1977/78: 8 MSEK; 1978/79: 12 MSEK; and 1979/80: 16 MSEK.
2. For dissenting views by the Moderate Party, see the following chapter.
3. Letter ('Biståndsframställning från ANC (Sydafrika)'/'Request for assistance from ANC') from Iwo Dölling,
   Swedish ambassador to Zambia, to the Ministry for Foreign Affairs, Swedish embassy, Lusaka, 24 April 1975
   (SDA). According to ANC, in early 1975 the movement catered for 250 people in Zambia, 210 in Tanzania
   and a total of about 100 in Botswana, Lesotho and Swaziland (ibid.).
4. ANC: 'Memorandum submitted by the African National Congress of South Africa to SIDA in support of a
   request for assistance for the year 1977-78', [no place or date, but forwarded to the Ministry for Foreign
   Affairs with covering letter ('Biståndsframställning från ANC (Sydafrika)'/'Request for assistance from ANC')
   from Anders Möllander, Swedish embassy, Lusaka, 14 April 1977] (SDA). Also Marianne Sundh: Memorandum ('Biståndssamarbetet med African National Congress of South Africa, ANC, under budgetåret 1976/77
   och framställning om stöd under budgetåret 1977/78'/'The aid cooperation with ANC during the financial
   year 1976/77 and request for support during 1977/78'), CCHA/SIDA, Stockholm, 6 May 1977 (SDA). In
   April 1977, ANC estimated that it had the following number of people under its care in Southern Africa:
   3,000 in Angola, 500 in Swaziland, 350 in Tanzania, 300 in Zambia, 150 in Mozambique, 150 in Botswana
   and 150 in Lesotho (ibid.). At the time, the great majority of the refugees in Swaziland and Mozambique were
   in temporary transit.
5. Angola, Botswana, Lesotho, Mozambique, Swaziland, Tanzania and Zambia.
6. See the chapter 'Cold War, Total Strategy and Expanded Assistance' on Namibia above.
7. 'Agreed minutes of discussions on the cooperation between the African National Congress of South Africa
   (ANC) and Sweden, 1977/78', Lusaka, 2 September 1977 (SDA).
8. Ibid.

with the assistance to MPLA. After the Swedish government's recognition in mid-February 1976 of the People's Republic of Angola, he would also take an active part in the establishment of an embassy in Luanda, as well as in paving the way for assistance to ANC and SWAPO in the newly independent republic.

The question of a representation in Angola was raised by Tambo in discussions with Bjurner in Lusaka in early May 1976. The Acting ANC President had visited Angola in March. During the visit, he had not only been assured of the new government's full political support, but had in a spectacular way also experienced the turning tide in Southern Africa when on 27 March 1976 he, together with the MPLA leader Lúcio Lara, on the border with Namibia witnessed the retreat from Angola of the South African Defence Force.[1] At a time when ANC was still facing restrictions in Tanzania and Zambia—as well as in Mozambique—Angola offered the movement significant space to break out of its isolation, including facilities for radio broadcasts to South Africa. The Luanda government, Tambo said, welcomed an ANC representation. In the absence of financial resources, it was, however, not clear when the movement would be able to establish an office.[2]

ANC appointed in the meantime Cassius Make and Max Moabi to represent the movement in Angola. In early June 1976, they met an official delegation from Sweden.[3] During its visit to Luanda, the delegation raised the question of possible assistance to ANC and SWAPO with President Agostinho Neto's foreign policy adviser Paulo Jorge, who—as noted in the context of Namibia—welcomed such support, stating that "nothing prevented any of the movements [...] from receiving goods in Angola".[4]

Visiting Luanda at the same time, SIDA's Carin Norberg from the embassy in Lusaka opened discussions with Make and Moabi on how Sweden best could assist the local ANC representation.[5] As the exchange of views took place before the Soweto events and the ensuing exodus, the two representatives were still restrained. Stating that the organization in Angola should "mainly dedicate itself to information [activities]", Make estimated that the number of ANC members would only increase to around ten. While they certainly would need food and other basic commodities, the most pressing request to Sweden, however, concerned equipment and furniture for an ANC mission.[6]

ANC was allocated office space by the MPLA government in mid-June 1976.[7] Expressing Angola's recognition of the movement as the legitimate representative of the South African majority, the first office was situated in the building previously

---

1. Tambo would often refer to this significant event in the history of the Southern African liberation struggles. It should be noted that the MPLA government as a gesture towards ANC had symbolically invited a group of MK soldiers to oversee SADF's withdrawal (Letter ('Nytt bistånd till ANC (SA)'/'Renewed assistance to ANC') from Anders Bjurner, Swedish embassy, to the Ministry for Foreign Affairs, Luanda, 13 November 1976) (SDA). In quite a different context, twenty years later Lara brought back the memory of the historic occasion. Openly critical of South Africa's policy towards Angola under President Nelson Mandela, in discussions with the author in April 1996 the veteran MPLA leader was of the opinion that the relations with the new government in Pretoria would have been much better had it been led by Oliver Tambo, "who shared our views and from the very beginning was together with us in the struggle" (Conversation with Lúcio Lara, Luanda, 16 April 1996).
2. Letter ('Samtal med O. Tambo, ANC's t.f. ordförande'/'Conversation with O. Tambo, ANC Acting President') from Anders Bjurner, Swedish embassy, to the Ministry for Foreign Affairs, Lusaka, 21 May 1976 (MFA).
3. Ann Wilkens: Memorandum ('Samtal med Paulo Jorge om stöd till befrielserörelser verksamma i Angola'/'Conversation with Paulo Jorge on support to liberation movements active in Angola'), Ministry for Foreign Affairs, Stockholm, 23 June 1976 (MFA).
4. Ibid.
5. Carin Norberg: 'Reserapport från besök i Angola 7-14 juni 1976' ('Travel report from visit to Angola 7-14 June 1976'), Swedish embassy, Lusaka, 12 July 1976 (SDA).
6. Ibid.
7. Ibid.

housing the Pretoria regime's consulate.[1] Together with Make and Moabi, Norberg was thus in a position to draft a preliminary list of requirements for ANC's Luanda representation.[2] The list—covering furniture, office equipment and two vehicles, but not as yet daily necessities for the ANC members—was formally submitted as a request to Sweden in a letter from Thomas Nkobi the following month.[3] Subsequently accommodated within the assistance for 1976/77[4], the swift action in favour of ANC's representation in Angola—taking place even before a Swedish embassy had been officially opened[5]—represents an early example of the pragmatic cooperation which over the years developed between SIDA and ANC's Treasury Department, where the opinion of Swedish officials was generally trusted by Nkobi and they in a spirit of common purpose *de facto* often acted on his behalf.[6]

Despite the predictions made by Make and Moabi, Angola soon became the most important Southern African host country for ANC refugees, who under Umkhonto we Sizwe were given military instruction at a number of camps allocated by the MPLA government.[7] Barrell estimates that MK over the ten-year period after 1977 trained on average 1,250 recruits each year.[8] "Basic training, lasting about six months, occurred mainly in Angola, where the ANC usually had

---

1. Letter ('Nytt bistånd till ANC (SA)'/'Renewed assistance to ANC') from Anders Bjurner, Swedish embassy, to the Ministry for Foreign Affairs, Luanda, 13 November 1976 (SDA).
2. Carin Norberg: 'Reserapport från besök i Angola 7-14 juni 1976' ('Travel report from visit to Angola 7-14 June 1976'), Swedish embassy, Lusaka, 12 July 1976 (SDA).
3. Letter from Thomas Nkobi, Acting Treasurer General, to the Swedish embassy, ANC, Lusaka, 13 July 1976 (SDA).
4. 'Agreed minutes of discussions on cooperation between Sweden and the African National Congress of South Africa', Lusaka, 1 September 1976 (SDA). Anders Bjurner, then chargé d'affaires at the Swedish embassy in Lusaka, headed the Swedish delegation, while Thomas Nkobi led the ANC team.
5. The Swedish embassy in Luanda was opened in October 1976.
6. This will be further illustrated below. Interviewed in 1996, Roland Axelsson, SIDA's former regional coordinator of humanitarian assistance, noted how he as early as at the end of the 1970s "was very much trusted and allowed to study [both SWAPO's and ANC's] systems of financial management. [...] Thomas Nkobi, Hifikepunye Pohamba [of SWAPO] and all their co-workers supported me one hundred per cent. They trusted me, but it was, of course, in their interest that their people were fed and that the money was correctly spent" (Interview with Roland Axelsson, pp. 253-54). ANC often formally acknowledged the assistance and advice given by Swedish officials. Submitting the movement's request for 1978/79, in April 1978, for example, Nkobi wrote in his covering letter: "The National Executive Committee of the ANC wishes to place on record its sincere appreciation for the cordial relations that exist between members of our organisation and officials of SIDA in Lusaka. We wish to make special mention of Ms. Elisabeth Michanek, Mr. Anders Möllander, Mr. P[er] Kökeritz and Mr. R[oland] Axelsson. We have enjoyed [...] maximum cooperation, assistance and advice at all times from the above mentioned" (Letter from Thomas Nkobi, Treasurer General, to the Swedish embassy, ANC, Lusaka, 10 April 1978) (SDA). An official of the Foreign Ministry, Möllander then served as first secretary at the embassy. Kökeritz headed the SIDA office, where Michanek and Axelsson were particularly involved with humanitarian assistance.
7. Between 1976 and 1989—when they were closed as a result of the December 1988 New York accords on Namibia, signed by Angola, Cuba and South Africa—ANC/MK used a number of camps in Angola. The first was the Gabela camp in the province of Kwanza Sul, which was used from late 1976 until 1977. Transit facilities were also established outside Luanda and Benguela in 1976-77. ANC's first major training camp was set up at Novo Catengue in the Benguela province in May 1977. Often referred to as 'the University of the South', it was a former Portuguese army camp under Cuban administration. A first contingent of 560 recruits from the 1976 uprising—christened the 'June 16 Detachment'—began training there in 1977. Novo Catengue was abandoned after a South African air strike in March 1979, which killed one Cuban and two MK soldiers. The bulk of the trainees were then transferred to the Pango camp, established on an old coffee estate in the province of Kwanza Norte. In the same area, the Funda, Fazenda and Quibaxe camps had been opened in 1977-78. In 1979—at the same time as Pango—the Viana transit camp outside Luanda and the Caxito training camp north of the capital were also set up. A large camp was, finally, established at Caculama, some 60 kilometres east of Malanje, in January 1981. Swedish funds were later set aside for agricultural activities at the Caculama camp. In addition to training camps, ANC/MK was also running a detention centre in Angola. Known as Camp 32 or Quatro, it was established in 1979, not far from Quibaxe in Kwanza Norte. With regard to military instruction, it could be noted that Cuban officers assisted ANC from the beginning. Instructors from the Soviet Union started to arrive in 1979.
8. Barrell op. cit., p. 42.

about five camps operating at any one time".[1] During this period, Swedish commodity aid in the form of food, clothes and other basic necessities for the freedom fighters was constantly growing. In this context, it should be noted that the ANC members in the Angolan camps due to the host country's war-torn economy faced particularly harsh conditions. Garth Strachan, who was in Angola from the late 1970s until the early 1980s, later recalled how

> there were very long periods of time when the conditions were extremely bad. I remember someone saying that even Robben Island had been easier than the camps. [...] I think that it was well known, at least in my experience, that the support was coming from friendly countries. The food was from the Soviet Union and some of the East bloc countries. But we were always told that the financial support for the food that was being purchased, as well as for the clothes and the soap and all those things, was from Holland and Sweden.[2]

Considerable quantities of food were also delivered directly by Sweden in favour of the ANC/MK camps. As early as in 1977/78—when, as noted above, one third of the total ANC allocation was set aside for daily necessities in Angola—the food supplies shipped to ANC amounted to 60 tons, with rice, tinned meat, tinned fish, sugar and dried milk as major items.[3] Two years later, the supplies had increased to 106 tons.[4] The trend accelerated in the 1980s. Between July and December 1983—at a time when ANC estimated that it catered for 8,900 people in Angola[5]—the food shipped by SIDA and delivered to ANC in Luanda amounted to no less than 436 tons.[6] This corresponded to almost 50 kilograms per person, or a daily individual ration of a quarter of a kilo.

Mozambique and Onward Flights

While Angola became of crucial importance from mid-1976, independent Mozambique would play a far less prominent role. Like MPLA, FRELIMO was aligned with ANC within the so called Khartoum alliance.[7] When the Mozambican liberation movement assumed state power in June 1975—proclaiming the People's

1. Ibid. One of the early ANC/MK trainees in Angola was Solomon Mahlangu, who came to personify the new generation of freedom fighters. He had left South Africa after the 1976 Soweto uprising. Returning via Swaziland in June 1977, he was involved a few days later in a shootout with the police in central Johannesburg. Arrested and subsequently sentenced to death, Mahlangu was hanged on 6 April 1979. Shortly before he was sent to the gallows, he wrote: 'My blood will nourish the tree which will bear the fruits of freedom'. A legend for the black youth, ANC gave his name to the Solomon Mahlangu Freedom College (SOMAFCO) in Tanzania.
2. Interview with Garth Strachan, p. 193. For descriptions of the conditions in the ANC/MK camps in Angola, see Kasrils op. cit., pp. 136-54 and 169-89, and Barrell op. cit., pp. 43-45.
3. Letter ('Bistånd till ANC (SA) 1977/78'/'Assistance to ANC 1977/78') from Carin Norberg, Swedish embassy, to SIDA, Luanda, 28 November 1977 (SDA). It could as a curiosity be noted that SIDA at the same time delivered 500 pairs of "woollen knee-length socks for men [...] in dark colours (grey, brown, green)" ('Inköpsanmodan'/'Procurement request' attached to ibid.). Clothes were also supplied by the Swedish government outside the bilateral cooperation programme with ANC. In 1978, for example, 2,000 pairs of trousers were donated to ANC in Angola (Letter ('Beredskapslager av byxor till befrielserörelserna'/'Trousers from the government's stores to the liberation movements') from SIDA Stockholm to the SIDA offices in Dar es Salaam, Luanda, Lusaka and Maputo, Stockholm, 21 December 1978) (SDA).
4. Letter ('Purchasing programme ANC-Angola 1979/80') from SIDA to the Swedish embassy in Luanda, Stockholm, 29 November 1979 (SDA). In addition to food, the SIDA supplies to ANC in Angola in 1979/80 included huge quantities of soap, toothpaste, shoes and clothes, *inter alia* in the form of ladies' underwear to the female ANC-MK members (ibid.).
5. Tor Sellström: Memorandum ('Humanitärt bistånd till African National Congress of South Africa (ANC), budgetåret 1984/85'/'Humanitarian assistance to ANC during the financial year 1984/85'), SIDA, Stockholm, 13 March 1984 (SDA).
6. Letter ('Matleveranser till ANC Angola'/'Food deliveries to ANC Angola') with attached 'Statement of material procurement' from SIDA to the Swedish embassy in Luanda, Stockholm, 9 January 1984 (SDA).
7. ANC/MK cadres—among them Josiah Jele and Lennox Lagu—had during the Mozambican liberation struggle been attached to FRELIMO.

Republic of Mozambique—ANC had thus well-founded expectations that it would be welcome to open an office and start project activities in the country. Bordering Swaziland and South Africa—with both the Johannesburg and Durban areas less than 500 kilometres away—southern Mozambique and the capital Maputo offered, in addition, unprecedented possibilities for armed operations against the apartheid regime. At a time when ANC had established a precarious presence in Swaziland and was trying to link up with the emerging internal South African opposition, Mozambique's independence was of enormous potential importance.

As was the case with MPLA, the Swedish government maintained an open and frank dialogue with FRELIMO. When in mid-April 1975 its Vice-President Marcelino dos Santos visited Stockholm to discuss the future bilateral relations with Sweden, Prime Minister Palme—referring to a recent meeting with Oliver Tambo—emphasized that it was "important to show solidarity [also with ANC], even if the liberation of the South African people to all appearances would take a long time".[1] In his reply, dos Santos confirmed that independent Mozambique would extend political support to the movement, although the country's exposed position made it difficult to make "too many statements" regarding South Africa.[2]

Two months later, representatives of the Swedish government and ANC met in Lusaka for a first round of negotiations regarding the assistance programme in 1975/76.[3] On this occasion, ANC proposed financial support for the establishment of a vehicle workshop in the Mozambican capital. Against the background of the close relations between ANC and FRELIMO, as well as of the assurances given by Marcelino dos Santos, the proposal was accepted.[4]

The Mozambican government, however, did not give the proposed project its blessing.[5] Meeting Anders Bjurner in Lusaka in May 1976—that is, when he first raised the question of Swedish support to ANC in Angola—Oliver Tambo was decidedly "restrained" with regard to Mozambique, giving the impression that he "was not fully convinced about ANC's possibilities there".[6] Although he underlined the old bonds with FRELIMO, Tambo "seemed to be of the opinion that Mozambique was overly cautious vis-à-vis South Africa". Stating that there at the most were some twenty ANC members in the country, the Acting President critically noted that in addition there was "a great number of South African refugees, [...] but the Mozambican authorities do not allow us to see them".[7]

Mozambique's cautious stand vis-à-vis ANC and South Africa should be seen in the light of its wider international and regional commitments. In accordance with UN and OAU resolutions, after independence the FRELIMO government gave precedence to the liberation struggle in Rhodesia. Imposing sanctions against the Smith regime, accommodating ZANU and receiving tens of thousands of refugees

---

1. Ann Wilkens and Mikael Dahl: Memorandum ('Besök av FRELIMO-delegation hos statsministern'/'Visit by FRELIMO delegation to the Prime Minister'), Ministry for Foreign Affairs, Stockholm, 14 May 1975 (SDA). The meeting between dos Santos and Palme took place on 18 April 1975.
2. Ibid. The Mozambican economy was closely intertwined with South Africa's. There were, for example, some 150,000 Mozambican migrant labourers in the apartheid republic.
3. Due to the unsettled political situation in Southern Africa at the time, the 1975 aid negotiations between Sweden and ANC were held on two occasions, namely in June and in September.
4. 'Agreed minutes of discussions on cooperation 1975/76 between Sweden and [the] African National Congress, South Africa, ANC', Lusaka, 12 September 1975 (SDA).
5. As late as in August 1976, ANC was confident that the Mozambican authorities would support the project proposal ('Agreed minutes of discussions on cooperation between Sweden and the African National Congress', Lusaka, 1 September 1976) (SDA).
6. Letter ('Samtal med O. Tambo, ANC's t.f. ordförande'/'Conversation with O. Tambo, ANC Acting President') from Anders Bjurner, Swedish embassy, to the Ministry for Foreign Affairs, Lusaka, 21 May 1976 (MFA).
7. Ibid.

from the neighbouring country, during the second half of the 1970s Mozambique paid a high price for its principled stand. In strictly economic terms, it has been estimated that sanctions against Rhodesia between 1976 and 1980 cost the country in excess of 500 MUSD in lost transit revenue alone.[1] To this should be added enormous losses as a result of direct Rhodesian military attacks and increasingly devastating operations carried out by RENAMO.[2] Although close to ANC, in this situation the government in Maputo tried to avoid open conflicts with the apartheid regime.

The restrictive attitude towards ANC was soon evident to the Swedish authorities. In September 1976—at the same time as a ZANU delegation visited Sweden to discuss humanitarian assistance[3]—SIDA's Bo Westman at the embassy in Maputo reported that the question of the proposed vehicle workshop had been raised with the Mozambican Foreign Ministry, but no reply had been given.[4] In marked contrast to Angola, the Maputo government under Machel would not only be reluctant towards ANC projects, but did not grant the movement recognized office facilities.[5] Also in September 1976, Westman informed the authorities in Stockholm that "an ANC office in the proper sense of the word does not yet exist in Maputo".[6] Nevertheless, with the government's consent two ANC representatives—Lennox Lagu and Jacob Zuma—were based in the Mozambican capital.[7] The Swedish embassy entered into contact with them at an early stage. To facilitate their work, in July 1976, for example, it was decided to supply them with a Land Rover.[8]

As a result of the post-Soweto repression, from mid-1976 hundreds of young South Africans would via Swaziland end up in Mozambique, where the majority sought contact with ANC.[9] However, neither the FRELIMO government nor ANC wished them to stay, in the former case for security reasons and in the latter due to the fact that they could not be properly cared for, particularly with regard to military training. After unavailing requests to OAU[10], during the annual negotiations with Sweden in late August 1976 ANC therefore enquired whether funds could be

---

1. Phyllis Johnson and David Martin (eds): *Destructive Engagement: Southern Africa at War*, Zimbabwe Publishing House, Harare, 1986, p. 17. The March 1976 closure of the border with Rhodesia deprived Mozambique of about one third of its foreign currency revenue in the form of rail and port charges (ibid.).
2. In Portuguese, *Resistência Nacional Moçambicana*, or Mozambique National Resistance (MNR).
3. See the chapter 'Patriotic Front: ZANU and ZAPU towards Independence'.
4. Letter ('Uppgifter om ANC/SA'/'Information re ANC') from Bo Westman, Swedish embassy, to CCHA/SIDA, Maputo, 20 September 1976 (SDA).
5. As noted in the chapter on Mozambique, some observers have claimed that at the time there existed a secret non-aggression treaty between FRELIMO and the Pretoria government. South Africa was said to have agreed not to intervene in Mozambique, while the Maputo government was said to have agreed not to allow ANC to operate from its territory. Eventually, however, Mozambique would become ANC's main operational bridgehead. Quoting Joe Slovo—who in 1980 set up a Special Operations Unit in Maputo—Barrell states that "ANC had an understanding with the FRELIMO government under which it was free to conduct military operations into South Africa provided it did so indirectly via Swaziland and not directly across Mozambique's borders" (Barrell Ph. D. op. cit., chapter three, p. 33).
6. Letter ('Uppgifter om ANC/SA'/'Information re ANC') from Bo Westman, Swedish embassy, to CCHA/SIDA, Maputo, 20 September 1976 (SDA).
7. After detention in Swaziland, Zuma had in May 1976 been expelled to Mozambique.
8. Letter ('Uppgifter om ANC/SA'/'Information re ANC') from Bo Westman, Swedish embassy, to CCHA/SIDA, Maputo, 20 September 1976 (SDA).
9. The other main escape route went via Botswana. Although most of the so called 'Soweto refugees' had never been active within ANC structures in South Africa, they were primarily attracted to the movement due to its commitment to armed struggle. In exile, many of them expressed the wish to join Umkhonto we Sizwe. Barrell estimates that some 4,000 young blacks left South Africa over the eighteen months between July 1976 and December 1977. About 3,000 of them joined ANC and most of these MK (Barrell Ph. D. op. cit., chapter three, p. 3).
10. Anders Bjurner: Memorandum ('Förhandlingsprotokoll för bistånd till ANC (Sydafrika) 1976/77'/'Agreed minutes regarding assistance to ANC 1976/77'), Swedish embassy, Lusaka, 3 September 1976 (SDA). According to Bjurner, the ANC delegation—led by Thomas Nkobi—"did not hide its disappointment concerning [OAU's] lack of willingness to assist" (ibid.).

made available to transport the refugees by air to Tanzania. The Swedish delegation was positive to the proposal, recommending that unutilized allocations made earlier for the vehicle workshop and other activities in Mozambique could be used.[1] It was agreed to set aside an amount of 100,000 SEK for the purpose.[2]

This marked the beginning not only of a major post-Soweto operation, but also of close Swedish involvement in a number of emergency evacuations by air of ANC members from one area to another in Southern Africa during the 1980s. The transport component within the regular cooperation programme would in the case of ANC thus mainly be used to move people rather than—as in the cases of ZANU, ZAPU and SWAPO—for the procurement of vehicles to move goods.[3]

The original ANC allocation for the period 1 July 1976-30 June 1977 was 3 MSEK. Due to rapidly increasing numbers of refugees in Botswana and Mozambique in need of daily necessities and onward transportation, in October 1976 the movement submitted an additional request for 4.2 MSEK. It covered costs for the transfer of 300 people from Mozambique to Tanzania, 400 from Mozambique to Angola and 300 from Botswana to Tanzania.[4] Due to agreements with ZANU and ZAPU of Zimbabwe, as well as with SWAPO of Namibia, the overall Swedish budget for humanitarian assistance in Southern Africa was, however, at that time almost fully committed.

In this situation—reflecting the broad Nordic consensus on apartheid South Africa—Fälldin's non-socialist government approached Odvar Nordli's Social Democratic government in Norway, proposing that they together should meet the urgent

---

1. 'Agreed minutes of discussions on cooperation between Sweden and the African National Congress of South Africa', Lusaka, 1 September 1976 (SDA).
2. Ibid.
3. In the early stages of the cooperation, Sweden supplied the ANC offices in Southern Africa with a large number of station wagons, cross-country vehicles and heavy-duty trucks. In 1977/78, for example, 12 vehicles were purchased ('Agreed minutes of discussions on the cooperation between Sweden and the African National Congress of South Africa (ANC) 1978/79', Lusaka, 26 May 1978) (SDA). In both 1978/79 and 1979/80, no allocation was, however, made for the procurement of vehicles since—as stated by ANC—"funds for this item can be obtained elsewhere" (ibid. and 'Agreed minutes from discussions on the cooperation between the African National Congress of South Africa (ANC) and the Swedish International Development Authority (SIDA)', Lusaka, 18 May 1979) (SDA). As ANC was supported in this respect by the Soviet Union, Norway and other donors, the 'vehicle component' within the Swedish assistance to ANC would during the 1980s only represent between 1.5 and 3.5 per cent of the overall annual allocations ('Agreed minutes' for the period 1980/81-1989/90) (SDA). Compared with the assistance to SWAPO, this was a very small share (cf. the chapter 'Transport, Home Front, Churches and Trade Unions' on Namibia). Nevertheless, the contributions towards the procurement of vehicles during the decade amounted in total to 11.6 MSEK. In 1986/87 alone, ANC purchased no less than 16 vehicles under the Swedish assistance programme ('Minutes from consultative talks in Lusaka, 2-5 December 1986, between the African National Congress of South Africa (ANC) and SIDA concerning humanitarian assistance', Lusaka, 5 December 1986) (SDA). In addition, hundreds of smaller vehicles were bought by ANC organizers in South Africa under the 'home front component'. In the case of SWAPO, a transport study was carried out by SIDA in 1982-83. In order to "render the utilization of the total vehicle fleet [in exile] more effective", it was agreed in May 1986 to launch a similar study for ANC ('Agreed minutes [from] consultations in Lusaka, May 1986, between the African National Congress of South Africa and Sweden concerning humanitarian assistance', Lusaka, 9 May 1986) (SDA). A first inventory was made by Hans Abrahamsson in December 1986. Focusing on ANC in Lusaka, he found that between 80 and 90 per cent of some 100 vehicles were in working order, that is, an incomparably better situation than the one prevailing in SWAPO. At the same time, however, he noted that there was scope for improvement, recommending Swedish technical assistance in the form of a transport planner (Hans Abrahamsson: Memorandum ('Transport management support to ANC-Lusaka: Findings and recommendations from field visit [2-5 December 1986]'), Gothenburg, 9 December 1986) (SDA). The proposal was positively received by ANC, but only in early 1990—after ANC's unbanning and pending the return to South Africa—did SIDA manage to recruit a suitable person ('Agreed minutes from consultations held in Lusaka, May 1990, between the African National Congress of South Africa and Sweden concerning humanitarian assistance', Lusaka, 18 May 1990) (SDA). In addition to the supply of vehicles—notably for the movement's agricultural projects—the direct Swedish support to ANC's transport sector was from 1985 mainly channelled to the Alpha mechanical workshop in Lusaka (see below).
4. Ann Wilkens: Memorandum ('Tilläggsframställning från African National Congress of South Africa'/'Additional request from ANC'), CCHA/Ministry for Foreign Affairs, [Stockholm], 2 December 1976 (SDA).

request.[1] The Norwegian government had until then not extended direct official support to ANC. Received in a positive spirit, the approach subsequently led to a change in this regard. In July 1977, the Norwegian government made a first allocation of 2 MNOK to ANC.[2] From then on, Sweden and Norway coordinated their support to the movement, in particular with regard to 'daily necessities' in Southern Africa.[3]

Meanwhile, on 27 January 1977 Sweden decided to grant ANC an additional amount of 2.5 MSEK, increasing the allocation for 1976/77 to 5.5 million.[4] Used in accordance with the ANC request of October 1976, the actual distribution of the funds was coordinated by Nkobi, Moonsamy and Reddy Mazimba, ANC's Chief Representative to Tanzania, with SIDA's Anna Runeborg at the embassy in Dar es Salaam.[5] Years later, Mazimba—then using the name Mampane—recalled:

> In 1976, I was promoted to ANC Chief Representative in Tanzania. At that time, we had a lot of young people coming to Dar es Salaam as a result of the Soweto uprising. I would go to the airport and divide them. Those who went for military training on one side and those who went for academic studies on the other. [...] That activity made me be more in contact with Anna Runeborg. Thomas Nkobi [...] gave me instructions to organize charter flights to fly our MK personnel out of Tanzania to Angola. I would then go to Anna and say: 'Anna, here is my problem'. She was helpful all the time. [...]
>
> At that time, there was a war in the Shaba province of Zaire. From Dar es Salaam to Luanda you had to fly over the Shaba province. But we decided that the flight[s] must go from Dar es Salaam to Ndola, Zambia. We would go down there, and from Ndola we would continue to Angola to avoid the Shaba province. That added to the price, but SIDA covered the costs. Everything, the flights and everything.[6]

Support to the transfer and resettlement of refugees—mainly to Tanzania and Angola—continued in 1977/78, when one million out of the total ANC allocation of 8 MSEK was set aside for this purpose.[7] At the annual negotiations in Lusaka in August 1977, the parties agreed that "the amount [...] for transport under each [host] country [in Southern Africa would] include air fares [and] costs for train and car transport".[8]

At a particularly critical juncture—after the independence of Angola and Mozambique and responding to the post-Soweto exodus—the Swedish government

---

1. Ibid. ANC's Stockholm representative, Sobizana Mngqikana, visited Oslo for the same reason in November 1976 (Østbye in Eriksen (ed.) op. cit., p. 141).
2. On the beginnings of the Norwegian assistance to ANC, see Østbye in Eriksen (ed.) op. cit., pp. 131-43.
3. During the aid negotiations with Sweden in late August 1977—that is, immediately after the Norwegian government's positive decision—the ANC delegation, led by Secretary General Alfred Nzo, expressed the hope that "Swedish and Norwegian assistance [...] would set an example for [the] Nordic and other countries" ('Agreed minutes of discussions on the cooperation between the African National Congress of South Africa (ANC) and Sweden 1977/78', Lusaka, 2 September 1977) (SDA).
4. Ministry for Foreign Affairs: Decision ('Stöd till African National Congress of South Africa'/'Support to ANC'), signed by Ola Ullsten, Stockholm, 27 January 1977 (SDA). See also Marianne Sundh: Memorandum ('Biståndssamarbetet med African National Congress of South Africa, ANC, under budgetåret 1976/77 och framställning om stöd under budgetåret 1977/78'/'The aid cooperation with ANC during the financial year 1976/77 and request for support during 1977/78'), CCHA/SIDA, [Stockholm], 6 May 1977 (SDA).
5. For example, Anna Runeborg: Memorandum ('Minnesanteckningar från möte på ANC/SA's kontor den 5 maj 1977 beträffande 1977/78 års framställning'/'Notes from meeting at the ANC office on 5 May 1977 regarding the request for 1977/78'), Swedish embassy, Dar es Salaam, [no date, but attached to Runeborg's covering letter ('ANC/SA's framställning 1977/78'/'ANC's request 1977/78') on 6 May 1977] (SDA).
6. Interview with Reddy Mampane, p. 143. Reddy (Jan) Mampane (aka Mazimba) was in 1996 appointed South African ambassador to Angola.
7. Marianne Sundh: Memorandum ('Information om biståndssamarbetet med African National Congress of South Africa (ANC) budgetåren 1976/77 och 1977/78'/'Information on the aid cooperation with ANC during the financial years 1976/77 and 197/78'), CCHA/SIDA, [Stockholm], 28 October 1977 (SDA).
8. 'Agreed minutes of discussions on the cooperation between the African National Congress of South Africa (ANC) and Sweden 1977/78', Lusaka, 2 September 1977 (SDA).

actively intervened on ANC's behalf, supporting the establishment of its representation in Luanda[1], financing the onward transportation of recruits to Angola and delivering food and other daily necessities to the camps in that country. Initiated under Palme's Social Democratic government and consolidated by Fälldin's non-socialist coalition, this significant contribution to ANC's re-emergence as a significant actor in South African politics—from late 1976 increasingly expressed through armed operations[2]—has not been documented in studies on the South African struggle.[3] Extended on a humanitarian basis, it was at the time acknowledged by the ANC leadership as being "of decisive importance".[4] In an unsettled Southern African political environment and a divided Cold War context, a flexible interpretation of humanitarian assistance paved the way for special relations.[5]

Information and Publicity

Early involvement with ANC information and publicity: Dummy of the first issue of *Mayibuye*, 1975

To the relationship contributed the fact that Sweden at an early stage responded positively to ANC's calls for assistance to break out of its isolation through intensified information and publicity. In the light of the limitations experienced in the Southern African host countries, by the mid-1970s ANC had—as stated by Oliver Tambo during his visit to Sweden in October 1975—come to the conclusion that it must develop an active policy in this regard.

In fact, as early as in February 1975 ANC had included funds for "information, publicity and propaganda" in its request for assistance during 1975/76.[6] Financial support was notably sought for the regular production of *Mayibuye*—a "bulletin of the ANC, South Africa"—of which a roughly designed dummy was sub-

1. As a reflection of ANC's improving standing in Sweden, Foreign Affairs officials in other African countries became at the time overly keen to assist the movement. When Thabo Mbeki, Chief Representative to Nigeria, with small resources was setting up an ANC office in Lagos in mid-1977, first secretary Staffan Åberg at the Swedish embassy "promised to assist [him] by transmitting urgent messages [...] to other African capitals" (Letter ('ANC (Sydafrika) öppnar Lagos-kontor'/'ANC opens Lagos office') from Staffan Åberg, Swedish embassy, to the Ministry for Foreign Affairs, Lagos, 22 June 1977) (MFA). The initiative was not well received at the Foreign Ministry in Stockholm. Stating that the Nigerian authorities should be in a better position to assist and that the most natural way for ANC to communicate with other African governments would be through their embassies, Åberg was asked to withdraw his commitment (Cable from the Ministry for Foreign Affairs to the Swedish embassy in Lagos, Stockholm, 6 July 1977) (MFA).
2. Barrell Ph. D. op. cit., chapter three, p. 1 and passim.
3. Practically without exception, studies on the Southern African liberation movements fail to address the crucial issue of the material conditions of the struggle. In the case of the movements' armed forces, Napoleon's dictum that 'armies do not march on empty stomachs' was, however, as important—if not more—as the question of arms' supplies.
4. 'Agreed minutes of discussions on the cooperation between the African National Congress of South Africa (ANC) and Sweden 1977/78', Lusaka, 2 September 1977 (SDA).
5. During the aid negotiations between Sweden and ANC in August 1976, it was agreed as a guiding principle that "great flexibility and urgency was important" with regard to the cooperation ('Agreed minutes of discussions on cooperation between Sweden and the African National Congress of South Africa', Lusaka, 1 September 1976) (SDA).
6. 'Agreed minutes of discussions on cooperation 1975/76 between Sweden and [the] African National Congress, South Africa, ANC', Lusaka, 12 September 1975 (SDA).

mitted.[1] While the ANC allocations during the initial years had been entirely earmarked for commodity aid in the form of daily necessities for the members in Tanzania and Zambia, this policy was radically changed during the aid negotiations in Lusaka in mid-1975. Noting that "all fields suggested [by ANC] for Swedish assistance were in principle accepted"[2], a budget post for "miscellaneous" items was established for 1975/76.[3] Representing no less than 419,000 SEK of the total allocation of 1 million[4], it was *inter alia* used for support towards ANC's information efforts.

In 1975, Sweden thus became involved in the preparatory production stages of *Mayibuye*, which subsequently appeared as "the fortnightly journal of the African National Congress".[5] Under the 'home front component', ANC would later use Swedish funds to distribute *Mayibuye*, *Voice of Women*—the journal of the ANC Women's Secretariat[6]—and other publications inside the apartheid republic.[7]

In the process of "re-organising and radically upgrading the level, scope and effectiveness of [its] information services"[8], in early May 1976 ANC gave considerably more attention to this activity in its submission for 1976/77. The request contained a particular section on information, publicity and propaganda, drafted by Oliver Tambo.[9] During a meeting with Anders Bjurner shortly thereafter, the Acting ANC President described information as "absolutely the most important [component]". Stating that it was an area which in the past had been given "insufficient attention", he explained that the ANC leadership was busy preparing the launch of an "information offensive" against South Africa and that the request to Sweden formed part of that initiative. At the level of the National Executive Committee, Tambo himself was responsible for information matters, assisted by Thabo Mbeki.[10]

As part of the 'détente exercise', the Zambian government had in late 1975 stopped ANC's 'Radio Freedom' broadcasts to South Africa. At the time of submitting its 1976/77 request, only Tanzania allowed the movement access to its radio services. A similar offer had, however, been made by the Angolan government, and

---

1. Letter ('Biståndsframställning från ANC (Sydafrika)'/'Request for assistance from ANC') from Iwo Dölling, Swedish ambassador to Zambia, to the Ministry for Foreign Affairs, Swedish embassy, Lusaka, 24 April 1975 (SDA).
2. 'Agreed minutes of discussions on cooperation 1975/76 between Sweden and [the] African National Congress, South Africa, ANC', Lusaka, 12 September 1975 (SDA). Anders Bjurner and Thomas Nkobi led their respective delegations.
3. Ibid.
4. Ibid.
5. ANC's official organ was *Sechaba*, of which the first issue appeared in January 1967. While the manuscripts were compiled in London and a London address was formally given for correspondence, *Sechaba* was from the beginning financially supported by and printed in the German Democratic Republic (Schleicher op. cit., pp. 55-60).
6. As noted in the chapter 'SACTU, Unions and Sanctions', *Voice of Women* was from 1979 financially supported by LO. After the unbanning of ANC, Swedish funds were used to launch *Mayibuye* as ANC's main public organ in South Africa, with a targeted edition of 50,000 copies ('Agreed minutes from consultations held in Benoni, South Africa, May 1991, between the African National Congress of South Africa (ANC) and the government of Sweden concerning humanitarian assistance', Johannesburg, 19 May 1991) (SDA).
7. 'Report on the home front', attached to 'Agreed minutes [from] consultations in Lusaka, March 1983, between the African National Congress of South Africa, ANC, and Sweden concerning humanitarian assistance', Lusaka, 25 March 1983 (SDA).
8. 'Memorandum submitted by the African National Congress (SA) to SIDA in support of a request for assistance for the year 1976/77', ANC, Lusaka, [no date, but May 1976] (SDA).
9. Letter ('Samtal med O. Tambo, ANC's t.f. ordförande'/'Conversation with O. Tambo, ANC Acting President') from Anders Bjurner, Swedish embassy, to the Ministry for Foreign Affairs, Lusaka, 21 May 1976 (MFA).
10. Ibid.

ANC was confident that further breakthroughs would be forthcoming.[1] Against this background, in May 1976 the general outline of ANC's information plans was optimistic and comprehensive, covering its own publications as well as radio broadcasts from friendly countries.[2] Assistance from Sweden was requested for both printing and radio equipment.[3]

ANC's submission was discussed during the aid negotiations in Lusaka in late August 1976, where the Swedish delegation in general terms "expressed [a] positive interest" in supporting the proposed information activities.[4] As neither Tambo nor Mbeki was in Lusaka at the time[5], it was, however, decided to postpone more detailed discussions until later.[6] An amount of 281,000 SEK of the initial ANC allocation of 3 MSEK for 1976/77 was in the meantime set aside as a particular 'information component'.[7] Swedish support to ANC's Department of Information and Publicity—until 1989 led by Thabo Mbeki—would from then on become a regular feature in the cooperation programme. The component was in 1977/78 increased to 430,000 SEK[8] and in 1978/79 to 600,000 SEK.[9] By 1984/85, it had reached the level of 1.9 MSEK.[10]

Utilization of the 1976/77 grant for information was discussed in mid-October 1976 between Mbeki and SIDA's Carin Norberg in Lusaka, where Tambo's assistant proposed that Sweden in addition to telex equipment should supply ANC with four short wave radio units for internal communications, to be set up in Dar es Salaam, Luanda, Lusaka and Maputo.[11] Formalized through a written request, ANC also included training of two radio operators in the proposal.[12] For implementation, SIDA subsequently procured the services of the official consultancy firm SWEDTEL[13]—which in 1972 had assisted PAIGC of Guinea-Bissau with

---

1. Negotiations regarding broadcasting facilities had been initiated with the governments of Congo (Brazzaville), India, Madagascar and Mozambique ('Memorandum submitted by the African National Congress (SA) to SIDA in support of a request for assistance for the year 1976/77', Lusaka, [no date, but May 1976]) (SDA).
2. In its memorandum to the Swedish government, ANC stated in May 1976 that during 1976/77 it would a) set up a coordinating information centre; b) raise its regular, external publications to four; c) produce and distribute within South Africa two publications, one aimed at the white population and one at the black majority; and d) increase the centres of radio broadcasts to South Africa. The proposed information centre played a particularly important role. It would "ideally be based in Lusaka". However, due to the 'détente exercise' ANC noted that "prevailing circumstances have led [us] to consider Dar es Salaam as a suitable alternative" (ibid.). A research committee—later division—was at about the same time established in London. It was led by Pallo Jordan, who in 1989 became ANC Director of Information and Publicity and in 1994 was appointed Minister of Posts, Telecommunications and Broadcasting.
3. Ibid.
4. 'Agreed minutes of discussions on cooperation between Sweden and the African National Congress of South Africa', Lusaka, 1 September 1976 (SDA).
5. Only rarely did Oliver Tambo formally take part in the annual aid negotiations with Sweden. He was, however, very well informed on the cooperation programme and would often follow it up in discussions with the Swedish embassies in Southern Africa. Comprehensive reviews of the programme were, in addition, held with Tambo during his frequent visits to Sweden.
6. Anders Bjurner: Memorandum ('Förhandlingsprotokoll för bistånd till ANC (Sydafrika) 1976/77'/'Agreed minutes regarding assistance to ANC'), Swedish embassy, Lusaka, 3 September 1976 (SDA).
7. 'Agreed minutes of discussions on cooperation between Sweden and the African National Congress of South Africa', Lusaka, 1 September 1976 (SDA).
8. 'Agreed minutes of discussions on the cooperation between the African National Congress of South Africa (ANC) and Sweden 1977/78', Lusaka, 2 September 1977 (SDA).
9. 'Agreed minutes of discussions on the cooperation between the African National Congress of South Africa (ANC) and Sweden 1978/79', Lusaka, 26 May 1978 (SDA).
10. 'Agreed minutes [from] consultations in Lusaka, April 1984, between the African National Congress of South Africa and Sweden concerning humanitarian assistance', Lusaka, 6 April 1984 (SDA).
11. Carin Norberg: Memorandum ('Minnesanteckningar från samtal med Thabo Mbeki, ANC (SA), 14 oktober 1976'/'Notes from conversation with Thabo Mbeki of ANC, 14 October 1976'), Swedish embassy, Lusaka, [no date] (SDA).
12. Letter from Thomas Nkobi to the Swedish embassy, ANC, Lusaka, 20 October 1976 (SDA).
13. Swedish Telecommunication Consulting AB (SWEDTEL): 'Offert avseende radioprojekt för ANC i Zambia m.fl.' ('Tender for ANC radio project in Zambia etc.'), Stockholm, 22 December 1976 (SDA).

Broadcasting to South Africa:
From ANC's 'Radio Freedom'
in Lusaka, mid-1981
(Photo: Georg Dreifaldt)

the delivery of a mobile radio station[1]—and the project was implemented in early 1977.[2] Information was thus not only included as a separate component in the ANC assistance, but it also paved the way for concrete projects carried out by third parties, a feature which during the 1980s would be increasingly common.

In its annual request, ANC noted in April 1977 that "the decision to set up an information centre is now in the stage of implementation".[3] At the same time, it conceded that "only one country—Tanzania—provides time on its radio programme for ANC broadcasts".[4] While ANC's publications started to have an important international impact[5], in early 1977 the movement—due to several host countries' reluctance—was still not in a position to effectively launch its broadcasts to South Africa. As a result of the demise of détente and the Soweto watershed, this situation, however, changed. In April 1978, Tambo and Nkobi could inform the Swedish embassy in Lusaka that 'Radio Freedom'—'the voice of the African National Congress and Umkhonto we Sizwe'—had established regular transmissions from Luanda and Lusaka in addition to Dar es Salaam.[6] Similar facilities were in 1979 granted by the government of the Democratic Republic of Madagascar[7] and later by the government of Ethiopia.

Besides equipment to the various 'Radio Freedom' units, Swedish assistance in the form of cash support and daily necessities was extended to ANC's radio crews,

---

1. See the chapter 'PAIGC of Guinea-Bissau: Breaking the Ground'.
2. Eventually, the project costs amounted to 347,000 SEK (SIDA: 'ANC (South Africa): Cooperation programme with Sweden 1976/77', attached to Marianne Sundh: Memorandum ('Information om biståndssamarbetet med African National Congress of South Africa (ANC) budgetåren 1976/77 och 1977/78'/'Information on the aid cooperation with ANC during the financial years 1976/77 and 1977/78'), CCHA/SIDA, Stockholm, 28 October 1977) (SDA).
3. 'Memorandum submitted by the African National Congress of South Africa to SIDA in support of a request for assistance for the year 1977/78', ANC, Lusaka, [no date, but attached to letter ('Biståndsframställning från ANC (Sydafrika)'/'Request for assistance from ANC') from Anders Möllander, Swedish embassy, to the Ministry for Foreign Affairs, Lusaka, 14 April 1977] (SDA).
4. Ibid.
5. It was in 1977 that ANC began to publish its *Weekly News Briefing*, compiled and edited in London by Gill Marcus. Later financially supported by Sweden, the publication played a significant role. As noted by Shubin, "[f]or the first time ANC activists and supporters all over the world were [now] able to get speedy and concise information about developments in South Africa [, as well as] up-to-the-minute information about ANC positions on major issues" (Shubin op. cit., p. 184).
6. Elisabeth Michanek: Memorandum ('Möte med Oliver Tambo den 11 april 1978'/'Meeting with Oliver Tambo on 11 April 1978'), Swedish embassy, Lusaka, 20 April 1978 (ANC).
7. 'Agreed minutes from discussions on the cooperation between the African National Congress of South Africa (ANC) and the Swedish International Development Authority (SIDA)', Lusaka, 18 May 1979 (SDA).

including those in Antananarivo and Addis Ababa.[1] As in the case of ANC's official publications, funds set aside under the 'home front component' were, finally, used for underground dissemination of the broadcasts in South Africa. Radios, cassette recorders and duplicating equipment were procured. In January 1986, for example, ANC reported on the component that "[w]e have [...] formed radio clubs inside the country, where our units are able to monitor 'Radio Freedom', dub our pro-grammes, reproduce the dubbed material and distribute it as propaganda".[2]

Attention to the Internal Struggle

More than anything, it was the Swedish government's readiness to support ANC's struggle inside South Africa and the introduction in 1977/78 of a specific 'home front component' under the regular cooperation programme which cemented the relationship. This support was exceptional, both from a Swedish and an ANC point of view. Official funds for activities inside Namibia were within the bilateral aid programme also extended to SWAPO.[3] However, they did not assume the same magnitude or significance as in the case of South Africa. And while ANC intermit-tently received cash contributions from Eastern European countries and a number of Western NGOs, only the Swedish government would on a regular, continuous basis explicitly grant the movement budgetary support for its internal political work.[4] In 1995, Kay Moonsamy commented:

> The humanitarian assistance [from Sweden] covered food, clothing, shelter, upkeep and the running of ANC offices throughout the world, but, much more, it also included a component which was simply called the [h]ome [f]ront. [...] In fact, it was the first item on the agenda at the [annual] negotiations. [...]
>
> That is when one could say, yes, here is a country and a people who support our cause, because the millions that were given [under this] component [...] were given without any strings attached whatsoever. It was budgetary support. That is important, because those funds did a lot. It was under the heading humanitarian assistance, but the [h]ome [f]ront allocation was for underground activities, for organizers, meetings, publication of leaflets, pamphlets and so on. That is, to move the struggle forward.[5]

Swedish assistance to ANC was initially seen as temporary. At the level of lower and middle-rank aid officials in Stockholm and at the embassies in Southern Africa, the movement, however, enjoyed widespread sympathy, often expressed in favour of assistance to facilitate its re-establishment in South Africa. For example, com-menting on ANC's 1972 request for assistance in Tanzania and Zambia, the Lusaka embassy recommended official support as it indirectly would release funds for the movement's activities inside the apartheid republic. At the same time, Anders Möllander, then assistant CCHA secretary, raised the question whether "we in

1. Swedish support to ANC in Madagascar and Ethiopia was introduced in 1982/83 ('Agreed minutes of discus-sions in Lusaka, May 1982, between the African National Congress of South Africa, ANC, and the Swedish International Development Authority, SIDA, concerning humanitarian assistance', Lusaka, 24 May 1982) (SDA).
2. Letter ('Submission of budgets for 1986/87 and consolidation of projects 1985/86') from Thomas Nkobi, Treasurer General, to the Swedish embassy, ANC, Lusaka, 10 January 1986 (SDA).
3. See the chapter 'Transport, Home Front, Churches and Trade Unions' on Namibia.
4. As will be further illustrated below, during the 1980s Norway was together with Sweden ANC's largest donor with regard to daily necessities in the Southern African 'forward areas'. Official Norwegian funds were, how-ever, not extended to ANC for activities inside the apartheid republic (Østbye in Eriksen (ed.) op. cit., p. 171).
5. Interview with Kay Moonsamy, p. 162.

some way can support the 'infiltration' of ANC members into the South African homelands? By covering [their] travel costs? Through equipment? [Or] education?"[1]

Since ANC had only requested Swedish assistance for daily necessities for its exiled members, in 1972 Möllander's question was theoretical. It would remain so until mid-1975, when SWAPO's resident representative Ben Amathila approached SIDA concerning the possibilities of support for political organizers in Namibia, including their salaries.[2] In a memorandum discussed with Ann Wilkens at the Foreign Ministry, SIDA's Astrid Bergquist—the CCHA secretary—argued that since the objective of the cooperation with the nationalist movements was to contribute towards political liberation, it would be justified to "stretch the concept of humanitarian assistance" and also grant SWAPO financial resources for "straightforward political work".[3] Although the recommendation *inter alia* implied that the Swedish government would cover the salary costs of foreign political cadres working 'beyond the enemy lines'—and not within liberated areas—it was accepted. In August 1975, a 'home front component' was introduced in the Swedish support to SWAPO for the financial year 1975/76.[4]

In the case of ANC, a first appeal for Swedish support in South Africa was made in March 1976, when it proposed that "maintenance of political officials and their families" inside the country should be indirectly covered as part of humanitarian assistance to the movement in Swaziland.[5] In spite of the detention and subsequent expulsion from the country of Mbeki and Zuma, in discussions with the Swedish embassy in Lusaka Tambo and Nkobi emphasized the importance of such a flexible approach.[6] Their views were accepted by CCHA[7] and the government. At the official aid negotiations in late August 1976, it was agreed to also give the humanitarian assistance to ANC a 'stretched' interpretation and include both Swaziland and Lesotho in the cooperation programme for 1976/77.[8] Since Sweden had no official representation in these countries, it was further agreed that the support should be extended on a cash basis.[9] Finally, in a press release issued by the Swedish embassy in Lusaka after the talks, ANC was explicitly acknowledged as "*the* national liberation movement of South Africa".[10]

At the very time when ANC achieved a significant breakthrough, the Social Democratic Party lost the parliamentary elections in Sweden. In October 1976, it handed over the reins of government to the Centre Party leader Thorbjörn Fälldin's non-socialist tripartite coalition. In addition to the Liberal Party, it included the

---

1. Handwritten notes from Anders Möllander, SIDA, to Gun-Britt Andersson, Ministry for Foreign Affairs, on Olof Milton: Memorandum ('Behovet av svenskt stöd till ANC-medlemmar i exil'/'The need for Swedish support to ANC members in exile'), Swedish embassy, Dar es Salaam, 28 August 1972 (SDA).
2. See the chapter 'Transport, Home Front, Churches and Trade Unions' on Namibia.
3. Astrid Bergquist: Memorandum ('Samtal med Ben Amathila, SWAPO's representant, angående 1975/76 års bistånd till SWAPO'/'Conversation with Ben Amathila, the SWAPO representative, regarding the assistance to SWAPO in 1975/76'), SIDA, Stockholm, 12 August 1975 (SDA).
4. 'Agreed minutes of discussion[s] on cooperation between Sweden and South West Africa People's Organization (SWAPO)', Lusaka, 26 August 1975 (SDA).
5. Marianne Sundh: Memorandum ('Framställning från ANC (SA) om ytterligare stöd 1975/76'/'Request from ANC (SA) for additional support in 1975/76'), CCHA/SIDA, Stockholm, 6 May 1976 (SDA).
6. Ibid.
7. CCHA: 'Protokoll [från sammanträde 18 maj 1976]' ('Minutes [from meeting 18 May 1976]'), SIDA, [Stockholm], 18 May 1976 (SDA).
8. 'Agreed minutes of discussions on cooperation between Sweden and the African National Congress of South Africa', Lusaka, 1 September 1976 (SDA).
9. Quarterly payments were made by Sweden "to accounts suggested by ANC" (ibid.).
10. Embassy of Sweden: 'Swedish support to ANC (South Africa)', Press release, Lusaka, 1 September 1976 (SDA).

conservative Moderate Party, the only parliamentary party which consistently had opposed official assistance to the Southern African liberation movements. As earlier noted, the change of government raised concerns that the Swedish support would be negatively affected. In the case of ANC, both Prime Minister Fälldin's Centre Party and—above all—the Liberal Party had, however, during their many years in opposition advocated increased assistance.[1]

The initial apprehensions felt by ANC, ZANU, ZAPU and SWAPO were soon dissipated. Solid aid relations were maintained. In early February 1977, for example, Foreign Minister Karin Söder's political adviser and Centre Party colleague Pär Granstedt paid a visit to Dar es Salaam, where he assured the local ANC representatives that the government would not only continue where its Social Democratic predecessor had left off, but increase the official support.[2]

A direct dialogue was also opened between Oliver Tambo and the Liberal Cooperation Minister Ola Ullsten. Meeting in Lusaka later in February, the ANC leader stated that it was important to establish links with the new government in Stockholm and that it was "gratifying" to hear that it would continue the policy initiated by the Social Democratic Party.[3] Briefing the Swedish delegation, he gave an overview of the situation in Southern Africa from an ANC perspective. According to Tambo, "war was inevitable" in Zimbabwe and South Africa. The campaign against the apartheid regime—which would be both "bitter and hard"—had just begun, and it was ANC's role to "mobilize the South African people for the armed struggle".[4] Noting that the cooperation with SIDA was "very positive", the ANC leader stressed the need for assistance in favour of the movement's work inside South Africa.[5]

Shortly thereafter, ANC submitted its request for continued Swedish assistance during the financial year 1977/78. Stating that "it was a matter of great encouragement [...] to have had the opportunity of meeting the Swedish delegation [...] led by [...] Ola Ullsten", the submission continued:

> SIDA has for years given us assistance to cater for the very essential daily needs of our people [in exile]. However, the present upheavals and revolt by our youth and people [in South Africa have] added greater responsibility on the ANC to expand its underground machinery. To cope with the recent developments, we need many more full-time organizers inside the country. [They] need to be maintained. There is also an increased need for transport to enable [the] organizers to cover the length and breadth of our country. Funds are desperately required for [our] functionaries' [...] food, clothing and rental requirements, travelling expenses, such as train and air fares, petrol and maintenance of vehicles, etc. In addition, [our] propaganda work must be intensified. The need for clandestinely produced printed material, tape recorders and tapes has increased.[6]

---

1. See the chapter 'ANC of South Africa: No Easy Walk'.
2. Anders Möllander: Memorandum ('Samtal med ANC (SA)-representanter'/'Conversation with ANC representatives'), Swedish embassy, Dar es Salaam, 11 February 1977 (MFA).
3. Elisabeth Michanek: Draft memorandum ('Möte med ANC's (SA) president Oliver Tambo den 28 februari 1977'/'Meeting with ANC President Oliver Tambo on 28 February 1977'), Swedish embassy, Lusaka, 7 March 1977 (MFA).
4. Ibid.
5. Ibid. With regard to the Inkatha leader Gatsha Buthelezi, Tambo was of the opinion that "[h]e is no real puppet". Discussing the general situation in Southern Africa, he expressed satisfaction with the Swedish development assistance to South Africa's neighbours, notably Lesotho and Swaziland. "Their strength is our strength", he said. In the case of Zambia, the ANC President noted, however, that ANC was still facing restrictions. While the National Executive Committee would remain in Lusaka, ANC was therefore considering whether the Revolutionary Council should be moved to Luanda (ibid.). A decision to that effect was subsequently taken.
6. 'Memorandum submitted by the African National Congress of South Africa to SIDA in support of a request for assistance for the year 1977/78', ANC, Lusaka [no date, but attached to letter ('Biståndsframställning från ANC (Sydafrika)'/'Request for assistance from ANC') from Anders Möllander, Swedish embassy, to the Ministry for Foreign Affairs, Lusaka, 14 April 1977)] (SDA).

Without specifying a budget, ANC concluded that "[a]ny help in easing this burden will be greatly appreciated".[1]

ANC's emphasis on internal political work was a prelude to a major strategic review carried out in 1978-79. Lacking an established political base within South Africa, the movement had been largely unable to exploit the rise of black consciousness, the emergence of militant trade unions and the Soweto events. As noted by Barrell, "ANC's response to [the] political upsurge was [to continue] to give priority to armed struggle and the recruitment of cadres for military training, rather than building up [an] internal political organisation".[2] Armed struggle, it was argued, would create the conditions for and develop a popular political base, not the other way around. After the Soweto events—which had taken place without any previous military ANC activity—this long held view was, however, increasingly questioned.[3] At the end of 1977, ANC's Revolutionary Council—headed by Tambo—thus decided to set up a specialized committee for political work, called the Internal Policy and Reconstruction Department (IPRD).[4]

IPRD was considerably strengthened in early 1978, when Mac Maharaj—who was released from Robben Island in December 1976 and went into exile in July 1977—was appointed head of the department. With recent experiences from South Africa, the veteran ANC leader soon "accused [military] leaders like Joe Modise and Joe Slovo of having not only ignored the urgency of political reconstruction by political means, but of repeatedly frustrating attempts to achieve it".[5] In turn, his strategic understanding appeared to be borne out by relevant contemporary experiences. Led by Oliver Tambo, in October 1978 a high-powered ANC delegation[6] visited the recently re-united Vietnam, touring all parts of the country, exchanging views with the Vietnamese Workers Party and discussing with the legendary General Vo Nguyen Giap. Undertaken "to draw such lessons as might be creatively applied to ANC's struggle"[7], the visit had far-reaching consequences. As propositions and experiences applicable to the South African struggle, the delegation identified *inter alia* that "the political struggle is primary"; that "revolutionary armed struggle itself can only succeed if it grows out of [a] mass political base"; and that the Vietnamese had "at all times [worked] to create legal and semi-legal organisations", with the objective of forming "the broadest national front [possible]".[8]

The concerns raised by Maharaj[9] and the findings from the visit to Vietnam were discussed during a joint meeting of ANC's National Executive Committee and the Revolutionary Council in Luanda at the end of December 1978. Concluding that "the Vietnamese experience reveals certain shortcomings on our part and draws attention to areas of crucial importance which we [have] tended to neglect"[10], it decided to set up a Politico-Military Strategy Commission to review

1. Ibid.
2. Barrell Ph. D. op. cit., chapter three, p. 34.
3. Among the early critics was Pallo Jordan, then based in London (ibid., p. 10).
4. Intermittently called the Department of Internal Reconstruction and Development (IRD).
5. Barrell Ph. D. op. cit., chapter four, p. 6.
6. In addition to Tambo, the delegation included Joe Modise (Commander of the Revolutionary Council's Central Operations Headquarters), Joe Slovo (his deputy), Moses Mabhida (Secretary of the Revolutionary Council), Cassius Make (Assistant Secretary) and Thabo Mbeki. A rising star in the National Executive Committee, Mbeki had in January 1978 been appointed Political Secretary in the President's Office and Head of ANC's Political Commission.
7. Barrell Ph. D. op. cit., chapter four, p. 8.
8. Cited in Karis and Gerhart op. cit., p. 303.
9. As well as by other senior ANC leaders recently joining the movement in exile, among them notably Joe Gqabi.
10. Cited in Karis and Gerhart op. cit., p. 302.

ANC's options.[1] After extensive consultations, the central recommendations contained in the commission's final report—known within ANC as the 'Green Book'
due to the colour of its cover—were approved in August 1979. Although 'parallel-
ism' of military and political approaches subsequently remained, this marked a
"seminal"[2] strategic re-orientation in favour of political mass mobilization and—
presaging UDF[3]—of the creation of "a nation-wide popular liberation front".[4]
While the seizure of state power ultimately was seen as the result of a military confrontation with the apartheid forces, the armed activities until the establishment of
a popular revolutionary base were to play a secondary role. At a time when Pretoria was launching its 'total strategy' doctrine, they would primarily focus on propaganda, notably in support of a campaign to popularize ANC's non-racial vision for
South Africa contained in the Freedom Charter.[5] As stated in the 'Green Book':

> At the present moment, we are at the stage when the main task is to concentrate on political
> mobilisation and organisation so as to build up political revolutionary bases throughout the
> country. In as much as the growth of the armed struggle depends on the rate of advance of the
> political struggle, the armed struggle is secondary at this time. [...]
>
> [W]e must work for the political mobilisation and organisation of the masses of our people
> into active struggle as a matter of priority. We must aim to attract all forces—at national,
> regional and local levels—who have [the] potential to confront the regime in the struggle
> against racism and for one united non-racial South Africa. We must bring about the broadest
> possible unity of all national groups, classes and strata, organisations, groups and prominent
> personalities around local and national issues. This means [that] we must combine illegal with
> legal and semi-legal activity to ensure such mass mobilisation and to establish our presence and
> influence wherever the people are.[6]

The Home Front Component

ANC's submission for assistance in 1977/78 did not make any reference to military
activities. However, it must have been evident—not least from Tambo's discussions
with Ullsten in February 1977—that support for ANC's 'underground machinery'
implied 'mobilization for the armed struggle'. This notwithstanding, it was received
in a positive spirit by the Swedish authorities.[7] Thus, in what amounted to a unique
expression of political support Prime Minister Fälldin's government—remarkably
including the Moderate Party—not only responded to ANC's request by increasing
the annual allocation from 5.5 to 8 MSEK, but also included a specific 'home front

---

1. The commission was composed of the members of the delegation to Vietnam except for Cassius Make, who
   was replaced by Joe Gqabi. Maharaj was a notable absentee. Apparently, he preferred to devote himself to
   IPRD's practical work (Barrell Ph. D. op. cit., chapter four, p. 13).
2. Karis and Gerhart op. cit., p. 305.
3. United Democratic Front (see below).
4. The 'Green Book', cited in Karis and Gerhart op. cit., p. 730.
5. Barrell Ph. D. op. cit., chapter four, p. 18. The strategic re-orientation was reflected in ANC's general discourse and propaganda. While 1979 had been declared 'The Year of the Spear', 1980 became 'The Year of the
   Charter'. It will be seen below that Swedish funds under the 'home front component' were set aside for "bulletins in local languages". They were largely dedicated to the Freedom Charter.
6. The 'Green Book', cited in Karis and Gerhart op. cit., pp. 731 and 729-30. It should also be noted that ANC
   made tactical concessions with regard to its socialist objectives. Thus, the 'Green Book' explained, "[i]n the
   light of the need to attract the broadest range of social forces [...], a direct or indirect commitment at this
   stage to a continuing revolution which would lead to a socialist order may unduly narrow this line-up [...].
   ANC is not a party, and its direct or open commitment to socialist ideology may undermine its basic character
   as a broad national movement" (ibid., p. 724).
7. Pär Granstedt, Foreign Minister Karin Söder's political adviser and Centre Party colleague, later commented:
   "[O]f course, [the Swedish assistance] was in a way support for the armed struggle. I do not think that we
   wanted to prevent that. Giving humanitarian support to a liberation movement involved in armed struggle
   was in a way support for that struggle. But, we were satisfied that it was not directly used for arms or military
   operations" (Interview with Pär Granstedt, p. 271).

component' in the 1977/78 programme. At the same time as action against Swedish investments in South Africa was initiated[1] and official support to SACTU started[2], the Centre and Liberal parties clearly demonstrated that their long-standing advocacy of ANC had not changed.

Invited by Cooperation Minister Ullsten, in late August 1977—immediately after the UN/OAU anti-apartheid conference in Lagos, where Ullsten represented the Swedish government—Tambo again visited Sweden. Apart from addressing the Liberal Party congress[3] and holding a series of bilateral meetings with various organizations[4], the recently confirmed ANC President[5] discussed the movement's request for 1977/78 at the Foreign Ministry and SIDA.[6] A few days later, formal aid negotiations took place in Lusaka. Respectively led by SIDA's Kurt Kristiansson and ANC Secretary General Alfred Nzo[7], they represent a turning point in the relations between Sweden and ANC.[8] By setting aside 600,000 SEK of a total allocation of 8 million—corresponding to 7.5 per cent—in favour of "internal work in South Africa", the government committed itself to financially supporting the liberation movement with regard to underground "information, political mobilization, humanitarian relief and legal aid" inside the apartheid state during 1977/78.[9]

Nine months later, the 'home front component'—as it was subsequently to be called—was raised to no less than 4 million of an ANC allocation for 1978/79 of

---

1. In early June 1977, two commissions were appointed to look into the question of legislated restrictions with regard to Sweden's economic relations with South Africa and Namibia (see the chapter 'SACTU, Unions and Sanctions').
2. Also in June 1977, a decision was taken to extend official support to the SACTU office in Dar es Salaam (see ibid.).
3. Marika Fahlén: Memorandum ('Inför Oliver Tambo's besök i Sverige 26-30 augusti 1977'/'In view of Oliver Tambo's visit to Sweden, 26-30 August 1977'), Ministry for Foreign Affairs, Stockholm, 23 August 1977 (MFA). Reflecting the broad anti-apartheid consensus in Sweden, Tambo and ANC were regularly invited to the congresses of both the Liberal and the Social Democratic parties, whether in opposition or in government. One year later—in September 1978—the ANC President thus attended the Social Democratic Party congress. At the meetings of both the Liberals in 1977 and the Social Democrats in 1978, Tambo was accompanied by Pallo Jordan, ANC's head of research (Marika Fahlén: Memorandum ('Samtal med ANC-ledaren Oliver Tambo'/'Conversation with the ANC leader Oliver Tambo'), Ministry for Foreign Affairs, Stockholm, 27 September 1978) (SDA).
4. Notably with the Social Democratic Party and Olof Palme, just before his departure to Southern Africa (cf. the previous chapter).
5. On the recommendation of the leaders on Robben Island, in July 1977 Tambo was invested with full authority as President of the African National Congress.
6. Marianne Sundh: 'Kallelse: Besök av Oliver Tambo, President för African National Congress of South Africa' ('Summons: Visit by Oliver Tambo, President of ANC'), SIDA, Stockholm, 25 August 1977 (SDA).
7. The other members of the Swedish delegation were Marika Fahlén from the Ministry for Foreign Affairs, Marianne Sundh from SIDA and Roland Axelsson, Per Kökeritz, Elisabeth Michanek and Anders Möllander from the Swedish embassy in Lusaka. In addition to Nzo, ANC was represented by Thomas Nkobi, M. Moosajee and Jimmy Phambo. It could as a curiosity be noted that Kurt Kristiansson, the leader of the Swedish delegation, as chairman of the National Council of Swedish Youth together with the then ANC Secretary General Duma Nokwe on 1 March 1963 had launched a Swedish consumer boycott against apartheid. Unbeknown to his Swedish hosts, Nokwe was at the time on his way to the Soviet Union to request assistance for the armed struggle (see Sellström Volume I, pp. 190-94). In a different context, a decade and a half later Kristiansson would be discussing official Swedish support to ANC's underground structures with Alfred Nzo, Nokwe's successor as Secretary General.
8. It should be underlined that the decision taken by the non-socialist government to support ANC's internal underground structures was taken at a time when the Swedish NGO solidarity movement was still debating how best to promote the cause of the liberation movement. As noted in an internal discussion paper by Sören Lindh in 1982, it was only after "prolonged [and] sometimes devastating discussions" that the Africa Groups in 1976 adopted a programme which gave priority to South Africa, Namibia and Zimbabwe. And it was not until 1978—after two additional years of what he characterized as "a concentrated [period] of birth and preparations of ideas and initiatives"—that AGIS seriously started to work in favour of ANC (Sören Lindh: 'AGIS' organisatoriska historia: En subjektiv beskrivning' ('The history of AGIS' organization: A subjective description'), AGIS, winter conference 1982, [no place or date] (AGA).
9. 'Agreed minutes of discussions on the cooperation between the African National Congress of South Africa (ANC) and Sweden 1977/78', Lusaka, 2 September 1977 (SDA).

12 MSEK.[1] And in May 1979—when the strategic re-orientation expressed in the 'Green Book' had been accepted in principle by ANC's National Executive Committee[2]—it was further increased to 5.5 out of 16 MSEK, corresponding to 34.5 per cent of the official Swedish assistance to ANC in 1979/80.[3]

Official Swedish support to ANC's underground activities would from then on become a permanent feature of the assistance programme. In fact, regularly representing around one third of the annual grants to the South African liberation movement, over the years in exile the politically motivated 'home front component' was together with the more strictly—but flexible—humanitarian budget for 'daily necessities' by far the largest item. Its significance from 1977/78 until the unbanning of ANC and the legal re-establishment of the movement in South Africa in the early 1990s appears from the following table:[4]

The 'home front component' in Sweden's assistance to ANC
(in thousands of SEK)

Financial year	Total allocation	Home front	Percentage
1977/78	8,000	600	7.5
1978/79	12,000	4,000	33.3
1979/80	16,000	5,520	34.5
1980/81	20,000	7,100	35.5
1981/82	23,000	8,100	35.2
1982/83	27,000	9,500	35.2
1983/84	32,000	10,850	33.9
1984/85	37,000	12,000	32.4
1985/86	48,000	17,000	35.4
1986/87	59,500	20,000	33.6
1987/88	64,000	22,000	34.4
1988/89	71,000	23,000	32.4
1989/90	85,000	24,000	28.2
1990/91	97,500	26,500	27.2
1977/78–90/91	600,000	190,170	31.7

Apart from funds for information activities[5], from mid-1977 until ANC's unbanning a total amount of 190 MSEK was in the form of cash support directly disbursed by Sweden towards the movement's internal work.[6] For which activities were the resources used? How were the funds paid and accounted for? Were any problems encountered? What was the impact of these contributions?

---

1. 'Agreed minutes of discussions on the cooperation between Sweden and the African National Congress of South Africa (ANC) 1978/79', Lusaka, 26 May 1978 (SDA).
2. Formally approved in August 1979, the recommendations contained in the 'Green Book' had in principle been accepted by the National Executive Committee in March.
3. 'Agreed minutes from discussions on the cooperation between the African National Congress of South Africa (ANC) and the Swedish International Development Authority (SIDA)', Lusaka, 18 May 1979 (SDA).
4. Based on original allocations and additional grants as budgeted during the annual aid negotiations between Sweden and ANC during the period.
5. The information budget was partly used for internal activities.
6. From 1975/76 until Namibia's independence in 1990, an amount of 89 MSEK was correspondingly extended to SWAPO. It represented 13 per cent of the 669 MSEK directly disbursed by the Swedish government to the Namibian organization (see the chapter 'Transport, Home Front, Churches and Trade Unions' on Namibia). Combining the 'home front' allocations to ANC and SWAPO, via the two liberation movements Sweden thus channelled a total amount of 279 MSEK in favour of their underground campaigns against apartheid South Africa. To this should be added substantial resources indirectly transferred via NGOs.

When the 'home front component' was introduced, it was in general terms allocated for 'information, political mobilization, humanitarian relief—notably in favour of families of imprisoned ANC members—and legal aid'. No further specification was made. Nor did Sweden request any particular financial reports on the utilization of the funds, which as pure budgetary support were transferred to an ANC bank account in London.[1]

This open-ended policy was over the following years maintained under the Fälldin and Ullsten governments. At the time of ANC's strategic review, it was clearly understood that the main purpose of the allocation was to support ANC's underground efforts in South Africa. The agreement reached in May 1978 to radically increase the 'home front component' from 600,000 to 4 million SEK—establishing it at the level of one third of the total allocation, a share which would be maintained until the end of the 1980s—was made in response to ANC's submission for 1978/79. It stressed "the key question of expanding our network of organisers, who need transport, safe houses, visible means of subsistence and so on".[2] ANC, however, hastened to add that

> none of the [...] items [for which Swedish assistance is sought] relates to activities of a military nature. They are aimed at the mobilisation and political guidance of the people in their resistance to the forces of domination and their struggle to assert their humanity and transform South Africa into the motherland of all who live in it.[3]

The assistance to ANC's internal work—later somewhat cryptically characterized by SIDA's Roland Axelsson as "humanitarian in the political sense of the word"[4]—was in May 1979 increased to 5.5 MSEK. While this agreement was reached in the absence of any specific considerations, detailed stipulations or financial reporting requirements[5], one year later the Swedish authorities raised for the first time the need for defining a basic framework for the 'home front component'. This, in turn, was largely prompted by the IUEF affair, which in early 1980 had come as a severe warning with regard to activities inside South Africa.

In the case of ANC, however, the policy of supporting internal activities was not called into question. On the contrary, one of the main consequences of 'Operation Daisy' was, as earlier noted, that the organization's primacy in this respect was further strengthened. The significance of the 'home front component' was at the same time emphasized. Commenting on ANC's request for Swedish assistance in 1980/81, SIDA's representative to Zambia, Lars-Olof Edström, underscored in March 1980

> the importance of supporting [ANC's] increasingly central internal work. [We are of the opinion that] the developments during the last year show that [it] must be given priority. ANC is no

---

1. 'Agreed minutes of discussions on the cooperation between the African National Congress of South Africa (ANC) and Sweden 1977/78', Lusaka, 2 September 1977 (SDA).
2. 'African National Congress (SA) to SIDA in support of a request for assistance for the year 1978/79', attached to letter from Thomas Nkobi to the Swedish embassy, ANC, Lusaka, 10 April 1978 (SDA).
3. Thomas Nkobi: 'Supplementary memorandum to SIDA', ANC, Lusaka, 24 April 1978 (SDA). In the light of ANC's review exercise, it is not without interest to note that the movement in its 1978/79 request to Sweden in April 1978 stated that "[i]t is [...] crucial and of urgent importance that we considerably upgrade the level and intensity of organisational and propaganda work in the [rural] areas. This involves the division of the countryside into geo-political regions and zones, each manned with organisational and propaganda units which are [...] adequately and materially equipped to perform, or create conditions for performing, defined tasks pursuant to the objectives we have outlined" (ibid.).
4. Interview with Roland Axelsson, p. 255.
5. Apart from the budgeting exercise, there is no indication that the 'home front component' was discussed during the aid negotiations in May 1979, respectively led by SIDA's Assistant Director General Curt Ström and ANC Secretary General Alfred Nzo ('Agreed minutes from discussions on the cooperation between the African National Congress of South Africa (ANC) and the Swedish International Development Authority (SIDA)', Lusaka, 18 May 1979) (SDA).

longer an exile organization [, but] very active inside South Africa. Support to the internal work must accordingly constitute an essential part of the Swedish assistance.[1]

After preliminary contacts with the ANC leadership in Lusaka, Edström suggested at the same time more transparent budgeting and reporting procedures regarding the 'home front component'. Without ANC "giving away" information on "channels and contacts", they should focus on the different purposes of the support.[2]

Edström's proposal was accepted by both ANC and the authorities in Stockholm. During the annual aid negotiations in May 1980—where the Swedish delegation in its introductory remarks notably stated that "Swedish foreign policy regarding Southern Africa aimed at a concentrated effort to bring about political change in Namibia and South Africa"[3]—it was agreed to subdivide the 'home front component' into eight categories, each with a separate indicative budget. These categories—which were to be maintained throughout the 1980s—were:

- assistance to dependants,
- bulletins in local languages,
- legal aid,
- organizational activities,
- printing equipment,
- publicity,
- support for legal organizations, and
- transport.[4]

Under a total 'home front' budget of 7.1 MSEK, 'support for legal organizations' with an allocation of 2 million was by far the largest sub-item.[5]

As a clearer subdivision of the 'home front component' was established—and its share of one third of the overall ANC allocation became the norm[6]—over the following years the accounting of the support was also to be defined. When the component was introduced in mid-1977, it was agreed that the Swedish funds should be transferred to a bank account held by ANC in London. From there, ANC couriers took over, carrying the money to South Africa for distribution to the various

---

1. Letter ('ANC-biståndet 1980/81'/'The ANC assistance in 1980/81') from Lars-Olof Edström to SIDA, Swedish embassy, Lusaka, 13 March 1980 (SDA). This opinion was at the same time conveyed to the Swedish government by the leaders of the Frontline States. After discussions with President Nyerere, David Wirmark, the Swedish ambassador to Tanzania, wrote in March 1980 to the Foreign Ministry and SIDA that "the work within South Africa will be decisive [...]. [The] conclusion is thus that it is important to support [ANC's] activities inside [the country]" (Cable ('Ert brev 11 februari ang. humanitära biståndet till södra Afrika under 1980-talet'/'Your letter of 11 February re [the] humanitarian assistance to Southern Africa in the 1980s') from David Wirmark to the Ministry for Foreign Affairs and SIDA, Swedish embassy, Dar es Salaam, 21 March 1980) (SDA).
2. Ibid.
3. 'Minutes from discussions on the cooperation between the African National Congress of South Africa (ANC) and the Swedish International Development Authority (SIDA), May 1980', Lusaka, 29 May 1980 (SDA). Lars-Olof Edström led the Swedish delegation and Thomas Nkobi the ANC team.
4. Ibid.
5. Ibid.
6. The rule of thumb by which one third of the official assistance was set aside for ANC's internal work subsequently guided the cooperation. It was maintained by Palme's Social Democratic government, which in October 1982 was returned to power. It could be noted that ANC during the aid negotiations in May 1986 emphasized the need for a radical increase of the 'home front component' and, uncommonly, "questioned the Swedish position regarding the special 'ceiling' set for this support" ('Agreed minutes [from] consultations in Lusaka, May 1986, between the African National Congress of South Africa and Sweden concerning humanitarian assistance', Lusaka, 9 May 1986) (SDA). While the budget was raised from 17 to 20 MSEK, its share of the overall assistance remained, however, at the level of one third, or 33.6 per cent (see the table above).

end users. While the couriers were accountable to the movement[1], the Swedish authorities had no influence or control over the actual utilization of the assistance. It was against this background considered essential to establish mutually acceptable reporting routines.

The issue was, for example, raised by the Liberal Under-Secretary of State for Foreign Affairs Hans Blix in discussions with Oliver Tambo and Thomas Nkobi in Stockholm in March 1981. Stating that "in order to avoid that the [overall] assistance to ANC [is] called into question", he emphasized that "the [Swedish] government at all times must be in a position to confirm that it is exclusively humanitarian", a view which was shared by the ANC leaders.[2] Apart from general, narrative accounts[3], a reporting formula with regard to the 'home front' was, however, only finalized in 1982-83. The CCHA secretariat expressed in the meantime the opinion that "the internal assistance is based on trust and must be kept secret", adding that it "meets great demands and constitutes an appropriate way for Sweden to support [ANC's home front] activities".[4]

While drawing the same conclusion, a year later—in April 1982—the secretariat, however, noted that ANC's general reports had "important shortcomings".[5] During the following negotiations—where the 'home front component' was increased to 9.5 out of 27 MSEK—it was thus agreed for the first time that SIDA would receive "a written yearly detailed report on activities carried out [by ANC] inside the country".[6] Such a report was accordingly submitted at the negotiations in Lusaka in March 1983.[7] Since the form and content of the annual report were highly sensitive[8], it was at the same time agreed that "vouchers will be submitted only if that can be done without ANC security being affected".[9] These general guidelines were subsequently applied to the 'home front component' until the end in 1990/91.

---

1. Ulla Ström: Memorandum ('Minnesanteckningar från diskussioner mellan SIDA och ANC i Lusaka 14 maj 1981'/'Notes from discussions between SIDA and ANC in Lusaka, 14 May 1981'), SIDA, Stockholm, 3 June 1981 (SDA).
2. Henrik Salander: Memorandum ('Biståndsdiskussioner'/'Discussions on assistance'), Ministry for Foreign Affairs, Stockholm, 24 March 1981 (MFA).
3. In November 1981, Nkobi submitted a general report on ANC's internal work and the Swedish assistance ('Brief report [on] SIDA's allocation to the African National Congress for the period 1980/81 ended 30th June', ANC, Lusaka, 18 November 1981) (SDA). Usually drafted by Tambo, Nzo or Nkobi, ANC's annual requests and reports to Sweden are unique sources of information with regard to the movement's general policy and underground activities in South Africa. For example, while underlining "the necessity to combine armed struggle with mass struggle" as early as in November 1981 Nkobi highlighted for particular attention the fields of sports and culture, the latter specified as "painting, dance, music, poetry etc" (ibid.).
4. Henrik Salander: Memorandum ('Bidrag till African National Congress (ANC) i Sydafrika 1981/82'/'Contribution to ANC in South Africa 1981/82'), CCHA/Ministry for Foreign Affairs, [Stockholm], 27 April 1981 (SDA).
5. Dag Ahlander: Memorandum ('Bidrag till African National Congress (ANC) i Sydafrika 1982/83'/'Contribution to ANC in South Africa 1982/83'), CCHA/Ministry for Foreign Affairs, [Stockholm], 29 April 1982 (SDA).
6. 'Agreed minutes of discussions in Lusaka, May 1982, between the African National Congress of South Africa, ANC, and the Swedish International Development Authority, SIDA, concerning humanitarian assistance', Lusaka, 24 May 1982 (SDA). The delegations were respectively led by SIDA's Director General Anders Forsse and ANC's Secretary General Alfred Nzo.
7. ANC: 'Report on the home front', attached to 'Agreed minutes [from] consultations in Lusaka, March 1983, between the African National Congress of South Africa, ANC, and Sweden concerning humanitarian assistance', Lusaka, 25 March 1983 (SDA).
8. Financing of ANC's internal work was not only a sensitive issue vis-à-vis Sweden, but for security reasons also within the organization. In 1995, Strachan noted that "[t]he ANC Treasurer General's [O]ffice was remarkably good at keeping quiet about the lines of supply [...]. [W]e had millions of Rands passing through our hands for the struggle inside the country, for example, for MK soldiers moving into South Africa. It was an incredibly tightly kept secret" (Interview with Garth Strachan, p. 193).
9. 'Agreed minutes [from] consultations in Lusaka, March 1983, between the African National Congress of South Africa, ANC, and Sweden concerning humanitarian assistance', Lusaka, 25 March 1983 (SDA).

Questions and Scope

Funds for ANC's internal work were handled by the movement itself. Neither in exile nor in South Africa was there any Swedish involvement in the planning or actual utilization of the assistance.[1] Thus, the Swedish authorities were not in a position to monitor the support. Apart from general political reports from the legation in Pretoria[2], it was likewise impossible to independently assess its effects.[3] On both accounts, the Swedish government relied on ANC.

The main activity for which ANC utilized the official Swedish assistance inside South Africa will be illustrated below. In the meantime, it could be noted that the 'home front component' due to security concerns, internal ANC compartmentalization and phased disbursements—where funds over long distances passed through the hands of several middlemen—was surrounded by a high degree of uncertainty, both with regard to possible misappropriation and use for military purposes. To this should be added that evidence of expenditure was lost when people were detained and equipment impounded.[4] With regard to misuse of funds, Garth Strachan, who from Lusaka and Harare was closely involved with ANC's internal work, later stated that

> it will be very difficult to say how much corruption there was [, but] one has to ask the question: Was there any alternative? [...] The only alternative was not to supply the money. [...] [I]t took a great deal of courage to provide money and support, knowing full well that the lines of accountability were not strong and therefore open to abuse. It meant that Sweden was supporting the struggle while knowing that there would be some corruption.[5]

Looking back, Bengt Säve-Söderbergh, between 1985 and 1991 Under-Secretary of State for International Development Cooperation, was similarly of the opinion that

> [g]etting involved in activities like these always constitutes a risk. If you want change, you must take risks. But, on the whole, we judged on balance and demanded what was reasonable.[6]

Finally, SIDA's former Director General Carl Tham recalled in 1997:

> [T]here was a kind of war-like situation, particularly in the 1980s. We were happy if the money came to the support of the people that we wanted to assist. We had no indication of any misuse, that is, that money came into private pockets. I am not saying that it did not happen. Maybe it did, but we never received any indication to that effect.[7]

The ANC headquarters in Lusaka—more specifically the Office of the Treasurer General—depended on long and complicated lines of accounting. To a large extent,

---

1. In the case of South Africa, this was in contrast to the support to UDF and other anti-apartheid organizations, where—as will be seen below—the Swedish legation in Pretoria played a prominent role.
2. In January 1981, for example, the Swedish envoy Gustaf Hamilton reported to the Foreign Ministry in Stockholm that "ANC's role in the resistance struggle is strong and has further increased during the past year. The movement is present in most contexts, while [BCM] has receded" (Letter ('Sydafrika inför 1981'/'South Africa facing 1981') from Gustaf Hamilton, Swedish legation, to the Ministry for Foreign Affairs, Pretoria, 5 January 1981) (MFA).
3. To a certain extent, the situation in this regard was comparable to the support earlier extended to the liberated areas of Guinea-Bissau, Mozambique and Angola. Although the substantial assistance to PAIGC, for example, was in the form of commodity aid, there was no permanent Swedish presence in Guinée-Conakry—the main host country—and SIDA was in no position to monitor the utilization of the support inside Guinea-Bissau.
4. See, for example, [Thomas Nkobi]: 'Brief report [on] SIDA's allocation to the African National Congress for the period 1980/81 ended 30th June', ANC, Lusaka, 18 November 1981 (SDA).
5. Interview with Garth Strachan, p. 195.
6. Interview with Bengt Säve-Söderbergh, p. 339.
7. Interview with Carl Tham, p. 344. The question of misappropriation within the official cooperation will be further addressed below.

ANC and the Swedish authorities were here placed in a similar dilemma, namely how to financially support the anti-apartheid opposition in South Africa while at the same time keeping non-authorized expenditures at bay. In the absence of vouchers and other internal documentary evidence, 'reasonable' control was carried out by estimating the costs of salaries, vehicles, equipment, transport and other items included in the progress reports received by ANC in Lusaka. They, in turn, formed the basis of the accounts submitted to Sweden. Roland Axelsson, SIDA's Lusaka-based regional coordinator of humanitarian assistance, later explained that

> [e]ach year we got what I would call half financial statements [...], but they were not so detailed. However, all the material that ANC bought for the money, like small cars, duplicating machines, simple office equipment and so on [was] listed, even if there was no detailed purchase price for each item. We could anyhow estimate how much they would have [cost].[1]

Above all, it was of the utmost importance to Sweden that official funds were not used for military purposes. Trying to implicate the Swedish government in the armed activities of Umkhonto we Sizwe, during the 1980s the Pretoria regime asserted on several occasions that this was the case. For example, after the December 1982 raid on ANC in Maseru, Lesotho, the South African security police claimed to have seized documents showing such an involvement.[2] The same allegation was made in connection with the bombing of ANC's office in Harare, Zimbabwe, in May 1986.[3]

Although Swedish funds—both in the 'forward areas' and in South Africa—certainly benefited the liberation movement's armed wing[4], the apartheid government was, however, never in a position to present conclusive evidence that official Swedish support in breach of the agreements with ANC was diverted to military activities.[5] Those immediately involved on behalf of ANC and Sweden have also repudiated South Africa's allegations to that effect. Broadening the horizon to the Nordic countries, in 1995 Reddy Mampane emphatically stated:

> I know very well that the Nordic countries did not give ANC weapons. They did not. They gave us humanitarian assistance, including food, medicines and so forth, but also funds to make it possible to travel, to go into the country and to organize the machinery there. But no

---

1. Interview with Roland Axelsson, p. 255. Axelsson also touched upon a related problem, namely in whose name ownership of vehicles and other items purchased under the 'home front component' was formally registered. For security reasons, it was obviously not ANC. To the author's knowledge, this question has never been followed up by the organization or, in similar circumstances, by any other Southern African liberation movement.

2. Neil Hooper: 'R 10-m: That's what the Swedes hand over each year to ANC and SWAPO' in *Sunday Times*, 13 February 1983.

3. Interview with Reddy Mampane, p. 148. Pretoria's allegations were regularly discussed at the annual aid negotiations between Sweden and ANC. In May 1987, for example, the Swedish delegation "underlined the importance of timely and accurate reporting [...] since the apartheid regime was trying to propagandize that Swedish assistance was being utilized for non-humanitarian activities" ('Agreed minutes [from] consultations in Lusaka, May 1987, between the African National Congress of South Africa and Sweden concerning humanitarian assistance', Lusaka, 8 May 1987) (SDA).

4. Cf. Axelsson: "It happened [...] that [Swedish] funds were used to feed military people. They had to live, too" (Interview with Roland Axelsson, p. 253). It could be noted that the Swedish embassy in Gaborone in March 1980 reported that "the main part" of the assistance to ANC in Lesotho was being used for activities inside South Africa. Although the activities stated by ANC were of a humanitarian character, this was in breach of the agreement in force and should therefore be raised with the headquarters in Lusaka. At the same time, however, the embassy was of the opinion that ANC in Lesotho was "a well functioning channel for activities [...] in South Africa". Against this background, it argued in favour of increased support via Lesotho for the movement's internal work (Sten Rylander: Memorandum ('ANC's framställning om bistånd 1980/81'/'ANC's request for assistance in 1980/81'), Swedish embassy, Gaborone, 28 March 1980) (SDA).

5. Commenting on the wider Nordic assistance to ANC, South Africa's former Foreign Minister 'Pik' Botha stated in 1995: "I cannot escape from either the suspicion or the assumption that the Nordic governments despite the basis on which they gave aid—that it should not be of a military nature—knew that some of it did go for military purposes" (Interview with Roelof ('Pik') Botha, p. 115).

weapons. That I know for a fact, because I was dealing with that, especially when I was in Zimbabwe as the ANC Chief Representative.[1]

Working closely with Thomas Nkobi and his staff in Lusaka—as well as with the different ANC offices in Southern Africa—Roland Axelsson, an auditor by profession, likewise affirmed in 1996 with regard to the 'home front component' that

> no [Swedish] funds were used for military purposes. [...] Not for making bombs and other things. Absolutely not.[2]

Satisfied that it was used for non-military activities, both the non-socialist and Social Democratic governments would throughout the 1980s with acceptable reports as *quid pro quo*[3] from year to year raise the 'home front component', which in 1990/91 eventually reached the level of 26.5 MSEK. Apart from 'assistance to dependants' and 'legal aid', the funds were within the agreed sub-categories primarily used for organization and political mobilization. Within this broader activity, financial and logistical support to underground operatives played a particularly significant role. Based on ANC's written reports to SIDA, the number of internal organizers supported by Sweden may illustrate the scope of the assistance.

According to the Internal Policy and Reconstruction Department, in 1979 the total number of ANC operatives in the whole of South Africa was only around 70.[4] Maharaj later estimated that the organized underground structures at that time comprised between 300 and 500 individuals, mainly working in the larger urban centres.[5] In its progress report to Sweden on the utilization of the 'home front component' during the financial year 1982/83, ANC, however, stated that by 1982 it had been able to increase the number of organizers to 650, with 300 in the Transvaal, 200 in the Cape, 100 in the Orange Free State and 50 in Natal. Each of them was paid a monthly salary of 200 South African Rands (SAR). In addition, 100,000 SAR out of the Swedish contribution had been set aside for transport, accommodation, food and other costs for 200 couriers travelling within South Africa and from South Africa to meetings with ANC abroad.[6]

Two years later—in May 1985—the movement stated that "we have an average of eight fully operational [...] underground propaganda structures in each province of South Africa", listing the equipment procured with Swedish funds for their

---

1. Interview with Reddy Mampane, pp. 147-48. At about the same time, Indres Naidoo was of the contradictory opinion that "probably 50 per cent [of the Swedish 'home front component'] went directly to the armed struggle" (Interview with Indres Naidoo, p. 179). Based in Mozambique, Naidoo was in the early and mid-1980s attached to ANC's IPRD department. His recollection most probably refers to the logistics and organization of the armed underground structures, not to their activities as such.
2. Interview with Roland Axelsson, pp. 253 and 255.
3. There was in general a marked deterioration with regard to the agreed reporting routines after ANC's unbanning in early 1990, when the movement was facing at the same time the challenges of re-establishing itself in South Africa and maintaining its socio-political responsibilities and projects in exile. In a strongly worded letter to Thomas Nkobi, SIDA's Deputy Director General Jan Cedergren noted in October 1990 "with great concern [...] that in spite of our agreement [...] ANC is not prepared to submit financial reports or activity reports concerning the Swedish support to home activities" (Letter ('Swedish support to home activities') from Jan Cedergren to Thomas Nkobi, SIDA, Stockholm, 11 October 1990) (SDA). A report was subsequently submitted. As ANC re-established itself inside South Africa, no particular 'home front component' was included in the Swedish assistance for 1991/92.
4. As quoted by Shubin op. cit., p. 201.
5. Barrell Ph. D. op cit., chapter five, p. 4.
6. ANC: 'Report on the home front', attached to 'Agreed minutes [from] consultations in Lusaka, March 1983, between the African National Congress of South Africa, ANC, and Sweden concerning humanitarian assistance', Lusaka, 25 March 1983 (SDA).

work.[1] And in its request for continued assistance in 1986/87, ANC reported that the number of full-time organizers at the end of 1985 had grown to 780.[2] While monthly allowances paid to organizers active within legal organizations and salaries for full-time underground operatives by 1986 respectively had been raised to 400 and 500 SAR—with additional contributions for transport of between 300 and 400[3]—in May 1989, finally, ANC accounted for no less than 1,225 underground organizers in its report on the 'home front component'. Of these, 420 were active in the Transvaal, 230 in the Orange Free State, 225 in the Western Cape, 200 in the Eastern Cape and 150 in Natal.[4]

Although Sweden only acted as a donor, its financial contributions towards ANC's internal organization and political work were of significant consequence. As stated by the liberation movement in a political overview submitted to the bilateral talks in May 1986:

> In all the areas in which the underground operates, its efficiency depends to a large measure on the presence of full-time operatives, professional revolutionaries whose sole occupation is [the] struggle. Such operatives have to be maintained by the movement. Their families depend on us for their daily subsistence. They have to set up viable projects for their cover and for their underground work. To be in constant touch with the people, they have to have adequate means of transportation, a vast network of accommodation and other facilities [...].[5]

More than any other component within Sweden's official cooperation with ANC, the support to the movement's internal work was kept strictly confidential.[6] Known on both sides only to the decision makers and the officials directly concerned, it has never been documented. While the military support granted by the Eastern European countries prompted the United States and its Western allies to brand ANC as 'Soviet-backed', the political dimension of the Swedish assistance has been over-

---

1. ANC: 'Progress report for SIDA relating to work inside South Africa for the financial year 1984 to May 1985', attached to 'Agreed minutes [from] consultations in Lusaka, May 1985, between the African National Congress of South Africa and Sweden concerning humanitarian assistance', Lusaka, 30 May 1985 (SDA).
2. Letter ('Submission of budgets for 1986/87 and consolidation of projects 1985/86') with attachments from ANC to the Swedish embassy, ANC, Lusaka, 10 January 1986 (SDA).
3. ANC: 'Annual report to SIDA for the year 1986', attached to letter ('Humanitarian assistance 1987/88') with attachments from ANC to the Swedish embassy, Lusaka, 19 January 1987 (SDA).
4. ANC: 'Report to SIDA: Our financial responsibility', [Lusaka], 23 May 1989 (SDA).
5. ANC: 'The current political situation', attached to 'Agreed minutes [from] consultations in Lusaka, May 1986, between the African National Congress of South Africa and Sweden concerning humanitarian assistance', Lusaka, 9 May 1986 (SDA).
6. Under the vote 'Humanitarian assistance in Southern Africa', the total amounts allocated to the liberation movements were indicated in the Swedish budget. The actual distribution of the funds was, however, not specified. While the Swedish embassy in Lusaka after negotiations with ANC and SWAPO in a press release in May 1982 stated that the grants for 1982/83 respectively were 27 and 43 MSEK, the purpose of the support was only in general terms given as "mainly for [...] daily necessities [...], educational, medical and farming equipment" (Swedish embassy: 'Press release', attached to 'Agreed minutes of discussions in Lusaka, May 1982, between the African National Congress of South Africa, ANC, and the Swedish International Development Authority, SIDA, concerning humanitarian assistance', Lusaka, 24 May 1982) (SDA). The 'home front components' were not mentioned. On the basis of the overall figures, the South African press, however, turned strongly against the Swedish government. When the ANC allocation for 1983/84 was announced, *The Star*, for example, characterized Sweden as "ANC's biggest Western 'sugar daddy'" (Stephen McQuillan: 'Sweden aids both ANC and Escom' in *The Star*, 18 July 1983). With regard to the strict confidentiality with which the 'home front component' was treated, it could be noted that the centrally placed Swedish solidarity activist Bertil Högberg, occupying prominent positions within BF, ISAK and AGIS and in close contact with SIDA, in November 2000 stated that "I was not aware of the extent of [this assistance]" (Letter from Bertil Högberg to the author, Uppsala, 17 November 2000).

looked.[1] It is thus not surprising that South African anti-apartheid academics have characterized it as "peacenik".[2]

Respectively set in a Cold War context and focusing on the Swedish support to ANC in exile, both characterizations, however, downplay the role played by Sweden with regard to the movement's underground efforts inside the apartheid republic. Extended from mid-1977—only four years after the modest beginnings in Tanzania and Zambia—the 'home front component' made it considerably less difficult to implement and sustain the strategic decisions reached in 1979, which—as noted by Barrell—"paved the way for the ANC's rise in coming years to a position of pre-eminence".[3] Interviewed in 1995, ANC's Mampane concluded that

> the SIDA support which was channelled to the [h]ome [f]front had a tremendous impact on the reorganization of the internal structures. In order to create an underground machinery, we had to get cadres into the country, organize the people and set up good communications. To do this, we needed funds, and the money which was channelled by Sweden represented, I think, the bulk of the resources which assisted ANC to be able to operate.[4]

Before turning attention to ANC in exile, it should be recalled that from the late 1970s substantial amounts were indirectly extended by the Swedish government to the South African trade unions and, later, to COSATU. In addition, as early as in October 1983—only two months after its launch—a first transfer of funds to the United Democratic Front (UDF) was made via the International Centre of the Swedish Labour Movement.[5] As will be seen below, apart from regular contributions to various affiliated organizations, slightly below 50 MSEK was subsequently disbursed in favour of UDF. When Treasurer General Nkobi in his introductory remarks to the official aid negotiations stated in May 1987 that Sweden and ANC were "in the same trenches"[6], his critical comments of April 1978—implying that official funds through IUEF had been used against ANC[7]—were long since a thing of the past.

The special relations which developed between Sweden and ANC from the mid-1970s were consolidated around 1980. From then on, no official voices were raised in Sweden in favour of competing South African organizations. Whether under

---

1. Reflecting on a meeting with Ronnie Kasrils in Harare in the mid-1980s—where the leading SACP member and MK head of military intelligence said that "[the Swedes] give us more money than anyone else"— Howard Barrell wrote in October 1999: "I had been introduced to a simple fact about the South African liberation struggle, one I should easily have guessed at, but which had got hidden, I suppose, under a determination not to know what I didn't need to know. It was mainly the Swedes who were keeping me, and thousands like me, alive in exile. It was largely Swedish money that I and hundreds of others were sending [...] inside the country to fund various activities against the government" (Howard Barrell: ''Stockholm gold' for the masses' in *Mail & Guardian*, 29 October-4 November 1999).
2. Peter Vale and John Daniel: ''Upstairs-Downstairs': Understanding the 'new' South Africa in the 'new' world' [no place or date, but 1993]. While Sweden never supported the armed struggle, it could be noted that funds channelled to the 'home front' and to the maintenance of MK cadres in Angola and Uganda in total amounted to 285 MSEK, representing slightly less than one third of the overall disbursements to the liberation movement. To this could be added indirect support in the form of 'daily necessities' to underground members in the 'forward areas' (cf. below).
3. Barrell op. cit., p. 37.
4. Interview with Reddy Mampane, p. 147. Cf. Strachan, who in the 1980s served as administrative secretary to the ANC Revolutionary Council and the Politico-Military Council: "The only form of support that to the best of my knowledge was not given was literally the military hardware itself. But without these other elements, the armed struggle would not have been possible anyway" (Interview with Garth Strachan, p. 193).
5. The early Swedish assistance to UDF has also been overlooked. In his otherwise comprehensive history of the front, Seekings incorrectly states that it only started after a meeting between ANC and UDF in Stockholm in January 1986 (Jeremy Seekings: *The UDF: A History of the United Democratic Front in South Africa, 1983-1991*, David Philip, Cape Town; James Currey, Oxford; and Ohio University Press, Athens, 2000, p. 169).
6. 'Agreed minutes [from] consultations in Lusaka, May 1987, between the African National Congress of South Africa and Sweden concerning humanitarian assistance', Lusaka, 8 May 1987 (SDA).
7. See the preceding chapter.

non-socialist or Social Democratic governments, ANC was *de facto* seen as a 'government-in-waiting' and from a protocol point of view accorded a status similar to that of independent states.[1] For example, when in early March 1981 Tambo led a high-level delegation to Sweden[2], meetings with Prime Minister Fälldin, Foreign Minister Ullsten and Archbishop Sundby were included in the official programme in addition to discussions with the Social Democratic opposition leader Palme, LO, CSM, AGIS, ISAK and other organizations.[3]

ANC reciprocated by similarly according Sweden special honours. While the first speaker at the movement's 70th anniversary celebrations in Lusaka in January 1982 represented OAU, he was followed by the Swedish ambassador, Göran Hasselmark.[4] Representatives of the Non-Aligned Movement, SWAPO, the Soviet Union and the Zambian ruling party UNIP subsequently addressed the meeting.[5] The support to ANC's internal work was of significance in this context. As stated by Oliver Tambo to the Social Democratic Foreign Minister Lennart Bodström[6] during the Non-Aligned Conference in New Delhi, India, in March 1983: "Without the Swedish assistance ANC could hardly operate".[7]

---

1. Cf. Mabuza, ANC's Chief Representative to the Nordic countries (1979-88): "It was unbelievable how we were recognized. This might sound a little bit presumptuous and arrogant, but we were better treated and recognized than some of the real, accredited ambassadors in all the Nordic countries" (Interview with Lindiwe Mabuza, p. 135).
2. The ANC delegation included Thomas Nkobi, Thabo Mbeki, Rebecca Matlou (aka Sankie Mthembi-Mahanyele) and Thozamile Botha, the latter representing SACTU. Lindiwe Mabuza also formed part of the delegation.
3. Anders Bjurner: 'Preliminärt program: Besök av ANC's president Oliver Tambo'/'Preliminary programme: Visit by ANC President Oliver Tambo', Ministry for Foreign Affairs, 25 February 1981 (MFA). Accompanied by Mbeki, Eddie Funde from the Youth Secretariat, Raymond Mokoena from the International Department and Dulcie September from the Treasury, Tambo was in May 1983 received in the same way by the Social Democratic government. In addition to discussions with Prime Minister Palme, Foreign Minister Bodström and the leaders of the opposition parties, the ANC delegation thus held meetings with SIDA, CCHA, LO/TCO, AIC and the parliamentary Standing Committee on Foreign Affairs (Anders Bjurner: 'Besöksprogram för O. Tambo, ANC's ordförande'/'Programme for the visit by O. Tambo, ANC President', Ministry for Foreign Affairs, 22 April 1983) (MFA). Forming part of a Nordic tour, the visit to Sweden took place from 3 to 5 May 1983.
4. Foreign Minister Ola Ullsten was at the time visiting Zambia, where in connection with ANC's celebrations he held discussions with the leadership of the movement ('Statement by the Minister for Foreign Affairs, Mr. Ola Ullsten, on the occasion of the 70th anniversary of the African National Congress', 7 January 1982, in Ministry for Foreign Affairs: *Documents on Swedish Foreign Policy: 1982*, Stockholm, 1985, pp. 196-97).
5. ANC: 'Programme on the occasion of the 70th anniversary of the African National Congress, United Nations Institute for Namibia, Lusaka, 9 January 1982' (MFA). ANC's statement— delivered at a number of venues all around the world—was read in Lusaka by MK Commander Joe Modise, democratic South Africa's first Minister of Defence. As was customary in ANC's official statements at the time, the socialist countries were characterized as "the mainstay of [the] world revolutionary process" ('Statement of the National Executive Committee of the African National Congress on the occasion of the 70th anniversary of the formation of the [ANC], 8 January 1982') (MFA).
6. When the Social Democratic Party returned to power in October 1982, Bodström succeeded the Liberal Ola Ullsten as Foreign Minister.
7. Axel Edelstam: Memorandum ('Utrikesministerns samtal med Oliver Tambo, ledare för ANC'/'The Foreign Minister's conversation with Oliver Tambo, leader of ANC'), Swedish embassy, New Delhi, 17 March 1983 (MFA). The apartheid regime was according to Tambo aware of the role played by Sweden. He therefore warned of possible South African attempts to sabotage the Swedish assistance (ibid.). It could also be noted that the ANC President as early as in March 1983—that is, one year before the Nkomati Accord—predicted that actions would be taken against ANC's presence in Mozambique: "If Mozambique does not deal with ANC, South Africa will", he told Bodström (ibid.).

Attacks and Assistance in the Forward Areas: Swaziland and Mozambique

Daily Necessities on the Frontline

Most elements in Sweden's anti-apartheid policy had been put in place by 1980. Comprehensive trade sanctions would not be imposed until 1987, but the investment ban of July 1979 was a significant—and, from the point of view of traditional Swedish security policy, exceptional—first step towards unilateral action outside the United Nations framework. In the beginning questioned by certain domestic political actors and internationally aligned media voices, by then, too, the officially initiated assistance to ANC enjoyed solid support. At the level of the popular movements, the Africa Groups firmly backed ANC, and—with the notable exception of the Moderates—all political parties represented in parliament promoted direct cooperation with the organization. Around 80 per cent of the Swedish MPs belonged to these parties.[1] While the Moderate Party opposed the very principle of

Bombs against the ANC office in Stockholm, September 1986: Lindiwe Mabuza arriving on the scene (Photo: Lasse Hedberg/ Pressens Bild)

---

1. See Appendix II.

supporting any liberation movement[1], no representative voices advocated government assistance to 'alternative' anti-apartheid forces.[2]

By 1980, the overall structure of the official ANC support was, in addition, near
completion. During the 1980s, roughly one third of the steadily growing annual
grants was set aside for direct refugee assistance in Southern Africa; one third for
administration, capacity-building and various projects in exile; and the remaining
third for internal political work.[3] The 'home front component' was discussed in the
previous chapter. Focusing on the so called 'forward areas' until ANC's unbanning
and homecoming, the humanitarian support extended in the form of 'daily necessities' will be presented below.

---

1. The Moderate Party formed part of Fälldin's first and second non-socialist coalition governments, that is,
   from October 1976 until October 1978 and between October 1979 and May 1981. Opposing the dominant
   Centre-Liberal policy of increased assistance to the nationalist movements in Zimbabwe, Namibia and South
   Africa, in January 1978, for example, the Moderate MP Allan Åkerlind demanded in a parliamentary motion
   that "no development aid shall be accorded so called liberation movement[s]" (Swedish Parliament 1977/78:
   Motion No. 532, Riksdagens Protokoll 1977/78, p. 1). A backbencher on the extreme right of his party, two
   years later Åkerlind not only requested that official assistance to the liberation movements should be "completely discontinued", but also that humanitarian support in favour of Southern African refugees should be
   terminated (Swedish Parliament 1979/80: Motion No. 1626, Riksdagens Protokoll 1979/80, p. 1). In 1982,
   his colleague Tore Nilsson introduced a parliamentary motion in which he argued that "training of [ANC]
   terrorists is conducted by [the Palestine Liberation Organization]" and that "ANC only enjoys support from
   a very minimal part of the African population in [South Africa]" (Swedish Parliament 1981/82: Motion No.
   1249, Riksdagens Protokoll 1981/82, p. 7). While the Moderate Party was the home of dissenting Swedish
   voices, it should be noted that Carl Bildt—the future party leader (1986-99) and Prime Minister (1991-94)—
   at an early stage took stands which went contrary to the views of many of his colleagues. Although opposed
   to the proposed ban against new investments in South Africa, in an internal memorandum on the non-socialist government's Southern African policy, in October 1977 he generally supported its pro-active approach,
   noting that it had "goodwill" effects and could counter the "undesirable" influence of the East bloc countries
   (Carl Bildt: Memorandum ('Synpunkter på PM om Sveriges södra Afrika-politik'/'Comments on memorandum re Sweden's Southern Africa policy'), Ministry for Economic Affairs, Stockholm, 4 October 1977)
   (MFA). More significant is that Bildt in June 1984 joined fellow MPs from the Left Party Communists (Eva
   Hjelmström), the ruling Social Democratic Party (Jan Bergqvist), the Centre Party (Pär Granstedt) and the
   Liberal Party (Björn Molin) in submitting a request to SIDA for financial support towards the establishment
   of an Association of West European Politicians (later Parliamentarians) for Action against Apartheid
   (AWEPAA) (Bergqvist et al.: 'Till SIDA'/'To SIDA', [Stockholm], 8 June 1984) (SDA). Together with Oswald
   Söderquist of the Left Party Communists, Hans Göran Franck of the Social Democratic Party and Granstedt,
   Bildt subsequently served as a member of the organization's coordinating committee in Sweden (Franck et al.:
   'Till SIDA'/'To SIDA', Stockholm, 19 December 1985) (SDA). Bildt's anti-apartheid involvement was largely
   ignored by the Moderate pro-South African backbenchers. As late as in 1996, Birger Hagård, for example,
   claimed that he did not know of AWEPAA or that his party leader had been active within the association
   (Interview with Birger Hagård, p. 274). Founded by parliamentarians from 14 countries, AWEPAA was formally established in Copenhagen, Denmark, in November 1984. In addition to economic sanctions, among its
   original objectives was the "promotion of support to the oppressed people of South Africa and Namibia and
   their national liberation movements" (AWEPAA: 'Rules and regulations', [Copenhagen], 3 November 1984)
   (SDA). As treasurer, Pär Granstedt of the Swedish Centre Party formed part of its executive committee,
   headed by Jan Nico Scholten from the Netherlands. With a grant of 110,000 SEK—corresponding to 12.5 per
   cent of its budget—the Swedish government was from the beginning in 1985 AWEPAA's main donor
   (AWEPAA: 'Financial report 1985', The Hague, [no date]) (SDA). At the end of that year, 108 out of 349
   Swedish MPs had joined the organization (Franck et al.: 'Till SIDA'/'To SIDA', Stockholm, 19 December
   1985) (SDA). See also the interview with Pär Granstedt, p. 272.
2. In January 1984, the former Education Minister Jan-Erik Wikström and four fellow Liberal MPs submitted
   an extraordinary parliamentary motion in favour of ANC, SACTU *and* PAC (see the chapter "Looking for
   Alternatives': Pan Africanist Congress'). Acknowledging that ANC and UDF "possibly are the strongest political forces within the anti-apartheid resistance", in January 1988 Margaretha af Ugglas and seven Moderate
   Party MPs—among them Gunnar Hökmark—warned against 'unilateral support" to the two organizations.
   While they did not suggest any alternatives, in their motion the future Foreign Minister (1991-94) and her
   colleagues expressed the opinion that "the development towards a democratic South Africa naturally
   demands that a host of different political opinions [...] must be allowed and [made able] to grow" (Swedish
   Parliament 1987/88: Motion No. U 503, Riksdagens Protokoll 1987/88, p. 15). In January 1993, Karin Falk-
   mer of the ruling Moderate Party requested the parliament to reject the Bildt government's proposal concerning continued financial assistance to ANC, advocating instead support to the little known Get Ahead
   Foundation and the Urban Foundation in South Africa (Swedish Parliament 1992/93: Motion No. U 205,
   Riksdagens Protokoll 1992/93, p. 11).
3. Cf. the tables on the ANC allocation in 1987/88 below.

In the meantime, it should as a general, introductory comment be noted that the Swedish authorities from the beginning found ANC to be a reliable partner, which under difficult circumstances was capable of handling and reporting on funds disbursed in several Southern African countries. In a memorandum on ANC's request for assistance in 1981/82, the CCHA secretariat concluded that

> the impressions so far are unequivocal: ANC has a well functioning administration [and] the funds allocated have been put to good use.[1]

Five years later—in April 1986—SIDA's Director General Carl Tham stated in a submission to the Ministry for Foreign Affairs that

> the [past] experiences of [the] cooperation with ANC are good. [...] ANC has been an efficient channel for Swedish humanitarian support to the victims of the apartheid policy. Despite the fact that [it] is a liberation movement [engaged] in [a] struggle, [ANC] has in a competent way administered [our] assistance.[2]

As a result of ANC's growing pains, administrative problems emerged towards the end of the 1980s. Throughout the decade, accounting deficiencies in the 'forward areas'—mainly due to South African attacks—did not, however, undermine the trust placed in the movement. On the contrary, the official grants were constantly raised. Over and above the annual allocations, extraordinary contributions were also granted. The broad political support enjoyed by ANC—and SWAPO of Namibia—was notably demonstrated by the fact that the Swedish parliament on more than one occasion voted to increase the budgetary proposals submitted by the government.[3]

In the 1980s, the allocations and disbursements to SWAPO exceeded those to ANC.[4] Nevertheless, despite considerably more complicated and exposed environments—where most of the South African refugees, as opposed to their Namibian brothers and sisters, lived outside established settlements—the Swedish per capita support to ANC was on average twice as high as that extended to SWAPO. It was also more inclusive. Beginning in 1973 with humanitarian support to both civilian and military cadres in Tanzania and Zambia, assistance in the form of daily necessities was from the late 1970s in addition to the Angolan camps extended to the movement in Mozambique, Botswana, Lesotho and Swaziland, that is, ANC 'forward areas' with a significant underground MK presence.

As a second general comment, it could be noted that the mere size of the Swedish assistance at an early stage caused mutual concerns, an issue which after ANC's unbanning would become particularly problematic. In the mid-1980s, Norway joined Sweden in extending direct official support to ANC in the 'forward areas'. Closely coordinating their contributions, the two countries thereby played unique roles with regard to the maintenance of thousands of ANC members and their fami-

---

1. Henrik Salander: Memorandum ('Bidrag till African National Congress (ANC) i Sydafrika 1981/82'/'Contribution to ANC in South Africa 1981/82'), CCHA/Ministry for Foreign Affairs, [Stockholm], 27 April 1981 (SDA).
2. Letter ('Humanitärt bistånd till African National Congress of South Africa (ANC), budgetåret 1986/87'/ 'Humanitarian assistance to ANC during the financial year 1986/87') from Carl Tham to the Ministry for Foreign Affairs, SIDA, Stockholm, 16 April 1986 (SDA).
3. This was, for example, the case in 1983/84. While the Social Democratic government proposed an overall budget for humanitarian assistance in Southern Africa of 140 MSEK—of which half was earmarked for ANC and SWAPO—the parliamentary debate resulted in an increase of 20 million and a final vote of 160 MSEK (Sten Rylander: Memorandum ('Det humanitära biståndet i södra Afrika 1983/84'/'The humanitarian assistance in Southern Africa 1983/84'), Ministry for Foreign Affairs, Stockholm, 17 August 1983) (SDA).
4. In 1986/87, the disbursements to ANC exceptionally exceeded those to SWAPO. Cf. the attached tables.

lies.[1] At the end of the 1970s and in the early 1980s, it was, however, only the Swedish government which on a regular, planned basis granted such assistance. Stating that "ANC's strong position today would not have been possible without [this] support", in discussions with Foreign Minister Ullsten Tambo commented in March 1981 that Sweden's dominant position in this regard "perhaps [implied] a dangerous [dependency] situation".[2]

While the Swedish government in order to avoid becoming "too big a donor"[3] on ANC's behalf actively tried to prevail upon other countries to assist, apart from Norway the response from the international community was lukewarm to negative. Noting that Sweden alone in 1982/83 had covered 40 per cent of the basic needs of an ANC population in Southern Africa of 11,000[4], in its request for 1984/85 the movement raised this issue. Implicitly criticizing not only the Western powers, but also the United Nations, the Eastern European governments, international NGOs and many national solidarity groups, ANC concluded:

> Although the whole world has on numerous occasions in various forums condemned South Africa and pledged support to the ANC, few countries have given us more than just moral and political support. [...] Few donors are keen on giving assistance for daily necessities largely because such assistance leaves no living proof. It is all consumed. Hence, most donors prefer to go into projects that the whole world can see.[5] [...]

> [A]s far as humanitarian assistance goes, SIDA is our major donor. [...] We wish to place it on record that [the support] is indelibly etched in our minds. It has helped restore our dignity and has prevented us from being reduced to the level of beggars—the lot of refugees the world over. Indeed, with the confidence that we do not have to spend time thinking [about] what we shall eat tomorrow, we have been able to concentrate with oneness of mind on the struggle for the liberation of our country. Moreover, it would not have been possible for us to mount the kind of projects we have if we did not have some of our basic needs partially satisfied. And so, it is without shame that once again we approach SIDA for humanitarian assistance.[6]

Before turning in more detail to the humanitarian non-project aid, it should as a third comment, finally, be noted that the administrative routines established for the cooperation strengthened the day-to-day contacts between the Swedish officials in Southern Africa and the local ANC communities. This, in turn, contributed to increased mutual understanding and a broadening of the 'special relationship'.

---

1. In reaction to various attacks on Sweden's support to ANC, the movement declared in January 1993 that "ANC, during decades of illegality, bannings, banishment and exile found firm friends in the international community, not least among them Sweden. Both the Swedish people and government took the cause of freedom and justice for all South Africans to their hearts. They provided humanitarian assistance without which thousands of people would not have had food, clothing, education or shelter" (ANC: 'Press statement on aid from Sweden', Department of Information and Publicity, Marshalltown, 5 January 199[3]).
2. Anders Bjurner: Memorandum ('Samtal mellan utrikesministern och ANC's ordförande Oliver Tambo'/'Conversation between the Foreign Minister and ANC President Oliver Tambo'), Ministry for Foreign Affairs, Stockholm, 4 March 1981 (MFA).
3. CCHA: Memorandum ('Riktlinjer för humanitärt bistånd i södra Afrika'/'Guidelines for humanitarian assistance in Southern Africa'), SIDA, Stockholm, 10 December 1984 (SDA).
4. ANC: 'SIDA humanitarian assistance to the African National Congress of South Africa for the year 1983/84 and submissions for the year 1984/85', ANC, Lusaka, 5 January 1984 (SDA).
5. While donors remained reluctant to support ANC's current and administrative costs—but Norway from the start had supported infrastructural developments at SOMAFCO and Dakawa—at the end of 1984 no less than 200 organizations were in an uncoordinated manner making deliveries to the movement's Tanzanian settlements, which at the time accommodated around 2,000 people. As a result, ANC was, for example, faced with the problem of having to cope with more than 40 different makes of vehicles, often supplied without spare parts (Roland Axelsson: Memorandum ('Anteckningar från sammanträde och diskussioner i Tanzania avseende ANC, 6-10 december 1984'/'Notes from consultation and discussions in Tanzania regarding ANC, 6-10 December 1984'), Swedish embassy, Lusaka, 9 January 1985) (SDA).
6. ANC: 'SIDA humanitarian assistance to the African National Congress of South Africa for the year 1983/84 and submissions for the year 1984/85', ANC, Lusaka, 5 January 1984 (SDA).

Initially, ANC preferred commodity aid to cash support.[1] At the bilateral negotiations in August 1977, it was, however, agreed to introduce a system of quarterly
payments in advance to the movement's local representations.[2] The following year,
it was decided that funds disbursed should be accounted for in the form of quarterly financial reports, to be "submitted not later than three months after the end of
each quarter to the Swedish [embassies] in Tanzania, Botswana, Mozambique,
Angola and Zambia [...]".[3]

By decentralizing responsibility for local funds in favour of 'daily necessities'
and 'office administration'[4], from the late 1970s the Swedish missions and the
ANC representations in the Southern African region became jointly involved with
the cooperation programme. On both sides, officials based in the forward areas
often took part in the annual aid negotiations. As the beneficiaries in their respective countries were individuals with different problems and needs—not living in
camps or settlements which could be supplied through bulk deliveries of food and
commodity aid—the system brought the parties together.[5] As earlier in Tanzania
and Zambia[6], this not only led to frequent contacts, but in many cases to close personal relations. In times of problems or threats, ANC representatives and ordinary
members approached Swedish officials for advice, support or protection.

Range and Numbers

Although Sweden at an early stage supported ANC inside South Africa, as a result
of the post-Soweto refugee flows humanitarian non-project aid in exile became the
centrepiece of the cooperation. From 1977/78, support in the form of daily necessities was channelled to ANC in Angola, Botswana, Lesotho, Mozambique, Swaziland, Tanzania and Zambia. Administrative support to the movement's local
representations was also extended.[7]

ANC's position in these countries was far from uniform. With government support in Angola, Tanzania and Zambia, the movement would towards the end of the
1970s establish military camps or civilian settlements where refugees in relative
safety from South African attacks could be collectively accommodated and supplied. In Botswana, Lesotho, Swaziland and Mozambique, this was never the case.
In these countries, ANC members would in environments exposed to strikes by the

1. Anders Bjurner: Memorandum ('Förhandlingsprotokoll för bistånd till ANC (Sydafrika) 1975/76'/'Agreed
   minutes re assistance to ANC in 1975/76'), Swedish embassy, Lusaka, 18 September 1975 (SDA).
2. 'Agreed minutes of discussions on the cooperation between the African National Congress of South Africa
   (ANC) and Sweden 1977/78', Lusaka, 2 September 1977 (SDA). On the system of quarterly payments in
   advance, see the chapter 'FRELIMO of Mozambique: Clearing a Way'. See also the interview with Roland
   Axelsson, p. 253.
3. 'Agreed minutes of discussions on the cooperation between Sweden and the African National Congress of
   South Africa (ANC) 1978/79', Lusaka, 26 May 1978 (SDA). In the cases of Lesotho and Swaziland—where
   there were no official Swedish representations—it was agreed that the quarterly reports should be submitted
   to the embassies in Lusaka (later Gaborone) and Maputo, respectively (ibid.).
4. Consolidated annual reports were compiled by ANC's Treasury Department.
5. With its military camps, Angola was an exception in this regard. Although huge quantities of food and other
   basic necessities were delivered from Sweden, the contacts between the Swedish embassy and the ANC/MK
   representation in Luanda remained limited.
6. In the early 1980s, the Swedish embassy in Lusaka arranged soccer matches between the Swedish community
   and ANC (Author's recollection).
7. 'Agreed minutes of discussions on the cooperation between the African National Congress of South Africa
   (ANC) and Sweden 1977/78', Lusaka, 2 September 1977 (SDA).

apartheid regime and shifting attitudes of the host governments on an individual basis precariously settle among the local populations. From the point of view of humanitarian assistance, it was considerably more complicated to meet the needs of the latter than of the former.

While the substantial amounts granted towards daily necessities in the main host countries of Angola, Tanzania and Zambia should not be ignored[1], the presentation below focuses on the cooperation with ANC in Swaziland and Mozambique. Sweden's relations with the movement in Lesotho, Botswana and independent Zimbabwe will be discussed in the following chapter.

According to ANC's estimates, at the beginning of the 1980s the movement catered for a total of 8,800 people in Southern Africa.[2] At the time of its unbanning ten years later, the number had grown to almost 25,000.[3] The budget component for daily necessities under the Swedish assistance underwent a corresponding increase. During the financial year 1980/81, an amount of 9.4 MSEK was set aside for this purpose.[4] In 1990/91—when the overall budget had reached 103 million and support was extended to ANC in twelve African countries[5]—the component amounted in total to 33 MSEK.[6] On the basis of ANC's figures, in the early 1980s the Swedish per capita contribution towards the maintenance of its members was thus 1,070 SEK and one decade later 1,320 SEK.[7] In the forward areas, it was considerably higher.

From modest beginnings in 1973, over the years Sweden would allocate under the bilateral cooperation programme with ANC around 250 MSEK—in current figures—in favour of the movement's exiled members in Southern Africa. Summarized

1. In 1979/80, 5 million out of the total allocation of 6.5 MSEK for daily necessities—corresponding to 77 per cent—was earmarked for Angola (3.2 MSEK), Tanzania (1.0) and Zambia (0.8) ('Agreed minutes from discussions on the cooperation between the African National Congress of South Africa (ANC) and the Swedish International Development Authority (SIDA)', Lusaka, 18 May 1979) (SDA). Ten years later—when humanitarian assistance was extended to ANC in twelve African countries—the three countries' combined share of the 27 MSEK budgeted in favour of daily necessities was 19 million, or 71 per cent. With 9.0 million, Angola was still the most important host country, followed by Tanzania (8.0) and Zambia (2.0 MSEK) ('Agreed minutes from consultations held in Lusaka, May 1989, between the African National Congress of South Africa and Sweden concerning humanitarian assistance', Lusaka, 26 May 1989) (SDA).

2. Henrik Salander: Memorandum ('Bidrag till African National Congress (ANC) i Sydafrika 1981/82'/'Contribution to ANC in South Africa 1981/82'), CCHA/Ministry for Foreign Affairs, [Stockholm], 27 April 1981 (SDA).

3. 'Agreed minutes from consultations held in Lusaka, May 1990, between the African National Congress of South Africa and Sweden concerning humanitarian assistance', Lusaka, 18 May 1990 (SDA) and Per Sjögren: Memorandum ('Förhandlingar med ANC i Lusaka 15-18 maj 1990'/'Negotiations with ANC in Lusaka 15-18 May 1990'), Ministry for Foreign Affairs, Stockholm, 12 June 1990 (SDA). In late 1991, UNHCR estimated the total number of South African refugees at 30,000. In addition to people under ANC's care, this figure included members of other organizations, as well as non-affiliated individual exiles (Birgitta Sevefjord: Memorandum ('Minnesanteckningar från möte med UNHCR'/'Notes from meeting with UNHCR'), Swedish embassy, Dar es Salaam, 15 November 1991) (SDA).

4. 'Minutes from discussions on the cooperation between the African National Congress of South Africa (ANC) and the Swedish International Development Authority (SIDA), May 1980', Lusaka, 29 May 1980 (SDA).

5. By that time, the Swedish assistance to ANC also included Ethiopia, Kenya, Madagascar, Uganda and Zimbabwe. Namibia was added to the list in 1991/92.

6. 'Agreed minutes from consultations held in Lusaka, May 1990, between the African National Congress of South Africa and Sweden concerning humanitarian assistance', Lusaka, 18 May 1990 (SDA).

7. In the case of SWAPO, the annual Swedish support per capita was around 500 SEK. Practically all Namibian refugees were accommodated in settlements and supplied with bulk commodity aid. To this should be added that SWAPO benefited from a much broader international support than ANC.

for the main host countries, the accumulated budgeted amounts for the period
1972/73-1991/92 appear in the following overview:[1]

'Daily necessities' in Sweden's assistance to ANC
(in thousands of SEK)

Host country	Budgeted amount	Percentage
Angola	85,200	34.5
Tanzania	72,300	29.2
Zambia	25,500	10.3
Botswana	18,300	7.4
Mozambique	11,400	4.6
Swaziland	10,700	4.3
Uganda	9,500	3.9
Lesotho	7,600	3.1
Zimbabwe	3,000	1.2
Other countries	3,800	1.5
All countries	247,300	100.0

A wide interpretation of 'daily necessities' was applied from the late 1970s, particularly with regard to individual beneficiaries outside ANC's camps and settlements.
In 1977/78—when the parties formally agreed that "flexibility should be maintained within the programme of cooperation"[2]—a house was, for example, purchased for the movement in Swaziland.[3] In addition to food, clothes and medicines,
as early as in 1978/79 it was agreed that the component could cover "rent, water,
electricity, house repairs, furniture [and] transport costs, such as petrol, oil, car
maintenance [as well as] air, bus and train fares".[4] Eventually accommodating
practically all the expenses of the recipient ANC members—from cooking gas and
shoe repairs to school fees and funeral costs—entertainment, superfluous goods and
military items were, however, excluded.[5] It is in this context relevant to emphasize
that ANC's representatives in Southern Africa, as well as the officials at the headquarters in Lusaka, also benefited from the support.

1. The table is based on the original estimates established during the annual negotiations between Sweden and
   ANC. It should be noted that, due to unforeseen political developments, reallocations were often made
   between the country budgets. Extraordinary allocations would be extended by the Swedish government for
   the same reason. These adjustments and additions are not reflected in the table, which, nevertheless, gives an
   accurate account of the support towards 'daily necessities' in ANC's main host countries. With regard to the
   individual countries, it should also be borne in mind that Uganda was only included in 1989/90, when thousands of ANC/MK cadres were evacuated from Angola and accommodated there. In the case of Zimbabwe,
   substantial amounts were separately set aside in favour of ANC members from the region who visited the
   country for political meetings, medical attention or other purposes. 'Other countries', finally, refer to Ethiopia
   (1,300), Madagascar (1,100), Kenya (800) and Namibia (600). Assistance to the ANC offices in Africa, Sweden and elsewhere—notably in the United States—is not included in these figures.
2. 'Agreed minutes of discussions on the cooperation between the African National Congress of South Africa
   (ANC) and Sweden 1977/78', Lusaka, 2 September 1977 (SDA).
3. Ibid.
4. 'Agreed minutes of discussions on the cooperation between Sweden and the African National Congress of
   South Africa (ANC) 1978/79', Lusaka, 26 May 1978 (SDA).
5. Cf. below. Also ANC: 'Annual request to SIDA 1990/91: General summary', ANC, Lusaka, 15 February 1990
   (SDA). With regard to non-essential items, it could be noted that the local Swedish missions in the early 1980s
   often showed a permissive attitude. For the quarter period January to March 1982, for example, the embassy
   in Maputo accepted that 10 per cent of the grant to ANC in Mozambique had been spent on cigarettes (Bo
   Westman: Memorandum ('Reports and payments ANC/Maputo [and] Swaziland'), Swedish embassy,
   Maputo, 20 April 1982) (SDA). Similar expenditures in breach of the spirit of the cooperation were soon rectified, notably through Roland Axelsson's regular visits to the different Southern African countries from late
   1984.

As was the case with regard to the other Southern African liberation movements, Sweden was in no position to determine the number of people in the liberated areas or refugees in the independent host countries.[1] In the case of ANC, more or less accurate estimates were, in addition, complicated by a number of factors. Contrary to the mass departures from Zimbabwe and Namibia into settlements run by ZANU, ZAPU and SWAPO, those who sought contact with ANC in exile left South Africa on an individual basis. Crossing the borders into Botswana, Lesotho, Swaziland and Mozambique—and later Zimbabwe—they were normally not recognized by UNHCR as *bona fide* refugees, but seen as people in transit. Without legal protection and as a result of South African pressure or attacks, they were often forced to leave.[2] Swedish support was regularly granted towards their onward transportation.

Most exiles would eventually return to South Africa after ANC's unbanning. At the same time, however, there was a parallel outward flow of people from the hostilities with Inkatha in Natal and the Johannesburg area. In fact, the magnitude of the exodus in early 1990—which reached as far as Tanzania—was only surpassed by that which took place after the 1976 Soweto events.[3] Assistance in the form of daily necessities would over the years thus be extended to constantly fluctuating populations, regularly motivating reallocations within the ANC budget. This notwithstanding, the utilization rate remained very high, as a rule approaching 100 per cent.

Implemented under difficult circumstances, during the 1980s the support to ANC in the forward areas—notably in Swaziland and Lesotho—called for extraordinary routines. As Thomas Nkobi and his staff at ANC's Treasury Department in Lusaka were unable to visit these countries, the administration of the cooperation was largely delegated to SIDA. Often acting on Nkobi's behalf, from late 1984 SIDA's regional coordinator Roland Axelsson would in this context play a particularly prominent and crucial role.

South Africa in Southern Africa

The political significance and the administrative problems of the support in the forward areas should be viewed against Pretoria's 'total strategy' and its mixture of sticks and carrots towards the neighbouring states.

---

1. Reliable estimates were particularly problematic in the forward areas. In the case of Lesotho, for example, the Maseru government stated in late 1983 that there were 11,500 South African refugees in the country. Only 1,300 were, however, registered with UNHCR. At the same time, ANC claimed that it catered for a local population of 1,200. Nevertheless, the three figures could be more or less accurate. While non-resident South Africans were seen by the government as refugees, UNHCR only listed those who had registered as such. Fearing exposure, the majority of those who contacted ANC did not register with UNHCR. The figures given by UNHCR and ANC thus referred to different categories (Tor Sellström: Memorandum ('Humanitärt bistånd till African National Congress of South Africa (ANC) budgetåret 1984/85'/'Humanitarian assistance to ANC during the financial year 1984/85'), SIDA, Stockholm, 13 March 1984) (SDA).
2. South Africa's strikes against ANC members in Botswana, Lesotho, Swaziland and Mozambique—later also in Zambia and Zimbabwe—normally claimed victims among the local populations. Rather than a consequence of incompetence, this was a calculated tactic to convince the national communities that an ANC presence in their midst represented a direct security risk. The objective was that ANC should be frozen out. In leaflets left behind after a South African raid on ANC in Harare in 1986, it was, for example, stated: "South African troops have carried out an attack against offices and houses used by ANC gangsters in your country. [...] For your own safety, you should not allow ANC gangsters to occupy houses and offices [...] from where they can plan [...] vicious, cowardly acts against innocent people in our country. If this happens, it is our right to seek out and destroy [them] wherever they may be" (Author's collection).
3. Roland Axelsson: Memorandum ('Anteckningar från besök i Tanzania 29 mars-3 april 1990'/'Notes from visit to Tanzania, 29 March-3 April 1990'), Swedish embassy, Lusaka, 9 April 1990 (SDA).

Apartheid's military operations and destabilization policies have been noted in the context of Angola and Namibia.[1] As a general background to the presentation below, it should be recalled that the 'total strategy' against what was perceived as a 'Communist onslaught' was adopted as official state policy after the accession to the premiership of former Defence Minister P.W. Botha in September 1978.[2] Largely emboldened by the British and US governments under Margaret Thatcher and Ronald Reagan[3], it caused enormous material damage and untold human suffering in Southern Africa. In purely monetary terms, the UN Economic Commission for Africa calculated in 1989 that the region's economic losses due to South Africa's cross-border operations over the 1980-88 period exceeded 60 billion USD. The number of war-related deaths was for the same period estimated at 1.5 million, of which almost 1 million were children.[4]

With the overall objective to establish a *cordon sanitaire* vis-à-vis the independent African states, 'total strategy' included in addition to direct military attacks and covert operations against ANC and SWAPO a number of elements aiming at stemming the anti-apartheid tide, destabilizing the Frontline States and forcing them into acquiescent, subordinate relations. As stated by Hanlon,

> South Africa's white leadership [...] concluded that the best way to preserve minority rule [was] to fight [the] war outside South Africa [and] to open up a 'second front' in the neighbouring states. The goal [was] nothing less than control of the neighbours. Pretoria intend[ed] to keep them in thrall and thus to create a buffer against both the southward tide of majority rule and against international campaigns for sanctions.[5]

Pursuing this cause, Pretoria sponsored and supplied UNITA of Angola, RENAMO of Mozambique[6], LLA of Lesotho[7] and other "surrogate forces"[8] waging armed

---

1. See the chapter 'Cold War, Total Strategy and Expanded Assistance' on Namibia.
2. In August 1979, the South African State Security Council (SCC) established a coordinating body, which in addition to SADF, the South African Police and the National Intelligence Service included the Departments of Foreign Affairs, Finance and Trade and Industry, as well as South African Railways and the South African Broadcasting Corporation (TRC op. cit. (Vol. II), p. 87). "Guidelines" for cross-border operations were also issued by SCC in 1979 (ibid., p. 145).
3. Leading the British Conservative Party, Thatcher became Prime Minister in 1979. Reagan—the Republican candidate—won the US presidential elections in late 1980. The terms of office of Botha, Thatcher and Reagan largely overlapped. Botha served as Prime Minister and—from 1984—as President of South Africa between 1978 and 1989. While Thatcher's premiership lasted from 1979 to 1990, Reagan held the US presidency between 1981 and 1989.
4. UN Economic Commission for Africa op. cit., p. 6.
5. Hanlon op. cit., p. 1.
6. Set up in the mid-1970s by the Smith regime in Rhodesia to combat ZANU and destabilize the FRELIMO government in Mozambique, in March 1980—immediately after the independence elections in Zimbabwe—RENAMO was together with Bishop Muzorewa's 'auxiliaries' and a large number of Rhodesian military and security personnel transferred in a clandestine operation to South Africa. All in all, some 5,000 Rhodesians were recruited into SADF. RENAMO was subsequently based in northern Transvaal, with operational headquarters near Phalaborwa. On the SADF payroll, the RENAMO President Afonso Dhlakama, six senior officers and their families were hosted on a farm north of Pretoria (TRC op. cit. (Vol. II), pp. 89 and 93).
7. Lesotho Liberation Army. Although officially based in Botswana, the LLA leader Ntsu Mokhehle—future Prime Minister of Lesotho (1993-98)—spent long periods in South Africa in the early 1980s. According to the South African Truth and Reconciliation Commission, he was *inter alia* given accommodation at Vlakplaas, the secret base of apartheid's death squads (ibid., p. 96).
8. Ibid., pp. 88-92.

struggle against the Frontline States.[1] Road and rail networks; oil tanks; electricity, water, fuel and communications lines; factories, schools and clinics; and other economic and social facilities across Southern Africa were attacked.[2] At the same time as direct and indirect military sticks were wielded—and the infrastructure of the target countries was being ruined—economic carrots were also dangled. At the end of the 1970s, the Botha regime launched the idea of a 'Constellation of States' (CONSAS) which around a South African hub would include the 'independent' bantustans; Botswana, Lesotho and Swaziland; acquiescent Malawi, Namibia under a DTA dispensation and Zimbabwe ruled by Bishop Muzorewa. Proposing a number of joint projects, it was assumed that 'home brewed' South African capitalism would be more attractive than 'foreign' socialist alternatives.

Euphemistically advocating "regional solutions to regional problems", the CONSAS concept was coupled with policies of enticing the proposed member states into non-aggression pacts with Pretoria in order to promote "mutual defence against a common enemy".[3] The objective was, as noted by Davies, to make "South Africa [...] internationally recognised as the *de facto* 'regional power' with whom the major powers would have to deal".[4]

Based on the false assumptions that the independent Southern African states feared socialism more than apartheid and that Bishop Muzorewa commanded a popular majority[5], the CONSAS proposal was, however, shattered by the outcome of the independence elections held in Zimbabwe in late February 1980. As subsequently noted by Deon Geldenhuys, a leading South African academic interpreter of the overall objectives of 'total strategy',

> Robert Mugabe's victory in the 1980 independence election was greeted with disbelief and alarm in South Africa's ruling circles. Mugabe used to be portrayed as the archetype Marxist terrorist chief, and prior to his assumption of power dire warnings were sounded [...] about the havoc a Patriotic Front regime would wreak not only in Zimbabwe, but [in] Southern Africa generally.[6]

Moreover, three weeks later—on 1 April 1980—the Southern Africa Development Coordination Conference (SADCC) was formed in Lusaka. With "the reduction of economic dependence, particularly, but not only, on the Republic of South Africa"

---

1. UNITA, in particular, also carried out military operations against ANC. In fact, in 1998 the Truth and Reconciliation Commission concluded that "considerably more MK combatants were killed in [...] 'UNITA ambushes' [in Angola] than by the SADF [...]. This was, indeed, the single largest cause of unnatural deaths amongst ANC members in exile" (ibid., p. 95).

2. In Mozambique, the Cabora Bassa electricity network was so frequently sabotaged that it was inoperative for more than a decade. The pipeline, road and railway from Beira to Zimbabwe were other 'standing targets'. Between 1982 and 1987, the pipeline was ruptured on no less than thirty-seven occasions (ibid., p. 155).

3. Robert Davies: *South African Strategy towards Mozambique in the Post-Nkomati Period: A Critical Analysis of Effects and Implications*, Research Report No. 73, Scandinavian Institute of African Studies, Uppsala, 1985, p. 10.

4. Ibid.

5. The apartheid government channelled in excess of 12 million South African Rands in support of Bishop Muzorewa's UANC in the 1980 Zimbabwe independence elections. Approximately half of the amount came from state coffers, while the rest was raised from the private sector by Foreign Minister 'Pik' Botha (TRC op. cit. (Vol. II), p. 88).

6. Deon Geldenhuys: 'The Destabilisation Controversy: An Analysis of a High-Risk Foreign Policy Option for South Africa' in William Gutteridge (ed.): *South Africa: From Apartheid to National Unity, 1981-1994*, Dartmouth Publishing, Aldershot, 1995, p. 17. Geldenhuys' often quoted article was first published in *Politikon*, the South African Journal of Political Science, in December 1982.

as its main objective[1], in addition to the Frontline States of Angola, Botswana, Mozambique, Tanzania and Zambia among the nine constituent members were to Pretoria's great shock also Lesotho, Malawi[2], Swaziland and Zimbabwe, the latter before its formal independence.

Forced to abandon the CONSAS idea, these setbacks precipitated the apartheid regime's embarking on a generalized and indiscriminate course of regional destabilization. The more immediate aims of the overt and covert actions were

- that regional states both refuse to permit liberation movements to operate from their territories and take steps to prevent these movements from operating clandestinely,

- that regional states do not develop strong economic or, more particularly, military ties with socialist countries,

- that regional states maintain and even deepen their economic links with South Africa and refrain from supporting calls for sanctions [...], and

- that regional states 'moderate' their criticisms of apartheid.[3]

A prerequisite for official Swedish assistance to ANC was that it was acceptable to the host countries. Sweden maintained close relations with most of the SADCC states[4], and—as earlier noted—clearance concerning support to the liberation movements was as a rule requested and accepted.[5] Events following upon the Zimbabwe elections would, however, cause concern in this regard. Whereas Swaziland—with which Sweden maintained only limited relations—had never openly supported ANC and the Swazi police from the mid-1970s intervened against its members, restrictions against the movement were as a result of South African pressure in early 1980 also imposed by Botswana, Mozambique and, to a certain extent, Zambia, all of them Frontline States with close Swedish links. At a time when the Swedish ANC assistance had reached a level of 20 MSEK and the framework of the cooperation had been defined, Pretoria was forcing several Southern African states to distance themselves from the movement.

---

1. SADCC: 'Southern Africa: Toward Economic Liberation', Lusaka, 1 April 1980.

2. The fact that Malawi joined SADCC was particularly remarkable. Under President Kamuzu Banda, the country had since independence in July 1964 embarked on a unique course among the African states, establishing close relations with the white minority regimes in South Africa, Rhodesia and the Portuguese colonies. Swedish development assistance was for this reason not extended to Malawi, nor was a diplomatic mission opened in the country.

3. Davies op. cit., p. 11.

4. Sweden extended bilateral development assistance to all the SADCC states except Malawi. Together with the other Nordic countries, it would from the outset also become one of SADCC's leading donors. According to OECD, the Swedish share of total aid disbursements from its member states to the nine SADCC countries was in the period 1981- 85 no less than 14.2 per cent. The Nordic share was at the same time 29.9 per cent (Sellström Volume I, pp. 54-55). By 1980, Sweden had diplomatic missions in all the SADCC capitals barring Lilongwe (Malawi), Maseru (Lesotho) and Mbabane (Swaziland). An embassy was opened in Maseru in July 1985.

5. During the 'détente exercise' in the mid-1970s, Swedish financial assistance towards land acquisitions by ANC, SWAPO and ZANU was for security reasons not supported by Zambia. There was, however, no fundamental conflict between the Swedish and Zambian governments. Interviewed in 1995, the former President Kenneth Kaunda stated that his government was "very happy" to accept Swedish—and Nordic—assistance to the Southern African liberation movements based in the country. He added that "if the Nordic countries for any reason had given them armed support, we would not have had any objections at all. Not with the Nordic countries" (Interview with Kenneth Kaunda, p. 241).

In the case of Botswana—where the movement had less than 100 permanent members[1]; there was no official ANC office[2]; and the Swedish budget for 'daily necessities' in 1979/80 only amounted to 300,000 SEK[3]—"in rather unpleasant ways"[4] in mid-March 1980 the police carried out preventive raids against South African and other refugees, moving them to Dukwe, some 140 kilometres west of Francistown.[5] Joe Gqabi, a member of the National Executive Committee, ANC's 'senior official' and Sweden's main contact in the country, was forced to leave three months later.[6] In addition to detentions, in early 1981 South African refugees were, finally, handed over to the apartheid authorities, which provoked strong protests from UNHCR and a critical *démarche* from Sweden to the Masire government.[7] As stated by Thabo Mbeki during a regional meeting with SIDA representatives in Lusaka in September 1981, Botswana had from early 1980 in response to South African pressure embarked on a "movement backwards".[8]

Although enforced with less zeal, restrictive measures were at the same time carried out by the Mozambican government. Swedish assistance to ANC in Mozam-

---

1. Letter ('Samtal med befrielserörelser i Gaborone'/'Conversations with liberation movements in Gaborone') with attachments from Irene Larsson, Swedish ambassador to Botswana, to the Ministry for Foreign Affairs, Swedish embassy, Gaborone, 12 March 1979 (SDA) and Sten Rylander: Memorandum ('ANC's framställning om bistånd 1980/81'/'ANC's request for assistance in 1980/81'), Swedish embassy, Gaborone, 28 March 1980 (SDA).

2. As late as in 1980, there were no official ANC offices in Botswana, Lesotho, Swaziland or Mozambique (Birgitta Berggren: Memorandum ('Besök på SIDA den 14 april 1980 av President Oliver Tambo, African National Congress, South Africa'/'Visit at SIDA 14 April 1980 by President Oliver Tambo, ANC'), SIDA, 23 April 1980) (SDA).

3. 'Agreed minutes from discussions on the cooperation between the African National Congress of South Africa (ANC) and the Swedish International Development Authority (SIDA)', Lusaka, 18 May 1979 (SDA).

4. Sten Rylander: Memorandum ('ANC's framställning om bistånd 1980/81'/'ANC's request for assistance in 1980/81'), Swedish embassy, Gaborone, 28 March 1980 (SDA).

5. Ibid. The camp at Dukwe had been established in the 1970s to accommodate refugees from Zimbabwe.

6. Irene Larsson: Memorandum ('Botswanas politik visavi flyktingar och befrielserörelser'/'Botswana's policy towards refugees and liberation movements'), Swedish embassy, Gaborone, 12 June 1980 (SDA) and Sten Rylander: Memorandum ('Befrielserörelser och flyktingar i Botswana: Samtal med ANC och SWAPO'/'Liberation movements and refugees in Botswana: Conversations with ANC and SWAPO'), Swedish embassy, Gaborone, 9 September 1981 (SDA). Gqabi subsequently moved to Zimbabwe. Serving as ANC's *de facto* representative, he maintained close relations with the Swedish embassy in Harare, often staying in the residence of SIDA's Ola Jämtin. After several attempts on his life, in late July 1981 Gqabi was assassinated by South African agents.

7. Sten Rylander: Memorandum ('Befrielserörelser och flyktingar i Botswana: Samtal med ANC och SWAPO'/ 'Liberation movements and refugees in Botswana: Conversations with ANC and SWAPO'), Swedish embassy, Gaborone, 9 September 1981 (SDA). According to Thabo Mbeki—whose younger brother Jama was detained in Botswana in mid-1981, accused of being involved in the murder of a South African agent, and who shortly thereafter visited the country for discussions with the government—the authorities had not only invented charges against ANC members, but in several cases also tortured them (ibid.). It should be noted that the relations between ANC and Botswana improved after a meeting between Oliver Tambo and President Quett Masire in Gaborone in August 1981 (ibid.). Jama Mbeki was set free on bail. He later disappeared in unclear circumstances. According to Mbeki's biographer Gevisser, he was possibly murdered in Lesotho in 1983 (Mark Gevisser: 'The family man', Part one of a six-part 'Thabo Mbeki story' in *Sunday Times*, 16 May 1999).

8. Sten Rylander: Memorandum ('Befrielserörelser och flyktingar i Botswana: Samtal med ANC och SWAPO'/'Liberation movements and refugees in Botswana: Conversations with ANC and SWAPO'), Swedish embassy, Gaborone, 9 September 1981 (SDA). Viewing the developments with "serious concern", the SWAPO leader Aaron Mushimba stated at the same time that Botswana was "drifting" (ibid.).

bique had mostly been used for onward transportation of refugees arriving after the Soweto uprising. For the financial year 1979/80, 500,000 SEK had been set aside for daily necessities in the country, mainly targeting people in transit.[1] ANC and FRELIMO had close and long-standing relations. Following sharp warnings from Pretoria, after ZANU's electoral victory in Zimbabwe some 40 ANC members were, however, requested to leave with immediate effect, while the bulk of the South African refugees were moved to the Nampula province in the northern parts of the country.[2]

ANC's situation in Mozambique was discussed in March 1980 by Presidents Tambo and Machel. The talks made it clear that "Mozambique [was] not ready to grant ANC [any] support over and above what was [already] extended".[3] In March 1980, SIDA's Bo Westman at the Swedish embassy in Maputo reported that "Zimbabwe's independence has [...] not improved ANC's possibilities to wage armed struggle [from Mozambique]".[4] This impression seemed the following month to be confirmed by Oliver Tambo, who during discussions with the authorities in Stockholm regretted that the FRELIMO government due to South African threats was restricting ANC's freedom of movement.[5]

While the government of Chief Leabua Jonathan in the exposed enclave of Lesotho

1. 'Agreed minutes from discussions on the cooperation between the African National Congress of South Africa (ANC) and the Swedish International Development Authority (SIDA)', Lusaka, 18 May 1979 (SDA).

2. Bo Westman: Memorandum ('Humanitarian assistance to Southern Africa during the [19]80s'), Swedish embassy, Maputo, 10 March 1980 (SDA). ANC was promised land in Nampula province. During the 1981 aid negotiations between Sweden and ANC, an initial amount of 100,000 SEK was set aside for development of a proposed site ('Agreed minutes of discussions in Lusaka, May 1981, on the cooperation between the African National Congress of South Africa, ANC, and the Swedish International Development Authority, SIDA', Lusaka, 18 May 1981) (SDA). Similar allocations were made for 1982/83 and 1983/84. By early 1982, some 300 ANC refugees had been moved to Nampula, where those who could not continue to Tanzania and Angola faced an "extremely difficult situation" (Bo Westman: Memorandum ('ANC in Maputo and Swaziland'), Swedish embassy, Maputo, 23 April 1982) (SDA). Due to South African attacks and RENAMO operations, the Mozambican authorities would, however, reconsider the idea of a permanent ANC settlement in the country. As late as in February 1983, the proposed project had not got off the ground (Tor Sellström: Memorandum ('Biståndsframställningar från ANC och SACTU 1983/84'/'Requests for assistance from ANC and SACTU in 1983/84'), Swedish embassy, Maputo, 9 February 1983) (SDA). To ANC's great disappointment, the Nampula farm never became a reality. It should, however, be noted that the movement was allowed to establish a piggery project in Matola on the outskirts of Maputo. Surprisingly, it was not closed down after the Nkomati Accord, but continued with Swedish support throughout the 1980s (Roland Axelsson: Memorandum ('Anteckningar från besök i Maputo 5-6 april 1990'/'Notes from visit to Maputo, 5-6 April 1990'), Swedish embassy, Lusaka, 17 April 1990) (SDA).

3. Bo Westman: Memorandum ('Humanitarian assistance to Southern Africa during the [19]80s'), Swedish embassy, Maputo, 10 March 1980 (SDA). Westman based his assessment on information given by ANC's local representatives.

4. Ibid.

5. Birgitta Berggren: Memorandum ('Minnesanteckningar från samtal på SIDA den 14 april 1980 med president Oliver Tambo, African National Congress, South Africa'/'Notes from conversations at SIDA 14 April 1980 with President Oliver Tambo, ANC'), SIDA, Stockholm, 21 April 1980 (SDA). The FRELIMO government maintained complex and contradictory relations with ANC. At the same time as South African refugees seeking contact with the movement either were moved from the Maputo area or had to leave the country, many skilled ANC members were given official employment. Prominent representatives—among them Ruth First and Albie Sachs—worked for the Mozambican government. In addition to ANC officials such as Lennox Lagu and Jacob Zuma, many SACP and SACTU cadres also lived in the country. Above all, with the Machel government's tacit consent, Joe Slovo set up an underground MK Special Operations Unit in Maputo in 1980 (Barrell Ph. D. op. cit., chapter three, p. 33).

in marked contrast to Swaziland firmly resisted Pretoria's pressure[1], even Zambia—hosting the ANC headquarters—in early 1980 through the Ministry of Defence warned the movement to limit its activities. Not more than twenty ANC officials would be allowed to remain.[2] According to Thabo Mbeki, the directive was, however, not authorized by President Kaunda, and by mid-1980 the restrictions had been lifted.[3]

In spite of the generally worsening security conditions in the region, the Fälldin government did not suspend the ANC assistance in the forward areas. This stand was confirmed after discussions with Oliver Tambo in mid-April 1980. Visiting Stockholm to address an ICSA conference, in meetings with the Prime Minister[4] and SIDA[5], the ANC leader convincingly pleaded for continued support also in the exposed neighbouring states to South Africa. At the official aid negotiations in Lusaka the following month, the budgeted amounts for daily necessities in Botswana, Lesotho, Swaziland and Mozambique during 1980/81 were thus not only maintained, but substantially increased.[6]

In a complex set of relations vis-à-vis the host countries and the South African liberation movement, Sweden assumed a pro-active—and sometimes interventionist—role in favour and on behalf of the latter. In combination with the 'home front

1. The friendly relationship between Lesotho and South Africa deteriorated radically towards the end of the decade. Chris Hani had settled in Lesotho in 1974. After the Soweto uprising, the country became an important sanctuary and transit country for South African refugees. Swedish assistance in the form of daily necessities was extended to ANC in Lesotho from the financial year 1976/77, when an amount of 70,000 SEK was allocated ('Agreed minutes of discussions on cooperation between Sweden and the African National Congress of South Africa', Lusaka, 1 September 1976) (SDA). According to Hani, there were at the end of 1979 around 200 ANC members and an additional 800 sympathizers in the country (Sten Rylander: Memorandum ('Lesotho och ANC's verksamhet i Sydafrika'/'Lesotho and ANC's activities in South Africa'), Swedish embassy, Gaborone, 9 November 1979) (SDA). Against this background, the Swedish budget was regularly increased, reaching no less than 1 MSEK in 1981/82 ('Agreed minutes of discussions in Lusaka, May 1981, on the cooperation between the African National Congress of South Africa, ANC, and the Swedish International Development Authority, SIDA', Lusaka, 18 May 1981) (SDA). Visiting Sweden shortly after the independence elections in Zimbabwe, Oliver Tambo stressed the positive role played by the Jonathan government in spite of mounting South African pressure (Birgitta Berggren: Memorandum ('Minnesanteckningar från samtal på SIDA den 14 april 1980 med president Oliver Tambo, African National Congress, South Africa'/ 'Notes from conversations at SIDA 14 April 1980 with President Oliver Tambo, ANC'), SIDA, Stockholm, 21 April 1980) (SDA). By early 1981, Lesotho, too, had, however, been forced by Pretoria to reconsider its support for ANC. Hani was asked by Foreign Minister Charles Molapo to leave the country. While the decision was revoked by Prime Minister Jonathan (Cable from Irene Larsson, Swedish ambassador to Botswana and Lesotho, to the Ministry for Foreign Affairs, Gaborone, 28 April 1981) (SDA), towards the end of 1981 the ANC leadership in Lusaka also suggested that due to the worsening security situation Hani should leave (Letter ('Lesotho') from Göran Hasselmark, Swedish ambassador to Zambia, to the Ministry for Foreign Affairs, Lusaka, 18 November 1981) (MFA). He was eventually forced to abandon Lesotho in May 1982 (Karl-Göran Engström: Memorandum ('ANC Lesotho'), Swedish embassy, Gaborone, 22 November 1982) (SDA). Seven months later—on 9 December 1982—more than a hundred South African commandos descended on Maseru, killing thirty South African refugees and twelve Lesotho nationals. As in Swaziland and—to a lesser extent—Botswana, the Swedish support would from then on largely assume the character of humanitarian contingency assistance.
2. Göran Hasselmark: Memorandum ('ANC i Zambia'/'ANC in Zambia'), Swedish embassy, Lusaka, 29 July 1980 (SDA).
3. Ibid.
4. Göran Zetterqvist: Memorandum ('Besök av ANC's president hos statsministern'/'The ANC President visiting the Prime Minister'), Ministry for Foreign Affairs, Stockholm, 21 April 1980 (SDA). The meeting between Fälldin and Tambo was *inter alia* attended by Thabo Mbeki. It took place on 14 April 1980. During the discussion, Fälldin "emphasized that Sweden would continue to intensify its support for the liberation struggle in South Africa, politically as well as [in the form of] assistance" (ibid.).
5. Birgitta Berggren: Memorandum ('Besök på SIDA den 14 april 1980 av President Oliver Tambo, African National Congress, South Africa'/'Visit at SIDA 14 April 1980 by President Oliver Tambo, ANC'), SIDA, Stockholm, 23 April 1980 (SDA).
6. 'Minutes from discussions on the cooperation between the African National Congress of South Africa (ANC) and the Swedish International Development Authority (SIDA), May 1980', Lusaka, 29 May 1980 (SDA). Led by Nkobi, Mbeki formed part of the ANC delegation.

component', this, in turn, consolidated the mutual bonds.[1] Presenting the cooperation between Sweden and ANC in the forward areas, the following overview
attempts to illustrate some of the main developments in this regard.

Apartheid's Second Front

With the opening of 'apartheid's second front'[2], Pretoria would from the late 1970s
wreak havoc over Southern Africa.[3] Embarking on a rearguard action against inevitable political change, the apartheid regime reacted to the outcome of the independence elections in Zimbabwe by unleashing unprecedented assaults on the region's
independent states, ANC and SWAPO. An account of Pretoria's wars falls outside
the scope of this study.[4] In the context of Sweden's assistance to ANC, it should,
however, be borne in mind that the movement—which before 1980 had certainly
not been spared covert actions against its exiled members[5]—in the early and mid-
1980s increasingly became the target of cross-border operations.

In addition to large-scale military attacks on Matola outside Maputo in January
1981[6], Maseru in December 1982 and Gaborone in June 1985—which together
claimed the lives of 54 ANC members and 17 local citizens or permanent residents,
many of whom were children[7]—leading representatives of the movement fell victim
to assassinations carried out by Pretoria's secret death squads. Joe Gqabi, ANC's
senior official in Zimbabwe, was killed in Harare in July 1981 and Ruth First in
Maputo a year later. Cassius Make (aka Job Tlhabane)—with whom Swedish
assistance to Angola had been discussed in 1976—was gunned down outside Manzini, Swaziland, in July 1987. Casting the net outside Southern Africa, in March
1982 ANC's London office was bombed by South African operatives—notably

1. Cf. the interview with Thabo Mbeki, pp. 155-56.
2. Hanlon op. cit.
3. It should be noted that at the end of the 1970s ANC and Pretoria embarked on opposite paths. While ANC's
   1978-79 strategic review concluded that primacy should be given to political mobilization inside South
   Africa, the apartheid regime chose to go to war outside its borders.
4. See, for example, Gavin Cawthra: *Brutal Force: The Apartheid War Machine*, International Defence and Aid
   Fund for Southern Africa, London, 1986; Joseph Hanlon: *Beggar Your Neighbours: Apartheid Power in
   Southern Africa*, Catholic Institute for International Relations, London, with James Currey and Indiana University Press, London and Bloomington, 1986; and Johnson and Martin (eds) op. cit. On South Africa's covert
   operations, cf. also Pauw (1991) op. cit., Pauw (1997) op. cit. and TRC op. cit.
5. The first cross-border assassinations carried out by Pretoria occurred in February 1974, when—within two
   weeks of each other—SASO's Abraham Onkgopotse Tiro and ANC's John Dube (aka Boy Mvemve), Deputy
   Chief Representative to Zambia, were killed by letter bombs in Botswana and Zambia, respectively. A
   detailed catalogue of external "assassinations, ambushes and abductions" is found in TRC op. cit. (Vol. II),
   pp. 97-134. Cross-border "military operations, raids, sabotage and arson" are presented in ibid., pp. 144-63.
   In his first study on apartheid's death squads, Pauw, too, lists "political assassinations of anti-apartheid activists". Covering the period 1971-91, his list includes murders committed both inside and outside South Africa.
   Although far from comprehensive, it is for the purpose of the discussion above relevant to note that more
   politically motivated assassinations during the period were carried out outside South Africa than within the
   country. Out of the 225 people listed, 138 were killed in cross-border operations—mainly in the forward
   areas—and 87 inside the apartheid republic (Pauw (1991) op. cit., pp. 270-86).
6. Several of the sixteen ANC cadres killed in the Matola raid were known to the Swedish government and solidarity movement. Invited by the Africa Groups, William Khanyile, for example, had a year earlier—in January-February 1980—visited Sweden. Representing SACTU, he travelled the country, where in meetings with
   local trade unions he raised the issue of comprehensive sanctions against the apartheid regime (cf. the chapter
   'SACTU, Unions and Sanctions'). Three of the attackers—all of them Rhodesians recruited into SADF—died
   during the raid. One of them had his helmet decorated with a swastika and the words 'Follow Me'. The helmet was subsequently brought to Sweden, where it was exhibited by the ANC office in Stockholm.
7. Six ANC members and three Lesotho nationals were killed during yet another large-scale raid on Maseru in
   December 1985. In May 1986, SADF launched simultaneous attacks on Gaborone, Harare and Lusaka.
   While there were no ANC casualties, three nationals died and around twenty were injured.

including Craig Williamson[1] —and in September 1986 its Stockholm premises were similarly targeted. Dulcie September, ANC Chief Representative to France, was shot in Paris in March 1988.

While these actions were widely covered by South African and international media, covert actions carried out against ANC officials and structures in the forward areas were seldom registered. After a number of attempts on his life, in January 1978[2], for example, Bafana Duma, ANC's representative in Swaziland, lost one arm and suffered serious facial injuries through an explosive device placed inside a post office box in Manzini.[3] Four years later—in June 1982—the movement's acting head in the country, Petrus Nyawose, was killed together with his wife in a car explosion outside their flat, also in Manzini.[4] In addition, ANC offices in the region were regularly attacked. Apart from the above mentioned raids on Maseru and Gaborone, this was, for example, the case in Maputo in October 1983 and in Harare in May 1986, as well as in May 1987.

Targeting ANC's representatives and offices, apartheid's operations seriously affected the implementation of the Swedish assistance, particularly in the so called BLS countries.[5] Over the years, many senior ANC officials with whom the local support initially had been designed were killed, maimed or—as in the case in 1980 of Joe Gqabi in Botswana and in 1982 of Chris Hani in Lesotho and Stanley Mabizela in Swaziland[6]—forced to leave. In their stead, representatives with less experience and authority were appointed. When they, too, were assassinated, abducted or expelled, locally based 'caretakers' with only weak lines of communication to ANC in Lusaka were nominated to act on the movement's behalf.

In the process, serious administrative problems emerged. In addition to documents lost in South African attacks, disbursement and distribution routines were disrupted and misappropriations occurred. As a result, from the early 1980s ANC's reports on the assistance in the forward areas were often incomplete or defective. This notwithstanding, on the basis of ANC's requests Sweden would throughout the decade[7] extend official humanitarian support in the form of daily necessities for its members and their dependants in the forward areas.

---

1. As noted, the Swede Bertil Wedin—later mentioned in connection with the Palme assassination—was at the time working for Williamson in London (cf. the chapter 'MPLA of Angola: A Rockier Road').

2. The report by the Truth and Reconciliation Commission states that the assassination attempt took place in January 1977 (TRC op. cit. (Vol. II), p. 101). The actual date was 23 January 1978 (Bo Westman: Memorandum ('Bombattentat mot ANC-medlem i Swaziland'/'Bomb attack on ANC member in Swaziland'), Swedish embassy, Maputo, 21 February 1978) (SDA). See also 'Hunt is on for bomber—PM' in *The Times of Swaziland*, 30 January 1978.

3. The assassination attempt was carried out by the Ermelo security police in South Africa (TRC op. cit. (Vol. II), p. 101).

4. The operation was sanctioned by the Pretoria government and the killers were awarded the official medal 'Police Star for Outstanding Service' (ibid., p. 106). Two years before—in May 1980—Nyawose had formed part of the ANC delegation to the annual aid negotiations with Sweden in Lusaka ('Minutes from discussions on the cooperation between the African National Congress of South Africa (ANC) and the Swedish International Development Authority (SIDA), May 1980', Lusaka, 29 May 1980) (SDA).

5. That is, Botswana, Lesotho and Swaziland.

6. Following the security pact between South Africa and Swaziland—signed in February 1982—Mabizela was forced to leave (Bo Westman: Memorandum ('ANC in Maputo and Swaziland'), Swedish embassy, Maputo, 23 April 1982) (SDA). He subsequently served as ANC's Chief Representative to Tanzania and, later, to Zimbabwe.

7. The support to ANC in Lesotho was brought to an end in 1989.

In the cases of Swaziland and—from 1986—Lesotho, the assistance to ANC was, in addition, granted contrary to the policies pursued by the host countries. From the point of view of international relations, the Swedish government's stand was in this regard remarkably interventionist. It is, in fact, doubtful whether Sweden in the Cold War period anywhere else so decidedly supported a political movement which was opposed by third party governments with whom bilateral diplomatic relations were maintained.[1]

The stand was also remarkably indulgent towards ANC. After Hani's forced departure from Lesotho, in November 1982 the Swedish ambassador Karl-Göran Engström reported, for example, that local financial control was inadequate; that the quarterly accounts received from the new representation "cannot be approved"; and—against this background—that "we do not intend to disburse more funds until [...] the situation [...] is clarified".[2] As the livelihood of scores of ANC rank and file members in Lesotho thereby would be affected, the authorities in Stockholm, however, took a different position. After consultations with the Ministry for Foreign Affairs, SIDA replied that "[i]t is our opinion that funds for the time being may be disbursed, despite deficient reporting".[3]

While it stressed the need for "satisfactory information" concerning the humanitarian content of the assistance[4], the reply from Stockholm may illustrate both the overall trust established vis-à-vis ANC and the forbearance towards the movement's precarious situation and needs in the forward areas. In Swaziland, Mozambique and Lesotho, the problems would, however, be considerably compounded when in 1982, 1984 and 1986, respectively, they succumbed to Pretoria's pressure and entered into formal security arrangements with the apartheid regime, largely targeting ANC.[5] In the process, Sweden had to weigh the humanitarian assistance to the South African liberation movement against its bilateral relations with these countries.

Swaziland

The small Kingdom of Swaziland—sandwiched between Mozambique and South Africa—was of great strategic importance to ANC. Despite close historical links to

---

1. With similarities to the ANC 'home front component', official assistance was concurrently channelled to Lech Walesa's Solidarity opposition movement against the Communist regime in Poland. In contrast to the ANC support, it was, however, neither governed by an official agreement, nor extended in third countries averse to it. Of less magnitude, the same could be said about the support to various opposition movements in Latin America.
2. Karl-Göran Engström: Memorandum ('ANC Lesotho'), Swedish embassy, Gaborone, 22 November 1982 (SDA).
3. Letter ('Utbetalningar ANC-Lesotho'/'Disbursements ANC-Lesotho') from Ulla Ström to the Swedish embassy in Gaborone, SIDA, Stockholm, 20 December 1982 (SDA).
4. Ibid. At the bilateral negotiations in May 1982, the Swedish assistance to ANC in Lesotho was increased from 1.0 to 1.2 MSEK. After Angola (5.0) and Tanzania (2.4)—but notably before Zambia (1.0)—with regard to daily necessities, Lesotho in 1982/83 thus occupied a prominent third position among ANC's host countries.
5. In February 1984—one month before the Nkomati Accord with Mozambique—South Africa also negotiated with Angola. Arranged by the US government, an agreement on troop withdrawals was reached in principle in Lusaka. Extremely limited and from the outset a dead letter, it did not, however, concern ANC, but primarily SWAPO and UNITA.

the Swazi royal house[1], the movement's position there was, however, far from secure. In the period preceding the June 1976 Soweto uprising, members of the organization were abducted and taken to South Africa. Thabo Mbeki—then ANC Acting Chief Representative to Swaziland—Jacob Zuma and Albert Dhlomo were detained and expelled to Mozambique. Intervening on ANC's behalf, the detention of Mbeki and his colleagues prompted the Swedish government to express its concern to the Swazi authorities.[2]

With a token amount of 5,000 SEK, official assistance for 'daily necessities' was extended to ANC in Swaziland from the financial year 1976/77.[3] Scores of young people fleeing from the post-Soweto repression would at the same time cross the border into the country. In spite of increasing South African attacks and interventions by the Swazi police[4], on ANC's request the annual allocations were therefore regularly raised, reaching 500,000 SEK in 1980/81.[5] The funds were paid out in cash to ANC's representatives on a quarterly basis through visits by SIDA officials from the embassy in Maputo.

In the light of escalating conflicts between the Swazi government and the South African liberation movement, in the aftermath of Zimbabwe's independence the authorities in Stockholm found it necessary to raise the issue of ANC support with the Mbabane government. However, rather than being asked to obtain Swaziland's formal acceptance, ambassador Finn Bergstrand in Maputo—also accredited to Swaziland—was in July 1981 instructed by the Foreign Ministry to merely notify the Swazi authorities of the assistance. Referring to "our principle of always informing the host country [of] support to a liberation movement", the instruction read:

> The Swazi authorities should be aware [of the fact] that we [extend] humanitarian support to ANC in Swaziland. It has been the belief of the [Foreign Ministry] and SIDA that the Swazis were aware of the [...] assistance. Should this not be the case, they ought to be informed at an appropriate level.[6]

1. Under Queen Regent Labotsibeni—Sobhuza's grandmother—the Swazi royal house was closely associated with the formation of ANC in 1912 (cf. Peter Walshe: *The Rise of African Nationalism in South Africa: The African National Congress 1912-1952*, C. Hurst & Company, London, and University of California Press, Berkeley and Los Angeles, 1970, pp. 30-40. On Sobhuza and ANC, see also Hilda Kuper: *Sobhuza II: Ngwenyama and King of Swaziland*, Duckworth, London, 1978, passim). In his autobiography, Nelson Mandela describes Sobhuza as "an enlightened traditional leader and also a member of the ANC" (Mandela op. cit., p. 482). After Mandela's imprisonment on Robben Island, Winnie Mandela placed their daughters Zenani and Zindzi at boarding schools in Swaziland, where Zenani in 1977 married Prince Thumbumuzi, a son of King Sobhuza. Walter and Albertina Sisulu's son Zwelakhe and daughter Lindiwe also studied and lived in the country, as did children of other South African nationalist leaders. The relations between ANC and Swaziland were thus complex and contradictory. This could be illustrated by the following anecdote, related by Stanley Mabizela to the author in the early 1980s: After a shootout between the Swazi police and ANC freedom fighters, Sobhuza summoned his police commissioner and Mabizela to the royal kraal. After hearing the two parties' versions of the events, Sobhuza was most upset. Calling the Swazi Commissioner of Police "a dog" and ordering him to leave by crawling backwards, he turned to Mabizela and said: "What shall I tell Labotsibeni?" (Author's recollection. Labotsibeni died in 1925).
2. See the chapter 'ANC of South Africa: No Easy Walk'.
3. 'Agreed minutes of discussions on cooperation between Sweden and the African National Congress of South Africa', Lusaka, 1 September 1976 (SDA). The amount of 5,000 SEK could be compared with the allocations of 70,000 and 100,000 SEK extended to ANC in Lesotho and Botswana, respectively (ibid.).
4. The assassination attempt in January 1978 against the ANC representative Bafana Duma has been mentioned. In August 1978, the Swazi police raided a number of ANC residences, detaining eleven members and impounding their vehicles (Bo Westman: Memorandum ('Interview with ANC representative in Swaziland'), Swedish embassy, Maputo, 6 September 1978) (SDA).
5. 'Minutes from discussions on the cooperation between the African National Congress of South Africa (ANC) and the Swedish International Development Authority (SIDA), May 1980', Lusaka, 29 May 1980 (SDA).
6. Cable ('Utbetalning av stöd till ANC'/'Disbursement of support to ANC') from the Ministry for Foreign Affairs to the Swedish embassy in Maputo, Stockholm, 20 July 1981 (SDA).

Before any concrete steps were taken, the question was, however, raised with ANC. In a meeting in Zimbabwe the following month, Thabo Mbeki told Anders Bjurner from the Foreign Ministry that although some Swazi cabinet ministers were clearly "hostile" towards the movement, King Sobhuza himself had given ANC permission to remain and work in the country. Mbeki also said that ANC's "main contact person" was the Swazi Deputy Prime Minister Ben Nsibandze, recommending that confirmation was sought directly from him.[1] Ambassador Bergstrand was against this background instructed to "inform" Nsibandze of the Swedish assistance. Aware of its sensitivity, the authorities in Stockholm added that—"without dramatizing the issue"—Bergstrand "should receive confirmation that Swaziland does not oppose [humanitarian] support from Sweden to ANC".[2]

Bergstrand was received by Nsibandze in early November 1981. While the Deputy Prime Minister "did not react" to the information about the Swedish support—neither accepting nor rejecting it—he emphasized that "South Africa accused Swaziland of [...] not taking sufficiently effective measures to avoid becoming a launching site and a transit territory for perpetrators of attacks [against the republic]".[3] As in June 1976—when the Swazi authorities in similar circumstances had made it clear that the country could not become "a springboard for guerrilla activities"[4]—it could hardly be said that Swaziland welcomed assistance to ANC.

The authorities in Stockholm, however, interpreted Nsibandze's attitude differently. Responding to Bergstrand's report from the meeting, quite remarkably the Ministry for Foreign Affairs concluded that "no further steps are presently needed to assure us that the Swazi authorities are in agreement with Sweden's support to ANC".[5] At the annual negotiations six months later, it was on ANC's request agreed to raise the allocation for daily necessities in Swaziland from 600,000 SEK in 1981/82 to 700,000 SEK in 1982/83.[6]

By endorsing the allocation, Prime Minister Fälldin's Centre-Liberal government gave *de facto* precedence to the relations with ANC over those with Swaziland, a SADCC member to whom Sweden also extended bilateral development assistance. This was further accentuated by the Social Democratic government under Olof Palme, which returned to power in October 1982. Although Sweden as a principle had maintained that aid should not be used as a foreign policy tool to award or punish recipient developing countries, it decided to phase out the bilateral aid to Swaziland. Elaborating on the decision taken, in a letter to the Swedish embassy in Maputo the Foreign Ministry explained in January 1983 that

> we have [now] more grounds than in the past to question Swaziland's policy in a wider Southern African context. I am particularly thinking of [its] attitude towards ANC and the questionable, dubious contacts with South Africa [...]. Developments in Swaziland have simply gone in

---

1. Cable ('Om stöd till ANC i Swaziland'/'Re support to ANC in Swaziland') from the Ministry for Foreign Affairs to the Swedish embassy in Maputo, Stockholm, 1 September 1981 (SDA).
2. Ibid.
3. Finn Bergstrand: Memorandum ('Swaziland och ANC'/'Swaziland and ANC'), Swedish embassy, Maputo, 3 November 1981 (SDA).
4. Letter ('ANC i Swaziland') from Åke Fridell to the Ministry for Foreign Affairs, Swedish legation, Pretoria, 7 June 1976 (MFA).
5. Cable ('Re Swaziland och ANC') from the Ministry for Foreign Affairs to the Swedish embassy in Maputo, Stockholm, 20 November 1981 (SDA).
6. 'Agreed minutes of discussions in Lusaka, May 1982, between the African National Congress of South Africa, ANC, and the Swedish International Development Authority, SIDA, concerning humanitarian assistance', Lusaka, 24 May 1982 (SDA). SIDA's Director General Anders Forsse led the Swedish delegation.

the wrong direction with regard to the overriding objectives of [Sweden's] foreign and aid policy in [the region]".[1]

In the period between Bergstrand's meeting with Nsibandze and the decision a year later to phase out the bilateral assistance[2], significant developments had taken place. Shortly after the talks—on 1 December 1981—armed clashes took place between Swazi military forces and ANC members.[3] Although kept secret for more than two years[4]—but hinted at by Deputy Prime Minister Nsibandze and made evident through the actions of the Swazi police and army—in February 1982, Swaziland became the first independent Southern African country to give in to Pretoria's 'total strategy' by concluding a mutual security pact with the apartheid state. Targeting ANC[5], it *inter alia* laid down that

> the contracting parties shall live in peace and [...] not allow any activities within their respective territories directed towards the commission of any act which involves a threat or use of force against each other's territorial integrity. [...] The parties undertake to combat terrorism, insurgency and subversion individually and collectively, and shall call upon each other wherever possible for such assistance and steps as may be deemed necessary or expedient to eliminate this evil.[6]

In August 1982, finally, the Swazi regent King Sobhuza II died. With his death, the remaining threads in the umbilical cord between ANC and Swaziland were cut off.[7] In the following political turmoil, developments went from bad to worse. After the assassination of ANC's Acting Chief Representative in Swaziland, Petrus Nyawose, in June 1982, in October his successor, Nkosi Mvemwe, stated that she was heading towards a "nervous breakdown" and that the approximately 400 South African

---

1. Cited in Samuel Falle and Karlis Goppers: *Looking Both Ways: Swaziland between South Africa and SADCC, An Evaluation of Sweden's Development Cooperation with Swaziland*, SIDA Evaluation Report 1987:6, SIDA, Stockholm, 1988, p. 9. The decision to phase out bilateral aid to Swaziland was largely based on consultations with ANC and the government of Mozambique. As noted above, ANC was in general supportive of Swedish development assistance to the SADCC states. Albeit expressing concerns with regard to developments in the neighbouring country, as late as in January 1982 the Maputo government, too, recommended Sweden to maintain its assistance to Swaziland (Finn Bergstrand: Memorandum ('ANC och Swaziland'/'ANC and Swaziland'), Swedish embassy, Maputo, 27 January 1982) (SDA). The attitudes, however, rapidly changed after the death of King Sobhuza in August 1982. In the case of ANC, President Tambo turned from forbearance to rejection. During a meeting at the Ministry for Foreign Affairs in May 1983—after the Swedish decision to end the bilateral aid relationship—he stated that Swaziland had been "reduced to a glorified bantustan" which did not "deserve" development assistance (Anders Bjurner: Memorandum ('Överläggningar med Oliver Tambo, ANC's president'/'Deliberations with Oliver Tambo, ANC President'), Ministry for Foreign Affairs, Stockholm, 9 June 1983) (MFA). The meeting with Tambo took place on 3 May 1983.
2. While bilateral aid was phased out over the following years, Sweden supported regional SADCC projects in the country. In particular, it co-financed the rehabilitation and upgrading of the main road from central Swaziland to the Mozambican border.
3. Finn Bergstrand: Memorandum ('ANC och Swaziland'), Swedish embassy, Maputo, 7 December 1981 (SDA). See also 'Exército suázi combate ANC' ('The Swazi army combats ANC') in *Notícias*, 4 December 1981.
4. It was only on 31 March 1984—two weeks after the Nkomati Accord—that the Swazi and South African governments decided to make their security pact publicly known (cf. Johnson and Martin (eds) op. cit., pp. 337-38).
5. It should be noted that Swaziland before the security pact maintained close and friendly relations with South Africa. Unlike Mozambique—and, to a lesser extent, Lesotho—the country was never exposed to the crippling effects of surrogate forces sponsored by Pretoria.
6. Letters of exchange between Swaziland and South Africa, authorized by King Sobhuza, Kwaluseni, Swaziland, 17 February 1982 (MFA). The full text of the agreement is reproduced in Johnson and Martin (eds) op. cit., pp. 332-37. Not surprisingly, the security pact with South Africa and the clampdown on ANC led to severe tensions within the SADCC community. In an editorial comment, *Sunday Times* of Zambia stated in May 1984 that "Swaziland is really becoming an embarrassing thorn in the flesh for independent Africa in its activities against the liberation struggle in Southern Africa in general and the African National Congress of South Africa in particular. [...] She is a lost sheep" (*Sunday Times*, 6 May 1984). The author recalls that Angolan officials to a SADCC meeting in the early 1980s were detained upon arrival in Swaziland.
7. Representing ANC, Oliver Tambo was present at the funeral of King Sobhuza on 3 September 1982.

refugees in the country—the majority of whom belonged to ANC—were facing a "difficult situation".[1]

In "the biggest operation against the ANC ever mounted in Swaziland"[2], two months later—on 16 December 1982, ironically the day of Umkhonto we Sizwe—Mvemwe's fears were confirmed. Immediately following on the SADF attack on the Lesotho capital Maseru[3], in one major swoop the Swazi police arrested around 90 South African exiles, many of whom were residents in the country. Although most of them were released, 15 to 20 ANC and SACTU members were taken to a detention camp, while a similar number of MK freedom fighters were expelled to Mozambique.[4]

The period from Sobhuza's death to the coronation of his young successor Mswati III in April 1986 has been characterized as an "anarchic interregnum", during which Swaziland "was ruled by a corrupt, self-seeking clique [whose] policy was excessively pro-South African".[5] With regard to ANC and the Swedish assistance, it should be noted that it was in this period that apartheid's death squads in collusion with Swazi police[6] firmly turned against the movement, embarking on covert operations that would continue throughout the 1980s. In Swaziland—more than in any other forward area—detentions, expulsions, bombings, abductions and assassinations became legion.

Sweden did not phase out the humanitarian support to ANC in Swaziland. On the contrary, the allocations towards daily necessities were regularly increased, eventually reaching the level of 1.4 MSEK in 1989/90.[7] From late 1982, the cooperation was, however, seriously disrupted by the actions against the movement. Visiting Swaziland shortly after the December 1982 raids, SIDA's Tor Sellström from the embassy in Maputo concluded that there simply was "no counterpart to whom Swedish funds could be channelled".[8] As both ANC and SACTU were prevented from working openly and their representatives had been detained, in consultations with Lennox Lagu, ANC's Chief Representative to Mozambique, it was agreed in January 1983 to suspend the payments to the two organizations in Swaziland.[9]

Whereas this decision obviously affected a number of rank and file members and their dependants, the funds originally set aside for daily necessities in Swaziland were together with extraordinary grants used instead to maintain and evacuate ANC people by air from Maputo to Luanda. Fleeing from Lesotho after the SADF attack in early December 1982 and from Swaziland after the police raids one week later, large groups of refugees arriving in Mozambique could not be properly catered for. Noting that the sudden influx was causing "serious accommodation

---

1. Tor Sellström: Memorandum ('ANC Swaziland'), Swedish embassy, Maputo, 27 October 1982 (SDA).
2. James Dlamini: 'Massive swoop on ANC' in *The Times of Swaziland*, 17 December 1982.
3. The SADF attack on Maseru took place on 8 December 1982. Two days earlier, the Swazi Senator J.S. Mavimbela had strongly turned against ANC, stating that "it was a mistake from the very beginning to allow these people to roam around us. They live in flats and ordinary houses everywhere, and many of them are guerrillas" (cited in James Dlamini: 'Get tough with refugees' in *The Times of Swaziland*, 7 December 1982). In his message of condolence to the Lesotho government, the Swazi Foreign Minister Richard Dlamini stated that the raid "makes us even more determined not to allow [that our] peace, stability and progress [...] [is] endangered by people who come to our [k]ingdom under the camouflage of refugees" ('Minister sends message of condolence to Lesotho' in *The Times of Swaziland*, 14 December 1982).
4. Tor Sellström: Memorandum ('ANC Swaziland'), Swedish embassy, Maputo, 3 January 1983 (SDA).
5. Falle and Goppers op. cit., p. 21.
6. According to the Truth and Reconciliation Commission, Swazi police officers were paid by South Africa for their collaboration (TRC op. cit. (Vol. II), p. 128).
7. 'Agreed minutes from consultations held in Lusaka, May 1989, between the African National Congress of South Africa and Sweden concerning humanitarian assistance', Lusaka, 26 May 1989 (SDA).
8. Tor Sellström: Memorandum ('ANC Swaziland'), Swedish embassy, Maputo, 3 January 1983 (SDA).
9. Ibid.

and food problems", on 7 January 1983 Lennox Lagu submitted an emergency request to Sweden, appealing for "assistance to enable us to transport these young people to Luanda for resettlement".[1]

In response to Lagu's request, an extraordinary allocation of 200,000 SEK was immediately granted by the authorities in Stockholm.[2] As early as on 11 January, 40 people could thus be flown to Angola.[3] A second group of 40 ANC members were evacuated the following week.[4] While UNHCR until the late 1980s remained remarkably indifferent to the fate of ANC and other South African exiles in highly exposed situations in Southern Africa, similar urgent evacuations financed through reallocations and emergency grants were on short notice later organized by Sweden from Botswana and, above all, Lesotho.[5]

Those detained in Swaziland were eventually released, and—without further consultations with the host country—the Swedish assistance resumed.[6] However, following the March 1984 Nkomati Accord between Pretoria and Maputo, the relations between ANC and the Swazi government again deteriorated sharply. Given only six weeks warning to cope with the implications of the accord, more than a hundred MK cadres waiting in Mozambique for deployment into South

---

1. Lennox Lagu: 'Application for emergency assistance', ANC, Maputo, 7 January 1983 (SDA). The same appeal was without success made to the Mozambican government, OAU and UNHCR (Letter from Thomas Nkobi, Treasurer General, to the Swedish embassy in Lusaka, ANC, Lusaka, 21 February 1983) (SDA).

2. Letter ('Extrabistånd till ANC Moçambique'/'Extraordinary assistance to ANC Mozambique') from Tor Sellström to SIDA, Swedish embassy, Maputo, 12 January 1983 (SDA). The authorities in Stockholm reached a decision over a Saturday-Sunday weekend (ibid.).

3. Ibid.

4. Letter ('Extrabistånd till ANC Moçambique (II)'/'Extraordinary assistance to ANC Mozambique (II)') from Tor Sellström to SIDA, Swedish embassy, Maputo, 19 January 1983 (SDA).

5. After the January 1983 evacuations from Lesotho and Mozambique, Thomas Nkobi wrote that "[t]he concern shown by the government and people of Sweden has saved lives. Had the UNHCR responded to our request for assistance to remove our people from Lesotho, many [more] lives would have been saved. However, this UN agency has [such] an archaic, bureaucratic way of functioning that it takes ages before anything is actually done" (Letter from Thomas Nkobi to the Swedish embassy in Lusaka, ANC, Lusaka, 21 February 1983) (SDA). Over the years, ANC encountered considerable problems with regard to UNHCR. As early as in May 1979, it formally stated during the annual aid negotiations with Sweden that "[t]he cooperation with UNHCR is not satisfactory" ('Agreed minutes from discussions on the cooperation between the African National Congress of South Africa (ANC) and the Swedish International Development Authority (SIDA)', Lusaka, 18 May 1979) (SDA). Recalling that UNHCR's stand "had proved to be fatal in connection with the massacre in Maseru in December 1982", five years later the movement stressed that it "continued to experience serious problems when it comes to airlifting refugees coming out of South Africa" ('Agreed minutes [from] consultations in Lusaka, April 1984, between the African National Congress of South Africa and Sweden concerning humanitarian assistance', Lusaka, 6 April 1984) (SDA). As the Swedish government was represented on UNHCR's Executive Committee, ANC at the same time "appealed to Sweden to continue to use its influence with a view to increasing the support and assistance from this agency" (ibid.). Sweden had earlier raised the issue with the UN organization (Sten Rylander: Memorandum ('Överläggningar med African National Congress (ANC) om humanitärt bistånd i södra Afrika'/'Deliberations with ANC on humanitarian assistance in Southern Africa'), Ministry for Foreign Affairs, Stockholm, 16 April 1984) (SDA). Since only marginal improvements were noted, after the events in Lesotho at the end of 1985 (see below) it was eventually decided to allocate UNHCR a specific grant of 2 MSEK "to be utilized for evacuation of refugees in Southern Africa in 1986" ('Agreed minutes [from] consultations in Lusaka, May 1986, between the African National Congress of South Africa and Sweden concerning humanitarian assistance', Lusaka, 9 May 1986) (SDA).

6. Letter ('ANC i Swaziland och Moçambique'/'ANC in Swaziland and Mozambique') from Tor Sellström to SIDA, Swedish embassy, Maputo, 22 February 1983 (SDA). According to ANC's Nkosi Mvemwe, there were towards the end of 1983 around 200 ANC refugees registered with UNHCR in Swaziland. In addition to UNHCR, they were assisted by the Swaziland Council of Churches and SIDA. Around two thirds of the Swedish contribution was used for food, clothes etc., while the balance was set aside for rents, petrol and transport costs (Kaj Persson: Memorandum ('Samtalsnedteckningar från möte med ANC-representanten i Swaziland, Mrs. Mvemwe, den 4 december 1983'/'Notes from conversation with Mrs. Mvemwe, ANC representative in Swaziland, 4 December 1983'), Ministry for Foreign Affairs, Stockholm, 20 December 1983) (SDA). The meeting with Mvemwe took place in Mbabane in a tense political atmosphere. According to the notes by Kaj Persson, "during the entire conversation she had her car keys ready at hand, talking about her chances to avoid 'accidents'" (ibid.). The author took part in the meeting.

Africa "were hurriedly spirited [by ANC] across the border into Swaziland".[1] Once
inside the country, "cases of indiscipline by MK members [...] led to shootouts with
[the] Swazi security forces"[2], which prompted Prince Bhekimpi, the Prime Minister
of Swaziland, to issue a virtual declaration of war on ANC.[3]

The security pact with South Africa notwithstanding, in early April 1984 Sweden agreed to allocate 600,000 SEK to ANC in Swaziland during the financial year
1984/85.[4] Nevertheless, due to the turbulent developments in the aftermath of the
Nkomati Accord, in late June 1984 ANC's former treasurer in Mozambique, Robert Conco ('Malume')[5], instructed the Swedish embassy in Maputo to once again
suspend the assistance.[6]

Humanitarian Support Underground

By mid-1984, it appeared that Sweden could no longer extend humanitarian assistance to ANC in Swaziland. The host government was clearly hostile to the movement. Senior officials based at the headquarters in Lusaka could not visit the
country, and ANC itself requested the Swedish authorities to withhold payments
until the general political situation had been clarified. At about the same time,
SIDA, however, proceeded to strengthen the administration of the humanitarian
support to Southern Africa in general and to ANC and SWAPO in particular. As
part of this exercise, a post for regional coordination was established at the Swedish embassy in Lusaka. Roland Axelsson—a senior SIDA official, an auditor by
profession and a person who since the early 1970s had worked closely with the
Southern African liberation movements in both Tanzania and Zambia[7]—was subsequently appointed, taking up his position in October 1984.[8]

Regularly visiting the countries where Sweden extended assistance to ANC and
SWAPO, Axelsson would over the following seven years not only establish a
number of financial control and reporting mechanisms, but in general introduce a
high degree of administrative homogeneity and stability into the cooperation with

---

1. Barrell Ph. D. op. cit., chapter seven, p. 31.
2. Ibid., p. 32. Some 80 ANC members were subsequently deported (ibid.).
3. 'Address by H.E. The Right Honourable Prime Minister of the Kingdom of Swaziland, Prince Bhekimpi, on
   the status of ANC refugees'. The statement was submitted to the Swedish government by the Swazi embassy
   in London on 24 April 1984 (MFA). By then, too, the 1982 security pact between South Africa and Swaziland
   had been made public. Eight months later, the deputy head of the Swazi security police, Petrus Shiba, was
   assassinated. Although the circumstances were unclear, ANC was blamed for the murder. At a press conference, Majaji Simelane, head of Swaziland's police force, stated: "Since the ANC have made an undeclared war
   against us, we are going to track them down no matter [...] the consequences. We have no record of killing,
   but this time we are ready for casualties" (*The Swazi Observer*, 10 December 1984, cited in memorandum
   attached to letter ('ANC i Swaziland') from Malin Kärre to the Ministry for Foreign Affairs, Swedish
   embassy, Maputo, 14 January 1985) (SDA). At the same time, the Swazi newspapers published a 'wanted' list
   of 23 ANC members allegedly staying illegally in the country (ibid.).
4. 'Agreed minutes [from] consultations in Lusaka, April 1984, between the African National Congress of South
   Africa and Sweden concerning humanitarian assistance', Lusaka, 6 April 1984 (SDA).
5. Together with other senior ANC officials, such as Ronnie Kasrils, Lennox Lagu and Joe Slovo, Conco was
   forced to leave Mozambique as a result of the Nkomati Accord.
6. Jan Robberts: Memorandum ('ANC Swaziland och Moçambique'/'ANC Swaziland and Mozambique'),
   Swedish embassy, Maputo, 29 June 1984 (SDA).
7. Cf. the interview with Roland Axelsson, p. 252.
8. Minutes from consultative talks in Lusaka, October-November 1984, between the African National Congress of South Africa (ANC) and SIDA concerning humanitarian assistance', Lusaka, 1 November 1984
   (SDA). In addition to the annual aid negotiations, so called 'consultative talks' (*programsamtal*) were from
   1983 introduced as a major mid-term planning instrument in the cooperation between Sweden, ANC and
   SWAPO.

the two liberation movements.[1] In close contact with Thomas Nkobi, in situations where the ANC Treasurer General or his senior staff for political reasons were prevented from intervening, Axelsson, in addition, often acted *de facto* as his personal troubleshooter. This was particularly the case in the forward areas. Guided by the objective that the humanitarian assistance must reach those for whom it was intended, in exposed and difficult environments Axelsson constantly adjusted the disbursement and distribution routines, set up bogus holding organizations and—as will be seen below—even dismissed and appointed ANC caretakers to facilitate the support.[2]

In the case of Swaziland—where the Swedish assistance during the second half of 1984 "due to the deportation of all ANC leaders"[3] had temporarily been channelled via the Ephesus House Committee[4]—Axelsson established that in addition to a number of ANC refugees in transit there only remained 137 *bona*

---

1. Of the opinion that "there is too much snooping around in Stockholm", from the beginning Axelsson also insisted upon strict confidentiality regarding the administration of the humanitarian assistance (Letter ('Vårt bistånd till befrielserörelserna'/'Our assistance to the liberation movements') from Roland Axelsson to the Swedish embassy in Gaborone, Swedish embassy, Lusaka, 4 December 1984) (SDA).

2. Although focusing on the Swedish assistance to ANC and SWAPO, Axelsson's reports from his meetings with the two liberation movements in Southern Africa are unique with regard to day-to-day routines, setbacks and successes during the second half of the 1980s. In particular, his quarterly memoranda to SIDA from visits to ANC in the forward areas over seven years have no parallel. With a wealth of detailed financial information, as befits a trained auditor Axelsson describes in a matter-of-fact way the material conditions faced by the liberation movement's local representatives and non-combatant members.

3. 'Agreed minutes [from] consultations in Lusaka, May 1985, between the African National Congress of South Africa and Sweden concerning humanitarian assistance', Lusaka, 30 May 1985 (SDA).

4. Originally set up in the early 1960s by the Swaziland-Scandinavian Committee to provide bursaries for South African exiles, Ephesus House was in the mid-1970s reorganized under the umbrella of IUEF. An Ephesus House Bursary Committee was established. After South Africa's penetration of IUEF and its subsequent dissolution, the Ephesus House Committee continued to function as an independent organization. Professor John Daniel of the University of Swaziland served as chairman of the committee, while Felicia Forrest as chief executive officer was responsible for the office in Manzini. Via AET and WUS, the Scandinavian governments supported the organization. Norway, in particular, extended substantial amounts in the form of direct assistance. In 1984, for example, the Norwegian government granted no less than 750,000 NOK in favour of some 100 South African students at the primary, secondary and tertiary levels (Roland Axelsson: Memorandum ('Anteckningar från möten på norska ambassaden i Harare 14-15 mars 1985'/'Notes from meetings at the Norwegian embassy in Harare, 14-15 March 1985'), Swedish embassy, Lusaka, 21 March 1985) (SDA). While Norway did not extend direct, regular support to ANC in Swaziland, the assistance via Ephesus House largely benefited the resident members of the movement. Accused of working for ANC, in early 1985 Daniel and Forrest—both South African—were deported. In the case of Forrest, she was initially detained by the Swazi police. As later noted by the South African Truth and Reconciliation Commission, "[h]er feared handover to the South African security police was [, however,] prevented by the vigorous intervention of the Norwegian embassy in Harare, which sent a senior official to Swaziland" (TRC op. cit. (Vol. II), p. 159). The official was Knut Vollebæk, future (1997) Foreign Minister of Norway. In mid-October 1986, finally, Ephesus House was raided by South African operatives led by the death squad commander Eugene de Kock. During the raid, women were assaulted and registers, files and photographs were removed. Together with three of his colleagues, de Kock later submitted an amnesty application for the raid to the Truth and Reconciliation Commission. It is in the context of this study of interest to note that the raiding party—acting on 'information' extracted from Glory Sedibe ('September'), a leading MK intelligence officer abducted from Swaziland by de Kock in June 1986—was led by the false belief that Ephesus House was a SIDA office (Letter ('Brådskande: Amnesty hearings betr. attack på SIDA kontor i Swaziland på 1980-talet'/'Urgent: Amnesty hearings re attack on SIDA office in Swaziland in the 1980s') from Claes Norrlöf to Sida Stockholm, Swedish embassy, Pretoria, 4 August 2000) (SDA). Arguing political motives for their action, during amnesty hearings in Pretoria in mid-August 2000 the four applicants stated that "it was well known that SIDA supported ANC" (Letter ('Sannings- och försoningskommissionen: Hearing med anknytning till SIDA's kontor i Manzini, Swaziland, 1986'/'Truth and Reconciliation Commission: Hearing with connections to the SIDA office in Manzini, Swaziland, 1986') from Karin Höglund to the Ministry for Foreign Affairs, Swedish embassy, Pretoria, 28 September 2000) (MFA). In February 2001, they were granted amnesty for the operation (TRC statement, 6 February 2001).

fide recipients.[1] While the earlier routine of transfers by the Swedish embassy in Maputo was brought to an end and ANC opposed further disbursements via Ephesus House[2], it was agreed at the bilateral consultative talks in October-November 1984 to administer the Swedish assistance from Lusaka.[3] Shortly thereafter, Thomas Nkobi appointed the resident ANC member Elisabeth Tryon as caretaker of the support. Referred to as 'Dolly Page', she opened a bank account under the designation 'SIDA Housing Project'.[4] In turn appearing as 'Ronald Smith', Axelsson visited her in early February 1985, when they agreed on routines for payments and quarterly financial reports.[5] A governing board for the 'SIDA Housing Project' was also established, with Axelsson as chairman. Thus started—after two years of considerable problems—the second, 'underground' phase of the Swedish government's humanitarian support to ANC in Swaziland.

Meeting for consultative talks in November 1985, ANC and SIDA "concluded that the [...] system [...] was functioning satisfactorily".[6] The number of ANC members in Swaziland receiving Swedish assistance was at the time around 110, all of them registered as refugees.[7] As in Botswana and Lesotho, the bulk of the assistance was extended in the form of individual monthly allowances. Regularly adjusted to the local living costs, in the case of Swaziland they were, for example, reviewed by Nkobi and Axelsson in January 1986. In addition to contributions towards rents[8], electricity, paraffin and water, the allowance rate for single adults was then established at 150 Swazi Emalangeni per month, whereas couples were to receive 250 and children 60 Emalangeni.[9] On an annual basis, the Swedish contribution towards daily necessities for individual ANC members in Swaziland was thus at the time on average 1,880 Emalangeni—or South African Rands[10]—which corresponded to approximately 5,500 SEK.[11] As earlier noted, this was almost five times more than the per capita support to all ANC exiles, and ten times higher than that extended to the SWAPO refugees in the settlements in Angola and Zambia.

1. In a comment to SIDA on ANC's request for Swedish assistance in 1985/86, after his first visit to the forward areas Axelsson wrote in January 1985 that "the numbers given on refugees are, as usual, too high". Whereas ANC estimated that it catered for 1,400 people in Lesotho and 700 in Swaziland, Axelsson concluded that the number of "civilian refugees" in both countries did not exceed 200. Although clearly inflated, ANC's estimates, however, made provision for refugees in transit (Roland Axelsson: Memorandum ('Kommentar till ANC request [19]85/86'/'Comment on ANC's request for 1985/86'), Swedish embassy, Lusaka, 21 January 1985) (SDA).
2. 'Minutes from consultative talks in Lusaka, October-November 1984, between the African National Congress of South Africa (ANC) and SIDA concerning humanitarian assistance', Lusaka, 1 November 1984 (SDA) and letter ('Månadsbrev januari 1985: ANC'/'Monthly letter January 1985: ANC') from Roland Axelsson to SIDA, Swedish embassy, Lusaka, 25 January 1985 (SDA).
3. 'Minutes from consultative talks in Lusaka, October-November 1984, between the African National Congress of South Africa (ANC) and SIDA concerning humanitarian assistance', Lusaka, 1 November 1984 (SDA).
4. Within the bilateral development assistance to Swaziland, SIDA was in the early 1980s supporting the construction of primary schools. All over the country there were building signs indicating the support from SIDA (Author's recollection).
5. Roland Axelsson: Memorandum ('Anteckningar från besök i Swaziland 1-5 februari 1985'/'Notes from visit to Swaziland, 1-5 February 1985'), Swedish embassy, Lusaka, 22 February 1985 (SDA).
6. 'Minutes from consultative talks in Lusaka, 19-22 November 1985, between the African National Congress of South Africa (ANC) and SIDA concerning humanitarian assistance', Lusaka, 21 November 1985 (SDA).
7. Ibid.
8. The ceiling for contributions towards rental costs was 300 Emalangeni per month.
9. 'Guidelines for payments to be made in Swaziland', signed on behalf of ANC and SIDA by Thomas Nkobi and Roland Axelsson, Lusaka, 29 January 1986 (SDA). The agreement further stated that "[p]eople who receive other allowances, e.g. from UNHCR, have these deducted from the SIDA allowances to ensure that everyone is paid at the same rate. [...] Persons who are employed are not entitled to any allowance" (ibid.).
10. The Swazi and South African currencies were at parity.
11. Based on letter ('Månadsbrev februari 1986: ANC'/'Monthly letter February 1986: ANC') from Roland Axelsson to SIDA, Swedish embassy, Lusaka, 6 February 1986 (SDA).

The Swazi 'anarchic interregnum' ended with King Mswati's accession to the throne in April 1986. South African attacks against ANC continued, however, unabated. Comparing Swaziland to a "bantustan"[1], the movement would during the second half of the 1980s ceaselessly face serious problems. Due to threats by South African agents, in early 1987 Dolly Page was forced to leave.[2] As eleven ANC members were killed and others abducted during the first half of 1987[3], in her stead caretakers were subsequently appointed. Although Roland Axelsson regularly visited Swaziland on a quarterly basis to follow up the assistance, these developments—increasingly widening the gap between ANC in Swaziland and the headquarters in Lusaka—would towards the end of 1988 eventually lead to an acute crisis.

Visiting Swaziland in October 1988, Axelsson found that the then caretaker, Sebenzile Motsa, had broken down under the pressure. Due to mismanagement, the assistance had not reached the designated beneficiaries, with serious personal economic and social problems as a consequence.[4] Supported by ANC's 'elders' in Swaziland and in Nkobi's absence "given a free hand to act according to my judgment" by Kay Moonsamy in Lusaka[5], in an unprecedentedly interventionist move the Swedish official dismissed Motsa and appointed Dorcas Mokoena as the movement's new caretaker.[6] After recovering cheque books and other documents from the former representative, Axelsson then convened a board meeting of the 'SIDA Housing Project', where he himself was confirmed as chairman, Mokoena became the treasurer and Cynthia Mohale of Ephesus House the secretary.[7]

Subsequently endorsed by ANC's Treasurer General, the administrative set-up was, however, far from tested. At the annual aid negotiations in Lusaka in May 1989, the parties concluded that "it had been difficult to find reliable unofficial representatives to take care of the [Swedish] funds", hoping that "the new system would prove to be an efficient and secure way of providing and controlling funds for all the refugees concerned". At the same time, it was noted that if this was not to be the case, "funds for daily necessities [in Swaziland] would no longer be made available by Sweden".[8] In the meantime, no less than 1.4 MSEK was set aside for the purpose during the financial year 1989/90.[9]

Shortly thereafter—in June 1989—Nkobi asked Axelsson to cancel his scheduled visit to Swaziland due to security problems.[10] In addition to concerns for Axelsson's personal safety, it had come to light that South Africa was intensifying its penetration of ANC's structures in Swaziland and that the 'SIDA Housing Project' was one of the targets. According to Nkobi, the recently appointed care-

1. Thomas Nkobi cited in Kaj Persson: Memorandum ('Samtal med företrädare för ANC'/'Conversation with ANC representatives'), Ministry for Foreign Affairs, Stockholm, 10 December 1986 (MFA).
2. Roland Axelsson: Memorandum ('Anteckningar från besök i Swaziland 23-25/3 1987'/'Notes from visit to Swaziland, 23-25 March 1987'), Swedish embassy, Lusaka, 2 April 1987 (SDA).
3. Elisabeth Dahlin: Memorandum ('Humanitärt bistånd till African National Congress of South Africa (ANC) budgetåren 1988/89-1989/90'/'Humanitarian assistance to ANC during the financial years 1988/89-1989/90'), SIDA, Stockholm, 19 October 1987 (SDA).
4. Roland Axelsson: Memorandum ('Anteckningar från besök i Swaziland 5-7 oktober 1988'/'Notes from visit to Swaziland, 5-7 October 1988'), Swedish embassy, Lusaka, 29 October 1988 (SDA).
5. Ibid. Axelsson contacted Moonsamy over the telephone.
6. Ibid.
7. Ibid.
8. 'Agreed minutes from consultations held in Lusaka, May 1989, between the African National Congress of South Africa and Sweden concerning humanitarian assistance', Lusaka, 26 May 1989 (SDA).
9. Ibid.
10. Letter ('Månadsbrev juni 1989: ANC'/'Monthly letter June 1989: ANC') from Roland Axelsson to SIDA, Swedish embassy, Lusaka, 9 June 1989 (SDA).

taker was involved. Axelsson then froze the Swazi bank account.[1] As so many times before, innocent ANC members were once again affected.

At that time, there remained fewer than 100 *bona fide* ANC recipients in the country. Weighing the security aspects against the small number of refugees, the Swedish delegation to the consultative talks in November-December 1989 concluded that "all disbursements of funds to Swaziland should cease at the latest by [30 June] 1990".[2] Led by Thomas Nkobi, the ANC delegation, however, expressed "grave concern" with regard to SIDA's stand, in an unusually harsh comment adding that it amounted to "a departure from [the] normal ANC-SIDA cooperation".[3] Participating in the talks, Eva Belfrage later wrote that ANC had reacted to the Swedish opinion "with disappointment and dismay".[4]

Axelsson, too, was in favour of continued assistance to ANC in Swaziland.[5] As the 1989/90 allocation was never called into question, it was, eventually, agreed to yet again introduce a new disbursement system. In early 1990, another bank account—'SRA Housing Project'[6]—was opened, out of which monthly cheques were distributed to the beneficiaries. In Swaziland, Lindiwe Sisulu-Guma, the daughter of the veteran ANC leader Walter Sisulu, was made responsible for the assistance, which by April 1990 only involved around 70 people.[7]

At about the same time, it was discovered that Cynthia Mohale, chief executive officer at Ephesus House and secretary on the former board of the 'SIDA Housing Project', had been involved in fraudulent activities. According to Axelsson's estimates, she had embezzled around 15,000 Emalangeni of SIDA's assistance to ANC.[8] As she had misappropriated funds at Ephesus House too[9], at the aid negotiations in May 1990 ANC informed SIDA that legal proceedings were being instituted against her.[10] By that time, the movement had been unbanned. Although 1.2 MSEK was set aside for daily necessities in Swaziland during 1990/91[11] and 0.5 MSEK for 1991/92[12], the bulk of the funds was soon reallocated towards more pressing needs in South Africa. When in November 1991 Lena Johansson—Axelsson's successor as SIDA's coordinator of humanitarian assistance—together with ANC's former caretaker Dolly Page (aka Elisabeth Tryon) visited Swaziland, they

1. Ibid.
2. 'Minutes from consultative talks in Lusaka, 27 November-1 December 1989, between the African National Congress of South Africa (ANC) and the Swedish International Development Authority (SIDA) concerning humanitarian assistance', Lusaka, 1 December 1989 (SDA). The Swedish delegation was led by Lena Johansson, head of section at the SIDA headquarters in Stockholm.
3. Ibid.
4. Eva Belfrage: Memorandum ('Rapport från programsamtal mellan ANC och SIDA i Lusaka 27/11-1/12 1989'/'Report on consultative talks between ANC and SIDA in Lusaka, 27 November-1 December 1989'), SIDA, Stockholm, 11 December 1989 (SDA).
5. Cf. Axelsson's later statement: "[I]n Swaziland, we never stopped the assistance completely. SIDA wanted to stop it several times, but I managed to convince them that it should go on" (Interview with Roland Axelsson, p. 255).
6. The letters SRA stood for SIDA, Roland and Axelsson.
7. Roland Axelsson: Memorandum ('Anteckningar från besök i Swaziland 15-23 januari och 7-8 april 1990 samt från relevanta diskussioner i Lusaka och Harare'/'Notes from visits to Swaziland, 15-23 January and 7-8 April 1990, and from relevant discussions in Lusaka and Harare'), Swedish embassy, Lusaka, 20 April 1990 (SDA). With an allocation of 1.4 MSEK for daily necessities in Swaziland, in 1989/90 the average Swedish per capita contribution amounted to the quite staggering amount of 20,000 SEK.
8. Ibid.
9. AET: 'Evaluation of Swaziland refugee education project', a draft report kindly submitted to the author, London, 1 May 1997 (NAI).
10. 'Agreed minutes from consultations held in Lusaka, May 1990, between the African National Congress of South Africa and Sweden concerning humanitarian assistance', Lusaka, 18 May 1990 (SDA).
11. Ibid.
12. 'Agreed minutes from consultations held in Benoni, South Africa, May 1991, between the African National Congress of South Africa (ANC) and the government of Sweden concerning humanitarian assistance', Johannesburg, 19 May 1991 (SDA).

ARO solidarity workers received
by President Samora Machel in
Maputo, March 1979 (from left):
Bertil Odén, Elisabet Odén,
Thomas Kjellson, Gabor Tiroler
and Ninni Uhrus (Courtesy
of Bertil Odén)

confirmed ANC's decision that no further support should be channelled to South
African exiles in the country as from January 1992.[1]

Mozambique

To all parties involved, Mozambique was radically different from Swaziland.
Although the government of the former Portuguese colony since independence in
1975 had adopted a cautious stand vis-à-vis South Africa, and ANC had not been
allowed to establish military camps or civilian settlements in the country, there
were strong historical bonds between FRELIMO and the Congress Alliance. At the
time of the ZANU victory in Zimbabwe—to which Mozambique more than any
other Frontline State had contributed—not only ANC, but also SACP and SACTU
had a significant *de facto* presence in Maputo. Several South African exiles had
been given official employment there, and with the government's tacit consent an
underground MK Special Operations Unit was allowed from 1980.[2]

To Sweden, FRELIMO and Mozambique had a special significance, both at the
official and at the NGO levels. The organization led by President Samora Machel
was the first Southern African liberation movement to which official Swedish support was extended.[3] At independence, the humanitarian support was replaced by
development assistance. By 1980/81, it amounted to 180 MSEK, placing Mozambique behind Tanzania as the second most important recipient of Swedish bilateral
aid in Africa.[4] As a leading SADCC member, Mozambique would from 1980 also
receive substantial resources in the form of regional assistance. Since the 1960s,
FRELIMO had similarly played a particularly prominent role within the Swedish

---

1. Lena Johansson: Memorandum ('Besök i Swaziland, ANC'/'Visit to Swaziland, ANC'), Swedish legation, Pretoria, 14 November 1991 (SDA).
2. As earlier noted, ANC was allowed to run a piggery project in Matola. In the case of SACP, by 1982 most of
   its leadership was concentrated in Maputo. Moses Mabhida, the General Secretary, Chris Hani, John Nkadimeng, Joe Slovo and other leading SACP officials were, however, required to leave after the Nkomati Accord.
   For the rest of the 1980s, Lusaka became the SACP headquarters.
3. See the chapter 'FRELIMO of Mozambique: Clearing a Way'.
4. Sida op. cit. (1997 b).

solidarity movement.[1] This continued after independence, when the Africa Groups under ARO recruited qualified solidarity workers for placement in the country.[2]

In spite of the Mozambican authorities' reluctance to allow permanent ANC settlements or project activities, against the background of Sweden's support to FRELIMO it was only natural that they would agree to strictly humanitarian assistance to the movement. As noted above, after the 1976 Soweto uprising the Swedish assistance would mainly be used for onward transportation of refugees to Tanzania and, above all, to Angola. Increasing amounts were, however, also set aside in favour of the members of the Congress Alliance who were allowed to stay. In 1980/81, for example, the allocation towards 'daily necessities' to ANC in Mozambique was 750,000 SEK, which could be compared to the 500,000 SEK extended for the same purpose to ANC in Swaziland.[3]

To the apartheid regime, Mozambique represented a real threat. Embarking on a socialist path, an outspoken opponent of racism and committed to promoting regional cooperation against South Africa, the FRELIMO government was soon singled out for both overt and covert aggression. Since the Mozambican railways and ports offered an alternative to dependence on South African routes for five of its landlocked SADCC partners[4], within Pretoria's 'total strategy' the transport network was particularly targeted for direct military attacks by SADF and sabotage operations by RENAMO. As noted by Ohlson,

> if the transport routes through Mozambique and the ports of Maputo, Beira and Nacala were to be blocked, then the whole region would become hostage to South Africa's intentions. Mozambique would have to change its policies towards South Africa and [...] cease to be a threat, ideologically, economically or otherwise.[5]

In his normative study on destabilization, Geldenhuys summarized in late 1982 South Africa's policy towards Mozambique as follows:

> What Pretoria essentially desires is a friendly, cooperative neighbour, instead of a Marxist state threatening its security. To achieve these objectives, support for [RENAMO] and the severe manipulation of economic ties are the two obvious means to employ.[6]

Apartheid's onslaught on Mozambique—later described by a leading US official as "one of the most brutal holocausts against ordinary human beings since World War II"[7]—would from around 1980 largely develop along these lines. Closely involved in development assistance to Mozambique—not least in the transport and communications sector—and with aid workers based in most parts of the country[8], the Swedish authorities were well placed to assess the disastrous effects of Pretoria's operations, which by 1983 had generated a deep structural crisis.

---

1. See the chapter 'FRELIMO of Mozambique: Clearing a Way'.
2. Ibid.
3. 'Minutes from discussions on the cooperation between the African National Congress of South Africa (ANC) and the Swedish International Development Authority (SIDA), May 1980', Lusaka, 29 May 1980 (SDA).
4. Botswana, Malawi, Swaziland, Zambia and Zimbabwe.
5. Ohlson op. cit., p. 60.
6. Geldenhuys in Gutteridge (ed.) op. cit., p. 24.
7. US Deputy Assistant Secretary of State for Africa Roy Stacy cited in Ohlson op. cit., p. 63.
8. Closely following the developments in Mozambique, Thabo Mbeki, in particular, would often consult SIDA officials based in Mozambique. For example, in connection with the official aid negotiations in Lusaka in April 1984—that is, immediately after the Nkomati Accord—he had longer discussions with SIDA's Evelyn Forsman from the embassy in Maputo (Author's recollection).

Assisting ANC in the country, Sweden could also appreciate the FRELIMO government's predicament vis-à-vis the South African liberation movement. After the South African raid on Matola in January 1981 and the assassination of Ruth First in August 1982, an official Swedish delegation—led by Gösta Edgren, Under-Secretary of State for International Development Cooperation—was, for example, in Maputo for bilateral aid negotiations with Mozambique when in late May 1983 the South African air force carried out yet another attack on alleged ANC bases on the outskirts of the capital. Whereas the South African Minister of Defence, General Magnus Malan, announced that the strike was a success and that six ANC bases, a missile battery and forty-one ANC 'terrorists' had been 'eliminated', the delegation could on the spot conclude that this was pure invention.[1] Instead, the 'targets' hit were the homes of ordinary citizens, as well as the crèche of a jam factory. Along with a South African refugee, five Mozambican civilians, among them a child, were killed in the widely publicized cross-border operation.[2]

Swastika-decorated helmet found after SADF's attack on ANC in Matola, Mozambique, January 1981 (Photo: Georg Dreifaldt)

By that time, the Mozambican government had already found it necessary to come to terms with South Africa as a way of ending the onslaught. Secret bilateral talks had started in early 1983. Although the issue of ANC—in addition to that of RENAMO—featured prominently, FRELIMO, however, did not keep the movement informed of the negotiations. When in February 1983 Nelson Mandela was awarded the honorary title 'Citizen of Rome', ANC thus appointed the veteran Mozambican politician Marcelino dos Santos to represent him at the ceremony in Italy. Covering the event, the official Mozambican newspaper *Notícias* carried the headline 'Mozambique will always be loyal to ANC'.[3] With other expressions of support, such statements would after the Nkomati Accord add to ANC's bitterness.

The talks between South Africa and Mozambique—held in Swaziland and respectively led by Foreign Minister 'Pik' Botha and Jacinto Veloso, Minister of Economic Affairs in the President's Office—resulted in a breakthrough in mid-December 1983. ANC had shortly before been notified by the Mozambican author-

1. Based in Maputo and forming part of the Swedish delegation, together with Malin Kärre—also from the local embassy—the author visited the scenes of the air strike immediately thereafter. "Reject[ing] terror as a means of settling conflicts", the attack was "utterly condemned" by Foreign Minister Lennart Bodström ('Statement by the Minister for Foreign Affairs, Mr. Lennart Bodström', occasioned by the South African attack on Mozambique', 24 May 1983, in Ministry for Foreign Affairs: *Documents on Swedish Foreign Policy: 1983*, Stockholm, 1987, p. 194).

2. In an internal communication to the South African army chief Lieutenant General Geldenhuys, the SADF head Lieutenant General Viljoen subsequently described the attack as "not merely a disappointment, but a shock [...]. [O]ur image and credibility with [the] government and abroad has been seriously damaged" (cited in TRC op. cit. (Vol. II), p. 147).

3. 'RPM será sempre solidária com ANC' ('The People's Republic of Mozambique will always be loyal to ANC') in *Notícias*, 18 February 1983.

ities that no more than 50 members would be allowed in the country.[1] As it became increasingly evident that a formal agreement between Pretoria and Maputo was being prepared—and that ANC in all likelihood would be further affected—the Swedish ambassador to Mozambique, Bo Kälfors, turned to Stockholm for advice. In a far less interventionist instruction than the one issued to his predecessor Finn Bergstrand with regard to Swaziland two years earlier, on 24 February 1984 the Ministry for Foreign Affairs asked Kälfors to inform the Mozambican Foreign Minister Joaquim Chissano that

> [w]e obviously do not have any reason to criticize Mozambique for having initiated [...] nego-
> tiations [with South Africa]. [...] At the same time [, however,] we assume that ANC refugees
> also in the future will be received in accordance with [the relevant] international conventions
> and that Sweden henceforth, too, will be able to extend its humanitarian assistance to ANC in
> Mozambique. The issue of which security [...] Mozambique may require with regard to ANC's
> localization in the country is in our view entirely a question for the Mozambican government
> to determine in agreement with ANC.[2]

While two days later these views were conveyed by Kälfors to Chissano, on 28 February 1984 ANC President Oliver Tambo met the Swedish ambassador. Explaining that he after quite some time in the Mozambican capital had not been received by President Samora Machel until 26 February, Tambo was "worried".[3] Stating that the talks between Pretoria and Maputo had taken ANC "by surprise" and—less than entirely truthfully—that the movement had never carried out military operations from the country, he, however, appreciated that Mozambique due to the South African onslaught had been forced to negotiate "under the barrel of the gun". Although Machel had assured him that the deportation of ANC members—notably Joe Slovo—had not been discussed with the Pretoria regime, Tambo, nevertheless, concluded that with regard to Mozambique it was now a question of "South Africa in and ANC out".[4]

In the absence of any prominent African leader—barring Prime Minister Bhekimpi of Swaziland—an 'Agreement on non-aggression and good neighbourliness between the government of the People's Republic of Mozambique and the government of the Republic of South Africa' was signed on the banks of the Nkomati river by President Machel and Prime Minister Botha on 16 March 1984. Known as the 'Nkomati Accord', the pact not only constituted a severe setback to ANC, but it also provoked serious criticism among the Frontline States. Although the accord—which in principle targeted RENAMO in Mozambique and ANC in South Africa—contrary to the security pact between South Africa and Swaziland did not make provision for operations by the contracting parties on each other's territories, it committed the parties to

> forbid and prevent in their respective territories the organisation of irregular forces or armed
> bands [...] whose objective is to carry out [...] acts [which are] likely to endanger mutual peace
> and security;

1. Kaj Persson: Memorandum ('Samtalsanteckningar från möte 1 december [1983] med ANC's [...] Robert
   Conco'/'Notes from conversation with ANC's Robert Conco on 1 December 1983'), Ministry for Foreign
   Affairs, Stockholm, 15 December 1983 (SDA). There were at the time between 300 and 400 South African
   refugees in transit in Mozambique (ibid.). According to Shubin, ANC members were occupying around 30
   houses and flats in Maputo (Shubin op. cit., p. 252).
2. Cable from the Ministry for Foreign Affairs to the Swedish embassy in Maputo, Stockholm, 24 February
   1984 (MFA).
3. Cable ('Samtal med Oliver Tambo'/'Conversation with Oliver Tambo') from Bo Kälfors, Swedish ambassador
   to Mozambique, to the Ministry for Foreign Affairs, Swedish embassy, Maputo, 28 February 1984 (MFA).
4. Ibid.

eliminate from their respective territories bases, training centres, places of shelter, accommodation and transit for elements who intend to carry out [such] acts; and

exercise strict control [...] over [such] elements.[1]

In the case of ANC, the reaction was immediate. On behalf of the National Executive Committee, Secretary General Alfred Nzo issued on the very same day a statement which declared that

the Botha regime has sought to reduce the independent countries of our region to the level of its bantustan creations by forcing them to [...] enter into so called non-aggression pacts [...]. Such accords, concluded as they are with a regime which has no moral or legal right to govern our country, cannot but help to perpetuate the illegimate rule of the [...] white settler minority.[2]

At a time when its assistance to ANC in Mozambique amounted to 1.5 MSEK[3]—in the non-military field by far exceeding that of any other donor—Sweden would closely follow the post-Nkomati developments. On 19 March 1984, for example, the accord and its possible consequences were discussed by Thabo Mbeki and the Swedish ambassador to Zambia, Jan Ölander. Stating that ANC was "extremely disappointed with Mozambique", Mbeki also expressed concern with regard to the future of SADCC.[4] Although less bluntly, a couple of days later he conveyed the same message to a large audience attending an International Hearing on South African Aggression against the Neighbouring States, jointly organized by the Norwegian Council for Southern Africa, the Africa Groups of Sweden and the Danish Association for International Cooperation[5] in Oslo from 22 to 24 March 1984.[6] Met with sympathy, ANC's views were reflected by the conference panel, which *inter alia* included socialist and non-socialist members of parliament from Denmark, Norway and Sweden. Thus, the final declaration noted that "[t]he recent negotiations and agreements [...] cannot hide the fact that a lasting peace in Southern Africa is impossible as long as the apartheid system exists".[7]

ANC's disappointment turned into dismay when on 24 March the Mozambican authorities in a surprise move started to raid the residences of its members in Maputo.[8] Carried out by armed personnel over two days, some of the Mozambican security officials wore gas masks. This was ostensibly in case of resistance, but—according to Joe Slovo—"ANC activists were convinced that the [...] masks cov-

---

1. 'Nkomati Accord'. The full text of the agreement is reproduced in Johnson and Martin (eds) op. cit., pp. 323-26.
2. 'ANC on the Nkomati Accord', 16 March 1984, in *Sechaba*, May 1984, pp. 3-4.
3. 'Agreed minutes [from] consultations in Lusaka, March 1983, between the African National Congress of South Africa, ANC, and Sweden concerning humanitarian assistance', Lusaka, 25 March 1983 (SDA).
4. Cable ('ANC om läget i södra Afrika'/'ANC on the situation in Southern Africa') from Jan Ölander, Swedish ambassador to Zambia, to the Ministry for Foreign Affairs, Swedish embassy, Lusaka, 19 March 1984 (MFA). Ölander also informed Mbeki of the decision to arrange a meeting in Sweden between the Foreign Ministers of the Nordic countries and the Frontline States, as well as of Lesotho. Through Mbeki, ANC was invited to submit comments on the proposed agenda (ibid.).
5. In Danish, *Mellemfolkeligt Samvirke*.
6. Held less than a week after the Nkomati Accord, the important Oslo hearing arranged by the NGO solidarity movement in Norway with support from its counterparts in Denmark and Sweden became more topical than originally envisaged. In addition to prominent international speakers—among them the British historian Basil Davidson and Bishop Desmond Tutu, the General Secretary of the South African Council of Churches, who later in the year was awarded the Nobel Peace Prize—politicians, officials and activists from Norway, Sweden and the other Nordic countries attended in large numbers. At the final session, there were some 1,200 people present (cf. Nina Drolsum: 'The Norwegian Council for Southern Africa (NOCOSA): A Study in Solidarity and Activism' in Eriksen (ed.) op. cit., pp. 230-32).
7. Declaration of the Panel at the International Hearing on South African Aggression against the Neighbouring States, Oslo, 22-24 March 1984' (AGA).
8. Cable ('ANC-hus genomsökta i Maputo'/'ANC houses searched in Maputo') from the Swedish embassy to the Ministry for Foreign Affairs, Maputo, 26 March 1984 (MFA).

ered the faces of South Africans".[1] Impounding light arms[2], foreign and local currency, as well as personal belongings, the scars from the operation would never
fully heal.[3] In a personally phrased letter to SIDA, Stan Mabizela, ANC's Chief
Representative to Tanzania—whose wife Tiksie at the time was working at the
Mozambican Central Bank in Maputo—wrote in May 1984 that we

> are shocked by the behaviour of FRELIMO towards the ANC community in Maputo. They
> applied the terms of the [Nkomati Accord] with what may be called religious zeal. They raided
> our houses at gunpoint and [with] fixed bayonets! Tiksie is shattered as she had great faith in
> Samora. [...] Over 150 of our civilian population have arrived in Dar es Salaam from Maputo,
> putting a great strain on us in terms of housing in particular. A big tent city has shot up in the
> wilderness of Dakawa.[4]

Soon after the raids, the Mozambican authorities presented ANC with the conditions which would regulate the movement's future presence in the country.[5] President Machel's assurances to Oliver Tambo notwithstanding, the number of ANC
activists was limited to ten. No senior political or military officials could form part
of this group. All other ANC members had to leave[6], although they were not to go
to Swaziland, Lesotho or Zimbabwe. While ten senior ANC officials based abroad
would be allowed to enter Mozambique on short notice, only the ANC President
and the Secretary General had, finally, the right to visit the country at any time.[7]

As noted by Tambo in his meeting with ambassador Kälfors, this effectively
meant that ANC was forced to abandon the particularly important forward area of
Mozambique. While Jacob Zuma remained in Maputo as Chief Representative, in
April 1984 virtually all senior ANC officials—among them Lennox Lagu and Joe
Slovo—left the country along with political and military rank and file cadres, in the
former case primarily for Zambia and Tanzania and in the latter for Angola. Swedish funds were largely used for the evacuation.[8]

Adjusting to Nkomati

On account of its historical relations with FRELIMO and the strategic importance
of Mozambique, the Nkomati Accord was a major reversal to ANC. According to
the Soviet scholar and activist Vladimir Shubin, it was regarded by the movement

---

1. Information by Slovo quoted in Shubin op. cit., p. 256.
2. A gun previously given by the Mozambican government to Slovo for self-protection was, for example, confiscated (Cable ('ANC-hus genomsökta i Maputo'/'ANC houses searched in Maputo') from the Swedish
   embassy to the Ministry for Foreign Affairs, Maputo, 26 March 1984) (MFA).
3. During the aid negotiations with Sweden in May 1988, ANC expressed "deep distrust" towards Mozambique
   (Karin Roxman: Memorandum ('Rapport från överläggningar med ANC den 9-12 maj 1988'/'Report from
   deliberations with ANC, 9-12 May 1988'), Ministry for Foreign Affairs, Stockholm, 31 May 1988) (MFA).
   Visiting Sweden at the end of the year, Mbeki was similarly critical of President Chissano's policies vis-à-vis
   South Africa and ANC (Sten Rylander: Memorandum ('Thabo Mbeki besöker statssekreterare Säve-Söderbergh'/'Thabo Mbeki visits Under-Secretary of State Säve Söderbergh'), Ministry for Foreign Affairs, Stockholm, 2 January 1989) (SDA).
4. Letter from Stanley Mabizela to SIDA, ANC, Dar es Salaam, 18 May 1984 (SDA).
5. Letter ('ANC i Moçambique efter avtalet'/'ANC in Mozambique after the accord') from Bo Kälfors, Swedish
   ambassador to Mozambique, to the Ministry for Foreign Affairs, Swedish embassy, Maputo, 3 April 1984
   (SDA). The conditions were submitted to ANC on 29-30 March 1984 (ibid.).
6. ANC members with residence and work permits were exempted (ibid.).
7. Ibid.
8. In breach of the conditions set by Mozambique, more than a hundred MK freedom fighters were at the same
   time spirited across the southern border with Swaziland. While some clashed with the Swazi police and armed
   forces, many managed to make their way into South Africa. At a time when UDF emerged as a major political
   force, the level of ANC's armed activity inside the country increased after the Nkomati Accord (Shubin op.
   cit., p. 263).

as "the most serious blow [...] since its banning in 1960".[1] Meeting representatives from the Swedish government for annual aid negotiations in Lusaka in early April 1984, ANC, naturally, paid particular attention to the Nkomati Accord and its relations with Mozambique. Denouncing the raids carried out against its members and the curtailing of its presence in the country, ANC Secretary General Alfred Nzo—who on behalf of the National Executive Committee on the day of the accord had compared Mozambique to a South African bantustan—stated, however, that the organization "was not going to take an anti-Mozambique posture".[2]

Despite the unsettling events, ANC was confident that a *modus vivendi* could be established with the FRELIMO government, pleading continued assistance. Since the Swedish authorities following ambassador Kälfors' February meeting with the Mozambican Foreign Minister Chissano had not been notified to the contrary, it was agreed to tentatively set aside no less than one million SEK towards daily necessities for ANC members in Mozambique during 1984/85.[3] As the extent of the security arrangement between Pretoria and Maputo became evident—and by mid-1984 there only remained some 100 ANC refugees in the country[4]—soon, however, the parties decided to reallocate the entire allocation in favour of Tanzania, where many ANC members had to be accommodated.[5] For 1985/86, a limited amount of 200,000 SEK was budgeted for ANC in Mozambique.[6]

In ANC's view, the Nkomati Accord largely became a reality due to Pretoria's "tactic of dealing with the Frontline States piecemeal".[7] As the pace of events in Southern Africa rapidly escalated from mid-1983, the independent countries had not been able to come together to coordinate their policies towards South Africa, ANC and SWAPO.[8] At the end of April 1984, however, a summit meeting of the Frontline States was convened by President Nyerere in Arusha, Tanzania. Attended by both President Machel and Oliver Tambo, the meeting assessed the situation in the region. Although the final communiqué only contained a cautious formulation on the Nkomati Accord—expressing "the hope that the South African government [would] live up to the commitment to cease its acts aim[ing] at the destabilisation of

---

1. Ibid., p. 254. It should be noted that the ANC leadership at about the same time had to deal with a serious mutiny in the MK camps in Angola.
2. 'Agreed minutes [from] consultations in Lusaka, April 1984, between the African National Congress of South Africa and Sweden concerning humanitarian assistance', Lusaka, 6 April 1984 (SDA).
3. Ibid.
4. 'Minutes from consultative talks in Lusaka, October-November 1984, between the African National Congress of South Africa (ANC) and SIDA concerning humanitarian assistance', Lusaka, 1 November 1984 (SDA).
5. 'Agreed minutes [from] consultations in Lusaka, May 1985, between the African National Congress of South Africa and Sweden concerning humanitarian assistance', Lusaka, 30 May 1985 (SDA). A major consideration behind the decision to transfer the entire 1984/85 ANC Mozambican allocation to Tanzania was that the government of Norway in 1985 allocated funds for the movement in Mozambique (Roland Axelsson: Memorandum ('Anteckningar från möten på norska ambassaden i Harare 14-15 mars 1985'/'Notes from meetings at the Norwegian embassy in Harare, 14-15 March 1985'), Swedish embassy, Lusaka, 21 March 1985) (SDA). As in Botswana and Lesotho, Sweden and Norway would from the mid-1980s coordinate their assistance to ANC in Mozambique.
6. With an allocation of 400,000 NOK, the government of Norway was during the calendar year 1985 the major donor to ANC in Mozambique. The official Swedish contribution for 1985/86 amounted to 200,000 SEK. Since there were around 100 ANC recipients, on a per capita basis the combined annual Norwegian-Swedish support to the members in Mozambique was at the time approximately 6,000 SEK ('Minutes from consultative talks in Lusaka, 19-22 November 1985, between the African National Congress of South Africa (ANC) and SIDA concerning humanitarian assistance', Lusaka, 21 November 1985) (SDA). According to a later statement by ANC's Indres Naidoo, the bulk of the beneficiaries were underground MK cadres, among them Siphiwe ('Guebuza') Nyanda, Chief of Staff in the South African National Defence Force after the democratic elections in 1994 (Interview with Indres Naidoo, p. 179).
7. 'Agreed minutes [from] consultations in Lusaka, April 1984, between the African National Congress of South Africa and Sweden concerning humanitarian assistance', Lusaka, 6 April 1984 (SDA).
8. Ibid.

Oliver Tambo, Lindiwe Mabuza and Josef Dube briefing SIDA and CCHA on the Nkomati Accord, Stockholm, May 1984: Chairing the Swedish delegation is Lars-Olof Edström (in light jacket). Taking notes next to him is the author. Also in the picture are Ingalill Colbro, Gunnar Helander, Lars-Olof Höök, Kurt Kristiansson and Elisabeth Michanek (Photo: Paul Rimmerfors)

Mozambique" and the "appreciation of Mozambique's commitment to continued moral, political and diplomatic support for the ANC"[1]—it, however, identified "the abolition of apartheid by whatever means are necessary" as the shared objective of the Frontline States and the liberation movements.[2]

Above all, beyond the public statements Presidents Nyerere of Tanzania and Kaunda of Zambia, as well as Prime Minister Mugabe of Zimbabwe, criticized Mozambique for signing the accord and, notably, for its harsh clampdown on ANC. While he was of the opinion that "Mozambique has become closer to South Africa than any other country in the region with the exception of Swaziland", visiting Sweden shortly after the Frontline States' meeting Oliver Tambo was thus confident that "Arusha [had] stemmed the tide".[3]

Eventually, it was the apartheid regime's failure to honour the Nkomati Accord—making it clear that Pretoria from the outset had negotiated in bad faith—which rallied the Frontline States behind Mozambique and the South African liberation movement. While the Mozambican government effectively restricted ANC's presence, its South African counterpart continued to support RENAMO. As later stated by Craig Williamson, "what had been an official project became a covert one".[4] A two-year stockpile of weaponry was, for example, delivered to RENAMO

1. 'Frontline States summit meeting Arusha, Tanzania, April 29, 1984: Final communiqué', attached to *ANC Weekly News Briefing*, No. 18, 1984.
2. Ibid.
3. Tor Sellström: Memorandum ('Möte med ANC's ordförande Oliver Tambo, SIDA, 14 maj 1984'/'Meeting with ANC President Oliver Tambo at SIDA on 14 May 1984'), SIDA, Stockholm, 16 May 1984; quotations in English in the original (SDA). The meeting was held to brief the members of the SIDA board and CCHA on the developments in Southern Africa in general and the Nkomati Accord in particular. Tambo was accompanied by Josef Dube and Lindiwe Mabuza. The author served as secretary to the meeting. The ANC President was unusually blunt with regard to Swaziland. Describing the country as "a province of South Africa", he advised his Swedish hosts that the Swazis "ought to be reminded that they have moved into the wrong camp" (ibid.). Ending his overview, he stated that ANC in the light of the Swazi and Mozambican security arrangements with Pretoria had concluded that "the armed struggle has to be centered more inside South Africa than it has been so far" (ibid.).
4. TRC op. cit. (Vol. II), p. 94.

in the two months preceding the signing of the agreement[1], and from 1985 the war against the FRELIMO government intensified. Following the death of President Samora Machel in a mysterious plane crash on South African territory in mid-October 1986, it would peak with disastrous effects during 1987-89.

It should, meanwhile, be noted that at the time Prime Minister Olof Palme was actively involved in two important initiatives to check apartheid's heavy-handed diplomatic thrust into Southern Africa, facilitating instead a common stand by the Frontline States, ANC, SWAPO and some of its main international supporters. Whereas the Pretoria government—encouraged by the recent security agreements—in an extraordinary display of political arrogance in April 1984 made "a friendly proposal to Sweden" to enter into joint ventures with South African companies in Mozambique[2], in June the Social Democratic government hosted a meeting in Stockholm of the Foreign Ministers of the Nordic countries, the Frontline States and Lesotho. On behalf of the Socialist International, Palme was, in addition, closely involved in preparing a conference between the Socialist Group of the European Parliament, the Frontline States, ANC and SWAPO, held in Arusha in early September.[3]

Although the Nordic countries at the level of the United Nations had coordinated their policies towards South Africa since the early 1960s—in March 1978 eventually adopting a common Programme of Action against Apartheid, or the so called Oslo plan[4]—until the Stockholm meeting in June 1984 they had not held joint political consultations with the Frontline States as a group. Complementing a parallel North-South initiative vis-à-vis SADCC in the economic and cultural

---

1. Ibid. The real extent of South Africa's backing of RENAMO and other surrogate forces in the region may never be known. Practically all relevant files were destroyed during the transition period in the early 1990s. In 1993 alone, no less than 44 tons of paper-based and microfilm records were incinerated, including the entire archive of the Military Intelligence's Directorate of Special Tasks, that is, the branch which directed Pretoria's proxy wars in Angola, Lesotho, Mozambique and Zimbabwe (Verne Harris: "They Should Have Destroyed More': The Destruction of Public Records by the South African State in the Final Years of Apartheid, 1990-94' in *Transformation*, No. 42, 2000, pp. 29-56).

2. The proposal was made by South Africa's Deputy Foreign Minister Louis Nel to the Swedish envoy Arne Helleryd in Cape Town on 25 April 1984 (Letter ('Sydafrika vill ha samtal med Sverige'/'South Africa wants discussions with Sweden') from Arne Helleryd to the Ministry for Foreign Affairs, Swedish legation, Cape Town, 26 April 1984) (MFA). Repeatedly reverting to the issue, in October 1984 Helleryd eventually responded to Nel by submitting a formal note. Explaining that "the Swedish government finds [...] that the existing diplomatic channels are sufficient to serve the purpose of the exchange of views between our two governments", the note concluded that Sweden "is [thus] not prepared to enter into direct discussions with the government of the Republic of South Africa". With regard to South African-Swedish joint ventures in the region, Helleryd further stated: "As to Swedish development aid to [the] Southern African states, the Swedish government prefers to discuss such issues exclusively and directly with the receiving state. [It is], consequently, not interested in opening up trilateral talks with the Republic of South Africa on development projects" (Cable ('Samtal med Sydafrika'/'Discussions with South Africa') from Arne Helleryd to the Ministry for Foreign Affairs, Swedish legation, Pretoria, 2 November 1984) (MFA).

3. Palme played a particularly prominent role at the Arusha conference. As later noted by Bengt Säve-Söderbergh, his attendance was largely motivated by his concern for ANC in the post-Nkomati period. Interviewed in 1997, Säve-Söderbergh explained: "I was in charge of organizing [the] conference [...] in Arusha [...] and went there to prepare it with Salim [Ahmed] Salim. I came back and said to Palme: 'The only negative thing that I can report to you is that the conference will take place one week before the [Social Democratic Party] congress of September 1984. But if that can be dealt with, it would be immensely important if you at an early stage could announce your attendance, because then all the others would also attend. Your name is so important in this connection'. The [Swedish] 1985 elections were coming closer and most people advised him not to go to Africa one week before the party congress. But he said: 'Give me a week to think about it'. He came back a week later and said: 'I will not follow the advice given by most people. I will go. If friendships ever count, it is when your friends are in trouble, and this time my old friend Oliver Tambo is in trouble" (Interview with Bengt Säve-Söderbergh, pp. 337-38).

4. See the chapter 'SACTU, Unions and Sanctions'.

fields[1], in the light of Pretoria's continuous destabilization policies the meeting was proposed by the Swedish government in late 1983.[2] The original idea was to bring together the five Nordic countries, the six Frontline States[3] and ANC and SWAPO for informal discussions. The Danish and Norwegian governments were, however, uncomfortable with the proposed participation of the two liberation movements.[4] Eventually, therefore, they were not invited.[5] On account of its firm anti-apartheid stand, the government of Lesotho was, on the other hand, asked to join.[6]

No formal communiqué was issued from the Stockholm meeting. Nevertheless, summing up the deliberations in a joint statement to the press, the Swedish Foreign Minister Lennart Bodström indirectly expressed common views that were critical of the Nkomati Accord. According to Bodström,

> [w]e agree that the fundamental cause of the conflict in Southern Africa is the policy of apartheid. No significant changes in that policy can be discerned. [...] South Africa's policy of destabilization continues, even if its tactics have changed. The aim is to preserve apartheid. We can see no lasting peace in Southern Africa as long as apartheid remains.

> Contacts between South Africa and the states in its vicinity are necessary for geographical reasons and due to the economic dependence of [the] neighbouring states [...]. However, such contacts cannot be invoked as a pretext for attempts to break the international isolation of the apartheid regime. [...] The importance of increasing international pressure on South Africa was confirmed. [...] We [thus reiterate] the need for continuing support for South Africa's neighbouring states and for the liberation movements, especially in the light of the most recent developments.[7]

1. Against a background of stalled multilateral negotiations on a New International Economic Order (NIEO), in 1982 the Finnish Prime Minister Kalevi Sorsa proposed to his Nordic colleagues the idea of identifying a group of developing countries with which the Nordic countries could enter into an inter-regional NIEO relationship, or a 'mini-NIEO', as the proposal was called in Norway. Due to their aid involvement and anti-apartheid policies, it was logical that they would primarily consider the SADCC members as possible partners. A formal decision to this effect was taken in December 1984 by the Nordic Prime Ministers at their annual meeting in Reykjavik, Iceland, and in January 1986 a 'Joint Declaration on Expanded Economic and Cultural Cooperation'—popularly known as the 'Nordic-SADCC Initiative'—was signed by the five Nordic and the nine SADCC governments in Harare, Zimbabwe (cf. Tor Sellström: 'Some Factors behind Nordic Relations with Southern Africa' and Tom Østergaard: 'Aiming beyond Conventional Development Assistance: An Analysis of Nordic Aid to the SADCC Region' in Bertil Odén and Haroub Othman (eds): *Regional Cooperation in Southern Africa: A Post-Apartheid Perspective*, The Scandinavian Institute of African Studies, Uppsala, 1989, pp. 19-20 and 159-68).
2. 'In December, the Minister for Foreign Affairs, Mr. Lennart Bodström, invited the Foreign Ministers of the six Frontline States in Southern Africa to a meeting in Stockholm on 26-27 April 1984' in Ministry for Foreign Affairs: *Documents on Swedish Foreign Policy: 1983*, Stockholm, 1987, pp. 196-97. The meeting was later postponed from April to June 1984.
3. Zimbabwe joined the group of Frontline States upon independence in 1980.
4. Bjarne Lindstrøm: Memorandum ('Frontlinjestatsmøtet: Spørsmål om deltagelse av frigjøringsbevegelsene'/ 'The meeting with the Frontline States: The question of participation by the liberation movements'), Ministry of Foreign Affairs of Norway, Oslo, 9 April 1984 (MFA). Both Denmark and Norway preferred that the meeting would be limited to independent states. In the case of Norway, it was further argued that "if SWAPO and ANC participate [...] PAC should also take part" (ibid.).
5. ANC was, however, invited to submit comments on the proposed agenda, and in mid-May 1984—one month before the meeting—Oliver Tambo visited Sweden to state the movement's views on the Nkomati Accord and the situation in Southern Africa.
6. A second meeting of the Foreign Ministers of the Nordic countries and the Frontline States was held in Arusha, Tanzania, in January 1988. At that time, Lesotho was ruled by a military council and not invited.
7. 'Summary press statement by the chairman, following the meeting of Foreign Ministers of the Nordic countries, the Frontline States and Lesotho', 21 June 1984, in Ministry for Foreign Affairs: *Documents on Swedish Foreign Policy: 1984*, Stockholm, 1988, p. 183. In the case of Sweden and Mozambique, it could be noted that the Swedish bilateral aid allocation for 1984/85 for the first time since the country's independence in 1975 was not increased, but maintained at the 1983/84 level of 255 MSEK (Sida op. cit. (1997 b), p. 46).

Attending the Socialist International conference in Arusha in September 1984—where Western European Social Democratic politicians[1] for the first time jointly shared ideas with the leaders of the Frontline States, ANC and SWAPO[2]—Olof Palme echoed these words.[3] In private discussions with the Mozambican President, he appears to have been considerably more outspoken. Supporting Oliver Tambo—and conveying "what we could not say"—according to ANC's Lindiwe Mabuza, Palme's initial comment to Machel concerning the agreement with South Africa was simply: "How could you?"[4]

Interviewed in 1996, the former Mozambican Security Minister Sérgio Vieira confirmed that "a sort of misunderstanding [had] occurred". Stating that Palme and others attending the Arusha conference "actually had not read the documents", Vieira added that they after "very long discussions [...] eventually [...] understood our position and decision". When Machel asked whether "the Mozambicans [should] appear to the international community as war-mongers or [...] let the South Africans show that they do not respect peace", Palme had replied "that no country can oppose an effort for peace".[5]

The Nkomati Accord was a dramatic event in the history of the South and Southern African liberation struggles. To outside supporters of both Mozambique's right to national self-determination and ANC's quest for freedom, it was controversial. While the expulsion of the liberation movement was clearly a setback[6], it should be noted, however, that the greatest upsurge of the internal anti-apartheid opposition took place under the UDF umbrella *after* the accord.[7] Although the two developments were not interconnected[8], with regard to ANC one of the effects of the Nkomati Accord was to reinforce the shift in strategy which the movement had initiated in 1978-79. In order to direct the uprisings in the South African townships, greater emphasis was placed on internal political work rather than on armed operations from abroad. With the introduction of international sanctions and South Africa's economic decline, this, eventually, paved the way for the demise of the apartheid regime. Contrary to Pretoria's designs, the agreement with Mozam-

---

1. In addition to Palme, among the European participants were, for example, Lionel Jospin of France, Anker Jørgensen of Denmark and Mário Soares of Portugal.
2. Barring the Angolan President José Eduardo dos Santos, the leaders of all the Frontline States—that is, Kenneth Kaunda of Zambia, Samora Machel of Mozambique, Quett Masire of Botswana, Robert Mugabe of Zimbabwe and Julius Nyerere of Tanzania—were in attendance together with Sam Nujoma of SWAPO and Oliver Tambo of ANC.
3. Cf. Olof Palme in The Socialist International op. cit., pp. 35-42.
4. Interview with Lindiwe Mabuza, p. 142.
5. Interview with Sérgio Vieira, p. 57.
6. See the foreword by President Nyerere to Johnson and Martin (eds) op. cit., p. x.
7. Ibid., p. xi.
8. Some of the Mozambican government representatives directly involved in the negotiations leading up to the Nkomati Accord later rationalized the expulsion of ANC as a means to push the movement towards an intensification of the internal struggle. Interviewed in 1996, Veloso, notably, stated that the accord "had advantages for the liberation of South Africa". Adding that "at the time, it appeared to us that the accord also would set a precedent for an internal agreement between the black population and the established white power", he went as far as asserting that it "lit the light at the end of the tunnel for democracy in South Africa" and that "[t]he final downfall of apartheid started with the Nkomati Accord" (Interview with Jacinto Veloso, p. 54). Less adamant in this respect, his colleague Sérgio Vieira noted at the same time that "I do not think that the Nkomati Accord was a fundamental element, but it was important for the isolation of the apartheid regime. [...] South Africa was all the time arguing that they were going to be invaded by the Russians, the Chinese and the Communist hordes through Mozambique. After Nkomati, they could not come with that kind of mythology. [The accord] helped to further erode the apartheid system and strengthen the internal struggle" (Interview with Sérgio Vieira, p. 57).

bique did not constitute a final blow to ANC.[1] It is in this context not without relevance to note that Sweden and ANC during their negotiations in early April 1984 agreed to raise the 'home front component' by more than 40 per cent, or from 12 MSEK in 1984/85 to 17 MSEK in 1985/86.[2]

ANC was in the meantime forced to keep a low profile in Mozambique. Although allowing limited Swedish and Norwegian humanitarian assistance to its remaining members in the country, it was only in connection with the funeral of the SACP General Secretary Moses Mabhida in late March 1986 that the Mozambican authorities again publicly showed their solidarity with the South African liberation movement.[3] Nevertheless, ANC's regained recognition by the FRELIMO government—taking place after the military coup in Maseru and its expulsion from Lesotho—would be both precarious and short-lived. Chief Representative Jacob Zuma and the members of his rump mission[4] were constantly exposed to South African threats. Denied security protection by the Mozambican government, they sometimes stayed overnight in residences occupied by Swedish embassy officials.[5] In October 1986, the embassy, finally, decided that part of the allocation to ANC in Mozambique would be used to accommodate "those who are most exposed" in local hotels.[6]

After the death of President Machel in mid-October 1986, the apartheid regime increased its demands on Mozambique. In December, President P.W. Botha conveyed a letter to his newly appointed Mozambican counterpart, the former Foreign Minister Joaquim Chissano, requesting the deportation of five of ANC's ten resident officials in Maputo. In addition to Jacob Zuma, the targeted representatives were Keith Mokoape, Indres Naidoo, Bobby Pillay and Sue Rabkin, all of them closely linked to Umkhonto we Sizwe. On behalf of ANC, President Tambo agreed that the five should be recalled to Lusaka.[7] Noting that the withdrawal "not only amounts to a political setback, but [...] to personal tragedies for people who for

1. Cf. Abrahamsson and Nilsson op. cit., pp. 107-10. In August 1984, professor Hendrik van der Merwe of the University of Cape Town visited the ANC headquarters in Lusaka. Maintaining close relations with important representatives of the ruling National Party, he wanted to ascertain the liberation movement's views with regard to a possible negotiated settlement in South Africa. Invited to Sweden to attend the ruling Social Democratic Party congress, Secretary General Alfred Nzo informed the Swedish Foreign Minister Lennart Bodström about the visit the following month (Anders Möllander: Memorandum ('Samtal med sydafrikanska ANC's generalsekreterare Nzo'/'Conversation with Secretary General Nzo of ANC of South Africa'), Ministry for Foreign Affairs, Stockholm, 20 September 1984) (SDA). From the very beginning, ANC would normally update the Swedish government about 'the talks about talks' that were initiated behind the public arena in the mid-1980s. Despite the setbacks in Mozambique and other forward areas, as early as in February 1985—less than a year after the Nkomati Accord—in this context Roland Axelsson reported from a meeting with Thabo Mbeki that he had "rarely seen him so optimistic and upbeat" (Letter ('Månadsbrev februari 1985: ANC'/ 'Monthly letter February 1985: ANC') from Roland Axelsson to SIDA, Swedish embassy, Lusaka, 22 February 1985) (SDA). Cf. also Roland Axelsson: Memorandum ('Anteckningar från möte med Thabo Mbeki, ANC, 1985 01 29'/'Notes from meeting with Thabo Mbeki, ANC, 29 January 1985'), Swedish embassy, Lusaka, 31 January 1985 (SDA).
2. See the table in the previous chapter 'From Beds in Exile to Organizers at Home'.
3. Following a meeting between Oliver Tambo and Samora Machel earlier in the month, the funeral of Mabhida on 29 March 1986 was accorded the highest protocollary attention. Both Tambo and Machel addressed the ceremony, which was also attended by high-ranking UDF officials from South Africa, among them President Archibald Gumede and Curnick Ndlovu, its National Chairman.
4. Following the Nkomati Accord, ANC was allowed ten representatives in Mozambique. The host country—and South Africa—would, however, only allow eight of the ten officials proposed by the movement (Willy Petterson: Memorandum ('ANC i Moçambique'/'ANC in Mozambique'), Swedish embassy, Maputo, 23 October 1986) (SDA).
5. Ibid.
6. Ibid.
7. Malin Kärre: Memorandum ('ANC i Maputo'/'ANC in Maputo'), Swedish embassy, Maputo, 7 January 1987 (SDA).

many years have lived in Mozambique and formed families [there]", Malin Kärre, first secretary at the Swedish embassy, was critical of the arrangement.[1]

Given respite to celebrate ANC's 75th anniversary[2], the five plus Mohamed Timol—another ANC member listed by the South Africans—left Maputo on 9 January 1987. With some 500 people in attendance, the anniversary celebrations on the eve of the departure turned into an emotional, but militant send-off. ANC's outgoing Chief Representative Jacob Zuma[3]—the future Deputy President of South Africa, who eleven years earlier had been forced out of Swaziland too—addressed the audience. Neither FRELIMO nor the Mozambican government were, however, represented by any high-ranking member or official. Reporting on the events, in a letter to the Foreign Ministry in Stockholm Kärre did not hide her criticism. Stating the opinion that Mozambique should have stood up more forcefully for ANC, she characterized the departure of Zuma and his colleagues as "humiliating".[4]

Contrary to the situation in Botswana, Lesotho and Swaziland, ANC was, nevertheless, allowed to maintain a diplomatic mission in Mozambique. As Pretoria's backing of RENAMO continued and South African refugees kept on crossing into the country, the host government also accepted Swedish—and Norwegian—assistance in the form of daily necessities for people under the movement's care. In 1987/88—when the number of refugees was estimated at 150[5]—850,000 SEK was set aside for ANC in Mozambique.[6] On a per capita basis, this corresponded to some 5,700 SEK, that is, an annual provision comparable to the one extended by Sweden to ANC members in neighbouring Swaziland.[7] Three years later—when there was a marked increase of people fleeing from the hostilities with Inkatha in Natal[8]—the allocation reached 1 MSEK.[9] In spite of the Nkomati drama, over the fifteen years from the country's independence until ANC's unbanning the Swedish government remained the movement's principal donor in Mozambique.

---

1. Ibid.
2. Interview with Indres Naidoo, p. 180. According to Naidoo, "[t]he Mozambicans did not insist that we leave, but it was quite clear that they would like us to go. [Our presence] was too dangerous for all concerned" (ibid.).
3. Zuma was replaced by Sipho Dlamini, former staff member of the Centre of African Studies at the Eduardo Mondlane University in Maputo.
4. Letter ('ANC i Maputo') from Malin Kärre to the Ministry for Foreign Affairs, Swedish embassy, Maputo, 12 January 1987 (MFA).
5. Roland Axelsson: Memorandum ('Anteckningar från besök i Maputo 8-11 oktober 1988'/'Notes from visit to Maputo, 8-11 October 1988'), Swedish embassy, Lusaka, 30 October 1988 (SDA).
6. 'Agreed minutes [from] consultations in Lusaka, May 1987, between the African National Congress of South Africa and Sweden concerning humanitarian assistance', Lusaka, 8 May 1987 (SDA).
7. In consultations between Axelsson, Nkobi and ANC's Maputo office, in the late 1980s it was agreed to introduce a routine of individual, monthly allowances to the members in Mozambique. Set in US Dollars, the basic rate for adults was 52 USD per month, while children received 22 USD. A biannual clothing allowance was also granted. It amounted to 160 USD for adults and 90 USD for children (Roland Axelsson: Memorandum ('Anteckningar från besök i Maputo 5-6 april 1990'/'Notes from visit to Maputo, 5-6 April 1990'), Swedish embassy, Lusaka, 17 April 1990) (SDA).
8. Ibid.
9. 'Agreed minutes from consultations held in Lusaka, May 1990, between the African National Congress of South Africa and Sweden concerning humanitarian assistance', Lusaka, 18 May 1990 (SDA).

Lesotho, Botswana, Zimbabwe and a Note on Security

Lesotho

Completely surrounded by South Africa, of all the SADCC states Lesotho was the most vulnerable. With more than half of the adult population employed by mines, farms and factories in the apartheid republic and all of the foreign trade passing via its mighty neighbour, the tiny mountain kingdom was in an invidious position, "caught between the millstones of white South Africa and black nationalism".[1] Opting for close cooperation with Pretoria upon independence in 1966, during the 1970s the government under Prime Minister Leabua Jonathan embarked, however, on an increasingly defiant anti-apartheid course. While Chris Hani as early as in 1974 had been welcome to settle there, after the 1976 Soweto uprising Lesotho became an important sanctuary and transit point for thousands of South African refugees. By 1983, the Jonathan government estimated that Lesotho accommodated some 11,500 people who had fled from political persecution in South Africa. Many of them were aligned with ANC and the wider Congress Alliance, while others expressed allegiance to BCM and PAC.

When the Pretoria regime formulated its 'total strategy', the dislodging of Chief Jonathan was high on the agenda. In fact, the first military operations carried out by Ntsu Mokhehle's surrogate Lesotho Liberation Army inside the country occurred as early as in May 1979.[2] Broadening the attacks to include South African exiles, after the Zimbabwe independence elections they culminated in December 1982 in the SADF-led raid on ANC in the capital Maseru, during which 30 South Africans and 12 Lesotho nationals were killed. It did not, however, end Jonathan's resolve to resist South Africa. On the contrary, by consolidating the links with ANC, calling for international sanctions and establishing diplomatic relations with the Soviet Union, the People's Republic of China and the People's Republic of Korea, on most core issues his stand was diametrically opposed to South Africa's.[3]

As his course was far from supported by the country's political and military élite—and Pretoria's destabilization continued—in January 1986, Prime Minister Jonathan was deposed by Major-General Justin Lekhanya in the first military coup ever to take place in Southern Africa. Shortly thereafter—in late March 1986—the new government[4] followed Swaziland (1982) and Mozambique (1984) by entering into a security arrangement with South Africa. Emphasizing "their adherence to the principles of mutual respect and non-interference in the internal affairs of sovereign states", the parties notably "reaffirmed that they will not allow their territories to

---

1. Rok Ajulu and Diana Cammack: 'Lesotho, Botswana, Swaziland: Captive States' in Johnson and Martin (eds) op. cit., p. 139.
2. Ibid., p. 145.
3. The subsequent military cooperation with North Korea provoked particular opposition within Lesotho's armed forces.
4. Effectively ruled by a five-man Military Council under Lekhanya, nominal executive power passed from Chief Jonathan to his uncle, King Moshoeshoe II.

be used for the planning and execution of acts of terrorism against the other".[1] Targeting ANC, the agreement signalled the end of the movement's official presence in Lesotho. It also meant that the official Swedish assistance to ANC—as earlier in Swaziland—entered into a complex 'underground' phase.

As a general background to the presentation below, it should be noted that Sweden's relations with Lesotho were considerably closer than those with Swaziland, a country with which it was often compared. Mainly on a multilateral basis, Swedish development assistance to the two kingdoms had started in the late 1960s. In both cases, the chief objective of the support was to strengthen their political and economic independence vis-à-vis South Africa. While the Swazi government opted to stay close to the apartheid regime—in 1982 eventually entering into a secret security arrangement with Pretoria—the government in Maseru, however, chose a different path. At about the same time as Sweden decided to phase out its assistance to Swaziland, in 1983 Lesotho was included as one of the so called 'programme countries'. Chief Jonathan's anti-apartheid stand, the fact that Lesotho welcomed South African refugees and ANC's favourable opinion[2] were in this respect decisive elements. In 1994, an independent evaluation of SIDA's aid cooperation with Lesotho concluded that

> Sweden's support to Lesotho was guided by the political objectives of opposing apartheid and assisting [the country] to retain its political independence.[3]

From 1983, the political interaction between the Social Democratic government in Sweden and the Jonathan regime in Lesotho developed rapidly. Including SIDA's Director General Anders Forsse, the Swedish delegation to the SADCC conference in Maseru in January 1983 was, for example, led by Foreign Minister Lennart Bodström.[4] Later in the year, Lesotho's Minister of Planning, Employment and Economic Affairs, Evaristus Sekhonyana, visited Stockholm, where he notably sought assistance in the form of a civilian passenger aircraft with the capacity to link Lesotho with the other SADCC countries.[5] It was listed as a regional SADCC project, and his plea was supported. With the explicit proviso that the aircraft in case

---

1. Cited in cable ('Ordföranden i Lesotho's militärråd besöker Sydafrika'/'The chairman of Lesotho's military council visits South Africa') from Jan Lundvik, Swedish envoy to South Africa, to the Ministry for Foreign Affairs, Swedish legation, Pretoria, 2 April 1986 (MFA).
2. In discussions on the situation in Southern Africa at the Foreign Ministry in Stockholm, in May 1983 ANC President Oliver Tambo stated, for example, that it was "particularly important to assist Lesotho", which he described as the liberation movement's "most advanced vantage point in Southern Africa" (Dag Ahlander: Memorandum ('Samtal med ANC-ledaren Oliver Tambo'/'Conversation with the ANC leader Oliver Tambo'), Ministry for Foreign Affairs, Stockholm, 4 May 1983) (SDA).
3. Tyrell Duncan, Frank Baffoe and Karin Metell: *Support against Apartheid: An Evaluation of 28 Years of Development Assistance to Lesotho*, SIDA Evaluation Report 1994:3, SIDA, Stockholm, 1994, p. 9. Bilateral Swedish assistance was mainly extended for public administration; agriculture, forestry and land conservation; telecommunications; labour intensive construction; and civil aviation. Expressed in current figures, at the end of 1991 the cumulative aid disbursements from Sweden to Lesotho exceeded 500 MSEK (ibid.).
4. Due to the tense situation in Maseru following the December 1982 SADF raid, Bodström was accompanied by two Swedish security policemen. In his memoirs, the former Foreign (1982-85) and Education (1985-89) Minister notes that "it was the only time during my period in government that this was deemed necessary" (Lennart Bodström: *Mitt i Stormen*/'In the Midst of the Storm', Hjalmarson & Högberg Bokförlag, Stockholm, 2000, p. 201).
5. Duncan, Baffoe and Metell op. cit., p. 72. At the time, South Africa had started to interfere with Lesotho's air services, which were all routed via Johannesburg.

of need should also be used to evacuate South African refugees, in September 1985 Sweden delivered a Fokker F-27 to Lesotho Airways.[1]

As already noted, Lesotho was also invited to take part in the meeting between the Foreign Ministers of the Nordic countries and the Frontline States, hosted by Bodström in the Swedish capital in June 1984. While Sweden's diplomatic relations with the country until then had been conducted from Botswana, at about the same time it was, finally, decided to establish an official mission in Maseru. Headed by chargé d'affaires Martin Wilkens, an embassy was formally opened in July 1985.[2] Apart from Malawi and Swaziland, there were thus Swedish embassies with SIDA offices in all the SADCC countries.[3]

It is in this context relevant to note that King Moshoeshoe II—contrary to the Swazi royal house—played an active and important role for the development of closer links with Sweden. Following Lesotho's independence in 1966, relations between Prime Minister Jonathan and the constitutional monarch were initially extremely strained. For a short period in the early 1970s, Moshoeshoe was even forced into exile, which he spent in the Netherlands.[4] By the early 1980s, however, the fences between the Prime Minister and the King had largely been mended. In addition to shared views with regard to Lesotho's historical role as a country of asylum[5], Moshoeshoe was keenly aware of his country's dependence on South Africa and interested in new ideas regarding the development of Lesotho and the Southern African region as a whole. Favouring an alternative road to the strategies advocated on both sides of the Iron Curtain[6], his attention was drawn to the so called 'Swedish model'. Although Sweden was a monarchy, the academically inclined King entered into direct contacts with the Swedish aid authorities and development oriented research institutions.

In November 1983, for example, Moshoeshoe participated at a seminar on 'Communications for development' in Uppsala, organized by the Dag Hammarskjöld Foundation together with the Swiss-based International Foundation for Development Alternatives. During the seminar, he established relations with the Swedish Foreign Minister Lennart Bodström and SIDA's former Director General

---

1. Along with training, technical assistance and spare parts, the cost of the 'Swedish plane' amounted to no less than 42 MSEK, which was debited against the budget allocation for regional development in Southern Africa (Duncan, Baffoe and Metell op. cit., p. 131). The training took place in Finland, and for a long time the Finn Aimo Ahjolinna was, as chief pilot of the Fokker plane, attached by Sweden to Lesotho Airways. At the time of delivery in September 1985, Lesotho had no direct air connections with any SADCC country except Swaziland. Honoured by the presence of King Moshoeshoe, the arrival of the plane was hailed as a significant contribution to the country's survival as a sovereign state. Together with the Swedish ambassador Karl-Göran Engström, the author travelled with the plane on its final leg from Gaborone, Botswana.
2. 'Minutes from consultative talks in Lusaka, 19-22 November 1985, between the African National Congress of South Africa (ANC) and SIDA concerning humanitarian assistance', Lusaka, 21 November 1985 (SDA).
3. The decision to establish an embassy in Maseru was highly appreciated. In order to give the Swedish authorities a general introduction to Lesotho, in February 1985 a delegation was taken on a week-long tour by helicopter around the country. A mini-seminar on Swedish assistance and issues in development was also hosted by King Moshoeshoe at the Royal Palace in Maseru. Led by Gösta Edgren, Under-Secretary of State for International Development Cooperation in the Ministry for Foreign Affairs, Karl-Göran Engström, the Swedish ambassador to Botswana and Lesotho, Sten Rylander from the Foreign Ministry, Lennart Wohlgemuth from SIDA and the author—also representing SIDA—formed part of the official delegation. Roy Johansson Unge, SIDA's representative to Lesotho, was attached to the mission (Author's recollection).
4. Moshoeshoe was allowed to return after undertaking not to interfere in political affairs.
5. Lesotho (Basutoland) emerged as a national entity from the 1820s, when King Moshoeshoe I rallied the remnants of various ethnic groups seeking refuge in his territory from the inter-African 'wars of calamity' (*mfecane* or *difaquane*). See, for example, Elizabeth Eldredge: *A South African Kingdom: The Pursuit of Security in Nineteenth-Century Lesotho*, Cambridge University Press, Cambridge, 1993.
6. Cf. His Majesty King Moshoeshoe of Lesotho: 'Alternative Strategies for Development: A Clarion Call!' in *Another Development for SADCC*, Foundation for Education with Production/Dag Hammarskjöld Foundation, Serowe, Botswana, 1987, pp. 8-16.

Royal contacts with researchers and diplomats: King Moshoeshoe II with Sven Hamrell of the Dag Hammarskjöld Foundation (left) and Sten Rylander of the Foreign Ministry, Uppsala, November 1983 (Photo: Harald Hamrell)

Ernst Michanek, as well as with the future UN Commissioner for Namibia and President of Finland, Martti Ahtisaari, and the future Foreign Minister of Norway, Thorvald Stoltenberg.[1]

Two years later—in mid-November 1985, that is, at the time of the South African squeeze which the following month saw yet another raid against ANC and in January 1986 culminated in Lekhanya's military coup—King Moshoeshoe himself hosted a seminar at the Royal Palace in Maseru on 'Another development for SADCC'.[2] Sponsored by the Dag Hammarskjöld Foundation and jointly organized by the Foundation for Education with Production, Botswana, and the Institute of Southern African Studies at the National University of Lesotho, it further strengthened his links with Sweden.[3] After the January 1986 coup, the King was vested with legislative and executive powers. Albeit soon reduced to a formality, this provision largely explains why the Swedish government—much like ANC[4]—in spite of

1. Dag Hammarskjöld Foundation: '[Programme of] the 1983 Dag Hammarskjöld/IFDA seminar on communications for development', Uppsala, 10-13 November 1983, and author's conversation with Sven Hamrell, former Director of the Dag Hammarskjöld Foundation, Uppsala, 2 January 2001.
2. Ibid. The seminar was held 18 and 22 November 1985. With the theme 'Another development for Lesotho?', a sequel was sponsored by the Dag Hammarskjöld Foundation in Maseru in December 1987. Moshoeshoe took an active part in the deliberations. Among other participants from Lesotho were cabinet members Khalaki Sello and Michael Sefali (*Another Development for Lesotho?: Alternative Development Strategies for the Mountain Kingdom*, Foundation for Education with Production/Dag Hammarskjöld Foundation, Serowe, Botswana, 1989).
3. In 1986, King Moshoeshoe II became a member of the International Honorary Committee of the Dag Hammarskjöld Foundation.
4. The coup in Lesotho was discussed by Olof Palme and Oliver Tambo during their very last meeting on 21 February 1986, one week before the assassination of the Swedish Prime Minister. Although the ANC President deplored that the movement had "lost a good friend in [Leabua] Jonathan", he, however, expressed confidence in King Moshoeshoe, who he described as "a supporter of ANC's programme, the Freedom Charter" (Anders Möllander: Memorandum ('ANC's president Oliver Tambo hos statsministern'/'ANC President Oliver Tambo with the Prime Minister'), Ministry for Foreign Affairs, Stockholm, 26 February 1986) (MFA). In a long exchange in Lusaka with Kurt Kristiansson—SIDA's newly appointed representative to Lesotho and close to Tambo since the beginning of the 1960s—in early May 1986, he again called for moderation, characterizing the King as "an honest, perspicacious, purposeful and determined" political actor. Adding that "we know most of [the cabinet members] well" and that "we have many friends there", Tambo emphasized that with regard to the new situation in Lesotho it was of importance to "keep it cool" (Kurt Kristiansson: Memorandum ('Samtal med Oliver Tambo'/'Conversation with Oliver Tambo'), Swedish embassy, Maseru, 24 March 1986) (SDA). Two of the new ministers were known ANC supporters. Khalaki Sello, appointed Minister of Law, Public Service and Constitutional and Parliamentary Affairs, had in 1962 even been jailed for two years for ANC membership. Michael Sefali, who became Minister of Planning and Economic Affairs, had received his academic training in the Soviet Union. A founder member of the tiny and ephemeral Communist Party of Lesotho, as head of the Institute of Southern African Studies at the National University of Lesotho he had often denounced South Africa's destabilization policies. Both Sello and Sefali were close to King Moshoeshoe.

the military takeover and subsequent events did not sever its recently established diplomatic relations with Lesotho.[1]

Special Flights

Swedish assistance to ANC in Lesotho started in 1976/77, when an amount of 70,000 SEK was set aside for daily necessities.[2] Efficiently administered by Chris Hani, the allocation had grown to 1.2 MSEK when in mid-1982 he left the country.[3] Lesotho thereby occupied third position among the countries to which Swedish non-project aid in favour of ANC was channelled, after Angola and Tanzania, but—notably—before Zambia.[4] Although Hani's departure led to a marked deterioration with regard to the local administration of the support, it was not only maintained, but due to the consequences of the South African raid on Maseru in December 1982 increased.

In 1983/84, 1.3 MSEK was allocated for daily necessities in Lesotho.[5] The following year—when the number of resident *bona fide* ANC beneficiaries in the country was around 200, with another 50 to 60 in transit[6]—the allocation was raised to 1.5 MSEK.[7] After consultations with Thomas Nkobi, Roland Axelsson and Japhet Ndlovu, ANC's Chief Representative to Lesotho, agreed at the same time on a system of individual allowances. A basic, monthly contribution for adults was set at 120 Maloti—or South African Rands[8]—whereas children received 50 Maloti.[9] In the case of Lesotho, the individual allowances were high from the beginning. As early as in mid-1984, the Swedish contribution to the adult ANC recipients was on an annual basis no less than 7,200 SEK.[10]

From mid-1985, however, it was the physical safety of the ANC refugees rather than their daily expenses which would be of main concern. Increasing the pressure on Chief Jonathan's government, in August the South African Foreign Minister

---

1. Relations between General Lekhanya and King Moshoeshoe soon soured, eventually leading to the King's second exile in March 1990. He was succeeded by his son, who was crowned as King Letsie III in November 1990. Allowed to return to Lesotho in July 1992, Moshoeshoe was killed in a car accident in January 1996.
2. 'Agreed minutes of discussions on cooperation between Sweden and the African National Congress of South Africa', Lusaka, 1 September 1976 (SDA).
3. 'Agreed minutes of discussions in Lusaka, May 1982, between the African National Congress of South Africa, ANC, and the Swedish International Development Authority, SIDA, concerning humanitarian assistance', Lusaka, 24 May 1982 (SDA).
4. Ibid.
5. 'Agreed minutes [from] consultations in Lusaka, March 1983, between the African National Congress of South Africa, ANC, and Sweden concerning humanitarian assistance', Lusaka, 25 March 1983 (SDA).
6. 'Minutes from consultative talks in Lusaka, October-November 1984, between the African National Congress of South Africa (ANC) and SIDA concerning humanitarian assistance', Lusaka, 1 November 1984 (SDA).
7. 'Agreed minutes [from] consultations in Lusaka, April 1984, between the African National Congress of South Africa and Sweden concerning humanitarian assistance', Lusaka, 6 April 1984 (SDA).
8. As in the case of Swaziland, the Lesotho currency was on a par with South Africa's.
9. 'Minutes from consultative talks in Lusaka, October-November 1984, between the African National Congress of South Africa (ANC) and SIDA concerning humanitarian assistance', Lusaka, 1 November 1984 (SDA).
10. The corresponding support in Swaziland amounted in 1986 to approximately 5,500 SEK. In Lesotho's case, it should be noted that the Norwegian government also extended assistance towards daily necessities for ANC's members. With an allocation of 1.5 MNOK for this purpose in the calendar year 1985, it approximated the assistance from Sweden (Roland Axelsson: Memorandum ('Anteckningar från möte på norska ambassaden i Harare 1985 08 30'/'Notes from meeting at the Norwegian embassy in Harare, 30 August 1985'), Swedish embassy, Lusaka, 23 September 1985) (SDA). Assuming that at the time there were as many as 250 *bona fide* ANC beneficiaries in Lesotho, on an annual basis each of them would on average have received the quite remarkable amount of 12,000 SEK from the two Scandinavian governments. In fact, the number of ANC members financially supported was considerably lower. As funds set aside by Sweden and Norway for daily necessities had to be reallocated in favour of evacuation operations, there was, however, no corresponding increase of the individual allowances.

'Pik' Botha delivered a list of ANC members in Lesotho who according to Pretoria should be deported from the country.[1] With the December 1982 Maseru massacre in fresh memory, through contacts with Oliver Tambo it was agreed to evacuate them to Tanzania.[2] The practicalities of the evacuation and the question of the movement's continued presence in Lesotho were discussed with an ANC delegation led by Jacob Zuma.[3]

An evacuation from the enclave of Lesotho was far from easy. The small Fokker aircraft delivered by Sweden in September 1985 had not yet entered into regular service, and there were no direct flights to Zambia, Tanzania or any other friendly country. The only connections operated by Lesotho Airways were with Johannesburg and Manzini, Swaziland, two transit points that for security reasons were to be avoided. While UNHCR could charter planes to evacuate exposed refugees, its administrative routines were, however, remarkably slow.[4] At the time, no less than 110 South Africans were already on the waiting list for resettlement in a third country, while another 70 were being processed by the UN organization and potential third countries.[5]

With other exposed South African refugees, the ANC members targeted by Pretoria were trapped in Lesotho, often staying together in bigger groups.[6] The situation turned critical in November 1985, when rumours started to circulate that the apartheid regime around 1 December would carry out military operations against them.[7] Visiting Maseru in mid-November, Kaj Persson from the Swedish Foreign Ministry and Margareta Husén from SIDA confirmed that the political climate was tense, and that the Lesotho government, ANC and UNHCR all considered the danger of a South African attack as real.[8] Characterizing the increasing influx of South African asylum seekers as building up "a political powder keg", the Swedish officials concluded that they ought to be transferred to a third country as soon as possible.[9]

After their visit to Lesotho, Persson and Husén attended the annual consultative talks between Sweden and ANC, held in Lusaka on 19-22 November 1985. During the meeting, the Swedish delegation "expressed [...] concern about the security situation for the refugees in Lesotho", proposing that the Fokker aircraft donated by

1. Martin Wilkens: Memorandum ('Sydafrikanska flyktingar i Lesotho'/'South African refugees in Lesotho'), Swedish embassy, Maseru, 3 October 1985 (MFA).
2. Ibid.
3. Roland Axelsson: Memorandum ('Anteckningar från besök i Maseru 1985 09 28-10 03'/'Notes from visit to Maseru, 28 September to 3 October 1985'), Swedish embassy, Lusaka, 15 October 1985 (SDA).
4. According to the South African Truth and Reconciliation Commission, Pretoria's actions were "facilitated by an informer network in the Maseru office of [...] UNHCR" (TRC op. cit. (Vol. II), p. 98).
5. Roland Axelsson: Memorandum ('Anteckningar från besök i Maseru 1985 09 28-10 03'/'Notes from visit to Maseru, 28 September to 3 October 1985'), Swedish embassy, Lusaka, 15 October 1985 (SDA).
6. During a visit to Maseru in late September-early October 1985, Roland Axelsson was taken by Japhet Ndlovu to a transit centre which under primitive conditions housed 71 male ANC members. Fifteen of them were sleeping on the concrete floor. In a subsequent report to SIDA, Axelsson wrote in his matter-of-fact way that "I 'instructed' [the ANC representative] to immediately purchase mattresses" (ibid.).
7. Roy Unge: 'Tankar och händelser i Lesotho, november 1985-december 1986' ('Reflections and events in Lesotho, November 1985-December 1986'), [no place], 1987, p. 1. SIDA's Roy [Johansson] Unge played a particularly prominent role in the 1985-86 drama. His contribution was acknowledged by ANC Secretary General Alfred Nzo, who during the May 1986 aid negotiations with Sweden on behalf of the movement expressed "gratitude [...] in particular [to] the SIDA representative in Lesotho for the assistance rendered during the critical period in that country" ('Agreed minutes [from] consultations in Lusaka, May 1986, between the African National Congress of South Africa and Sweden concerning humanitarian assistance', Lusaka, 9 May 1986) (SDA). In 1987, Unge summarized his experiences in a 55-page document, which he later kindly copied to the author. It is referenced below as 'Unge: Reflections'.
8. Kaj Persson: Memorandum ('Programsamtal med ANC 1985/86'/'Consultative talks with ANC 1985/86'), Ministry for Foreign Affairs, Stockholm, 11 December 1985 (SDA).
9. Ibid.

Sweden could be chartered for an emergency operation. Against this background, the parties agreed to raise the 1985/86 Lesotho budget to 2 MSEK.[1]

Immediately thereafter, Japhet Ndlovu paid a short visit to Lusaka, emphasizing the seriousness of the situation. Returning to Maseru, on 25 November he submitted a request from ANC's National Executive Committee to the Lesotho government, asking "for permission and assistance for an urgent airlifting of [more than 123] refugees, who have to be transferred to Morogoro, Tanzania".[2] Stating that "it is strongly felt by the ANC that the prolonged presence of these [refugees] [...] poses serious security problems", Ndlovu added that the difficult situation was "a result of hard-to-explain bottlenecks in the process of transferring them through the established UNHCR [...] procedures".[3] He therefore asked the Lesotho authorities to issue the refugees with proper travel documents, stressing that the evacuation should take place before 1 December 1985.[4]

Using Swedish funds[5], the ANC headquarters in Lusaka had in the meantime chartered a Boeing 707 from Zambia Airways.[6] It landed at Moshoeshoe I International Airport outside the Lesotho capital on 26 November. At that time, no travel documents had been processed. After a telephone conversation between ANC Secretary General Alfred Nzo and the Lesotho Foreign Minister Vincent Makhele, around 145 refugees—among them Japhet Ndlovu—were, however, allowed to board the aircraft, which immediately took off for Zambia.[7] One hour later, it was back in Maseru. While flying over South African territory, the authorities in Pretoria had tried to force the plane to land in Johannesburg. The chief pilot from Zambia Airways had, however, refused, preferring instead to return with his sensitive cargo.[8]

The following days were "panicky"[9] and "chaotic".[10] While the situation with regard to a possible new departure remained unclear—and anonymous bomb threats were made against the Zambian aircraft—the "atmosphere among the ANC refugees became more and more tense".[11] On 1 December 1985—the date around which the rumoured South African attack would take place—the chartered plane, eventually, had to fly back to Zambia without any evacuees.[12] According to SIDA's

1. 'Minutes from consultative talks in Lusaka, 19-22 November 1985, between the African National Congress of South Africa (ANC) and SIDA concerning humanitarian assistance', Lusaka, 21 November 1985 (SDA).
2. Letter from Japhet Ndlovu, ANC Chief Representative to Lesotho, to the Secretary for the Interior, Maseru, 25 November 1985, attached to letter ('Flyktingar från Sydafrika'/'Refugees from South Africa') from Roy J. Unge to SIDA, Swedish embassy, Maseru, 27 November 1985 (SDA).
3. Ibid.
4. Ibid.
5. Letter ('Månadsbrev: November-december 1985'/'Monthly letter: November-December 1985') from Roland Axelsson to SIDA, Swedish embassy, Lusaka, 9 December 1985 (SDA).
6. A list of 140 ANC members considered to be particularly exposed was on 24 November sent by Ndlovu to ANC Lusaka through Sten Rylander from the Swedish Foreign Ministry (Letter ('Flyktingar från Sydafrika'/ 'Refugees from South Africa') from Roy J. Unge to SIDA, Swedish embassy, Maseru, 27 November 1985) (SDA). Rylander had visited Maseru to attend the seminar on 'Another development for SADCC'.
7. Ibid.
8. Ibid. and Unge: Reflections, pp. 2-3. The ANC headquarters in Lusaka subsequently alleged that the UNHCR representative to Lesotho, Kolude Doherty of Nigeria, had informed the British and US ambassadors about the flight. They, in turn, were said to have informed the South African authorities (Cable ('Misslyckat försök att transportera ANC-flyktingar från Lesotho till Zambia'/'Failed attempt to transport ANC refugees from Lesotho to Zambia') from the Swedish embassy to the Ministry for Foreign Affairs, Lusaka, 4 December 1985) (SDA).
9. Letter ('Attempted airlift of ANC student refugees') from Japhet Ndlovu to Prime Minister Leabua Jonathan, Maseru, 29 November 1985, attached to letter ('Flyktingar från Sydafrika: Kapitel 2'/'Refugees from South Africa: Chapter 2') from Roy Johansson Unge to SIDA, Swedish embassy, Maseru, 16 December 1985 (SDA).
10. Unge: Reflections, p. 3.
11. Ibid.
12. Ibid.

Roy Unge, at the time acting chargé d'affaires at the Swedish embassy, this, in turn, caused "panic within the government in Maseru, as well as among the refugees and at the ANC headquarters in Lusaka, [who asked w]hat could be done to quickly get the 140 people whose lives were in danger out [of the country]".[1]

The Fokker aircraft delivered by Sweden to Lesotho Airways could only carry 40 passengers. This notwithstanding, under the prevailing circumstances it was agreed by the Lesotho government and ANC to use the plane for a spaced evacuation operation under the auspices of UNHCR. With financial support from Norway and Sweden[2] and a crew from Finland, on 5 December 1985 the plane successfully evacuated a first group of 40 refugees to Zambia.[3] A second flight took place on 7-8 December[4], and a third on 11 December.[5] The fourth and final emergency flight—scheduled for 13 December—was, however, stopped by Pretoria. In a note blatantly contradicting the earlier demands that refugees should leave, the South African Foreign Ministry accused the Lesotho government of ferrying out "'ANC terrorists' for further military training", adding that it had "reliable information that ANC was planning an imminent attack on South Africa".[6] At a time when 120 ANC refugees had been evacuated, the apartheid regime denied Lesotho Airways further permission to fly over South African territory.[7]

It was, however, South Africa that was planning a military operation.[8] During the night between 19 and 20 December 1985, a death squad commando from Vlakplaas led by Eugene de Kock[9] attacked two houses in Maseru, killing six ANC members and three Lesotho citizens. Among those assassinated were Morris Seabelo[10], a senior MK commander formerly based in Angola, and a young female

---

1. Ibid., p. 4.
2. The Norwegian government had channelled direct assistance to ANC in Lesotho since the early 1980s. Contrary to Sweden, Norway did not maintain an official representation in the country. It was against this background agreed by the two Scandinavian donors in late 1985 to pool their support to ANC within a 'Lesotho Welfare Fund', monitored by SIDA (Cable ('Støtte til Lesotho Welfare Fund'/'Support for Lesotho Welfare Fund') from Knut Vollebæk, Norwegian embassy in Harare, to Roy Johansson [Unge], Swedish embassy in Maseru, Harare, 8 October 1985) (SDA). The coordinated effort continued throughout the 1980s. When in September 1988 Roland Axelsson established a new, 'underground' bank arrangement for the joint assistance, it was called 'S. N. Distributors', where the capital letters stood for Sweden and Norway (Roland Axelsson: Memorandum ('Anteckningar från besök i Maseru 28/1-1/2 1989'/'Notes from visit to Maseru, 28 January-1 February 1989'), Swedish embassy, Lusaka, 15 February 1989) (SDA). As will be seen below, in 1988/89 the Swedish assistance to ANC in Lesotho amounted to 600,000 SEK. The official Norwegian allocation for the calendar year 1989 was 250,000 NOK (Letter ('ANC Lesotho: Støtte til daglig underhold'/'ANC Lesotho: Support for daily necessities') from Mette Ravn, Ministry of Foreign Affairs of Norway, to SIDA, Oslo, 30 January 1989) (SDA). Sweden and Norway were the only countries to extend regular, humanitarian non-project aid to ANC in Lesotho.
3. Unge: Reflections, p. 4.
4. The second flight went via Gaborone, Botswana. At the same time carrying out scheduled commercial flights from Maseru, upon arrival in Johannesburg on 8 December 1985 the Lesotho Airways Fokker was received by South African soldiers. No refugees were, however, on board the plane, which therefore was allowed to continue its regular service (ibid., p. 5).
5. Ibid.
6. Cited in ibid., pp. 5-6.
7. Ibid., p. 5. Japhet Ndlovu remained as ANC Chief Representative in Lesotho.
8. The head of the Swedish embassy, Martin Wilkens, adopted a stand which was contrary not only to the assessment of the Maseru government and ANC, but also to the views held by the authorities in Stockholm. Wilkens was not in Lesotho when the evacuation of the refugees started. Upon his return, he, however, wrote a letter to the Swedish Foreign Ministry in which he strongly questioned the entire operation. Characterizing the decision taken by ANC—and supported by Sweden—as "rash and unprepared", as late as on 14 December 1985 he added that "[n]othing appeared in Maseru that indicated that the danger for the refugees was really acute" (Letter ('Sydafrikanska flyktingar i Lesotho'/'South African refugees in Lesotho') from Martin Wilkens, Swedish chargé d'affaires, to the Ministry for Foreign Affairs, Swedish embassy, Maseru, 14 December 1985) (MFA).
9. TRC op. cit. (Vol. II), p. 109.
10. Ibid.

member of ANC's cultural ensemble *Amandla* who had earlier performed in Sweden.[1]

The rumours of South African attacks proved to be real, and the situation for the remaining members of the ANC community became extremely unsafe. Although a citizen of Lesotho and employed by the Swedish embassy, Limpho Hani—the wife of Chris Hani; since March 1983 Commissar and Second-in-Command of Umkhonto we Sizwe—chose to move with their three daughters to the residence of Roy and Gunnel Unge, where they would stay for more than a month.[2] The Lesotho government, in the meantime, turned the funeral of those killed in the South African raid into a major manifestation of support for ANC.

Attended by thousands of people, the funeral took place on 29 December 1985. King Moshoeshoe, Prime Minister Jonathan and ANC Treasurer General Nkobi were the main speakers.[3] While Moshoeshoe in his speech read at length from ANC's Freedom Charter, Jonathan quoted a recent message from Pretoria in which the South African government requested bilateral talks with Lesotho. He, however, rejected the idea, stating that there was no point in such a meeting. President Botha should talk with Nelson Mandela instead.[4] In an indirect way, the imprisoned ANC leader was also present at the ceremony. At the end of his speech, Thomas Nkobi read out a telex received from Nelson and Winnie Mandela. It said:

> Whilst we continue to shed oceans of tears and rivers of blood, we accept the declaration of war and the painful reality that our pride and honour call on us to respond likewise. [...] [O]n our blood, we shall walk to freedom. [...] Like all struggling movements, we do not doubt our victory. On behalf of the internal wing of the struggle, the leaders inside South Africa—behind bars in Pollsmoor [and on] Robben Island—the detainees, the banned and exiled, and our country as a whole, we wish to express our deepest sympathies.[5]

The following day, a unanimous UN Security Council condemned South Africa's violation of Lesotho's sovereignty and the raid against ANC.[6] In defiance, however, Pretoria imposed on 1 January 1986 a *de facto* border blockade on Lesotho. Serious shortages of petrol, food, medical supplies and other basic necessities soon

---

1. Unge: Reflections, p. 11.
2. Ibid., p. 8. As earlier noted, Limpho Hani was employed by the SIDA office in Maseru in late 1984. Constantly watched by the South African security forces, in late 1988 it was, however, recommended that her employment should be brought to an end. As later stated by SIDA's security adviser, it had become "a threatening factor" (Author's conversation with Staffan Marelius, Stockholm, 28 February 1996). By that time, several incidents of attempted sabotage against the Swedish embassy in Maseru had taken place. The brakes of an official car had, for example, been tampered with (Interview with Roland Axelsson, p. 254). Before terminating her employment, the sensitive issue was discussed with ANC in general and Chris Hani in particular. Although a decision would affect the livelihood of his wife and their three children, the leading MK official understood the Swedish concerns. In a meeting in Lusaka in December 1988, he thus stated that "good relations between [ANC] and Sweden were of primary importance" (Dag Ehrenpreis: Memorandum ('Samtal med Chris Hani'/'Conversation with Chris Hani'), SIDA, Stockholm, 16 December 1988) (SDA). Limpho Hani herself was, however, bitter about her subsequent notice (see, for example, Roland Axelsson: Memorandum ('Anteckningar från besök i Maseru 28 juni-2 juli 1989'/'Notes from visit to Maseru, 28 June-2 July 1989'), Swedish embassy, Lusaka, 5 July 1989) (SDA).
3. Together with the Zambian Foreign Minister Lameck Goma, Nkobi travelled to Maseru in a plane chartered by President Kaunda for the occasion.
4. It could be noted that the first direct contact between the Pretoria regime and Mandela had taken place the previous month. Unbeknown to the outside world, in November 1985 the South African Minister of Justice 'Kobie' Coetsee met the ANC leader at the Volks Hospital in Cape Town (on the ensuing secret talks, see Allister Sparks: *Tomorrow Is Another Country: The Inside Story of South Africa's Negotiated Revolution*, Struik Book Distributors, Sandton, 1994).
5. Cited in Unge: Reflections, pp. 14-15.
6. Hanlon op. cit. ('Beggar'), p. 118. In his condemnation of the attack, the Swedish Foreign Minister Sten Andersson had on 20 December urged the Security Council to decide on mandatory sanctions against the apartheid regime ('Statement by Mr. Sten Andersson, Minister for Foreign Affairs, on the South African attack on refugees in Lesotho', Ministry for Foreign Affairs, Stockholm, 20 December 1985) (MFA).

developed. Popular discontent turned into desperation, which in turn paved the way for the intervention on 20 January by the Lesotho Paramilitary Force against Chief Leabua Jonathan. Led by Major-General Lekhanya, the first military government in Southern Africa was installed. It would, as noted above, enter into a security agreement with South Africa at the end of March 1986.

Problems and Suspension

The military takeover signalled the end of ANC's official presence in Lesotho. As a condition for lifting its blockade, South Africa immediately demanded the deportation of around 80 South African refugees.[1] While some of those listed had been evacuated in December and most of the others were already being processed by UNHCR for resettlement in third countries, this request was soon met. On 25 January 1986, a first batch of 57 left.[2] "[A]s soon as the plane was in the air, South Africa raised its border gates and normal traffic began to flow".[3]

Many more left over the following months. At the same time, there was a steady influx of new refugees from the repression under the South African state of emergency.[4] In addition, in an arrangement not dissimilar to that in Mozambique, ANC was initially allowed to maintain its representative and some other officials in Lesotho. In May 1986, however, Pretoria increased the pressure on the Lekhanya government to expel Japhet Ndlovu and a number of ANC, BCM and PAC members. Among them were people who had lived in Lesotho for many years.[5] Yielding to South Africa's demands and arguing that they were illegal immigrants, in early June Radio Lesotho announced that

> [t]he government has issued a warning to the effect that it has come to its notice that certain people have entered Lesotho unlawfully. [S]uch people should report their presence at the Ministry of Interior and Chieftainship Affairs before 17 June [1986]. Otherwise, they should return to their respective countries.[6]

The announcement went on to name 46 people, among them ANC Chief Representatve Ndlovu and the organization's local treasurer, Joseph Mjiba.[7] In their respective capacities, they had for a long time been responsible for the administration of the support from Sweden. Now, the cooperation was coming to an end. This, however, was not without additional incidents. When on 14 June Ndlovu and other exiles under the auspices of UNHCR were about to embark on a regular flight from Maseru, he was ordered by the Lesotho security police to remain behind, as "the South Africans had some questions [for him]".[8] Ndlovu was subsequently detained at the airport. As in December 1985, in this sensitive situation SIDA's Roy Unge again managed to charter Lesotho Airways' Fokker aircraft, which the following

---

1. Unge: Reflections, p. 23.
2. Ibid., p. 24.
3. Hanlon op. cit. ('Beggar'), p. 119.
4. A partial state of emergency had been declared by Pretoria in July 1985. It was made nationwide in June 1986. According to UNHCR, close to 200 South African refugees—out of which 90 per cent belonged to ANC—were registered during the first half of 1986 (Roland Axelsson: Memorandum ('Anteckningar från besök i Lesotho 11-15 september 1986'/'Notes from visit to Lesotho, 11-15 September 1986'), Swedish embassy, Lusaka, 25 September 1985) (SDA).
5. Japhet Ndlovu, for example, had lived in the country for 23 years. He was married to a woman from Lesotho and their three children were born there (Unge: Reflections, p. 33).
6. Cited in ibid.
7. Ibid., pp. 33-34.
8. Ibid., p. 34.

day left for Zimbabwe with Ndlovu and nineteen others on board.[1] Thus ended ANC's official presence in Lesotho. The Swedish assistance was, however, not suspended. In spite of considerable problems, it would continue for another three and a half years.

The problems started at once. Before his departure, Ndlovu had appointed Simon Makheta—a naturalized Lesotho citizen—as temporary 'caretaker' of the Swedish and Norwegian assistance. In mid-July, however, the ANC headquarters in Lusaka informed SIDA that the movement could not endorse the appointment, requesting that no disbursements should be made through him.[2] As it turned out, the issue was academic. On 22 July 1986—at the same time as three young ANC members registered with UNHCR were shot to death—Makheta was abducted from his home in Maseru.[3]

This was the beginning of a chain of negative events involving subsequent 'care-takers' and, by extension, the entire humanitarian assistance to the ANC refugees in Lesotho. In the process, large amounts of Swedish and Norwegian funds were either unaccounted for, lost or misappropriated.[4] Thus—according to a later statement by him—when Makheta was abducted, the kidnappers also seized financial statements and vouchers to SIDA for some 19,000 Maloti.[5] As Makheta had not been endorsed as 'caretaker' by ANC and it at the time was impossible to verify his story, it was agreed to write off the amount.[6]

Following Makheta's disappearance, the Secretary General of the Christian Council of Lesotho, Father Michael Worsnip—who had officiated at the funeral of the raid victims at the end of December 1985 and was close to ANC—was as a gap-filling measure temporarily charged by the Swedish embassy to administer the

1. Ibid., pp. 35-36. Also Roy J. Unge: Memorandum ('Angående slutet på ANC's officiella representation i Lesotho'/'Regarding the end of ANC's official representation in Lesotho'), [no place, but Swedish embassy, Maseru], 16 June 1986 (SDA). Eleven of the evacuees were ANC members, while the others were affiliated to PAC or different BCM organizations (ibid.). Ndlovu was subsequently appointed ANC Deputy Chief Representative to Zambia. After the democratic elections in South Africa, he returned to Lesotho, this time as high commissioner representing the government of Nelson Mandela.
2. Cable ('Re Simon Makheta i Lesotho') from Roland Axelsson to SIDA Stockholm and SIDA Maseru, Swedish embassy, Lusaka, 16 July 1986 (SDA). According to the cable, ANC was of the opinion that Makheta "is a businessman with a dubious economy" (ibid.).
3. Roy J. Unge: Memorandum ('Anteckningar från telefonsamtal med generalsekreteraren i Christian Council of Lesotho 86 07 25'/'Notes from telephone conversation with the Secretary General of the Christian Council of Lesotho, 25 July 1986'), [no place, but Swedish embassy, Maseru], 25 July 1986 (SDA). Also Unge: Reflections, p. 37. Makheta—whose daughter was studying in Sweden—turned up in Maseru in February 1987. Visiting the Swedish embassy, he said that he had been abducted by eleven armed men, four of them from the South African police. Taken to South Africa, he had been held at various police stations. In October 1986, he had been interrogated by security officers in Ladybrand. Among the issues raised was the question of Sweden's relations with ANC. According to Makheta, his interrogators were well informed concerning the Swedish embassy and its assistance to ANC in Lesotho. They were said to have shown him a photograph of the Swedish chargé d'affaires Martin Wilkens together with SIDA's Kurt Kristiansson and Roy Unge, and knew who was who among the three (Martin Wilkens: Memorandum ('Kidnappade ANC-representanten Simon Makheta'/'The abducted ANC representative Simon Makheta'), Swedish embassy, Maseru, 13 March 1987) (MFA). Makheta's account was at the time viewed with incredulity (see, for example, "'Kidnapped' refugee reappears in Lesotho' in *The Star*, 4 March 1987). It was, however, later borne out in an amnesty submission to the South African Truth and Reconciliation Commission by the Special Branch operative Henri van der Westhuizen, who also confirmed that the three young ANC refugees had been killed by a joint commando from Vlakplaas and Ladybrand (TRC op. cit. (Vol. II), p. 130; Makheta is there presented as Simon Moghetla, alias Joseph Mothopeng).
4. By September 1987, a total, accumulated amount of 63,300 Maloti—corresponding to some 175,000 SEK—was unaccounted for (Roland Axelsson: Memorandum ('Anteckningar från besök i Lesotho 12-18 september 1987'/'Notes from visit to Lesotho, 12-18 September 1987'), Swedish embassy, Lusaka, 18 September 1987) (SDA).
5. Ibid.
6. Ibid.

ANC Chief Representative
Japhet Ndlovu outside
the Swedish embassy in
Maseru in early 1986
(Photo: Jan Sundfeldt)

assistance.[1] He was, however, expelled from Lesotho in mid-September 1986.[2] With his deportation, another 22,000 Maloti was left without records.[3] In this situation it is not surprising that SIDA's Kurt Kristiansson already in mid-August reported that "there is next to chaos when it comes to disbursements of [Swedish] funds to ANC refugees in Lesotho", stressing that the local SIDA office "on its own neither can, nor should carry [them] out".[4]

The message was conveyed to ANC in Lusaka, which in early September for the first time since Ndlovu's departure nominated a properly authorized 'caretaker'. This, however, was far from a permanent solution. Allegedly harassed by South African security forces, the person in question, Kananelo Tlebere—working at the Lesotho National Development Corporation—suddenly left Lesotho in mid-November 1986.[5] Contrary to his two unauthorized predecessors, Tlebere had not distributed any of the funds received from Sweden in favour of the remaining ANC exiles in Lesotho. They amounted in total to 18,000 Maloti.[6]

The case of the first formal caretaker in Lesotho stands out as one of the very rare instances of probable theft in the long cooperation between Sweden and ANC, stretching over two decades and involving almost 900 MSEK.[7] As such, it was seriously followed up by the cooperating parties. In October 1987, Tlebere was eventu-

1. On Japhet Ndlovu's advice, Worsnip had been assisting Makheta (Roland Axelsson: Memorandum ('Anteckningar från besök i Lesotho 11-15 september 1986'/'Notes from visit to Lesotho, 11-15 September 1986'), Swedish embassy, Lusaka, 25 September 1986) (SDA).
2. Unge: Reflections, pp. 37-38. In December 1986, the Christian Council of Lesotho was ordered by the Lekhanya government not to concern itself with South African refugees in general and ANC in particular (ibid., p. 39).
3. Roland Axelsson: Memorandum ('Anteckningar från besök i Lesotho 12-18 september 1987'/'Notes from visit to Lesotho, 12-18 September 1987'), Swedish embassy, Lusaka, 18 September 1987 (SDA).
4. Kurt Kristiansson: Memorandum ('ANC's situation i Lesotho'/'ANC's situation in Lesotho'), Swedish embassy, Maseru, 19 August 1986 (SDA).
5. Unge: Reflections, p. 38.
6. Roland Axelsson: Memorandum ('Anteckningar från besök i Lesotho 12-18 september 1987'/'Notes from visit to Lesotho, 12-18 September 1987'), Swedish embassy, Lusaka, 18 September 1987 (SDA).
7. Cf. the interview with Roland Axelsson, p. 253. As noted by Axelsson, however, Tlebere "was not an ANC leader [, but] an outsider who used the liberation movement" (ibid.).

ally located in Zimbabwe[1], and in February 1988 he was confronted there by Roland Axelsson.[2] At that time—one and a half years after his departure from Lesotho—he denied any foul play, stating that he, in fact, had both distributed the funds received and reported to the "ANC structures". This was contradicted by ANC Treasurer General Thomas Nkobi, who described Tlebere as "dangerous" and informed Axelsson that the movement's security services were looking into the case.[3] No record has been found indicating if and how the matter was finally settled.

In December 1986—when developments in Lesotho had gone from bad to worse[4] and ANC in discussions with Swedish officials described the conditions in the country as more hostile than those in Swaziland, characterizing both countries as "bantustans"[5]—the movement appointed a new caretaker.[6] He was under strict confidentiality in January 1987 introduced to Roland Axelsson and the Maseru embassy as 'Mr. Ngidi' (aka 'Karabo').[7] At that time, there remained only around 50 ANC people in the country who were supported by Sweden and Norway.[8] While Axelsson reviewed the disbursement and reporting routines, the difficulties in Lesotho—in the SIDA official's opinion the "main problem country"[9]—did not, however, subside. In early 1987, they would, on the contrary, provoke divergent opinions within the Swedish embassy in Maseru and an unusual exchange with the authorities in Stockholm.

Stating that the Maseru government "obviously does not want an ANC presence in the country, whether official or clandestine", in a letter to the Foreign Ministry the Swedish chargé d'affaires Martin Wilkens in January 1987 expressed concern with regard to the ANC assistance and its possible negative impact on the bilateral relations between Sweden and Lesotho.[10] Fearing that "we [...] soon may end up in a situation where [it] manifestly goes against the will of the Lesotho government", he was of the opinion that the links with the host government should not be exposed to "such hazards" and that the Swedish authorities should find "alternative ways to channel the [support] to ANC in Lesotho". In the latter context,

1. Roland Axelsson: Memorandum ('Anteckningar från besök i Harare 21 oktober 1987'/'Notes from visit to Harare, 21 October 1987'), Swedish embassy, Lusaka, 26 October 1987 (SDA).
2. Roland Axelsson: Memorandum ('Fallet Kananelo Tlebere'/'The case of Kananelo Tlebere'). Swedish embassy, Lusaka, 12 February 1988 (SDA).
3. Ibid.
4. Together with their wives, the former Foreign and Information Ministers Vincent Makhele and Desmond Sixishe were brutally assassinated outside Maseru in mid-November 1986. Serving under Prime Minister Jonathan, both of them were close to ANC. They also maintained good relations with Sweden. Sixishe had on 20 January 1986—that is, the day of the military takeover—inquired about political asylum in Sweden. The response from the Foreign Ministry in Stockholm was that he was welcome, but that formally he had to apply for asylum from a country other than Lesotho (Unge: Reflections, p. 41). It was, however, impossible for him to leave the country. After the coup, Makhele and Sixishe were instead detained for a couple of weeks. Fearing for his life, in late August Sixishe again contacted the Swedish embassy. Taken to Roy Unge's residence together with his family, he was given the same response as in January. According to Unge, the Swedish chargé d'affaires Martin Wilkens "did not want to believe the seriousness of [...] the situation, doing everything in order that Sixishe [...] would abandon the idea of asylum" (ibid., p. 43).
5. Thomas Nkobi cited in Kaj Persson: Memorandum ('Samtal med företrädare för ANC'/'Conversation with ANC representatives'), Ministry for Foreign Affairs, Stockholm, 10 December 1986 (SDA).
6. Unge: Reflections, p. 39.
7. Roland Axelsson: Memorandum ('Anteckningar från besök i Lesotho 27-29 januari 1987'/'Notes from visit to Lesotho, 27-29 January 1987'), Swedish embassy, Lusaka, 26 February 1987 (SDA). In his notes, Axelsson—who carried contact addresses given to him by Thomas Nkobi in Lusaka—describes how under difficult circumstances he tried to arrange meetings with both 'Ngidi' and 'Karabo' before finding out that they were one and the same person.
8. Ibid.
9. Ibid.
10. Letter ('Sveriges bistånd till ANC i Lesotho'/'Sweden's assistance to ANC in Lesotho') from Martin Wilkens, chargé d'affaires, to the Ministry for Foreign Affairs, Swedish embassy, Maseru, 1 January 1987 (SDA).

Wilkens not only stressed that "the embassy does not have a clear picture of the real destination of the Swedish money", but questioned in general terms as "extraordinary" the fact that it was "distributing public funds for the maintenance of people [...] who we don't know and whose needs [...] have never been assessed by a Swedish authority".[1]

The initial reaction in Stockholm to the letter was to wait and see. In the meantime, Kurt Kristiansson, SIDA's representative to Lesotho, distanced himself from most of its contents, writing to the Foreign Ministry that Wilkens' information "is unfortunately not entirely correct".[2] Although he confirmed that those responsible for the assistance at the Maseru embassy did not personally know all the ANC beneficiaries, he underlined that Japhet Ndlovu before his departure had submitted a list with names—albeit "not always the real [ones]"—and other relevant data. Adding that "we must trust the ANC representative", Kristiansson, however, did not comment on the possible consequences of the ANC support on Sweden's relations with Lesotho.[3] Roland Axelsson was in this respect less restrained. After a visit to Lesotho at the end of January 1987, SIDA's regional coordinator strongly rejected Wilkens' viewpoints, stating that

> if our aid to ANC [...] one day should [...] be detrimental to the relations between Sweden and Lesotho—as feared by Martin [Wilkens]—I think that our relations with ANC are worth the damage. Lesotho is, after all, only a small country, [which is] dependent on South Africa and cannot in the slightest way influence developments in Southern Africa, whereas ANC is the leading movement for the abolition of apartheid and the introduction of democracy [...]. There should be no doubt concerning which relationship is the most important.[4]

The Ministry for Foreign Affairs reacted to the letters from Wilkens and Kristiansson in early April 1987, one month before the annual negotiations with ANC. While acknowledging that assistance to the movement in Lesotho was "a sensitive subject", Assistant Under-Secretary Tom Tscherning dismissed the arguments raised by the chargé d'affaires, supporting those put forward by SIDA's representative. Emphasizing that "the selection of beneficiaries must fall upon ANC", he concluded that "they are as well identified as may be considered possible and appropriate".[5] Adding that "the cooperation with ANC to a considerable extent is based on mutual trust", Tscherning, finally, noted that the crucial question of the host government's acceptance had been raised with Michael Sefali, Lesotho's Minister of Planning and Economic Affairs, during his visit to Stockholm in mid-January 1987. During the discussions, "our humanitarian assistance to ANC did not appear as news to Sefali, who also did not raise any objections against the [support]."[6]

Continued Swedish support in the form of daily necessities to ANC in Lesotho was against this background discussed during the bilateral negotiations in Lusaka in May 1987. Although the parties noted that "due to several incidents—including kidnappings, shootings and arrests—the reporting of the [assistance] had been unsatisfactory and [that] the new [administrative] system had not been functioning

1. Ibid.
2. Letter ('Sveriges bistånd till ANC i Lesotho'/'Sweden's assistance to ANC in Lesotho') from Kurt Kristiansson, SIDA representative, to the Ministry for Foreign Affairs, Swedish embassy, Maseru, 6 February 1987 (SDA).
3. Ibid.
4. Roland Axelsson: Memorandum ('Anteckningar från besök i Lesotho 27-29 januari 1987'/'Notes from visit to Lesotho, 27-29 January 1987'), Swedish embassy, Lusaka, 26 February 1987 (SDA).
5. Letter ('Humanitärt bistånd till ANC i Lesotho'/'Humanitarian assistance to ANC in Lesotho') from Tom Tscherning, Ministry for Foreign Affairs, to the Swedish embassy in Maseru, Stockholm, 6 April 1987 (SDA).
6. Ibid.

very well", an amount of 500,000 SEK was budgeted for 1987/88.[1] This decision, in turn, was largely based on ANC's undertaking that "the situation [in Lesotho] would [...] be closely monitored by the [...] Treasurer General's Office".[2] It was, however, only at the end of September 1987—almost five months later—that ANC authorized Pitso Lithobane as yet another "contact person for receiving and distributing humanitarian assistance".[3] Assisted by Limpho Hani, disbursements in favour of the beneficiaries in Lesotho were in the meantime administered by the SIDA office in Maseru.

At the aid negotiations in May 1988, the parties once again noted that "[d]ue to the security situation [...] problems had continued to occur with regard to financial reporting on the utilization of funds for daily necessities in Lesotho".[4] This notwithstanding, it was not only agreed to maintain the support, but to increase the budget from 500,000 to 600,000 SEK in 1988/89.[5] A couple of months later, Axelsson introduced yet another administrative routine for the Swedish—and Norwegian—funds. As before in Swaziland, he opened a bank account in the name of a bogus organization, named 'S.N. Distributors' after the donors.[6] Initially working well, when Axelsson in late June 1989 paid one of his regular visits to Maseru he found, however, that his postbox had been emptied and that a number of cheques posted earlier to various beneficiaries had been stolen.[7] Twenty-seven ANC families in Lesotho were thereby left without support.[8]

This was the end of the official Swedish assistance to ANC in Lesotho. As later noted by Axelsson,

[i]t was too dangerous to work there any longer. The South Africans had infiltrated everywhere. We could not get the money to the families who needed the support. And we could not find a reliable person to assist us. [...] I had to convince Thomas Nkobi that it was necessary [to stop].[9]

Meeting for consultative talks in Lusaka in November 1989, SIDA and ANC formally confirmed the decision taken by Axelsson and Nkobi.[10] After three and a half years of trials and tribulations, increasing security problems, funds repeatedly lost and reports missing, Lesotho was no longer included among the countries to which Swedish assistance in the form of daily necessities was extended. In fact, before ANC's unbanning and return to South Africa, it was only in Lesotho that the support was brought to an end.

---

1. 'Agreed minutes [from] consultations in Lusaka, May 1987, between the African National Congress of South Africa and Sweden concerning humanitarian assistance', Lusaka, 8 May 1987 (SDA). The delegations from ANC and Sweden were respectively led by Thomas Nkobi and Lars-Olof Edström.
2. Ibid.
3. Letter ('Contact name in Lesotho') from Thomas Nkobi to Roland Axelsson, ANC, Lusaka, 25 September 1987 (SDA).
4. 'Agreed minutes [from] consultations in Lusaka, May 1988, between the African National Congress of South Africa and Sweden concerning humanitarian assistance', Lusaka, 11 May 1988 (SDA). Jan Cedergren, Deputy Director General of SIDA, led the Swedish delegation, while Thomas Nkobi headed the ANC team.
5. Ibid.
6. Roland Axelsson: Memorandum ('Anteckningar från besök i Maseru 28/1-1/2 1989'/'Notes from visit to Maseru, 28 January-1 February 1989'), Swedish embassy, Lusaka, 15 February 1989 (SDA). The system was introduced in September 1988. Individual cheques were drawn from the account and distributed by post to the ANC beneficiaries.
7. Roland Axelsson: Memorandum ('Anteckningar från besök i Maseru 28 juni-2 juli 1989'/'Notes from visit to Maseru, 28 June-2 July 1989'), Swedish embassy, Lusaka, 5 July 1989 (SDA).
8. Ibid.
9. Interview with Roland Axelsson, p. 255.
10. Eva Belfrage: Memorandum ('Rapport från programsamtal mellan ANC och SIDA i Lusaka 27/11-1/12 1989'/'Report on consultative talks between ANC and SIDA in Lusaka, 27 November-1 December 1989'), SIDA, Stockholm, 11 December 1989 (SDA).

Botswana

Of the three BLS countries, Botswana was by far Sweden's most important cooperating partner. After an initial period of mainly multilateral aid, as early as in 1971—twelve years before Lesotho—it was included among the priority countries for Swedish bilateral development assistance. While an embassy with a SIDA office was established in the capital Gaborone, over the following years Sweden became one of Botswana's main donors.[1]

Surrounded by minority-ruled Rhodesia, Namibia and South Africa, from its independence in 1966 Botswana—later a founding member of the Frontline States group—assumed an important position as transit territory and safe haven for thousands of refugees from these countries. Although not allowed to establish settlements or embark on permanent projects there, ZAPU of Zimbabwe, SWAPO of Namibia, as well as BCM and PAC of South Africa, had, in addition, political representatives in the country. In the case of ANC, Thabo Mbeki spent the greater part of 1973 and 1974 in Botswana, where he, as noted above[2], obtained President Seretse Khama's permission to set up an ANC office. In November 1975, the President's Office notified Sweden that the Botswana government approved of official humanitarian support to the movement.[3]

Without any particular complications, Swedish support to ANC in Botswana was on a regular basis extended from the financial year 1975/76, when a modest amount of 33,500 SEK was allocated towards 'foodstuff and other daily necessities'.[4] At the time of Zimbabwe's independence in April 1980, the allocation had grown to 300,000 SEK.[5]

By comparison with Swaziland's pro-South African stand and Lesotho's challenging posture, in the early to mid-1980s Botswana would in its relations with the apartheid neighbour follow a middle course. Resolutely rejecting a security arrangement with Pretoria[6], in reaction to South African pressure and military raids the authorities, however, intervened against ANC and other nationalist organizations. As South Africa reacted to the outcome of the independence elections in Zimbabwe by launching its regional destabilization offensive—including cross-border operations into Botswana[7]—the government moved South African and other exiles to the Dukwe refugee camp. Joe Gqabi, ANC's Chief Representative, was forced to leave the country in June 1980. Furthermore, in early 1981 a number of South African refugees were handed over to the apartheid police[8], prompting Swedish protests

---

1. During the period from 1968/69 to 1994/95, the Swedish assistance to Botswana amounted—in fixed prices (1995)—to a total of 3.2 billion SEK (Sida op. cit., p. 29).
2. See the chapter 'ANC of South Africa: No Easy Walk'.
3. Letter ('Bistånd till ANC Sydafrika i Botswana'/'Assistance to ANC South Africa in Botswana') from Bo Källfors, Swedish ambassador to Botswana, to the Ministry for Foreign Affairs, Swedish embassy, Gaborone, 14 November 1975 (SDA). ANC was later allowed to run a small agricultural project outside Gaborone.
4. 'Agreed minutes of discussions on cooperation 1975/76 between Sweden and [the] African National Congress, South Africa, ANC', Lusaka, 12 September 1975 (SDA).
5. 'Agreed minutes from discussions on the cooperation between the African National Congress of South Africa (ANC) and the Swedish International Development Authority (SIDA)', Lusaka, 18 May 1979 (SDA).
6. South Africa never managed to force Botswana into a non-aggression treaty.
7. In November 1981, a death squad commando from Vlakplaas carried out an attack on ANC exiles in Gaborone (see below).
8. According to later findings by the South African Truth and Reconciliation Commission, "though not an agent", Simon Hirshfeldt, at the time Botswana's Commissioner of Police, "worked closely with the [South African] security police" (TRC op. cit. (Vol. II), p. 98).

and Thabo Mbeki to conclude that Botswana had embarked on a "movement backwards".

While the Botswana government firmly opposed any movement of arms by Umkhonto we Sizwe into or via the country[1], at no point, however, did it request Sweden to suspend its non-military support to ANC. Situated next to the South African border—only some 350 kilometres from Johannesburg and Pretoria—Gaborone would also become a centre and meeting place for anti-apartheid intellectuals, artists, musicians and writers. On ANC's initiative, in July 1982 the National Museum of Botswana and the local *Medu* Cultural Ensemble notably organized a conference-cum-festival on 'Culture and Resistance' in the capital. Hundreds of cultural workers from South Africa joined exiled colleagues there for a major manifestation. Supported by Sweden and other Nordic countries, it was, as later noted by Lindiwe Mabuza, of significant political importance as "we for the first time as South African artists were able to declare that we were going to be active in the cultural boycott".[2] Benefiting from easy access to South Africa and the host country's support, other ANC-aligned structures were at about the same time established in Gaborone. This was, for example, the case with the information agency Solidarity News Service, which was set up in 1983 and with official Swedish funds was supported by the Africa Groups from 1984.[3]

By 1985, however, the apartheid regime decided to move against Botswana. After the Gaborone home of the exiled South African journalist Nat Serache had been blown up on 13 February[4], on 14 May a car bomb killed Vernon Nkadimeng—the son of SACTU's General Secretary John Nkadimeng—[5] and, using mortars and machine guns, on 14 June South African commandos attacked ten houses in the capital supposedly accommodating 'ANC terrorists'. Leaving twelve people killed[6], the apartheid operatives returned a year later. In a coordinated, airborne action, on 19 May 1986 attacks were carried out against Botswana, Zambia and Zimbabwe.[7]

---

1. In 1982, notably, Joe Modise, Commander of MK and South Africa's future Defence Minister, was together with Cassius Make, Assistant Secretary of ANC's Revolutionary Council, arrested, charged and sentenced to a year's imprisonment in Botswana for illegal possession of arms (Shubin op. cit., p. 231).

2. Interview with Lindiwe Mabuza, p. 139.

3. CCHA: 'Protokoll [från sammanträde 7 juni 1984]' ('Minutes [from meeting 7 June 1984]'), SIDA, [Stockholm], 14 June 1984 (SDA).

4. Patrick Laurence: 'Former Mail man bombed in Botswana' in *Rand Daily Mail*, 14 February 1985. Also letter ('Attentat mot ANC-medlemmar i Gaborone'/'Attack against ANC members in Gaborone') from Karl-Göran Engström, Swedish ambassador to Botswana, to the Ministry for Foreign Affairs, Swedish embassy, Gaborone, 18 February 1985 (SDA).

5. Cf. TRC op. cit. (Vol. II), p. 108.

6. The Truth and Reconciliation Commission later noted: "So negative was the general reaction to the raid that an elaborate propaganda exercise had to be mounted to justify the operation. This was orchestrated by Craig Williamson [...]. In a discussion with the commission, Eugene de Kock stated that some of the weapons displayed as captured in [Gaborone] were in fact borrowed from him by Williamson" (ibid., p. 150). Asked to comment on the fact that a six-year-old child was killed by the South African commandos, after the attack Williamson, at the time heading the intelligence section of the Security Branch, stated that "the responsibility for innocent civilian deaths must be laid primarily at the door of the ANC" ('Justifying Gaborone' in *Financial Mail*, 28 June 1985, p. 62).

7. While the operation in the case of Botswana targeted an ANC transit facility in Gaborone, no South African exiles were killed. A citizen of Botswana—the successful football player Jabulani Masila—was, however, shot to death and many others were wounded (TRC op. cit. (Vol. II), pp. 150-51).

And the following month—on 14 June—a death squad commando again descended on the Botswana capital.[1]

As planned by Pretoria, these attacks forced the Botswana government to move against ANC. Although less dramatically than in Swaziland and Lesotho, this, in turn, affected the Swedish support. Largely mirroring the developments in Lesotho after the January 1986 military coup, the problems encountered in Botswana in this regard will here, finally, be summarized.

Already in 1984, ANC had been asked to withdraw its Gaborone representative.[2] Unofficially represented by Koos Segola—exiled in the country since 1962[3]—a new Chief Representative, Thami Sindelo, arrived in April 1985.[4] He took up his position at a particularly sensitive moment. In March 1985, the Pretoria government demanded that seventeen ANC members should be deported[5], and soon after Sindelo's arrival the Botswana police started to search houses occupied by South African refugees in and around Gaborone.[6] On 14 June, finally, the apartheid commandos struck, killing nine South Africans, two young local women and a Somali refugee.[7]

At the time of the raid, ANC catered for around one hundred people in Botswana, of whom about half were refugees in transit.[8] As in the other forward areas, only Sweden and Norway channelled official support to the movement. In the case of Botswana, it was very similar, both with regard to quantity and purpose. While the Swedish ANC budget for daily necessities in the country in 1984/85 amounted to 1 MSEK[9], the contribution from the Norwegian government for the calendar year 1985 was 1 MNOK.[10] Due to the raid, ANC's financial reporting to the two donors was also affected. Receipts and other relevant documents had either been stolen or destroyed, making it impossible for the movement to submit proper accounts of expenditure incurred during the previous months.[11]

---

1. One ANC member was killed during the June 1986 raid. Among those wounded was Thabiseng Theresa Mabuza, an eleven-year-old schoolgirl whose dream it was to become a classical dancer. Shot in the stomach, her spinal cord was irreparably damaged and she became paraplegic. She was initially treated in Botswana and later in Zimbabwe, USA and Sweden, but remained paralyzed from the waist down (Letter with medical report ('Miss Theresa Mabuza') from Tor Sellström to SIDA, Swedish embassy, Harare, 5 January 1988) (SDA). In September 1987, she attended the important International Conference on Children, Repression and the Law in Apartheid South Africa, held in Harare, where she informed the participants about the South African commando raid. The Swedish singer and activist Mikael Wiehe also attended the conference. Deeply impressed by the encounter with the girl, he subsequently included her traumatic experience in the song 'Weekend i Harare', released in 1988.
2. Roland Axelsson: Memorandum ('Anteckningar från besök i Botswana 5-8 februari 1985'/'Notes from visit to Botswana, 5-8 February 1985'), Swedish embassy, Lusaka, 4 March 1985 (SDA).
3. Ibid.
4. Letter ('Lägesrapport ANC Botswana'/'Status report [on] ANC Botswana') from Ingrid Löfström Berg to SIDA, Swedish embassy, Gaborone, 29 April 1985 (SDA).
5. Ibid. At the time based in Botswana, the prominent poet Mongane Wally Serote was on Pretoria's list. Eight of the ANC members listed had already left the country (ibid.).
6. Ibid.
7. Among the South Africans killed was the painter Thami Mnyele.
8. Roland Axelsson: Memorandum ('Anteckningar från möte med ANC i Gaborone 1985 08 26'/'Notes from meeting with ANC in Gaborone, 26 August 1985'), Swedish embassy, Lusaka, 23 September 1985 (SDA).
9. 'Agreed minutes [from] consultations in Lusaka, April 1984, between the African National Congress of South Africa and Sweden concerning humanitarian assistance', Lusaka, 6 April 1984 (SDA).
10. Roland Axelsson: Memorandum ('Anteckningar från möte med NORAD i Gaborone 1985 08 26'/'Notes from meeting with NORAD in Gaborone, 26 August 1985'), Swedish embassy, Lusaka, 19 September 1985 (SDA). Combining the Swedish and Norwegian allocations, in 1985 the per capita support to ANC in Botswana was no less than 20,000 SEK. Large amounts were, however, used for administration, transport and emergency evacuations. Although still very significant, the support to the individual ANC members was therefore considerably lower.
11. Ibid. and Roland Axelsson: Memorandum ('Anteckningar från möte med ANC i Gaborone 1985 08 26'/'Notes from meeting with ANC in Gaborone, 26 August 1985'), Swedish embassy, Lusaka, 23 September 1985 (SDA). According to Craig Williamson, the South African commandos seized "deposit and payment records, [as well as] bank statements and receipt books, [amounting to] the records of the ANC's Botswana machinery since 1977" ('Justifying Gaborone' in *Financial Mail*, 28 June 1985, p. 62).

For the quarter period 1 July-30 September 1985—that is, after the raid—SIDA, however, subsequently discovered "several irregularities", including "forgery of receipts [for] at least 9,000 [Botswana] Pula".[1] In countries where there were official ANC representations, misappropriations of Swedish funds had been extremely rare. SIDA therefore reacted to the unusual incident by demanding an investigation into the Botswana office's financial administration.[2] The request was immediately supported by Thomas Nkobi, who in late January 1986 sent his troubleshooter Doodles Gaboo, Administrative Secretary at the Treasury Department, to Gaborone.[3]

Going through the books, Gaboo could confirm the irregularities, establishing that "the embezzled sum amount[ed] to approximately 15,000 Pula".[4] Only Swedish funds were involved.[5] Emphasizing that it would "soon take steps in order to prevent a repetition", the headquarters in Lusaka, in the meantime, intervened by setting up a local ANC Botswana committee comprising the representative, the acting treasurer and a senior member to be "in collective charge of [the] finances".[6] Less than one and a half months later, the situation, however, dramatically changed. In early March 1986—even before the military authorities in Lesotho— the Masire government gave in to South Africa's pressure, deciding to deport the ANC Chief Representative Thami Sindelo and his deputy.[7] As earlier in Swaziland and—from June 1986—in Lesotho, ANC was left without an official representation.[8]

Albeit of far-reaching political significance, in the case of Botswana—where the government contrary to the situation in Lesotho and Swaziland was generally supportive towards the liberation movement and strongly opposed incursions by South African security forces—the closure of the ANC office would, however, only have a marginal effect on the Swedish assistance. Due to easy access from Lusaka, the ANC headquarters were in a position to identify capable administrators of the support. On behalf of Thomas Nkobi, in April 1986 Doodles Gaboo appointed Barry-Guilder as caretaker.[9] Formerly attached to the Gaborone-based Solidarity News

---

1. ANC-SIDA: 'SIDA contribution to ANC Botswana', [no place, but Lusaka], 14 January 1986 (SDA). This corresponded to a little more than 40,000 SEK.

2. Ibid.

3. Letter ('ANC Botswana') from Ingrid Löfström Berg to SIDA, Swedish embassy, Gaborone, 23 January 1986 (SDA).

4. Roland Axelsson: 'Minutes of quarterly meeting ANC-SIDA', Swedish embassy, Lusaka, 3 March 1986 (SDA). In Swedish Kronor, the embezzled amount was around 67,500 SEK.

5. Ibid.

6. Ibid. The forgeries were committed by rank and file members and did not involve ANC's local officials (Roland Axelsson: Memorandum ('Anteckningar från besök i Gaborone den 19-21 april 1986'/'Notes from visit to Gaborone, 19-21 April 1986'), Swedish embassy, Lusaka, 22 May 1986) (SDA).

7. Cable ('ANC-representanterna lämnar Botswana'/'The ANC representatives leave Botswana') from Göran Zetterqvist, Swedish ambassador to Botswana and Lesotho, Swedish embassy, Gaborone, 5 March 1986 (SDA). While the government in Gaborone at the same time announced that the information agency Solidarity News Service—supported by the Africa Groups and attacked during the June 1985 raid—would not be allowed to resume its activities, it should be noted that the decision to deport the ANC representative was not extended to include the PAC or SWAPO representatives (ibid.).

8. Although ANC was allowed to maintain an office in Maputo, in January 1987 its Chief Representative to Mozambique, Jacob Zuma, was forced to leave. By early 1987, there were no longer any official ANC representatives in the forward areas of Botswana, Lesotho, Mozambique or Swaziland.

9. Roland Axelsson: Memorandum ('Anteckningar från besök i Gaborone den 19-21 april 1986'/'Notes from visit to Gaborone, 19-21 April 1986'), Swedish embassy, Lusaka, 22 May 1986 (SDA).

Service and working in tandem with Richard Whiteing, he would together with the Swedish embassy[1] and Roland Axelsson over the following years administer the assistance to the satisfaction of all parties concerned.[2] Advised by ANC's Treasury Department and SIDA, from the very beginning Guilder introduced a compartimentalized routine under which the ANC beneficiaries received a monthly cash allowance.[3] Subsequently adjusted, the initial rate for adults was 225 Pula and for children 75 Pula. Reports to SIDA were also submitted on a monthly basis.[4]

In spite of the developments in 1985-86, during the aid negotiations in May 1986—when there were still around a hundred permanent ANC refugees and family dependants in the country[5]—Sweden and ANC increased the allocation for daily necessities in Botswana from 1.25 MSEK in 1985/86[6] to 1.75 MSEK in 1986/87.[7] From the point of view of Swedish support, Botswana in the process replaced Lesotho as the third most important country to which ANC assistance was extended.[8] With a regular inflow of refugees from South Africa, this position was maintained until the unbanning of the movement. For the financial year 1989/90, no less than 2.9 MSEK was set aside for ANC and its members in Botswana.[9]

Zimbabwe

A condition for Swedish assistance to ANC and other Southern African liberation movements was that it was acceptable to the host countries. In some cases—notably in Swaziland, as well as in Lesotho after the 1986 military coup—it is doubtful whether a formal approval would have been given. The security agreements with South Africa targeted the very same organization which was supported by Sweden. Towards the end of the 1980s, the authorities in these 'captive' states were, in addition, increasingly hostile towards ANC. Instead of seeking official authorization—thereby risking a negative response—in this situation the Swedish government chose, as earlier noted, to 'inform' or 'notify' individual cabinet members known to

---

1. Although the relations with Guilder and the local ANC community were frequent and close, the embassy in central Gaborone was not used as a meeting point. As later stated by Axelsson, "[w]e always tried to be careful. For instance, in Gaborone we never met ANC in the Swedish embassy. We had to arrange some other place where we could meet. We knew that the embassy was always watched. And we never used diplomatic cars. We always used other cars, both to and from such meetings" (Interview with Roland Axelsson, p. 255).
2. In Botswana, there was thus no need for bogus arrangements such as those introduced by Roland Axelsson in Swaziland and Lesotho. While Guilder left Botswana in 1989, Whiteing remained. Replacing Guilder, ANC appointed Dennis Mothusi as caretaker (Roland Axelsson: Memorandum ('Anteckningar från besök i Botswana 23-27 januari 1990'/'Notes from visit to Botswana, 23-27 January 1990'), Swedish embassy, Lusaka, 20 February 1990) (SDA). Only at the end of 1990—almost a year after ANC's unbanning—did the Botswana government welcome ANC to once again establish an official representation in the country (Cable ('ANC i Botswana') from Folke Löfgren, Swedish ambassador to Botswana and Lesotho, to the Ministry for Foreign Affairs, Swedish embassy, Gaborone, 18 September 1991) (MFA).
3. The assistance to ANC in Botswana was exceptional in that payments for daily necessities were made in cash (Interview with Roland Axelsson, p. 253).
4. Roland Axelsson: Memorandum ('Anteckningar från besök i Gaborone den 19-21 april 1986'/'Notes from visit to Gaborone, 19-21 April 1986'), Swedish embassy, Lusaka, 22 May 1986 (SDA). On an annual basis, the Swedish support to ANC's adult members in Botswana thus amounted to the quite extraordinary amount of 12,000 SEK. In addition to the Norwegian assistance, to this should be added allowances for rents, energy, school fees etc.
5. Ibid.
6. 'Agreed minutes [from] consultations in Lusaka, May 1985, between the African National Congress of South Africa and Sweden concerning humanitarian assistance', Lusaka, 30 May 1985 (SDA).
7. 'Agreed minutes [from] consultations in Lusaka, May 1986, between the African National Congress of South Africa and Sweden concerning humanitarian assistance', Lusaka, 9 May 1986 (SDA).
8. Ibid.
9. 'Agreed minutes from consultations held in Lusaka, May 1989, between the African National Congress of South Africa and Sweden concerning humanitarian assistance', Lusaka, 26 May 1989 (SDA).

be sympathetic towards ANC about the support. They, in turn, 'took note of' the Swedish position, but did not formally endorse it.

Internationally acknowledged as an important donor in the humanitarian field and actively intervening on ANC's behalf, in no Southern African country was the Swedish government ever requested to suspend its assistance.[1] In spite of excellent bilateral relations and insistent promotion of ANC, it would in one case, however, take years before Sweden was given the green light to assist the movement. That was in Zimbabwe.

ZANU's comfortable victory in the Zimbabwe independence elections shattered in early 1980 Pretoria's prospects of forming a regional 'Constellation of States' in defence of white South Africa. Hailed as "a moment of triumph", in a statement issued shortly after the announcement of the election results ANC's National Executive Committee noted that "the strategic situation has shifted against the enemy of the whole continent of Africa", expressing confidence that "the people of the new Republic of Zimbabwe [...] will steadfastly support the revolutionary struggle of our people until final victory".[2]

ANC was, however, also aware of the new state's close links with South Africa, which had been reinforced during fifteen years of international sanctions. In a meeting at the SIDA headquarters in Stockholm just before the independence celebrations in Salisbury (now Harare), President Tambo underlined "the extremely hard pressure" that Robert Mugabe, ZANU's leader and Prime Minister elect, was exposed to by the apartheid regime. In this difficult situation, Tambo added, it was "understandable that Mugabe had to manoeuvre with caution".[3] At the same time, both the ANC leader and his Swedish hosts were clearly sensitive to the fact that the relations between ZANU and the South African liberation movement were far from cordial.

As earlier noted[4], ZANU did not form part of the Khartoum alliance of so called 'authentic' liberation movements supported by the Soviet Union and its allies. Whereas ANC since the mid-1960s had been closely linked to Joshua Nkomo's ZAPU, Mugabe's victorious organization had been associated with PAC.[5] Lumped together with the latter, Tambo had in a NEC report to ANC's 1969 consultative conference in Morogoro even characterized ZANU as a "spurious stooge

1. The decision to end the support in Lesotho was taken jointly by ANC and Sweden.
2. Alfred Nzo: 'Victory in Zimbabwe', Statement on behalf of the ANC National Executive Committee, in *Mayibuye*, No. 3, 1980, pp. 5-6. It is in the context of ANC's relations with ZANU at the time significant that neither the victorious movement nor Robert Mugabe, the Prime Minister elect, were mentioned in the long statement. It quoted instead the "spokesmen of the new Zimbabwe" (p. 5). It could also be noted that the prime lesson for ANC was the primacy of armed struggle: "Of strategic importance has once again been the vindication of armed struggle as an effective weapon for winning genuine power [...]. This is the crux of the whole question" (p. 6).
3. Birgitta Berggren: Memorandum ('Minnesanteckningar från samtal på SIDA den 14 april 1980 med president Oliver Tambo, African National Congress/South Africa'/'Notes from conversation at SIDA on 14 April 1980 with President Oliver Tambo, ANC'), SIDA, Stockholm, 21 April 1980 (SDA).
4. See the Prologue.
5. Towards the end of the liberation struggle in Zimbabwe, ZANU had invited MK cadres to join ZANLA. But, as noted by Shubin, "this proposal was ultimately not accepted by the ANC, presumably because ZANU maintained traditionally close relations with the PAC. In any event, the ANC wanted first to discuss this issue with ZAPU, whose leadership was apparently opposed to it" (Shubin op. cit., p. 207). In fact, at the end of the 1970s there were about 100 MK fighters inside Zimbabwe under ZIPRA's command (Barrell Ph. D. op. cit., chapter five, p. 34). In addition, "a large number"—perhaps 200—were infiltrated from Zambia with returning ZAPU members during the repatriation exercise in early 1980. Moving into the designated assembly points, most of them were after independence identified by the Mugabe government, rounded up and sent back across the Zambezi (David Martin and Phyllis Johnson: 'Zimbabwe: Apartheid's Dilemma' in Johnson and Martin (eds) op. cit., pp. 46 and 351). This added to the distrust and strain between ANC and ZANU.

organization", created and maintained by "the imperialists".[1] At the time of Zimbabwe's independence in April 1980, ANC had thus to make a serious political effort to bridge the confidence gap vis-à-vis Robert Mugabe's movement in order to establish a presence in the strategically important country.[2] While Zimbabwe held the Soviet Union and its allies at arm's length, contrary to the situation in Angola and Mozambique ANC was in this context largely dependent on the good offices of Sweden. From the very beginning, Thabo Mbeki would here play a particularly crucial role.

After independence in mid-April 1980, SIDA's Ola Jämtin at the embassy in Lusaka was transferred to Harare (Salisbury) to set up a Swedish mission and coordinate development assistance to Zimbabwe, which as a result of the humanitarian support to ZANU and ZAPU from its birth was confirmed as a 'programme country'.[3] Responsible for Sweden's cooperation with the Southern African liberation movements, Jämtin had since his posting to Lusaka in mid-1979 established close personal relations with Mbeki. On Midsummer's Day 1980—the eve of his departure to Zimbabwe—his farewell party was, for example, in addition to Hidipo Hamutenya of SWAPO attended by the future President of South Africa.[4]

Jämtin had barely settled into his new environment, when a couple of weeks later Mbeki showed up at his Harare residence. The Swedish official later recalled:

> One night, coming back rather late [...], Toko, who took care of the house and stayed in the [...] servants quarters [...], came [...] to tell [me] about some strange visititors sitting in his kitchen. Toko had not known how to handle the situation when earlier in the evening the two [...] unknown Africans [had] knocked on his door. [...]

> When we sat down inside my house, Thabo told me that they had come to introduce ANC to the new Zimbabwean administration. [To] sound them out, sort of, and—as I remember it—work towards an open and constructive relationship between Zimbabwe and ANC. It was a very nice surprise for me to have Thabo visiting. [...] [He] and his colleague [...][5] were planning to stay for one week. [...]

> [In the] morning, we had breakfast together before we were to drive to town. We saw a pick-up [truck] coming up the driveway [...], loaded with [...] tools [...]. Two white men stepped out

1. Tambo op. cit., p. 74. Convinced of ZAPU's primacy within the Patriotic Front, many ANC representatives reacted with incredulity to the election results in Zimbabwe. Based at the Swedish embassy in Lusaka, the author recalls how SWAPO's Libertine Amathila on the morning of the announcement virtually came there dancing, while ANC's Billy Modise—working at the UN Institute for Namibia—later in the day was clearly subdued. Closer to the events in Zimbabwe, Thabo Mbeki was, however, neither surprised, nor negative. In addition to various sources of information, he—as well as Oliver Tambo—was well aware of the fact that Sweden supported ZANU and ZAPU on equal terms. Together with Anders Möllander and/or Ola Jämtin, the author visited Zimbabwe on several occasions before the independence elections at the end of February 1980 (cf. the chapter 'Patriotic Front: ZANU and ZAPU towards Independence'). Returning to Lusaka, Mbeki regularly asked the Swedish officials about their assessment of the relative strength of the two Patriotic Front partners. Informed that the overwhelming impression was a landslide victory for ZANU, he seemed to concur. While the Soviet Union, GDR and other East European countries strongly questioned this impression, representatives of the Cuban embassy were, similarly, understanding (Author's recollection).
2. In his doctoral dissertation on ANC's diplomacy and international relations, Scott Thomas claims that "ANC's links with ZAPU did not harm its representation in Zimbabwe", incorrectly stating that "[i]n 1979, even before Zimbabwe's formal independence, the ANC opened an office in Harare" (Thomas op. cit., p. 147). However, an officially recognized ANC mission was not established in the Zimbabwean capital until 1985.
3. See the chapter 'Patriotic Front: ZANU and ZAPU towards Independence'.
4. Ola Jämtin: 'Minnen från kontakter med ANC 1979-1981: Lusaka, Zambia, och Salisbury, Zimbabwe'/ 'Memories from contacts with ANC 1979-1981: Lusaka, Zambia, and Salisbury, Zimbabwe', Stockholm, 6 February 1997. Written in English, Jämtin's recollections were kindly submitted for this study. The farewell party was held at the author's residence. Jämtin notes that Mbeki and Hamutenya "joined together in the performance of a Southern African song and dance number, which greatly contributed to a nice atmosphere and ha[s] stayed in my memor[y] ever since" (ibid.).
5. Jämtin does not recall the name of Mbeki's colleague (ibid.).

of the [truck]. To me they looked very much like workers sent out to do repair[s] [, but] I had not ordered any since I did not have any problems with my house. [As] they went to my door, I stood up from the table to meet and assist them in finding the right house for their assignment. [But] [t]o my almost shocking surprise, they did not ask about any repair[s]. Instead, one of them immediately presented me with a small piece of paper on which the names of my guests were written [, saying]: 'Sir, we are from the [...] security police. Are these people in your house now?'

[T]he still heavily white-[dominated] security service [in Zimbabwe] represented to me [a force which] until rather recently [had] collaborated with their colleagues in South Africa. [...] [T]hat was not the right type of reception the ANC should be given when the organisation [...] wanted to come for discussions. What could I do?

Having [...] clearly underlined that the house [belonged to] the Swedish government and [was] under diplomatic immunity, [I thought] that I perhaps should consult my ambassador [...]. [S]ince the visitors welcome[d] the meeting, I, however, saw it possible to let them in. We then continued our breakfast, also offering coffee to [the] security men. [...] They politely turned down the offer, [but] stayed [until] they had reached an agreement with [...] Mbeki about keeping in regular contact during the week, and that Thabo and his friend should not leave Salisbury.

During the week that followed, Thabo asked me [on] several [occasions] to drive him or both of them to different addresses and meetings. We always agreed on [a] time when I should pick them up, or that they would be taken back by the [people they were meeting]. Everything passed without [any] problems. A few weeks [later], the first [...] ANC representative showed up in Salisbury.[1]

During his first visit to Zimbabwe, Mbeki held a series of meetings with leading government and ZANU representatives, and it was in principle agreed that an official ANC delegation led by President Tambo should attend the Heroes' Day celebrations in Harare on 11-12 August 1980.[2] This was later confirmed. Emphasizing that "[t]he significance of the visit cannot be overestimated", in a subsequent interview in ANC's journal *Mayibuye* Tambo noted that

we reached a remarkable identity of views. The visit was in every respect most successful. What is more, our discussions left us with no doubt [...] that the Zimbabwe leadership stands firmly in solidarity with our struggle, which it regards as the struggle of all Zimbabweans.[3]

One month later, Oliver Tambo and Thabo Mbeki informed the Swedish embassy in Lusaka about the discussions in Harare. In their view, the results were "beyond expectation".[4] The Mugabe government had invited ANC to immediately establish a presence in Zimbabwe. An official representation would be opened in the capital before the end of the year, and suitable premises were already being identified. As there was an increasing inflow of refugees from South Africa, it could also be necessary to establish a second office in Bulawayo and to procure land to accommodate them. While no military bases were allowed, the ANC leaders further stated that the movement—"as earlier had been the case from Tanzania to Zambia"—was planning to transfer certain central functions to Zimbabwe in order to be "close[r] to the scene". The Department of Information and Publicity—headed by Mbeki— was a case in point.[5]

1. Ibid.
2. Helena Ödmark: Memorandum ('ANC etablerar [närvaro] i Zimbabwe'/'ANC establishes presence in Zimbabwe'), Swedish embassy, Salisbury, 25 July 1980 (SDA).
3. 'ANC Visit to Zimbabwe', Interview with Comrade O. R. Tambo, in *Mayibuye*, [no number], 1980, p. 1.
4. Cable ('Svenskt bistånd åt ANC-kontor i Salisbury'/'Swedish assistance for ANC office in Salisbury') from Ulf Waldén to the Ministry for Foreign Affairs, Swedish embassy, Lusaka, 17 September 1980 (SDA).
5. Ibid.

At a time when ANC was facing restrictions in several Southern African countries, the prospects of establishing a solid political base in newly independent Zimbabwe were both opportune and inspiring. To be able to do so, Tambo said, the movement needed financial support from Sweden.[1]

The signals received from Harare were, however, less enthusiastic. In a meeting with the Swedish ambassador Bo Heinebäck and Tom Vraalsen from the Norwegian Ministry of Foreign Affairs, the veteran ZANU leader Simon Muzenda—who combined the portfolios of Deputy Prime Minister and Foreign Minister—was with regard to ANC in early September 1980 "cautious and doubtful".[2] Stating that "it is only now that we are beginning to have contacts with them", he stressed that no decision had been taken as to when an ANC office could be opened.[3]

With conflicting messages from the two friendly parties, in early October 1980 the Foreign Ministry in Stockholm issued an instruction to the Swedish embassies in Lusaka and Harare. Noting that it in principle had "no objections against ANC reallocating available [Swedish] funds in favour of an office in Zimbabwe", it, however, strongly emphasized that "it must be made clear to ANC that before a Swedish contribution may be used, Zimbabwe has to give its explicit consent".[4] What was important to Sweden, the instruction declared, was "that we receive an authoritative, clear statement from the government of Zimbabwe".[5] Adding that "we hope [...] that ANC understands the importance we attach to avoiding any misunderstandings in our relations with Zimbabwe in this regard", the Foreign Ministry motivated the decision by referring to "the earlier strained links between ANC and ZANU, as well as [to] the controversial nature of the issue at the level of the [Mugabe] government".[6] The following year—in early July 1981; shortly before the assassination of Joe Gqabi—the Fälldin government specified that the decision not only applied to an office, but also to 'daily necessities' for ANC refugees in the country.[7]

The Swedish position was conveyed to Thabo Mbeki in Lusaka. While in the light of earlier relations between his movement and ZANU he was "understanding", he, however, added that the strains "were history" and that ANC expected an official approval by the Zimbabwe government within three to four weeks.[8] On the very same day, the cautious Swedish approach was, however, validated by ambassador Heinebäck in Harare. After discussions with Emmerson Munangagwa, Zimbabwe's Minister of State for Security, he reported that Mugabe's government "found no reason to embrace ANC".[9] According to Munangagwa, it was only after ZANU's electoral victory that ANC had shown interest in bilateral relations.

1. Ibid.
2. Bo Heinebäck: Memorandum ('Samtal med utrikesminister Muzenda om södra Afrika'/'Conversation with Foreign Minister Muzenda about Southern Africa'), Swedish embassy, Salisbury, 4 September 1980 (MFA).
3. Ibid.
4. Cable ('Svenskt stöd för ANC-kontor i Zimbabwe'/'Swedish support for [an] ANC office in Zimbabwe') from the Ministry for Foreign Affairs to the Swedish embassies in Lusaka and Salisbury, Ministry for Foreign Affairs, Stockholm, 6 October 1980 (SDA).
5. Ibid.
6. Ibid.
7. Cable ('Bistånd till ANC i Zimbabwe'/'Assistance to ANC in Zimbabwe') from the Ministry for Foreign Affairs to the Swedish embassies in Lusaka and Salisbury, Ministry for Foreign Affairs, Stockholm, 3 July 1981 (SDA).
8. Cable ('Om stöd ANC-kontor i Salisbury'/'Re support [to] ANC office in Salisbury') from Göran Hasselmark, Swedish ambassador to Zambia, to the Ministry for Foreign Affairs, Swedish embassy, Lusaka, 14 October 1980 (MFA).
9. Bo Heinebäck: Memorandum ('Samtal om ANC'/'Conversation on ANC'), Swedish embassy, Salisbury, 14 October 1980 (SDA).

Although it was correct that the issue of an ANC office had been raised, the informal representative who had been sent to Harare—that is, Joe Gqabi—was, however, in the country "without [...] authorization".[1]

Insistence and Reluctance

Following the instructions from Stockholm, no Swedish financial support was extended to ANC in Zimbabwe. From his arrival in mid-1980, Joe Gqabi was, however, on a personal basis assisted by Ola Jämtin. Looking back, Jämtin stated in 1997:

> [After Thabo Mbeki], [t]he second ANC man on the scene was Joe Gqabi. [He was] a mystery to me, though we came to establish a relationship [...]. Joe [w]ould call me in my office, suggesting that we meet at a certain time at 'the usual place' or 'the place', meaning different places, an Italian restaurant or the restaurant in the [Harare] gardens. [He] was very security conscious.[2] He preferred to stay at different addresses, [ir]regularly moving between houses. It also happened [that] he stayed overnight at my house. His car [w]ould be parked well hidden, not to be seen from the road, which Joe saw as a great advantage. He, of course, came without prior arrangement. He knew [that] the room was always [there] for him.[3]

Until mid-1982, the Swedish ambassador Bo Heinebäck and SIDA's resident representative Jan Cedergren—both of them having established cordial relations with the ZANU leadership during the liberation struggle[4]—would on ANC's behalf untiringly raise the outstanding question of the movement's status with the Zimbabwe government. In February 1981, for example, it was discussed in a meeting between Cedergren and Deputy Prime Minister Muzenda. Taking place shortly after South Africa's Matola raid on ANC in Mozambique, Muzenda was for reasons of national security still very hesitant about an official representation of the movement. Stating that Zimbabwe's security forces were "totally infiltrated and full of South Africans", open activities by ANC and PAC would in his view be tantamount to "suicide".[5] While regretting the divisions within PAC, Muzenda was at the same time suspicious of ANC's relations with ZAPU.[6]

As if to underline Muzenda's doubts, on 23 February 1981 Joe Gqabi was exposed to a first assassination attempt.[7] And in early May, South Africa's Minister of Law and Order, Louis le Grange, threatened to attack alleged ANC bases in

---

1. Ibid.
2. Gqabi became in 1981 head of intelligence and Deputy Director of ANC's Department of Intelligence and Security, led by Mzwai Piliso. Reddy Mazimba, his successor as representative to Zimbabwe, was head of security.
3. Ola Jämtin: 'Minnen från kontakter med ANC 1979-1981: Lusaka, Zambia, och Salisbury, Zimbabwe'/ 'Memories from contacts with ANC 1979-1981: Lusaka, Zambia, and Salisbury, Zimbabwe', Stockholm, 6 February 1997. Gqabi's movements were closely monitored by Zimbabwe's security police. Two days after his assassination, they came to Jämtin's residence, asking: "Where did he use to sleep?" In his recollections, Jämtin writes: "Of course, the room that Joe had used was totally empty. [There was] just the bed, a chair, [a] table and a filing cabinet that [he] had placed there. [It was] also empty! The police found one simple piece of paper stamped with some text, took it and left the house without one more word" (ibid.).
4. See the chapter 'Patriotic Front: ZANU and ZAPU towards Independence'.
5. Jan Cedergren: Memorandum ('ANC i Zimbabwe'), Swedish embassy, Salisbury, 23 February 1981 (SDA).
6. Ibid.
7. Mike Overmeyer: 'Bomb was wired to car wheel say police' in *The Herald*, 24 February 1981.

Zimbabwe.[1] His statement was followed up in June by Prime Minister P.W. Botha, who declared that South Africa would take action against Zimbabwe if ANC or other "hostile movements" were allowed to open offices there.[2] Finally, on the evening of 31 July 1981 Joe Gqabi was killed by a South African hit squad outside his house in Harare.[3] Defying the apartheid regime, ten days later the Zimbabwe government honoured his memory with a solemn state funeral, addressed by both Prime Minister Robert Mugabe and ANC President Oliver Tambo. Representatives of very few Western countries attended the ceremony, and only at junior level. The Swedish government was represented by ambassador Heinebäck and Gqabi's friend Ola Jämtin, who laid a wreath on the grave.[4]

The assassination of Gqabi formed part of a generalized South African offensive. As noted by Hanlon, "[b]y early 1981, South Africa's State Security Council had clearly decided to hit Zimbabwe hard. There was substantial sabotage and Zimbabwe was subjected to *de facto* sanctions. The main goal seemed simply to show Prime Minister Mugabe who was boss in the region, and to cause as much disruption as possible without overt military intervention".[5] Making use of a fifth column of white Zimbabweans, a series of covert operations were launched instead. Two weeks after the murder of ANC's representative, the army arsenal at the Inkomo Barracks some 30 kilometres from the capital was blown up. And on 18 December 1981, a bomb shattered the ZANU headquarters in downtown Harare, killing seven people and injuring 124, mostly Christmas shoppers.[6] The bomb went off at the time when Mugabe and many cabinet members were scheduled to attend a ZANU meeting. Fortuitously, it was delayed. Had the meeting occurred according to plans, the Prime Minister and almost the entire ZANU leadership would have been killed.[7]

The issue of an officially recognized ANC mission was against this background kept on ice. Following a visit by ANC's Secretary General Alfred Nzo, it was, however, agreed by the Zimbabwe government that the movement informally could

---

1. Government of Zimbabwe: 'Minister replies to South Africa', Press statement, Department of Information, Salisbury, 11 May 1981 (SDA).
2. Tendai Dumbutshena: 'We won't be dictated to: Mugabe' in *Daily Mail*, 10 June 1981. Botha's threat was made in the midst of mounting South African pressure on Zimbabwe and in connection with a 'Namibia solidarity week' organized by ZANU and attended by SWAPO President Sam Nujoma. In reaction to the statements made by le Grange and Botha, the Harare government declared that no military bases were allowed in the country, but that Zimbabwe had a moral, humanitarian and political obligation to receive people fleeing from apartheid oppression. Thus, Prime Minister Mugabe stated: "We are entitled to give political support to the liberation movements in South Africa and Namibia. It is our duty under the OAU Charter" (cited in ibid.).
3. The South African Truth and Reconciliation Commission later established that Gqabi "was assassinated by South African agents operating in collusion with a group of Zimbabwean agents [based] inside Zimbabwe's CIO" (TRC op. cit. (Vol. II), p. 104). Gqabi's house should have been protected by the Zimbabwean security police. While the ANC leader himself rarely spent the night in the house, his young assistant Geraldine Fraser did. Arguing that the murder was an 'inside job', the security police arrested Fraser, kept her in solitary confinement and interrogated her for seventeen days. She was later expelled to Zambia (Jan Cedergren: Memorandum ('Zimbabwe och ANC: Lägesrapport'/'Zimbabwe and ANC: Status report'), Swedish embassy, Salisbury, 29 October 1981 (SDA) and Shelagh Gastrow: *Who's Who in South African Politics*, No. 5, Ravan Press, Johannesburg, 1995, p. 70). Subsequently undergoing military training in Angola and becoming a member of SACP's Politburo, Geraldine Fraser-Moleketi was in 1995 appointed Deputy Minister of Welfare.
4. Bo Heinebäck: Memorandum ('Statsbegravning för ANC-representanten Joe Gqabi'/'State funeral for the ANC representative Joe Gqabi'), Swedish embassy, Salisbury, 13 August 1981 (SDA). The funeral took place on 9 August 1981.
5. Hanlon op. cit. ('Beggar'), p. 173.
6. Ibid., p. 175.
7. Ibid. Shortly afterwards, Mugabe's head of close security, Geoffrey Price, fled to South Africa. A conspicuous example of the cost of post-independence reconciliation, Price had in 1979-80 been closely involved in Bishop Muzorewa's election campaign.

place a contact person in Gqabi's stead.[1] Known as Pila Pola, he would at ANC's expense be staying at a hotel in central Harare, closely watched by the security police.[2] His contacts with the Swedish embassy were considerably looser than those maintained by his predecessor.[3] Nevertheless, while the Mugabe government was "lying very low"[4], its non-socialist counterpart in Stockholm continued on ANC's behalf to insist on a more permanent solution. During an official visit to Zimbabwe, in early January 1982 Foreign Minister Ola Ullsten raised the issue of Swedish support to an ANC office directly with Robert Mugabe. Not dismissive, the Zimbabwe Premier welcomed the proposal as and when the general security conditions so would allow.[5]

Once again, however, Simon Muzenda was lukewarm to the idea. Asked to follow up the discussion between Mugabe and Ullsten, at the end of January ambassador Heinebäck came back to him. Stating that he himself had been in the same position and that there were no doubts with regard to the humanitarian character of Sweden's assistance[6], the Deputy Prime Minister was, nevertheless, evasive. In addition to national security concerns, Muzenda for the first time introduced PAC into the equation. Like PAC, ZANU had once been "the underdog". Zimbabwe, he said, acted in accordance with OAU decisions and supported both ANC and PAC. Why did Sweden not follow the same line?[7]

Drawing conclusions from the meeting, in a subsequent report to the Foreign Ministry in Stockholm Heinebäck commented that "we should not [continue to] create the impression that we want to interfere in [Zimbabwe's] delicate process of at the same time [having to] develop a *modus vivendi* with South Africa and its liberation movements".[8] Emphasizing that the government of Zimbabwe was "significantly more sceptical than ourselves of the recipient of our assistance", he added that in this regard there was a risk of sowing "irritation into our general, bilateral relations". While hoping that "our new 'reminders' [...] during the last weeks may

1. Jan Cedergren: Memorandum ('Zimbabwe och ANC: Lägesrapport'/'Zimbabwe and ANC: Status report'), Swedish embassy, Salisbury, 29 October 1981 (SDA).
2. Ibid. A leading MK member, Pola was also known as Judson Khuzwayo. In early May 1985, he died in a car accident on the road between Harare and Lusaka.
3. Shortly after his arrival, Pola asked the Swedish embassy to supply him with a letter bomb detector, a request which ultimately was not granted (ibid.). In May 1982, both the SIDA representative to Zimbabwe, Jan Cedergren, and Pila Pola took part in the aid negotiations between Sweden and ANC in Lusaka ('Agreed minutes of discussions in Lusaka, May 1982, between the African National Congress of South Africa, ANC, and the Swedish International Development Authority, SIDA, concerning humanitarian assistance', Lusaka, 24 May 1982) (SDA).
4. Jan Cedergren: Memorandum ('Zimbabwe och ANC: Lägesrapport'/'Zimbabwe and ANC: Status report'), Swedish embassy, Salisbury, 29 October 1981 (SDA).
5. Cable ('Bidrag till ANC's kontor i Salisbury'/'Contribution towards ANC's office in Salisbury') from the Ministry for Foreign Affairs to the Swedish embassy in Salisbury, Ministry for Foreign Affairs, Stockholm, 18 January 1982 (SDA). The meeting between Mugabe and Ullsten took place on 5 January 1982. Ten days later, Ullsten informed Thomas Nkobi in Stockholm that Swedish assistance would be extended as soon as ANC's office had been formally established (Anders Bjurner: Memorandum ('Besök av ANC-ledare hos utrikesministern'/'ANC leader visiting the Foreign Minister'), Ministry for Foreign Affairs, Stockholm, 18 January 1982) (MFA).
6. On Muzenda and Swedish assistance to ZANU in Zambia in the mid-1970s, see the chapter 'Patriotic Front: ZANU and ZAPU towards Independence'.
7. Cable ('Bidrag till ANC's kontor i Salisbury'/'Contribution to ANC's office in Salisbury') from Bo Heinebäck, Swedish ambassador to Zimbabwe, to the Ministry for Foreign Affairs, Swedish embassy, Salisbury, 25 January 1982 (MFA). During the conversation, Muzenda told Heinebäck that ANC was "completely" dependent on the Soviet Union, adding that "the Russians are no joke in this region, you know" (ibid.). Whereas after Zimbabwe's independence Muzenda and other ZANU leaders had been critical of the divisions within PAC, the relations with the former ally considerably improved when in January 1981 John Pokela took over the chairmanship of the movement. By 1981, both ANC and PAC had 'unofficial' representatives in Harare.
8. Ibid.

carry the issue forward to the benefit of ANC", the Swedish ambassador wanted to bring the matter to a close.[1]

Shortly thereafter, the issue of ANC's status in Zimbabwe dramatically assumed a new dimension when in February 1982 the government discovered arms caches on farms belonging to ZAPU. Allegedly, ANC weaponry was involved.[2] Marking the beginning of a fratricidal military campaign against Joshua Nkomo's movement in Matabeleland[3], it also led to a crackdown on ZAPU's traditional ally ANC. MK cadres who had stayed underground in the country were rounded up, a number of them were jailed and some tortured.[4] Tight restrictions were placed on ANC. Quoting Garth Strachan—who from the mid-1980s would be based in Harare[5]—Barrell notes that the movement "was not allowed to set up even 'minimal bases' for the transit of men and material from Zambia".[6]

While the Swedish authorities maintained close relations with ZANU, ZAPU and ANC, they were far removed from the military aspects of the conflict. In accordance with ambassador Heinebäck's recommendations, they had, in addition, before the discovery of ZAPU's arms caches already decided to downplay the issue of ANC's representation in Zimbabwe. On his own initiative, in early May 1982 Muzenda, however, contacted Heinebäck, somewhat "unclearly" conveying that it would be "helpful if [Sweden] helped both" in Zimbabwe, that is, ANC and PAC.[7] Against this background, the Swedish ambassador approached Zimbabwe's Foreign Minister, Witness Mangwende. "Emphatically" stressing that unilateral support to ANC was "out of the question", he appeared "unpleasantly affected" by the approach, "almost turning his back" on Heinebäck.[8]

Reacting to Heinebäck's report, later in the month the Foreign Ministry in Stockholm concluded that "neither you, nor any other Swedish representative, should with the Zimbabwe authorities [...] [henceforth] raise the question of Swedish support to ANC in [the country], but instead wait and see if there are possible queries or a confirmation".[9] For the following three years, this instruction effectively pushed Sweden's insistence on direct support into the background.

In the meantime, ANC in Zimbabwe was assisted in indirect ways. As no official political representatives were allowed, President Tambo, for example, asked whether professionals belonging to the movement could be placed there under SIDA's auspices. Seconded to the Swedish bilateral cooperation programme with

---

1. Ibid.
2. Letter ('Relationerna ANC-ZAPU-ZANU'/'The relations between ANC, ZAPU and ZANU') from Lars Tillfors to the Ministry for Foreign Affairs, Swedish embassy, Harare, 7 May 1982 (SDA). Cf. Barrell Ph. D. op. cit., chapter six, p. 12.
3. For an account of the military campaign in Matabeleland, see Catholic Commission for Justice and Peace in Zimbabwe (CCJPZ) and Legal Resources Foundation (LRF): 'Breaking the Silence-Building True Peace: A Report on the Disturbances in Matabeleland and the Midlands 1980 to 1988', Harare, February 1997. A comprehensive narrative of the events is given by Katri Pohjolainen Yap in her Ph.D. dissertation 'Uprooting the Weeds: Power, Ethnicity and Violence in the Matabeleland Conflict 1980-1987', University of Amsterdam, Amsterdam, 2001. Cf. also Peter Godwin: *Mukiwa: A White Boy in Africa*, Macmillan, London, 1996.
4. Barrell Ph. D. op. cit., chapter six, p. 12.
5. Strachan served as secretary to ANC's Regional Politico-Military Committee in Zimbabwe.
6. Barrell Ph. D. op. cit., chapter six, pp. 12-13.
7. Letter ('Svenskt stöd till ANC's verksamhet i Zimbabwe'/'Swedish support to ANC's activities in Zimbabwe') from Bo Heinebäck to the Ministry for Foreign Affairs, Swedish embassy, Harare, 11 May 1982 (SDA).
8. Ibid. In his letter, ambassador Heinebäck underlined the "mean treatment presently accorded ANC in Zimbabwe" (ibid.). It should be recalled that Sweden during the last stages of the liberation struggle in Zimbabwe supported ZANU and ZAPU on an equal basis (cf. the chapter 'Patriotic Front: ZANU and ZAPU towards Independence').
9. Cable ('Svenskt stöd till ANC i Zimbabwe'/'Swedish support to ANC in Zimbabwe') from the Ministry for Foreign Affairs to the Swedish embassy in Harare, Ministry for Foreign Affairs, Stockholm, 28 May 1982 (MFA).

Zimbabwe, they could, he argued, both contribute to the country's development efforts and gain valuable experience for a future democratic South Africa. They, of course, would also serve as important contacts for ANC.

In March 1983, Tambo notably made an appeal in favour of Jaya Appalraju, a development planner who at the time was working on a UN contract at the Ardhi Institute in Dar es Salaam.[1] Appalraju had studied in Lund from the late 1960s to the early 1970s and was a Swedish citizen. From his student days, he knew some of the leading ZANU politicians, among them Sydney Sekeramayi, at the time Minister of Lands, Resettlement and Rural Development. After consultations with Zimbabwe, Appalraju was subsequently employed under a SIDA contract as a programme director by the Ministry of Local Government, Rural and Urban Development. He settled in Harare in July 1984[2] and stayed there for the following ten years. He would, in particular, be closely involved with ANC's planning for a post-apartheid South Africa.[3]

It could, finally, be noted that other indirect efforts were made to support ANC in Zimbabwe. In May 1984, for example, the local SIDA office decided to grant Zimbabwe Publishing House 18,000 SEK for the publication and distribution of a history of ANC written by Francis Meli, the editor of *Sechaba*.[4]

Final Clearance

Issued by the Fälldin government, the instruction not to insist on the establishment of an official ANC office in Zimbabwe was upheld by Olof Palme's Social Democratic government, which returned to power in October 1982. Whereas the government of Norway—which supported both ANC and PAC—in 1984 started to channel humanitarian assistance to ANC refugees in the country[5], in the case of Sweden the positions appeared for a long time to be blocked. In discussions between Oliver Tambo and Prime Minister Robert Mugabe, it was, however, in early 1985 agreed that ANC's *de facto* presence should be made official and that a proper representation would be set up.[6] Reddy Mazimba (aka Mampane), ANC's

1. Letter ('En begäran från Oliver Tambo'/'A request from Oliver Tambo') from David Wirmark, Swedish ambassador to Tanzania, to the Ministry for Foreign Affairs, Swedish embassy, Dar es Salaam, 4 March 1983 (SDA). Cf. Appalraju: "[T]here were serious constraints in the support of the Frontline States to the liberation movement, so Oliver Tambo considered my function and role as a technical person ideal. I could operate in a supportive role for ANC and also be a fully-fledged civil servant in my own right, rather than—as was suggested [...]—joining the [ANC] Treasury [Department]. He opposed that and suggested that I move to Zimbabwe" (Interview with Jaya Appalraju, p. 105).
2. Interview with Jaya Appalraju, p. 105.
3. See the chapter 'Banning of Trade and Planning for Post-Apartheid'. After his return to South Africa, Appalraju was appointed in 1995 Executive Director of Matla Trust, succeeding Billy Modise, a close friend from university days in Lund. Appalraju died prematurely in 1996.
4. Decision ('Publikationsstöd till bok om ANC's historia'/'Support for the publication of a book on ANC's history'), ZIM-DCO-23/84, SIDA, Harare, 28 May 1984 (SDA). Meli's book—*South Africa Belongs to Us: A History of the ANC* (Zimbabwe Publishing House, Harare)—appeared in 1988.
5. Roland Axelsson: Memorandum ('Anteckningar från möten på norska ambassaden i Harare 14-15 mars 1985'/'Notes from meetings at the Norwegian embassy in Harare, 14-15 March 1985'), Swedish embassy, Lusaka, 21 March 1985 (SDA). It is not known how the clearance for Norway's assistance was conveyed. It should be noted that it was for daily necessities, not for administrative support to ANC's office (Roland Axelsson: Memorandum ('Anteckningar från besök, Harare 15-17/9 1986'/'Notes from visit to Harare, 15-17 September 1986'), Swedish embassy, Lusaka, 13 October 1986) (SDA).
6. Letter ('Samtal med Oliver Tambo'/'Conversation with Oliver Tambo') from Lars Norberg, Swedish ambassador to Zimbabwe, to the Ministry for Foreign Affairs, Swedish embassy, Harare, 5 February 1985 (SDA).

former representative to Tanzania, was subsequently appointed Chief Representative to Zimbabwe.[1]

Against this background, the new Swedish ambassador, Lars Norberg, ventured to re-introduce the dormant issue of support to an ANC office. Deputy Prime Minister Muzenda, however, remained as negative as in the past.[2] Nevertheless, acting on behalf of Premier Mugabe, in May 1985 Permanent Secretary Eleck Mashingaidze of the Foreign Ministry contacted Norberg.[3] Stressing that the government of Zimbabwe in accordance with OAU decisions gave ANC and PAC equal treatment, he told the ambassador that "a written consent to direct Swedish support to ANC in Zimbabwe was out of the question". On the other hand, he explained, the government was "of course" not against assistance to an ANC office as long as it was handled "discreetly" and in such a way that Zimbabwe would not be seen to depart from the OAU policy.[4]

Thus informed, after consultations with SIDA's local representative Dag Ehrenpreis, Norberg recommended on 28 May 1985 that

> direct Swedish support is extended to ANC's office in Harare in order to make it possible for the organization to carry out activities to the extent allowed by the government of Zimbabwe. [...] It is important that this sensitive question is treated with utmost discretion and that [the] support is not reported in publicly available documents.[5]

The authorities in Stockholm immediately endorsed the recommendation. Annual aid negotiations were held with ANC in Lusaka on 29-30 May. During the talks, the Swedish delegation clarified that "[r]ecent contacts [with] the Zimbabwean government had opened possibilities of allocating funds to ANC [in] Zimbabwe".[6] Tentatively setting aside an amount of 100,000 SEK, the parties agreed that "this allocation should be treated with special caution".[7]

After five years of trials and tribulations, from 1985/86 official Swedish support to ANC in Zimbabwe was finally introduced. SIDA's Roland Axelsson visited Harare in August 1985. By that time, Reddy Mazimba had taken up the position as Chief Representative, and a total of eight people were busy at a temporary office in downtown Harare.[8] The movement had also procured land outside Bulawayo to start an agricultural project, in which another six members were involved.[9] Apart from residents, students and people in transit, there were some 40 ANC exiles in

---

1. Mazimba had in the late 1970s worked closely with the Swedish embassy in Dar es Salaam. According to him, "that [was] why I was sent to Harare" (Interview with Reddy Mampane, p. 147). In the beginning, ANC had a low profile in Zimbabwe. Mazimba and Appalraju had been together in Tanzania—which also recognized PAC—and with small means they soon established ANC's authority over the rival movement. On ANC and PAC in Zimbabwe, see ibid.

2. Cable ('ANC i Zimbabwe') from Lars Norberg, Swedish ambassador to Zimbabwe, to the Ministry for Foreign Affairs, Swedish embassy, Harare, 28 May 1985 (SDA).

3. Ibid.

4. Ibid.

5. Ibid.

6. 'Agreed minutes [from] consultations in Lusaka, May 1985, between the African National Congress of South Africa and Sweden concerning humanitarian assistance', Lusaka, 30 May 1985 (SDA).

7. Ibid.

8. Roland Axelsson: Memorandum ('Anteckningar från möte med ANC i Harare 1985 09 02'/'Notes from meeting with ANC in Harare, 2 September 1985'), Swedish embassy, Lusaka, 23 September 1985 (SDA).

9. Ibid. Later known as the Vukani co-operative, the 10-hectare farm was mainly dedicated to poultry and vegetables. No direct official Swedish assistance was channelled to this project.

the country.[1] They were mainly supported by Norway, which for the calendar year 1985 had allocated 200,000 NOK for the purpose.[2]

Over the following years, the contribution towards 'daily necessities' was continuously raised, reaching 400,000 SEK in 1987/88.[3] More important, however, was the direct assistance to ANC's political representation, the issue that had originally stalled the cooperation. For the financial year 1985/86, 350,000 SEK was allocated towards the purchase of proper office facilities. The full amount was transferred in mid-February 1986.[4] The timing and significance of the support would soon be dramatically evident. In a simultaneous attack on Gaborone, Harare and Lusaka, on 19 May 1986 South African commandos aided by local agents blew up ANC's temporary office in Angwa Street.[5] While no people were killed, the building was shattered. Although combined with unforeseen internal complications[6], with the Swedish funds the movement could, however, in mid-September

1. Ibid.
2. Ibid. Norway and Sweden were the only Western countries to extend official, direct support to ANC in Zimbabwe. With regard to 'daily necessities', it should be noted that the Norwegian assistance not only preceded that from Sweden, but that it regularly exceeded the Swedish contribution. In 1988, for example, Norway allocated no less than 1.2 MNOK to the movement's members in the country (Roland Axelsson: Memorandum ('Anteckningar från besök i Harare 2-6/2 1988'/'Notes from visit to Harare, 2-6 February 1988'), Swedish embassy, Lusaka, 11 February 1988) (SDA).
3. 'Agreed minutes [from] consultations in Lusaka, May 1987, between the African National Congress of South Africa and Sweden concerning humanitarian assistance', Lusaka, 8 May 1987 (SDA).
4. Letter ('Zimbabwe: Kommentarer till ANC's framställning 1986/87'/'Zimbabwe: Comments on ANC's request for 1986/87') from Tor Sellström to SIDA, Swedish embassy, Harare, 19 February 1986 (SDA). The author was based in Harare from January 1986 until December 1990.
5. TRC op. cit. (Vol. II), p. 151. Appearing before the commission, in December 1997 South Africa's former Defence Minister Magnus Malan confirmed that the operation was endorsed by President P.W. Botha, adding that "[t]he State President told me to keep quiet about this" (ibid.). In reality, however, the Pretoria regime was far from silent. On 20 May—the day after the attack—the South African legation in Stockholm submitted a long note to the Swedish Ministry for Foreign Affairs, giving "background information concerning the attacks on the ANC targets in Zimbabwe, Botswana and Zambia by small elements of the South African Armed Forces which were carried out on 19 May 1986" (*Aide-mémoire* [no title], South African legation, Stockholm, 20 May 1986) (MFA). Officially acknowledging the cross-border operations, in the case of Zimbabwe it was argued that the ANC office in Harare had been coordinating "the infiltration, accommodation, transport and expatriation of the terrorists who were responsible for [the placement of] landmines in [...] Northern Transvaal" (ibid.). At a time when the relations between South Africa and Sweden were becoming tense, the note was seen as a warning against any assistance to ANC. Reddy Mazimba—whose residence was also blown up during the raid—later commented: "[W]hen our office in Harare was bombed, a very interesting thing happened. This was on 19 May 1986, at one o'clock in the morning. [T]he very same day, *The Citizen* in Johannesburg wrote that Reddy Mazimba [...] was dead! They took that to the Swedish legation in Pretoria, which transmitted it to the Swedish embassy in Harare. The ambassador called me and said: 'Do you see how they talk about us down there?' This was a way of saying that 'Sweden gives ANC weapons'" (Interview with Reddy Mampane, p. 148).
6. Anticipating funds from Sweden, ANC had in August 1985 purchased a house to be used as office-cum-residence. For unclear reasons, Chief Representative Mazimba, however, disposed of the property in March 1986. Reacting strongly to the information, in late April—three weeks before the South African attack—Thomas Nkobi wrote to Roland Axelsson, stating that Mazimba had "acted beyond his authority" and that the ANC headquarters in Lusaka had taken "immediate steps [...] to remedy this irregularity" (Letter ('Swedish grant [of] 350,000 [SEK] for purchase of premises in Zimbabwe') from Thomas Nkobi, Treasurer General, to SIDA, ANC, Lusaka, 30 April 1986) (SDA). The incident was discussed during the negotiations between Sweden and ANC in May 1986, where it was decided that "ANC should repossess the house" ('Agreed minutes [from] consultations in Lusaka, May 1986, between the African National Congress of South Africa and Sweden concerning humanitarian assistance', Lusaka, 9 May 1986) (SDA). As this was not possible, with Jaya Appalraju's assistance the property in Lincoln Road was at a very sensitive moment identified instead. This house, however, had serious structural faults, and over the following years an additional amount of 700,000 SEK was as a follow-up to the original Swedish commitment disbursed for repairs and reconstruction ('Agreed minutes' 1986-90).

1986 buy a property in Lincoln Road, which was converted into a permanent office.[1]

By 1986, Zimbabwe had become of central importance to ANC. At a time when the movement was facing serious restrictions or persecution in the forward areas of Botswana, Lesotho, Mozambique and Swaziland, the hitherto hesitant Frontline State offered unprecedented possibilities for contacts with the internal South African opposition.[2] Visiting Harare in February 1986, Thabo Mbeki—who six years earlier had initiated ANC's contacts with ZANU—underlined that the political relationship with the government was good.[3] Stating that "ANC does not want a big community in Zimbabwe", he primarily looked upon the country as an important "meeting place".[4]

This is also the role that Zimbabwe would play towards the end of the 1980s.[5] In addition to regularly hosting encounters between the ANC leadership and a vari-

---

1. Roland Axelsson: Memorandum ('Inköp av nytt ANC-kontor i Harare'/'Purchase of a new ANC office in Harare'), Swedish embassy, Lusaka, 13 October 1986 (SDA). As noted by Appalraju, the ANC office in Harare had, however, "always a very slim and low profile [...]. We worked in terms of committees. There were groups of people outside the formal ANC representation who were doing a lot of the work, whether it was in education or [in] health or keeping the various departments afloat, as well as working on the PASA project" (Interview with Jaya Appalraju, p. 106).

2. This, in turn, provoked a series of apartheid attacks on ANC in Zimbabwe. In May 1987, for example, Tsitsi Chiliza, a Zimbabwean citizen and the wife of an ANC member, was killed by a booby-trapped television set intended for Jacob Zuma (TRC op. cit. (Vol. II), p. 141). A couple of days later, the relocated ANC office in Harare was hit by a rocket (ibid., p. 159). Jeremy Brickhill, a ZAPU member married to ANC's Joan Freeman, was severely crippled in a bomb blast which in October 1987 injured seventeen people in a shopping centre in central Harare ('Bomb blast injures 17' in *The Herald*, 14 October 1987). In January 1988, another car bomb left three ANC members wounded in Bulawayo (Saul Ndlovu: 'The Blast that Shook Bulawayo' in *Prize Africa*, April 1988, pp. 16-17). And in April 1990, the Anglican priest and ANC member Michael Lapsley was dismembered by a letter bomb delivered to his house in the capital (Funny Mushava: 'Priest injured in Harare bomb blast' in *The Herald*, 30 April 1990). Infiltrated by South Africa, after many of these attacks the Zimbabwean security forces tried to implicate ANC itself. After the bomb blast in Bulawayo in January 1988, Johnny Makatini and Thabo Mbeki were, for example, immediately requested to go to Zimbabwe for clarifications. From the early morning until late at night, they were questioned at a Harare hotel by two—black—CIO officials about ANC's possible role. When around midnight the discussions were eventually coming to a close, Mbeki called the author to come to the hotel with a bottle of whisky. Introduced by Makatini and Mbeki as a 'Malawian business friend', the author took part in the concluding small talk. As the whisky bottle was being emptied, there was a telephone call for the senior CIO official. Noticeably upset, he asked the author to leave the room. A couple of minutes later, the Zimbabweans left. Invited back, the author was told by the ANC leaders that the incoming call was from the CIO headquarters, conveying the news that the Bulawayo attack had been coordinated by senior—white—Zimbabwean security officials (Author's recollection).

3. Tor Sellström: Memorandum ('Zimbabwe: Kommentarer till ANC's framställning 1986/87'/'Zimbabwe: Comments on ANC's request for 1986/87'), Swedish embassy, Harare, 19 February 1986 (SDA).

4. Ibid. Beyond Sweden's political and humanitarian concern, by 1986 ANC had also reached an understanding with Mugabe's government on clandestine military activities. According to Barrell, "whereas the movement of ANC political personnel through Zimbabwe was subject to few restrictions, military movement was covered by a secret understanding [...] to which only a few top officials on either side were party. Its basic terms were that Zimbabwe would turn a blind eye to a limited flow of ANC weapons and military personnel [...], but [that] it should be kept informed in outline of what was being planned and done. ANC should appoint a 'military attaché' [...] to facilitate this communication. It [subsequently] did, [seconding] a man who used the *nom de guerre* 'Manchecker'", aka Julius Madiba (Barrell Ph. D. op. cit., chapter eight, pp. 26-27). Cf. Chief Representative Mazimba: "[A] meeting took place between Joe Modise, our Army Commander, and Rex Nhongo, the Commander of the Zimbabwean armed forces, to discuss how Zimbabwe could assist us to cross the border into South Africa. A decision was taken that one of the bedrooms in my house should be turned into an armoury. A truck would leave Lusaka full of weapons and drive to Harare and I would tell the Zimbabweans that it was coming. There would not be any search. It would get into my yard and off-load all kinds of weapons and explosives into the bedroom. My house was guarded by the Zimbabwean para-military [forces] around the clock. It was used like that, because the Zimbabweans said that nobody would expect to find weapons in the Chief Representative's house" (Interview with Reddy Mampane, p. 147).

5. On Zimbabwe's importance for ANC, see the interview with Jaya Appalraju, pp. 105-06.

ety of broadly based internal South African groups[1], the Zimbabwe government staged a number of significant anti-apartheid conferences.[2] It also facilitated important cultural manifestations against South Africa, such as prominent international films[3], music and sporting events.[4] In the process, Zimbabwe became a leading arena for the wider international struggle against the white minority regime in Pretoria.[5]

While the allocation for 'daily necessities' in 1989 benefited some 120 permanent ANC refugees in the country[6], the Swedish assistance to ANC in Zimbabwe was considerably wider. In addition to a number of activities under the so called PASA project[7], support was thus extended towards secondary education, computer courses, agricultural training, a 'visitors' fund' and medical treatment for ANC's members in the region.[8]

Security

In the unsettled transition period after Zimbabwe's independence in 1980, Swedish embassy officials would be watched by local and, possibly, South African security agents.[9] Working with Gqabi and Mbeki, SIDA's Ola Jämtin, in particular, caught

---

1. Cf., for example, the interview with ZANU's Didymus Mutasa, p. 220. Many of the encounters organized by Mutasa through Cold Comfort Farm were financed by Sweden (ibid.).
2. The International Conference on Children, Repression and the Law in Apartheid South Africa, held in Harare in September 1987 and partly financed by Sweden, could here be mentioned. Attended *inter alia* by Robert Mugabe, Oliver Tambo and Lisbet Palme—the widow of the slain Swedish Prime Minister—apart from its wider repercussions, the conference substantially consolidated ANC's position in Zimbabwe (Mono Badela: 'Just one more rally against apartheid? Not really. Ask Adrian Vlok' in *Weekly Mail*, 2-8 October 1987).
3. Both the award-winning 'Cry Freedom' about the life of Steve Biko and 'A World Apart' about Ruth First, the wife of Joe Slovo, were shot in Zimbabwe. For her role in the latter, Linda Mvusi, an ANC member based in Harare, shared the 1988 Cannes film festival's Best Actress Award, the first South African to receive such an honour.
4. With Miriam Makeba, Hugh Masekela, Ladysmith Black Mambazo and other famous South African artists, the US singer Paul Simon staged his 'Graceland' concert in Harare in February 1987. The Swedish 'Frontline Rock' tour around Zimbabwe and Zambia took place in March-April 1987. Initiated by Caiphus Semenya and Letta Mbulu, South African Artists United's musical 'Buwa' was, finally, launched in the Zimbabwe capital in January 1987.
5. In general, Zimbabwe offered considerably better communications with South Africa than Zambia. In this context, however, the author recalls the emotional moment when on 5 November 1987 Thabo Mbeki's father, the former ANC Chairman Govan Mbeki, as the first Rivonia trialist was released from Robben Island and taken to a hotel in Port Elizabeth. For the occasion, Thabo Mbeki travelled to Harare, where he stayed at the Sheraton. Cheerfully and at the same time solemnly meeting in his room, Thabo and his brother Moeletsi, Max Sisulu, Reddy Mazimba and the author tried to contact Govan Mbeki. While there were no problems with the telephone lines, repeated attempts were, however, frustrated. At the hotel in Port Elizabeth, the Special Branch took the calls. When Mazimba tried—introducing himself and asking to talk to the ANC leader— the responsible security officer jumped, stating that "we want you here!" Despite various efforts, on that special evening Thabo and Moeletsi Mbeki could not—after twenty-five years of separation—talk to their supposedly released father (Author's recollection).
6. Roland Axelsson: Memorandum ('Anteckningar från besök i Harare 28-31 mars 1989'/'Notes from visit to Harare, 28-31 March 1989'), Swedish embassy, Lusaka, 3 April 1989 (SDA).
7. Planning for a Post-Apartheid South Africa (PASA). See below.
8. Letter ('Rapport om ANC i Zimbabwe, oktober 1991'/'Report on ANC in Zimbabwe, October 1991') from Birgitta Berggren, SIDA's representative to Zimbabwe, to SIDA, Swedish embassy, Harare, 14 October 1991 (SDA).
9. As noted by the Truth and Reconciliation Commission, "Zimbabwe was [...] extensively penetrated by [South Africa] and double agents operating from within Zimbabwe's security service. [...] [At the time of independence,] a fifth column of South African agents remained intact inside Zimbabwe, strategically located within the military, the police and the CIO" (TRC op. cit. (Vol. II), pp. 99 and 90).

their attention. As in connection with later South African raids in Zimbabwe[1], Jämtin opened his diplomatic residence to ANC. Together with Roland Axelsson, Roy Unge in Lesotho and other officials he would be at the centre of the movement's efforts to establish itself, or remain, in the forward areas. As a follow-up to the presentation above, it is here, finally, relevant to briefly comment on the security aspects concerning those responsible for the official Swedish ANC assistance in the forward areas.

Although Sweden worked closely with ANC in countries where the movement was highly exposed; ANC representatives and projects were attacked[2]; and the South African security police monitored the assistance[3], during two decades of cooperation no Swedish official was ever wounded or killed in South African operations.[4] Asked if he was aware of any plans directed against Swedes who assisted ANC in Southern Africa, Craig Williamson stated in 1996 that "when we did our cross-border operations, we tried to avoid to have any international people hit due to the political problems involved".[5] Nevertheless, in addition to innocent citizens of the Southern African host countries, international aid workers were over the years killed, wounded or abducted in South African attacks on ANC. In September 1987, an attempt was made in Harare on the life of Conny Braam, chairperson of the Dutch Anti-Apartheid Movement.[6]

In the light of the frequent and close contacts between Swedish officials and exposed ANC members in the forward areas, it was, probably, luck more than anything else which saved the cooperation from a major casualty.[7] Concentrating on secrecy with regard to information, for many years the authorities in Stockholm downplayed the issue of physical security. Looking back, SIDA's Birgitta Berggren, former secretary to the Consultative Committee on Humanitarian Assistance and head of the aid agency's Southern Africa section, commented in 1996:

> Working with these questions, you were generally on the alert. Of course, there were problems at times, but nothing really serious as far as I can remember. When SIDA people travelled via

1. Before the May 1986 raid on Harare, the author was asked by ANC's Chief Representative Reddy Mazimba to accommodate Secretary General Alfred Nzo. In a later interview, Mazimba recalled: "We always used to get some information that BOSS was coming to raid us and took precautions. [...] Alfred Nzo, our Secretary General and presently Minister of Foreign Affairs, was in Harare and I explained the situation to him. We went around to all our residences and told the people to get out of the houses. Some of them went to sleep at the police station and so forth. [...] At one o'clock, we heard an explosion. [...] We woke up without an office! We then drove to Ashdown Park, where [my] house was also finished. In this situation, who was on our side? Who was on the side of the South African liberation movement, ANC? The Scandinavian countries—SIDA, in particular, the Norwegian People's Aid, NORAD and others. The Lutheran World Federation in Harare even made space at their office to let us operate from there. Other countries were not there. They were on the side of the regime. Countries like the United States, Britain and so on, oiling apartheid to continue murdering our people" (Interview with Reddy Mazimba, p. 148).
2. Many examples could here be quoted. In the false belief that Ephesus House in Manzini, Swaziland, was a SIDA office, in October 1986 it was raided by a South African commando led by Eugene de Kock. And in April 1989, ANC's Chongela farm in Zambia was attacked by agents recruited by de Kock. During the operation, the farm manager, Sadhan Naidoo, and another ANC member, Moss Mthunzi, were killed (TRC op. cit. (Vol. II), p. 122). As will be seen below, the Chongela farm was one of the priority projects in Sweden's cooperation with ANC. It was regularly visited by Swedish officials and consultants.
3. Author's conversations with Major General Hendrik Vermeulen in Uppsala, 29 February 1996, and with Craig Williamson in Pretoria, 23 April 1996.
4. In early December 1984, the Swedish solidarity worker Per Martinsson was killed in a RENAMO ambush on a vehicle convoy in southern Mozambique. Martinsson was recruited by ARO ('Mordet på Per Martinsson'/ 'The Assassination of Per Martinsson' in *Afrikabulletinen*, No. 1, 1985, p. 23).
5. Interview with Craig Williamson, p. 202.
6. TRC op. cit. (Vol. II), p. 116. In the case of Braam, the technique of poisoned clothes was applied. Reverend Frank Chikane, Secretary General of the South African Council of Churches, was exposed two years later to a similar assassination attempt.
7. It is open to speculation what effect the death of a Swedish diplomat or aid official would have had. It is, however, not farfetched to imagine that it could have led to a considerably lower profile in the forward areas.

South Africa and the luggage passed through Jan Smuts airport in Johannesburg, it was very likely that it was checked. It also happened that letters in a suitcase were torn and put back. It was part of the situation. I do not think that one took it that seriously. You had to expect it, and be very cautious, never leaving any documents in your hotel room and always carrying what was important in your hand luggage. That was normal precaution. It was not all that dramatic, really.[1]

In the mid-1980s, when Pretoria's attacks on ANC were legion and a tense atmosphere characterized the diplomatic relations with South Africa—described in early 1987 by Sweden's envoy Jan Lundvik as "confrontational"[2]—the issue of protective security would, however, be raised, both with regard to Swedish officials working with the movement and the movement itself. Against the background of a number of incidents in the first half of the decade, it is surprising that this was not done earlier. While the Swedish involvement with Mbeki and Gqabi in Harare in 1980-81 generally brought Swedish officials in contact with antagonistic interests, a South African commando raid on ANC members in Gaborone had in November 1981 drawn direct attention to the close personal links existing between Sweden and the South African liberation movement.

In one of the first cross-border operations carried out by the Vlakplaas-based death squads, on the night of 26 November 1981 a commando led by Dirk Coetzee descended on a house in the Botswana capital occupied by the ANC member Joyce Dipale, a friend of SIDA's resident representative Sten Rylander and his wife Berit.[3] Shot point-blank, Dipale and Lilian Keagle, a Botswana woman, survived the attack. Fearing that the assailants would return, with three bullets in her back and bleeding profusely Dipale managed to reach the Rylanders' residence.[4] Taken by Sten and Berit Rylander to the local hospital[5], she was later sent to Canada for treatment.[6]

In the mid-1980s—against a background of generally deteriorating conditions in Southern Africa, mainly illustrated by RENAMO's operations in Mozambique—SIDA embarked on a review of its routines. A regional security adviser was appointed. In one of his first submissions, Staffan Marelius raised the issue of personal contacts with ANC and SWAPO. Proposing a number of "practical measures [...] to protect those officials at the embassies who administer [support to] the liberation movements", he recommended *inter alia* that meetings only should take place at the Swedish missions, not in private homes or in public places.[7] While visits to the movements' offices and houses were to be avoided, he further stressed that diplomatic residences should "not be put at [their] members' disposal".[8]

1. Interview with Birgitta Berggren, p. 261.
2. Cable ('Förbindelserna med Sydafrika'/'The relations with South Africa') from Jan Lundvik, Swedish envoy to South Africa, to the Ministry for Foreign Affairs, Swedish legation, Pretoria, 6 February 1987 (MFA).
3. TRC op. cit. (Vol. II), pp. 105-06.
4. Visiting Botswana, Lennart Wohlgemuth, the head of SIDA's Southern Africa section, was at the time staying with the Rylanders.
5. Cable ('Incident involverande biståndskontorschefen och ANC-medlem'/'Incident involving the SIDA representative and an ANC member') from Karl-Göran Engström, Swedish ambassador to Botswana, to the Ministry for Foreign Affairs, Swedish embassy, Gaborone, 1 December 1981 (MFA).
6. Dipale subsequently suffered a stroke and lost the power of speech (Bernstein (1994) op. cit., pp. 215-19). Attending a TRC hearing in Johannesburg on the attack, she was in January 1997—fifteen years later—still unable to testify (Robert Brand: 'Coetzee an 'inept bungler" in *The Star & SA Times International*, 22 January 1997).
7. Staffan Marelius: Memorandum ('Skyddsåtgärder för befrielserörelsehandläggare vid biståndskontor'/'Protective measures for officials at the [SIDA missions] administering support to the liberation movements'), Swedish embassy, Gaborone, 5 September 1985 (SDA). Drawing a completely opposite conclusion, in Botswana SIDA's regional coordinator of humanitarian assistance Roland Axelsson avoided—as noted above—meetings at the embassy as "[w]e knew that [it] was always watched".
8. Ibid.

Although welcoming a discussion on protective security, Marelius' restrictive recommendations were opposed by SIDA's officials in the region. In a comment which largely reflected a common understanding, SIDA's senior representative to Zimbabwe, Torsten Johansson—who in the 1970s had been in close contact with Chris Hani in Lesotho[1]—emphasized that

> [w]e must be able to receive members of the liberation organizations in our residences. Our solidarity cannot merely [be expressed] through [...] financial contributions. [Swedish] officials must be aware that solidarity implies to share the risks [...] with those who we assist. There are many examples of officials who at critical moments have saved people by giving them sanctuary, if only for a night. We thus oppose [any] interdiction against receiving people in need at our residences![2]

The recommendations made by Marelius would, in addition, have hampered the implementation of a number of projects agreed with the liberation movements. Against this background, no binding instructions concerning Swedish officials' social intercourse with ANC and SWAPO were ever issued. While tensions during the second half of the 1980s mounted in the region, it became, on the contrary, increasingly common that Swedish diplomatic residences at critical moments were opened to ANC representatives. This, in turn, reflected the special political relationship established with the South African liberation movement. When, for example, in 1987 Jan Lundvik, Sweden's representative in Pretoria, cautioned against "repeated anonymous threats [made] against Swedish missions in [Southern Africa]"[3], Bo Kälfors, his colleague in Maputo, reacted by stating that

> [c]arefulness could be observed without in any way suspending our solidarity and support for ANC, which [...] leads the struggle for a free and democratic South Africa. We must not allow ourselves to be frightened by South Africa's policy of violence and brutality.[4]

At that time—a year after the assassination of Prime Minister Olof Palme and the bombing of ANC's Stockholm office—there were, nevertheless, serious reasons to heed Lundvik's warnings. In Maseru, an attempt to sabotage the brakes of a Swedish diplomatic vehicle had been discovered[5], and in the Swazi capital Mbabane Roland Axelsson's car was hit by a lorry under unclear circumstances.[6] Following a break-in at the Swedish embassy in Lusaka, in May 1988 the annual negotiations with ANC were for reasons of security, finally, held at the Zambian Central Bank.[7]

Concluding this comment on matters relating to protection from possible South African attacks, it should be noted that a particular budget post for 'security' was introduced from the financial year 1987/88 within the regular allocation to ANC. In addition to personal protection for the movement's resident representative Lindiwe

---

1. Based in Gaborone as SIDA's representative to Botswana and Lesotho, Johansson—a keen amateur aviator—had on his flights between the two countries often carried messages to and from Hani (Author's recollection from conversations with Johansson and Hani).
2. Letter ('Skyddsåtgärder för befrielsehandläggare vid biståndskontor'/'Protective measures for officials [at the SIDA missions] administering support to the liberation movements') from Torsten Johansson to SIDA, Swedish embassy, Harare, 6 November 1985 (SDA).
3. Cable ('Förbindelserna med Sydafrika'/'The relations with South Africa') from Jan Lundvik, Swedish envoy to South Africa, to the Ministry for Foreign Affairs, Swedish legation, Pretoria, 6 February 1987 (MFA).
4. Bo Kälfors: Memorandum ('Sydafrikansk reaktion på skriverier i svensk press om dödade ambassadchauffören; hotbilden i Maputo'/'South Africa's reaction to writings in the Swedish press about the killing of the embassy driver; the threat scenario in Maputo'), Swedish embassy, Maputo, 18 June 1987 (MFA). In unclear circumstances, the Mozambican driver employed by the Swedish embassy in Maputo was together with his wife assassinated on 10 June 1987 (ibid.).
5. Interview with Roland Axelsson, pp. 254-55.
6. Ibid., p. 254.
7. Jan Cedergren: Memorandum ('Rapport från överläggningar med ANC den 9-12 maj 1988'/'Report from deliberations with ANC, 9-12 May 1988'), Ministry for Foreign Affairs, Stockholm, 31 May 1988 (SDA).

ANC Head of Security
Joe Nhlanhla with
SIDA's Lena Johansson
during a visit to Stock-
holm in early 1990
(Courtesy of
Lena Johansson)

Mabuza, after the bombing of the ANC office in Stockholm in September 1986 it
was agreed to install security equipment at the office. If proven adequate, it was at
the same time decided to supply similar devices to ANC's offices in Southern
Africa.[1] After a joint positive assessment, at the negotiations in May 1987 the parties for the first time set aside funds for security equipment in the countries where
ANC maintained official representations.[2]

Also benefiting Swedish officials working with ANC[3], the contribution towards
security rapidly grew over the following years, to the extent that it by 1989 had
become one of the priority areas within the bilateral cooperation programme.[4]
Designed by Joe Nhlanhla, ANC's Secretary for Intelligence and Security, and
implemented by the Swedish private company AB Danmex, the comprehensive support focused on ANC's headquarters in Zambia, but it also covered offices and residences in Angola, Botswana, Mozambique, Tanzania, Uganda and Zimbabwe.[5]
Several tons of equipment were sent by air to these countries, where it was cleared
through the local Swedish embassies.[6] Among the items supplied by Sweden were
letter bomb, explosive and metal detectors; debugging equipment and voice scram-

---

1. 'Minutes of quarterly meeting ANC-SIDA', Swedish embassy, Lusaka, 6 March 1987 (SDA).
2. 'Agreed minutes [from] consultations in Lusaka, May 1987, between the African National Congress of South
   Africa and Sweden concerning humanitarian assistance', Lusaka, 8 May 1987 (SDA).
3. Mainly through the supply of car alarm systems.
4. 'Minutes from consultative talks in Lusaka, 27 November-1 December 1989, between the African National
   Congress of South Africa (ANC) and the Swedish International Development Authority (SIDA) concerning
   humanitarian assistance', Lusaka, 1 December 1989 (SDA).
5. AB Danmex: 'Delivery status 1991.01.08 for equipment and remaining shipments', [no place], 8 January
   1991 (SDA).
6. The total weight of the first consignment was almost 5 tons ([Stig Dahn]: Memorandum ('Kort bakgrund'/
   'Brief background'), [no place or date, but early 1991]) (SDA). Dahn, a former Swedish police officer, was on
   behalf of AB Danmex responsible for the security support.

blers; cordless telephones and walkie-talkies; surveillance cameras and intercom systems; bullet-proof windows; car alarms and home security systems.[1]

From the start in 1987/88 until 1989/90, the budget for security increased from 600,000 SEK to 4 MSEK, representing by far the single largest sub-item under the heading 'administration and information' within the overall Swedish allocation to ANC.[2] The component was not only retained, but considerably increased when the bulk of the Swedish assistance after ANC's unbanning was transferred to South Africa. For 1993/94—the last year of official assistance to the movement—no less than 8 MSEK was allocated in favour of security at the ANC headquarters in Johannesburg and regional offices around the country.[3] This, in turn, corresponded to more than 6 per cent of the ANC grant of 127 MSEK.[4] In exile and in South Africa, between 1987/88 and 1993/84 a total amount of 23.9 MSEK was channelled by the Swedish government towards the physical protection of ANC's offices and officials.

1. ANC: 'Technical progress report to Stig Dahn: 1990-1991', ANC, Lusaka [no date] (SDA). Most of the office equipment was later transferred to South Africa. It should be noted that SIDA through equipment and training courses in the early 1990s also financed ANC's computerization programme at its headquarters in Lusaka.
2. 'Agreed minutes from consultations held in Lusaka, May 1989, between the African National Congress of South Africa and Sweden concerning humanitarian assistance', Lusaka, 26 May 1989 (SDA). In 1989/90, the security component represented 4.7 per cent of the total allocation (ibid.).
3. 'Agreed minutes from consultations held in Johannesburg, South Africa, November 1993, between the African National Congress of South Africa (ANC) and [the] Swedish International Development Authority (SIDA) concerning humanitarian assistance', Johannesburg, 2 December 1993 (SDA).
4. Ibid.

Closer and Broader Cooperation: Projects in Exile, Mineworkers, UDF and Civics in South Africa

Country Programming and Projects

The Swedish government's direct assistance to ANC was from the early 1980s divided in roughly equal parts between a 'home front component'; 'daily necessities' for its members in Southern Africa; and support for administration, programmes and projects coordinated at the headquarters in Lusaka. An overview of the latter will be presented in the text below, which in addition focuses on the indirect, but substantial involvement with the major ANC-aligned civic and trade union movements in South Africa. Before turning to the assistance after ANC's unbanning in 1990, the chapter, finally, includes brief comments on Washington's and Pretoria's views on Sweden's relations with the future ruling party in the mid-1980s.

After Zimbabwe's independence, there remained in Southern Africa only two liberation movements to which official Swedish support was extended, namely, SWAPO of Namibia and ANC of South Africa. As the annual allocations were regularly increased and the cooperation with the two expanded, in the early 1980s it was decided to introduce administrative routines for the support similar to those applying with regard to Sweden's independent partner countries. The cooperation with both SWAPO and ANC would be governed by so called 'country programming', based on long-term commitments and rolling budgets, which in addition to formal, annual negotiations included quarterly follow-up meetings and consultative talks—comparable to mid-term reviews—once a year. Gradually introduced from 1982/83, this administrative system for reporting and planning was fully established by the end of 1984.

In the case of SWAPO, the decision was conveyed in May 1982.[1] At the aid negotiations with ANC during the same month, the Swedish delegation, likewise, noted that "the substantial support [...] was becoming increasingly similar to the [...] cooperation between the so called programme countries and Sweden. It seemed appropriate, therefore, to apply procedures similar to those concerning [the] programme countries".[2] Positively acknowledged by the South African liberation movement[3], from the point of view of aid relations the decision not only implied that it was recognized *de facto* on a par with the independent core countries receiv-

---

1. See the chapter 'With SWAPO to Victory'.
2. 'Agreed minutes of discussions in Lusaka, May 1982, between the African National Congress of South Africa, ANC, and the Swedish International Development Authority, SIDA, concerning humanitarian assistance', Lusaka, 24 May 1982 (SDA).
3. In its request for assistance in 1984/85, ANC noted: "We felt greatly honoured when SIDA informed us that they regard the ANC as the *de facto* government of South Africa and were going to negotiate with us at governmental level. This was an expression of confidence in us and in the justice of our cause" (ANC: 'SIDA humanitarian assistance to the African National Congress of South Africa for the year 1983/84 and submissions for the year 1984/85', ANC, Lusaka, 5 January 1984) (SDA).

Country programming and formal negotiations with South Africa's 'government-in-waiting':
Lena Johansson and Thomas Nkobi signing agreed minutes from consultative talks between
Sweden and ANC, Lusaka, December 1989 (Courtesy of Lena Johansson)

ing Swedish development assistance—notably its host countries in Southern Africa—but, above all, that on a steady basis it could make activity plans for more than a year at a time. This was different from the *ad hoc* support irregularly received from many Eastern European countries.[1]

Initially, the country programming technique would in SWAPO's case lead to increasing unspent balances and serious concerns with regard to the movement's overall administrative capacity.[2] During the first half of the 1980s, similar bottlenecks were not encountered within the cooperation with ANC. The difference in this regard was mainly due to the scope of the respective assistance programmes. From the late 1970s, various activities involving third parties—notably at the Kwanza Sul settlement in Angola—made the transition from commodity aid to projects burdensome for SWAPO.[3] In marked contrast, as late as in 1984 90 per cent of the Swedish ANC support was still extended in cash. There was no technical assistance, and in addition to food deliveries from SIDA to the camps in Angola the only bilateral project activities were in favour of the movement's farms in Tanzania and Zambia.[4] It was also largely in respect of the latter that administrative shortcomings subsequently would appear. In the meantime, the utilization rate of the assistance was until the mid-1980s around 100 per cent.[5]

In the case of ANC, between 1982 and 1984 a lot of attention was paid to financial administration in general, as well as to project preparation, accounting and auditing. Visiting Lusaka from the SIDA headquarters in Stockholm, together

---

1. The German Democratic Republic, for example, often made *ad hoc* donations in cash and kind to the Southern African liberation movements in connection with visits to the country or with certain political events (Schleicher op. cit., passim).
2. See the chapter 'With SWAPO to Victory'.
3. Ibid.
4. Tor Sellström: Memorandum ('Humanitärt bistånd till African National Congress of South Africa (ANC), budgetåret 1984/85'/'Humanitarian assistance to ANC during the financial year 1984/85'), SIDA, Stockholm, 13 March 1984 (SDA).
5. Ibid.

with Thomas Nkobi, Kay Moonsamy and Dulcie September[1], Roland Axelsson—then at SIDA's finance division—established detailed procedures in January 1983 regarding financial reporting of the assistance.[2] They laid down that annual, consolidated statements should be drawn up and signed by an ANC Chief Internal Auditor.[3] At the time, no such position existed. Later in the year, it was, however, created.[4] The problems encountered in the forward areas notwithstanding, in a letter to the Ministry for Foreign Affairs, SIDA's Director General Carl Tham noted in April 1986 that ANC's rendering of accounts had since "continuously improved".[5]

To this contributed Treasurer General Nkobi's personal dedication and the fact that close working relations between his department and SIDA were established towards the mid-1980s. Preparing for the first bilateral consultative talks—held in Lusaka three months later[6]—in September 1983 Nkobi visited the aid agency in Stockholm to better familiarize himself with its routines and requirements.[7] A year later—when proper project activities were still in their infancy—two officials from the Treasury Department, Jacob Chilwane and Bunny Mackay, respectively Project Coordinator and Head of Agricultural Projects, were invited for a similar study visit.[8] After his arrival in Lusaka in October 1984, SIDA's regional coordinator Roland Axelsson, finally, introduced a monitoring system of quarterly review meetings with Nkobi and his staff. Comprehensively covering all aspects of the Swedish assistance to ANC, the first of these regular meetings was held in mid-January 1985.[9]

Whereas SWAPO's initially much weaker financial administrative capacity improved considerably during the second half of the 1980s, in spite of these efforts—and the fact that project activities played a far less prominent role in the overall assistance to ANC—as early as in December 1986 it was, however, noted that the financial reporting from the South African movement was lagging behind. During consultative talks in Lusaka, the SIDA delegation emphasized that "such a

---

1. As Administrative Secretary at ANC's Treasury Department, September was in the early 1980s closely involved with the Swedish assistance. Largely due to this experience, in April 1983 the ANC National Executive Committee decided to appoint her Chief Representative to the Nordic countries, based in Stockholm (Letter from Josiah Jele to the Director[-General] of SIDA, ANC, Lusaka, 4 May 1983) (SDA). The decision was, however, reversed, and Lindiwe Mabuza continued to represent the movement. A couple of years later, Dulcie September became ANC's Chief Representative to France, where in March 1988 she was assassinated outside her office.
2. Roland Axelsson: Memorandum ('Memorandum re ANC [on] rendering of accounts to SIDA, internal control and ANC internal audit department'), [Swedish embassy], Lusaka, 26 January 1983 (SDA).
3. Ibid.
4. Tor Sellström: Memorandum ('Programsamtal med ANC'/'Consultative talks with ANC'), SIDA, Stockholm, 14 October 1983 (SDA).
5. Letter ('Humanitärt bistånd till African National Congress of South Africa (ANC), budgetåret 1986/87'/ 'Humanitarian assistance to ANC [during] the financial year 1986/87') from Carl Tham, Director General, to the Ministry for Foreign Affairs, SIDA, Stockholm, 16 April 1986 (SDA).
6. Kaj Persson: Memorandum ('Programsamtal med ANC'/'Consultative talks with ANC'), Ministry for Foreign Affairs, Stockholm, 9 January 1984 (SDA). The delegations to the first 'programme deliberations' were led, respectively, by Brita Östberg, SIDA's representative to Zambia, and Thomas Nkobi.
7. Tor Sellström: Memorandum ('Programsamtal med ANC'/'Consultative talks with ANC'), SIDA, Stockholm, 14 October 1983 (SDA).
8. 'Minutes from consultative talks in Lusaka, October-November 1984, between the African National Congress of South Africa (ANC) and SIDA concerning humanitarian assistance', Lusaka, 1 November 1984 (SDA).
9. Roland Axelsson: Memorandum ('Minutes of quarterly meeting ANC-SIDA'), Swedish embassy, Lusaka, 21 February 1985 (SDA). In a preamble to the minutes, it was noted that "[w]e all agreed that the introduction of [quarterly] meetings should give both parties better opportunities to discuss outstanding problems and to inform each other of recent development[s], as well as of budget utilization etc." (ibid.). Thomas Nkobi regularly represented ANC at the quarterly review meetings.

delay is looked upon very seriously".[1] The main culprit in this regard was ANC's Department of Information and Publicity, led by Thabo Mbeki.[2] Still in December 1987, "[b]oth delegations regretted that no accounts have been rendered to SIDA for funds allocated for information and publicity since November 1985".[3] Against this background, it was "agreed to reduce the [information] budget for 1987/88 by 50 per cent"[4], a measure which stands out as exceptional in the cooperation between Sweden and ANC.[5]

As the political demands on ANC were growing rapidly towards the end of the 1980s—leading *inter alia* to the establishment of new departments at the headquarters in Lusaka and a number of new offices around the world—both the Office of the Treasurer General and SIDA expressed concerns with regard to the movement's capacity to efficiently administer the assistance received. After leading the Swedish delegation to the annual negotiations in May 1988, SIDA's Deputy Director General Jan Cedergren noted in an internal memorandum that

> [i]t is important to carefully study ANC's future administrative capacity. For natural reasons, the movement suffers from certain growing pains and a too slow administrative and organizational adjustment to the new requirements [...]. This has, in particular, a bearing on the project activities within the [cooperation] programme. Sweden is still ANC's predominant donor, although the support from others is also increasing. This fact, as well as the close and long-standing cooperation, gives [us] both a responsibility and a possibility to constructively raise different problems in the [bilateral] dialogue with ANC.[6]

Treasurer General Nkobi generally supported these views.[7] In a submission to the government of Norway regarding continued assistance to the ANC Development Centre at Dakawa, Tanzania, he stated, for example, in April 1989 that "we are [...] overstretched in our project planning and management responsibilities", concluding that "[i]t has become imperative that we strengthen our [...] management".[8]

---

1. 'Minutes from consultative talks in Lusaka, 2-5 December 1986, between the African National Congress of South Africa (ANC) and SIDA concerning humanitarian assistance', Lusaka, 5 December 1986 (SDA).
2. 'Agreed minutes [from] consultations in Lusaka, May 1987, between the African National Congress of South Africa and Sweden concerning humanitarian assistance', Lusaka, 8 May 1987 (SDA).
3. 'Minutes from consultative talks in Lusaka, 8-11 December 1987, between the African National Congress of South Africa (ANC) and SIDA concerning humanitarian assistance', Lusaka, 11 December 1987 (SDA). Cedergren led the Swedish delegation and Nkobi the ANC team.
4. Ibid.
5. During the negotiations in May 1988, it was positively noted that "[t]he major part of the [outstanding] accounting had now been submitted [by DIP] to SIDA" ('Agreed minutes [from] consultations in Lusaka, May 1988, between the African National Congress of South Africa and Sweden concerning humanitarian assistance', Lusaka, 11 May 1988) (SDA).
6. Jan Cedergren: Memorandum ('Rapport från överläggningar med ANC den 9-12 maj 1988'/'Report from deliberations with ANC, 9-12 May 1988'), Ministry for Foreign Affairs, Stockholm, 31 May 1988 (SDA).
7. Billy Modise, who in 1988 took up the position as ANC Chief Representative to Sweden, held a different view. Looking back in 1995, he stated: "Where the parties might have been differing was on how the support should be channelled and on the accounting of that support". Albeit mainly addressing the issue of assistance to the internal struggle in South Africa, he continued: "The government of the Social Democrats used to give straightforward support and understood why receipts in a township perhaps had not been kept. The controls that normally any lender of money exercises were not set that strongly. But they controlled. However, as time went on, the whole process became bureaucratized. They had to check how every Krona was used. At times, this interfered with the political work, because it was, in fact, true that many of the activities were funded in a manner where there were no receipts. It just had to be based on trust" (Interview with Billy Modise, p. 160). In turn, Bengt Säve-Söderbergh, Social Democratic Under-Secretary of State for International Development Cooperation in the Ministry for Foreign Affairs between 1985 and 1991, was in 1997 of the opinion that "ANC [...] was not the best when it comes to accounting and reporting. I think that all organizations that are being built up—whether it is a liberation movement or a sports club—should be trained in these fields. It is [...] part of democracy-building" (Interview with Bengt Säve-Söderbergh, p. 339).
8. Thomas Nkobi: 'MFA/NPA/ANC workshop: ANC Development Centre, Dakawa', 27-28 April 1989 [no place or date] (SDA).

Various initiatives were taken in 1988-89 to improve the situation. In the case of Sweden, a detailed 'Manual for reports and requests' was drafted by SIDA in early 1988 and approved by ANC.[1] As a number of specialized seminars and training courses were organized, during the consultative talks in November-December 1988 it was, more importantly, agreed that

> a study should be undertaken with the view to assess [ANC's] existing administrative capacity and identify manpower needs in order to improve the administration, management and professional performance in the various structures and projects of [the movement's] external organization.[2]

Comprehensively covering a general "survey of the structure of [ANC's] external organization"—including "staffing, workload[s] and responsibilities"—as well as a review of the bilateral administrative routines between Sweden and ANC[3], the sensitive and strategic study was jointly carried out by the liberation movement[4] and the Swedish National Institute for Civil Service Training and Development.[5] The findings[6] and recommendations were discussed at a workshop in Lusaka in mid-May 1989.

During the following aid negotiations, ANC's Assistant Secretary General Henry Makgothi commended the study. Noting that "[t]he fact that Sweden and the ANC were engaged in this joint exercise was another example of the mutual confidence that had been built up over the years", for 1989/90 the parties agreed to make "[s]pecial reference [...] to the work now being initiated regarding support for administrative development".[7] The focus on management and administration had immediate results. Before the consultative talks in November-December 1989, SIDA thus received—"for the first time ever"—proper, written reports on "most of the projects" supported.[8]

While ANC's shortcomings did not affect the utilization rate of the assistance[9], at the end of the 1980s the joint concerns with regard to financial and general admi-

---

1. ANC-SIDA: 'Manual for reports and requests', [no place or date, but Lusaka, May 1988] (SDA).

2. Patrick Fitzgerald, Enos Ngutshana, Göran Andersson and Bosse Hammarström: 'ANC Administrative Study', May 1989, p. 1 (SDA).

3. Berit Rylander: 'Terms of reference: Study on ANC administrative capacity and educational needs, and study on administrative routines for ANC/SIDA cooperation', SIDA, Stockholm, 10 March 1989 (SDA). The survey did not include ANC's military organization.

4. The ANC members of the study team were Patrick Fitzgerald and Enos Ngutshana, respectively representing the Departments of Arts and Culture and Manpower Development.

5. In Swedish, *Statens Institut för Personalutveckling* (SIPU), a public agency. SIPU was represented by Göran Andersson and Bosse Hammarström.

6. The study concluded that SIDA, "compared to other donors [...], is relatively demanding" (Fitzgerald, Ngutshana, Andersson and Hammarström op. cit., p. 25).

7. 'Agreed minutes from consultations held in Lusaka, May 1989, between the African National Congress of South Africa and Sweden concerning humanitarian assistance', Lusaka, 26 May 1989 (SDA).

8. Eva Belfrage: Memorandum ('Rapport från programsamtal mellan ANC och SIDA i Lusaka 27/11-1/12 1989'/'Report from consultative talks between ANC and SIDA in Lusaka, 27 November-1 December 1989'), SIDA, Stockholm, 11 December 1989 (SDA).

9. On the contrary. During the consultative talks between SIDA and ANC in November-December 1989, it was noted that a mere 325,000 SEK remained unutilized from the 1988/89 allocation of 71 MSEK, representing less than 0.5 per cent ('Minutes from consultative talks in Lusaka, 27 November-1 December 1989, between the African National Congress of South Africa (ANC) and the Swedish International Development Authority (SIDA) concerning humanitarian assistance', Lusaka, 1 December 1989) (SDA).

nistration referred mainly to the liberation movement's overall capacity to adapt to the rapidly changing political realities and prepare for a democratic transition in South Africa. Conscious of this challenge and as a follow-up to the administrative study, in late October 1989 Nkobi submitted a request for Swedish support concerning consultancy services and training in respect of "financial administration and budgeting [...], projects [...], computerized accounts [and] auditing".[1]

Sweden's assistance in these fields after ANC's unbanning and homecoming in 1990 will be covered below. Before addressing the question of project support in exile, it should, finally, be noted that the demands on ANC as a result of the close dialogue on administrative capacity increased sharply. Reacting to ANC's draft request for assistance in 1990/91, in mid-January 1990—at a time when Walter Sisulu, Govan Mbeki, Ahmed Kathrada and other released Rivonia trialists were due to visit Stockholm[2]—Cedergren commented in a cable to the Swedish embassy in Lusaka that

> [t]he request is extremely weak [...] and can [...] not be prepared and presented to the government. ANC should be urged to as soon as possible submit a new request, which follows the guidelines [...] agreed upon. [...] ANC can no longer be excused [by stating] that they do not know what SIDA requires [...]. In September [1989], a full week was spent together with the Treasury and [other] departments concerned dedicated to this question. While the Departments of [Arts and] Culture and Information [and Publicity] have respected the agreement on the format of the request, others have generally ignored it. We [thus] ask the SIDA office to convey our concerns to the ANC leadership and stress the importance of a [...] serious submission.[3]

A month later—after its unbanning—the movement came back to SIDA with a detailed, 42-page request, which in the introduction self-critically stated that "lack of trained cadres on management and administration has hampered our organizational and administrative tasks". Acknowledging that "[a]cute problems still exist", ANC asked for continued assistance in order to "tackle these [...] with great vigour and determination".[4] Over the following months, the leadership returned to South Africa. While Swedish support was soon extended towards the establishment of the movement inside the country, the administrative reforms embarked upon in exile came to an end, with—as will be seen below—considerable difficulties as a result.

A combination of political challenges and social responsibilities vis-à-vis increasing refugee populations led from the mid-1980s to 'growing pains' and an 'overstretching' of ANC's administrative capacity. In the case of the Swedish assistance, this did not translate into widespread mismanagement or misappropriation of funds.[5] In some instances, however, it did hamper or slow down ambitiously planned

1. Letter ('Administration development fund') from Thomas Nkobi, Treasurer General, to SIDA, ANC, Lusaka, 26 October 1989 (SDA).
2. Per Sjögren: Memorandum ('ANC-besök till Sverige'/'ANC visit to Sweden'), Ministry for Foreign Affairs, Stockholm, 16 January 1990 (SDA).
3. Cable from Jan Cedergren to the Swedish embassy in Lusaka, SIDA/Ministry for Foreign Affairs, Stockholm, 16 January 1990 (SDA).
4. ANC: 'Annual request to SIDA 1990/91', [no place or date, but delivered to the Swedish embassy in Lusaka on 15 February 1990] (SDA).
5. Cf. the interview with Roland Axelsson, p. 253.

activities. In his report to the ANC National Congress in Durban, Nkobi stated in July 1991:

> It must be appreciated that in the conditions of exile the administrative skills were not available to manage the enormous growth of the budget requirements. The movement itself did not realise the importance of training cadres with the necessary administrative skills. This lack [...] is still with us today.[1]

Struggling to overcome these shortcomings, Nkobi would in this respect continuously seek advice and assistance from SIDA. Looking back on two decades of close cooperation, in his opening statement to the final aid negotiations between Sweden and ANC—held in Johannesburg in November 1993—he singled out "the support given [...] to draw up accounting and administrative manuals" as a particularly important contribution.[2]

Objectives and Structure

Addressing the ANC congress in Durban in July 1991—the first to be held on South African soil since the 1950s—Thomas Nkobi explained that the movement's project activities in exile "were conceived as integral to the struggle" and that they had five principal objectives, namely:

- to create self-sufficiency;
- to develop human resources;
- to generate income, where possible;
- to prepare cadres for their reintegration in a democratic South Africa; and
- to begin the creation of alternative educational and other institutions in preparation for a post-apartheid South Africa.[3]

In the context of Sweden, the issue of planning and preparing for a post-apartheid society will be discussed in the concluding chapter on the cooperation with ANC. Here, it remains to present the main project activities supported in the host countries in Southern Africa, as well as in Sweden itself.

The distribution of funds and the general profile of the official Swedish assistance to SWAPO of Namibia in 1987/88 has been given above.[4] For purposes of comparison, the corresponding data for ANC during that randomly chosen year—when the available resources in total amounted to 68.8 MSEK[5]—were as follows:[6]

---

1. ANC: 'Report of the Office of the Treasurer General', ANC National Congress, Durban, July 1991, p. 2.
2. 'Agreed minutes from consultations held in Johannesburg, South Africa, November 1993, between the African National Congress of South Africa (ANC) and [the] Swedish International Development Authority (SIDA) concerning humanitarian assistance', Johannesburg, 2 December 1993 (SDA). Nkobi further stated that "there could be no complete history of the struggle in South Africa without mention[ing] the invaluable assistance [from] Sweden and other Nordic countries" (ibid.).
3. ANC: 'Report of the Office of the Treasurer General', ANC National Congress, Durban, July 1991, p. 20.
4. See the chapter 'With SWAPO to Victory'.
5. Made up of an outgoing balance from 1986/87 of 4.8 million and an allocation for 1987/88 of 64 MSEK. Slightly larger, the corresponding SWAPO budget amounted to 77.6 MSEK.
6. 'Minutes from consultative talks in Lusaka, 8-11 December 1987, between the African National Congress of South Africa (ANC) and SIDA concerning humanitarian assistance', Lusaka, 11 December 1987 (SDA).

ANC: SIDA budget 1987/88
(in thousands of SEK)

Country / Sector / Activity	Budgeted amount	Percentage
A) ZAMBIA	(12,300)	(17.9)
Administration	1,700	2.5
Agriculture (Alpha farm)	800	1.2
Culture	1,000	1.4
Daily necessities	1,900	2.8
Information	1,700	2.5
Mechanical workshop	600	0.9
Post-apartheid planning	1,400	2.0
Security	600	0.9
Transport	2,600	3.7
B) SWEDEN	(8,600)	(12.5)
Administration/office	1,100	1.6
Agricultural training	3,000	4.4
Education	4,500	6.5
C) TANZANIA	(9,000)	(13.1)
Agriculture (Mazimbu farm)	3,100	4.5
Daily necessities	5,900	8.6
D) SOUTH AFRICA	(22,000)	(32.0)
Home front activities	22,000	32.0
E) OFFICES/DAILY NECESSITIES	(16,550)	(24.0)
Angola	11,200	16.3
Botswana	1,900	2.8
Ethiopia	200	0.3
Lesotho	500	0.7
Madagascar	100	0.1
Mozambique	850	1.2
Swaziland	1,200	1.7
Zimbabwe	600	0.9
F) OTHER	(350)	(0.5)
SACTU	350	0.5
TOTAL	68,800	100.0

In 1987/88, the assistance to ANC thus had the following general profile:[1]

Component	MSEK	Percentage
Humanitarian aid/Daily necessities	24.4	35.5
Home front	22.0	32.0
Education, training and planning	8.9	12.9
Administration	5.1	7.4
Agriculture	3.9	5.7
Transport	3.2	4.6
Other (Culture and SACTU)	1.3	1.9
TOTAL	68.8	100.0

---

1. The table is—as earlier in the case of SWAPO—somewhat arbitrary. Different components overlap and some activities could be moved from one component to another. Training in agricultural skills, for example, is registered under 'Education, training and planning', but could alternatively be referred to as 'Agriculture'.

When compared to the SWAPO assistance, it could be noted that the Swedish support to ANC with regard to strictly humanitarian aid, education and agriculture was remarkably similar. With only marginal proportional differences between the three components, together they represented in the case of SWAPO 54.9 per cent of the available resources, while their share of the ANC budget was 54.1 per cent. Striking contrasts appear, however, in respect of the 'home front component', administration (including information), transport and construction/infrastructure. Whereas the latter two components in SWAPO's case received 25.7 per cent of the funds, within the ANC budget their combined share was merely around 5 per cent.[1] Much greater prominence was given instead to the 'home front' and general administration, core political components which under the SWAPO budget accounted for 19.4 per cent, but in the cooperation with ANC amounted to no less than 39.4 per cent, or more than twice as much.

This, in turn, was both a consequence of the flexibility of the Swedish assistance and of the fact that other donors—notably the government of Norway—towards the end of the 1970s pledged support to the infrastructural development of the Solomon Mahlangu Freedom College (SOMAFCO) at Mazimbu outside Morogoro, Tanzania. Official Norwegian assistance to ANC could not be used inside South Africa[2], but would be dominant with regard to construction activities at SOMAFCO and, later, at the neighbouring Dakawa Development Centre, the movement's largest civilian settlements in exile.[3]

While Sweden and ANC in May 1979 agreed to set aside 1 MSEK towards the school project at Mazimbu[4], the following year—at the same time as Sweden embarked upon a major building programme at SWAPO's Kwanza Sul settlement in Angola[5]—it was noted that "[t]he donor response to [...] [SOMAFCO] had been encouraging". The Swedish funds had "consequently been directed towards other, more pressing needs".[6] The same conclusion was reached during the aid negotiations in May 1981.[7] Whereas significant amounts were channelled indirectly via Swedish NGOs—and direct support was extended both in the form of 'daily necessities' and for agricultural development—within the bilateral cooperation programme no official funds were from then on allocated in favour of the general construction programmes at the ANC settlements in Tanzania.

---

1. Within the cooperation with ANC, no funds were, strictly speaking, allocated towards construction activities or infrastructural development. Under the heading 'Offices/Daily necessities', significant amounts were, however, in addition to procurement of office premises allocated for reconstruction and/or repair works, notably in Harare. 'Agriculture', similarly, included dam construction and other infrastructural undertakings. This notwithstanding, there were no specific building programmes comparable to those carried out at SWAPO's Kwanza Sul settlement.
2. Østbye in Eriksen (ed.) op. cit., p. 171.
3. On the Norwegian contribution towards the establishment and development of SOMAFCO and Dakawa, see ibid., pp. 149-54. Over the years, the government of Norway was by far the largest donor with regard to fixed installations at these two settlements. According to Nkobi's report to the ANC congress in Durban in July 1991, Norway had covered no less than around 60 per cent of the infrastructure at Dakawa (ANC: 'Report of the Office of the Treasurer General', ANC National Congress, Durban, July 1991, pp. 29-32). While Sweden was ANC's main donor regarding its political work inside South Africa, Norway was the principal supporter of the two Tanzanian settlements. When it comes to 'daily necessities', Sweden and Norway together were, finally, the largest contributors to the ANC refugees in all the Southern African countries.
4. 'Agreed minutes from discussions on the cooperation between the African National Congress of South Africa (ANC) and the Swedish International Development Authority (SIDA)', Lusaka, 18 May 1979 (SDA).
5. See the chapter 'Cold War, Total Strategy and Expanded Assistance'.
6. 'Minutes from discussions on the cooperation between the African National Congress of South Africa (ANC) and the Swedish International Development Authority (SIDA), May 1980', Lusaka, 29 May 1980 (SDA).
7. 'Agreed minutes of discussions in Lusaka, May 1981, on the cooperation between the African National Congress of South Africa, ANC, and the Swedish International Development Authority, SIDA', Lusaka, 18 May 1981 (SDA).

Most components within Sweden's assistance to ANC have been covered above. Before a summary of the cooperation in the fields of agriculture and education is made, it should be recalled that the bulk of the humanitarian commodity aid during the 1980s was channelled to the Umkhonto we Sizwe camps in Angola. As noted in the table above, in 1987/88—when ANC reported that it catered for a population of 12,500 in the country[1]—as much as 16.3 per cent of the grant was set aside for this purpose. In fact, under the heading 'daily necessities' more funds—amounting to 85.2 MSEK, or over a third of the total—would over the years be allocated to ANC in Angola than in any other country.[2]

Although initiated at an early and critical stage at the time of the June 1976 Soweto uprising[3], in sharp contrast to the situation in all the other Southern African countries the Swedish embassy's relations with ANC in Angola were, however, weak. Demands for reports on the assistance would also cause unusual strains in the mid-1980s. In the case of Angola—the movement's main military training ground—it was not the host government's opposition, but ANC's own reluctance and secretiveness, which stood in the way.

Non-Transparency in Angola

In a comment to ANC's request for continued assistance in 1980/81, Bengt Svensson, SIDA's representative to Angola, noted in April 1980 that Sweden was the movement's largest donor in the country.[4] Emphasizing that the local ANC representation—headed by the NEC member Mziwandile ('Mzwai') Piliso[5]—"in a detailed and exemplary manner every quarter punctually reported on the utilization of the [Swedish] contribution", he, however, added that

> [t]he contacts between ANC and the embassy are not characterized by the [same] openness as in the case of [...] SWAPO. [...] [A] possible [reason could be] that the activities partly are of such nature that [the movement] on good grounds does not want to [expose] them. [...] [T]he movement has until now not shown any interest in informing the [SIDA] office about [its] project activities, nor have we been allowed to visit [its] camps or [had the opportunity] to engage in deeper political discussions.[6]

In addition to approval by the host governments, it was a prerequisite that Swedish aid officials could visit the activities supported. In April 1982, the delegation to the impending negotiations with the movement was thus instructed by the Foreign Ministry to raise the question of a visit to the ANC camps.[7] During the delibera-

---

1. 'Minutes from consultative talks in Lusaka, 8-11 December 1987, between the African National Congress of South Africa (ANC) and SIDA concerning humanitarian assistance', Lusaka, 11 December 1987 (SDA).
2. Cf. the table ''Daily necessities' in Sweden's assistance to ANC' in the chapter 'Attacks and Assistance in the Forward Areas: Swaziland and Mozambique'.
3. See the chapter 'From Beds in Exile to Organizers at Home'.
4. Svensson did not discuss military assistance.
5. Due to the war situation, ANC treated Angola as a 'military zone'. As Regional Commander, Piliso was responsible for all MK camps in the country. In 1981, he was appointed Director of the ANC Department of Intelligence and Security, with Joe Gqabi as his deputy (ANC: 'Further submissions and responses by the African National Congress to questions raised by the Commission for Truth and Reconciliation', ANC, Johannesburg, 12 May 1997).
6. Bengt Svensson: Memorandum ('ANC's framställning om bistånd 1980/81: Bk's yttrande'/'ANC's request for assistance in 1980/81: Comments by the SIDA office'), Swedish embassy, Luanda, 15 April 1980 (SDA).
7. Dag Ahlander: Memorandum ('Riktlinjer inför förhandlingar med befrielserörelserna ANC och SWAPO i maj 1982'/'Guidelines for negotiations with the liberation movements ANC and SWAPO in May 1982'), Ministry for Foreign Affairs, Stockholm, 29 April 1982 (SDA).

tions, it was—in very general terms— "agreed that Swedish representatives would visit ANC projects there".[1]

While the ANC office in Luanda in January 1983 submitted a request for agricultural equipment to a proposed farm on land allocated by the Angolan government in the Malanje province[2], only in late February—almost a year after the agreement—could SIDA's Bengt Svensson and Christina Regnell eventually pay a visit to an ANC project, namely the Viana transit camp, situated some 20 kilometres east of the capital. Opened in 1979, it accommodated at the time between 200 and 300 people.[3] This was a far cry from the thousands of ANC members in Angola to whom since 1976 a total of 21.5 MSEK had been extended.[4] During the annual negotiations with ANC in Lusaka the following month, the Swedish delegation again "emphasized the importance of visits to the ANC refugee settlements in Angola". And again "both parties agreed that such visits should take place", this time setting 30 June 1983 as a deadline.[5]

Although the allocation for 'daily necessities' was increased, ANC, however, did not reciprocate by arranging the agreed visits. Towards the end of his term, in a letter to SIDA's Director General Anders Forsse, Bengt Svensson noted in August 1983 that since his arrival in Angola in 1979 there had been "significant differences" between the Swedish embassy's relations with SWAPO and ANC. In his view, "SWAPO is [...] characterized by an openness that borders on carelessness. It is never difficult to visit the big camp in Kwanza Sul, although it requires military escort in the present security situation".[6] With regard to ANC, however, he stated that

> in spite of the agreements at the negotiations in Lusaka and [our] insistence, we have not managed to see what happens to that part of our assistance which is utilized beyond ANC's Luanda office. The objections to our requests in this regard have not been particularly [...] convincing. During my remaining time here, I will, of course, do what I can to try to find a solution [...], but I have no great hopes.[7]

Having insisted on visits to ANC's Angolan 'refugee settlements', in the light of the request in favour of the farm in Malanje, SIDA and the Foreign Ministry in Stockholm made support conditional on "insights into [the project]".[8] This opinion was conveyed to ANC during the consultative talks in Lusaka in December 1983. Initially, it was far from well received. Showing an uncharacteristic unwillingness to

1. 'Agreed minutes of discussions in Lusaka, May 1982, between the African National Congress of South Africa, ANC, and the Swedish International Development Authority, SIDA, concerning humanitarian assistance', Lusaka, 24 May 1982 (SDA). An amount of 300,000 SEK was at the same time tentatively set aside in support of an ANC farm in Angola. The delegations from Sweden and ANC were, respectively, headed by SIDA's Director General Anders Forsse and ANC's Secretary General Alfred Nzo.
2. 'ANC (SA) farm project: Funding request', attached to letter ('Veckobrev ANC vecka 1 1983'/'Weekly letter [on] ANC, week 1, 1983') from Laila Jensen to SIDA, Swedish embassy, Luanda, 5 January 1983 (SDA). SIDA had earlier delivered two tractors to ANC in Angola (ibid.).
3. Bengt Svensson: Memorandum ('Besök vid ANC flyktingläger samt planerat projekt i Viana: Årsförhandlingar'/'Visit to ANC refugee camp and planned project in Viana: Annual negotiations'), Swedish embassy, Luanda, 1 March 1983 (SDA).
4. Agreed minutes 1976/77-1982/83.
5. 'Agreed minutes [from] consultations in Lusaka, March 1983, between the African National Congress of South Africa, ANC, and Sweden concerning humanitarian assistance', Lusaka, 25 March 1983 (SDA).
6. Letter ('Tankar om vårt bistånd till SWAPO och ANC: Nkosi Sikelel' iAfrika'/'Reflections on our assistance to SWAPO and ANC: Nkosi Sikelel' iAfrika') from Bengt Svensson to SIDA's Director General, Swedish embassy, Luanda, 11 August 1983 (SDA).
7. Ibid.
8. Tor Sellström: Letter ('ANC's jordbruksprojekt i Malanje samt reallokeringar inom den lokala ANC-budgeten'/'ANC's agricultural project in Malanje and reallocations within the local ANC budget') to the Swedish embassy in Luanda, SIDA, Stockholm, 22 November 1983 (SDA).

cooperate, Treasurer General Nkobi criticized the Swedish stand, stating that it "amounted to a lack of confidence".[1] Eventually, however, it was once again agreed that a visit should be arranged. The same agreement was reached during the aid negotiations in April 1984, where the delegation from Sweden reiterated that "a prerequisite for [...] support to ANC projects in the independent countries of Southern Africa was that SIDA could visit the [activities]".[2]

In late September 1984—after eight years of support to ANC in Angola—a visit to one of the major camps outside Luanda finally took place, albeit not as a result of arrangements made by the headquarters in Lusaka. Nor was the visit undertaken by a government official. While on a mission to the SWAPO settlement in Kwanza Sul, SIDA's consultant Josef Jonsson from the Swedish University of Agricultural Sciences in Uppsala (SLU)[3] was instead asked at short notice by the local ANC office to make a general assessment of the farm in the Malanje province, situated close to the movement's main military training base at Cucalama some 500 kilometres east of Luanda.[4]

In his subsequent report to SIDA, Jonsson was deeply impressed. With some equipment from the Soviet Union, around 60 ANC members—most of them living in tents—had recently started production on 40 of the huge farm's 15,000 hectares. Noting that the site had "an enormous potential", he particularly stressed "the initiative, interest and dedication to work" displayed by his hosts.[5] Against this background, he strongly recommended Swedish assistance in the form of infrastructural development, agricultural equipment and, possibly, advisers.[6]

Positively assessed by both ANC and the Swedish authorities[7], the first ever visit to an ANC inland site in Angola would, however, ironically end in an anticlimax. Due to escalating attacks by Jonas Savimbi's UNITA movement, the already precarious security situation in the Malanje province soon deteriorated further.[8] After a

---

1. Kaj Persson: Memorandum ('Programsamtal med ANC'/'Consultative talks with ANC'), Ministry for Foreign Affairs, Stockholm, 9 January 1984 (SDA).
2. 'Agreed minutes [from] consultations in Lusaka, April 1984, between the African National Congress of South Africa and Sweden concerning humanitarian assistance', Lusaka, 6 April 1984 (SDA). By that time, however, a major mutiny in some of the MK camps had been shaking the movement in Angola since January 1984. Severely suppressed by the Angolan military and ANC, the troubles continued throughout the first half of the year (cf., for example, Kasrils op. cit., pp. 248-60 and Stephen Ellis: 'Mbokodo: Security in ANC Camps, 1961-1990' in *African Affairs*, No. 93, 1994, pp. 279-98). With reference to violation of human rights in SWAPO (see the chapter 'The Shipanga Affair and Beyond: Humanitarian Assistance and Human Rights'), it should in the context of ANC—where similar abuses occurred, albeit on a much lesser scale—be noted that the Swedish authorities were cut off from the events. In the case of ANC, there were no contacts with the mutineers, nor with the camps where the tragic developments took place.
3. In Swedish, *Sveriges Lantbruksuniversitet*. Jonsson would for two decades play a prominent role as agricultural adviser to both SWAPO and ANC.
4. Letter ('ANC-farmen i Malanje'/'The ANC farm in Malanje') from Gunvor Ngarambe to SIDA, Swedish embassy, Luanda, 3 October 1984 (SDA).
5. Jonsson stated that "it was a dream situation for an adviser. All advice was noted, both in writing and on cassette tapes".
6. Josef Jonsson: Memorandum ('Rapport från besök på ANC's farm 1984-09-27'/'Report from visit to the ANC farm, 27 September 1984'), Luanda, [no date], September 1984 (SDA).
7. 'Minutes from consultative talks in Lusaka, October-November 1984, between the African National Congress of South Africa (ANC) and SIDA concerning humanitarian assistance', Lusaka, 1 November 1984 (SDA).
8. Under constant pressure from UNITA in Malanje and urged thereto by the Angolan host government, in mid-1983 Umkhonto we Sizwe embarked on a counteroffensive. Led by Chris Hani, Lennox Lagu and Timothy Mokoena, the military campaign was initially successful. Towards the end of the year, ANC/MK would, however, register increasing casualties. As acknowledged by Kasrils, this in turn led "[a] good half of the MK contingent [to] beg[in] exhibiting signs of defiance", thus providing the background to the following mutiny (Kasrils op. cit., pp. 249-50). While it in this light is easy to understand why the ANC leadership in Lusaka was reluctant towards official visits, it is puzzling that the representation in Luanda in September spontaneously invited Josef Jonsson to the main theatre of the war and the internal struggles.

first delivery of agricultural equipment, the assistance to the Cucalama farm had to be phased out. SIDA's Roland Axelsson later commented:

> [W]e purchased quite a lot of equipment that was sent to the ANC farm in Malanje. Josef Jonsson was there, overseeing the arrival of the equipment. But after a few months, the ANC people had to leave. The area was not secure. Some people were killed and others were frightened. So, the Swedish assistance was unfortunately of very little use.[1]

The controversial issue of visits to the settlements in Angola was in the process removed from the agenda. Sweden would thereafter no longer insist on firsthand insights into the utilization of the support. Considerable resources were, however, continuously extended to ANC in Angola until the evacuation of the bulk of the MK cadres in 1989, as well as for the movement's remaining population in the country. For 1988/89, no less than 12.5 MSEK was allocated to ANC in Angola, representing more than 46 per cent of the funds set aside for this purpose in altogether ten host countries in Southern Africa.[2] While the Swedish authorities stayed in close contact with the local ANC communities in all these countries, apart from comparatively weak contacts with the Luanda office and odd visits to projects in the vicinity of the capital, in the case of Angola—a 'military zone' and the main recipient of the humanitarian support—the extraordinary fact, therefore, is that no official follow-up or assessment of the commodity aid to the movement's main centres was ever made.[3]

Farms and Agricultural Training

With the introduction of country programming, comprehensive project activities—including technical assistance, consultancy services and training—would from the mid-1980s play an increasingly important role in the assistance to ANC. Going back to where it all started[4], after a ten-year hiatus the Swedish delegation to the annual negotiations in Lusaka stated in April 1984 that "support could be given to ANC projects, with preference [...] to [activities] aiming at a higher degree of self-reliance, particularly in the field of agriculture".[5] For 1984/85, an amount of 3.6 MSEK was budgeted for agricultural support in Tanzania and Zambia.[6] Following ANC requests, over and above the core allocation 2 MSEK was at the same time set

---

1. Interview with Roland Axelsson, p. 254.
2. 'Agreed minutes [from] consultations in Lusaka, May 1988, between the African National Congress of South Africa and Sweden concerning humanitarian assistance', Lusaka, 11 May 1988 (SDA). As the war in Angola effectively thwarted ANC's local plans to become self-sufficient with regard to food supplies, from the mid-1980s Swedish funds would be used to airfreight meat, vegetables and other fresh provisions from Zambia. Increasingly, the supplies were provided from ANC's own farms.
3. After ANC's evacuation from Angola, the majority of the MK cadres were accommodated in Uganda, where they would continue to receive Swedish support in the form of 'daily necessities'. Also here, ANC initially opposed follow-up visits. In November 1990, this prompted SIDA's Deputy Director General Jan Cedergren to address a protest to Thomas Nkobi, stating that "it is the first time [that] SIDA has ever been denied a visit to a liberation movement settlement supported by Sweden" (Letter ('Swedish cooperation with ANC 1990/91: Allocation for Uganda') from Jan Cedergren to Thomas Nkobi, SIDA, Stockholm, 30 November 1990) (SDA). While ANC's Treasurer General—now placed in Johannesburg—must have recalled that this was not entirely true, a visit to Uganda was subsequently arranged. Combining the figures for Angola and Uganda, from the mid-1970s the Swedish government granted 94.7 MSEK towards the maintenance of ANC's military cadres. This corresponded to 38.4 per cent of the total funds allocated for 'daily necessities' and to 10.6 per cent of all the funds disbursed to the liberation movement.
4. Initially seeing the humanitarian assistance to ANC as temporary, the Swedish authorities—as noted above—had in February 1973 expressed interest "in following ANC's plans and measures to start agricultural production" (see the chapter 'From Beds in Exile to Organizers at Home').
5. 'Agreed minutes [from] consultations in Lusaka, April 1984, between the African National Congress of South Africa and Sweden concerning humanitarian assistance', Lusaka, 6 April 1984 (SDA).
6. Ibid.

aside for assistance in the field of education.[1] Apart from certain specific projects—notably the Alpha mechanical workshop in the Zambian capital[2]—agriculture and education would from then on become priority areas within the bilateral cooperation programme.

As earlier noted, in the mid-1970s Tanzania and Zambia were opposed to permanent ANC settlements.[3] Nevertheless, against the background of increasing numbers of South African refugees in the wake of the Soweto uprising, towards the end of the decade the Nyerere and Kaunda governments changed their attitude. In 1977, Tanzania granted the movement land on an abandoned sisal estate at Mazimbu, Morogoro, where the SOMAFCO school complex was subsequently established.[4] Additional areas were allocated five years later at Dakawa, some 55 kilometres north of Mazimbu. At both Mazimbu and Dakawa, ANC would clear the land for crop production and animal husbandry.

While the Zambian government similarly had not provided space for social projects and self-reliant agriculture, by 1978 it too, however, agreed to ANC landholdings in the country. In ANC's request for Swedish assistance during 1978/79, the movement therefore included the "purchase [of] a farm which has already been extensively developed", estimating the costs at less than 1 MSEK.[5] Like its Social Democratic predecessor, the Fälldin government was positive to the proposal. During the aid negotiations in May 1978, it was agreed that unutilized funds could be set aside for a "farm which ANC plans to buy in Zambia".[6] The property in question was the 1,300-hectare Chongela farm, situated in a prime agricultural region some 40 kilometres north of Lusaka.

Including buildings, machinery, cattle and other assets[7], the Chongela farm was purchased for the equivalent amount of 800,000 SEK in August 1978.[8] It was taken over by ANC two months later.[9] At the same time, it was agreed that Josef

---

1. Ibid.
2. In the late 1970s, raw materials had been supplied to ANC's Star Furniture company in Lusaka. Much more comprehensive and important was the assistance to the Alpha mechanical workshop. Purchased in 1985 for the equivalent of 2.8 MSEK ('Agreed minutes [from] consultations in Lusaka, May 1985, between the African National Congress of South Africa and Sweden concerning humanitarian assistance', Lusaka, 30 May 1985) (SDA), the original objective was that it should service the movement's vehicle fleet. Training of ANC members in auto-mechanics was an additional aim. Although constantly struggling with a lack of spare parts, the workshop was eventually in a position to take on commercial jobs, becoming profitable and generating local funds in 1989 ('Agreed minutes from consultations held in Lusaka, May 1989, between the African National Congress of South Africa and Sweden concerning humanitarian assistance', Lusaka, 26 May 1989) (SDA). The Dane Kaj Jansson was recruited by SIDA in 1985 as workshop manager and senior training officer. In 1989, Ole Mortensen—also from Denmark—was seconded as auto-electrician. Between 1985 and 1992, around 12 MSEK was disbursed from Sweden to the project, mainly for technical assistance, equipment, tools and spare parts (see also ANC: 'Report of the Office of the Treasurer General', ANC National Congress, Durban, July 1991, p. 21).
3. See the chapter 'From Beds in Exile to Organizers at Home'.
4. On the background to SOMAFCO, see the interview with Reddy Mampane, pp. 143-46.
5. Letter with submission ('African National Congress (SA) to SIDA in support of a request for assistance for the year 1978/79') from Thomas Nkobi, Treasurer General, to SIDA, ANC, Lusaka, 10 April 1978 (SDA).
6. 'Agreed minutes of discussions on the cooperation between Sweden and the African National Congress of South Africa (ANC) 1978/79', Lusaka, 26 May 1978 (SDA). Ove Heyman, ambassador to Zambia, led the Swedish delegation and Thomas Nkobi the ANC team.
7. Not without a certain irony, the seller of the property—an elderly lady of East European origin—generously decided to include some old muskets in the sale (Author's recollection from conversations with Elisabeth Michanek).
8. Decision No. 94/78, SIDA, Lusaka, 18 August 1978 (SDA). Prepared by Elisabeth Michanek, the decision was signed by Lars-Olof Edström. The figure of 0.8 MSEK included costs for consultancy services and technical assistance. The actual selling price of the farm itself was 135,000 Zambian Kwacha, corresponding to 550,000 SEK (Josef Jonsson and Erik Bergstrand: 'Inventory: Chongela farm, 9 September 1985', Lusaka, 17 September 1985) (SDA).
9. ANC: 'Interim report and budget follow-up as per 23 October 1978 for Chongela estate farm No. 2058', ANC, Lusaka, [no date, but submitted to the Swedish embassy on 23 October 1978] (SDA).

Training in
mechanics: Alvar
Nilsson (left) with
ANC cadres at the
Mazimbu farm,
Tanzania, in the
late 1980s (Photo:
Josef Jonsson)

Jonsson from SLU should assist the movement in drawing up a development plan
during a three-month period.[1] Serving as a consultant-cum-adviser to SIDA and
ANC, this marked the beginning of his long involvement with the liberation movement over the following fifteen years. During this period, he would establish particularly close and trusting relations with Treasurer General Nkobi.

As ANC also had a vegetable farm at Makeni on the outskirts of Lusaka[2], when
in August 1985 a Swedish contribution of 1.3 MSEK was used to more than double
the extension of Chongela through the purchase of the adjacent 1,600-hectare
Alpha estate, this expanded the movement's main agricultural enterprise in exile to
a total of almost 3,000 hectares.[3]

From 1985, Swedish project support to ANC in the field of agriculture focused
on the Mazimbu and Dakawa farms in Tanzania and on the Chongela, Alpha and
Makeni farms in Zambia.[4] Until the phasing out of the assistance to the external
activities in 1992, a total of 27 MSEK was extended to these farms in the form of
infrastructure, vehicles, machinery, equipment, livestock, seeds, consultancy services and other inputs.[5] Another 10.5 MSEK was used for agricultural training in
Africa and in Sweden, bringing the total sector support to 38 MSEK.[6]

The overwhelming majority of the ANC cadres came from urban backgrounds.
Very few had been trained in agricultural sciences and almost none had any experience of managing large, modern farming enterprises. At practically all levels, there

1. Decision No. 94/78, SIDA, Lusaka, 18 August 1978 (SDA).
2. In addition to supplying the ANC community in Lusaka with fresh vegetables, products from the Makeni plot
   were sold at the 'Soweto' market close to the Lusaka city centre (Author's recollection).
3. Roland Axelsson: Memorandum ('Humanitärt bistånd till African National Congress of South Africa (ANC)
   budgetåret 1986/87: Förberedande direktionsbehandling (D 1)'/'Humanitarian assistance to ANC during the
   financial year 1986/87: Preparatory discussion by [SIDA's] management committee (D 1)'), Swedish embassy,
   Lusaka, 17 September 1985 (SDA).
4. In 1988, the Angolan government donated the so called Lillie's farm to ANC. Situated some 40 kilometres
   south of Luanda, the soil, however, was not conducive to farming. Nevertheless, the movement tried hard to
   start production there, and in May 1990 it was agreed to allocate 0.5 MSEK to the farm ('Agreed minutes
   from consultations held in Lusaka, May 1990, between the African National Congress of South Africa and
   Sweden concerning humanitarian assistance', Lusaka, 18 May 1990) (SDA).
5. Agreed minutes for the period 1984/85-1991/92. Around 16 MSEK was channelled to the farms in Tanzania
   and 11 MSEK to the farms in Zambia.
6. Ibid. The figure includes the support to Lillie's farm in Angola.

was from the beginning a marked need of technical assistance and training. In his report to the 1991 Durban congress, Nkobi emphasized that in exile

> [t]he shortage of qualified personnel has been the most serious constraint, which in many instances has hampered smooth development and necessitated the recruitment of non-South African professionals and skilled personnel for most projects.[1]

This was particularly true for agriculture.[2] Whereas ANC could initially count on indispensable technical assistance from international NGOs—notably from Denmark and Sweden[3]—when the activities expanded in the mid-1980s, the shortcomings soon became evident. During the aid negotiations between Sweden and ANC in May 1986, it was noted that "almost no disbursements had been made out of the funds allocated for agricultural equipment to the farms in Tanzania".[4] Against this background, the ANC delegation stated that the movement "would appreciate SIDA assistance in planning and implementing a comprehensive training programme within the agricultural sector".[5]

The proposal was well received. Beginning in 1986/87 under Josef Jonsson's coordination, SLU would in addition to general advisory services organize a number of courses in Sweden, as well as on-the-job training at ANC's farms in Tanzania and Zambia. Within the overall programme, the Swedish Co-operative Centre (SCC)—a non-governmental, non-profit association for the provision of support to self-help initiatives[6]—would at the same time focus in particular on technical assistance and training with respect to dairy farming and milk production.[7] At a time when the Swedish trade union movement was supporting the United Democratic Front and bilateral discussions on a post-apartheid South Africa had been initiated, the institutional involvement by SLU and SCC with ANC in the non-traditional field of agriculture broadened the liberation organization's resource and solidarity base in Sweden.[8]

The twin objectives of the ANC farms were to supply the refugee populations with fresh food and to generate income. Between the social and the commercial intentions, there were, however, contradictions. While the Mazimbu and Dakawa

---

1. ANC: 'Report of the Office of the Treasurer General', ANC National Congress, Durban, July 1991, p. 26.
2. In a study ('Staff development programme for ANC agriculture projects'), it was estimated as late as in 1987 that there was a need for around 50 trained agriculturalists to manage the movement's farms. At the time, however, only some 20 ANC members had the necessary qualifications (Josef Jonsson: Memorandum ('Upplevelser och reflexioner angående SIDA's stöd till ANC's jordbruksprojekt i Mazimbu, Tanzania'/'Experiences and reflections concerning the SIDA support to ANC's agricultural project at Mazimbu, Tanzania'), [no place], 17 April 1988) (SDA).
3. For many years, Danchurchaid seconded a manager to the Mazimbu farm in Tanzania. He was later joined by a senior horticulturalist. By 1987, however, the Danish NGO had decided to phase out its technical assistance (ibid.). In the case of the Swedish solidarity movement, in early 1980 ARO proposed that two specialists in animal husbandry—Anders Emnéus and Britt Svensson—should be placed at the Chongela farm in Zambia. In desperate need of trained personnel, the proposal was characterized by Thomas Nkobi as a "fantastic offer" (Letter ('Swedish workers for the farm') from Thomas Nkobi, Treasurer General, to the Swedish embassy, ANC, Lusaka, 20 March 1980) (SDA). Arriving in January 1981, due to problems with work permits they had to leave Zambia after a couple of months (Note by Roland Axelsson on copy of a letter from ARO to the Zambian embassy in Stockholm, Stockholm, 17 November 1980) (SDA). Subsequently joining the Swedish Co-operative Centre, Emnéus and Svensson would be seconded to Mazimbu from late 1986 as advisers in dairy farming.
4. 'Agreed minutes [from] consultations in Lusaka, May 1986, between the African National Congress of South Africa and Sweden concerning humanitarian assistance', Lusaka, 9 May 1986 (SDA).
5. Ibid.
6. In Swedish, *Kooperation Utan Gränser*, set up by the major national co-operative unions.
7. 'Agreed minutes [from] consultations in Lusaka, May 1986, between the African National Congress of South Africa and Sweden concerning humanitarian assistance', Lusaka, 9 May 1986 (SDA).
8. Under the bilateral programme, SCC later organized courses for ANC in co-operative training and development ('Agreed minutes from consultations held in Lusaka, May 1989, between the African National Congress of South Africa and Sweden concerning humanitarian assistance', Lusaka, 26 May 1989) (SDA).

Selecting millet for seeds: ANC farm manager Sadhan Naidoo with the Swedish adviser
Anders Tuvesson in Zambia in the late 1980s (Photo: Josef Jonsson)

farms managed to increasingly satisfy the needs of the movement's members in
Tanzania[1]—and meat, vegetables and other produce from the Zambian farms were
airlifted from the mid-1980s to the camps in Angola[2]—it was considerably harder
to turn them into economically viable units. Largely due to political interference, in
the case of the Mazimbu farm—where Sweden remained the only donor[3]—Josef
Jonsson and the embassy in Dar es Salaam concluded, for example, in early 1988 that
"it is operating badly in practically all respects".[4] And at the negotiations in May
1989, the Swedish delegation "expressed grave concern [about] the current development", in addition to a "lack of experienced and competent farm management"
emphasizing in particular the absence of "economic autonomy" and "interference in
the technical operations".[5]

The criticism mainly concerned the farms in Tanzania. Although the general situation in Zambia in these respects was much more positive, in April 1989 the
Chongela farm was, however, attacked by South African agents. During the attack,
the farm manager, Sadhan Naidoo, and the workshop manager, Moss Mthunzi—
who worked closely with Josef Jonsson and the Swedish adviser Anders Tuvesson[6]—

---

1. In early 1985, the ANC population at Mazimbu was around 1,400, with another 500 at Dakawa (Margareta
   Husén: Memorandum ('Humanitärt bistånd till African National Congress of South Africa (ANC) budgetåret
   1985/86'/'Humanitarian assistance to ANC in 1985/86'), SIDA, Stockholm, 18 March 1985) (SDA). By mid-
   1991, the total population had increased to 4,500 (Birgitta Sevefjord: Memorandum ('Lägesrapport från
   ANC's läger i Mazimbu och Dakawa'/'Status report on the ANC settlements at Mazimbu and Dakawa'),
   Swedish embassy, Dar es Salaam, 2 October 1991) (SDA).
2. In 1986/87, about 40 per cent of the allocation to ANC in Angola was used to airfreight food from Zambia
   (Roland Axelsson: 'Minutes of quarterly meeting ANC-SIDA', Swedish embassy, Lusaka, 9 October 1986)
   (SDA).
3. Eva Nauckhoff: Memorandum ('ANC-biståndet till Mazimbu'/'The ANC assistance to Mazimbu'), Swedish
   embassy, Dar es Salaam, 15 April 1988 (SDA).
4. Ibid.
5. 'Agreed minutes from consultations held in Lusaka, May 1989, between the African National Congress of
   South Africa and Sweden concerning humanitarian assistance', Lusaka, 26 May 1989 (SDA).
6. Attached to the SLU training programme, Tuvesson was for longer periods based at the Chongela farm.

were assassinated.[1] This was a severe setback, effectively delaying the decision reached by the ANC leadership "that [...] the farms should become more commercial and income-generating".[2]

At the time of ANC's unbanning in early 1990, there remained considerable problems with regard to the farms in Tanzania and Zambia. In the light of largely conflicting policy objectives and a shortage of qualified manpower, the movement, however, managed surprisingly well in the difficult area of large-scale agriculture. In Zambia, maize, sorghum, sunflower and soya beans together with other crops were grown at Chongela and Alpha, which in 1990 also produced 150 tons of vegetables. In addition to a large poultry section and a piggery[3], the cattle herd in 1990 exceeded a thousand head, out of which 175 were slaughtered. During the same year, 35,000 litres of milk were supplied to the movement.[4] With a largely similar profile, the Mazimbu farm in Tanzania was at the same time able to provide the local ANC community with 45 per cent of its needs.[5] In May 1989, SCC noted that the dairy unit "functions [...] irreproachably"[6], and during the aid negotiations with ANC in South Africa in May 1991 the Swedish delegation expressed the opinion that Mazimbu "in several aspects is the most modern farm in Tanzania".[7]

Education and Asylum Seekers in Sweden

Educational support to South African refugees had since the mid-1960s played a prominent part in Swedish humanitarian assistance. Sweden was also the largest donor to a number of international scholarship programmes, such as AET, IUEF, UNETPSA and WUS. Via the churches, educational support was in addition channelled through LWF and WCC. Although ANC at an early stage suggested that placement in Sweden of students should be included in the bilateral cooperation programme, due to SIDA's reluctance to administer individual scholarships and to the high costs involved[8], the idea, however, did not materialize until the mid-1980s.

Together with SWAPO's Hadino Hishongwa, in December 1982 ANC's Chief Representative Lindiwe Mabuza made a direct appeal to the Swedish government "to allow some of our students to take up academic and professional studies [in the country]".[9] The proposal soon found political support. In January 1984, for example, Pär Granstedt and a group of fellow MPs from the Centre Party introduced a parliamentary motion in which they stressed the importance of "expanding the

1. TRC op. cit. (Vol. II), p. 122.
2. 'Minutes from consultative talks in Lusaka, 27 November-1 December 1989, between the African National Congress of South Africa (ANC) and the Swedish International Development Authority (SIDA) concerning humanitarian assistance', Lusaka, 1 December 1989 (SDA).
3. The main breeding boars were called 'Verwoerd', 'Vorster' and 'Botha' (Author's recollection).
4. ANC: 'Report of the Office of the Treasurer General', ANC National Congress, Durban, July 1991, p. 22.
5. Ibid., p. 20.
6. SCC: 'Request for funds supporting co-operative development within [the] African National Congress', [Stockholm], 9 May 1989 (SDA).
7. 'Agreed minutes from consultations held in Benoni, South Africa, May 1991, between the African National Congress of South Africa (ANC) and the government of Sweden concerning humanitarian assistance', Johannesburg, 19 May 1991 (SDA). The subsequent vandalism at Mazimbu will be referred to below.
8. Astrid Dufborg/Lennart Wohlgemuth: Memorandum ('Instruktion för förhandling med ANC om bistånd på undervisningsområdet'/'Instruction regarding negotiation with ANC on assistance in the field of education'), SIDA, Stockholm, 18 May 1984 (SDA).
9. Letter with background memorandum ('Placement of South African and Namibian students by ANC and SWAPO in Swedish academic institutions') from Lindiwe Mabuza to Anita Gradin, Minister of Immigration, ANC, Stockholm, 8 December 1982 (SDA). With regard to later problems concerning asylum seekers (see below), it is noteworthy that Hishongwa and Mabuza proposed that "[t]o avoid students remaining in Sweden after completing their studies [...], the students, ANC and SWAPO could have an agreement signed that [they] shall [...] return to the country where he/she was sent from" (ibid.).

Swedish support to [...] include scholarships". ANC and SWAPO, they noted, "could mainly send students [...] to the [Eastern European] countries, [but it] should be important [for them] to gain experience from other social systems too".[1]

After discussions with SIDA's Brita Östberg in Lusaka, Henry Makgothi, ANC Secretary of Education and Culture, had already before the Centre Party motion formally submitted a request for a visit to Sweden "in order to study the opportunities available [...] and to have more concrete discussions", particularly with regard to teacher training and adult education, as well as tuition in vocational, administrative and management skills.[2] In early 1984, several concurrent developments paved the way for a more positive stand vis-à-vis direct educational support.[3] Preparing for the forthcoming annual aid negotiations, this, in turn, led the Foreign Ministry and SIDA in March to tentatively allocate 2 MSEK outside the core allocation for "a separate scholarship and education programme in Sweden".[4] ANC was informed about the decision the following month.

Emphasizing that it had not been involved in the decision process, SIDA's education division, however, "categorically rejected all proposals concerning individual scholarships".[5] Provided that it was granted additional resources in the form of an administrator, the division was, nevertheless, positive to educational support as long as it focused on "one coherent course for a group of ANC people".[6] On this basis, initial discussions were held in late May 1984 between SIDA's Lennart Wohlgemuth and ANC's Mohammed Tikly, Director at SOMAFCO, leading in principle to an agreement on "long-term educational cooperation".[7] With regard to activities in Sweden, a total of 33 MSEK between 1984/85 and 1991/92 would subsequently be allocated to bilateral sector support.[8]

In September 1984, Mats Karlsson was recruited by SIDA to prepare the educational assistance to ANC[9], and in October a field mission to SOMAFCO was undertaken. With a pronounced lack of qualified ANC teachers, the settlement in

---

1. Swedish Parliament 1983/84: Motion No. 1543, Riksdagens Protokoll 1983/84, p. 1. In a comment to the motion, Kaj Persson of the Foreign Ministry wrote to SIDA that it was "entirely in line with our thinking" (Letter from Kaj Persson to SIDA, Ministry for Foreign Affairs, Stockholm, 30 January 1984) (SDA). It could in the context of the Centre Party's views be noted that ANC often emphasized the significance of closer links with the wider Swedish society. During the consultative talks in November-December 1989, for example, "[t]he ANC delegation stated its view that education in Sweden still remains an important part of the overall training of ANC members. A major motive [...] was to increase the relations between ANC and Sweden" ('Minutes from consultative talks in Lusaka, 27 November-1 December 1989, between the African National Congress of South Africa (ANC) and the Swedish International Development Authority (SIDA) concerning humanitarian assistance', Lusaka, 1 December 1989) (SDA).
2. Letter from Henry Makgothi to Brita Östberg, SIDA representative to Zambia, ANC, Lusaka, 3 January 1984 (SDA).
3. Under the cooperation programme with SWAPO, 2 MSEK had in March 1983 been set aside for educational planning (see the chapter 'With SWAPO to Victory').
4. Kaj Persson: Memorandum ('Förslag till riktlinjer inför överläggningar med ANC i Lusaka den 2-6 april 1984'/'Proposed guidelines for deliberations with ANC in Lusaka, 2-6 April 1984'), Ministry for Foreign Affairs, Stockholm, 29 March 1984 (SDA).
5. Astrid Dufborg/Lennart Wohlgemuth: Memorandum ('Instruktion för förhandling med ANC om bistånd på undervisningsområdet'/'Instruction regarding negotiation with ANC on assistance in the field of education'), SIDA, Stockholm, 18 May 1984 (SDA).
6. Ibid.
7. 'Agreed minutes from ANC-SIDA talks on educational cooperation, 22-28 May 1984', Stockholm, 28 May 1984 (SDA).
8. Agreed minutes 1984/85-1991/92. Education was included from 1985/86 in the core allocation to ANC.
9. Recently graduated from university, this was the beginning of Karlsson's international career. Joining the Ministry for Foreign Affairs in 1987, he became its chief economist in 1991 and in 1994 Under-Secretary of State for International Development Cooperation. In 1999, Karlsson was appointed Vice-President of the World Bank, responsible for external and UN affairs.

Margareta Bergknut of ARO teaching at ANC's primary school, Solomon Mahlangu Freedom College, Tanzania, in the early 1980s (Photo: Magnus Bergmar)

Tanzania was relying to a large extent on personnel seconded by international NGOs, among them ARO of Sweden.[1] Rather than for higher education in general, the movement had against this background decided to use the Swedish assistance to develop its own manpower resources, linking this directly to the shortages at SOMAFCO.[2] After discussions with Henry Makgothi, Mohammed Tikly and other ANC officials, the visiting SIDA delegation agreed that "two groups of trainees— one [consisting of] primary and the other [of] pre-school [teachers]—will undergo a

1. The direct training support was largely supplementary to a number of projects implemented by Swedish NGOs with official funds or with their own resources. With regard to education and health at SOMAFCO, *Rädda Barnen* (RB)—the Swedish section of Save the Children—was involved from the very beginning. On behalf of RB, Gunilla Larsson visited the settlement in early 1979, pledging support for the construction of a crèche and a nursery school. Following the visit, it sent 9 tons of clothes to SOMAFCO (Letter ('Package *Rädda Barnens Riksförbund*, Stockholm') from Reddy Mazimba, ANC Chief Representative, to the Swedish embassy, ANC, Dar es Salaam, 25 July 1979) (SDA). Subsequently contributing 6.3 MSEK over three years towards the establishment of the Charlotte Maxeke Children's Centre, among the Swedish NGOs RB was the most important donor in the early 1980s (Dag Ahlander: Memorandum ('Bidrag till African National Congress (ANC) i Sydafrika 1982/83'/'Contribution to ANC [in] 1982/83'), Ministry for Foreign Affairs, Stockholm, 29 April 1982) (SDA). The Recruitment Organization of the Africa Groups (ARO), the Centre Party Youth League (CUF), the Swedish Union of Secondary School Students (SECO) and the Swedish Teachers Association (*Sveriges Lärarförbund*—SL) soon followed suit, extending technical assistance (ARO), support for the construction of a library (CUF), a laboratory (SECO) and a teachers' block (SL). Representing ARO, Margareta and Knut Bergknut worked at SOMAFCO as primary and secondary school teachers between 1982 and 1985 (ANC: 'SOMAFCO: Official Opening 21-23 August 1985-Progress Report/Special Edition', ANC, Amsterdam, 1985, p. 32). In 1985, the secondary schools in the Nordic countries dedicated a joint Operation Day's Work to the ANC schools in Tanzania, as well as to alternative schools in Zimbabwe. In the case of ANC, more than 20 MSEK was raised, of which close to 8 MSEK in Sweden alone (Roger Hällhag: Letter ('COSAS') to AIC, Stockholm, 27 May 1985) (SDA). Cf. also the interviews with Rica Hodgson (p. 133) and Lindiwe Mabuza (p. 139).

2. Although highly relevant to a self-reliant policy at SOMAFCO, the different professional categories identified for training in Sweden—pre-school and primary school teachers and later auxiliary nurses and office machine technicians—enjoyed low status among the ANC refugees. Initially, therefore, the movement encountered some difficulties in recruiting suitable candidates for the courses (Margareta Husén: Memorandum ('Humanitärt bistånd till African National Congress of South Africa (ANC), budgetåret 1986/87'/'Humanitarian assistance to ANC in 1986/87'), SIDA, Stockholm, 10 March 1986) (SDA). The low status of their functions probably contributed to the fact that several trainees decided to seek political asylum in Sweden instead of returning to Tanzania and other countries in Southern Africa (see below).

year's training in Sweden in order to improve and strengthen the staffing [situation at] SOMAFCO".[1] A formal decision to this effect was signed in Lusaka in January 1985.[2] The following month, five students in each category arrived in Sweden for a teacher training programme implemented by Linköping university in cooperation with Marieborg folk high school in Norrköping, both in the south-eastern province of Östergötland. Over the following years, a total of 21 ANC trainees successfully completed their studies.[3] The majority took up positions as teachers at SOMAFCO or were granted scholarships to pursue further studies.[4]

Positively assessed by both parties[5], it was later in 1985 suggested that the education support should be extended to include auxiliary nurses and office machine technicians.[6] Discussed during the consultative talks between SIDA and ANC in November 1985[7], the proposal was endorsed. Towards the end of 1986—at about the same time as SLU and ANC embarked on an agricultural training programme— the Thapper school of nursing[8] and Ingelsta high school, both in Norrköping, began to train or upgrade ANC students from these categories. In addition to a number of seminars and short courses—notably in international procurement— arranged for the Office of the Treasurer General[9], at the end of the decade Sandö U-Centre in northern Sweden, finally, followed up its earlier cooperation with SWAPO[10] by training ANC officials in different administrative skills.[11]

Bilateral education support to ANC started with the teacher training programme at Linköping university. Three courses were held between 1985 and 1988. In January 1989, however, the movement decided to discontinue the programme, arguing *inter alia* that the tailor-made instruction did not furnish the students with

---

1. 'Agreed minutes from the ANC-SIDA consultations on educational cooperation, 23-25 October, held at Mazimbu, Tanzania', Mazimbu, 26 October 1984 (SDA). The members of the Swedish delegation were Gunilla Rosengart (SIDA), Mats Karlsson (SIDA), Sven Andersson (University of Linköping) and Anders Grunnesjö (University of Linköping). Lindiwe Mabuza, ANC's representative to Sweden, accompanied the delegation (ibid.).

2. Margareta Husén: Memorandum ('Humanitärt bistånd till African National Congress of South Africa (ANC) budgetåret 1985/86'/'Humanitarian assistance to ANC in 1985/86'), SIDA, Stockholm, 18 March 1985 (SDA).

3. Department of Teacher Training, University of Linköping: 'SIDA-ANC Education Cooperation Programme: Final Report on the Third SOMAFCO Teacher Training Programme', Linköping, March 1990, Appendix 2, p. 2 (SDA).

4. Berit Rylander: Memorandum ('Genomgång av undervisningsstödet till ANC och SWAPO, Luanda, Lusaka, Dar es Salaam, Mazimbu, 17-28/2 1989'/'Review of the education support to ANC and SWAPO, Luanda, Lusaka, Dar es Salaam [and] Mazimbu, 17-28 February 1989'), SIDA, Stockholm, 31 March 1989 (SDA). The agreement on teacher training included advisory assistance to the schools at SOMAFCO.

5. 'Agreed minutes from discussions on the ANC-SIDA educational cooperation, held at SOMAFCO, Mazimbu, Tanzania, 28-29 October 1985', Mazimbu, 29 October 1985 (SDA).

6. Ibid.

7. 'Minutes from consultative talks in Lusaka, 19-22 November 1985, between the African National Congress of South Africa (ANC) and SIDA concerning humanitarian assistance', Lusaka, 21 November 1985 (SDA).

8. In Swedish, *Thapperska skolan*.

9. In the process of establishing a Procurement Section, in May 1986 ANC requested SIDA to arrange "comprehensive procurement/shipping seminars" ('Agreed minutes [from] consultations in Lusaka, May 1986, between the African National Congress of South Africa and Sweden concerning humanitarian assistance', Lusaka, 9 May 1986) (SDA). Beginning in 1987, several courses in international procurement were organized. Initially led by officials from SIDA's procurement division in Stockholm, from 1989 they were administered by the Swedish company Afri Scan Group (ASG) in Dar es Salaam (Roland Axelsson: Memorandum ('Anteckningar från besök i Tanzania 27/2-4/3 1989'/'Notes from visit to Tanzania, 27 February-4 March 1989'), Swedish embassy, Lusaka, 7 March 1989) (SDA).

10. See the chapter 'With SWAPO to Victory'.

11. In 1990, for example, 15 ANC administrators were received at Sandö ('Agreed minutes from consultations held in Lusaka, May 1990, between the African National Congress of South Africa and Sweden concerning humanitarian assistance', Lusaka, 18 May 1990) (SDA).

internationally recognized academic certificates.[1] While other training courses were not affected, ANC's stand in this regard should, in addition, be seen in the light of unforeseen political problems. During the second half of the 1980s, a number of ANC trainees in Sweden denounced the movement, eventually seeking asylum in the country. Closely followed by the media and causing strains in the relations between Sweden and the South African liberation movement, the prolonged 'defection saga' should here, finally, be noted.

At the time of designing the first training course, it was made clear that

> ANC's interest in Sweden and the support from the Swedish people for the struggle in Southern Africa are factors that motivate this type of cooperation. The students should therefore, during the course, have [the] opportunity for broad contacts with the Swedish society and [the] Swedish people.[2]

Cooperation with local solidarity groups was, in particular, envisaged. While the majority of the trainees over the years took an active part in support activities for ANC, in early 1986—at the end of the first teacher training course—two students, however, refused to return to Tanzania, applying instead for political asylum in Sweden. Later granted permanent residence by the Swedish Immigration Board (SIV)[3], this caused the ANC leadership to "express concern" during the annual aid negotiations in May 1986.[4] It was, nevertheless, agreed to expand the training scheme.

Of some 50 ANC teacher students—recruited in Tanzania and Zambia— another ten applied for asylum between August 1986 and June 1988.[5] Most of the applications were turned down. The students, however, successfully appealed against the decisions[6], laying the basis for a drawn-out process. Initially taking place beyond the headlines—but causing strong protests by ANC's local representa-

---

1. Berit Rylander: Memorandum ('Genomgång av undervisningsstödet till ANC och SWAPO, Luanda, Lusaka, Dar es Salaam, Mazimbu, 17-28/2 1989'/'Review of the education support to ANC and SWAPO, Luanda, Lusaka, Dar es Salaam [and] Mazimbu, 17-28 February 1989'), SIDA, Stockholm, 31 March 1989 (SDA). Focusing on teacher training at SOMAFCO, the agreement with Linköping university was, however, renewed in September 1989 (Department of Teacher Training, University of Linköping: 'SIDA-ANC Education Cooperation Programme: Progress Report [on] Upgrading of Primary School Teachers from ANC and Support Services to SOMAFCO, 1989-1991', Linköping, June 1991, p. 1) (SDA).
2. Department of Teacher Training, University of Linköping: 'SIDA-ANC Education Cooperation Programme: Final Report on the Third SOMAFCO Teacher Training Programme', Linköping, March 1990, p. 1 (SDA).
3. Ulla Ström: Memorandum ('ANC-stipendiater i Sverige'/'ANC scholarship holders in Sweden'), Ministry for Foreign Affairs, Stockholm, 30 June 1988 (SDA). From the documentation available, it is not clear on what specific grounds the applications for asylum were made. It appears, in addition, that the positive decision regarding the first two asylum seekers was taken without consultations with SIDA or the Ministry for Foreign Affairs. The Immigration Board was located in Norrköping, i.e. the town where the ANC students were staying.
4. 'Agreed minutes [from] consultations in Lusaka, May 1986, between the African National Congress of South Africa and Sweden concerning humanitarian assistance', Lusaka, 9 May 1986 (SDA). The issue was far from novel to the ANC leadership. In a letter to the South African Students Union in the Soviet Union, in June 1979 Secretary General Nzo "deplored the fact that some students were abandoning any commitment to the ANC as soon as they reached their places of study" (Shubin op. cit., p. 173). Almost half of the ANC students who went to the Soviet Union after the Soweto revolt did not complete their courses, "either because of academic failure or because of violations of discipline" (ibid., p. 172).
5. Ulla Ström: Memorandum ('ANC-stipendiater i Sverige'/'ANC scholarship holders in Sweden'), Ministry for Foreign Affairs, Stockholm, 30 June 1988 (SDA). Another ANC member later joined the group, bringing the total number to thirteen.
6. Ibid.

tive Lindiwe Mabuza[1] and close contacts between SIDA, the Foreign Ministry and the Immigration Board[2]—by mid-1989 the issue came to a head.

As ANC assured the Swedish government that "there will be no retribution against [the asylum seekers]"[3]; only one had formally decided to leave the movement[4]; they admitted to applying for training in Sweden in order to stay there[5]; SIV found that a former ANC member had been actively lobbying the students to do so[6]; and the Foreign Ministry concluded that there were "good prospects for asylum" in Tanzania and Zambia[7], in July 1989 it was decided that they should be sent back to these first countries of refuge.[8] Once again, however, the decision was contested.[9] More importantly, at a time when extreme right circles in Sweden had gone on an offensive against the official assistance to ANC[10], what essentially amounted to a question of existential opportunities for a group of young South African refugees would assume political dimensions.

Intensively courted by the Swedish conservative press, the 'defectors'—facing the reality of being sent back to Africa against their immediate will[11]—were not only quoted as denouncing alleged widespread ANC practices of assassination, torture and rape, but also as levelling similar accusations against Tanzania and Zam-

---

1. Ulla Ström: Memorandum ('ANC-stipendiater i Sverige'/'ANC scholarship holders in Sweden'), Ministry for Foreign Affairs, Stockholm, 14 October 1987 (SDA).
2. The issue was regularly discussed during the annual negotiations and consultative talks between Sweden and ANC. See, for example, 'Minutes from consultative talks in Lusaka, 8-11 December 1987, between the African National Congress of South Africa (ANC) and SIDA concerning humanitarian assistance', Lusaka, 11 December 1987 (SDA).
3. Letter from Thomas Nkobi to Foreign Minister Sten Andersson, ANC National Executive Committee, ANC, Lusaka, 28 November 1988 (MCA). In the letter on the issue of political asylum, Nkobi emphasized "the possible negative effects of such a development on our extremely warm and fraternal relations" (ibid.).
4. Billy Modise: 'Statement by the African National Congress office in Stockholm', ANC, Stockholm, 17 August 1989 (AGA).
5. Anna Maria Rehnberg: 'Tre avhoppare från ANC får uppskov'/'Three ANC defectors are granted adjournment' in *Svenska Dagbladet*, 24 August 1989. In a comment on the 'defection saga', Bruno Beijer, first secretary at the Swedish embassy in Dar es Salaam, described in general the "scholarship disease" prevailing at SOMAFCO in the late 1980s. Scholarships, he noted, were "*the* way to leave Mazimbu" and a frustrating refugee existence (Letter ('ANC-stipendiater i Sverige'/'ANC scholarship holders in Sweden') from Bruno Beijer to the Ministry for Foreign Affairs, Swedish embassy, Dar es Salaam, 16 September 1988) (SDA).
6. Ulla Ström: Memorandum ('ANC-stipendiater i Sverige'/'ANC scholarship holders in Sweden'), Ministry for Foreign Affairs, Stockholm, 30 June 1988 (SDA).
7. Anders Bjurner: Memorandum ('Avhoppade ANC-stipendiater'/'Defecting ANC scholarship holders'), Ministry for Foreign Affairs, Stockholm, 25 April 1989 (MFA).
8. Letter from Berit Rylander to ANC, SIDA, Stockholm, 21 July 1989 (SDA) and cable ('Avhoppade ANC-are'/ 'Defecting ANC members') from the Ministry for Foreign Affairs to the Swedish embassies in Lusaka and Dar es Salaam and the legation in Pretoria, Stockholm, 18 August 1989 (SDA).
9. The Liberal MP Ingela Mårtensson brought the issue to the Parliamentary Committee on the Constitution (Anna Maria Rehnberg: 'Tre avhoppare från ANC får uppskov'/'Three ANC defectors are granted adjournment' in *Svenska Dagbladet*, 24 August 1989).
10. In 1989, a marginal Sweden-South Africa Society (*Sverige-Sydafrikasällskapet*) became increasingly vociferous. Many of its members belonged to extreme right or neo-Nazi groups. The secretive society had also close links with the journal *Contra* (cf. the chapter 'MPLA of Angola: A Rockier Road'). Tommy Hansson, for example, was an active member, regularly contributing articles to its bimonthly publication *Sydafrika-Nytt* ('News from South Africa'). The issue of the ANC students was immediately highlighted. In an article published in October 1989, Hansson denounced both the Swedish government and ANC, stating that "the South African government has assured [them] that they are welcome back" (Tommy Hansson: 'Avhoppade ANC-medlemmar till Sydafrika-Nytt: 'Obegripligt att Sverige Stöder Diktatur, Korruption och Maktmissbruk'/ 'Defecting ANC Members to News from South Africa: 'Incomprehensible that Sweden Supports Dictatorship, Corruption and Power Abuse" in *Sydafrika-Nytt*, No. 5, 1989, pp. 4-5). Hansson also castigated ANC in the conservative journal *Svensk Tidskrift*, which was close to the Moderate Party. In an article published in early 1986, for example, he described ANC as a "terrorist organization", advocating instead support for Gatsha Buthelezi and Inkatha (Tommy Hansson: 'Stöd Ej ANC's Terrorpolitik'/'Don't Support ANC's Terror Policies' in *Svensk Tidskrift*, No. 1, 1986, pp. 67-68).
11. Some of the asylum seekers had established relationships with Swedish partners (Cecilia Höglund: Memorandum ('ANC-stipendiater som valt att stanna i Sverige'/'ANC scholarship holders who have opted to stay in Sweden'), Ministry for Foreign Affairs, Stockholm, 10 September 1987) (MFA).

bia.[1] While the erstwhile solidarity activist Claes-Adam Wachtmeister[2]—attached to the Swedish Institute of International Affairs—characterized the Foreign Ministry's opinion that these countries would protect the ANC members as "exceptionally naive"[3], the conservative daily *Svenska Dagbladet* went as far as asserting that extradition would lead to "certain death".[4] Generally questioning the Social Democratic government's policy towards South Africa, the newspaper—close to the Moderate Party—demanded that the assistance to ANC should be "reconsidered".[5]

This, in turn, provoked strong reactions from the Swedish solidarity movement[6], the local ANC office[7] and the resident ANC community in Sweden.[8] Stating that it was "disturbed by the media coverage of the deserters", in mid-August 1989 ANC's Regional Political Committee in Stockholm declared that

> [w]e denounce [the] deserters and their slanderous campaigns. Many of us have lived in Sweden for years, others have worked in Tanzania and in Zambia. We know that the deserters are distorting the truth because they fear the rigours of life in Africa and would like to stay in the comfort of this country. Their actions are strengthening the apartheid regime.[9]

ANC had in early 1989 decided not to send any more students to Sweden if the asylum seekers were allowed to stay.[10] Brought to the attention of the Parliamentary Committee on the Constitution, the case would, however, only be finalized a year later. In the meantime, therefore, the education support continued, although during the consultative talks in November-December 1989 the parties "strongly emphasized the importance of careful selection, preparation and follow-up of [the] trainees [going] to Sweden".[11]

After four years, the drawn-out 'defection saga' finally came to a close at the beginning of 1990, when the Swedish government decided to grant residence permits to most of the asylum seekers. Explaining that it had been taken on "humanitarian grounds", the decision was conveyed to the ANC leadership by Cooperation

---

1. There was a strong Swedish presence in both Tanzania and Zambia and the credibility of the accusations was low. As earlier noted, several NGOs worked closely with ANC in the two countries. In the case of Mazimbu and Dakawa, no less than around 300 people working for Swedish NGOs and SIDA stayed in the settlements or visited them during 1987 (Roland Axelsson: Memorandum ('Anteckningar från besök i Tanzania 27/2-4/3 1989'/'Notes from visit to Tanzania, 27 February-4 March 1989'), Swedish embassy, Lusaka, 7 March 1989) (SDA).
2. Serving as vice-chairman of the Swedish South Africa Committee in the early 1960s, Wachtmeister drafted a proposal justifying support of the armed struggle (Sellström Volume I, pp. 219 and 221).
3. Claes-Adam Wachtmeister: 'Svenskt bryderi inför Sydafrikaflyktingar' ('Swedish confusion towards South African refugees'), Utrikespolitiska Institutet, Stockholm, 29 September 1989 (NAI).
4. Michael Kruger: 'Utvisade ANC-avhoppare blir dödsdömda' ('Expelled ANC defectors will be sentenced to death') in *Svenska Dagbladet*, 24 August 1989.
5. Ibid.
6. See, for example, Birgit Jödahl: 'ANC, Våldet, Avhoppare och Media: 'Spelar i Händerna på Sydafrikas Regim'' ('ANC, Violence, Defectors and Media: 'Playing into the Hands of the South African Regime'') in *Afrikabulletinen*, No. 5, 1989, pp. 16-17.
7. Billy Modise: 'Statement by the African National Congress office in Stockholm', ANC, Stockholm, 17 August 1989 (AGA). Modise had in 1988 succeeded Lindiwe Mabuza as Chief Representative.
8. Statement [no title] by the ANC Regional Political Committee, Stockholm, 15 August 1989 (AGA).
9. Ibid.
10. Berit Rylander: Memorandum ('Genomgång av undervisningsstödet till ANC och SWAPO, Luanda, Lusaka, Dar es Salaam, Mazimbu, 17-28/2 1989'/'Review of the education support to ANC and SWAPO, Luanda, Lusaka, Dar es Salaam [and] Mazimbu, 17-28 February 1989') (SDA). Although on a smaller scale, ANC faced similar problems in Norway. In October 1989, Thandi Rankoe, the movement's representative in Oslo, "expressed concern at the growing problem of people going to Scandinavia and not returning to base" (Henry Makgothi: Internal ANC memorandum to Alfred Nzo and Thomas Nkobi, ANC, Lusaka, 17 November 1989) (MCA).
11. 'Minutes from consultative talks in Lusaka, 27 November-1 December 1989, between the African National Congress of South Africa (ANC) and the Swedish International Development Authority (SIDA) concerning humanitarian assistance', Lusaka, 1 December 1989 (SDA).

Minister Lena Hjelm-Wallén during a visit to Zambia in early February.[1] Reacting to the news, Treasurer General Thomas Nkobi stated that he "appreciated the sensitivity of the issue" and that he saw the decision as "an expression of the humanitarian society in Sweden".[2] As Hjelm-Wallén and Nkobi agreed that careful selection of future trainees was essential, the controversial question was thus undramatically brought to an end. ANC was unbanned shortly thereafter, and at the aid negotiations in May 1990 it was agreed to substantially expand the training programmes in Sweden, for which no less than 8.5 MSEK was allocated during 1990/91.[3] Over the following years, no further cases were recorded of ANC students seeking asylum in the country.[4]

NUM, LO/TCO and the E-Plan

The training in Sweden of ANC support staff was primarily designed to alleviate the movement's manpower shortages in exile. However, indirect official support to education schemes inside South Africa would from the early 1980s have an incomparably greater political impact.[5] This was particularly the case with the so called 'E-plan', which effectively contributed to the spectacular growth of the National Union of Mineworkers (NUM). NUM, in turn, played a prominent role in the unity process leading to the formation of the Congress of South African Trade Unions (COSATU).[6]

---

1. Kaj Persson: Memorandum ('Biståndsminister Hjelm-Walléns samtal med ANC-ledningen'/'Cooperation Minister Hjelm-Wallén's conversation with the ANC leadership'), Swedish embassy, Lusaka, 8 February 1990) (SDA).

2. Ibid.

3. 'Agreed minutes from consultations held in Lusaka, May 1990, between the African National Congress of South Africa and Sweden concerning humanitarian assistance', Lusaka, 18 May 1990 (SDA).

4. During the three-year period 1991/92-1993/94, a total of no less than 208.6 MSEK was disbursed from Sweden in favour of various education schemes for South Africans. For a comprehensive discussion of this support, see Zelda Groener, Ihron Rensburg and Joel Samoff: 'Contested Transitions: A Review of Swedish Support to the Education of South Africans', Final report prepared for SIDA's education division, Samoff Services, [no place], September 1994 (SDA).

5. Via the churches, official Swedish assistance was extended from the late 1970s to various education programmes of a humanitarian nature. Although much wider in scope, the Asingeni Relief Fund—set up by the South African Council of Churches (SACC) at the outbreak of the Soweto uprising—included support in the form of study grants. Assistance to the fund was from late 1976 channelled via the Church of Sweden Aid (CSA) (cf. Ryman op. cit., p. 213). It was *inter alia* to discuss future cooperation with CSA that Bishop Tutu—who in 1978 had been appointed General Secretary of SACC—in August 1979 paid his first of many visits to Sweden (Birgitta Berggren: Memorandum ('Minnesanteckningar från samtal med biskop Desmond Tutu, South African Council of Churches, den 30 augusti 1979'/'Notes from conversation with Desmond Tutu, SACC, 30 August 1979'), SIDA, Stockholm, 31 August 1979) (SDA). At the end of the 1970s, the Church of Sweden Mission (CSM) also started to support practical training of unemployed black youth through the South African Institute of Race Relations (SAIRR). In addition, significant amounts were channelled by CSM to SAIRR's scholarship scheme in favour of internally banned persons (see, for example, Elisabeth Michanek: Memorandum ('Ansökan från Svenska Kyrkans Mission om stöd till stipendier för bannlysta i Sydafrika'/'Request from the Church of Sweden Mission for support to scholarships for banned [people] in South Africa'), SIDA/CCHA, [Stockholm], 29 November 1983) (SDA). The support was administered from the mid-1980s by the Swedish Ecumenical Council (SEN). Granted a SIDA contribution of 3.7 MSEK, in 1989, for example, SEN extended individual scholarships to 125 political activists in South Africa (Magdalena Ginste: Memorandum ('Ansökan från Svenska Ekumeniska Nämnden om medel för stipendier till politiskt förföljda i Sydafrika'/'Request from the Swedish Ecumenical Council for funds towards scholarships for politically persecuted [persons] in South Africa'), SIDA/CCHA, [Stockholm], 29 November 1988) (SDA).

6. As well as for the launch of the Mineworkers Union of Namibia (MUN) (see the chapter 'Transport, Home Front, Churches and Trade Unions' on Namibia).

Several of its leaders—notably Cyril Ramaphosa[1]—were also active within the mass democratic movement. Swedish support to COSATU has been presented in an earlier chapter.[2] Here, the little known involvement with NUM and UDF will be addressed.[3]

As noted by Wickman in her overview of LO/TCO's cooperation with the South African labour movement, among the industrial unions NUM was by far the single most important recipient of Swedish support. Until 30 June 1996—that is, two years after the democratic elections—37.8 MSEK was channelled to the mineworkers' organization, while the second placed National Union of Metalworkers of South Africa (NUMSA) received 19.6 million.[4]

That NUM received almost twice as much financial support as NUMSA may appear surprising. The majority of the Swedish-owned manufacturing firms were active in the metal industry[5], and labour links between the parent companies in Sweden and their subsidiaries in South Africa had already been established in the mid-1970s. No similar connections existed between the mines and the mineworkers in the two countries.[6] For many years, there were few openings for organized contacts with the black miners in the apartheid republic. A general strike organized by the then powerful African Mineworkers Union had in 1946 been crushed in blood[7], leading to de-recognition of their union rights. In fact, while the 1979 Wiehahn Commission recommended approval of registered black unions, due to the mining industry's strategic role in the South African economy, it was only in 1981

---

1. Born in 1952, Ramaphosa grew up in Soweto. In 1972, he began law studies at the University of the North, where he joined the South African Students Organization (SASO), also chairing the local branch of the Student Christian Movement. Detained for a year in 1974 after a pro-FRELIMO rally at the university, on his release he became active in Steve Biko's Black People's Convention (BPC). At about the same time, he was articled to a law firm in Johannesburg. Following the outbreak of the June 1976 Soweto uprising, he was once again detained, this time for six months at the infamous John Vorster Square prison. After graduation in 1981, Ramaphosa joined the Council of Unions of South Africa (CUSA) as a legal adviser, paying particular attention to the situation of the black mineworkers. (The BCM-inspired CUSA was a member of ICFTU. In the context of Ramaphosa's future close contacts with Sweden and the Nordic countries, it should be noted that LO of Norway via ICFTU contributed 100,000 NOK towards his employment with CUSA. See Vetlesen (1998) op. cit., p. 57.) In August 1982, CUSA resolved to form a National Union of Mineworkers (NUM). At its inaugural congress in December 1982, Ramaphosa became its General Secretary. He maintained this position until 1991, when at the ANC congress in Durban in July he ousted Alfred Nzo as Secretary General of the movement. Actively working for trade union unity, under Ramaphosa's leadership NUM left the black exclusivist CUSA in mid-1984. As convener of its inaugural meeting, he was in December 1985 chosen to deliver the keynote address at the launch of COSATU. Openly assuming ANC positions, in February 1987 he was instrumental behind NUM's adoption of the principles outlined in the Freedom Charter, which in July, on the mineworkers' initiative, were embraced by COSATU as well. After leading NUM through the national strikes in 1987, the young Ramaphosa, finally, became a major figure in the South African drama. Later described by Nelson Mandela as "probably the most accomplished negotiator in the ranks of the ANC" (Mandela op. cit., p. 583), as leader of the National [Mandela] Reception Committee, ANC Secretary General and head of the movement's negotiating team, he constructively contributed to apartheid's demise. Widely tipped as a potential Deputy President in 1994, Mandela, however, ultimately opted for Thabo Mbeki. Ramaphosa, instead, became Chairman of the Constitutional Assembly. Re-elected ANC Secretary General in late 1994, soon thereafter he left the political arena, joining black business as Deputy Executive Chairman of New Africa Investments Limited.
2. See the chapter 'SACTU, Unions and Sanctions'.
3. Very few students of the South African trade union and mass democratic movements in the 1980s have looked into the question of funding—whether internal or external—and, thus, the material conditions for the struggle. Southall's study on international labour and the unions (op. cit.) stands out as a positive exception, while Seekings's history of UDF, for example, is largely silent—or even inaccurate—in this regard (op. cit.).
4. Cf. the chapter 'SACTU, Unions and Sanctions'. As noted there, until 30 June 1996 LO/TCO had in total channelled almost 200 MSEK to the South African trade unions. With 54 MSEK, COSATU was the largest recipient (ibid.). Around 90 per cent of the funds were allocated by the Swedish government.
5. See the chapter 'Isolation versus Involvement: Companies, Churches and Labour in the 1970s'.
6. This, in turn, largely explains why the Swedish Mineworkers Union was decidedly more positive towards economic sanctions than *Metall*.
7. Striking for better pay and working conditions, between 60,000 and 70,000 black miners were ferociously attacked by the police. Twelve miners were killed and no less than 1,200 wounded (Lodge op. cit., p. 20).

that certain rights were extended to the miners.[1] It was against this background, finally, that the BCM-inspired Council of Unions of South Africa (CUSA) in August 1982 decided to form a National Union of Mineworkers.

Bilateral relations between the Swedish Mineworkers Union and NUM were in general facilitated by the LO/TCO support extended via ICFTU to CUSA. As earlier noted, LO/TCO had, in addition, from the late 1970s embarked on an education project in Lesotho which targeted migrant labourers working on contract for the South African mining corporations. On behalf of ICFTU and LO/TCO, from 1979 the Swede Ove Johansson was based in Maseru, where he assisted and closely followed the unionization efforts on the South African mines.[2] Many workers from the independent kingdom played leading roles in this regard. James Motlatsi, NUM's first President, working in close tandem with Cyril Ramaphosa and later a frequent visitor to Sweden[3], was, for example, from Mohales Hoek in Lesotho.[4]

Above all, however, it was direct contacts between Stig Blomqvist, Motlatsi and Ramaphosa which paved the way for the substantial Swedish support to the recently founded NUM.[5] This, in turn, was largely coincidental. Seconded by the Swedish Mineworkers Union, Blomqvist—himself a miner—had in 1981 joined the Miners International Federation (MIF) to organize trade union education projects in Latin America.[6] After harsh experiences in Colombia, Peru and Guyana[7], he was in 1983 transferred to Zimbabwe, where in June—just two months before meeting Motlatsi and Ramaphosa—he established a base in Harare. Financially supported by LO/TCO, covering Southern Africa and working alone, together with 'Palle' Carlsson—the Swedish trade union council's representative in Namibia in the late 1970s[8]—Blomqvist is another 'unsung pioneer' in Sweden's involvement for human dignity and democracy in the region.[9]

---

1. In 1981, the Chamber of Mines declared that it would only bargain with registered unions which represented 30 per cent or more of the workforce throughout the entire industry. It also denied union officials access to the miners' hostels. After a number of strikes and extensive rioting by between 30,000 and 40,000 workers in 1981-82, NUM was, however, recognized *de facto* in October 1982 (Southall op. cit., pp. 73-74).
2. See the chapter 'SACTU, Unions and Sanctions'.
3. Interviewed in 1997, Stig Blomqvist recalled: "In the beginning, NUM was working from one room, where Ramaphosa and Motlatsi were also sleeping. As a team, they were perfect. [...] Motlatsi was not talking, but in the mines he was talking a lot. He is the best agitator I know. [...] He is better than Cyril even" (Interview with Stig Blomqvist, p. 268). According to Motlatsi, from 1985 he visited Sweden "every year, maybe once or twice or sometimes even three times" (Interview with James Motlatsi, p. 166).
4. Interview with Stig Blomqvist, p. 268. Like many young men in Lesotho, after finishing school Motlatsi went to work in 1970 on the mines in South Africa. He served his first contract at Welkom in the Orange Free State, going to the Western Deep Levels mine in Carletonville west of Johannesburg in 1974. Motlatsi and Ramaphosa started to work together in 1982.
5. NUM held its inaugural congress in December 1982.
6. Interview with Stig Blomqvist, pp. 266-67.
7. Ibid., p. 267.
8. See the chapter 'Transport, Home Front, Churches and Trade Unions' on Namibia above.
9. As noted, Ben Ulenga, former Secretary General of the Mineworkers Union of Namibia, stated in 1995: "I was [...] lucky to link up with a guy called Stig Blomqvist, who was in Zimbabwe. He was a person who was very much down to earth. He understood what was happening. He was the best, as far as I am concerned" (Interview with Ben Ulenga, p. 100). A year later, the NUM President James Motlatsi said that "Stig Blomqvist [...] was really a driving force. Stig is my personal friend. I cannot go to Sweden without seeing him" (Interview with James Motlatsi, p. 167). Banned from entering South Africa, it was only in February 1987 that Blomqvist managed to get a visa to the country. Attending NUM's fifth congress in Soweto, the union delegates overwhelmingly showed him their appreciation. "They carried me on their shoulders around the congress hall", he later recalled (Interview with Stig Blomqvist, p. 268). Together with Motlatsi he also visited the Western Deep Levels gold mine in Carletonville. The visit left him with new impressions. Addressing some 15,000 workers, they responded: "Thank you very much for what you have done for us, but we don't want money. [W]e want guns!" (Interview with James Motlatsi, pp. 167-68). But Blomqvist explained: "I am sorry, I cannot do that. The Swedish people do not believe in a violent change of society. We believe in peaceful methods, including strikes, but not in violence". According to him, "they accepted that" (Interview with Stig Blomqvist, p. 268).

The first meeting between Blomqvist and the NUM leaders took place in Harare in early August 1983. Blomqvist later recalled how

> [o]ne day I was approached by a man called Cyril Ramaphosa. He called me from Johannesburg and said that he was the General Secretary of a newly formed National Union of Mineworkers (NUM). He asked me if I was willing to get the union moving through education activities. [...] I then met Ramaphosa and [...] Motlatsi at the airport in Harare. I first took them to the trade union office in town and introduced them to Geoffrey Mutandare, the chairman of the Mineworkers Union of Zimbabwe. Mutandare was joking and said: 'We must have a party for our friends from South Africa'. But Cyril said: 'No. We have not come here for a party. We have come here for work'. That showed me what kind of man he was. That was enough for me.
>
> We then went to my house, and I told them about the low cost education which I had been introducing in the unions. Ramaphosa said: 'It sounds good'. [...] [He then] presented his plans and wrote down the layout on a paper. He showed his capacity. How he can form ideas into an almost perfect layout. Because it was he who did that, not I.
>
> We designed the whole structure of NUM's education activity that night. It is still there today, [s]o it was not a bad job. Cyril [...] also worked out a preliminary budget for one year. I then phoned the former director of the LO/TCO Council of International Trade Union Cooperation, Jan-Erik Norling. [...] I said to him: 'Can you get the money?' And Norling [replied]: 'You can go ahead with the planning. I will get the money'. He took a risk that nobody else in Sweden in those days would have taken.[1]

Interviewed in 1996, Motlatsi similarly remembered the first meeting with Blomqvist:

> I and Cyril Ramaphosa flew to Harare, Zimbabwe, where we met Stig Blomqvist [...], who was a regional educator for the Miners International Federation [...]. We had a meeting overnight, and he contacted [Sweden][2] by telephone the very same day. In the morning, he told us that there was a possibility of getting financial assistance [...].[3]

On their return to Johannesburg, Motlatsi and Ramaphosa immediately drafted a detailed project memorandum, which was approved by NUM's National Executive Committee.[4] Noting that the NUM membership had grown from 14,000 in December 1982 to 40,000 in August 1983[5] and that the union was "constantly inundated by requests from miners", the memorandum warned against "the dangers of growing too big too quickly", adding that "unguided rapid growth could eventually lead to the union's demise".[6] Against this background, a consolidation plan had earlier been drafted. Focusing on organization at the shaft level, the main component of the strategy was education, with the following primary objectives:

- providing basic skills,
- arousing interest and strengthening loyalty towards trade unionism,
- putting labour problems in their broader social and economic setting, and
- training workers for responsible tasks in the workplace and [the] community.[7]

---

1. Interview with Stig Blomqvist, pp. 267-68.
2. In Motlatsi's recollection, Blomqvist contacted Anders Stendalen of the Swedish Mineworkers Union. According to Blomqvist, he, however, called Jan-Erik Norling of the LO/TCO council.
3. Interview with James Motlatsi, p. 165.
4. Letter ('Education project') from Cyril Ramaphosa to Stig Blomqvist, NUM, Johannesburg, 15 September 1983 (LMA). Ramaphosa addressed Blomqvist as "dear brother Stig" (ibid.). Looking back, Motlatsi later said that "our relationship with the Swedish miners went beyond a normal friendship. [...] We were not treated like friends, but like brothers" (Interview with James Motlatsi, p. 166).
5. The total workforce in the South African mining industry was at the time around 750,000.
6. NUM National Executive Committee: Memorandum ('Education and training project'), NUM, Johannesburg, 2 August 1983 (SDA).
7. Ibid.

These objectives were to be achieved over a two-year period through the training of 600 study circle leaders, who—guided by workers' education instructors in the different mining regions of the country—would reach 15,000 members.[1]

Known as the 'E-plan'—which simply stood for 'education', but "was confusing to the police"[2]—Motlatsi later presented it as follows:

> The 'E-plan' worked like this: We took it to the union leaders and [they] identified the activists. [...] After educating the activists, they [, in turn,] went to the hostels, where they ran courses in the rooms when the workers had the time. It was an informal education. We realised that unless we moved in that direction, we would not be able to educate the masses. [...] [B]ecause most of the mineworkers were illiterate, it was not as easy as one could have thought. But through [foreign] assistance[3] and the plans of mass education, we succeeded in recruiting thousands and thousands of miners between 1982 and the 1987 national strike.[4]

Accompanied by Blomqvist[5], Ramaphosa paid his first visit to Sweden in October 1983. In addition to discussions with LO/TCO on the requested education support, the NUM General Secretary gave a press conference at the LO headquarters in Stockholm.[6] Well attended and widely covered, it marked the beginning of Ramaphosa's high profile in the country. As would be the case during subsequent visits, the internally based labour leader was decidedly outspoken. After describing NUM's main enemies as "the government, the employers and the white trade unions", he was asked if he did not fear reprisals on his return to South Africa. In response, Ramaphosa stated:

> I am not afraid. Like so many workers and trade union leaders, I have already been detained. But I am not doing anything illegal. I am, quite simply, merely telling the truth.[7]

1. Ibid. The following remark should be noted: "All efforts will be made to get mine managements to agree to the use of their training centres or other suitable venues, [f]ailing which churches in the surrounding areas will have to be used" (ibid.). On the Swedish labour movement and the mobilizing instrument of study circles, see Sellström Volume I, pp. 37-38.
2. Interview with Stig Blomqvist, p. 268. Proposed and coordinated by Nelson Mandela, ANC had in 1953 adopted a so called 'M-plan' for organization in the townships. Based on a system with street-cells, it bore similarities to NUM's 'E-plan'. According to Blomqvist, "[t]he whole [plan] [...] was built on the cell-system—the [C]ommunist-inspired system—and the Swedish study circle activity. We started cells which could operate in a country where nothing was allowed [...]. It also worked in the closed hostels" (Interview with Stig Blomqvist, p. 268).
3. While most of the financial assistance came from Sweden, NUM was also supported by the labour movements in Denmark and Norway, subsequently joined by the unions in Holland (Interviews with James Motlatsi, p. 165, and Stig Blomqvist, p. 268). With regard to outside assistance, Blomqvist—who was seconded to the mineworkers' international—later stated: "Cyril told me that he had been running around the world, to the Americans, to the Germans, everybody, trying to get assistance. But they did not get anything practical which was useful to them. What they got was peanuts. Nothing to start a mass movement with. And that is what we are talking about, the start of a mass movement. [...] The big Western powers did nothing for the development of [this] movement in South Africa. That is my judgement. It was only the Nordic countries and Holland. They should have full credit for that. Nobody else, especially not the Germans. They have not done anything, other than invite people for seminars where they tried to brainwash them. [...] I fought against it [...]. I was fighting, because I saw that the Americans and the Germans wanted to control others with their money. Everything they assisted was connected to their own countries. They used the trade union movement for political purposes" (Interview with Stig Blomqvist, p. 268-69). Asked if there were any conditions attached to the Swedish and Scandinavian support, Motlatsi responded in 1996: "No. We did not really encounter any political conditions whatsoever". At the same time, the NUM President explained that we "learned that it is important to keep labour autonomous from the political party" (Interview with James Motlatsi, pp. 167-68).
4. Interview with James Motlatsi, pp. 165-66.
5. Letter from Cyril Ramaphosa to LO/TCO, NUM, Johannesburg, 20 September 1983 (LMA).
6. Hans Fogelström: Circular ('Besök från Sydafrika'/'Visit from South Africa'), LO, [Stockholm], 5 October 1983 (LMA).
7. Cited in Thorwald Olsson: 'Svart gruvfack i Sydafrika: De vita arbetarna vår värsta fiende' ('Black miners' union in South Africa: The white workers [are] our worst enemy') in *Dagens Nyheter*, 12 October 1983. Characterizing Swedish moral and material support as "vital", Ramaphosa hoped that NUM would have half a million members by 1990 (ibid.).

Following Ramaphosa's visit, in mid-December 1983 LO/TCO submitted a request to the Consultative Committee on Humanitarian Assistance (CCHA), proposing that an available balance of 735,000 SEK out of funds earlier granted should be channelled through MIF to NUM's education plan.[1] The request was approved the following month.[2] At a time when official assistance to UDF was extended via AIC, together with the support directly allocated to ANC under the 'home front component' Sweden would thereby be closely involved with the main labour, community and political actors in the mounting South African struggle during the 1980s.

LO/TCO and the Mineworkers Union were from the outset impressed by NUM's achievements. In a letter to SIDA, Jan-Erik Norling of the trade union council wrote in November 1984 that "NUM's [...] breakthrough into the South African mining industry is one of the most important [developments] [...] in the struggle against apartheid. I would also like to stress that we have great confidence in the organization and its leaders. In the light of its short existence, one cannot but admire them".[3] As earlier noted, Anders Stendalen, chairing both the Swedish Mineworkers Union and the Miners International Federation[4], expressed a similar opinion.[5] In response, in mid-November 1984 CCHA almost doubled LO/TCO's allocation to NUM from 735,000 SEK to 1.3 MSEK.[6] Broadened to include legal aid and a health and safety programme, the Swedish support to NUM was over the following years regularly increased.

Miners' Solidarity

While NUM—"breathing down the necks of the mining bosses"[7]—registered continuous growth[8], from mid-1984 the direct contacts with Sweden developed. In February 1985, for example, LO/TCO's Sven Fockstedt visited the union in South Africa[9], and during the same month Motlatsi and Ramaphosa again travelled to Sweden. Later in the year the relations assumed a regional dimension, when in November Blomqvist, LO/TCO and NUM took active part in the formation of a

---

1. Letter ('Stöd till National Union of Mineworkers (Sydafrika)'/'Support to NUM') from Jan-Erik Norling to CCHA, LO/TCO Council of International Trade Union Cooperation, Stockholm, 13 December 1983 (SDA).
2. Letter ('Stöd till National Union of Mineworkers'/'Support to NUM') from Lars-Olof Edström to LO/TCO, SIDA, 10 January 1984 (SDA). The 'E-plan' was formally launched through a seminar for workers' education instructors held from 15 to 24 January 1984 (Letter ('Stöd till National Union of Mineworkers (Sydafrika)'/ 'Support to NUM') from Jan-Erik Norling to SIDA, LO/TCO Council of International Trade Union Cooperation, Stockholm, 29 October 1984) (SDA).
3. Letter from Jan-Erik Norling to SIDA, LO/TCO Council of International Trade Union Cooperation, Stockholm, 9 November 1984 (SDA).
4. Representing one of the strongest mining industries in the world, James Motlatsi was in 1988 elected Vice-President of MIF. While NUM was a member of MIF, it remained highly critical of the Western-aligned ICFTU, where LO and TCO played prominent roles. In discussions with the Swedish legation in Pretoria, in November 1984, for example, Ramaphosa strongly turned against ICFTU's "anti-Communism" (Cable ('Ansökan från LO/TCO för stöd till NUM'/'Request from LO/TCO for support to NUM') from the Swedish legation to the Ministry for Foreign Affairs, Pretoria, 12 November 1984) (SDA). As will be seen below, during his visits to Sweden Ramaphosa also endorsed SACTU.
5. Cf. the chapter 'SACTU, Unions and Sanctions'.
6. Elisabeth Michanek: Memorandum ('Ansökan från LO/TCO's biståndsnämnd om bidrag till National Union of Mineworkers i Sydafrika'/'Request from the LO/TCO Council of International Trade Union Cooperation for contribution to NUM'), SIDA/CCHA, [Stockholm], 13 November 1984 (SDA).
7. NUM: 'This Is the National Union of Mineworkers: A Union Preparing a Better Future for Miners', NUM, [no place or date, but Johannesburg, 1985] (LMA).
8. By early 1985, the membership had grown to 110,000. With 260,000 members in late 1987, NUM was by far COSATU's largest affiliate, representing twice as many workers as NUMSA (Southall op. cit., pp. 284-85).
9. Sven Fockstedt: 'Facklig kamp i Sydafrika: Anteckningar från ett studiebesök, 26 januari-16 februari 1985'/ 'Trade union struggle in South Africa: Notes from a study visit, 26 January-16 February 1985', LO/TCO, [no place or date, but Stockholm, 1985] (SDA).

Trade union cooperation
(from left): President
James Motlatsi of the
South African National
Union of Mineworkers,
General Secretary Cyril
Ramaphosa and Anders
Stendalen, chairman of
the Swedish Mineworkers
Union, Stockholm,
February 1985
(Courtesy of Anders
Stendalen)

Southern African Mineworkers Federation, bringing together the miners in Botswana, Lesotho, Namibia, South Africa, Swaziland, Zambia and Zimbabwe.[1]

It was, however, the disaster at the Kinross mine east of Johannesburg in September 1986[2] and the national strike in August 1987[3] which really turned NUM into a household name among the Swedish mineworkers.[4] On both occasions, they launched broad solidarity actions. Immediately after the outbreak of the strike in August 1987, LO and the miners' union "appealed for massive support from both the labour movement and the general public in favour of the South African mineworkers".[5] Led by Anders Stendalen, at the same time the Swedish mineworkers started a massive fund-raising campaign.[6] Continuing after the conflict, by 31 December 1987 they had raised no less than 3.4 MSEK in favour of NUM.[7]

---

1. The regional organization was formed on MIF's initiative. It could as a curiosity be noted that Morgan Tsvangirai of Zimbabwe and Ben Ulenga of Namibia—future leaders of the political opposition in their respective countries—were closely involved with NUM in the setting up of the federation.
2. Close to 200 mineworkers were killed during the accident at Kinross. Assisting NUM, in the wake of the disaster safety experts were seconded from Sweden and the other Nordic countries (Interview with James Motlatsi, p. 166).
3. Between 1975 and 1986, profits in the South African mining industry rose in real terms by 44%. Against this background, NUM demanded a general wage increase of 30%. The Chamber of Mines, however, offered no more than 15 to 23%. Negotiations between the parties deadlocked in July 1987, and on 9 August some 340,000 mineworkers downed tools in the biggest strike ever to take place in South Africa. What followed over the next three weeks was a nationwide trial of strength between the mining companies and the state on the one hand and the miners on the other. Around 45,000 workers were dismissed, 400 arrested, 500 seriously injured and 9 killed during the confrontations. On 28 August 1987, NUM was ultimately forced to accept the original offer from the Chamber of Mines. Although this was a battle lost, NUM had by no means been broken. On the contrary, its organization and cohesion were strengthened during the conflict (cf. the interview with James Motlatsi, p. 166). During his visit to Sweden in October 1987, Ramaphosa concluded that "[t]he confrontation between the mining bosses, the state and the miners was a necessary stage on the road to a free and democratic non-racial South Africa. The miners' strike and other strikes embarked upon by COSATU unions have firmly placed the South African working class in the frontline in the struggle against racial tyranny and economic exploitation" (Cyril Ramaphosa: 'Olof Palme Prize address', Stockholm, 24 October 1987) (LMA).
4. Anders Stendalen later commented that "I don't think that we ever had such a strong response among our members to any campaign as the one we carried out for [...] South Africa" (Anders Stendalen cited in 'Landet som Skakat Oss'/'The Country Which Shook Us', *SIDA Rapport*, No. 3, 1994, p. 21).
5. Stig Malm, chairman: Circular ('Solidaritetsaktion för gruvarbetarna i Sydafrika'/'Solidarity action for the mineworkers in South Africa'), LO, Stockholm, 14 August 1987 (LMA).
6. Letter ('Svenska Gruvindustriarbetareförbundets stödaktion för gruvarbetarna i Sydafrika'/'The Swedish Mineworkers Union's support action for the mineworkers in South Africa') from Anders Stendalen, chairman, to AIC, Grängesberg, 19 August 1987 (LMA).
7. *AIC-Bulletinen*, No. 6/1987-1/1988, p. 24.

Effectively contributing to the successful campaign was that NUM—as earlier had been the case with UDF[1]—was singled out for special honours by the social democratic movement.[2] Shortly after the strike in South Africa, the International Centre of the Swedish Labour Movement (AIC) decided to grant NUM and Cyril Ramaphosa the first ever Olof Palme Prize for International Understanding and Common Security on account of "the courage and wisdom displayed by the members of South Africa's black mineworkers' union in their solidarity struggle for human rights and dignity, with [Ramaphosa] as [their] leader".[3]

Together with Motlatsi and other NUM officials, Ramaphosa was allowed to travel to Sweden to receive the prize. Amounting to 100,000 SEK, it was delivered by Lisbet Palme—the widow of the slain Prime Minister—during a ceremony in Stockholm on 24 October 1987. In his address on NUM's behalf, Ramaphosa was both defiant and confident. Openly identifying with the banned ANC, calling for sanctions, censuring the major Western powers and outlining the tasks involved in working towards a post-apartheid South Africa, in his vote of thanks he stated:

[This] is the first time that a prize has been given to South African workers as a group, and it is the first time that South African miners—who are the most important creators of our country's wealth—have been honoured and recognized for their contribution to our liberation struggle. It is an undisputable fact that miners constitute the backbone of [the] resistance to apartheid rule. [...]

The prize is [...] a declaration of solidarity and a gesture of encouragement to [the] South African miners, who have just emerged from the most historic strike in [the country]. During the strike, it was important for us to know that we had [the] support of the Swedish people, the Swedish LO and the Swedish miners. [...] Sweden has become a torchbearer, and must be applauded for taking a stand against apartheid. [...]

There is no longer any doubt that it is the working people in South Africa—as part of the Mass Democratic Movement [and] under the proven leadership of the African National Congress— who hold the key to victory over apartheid and exploitation. [...] The South African problem cannot be resolved without [a] total dismantling of apartheid and the handing over of state power to the legitimate leaders of our people, Nelson Mandela and Oliver Tambo. [...]

Disappointingly, the major leaders of [the] Western powers, such as Great Britain, West Germany and USA, still refuse to support our struggle. [...] The truth of the matter is that Thatcher and Reagan love Botha and support apartheid. Thatcher, Reagan and Kohl are seen by

---

1. In May 1984—only nine months after its formation—the United Democratic Front was granted the 'Let Live Prize' by the Malmö-based social democratic newspaper *Arbetet*.

2. On one of their visits to Sweden in the mid-1980s, Ramaphosa and Motlatsi were introduced to Prime Minister Palme. According to Stendalen—who served as intermediary—it was the first time that Palme held direct, substantial discussions with prominent leaders representing the internal trade union movement (Author's telephone conversation with Anders Stendalen, 3 May 2001).

3. Elli-Kari Höjeberg: 'Ramaphosa: Gruvorna Var i Våra Händer' ('Ramaphosa: The Mines Were in Our Hands') in *AIC-Bulletinen*, No. 6/1987-1/1988, p. 24. It should be underlined that Ramaphosa in this interview—appearing in a LO-supported publication—firmly defended SACTU. Stating that it was "insulting" when SACTU was criticized for being a member of the Communist-dominated WFTU, he declared that the organization was "a vital part of our liberation struggle" and that it had played a "decisive role in the efforts towards trade union organization in South Africa, not only in the 1950s, but also when COSATU was formed in 1985". As earlier noted, LO rejected SACTU, but was a leading COSATU donor. At the same time, the Social Democratic government extended official Swedish support to SACTU, albeit via ANC. In this regard, the NUM General Secretary was clearly critical of LO's position. Stressing that "you interfere in our internal affairs when [you] try to drive a wedge between us and SACTU", Ramaphosa added: "Although we receive support from Western trade unions, it does not mean that you can dictate the terms [...]. COSATU will always defend SACTU, in the same way that SACTU defends us" (ibid., p. 27). On LO/TCO, NUM and SACTU, see also the interviews with James Motlatsi (p. 167) and Stig Blomqvist (p. 269).

Lisbet Palme handing Cyril
Ramaphosa the first Olof
Palme Prize, awarded to
the National Union of Mine-
workers of South Africa,
Stockholm, October 1987
(Photo: Aftonbladet Bild)

oppressed South Africans as the butchers of the 1980s.[1] The money South Africa earns
through trade with their countries enables the government to buy weapons for the army and
the police in order to kill hundreds of children and women in the townships of Soweto. [...]

We are [, however,] so certain of our victory that our people have started thinking, discussing
and working towards a post-apartheid society.[2] Our task, therefore, is to prepare, organize,
mobilize, study, agitate and move forward to people's power in reality and not in slogans only.

In preparation for a post-apartheid South Africa, the National Union of Mineworkers has
decided that the Olof Palme Prize money should be used to establish a scholarship to be known
as the 'Olof Palme-NUM Scholarship'. [It] will [enable] people to acquire skills in the mining
industry, so that after apartheid is abolished we should have our own mining engineers, sur-
veyors, geologists, rock mechanics experts and mine managers, who will be sufficiently qualified to run our mines, as set out in the Freedom Charter.[3]

Later elected ANC Secretary General, through NUM and COSATU the former
BCM activist Cyril Ramaphosa was a crucial actor in the decisive political process
of bringing the powerful South African labour movement into an alliance with
ANC in exile. The labour support channelled by the Nordic trade unions was in
this regard not without significance. Retroactively assessing the support, in 1996
NUM President James Motlatsi stated that

[t]he importance of the assistance [...] lies in the fact that we succeeded in mobilizing the rank
and file through education, and that we were able to sustain quite a number of painful strikes,

1. On his first official visit to democratic South Africa, in September 1995 the German Chancellor Helmut Kohl
   unabashedly stated that "German companies showed a lasting and ongoing commitment in South Africa,
   even in later, difficult, times. They provided and preserved work for many, especially discriminated population groups, thus giving them hope for a better future" ('Speech by Dr. Helmut Kohl, Chancellor of the Federal Republic of Germany, before the members of the two houses of the South African parliament', Cape
   Town, 11 September 1995) (NAI). For comments on this statement, see, for example, the interviews with
   Reddy Mampane (p. 148), Kay Moonsamy (pp. 163 and 165) and Beyers Naudé (p. 185).
2. Prime Minister Palme and ANC President Tambo had in early 1986 raised the issue of Swedish planning support towards a post-apartheid dispensation (see the chapter 'Banning of Trade and Planning for Post-Apartheid').
3. Cyril Ramaphosa: 'Olof Palme Prize address', Stockholm, 24 October 1987 (LMA). NUM and Ramaphosa
   subsequently called on trade unions around the world to contribute to the 'Olof Palme-NUM Scholarship' (cf.
   Vetlesen (1998) op. cit., pp. 27-28). On NUM's initiative, COSATU had in July 1987 adopted the principles
   of ANC's Freedom Charter.

sit-ins and dismissals without demoralizing those who were still working. [...] It was also very important that we were able to interact with the entire world. [...] [T]hrough the education assistance, we were able to extend friendship with sister unions all over the world. That also made a proper communication possible between the liberation movement, namely ANC, and the mass democratic movement inside the country. It made it possible to have public and underground meetings, so I would say that the Nordic countries played an important role. Indeed, we are where we are today because of the role they played.[1]

The United Democratic Front

With the growth and consolidation of the trade union movement and the emergence of numerous student, youth and community organizations all over South Africa[2], in the late 1970s and the early 1980s the internal anti-apartheid opposition underwent a significant revival. At the same time, cooperation and coordination between workers', students' and community-based organizations increased. Many of them had, however, a limited membership. In the absence of a political organization which on a national scale could coordinate the opposition, their impact was fragmented and restricted. This would radically change following the launch in Cape Town on 20 August 1983 of the United Democratic Front (UDF), an historic event which signalled the beginning of a protracted popular rebellion and, eventually, the end of apartheid rule.[3]

This is not the place to elaborate on the origins of UDF, nor to closely follow its course during the 1980s. Suffice it here initially to note that while ANC's strategic review in the late 1970s—toning down the movement's 'commitment to a socialist order'—made a call for the establishment of 'a nationwide popular liberation front'[4] and many underground ANC members actively pursued this cause, UDF was "not a creation of the African National Congress".[5] Instead, it was the end result of several parallel developments, where opposition to the Pretoria regime's plans to win over coloured and Indian allies by creating separate parliamentary assemblies for these groups' so called 'own affairs' was of decisive consequence. When in mid-1982 Prime Minister P.W. Botha laid down guidelines for a new, tricameral constitutional dispensation, they immediately set in motion soul-searching debates within a wide range of coloured and Indian organizations, as well as among the churches. Excluding the African majority and attempting to divide the coloured and Indian communities by co-opting their middle class strata—"making

---

1. Interview with James Motlatsi, p. 168.
2. Of particular importance in the immediate post-BCM period was the Congress of South African Students (COSAS), which was established in June 1979 and soon had branches at secondary schools and technical colleges all over the country. Initially BCM-inspired and set up to replace the banned South African Students Movement (SASM), as early as in 1980 it declared its support for ANC's Freedom Charter, the first mass organization in South Africa since the 1960s to do so. The COSAS President, Ephraim Mogale, was a clandestine ANC member, eventually convicted of 'furthering the aims of ANC'. With the guiding principle that ANC was the 'authentic liberation movement', COSAS upheld firm non-racial views. In addition to educational campaigns, in the early 1980s it launched a number of nationwide political protest and boycott actions. From the very beginning, COSAS, finally, formed part of the United Democratic Front, becoming one of its strongest national affiliates. COSAS was banned in August 1985.
3. On UDF, its affiliate organizations and the popular struggles in the 1980s, see Gregory F. Houston: *The National Liberation Struggle in South Africa: A Case Study of the United Democratic Front, 1983-1987*, Ashgate Publishing, Aldershot, 1999; Ineke van Kessel: *'Beyond Our Wildest Dreams': The United Democratic Front and the Transformation of South Africa*, University Press of Virginia, Charlottesville and London, 2000; and Seekings op. cit.
4. See the chapter 'From Beds in Exile to Organizers at Home'.
5. Mac Maharaj cited in 'UDF: An Historical Development' in *Sechaba*, March 1984, p. 17. The interview with Maharaj—heading ANC's Internal Policy and Reconstruction Department—was first published in *Mayibuye*, No. 10, 1983.

them shareholders in apartheid [and] partners in their own oppression"[1]—the tricameral dispensation forced a stand with regard to participation or opposition.[2] It became, as stated by the Swedish political scientist Per Strand, "a constitution for conflict".[3]

More than any other, Reverend Allan Boesak, the Cape Town-based coloured President of the World Alliance of Reformed Churches[4], has been credited with the idea of UDF.[5] In an address to a conference of the Transvaal Anti-South African Indian Council in Johannesburg, in January 1983 he rejected the tricameral proposals, stating that

> [t]here is [...] no reason why the churches, civic associations, trade unions, student organizations and sport bodies should not unite on this issue, pool [their] resources, inform people of the fraud that is about to be perpetuated in their name and [...] expose [the] plans for what they are.[6]

As later noted by the UDF activist Cassim Saloojee, Boesak's speech "just created one helluva sensation".[7] The conference endorsed Boesak's suggestion, and set up a steering committee to establish a united front. This was followed by the election of an interim executive and the establishment over the following months of regional structures. Attended by delegates of no less than 565 organizations[8], in August 1983, this process, finally, culminated in the launch at Rocklands Community Centre in Mitchell's Plain—a coloured settlement on the Cape Flats—of a national United Democratic Front under the banner 'UDF Unites-Apartheid Divides'.

Although ANC in exile was not directly involved in these developments—and UDF only adopted the Freedom Charter in 1987—the front's 'Charterist' orientation was evident from the outset. According to Seekings, "with a few exceptions, all [organizations represented] were led by activists who considered themselves supporters or even members of the ANC".[9] This, in turn, was reflected in the appointment of national UDF representatives, as well as in the front's general policy principles. The three national co-presidents elected were all closely associated with the banned ANC, namely, the Natal leader Archie Gumede, the Transvaalbased representative Albertina Sisulu—the wife of prisoner for life Walter Sisulu—and the

---

1. Houston op. cit., p. 60.
2. The tricameral dispensation was enacted by the white-only South African parliament in 1983, coming into effect in September 1984. Separate elections for the coloured and Indian chambers were held in August 1984. The results indicated a widespread opposition to the new dispensation. According to official figures, the participation in the coloured election was around 30 and in the Indian election 20 per cent. UDF put the figures at 17.5 and 15.5 per cent, respectively (Houston op. cit., p. 72).
3. Per Strand: *Decisions on Democracy: The Politics of Constitution-Making in South Africa, 1990-1996*, Uppsala University, Uppsala, 2000, p. 89.
4. Influenced by Steve Biko's black consciousness philosophy, Boesak—representing the coloured *Sendingkerk* branch of the official Dutch Reformed Church (DRC)—had in October 1981 been elected Chairman of the Alliance of Black Reformed Christians in Southern Africa. In that capacity, in August 1982 he attended a meeting of the World Alliance of Reformed Churches in Ottawa, Canada, successfully introducing a resolution which declared apartheid a heresy. This led to the suspension of DRC from the Calvinist alliance and the election of Boesak as President, making him the spiritual leader of some 150 churches in more than 70 countries.
5. See, for example, the interview with Mac Maharaj in *Sechaba*, March 1984, where the ANC leader stated that Boesak "caught the right moment in the history of our people, interpreted correctly the conditions that have matured and made a stirring call for unity [...] in a United Democratic Front" (p. 17). Also *UDF News*, No. 1, August 1983, noting that it was "Allan Boesak's call for unity and joint action against the government's new plans [that] planted the seed that is growing into a massive national United Democratic Front" (p. 3).
6. Boesak cited in Houston op. cit., p. 62.
7. Saloojee cited in Seekings op. cit., p. 49.
8. Ibid., p. 59. A parallel mass meeting was attended by well over 10,000 people.
9. Ibid.

Western Cape trade unionist Oscar Mpetha.[1] Among the central principles which similarly indicated close affinity with the liberation movement were, in addition, the following:

– an unshakeable conviction in the creation of a non-racial, unitary state in South Africa, undiluted by racial or ethnic considerations as formulated in the bantustan policy, and

– an adherence to the need for unity in struggle through which all democrats, regardless of race, religion or colour, shall take part together.[2]

These principles also defined UDF's stand vis-à-vis so called 'non-collaborationist' organizations opposed to alliances with white South Africans and non-white middle class organizations alike, such as the white student organization NUSAS and the black Western Cape Traders Association, which both joined the front. Rejecting UDF's multi-racial views, in June 1983 the BCM-inspired AZAPO and the Cape Town-centred Unity Movement formed an alternative alliance called the National Forum, which adopted a socialist 'Manifesto of the Azanian People', but failed to mobilize mass support.[3] While the relations between UDF and the National Forum were initially tense, it was, however, the rejection of the bantustan policy which, more importantly, defined the front vis-à-vis Inkatha, soon leading to open hostilities between the two in Natal, as well as in the Johannesburg area.[4]

Largely formed in opposition to Pretoria's constitutional plans, UDF was during its first year mainly re-active, launching high-profile national campaigns against the tricameral dispensation. Initially, coloured and Indian organizations would therefore be at the forefront. Beginning with the uprising in the metropolitan Vaal Triangle in September 1984[5], the focus, however, shifted from the constitutional sphere to local issues in the black townships, where protests around schools and rents evolved into a challenge of the authorities. Although the township rebellion was primarily spontaneous and UDF's impact mostly indirect, from then on the front played a leading role in the protracted insurrection against the apartheid state, heeding ANC's call to make South Africa 'ungovernable'.[6] Advancing the slogan

---

1. At the executive level, Popo Molefe was appointed UDF National General Secretary and Patrick Lekota—nicknamed 'Terror' due to his soccer-playing skills—National Publicity Secretary.

2. Houston op. cit., p. 64.

3. The launch of the National Forum was attended by over 800 people, reportedly representing 164 organizations (Seekings op. cit., p. 68).

4. As noted in the chapter 'Gatsha Buthelezi and Inkatha', relations between ANC and Inkatha had broken down at the end of 1979.

5. In September 1984, a major rebellion broke out in the townships of the Vaal Triangle region in Transvaal. The main cause of the uprising was increases in rent and service charges imposed by the community councils, seen as government stooges. Joined by students and workers, the protests soon spread to the Orange Free State, the Cape province and Natal. After deploying the South African Defence Force against the rebellion, in July 1985 the government responded by declaring a state of emergency in 36 magisterial districts. It was extended in October 1985, covering *inter alia* the Western Cape. Lifted in March 1986, the partial legislation was followed three months later by a nationwide state of emergency, subsequently re-imposed until mid-1990.

6. On the relations between ANC in exile and UDF in South Africa, the following comment by Raymond Suttner—a leading internal member of ANC, SACP and UDF Transvaal—could be noted: "Throughout the existence of the UDF, many of us understood ourselves to be carrying out the strategic perspectives of the ANC, though on a day-to-day basis what that meant was decided by activists on the ground, and very often UDF affiliates came up with ideas or solutions that the ANC could never have envisaged. Activists would carefully scrutinise ANC statements, but they had to work out how to apply these in their specific conditions. [...] [I]t often turned out quite differently from what [the] strategists in Lusaka or [at the] Johannesburg UDF [headquarters] had expected or hoped" (Raymond Suttner: 'Reviews' in *News from the Nordic Africa Institute*, No. 1, 2001, p. 41).

'Forward to People's Power', in the process UDF strongly denounced Pretoria's main international supporters. After the June 1986 imposition of a nationwide state of emergency, followed by intensified popular rebellion and escalating repression[1], in October 1987—at a time when the front openly identified with ANC—it suspended relations with the British government.[2] After consultations with ANC, a corresponding decision was at the same time taken with regard to the United States.[3]

Before discussing Sweden's relations with UDF, it should be noted that towards the end of the 1980s the front received considerable financial resources from the European Community towards a number of project activities.[4] They were channelled via the Kagiso Trust, set up in May 1986 by the South African Council of Churches and the Southern African Catholic Bishops Conference.[5] In October 1986, however, the apartheid regime declared UDF an 'affected organization', which meant that it was prohibited from receiving foreign funds.[6] While various ways and means to circumvent this legislation were eventually found, the situation became much more complicated when in February 1988 the front and 17 other organizations were banned altogether. Forced underground and in danger of losing authority over its constituency—notably the youth organizations—it, nevertheless, continued to operate. Joining forces with COSATU, it regrouped under the guise of a Mass Democratic Movement. Amidst a general revival of overt defiance and protest, at the end of 1989 UDF unilaterally declared itself 'unbanned', a *de facto* stand which was formalized by the government in February 1990.

With the parallel unbanning of ANC and Nelson Mandela's release, the historic role played by UDF came to a close. Uncertain about its future and lapsing into inactivity, in early March 1991 the front decided to dissolve.[7] On its eighth anniversary, the United Democratic Front—having in crucial ways inspired and mobilized people across South Africa to confront the apartheid state—was disbanded

---

1. Between June 1986 and June 1987, over 25,000 people were detained in South Africa (TRC op. cit. (Vol. III), p. 25).
2. Cable ('UDF bryter förbindelserna med Storbritannien'/'UDF breaks relations with Great Britain') from the Swedish legation to the Ministry for Foreign Affairs, Pretoria, 29 October 1987 (SDA).
3. Letter ('UDF bryter med Storbritannien och USA'/'UDF breaks with Great Britain and USA') from Anders Möllander to the Ministry for Foreign Affairs, Swedish legation, Pretoria, 12 November 1987 (SDA). Extremely discontented with the American, British and West German policy towards South Africa, during consultative talks between Sweden and ANC Treasurer General Thomas Nkobi had in November 1985 stated that "sabotage actions against British economic interests in South Africa would be initiated" (Kaj Persson: Memorandum ('Programsamtal med ANC 1985/86'/'Consultative talks with ANC [for] 1985/86'), Ministry for Foreign Affairs, Stockholm, 11 December 1985) (SDA).
4. In addition to AIC of Sweden and the European Community, during the second half of the 1980s NOVIB of the Netherlands was among UDF's main donors.
5. Although not a member of the European Community and with direct links to UDF, Sweden too would support the Kagiso Trust. In November 1987, for example, the Consultative Committee on Humanitarian Assistance endorsed a proposal to allocate no less than 7.3 MSEK to Kagiso via CSA in cooperation with AGIS, CSM and Diakonia (Lena Johansson: Memorandum ('Möte med Kagiso-fonden, London, 12 januari 1988'/'Meeting with the Kagiso Trust in London on 12 January 1988'), SIDA, Stockholm, 26 January 1988) (SDA).
6. The ban on foreign funding—in addition to UDF affecting *inter alia* NUSAS and the Christian Institute—was only repealed in mid-April 1991 ('Foreign money ban lifted' in *Weekend Argus*, 13 April 1991).
7. Letter ('United Democratic Front, UDF') from Anders Möllander to AIC, Swedish legation, Pretoria, 7 March 1991 (OPA).

in August 1991. Joining ANC, many of its leaders would subsequently occupy prominent positions in the new South Africa.

Describing the workings of UDF, in the late 1980s the South African political scientist Tom Lodge concluded that it functioned "more in the fashion of a social movement than a deliberately contrived political machine".[1] With a federative structure, the front was established at the national, regional and local levels. The National Executive Committee was responsible for coordinating the implementation of UDF's policy and programme. To this end, it worked through ten regional structures, each with its own executive committee. However, they were accountable to the organizations affiliated at the local level. Among themselves, the regional committees therefore often took different stands on account of specific regional or sub-regional issues.

In his history of UDF, Jeremy Seekings has presented the front as follows:

> [A]t the national level, it comprised a federation of regional [...] bodies, each of which was a front or umbrella structure for highly diverse affiliated organisations. The affiliates ranged from student groups to civic associations, overtly political organisations to sport clubs. They existed independently of, and remained formally autonomous from, the UDF. Indeed, the UDF's structures were formally accountable to the affiliates. The UDF was not a party, did not have branches and never allowed for individual or personal membership. But it had its own discrete structures at national, regional and sub-regional levels. These structures organised events and campaigns, produced media, helped to build affiliates at both the local level and in the different 'sectors' (such as students, 'youth', women and civic associations) and channelled funds, as well as playing a general coordinating role for the UDF's affiliates.[2]

At its peak in 1987, UDF had approximately 700 affiliates with a combined membership of close to two million people.[3] Some of the affiliates—such as COSAS, SAAWU[4] and the Federation of South African Women—had their own national structures, while the great majority were restricted to a specific area, city or township. Among the latter were, for example, the Johannesburg Democratic Action Committee (JODAC) and the Durban Housing Areas Action Committee (DHAC).

The presentation below focuses on Sweden's relations with UDF *per se*, while the substantial support channelled to many of its affiliates via international[5] and Swedish NGOs falls outside the narration.[6] It should, however, be noted that the official assistance from Sweden registered a major expansion from the mid-1980s; that it involved an increasing number of Swedish popular organizations; and that

---

1. Lodge cited in Seekings op. cit., p. 15.
2. Ibid.
3. Houston op. cit., pp. 104 and 90.
4. South African Allied Workers Union.
5. Official Swedish support was channelled, for example, via the London-based Catholic Institute for International Relations (CIIR) to the Release Mandela Campaign (RMC) from mid-1984 (cf. Elisabeth Michanek: Memorandum ('Ansökan från Catholic Institute for International Relations avseende stöd till Release Mandela Campaign'/'Request from CIIR re support to RMC'), SIDA/CCHA, [Stockholm], 25 May 1984) (SDA). In addition, from 1985-86 CIIR administered Swedish assistance in favour of the End Conscription Campaign (ECC) (Letter from Ian Linden, General Secretary, to SIDA, CIIR, London, 24 September 1985) (SDA), as well as to the Johannesburg Democratic Action Committee (JODAC) (Letter from Ian Linden to SIDA, CIIR, London, 24 July 1986) (SDA). For a presentation of these and other UDF affiliates, see Hennie Kotzé and Anneke Greyling: *Political Organisations in South Africa A-Z*, Tafelberg Publishers, Cape Town, 1994.
6. Examples of South African organizations and publications receiving official Swedish support are given in an accompanying appendix. To these should be added a number of international NGOs which, in turn, assisted various anti-apartheid structures.

the overwhelming majority of the recipients were affiliated to or aligned with UDF.[1] While the Swedish authorities from the mid-1960s until the democratic elections in 1994 in current figures in total, directly and indirectly, transferred some 2.5 billion SEK as anti-apartheid support, no less than 1.9 billion—representing more than 75 per cent—was disbursed between 1985/86 and 1992/93. As summarized by SIDA, the overall distribution is reflected in the following chart:

Distribution of Swedish assistance to South Africa 1985/86-1992/93

(total disbursements: 1.9 billion SEK)

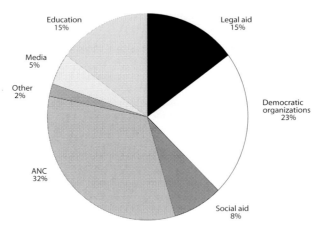

Source: *Sydafrika: Bistånd för Frihet*, SIDA, 1994

---

1. Following the 'IUEF affair', the Swedish authorities would in the case of requests in favour of internally based South African organizations as a rule seek ANC's opinion. While the movement, naturally, was positive towards Charterist-inspired initiatives, as noted by Strachan it "did not jettison or sabotage project proposals or support applications from organizations which did not hold the same ideological or political view as ANC" (Interview with Garth Strachan, p. 195). Official support to the Institute for a Democratic Alternative in South Africa (IDASA) could be quoted in this context. After resigning as MPs and leaders of the Progressive Federal Party (PFP), in May 1986 Frederik van Zyl Slabbert and Alex Boraine launched IDASA "to assist in creating a climate for true negotiation on the road to a non-racial democracy" (Kotzé and Greyling op. cit., p. 180). Initial support was received from the Norwegian government, and before the official launch it was proposed that Slabbert and Boraine should visit the Nordic countries to discuss the initiative (see the interview with Alex Boraine, p. 108, and cable ('Institute for Democratic Alternatives') from Jan Lundvik, Swedish envoy to South Africa, to the Ministry for Foreign Affairs, Swedish legation, Cape Town, 28 April 1986) (SDA). In meetings with the former PFP leaders, it was at the same time agreed that Sweden should raise the question of possible financial assistance with ANC (ibid.). They, in turn, contacted the liberation movement regarding the political aspects of the initiative. In the case of Sweden, the issue of support was raised with ANC during the annual negotiations in Lusaka in early May. It was followed up with Thomas Nkobi, who on 20 May 1986 paid a short visit to Stockholm and conveyed a positive decision (Cable ('Om Slabbert-Boraine's institut, IDASA'/'Re IDASA') from the Ministry for Foreign Affairs to the Swedish legations in Pretoria and Cape Town, Stockholm, 22 May 1986) (SDA). After discussions in Sweden with Slabbert and Boraine, it was subsequently agreed that official support to IDASA should be channelled via the Swedish International Liberal Center (SILC), the Liberal Party's branch for international solidarity (in Swedish, *Liberalt Utvecklingscentrum*, LUC). Covering around 20 per cent of IDASA's annual budgets, via SILC the Swedish Social Democratic government soon became IDASA's principal donor. Between 1986/87 and 1990/91, some 10.5 MSEK was channelled to the organization (Christina Regnell: Memorandum ('Ansökan från Liberalt Utvecklingscentrum, LUC, om stöd till IDASA och Five Freedoms Forum 1991'/'Request from SILC for support to IDASA and Five Freedoms Forum 1991'), SIDA/CCHA, [Stockholm], 5 December 1990) (SDA). To this should be added additional funds for particular events and projects, such as the historic encounter arranged by IDASA in Dakar, Senegal, in July 1987 between a group of predominantly Afrikaans-speaking South Africans and ANC in exile. This and other bridge-building meetings between various groups of white South Africans and the liberation movement towards the end of the 1980s and in the early 1990s were regularly supported by Sweden and the other Scandinavian countries (Interview with Alex Boraine, pp. 109-10).

The direct assistance to ANC during the seven-year period thus corresponded to around one third of the total. With almost 700 MSEK, indirect support to 'democratic organizations', 'social aid' and 'media' represented a slightly bigger share. The Swedish trade union support falls mainly within these general categories.[1] Included here are also the resources extended in favour of UDF, UDF-affiliated local organizations and UDF-aligned information agencies and publications.[2] Turning to the assistance granted via the International Centre of the Swedish Labour Movement[3] to the United Democratic Front, it should be borne in mind that the combined involvement with the front and its affiliates was considerably broader. Over the years, it was, however, only AIC which on a bilateral basis channelled official funds to UDF[4], from 1983 entering into a close relationship with the principal vehicle of the mounting—and eventually decisive—popular anti-apartheid South African rebellion. This, in turn, paved the way for a substantial voter education programme in the early 1990s.

A Swift Response: AIC, UDF and the Civics

The response by AIC and the Swedish authorities to the formation of UDF was swift. Visiting Stockholm one month after the national launch, on 23 September 1983 UDF's Auret van Heerden submitted an application for funds to the labour

---

1. As earlier noted, substantial amounts of the trade union assistance were set aside for education and legal aid.
2. Between 1985/86 and 1992/93, around 95 MSEK was channelled in favour of the anti-apartheid media in South Africa. Support to the 'alternative press' started, however, soon after its emergence around 1980 (on this subject, see Keyan Tomaselli and P. Eric Louw (eds): *The Alternative Press in South Africa*, Anthropos Publishers, Bellville, and James Currey, London, 1991, and Les Switzer and Mohamed Adhikari (eds): *South Africa's Resistance Press: Alternative Voices in the Last Generation under Apartheid*, Ohio University Center for International Studies, Athens, 2000). While publications such as *FOSATU Worker News*, *COSATU News* and *UDF News* received Swedish support within the general assistance to the issuing organizations, from the early 1980s more targeted support would be extended to a great number of 'community papers', 'left-commercial' newspapers, news agencies, typesetting projects and printers. As a rule holding themselves accountable to UDF, among the many anti-apartheid publications assisted were *The Eye*, *Grassroots*, *Indicator*, *Namaquanuus*, *New Nation*, *Saamstaan*, *Saspu National*, *South*, *Speak*, *Ukusa*, *Vrye Weekblad*, *Weekly Mail* and *Work in Progress*. On the production side, the Set Bold typesetting project could be mentioned. Considerable resources via Swedish or international NGOs were also channelled to other information projects, such as the Film Resource Unit and the Video News Services. Largely complementary to the core UDF support channelled by AIC, the attention paid by the Africa Groups to information projects in South Africa should in this context be underlined. With funds allocated by SIDA, from the mid-1980s the solidarity movement focused its internal support on three areas, namely, health, land issues and media. Within the latter area, AGIS supported *inter alia* training of black journalists at *Vrye Weekblad* and *Weekly Mail*, as well as at the local Cape Town *Bush Radio* station. Production and distribution of the Afrikaans-speaking publications *Namaquanuus* and *Saamstaan* were also supported (AGIS: 'Afrikagruppernas årsmöte 1993'/'Annual AGIS' meeting 1993', [no date or place]) (AGA). From the late 1980s, official funds were, in addition, extended via AGIS to the Press Trust of South Africa and other anti-apartheid information services (Letter ('Ansökan från Afrikagrupperna i Sverige, AGIS, om stöd till Press Trust of South Africa'/'Request from AGIS for support to the Press Trust of South Africa') from Eva Belfrage, SIDA, to the Africa Groups, SIDA/CCHA, [Stockholm], 14 December 1989) (SDA).
3. On AIC, see the chapter 'Transport, Home Front, Churches and Trade Unions' on Namibia.
4. Cable ('Re UDF och Boesak'/'Re UDF and Boesak') from the Ministry for Foreign Affairs to the Swedish legations in Pretoria and Cape Town, Stockholm, 12 March 1987 (SDA). After the unbanning of ANC and UDF, via AIC the Swedish government remained the sole donor to the front's central structures (Lena Johansson: Memorandum ('Årsansökan från Arbetarrörelsens Internationella Centrum om stöd till UDF i Sydafrika'/'Annual request from AIC for support to UDF in South Africa'), SIDA/CCHA, [Stockholm], 24 September 1990) (SDA).

movement's international coordinating body. Focusing on support to the front's central administration in the form of salaries, office rental, equipment and recurrent costs, as well as on the production and distribution of *UDF News* and propaganda material such as pamphlets, posters and stickers[1], it was received in a positive spirit. After deciding to grant UDF 200,000 SEK from its own International Solidarity Fund, four days later AIC formally approached the official Consultative Committee on Humanitarian Assistance with an initial request for 1.55 MSEK, giving priority to the front's planned training and information activities.[2]

Noting that ANC was the most important recipient of official Swedish antiapartheid assistance, but that "the bulk of the support [goes] to activities in exile", in the request AIC's Secretary General Bengt Säve-Söderbergh expressed the opinion that "support to UDF [in South Africa] is a good complement". He also asked for "urgent attention" to the submission.[3] This recommendation was, indeed, followed. On 30 September—three calendar days later and only a week after the original UDF request—the CCHA secretariat endorsed the proposal.[4] What is more, while a formal decision was not taken until 1 November 1983[5], after contacts with UDF in South Africa—and with NUM's General Secretary Cyril Ramaphosa in Stockholm[6]—it was at the end of October agreed to transfer a first instalment of 500,000 SEK.[7] Via AIC, official financial support was thus extended to UDF two months after its formation.[8] By that time, further applications had already been submitted by the front. Treated in a similarly swift and positive way, from as early as in 1983-84 Sweden became UDF's main foreign donor.[9]

---

1. 'Application for funds for the United Democratic Front', attached to letter from Auret van Heerden to the International Solidarity Fund of the Swedish Labour Movement, [no place, but Stockholm], 23 September 1983 (SDA).

2. 'Ansökan om bidrag till utbildnings- och informationsverksamheten för United Democratic Front (UDF) i Sydafrika' ('Request for contribution towards UDF's training and information activities') from AIC to SIDA, Stockholm, 27 September 1983 (SDA).

3. Ibid.

4. Elisabeth Michanek: Memorandum ('Ansökan från AIC om bidrag för stöd till utbildnings- och informationsverksamhet vid United Democratic Front i Sydafrika'/'Request from AIC for contribution towards support for UDF's training and information activities'), SIDA/CCHA, [Stockholm], 30 September 1983 (SDA).

5. SIDA: Decision, Office of the Director General, No. 499/1983, Stockholm, 1 November 1983 (SDA). Support to UDF had been recommended by CCHA at its meeting on 13 October 1983 (ibid.). Through a letter of exchange, a formal agreement between UDF and AIC was respectively signed in Johannesburg on 10 January and in Stockholm on 25 January 1984 (OPA).

6. Ramaphosa visited LO/TCO in Stockholm in early October 1983. At that time, AIC and LO/TCO shared offices. Säve-Söderbergh later commented: "It was very convenient, because Cyril Ramaphosa and many others who were involved in both the trade unions and UDF were often there. So, I knew what the situation was" (Interview with Bengt Säve-Söderbergh, p. 339).

7. Kaj Persson: Memorandum ('Humanitärt bistånd till södra Afrika'/'Humanitarian assistance to Southern Africa'), Ministry for Foreign Affairs, Stockholm, 26 October 1983 (SDA). It could be noted that the first payments to UDF were made via an account held be IDAF's Horst Kleinschmidt in London (ibid.).

8. In 1997, Säve-Söderbergh said that he "initially had problems with some SIDA bureaucrats" regarding the support to UDF, adding that "[t]his was new to them and they did not really know what to do" (Interview with Bengt Säve-Söderbergh, p. 340). In the light of the extraordinary speed with which AIC's original request was processed, this is hardly borne out by the documents consulted.

9. This is ignored by Seekings in his history of UDF. Although the study was financially supported by AIC (Seekings op. cit., p. ix)—and relevant information should have been easy to obtain—he states that a meeting in Stockholm in January 1986 between ANC and UDF "was also important in that it led to Swedish funding of [the front]" (ibid., p. 169). By that time, however, some 6.3 MSEK had already been disbursed by AIC to UDF's central structures, from 1984 corresponding to half or more of the core budget.

While the UDF leadership in South Africa from the very beginning entered into contact with the Swedish legation,[1] in Sweden, it was AIC's Säve-Söderbergh who more than any other paved the way for an active involvement with the front. Looking back in 1997, Säve-Söderbergh—who in 1985 was appointed Under-Secretary of State for International Development Cooperation in the Ministry for Foreign Affairs—said that he had been

> convinced that nothing decisive would take place until you really had actions going on inside the country. [...] In 1983, [however,] a very important thing happened in South Africa—which went almost unnoticed by many people—namely the founding of the United Democratic Front [...]. I realized that it was a very important event. In those days, there was still some hesitation among [the] solidarity groups and also within ANC regarding the situation inside South Africa. But I immediately initiated working relations with UDF [...,] seizing the moment and going full blast [...]. If there is any crucial matter where I personally affected developments, I would say that it was with regard to UDF. [...] A few months later, I moved back to the Foreign Ministry, where, of course, I could follow and influence things quite a lot.[2]

Via the Swedish legation in Pretoria, in mid-October 1983 Beyers Naudé—the banned leader of the Christian Institute, patron of the front and as early as in March 1981 described by the legation as "our principal contact"[3]—submitted another application for "urgent financial assistance" to the popular, UDF-aligned Charterist movement, this time in favour of some twenty local and regional youth organizations recently established in different parts of South Africa. Among them were the Cape Youth Congress (CAYCO), the Port Elizabeth Youth Congress (PEYCO), the Natal Youth Congress (NAYCO) and the Soweto Youth Congress (SOYCO).[4] Referred by SIDA to AIC for consideration, together with other UDF-

---

1. See, for example, the interview with Trevor Manuel, p. 149. While some of the leading UDF patrons—among them Beyers Naudé and Desmond Tutu—had long-standing previous relations with Sweden, this was not the case with the front's national and regional executive officers. Earlier influenced by or active within BCM-aligned organizations, it was with the formation of UDF that younger activists such as Azhar Cachalia, 'Terror' Lekota, Trevor Manuel, Popo Molefe, Eric Molobi, Mohammed Valli Moosa and Murphy Morobe entered into closer contact with the Swedish legation, AIC and Sweden in general. Based in Cape Town, Manuel, for example, had no contacts with the Swedish authorities or with the Swedish support to the anti-apartheid struggle before 1984. Via the churches, there were, however, indirect connections also with AGIS and the wider Swedish solidarity movement. Interviewed in 1995, the then Minister of Trade, Industry and Tourism explained: "I was working in civic organizations on a full-time basis from 1981, but we had very little access to resources. For campaigns, we used to go around the townships, but also to the churches. I later came to understand that we then also used facilities that were extended by the Nordic countries. On the Cape Flats, the Lutheran Centre in Belgravia was, for example, a meeting point which was very widely used. But I did not immediately understand the connection. Not until later. [...] One of the individuals who repeatedly came through was a man from Sweden called Magnus Walan. I do not remember when I first met Magnus, but it would have been before my long stint in jail. It was probably with the Swedish priest Per Svensson at the Lutheran Centre in Belgravia in early 1985 or something like that" (Interview with Trevor Manuel, pp. 149 and 151). Walan was a leading member of AGIS and ISAK.
2. Interview with Bengt Säve-Söderbergh, pp. 336-37 and 339-40.
3. Letter ('Internbistånd till Sydafrika'/'Internal assistance to South Africa') from Per Lindström, Swedish legation, to the Ministry for Foreign Affairs, Pretoria, 16 March 1981 (SDA).
4. Letter from C.F. Beyers Naudé to SIDA, Johannesburg, 12 October 1983 (SDA). As noted by Kotzé and Greyling, "[y]outh organisations were the cutting edge of the UDF" (Kotzé and Greyling op. cit., p. 260). Initiated by COSAS and inspired by UDF, in 1983 a great number of local and regional youth congresses were formed all over South Africa. Eventually reduced to ten, after the banning of COSAS they, in turn, established the national South African Youth Congress (SAYCO) in Cape Town in March 1987. Adopting the Freedom Charter, led by Peter Mokaba—UDF Publicity Secretary in Northern Transvaal and future President of the ANC Youth League—and with a membership of between 600,000 and 700,000, SAYCO was a major force in the anti-apartheid struggle in the late 1980s. In terms of the state of emergency, it was restricted in February 1988. With the exception of one member, SAYCO's entire National Executive Committee was at the same time arrested. In its stead, a South African Students Congress (SASCO) was launched. Together with ANC, PAC, SACP, UDF and other political organizations, SAYCO was unbanned in February 1990. Towards the end of 1991, it was incorporated into the ANC Youth League.

supporting projects[1] the application was included in March 1984 in a comprehensive submission to CCHA, amounting to no less than 7.6 MSEK.[2]

Partly overlapping with other activities supported by Sweden, at its regular meeting the following month the consultative committee decided to recommend a grant of 6.1 MSEK.[3] Subsequently endorsed by the Social Democratic government[4], this not only placed UDF among the major recipients of official Swedish humanitarian assistance[5], but consolidated the social democratic labour movement's involvement with the front and its wider popular base. Before too long, UDF would be widely quoted in Sweden. On AIC's initiative[6], the social democratic newspaper *Arbetet* decided in early 1984 to award the front its 'Let Live Prize'. It was presented by Foreign Minister Lennart Bodström[7] to Murphy Morobe and Cassim Saloojee on 27 May 1984.[8] Together with ANC, NUM and the core trade union movement, shortly after its formation UDF thus emerged as one of the central bene-ficiaries of Sweden's pro-active support to the struggle against the apartheid regime.

It should be noted that UDF was keen to avoid becoming financially dependent on foreign funding and that the Swedish—or Nordic—'model' was initially looked upon with a fair amount of scepticism. In a meeting with the Swedish envoy Arne Helleryd, the Cape Town-based UDF national executive member Trevor Manuel stated in March 1985 that UDF could possibly raise substantial amounts abroad, but that it wanted to steer clear of any outside dependency. Instead, Manuel said, the organization intended to make do with whatever resources it could raise from its affiliates and other sources inside South Africa.[9] Commenting on UDF's initial years, in an interview in 1995 the then Minister of Trade, Industry and Tourism graphically illustrated the early self-reliant approach and subsequent developments:

---

1. Such as the Set Bold Typesetting Unit, the Alternative Distribution and Printing Service and the Centre for Applied Legal Studies, all in Johannesburg.
2. Bengt Säve-Söderbergh: Memorandum ('Stöd till organisationer och projekt i Sydafrika'/'Support to organizations and projects in South Africa'), AIC, Stockholm, 16 March 1984 (SDA).
3. Elisabeth Michanek: Memorandum ('Ansökan från AIC om bidrag för stöd till projekt i Sydafrika'/'Request from AIC for contribution towards projects in South Africa'), SIDA/CCHA, [Stockholm], 2 April 1984 (SDA). The downward adjustment was made with regard to maintenance of individual apartheid opponents, a programme which via CSA, IDAF and other channels already received considerable official Swedish support.
4. Ministry for Foreign Affairs: 'Regeringsbeslut' ('Government decision'), Stockholm, 17 May 1984 (SDA).
5. The direct allocation to ANC for 1984/85 was 37 MSEK, out of which 12 MSEK was under the 'home front' component. As noted above, 'support for legal organizations' was by far the largest sub-item within this component (see the chapter 'From Beds in Exile to Organizers at Home'). Although probably unbeknown to the recipients, official Swedish support to UDF and its affiliates was thus also extended via ANC.
6. Interview with Bengt Säve-Söderbergh, p. 340.
7. See 'Speech by the Minister for Foreign Affairs, Mr. Lennart Bodström, at the presentation in Malmö of the 'Let Live Prize' to the United Democratic Front', 27 May 1984, in Ministry for Foreign Affairs: *Documents on Swedish Foreign Policy: 1984*, Stockholm, 1988, pp. 184-86.
8. 'Fortsatt kamp sida vid sida' ('Continued struggle side by side') in *Arbetet*, 28 May 1984. Cf. the interview with Bengt Säve-Söderbergh (p. 340), where he, however, wrongly recalls that Morobe was accompanied by Azhar Cachalia, not Saloojee. It should in this context be noted that later in the year the Norwegian Nobel Committee granted the Nobel Peace Prize to Bishop Desmond Tutu, who was not only General Secretary of the South African Council of Churches (SACC), but also a leading UDF patron. As in the case of Albert Luthuli and ANC in 1961, this, in turn, broadened UDF's audience in the Nordic countries. The Swedish CSM missionary Axel-Ivar Berglund—Tutu's former colleague at SACC—had for many years campaigned in favour of awarding him the coveted prize (Conversation with Axel-Ivar Berglund, Uppsala, 2 February 2000). Finally, in January 1987 the UDF activist Frank Chikane—who three months later succeeded Tutu as SACC General Secretary—was awarded the Swedish free churches' Diakonia Peace Prize at a ceremony in Stockholm (Sven Öste: 'Efter fredspriset väntar skilsmässan'/'After the peace prize awaits separation' in *Dagens Nyheter*, 12 January 1987).
9. Letter ('UDF') from Arne Helleryd, Swedish envoy to South Africa, to the Ministry for Foreign Affairs, Swedish legation, Cape Town, 29 March 1985 (SDA).

In the early period, a lot was done from resources collected from the workers. [...] We stood at the [factory] gate[s] and collected dues [...]. There was a frugality about the involvement, with people of a very strong character [and] a commitment that certainly had no relation to any pecuniary advantage [...]. [...] When we launched UDF, activists [...] were involved in the cooking of the meals. We hired mattresses and people slept in schools, church halls, mosques or whatever space we could find to accommodate them. But at the COSATU launch in Durban in 1985, people stayed in hotels. For me that was a big shift. [...]

We spent a fair amount of time in prison[1] debating with some concern the ease with which money suddenly had become available. [...] At that time, the European [Community] [...] started its twin-track strategy, and we had the establishment of the Kagiso Trust with project financing in South Africa. [...] I [...] recall when we prepared [the Conference for a Democratic Future]. It was scheduled for September 1988 and was to be held in Cape Town. I was fresh out of jail and was asked by the UDF people to be involved. [...] When the conference eventually took place in Johannesburg at the end of 1989 [...] we all stayed in hotels. In the early period of UDF, we stayed in houses even for executive meetings, but when we came out of jail there was a shift to hotels and a shift from driving to flying. [...] [T]here was a turning point which I still find a bit disconcerting. [...] I think that we were spoilt in a way that it was virtually impossible to retreat from.[2]

Thus concerned with the crucial question "How does an organization function when the tap can be closed off?"[3], in the interview Manuel also illustrated the initial misgivings felt by many UDF activists with regard to possible foreign political influence and aid conditionalities. Although noting that Sweden and the other Nordic countries in the bipolar Cold War context "presented themselves as a fairly safe route" and that they together with the World Council of Churches "were the channels used for [UDF's] resources"[4], he explained:

In 1984, UDF won a Swedish prize and extensive offers were made for people to spend time in Sweden and in the other Nordic countries, going there for training and for an examination of the way in which [s]ocial [d]emocracy functions.[5] This was debated in UDF in the early days. There was some suspicion about elements in the Nordic countries, such as the general improvement in living standards, the role of the trade unions and the change from what we narrowly understood as a necessary, very militant position [...]. Almost an emasculation of a tradition.

Looking back, I can say that the issues that were then strongly in focus in South Africa were [...] related to the question of ownership of the means of production. Our view was that the general improvements and the general conduct of [s]ocial [d]emocracy—capitalism with a good face—had numbed the sense of the workers about the question of who should own the means of production. [...] They were not big public debates, but amongst us there were at the

---

1. Manuel was jailed from August 1986 until July 1988 and from September 1988 to February 1989.
2. Interview with Trevor Manuel, pp. 150-51.
3. Ibid., p. 152.
4. Ibid., p. 149.
5. Manuel's recollection in this regard seems exaggerated. In cooperation with ANC and the Workers Educational Association (ABF), AIC would between 1987 and 1991 organize five comprehensive study visits to Sweden (Monica Andersson: Memorandum ('PM om insatser i södra Afrika, 920203'/'Re projects in Southern Africa, 3 February 1992'), Social Democratic Party, [no place or date, but Stockholm, 3 February 1992]) (OPA). While many leading UDF representatives visited the country from the mid-1980s, this programme targeted ANC members in exile. Over the years, it involved some 50 people (ibid.). One of them was the ANC/SACP member Indres Naidoo, who formed part of the first group and in 1987 spent three months in Sweden. Looking back in 1995, he made a positive assessment of the visit (Interview with Indres Naidoo, pp. 180-81). Focusing on issues of local government, the programme was far from sectarian. As noted by Naidoo, the agreement between ANC and AIC-ABF was that the visitors "should spend time with all [the Swedish] political parties [...] [T]hat agreement was kept" (ibid., p. 181). Nevertheless, Manuel's impression is correct inasmuch as the explicit "objective of the [...] labour movement [was] to present the Swedish model to the South African friends" ('ANC-aktivister Här för att Lära om Svenska Modellen'/'ANC Activists Here to Learn about the Swedish Model' in *AIC-Bulletinen*, No. 6/1987-1/1988, p. 27, and letter/request [no title] from Margareta Grape-Lantz to CCHA/SIDA, AIC, Stockholm, 18 May 1987) (SDA).

time certainly debates about whether the Nordic support was not a very careful plan to have us focus on reform rather than on revolution.[1]

In the case of Sweden, UDF's doubts regarding ideological ownership and conditionalities would essentially be clarified—or relegated to the background—through discussions with COSATU, NUM and other leading trade union structures, but, above all, with the ANC leadership in exile. In addition, by 1985 the demands on the front had grown to the extent that it could no longer rely upon financial resources raised internally. Involved in UDF's budgetary work, Manuel later noted that

> very early in 1985, we realized that even the resources of the budget that I had spent so many nights putting together were just gone. I do not know whether it would even have carried us until the ANC conference [in Zambia] in mid-1985, because by then you had had the shootings in Uitenhage[2] and a number of other events. During that period, I became intensely aware of the general support from the Nordic countries. [...] [Under] the state of emergency, survival became imperative to the kind of fund-raising that we had done in the early 1980s.[3]

From mid-1986—coinciding with the nationwide state of emergency and at a time when the European Community started to allocate funds to its project activities—UDF substantially raised the core budget and its requests to Sweden for assistance. In spite of the concerns mentioned by Manuel, they would, as before, be submitted to the social democratic movement's AIC, which during the second half of the 1980s was to channel considerable resources from the Swedish government to the mounting South African anti-apartheid rebellion. In addition to UDF *per se*, AIC would at the same time be increasingly involved with a number of its affiliates.

UDF's core budget for the period 1 July 1986 to 30 June 1987—"prepared with the view to vastly increase [its] programmes, work and size nationally"—amounted to 2.9 million South African Rands[4], which corresponded to 8.2 MSEK. Submitted to AIC for consideration, in its subsequent request to CCHA the Swedish labour movement NGO noted in September 1986 that "it cannot be deemed advisable either for UDF or for AIC/SIDA to be [the front's] sole donor".[5] This consideration notwithstanding, the application for official funds to UDF amounted to 6 MSEK, representing no less than 73 per cent of the organization's estimated financial

---

1. Interview with Trevor Manuel, pp. 149-50. Cf. the following comment by Raymond Suttner: "[T]he former socialist countries and Cuba, Vietnam and Nicaragua [...] provided fruit for ideological and theoretical advances, whatever one may think now of the weaknesses of the socialist project and even its failures. It was for many people in South Africa a source for inspiration, for debate, for vision of the new era, examples that showed that it was possible to defeat imperialist and oppressive forces. The Nordic countries did not offer the vision of revolutionary transformation which was vital to the moral and political energies of the liberation movement for much of its existence" (Suttner in Robben Island Museum, Mayibuye Centre and Nordic Africa Institute op. cit., p. 88). Suttner, however, added: "[T]his is not necessarily something we should criticize. I think it is worthy of credit that they accepted that it was we who had to develop our strategy and [that] they made their contribution within that framework. They were partisans of our cause, though in different ways" (ibid.). On this point, see also the interview with Garth Strachan, pp. 192-93.
2. On 21 March 1985—the anniversary of the 1960 Sharpeville shootings—police opened fire on a funeral procession in the Uitenhage township of Langa, killing 20 of the mourners. Provoking demonstrations and boycotts all over the country, in July 1985 the government declared a state of emergency.
3. Interview with Trevor Manuel, pp. 149-50. He, however, added that under "the conditions imposed by the state of emergency, all financial accounting went out through the window, and I think that there was a measure of corruption. Whether this was per force of circumstance or by design remains a moot point, but there was just too much money around. I also think that a great deal of personal enrichment took place" (ibid., p. 150). In this context, the case of Allan Boesak and his Foundation of Peace and Justice features prominently. It will be commented upon below.
4. United Democratic Front: 'Budget as of 1 July 1986 to 30 June 1987', [no place, but Johannesburg], 8 May 1986 (OPA).
5. AIC: 'Ansökan om bidrag för insatser i Sydafrika' ('Request for contribution towards projects in South Africa'), Stockholm, 9 September 1986 (SDA).

requirements in 1986/87. At the same time, AIC applied *inter alia* for funds in favour of continued assistance to the South African youth congresses, Allan Boesak's Foundation for Peace and Justice and the UDF-aligned newspapers *Speak* and *New Nation*, bringing the total request to 9.7 MSEK.[1]

Endorsed by CCHA[2], AIC's submission was in its entirety approved by Cooperation Minister Lena Hjelm-Wallén in early November 1986.[3] When in August 1987 AIC again turned to CCHA with a request for funds—now amounting to 11.2 MSEK[4]—to UDF and affiliated organizations during 1987/88, it was similarly supported.[5] Of the requested amount, 8 MSEK referred to UDF, representing 50 per cent its national budget.[6] With increasing allocations, AIC would over the following years until the disbanding of UDF in August 1991 continue to account for around half of the front's national expenditure, covering administration, salaries, vehicles and, in general, recurrent costs.[7] In addition to resources raised within the labour movement itself, during the front's seven years a total of 47.7 MSEK was channelled via AIC by the Swedish government to UDF's core structures.[8] To this should be added substantial transfers in favour of the Cape Democrats, COSAS, COTRALESA[9], Natal Indian Congress, SAYCO[10], Soweto Civic Association, Transvaal Indian Congress, Tumahole Civic Association, United Committee of Concern and many other UDF-affiliated national, regional and local organizations.[11]

---

1. Ibid. and AIC: 'Kompletterande ansökan om bidrag för insatser i Sydafrika' ('Complementary request for contribution towards projects in South Africa'), Stockholm, 12 September 1986 (SDA).
2. Margareta Husén: Memorandum ('Ansökan från Arbetarrörelsens Internationella Centrum om bidrag för insatser i Sydafrika'/'Request from AIC for contribution towards projects in South Africa'), SIDA/CCHA, [Stockholm], 17 October 1986 (SDA).
3. Ministry for Foreign Affairs: 'Regeringsbeslut' ('Government decision'), Stockholm, 6 November 1986 (SDA).
4. AIC: Memorandum [no title], Stockholm, 19 August 1987 (SDA).
5. Ministry for Foreign Affairs: 'Regeringsbeslut' ('Government decision'), Stockholm, 1 October 1987 (SDA).
6. AIC: Memorandum [no title], Stockholm, 19 August 1987 (SDA).
7. Lena Johansson: Memorandum ('Årsansökan från Arbetarrörelsens Internationella Centrum om stöd till UDF i Sydafrika'/'Annual request from AIC for support to UDF in South Africa'), SIDA/CCHA, [Stockholm], 24 September 1990 (SDA).
8. CCHA documents for the period 1983-91 (SDA).
9. The assistance to COTRALESA, the Congress of Traditional Leaders of South Africa, should be emphasized. Formed in September 1987 by chiefs of KwaNdebele and Moutse, it opposed 'independence' for the homelands, campaigned for the abolition of the bantustan system and supported the granting of South African citizenship to all inhabitants in the country. In a letter of thanks to the Swedish legation in Pretoria for assistance received, COTRALESA stated in mid-1989 that "many chiefs and headmen [had been] forced out of their areas [due to] the unacceptable policy of separate development. [...] This made them [...] come together and discuss their fate. They [...] agreed upon forming an organisation that will unite chiefs, headmen and subchiefs. [...] COTRALESA has committed itself to the struggles waged by all communities, particularly those under chiefs. [It] will continue with the struggle for liberation" (Letter ('Financial assistance towards COTRALESA's meeting held on the 11th June 1989') from COTRALESA to the Swedish legation, Marshalltown, 19 June 1989) (OPA). On UDF's recommendation, Swedish support to COTRALESA was extended from 1988/89 (Margareta Grape-Lantz: Memorandum ('Ansökan om humanitärt bistånd till Sydafrika'/'Request for humanitarian assistance to South Africa'), AIC, 5 July 1989) (SDA). Increasingly associated with UDF and the Mass Democratic Movement, in July-August 1989 the organization held discussions with ANC in Lusaka. Although it also met the government for bilateral talks on several occasions, after ANC's unbanning COTRALESA came out in open support of the liberation movement, representing an important political counterweight to Gatsha Buthelezi's KwaZulu-based Inkatha. After a visit to her husband Walter Sisulu at Pollsmoor Prison, in June 1989 the UDF leader Albertina Sisulu conveyed a firm message of encouragement to the chiefs' initiative ('Message from Albertina Sisulu' attached to letter ('COTRALESA') from Anders Möllander to AIC, Swedish legation, Pretoria, 26 June 1986) (SDA).
10. Official support to SAYCO was in addition extended through the National Council of Swedish Youth (Tomas Johansson, Secretary General: Memorandum ('Ansökan om humanitärt bistånd till South African Youth Congress'/'Request for humanitarian assistance to SAYCO'), LSU, Stockholm, 16 October 1989) (SDA).
11. Via AIC, official funds were also channelled to a number of legal organizations in South Africa, such as the Centre for Applied Legal Studies, the National Association of Democratic Lawyers and Lawyers for Human Rights (CCHA documents for the period 1983-91) (SDA).

Following a request by Nelson Mandela during his visit to Sweden in March 1990, the Social Democratic Party, AIC and the wider Swedish labour movement would together with many of these organizations be closely involved with voter education and election training in South Africa.[1] It should, nevertheless, be noted that UDF's decision to disband in August 1991 was received with regret. In a letter to the German Social Democratic Party and the Friedrich Ebert Foundation, in June 1992 AIC's Jan Hodann wrote that "AIC had hoped that UDF should continue to exist at least for some years after ANC became legal [...] in order to have a non-party structure [...] for support in the struggle against apartheid".[2] "In the meanwhile", Hodann noted,

> we turned our attention to the [c]ivic [m]ovement, [which] had been part of UDF [...]. In AIC, there was a general understanding that we should transfer our work to the civics. The Social Democratic Party should continue the relations with ANC and [LO/TCO its relations with] COSATU and other independent unions.[3]

Largely based on its own historical experiences, in the early 1990s the Swedish labour movement thus envisaged a continued involvement with the Charterist alliance at three mutually supportive levels, namely, popular ('civics'), labour (COSATU) and party (ANC). Seen as important both for the ultimate defeat of the apartheid regime and for the establishment of a future sustainable democracy was, in this context, the relative autonomy of the alliance's constituent parts.[4]

The Role of the Swedish Legation

As Sweden and ANC established a 'special relationship' outside South Africa and in the early 1980s there were still weak lines of communication between the exiled ANC leadership and the internal opposition, the Swedish legation in Pretoria would throughout the decade play an active role as a 'clearing house' for assistance to UDF, its affiliates and a range of aligned organizations. In close contact with the civic movement—as well as with prominent banned ANC representatives and veteran anti-apartheid activists, such as Winnie Mandela[5] and Beyers Naudé—the legation not only acted as an extended branch of AIC, AGIS, LO/TCO and many other Swedish NGOs, but would in a difficult environment also promote meetings between UDF and ANC in Sweden.

---

1. See the chapter 'Free at Last' and the interview with Pierre Schori, p. 336.
2. Letter [no title] from Jan Hodann to Wolfgang Weege (SPD) and Efried Adam (Friedrich Ebert Foundation), AIC, Stockholm, 30 June 1992; original in English (OPA).
3. Ibid.
4. Contrary to the situation in Zimbabwe and Namibia, after the 1994 democratic elections the South African trade union movement defended its independence vis-à-vis ANC. Interviewed in 1996, James Motlatsi, President of the National Union of Mineworkers, stated that "we have learned [from the Nordic countries] that it is important to keep labour autonomous from the political party. Rather than going the way which Namibia went when NUNW affiliated to SWAPO, we took another approach. We opted for an alliance with ANC, an alliance in which we will remain autonomous and which will be reviewed time and again. [...] We are not married to the party. No ways! We are keeping our autonomy and that in itself is very important, not only for today, but even for the future of the labour movement in this country" (Interview with James Motlatsi, p. 168).
5. In late December 1984, for example, Birgitta Karlström Dorph from the legation visited Winnie Mandela in Brandfort, the small town in the Orange Free State to which she had been banished in 1977. Among the many questions discussed were Nelson Mandela's situation at Pollsmoor Prison, the Nkomati Accord and the war in Angola (Cable ('Samtal Winnie Mandela'/'Conversation [with] Winnie Mandela') from the Swedish legation to the Ministry for Foreign Affairs, Pretoria, 2 January 1985) (SDA).

Secretly coordinating UDF
assistance: Birgitta Karlström
Dorph of the Swedish legation
in Pretoria with Dr. Beyers
Naudé in Johannesburg
in the mid-1980s
(Courtesy of
Birgitta Karlström Dorph)

Based in Pretoria, but visiting anti-apartheid organizations and projects all over South Africa, Bengt Herrström[1], Cecilia Höglund and, above all, Birgitta Karlström Dorph played decisive roles in these regards.[2] Their pro-active involvement was acknowledged by AIC, which in a report to CCHA on the assistance channelled in 1986/87-1987/88 to UDF and other organizations emphasized the legation's importance and a remarkably 'symbiotic relationship' between the NGO and the Swedish diplomatic mission. AIC's view deserves to be quoted at some length:

> The humanitarian projects implemented by [AIC] in South Africa are in essential aspects different from corresponding undertakings in Latin America. In Latin America, we are in an entirely different position when it comes to [our] possibilities and requirements to monitor the projects through direct contacts and visits to the countries where they are being implemented. In other words, we are [there] able to base ourselves on our own experiences and assessments. The conditions in South Africa are completely different. [We have] no possibilities to establish primary contacts with the recipient organizations through visits [to the country]. With regard to assessments and judgements of [their] strength and capacity, we are [therefore] entirely dependent on the assistance extended to us by the legation in Pretoria.

> The legation has [...] carried out tasks which go far beyond [those] of a referral or supervising authority. Its function has in reality been comparable to that of a field office. [It] has assisted us through continuous contacts with recipient organizations, and disbursements have only taken place on instruction from the legation.

> Our experiences from the cooperation with the legation [are] exceptionally good. [...] The assistance channelled by AIC could not have been realized without [its] efforts. [...] Such a

---

1. Based at the Pretoria legation from 1984 to 1988, Herrström was mainly responsible for contacts with the trade unions.
2. As noted in the SWAPO chapter 'Transport, Home Front, Churches and Trade Unions', Karlström Dorph—who served as counsellor at the Swedish legation in Pretoria between 1982 and 1988—also regularly visited Namibia to follow up the Swedish assistance. In South Africa, she was in particularly close contact with Beyers Naudé. Interviewed in 1995, the legendary founder of the banned Christian Institute and UDF patron commented: "[F]or a long period, I regularly met with Birgitta Karlström Dorph from the Swedish legation. I had long and meaningful discussions with her. I reported to her in full about what was happening. I heard which information she and the legation needed, gathered the information and then, at a given point, reported back to her. Apart from many other qualifications, Birgitta had the gift of winning the trust of the black community through her person and through her commitment. [...] Whenever Birgitta promised anything, she kept her word. When she could not, she was very clear to say: 'I cannot promise anything, but I will see what I can do'. Among those who came to know her personally in South Africa, there is a deep and lasting respect for her person and her commitment" (Interview with Beyers Naudé, p. 184).

division of functions between a [government] authority and a non-governmental organization is, of course, from an objective point of view remarkable, but in the case of South Africa justi- fied. Without this symbiotic relationship, it would not be possible to carry out the projects which both the state and AIC not only consider desirable, but necessary in order to support the struggle against apartheid.[1]

MESSAGE OF CONDOLENCES TO:
1. MRS. PALME
2. HIS MAJESTY THE KING OF SWEDEN AND
3. PARLIAMENT

Reacting to the assassination of Olof Palme: Message of condolences from the Delmas treason trialists, March 1986

By actively identifying and proposing projects for support, the efforts by Karlström Dorph and other representatives at the Pretoria mis- sion[2] largely paved the way for the extraordi- nary NGO involvement during the second half of the 1980s.[3] Although the rank and file members of most of the South African organi- zations assisted for reasons of security were kept unaware of the connection[4], at the level of the political leadership the Swedish contri- butions were widely recognized. Many exam- ples could here be quoted. A particularly warm acknowledgement was after the assassi- nation of Prime Minister Palme smuggled out of prison to Karlström Dorph in early March 1986 by 'Terror' Lekota, Popo Molefe and other UDF representatives standing accused of high treason in the so called 'Delmas 22 Trial'.[5] Addressed to Mrs. Palme, the Swedish King and parliament, the handwritten note of condolences *inter alia* stated that

---

1. Margareta Grape-Lantz: Memorandum ('Rapport om AIC's insatser i Sydafrika avseende anslag beviljade för 1986/87 och 1987/88'/'Report on AIC's projects in South Africa with regard to grants allocated for 1986/87 and 1987/88'), AIC, Stockholm, 13 February 1989 (SDA). While the wider solidarity movement advocated isolation of the apartheid regime, the demand to close the Pretoria mission never became an issue in Sweden. The role it played was, simply, of decisive importance to most NGOs actively involved inside South Africa. It could be noted that Sweden at the United Nations upheld the 'universality principle' and in the 1960s and early 1970s voted against South Africa's exclusion from the world organization. In November 1974, however, the UN General Assembly ruled that the South African delegation could not participate in the proceedings of the assembly (cf. the interview with Roelof 'Pik' Botha, p. 117).
2. Anders Möllander joined the legation as counsellor in 1987.
3. In the field of culture alone, around 25 groups, organizations and projects would eventually receive official support, mainly via Swedish Travelling Exhibitions (STE; in Swedish, *Riksutställningar*). As later noted by STE's coordinator Christina Björk, the recipients were often suggested by the legation in Pretoria (Sida: *Nyck- lar till den Nya Nationen: Kultursamarbete mellan Sverige och Sydafrika* ('Keys to the New Nation: Cul- tural Cooperation between Sweden and South Africa'), Sida, Stockholm, 1998, p. 3).
4. See, for example, the interviews with Trevor Manuel and Beyers Naudé. Manuel noted that "[t]he source of [the] support was seen as covert and we would not do anything to jeopardise it", concluding that "I do not think that the message of support really got through to the people" (p. 151). In 1995, Naudé similarly stated that "the fear that the security police, the phone-tapping and everything else" could put it at risk meant that the broader community of beneficiaries was kept unaware of the Swedish—and Nordic—support, but that it "now should be brought much more into the open" (p. 184). Cf. also Naudé in Åberg op. cit., pp. 125-26.
5. Following the September 1984 Vaal Triangle uprising, Lekota, Molefe and twenty other internal leaders were detained. They were charged with high treason in June 1985, accused of conspiring with ANC and SACP to promote national unrest in order to overthrow the government. Imprisoned in Delmas, a small town in East- ern Transvaal, they faced possible death sentences. After a marathon trial, the presiding judge found in November 1988 that UDF had acted as the internal wing of the banned ANC. Lekota was sentenced to twelve years imprisonment and Molefe to ten. However, those convicted were granted leave to appeal, and in December 1989 the South African Appeal Court quashed all the convictions. In 1994, Lekota was appointed Premier of the Free State Province, while Molefe assumed the same position in the North West Province.

[u]nder [Palme's] leadership, Sweden made [an] invaluable contribution to the struggles of [the] oppressed peoples of the world. And for us in South Africa, the people of Sweden [became] under the leadership of Mr. Palme [a] reliable all[y] in the fight against apartheid. Not only did his government repeatedly and unequivocally express its abhor[r]ence of the racist policies of the present government of South Africa, but it selflessly gave to our people moral and material support.[1]

Directly cooperating with ANC and via AIC supporting UDF, from the mid-1980s the authorities in Stockholm and the legation in Pretoria would, in addition, act as go-betweens for talks between the internal UDF and ANC in exile, facilitating a number of encounters in Sweden. This was notably the case in January 1986, when senior UDF representatives for the first time met the ANC leadership under President Oliver Tambo[2] in Stockholm for consultations which were to have "a considerable effect on the [united front]".[3] Although various UDF leaders had been in contact with ANC since its formation in 1983[4], "not until January 1986 was there a substantial and detailed dialogue on strategies and tactics [between the two organizations]".[5]

After initial discussions in Harare in December 1985 between ANC and Jay Naidoo, General Secretary of the recently formed COSATU[6], by early 1986 the basis was thereby being laid for more coordinated action by the dominant South African labour, civic and liberation movements.[7] Led by Secretary General Alfred Nzo, during the annual aid negotiations with Sweden in May 1986 the ANC delegation characterized the internal political situation as "extremely hopeful".[8]

On its return to South Africa from Sweden, the UDF delegation issued a statement to the press, briefly noting that talks had been held with ANC.[9] Representing the front, two months later Allan Boesak attended the funeral of Olof Palme in Stockholm. In that connection, on 14 March 1986 he was together with ANC Pre-

---

1. 'Message of condolences from the Delmas treason trialists', attached to letter ('Kondoleanser'/'Condolences') from the Swedish legation to the Ministry for Foreign Affairs, Pretoria, 11 March 1986 (MFA). In order to protect the contacts with the 'Delmas 22', Anders Möllander of the Foreign Ministry noted on the letter that "it must not be stated that the message has been delivered via the legation" (ibid.). On the political significance of the message, see the interview with Lindiwe Mabuza, p. 142.

2. UDF was represented by Cheryl Carolus, Yunus Mahomed, Mohammed Valli Moosa, Arnold Stofile and Raymond Suttner, while the ANC delegation in addition to Tambo included Alfred Nzo, Thomas Nkobi, Mac Maharaj, Thabo Mbeki and Aziz Pahad. In late February 1986, Mahomed returned to Sweden to represent UDF at the People's Parliament against Apartheid, where he again met Oliver Tambo, Thabo Mbeki and other leading ANC representatives.

3. Seekings op. cit., p. 166.

4. According to Manuel, "[e]ven the launch of UDF was done [...] through the dispatch of an individual to Botswana for an ANC hook-up to get some hard cash that we could use" (Interview with Trevor Manuel, p. 149).

5. Seekings op. cit., p. 166. For a presentation of the issues discussed during the historic Stockholm meeting, see ibid., pp. 166-69.

6. More substantial discussions between COSATU, ANC and SACTU were held in Lusaka in March 1986.

7. According to Seekings, during the talks in Stockholm "[t]he ANC leaders urged the UDF to [carry out] campaigns for the establishment of non-racial local government [structures] [...]. [The front] should also work with COSATU [and in general] seize the initiative at this time of crisis for the government". To weaken the enemy camp politically, UDF should, in addition, "expand the democratic movement among white South Africans" (Seekings op. cit., p. 167).

8. 'Agreed minutes [from] consultations in Lusaka, May 1986, between the African National Congress of South Africa and Sweden concerning humanitarian assistance', Lusaka, 9 May 1986 (SDA). In a document submitted to the Swedish delegation ANC went even further, not only stating that "[t]he historic initiative is in our hands", but that "the collapse of the apartheid system is imminent". COSATU's role was in this context particularly emphasized: "ANC views the formation of COSATU as one of the most significant developments in the history of our struggle" (ANC: 'The current political situation', [no place, but Lusaka], 30 April 1986, attached to ibid.).

9. Cable ('Samtal UDF-ANC i Stockholm'/'Discussions between UDF and ANC in Stockholm') from the Swedish legation to the Ministry for Foreign Affairs, Pretoria, 12 February 1986 (SDA).

sident Tambo and SWAPO President Nujoma received by the slain Premier's successor, Ingvar Carlsson.[1] Although UDF was still formally legal, the attention by the Social Democratic government incensed the Pretoria regime. Following other visits by UDF representatives to Sweden, in October 1986 the South African legation in Stockholm reacted by submitting a strongly worded note to the Foreign Ministry, declaring *inter alia* that

> [t]he visible organising presence of the yellow UDF [tee] shirt at [...] emotion and hate-charged rallies [, and] the deterioration of these occasions into barbaric riots accompanied by the summary execution by torture, burning and desecration of so called 'collaborators', 'puppets' and other political opponents, have shocked and revolted the South African and wider community. Sinister subliminal coercion in UDF publications has done little to dispel the outrage which civilized South Africans feel regarding the organisation.[2]

Concluding that "[n]o government can allow such a situation to continue indefinitely"[3]—and delivered at a time when the relations between Sweden and South Africa were heading towards an all-time low—the protest did not deter the Swedish authorities from extending continued assistance to UDF. While the front took preventive measures in case of a possible banning order[4], in November 1986 a substantially increased grant was allocated via AIC. Official meetings with UDF officials, as well as bilateral talks between the internal front and ANC in exile, were, in addition, arranged on an increasing scale towards the end of the 1980s.[5]

The Boesak Case

Due to the generally worsening situation in South Africa, the state of emergency, detentions, bannings of UDF affiliates, prohibition of foreign funding and indiscriminate violence by so called 'third forces' sponsored by the Pretoria regime, during the second half of the 1980s it became considerably more difficult to follow up the UDF assistance and other projects. Regretting that it was not in a position to report on AIC's support to the UDF-affiliated media structures MARS[6] and ADAP[7], in January 1988, for example, the Swedish legation in Pretoria noted that

1. Stefan Noreén: Memorandum ('Statsminister Carlssons samtal med Oliver Tambo, ANC, Sam Nujoma, SWAPO, och Allan Boesak, United Democratic Front i Sydafrika, i Rosenbad'/'Prime Minister Carlsson's conversation with Oliver Tambo, ANC, Sam Nujoma, SWAPO, and Allan Boesak, UDF, at Rosenbad'), Cabinet Office, Stockholm, 24 March 1986 (SDA).
2. Diplomatic note [no title] from the South African legation to the Ministry for Foreign Affairs, Stockholm, 15 October 1986 (MFA).
3. Ibid.
4. In February 1986, UDF started to deliver copies of its entire national archives to the Swedish legation for safekeeping in Sweden (Letter ('UDF's arkiv'/'UDF's archives') from Birgitta Karlström Dorph to AIC, Swedish legation, Pretoria, 11 February 1986) (SDA).
5. In mid-March 1987, for example, UDF President Archie Gumede held discussions in Stockholm with Foreign Minister Sten Andersson (Anders Möllander: Memorandum ('Utrikesministern tar emot ledare för den sydafrikanska antiapartheidorganisationen UDF'/'The Foreign Minister receives leaders of the South African antiapartheid organization UDF'), Ministry for Foreign Affairs, Stockholm, 2 April 1987) (SDA). The following month, Beyers Naudé and Thabo Mbeki met at the Lusaka residence of first secretary Erik Backman for consultations on UDF matters (Cable ('Beyers Naudé samtalar med ANC'/'Beyers Naudé talks to ANC') from the Swedish embassy to the Ministry for Foreign Affairs, Lusaka, 29 April 1987) (SDA). Immediately after the December 1988 New York accords on Namibia—which directly affected ANC in Angola—Mbeki and UDF's Morobe and Valli Moosa also met in Stockholm for discussions on the developments in South and Southern Africa (Sten Rylander: Memorandum ('Thabo Mbeki besöker statssekreterare Säve-Söderbergh'/'Thabo Mbeki visits Under-Secretary of State Säve-Söderbergh'), Ministry for Foreign Affairs, Stockholm, 2 January 1989) (SDA).
6. Media and Resource Services.
7. Alternative Distribution and Printing Services.

[these] organizations have disbanded after the authorities seized their documents and the [building] was burnt down. Some equipment had earlier been destroyed by unknown men. Those who worked [there] are now dispersed [and] most of them seem to have gone abroad. I think that it will be very difficult to obtain [proper financial] accounts. We should perhaps close the case.[1]

While the statement illustrates the realities under which support to anti-apartheid organizations in South Africa was extended in the 1980s, on balance the administrative problems were surprisingly few. In the case of AIC and the wider UDF umbrella, major reporting difficulties were limited to SAYCO[2] and—in 1990—to COTRALESA.[3] Coordinated by UDF's Treasurer Azhar Cachalia, the Swedish support to the front's central structures was well accounted for.

As noted by South Africa's future Finance Minister Trevor Manuel, there was, however, also "a measure of corruption". In 1995, he expressed the opinion that from the mid-1980s there "was just too much money around" and that "a great deal of personal enrichment took place".[4] This affected the Swedish assistance via AIC to *New Nation*, a UDF-aligned newspaper launched by the Southern African Catholic Bishops Conference in Johannesburg in January 1986[5], and, above all, to the Cape Town-based Foundation for Peace and Justice (FPJ), set up by Reverend Allan Boesak in May 1986.

The case of FPJ and Boesak became world news in October 1994 when it was revealed that the charismatic UDF founder, leader of ANC's election campaign in the Western Cape and South Africa's ambassador-designate to the United Nations in Geneva was suspected of misappropriation of donor funds, primarily from Denmark and Sweden.[6] Strongly rejected by Boesak—as well as by ANC—the suspicions led to police investigations[7] and, eventually, to criminal charges. In March 1999, he was found guilty of theft and fraud amounting to a total of 1.3 million

---

1. Letter from Birgitta Karlström Dorph to AIC, Swedish legation, Pretoria, 21 January 1988, quoted in Margareta Grape-Lantz: Memorandum ('Rapport om AIC's insatser i Sydafrika avseende anslag beviljade för 1986/87 och 1987/88'/'Report on AIC's projects in South Africa with regard to grants allocated for 1986/87 and 1987/88'), AIC, Stockholm, 13 February 1989 (SDA).
2. Ibid. It should be recalled that SAYCO was restricted and that its entire leadership—barring one member—was detained in February 1988.
3. Letter ('COTRALESA') from Anders Möllander to AIC, Swedish legation, Pretoria, 18 July 1990 (SDA).
4. Interview with Trevor Manuel, p. 150.
5. Swedish assistance to *New Nation* was extended via AIC from mid-1986, when an amount of 1.4 MSEK was allocated *inter alia* for the setting up of a news agency. Shortly thereafter, its chief editor Zwelakhe Sisulu—the son of Walter and Albertina Sisulu—was detained, until December 1988 spending a total of nineteen months in solitary confinement without trial. During his imprisonment, a consultant administrator working for the newspaper deposited the Swedish grant with a stockbroker, who invested the money in shares. The irregularity was discovered in early 1988, when the consultant had already left South Africa (Letter ('New Nation') from Birgitta Karlström Dorph to AIC, Swedish legation, Pretoria, 14 March 1988) (SDA). Eventually, *New Nation*'s lawyer managed to contact the consultant in London and recover three quarters of the funds (Anders Möllander: Memorandum ('New Nation: Förskringring?'/'New Nation: Fraud?'), Swedish legation, Pretoria, 7 September 1988) (SDA).
6. Johan Wallquist: 'Biståndet hamnade i pastorns ficka' ('The aid ended up in the pastor's pocket') in *Expressen*, 25 October 1994, and Gaye Davis: 'Boesak's peace trustees resign' in *Weekly Mail & Guardian*, 28 October-3 November 1994. Set up as an 'extended ministry' of Boesak's Bellville *Sendingkerk* congregation, FPJ received contributions from reformed churches in the Federal Republic of Germany, the Netherlands, Switzerland, USA and other countries. Over the years, however, the bulk of the assistance came from the Scandinavian countries via Danchurchaid of Denmark, the Church of Norway Council on Ecumenical and International Relations and AIC of Sweden. The Stockholm-based *Immanuelskyrkan* of the Mission Covenant Church also supported FPJ. Via AIC, official Swedish funds—in total amounting to around 6 MSEK—were, as noted above, granted from 1986/87.
7. The investigations were instigated on Archbishop Desmond Tutu's initiative.

South African Rands—of which more than half had been granted by AIC[1]—and sentenced to six years in prison by the Cape High Court.[2]

Financial contributions raised internationally by Boesak for humanitarian assistance to disadvantaged communities in the Cape region had been used instead for his residence in an up-market Capetonian suburb and other personal purposes. The 'Boesak affair' was a major political casualty for ANC and the post-1994 Mandela government. In the history of the Swedish humanitarian assistance to Southern Africa, it also stands out as a glaring exception. During Sweden's long and broad involvement, there are no similar cases of fraud by a trusted political leader for his or her personal enrichment. In the light of the extensive documentation on Sweden's relations with Allan Boesak and FPJ[3], it appears, however, that the unfortunate developments could have been avoided. Although he was a key political actor in the anti-apartheid struggle, the accumulated evidence concerning his frail administrative integrity is so convincing that direct financial assistance seems to have been questionable from the mid-1980s.

Thus, from an early stage ANC[4], UDF[5], Kagiso Trust[6] and the Swedish legation in Pretoria[7] repeatedly raised concerns with regard to Boesak's economic transactions and handling of funds. Although these were shared by AIC, during frequent

---

1. In addition to grants from Sweden, the embezzlement included contributions from the World Alliance of Reformed Churches—of which Boesak was the President until 1990—and from the US musician Paul Simon and his 1988 'Graceland' concert tour. Representatives from SIDA and AIC gave evidence during the 1998-99 trial.
2. Leif Norrman: 'Boesak fick sex år' ('Boesak got six years') in *Dagens Nyheter*, 25 March 1999. FPJ's accountant Freddie Steenkamp was in November 1997 also sentenced to six years imprisonment for his involvement in the affair. In May 2000, the Supreme Court of Appeal in Bloemfontein halved Boesak's sentence to three years, which he thereafter started to serve at Malmesbury Prison.
3. A remarkable number of letters and memoranda were dedicated to Boesak and FPJ during the period 1986-89.
4. During a stopover in Stockholm after ANC's historic visit to Washington, in talks with Foreign Ministry officials in February 1987 Thabo Mbeki was highly critical of Allan Boesak's economic transactions, stating that the UDF leader was closely involved in the US Coca Cola company's so called 'disinvestment' initiative. According to Mbeki, through Boesak's assistance the company had moved the production to Swaziland, while the plants in South Africa with loans from the company and binding buy-back options had been 'sold' to black businessmen. As Coca Cola's guest, Boesak was in the United States at the time of ANC's official visit. He "had appeared at the Riverside Church in New York, but left before Tambo's speech" (Anders Möllander: Memorandum ('Samtal med ANC-ledare'/'Conversation with ANC leader'), Ministry for Foreign Affairs, Stockholm, 10 February 1987) (MFA). On 21 January 1987, President Tambo delivered the first 'Olof Palme Memorial Lecture on Disarmament and Development' in the Riverside Church. The address is reproduced in Tambo op. cit., pp. 235-45.
5. When in June 1987 the Swedish legation contacted UDF for information on funds disbursed to Boesak, it was told that "Boesak raises so much money that he perhaps does not really keep track of where it comes from or [to whom] he pays it out" (Cable ('Boesak och AIC'/'Boesak and AIC') from the Swedish legation to the Ministry for Foreign Affairs, Pretoria, 8 June 1987) (SDA).
6. In discussions with Kagiso's Executive Director Achmed Dangor, Karlström Dorph was in August 1987 informed that Boesak—a member of the Kagiso board—had only attended one meeting. He had then submitted "a number of applications [which] he immediately wanted to have endorsed [...] and the money transferred to his account in Cape [Town]". When the board stated that requests had to be processed "in due order", Boesak "was not satisfied". He had from then on not taken part in any board meeting (Cable ('Kagiso') from the Swedish legation to the Ministry for Foreign Affairs, Pretoria, 27 August 1987) (SDA).
7. The legation stated its misgivings on many occasions. In September 1987, for example, it noted that Boesak—who, however, put the blame on the UDF Cape leadership, described by him as "young, inexperienced and apparently unable to budget"—could not submit a satisfactory report on AIC's grant to FPJ for 1986/87 (Cable [no title] from the Swedish legation to the Ministry for Foreign Affairs, Cape Town, 4 September 1987) (SDA). Two months later, the Swedish envoy Jan Lundvik reported after another meeting with Boesak in Cape Town that he had been unable to obtain a financial statement (Cable [no title] from the Swedish legation to the Ministry for Foreign Affairs, Swedish legation, Cape Town, 10 November 1987) (SDA). While the Foreign Ministry in Stockholm in March 1988 emphasized that "the requirements with regard to financial accounts are the same for Boesak as for other recipients of Swedish humanitarian assistance" (Cable [no title] from the Ministry for Foreign Affairs to the Swedish legation in Pretoria, Stockholm, 30 March 1988) (SDA), doubts and a lack of transparency between FPJ and UDF's Cape structures, however, persisted (Cable ('Utbetalning Boesak/UDF'/'Disbursement to Boesak/UDF') from the Swedish legation to the Ministry for Foreign Affairs, Cape Town, 25 April 1988) (SDA).

visits to Sweden[1]—where he enjoyed wide support and maintained privileged relations with the Social Democratic Party, the solidarity movement and the churches[2]—Boesak, however, continuously managed to stave off the doubts.[3] Despite reports and formal requests which were lacking[4], after discussions in Stockholm[5] AIC decided in August 1988 to proceed with payments to FPJ.[6] As late as in November 1993—almost seven years after the initial question marks—its successor OPIC[7] stated in a submission to SIDA that it found it "desirable to continue the budgetary support to FPJ", requesting a financial contribution of 1.6 MSEK for the financial years 1993/94-1994/95.[8]

Less than six months after the April 1994 elections in South Africa, SIDA, however, decided to audit the foundation, a move which together with an earlier initiative by Danchurchaid initiated the process towards the conviction of Allan Boesak. No longer reflecting a 'symbiotic relationship', in the case of the controversial Foundation for Peace and Justice the Swedish authorities decided to intervene, albeit belatedly and when the financial, political and moral damage had already been done.

US and South African Views on ANC and Sweden

Through external destabilization operations and security arrangements such as the Nkomati Accord imposed on Mozambique, the increasingly militarized Pretoria government tried in the early 1980s to isolate ANC and push the movement out of the neighbouring states. In South Africa itself, this policy was coupled with constitutional engineering designed to keep the black majority excluded from political participation, a process which culminated in the tricameral constitution. As the

---

1. In 1986-87 alone, Boesak paid three high-profile visits to Sweden (Ulf Hagman: 'Boesak kritiserar svenska företag'/'Boesak criticizes Swedish companies') in *Svenska Dagbladet*, 17 June 1987.
2. It could be noted, for example, that ISAK's chairman Lennart Renöfält was from the Mission Covenant Church Youth (*Svenska Missionsförbundets Ungdom*). The Mission Covenant Church of Sweden was affiliated to the World Alliance of Reformed Churches, of which Boesak was the President and spiritual leader.
3. During a visit to Sweden in October 1986, Boesak submitted a request to AIC for funds towards his personal security, including a reinforced BMW vehicle and equipment for his residence and office. The requested amount of 410,000 SEK was to be transferred to FPJ. In connection with another visit in June 1987, AIC decided to support the request, allocating 250,000 SEK from its own International Solidarity Fund. At the same time, it turned to the Ministry for Foreign Affairs—not to CCHA or SIDA, as was the established procedure—for the remaining 160,000 SEK (Letter ('Ansökan om stöd till Sydafrika'/'Request for support to South Africa') from Margareta Grape-Lantz to the Ministry for Foreign Affairs, AIC, Stockholm, 16 June 1987) (MFA). The submission was referred to the Swedish legation in Pretoria for comments. While stating that Boesak was "in a very exposed position", the legation, however, did not favour the granting of official funds. In a meeting with Boesak, it pointed out the political risk that he could be criticized for "using donor funds for a luxury car whilst people are suffering" (Cable ('Säkerhetsanordningar för Allan Boesak'/'Security arrangements for Allan Boesak') from the Swedish legation to the Ministry for Foreign Affairs, Pretoria, 29 July 1987) (SDA). It should be noted that Boesak eventually bought the specially equipped BMW, but that he soon sold it and pocketed the money. During the trial at the Cape High Court, he quite remarkably argued in November 1998 that the car was a personal gift from Prime Minister Carlsson, who in the late 1980s chaired the AIC-administered solidarity fund (Wolfgang Hansson: 'Sveriges gåva: En lyxig BMW'/'Sweden's gift: A luxurious BMW' in *Aftonbladet*, 10 November 1998).
4. Cable ('Bidrag till Boesak'/'Contribution to Boesak') from the Ministry for Foreign Affairs to the Swedish legation in Pretoria, Stockholm, 15 April 1988 (SDA).
5. Boesak also raised the issue of financial support directly with Prime Minister Carlsson (ibid.).
6. Letter [no title] from Margareta Grape-Lantz to the Ministry for Foreign Affairs, AIC, Stockholm, 16 August 1988 (SDA).
7. Olof Palme International Center.
8. Letter with attached memorandum ('Årsansökan till SIDA rörande Olof Palmes Internationella Centrum's verksamhet i Sydafrika'/'Annual request to SIDA concerning OPIC's activities in South Africa') from Jan Hodann to SIDA, AIC, Stockholm, 19 November 1993 (SDA).

South African economy entered into a prolonged period of recession[1]—and the war against SWAPO further drained the resources—the attempts to salvage the white minority regime backlashed. As ANC intensified its internal underground work, the political campaigns by UDF and the wider labour and civic movements eventually made the apartheid state 'ungovernable'.

In the meantime, Pretoria's two-pronged policy to isolate ANC and keep the black majority disenfranchised continued to enjoy support from the major Western powers. By the mid-1980s, this brought the United States and Great Britain on a diplomatic collision course with the Swedish government.[2] Learning about a forth-coming visit to Sweden by ANC President Oliver Tambo, in early May 1984—that is, shortly after the Nkomati Accord—second secretary Jimmy Kolker from the US embassy in Stockholm contacted Anders Bjurner at the Foreign Ministry. Stressing that his government's views differed from those held by Sweden, in what amounted to a thinly veiled protest he delivered a note which clarified Washington's position. It stated *inter alia* that

> [w]e cannot have a productive relationship of any sort with an organization committed to ter-rorism and cross-border violence. One that uses a foolish Marxist optic for defining contempo-rary reality and proclaims the US as the main villain of the piece. [...] If we are defined as the enemy, we will defend ourselves. If the ANC remains dedicated to destructive violence, polari-zation and Marxist clichés, it will reinforce its isolation and irrelevance, and we will draw the necessary conclusions. [...]

> The reverse is also true. As and if the ANC enters the bargaining arena—indirectly and tacitly if necessary, overtly if the [South African government] permits it—its relations with us could [...] develop in a more positive direction. [...] The ANC has a choice between Armageddon and serious relevance to change in South Africa.[3]

Thus identifying the banned liberation movement—not the apartheid regime—as terrorist, guilty of cross-border operations and bearing the responsibility for initia-tives towards possible negotiations, the US stand was diametrically opposed to that

---

1. Switzer—quoting Anton Lowenberg and William Kaempfer—notes that South Africa's annual   industrial growth between 1964 and 1974 averaged 6.3 to 7.4%. It declined to 5.1% between 1974 and 1980. In the crucial period 1980-84, it was, however, negative, or -0.1%. Real GDP per capita also declined, showing a negative rate by the early 1980s (Les Switzer: 'South Africa's Resistance Press in Perspective' in Switzer and Adhikari (eds) op. cit., p. 9). The downward economic spiral became acutely critical in September 1985, when a number of major international banks refused to grant South Africa further extensions on debt repay-ments, forcing it to default on its foreign debt. As the value of the South African Rand against the US Dollar plummeted from 1.29 in 1980 to 0.35, this immediately prompted South Africa's leading businessmen to enter into talks with ANC. Led by Gavin Relly, chairman of the Anglo-American Corporation—the country's largest company—in mid-September 1985 a first round of talks was held with the liberation movement in Zambia. Together with the South African insurrection and subsequent international sanctions, this, in turn, decisively turned the tide against the apartheid regime. It is in this context not without interest to note that Olof Palme in his very last recorded meeting with Oliver Tambo on 21 February 1986 mentioned that Relly had visited him as early as in 1983 (Anders Möllander: Memorandum ('ANC's president Oliver Tambo hos statsministern'/'ANC President Oliver Tambo with the Prime Minister'), Ministry for Foreign Affairs, Stock-holm, 26 February 1986) (MFA).
2. The US policy of 'constructive engagement' with the Pretoria regime was widely supported by the Western countries. At the 1985 SADCC conference in Swaziland, the leader of the French delegation complained to the Swedish delegation about the Nordic countries' call for sanctions, the support to ANC and SWAPO and, in general, their supposedly 'idealistic' view of development assistance to the majority-ruled Southern African countries. "It is so easy for you Nordics", he said. "You have no interests at stake". With reference to what he evidently saw as an irrelevant group of Frontline States, he added: "You are just another Backline State" (Author's recollection, also noted in Sellström in Odén and Othman (eds) op. cit., p. 15). In November 1986, President Botha made an official visit to France.
3. Note [no place or date] delivered by Jimmy Kolker, US embassy in Stockholm, attached to Anders Bjurner: Memorandum ('USA och befrielserörelsen ANC'/'USA and the liberation movement ANC'), Ministry for For-eign Affairs, Stockholm, 9 May 1984 (SDA).

of Sweden.[1] Despite Pretoria's occupation of Namibia, repeated military campaigns into Angola, continued assistance to RENAMO in Mozambique, wanton attacks on the Frontline States and unprecedented violence against the popular movement in South Africa itself, together with the British government under Margaret Thatcher the Reagan administration in the mid-1980s steadfastly underpinned the anachronistic apartheid regime.[2]

In his last public speech—delivered on 21 February 1986 to the People's Parliament against Apartheid—Prime Minister Palme characterized this stand as "madness", making the often quoted statement that "[i]f the world decides to abolish apartheid, apartheid will disappear".[3] Soon thereafter, Foreign Minister Sten Andersson emphasized the particular complicity and responsibility shared by the two leading Western countries. Addressing a meeting on South Africa at the University of Stockholm, in early April 1986 he concluded that

> [t]he states now hindering a consensus are the United States and the United Kingdom. Those two nations have a unique chance to change the course of history—such as it looks like being—to stop a disaster in South Africa. They should assume their responsibility and consent to mandatory sanctions for all UN member states.[4]

Attending the World Conference on Sanctions against Racist South Africa—organized in Paris in June 1986 by the United Nations in cooperation with OAU and the Non-Aligned Movement—two months later Andersson stated that he was "greatly disappointed that the UK and the USA have decided not to participate". Stressing that "to fight for an opinion is a democratic right, but to escape from a debate where international peace and security are at stake is a sign of weakness", he again called for mandatory sanctions, adding that "the white minority regime must be brought to agree to the demands from, amongst others, the UDF and the ANC for a free South Africa in which all are equals".[5]

---

1. The nationalist movements in Namibia and South Africa were in the US and British governments' Cold War perspective commonly seen as 'Soviet-backed', 'Communist' or 'terrorist'. In March 1982, the US Senate held a series of hearings on "the role of the Soviet Union—through its puppets in Cuba and East Germany—in fomenting and supporting terrorism in [S]outhern Africa". Notably preoccupied with SWAPO and ANC, the hearings were based on the premise that "these three countries [...] under the overall control of the Politburo in Moscow [are] actively and successfully trying to infiltrate and manipulate so-called national liberation movements [in the region]" (*The Role of the Soviet Union, Cuba and East Germany in Fomenting Terrorism in Southern Africa*, op. cit.,Volume I, p. 1). Testimonies to this effect were given *inter alia* by the US Assistant Secretary of State for African Affairs, Chester Crocker, and by the former SWANU and SWAPO leaders Jariretundu Kozonguizi and Andreas Shipanga. The substantial and long-standing official Swedish and Nordic support to ANC and SWAPO was not mentioned in the extensive documentation from the hearings, published in two volumes of a total of over 1,800 pages.

2. Not until early 1987 was Oliver Tambo invited to the United States for consultations, held with Secretary of State George Shultz in Washington on 28 January. Johnny Makatini, Thabo Mbeki, Barbara Masekela and Neo Mnumzana accompanied the ANC President. Reflecting the close relationship with Sweden, Tambo himself, Makatini or Mbeki from the mid-1980s would as a rule brief the Swedish government on talks held with the major Western powers or the Soviet Union. In the case of the Washington meeting, as early as on 6 February 1987 Mbeki informed Foreign Minister Andersson of the issues discussed (Anders Möllander: Memorandum ('Den sydafrikanska befrielserörelsen ANC's informationschef Thabo Mbeki hos utrikesministern'/ 'ANC's head of information Thabo Mbeki with the Foreign Minister'), Ministry for Foreign Affairs, Stockholm, 10 February 1987) (MFA). The following month, Tambo gave ambassador Ölander in Lusaka a copy of ANC's preparatory notes for and report from the meeting (attached to letter ('ANC's Tambo möter Shultz'/ 'ANC's Tambo meets Shultz') from Jan Ölander to the Ministry for Foreign Affairs, Swedish embassy, Lusaka, 10 March 1987) (SDA).

3. Olof Palme: 'South Africa and the Nordic Countries: Speech to the Swedish People's Parliament against Apartheid', 21 February 1986, in *Development Dialogue*, No. 1, 1987, p. 72.

4. 'Address by the Minister for Foreign Affairs, Mr. Sten Andersson, at an open meeting at the University of Stockholm, Frescati, concerning South Africa', 10 April 1986, in Ministry for Foreign Affairs: *Documents on Swedish Foreign Policy: 1986*, Stockholm, 1990, p. 213.

5. 'Speech by the Minister for Foreign Affairs, Mr. Sten Andersson, at the World Conference on Sanctions against Racist South Africa in Paris', 17 June 1986 (Press release) in ibid., pp. 218-19.

While the content and details of the official bilateral Swedish support to ANC, UDF and the South African labour and civic movements were confidential, the government's high-profile, dissident 'non-Western' stand would, not surprisingly, enrage the embattled Pretoria regime. From mid-1985—coinciding with a tightening of the Swedish 1979 sanctions legislation—the official bilateral contacts deteriorated sharply.[1] In November 1985, Francis Drake, head of the South African legation in Stockholm, submitted an *aide mémoire* to the Foreign Ministry, stressing that

> [t]he South African [g]overnment regards the fact that the ANC is [...] permitted to maintain an office in Sweden and to further its aims with approval of the Swedish [g]overnment as being irreconcilable with [its] known opposition to terrorism.[2]

Arguing that the "South African [g]overnment is actively engaged in a programme of constitutional and social reform aimed at extending democratic rights to all and to eliminating racial discrimination", blinded by the beam in its own eye the protest went on to state that "[t]his is an age of terrorism". Under the leadership of Joe Slovo—"known to be a full [C]olonel in the KGB, the security service of the Soviet Union"—ANC, it declared, "has established links with [...] such organisations as the [Palestine] PLO [and the West German] Baader-Meinhof gang [and the] Red Army Faction [...] to coordinate the training of terrorists and the execution of their activities".[3] Against this background, Pretoria's representative concluded:

> There is little doubt that the ANC is a revolutionary organisation which is destabilising the entire Southern African sub-continent as part of a global drive against [W]estern influence. [...] It is clear that the ANC has every intention of continuing on the path of confrontation, terrorism and violence, threatening lives and property not only in the Republic of South Africa, but also in other countries. [...] [In fact,] the ANC not only poses a threat to the security of the people of [S]outhern Africa. [I]t also poses a similar threat in other parts of the world. [...] [T]errorism is a global manifestation and should effectively be treated as such [...].[4]

While such outlandish views in Sweden found an echo among fringe groups on the extreme right[5], in South Africa they were accompanied by increasingly aggressive diatribes. In February 1987, Jan Lundvik, Sweden's envoy to the country, reported to the Foreign Ministry in Stockholm that there was a general "atmosphere of confrontation".[6] This was expressed *inter alia* through "repeated anonymous threats

---

1. As noted in the chapter 'Black Consciousness, IUEF and 'Operation Daisy", the possibility of a South African connection to the assassination of Olof Palme had fifteen years later not been ruled out, either by the Swedish authorities or by ANC. The Swedish Prime Minister was killed on 28 February 1986. Six months later—on 8 September 1986—the ANC office in Stockholm was the target of a similarly unsolved attack (see, for example, 'Bombdåd mot ANC-kontor'/'Bombing of ANC office' in *Dagens Nyheter* and 'Ett under hon lever'/'A miracle that she is alive' in *Arbetet*, 9 September 1986). In September 1987, three Swedish aid workers were kidnapped and one of them killed by UNITA in Angola (see above 'MPLA of Angola: A Rockier Road').
2. *Aide mémoire* from the South African legation in Stockholm, 13 November 1985, attached to memorandum ('Sydafrika om ANC'/'South Africa on ANC') by Irene Larsson and Anders Möllander, Ministry for Foreign Affairs, Stockholm, 27 November 1985 (SDA).
3. Ibid. Apart from everything else, it can hardly be said that the Baader-Meinhof group or the Red Army Faction existed at all in the mid-1980s.
4. Ibid.
5. The South African legation in Stockholm was in close contact with Swedish extreme right and neo-Nazi elements. Using arguments similar to those expressed by Drake, they became increasingly active from the mid-1980s. In early 1986, *Contra*'s Tommy Hansson even published his immoderate views in the Moderate Party-aligned review *Svensk Tidskrift*. Initially advocating support for Buthelezi's Inkatha movement, as apartheid was heading towards its end they, however, shifted their allegiance to the all-white National Party. After a visit to South Africa in August 1988, Hansson concluded that he "personally would like to recommend a Western association with [this party]" (Hansson (1989) op. cit., p. 213).
6. Cable ('Förbindelserna med Sydafrika'/'The relations with South Africa') from Jan Lundvik to the Ministry for Foreign Affairs, Swedish legation, Cape Town, 6 February 1987 (MFA).

against Swedish missions in [Southern Africa]", as well as various statements made by South African diplomats. Noting that there were "good reasons to believe" that Pretoria in the case of a trade boycott would break diplomatic relations, Lundvik recommended the Foreign Ministry to prepare a "contingency plan".[1] Interpreting the developments in the same way, the Swedish authorities requested the legation to "already now weed out all sensitive documents that are not needed for [your] routine activities and prepare to transport them by air to Stockholm".[2] Instructions with regard to radio and encoding equipment were also issued.[3]

As it eventually turned out, the bilateral relations were never suspended and the full contingency plan was accordingly not implemented. The confrontational atmosphere, however, prevailed. In an editorial published soon thereafter, *The Citizen*—mouthpiece of the apartheid government—bluntly told Sweden "to go to hell".[4] Under the headline 'Sweden again', the call was followed up in early April 1987 by the newspaper in another leading comment, which caustically declared that

> the Swedes should stop mucking about in a sub-continent in which they have no real stake and in which they have had a deplorable record of involvement. [...] One day, when Sweden's hostility becomes too dangerous and its direct interference in our internal affairs becomes too much to bear, it should not be surprised if 'Swedes go home' becomes a popular slogan.[5]

Responding to these and other attacks on the Social Democratic government's stand, in a speech in Gothenburg Pierre Schori, Under-Secretary of State for Foreign Affairs, commented the following month that

> we can take this, since the suggestion comes from a government which has created a hell on earth for the majority of its citizens. It does not worry us, and we take it as a sign that we are doing the right thing. [...] What is more important [...] is that all those fighting against apartheid and for a free and democratic South Africa give their blessing to our action. On May Day, Mr. Oliver Tambo was in Stockholm. On Soweto Day, 16 June, Dr. Allan Boesak will be here. We are pleased to be able to note that our contacts are with [the] representatives of a democratic and free South Africa. Not with Mr. Botha and his entourage. [...]

> Our task is not to condemn or to express a view on how the oppressed wage their struggle. Our task is to use the means we have at our disposal to seek to ensure that the transition to a democratic society, with equal rights for all, takes place as quickly and with as little bloodshed as possible. I think that we in Sweden should feel some pride in the fact that for over two decades we have lent active support to this historic struggle for freedom, the end of which is now finally in sight.[6]

---

1. Ibid. Swedish legislation banning trade with South Africa was passed on 4 June 1987, becoming effective on 1 July 1987.
2. Cable ('Om förbindelserna med Sydafrika'/'On the relations with South Africa') from the Ministry for Foreign Affairs to the Swedish legations in Pretoria and Cape Town, Stockholm, 24 February 1987 (MFA).
3. Ibid.
4. 'Go to hell', editorial in *The Citizen*, 3 March 1987.
5. 'Sweden again', editorial in *The Citizen*, 8 April 1987.
6. 'Speech by the Under-Secretary of State for Foreign Affairs, Mr. Pierre Schori, in Gothenburg on Sweden's policy towards South Africa', 5 May 1987, in Ministry for Foreign Affairs: *Documents on Swedish Foreign Policy: 1987*, Stockholm, 1990, pp. 207 and 211.

Culture and Popular Initiatives:
From Frontline Rock to the People's Parliament

Popular Explosion

The assistance extended via and by various popular movements and non-governmental organizations to ANC, NUM, UDF and other structures inside the apartheid republic was treated confidentially. From the point of view of information and further mobilization this was an important limitation. Through persistent public anti-apartheid opinion work by AGIS and ISAK, as well as silent identification and involvement by SIDA of an increasing number of NGOs as channels for official support[1], the issue of South Africa would, however, assume dimensions of national concern[2] and the assistance to ANC and the internal forces come close to "a collective secret".[3]

While ANC President Tambo later characterized the relations with Sweden as "a natural system [...] from people to people"[4]; Prime Minister Carlsson emphasized that the "deeply rooted and impressively broad [popular] commitment" was "both an explanation and a prior condition for [the government's] active policy"[5]; and the national board of the Africa Groups noted that "the majority of [our] demands and our global view [...] are [...] shared with most of the established [political] parties and popular movements"[6], by the mid-1980s there was in Swe-

---

1. Cf. the interview with Birgitta Berggren, p. 258.
2. Although the Norwegian government did not extend official assistance to ANC, UDF or other organizations inside South Africa, the popular opinion was similar in the neighbouring country. In a comparative study on their policies vis-à-vis South Africa of Canada, Great Britain, Israel, Japan, Scandinavia and West Germany, the US scholar Richard Payne noted in 1990 that "[p]erhaps no other international conflict is of greater interest to the Scandinavians than apartheid" (Richard J. Payne: *The Nonsuperpowers and South Africa: Implications for US Policy*, Indiana University Press, Bloomington and Indianapolis, 1990, p. 163).
3. Interview with Birgitta Berggren, p. 258.
4. Tambo in Hadjor (ed.) op. cit., p. 258.
5. 'Excerpt on [S]outhern Africa from a speech by the Prime Minister, Mr. Ingvar Carlsson, at the Workers Educational Association Anniversary Conference', 16 November 1987, in Ministry for Foreign Affairs: *Documents on Swedish Foreign Policy: 1987*, Stockholm, 1990, p. 217.
6. AGIS: 'Afrikagruppernas verksamhetsberättelse 1985/86'/'The Africa Groups' activity report for 1985/86' [no place or date], p. 4 (AGA). Advocating unilateral comprehensive sanctions, with regard to Sweden's economic relations with apartheid South Africa the demands and views of AGIS—and ISAK—were, however, clearly different. On the generally 'corporatist' character of the Swedish polity, see Sellström Volume I, p. 37. With regard to South Africa, the following observation by Payne could be noted: "Almost every conceivable aspect of social, economic and political life has its formal organization, and the relationship between [interest groups] and the government is formalized through rules and practices of communication prior to making foreign policy and through representation in the plethora of consultation and decision-making bodies. In Sweden [...], interest groups and anti-apartheid organizations are generally regarded as essential participants in the foreign policy process and relevant groups as well as government ministries and agencies are given preparatory drafts of proposed legislation for comment, which helps to reinforce cooperation and consensus-building. The various anti-apartheid organizations carry their own legacy of past involvement in the formulation of particular policies, a busy schedule of ongoing consultations and a well-justified expectation that their opinions will be solicited and taken into consideration in the future" (Payne op. cit., p. 152).

Galloping solidarity:
Bengt Nordenbrand
with ANC pioneer on
Never Despair, Täby,
June 1988 (Photo:
Börje Söderberg)

den a veritable "explosion"[1] of anti-apartheid initiatives and activities.[2] As earlier noted, a closer presentation of this rich popular involvement falls outside the scope of the study, a lacuna which hopefully will be covered in future works. Instead, the concluding chapters on Sweden's official relations with ANC and South Africa will discuss the third and final sanctions debate in the 1980s, the planning initiated in 1986 with the liberation movement for a post-apartheid dispensation and the bilateral links from its unbanning in 1990 until the democratic elections in 1994.

This said, in order to place the main subjects within their proper context and to illustrate the role played by the broader popular Swedish anti-apartheid movement—as well as the growing consensus between the state and the civil society and their points of divergence—comments will here be made on two particular events which in the mid-1980s not only summarized three decades of NGO involvement, but served as platforms for intensified solidarity campaigns, namely, the musical

1. Interview with Lindiwe Mabuza, p. 139.
2. Many extraordinary examples could here be given. One of the more spectacular individual contributions to ANC was made by the computer expert and racehorse owner Bengt Nordenbrand from Stockholm. Outraged by television coverage of police brutality against black children in South Africa, in 1986 he decided on his daughter's advice to donate half of his thoroughbred's winnings to ANC's SOMAFCO school in Tanzania. The initiative was formalized through an agreement with the movement's resident representative, Lindiwe Mabuza. Appropriately called *Never Despair*, the horse—which had been among the top ten in Scandinavia—was to race in ANC's black, green and gold colours. Eventually fracturing a leg, during his active career *Never Despair* contributed 50,000 SEK to the ANC school (Ylva Ericson: 'Det Är Aldrig För Sent att Börja'/'It Is Never Too Late to Begin' in *Hästjournalen*, No. 7, 1995, pp. 36-37). Nordenbrand's initiative made a profound impression on the ANC leadership. President Tambo himself entered into direct contact with him, and in early 1987 Nordenbrand was invited by ANC to Tanzania, Zambia and Zimbabwe (Letter from Bengt Nordenbrand to the author, Oslo, 30 June 1987) (NAI). The donation also made headlines in the alternative South African press. Reporting from Harare, Howard Barrell published several articles on *Never Despair* in *Weekly Mail* (see 'ANC stakes all on weak-kneed trot' in *Weekly Mail*, 14-20 November 1986, and 'Never Despair: The horse can't run, but can he swim!' in *Weekly Mail*, 27 March-2 April 1987). Through his ANC contacts, Nordenbrand became further involved in the anti-apartheid cause. In addition to *Never Despair* and the funds to SOMAFCO, he personally contributed towards the maintenance of an orphaned South African child in Sweden (see photo) and financed the studies in bio-chemistry of a young ANC student in Britain (Letter ('*Never Despair*') from Tor Sellström to the Swedish embassy in Pretoria, Uppsala, 22 September 1995) (NAI). It could be noted that when in 1995 ANC was balancing its books with regard to assets obtained in exile, *Never Despair* caused considerable confusion (ibid.). While the horse itself was never formally registered as ANC property, the original idea was that it would retire in a free South Africa. As stated by Nordenbrand to Barrell: "[W]hen South Africa is liberated, *Never Despair* will come to Soweto [...] and all the little children will have rides on him" (Howard Barrell: 'Never Despair: The horse can't run, but can he swim!' in *Weekly Mail*, 27 March-2 April 1987). Nordenbrand visited South Africa in late 1995. *Never Despair*, however, never made the journey to Soweto.

gala for ANC in Gothenburg in November 1985 and its sequel of artistic involvement, as well as the Swedish People's Parliament against Apartheid in Stockholm in February 1986. Respectively organized by concerned rock musicians and jointly by ISAK and SFN[1], on both occasions Prime Minister Palme played a prominent role. The gala and the popular assembly consolidated the anti-apartheid cause, bringing a number of national organizations into direct contact and cooperation with their counterparts in South Africa and cementing the demands for comprehensive sanctions. The wider field of culture was in this context of particular importance.[2]

Culture and Music

Cultural workers had from the beginning been in the forefront of the anti-apartheid movement in Sweden. Together with the former South Africa CSM missionary Gunnar Helander, the young writer Per Wästberg—later an acclaimed novelist, President of International PEN and a member of the Swedish Academy[3]—had in September 1959 launched the very first organized expression of solidarity with the disenfranchised black majority, the Swedish Fund for the Victims of Racial Oppression in South Africa.[4]

While several members of the visiting black South African musical group *The Golden City Dixies* at about the same time were granted political asylum in Sweden—subsequently appearing at the 1960 First of May demonstrations in Stock-

---

1. *Svenska FN-förbundet*, or the United Nations Association of Sweden.
2. Swedish sports organizations and individual representatives were comparatively late in joining the anti-apartheid campaign. It was only in November 1985 that the Swedish Sports Confederation (in Swedish, *Sveriges Riksidrottsförbund*; RF) decided to put an end to further contacts with South Africa (Kerstin Törngren: 'Idrotten Kommer på Upploppet'/'Sports Are Coming at the Finish' in *Afrikabulletinen*, No. 1-2, 1986, p. 30). Once the decision had been taken, however, RF would with official funds from SIDA become a major supporter of SAN-ROC, the London-based South African Non-Racial Olympic Committee led by Sam Ramsamy. While official Swedish support had earlier been channelled via IDAF, from 1986—when a contribution of 500,000 SEK was granted—direct relations were established between RF and SAN-ROC (Lena Johansson: Memorandum: 'Ansökan från Sveriges Riksidrottsförbund om stöd till South African Non-Racial Olympic Committee, SAN-ROC'/'Request from the Swedish Sports Confederation for support to SAN-ROC', SIDA/CCHA, [Stockholm], 6 September 1988) (SDA). The grant was raised during the following two years to 550,000 and 600,000, respectively (ibid.). It was in 1988 extended in favour of the International Campaign Against Apartheid Sport (ICAAS), of which Ramsamy was the Executive Director. Also supported by Norway, in 1988 the Swedish contribution to ICAAS represented 66 per cent of its expenditure. In its annual report, the organization noted that "[i]f it hadn't been for the Scandinavian countries, especially Sweden and Norway, we would not be able to operate effectively. The Swedish Sports Confederation is still our largest donor" (Letter ('Budget for 1989') with attachments from Sam Ramsamy to RF, ICAAS, London, 3 January 1989) (SDA). Opened by Prime Minister Ingvar Carlsson, in September 1990 RF hosted the Fourth International Conference Against Apartheid in Sport in Stockholm, where it was resolved that South Africa's sporting isolation should be ended (Kotzé and Greyling op. cit., p. 263). It could be noted that it was not until 1986 that AGIS and ISAK in their public opinion work actively started to enlist Swedish sportsmen and women (AGIS: 'Afrikagruppernas verksamhetsberättelse 1986/87'/'The Africa Groups' activity report for 1986/87' [no place or date], p. 3) (AGA). The campaign was largely successful. Referring to the stand taken by Swedish artists and musicians, in May 1987 a group of prominent active sport representatives—among them Agneta Andersson and Anna Olsson, gold medalists in canoeing at the 1984 Los Angeles Olympic Games—issued an appeal in favour of the formation of an organization called Athletes Against Apartheid (in Swedish, *Idrottare Mot Apartheid*) (Agneta Andersson et al.: 'Gå med i Idrottare Mot Apartheid'/'Join Athletes Against Apartheid', Stockholm, 11 May 1987) (SDA). While the organization was subsequently launched, there were also those who actively opposed any break with South Africa. This was notably the case with Ragnar Skanåker—gold medalist in pistol-shooting at the 1972 Munich Olympics—who was an active member of the extreme pro-apartheid Sweden-South Africa Society (cf. 'Profilen'/'The Profile' in *Sydafrika-Nytt*, No. 5, 1990, p. 6, where Skanåker stated that he "had done everything possible to help my South African colleagues to rejoin the sporting community").
3. Wästberg joined the Swedish Academy in 1997.
4. Sellström Volume I, pp. 137-46. Helander, too, was a prolific writer. For a presentation and analysis of his novels set in South Africa, see Frederick Hale: *A Swedish Pen Against Apartheid: The South African Novels of Gunnar Helander*, African Renaissance Publishers, Cape Town, 2001.

holm[1]—the following year the well established author Sara Lidman went to South Africa to write an account of "[the] treachery and supposed excellence of the so-called Free World".[2] Establishing close contacts with the future Nobel literature laureate Nadine Gordimer[3], members of the *Drum* magazine collective and ANC, in February 1961 she was detained and charged under the racial Immorality Act for "wrongfully [...] having had or attempting to have unlawful carnal intercourse" with Peter Nthite, former organizing secretary of the ANC Youth League and one of the accused in the ongoing Treason Trial.[4] As later stated by Wästberg, this caused a "tremendous commotion" in Sweden[5], not least among her fellow cultural workers.[6] In 1962, finally, a Swedish Committee for African Art and Craft led by Signe Höjer started to support the Rorke's Drift Art and Craft Centre, set up at CSM's Oscarsberg mission station in Zululand. It was the first specific project in South Africa to receive official Swedish assistance.[7]

Already in the early 1960s, there was a marked interest by Swedish writers, artists and cultural promoters in South Africa. Introducing African music and culture to the Swedish public, at the same time visiting exiled anti-apartheid musicians such as the singer Miriam Makeba and the trumpet player Hugh Masekela inspired the emerging solidarity movement.[8] Bridging the 1960s' pre-Vietnam and the 1980s' post-Vietnam NGO movement, it was largely on the wider cultural front that firm opposition to apartheid was maintained throughout the years, paving the way for boycott demands and initiatives towards extended popular mobilization.[9]

Despite a lull in the attention paid to the South African struggle by the popular movements in the early to mid-1970s[10], there was a direct connection between the

---

1. Sellström Volume I, pp. 125 and 144.
2. Ibid., p. 152.
3. Gordimer was awarded the Nobel Prize for literature in 1991.
4. The apartheid regime's charge sheet quoted in Birgitta Holm: *Sara Lidman: I Liv och Text* ('Sara Lidman: In Life and Text'), Albert Bonniers Förlag, Stockholm, 1998, p. 232.
5. Letter from Per Wästberg to the author, Stockholm, 9 April 1997.
6. See Sellström Volume I, pp. 152-55. Holm's biography of Lidman was not available at the time of writing the first volume. In her study, Holm describes how the Swedish UN Secretary General Dag Hammarskjöld personally intervened in favour of Lidman's release and subsequent deportation from South Africa. In a cable to their mutual Swedish friend Jytte Bonnier, he wrote from New York on 10 February 1961: "Have sent personal message to [P]rime [M]inister [Verwoerd] explaining as well as possible [the] situation and pleading for his personal attention. This, of course, in no way can be given publicity as I have been able to send such a message only in [a] personal capacity, anything else being beyond my competence" (quoted in Holm op. cit., p. 234).
7. See the chapter 'Gatsha Buthelezi and Inkatha'.
8. Lindiwe Mabuza, ANC's former Chief Representative to Sweden, stated in 1996: "I remember it as if it was yesterday—reading the newspapers [in South Africa]—[how] Swedish artists went to meet Miriam Makeba at the airport. They had created Miriam Makeba hats and welcomed her, because she was an artist who represented the politics that they supported. It was always there" (Interview with Lindiwe Mabuza, p. 141).
9. Mikael Wiehe—the main promotor of the November 1985 ANC musical gala—has explained how in his youth he was inspired by Per Wästberg's first book on South Africa, *På Svarta Listan* ('On the Black List'), published in 1960 (Grim Berglund: 'Rockkonsert för ANC: Solidaritetsarbete Är Förbannat Roligt'/'Rock Concert for ANC: Solidarity Work Is Damned Fun' in *Rapport från SIDA*, No. 3, 1986, p. 2).
10. ANC's London-based cultural group *Mayibuye*—including *inter alia* Barry Feinberg and the future political and military leaders Pallo Jordan and Ronnie Kasrils—toured Sweden in March 1976. It also appeared on Swedish television ('Mayibuye's Sånger ANC's Röst'/'Mayibuye's Songs ANC's Voice' in *Afrikabulletinen*, No. 33, 1976, p. 15). South African artists would in addition take part in cooperation projects between Sweden and the Frontline States. In 1980, this was, for example, the case with the actor John Kani and the composer Jonas Gwangwa, who played prominent parts in the Swedish-Zambian screen adaption of Doris Lessing's famous novel 'The Grass Is Singing' (in Swedish, *Gräset Sjunger*). Directed by Michael Raeburn, shot in Zambia and featuring the US actress Karin Black, the film was launched with the original book title in 1981. In the United States, it was distributed under the title 'Killing Heat'. As earlier noted, Swedish support was channelled in July 1982 to the conference-cum-festival on 'Culture and Resistance', organized in Botswana on ANC's initiative. Following this important event, ANC set up a specific Department of Arts and Culture. Headed by Barbara Masekela, it would from 1983 receive *ad hoc* official Swedish support outside the ANC allocation. On ANC's request, the assistance was from 1986/87 included under the regular cooperation.

individual commitment displayed by renowned Swedish artists and writers—from
Bror Hjorth to Peter Weiss[1]—in the previous decade and the collective efforts and
initiatives embarked upon in the mid-1980s. Actively encouraged by ANC's resident representative Lindiwe Mabuza—in her own right an acknowledged poet and
writer[2]—a strong cultural dimension was re-introduced into the anti-apartheid
campaigns from the late 1970s.[3] ANC's cultural ensemble *Amandla*—set up among
MK trainees in Angola—would here play a particularly important role. Led by the
composer and trombonist Jonas Gwangwa, from 1980 the group made several
tours around Sweden and the other Nordic countries. In Sweden, these tours were
mainly organized by the Africa Groups.[4] On behalf of ANC, records by the group
were also produced.[5] Mabuza later recalled:

> Culture was a weapon in the struggle, but it was more than that. Culture was the best way of
> talking about the soul of the people, the feelings of the people. [...] Through culture, we were
> injecting our sensitivities into the audience. Whoever was part of that felt that their decision to
> support us was correct. [...]

> I was able to convince the Nordic countries to bring *Amandla* there. By that time, *Amandla*
> was not even formed! It was a notion. Once they said yes, I painted the concept that it was an
> ANC cultural group that would perform on stage and win the people in Scandinavia. When
> that was accepted by the [Nordic solidarity movements], we built *Amandla*. [It] was built from
> our base in Angola, which was associated with the military. This shows the dynamics. [W]e
> said: 'Where do we find the people who are sufficiently disciplined and organized?' We went to
> the military camps, where the culture of South Africa continued to thrive. The culture of liber-
> ation. [...]

1. Visitors to the Bror Hjorth Museum in Uppsala—housed in the sculptor's former residence-cum-atelier—will
   notice his call for a boycott of South African goods, designed in support of SUL's 1963 campaign (see Sellström Volume I, pp. 190-98). In 1966, the South Africa Committee in Lund assembled a portfolio with works
   by six artists (Gert Aspelin, Jörgen Fogelquist, Thormod Larsen, Lage Lindell, Pär Gunnar Thelander and
   Lars-Erik Ström). Produced in 200 copies with a foreword by Peter Weiss and an allegory by Sara Lidman, it
   was sold for 300 SEK. The funds raised were donated to ANC, the Anti-Apartheid Movement in London and
   the national Swedish South Africa Committee ('Konstnärer Gör Grafikmapp för Sydafrikakommittén i Lund'/
   'Artists Make Prints Portfolio for the South Africa Committee in Lund' in *Syd- och Sydvästafrika*, No. 3,
   1966, p. 8).
2. In the mid-1980s, Mabuza was assisted at the Stockholm office by South Africa's future Minister of
   Housing Sankie Mthembi-Mahanyele, at the time known as Rebecca Matlou. She was in particular
   involved with the *Amandla* tours in Scandinavia. Also a prominent writer, in 1985 her short story 'One
   Never Knows' was accorded honourable mention in a competition organized by SIDA for African female
   writers. ANC's Ponkie Khazamula won the contest with her contribution 'I Won't Be Moved' (SIDA:
   Whispering Land: An Anthology of Stories by African Women, Office of Women in Development, Stockholm, 1985). Cf. the interviews with Sankie Mthembi-Mahanyele (pp. 168-72) and Lindiwe Mabuza (p.
   139).
3. Mabuza noted in 1999: "Within the ANC, there had always been recognition of culture as a potent weapon
   of struggle. One of our aims was to ensure that [the] ANC would be regarded by all as a popular and serious
   people's organization. In Scandinavia, culture certainly became the centrepiece of all our work. We found that
   political ideas packaged and presented through a universally appealing medium of culture struck a resonant
   chord even amongst those not politically involved. It also showed a dimension of the ANC as an organization
   concerned with diverse aspects of life, contrary to the image of heartless 'terrorists'"(Mabuza in Robben
   Island Museum, Mayibuye Centre and Nordic Africa Institute op. cit., p. 98).
4. At AGIS, Lena Johansson was actively involved in the *Amandla* tours.
5. Recorded in studios in Luanda and Lusaka, in 1980, for example, A Disc, a record company of the Swedish
   labour movement, produced the album 'Amandla' on ANC's behalf. In 1983, Afrogram—the label of the
   Africa Groups—similarly issued 'Amandla: First Tour Live', recorded at the Old Swedish Musical Academy in
   Stockholm in October 1980.

ANC's *Amandla* cultural ensemble performing the gumboot dance in Gothenburg during one of its tours in Sweden in the 1980s (Courtesy of ISAK)

[B]ut to form *Amandla*, we needed to start from zero. They did not have any instruments. They did not have uniforms and we did not have the money to bring them to Europe.[1] Once the four Nordic countries said yes, we went to Holland, because there was a strong anti-apartheid movement there. We also went to Germany. [...] I started [in Sweden] in 1979, but in 1980 we were already able to bring *Amandla*. The second tour was in 1983. By [then] they were nearly professional. [...]

What happened was that the creativity of our soldiers came out. They created the script. They were able to explain the formation of ANC and what had happened in the different phases of our struggle. This was the best bullet we had, because where you did not convince people with your political argument, *Amandla* did that in two hours. It was graphic. It was for everybody to hear and see.[2]

1. Outside the annual ANC allocation, SIDA's education division decided in May 1980 to cover the costs for the procurement of traditional ethnic costumes, musical instruments and other items required for the European launch of *Amandla* (Letter ('Regionalt kulturstöd åt ANC'/'Regional cultural support to ANC') from Roland Axelsson to SIDA, Swedish embassy, Lusaka, 5 May 1981) (SDA). While the equipment was collected on an *ad hoc* basis, it was only in April the following year that ANC's Treasury Department submitted a comprehensive request in favour of the ensemble's requirements (Letter from Thomas Nkobi to the Swedish embassy, ANC, Lusaka, 28 April 1981) (SDA).
2. Interview with Lindiwe Mabuza, pp. 140-41. She went on to say: "*Amandla* was seen by ambassadors from other countries and they were sending reports to their [...] governments: 'Here are the Swedes at it again. This time it is on the cultural front'. Which government was to say that Sweden was doing something wrong by assisting us in that way?" (ibid., p. 141). Organized by the Africa Groups, *Amandla*'s first visit to Sweden took place in October-November 1980, performing in Gothenburg, Stockholm, Umeå, Uppsala and Västerås ('Sång-och Danstrupp Hit!'/'Song and Dance Troupe Coming Here!' in *Afrikabulletinen*, No. 54, 1980, p. 19). The second visit in 1983 was sponsored in addition to AGIS by *inter alia* AIC (Letter ('Main organizers and organizations connected with [the] *Amandla* tour, 1983') from Lindiwe Mabuza, ANC, Stockholm, 30 January 1984) (OPA). On *Amandla* and Norway, see Drolsum in Eriksen (ed.) op. cit., p. 259.

The encounters with *Amandla*, contacts with UDF-aligned initiatives inside South Africa—initially the *Action Workshop* theatre group in Cape Town[1]—and public pro-ANC stands by younger musical groups such as *Imperiet*[2] would in the mid-1980s lead Swedish cultural workers of different generations and orientations to form their own anti-apartheid organizations and join the broader organized solidarity movement.[3] Mainly inspired by graphic art practitioners, in January 1985 the organization Artists Against Apartheid[4] was launched, soon followed by Musicians Against Apartheid.[5] Both joined the Isolate South Africa Committee, actively advocating a boycott of the Pretoria regime and support to ANC and SWAPO.[6] As later noted by Lindiwe Mabuza, "after all the years developing these structures [, the different artistic and cultural expressions of solidarity] would just explode in the [...] gala for ANC in Gothenburg in November 1985".[7]

1. Swedish Travelling Exhibitions' (STE) involvement with internally based cultural organizations, art schools, artists and musicians started after contacts between Christina Björk and *Action Workshop* in 1984 (Sida (1998) op. cit., p. 3). Through Björk's commitment, assistance from the Swedish legation and funds from SIDA, an increasing number of South African recipients would from the mid-1980s be included under the cultural support channelled by STE. Among them in 1989 were Alexandra Art Centre, Federal Union of Black Artists, Free Filmmakers, Letsema Art Project, Media and Silkscreen Project, Thupelo Art Project, Union Artists, Video News Services and the Weekly Mail Film Festival (Letter ('Ansökan'/'Request') from *Riksutställningar* to CCHA, Stockholm, 5 July 1989, and Lena Johansson: Memorandum ('Årsansökan från Riksutställningar om stöd till kulturell verksamhet i Sydafrika'/'Annual request from Swedish Travelling Exhibitions for cultural activities in South Africa'), CCHA/SIDA, [Stockholm], 20 September 1989) (SDA). Between 1985 and 1991, the official Swedish support to cultural activities in South Africa amounted in total to around 16 MSEK (Åberg op. cit., p. 92).
2. Led by Joakim Thåström, in 1985 the popular rock group *Imperiet* ('The Empire') dedicated the album '2:a Augusti 1985' ('Second of August 1985') to ANC. Without any strings attached, 10 SEK of each album sold was channelled to the liberation movement. For the significance of this initiative vis-à-vis the Swedish youth, see Herman Andersson: 'Imperiet och ANC' ('Imperiet and ANC') in *Afrikabulletinen*, No. 6, 1985, p. 3. Representing a younger musical generation, Thåström and *Imperiet* featured prominently at the November 1985 ANC gala.
3. The Church of Sweden Mission, AGIS and others had promoted South African music and ANC liberation songs since the late 1970s, soon leading to a proliferation of choral groups all over the country. At the local level, churches, schools and solidarity groups formed hundreds of choirs singing in South African languages. This, in turn, had a major mobilizing effect on the Swedish anti-apartheid opinion. A similar development took place in Norway. An impressed Walter Sisulu later commented that "they sing Nkosi Sikelele better than we do!" (Interview with Walter Sisulu p. 191). In March 1990, a giant choir of several hundred members performed South African songs for Nelson Mandela at the Globe Arena gala (see below).
4. In Swedish, *Konstnärer Mot Apartheid*. The first initiative to formally bring national anti-apartheid artists and sports representatives together had been taken in the United States in 1983, when the singer Harry Belafonte and the tennis player Arthur Ashe set up Artists and Athletes Against Apartheid. In 1985, the musician Stephen van Zandt ('Little Steven') took this initiative a step further through the formation of United Artists Against Apartheid. In the case of Great Britain, in April 1986 Jerry Dammers and Dali Tambo—the son of the ANC President— launched a similar national coordinating body called Artists Against Apartheid (William Campschreur and Joost Divendal (eds): *Culture in Another South Africa*, Zed Books, London, 1989, pp. 179-80).
5. In Swedish, *Artister Mot Apartheid*, also translated as Performing Artists Against Apartheid. It should be noted that individual Swedish writers—among them Sara Lidman and Per Wästberg—had from the 1950s denounced apartheid and colonialism, actively introducing Southern African voices to the general public (see Sellström Volume I, pp. 111-17). In the case of South Africa, formalized relations were established in 1988 between Swedish PEN and the Congress of South African Writers (COSAW), set up in June 1987. A first official grant of 340,000 SEK was then channelled to the organization. On the Swedish side, the cooperation was subsequently taken over by the Swedish Union of Authors (*Sveriges Författarförbund*), which in 1990 was granted 950,000 SEK in support of COSAW (Lena Johansson: Memorandum ('Ansökan från Sveriges Författarförbund om stöd till projekt i Sydafrika'/'Request from the Swedish Union of Authors for support to projects in South Africa'), SIDA/CCHA, [Stockholm], 24 September 1990) (SDA).
6. From the mid-1980s, ISAK launched successful campaigns against the appearance in Sweden of a number of international artists who were blacklisted by the United Nations due to their South African contacts. Frank Sinatra, for example, had to cancel a planned concert tour (ISAK: 'Vad gjorde Isolera Sydafrika Kommittén 1986-87?'/'What did the Isolate South Africa Committee do in 1986-87?', activity report by the ISAK board, [no place or date]) (ISA). According to Per Wästberg, "Sweden followed the [cultural] boycott of South Africa more strictly than any other country" (Interview with Per Wästberg, p. 357).
7. Interview with Lindiwe Mabuza, p. 139.

Gala for ANC

Staged on 29-30 November 1985 in the form of two concerts at the Scandinavium arena in Gothenburg in front of some 25,000 people[1], the ANC gala brought twenty of Sweden's leading rock and popular musicians[2] together in a major manifestation of support for ANC.[3] Partly inspired by the international 'Band Aid' and 'Live Aid' concerts launched in 1984 by the Irish singer Bob Geldof for the drought victims in Ethiopia[4], by taking a clear political stand the Swedish artists went an important step further, actively setting out to raise awareness and funds for the South African liberation movement. As stated shortly before the gala by Mikael Wiehe, its main promoter and a veteran representative of the post-1968 'progrock' musical movement:

> I am terribly tired of the melancholy [prevailing with regard to] solidarity work. [...] In Sweden, music and politics have been connected since the musical movement started fifteen years ago. [...] [W]e must bring the positive force of the struggle to the fore. Solidarity work knits [people] together. It is voluntary and damned fun.[5]

One of the main factors behind the success and subsequent impact of the ANC gala on the Swedish youth was, as indicated by Wiehe, that it brought popular musicians from different backgrounds together for a political cause. Tomas Ledin—who together with Wiehe more than anybody else would become associated with the effort and whose contribution was greatly acknowledged by ANC[6]—recalled in 1997:

> [T]he initiative came from Mikael Wiehe together with Björn Afzelius and Dan Hylander. [...] The Swedish rock scene was—in the media anyway—divided between commercial rock n' roll and alternative, more political rock n' roll. I was in their eyes in the commercial world, so they wanted to create a bridge. If we were the foundation, we could together get everybody involved. This was the idea. [...]

> I was aware of the situation in South Africa [...], but I did not know in detail what ANC really stood for. [...] [However,] I realized quite soon that if we were going to make a difference, ANC was the right organization to support. [...] There were, of course, those who said that it was too much to the left and that one should not go along with something so political. But [after some research] I felt that I had no problem in supporting [ANC]. [...] It was important to

---

1. Tommy Rander of the record company Transmission was responsible for organizing the event. He also planned and administered the subsequent 'Frontline Rock' tours in Southern Africa and Sweden together with ANC and AGIS.
2. Björn Afzelius, Py Bäckman, Eva Dahlgren, Anders Glenmark, Hansson de Wolfe United, Dan Hylander, Imperiet, Tommy Körberg, Tomas Ledin, Peps Persson, Mikael Rickfors, Mats Ronander, Anne-Lie Rydé, Totta's Bluesband, Mikael Wiehe and Jerry Williams. Sanne Salomonsen from Denmark was invited to join the Swedish artists.
3. Local concerts for ANC were held around the country on a smaller scale.
4. Interview with Tomas Ledin, p. 300.
5. Cited in Grim Berglund: 'Rockkonsert för ANC: Solidaritetsarbete Är Förbannat Roligt'/'Rock Concert for ANC: Solidarity Work Is Damned Fun' in *Rapport från SIDA*, No. 3, 1985, p. 2.
6. Ledin and Wiehe jointly wrote the lead song 'Berg är till för att flyttas' ('Mountains are to be moved'). Eight years later—in December 1993—ANC invited Ledin and Wiehe to Oslo to meet Nelson Mandela when he received the Nobel Peace Prize. They were also invited to South Africa to attend Mandela's presidential inauguration in May 1994. Ledin later stated: "[I]t was quite spectacular. I had [the Swedish Foreign Minister] Sten Andersson to the right [...] and a couple of rows above were Fidel Castro and Yasser Arafat. From our part of the world, it was Mikael and I. Quincy Jones was there from the US [...]. It was quite something" (Interview with Tomas Ledin, p. 303). Together with the Finnish singer Arja Saijonmaa and the Norwegian solidarity choir *Inkululeko*, in February 1999 Ledin and Wiehe appeared during a conference on Robben Island on 'Nordic Solidarity with the Liberation Struggles in Southern Africa and Challenges for Democratic Partnerships into the 21st Century'.

create a platform that a lot of artists could support. The strategy was that Mikael Wiehe and I jointly could bring a lot of artists together if we had a platform that was humanitarian. [...]

What was great was that during the [preparatory] work artists kept calling, wanting to join. More artists were added all the time, which, of course, was good for the spirit of the project. [...] There were only a few who said that they did not want to participate. I do not think that it was for political reasons, but more for personal artistic reasons.[1]

While the concerts were organized by the rock artists themselves, so important was the event that it brought Johnny Makatini, ANC's Secretary for International Affairs, and Prime Minister Olof Palme to Gothenburg. Far from being allowed to 'steal the show', both of them were invited on stage as fellow participants. Together with Barbara Masekela, Director of ANC's Department of Arts and Culture, Lindiwe Mabuza and other members living in Sweden, Makatini joined an *ad hoc* choir which opened the gala by singing the movement's song of thanks 'When freedom we have won'. It was included as the first entry on the live double album issued from the event.[2]

To loud cheers, Palme was, similarly, introduced by Wiehe to the capacity crowd as "one of the most prominent artists of the land".[3] In his brief address, the Premier recalled how in the late 1940s "as his first political act" he had raised funds for black South African students through donating blood. He further underlined the importance of outside pressure against the apartheid regime, introducing a dictum which three months later in a more general sense he was to repeat to the People's Parliament against Apartheid. "If the youth of the world decides to get rid of apartheid", he said, "then apartheid will disappear". Stating that the government had been "inspired by your action", Palme, finally, announced that a decision had been taken the previous day to increase the annual official allocation to ANC through an additional grant of 5 MSEK. "[W]e have a common responsibility", he concluded, "we have to work in our own separate ways [and] together [call for] the release of Nelson Mandela, an end to the state of emergency, elimination of apartheid [and] freedom for Africa".[4]

To raise as much money as possible, the musicians, promoters, technicians and everybody else worked for free.[5] In addition to receipts from the concerts—including television rights—funds were mainly raised through the sale of a live recording, issued only a week later. As the double LP—subsequently released on CD—was still selling in the late 1990s[6], it is difficult to estimate the total proceeds of the gala. While Ledin in March 1997 estimated the amount to between 10 and 12 MSEK[7], as early as in February 1987 Mabuza reported to Treasurer General Nkobi on the

---

1. Interview with Tomas Ledin, pp. 300-301. Ledin also noted how the gala increased the awareness among the musicians of the international implications of the cultural boycott against apartheid (ibid., p. 302).
2. Björn Afzelius et al.: 'ANC-Galan: Svensk Rock mot Apartheid' ('The ANC Gala: Swedish Rock against Apartheid'), Committee of November 29th/Amalthea, 1985. Becoming a gold album, the double LP was later released on compact disc.
3. Cited from the compact disc 'Olof Palme: En Levande Vilja' ('Olof Palme: A Living Will'), Sveriges Social-demokratiska Arbetareparti/Amigo, Stockholm, 1996.
4. 'Ungdomen och Sydafrika: Anförande på ANC-galan i Göteborg den 29 november 1985' ('The youth and South Africa: Address at the ANC gala in Gothenburg, 29 November 1985') in Olof Palme: *En Levande Vilja* ('A Living Will'), Tiden, Stockholm, 1987, pp. 388-89.
5. Interview with Tomas Ledin, p. 301.
6. Ibid.
7. Ibid.

Golden results: ANC Chief Representative Lindiwe Mabuza (third from right), Agnes Mackay and Eddie Funde with Swedish artists from the solidarity rock gala held in Gothenburg in November 1985 (Photo: Per Björn/ Aftonbladet Bild)

transfer of 9.25 MSEK to ANC's London account.[1] This substantial voluntary contribution[2] was extended as budgetary support, with no strings attached.[3] As explained by Wiehe:

> It is important to us that ANC receives the money without restrictions. It shows that we are at the same level, [which is] a vital prerequisite and a natural approach in solidarity work. [I]f we support their liberation struggle, it is important that they, too, stand free vis-à-vis us.[4]

This attitude—and the gala as such—incensed conservative circles in Sweden. Accommodated by Margaretha af Ugglas at the Moderate Party-aligned journal *Svensk Tidskrift*, Tommy Hansson of the extreme right *Contra* group and later a leading member of the pro-Pretoria Sweden-South Africa Society would thus in early 1986 claim that

> Swedish artists [...] through the two galas arranged in Gothenburg [...] have made it possible for ANC to murder and mutilate still more innocent South Africans, black, white and coloured.[5]

---

1. Letter ('Transfers') from Lindiwe Mabuza, Chief Representative, to Treasurer General Thomas Nkobi, ANC, Stockholm, 18 February 1987 (MCA).
2. The amount corresponded to 14 per cent of the official disbursements via SIDA to ANC in 1986/87 (cf. Appendix XIV).
3. Interview with Tomas Ledin, p. 301.
4. Cited in Grim Berglund: 'Rockkonsert för ANC: Solidaritetsarbete Är Förbannat Roligt'/'Rock Concert for ANC: Solidarity Work Is Damned Fun' in *Rapport från SIDA*, No. 3, 1985, p. 2.
5. Tommy Hansson: 'Stöd Ej ANC's Terrorpolitik'/'Don't Support ANC's Terror Policies' in *Svensk Tidskrift*, No. 1, 1986, p. 67.

Broadening and consolidating the support for ANC and its struggle for human rights, where it mattered most the November 1985 gala was, however, greatly appreciated. Leading the ANC delegation to the People's Parliament against Apartheid in Stockholm in February 1986, in his address to the assembly Oliver Tambo explicitly referred to "the contribution [made] by the Swedish cultural workers", seen as "an expression of their unconditional commitment to ANC and the struggle for a free South Africa". Emphasizing the consensus reached in this regard by the official authorities and the NGO movement, the ANC President further stated the opinion that

> when the government through Prime Minister Olof Palme decided to raise the funds collected for ANC by the cultural workers, it merely confirmed that there in Sweden is great unity concerning apartheid and that the invaluable support extended to [us] by the government is an expression of the will of the entire Swedish people. [...] [I]t gives us strength and encouragement [, reflecting] the unity that we, too, are pursuing in our struggle.[1]

Meanwhile, it should be noted that the initiative was far from a one-off affair. Instead, in 1986-87 it set in motion a chain of important events on the cultural front, which together with the people's assembly strengthened the demands in Sweden for complete isolation of the apartheid regime, particularly among the youth.

In acknowledgment of their contribution, ANC invited the artists to Southern Africa. With financial assistance from SIDA, along with Tommy Rander—the chief organizer of the gala—in March 1986 Py Bäckman, Eva Dahlgren, Dan Hylander and Tomas Ledin of the 'Committee of November 29th'[2] spent two weeks in Tanzania, Zambia and Zimbabwe, familiarizing themselves "in the flesh" with the liberation movement by *inter alia* visiting the SOMAFCO school.[3] In addition to press conferences and a television appearance in Harare, they were interviewed by ANC's 'Radio Freedom' in Lusaka.[4] As later stated by Ledin,

> [w]e were not aware of the significance of [our initiative] until we came there. We then understood that it was important to keep spirits up. It was in every aspect a fantastic experience. It was also very moving, because we were not aware that what we had done in Sweden had had such an impact.[5]

Although the Swedes did not perform on stage during the trip, they met and exchanged ideas with ANC cultural workers and local artists. These encounters led them to embark on an ambitious cooperation project, notably involving exchange tours in the respective regions between musicians from Scandinavia and Southern

1. 'Anförande av ANC's president Oliver Tambo' ('Address by ANC President Oliver Tambo') in ISAK and SFN: *Svensk Folkriksdag mot Apartheid 21-23 februari 1986* ('Swedish People's Parliament against Apartheid, 21-23 February 1986'), Stockholm, 1986, pp. 122-23.
2. To administer the recordings, funds etc., the artists and organizers involved in the ANC gala formed a 'Committee of November 29th'.
3. Interview with Tomas Ledin, pp. 301-302.
4. Interview with Eva Dahlgren in Steffo Törnquist: 'Alla talar om ANC-galan' ('Everybody talks about the ANC gala') in *Expressen*, 11 April 1986. Tomas Ledin was video-taping during the trip. A 20-minute edited version of his film was later shown on Swedish television (ibid. and the interview with Tomas Ledin, p. 302).
5. Interview with Tomas Ledin, p. 301.

Africa.[1] Assisted by the Africa Groups and the ANC representation in Stockholm, in October 1986 a first 'Frontline Rock' concert tour was organized in Sweden as a North-South bridging exercise. Performing in Gothenburg, Malmö, Sandviken, Stockholm and Örebro, an *ad hoc* cast composed of Zimbabwe's Lovemore Majaivana[2] and his *Zulu Band*, members of ANC's *Amandla* group[3], Py Bäckman, Dan Hylander, Tomas Ledin, Peps Persson, Mikael Wiehe and other Scandinavian musicians[4] brought the message of solidarity with Southern and South Africa a step further.[5] Coordinated by Tommy Rander, on behalf of ANC and the 'Committee of November 29th' a live album from the Gothenburg concert was also produced.[6]

Rock and Cooperation on the Frontline

What in this context was to confirm ANC's standing among the youth in Sweden was the well attended and highly publicized second leg of the Frontline Rock tour, staged in Zambia and Zimbabwe in March-April 1987. Financed by the November 29 Committee through the proceeds from the Gothenburg gala, it was not conceived as a fund-raising exercise, but as an expression of support for ANC and the two Frontline States in the ongoing regional conflict.[7] In the case of Zimbabwe, this initially met with unexpected opposition from the Ministry for Youth, Sports and Culture, which not only demanded that PAC should be put on a par with ANC, but also requested a share in the assumed commercial receipts.[8] This was not acceptable to the Swedish artists, who in late February—one month before the scheduled start of the tour—adamantly declared "to whom it may concern" that

> [i]t has come to our attention that economic and political demands have been made on the Frontline Rock project. We wish to inform any interested party—especially in Zimbabwe—[that] there are two fundamental principles from which [we] will not deviate [, namely that] we do not [recognize] any other liberation movement in South Africa beside[s] the ANC [and that] we are mostly interested in promoting and—if possible—elevat[ing] the material conditions for

1. Committee of November 29th: 'Information sheet', [no place], 23 July 1986 (Author's collection). The cooperation covered in addition assistance in the form of technical equipment, notably a PA-system donated to ANC and used *inter alia* for the 'Buwa' musical. Soon thereafter, direct contacts with musicians in South Africa also led to technical support. Towards the end of 1986, the Swedish cultural umbrella organization *Kontaktnätet* (The Swedish Network)—representing some 35,000 members—entered into relations with the UDF-aligned Musical Action for People's Power (MAPP) in Cape Town, financing a sound system (Åberg op. cit., pp. 85-87). Via the Swedish record company Amalthea—which on behalf of the 'Committee of November 29th' had produced the double album from the ANC gala—closer links with the Cape Town-based alternative company Shifty Records were soon established. In 1987/88, SIDA granted *Kontaktnätet* 1.2 MSEK in favour of Shifty Records, mainly for a mobile recording studio (Lena Johansson: Memorandum ('Årsansökan från Kontaktnätet om stöd till musikrörelsen i Sydafrika och erfarenhetsutbyte'/'Annual request from the Swedish Network for support to the musical movement in South Africa and exchange of experiences'), SIDA/CCHA, [Stockholm], 20 February 1989) (SDA). Over the following two years, SIDA granted another 0.7 MSEK (ibid. and Lena Johansson: 'Årsansökan från Kontaktnätet om fortsatt stöd till projekt i Sydafrika'/'Annual request from the Swedish Network for continued support to projects in South Africa'), SIDA/CCHA, [Stockholm], 24 September 1990) (SDA).
2. Born Tshuma, Majaivana was the Ndebele artistic name for 'The Jiving Man', a popular singer in Zimbabwe at the time.
3. Mmabatho Nhlanhla, Beauty Khuzwayo and Thuthu Radebe.
4. Notably the Danish guitarist Henrik Strube.
5. For the coverage given to the Swedish tour in Zimbabwe, see Andy Moyse: 'Frontline Rock' in *Parade*, [no number], December 1986, pp. 25-29 and 43. Cf. also the interview with Tomas Ledin, p. 302, and Mikael Frohm: 'Dom bildar front på ANC-soarén!'/'They are the front for the ANC entertainment!' in *Arbetet*, 3 October 1986.
6. Lovemore Majaivana et al.: 'Frontline Rock', ANC & Committee of November 29th/Transmission, 1987.
7. In May 1986, South Africa launched simultaneous attacks on ANC in Botswana, Zambia and Zimbabwe.
8. Cable ('Frontline Rock-turné i Zimbabwe och Zambia'/'Frontline Rock tour in Zimbabwe and Zambia') from Tommy Rander on behalf of the 'Committee of November 29th' to the Ministry for Foreign Affairs, Stockholm, and the Swedish embassy, Harare, Gothenburg, 6 March 1987 (Author's collection).

the musicians in Zambia and Zimbabwe. We will not [...] take suggestions that compromise any of these principles serious[ly].[1]

On behalf of the organizing committee, Tommy Rander, its chairperson, further stated:

> If anyone, any body [...], interest [group] or party makes economic demands on the Frontline Rock project, we would be forced to enquire about the legal grounds for such a demand [and]—if necessary—[consider] the cancellation of the entire project, [at] present and [in the] future.[2]

While Rander at that time had agreed with the Zimbabwe army command that a benefit show for the soldiers protecting the Beira corridor in Mozambique against RENAMO would be included in the tour[3], through diplomatic interventions by the ANC headquarters in Lusaka and the Swedish embassy in Harare[4] these complications were eventually solved to the satisfaction of the musicians.

Preceded by the launch in Zambia and Zimbabwe of the album recorded from the first leg of the Frontline Rock project, as well as by video screenings on national television in the two countries from the November 1985 Gothenburg gala and the October 1986 tour[5], the Swedish artists' highly successful ANC solidarity peregrination took place from 24 March to 5 April 1987. Joined by the Danish guitarists Henrik Strube and Lars Krarup, during an intense roadshow Annie Bodelsson, Py Bäckman, Dan Hylander, Per Melin and Peps Persson performed for free or nominal entrance fees together with Lovemore Majaivana and ANC's *Thami Mnyele Quartet*[6] at ten different locations, from Kambuzuma township outside Harare via Masvingo and Mutare in Zimbabwe to Kitwe and Ndola on the Zambian Copperbelt. Major shows were also held in Harare, Bulawayo and Lusaka. In addition to ANC technicians and a sound crew from Sweden, the travelling musical party was accompanied by both local and Swedish journalists[7], who reported to their respec-

---

1. Cable ('Regarding Frontline Rock') from Tommy Rander on behalf of the 'Committee of November 29th' to ANC, Lusaka, and the Swedish embassy, Harare, Gothenburg, 21 February 1987; original in English (Author's collection).
2. Ibid.
3. Ibid. This benefit concert was subsequently staged in Mutare on 4 April 1987. The original idea was to arrange a concert inside Mozambique, but it had to be abandoned for practical and security reasons (Author's recollection). After the last performance in Harare on 5 April—which was also free of charge—Frontline Rock donated 1,200 Zimbabwe Dollars to Major General Jevan Maseko in favour of the troops in the Beira corridor (*The Herald*, 7 April 1987). The Swedish artists' pro-ANC and general political stand was in stark contrast to parallel international initiatives. When in February 1987 the US singer Paul Simon—at the time questioned by ANC, UN and the worldwide anti-apartheid movement for his contacts with South Africa—staged his 'Graceland' concert in Harare, a cheque of 15,000 Zimbabwe Dollars was, for example, presented to Sally Mugabe in favour of a leprosy project and the Zimbabwe Jairos Jiri Association for the physically handicapped. Surrounded by considerable international attention, Simon's 'Graceland' appearances in Harare on 14-15 February 1987—surprisingly joined by Miriam Makeba and Hugh Masekela—were received with mixed feelings. For a call to boycott the essentially commercial event, see Phineas Ndlovu: 'There is no grace in Graceland' in *The Herald*, 14 February 1987.
4. As a reflection of the wider understanding between the Swedish NGO movement and the government, it could be noted that Rander and the 'Committee of November 29th' sought and received support for its stand from Pierre Schori, Under-Secretary of State for Foreign Affairs. The above quoted cable of 6 March 1987 from Rander to the Ministry for Foreign Affairs was addressed to Schori, who forwarded it to the embassy in Harare.
5. 'On the Frontline' in *Parade*, [no number], March 1987, p. 50.
6. The quartet was named after the talented South African painter Thami Mnyele, killed in an apartheid raid on Botswana's capital Gaborone in June 1985.
7. In addition to locally based correspondents, the journalists from Sweden were Anders Edgren, Erland Huledal and Mia Gerdin. Working for the national radio network, Gerdin produced a highly entertaining coverage of the roadshow for Swedish Radio's youth programme *Mareld* ('Seafire'), presented on Programme One (P1) on 15 April 1987.

tive readers and listeners on the concerts staged, the political message carried and the enthusiastic reception encountered all the way.[1]

Taking place at a time when the final national sanctions debate was at its peak and the government and the South African liberation movement through the PASA programme were reaching out to a number of institutions and organizations, the politically motivated solidarity effort by the rock artists consolidated ANC's broader popular support in Sweden. The popularity of the artists involved—as well as their personal experiences and subsequent productions[2]—clearly influenced the younger generation. In an article in SIDA's magazine *Rapport*, they were described as "possibly Sweden's best known aid workers, although [the fact] that they are just [that] might perhaps not be so well known".[3] Impressed by the encounter with ANC and the realities in Southern Africa, Dan Hylander summarized the artists' feelings by underlining that "[t]here are, after all, more important things than selling records".[4]

It is in this context not without significance that the commitment shown by the Swedish artists partly inspired Caiphus Semenya and other exiled musicians to set up the organization South African Artists United (SAAU), which with financial assistance from Norway and Sweden and technical support from the 'Committee of November 29th' in mid-1986 launched a seminal musical drama project.

Although it welcomed an increasing anti-apartheid involvement by Western cultural workers, in its manifesto SAAU regretted that the developments so far also had

> kindled opportunistic tendencies among certain artists, who have seen this [process] as a vehicle to generate publicity for themselves in the guise of helping the fight against apartheid. These artists have contributed to a general confusion of the issues that the people of [South Africa are] fighting for. [For example,] some American artists ignorantly portray the struggle as a civil rights' movement. [...] [Others, however,] have given visible concrete support, like the Swedish artists who came together and organized [...] *Svensk Rock mot Apartheid*, which was a fund-raiser for the ANC. The event was a great success, and the people of [South Africa] thank all the artists who participated in that historic event.[5]

At the same time, Semenya and his colleagues—among them several prominent singers, players and composers such as Jonas Gwangwa, Hugh Masekela and Letta Mbulu, all anti-apartheid artists who had been forced into exile in the 1960s—noted that

---

1. In the case of Zimbabwe, see, for example, David Masunda: 'The music of freedom moves thousands' in *The Herald*, 10 April 1987; 'Frontline Rock' in *Parade*, [no number], May 1987, pp. 25-27; and Donatus Bonde: 'Jive by Daylight, Rock by Moonlight' in *Moto*, No. 54, 1987, pp. 29-30. Among the many newspaper articles published in Sweden, the following two could be mentioned: Erland Huledal: 'Kultur(k)rocken som alla älskar' ('The cultural rock collision which everybody loves') in *Göteborgs-Tidningen*, 19 April 1987, and Anders Edgren: 'Segertåget genom Afrika' ('The triumphal procession through Africa') in *Aftonbladet*, 20 April 1987.

2. Influenced by a wayside encounter outside Masvingo, Peps Persson—the Swedish master of reggae music—composed the popular 'Samma sång' ('The same song'), included in his album 'Fram med Pengarna!' ('Out with the Money!'), Sonet Grammofon, 1988.

3. Erland Huledal: 'Det Finns Viktigare Saker än att Sälja Skivor' ('There Are More Important Things Than Selling Records') in *Rapport från SIDA*, No. 5, 1987, p. 25.

4. Ibid. Through their musical initiatives, several of the Swedish artists became more generally involved in anti-apartheid information and opinion work. In September 1987, for example, Mikael Wiehe attended the International Conference on Children, Repression and the Law in South Africa, held in Harare.

5. South African Artists United: 'Musical project', Manifesto and project proposal submitted by Caiphus Semenya to the Swedish embassy in Harare on 4 September 1986 [no place or date] (Author's collection).

there is a very important component missing. This [...] is [made up of] the exiled South African artists who have been living in [the] Western metropolises for years and have been educating their audiences long before the South African struggle became a popular issue. These artists [have been] subjected to very little coverage or none at all from the [...] news media and the major record companies, who [in the past] were reluctant to support their cause [...]. They are the true vanguard of [the] artists against apartheid [...]. [...] [Their] visibility should be prominent. [...] With them in the forefront, a lot of confused issues will be clarified.[1]

Against this background, the SAAU manifesto declared:

> It is now more than ever [...] important that a group made up of professional [South African] singers, musicians, actors, dancers and poets be put together to form a collective, unified polit-ical voice. This group will be the nucleus of a theatrical musical show which will be both enter-taining and educational, because its theme will [have] a clear political message. Also young promising amateurs will be included in the project. The [...] aim [is] to ensure that revolution-ary theatre, music, dance, art and literature follow the correct path of development and pro-vide better assistance [to] the overthrow of the fascist South African regime and the accomplishment of the task of national liberation.[2]

Thus claiming a leading political role in the international effort against apartheid, SAAU, however, did not openly advocate support for ANC. This partly followed from the mobilization of exiled South African artists from different political backgrounds, but was above all due to the fact that from the start it included younger popular artists who lived and were professionally active inside the apart-heid republic, such as Stella Khumalo and Condry Ziqubu. Nevertheless, sup-ported by the ANC leadership in exile, the guiding principle was unmistakenly Charterist: "[T]he [organization] will adhere to the [...] goals of our struggle, [namely] to create a non-racial, democratic, unitary state, where all will live in peace as equal citizens".[3]

SAAU was mainly the brainchild of the well-known California-based South African singer and composer Caiphus Semenya[4], who through the good offices of ANC's representative Lindiwe Mabuza in connection with the Swedish People's Parliament against Apartheid in February 1986 had performed during a gala show staged at the Concert Hall in Stockholm. During his stay, Semenya also entered into contact with the Africa Groups, the November 29 Committee and the official aid authorities, paving the way for cooperation with regard to his and SAAU's major initiative, the 'Buwa' ('Speak out') musical drama. Coinciding with the Frontline Rock plans, Semenya's intention was to assemble artists from the South African diaspora and the apartheid republic in Harare to finalize, rehearse and launch the project before taking it on a fund-raising world tour.[5]

---

1. Ibid.
2. Ibid.
3. Ibid.
4. Together with the US musician Quincy Jones, Semenya was nominated in 1985 for an Oscar for the music to the film 'The Color Purple'.
5. Letter ('Projektframställning från South African Artists United avseende sydafrikansk musikal'/'Project request from SAAU regarding a South African musical') from Tor Sellström to SIDA, Swedish embassy, Harare, 9 September 1986 (SDA). Interviewed in early 1987, Semenya stated: "We chose Harare because it is close to our home and our [performances] here will be used as a springboard for the show that will be seen in [the] Scandinavian countries before going on a worldwide tour" ('Buwa: A Musical Drama on Apartheid' in *Moto*, No. 52, 1987, p. 29). As in the case of the Swedish Frontline Rock project, prominent Zimbabwean artists took part in 'Buwa'. This was notably the case of the veteran female singer Dorothy Masuka, who at the last moment replaced Miriam Makeba in one of the leading roles.

After submitting a project outline to the Swedish embassy in Harare, in September 1986 Semenya returned to Sweden for further discussions with SIDA and potentially interested NGOs, among them the International Centre of the Swedish Labour Movement (AIC). With strong support from Lindiwe Mabuza, the proposal was well received. Although cultural assistance did not form part of the labour movement's core activities, due to the political significance of the initiative AIC decided to grant SAAU 40,000 SEK from its own International Solidarity Fund.[1] On AIC's request, SIDA agreed at the same time to allocate 210,000 SEK, bringing the combined Swedish contribution to 250,000 SEK.[2] A similar formula for support was shortly thereafter found in Norway, where AIC's counterpart AIS[3] with its own funds and an official grant from the Ministry of Foreign Affairs added 240,000 NOK.[4]

Semenya had by mid-1986 practically finalized the script for 'Buwa', as well as secured the participation of some 40 prominent South African musicians, dancers and actors.[5] Gathering in Harare from various corners of the world[6], from late October 1986 their stay and rehearsals—soon becoming 'the talk of the town'[7]—were financially covered by the Swedish and Norwegian contributions. In the case of Sweden, the participation was extended when in November three sound and light technicians who had assisted the first leg of the Frontline Rock project were seconded by the 'Committee of November 29th' to join the cast.[8]

After a jam-packed jamboree at the Skyline Motel outside Harare on New Year's Eve[9], the defiant drama—described by *Weekly Mail* as "[o]ne of the most ambitious South African musical ventures [that] has emerged from the shadow of secrecy across the border"[10]—was successfully launched at the Seven Arts Theatre in the Zimbabwean capital on 10 January 1987. Attracting huge crowds of anti-

---

1. Letter with annotations ('Förslag till beslut per capsulam'/'Proposed per capsulam decision') from Elisabeth Michanek to the board members of the International Solidarity Fund, AIC, Stockholm, 9 October 1986 (OPA).

2. SIDA: Decision, Education division, No. 344/1986, Stockholm, 11 October 1986 (SDA).

3. *Arbeiderbevegelsens Internasjonale Støttekomité*, or the International Support Committee of the Norwegian Labour Movement.

4. 'Letter of intent', signed by Tor Halvorsen (AIS) and Caiphus Semenya (SAAU), Oslo, 27 October 1986 (OPA). The Swedish and Norwegian contributions were administered by the Harare office of the Norwegian People's Aid (in Norwegian, *Norsk Folkehjelp*) (ibid.).

5. Semenya had worked on the script for more than two years. Interviewed after the preview, he explained that 'Buwa' was "the culmination of ten years [of] dreaming, planning and scheming. [...] But [...] it was only a dream. [...] [T]hanks to initial funding from Swedish and Norwegian aid organisations, we're [now] making that dream a reality" (Gwen Ansell: 'Musicians struggle against South African apartheid' in *Botswana Daily News*, 19 January 1987).

6. Among the top South African artists who had originally agreed to participate, Miriam Makeba and Dollar Brand (Abdullah Ibrahim) were the most notable absentees.

7. And further afield. The rehearsals—taking place in an abandoned supermarket on the outskirts of Harare—were often visited by leading ANC representatives from Lusaka, among them notably Treasurer General Thomas Nkobi, who recalled the vibrant 1950s in Sophiatown (Author's recollection).

8. Anders Hagström, Jimmy Olsson and Lars Lanhed.

9. Cf. Ray Mawerera: 'Music Magic' in *Parade*, [no number], February 1987, pp. 23 and 35.

10. Andrew Robinson: 'SA exiles speak their minds' in *Weekly Mail*, 23-29 January 1987. *The Herald* of Harare presented 'Buwa' as "probably the most ambitious musical to have been undertaken by Southern African artists" (David Masunda: 'Harare launch for black SA musicians' showcase' in *The Herald*, 27 December 1986).

apartheid activists and music lovers from Zambia, Botswana and South Africa[1], on public demand the intended one-off show was extended over the following three nights.[2] Also attended by Oliver Tambo and several Zimbabwean cabinet members[3], the musical journey through South Africa's political history—prominently featuring the role of Nelson Mandela[4]—contributed to lessening the distance between ANC and ZANU.

The popular initiatives launched in 1986-87 by the South African artists through 'Buwa' and their Swedish colleagues through 'Frontline Rock' had a significant impact with regard to Zimbabwe's increasingly active role as an important meeting ground for ANC in the final stages of the anti-apartheid struggle.[5] Inside the republic, the cultural boycott was at the same time sorely felt. Commenting on the wider significance of 'Buwa', *Weekly Mail*, for example, tersely noted that "[i]t's a shame South Africa will miss it".[6]

Official Support to ANC's Cultural Department

After virtually exploding onto the Southern African scene, SAAU's musical drama—subsequently affected by internal contradictions and defections[7]—was in late 1987 taken on a less successful international fund-raising tour, eventually having its formal première in Harare in November 1988. Although Semenya's initiative in the final event did not reap the laurels and funds expected, from the point of view of the main subject of this study it had an impact. Together with the parallel Frontline Rock project, it not only brought the Swedish NGO community into closer contacts with ANC's Department of Arts and Culture (DAC), but also SIDA and, in general, the official authorities. This was from 1986/87 expressed through the inclusion in the regular ANC cooperation programme of a specific budget post for cultural activities.[8] Above all, however, the wider field of culture would over the following years feature prominently within the post-apartheid planning programme discussed in the following chapter. In the meantime, a brief comment should be made on the official Swedish cultural support extended within the overall assistance to ANC in the late 1980s.

1. For many South Africans, 'Buwa' offered a rare opportunity to meet exiled family members. After decades of separation, the aged, but unbroken Thomas Masekela—the father of Barbara and Hugh Masekela and a keen amateur sculptor—travelled to Harare to join the Director of ANC's Department of Arts and Culture and the world-famous trumpet player (Author's recollection).
2. With a capacity of 800, the Seven Arts Theatre received in total well over 3,000 people for the extended preview.
3. *The Herald*, 16 January 1987. Among the ZANU ministers and politicians who attended the New Year's jamboree or the 'Buwa' preview were Ernest Kadungure, David Karimanzira, Witness Mangwende, Maurice Nyagumbo and Sydney Sekeramayi. A former student of Lund University, Sekeramayi—then Minister of Health—had in March 1986 met Dan Hylander, also from Lund, and the other visiting representatives of the 29 November Committee (Author's recollection).
4. Among the many highlights of 'Buwa' was Hugh Masekela's 'Mandela: Bring him back home!', staged before the artist—controversially—joined Paul Simon's 'Graceland' concert.
5. Cf. the interviews with ANC's Jaya Appalraju (p. 106) and ZANU's Didymus Mutasa (p. 220).
6. Andrew Robinson: 'SA exiles speak their minds' in *Weekly Mail*, 23-29 January 1987.
7. Notably by Jonas Gwangwa, Hugh Masekela and internally based South African artists, who were committed to other engagements.
8. Budget attached to 'Minutes from consultative talks in Lusaka, 2-5 December 1986, between the African National Congress of South Africa (ANC) and SIDA concerning humanitarian assistance', Lusaka, 5 December 1986 (SDA). In the adjusted annual budget for 1986/87, the allocation for cultural activities amounted to 539,000 SEK (ibid.).

Headed by Barbara Masekela[1], DAC was established by ANC as a follow-up to the July 1982 Botswana conference on 'Culture and Resistance'. Official Swedish support to the department was initially extended on an *ad hoc* basis, outside the annual allocation to the movement.[2] While SIDA during the second half of the 1980s continued to support extraordinary requests in favour of various cultural initiatives[3], at the annual aid negotiations in Lusaka in May 1986 ANC, however, suggested that cultural projects should be included in the regular cooperation programme.[4] This was welcomed by the Swedish authorities. Between 1986/87 and 1989/90, a total of 4.1 MSEK was allocated to DAC for the purpose.[5]

The bulk of these resources was used for the training of textile artists, as well as for the setting up of a textile printing workshop at ANC's Dakawa Development Centre in Tanzania. Originally envisaged as one of many activities at a planned, comprehensive Dakawa Cultural Centre, it would later turn out that the project became "the first, and only, aspect to be implemented".[6] As such, however, it was largely successful. While ANC trainees under the auspices of Artists Against Apartheid went to Sweden for studies, from 1987 the Swedish consultant Malin Sellman—who had previously worked at the Rorke's Drift Arts and Craft Centre in South Africa—started to develop the workshop, which eventually produced items of sufficient quality to be shown at art and handicraft exhibitions in Scandinavia and the Netherlands.[7]

Like other ANC projects in exile, the Dakawa textile printing workshop was caught up in the events that followed the unbanning of the movement and the release of Nelson Mandela. In this case, however, Barbara Masekela and her staff managed to move the activity to South Africa. Looms and other equipment bought in Sweden were shipped to the country, where Malin Sellman and previously Tanzania-based South African artists such as Vusi Khumalo and Tebogo Ditlhakanyane in mid-1991 set up a new Dakawa Art and Craft Community Centre in the Eastern Cape university town of Grahamstown, largely chosen because of its annual arts

---

1. Born in Johannesburg in 1941, after matriculation in Durban—where she had been introduced to ANC President-General Albert Luthuli—Masekela initially worked for the *New Age* newspaper before enrolling at the Lesotho campus of the University of Botswana, Lesotho and Swaziland. In 1963, she left for Ghana, eventually moving to the United States, where in 1965 she took up studies at Fordham University, New York. After a spell at the University of Zambia, in 1969 she returned to the United States. Joining Lindiwe Mabuza at Ohio University in 1970, she completed her BA degree, majoring in English literature. She then moved to the English department at Rutgers University, where she lectured until 1982. In the meantime, she completed her MA degree. Working closely with Johnny Makatini, ANC's representative to the United Nations, while in New York she was appointed chairperson of the movement's Regional Political Committee for the US, addressing anti-apartheid meetings all over the country. An acknowledged poet in her own right, in addition to women's issues Masekela—the sister of Hugh Masekela—was particularly concerned with the cultural boycott of South Africa. In August 1982, she moved to Zambia to work full-time for ANC. When ANC the following year decided to form a Department of Arts and Culture, she became its first Director. Under her leadership, the department would over the following years have a major impact on the international academic and cultural isolation of the Pretoria regime. Following ANC's unbanning in February 1990, she accompanied Nelson Mandela on his tours to the United States, India and other countries, eventually becoming Head of Staff in his office. Serving on ANC's negotiations' commission, in July 1991 Masekela was elected to the movement's National Executive Committee. In 1995, finally, she took up the position as South Africa's first black ambassador to France.
2. This was, for example, the case with *Amandla*'s visit to Sweden in 1983.
3. In early 1986, SIDA decided to support ANC's cultural journal *Rixaka* (Letter ('Rixaka funding document') from Barbara Masekela to SIDA, ANC, Lusaka, 26 February 1986) (SDA).
4. 'Agreed minutes [from] consultations in Lusaka, May 1986, between the African National Congress of South Africa and Sweden concerning humanitarian assistance', Lusaka, 9 May 1986 (SDA).
5. Agreed minutes for the period.
6. Séan Morrow: 'Dakawa Development Centre: An African National Congress Settlement in Tanzania, 1982-1992' in *African Affairs*, No. 389, October 1998, p. 518.
7. Ibid., p. 519.

festival. Officially opened by ANC's Deputy President Walter Sisulu on 17 October 1992[1], Sweden would continue to support the centre in the early 1990s.

The People's Parliament against Apartheid

Looking back on her years in Sweden, in 1999 Lindiwe Mabuza concluded that "[i]f the ANC [g]ala [...] marked the ultimate or pinnacle in cultural expression of solidarity, then the political climax would have [...] been the Swedish People's Parliament against Apartheid".[2] Leading ANC's delegation to the popular assembly in Stockholm, in his address to what he characterized as a "pioneering" and "epochmaking" initiative[3] President Tambo, similarly, expressed that

> [i]t is hard to find words to describe what I feel [...]. Never in the history of our struggle have we witnessed an event such as this People's Parliament. A whole nation has gathered in [the] capital [...] to discuss developments [which are] taking place at the opposite end of the globe.[4]

Originally suggested at a forum organized in 1982 by the United Nations Association of Sweden (SFN)[5], the idea of convening a national anti-apartheid 'parliament' with delegates from the Swedish popular movements[6] was pursued over the following years in consultations between SFN and the Isolate South Africa Committee (ISAK). By early 1985—at a time when more than 40 national organizations had joined ISAK[7] and 30 out of 279 municipal authorities were boycotting South African products[8]—the idea had developed into a concrete proposal.

Following preparations by a committee with representatives from *inter alia* the Africa Groups (AGIS), the Co-operative Union and Wholesale Society (KF), the Trade Union Confederation (LO), the Centre Party Women's League, the Liberal Party Youth League and church organizations[9], ISAK and SFN issued invitations to a *folkriksdag*, to be held at the People's Hall[10] in Stockholm from 21 to 23 February 1986. The objective was to "comprehensively strengthen the solidarity and opinion work for the liberation struggle in Southern Africa".[11] Local, regional and national Swedish organizations were invited. To mark the popular character and the difference vis-à-vis the official Swedish parliament, "political parties and their local organizations" were excluded from the civil society deliberations.[12]

Guided by the ISAK and SFN chairmen Lennart Renöfält and Jan Bergqvist, after intense voluntary work by the core organizations involved, their own financial

---

1. Shelagh Stow: 'Craft project triumph over oppression' in *Eastern Province Herald*, 19 October 1992.
2. Mabuza in Robben Island Museum, Mayibuye Centre and Nordic Africa Institute op. cit., p. 97.
3. 'Anförande av ANC's president Oliver Tambo' ('Address by ANC President Oliver Tambo') in ISAK and SFN op. cit., p. 124.
4. Ibid., p. 118.
5. Letter ('Ansökan om medel för [en] Folkriksdag mot Apartheid, 21-23 februari 1986'/'Request for funds for [a] People's Parliament against Apartheid, 21-23 February 1986') from ISAK and SFN to SIDA, Stockholm, 3 May 1985 (SDA).
6. On the role of the popular movements in 'Organization-Sweden', see Sellström Volume I, pp. 37-38.
7. For a brief presentation of ISAK, see the chapter 'SACTU, Unions and Sanctions'.
8. ISAK and AGIS: 'Anti-Apartheid Work in Sweden', [Stockholm], July 1985 (ISA).
9. ISAK and SFN op. cit., pp. 173-74.
10. In Swedish, *Folkets Hus*.
11. ISAK and SFN op. cit., p. 11.
12. Ibid., p. 12. Youth and women's branches of the political parties were, however, welcome to take part. The youth leagues of all the Swedish parliamentary parties—also including the Moderate youth—were represented.

inputs and official contributions through SIDA[1], the assembly was held in late February 1986, three months after the ANC musical gala in Gothenburg. With more than 1,000 delegates from some 700 organizations from Lund in the south to Kiruna in the north[2], the Swedish People's Parliament against Apartheid reflected a significant national opinion. Representing the culmination of three decades of popular mobilization against apartheid, it was the broadest manifestation of its kind ever to be staged in Sweden, by far surpassing any event organized against the Vietnam war or other international issues in the 1970s and the early 1980s.

As such, it attracted considerable international attention. Messages of encouragement were received from the United Nations Secretary General Javier Pérez de Cuéllar, the Indian Prime Minister Rajiv Gandhi on behalf of the Non-Aligned Movement, the Senegalese President Abdou Diouf for the Organization of African Unity and the Zambian President Kenneth Kaunda in the name of the Frontline States.[3] In addition to Prime Minister Olof Palme, ANC's Oliver Tambo[4], UDF's Yunus Mohamed[5] and SWAPO's Foreign Affairs Secretary Theo-Ben Gurirab[6], amongst others Joseph Garba of the UN Anti-Apartheid Committee, Sundie Kazunga of the UN Council for Namibia and Bishop Trevor Huddleston of the British Anti-Apartheid Movement were invited to address the opening session.

The actual 'parliamentary' proceedings were held in six different commissions[7], which brought their conclusions to a final plenary session. Here, the delegates were in agreement that the apartheid system should be condemned as "a crime against humanity and a threat to world peace", stressing that it represented "the worst expression of racism in our time". As "a shameful relic of the colonial era", the general declaration stated, "apartheid has institutionalized a colonial and racist system which both in theory and practice closely follows in the footsteps of Nazi Germany".[8] For the purpose of this study, it should more specifically be noted that the Swedish NGOs—with the notable exception of the Moderate Party Youth League—strongly pronounced themselves in favour of ANC and demanded an immediate end to Sweden's economic, cultural and other relations with the apartheid state.

With regard to the path of the South African struggle, the popular assembly stated the opinion that "[t]he Freedom Charter [...] remains the basic document", declaring "its support for [...] the direction of the liberation struggle expressed therein".[9] Thus disregarding the views held by PAC, AZAPO and other non-Char-

---

1. Through SIDA, the Swedish government contributed 175,000 SEK to the estimated costs of 360,000 SEK (Elisabeth Michanek: Memorandum ('Ansökan från Isolera Sydafrikakommittén och Svenska FN-förbundet om medel för en Folkriksdag mot Apartheid'/'Request from ISAK and SFN for funds towards a People's Parliament against Apartheid'), SIDA/CCHA, [Stockholm], 29 May 1985, and CCHA: 'Protokoll [från sammanträde 6 juni 1985]'/'Minutes [from meeting 6 June 1985]', SIDA, Stockholm, 12 June 1985) (SDA).
2. ISAK and SFN op. cit., pp. 22 and 176-93.
3. Ibid., pp. 5 and 166-71.
4. Tambo was accompanied *inter alia* by Thabo Mbeki, Lindiwe Mabuza and Jacob Chilwane.
5. The future South African Minister of Sports and Recreation Steve Tshwete—who had recently joined ANC in exile—represented UDF together with Mohamed.
6. SWAPO was represented by Theo-Ben Gurirab, Hidipo Hamutenya and—from its internal wing—Nico Bessinger.
7. The commissions discussed a) South Africa as a threat to world peace, b) Apartheid oppression and the struggle for freedom in South Africa, c) Freedom for Namibia, d) Development aid as a component of the struggle against apartheid: Support to the Frontline States, e) Isolating apartheid: Economic sanctions, and f) No collaboration with apartheid: Opinion work, culture and sports.
8. ISAK and SFN op. cit., p. 22.
9. ISAK and SFN op. cit., p. 41.

terist organizations[1], the People's Parliament confirmed ANC's hegemonic position in Sweden. Calling for increased official and NGO assistance to the movement, ANC was characterized as "the leading force in the struggle against apartheid" and was together with SWAPO of Namibia "wholeheartedly" supported.[2] In addition, the assembly advocated assistance to UDF and COSATU, as well as to "the underground trade union federation SACTU".[3] With regard to the forms of the struggle, the final declaration further emphasized "the right [of the South African people] to determine [...] which methods to adopt in order to defend and liberate itself from the oppression of the apartheid system. The apartheid regime, not the liberation movement", it concluded, "bears the full burden of responsibility for the violent confrontation which is now escalating".[4]

While these positions were not in contradiction with the policy which had been pursued for more than a decade by the Swedish government, it was with regard to Sweden's continuing economic relations with South Africa and the firm demand for complete isolation of the regime that the People's Parliament against Apartheid and the subsequent NGO opinion work would have a direct impact. The economic relations and the third, final national sanctions debate will be presented in the next chapter. In the meantime, it remains to be underlined that the popular forum characterized the Swedish trade relations with South Africa as "morally reprehensible [...], increasingly unacceptable and offensive".[5] Similarly rejecting the 'hibernation' of Swedish companies in the apartheid republic—allowed under the 1979 legislation against new investments—the delegates requested the Social Democratic government to impose a total boycott without delay.[6]

Although the delegates noted "the positive role played by Sweden at the United Nations to achieve a broad agreement on measures to isolate apartheid"[7]—an opinion shared by ANC President Oliver Tambo[8]—in the light of the Western powers' opposition to a binding Security Council resolution they urged the government to take unilateral action. Stressing that a boycott "must be seen as a foreign policy issue and not as a technical trade consideration"[9], the Swedish People's Parliament against Apartheid requested the government

---

1. Neither PAC nor AZAPO were invited to the People's Parliament. In his address to the assembly, UDF's Yunus Mohamed stated that "[o]rganizations like PAC and the Unity Movement do not enjoy any support worth mentioning [in South Africa]" (ibid., p. 134). However, a few individual delegates representing the Christian Democratic Youth (*Kristen Demokratisk Ungdom*) advocated support for PAC too (ibid., p. 94).
2. Ibid., pp. 25 and 44. Representing a distinct minority opinion, delegates from the Moderate Party Youth League, however, strongly denounced ANC. In a statement of dissent, they argued that "we cannot give our support to ANC, an organization which merely will replace today's oppression with another kind of oppression. We condemn ANC's violent actions, which increasingly affect the civilian population. The [assertion] that ANC has a broad political base is [...] not in accordance with the truth. The political influence of the Communist Party is completely dominant among ANC's leaders". Against this background, the Moderate youth members demanded that "no Swedish support shall be given to ANC" (ibid., p. 95).
3. Ibid., pp. 44-46.
4. Ibid., p. 24.
5. Ibid., pp. 70 and 77.
6. Also in this respect, the representatives from the Moderate Party Youth League submitted statements of dissent, instead of isolation advocating a policy of 'constructive engagement' (ibid., pp. 101-104).
7. Ibid., p. 70.
8. In Prime Minister Palme's presence, Tambo stated in his speech: "I want to use this opportunity to express our appreciation of the measures already taken by Sweden to isolate South Africa [...]. [The Swedish stand] is of great international significance, since it serves as an example for other countries, showing that sanctions can and must be imposed, unilaterally if necessary. We wish that Sweden continues to play a pioneering role in the struggle against apartheid. It appears to us [, however,] that the Swedish companies' reluctance to withdraw from South Africa amounts to a deliberate rejection of the Swedish people's demands [...]. Perhaps the time has come to force these companies to end their destructive participation in the apartheid system. It is encouraging that a broad popular campaign with this objective in mind has already been launched. The initiatives taken to stop the trade with South Africa pave the way for further actions in this regard" (ibid., p. 122).
9. Ibid., p. 77.

– to promptly draft [...] a plan for the phasing out of the activities and investments of Swedish companies in South Africa and Namibia,

– to prepare a bill [...] prohibiting the companies' activities [there], and

– to immediately present a bill bringing all trade with South Africa to an end.[1]

In addition to strict isolation in the fields of culture and sports[2], these were demands that AGIS and ISAK had raised since the early 1980s and from then on would be made by the broader Swedish anti-apartheid movement. What in this context stands out as exceptional by international comparison is the fact that the NGO boycott campaign was encouraged and largely financed through official funds. In January 1987—in the midst of the parliamentary sanctions debate—Margareta Winberg[3] and Torgny Larsson, MPs for the ruling Social Democratic Party, submitted a motion proposing that the Africa Groups and the Isolate South Africa Committee instead of *ad hoc* project contributions should be accorded general official grants on an annual basis.[4] The proposal was endorsed. In the case of ISAK alone, between 1985/86 and 1991/92 the Swedish authorities granted the organization a total of 5.8 MSEK, mainly for national and international information activities with regard to boycott issues.[5]

Olof Palme's Last Appearance

The Swedish People's Parliament against Apartheid will, finally, be remembered as the last public forum attended by Olof Palme. To stress the popular character of the event, the organizers had decided not to invite political parties represented in the national parliament or any official authority, institution or spokesperson. On account of his lifelong personal commitment to the anti-apartheid cause—most recently through his backing of the rock artists' November 1985 ANC gala—an exception was, however, made in the case of the Prime Minister himself. Palme was asked to address the opening session on 21 February 1986. Exactly one week later—at midnight on 28 February—he was gunned down by an assassin three blocks away from the People's Hall in Stockholm where the popular assembly had taken place.

As has been evident throughout this study, Palme was during his entire political career concerned and closely involved with the struggles for national liberation, majority rule and democracy in Southern Africa. Actively advocating support for the liberation movements—in this respect having a decisive impact on the Swedish Social Democratic Party and the Socialist International[6]—South Africa and Namibia had always featured prominently. When in February 1986 he added his voice to those of ANC's Oliver Tambo, UDF and SWAPO at the NGO *folkriksdag*,

---

1. Ibid., pp. 71 and 77.
2. Ibid., pp. 84-85.
3. In 1994, Winberg joined the Swedish government as Minister of Agriculture.
4. Swedish Parliament 1986/87: Motion No. U 226, Riksdagens Protokoll 1986/87, p. 14.
5. Letter ('Slutrapportering av bidrag till ISAK'/'Final report on contributions to ISAK') from Helene Wede to ISAK, SIDA, Stockholm, 14 February 1992 (SDA).
6. Cf. the following statement made by Gro Harlem Brundtland, Prime Minister of Norway and chairperson of the Norwegian Labour Party: "The active support given by Olof Palme and Sweden to the liberation movements in the 1960s is probably one of Palme's most important political contributions to further North-South dialogue. Twenty years later, this support may seem obvious. We must remember, however, that in the 1960s the liberation movements were considered of a dubious nature in the Western world, even far into the social democratic movement. Olof Palme took the lead in supporting the liberation and freedom of those Third World countries that did not benefit from peaceful decolonization within the UN framework. In the 1960s, Palme's political leadership in this context was courageous and [...] had far-reaching consequences" (Gro Harlem Brundtland: 'The Scandinavian Perspective on the North-South Dialogue' in Hadjor (ed.) op. cit., p. 15).

it followed naturally from his 'first political act' in favour of South African students in the late 1940s; his anti-colonial message to Swedish youth associations at Sånga-Säby in November 1953[1]; his First of May speech against racism and apartheid in Kramfors in 1964[2]; his chairmanship of the Namibia conference in Oxford in 1966[3]; and his 'crusade' against the white minority regimes in Southern Africa in 1977.[4]

Characterizing apartheid and international support of the racist minority regime as "an incredible example of [...] insanity" and as "a classic example of madness of which nothing can come but evil"[5], in his militant speech Palme stated:

> Fundamentally, [the issue of apartheid] is a profoundly emotional question [...] which goes to the depths of our feelings because it is such an uncommonly repugnant system. [...] [O]n account of people's colour, [apartheid] abandons them to poverty. This system will be to the discredit of the world for as long as it persists. [...]

> What we are now witnessing in South Africa is a vicious circle of increased violence in defence of a system that is already doomed. It is only shortsightedness, a disinclination to see reality as it is, that makes the white minority cling firmly to power through continued oppression of its own population and terrorism towards neighbouring countries. The white people must be aware of their own interests in negotiating a peaceful solution, while such a solution is still at all possible. [...]

> [T]he reaction of the rest of the world is of great importance. Pressure on the regime must increase. It must be made clear to the minority regime that it has no support in the outside world. [...] [The] system can live on because it gets [such] support. [However, i]f the support is pulled away and turned into resistance, apartheid cannot endure. If the world decides to abolish apartheid, apartheid will disappear. [...]

> [G]iven the vested interests of finance and of the superpowers, there is [one] classic way forward, namely that of mobilizing popular opinion in support of human dignity. And that is the essential importance of a popular assembly like this [...]. [B]y declaring our support for the struggle [of the black population and] by helping to isolate the apartheid regime, we must live up to our responsibility for bringing this repulsive system to an end.[6]

Having known each other for more than twenty years[7], the People's Parliament against Apartheid marked the end of the close cooperation and deep friendship between Palme and Tambo.[8] In addition to discussions at the NGO assembly itself, during the ANC President's stay they also met for bilateral talks. The last recorded meeting between the two took place at the Prime Minister's Office on 21 February 1986. Tambo was accompanied by Thabo Mbeki and Lindiwe Mabuza, while

---

1. See Sellström Volume I, pp. 95-96.
2. Ibid., p. 225.
3. Ibid., pp. 273-77.
4. Palme's 1977 'crusade' is presented in the chapter 'SACTU, Unions and Sanctions'.
5. Palme op. cit. in *Development Dialogue*, No. 1, 1987, p. 73.
6. Palme op. cit. in *Development Dialogue*, No. 1, 1987, pp. 64-73. When in September 1996 the South African death squad commander Eugene de Kock stated that the apartheid regime was behind the assassination of Olof Palme, several Swedish newspapers linked the killing to Palme's speech to the People's Parliament (cf. Wolfgang Hansson: 'Palme: De vitas stora hot'/'Palme: The great threat to the whites' in *Aftonbladet*, 27 September 1996; Kaa Eneberg: 'Eldigt tal om bojkott retade regimen'/'Fiery speech on boycott provoked the regime' in *Dagens Nyheter*, 27 September 1996; and Anders Leopold: 'Mordagenten satt i publiken'/'The assassin was in the audience' in *Expressen*, 27 September 1996). Not until early 1998—twelve years after the assassination—did the official Palme Inquest study ISAK's documentation from the popular assembly, including lists of the participants (*Granskningskommissionens Betänkande* op. cit., p. 447).
7. Palme op. cit. in *Development Dialogue*, No. 1, 1987, p. 64. As far as can be reliably established, Palme and Tambo met for the first time in Stockholm in August 1962 (Sellström Volume I, p. 111).
8. On the friendship between Palme and Tambo, see the interviews with ANC's Lindiwe Mabuza (p. 141) and the Social Democratic Party's Bengt Säve-Söderbergh (p. 338).

Meeting for the last time: ANC President Oliver Tambo and Prime Minister Olof Palme
during the Swedish People's Parliament against Apartheid, Stockholm, February 1986
(Photo: Jim Elfström/IKON, Svenska kyrkans bildbyrå)

Bengt Säve-Söderbergh, Under-Secretary of State for International Development
Cooperation, Anders Möllander and Stefan Noréen, first secretaries at the Foreign
Ministry, and Gunnar Stenarv, international secretary of the Social Democratic
Party, joined Palme.[1] Among the questions discussed were the situation in Lesotho
after the military takeover the previous month and the rumours about a release of
Nelson Mandela.[2] Seeing a faint light at the end of the tunnel, during their final
encounters in Stockholm Palme and Tambo, finally, agreed on the importance of
Swedish support for a broad, preparatory ANC project towards a post-apartheid
dispensation.

Four years later, Mandela was eventually released. He soon went to Sweden to
consult with Tambo, then hospitalized at the Ersta clinic in Stockholm.[3] Palme,
however, did not live to meet the legendary ANC leader whose freedom he so persistently had demanded since 1964[4], or to experience the transition towards
democracy in the land of apartheid. One and a half decades later, one of the 'trails'
in the unsolved Palme assassination remained South African.[5] In a semi-official
biographical sketch of Thabo Mbeki, a team close to the future President stated

1. Anders Möllander: Memorandum ('ANC's president Oliver Tambo hos statsministern'/'ANC President Oliver
   Tambo with the Prime Minister'), Ministry for Foreign Affairs, Stockholm, 26 February 1986 (MFA).
2. Ibid.
3. Suffering from a cerebral haemorrhage, in August 1989 Tambo entered a London hospital. In early January
   1990—one month before ANC's unbanning and Mandela's release—he was moved to Ersta, a clinic specializing in the rehabilitation of patients with brain damage. Staying there until the end of April 1990, after thirty
   years of exile Tambo subsequently returned to South Africa. He died in April 1993. On Tambo's contacts
   with the Swedish government during his stay at the Ersta clinic, see the interview with the former Cooperation and Foreign Minister Lena Hjelm-Wallén: "I remember what it was like to be there, just sitting with him,
   holding his hand. He was lonely at Ersta and we tried to visit him as much as possible. Not many governments were so close to a leader of a liberation movement" (pp. 293-94).
4. Cf. Palme's 1964 Labour Day speech in Kramfors in Sellström Volume I, p. 225.
5. See the chapter 'Black Consciousness, IUEF and Operation Daisy'.

in 1998 that "to this day suspicions persist that Olof Palme was assassinated because of his support for the ANC".[1]

Meanwhile, the news of Palme's death was received with grief and anger by ANC. In a message of condolence to Palme's successor Ingvar Carlsson—published in the movement's organ *Sechaba*—President Tambo wrote:

> We have received with extreme shock and heartfelt grief news of the death of our very dear brother, the Prime Minister of Sweden, Olof Palme, a death that came as a lightning bolt out of the cloudless skies. The unspeakable crime of his assassination has sent a stunning shockwave throughout the ranks of the leadership and membership of the African National Congress and the millions of our people.[2] We had come to know him not only as a leader of the Swedish people and an international statesman, but also as one of us, a fellow combatant who [...] made an inestimable contribution to the struggle for the liberation of South Africa.
>
> The murderer's gun that fired the fatal shot was aimed directly against the ANC and our people as well [...]. We who saw him only a week ago—drawing strength from his confidence in the proximity of our victory—know it in our hearts that [...] his [last] thoughts were about those who are struggling for their emancipation, for a decent life in conditions of liberty and for a world free of wars. From Vietnam to Nicaragua, from El Salvador to Palestine, from Sahara to South Africa, across the face of the globe, the flags hang limp and at half mast in loving memory of this giant of justice who had become a citizen of the world, a brother and comrade to all who are downtrodden.[3]

---

1. Mbeki op. cit., p. xix.
2. Based at the Swedish embassy in Harare at the time, the author recalls how ANC members living in Zimbabwe spontaneously would phone to communicate their grief, both to the embassy and to the staff members' private residences.
3. 'ANC Pays Tribute to Olof Palme' in *Sechaba*, April 1986, p. 22. While 'Terror' Lekota, Popo Molefe and other UDF leaders facing possible death sentences in the 'Delmas 22 Trial' in early March 1986 smuggled out a similar message, Lindiwe Mabuza, ANC's resident Chief Representative to Sweden, dedicated a longer epic to Olof Palme. With a preface by Oliver Tambo, it was published in 1987 in a bilingual English-Swedish edition under the title *To Sweden from ANC* by the Social Democratic Party (Lindiwe Mabuza: *Till Sverige från ANC*, Socialdemokraterna, Stockholm, 1987). During his official visit to the United States in January 1987, President Tambo delivered the first 'Olof Palme Memorial Lecture on Disarmament and Development' in the Riverside Church, New York.

Banning of Trade and Planning
for Post-Apartheid

Increasing Commodity Exchange

The final Swedish sanctions debate focused in the mid-1980s on the trade relations with South Africa. Under Ola Ullsten's minority government, Sweden had in July 1979 become the first country with significant interests in the apartheid economy to ban new investments, allowing, however, already established subsidiaries to 'hibernate' in the country.[1] Although commodity trade was not affected, the legislation was controversial from the outset. Firmly opposed by the export-oriented business community and the Moderate Party, the law was at the same time found wanting not only by the anti-apartheid solidarity movement, but also by the political parties which had promoted it, including the opposition Social Democratic Party. In October 1980, the Centre leader Thorbjörn Fälldin's second non-socialist coalition government therefore decided to assess the so called 'South Africa law'.[2] And in December 1981—during his third coalition cabinet[3]—a parliamentary commission was appointed to undertake the review.

Chaired by ambassador Sverker Åström[4], the commission presented its findings to Olof Palme's Social Democratic government in June 1984. Although it noted that the 1979 unilateral ban on new investments—a significant departure from Sweden's traditional foreign and security policy—"undoubtedly [had] played a role [...] as an encouragement and a signal [...] to the apartheid opponents in South Africa", it was "forced" to conclude that "one of the most important [aspects] of the law, [namely,] to serve as a model for similar measures in other countries, only had been achieved to a very limited extent".[5] This notwithstanding, the commission considered an abrogation of the legislation "out of the question"[6], suggesting instead a number of areas where it could be tightened up.[7]

---

1. See the chapter 'SACTU, Unions and Sanctions'.
2. The law also applied to Namibia. On Sweden's insignificant economic exchange with this country, see the chapter 'SWAPO of Namibia: Tentative Steps towards Firm Relations'.
3. Excluding the Moderate Party, Fälldin's Centre and Liberal coalition ruled from May 1981 until October 1982, when the Social Democratic Party under Olof Palme returned to power.
4. Ulla Ström from the Ministry for Foreign Affairs—previously administering Sweden's assistance to ANC at SIDA—served as secretary to the commission.
5. SOU (1984) op. cit., pp. 108-109. In spite of the 1978 Nordic Programme of Action against Apartheid, Denmark and Finland did not legislate against investments in South Africa and Namibia until May and November 1985, respectively. In May 1986, Denmark, however, became the first Nordic country to introduce a comprehensive trade boycott.
6. SOU (1984) op. cit., p. 109.
7. Representing the Moderates, the future party leader Bo Lundgren (1999-) took a dissenting stand, advocating outright abrogation of the 1979 legislation (ibid., p. 221).

Largely based on the commission report, between March 1985 and May 1986 the Swedish parliament endorsed four new government bills against apartheid South Africa, covering *inter alia* leasing arrangements, technology transfers and trade licenses.[1] Paving the way for a comprehensive trade boycott, the legislation included a far-reaching ban on the importing of South African agricultural products, including wine[2], as well as according the right to municipal and regional councils to impose local boycotts. These were demands which had been raised for a long time by AGIS and ISAK[3] and at the level of parliament notably by the Centre Party.[4]

In stark contrast to these measures and, above all, to the rapidly increasing official allocations to ANC[5], bilateral trade relations continued, however, unfettered by any legal restrictions. While the total value of Swedish exports to South Africa in 1978 amounted to 411 MSEK, from 1979—when the investment ban was declared—it would, in current figures, register a spectacular growth, reaching 1,017 MSEK in 1981 and no less than 1,575 MSEK in 1984, an increase of almost 300 per cent.[6] Although less pronounced, imports from the apartheid republic showed a similar trend, increasing from 177 MSEK in 1978 to 388 MSEK in 1984, or by more than 100 per cent.[7] This extraordinary development is illustrated in the following graph:

---

1. For information on the Swedish sanctions laws, see Appendix VII. In June 1982, the Fälldin government restricted the granting of visas to Sweden for South Africans representing the apartheid regime.

2. In 1948, Sweden was the world's second largest buyer of South African fruit, and in 1984 fruit and vegetables still accounted for 28 per cent of the value of the imports from South Africa ('Press release' [in English], Ministry for Foreign Affairs, Stockholm, 2 September 1985) (SDA). The decision to prohibit the importing of agricultural products was based on the fact that these were largely supplied through prison labour, a system which in South Africa had been officially in force since the early 1930s. Until 1985, the Social Democratic government argued that obligations under the international General Agreement on Tariffs and Trade (GATT)—in addition to a binding UN Security Council resolution—excluded unilateral Swedish boycott measures. Following intense information work by AGIS, ISAK and other actors, eventually, however, it paid heed to the GATT clause which allowed for exemption in the case of prisoners or forced labour being used in a production process (Ministry for Foreign Affairs: *Prohibition of Imports of Agricultural Produce from South Africa*, Stockholm, December 1985, pp. 23-28).

3. Cf. the interview with AGIS' Sören Lindh, p. 308. South African fruit and other agricultural produce were particularly targeted during the Swedish consumer boycotts in the early 1960s (see Sellström Volume I, pp. 181-98).

4. Beginning in January 1981, Pär Granstedt of the Centre Party submitted parliamentary motions to make it legally possible for local councils to boycott South African products (Swedish Parliament 1981/82: Motion No. 931, Riksdagens Protokoll 1981/82, pp. 7-8). Pushed by the first generation South Africa Committees, many councils had in the early 1960s unilaterally decided to refuse goods from the apartheid republic. By June 1965, no less than 20 of Sweden's 24 regional councils boycotted South Africa (Sellström Volume I, p. 223).

5. Between 1976/77 and 1983/84, the official annual allocations to ANC were raised from 5.5 to 32 MSEK, an increase of 480 per cent.

6. See Appendix VI: 'Swedish commodity trade with South Africa 1950-1990'. As earlier noted, the increase was largely due to transactions between Swedish parent companies and their South African subsidiaries in order to circumvent the investment ban.

7. Ibid. Imports from South Africa peaked in 1985, when they reached 413 MSEK. After the ban on agricultural products—effective from 1 January 1986—they rapidly fell. In 1986, Sweden imported South African goods for a total value of 146 MSEK, representing a decrease from the previous year of 65 per cent (ibid.).

Sweden's commodity trade with South Africa 1950–1990
(current amounts in millions of SEK)

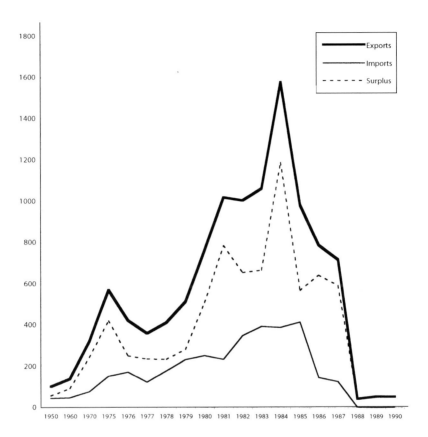

Source: Statistiska Centralbyrån

Although South Africa played a marginal role in Sweden's total commodity exchange—in 1984 merely accounting for 0.6 per cent of its exports and 0.2 per cent of its imports—the trade was highly advantageous. In 1984, the surplus in Sweden's favour amounted to no less than 1,187 MSEK, representing 4.9 per cent of the overall positive trade balance.[1] While this influenced both the Swedish export companies and part of the trade union movement—notably the Metalworkers Union[2]—it was, however, not raised as a fundamental political argument in the mid-1980s boycott debate. This centred instead on security, foreign and trade policy principles, in particular Sweden's adherence to the UN Charter and membership of the General Agreement on Tariffs and Trade (GATT). Focusing its attention on

---

1. Statistiska Centralbyrån: *Statistisk Årsbok för Sverige: 1988* ('Statistical Abstract of Sweden: 1988'), Statistics Sweden, Stockholm, 1987, table 135, pp. 142-43.

2. The role played by *Metall* was discussed in the chapter 'SACTU, Unions and Sanctions'. As noted, the issue of job security—both in Sweden and in South Africa—was a central concern raised against a comprehensive boycott.

the parliamentary parties, the following presentation summarizes the debate, which after considerable tensions ended in a decision on a comprehensive trade embargo from 1 July 1987.

Social Democratic Wavering

Although—with the exception of the Moderate Party—there was a broad parliamentary majority in favour of official assistance to ANC, in the early to mid-1980s the political parties were less united with regard to the liberation movement's call for economic isolation of the apartheid regime.[1] In January 1981, for example, the Centre Party MP Sven Johansson sided with the Moderate Party in opposing the investment ban and, thus, his own government, stating in a parliamentary motion that "isolation of South Africa leads nowhere".[2] The Liberals were also divided. In 1984, a principled exchange took place in the journal *Liberal Debatt* between Olle Wästberg, representing the Liberal Party on the parliamentary South Africa review commission, and Ernst Klein, head of the foreign desk at the newspaper *Expressen*. While Wästberg advocated firmer measures against South Africa—arguing that "Swedish companies take part in a brutal racial oppression"[3]—Klein demanded that the "policy of isolation [should be] abandoned".[4]

As in the case of the Centre MP Sven Johansson, Klein thus added his voice to that of the Moderate Party. Against a background of mounting popular boycott demands, this opposition, in turn, became particularly active in the mid-1980s, after the presentation of the South Africa review commission's report. In November 1984, the future Prime Minister Carl Bildt, his colleague and future Foreign Minister Margaretha af Ugglas, Bo Lundgren and other Moderate Party MPs rejected the 1979 investment ban and the Social Democratic government's bill to tighten up the legislation.[5] Over the following years, Bildt would with equal determination oppose all proposals for a unilateral trade boycott.[6]

In this respect, it was above all the Moderate Party chairman Ulf Adelsohn[7] who through a number of spectacular statements was in the public limelight. Visiting a mining company in the central parts of Sweden in August 1985, against the

---

1. In his Ph. D. dissertation from 1991, Nordenmark gives a schematic picture of the parliamentary situation in the mid-1980s. According to him, the Left Party Communists, the Centre Party and the Liberal Party were in favour of comprehensive sanctions, while the ruling Social Democratic Party together with the Moderate Party were against (Nordenmark op. cit., figure 8, p. 118). While the Left Party Communists since the late 1970s advocated unilateral economic isolation and the Moderate Party opposed such measures, with regard to the non-socialist 'middle' parties and the ruling party the situation was, however, much more complex.
2. Swedish Parliament 1980/81: Motion No. 1590, Riksdagens Protokoll, p. 11.
3. Olle Wästberg: 'Sluta Delta i Apartheidpolitiken!' ('Stop Participating in Apartheid's Policy!') in *Liberal Debatt*, No. 5, 1984, pp. 34-36.
4. Ernst Klein: 'Sydafrikas Framtid Är Svart' ('South Africa's Future Is Black') in *Liberal Debatt*, No. 6, 1984, pp. 38-41.
5. Swedish Parliament 1984/85: Motion No. 166, Riksdagens Protokoll, pp. 10-20.
6. See, for example, Swedish Parliament 1986/87: Motion No. U112, Riksdagens Protokoll, pp. 5-14.
7. Adelsohn chaired the Moderate Party between 1981 and 1986.

opinion held by the managing director[1] he reluctantly conceded that he "possibly" could accept a UN-supported boycott, adding, however, that "[i]f we boycott their products, the poor Negroes in South Africa will be without jobs".[2] The comment was made during the run-up to the September 1985 national elections, and Adelsohn's insensitivity towards the South African liberation struggle was quickly capitalized upon by the ruling party. Four days later, the Foreign Affairs' Under-Secretary of State Pierre Schori published an article in *Aftonbladet* in which he emphasized that the Moderate Party "fortunately" did not represent Sweden, which under Social Democratic rule, he added, "always and without hesitation will stand on the side of freedom in South Africa".[3]

With regard to the issue of a unilateral trade boycott, the Social Democratic government would, however, show a great amount of hesitancy. As leader of the opposition, Olof Palme had in March 1977 stated that "free human beings are more important than free movements of capital"[4], and in May 1983 Foreign Minister Lennart Bodström concluded that "since apartheid [...] is mainly an economic system, it is by economic measures that it must be attacked".[5] Nevertheless, on account of Sweden's policy of non-alignment, the government maintained that comprehensive sanctions could only be introduced following a decision by the UN Security Council.[6]

In the light of the rapidly deteriorating situation in South and Southern Africa; international reactions, particularly in neighbouring Denmark and Norway; and mounting political pressure at home, it became increasingly difficult to uphold this traditional foreign and security principle. In mid-1986, the boycott debate thus landed Ingvar Carlsson—Palme's successor as party leader and Prime Minister—with his first political crisis.

Several developments led to this situation. In July 1985, the South African President P.W. Botha imposed a state of emergency. Delivering his so called 'Rubicon speech'[7], in August he proceeded to rule out any significant reforms of the racist political system. And in September, Finance Minister Barend du Plessis unilaterally

---

1. Facing strong competition from South Africa, Ulf Juvél, the managing director of the Persberg company, told Adelsohn that he was not against a Swedish boycott.

2. Cited in Kalle Jungkvist: 'Ett uttalande det blir bråk om' ('A statement which will cause trouble') in *Aftonbladet*, 13 August 1985.

3. Pierre Schori: 'Äntligen reagerar världen mot Sydafrika' ('Finally the world reacts against South Africa') in *Aftonbladet*, 17 August 1985.

4. Cited in Schori (1994) op. cit., p. 27.

5. 'Speech by the Minister for Foreign Affairs, Mr. Lennart Bodström, on Africa Day in Stockholm, concerning Southern Africa', 24 May 1983, in Ministry for Foreign Affairs: *Documents on Swedish Foreign Policy: 1983*, Stockholm, 1987, p. 193.

6. Closely involved with the South African liberation struggle since the 1960s, Mats Hellström, Social Democratic Minister for Foreign Trade (1983-86), persistently rejected the idea of a unilateral Swedish trade ban. See, for example, Anders Mellbourn: 'Sverige avvaktar' ('Sweden waits and sees') in *Dagens Nyheter*, 27 July 1985.

7. President Botha's much awaited August 1985 address to the National Party congress in Durban became known as the 'Rubicon speech' following hints by Foreign Minister 'Pik' Botha that the President would announce far-reaching reforms, leading to an end to apartheid and, thus, to 'a crossing of the Rubicon'. In his speech, however, P.W. Botha rejected significant reforms and the inclusion of the black population in the national political system, angrily denouncing 'foreign interference' in South Africa's internal affairs.

announced a freeze on the country's foreign loan repayments, turning South Africa into "the first major country in the world to default".[1] Reflecting the apartheid regime's deep political and economic crisis, as a result the pressure for international sanctions immediately increased. Against President Reagan's policy of 'constructive engagement', the US Congress submitted draft legislation which aimed at severely curtailing the United States economic relations with South Africa. Similar measures were introduced by the Commonwealth, the European Community and a number of individual countries around the world.[2]

Meanwhile, in Sweden the demands for a trade ban intensified. While the labour movement through LO and the churches via the Swedish Ecumenical Council in August 1985 issued a joint call for a boycott[3]; the congress of the LO-affiliated Public Employees Union[4] passed a resolution to that effect[5]; and the independent Dockworkers Union[6] refused to handle South African goods during September[7], important branches of the ruling Social Democratic Party—notably the Youth League, the Women's League and the Brotherhood Movement—increased the pressure for unilateral action.

In addition to the public opinion effects of the People's Parliament against Apartheid, of more significant political consequence was the common position taken by the opposition Liberal and Centre parties. Supporting the demands for a comprehensive boycott raised by the Left Party Communists since the late 1970s, in June 1986 the boards of the two non-socialist parties requested an end to all trade with South Africa.[8] As in the case of the 1979 investment legislation—where Norway had served as an example[9]—this stand was largely influenced by developments at the Nordic level. As the first signatory of the 'Oslo plan', on 30 May 1986 Denmark—at the time a member of the UN Security Council—thus adopted a compre-

---

1. Joseph Hanlon and Roger Omond: *The Sanctions Handbook*, Penguin Books, Harmondsworth, 1987, p. 210.

2. The principal Commonwealth and EC measures on South Africa were adopted in September 1986. Overriding President Reagan's veto, the US Congress passed a Comprehensive Anti-Apartheid Act in October 1986. In the latter case, it was not only designed to put pressure on the apartheid regime, but also on ANC and PAC. The act laid down that "United States policy toward the African National Congress, the Pan African Congress (*sic*) and their affiliates shall be designed to bring about a suspension of violence that will lead to the start of negotiations [for] a non-racial and genuine democracy in South Africa. The United States shall work toward this goal by encouraging [ANC, PAC] and their affiliates to 1) suspend terrorist activities [...]; 2) make known their commitment to a free and democratic post-apartheid South Africa; 3) agree to enter into negotiations with the South African government and other groups [...]; [and] 4) reexamine their ties to the South African Communist Party" ('US Comprehensive Anti-Apartheid Act of 1986' in Merle Lipton: 'Sanctions and South Africa: The Dynamics of Economic Isolation', Special report No. 1119, The Economist Intelligence Unit, London, January 1988, p. 139).

3. Cecilia Steen-Johnsson: 'Kyrkan stöder LO' ('The church supports LO') in *Dagens Nyheter*, 24 August 1985.

4. In Swedish, *Statsanställdas Förbund*.

5. Per Carleson: 'Facklig protest mot Sydafrika' ('Trade union protest against South Africa') in *Dagens Nyheter*, 20 August 1985.

6. In Swedish, *Svenska Hamnarbetareförbundet*. Founded in 1972, the Dockworkers Union was not affiliated to LO.

7. Anders Nordström: 'Blockad mot Sydafrika' ('Embargo on South Africa') in *Dagens Nyheter*, 24 August 1985.

8. Nordenmark op. cit., p. 116.

9. See the chapter 'SACTU, Unions and Sanctions'.

hensive ban on trade with the apartheid republic.[1]

Challenged on all fronts, except by the Moderate Party and the Swedish business community, Ingvar Carlsson's Social Democratic government, however, continued to reject the idea of a trade boycott, in addition to a binding UN resolution arguing that "a unilateral Swedish [decision] would be in contravention of the GATT instrument".[2] This, in turn, unleashed massive criticism, not only domestically, but also in the Nordic countries and from a number of prominent South African apartheid opponents.

Inspired by the Danish parliament's boycott decision, in early June 1986 the LO-owned social democratic newspaper *Aftonbladet* called upon Sweden to follow suit.[3] When the Norwegian Labour government through Prime Minister Gro Harlem Brundtland announced the following month that it, too, would introduce a boycott bill, on 24 July her colleague Ingvar Carlsson, however, stated that Sweden "as a small neutral country could not budge from [its obligations under] international law and [...] agreements", cryptically adding that this "perhaps was easier for Norway, which formed part of NATO".[4]

The reaction to the statement was immediate and damning. While Anna Lindh, chairperson of the Social Democratic Youth League[5], commented that it would be "humiliating" if Sweden did not join the other Scandinavian countries[6], in an editorial *Aftonbladet* rejected Carlsson's arguments, concluding that "[t]he government should immediately impose a total Swedish economic boycott on South Africa".[7] Similar criticism and demands were raised by the editors of *Arbetet* and five other

---

1. At the time, Denmark had a non-socialist coalition government, with Poul Schlüter from the Conservatives as Prime Minister. With regard to the ensuing Swedish debate, it should be noted that it was the Danish parliamentary opposition—led by the Social Democratic Party—which introduced the boycott bill, and that the MPs from the ruling coalition abstained from voting when it was adopted (Christopher Munthe Morgenstierne: 'Denmark: A Flexible Response', Draft, [Copenhagen], January 1999, p. 70). In Norway, however, it was Prime Minister Gro Harlem Brundtland's Labour government which in July 1986 announced the introduction of a boycott bill. It was submitted in November and adopted in mid-March 1987, two months before the Swedish parliament's decision. The process in Finland was parallel to that in Sweden. In both countries, legislation prohibiting trade with South Africa and Namibia was passed in May 1987. Entering into effect on 1 July 1987, from that time all the Nordic countries except Iceland boycotted trade with the apartheid republic. The pre-boycott commercial relations between the Nordic countries and South Africa showed notable variations. While Iceland's exchange in 1985 was insignificant—with imports of a total value of 0.9 MUSD and exports of 0.1 MUSD—trade with South Africa was also marginal in the other four countries, only representing between 0.6 per cent (Denmark) and 0.2 per cent (Finland) of their respective foreign trade. In absolute figures, Denmark—the first Nordic country to introduce a boycott—had the largest exchange. In 1985, the value of Denmark's exports to South Africa was 58 MUSD. At the same time, however, the imports—mainly in the form of coal—amounted to no less than 159 MUSD. Apart from Iceland, Denmark was thereby the only Nordic country with a negative trade balance vis-à-vis South Africa. In the case of Sweden—the largest Nordic market—the exports amounted in 1985 to 114 MUSD and the imports to 48 MUSD. The corresponding figures for Norway were 69 and 33 MUSD, and for Finland 51 and 17 MUSD (The Nordic Council of Ministers and the Nordic Statistical Secretariat: *Yearbook of Nordic Statistics: 1986*, Copenhagen/Stockholm, 1987, tables 122 and 123, pp. 196-98). With regard to Norway, it should, finally, be noted that the shipping of crude oil to South Africa by Norwegian tankers played a more prominent role than that of bilateral commodity trade (see Eriksen and Krokan in Eriksen (ed.) op. cit., pp. 193-210).

2. 'Speech by the Prime Minister, Mr. Ingvar Carlsson, at the congress of the League of Christian Social Democrats at Solna', 1 August 1986, in Ministry for Foreign Affairs: *Documents on Swedish Foreign Policy: 1986*, Stockholm, 1990, p. 30.

3. 'Handelsbojkott mot Sydafrika' ('Trade boycott against South Africa'), editorial in *Aftonbladet*, 4 June 1986. See also the call 'Heja Danmark!' ('Well done Denmark!') in the syndicalist paper *Arbetaren*, 13 June 1986.

4. Cited in Claes Leo Lindwall: 'Ingvar Carlsson: Sanktioner är folkrättsbrott' ('Ingvar Carlsson: Sanctions contravene international law') in *Dagens Nyheter*, 25 July 1986. Denmark, too, was a NATO member.

5. Lindh became Minister of the Environment in 1994 and Minister for Foreign Affairs in October 1998.

6. Cited in Hans Jonsson: 'Bojkotta Sydafrika nu' ('Boycott South Africa now') in *Aftonbladet*, 25 July 1986.

7. 'Bojkotta Sydafrika nu' ('Boycott South Africa now'), editorial in *Aftonbladet*, 25 July 1986.

major social democratic newspapers.[1] Outside the labour movement, the reactions were equally harsh. Pär Granstedt of the Centre Party joined Anna Lindh in characterizing the government's position as "humiliating"[2], and in a speech in Kalix in the north of the country the Centre leader and former Foreign Minister Karin Söder[3] introduced a painful element into the debate, arguing that "[Swedish] non-participation in a Nordic boycott would be a very bad way [in which to honour] the legacy of Olof Palme".[4] Less outspoken, on behalf of the Liberal Party Birgit Friggebo advocated a unilateral boycott, whereas the Moderate Party's Carl Bildt stated that he "in principle totally support[ed] the government's South Africa policy".[5]

Over the following days, other Swedish voices joined the critics. As Prime Minister Carlsson and Foreign Minister Andersson at a press conference on 27 July reiterated the government's opinion that a trade ban only could follow upon a UN Security Council decision[6], in a speech in Visby Lars Werner, the chairman of the Left Party Communists, described it as tantamount to giving "Reagan and Thatcher a right of veto against a comprehensive boycott".[7] At the opposite end of the political spectrum, Alf Svensson, the leader of the Christian Democratic Union, argued in a similar vein that it was "unacceptable to defend Sweden's passivity by referring to the major trading powers", adding that it was "embarrassing that the Prime Minister acted as a brake block".[8] At the end of July, finally, Bertil Werkström, Archbishop of the Church of Sweden, stated that he was "very disappointed with the government's hesitancy".[9]

Although Sweden since the late 1960s had led the Nordic countries' opposition to apartheid, Social Democratic representatives in Denmark and Norway would also censure Carlsson and his cabinet. In late July 1986, the Norwegian Trade Minister Kurt Mosbakk deplored the official Swedish stand[10], in Denmark joined *inter alia* by the former Justice Minister Ole Espersen.[11] To these critical fraternal reactions were added those of a number of prominent South African apartheid opponents, closely involved with the Swedish humanitarian assistance. Interviewed in Cape Town, UDF's Allan Boesak stated his disappointment, wondering why the Swedish government—which until then "had been standing there all alone"—was "hesitating now that South Africa is at such a sensitive juncture?"[12] COSATU's General Secretary Jay Naidoo also expressed his "disappointment"[13], whereas Winnie Mandela referred to Olof Palme, venturing the opinion that "I am convinced that the deceased Swedish Prime Minister a long time ago would have taken

---

1. Thomas Sjöberg: 'Carlsson pressad av bojkott-kraven' ('Carlsson is under pressure from the boycott demands') in *Aftonbladet*, 26 July 1986.
2. Cited in 'Nya krav på handelsbojkott' ('New demands for a trade boycott') in *Arbetet*, 27 July 1986.
3. A strong supporter of Nordic cooperation, Söder chaired the Centre Party in 1985-86.
4. Cited in Sigge Sigfridsson: 'Karin Söder: Ni missbrukar arvet efter Olof Palme' ('Karin Söder: You are mistreating the legacy of Olof Palme') in *Aftonbladet*, 28 July 1986.
5. Ibid.
6. Jan Axelsson: 'Utrikesnämnden möts om Sydafrikapolitiken' ('The Advisory Council on Foreign Affairs will meet concerning the South Africa policy') in *Folket*, 28 July 1986.
7. Cited in 'Falskt, oansvarigt, passivt' ('False, irresponsible, passive') in *Svenska Dagbladet*, 29 July 1986.
8. Cited in 'Generande' ('Embarrassing') in *Göteborgs-Posten*, 29 July 1986.
9. Cited in Sigge Sigfridsson and Paul Ronge: 'Ska Malm tvinga fram en bojkott?' ('Will Malm force a boycott?') in *Aftonbladet*, 31 July 1986.
10. 'Norsk besvikelse' ('Norwegian disappointment') in *Dagens Nyheter*, 29 July 1986.
11. Björn Persson: 'Statsministerns första motgång' ('The Prime Minister's first setback') in *Aftonbladet*, 29 July 1986. Denmark did not extend direct official assistance to ANC.
12. Cited in 'Pastor Allan Boesak i Sydafrika: Vi är besvikna' ('Pastor Allan Boesak in South Africa: We are disappointed') in *Expressen*, 28 July 1986.
13. Cited in Mono Badela: 'Carlsson förstör Sveriges rykte' ('Carlsson ruins Sweden's reputation') in *Aftonbladet*, 30 July 1986.

action against the South African racist regime".[1] According to *Aftonbladet*, in a particularly severe comment Archbishop Desmond Tutu, finally, said that

> the oppressed in South Africa are extremely disappointed with the new Swedish Prime Minister's indecision. He is actually ruining the Scandinavian peoples' fine record.[2]

Pressures, Turnabout and Final Embargo

Coming to the fore less than six months after the assassination of Olof Palme, for Prime Minister Ingvar Carlsson the boycott debate during the parliamentary recess in the Swedish summer of 1986 was a baptism of fire. During a press conference in early August, he bitterly commented that he had expected attacks from the non-socialist parties and an end to his introductory "political honeymoon", but not around a foreign policy issue which apart from the Moderate Party had traditionally been characterized by a broad consensus.[3] Particularly upset by the comparisons made to Palme—who, it should be underlined, equally opposed a unilateral Swedish decision outside the UN framework—Carlsson described the Centre and Liberal parties' criticism as "shabby", emphasizing that the boycott issue must not be turned into "a running contest" between the parties.[4]

While leading Social Democrats came out in defence of the government's policy[5]; Carlsson personally contacted Allan Boesak to explain the official Swedish position[6]; and a close dialogue was maintained with ANC[7], on 1 August 1986 the beleaguered Prime Minister went on a counteroffensive. The occasion was the congress of the Social Democratic Christian Brotherhood Movement, one of the most outspoken pro-boycott branches of the wider Swedish labour movement. Here, however, he once again rejected the demands for unilateral action, stating *inter alia* that

> [f]or long periods—when South Africa was not front-page news—we were [...] always to the fore [...]. Now, after a week's confused discussion, it seems as if in some quarters twenty-five years of purposeful and insistent work in the name of solidarity have been completely swept away. Instead, an attempt has been made to give [...] the impression that Sweden stands aloof from the policy of sanctions against South Africa, when the truth is that we have often taken

1. Cited in ibid.
2. Cited in ibid.
3. Paul Ronge: 'Tarvligt jämföra med Olof Palme' ('Shabby to compare with Olof Palme') in *Aftonbladet*, 2 August 1986.
4. Ibid. In particular, Carlsson expressed disappointment with the Centre Party leader Karin Söder. With regard to the criticism raised by the Swedish 'middle parties', the fact should be noted that they as examples used Social Democratic boycott initiatives in Denmark and Norway, ignoring that these were opposed by their respective non-socialist sister parties.
5. See, for example, Pierre Schori's article 'Svart blir vitt—Vitt blir svart' ('Black becomes white—White becomes black') in *Aftonbladet*, 31 July 1986, where the Under-Secretary of State for Foreign Affairs *inter alia* stated: "To all of those who only now [...] are demanding radical measures against South Africa we say 'Welcome on board', but don't let yourselves be tempted by opportunism or guided by ignorance. Only a well thought-out, long-term policy will produce results".
6. Per Wendel: 'Carlsson får stöd' ('Carlsson gets support') in *Expressen*, 1 August 1986.
7. Johnny Makatini, ANC's Secretary for International Affairs and Chief Representative to the United Nations, visited Stockholm for consultations with Foreign Minister Sten Andersson on no less than three occasions between June and September 1986. Cf. 1) Anders Möllander: Promemoria ('Utrikesministerns samtal med ANC's utrikeschef Johnny Makatini'/'The Foreign Minister's conversation with ANC's Head of Foreign Affairs, Johnny Makatini'), Ministry for Foreign Affairs, Stockholm, 5 June 1986 (SDA); 2) Anders Möllander: Promemoria ('Utrikesministerns samtal med utrikeschefen i den sydafrikanska befrielserörelsen ANC, Johnston Makatini'/'The Foreign Minister's conversation with the Head of Foreign Affairs of the South African liberation movement ANC, Johnston Makatini'), Ministry for Foreign Affairs, Stockholm, 19 August 1986 (SDA); and 3) Anders Möllander: Promemoria ('ANC's utrikeschef Johnny Makatini besöker utrikesministern'/'ANC's Head of Foreign Affairs Johnny Makatini visits the Foreign Minister'), Ministry for Foreign Affairs, Stockholm, 30 September 1986 (SDA).

up the cudgel for just such a policy and that we have consequently already introduced a number of sanctions [laws].[1] [...]

I want to protest strongly against the past week's statements in various quarters to the effect that there is no hope of gaining a hearing for UN sanctions. [...] I [...] consider [it] both rash and irresponsible to give up [...] the possibility of a decision on stricter sanctions in the UN Security Council. That attitude would be defeatist and dangerous. The Swedish government will on the contrary exploit to the full the increased chances of [such a decision]. [...] An important reason for us to keep steadfastly to this line is that we, as a small neutral country, have an extremely important interest in [the fact that] respect for international law and international agreements [is] being maintained. As a neutral country, we have only ourselves and international law to rely on [...].[2]

Nevertheless, at the same time the Premier noted that "if the United States and the United Kingdom do not cease to resist a decision on sanctions in the UN Security Council, we shall try other measures".[3] Thus leaving an opening for unilateral action, this stand was supported by the LO chairman Stig Malm, who added the opinion that "we in the case of South Africa should totally not give a damn about the GATT regulations".[4]

The Nordic Prime Ministers met in Odense, Denmark, two weeks later. On behalf of Sweden finding himself in an unfamiliar back seat position with regard to South Africa, Ingvar Carlsson[5] had in principle to agree with a joint decision that prohibition of trade with South Africa and Namibia should be introduced by all before the end of 1986.[6] The issue was followed up by Foreign Minister Sten Andersson in discussions with ANC President Tambo, Secretary General Nzo and International Secretary Makatini during the summit meeting of the Non-Aligned Movement in Harare in early September. While Andersson still argued that Sweden's policy of neutrality required a UN Security Council decision "in some form", but that the government in such a case was ready "to go all the way", the comments by Tambo—well aware of the recent Swedish debate and largely echoing his words to the People's Parliament against Apartheid—were that

ANC would already earlier have liked to see Sweden move still further towards a total boycott of the apartheid regime, but that there should be no doubt concerning the sincerity with which [the movement] valued Sweden's role and support. [...] Sweden was [its] closest friend in Europe. [It] had been at the forefront and had served as a catalyst vis-à-vis other countries with regard to legislation against South Africa and other measures to isolate [the regime]. [...]

---

1. As recently as on 1 July 1986, legislation extending the 1979/1985 investment ban had been introduced.
2. 'Speech by the Prime Minister, Mr. Ingvar Carlsson, at the congress of the League of Christian Social Democrats at Solna, 1 August 1986, in Ministry for Foreign Affairs: *Documents on Swedish Foreign Policy: 1986*, Stockholm, 1990, pp. 29-31.
3. Ibid., p. 32.
4. Cited in Paul Ronge: 'Målet är total bojkott' ('The aim is a total boycott') in *Aftonbladet*, 1 August 1986.
5. As well as his Finnish colleague, the Social Democratic Prime Minister Kalevi Sorsa. In the case of Finland, the Transport Workers Union had in October 1985 started a blockade of goods being shipped to and from South Africa. Soon joined by other unions and supported by SAK—the Finnish trade union confederation—by 1986 the blockade had reduced trade with the apartheid republic to "a mere trickle" (cf. Timo-Erkki Heino: *Politics on Paper: Finland's South Africa Policy 1945-1991*, Nordiska Afrikainstitutet, Uppsala, 1992, pp. 83-94).
6. 'Företagen måste lämna Sydafrika' ('The companies must leave South Africa'), editorial in *Aftonbladet*, 12 August 1986. The social democratic newspaper immediately raised the issue of the Swedish companies which under the 1979 investment law were allowed to remain in South Africa, arguing that they also "must go, or else a trade boycott will be cosmetic" (ibid.).

[However,] in ANC's opinion [the time had now come for] individual countries and regions—among them the Nordic [countries]—to speedily take further unilateral action.[1]

To prepare for a boycott decision, following the Nordic Prime Ministers' meeting in Denmark the government had in August 1986 set up an inter-ministerial working group to assess the effects on the economy, notably with regard to employment at Swedish export and import companies.[2] Led by Carl Johan Åberg, Under-Secretary of State at the Foreign Ministry's Department of Trade, it presented its findings in late November, estimating that between 500 and 800 jobs would be affected.[3] By that time, the Social Democratic government in Norway had already submitted its boycott bill. Whether as a consequence of a UN decision or as a result of Nordic agreements, a trade embargo was thus in the offing and a number of measures would have to be introduced in order to cushion its effects. This issue—as well as the employment situation at the Swedish owned companies in South Africa[4]—was raised in particular by the Metalworkers Union.

Three months later, contingency turned into reality when on 20 February 1987 the United States and Great Britain once again vetoed a draft resolution on selective mandatory sanctions, submitted to the UN Security Council by Zambia and other non-aligned council members. The Federal Republic of Germany also voted against the resolution, while France and Japan abstained.[5] Directly or indirectly, South Africa's major trading partners continued to block even selective UN measures to commercially isolate the apartheid regime.

After investing much hope, prestige and diplomatic work in support of the draft resolution, the outcome of the Security Council's deliberations was "a source of great disappointment" to the Social Democratic government.[6] As the Left Party Communists, the Centre Party and the Liberal Party immediately renewed their demands for unilateral action, on 2 March the ruling party convened its National Board for an extraordinary meeting. Although according to Foreign Trade Minister Anita Gradin[7] there were "divergent views" and the decision was taken with "a very big amount of hesitation"[8], the party leadership, nevertheless, resolved to put "commitment before principles" and as a "unique" measure submit a parliamentary bill on a Swedish trade ban.[9] Representing "a complete turnabout" vis-à-vis traditionally held positions[10], the bill was after a brief cabinet meeting introduced

1. Mikael Dahl: Promemoria ('Utrikesministerns samtal den 2 september 1986 med Oliver Tambo vid de allians-fria staternas möte i Harare'/'The Foreign Minister's conversation with Oliver Tambo during the meeting of the non-aligned states in Harare, 2 September 1986'), Ministry for Foreign Affairs, Stockholm, 11 September 1986 (MFA).
2. In 1986, no less than around 350 Swedish companies held licenses for exports to South Africa, while just over 30 carried out registered imports from the country. The ten largest exporters—of which several had subsidiaries in South Africa—accounted for more than half of the total export value (Ministry for Foreign Affairs: *Prohibition of Trade with South Africa and Namibia*, Stockholm, March 1987, pp. 28-29).
3. 'Report on a possible Swedish boycott against South Africa', 27 November 1986 (press release), in Ministry for Foreign Affairs: *Documents on Swedish Foreign Policy: 1986*, Stockholm, 1990, pp. 322-23.
4. By law, the Swedish owned companies in South Africa had to report on their operations. At the end of 1985, there remained ten Swedish subsidiaries in the republic, having a total workforce of 2,400. About half of the employees were black. At eight of the ten companies, the workers were organized in trade unions ('Governmental report to parliament regarding the operations of Swedish companies in South Africa and Namibia during 1985', 17 December 1986 (press release), in Ministry for Foreign Affairs: *Documents on Swedish Foreign Policy: 1986*, Stockholm, 1990, pp. 328-29).
5. United Nations: *Yearbook of the United Nations: 1987*, Department of Public Information, United Nations, New York, 1992, pp. 134-35.
6. Ministry for Foreign Affairs: *Prohibition of Trade with South Africa and Namibia* op. cit., p. 23.
7. Gradin served as Minister for Foreign Trade between 1986 and 1991.
8. Indirect quote in Nordenmark op. cit., p. 135.
9. Ibid.
10. Ibid., p. 119.

only ten days later.[1] Despite firm opposition by the Moderate Party, on 22 May 1987 it was adopted with an overwhelming majority of 234 votes in favour and 66 against.[2]

Entering into effect on 1 July 1987[3], after two and a half decades of popular demands, three major national debates and considerable Social Democratic anguish, Sweden eventually decided to complement its official assistance to ANC, SWAPO and the wider apartheid opposition with comprehensive legislation against bilateral trade with the Pretoria regime.[4]

The 1987 trade embargo applied in principle to imports of all goods of South African or Namibian origin and exports of goods to South Africa and Namibia.[5] A general exception was, however, made "in the case of publications and news matter, since it is obviously of great importance that there continue to be a flow of information to and from South Africa".[6] Articles intended for humanitarian or medical purposes were also exempted.[7] Finally, the legislation covered "certain [...] activities liable to promote breaches of the prohibition of imports and exports, [such as] the loading, unloading and transport of goods, the supply of means of transport and the provision of orders relating to such activities, whether directly or through intermediaries".[8]

The Africa Groups, the Isolate South Africa Committee and other constituent parts of the wider solidarity movement greeted the boycott decision with satisfaction. In an editorial in *Afrikabulletinen*, AGIS commented:

> Finally a Swedish trade boycott! After years of demands and pressure from the South African and Namibian peoples, from the Frontline States and from all of us in the solidarity movement. We welcome the decision taken by the government, with pleasure giving it a fair amount of praise. But it is our work, our demands [and their] dissemination among the Swedish peo-

---

1. Government Bill 1986/87: 110, in Ministry for Foreign Affairs: *Prohibition of Trade with South Africa and Namibia* op. cit.
2. Tor Sellström: 'Sanctions against South Africa: The Case of Sweden' in *Southern Africa Political and Economic Monthly*, No. 1, September 1987, p. 12.
3. To enable the companies concerned to wind up their business connections, the full embargo entered into force on 1 October 1987.
4. Not without historical irony, it should be noted that when the Nordic and other Western countries in 1986-87 decided to sever trade relations with South Africa, opposite policies were embraced by the Soviet Union and its Eastern allies. As evidence of close and long-standing contacts between Moscow and Pretoria in the highly secretive trade of diamonds, gold and platinum surfaced in early 1987 ('Diamonds forever' in *Financial Mail*, 6 February 1987, pp. 115-16; cf. Shubin op. cit., pp. 373-77), towards the end of that year the Soviet-made Niva four-wheel drive vehicle was, for example, introduced on the South African market (Letter ('Sovjetiska bilar till Sydafrika'/'Soviet vehicles to South Africa') from Jan Lundvik, Swedish envoy to South Africa, Swedish legation, Pretoria, 11 December 1987) (MFA).
5. The decisive factor with regard to imports was the country of origin. It made no difference whether the goods came directly from South Africa, Namibia or via a third country. It could be noted that Sweden's stand on South Africa from the early 1980s affected the official aid programmes to Southern Africa in general, including the support to ANC and SWAPO. In the case of ANC, the annual agreements stipulated that "Swedish funds should not be used for procurement of goods and services originating from South Africa when alternatives to such procurement exist" ('Agreed minutes [from] consultations in Lusaka, May 1985, between the African National Congress of South Africa and Sweden concerning humanitarian assistance', Lusaka, 30 May 1985) (SDA). This policy was made unconditional in May 1987, when the parties agreed that "Swedish funds should not be used for procurement of goods and services originating from South Africa" ('Agreed minutes [from] consultations in Lusaka, May 1987, between the African National Congress of South Africa and Sweden concerning humanitarian assistance', Lusaka, 8 May 1987) (SDA). It goes without saying that this stipulation did not apply to the 'home front component' or other official assistance channelled to the anti-apartheid opposition inside South Africa.
6. Ministry for Foreign Affairs: *Prohibition of Trade with South Africa and Namibia* op. cit., p. 38.
7. Ibid.
8. Ibid., pp. 2-3. In addition to the effects of the trade boycotts in the other Nordic countries, this eventually forced the Gothenburg-based Transatlantic Shipping Company to close down. Originally established in 1904, Transatlantic's regular shipping service between South Africa, Sweden and the Nordic countries had from the early 1960s been particularly targeted by the popular boycott movement (see Sellström Volume I, pp. 190-98 and 209-14).

'Shell is oiling apartheid – Boycott Shell': The Isolate South Africa Committee campaigning in Luleå, May 1989 (Photo: Roland S. Lundström)

ple, [...] our demonstrations, lobbying and letters to the press, which have forced the politicians to act. Today, we in the solidarity movement may therefore be entitled to feel a bit proud.[1]

At the same time, AGIS and ISAK underlined that there was no reason for complacency. The Swedish companies in South Africa were still allowed to operate. In their view, the legislation also had serious loopholes, in particular since it did not apply to firms operating under foreign legislation in third countries and excluded services.[2] Against this background, AGIS called for "a continuation of the work in favour of a total boycott", adding that

> [w]e must at the same time be aware [of the fact] that apartheid cannot be crushed through sanctions alone, however international and complete they might be. [Sanctions] may contribute to a weakening of the apartheid regime, facilitating the struggle against it. But the final blow must be delivered by the South African and Namibian peoples themselves. It is therefore important that we continue to support ANC, SWAPO and the Frontline States, who are severely affected by South Africa's terror.[3]

1. 'Kommentaren' ('The Comment') in *Afrikabulletinen*, No. 2, 1987, [p. 1].
2. See, for example, AGIS: 'Sweden and South Africa: The Two Faces', [Stockholm], 1 July 1987, an information pamphlet written by Madi Gray, and ISAK: 'Vad gjorde Isolera Sydafrika Kommittén 1986-87?' ('What did the Isolate South Africa Committee do in 1986-87?'), activity report by the ISAK board, [no place or date] (ISA). These weaknesses were similarly noted by the government. At the same time as the boycott bill was submitted, it appointed a parliamentary commission to study "the possibility of extending the embargo to Swedish owned subsidiaries in other countries" and "the necessity of further restrictions and prohibitions [with regard to] trade in services" (Ministry for Foreign Affairs: *Prohibition of Trade with South Africa and Namibia* op. cit., pp. 47-49).
3. 'Kommentaren' ('The Comment') in *Afrikabulletinen*, No. 2, 1987 [p. 1]. As earlier noted, this opinion differed quite substantially from that held by the anti-apartheid movement in many Western countries, which emphasized the primacy of economic isolation (cf. the chapter 'Isolation versus Involvement: Companies, Churches and Labour in the 1970s'). For a case in point, see the discussion paper 'Contextualizing Scandinavian support for the South African liberation struggle' by the Danish history student Gorm Gunnarsen, submitted to a symposium on 'History for Democracy' held at Robben Island, Cape Town, in February 2000 (NAI).

While AGIS intensified its solidarity activities; ISAK embarked on new boycott campaigns[1]; and Sweden eventually legislated against trade in services[2], it should, nevertheless, be noted that the 1987 embargo—as illustrated in the graph above—practically brought the commodity exchange with the apartheid republic to a standstill. Amounting to a total value of 1,575 MSEK, Swedish exports to South Africa had in 1984 reached an all-time peak. From 717 MSEK in 1987, after the introduction of the boycott legislation they, however, dropped drastically to a mere 43 MSEK in 1988[3], representing an insignificant 0.01 per cent of the country's direct total sales abroad, almost exclusively made up of medical supplies and other humanitarian goods. Corresponding developments were registered with regard to imports. Peaking at 413 MSEK in 1985, following the January 1986 ban on agricultural products and the July 1987 general embargo, they plummeted to 2 MSEK in 1988, representing a share of Sweden's total imports too small to be measured in a meaningful way.

With regard to commodity trade, by 1988 the historical relations between Sweden and South Africa had come to an end.[4] Amounting to 64 MSEK in 1987/88, at the same time the direct, official allocation to ANC exceeded the total value of the commodity exchange.[5] Over the following four years it would almost double, reaching 120 MSEK in 1991/92.[6]

The PASA Initiative

In connection with the People's Parliament against Apartheid, Tambo raised with Palme the possibility of support towards ANC's planning for a post-apartheid dis-

---

1. Continuously monitoring all possible contacts between Sweden and South Africa, ISAK—which at the time had more than 60 member organizations—would in June 1986 join the broad international campaign against the British-Dutch Shell Oil company (cf. ISAK: 'Shell Smörjer Apartheid'/'Shell Fuels Apartheid', Stockholm, February 1989) (ISA). While the campaign in Australia, Britain, Canada, Holland, USA and the Nordic countries—notably in oil-producing Norway—helped to boost the anti-apartheid movement, in Sweden it largely backfired. Targeting individual Shell service stations all around the country, against the explicit policy of the ISAK board, in around twenty cases peaceful dissuasion turned into violent action and sabotage (Dick Emanuelsson: 'Men kampanjen mot Shell fortsätter'/'But the campaign against Shell continues' in *Norrskensflamman*, 27 November 1987). This, in turn, prompted the Liberal Party Youth League to withdraw from the organization (Lars Malvin Karlsson: 'Hej Då ISAK!'/'Goodbye ISAK!' in *Amandla*, Nos. 2-3, 1995, p. 20). In the late 1980s, the organizers of the international anti-Shell campaign could hardly have imagined that the headquarters of the unbanned ANC in 1990 would be housed in Shell House, Johannesburg.
2. In connection with Nelson Mandela's first visit to Sweden, on 15 March 1990 the commodity embargo was extended to include services. Arguably, Sweden had thereby imposed tighter sanctions against South Africa than any other country. Together with Finland the last Nordic country to ban trade with the apartheid republic, Sweden was the last to lift its embargo. While Finland did so in June 1991, Denmark in March 1992 and Norway in March 1993, at ANC's request it was only in September-November 1993 that the Swedish boycott legislation was abrogated by Carl Bildt's non-socialist government ('Lifting of sanctions against South Africa and introduction of measures to promote trade with South Africa', 13 September 1993 (press release), in Ministry for Foreign Affairs: *Documents on Swedish Foreign Policy: 1993*, Stockholm, 1994, pp. 433-34).
3. Cf. the accompanying Appendix VI.
4. On Sweden's early economic links with South Africa, see Sellström Volume I, pp. 122-24.
5. 'Agreed minutes [from] consultations in Lusaka, May 1987, between the African National Congress of South Africa and Sweden concerning humanitarian assistance', Lusaka, 8 May 1987 (SDA).
6. 'Agreed minutes from consultations held in Benoni, South Africa, May 1991, between the African National Congress of South Africa (ANC) and the government of Sweden concerning humanitarian assistance', Johannesburg, 19 May 1991 (SDA).

pensation[1], later known as PASA.[2] As cracks in the apartheid wall were becoming increasingly visible, a number of research projects on a future democratic South Africa had by then been initiated at various universities around the world, notably in Great Britain and in the Netherlands. Often led by South African exiles with close links to the liberation movement, these initiatives were not co-ordinated by ANC and—partly due to the academic boycott—only loosely connected with similar projects and the broader opposition inside South Africa. Against this background, in January 1986 the ANC leadership decided to embark on a policy-oriented PASA programme. At an agitated meeting of the National Executive's Working Committee[3] Pallo Jordan, Secretary of ANC's Department of Economics and Planning[4], later explained:

> PASA arose as a result of NEC decisions. I refer [the] members of the NEC to a meeting [...] in early 1986. There was a report from myself and Cde. President [Tambo] [...]. It was that meeting that took a decision that the ANC needs to launch a comprehensive programme of research on a post-apartheid South Africa, if only because all sorts of other forces are engaged in it and might end up writing our agenda. Subsequent to that meeting, the President attended the Swedish People's Parliament where] he entered into discussion with the Swedes, who undertook to look into the possibilities of funding the project. They later agreed.[5]

Following the exchange of views between Tambo and Palme, Swedish support to the initiative was "frequently discussed" during the annual aid negotiations in Lusaka in May 1986[6], where ANC[7] in particular emphasized the financial needs of its recently established Department of Legal and Constitutional Affairs.[8] While it announced that a comprehensive request in favour of PASA would be submitted later in the year[9], initially, however, both the initiative and Sweden's role were far from uncomplicated.[10] Combined with a number of practical problems, formal PASA structures were not established until 1988. Nevertheless, from 1987 the programme would be actively pursued.

---

1. 'Introductory remarks by the head of the Swedish delegation', attached to 'Agreed minutes [from] consultations in Lusaka, May 1986, between the African National Congress of South Africa and Sweden concerning humanitarian assistance', Lusaka, 9 May 1986 (SDA). Carl Olof Cederblad, Director at the Ministry for Foreign Affairs, led the Swedish delegation.
2. PASA was an acronym for Post-Apartheid South Africa.
3. In the absence of President Tambo normally chaired by Secretary General Nzo, the National Working Committee (NWC) coordinated ANC policy between regular meetings of the full National Executive Committee (NEC).
4. ANC had in the 1970s set up a research unit within the Department of Information and Publicity, led by Jordan from 1980. When in October 1986 the movement decided to establish a separate Department of Economics and Planning, Jordan became its Secretary (Letter ('Månadsbrev oktober 1986: ANC'/'Monthly letter October 1986: ANC') from Roland Axelsson to SIDA, Swedish embassy, Lusaka, 10 October 1986) (SDA).
5. ANC: 'Minutes of NWC' , [no place or date, but Lusaka and—according to Shubin op. cit., p. 393—22 February 1988] (MCA).
6. Carl Olof Cederblad: Memorandum ('Förhandlingsrapport från överläggningar med ANC rörande humanitärt bistånd 1986/87'/'Report from negotiations with ANC concerning humanitarian assistance 1986/87'), Ministry for Foreign Affairs, Stockholm, 6 June 1986 (SDA).
7. The ANC delegation was led by Alfred Nzo, seconded by Thomas Nkobi. Neither Pallo Jordan nor Zola Skweyiya took part in the deliberations.
8. Headed by Zola Skweyiya, ANC's Department of Legal and Constitutional Affairs was set up in January 1986. At the centre of the PASA programme, Skweyiya was after the 1994 democratic elections appointed Minister of Public Service and Administration.
9. Carl Olof Cederblad: Memorandum, June 1986, op. cit.
10. There were at the time not only strong voices at the level of ANC's leadership who questioned the idea of negotiations with the apartheid regime, but also the Social Democratic 'Swedish model' and, hence, close political links with Sweden concerning the PASA programme. It could be noted that the Soviet Union in March 1987—that is, before the August Bommersvik workshop in Sweden—organized a 'Social Scientists Seminar' for ANC in Moscow, chaired by its former ambassador to Zambia, Vassily Solodovnikov, then representing the Afro-Asian Solidarity Committee. Pallo Jordan headed the ANC team to the seminar (ANC: 'Report of the Social Scientists Seminar', [no date or place]) (MCA).

Launched by ANC, sanctioned by Zimbabwe[1] and facilitated by Sweden, the broad, consultative PASA programme was to have a significant impact on post-1990 South Africa. Together with parallel contacts with the Pretoria government on 'talks about talks'—inside South Africa conducted by Nelson Mandela and outside primarily by Thabo Mbeki[2]—it would through a participatory process largely define the positions and policies held by ANC, UDF, COSATU and the mass democratic movement during the negotiations for a democratic dispensation. While this was crucially the case in respect of constitutional affairs, it also applied to a range of fundamental socio-economic issues. By challenging old ideological moulds and linking up with the vibrant internal civic and trade union movements, through PASA ANC embarked on a comprehensive policy exercise which before the 1994 elections resulted in the publication of its *Reconstruction and Development Programme*, a political manifesto for change popularly known as RDP.[3]

Whereas Sweden's involvement with PASA is outlined below, a detailed discussion of the rich programme falls outside the scope of this study.[4] Here again, it is hoped that future investigations will shed light on its course and content, the impact it had on ANC, SACP and the exiled partners' alliance with UDF, COSATU and the civic movement, as well as on the alliance's policies after the unbannings in February 1990. It should in this context be recalled that ANC initiated substantial discussions on strategy and tactics with UDF in Stockholm in January and with COSATU in Lusaka in March 1986[5], that is, about the same time as the PASA initiative was launched. And by mid-1986, leading ANC representatives declared that the movement—subject to certain core conditions—was positive towards political negotiations with the apartheid regime.[6]

In the meantime, the following general remarks made in 1995 by ANC's Jaya Appalraju—a pivotal PASA promoter and organizer based in Harare—should be noted:

---

1. By far the most of the consultative PASA meetings between ANC and activists and professionals from South Africa took place in Zimbabwe. As later stated by Jaya Appalraju, who on ANC's behalf played a central role in the organization of the meetings, "Zimbabwe was crucial, and, whenever possible, we involved and interacted with the Zimbabweans. [...] [PASA] was broadly supported by the Zimbabwe government. They sanctioned the project. For example, we had to get people into Zimbabwe on bantustan passports and so forth. We had to explain [...] what it was all about and that we had to get so-and-so into the country over a weekend or a couple of days to hold intensive workshops or all-night sessions. The Zimbabwe government was very supportive in that respect. The University of Zimbabwe, the Cold Comfort Farm Trust and various institutions assisted us in making that possible. [...] [T]hey interacted tremendously with us, assisted us and facilitated the process" (Interview with Jaya Appalraju, pp. 105-06).
2. The inside story of South Africa's negotiated revolution has been narrated by Allister Sparks in Sparks op. cit.
3. ANC: *The Reconstruction and Development Programme*, ANC, Johannesburg, 1994.
4. In addition to the priority areas mentioned in the text, the PASA programme covered a wide spectrum of topics for a democratic South Africa, from language policy to science and technology.
5. See the chapter 'Closer and Broader Cooperation: Projects in Exile, Mineworkers, UDF and Civics in South Africa'.
6. James Stuart (aka Hermanus Loots) cited in Anders Möllander: Memorandum ('Besök av medlemmen i sydafrikanska ANC's exekutivkommitté, James [Stuart]'/'Visit by the ANC NEC member James [Stuart]'), Ministry for Foreign Affairs, Stockholm, 23 October 1986 (MFA). Invited to Sweden by the Africa Groups to attend a Namibia seminar, Stuart was together with Lindiwe Mabuza received at the Foreign Ministry on 20 October 1986. On behalf of ANC's National Executive Committee, during the meeting he stated *inter alia* that the movement was "very positive" towards negotiations, as "only a [negotiated solution] could shorten the struggle and [thus reduce] the sufferings". While ANC was not prepared to abandon the armed struggle, to pave the way for negotiations it demanded a) a release of all political prisoners; b) a repeal of the banning of political organizations; c) an end to the state of emergency; and d) an agreement that negotiations would be held directly between the government, ANC and "other parties". With regard to the PASA process, Stuart expressed the opinion that ANC would soon take a decision in favour of "a multi-party system" and a "mixed economy" (ibid.). These were, indeed, early signals of far-reaching change. Looking at the developments from a Soviet perspective, Shubin writes that the ANC National Executive only took a conditional stand on negotiations in late 1987 (Shubin op. cit., p. 321).

There were a few of us in different fields pushing ANC for resources and [...] some manpower behind the planning and thinking about a post-apartheid situation [once] Zimbabwe had changed. Although the objective circumstances did not allow us to rationalize when this would take place, the momentum put pressure on ANC to start to think about what should be done [...]. Tambo raised this issue very strongly in various informal gatherings [...].

We insisted that [the PASA programme] had to be [carried out] not by ANC alone, but in collaboration with groups inside the country. They were in the frontline, facing the issues [on] a day-to-day basis, fighting for rents, water etc. [W]e had to translate this into some sort of long-term demands. We worked under very difficult circumstances with activists on the ground from all over [South Africa]. [...] For us outside [...], this was an important learning period. [...]

[T]he PASA project [...] was a major initiative [and] [t]he Harare Declaration[1], which this thinking sort of led up to, was a landmark for the way in which the process unfolded after that. We did not really know where the process was leading to ourselves, but it was intensive and it grew. It was a groundswell, and after a while it was not clandestine any more. Businessmen would come out and declare that they were consulting with ANC. We could agree on a lot of issues and disagree on others, and for the first time the [South African] media were giving us a lot of legitimate coverage. [...] [PASA] was, I think, the foundation of the democratic process in this country. In some respects, the post-apartheid discussion that we are in at the moment was started in that consultative process.[2]

Initially interpreted differently by the Swedish authorities and the ANC officials with regard to the balance between strict research and broader policy studies, as well as concerning the role and extent of Sweden's involvement, it would take some time before the PASA programme eventually was designed, mutually understood, established and supported. More than any other ANC leader, Thabo Mbeki—at the same time closely involved in indirect exploratory talks with the Pretoria regime—would in this context play an active and decisive role.

Capacity-Building and Research Support

In addition to various international scholarship programmes and multilateral support to centres such as the Lusaka-based UN Institute for Namibia[3], Swedish bilateral assistance to strengthen the Southern African liberation movements with regard to socio-economic planning was extended from 1977/78. Outside the core programme administered by SIDA, in that year the Swedish Agency for Research Cooperation with Developing Countries (SAREC) decided to grant ZAPU 200,000 SEK for the establishment of a Zimbabwe Research and Information Centre, also based in Lusaka.[4]

As ANC, SWAPO and ZANU equally expressed interest in research support from SAREC, this decision prompted an internal Swedish discussion on short-term relief and long-term planning. While it was agreed that academically oriented research projects also in the future should be financed and administered by SAREC[5], the Swedish aid officials were positive to the inclusion of forward-looking

---

1. On the Harare Declaration, see below.
2. Interview with Jaya Appalraju, pp. 105-06.
3. See the chapter 'Transport, Home Front, Churches and Trade Unions' on Namibia.
4. See the chapter 'Patriotic Front: ZANU and ZAPU towards Independence'. Also Marika Fahlén: Memorandum ('Långsiktigt bistånd till befrielserörelserna: Forskning'/'Long-term assistance to the liberation movements: Research', Ministry for Foreign Affairs, Stockholm, 2 November 1978 (SDA).
5. The official support channelled by SAREC in favour of the Southern African liberation movements is not included in the accompanying disbursement tables. This is mainly due to the fact that the support was normally extended to projects submitted by individual scholars, based at various universities and research centres in Africa and Europe.

policy studies within the ongoing support programmes to the liberation movements.[1]

Proposing a shift in emphasis from a re-active to a more pro-active approach, in an internal discussion paper SIDA's Assistant Director General Curt Ström argued provocatively in January 1978 that

> [t]he Swedish support to refugees and liberation movements in Southern Africa is a palliative which in the short term mitigates distress, but does not really change anything. It does not contribute to challenging the power structure which is the cause of the prevailing oppression. It is humanitarian, but lacks clear objectives.[2]

Against this background, Ström expressed the opinion that the liberation movements should work out "long-term, constructive projects" and that Sweden must "actively support [their] preparations".[3] This conclusion was supported by Thord Palmlund, Under-Secretary of State for International Cooperation, who on behalf of the Ministry for Foreign Affairs stated that the government was willing to support "activities which are likely to be of significance for and after the transition to majority rule", including socio-economic and administrative studies, theoretical and vocational training, assessment of labour markets, ownership conditions and other relevant issues in the respective countries.[4] At the same time, Palmlund stressed that support to such activities should not encroach upon the humanitarian support, but be additional to the ongoing cooperation with the nationalist movements.[5]

In the case of ANC, discussions on research support were initiated immediately thereafter. In late March 1978, Marika Fahlén from the Foreign Ministry and Marianne Sundh from SIDA visited London for a preliminary exchange of views with Frene Ginwala, Gill Marcus and Francis Meli, who were all centrally involved in research and information work.[6] The discussions were followed up during the annual aid negotiations in Lusaka in May, where ANC gave information about its plans for "long-term projects" and "stressed the need for [...] know-how in different fields".[7] Noting that a research centre could become "a potentially [...] important sub-department" of ANC's Department of Information and Publicity, but was

---

1. This issue had featured prominently long before the 1969 decision to extend direct, official support to PAIGC and the Southern African liberation movements. The Swedish support from 1965 to FRELIMO's Mozambique Institute in Dar es Salaam should be brought to mind (cf. Sellström Volume I, pp. 453-59, and the earlier chapter 'FRELIMO of Mozambique: Clearing a Way'). In the case of Namibia, Olof Palme had in his main address to the 1966 Oxford conference emphasized that "[t]he time for planning, preparations and constructive thinking [...] has already come" (Sellström Volume I, p. 275). Finally, with regard to South Africa, it should be recalled that Prime Minister Ullsten in January 1979 expressed the opinion that "[w]e should [...] make available resources for research and studies on South African society and on the role of South Africa in the regional and global context. Such studies could also include methods and means for preparing and engaging the South African population in the process of transition to majority rule. We should not lose any time in taking up this task" (see the chapter 'SACTU, Unions and Sanctions').
2. Curt Ström: Memorandum ('Biståndets roll i södra Afrika-politiken'/'The role of aid in [Sweden's] Southern Africa policy'), SIDA, Stockholm, 5 January 1978 (SDA). A specific 'home front component' had been included from 1 July 1977 in the official cooperation programme with ANC (see the chapter 'From Beds in Exile to Organizers at Home').
3. Curt Ström: Memorandum ('Biståndets roll i södra Afrika-politiken'/'The role of aid in [Sweden's] Southern Africa policy'), SIDA, Stockholm, 5 January 1978 (SDA).
4. Letter ('Långsiktigt bistånd till södra Afrika'/'Long-term assistance to Southern Africa') from Thord Palmlund to the Swedish embassy in Luanda, Ministry for Foreign Affairs, Stockholm, 10 February 1978 (SDA).
5. Ibid.
6. Letter ('ANC Sydafrika'/'ANC South Africa') from Marika Fahlén to the Swedish embassy in Lusaka, Ministry for Foreign Affairs, Stockholm, 5 April 1978 (SDA) and Marika Fahlén: Memorandum ('Bidrag till African National Congress, ANC Sydafrika'/'Contribution to ANC'), Ministry for Foreign Affairs, Stockholm, 26 April 1978 (SDA).
7. 'Agreed minutes of discussions on the cooperation between Sweden and the African National Congress of South Africa (ANC) 1978/79', Lusaka, 26 May 1978 (SDA).

still in its "formative stage", in July 1978 the movement submitted a request to SAREC for support towards "research premises, [...] reference material" and other needs at the headquarters in Lusaka.[1]

The request was discussed during a visit to Lusaka by SAREC's Lennart Båge and Anders Johnson.[2] The official Swedish research aid agency[3] would over the next decade be associated directly and indirectly with several projects launched by ANC scholars in exile.[4] In addition to initial core support to ANC's research unit in Lusaka, assistance was extended *inter alia* to the Centre of African Studies at the Eduardo Mondlane University in Maputo, where—until her violent death in August 1982—Ruth First together with a group of prominent ANC academics carried out a number of important studies on South and Southern Africa.[5] Via SAREC, support was also extended to various research projects in Great Britain. Beginning in 1985, a project on 'Economic Change, Social Conflict and Education in Contemporary South Africa', coordinated by Harold Wolpe and administered by the Ruth First Memorial Trust in London, was among those supported.[6] Finally, over and above the bilateral PASA programme Swedish funds were, for example, via the Commonwealth Secretariat from 1989 channelled to a major project on democratic South Africa's future constitution, led by Albie Sachs at the University of London.[7]

---

1. Letter ('Research project grant application') from Sizakele Siqxashe to the Swedish embassy in Lusaka, ANC Department of Information and Publicity, Lusaka, 31 July 1978 (SDA).
2. Author's recollection. At the time, the author represented SAREC at the Swedish embassy in Lusaka.
3. In 1995, SIDA and SAREC were amalgamated within the new Swedish International Development Cooperation Agency, Sida.
4. Official support via SIDA was at about the same time extended to a number of international NGOs which specialized in the study and monitoring of South Africa's external links in various strategic areas. From the start in 1979, this was the case with the World Campaign against Military and Nuclear Collaboration with South Africa, set up in Oslo by Abdul Minty, former Secretary General of the British Anti-Apartheid Movement who after the democratic elections would be appointed Deputy Director General in the South African Department of Foreign Affairs. This was also the case with the Amsterdam-based Shipping Research Bureau (SRB), which focused on the oil embargo against South Africa. Set up in 1980, it was similarly supported by SIDA from the very beginning. The history of SRB was published in 1995 (Richard Hengeveld and Jaap Rodenburg (eds): *Embargo: Apartheid's Oil Secrets Revealed*, Amsterdam University Press, Amsterdam). According to the study, SIDA "was one of the pillars without which the SRB's fragile structure would have collapsed in the initial phase" (p. 375). On the early Swedish support to SRB, see also the interview with Birgitta Berggren (p. 259). Successfully monitoring the supply of oil and petroleum products to the Pretoria regime, SRB was feared and profoundly disliked by the international shipping companies. In 1996, Berggren recalled: "The facts which [SRB] presented and gave publicity to were absolutely devastating. The shipping companies contacted the Ministry for Foreign Affairs and parliamentarians in Sweden in order to stop the support from SIDA" (ibid.). Contrary to the situation in Norway, there were no Swedish-owned companies or tankers which supplied oil to South Africa. Nevertheless, soon after the first SIDA contribution, both the Swedish Employers Confederation and the Swedish Shipowners Association protested without success against the official support (Anders Bjurner: Memorandum ('Svenskt bidrag till kartläggning av skeppningar av olja till Sydafrika'/'Swedish contribution towards mapping of oil shipments to South Africa'), Ministry for Foreign Affairs, 17 December 1980) (SDA).
5. Among the South African scholars at the Maputo Centre of African Studies were Robert Davies, Sipho Dlamini, Helena Dolny, Alpheus Manghezi and Dan O'Meara.
6. Letter [no title] from Margareta Husén to the Swedish embassy in Dar es Salaam, SIDA, Stockholm, 7 October 1986 (SDA).
7. Lena Johansson: Memorandum ('Ansökan från Commonwealth Secretariat om stöd till forskningsprojekt'/'Request from the Commonwealth Secretariat for support to a research project'), SIDA/CCHA, [Stockholm], 20 September 1989 (SDA). With Sachs as its founding Director, in 1989 the South Africa Constitution Studies Centre was established at the Institute of Commonwealth Studies at the University of London. The core programme was financed by the Swedish government and the Ford Foundation of the United States. In 1992, the centre moved to the University of the Western Cape, where Sachs was made Professor Extraordinary. He was also appointed Honorary Professor at the University of Cape Town. As an ANC NEC member and leading representative of the organization's Constitutional Committee, Sachs took an active part in the negotiations for a democratic dispensation. After the 1994 elections, the internationally renowned intellectual, author and activist became a member of the Constitutional Court of South Africa.

Joint Preparations and ANC Criticism

What Oliver Tambo had in mind when in February 1986 he raised the PASA proposal with Olof Palme was a policy-oriented ANC programme, drawing on various
relevant international examples and carried out in close cooperation with the mass
democratic movement in South Africa. As noted from the statement by Pallo Jordan quoted above, this was not least important in order to affirm the movement's
primacy in the unfolding post-apartheid debate. In turn, the proposal was strongly
supported by the Swedish government, which through various channels already
extended substantial assistance to the ANC-aligned UDF, COSATU and a large
number of their affiliates. In November 1986, the instruction issued by the Foreign
Ministry to the delegation to the consultative talks with ANC the following month
laid down that "[s]upport towards planning of a post-apartheid South Africa
should become a central component of the cooperation", adding that "[t]he issue is
of such a central political nature that it shall be accorded priority".[1]

During the subsequent talks, the representatives from ANC and Sweden agreed
that PASA was "a matter of priority for both parties". As "possible ways to prepare
a concrete project proposal" were discussed, the Swedish delegation "offered to
host a [preparatory] seminar in Sweden before the [...] annual [aid] consultations in
May 1987". In the meantime, it was decided to tentatively set aside 500,000 SEK
for the initiative in 1986/87.[2] On behalf of the movement, three months later Thomas Nkobi for the first time formally submitted a rough PASA request, containing
activity plans from the Departments of Economics and Planning; Legal and Constitutional Affairs; and Manpower Development.[3] Covering an extensive list of subjects, in the short-term perspective the respective plans envisaged *inter alia* Swedish
support for an overall socio-economic analysis, a seminar on constitutional alternatives and studies of labour market policies in the Western countries, notably Sweden.[4]

The most concrete submission was that from the Department of Legal and Constitutional Affairs, which intended to invite no less than 180 participants to a seminar to be held in Lusaka in May 1987. The objective was to "bring together South
Africans from all [walks] of life for the purpose of discussing constitutional options

---

1. Kaj Persson: Memorandum ('SIDA's instruktion inför programsamtal med ANC: Synpunkter'/'Instruction to
   SIDA for the consultative talks with ANC: Considerations'), Ministry for Foreign Affairs, Stockholm, 3
   November 1986 (SDA).
2. 'Minutes from consultative talks in Lusaka, 2-5 December 1986, between the African National Congress of
   South Africa (ANC) and SIDA concerning humanitarian assistance', Lusaka, 5 December 1986 (SDA). The
   ANC and Swedish delegations were respectively led by Thomas Nkobi and SIDA's Lars-Olof Edström. To dis-
   cuss the proposed seminar, a separate meeting was held with ANC's Department of Legal and Constitutional
   Affairs (Kaj Persson: Memorandum ('Programsamtal med ANC, 2-5 december 1986'/'Consultative talks with
   ANC, 2-5 December 1986'), Ministry for Foreign Affairs, Stockholm, 11 December 1986) (SDA).
3. Letter ('Post-apartheid planning for a future democratic South Africa') with attachments from Thomas
   Nkobi, Treasurer General, to the Swedish embassy in Lusaka, ANC, Lusaka, 11 February 1987 (SDA). In the
   letter, Nkobi noted that submissions from the Departments of Education and Health would be forthcoming
   (ibid.).
4. Kaj Persson: Memorandum ('Bistånd till ANC's planeringsverksamhet'/'Assistance to ANC's planning activities'), Ministry for Foreign Affairs, Stockholm, 4 March 1987 (SDA). Noting that "the South African [labour
   market] machinery [...] is of [W]estern origin", in its submission the ANC Department of Manpower Development proposed that "a study is [...] conducted [on] the type of practical training that can be offered in the
   various countries of the [W]est". In respect of Sweden, the department generally "envisage[d] cooperation [...]
   in the field of planning of the labour resources of South Africa. As Sweden has a profound experience in this
   field, it [is] one of the [countries] where planning officers [...] could be sent to learn the methods of [labour
   market] planning [....], as well as research into how [these] can be applied to [the] South African situation"
   (ANC Department of Manpower Development: 'Proposal for Cooperation with SIDA', submission attached
   to letter ('Post-apartheid planning for a future democratic South Africa') from Thomas Nkobi to the Swedish
   embassy in Lusaka, ANC, Lusaka, 11 February 1987) (SDA).

acceptable to all", thereby initiating a process towards "a consensus on constitutional proposals [...] for a future democratic South Africa".[1] As the constitutional debate would be at the very centre of South Africa's transition towards democracy, it is relevant to quote the following introductory paragraph from ANC's submission:

> Over a number of years, a considerable number of specialists and 'think tanks'—commissioned both by the apartheid authorities and [...] various [W]estern governments, non-governmental organisations, institutions of higher learning etc.—have been hard at work drafting constitutional proposals and models for a post-apartheid South Africa. [However,] [i]t behoves the ANC as the leading force, [...] organiser of the struggle against apartheid and [...] the legitimate representative and champion of the oppressed to seize the initiative in this constitutional debate [...], [f]ocusing the thinking of our people [and] involving them with [the] aim of increasing and sharpening their political consciousness [...].
>
> [Against this background, ANC will] study and follow up all constitutional and legal developments inside South Africa, both those initiated by the apartheid regime [and] by any other government, non-governmental organisation or individual who for whatever reason deem it their duty to work in that field.[2]

While ANC used the initial allocation of 500,000 SEK to launch the PASA initiative, the formal submission was discussed during the aid negotiations in May 1987. Recalling the Swedish offer from December 1986, it was agreed that a comprehensive "brainstorming" seminar would be held in Sweden in August 1987, where "ANC participants from outside and inside South Africa would discuss the future [...] activities, [define] possible areas [...] and [establish] a [planning] programme".[3] In preparation, ANC arranged over the following months a number of workshops and conferences. A first seminar on constitutional options was held in Harare in July. In addition to the core issue, it identified a number of closely related areas for further studies, such as local government, land, gender and affirmative action, which subsequently would be included in the PASA programme.[4]

Preparatory meetings with Sweden were held in Lusaka in June and in Harare in July 1987. In addition to a host of other tasks, Thabo Mbeki—who had accompanied Tambo to the talks with Palme in February 1986—took from the very beginning an active part in the design and orientation of the programme. Representing ANC's National Executive Committee, together with Bunny Mackay, Ted Pekane, Max Sisulu and Manto Tshabalala[5] he attended the meeting in Lusaka which in late June 1987 established the general framework of the forthcoming seminar. In consultations with Göran Andersson of SIPU[6], Roland Axelsson from the local embassy and Tor Sellström from Harare, it was agreed that it "should be seen as a

1. ANC Department of Legal and Constitutional Affairs: 'Project proposal document: Seminar on a future constitution for a democratic South Africa', submission attached to letter ('Post-apartheid planning for a future democratic South Africa') from Thomas Nkobi to the Swedish embassy in Lusaka, ANC, Lusaka, 11 February 1987 (SDA).
2. Ibid.
3. 'Agreed minutes [from] consultations in Lusaka, May 1987, between the African National Congress of South Africa and Sweden concerning humanitarian assistance', Lusaka, 8 May 1987 (SDA). Again, the ANC and Swedish delegations were respectively led by Thomas Nkobi and Lars-Olof Edström.
4. ANC: 'Constitutional options for a non-racial democratic South Africa', [no place or date], project proposal submitted after the August 1987 Bommersvik seminar in Sweden (SDA).
5. Mackay was at the time Head of Agricultural Projects in the Office of the Treasurer General. Pekane represented the Department of Legal and Constitutional Affairs, Sisulu the Department of Economics and Planning and Tshabalala the Department of Health. Later in 1987, Mackay was appointed Head of ANC's Post-Apartheid Committee and Tshabalala Administrative Secretary. After serving as Deputy Minister of Justice from 1996, Tshabalala became in 1999 Minister of Health in President Mbeki's first cabinet.
6. The Swedish National Institute for Civil Service Training and Development (SIPU) was responsible for the practical arrangements of the Bommersvik meeting.

starting point [for a] dialogue"; that the main objective was to "design a comprehensive [ANC] project proposal on [...] possible [...] options for [...] post-apartheid
reconstruction"; that ANC should hold separate, internal sessions with the participants from South Africa; that a joint ANC-Swedish secretariat should coordinate
the proceedings; and that Sweden should assist by seconding relevant experts and
policy makers.[1]

Further consultations between ANC, representatives from South Africa and
Sweden were held in Harare at the end of July. During these meetings, six priority
areas were identified, namely, a) state, structure of government and constitutional
affairs; b) mass media and culture; c) health, education and social services; d) local
government and planning; e) economy, agriculture and energy; and f) women and
children.[2] To cover these subjects and the main regions in South Africa, ANC concluded that ten resource persons from within the country in addition to twelve officials and researchers based in exile should be invited.[3] In order to protect the
participants from South Africa from possible legal consequences, it was resolved
that no publicity should be given to the event. While the seminar in the subsequent
documentation was presented as a general 'Workshop on Research Priorities for
Developing Countries', it was in this context, finally, agreed that the Swedish
organizers "on behalf of Stockholm university" should send individual invitations
to those coming from South Africa, asking them "to attend a summer workshop on
new trends in education with production".[4]

Preceded by two days of discussions between the internally based and exiled
South Africans, the PASA seminar took place between 17 and 24 August 1987 at
the Bommersvik training centre of the Social Democratic Youth League, some 70
kilometres southwest of Stockholm. Although the meeting was sanctioned by ANC
President Tambo and the agenda and objectives had been thoroughly discussed, initially a great deal of uncertainty prevailed. As stated in ANC's notes from the internal, preparatory deliberations, not only had a great deal of criticism been raised by
various structures of the movement—notably the Women's Secretariat and the
Youth League, who felt that they had not been properly consulted—but "[t]he
Swedish participation was [also] a controversial subject".[5]

The criticism was addressed by Mbeki, Jordan and other leading ANC representatives arriving on the eve of the seminar.[6] Nevertheless, wary of dominant overtures in favour of a 'Swedish, or Nordic, model' and the linking of exclusively
Social Democratic recipes and resources to what potentially could become a divi-

---

1. Cable ('Möte med ANC ang Planning for Post-Apartheid South Africa'/'Meeting with ANC re Planning for Post-Apartheid South Africa') from Jan Ölander, Swedish ambassador to Zambia, to the Ministry for Foreign Affairs, Swedish embassy, Lusaka, 25 June 1987 (SDA) and ANC: 'Report on a meeting in preparation of the proposed seminar on the planning for [a] post-apartheid South Africa', [no place or date] (MCA).

2. ANC: 'Minutes of the Harare consultative meeting, 25-26 July 1987', [no further specification of place or date] (MCA). The ANC team included Pallo Jordan and Thabo Mbeki.

3. Among them were Paul Daphne (Natal), John Levi Engelbrecht (Western Cape), Randi Erentzen (Western Cape) and Mathole Motshekga (Transvaal). At the time, Daphne coordinated a Social Policy Research Project, set up in Durban in early 1987. It was, however, underlined that adequate structures—"accountable to the broad democratic movement"—must be established in all the regions of South Africa. An *ad hoc* committee composed of Daphne, Engelbrecht and Motshekga was charged with this task (ibid.).

4. Cable ('Planning for post-apartheid South Africa') from Tor Sellström to the Ministry for Foreign Affairs and SIDA, Swedish embassy, Harare, 28 July 1987 (SDA).

5. ANC: 'Meeting to brief comrades Zola [Skweyiya] and Max [Sisulu], 15 August 1987' and 'Meetings of the ANC delegation on 17 and 22 August 1987' [no further specification of place or date] (MCA).

6. In addition to Thabo Mbeki and Pallo Jordan, among the ANC representatives who took part at the Bommersvik seminar were Jaya Appalraju, Lindiwe Mabuza, Bunny Mackay, Barbara Masekela, Ted Pekane, Max Sisulu, Zola Skweyiya and Manto Tshabalala. Mbeki, Jordan, Mackay and Tshabalala represented ANC on the joint steering committee (ibid.).

sive programme[1], the South African participants agreed that "[t]he project should not be tied to [...] Swedish funding only" and that "[o]ther donors should be involved".[2] Welcoming advice and financial support, the ownership of the initiative, they emphasized, should belong to ANC in cooperation with the broader South African mass democratic movement.[3]

While the Social Democratic hosts, naturally, advocated post-apartheid policies based on Swedish experiences—also advising against a too academic approach and arguing in favour of a policy-oriented PASA agenda[4]—this opinion was respected. In her opening address, Cooperation Minister Lena Hjelm-Wallén noted that "[i]t is [our] ambition to present [...] a balanced picture of various spheres of [the] Swedish society and policies [, where] [t]here will be emphasis not only on positive achievements, but also on shortcomings. [The] Swedish experience", she continued, "although useful as a source of ideas and suggestions, cannot pretend to be universally applicable". Against this background, the seminar "should rather be seen as a forum for your own discussion[s], in which Swedish experts will be happy to share their [views]".[5] In a later, internal comment to the Bommersvik seminar, SIDA's Deputy Director General Lars-Olof Edström—who chaired the opening session—similarly stressed that "[o]ur role is to give financial support to the movement's own work".[6]

The Swedish government accorded great importance to the PASA initiative. At Bommersvik, in addition to Hjelm-Wallén's participation this was illustrated by the fact that Prime Minister Carlsson—by then relieved of the contentious boycott issue—paid a visit to the seminar.[7] In spite of the summer holiday season, a number of high-ranking officials, academics and politicians would also take an active part in the proceedings, either by submitting papers for discussion[8] or by serving as resource persons in the six working groups into which the participants were divided to reflect upon the priority areas.[9]

1. Author's recollection.
2. ANC: 'Meetings of the ANC delegation on 17 and 22 August 1987' (MCA).
3. This was in marked contrast to SWAPO's approach. As noted in the chapter 'With SWAPO to Victory', Swedish bilateral assistance to the movement's socio-economic plans for independent Namibia started in mid-1988. A 'brainstorming seminar' similar to the ANC Bommersvik workshop was held in Sollentuna outside Stockholm in December 1988. With a radically weaker research base at its disposal, contrary to ANC SWAPO did not, however, primarily ask for guidance, but requested Sweden to carry out strategic studies on Namibia's transport and communications sector, as well as on the establishment of a central bank. Similar requests on its behalf were submitted to the other Nordic countries.
4. Lena Johansson: Memorandum ('Minnesanteckningar från samråd SIDA/UD om humanitärt bistånd i södra Afrika, 19 januari 1988'/'Notes from consultations between SIDA and the Foreign Ministry regarding humanitarian assistance in Southern Africa, 19 January 1988'), SIDA, Stockholm, 20 January 1988 (SDA).
5. 'Opening speech by Lena Hjelm-Wallén on 17 August 1987 at [the] Bommersvik workshop' (MCA).
6. Letter ('Handläggning av Post-Apartheid South Africa'/'Administration of PASA') from Lars-Olof Edström to the Swedish embassy in Harare, SIDA, Stockholm, 9 November 1987 (SDA).
7. The Swedish trade embargo on South Africa entered into force the previous month.
8. Two general discussion papers were presented. Sverker Gustavsson, Under-Secretary of State in the Ministry of Education, submitted a paper on 'Popular rule and the transformation of the Swedish society', while Jan O. Karlsson, his counterpart at the Ministry of Finance, contributed a study on 'Economic policy options: The development of the Swedish welfare policy' (ANC/SIPU: 'Report on workshop on research priorities for developing countries', [no place or date, but Lusaka/Stockholm in early 1988]) (SDA).
9. The Swedish resource persons were: Björn Beckman of the University of Stockholm (State, structure of government and constitutional affairs), Jan Sandquist and Bo Kärre of SIDA (Mass media and culture), Ernst Michanek, former Director General, and Lennart Wohlgemuth of SIDA (Health, education and social services), Ove Andersson of Swedeplan (Local government and planning), Bertil Odén of SIDA (Economy, agriculture and energy) and Maj-Lis Lööw, MP and President of the Social Democratic Women's League (Women and children) (ibid.).

The Bommersvik deliberations were later summarized in a 40-page joint report by ANC and SIPU, the latter acting on behalf of the Swedish authorities.[1] With regard to the general orientation of ANC's post-apartheid planning work, the following extract from the report could be quoted:

> All working groups agreed that a coordinated research effort would provide a unifying ideological concern that links the various sectors [...] into a coherent whole, serving not only the short-term goals in socio-economic development, but also the long-term aspirations of [the] people. Moreover, [they] emphasised the importance of popular participation in research programmes and the accountability of research units to the people. All working groups saw [such] units as sources of guidance to non-governmental community organisations and the people as a whole. Thus, it was recommended that [the] character [of the planning process] will be [that of] a policy-oriented, problem-solving search for knowledge and information, whose content will seek to further the formulation of economic policies and programmes.[2]

After the closure of the seminar, a deputation led by Mbeki and Jordan submitted a preliminary report to Bengt Säve-Söderbergh, Under-Secretary of State for International Cooperation. Dividing the future work into eight subject areas[3], the ANC and South African participants estimated that the financial requirements for a comprehensive PASA programme—covering all the regions in the country—during an initial year would be no less than 21 MSEK.[4] However, while it would take time to establish an adequate PASA structure and it was acknowledged "that funds for this gigantic task can never be sufficient", in order to proceed ANC asked for interim support amounting to 600,000 SEK[5], a request which was subsequently granted.[6]

Whereas the initiative taken by Tambo and Palme in February 1986; followed up at Bommersvik one and a half years later; and complemented by various parallel South African and international projects[7] coincided with an internal process linking up an increasing number of scholars with community-based organizations—characterized by Mathole Motshekga as "development of policy with research as an instrument"[8]—the ANC-led PASA programme itself, however, was initially fraught with difficulties. Shortly after the meeting in Sweden, ANC conceded in an internal report that

> it is doubtful whether, in fact, the mass democratic movement has been briefed thoroughly on this project. [I]n this event, [it] might therefore not achieve the objectives for which it is intended. For these reasons, it is [...] recommended that a special meeting soon [is] convened between the ANC [National Executive Committee] and the leadership of the mass democratic movement. This should clear the air and at the same time facilitate the establishment of [an] internal coordinat[ing] structure on a firm and more representative basis.[9]

---

1. The original draft was edited by ANC and submitted to SIPU in December 1987 (Letter [no title] from Elisabeth Dahlin to the Swedish embassy in Lusaka, SIDA, Stockholm, 18 December 1987) (SDA).
2. ANC/SIPU: 'Report on workshop on research priorities for developing countries' (SDA).
3. It was decided to treat education, health and social services as separate areas of study.
4. ANC: 'Presentation of project document to the Ministry [for] Foreign Affairs on 24 August 1987' [no further specification of place or date] (MCA).
5. Ibid.
6. Adjusting the budget for 1987/88, at the consultative talks in December 1987 it was agreed to set aside 1.8 MSEK for post-apartheid planning ('Minutes from consultative talks in Lusaka, 8-11 December 1987, between the African National Congress of South Africa (ANC) and SIDA concerning humanitarian assistance') (SDA).
7. Notably the South African Economic Research and Training (SAERT) project, based at the University of Amsterdam, Holland. SAERT was closely linked to ANC's PASA programme.
8. Cited in Bertil Odén: Memorandum ('PASA efter möte med National Research Committee i Harare, 23 september 1988'/'PASA after meeting the National Research Committee in Harare on 23 September 1988'), SIDA, Stockholm, 4 October 1988 (SDA).
9. ANC: 'Presentation of project document to the Ministry [for] Foreign Affairs on 24 August 1987' (MCA).

During a follow-up meeting with SIDA, ANC stated in December 1987 that "UDF and COSATU have been briefed on [the] project".[1] Although the National Executive Committee—ANC's highest organ—originally had endorsed the planning initiative, in February 1988, however, NEC's Working Committee called PASA into question. In the absence of Tambo and at a time when Mbeki was involved in secret 'talks about talks' with prominent Afrikaner representatives in England[2], senior NEC members critically observed that "[t]here is a loss of control [as] more and more workshops [are] being organised which involve people from home".[3] In this regard, Chris Hani and Joe Slovo—both holding leading positions in the South African Communist Party—expressed particularly strong views.

Concerning Mbeki's talks, Hani—according to the minutes with "general acclamation of approval"—stated that "[i]t is very disturbing that a member of the NEC leaves to hold discussion[s] with Afrikaner intellectuals without prior consultations", asking "[o]n whose authority Cde. Thabo has entered into [these talks]?" Far from satisfied with the explanations given, he concluded:

> Let the minutes record that we register our extreme displeasure [with the fact] that Cde. Thabo has unilaterally gone to London without any consultation and without a mandate from the NEC.[4]

Hani's criticism prompted Joe Nhlanhla, ANC's Secretary of Intelligence and Security, to comment that "[t]his is part of a bigger problem. There are lots of people who are meeting people from home without any consultation, let alone coordination". In this context, Joe Slovo raised the PASA programme, wanting "to know and receive answers". More specifically, he asked: "Who controls it? Where do the finances come from? Who appointed the people who serve on it?" While Pallo Jordan reminded the participants that in early 1986 the National Executive Committee had approved the initiative and that the subsequent developments had regularly been reported upon, he noted that in the process there "had emerged a consensus that PASA would be an autonomous structure in which ANC had an input, but was not explicitly running it. This", he added, "was to afford people from home a measure of protection". Referring to the Bommersvik seminar, Slovo, nevertheless, insisted:

> Who took the decision on the people who went to Sweden? Even if it is autonomous, PASA is using our personnel, our office space [and] our equipment. It is understandable that it is autonomous, but we must appoint the personnel. We discuss [and then we] formally set up the structures.[5]

In this, Slovo was supported by Hani, who stressed that "[t]he principle of accountability must be maintained. Some of us will later ask what our priorities [were]? We might [then] be opening a can of worms". In his reply, Jordan stood his ground, arguing that "[o]nce it was decided that a [PASA] project was necessary, we needed

---

1. ANC: 'Consultative meeting on PASA between the SIDA and the ANC delegations', [no place], 10 December 1987 (SDA).
2. Between November 1987 and May 1990, Mbeki led small ANC delegations to twelve secret meetings with representatives of the South African Afrikaner establishment at Mells, close to Bath in England (Sparks op. cit., pp. 80-86). The IDASA-sponsored Dakar meeting between ANC—also led by Mbeki—and white South Africans was held in August 1987.
3. Joe Nhlanhla cited in ANC: 'Minutes of NWC', [Lusaka, 22 February 1988] (MCA).
4. Ibid.
5. Ibid.

people to administer it [...]. We cannot expect [the National Working Committee] to endorse every little decision".[1]

ANC Secretary General Alfred Nzo chaired the meeting. Summing up the "fiery discussion"[2], he stated:

> In fairness, we must say that documents [on PASA] were circulated [and] [w]e expected that they were read. [...] I was invited to a meeting of the PASA secretariat [where] it was decided [...] that it should fall under the President's Office. [...] [However,] I suggest [...] that the matter be discussed by the NEC. In preparation for that, we can request the PASA secretariat to prepare a report, plus a financial statement. [...] We can then take firm decisions consciously [...] and not just [as matters] evolve.[3]

Formalization and Structures

Albeit for different reasons, in order to allocate operational funds to the PASA programme the Swedish authorities also wished to see a clearer administrative structure. According to ANC's notes from a joint meeting held in December 1987:

> SIDA feels that [...] PASA must be properly handled. In order to continue its support [...], SIDA needs to know what the ANC wants to do and how it intends implementing [the] project. [...] A structure to handle [the] activities should be established. SIDA will continue [its] assistance after the ANC has taken a firm stand on the issue.[4]

As ANC's Post-Apartheid Interim Committee under Mackay and Tshabalala with support from Tambo, Mbeki, Jordan and other leading officials despite the criticism aired at NEC's Working Committee continued to arrange workshops and meetings with representatives from South Africa—largely financed by Sweden through the regular cooperation programme—it was, however, only towards the end of 1988 that a proper PASA structure eventually began to take form.

This notwithstanding, concerning the process of post-apartheid planning itself, major advances were achieved, notably with regard to the core issue of a legal framework for a future democratic South Africa. After a long consultative process—notably involving the UDF-affiliated National Association of Democratic Lawyers (NADEL)[5]—in August 1988 ANC was in a position to table a set of constitutional guidelines "for consideration by all the people of our country".[6] As noted by Mbeki, the guidelines—widely distributed in South Africa and summarized by some of the major national newspapers—were not to be seen as a final ANC product, but as an input into an ongoing democratic discussion and planning

---

1. Ibid.
2. Shubin op. cit., p. 326.
3. ANC: 'Minutes of NWC', [Lusaka, 22 February 1988] (MCA).
4. ANC: 'Consultative meeting on PASA between the SIDA and the ANC delegations', [no place], 10 December 1987 (SDA).
5. NADEL was one of the organizations receiving Swedish support via AIC (see the chapter 'Closer and Broader Cooperation: Projects in Exile, Mineworkers, UDF and Civics in South Africa'). In connection with bilateral ANC consultations in Harare in February 1989, representatives from NADEL contributed to a parallel PASA meeting between ANC and Sweden (Kaj Persson: Memorandum ('Minnesanteckningar från möte om post-apartheid-projektet om Sydafrika'/'Notes from a meeting concerning the South African post-apartheid project'), Swedish embassy, Lusaka, 14 February 1989) (SDA). With regard to ANC's work towards a future democratic dispensation, it could be noted that CCHA in mid-1991 granted the Raoul Wallenberg Institute in Lund 4.9 MSEK in support of the movement's Constitutional Committee (Ingalill Colbro: Memorandum ('Ansökan om stöd från Raoul Wallenberg-institutet'/'Request for support from the Raoul Wallenberg Institute'), SIDA/CCHA, [Stockholm], 28 May 1991) (SDA).
6. ANC: 'Mass action for people's power!', Statement of the National Executive Committee presented by Oliver Tambo, Lusaka, 8 January 1989.

process.[1] As such, they were considered "a priority" for the future post-apartheid work.[2]

The declared ambition at the Bommersvik seminar was to facilitate the formation of planning units in all the regions of South Africa; an internal coordinating body; and an overall PASA centre based close to the ANC headquarters in Lusaka. While internal regional units were set up and the University of the Western Cape (UWC) was identified to coordinate the activities[3], it proved, however, considerably more difficult to launch a formally autonomous structure in exile. Initially, it was hoped that it could be accommodated at the University of Zambia (UNZA). In spite of promising contacts between Oliver Tambo and President Kaunda[4], the UNZA senate, however, did not support the proposal, arguing that the political content was "disconcerting" and that the approach was not sufficiently "academic".[5]

Nevertheless, by the end of 1988 ANC's efforts had resulted in the formation of both an internal and an external PASA structure. Based at UWC in Cape Town and led by Randi Erentzen, in South Africa a Centre for Development Studies (CDS) was formally registered as an independent trust with a board initially representing seven regions in the country.[6] Under the Zambian Company's Act, a South African Studies Project (SASPRO) was at about the same time set up in Lusaka, governed by a board of directors including *inter alia* Thabo Mbeki.[7] Thus constituted and between them coordinating the planning work, in February 1989 SASPRO and CDS invited Swedish officials to a meeting in Harare to discuss their activity plans and prepare a budget for financial support.[8] Following these consultations, the next month ANC/SASPRO submitted a formal funding request to Sweden, covering the period July 1989-June 1991 and amounting to approximately 12 MSEK.[9]

---

1. Sten Rylander: Memorandum ('Thabo Mbeki besöker statssekreterare Säve-Söderbergh'/'Thabo Mbeki visits Under-Secretary of State Säve Söderbergh'), Ministry for Foreign Affairs, Stockholm, 2 January 1989 (SDA).
2. ANC: 'Report on research' [no place or date], attached to letter ('Post-apartheid South Africa') from Kaj Persson to the Ministry for Foreign Affairs, Swedish embassy, Lusaka, 14 February 1989 (SDA).
3. In January 1987, Gert Johannes 'Jakes' Gerwel became Vice-Chancellor of the University of the Western Cape. Designating the university as a vehicle for change, he soon took an active interest in the PASA programme, in mid-1988 visiting ANC in Lusaka and Sweden for discussions (Jan Cedergren: 'Rapport från överläggningar med ANC den 9-12 maj 1988'/'Report from deliberations with ANC, 9-12 May 1988'), Ministry for Foreign Affairs, Stockholm, 31 May 1988 (SDA). Following the April 1994 general elections in South Africa, Gerwel was appointed Director General in the Office of President Mandela.
4. Formally, President Kaunda was the Chancellor of UNZA.
5. Bertil Odén: Memorandum ('Aktuella läget för PASA'/'PASA status report'), Swedish embassy, Lusaka, 14 September 1988 (SDA). Formerly with SIDA, at the time Odén was attached to the Nordic Africa Institute. Since the August 1987 Bommersvik seminar closely following the PASA initiative, he served as an adviser to the Swedish aid authorities. At the end of 1988, ANC registered SASPRO as an independent company in Zambia, at the same time seeking an agreement with UNZA. However, the proposed association never materialized. Shortly before the decision to transfer SASPRO to South Africa, in February 1990 Mbeki—a member of the SASPRO board—critically commented that UNZA "had been acting too slowly" (Cable ('Möte med ANC om humanitärt bistånd till Sydafrika'/'Meeting with ANC on humanitarian assistance to South Africa') from the Ministry for Foreign Affairs to the Swedish missions in Cape Town, Pretoria and Lusaka, Stockholm, 14 February 1990) (SDA).
6. ANC: 'Report on research' [no place or date], attached to letter ('Post-apartheid South Africa') from Kaj Persson to the Ministry for Foreign Affairs, Swedish embassy, Lusaka, 14 February 1989 (SDA).
7. Ibid. and Dag Ehrenpreis: Memorandum ('Forskning om Sydafrika efter apartheid: PASA'/'Research on South Africa after apartheid: PASA'), SIDA, Stockholm, 12 January 1989 (SDA).
8. At the meeting held at the Jameson Hotel on 6 February 1989, ANC/SASPRO was represented by Thabo Mbeki, Steve Tshwete, Zola Skweyiya, Bunny Mackay and Manto Tshabalala. Led by Randi Erentzen, the internal CDS team included Bill Jardine, Marian Lacey, Ace Magasitule and Mathole Motshekga. Nano Mathlape from SAERT in Amsterdam also formed part of the PASA delegation. The Swedish representatives were Kaj Persson from the embassy in Lusaka, Tor Sellström (SIDA) and Per-Arne Ströberg (SAREC) from the embassy in Harare (Kaj Persson: Memorandum ('Minnesanteckningar från möte om post-apartheid-projektet om Sydafrika'/'Notes from a meeting concerning the South African post-apartheid project'), Swedish embassy, Lusaka, 14 February 1989) (SDA).
9. SASPRO Limited: 'Project document: SASPRO', request signed by Bunny Mackay and forwarded to the Swedish embassy in Lusaka, SASPRO, Lusaka, 11 March 1989 (SDA).

The request was discussed during the annual aid negotiations in Lusaka in May, where the ANC delegation noted that

> [c]ontrary to expectations of all involved, the [PASA] process had been longer than envisaged and the first phase since the Bommersvik meeting in August 1987 deliberately slow. This [was] due to the process-oriented nature of the project as opposed to clear-cut, academic[ally] tailored research. The series of consultations and workshops held throughout South Africa and externally [...] aimed at elaborating on areas scantily covered or omitted at Bommersvik. [...] [However,] [w]ith the completion of the preparatory work [...], PASA was now ready for actual funding [...]. The urgency of a quick decision [...] should be seen in relation to the dynamic momentum set in motion by the preparatory process.[1]

While the Swedish delegation raised "some questions and points for clarification", at the negotiations it was, however, only decided to set aside 400,000 SEK in favour of PASA during the financial year 1989/90.[2] After receiving additional information, in September 1989, it was, finally agreed that no less than 13.1 MSEK should be extended over the two-year period 1989/90-1990/91, with 5 million in favour of SASPRO and slightly more than 8 million to CDS.[3]

As ANC and SIDA discussed how the financial resources should be disbursed, in February 1990 the unbanning of the movement radically altered the conditions of the support. Whereas it was decided to channel the assistance to CDS via the Dag Hammarskjöld Foundation in Uppsala[4], as early as in March 1990 ANC resolved to disband the SASPRO structure in Zambia[5], which over the period June-September was transferred to South Africa and largely became amalgamated with CDS.[6] Swedish support towards post-apartheid planning would at the same time involve an increasing number of organizations, both in Sweden and in South Africa. In discussions with Thabo Mbeki, in April 1990 it was, for example, proposed to arrange a seminar in South Africa on Swedish economic and social experiences together with ANC, UDF and COSATU.[7]

Subsequently held in Witkoppen outside Johannesburg in October 1990—shortly after the publication of ANC's discussion document on economic policy, which emphasized the liberation movement's "basic perspective [...] of a mixed economy"[8]—the seminar on 'Economic Policy, Democracy and Social Welfare: The

---

1. 'Agreed minutes from consultations held in Lusaka, May 1989, between the African National Congress of South Africa and Sweden concerning humanitarian assistance', Lusaka, 26 May 1989 (SDA).
2. Ibid. During the three-year period 1987/88-1989/90, a total amount of 4.1 MSEK was allocated by Sweden towards ANC's preparatory PASA work (Bertil Odén: Memorandum ('Ansökan från The South African Studies Project (SASPRO) om stöd till forskningsprogram om det framtida Sydafrika'/'Request from SASPRO for support to a research programme on future South Africa'), SIDA/CCHA, [Stockholm], 20 September 1989) (SDA).
3. Odén ibid.
4. In 1990/91, slightly more than 2 MSEK was transferred via the Dag Hammarskjöld Foundation (DHF) to CDS (Anita Theodossiadis: 'Planeringsöversikt humanitärt bistånd södra Afrika'/'Planning summary [of] humanitarian assistance [to] Southern Africa', SIDA/CCHA, [Stockholm], 16 September 1991) (SDA). A formal agreement between CDS and DHF was only signed in July 1991 (Information from DHF, Uppsala, 2 May 2001).
5. Eva Belfrage: Memorandum ('Anteckningar från besök av ANC den 28 mars 1990'/'Notes from visit by ANC on 28 March 1990'), SIDA, Stockholm, 30 March 1990 (SDA).
6. Per Sjögren: Memorandum ('Förhandlingar med ANC i Lusaka 15-18 maj 1990'/'Negotiations with ANC in Lusaka, 15-18 May 1990'), Ministry for Foreign Affairs, Stockholm, 12 June 1990 (SDA).
7. Per Sjögren: Memorandum ('Seminarium'/'Seminar'), Ministry for Foreign Affairs, Stockholm, 6 April 1990 (SDA).
8. ANC: 'Discussion document on economic policy', ANC, Marshalltown, September 1990. Submitted for discussion by ANC's Department of Economic Policy, this important document was the outcome of two PASA workshops held in Harare in April-May and September 1990.

Swedish Option'[1] resulted *inter alia* in follow-up study visits to Sweden[2], as well as in financial support towards a number of policy workshops in South Africa.[3] The official assistance to ANC after its unbanning will be discussed below.[4] Meanwhile, it could be noted that the PASA project soon was to cover electoral training and voter education. With Swedish funds, CDS thus launched a nationwide 'Civic Education Programme on Elections' in November 1991.[5]

With regard to the original PASA initiative, the Swedish government mainly acted as a facilitator, supporting ANC's own planning work.[6] It is against this background difficult to assess Sweden's possible influence. According to ANC's Jaya Appalraju, it was considerable. Interviewed in September 1995, he noted:

> In [the] consultative discussions on the post-apartheid project, Swedish involvement and Swedish thinking was always sought after, whether it was on the question of constitutional development or in education. We always made sure that somebody had actually researched what was Swedish policy, or Scandinavian policy, towards the various issues of women, welfare, macro-economic growth and so forth. Besides financial resources, I think that inputs from the Scandinavian governments in terms of their own historical experience always featured in our discussions. [...]
>
> From the Bommersvik PASA meeting in 1987, our economists really started to look much more closely at the history of Swedish policy-making, comparing and critically assessing the

---

1. Organized by ANC, COSATU and UDF in cooperation with SIPU of Sweden, among the Swedish resource persons addressing the seminar were Bengt Säve-Söderbergh, Under-Secretary of State for International Cooperation; Jan O. Karlsson, then economic adviser in the Prime Minister's Office; Anders Mellbourn of the liberal newspaper *Dagens Nyheter*; Ernst Michanek, former Director General of SIDA; and Bengt Rydén, General Manager of the Stockholm Stock Exchange. Göran Andersson represented SIPU ('Economic policy, democracy and social welfare: The Swedish option—Reports from the seminar at Indaba Hotel, Witkoppen, 24-26 October 1990', attached to letter ('Seminariet i Sydafrika om svenska erfarenheter av politisk ekonomi, demokrati och social välfärd i oktober 1990'/'The seminar in South Africa on Swedish experiences regarding political economy, democracy and social welfare in October 1990') from Christina Hoffman to the Ministry for Foreign Affairs, Swedish legation, Pretoria, 6 March 1991) (MFA).
2. To study the national elections, a delegation of six people was invited to Sweden in September 1991. Four of them—led by the future Deputy Minister of Home Affairs Penuell Maduna—represented ANC and the other two PAC and the New Unity Movement (SIPU: 'The Swedish electoral system: South African study visit to Stockholm, 3-17 September 1991', SIPU, Stockholm, 1991) (SDA).
3. In April 1991, 1.1 MSEK was allocated to ANC and COSATU for a series of workshops on economic policy (Ingalill Colbro: Memorandum ('Ansökan om stöd till ANC för en seminarieserie'/'Request for support to ANC for a series of seminars'), SIDA/CCHA, [Stockholm], 4 April 1991) (SDA).
4. With regard to PASA, it could be mentioned that SIDA through CDS in October 1990 supported a national consultative conference on 'Local Government and Planning for a Democratic South Africa', held in Johannesburg shortly before the above-mentioned seminar on economic policy. In addition to ANC policy papers presented by *inter alia* Jaya Appalraju, Thozamile Botha and Zola Skweyiya, the conference discussed relevant experiences from Great Britain, India, Nicaragua, Sweden and Zimbabwe. The paper on Sweden—focusing on local government and urban land use—was presented by Ann Schlyter from the University of Lund (CDS: *Local Government and Planning for a Democratic South Africa*, University of the Western Cape, Bellville, 1991).
5. Letter [no title] from Randi Erentzen to the Dag Hammarskjöld Foundation, Centre for Development Studies, University of the Western Cape, Bellville, 31 October 1991 (SDA).
6. The role of facilitator also included the arranging of meetings between ANC and third parties. In July 1992, for example, SIDA financed an encounter in Mariefred, Sweden, between the South African liberation movement and representatives from the Czech Republic, Hungary, Poland and Slovakia, organized by the Nordic Africa Institute. Alfred Nzo, former Secretary General and South Africa's future Foreign Minister; Penuell Maduna of the Constitutional Committee; and Mongane Wally Serote, heading the Department of Arts and Culture, represented ANC (Zdenek Cervenka: *African National Congress Meets Eastern Europe: A Dialogue on Common Experiences*, Current African Issues No. 15, Nordiska Afrikainstitutet, Uppsala, November 1992).

impact on both the economy and the politics of Sweden. It definitely had and still has a major influence [...].[1]

Billy Modise—who as ANC Chief Representative to Sweden closely followed the PASA work in the late 1980s—stated at the same time that

[t]he bottom line is that the struggle was ours, as ANC, but Sweden was very central in that struggle. They took it onto themselves much more than a normal government would do. Secondly, because its leadership at all levels spent time discussing the struggle with our leaders— the Tambos of this world—Sweden was in its own way able to influence them how they should handle things. In the minds of our leaders, Sweden helped to confirm that the basis of the struggle was to create democracy. The interaction between Sweden and ANC strengthened the democratic urge of the ANC leadership.[2]

---

1. Interview with Jaya Appalraju, p. 106. One and a half years after the South African democratic elections, Appalraju added: "We hope that this is reinforced, because now the field has been opened so considerably and there are so many other views that have come in and to some extent have diverted us from our initial ideas of where we should be going. I think that we are now going through a moment of resignation from this tremendous amount of input, discussion and debate about what should be done, for instance with the South African economy" (ibid.). Asked whether in his opinion there was a hidden political agenda behind the Swedish support, Appalraju commented: "Even if there was, I do not think that we ever felt it. There were no strings attached to the support we received. In fact, we were extremely free in the way we used the support and we understood very well that we were to deal with an extremely complex capitalist economy in South Africa. Nobody was going to convince us that we were going to have to prepare for an essentially planned economy. We had to deal with the realities of that complex and monopolized situation. Even if there had been an agenda, it would not have been relevant under our circumstances, because we had to look very carefully at the objective realities. [...] [This] was very different from [the support received] from a lot of other countries" (ibid., pp. 106-07).
2. Interview with Billy Modise, p. 160.

Free at Last

The Last Mile

The Thirty Years' War in Southern Africa entered its final phase with the unbanning of ANC, PAC, SACP, UDF and a number of anti-apartheid organizations on 2 February 1990.[1] Nelson Mandela was released nine days later and on 21 March—exactly 30 years after the Sharpeville massacre—independent Namibia was born under a SWAPO government. Coinciding with the demise of the Soviet Union and an end to the Cold War[2], these events augured fundamental changes. In South Africa itself, the road towards a non-racial, democratic dispensation was, however, far from open. On the contrary, the four-year period from ANC's legalization and Mandela's release to the democratic elections in April 1994 would be dominated by political attempts to divide the Congress Alliance and marginalize ANC, as well as by unprecedented violence, rampant corruption and, in general, widespread uncertainty about the country's future.[3]

When compared to the independence process in Namibia[4], it should be recalled that the point of departure in South Africa was radically different. While in the Namibian case there was a strong external involvement, an existing blueprint for the transition process in the form of UN Security Council Resolution 435 and a considerable deployment of international civilian and military personnel under UNTAG to oversee the agreed schedule towards elections, constitution-making and the transfer of power[5], in South Africa the course was pursued by domestic actors. Apart from general commitments towards a negotiated solution, there was at the outset no legal instrument, or 'road map', which defined the final objective, offered a timetable or regulated the proceedings, nor was there an independent external administrative or military presence to supervise and protect the process.[6]

---

1. In his landmark speech at the opening session of the South African parliament, President de Klerk announced the lifting of restrictions on 33 political organizations and 374 individual activists.
2. The Berlin wall—arguably the prime symbol of the Cold War—started to be taken down in early November 1989, at the same time as independence elections were held in Namibia. In his address on 2 February 1990, de Klerk stated that "[t]he events in the Soviet Union and Eastern Europe [...] weaken the capability of [the] organisations [which are unbanned]". This, he said, was one of "[t]he most important facets of the advice received by the government in this connection" ('Address by State President F.W. de Klerk at the opening of the second session of the ninth parliament of the Republic of South Africa', Cape Town, 2 February 1990) (NAI).
3. From the start of the negotiations in mid-1990 to the elections in April 1994, no less than 14,000 people were killed in politically related incidents in South Africa (TRC op. cit. (Vol. II), p. 584). For an account of the violent events, see Daniel Reed: *Beloved Country: South Africa's Silent Wars*, BBC Books, London, 1994. The most dramatic political assassination was that of Chris Hani, the popular ANC leader-cum-General Secretary of the Communist Party, who was shot by white extremists outside his home in Johannesburg in April 1993.
4. As well as to the 1979-80 process in Zimbabwe, which was formally administered by the United Kingdom and supervised by contingents from the Commonwealth (see the chapter 'Patriotic Front: ZANU and ZAPU towards Independence').
5. Cf. the chapter 'With SWAPO to Victory'.
6. There were, however, several international observer teams in the country. The UN Observer Mission in South Africa (UNOMSA) was set up in September 1992.

Beginning through secret 'talks about talks' between the Pretoria government and ANC[1], in South Africa the transition from white minority rule towards a political dispensation yet to be defined was chartered in difficult internal multi-party negotiations, extended over several years and taking place in a situation of near civil war. As a brief guide to the following presentation, the main events along this road are summarized in the box below. It should be added that the political scene in Namibia was considerably less complicated than that prevailing in South Africa. Whereas SWAPO was seen by all parties involved as the dominant nationalist organization, with regard to ANC this was initially far from being the case. Although violently opposed by Inkatha and contested by PAC, AZAPO and others, the wider Congress Alliance led by Mandela would, however, soon establish its authority and eventually appear as the regime's undisputed counterpart.

1988 (December)	New York accords between Angola, Cuba and South Africa
1989 (Jan–Oct)	President P.W. Botha suffers a stroke, resigns and is replaced by F.W. de Klerk
1989 (August)	ANC–OAU Harare declaration
1989 (October)	Walter Sisulu and other Rivonia prisoners released
1989 (November)	SWAPO victory in the Namibian elections and fall of the Berlin wall
1990 (February)	Unbanning of ANC, PAC, SACP, UDF and release of Nelson Mandela
1990 (March)	Independence of Namibia
1990 (May)	Groote Schuur talks between ANC and the South African government
1990 (August)	ANC suspends the armed struggle
1991 (December)	First session of the Convention for a Democratic South Africa (CODESA)
1992 (March)	Whites-only referendum endorses negotiation process
1992 (June)	ANC withdraws from CODESA following the Boipatong massacre and evidence of 'third force' operations
1993 (April)	Negotiations resume through the Multi-Party Forum
1993 (July)	Agreement on democratic elections 27 April 1994
1993 (September)	Mandela calls for the lifting of economic sanctions
1993 (November)	Agreement on a non-racial, democratic interim constitution
1993 (December)	Legislation passed on a Transitional Executive Council
1994 (April)	ANC wins democratic elections
1994 (May)	Nelson Mandela sworn in as President of South Africa

Although the imprisoned Nelson Mandela and Thabo Mbeki together with other ANC leaders in exile had embarked upon exploratory talks with the Pretoria regime, the pace of the final events and the announcement made on 2 February 1990 by President F.W. de Klerk would largely take the liberation movement off guard. Catering for thousands of refugees in various settlements in Africa; having recently established a veritable "diplomatic empire"[2] around the world; and at the

---

1. From mid-1985 until its legalization, internally through Mandela and in exile ANC held no fewer than around 75 meetings with government officials and representatives of the South African white community (Ohlson op. cit., p. 97).
2. Rantete op. cit., p. 4. Cf. below.

time involved in the clandestine 'Operation Vula'[1], the unbanning of ANC would, as noted by Scott Thomas, confront the organization with a combined 're-entry' and 're-emergence' problem[2] of how to transfer the centre of its activities, its political leadership and its trained exiled cadres to South Africa, where in an uncertain situation after three decades of underground work it was to operate openly as a legal entity. The overall challenge has been summarized as follows by Roger Southall:

> For the ANC, particularly, these proved enormously difficult times as it sought to restore itself as a legal, mass movement in the face of not just the exuberant and often conflicting aspirations of its impatient supporters, but also hugely successful forays launched against it by an array of opponents, most notably Inkatha and powerful elements within the security forces. And all the time it was struggling to adjust to its new situation, provide for the return of thousands of exiles, develop its infrastructure, develop its policies for a post-apartheid South Africa and, not least, prepare itself and its cohorts for participation in forthcoming constitutional negotiations with the government concerning the creation of a non-racial, democratic South Africa. The entire process severely stretched the organisational capacity of the ANC.[3]

The Swedish government assisted ANC from the very beginning in its efforts to overcome these difficulties, in the process becoming closely involved with the denouement of the apartheid drama. In fact, with the parallel exit from the scene of the Soviet Union and its Eastern European allies[4], the direct official support from Sweden to ANC would from 1990 arguably assume a more strategic importance than ever before, in particular with regard to infrastructure, administration, electoral preparations and planning for a future dispensation. ANC's dependency on Swedish financial resources became at the same time a source of mutual concern. Together with the questions of maintaining economic sanctions, ending the external support and extending assistance exclusively to one political actor, it would largely occupy the dialogue between Sweden and ANC during the troubled South African transition period. These issues—from October 1991 addressed by Carl Bildt's non-socialist government[5]—will be discussed below.

Setbacks and Breakthroughs

ANC in exile would towards the close of the 1980s experience mixed fortunes. After a quarter-century period when Great Britain and the United States persistently had left the liberation movement out in the cold, in September 1986 Oliver Tambo for the first time met Foreign Secretary Sir Geoffrey Howe and other members of the British government.[6] Four months later, he was received by the US Secretary of State George Shultz. As the Commonwealth, the European Community and the United

---

1. Coordinated by Mac Maharaj and subsequently assisted by the Soviet Union, the operation *Vulindlela*—Zulu for "opening a way"—was launched in 1988 to infiltrate senior ANC/MK leaders into South Africa. The highly secret initiative was uncovered by the South African security forces in July 1990, shortly before ANC's announcement that it was to suspend the armed struggle (cf. Barrell Ph. D. op. cit., chapter nine, pp. 45-48, Kasrils op. cit., pp. 301-43 and Shubin op. cit., pp. 332-39. From May to October 1995, ANC's journal *Mayibuye* published a six-part story on the operation, entitled 'Talking to Vula' and written by Tim Jenkin).
2. Thomas op. cit., p. 235.
3. Southall op. cit., p. 305.
4. On the Soviet Union and South Africa after ANC's unbanning, see Shubin op. cit., pp. 366-90.
5. In September 1991, the Social Democratic Party was defeated in the national elections by a non-socialist coalition led by the Moderate Party, which as junior partners included the Centre and Liberal parties and the Christian Democrats. The coalition governed until September 1994, when the Social Democrats under Ingvar Carlsson returned to power.
6. Thomas op. cit., p. 205.

States Congress introduced selective economic sanctions against Pretoria, ANC was thus increasingly recognized by the Western powers as a significant political actor, albeit reluctantly and with reservations. This, in turn, facilitated the opening of ANC missions in Washington and in other capitals around the world.

At the same time, however, the Western powers demanded that ANC should suspend its armed struggle. As long as Pretoria's violent campaigns in South Africa and in the Southern African region continued unabated, this was not acceptable. Although ANC as early as in October 1986 had stated in principle its positive attitude towards political negotiations[1], under the prevailing circumstances the threat of force was in addition to international sanctions a crucial bargaining asset which the liberation movement could not surrender.[2]

As a consequence of diplomatic talks between the United States and the Soviet Union on the situation in Angola and Namibia—which in December culminated in the New York accords between Angola, Cuba and South Africa[3]—towards the end of 1988 ANC was, however, forced to close its military camps in Angola and evacuate its troops to Tanzania and Uganda. Although the independence of Namibia was worth the sacrifice of having to relocate the bulk of its army even further from South Africa, "in the short term [this] created serious problems"[4], leading to heated debates at the level of the ANC leadership. The setback was at about the same time compounded by the possibility of also having to withdraw from Zambia, which hosted the ANC headquarters. Addressing these challenges, in a meeting of NEC's Working Committee President Tambo concluded in mid-November 1988 that

> [w]hen [these governments] say [that] we must move, we will have to move. [...] When a government takes that decision, it has to be implemented and we cannot give excuses. [...] Our people must be made to understand that if Zambia wants to do that, they will do it.

> We are moving from the West, virtually demolishing our army and retreating from strategic positions. When the whole army is moving from [Angola], who will say no to an order to

---

1. Cf. above. In a report submitted in May 1987 to the official aid negotiations with Sweden, ANC stated: "We reiterate our commitment to seize any opportunity that may arise to participate in a negotiated resolution of the conflict in our country. This shall be done in the interests of the masses of our people and those of Southern Africa as a whole, with the specific aim of creating a democratic, non-racial and united South Africa" ('Progress report to SIDA', attached to 'Agreed minutes [from] consultations in Lusaka, May 1987, between the African National Congress of South Africa and Sweden concerning humanitarian assistance', Lusaka, 8 May 1987) (SDA).

2. It was only in August 1990—six months after its legalization—that ANC decided to suspend the armed struggle. The issue of political negotiations with the Pretoria regime was, however, controversial until the very end. Many examples could here be quoted. As late as in January 1989, ANC's official organ *Sechaba* published a discussion article by Sizwe Mkhwanazi in which he argued that "[t]he armed seizure of political power is the strategic objective of the vanguard of the South African liberation movement, the ANC. [...] We are not engaging in armed struggle as a pressure tactic for the enemy to come to the negotiating table. We are fighting to seize power [and w]e have to admit openly that negotiations [...] would represent something like an abortion of our revolution" (Sizwe Mkhwanazi: 'Our Vanguard and the Seizure of Power' in *Sechaba*, No. 1, 1989, pp. 22 and 23). And in April 1989—only four months prior to the Harare Declaration—SACP called for mass insurrection in its new programme 'The Path to Power', adopted at its seventh congress in Havana, Cuba. Noteworthy—by his biographer Gevisser described as "schizophrenia"—is that Thabo Mbeki formed part of the drafting committee and that he chaired the SACP congress, held at a time when he was closely engaged in diplomatic 'talks about talks'. After the unbannings in February 1990, Mbeki made the decision to let his SACP membership lapse (Mark Gevisser: 'The bag-carrier' and 'The deal-maker', Parts four and five of a six-part 'Thabo Mbeki story' in *Sunday Times*, 6 and 13 June 1999).

3. See the chapters 'SWAPO of Namibia: Tentative Steps towards Firm Relations' and 'With SWAPO to Victory'.

4. Shubin op. cit., p. 343.

move? Everybody must move. Things have changed, comrades, [and] our people must under-stand that. What we will do is to minimize [the] discomfort, but move we must.[1]

With reference to the developments in Mozambique after the March 1984 Nko-mati Accord, the ANC President, finally, added: "We must move before the Maputo kind of situation overtakes us".[2]

While ANC never had to leave Zambia, at a press conference in Lusaka in mid-January 1989 Tambo announced that the movement was withdrawing its military forces from Angola "in order to prevent South Africa from using ANC's presence [there] to block the liberation process [in Namibia]".[3] Assisted by the Soviet Union[4], in a major operation up to 10,000 MK cadres were subsequently airlifted to Tanzania and, above all, to Uganda, which under President Yoweri Museveni in 1989 became one of ANC's main host countries.[5] From 1 July 1989, Uganda was also included among the countries to which official Swedish ANC assistance was extended. At the aid negotiations in Lusaka in May 1989, it was decided to set aside 1 MSEK in favour of daily necessities for the MK evacuees in that country during the financial year 1989/90.[6] With new arrivals, as early as in November 1989 it was agreed to increase the allocation to 3 MSEK[7] and in May 1990—that is, after ANC's unbanning—an amount of 4.5 MSEK was initially budgeted for Uganda.[8] As the allocation for daily necessities in Angola was correspondingly reduced[9], considerable increases were at the same time made with regard to Tanza-nia. For 1990/91, no less than 12 MSEK was allocated towards daily necessities through the ANC office in Dar es Salaam.[10]

While in the latter case there were established routines to oversee the assistance, in Uganda, however, it was only in May 1991 that SIDA's Lena Johansson could visit the main ANC/MK camp. The difficulties in monitoring the support had by

1. ANC: 'Minutes of meeting of NWC held on 17 November 1988', Office of the Secretary General, Lusaka, [no further date] (MCA). Shubin states that the meeting took place on 1 November (Shubin op. cit., p. 343), but the minutes are dated as indicated.
2. Ibid.
3. Cable ('ANC's militära gren lämnar Angola'/'ANC's military wing leaves Angola') from Kaj Persson to the Ministry for Foreign Affairs, Swedish embassy, Lusaka, [20 January 1989] (SDA). Tambo did not say where the MK cadres were to be hosted (ibid.).
4. Shubin op. cit., p. 350.
5. Military hardware and other equipment were transported by sea to Tanzania and by air to Uganda (ibid.).
6. 'Agreed minutes from consultations held in Lusaka, May 1989, between the African National Congress of South Africa and Sweden concerning humanitarian assistance', Lusaka, 26 May 1989 (SDA). The ANC dele-gation was led by Secretary General Alfred Nzo. Sten Rylander, Assistant Under-Secretary at the Ministry for Foreign Affairs, headed the Swedish team.
7. 'Minutes from consultative talks in Lusaka, 27 November-1 December 1989, between the African National Congress of South Africa (ANC) and the Swedish International Development Authority (SIDA) concerning humanitarian assistance', Lusaka, 1 December 1989 (SDA).
8. 'Agreed minutes from consultations held in Lusaka, May 1990, between the African National Congress of South Africa and Sweden concerning humanitarian assistance', Lusaka, 18 May 1990 (SDA).
9. As noted above, in May 1990 it was agreed to allocate 0.5 MSEK to ANC's so called Lillie's farm south of Luanda. While the soil was not conducive to agriculture, at the time unbeknown to the Swedish authorities the farm, however, was of significant political importance with regard to ANC's situation in Angola. At a meeting of ANC's National Working Committee, in December 1988 it was under Oliver Tambo's chairman-ship resolved that "[t]he farm [...] will become more important in providing a legend for our continued presence [...] as refugees, since the UNHCR will [now] be inclined to monitor us more carefully. [...] [It] should [...] help [us] in providing [a] suitable legend for [the] ANC comrades remaining in Angola" (ANC: 'Meeting of NWC held on 12 December 1988', Office of the Secretary General, Lusaka, [no further date]) (MCA).
10. 'Agreed minutes from consultations held in Lusaka, May 1990, between the African National Congress of South Africa and Sweden concerning humanitarian assistance', Lusaka, 18 May 1990 (SDA).

then provoked strong Swedish protests.[1]

Despite the withdrawal from Angola, on the diplomatic front ANC could, however, towards the end of the 1980s register a number of successes. Increasingly acknowledged as a leading South African representative, the movement was welcome to set up offices in countries which earlier had shied away from it. In Africa, for example, this was the case in Kenya, where in June 1988 it opened a mission which was even accorded diplomatic status.[2] By early 1989, there were no fewer than about thirty ANC missions around the world[3], with advanced plans for the establishment of another ten.[4] To coordinate this rapidly growing diplomatic network, with support from the Norwegian government the ANC leadership held a major strategy conference for its chief representatives and regional treasurers at Gran outside Oslo in mid-March 1989, attended by no less than 88 delegates.[5]

Sweden was closely associated with this expansion. In addition to the Stockholm office, from 1989/90 support was extended to twelve ANC representations in Africa.[6] The agreement was that administrative support was only to be given in countries where Swedish assistance was channelled to ANC refugees or projects. When in mid-1989 the movement faced financial constraints regarding the opening of its US mission in Washington—to be headed by Lindiwe Mabuza, the former Chief Representative to Sweden—an exception to this rule was, however, made. Following a special ANC appeal, at the annual negotiations in May 1989 it was decided to set aside 400,000 SEK for the Washington office.[7] When ANC soon thereafter found it necessary to procure new premises, another 1.6 MSEK was allocated.[8]

1. One possible reason for the reluctance shown by ANC—and the Kampala government—to let the Swedish authorities visit the MK camps in Uganda was that they included prisoners held by the liberation movement. In December 1988, a special meeting of ANC's National Working Committee—attended *inter alia* by Oliver Tambo, Alfred Nzo and Thomas Nkobi—had decided that ANC's detainees at Camp 32, or Quatro, in Angola should be transferred to Uganda (ANC: 'Minutes of special meeting of NWC held 21 December 1988', Office of the Secretary General, Lusaka, [no further date]) (MCA). The subsequent prison transport—according to Shubin implemented without Soviet assistance (Shubin op. cit., pp. 344-45)—was far from an edifying affair. In June 1989, SIDA's Georg Dreifaldt reported from Luanda how the detainees had been held in containers for up to two days before being flown out from Angola by commercial air carriers (Georg Dreifaldt: Memorandum ('Samtal med ANC's Chief Representative Uriah Mokeba'/'Conversation with ANC Chief Representative Uriah Mokeba'), Swedish embassy, Luanda, 6 June 1989) (SDA). In mid-May 1991—just prior to the first SIDA visit to Uganda—Joe Nhlanhla, ANC's Intelligence and Security Secretary, told the Swedish authorities that it had been decided to release the last 31 detainees held by the movement (Cable ('ANC's politiska fångar'/'ANC's political prisoners') from Anders Möllander to the Ministry for Foreign Affairs, Swedish legation, Pretoria, 15 May 1991) (MFA).
2. Roland Axelsson: Memorandum ('Anteckningar från besök i Nairobi, 28-31 oktober 1988'/'Notes from visit to Nairobi, 28-31 October 1988'), Swedish embassy, Lusaka, 2 November 1988 (SDA).
3. SIDA/CCHA: Memorandum ('Humanitärt bistånd till African National Congress of South Africa (ANC) budgetåret 1989/90'/'Humanitarian assistance to ANC [during] the financial year 1989/90'), SIDA, Stockholm, 21 March 1989 (SDA). As ANC has often been presented as a Soviet proxy, it should be noted that it was only in November 1987 that Simon Makana as Chief Representative to the Soviet Union formally opened a mission in Moscow (Shubin op. cit., pp. 310-11).
4. ANC: 'Conference of Chief Representatives and Regional Treasurers [at] Gran, Norway', ANC, Lusaka, 1989 (MCA).
5. Ibid. See also Østbye in Eriksen op. cit., p. 154.
6. 'Agreed minutes from consultations held in Lusaka, May 1989, between the African National Congress of South Africa and Sweden concerning humanitarian assistance', Lusaka, 26 May 1989 (SDA). Support to the ANC office in Windhoek was added in 1990.
7. Ibid.
8. 'Minutes from consultative talks in Lusaka, 27 November-1 December 1989, between the African National Congress of South Africa (ANC) and the Swedish International Development Authority (SIDA) concerning humanitarian assistance', Lusaka, 1 December 1989 (SDA). The allocation was treated as a loan. It was agreed that the funds "for procuring an office building in Washington [were given on] condition [...] that the full amount [is] later raised in the [United States] and [is] paid back to [...] a Swedish budgetary contribution to the ANC" (ibid.).

ANC's diplomatic offensive would in August 1989 lead to the 'Harare Declaration', which in turn paved the way for the democratic opening in South Africa. Before turning to these events, it should be noted that the intense activities in 1988-89 took a heavy toll on the leadership. At the end of 1988, Johnny Makatini, ANC's Secretary for International Affairs, passed away in Lusaka, and in August 1989 President Tambo entered a London hospital, suffering from a cerebral haemorrhage. In early January 1990, he was moved for further treatment to the Ersta clinic in Stockholm. Until the release of Nelson Mandela, Thabo Mbeki—who succeeded Makatini as chief diplomat—would thereby serve as *de facto* leader of the liberation movement during the crucial months from the adoption of the Harare Declaration to ANC's unbanning.

From Harare via Stockholm to Mandela's Release

The Harare Declaration represents a turning point in the South and Southern African drama. Based on a discussion paper drafted by ANC, after extensive consultations with the Frontline States and other friendly governments, the document— formally entitled 'Declaration on the Question of South Africa'—was adopted by the OAU Ad Hoc Committee on Southern Africa at a meeting in the Zimbabwean capital on 21 August 1989, one week after P.W. Botha's resignation as President. Four months later—on 9 December—it was endorsed by the Conference for a Democratic Future in South Africa, held in Johannesburg with representatives from hundreds of organizations from the Mass Democratic Movement. On 14 December, finally, a slightly modified version was approved by the UN General Assembly.[1]

Through the declaration, in a statement of principles the OAU Committee made it known that

> [w]e believe that a conjuncture of circumstances exists which, if there is a demonstrable readiness on the part of the Pretoria regime to engage in negotiations genuinely and seriously, could create the possibility to end apartheid through negotiations. [...] We would therefore encourage the people of South Africa, as part of their overall struggle, to get together to negotiate an end to [...] apartheid [...] and agree on all the measures that are necessary to transform their country into a non-racial democracy. We support the position held by the majority of the people of South Africa that these objectives, and not the amendment or reform of the apartheid system, should be the aims of the negotiations.[2]

Adding that the outcome of such a process should be a new constitutional order— "a united, democratic and non-racial state [in which] all its people shall enjoy common and equal citizenship and nationality, regardless of race, colour, sex or creed"—and demanding that the South African government in order to create the necessary climate for negotiations "at the very least" should "release all political prisoners [...], lift all bans and restrictions [...], remove all troops from the townships [and] end the state of emergency"[3], the declaration was a major success for ANC.[4]

---

1. 'Declaration on Apartheid and Its Destructive Consequences in Southern Africa', United Nations General Assembly, New York, 14 December 1989 (NAI).
2. 'Declaration of the OAU Ad Hoc Committee on Southern Africa on the Question of South Africa', Harare, 21 August 1989 (NAI).
3. Ibid. Steps towards negotiations that coincided with ANC's views were outlined in the declaration.
4. While PAC and BCM-aligned organizations advocated black exclusivist policies, Inkatha stood for a federal constitutional dispensation.

Replacing P.W. Botha, Frederik Willem (F.W.) de Klerk was sworn in as South Africa's President on 20 September 1989. Although his programme fell short of doing away with apartheid and introducing a non-racial democracy, de Klerk, nevertheless, came into power with a proposal for change. Under heavy internal and external pressure to proceed along the lines spelt out in the Harare Declaration, on 15 October he released Walter Sisulu and—barring Nelson Mandela—the remaining ANC Rivonia trialists, as well as Jeff Masemola of PAC.[1] In his memoirs, Mandela later wrote:

> It was a day we had yearned for and fought for over so many years. De Klerk had lived up to his promise, and the men were released under no bans. They could speak in the name of the ANC. It was clear that the ban on the organization had effectively expired, a vindication of our long struggle and our resolute adherence to principle.[2]

However, it was only on 2 February 1990 that de Klerk announced the formal unbanning of ANC. Mandela himself had to wait another nine days before he, too, as a free man could walk through the Victor Verster prison gates at Paarl and at a tumultuous ceremony at the Grand Parade in Cape Town address the people of South Africa after more than 27 years behind bars.

After a meeting with ANC, UDF and COSATU in Lusaka and via visits to Tanzania, Holland and Norway, from 1 to 5 February 1990 Walter Sisulu, Govan Mbeki and four senior leaders released in October 1989[3] went to Sweden for consultations with Oliver Tambo, whom they had not met for almost three decades. Accompanied by Thabo Mbeki, ANC Assistant Secretary General Henry Makghoti and Intelligence and Security Secretary Joe Nhlanhla[4], on 2 February—the very day of the unbanning of ANC and SACP—they were joined *inter alia* by Alfred Nzo and Joe Slovo, arriving from Moscow.[5] While the original programme was similar to that of an official visit by a high-level foreign mission[6], due to their presence in Stockholm on the historic Second of February the internal discussions and the consultations with the Swedish government, aid authorities and solidarity organizations assumed a particular significance.[7] As Nelson Mandela the following month

1. In addition to Sisulu and Masemola, the following were set free: Ahmed Kathrada, Raymond Mhlaba, Wilton Mkwayi, Andrew Mlangeni, Oscar Mpetha and Elias Motsoaledi. As earlier noted, Govan Mbeki was released at the end of 1987.

2. Mandela op. cit., p. 542. Two weeks later, a huge rally was held in Soweto to welcome back the released senior leaders. Accepted by the government, it was the first open ANC meeting in South Africa in over 25 years.

3. Joined by their wives—and in the case of Mkwayi, his daughter—Raymond Mhlaba, Wilton Mkwayi, Andrew Mlangeni and Elias Motsoaledi accompanied Sisulu and Mbeki (Per Sjögren: Memorandum ('ANC-delegation besöker Sverige 1-5 februari 1990'/'ANC delegation visits Sweden 1-5 February 1990'), Ministry for Foreign Affairs, Stockholm, 26 January 1990) (SDA).

4. Ibid. Billy Modise, ANC's Chief Representative to Sweden, also formed part of the delegation.

5. Shubin op. cit., p. 365.

6. In addition to internal deliberations and talks with President Tambo, the programme included discussions with Prime Minister Ingvar Carlsson, Foreign Minister Sten Andersson and SIDA's Director General Carl Tham, as well as meetings with the parliamentary Standing Committee on Foreign Affairs, the Consultative Committee on Humanitarian Assistance and the Africa Groups and other anti-apartheid solidarity organizations. During the visit, the 'Sisulu group' also held several press conferences, visited the grave of Olof Palme and participated at a public meeting held at the People's Hall in Stockholm ('Programme for the visit to Sweden of the ANC delegation, 1-5 February 1990', Ministry for Foreign Affairs, Stockholm, 30 January 1990) (SDA).

7. Closely following the developments in South Africa, the unbanning of ANC and the release of Mandela did not come as a surprise to the Swedish authorities. In a background memorandum to the visit of the 'Sisulu group', Per Sjögren of the Foreign Ministry wrote on 26 January that "at the opening of [the South African] parliament on 2 February, President de Klerk will possibly announce some initiative" (Per Sjögren: Memorandum ('ANC-delegation besöker Sverige 1-5 februari 1990'/'ANC delegation visits Sweden 1-5 February 1990'), Ministry for Foreign Affairs, Stockholm, 26 January 1990) (SDA).

Walter Sisulu and Lisbet Palme singing the ANC anthem in Stockholm in
February 1990: On Sisulu's right is Alfred Nzo and behind him Anders Bjurner,
Foreign Minister Sten Andersson and Ulla Ström (Photo: Bertil Ericson/
Pressens Bild)

also led a large delegation to Stockholm—and Oliver Tambo remained there for
treatment—from the beginning of the South African transition, the Swedish government's contacts with both the internally based and the exiled ANC leadership
were exceptional.[1]

Immediately after de Klerk's speech, the ANC leaders assembled in Stockholm
held a press conference in which they characterized the legalization of the movement and "other organizations"[2], as well as the suspension of the death sentence
and further initiatives, as "important announcements which go a long way towards
creating a climate conducive to negotiations".[3] Urging Pretoria to release Nelson
Mandela "without further delay", at the same time they asked the international
community to maintain the pressure on the apartheid regime: "We [...] expect that

1. At about the same time, "Soviet relations with the ANC and its allies started to cool and even to deteriorate"
   (Shubin op. cit., p. 369). Although Shubin gives a different picture and the Soviet Union continued to extend
   military assistance, the relations had, in fact, been under pressure since 1987. In a meeting in Lusaka with
   SIDA's Elisabeth Dahlin, Johnny Makatini, for example, expressed in February 1988 his disappointment with
   the authorities in Moscow, stating that "you think that you know where your friends are, but then it turns out
   that you did not know at all". In particular, Makatini referred to his visit to Moscow in connection with
   ANC's 75th anniversary celebrations in January 1987. Complaining that the Soviet officials had been "markedly uninformed on the question of South Africa", he told Dahlin that "we clashed on every single detail and
   [...] I had to explain [the situation] from the very beginning" (Elisabeth Dahlin: Memorandum ('Anteckningar
   från samtal med Johnny Makatini, utrikespolitisk talesman, ANC, 4/2 1988, Lusaka'/'Notes from conversation with Johnny Makatini, foreign affairs' spokesman [of] ANC, 4 February 1988, Lusaka'), SIDA, Stockholm, [no date, but registered on 9 February 1988]) (SDA). In his account of Makatini's visit, Shubin does not
   mention any strains. On the contrary, according to him Makatini criticized the United States and Britain for
   having hidden agendas vis-à-vis ANC (Shubin op. cit., pp. 309-10). In a meeting in Lusaka with the Soviet
   Foreign Minister Eduard Shevardnadze in March 1990—while he was stopping over on his way to the
   Namibian independence celebrations in Windhoek—an ANC delegation comprising *inter alia* Alfred Nzo,
   Thomas Nkobi, Thabo Mbeki, Joe Modise and Joe Slovo asked quite forcefully through Mbeki that "[t]he
   USSR should continue to be seen as not beginning to establish links with a system on its way out. [...] We
   wouldn't want a negative perception of the USSR among our people" (ANC: 'Report on the ANC meeting
   with the Soviet Foreign Minister, 20 March 1990', Lusaka, [20 March 1990]) (MCA).
2. The brief statement did not mention SACP, PAC or any other organization. On 2 February, SACP also issued
   a positive statement ('Statement from the International Committee of the South African Communist Party',
   [no place], 2 February 1990) (NAI).
3. 'Statement by the President of the ANC, Oliver Tambo, and other leaders of the ANC currently visiting Sweden', Stockholm, 2 February 1990 (NAI).

'What now?': ANC Secretary General Alfred Nzo, President Oliver Tambo and Secretary of International Affairs Thabo Mbeki after the unbanning of the organization, Stockholm, February 1990 (Photo: Jan Collsiöö/Pressens Bild)

no country committed to ending white minority domination in South Africa will do anything to lessen [its] isolation".[1]

As it embarked on internal discussions on how best to bring about "a disciplined and ordered restructuring" of the movement[2], on the same day the ANC delegation led by Sisulu held a first meeting with Foreign Minister Andersson, Foreign Trade Minister Gradin, Under-Secretary of State Säve-Söderbergh and SIDA's Director General Tham on the possible consequences of de Klerk's announcement for the relations with Sweden. While the consultations mainly focused on the importance of keeping economic sanctions in place[3], the following day more substantial discussions on the assistance were held between Thabo Mbeki and Billy Modise from ANC, Säve-Söderbergh and Per Sjögren from the Foreign Ministry and Tham and Lena Johansson from SIDA.[4] The overall conclusion was that the unfolding events in South Africa "increased the importance of an intensified aid dialogue between [Sweden] and the democratic movement in South Africa", and that it should concentrate on support

> to promote the political democratization process, as well as to [strengthen] the democratic opposition with regard to the building of a future democratic [society].[5]

1. Ibid.
2. 'ANC press statement issued by Secretary General Alfred Nzo', [Stockholm], Sweden, 5 February 1990 (NAI).
3. Cable ('Utrikes- och utrikeshandelsministerns samtal med ANC-ledningen 2.2 1990'/'Conversation between the Foreign and the Foreign Trade Ministers and the ANC leadership [on] 2 February 1990') from the Ministry for Foreign Affairs to various Swedish embassies and missions, Stockholm, 2 February 1990 (SDA).
4. At the time visiting Lusaka, in a parallel meeting with Treasurer General Thomas Nkobi, Barbara Masekela and others, on 2 February 1990 Cooperation Minister Lena Hjelm-Wallén also discussed the future aid relations with ANC (Kaj Persson: Memorandum ('Biståndsminister Hjelm-Walléns samtal med ANC-ledningen'/ 'Cooperation Minister Hjelm-Wallén's conversation with the ANC leadership'), Swedish embassy, Lusaka, 8 February 1990) (SDA).
5. Cable ('Möte med ANC om humanitärt bistånd till Sydafrika'/'Meeting with ANC on humanitarian assistance to South Africa') from the Ministry for Foreign Affairs to the Swedish missions in Cape Town, Pretoria and Lusaka, Stockholm, 14 February 1990 (SDA).

Once the fragile negotiation process was on track, this reorientation from external humanitarian to internal political support would become the main thrust of the Swedish assistance to ANC and its allies. At the meeting on 3 February 1990, it was, in the meantime, agreed that Sweden as soon as possible should assist the National Reception Committee (NRC), set up in South Africa to facilitate the work by the released 'Sisulu group' and, eventually, by Nelson Mandela. A request to that effect had during a recent visit to Stockholm been submitted by the NRC Chairman Cyril Ramaphosa.[1]

Strongly endorsed by Thabo Mbeki—who described it as being of "central importance"[2]—the proposal was swiftly processed. After identifying the Swedish Ecumenical Council (SEN) as an appropriate channel, as early as on 16 February 1990 no less than 5 MSEK was allocated to NRC outside the regular cooperation programme with ANC.[3] The contribution would over a period of twelve months be used *inter alia* for the released ANC leaders' "life and welfare", covering housing, daily necessities, health, travel and other expenses; offices, equipment and current administrative costs; and security arrangements—including personnel—in their respective residences and places of work.[4] Before the phased return of its external leaders, under Sisulu's coordination and in close cooperation with the mass democratic movement, ANC was thus after its unbanning in a better position to rebuild its structures inside South Africa.[5]

After Mandela's release on 11 February 1990, preparations were immediately set in motion for discussions with the ANC leadership in Lusaka and President Tambo in Stockholm. On 1-2 March, Mandela, Govan Mbeki, Walter Sisulu and the other Rivonia trialists attended an extended NEC meeting in the Zambian capital where a number of far-reaching decisions were made. In addition to reaffirming its decision to meet the South African government to discuss the removal of remaining obstacles in the way of negotiations, Mandela was formally appointed Deputy President of ANC[6] and Mbeki and Sisulu reinstated as members of the National Executive Committee. The meeting further decided that "the headquarters [...] of the ANC will be opened in Johannesburg without delay" and that "some [NEC] members [...] will be selected and sent home as soon as the necessary arrangements are made".[7] Finally, it confirmed that Mandela before his return to

1. Ibid.
2. Ibid.
3. Letter ('Ansökan från Svenska Ekumeniska Nämnden om stöd till National Reception Committee, Released Rivonia Prisoners'/'Request from the Swedish Ecumenical Council for support to NRC, Released Rivonia Prisoners') from Lena Johansson to SEN, SIDA, Stockholm, 16 February 1990 (SDA).
4. Cable [no title] from the Ministry for Foreign Affairs to the Swedish legation in Pretoria, Stockholm, 7 February 1990 (SDA) and agreement ('Avtal om stöd till Svenska Ekumeniska Nämnden om stöd till National Reception Committee, Released Rivonia Prisoners'/'Agreement on support to the Swedish Ecumenical Council regarding assistance to NRC, Released Rivonia Prisoners'), SIDA/CCHA, Stockholm, 16 February 1990 (SDA). Swedish financial support was also extended to Govan Mbeki when he was released at the end of 1987 (Letter ('Stöd till boende'/'Housing support') from Birgitta Karlström Dorph to SIDA, Swedish legation, Pretoria, 17 December 1987) (SDA).
5. It should be recalled that the so called 'home front' component within Sweden's regular assistance to ANC amounted to 24 MSEK in 1989/90. It was raised to 26.5 MSEK in 1990/91 (cf. the chapter 'From Beds in Exile to Organizers at Home').
6. It was only at the ANC congress in Durban in July 1991 that Mandela formally replaced Tambo as President of ANC, for the first time occupying the highest office in the organization. Walter Sisulu was at the same time elected Deputy President and Cyril Ramaphosa Secretary General.
7. ANC: 'Press statement of the National Executive Committee of the African National Congress', Lusaka, 2 March 1990 (NAI).

Re-united at last: Nelson
Mandela and Oliver Tambo
at Haga Palace,
Stockholm, March 1990
(Photo: Anders Holmström/
Pressens Bild)

South Africa would go to Zimbabwe, Tanzania and Sweden.[1] Accompanied by his
wife Winnie and a huge delegation[2], Nelson Mandela visited Stockholm and Uppsala in mid-March 1990.[3] It was to be the first of three visits to Sweden before he in
May 1994 was sworn in as President of South Africa.[4] Although still denied citizenship in the land of his birth, in March 1990 he was, however, already treated as
a head of state. Staying at Haga Palace just north of Stockholm[5]—where after 28
years he was reunited with his old friend and close comrade Oliver Tambo[6]—in
addition to internal ANC deliberations and talks with the Swedish government,
during his tremendously popular, week-long visit he addressed the parliament[7],

---

1. Ibid.
2. Among the ANC officials in exile and the internally based activists who accompanied Nelson and Winnie
   Mandela were Chris Hani, Dennis Goldberg, John Gomomo, Ahmed Kathrada, Trevor Manuel, Thabo and
   Zanele Mbeki, Billy and Yolisa Modise (based in Stockholm), Mohammed Valli Moosa, Ruth Mompati,
   Mendi Msimang, Joe Nhanhla, Sankie Nkondo, Alfred Nzo, Aziz Pahad, Cyril Ramaphosa and Adelaide
   Tambo. In Stockholm, they were joined by other prominent South Africans, such as Miriam Makeba.
3. In a preparatory meeting with the Swedish envoy Jan Lundvik on 20 February 1990, Mandela—a lawyer by
   profession—expressed particular interest in the Swedish *ombudsman* institution, that is, the public office for
   complaints by ordinary citizens against the government or the official administration (Cable ('Samtal med
   Mandela'/'Conversation with Mandela') from Jan Lundvik to the Ministry for Foreign Affairs, Swedish legation, Cape Town, 21 February 1990) (SDA).
4. Mandela returned to Stockholm in May 1992 and—after receiving the Nobel Peace Prize in Oslo—together
   with President F.W. de Klerk in December 1993. While his host in March 1990 was the Social Democratic
   Prime Minister Ingvar Carlsson, on the latter two occasions he was received by Carl Bildt of the Moderate
   Party. Bildt succeeded Carlsson as Premier in October 1991.
5. Haga Palace is traditionally used for the accommodation of visiting royalty and heads of state.
6. Mandela had last met Tambo during his Africa tour in 1962. In his memoirs, Mandela notes: "Seeing my old
   friend and law partner [in Stockholm] was the reunion I most looked forward to. Oliver was not well, but
   when we met we were like two young boys in the veld who took strength from our love for each other. We
   began by talking of old times, but when we were alone, the first subject he raised was the leadership of the
   organization. 'Nelson', he said, 'you must now take over as President of the ANC. I have been merely keeping
   the job warm for you'. I refused, telling him that he had led the organization in exile far better than I ever
   could have. It was neither fair nor democratic for a transfer to occur in such a manner. [...] It was a sign of his
   humility and selflessness that he wanted to appoint me President, but it was not in keeping with the principles
   of the ANC" (Mandela op. cit., p. 564).
7. Returning to Sweden in March 1999, Mandela recalled that "[w]hen I spoke in the Swedish parliament nine
   years ago, [...] [i]t was [...] the first time ever that I had the opportunity to speak in a [national assembly], the
   highest institution of democracy" ('Speech by President Nelson Mandela during a visit to the Swedish parliament, 18 March 1999') (NAI).

held a religious service in Uppsala Cathedral and attended a mass rally at the Globe Arena in Stockholm, organized by AGIS and ISAK together with a host of organizations in an *ad hoc* 'Committee for the Release of Nelson Mandela'.[1]

Meeting a cross-section of the Swedish public, the man who only one month earlier had been known as 'the world's longest serving political prisoner' was surprisingly well informed about Sweden and its history of involvement with the antiapartheid cause. While he, for example, in acknowledgement of the Swedish mineworkers' support for NUM in the 1980s invited their leader Anders Stendalen to bilateral talks at Haga Palace[2], at the service in Uppsala Cathedral on 13 March 1990—led by Archbishop Bertil Werkström[3]—Mandela went back to the 1940s and 1950s, stating that

> we are pleased to be here today, because this gives us the rare opportunity to extend our profound gratitude to the Church of Sweden itself. We know, and are moved by the fact that among the first to sound the warning bells about the situation in South Africa were Swedish men and women of conscience who had served as missionaries among our people. Conscious of the dictates of their faith to take sides with the hungry, the poor and the oppressed, they spread the word about [...] apartheid [...]. And when the time came, the church was in the front ranks in the effort to isolate this evil.[4]

As the South African state of emergency was still in place, hundreds of political prisoners were locked up in jail and no agenda for negotiations had yet been established, Mandela's main political message was, however, to maintain and, if possible, increase the isolation of the apartheid regime.[5] By that time, Sweden was arguably applying more comprehensive economic sanctions than any other Western country and the message was well understood. In his speech at the official dinner for the visiting delegation—in addition to the Swedish guests[6] including Neil

---

1. Through SIDA, the Swedish government granted AGIS and ISAK one million SEK to organize the gala at the Globe Arena and other public activities in connection with Mandela's visit (AGIS: Memorandum ('Lägesrapport för bidrag erhållet av Kommittén för Nelson Mandelas Frigivning, mars 1990'/'Status report concerning contribution received by the Committee for the Release of Nelson Mandela' [in] March 1990'), Africa Groups of Sweden, Stockholm, 2 June 1991) (SDA). In addition to some 60 NGOs, all the parliamentary parties except the Moderate Party—and its youth league—formed part of the Committee for the Release of Nelson Mandela (Information leaflet on the Globe Arena rally ('För ett fritt Sydafrika'/'For a free South Africa'), [no place or date, but Stockholm in March 1990]) (ISA).
2. Author's telephone conversation with Stendalen, 3 May 2001.
3. Stressing that the struggle for democracy in South Africa was far from over, in his sermon Archbishop Werkström stated: "To apply comprehensive sanctions on South Africa is a matter of justice, just as it once was a matter of justice to abolish the slave trade. In neither case can the church afford merely to be an onlooker" ('Homily by the Archbishop of the Church of Sweden [on] the occasion of a thanksgiving service held at Uppsala Cathedral during Mr. Nelson Mandela's visit to Sweden, Tuesday 13 March 1990') (CSA).
4. 'Statement of the Deputy President of the African National Congress, Nelson Mandela, at the religious service at the Cathedral of Uppsala, Sweden, 13 March 1990' (CSA). On the early anti-apartheid involvement by the Church of Sweden Mission, see Sellström Volume I, pp. 130-36 and passim.
5. In early 1990, ANC's domestic gains were initially balanced by setbacks in both the East and the West. In January, the South African Foreign Minister 'Pik' Botha paid an official visit to Hungary, which before the fall of the Berlin wall had been a staunch supporter of ANC. Clearly indicating a shift with regard to the international relations of ANC—and SACP—the visit was sharply criticized. On 21 January 1990, an extended meeting of ANC's National Executive Committee "expressed its grave concern at the unfriendly act of the government of Hungary, which against the interests of the overwhelming majority of the people of our country, its own international commitments and in contemptuous disregard of our [...] representations [has] received representatives of the apartheid regime" ('Statement of the extended meeting of the National Executive Committee of the African National Congress', Lusaka, 21 January 1990) (NAI). After Nelson Mandela's release, the British government argued forcefully against any further international measures to isolate the Pretoria regime. Meeting in Lusaka in mid-February 1990, NEC "strongly condemn[ed] the position taken by the British government on this issue" ('Statement of the National Executive Committee of the African National Congress, Lusaka, 16 February 1990') (NAI).
6. Several representatives from AGIS and ISAK were invited to the official dinner. While Lars Werner, the leader of the Left Party Communists, also took part, it could be noted that the future Prime Minister Carl Bildt and the other leaders of the non-socialist Swedish opposition parties were absent.

Kinnock, the leader of the opposition British Labour Party, the Foreign Ministers of Denmark, Finland and Iceland[1] and a prominent representative from Norway[2]— Prime Minister Ingvar Carlsson concluded that "now is not the time to lift sanctions. On the contrary, existing sanctions must be effectively maintained".[3]

While the Swedish parliament the following day extended the embargo on South Africa to also include trade in services[4], at the huge, televised Globe Arena gala[5] Mandela, finally, graphically illustrated the importance of maintaining economic pressure by stating that "it would be foolish to extinguish the fire just when the water is about to boil".[6] Until the ANC leader in an address to the UN General Assembly in September 1993 eventually called upon the international community to lift the sanctions, this statement would often be quoted during the ensuing Swedish debate.

The Struggle and Assistance Continue

Before Mandela's visit, various possible South African scenarios and consequences with regard to the future official assistance to ANC and the democratization process had been discussed by the Swedish authorities. An overriding conclusion from these deliberations was that once the apartheid system had been abolished, "support to a political party cannot be granted".[7] Introduced by Prime Minister Carlsson's Social Democratic government, the question of whether and under which circumstances ANC could be considered a liberation movement eligible for official support would—together with the issue of maintaining or lifting sanctions—subsequently be hotly debated under the Moderate Party leader Carl Bildt's government.

In early 1990, these questions were, however, far from heading the agenda. Although ANC had been unbanned and Mandela was a free man, apartheid—from the point of view of international law forming the very basis for Sweden's humanitarian assistance—was firmly in place and South Africa's political future highly uncertain. No formal negotiations with the Pretoria regime had been initiated. Visiting Sweden together with Mohammed Tikly, the head of ANC's Projects Department, in late March Treasurer General Thomas Nkobi underlined that the prevailing conditions did not allow for a quick return of the exiled population. On the contrary, due to the unrest in Natal, there was a steady outflow of refugees seeking

---

1. Uffe Ellemann-Jensen from Denmark, Pertti Paasio from Finland and Jon Baldvin Hannibalsson from Iceland.
2. Knut Vollebæk, at the time Norwegian State Secretary of Foreign Affairs.
3. 'Speech by the Prime Minister, Mr. Ingvar Carlsson, at a dinner for Mr. Nelson Mandela', 14 March 1990, in Ministry for Foreign Affairs: *Documents on Swedish Foreign Policy: 1990*, Stockholm, 1991, p. 31.
4. Cf. Appendix VII. At a meeting in Turku, Finland, the Nordic countries decided on 6-7 March 1990 to lift the economic sanctions against Namibia ('Statement on South Africa and Namibia, issued at the meeting of [the] Nordic foreign ministers in Turku', 7 March 1990, in Ministry for Foreign Affairs: *Documents on Swedish Foreign Policy: 1990*, Stockholm, 1991, pp. 102-103).
5. Addressed by both Mandela and Prime Minister Carlsson, the sold out gala at the Globe Arena in Stockholm on 16 March 1990 was attended by more than 12,000 people ('Släck inte Elden när Grytan just Börjar Koka'/ 'Don't Extinguish the Fire When the Pot Starts to Boil' in *Södra Afrika Nyheter*, Nos. 6-7, 1990).
6. Mandela cited in ibid.
7. Per Sjögren: Memorandum ('Biståndspolitiska överväganden avseende det humanitära stödet till ANC och i Sydafrika'/'Aid policy considerations regarding the humanitarian support to ANC and South Africa'), Ministry for Foreign Affairs, Stockholm, 8 March 1990 (MFA).

assistance from ANC. The thrust of the Swedish assistance should thus be maintained in 1990/91.[1] Meeting for annual negotiations in Lusaka on 15-18 May 1990, this was confirmed by the delegations, respectively led by ANC Secretary General Alfred Nzo and SIDA's Deputy Director General Jan Cedergren.[2] At that time, the movement had already sent an advance party from the headquarters in Zambia to South Africa.[3] More importantly, on 2-4 May a first, promising direct encounter on 'talks about talks' had been held with the Pretoria government at Groote Schuur in Cape Town, the former official residence of South Africa's Premiers.[4] Although against this background Sweden in principle was ready to consider the assistance "in a more flexible manner [...] both regarding [...] content and modality", ANC, however, conveyed its decision that "external projects [would] remain in operation for the foreseeable future, especially those concerned with education, training and agriculture".[5] To this should be added the movement's direct responsibility for an estimated 20,000 members in exile and for "a continuous influx of refugees".[6]

Agreeing on a budget for the period 1 July 1990-30 June 1991, only minor changes were thus made in the ongoing cooperation programme. Raised from 85 MSEK in 1989/90 to 97.5 MSEK[7]—an increase of 15 per cent—and with an estimated unspent balance of 5.5 million, the available allocation amounted in 1990/91

1. Eva Belfrage: Memorandum ('Anteckningar från besök av ANC den 28 mars 1990'/'Notes from visit by ANC on 28 March 1990'), SIDA, Stockholm, 30 March 1990 (SDA).
2. This was one of the rare occasions when Thomas Nkobi did not participate at the bilateral aid negotiations. In his absence, Alfred Nzo—who had just returned to Lusaka from the Groote Schuur meeting—stated that "[w]ithout Swedish assistance, the struggle would not have reached its advanced present position" ('Agreed minutes from consultations held in Lusaka, May 1990, between the African National Congress of South Africa and Sweden concerning humanitarian assistance', Lusaka, 18 May 1990) (SDA).
3. Penuell Maduna, Mathews Phosa and Jacob Zuma. Flying to South Africa on 21 March 1990, the day of the independence celebrations in Namibia, on ANC's behalf they prepared for the Groote Schuur meeting.
4. On 27 April 1990, Thabo Mbeki, Joe Modise, Ruth Mompati, Alfred Nzo and Joe Slovo boarded a plane put at their disposal by the Zambian President Kenneth Kaunda to attend the historic talks at Groote Schuur. Led by Nelson Mandela, the ANC team included in addition Cheryl Carolus (UDF), Archie Gumede (UDF), Ahmed Kathrada, Beyers Naudé (UDF) and Walter Sisulu. President de Klerk headed the government delegation. After three days of talks, on 4 May 1990 the parties signed the 'Groote Schuur Minute', agreeing on "a common commitment towards the resolution of the existing climate of violence and intimidation from whatever quarter, as well as a commitment to stability and to a peaceful process of negotiations" ('The Groote Schuur Minute') (NAI). While constitutional issues were not discussed, it was further agreed to establish "[e]fficient channels of communication [...] in order to curb violence" (ibid.). Three months later—on 6 August 1990—the two sides met again in Pretoria, where Mandela announced a unilateral suspension of ANC's armed struggle. Thus, "the way [was] open to proceed towards negotiations on a new constitution" ('The Pretoria Minute') (NAI). While PAC refused to follow ANC—and Mandela's commitment "was a major concession for which he got little in return, [stirring] the first ripples of concern among ANC radicals who thought [that] he was giving away too much" (Sparks op. cit., p. 124)—multi-party talks on a new South African dispensation were opened in the midst of escalating violence in December 1991. Known as the Convention for a Democratic South Africa (CODESA), ANC's core Negotiations Commission to the subsequent talks comprised the following representatives: President Nelson Mandela, Deputy President Walter Sisulu, Secretary General Cyril Ramaphosa, Barbara Masekela, Thabo Mbeki, Mohammed Valli Moosa, Joe Slovo and Jacob Zuma (ANC: *Negotiations Bulletin*, No. 1, 15 October 1991) (NAI).
5. 'Agreed minutes from consultations held in Lusaka, May 1990, between the African National Congress of South Africa and Sweden concerning humanitarian assistance', Lusaka, 18 May 1990 (SDA).
6. Ibid. After the unbanning, ANC set up a committee to plan for the return of its members in exile. According to a preliminary census, in May 1990 the population was "20,000 plus" (ibid.).
7. After Namibia's independence in March 1990, the official Swedish budget allocation for humanitarian assistance in Southern Africa was almost exclusively used for direct or indirect support to the anti-apartheid struggle in South Africa. In 1990/91, a total of 255.3 MSEK was disbursed towards this purpose. While 90 MSEK was paid out in favour of ANC (see the accompanying disbursement table), the remaining 165 million was channelled via a range of international and Swedish NGOs. The most important among the former were IDAF, which received no less than 57 MSEK for legal assistance, and WUS (25) and AET (11.8) for scholarship programmes. With total contributions of 13 MSEK, in Sweden AIC was the principal channel, followed by Diakonia (9.1), SEN (5.2) and CSM (4.4) (Anita Theodossiadis: 'Planeringsöversikt humanitärt bistånd södra Afrika'/'Planning summary [of] humanitarian assistance [to] Southern Africa', SIDA/CCHA, [Stockholm], 16 September 1991) (SDA).

to a total of 103 MSEK. Of this, 33 MSEK was set aside for 'daily necessities' in twelve host countries; 18.3 million for continuing programmes regarding 'training and culture'; 15.6 for 'administration and information' in exile; 8 for 'projects', mainly in agriculture; 1.6 for 'other activities'—notably including 700,000 SEK in favour of SACTU—and 26.5 MSEK towards the 'home front'.[1]

Although the latter component was used by ANC for its organizational efforts in South Africa, from 1 July 1991—when the return of the exile population had started, the movement was preparing for its first congress after the unbanning and formal multi-party negotiations were about to be opened—the distribution of the official funds would be radically different. For 1991/92, no less than 71.8 MSEK—corresponding to around 60 per cent of the available resources—was budgeted for ANC's domestic political work.[2]

Meanwhile, in South Africa ANC faced tremendous challenges. With several key leaders in detention[3] and although the movement enjoyed massive support, as late as in October 1990 its Organizing Committee noted in an internal report that "we have not been able to translate [this] into structured organisational allegiance".[4] Having divided the country into 14 regions and set an overall target of one million members after its unbanning, by mid-October 1990 only 5 regional interim structures had been established and the signed up national membership was merely 155,000. Against this background, the committee noted that "[t]he picture that emerges [...] is not what we would wish it to be".[5]

In turn, the problems faced by Walter Sisulu and his colleagues with regard to the rebuilding of ANC were largely due to objective factors, notably official hostility and violence, both in South Africa 'proper' and in the homelands. The situation was particularly bad in KwaZulu-Natal, "where association, let alone actual membership, is an invitation to the Inkatha warlords and their surrogates". In Bophuthatswana, the Organizing Committee stated, "harassment has reached such a high pitch that practically all branches launched have been immobilised. Members are arrested and dismissed from their [places of] work".[6]

Although ANC had been recognized *de facto* by the Pretoria regime as *the* crucial negotiating counterpart on a road towards a new South Africa, the political arena was far from democratic. In addition to legacies of three decades of banning and being subjected to widespread institutional animosity and outright violence, with very limited financial, administrative and personnel resources the movement in 1990-91 was, indeed, facing an uphill struggle. These challenges impressed high-ranking Swedish aid officials visiting the country.

In October 1990, Bengt Säve-Söderbergh, Under-Secretary of State for International Cooperation, led a delegation to a seminar on economic policy, organized with ANC, COSATU and UDF outside Johannesburg. Together with *inter alia* Jan Cedergren and Per Wästberg, four months later—in mid-February 1991—SIDA's

---

1. 'Agreed minutes from consultations held in Lusaka, May 1990, between the African National Congress of South Africa and Sweden concerning humanitarian assistance', Lusaka, 18 May 1990 (SDA).
2. See the table below.
3. Among them Mac Maharaj and Siphewe Nyanda ('Gebuza'), who were detained in July 1990 when Operation Vula was uncovered by the security police.
4. ANC: 'Report of the Organising Committee' [no place or date, but South Africa in October 1990] (MCA).
5. Ibid.
6. Ibid.

Confirming a special relation-
ship: Nelson Mandela and SIDA's
Director General Carl Tham in
Johannesburg, February 1991
(Courtesy of Per Wästberg)

Director General Carl Tham paid an extensive visit to South Africa, which covered the townships of Johannesburg and Cape Town and included talks with Mandela, Joe Slovo and a range of representatives from the trade unions, the mass demo-cratic movement, the alternative media and leading civic organizations, as well as a meeting with South Africa's Deputy Foreign Minister Leon Wessels. In a subse-quent 20-page report from the visit—his first ever to South Africa—Tham vividly described his impressions from the encounter with apartheid and engineered pov-erty. In South Africa, he wrote,

> we are exposed to poverty which is created by design and differences between rich and poor which have been calculated. It is not the outcome of a general state of affairs or unusually unfavourable conditions, but [the result] of a conscious, explicit policy, which, furthermore, is implemented with great efficiency. Not until you see it with your own eyes can you understand how the system has managed to keep the whites in a dream world, completely isolated from the poverty and misery upon which their own wealth and comfort is built.[1]

Denouncing the Western countries' historical responsibility for the establishment and maintenance of the racist system—as well as the contemporary British and German support to Inkatha—Tham strongly warned against the misconception that apartheid was dead, or dying. Sweden, he said, "must not be confused by [such] insidious [assertions]. The policy [pursued] by de Klerk must be judged on the basis of what it actually is, and not for what he would like it to be".[2] The road towards democracy and material improvements for South Africa's black majority would be long and arduous. In the meantime, Tham concluded that

---

1. Carl Tham: Memorandum ('Rapport från besök i Sydafrika 12-18 februari 1991'/'Report from visit to South Africa, 12-18 February 1991'), SIDA, Stockholm, 28 February 1991 (SDA).
2. Ibid.

Meeting in South Africa after
close contacts in Mozam-
bique: Joe Slovo (left) and
Jan Cedergren at ANC's
headquarters, Johannes-
burg, February 1991
(Courtesy of Per Wästberg)

ANC's situation is not easy. [...] We must realize [the] obvious [fact] that it is ANC—and not
the government, controlling [a] gigantic security apparatus—which is negotiating from a disadvantageous position. As close friends, we should not hesitate to put forward advice or criticism [...], but we must also understand the [extent] of the difficulties confronted [by the
movement]. We should not abandon our policy that sanctions only may be lifted when ANC
so thinks it fit, and not be impressed by the evident fact that those European countries which
never wanted to impose sanctions now eagerly will use every opportunity to abolish them.[1]

Sweden and ANC in South Africa

In consultations with ANC, in early 1991 it was agreed that the direct assistance
should include "organizational development and support for the negotiation process".[2] According to the instruction to the Swedish delegation attending the annual
aid negotiations in May 1991, "[t]he main orientation of the [...] assistance is to
concentrate on [...] activities in South Africa, including support for ANC's organizational [efforts], negotiations and education".[3] At the same time, it was decided to
increase the bilateral allocation from 97.5 MSEK in 1990/91 to 120 MSEK in
1991/92—or by 23 per cent—"in recognition of the needs facing the ANC in order
to establish itself inside [the country] and to be able to participate fully and effectively in the transformation of South Africa".[4]

Although the Social Democratic government in February 1991 had informed
the movement that "Swedish support [...] could not continue once the ANC as a
political party participates in democratic elections or a democratic constitution for

1. Ibid. From his influential position as Director General of SIDA, Tham consistently advocated continued
   assistance to ANC. Interviewed in 1997, he explained: "It was obvious to me that de Klerk supported the
   forces which were against [the movement] and that the whole process from 1991 with all the killings was part
   of a political struggle to weaken ANC" (Interview with Carl Tham, p. 344).
2. Ingalill Colbro: Memorandum ('Humanitärt bistånd till African National Congress of South Africa (ANC)
   budgetåret 1991/92'/'Humanitarian assistance to ANC [during] the financial year 1991/92'), SIDA/CCHA,
   [Stockholm], 4 April 1991 (SDA).
3. Lena Sundh: Memorandum ('Instruktion inför överläggningar med ANC om humanitärt biståndssamarbete'/
   'Instruction in view of deliberations with ANC concerning humanitarian cooperation'), Ministry for Foreign
   Affairs, Stockholm, 17 April 1991 (SDA).
4. 'Agreed minutes from consultations held in Benoni, South Africa, May 1991, between the African National
   Congress of South Africa (ANC) and the government of Sweden concerning humanitarian assistance', Johannesburg, 19 May 1991 (SDA).

For the first time in South Africa: Aid negotiations between Sweden and ANC in Benoni, May 1991. Shaking hands are Under-Secretary Bengt Säve-Söderbergh and ANC Treasurer General Thomas Nkobi. On the left is Kay Moonsamy and on the right Walter Sisulu (Courtesy of Ingalill Colbro)

South Africa [is] adopted"[1], at the following aid negotiations in Benoni outside Johannesburg—the first ever to be held in South Africa; respectively led by Säve-Söderbergh and Nkobi—the cooperation programme was thus radically restructured.

An overview of Sweden's direct support to ANC inside South Africa from 1 July 1991 will be given below. The change in emphasis from external to internal assistance motivated in the meantime a corresponding transfer of administrative responsibility from the Swedish embassy in Lusaka to the legation in Pretoria. In June 1991, it was agreed that Lena Johansson—Roland Axelsson's successor as SIDA's Lusaka-based regional coordinator of humanitarian assistance—should move to Pretoria as from September. The task of external coordination was at the same time given to her colleague Birgitta Sevefjord at the Swedish embassy in Dar es Salaam.[2]

Reflecting the changing focus of the assistance, it should here be noted that SIDA on CCHA's recommendation outside the bilateral cooperation programme in mid-June 1991—less than four weeks after the annual aid negotiations—decided to grant ANC an extraordinary contribution of 3.5 MSEK in support of its upcoming

1. Ibid.
2. Christina Regnell: Memorandum ('Framtida bistånd till Sydafrika: Riktlinjer'/'Future assistance to South Africa: Guidelines'), SIDA, Stockholm, 14 June 1991 (SDA). Cf. Lena Johansson: Memorandum ('ANC-handläggning i Lusaka, Zambia'/'ANC administration in Lusaka, Zambia'), Swedish embassy, Lusaka, 23 May 1991 (SDA). Initially, the South African government protested against the placement of Johansson in Pretoria (Bengt Herrström: Memorandum ('Sydafrikas ambassadör besöker tjf polchefen'/'South Africa's [envoy] visits the acting head of the Political Department'), Ministry for Foreign Affairs, Stockholm, 10 October 1991) (MFA). In September 1991, she could, however, take up her position as first secretary.

congress, to be held in Durban the following month.[1] By that time, considerable media attention was being given to Sweden's cooperation with ANC, both internationally and in South Africa.[2] This, in turn, prompted the Foreign Ministry to draft a memorandum through which the Swedish officials were reminded that

> [t]he decision on [support] to the [ANC] congress is classified as confidential. If we answer [questions in this regard], we [would] [...] enter into details concerning our cooperation with ANC which perhaps it is not advisable to disclose. When we [...] [address such] questions, we may possibly state that we can give information in general and in broad terms, but that we are not willing to discuss whether and with what amounts individual projects and activities have been supported.[3]

However, at the July congress in Durban—the first to be held on South African soil in more than 30 years[4]—ANC itself disclosed the sources of the support received. With regard to the actual assembly, in his report Treasurer General Nkobi noted that SIDA through its grant of 3.5 MSEK was "the main donor and the highest contributor".[5] Support for the congress amounting to 1.25 MNOK had, in addition, been extended by the government of Norway.[6]

More revealing were the figures given by Nkobi's office with regard to ANC's comprehensive financial situation in South Africa and in exile. For the period 1 March-31 December 1990, the movement's total income for internal activities amounted to 11.3 million South African Rands, of which no less than 86.6 per cent—or 9.8 MSAR—was in the form of grants, 5.3 per cent as membership fees, 3.7 per cent as donations and the remaining 4.4 per cent described as "other income".[7] As the funds channelled by SIDA under the 'home front component' during the same period amounted to 21.2 MSEK[8]—approximately corresponding to 9.4 MSAR[9]—it follows that ANC in South Africa at the time of its legalization

---

1. SIDA: Decision ('Ansökan från ANC om extrabidrag till rörelsens förestående kongress'/'Request from ANC for [an] extraordinary grant towards the movement's forthcoming congress'), Office of the Director General, No. 99/1991, Stockholm, 17 June 1991 (SDA). Thus, the direct core support to ANC in 1991/92 amounted in total to 123.5 MSEK, up by 27 per cent from the previous year. It should be recalled that SIDA in August 1991 following a joint request by ANC and PAC set aside 250,000 SEK to a Patriotic Front conference. For reasons discussed in the chapter 'Looking for Alternatives: Pan Africanist Congress', the allocation was never disbursed.
2. At the time, the South African press often contained more or less fanciful 'reports' on Sweden's ANC assistance. In early July 1991, *Finance Week*, for example, stated that the support agreed for 1991/92 amounted to 270 million South African Rands (or more than 600 MSEK), of which 150 million (some 340 MSEK) was said to be earmarked for internal activities (Cable ('Sveriges bidrag till ANC'/'Sweden's contribution to ANC') from the Swedish legation to the Ministry for Foreign Affairs, Pretoria, 12 July 1991) (SDA).
3. Lena Sundh: Memorandum ('Sveriges bistånd till ANC'/'Sweden's assistance to ANC'), Ministry for Foreign Affairs, Stockholm, 12 July 1991 (SDA).
4. The ANC assembly was called both a 'congress' and a 'conference'. In the official documentation, it was presented as ANC's 'national congress'. At the time, the movement had managed to set up a total of 936 local branches in all of its 14 administrative regions. The signed up national membership—which in October 1990 was 155,000—had by February 1991 increased to 289,000 and by June 1991 to 521,000 (Rantete *op. cit.*, pp. 14-15). The Durban congress led to major changes at the level of the ANC leadership. Nelson Mandela replaced Oliver Tambo as President and Walter Sisulu was elected Deputy President. Succeeding Alfred Nzo, Cyril Ramaphosa was at the same time appointed Secretary General, with Jacob Zuma as his deputy. While Tambo became National Chairman, among ANC's top three officials it was only Treasurer General Thomas Nkobi who retained his position. In the elections to the National Executive Committee, Chris Hani received the highest number of votes, followed by Thabo Mbeki and Joe Slovo.
5. ANC: 'Report of the Office of the Treasurer General', ANC National Congress, Durban, July 1991, p. 18.
6. Ibid. Expressed in South African Rands, the Swedish and Norwegian contributions were, respectively, around 1.5 million and 520,000 (ibid.).
7. Ibid., p. 4. 'Donations' referred mainly to private and corporate contributions raised in South Africa. 'Other income' included sales, interest received etc.
8. Calculated on a monthly basis and based on the table included in the chapter 'From Beds in Exile to Organizers at Home'.
9. Based on an exchange rate of 1 SAR=2.25 SEK.

was heavily dependent on Swedish assistance. In fact, while ANC reported that "[t]here has not been any support received [from NGOs] since the organisation moved into the country"[1], in 1990 the official assistance from Sweden represented a staggering share of 96 per cent of all grants received and 83 per cent of the movement's total internal financial resources.[2]

According to the information submitted by the Office of the Treasurer General, Sweden's dominance as ANC's main donor was striking also when taking its external projects and activities into account. During the calendar year 1990, the movement's consolidated income was 79.7 MSAR, approximately corresponding to 180 MSEK.[3] Although the available statistics from Sweden refer to its financial year from 1 July to 30 June, on the basis of the actual disbursements in 1989/90 and 1990/91[4] it could be estimated that some 85 MSEK was paid out in favour of ANC in 1990. Accordingly, in that year the support from the Swedish government alone represented around 47 per cent of the movement's total income, or more than half of the grants received.

The relative share of the Swedish assistance was not explicitly spelt out in the Treasurer General's report, which only in general terms indicated that ANC's main donors in July 1991 were Sweden, Norway, Finland, Denmark[5], Australia[6] and Italy.[7]

While the Nordic countries thus featured prominently[8], the report strongly warned against continued dependence on foreign funding, stressing that "[a]s the oppressed and struggling people we must finance our [own] liberation", raising the crucial issue of the movement's "financial viability [...] in the long term".[9] Forcefully arguing in favour of self-sufficiency, Nkobi stated:

> We must struggle to end our dependence on external forces. We have the national responsibility and duty to create and sustain alternative, reliable sources of funds, and the only sources [...] that will be reliable [are] those that come from our people. We must recognise the reality that external sources of financial and other support are not stable. [...] Unless we are self-sufficient in our work, we shall be vulnerable to external pressures, which we cannot afford at this decisive moment of our struggle. [...] It is imperative that the National Executive Committee

1. ANC: 'Report of the Office of the Treasurer General', ANC National Congress, Durban, July 1991, p. 19.
2. The lion share of the resources raised by Mandela during his world tours was as a result of technical problems not readily available. This was notably the case with some 5 million USD from a number of sources in the United States (Rantete op. cit., p. 30, note 64).
3. Of the total income, 90.7 per cent—72.3 MSAR—was in the form of grants (ANC: 'Report of the Office of the Treasurer General', ANC National Congress, Durban, July 1991, p. 10). At the same time, ANC estimated that the value of its total external assets in the form of land, buildings, vehicles, equipment etc. amounted in December 1990 to 655 MSAR, or close to 1.5 billion SEK (ibid., pp. 1 and 11-12).
4. Cf. the accompanying disbursement table (Appendix XIV).
5. With regard to Denmark, the report stated that "ANC has at long last established direct links with the Danish government", which in 1991 allocated 15 million Danish Kroner for "assistance towards the establishment of democratic structures inside South Africa" (ANC: 'Report of the Office of the Treasurer General', ANC National Congress, Durban, July 1991, p. 18).
6. For the period 1990-93, an amount of 15 million Australian Dollars had been allocated towards projects and activities in exile, as well as for repatriation of ANC refugees (ibid.).
7. In 1987, the Italian government started an assistance programme with ANC, amounting to 2 MUSD (ibid., p. 19).
8. In late September 1991, it was announced that the US government was to donate 12.5 MSAR to ANC and 7 MSAR to the Inkatha Freedom Party—respectively corresponding to 28 and 16 MSEK—"to help the two organisations prepare for negotiations" ('ANC and IFP get R19.5m from US' in *The Sowetan*, 27 September 1991). Two months earlier, the Pretoria regime had conceded that it had been running a slush fund for Inkatha.
9. ANC: 'Report of the Office of the Treasurer General', ANC National Congress, Durban, July 1991, p. 3.

actively participates in, and fully supports, the activities of the [Office of the Treasurer General] in its efforts to transform the movement into a self-sustaining organisation.[1]

Shortly thereafter—in September 1991—the Social Democratic Party lost the parliamentary elections in Sweden to a non-socialist coalition led by the Moderate Party, traditionally standing outside the broad social-liberal anti-apartheid movement and strongly opposed to economic sanctions against South Africa.[2] As if he could foresee this significant political change, the Treasurer General, finally, cautioned the Durban congress that

[t]he amount of funds received for [...] our projects and other activities can be, and is, influenced by changes of government, pressure exerted by some governments and organisations upon progressive and friendly forces, and by the social, political and economic interests of the leaders of some countries and organisations.[3]

While, indeed, it was ironic that the Swedish government during the last leg of ANC's protracted struggle would be led by a party which consistently had shunned the liberation movement—as late as in March 1990 even keeping away from the popular celebrations in connection with Nelson Mandela's visit—the bilateral, exclusive assistance to ANC would, however, not be immediately affected by the change in Stockholm. Nor would the sanctions be lifted. As the Bildt administration upheld the agreements made by its Social Democratic predecessor, in October 1991 the Moderate Foreign Minister Margaretha af Ugglas—having considerable personal economic interests in South Africa and known as a staunch opponent of sanctions—surprised friends and opponents alike by stating in the Swedish parliament that

Sweden's long-standing support for the struggle against apartheid will continue. Our sanctions are an important aspect of this work. Actual developments [...] will determine if and when Sweden can revoke its sanctions. A decision to this effect must be based on a comprehensive assessment of the political situation in South Africa [, but t]here must be clear evidence of profound and irreversible change.[4]

The orientation and content of the ANC programme were also maintained. In view of the forthcoming consultative talks concerning the assistance in 1992/93, a SIDA

---

1. Ibid. In the midst of ensuing discussions on financial dependency, at the consultative talks between Sweden and ANC in November 1991—that is, only four months later—Nkobi, however, pleaded for a redoubling of the official Swedish support. In his introductory address, Nkobi stated: "SIDA has supported the ANC through all the dark years of exile, and [has] largely contributed to bringing us where we are today. Down the years, you have shown confidence in the ANC as the torch-bearer of democracy. We can now see a light at the end of the tunnel. However, for us to complete the last part of our journey, to bring our people to the dawn of liberation, it is essential that support to our organisation [is] increased. We are therefore appealing to SIDA, the government and the people of Sweden, to double their contribution for 1992/93, [in order] to ensure the achievement of our goal of a non-racial, non-sexist, democratic South Africa in the shortest possible time" ('Address by the Treasurer General to the ANC-SIDA talks, 19 November 1991', attached to 'Agreed minutes from consultations held in Benoni, South Africa, November 1991, between the African National Congress of South Africa (ANC) and the Swedish International Development Authority (SIDA) concerning humanitarian assistance', Johannesburg, 23 November 1991) (SDA).
2. As Prime Minister elect, Carl Bildt formed a cabinet in which his party colleague Margaretha af Ugglas became Foreign Minister and Alf Svensson, the leader of the Christian Democrats, Minister for International Development Cooperation. The Centre and Liberal parties were part of the coalition. Contrary to the situation in 1976-82, the non-socialist government which ruled between 1991 and 1994 was, however, dominated by the Moderate Party, which had more parliamentary seats than the two 'middle' parties together.
3. ANC: 'Report of the Office of the Treasurer General', ANC National Congress, Durban, July 1991, p. 3.
4. 'Reply by the Minister for Foreign Affairs, Mrs. Margaretha af Ugglas, to a question from Mr. Hans Göran Franck concerning South Africa', 22 October 1991, in Ministry for Foreign Affairs: *Documents on Swedish Foreign Policy: 1991*, Stockholm, 1992, p. 332.

Aid negotations in Benoni, South Africa, November 1991: Nelson Mandela and Thomas Nkobi with the Swedish delegation (from left): Tarja Roghult, Ingalill Colbro, Birgitta Sevefjord, Kaj Persson, Johan Brisman, Lena Johansson and Anders Möllander (Courtesy of Ingalill Colbro)

memorandum serving as an instruction to the Swedish delegation[1] confirmed in October 1991 that the support "should focus on strategic areas, namely organizational development and the negotiation process inside the country".[2] Although the delegation was requested to "reiterate [its] concern [...] regarding [the] vulnerability [which follows from] strong aid dependency", at the same time, however, it should

> express willingness to extend continued support towards ANC's organizational [efforts] and its administration in South Africa. The running and maintenance of all its departments should fall under this heading.[3]

The continuity of the Swedish government's support was appreciated by Nelson Mandela[4], Cyril Ramaphosa[5], Thomas Nkobi and the ANC delegation to the talks held in Benoni, Johannesburg, in mid-November 1991, shortly before the initial session of the multi-party CODESA negotiations.[6] While plans for 1992/93 were drawn up in the midst of rapid developments and, in general, a fluid political climate, at the talks the Swedish delegation—led by SIDA's Assistant Director General

1. SIDA: Decision ('Riktlinjer för överläggningar med African National Congress, ANC, avseende budgetåret 1992/93'/'Guidelines for deliberations with ANC concerning the financial year 1992/93'), Office of the Director General, No. 176/1991, Stockholm, 8 November 1991 (SDA).
2. Ingalill Colbro: Memorandum ('Bakgrundspromemoria för överläggningar med ANC, november 1991'/ 'Background memorandum for deliberations with ANC [in] November 1991'), SIDA, Stockholm, 23 October 1991 (SDA).
3. Ibid.
4. Letter ('Samtal med Nelson Mandela'/'Conversation with Nelson Mandela') from Anders Möllander to the Ministry for Foreign Affairs, Swedish legation, Pretoria, 27 November 1991 (SDA).
5. The meetings with President Mandela and Secretary General Ramaphosa were arranged outside the consultative talks on aid cooperation (Kaj Persson: Memorandum ('Programsamtal med ANC'/'Consultative talks with ANC'), Ministry for Foreign Affairs, Stockholm, 2 December 1991) (SDA).
6. In December 1991, the multi-party negotiating forum Convention for a Democratic South Africa met for the first time to discuss South Africa's future constitution. Boycotted by the pro-apartheid Conservative Party, as well as by AZAPO and PAC, it was attended by a wide range of political organizations. ANC and the National Party dominated the proceedings.

Johan Brisman[1]—correspondingly received confirmation on a number of central issues. With regard to ANC's reliance on foreign funding, it was established that the Swedish budgetary support covered one third of the total expenditure on administration, benefiting 22 departments at the headquarters in Johannesburg, 14 regional offices and the women's and youth leagues.[2] In its request for continued assistance, ANC shortly thereafter indicated that Sweden financed the salaries of 200 of its 430 national and regional officials.[3] Secondly, it was noted that ANC's National Executive Committee in November 1991 had decided to phase out the movement's external projects by July 1992.[4] Finally, in a separate meeting Mandela underlined that the organization would not register as a political party, but continue "as a front" until apartheid's conclusive demise.[5]

New Swedish Signals

In early 1992, the Bildt government started more actively to question the South Africa policy. After the launch of the CODESA talks and in response to the endorsement of negotiations by South Africa's white electorate[6]—as well as being

---

1. In addition to Brisman, the following formed part of the Swedish delegation: Kaj Persson from the Foreign Ministry; Ingalill Colbro and Tarja Roghult from SIDA; Birgitta Sevefjord from the embassy in Dar es Salaam; and Christina Hoffman de Vylder, Lena Johansson, Anders Möllander and Ingemar Stjernberg from the legation in Pretoria. Led by Thomas Nkobi, around 25 officials from the headquarters in Johannesburg, Stockholm and various offices in Africa represented ANC.

2. Ingalill Colbro: Memorandum ('Rapport från överläggningar med ANC, november 1991'/'Report from deliberations with ANC [in] November 1991'), SIDA, Stockholm, 5 December 1991 (SDA) and 'Agreed minutes from consultations held in Benoni, South Africa, November 1991, between the African National Congress of South Africa (ANC) and the Swedish International Development Authority (SIDA) concerning humanitarian assistance', Johannesburg, 23 November 1991 (SDA). On a monthly basis, 850,000 SAR was transferred to ANC's regional structures. Swedish funds were largely used for this purpose (ibid.).

3. SIDA: Memorandum ('Det svenska biståndet till ANC samt ANC's framställning för 1992/93'/'The Swedish assistance to ANC and ANC's request for 1992/93'), [Stockholm], 13 April 1992 (SDA) and ANC: 'Submission to SIDA for [the] financial year July 1992-June 1993', [no place or date] (SDA). In its request, the movement noted: "In this uncertain period, the ANC remains heavily dependent upon financial support from SIDA [...]. Although the ANC is urgently undertaking measures to ensure self-sufficiency by the middle of 1993, it must accept that without the SIDA contribution [...] the administration and infrastructure [...] would have to close down. The predictable consequences of such a collapse would be the derailing of peaceful democratic discourse within South Africa and the loss of any hope for a legitimate and prosperous government for decades to come" (ibid.).

4. Colbro: Memorandum, 5 December 1991, and 'Agreed minutes', 23 November 1991.

5. Letter ('Samtal med Nelson Mandela'/'Conversation with Nelson Mandela') from Anders Möllander to the Ministry for Foreign Affairs, Swedish legation, Pretoria, 20 November 1991 (SDA). In bilateral talks with ANC, in January-February 1993 the National Party/Pretoria government intensified its pressure on the liberation movement to register as a political party. ANC, however, "confirmed that it would not change its status until a new constitution is adopted" (ANC: _Negotiations Bulletin_, No. 20, 9 February 1993).

6. In a whites-only referendum held on 17 March 1992, nearly 70 per cent of the votes cast were in favour of continued negotiations towards a post-apartheid dispensation. In an internal memorandum to the movement's missions abroad, ANC commented on the outcome as follows: "Euphoria has set in on the part of many countries that the landslide vote has now definitely cleared the path for an absolute change. We in the ANC and the democratic movement [...] cannot assume that [...] a political solution is guaranteed. The only guarantee would be the signing of agreements [on an] interim transitional government [...]. It is at that point that we can conclude [that] the process [is] irreversible and thus call for the lifting of all restrictions (except the arms embargo)" (ANC: 'Perspectives on ANC's international work', Department of International Affairs, [no place or date, but Johannesburg in March 1992]) (SDA).

exposed to domestic criticism[1] and indirect external pressure[2]—in mid-March Foreign Minister af Ugglas declared that the reform process "brings to the fore the question of the date for the dismantling of sanctions against South Africa".[3] More importantly, although the conditions and cut-off points earlier established were far from being at hand[4]—and the ministry's own legal experts did not unequivocally support such a view[5]—at the same time leading foreign affairs' representatives began to express doubts about the ANC support. While SIDA's Carl Tham and committee members such as Karl-Axel Elmquist and Per Wästberg during a CCHA meeting forcefully advocated continued official assistance[6], Anders Bjurner from

1. Led by Peter Wallenberg, the International Council of Swedish Industry (NIR) had consistently lobbied against sanctions, as well as opposed official assistance to ANC (cf. the chapter 'Isolation versus Involvement: Companies, Churches and Labour in the 1970s'). Thus sharing views with the Moderate Party, NIR's campaign intensified after the formation of the non-socialist government in October 1991. Interviewed in March 1992, Wallenberg declared that the Swedish sanctions "[had] done more harm to ourselves than to South Africa" and that in South Africa "it [was] the blacks who [had] taken the punch". Criticizing the Bildt government for "dragging its feet" with regard to a repeal of the sanctions legislation, he also turned against the assistance to ANC, implying that Buthelezi's Inkatha was an alternative. In an often quoted statement, the powerful industrialist said: "[W]e have supported one of [mainly] two black movements, and have not given anything to the other. [...] I wonder what we would think if someone was busy giving out a lot of money to the Lapps so that they could create [massive] problems for the Swedish government. [...] I guess that it would provoke incredible outcries" (Peter Wallenberg cited in Mikael Johansson and Bo Lundström: 'Sydafrikasanktionerna kostade miljarder'/'The South Africa sanctions cost billions' in *Svenska Dagbladet*, 29 March 1992). (On Wallenberg's meeting with Nelson Mandela in Stockholm two months later, see below.) In the hardening political climate in early 1992, the conservative newspaper *Svenska Dagbladet* also censured the ANC support. Shortly after a visit to Sweden by Mandela, Nkobi, Thabo Mbeki and other leading ANC representatives, in an editorial comment the paper argued in late May 1992 that the organization "in today's South Africa from all aspects but formally is a [political] party", adding that "[i]t would [...] be extraordinary if a [non-socialist] Swedish government should continue to give away hundreds of millions [...] to a party which from an ideological point of view is [...] a cross between [the Communist Party Marxist-Leninists (Revolutionaries)] and the Social Democrats" ('Tagande av svenskt stöd'/'Receiving Swedish support' in *Svenska Dagbladet*, 23 May 1992). Nevertheless, only four days later the government announced that it had decided to grant ANC 110 MSEK for the financial year 1992/93 (Ministry for Foreign Affairs: Press release ('ANC får fortsatt svenskt stöd'/'ANC receives continued Swedish support'), Stockholm, 27 May 1992) (MFA).

2. Finland repealed its sanctions against South Africa as early as in June 1991 and Denmark—which revoked its investment ban in January 1992—followed suit after the white referendum in March 1992. These examples were used *inter alia* by the Swedish Metalworkers Union in favour of a similar decision in Sweden (see the chapter 'SACTU, Unions and Sanctions').

3. Ministry for Foreign Affairs: Press release ('The Minister for Foreign Affairs, Mrs. Margaretha af Ugglas, says: 'The victory of the supporters of reform in South Africa is gratifying"), Stockholm, 18 March 1992 (MFA). Looking back, Pierre Schori noted that "Carl Bildt [...] in May 1992 [...] expressed the view that sanctions could [...] be abolished within a fortnight. This moved me to reply [in parliament] that it was developments in South Africa, not the Moderates' concern for Swedish business, which would decide when we were able to repeal our sanctions" (Schori (1994) op. cit., p. 32).

4. That is, a) when ANC as a political party would participate in democratic elections or b) when a democratic constitution for South Africa had been adopted (see above).

5. In an internal memorandum, the Legal Department of the Ministry for Foreign Affairs discussed in January 1992 the principles of international law determining intervention in the affairs of another state in the context of foreign aid to political organizations. The conclusion reached was that the main determinants were the extent and degree of democratic development in the state in question. Thus, "if the state [...] is *clearly* undemocratic, [...] aid should not amount to proscribed intervention. [On the contrary,] such aid could rather be considered in line with the principles of peoples' right to self-determination. [And t]o promote a people's development towards independence and self-determination is entirely compatible with international law" (Harry Landau: Memorandum ('Frågan om förenlighet av svenskt bistånd till politiska partier i främmande stat och non-interventionsprincipen'/'The question of compatibility between Swedish assistance to political parties in a foreign state and the principle of non-intervention'), Ministry for Foreign Affairs, Stockholm, 29 January 1992) (MFA). Cf. the exchange below between the Swedish government and the Social Democratic opposition.

6. According to the notes from the meeting, Wästberg, for example, was of the opinion that "there at the moment is no assistance to South Africa which is more important than that to ANC" (Ingalill Colbro: Memorandum ('Minnesanteckningar från Beredningen för Humanitärt Biståndts möte 19 mars 1992 om framtida bistånd till ANC'/'Notes from the CCHA meeting on 19 March 1992 concerning future assistance to ANC'), SIDA, Stockholm, 19 March 1992) (SDA).

the Foreign Ministry was less convinced.[1]

Both with regard to the maintenance of sanctions and the continuation of the ANC assistance, divergent views would from then on increasingly characterize the relations between SIDA and the Foreign Ministry, as well as between the Social Democratic opposition and the non-socialist government. Reflecting on the developments from his position in Windhoek, one year later—in May 1993—Sten Rylander, the Swedish ambassador to Namibia, critically wrote to the ministry in Stockholm that

> [w]hat I see today is a timorous hesitation with regard to the handling of the ANC assistance, as well as over-enthusiastic and commercially driven attempts to revoke the sanctions. [This] has [...] led to an unnecessary party politicization of the issues [...].[2]

Eventually, however, Sweden would only lift its trade embargo in September 1993[3], following an agreement on a Transitional Executive Council (TEC), a *de facto* interim government which was formally endorsed by the South African parliament in December. While most countries by then had already done so, in an address to the UN General Assembly Nelson Mandela in September also called upon the world to end the economic isolation of his country. Albeit somewhat exaggerated, Prime Minister Carlsson's statement to Mandela in Stockholm of March 1990 that "Sweden was the first to employ sanctions in support of the liberation struggle [and has] nothing against being the last to repeal them"[4], in a Western context—and remarkably under a Moderate-led government—this would largely be the case.

Eventually, too, the direct, official aid cooperation with ANC would not be brought to an end until 27 January 1994, only three months ahead of the South African elections. More significantly, despite internal Swedish contradictions, certain bilateral strains and the 'timorousness' noted by Rylander, due to the massive support enjoyed by the movement the essentially political, exclusive assistance to ANC in South Africa was under Carl Bildt's non-socialist government not only maintained, but for all practical purposes considerably expanded and increased. In this respect, too, the role played was exceptional.

The interaction with and assistance to ANC in South Africa from mid-1992 until its electoral victory in April 1994 will occupy the last pages of this study. Before turning to the final demise of white minority rule and apartheid, the issue

---

1. Bjurner argued *inter alia* that Sweden's "enormous dominance" was "doubtful", asking why ANC's participation in the negotiation process could not be supported with official South African funds. Clarification in that respect, he said, would make it easier to "present the whole case [of ANC support] to the Foreign Minister" (ibid.). It should be recalled that Foreign Ministry officials in 1989-90—that is, under a Social Democratic government—had argued that the humanitarian assistance to SWAPO must be discontinued and that Sweden should be neutral vis-à-vis the independence elections in Namibia (see the chapter 'With SWAPO to Victory').

2. Letter ('Om samarbetet med ANC och de framtida relationerna med Sydafrika: En kommentar utifrån namibiska perspektiv'/'On the cooperation with ANC and the future relations with South Africa: A comment from a Namibian perspective') from Sten Rylander, Swedish ambassador to Namibia, to the Ministry for Foreign Affairs, Windhoek, 10 May 1993 (MFA). Strongly arguing in favour of continued ANC assistance, Rylander observed that "[t]o promote the [very] force which advocates political rights and an end to the discrimination of the black population [...] cannot be considered tantamount to undue intervention in [South Africa's] internal affairs. It can in no way be compared to the interference support to a political party in an established democracy would imply" (ibid.).

3. Press release: 'Lifting of sanctions against South Africa and introduction of measures to promote trade with South Africa', 13 September 1993, in Ministry for Foreign Affairs: *Documents on Swedish Foreign Policy: 1993*, Stockholm, 1994, pp. 433-34.

4. Cited in Schori (1994) op. cit., p. 32.

and the lands where it all modestly started in early 1973—humanitarian assistance to the movement in East and Central Africa—should, however, first be revisited.[1]

Phasing out the External Projects

As in the case of SWAPO in Angola[2], the winding up of the assistance to ANC's main settlements in exile would not be without complications. While the principal problems encountered in the former case resulted from the void left at Kwanza Sul after the repatriation of the Namibian refugees and the Angolan host government's inability to protect the vacated site, in the latter they were a consequence of a combination of factors. Foremost among these were the early return to South Africa of ANC's political leaders and core officials; the Pretoria regime's drawn-out opposition to a massive repatriation exercise[3]; the uncertainties prevailing with regard to overall domestic developments; and the fact that there was a constant influx of people fleeing from the hostilities in KwaZulu-Natal and the Greater Johannesburg area.

This led to a breakdown of the administration at the settlements in Tanzania, as well as to widespread indiscipline, theft and violence both there and in Zambia. The Swedish authorities would in this respect strongly state their dissatisfaction to the ANC leadership in Johannesburg. With regard to Uganda and the MK evacuees from Angola, the situation was different. However, as SIDA could only in May 1991 follow up the assistance, the humanitarian support in that country, too, would be a subject of concern. As closer cooperation developed in South Africa, the dialogue thus became sharper with regard to the activities supported in exile.

After ANC's withdrawal from Angola, Sweden decided in May 1989 to allocate 1 MSEK to the movement in Uganda for the financial year 1989/90, an amount which at the consultative talks in November was raised to 3 MSEK. As earlier noted, for the first time Uganda was thereby included among the countries to which official ANC assistance was channelled. As it was a prerequisite that SIDA officials could follow up the activities supported, in October 1989 Roland Axelsson travelled to the country. He was, however, denied access to the two camps outside Masaka and Mbarara put at ANC's disposal by the Museveni government.[4]

In March 1990—shortly after ANC's unbanning—Axelsson made a new attempt. Told by ANC's resident Deputy Chief Representative Leonard Maleko

---

1. The termination of the ANC support in the 'forward areas' and in Angola has been discussed above. It remains to comment on the assistance in the movement's historical host countries, that is, Tanzania and Zambia, as well as—from 1989—Uganda.
2. See the chapter 'With SWAPO to Victory'. As noted there, following SWAPO's return to Namibia a veritable cannibalization of its former Angolan settlement in Kwanza Sul took place.
3. Rejecting a general amnesty in favour of the South Africans in exile, the Pretoria regime was for a long time opposed to UNHCR and a UN-sponsored repatriation exercise. On an individual basis, all returnees were instead vetted before they were given 'indemnity'. Finally, it was only in August 1991 that an agreement was signed between the South African government and UNHCR on the voluntary repatriation and reintegration of refugees.
4. Roland Axelsson: Memorandum ('Anteckningar från besök i Uganda 27-28 mars 1990'/'Notes from visit to Uganda, 27-28 March 1990'), Swedish embassy, Lusaka, 5 April 1990 (SDA). ANC's first Chief Representative to Uganda was Thenjiwe Mtintso, who arrived there in January 1989. The camp at Masaka was situated some 150 kilometres southwest of the capital Kampala and the one outside Mbarara another 150 kilometres to the west. According to ANC, in October 1989 there were around 2,000 MK evacuees from Angola in the two camps (ibid.).

that it was "impossible" to go to the camps, this visit, too, was unsuccessful.[1] SIDA's regional coordinator was, nevertheless, allowed to verify ANC's financial records held at the office in Kampala. Finding them wanting, he issued "an ultimatum" to Thomas Nkobi that he must be given authority to visit the camps before June 1990. If not, he added, "I cannot take responsibility for the disbursement of further Swedish funds".[2]

The issue was discussed during the last aid negotiations held in Lusaka in May 1990. While the ANC delegation led by Secretary General Nzo reported that the Ugandan government was "sensitive about visitors to the ANC settlement[s]", it, however, undertook to "make strenuous efforts to obtain clearance for a visit by a SIDA representative", who should be accompanied by an official from the Office of the Treasurer General.[3] Although no substantial follow-up of the assistance had been made, on the basis of this assurance the Swedish delegation—headed by SIDA's Jan Cedergren—agreed to set aside no less than 4.5 MSEK for 'daily necessities' in Uganda in 1990/91.[4]

When Axelsson returned to the country in October 1990, he was, however, once again refused entry to the ANC camps.[5] Furthermore, "the ANC office in Kampala was not even aware of the conditions set for [the] payment of SIDA funds [and] it seems that the Uganda government had not been approached about a possible [...] visit".[6] Against this background, in late November Cedergren sent a strong protest to Thomas Nkobi at the ANC headquarters in Johannesburg, stating that this "is the first time [that] SIDA has ever been denied a visit to a liberation movement settlement supported by Sweden"[7]; requesting "a confirmation in writing that the Uganda government actually refuses such a visit"; and stressing that "[actual] SIDA support to ANC refugees in Uganda would be pending such [a] confirmation".[8]

At a time when the ANC leadership had returned to South Africa and the first signs of administrative breakdowns started to appear in Tanzania, the problems encountered with regard to Uganda were far from conducive to a continuation of

---

1. Ibid. Thousands of freedom fighters were also moved from Angola to Tanzania, where they were settled outside Tanga some 280 kilometres north of Dar es Salaam, as well as at Iringa, around 500 kilometres west of the capital. Smaller numbers were placed at Mazimbu and Dakawa. This, in turn, led to "irritating" restrictions concerning regular visits to ANC's main settlements in the country. SIDA's Birgitta Sevefjord was notably denied access to SOMAFCO/Mazimbu (Roland Axelsson: Memorandum ('Anteckningar från besök i Tanzania 29 mars-3 april 1990'/'Notes from visit to Tanzania, 29 March-3 April 1990'), Swedish embassy, Lusaka, 9 April 1990) (SDA).
2. Roland Axelsson: Memorandum ('Anteckningar från besök i Uganda 27-28 mars 1990'/'Notes from visit to Uganda, 27-28 March 1990'), Swedish embassy, Lusaka, 5 April 1990 (SDA).
3. 'Agreed minutes from consultations held in Lusaka, May 1990, between the African National Congress of South Africa and Sweden concerning humanitarian assistance', Lusaka, 18 May 1990 (SDA).
4. Ibid. In addition, 700,000 SEK was tentatively allocated to agricultural activities in Uganda (ibid.).
5. Letter ('Swedish cooperation with ANC 1990/91: Allocation for Uganda') from Jan Cedergren to Thomas Nkobi, SIDA, Stockholm, 30 November 1990 (SDA).
6. Ibid.
7. As earlier discussed, for many years Swedish officials were not granted access to the ANC camps in Angola (cf. the chapter 'Closer and Broader Cooperation: Projects in Exile, Mineworkers, UDF and Civics in South Africa'). Similarly, in 1976-77 authority was not given by the Zambian government to visit the SWAPO settlement at Nyango, initially declared a 'security area' (cf. the chapter 'Transport, Home Front, Churches and Trade Unions'). This notwithstanding, in both cases Swedish humanitarian assistance towards 'daily necessities' was extended.
8. Letter ('Swedish cooperation with ANC 1990/91: Allocation for Uganda') from Jan Cedergren to Thomas Nkobi, SIDA, Stockholm, 30 November 1990 (SDA).

large scale assistance to the movement in exile.[1] In April 1991, the Ugandan government, however, eventually agreed to a visit to the ANC/MK 'Dr. Hugo Nkabinde camp', then housing around 2,500 people.[2] At the end of the following month—shortly after the annual negotiations held in Benoni, South Africa—SIDA's Lena Johansson and ANC's Ismail Coovadia travelled to Uganda, where a visiting programme was set up by the movement's Chief Representative, the former ANC National Commissar and SOMAFCO Director Andrew Masondo.

During the visit, Johansson and Coovadia noted that the conditions in the camp were "poor", but that the ANC office was "well managed". A number of initiatives had been taken to improve the situation for the ANC/MK population in the country, in total estimated at around 3,000.[3] Against this background, the SIDA representative recommended that the 4 MSEK tentatively set aside earlier in the month for ANC in Uganda during 1991/92 should be made available[4], a proposal which was endorsed by the authorities in Stockholm.[5]

The joint SIDA-ANC visit was followed up by Birgitta Sevefjord from the Swedish embassy in Dar es Salaam in early November 1991. Her impressions were even more positive. Noting that the South Africans in Uganda depended exclusively on financial support from the Swedish government and that they, in addition, received clothes and other items only from the Swedish NGO *Praktisk Solidaritet*, Sevefjord in particular underlined their spirit of self-reliance. Although most of the refugees were housed in primitive earthen structures, she found that "almost all of them take part in some form of [outdoor] education", adding that "[e]verything I observed was in good order, clean, neat and well managed".[6] Concluding that "compared to Tanzania, it was like coming to another planet", she was in favour of continued assistance.[7] As ANC at the same time decided to bring its external

1. ANC had at the annual negotiations in May 1990 explained that its external projects would continue "for the foreseeable future". Following this decision, preparations were initiated to organize a donors' conference with the main objective to raise funds for the Mazimbu and Dakawa settlements. Swedish support for the conference was sought *inter alia* by Thomas Nkobi during a visit to Stockholm in late November 1990. Increasingly involved with ANC inside South Africa, by that time, however, the Swedish authorities had begun to question the relevance of major initiatives—focusing on infrastructural development and involving large investments—in favour of the refugee population in exile, considered likely to be repatriated in a not too distant future. Following Nkobi's visit, on behalf of SIDA Cedergren conveyed the conclusion that it was "reluctant to support the development centre [at] Dakawa" (Letter ('Request for support: ANC Development Centre, Dakawa, Tanzania') from Jan Cedergren to Thomas Nkobi, SIDA, Stockholm, 18 December 1990) (SDA). Contrary to the situation in December 1987—when ANC under the theme 'Peoples of the World against Apartheid for a Democratic South Africa' convened a similar conference in Arusha, Tanzania, attended by Lisbet Palme and a large Swedish delegation (ANC: 'Conference report' and attached documents, [no place or date]) (SDA)—the conference itself was also accorded low priority. Coordinated by the Norwegian People's Aid and eventually held in Arusha in early February 1991, the official conference involvement was limited to a financial grant of 200,000 SEK to the Norwegian NGO (Letter ('ANC donors conference') from Jan Cedergren to Thomas Nkobi, SIDA, Stockholm, 14 December 1990) (SDA) and a rather low-key attendance by a delegation formed by Anders Oljelund, ambassador to Tanzania, Lena Sundh of the Foreign Ministry, Ingalill Colbro of SIDA, Lena Johansson from the embassy in Lusaka and Birgitta Sevefjord from Dar es Salaam (Lena Sundh: Memorandum ('ANC's givarkonferens i Arusha 6-8 februari 1991'/'ANC's donor conference in Arusha, 6-8 February 1991'), Ministry for Foreign Affairs, Stockholm, 22 February 1991) (SDA).
2. Lena Johansson: Memorandum ('Tjänsteresa Uganda'/'Duty trip [to] Uganda'), Swedish embassy, Lusaka, 28 May 1991 (SDA). By then, ANC's two earlier camps in Uganda had been amalgamated into a new camp established some 120 kilometres northwest of Kampala.
3. Ibid.
4. Ibid.
5. Letter ('Swedish assistance to ANC-Uganda') from Jan Cedergren to Thomas Nkobi, SIDA, Stockholm, 6 June 1991 (SDA).
6. Letter ('Reserapport från Uganda'/'Travel report from Uganda') from Birgitta Sevefjord to SIDA, Swedish embassy, Dar es Salaam, 13 November 1991 (SDA).
7. Ibid.

projects to a close, by mid-1992 the Swedish non-military support to the MK contingent in Uganda was, however, phased out.

Meanwhile, in Tanzania and Zambia—historically housing the bulk of ANC's civilian population in exile—the conditions deteriorated rapidly.[1] In both countries, the return to South Africa of ANC's political leaders and core officials—called upon to establish and staff the headquarters in Johannesburg—created a serious void.[2] In a situation of continuous inflows of new refugees[3], the remaining, largely inexperi-enced, administrative cadres were increasingly incapable of running the movement's large and complex settlements, particularly at Mazimbu and Dakawa. As social programmes were affected—and the Pretoria government only agreed with UNHCR in August 1991 on an organized, massive repatriation exercise[4], which, furthermore, proved to be remarkably slow[5]—a mood of generalized "resignation" set in among the ANC refugees.[6]

---

1. Signs of administrative breakdown were noted as early as in February 1991. Visiting the ANC settlements in Tanzania in connection with the above-mentioned Arusha conference, Ingalill Colbro, Lena Johansson and Birgitta Sevefjord reported that "the administration of Mazimbu has deteriorated [and] [t]he mood among the people seem[s] to have gone down" (Colbro, Johansson and Sevefjord: Memorandum ('Visit at Mazimbu and Dakawa: ANC's donors' conference'), [no place], 8 February 1991) (SDA). Returning to Mazimbu the following month, Sevefjord found that the situation had deteriorated further. The rate of theft and assault had increased, and ANC's farm manager Tom Zwane feared that "[a]nyday from now someone will be killed" (Letter [no title] from Birgitta Sevefjord to SIDA, Swedish embassy, Dar es Salaam, 6 March 1991) (SDA). Widespread indiscipline among the ANC population in Zambia was also noted over the following months (Cable ('Situationen bland kvarvarande ANC-medlemmar i Lusaka'/'The situation among the remaining ANC members in Lusaka') from the Swedish embassy to the Ministry for Foreign Affairs, Lusaka, 11 July 1991) (SDA).
2. Sweden actively supported the return of the ANC officials. In order to repatriate a core of 500 people, in September 1990 an extraordinary amount of 850,000 SEK was granted, covering the estimated costs of five chartered flights from Zambia and Tanzania. The first flight from Lusaka took off on 6 March 1991, with 91 ANC members on board. SIDA's Lena Johansson accompanied the group. On 18 April 1991, the first flight from Dar es Salaam similarly brought 121 people to Johannesburg (Cable ('Repatriering av ANC-medlemmar'/'Repatriation of ANC members') from the Swedish embassy to the Ministry for Foreign Affairs, Lusaka, 18 March 1991 (SDA) and Birgitta Sevefjord: Memorandum ('Repatrieringsflyg DSM-Johannesburg den 18 april 1991'/'Repatriation flight Dar es Salaam-Johannesburg, 18 April 1991'), Swedish embassy, Dar es Salaam, 23 April 1991) (SDA).
3. As late as in October 1991—when there were around 4,500 people at Mazimbu and Dakawa—Sevefjord reported that "there is a continuous inflow, but no outflow" (Birgitta Sevefjord: Memorandum ('Lägesrapport från ANC's läger i Mazimbu och Dakawa'/'Status report regarding the ANC camps at Mazimbu and Dakawa'), Swedish embassy, Dar es Salaam, 2 October 1991) (SDA). New groups of South African refugees were at the same time coming to Zambia (Letter ('Reserapport från Zambia'/'Travel report from Zambia') from Birgitta Sevefjord to SIDA, Swedish embassy, Dar es Salaam, 29 October 1991) (SDA).
4. At the time, UNHCR estimated that there were in total 40,000 ANC refugees in Africa, including 11,000 in Tanzania (Anders Oljelund: Memorandum ('Repatriering av ANC-are till Sydafrika'/'Repatriation of ANC [refugees] to South Africa'), Swedish embassy, Dar es Salaam, 1 October 1991) (SDA). At the consultative talks in November 1991, ANC reported that around 7,000 exiles had returned (Kaj Persson: Memorandum ('Programsamtal med ANC'/'Consultative talks with ANC'), Ministry for Foreign Affairs, Stockholm, 2 December 1991) (SDA).
5. Soon after the formal agreement with South Africa, Sweden granted 12.5 MSEK to UNHCR for the repatriation exercise ('Minutes of the quarterly meeting ANC/SIDA', Johannesburg, 25 September 1991) (SDA). The first UNHCR flight to South Africa (Durban) left Dar es Salaam on 11 December 1991 (Letter ('Veckobrev: ANC'/'Weekly letter: ANC') from Ingalill Colbro to the Swedish legation in Pretoria, SIDA, Stockholm, 16 December 1991) (SDA). The repatriation operation was, however, slow, and as late as in March 1992 there remained hundreds of registered returnees in Tanzania and Zambia. Critically commenting on the situation, SIDA's Birgitta Sevefjord noted that "UNHCR acts in an amazingly unprofessional way" and that "the cooperation with ANC is bad" (Letter ('Tillägg till reserapporten från Zambia inför samtalen i Johannesburg 24 mars 1992'/'Addendum to the travel report from Zambia in view of the talks in Johannesburg on 24 March 1992') from Birgitta Sevefjord to SIDA, Swedish embassy, Dar es Salaam, 25 March 1992) (SDA).
6. Ingalill Colbro: Memorandum ('Humanitärt bistånd till African National Congress of South Africa (ANC) budgetåret 1991/92'/'Humanitarian assistance to ANC [during] the financial year 1991/92'), SIDA/CCHA, [Stockholm], 4 April 1991 (SDA).

To this should be added sharp divisions between, on the one hand, those of the older exiled population who yearned to go back to South Africa and, on the other, those who had recently left the country and feared a return. Fleeing from the fighting in rural Natal and the battles in the townships of Transvaal, many in the latter category—mainly youngsters steeped in hard environments of rebellion and violence—had, in addition, little previous political experience of either ANC or organized community life.[1] Together with a number of frustrated, demobilized former MK soldiers, it was primarily within this category that gangs were formed, which in 1991-92 became associated with drugs, theft, violence and, in general, a climate of indiscipline and insecurity in the settlements.[2] Similar developments took place in Zambia.[3]

It would lead too far to go into details with regard to these events, which constitute an unfortunate epilogue to ANC's long and proud history of efficient administration in exile and successful cooperation with the two host countries and a range of international donors.[4] Suffice it to note that in the case of Sweden and other friendly countries it prompted appeals for intervention to the ANC leadership in Johannesburg.[5] Pending a massive operation through UNHCR, funds were also allocated to repatriate particularly vulnerable groups, notably children.[6]

In the meantime, a wave of vandalization took place at the settlements in Tanzania. In the absence of a recognized and effective leadership, ANC inhabitants, local workers and residents—as well as members of the Tanzanian armed forces

---

1. The security situation at the ANC settlements in Tanzania deteriorated considerably in mid-June 1991, when increasing incidents of rape and assault were reported. According to Sevefjord, the attacks were mainly carried out by "young men who have recently arrived from Natal and who have [...] the bad taste to call themselves Inkatha" (Birgitta Sevefjord: Memorandum ('Rapport om säkerhetsläget och social oro i Mazimbu och Dakawa'/'Report on the security situation and social insecurity at Mazimbu and Dakawa'), Swedish embassy, Dar es Salaam, 26 June 1991) (SDA).

2. Ibid. Many demobilized MK soldiers contacted the Swedish embassy in Dar es Salaam for possible scholarships (ibid.).

3. In Zambia, the developments culminated in May 1992 in the assassination of a resident white farmer and his wife (Cable ('ANC-medlemmar inblandade i morddrama på farmare i Zambia'/'ANC members involved in assassination drama of farmer in Zambia') from the Swedish embassy to the Ministry for Foreign Affairs, Lusaka, 27 May 1992) (SDA).

4. In his report to the July 1991 congress, Treasurer General Thomas Nkobi estimated that the value of ANC's fixed and moveable assets at Mazimbu exceeded 250 MSAR, or more than 560 MSEK. The corresponding estimate for Dakawa was 70 MSAR (around 160 MSEK) (ANC: 'Report of the Office of the Treasurer General', ANC National Congress, Durban, July 1991, p. 26). While a host of international donors over the years contributed to the development of the SOMAFCO school and, in general, to the Mazimbu settlement, in the case of Dakawa the government of Norway was by far the largest donor. In fact, between 1985 and 1991 Norway financed more than 50 per cent of the infrastructure and the buildings at Dakawa (ibid., pp. 29-32).

5. Cf., for example, cable ('ANC i Zambia och Tanzania'/'ANC in Zambia and Tanzania') from the Ministry for Foreign Affairs to the Swedish legation in Pretoria, Stockholm, 16 July 1991 (SDA). It should be noted that Winnie Mandela—at the time heading ANC's Department of Social Welfare—visited the settlements in Tanzania in late October 1991. By then, however, the frustration among the refugees was such that she was received by vociferous protests and demonstrations. Mandela herself contributed to the tensions by stating that ANC would not organize any further repatriation flights from Tanzania. At Dakawa, her meeting with the ANC residents aborted after five minutes and she had to be protected by Tanzanian police (Birgitta Sevefjord: Memorandum ('Minnesanteckningar från möte med UNHCR'/'Notes from a meeting with UNHCR'), Swedish embassy, Dar es Salaam, 15 November 1991) (SDA). In early November, the ANC headquarters in Johannesburg decided against this background to organize a flight from Dar es Salaam. It carried *inter alia* all the remaining primary school children (ibid.).

6. Although this was not the original intention, children, sick and elderly people were, for example, included among those repatriated with the five SIDA-financed charter flights mentioned above (Birgitta Sevefjord: Memorandum ('Repatrieringsflyg DSM-Johannesburg den 18 april 1991'/'Repatriation flight Dar es Salaam-Johannesburg, 18 April 1991'), Swedish embassy, Dar es Salaam, 23 April 1991) (SDA).

deployed to protect the sites—went on a veritable thieving spree.[1] Visiting Mazimbu in mid-March 1992, Birgitta Sevefjord from the Swedish embassy in Dar es Salaam observed how "many residences have been vandalized. In the four rows of houses that I [went to], everything had been taken away, including all the switches [and] the toilets".[2]

This, indeed, was a sad comment to many years of cooperation between ANC and the international community—foremost the Nordic countries—to establish and equip Mazimbu as a model refugee settlement.[3] Although the situation in this respect was considerably better with regard to the ANC farms—which were kept in operation after July 1992—following a visit to Zambia one year later, SIDA's consultant Josef Jonsson similarly noted that "capital waste has continued due to vandalism and under-utilization of the investments made".[4]

Facing an impossible equation of having at the same time to address the internal political challenges and maintain its external settlements, in November 1991—after the agreement between the South African government and UNHCR and shortly before the CODESA talks—ANC's National Executive Committee decided, finally, to wind up the projects in exile by mid-1992. The implementation of this decision was notably followed up at a solemn ceremony in Tanzania on 12 July 1992, where Oliver Tambo officially handed over the Mazimbu and Dakawa settlements to President Ali Hassan Mwinyi.[5] Perhaps more than anything else, this symbolized ANC's definite homecoming after more than three decades in exile.

Carried out in the presence of the ambassadors and heads of mission from the Nordic countries, in the case of Sweden the handover also represented an end to the humanitarian assistance initiated on a modest scale in the same country almost twenty years earlier. Although it remained to phase out ANC's agricultural projects in Zambia, from then on the official support was channelled to the movement inside South Africa, where—in spite of doubts and intense discussions—it would assume a markedly political character.

---

1. Birgitta Sevefjord: Memorandum ('ANC i Tanzania: Rapport inför samtalen i Johannesburg 24 mars'/'ANC in Tanzania: Report in view of the talks in Johannesburg on 24 March'), Swedish embassy, Dar es Salaam, 14 March 1992 (SDA).
2. Ibid.
3. Cf. the fate of SWAPO's Kwanza Sul settlement in Angola.
4. Josef Jonsson: Memorandum ('Besök till ANC-farmerna i Chisamba 1993 03 31'/'Visit to the ANC farms at Chisamba on 31 March 1993'), Lusaka, 4 April 1993 (SDA).
5. ANC's handover of the settlements in Tanzania was surrounded by controversy. Thus, in early March 1992 it was announced by the Tanzanian press that ANC had decided to hand the sites over to the ruling—and only—party, Chama Cha Mapinduzi (CCM), not to the government. Having made huge investments in the settlements, through their resident ambassadors the Nordic countries immediately approached the Tanzanian Foreign Minister Ahmed Hassan Diria for clarification. A meeting with a visiting ANC delegation led by Thomas Nkobi was also held (Birgitta Sevefjord: Memorandum ('Ang. överlämnandet av Mazimbu och Dakawa till CCM'/'Re. the handover of Mazimbu and Dakawa to CCM'), Swedish embassy, Dar es Salaam, 11 March 1992) (SDA). As these contacts seemed to confirm the press reports, the Nordic countries jointly registered their disapproval, stating that "[i]t had never been intended that the financial assistance to ANC from [the] Nordic governments and solidarity organizations was to become an ANC possession of a kind that it could give away to sister parties" (*Aide mémoire*: 'Summing up of discussions with Minister Diria on ANC', Swedish embassy, Dar es Salaam, 5 March 1992) (MFA). At the same time, they declared the opinion that "the government of Tanzania was the natural proprietor of the camps when they no longer served ANC" (ibid.). The issue would attract a lot of attention. As late as in mid-June 1992, SIDA's resident representative Bo Westman recalled in a letter to the Tanzanian government that Sweden and the other Nordic countries had "voiced deep concern [about] the camps being handed over to a political party" (Letter ('The ANC camps in Mazimbu and Dakawa') from Bo Westman to Crispin Mbapila, Principal Secretary, Ministry of Foreign Affairs and International Cooperation, Swedish embassy, Dar es Salaam, 15 June 1992) (SDA). Similar messages were conveyed by the other Nordic embassies (letters attached to ibid.). As noted in the text above, eventually, however, the settlements were transferred to the Tanzanian government. In the case of SOMAFCO, it was attached to the Sokoine University of Agriculture in nearby Morogoro.

Liberation Movement or Political Party?

In mid-May 1992—when the CODESA talks had ended in an impasse and only one week ahead of the scheduled aid negotiations on Swedish assistance—Nelson Mandela led a high-level ANC delegation to Stockholm.[1] Taking place at a time when Foreign Minister af Ugglas had indicated that the economic isolation of South Africa might be brought to an end and powerful business representatives, as well as conservative press voices, strongly questioned the ANC support, the first bilateral deliberations between the ANC President and Prime Minister Carl Bildt would be of significant importance.

The meeting between Mandela and Bildt—joined *inter alia* by Cooperation Minister Alf Svensson and Lars-Åke Nilsson, Under-Secretary of State for Foreign Affairs[2]—took place on 20 May 1992. After a general exchange of views on the political situation in South Africa, it focused on the twin issues of sanctions and assistance.

With regard to sanctions, Bildt dissipated the doubts possibly caused by his colleague af Ugglas by stating that they "should be kept in place until the parties [in South Africa] had agreed on an interim government".[3] Noting that this position was in accordance with ANC policy, Mandela commented that "it was a source of concern [...] that friends [like Sweden] became disadvantaged now that many countries [unilaterally] were lifting their [restrictions]".[4] ANC had internally started to discuss the possibility of certain "accommodations", and Sweden "should not have to wait too long" before the sanctions could be phased out.[5] At any rate, he concluded, "whatever measures [the government] would take in this regard could never change the fact that Sweden had been strongly engaged in the struggle against apartheid".[6]

Turning to the question of ANC assistance, Bildt initially noted that "it was largely of a political nature, although it was called humanitarian". While this was "nothing that Sweden should be ashamed of", he, however, stressed that direct official support to a political party in a democratic South Africa would not be extended. He also pointed at "the risk ANC was running of becoming too dependent on a single donor", in this context indicating that there were other ways and means for Sweden to support the process towards democracy. This, in turn, was followed up by Mandela, who stated that his organization was interested in support for voter education and electoral training, which should not be restricted to

---

1. Among those who accompanied Mandela were Thomas Nkobi, Thabo Mbeki and Aziz Pahad, ANC's Deputy Director of International Affairs.
2. It should be noted that Foreign Minister Margaretha af Ugglas did not participate in the meeting (Cabinet Office: 'Talks between the government of Sweden and the African National Congress', [Stockholm], 20 May 1992) (MFA).
3. Bengt Herrström: Draft memorandum ('Nelson Mandelas samtal med regeringen'/'Nelson Mandela's conversation with the government'), Ministry for Foreign Affairs, Stockholm, [no date, but registered on 21 May 1992] (MFA).
4. Ibid.
5. Ibid. During his stay in Sweden, Mandela also had a lunch meeting with Peter Wallenberg, the powerful industrialist who represented several Swedish companies with interests in South Africa. As earlier noted, Wallenberg was a firm opponent of sanctions and far from a supporter of ANC, or even black majority rule. This notwithstanding, according to Åke Magnusson—who attended the luncheon—the ANC President told Wallenberg that "Swedish industry would be rewarded for supporting the struggle and that he would love to do business with friends rather than with enemies" (Interview with Åke Magnusson, p. 320).
6. Bengt Herrström: Draft memorandum ('Nelson Mandelas samtal med regeringen'/'Nelson Mandela's conversation with the government'), Ministry for Foreign Affairs, Stockholm, [21 May 1992] (MFA).

ANC members, but directed to "all who needed it".[1] As will be seen below, the assistance subsequently extended via AIC/OPIC would be designed in such a way.[2]

On 27 May—one week after the talks between Bildt and Mandela—the non-socialist government decided to grant ANC 110 MSEK for the period 1 July 1992-30 June 1993[3], thereby turning down the calls for a termination of the support made *inter alia* by the conservative newspaper *Svenska Dagbladet*[4] and in the main continuing the policy inherited from its Social Democratic predecessor. Brought down from 120 MSEK in 1991/92—or by 8 per cent—this, however, meant that for the first time ever the regular, annual allocation was reduced. While this was motivated by the fact that "the ANC refugees have returned home"[5], as the support was almost exclusively for the movement and its efforts in South Africa "no direct comments" in this regard were made by ANC at the following negotiations.[6] In fact, compared with the 1991/92 allocation, the resources set aside for ANC's internal work under the direct, official Swedish support in 1992/93 increased from 71.8 to 97.7 MSEK, or by more than a third.[7]

Respectively led by ANC's Treasurer General Thomas Nkobi and SIDA's Assistant Director General Johan Brisman, aid negotiations between the parties were held in Johannesburg at the end of May 1992, almost ten years to the day since Sweden was last represented by a non-socialist government.[8] Noting that the deliberations constituted a continuation of the high-level talks in the Swedish capital a week earlier, in his introductory overview ANC Deputy President Walter Sisulu stated that it was "thanks to Sweden that [South Africa] now stood at the brink of an epochal transformation".[9] However, as no fundamental breakthrough had taken place, there was "as yet no reason [for ANC] to change its character". While ANC "was acutely aware of and respected the positions of the Swedish government in respect of aid to political parties"[10], it was hoped that the support to the liberation movement could continue along established lines.

As indicated above, this would also be the case. On behalf of the Swedish delegation, Brisman explained that

> [t]he main thrust of the Swedish assistance [in 1992/93] should be to continue to support the process towards democracy in South Africa through [...] the negotiation efforts of the ANC. Continued support to [...] ANC's administration, as well as support to information and educa-

---

1. Ibid.
2. Following consultations in March 1992 between ANC and the Social Democratic Party, at the time of Mandela's visit AIC had already submitted a request to CCHA for support towards voter education and election training (see below).
3. Ministry for Foreign Affairs: Press release ('ANC får fortsatt svenskt stöd'/'ANC receives continued Swedish support'), Stockholm, 27 May 1992 (MFA).
4. Cf. the editorials 'Finansiärens talan' ('The claim of the donor') and 'Tagande av svenskt stöd' ('Receiving Swedish support') in *Svenska Dagbladet*, 20 and 23 May 1992. In the former—published on the very day of the meeting between Bildt and Mandela—the Moderate-aligned newspaper argued that in the ANC leadership there were "orthodox Communists who regret the collapse of the Soviet Union and wish to [nationalize] the South African economy". Against this background, it stated, "it would be unfortunate if Swedish aid to South Africa would be used to introduce the same system [there] as the [support] to the Baltic states is to assist in dismantling".
5. Ministry for Foreign Affairs: Press release ('ANC får fortsatt svenskt stöd'/'ANC receives continued Swedish support'), Stockholm, 27 May 1992 (MFA).
6. Kaj Persson: Memorandum ('Överläggningar med ANC om biståndssamarbete'/'Deliberations with ANC concerning aid cooperation'), Ministry for Foreign Affairs, Stockholm, 1 June 1992 (MFA).
7. See the table below.
8. At the time of the aid negotiations in Lusaka in May 1982, Sweden had a Liberal-Centre coalition government led by Thorbjörn Fälldin. It did not include the Moderate Party.
9. 'Agreed minutes from consultations held in Johannesburg, South Africa, May 1992, between the African National Congress of South Africa (ANC) and Sweden concerning humanitarian assistance', Johannesburg, 30 May 1992 (SDA).
10. Ibid.

tional activities geared towards democracy and [a] market economy, would also form an important part of the cooperation.[1]

With regard to the ongoing cooperation programme, two major observations were, however, made. Stating that "Sweden [had] linked its support to the ANC external missions mainly to the presence of refugees in [the] countries [concerned]", as a consequence of the repatriation process "[this] would have to be phased out". As from 1 July 1993, "no support would be given to the ANC external missions".[2] While the issue of whether and under what circumstances ANC should be seen as a political party was not explicitly raised, in the view of the Swedish delegation there was "a need to agree [...] upon a budget [for 1992/93] which was so structured that [...] ANC's dependence on Swedish support would gradually decrease".[3]

Based on these positions and general guidelines, a cooperation programme for 1992/93 was established. The support in South Africa is presented below. Subsequently endorsed by the authorities in Stockholm, it may thus be concluded that the non-socialist coalition government in no decisive way embarked on a new Swedish course vis-à-vis ANC.

This said, by introducing ideologically normative considerations into the dialogue, a break with the past was made. While Sweden—whether under Social Democratic or non-socialist rule—traditionally had maintained that it was for the liberation movements and peoples themselves to define their future, the emphasis of May 1992 on a South African 'market economy' stands out as exceptional. What is more, in addition to conveying "the firm belief that economic growth was best achieved through market oriented policies", at the negotiations in Johannesburg this opinion was for the first time presented as a fundamental tenet of Sweden's aid policy. It was thus recorded in the agreed minutes that

[t]he Swedish government had as a basic principle in its development cooperation the promotion of democracy and the development of market economic systems.[4]

Dominance and Reactions

Sweden's bilateral support to ANC in South Africa from 1 July 1991 until 27 January 1994—when it formally ended—is summarized in the following table:[5]

---

1. Ibid.
2. Ibid. On this point, the parties agreed to disagree. In ANC's view, it was still too early to phase out the support to its offices abroad (Kaj Persson: Memorandum ('Överläggningar med ANC om biståndssamarbete'/ 'Deliberations with ANC concerning aid cooperation'), Ministry for Foreign Affairs, Stockholm, 1 June 1992) (MFA).
3. 'Agreed minutes from consultations held in Johannesburg, South Africa, May 1992, between the African National Congress of South Africa (ANC) and Sweden concerning humanitarian assistance', Johannesburg, 30 May 1992 (SDA).
4. Ibid.
5. Based on original budget allocations and re-allocations made during the period.

SIDA budget allocations to ANC in South Africa 1991/92–1993/94
(in thousands of SEK)

Component	91/92	92/93	93/94*	TOTAL
Core administration	24,000	19,000	15,700	58,700
1991 conference	3,500	–	–	3,500
Financial administration	–	4,000	4,500	8,500
Human resources development	4,000	5,600	3,600	13,200
Transport	3,000	5,900	4,700	13,600
Information and publicity	4,800	10,600	11,800	27,200
Telecommunications network	–	–	7,300	7,300
Printing press	–	–	4,000	4,000
Security	2,500	4,200	8,000	14,700
Education	15,000	13,000	1,200	29,200
Social welfare	–	2,100	5,900	8,000
Women's league	2,000	2,200	4,700	8,900
Youth league	3,000	4,600	3,500	11,100
Negotiation process	10,000	20,000	10,600	40,600
TEC support	–	–	2,500	2,500
Peace desk	–	–	2,400	2,400
Democratization campaigns	–	6,500	12,000	18,500
Economic policy studies	–	–	2,500	2,500
Women's emancipation	–	–	1,800	1,800
Other	–	–	1,000	1,000
TOTAL	71,800	97,700	107,700	277,200

* 1 July 1993 – 27 January 1994 (including balances)

After winning the parliamentary elections in September 1991, Carl Bildt's non-socialist coalition was in power in Sweden during practically the whole of this period, when a total of 277 MSEK was allocated. Almost exclusively, the assistance was extended in the form of budgetary support, with few project components and a high utilization rate.[1] It may therefore be compared to the comprehensive amount of 896 MSEK which—in current, audited figures—was disbursed through SIDA as official assistance to ANC from the start in 1973 until the end in 1994.[2] No less than a third—or some 31 per cent—was thus extended under the Moderate Party leader's administration. From the table above, it also appears that the largest amounts during the final period were set aside for ANC's organization (24%)[3] and its negotiation efforts (15.5%)[4], followed by education and training (15%)[5] and

---

1. For technical reasons, the recorded utilization rate was low in 1992/93, but high in 1993/94.
2. See Appendix XIV.
3. 'Core administration' and 'financial administration' in the table above. 'Transport' and 'security' could be added here. During the two and a half years, a total of 14.7 MSEK was set aside for protective security. It covered *inter alia* a) the supply and installation of an alarm system at the ANC headquarters in Johannesburg, as well as at the residences of a number of the movement's top officials; b) security arrangements at the 14 regional offices; and c) a radio communication system between the headquarters and the regional offices ('Resultatredovisning Sydafrika'/'Report on results [in] South Africa', attached to SIDA: Memorandum ('Bakgrundspromemoria inför långsiktigt utvecklingssamarbete med Sydafrika'/'Background memorandum in view of long-term development cooperation with South Africa'), Stockholm, 17 January 1995) (SDA). On Swedish support in respect of security, see also the chapter 'Lesotho, Botswana, Zimbabwe and a Note on Security'.
4. 'Negotiation process' and 'TEC support'.
5. 'Human resources development' and 'education'.

information and publicity (14%).[1]

While the actual distribution and the details of the assistance were kept confidential, it was no secret that the Swedish government supported the movement. When in early January 1993 UNDP for the first time published information on international aid flows to South Africa—showing that Sweden in 1992 was the third largest donor after the European Community and the United States[2]—the ANC assistance was in general terms confirmed by both the legation in Pretoria and the movement itself.[3] Made at a critical juncture—when the CODESA talks had broken down and the relations between the Pretoria regime and ANC were uneasy—the announcements caused a furore in South Africa. As before, the English-speaking pro-Pretoria newspaper *The Citizen* led the way.[4] In an editorial entitled 'Keep out', it commented:

> We were angry that the Swedes backed the ANC when it was a terrorist organisation, and we are even more outraged that they should do so now that apartheid laws have been abolished and we are in a transition to a new South Africa. [...]
>
> By singling out the ANC and ignoring the rest, Sweden is showing not only partiality, but is interfering in this country's affairs. [...] We won't tell Sweden to go to hell this time. We'll tell it to keep its damn nose out of our affairs.[5]

Although less crude, the reactions of several prominent South African politicians were equally strong. Zach de Beer, the leader of the Democratic Party, characterized the Swedish ANC support as "surely the [most] gross form of interference in the internal affairs of [another country]".[6] Similarly, Frank Mdlalose, the National Chairman of the Inkatha Freedom Party, concluded that Sweden contrary to the United States was not in favour of democracy, but merely of "those it would like to see in power".[7] Other statements to this effect were made over the following months. Broadening the horizon to the Nordic countries, in a temperamental address in August 1993 Foreign Minister 'Pik' Botha, for example, castigated the Scandinavians as

---

1. 'Information and publicity' plus 'telecommunications network' and 'printing press'. The assistance in the field of information and publicity covered the production of ANC's journal *Mayibuye*. It could in this context be recalled that Sweden as early as in 1975 was involved in the preparatory stages of the publication of *Mayibuye* in exile (cf. the chapter 'From Beds in Exile to Organizers at Home').
2. According to the UNDP report, the main donors in 1992 were the European Community (108 MUSD), USA (80), Sweden (57), United Kingdom (27) and Germany (18). The international aid was almost exclusively channelled to South African NGOs, including political organizations. It amounted in total to 343 MUSD, of which the Swedish contribution represented 16.5 per cent (quoted from 'SA now one of world's biggest recipients of project aid, says UN' in *Business Day*, 6 January 1993). Swedish statistics show that a total of 263 MSEK was disbursed as official humanitarian assistance to South Africa during the financial year 1991/92. Of this, 106 MSEK (40.5%) was channelled as direct support to ANC. The remaining amount was extended to various South African recipients via international (82 MSEK/31%) and Swedish (75 MSEK/28.5%) non-governmental organizations (Kaj Persson: 'Humanitärt bistånd till Sydafrika: Viktigare förmedlande organisationer'/'Humanitarian assistance to South Africa: Principal intermediaries', Ministry for Foreign Affairs, Stockholm, 22 January 1993) (SDA).
3. ANC: 'Press statement on aid from Sweden', Department of Information and Publicity, Marshalltown, 5 January 199[3].
4. Cf. the chapter 'Closer and Broader Cooperation: Projects in Exile, Mineworkers, UDF and Civics in South Africa'.
5. 'Keep out' in *The Citizen*, 7 January 1993.
6. de Beer cited in 'Swedish aid to ANC is slammed' in *The Citizen*, 6 January 1993.
7. Mdlalose cited in 'IFP hits Sweden's aid to ANC' in *The Citizen*, 13 January 1993. PAC was, similarly, upset. Looking back in 1995, PAC MP Gora Ebrahim stated: "We are disappointed. We had all negotiated and we were going for an election. At that crucial moment, the Swedish government made a very substantial donation to ANC for election purposes. Naturally, that influenced the election results, and we regard that as gross interference" (Interview with Gora Ebrahim, p. 121).

bleak and overfed Norther[n]lings [in states] where even [the] citizens' funerals are paid for by the government.[1]

Meanwhile, the confirmation of the ANC support led to further strains between the Swedish and South African governments. On 7 January 1993, Claes Hammar, counsellor at the Swedish legation, was called to the Department of Foreign Affairs in Pretoria "for clarifications".[2] Characterizing the assistance as "gross interference", the responsible official, Bela Harrison, declared that this—combined with the fact that Sweden had not lifted its economic sanctions —was "seen in a most serious light".[3] Sweden, she said, was "partisan", an impression which she illustrated by the fact that it did not extend support to other political organizations, "such as [Inkatha] and PAC".[4] Against this background, the South African government expected "an immediate written explanation", pending which "appropriate action" was being considered.[5]

The Swedish legation assessed the situation—and the threat of action—as being "serious".[6] Two months later, Foreign Under-Secretary of State Lars-Åke Nilsson travelled to South Africa for discussions with both the government and ANC, as well as with a number of leading business representatives.[7] On his return to Sweden in mid-March 1993, he followed up the talks with the South African envoy Eugene Myburgh. During their meeting, Nilsson stated that in South Africa he "had emphasized to ANC that the [Swedish] assistance must be non-partisan".[8] "Already now", he told Myburgh, "we see ANC as a *de facto* political party". Although no decision to that effect had been taken, he also declared that "as developments are unfolding, the support [will] cease on 1 July 1993 at the latest".[9]

While Nilsson's contacts with the South African authorities might have appeased Pretoria, the effect was the opposite with regard to ANC.[10] In fact, although Sweden remained its largest supporter, from early 1993 the government had introduced a considerable degree of uncertainty into the relationship. This came notably to the fore in the discussions held between Nilsson and ANC in Johannesburg.

---

1. Botha cited in 'Mistake to keep out traditional leaders: Pik' in *The Citizen*, 10 August 1993. Botha had as a young diplomat served at the South African embassy in Stockholm from mid-1956 until early 1960 (Sellström Volume I, p. 112). In 1995, he recalled how his arrival in Sweden was "a very sudden introduction into a very critical world" (Interview with Roelof 'Pik' Botha, p. 111).
2. Cable ('Utrikesministeriet kräver förklaring om Sveriges bistånd till Sydafrika och hotar med åtgärder'/'The Foreign Department requests clarification regarding Sweden's assistance to South Africa and threatens with action') from Ingemar Stjernberg, Swedish envoy to South Africa, to the Ministry for Foreign Affairs, Pretoria, 8 January 1993 (MFA).
3. Ibid.
4. Ibid. Although from different perspectives, both Inkatha and PAC were highly critical of negotiations based on an understanding between the South African government and ANC.
5. Ibid.
6. Ibid. It was, in particular, expected that the Pretoria government would restrict SIDA's presence in the country (ibid.).
7. Lars-Åke Nilsson: Memorandum ('Intryck från Sydafrika'/'Impressions from South Africa'), Ministry for Foreign Affairs, Stockholm, 16 March 1993 (MFA).
8. Bengt Herrström: Memorandum ('Sydafrikas ambassadör besöker departementet'/'South Africa's [envoy] visits the Ministry'), Ministry for Foreign Affairs, Stockholm, 18 March 1993 (MFA).
9. Ibid.
10. Uncharacteristic strains also appeared between the Foreign Ministry and SIDA. In his report to Prime Minister Bildt, Foreign Minister af Ugglas and Cooperation Minister Svensson, after the visit to South Africa Nilsson complained that "the [SIDA] office in Pretoria to an extremely limited extent has informed ANC about the guidelines for future Swedish support. My impression [is] that [SIDA's] Lena Johansson has locked herself into a continuation of the support in its present forms" (Lars-Åke Nilsson: Memorandum ('Intryck från Sydafrika'/'Impressions from South Africa'), Ministry for Foreign Affairs, Stockholm, 16 March 1993) (MFA). SIDA, however, administered the assistance according to the official agreement between the parties.

During his stay in South Africa, on 9 March 1993 Lars-Åke Nilsson raised the issue of the ongoing bilateral cooperation with ANC's National Chairman Oliver Tambo[1], Treasurer General Thomas Nkobi and a number of other leading ANC officials.[2] The Swedish government had the previous day in a parliamentary submission proposed that the 1987 trade embargo should be lifted. During the meeting with ANC, the Foreign Under-Secretary of State expressed, in addition, the opinion that developments in South Africa were approaching a point where "the present forms of support must [...] come to a halt".[3]

Although multi-party planning talks had resumed by that time, the South African transition process was, however, far from irreversible, and on both accounts the ANC delegation begged to differ. While Aziz Pahad, ANC's Deputy Director of International Affairs, commented that the Swedish government's decision on sanctions was the "wrong signal" to send, Nkobi went further. ANC, he said, had noticed "several signs [of] a relaxed support from the Scandinavian countries".[4] The movement had against this background decided to send a delegation for consultations with "different structures in Sweden" and in the neighbouring countries.[5]

One month later, Nkobi himself led an ANC team to the Nordic countries. It included Patrick Lekota, Penuell Maduna and Aziz Pahad.[6] In addition to a number of other meetings—notably with the opposition Social Democratic Party[7]—their stay in Stockholm included on 19 April 1993 a visit to the Ministry for Foreign Affairs. However, despite the talks held in Johannesburg the previous month the delegation was not received by Foreign Minister af Ugglas, nor by Under-Secretary of State Nilsson. In their absence, the talks at the Foreign Ministry were chaired instead by ambassador Anders Oljelund, deputy head of the political department.[8]

The meeting took place at an exceptionally critical moment. Chris Hani had been assassinated the week before and there was an acute risk that the South African transition process would come to a violent close. After stating the opinion that "the situation in South Africa apparently has not been entirely understood by some of ANC's old friends, including Sweden", Nkobi and his team stressed that the organization was facing "a gigantic task" in order to secure a non-racial, demo-

1. O.R. Tambo died on 24 April 1993. As far as can be ascertained, the meeting on 9 March was his last with a high-ranking Swedish government official. The former ANC President had since the early 1960s been in close and regular contact with Sweden and was more than anybody else responsible for the 'special relationship' which subsequently developed. While Tambo, tragically, did not live to experience the final demise of the apartheid regime, it must have been disappointing to note that Swedish support appeared to falter when success was so near.
2. In addition to Tambo and Nkobi, among those present at the meeting were Penuell Maduna, Popo Molefe, Aziz Pahad and Zola Skweyiya. Nozipho Diseko—who in mid-1991 had replaced Billy Modise as the movement's Chief Representative to Sweden—also formed part of the ANC delegation.
3. Cable ('Kabinettsekreterarens samtal med ANC tisdagen den 9 mars'/'The Under-Secretary of State's conversation with ANC, Tuesday 9 March') from the Swedish legation to the Ministry for Foreign Affairs, Pretoria, 10 March 1993 (MFA).
4. Ibid. In 1993, the direct official ANC assistance from Norway was 22 million Norwegian Kroner. While Denmark extended indirect support of 12 million Danish Kroner, Finland had at the time phased out its bilateral cooperation (Kaj Persson: Memorandum ('Övriga nordiska länders Sydafrika-bistånd'/'Assistance to South Africa from the other Nordic countries'), Ministry for Foreign Affairs, Stockholm, 29 April 1993) (MFA).
5. Cable ('Kabinettsekreterarens samtal med ANC tisdagen den 9 mars'/'The Under-Secretary of State's conversation with ANC, Tuesday 9 March') from the Swedish legation to the Ministry for Foreign Affairs, Pretoria, 10 March 1993 (MFA).
6. Kaj Persson: Memorandum ('Sammansättning av ANC-delegation'/'Composition of ANC delegation'), Ministry for Foreign Affairs, Stockholm, 14 April 1993 (MFA).
7. Letter ('Samtal med ANC-företrädare'/'Conversation with ANC representatives') from Claes Hammar to the Ministry for Foreign Affairs, Swedish legation, Pretoria, 5 May 1993 (SDA).
8. Also present at the meeting were Kaj Persson, Ann Wilkens and Staffan Wrigstad.

cratic and peaceful solution to the ongoing drama.[1] The South African people were
not yet free, and ANC continued therefore to function as a national liberation
movement, not as a political party. However, while the ruling National Party could
draw upon public funds and the movement's support from both "the former East
bloc countries and many Western democracies" had ceased, it was in dire financial
straits. Against this background, Nkobi concluded, "it would be tantamount to
disaster to leave ANC without assistance".[2]

Although not in a position to convey its views to the Moderate Party's repre-
sentatives, the ANC delegation was, however, received by the leaders of the ruling
coalition's Christian Democratic and Liberal parties, Cooperation Minister Alf
Svensson and Social Minister Bengt Westerberg. These talks were encouraging.[3]
Instead of shutting the door on a constructive dialogue regarding continued aid
relations, Svensson and Westerberg were—as later expressed by Alf Samuelsson,
Christian Democratic Under-Secretary of State for International Development
Cooperation—open to "a non-partisan formula during the last mile".[4] In discussions with Cooperation Minister Svensson, it was agreed that ANC should work
out a plan on how to progressively phase out the direct official support with a view
to possibly replacing it with indirect assistance through ANC-aligned structures. To
better inform himself about the process in South Africa and discuss how and when
such a transformation could take place, Samuelsson, it was decided, should visit
the country as soon as possible.[5]

In Sweden—where popular support for ANC was overwhelming and the movement enjoyed broad parliamentary backing—the initiative concerning future assistance was thereby brought back to the sphere of aid. The Moderate Party—which in
this context assumed a minority position—had to retreat.[6] While Nkobi expressed
doubts with regard to the proposed transformation formula[7], the threat of a sudden termination of the Swedish assistance had, however, been averted. This, in
turn, had been building up as the end of the financial year 1992/93 was approaching, and, thus, the expiry date of 30 June of the agreement in force.

When in mid-June 1993 Samuelsson subsequently led a broad aid delegation to
South Africa[8], SIDA's Assistant Director General Johan Brisman commented in a
review meeting with ANC in Johannesburg that "the question of how long the support to the ANC would continue [...] was still unclear" [, but] a decision could pos-

---

1. Ann Wilkens: Memorandum ('Överläggningar med ANC-delegation'/'Deliberations with ANC delegation'),
   Ministry for Foreign Affairs, Stockholm, 26 April 1993 (SDA).
2. Ibid.
3. On his return to South Africa, Nkobi noted in particular the positive talks held with the Social Democratic
   Party, Alf Svensson and Bengt Westerberg. It could be noted that his general impression was that "it was the
   [political] parties and the Swedish parliament that decided with regard to the ANC support, rather than the
   government" (Letter ('Samtal med ANC-företrädare'/'Conversation with ANC representatives') from Claes
   Hammar to the Ministry for Foreign Affairs, Swedish legation, Pretoria, 5 May 1993) (SDA).
4. 'Minutes of meeting between representatives of the ANC and of the Swedish government, SIDA, Swedecorp
   and BITS', Johannesburg, 16 June 1993 (SDA).
5. Letter ('Samtal med ANC-företrädare'/'Conversation with ANC representatives') from Claes Hammar to the
   Ministry for Foreign Affairs, Swedish legation, Pretoria, 5 May 1993 (SDA).
6. For a summary of the Swedish debate in mid-1993, see 'Disagreement on Sweden's Aid to ANC in South
   Africa Remains' in Development Today, No. 9, 1993, p. 9.
7. Letter ('Samtal med ANC-företrädare'/'Conversation with ANC representatives') from Claes Hammar to the
   Ministry for Foreign Affairs, Swedish legation, Pretoria, 5 May 1993 (SDA).
8. On the visit—which included representatives from official Swedish aid agencies other than SIDA—see Ingemar Stjernberg: Memorandum ('Protokoll från ANC rörande möten med svenska delegationer i juni 1993'/
   'Minutes from ANC regarding meetings with Swedish delegations in June 1993'), Swedish legation, Pretoria,
   16 July 1993 (SDA) and Johan Brisman: 'Reserapport' ('Travel report'), SIDA, Stockholm, 21 June 1993
   (SDA).

sibly [be made] only in September 1993".[1] Eventually, it was not until early November that the issue was finally resolved, and then—quite paradoxically—in favour of a considerably increased direct ANC allocation. The government initiative taken in March to lift the trade embargo was in the meantime kept on ice by the Swedish parliament. The 1987 legislation was only revoked in September 1993.

Administrative Weaknesses and Support

The last leg towards a final aid agreement with ANC was far from uncomplicated. In addition to intense political discussions in Sweden, the way was paved *inter alia* through a number of SIDA visits to Johannesburg[2] and, in general, a close dialogue with the movement. This focused in particular on ANC's administration, which by mid-1993—as the organization led by Mandela increasingly assumed semi-official functions and its capacity in the process was being severely stretched—had become a "problem child".[3] As ANC's National Executive Committee could not "relate its political activities to [the movement's] financial realities"[4], severe bottlenecks and shortcomings appeared, notably in the Office of the Treasurer General. This, in turn, motivated both extraordinary SIDA support and criticism.

At Thomas Nkobi's personal request, SIDA had in early 1992 seconded Roland Axelsson to assist with the establishment of proper financial and other administrative procedures for the rapidly growing organization. Axelsson carried out this task at the ANC headquarters in Johannesburg in March-April 1992.[5] During a follow-up visit one year later, he, however, found that many of his recommendations had been ignored.[6] As ANC at the same time—and at a very critical moment concerning future assistance—lagged behind with regard to its reporting requirements to SIDA, on behalf of the aid agency Brisman sent a particularly frank letter to Treasurer General Nkobi. Together with the fact that ANC had invited Axelsson to review its entire administrative set-up—notably the strategic finance department—Brisman's letter and Nkobi's reply may serve to illustrate the nature and spirit of the close relationship which in spite of the Moderate Party's positions had developed between ANC and SIDA.[7]

In his letter to Nkobi—addressed as "Dear Thomas"—SIDA's Assistant Director General[8] wrote on 24 May 1993:

> In our cooperation, we have over the years taken note of ANC's difficulties in providing proper financial follow-ups, audited reports, activity reports and [in implementing] recommendations on how to improve administrative routines. We do understand the difficulties involved in building an efficient [...] organization in the present situation, and I think [that] you recognize

---

1. '[Minutes from] a special review meeting ANC/SIDA', Johannesburg, 14 June 1993 (SDA).
2. In order to "initiate internal studies on a phasing out/termination of the ANC assistance and to sketch proposals for alternative areas of support when [it] comes to an end", SIDA's Birgitta Sevefjord, for example, spent two weeks with ANC in June 1993 (Birgitta Sevefjord: 'Reserapport'/Travel report', SIDA, Stockholm, 25 June 1993) (SDA).
3. Ibid.
4. Ibid.
5. Roland Axelsson: 'Report to ANC regarding my visit to [the] ANC head office during the period [12-23 April 1993]', SIDA, Stockholm, 3 May 1993 (SDA).
6. Ibid. With regard to ANC's archival routines, Axelsson noted: "My recommendations [from] 1992 in this field have been fully ignored by ANC. I have not been able to find any interest whatsoever in establishing a system for central registration and filing of documents" (ibid.).
7. As noted in the chapter 'From Beds in Exile to Organizers at Home', Nkobi and Axelsson had on behalf of ANC and SIDA been involved in the cooperation from the very beginning.
8. In September 1994, Brisman became counsellor at the Swedish embassy in Pretoria. In that position, he coordinated the transition from Swedish humanitarian assistance to development cooperation with South Africa.

the understanding we have shown over the years [when] you were in exile and [after] your transition into South Africa.

It is with great concern [that] we now take note of a negative development within ANC when it comes to certain aspects of the financial and administrative procedures applied. To help you in reversing the trend, we [...] made Mr. Roland Axelsson available to assist in developing methods to facilitate [such] procedures. We are sad to notice that so far very little action seems to [have been] taken on his recommendations. [...]

I believe that our relations are founded on such a strong base of mutual understanding and trust that you will not be offended by the straightforward language used in this letter.[1]

Similarly addressing Brisman as "Dear Johan", ANC's Treasurer General replied as follows on 1 June 1993:

Let me hasten to reassure you that the frank language of the letter cannot offend me, or in any way damage the relations of mutual understanding and trust that have been developed over the years between SIDA and the ANC. On the contrary, I consider that it is especially in this period of heightened responsibility for the ANC that its tried and trusted friends should be able to discuss matters with us in a straightforward manner.

Your concerns are sincerely appreciated, particularly as they emanate from a source which demonstrably desires to see the ANC overcoming the difficulties involved in building an efficient civil organisation. The report of my dear friend Roland Axelsson is also forthright and unequivocal, and I thank him for [that] for the same reasons. [...]

Some of the recommendations that Roland had made [during] the earlier visit had not been implemented at the time of his second visit, but this has been due more to the absence of skills and supervision, rather than neglect. [...] The groundwork is [, however,] being prepared to [assure] you that we have, in the near future, a budgetary system of monitoring and controlling expenditures, which of necessity will entail a change in the administrative structure affecting all departments. At the same time, the financial records will be brought up to date on a day by day basis. [...]

In these circumstances, I can only reiterate our request that we [once again] be availed the support of Roland Axelsson [...]. I repeat that if the impression might have been created that we do not heed his advice, it is largely owing to [a] lack of skills and inadequate supervision and the manner in which we have defined our [political] priorities.[2]

Based on Nkobi's letter and request, it was decided to once again second Axelsson to his department.[3] While Axelsson's third working period at the ANC headquarters in Johannesburg resulted *inter alia* in the production of an important internal administrative manual[4], ANC, however, was at the same time still lagging behind with regard to audited financial reports to SIDA. As late as in October 1993—at a time when the Swedish government had not yet taken a decision on renewed ANC assistance—despite repeated requests the Swedish authorities had, for example, not

1. Letter ('Financial and other administrative procedures within ANC') from Johan Brisman to Thomas Nkobi, SIDA, Stockholm, 24 May 1993 (SDA).
2. Letter ('Financial and administrative routines within the ANC') from Thomas Nkobi to Johan Brisman, ANC, Johannesburg, 1 June 1993 (SDA).
3. Letter ('Financial and administrative procedures within ANC') from Johan Brisman to Thomas Nkobi, SIDA, Stockholm, 4 June 1993 (SDA).
4. Letter ('Concerning outstanding financial reports') from Johan Brisman to Thomas Nkobi, SIDA, Stockholm, 8 October 1993 (SDA). Axelsson visited Johannesburg in June-July and in September 1993.

received a proper, comprehensive financial statement regarding the 1991/92 allocation.[1] Against this background, SIDA decided to momentarily suspend further disbursements, as well as to threaten with an external audit of some of the activities
concerned, notably the support extended to ANC's foreign missions.[2]

It should here be noted that when in November 1993 Sweden decided to grant
ANC 95 MSEK for the period until 27 January 1994[3], it was concluded in consultation with Nkobi that "extraordinary efforts [would] have to be made [...] [i]n
order to properly utilize such a large amount of money in such a short period of
time".[4] To this end, it was proposed that SIDA should recruit a qualified person,
"who with a special mandate could assist [ANC's] various departments [...] in identifying activities that could be financed from Sweden [, as well as] preparing budgets and requests and [...] structuring the costs in such a way [as to] make maximum
use of the [...] funds".[5] The proposal was endorsed by ANC Secretary General
Cyril Ramaphosa, and in December 1993-January 1994 Georg Dreifaldt—who as
a veteran AGIS member and a SIDA official in Angola and Namibia was well
known to the organization—carried out this critical task.[6] Bringing their long-
standing cooperation with the liberation movement to an end, in mid-April 1994—
just before the democratic elections—on SIDA's behalf Axelsson and Dreifaldt also
visited ANC in Johannesburg "to reach a final financial settlement as far as [Swe-
den's] cooperation [...] was concerned".[7]

Voter Education and Election Training

After drawn-out and difficult negotiations, it was in July 1993 agreed by the main
South African political actors—notably ANC and the ruling National Party—that
the first ever non-racial elections in the country should be held on 27-29 April
1994.[8] Close cooperation between Sweden and ANC with regard to voter education and electoral training had by then already been established. At a time when the
direct official assistance was increasingly being questioned by the Moderate Party,
the uncertainties surrounding the bilateral relationship were thus partly offset by
considerable indirect support to 'level the playing field' pending a democratic election campaign. This was a crucial element in the country of apartheid, where an
estimated 18 million people had never been allowed to vote and ANC was hugely
disadvantaged when compared to the National Party and other established political

1. Ibid.
2. Ibid.
3. Formally, the allocation was granted for the period 1 July 1993-27 January 1994.
4. Letter ('Cooperation between the ANC and Sweden through SIDA during fiscal year 1993/94') from
   Johan Brisman to ANC Secretary General Cyril Ramaphosa, Johannesburg, 17 November 1993 (SDA).
5. Ibid.
6. Roland Axelsson: 'Report on final financial accounts of SIDA's support to ANC', RAX Consulting AB,
   Stockholm, 2 May 1994 (SDA). Axelsson had by that time left SIDA and set up a private auditing company.
7. Ibid.
8. Chief Buthelezi's Inkatha Freedom Party only agreed to participate in the elections on 19 April 1994,
   one week before the historic event. Eventually, it was decided to open the polling stations on 26 April
   1994.

opponents. Several Swedish organizations would participate in this effort.[1] However, the early and dominant role played by the Social Democratic Party and the wider labour movement was in this context particularly prominent.

Swedish electoral support to South Africa has been discussed elsewhere.[2] In the light of its significance, it merits, however, a brief comment in this study as well. While official financial resources were channelled to the ANC-aligned independent Matla Trust[3] and COSATU[4], the following summary focuses on the assistance extended via the Olof Palme International Center (OPIC)[5] to the South African Voter Education and Elections Training Unit (VEETU). This is motivated *inter alia* by ANC's post-electoral assessment that "[w]e could not have won this election without the work that VEETU did".[6]

---

1. Before the elections, AGIS and ISAK, for example, raised around 1 MSEK in favour of ANC and voter education for women (AGIS: 'Afrikagruppernas verksamhetsberättelse för [19]93/94'/'Activity report by the Africa Groups for 1993/94'), [no place or date] (AGA). It should in this context, however, also be noted that there were neo-Nazi groups in Sweden who not only defended apartheid in theory, but actively supported South African white supremacist organizations that were preparing for armed campaigns against democratic elections and majority rule. While working on a project in South Africa, in late 1993 the Swedish author and film-maker Lasse Berg thus came across two young Swedes who had joined the Afrikaner Weerstandsbeweging (Afrikaner Resistance Movement; AWB), led by Eugene Terre'Blanche. Both of them had a military background and formed part of a 'foreign legion' set up by Terre'Blanche as a 'security force' at AWB's head office in Ventersdorp in the Orange Free State. Berg managed to interview one of the Swedes, who introduced himself as 'Lieutenant Erik'. The interview was screened on Swedish television in mid-December 1993. Dressed in AWB's uniform and covered by a balaclava, the young Swede stated that he "had gone to South Africa to fight on the side of the whites. [...] We see the struggle as being international. Communism in Sweden or Communism here is the same thing [...]. If a country shall live in harmony, a basic requirement is that [the races] live apart. [...] We have come here to fight on the side of AWB. I believe that there will be a war [...] between ANC and AWB [...] and I am prepared to give my life for [our] cause" (Transcript of interview in Lasse Berg and Anders Ribbsjö: 'Löjtnant Erik: På Äventyr i Vita Afrika'/'Lieutenant Erik: Adventures in White Africa', Documentary film, TV 1, 20 December 1993). In March 1994, several hundred armed AWB members took part in a failed attempt to defend the rule of Lucas Mangope in the Bophuthatswana bantustan. The organization was also behind a spate of bombings and killings just before the April 1994 elections. However, its support among South Africa's whites dwindled rapidly as the reality of political change became clear. The fate of 'Lieutenant Erik' and his Swedish brother-in-arms is not known.

2. In November 1995, the Olof Palme International Center published an independent evaluation in English of its support to the Voter Education and Elections Training Unit, undertaken jointly by Annika Lysén and Jean Fairbairn (Lysén and Fairbairn: 'Evaluation of the OP[I]C/SDP Project within the Voter Education and Elections Training Unit', OPIC, Stockholm). Chosen as a case study, the Swedish labour movement's support to VEETU has also been analyzed by Anna Brodin in her Ph.D. dissertation *Getting Politics Right: Democracy Promotion as a New Conflict Issue in Foreign Aid Policy* (Department of Political Science, University of Gothenburg, Gothenburg, 2000).

3. During the financial year 1993/94, 3.2 MSEK was disbursed to the Matla Trust. As in the case of voter education through COSATU, the Swedish contribution, however, did not exceed 10 per cent of the organization's budget for the purpose ('Resultatredovisning Sydafrika'/'Report on results [in] South Africa', attached to SIDA: Memorandum ('Bakgrundspromemoria inför långsiktigt utvecklingssamarbete med Sydafrika'/'Background memorandum in view of long-term development cooperation with South Africa'), Stockholm, 17 January 1995) (SDA). After his assignment as ANC Chief Representative to Sweden, Billy Modise was appointed Executive Director of the Matla Trust in mid-1991. When in early 1995 he took up the position as South Africa's high commissioner to Canada, he was succeeded by Jaya Appalraju. During the transition years, the ANC-aligned trust was thus successively led by two former students of Lund university.

4. Via the LO/TCO Council of International Trade Union Cooperation, an amount of 1 MSEK was channelled in 1993/94 from SIDA to COSATU for voter education (ibid.). In addition to various democracy programmes implemented through Swedish NGOs that were firmly established in South Africa, it could be noted that SIDA before the 1994 elections allocated 2 MSEK to the Pentecostal Mission Aid (in Swedish, *Pingstmissionens U-landshjälp*) towards election training (ibid.).

5. Incorporating the Peace Forum of the Labour Movement (in Swedish, *Arbetarrörelsens Fredsforum*), in 1992 the International Centre of the Swedish Labour Movement (AIC) became the Olof Palme International Center (OPIC). In its cooperation with the Southern African liberation movements, AIC had from the start in 1978 paid attention to technical support and management training for democratic elections (see the chapter 'Cold War, Total Strategy and Expanded Assistance' on Namibia). In 1995, Bengt Säve-Söderbergh—its first Secretary General (1978-85)—was appointed head of the Stockholm-based International Institute for Democracy and Electoral Assistance (International IDEA). Carl Tham, SIDA's former Director General, became head of OPIC in 1999.

6. Quoted in Brodin op. cit., p. 218.

When democratic elections in South Africa were still a distant prospect, the pros and cons of various electoral systems and, in general, the necessity of future voter education and management training schemes had been discussed within the PASA programme. As far as can be ascertained, the first time that a senior ANC official directly approached Sweden for electoral assistance was, however, immediately before ANC's unbanning in early February 1990, when Treasurer General Nkobi raised the issue with Cooperation Minister Lena Hjelm-Wallén.[1] Visiting Sweden the following month, Nelson Mandela "asked the Social Democratic Party [...] to help ANC with the preparations for [a] forthcoming election campaign".[2] According to Pierre Schori—at the time Social Democratic Under-Secretary of State for Foreign Affairs—"[t]here were many with a lot of money who wanted to do that. [...] But Mandela wanted Sweden to be the main sponsor, politically as well as practically. We then set up one of the largest popular education projects ever in South Africa".[3]

Mandela's appeal was explicitly addressed to the Social Democratic Party (SDP). ANC later explained that the movement "preferred SDP to take on the project [...] because [it] wanted to share the experiences of a democratic [political party] organization [and] SDP had been involved in similar projects in other parts of the world, such as Nicaragua, Chile and Namibia".[4] However, as a massive voter education campaign in South Africa was beyond SDP's financial means and official funds could not be granted directly to a Swedish political party[5], eventually the assistance was with funds from SIDA formally extended via the broader OPIC, of which SDP was a prominent member. Nevertheless, as noted by Brodin, "[t]he distinction between [OPIC] and SDP [was] hard to make since most of the agreements were signed [by the party]".[6] Apart from OPIC's Jan Hodann and Birgitta Silén[7], those actively involved on the Swedish side were mainly party officials, such as Monica Andersson, Conny Fredriksson and Bo Toresson.[8]

---

1. Kaj Persson: Memorandum ('Biståndsminister Hjelm-Walléns samtal med ANC-ledningen'/'Cooperation Minister Hjelm-Wallén's conversation with the ANC leadership'), Swedish embassy, Lusaka, 8 February 1990 (SDA).
2. Interview with Pierre Schori, pp. 335-36.
3. Ibid., p. 336.
4. 'Report from [a] meeting [between the] ANC Elections Commission, the Centre for Development Studies, the Education Resource and Information Project, the Voter Education and Elections Training Unit and the Swedish Social Democratic Party at Shell House, Johannesburg, 20 April 1993', [no place, but Johannesburg], 5 May 1993 (OPA).
5. In her study, Brodin states that "[i]t was not possible for [SIDA] to fund a project in which the ANC would be the only recipient" (Brodin op. cit., p. 214). In the light of Sweden's massive and long-standing bilateral support to the South African liberation movement, this is a surprising conclusion. Instead, the initial problem was—as Brodin also mentions—that SIDA at the time could not extend official funds to a Swedish party for direct political support to a sister organization. That would change later. From the financial year 1995/96, parties represented in the Swedish parliament could on the basis of their respective parliamentary strength apply for official funds in favour of aid projects which promoted a democratic course, including bilateral support to political organizations. However, the funds could not be used for election purposes.
6. Ibid., p. 233. This was notably the case with the main agreement of June 1993, which was formally entered into between SDP and ERIP ('Cooperation agreement between the Swedish Social Democratic Party and [the] Education Resource and Information Project concerning voter education and election training in South Africa', Stockholm, 2 June 1993-Cape Town, 9 June 1993) (OPA). The agreement was signed on behalf of SDP by Monica Andersson, deputy international secretary. Garth Strachan represented ERIP.
7. Silén was seconded from SDP to OPIC.
8. At the time, Fredriksson was international secretary and Andersson deputy international secretary of the Social Democratic Party. Toresson served as party secretary between 1982 and 1993.

Mandela's early initiative was followed up by ANC in discussions with the Swedish labour movement, both in Sweden and in South Africa.[1] In the course of these discussions, the movement proposed that the Centre for Development Studies (CDS)—that is, the internal PASA structure which had been set up at the University of the Western Cape and in November 1991 with Swedish support had launched a 'Civic Education Programme on Elections'[2]—should act as a counterpart to OPIC for possible assistance. The proposal was accepted, and in May 1992—when the Social Democratic Party was in opposition in Sweden and democratic elections were still far from being assured in South Africa—OPIC submitted a request to SIDA for 4.1 MSEK towards a voter education programme, which, it emphasized, should be "non-partisan".[3]

The application was approved by SIDA in June 1992.[4] To be used for purposes of an "entirely political" character[5], the Social Democratic Party was at about the same time granted 500,000 SEK from the labour movement's own International Solidarity Fund in direct favour of ANC and its planned election campaign.[6] Although separate, both the 'non-partisan' OPIC project and the 'partisan' SDP initiative were on the Swedish side subsequently administered by the same people[7], which led to a fair amount of confusion. A similar lack of clarity characterized the scene in South Africa, where the boundary line between the ANC-inspired CDS and the liberation movement itself was not easily discernible.[8]

This and other issues were discussed at a strategy conference convened by CDS in September 1992. Attended by a broad spectrum of South African NGOs, as well as by representatives of ANC and the Swedish Social Democratic Party, the conference not only resulted in a new organizational set-up for the ANC-led voter initiative, but also in a radically different approach to the whole issue of preparatory

---

1. In September 1991, for example, Zola Skweyiya and Brigitte Mabandla from ANC's Legal and Constitutional Committee visited Stockholm to discuss Swedish support for a voter education programme with OPIC and the Social Democratic Party (Lysén and Fairbairn op. cit., pp. 6 and 13). In March 1992, OPIC's Jan Hodann and SDP's Monica Andersson and Bo Toresson travelled to South Africa to follow up the proposal (Brodin op. cit., p. 214).
2. See the preceding chapter.
3. AIC: 'Ansökan om bidrag till valutbildning i Sydafrika' ('Request for contribution towards voter education in South Africa'), Stockholm, 7 May 1992 (OPA). The application was signed by Margareta Grape. Drawing conclusions from a parallel submission, both Brodin (op. cit., p. 214) and Lysén and Fairbairn (op. cit., p. 6) refer in this context to an application from SDP, signed by Monica Andersson and dated 30 April 1992. It was, however, Grape's request on behalf of AIC/OPIC that was processed by the Swedish authorities (SIDA: Decision ('Ansökan från Arbetarrörelsens Internationella Centrum om stöd till valutbildning'/'Request from AIC for support towards voter education'), Regional secretariat for Southern Africa, No. 62/1992, Stockholm, 5 June 1992) (SDA).
4. SIDA: Decision, Stockholm, 5 June 1992 (SDA).
5. Jan Hodann: Memorandum ('Anslag till Sydafrika'/'Grant to South Africa'), OPIC, Stockholm, 23 November 1992 (OPA).
6. Ibid. and Monica Andersson: Memorandum ('Ansökan om stöd till ANC'/'Request for support to ANC'), SDP, Stockholm, 12 November 1992 (OPA). SDP's bilateral support to ANC was highly appreciated. Interviewed in 1995, Garth Strachan—former Director of ERIP and a member of SACP's Central Committee—noted: "I left VEETU four months before the elections. I then worked with ANC for the campaign in the Western Cape. Here, there was Swedish Social Democratic Party support. That was invaluable in terms of advice, guidance and for gaining a strategic understanding of an election process. It was absolutely invaluable. What I recall as being most important was the meetings with the ANC leadership—Nelson Mandela, Walter Sisulu and others—but also with the regional leadership. The biggest problem for ANC [...] was a lack of understanding of what an election is. The politicians thought that they could lead the election, but there was no understanding of the management component. I think that the Swedish Social Democrats went a very long way in assisting ANC to reach a proper understanding of what an election is, of its component parts, its political parts, its management parts. ANC could have made very serious mistakes, but the potential for those mistakes was very much minimized by the support from Sweden" (Interview with Garth Strachan, p. 197).
7. Jan Hodann: Memorandum ('Anslag till Sydafrika'/'Grant to South Africa'), OPIC, Stockholm, 23 November 1992 (OPA). Both projects were coordinated by SDP's Bo Toresson (ibid.).
8. See Brodin op. cit., p. 233.

work for democratic elections. Thus, while it was decided to transfer the coordinating function from CDS to the Education Resource and Information Project (ERIP)—set up in Cape Town in the mid-1980s by Trevor Manuel, Cheryl Carolus and other UDF leaders[1]—it was further agreed that voter education in order to be effective should be carried out in cooperation with the constituent parts of the mass democratic movement. In addition, it was convincingly argued, there was an acute need for election management training "if democratic elections are to be conducted on an equal and fair basis".[2] This, in turn, gave birth to VEETU and, eventually, to a new request for Swedish assistance.

What became known as VEETU was a consortium of four training NGOs with close links to ANC, namely, ERIP in Cape Town, the Human Awareness Programme in Johannesburg, the Centre for Community and Labour Studies in Durban and Afesis in East London. Led by Garth Strachan, ERIP was responsible for national coordination, as well as for actual design of the project.[3] This would focus on training in election management and skills development, covering *inter alia* election strategy, information, public relations, logistics and canvassing, as well as on voter education in favour of particularly disadvantaged groups, such as farm workers and women.[4]

Although ANC was initially reluctant about the idea[5], VEETU's services were, in addition, available to all organizations without previous electoral experience. As later noted by Strachan, "there was an agreement with the Swedes that we would train all the political parties which hitherto had not participated in an election".[6] Apart from ANC and its immediate allies, the client organizations thus included PAC, the Muslim Front, trade unions, civic and women's organizations, as well as a range of locally based NGOs. The Inkatha Freedom Party was also invited to join the programme.[7] However, "in spite of repeated written and face to face requests to provide [Inkatha] with training, they never agreed to that".[8]

VEETU was established at a time when the CODESA negotiations had broken down and democratic elections seemed distant. It was only in July 1993 that agreement on an election date was ultimately reached. This notwithstanding, the training and education needs were enormous. As early as in January 1993, the ambitious programme was therefore launched in earnest.[9] Initially, the costs were mainly covered by the Swedish contribution of June 1992, as well as by a grant from the Danish government.[10] These resources were, however, far from sufficient. On VEETU's behalf,

---

1. Interview with Garth Strachan, p. 195.
2. Quoted in Lysén and Fairbairn op, cit., p. 8. Strachan later commented: "When I became [D]irector of ERIP in 1992, we were asked by [CDS] to do voter education for the forthcoming elections. We agreed to do it, but in meetings with people from [OPIC]—specifically delegations led by Bo Toresson—we put forward the idea that as much as voter education was important, unless you provided elections training support you would never level the playing field in South Africa. Because you are asking a sector of the democratic movement with no experience of elections whatsoever to compete on an equal footing with the National Party, which [...] had the monopoly of the media [...] and a huge, highly sophisticated and experienced election machine. Toresson and his colleagues not only quickly came to see the logic of what we were saying, but also very swiftly linked up with ANC [in this regard]" (Interview with Garth Strachan, p. 196).
3. Ibid.
4. Ibid. and Brodin op. cit., p. 217.
5. Brodin op. cit., p. 214.
6. Interview with Garth Strachan, p. 196. Cf. Lysén and Fairbairn op. cit., pp. 37-39.
7. Lysén and Fairbairn op. cit., p. 10.
8. Interview with Garth Strachan, p. 196.
9. VEETU: 'Interim progress report as at 22 January 1993', [no place or date] (OPA).
10. Ibid.

in December 1992 OPIC thus submitted a new request to SIDA, amounting to 10.4 MSEK. Taking unspent balances into account, in February 1993 the official aid agency approved the application, granting an amount of 9.2 MSEK.[1] Finally, in June 1993 a new agreement on Swedish support to VEETU was signed, formally between SDP and ERIP.[2]

Among several voter training initiatives, VEETU stands out as a major undertaking. From January 1993 until the South African general elections in April 1994 the organization held no fewer than 467 workshops, in total attended by more than 77,000 participants.[3] During the same period, some 2.2 million potential voters were reached by its education programme.[4] The Swedish input into this effort was significant. From a quantitative point of view, the funds extended via OPIC represented around 33 per cent of the total VEETU budget.[5] Arguably more important was the qualitative aspect. Interviewed in Cape Town in 1995, ERIP's former Director Garth Strachan concluded:

> [VEETU] was a massive project. It would never have been possible without the Olof Palme International Center. It was not just the financial support. During the seven months before the elections, I cannot recall a period longer than two weeks when somebody from [OPIC] was not here to give advice, support and, in a sense, knowledge and experience of elections in Sweden and other countries. In a way, I think that the massive effort [...] was seen by the Swedish people as a sort of natural culmination of a long process of support for the coming into fruition of democracy. It was the final contribution that should be made [...].[6]

Final Contribution and Freedom at Long Last

In the midst of a heated national debate and after considerable delays, on 11 November 1993 the Swedish government decided to grant ANC a final contribution of 95 MSEK.[7] While the decision had retroactive effect from 1 July 1993, it laid down that the long-standing official assistance to the South African liberation movement should come to an end on 27 January 1994, three months before the set election date.[8] This was explained as follows in a letter from Cooperation Minister Svensson to ANC President Mandela:

---

1. SIDA: Decision ('Ansökan från Olof Palmes Internationella Centrum om stöd till valutbildning i Sydafrika, steg II'/'Request from OPIC for support towards voter education in South Africa, phase II'), Regional secretariat for Southern Africa, No. 18/1993, Stockholm, 22 February 1993 (SDA).
2. 'Cooperation agreement between the Swedish Social Democratic Party and [the] Education Resource and Information Project concerning voter education and election training in South Africa', Stockholm, 2 June 1993-Cape Town, 9 June 1993 (OPA).
3. Lysén and Fairbairn op. cit., p. 1. In their evaluation study, the authors estimate that some 60% of the workshops carried out for VEETU's clients benefited ANC and its allies, 29% COSATU, 5% PAC and 6% other organizations (ibid., p. 10).
4. Ibid., p. 1.
5. Ibid., pp. 1 and 58. Among VEETU's main donors were the governments of Denmark (16%) and the Netherlands (11%), as well as the Dutch NGOs Holland Committee on Southern Africa, Interfund and Novib, which together contributed 20% (ibid.). Germany, Great Britain and the United States shied away from VEETU and its links to ANC. Strachan noted in 1995 that "[t]here were governments that categorically refused to give [any] money. The British, the Americans and the Germans. I met their ambassadors on a number of occasions" (Interview with Garth Strachan, p. 196).
6. Ibid. VEETU was initially established to operate until the national elections. However, the Swedish partners insisted that the unit should continue its work and cover the scheduled local elections as well. They were held on 1 November 1995, barring in KwaZulu/Natal and the Cape Town metropolitan area, where they took place in May 1996. The contribution via OPIC to VEETU's training and education efforts for the local polls was even more prominent, in financial terms amounting to 14.3 MSEK (Lysén and Fairbairn op. cit., p. 1). This corresponded to 49% of the total grants received (ibid., p. 58).
7. Ministry for Foreign Affairs: 'Regeringsbeslut: Begäran om humanitärt bistånd till ANC budgetåret 1993/94' ('Cabinet decision: Request for humanitarian assistance to ANC [during] the financial year 1993/94'), Stockholm, 11 November 1993 (SDA). The decision was signed by Cooperation Minister Alf Svensson.
8. Ibid.

Sweden and the ANC have benefited from far-reaching and close [...] cooperation for more than [twenty] years. From a Swedish point of view, this has been a natural consequence of our active repudiation of apartheid and our support for ANC['s] efforts to abolish this system. As a result of your long and patient struggle, the ANC has a special position in Sweden. We have supported you in the difficult years when oppression and persecution were at their worst and international support was at a low point. [...] [C]ooperation between us has expanded and developed, and as time passed it was increasingly treated on the same basis as development cooperation between Sweden and independent countries in the region. [...]

When the ANC regained its legal status in South Africa in 1990, Sweden considered that it should obviously continue to support [the movement] in rebuilding [its] organization and in the negotiation process to achieve a democratic South Africa. At the same time, Sweden made it clear that direct [...] cooperation [...] could only continue until the ANC became a political party, participating in democratic elections. This position was subsequently reiterated at all major meetings between [the parties] and is in accordance with Swedish practice and [...] international law. As far as Sweden is concerned, we consider that the election campaign may be said to commence three months prior to the election, that is to say on 27 January 1994. At this point, direct [...] cooperation between Sweden and the ANC must cease.

The Swedish government has today decided on extensive and flexible support for the ANC [during the financial] year 1993/94, until the point when direct support has to be terminated. Our aim is that [it] should continue to provide active support for the ANC and help to reduce the financial imbalance in the negotiation process. Other forms of Swedish humanitarian assistance to the democratization process in South Africa will not be affected by this decision [...].[1]

Although the amount granted for the seven months between 1 July 1993 and 27 January 1994 *de facto* represented a considerable increase of the 1992/93 allocation[2], the decision by the non-socialist government was severely criticized by the opposition Social Democratic Party and various organizations. Informed of the government's stand, in a letter to Prime Minister Carl Bildt the Social Democratic leader Ingvar Carlsson wrote on 10 November:

We have [studied] the draft cabinet decision on Sweden's support to ANC for the financial year 1993/94. In this connection, I wish to convey the Social Democratic position.

First and foremost, I want to express the disappointment we feel concerning the way in which the government has handled this issue. [It] has focused its attention on a phasing out of the assistance, rather than on designing [the support] in the best way to secure the democratization process. This [constitutes] an unfortunate end to several decades of very close Swedish cooperation with the organization which has been the bearer of the democracy efforts in South Africa. [...].We do not share the government's view of ANC as a political party. ANC is a broad civic movement, [representing a] force which possibly can guarantee a transition to democracy. It is this movement which [...] may limit the use of violence by different extremist [organizations]. The election which is forthcoming is an election on democracy, not an election in a democracy. The country has still no democratic constitution and the correlation of forces is deeply unbalanced. We are therefore of the opinion that the government's decision to end the cooperation with ANC on 27 January is unfortunate. [It] should have granted ANC the full amount for utilization during the entire financial year 1993/94.[3]

---

1. Letter ('Development cooperation between Sweden and the ANC') from Alf Svensson to Nelson Mandela, Ministry for Foreign Affairs, Stockholm, 11 November 1993 (MFA).
2. The ANC allocation for 1992/93 was 110 MSEK. On a monthly basis, the grant for 1993/94 represented an increase of almost 50 per cent. As indicated in the table above, the Swedish assistance in 1993/94 was, in addition, substantially broader than during the two previous years.
3. That is, until 30 June 1994. Letter [no title] from Ingvar Carlsson to Carl Bildt, Socialdemokraterna, Stockholm, 10 November 1993 (MFA).

In a subsequent radio debate between SDP's Pierre Schori and Alf Svensson, leader of the Christian Democrats and as Minister for International Development Co-operation and Human Rights responsible for the cabinet decision[1], the former publicly censured the government's stand, emphasizing the argument that the South African election was "not an election in a democracy, but [...] for democracy".[2] In response, Svensson declared on behalf of the Bildt government that "we are completely astounded. [...] I believe that the Social Democrats are unique in the world [...] when they now assert that support should be extended to a political party in another country".[3]

Thus, when on 16 November 1993—less than a week after the government decision—the last ever aid negotiations with ANC were held in Johannesburg, there were strongly divergent views between the ruling non-socialist coalition and the parliamentary opposition. To ANC itself, however, the Swedish stand did not come as a surprise. In several interviews and in a meeting with Kaj Persson from the Foreign Ministry, National Chairman Thabo Mbeki expressed his "understanding", registering, in addition, the positive fact that the movement had been granted the full amount requested for 1993/94.[4]

Ultimately, neither the government decision nor the Swedish debate cast gloomy shadows over the historic, final negotiations, held on the eve of the approval of a draft South African constitution and respectively led by Thomas Nkobi and Johan Brisman.[5] On the contrary, while the ANC delegation in general was certain that "27 April would result in a government of the people", in a more personal capacity Nkobi "expressed pleasure [at the fact] that he had been present in the first contacts between SIDA and the ANC, and that he was still participating at this final meeting".[6] In a solemn and optimistic atmosphere, a detailed budget was established for the final Swedish allocation of 95 MSEK.

As noted, during the hectic pre-election period Georg Dreifaldt assisted ANC with the utilization of the grant, and in mid-April he and Roland Axelsson returned to Johannesburg to examine the movement's preliminary financial statement concerning Swedish assistance from 1 July 1993 until 27 January 1994. When the books were balanced, it was established that 21 MSEK remained unspent.[7] As 6.5 MSEK was committed to cover costs incurred before the final deadline, Axelsson, however, recommended SIDA to make a final disbursement to ANC of this

---

1. Svensson also served as Deputy Minister for Foreign Affairs.
2. Transcript attached to memorandum ('Inslag i Lunchekot 1993-11-13: Politisk strid om Sveriges stöd till ANC'/'Feature of [radio programme] on 13 November 1993: Political dispute regarding Sweden's support to ANC'), Ministry for Foreign Affairs, Stockholm, 15 November 1993 (MFA).
3. Ibid.
4. Kaj Persson: Memorandum ('Överläggningar med ANC om biståndssamarbetet'/'Deliberations with ANC concerning the aid cooperation'), Ministry for Foreign Affairs, Stockholm, 14 December 1993 (MFA). The meeting between Persson and Mbeki took place in Johannesburg on 15 November 1993, the day preceding the official talks (ibid.).
5. In addition to Brisman, the Swedish participants at the last aid negotiations with ANC were Gunilla von Bahr, Claes Hammar, Lena Johansson and Sara Lindgren from the Swedish embassy in Pretoria, Kaj Persson from the Foreign Ministry and Tarja Roghult and Birgitta Sevefjord from SIDA. More than twenty officials formed part of the ANC delegation. In an opening statement, Thabo Mbeki outlined the political situation in the country. It could as a curiosity be noted that he estimated that ANC would receive between 55 and 60 per cent of the votes in the forthcoming elections ('Agreed minutes from consultations held in Johannesburg, South Africa, November 1993, between the African National Congress of South Africa (ANC) and [the] Swedish International Development Authority (SIDA) concerning humanitarian assistance', Johannesburg, 2 December 1993) (SDA).
6. Ibid.
7. Kaj Persson: Memorandum ('Utbetalning till ANC'/'Disbursement to ANC'), Ministry for Foreign Affairs, Stockholm, 22 June 1994 (MFA).

amount.[1] Meanwhile, at a ceremony in Johannesburg on 11 May 1994—the day after President Mandela's inauguration—Secretary General Cyril Ramaphosa handed over ANC's externally audited financial report for 1992/93 and 1993/94 to SIDA's Director General Carl Tham.[2] Together with outstanding accounts concerning earlier Swedish assistance to ANC in Swaziland and Zimbabwe, it was examined by Axelsson, who in June 1994 concluded:

> I have scrutinized the audited statements and find them satisfactory. [...] I thus recommend SIDA to accept that the total financial support to ANC through the years has been fully accounted for and that the use of the contributions has—from an audit and control point of view—been satisfactorily reported on.[3]

After a considerable delay due to late invoicing and other technicalities, in October 1994 SIDA, finally, transferred the above-mentioned amount of 6.5 MSEK.[4] Twenty-one years of close cooperation between Sweden and ANC had thereby formally come to an end. From the start in 1973, in current figures a total of 896 MSEK had been disbursed as direct official assistance to the South African liberation movement.[5]

In connection with the peace prize jointly awarded to them by the Norwegian Nobel Committee, in December 1993 Nelson Mandela and F.W. de Klerk paid a short visit to Stockholm. While this was Mandela's third visit to the country, it was the first time ever that a South African head of state was received in Sweden.[6] Three months later, Margaretha af Ugglas became the first Swedish Foreign Minister to go to South Africa.[7] Before the general elections, the bilateral relations between the countries were thus being normalized.[8]

There was at the same time widespread concern with regard to the continuing violence in South Africa and the prospects of free and fair polls. SIDA would against this background allocate considerable resources in favour of various peace and election monitoring initiatives.[9] Particularly significant among the former was PEMSA—Peace Monitoring in South Africa—a cooperation project between seventeen Swedish and three South African NGOs which was initiated in August 1993.[10] During its most active phase from January to July 1994, a total of 66 Swedish

---

1. Roland Axelsson: 'Report on final financial accounts of SIDA's support to ANC', RAX Consulting AB, Stockholm, 2 May 1994 (SDA).
2. Cf. 'Goodbye and Hello from Sweden' in *Mayibuye*, No. 5, 1994, p. 17. The audit was performed by H. Daniels & Co., chartered accountants based in Cape Town.
3. Roland Axelsson: 'Addendum to report on final financial accounts of SIDA's support to ANC', RAX Consulting AB, Stockholm, 14 June 1994 (SDA).
4. SIDA: Decision ('Slututbetalning till ANC 1993/94'/'Final disbursement to ANC 1993/94'), Regional secretariat for Southern Africa, No. 146/1994, Stockholm, 3 October 1994 (SDA). The remaining unspent balance of 14.5 MSEK as of 27 January 1994 was reallocated in favour of ANC-aligned NGOs.
5. See Appendix XIV.
6. In his memoirs, de Klerk complains that his reception in Norway "was reserved in comparison with the effusive and unrestrained welcome that was accorded to Mandela" (de Klerk op. cit., p. 297). In Sweden, the two laureates were received by King Carl Gustav XVI and Prime Minister Carl Bildt. They also attended a luncheon hosted by Peter Wallenberg (ibid., p. 300).
7. 'Minister's visit ends SA-Sweden stand-off' in *The Citizen*, 14 February 1994.
8. Diplomatic relations at ambassadorial level had been established on 1 November 1993.
9. A total amount of close to 60 MSEK was granted for these purposes (SIDA: Memorandum ('Bakgrundspromemoria inför långsiktigt utvecklingssamarbete med Sydafrika'/'Background memorandum in view of long-term development cooperation with South Africa'), Stockholm, 17 January 1995) (SDA).
10. On PEMSA, see Jonas Ewald and Håkan Thörn: *Peace Monitoring in South Africa*, The Swedish UN Association, Stockholm, 1994. This evaluation report in English is an abbreviated version of the original Swedish text (*Fredsövervakning i Sydafrika*, Svenska FN-förbundet, Stockholm, 1994).

History in the making:
Cooperation Minister Alf
Svensson (right) and Kaj
Persson of the Foreign
Ministry observing the
elections in Soweto,
April 1994
(Courtesy of Kaj Persson)

peace monitors worked within the project.[1] Attached to different organizations and programmes, the actual elections at the end of April were, finally, observed by around 200 Swedes, one of them being Cooperation Minister Alf Svensson.[2]

Bringing a formal end to apartheid, white minority rule and the Thirty Years' War in the region, the peaceful and joyous elections in South Africa on 26-29 April 1994 will be inscribed in the history books as a seminal, democratic triumph at the end of the troubled 20th century. Reflecting on the "fantastic impossibility" of apartheid, ANC and the "great struggle of people to be free", in a little known introduction to South Africa published in 1957—three years before Sharpeville and the bannings of ANC and PAC—the prominent South African author and Liberal politician Alan Paton had predicted:

> In 1960, the massive wall may show a crack. In 1970, the crack may have become a breach. In 1980, the waters may be pouring through. [And] in 2000, the river may be flowing quietly to the sea, with only a few ruins left of its former impediment, to be preserved as historical monuments of the folly of mankind.[3]

Paton described ANC as "the largest African organization".[4] The South African majority could, however, only confirm this at democratic polls in late April 1994, almost four decades later. To the informed observer, the outcome held few surprises. The results—when they were eventually announced after days of complicated counting—gave the African National Congress an overwhelming 62.6 per cent of the national vote. The National Party came second with 20.4 per cent and

1. Ibid., p. 9.
2. SIDA: Memorandum ('Bakgrundspromemoria inför långsiktigt utvecklingssamarbete med Sydafrika'/'Background memorandum in view of long-term development cooperation with South Africa'), Stockholm, 17 January 1995 (SDA). Representing AWEPA, the author served as an election observer in the war-torn region of the Natal Midlands.
3. Alan Paton: *South Africa and Her People*, Lutterworth Press, London, 1957, pp. 136-38.
4. Ibid., p. 134.

Inkatha third with 10.5 per cent, followed by the Freedom Front (2.2 per cent), the Democratic Party (1.7 per cent) and PAC (1.3 per cent).[1]

Two weeks later—on 10 May 1994—Nelson Mandela was sworn in as President of South Africa and head of an ANC-led Government of National Unity, with Thabo Mbeki as First Deputy and F.W. de Klerk as Second Deputy President. Attended by 100,000 people, the inauguration at the Union Buildings in Pretoria "blended formal ceremonialism with the vitality of a Woodstock rock concert".[2] More than 6,000 guests from around 140 countries had come to celebrate the historic occasion, among them the former Presidents of Tanzania and Zambia, Julius Nyerere and Kenneth Kaunda; the US Vice President Al Gore; Prince Philip and the British Foreign Secretary Douglas Hurd; the Israeli President Ezer Weizman and the PLO leader Yasir Arafat, as well as the Cuban President Fidel Castro.[3]

While Denmark was represented by Prime Minister Poul Nyrup Rasmussen and Finland by President Martti Ahtisaari, Sweden—for many years ANC's main donor—kept a remarkably low profile. Conspicuously absent from the ceremony were the Moderate Prime Minister Carl Bildt, the Moderate Foreign Minister Margaretha af Ugglas and the Christian Democratic Cooperation Minister Alf Svensson. Instead, the government was represented by the Liberal Social Minister Bengt Westerberg, who in addition served as Deputy Prime Minister. SIDA's Director General Carl Tham was also present, together with Sten Andersson from the opposition Social Democratic Party and a host of Swedish anti-apartheid activists and NGO representatives.[4]

Four months later, the non-socialist coalition lost the parliamentary elections in Sweden. With Ingvar Carlsson as Prime Minister, the Social Democratic Party returned to power.[5] Leading a delegation which included officials who had been closely involved with ANC since the early or mid-1970s—such as Anders Bjurner and Bo Heinebäck[6]—in February 1995, Carlsson paid an official visit to the new South Africa. In addition to political talks, on 20 February, finally, he and President Mandela signed a first bilateral agreement on development cooperation. Sweden would from 1 July 1995 until 31 December 1996 make available 345 MSEK as a grant, primarily for projects and programmes which promoted democracy and human rights, education, public administration and a balanced development in the urban sector.[7] As had earlier been the case in Guinea-Bissau, Mozambique, Angola, Zimbabwe and Namibia, the humanitarian support to the victorious nationalist movement was transformed into development assistance, and South Africa was included among the core countries for Swedish aid.[8]

---

1. Another 13 political parties received a total of 1.3 per cent of the popular vote.
2. Sparks op. cit., p. 228.
3. Leif Norrman: 'Mandela svor presidenteden' ('Mandela swore the presidential oath') in *Dagens Nyheter*, 11 May 1994.
4. ANC had, for example, invited the Swedish rock artists Tomas Ledin and Mikael Wiehe to the inauguration ceremony (cf. the interview with Tomas Ledin, p. 303).
5. Carlsson resigned in 1996. He was replaced as party leader and Prime Minister by Göran Persson.
6. Heinebäck had become Sweden's first ambassador to democratic South Africa in 1994.
7. 'Development cooperation agreement between the government of Sweden and the government of the Republic of South Africa, 1 July 1995-31 December 1996', Cape Town, 20 February 1995 (SDA).
8. During the financial year 1994/95, 220 MSEK was allocated to a number of South African NGOs and institutions (SIDA: Memorandum ('Utvecklingssamarbete med Sydafrika 1 juli 1995-31 december 1998'/'Development cooperation with South Africa 1 July 1995-31 December 1998'), Stockholm, 19 January 1995) (SDA).

Epilogue

A Disproportionate International Impact...

In a travesty of William Shakespeare's *Hamlet*, the South African Broadcasting Corporation complained in 1967:

> Through these ten years past, in the temper of their indignation,
> Denmark and her Nordic neighbours have led Europe's crusade
> against our country.
> Norway's parliament lends succour to refugees from our land.
> Sweden's men-of-letters break down the pales and forts of reason.
> In their censure, they find general corruption in each of our particular faults,
> and they assail our policies with blasts from hell.
> The Danish government sets funds aside to counter race discrimination.
> Nordic navvies, in the ports of Scandinavia, withdraw their hand
> and our cargoes remain within their holds.[1]

Forming part of a Nordic undertaking, this study attempts to document the involvement of Sweden in the Southern African struggles against colonialism, occupation and white minority rule. While Volume I set out to identify the actors and factors behind the involvement, the ambition of the present volume is to illustrate the Swedish participation. Focusing on official assistance to the nationalist movements, it is hoped that the study together with the monographs on Denmark, Finland and Norway[2], as well as the accompanying interview volume[3], will contribute to a broader understanding of the international aspects of the Thirty Years' War in the region, a significant chapter in the quest for national self-determination, democracy and human rights towards the end of the troubled 20th century.

Primarily written for the general reader interested in the relations between Sweden and the Southern African liberation movements, the presentation should also provide material for more theoretical enquiries, for example, with regard to Swedish foreign policy in the Cold War era; regional developments in a bipolar world; and the diplomatic initiatives, political alliances and material conditions of the different movements.

Shunned as 'Communist' or 'terrorist' during the Cold War, the Southern African liberation movements were generally considered of a dubious nature in the West. From 1969—before the fall of the Portuguese empire—the US government based its policy towards the region on the premise that "[t]he whites are here to stay and [that] the only way that constructive change can come about is through them". It was also asserted that "[t]here is no hope for the blacks to gain the political rights they seek through violence [, as] this will only lead to chaos and increased opportunities for the Communists".[4] Twenty years later—when Angola, Mozambique and Zimbabwe had won their independence and the Pretoria regime

---

1. SABC Survey, 'Current Affairs', Johannesburg, 13 October 1967.
2. Morgenstierne op. cit. (Denmark; forthcoming), Eriksen (ed.) op. cit. (Norway) and Soiri and Peltola op. cit. (Finland).
3. Sellström (ed.) op. cit.
4. *The Kissinger Study on Southern Africa* op. cit., p. 66.

Joint Nordic-South African appearance at the UN World Summit for Social Development, Copenhagen, March 1995 (from left): Ingvar Carlsson (Sweden), Martti Ahtisaari (Finland), Nelson Mandela (South Africa), Poul Nyrup Rasmussen (Denmark), Gro Harlem Brundtland (Norway) and David Oddsson (Iceland) (Photo: Anders Gunnartz)

was increasingly seen to be doomed—the British Prime Minister Margaret Thatcher at the 1987 Commonwealth summit meeting in Vancouver, Canada, characterized ANC as "terrorist", adding that anyone who thought that it was going to rule the country was "living in cloud cuckoo land".[1]

Siding with Portuguese colonialism, Rhodesian settlers and apartheid South Africa, the leading Western powers' policies towards Southern Africa led to untold human suffering, as well as to serious economic and political consequences throughout the region and beyond. Reflecting on the drawn-out drama as Nelson Mandela was sworn in as President in Pretoria in May 1994, Carl Tham, the Director General of the Swedish International Development Authority, noted that

> Mandela is now hailed and admired by those Western democracies that for decades underpinned the apartheid regime and only in the 1980s, reluctantly and insufficiently, applied pressure against it. [...] It is difficult not to think of all the victims of the oppression, and that they might have been saved through an early decisive international action, for example, after the Sharpeville massacre in 1960. If the democracies in the Western world then had decided to crush apartheid, much would have looked different, not only in South Africa.[2]

Sweden's involvement—from the anti-apartheid writings in the 1950s of committed 'men-of-letters' via the re-active official support to the victims of racism and colonialism in the 1960s to the increasingly pro-active, direct cooperation with the national liberation movements from 1969—has here been discussed. Borne along by a broadly based solidarity movement, in purely monetary terms—and in current

---

1. Cited in Freeman op. cit., p. 209. At the same time, Thatcher declared that she would never talk to any ANC leaders and denied that British officials had met with representatives of the movement. However, her Foreign Secretary, Geoffrey Howe, had recently held discussions with ANC President Oliver Tambo.
2. Tham op. cit., p. 290.

figures—Social Democratic and non-socialist governments would until the 1994 democratic elections in South Africa channel a total of 4 billion Swedish Kronor as official humanitarian assistance to Southern Africa. Of this amount, 1.7 billion—over 40 per cent—was extended under bilateral agreements to FRELIMO of Mozambique, MPLA of Angola, ZANU and ZAPU (Patriotic Front) of Zimbabwe, SWAPO of Namibia and ANC of South Africa, that is, to the movements which eventually became victorious in their respective countries.

In practically all fields barring the supply of arms, military training and the armed struggle as such, Sweden would—in the words of the Canadian scholar David Ross Black—"have a disproportionate impact".[1] As noted with regard to Namibia and South Africa by his US academic colleague and Southern African expert William Minter,

> in the 1980s the international right wing was fond of labeling SWAPO and ANC as 'Soviet-backed'. In empirical terms, [however,] the alternate, but less dramatic, labels 'Swedish-backed' or 'Nordic-backed' would have been equally or even more accurate, especially in the non-military aspects of international support.[2]

While some Western governments—notably in The Netherlands[3] and Italy—eventually joined Sweden and the Nordic countries in extending direct or indirect assistance to the liberation movements, there emerged over the years a growing frustration with the fact that so few were ready to grant official support even to international humanitarian organizations. As stated by the Liberal Foreign Minister Ola Ullsten in the non-socialist government's declaration on foreign policy in March 1981, "[i]f it is the influence of the Soviet Union that they fear in the region, then there are even stronger reasons to take a stand for black Africa".[4] And addressing a conference in London, the Social Democratic Cooperation Minister Lena Hjelm-Wallén emphasized in June 1988:

> As regards humanitarian assistance generally in Southern Africa [...], it should be stressed that we all have an international obligation to try to see to it that the flow [...] will continue and increase. The needs are growing and very obvious. [...] There is [, however,] a clear case for a better burden-sharing when it comes to donor support for institutions and organizations such as the Africa Educational Trust (AET), [the] World University Service (WUS), [the] Commonwealth Fund for Technical Cooperation (CFTC) and the anti-apartheid funds within the United Nations system, as well as [for] organizations involved in providing legal protection [...] such as the International Defence and Aid Fund (IDAF).
>
> I am sure that many of you are not aware that the Swedish share of the financing of most of these organizations exceeds 50 per cent. And many of us, on our [part], are indeed surprised to learn that these excellent organizations—most of which are based in London—still receive very minimal official contributions from the United Kingdom and other OECD countries.[5]

---

1. David Ross Black: 'Australian, Canadian and Swedish Policies toward Southern Africa: A Comparative Study of 'Middle Power Internationalism'', Ph.D. dissertation, Dalhousie University, Halifax, Nova Scotia, 1991, p. 347.
2. William M. Minter: Review of *The Impossible Neutrality* by Pierre Schori in *Africa Today*, No. 43, 1996, p. 95.
3. In 2000, the Archives Commission Netherlands-Southern Africa decided to launch a project to document the Dutch involvement in the Southern African liberation struggles.
4. Swedish Parliament 1981: Debate on foreign and trade policy, 18 March 1981, Riksdagens Protokoll 1981, p. 44.
5. 'Sweden's role in Southern Africa': Statement by H.E. Mrs. Lena Hjelm-Wallén, Minister for International Development Cooperation, at the [conference on] 'Peace and Development in the Frontline States', organized by War on Want, London, 9 June 1988 (MFA). The contributions by AET, CFTC, IDAF and WUS are only indirectly referred to in the text. Although the Swedish government was a principal donor and many Swedes worked closely with them—notably at IDAF—as international NGOs they fall outside the main scope of this study.

The Southern African struggles were fought and won by the peoples of the region themselves. However, the diplomatic, political and material contribution from Sweden was—as noted by several nationalist representatives in the interviews for this study—of critical importance, not least to assert the liberation movements' independence in the Cold War context. While President Joaquim Chissano of Mozambique in the case of FRELIMO stated that "[w]e found a middle point in Sweden which we could refer to" and that the support "proved our policy in terms of relationships"[1], on behalf of ANC Thabo Mbeki of South Africa argued that

> [t]he position of Sweden created more space than the African or non-aligned position. It created space for ANC to be able to deal with the rest of the Western world. And not just the Western world, but even with regard to the Eastern world and the relationship of ANC with those countries.[2]

In Mbeki's view,

> the particular role of Sweden [...] was to say that the people have got the right and the duty to rebel against oppression, and that the concept of emancipation of a people cannot be reduced to a protest movement. [It] concerns the right to self-determination of small nations. That is something which is legitimate, which is necessary and which must be supported. [A] second element [...] is that as part of the recognition of that right [...], you support the people who are engaged in the struggle. You do not define what they should be.[3]

Although part of the rich North, Sweden itself was a small, non-aligned country which in the divided Cold War world jealously defended its right to self-determination and self-definition. Without a colonial past and a principled supporter of the UN Charter, in addition to strictly humanitarian concerns, assistance to the Southern African quest for national liberation was from the late 1960s increasingly seen by a broad social-liberal majority as an integral component of Sweden's policy of active neutrality. In 1978, for example, David Wirmark of the Liberal Party argued that SWAPO's struggle in Namibia and the Swedish support to the movement had "the same objectives".[4] Olof Palme, in particular, has been identified with this position.[5] Addressing the Social Democratic Party congress in 1984, he said:

> Our international involvement concerns important principles [, namely,] respect for the right to self-determination, social and economic justice, peace and liberty. But it is also about self-interest. Sweden is part of the world. We cannot isolate ourselves. Working for peace and international solidarity, we assume responsibility for Sweden too. [...]
>
> International law is of particular importance for small nations. We [...] therefore react [...] strongly against violations in this regard. [...] Our defence of other people's right to by themselves form their own future does [, however,] not mean that we can ensure a certain [political course] or a specific social system in those countries, once self-determination has been achieved. We support people's right to independence, but cannot give any assurances of what will happen thereafter. People themselves form their destinies.[6]

Palme, Ullsten, Wirmark and other politicians who were to play prominent roles with regard to Sweden's cooperation with the liberation movements had their first encounters with the Southern African nationalist leaders in the 1950s or early

---

1. Interview with Joaquim Chissano, p. 39.
2. Interview with Thabo Mbeki, p. 154.
3. Ibid., p. 153.
4. David Wirmark: 'Kamp och bistånd med samma mål' ('Struggle and assistance with the same objectives') in *Svenska Dagbladet*, 5 December 1978. See the chapter 'The Shipanga Affair and Beyond: Humanitarian Assistance and Human Rights'.
5. Cf. the interview with Thabo Mbeki, p. 153.
6. Olof Palme: *Palme Själv* ('Palme Himself'), Selected texts, Tidens Förlag, Stockholm, 1996, pp. 199-201.

1960s. When during the latter decade the movements—due to the intransigence of the white minority regimes and the stand of the Western powers—embarked on armed struggle and in the process were supported by the Soviet Union, the People's Republic of China and their respective allies, there was in Sweden a generation of centrally placed policy-makers who were able to look beyond 'the Communist spectre' and relate to the nationalist core of the struggles.

Of particular importance in this context were the early relations established with Tanzania and Zambia, the movements' main host countries and Sweden's principal cooperating partners in the region. Advice was often sought from Presidents Julius Nyerere and Kenneth Kaunda. Also following a non-aligned course, they made far-reaching contributions. Invited to the 1976 Labour Day celebrations in Stockholm, Nyerere, for example, stated:

> The freedom fighters of Rhodesia, just like FRELIMO and MPLA, will get support from the independent states of Africa. But we in Africa do not manufacture guns. So, they will get arms from the Communist countries, and from those Third World countries which have them. [...]
>
> In the past, Sweden and some other supporters of national independence have understood this. I ask you to understand it now. The political campaigning against the freedom movements is intensifying, [and] the very horrors of war will be used to confuse the issue. The misery of the injured and the innocent will be presented as propaganda. And you will be asked not to support those who have taken up arms and caused such suffering. [...]
>
> Colonialism and racialism are evil, [and] the freedom cause is just. But the freedom fighters are not angels. They are men and women made angry and desperate by humiliation and oppression.
>
> The independent countries of Africa are not great examples of justice and personal freedom. There is no guarantee that Zimbabwe and Namibia will be great non-racial democracies from the moment of their birth. But independence brings a chance to struggle against the poverty and economic oppression which underlies a lack of personal freedom. It gives a chance for the real struggle for human justice to begin.[1]

Concerned with the overriding historical contradiction between, on the one hand, colonialism and minority rule, and, on the other, national self-determination and majority rights, this study on solidarity and assistance is also about 'the right to begin'. Although outside the primary scope—and thus 'another story'—it could be recorded that the veteran ANC leader Walter Sisulu after the demise of apartheid noted with regard to Sweden that

---

1. 'President Nyerere's speech at the May Day rally [in] Stockholm [on] 1 May 1976', Ministry of Information and Broadcasting, Dar es Salaam, 1 May 1976 (NAI). As surmised by Nyerere, Zimbabwe—formally a multi-party state—would upon independence not develop into a 'great non-racial democracy'. The political situation in the country deteriorated considerably towards the end of the 1990s. As Robert Mugabe from the mid-1970s was seen generally in Sweden in the same positive light as later Nelson Mandela, it is relevant to note that the ZANU leader's support rapidly waned. Thus, in a series of articles in *Dagens Nyheter* in December 1997-January 1998 Per Wästberg—who in the 1960s opened the eyes of the Swedish public to the nationalist cause in Zimbabwe and formed part of an Amnesty group which 'adopted' Mugabe—criticized the ZANU government in no uncertain terms (see, for example, Per Wästberg: 'Gamarna flockar sig kring bytet' ('The vultures flock round the prey') in *Dagens Nyheter*, 28 December 1997). As the rule of law continued to break down, in April 2000 the Social Democratic Foreign Minister Anna Lindh wrote to her counterpart, ZANU's Stanislaus Mudenge, that "Sweden—as a long-standing friend of Zimbabwe; having supported the liberation struggle from the earliest hour—is alarmed by the way groups are now being pitched against each other, the rule of law [is] being set aside and [there is a] brutal return to politics of violence and intimidation. This dismay is shared by the many people and organizations in our country who supported liberation in Southern Africa" (Letter from Anna Lindh to Stanislaus Mudenge, Ministry for Foreign Affairs, Stockholm, 19 April 2000) (MFA). In January 2001, the Swedish government decided to cut back on the official development assistance to Zimbabwe.

[w]e [still] need each other. We have a greater job to do, and this time not for a particular country, but on a global basis. [...] The first stage without the second is not worth it.[1]

... but Conspicuous Domestic Silence

The close cooperation with the liberation movements in Southern Africa represents a unique, active chapter in contemporary Swedish international affairs. Carl Tham, who from 1985 as head of the official aid agency SIDA was responsible for the implementation of the assistance, has characterized the support to ANC as "one of the most important foreign policy and cooperation efforts carried out by Sweden".[2] Quite remarkably, however, little evidence of the involvement and the underlying considerations is to be found in reminiscences published by centrally placed Swedish politicians.[3] Thus, in their memoirs the former Centre Party Premier Thorbjörn Fälldin (1976-78 and 1979-82) and his Social Democratic successor Ingvar Carlsson (1986-91 and 1994-96)—both personally committed and playing prominent official roles in this regard—only make brief, general references to their encounters with Southern Africa as youth leaders in the early 1960s.[4] Similarly, the former Social Democratic cabinet members Mats Hellström and Thage G. Peterson only mention Southern Africa in passing.[5]

More noteworthy is that the Swedish academic community has not paid attention to the 'disproportionate impact' Sweden had in Southern Africa during the last decades of the 20th century. Apart from a limited number of dissertations on economic sanctions[6] and voter education and electoral training in South Africa[7] there are no comprehensive studies of Sweden's historical links with the region; no sociological inquiries into the emergence, growth and significance of the wider solidarity movement; and, most notably, no serious efforts in the fields of political science, international affairs or peace and conflict studies to contextualize, compare and analyze the regional role played by Sweden vis-à-vis other international actors or arenas.

In the light of the fact that approximately half of Sweden's overall official development aid has traditionally been channelled to Southern Africa, the academic silence becomes even more conspicuous. In his comparative study of Australia, Canada and Sweden, Ross Black noted in 1991 that in Sweden in the 1980s there was "an unusually strong domestic base of popular interest and engagement", leading to "the emergence of a relatively large cadre of citizens with direct experience of, and dedication to, the people and countries of the region. [...] Collectively, they gave Southern African issues a higher degree of domestic political salience [...] than in virtually any other Western country".[8]

---

1. Interview with Walter Sisulu, p. 191.
2. Tham op. cit., p. 290. Also Tham in Kaa Eneberg: 'Biståndet en svensk succé' ('The assistance a Swedish success') in *Dagens Nyheter*, 3 July 1994. Cf. the interview with David Wirmark, p. 351.
3. Cf. Sellström Volume I, pp. 20-21, where, however, the important contribution made by Pierre Schori is underlined. In his memoirs, the former Foreign Minister Lennart Bodström (1982-85) includes a brief passage on Southern Africa (Bodström op. cit., pp. 200-03). Of a very general nature, it does not shed new light on the Social Democratic government's policy vis-à-vis the region.
4. Thorbjörn Fälldin: *En Bonde Blir Statsminister* ('A Farmer Becomes Prime Minister'), Albert Bonniers Förlag, Stockholm, 1998, pp. 222-23, and Ingvar Carlsson: *Ur Skuggan av Olof Palme* ('From the Shadow of Olof Palme'), Hjalmarson & Högberg Bokförlag, Stockholm, 1999, pp. 130-32.
5. Mats Hellström: *Politiskt Liv* ('Political Life'), Hjalmarson & Högberg Bokförlag, Stockholm, 1999, pp. 13-14, and Peterson op. cit., pp. 75-77, 79-81 and 422-24.
6. Nordenmark op. cit.
7. Brodin op. cit.
8. Ross Black op. cit., pp. 308 and 314.

Nevertheless, when in 1998 a major inter-disciplinary research project was launched on 'Sweden during the Cold War'—financially supported *inter alia* by the Foreign Ministry and the Swedish Institute of International Affairs; coordinated by the departments of political science, history and contemporary affairs at the universities of Gothenburg, Stockholm and Södertörn; and covering some 20 different subjects—the involvement with Southern Africa was not included.[1] At the same time, Swedish secondary school textbooks in social studies remained silent on the substantial popular and official interaction with the region. In a review of 46 books used in the late 1990s, Mai Palmberg of the Nordic Africa Institute found that it was mentioned in only 3 of the 26 books discussing South Africa, and then only in the context of economic sanctions.[2] On this basis, she concluded:

> [T]he great Swedish support to the South African struggle against apartheid has not become a fact worth mentioning in the textbooks. This is quite remarkable. It should [...] have been natural to connect events happening far away with what has engaged tens of thousands of people in Sweden. It would [...] have been possible to point out the importance that also a small country like Sweden can have. But the textbooks are silent.[3]

Hopefully, social scientists and textbook authors will in the future give due attention to the popular and official commitment to the cause of national liberation in Southern Africa. If this study can contribute in this regard, it has achieved one of its main objectives.

---

1. 'Nyhetsbrev från forskningsprogrammet *Sverige under Kalla Kriget* (SUKK)' ('Newsletter from the research programme 'Sweden during the Cold War'), 2000:2 [no place or date, but early 2001].
2. Mai Palmberg: *Afrikabild för Partnerskap?: Afrika i de Svenska Skolböckerna* ('Image of Africa for Partnership?: Africa in the Swedish Textbooks'), Nordiska Afrikainstitutet, Uppsala, 2000, p. 200.
3. Ibid.

Bibliography

Published sources

1. Books

Abrahamsson, Hans and Anders Nilsson, 1995, *Mozambique: The Troubled Transition*, Zed Books, London and New Jersey.

Abrahamsson, Hans, 1997, *Seizing the Opportunity: Power and Powerlessness in a Changing World Order—The Case of Mozambique*, Department of Peace and Development Research, University of Gothenburg.

Adler-Karlsson, Gunnar, 1970, *Västerns Ekonomiska Krigföring 1947–1967*, Rabén och Sjögren, Stockholm.

Afrikagrupperna i Sverige, 1972, *Afrika: Imperialism och Befrielsekamp*, Lund.

Afrikagrupperna i Sverige, 1977, *Befrielsekampen i Afrika*, Stockholm.

Ahlmark, Per, 1994, *Vänstern och Tyranniet*, Timbro, Stockholm.

Ahlsén, Bengt, 1972, *Portugisiska Afrika: Beskrivning av ett Kolonialimperium och dess Sönderfall*, Svenska Utbildningsförlaget Liber AB, Stockholm.

Allie, Najwah, 1991, *Directory of South African Trade Unions: A Complete Guide to All South Africa's Trade Unions*, SALDRU, Cape Town.

ANC, 1994, *The Reconstruction and Development Programme*, ANC, Johannesburg.

Andreassen, Knut and Birgitta Dahl, 1971, *Guinea-Bissau: Rapport om ett Land och en Befrielserörelse*, Prisma, Stockholm.

Andreassen, Knut, 1973, *Kamrater i Angola*, Hermod, Malmö.

Andresen, Trond and Steinar Sætervadet, 2000, *Fra Dugnad till Bistand: Namibiaforeningen gjennom 20 År*, Namibiaforeningen, Elverum.

Anglin, Douglas G. and Timothy M. Shaw, 1979, *Zambia's Foreign Policy: Studies in Diplomacy and Dependence*, Westview Press, Boulder, Colorado.

Anglin, Douglas G., Timothy M. Shaw and Carl G. Widstrand, (eds.), 1978, *Conflict and Change in Southern Africa: Papers from a Scandinavian–Canadian Conference*, University Press of America, Washington.

Another Development for Lesotho?: Alternative Development Strategies for the Mountain Kingdom, 1989, Foundation for Education with Production/Dag Hammarskjöld Foundation, Serowe, Botswana.

Another Development for SADCC, 1987, Foundation for Education with Production/Dag Hammarskjöld Foundation, Serowe, Botswana.

Ansprenger, Franz, 1975, *Die Befreiungspolitik der Organisation für Afrikanische Einheit (OAU), 1963 bis 1975*, Studien zum Konflikt im Südlichen Afrika, Chr. Kaiser Verlag, Munich.

Bakkevig, Trond, 1995, *Den Norske Kirke og Kampen mot Apartheid*, Mellomkirkelig Råd, Oslo.

Barber, James and John Barratt, 1990, *South Africa's Foreign Policy: The Search for Status and Security 1945–1988*, Cambridge University Press, Cambridge.

Barrell, Howard, 1990, *MK: The ANC's Armed Struggle*, Penguin Forum Series, Penguin Books, Harmondsworth.

Baskin, Jeremy, 1991, *Striking Back: A History of COSATU*, Verso, London and New York.

Bauer, Gretchen, 1998, *Labor and Democracy in Namibia, 1971–1996*, Ohio University Press, Athens, and James Currey, London.

Bernstein, Hilda, 1978, *No. 46—Steve Biko*, International Defence & Aid Fund, London.

Bernstein, Hilda, 1994, *The Rift: The Exile Experience of South Africans*, Jonathan Cape, London.

Bhebe, Ngwabi and Terence Ranger, (eds.), 1995, *Soldiers in Zimbabwe's Liberation War*, Volume I, University of Zimbabwe Publications, Harare.

Bhebe, Ngwabi and Terence Ranger, (eds.), 1995, *Society in Zimbabwe's Liberation War*, Volume II, University of Zimbabwe Publications, Harare.

Bhebe, Ngwabi, 1999, *The ZAPU and ZANU Guerrilla Warfare and the Evangelical Lutheran Church in Zimbabwe*, Mambo Press, Gweru, in association with Studia Missionalia Upsaliensia, Uppsala.

Biko, Steve, 1979, *I Write What I Like*, Heinemann Educational Books, London, Ibadan and Nairobi.

Bodström, Lennart, 2000, *Mitt i Stormen*, Hjalmarson & Högberg Bokförlag, Stockholm.

Bridgland, Fred, 1986, *Jonas Savimbi: A Key to Africa*, Mainstream Publishing Company, Edinburgh.

Brodin, Anna, 2000, *Getting Politics Right: Democracy Promotion as a New Conflict Issue in Foreign Aid Policy*, Department of Political Science, University of Gothenburg, Gothenburg.

Brundenius, Claes, Kenneth Hermele and Mai Palmberg, 1980, *Gränslösa Affärer: Om Svenska Företag i Tredje Världen*, Liber Förlag, Stockholm.

Bushin, Vladimir, 1989, *Social Democracy and Southern Africa (1960s–1980s)*, Progress Publishers, Moscow.

Cabral, Amílcar, 1969, *Revolution in Guinea: An African People's Struggle,* Stage 1, London.

Campschreur, William and Joost Divendal (eds.), 1989, *Culture in Another South Africa*, Zed Books, London.

Cann, John P., 1997, *Counterinsurgency in Africa: The Portuguese Way of War, 1961–1974*, Greenwood Press, Westport, Connecticut and London.

Carlsson, Ingvar, 1999, *Ur Skuggan av Olof Palme*, Hjalmarson & Högberg Bokförlag, Stockholm.

Carter, Gwendolen M. and Patrick O'Meara, (eds.), 1979, *Southern Africa: The Continuing Crisis*, The Macmillan Press, London and Basingstoke.

Catholic Institute for International Relations (CIIR) and British Council of Churches (BCC), 1986, *Namibia in the 1980s*, CIIR/BCC, London.

Caute, David, 1983, *Under the Skin: The Death of White Rhodesia*, Allen Lane, London.

Cawthra, Gavin, 1986, *Brutal Force: The Apartheid War Machine*, International Defence and Aid Fund for Southern Africa, London.

Centre for Development Studies (CDS), 1991, *Local Government and Planning for a Democratic South Africa*, University of the Western Cape, Bellville.

Chabal, Patrick, 1983, *Amílcar Cabral: Revolutionary Leadership and People's War*, African Studies Series, Cambridge University Press, Cambridge.

Chaliand, Gérard, 1964, *Guinée 'Portugaise' et Cap Vert en Lutte pour Leur Indépendence*, Maspero, Paris.

Chan, Stephen, 1990, *Exporting Apartheid: Foreign Policies in Southern Africa 1978–1988*, Macmillan Publishers, London and Basingstoke.

Christie, Iain, 1988, *Machel of Mozambique*, Zimbabwe Publishing House, Harare.

Cilliers, J.K., 1985, *Counter-Insurgency in Rhodesia*, Croom Helm, London, Sydney and Dover, New Hampshire.

Ciment, James, 1997, *Angola and Mozambique: Postcolonial Wars in Southern Africa*, Facts on File, New York.

Cliffe, Lionel, (ed.), 1994, *The Transition to Independence in Namibia*, Lynne Rienner Publishers, Boulder and London.

Clutton-Brock, Guy and Molly, 1972, *Cold Comfort Confronted*, Mowbrays, London and Oxford.

Cooper, Allan D., (ed.), 1988, *Allies in Apartheid: Western Capitalism in Occupied Namibia*, Macmillan Press, London.

Correia, Pedro Pezerat, 1991, *Descolonização de Angola: A Jóia da Corona do Império Português*, Inquérito, Lisbon.

Crocker, Chester, 1992, *High Noon in Southern Africa: Making Peace in a Rough Neighborhood*, W. W. Norton & Company, New York.

Cronje, Gillian and Suzanne, 1979, *The Workers of Namibia*, International Defence and Aid Fund for Southern Africa, London.

Daly, Reid, 1982, *Selous Scouts: Top Secret War*, Galago Publishing, Alberton.

Davidson, Basil, 1969, *Frihetskampen i Guinea-Bissau*, Natur och Kultur, Stockholm.

Davidson, Basil, 1972, *In the Eye of the Storm: Angola's People*, Longman, London.

Davies, Rob, Dan O'Meara and Sipho Dlamini, 1984, *The Struggle for South Africa: A Reference Guide to Movements, Organizations and Institutions*, Zed Books, London.

Dobell, Lauren, 1998, *SWAPO's Struggle for Namibia, 1960–1991: War by Other Means*, Basel Namibia Studies Series No. 3, P. Schlettwein Publishing, Basel.

Dreyer, Ronald, 1994, *Namibia and Southern Africa: Regional Dynamics of Decolonization 1945–1990*, Kegan Paul International, London and New York.

Drolsum, Nina, 1999, *For et Fritt Afrika: Solidaritet mot Kolonialisme og Apartheid for Menneskeverd og Rettferdighet—Fellesrådet 1967–2000*, Fellesrådet for Afrika, Solidaritet Forlag, Oslo.

Egerö, Bertil, 1987, *Mozambique: A Dream Undone: The Political Economy of Democracy, 1975–84*, Nordiska Afrikainstitutet, Uppsala.

Ehnmark, Anders and Jean Hermanson, 1973, *Exemplet Guinea-Bissau: Ett Reportage om en Befrielserörelse*, Bokförlaget PAN/Norstedts, Stockholm.

Ehnmark, Anders, (ed.), 1968, *Guerilla*, Bokförlaget PAN/Norstedts, Stockholm.

Ehnmark, Anders, 1993, *Resan till Kilimanjaro: En Essä om Afrika efter Befrielsen*, Norstedts, Stockholm.

Eldredge, Elizabeth, 1993, *A South African Kingdom: The Pursuit of Security in Nineteenth-Century Lesotho*, Cambridge University Press, Cambridge.

Engellau, Patrik, 1980, *Genom Ekluten*, Atlantis, Stockholm.

Eriksen, Tore Linné, (ed.), 2000, *Norway and National Liberation in Southern Africa*, Nordiska Afrikainstitutet, Uppsala.

Ewald, Jonas and Håkan Thörn, 1994, *Peace Monitoring in South Africa*, The Swedish UN Association, Stockholm.

Flower, Ken, 1987, *Serving Secretly: An Intelligence Chief on Record—Rhodesia into Zimbabwe 1964 to 1981*, Juhn Murray, London.

Freeman, Linda, 1997, *The Ambiguous Champion: Canada and South Africa in the Trudeau and Mulroney Years*, University of Toronto Press, Toronto, Buffalo and London.

Fälldin, Thorbjörn, 1998, *En Bonde Blir Statsminister*, Albert Bonniers Förlag, Stockholm.

Föreningen Verdandis Zambiagrupp, 1972, *Zambia: Ett Gränsfall*, Folkuniversitetets förlag/Föreningen Verdandi, Stockholm.

Gastrow, Shelagh, 1995, *Who's Who in South African Politics*, No. 5, Ravan Press, Johannesburg.

Gevisser, Mark, 1996, *Portraits of Power: Profiles in a Changing South Africa*, David Philip Publishers, Cape Town, in association with *Mail & Guardian*, Johannesburg.

Godwin, Peter, 1996, *Mukiwa: A White Boy in Africa*, Macmillan, London.

Groth, Siegfried, 1995, *Namibia: The Wall of Silence*, Peter Hammer Verlag, Wuppertal.

Gustavsson, Rolf, (ed.), 1971, *Kapitalismens Utveckling i Afrika: Studier i Afrikas Moderna Ekonomiska Historia*, Cavefors, Lund.

Gutteridge, William (ed.), 1995, *South Africa: From Apartheid to National Unity, 1981–1994*, Dartmouth Publishing, Aldershot.

Hadjor, Kofi Buenor, (ed.), 1988, *New Perspectives in North–South Dialogue: Essays in Honour of Olof Palme*, I. B. Tauris Publishers, London.

Hadland, Adrian and Jovial Rantao, 1999, *The Life and Times of Thabo Mbeki*, Zebra Press, Rivonia.

Hale, Frederick, 2001, *A Swedish Pen Against Apartheid: The South African Novels of Gunnar Helander*, African Renaissance Publishers, Cape Town.

Hallencreutz, Carl Fredrik, 1998, *Religion and Politics in Harare 1890–1980*, Studia Missionalia Upsaliensia No. LXXIII, Swedish Institute of Missionary Research, Uppsala.

Hanlon, Joseph and Roger Omond, 1987, *The Sanctions Handbook*, Penguin Books, Harmondsworth.

Hanlon, Joseph, 1986, *Apartheid's Second Front: South Africa's War against Its Neighbours*, Penguin Books, Harmondsworth.

Hanlon, Joseph, 1986, *Beggar Your Neighbours: Apartheid Power in Southern Africa*, Catholic Institute for International Relations, London, with James Currey and Indiana University Press, London and Bloomington.

Hansson, Tommy, 1989, *Slaveri i Vår Tid: En Handbok i Totalitär Socialism*, Contra Förlag, Stockholm.

Hansson, Tommy, 1993, *Åter till det Kalla Kriget*, Contra Förlag, Stockholm.

Harlin, Tord, 1991, *Trons Öga*, Verbum, Stockholm.

Hastings, Adrian, 1974, *Wiriyamu*, Gummessons Bokförlag, Falköping.

Heino, Timo-Erkki, 1992, *Politics on Paper: Finland's South Africa Policy 1945–1991*, Nordiska Afrikainstitutet, Uppsala.

Heldal, Inger A., (ed.), 1996, *From Cape to Cape Against Apartheid: Norwegian Support for Democracy in South Africa*, Mayibuye Books, Cape Town.

Hellberg, Carl-Johan, 1997 *Mission, Colonialism and Liberation: The Lutheran Church in Namibia 1840–1966*, New Namibia Books, Windhoek.

Hellström, Mats, 1999, *Politiskt Liv*, Hjalmarson & Högberg Bokförlag, Stockholm.

Hengeveld, Richard and Jaap Rodenburg (eds.), 1995, *Embargo: Apartheid's Oil Secrets Revealed*, Amsterdam University Press, Amsterdam.

Henriksen, Thomas H., 1978, *Mozambique: A History*, Rex Collings, London, with David Philip, Cape Town.

Herlitz, Gillis, 1981, *Dagbok från Zimbabwe: Rapport från en Stats Födelse*, Nordiska Afrikainstitutet, Uppsala.

Heywood, Annemarie, 1994, *The Cassinga Event*, Archeia No. 18, National Archives of Namibia, Windhoek.

Hishongwa, Ndeutala, 1992, *The Contract Labour System and Its Effects on Family and Social Life in Namibia: A Historical Perspective*, Gamsberg Macmillan, Windhoek.

Holm, Birgitta, 1998, *Sara Lidman: I Liv och Text*, Albert Bonniers Förlag, Stockholm.

Houston, Gregory F., 1999, *The National Liberation Struggle in South Africa: A Case Study of the United Democratic Front, 1983–1987*, Ashgate Publishing, Aldershot.

Hyslop, Jonathan, (ed.), 1999, *African Democracy in the Era of Globalisation*, Witwatersrand University Press, Johannesburg.

Häggman, Bertil, 1987, *Frihetskämpar: Motstånd på Kommunistiskt Territorium*, Contra Förlag, Stockholm.

International Defence and Aid Fund for Southern Africa (IDAF), 1989, *Namibia: The Facts*, IDAF Publications, London.

Irogbe, Kema, 1997, *The Roots of United States Foreign Policy toward Apartheid South Africa, 1969–1985*, The Edwin Mellen Press, Lewiston, Queenston and Lampeter.

Isaacman, Allan and Barbara Isaacman, 1983, *Mozambique: From Colonialism to Revolution, 1900–1982*, Westview Press, Boulder, Colorado.

ISAK and SFN, 1986, *Svensk Folkriksdag mot Apartheid 21–23 februari 1986*, Stockholm.

Israel, Joachim, 1998, *Ett Upproriskt Liv*, Norstedts Förlag, Stockholm.

Johnson, Phyllis and David Martin (eds.), 1986, *Destructive Engagement: Southern Africa at War*, Zimbabwe Publishing House, Harare.

Kapuscinski, Ryszard, 1988, *Another Day of Life*, Picador/Pan Books, London.

Karis, Thomas G. and Gail M. Gerhart, 1997, *From Protest to Challenge: A Documentary History of African Politics in South Africa, 1882–1990; Volume 5: Nadir and Resurgence, 1964–1979*, Indiana University Press, Bloomington & Indianapolis.

Kasrils, Ronnie, 1993, *'Armed and Dangerous': My Undercover Struggle against Apartheid*, Heinemann, Oxford.

Kastlund, Åke, 1967, *Resa genom Svart och Vitt*, Svenska Kyrkans Diakonistyrelses Bokförlag, Stockholm.

Katjavivi, Peter, 1988, *A History of Resistance in Namibia*, James Currey, London, OAU, Addis Ababa and Unesco Press, Paris.

Katjavivi, Peter, Per Frostin and Kaire Mbuende, (eds.), 1989, *Church and Liberation in Namibia*, Pluto Press, London (UK) and Winchester (USA).

Kessel, Ineke van, 2000, *'Beyond Our Wildest Dreams': The United Democratic Front and the Transformation of South Africa*, University Press of Virginia, Charlottesville and London.

Kissinger, Henry, 1999, *Years of Renewal*, Simon & Schuster, New York.

The Kissinger Study on Southern Africa, 1975, Spokesman Books, Nottingham.

de Klerk, F. W., 1998, *The Last Trek: A New Beginning*, Macmillan, London and Basingstoke.

Kotzé, Hennie and Anneke Greyling, 1994, *Political Organisations in South Africa A-Z*, Tafelberg Publishers, Cape Town.

Kuper, Hilda, 1978, *Sobhuza II: Ngwenyama and King of Swaziland*, Duckworth, London.

Langley, J. Ayo, 1979, *Ideologies of Liberation in Black Africa, 1856–1970: Documents on Modern African Political Thought from Colonial Times to the Present*, Rex Collings, London.

Lara, Lúcio, 1998, *Um Amplo Movimiento...: Itinerário do MPLA através de Documentos e Anotações*, Volume I – Until February 1961, LitoTipo, Luanda.

Legum, Colin and John Drysdale, 1970, *Africa Contemporary Record: Annual Survey and Documents 1969–1970*, Africa Research Limited, Exeter.

Leijnse, Emma, 2000, *Solidaritetens Ansikte: Historien om Emmaus Björkå*, Leijnse Förlag, Stockholm.

Leys, Colin and John Saul, 1995, *Namibia's Liberation Struggle: The Two-Edged Sword*, James Currey, London, and Ohio University Press, Athens.

Lindmarker, Ingmar, 1971, *Det Vita Afrika: Sydafrika och Dess Grannar*, Gebers/Almqvist & Wiksell, Stockholm.

Lodge, Tom, 1983, *Black Politics in South Africa Since 1945*, Longman, London and New York.

Lopes, Carlos, 1987, *Guinea Bissau: From Liberation Struggle to Independent Statehood*, Westview Press, Boulder, Colorado and Zed Books, London and New Jersey.

LO-TCO, 1975, *South Africa: Black Labour–Swedish Capital*, A Report by the LO/TCO Study Delegation to South Africa 1975, LO-TCO, Uppsala.

LO-TCO, 1975, *Sydafrika: Svart Arbetskraft–Svenskt Kapital*, LO-TCO, Uddevalla.

Lubowski, Molly and Marita van der Vyver, [no year], *Anton Lubowski: Paradox of a Man*, Queillerie Publishers, Strand.

Luckhardt, Ken and Brenda Wall, 1980, *Organize or Starve!: The History of the South African Congress of Trade Unions*, Lawrence and Wishart, London.

Lundahl, Mats and Lena Moritz, 1996, *Det Nya Sydafrika: Ekonomi och Politik efter Apartheid*, SNS Förlag, Stockholm.

Mabuza, Lindiwe, 1987, *To Sweden from ANC/Till Sverige från ANC*, Socialdemokraterna, Stockholm.

MacQueen, Norrie, 1997, *The Decolonization of Portuguese Africa: Metropolitan Revolution and the Dissolution of Empire*, Longman, London and New York.

Magnusson, Åke, 1969, *Moçambique*, Nordiska Afrikainstitutet, Uppsala.

Magnusson, Åke, 1974, *Sverige–Sydafrika: En Studie av en Ekonomisk Relation*, The Scandinavian Institute of African Studies, Uppsala.

Magnusson, Åke, 1979, *Sydafrika i Världen*, Nordiska Afrikainstitutet, Uppsala.

Mandela, Nelson, 1994, *Long Walk to Freedom: The Autobiography of Nelson Mandela*, Macdonald Purnell, Randburg.

Marcum, John, 1969, *The Angolan Revolution: The Anatomy of an Explosion (1950–1962)*, Volume I, The MIT Press, Cambridge, Massachusetts, and London, England.

Marcum, John, 1978, *The Angolan Revolution: Exile Politics and Guerrilla Warfare (1962–1976)*, Volume II, The MIT Press, Cambridge, Massachusetts, and London, England.

Maré, Gerhard, 1992, *Brothers Born of Warrior Blood: Politics and Ethnicity in South Africa*, Ravan Press, Johannesburg.

Maree, Johann, (ed.), 1987, *The Independent Trade Unions, 1974–1984: Ten Years of the South African Labour Bulletin*, Ravan Press, Johannesburg.

Martin, David and Phyllis Johnson, 1981, *The Struggle for Zimbabwe*, Faber and Faber, London and Boston.

Martin, David and Phyllis Johnson, 1985, *The Chitepo Assassination*, Zimbabwe Publishing House, Harare.

Massie, Robert Kinloch, 1997, *Loosing the Bonds: The United States and South Africa in the Apartheid Years*, Nan A. Talese/Doubleday, New York.

Mbeki, Thabo, 1998, *Africa: The Time Has Come*, Selected speeches, Tafelberg Publishers, Cape Town/Mafube Publishing, Johannesburg.

Mbuende, Kaire, 1986, *Namibia, the Broken Shield: Anatomy of Imperialism and Revolution*, Liber Förlag, Malmö.

McLaughlin, Janice, 1996, *On the Frontline: Catholic Missions in Zimbabwe's Liberation War*, Baobab Books, Harare.

Meli, Francis, 1988, *South Africa Belongs to Us: A History of the ANC*, Zimbabwe Publishing House, Harare.

Minter, William, 1988, *Operation Timber: Pages from the Savimbi Dossier*, Africa World Press, Trenton, New Jersey.

Mutasa, Didymus, 1974, *Rhodesian Black behind Bars*, Mowbrays, London and Oxford.

Mzala [Jabulani Nxumalo], 1988, *Gatsha Buthelezi: Chief with a Double Agenda*, Zed Books, London and New Jersey.

Möllander, Anders, 1982, *Sverige i Södra Afrika: Minnesanteckningar 1970–80*, SIDA, Stockholm.

Newitt, Malyn, 1995, *A History of Mozambique*, Hurst & Company, London.

Ngavirue, Zedekia, 1997, *Political Parties and Interest Groups in South West Africa (Namibia): A Study of a Plural Society*, P. Schlettwein Publishing, Basel, Switzerland.

Nilsson, Karl N. Alvar, 1998, *Överklass, Nazism och Högerextremism: 1945–1995*, Carlsson Bokförlag, Stockholm.

Nkomo, Joshua, 1984, *The Story of My Life*, Methuen, London.

Nordenmark, Ove, 1991, *Aktiv Utrikespolitik: Sverige–Södra Afrika, 1969–1987*, Acta Universitatis Upsalienses No. 111, Almqvist & Wiksell International, Stockholm.

Nujoma, Sam, 2001, *Where Others Wavered: The Autobiography of Sam Nujoma*, Panaf Books, London.

Odén, Bertil and Haroub Othman (eds.), 1989, *Regional Cooperation in Southern Africa: A Post-Apartheid Perspective*, The Scandinavian Institute of African Studies, Uppsala.

Ohlson, Thomas, 1998, *Power Politics and Peace Politics: Intra-State Conflict Resolution in Southern Africa*, Department of Peace and Conflict Research, Uppsala University, Uppsala.

Olukoshi, Adebayo O., 1998, *The Politics of Opposition in Contemporary Africa*, Nordiska Afrikainstitutet, Uppsala.

PAIGC, 1970, *O Nosso Livro*, Wretmans Boktryckeri, Uppsala.

Palm, Göran, (ed.), 1971, *Vår Kamp Er Kamp*, Bokförlaget PAN/Norstedts, Stockholm.

Palmberg, Mai, (ed.), 1983, *The Struggle for Africa*, Zed Press, London.

Palmberg, Mai, 2000, *Afrikabild för Partnerskap?: Afrika i de Svenska Skolböckerna*, Nordiska Afrikainstitutet, Uppsala.

Palme, Olof, 1987, *En Levande Vilja*, Tiden, Stockholm.

Palme, Olof, 1996, *Palme Själv*, Selected texts, Tidens Förlag, Stockholm.

Paton, Alan, 1957, *South Africa and Her People*, Lutterworth Press, London.

Pauw, Jacques, 1991, *In the Heart of the Whore: The Story of Apartheid's Death Squads*, Southern Book Publishers, Halfway House.

Pauw, Jacques, 1997, *Into the Heart of Darkness: Confessions of Apartheid's Assassins*, Jonathan Ball Publishers, Johannesburg.

Payne, Richard J., 1990, *The Nonsuperpowers and South Africa: Implications for US Policy*, Indiana University Press, Bloomington and Indianapolis.

Peltola, Pekka, 1995, *The Lost May Day: Namibian Workers Struggle for Independence*, The Finnish Anthropological Society in association with the Nordic Africa Institute, Jyväskylä.

Peterson, Thage G., 1999, *Resan mot Mars: Anteckningar och Minnen*, Albert Bonniers Förlag, Stockholm.

Pityana, Barney, Mamphela Ramphele, Malusi Mpumlwana and Lindy Wilson (eds.), 1991, *Bounds of Possibility: The Legacy of Steve Biko & Black Consciousness*, David Philip Publishers, Cape Town, and Zed Books, London and New Jersey.

Pogrund, Benjamin, 1990, *How Can Man Die Better...: Sobukwe and Apartheid*, Peter Halban Publishers, London.

Rantete, Johannes, 1998, *The African National Congress and the Negotiated Settlement in South Africa*, J. L. van Schaik Publishers, Pretoria.

Reed, Daniel, 1994, *Beloved Country: South Africa's Silent Wars*, BBC Books, London.

Reynolds, Andrew, (ed.), 1994, *Election '94 South Africa: The Campaigns, Results and Future Prospects*, James Currey, London; David Philip, Cape Town and Johannesburg; and St. Martin's Press, New York.

Riley, Eileen, 1991, *Major Political Events in South Africa 1948–1990*, Facts on File, Oxford and New York.

Robinson, Richard A.H., 1979, *Contemporary Portugal: A History*, George Allen and Unwin, London.

Rocha, Carlos, 1978, *Contribuição à História Económica de Angola*, INA, Luanda.

The Role of the Soviet Union, Cuba and East Germany in Fomenting Terrorism in Southern Africa, Volume I, 1982, Hearings before the Subcommittee on Security and Terrorism, Committee on the Judiciary, United States Senate, US Government Printing Office, Washington.

Rudebeck, Lars, 1974, *Guinea-Bissau: A Study of Political Mobilization*, Scandinavian Institute of African Studies, Uppsala.

Ryan, Colleen, 1990, *Beyers Naudé: Pilgrimage of Faith*, David Philip, Cape Town; Wm. B. Eerdmans, Grand Rapids; and Africa World Press, Trenton.

Ryman, Björn, 1997, *Lutherhjälpens Första 50 År*, Verbum Förlag, Stockholm.

Rösiö, Bengt, 1988, *Yrke: Diplomat*, Norstedts Förlag, Stockholm.

Saul, John S., 1993, *Recolonization and Resistance: Southern Africa in the 1990s*, Africa World Press, Trenton.

Saunders, Christopher and Nicholas Southey, 2000, *Historical Dictionary of South Africa*, Second edition, The Scarecrow Press, Lanham, Maryland, and London.

Schleicher, Hans-Georg and Ilona, 1998, *Special Flights: The GDR and Liberation Movements in Southern Africa*, SAPES Books, Harare.

Schleicher, Ilona and Hans-Georg, 1997, *Die DDR im Südlichen Afrika: Solidarität und Kalter Krieg*, Institut für Afrika-Kunde, Hamburg.

Schori, Pierre, 1992, *Dokument Inifrån: Sverige och Storpolitiken i Omvälvningarnas Tid*, Tidens Förlag, Stockholm.

Schori, Pierre, 1994, *The Impossible Neutrality—Southern Africa: Sweden's Role under Olof Palme*, David Philip Publishers, Cape Town.

Seekings, Jeremy, 2000, *The UDF: A History of the United Democratic Front in South Africa, 1983–1991*, David Philip, Cape Town; James Currey, Oxford; and Ohio University Press, Athens.

Sellström, Tor, (ed.), 1999, *Liberation in Southern Africa—Regional and Swedish Voices: Interviews from Angola, Mozambique, Namibia, South Africa, Zimbabwe, the Frontline and Sweden*, Nordiska Afrikainstitutet, Uppsala.

Sellström, Tor, 1999, *Sweden and National Liberation in Southern Africa. Volume I: Formation of a Popular Opinion (1950–1970)*, Nordiska Afrikainstitutet, Uppsala.

Shamuyarira, Nathan M., (ed.), 1972, *Essays on the Liberation of Southern Africa*, University of Dar es Salaam, Studies in Political Science, No. 3, Tanzania Publishing House, Dar es Salaam.

Shipanga, Andreas, 1989, *In Search of Freedom*, The Andreas Shipanga Story as told to Sue Armstrong, Ashanti Publishing, Gibraltar.

Shubin, Vladimir, 1999, *ANC: A View from Moscow*, Mayibuye History and Literature Series No. 88, Mayibuye Books, University of the Western Cape, Bellville.

Sibeko, Archie (Zola Zembe) with Joyce Leeson, 1996, *Freedom in Our Lifetime*, Indicator Press, Durban.

SIDA, 1985, *Whispering Land: An Anthology of Stories by African Women*, Office of Women in Development, Stockholm.

Sida, 1998, *Nycklar till den Nya Nationen: Kultursamarbete mellan Sverige och Sydafrika*, Sida, Stockholm.

Sida-seniorerna, 1999, *... Och Världen Växte: Biståndet Som Vi Minns Det*, Sida-seniorerna, Uppsala.

Simons, Jack and Ray, 1969, *Class and Colour in South Africa 1850–1950*, Penguin African Library, Harmondsworth.

Sithole, Masipula, 1999, *Zimbabwe: Struggles-within-the-Struggle (1957–1980)*, Rujeko Publishers, Harare.

Soggot, David, 1986, *Namibia: The Violent Heritage*, Rex Collings, London.

Soiri, Iina and Pekka Peltola, 1999, *Finland and National Liberation in Southern Africa*, Nordiska Afrikainstitutet, Uppsala.

Southall, Roger, 1995, *Imperialism or Solidarity?: International Labour and South African Trade Unions*, UCT Press, Rondebosch.

Sparks, Allister, 1994, *Tomorrow Is Another Country: The Inside Story of South Africa's Negotiated Revolution*, Struik Book Distributors, Sandton.

Steenkamp, William, 1983, *Borderstrike: South Africa into Angola*, Butterworths Publishers, Durban.

Stiff, Peter, 1987, *See You in November*, Galago Paperback, Alberton.

Stockwell, John, 1978, *In Search of Enemies: A CIA Story*, W.W. Norton, New York.

Stokke, Olav and Carl Widstrand, (eds.), 1973, *The UN-OAU Conference on Southern Africa, Oslo, 9–14 April 1973*, Scandinavian Institute of African Studies, Uppsala.

Stokke, Olav, 1978, *Sveriges Utvecklingsbistånd och Biståndspolitik*, Scandinavian Institute of African Studies, Uppsala.

Strand, Per, 2000, *Decisions on Democracy: The Politics of Constitution-Making in South Africa, 1990–1996*, Uppsala University, Uppsala.

Sundqvist, Sven-Ivan, 1974, *Sydafrikas Guldålder*, Askild & Kärnekull, Borås.

Switzer, Les and Mohamed Adhikari (eds.), 2000, *South Africa's Resistance Press: Alternative Voices in the Last Generation under Apartheid*, Ohio University Center for International Studies, Athens.

Tambo, Oliver, 1987, *Preparing for Power: Oliver Tambo Speaks*, Compiled by Adelaide Tambo, Heinemann, London.

Tham, Carl, 1994, *När Tiden Vänder*, Norstedts Förlag, Stockholm.

Thomas, Scott, 1996, *The Diplomacy of Liberation: The Foreign Relations of the ANC since 1960*, Tauris Academic Studies, I.B. Tauris Publishers, London and New York.

Thorud, Johan, 1972, *Geriljasamfunnet: Guinea-Bissaus Kamp mot Portugal*, Tiden, Oslo.

Tomaselli, Keyan and P. Eric Louw (eds.), 1991, *The Alternative Press in South Africa*, Anthropos Publishers, Bellville, and James Currey, London.

Truth and Reconciliation Commission of South Africa Report, 1998, Juta & Co. Ltd, Kenwyn, Cape Town.

Tutu, Desmond, 1997, *The Essential Desmond Tutu*, compiled by John Allen, David Philip Publishers and Mayibuye Books, Cape Town.

Tvedten, Inge, 1992, *Country Analysis: Angola*, SIDA, Stockholm.

Tvedten, Inge, 1997, *Angola: Struggle for Peace and Reconstruction*, Westview Press, Boulder, Colorado and Oxford.

United Nations Institute for Namibia (UNIN), 1987, *Namibia: A Direct United Nations Responsibility*, UNIN, Lusaka.

Walker, Walter, 1978, *The Bear at the Back Door: The Soviet Threat to the West's Lifeline in Africa*, Foreign Affairs Publishing Co., Surrey.

Walshe, Peter, 1970, *The Rise of African Nationalism in South Africa: The African National Congress 1912–1952*, C. Hurst & Company, London, and University of California Press, Berkeley and Los Angeles.

Webb, Pauline, (ed.), 1994, *A Long Struggle: The Involvement of the World Council of Churches in South Africa*, WCC Publications, Geneva.

Vetlesen, Vesla, 1998, *Frihet for Sør-Afrika: LO og Kampen mot Apartheid*, Tiden Norsk Forlag, Oslo.

White, Jon Manchip, 1969, *The Land God Made in Anger: Reflections on a Journey through South West Africa*, George Allen and Unwin, London.

Winter, Gordon, 1981, *Inside BOSS, South Africa's Secret Police*, Penguin Books, Harmondsworth.

Wirmark, David, (ed.), 1975, *The Rich and the Poor: New Approaches towards a Global Development Strategy*, Bokförlaget Folk och Samhälle, Stockholm.

Woods, Donald, 1978, *Biko*, Paddington Press, New York and London.

Wästberg, Per, 1995, *I Sydafrika: Resan mot Friheten*, Wahlström & Widstrand, Stockholm.

ya Nangolo, Mvula and Tor Sellström, 1995, *Kassinga: A Story Untold*, Namibia Book Development Council, Windhoek.

Zartman, William, 1989, *Ripe for Resolution: Conflict and Intervention in Africa*, Oxford University Press, New York.

Åberg, Ingrid Puck, 1992, *Att Skapa Något Slags Hopp: Om Svenskt Humanitärt Bistånd i Södra Afrika*, SIDA, Stockholm.

Åström, Sverker, 1987, *Sweden's Policy of Neutrality*, The Swedish Institute, Stockholm.

2. Other publications and documents[1]

AET, 'Evaluation of Swaziland refugee education project', Draft report, London, 1 May 1997.

Afrikagrupperna i Sverige, *För ett Fritt Angola: En Analys av MPLA, FNLA och UNITA*, Afrikagruppernas Skriftserie, No. 4, Stockholm, August 1975.

Afrikagrupperna i Sverige, *Sweden and South Africa*, Afrikagrupperna, Stockholm, September 1985.

ANC, 'Further submissions and responses by the African National Congress to questions raised by the Commission for Truth and Reconciliation', ANC, Johannesburg, 12 May 1997.

ANC, 'Mass action for people's power!', Statement of the National Executive Committee presented by Oliver Tambo, Lusaka, 8 January 1989.

ANC, 'Press statement on aid from Sweden', Department of Information and Publicity, Marshalltown, 5 January 199[3].

ANC, 'Report of the Office of the Treasurer General', ANC National Congress, Durban, July 1991.

ANC, 'SOMAFCO: Official Opening 21–23 August 1985—Progress Report/Special Edition', ANC, Amsterdam, 1985.

ANC, 'Statement to the Truth and Reconciliation Commission', ANC Department of Information and Publicity, Johannesburg, August 1996.

ANC, *Documents of the Second National Consultative Conference of the African National Congress: Zambia, 16–23 June 1985*, ANC, London, [no year].

Andersson, Anders, 'Dilemmas with Sanctions: The Policy of the Black South African Trade Unions and *Svenska Metall* towards Sanctions and Disinvestment against South Africa 1979–1993', Department of History, Gothenburg University, September 1999.

Andersson, Gun-Britt, *Befrielse i Södra Afrika*, Världspolitikens Dagsfrågor, No. 3, 1973, Utrikespolitiska Institutet, Stockholm, 1973.

Asmal, Kader and Louise, 'Anti-apartheid Movements in Western Europe', United Nations Unit on Apartheid, Notes and Documents, No. 4/74, United Nations, New York, March 1974.

Barrell, Howard, 'Conscripts to Their Age: African National Congress Operational Strategy, 1976–1986', St Antony's College, University of Oxford, 1993.

Catholic Commission for Justice and Peace in Zimbabwe and Legal Resources Foundation, 'Breaking the Silence-Building True Peace: A Report on the Disturbances in Matabeleland and the Midlands 1980 to 1988', Harare, February 1997.

Cervenka, Zdenek, *African National Congress Meets Eastern Europe: A Dialogue on Common Experiences*, Current African Issues No. 15, Nordiska Afrikainstitutet, Uppsala, November 1992.

Compact disc: 'Olof Palme: En Levande Vilja', Sveriges Socialdemokratiska Arbetareparti/Amigo, Stockholm, 1996.

Dag Hammarskjöld Foundation, '[Programme of] the 1983 Dag Hammarskjöld/IFDA seminar on communications for development', Uppsala, 10–13 November 1983.

Davies, Robert, *South African Strategy towards Mozambique in the Post-Nkomati Period: A Critical Analysis of Effects and Implications*, Research Report No. 73, Scandinavian Institute of African Studies, Uppsala, 1985.

Duncan, Tyrell, Frank Baffoe and Karin Metell, *Support against Apartheid: An Evaluation of 28 Years of Development Assistance to Lesotho*, SIDA Evaluation Report 1994:3, SIDA, Stockholm, 1994.

Egerö, Bertil, *South Africa's Bantustans: From Dumping Grounds to Battlefronts*, Discussion Paper No. 4, Nordiska Afrikainstitutet, Uppsala, 1991.

Falle, Samuel and Karlis Goppers, *Looking Both Ways: Swaziland between South Africa and SADCC*, An Evaluation of Sweden's Development Cooperation with Swaziland, SIDA Evaluation Report 1987:6, SIDA, Stockholm, 1988.

Folkpartiet, *Stöd åt Motståndsrörelser*, Rapport från en arbetsgrupp inom Folkpartiet, Bokförlaget Folk och Samhälle, Stockholm, 1969.

Hallencreutz, Carl F. and S. Axelson, (eds.), *Annual Report 1992 of Uppsala Studies of Mission*, Faculty of Theology, University of Uppsala, Uppsala, 1993.

---

1. Excluding documents held at the archives consulted (see 1. Archives below)

Heldal, Inger A., (ed.), *Sammen for Demokrati: Norsk Støtte til Kampen mot Apartheid*, PDC Aurskog, Oslo, 1996.

Högberg, Bertil, Bertil Odén and Vita Sigurdson, *Nordic Organisations in Independent Namibia: Report from a Conference in Sigtuna, 9–10 March, 1989*, The Scandinavian Institute of African Studies in cooperation with Nordic Non-Governmental Organisations, Uppsala, September 1989.

International Peace Academy/Arnold Bergstraesser Institut, *The Namibian Peace Process: Implications and Lessons for the Future*, Report on the Freiburg Symposium, 1–4 July 1992, Freiburg, 1994.

International University Exchange Fund (IUEF), 'Annual Report 1978–79', IUEF, Geneva, 1979.

International University Exchange Fund (IUEF), 'Statutes', IUEF, Geneva, June 1978.

Lipton, Merle, 'Sanctions and South Africa: The Dynamics of Economic Isolation', Special report No. 1119, The Economist Intelligence Unit, London, January 1988.

Lysén, Annika and Jean Fairbairn, 'Evaluation of the OP[I]C/SDP Project within the Voter Education and Elections Training Unit', OPIC, Stockholm, November 1995.

Magnusson, Åke, *Swedish Investments in South Africa*, Research Report No. 23, The Scandinavian Institute of African Studies, Uppsala, 1974.

Morgenstierne, Christopher Munthe, 'Denmark: A Flexible Response', Draft, [Copenhagen], January 1999.

The Mozambique Institute, *Mozambique and the Mozambique Institute 1972*, Dar es Salaam, [no date].

Mozambique Institute, 'Mozambique Institute: 1965', [no place or date].

Narum, Ragnhild, 'Norge og Rasekonflikten i Sør-Afrika', University of Oslo, Oslo, 1998.

Näringslivets Internationella Råd (NIR), *Sydafrika och Svenskt Näringsliv*, NIR, Lund, 1983.

Odén, Bertil, Henning Melber, Tor Sellström and Chris Tapscott, *Namibia and External Resources: The Case of Swedish Development Assistance*, Research Report No. 96, Nordiska Afrikainstitutet, Uppsala, 1994.

Pohjolainen Yap, Katri, 'Uprooting the Weeds: Power, Ethnicity and Violence in the Matabeleland Conflict 1980-1987', University of Amsterdam, Amsterdam, 2001.

Robben Island Museum, Mayibuye Centre and Nordic Africa Institute, *Conference Report: Nordic Solidarity with the Liberation Struggles in Southern Africa, and Challenges for Democratic Partnerships into the 21st Century*, Robben Island, 11–14 February 1999.

Ross Black, David, 'Australian, Canadian and Swedish Policies toward Southern Africa: A Comparative Study of 'Middle Power Internationalism', Dalhousie University, Halifax, Nova Scotia, 1991.

Rudebeck, Lars, 'Some Facts and Observations on Relations between the Nordic Countries and the Officially Portuguese-speaking Countries of Africa', Paper presented to a conference on the Portuguese-speaking countries in Africa organized by the *Stiftung Wissenschaft und Politik*, Ebenhausen, West Germany, February 1986.

SADCC: 'Southern Africa: Toward Economic Liberation', Lusaka, 1 April 1980.

SIDA, *Verkstad i Exil: SWAPOs Fordonverkstad i Angola*, SIDA, Bistånd Utvärderat No. 1/89, Stockholm, 1989.

The Socialist International, *The Arusha Conference*, Conference on Southern Africa of the Socialist International and the Socialist Group of the European Parliament with the Front Line States, ANC and SWAPO, Arusha, Tanzania, 4–5 September 1984, The Socialist International, London, 1985.

Svedberg, Peter, Anders Olofsgård and Björn Ekman, *Evaluation of Swedish Development Cooperation with Guinea-Bissau*, Secretariat for Analysis of Swedish Development Assistance (SASDA), Report No. 3, Ds 1994:77, Ministry for Foreign Affairs, Stockholm, 1994.

The Swedish People's Parliament against Apartheid in Stockholm, 21–23 February 1986, Final document, English translation [no place or date].

United Nations Centre Against Apartheid, 'No neutrality towards the struggle in Southern Africa', Statement made by Mr. Olof Palme at the meeting of the Security Council on 25 March 1977, United Nations, New York, April 1977.

United Nations Economic Commission for Africa, *South African Destabilization: The Economic Cost of Frontline Resistance to Apartheid*, United Nations, New York, October 1989.

United Nations, *Yearbook of the United Nations* (1960–1989), Department of Public Information, United Nations, New York.

Wickman, Solveig, *Sydafrika: Fackligt Bistånd*, Förlaget Trädet/LO/TCO's Biståndsnämnd, Stockholm, 1996.

3. Official records

The main Swedish public documents consulted are:

Code of Statutes (*Svensk Författningssamling*): 1969–1990

Government Bills (*Propositioner*): 1962–1990

Government Statements on Foreign Policy to the Swedish Parliament (*Regeringens utrikespolitiska deklarationer*): 1950–1994

Parliamentary Committee Reports (*Utskottsbetänkanden*): 1965–1975

Parliamentary Motions/Members' Bills (*Motioner*): 1965–1995

Official Government Reports (*Statens Offentliga Utredningar*): 1970–1995

4. Other official records

Hagård, Birger, 'Anmälan till Konstitutionsutskottet', Stockholm, 5 November 1996, published in Swedish Parliament/Konstitutionsutskottets betänkande, No. 1997/98: KU 25, Part II, Stockholm, 1998.

Kommerskollegium, *Handel: Berättelse för år 1950*, Volume I, Sveriges Officiella Statistik, Norstedt & Söner, Stockholm, 1952.

(Royal) Ministry for Foreign Affairs, *Documents on Swedish Foreign Policy* (1965–1993), Stockholm.

Ministry for Foreign Affairs, *Prohibition of Investments in South Africa and Namibia and Other Measures against Apartheid*, Stockholm, 1985.

Ministry for Foreign Affairs, *Prohibition of Imports of Agricultural Produce from South Africa*, Stockholm, December 1985.

Ministry for Foreign Affairs, *Prohibition of Trade with South Africa and Namibia*, Stockholm, March 1987.

The Nordic Council of Ministers and the Nordic Statistical Secretariat, *Yearbook of Nordic Statistics: 1986*, Copenhagen/Stockholm, 1987.

Sida, 'Sida's International Development Cooperation: Statistical Summary of Operations 1997', Sida, Stockholm, 1997 (Sida b).

SIDA, *Bistånd i Siffror och Diagram*, Stockholm, January 1995.

Sida, *Development in Partnership: Sida and Swedish Bilateral Development Cooperation in Africa*, Sida, Stockholm, 1997.

Statistiska Centralbyrån, *Handel: Berättelse för år 1960*, Volume II, Stockholm, 1963.

Statistiska Centralbyrån, *Utrikeshandel 1980*, Liber/Allmänna Förlaget, Stockholm, 1982.

Statistiska Centralbyrån, *Statistisk Årsbok för Sverige: 1988*, Statistics Sweden, Stockholm, 1987.

5. Periodicals

A Voz da Revolução
Africa News
Africa Report
Africa Today
African Affairs
Afrikabulletinen
AIC-Bulletinen
Amandla
ANC Weekly News Briefing
Angola-Rapport
Contra
Development Dialogue
Development Today
Expresso
Fackföreningsrörelsen
Film & TV
Foreign Affairs
Forum for Utviklingsstudier
Fönstret
Gnistan
Hästjournalen
Internasjonal Politikk
Journal of Contemporary African Studies
Journal of Southern African Studies
Kommentar
Liberal Debatt
Lutherhjälpen
Maji Maji
Mayibuye
Moto
Mozambique Revolution
New Left Review
News from the Nordic Africa Institute

Parade
Phambili
Prize Africa
Rapport från SIDA
Review of African Political Economy
Searchlight South Africa
Sechaba
SIDA Rapport
SIF-Tidningen
Southern Africa Political and Economic
    Monthly
Southern Africa Report
Statsanställd
SWAPO News and Views
Svensk Missionstidskrift
Svensk Tidskrift
Syd- och Sydvästafrika
Sydafrika-Nytt
Södra Afrika Informationsbulletin
Södra Afrika Nyheter
TCO-Tidningen
The African Communist
The Namibian Review
Tiden
Transformation
UDF News
UN Secretariat News
Weekend Argus
West Africa
Vi
Zimbabwe Chimurenga
Zimbabwe News

6. Newspapers

The main source consulted for newspaper articles is the Press Archive of the Uppsala University Library, which holds cuttings from around 50 Swedish daily papers since 1945. The cuttings are organized according to subjects and countries. Swedish newspapers have also been studied at the Uppsala University Library (*Carolina Rediviva*) and selected Norwegian press reports at the Oslo University Library.

a) Swedish newspapers

Aftonbladet
Arbetaren
Arbetet
Barometern
Blekinge Läns Tidning
Dagen
Dagens Nyheter
Expressen
Folket
Gotlands Allehanda
Gotlands Tidningar
Göteborgs-Posten
Göteborgs-Tidningen

Kvällsposten
Norrköpings Tidningar
Norrskensflamman
Nya Wermlands-Tidningen
Stockholms-Tidningen
Sundsvalls Tidning
Svenska Dagbladet
Sydsvenska Dagbladet
Tidsignal
Upsala Nya Tidning
Vestmanlands Läns Tidning
Östersunds-Posten
Östgöta-Correspondenten

b) International newspapers

Botswana Daily News, Botswana
Business Day, South Africa
Daily Mail, Zimbabwe
Daily News, Tanzania
Diário de Notícias, Portugal
Eastern Province Herald, South Africa
Financial Mail, South Africa
Financial Times, Great Britain
Jornal de Angola, Angola
Mail & Guardian (Weekly Mail and *Weekly Mail & Guardian)*, South Africa
Mannheimer Morgen, Germany
Morgenavisen/Jyllands-Posten, Denmark
Notícias, Mozambique
Rand Daily Mail, South Africa
Saint Louis Post, United States
Sunday Express, South Africa

Sunday News, Tanzania
Sunday Times, South Africa
The Citizen, South Africa
The Economist, Great Britain
The Herald, Zimbabwe
The Namibian, Namibia
The Observer, Great Britain
The Sowetan, South Africa
The Star & SA Times International, South Africa
The Star International Weekly, South Africa
The Star, South Africa
The Sunday Times Magazine, South Africa
The Swazi Observer, Swaziland
The Times of Swaziland, Swaziland
Times of Zambia, Zambia
Zambia Daily Mail, Zambia

Primary sources

1. Archives

The Nordic Africa Institute (NAI) holds a substantial amount of documents on and by the Southern African liberation movements, including stencilled information bulletins published in Swedish from the 1960s. Other documents cited or consulted are upon written request and subject to approval by the repository archive available at the institute for bona fide students. For the benefit of the non-Swedish reader/student, the title of the Swedish documents are in the footnotes given an English translation. The main archives, organizations or private collections holding the documents are within brackets given an abbreviated reference, such as (MFA) for the Ministry for Foreign Affairs. The Swedish documentary sources thus referenced are:

(AGA)   Africa Groups in Sweden (*Afrikagrupperna i Sverige*) (The documentation has been transferred to the Labour Movement Archives and Library–LMA)
(AJC)   Anders Johansson (private collection)
(BHC)   Bertil Högberg (private collection)
(CSA)   Church of Sweden Mission Archives (*Svenska Kyrkans Missions Arkiv*), Uppsala
(ISA)   Isolate South Africa Committee (*Isolera Sydafrika-Kommittén*) (The documentation has been transferred to the Labour Movement Archives and Library–LMA)
(JIC)   Joachim Israel (private collection)
(MFA)   Ministry for Foreign Affairs (*Utrikesdepartementet*), Stockholm
(LMA)   Labour Movement Archives and Library (*Arbetarrörelsens Arkiv och Bibliotek*), Stockholm
(NAI)   Nordic Africa Institute (*Nordiska Afrikainstitutet*), Uppsala
(OPA)   Olof Palme International Center, Stockholm
(SDA)   Swedish International Development Cooperation Agency (*Styrelsen för Internationellt Utvecklingssamarbete*), Stockholm
(UPA)   Archives of the Popular Movements in Uppland County (*Folkrörelsearkivet för Uppsala Län*), Uppsala

In addition, the following two archives in Southern Africa are similarly referenced:

(MCA)   Mayibuye Centre for History and Culture in South Africa, Cape Town, South Africa
(MHA)   Historical Archive of Mozambique (*Arquivo Histórico de Moçambique*), Maputo, Mozambique

At the time of data collection, the documentation held at the active—or recently active—non-governmental organizations (AGA, ISA and OPA) had not been organized and/or classified for easy reference. The same applies, naturally, to the three private collections (AJC, BHC and JIC). With regard to the major Swedish archives consulted (CSA, MFA, LMA, SDA and UPA), the information below should, however, guide the interested student via the principal records to the individual document cited. This said, it should be noted that the documents held at the Ministry for Foreign Affairs (MFA) and at the Swedish International Development Cooperation Agency (SDA) are restricted. Secondly, the files, series or archives indicated contain a considerable amount of documents. Only the ten MFA files comprise around 400 dossiers with up to 200 pages each. The SDA series are considerably vaster. The single archive on the LO/TCO Council of International Trade Union Cooperation at LMA consists, similarly, of several hundred volumes.

Due to the amount of documents involved and to the diverse classification systems used, it has not proved meaningful to further subdivide the documentation for direct reference in the footnotes. Bearing in mind the country discussed, the organization referred to and the date of the document cited, it should, nevertheless, not be too difficult to locate an individual source. Regarding the more recent MFA and SDA sources—roughly covering the period 1990–1994—a large amount of active documents have, finally, been consulted during meetings with Foreign Ministry and Sida officials, i.e. before filing. They are in the footnotes also referenced as (MFA) or (SDA), respectively. The volumes, files, series and archives studied at the main repositories are:

a) Church of Sweden Mission Archives (CSA)

Files: Correspondence on South Africa, Rhodesia (Zimbabwe) and South West Africa (Namibia): 1955–1980

b) Ministry for Foreign Affairs (MFA)

Files: HP 1 / By and By[1]   British territories in Africa: 1962–1980
HP 1 / Dpk   Portuguese territories: 1968–1975
HP 1 / Yan   Angola: 1975–1978 and 1986–1988
HP 1 / Ymo   Mozambique: 1975–1986
HP 1 / Ysy   South Africa: 1958–1994
HP 21 / Ysy   Questions regarding national minorities; South Africa: 1961–1979
HP 48 / M   United Nations mandates: 1964–1974
HP 53 / Ysy   Protectorates, mandates and possessions; South Africa: 1974–1978
U 30 / By   Humanitarian aid: British territories in Africa: 1965–1974
U 30 / Dpk   Humanitarian aid: Portuguese territories: 1968–1974

c) Labour Movement Archives and Library (LMA)

Archives: 2600   International Centre of the Swedish Labour Movement (*Arbetarrörelsens Internationella Centrum*) (AIC): 1978–1984

3115   LO/TCO Council of International Trade Union Cooperation: 1976–1990

Pierre Schori   Private archive

d) Swedish International Development Cooperation Agency (SDA)

Volumes: 1171–1226:   Documents on Swedish humanitarian assistance to Southern Africa: 1965–1972

Series: 1.11   Refugee and humanitarian assistance: 1972–1994. (Before 1 July 1972, the series carried the designation 4.4)
Sub-divided according to organizations, this is the main SIDA series on Swedish and international NGOs channelling humanitarian assistance to Southern Africa. (Example: 1.11.1/AGIS)

1.12   Assistance to liberation movements: 1972–1994. (Before 1 July 1972, the series equally carried the designation 4.4)
Followed by the name of a liberation movement, this is the main SIDA series on Swedish humanitarian assistance to Southern Africa (Example: 1.12.1/ANC)

1.13   Contributions to Swedish NGOs: 1972–1994 (Before 1 July 1972, the series was 4.6)

2.6.2   Assistance to Southern African liberation movements: 1972–1978. This series was in use during the period 1972–1978. Within the series, each liberation movement had an individual designation. (Example: 2.6.2.3: Assistance to FRELIMO)

9.3   Consultative Committee on Humanitarian Assistance: 1970–1994

e) Archives of the Popular Movements in Uppland County (UPA)

Archives: Laboremus: Documents 1960–1965
Swedish FRELIMO Group: Documents 1966–1970
South Africa Committee: Documents 1963–1968

The documents cited from the Historical Archive of Mozambique (MHA) were kindly identified by its director, Mrs. Inês Nogueira da Costa. The ANC box files consulted at the Mayibuye Centre in Cape Town (MCA) are as follows:

Box files: 1   South Africa United Front: 1961
            3   ANC Women's Section/Correspondence with Sweden: 1979–1981
           15   Notes and correspondence on foreign funding in South Africa: 1985–1987
           19   Bommersvik, Sweden: Workshop on post-apartheid research priorities: 1987
           26   Report from workshop in Sweden on research priorities, August 1987
           51   ANC National Executive Committee: Records 1986–1990
           52   ANC National Executive Committee: Records 1990–1991
           59   ANC Department of Research: Minutes of Harare consultative meeting:
                July 1987
           60   Office of the ANC Treasurer General: 1984–1991
           64   International relations – Scandinavia: 1986–1990
           69   Correspondence with ANC offices – Scandinavia: 1987–1990

2. Interviews

Over eighty interviews were carried out for the study. They are listed below. The interviews have
been published by the Nordic Africa Institute in Tor Sellström (ed.): *Liberation in Southern
Africa—Regional and Swedish Voices: Interviews from Angola, Mozambique, Namibia, South
Africa, Zimbabwe, the Frontline and Sweden* (1999).

Angola   Paulo Jorge, Luanda, 15 April 1996
                Lúcio Lara, Luanda, 16 April 1996
                Ruth Neto, Luanda, 16 April 1996
                Miguel N'Zau Puna, Luanda, 17 April 1996
                Alberto Ribeiro-Kabulu, Harare, 5 May 1996
                Holden Roberto, Luanda, 17 April 1996
                Jorge Valentim, Luanda, 18 April 1996

Mozambique   Joaquim Chissano, Maputo, 2 May 1996
                Janet Mondlane, Maputo, 30 April 1996
                Jorge Rebelo, Maputo, 1 May 1996
                Marcelino dos Santos, Maputo, 3 May 1996
                Jacinto Veloso, Maputo, 29 April 1996
                Sérgio Vieira, Maputo, 29 April 1996

Namibia   Ottilie Abrahams, Windhoek, 16 March 1995
                Ben Amathila, Stockholm, 19 May 1995
                Hadino Hishongwa, Windhoek, 15 March 1995
                Peter Katjavivi, Windhoek, 20 March 1995
                Charles Kauraisa, Windhoek, 20 March 1995
                Dirk Mudge, Kalkfeld, 18 March 1995
                Aaron Mushimba, Windhoek, 16 March 1995
                Mishake Muyongo, Windhoek, 17 March 1995
                Festus Naholo, Windhoek, 15 March 1995
                Zedekia Ngavirue, Windhoek, 17 March 1995
                Hifikepunye Pohamba, Windhoek, 15 March 1995
                Andreas Shipanga, Windhoek, 20 March 1995
                Andimba Toivo ya Toivo, Windhoek, 17 March 1995
                Ben Ulenga, Windhoek, 16 March 1995

South Africa   Jaya Appalraju, Johannesburg, 14 September 1995
                Alex Boraine, Cape Town, 12 September 1995
                Roelof ('Pik') Botha, Cape Town, 12 September 1995
                Gora Ebrahim, Harare, 22 July, 1995
                Gerald Giose, Cape Town, 6 December 1995
                John Gomomo, Stockholm, 6 September 1996
                Rica Hodgson, Johannesburg, 19 September 1995

Lindiwe Mabuza, Bonn, 14 March 1996
Reddy Mampane, Johannesburg, 17 September 1995
Trevor Manuel, Cape Town, 8 September 1995
Thabo Mbeki, Cape Town, 8 September 1995
Billy Modise, Johannesburg, 15 September 1995
Kay Moonsamy, Johannesburg, 14 September 1995
James Motlatsi, Johannesburg, 25 April 1996
Sankie Mthembi-Mahanyele, Cape Town, 7 September 1995
Indres Naidoo, Cape Town, 7 December 1995
Beyers Naudé, Johannesburg, 15 September 1995
Barney Pityana, Uppsala, 23 January 1997
Walter Sisulu, Johannesburg, 15 September 1995
Garth Strachan, Cape Town, 10 September 1995
Craig Williamson, Pretoria, 23 April 1996

Sweden

Roland Axelsson, Stockholm, 31 October 1996
Birgitta Berggren, Stockholm, 27 March 1996
Tore Bergman, Uppsala, 10 February 1997
Stig Blomqvist, Bro, 29 January 1997
Pär Granstedt, Stockholm, 3 June 1996
Birger Hagård, Stockholm, 9 October 1996
Sven Hamrell, Uppsala, 10 April 1996
Gunnar Helander, Västerås, 12 February 1996
Carl-Henrik Hermansson, Stockholm, 22 November 1996
Lena Hjelm-Wallén, Stockholm, 14 January 1997
Anders Johansson, Eskilstuna, 19 November 1996
Tomas Ledin, Stockholm, 18 March 1997
Sören Lindh, Stockholm, 4 February 1997
Stig Lövgren, Sollentuna, 21 February 1996
Åke Magnusson, Stockholm, 27 January 1997
Ernst Michanek, Stockholm, 19 March 1996
Hillevi Nilsson, Stockholm, 4 February 1997
Pierre Schori, Stockholm, 28 June 1996
Bengt Säve-Söderbergh, Stockholm, 14 January 1997
Carl Tham, Stockholm, 14 January 1997
David Wirmark, Stockholm, 20 February 1996
Per Wästberg, Stockholm, 28 February 1996

Zimbabwe

Canaan Banana, Harare, 3 June 1996
Dumiso Dabengwa, Harare, 27 July 1995
Kumbirai Kangai, Harare, 19 July 1995
Didymus Mutasa, Harare, 25 July 1995
Abel Muzorewa, Harare, 26 November 1996
John Nkomo, Harare, 21 July 1995
Sydney Sekeramayi, Harare, 27 July 1995
Ndabaningi Sithole, Harare, 25 July 1995
Josiah Tungamirai, Harare, 7 June 1996

Others

Kenneth Kaunda, Lusaka, 15 July 1995
Salim Ahmed Salim, Copenhagen, 16 November 1995
Vladimir Shubin, Cape Town, 12 September 1995

Appendices

Appendix I:
Conversion table SEK/USD 1950–1995

Year	1 USD	1 SEK
1950	5.18 SEK	0.19 USD
1955	5.18 SEK	0.19 USD
1960	5.17 SEK	0.19 USD
1965	5.17 SEK	0.19 USD
1970	5.19 SEK	0.19 USD
1975	4.17 SEK	0.24 USD
1980	4.23 SEK	0.24 USD
1985	8.61 SEK	0.12 USD
1990	5.91 SEK	0.17 USD
1995	7.13 SEK	0.14 USD

Source: Riksbanken Infocenter

Appendix II:
Parliamentary elections in Sweden – Distribution of votes (%)

Year	LPC	SDP	CP	LP	MP	O
1948	6.3	46.1	12.4	22.8	12.3	0.1
1952	4.3	46.1	10.7	24.4	14.4	0.1
1956	5.0	44.6	9.4	23.8	17.1	0.1
1958	3.4	46.2	12.7	18.2	19.5	0.0
1960	4.5	47.8	13.6	17.5	16.5	0.1
1964	5.2	47.3	13.2	17.0	13.7	3.6
1968	3.0	50.1	15.7	14.3	12.9	4.1
1970	4.8	45.3	19.9	16.2	11.5	2.2
1973	5.3	43.6	25.1	9.4	14.3	2.4
1976	4.8	42.7	24.1	11.1	15.6	1.8
1979	5.6	43.2	18.1	10.6	20.3	2.2
1982	5.6	45.6	15.5	5.9	23.6	3.8
1985	5.4	44.7	12.4	14.2	21.3	2.0
1988	5.8	43.2	11.3	12.2	18.3	9.1
1991	4.5	37.6	8.5	9.1	21.9	18.4
1994	6.2	45.3	7.7	7.2	22.4	11.3

LPC—Left Party Communists, SDP—Social Democratic Party, CP—Centre Party, LP—Liberal Party, MP—Moderate Party, O—others, such as the Green Party and the Christian Democrats

Appendix III:
Governments in Sweden 1951–1994

Year	Prime Minister	Party	Coalition Partners
1951	Tage Erlander	SDP	CP
1957	Tage Erlander	SDP	
1969	Olof Palme	SDP	
1976	Thorbjörn Fälldin	CP	LP, MP
1978	Ola Ullsten	LP	
1979	Thorbjörn Fälldin	CP	LP, MP
1981	Thorbjörn Fälldin	CP	LP
1982	Olof Palme	SDP	
1986	Ingvar Carlsson	SDP	
1991	Carl Bildt	MP	CP, LP, CD

SDP—Social Democratic Party, CP—Centre Party, LP—Liberal Party, MP—Moderate Party, CD—Christian Democrats

Appendix IV:
Swedish exports to Southern Africa and Portugal 1950–1970
(percentage share of total exports)

Area/Country	1950	1960	1970
Southern Africa*	1.9	1.3	1.1
----- South Africa	1.8	1.0	0.9
----- region less South Africa*	0.1	0.3	0.2
Portugal	0.5	0.5	0.6
Southern Africa and Portugal	2.4	1.8	1.7

* Includes Northern Rhodesia/Zambia and Nyasaland/Malawi.

Source: Kommerskollegium (1950) and Statistiska Centralbyrån (1960 and 1970)

Appendix V:
Swedish imports from Southern Africa and Portugal 1950–1970
(percentage share of total imports)

Area/Country	1950	1960	1970
Southern Africa*	1.5	1.1	0.6
----- South Africa	0.7	0.3	0.2
----- region less South Africa*	0.8	0.8	0.4
Portugal	0.4	0.3	0.8
Southern Africa and Portugal	1.9	1.4	1.4

* Includes Northern Rhodesia/Zambia and Nyasaland/Malawi. Traditionally, Sweden imported a lot of copper from Zambia.

Source: Kommerskollegium (1950) and Statistiska Centralbyrån (1960 and 1970)

Appendix VI:
Swedish commodity trade with South Africa 1950–1990
(current amounts in millions of SEK)

Year	Exports	Share*	Imports	Share*	Surplus
1950	101	1.8	44	0.7	57
1960	139	1.0	47	0.3	92
1970	320	0.9	78	0.2	242
1975	570	0.8	151	0.2	419
1976	421	0.5	171	0.2	250
1977	358	0.4	123	0.1	235
1978	411	0.4	177	0.2	234
1979	513	0.4	232	0.2	281
1980	761	0.6	252	0.2	509
1981	1,017	0.7	233	0.2	784
1982	1,002	0.6	348	0.2	654
1983	1,059	0.5	392	0.2	667
1984	1,575	0.6	388	0.2	1,187
1985	981	0.4	413	0.2	568
1986	787	0.3	146	0.1	641
1987	717	0.3	127	0.1	590
1988**	(43)	0.01	(2)	–	(41)
1989	(54)	0.02	–	–	(54)
1990	(54)	0.02	(2)	–	(52)

* Percentage share of total Swedish exports/imports.
** Figures for 1988–90 refer to items exempted from the 1987 trade boycott, such as medical supplies and other humanitarian goods.

Source: Statistiska Centralbyrån

Appendix VII:
Swedish sanctions against Rhodesia, Namibia and South Africa

Rhodesia: Blockade
Passed on: 28 May 1969
Valid from: 1 July 1969
Scope: Economic blockade
Government: Social Democratic Party (PM: Olof Palme)

South Africa: Arms
Passed on: 15 December 1977
Valid from: 1 January 1978
Scope: Prohibition of arms sales
Government: Coalition of Centre, Liberal and Moderate parties (PM: Thorbjörn Fälldin)

Namibia/South Africa: New investments
Passed on: 7 June 1979
Valid from: 1 July 1979
Scope: Prohibition of new investments
Government: Liberal Party (PM: Ola Ullsten)

Namibia/South Africa: Visa regulations
Passed on: 10 June 1982
Valid from: 1 July 1982
Scope: Restriction of visas to persons in official capacity
Government: Coalition of Centre and Liberal parties (PM: Thorbjörn Fälldin)

Namibia/South Africa: Leasing
Passed on: 7 March 1985
Valid from: 1 April 1985
Scope: Extension of 1979 legislation to include leasing
Government: Social Democratic Party (PM: Olof Palme)

Namibia/South Africa: Agricultural trade
Passed on: 17 December 1985
Valid from: 1 January 1986
Scope: Prohibition of importation of agricultural products
Government: Social Democratic Party (PM: Olof Palme)

Namibia/South Africa: Local boycotts
Passed on: 17 December 1985
Valid from: 1 January 1986
Scope: Granting of right to municipal and regional councils to impose boycotts
Government: Social Democratic Party (PM: Olof Palme)

Namibia/South Africa: Technology transfers and trade licences
Passed on: 15 May 1986
Valid from: 1 July 1986
Scope: Extension of 1979/1985 legislation to include technical cooperation,
                  including patents and licensing of trade
Government: Social Democratic Party (PM: Ingvar Carlsson)

Namibia/South Africa: Trade boycott
Passed on: 4 June 1987
Valid from: 1 July 1987
Scope: Prohibition of trade
Government: Social Democratic Party (PM: Ingvar Carlsson)

South Africa: Services
Passed on: 15 March 1990
Valid from: 1 April 1990
Scope: Extension of 1987 legislation to include services
Government: Social Democratic Party (PM: Ingvar Carlsson)

Appendix VIII:
PAIGC – Disbursements through SIDA
(current amounts in thousands of SEK)

Year	Amount
1969/70*	–
1970/71	1,650
1971/72	3,550
1972/73	8,340
1973/74	15,525
1974/75	16,115
1975/76**	6,810
1976/77**	1,565
TOTAL	53,555

* Payments for deliveries made in 1969/70 registered in 1970/71.
** Payments registered after the independence of Guinea-Bissau.

Source: SIDA's audited annual accounts

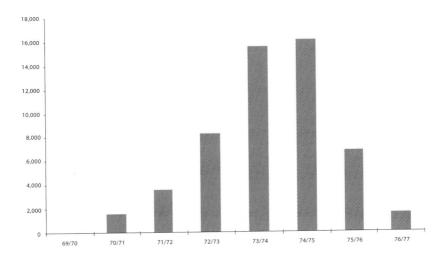

Appendix IX:
FRELIMO – Disbursements through SIDA
(current amounts in thousands of SEK)

Year	Amount*
1969/70	–
1970/71	–
1971/72	480
1972/73	920
1973/74	3,500
1974/75	12,165
1975/76**	5,850
1976/77**	50
TOTAL	22,965

* From 1965, 1.7 million SEK was disbursed to the
Mozambique Institute. The figures do not include allocations
outside the regular bilateral assistance programme.
** Payments registered after the independence of Mozambique.

Source: SIDA's audited annual accounts

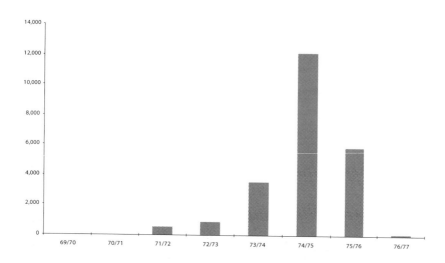

Appendix X:
MPLA – Disbursements through SIDA
(current amounts in thousands of SEK)

Year	Direct*	Other**	Total
1969/70	–	–	–
1970/71	–	–	–
1971/72	460	–	460
1972/73	100	–	100
1973/74	940	650	1,590
1974/75	770	–	770
1975/76	5,440	1,500	6,940
1976/77***	70	1,150	1,220
TOTAL	7,780	3,300	11,080

* Disbursements under the regular bilateral assistance programme.
** Multi-bilateral aid to the MPLA school at Dolisie, Congo, through UNESCO.
*** Payments registered after the independence of Angola.

Source: SIDA's audited annual accounts

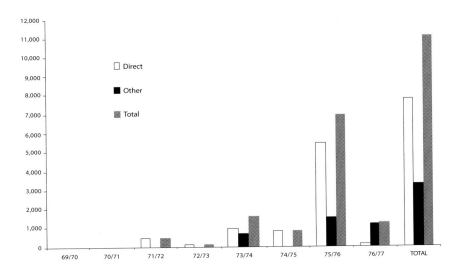

Appendix XI:
ZANU – Disbursements through SIDA
(current amounts in thousands of SEK)

Year	Amount*
1969/70**	50
1970/71**	70
1971/72	–
1972/73**	70
1973/74	290
1974/75	620
1975/76	25
1976/77	260
1977/78	2,390
1978/79	7,070
1979/80	16,340
1980/81***	18,340
TOTAL	45,525

* Excluding allocations outside the regular bilateral
  assistance programme.
** Formally to the Zimbabwe Welfare Trust.
*** Registered after the independence of Zimbabwe.
  Balanced with payments to ZAPU.

Source: SIDA's audited annual accounts

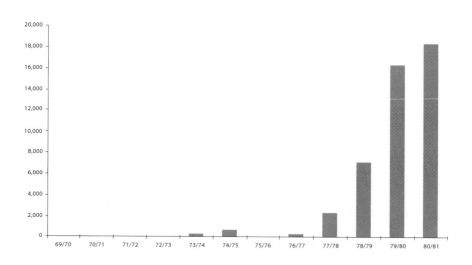

Appendix XII:
ZAPU – Disbursements through SIDA
(current amounts in thousands of SEK)

Year	Amount*
1969/70	–
1970/71	–
1971/72	–
1972/73	50
1973/74	–
1974/75	50
1975/76	–
1976/77	–
1977/78	2,500
1978/79	7,960
1979/80	14,020
1980/81**	18,340
TOTAL	42,920

* Excluding allocations outside the bilateral
assistance programme.
** Registered after the independence of Zimbabwe.
Balanced with payments to ZANU.

Source: SIDA's audited annual accounts

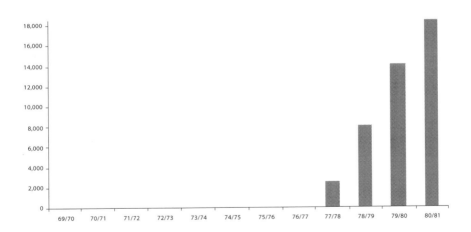

Appendix XIII:
SWAPO – Disbursements through SIDA
(current amounts in thousands of SEK)

Year	Amount*	Year	Amount*
1969/70	–	1980/81	36,210
1970/71	30	1981/82	36,460
1971/72	45	1982/83	48,935
1972/73	55	1983/84	37,850
1973/74	225	1984/85	45,705
1974/75	850	1985/86	111,875
1975/76	1,750	1986/87	62,185
1976/77	5,380	1987/88	68,395
1977/78	12,250	1988/89	82,040
1978/79	14,480	1989/90	59,515
1979/80	26,545	1990/91**	17,995
TOTAL			668,775

* Excluding allocations outside the regular bilateral assistance programme.
** Payments registered after the independence of Namibia. Additional
  commitments of 2.7 MSEK disbursed between 1991/92 and 1993/94, bringing
  the official support to 671.5 MSEK.

Source: SIDA's audited annual accounts

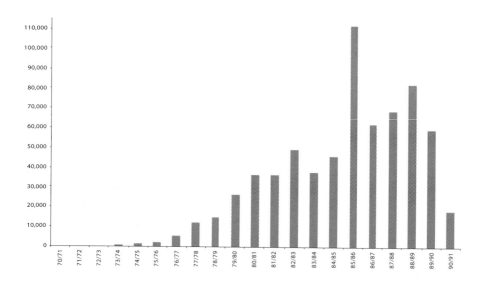

Appendix XIV:
ANC – Disbursements through SIDA
(current amounts in thousands of SEK)

Year	Amount*	Year	Amount*
1969/70	–	1982/83	30,090
1970/71	–	1983/84	28,900
1971/72	–	1984/85	32,560
1972/73	35	1985/86	49,060
1973/74	215	1986/87	64,555
1974/75	320	1987/88	56,780
1975/76	790	1988/89	75,965
1976/77	4,250	1989/90	80,405
1977/78	8,780	1990/91	90,030
1978/79	12,110	1991/92	105,730
1979/80	15,710	1992/93	53,325
1980/81	21,270	1993/94	134,630
1981/82	23,755	1994/95**	6,485
TOTAL			895,750

* Excluding allocations outside the regular bilateral assistance programme.
** Registered after the elections in South Africa in April 1994.

Source: SIDA's audited annual accounts

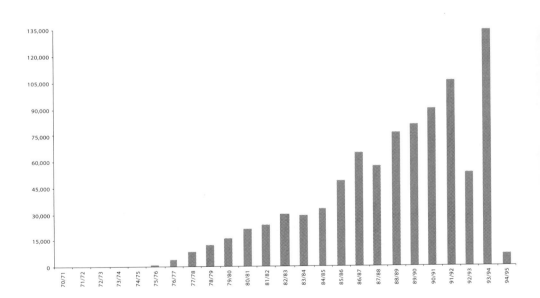

Appendix XV:
Total disbursements through SIDA to the Southern African liberation movements
and PAIGC 1969–1995
(current amounts in thousands of SEK)*

Year	PAIGC	FRELIMO	MPLA	ZAPU	ZANU	SWAPO	ANC	TOTAL
1969/70	–	–	–	–	50	–	–	50
1970/71	1,650	–	–	–	70	30	–	1,750
1971/72	3,550	480	460	–	–	45	–	4,535
1972/73	8,340	920	100	50	70	55	35	9,570
1973/74	15,525	3,500	940	–	290	225	215	20,695
1974/75	16,115	12,165	770	50	620	850	320	30,890
1975/76	6,810	5,850	5,440	–	25	1,750	790	20,665
1976/77	1,565	50	70	–	260	5,380	4,250	11,575
1977/78	–	–	–	2,500	2,390	12,250	8,780	25,920
1978/79	–	–	–	7,960	7,070	14,480	12,110	41,620
1979/80	–	–	–	14,020	16,340	26,545	15,710	72,615
1980/81	–	–	–	18,340	18,340	36,210	21,270	94,160
1981/82	–	–	–	–	–	36,460	23,755	60,215
1982/83	–	–	–	–	–	48,935	30,090	79,025
1983/84	–	–	–	–	–	37,850	28,900	66,750
1984/85	–	–	–	–	–	45,705	32,560	78,265
1985/86	–	–	–	–	–	111,875	49,060	160,935
1986/87	–	–	–	–	–	62,185	64,555	126,740
1987/88	–	–	–	–	–	68,395	56,780	125,175
1988/89	–	–	–	–	–	82,040	75,965	158,005
1989/90	–	–	–	–	–	59,515	80,405	139,920
1990/91	–	–	–	–	–	17,995	90,030	108,025
1991/92	–	–	–	–	–	50	105,730	105,780
1992/93	–	–	–	–	–	1,730	53,325	55,055
1993/94	–	–	–	–	–	870	134,630	135,500
1994/95	–	–	–	–	–	–	6,485	6,485
TOTAL	53,555	22,965	7,780	42,920	45,525	671,425	895,750	1,739,920

* Excluding allocations for emergencies, cultural activities, information, research etc. outside the regular bilateral assistance programmes.

Source: SIDA's audited annual accounts

Total disbursements through SIDA to the Southern African liberation movements and PAIGC 1969–1995

(current amounts in thousands of SEK)

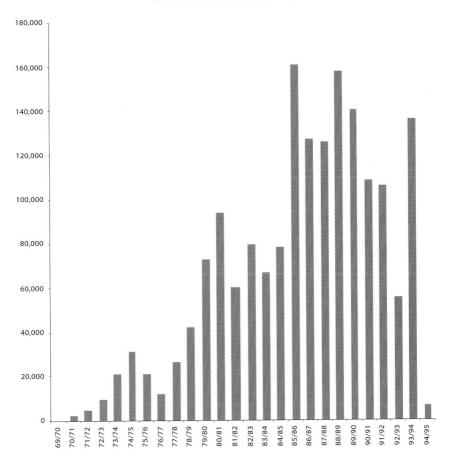

Source: SIDA's audited annual accounts

Appendix XVI:
South African organizations and publications supported by Sweden
A selected list

Adult Learning Project
Adult Literacy and Advice Centre
Africa Press
African Music and Drama Association
Agenda Press Service
Akanani Rural Development Association
Alexandra Art Centre
Alexandra Civic Organization
Alexandra Health Clinic
Art Foundation
Asingeni Fund
Bellville Community Health Project
Black Health Workers' Union of South Africa
Black Sash
Border Rural Committee
Bush Radio
Call of Islam
Cape Democrats
Career Information Centre
Centre for Applied Legal Studies
Centre for Development Studies
Centre for Health and Social Studies
Centre for the Art of Living
Centre for the Study of Health Policy
Child Guidance Clinic
Christian Institute of South Africa
Civic Association of Southern Transvaal
Community Arts Project
Community Law Centre
Community Property Organization
Community Research and Information Centre
Congress of South African Students
Congress of South African Trade Unions and affiliated
  unions
Congress of South African Writers
Congress of Traditional Leaders of South Africa
Consumer Cooperative Society, Soweto
Council of Unions of South Africa
Cradock Community Centre
Cultural Workers Congress
Durban Housing Committee
East Rand Community Advice Bureau
Eastern Cape Development and Funding Forum
Eastern Cape News Agencies
Eastern Cape Youth Congress
Ecumenical Action Against Racism
Ecumenical Bursary Fund
Ecumenical Centre Trust
Education Charter Campaign
Education Resource and Information Centre
Educational Development Trust Training Service Unit
Eldorado Park Advice Office
End Conscription Campaign
English Language Project
Environmental and Development Agency
Evaluation and Planning Centre, Durban
Federation of South African Trade Unions and
  affiliated unions
Film and Allied Workers Organization
Film Resource Unit
Five Freedoms Forum
Foundation for Peace and Justice
Free Filmmakers
Grahamstown Rural Committee
Health Care Trust
Health Information Centre and Technical Advice
  Group

Health Service Development Unit
Health Workers Association
Human Rights Trust
Ikageng Education and Community Center
Institute for Contextual Theology
Institute for Democratic Alternatives in South Africa
Interchurch Media Programme
Isinamva Development Centre
Johannesburg Democratic Action Committee
Kagiso Trust
Kathelong Art Centre
Khanya College
Khanyisa Literacy Project
Koinonia
Lawyers for Human Rights
Learn and Teach
Legal and Relief Aid
Legal Resource Centre
Letsema Art Project
Lutheran Youth Centre
Market Theatre
Masisizane secretary school
Matla Trust
Mayibuye Centre
Media and Resource Services
Media and Silkscreen Project
Media Workers Association of South Africa
Mission of the Churches for Community
  Development
Muldersdrift Health Development Programme
Musical Action for People's Power
Namaquanuus
Natal Indian Congress
National Association of Democratic Lawyers
National Education Crisis Committee
National Land Committee
National Literacy Co-operation
National Reception Committee
National Union of South African Students
New African
New African Theatre Trust
New Nation
New World Foundation
Nkwenkwe Art Center and Development Project
Open School
Organization for Appropriate Social Service
  in South Africa
Orlando Children's Home
Peace Coordination Trust
People Opposing Women's Abuse
Philani Nutrition Centre
Pietermaritzburg Agency for Christian Social
  Awareness
Popular History Trust
Press Trust of South Africa
Ravan Press
Release Mandela Campaign
Riverlea Resource Centre
Riverlea Youth Congress
Saamstaan Publikasies
Saspu National
Set Bold
Shifty Records
Sibekokuhle Women's Project
Skotaville Publishers
Solidarity News Service
South

South African Artists United
South African Committee for Higher Education
South African Council of Churches
South African History Archives
South African Institute of Race Relations
South African Legal Defence Fund
South African Medical Scholarships Trust
South African National Civics Organization
South African Non-Racial Olympic Committee
South African Prisoners' Education Trust
South African Students' Education Trust
South African Studies Project
South African Youth Congress
Southern African Advanced Education Project
Southern Cape Land Committee
Soweto Civic Association
Soyikwa Theatre Group
Speak
Student Emergency Fund
Student Union for Christian Action
Students' Teaching and Education Programme
Taurus Publishers
The Eye
The Voice
Theology Exchange Programme

Thupelo Art Project
Transvaal Indian Congress
Transvaal Rural Action Committee
Tumahole Civic Association
TURRET Correspondence College
Umthombo Wolwazi Literacy Centre
Union of Black Journalists
United Committee of Concern
United Democratic Front and affiliates
Urban Research Services
Use, Speak, Write English
Weekly Mail
Western Cape Media Trainers Forum
Western Cape Teachers Union
Video News Services
Winterveld Community Center
Witwatersrand Workers' Library
Women's Development and Staff Training
Workers' College Durban
Voter Education and Election Training Unit
Vrye Weekblad
Vuyani Educare Centre
Young Workers Education Project
Zimele Trust Fund

Name Index